CHILTON®

CHRYSLER
SERVICE MANUAL
2012 EDITION
VOLUME I

CENGAGE
Learning®

Australia • Brazil • Japan • Korea • Mexico • Singapore • Spain • United Kingdom • United States

CHILTON®
Chrysler Service Manual
2010 Edition
Volume I

**Vice President,
Technology Professional
Business Unit:**
Gregory L. Clayton

**Publisher,
Technology Professional
Business Unit:**
David Koontz

Director of Marketing:
Beth A. Lutz

Senior Production Director:
Wendy Troeger

Production Manager:
Sherondra Thedford

Marketing Manager:
Jennifer Barbic

Marketing Coordinator:
Rachael Torres

Editorial Assistant:
Lisa Staib

Chilton Content Specialist:
Paula Baillie

Graphical Designer:
Melinda Possinger

Art Director:
Benj Gleeksman

Sr. Content Project Manager:
Mike Tubbert

Senior Editors:
Eugene F. Hannon, Jr., A.S.E.
Ryan Lee Price
Richard J. Rivele
Christine L. Sheeky

Editors:
Julia Gillis
Kyla Nyjordet
David G. Olson
Lance Williams

For product information and technology assistance, contact us at
Professional & Career Group customer Support, 1-800-648-7450.
For permission to use material from this text or product, submit all requests online at
www.cengage.com/permissions.
Further permissions questions can be e-mailed to
permissionrequest@cengage.com.

ISBN-13: 978-1-4354-6159-8
ISBN-10: 1-4354-6159-2
ISSN: 1551-4412

Chilton
5 Maxwell Drive
Clifton Park, NY 12065-2919
USA

Cengage Learning is a leading provider of customized learning solutions with office locations around the globe, including Singapore, the United Kingdom, Australia, Mexico, Brazil, and Japan. Locate your local office at: **international.cengage.com/region**

Cengage Learning products are represented in Canada by Nelson Education, Ltd.

NOTICE TO THE READER

Publisher does not warrant or guarantee any of the products described herein or perform any independent analysis in connection with any of the product information contained herein. Publisher does not assume, and expressly disclaims, any obligation to obtain and include information other than that provided to it by the manufacturer.

The reader is expressly warned to consider and adopt all safety precautions that might be indicated by the activities described herein and to avoid all potential hazards. By following the instructions contained herein, the reader willingly assumes all risks in connection with such instructions.

The publisher makes no representations or warranties of any kind, including but not limited to, the warranties of fitness for particular purpose or merchantability, nor are any such representations implied with respect to the material set forth herein, and the publisher takes no responsibility with respect to such material. The publisher shall not be liable for any special, consequential, or exemplary damages resulting, in whole or part, from the readers' use of, or reliance upon, this material.

Printed in the United States of America
1 2 3 4 5 6 7 17 16 15 14 13 12

Table of Contents

Model Index

USING THIS INFORMATION

Organization

To find where a particular model section or procedure is located, look in the Table of Contents. Main topics are listed with the page number on which they may be found. Following the main topics is an alphabetical listing of all of the procedures within the section and their page numbers.

Manufacturer and Model Coverage

This product covers 2010-2011 Chrysler models that are produced in sufficient quantities to warrant coverage, and which have technical content available from the vehicle manufacturers before our publication date. Although this information is as complete as possible at the time of publication, some manufacturers may make changes which cannot be included here. While striving for total accuracy, the publisher cannot assume responsibility for any errors, changes, or omissions that may occur in the compilation of this data.

Part Numbers & Special Tools

Part numbers and special tools are recommended by the publisher and vehicle manufacturer to perform specific jobs. Before substituting any part or tool for the one recommended, you must be completely satisfied that neither your personal safety, nor the performance of the vehicle will be endangered.

ACKNOWLEDGEMENT

Portions of materials contained herein are sourced from Chrysler Group LLC.

PRECAUTIONS

Before servicing any vehicle, please be sure to read all of the following precautions, which deal with personal safety, prevention of component damage, and important points to take into consideration when servicing a motor vehicle:

• Always wear safety glasses or goggles when drilling, cutting, grinding or prying.

• Steel-toed work shoes should be worn when working with heavy parts. Pockets should not be used for carrying tools. A slip or fall can drive a screwdriver into your body.

• Work surfaces, including tools and the floor should be kept clean of grease, oil or other slippery material.

• When working around moving parts, don't wear loose clothing. Long hair should be tied back under a hat or cap, or in a hair net.

• Always use tools only for the purpose for which they were designed. Never pry with a screwdriver.

• Keep a fire extinguisher and first aid kit handy.

• Always properly support the vehicle with approved stands or lift.

• Always have adequate ventilation when working with chemicals or hazardous material.

• Carbon monoxide is colorless, odorless and dangerous. If it is necessary to operate the engine with vehicle in a closed area such as a garage, always use an exhaust collector to vent the exhaust gases outside the closed area.

• When draining coolant, keep in mind that small children and some pets are attracted by ethylene glycol antifreeze, and are quite likely to drink any left in an open container, or in puddles on the ground. This will prove fatal in sufficient quantity. Always drain the coolant into a sealable container.

• To avoid personal injury, do not remove the coolant pressure relief cap while the engine is operating or hot. The cooling system is under pressure; steam and hot liquid can come out forcefully when the cap is loosened slightly. Failure to follow these instructions may result in personal injury. The coolant must be recovered in a suitable, clean container for reuse. If the coolant is contaminated it must be recycled or disposed of correctly.

• When carrying out maintenance on the starting system be aware that heavy gauge leads are connected directly to the battery. Make sure the protective caps are in place when maintenance is completed. Failure to follow these instructions may result in personal injury.

• Do not remove any part of the engine emission control system. Operating the engine without the engine emission control system will reduce fuel economy and engine ventilation. This will weaken engine performance and shorten engine life. It is also a violation of Federal law.

• Due to environmental concerns, when the air conditioning system is drained, the refrigerant must be collected using refrigerant recovery/recycling equipment. Federal law requires that refrigerant be recovered into appropriate recovery equipment and the process be conducted by qualified technicians who have been certified by an approved organization, such as MACS, ASI, etc. Use of a recovery machine dedicated to the appropriate refrigerant is necessary to reduce the possibility of oil and refrigerant incompatibility concerns. Refer to the instructions provided by the equipment manufacturer when removing refrigerant from or charging the air conditioning system.

• Always disconnect the battery ground when working on or around the electrical system.

• Batteries contain sulfuric acid. Avoid contact with skin, eyes, or clothing. Also, shield your eyes when working near batteries to protect against possible splashing of the acid solution. In case of acid contact with skin or eyes, flush immediately with water for a minimum of 15 minutes and get prompt medical attention. If acid is swallowed, call a physician immediately. Failure to follow these instructions may result in personal injury.

• Batteries normally produce explosive gases. Therefore, do not allow flames, sparks or lighted substances to come near the battery. When charging or working near a battery, always shield your face and protect your eyes. Always provide ventilation. Failure to follow these instructions may result in personal injury.

• When lifting a battery, excessive pressure on the end walls could cause acid to spew through the vent caps, resulting in personal injury, damage to the vehicle or battery. Lift with a battery carrier or with your hands on opposite corners. Failure to follow these instructions may result in personal injury.

• Observe all applicable safety precautions when working around fuel. Whenever servicing the fuel system, always work in a well-ventilated area. Do not allow fuel spray or vapors to come in contact with a spark, open flame, or excessive heat (a hot drop light, for example). Keep a dry chemical fire extinguisher near the work area. Always keep fuel in a container specifically designed for fuel storage; also, always properly seal fuel containers to avoid the possibility of fire or explosion. Do not smoke or carry lighted tobacco or open flame of any type when working on or near any fuel-related components.

• Fuel injection systems often remain pressurized, even after the engine has been turned OFF. The fuel system pressure must be relieved before disconnecting any fuel lines. Failure to do so may result in fire and/or personal injury.

• The evaporative emissions system contains fuel vapor and condensed fuel vapor. Although not present in large quantities, it still presents the danger of explosion or fire. Disconnect the battery ground cable from the battery to minimize the possibility of an electrical spark occurring, possibly causing a fire or explosion if fuel vapor or liquid fuel is present in the area. Failure to follow these instructions can result in personal injury.

• The EPA warns that prolonged contact with used engine oil may cause a number of skin disorders, including cancer! You should make every effort to minimize your exposure to used engine oil. Protective gloves should be worn when changing oil. Wash your hands and any other exposed skin areas as soon as possible after exposure to used engine oil. Soap and water, or waterless hand cleaner should be used.

• Some vehicles are equipped with an air bag system, often referred to as a Supplemental Restraint System (SRS) or Supplemental Inflatable Restraint (SIR) system. The system must be disabled before performing service on or around system components, steering column, instrument panel components, wiring and sensors. Failure to follow safety and disabling procedures could result in accidental air bag deployment, possible personal injury and unnecessary system repairs.

• Always wear safety goggles when working with, or around, the air bag system. When carrying a non-deployed air bag, be sure the bag and trim cover are pointed away from your body. When placing a non-deployed air bag on a work surface, always face the bag and trim cover upward, away from the surface. This will reduce the motion of the module if it is accidentally deployed.

• Electronic modules are sensitive to electrical charges. The ABS module can be damaged if exposed to these charges.

• Brake pads and shoes may contain asbestos, which has been determined to be a cancer-causing agent. Never clean brake surfaces with compressed air. Avoid inhaling brake dust. Clean all brake surfaces with a commercially available brake cleaning fluid.

• When replacing brake pads, shoes, discs or drums, replace them as complete axle sets.

• When servicing drum brakes, disassemble and assemble one side at a time, leaving the remaining side intact for reference.

• Brake fluid often contains polyglycol ethers and polyglycols. Avoid contact with the eyes and wash your hands thoroughly after handling brake fluid. If you do get brake fluid in your eyes, flush your eyes with clean, running water for 15 minutes. If eye irritation persists, or if you have taken brake fluid internally, immediately seek medical assistance.

• Clean, high quality brake fluid from a sealed container is essential to the safe and proper operation of the brake system. You should always buy the correct type of brake fluid for your vehicle. If the brake fluid becomes contaminated, completely flush the system with new fluid. Never reuse any brake fluid. Any brake fluid that is removed from the system should be discarded. Also, do not allow any brake fluid to come in contact with a painted or plastic surface; it will damage the paint.

• Never operate the engine without the proper amount and type of engine oil; doing so will result in severe engine damage.

• Timing belt maintenance is extremely important! Many models utilize an interference-type, non-freewheeling engine. If the timing belt breaks, the valves in the cylinder head may strike the pistons, causing potentially serious (also time-consuming and expensive) engine damage.

• Disconnecting the negative battery cable on some vehicles may interfere with the functions of the on-board computer system (s) and may require the computer to undergo a relearning process once the negative battery cable is reconnected.

• Steering and suspension fasteners are critical parts because they affect performance of vital components and systems and their failure can result in major service expense. They must be replaced with the same grade or part number or an equivalent part if replacement is necessary. Do not use a replacement part of lesser quality or substitute design. Torque values must be used as specified during reassembly.

CHRYSLER AND DODGE

300 • Charger

1

SPECIFICATIONS AND MAINTENANCE CHARTS

ENGINE AND VEHICLE IDENTIFICATION

	Engine							Model Year	
Code ①	Liters (cc)	Cu. In.	Cyl.	Fuel Sys.	Engine Type	Eng. Mfg.		Code ②	Year
D	2.7	167	6	SFI	Gas	Chrysler		A	2010
V	3.5	214	6	SFI	Gas	Chrysler		B	2011
G	3.6	220	6	SFI	Gas	Chrysler			
T	5.7	348	8	SFI	Gas	Chrysler			
W	6.1	370	8	SFI	Gas	Chrysler			

① 8th position of VIN

② 10th position of VIN

25766_300C_C0001

GENERAL ENGINE SPECIFICATIONS

All measurements are given in inches.

Year	Model	Engine Displacement Liters	Engine ID/VIN	Fuel System Type	Net Horsepower @ rpm	Net Torque @ rpm (ft. lbs.)	Bore x Stroke (in.)	Com-pression Ratio	Oil Pressure @ rpm
2010	300/	2.7	D	MPI	178@5500	190@4000	3.39x3.09	9.67:1	45-105@3000
	Charger	3.5	V	MPI	250@6400	250@3800	3.78x3.19	10:01	45-105@3000
		5.7	T	MPI	358@5150	389@4250	3.92x3.58	10.5:1	25-110@3000
		6.1	W	MPI	425@6000	420@4800	4.05x3.58	10.3:1	25-110@3000
2011	300/	3.6	G	MPI	288@6350	260@4800	3.78x3.27	10.2:1	①
	Charger	5.7	T	MPI	358@5150	389@4250	3.92x3.58	10.5:1	25-110@3000

① 30-139@1201-3500

25766_300C_C0002

ENGINE TUNE-UP SPECIFICATIONS

Year	Engine Displacement Liters	Engine ID/VIN	Spark Plug Gap (in.)	Ignition Timing (deg.)		Fuel Pump (psi)	Idle Speed (rpm)		Valve Clearance	
				MT	AT		MT	AT	Intake	Exhaust
2010	2.7	D	0.051	NA	NA	53-63	NA	NA	①	②
	3.5	V	0.051	NA	NA	53-63	NA	NA	①	②
	5.7	T	0.040	NA	NA	53-63	NA	NA	③	④
	6.1	W	0.051	NA	NA	53-63	NA	NA	⑤	⑥
2011	3.6	G	0.04	NA	NA	53-63	NA	NA	⑦	⑧
	5.7	T	0.04	NA	NA	53-63	NA	NA	③	④

NA: Not Available

① 0.0009-0.0026

② 0.002-0.0037

③ 0.0008-0.0025

④ 0.0009-0.0025

⑤ 0.0008-0.0025

⑤ 0.0010-0.0028

⑦ 0.0009-0.0024

⑧ 0.0012-0.0027

25766_300C_C0003

CAPACITIES

Year	Model	Engine Displacement Liters	Engine ID/VIN	Engine Oil with Filter (qts.)	Transmission (pts.) Auto.	Transmission (pts.) Manual	Drive Axle (pts.) Front	Drive Axle (pts.) Rear	Transfer Case (pts.)	Fuel Tank (gal.)	Cooling System (qts.)
2010	300/	2.7	D	6.0	③	NA	1.26	①	2.11	18.0	9.9
	Charger	3.5	V	6.0	③	NA	1.26	①	2.11	②	11.1
		5.7	T	7.0	③	NA	1.26	①	2.11	19.0	14.7
		6.1	W	7.0	③	NA	1.26	①	2.11	19.0	15.2
2011	300/	3.6	G	6.0	10.6/16.2	NA	1.26	①	2.11	19.0	10.4
	Charger	5.7	T	7.0	10.6/16.2	NA	1.26	①	2.11	19.0	14.7

NOTE: All capacities are approximate. Add fluid gradually and ensure a proper fluid level is obtained.

① 198mm RII Rear Axle: 3

  200mm RII Rear Axle: 2.35

  215mm RII Rear Axle: 2.54

  226mm RII Rear Axle: 2.75 (Limited Slip Rear Axles require the addition of 4 oz. of Limited Slip Additive

② With AWD: 19

  Without AWD: 18

③ 42RLE: 4.0/8.8

  NAG 1: 5.3/8.1

25766_300C_C0004

FLUID SPECIFICATIONS

Year	Model	Engine Disp. Liters	Engine Oil	Manual Trans.	Auto. Trans.	Drive Axle Front	Drive Axle Rear	Transfer Case	Power Steering Fluid	Brake Master Cylinder	Cooling System
2010	300/	2.7	①	NA	ATF+4	②	③	④	⑤	⑥	⑦
	Charger	3.5	⑧	NA	ATF+4	②	③	④	⑤	⑥	⑦
		5.7	①	NA	ATF+4	②	③	④	⑤	⑥	⑦
		6.1	⑨	NA	ATF+4	②	③	④	⑤	⑥	⑦
2011	300/	3.6	⑩	NA	ATF+4	②	③	④	⑪	⑥	⑦
	Charger	5.7	①	NA	ATF+4	②	③	④	⑪	⑥	⑦

DOT: Department Of Transpotation

① API Certified SAE 5W-20

② SAE 75W-90

③ 198 mm, 200 mm and 215 mm RII Rear Axle: Synthetic Gear Lubricant SAE 75W-140

  226 mm RII Rear Axle: Synthetic Gear Lubricant SAE 75W-90

④ Transfer Case Lubricant

⑤ Power Steering Fluid +4

⑥ Brake Fluid DOT 3, SAE J1703

⑦ Antifreeze/Coolant 5 Year/100,000 Mile Formula HOAT (Hybrid Organic Additive Technology)G

⑧ API Certified SAE 10W-30

⑨ Full Synthetic SAE 5W-40 or equivalent

⑩ API SAE 5W-30

⑪ Hydraulic Power Steering Fluid

25766_300C_C0005

VALVE SPECIFICATIONS

Year	Engine Displacement Liters	Engine ID/VIN	Seat Angle (deg.)	Face Angle (deg.)	Spring Test Pressure (lbs. @ in.)	Spring Free-Length (in.)	Spring Installed Height (in.)	Stem-to-Guide Clearance (in.)		Stem Diameter (in.)	
								Intake	Exhaust	Intake	Exhaust
2010	2.7	D	45-45.5	44.5-45.5	56-64@ 1.4961	1.797	1.496	0.0009-0.0026	0.002-0.0037	0.2337-0.2344	0.2326-0.2333
	3.5	V	45-45.5	44.5-45	①	②	③	0.0009-0.0026	0.002-0.0037	0.2730-0.2737	0.2719-0.2726
	5.7	T	44.5-45	45-45.5	92.8-102@ 1.77	2.189	1.810	0.0008-0.0025	0.0009-0.0025	0.312-0.3130	0.312-0.3130
	6.1	W	④	44.5-45	⑤	⑥	⑦	0.0008-0.0025	0.0010-0.0028	0.312-0.3130	0.312-0.3130
2011	3.6	G	44.5-45	45-45.5	63-69@ 1.57	2.067	1.575	0.0009-0.0024	0.0012-0.0027	0.2346-0.2354	0.2343-0.2351
	5.7	T	44.5-45	45-45.5	92-102@ 1.77	2.189	1.810	0.0008-0.0025	0.0009-0.0025	0.312-0.313	0.312-0.313

① Intake: 69.5-80.5@1.4961

　Exhaust: Yellow 70.5-79.5@1.496

　Exhaust: White 80-90@1.496

② Intake (Approx): 1.7195

　Exhaust (Approx): Yellow 1.8543

　Exhaust (Approx): White 1.9015

③ 1.4961 (Spring seat to bottom retainer-intake and exhaust)

④ Intake: 45.5-46

　Exhaust:45-45.5

⑤ Intake: 95-102@ 1.87

　Exhaust: 95-102@ 1.772

⑥ Intake (Approx): 2.133

　Exhaust (Approx): 2.023

⑦ Intake: 1.870 (Spring seat to bottom of retainer)

　Exhaust: 1.772 (Spring seat to bottom of retainer)

CAMSHAFT SPECIFICATIONS

All measurements in inches unless noted

Year	Engine Displacement Liters	Engine Code/VIN	Journal Diameter	Brg. Oil Clearance	Shaft End-play	Runout	Journal Bore	Lobe Height Intake	Lobe Height Exhaust
2010	2.7	D	0.9449-0.9441	0.0020-0.0035	0.0051-0.11	NA	NA	NA	NA
	3.5	V	1.6905-1.6913	0.003-0.0047	0.001-0.014	NA	NA	NA	NA
	5.7	T	①	②	0.0031-0.0114	NA	NA	NA	NA
	6.1	W	③	④	0.0031-0.0114	NA	NA	NA	NA
2011	3.6	G	⑤	⑥	0.003-0.10	NA	NA	NA	NA
	5.7	T	①	②		NA	NA	NA	NA

NA: Not Available

① No. 1: 2.29
No. 2: 2.28
No. 3: 2.26
No. 4: 2.24
No. 5: 1.72

② No. 1: 0.0015-0.003
No. 2: 0.0019-0.0035
No. 3: 0.0015-0.003
No. 4: 0.0019-0.0035
No. 5: 0.0015-0.003

③ No. 1: 2.29
No. 2: 2.27
No. 3: 2.26
No. 4: 2.24
No. 5: 1.72

④ No. 1: 0.0015-0.003
No. 2: 2.27
No. 3: 2.26
No. 4: 2.24
No. 5: 1.72

⑤ No. 1: 1.2589-1.2596
No. 2, 3, 4: 0.9440-0.9447

⑥ No. 1: 0.00010-0.0026
No. 2, 3, 4: 0.0009-0.0025

25766_300C_C0007

CRANKSHAFT AND CONNECTING ROD SPECIFICATIONS

All measurements are given in inches.

Year	Engine Displacement Liters	Engine ID/VIN	Crankshaft Main Brg. Journal Dia.	Crankshaft Main Brg. Oil Clearance	Crankshaft Shaft End-play	Thrust on No.	Connecting Rod Journal Diameter	Connecting Rod Oil Clearance	Connecting Rod Side Clearance
2010	2.7	D	2.4997-2.5004	0.0012-0.0022	0.002-0.010	NA	2.1067-2.1060	0.0012-0.0026	0.0004
	3.5	V	2.519-2.5200	0.0013-0.0024	0.002-0.010	NA	2.282-2.2830	0.0014-0.0029	0.0004
	5.7	T	2.5585-2.5595	0.0009-0.0020	0.002-0.0110	NA	2.1260	0.0007-0.0023	0.0001
	6.1	W	2.5585-2.5595	0.0009-0.0020	0.002-0.0110	NA	2.125-2.1260	0.0007-0.0029	0.0001
2011	3.6	G	2.8310-2.8380	0.0009-0.0020	0.0020-0.0114	NA	2.3193-2.3263	0.0009-0.0025	0.0002
	5.7	T	2.5585-2.5595	0.0009-0.0020	0.002-0.0110	NA	2.1260	0.0007-0.0023	0.0001

NA: Not Available

25766_300C_C0008

PISTON AND RING SPECIFICATIONS

All measurements are given in inches.

Year	Engine Displacement Liters	Engine ID/VIN	Piston Clearance	Ring Gap			Ring Side Clearance		
				Top Compression	Bottom Compression	Oil Control	Top Compression	Bottom Compression	Oil Control
2010	2.7	D	NA	0.008-0.0140	0.0146-0.0249	0.010-0.0300	0.0013-0.0032	0.0016-0.0031	0.0020-0.008
	3.5	V	NA	0.008-0.0140	0.0078-0.0157	0.010-0.0300	0.0016-0.0031	0.0016-0.0031	0.0015-0.0073
	5.7	T	0.012-0.0230	0.015-0.0210	0.009-0.0200	0.0059-0.0259	0.001-0.0035	0.001-0.0031	0.002-0.008
	6.1	W	0.00096-0.0020	0.0118-0.0157	0.0137-0.0236	0.0079-0.0280	0.0007-0.0026	0.0007-0.0022	0.0007-0.0091
2011	3.6	G	0.0001-0.0004	0.010-0.0160	0.012-0.0180	0.006-0.0260	0.0010-0.0033	0.0012-0.0031	0.0003-0.0068
	5.7	T	0.012-0.0230	0.015-0.0210	0.009-0.0200	0.0059-0.0259	0.001-0.0035	0.001-0.0031	0.002-0.008

NA: Not Available

25766_300C_C0009

TORQUE SPECIFICATIONS

All readings in ft. lbs.

Year	Engine Disp. Liters	Engine ID/VIN	Cylinder Head Bolts	Main Bearing Bolts	Rod Bearing Bolts	Crankshaft Damper Bolts	Flywheel Bolts	Manifold		Spark Plugs	Oil Pan Drain Plug
								Intake	Exhaust		
2010	2.7	D	①	9	NA	125	NA	9	17	15	20
	3.5	V	②	21	NA	70	70	③	17	20	20
	5.7	T	④	⑤	⑥	129	70	9	18	13	20
	6.1	W	⑦	⑧	⑨	129	70	9	23	13	20
2011	3.6	G	⑩	9.5	⑥	⑪	70	⑫	NA	13	20
	5.7	T	⑤	⑤	⑥	129	70	9	18	13	20

NA: Not Available

① Step 1: Bolts 1-8 35 ft. lbs. (48 Nm)
  Step 2: Bolts 1-8 55 ft. lbs. (75 Nm)
  Step 3: Bolts 1-8 55 ft. lbs. (75 Nm)
  Step 4: Bolts 1-8 +90 degrees (Do NOT use a torque wrench for this step)
  Step 5: Bolts 9-11 21 ft. lbs. (28 Nm)
② Step 1: 45 ft. lbs. (61 Nm)
  Step 2: 65 ft. lbs. (88 Nm)
  Step 3: 65 ft. lbs. (88 Nm)
  Step 4: +1/4 turn
③ Lower: 21 ft. lbs.
  Upper: 9 ft. lbs.
④ Step 1: M12 25 ft. lbs. (34 Nm)
  M8 15 ft. lbs. (20 Nm)
  Step 2: M12 40 ft. lbs. (54)
  M8: 15 ft. lbs. (20 Nm)
  Step 3: M12 +90 degrees
  M8 25 ft. lbs. (34 Nm)
⑤ 20 ft. lbs. (27 Nm) + 90 additional degrees
⑥ 15 ft. lbs. (21 Nm) + 90 additional degrees

⑦ Step 1 Bolts 1-10: 25
  Step 1 Bolts 11-15: 15
  Step 2 Bolts 1-10: 40
  Step 2 Bolts 11-15: 15
  Step 3 Bolts 1-10: Rotate bolts 90 degrees
  Step 4 bolts 11-15: 25
⑧ M-12 Bolts: 21 plus 90 degree turn
  Crossbolts M-8 Bolts: 16
⑨ 33 plus 60 degree turn
⑩ Step 1: All to 22 ft. lbs. (30 Nm)
  Step 2: All to 33 ft. lbs. (45 Nm)
  Step 3: All +75 degree turn. (Do not use a torque wrench for this step)
  Step 4: All +50 degree turn. (Do not use a torque wrench for this step)
  Step 5: Loosen all fasteners in reverse of sequence
  Step 6: All to 22 ft. lbs. (30 Nm)
  Step 7: All to 33 ft. lbs. (45 Nm)
  Step 8: All +70 degree turn. (Do not use a torque wrench for this step)
  Step 9: All +70 degree turn. (Do not use a torque wrench for this step)
⑪ 30 + 105 degree turn
⑫ Upper and Lower (M6 Bolts): 6

25766_300C_C0010

WHEEL ALIGNMENT

Year	Model		Caster Range (+/-Deg.)	Caster Preferred Setting (Deg.)	Camber Range (+/-Deg.)	Camber Preferred Setting (Deg.)	Toe-in (in.)
2010	300/	FL	3.5-5.5	4.5	0.50-0.80	0.15	NA
	Charger	FR	4.10-6.10	5.10	-0.70-0.30	-0.25	NA
	AWD	RL	NA	NA	-1.20-+0.10	-0.55	NA
		RR	NA	NA	-1.20-+0.10	-0.55	NA
	300/	FL	8	7.0-9.0	0.50-0.80	0.15	NA
	Charger	FR	9	8-10	-0.90-+0.40	-0.25	NA
	RWD	RL	NA	NA	-1.20-+0.10	-0.55	NA
		RR	NA	NA	-1.20-+0.10	-0.55	NA
	300/	FL	8.3	7.3-9.3	-1	-0.05	NA
	Charger	FR	9.3	8.3-10.3	-0.90-+0.10	-0.35	NA
	SRT8	RL	NA	NA	-1.20-+0.10	-0.55	NA
		RR	NA	NA	-1.20-+0.10	-0.55	NA
2011	300/	FL	3.5-5.5	4.50	-0.55-0.55	0	NA
	Charger	FR	4.10-6.10	5.10	-0.95-0.15	-0.40	NA
	AWD	RL	NA	NA	-1.3 - -0.20	-0.75	NA
		RR	NA	NA	-1.3 - -0.20	-0.75	NA
	300/	FL	NA	NA	NA	NA	NA
	Charger	FR	NA	NA	NA	NA	NA
	RWD	RL	7-9	8	-1.40- -0.30	-0.85	NA
		RR	7.70-9.70	8.70	-1.80- -0.70	-1.25	NA

25766_300C_C0011

TIRE, WHEEL AND BALL JOINT SPECIFICATIONS

Year	Model	OEM Tires Standard	OEM Tires Optional	Tire Pressures (psi) Front	Tire Pressures (psi) Rear	Wheel Size	Ball Joint Inspection	Lug Nut (ft. lbs.)
2010	300/	245/45ZR20	NA	①	①	NA	0.059	110
	Charger	255/45ZR20	NA	①	①	NA	0.059	110
2011	300/	245/45ZR20	NA	①	①	NA	0.059	110
	Charger	255/45ZR20	NA	①	①	NA	0.059	110

OEM: Original Equipment Manufacturer

PSI: Pounds Per Square Inch

NA: Information not available

① Refer to the Vehicle Cirtification Label for specifications

25766_300C_C0012

BRAKE SPECIFICATIONS

All measurements in inches unless noted

| Year | Model | | Brake Disc | | | Brake Drum Diameter | | | Minimum Pad/Lining Thickness | | Brake Caliper | |
			Original Thickness	Minimum Thickness	Max. Runout	Original Inside Diameter	Max. Wear Limit	Maximum Machine Diamter	Front	Rear	Bracket Bolts (ft. lbs.)	Mounting Bolts (ft. lbs.)
2010	300	F	①	②	③	NA	NA	NA	0.040	0.040	④	⑤
		R	①	②	③	NA	NA	NA	0.040	0.040	④	⑥
	Charger	F	①	②	③	NA	NA	NA	0.040	0.040	④	⑤
		R	①	②	③	NA	NA	NA	0.040	0.040	④	⑥
2011	300	F	①	②	③	NA	NA	NA	0.040	0.040	④	⑤
		R	①	②	③	NA	NA	NA	0.040	0.040	④	⑥
	Charger	F	①	②	③	NA	NA	NA	0.040	0.040	④	⑤
		R	①	②	③	NA	NA	NA	0.040	0.040	④	⑥

F: Front

R: Rear

NA: Information not available

① Base (17 inch) Front:1.097-1.107
  Base (17 inch) Rear: 0.389-0.399
  Premium (18 inch) Front: 1.097-1.107
  Premium (18 inch) Rear: 0.861-0.871
  SRT8 Front: 1.256-1.264
  SRT8 Rear: 1.098-1.106

② Base (17 inch) Front: 1.040
  Base (17 inch) Rear: 0.335
  Premium (18 inch) Front: 1.040
  Premium (18 inch) Rear: 0.807
  SRT8 Front: 1.181
  SRT8 Rear: 1.024

③ Non SRT8: 0.0014
  SRT8: 0.0012

④ Front: 70
  Rear: 85

⑤ SRT8: 96

⑥ SRT8: 140

25766_300C_C0013

SCHEDULED MAINTENANCE - NORMAL
2010 Dodge Charger, Chrysler 300

TO BE SERVICED	TYPE OF SERVICE	6	12	18	24	30	36	42	48	54	60	66	72	78	84	90	96	102
Engine oil & filter	Replace	✓	✓	✓	✓	✓	✓	✓	✓	✓	✓	✓	✓	✓	✓	✓	✓	✓
Rotate tires, inspect tread wear, measure tread depth and check pressure	Rotate	✓	✓	✓	✓	✓	✓	✓	✓	✓	✓	✓	✓	✓	✓	✓	✓	✓
Air conditioner filter	Replace		✓		✓		✓		✓		✓		✓		✓		✓	
Brake system components	Inspect/ Service		✓		✓		✓		✓		✓		✓		✓		✓	
Exhaust system & heat shields	Inspect		✓		✓		✓		✓		✓		✓		✓		✓	
Inspect front suspension, tie rod ends and boot seals for cracks or leaks and all parts for damage, wear, improper looseness or end play.	Inspect		✓		✓		✓		✓		✓		✓		✓		✓	
CV Joints	Inspect		✓		✓		✓		✓		✓		✓		✓		✓	
Rear/front axle fluid level	Inspect			✓			✓			✓	✓		✓			✓		
Engine air filter	Replace					✓					✓					✓		
Adjust parking brake on vehicles with four-wheel disc brakes	Adjust					✓					✓					✓		
Engine coolant	Replace																	✓
Spark plugs	Replace																	✓
Spark plugs (5.7L only)	Replace					✓					✓					✓		
PCV valve	Inspect/ Service															✓		
Auto transmisison fluid & filter	Replace																	✓
Accessory drive belt	Inspect	✓	✓	✓	✓	✓	✓	✓	✓	✓	✓	✓	✓	✓	✓	✓	✓	✓
Accessory drive belt	Replace	at 120,000 miles if not previously serviced																
Rear axle fluid	Replace								✓							✓		
Timing belt (3.5L)	Replace																	✓
Transfer case fluid	Replace															✓		
Battery	Inspect/ Service	✓	✓	✓	✓	✓	✓	✓	✓	✓	✓	✓	✓	✓	✓	✓	✓	✓
Fluid levels (all)	Top off	✓	✓	✓	✓	✓	✓	✓	✓	✓	✓	✓	✓	✓	✓	✓	✓	✓
Horn, exterior lamps, turn signals and hazard warning light operation	Inspect	✓	✓	✓	✓	✓	✓	✓	✓	✓	✓	✓	✓	✓	✓	✓	✓	✓

*Oil Change Indicator System

On Electronic Vehicle Information Center (EVIC) equipped vehicles, "Oil Change Required" is displayed in the EVIC and a single chime sounds, indicating that an oil change is necessary. On non-EVIC equipped vehicles, "Change Oil" flashes in the instrument cluster and a single chime sounds indicating that an oil change is necessary. Illumination of the oil change message is based on the operating conditions of the vehicle. When the message is illuminated, the vehicle must be serviced within 500 miles.

The oil change indicator will not monitor the time since the last oil change. Change the oil if it has been more than 6 months since the last oil change, even if the oil change indicator message is not illuminated.

Under no circumstances should oil change intervals exceed 6,000 miles or 6 months, whichever comes first.

To reset the oil change indicator, perform the following procedure:

1. Turn the ignition switch to the ON position. Do not start the engine.

2. Fully press the accelerator pedal 3 times within 10 seconds.

3. Turn the ignition switch to the LOCK position.

If the indicator message illuminates when the vehicle is started, repeat the procedure.

25766_300C_C0014

SCHEDULED MAINTENANCE - SEVERE
2010 Dodge Charger, Chrysler 300

TO BE SERVICED	TYPE OF SERVICE	VEHICLE MILEAGE INTERVAL (x1000)																
		6	12	18	24	30	36	42	48	54	60	66	72	78	84	90	96	102
Engine oil & filter	Replace	✓	✓	✓	✓	✓	✓	✓	✓	✓	✓	✓	✓	✓	✓	✓	✓	✓
Rotate tires, inspect tread wear, measure tread depth, check pressure	Rotate	✓	✓	✓	✓	✓	✓	✓	✓	✓	✓	✓	✓	✓	✓	✓	✓	✓
Air conditioner filter	Replace		✓		✓		✓		✓		✓		✓		✓		✓	
Brake system components	Inspect/Service						✓		✓		✓		✓		✓		✓	
Exhaust system & heat shields	Inspect		✓		✓		✓		✓		✓		✓		✓		✓	
Inspect front suspension, tie rod ends & boot seals for cracks or leaks & all parts for damage, wear, improper looseness or end play.	Inspect		✓		✓		✓		✓		✓		✓		✓		✓	
CV Joints	Inspect		✓		✓		✓		✓		✓		✓		✓		✓	
Front axle fluid	Replace								✓								✓	
Rear/front axle fluid level	Inspect			✓			✓			✓			✓			✓		
Engine air filter	Inspect/Service		✓		✓		✓		✓		✓		✓		✓		✓	
Adjust parking brake on vehicles with four-wheel disc brakes	Adjust					✓					✓					✓		
Engine coolant	Replace										✓							✓
Spark plugs	Replace																	✓
Spark plugs (5.7L only)	Replace					✓					✓					✓		
PCV valve	Inspect/Service															✓		
Auto transmisison fluid & filter	Replace										✓							
Accessory drive belt	Inspect	✓	✓	✓	✓	✓	✓	✓	✓	✓	✓	✓	✓	✓	✓	✓	✓	✓
Accessory drive belt	Replace	at 120,000 miles if not previously serviced																
Rear axle fluid	Replace								✓							✓		
Timing belt (3.5L)	Replace																	✓
Transfer case fluid	Replace										✓							
Battery	Inspect/Service	✓	✓	✓	✓	✓	✓	✓	✓	✓	✓	✓	✓	✓	✓	✓	✓	✓
Fluid levels (all)	Top off	✓	✓	✓	✓	✓	✓	✓	✓	✓	✓	✓	✓	✓	✓	✓	✓	✓
Horn, exterior lamps, turn signals and hazard warning light operation	Inspect	✓	✓	✓	✓	✓	✓	✓	✓	✓	✓	✓	✓	✓	✓	✓	✓	✓

*Oil Change Indicator System

On Electronic Vehicle Information Center (EVIC) equipped vehicles, "Oil Change Required" is displayed in the EVIC and a single chime sounds, indicating that an oil change is necessary. On non-EVIC equipped vehicles, "Change Oil" flashes in the instrument cluster and a single chime sounds indicating that an oil change is necessary. Illumination of the oil change message is based on the operating conditions of the vehicle. When the message is illuminated, the vehicle must be serviced within 500 miles.

The oil change indicator will not monitor the time since the last oil change. Change the oil if it has been more than 6 months since the last oil change, even if the oil change indicator message is not illuminated.

Under no circumstances should oil change intervals exceed 6,000 miles or 6 months, whichever comes first.

To reset the oil change indicator, perform the following procedure:

1. Turn the ignition switch to the ON position. Do not start the engine.

2. Fully press the accelerator pedal 3 times within 10 seconds.

3. Turn the ignition switch to the LOCK position.

If the indicator message illuminates when the vehicle is started, repeat the procedure.

SCHEDULED MAINTENANCE - NORMAL
2011 Dodge Charger, Chrysler 300

TO BE SERVICED	TYPE OF SERVICE	VEHICLE MILEAGE INTERVAL (x1000)																
		8	16	24	32	40	48	56	64	72	80	88	96	104	112	120	128	136
Engine oil & filter	Replace	✓	✓	✓	✓	✓	✓	✓	✓	✓	✓	✓	✓	✓	✓	✓	✓	✓
Rotate tires, inspect tread wear, measure tread depth and check pressure	Rotate		✓		✓		✓		✓		✓		✓		✓		✓	
Brake system components	Inspect/ Service		✓		✓		✓		✓		✓		✓		✓		✓	
Exhaust system & heat shields	Inspect		✓		✓		✓		✓		✓		✓		✓		✓	
Inspect the front suspension, tie rod ends and boot seals for cracks or leaks and all parts for damage, wear, improper looseness or end play.	Inspect		✓		✓		✓		✓		✓		✓		✓		✓	
CV Joints	Inspect	✓	✓	✓	✓	✓	✓	✓	✓	✓	✓	✓	✓	✓	✓	✓	✓	✓
Engine air filter	Replace			✓					✓				✓				✓	
Adjust parking brake on vehicles equipped with four-wheel disc brakes.	Adjust			✓					✓				✓				✓	
Engine coolant	Replace										✓							
Spark plugs (3.6L)	Replace												✓					
Spark plugs (5.7L)	Replace			✓					✓				✓				✓	
PCV valve	Inspect/ Service												✓					
Auto transmission fluid & filter	Replace															✓		
Accessory drive belt	Inspect	✓	✓	✓	✓	✓	✓	✓	✓	✓	✓	✓	✓	✓	✓	✓	✓	✓
Accessory drive belt	Replace	at 120,000 miles if not previously serviced																
Horn, exterior lamps, turn signals and hazard warning light operation	Inspect	✓	✓	✓	✓	✓	✓	✓	✓	✓	✓	✓	✓	✓	✓	✓	✓	✓
Fluid levels (all)	Top off	✓	✓	✓	✓	✓	✓	✓	✓	✓	✓	✓	✓	✓	✓	✓	✓	✓
Air conditioner filter	Replace		✓		✓		✓		✓		✓		✓		✓		✓	
Front & rear axle fluid	Inspect/ Add			✓			✓			✓			✓			✓		
Transfer case fluid	Inspect/ Add				✓				✓				✓				✓	

*Oil Change Indicator System

On Electronic Vehicle Information Center (EVIC) equipped vehicles, "Oil Change Required" is displayed in the EVIC and a single chime sounds, indicating that an oil change is necessary. On non-EVIC equipped vehicles, "Change Oil" flashes in the instrument cluster and a single chime sounds indicating that an oil change is necessary. Illumination of the oil change message is based on the operating conditions of the vehicle. When the message is illuminated, the vehicle must be serviced within 500 miles.

The oil change indicator will not monitor the time since the last oil change. Change the oil if it has been more than 6 months since the last oil change, even if the oil change indicator message is not illuminated.

Under no circumstances should oil change intervals exceed 6,000 miles or 6 months, whichever comes first.

To reset the oil change indicator, perform the following procedure:

1. Turn the ignition switch to the ON position. Do not start the engine.

2. Fully press the accelerator pedal 3 times within 10 seconds.

3. Turn the ignition switch to the LOCK position.

If the indicator message illuminates when the vehicle is started, repeat the procedure.

25766_300C_C0016

SCHEDULED MAINTENANCE - SEVERE
2011 Dodge Charger, Chrysler 300

TO BE SERVICED	TYPE OF SERVICE	VEHICLE MILEAGE INTERVAL (x1000)																
		8	16	24	32	40	48	56	64	72	80	88	96	104	112	120	128	136
Engine oil & filter	Replace	✔	✔	✔	✔	✔	✔	✔	✔	✔	✔	✔	✔	✔	✔	✔	✔	✔
Rotate tires, inspect tread wear, measure tread depth and check pressure	Rotate	✔	✔	✔	✔	✔	✔	✔	✔	✔	✔	✔	✔	✔	✔	✔	✔	✔
Brake system components	Inspect/Service		✔		✔		✔		✔		✔		✔		✔		✔	
Exhaust system & heat shields	Inspect		✔		✔		✔		✔		✔		✔		✔		✔	
Inspect front suspension, tie rod ends & boot seals for cracks or leaks & all parts for damage, wear, improper looseness or end play.	Inspect		✔		✔		✔		✔		✔		✔		✔		✔	
CV Joints	Inspect			✔			✔			✔			✔			✔		
Engine air filter	Inspect/Service		✔		✔		✔		✔		✔		✔		✔		✔	
Engine coolant	Replace									✔								
Spark plugs (3.6L)	Replace												✔					
Spark plugs (5.7L)	Replace				✔				✔				✔				✔	
PCV valve	Inspect/Service												✔					
Auto transmision fluid & filter	Replace								✔								✔	
Accessory drive belt	Inspect	✔	✔	✔	✔	✔	✔	✔	✔	✔	✔	✔	✔	✔	✔	✔	✔	✔
Accessory drive belt	Replace	at 120,000 miles if not previously serviced																
Battery	Inspect/Service	✔	✔	✔	✔	✔	✔	✔	✔	✔	✔	✔	✔	✔	✔	✔	✔	✔
Fluid levels (all)	Top off	✔	✔	✔	✔	✔	✔	✔	✔	✔	✔	✔	✔	✔	✔	✔	✔	✔
Horn, exterior lamps, turn signals and hazard warning light operation	Inspect	✔	✔	✔	✔	✔	✔	✔	✔	✔	✔	✔	✔	✔	✔	✔	✔	✔
Pass. compartment air filter	Replace		✔		✔		✔		✔		✔		✔		✔		✔	
Rear axle fluid	Inspect/Add		✔		✔		✔		✔		✔		✔		✔		✔	
Transfer case fluid	Replace															✔		
Front & rear axle fluid	Inspect/Add		✔		✔		✔		✔		✔		✔		✔		✔	

*Oil Change Indicator System

On Electronic Vehicle Information Center (EVIC) equipped vehicles, "Oil Change Required" is displayed in the EVIC and a single chime sounds, indicating that an oil change is necessary. On non-EVIC equipped vehicles, "Change Oil" flashes in the instrument cluster and a single chime sounds indicating that an oil change is necessary. Illumination of the oil change message is based on the operating conditions of the vehicle. When the message is illuminated, the vehicle must be serviced within 500 miles.

The oil change indicator will not monitor the time since the last oil change. Change the oil if it has been more than 6 months since the last oil change, even if the oil change indicator message is not illuminated.

Under no circumstances should oil change intervals exceed 6,000 miles or 6 months, whichever comes first.

To reset the oil change indicator, perform the following procedure:

1. Turn the ignition switch to the ON position. Do not start the engine.
2. Fully press the accelerator pedal 3 times within 10 seconds.
3. Turn the ignition switch to the LOCK position.

If the indicator message illuminates when the vehicle is started, repeat the procedure.

25766_300C_C0017

PRECAUTIONS

Before servicing any vehicle, please be sure to read all of the following precautions, which deal with personal safety, prevention of component damage, and important points to take into consideration when servicing a motor vehicle:

• Never open, service or drain the radiator or cooling system when the engine is hot; serious burns can occur from the steam and hot coolant.

• Observe all applicable safety precautions when working around fuel. Whenever servicing the fuel system, always work in a well-ventilated area. Do not allow fuel spray or vapors to come in contact with a spark, open flame, or excessive heat (a hot drop light, for example). Keep a dry chemical fire extinguisher near the work area. Always keep fuel in a container specifically designed for fuel storage; also, always properly seal fuel containers to avoid the possibility of fire or explosion. Refer to the additional fuel system precautions later in this section.

• Fuel injection systems often remain pressurized, even after the engine has been turned **OFF**. The fuel system pressure must be relieved before disconnecting any fuel lines. Failure to do so may result in fire and/or personal injury.

• Brake fluid often contains polyglycol ethers and polyglycols. Avoid contact with the eyes and wash your hands thoroughly after handling brake fluid. If you do get brake fluid in your eyes, flush your eyes with clean, running water for 15 minutes. If eye irritation persists, or if you have taken brake fluid internally, IMMEDIATELY seek medical assistance.

• The EPA warns that prolonged contact with used engine oil may cause a number of skin disorders, including cancer. You should make every effort to minimize your exposure to used engine oil. Protective gloves should be worn when changing oil. Wash your hands and any other exposed skin areas as soon as possible after exposure to used engine oil. Soap and water, or waterless hand cleaner should be used.

• All new vehicles are now equipped with an air bag system, often referred to as a Supplemental Restraint System (SRS) or Supplemental Inflatable Restraint (SIR) system. The system must be disabled before performing service on or around system components, steering column, instrument panel components, wiring and sensors. Failure to follow safety and disabling procedures could result in accidental air bag deployment, possible personal injury and unnecessary system repairs.

• Always wear safety goggles when working with, or around, the air bag system. When carrying a non-deployed air bag, be sure the bag and trim cover are pointed away from your body. When placing a non-deployed air bag on a work surface, always face the bag and trim cover upward, away from the surface. This will reduce the motion of the module if it is accidentally deployed. Refer to the additional air bag system precautions later in this section.

• Clean, high quality brake fluid from a sealed container is essential to the safe and proper operation of the brake system. You should always buy the correct type of brake fluid for your vehicle. If the brake fluid becomes contaminated, completely flush the system with new fluid. Never reuse any brake fluid. Any brake fluid that is removed from the system should be discarded. Also, do not allow any brake fluid to come in contact with a painted surface; it will damage the paint.

• Never operate the engine without the proper amount and type of engine oil; doing so WILL result in severe engine damage.

• Timing belt maintenance is extremely important. Many models utilize an interference-type, non-freewheeling engine. If the timing belt breaks, the valves in the cylinder head may strike the pistons, causing potentially serious (also time-consuming and expensive) engine damage. Refer to the maintenance interval charts for the recommended replacement interval for the timing belt, and to the timing belt section for belt replacement and inspection.

• Disconnecting the negative battery cable on some vehicles may interfere with the functions of the on-board computer system(s) and may require the computer to undergo a relearning process once the negative battery cable is reconnected.

• When servicing drum brakes, only disassemble and assemble one side at a time, leaving the remaining side intact for reference.

• Only an MVAC-trained, EPA-certified automotive technician should service the air conditioning system or its components.

BRAKES

GENERAL INFORMATION

PRECAUTIONS

• Certain components within the ABS system are not intended to be serviced or repaired individually.

• Do not use rubber hoses or other parts not specifically specified for and ABS system. When using repair kits, replace all parts included in the kit. Partial or incorrect repair may lead to functional problems and require the replacement of components.

• Lubricate rubber parts with clean, fresh brake fluid to ease assembly. Do not use shop air to clean parts; damage to rubber components may result.

• Use only DOT 3 brake fluid from an unopened container.

• If any hydraulic component or line is removed or replaced, it may be necessary to bleed the entire system.

• A clean repair area is essential. Always clean the reservoir and cap thoroughly before removing the cap. The slightest amount of dirt in the fluid may plug an orifice and impair the system function. Perform repairs after components have been thoroughly cleaned; use only denatured alcohol to clean components. Do not allow ABS components to come into contact with any substance containing mineral oil; this includes used shop rags.

• The Anti-Lock control unit is a microprocessor similar to other computer units in the vehicle. Ensure that the ignition switch is **OFF** before removing or installing controller harnesses. Avoid static electricity discharge at or near the controller.

ANTI-LOCK BRAKE SYSTEM (ABS)

• If any arc welding is to be done on the vehicle, the control unit should be unplugged before welding operations begin.

SPEED SENSORS

REMOVAL & INSTALLATION

Front

AWD Models

See Figures 1 through 3.

1. Raise and support vehicle.
2. Remove the sensor cable routing clip from brake hose bracket.

➡**To release sensor connector from body wiring harness connector in following step, move retaining clip as**

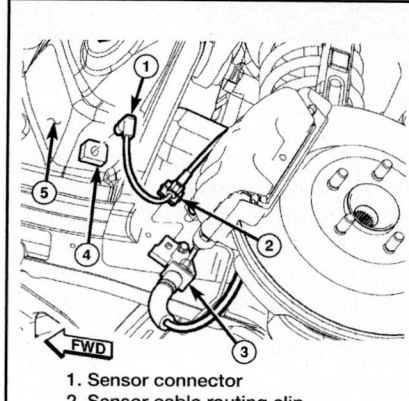

1. Sensor connector
2. Sensor cable routing clip
3. Brake hose bracket
4. Body wiring harness connector

1395

Fig. 1 Disconnecting the front wheel speed sensor

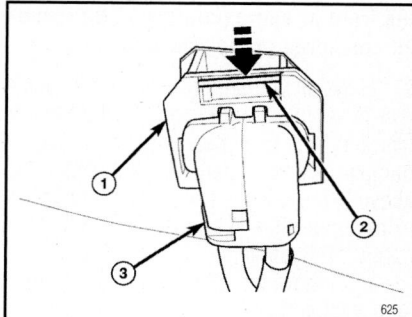

625

Fig. 2 Releasing the retaining clip (2) sensor connector (3) from the body wiring harness connector (1)

indicated here, then pull sensor connector outward.

3. Remove the sensor connector from body wiring harness connector.

4. Remove screw fastening wheel speed sensor to knuckle. Pull sensor head out of knuckle.

5. Remove the wheel speed sensor cable routing clip from knuckle.

6. Remove wheel speed sensor.

To install:

7. Install wheel speed sensor head into knuckle and install mounting screw. Tighten screw to 8 ft. lbs. (11 Nm).

8. Attach wheel speed sensor cable and routing clip to knuckle.

9. Attach sensor cable routing clip to brake hose bracket.

10. Connect the sensor connector to body wiring harness connector. When installing connector, make sure retaining clip on body connector is properly in place and sensor connect cannot be pulled out.

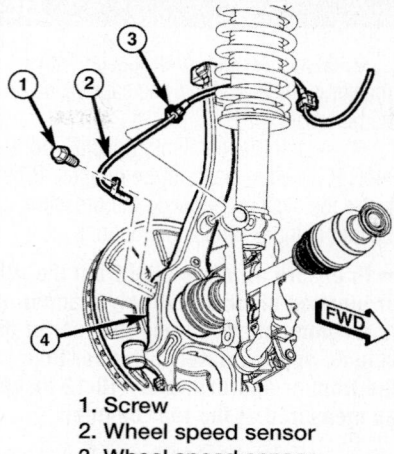

1. Screw
2. Wheel speed sensor
3. Wheel speed sensor cable routing clip
4. Knuckle

227

Fig. 3 Removing and installing the front (AWD) wheel speed sensor

11. Lower the vehicle.
12. Perform a verification test and clear any faults.

RWD Models

See Figures 4 through 6.

1. Raise and support the vehicle.
2. Remove the sensor cable routing clip from brake hose bracket.

➡**To release sensor connector from body wiring harness connector in following step, move retaining clip as indicated here, then pull sensor connector outward.**

3. Remove the sensor connector from body wiring harness connector.

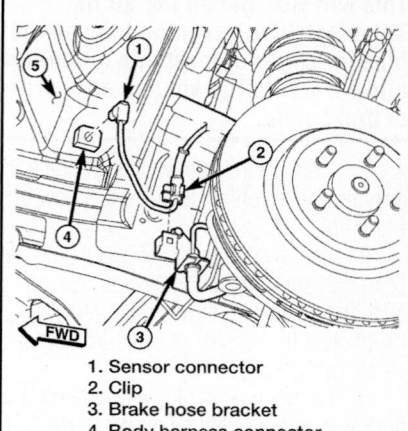

1. Sensor connector
2. Clip
3. Brake hose bracket
4. Body harness connector
5. –

357

Fig. 4 Removing the sensor cable and connector

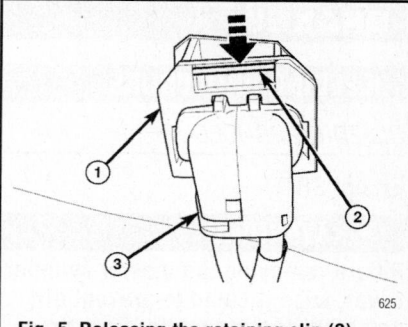

625

Fig. 5 Releasing the retaining clip (2) sensor connector (3) from the body wiring harness connector (1)

4. Remove the screw fastening wheel speed sensor to knuckle. Pull sensor head out of knuckle.

5. Remove the wheel speed sensor cable routing clip from brake hose routing bracket.

To install:

6. Install wheel speed sensor head into knuckle and install mounting screw. Tighten screw to 8 ft. lbs. (11 Nm).

7. Attach wheel speed sensor cable and routing clip to brake hose routing bracket.

8. Attach the sensor cable routing clip to brake hose bracket.

9. Connect the sensor connector to body wiring harness connector. When installing connector, make sure retaining clip on body connector is properly in place and sensor connect cannot be pulled out.

10. Lower vehicle.

11. Perform a verification test and clear any faults

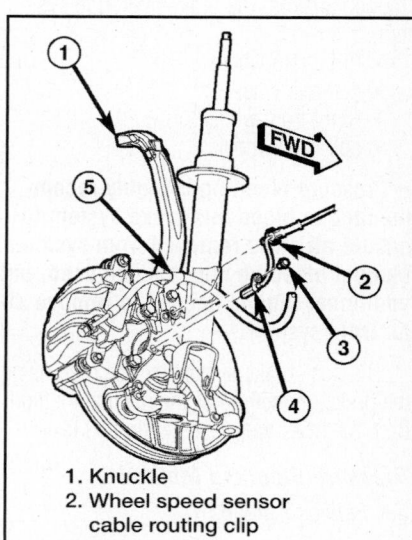

1. Knuckle
2. Wheel speed sensor cable routing clip
3. Screw
4. Sensor head
5. Brake hose routing bracket

251

Fig. 6 Removing and installing the wheel speed sensor (RWD)

BRAKES   **BLEEDING THE BRAKE SYSTEM**

BLEEDING PROCEDURE

BLEEDING PROCEDURE

Except SRT8

> ✳✳ **WARNING**
>
> **Before removing the master cylinder cover, wipe it clean to prevent dirt and other foreign matter from dropping into the master cylinder.**

> ✳✳ **WARNING**
>
> **Use only Mopar® brake fluid or an equivalent from a fresh, tightly sealed container. Brake fluid must conform to DOT 3 specifications.**

➡ **Do not pump the brake pedal at any time while having a bleeder screw open during the bleeding process. This will only increase the amount of air in the system and make additional bleeding necessary.**

➡ **Do not allow the master cylinder reservoir to run out of brake fluid while bleeding the system. An empty reservoir will allow additional air into the brake system. Check the fluid level frequently and add fluid as needed.**

The following wheel circuit sequence for bleeding the brake hydraulic system should be used to ensure adequate removal of all trapped air from the brake hydraulic system.

- Right rear wheel
- Left rear wheel
- Right front wheel
- Left front wheel

➡ **Pressure bleeding is highly recommended to bleed this brake system to ensure all air is removed from system. Manual bleeding may also be used, but additional time is needed to remove all air from system.**

The base brake system can be bled using the pressure method or the manual method. Both methods are presented in this text.

Pressure Bleeding Method

See Figures 7 and 8.

➡ **Follow the pressure bleeder manufacturer's instructions for use of pressure bleeding equipment.**

1. Remove filler cap from the top of fluid reservoir on master cylinder.

2. Install Adapter and Special Tool (master cylinder cap), in the caps place on the reservoir.

3. Attach Bleeder Tank, Special Tool C-3496-B, or equivalent, to the Adapter. Pressurize the system following the pressure bleeder manufacturer's instructions.

➡ **To ensure all air is bled from the ICU or junction block in a timely manner, it is recommended to raise the rear of the vehicle approximately 5°higher than the front or approximately 10-12 inches as measured at the rear bumper.**

4. Raise and support vehicle placing rear of vehicle approximately 5°higher than the front or if measured at the rear bumper, approximately 10-12 inches above level. It will be necessary to add extra support stands under vehicle to support this angle.

5. If installed, remove rubber dust caps from all four bleeder screws on calipers.

6. Starting at the first wheel circuit as listed earlier, attach a clear hose to the bleeder screw at that wheels brake caliper and feed the other end of hose into a clear jar containing enough fresh brake fluid to submerge the end of the hose.

> ✳✳ **WARNING**
>
> **Open the bleeder screw at least one full turn when instructed. Some air may be trapped in the brake lines or valves far upstream, as far as ten feet or more from the bleeder screw. If the bleeder screw is not opened sufficiently, fluid flow is restricted causing a slow, weak fluid discharge. This will NOT get all the air out. Therefore, it is essential to open the bleeder screw at least one full turn to allow a fast, large volume discharge of brake fluid.**

7. Open bleeder screw at least one full turn or more to obtain an adequate flow of brake fluid.

8. After 4 to 8 ounces of brake fluid has been bled through the brake hydraulic circuit, and an air-free flow (no bubbles) is maintained in the clear plastic hose and jar, close the bleeder screw.

9. Bleed the remaining wheel circuits in the same manner until all air is removed from the brake hydraulic system.

10. Check brake pedal travel. If pedal travel is excessive or has not improved, some air may still be trapped in the

hydraulic system. Re-bleed the brake system as necessary.

11. If equipped with antilock brakes, the hydraulic control unit may need to be bled, then re-bleed base brakes.

12. Reinstall all 4 bleeder screw dust caps.

13. Test drive vehicle to ensure brakes are operating properly and pedal feel is correct.

Manual Bleeding Method

See Figure 8.

➡ **To bleed the base brake system manually, an assistants help is required.**

➡ **To ensure all air is bled from the ICU or junction block in a timely manner, it is recommended to raise the rear of the vehicle approximately 5°higher than the front or approximately 10-12 inches as measured at the rear bumper.**

1. Raise and support vehicle placing rear of vehicle approximately 5°higher than the front or if measured at the rear bumper, approximately 10-12 inches above level. It will be necessary to add extra support stands under vehicle to support this angle.

2. Remove the rubber duct caps from all 4 bleeder screws.

3. Attach a clear hose to the bleeder screw at one wheel and feed the other end of the hose into a clear jar containing fresh brake fluid.

4. Have an assistant pump the brake pedal three or four times and hold it down before the bleeder screw is opened.

> ✳✳ **WARNING**
>
> **Open the bleeder screw at least one full turn when instructed. Some air may be trapped in the brake lines or valves far upstream, as far as ten feet or more from the bleeder screw. If the bleeder screw is not opened sufficiently, fluid flow is restricted causing a slow, weak fluid discharge. This will NOT get all the air out. Therefore, it is essential to open the bleeder screw at least one full turn to allow a fast, large volume discharge of brake fluid.**

5. While the pedal is being held down, open the bleeder screw at least 1 full turn. When the bleeder screw opens the brake pedal will drop all the way to the floor. Continue to hold the pedal all the way down.

6. Once the brake pedal has dropped, close the bleeder screw. The pedal can then be released.

7. Repeat steps 1-5 until all trapped air is removed from that wheel circuit (usually four or five times). This should pass a sufficient amount of fluid to expel all the trapped air from the brakes hydraulic system. Be sure to monitor brake fluid level in master cylinder fluid reservoir making sure it stays at a proper level. This will ensure air does not reenter brake hydraulic system through master cylinder.

➡️**Monitor the brake fluid level in the fluid reservoir periodically to make sure it does not go too low. This will ensure that air does not reenter the brake hydraulic system.**

8. Bleed the remaining wheel circuits in the same manner until all air is removed from the brake hydraulic system.

9. Check brake pedal travel. If pedal travel is excessive or has not improved, some air may still be trapped in the hydraulic system. Re-bleed the brake system as necessary.

10. If equipped with antilock brakes, the hydraulic control unit may need to be bled, then re-bleed base brakes.

11. Reinstall all 4 bleeder screw dust caps.

12. Test drive vehicle to ensure brakes are operating properly and pedal feel is correct.

SRT8

Use the following procedure to bleed the rear brake calipers of this vehicle. The front brake calipers may be bled using the same procedure as the standard model.

✳✳ WARNING

Before removing the master cylinder cover, wipe it clean to prevent dirt and other foreign matter from dropping into the master cylinder.

✳✳ WARNING

Use only Mopar® brake fluid or an equivalent from a fresh, tightly sealed container. Brake fluid must conform to DOT 3 specifications.

➡️**Do not pump the brake pedal at any time while having a bleeder screw open during the bleeding process. This will only increase the amount of air in the system and make additional bleeding necessary.**

➡️**Do not allow the master cylinder reservoir to run out of brake fluid while bleeding the system. An empty reservoir will allow additional air into the brake system. Check the fluid level frequently and add fluid as needed.**

➡️**Pressure bleeding is highly recommended to bleed this brake system to ensure all air is removed from system. Manual bleeding may also be used, but additional time is needed to remove all air from system.**

Although it is recommended that the base brake system be bled using the pressure method, the manual method can also be performed. Both methods are presented in this text.

Pressure Bleeding Method

➡️**Follow the pressure bleeder manufacturer's instructions for use of pressure bleeding equipment.**

1. Remove filler cap from the top of fluid reservoir on master cylinder.
2. Install the Adapter in the caps place on the reservoir.
3. Attach the Bleeder Tank Special Tool or equivalent, to the Adapter. Pressurize the system following the pressure bleeder manufacturer's instructions.

➡️**To ensure all air is bled from the ICU or junction block in a timely manner, it is recommended to raise the rear of the vehicle approximately 5° higher than the front or approximately 10-12 inches as measured at the rear bumper.**

4. Raise and support vehicle placing rear of vehicle approximately 5° higher than the front or if measured at the rear bumper, approximately 10-12 inches above level. It will be necessary to add extra support stands under vehicle to support this angle.

➡️**The following wheel circuit sequence for bleeding the brake hydraulic system should be used to ensure adequate removal of all trapped air from the brake hydraulic system.**

- Right rear wheel
- Left rear wheel
- Right front wheel
- Left front wheel

Rear Brakes
See Figures 7 and 8.

5. If installed, remove rubber dust caps from both bleeder screws on each caliper.

6. Starting at the first wheel circuit that needs to be bled, attach a clear hose to the inboard bleeder screw at that wheels brake caliper and feed the other end of hose into a clear jar containing enough fresh brake fluid to submerge the end of the hose.

✳✳ WARNING

Open the bleeder screw at least one full turn when instructed. Some air may be trapped in the brake lines or valves far upstream, as far as ten feet or more from the bleeder screw. If the bleeder screw is not opened sufficiently, fluid flow is restricted causing a slow, weak fluid discharge. This will NOT get all the air out. Therefore, it is essential to open the bleeder screw at least one full turn to allow a fast, large volume discharge of brake fluid.

7. Open inboard bleeder screw at least one full turn or more to obtain an adequate flow of brake fluid.

8. After 4 to 8 ounces of brake fluid has been bled through the brake hydraulic circuit, and an air-free flow (no bubbles) is maintained in the clear plastic hose and jar, close the bleeder screw.

9. Remove clear hose and install bleeder screw dust cap.

10. Attach a clear hose to the outboard bleeder screw at that same wheels brake caliper and feed the other end of hose into a clear jar containing enough fresh brake fluid to submerge the end of the hose.

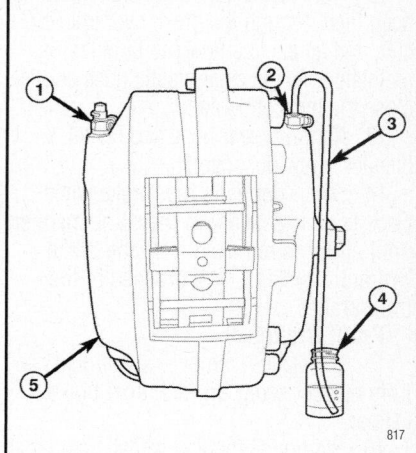

Fig. 7 Attaching hose (3) to the inboard bleeder screw (2) at the brake caliper. Feed the other end into a clear jar (4) with enough fluid to submerge the hose

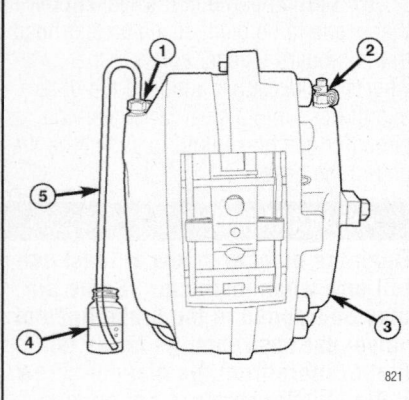

Fig. 8 Attaching hose (5) to the outboard bleeder screw (1) and feed the other end of the hose into a clear jar (4) with enough fluid to submerge the hose

✴✴ WARNING

Open the bleeder screw at least one full turn when instructed. Some air may be trapped in the brake lines or valves far upstream, as far as ten feet or more from the bleeder screw. If the bleeder screw is not opened sufficiently, fluid flow is restricted causing a slow, weak fluid discharge. This will NOT get all the air out. Therefore, it is essential to open the bleeder screw at least one full turn to allow a fast, large volume discharge of brake fluid.

11. Open outboard bleeder screw at least one full turn or more to obtain an adequate flow of brake fluid.

12. After 4 to 8 ounces of brake fluid has been bled through the brake hydraulic circuit, and an air-free flow (no bubbles) is maintained in the clear plastic hose and jar, close the bleeder screw.

13. Remove clear hose and install bleeder screw dust cap.

14. Bleed opposite rear brake wheel circuits as necessary in the same manner until all air is removed from the brake hydraulic system, then proceed to the front brakes.

Front Brakes

15. If installed, remove rubber dust cap from bleeder screw on each front brake caliper.

16. Starting at the first wheel circuit that needs to be bled, attach a clear hose to the bleeder screw at that wheels brake caliper and feed the other end of hose into a clear jar containing enough fresh brake fluid to submerge the end of the hose.

✴✴ WARNING

Open the bleeder screw at least one full turn when instructed. Some air may be trapped in the brake lines or valves far upstream, as far as ten feet or more from the bleeder screw. If the bleeder screw is not opened sufficiently, fluid flow is restricted causing a slow, weak fluid discharge. This will NOT get all the air out. Therefore, it is essential to open the bleeder screw at least one full turn to allow a fast, large volume discharge of brake fluid.

17. Open bleeder screw at least one full turn or more to obtain an adequate flow of brake fluid.

18. After 4 to 8 ounces of brake fluid has been bled through the brake hydraulic circuit, and an air-free flow (no bubbles) is maintained in the clear plastic hose and jar, close the bleeder screw.

19. Install bleeder screw dust cap.

20. Bleed opposite front brake wheel circuit as necessary in the same manner until all air is removed from the brake hydraulic system.

21. If equipped with antilock brakes, the hydraulic control unit may need to be bled, then re-bleed base brakes.

22. Once all brakes are bled, check brake pedal travel. If pedal travel is excessive or has not improved, some air may still be trapped in the hydraulic system. Re-bleed the brake system as necessary.

23. Test drive vehicle to ensure brakes are operating properly and pedal feel is correct.

Manual Bleeding Method

➡To bleed the base brake system manually, an assistants help is required.

➡To ensure all air is bled from the ICU or junction block in a timely manner, it is recommended to raise the rear of the vehicle approximately 5° higher than the front or approximately 10-12 inches as measured at the rear bumper.

1. Raise and support vehicle placing rear of vehicle approximately 5° higher than the front or if measured at the rear bumper, approximately 10-12 inches above level. It will be necessary to add extra support stands under vehicle to support this angle.

➡The following wheel circuit sequence for bleeding the brake hydraulic system should be used to ensure adequate removal of all trapped air from the brake hydraulic system.

- Right rear wheel
- Left rear wheel
- Right front wheel
- Left front wheel

Rear Brakes

See Figure 8.

2. If installed, remove rubber dust caps from both bleeder screws on each caliper.

3. Starting at the first wheel circuit that needs to be bled, attach a clear hose to the inboard bleeder screw at that wheels brake caliper and feed the other end of hose into a clear jar containing enough fresh brake fluid to submerge the end of the hose.

4. Have an assistant pump the brake pedal three or four times, then hold it down before the bleeder screw is opened.

✴✴ WARNING

Open the bleeder screw at least one full turn when instructed. Some air may be trapped in the brake lines or valves far upstream, as far as ten feet or more from the bleeder screw. If the bleeder screw is not opened sufficiently, fluid flow is restricted causing a slow, weak fluid discharge. This will NOT get all the air out. Therefore, it is essential to open the bleeder screw at least one full turn to allow a fast, large volume discharge of brake fluid.

5. While the pedal is being held down, open the inboard bleeder screw at least one full turn. When the bleeder screw opens the brake pedal will drop all the way to the floor. Continue to hold the pedal all the way down.

6. Once the brake pedal has dropped, close the bleeder screw. The pedal can then be released.

7. Repeat the above three steps until all trapped air is removed from that wheel circuit (usually four or five times). This should pass a sufficient amount of fluid to expel all the trapped air from the brakes hydraulic system. Be sure to monitor brake fluid level in master cylinder fluid reservoir making sure it stays at a proper level. This will ensure air does not reenter brake hydraulic system through master cylinder.

➡Monitor the brake fluid level in the fluid reservoir periodically to make sure it does not go too low. This will ensure that air does not reenter the brake hydraulic system.

8. Remove clear hose and install bleeder screw dust cap.

9. Attach a clear hose to the outboard bleeder screw at that same wheels brake caliper and feed the other end of hose into a clear jar containing enough fresh brake fluid to submerge the end of the hose.

10. Have an assistant pump the brake pedal three or four times, then hold it down before the bleeder screw is opened.

Open the bleeder screw at least one full turn when instructed. Some air may be trapped in the brake lines or valves far upstream, as far as ten feet or more from the bleeder screw. If the bleeder screw is not opened sufficiently, fluid flow is restricted causing a slow, weak fluid discharge. This will NOT get all the air out. Therefore, it is essential to open the bleeder screw at least one full turn to allow a fast, large volume discharge of brake fluid.

11. While the pedal is being held down, open the outboard bleeder screw at least one full turn. When the bleeder screw opens the brake pedal will drop all the way to the floor. Continue to hold the pedal all the way down.

12. Once the brake pedal has dropped, close the bleeder screw. The pedal can then be released.

13. Repeat the above three steps until all trapped air is removed from that wheel circuit (usually four or five times). This should pass a sufficient amount of fluid to expel all the trapped air from the brakes hydraulic system. Be sure to monitor brake fluid level in master cylinder fluid reservoir making sure it stays at a proper level. This will ensure air does not reenter brake hydraulic system through master cylinder.

➡Monitor the brake fluid level in the fluid reservoir periodically to make sure it does not go too low. This will ensure that air does not reenter the brake hydraulic system.

14. Remove clear hose and install bleeder screw dust cap.

15. Bleed opposite rear brake wheel circuits as necessary in the same manner until all air is removed from the brake hydraulic system, then proceed to the front brakes.

Front Brakes

16. If installed, remove rubber dust cap from bleeder screw on each front brake caliper.

17. Starting at the first wheel circuit that needs to be bled, attach a clear hose to the bleeder screw at one wheel and feed the other end of the hose into a clear jar containing fresh brake fluid.

18. Have an assistant pump the brake pedal three or four times and hold it down before the bleeder screw is opened.

✳✳ **WARNING**

Open the bleeder screw at least one full turn when instructed. Some air may be trapped in the brake lines or valves far upstream, as far as ten feet or more from the bleeder screw. If the bleeder screw is not opened sufficiently, fluid flow is restricted causing a slow, weak fluid discharge. This will NOT get all the air out. Therefore, it is essential to open the bleeder screw at least one full turn to allow a fast, large volume discharge of brake fluid.

19. While the pedal is being held down, open the bleeder screw at least one full turn. When the bleeder screw opens the brake pedal will drop all the way to the floor. Continue to hold the pedal all the way down.

20. Once the brake pedal has dropped, close the bleeder screw. The pedal can then be released.

21. Repeat steps 1-5 until all trapped air is removed from that wheel circuit (usually four or five times). This should pass a sufficient amount of fluid to expel all the trapped air from the brakes hydraulic system. Be sure to monitor brake fluid level in master cylinder fluid reservoir making sure it stays at a proper level. This will ensure air does not reenter brake hydraulic system through master cylinder.

➡Monitor the brake fluid level in the fluid reservoir periodically to make sure it does not go too low. This will ensure that air does not reenter the brake hydraulic system.

22. Install bleeder screw dust cap.

23. Bleed opposite front brake wheel circuit as necessary in the same manner until all air is removed from the brake hydraulic system.

24. If equipped with antilock brakes, the hydraulic control unit may need to be bled, then re-bleed base brakes.

25. Once all brakes are bled, check brake pedal travel. If pedal travel is excessive or has not improved, some air may still be trapped in the hydraulic system. Re-bleed the brake system as necessary.

26. Test drive vehicle to ensure brakes are operating properly and pedal feel is correct.

MASTER CYLINDER BLEEDING
See Figure 9.

✳✳ **WARNING**

When clamping master cylinder in vise, only clamp master cylinder by its mounting flange. Do not clamp master cylinder piston rod, reservoir, seal or body.

1. Clamp master cylinder in a vise.

✳✳ **WARNING**

When installing Adapters in master cylinder, do not overtighten. Damage to master cylinder could occur.

➡Bleeder Adapters are not interchangeable. To avoid mix-up, Bleeder Adapter 9748-1 is silver while Bleeder Adapter 9748-2 is black.

2. Attach special tools for bleeding master cylinder in following fashion: a.a. Thread Adapter, Special Tool 9748-2, into primary outlet port. Tighten Adapter to 10 ft. lbs. (14 Nm).

a. Thread Adapter (4), Special Tool 9748-1, into secondary outlet port. Tighten Adapter to 10 ft. lbs. (14 Nm).

b. Thread a Bleeder Tube, Special Tool 8358-1, into each Adapter. Tighten each tube to 10 ft. lbs. (14 Nm). Flex each bleeder tube and place open end into mouth of fluid reservoir as far down as possible.

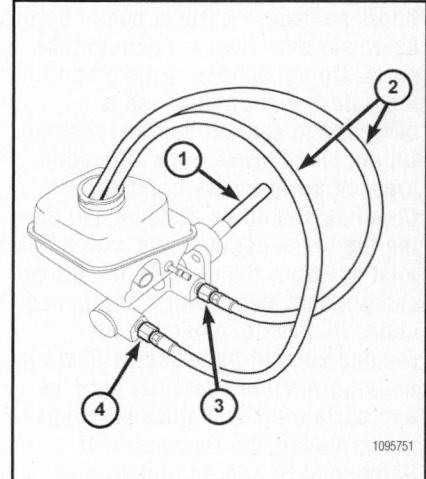

Fig. 9 Bleeding the master cylinder—bleeder tube (1), thread adapters (3 & 4)

➡**Make sure open ends of bleeder tubes stay below surface of brake fluid once reservoir is filled to proper level.**

3. Fill brake fluid reservoir to the MAX level with Mopar® brake fluid or equivalent conforming to DOT 3 specifications. Make sure fluid level is above tips of bleeder tubes in reservoir to ensure no air is ingested during bleeding.

4. Using a wooden dowel as a pushrod, slowly depress master cylinder pistons, then release pressure, allowing pistons to return to released position. Repeat several times until all air bubbles are expelled. Make sure fluid level stays above tips of bleeder tubes in reservoir while bleeding.

5. Remove bleeder tubes and adapters from master cylinder outlet ports, then plug outlet ports and install fill cap on reservoir.

6. Remove master cylinder from vise.

7. Install master cylinder on vehicle.

BLEEDING THE ABS SYSTEM

1. Before servicing the vehicle, refer to the Precautions Section.

The base brake's hydraulic system must be bled anytime air enters the hydraulic system. The ABS must always be bled anytime it is suspected that the HCU has ingested air.

Brake systems with ABS must be bled as two independent braking systems. The non-ABS portion of the brake system with ABS is to be bled the same as any non-ABS system.

The ABS portion of the brake system must be bled separately. Use the following procedure to properly bleed the brake hydraulic system including the ABS.

➡**During the brake bleeding procedure, be sure the brake fluid level remains close to the FULL level in the master cylinder fluid reservoir. Check the fluid level periodically during the bleeding procedure and add Mopar® DOT 3 brake fluid as required.**

✳✳ WARNING

When bleeding the brake system wear safety glasses. A clear bleed tube must be attached to the bleeder screws and submerged in a clear container filled part way with clean brake fluid. Direct the flow of brake fluid away from yourself and the painted surfaces of the vehicle. Brake fluid at high pressure may come out of the bleeder screws when opened.

When bleeding the ABS system, the following bleeding sequence must be followed to insure complete and adequate bleeding.

➡**Pressure bleeding is recommended to bleed the base brake system to ensure all air is removed from system. Manual bleeding may also be used, but additional time is needed to remove all air from system.**

2. .Make sure all hydraulic fluid lines are installed and properly torqued.

3. Connect the scan tool to the diagnostics connector. The diagnostic connector is located under the lower steering column cover to the left of the steering column.

4. Using the scan tool, check to make sure the ABM does not have any fault codes stored. If it does, clear them.

5. Bleed the base brake system.

6. Using the scan tool, select ECU VIEW, followed by ABS MISCELLANEOUS FUNCTIONS to access bleeding. Follow the instructions displayed. When finished, disconnect the scan tool and proceed.

7. Bleed the base brake system a second time. Check brake fluid level in the reservoir periodically to prevent emptying, causing air to enter the hydraulic system.

8. Fill the master cylinder fluid reservoir to the MAX level.

9. Test drive the vehicle to be sure the brakes are operating correctly and that the brake pedal does not feel spongy.

BRAKES
FRONT DISC BRAKES

✳✳ WARNING

Dust and dirt accumulating on brake parts during normal use may contain asbestos fibers from production or aftermarket brake linings. Breathing excessive concentrations of asbestos fibers can cause serious bodily harm. Exercise care when servicing brake parts. Do not sand or grind brake lining unless equipment used is designed to contain the dust residue. Do not clean brake parts with compressed air or by dry brushing. Cleaning should be done by dampening the brake components with a fine mist of water, then wiping the brake components clean with a dampened cloth. Dispose of cloth and all residue containing asbestos fibers in an impermeable container with the appropriate label. Follow practices prescribed by the Occupational Safety and Health Administration (OSHA) and the Environmental Protection Agency (EPA) for the handling, processing, and disposing of

dust or debris that may contain asbestos fibers.

BRAKE CALIPER

REMOVAL & INSTALLATION

Dual Piston

AWD Models
See Figures 10 and 11.

✳✳ CAUTION

Dust and dirt accumulating on brake parts during normal use may contain asbestos fibers from production or aftermarket brake linings. Breathing excessive concentrations of asbestos fibers can cause serious bodily harm. Exercise care when servicing brake parts. Do not sand or grind brake lining unless equipment used is designed to contain the dust residue. Do not clean brake parts with compressed air or by dry brushing. Cleaning should be done by dampen-

ing the brake components with a fine mist of water, then wiping the brake components clean with a dampened cloth. Dispose of cloth and all residue containing asbestos fibers in an impermeable container with the appropriate label. Follow practices prescribed by the Occupational Safety and Health Administration (OSHA) and the Environmental Protection Agency (EPA) for the handling, processing, and disposing of dust or debris that may contain asbestos fibers.

1. Before servicing the vehicle, refer to the Precautions Section.

2. Disconnect and isolate negative battery cable from battery post.

3. Using a brake pedal holding tool, depress brake pedal past its first inch of travel and hold it in this position. Holding pedal in this position will isolate master cylinder from hydraulic brake system and will not allow brake fluid to drain out of brake fluid reservoir while brake lines are open.

4. Raise and support vehicle.

5. Remove wheel mounting nuts, then tire and wheel assembly.

6. Remove banjo bolt (3) connecting flexible brake hose (1) to caliper (4). There are two sealing washers (2) (one on each side of hose fitting) that will come off when bolt is removed. Discard these washers; install NEW washers on installation.

7. While holding guide pins from turning, remove caliper guide pin bolts.

8. Remove brake caliper from brake adapter and pads.

To install:

✳✳ CAUTION

Always inspect brake pads before installing disc brake caliper and replace as necessary.

9. Completely retract caliper pistons back into bores of caliper. Use hand

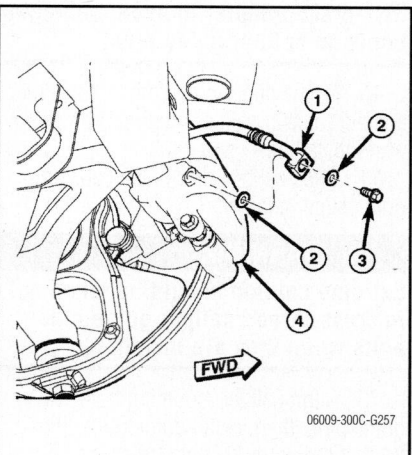

06009-300C-G257

Fig. 10 Brake line-to-caliper attachment

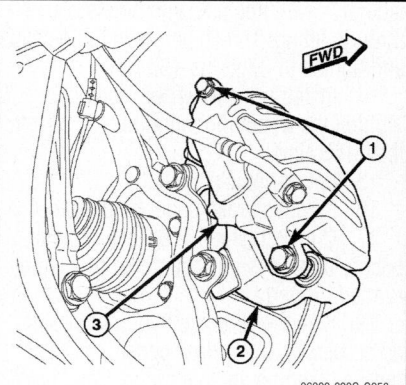

06009-300C-G258

Fig. 11 Caliper attachment. (1) caliper pins, (2) anchor plate, (3) caliper—dual piston caliper with AWD

pressure or a C-clamp may also be used to retract pistons, first placing a wood block over piston before installing C-clamp to avoid damaging piston.

✳✳ CAUTION

Use care when installing the caliper onto disc brake adapter to avoid damaging boots on caliper guide pins.

10. Push caliper guide pins into caliper adapter to clear caliper mounting bosses when installing.

11. Slide caliper over brake pads and onto caliper adapter.

✳✳ WARNING

Extreme caution should be taken not to cross-thread caliper guide pin bolts when they are installed.

12. Align caliper mounting holes with guide pins, then install guide pin bolts. While holding guide pins from turning, tighten bolts to 44 ft. lbs. (60 Nm).

13. Install banjo bolt attaching brake hose to caliper. Install NEW washers on each side of hose fitting as banjo bolt is placed through fitting. Thread banjo bolt into caliper and tighten to 37 ft. lbs. (50 Nm).

14. Install tire and wheel assembly. Tighten the wheel mounting nuts to 110 ft. lbs. (150 Nm).

15. Lower the vehicle.

16. Remove brake pedal holding tool.

17. Connect negative battery cable to battery post. It is important that this is performed properly.

18. Bleed the base brake hydraulic system as necessary. If a proper pedal is not felt during bleeding an area of repair then a base bleed system must be performed.

19. Road test the vehicle making several stops to wear off any foreign material on brakes and to seat brake shoes.

RWD Models

See Figure 12.

✳✳ CAUTION

Dust and dirt accumulating on brake parts during normal use may contain asbestos fibers from production or aftermarket brake linings. Breathing excessive concentrations of asbestos fibers can cause serious bodily harm. Exercise care when servicing brake parts. Do not sand or grind brake lining unless equipment used is designed to contain the dust residue. Do not clean brake parts with com-

pressed air or by dry brushing. Cleaning should be done by dampening the brake components with a fine mist of water, then wiping the brake components clean with a dampened cloth. Dispose of cloth and all residue containing asbestos fibers in an impermeable container with the appropriate label. Follow practices prescribed by the Occupational Safety and Health Administration (OSHA) and the Environmental Protection Agency (EPA) for the handling, processing, and disposing of dust or debris that may contain asbestos fibers.

1. Before servicing the vehicle, refer to the Precautions Section.

2. Disconnect and isolate negative battery cable from battery post.

3. Using a brake pedal holding tool, depress brake pedal past its first inch of travel and hold it in this position. Holding pedal in this position will isolate master cylinder from hydraulic brake system and will not allow brake fluid to drain out of brake fluid reservoir while brake lines are open.

4. Raise and support vehicle.

5. Remove wheel mounting nuts, then tire and wheel assembly.

6. Remove banjo bolt connecting flexible brake hose to caliper. There are two sealing washers (one on each side of hose fitting) that will come off when bolt is removed. Discard these washers; install NEW washers on installation.

7. While holding guide pins from turning, remove caliper guide pin bolts.

8. Remove brake caliper from brake adapter and pads.

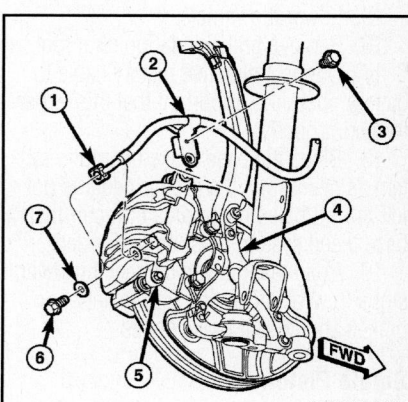

06009-300C-G256

Fig. 12 Dual piston caliper mounting. (1) banjo fitting, (2) hose, (3) bolt, (4) adaptor, (5) caliper pin, (6) banjo bolt, (7) washer

To install:

> ✳✳ **CAUTION**
>
> **Always inspect brake pads before installing disc brake caliper and replace as necessary.**

9. Completely retract caliper pistons back into bores of caliper. Use hand pressure or a C-clamp may also be used to retract pistons, first placing a wood block over piston before installing C-clamp to avoid damaging piston.

> ✳✳ **CAUTION**
>
> **Use care when installing the caliper onto disc brake adapter to avoid damaging boots on caliper guide pins.**

10. Push caliper guide pins into caliper adapter to clear caliper mounting bosses when installing.
11. Slide caliper over brake pads and onto caliper adapter.

> ✳✳ **WARNING**
>
> **Extreme caution should be taken not to cross-thread caliper guide pin bolts when they are installed.**

12. Align caliper mounting holes with guide pins, then install guide pin bolts. While holding guide pins from turning, tighten bolts to 44 ft. lbs. (60 Nm).
13. Install banjo bolt attaching brake hose to caliper. Install NEW washers on each side of hose fitting as banjo bolt is placed through fitting. Thread banjo bolt into caliper and tighten to 37 ft. lbs. (50 Nm).
14. Install tire and wheel assembly. Tighten the wheel mounting nuts to 110 ft. lbs. (150 Nm).
15. Lower the vehicle.
16. Remove brake pedal holding tool.
17. Connect negative battery cable to battery post. It is important that this is performed properly.
18. Bleed the base brake hydraulic system as necessary. If a proper pedal is not felt during bleeding an area of repair then a base bleed system must be performed.
19. Road test the vehicle making several stops to wear off any foreign material on brakes and to seat brake shoes.

Single Piston

See Figure 13.

> ✳✳ **CAUTION**
>
> **Dust and dirt accumulating on brake parts during normal use may contain**

asbestos fibers from production or aftermarket brake linings. Breathing excessive concentrations of asbestos fibers can cause serious bodily harm. Exercise care when servicing brake parts. Do not sand or grind brake lining unless equipment used is designed to contain the dust residue. Do not clean brake parts with compressed air or by dry brushing. Cleaning should be done by dampening the brake components with a fine mist of water, then wiping the brake components clean with a dampened cloth. Dispose of cloth and all residue containing asbestos fibers in an impermeable container with the appropriate label. Follow practices prescribed by the Occupational Safety and Health Administration (OSHA) and the Environmental Protection Agency (EPA) for the handling, processing, and disposing of dust or debris that may contain asbestos fibers.

1. Before servicing the vehicle, refer to the Precautions Section.
2. Disconnect and isolate negative battery cable from battery post.
3. Using a brake pedal holding tool, depress brake pedal past its first inch of travel and hold it in this position. Holding pedal in this position will isolate master cylinder from hydraulic brake system and will not allow brake fluid to drain out of brake fluid reservoir while brake lines are open.
4. Raise and support vehicle.
5. Remove wheel mounting nuts, then tire and wheel assembly.
6. Remove banjo bolt connecting flexi-

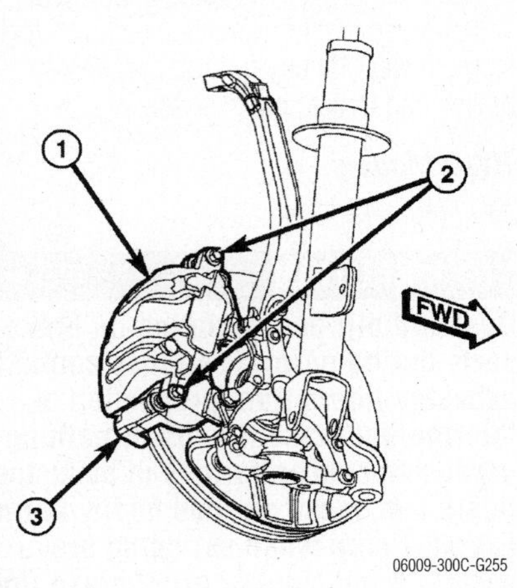

Fig. 13 Single piston caliper (1), mounting pins (2), adapter (3)

06009-300C-G255

ble brake hose to caliper. There are two sealing washers (one on each side of hose fitting) that will come off when bolt is removed. Discard these washers; install NEW washers on installation.
7. While holding guide pins from turning, remove caliper guide pin bolts.
8. Remove brake caliper from brake adapter and pads.

To install:

> ✳✳ **CAUTION**
>
> **Always inspect the brake pads before installing disc brake caliper and replace as necessary.**

9. Completely retract caliper piston back into bore of caliper. Use hand pressure or a C-clamp may be used to retract piston, first placing a wood block over piston before installing C-clamp to avoid damaging piston.

> ✳✳ **CAUTION**
>
> **Use care when installing caliper onto disc brake adapter to avoid damaging boots on caliper guide pins.**

10. Push caliper guide pins into caliper adapter to clear caliper mounting bosses when installing.
11. Slide caliper over brake pads and onto caliper adapter.

> ✳✳ **WARNING**
>
> **Extreme caution should be taken not to cross-thread caliper guide pin bolts when they are installed.**

12. Align caliper mounting holes with guide pins, then install guide pin bolts. While holding guide pins from turning, tighten bolts to 44 ft. lbs. (60 Nm).
13. Install banjo bolt attaching brake hose to caliper. Install NEW washers on each side of hose fitting as banjo bolt is placed through fitting. Thread banjo bolt into caliper and tighten to 37 ft. lbs. (50 Nm).
14. Install tire and wheel assembly. Tighten the wheel mounting nuts to 110 ft. lbs. (150 Nm).
15. Lower vehicle.
16. Remove brake pedal holding tool.
17. Connect negative battery cable to battery post. It is important that this is performed properly.
18. Bleed base brake hydraulic system as necessary. If a proper pedal is not felt during bleeding an area of repair then a base bleed system must be performed.
19. Road test vehicle making several stops to wear off any foreign material on brakes and to seat brake shoes.

DISC BRAKE PADS

REMOVAL & INSTALLATION

See Figures 14 and 15.

❋❋ CAUTION

Dust and dirt accumulating on brake parts during normal use may contain asbestos fibers from production or aftermarket brake linings. Breathing excessive concentrations of asbestos fibers can cause serious bodily harm. Exercise care when servicing brake parts. Do not sand or grind brake lining unless equipment used is designed to contain the dust residue. Do not clean brake parts with compressed air or by dry brushing. Cleaning should be done by dampening the brake components with a fine mist of water, then wiping the brake components clean with a dampened cloth. Dispose of cloth and all residue containing asbestos fibers in an impermeable container with the appropriate label. Follow practices prescribed by the Occupational Safety and Health Administration (OSHA) and the Environmental Protection Agency (EPA) for the handling, processing, and disposing of dust or debris that may contain asbestos fibers.

1. Before servicing the vehicle, refer to the Precautions Section.
2. Raise and support vehicle.
3. Remove wheel mounting nuts, then tire and wheel assembly.

➡In some cases, it may be necessary to retract caliper piston in its bore a small amount in order to provide sufficient clearance between shoes and rotor to easily remove caliper from knuckle. This can usually be accomplished before guide pin bolts are removed by grasping rear of caliper and pulling outward working with guide pins, thus retracting piston. Never push on piston directly as it may get damaged.

4. Remove lower caliper guide pin bolt. To do so, hold the guide pin (3) stationary while turning bolt (1).

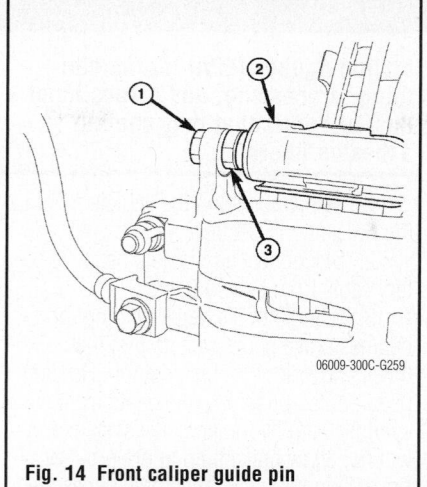

Fig. 14 Front caliper guide pin

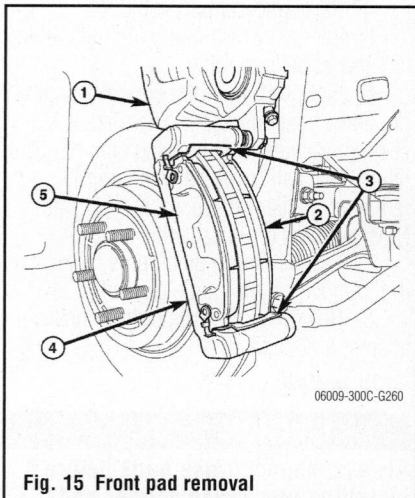

Fig. 15 Front pad removal

5. Rotate caliper upward (1), exposing brake pads (2 and 5). Use care not to overextend brake hose when doing this or damage may occur.
6. Remove inboard (2) and outboard (5) brake pads from caliper adapter (4).
7. If necessary, remove anti-rattle clips (3) from upper and lower abutments of adapter (4).

To install:

8. Completely retract caliper piston(s) back into bore(s) of caliper. To do so:
   a. Remove fluid reservoir cap.
   b. Use hand pressure or a C-clamp may be used to retract piston, first placing a wood block over piston(s) before installing C-clamp to avoid damaging piston(s).
   c. Install fluid reservoir cap.
9. If removed, attach anti-rattle clips to upper and lower abutments of adapter.
10. If equipped, remove the film from the brake pad double sticky isolator.
11. Install NEW inboard and outboard brake pads on caliper adapter. NEW inboard and outboard pads are interchangeable.
12. Push caliper guide pins into caliper adapter to clear caliper mounting bosses when installing.
13. Rotate caliper downward, aligning upper mounting boss with lower guide pin.
14. Install upper caliper guide pin bolt. While holding guide pin stationary, tighten bolt to 44 ft. lbs. (60 Nm).
15. Install tire and wheel assembly. Tighten wheel mounting nuts to 110 ft. lbs. (150 Nm).
16. Lower vehicle.
17. Pump brake pedal several times to set pads to caliper and brake rotor.
18. Check and adjust brake fluid level in reservoir.

❋❋ WARNING

When NEW brake pads have been installed, keep in mind that braking effectiveness might be somewhat reduced during the first brake applications following installation.

❋❋ WARNING

A burnish procedure must be performed anytime NEW brake pads or rotors are installed on a vehicle equipped with the Police Package. This procedure is particularly important in situations where high speed pursuit is a possibility. It is recommended that the procedure be performed by the Police agency operating the vehicle so it can be performed in a safe controlled environment. This information is covered in the Police Package Owner's Manual Supplement which was supplied when the vehicle was originally delivered.

19. Road test vehicle making several stops to wear off any foreign material on brakes and to seat brake shoes.

BRAKES   REAR DISC BRAKES

⁂ WARNING

Dust and dirt accumulating on brake parts during normal use may contain asbestos fibers from production or aftermarket brake linings. Breathing excessive concentrations of asbestos fibers can cause serious bodily harm. Exercise care when servicing brake parts. Do not sand or grind brake lining unless equipment used is designed to contain the dust residue. Do not clean brake parts with compressed air or by dry brushing. Cleaning should be done by dampening the brake components with a fine mist of water, then wiping the brake components clean with a dampened cloth. Dispose of cloth and all residue containing asbestos fibers in an impermeable container with the appropriate label. Follow practices prescribed by the Occupational Safety and Health Administration (OSHA) and the Environmental Protection Agency (EPA) for the handling, processing, and disposing of dust or debris that may contain asbestos fibers.

BRAKE CALIPER

REMOVAL & INSTALLATION
See Figures 16 and 17.

⁂ CAUTION

Dust and dirt accumulating on brake parts during normal use may contain asbestos fibers from production or aftermarket brake linings. Breathing excessive concentrations of asbestos fibers can cause serious bodily harm. Exercise care when servicing brake parts. Do not sand or grind brake lining unless equipment used is designed to contain the dust residue. Do not clean brake parts with compressed air or by dry brushing. Cleaning should be done by dampening the brake components with a fine mist of water, then wiping the brake components clean with a dampened cloth. Dispose of cloth and all residue containing asbestos fibers in an impermeable container with the appropriate label. Follow practices prescribed by the Occupational Safety and Health Administration (OSHA) and the Environmental Pro-

tection Agency (EPA) for the handling, processing, and disposing of dust or debris that may contain asbestos fibers.

1. Before servicing the vehicle, refer to the Precautions Section.
2. Disconnect and isolate negative battery cable from battery post.
3. Using a brake pedal holding tool, depress brake pedal past its first inch of travel and hold it in this position. Holding pedal in this position will isolate master cylinder from hydraulic brake system and will not allow brake fluid to drain out of brake fluid reservoir while brake lines are open.
4. Raise and support vehicle.
5. Remove wheel mounting nuts, then tire and wheel assembly.
6. Remove banjo bolt connecting flexible brake hose to caliper. There are two sealing washers (one on each side of hose fitting) that will come off when bolt is removed. Discard these washers; install NEW washers on installation.
7. While holding guide pins from turning, remove caliper guide pin bolts.
8. Remove brake caliper from brake adapter and pads.

To install:

⁂ CAUTION

Always inspect brake pads before installing disc brake caliper and replace as necessary.

9. Completely retract caliper piston back into bore of caliper. Use hand pressure or a C-clamp may be used to retract piston,

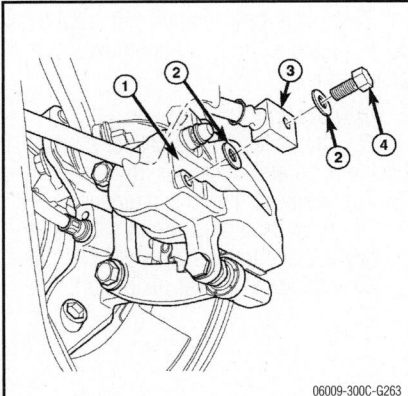

Fig. 16 Rear brake line (3) connection. (1) caliper, (2) washers, (4) banjo bolt

06009-300C-G263

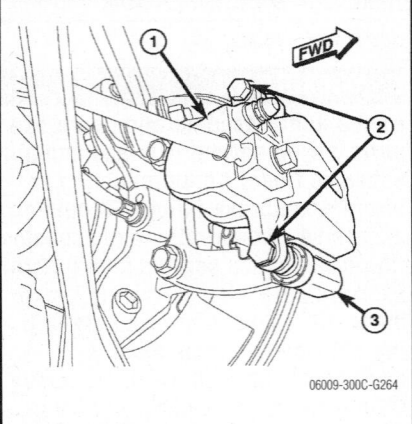

06009-300C-G264

Fig. 17 Rear caliper mounting. (1) caliper, (2) mounting pins, (3) adapter

first placing a wood block over piston before installing C-clamp to avoid damaging piston.

⁂ CAUTION

Use care when installing the caliper onto disc brake adapter to avoid damaging boots on caliper guide pins.

10. Push caliper guide pins into caliper adapter to clear caliper mounting bosses when installing.
11. Slide caliper over brake pads and onto caliper adapter.

⁂ WARNING

Extreme caution should be taken not to cross-thread caliper guide pin bolts when they are installed.

12. Align caliper mounting holes with guide pins, then install guide pin bolts. While holding guide pins from turning, tighten bolts to 23 ft. lbs. (31 Nm).
13. Install banjo bolt attaching brake hose to caliper. Install NEW washers on each side of hose fitting as banjo bolt is placed through fitting. Thread banjo bolt into caliper and tighten to 37 ft. lbs. (50 Nm).
14. Install tire and wheel assembly. Tighten the wheel mounting nuts to 110 ft. lbs. (150 Nm).
15. Lower the vehicle.
16. Remove brake pedal holding tool.
17. Connect negative battery cable to battery post. It is important that this is performed properly.
18. Bleed the base brake hydraulic sys-

tem as necessary. If a proper pedal is not felt during bleeding an area of repair then a base bleed system must be performed.

19. Road test vehicle making several stops to wear off any foreign material on brakes and to seat brake shoes.

DISC BRAKE PADS

REMOVAL & INSTALLATION

See Figures 18 and 19.

⁂ CAUTION

Dust and dirt accumulating on brake parts during normal use may contain asbestos fibers from production or aftermarket brake linings. Breathing excessive concentrations of asbestos fibers can cause serious bodily harm. Exercise care when servicing brake parts. Do not sand or grind brake lining unless equipment used is designed to contain the dust residue. Do not clean brake parts with compressed air or by dry brushing. Cleaning should be done by dampening the brake components with a fine mist of water, then wiping the brake components clean with a dampened cloth. Dispose of cloth and all residue containing asbestos fibers in an impermeable container with the appropriate label. Follow practices prescribed by the Occupational Safety and Health Administration (OSHA) and the Environmental Protection Agency (EPA) for the handling, processing, and disposing of dust or debris that may contain asbestos fibers.

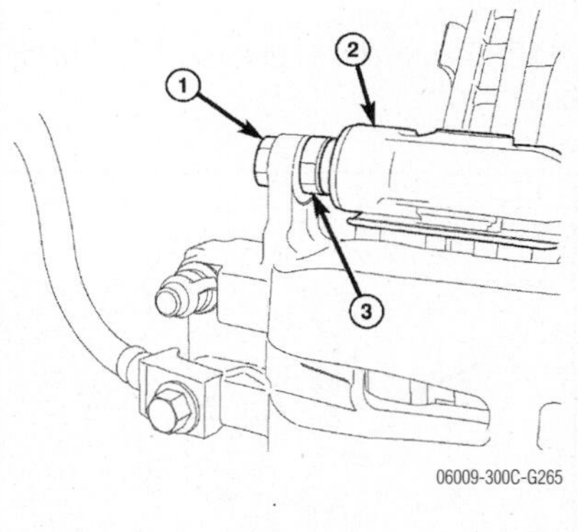

Fig. 18 Upper guide pin bolt (1) adapter (2), guide pin (3)—rear brakes

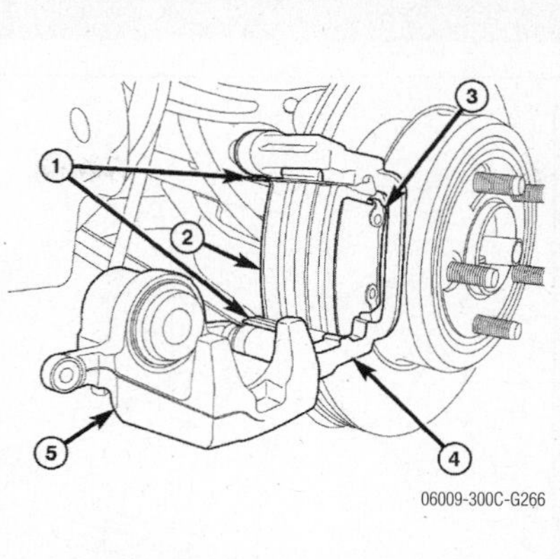

Fig. 19 Rear brake pad removal/installation. (1) anti-rattle clips, (2, 3) brake pads, (4) adapter, (5) caliper

1. Before servicing the vehicle, refer to the Precautions Section.
2. Raise and support vehicle.
3. Remove wheel mounting nuts, then tire and wheel assembly.

➡In some cases, it may be necessary to retract caliper piston in its bore a small amount in order to provide sufficient clearance between shoes and rotor to easily remove caliper from knuckle. This can usually be accomplished before guide pin bolts are removed by grasping rear of caliper and pulling outward working with guide pins, thus retracting piston. Never push on piston directly as it may get damaged.

4. Remove upper caliper guide pin bolt. To do so, hold the guide pin stationary while turning bolt.
5. Rotate caliper downward, exposing brake pads. Use care not to overextend brake hose when doing this or damage may occur.
6. Remove inboard and outboard brake pads from caliper adapter.
7. If necessary, remove anti-rattle clips from upper and lower abutments of adapter.

To install:

8. Completely retract the caliper piston back into bore of caliper. To do so:
   a. Remove the fluid reservoir cap.
   b. Use hand pressure or a C-clamp may be used to retract piston, first placing a wood block over piston before installing C-clamp to avoid damaging piston.
   c. Install the fluid reservoir cap.
9. If removed, attach anti-rattle clips to upper and lower abutments of adapter.
10. If equipped, remove the film from the brake pad double sticky isolator.
11. Install the NEW inboard and outboard brake pads on caliper adapter. NEW inboard and outboard pads are interchangeable.
12. Push caliper guide pins into caliper adapter to clear caliper mounting bosses when installing.
13. Rotate caliper upward, aligning upper mounting boss with upper guide pin.
14. Install upper caliper guide pin bolt. While holding guide pin stationary, tighten bolt to 23 ft. lbs. (31 Nm).
15. Install tire and wheel assembly. Tighten the wheel mounting nuts to 110 ft. lbs. (150 Nm).
16. Lower the vehicle.
17. Pump the brake pedal several times to set pads to caliper and brake rotor.
18. Check and adjust brake fluid level in reservoir.

⁂ CAUTION

If NEW brake rotors or pads have been installed, keep in mind that braking effectiveness might be somewhat reduced during the first brake applications following installation.

⁂ WARNING

A burnish procedure must be performed anytime NEW brake pads or rotors are installed on a vehicle equipped with the Police Package. This procedure is particularly important in situations where high speed pursuit is a possibility. It is recommended that the procedure be performed by the Police agency operating the vehicle so it can be performed in a safe controlled environment. This information is covered in the Police Package Owner's Manual Supplement which was supplied when the vehicle was originally delivered.

19. Road test vehicle making several stops to wear off any foreign material on brakes and to seat brake shoes.

PARKING BRAKE SHOES

REMOVAL & INSTALLATION

See Figures 20 through 23.

1. Before servicing the vehicle, refer to the Precautions Section.

➡**The following procedure may be used to remove shoes on either side of the vehicle.**

2. Raise and support vehicle.
3. Remove rear hub and bearing.
4. Completely back off parking brake shoe adjustment.
5. Remove parking brake shoe adjuster spring.
6. Remove shoe adjuster.
7. Remove upper brake shoe hold-down clip and pin.
8. Remove upper shoe from return spring and shoe actuator lever.
9. Remove return spring from lower shoe.
10. Remove shoe actuator lever from end of cable.
11. Remove lower brake shoe hold-down clip and pin.
12. Remove lower shoe.
13. Inspect springs, adjuster, lever and aluminum shoe anchor pin for wear or damage. Replace as necessary.

To install:

➡**The following procedure may be used to install shoes on either side of the vehicle.**

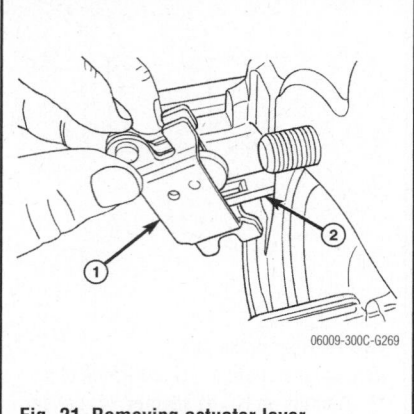

06009-300C-G269

Fig. 21 Removing actuator lever

➡**Inspect springs, adjuster, lever and aluminum shoe anchor pin for wear or damage prior to installation. Replace as necessary.**

14. Install lower brake shoe hold-down pin through rear of support.
15. Install lower shoe against support plate.
16. Install lower brake shoe hold-down clip.
17. Install shoe actuator lever on end of parking brake cable. Make sure actuator lever is positioned with word "UP" facing outward.
18. Install return spring to lower shoe.
19. Install upper shoe against support plate and onto shoe actuator lever.
20. Install upper brake shoe hold-down pin through rear of support and upper shoe.

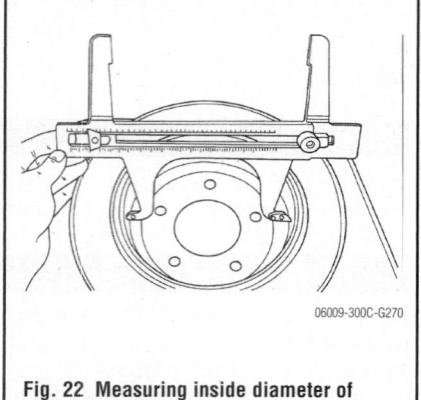

06009-300C-G270

Fig. 22 Measuring inside diameter of parking brake drum

21. Install upper brake shoe hold-down clip.
22. Attach return spring to upper shoe.
23. Install shoe adjuster. Place end of adjuster with star wheel upward.
24. Install parking brake shoe adjuster spring.
25. Using Brake Shoe Gauge, Special Tool C-3919, or equivalent, measure inside diameter of parking brake drum portion of rotor.
26. Place Gauge over parking brake shoes at widest point.
27. Using adjuster star wheel, adjust parking brake shoes until linings on both park brake shoes just touch jaws on gauge. This will give a good preliminary adjustment of parking brake shoes, before a final adjustment is made at end of this procedure.
28. Install hub and bearing with wheel speed sensor as well as all components necessary to access it.
29. Lower vehicle.
30. Perform final adjustment of parking brake shoes.

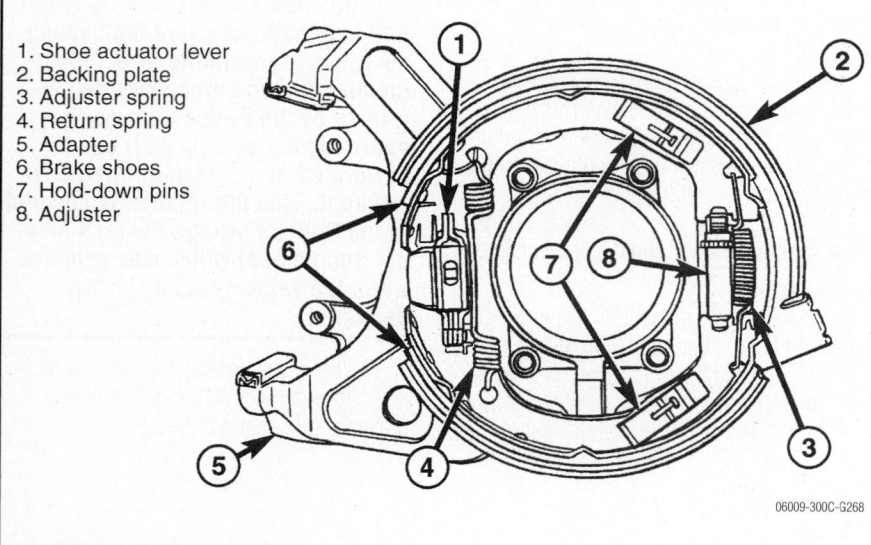

1. Shoe actuator lever
2. Backing plate
3. Adjuster spring
4. Return spring
5. Adapter
6. Brake shoes
7. Hold-down pins
8. Adjuster

06009-300C-G268

Fig. 20 Parking brake

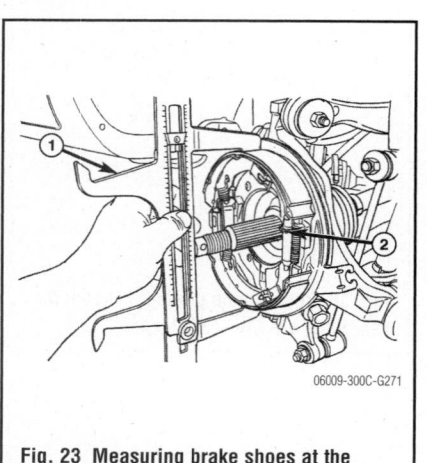

06009-300C-G271

Fig. 23 Measuring brake shoes at the widest point

CHASSIS ELECTRICAL   AIR BAG (SUPPLEMENTAL RESTRAINT SYSTEM)

GENERAL INFORMATION

✳✳ WARNING

These vehicles are equipped with an air bag system. The system must be disarmed before performing service on, or around, system components, the steering column, instrument panel components, wiring and sensors. Failure to follow the safety precautions and the disarming procedure could result in accidental air bag deployment, possible injury and unnecessary system repairs.

SERVICE PRECAUTIONS

Disconnect and isolate the battery negative cable before beginning any airbag system component diagnosis, testing, removal, or installation procedures. Allow system capacitor to discharge for two minutes before beginning any component service. This will disable the airbag system. Failure to disable the airbag system may result in accidental airbag deployment, personal injury, or death.

Do not place an intact undeployed airbag face down on a solid surface. The airbag will propel into the air if accidentally deployed and may result in personal injury or death.

When carrying or handling an undeployed airbag, the trim side (face) of the airbag should be pointing towards the body to minimize possibility of injury if accidental deployment occurs. Failure to do this may result in personal injury or death.

Replace airbag system components with OEM replacement parts. Substitute parts may appear interchangeable, but internal differences may result in inferior occupant protection. Failure to do so may result in occupant personal injury or death.

Wear safety glasses, rubber gloves, and long sleeved clothing when cleaning powder residue from vehicle after an airbag deployment. Powder residue emitted from a deployed airbag can cause skin irritation. Flush affected area with cool water if irritation is experienced. If nasal or throat irritation is experienced, exit the vehicle for fresh air until the irritation ceases. If irritation continues, see a physician.

Do not use a replacement airbag that is not in the original packaging. This may result in improper deployment, personal injury, or death.

The factory installed fasteners, screws and bolts used to fasten airbag components have a special coating and are specifically designed for the airbag system. Do not use substitute fasteners. Use only original equipment fasteners listed in the parts catalog when fastener replacement is required.

During, and following, any child restraint anchor service, due to impact event or vehicle repair, carefully inspect all mounting hardware, tether straps, and anchors for proper installation, operation, or damage. If a child restraint anchor is found damaged in any way, the anchor must be replaced. Failure to do this may result in personal injury or death.

Deployed and non-deployed airbags may or may not have live pyrotechnic material within the airbag inflator.

Do not dispose of driver/passenger/curtain airbags or seat belt tensioners unless you are sure of complete deployment. Refer to the Hazardous Substance Control System for proper disposal.

Dispose of deployed airbags and tensioners consistent with state, provincial, local, and federal regulations.

After any airbag component testing or service, do not connect the battery negative cable. Personal injury or death may result if the system test is not performed first.

If the vehicle is equipped with the Occupant Classification System (OCS), do not connect the battery negative cable before performing the OCS Verification Test using the scan tool and the appropriate diagnostic information. Personal injury or death may result if the system test is not performed properly.

Never replace both the Occupant Restraint Controller (ORC) and the Occupant Classification Module (OCM) at the same time. If both require replacement, replace one, then perform the Airbag System test before replacing the other.

Both the ORC and the OCM store Occupant Classification System (OCS) calibration data, which they transfer to one another when one of them is replaced. If both are replaced at the same time, an irreversible fault will be set in both modules and the OCS may malfunction and cause personal injury or death.

If equipped with OCS, the Seat Weight Sensor is a sensitive, calibrated unit and must be handled carefully. Do not drop or handle roughly. If dropped or damaged, replace with another sensor. Failure to do so may result in occupant injury or death.

If equipped with OCS, the front passenger seat must be handled carefully as well.

When removing the seat, be careful when setting on floor not to drop. If dropped, the sensor may be inoperative, could result in occupant injury, or possibly death.

If equipped with OCS, when the passenger front seat is on the floor, no one should sit in the front passenger seat. This uneven force may damage the sensing ability of the seat weight sensors. If sat on and damaged, the sensor may be inoperative, could result in occupant injury, or possibly death.

DISARMING THE SYSTEM

Disconnect and isolate the negative battery cable. Wait 2 minutes for the system capacitor to discharge before performing any service.

ARMING THE SYSTEM

To arm the system, connect the negative battery cable.

CLOCKSPRING CENTERING

➡ **See all applicable precautions before beginning service procedures.**

Disconnect and isolate the battery negative cable before beginning any airbag system component diagnosis, testing, removal, or installation procedures. Allow system capacitor to discharge for two minutes before beginning any component service. This will disable the airbag system. Failure to disable the airbag system may result in accidental airbag deployment, personal injury, or death.

The clockspring is mounted on the steering column behind the steering wheel. Its purpose is to maintain a continuous electrical circuit between the wiring harness and the driver's side air bag module. This assembly consists of a flat, ribbon-like electrically conductive tape that winds and unwinds with the steering wheel rotation.

Service replacement clock springs are shipped pre-centered and with a molded plastic locking pin that snaps into a receptacle on the rotor and is engaged between two tabs on the upper surface of the rotor case. The locking pin secures the centered clockspring rotor to the clockspring case during shipment, but the locking pin must be removed from the clockspring after it is installed on the steering column. This locking pin should not be removed until the clockspring has been installed on the steering column. If the locking pin is removed before the clockspring is installed on a steering column, the clockspring centering procedure must be performed.

➡️The clockspring cannot be repaired. If the clockspring is faulty, damaged, or if the driver airbag has been deployed, the clockspring must be replaced.

➡️Before starting this procedure, be certain to turn the steering wheel until the front wheels are in the straight-ahead position.

1. Place the front wheels in the straight-ahead position.
2. Remove the clockspring from the steering column.
3. Rotate the clockspring rotor clockwise to the end of its travel. Do not apply excessive torque.
4. From the end of the clockwise travel, rotate the rotor about two and one-half turns counterclockwise.

5. The engagement dowel and yellow rubber boot should end up at the bottom, and the arrows on the clockspring rotor and case should be in alignment. The clockspring is now centered.
6. The front wheels should still be in the straight-ahead position. Reinstall the clockspring onto the steering column.

DRIVE TRAIN

AUTOMATIC TRANSMISSION FLUID

DRAIN AND REFILL

Fluid/Filter Service

See Figure 24.

1. Run the engine until the transmission oil reaches operating temperature.
2. Raise and support vehicle.
3. Remove the bolts and retainers holding the oil pan to the transmission.
4. Remove the transmission oil pan and gasket from the transmission.
5. Remove the transmission oil filter and o-ring from the electro hydraulic control unit.
6. Clean the inside of the oil pan of any debris. Inspect the oil pan gasket and replace if necessary.
7. Install a new oil filter and o-ring into the electro hydraulic control unit.
8. Install the oil pan and gasket onto the transmission.
9. Install the oil pan bolts and retainers. Torque the bolts to 6 ft. lbs. (8 Nm).

10. Lower the vehicle and add 5.0 L (10.6 pts.) of transmission fluid to the transmission.
11. Check the oil level.

FILTER REPLACEMENT

Refer to DRAIN AND FILL.

TRANSFER CASE ASSEMBLY

REMOVAL & INSTALLATION

See Figures 25 and 26.

1. Before servicing the vehicle, refer to the precautions in the beginning of this section.
2. Raise and support the vehicle.
3. Remove the transfer case drain plug and allow the transfer case lubricant to drain into a suitable container.
4. Remove the exhaust.
5. Remove the rear propeller shaft.
6. Disconnect the temperature sensor harness connector and the clutch coil harness connector.
7. Raise transmission slightly with service jack to relieve load on crossmember and supports.
8. Remove bolts (2) securing rear support and cushion to transmission cross-member (3).
9. Remove bolts attaching the crossmember (1) to frame and remove crossmember (3).
10. Remove the front propeller shaft.

➡️The front (transmission) side of the PTU case flange is shown for clarity.

11. Remove the lower PTU case-to-transmission bolts from the lower half of the PTU case flange (2).
12. Slightly lower the rear of the transmission to gain access to the upper PTU-to-transmission bolts.
13. Support the PTU with a transmission jack.
14. Remove the upper PTU-to-transmission bolts from the upper half of the PTU case flange (1).
15. Remove the PTU.

To install:

16. Place the PTU on a transmission jack, and raise the PTU up to the rear transmission flange.
17. Align the PTU dowel pins with the holes in the rear transmission flange.

➡️The front (transmission) side of the PTU case flange is shown for clarity.

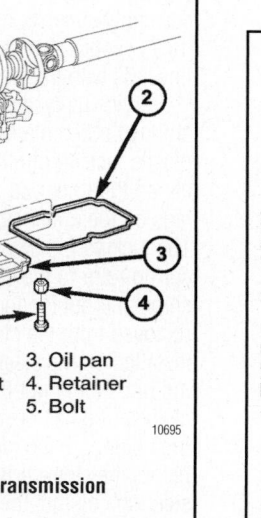

1. Oil filter
2. Oil pan gasket
3. Oil pan
4. Retainer
5. Bolt

10695

Fig. 24 Servicing the transmission fluid/filter

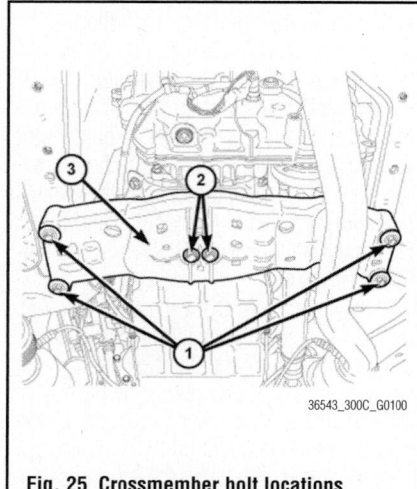

36543_300C_G0100

Fig. 25 Crossmember bolt locations

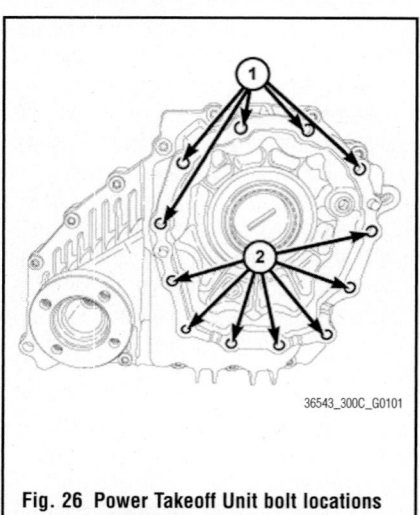

36543_300C_G0101

Fig. 26 Power Takeoff Unit bolt locations

18. Install the upper and lower PTU-to-transmission bolts into the upper and lower halves half of the PTU case flange. Tighten the PTU-to-transmission bolts to 41 ft. lbs. (55 Nm).

19. Raise the PTU and transmission up into position, and support with a suitable service jack. Remove the transmission jack.

20. Install the front propeller shaft.

21. Install the crossmember and install the bolts attaching the crossmember to frame.

22. Lower transmission with service jack onto crossmember and supports.

23. Install the bolts securing rear support and cushion to transmission crossmember.

24. Connect the temperature sensor harness connector and the clutch coil harness connector.

25. Install the rear propeller shaft.

26. Install the exhaust.

27. If the fluid was drained, fill the PTU with 33 oz. plus or minus 1.7 oz. (1.0L plus or minus 0.5L) of Mobil LT® fluid.

FRONT DRIVESHAFT

REMOVAL & INSTALLATION
See Figure 27.

1. Before servicing the vehicle, refer to the precautions in the beginning of this section.

2. Place gearshift lever in NEUTRAL and raise vehicle on hoist.

3. Remove driveshaft heat shield.

4. Apply alignment index marks on the driveshaft and front axle flanges.

5. Remove four front driveshaft-to-axle flange bolts.

6. Apply alignment index marks on the driveshaft and transfer case flanges.

7. Remove four front driveshaft-to-transfer case flange bolts.

8. Remove the driveshaft assembly.

To install:
9. Install the driveshaft into position.

10. Starting at transfer case end, align index marks. Install driveshaft-to-transfer case flange bolts.

11. Align index marks at front axle end of shaft, and loose-install driveshaft-to-front axle flange bolts.

12. Torque driveshaft-to-transfer case and axle flange bolts to 22 ft. lbs. (30 Nm).

13. Install driveshaft heat shield.

14. Lower the vehicle.

FRONT HALFSHAFT

REMOVAL & INSTALLATION
See Figures 28 through 30.

1. Before servicing the vehicle, refer to the precautions in the beginning of this section.

2. Raise and support vehicle.

3. Remove wheel mounting nuts, then tire and wheel assembly.

4. While holding link ball joint stem from rotating, remove nut fastening stabilizer link to shock clevis bracket. Slide link ball joint stem from clevis bracket.

5. Remove nut and pinch bolt fastening clevis bracket to bottom of shock assembly.

6. Remove nut and bolt attaching shock clevis bracket to lower control arm.

7. Pull lower end of clevis bracket outward away from lower control arm bushing, then slide it off shock assembly. It may be

necessary to use an appropriate prying tool to spread clamp area of clevis bracket allowing removal from shock assembly.

8. While a helper applies brakes to keep hub from rotating, remove hub nut from axle halfshaft.

➡ **In some cases, it may be necessary to retract caliper piston in its bore a small amount in order to provide sufficient clearance between shoes and rotor to easily remove caliper from knuckle. This can usually be accomplished before mounting bolts are removed, by grasping rear of caliper and pulling outward working with guide pins, thus retracting piston. Never push on piston directly as it may get damaged.**

9. Remove two bolts securing disc brake caliper and adapter to knuckle.

10. Remove disc brake caliper and adapter from knuckle as an assembly. Hang assembly out of way using wire or a bungee cord. Use care not to overextend brake hose when doing this.

11. Remove any clips retaining brake rotor to wheel studs.

12. Slide brake rotor off hub and bearing.

✳✳ CAUTION

In following step, use care not to damage ball joint seal boot while sliding the puller into place past seal boot.

13. Separate the upper ball joint stud from knuckle.

14. Remove the tool.

15. Remove nut from end of upper ball joint stud.

16. Remove clip fastening wheel speed sensor to knuckle.

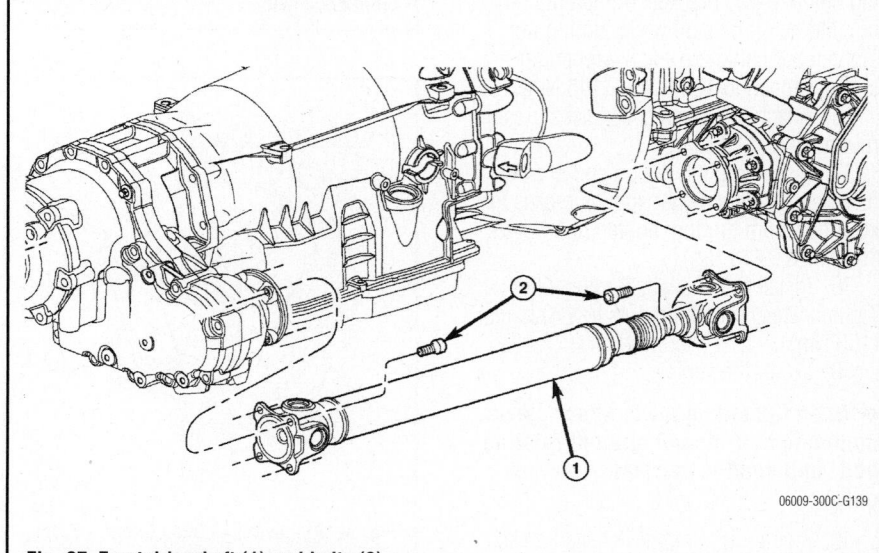

06009-300C-G139

Fig. 27 Front driveshaft (1) and bolts (2)

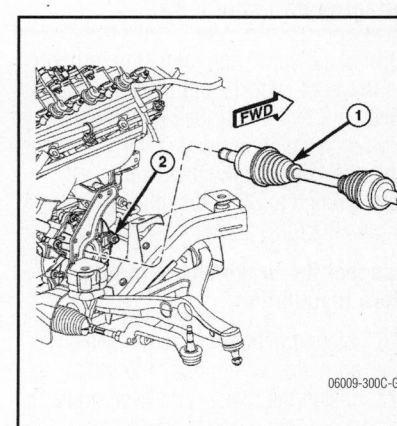

06009-300C-G147

Fig. 28 Right front halfshaft removal/installation

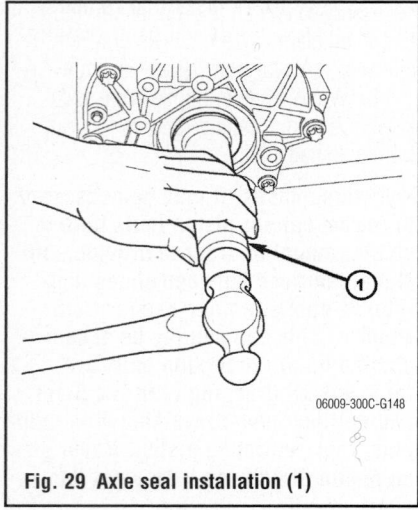

Fig. 29 Axle seal installation (1)

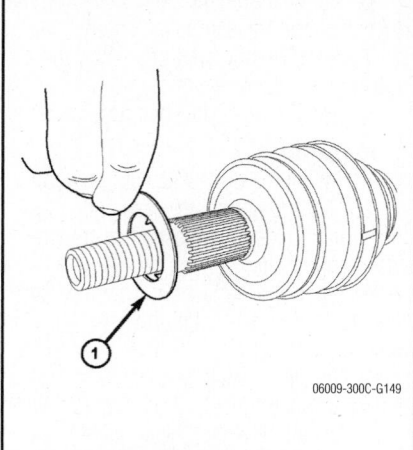

Fig. 30 Halfshaft isolation washer (1)

17. Disengage right halfshaft from axle and remove from vehicle.

18. Remove left halfshaft from vehicle.

To install:

19. Install left halfshaft assembly.

20. Using Tool C-4193-A, install new axle seal.

21. Install right halfshaft assembly.

➡**Before installing halfshafts into hub/bearing assemblies, ensure isolation washer is present on end of halfshaft. Inspect washer making sure it is not worn or damaged. Washer is bi-directional and can be installed in either direction on shaft.**

22. Install the halfshaft isolation washer.

23. Install the halfshaft into hub/bearing assembly.

24. Loosely install halfshaft hub nut, and do not tighten at this time.

✳✳ CAUTION

It is important to tighten nut as described in following step to avoid damaging ball stud joint.

25. Place upper ball joint stud through hole in top of knuckle and install nut. Tighten nut by holding ball joint stud with a hex wrench while turning nut with a wrench. Tighten nut using crow foot wrench on torque wrench to 35 ft. lbs. plus 90°turn (47 Nm plus 90°turn) torque.

➡**Inspect the brake shoes (pads) before installation.**

26. Clean the hub face to remove any dirt or corrosion where rotor mounts.

27. Install the brake rotor over studs on hub and bearing.

28. Install the disc brake caliper and adapter assembly over brake rotor.

29. Install the mounting bolts securing caliper adapter to knuckle. Tighten bolts to 125 ft. lbs. (169 Nm).

30. Pull lower end of shock assembly outward, then slide clevis bracket onto lower end. Slide clevis bracket onto shock assembly until bracket contacts collar on shock housing.

31. Install pinch bolt and nut fastening clevis bracket to bottom of shock assembly. Install pinch bolt from rear. Do not tighten at this time.

32. Slide clevis bracket over bushing mounted in lower control arm.

33. Install bolt and nut attaching shock clevis bracket to lower control arm. Do not tighten at this time.

34. Tighten pinch bolt attaching clevis bracket to shock assembly to 45 ft. lbs. (61 Nm).

35. Slide the stabilizer link ball joint stem into clevis bracket. Install nut fastening link to clevis bracket. Tighten nut by holding ball joint stud while turning nut. Tighten nut using crow foot wrench on torque wrench to 108 ft. lbs. (146 Nm).

36. Attach the wheel speed sensor cable routing clip at knuckle.

37. Install the hub nut on end of axle halfshaft. While a helper applies brakes to keep hub from turning, tighten hub nut to 157 ft. lbs. (213 Nm).

38. Install tire and wheel assembly. Tighten wheel mounting nuts to 110 ft. lbs. (150 Nm).

39. Lower the vehicle.

➡**When tightening lower shock clevis mounting bolt, do not attempt rotating bolt. Bolt shaft is serrated. Turn nut only.**

40. Tighten lower shock clevis bracket bolt nut to 128 ft. lbs. (174 Nm).

FRONT PINION SEAL

REMOVAL & INSTALLATION

See Figures 31 and 32.

1. Before servicing the vehicle, refer to the precautions in the beginning of this section.

2. Remove driveshaft and heat shield.

3. Using Tool 6958 (2), remove pinion flange nut.

4. Using Puller 1026 (1), remove pinion flange.

5. Remove pinion flange seal with suitable screwdriver and discard.

To install:

6. Using a seal driver, install new pinion flange seal.

7. Lightly tap pinion flange onto the shaft, just enough to start flange nut by hand.

8. Install pinion flange nut and torque to 350 ft. lbs. (475 Nm).

9. Install driveshaft and heat shield.

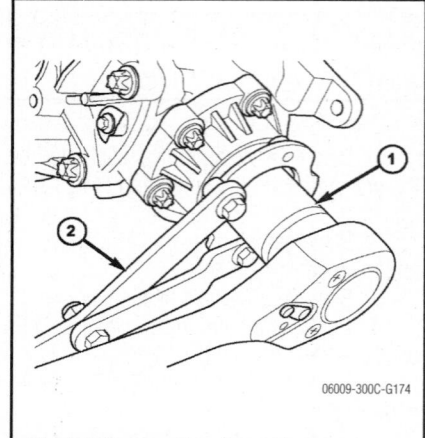

Fig. 31 Remove the pinion flange nut—Front drive axle

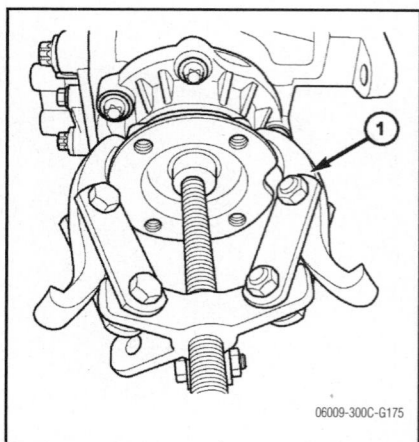

Fig. 32 Remove the pinion flange—Front drive axle

REAR AXLE HOUSING

REMOVAL & INSTALLATION

198mm Axle

1. Before servicing the vehicle, refer to the precautions in the beginning of this section.

➡**This procedure requires the compression of the rear suspension to ride height. A drive-on hoist should be used. If a drive-on hoist is not used, screw-style under-hoist jackstands are required to compress the rear suspension, facilitating rear halfshaft removal.**

> ⁂ **CAUTION**
>
> **Never grasp halfshaft assembly by the inner or outer boots. Doing so may cause the boot to pucker or crease, reducing the service life of the boot and joint. Avoid over angling or stroking the CV-joints when handling the halfshaft.**

2. With vehicle in neutral, position and raise vehicle on hoist.

3. Using 14mm hex, remove axle drain plug and drain rear axle fluid into container suitable for fluid reuse.

4. Install drain plug and torque to 44 ft. lbs. (60 Nm).

5. Remove rear exhaust system on dual-outlet exhaust models, otherwise, lower exhaust system at rear hanger(s) to provide adequate clearance.

6. Remove the driveshaft.

7. Remove the halfshafts.

8. Remove two rear axle-to-crossmember bolts.

9. Carefully lower rear axle. While lowering axle, separate driveshaft from axle and support with suitable rope or wire.

10. Remove axle assembly from vehicle and transfer to bench.

11. Using suitable screwdriver, remove axle seals and discard.

To install:

12. Install new axle seal(s).

➡**Use care when installing halfshaft to axle assembly. The halfshaft installation angle should be minimized to avoid damage to seal upon installation.**

13. Install the halfshafts.

14. Raise rear axle assembly into position. Align driveshaft index marks and start driveshaft coupler-to-axle bolt/nuts by hand.

15. Install two rear axle-to-crossmember bolts and torque to 162 ft. lbs. (220 Nm).

16. Install rear axle front mount isolator and torque bolt/nut to 48 ft. lbs. (65 Nm).

17. Again verify halfshaft inner joints are fully engaged to axle assembly.

18. Remove transmission jack.

19. If used, remove screw-type under-hoist jackstands.

20. Torque driveshaft coupler-to-axle flange bolt/nuts to 43 ft. lbs. (58 Nm).

21. Using a 14mm hex, remove rear axle fill plug. Fill axle with 1.5 qts. (1.4L) of Mopar® 75W-140 Synthetic Gear and Axle Lubricant. Install fill plug and torque to 44 ft. lbs. (60 Nm).

200mm Axle

1. Before servicing the vehicle, refer to the precautions in the beginning of this section.

➡**This procedure requires the compression of the rear suspension to ride height. A drive-on hoist should be used. If a drive-on hoist is not used, screw-style under-hoist jackstands are required to compress the rear suspension, facilitating rear halfshaft removal.**

> ⁂ **CAUTION**
>
> **Never grasp halfshaft assembly by the inner or outer boots. Doing so may cause the boot to pucker or crease, reducing the service life of the boot and joint. Avoid over angling or stroking the CV-joints when handling the halfshaft.**

2. With vehicle in neutral, position and raise vehicle on hoist.

3. Using 14mm hex, remove axle drain plug and drain rear axle fluid into container suitable for fluid reuse.

4. Install drain plug and torque to 44 ft. lbs. (60 Nm).

5. Remove rear exhaust system on dual-outlet exhaust models, otherwise, lower exhaust system at rear hanger.

6. Remove the rear driveshaft.

7. Remove the halfshafts.

8. Remove two rear axle-to-crossmember bolts.

9. Carefully lower rear axle. While lowering axle, separate driveshaft from axle and support with suitable rope or wire.

10. Remove axle assembly from vehicle and transfer to bench.

11. Using suitable screwdriver, remove axle seals and discard.

To install:

12. Install new axle seal(s) using Tool 9223.

➡**Use care when installing halfshaft to axle assembly. The halfshaft installation angle should be minimized to avoid damage to seal upon installation.**

13. Install the halfshafts.

14. Raise rear axle assembly into position. Align driveshaft index marks and start driveshaft coupler-to-axle bolt/nuts by hand.

15. Install two rear axle-to-crossmember bolts and torque to 162 ft. lbs. (220 Nm).

16. Install rear axle front mount isolator and torque bolt/nut to 48 ft. lbs. (65 Nm).

17. Again verify halfshaft inner joints are fully engaged to axle assembly.

18. Remove transmission jack.

19. If used, remove screw-type under-hoist jackstands.

20. Torque driveshaft coupler-to-axle flange bolt/nuts to 43 ft. lbs. (58 Nm).

21. Using a 14mm hex, remove rear axle fill plug. Fill axle with 1.5 qts. (1.4L) of Mopar® 75W-140 synthetic gear and axle lubricant. Install fill plug and torque to 44 ft. lbs. (60 Nm).

REAR DRIVESHAFT

REMOVAL & INSTALLATION

See Figures 33 through 36.

1. Before servicing the vehicle, refer to the precautions in the beginning of this section.

> ⁂ **CAUTION**
>
> **Driveshaft removal is a 2-person operation. Never allow driveshaft to hang from the center bearing, or while only connected to the transmission or rear axle flanges. A helper is required. If a driveshaft section is hung unsupported, damage may occur to the shaft, coupler, and/or center bearing from over-angulations. This may result in driveline vibrations and/or component failure.**

2. With vehicle in neutral, position on hoist.

3. Apply alignment index marks on the transmission and axle flanges and rubber couplers.

4. Remove crossmember.

5. Remove rear exhaust system.

6. Remove heat shield.

7. Remove driveshaft front coupler-to-flange bolts.

8. Remove driveshaft rear coupler-to-flange bolts.

9. Remove center bearing mounting bolts.

10. With the aid of a helper, remove driveshaft assembly.

11. Remove three coupler-to-driveshaft bolt/nuts.

12. Separate coupler and damper (if equipped) from driveshaft. Note orientation

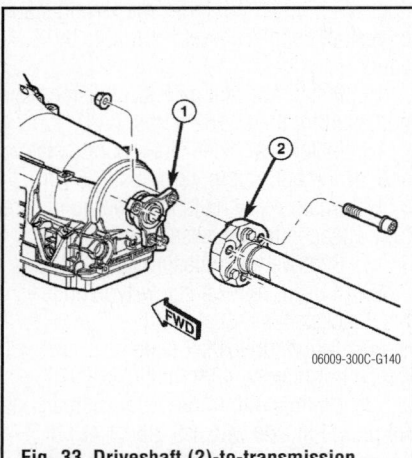

06009-300C-G140

Fig. 33 Driveshaft (2)-to-transmission flange (1) attachment

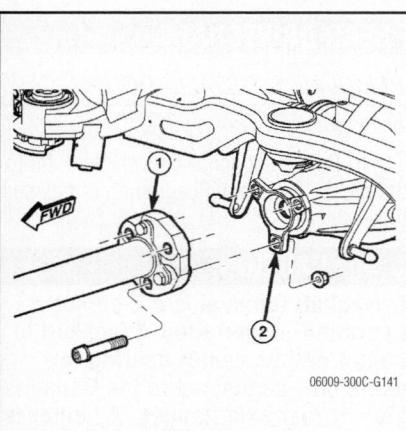

06009-300C-G141

Fig. 34 Driveshaft (1)-to-rear axle flange (2) attachment

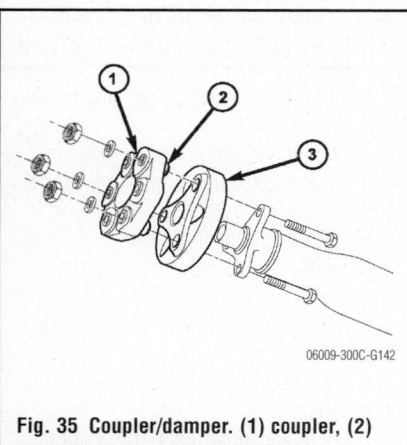

06009-300C-G142

Fig. 35 Coupler/damper. (1) coupler, (2) protruding sleeve, (3) damper

and direction of components. It is imperative that they are properly reinstalled.

To install:

13. If coupler and/or damper (V6 Models) were removed, align index marks and reinstall. Make sure protruding sleeve is properly seated into driveshaft or damper counter bores.

14. Install three bolts with washers and nuts and torque to 43 ft. lbs. (58 Nm).

15. Obtain helper and install driveshaft into position at axle. Align index marks placed upon removal. Install driveshaft rear coupler-to-axle flange bolt/nuts by hand. Do not torque at this time.

16. Install driveshaft into position at transmission flange. Align index marks placed upon removal. Install driveshaft front coupler-to-transmission flange bolt/nuts by hand. Do not torque at this time.

17. Loosely install center bearing-to-body bolts. Do not torque at this time.

18. Torque driveshaft front coupler-to-transmission flange bolt/nuts to 43 ft. lbs. (58 Nm).

19. Torque driveshaft rear coupler-to-axle flange bolt/nuts to 43 ft. lbs. (58 Nm).

➡️It is necessary to compress rear suspension to ride height before securing center bearing to body. Failure to compress suspension may result in objectionable noise and premature bearing wear.

20. Compress rear suspension with suitable jackstands.

21. Torque center bearing-to-body bolts to 20 ft. lbs. (27 Nm).

22. Install heat shield.

23. Install rear exhaust system.

24. Install the crossmember.

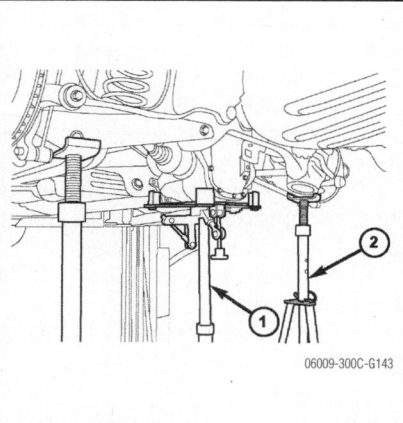

06009-300C-G143

Fig. 36 Compressing the rear suspension

REMOVAL & INSTALLATION

1. Before servicing the vehicle, refer to the precautions in the beginning of this section.

➡️**This procedure requires the compression of the rear suspension to ride height. A drive-on hoist should be used. If a drive-on hoist is not used, screw-style under-hoist jack stands are required to compress the rear suspension, facilitating rear halfshaft removal. Halfshaft inner and outer boots are not serviceable separately. Boot replacement requires entire shaft assembly replacement.**

✳️✳️ CAUTION

Unequal-length halfshafts are used. The left halfshaft is shorter than the right, and it is necessary to identify and tag halfshafts upon removal to ensure proper installation.

2. With vehicle in neutral, position and raise vehicle on hoist.

3. Using 14mm hex, remove axle drain plug and drain rear axle fluid into container suitable for fluid reuse.

4. Install drain plug and torque to:
   a. 198 Axle: 44 ft. lbs. (60 Nm).
   b. 210 Axle: 44 ft. lbs. (60 Nm).

5. Remove rear exhaust system on V8 equipped models.

6. Remove wheel/tire assembly from sides that shaft is to be removed.

7. Remove wheel hub nut and discard.

8. Apply alignment index marks to the propeller shaft rubber coupler and axle flange.

9. Remove three propeller shaft coupler-to-axle flange bolt/nuts.

10. Using suitable screwdriver, partially disengage halfshaft(s) from axle assembly.

11. If a drive-on hoist is used, position transmission jack to rear axle assembly. If a drive-on hoist is not used, compress rear suspension using screw-style under—hoist jack stands, then position transmission jack to rear axle assembly.

12. Remove rear axle forward mount isolator bolt/nut.

➡️**Access to rear axle-to-crossmember bolts is best achieved by use of short socket and a flexible-head ratchet.**

13. Remove two rear axle-to-crossmember bolts.

14. Carefully lower the rear axle. While lowering axle, separate propeller shaft from axle and support with suitable rope or wire.

15. Lower the axle just enough to remove halfshafts one at a time. Shift axle assembly in one direction, compressing one halfshaft while removing the other. Use caution to protect axle seal and journal.

To install:

16. Install new axle seals using the seal driver tool 9223 or equivalent.

17. Install halfshaft isolation washer. Washer is bidirectional, and can be installed in either direction.

18. Install halfshaft to wheel hub/knuckle assembly. Install new hub nut by hand.

19. Inspect slinger(s) for handling damage. Straighten as necessary to avoid contact with axle seal.

20. Lubricate halfshaft inner joint bearing journal with Mopar® gear and axle lubricant (75W-140). Using new circlip(s), install halfshaft to rear axle assembly. Use care not to damage axle seals. Verify proper installation by pulling outward on joint by hand.

21. Raise rear axle assembly into position. Align propeller shaft index marks (3) and start propeller shaft coupler-to-axle bolt/nuts by hand.

22. Install two rear axle-to-crossmember bolts and torque to 162 ft. lbs. (220 Nm).

23. Install rear axle front mount isolator as shown and torque bolt/nut to 48 ft. lbs. (65 Nm).

24. Again verify halfshaft inner joints are fully engaged to axle assembly.

25. Remove the transmission jack.

26. If used, remove screw-type underhoist jack stands.

27. Torque the propeller shaft coupler-to-axle flange bolt/nuts to 43 ft. lbs. (58 Nm).

28. Using a 14mm hex, remove rear axle fill plug : Fill axle with Mopar® 75W-140 synthetic gear and axle lubricant in the following quantities:
   a. 198 Axle: 1.5 qts. (1.4L)
   b. 210 Axle: 1.5 qts. (1.4L)

29. Install and torque fill plug to:
   a. 198 Axle: 44 ft. lbs. (60 Nm)
   b. 210 Axle: 44 ft. lbs. (60 Nm)
   c. For V8 models install exhaust system. Tighten band clamps to 45 ft. lbs. (61 Nm).

30. Lower the vehicle. Tighten halfshaft hub nut to 157 ft. lbs. (213 Nm) and install wheel center cap.

31. Install wheel/tire assembly and torque lug nuts to 110 ft. lbs. (150 Nm).

REAR PINION SEAL

REMOVAL & INSTALLATION

See Figures 37 through 40.

1. Before servicing the vehicle, refer to the precautions in the beginning of this section.

2. Remove rear axle assembly from vehicle.

3. Measure axle assembly rotating torque and record measurement for reuse on assembly.

4. Using flange holder C-3281(1) and 41mm socket, remove pinion flange nut and discard.

➡**Due to axle imbalance concerns, it is necessary to make sure pinion flange-to-shaft orientation is maintained. If alignment marks are not visible, apply appropriate marks before removing pinion flange.**

5. Using puller 1026 (1), remove pinion flange (2) from pinion shaft.

6. Using suitable tool, remove pinion seal and discard.

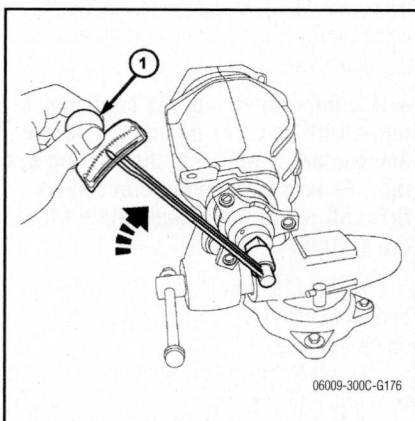

06009-300C-G176

Fig. 37 Measure axle assembly rotating torque

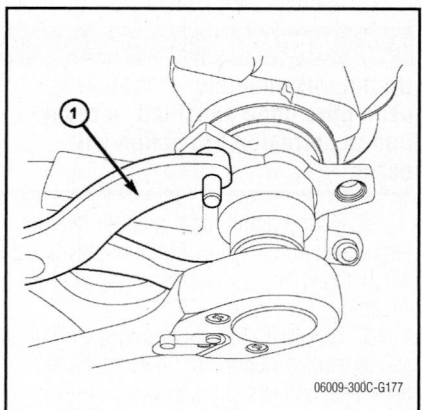

06009-300C-G177

Fig. 38 Remove flange nut

To install:

7. Apply light coating of gear lubricant to the lip of the pinion seal.

8. Using a seal driver, install pinion seal until tool bottoms on carrier.

9. Install pinion flange into position. Align index marks to maintain assembly balance.

10. Lightly tap on pinion flange until adequate pinion shaft threads are exposed.

11. Install new pinion flange nut. Using flange holder tool C-3281and 41mm socket, torque nut to 100 ft. lbs. (136 Nm).

12. Measure assembly turning torque. Axle assembly rotating torque must be should be equal to the reading recorded upon seal/flange removal.

13. If rotating torque is low, increase pinion flange nut torque in 60 inch lbs. (7 Nm) increments. Repeat until proper rotating torque is received.

14. Stake pinion flange nut (1) as shown.

15. Install rear axle assembly.

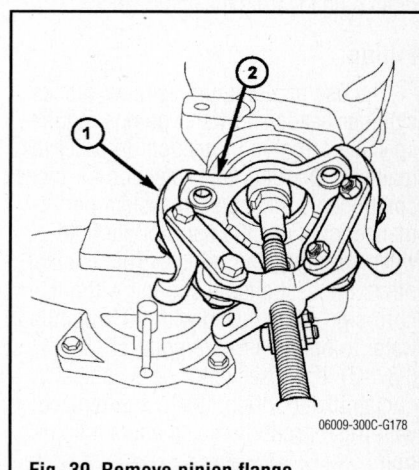

06009-300C-G178

Fig. 39 Remove pinion flange

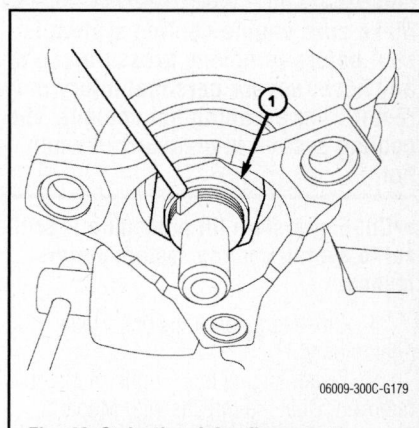

06009-300C-G179

Fig. 40 Stake the pinion flange nut

ENGINE COOLING

ENGINE COOLANT

DRAIN & REFILL PROCEDURE

Draining

✳✳ CAUTION

Do not remove cylinder block drain plugs or loosen radiator draincock with system hot and under pressure. Serious burns from coolant can occur.

DO NOT WASTE reusable coolant. If solution is clean, drain coolant into a clean container for reuse.

1. Remove radiator pressure cap.
2. Raise and secure vehicle.
3. If equipped, remove the underbody splash shield.
4. Loosen radiator petcock.
5. Drain coolant into a clean container.
6. If necessary, to perform a complete coolant drain of the engine, remove the drain plug (1) from the engine block.

Filling

The use of aluminum cylinder blocks, cylinder heads and water pumps requires special corrosion protection. In order to maintain the required protection for these components and cooling system performance, only use the appropriate fluid when servicing the vehicle. This coolant offers the best engine cooling without corrosion when mixed with 50% distilled water to obtain a freeze point of -35°F (-37°C). If it loses color or becomes contaminated, drain, flush, and replace with fresh properly mixed coolant solution.

✳✳ CAUTION

Make sure engine cooling system is cool before removing pressure cap or any hose. severe personal injury may result from escaping hot coolant. The cooling system is pressurized when hot.

➡**Cooling system fill procedure is critical to overall cooling system performance.**

1. Close radiator draincock. Hand tighten only.
2. Install engine block drain plugs, if removed. Coat the threads with Mopar® Thread Sealant with Teflon.

✳✳ CAUTION

When installing drain hose to air bleed valve, route hose away from accessory drive belts, accessory drive pulleys, and electric cooling fan motors.

➡**It may be necessary to install a bleed fitting on the 5.7L engine.**

3. Attach a 4–6 ft. (1.5 - 2 m) long 1/4 inch (6.35 mm) ID clear hose to bleeder fitting.

Bleed Valve Location
- 2.7L: Located on the water outlet connector at the front of engine.
- 3.5L: Located on the lower intake manifold, left of center and below the upper intake plenum.
- 5.7L: Located on the front of the water outlet housing at the front of engine.

4. Route hose away from the accessory drive belt, drive pulleys and electric cooling fan. Place the other end of hose into a clean container. The hose will prevent coolant from contacting the accessory drive belt when bleeding the system during the refilling operation.

➡**It is imperative that the cooling system air bleed valve be opened before any coolant is added to the cooling system. Failure to open the bleed valve first will result in an incomplete fill of the system.**

5. 5.7LENGINE: Install a threaded and barbed fitting (1/4 - 18 npt) into water pump housing.
6. Attach the Filling Aid Funnel to pressure bottle filler neck.
7. Using hose pinch-off pliers, pinch overflow hose that connects between the two chambers of the coolant bottle.
8. Open the bleed fitting.

✳✳ WARNING

Do not mix coolants. If coolant is used other than specified, a reduction in corrosion protection will occur.

9. Pour the antifreeze mixture into the larger section of Filling Aid Funnel (the smaller section of funnel is to allow air to escape).
10. Slowly fill the cooling system until a steady stream of coolant flows from the hose attached to the bleed valve.
11. Close the bleed valve and continue

filling system to the top of the Filling Aid Funnel.
12. Remove pinch-off pliers from overflow hose.
13. Allow the coolant in Filling Funnel to drain into overflow chamber of the pressure bottle.
14. Remove the Filling Aid Funnel. Install cap on coolant pressure bottle.
15. Remove hose from bleed valve.
16. 5.7L ENGINE: Install fitting into thermostat housing. Coat the threads with Mopar® Thread Sealant with Teflon.
17. Start engine and run at 1500 - 2000 RPM for 30 minutes.

➡**The engine cooling system will push any remaining air into the coolant bottle within about an hour of normal driving. As a result, a drop in coolant level in the pressure bottle may occur. If the engine cooling system overheats and pushes coolant into the overflow side of the coolant bottle, this coolant will be sucked back into the cooling system ONLY IF THE PRESSURE CAP IS LEFT ON THE BOTTLE. Removing the pressure cap breaks the vacuum path between the two bottle sections and the coolant will not return to cooling system.**

18. Shut off engine and allow it to cool down for 30 minutes. This permits coolant to be drawn into the pressure chamber.
19. With engine COLD, observe coolant level in pressure chamber. Coolant level should be within MIN and MAX marks. Adjust coolant level as necessary.

➡**The coolant bottle has two chambers. Coolant will normally only be in the inboard of the two. The outboard chamber is only to recover coolant in the event of an overheat or after a recent service fill.**

FLUSHING

Cleaning

Drain cooling system and refill with water. Run engine with radiator cap installed until upper radiator hose is hot. Stop engine and drain water from system. If water is dirty, fill system with water, run engine and drain system. Repeat until water drains clean.

Reverse Flushing

Reverse flushing of cooling system is the forcing of water through the cooling system. This is done using air pressure in the opposite direction of normal coolant flow. It is usually only necessary with very dirty systems with evidence of partial plugging.

Reverse Flushing Radiator

Disconnect radiator hoses from radiator inlet and outlet. Attach a section of radiator hose to radiator bottom outlet fitting and insert flushing gun. Connect a water supply hose and air supply hose to flushing gun.

✳✳ WARNING

Internal radiator pressure must not exceed 20 psi (138 kPa) as damage to radiator may result.

Allow the radiator to fill with water. When radiator is filled, apply air in short blasts. Allow radiator to refill between blasts. Continue this reverse flushing until clean water flows out through rear of radiator cooling tube passages. Have radiator cleaned more extensively by a radiator repair shop.

Reverse Flushing Engine

Drain the cooling system. Remove thermostat housing and thermostat. Install thermostat housing. Disconnect radiator upper hose from radiator and attach flushing gun to hose. Disconnect radiator lower hose from water pump and attach a lead-away hose to water pump inlet fitting.

✳✳ WARNING

On vehicles equipped with a heater water control valve, be sure heater control valve is closed (heat off). This will prevent coolant flow with scale and other deposits from entering heater core.

Connect water supply hose and air supply hose to flushing gun. Allow engine to fill with water. When engine is filled, apply air in short blasts, allowing system to fill between air blasts. Continue until clean water flows through the lead away hose.

Remove lead away hose, flushing gun, water supply hose and air supply hose. Remove thermostat housing and install thermostat. Install thermostat housing with a replacement gasket. Refer to Thermostat Replacement. Connect radiator hoses. Refill cooling system with correct antifreeze/water mixture.

Chemical Cleaning

In some instances, use a radiator cleaner (Mopar Radiator Kleen or equivalent) before flushing. This will soften scale and other deposits and aid flushing operation.

✳✳ WARNING

Follow the manufacturer's instructions when using these products.

ENGINE FAN

REMOVAL & INSTALLATION

1. Disconnect the negative battery cable.
2. Partially drain the cooling system.
3. 3.6L engine only, remove the air filter housing assembly.
4. Remove the upper radiator hose.
5. Detach the cooling fan electrical connector.
6. Remove the cooling fan mounting bolts.
7. Remove the radiator cooling fan assembly from vehicle.

To install:

8. Position the radiator cooling fan assembly in the vehicle.
9. Install the cooling fan mounting bolts and tighten them to 50 inch lbs. (6 Nm).
10. Attach the cooling fan electrical connector.
11. Install the upper radiator hose.
12. 3.6L engine only, install the air filter hosing assembly.
13. Fill the cooling system.
14. Operate the engine until it reaches normal operating temperature. Check cooling system and automatic transmission for correct fluid levels.

RADIATOR

REMOVAL & INSTALLATION

2.7L, 3.5L & 6.1L Engines

See Figures 41 and 42.

1. Disconnect the negative battery cable.
2. Drain the cooling system.
3. Disconnect the upper radiator hose.
4. Remove the upper radiator closure panels.
5. Remove the radiator fan assembly.
6. Raise and safely support the vehicle.
7. Remove the lower splash shield.
8. Disconnect the lower radiator hose.
9. Remove the lower condenser mount bolts.
10. Lower the vehicle.
11. Remove the upper radiator hose.

➡ **Bolts have a thread locker on them, use hand tools to remove the upper radiator mounting bolts.**

12. Remove the upper radiator mounting brackets and bolts.
13. Remove the upper condenser mounting bolts.
14. Separate the condenser assembly from radiator.
15. Tilt the radiator toward engine and remove radiator from vehicle.

To install:

16. Position the radiator into the engine compartment. Seat the radiator assembly lower rubber isolators into the mounting holes in radiator lower support.
17. Install radiator mounting bracket and bolts. Tighten the bolts to 106 inch lbs. (12 Nm).
18. Position the condenser on the radiator and install upper mounting bolts. Tighten bolts to 50 inch lbs. (6 Nm).
19. Install the lower condenser mounting bolts. Tighten bolts to 88 inch lbs. (10 Nm).
20. Install the lower radiator hose and clamp.

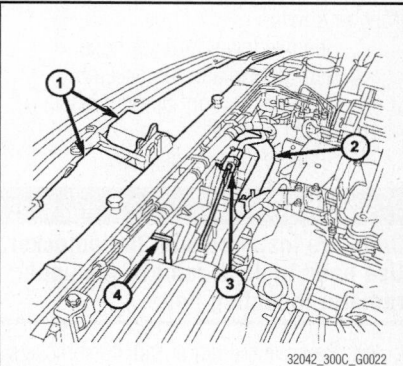

32042_300C_G0022

Fig. 41 View of the upper radiator closure panels (1), upper radiator hose (2), fan electrical connector (3) and fan assembly (4)

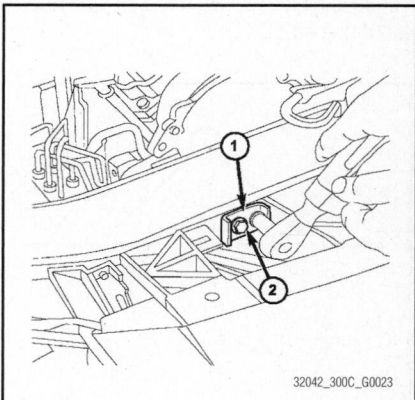

32042_300C_G0023

Fig. 42 Radiator mounting bracket (1) and bolts (2)

21. Install the radiator fan.

22. Install the upper radiator upper house. Align the hose so it does not interfere with the accessory drive belt or engine. Position hose clamp so it will not interfere with the hood.

23. Install the upper radiator closure panels.

24. Connect the negative battery cable.

25. Fill the cooling system with coolant.

26. Operate the engine until it reaches normal operating temperature. Check cooling system and automatic transmission for correct fluid levels.

3.6L Engine

See Figures 43 and 44.

1. Disconnect negative battery cable.
2. Remove the air intake assembly.
3. Drain cooling system.
4. Remove upper radiator hose.
5. Raise vehicle.
6. Remove the lower engine cover and front air shield.
7. Remove lower radiator hose.
8. Remove radiator fan assembly.
9. Remove the front bumper fascia.
10. Lower vehicle.
11. Remove the air deflectors.

✳✳ WARNING

Bolts are installed with threadlocker. Use hand tools to remove the upper radiator mounting bolts.

12. Remove the upper radiator brackets from the radiator supports.

13. Remove the lower condenser mounting bolts.

14. Remove the support bolt located between the cooler lines.

15. Using a suitable hanger. Support the condenser and remove the right side upper mounting bolt.

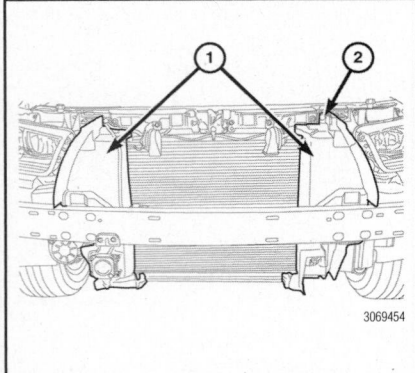

Fig. 43 Removing the air deflectors

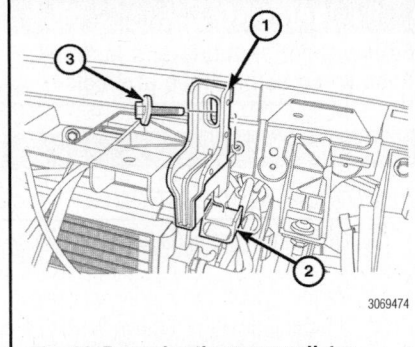

Fig. 44 Removing the upper radiator brackets

➡**To aid in removal. The upper shroud cover must be removed before the radiator. Leaving the cover on may cause the radiator to become jammed against the upper core support.**

16. Carefully remove the upper shroud cover by using a pick to pull the cover retaining hole away from the clip along the edge.

17. Tilt radiator toward engine for clearance from condenser.

18. Raise vehicle.

19. Using a suitable jack. Remove the lower radiator core support bolts.

20. Using care not to damage condenser or radiator fins. Lower the core support with the radiator.

21. Remove the radiator from the core support.

THERMOSTAT

REMOVAL & INSTALLATION

2.7L Engine

See Figure 45.

1. Disconnect negative cable from remote jumper terminal.
2. Drain cooling system.
3. Raise vehicle on hoist.
4. Remove right front wheel and belt splash shield.
5. Remove accessory drive belts.
6. Remove lower generator mounting bolt.
7. Lower vehicle.
8. Disconnect generator electrical connectors.
9. Disconnect AC clutch and AC pressure sensor electrical connectors. Reposition wiring harness.
10. Remove oil dipstick and tube. Plug hole in oil pan where dipstick tube mounts with water tight stopper.

✳✳ CAUTION

If hole for dipstick tube in oil pan is not plugged, coolant will enter oil pan. Serious engine damage can occur.

11. Remove remaining generator mounting bolts. Remove generator.

12. Remove radiator hose tube mounting bolt (3).

13. Disconnect hose clamps (1) at thermostat housing.

14. Remove thermostat housing bolts.

15. Remove thermostat and housing.

To install:

16. Clean gasket sealing surfaces.

➡**Install thermostat with the bleed valve located at the 12 o'clock position.**

17. Install the thermostat and gasket into the thermostat housing.

18. Install the thermostat and housing to cylinder block. Tighten attaching bolts to 105 inch lbs. (12 Nm).

19. Install radiator hose tube to thermostat and housing. Connect hose clamps at thermostat housing.

20. Install the radiator hose tube mounting bolt.

21. Install generator and attaching bolts.

➡**Before removing plug in oil pan, clean residual coolant from area.**

22. Remove the plug in oil pan and install engine oil dipstick tube.

23. Reconnect the AC clutch and AC pressure sensor connectors.

24. Reconnect the generator connectors.

25. Raise the vehicle on hoist.

26. Install the accessory drive belts.

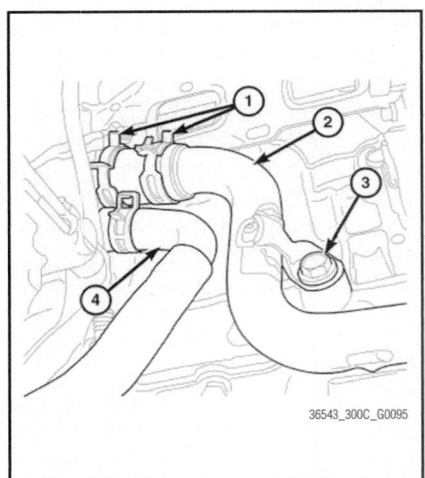

Fig. 45 Thermostat location—2.7L Engine

27. Install belt splash shield and right front wheel.
28. Lower the vehicle.
29. Reconnect negative battery cable.
30. Fill the cooling system.

3.5L Engine

See Figure 46.

1. Disconnect negative battery cable.
2. Raise the vehicle on hoist.
3. Remove belly pan.
4. Drain the cooling system.
5. Lower the vehicle on hoist.
6. Remove air box assembly.
7. Disconnect lower radiator hose from thermostat housing.
8. Remove the thermostat housing bolts.
9. Remove the thermostat housing, thermostat, and gasket.

➡**The OEM thermostat is staked in place at the factory. To ensure proper seating of replacement thermostat, carefully remove the bulged metal from the thermostat housing using a suitable hand held grinder. It is not necessary to re-stake the replacement thermostat into the thermostat housing.**

10. Clean gasket surfaces.

To install:

11. Position the gasket on thermostat and housing.
12. Install the thermostat housing, gasket and mounting bolts onto block. Tighten attaching bolts to 105 inch lbs. (12 Nm).
13. Install the radiator hose.
14. Install air box assembly.
15. Fill the cooling system.
16. Raise the vehicle on hoist.
17. Install belly pan.
18. Connect negative battery cable.

3.6L Engine

See Figure 47.

> ✳✳ **CAUTION**
>
> **Do not loosen radiator draincock with system hot and pressurized. Serious burns from coolant can occur.**

> ✳✳ **WARNING**
>
> **The Thermostat and housing is serviced as an assembly. Do not remove the thermostat from the housing, damage to the thermostat may occur.**

Do not waste reusable coolant. If solution is clean, drain coolant into a clean container for reuse.

If thermostat is being replaced, be sure that replacement is specified thermostat for vehicle model and engine type.

1. Disconnect negative battery cable at battery.
2. Remove the air intake assembly.
3. Drain cooling system.
4. Remove upper radiator hose clamp and upper radiator hose at thermostat housing.
5. Remove thermostat housing mounting bolts, thermostat housing and thermostat.

To install:

> ✳✳ **WARNING**
>
> **The Thermostat and housing is serviced as an assembly. Do not remove the thermostat from the housing, damage to the thermostat may occur.**

6. Clean mating areas of timing chain cover and thermostat housing.
7. Install a new gasket on to the thermostat housing.

8. Position thermostat housing on the water crossover.
9. Install two thermostat housing bolts. Tighten bolts to 9 ft. lbs. (12 Nm).
10. Install upper radiator hose on thermostat housing.
11. Fill cooling system.
12. Install the air intake system.
13. Connect negative battery cable to battery.
14. Start and warm the engine. Check for leaks.

5.7L Engine

See Figure 48.

1. Disconnect the negative battery cable.
2. Drain the cooling system.
3. Disconnect the radiator hose from thermostat housing.

➡**Thermostat O-ring is part of thermostat and is not serviced separately.**

4. Remove thermostat housing mounting bolts, thermostat housing and thermostat.

To install:

5. Clean the mating areas of timing chain cover and thermostat housing.

➡**Install thermostat with the bleed valve located at the 12 o'clock position.**

6. Install thermostat (spring side down) into recessed machined groove on timing chain cover with bleed valve located at the 12 o'clock position.
7. Position the thermostat housing on timing chain cover.
8. Install the two housing-to-timing chain cover bolts. Tighten bolts to 112 inch lbs. (13 Nm).

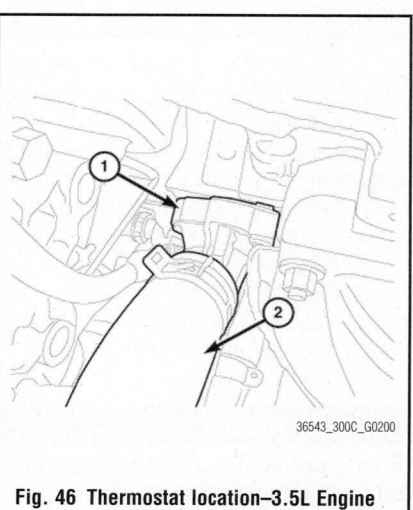

36543_300C_G0200

Fig. 46 Thermostat location–3.5L Engine

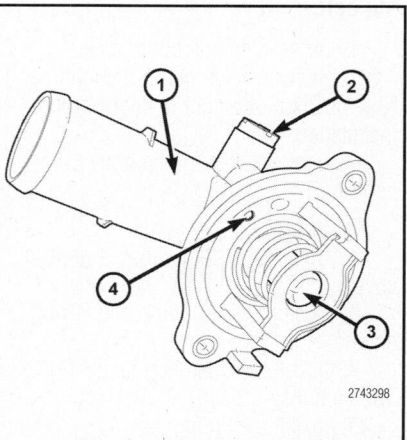

2743298

Fig. 47 View of the thermostat housing (1) and thermostat (3)—3.6L Engine

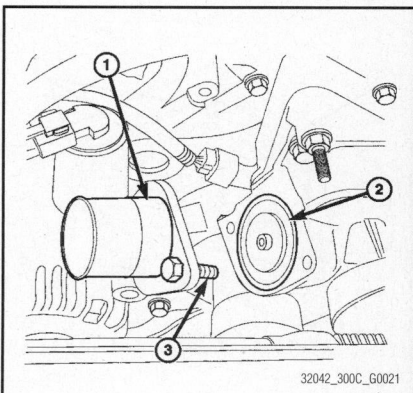

32042_300C_G0021

Fig. 48 Thermostat housing (1), thermostat (2) and retaining bolt (3)—5.7L engine

✳✳ CAUTION

Thermostat housing must be tightened evenly and thermostat must be centered into recessed groove in timing chain cover. If not, it may result in a cracked thermostat housing, damaged timing chain cover threads or coolant leaks.

9. Attach the lower radiator hose to thermostat housing.
10. Carefully lower the vehicle.
11. Fill the cooling system.
12. Connect the negative battery cable. Start and warm the engine. Check for leaks.

WATER PUMP

REMOVAL & INSTALLATION

2.7L Engine

See Figure 49.

1. Before servicing the vehicle, refer to the precautions.

✳✳ WARNING

Do not remove pressure cap with the system hot and pressurized. Serious burns from coolant can result.

2. Drain the cooling system.
3. Disconnect negative battery cable.
4. Remove the upper radiator hose.
5. Disconnect the cooling fan electrical connector.
6. Remove cooling fan mounting bolts.
7. Remove the radiator cooling fan assembly from vehicle.
8. Remove the radiator fan assembly.
9. Remove the accessory drive belt.

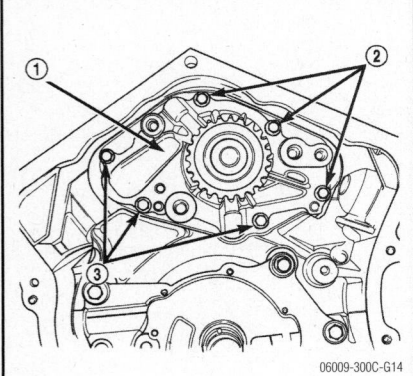

Fig. 49 Remove bolts (2 and 3) attaching water pump (1) to block—2.7L engine

➡ **The water pump is driven by the primary timing chain.**

10. Remove the timing chain and all chain guides.
11. Remove bolts attaching water pump to block.
12. Remove water pump and gasket.

To install:

13. Clean all sealing surfaces.
14. Install water pump and gasket. Tighten mounting bolts to 105 inch lbs. (12 Nm).
15. Install the timing chain guides and timing chain.
16. Install the accessory drive belts.
17. Position the radiator cooling fan assembly in vehicle.
18. Install cooling fan mounting bolts. Tighten to 50 inch lbs. (6 Nm)
19. Connect the cooling fan electrical connector.
20. Install the upper radiator hose.
21. Fill the cooling system.
22. Operate engine until it reaches normal operating temperature. Check cooling system and automatic transmission for correct fluid levels.

3.5L Engine

See Figure 50.

1. Before servicing the vehicle, refer to the precautions.

✳✳ WARNING

Do not remove pressure cap with the system hot and under pressure because serious burns from coolant can occur.

2. Drain the cooling system.
3. Remove the accessory drive belts.

➡ **The water pump is driven by the timing belt.**

4. Remove engine timing belt.
5. Remove water pump mounting bolts. Note position of longer bolts for proper installation.
6. Remove water pump body from engine.

To install:

7. Clean all O-ring surfaces on front cover.
8. Position water pump and O-ring to engine.
9. Install the mounting bolts. Tighten to 105 inch lbs. (12 Nm).
10. Install the timing belt.
11. Install the accessory drive belts.
12. Fill the cooling system.

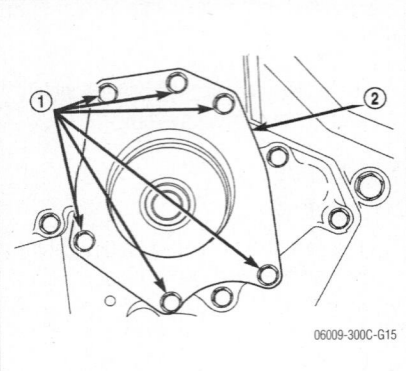

Fig. 50 Water pump mounting. (1) bolts, (2) pump—3.5L engine

3.6L Engine

See Figures 51 and 52.

➡ **The water pump on 3.6L engines is bolted directly to the engine timing chain case cover.**

1. Disconnect negative battery cable from battery.
2. Remove the air intake system and the air filter box cover as an assembly.
3. Drain the cooling system.
4. Remove the accessory drive belt.

✳✳ CAUTION

Constant tension hose clamps are used on most cooling system hoses. When removing or installing, use only tools designed for servicing this type of clamp. Always wear safety glasses when servicing constant tension clamps.

✳✳ WARNING

A number or letter is stamped into the tongue of constant tension clamps

5. If replacement is necessary, use only an original equipment clamp with matching number or letter.
6. Remove the lower heater hose at the water pump and position aside.
7. Remove the lower radiator hose from the water pump and position aside.
8. Remove idler pulley.
9. Remove the eleven water pump mounting bolts. Take notice to the four water pump bolts that bolt directly to the timing cover.

✳✳ WARNING

Do not pry on the water pump at the timing chain case/cover. The

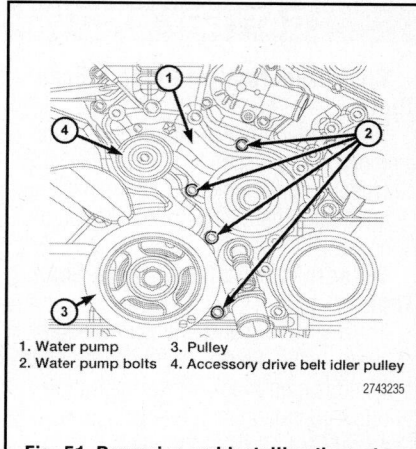

1. Water pump
2. Water pump bolts
3. Pulley
4. Accessory drive belt idler pulley

2743235

Fig. 51 Removing and installing the water pump

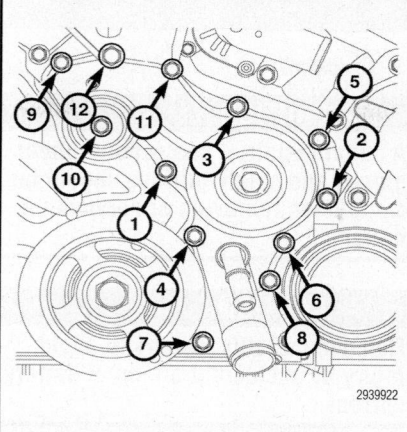

2939922

Fig. 52 Identifying the bolt tightening sequence

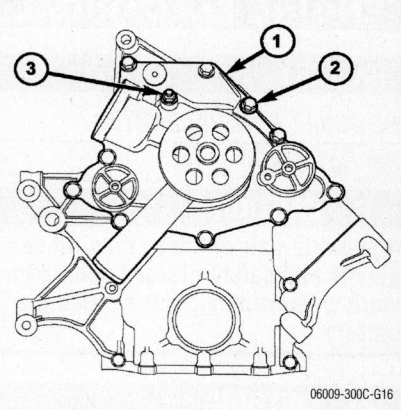

06009-300C-G16

Fig. 53 Water pump mounting (1) pump, (2) mounting bolts, (3) stud bolt

machined surfaces may be damaged resulting in leaks.

10. Remove water pump and discard gasket.

To install:
11. Clean mating surfaces.

➡**Take notice the lengths of the mounting bolts. Some M6 bolts mount directly to the timing cover.**

12. Using a new gasket, position water pump and hand tighten the M6 mounting bolts.
13. Hand tighten the idler pulley bolt.
14. Hand tighten the upper M8 and M10 water pump to engine block mounting bolts.

➡**Tightening the water pump fasteners in sequential order, will insure proper sealing surface.**

15. Tighten the bolts 1 - 12 in the sequence shown. Tighten the bolts to their respective torque:
    a. Tighten M6 mounting bolts to 9 ft. lbs. (12 Nm).
    b. Tighten M8 bolts to 18 ft. lbs. (25 Nm).
    c. Tighten M10 bolt to 41 ft. lbs. (55 Nm).
    d. Repeat the tightening sequence until the proper torque has been met.
16. Spin water pump to be sure that pump impeller does not rub against timing chain case/cover.

✳✳ **WARNING**

A number or letter is stamped into the tongue of constant tension clamps. If replacement is necessary, use only an original equipment clamp with matching number or letter.

17. Install the lower radiator hose.
18. Install the lower return heater hose.

✳✳ **WARNING**

When installing the serpentine accessory drive belt, belt must be routed correctly. If not, engine may overheat due to water pump rotating in wrong direction.

19. Install accessory drive belt.
20. Evacuate air and refill cooling system.
21. Install the air intake hose and resonator assembly at the air filter housing.
22. Connect the intake air temperature sensor.
23. Connect negative battery cable.
24. Check the cooling system for leaks.

5.7L Engine
See Figure 53.

1. Before servicing the vehicle, refer to the precautions.
2. Disconnect negative battery cable.
3. Drain the cooling system.
4. Disconnect negative battery cable.

5. Remove the upper radiator hose.
6. Disconnect the cooling fan electrical connector.
7. Remove cooling fan mounting bolts.
8. Remove the radiator cooling fan assembly from vehicle.
9. Remove the radiator fan assembly.
10. Remove the accessory drive belt.
11. Remove the thermostat.

➡**The water pump mounting bolts are different lengths. Note the location of the water pump mounting bolts.**

12. Remove water pump mounting bolts and remove water pump.

To install:
13. Install water pump and mounting bolts. Tighten mounting bolts to 20 ft. lbs. (28 Nm).
14. Make sure double ended bolt is in the proper location. Tighten double ended bolt to 20 ft. lbs. (28 Nm).
15. Position the radiator cooling fan assembly in vehicle.
16. Install cooling fan mounting bolts. Tighten to 50 inch lbs. (6 Nm)
17. Connect the cooling fan electrical connector.
18. Install the upper radiator hose.
19. Install the thermostat.
20. Install the accessory drive belt.
21. Install the radiator fan assembly.
22. Connect negative battery cable.
23. Fill the cooling system.
24. Pressure test cooling system.

ENGINE ELECTRICAL

BATTERY

REMOVAL & INSTALLATION
See Figure 54.

✳✳ CAUTION

A suitable pair of heavy duty rubber gloves and safety glasses should be worn when removing or servicing a battery.

✳✳ CAUTION

Remove metallic jewelry to avoid injury by accidental arcing of battery current.

1. Make sure ignition switch is in OFF position and all accessories are turned OFF.
2. Remove the rear compartment floor, trim panel to gain access to the battery.
3. Disconnect the battery negative cable (2) from the battery terminal.
4. Disconnect the battery positive cable (1) from the battery terminal.
5. Unlatch the battery retention strap (4).

✳✳ WARNING

Use care when disconnecting the battery vent tube from the battery. The vent tube nipple is made of plastic and is easily damaged if not disconnected properly.

6. Gently disconnect the battery vent tube from the battery nipple.
7. Remove the battery hold down clamp and remove the battery from the vehicle.

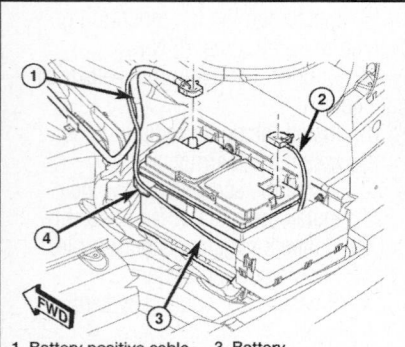

1. Battery positive cable   3. Battery
2. Battery negative cable   4. Battery retention strap

607

Fig. 54 Removing and installing the battery

To install:

✳✳ CAUTION

A suitable pair of heavy duty rubber gloves and safety glasses should be worn when removing or servicing a battery.

✳✳ CAUTION

Remove metallic jewelry to avoid injury by accidental arcing of battery current.

8. Position the battery in the battery tray.
9. Install the battery hold down clamp and bolt. Torque the bolt to 35 inch lbs. (4 Nm).

✳✳ WARNING

Use care when connecting the battery vent tube to the battery. The vent tube nipple is made of plastic and is easily damaged if not connected properly.

10. Gently connect the battery vent tube to the battery nipple.
11. Latch the battery retention strap.
12. Connect the battery positive cable.
13. Connect the battery negative cable.
14. Install the rear compartment floor trim panel.

BATTERY RECONNECT/RELEARN PROCEDURE

➡**This reconnection procedure is to be performed anytime the battery has been disconnected.**

1. Connect the battery negative cable to the battery post and tighten the clamp nut.
2. Install the rear compartment floor trim panel.

✳✳ WARNING

Once the battery has been connected, review and perform the following information as applicable.

Express Front Window(s)

➡**Make sure battery is fully charged before proceeding.**

➡**This needs to be completed every time the window glass is adjusted/removed, motor replaced, and or regulator replaced.**

BATTERY SYSTEM

Clear/Denormalize Using A Scan Tool

To clear/denormalize the door module memory, using a scan tool under the Miscellaneous menu look for Denormalization Window Command, and follow the directions.

Relearn/Normalize Using A Scan Tool

To relearn/normalize the door module memory, using a scan tool under the Miscellaneous menu look for Normalization Window command, and follow the directions.

Clear/Denormalize, Relearn/Normalize Without A Scan Tool

Hold up/down the window switch for at least 30 seconds until the DTC is set for stuck switch. This will clear the memory of the calibration information (CLEAR/DENORMAILIZE). Proceed to relearn/normalize.

3. Put a battery charger on vehicle.
4. If equipped with express-up/express-down, reset the express-up/down module for the door window glass. The window switch on the corresponding door must be used to control the window. Do not use the master switch for the passenger window.
5. To calibrate, start by moving the window to the middle position.
6. Drive the glass to the full-up position by pulling up on the window switch to its second detent and hold the switch until the glass is fully closed. Do not release the window switch. Continue to hold the window switch up for 2 seconds after the window glass is full closed.
7. Drive the glass to the full - down position by pushing down (depress) the window switch, (second detent if equipped with express-down) until the window glass is down for 2 seconds after the window glass is fully open. Do not release the window switch. Continue to hold the window switch down for 2 seconds after the window glass is fully open.
8. Check the operation of the express-up/ express-down feature.
9. If the express up/down doesn't work, repeat step # 3, waiting for 3 seconds.
10. Check that the window glass reverses when in the express-up mode by holding a pen in the path of the glass.
11. Once the proper operation of the express-up/express-down feature has been verified, clear all Diagnostic Trouble Codes (DTC's).

Electronic Stability Program (ESP)

If the vehicle is equipped with ESP, once the battery is reconnected, the Steering Angle Sensor (SAS) within the Antilock Brake Module (ABM) needs to be calibrated. The SAS requires calibration (initialization) using the scan tool anytime the battery or an ABS (ESP) component has been disconnected for any length of time. If the SAS is not calibrated following battery reconnection, the ESP/BAS indicator lamp will flash continuously with no DTCs.

12. To calibrate (initialize), perform the following:

a. Position the front wheels straight ahead and center the steering wheel.

b. Connect the scan tool to the vehicle.

c. Follow the directions on the scan tool.

ENGINE ELECTRICAL

ALTERNATOR

REMOVAL & INSTALLATION

2.7L Engine

See Figure 55.

> ❈❈ **CAUTION**
>
> **Disconnect negative cable from battery before removing battery output wire (B+ wire) from alternator. Failure to do so can result in injury or damage to electrical system.**

1. Before servicing the vehicle, refer to the precautions in the beginning of this section.
2. Disconnect negative battery cable.
3. Remove alternator drive belt.
4. Disconnect alternator field circuit plug.
5. Remove the B+ terminal nut and wire.
6. Remove 2 lower mounting bolts.
7. Remove the alternator.

To install:

8. Install the alternator.
9. Install upper bolt mounting bolt.
10. Install 2 lower mounting bolts.
11. Tighten bolts to 48 ft. lbs. (65 Nm).
12. Install the B+ terminal nut and wire. Tighten nut to 115 inch lbs. (13 Nm).

13. Connect alternator field circuit plug.
14. Install the alternator drive belt.
15. Connect negative battery cable.

3.5L Engine

See Figure 56.

> ❈❈ **CAUTION**
>
> **Disconnect negative cable from battery before removing battery output wire (B+ wire) from alternator. Failure to do so can result in injury or damage to electrical system.**

1. Before servicing the vehicle, refer to the precautions in the beginning of this section.
2. Disconnect negative battery cable.
3. Remove the alternator drive belt.
4. Remove bracket bolts.
5. Remove the upper mounting bolt.
6. Raise and support vehicle.
7. Remove middle splash pan.
8. Disconnect alternator field circuit plug.
9. Remove the B+ terminal nut and wire.
10. Remove lower mounting bolts.
11. Remove the alternator.

To install:

12. Install the alternator.
13. Install the lower mounting bolts. Loosen install the upper mounting bolt.

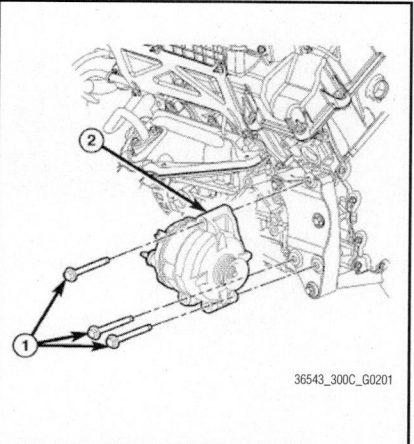

Fig. 55 Alternator bolt location—2.7L Engine

36543_300C_G0201

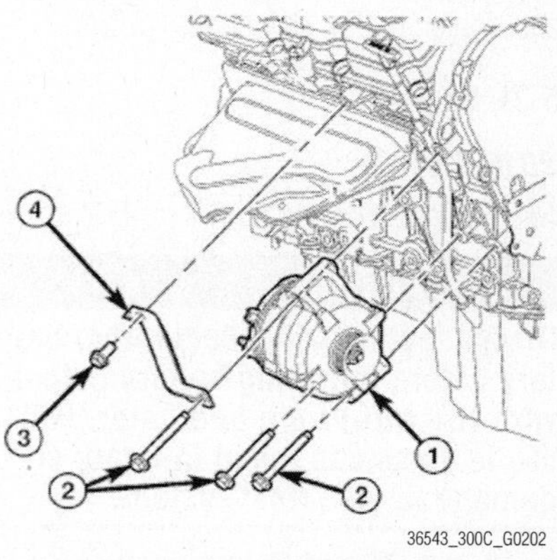

Fig. 56 Alternator (1), mounting bolts (2), bracket bolt (3) and bracket (4)—3.5L Engine

36543_300C_G0202

CHARGING SYSTEM

14. Tighten lower mounting bolts to 48 ft. lbs. (65 Nm).
15. Connect alternator field circuit plug.
16. Install the B+ terminal nut and wire. Tighten nut to 115 inch lbs. (13 Nm).
17. Install middle splash pan.
18. Lower the vehicle.
19. Remove the loose installed upper bolt.
20. Install bracket and bracket bolt.
21. Install upper mounting bolt and bracket.
22. Tighten the upper mounting bolt to 48 ft. lbs. (65 Nm).
23. Tighten the bracket bolt to 40 ft. lbs. (54 Nm).
24. Install the alternator drive belt.
25. Connect negative battery cable.

3.6L Engine

See Figures 57 through 59.

> ❈❈ **CAUTION**
>
> **Disconnect the negative battery cable before removing the battery output wire (B+ wire) from the generator. Failure to do so can result in injury or damage the electrical system.**

1. Disconnect and isolate the negative battery cable.

> ❈❈ **WARNING**
>
> **Do not let the tensioner arm snap back to the freearm position, sever damage may occur to the tensioner.**

2. Rotate the accessory drive belt tensioner counterclockwise until it contacts it's stop and remove the accessory drive belt, then slowly rotate the tensioner into the freearm position.
3. Remove the upper generator retaining bolts.
4. Remove the insulator cover from the B+ output terminal at the rear of the generator.
5. Remove the B+ terminal retaining nut at the rear of the generator and remove the B+ terminal.
6. Depress the field wire connector tab at the rear of the generator and disconnect the field wire connector.

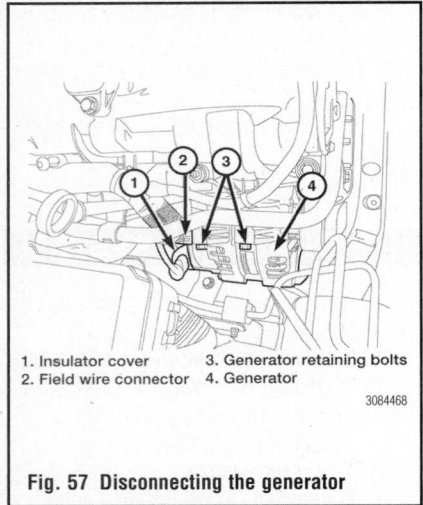

1. Insulator cover
2. Field wire connector
3. Generator retaining bolts
4. Generator

3084468

Fig. 57 Disconnecting the generator

7. Raise and support the vehicle.

8. Remove the belly pan retainers and remove the belly pan.

9. Remove the lower generator retaining bolt (1).

10. Remove the generator (2) from below the engine compartment.

To install:

→Position the generator, install all bolts to engine finger tight, then tighten fasteners to specification.

11. Position the generator to the engine and install the lower retaining bolt finger tight.

12. Lower the vehicle.

13. Install the upper generator retaining bolts and tighten to 18 ft. lbs. (25 Nm).

14. Snap the field wire connector into the rear of the generator.

15. Position the generator B+ terminal eyelet to the generator output stud, install the retaining nut and tighten to 10 ft. lbs. (13 Nm).

16. Install the insulator cover onto the B+ output terminal.

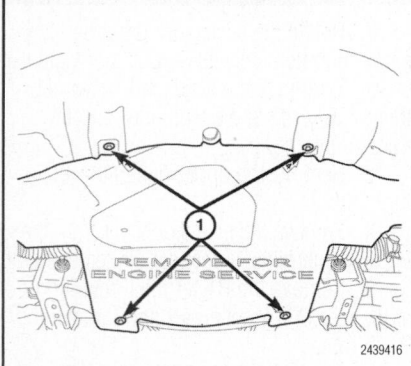

2439416

Fig. 58 Locating the belly pan retainers (1)

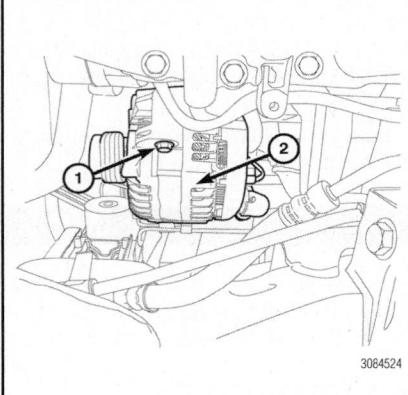

3084524

Fig. 59 Removing and installing the generator

17. Raise and support the vehicle.

18. Tighten the lower generator retaining bolt to 18 ft. lbs. (25 Nm).

19. Position the belly pan and install the belly pan retainers (1).

20. Lower the vehicle.

❈❈ WARNING

When installing a serpentine accessory drive belt, the belt MUST be routed correctly. The water pump will be rotating in the wrong direction if the belt is installed incorrectly, causing the engine to overheat.

❈❈ WARNING

Do not let the tensioner arm snap back to the freearm position, sever damage may occur to the tensioner.

21. Rotate the accessory drive belt tensioner counterclockwise until it contacts the stop and install the accessory drive belt onto the pulleys and slowly release the tensioner.

22. Connect the negative battery cable and tighten nut to 45 inch lbs. (5 Nm).

5.7L Engine

2010 Models

See Figures 60 and 61.

❈❈ CAUTION

Disconnect negative cable from battery before removing battery output wire (B+ wire) from alternator. Failure to do so can result in injury or damage to electrical system.

1. Before servicing the vehicle, refer to the precautions in the beginning of this section.

2. Disconnect negative battery cable at battery.

3. Remove the alternator drive belt.

4. Raise and support vehicle.

5. Unsnap plastic insulator cap from B+ output terminal.

6. Remove B+ terminal mounting nut at rear of alternator. Disconnect terminal from alternator.

7. Disconnect field wire connector at rear of alternator by pushing on connector tab.

8. Remove the alternator support bracket nut and bolt. Remove support bracket.

9. Remove the 2 alternator mounting bolts.

10. Remove the alternator from vehicle.

To install:

11. Position alternator to engine and install 2 mounting bolts.

12. Tighten bolts to 48 ft. lbs. (65 Nm).

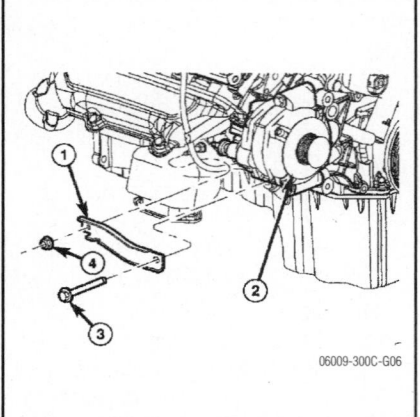

06009-300C-G06

Fig. 60 Alternator support bracket (1)— 5.7L engine

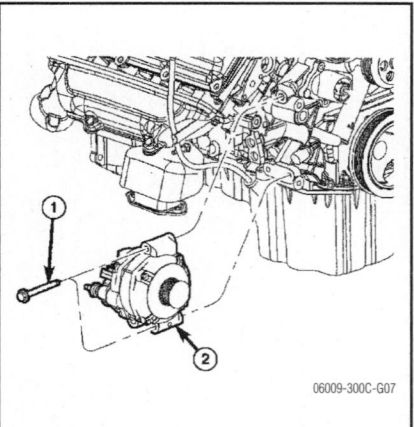

06009-300C-G07

Fig. 61 Alternator (2) installation—5.7L engine

13. Position support bracket to alternator and install bolt and nut. Tighten bolt/nut to 48 ft. lbs. (65 Nm).

14. Snap the field wire connector into rear of alternator.

15. Install the B+ terminal eyelet to alternator output stud.

16. Lower the vehicle.

❄❄ CAUTION

Never force a belt over a pulley rim using a screwdriver. The synthetic fiber of the belt can be damaged. When installing a serpentine accessory drive belt, the belt MUST be routed correctly. The water pump may be rotating in the wrong direction if the belt is installed incorrectly, causing the engine to overheat. Refer to belt routing label in engine compartment.

17. Install the alternator drive belt.

18. Install negative battery cable to battery.

2011 Models

See Figures 62 through 65.

❄❄ CAUTION

Disconnect the negative battery cable before removing the battery output wire (B+ wire) from the generator. Failure to do so can result in injury or damage the electrical system.

1. Disconnect and isolate the negative battery cable.

❄❄ WARNING

Do not let the tensioner arm snap back to the freearm position, sever damage may occur to the tensioner.

2. Rotate the accessory drive belt tensioner clockwise until it contacts the stop and remove the accessory drive belt, then slowly rotate the tensioner into the freearm position.

3. Raise and support the vehicle.

4. Remove the belly pan retainers and remove the belly pan.

5. Remove the transmission cooler line retaining clamp at the right crossmember and position the transmission cooler line aside.

6. Depress the field wire connector tab at the rear of the generator and disconnect the field wire connector.

7. Remove the insulator cover from B+ output terminal at the rear of the generator.

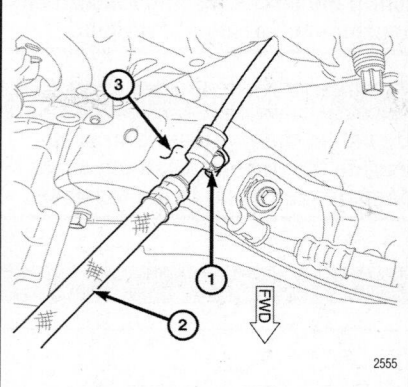

Fig. 62 View of the transmission cooler line retaining clamp (1), cooler line (2) and right crossmember (3)

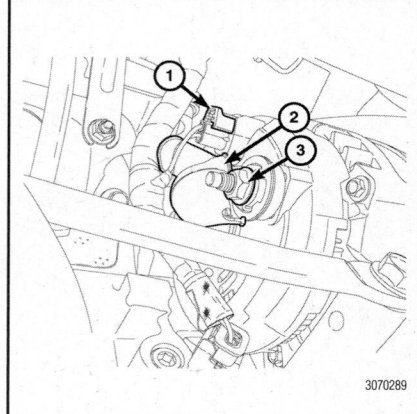

Fig. 63 Disconnecting the field wire connector tab (1), removing the insulator cover (2) and removing the retaining nut (3)

8. Remove the B+ terminal retaining nut at the rear of the generator and remove the B+ terminal.

9. Remove the generator support bracket to engine mount retaining nut.

10. Remove the generator support bracket retaining bolt and remove the support bracket.

11. Remove the remaining lower generator retaining bolt.

12. Lower the vehicle.

13. Remove the upper generator retaining bolt and remove the generator from the vehicle.

To install:

14. Position the generator and install the upper generator retaining bolt finger tight.

15. Raise and support the vehicle.

16. Position the generator B+ terminal eyelet to the generator output stud, install

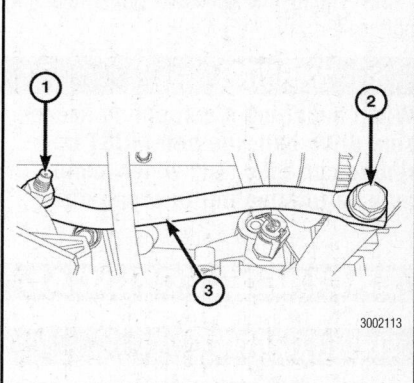

Fig. 64 Removing the generator support bracket to engine mount retaining nut (1), bolt (2) and support bracket (3)

the retaining nut and tighten to 10 ft. lbs. (13 Nm).

17. Install the insulator cover onto the B+ output terminal.

18. Snap the field wire connector into the rear of the generator.

19. Position the generator support bracket to the engine mount, install the retaining nut finger tight.

20. Position the generator support bracket to the generator and install the retaining bolt finger tight.

21. Install the remaining generator retaining bolt and tighten both lower retaining bolts to 48 ft. lbs. (65 Nm).

22. Tighten the generator support bracket to engine mount retaining nut to 21 ft. lbs. (28 Nm).

23. Position transmission cooler line and install the transmission cooler line retainer clamp to the right crossmember.

24. Position the belly pan and install the belly pan retainers.

25. Lower the vehicle.

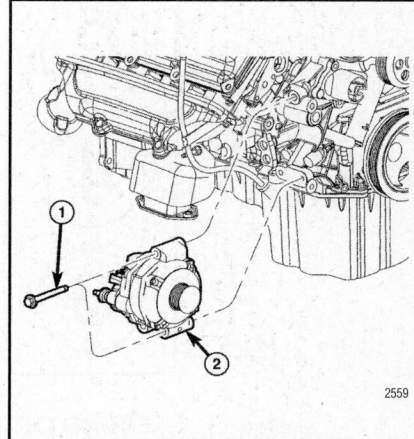

Fig. 65 View of the lower generator retaining bolt (1) and generator (2)

26. Tighten the generator upper retaining bolt to 48 ft. lbs. (65 Nm).

> ❊❊ **WARNING**
>
> **When installing a serpentine accessory drive belt, the belt MUST be routed correctly. The water pump may be rotating in the wrong direc-**

tion if the belt is installed incorrectly, causing the engine to overheat.

> ❊❊ **WARNING**
>
> **Do not let the tensioner arm snap back to the freearm position, sever damage may occur to the tensioner.**

27. Rotate the accessory drive belt tensioner clockwise until it contacts the stop, install the accessory drive belt onto the pulleys and slowly release the tensioner.

28. Connect the negative battery cable and tighten the nut to 45 inch lbs. (5 Nm).

ENGINE ELECTRICAL

FIRING ORDER

See Figures 66 and 67.

Refer to the accompanying illustrations.

IGNITION COIL

REMOVAL & INSTALLATION

2.7L Engine

1. Before servicing the vehicle, refer to the precautions in the beginning of this section.
2. Disconnect the negative battery cable.
3. Remove the upper intake manifold.
4. Prior to removing the ignition coils, spray compressed air around the coil area and spark plug to remove contaminates from around spark plug tube.
5. Disconnect the electrical connector from ignition coils.
6. Remove the fastener from each ignition coil assembly.

IGNITION SYSTEM

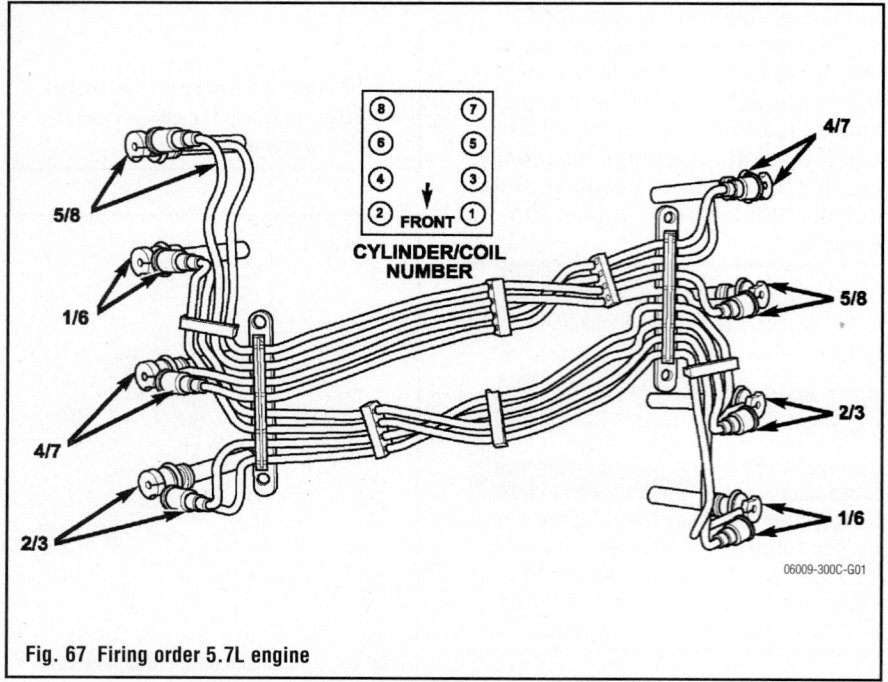

Fig. 67 Firing order 5.7L engine

7. Twist, lift and remove ignition coil from engine.

To install:

8. Align coil with top of spark plug.
9. Twist coil assembly down on to spark plug and install mounting bolt.
   a. Tighten bolt to 65 inch lbs. (7.5 Nm).
10. Connect the electrical connector to ignition coil.
11. Install the upper intake manifold.
12. Connect the negative battery cable and tighten nut to 45 inch lbs. (5 Nm).

3.5L Engine

See Figure 68.

1. Before servicing the vehicle, refer to the precautions in the beginning of this section.
2. Remove the engine cover.
3. Disconnect the negative battery cable.
4. Remove the intake manifold.
5. Unlock and disconnect electrical connector from ignition coils.

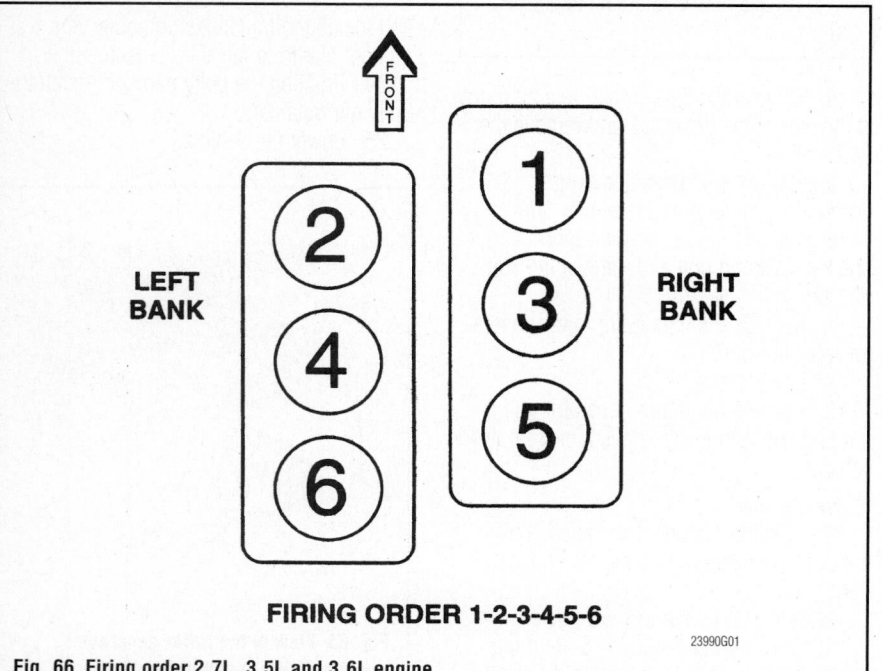

Fig. 66 Firing order 2.7L, 3.5L and 3.6L engine

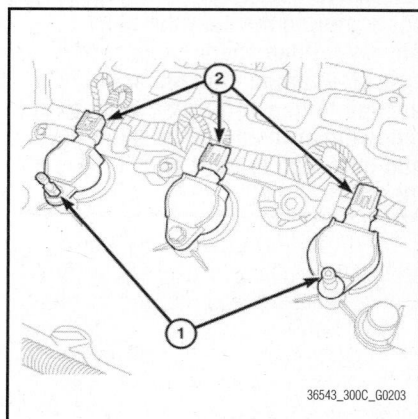

Fig. 68 Ignition coil (1, 2) location—3.5L Engine

6. Remove the mounting bolts and engine cover studs.

7. Prior to removing the ignition coils, spray compressed air around the coil area and spark plug to remove contaminates from around spark plug tube.

8. Twist, lift and remove ignition coil from engine.

To install:

9. Install the ignition coil.

10. Install engine cover studs in the two outside ignition coils on the front of the engine. Install bolts on the other ignition coils.

    a. Tighten the studs and bolts to 71 inch lbs. (8 Nm).

11. Connect the electrical connector and lock.

12. Install the intake manifold.

13. Connect negative battery cable and tighten nut to 45 inch lbs. (5 Nm).

14. Install engine cover.

3.6L Engine

See Figure 69.

1. Disconnect and isolate the negative battery cable.

2. Lift the engine cover retaining grommets off the ball studs and remove the engine cover.

3. If removing the ignition coils from cylinders 1, 3 or 5 on the right side of the engine, first remove the air inlet hose.

4. If removing the ignition coils from cylinders 2, 4 or 6 on the left side of the engine, first remove the air inlet hose, upper intake manifold and insulator.

➡**The left side ignition coils are shown, the right side ignition coils are similar.**

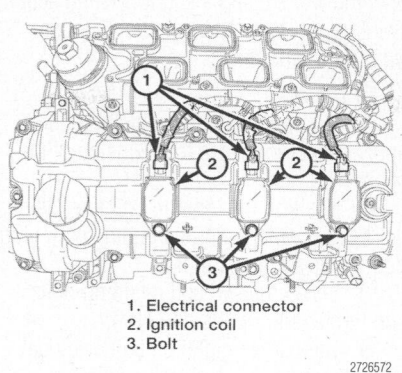

1. Electrical connector
2. Ignition coil
3. Bolt

Fig. 69 View of the ignition coil electrical connector (1), coil (2) and retaining bolts (3)

5. Unlock and disconnect the electrical connector from the ignition coil.

6. Remove the ignition coil retaining bolt.

7. Pull the ignition coil from cylinder head cover opening with a slight twisting action.

To install:

8. Using compressed air, blow out any dirt or contaminants from around the top of spark plug.

9. Check the condition of the ignition coil rubber boot. Inspect the opening of the boot for any debris, tears or rips. Carefully remove any debris with a lint free cloth.

✳✳ WARNING

Do not apply a silicone based grease such as Mopar® Dielectric Grease to the ignition coil rubber boot. The silicone based grease will absorb into the boot causing it to stick and tear.

---

10. Place a small, 360°bead of Fluostar 2LF lubricant along the inside opening of

the coil boot approximately 1 to 2 mm from the chamfer edge but not on the chamfered surface.

11. Position the ignition coil into the cylinder head cover opening. Using a twisting action, push the ignition coil onto the spark plug.

12. Install the ignition coil mounting bolt and tighten to 71 inch lbs. (8 Nm).

13. Connect and lock the electrical connector to the ignition coil.

14. If removed, install the insulator, upper intake manifold and air inlet hose.

15. Connect the negative battery cable and tighten nut to 45 inch lbs. (5 Nm).

5.7L Engine

2010 Models

See Figure 70.

A separate ignition coil, mounted to the valve cover is used for each cylinder. Each coil fires the two spark plugs at times predetermined by the Powertrain Control Module (PCM).

1. Before servicing the vehicle, refer to the precautions in the beginning of this section.

2. Unlock the electrical connector by pressing on tab while pulling electrical connector from the coil.

3. Remove two coil mounting bolts.

4. Carefully pull up coil from cylinder head opening with a slight twisting action. Twisting will help break loose boots from spark plugs.

5. Prior to removing the ignition coils, spray compressed air around the coil area and spark plug to remove contaminates from around spark plug tube.

To install:

6. Before installing coil(s), apply dielectric grease to inside of spark plug boots.

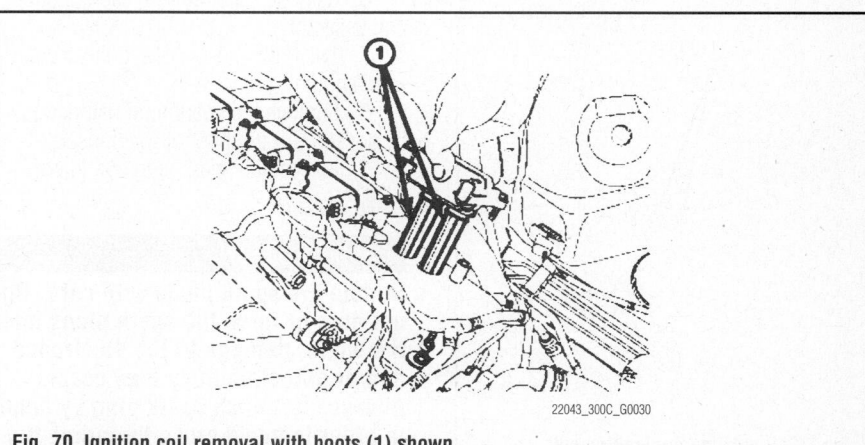

Fig. 70 Ignition coil removal with boots (1) shown

7. Position ignition coil into valve cover and push both spark plug boots onto each spark plug.

8. Install two coil mounting bolts and tighten to 106 inch lbs. (12 Nm).

9. Connect the electrical connector to the ignition coil and lock connector.

10. Connect negative battery cable and tighten nut to 45 inch lbs. (5 Nm).

2011 Models

See Figures 71 and 72.

1. Disconnect and isolate the negative battery cable.

2. Lift the engine cover retaining grommets off the ball studs and remove the engine cover.

3. Disconnect the ignition coil electrical connector by depressing the tab while pulling the electrical connector off the coil.

4. Remove the two ignition coil retaining bolts.

5. Carefully pull the ignition coil straight up and out of the cylinder head

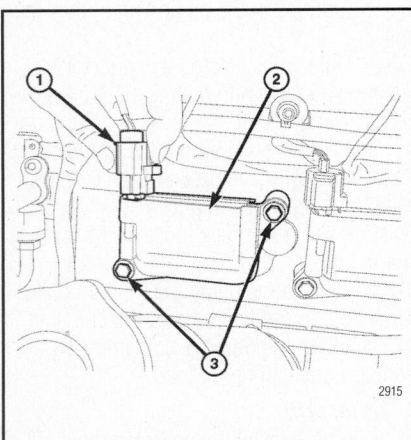

Fig. 71 Disconnecting the ignition coil electrical connector

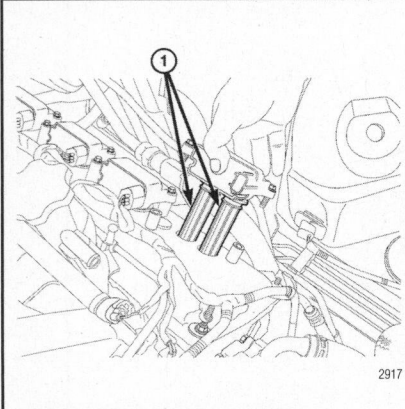

Fig. 72 Removing the ignition coil

opening while using a slight twisting action. Twisting will help break the boots loose from the spark plugs.

To install:

6. Before installing the ignition coil, apply dielectric grease to the inside of the spark plug boots.

7. Position the ignition coil into cylinder head opening and push both spark plug boots onto each spark plug.

8. Install the two coil retaining bolts and tighten to 9 ft. lbs. (12 Nm).

9. Connect the ignition coil electrical connector and lock the connector.

10. Position the engine cover and secure the retaining grommets onto the ball studs.

11. Connect the negative battery cable and tighten nut to 45 inch lbs. (5 Nm).

IGNITION TIMING

ADJUSTMENT

There are no adjustments necessary or possible.

SPARK PLUGS

REMOVAL & INSTALLATION

2.7L Engine

1. Before servicing the vehicle, refer to the precautions in the beginning of this section.

2. Disconnect the negative battery cable.

3. Remove the upper intake manifold.

4. Prior to removing the ignition coils, spray compressed air around the coil area and spark plug to remove contaminates from around spark plug tube.

5. Disconnect the electrical connector from ignition coils.

6. Remove fastener from each ignition coil assembly.

7. Twist, lift and remove ignition coil from engine.

8. Remove the spark plug using a quality socket with a rubber or foam insert.

9. Inspect the spark plug condition.

To install:

> **✵✵ CAUTION**
>
> **Handle the spark plugs with care. Do not drop or force the spark plugs into the wells, damage to the electrodes and/or porcelain body may occur. Always start each spark plug by hand in order to avoid cross-threading the**

spark plug in the cylinder head. Always tighten spark plugs to the specified torque. Too much or not enough torque will cause damage to the cylinder head and/or spark plug and may lead to poor engine performance.

10. To avoid cross threading, start the spark plug into the cylinder head by hand.
   a. Tighten spark plugs to 13 ft. lbs. (17.5 Nm).

11. Align coil with top of spark plug.

12. Twist coil assembly down on to spark plug and install mounting bolt.
   a. Tighten bolt to 65 inch lbs. (7.5 Nm).

13. Connect the electrical connector to ignition coil.

14. Install the upper intake manifold.

15. Connect the negative battery cable and tighten nut to 45 inch lbs. (5 Nm).

3.5L Engine

1. Before servicing the vehicle, refer to the precautions in the beginning of this section.

2. Remove the engine cover.

3. Disconnect the negative battery cable.

4. Remove the intake manifold.

5. Unlock and disconnect electrical connector from ignition coils.

6. Remove mounting bolts and engine cover studs.

7. Prior to removing the ignition coils, spray compressed air around the coil area and spark plug to remove contaminates from around spark plug tube.

8. Twist, lift and remove ignition coil from engine. Refer to Ignition Coil.

9. Remove the spark plug using a quality socket with a rubber or foam insert.

10. Inspect the spark plug condition.

To install:

> **✵✵ CAUTION**
>
> **Handle the spark plugs with care. Do not drop or force the spark plugs into the wells, damage to the electrodes and/or porcelain body may occur. Always start each spark plug by hand in order to avoid cross-threading the spark plug in the cylinder head. Always tighten spark plugs to the specified torque. Too much or not enough torque will cause damage to the cylinder head and/or spark plug and may lead to poor engine performance.**

11. To avoid cross threading, start the spark plug into the cylinder head by hand.

    a. Tighten spark plugs to 20 ft. lbs. (27 Nm).

12. Install ignition coil.

13. Install engine cover studs in the two outside ignition coils on the front of the engine. Install bolts on the other ignition coils.

    a. Tighten studs and bolts to 71 inch lbs. (8 Nm).

14. Connect electrical connector and lock.

15. Install intake manifold.

16. Connect negative battery cable and tighten nut to 45 inch lbs. (5 Nm).

17. Install engine cover.

3.6L Engine

1. Remove the ignition coil.

❋❋ WARNING

The spark plug tubes are a thin wall design. Avoid damaging the spark plug tubes. Damage to the spark plug tube can result in oil leaks.

2. Prior to removing the spark plug, spray compressed air into the cylinder head opening. This will help prevent foreign material from entering combustion chamber.

3. Remove the spark plug from the cylinder head using a quality thin wall socket with a rubber or foam insert.

4. Inspect the spark plug condition.

To install:

5. Check and adjust the spark plug gap with a gap gauging tool.

❋❋ WARNING

Special care should be taken when installing spark plugs into the cylinder head spark plug wells. Be sure the plugs do not drop into the plug wells as electrodes can be damaged.

❋❋ WARNING

The spark plug tubes are a thin wall design. Avoid damaging the spark

plug tubes. Damage to the spark plug tube can result in oil leaks.

❋❋ WARNING

Spark plug torque is critical and must not exceed the specified value. Overtightening stretches the spark plug shell reducing its heat transfer capability resulting in possible catastrophic engine failure.

6. Start the spark plug into the cylinder head by hand to avoid cross threading.

7. Tighten the spark plugs to 11–15 ft. lbs. (15–20 Nm).

8. Install the ignition coil

5.7L Engine

See Figure 73.

A separate ignition coil, mounted to the valve cover is used for each cylinder. Each coil fires the two spark plugs at times predetermined by the Powertrain Control Module (PCM).

1. Before servicing the vehicle, refer to the precautions in the beginning of this section.

2. Unlock the electrical connector by pressing on tab while pulling electrical connector from the coil.

3. Remove two coil mounting bolts.

4. Carefully pull up coil from cylinder head opening with a slight twisting action. Twisting will help break loose boots from spark plugs.

5. Prior to removing the ignition coils, spray compressed air around the coil area and spark plug to remove contaminates from around spark plug tube.

6. Remove spark plug from cylinder head using a quality socket with a rubber or foam insert. Also check condition of ignition coil O-ring and replace as necessary.

To install:

❋❋ CAUTION

Handle the spark plugs with care. Do not drop or force the spark plugs into

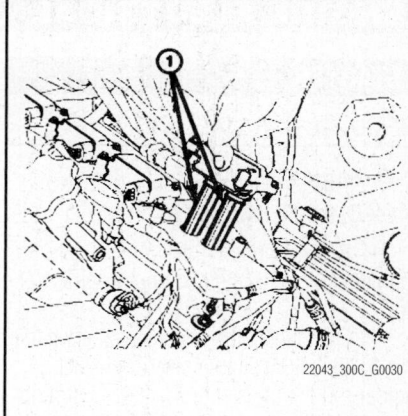

22043_300C_G0030

Fig. 73 Ignition coil removal with boots (1) shown

the wells, damage to the electrodes and/or porcelain body may occur. Always start each spark plug by hand in order to avoid cross-threading the spark plug in the cylinder head. Always tighten spark plugs to the specified torque. Too much or not enough torque will cause damage to the cylinder head and/or spark plug and may lead to poor engine performance.

7. To avoid cross threading, start the spark plug into the cylinder head by hand.

    a. Tighten spark plugs:

    • Up to 2010: to 13 ft. lbs. (17.5 Nm)

    • 2011: 18.5–22 ft. lbs. (25–30 Nm)

8. Before installing coil(s), apply dielectric grease to inside of spark plug boots.

9. Position ignition coil into valve cover and push both spark plug boots onto each spark plug.

    a. Install two coil mounting bolts and tighten to 106 inch lbs. (12 Nm).

10. Connect the electrical connector to the ignition coil and lock connector.

11. Connect negative battery cable and tighten nut to 45 inch lbs. (5 Nm).

STARTER

REMOVAL & INSTALLATION

2.7L Engine

See Figures 74 through 79.

1. Before servicing the vehicle, refer to the precautions in the beginning of this section.
2. Disconnect the negative battery cable.
3. Install a suitable steering wheel holder to lock the steering wheel in straight-ahead position.
4. Raise and safely support the vehicle.
5. Remove the underbody splash shield.
6. Remove the intermediate steering shaft center bolt.
7. Separate the intermediate steering shaft upper and lower shaft.
8. Disconnect the electrical connection from the starter.
9. Remove the 3 starter mounting bolts and wiring clip.
10. Pull the starter forward and down.
11. Maneuver the starter up and around exhaust.
12. Work starter past the intermediate steering shaft, then remove the starter from vehicle.

To install:

13. Work the starter up and past the transmission and exhaust.
14. Maneuver the starter up and past the intermediate shafts.
15. Angle the starter up toward engine.
16. Install the plastic retainer into starter dust shield. The dust shield has TOP marked on it and the plastic retainer goes in the hole.
17. Install the dust shield to the engine block using the plastic retainer to hold dust shield in place.
18. Install the starter and secure with the

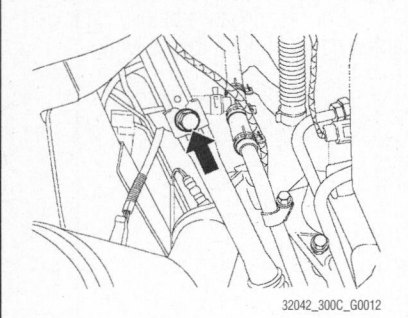

Fig. 74 Remove the intermediate steering shaft center bolt—2.7L and 3.5L engines

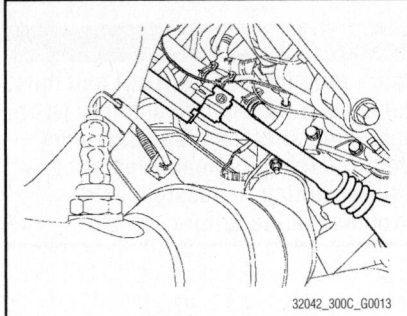

Fig. 75 Separate the intermediate steering shaft upper and lower shaft—2.7L and 3.5L engines

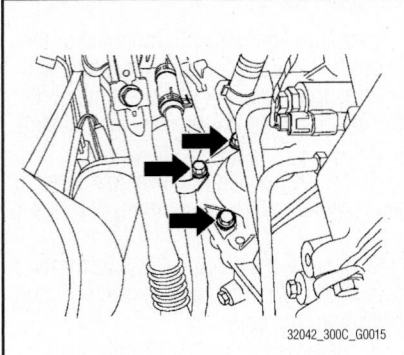

Fig. 76 Remove the 3 starter mounting bolts and wiring clip—2.7L and 3.5L engines

Fig. 77 Remove the starter from the vehicle—2.7L and 3.5L engines

retaining bolts. Torque the bolts to 40 ft. lbs. (54 Nm).

19. Attach the electrical connection to starter.
20. Match flats inside the intermediate shaft with that in the intermediate shaft extension, then slide the intermediate shaft onto extension.

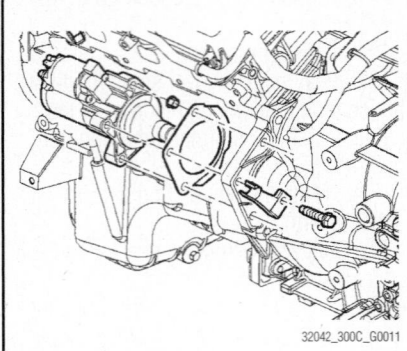

Fig. 78 Starter mounting—2.7L and 3.5L engines

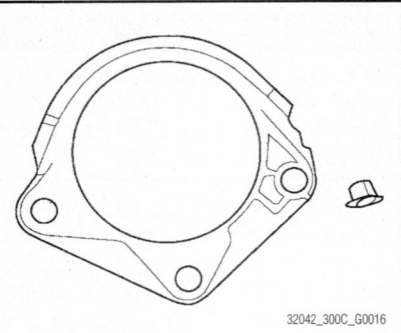

Fig. 79 Install the plastic retainer into starter dust shield. The dust shield has TOP marked on it and the plastic retainer goes in the hole—2.7L and 3.5L engines

21. Align the hole in the shafts.
22. Install the pinch bolt fastening intermediate shaft to intermediate shaft extension. Tighten the bolt to 32 ft. lbs. (43 Nm).
23. Install the underbody splash shield.
24. Carefully lower the vehicle.
25. Remove the steering wheel holder, then connect the negative battery cable.

3.5L Engine

See Figures 80 and 81.

➡**All Wheel Drive (AWD) procedure shown. Rear Wheel Drive (RWD) Similar.**

1. Disconnect and isolate negative battery cable at battery.
2. Remove the left side catalytic converter.
3. Remove battery cable nut (5) and battery cable (4) from solenoid stud (2).
4. Disconnect electrical connector (3) from starter solenoid terminal (1).

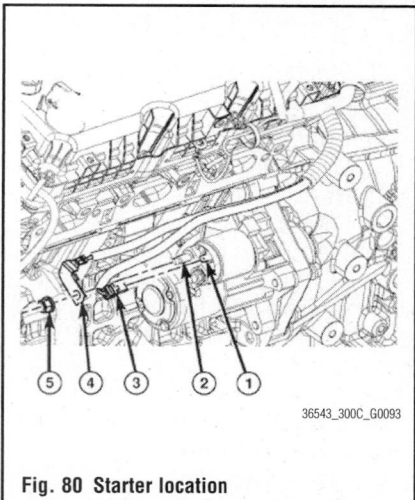

Fig. 80 Starter location

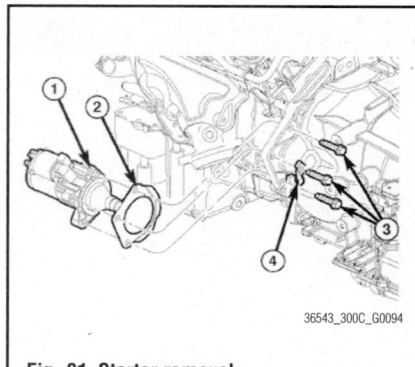

Fig. 81 Starter removal

5. Remove starter mounting bolts (3), the electrical harness mounting bracket (4) should remain in position.

6. Rotate and remove starter assembly (1) from transmission.

7. Remove starter motor dust shield (2).

To install:

8. Install starter motor dust shield.

9. Rotate and install starter assembly to transmission.

10. Install starter mounting bolts, and electrical harness mounting bracket. Tighten bolts to 40 ft. lbs. (54 Nm).

11. Connect electrical connector to starter solenoid terminal.

12. Install battery cable and nut to solenoid stud. Tighten nut to 97 inch lbs. (11 Nm).

13. Install left side catalytic converter.

14. Connect negative battery cable, tighten nut to 45 inch lbs. (5 Nm).

3.6L Engine

See Figure 82.

1. Disconnect and isolate the negative battery cable at the battery.

2. Secure the steering wheel.

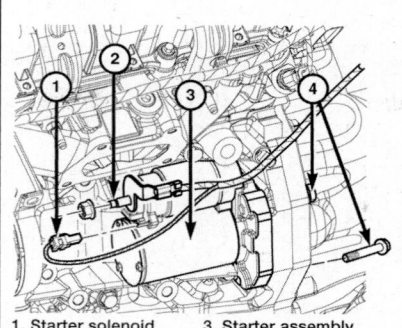

1. Starter solenoid	3. Starter assembly
electrical connector	4. Starter mounting bolts
2. Solenoid stud	

Fig. 82 Removing and installing the starter—3.6L engine

3. Remove the steering gear intermediate shaft.

4. Remove the starter solenoid heat shield.

5. Disconnect the starter solenoid electrical connector from starter solenoid terminal.

6. Remove the battery cable nut and battery cable from solenoid stud.

7. Remove the starter mounting bolts, the electrical harness mounting bracket should remain in position.

8. Rotate and remove starter assembly from transmission.

To install:

9. Position the starter inside the transmission.

10. Install the starter mounting bolts to the starter. Tighten the bolts to 40 ft. lbs. (55 Nm).

11. Connect the starter solenoid electrical connector to starter solenoid terminal.

12. Install the battery cable and nut to the solenoid stud. Tighten the nut to 8 ft. lbs. (11 Nm).

13. Install the starter solenoid heat shield.

14. Install the steering gear lower intermediate shaft.

15. Remove the steering wheel holder.

16. Connect the negative battery cable.

5.7L Engine

AWD Models

See Figure 83.

1. Before servicing the vehicle, refer to the precautions in the beginning of this section.

2. Disconnect and isolate the negative battery cable.

3. Raise and safely support the vehicle.

➡The steering gear assembly must be partially lowered to gain access to starter. Do not disconnect any hydraulic hoses or remove any steering linkage.

4. Remove the coupling bolt (pinch bolt) securing steering gear to steering column.

5. Remove the three steering gear mounting bolts and slightly lower the gear. Temporarily support the steering gear.

6. Remove the steering gear heat-shield.

7. Remove the 2 starter mounting bolts.

8. Move the starter motor towards front of vehicle far enough for nose of starter to clear. Always support the starter motor during this process. Do not let starter motor hang from wire harness.

9. Remove the battery cable-to-solenoid nut.

10. Remove the solenoid wire from solenoid stud.

11. Remove the starter motor.

To install:

12. Position the starter into transmission but do not install bolts.

13. Connect the solenoid wire to starter motor. The wire snaps onto the starter.

14. Position the battery cable to solenoid stud. Install and tighten battery cable eyelet nut to 97 inch lbs. (11 Nm). Do not allow starter motor to hang from wire harness.

15. Install and tighten both starter mounting bolts to 40 ft. lbs. (54 Nm)

16. Install the steering gear assembly and mounting bolts. Install steering column coupling bolt (pinch bolt) and tighten to 32 ft. lbs. (43 Nm).

17. Install the steering gear heat-shield.

18. Lower the vehicle.

19. Connect the negative battery cable.

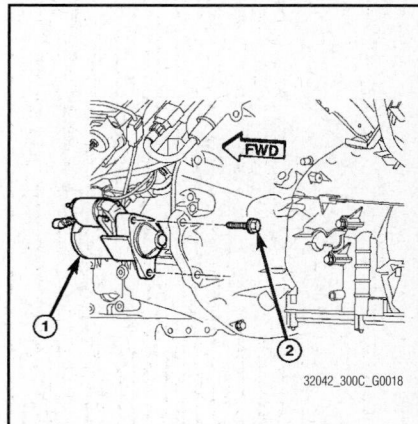

Fig. 83 Starter motor (1) and mounting bolt (2)—AWD vehicles

RWD Models

See Figure 84.

1. Before servicing the vehicle, refer to the precautions in the beginning of this section.

2. Disconnect and isolate the negative battery cable.

3. Raise and safely support the vehicle.

4. Remove the 3 starter mounting bolts.

5. Move the starter motor towards front of vehicle far enough for nose of starter to clear. Always support the starter motor during this process. Never let starter motor hang from wire harness.

6. Remove the battery cable-to-solenoid nut.

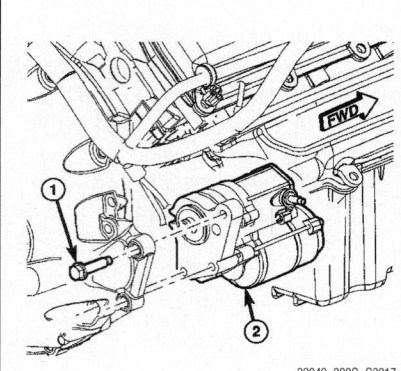

Fig. 84 View of the starter motor mounting bolts (1) and starter (2)—RWD vehicles

7. Remove the solenoid wire from solenoid stud.

8. Remove the starter motor from the vehicle.

To install:

9. Position the starter into transmission but do not install bolts.

10. Connect solenoid wire to starter motor. The wire snaps onto the starter.

11. Position the battery cable to solenoid stud. Install and tighten battery cable eyelet nut to 97 inch lbs. (11 Nm). Do not allow starter motor to hang from wire harness.

12. Install and tighten the three mounting bolts to 40 ft. lbs. (54 Nm).

13. Lower the vehicle.

14. Connect negative battery cable.

ENGINE MECHANICAL

➡**Disconnecting the negative battery cable may interfere with the functions of the on board computer systems and may require the computer to undergo a relearning process, once the negative battery cable is reconnected.**

ACCESSORY DRIVE BELTS

ACCESSORY BELT ROUTING

See Figures 85 through 88.

Refer to the accompanying illustrations.

INSPECTION

Inspect the serpentine drive belt for signs of glazing or cracking. A glazed belt will be perfectly smooth from slippage, while a good belt will have a slight texture of fabric visible. Cracks will usually start at the inner edge of the belt and run outward. All worn

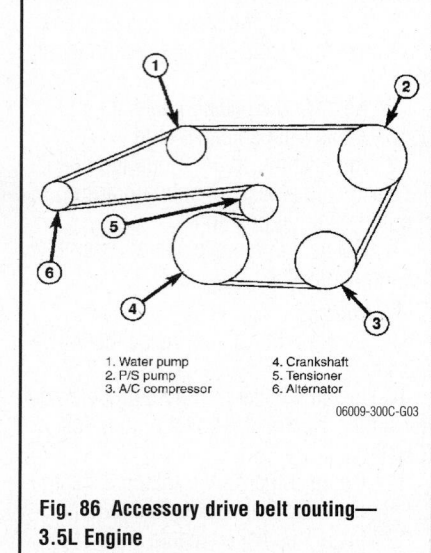

1. Water pump
2. P/S pump
3. A/C compressor
4. Crankshaft
5. Tensioner
6. Alternator

06009-300C-G03

Fig. 86 Accessory drive belt routing—3.5L Engine

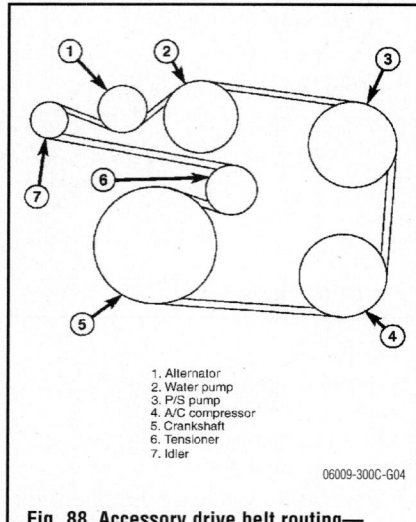

1. Alternator
2. Water pump
3. P/S pump
4. A/C compressor
5. Crankshaft
6. Tensioner
7. Idler

06009-300C-G04

Fig. 88 Accessory drive belt routing—5.7L Engine

or damaged drive belts should be replaced immediately.

ADJUSTMENT

The belts used on these vehicles are equipped with automatic tensioners which maintain tension. No adjustment is necessary or possible.

REMOVAL & INSTALLATION

✻✻ CAUTION

Do not let tensioner arm snap back to the freearm position. This may severely damage the tensioner.

1. Disconnect the negative battery cable from battery.

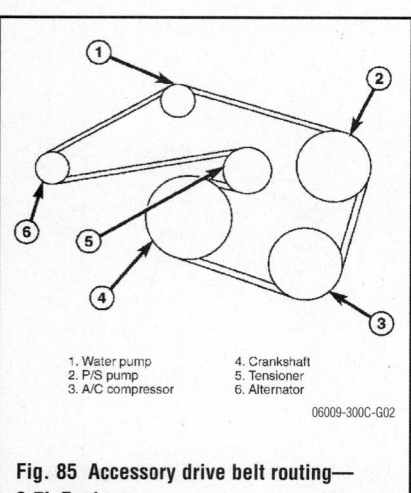

1. Water pump
2. P/S pump
3. A/C compressor
4. Crankshaft
5. Tensioner
6. Alternator

06009-300C-G02

Fig. 85 Accessory drive belt routing—2.7L Engine

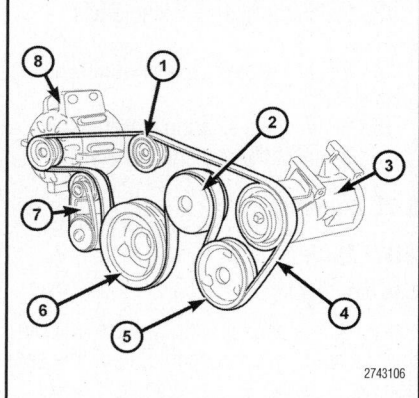

2743106

Fig. 87 Accessory drive belt routing (showing the idler puller (1), belt (4) and tensioner (7))—3.6L Engine

2. Rotate the belt tensioner counter-clockwise until it contacts its stop. Remove belt, then slowly rotate the tensioner into the freearm position.

To install:

3. Check condition of all pulleys.

✳✳ CAUTION

When installing the serpentine accessory drive belt, the belt MUST be routed correctly. If not, the engine may overheat due to the water pump rotating in the wrong direction.

4. Install a new belt. Route the belt around all pulleys except the idler pulley. Rotate the tensioner arm until it contacts its stop position. Route the belt around the idler and slowly let the tensioner rotate into the belt. Make sure the belt is seated onto all pulleys. The tensioner is equipped with an indexing tang on the back of the tensioner and an indexing stop on the tensioner housing. If a new belt is being installed, the tang must be within approximately 0.24-0.32 in. (6-8mm) of indexing stop (i.e. tang is approximately between the two indexing stops). A belt is considered new if it has been used 15 minutes or less.

5. With the drive belt installed, inspect the belt wear indicator

6. Connect the negative battery cable.

AIR CLEANER

REMOVAL & INSTALLATION

2.7L Engine

See Figure 89.

1. Disconnect negative battery cable.
2. Disconnect the charge air temperature sensor electrical connector.
3. Disconnect the clean air duct between throttle body and air filter housing.
4. Disconnect the makeup air (MUA) tube.
5. Remove mounting bolt.
6. Remove air filter housing.
7. Raise vehicle.
8. Partially remove front fascia to gain access to air filter resonator.
9. Remove mounting bolt.
10. Remove air cleaner resonator.

To install:

11. Position air cleaner resonator assembly in vehicle.
12. Install mounting bolt. Tighten bolt to 71 inch lbs. (8 Nm).

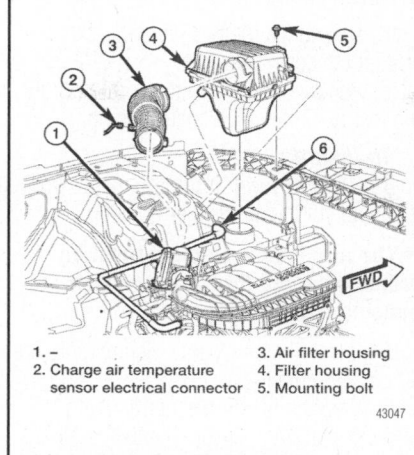

1. –
2. Charge air temperature sensor electrical connector
3. Air filter housing
4. Filter housing
5. Mounting bolt

43047

Fig. 89 Removing the air cleaner

13. Install front fascia.
14. Position air filter assembly in vehicle.
15. Install mounting bolt. Tighten to 44 inch lbs. (5 Nm).
16. Install makeup air (MUA) tube.
17. Install clean air duct between air filter housing and throttle body.
18. Tighten all clamps to 35 inch lbs. (4 Nm).

3.6L Engine

See Figures 90 and 91.

1. Remove the fresh air makeup hose at the air cleaner housing.
2. Remove the air cleaner housing cover retaining bolts.

✳✳ WARNING

Do not use compressed air to clean out the air cleaner housing without first covering the air inlet to the throttle body. Dirt or foreign objects could enter the intake manifold causing engine damage.

3. Lift the air cleaner housing cover off the housing and position aside.
4. Remove the air cleaner element.
5. Remove any dirt or debris from the bottom of the air cleaner housing.

To install:

6. Install a new air cleaner element into the air cleaner housing.
7. Position the air cleaner housing cover so that the alignment tabs insert into the lower housing.
8. Seat the cover onto the housing and install the retaining bolts and tighten to 35 inch lbs. (4 Nm).
9. Connect the fresh air makeup hose onto the air cleaner housing.

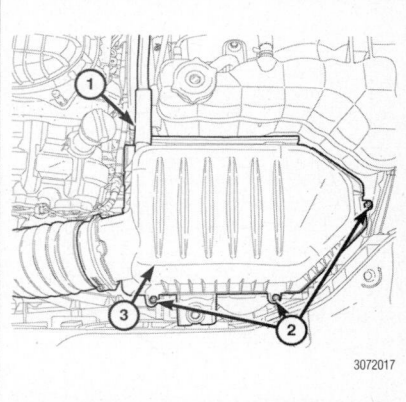

Fig. 90 View of the fresh air makeup hose (1), air cleaner housing cover retaining bolts (2) and housing (3)

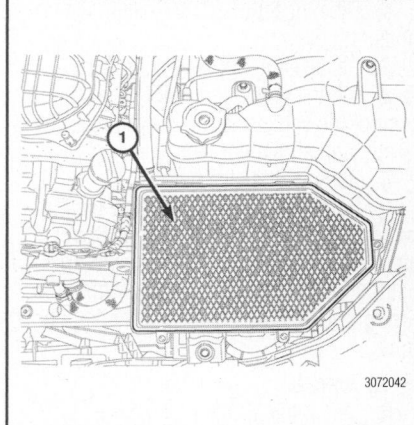

3072042

Fig. 91 Removing the air cleaner element (1)

6.1L Engine

1. Loosen clamp and disconnect air duct at throttle body.
2. Disconnect intake air temperature sensor electrical connector.
3. Remove makeup air hose.
4. Remove air cleaner housing retaining bolt and remove air cleaner housing.

To install:

5. Install the air filter housing into locating pin.
6. Install the hold down bolt into the air filter housing.
7. Install air duct to air cleaner cover and tighten hose clamp to 30 inch lbs. (3 Nm).
8. If any other hose clamps were removed from air intake system, tighten them to 30 inch lbs. (3.4 Nm).

FILTER/ELEMENT REPLACEMENT

2.7L Engine

See Figures 92 and 93.

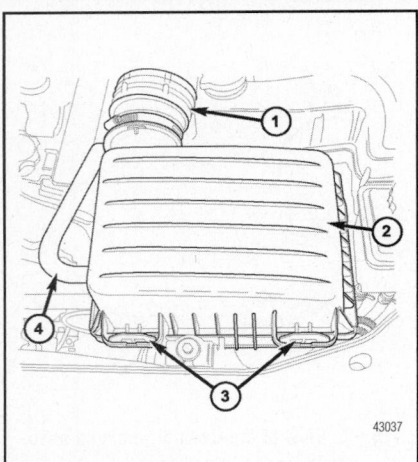

Fig. 92 View of the housing cover (2), housing cover tabs (3) and CCV hose (4)

1. Disconnect the CCV hose at the housing cover.
2. Release the housing cover tabs.
3. Lift the cover and pull toward the front of the vehicle to release the rear cover to housing alignment tabs.
4. Remove the element.
5. Remove any dirt or debris from the bottom of the air filter housing. Cover the air inlet to the throttle body, or do not use compressed air. Otherwise, dirt or foreign objects can enter the intake manifold.

To install:
6. Install the air filter element into air box .
   a. Position the cover so that the rear locking tabs insert into the lower housing.
7. Seat the cover onto element housing and assure that the front locking tabs engage.
8. Reconnect the CCV hose.

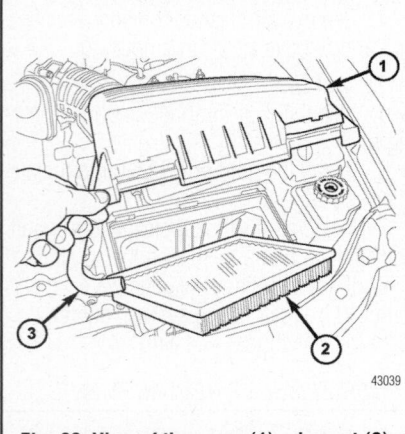

Fig. 93 View of the cover (1), element (2) and hose (3)

5.7L Engine
1. Disengage the two retaining clamps and lift the cover upwards.
2. Remove the air cleaner element from the inside of the air cleaner housing.

To install:
3. Clean any dirt or foreign matter from the inside of the air cleaner housing.

➡**The air cleaner element must be properly seated for the air cleaner housing cover to fit correctly.**

4. Install the air cleaner element into the air cleaner housing.
5. Position the air cleaner housing cover in place and secure the two retainer clips.

CAMSHAFT AND VALVE LIFTERS

INSPECTION

2.7L & 5.7L Engines
See Figure 94.

1. Inspect the camshaft bearing journals for damage and binding. If journals are binding, check the cylinder head for damage. Also check cylinder head oil holes for clogging.
2. Check the cam lobe and bearing surfaces for abnormal wear and damage. Replace camshaft if defective.

➡**If camshaft is replaced due to lobe wear or damage, always replace the rocker arms.**

3. Measure the lobe actual wear and replace camshaft if out of limit. Standard value is 0.001 in. (0.0254mm), wear limit is 0.010 (0.254mm).

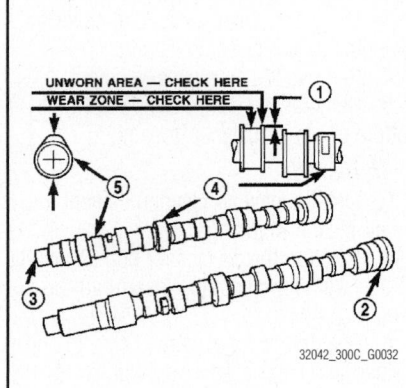

Fig. 94 Inspecting the camshaft

3.5L Engine
See Figure 95.

1. Inspect camshaft bearing journals (4) for damage and binding. If journals are binding, check the cylinder head for damage. Also check cylinder head oil holes for clogging.
2. Check the cam lobe (5) and bearing surfaces for abnormal wear and damage. Replace camshaft if defective.
3. Measure the lobe (5) actual wear and replace camshaft if out of limit. Standard value is 0.001 in. (0.0254 mm), wear limit is 0.010 in. (0.254 mm).

➡**If camshaft is replaced due to lobe wear or damage, always replace the rocker arms.**

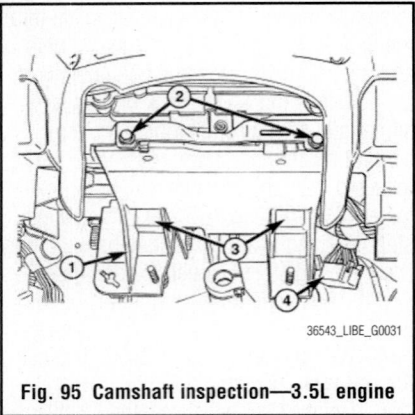

Fig. 95 Camshaft inspection—3.5L engine

REMOVAL & INSTALLATION

2.7L Engine
See Figures 96 through 101.

1. Before servicing the vehicle, refer to the precautions in the beginning of this section.
2. Remove the primary timing chain.
3. Remove secondary chain tensioner mounting bolts.

➡**Camshaft bearing caps have been marked during engine manufacturing. For example, number one exhaust camshaft bearing is marked "1E"**

4. Slowly loosen camshaft bearing cap bolts in the order shown.
5. Remove the camshaft bearing caps.
6. Remove intake camshaft, exhaust camshaft, secondary timing chain, and secondary timing chain tensioner together as an assembly.
7. Remove secondary timing chain tensioner and secondary timing chain from camshafts.
8. Remove rocker arms.

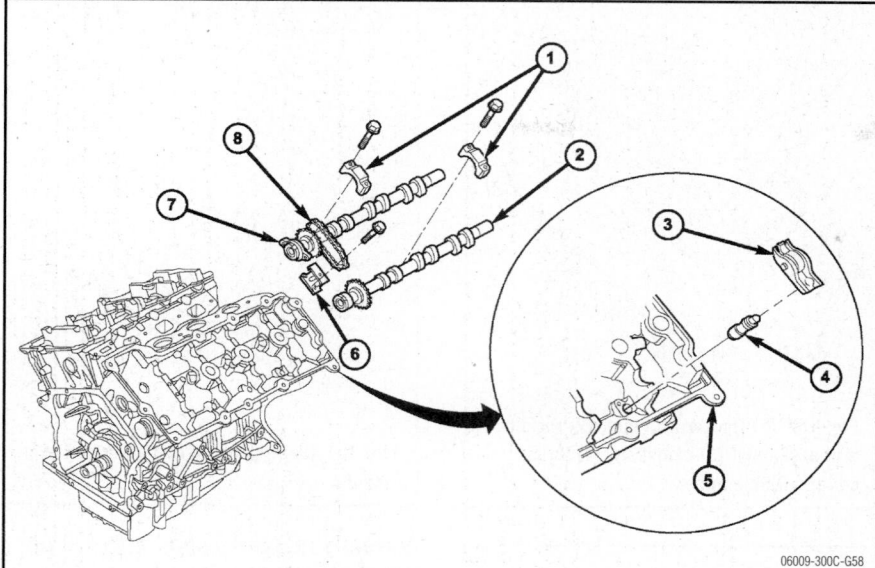

Fig. 96 Camshafts and related parts (1) bearing caps, (2) exhaust camshaft (3) rocker arm, (4) lash adjuster, (5) head, (6) secondary timing chain tensioner, (7) intake camshaft—2.7L engine

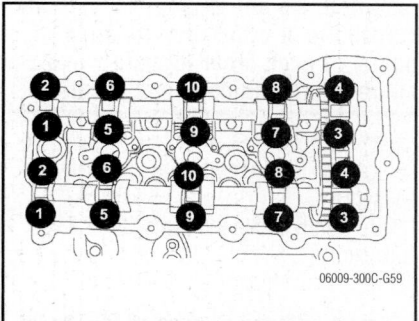

Fig. 97 Camshaft bearing cap loosening sequence—2.7L engine

➡If lash adjusters and rocker arms are to be reused, always mark position for reassembly in their original positions.

9. Remove lash adjuster(s).

To install:

10. Inspect camshaft bearing journals for damage and binding. If journals are binding, check the cylinder head for damage. Also check cylinder head oil holes for clogging.

11. Inspect camshaft sprockets for excessive wear. Replace camshafts if necessary.

12. Check the cam lobe surfaces for abnormal wear and damage. Replace camshaft if defective. Measure the actual wear and replace, if out of limits—standard value is 0.0254 mm (0.001 in.); wear limit is 0.254 mm (0.010 in.).

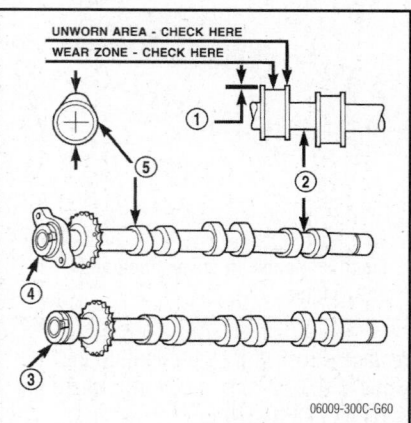

Fig. 98 Camshaft inspection points—2.7L engine

✳✳ CAUTION

When the timing chain is removed and the cylinder heads are installed, DO NOT rotate the camshafts or crankshaft without first locating the proper crankshaft position. Failure to do so will result in valve and/or piston damage.

13. Install hydraulic lash adjuster making sure adjusters are at least partially full of oil. This can be verified by little or no plunger travel when lash adjuster is depressed.

14. Install rocker arm(s) and cylinder head covers.

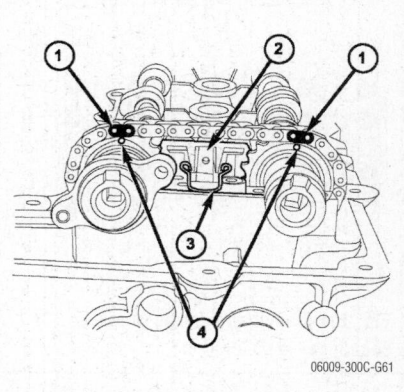

Fig. 99 Verify that plated links (1) are facing toward the front. Align the plated links (1) to the dots (4) on the camshaft sprockets—2.7L engine

15. Assemble camshaft chain on the cams. Verify that plated links are facing toward the front. Align the plated links to the dots on the camshaft sprockets.

16. If camshaft chain tensioner is already in the compressed and locked position, skip the next step.

17. When the camshaft chain tensioner is removed, it is necessary to compress and lock the tensioner using the following procedures:

    a. Place tensioner into a soft jaw vise.

    b. SLOWLY compress tensioner until fabricated lock pin or the equivalent can be inserted into the locking holes.

    c. Remove compressed and locked tensioner from the vise.

18. Insert the compressed and locked camshaft chain tensioner in-between the camshafts and chain.

19. Rotate the cams so that the plated links and dots are facing the 12:00 o'clock position.

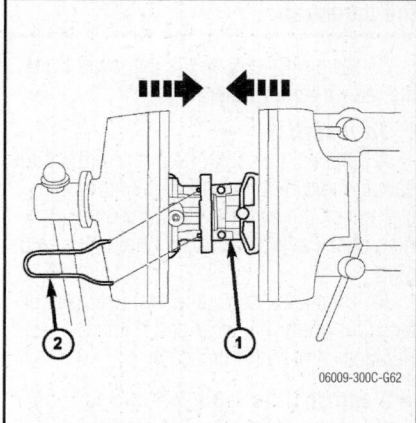

Fig. 100 Tensioner (1) and fabricated lock pin (2)—2.7L engine

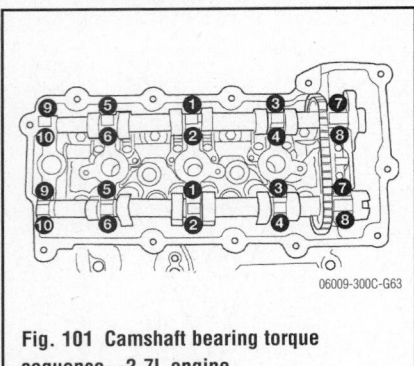

Fig. 101 Camshaft bearing torque sequence—2.7L engine

20. Install cams to cylinder head. Verify that rocker arms are correctly seated and in proper positions.

21. Install camshaft bearing caps. Verify that bearing caps are installed in same position as removed.

22. Tighten cam bearing cap bolts gradually in sequence shown in to 105 inch lbs. (12 Nm).

23. Install secondary chain tensioner (2) bolts and tighten to 105 inch lbs. (12 Nm).

24. Remove locking pin from secondary tensioners.

25. Measure camshafts end play.

26. Install the primary timing chain.

3.5L Engine

See Figures 102 and 103.

1. Before servicing the vehicle, refer to the precautions in the beginning of this section.

➡**Camshafts are removed from the rear of each cylinder head.**

2. Remove the cylinder head.

✳✳ **CAUTION**

Care must be taken not to nick or scratch the journals when removing the camshaft.

3. Carefully remove the camshaft from the rear of the cylinder head.

To install:

4. Inspect camshaft bearing journals for damage and binding. If journals are binding, check the cylinder head for damage. Also check cylinder head oil holes for clogging.

5. Check the cam lobe and bearing surfaces for abnormal wear and damage. Replace camshaft if defective.

➡**If camshaft is replaced due to lobe wear or damage, always replace the rocker arms.**

6. Measure the lobe actual wear and

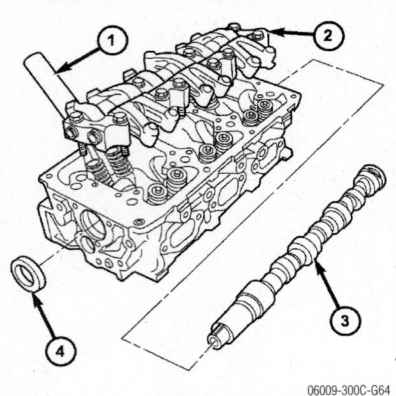

Fig. 102 (1) Rocker arm tool, (2) rocker arm assembly, (3) camshaft, (4) thrust collar—3.5L engine

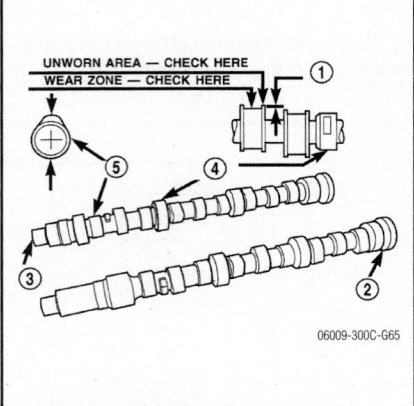

Fig. 103 Camshaft inspection points—3.5L engine

replace camshaft if out of limit. Standard value is 0.0254 mm (0.001 in.), wear limit is 0.254 mm (0.010 in.).

➡**Care must be taken not to scrape or nick the camshaft journals when installing the camshaft into position.**

7. Lubricate camshaft bearing journals, camshaft lobes and camshaft seal with clean engine oil and install camshaft into cylinder head.

8. Install the cylinder head.

3.6L Engine

Left Side

See Figures 104 through 107.

✳✳ **WARNING**

The magnetic timing wheels must not come in contact with magnets (pickup tools, trays, etc.) or any other strong magnetic field. This will destroy the timing wheels ability to

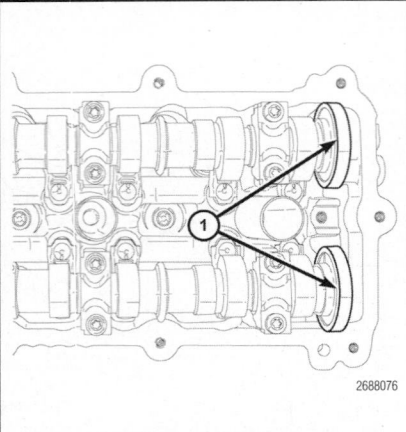

Fig. 104 Identifying the magnetic timing wheels

correctly relay camshaft position to the camshaft position sensor.

✳✳ **WARNING**

When the timing chain is removed and the cylinder heads are still installed, Do not forcefully rotate the camshafts or crankshaft independently of each other. Severe valve and/or piston damage can occur.

1. Remove the Left cylinder head cover, RH ignition coils, spark plugs and left cam phasers.

2. Gently rotate the camshafts CCW approximately 30°until the camshafts are in the neutral position (no valve load).

➡**Camshaft bearing caps should have been marked during engine manufacturing. For example, the number one exhaust camshaft bearing cap is marked "1E->". The caps should be installed with the notch forward.**

3. Slowly loosen the camshaft bearing cap bolts in the sequence shown.

✳✳ **WARNING**

DO NOT STAMP OR STRIKE THE CAMSHAFT BEARING CAPS. SEVERE DAMAGE WILL OCCUR TO THE BEARING CAPS.

➡**When the camshaft is removed the rocker arms may slide downward, mark the rocker arms before removing the camshaft.**

4. Remove the camshaft bearing caps and the camshafts.

To install:

5. Lubricate the camshaft journals with clean engine oil.

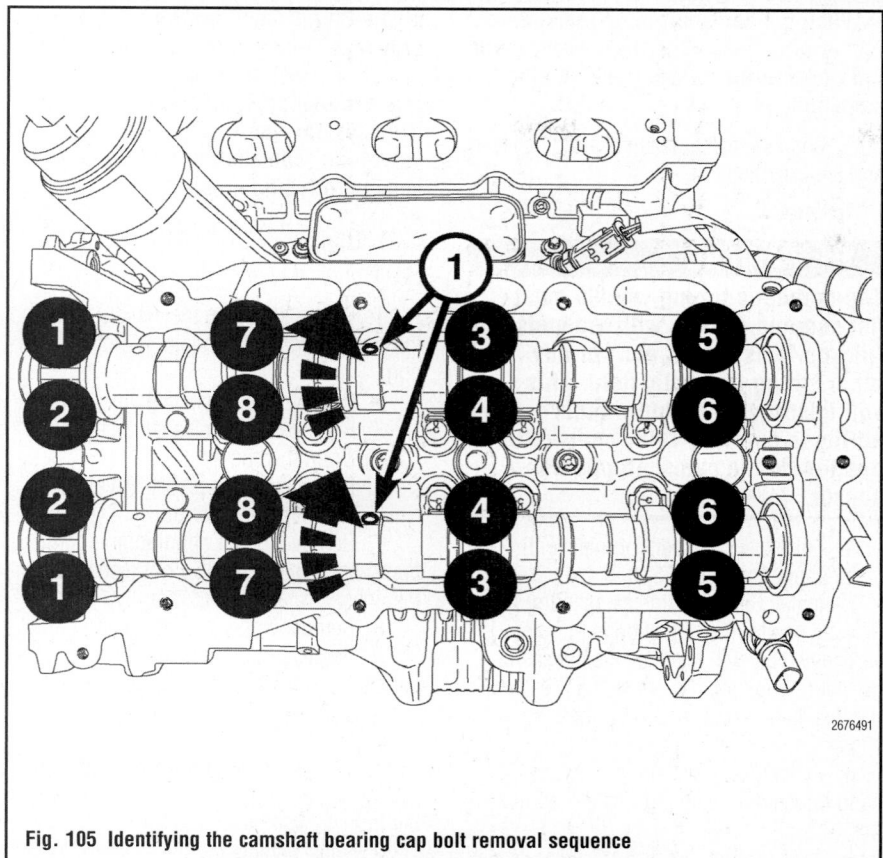

Fig. 105 Identifying the camshaft bearing cap bolt removal sequence

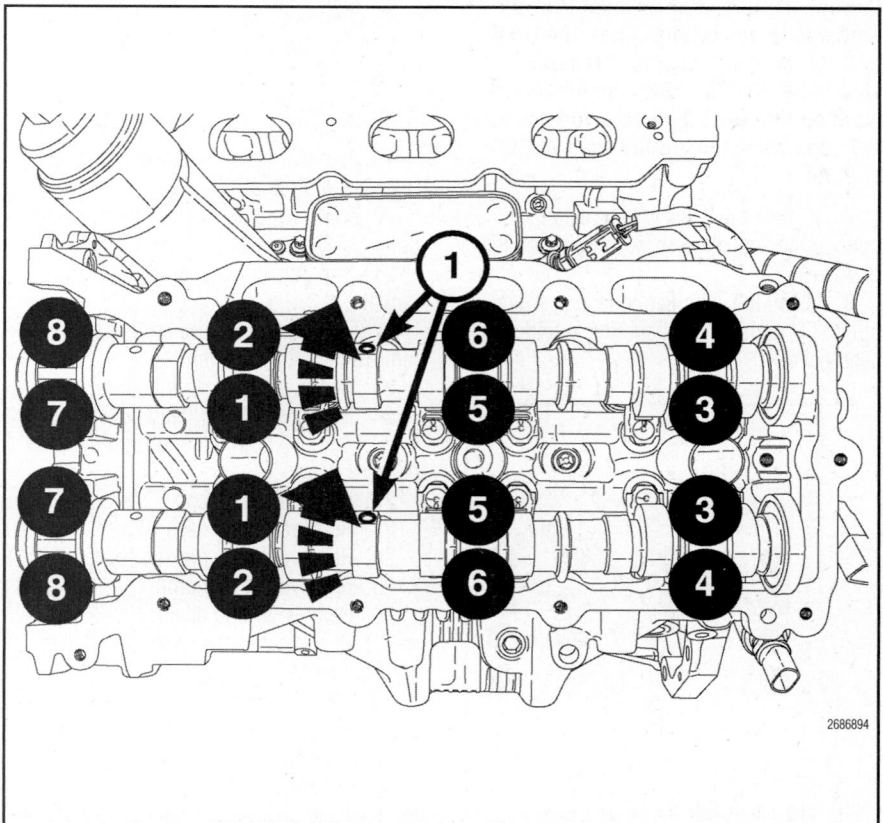

Fig. 106 Identifying the camshaft bearing cap tightening sequence and TDC position (1)

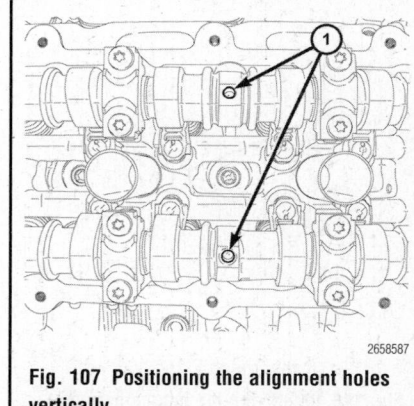

Fig. 107 Positioning the alignment holes vertically

6. Install the left side camshaft(s) approximately 30°CCW from the TDC position. This will place the camshafts at the neutral position (no valve load) easing the installation of the camshaft bearing caps.

7. Install the camshaft bearing caps and hand tighten the retaining bolts to 18 inch lbs. (2 Nm).

➡ Caps are identified numerically (1 through 4), intake or exhaust (I or E) and should be installed from the front to the rear of the engine. All caps should be installed with the notch forward so that the stamped arrows (<) on the caps point toward the front of the engine.

8. Tighten the bearing cap retaining bolts in the sequence shown to 84 inch lbs. (9.5 Nm).

9. Rotate the camshafts CW to TDC by positioning the alignment holes vertically.

10. Install the left cam phasers, spark plugs, RH ignition coils and the cylinder head cover.

➡ The Cam/Crank Variation Relearn procedure must be performed using the scan tool anytime there has been a repair/replacement made to a powertrain system, for example: flywheel, valvetrain, camshaft and/or crankshaft sensors or components.

Right Side

See Figures 108 through 110.

✳✳ WARNING

The magnetic timing wheels must not come in contact with magnets (pickup tools, trays, etc.) or any other strong magnetic field. This will destroy the timing wheels ability to correctly relay camshaft position to the camshaft position sensor.

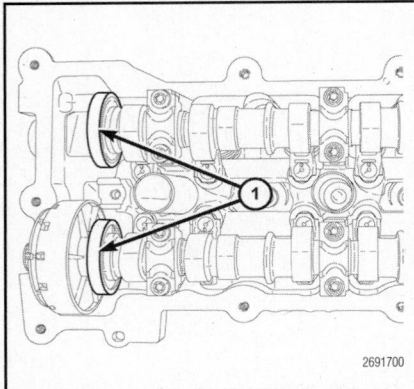

Fig. 108 Identifying the magnetic timing wheels (1)

✷✷ WARNING

When the timing chain is removed and the cylinder heads are still installed, Do not forcefully rotate the camshafts or crankshaft independently of each other. Severe valve and/or piston damage can occur.

1. Remove the Right cylinder head cover, LH ignition coils, spark plugs and right cam phasers.

➡Camshaft bearing caps should have been marked during engine manufacturing. For example, the number one exhaust camshaft bearing cap is marked "1E->". The caps should be installed with the notch forward.

2. Slowly loosen the camshaft bearing cap bolts in the sequence shown.

✷✷ WARNING

DO NOT STAMP OR STRIKE THE CAMSHAFT BEARING CAPS. SEVERE DAMAGE WILL OCCUR TO THE BEARING CAPS.

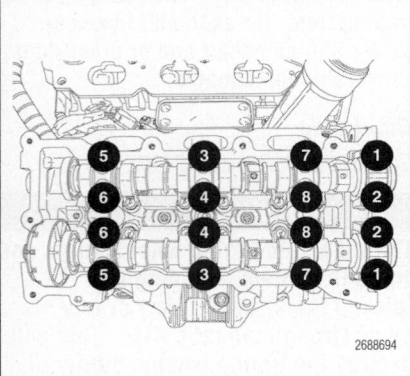

Fig. 109 Identifying the camshaft bearing cap removal sequence

➡When the camshaft is removed the rocker arms may slide downward, mark the rocker arms before removing the camshaft.

3. Remove the camshaft bearing caps and the camshafts.

To install:

✷✷ WARNING

The magnetic timing wheels must not come in contact with magnets (pickup tools, trays, etc.) or any other strong magnetic field. This will destroy the timing wheels ability to correctly relay camshaft position to the camshaft position sensor.

4. Lubricate camshaft journals with clean engine oil.

5. Install the right side camshaft(s) at TDC by positioning the alignment holes vertically. This will place the camshafts at the neutral position (no valve load) easing the installation of the camshaft bearing caps.

6. Install the camshaft bearing caps, hand tighten the retaining bolts to 18 inch lbs. (2 Nm).

➡Caps are identified numerically (1 through 4), intake or exhaust (I or E) and should be installed from the front to the rear of the engine. All caps should be installed with the notch forward so that the stamped arrows (<) on the caps point toward the front of the engine.

7. Tighten the bearing cap retaining bolts in the sequence shown to 84 inch lbs. (9.5 Nm).

8. Install the right cam phasers, spark plugs, LH ignition coils and the cylinder head cover.

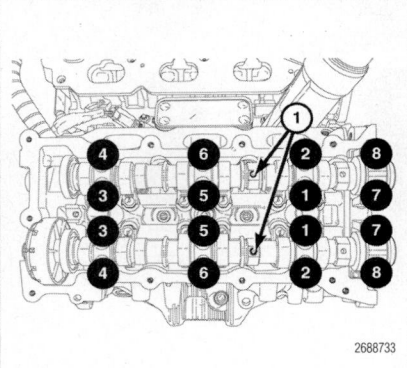

Fig. 110 Identifying the bearing cap retaining bolt tightening sequence

➡The Cam/Crank Variation Relearn procedure must be performed using the scan tool anytime there has been a repair/replacement made to a powertrain system, for example: flywheel, valvetrain, camshaft and/or crankshaft sensors or components.

5.7L Engine

See Figures 111 and 112.

1. Before servicing the vehicle, refer to the precautions in the beginning of this section.

2. Remove the negative battery cable.
3. Remove the air cleaner assembly.
4. Drain the coolant.
5. Remove the accessory drive belt.
6. Remove the alternator.
7. Remove the air conditioning compressor, and set aside. Do not disconnect the lines.
8. Remove upper radiator hose.
9. Remove upper radiator closure panels.
10. Disconnect cooling fan electrical connector.
11. Remove cooling fan mounting bolts.
12. Remove radiator cooling fan assembly from vehicle.
13. Raise vehicle.
14. Remove lower splash shield.
15. Remove lower radiator hose.
16. Remove lower condenser mount bolts.
17. Lower vehicle.
18. Remove upper radiator hose.
19. Remove upper radiator mounting brackets and bolts.
20. Remove upper condenser mounting bolts.
21. Separate condenser assembly from radiator.
22. Tilt radiator toward engine and remove radiator from vehicle.
23. Remove the intake manifold.
24. Remove cylinder head covers.
25. Remove both left and right cylinder heads
26. Remove the oil pan.
27. Remove timing case cover.
28. Remove the oil pick up tube.
29. Remove the oil pump.
30. Remove timing chain.
31. Remove camshaft tensioner/thrust plate assembly.
32. Remove the tappets and retainer assembly.
33. Install a long bolt into front of camshaft to aid in removal of the camshaft. Remove camshaft, being careful not to damage cam bearings with the cam lobes.

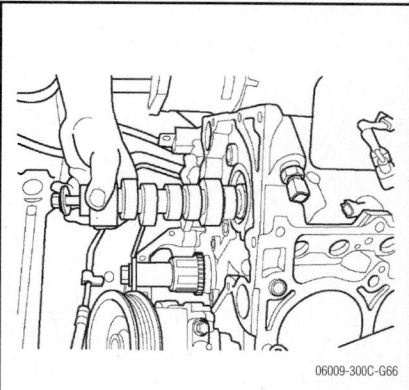

Fig. 111 Camshaft removal/installation—5.7L engine

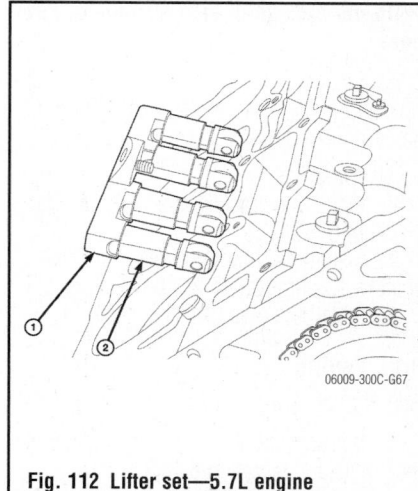

Fig. 112 Lifter set—5.7L engine

To install:

34. The cam bearings are not serviceable. Do not attempt to replace cam bearings for any reason.

35. Clean core hole in block.

➡**Do not apply adhesive to the new core hole plug. A new plug will have adhesive pre-applied.**

36. Install a new core hole plug at the rear of camshaft, using suitable flat faced tool. The plug must be fully seated on the cylinder block shoulder.

➡**The 5.7L LX engine uses a unique camshaft for use with the Multi Displacement System. When installing a new camshaft, the replacement camshaft must be compatible with the Multi Displacement System.**

37. Lubricate camshaft lobes and camshaft bearing journals and insert the camshaft.

38. Install camshaft Tensioner plate

assembly. Tighten bolts to 21 ft. lbs. (28 Nm).

39. Install timing chain and sprockets.

40. Measure camshaft end play. If not within limits (0.0031-0.0114 in.) install a new thrust plate.

41. Install the oil pump.

42. Install the oil pick up tube.

43. Each tappet reused must be installed in the same position from which it was removed. When camshaft is replaced, all of the tappets must be replaced.

➡**The 5.7L LX engine uses both standard roller tappets and deactivating roller tappets, for use with the Multi Displacement System. The deactivating roller tappets must be used in cylinders 1, 4, 6, 8. The deactivating tappets can be identified by the two holes in the side of the tappet body, for the latching pins.**

44. Install tappets and retaining yoke assembly.

45. Install both left and right cylinder heads.

46. Install pushrods.

47. Install rocker arms.

48. Install timing case cover.

49. Install the oil pan.

50. Install cylinder head covers.

51. Install intake manifold.

52. Position the air conditioning compressor on the engine.

53. Install the bolts that secure the air conditioning compressor and the automatic transmission cooler line bracket to the cylinder block. Tighten the bolts to 41 ft. lbs. (55 Nm).

54. Install the air conditioning compressor.

55. Install the alternator.

56. Install the accessory drive belt.

57. Position radiator into engine compartment. Seat the radiator assembly lower rubber isolators into the mounting holes in radiator lower support.

58. Install radiator mounting bracket and bolts. Tighten to 106 inch lbs. (12 Nm).

59. Position condenser on radiator and install upper mounting bolts. Tighten bolts to 50 inch lbs. (6 Nm).

60. Raise vehicle.

61. Install lower condenser mounting bolts. Tighten bolts to 88 inch lbs. (10 Nm).

62. Install lower radiator hose and clamp.

63. Lower vehicle.

64. Position radiator cooling fan assembly in vehicle.

65. Install cooling fan mounting bolts. Tighten to 50 inch lbs. (6 Nm)

66. Connect cooling fan electrical connector.

67. Install upper radiator upper hose. Align hose so it does not interfere with the accessory drive belt or engine. Position hose clamp so it will not interfere with the hood.

68. Install the air cleaner assembly.

69. Install the negative battery cable.

70. Refill coolant.

71. Refill engine oil.

72. Start engine and check for leaks.

CATALYTIC CONVERTER

REMOVAL & INSTALLATION

Left Side

See Figure 113.

1. Raise vehicle on hoist.

2. Hoist vehicle.

3. Disconnect downstream oxygen sensor electrical connectors.

4. Remove muffler and resonator assembly.

5. Remove ball flange nuts.

6. Remove catalytic converter ball flange nut.

7. Remove catalytic converter.

To install:

8. Install catalytic converter (3) onto exhaust manifold ball flange. Only finger tighten nuts at this time.

9. Install muffler and resonator assembly.

10. Install bolts and cross brace. Tighten bolts to 40 ft. lbs. (55 Nm).

11. Tighten manifold ball flange nut to 106 inch lbs. (12 Nm).

12. Check clearance between exhaust system and fuel tank. Clearance is .55 inches (14mm) for 5.7L engine and .62 inches (16mm) for V6 engine.

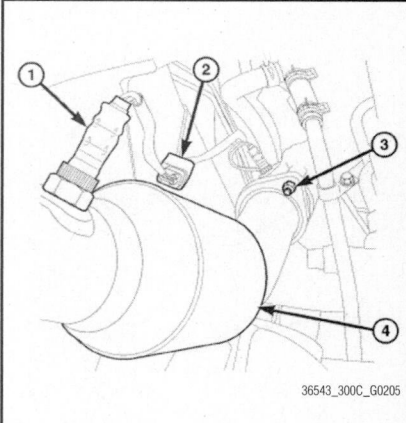

Fig. 113 Catalytic converter and related components—LH side

13. Check clearance at rear tunnel reinforcement. Clearance is .59 -.78 inches (15-20 mm)

14. Adjust clearance as necessary.

15. Tighten ball flange nuts to 25 ft. lbs. (34 Nm).

16. Lower vehicle.

17. Connect negative battery cable.

18. Start the engine and inspect for exhaust leaks. Repair exhaust leaks as necessary.

Right Side

See Figure 114.

1. Disconnect negative battery cable.
2. Raise vehicle on hoist.
3. Disconnect downstream oxygen sensor connectors.
4. Remove muffler and resonator.
5. For 2.7L/3.5L engine only - Remove nuts and cross-brace.
6. Remove catalytic converter to ball flange nuts.
7. Remove catalytic converter.

To install:

8. Install catalytic converter onto exhaust manifold ball flange. Only finger tighten nuts at this time.
9. Install muffler and resonator assembly.
10. Install bolts and cross brace. Tighten bolts to 40 ft. lbs. (55 Nm).
11. Tighten manifold ball flange nut to 106 inch lbs. (12 Nm).
12. Check clearance between exhaust system module and fuel tank. Clearance is .55 inches (14mm) for 5.7L engine and .62 inches (16mm) for 2.7/3.5L engine.
13. Check clearance at rear tunnel reinforcement. Clearance is .59 - .78 inches (15 - 20mm).
14. Adjust clearance as necessary.

15. Tighten ball flange nuts to 25 ft. lbs. (34 Nm).

16. Connect oxygen sensor connectors.

17. Lower vehicle.

18. Connect negative battery cable.

19. Start the engine and inspect for exhaust leaks. Repair exhaust leaks as necessary.

CRANKSHAFT FRONT SEAL

REMOVAL & INSTALLATION

3.5L Engine

See Figures 115 through 117.

For front seal service on the 2.7L and 5.7L engines, see Timing Chain Cover and Seal.

1. Before servicing the vehicle, refer to the precautions in the beginning of this section.
2. Remove the crankshaft sprocket.
3. Tap the dowel pin out of the crankshaft.

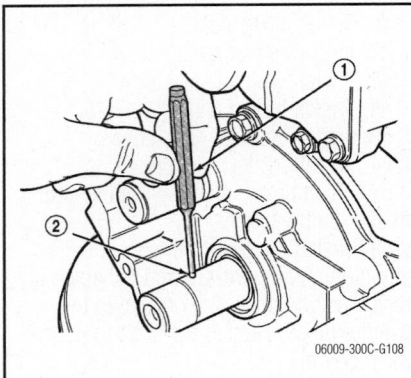

Fig. 115 Tap the dowel pin (2) out of the crankshaft—3.5L engine

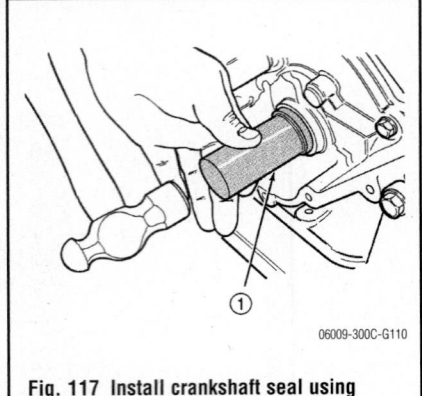

06009-300C-G110

Fig. 117 Install crankshaft seal using Special Tool 6342 (1)—3.5L engine

4. Remove crankshaft seal using Special Tool 6341A.

➡**Do not nick shaft seal surface or seal bore.**

5. Shaft seal lip surface must be free of varnish, dirt or nicks. Polish with 400 grit paper if necessary.

To install:

6. Install the crankshaft seal using Special Tool 6342.
7. Install the dowel pin into the crankshaft to 1.2 mm (0.047 in.) protrusion.
8. Install the crankshaft sprocket.

3.6L Engine

See Figures 118 and 119.

1. Remove the accessory drive belt and the crankshaft vibration damper.
2. Install the sleeve from Seal Remover 8511 around the flywheel key and onto the nose of the crankshaft.
3. Screw Seal Remover into the front crankshaft oil seal.
4. Install the extractor screw into the

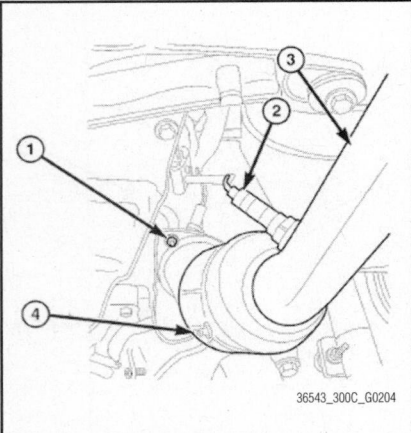

36543_300C_G0204

Fig. 114 Catalytic converter bolt location—RH side

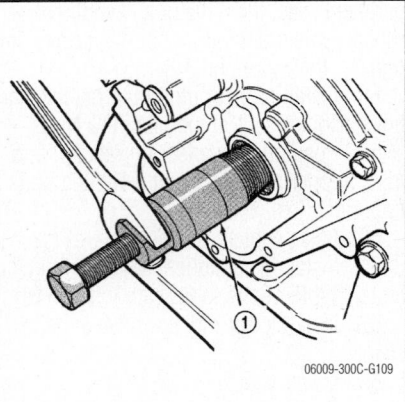

06009-300C-G109

Fig. 116 Remove crankshaft seal using Special Tool 6341A (1)—3.5L engine

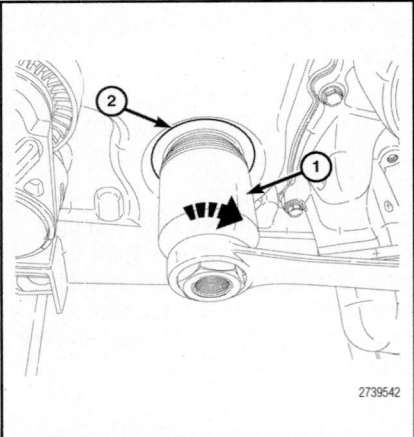

2739542

Fig. 118 View of the flywheel key (1) and sleeve (2)

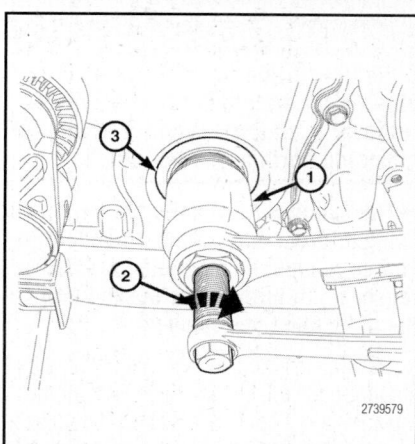

Fig. 119 View of the seal remover (1), extractor screw (2) and front oil seal (3)

Seal Remover. Hold the seal remover stationary and tighten the extractor screw against the sleeve until the front crankshaft oil seal is removed from the engine timing cover.

To install:

5. Position the front crankshaft oil seal into place on the engine timing cover.

6. Align the Front Crankshaft Seal Installer to the flywheel key on the crankshaft and against the front crankshaft oil seal.

❊❊ WARNING

Only tighten the crankshaft vibration damper bolt until the oil seal is seated in the cover. Overtightening of the bolt can crack the front timing cover.

7. Install and tighten the crankshaft vibration damper bolt until the Crankshaft oil seal is seated in the engine timing cover.

8. Install the crankshaft vibration damper and accessory drive belt

CYLINDER HEAD

REMOVAL & INSTALLATION

2.7L Engine

See Figures 120 through 127.

1. Before servicing the vehicle, refer to the precautions in the beginning of this section.

2. Perform fuel pressure release procedure before attempting any repairs.

3. Disconnect negative cable from battery.

4. Raise and safely support the vehicle.

5. Drain cooling system.

6. Remove accessory drive belt.

7. Remove the vibration damper.

8. Disconnect camshaft position sensor, and coolant temperature sensor connectors.

9. Remove upper intake manifold.

10. Disconnect coils, capacitors, and injector connectors.

11. Reposition harness out of the way.

12. Disconnect fuel feed line.

13. Remove lower intake manifold.

14. Remove the cylinder head cover.

15. Remove upper radiator hose.

16. Remove upper radiator closure panels.

17. Disconnect cooling fan electrical connector.

18. Remove cooling fan mounting bolts.

19. Remove radiator cooling fan assembly from vehicle.

20. Raise vehicle.

21. Remove lower splash shield.

22. Remove lower radiator hose.

23. Remove lower condenser mount bolts.

24. Lower vehicle.

25. Remove upper radiator mounting brackets and bolts.

26. Remove upper condenser mounting bolts.

27. Separate condenser assembly from radiator.

28. Tilt radiator toward engine and remove radiator from vehicle.

29. Disconnect Engine Coolant Temperature (ECT) sensor connector.

30. Remove radiator upper hose at tube.

31. Remove heater hose from heater tube at rear of engine.

32. Disconnect heater tube from retaining clip at rear of engine.

33. Disconnect electrical connector from coolant temperature sensor.

34. Remove screws attaching heater tube to outlet connector.

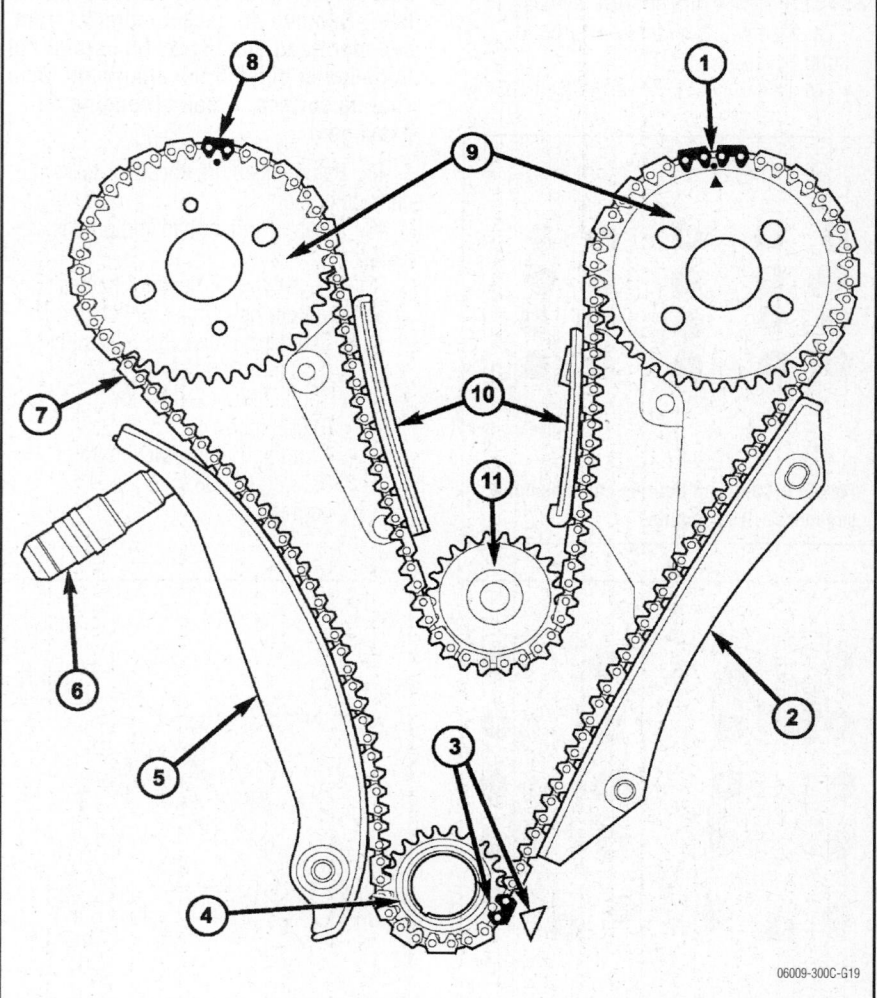

Fig. 120 Rotate crankshaft until crankshaft sprocket timing mark aligns with timing mark on oil pump housing (3)—2.7L engine

35. Disengage heater tube from outlet connector. To remove heater tube, move forward until the tube clears cylinder heads.

36. Remove coolant outlet.

37. Remove timing chain cover.

38. Rotate crankshaft until crankshaft sprocket timing mark aligns with timing mark on oil pump housing.

39. Remove primary timing chain.

40. Remove upper primary timing chain guides.

41. Remove camshaft bearing caps gradually in the sequence shown.

42. Remove camshafts and valvetrain components from cylinder head. Note component locations for reinstallation in original locations.

43. For left cylinder head removal:

a. Remove fastener securing engine oil dipstick tube to cylinder head. Remove engine oil dipstick tube.

b. Remove alternator.

44. For right cylinder head removal:

a. Remove cylinder head ground strap.

b. Disconnect EGR valve electrical

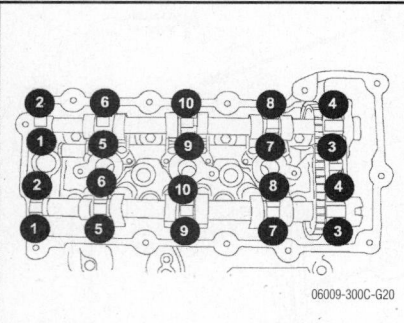

Fig. 121 Camshaft bearing cap loosening sequence—2.7L engine

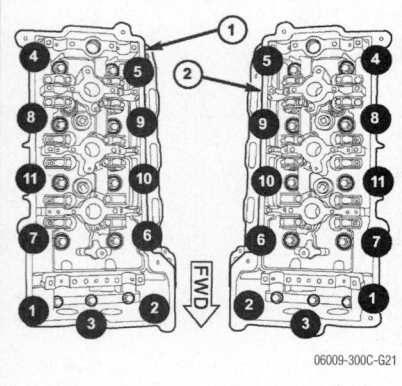

Fig. 122 Cylinder head bolt loosening sequence—2.7L engine

connector and remove EGR valve from head.

> ※ **CAUTION**
>
> **Ensure cylinder head bolts 1-3 are removed before attempting the removal of cylinder head, as damage to cylinder head and/or block may occur.**

45. Remove cylinder left head bolts and right head bolts in sequence shown.

46. Remove cylinder head(s).

47. Remove and discard cylinder head gasket.

To install:

To ensure engine gasket sealing, proper surface preparation must be performed, especially with the use of aluminum engine components and multi-layer steel cylinder head gaskets.

➡ **Multi-Layer Steel (MLS) head gaskets require a scratch free sealing surface. Remove all gasket material from cylinder head and block. Be careful not to gouge or scratch the aluminum head sealing surface. Clean all engine oil passages.**

48. Before cleaning, check for leaks, damage and cracks.

49. Clean cylinder head and oil passages.

50. Check cylinder head for flatness.

51. Cylinder head must be flat within:

- Standard dimension = less than 0.05 mm (0.002 inch.)
- Service Limit = 0.2 mm (0.008 inch.)
- Grinding Limit = Maximum of 0.2 mm (0.008 inch.) is permitted.

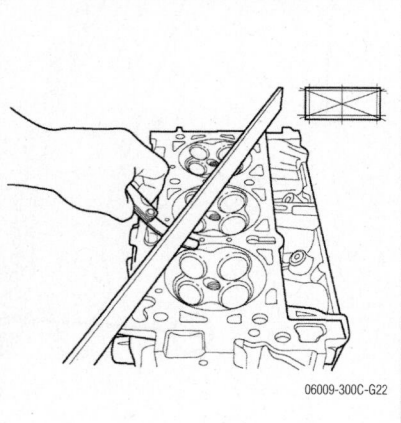

Fig. 123 Check cylinder head for flatness

> ※ **CAUTION**
>
> **0.20 mm (0.008 in.) MAX is a combined total dimension of the stock removal limit from cylinder head and block top surface (deck) together.**

➡ **The cylinder head bolts are tightened using a torque plus angle procedure. The bolts must be examined BEFORE reuse. If the threads are necked down the bolts must be replaced**

Necking can be checked by holding a straight-edge against the threads. If all the threads do not contact the scale, the bolt must be replaced.

> ※ **CAUTION**
>
> **When cleaning cylinder head and cylinder block surfaces, DO NOT use a metal scraper because the surfaces could be cut or ground. Use ONLY a wooden or plastic scraper.**

52. Clean sealing surfaces of cylinder head and block.

53. Install new head gasket over locating dowels.

54. Install cylinder head to block, assuring head is properly positioned over locating dowels.

55. Lubricate bolt threads with clean engine oil and install bolts.

56. Tighten bolts in sequence shown for left head and right head, using the following steps and torque values:

- Step 1: Bolts 1-8 to 35 ft. lbs. (48 Nm)
- Step 2: Bolts 1-8 to 55 ft. lbs. (75 Nm)
- Step 3: Bolts 1-8 to 55 ft. lbs. (75 Nm)
- Step 4: Bolts 1-8 to +90° turn. Do not use a torque wrench for this step.
- Step 5: Bolts 9-11 to 21 ft. lbs. (28 Nm)

57. For left cylinder head installation:

- Install engine oil dipstick tube.
- Install alternator.

58. For right cylinder head installation:

a. Install cylinder head ground strap.

b. Clean mounting surface and install EGR valve.

c. Install the EGR valve mounting bolts.

d. Inspect rubber silicone seals on intake manifold end of EGR tube.

e. Install upper tube into the intake manifold, being careful that the silicone rubber seals are correctly installed and undamaged..

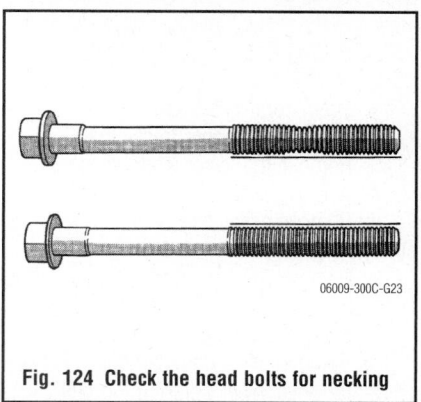

Fig. 124 Check the head bolts for necking

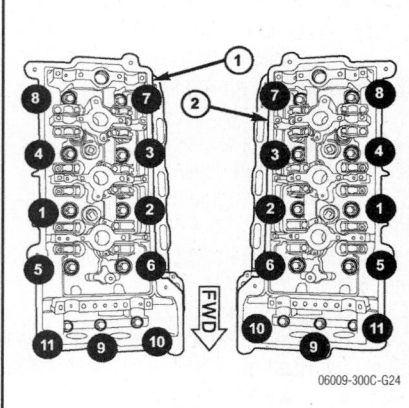

06009-300C-G24

Fig. 125 Cylinder head bolt torque sequence—2.7L engine

f. Install new gasket between the EGR valve and upper tube and install bolts.

g. Install the lower tube to exhaust manifold.

h. Install new gasket between the EGR valve and lower tube and install bolts.

i. Tighten the lower tube to EGR valve bolts to 95 inch lbs. (11 Nm).

j. Tighten the lower tube to exhaust manifold bolts to 275 inch lbs. (31 Nm).

k. Tighten the upper tube to EGR valve bolts to 95 inch lbs. (11 Nm).

l. Tighten EGR valve to cylinder head bolts to 23 ft. lbs. (31 Nm).

59. Install all valve train components and camshafts. Tighten camshaft bearing caps in sequence shown to 105 inch lbs. (12 Nm).

60. Install primary timing chain, guides and sprockets.

61. Inspect heater tube O-ring. Replace as necessary.

62. Lubricate O-ring with silicone type grease such as Mopar® dielectric grease.

63. Install the heater tube by inserting tube in between cylinder heads. Insert tube into outlet connector.

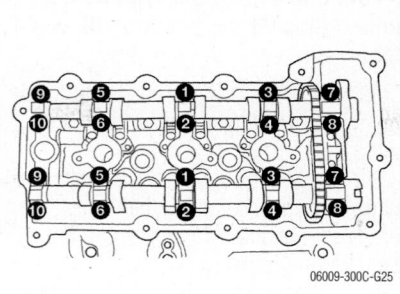

06009-300C-G25

Fig. 126 Camshaft bearing cap bolt torque sequence—2.7L engine

64. Attach heater tube to the retaining clip at rear of engine.

65. Install coolant outlet. Install attaching screws and tighten to 30 inch lbs. (3 Nm).

66. Position radiator into engine compartment. Seat the radiator assembly lower rubber isolators into the mounting holes in radiator lower support.

67. Install radiator mounting bracket and bolts. Tighten to 106 inch lbs. (12 Nm).

68. Position condenser on radiator and install upper mounting bolts. Tighten bolts to 50 inch lbs. (6 Nm).

69. Raise vehicle.

70. Install lower condenser mounting bolts. Tighten bolts to 88 inch lbs. (10 Nm).

71. Install lower radiator hose and clamp.

72. Lower vehicle.

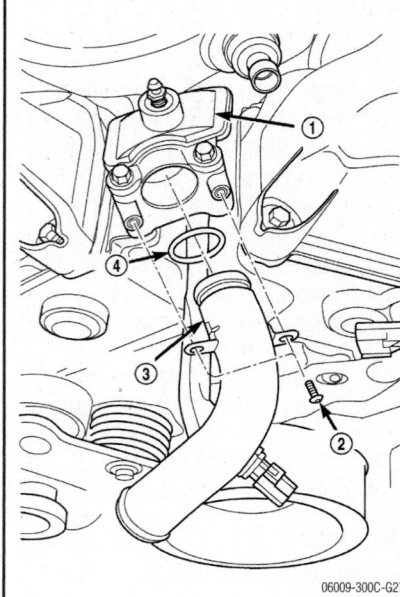

06009-300C-G27

Fig. 127 Coolant outlet installation—2.7L engine

73. Position radiator cooling fan assembly in vehicle.

74. Install cooling fan mounting bolts. Tighten to 50 inch lbs. (6 Nm)

75. Connect cooling fan electrical connector.

76. Install upper radiator upper hose. Align hose so it does not interfere with the accessory drive belt or engine. Position hose clamp so it will not interfere with the hood.

77. Install lower intake manifold.

78. Install the cylinder head cover.

79. Connect camshaft position sensor and coolant temperature sensor connectors.

80. Install timing chain cover.

81. Install crankshaft vibration damper.

82. Install upper intake manifold.

83. Connect oil pressure sensor connector.

84. Install accessory drive belt.

85. Fill the cooling system.

86. Connect negative battery cable.

87. Start engine and check for leaks.

3.5L Engine

Left Side

See Figures 128 and 129.

1. Before servicing the vehicle, refer to the precautions in the beginning of this section.

2. Perform the fuel relief procedure.

3. Disconnect the negative battery cable.

4. Drain cooling system.

5. Remove the upper intake manifold.

6. Remove the lower intake manifold

7. Remove the accessory drive belt.

8. Remove the belt tensioner.

9. Remove the accessory drive idler pulley.

10. Remove the power steering mounting bolts and set pump aside.

11. Remove the crankshaft damper.

12. Remove the lower outer timing belt cover.

13. Raise and support the vehicle.

14. Remove the front exhaust pipe to exhaust manifold mounting nuts.

15. Disconnect both oxygen sensor harness connectors.

16. Lower the vehicle.

17. Remove the outer timing belt cover.

18. Rotate the engine to TDC and align the timing marks.

19. Remove the timing belt tensioner, timing belt, then reset tensioner.

20. Remove the left cylinder head cover to cylinder head ground strap.

21. Remove the left cylinder head cover.

22. Remove the left rocker arm assembly.

23. Remove the left camshaft thrust plate.

24. Counterhold the left cam gear and remove the cam gear retaining bolt.

25. Push the camshaft out of the back of the cylinder head approximately 3.5 inches and remove the cam gear. Remove the front timing belt housing to cylinder head bolts.

26. Remove the cylinder head bolts in REVERSE of tightening sequence.

27. Remove the cylinder head.

28. Clean and inspect all mating surfaces.

To install:

To ensure engine gasket sealing, proper surface preparation must be performed, especially with the use of aluminum engine components and multi-layer steel cylinder head gaskets.

➡**Multi-Layer Steel (MLS) head gaskets require a scratch free sealing surface.**

Remove all gasket material from cylinder head and block. Be careful not to gouge or scratch the aluminum head sealing surface. Clean all engine oil passages.

❋❋ CAUTION

The cylinder head gaskets are not interchangeable between cylinder heads and are clearly marked right or left.

➡**The cylinder head bolts are tightened using a torque plus angle procedure. The bolts must be examined BEFORE reuse. If the threads are necked down the bolts must be replaced.**

Necking can be checked by holding a scale or straight-edge against the threads. If all the threads do not contact the scale the bolt must be replaced.

❋❋ CAUTION

When cleaning cylinder head and cylinder block surfaces, DO NOT use a metal scraper because the surfaces could be cut or ground. Use ONLY a wooden or plastic scraper.

29. Clean sealing surfaces of cylinder head and block.

❋❋ CAUTION

Ensure that the correct head gaskets are used and are oriented correctly on cylinder block.

➡**Before installing the cylinder head bolts, lubricate the threads with clean engine oil.**

30. Install the cylinder head over locating dowels and finger tighten the head bolts.

31. Tighten the cylinder head bolts in the following sequence, using the 4 step torque-turn method. Tighten according to the following torque values:
- Step 1: All to 45 ft. lbs. (61 Nm)
  a. Step 2: All to 65 ft. lbs. (88 Nm)
  b. Step 3: All (again) to 65 ft. lbs. (88 Nm)
  c. Step 4: + 90° turn. Do not use a torque wrench for this step.

32. Bolt torque after 90°turn should be over 90 ft. lbs. (122 Nm) in the tightening direction. If not, replace the bolt.

33. Install the inner timing cover to cylinder head bolts. Tighten bolts to 40 ft. lbs. (54 Nm).

34. Install camshaft sprocket. Counterhold the camshaft sprocket gear and tighten the camshaft sprocket bolt to 102 Nm plus a 90°turn (75 lbs. ft. plus a 90° turn).

35. Install the rear camshaft thrust plate and seal and the EGR valve.

36. Rotate the camshaft gear to its alignment mark and check the left camshaft gear and crankshaft gear timing alignment marks.

37. Install the timing belt and tensioner.

38. Install the timing belt outer cover.

39. Install the power steering reservoir.

40. Install the vibration damper.

41. Install the accessory drive belt tensioner.

42. Install the accessory drive belt idler pulley.

43. Install the right exhaust manifold.

44. Raise and support the vehicle.

45. Install the front exhaust pipe and connect the oxygen sensors.

46. Lower the vehicle.

47. Install the right rocker arm assembly.

48. Install the right cylinder head cover, ground strap and insulator.

49. Install lower intake manifold.

50. Install the fuel rail.

51. Install the upper intake manifold.

52. Connect the air cleaner element housing.

53. Fill the coolant system.

54. Connect the negative battery cable.

Right Side

See Figures 128 and 129.

1. Before servicing the vehicle, refer to the precautions in the beginning of this section.

2. Perform the fuel relief procedure.

3. Disconnect the negative battery cable.

4. Drain cooling system.

5. Remove the upper intake manifold.

6. Remove the lower intake manifold.

7. Remove accessory drive belt.

8. Remove accessory drive belt idler pulley.

9. Remove the power steering mounting bolts and set the pump aside.

10. Raise the vehicle.

11. Remove crankshaft damper.

12. Remove lower outer timing belt cover bolts.

13. Remove front exhaust pipe to exhaust manifold mounting nuts.

14. Disconnect both oxygen sensor harness connectors on each side.

15. Lower vehicle.

16. Remove the remaining outer timing belt cover bolts and cover.

17. Rotate the engine to TDC and align timing belt marks.

18. Remove the timing belt tensioner and reset the tensioner.

19. Remove the timing belt

20. Remove the right cylinder head cover to cylinder head ground strap and capacitor.

21. Remove the EGR valve and tube assembly.

22. Remove the right cylinder head cover.

23. Remove the right rocker arm assembly.

24. Remove the right rear camshaft thrust plate.

25. Counterhold the cam gear and remove the right cam gear retaining bolt.

26. Push the camshaft out of the back of the cylinder head approximately 3.5 inches and remove the right cam gear.

27. Remove the inner timing cover to cylinder head retaining bolts.

28. Remove the cylinder head bolts in REVERSE of tightening sequence.

29. Remove the cylinder head.

30. Clean and inspect all mating surfaces.

To install:

To ensure engine gasket sealing, proper surface preparation must be performed, especially with the use of aluminum engine components and multi-layer steel cylinder head gaskets.

➡**Multi-Layer Steel (MLS) head gaskets require a scratch free sealing surface.**

Remove all gasket material from cylinder head and block. Be careful not to gouge or

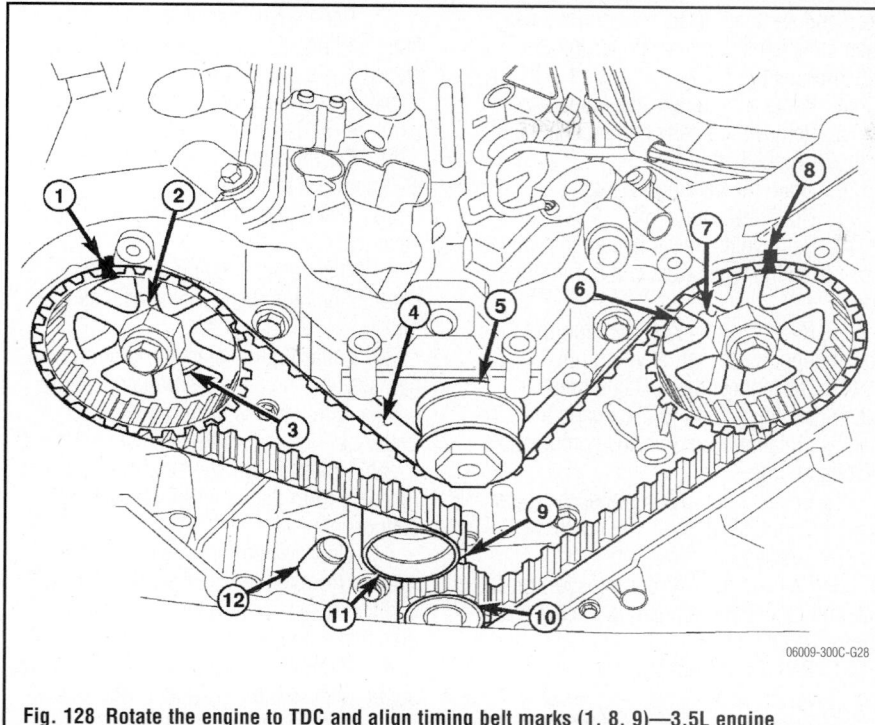

Fig. 128 Rotate the engine to TDC and align timing belt marks (1, 8, 9)—3.5L engine

scratch the aluminum head sealing surface. Clean all engine oil passages.

31. Before cleaning, check for leaks, damage and cracks.
32. Clean cylinder head and oil passages.
33. Check cylinder head for flatness.
34. Cylinder head must be flat within:
    - Standard dimension = less than 0.05 mm (0.002 inch.)
    - Service Limit = 0.2 mm (0.008 inch.)
    - Grinding Limit = Maximum of 0.2 mm (0.008 inch.) is permitted.

✳✳ WARNING
0.20 mm (0.008 in.) MAX is a combined total dimension of the stock removal limit from cylinder head and block top surface (deck) together.

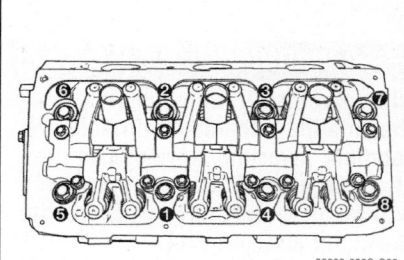

Fig. 129 Cylinder head bolt torque sequence—3.5L engine

✳✳ WARNING
The cylinder head gaskets are not interchangeable between cylinder heads and are clearly marked right or left.

➡ **The cylinder head bolts are tightened using a torque plus angle procedure. The bolts must be examined BEFORE reuse. If the threads are necked down the bolts must be replaced.**

Necking can be checked by holding a scale or straight-edge against the threads. If all the threads do not contact the scale the bolt must be replaced.

✳✳ WARNING
When cleaning cylinder head and cylinder block surfaces, DO NOT use a metal scraper because the surfaces could be cut or ground. Use ONLY a wooden or plastic scraper.

35. Clean sealing surfaces of cylinder head and block.

✳✳ WARNING
Ensure that the correct head gaskets are used and are oriented correctly on cylinder block.

➡ **Before installing the cylinder head bolts, lubricate the threads with clean engine oil.**

36. Install the cylinder head over locating dowels and finger tighten the head bolts.
37. Tighten the cylinder head bolts in the following sequence, using the 4 step torque-turn method. Tighten according to the following torque values:
    - Step 1: All to 45 ft. lbs. (61 Nm)
    - Step 2: All to 65 ft. lbs. (88 Nm)
    - Step 3: All (again) to 65 ft. lbs. (88 Nm)
    - Step 4: + 90°turn. Do not use a torque wrench for this step.
38. Bolt torque after 90°turn should be over 90 ft. lbs. (122 Nm) in the tightening direction. If not, replace the bolt.
39. Install the inner timing cover to cylinder head bolts. Tighten bolts to 40 ft. lbs. (54 Nm).
40. Install camshaft sprocket. Counterhold the camshaft sprocket gear and tighten the camshaft sprocket bolt to 75 ft. lbs. plus a 90°turn (102 Nm plus a 90°turn).
41. Install the rear camshaft thrust plate and seal and the EGR valve.
42. Rotate the camshaft gear to its alignment mark and check the left camshaft gear and crankshaft gear timing alignment marks.
43. Install the timing belt and tensioner.
44. Install the timing belt outer cover.
45. Install the power steering reservoir.
46. Install the vibration damper.
47. Install the accessory drive belt tensioner.
48. Install the accessory drive belt idler pulley.
49. Install the right exhaust manifold
50. Raise and support the vehicle.
51. Install the front exhaust pipe and connect the oxygen sensors.
52. Lower the vehicle.
53. Install the right rocker arm assembly.
54. Clean cylinder head and cover mating surfaces. Inspect and replace gasket and seals as necessary.
55. Install cylinder head cover bolts and tighten to 105 inch lbs. (12 Nm).
56. Install the ground strap retaining bolt to the cylinder head cover.
57. Install the wire harness track.
58. Install the ignition coils. Tighten mounting screws to 60 inch lbs. (6.7 Nm).
59. Connect the ignition coil electrical connectors.
60. Install the right cylinder head cover, ground strap and insulator.
61. Install lower intake manifold.
62. Install the fuel rail.
63. Install the upper intake manifold.
64. Connect the air cleaner element housing.

65. Fill the coolant system.
66. Connect the negative battery cable.

3.6L Engine

Left Side

See Figures 130 through 134.

> **⁑ WARNING**
>
> **The magnetic timing wheels must not come in contact with magnets (pickup tools, trays, etc.) or any other strong magnetic field. This will destroy the timing wheels ability to correctly relay camshaft position to the camshaft position sensor.**

1. Perform the fuel pressure release procedure.
2. Disconnect and isolate the negative battery cable.
3. Lift the engine cover retaining grommets off the ball studs and remove the engine cover.
4. Disconnect the electrical connector from the Inlet Air Temperature (IAT) sensor.
5. Loosen the clamp at the throttle body.
6. Loosen the clamp at the air cleaner housing.
7. Lift the air inlet hose assembly retaining grommet off the ball stud.
8. Remove the air inlet hose assembly.
9. Disconnect the fresh air makeup hose from the air cleaner housing.
10. Remove the air cleaner housing retaining bolt.
11. Remove the air cleaner housing.
12. Remove the fresh air makeup hose from the rear of the intake manifold.
13. Rotate the accessory drive belt tensioner counterclockwise until it contacts the stop and remove the accessory drive belt, then slowly rotate the tensioner into the freearm position.
14. Raise and support the vehicle.
15. Remove the belly pan retainers and remove the belly pan.
16. Drain the cooling system.
17. Drain the engine oil.
18. Remove the lower heater core return hose from the engine coolant pump housing.
19. Remove the heater core return tube lower support bracket retaining nut.
20. Disconnect the A/C compressor electrical connector and disengage the wire harness retainer from the A/C compressor discharge line.
21. Remove the A/C compressor lower retaining studs.
22. Lower the vehicle.
23. Remove the A/C compressor upper retaining bolts and reposition the A/C compressor aside.
24. Remove the coolant bottle return hose.
25. Remove the heater core purge hose from the coolant bottle.
26. Remove the coolant bottle retaining bolts.
27. Remove the coolant bottle.
28. Disconnect the heater core return hose.
29. Remove the heater core return tube upper support bracket retaining nut and remove the tube.
30. Remove the upper and lower intake manifolds and insulator.
31. Disconnect the left upstream oxygen sensor electrical connector from the main wire harness.
32. Loosen the lower down pipe flange bolts.
33. Remove the upper down pipe flange bolts and position the down pipe and catalytic converter aside.
34. Disconnect the Engine Coolant Temperature (ECT) sensor electrical connector.
35. Disconnect the ignition coil capacitor electrical connector.
36. Disconnect the injection/ignition electrical connector.
37. Disconnect the engine oil pressure/temperature sensor electrical connector.
38. Unfasten the injection/ignition wire harness and the oil pressure/temperature sensor wire harness from the retainer bracket on the rear of the left cylinder head.
39. Unfasten two starter wire harness retainers from the upper intake manifold support brackets.
40. Unfasten one main wire harness retainer from the left cylinder head cover and two retainers from the upper intake manifold support brackets.
41. Remove the bolts and remove the left upper intake manifold support brackets.
42. Remove the ignition coils.
43. Remove the cylinder head covers, lower and upper oil pans, crankshaft vibration damper and engine timing cover.

➡ **Take this opportunity to measure timing chain wear.**

> **⁑ WARNING**
>
> **When aligning timing marks, always rotate engine by turning the crankshaft. Failure to do so will result in valve and/or piston damage.**

44. Rotate the crankshaft clockwise to place the number one piston at TDC on the exhaust stroke by aligning the dimple on the crankshaft with the block/bearing cap junction. The left side cam phaser arrows should point toward each other and be parallel to the valve cover sealing surface. The right side cam phaser arrows should point away from each other and the scribe lines should be parallel to the valve cover sealing surface.

> **⁑ WARNING**
>
> **Always reinstall timing chains so that they maintain the same direction of rotation. Inverting a previously run chain on a previously run sprocket will result in excessive wear to both the chain and sprocket.**

45. Mark the direction of rotation on the timing chain using a paint pen or equivalent to aid in reassembly.

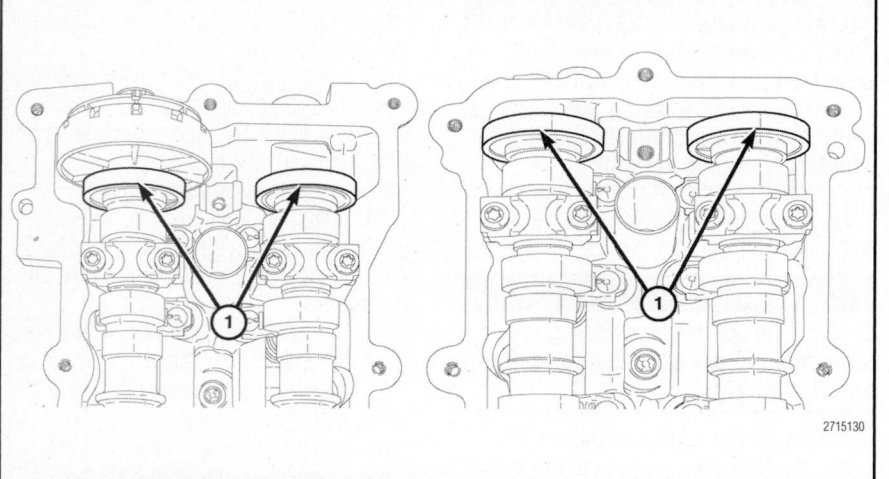

2715130

Fig. 130 Identifying the magnet timing wheels

When the timing chains are removed and the cylinder heads are still installed, DO NOT rotate the camshafts or crankshaft without first locating the proper crankshaft position. Failure to do so will result in valve and/or piston damage.

46. Reset the left cam chain tensioner by lifting the pawl, pushing back the piston and installing Tensioner Pin.

➡Minor rotation of a camshaft (a few degrees) may be required to install the camshaft phaser lock.

47. Install the LH Camshaft Phaser Lock.
48. Loosen both the intake oil control valve and exhaust oil control valve.
49. Remove the LH Camshaft Phaser Lock.
50. Remove the oil control valve from the left side exhaust cam phaser and pull the phaser off of the camshaft.
51. Remove the oil control valve from the left side intake cam phaser and pull the phaser off of the camshaft.
52. Remove the left cam chain tensioner arm.

53. Remove two T30 bolts and the left cam chain tensioner.
54. Remove two T30 bolts and the left cam chain guide.
55. Remove the left camshafts.

➡If the rocker arms are to be reused, identify their positions so that they can be reassembled into their original locations.

56. Remove the rocker arms.

➡If the hydraulic lifters are to be reused, identify their positions so that they can be reassembled into their original locations.

57. If required, remove the hydraulic lifters.
58. Using the sequence shown, remove the cylinder head retaining bolts.

☀☀ CAUTION

The multi-layered steel head gaskets have very sharp edges that could cause personal injury if not handled carefully.

☀☀ WARNING

Do not lay the cylinder head on its gasket sealing surface, due to the

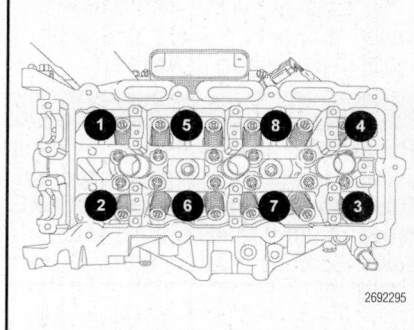

Fig. 132 Removing the cylinder head retaining bolts

design of the cylinder head gasket, any distortion to the cylinder head sealing surface may prevent the gasket from properly sealing resulting in leaks.

➡The head gasket crimps the locating dowels and the dowels may pull out of the engine block when the head gasket is removed.

59. Remove the cylinder head and gasket and discard the gasket.
60. If required, remove the Engine Coolant Temperature (ECT) sensor.
61. If required, remove the bolt and the ignition coil capacitor.
62. If required, remove the bolt and the engine wire harness retainer bracket.

To install:
63. If removed, install the Engine Coolant Temperature (ECT) sensor and tighten to 97 inch lbs. (11 Nm).
64. If removed, install the ignition coil capacitor with a M6 bolt and tightened to 89 inch lbs. (10 Nm).

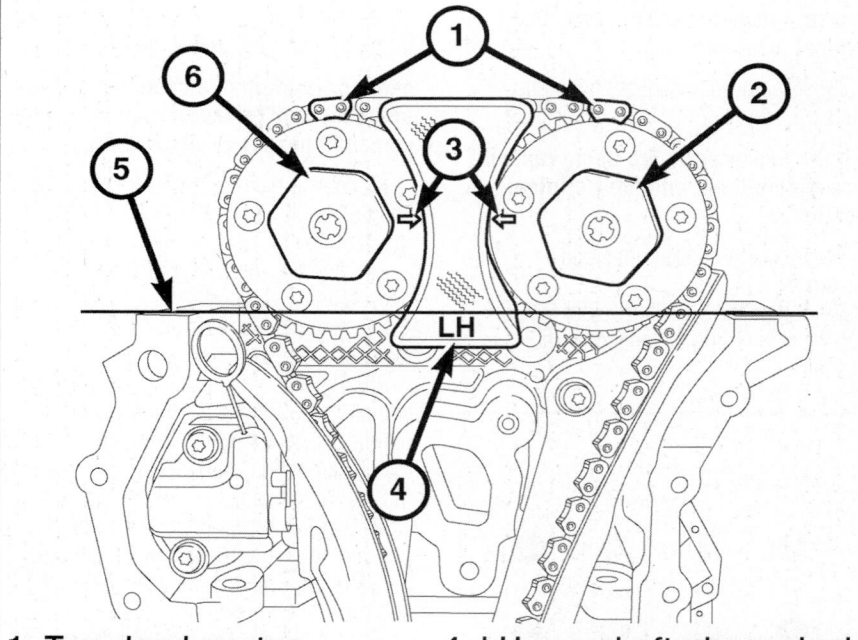

1. Top dead center
2. Exhaust oil control valve
3. –
4. LH camshaft phaser lock
5. –
6. Oil control valve

Fig. 131 Removing the phasers

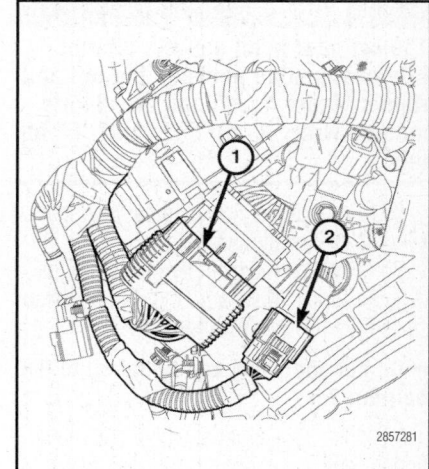

Fig. 133 Removing the ECT, ignition coil capacitor and engine wire harness bracket

65. If removed, install the engine wire harness retainer bracket with a T30 bolt and tightened to 9 ft. lbs. (12 Nm).

✳✳ WARNING

The cylinder head bolts are tightened using a torque plus angle procedure. The bolts must be examined BEFORE reuse. If the threads are necked down the bolts must be replaced.

66. Check cylinder head bolts for necking by holding a scale or straight edge against the threads. If all the threads do not contact the scale the bolt must be replaced.

✳✳ WARNING

When cleaning cylinder head and cylinder block surfaces, DO NOT use a metal scraper because the surfaces could be cut or ground. Use ONLY a wooden or plastic scraper.

67. Clean and prepare the gasket sealing surfaces of the cylinder head and block.

✳✳ WARNING

Non-compressible debris such as oil, coolant or RTV sealants that are not removed from bolt holes can cause the aluminum casting to crack when tightening the bolts.

68. Clean out the cylinder head bolt holes in the engine block.

✳✳ CAUTION

The multi-layered steel head gaskets have very sharp edges that could cause personal injury if not handled carefully.

✳✳ WARNING

The cylinder head gaskets are not interchangeable between the left and right cylinder heads and are clearly marked with "R" for right and "L" for left.

69. Position the new cylinder head gasket onto the locating dowels.

70. Position the cylinder head onto the cylinder block. Make sure the cylinder head seats fully over the locating dowels.

➡**Do not apply any additional oil to the bolt threads.**

71. Install the eight cylinder head bolts finger tight.

72. Tighten the cylinder head bolts in the sequence shown, following this 9 step torque plus angle method. Tighten according to the following torque values:

- Step 1: All to 22 ft. lbs. (30 Nm)
- Step 2: All to 33 ft. lbs. (45 Nm)
- Step 3: All + 75° Turn. Do not use a torque wrench for this step.
- Step 4: All + 50° Turn. Do not use a torque wrench for this step.
- Step 5: Loosen all fasteners in reverse of sequence shown
- Step 6: All to 22 ft. lbs. (30 Nm)
- Step 7: All to 33 ft. lbs. (45 Nm)
- Step 8: All + 70° Turn. Do not use a torque wrench for this step.
- Step 9: All + 70° Turn. Do not use a torque wrench for this step.

✳✳ WARNING

Do not rotate the camshafts more than a few degrees independently of the crankshaft. Valve to piston contact could occur resulting in possible valve damage. If the camshafts need to be rotated more than a few degrees, first move the pistons away from the cylinder heads by rotating the crankshaft counterclockwise to a position 30° BTDC. Once the camshafts are positioned at TDC rotate the crankshaft clockwise to return the crankshaft to TDC.

➡**If the hydraulic lifters are being reused, reassemble them into their original locations.**

73. If removed, install the hydraulic lifters.

➡**If the rocker arms are being reused, reassemble them into their original locations.**

74. Install the rocker arms and camshafts.

75. Rotate the camshafts clockwise to TDC by positioning the alignment holes vertically.

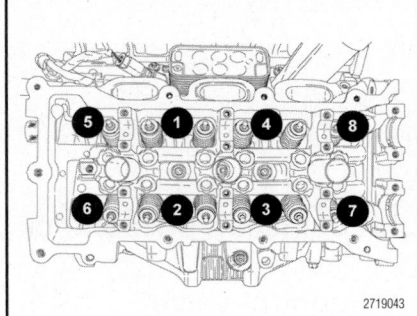

Fig. 134 Identifying the bolt installation sequence

76. Install the left cam chain guide with two bolts and tighten the T30 bolts to 9 ft. lbs. (12 Nm).

77. Install the left cam chain tensioner to the cylinder head with two bolts and tighten the T30 bolts to 9 ft. lbs. (12 Nm).

78. Reset the left cam chain tensioner by lifting the pawl, pushing back the piston and installing Tensioner Pin.

79. Install the left tensioner arm.

80. Press the left intake cam phaser onto the intake camshaft, install and hand tighten the oil control valve.

✳✳ WARNING

Always reinstall timing chains so that they maintain the same direction of rotation. Inverting a previously run chain on a previously run sprocket will result in excessive wear to both the chain and sprocket.

81. Drape the left side cam chain over the left intake cam phaser and onto the idler sprocket so that the arrow is aligned with the plated link on the cam chain.

82. While maintaining this alignment, route the cam chain around the exhaust and intake cam phasers so that the plated links are aligned with the phaser timing marks. Position the left side cam phasers so that the arrows point toward each other and are parallel to the valve cover sealing surface. Press the exhaust cam phaser onto the exhaust cam, install and hand tighten the oil control valve.

➡**Minor rotation of a camshaft (a few degrees) may be required to install the camshaft phaser or phaser lock.**

83. Install the LH Camshaft Phaser Lock and tighten the oil control valves to 110 ft. lbs. (150 Nm).

84. Remove the LH Camshaft Phaser Lock.

85. Remove the Tensioner Pin from the left cam chain tensioner.

86. Rotate the crankshaft clockwise two complete revolutions stopping when the dimple on the crankshaft is aligned the with the block/bearing cap junction.

87. While maintaining this alignment, verify that the arrows on the left side cam phasers point toward each other and are parallel to the valve cover sealing surface and that the right side cam phaser arrows point away from each other and the scribe lines are parallel to the valve cover sealing surface.

88. There should be 12 chain pins between the exhaust cam phaser triangle marking and the intake cam phaser circle marking.

89. If the engine timing is not correct, repeat this procedure.

90. Install the engine timing cover, crankshaft vibration damper, upper and lower oil pans and cylinder head covers.

91. Install the left upper intake manifold support brackets and tighten the stud finger tight.

92. Fasten two starter wire harness retainers to the upper intake manifold support brackets.

93. Fasten one main wire harness retainer to the left cylinder head cover and two retainers to the upper intake manifold support brackets.

94. Install the spark plugs and tighten to 13 ft. lbs. (18 Nm).

95. Install the ignition coils.

96. Connect the ignition coil capacitor electrical connector.

97. Connect the injection/ignition electrical connector.

98. Connect the engine oil pressure/temperature sensor electrical connector.

99. Fasten the injection/ignition wire harness and the oil pressure/temperature sensor wire harness from the retainer bracket on the rear of the left cylinder head.

100. Connect the Engine Coolant Temperature (ECT) sensor electrical connector.

101. Install the upper and lower intake manifolds.

102. Position the heater core return tube onto the upper support bracket, install the retaining nut and tighten to 9 ft. lbs. (12 Nm).

103. Connect the heater core return hose.

104. Position the A/C compressor, install the upper bolts finger tight.

105. Install the lower A/C compressor retaining studs finger tight

106. Tightened the A/C compressor upper bolts to 18 ft. lbs. (25 Nm).

107. Raise and support the vehicle.

108. Position the heater core return tube lower support bracket onto the A/C compressor lower retaining stud, install the nut and tighten both A/C compressor lower retaining nuts to 18 ft. lbs. (25 Nm).

109. Connect the A/C compressor electrical connector and fasten the wire harness retainer to the A/C compressor discharge line.

110. Connect the lower heater core return hose to the engine coolant pump housing.

111. Position the left down pipe onto the partially installed lower flange bolts.

112. Install the upper down pipe flange bolts and tighten to 17 ft. lbs. (23 Nm).

113. Tighten the lower down pipe flange bolts to 17 ft. lbs. (23 Nm).

114. Connect the left upstream oxygen sensor electrical connector to the main wire harness.

115. If removed, install the oil filter.

116. Position the belly pan and install the retainers.

117. Lower the vehicle.

118. Rotate the accessory drive belt tensioner counterclockwise until it contacts the stop and install the accessory drive belt, then slowly rotate the tensioner into position.

119. Connect the fresh air makeup hose to the rear of the intake manifold.

120. Position the coolant bottle into the engine compartment.

121. Install the coolant bottle retaining bolts and tighten to 9 ft. lbs. (12 Nm).

122. Connect the heater core purge hose to the coolant bottle.

123. Connect the coolant bottle return hose.

124. Position the air cleaner housing into the vehicle.

125. Install the air cleaner housing retaining bolt and tighten to 9 ft. lbs. (12 Nm).

126. Connect the fresh air makeup hose to the air cleaner housing.

127. Position the air inlet hose assembly onto the throttle body and the air cleaner housing.

128. Secure the air inlet hose assembly retaining grommet onto the ball stud.

129. Tighten the clamp at the air cleaner housing to 44 inch lbs. (5 Nm).

130. Tighten the clamp at the throttle body to 44 inch lbs. (5 Nm).

131. Connect the Inlet Air Temperature (IAT) sensor electrical connector.

132. Fill the crankcase with the specified type and amount of engine oil.

133. Fill the cooling system with the specified type and amount of engine coolant.

134. Position the engine cover and secure the retaining grommets onto the ball studs.

135. Connect the negative battery cable and tighten nut to 45 inch lbs. (5 Nm).

136. Run the engine until it reaches normal operating temperature and check for leaks.

➡The Cam/Crank Variation Relearn procedure must be performed using the scan tool anytime there has been a repair/replacement made to a powertrain system, for example: flywheel, valvetrain, camshaft and/or crankshaft sensors or components.

Right Side

See Figures 135 through 137.

✳✳ WARNING

The magnetic timing wheels must not come in contact with magnets (pickup tools, trays, etc.) or any

other strong magnetic field. This will destroy the timing wheels ability to correctly relay camshaft position to the camshaft position sensor.

1. Perform the fuel pressure release procedure.

2. Disconnect and isolate the negative battery cable.

3. Lift the engine cover retaining grommets off the ball studs and remove the engine cover.

4. Disconnect the electrical connector from the Inlet Air Temperature (IAT) sensor.

5. Loosen the clamp at the throttle body.

6. Loosen the clamp at the air cleaner housing.

7. Lift the air inlet hose assembly retaining grommet off the ball stud.

8. Remove the air inlet hose assembly.

9. Disconnect the fresh air makeup hose from the air cleaner housing.

10. Remove the air cleaner housing retaining bolt.

11. Remove the air cleaner housing.

12. Rotate the accessory drive belt tensioner counterclockwise until it contacts the stop and remove the accessory drive belt, then slowly rotate the tensioner into the freearm position.

13. Remove the generator.

14. Disconnect the vacuum line at the EVAP purge solenoid.

15. Disconnect the EVAP purge solenoid vacuum line at the intake manifold and remove the vacuum line.

16. Disconnect the PCV hose from the PCV valve and the intake manifold and remove hose.

17. Disconnect the brake booster vacuum hose and position aside.

18. Disconnect the electrical connector at the Manifold Absolute Pressure (MAP) Sensor.

19. Disconnect the electrical connector at the Electronic Throttle Control (ETC).

20. Disconnect the electrical connector at the Camshaft Position Sensor (CMP) and position harness aside.

21. Remove the upper and lower intake manifolds and insulator.

22. Raise and support the vehicle.

23. Remove the belly pan retainers and remove the belly pan.

24. Drain the cooling system.

25. Drain the engine oil.

26. Disconnect the right upstream oxygen electrical sensor connector from the main wire harness.

27. Loosen the lower down pipe flange bolts.

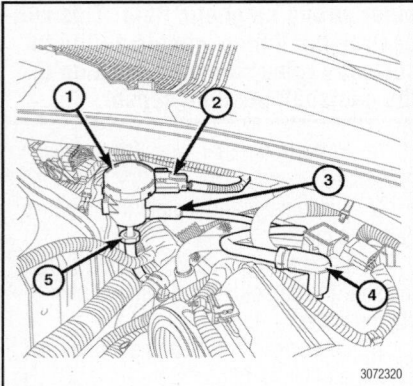

Fig. 135 View of the EVAP purge solenoid (1), vacuum line (3) and EVAP purge solenoid vacuum line (4)

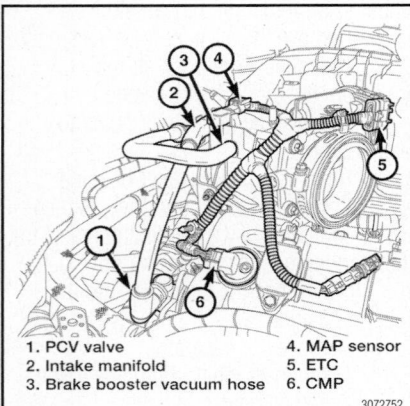

1. PCV valve
2. Intake manifold
3. Brake booster vacuum hose
4. MAP sensor
5. ETC
6. CMP

3072752

Fig. 136 Disconnecting the PCV hose, brake booster vacuum hose, MAP sensor, ETC and CMP sensor

28. Remove the upper down pipe flange bolts and position the down pipe and catalytic converter aside.
29. Remove the oil level indicator retaining bolt and remove the oil level indicator.
30. Remove the heater core supply tube support bracket retaining bolt and remove the heater core supply tube.
31. Disconnect the ignition coil capacitor electrical connector.
32. Remove the stud and remove the upper intake manifold support bracket (2).
33. Remove the cylinder head covers, lower and upper oil pans, crankshaft vibration damper and engine timing cover.

➡Take this opportunity to measure timing chain wear.

34. Lower the vehicle.
35. Remove the ignition coils.

✳✳ WARNING

When aligning timing marks, always rotate engine by turning the crank-

shaft. Failure to do so will result in valve and/or piston damage.

✳✳ WARNING

Always reinstall timing chains so that they maintain the same direction of rotation. Inverting a previously run chain on a previously run sprocket will result in excessive wear to both the chain and sprocket.

36. Rotate the crankshaft clockwise to place the number one piston at TDC on the exhaust stroke by aligning the dimple on the crankshaft with the block/bearing cap junction. The left side cam phaser arrows should point toward each other and be parallel to the valve cover sealing surface. The right side cam phaser arrows should point away from each other and the scribe lines should be parallel to the valve cover sealing surface.
37. Mark the direction of rotation on the timing chain using a paint pen or equivalent to aid in reassembly.

✳✳ WARNING

When the timing chains are removed and the cylinder heads are still installed, DO NOT rotate the camshafts or crankshaft without first locating the proper crankshaft position. Failure to do so will result in valve and/or piston damage.

38. Reset the right cam chain tensioner by pushing back the tensioner piston and installing Tensioner Pin.

➡Minor rotation of a camshaft (a few degrees) may be required to install the camshaft phaser lock.

39. Install the RH Camshaft Phaser Lock.
40. Loosen both the intake oil control valve and exhaust oil control valve.
41. Remove the RH Camshaft Phaser Lock.
42. Remove the oil control valve from the right side intake cam phaser and pull the phaser off of the camshaft.
43. Remove the oil control valve from the right side exhaust cam phaser and pull the phaser off of the camshaft.
44. Remove the right cam chain tensioner arm.
45. Remove two T30 bolts and the right cam chain tensioner.
46. Remove three T30 bolts and the right cam chain guide.
47. Remove the right camshafts.

➡If the rocker arms are to be reused, identify their positions so that they can

be reassembled into their original locations.

48. Remove the rocker arms.

➡If the hydraulic lifters are to be reused, identify their positions so that they can be reassembled into their original locations.

49. If required, remove the hydraulic lifters.
50. Using the sequence shown, remove the cylinder head retaining bolts.

✳✳ CAUTION

The multi-layered steel head gaskets have very sharp edges that could cause personal injury if not handled carefully.

✳✳ WARNING

Do not lay the cylinder head on its gasket sealing surface, due to the design of the cylinder head gasket, any distortion to the cylinder head sealing surface may prevent the gasket from properly sealing resulting in leaks.

➡The head gasket crimps the locating dowels and the dowels may pull out of the engine block when the head gasket is removed.

51. Remove the cylinder head and gasket. Discard the gasket.
52. If required, remove the bolt and the ignition coil capacitor.

To install:
53. If removed, install the ignition coil capacitor with an M6 bolt tightened to 89 inch lbs. (10 Nm).

✳✳ WARNING

The cylinder head bolts are tightened using a torque plus angle procedure. The bolts must be examined BEFORE reuse. If the threads are necked down the bolts must be replaced.

➡Typical cylinder head bolt shown.

54. Check the cylinder head bolts for necking by holding a scale or straight edge against the threads. If all the threads do not contact the scale the bolt must be replaced.

✳✳ WARNING

When cleaning cylinder head and cylinder block surfaces, DO NOT use a metal scraper because the surfaces could be cut or ground. Use ONLY a wooden or plastic scraper.

55. Clean and prepare the gasket sealing surfaces of the cylinder head and block.

✳✳ WARNING

Non-compressible debris such as oil, coolant or RTV sealants that are not removed from bolt holes can cause the aluminum casting to crack when tightening the bolts.

56. Clean out the cylinder head bolt holes in the engine block.
57. The multi-layered steel head gaskets have very sharp edges that could cause personal injury if not handled carefully.

✳✳ WARNING

The cylinder head gaskets are not interchangeable between the left and right cylinder heads and are clearly marked with "R" for right and "L" for left.

58. Position the new cylinder head gasket on the locating dowels.
59. Position the cylinder head onto the cylinder block. Make sure the cylinder head seats fully over the locating dowels.

➡**Do not apply any additional oil to the bolt threads.**

60. Install the eight cylinder head bolts finger tight.
61. Tighten the cylinder head bolts in the sequence shown, following this 9 step torque plus angle method. Tighten according to the following torque values:
- Step 1: All to 22 ft. lbs. (30 Nm)
- Step 2: All to 33 ft. lbs. (45 Nm)
- Step 3: All + 75°Turn Do not use a torque wrench for this step.
- Step 4: All + 50°Turn Do not use a torque wrench for this step.
- Step 5: Loosen all fasteners in reverse of sequence shown
- Step 6: All to 22 ft. lbs. (30 Nm)
- Step 7: All to 33 ft. lbs. (45 Nm)
- Step 8: All + 70°Turn Do not use a torque wrench for this step.
- Step 9: All + 70°Turn Do not use a torque wrench for this step.

➡**If the hydraulic lifters are being reused, reassemble them into their original locations.**

62. If removed, install the hydraulic lifters.

➡**If the rocker arms are being reused, reassemble them into their original locations.**

63. Install the rocker arms and camshafts.

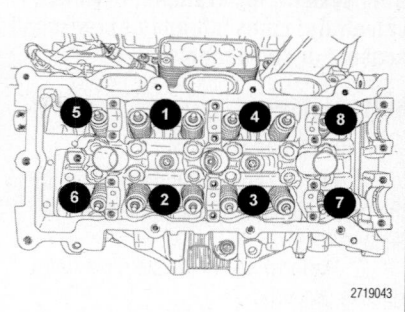

Fig. 137 Identifying the cylinder head bolt tightening sequence

✳✳ WARNING

Do not rotate the camshafts more than a few degrees independently of the crankshaft. Valve to piston contact could occur resulting in possible valve damage. If the camshafts need to be rotated more than a few degrees, first move the pistons away from the cylinder heads by rotating the crankshaft counterclockwise to a position 30°BTDC. Once the camshafts are positioned at TDC rotate the crankshaft clockwise to return the crankshaft to TDC.

64. Verify that the camshafts are set at TDC by positioning the alignment holes vertically.
65. Install the right cam chain guide with three bolts. Tighten the T30 bolts to 9 ft. lbs. (12 Nm).
66. Install the right cam chain tensioner to the engine block with two bolts. Tighten the T30 bolts to 9 ft. lbs. (12 Nm).
67. Reset the right cam chain tensioner by pushing back the tensioner piston and installing Tensioner Pin.
68. Install the right tensioner arm.

✳✳ WARNING

Always reinstall timing chains so that they maintain the same direction of rotation. Inverting a previously run chain on a previously run sprocket will result in excessive wear to both the chain and sprocket.

69. Press the right exhaust cam phaser onto the exhaust camshaft. Install and hand tighten the oil control valve.
70. Drape the right side cam chain over the right exhaust cam phaser and onto the idler sprocket so that the dimple is aligned with the plated link on the cam chain.
71. While maintaining this alignment, route the cam chain around the exhaust and

intake cam phasers so that the plated links are aligned with the phaser timing marks. Position the right side cam phasers so that the arrows point away from each other and the scribe lines are parallel to the valve cover sealing surface. Press the intake cam phaser onto the intake cam, install and hand tighten the oil control valve.

➡**Minor rotation of a camshaft (a few degrees) may be required to install the camshaft phaser or phaser lock.**

72. Install the RH Camshaft Phaser Lock and tighten the oil control valves and to 110 ft. lbs. (150 Nm).
73. Remove the RH Camshaft Phaser Lock.
74. Remove the Tensioner Pin from the RH cam chain tensioner.
75. Rotate the crankshaft clockwise two complete revolutions stopping when the dimple on the crankshaft is aligned the with the block/bearing cap junction.
76. While maintaining this alignment, verify that the arrows on the left side cam phasers point toward each other and are parallel to the valve cover sealing surface and that the right side cam phaser arrows point away from each other and the scribe lines are parallel to the valve cover sealing surface.
77. There should be 12 chain pins between the exhaust cam phaser triangle marking and the intake cam phaser circle marking.
78. If the engine timing is not correct, repeat this procedure.
79. Install the engine timing cover, crankshaft vibration damper, upper and lower oil pans and cylinder head covers.

➡**The left side ignition coils are shown, the right side ignition coils are similar.**

80. Install the spark plugs and tighten to 13 ft. lbs. (18 Nm).
81. Install the ignition coils.
82. Position the upper intake manifold support bracket and install the retaining stud finger tight.
83. Install the heater core supply tube with one bolt tightened to 9 ft. lbs. (12 Nm).
84. Position the oil level indicator, install the retaining bolt and tighten to 9 ft. lbs. (12 Nm).
85. Install the generator.
86. Rotate the accessory drive belt tensioner counterclockwise until it contacts the stop and install the accessory drive belt, then slowly rotate the tensioner into position.
87. Install the right down pipe onto the partially installed lower flange bolts (3).

88. Install the upper down pipe flange bolts and tighten all M8 bolts to 17 ft. lbs. (23 Nm).

89. Connect the right upstream oxygen sensor connectors (4) to the main wire harness.

90. Install the upper and lower intake manifolds.

91. Connect the electrical connector at the Camshaft Position Sensor (CMP).

92. Connect the electrical connector at the Electronic Throttle Control (ETC).

93. Connect the electrical connector at the Manifold Absolute Pressure (MAP) Sensor.

94. Connect the brake booster vacuum hose.

95. Connect the PCV hose to the PCV valve and to the intake manifold.

96. Connect the EVAP purge solenoid vacuum line to the intake manifold.

97. Connect the vacuum line to the EVAP purge solenoid.

98. Raise and support the vehicle.

99. If removed, install the oil filter.

100. Position the belly pan and install the retainers.

101. Lower the vehicle.

102. Position the air cleaner housing into the vehicle.

103. Install the air cleaner housing retaining bolt and tighten to 9 ft. lbs. (12 Nm).

104. Connect the fresh air makeup hose to the air cleaner housing.

105. Position the air inlet hose assembly onto the throttle body and the air cleaner housing.

106. Secure the air inlet hose assembly retaining grommet onto the ball stud.

107. Tighten the clamp at the air cleaner housing to 44 inch lbs. (5 Nm).

108. Tighten the clamp at the throttle body to 44 inch lbs. (5 Nm).

109. Connect the Inlet Air Temperature (IAT) sensor electrical connector.

110. Fill the crankcase with the specified type and amount of engine oil.

111. Fill the cooling system with the specified type and amount of engine coolant.

112. Position the engine cover and secure the retaining grommets onto the ball studs.

113. Connect the negative battery cable and tighten nut to 45 inch lbs. (5 Nm).

114. Run the engine until it reaches normal operating temperature and check for leaks.

➡**The Cam/Crank Variation Relearn procedure must be performed using the scan tool anytime there has been a repair/replacement made to a power-train system, for example: flywheel, valvetrain, camshaft and/or crankshaft sensors or components.**

5.7L Engine

See Figures 138 and 139.

1. Before servicing the vehicle, refer to the precautions in the beginning of this section.

2. Perform the fuel system pressure release procedure.

3. Disconnect the fuel supply line.

4. Disconnect the negative battery cable.

5. Drain cooling system.

6. Remove the air cleaner resonator and duct work.

7. Remove closed crankcase ventilation system.

8. Disconnect the exhaust at the exhaust manifolds.

9. Disconnect the evaporation control system.

10. Disconnect heater hoses.

11. Remove the power steering pump.

12. Disconnect coil on plug connectors.

❋❋ CAUTION

The ground straps must be installed in the same location as removed. The covers are machined to accept the ground straps in those locations only.

13. Remove cylinder head cover.

➡**The gasket may be used again, provided no cuts, tears, or deformation has occurred.**

14. Remove intake manifold and throttle body as an assembly.

15. Remove rocker arm assemblies and push rods. Identify to ensure installation in original locations.

16. Remove the head bolts from each cylinder head, using the sequence provided, and remove cylinder heads. Discard the cylinder head gasket.

To install:

17. Clean all surfaces of cylinder block and cylinder heads.

18. Clean cylinder block front and rear gasket surfaces using a suitable solvent.

19. Inspect the cylinder head for out-of-flatness, using a straight-edge and a feeler gauge. If tolerances exceed 0.0508mm (0.002 in.), replace the cylinder head.

20. Inspect the valve seats for damage. Service the valve seats as necessary.

21. Inspect the valve guides for wear, cracks or looseness. If either condition exists, replace the cylinder head.

22. Inspect pushrods. Replace worn or bent pushrods.

23. Clean all surfaces of cylinder block and cylinder heads.

24. Clean cylinder block front and rear gasket surfaces using a suitable solvent.

❋❋ CAUTION

The head gaskets are not interchangeable between left and right sides. They are marked "L" and "R" to indicate left and right sides.

❋❋ CAUTION

The head gaskets are marked "TOP" to indicate which side goes up.

25. Position new cylinder head gaskets onto the cylinder block.

26. Position cylinder heads onto head gaskets and cylinder block.

27. Tighten the cylinder head bolts in three steps using the sequence provided:

- Step 1: Snug tighten M12 cylinder head bolts, in sequence, to 25 ft. lbs. (34 Nm) and M8 bolts to 15 ft. lbs. (20 Nm).
- Step 2: Tighten M12 cylinder head bolts, in sequence, to 40 ft. lbs. (54 Nm) and verify M8 bolts to 15 ft. lbs. (20 Nm).
- Step 3: Turn M12 cylinder head bolts, in sequence, 90 degrees and tighten M8 bolts to 25 ft. lbs. (34 Nm).

28. Install pushrods and rocker arm assemblies in their original position, using pushrod retaining plate special tool 9070.

29. Install the intake manifold and throttle body assembly.

30. If required, adjust spark plugs to specifications. Install the plugs.

31. Connect the heater hoses.

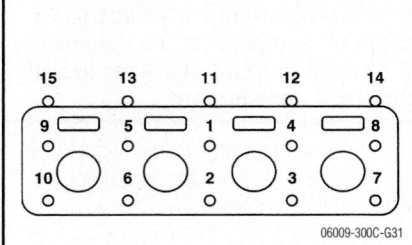

Fig. 138 Cylinder head bolt removal/tightening sequence—5.7L engine

06009-300C-G31

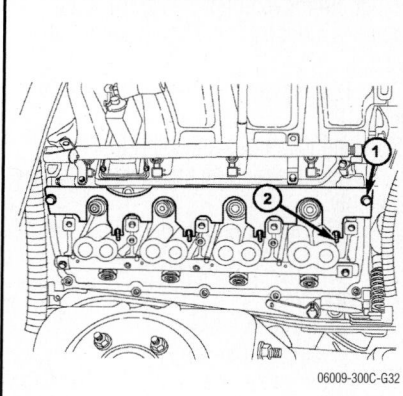

Fig. 139 Pushrod retaining plate—5.7L engine

32. Install the fuel supply line.
33. Install the power steering pump.
34. Install the drive belt.
35. Install the cylinder head cover.
36. Install ignition coil on plug, and torque fasteners to 105 inch lbs. (12 Nm)
37. Connect, ignition coil electrical connectors.
38. Install PCV hose.
39. Connect the evaporation control system.
40. Install the air cleaner.
41. Fill cooling system.
42. Connect the negative cable to the battery.
43. Start engine check for leaks.

ENGINE OIL & FILTER

REPLACEMENT

1. Run engine until achieving normal operating temperature.
   a. Position the vehicle on a level surface and turn engine off.
2. Hoist and support vehicle on safety stands.
3. Remove engine splash shields.
   a. Place a suitable drain pan under crankcase drain.
4. Remove drain plug from oil pan and allow oil to drain into pan. Inspect drain plug threads for stretching or other damage. Replace drain plug and gasket if damaged.
5. Remove oil filter.
6. Install drain plug in oil pan. Tighten plug to 20 ft. lbs. (27 Nm).
7. Install new oil filter.
8. Lower vehicle and remove oil fill cap. Fill crankcase with specified type and amount of engine oil.
9. Install oil fill cap.

10. Start engine and inspect for leaks.
11. Stop engine and inspect oil level.

Oil Filter Specification

All engines are equipped with a high quality full-flow, disposable type oil filter. When replacing oil filter, use a Mopar® filter or equivalent.

EXHAUST MANIFOLD

REMOVAL & INSTALLATION

3.5L Engine

Left Side

See Figure 140.

1. Before servicing the vehicle, refer to the precautions in the beginning of this section.
   a. Disconnect and isolate the negative battery cable.
2. Raise and support the vehicle.
   a. Separate the front exhaust pipe to manifold union.
3. Lower the vehicle.
4. Disconnect and remove the oxygen sensor from the exhaust manifold.
5. Remove the exhaust manifold shield retaining bolts, exhaust manifold, and discard gasket.

To install:

6. Inspect exhaust manifolds for damage or cracks.
7. Check manifold flatness.
8. Inspect the exhaust manifold gasket for obvious discoloration or distortion.
9. Check distortion of the cylinder head mounting surface with a straight-edge and thickness gauge.

➡**If replacing the exhaust manifold, tighten the exhaust outlet studs to manifold to 29 ft. lbs. (40 Nm).**

10. Position the exhaust manifold and gasket. Install the retaining bolts. Tighten 4 bolts starting at the center working outward to 17 ft. lbs. (23 Nm).
11. Install the exhaust manifold heat shields. Tighten the bolts to 105 inch lbs. (12 Nm).
12. Tighten the out most stud nuts to 73 inch lbs. (8 Nm).
13. Connect the oxygen sensor.
14. Raise and support the vehicle.
15. Connect the exhaust pipe to manifold union. Tighten the exhaust stud nuts to 25 ft. lbs. (34 Nm).
16. Connect the negative battery cable.

Right Side

See Figure 141.

1. Before servicing the vehicle, refer to the precautions in the beginning of this section.
2. Disconnect the negative battery cable.
3. Disconnect the upstream oxygen sensor electrical connector.
4. Raise and support the vehicle.
5. Remove the exhaust manifold to exhaust pipe flange retaining bolts.
   a. Lower the vehicle.
6. Remove the exhaust manifold heat shield and manifold.
7. Remove the oxygen sensor from the exhaust manifold.

To install:

8. Clean gasket surfaces.

➡**If replacing the exhaust manifold, tighten the exhaust outlet studs to 29 ft. lbs. (39 Nm).**

9. Position the exhaust manifold and gasket. Install the retaining bolts. Tighten 4 bolts starting at the center working outward to 17 ft. lbs. (23 Nm).

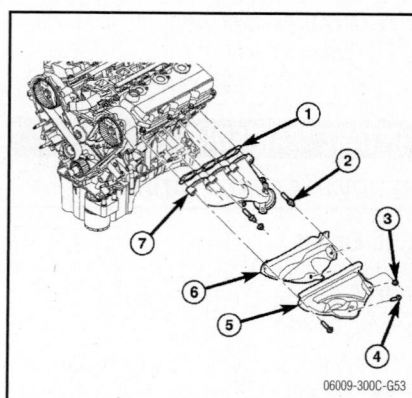

Fig. 140 Left side exhaust manifold (7), gasket (1) and related components—3.5L engine

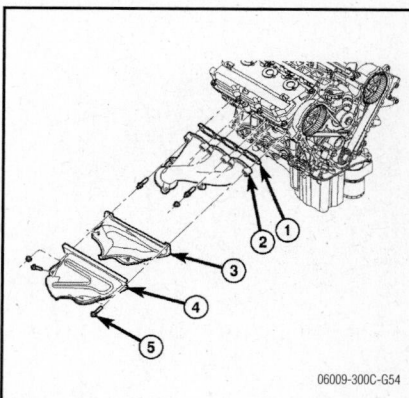

Fig. 141 Right side exhaust manifold (2), gasket (1) and related components—3.5L engine

a. Install the heat shields. Tighten the heat shield fasteners to 105 inch lbs. (12 Nm).

10. Tighten the 2 out most nuts to 73 inch lbs. (8 Nm).

a. Connect the oxygen sensor.

11. Raise and support the vehicle.

12. Connect the front exhaust pipe to exhaust manifold. Tighten the fasteners to 25 ft. lbs. (34 Nm).

13. Connect the negative battery cable.

3.6L Engine

The 3.6L aluminum cylinder heads are a unique design with left and right castings. The exhaust manifolds are integrated into the cylinder heads. If any damaged is found to the exhaust manifold portion, the cylinder head must be removed for repair or replacement.

5.7L Engine

See Figures 142 and 143.

1. Before servicing the vehicle, refer to the precautions in the beginning of this section.

2. Disconnect negative battery cable.

a. Raise vehicle.

b. Remove exhaust pipe to manifold bolts.

3. Remove engine mount to frame fasteners.

a. Using suitable jack, raise engine enough to remove manifolds.

✳✳ CAUTION

Do not damage engine harness while raising the engine.

4. Remove the engine mount.

5. Remove heat shield.

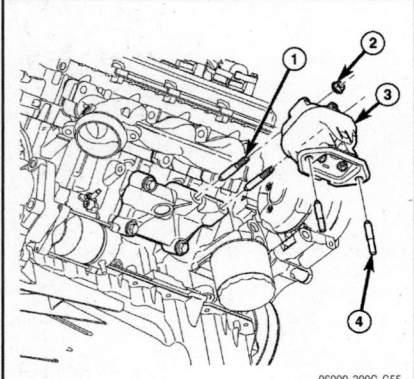

Fig. 142 Engine mount. (1) stud bolts, (2) nuts, (3) mount, (4) stud bolts—5.7L engine

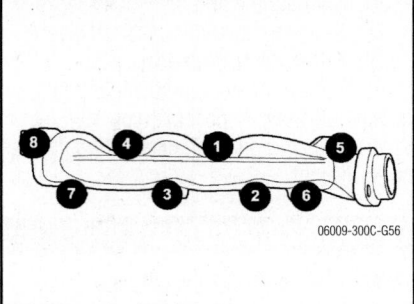

Fig. 143 Exhaust manifold loosening/tightening sequence—5.7L engine

6. Remove manifold bolts using sequence provided.

a. Remove manifold and gasket.

To install:

7. Clean mating surfaces on cylinder head and manifold. Wash with solvent and blow dry with compressed air.

8. Inspect manifold for cracks.

9. Inspect mating surfaces of manifold for flatness with a straight-edge. Gasket surfaces must be flat within 0.2 mm per 300 mm (0.008 inch per foot).

a. Install manifold gasket and manifold.

10. Install manifold bolts and tighten to 18 ft. lbs. (25 Nm).

a. Install heat shield and tighten nuts to 70 inch lbs. (8 Nm).

b. Install engine mounts. Torque to 70 ft. lbs. (95 Nm).

c. Lower engine.

✳✳ CAUTION

Do not damage engine harness while lowering the engine.

11. Install and tighten right and left side engine mount to frame fasteners. Torque to 70 ft. lbs. (95 Nm).

12. Install exhaust flange to pipe bolts.

13. Lower vehicle.

a. Connect negative battery cable.

INTAKE MANIFOLD

REMOVAL & INSTALLATION

2.7L Engine

Lower

See Figure 144.

1. Before servicing the vehicle, refer to the precautions in the beginning of this section.

2. Release fuel system pressure.

3. Disconnect negative battery cable located in trunk.

a. Remove upper intake manifold.

4. Disconnect injector electrical connectors.

5. Disconnect fuel supply hose from fuel rail.

6. Remove bolts attaching fuel rail.

7. Remove fuel rail and injectors as an assembly.

8. Remove manifold attaching bolts.

9. Remove lower manifold.

To install:

10. Check manifold for:
- Damage and cracks
- Gasket surface damage or warpage
- Damaged fuel injector ports

➡ **If the manifold exhibits any of these conditions, replace the manifold.**

11. Clean and inspect sealing surfaces of cylinder head and manifold. Gaskets can be reused provided they are free of cuts or tears.

12. Install lower manifold gasket.

13. Position manifold on cylinder head surfaces.

➡ **For ease of installing upper intake manifold, install a bolt 2-3 turns to the rearmost attaching hole of intake. This will properly position lower manifold.**

14. Install fuel rail with injectors and start bolts.

15. Install manifold attaching bolts and tighten in sequence shown in to 105 inch lbs. (12 Nm). Remove bolt used for aligning manifold.

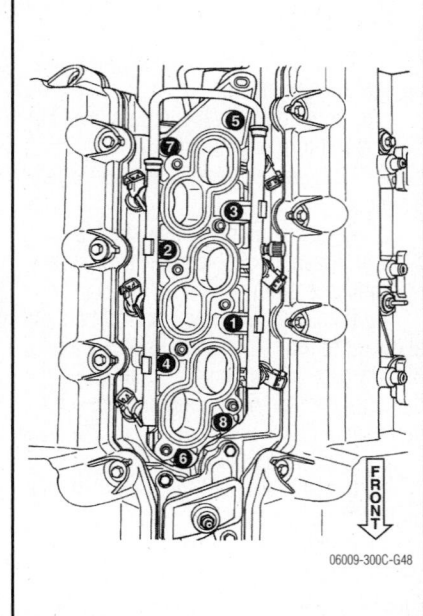

Fig. 144 Lower intake manifold loosening/tightening sequence—2.7L engine

a. Connect the fuel injector electrical connectors.

➡**Make sure fuel injectors are located in the correct location and position, as upper intake manifold interference could occur.**

16. Connect fuel supply hose to fuel rail.
17. Install upper intake manifold.

Upper

See Figure 145.

1. Before servicing the vehicle, refer to the precautions in the beginning of this section.
2. Disconnect negative battery cable.
3. Remove throttle body air inlet hose and air cleaner housing assembly.
4. Disconnect electrical connectors from the following components:
   • Manifold Absolute Pressure (MAP) Sensor
   • Electronic Throttle Control
   • Manifold Tuning Valve
5. Disconnect vapor purge hose, brake booster hose, positive crankcase ventilation (PCV) hose.
6. Remove manifold support brackets.
7. Remove manifold attaching bolts.
8. Remove the upper manifold.
9. Remove foam insulator.
10. Check manifold for:
    • Damage and cracks
    • Gasket surface damage or warpage
    • Damaged or clogged EGR ports
11. If the manifold exhibits any damaged or warped conditions, replace the manifold. Clean EGR ports as necessary.

To install:

12. Clean and inspect sealing surfaces. Gaskets can be reused, if free of cuts or tears.

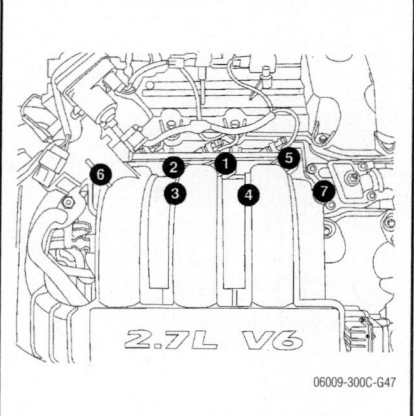

Fig. 145 Upper intake manifold loosening/tightening sequence—2.7L engine

➡**Make sure fuel injectors and wiring harnesses are in correct position to not interfere with upper manifold installation.**

13. Install the upper manifold gasket.
14. Position the upper manifold onto lower manifold.
15. Install manifold attaching bolts and tighten in sequence shown to 105 inch lbs. (12 Nm).
16. Connect PCV, brake booster, and vapor purge hoses.
17. Connect electrical connectors to the following components:
    • Manifold Absolute Pressure (MAP) Sensor
    • Electronic Throttle Control
    • Manifold Tuning Valve
18. Install throttle body air inlet hose and air cleaner housing assembly.

3.5L Engine

Lower

See Figures 146 and 147

1. Before servicing the vehicle, refer to the precautions in the beginning of this section.
2. Perform fuel pressure release procedure.
3. Drain the cooling system.
4. Disconnect the upper radiator hose from thermostat housing.
5. Remove the upper intake manifold.
6. Reposition power steering fluid reservoir and bracket.

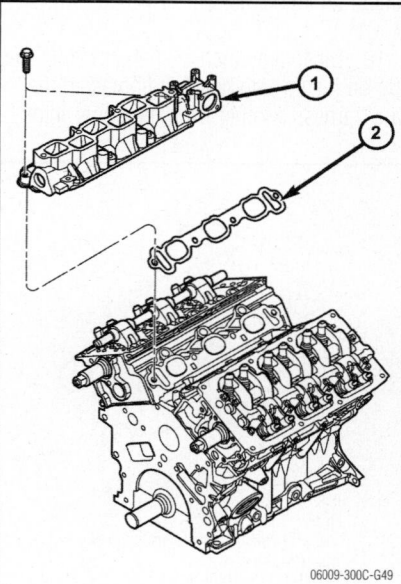

Fig. 146 Lower intake manifold (1) and gasket (2)—3.5L engine

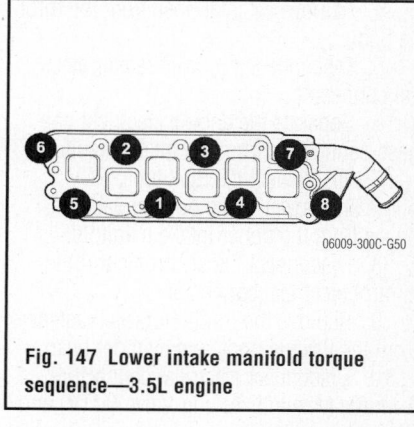

Fig. 147 Lower intake manifold torque sequence—3.5L engine

7. Disconnect the electrical connectors to fuel injectors and coolant temperature sensor.
8. Disconnect heater hose from the rear intake manifold.
9. Disconnect the coolant container hose at the rear intake manifold.
10. Disconnect the fuel supply hose from fuel rail.
11. Remove the bolts attaching fuel rail.
12. Remove fuel rail and injectors as an assembly.
13. Remove bolts attaching lower intake and remove intake manifold.

To install:

14. Clean all sealing surfaces.
15. Position new gaskets and intake manifold on cylinder head surfaces.
16. Install intake manifold bolts and gradually tighten in sequence shown until a torque of 21 ft. lbs. (28 Nm) is obtained.
17. Install fuel rail and injectors as an assembly.
18. Connect fuel supply hose to fuel rail.
19. Connect heater hose to rear lower intake manifold.
20. Connect coolant container hose to the rear lower intake manifold.
21. Connect electrical connectors to fuel injectors and coolant temperature sensor.
22. Install power steering fluid reservoir and bracket.
23. Install upper intake manifold.
24. Connect the upper radiator hose to thermostat housing.
25. Fill the cooling system.

Upper

See Figure 148.

1. Before servicing the vehicle, refer to the precautions in the beginning of this section.
2. Disconnect negative battery cable.
3. Disconnect the IAT sensor electrical connector.

4. Remove air inlet hose from the throttle body.

5. Disconnect the MAP sensor electrical connector.

6. Separate the engine electrical harness connectors from the intake manifold.

7. Disconnect the EGR tube, PCV, purge and power brake booster vacuum hoses from the upper intake manifold.

8. Disconnect the electronic throttle control electrical connector.

9. Remove the throttle bracket fasteners from the throttle body and cylinder head.

10. Disconnect electrical connectors from the Manifold Tuning Valve (MTV) and Short Runner Valve.

11. Remove the right intake manifold support brackets.

12. Remove the upper intake manifold retaining bolts, insulation foam pad and manifold. Clean all gasket sealing surfaces.

To install:

13. Clean and inspect gasket sealing surfaces.

14. Position new gasket.

15. Install the upper intake manifold insulator foam.

16. Install the upper intake manifold. Tighten bolts to 105 inch lbs. (12 Nm) starting in the center working outward in a cross sequence pattern.

17. Install the right manifold support brackets. Tighten fasteners to 105 inch lbs. (12 Nm).

18. Install the throttle bracket. Tighten fasteners to 105 inch lbs. (12 Nm) at the throttle body and 21 ft. lbs. (28 Nm) at the cylinder head.

19. Connect the manifold tuning valve and short runner valve electrical connectors.

20. Connect the electronic throttle control harness connector.

21. Connect the engine electrical connectors to the intake manifold.

22. Connect the EGR tube, PCV, purge and power brake booster vacuum hoses to the intake manifold.

23. Connect the MAP sensor harness connector.

24. Install the inlet hose and connect the IAT sensor harness connector.

25. Connect negative battery cable.

3.6L Engine

Upper

See Figures 149 through 153.

1. Disconnect and isolate the negative battery cable.

2. Lift the engine cover retaining grommets off the ball studs and remove the engine cover.

3. Disconnect the electrical connector from the Inlet Air Temperature (IAT) sensor.

4. Loosen the clamp at the throttle body.

5. Loosen the clamp at the air cleaner housing.

6. Lift the air inlet hose assembly retaining grommet off the ball stud.

7. Remove the air inlet hose assembly.

8. Disengage the brake booster hose retainer from the upper intake manifold.

9. Disconnect the electrical connectors from the Manifold Absolute Pressure (MAP) sensor and the Electronic Throttle Control (ETC).

10. Disengage the ETC harness from the clip on the throttle body and unfasten the wire harness retainer from the upper intake

manifold near the MAP sensor and reposition the wire harness.

11. Disconnect the following hoses from the upper intake manifold:
- Positive Crankcase Ventilation (PCV)
- Brake booster vacuum hose
- EVAP vapor purge line

12. Unfasten the wire harness retainer from the upper intake manifold support bracket stud retainer.

13. Remove the two nuts, loosen the stud and reposition the upper intake manifold support bracket.

14. Remove the heater core return tube upper support bracket retaining nut and reposition tube.

15. Remove the two nuts, loosen two stud retainers and reposition the two upper intake manifold support brackets.

➡The upper intake manifold attaching bolts are captured in the upper intake manifold. Once loosened, the bolts will have to be lifted out of the lower intake manifold and held while removing the upper intake manifold.

➡Exercise care not to inadvertently loosen the two fuel rail attachment bolts that are in close proximity of the upper intake manifold attaching bolts.

16. Remove the seven manifold attaching bolts and remove the upper intake manifold.

17. Remove and discard the six upper to lower intake manifold seals.

18. Cover the open intake ports to prevent debris from entering the engine.

19. If required, remove the insulator from the left cylinder head cover.

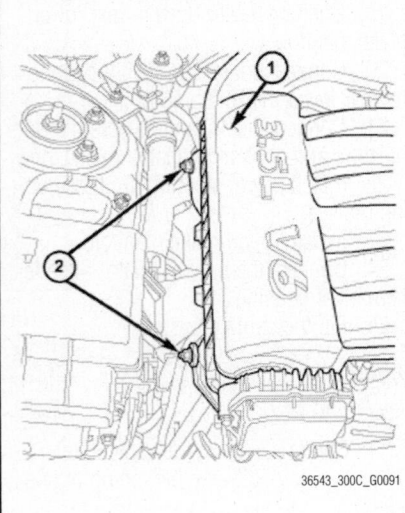

36543_300C_G0091

Fig. 148 Right upper intake manifold (1) support brackets (2)—3.5L engine

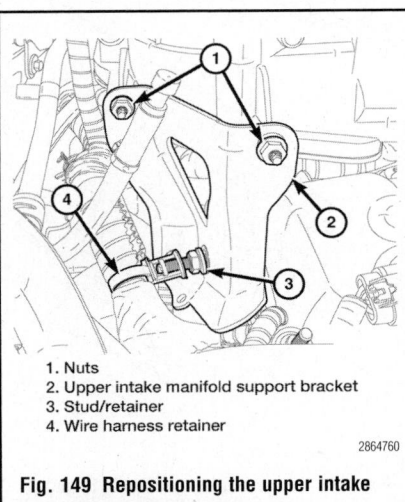

1. Nuts
2. Upper intake manifold support bracket
3. Stud/retainer
4. Wire harness retainer

2864760

Fig. 149 Repositioning the upper intake manifold support bracket

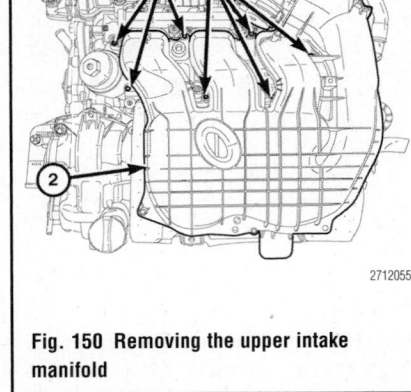

2712055

Fig. 150 Removing the upper intake manifold

To install:

➡ **Prior to installing the upper intake manifold, verify that the four fuel rail bolts were not inadvertently loosened. The bolts must tightened in the sequence shown to 62 inch lbs. (7 Nm).**

20. Clean and inspect the sealing surfaces. Install new upper to lower intake manifold seals.

➡ **Make sure the fuel injectors and wiring harnesses are in the correct position so that they don't interfere with the upper intake manifold installation.**

21. If removed, position the insulator onto the two alignment posts on top of the left cylinder head cover.

22. Lift and hold the seven upper intake attaching bolts clear of the mating surface. Back the bolts out slightly or if required, use an elastic band to hold the bolts clear of the mating surface.

23. Position the upper intake manifold onto the lower intake manifold so that the two locating posts on the upper intake manifold align with corresponding holes in the lower intake manifold.

24. Install the seven upper intake manifold attaching bolts. Tighten the bolts in the sequence shown to 71 inch lbs. (8 Nm).

25. Install two nuts to the upper intake manifold support bracket. Tighten the nuts to 89 inch lbs. (10 Nm) and tighten the stud to 15 ft. lbs. (20 Nm)

26. Engage the wire harness retainer to the stud.

27. Install the two upper intake manifold support brackets with two stud retainers and two nuts. Tighten the stud retainers to 15 ft. lbs. (20 Nm) and tighten the nuts to 89 inch lbs. (10 Nm).

28. Position the heater core return tube,

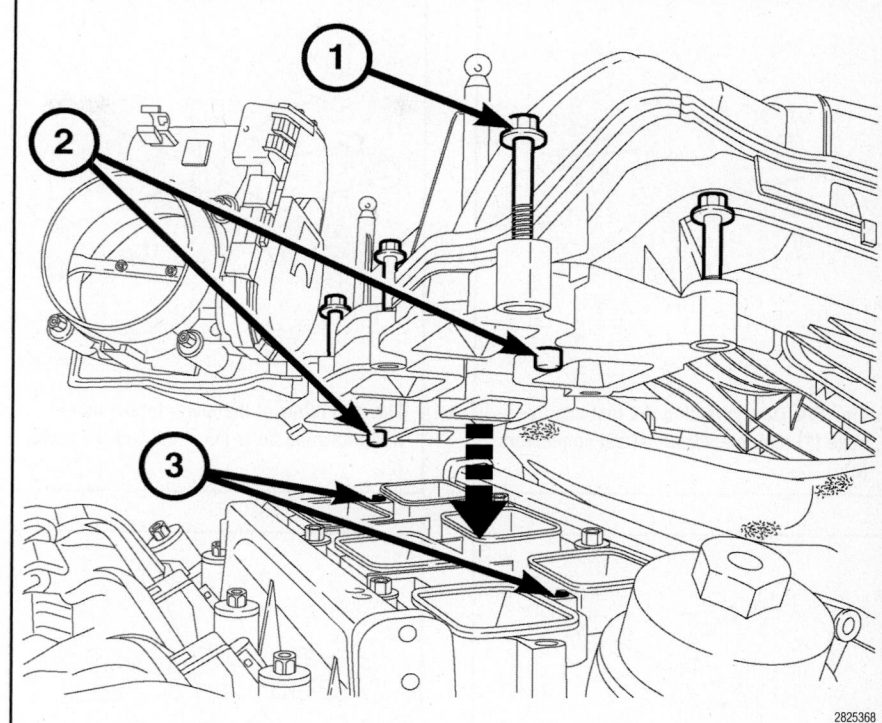

Fig. 152 Position the upper intake manifold onto the lower intake manifold so that the two locating posts (2) on the upper intake manifold align with corresponding holes (3) in the lower intake manifold. Install the upper intake manifold attaching bolts (1).

install the retaining nut and tighten to 9 ft. lbs. (12 Nm).

29. Connect the following hoses to the upper intake manifold:
- Positive Crankcase Ventilation (PCV)
- Brake booster vacuum hose
- EVAP vapor purge line

30. Connect the electrical connectors to the Manifold Absolute Pressure (MAP) sensor and the Electronic Throttle Control (ETC).

31. Secure the ETC harness to the clip on the throttle body and fasten the wire harness retainer to the upper intake manifold near the MAP sensor.

32. Fasten the brake booster vacuum hose retainer to the upper intake manifold.

33. Position the air inlet hose assembly (5) onto the throttle body and the air cleaner housing.

34. Secure the air inlet hose assembly retaining grommet onto the ball stud.

35. Tighten the clamp at the air cleaner housing to 44 inch lbs. (5 Nm).

36. Tighten the clamp at the throttle body to 44 inch lbs. (5 Nm).

37. Connect the Inlet Air Temperature (IAT) sensor electrical connector.

38. Position the engine cover and secure the retaining grommets onto the ball studs.

39. Connect the negative battery cable and tighten nut to 45 inch lbs. (5 Nm).

40. Start the engine and check for leaks.

Lower

See Figures 154 through 159.

1. Perform the fuel pressure release procedure.

2. Disconnect and isolate the negative battery cable.

3. Lift the engine cover retaining grom-

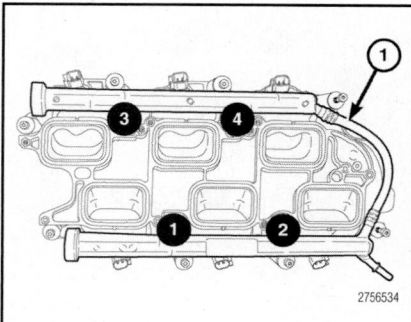

Fig. 151 Identifying the fuel rail bolt tightening sequence

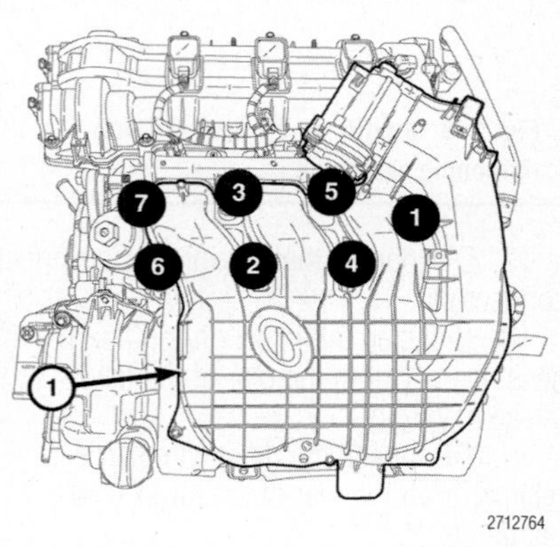

Fig. 153 Identifying the upper intake manifold attaching bolt tightening sequence

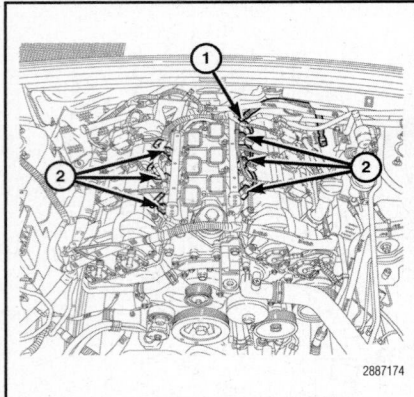

Fig. 154 Disconnecting the fuel supply hose (1) and injector electrical connectors (2)

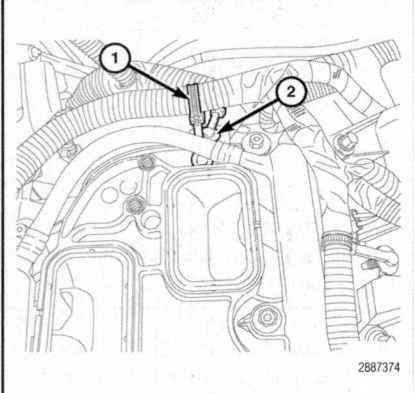

Fig. 155 Identifying the injection/ignition harness (1) and main wire harness retainers (2) from the lower intake manifold

mets off the ball studs and remove the engine cover.

4. Disconnect the electrical connector from the Inlet Air Temperature (IAT) sensor.

5. Loosen the clamp at the throttle body.

6. Loosen the clamp at the air cleaner housing.

7. Lift the air inlet hose assembly retaining grommet off the ball stud.

8. Remove the air inlet hose assembly.

⁂ CAUTION

The fuel system is under constant pressure even with engine off. Before servicing the fuel rail, fuel system pressure must be released.

9. Remove the upper intake manifold and support brackets.

10. Remove the insulator from the left cylinder head cover.

11. Disconnect the fuel supply hose from the fuel rail.

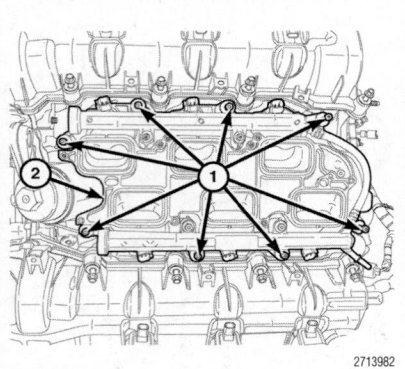

Fig. 156 View of the lower intake manifold attaching bolts (1) and lower manifold (2)

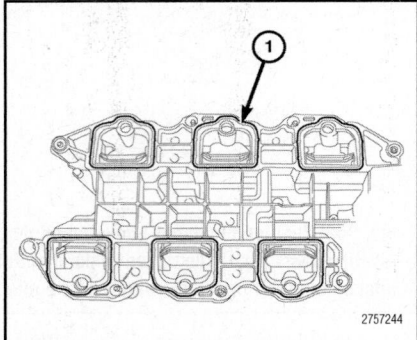

Fig. 157 Removing the 6 lower intake manifold cylinder head seals (1)

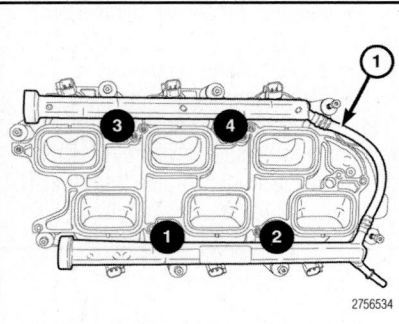

Fig. 158 Identifying the fuel rail bolt tightening sequence

12. Disconnect the fuel injector electrical connectors.

13. Unfasten the injection/ignition harness retainer from the rear of the lower intake manifold.

14. Disengage the main wire harness retainer from the rear of the lower intake manifold.

15. Remove the eight lower intake manifold attaching bolts.

16. Remove the lower intake manifold

with the fuel injectors and fuel rail as an assembly.

17. Remove and discard the six lower intake manifold to cylinder head seals.

18. If required, remove the fuel rail and fuel injectors from the lower intake manifold.

To install:

19. Clean and inspect the sealing surfaces. Install new lower intake manifold to cylinder head seals.

20. If removed, install the fuel injectors and the fuel rail to the lower intake manifold. Tighten the four bolts in the sequence shown to 62 inch lbs. (7 Nm).

21. Position the lower intake manifold onto the cylinder head surfaces.

22. Install the intake manifold retaining bolts and tighten in the sequence shown to 71 inch lbs. (8 Nm).

23. Fasten the main wire harness retainer to the rear of the lower intake manifold.

24. Fasten the injection/ignition harness retainer to the rear of the lower intake manifold.

25. Connect the fuel injector electrical connectors.

26. Connect the fuel supply hose to the fuel rail.

27. Install the insulator to the two alignment posts on top of the left cylinder head cover.

28. Install the upper intake manifold and support brackets.

29. Position the air inlet hose assembly onto the throttle body and the air cleaner housing.

30. Secure the air inlet hose assembly retaining grommet onto the ball stud.

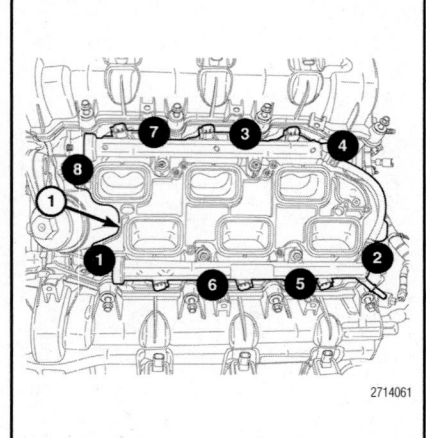

Fig. 159 Identifying the lower intake manifold bolt tightening sequence

31. Tighten the clamp at the air cleaner housing to 44 inch lbs. (5 Nm).

32. Tighten the clamp at the throttle body to 44 inch lbs. (5 Nm).

33. Connect the Inlet Air Temperature (IAT) sensor electrical connector.

34. Position the engine cover and secure the retaining grommets onto the ball studs.

35. Connect the negative battery cable and tighten nut to 45 inch lbs. (5 Nm).

36. Start the engine and check for leaks.

5.7L Engine

1. Before servicing the vehicle, refer to the precautions in the beginning of this section.

2. Remove engine cover.

3. Bleed fuel system.

4. Disconnect negative cable from battery.

5. Remove air inlet hose.

6. Remove ignition wires from on top of intake manifold.

7. Disconnect electrical connectors for the following components:
- Manifold Absolute Pressure (MAP) Sensor
- Fuel Injectors
- ETC (Electric Throttle Control)

8. Remove wire harness from intake manifold.

9. Disconnect brake booster hose, purge hose, and MUA hose (Make Up Air Hose).

10. Remove EGR tube from intake manifold.

11. Remove intake manifold retaining fasteners in a crisscross pattern starting from the outside bolts and ending at the middle bolts.

12. Remove intake manifold as an assembly.

To install:

➡ There is no approved repair procedure for the intake manifold. If severe damage is found during inspection, the intake manifold must be replaced.

Before installing the intake manifold thoroughly clean the mating surfaces. Use a suitable cleaning solvent, then air dry.

13. Inspect the intake sealing surface for cracks, nicks and distortion.

14. Inspect the intake manifold vacuum hose fittings for looseness or blockage.

15. Position intake manifold.

16. Install intake manifold retaining bolts, and tighten in sequence from the middle bolts towards the outside in a criss-cross pattern. Torque fasteners to 105 inch lbs. (12 Nm).

17. Install EGR tube.

18. Install wire harness on intake manifold.

19. Connect electrical connectors for the following components:
- Manifold Absolute Pressure (MAP) Sensor
- Fuel Injectors
- ETC (Electronic Throttle Control)

20. Install ignition wires.

21. Connect Brake booster hose, purge hose, and MUA hose (Make Up Air hose).

22. Install air inlet hose.

23. Connect negative cable to battery.

24. Install engine cover.

OIL PAN

REMOVAL & INSTALLATION

2.7L Engine

See Figures 160 and 161.

1. Before servicing the vehicle, refer to the precautions in the beginning of this section.

2. Disconnect negative battery cable located in trunk.

3. Remove engine oil indicator.

4. Raise and safely support the vehicle.

5. Remove lower splash shield retaining bolts and splash shield.

6. Drain engine oil and remove oil filter.

7. Remove the steering coupler bolt and separate coupler from rack.

8. Disconnect power steering pressure switch electrical connector.

9. Remove steering rack mounting bolts.

10. Remove power steering line support from frame.

11. Reposition rack out of the way.

12. Remove structural collar.

13. Remove alternator mounting bracket to oil pan lower bolt.

a. Remove air conditioning compressor bracket to oil pan lower bolt.

14. Remove lower timing chain cover to oil pan bolts.

✳✳ CAUTION

Assure removal of the four lower timing cover bolts, as damage to the timing cover and/or oil pan may occur.

15. Remove oil pan attaching bolts. Remove oil pan and gasket.

To install:

16. Clean oil pan and sealing surfaces. Inspect timing chain cover gaskets. Replace as necessary.

17. Apply a 1/8 inch bead of Mopar® Engine RTV GEN II, or equivalent, to the front T-joints (oil pan gasket to timing cover gasket interface) and the rear T-joints (oil pan gasket to crankshaft rear oil seal retainer gasket interface).

18. Install oil pan gasket to block.

➡ To prevent oil leaks at oil pan to timing chain cover, the following tightening sequence procedure must be performed.

19. Install oil pan and fasteners using the following tightening sequence:

a. Install oil pan bolts and nuts finger tight only—just tight enough to compress the gasket's rubber seal. Line up front of oil pan to be flush with front face of block.

b. Install lower timing chain cover bolts (1) and tighten to 105 inch lbs. (12 Nm).

c. Tighten oil pan bolts to 21 ft. lbs. (28 Nm).

d. Tighten oil pan nuts to 105 inch lbs. (12 Nm).

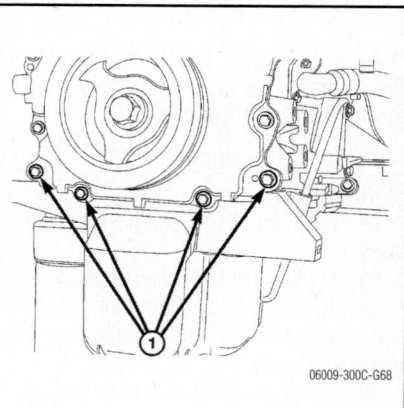

06009-300C-G68

Fig. 160 Lower timing chain cover-to-oil pan bolts (1)—2.7L engine

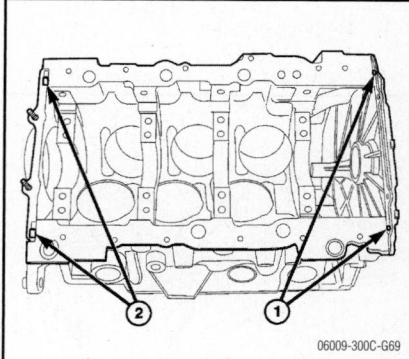

06009-300C-G69

Fig. 161 Apply a 1/8 inch bead of Mopar® Engine RTV GEN II, or equivalent, to the front T-joints (1) and the rear T-joints (2)—2.7L engine

20. Install lower bolt attaching the air conditioning compressor to oil pan. Tighten bolt to 21 ft. lbs. (28 Nm).

21. Install lower bolt attaching the alternator bracket to oil pan. Tighten bolt to 21 ft. lbs. (28 Nm).

22. Install oil filter and drain plug.

23. Install structural collar.

24. Position steering gear in place and install mounting bolts. Tighten bolts to 70 ft. lbs. (95 Nm).

25. Install the steering coupling lower pinch bolt at the gear using a new bolt. Tighten to 22 ft. lbs. (30 Nm).

26. Connect electrical connector to steering gear.

27. Install power steering line support and tighten.

28. Install lower splash shield and retaining bolts.

29. Lower vehicle.

30. Install engine oil level indicator.

31. Fill engine crankcase with proper oil to correct level.

32. Connect negative battery cable.

33. Start engine and check for leaks.

3.5L Engine

See Figures 162 through 166.

1. Before servicing the vehicle, refer to the precautions in the beginning of this section.

2. Disconnect negative battery cable.

3. Lock the steering wheel in the center position.

4. Remove engine oil indicator.

5. Raise and support the vehicle.

6. Remove the splash shield.

7. Drain engine oil and remove the oil filter.

8. Drain cooling system.

9. Raise and safely support the vehicle.

10. Disconnect coolant hoses from oil cooler.

11. Remove oil filter.

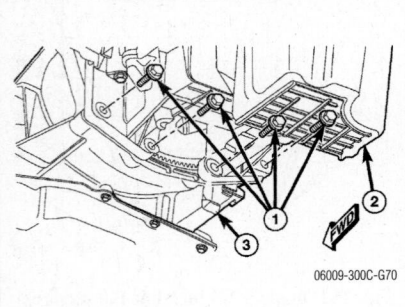

Fig. 162 Rear oil pan (2) to transmission (3) bolts (1)—3.5L engine

12. Remove oil cooler attaching fastener from center of oil cooler.

13. Remove oil cooler.

14. Separate the steering column coupler from the steering gear.

15. Remove steering gear to cradle mounting bolts and suspend steering gear aside.

16. Remove the flexplate access cover.

17. Remove the rear oil pan to transmission bolts.

18. Remove the two rear oil pan bolts.

19. Remove the remaining oil pan bolts.

20. Loosen the engine mount bolts at the cradle.

21. Raise and support the engine using a suitable floor jack with a block of wood at the transmission housing.

22. Remove the oil pan.

➡**A small amount of oil will remain in the oil pan. Use care when removing the oil pan from the engine.**

23. Clean all mating surfaces.

To install:

24. Clean oil pan and all gasket surfaces.

25. Apply a 1/8 inch bead of Mopar® Engine RTV GEN II, or equivalent, at the parting line of the oil pump housing and the rear seal retainer.

26. Install oil pan gasket to the engine block.

27. Install the oil pan while aligning the oil level indicator tube and attach fasteners finger tight.

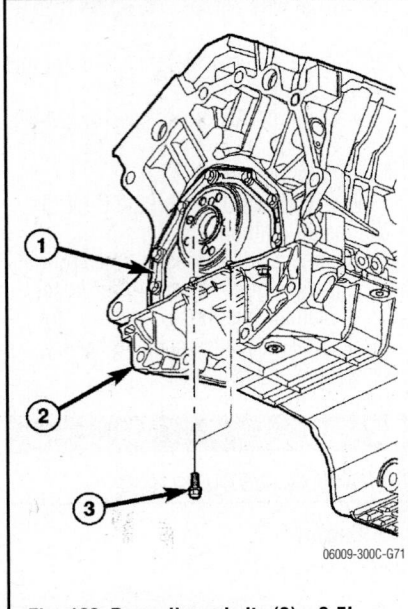

Fig. 163 Rear oil pan bolts (3)—3.5L engine

Fig. 164 Oil pan sealer application—3.5L engine

➡**Assure that the rear face of the oil pan is flush to the transmission bell housing when installing the oil pan.**

28. Pre-torque the horizontal rear oil pan to transmission bolts to 12 inch lbs. (1.4 Nm).

29. First tighten the M8 oil pan alignment bolt to 21 ft. lbs. (28 Nm), then tighten bolt to 21 ft. lbs. (28 Nm).

30. Tighten the remaining M8 bolts and M8 nuts to 21 ft. lbs. (28 Nm), and the M6 bolts to 105 inch lbs. (12 Nm).

31. Tighten the four M10 oil pan to transmission bolts to 40 ft. lbs. (55 Nm).

32. Lower the engine and remove the lifting fixture. Tighten the engine mount to cradle fasteners to 55 ft. lbs. (75 Nm).

33. Install the flexplate inspection cover and tighten the fastener to 97 inch lbs. (11 Nm)

34. Position oil cooler to fitting on oil pan.

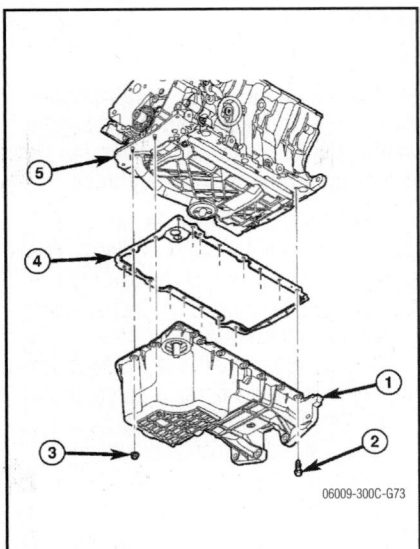

Fig. 165 Oil pan (1) and gasket (4) installation—3.5L engine

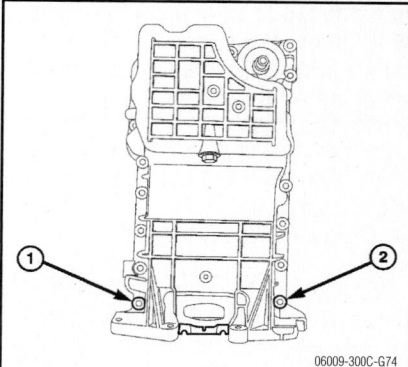

Fig. 166 First tighten the M8 (1) oil pan alignment bolt to 21 ft. lbs. (28 Nm), then tighten bolt (2) to 21 ft. lbs. (28 Nm)— 3.5L engine

➡Remove all oil and debris from the seal retainer surface. The cut out section of the oil cooler seal retainer flange (top) must be aligned with the tab on the oil pan. The oil cooler must be prevented from turning during the tightening sequence.

35. Install oil cooler attaching fastener and tighten to 55 ft. lbs. (75 Nm).
36. Install oil filter and tighten to 106 inch lbs. (12 Nm).
37. Connect coolant hoses to oil cooler.
38. Fill cooling system.
39. Install the engine oil filter.
40. Install the steering gear to cradle bolts and tighten the fasteners to 70 ft. lbs. (95 Nm).
41. Connect the steering gear coupler and tighten the fastener to 22 ft. lbs. (30 Nm).
42. Attach the splash shield.
43. Lower the vehicle.
44. Install the engine oil indicator.
45. Fill engine crankcase with proper oil to correct level.
46. Connect negative battery cable.

3.6L Engine

Lower

See Figure 167.

1. Raise and support the vehicle.
2. Remove the belly pan retainers and remove the belly pan.
3. Drain the engine oil.

➡The lower oil pan must be removed to access all of the upper oil pan retaining bolts.

4. Remove twelve bolts, two studs and two nuts from the flange of the lower oil pan.

> ✳✳ **WARNING**
>
> **Do not pry on the lower oil pan flange. There are no designated pry points for lower oil pan removal. Prying on only one or a few locations could bend the flange and damage the pan.**

5. Using a pry bar, apply side force to the lower oil pan in order to sever the sealant bond and remove the pan.
6. Remove all residual sealant from the upper and lower oil pans

To install:

> ✳✳ **WARNING**
>
> **Engine assembly requires the use of a unique sealant that is compatible with engine oil. Using a sealant other than Mopar® Threebond Engine RTV Sealant may result in engine fluid leakage.**

> ✳✳ **WARNING**
>
> **Following the application of Mopar® Threebond Engine RTV Sealant to the gasket surfaces, the components must be assembled within 20 minutes and the attaching fasteners must be tightened to specification within 45 minutes. Prolonged exposure to the air prior to assembly may result in engine fluid leakage.**

7. Clean the upper and lower oil pan mating surfaces with isopropyl alcohol in preparation for sealant application.
8. Apply a 2 to 3 mm wide bead of Mopar® Threebond Engine RTV Sealant to the lower oil pan.

Fig. 167 Removing the lower oil pan— 3.6L engine

> ✳✳ **WARNING**
>
> **Following assembly, the Mopar® Threebond Engine RTV Sealant must be allowed to dry for 45 minutes prior to adding oil and engine operation. Premature exposure to oil prior to drying may result in engine fluid leakage.**

9. Install two studs into the upper oil pan flange.
10. Install the lower oil pan to the upper oil pan with twelve bolts and two nuts tightened to 8 ft. lbs. (11 Nm).
11. Position the belly pan and install the retainers.
12. Lower the vehicle.
13. Fill the crankcase with the specified type and amount of engine oil.
14. Start and run the engine until it reaches normal operating temperature and check for leaks.

Upper

See Figures 168 through 172.

1. Disconnect and isolate the negative battery cable.
2. Lift the engine cover retaining grommets off the ball studs and remove the engine cover.
3. Disconnect the electrical connector from the Inlet Air Temperature (IAT) sensor.
4. Loosen the clamp at the throttle body.
   a. Loosen the clamp at the air cleaner housing.
5. Lift the air inlet hose assembly retaining grommet off the ball stud.
6. Remove the air inlet hose assembly.
7. Remove two bolts from the heater core inlet tube and reposition the tube.
8. Remove the bolt and remove the oil level indicator.
9. Raise and support the vehicle.
10. Remove the belly pan retainers and remove the belly pan.
11. Drain the engine oil.

➡The lower oil pan must be removed to access all of the upper oil pan retaining bolts.

12. Remove the lower oil pan.
13. Remove the lower intermediate coupling pinch bolt at the steering gear. Separate the lower intermediate shaft from the steering gear shaft.
14. Remove the steering gear mounting bolts and reposition the steering gear.
15. Remove the bolt and reposition the transmission cooling lines.

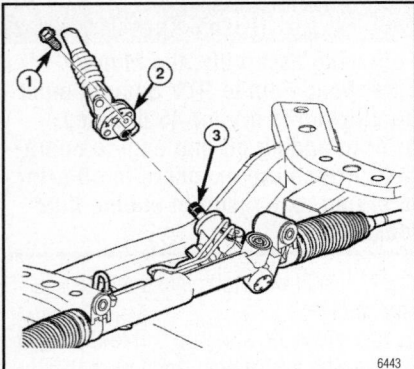

Fig. 168 Remove the lower intermediate coupling pinch bolt (1) at the steering gear. Separate the lower intermediate shaft (2) from the steering gear shaft (3).

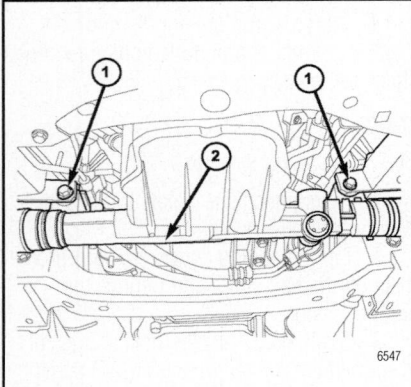

Fig. 169 Removing the steering gear mounting bolts (1) and repositioning the steering gear

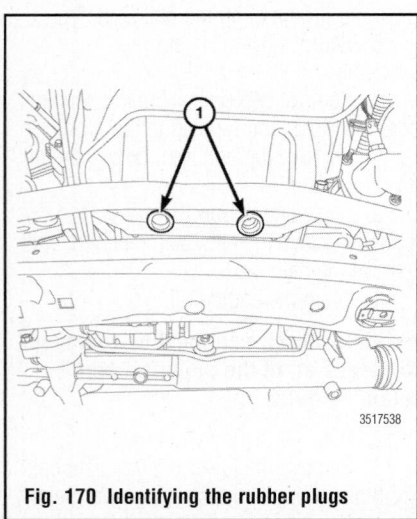

Fig. 170 Identifying the rubber plugs

16. Remove the two bolts from the rear engine mount isolator.

17. Using a suitable jack stand and a block of wood positioned under the transmission oil pan, raise the rear of the engine.

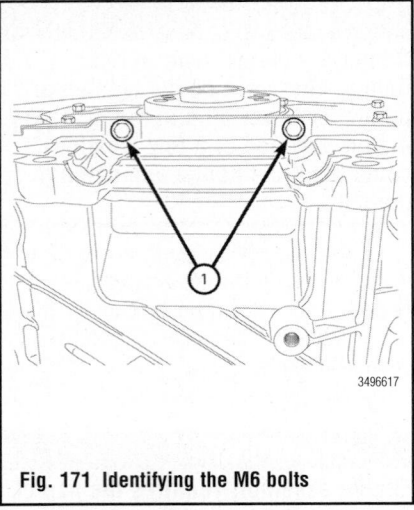

Fig. 171 Identifying the M6 bolts

18. Remove the four transmission to the engine oil pan bolts.

19. Remove the two rubber plugs covering the rear oil seal retainer flange bolts.

➡Shown with transmission removed for clarity.

✳✳ WARNING

There are two hidden M6 bolts that must be removed from the rear of the upper oil pan flange. If these bolts are not removed, the rear oil seal retainer flange will be severely damaged.

20. Remove two M6 bolts from the rear oil seal retainer flange.

21. Remove nineteen M8 oil pan mounting bolts.

22. Using the four indicated pry points, carefully remove the upper oil pan.

23. Remove all residual sealant from the upper and lower oil pans, timing chain cover, rear seal retainer and engine block mating surfaces.

To install:

✳✳ WARNING

Engine assembly requires the use of a unique sealant that is compatible with engine oil. Using a sealant other than Mopar® Threebond Engine RTV Sealant may result in engine fluid leakage.

✳✳ WARNING

Following the application of Mopar® Threebond Engine RTV Sealant to the gasket surfaces, the components must be assembled within 20 minutes and the attaching fasteners must

be tightened to specification within 45 minutes. Prolonged exposure to the air prior to assembly may result in engine fluid leakage.

24. Clean the upper and lower oil pans, timing chain cover, rear seal retainer and engine block mating surfaces with isopropyl alcohol in preparation for sealant application.

25. Apply a 2 to 3 mm wide bead of Mopar® Threebond Engine RTV Sealant to the upper oil pan as shown in the following locations:
- Oil pan to engine block flange
- Two timing cover to engine block T-joints
- Two rear seal retainer to engine block T-joints

✳✳ WARNING

Make sure that the rear face of the oil pan is flush to the transmission bell housing before tightening any of the oil pan mounting bolts. A gap between the oil pan and the transmission could crack the oil pan or transmission casting.

26. Install the oil pan to the engine block making sure the oil pan is flush to the transmission bell housing. Secure the oil pan to the engine block with nineteen M8 oil pan mounting bolts finger tight.

27. Install the four transmission to the engine oil pan bolts and tighten to 41 ft. lbs. (55 Nm).

28. Tighten the nineteen previously installed M8 oil pan mounting bolts to 18 ft. lbs. (25 Nm).

➡Shown with transmission removed for clarity.

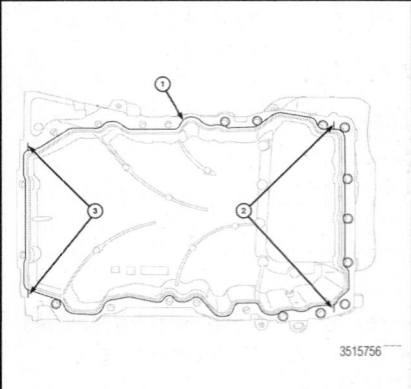

Fig. 172 Apply sealant to the oil pan-to-engine block flange (1), timing cover to engine block T-joints (2) and

29. Install the two M6 bolts to the rear oil seal retainer flange and tighten to 9 ft. lbs. (12 Nm).

30. Install the two rubber plugs covering the rear oil seal retainer flange bolts.

31. Lower the rear of the engine and install the two bolts to the rear engine mount isolator. Tighten the bolts to 35 ft. lbs. (47 Nm).

32. Install the transmission cooling lines and tighten the bolt to 9 ft. lbs. (12 Nm).

33. Lift the steering gear into the mounted position and install the steering gear mounting bolts. Tighten the bolts to 70 ft. lbs. (95 Nm).

34. Align the lower intermediate shaft with the input shaft and install the steering coupling. Install a NEW pinch bolt and tighten to 33 ft. lbs. (45 Nm).

35. Install the lower oil pan.

36. Position the belly pan and install the retainers.

37. Lower the vehicle.

38. Install the oil level indicator with bolt tightened to 9 ft. lbs. (12 Nm).

39. Position the heater core inlet tube and install two bolts tightened to 9 ft. lbs. n(12 Nm).

40. Fill the crankcase with the specified type and amount of engine oil.

41. Position the air inlet hose assembly onto the throttle body and the air cleaner housing.

42. Secure the air inlet hose assembly retaining grommet onto the ball stud.

43. Tighten the clamp at the air cleaner housing to 44 inch lbs. (5 Nm).

44. Tighten the clamp at the throttle body to 44 inch lbs. (5 Nm).

45. Connect the Inlet Air Temperature (IAT) sensor electrical connector.

46. Position the engine cover and secure the retaining grommets onto the ball studs.

47. Connect the negative battery cable and tighten nut to 45 inch lbs. (5 Nm).

48. Start and run the engine until it reaches normal operating temperature and check for leaks.

5.7L Engine

AWD Models

See Figures 173 and 174.

1. Before servicing the vehicle, refer to the precautions in the beginning of this section.

2. Disconnect the negative battery cable.

3. Remove the engine cover.

4. Remove the intake manifold.

5. Install engine lift fixture special tool

8984 and adapter 8984-UPD. See the Engine Removal and Installation procedure.

➡**Never use air tools when installing fasteners to engine.**

6. Raise vehicle.

7. Remove the belly pan.

8. Remove both left and right side engine mount to frame fasteners.

9. Drain engine oil and remove the oil filter.

10. Unbolt and lower the steering rack from the mounts. Do not remove power steering hoses, tie rod ends or disconnect steering column.

11. Remove the engine oil dipstick and tube from the oil pan.

12. Remove the left and right side exhaust at the manifolds.

13. Mark the front driveshaft to the flange at both ends to ensure correct installation.

14. Remove front driveshaft fasteners from the differential and transfer case. Remove the driveshaft from the vehicle.

15. Remove the left and right front drive axles.

16. Remove the differential support bracket from the differential to the engine block.

17. Unbolt the differential from the oil pan.

18. Rotate the differential so the drive flange is facing forward and the oil pan side is facing up. Remove the differential out through the opening at the rear of the cradle.

19. Remove the intermediate shaft from the oil pan.

20. Lower the vehicle.

21. Install engine support fixture special tool 8534. Do not attempt to fasten fixture to vehicle body, or attach the third support leg to the radiator support. See the Engine Removal & Installation procedure.

22. Raise engine using special tool 8534 and 8984 to provide clearance to remove oil pan.

23. Raise vehicle.

➡**Do not pry on oil pan or oil pan gasket. Gasket is integral to engine windage tray and does not come out with oil pan.**

➡**The horizontal M10 fasteners are 5 mm longer in length, and must be reinstalled in original locations.**

24. Remove the M10 fasteners (vertical and horizontal) from the rear of the oil pan to the transmission and engine.

25. Remove the oil pan mounting bolts and oil pan.

➡**When the oil pan is removed, a new oil pan gasket/windage tray assembly must be installed. The old gasket cannot be reused.**

26. Discard the integral windage tray and gasket and replace.

To install:

27. Clean the oil pan gasket mating surface of the block and oil pan.

➡**Mopar® Engine RTV must be applied to the 4 T-joints, (area where front cover, rear retainer, block, and oil pan gasket meet). The bead of RTV should cover the bottom of the gasket. This area is approximately 4.5 mm x 25 mm in each of the 4 T-joint locations.**

28. Apply Mopar® Engine RTV at the 4 T-joints.

➡**When the oil pan is removed, a new oil pan gasket/windage tray assembly must be installed. The old gasket cannot be reused.**

29. Install a new oil pan gasket/windage tray assembly.

30. If removed, reinstall the oil pump pickup tube with new O-ring. Tighten tube to pump fasteners to 21 ft. lbs. (28 Nm).

➡**The horizontal M10 fasteners are 5 mm longer in length, and must be reinstalled in original locations.**

31. Align the rear of the oil pan with the rear face of the engine block, and install the M10 and M6 oil pan fasteners finger tight. Using the following torque sequence, torque the M6 mounting bolts to 44 inch lbs. (5 Nm).

32. Using the following torque sequence, torque the M10 oil pan fasteners to 39 ft. lbs. (54 Nm).

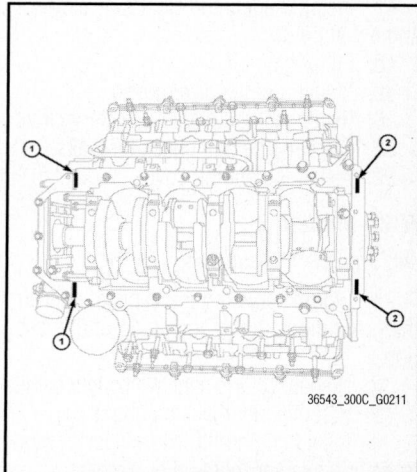

36543_300C_G0211

Fig. 173 Sealant application points (1, 2)

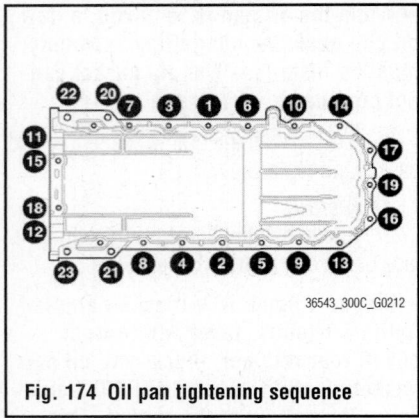

Fig. 174 Oil pan tightening sequence

33. Using the following torque sequence, torque the M6 oil pan fasteners to 106 inch lbs. (12 Nm).

34. Install the intermediate shaft to the oil pan. Torque fasteners to 21 ft. lbs. (28 Nm).

35. Install the front differential through the opening at the rear of the cradle, and attach to the oil pan.

36. Fasten the differential to the oil pan. Torque to 48 ft. lbs. (65 Nm).

37. Install the differential support bracket to the differential and the engine block.

38. Install the left and right front drive axles.

39. Install front driveshaft into the differential and transfer case.

40. Install the engine oil dipstick and tube.

41. Install the steering gear.

42. Lower the engine into mounts using special tool 8534.

43. Install both the left and right side engine mount studs and nuts. Torque to 70 ft. lbs. (95 Nm).

44. Remove special tool 8534.

45. Remove special tool 8984.

46. Install the intake manifold.

47. Install the left and right side exhaust at the manifolds.

48. Fill engine oil.

49. Install oil filter, if removed.

50. Reconnect the negative battery cable.

51. Start engine and check for leaks.

52. Install the engine cover.

RWD Models

See Figures 175 and 176.

1. Before servicing the vehicle, refer to the precautions in the beginning of this section.

2. Disconnect the negative battery cable.

3. Remove the intake manifold.

4. Install engine lift fixture special tool 8984 and adapter 8984-UPD. See the Engine Removal and Installation procedure.

※※ CAUTION

Never use air tools when installing fasteners to engine.

---

5. Raise vehicle.

6. Remove the belly pan.

7. Drain engine oil and remove the oil filter.

8. Unbolt and lower the steering rack from the mounts. Do not remove power steering hoses, tie rod ends or disconnect steering column.

9. Remove both left and right side engine hydro-mount to frame nuts, and studs.

   a. Remove the engine oil dipstick and tube from the oil pan.

10. Lower the vehicle.

11. Install engine support fixture special tool 8534. Do not use the third leg. See the Engine Removal and Installation procedure.

12. Raise engine using special tool 8534 and 8984 to provide clearance to remove oil pan.

➡ **Do not pry on oil pan or oil pan gasket. Gasket is integral to engine windage tray and does not come out with oil pan.**

➡ **The horizontal M10 fasteners are 5 mm longer in length, and must be reinstalled in original locations.**

13. Remove the M10 fasteners (vertical and horizontal) from the rear of the oil pan to the transmission and engine.

14. Remove the oil pan mounting bolts and oil pan.

➡ **When the oil pan is removed, a new oil pan gasket/windage tray assembly must be installed. The old gasket cannot be reused.**

15. Discard the integral windage tray and gasket and replace.

To install:

16. Clean the oil pan gasket mating surface of the block and oil pan.

➡ **Mopar® Engine RTV must be applied to the 4 T-joints, (area where front cover, rear retainer, block, and oil pan gasket meet). The bead of RTV should cover the bottom of the gasket. This area is approximately 4.5 mm x 25 mm in each of the 4 T-joint locations.**

17. Apply Mopar® Engine RTV at the 4 T-joints.

➡ **When the oil pan is removed, a new oil pan gasket/windage tray assembly must be installed. The old gasket cannot be reused.**

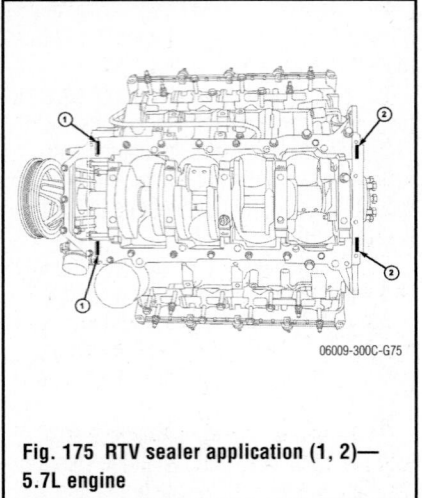

Fig. 175 RTV sealer application (1, 2)— 5.7L engine

18. Install a new oil pan gasket/windage tray assembly.

19. If removed, reinstall the oil pump pickup tube with new O-ring. Tighten tube to pump fasteners to 21 ft. lbs. (28 Nm).

➡ **The horizontal M10 fasteners are 5 mm longer in length, and must be reinstalled in original locations.**

20. Align the rear of the oil pan with the rear face of the engine block, and install the M10 and M6 oil pan fasteners finger tight. Using the accompanying torque sequence, torque the M6 mounting bolts to 44 inch lbs. (5 Nm).

21. Using the accompanying torque sequence, torque the M10 oil pan fasteners to 39 ft. lbs. (54 Nm).

22. Using the accompanying torque sequence, torque the M6 oil pan fasteners to 106 inch lbs. (12 Nm).

23. Lower the engine into mounts using special tool 8534.

24. Install both the left and right side engine mount studs and nuts. Torque the studs and nuts to 70 ft. lbs. (95 Nm).

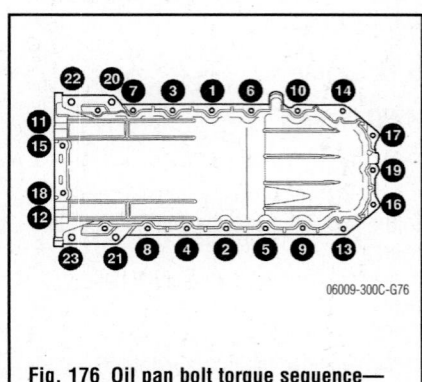

Fig. 176 Oil pan bolt torque sequence— 5.7L engine

25. Install the engine oil dipstick and tube.
26. Install the steering rack.
27. Remove special tool 8534.
28. Remove special tool 8984.
29. Install the intake manifold.
30. Fill engine oil.
31. Install oil filter, if removed.
32. Reconnect the negative battery cable.
33. Start engine and check for leaks.
34. Install the belly pan.

OIL PUMP

REMOVAL & INSTALLATION

2.7L Engine

See Figures 177 and 178.

1. Before servicing the vehicle, refer to the precautions in the beginning of this section.
2. Remove the crankshaft vibration damper.
3. Remove timing chain cover.
4. Remove the timing chain and sprockets.
5. Remove oil pan.
6. Remove oil pick-up tube and O-ring.
7. Ensure that crankshaft position is at 60°ATDC of No.1 cylinder, or crankshaft sprocket mark aligns with mark on oil pump. This position will properly locate oil pump upon installation.
8. Remove oil pump attaching bolts.
9. Remove oil pump.

To install:

✳✳ CAUTION

Crankshaft position must be at 60°ATDC of No.1 cylinder before installing oil pump. This position will properly locate oil pump. If not prop-

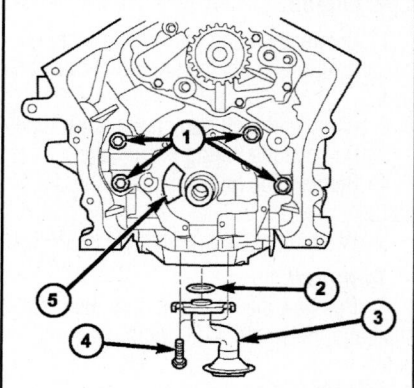

Fig. 177 Oil pump bolts (1), O-ring (2), pick-up tube (3), bolts (4), oil pump (5)— 2.7L engine

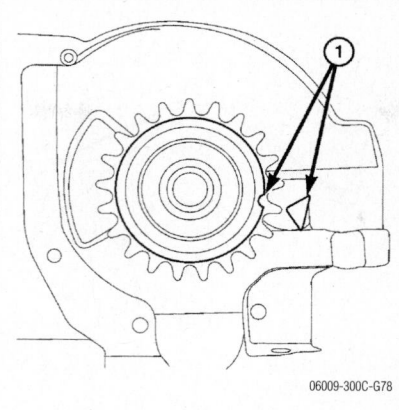

Fig. 178 Crankshaft at 60 degrees ATDC (1)—2.7L engine

erly located, severe damage to oil pump can occur.

10. Prime oil pump before installation by filling rotor cavity with engine oil.
11. If crankshaft has been rotated, it must be repositioned to 60° ATDC of No. 1 cylinder prior to oil pump installation.
12. Install oil pump carefully over crankshaft and into position.
13. Install oil pump attaching bolts. Tighten bolts to 21 ft. lbs. (28 Nm).
14. Install oil pick-up tube with new O-ring. Lubricate O-ring with clean engine oil before installation. Tighten attaching bolts to 21 ft. lbs. (28 Nm).
15. Install oil pan.
16. Install the timing chain and sprockets.
17. Install timing chain cover.
18. Install the crankshaft vibration damper.
19. Fill the crankcase with engine oil to correct level.

3.5L Engine

See Figure 179.

1. Before servicing the vehicle, refer to the precautions in the beginning of this section.
2. Drain the cooling system.
3. Remove the timing belt.
4. Remove the crankshaft sprocket.
5. Remove the oil pan.
6. Remove the oil pickup tube.
7. Remove the oil pump fasteners. Remove the oil pump and gasket from engine.

To install:

8. Prime oil pump before installation by filling rotor cavity with clean engine oil.
9. Install oil pump and gasket carefully

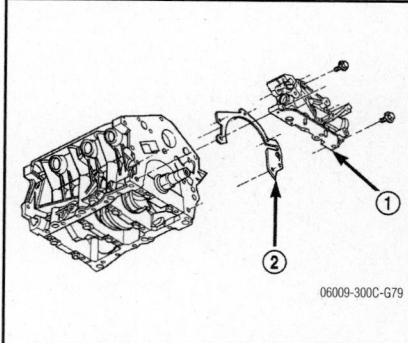

Fig. 179 Oil pump (1) and gasket (2)— 3.5L engine

over the crankshaft. Position pump onto block and tighten bolts to 21 ft. lbs. (28 Nm).

10. Install new O-ring on oil pickup tube.
11. Install oil pickup tube.
12. Install oil pan.
13. Install crankshaft sprocket.
14. Install timing belt.
15. Install the timing belt covers.
16. Install the crankshaft vibration damper. Torque to 70 ft. lbs. (95 Nm).
17. Install the accessory drive belt.
18. Fill the cooling system.
19. Fill engine crankcase with proper oil to the correct level.

3.6L Engine

See Figures 180 through 183.

1. Disconnect and isolate the negative battery cable.
2. Remove the upper oil pan.
3. Remove the oil pump pick-up.
4. Disconnect the engine wire harness from the oil pump solenoid electrical connector.

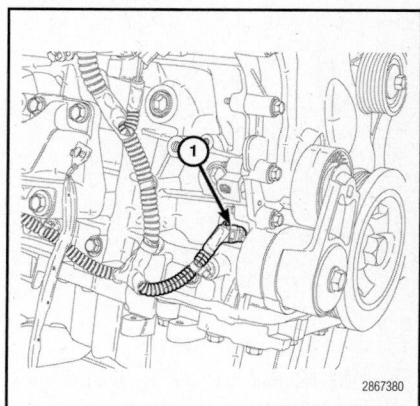

Fig. 180 Disconnecting the engine wire harness from the oil pump solenoid electrical connector

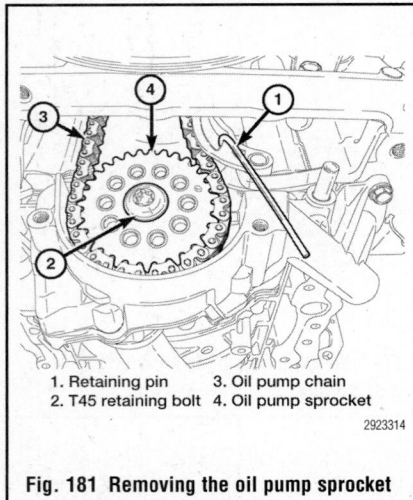

1. Retaining pin   3. Oil pump chain
2. T45 retaining bolt   4. Oil pump sprocket

2923314

Fig. 181 Removing the oil pump sprocket

5. Depress the connector retention lock tab to disengage the oil pump solenoid electrical connector from the engine block.

➡**Graphic shows the engine timing cover removed for clarity.**

6. Push the oil pump solenoid electrical connector into the engine block, rotate the connector slightly CW, push it past the primary chain tensioner mounting bolt and into the engine.

7. Push back the oil pump chain tensioner and insert a suitable retaining pin such as a 3 mm Allen wrench.

✳✳ WARNING

Always reinstall timing chains so that they maintain the same direction of rotation. Inverting a previously run chain on a previously run sprocket

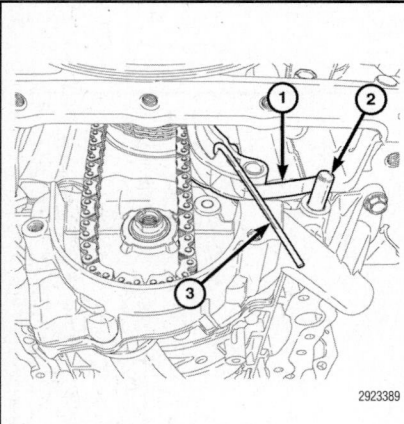

2923389

Fig. 182 Remove the retaining pin (3) and disengage the oil pump chain tensioner spring (1) from the dowel pin (2). Remove the oil pump chain tensioner from the oil pump

will result in excessive wear to both the chain and sprocket.

8. Mark the direction of rotation on the oil pump chain and sprocket using a paint pen or equivalent to aid in reassembly.

➡**There are no timing marks on the oil pump gear or chain. Timing of the oil pump is not required.**

9. Remove the oil pump sprocket T45 retaining bolt and remove the oil pump sprocket.

10. Remove the retaining pin and disengage the oil pump chain tensioner spring from the dowel pin.

11. Remove the oil pump chain tensioner from the oil pump.

12. Remove the four oil pump bolts and remove the oil pump.

To install:

13. Align the locator pins to the engine block and install the oil pump with four bolts (1). Tighten the bolts to 9 ft. lbs. (12 Nm).

14. Install the oil pump chain tensioner on the oil pump.

15. Position the oil pump chain tensioner spring above the dowel pin.

16. Push back the oil pump chain tensioner and insert a suitable retaining pin such as a 3 mm Allen wrench.

➡**There are no timing marks on the oil pump gear or chain. Timing of the oil pump is not required.**

➡**Always reinstall timing chains so that they maintain the same direction of rotation. Inverting a previously run chain on a previously run sprocket will result in excessive wear to both the chain and sprocket.**

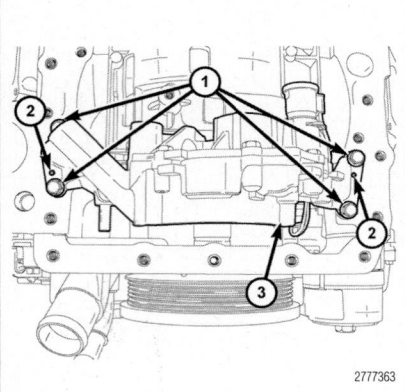

2777363

Fig. 183 Remove the four oil pump bolts (1) and remove the oil pump (2)

17. Place the oil pump sprocket into the oil pump chain. Align the oil pump sprocket with the oil pump shaft and install the sprocket. Install the T45 retaining bolt and tighten to 18 ft. lbs. (25 Nm).

18. Remove the retaining pin. Verify that the oil pump chain is centered on the tensioner and crankshaft sprocket.

19. Rotate the crankshaft CW one complete revolution to verify proper oil pump chain installation.

20. Position the oil pump solenoid electrical connector into the engine block. Rotate the connector so that it can be pushed past the primary chain tensioner mounting bolt. Then rotate the connector slightly CCW and push it into the engine block until it locks in place.

21. Verify that the oil pump solenoid electrical connector retention lock tab is engaged to the engine block.

22. Connect the engine wire harness to the oil pump solenoid electrical connector.

23. Install the oil pump pick-up.

24. Install the oil pan.

25. If removed, install the oil filter and fill the engine crankcase with the proper oil to the correct level.

26. Connect the negative battery cable and tighten nut to 45 inch lbs. (5 Nm).

✳✳ WARNING

A MIL or low oil pressure indicator that remains illuminated for more than 2 seconds may indicate low or no engine oil pressure. Stop the engine and investigate the cause of the indication.

27. Start and run the engine until it reaches normal operating temperature.

5.7L Engine

1. Before servicing the vehicle, refer to the precautions in the beginning of this section.

2. Remove the oil pan and pick-up tube.

3. Remove the timing chain cover.

4. Remove the four bolts, and the oil pump.

5. Wash all parts in a suitable solvent.

To install:

6. Position the oil pump onto the crankshaft and install the 4 oil pump retaining bolts.

7. Tighten the oil pump retaining bolts to 21 ft. lbs. (28 Nm).

8. Install the timing chain cover.

9. Install the pick-up tube and oil pan.

INSPECTION

2.7L & 3.5L Engine

See Figures 184 through 192.

The oil pump is replaced as an assembly; there are no subassembly components. In the event the oil pump is not functioning it must be replaced as an assembly.

➡**DO NOT inspect the oil relief valve assembly. If the oil relief valve is suspect, replace the oil pump.**

1. Disassemble oil pump.
2. Clean all parts thoroughly. Mating surface of the oil pump housing should be smooth. Replace pump cover if scratched or grooved.

   a. Lay a straightedge (1) across the pump cover (3) surface. For 2.7L and 3.5L engine, if a 0.001 in. (0.025 mm) feeler gauge can be inserted between cover and straight edge, cover should be replaced.
3. Measure thickness and diameter of outer rotor. For 2.7L engine, if outer rotor thickness measures 0.472 in. (12.005 mm) or less, or if the diameter is 3.382 in. (85.925 mm) or less, replace outer rotor. For 3.5L engine, if outer rotor thickness measures 0.563 in. (14.299 mm) or less, or if the diameter is 3.141 in. (79.78 mm) or less, replace outer rotor.
4. For 2.7L engine, if inner rotor measures 0.472 in. (12.005 mm) or less, replace inner rotor. For 3.5L engine, if inner rotor measures 0.563 in. (14.299 mm) or less, replace inner rotor.
5. Slide outer rotor (2) into body, press to one side with fingers and measure clearance between rotor and body. For 2.7L

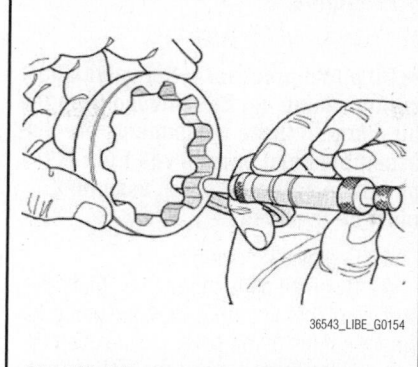

Fig. 185 Oil pump outer rotor thickness

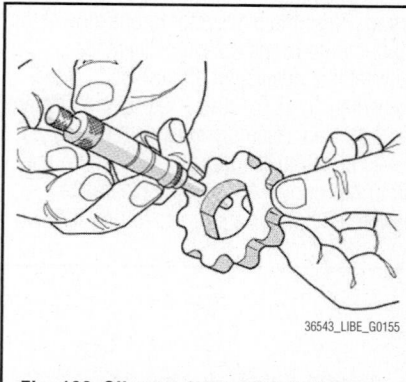

Fig. 186 Oil pump inner rotor thickness

engine, if measurement is 0.009 in. (0.235 mm) or more, replace body only if outer rotor is in specifications. For 3.5L engine, if measurement is 0.015 in. (0.39 mm) or more, replace body only if outer rotor is in specifications.
6. Install inner rotor into body. For 2.7L engine, if clearance between inner (3) and outer rotors (2) is 0.006 in. (0.150 mm) or more, replace both rotors. For 3.5L engine, if clearance between inner (3) and outer

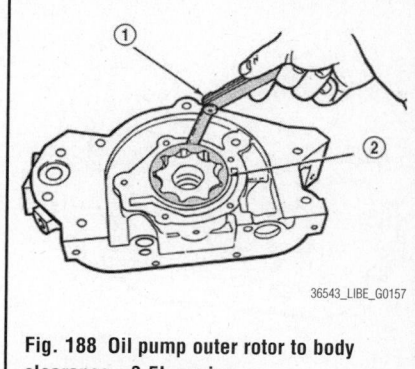

Fig. 188 Oil pump outer rotor to body clearance—3.5L engine

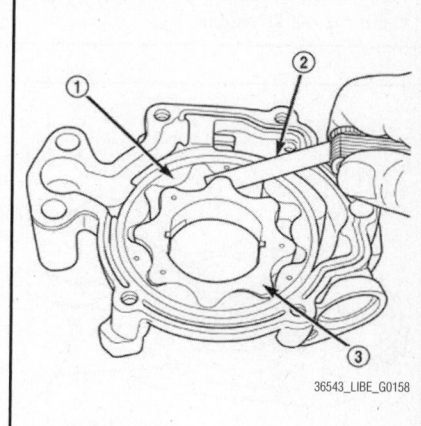

Fig. 189 Oil pump outer rotor to inner rotor clearance—2.7L engine

rotors (2) is 0.008 in. (0.20 mm) or more, replace both rotors.
7. Place a straightedge (1) across the face of the body, between bolt holes. For 2.7L engine, if a feeler gauge of 0.0038 in. (0.095 mm) or more can be inserted between rotors and the straightedge,

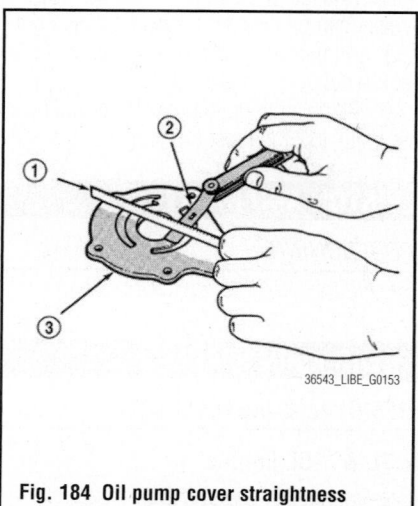

Fig. 184 Oil pump cover straightness

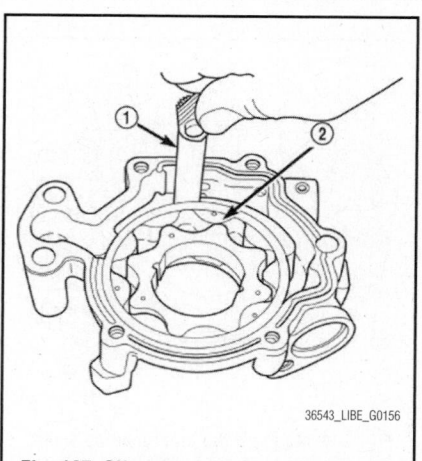

Fig. 187 Oil pump outer rotor to body clearance—2.7L engine

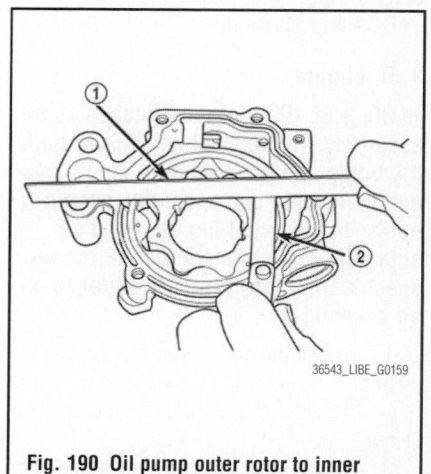

Fig. 190 Oil pump outer rotor to inner rotor clearance—3.5L engine

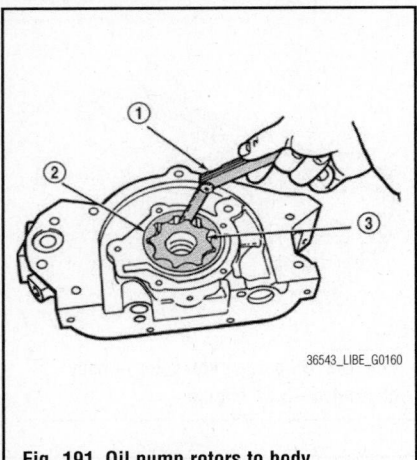

Fig. 191 Oil pump rotors to body clearance—2.7L engine

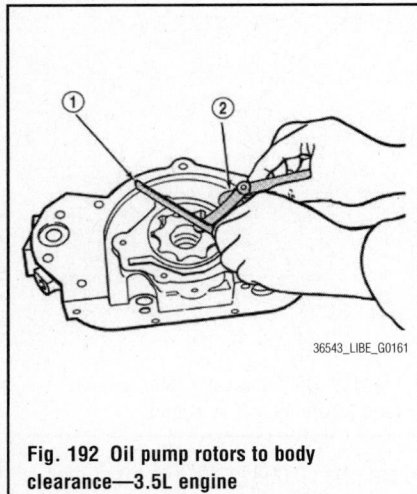

Fig. 192 Oil pump rotors to body clearance—3.5L engine

replace pump assembly ONLY if rotors are in specs. For 3.5L engine, if a feeler gauge of 0.003 in. (0.077 mm) or more can be inserted between rotors and the straightedge, replace pump assembly ONLY if rotors are in specs.

8. Assemble oil pump.

3.6L Engine

➡ **The 3.6L Oil pump is released as an assembly. The assembly includes both the pump and the solenoid. There are no serviceable sub-assembly components. In the event the oil pump or solenoid are not functioning or out of specification they must be replaced as an assembly.**

1. Inspect the solenoid wires for cuts or chaffing.
2. Inspect the condition of the connector O-ring seal.
3. Inspect the connector retention lock tab for fatigue or damage.

5.7L Engine

See Figures 193 through 196.

➡ **Oil pump pressure relief valve and spring should not be removed from the oil pump. If these components are disassembled and or removed from the pump the entire oil pump assembly must be replaced.**

1. Remove the pump cover.
2. Clean all parts thoroughly. Mating surface of the oil pump housing should be smooth. If the pump cover is scratched or grooved the oil pump assembly should be replaced.
3. Slide outer rotor into the body of the oil pump. Press the outer rotor to one side of the oil pump body and measure clearance between the outer rotor and the body. If the measurement is 0.235mm (0.009 in.) or more the oil pump assembly must be replaced.
4. Install the inner rotor in the into the oil pump body. Measure the clearance between the inner and outer rotors. If the

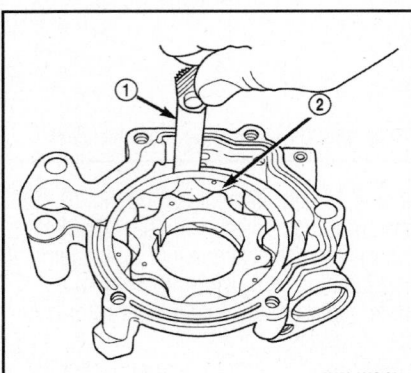

Fig. 193 Press the outer rotor to one side of the oil pump body and measure clearance between the outer rotor (2) and the body—5.7L engine

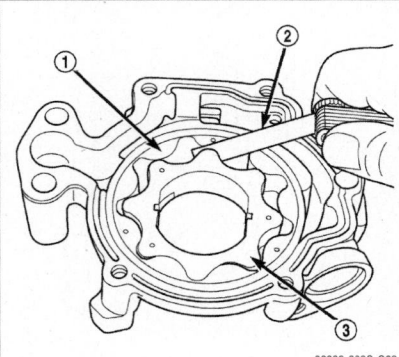

Fig. 194 Measure the clearance between the inner (3) and outer rotors (1)—5.7L engine

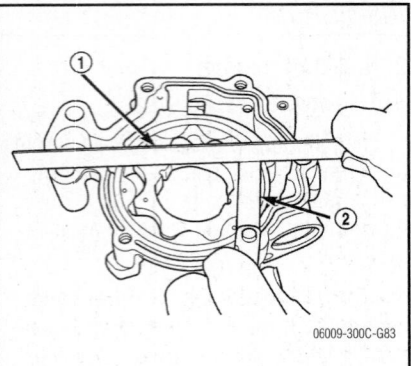

Fig. 195 If a feeler gauge (2) of 0.095 mm (0.0038 in.) or greater can be inserted between the straightedge and the rotors, the pump must be replaced—5.7L engine

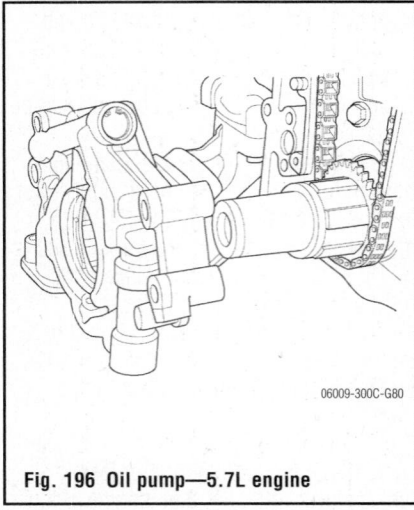

Fig. 196 Oil pump—5.7L engine

clearance between the rotors is 0.150 mm (0.006 in.) or more the oil pump assembly must be replaced.

5. Place a straight-edge across the body of the oil pump (between the bolt holes), if a feeler gauge of 0.095 mm (0.0038 in.) or greater can be inserted between the straightedge and the rotors, the pump must be replaced.

6. Reinstall the pump cover. Torque fasteners to 132 inch lbs. (15 Nm).

PISTON AND RING

POSITIONING

See Figures 197 through 200.

REAR MAIN SEAL

REMOVAL & INSTALLATION

2.7L & 3.5L Engine

See Figures 201 through 203.

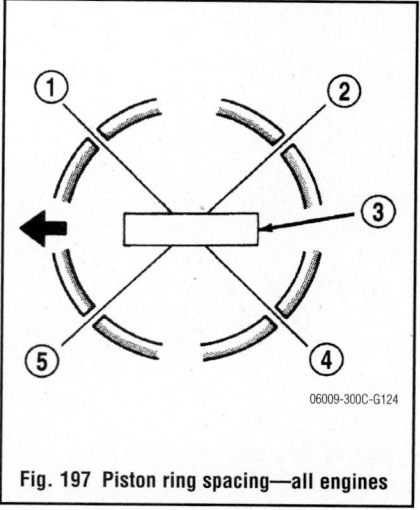

Fig. 197 Piston ring spacing—all engines

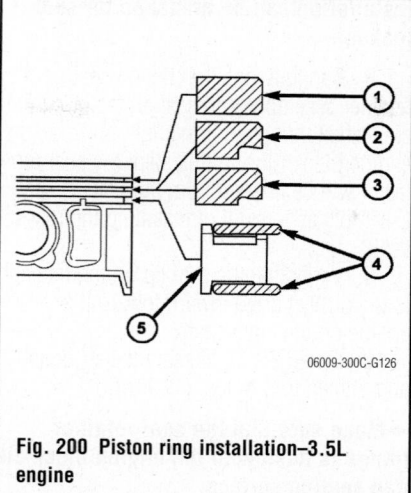

Fig. 200 Piston ring installation–3.5L engine

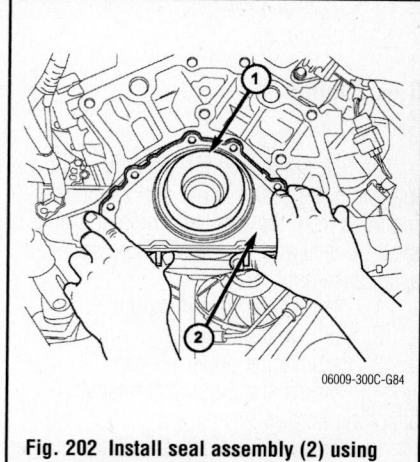

Fig. 202 Install seal assembly (2) using special tool 6926-1(1)—2.7L engine

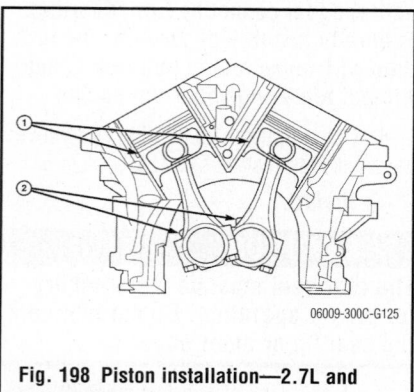

Fig. 198 Piston installation—2.7L and 3.5L engines

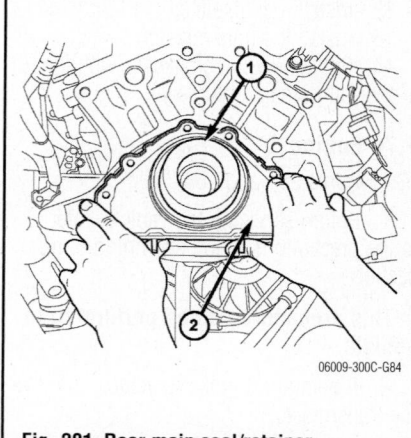

Fig. 201 Rear main seal/retainer assembly—2.7L engine

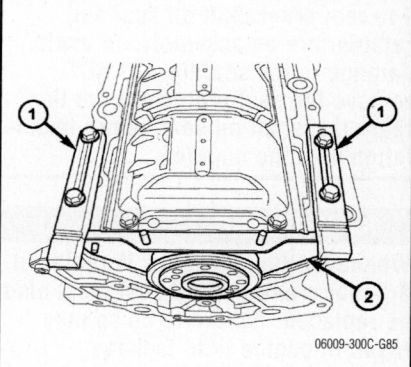

Fig. 203 Attach Special Tools 8225 (1) to pan rail using the oil pan fasteners—2.7L engine

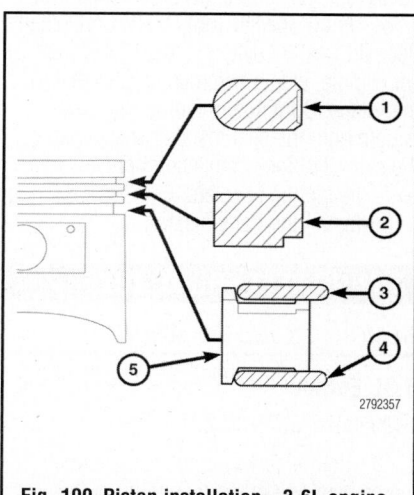

Fig. 199 Piston installation—3.6L engine

1. Before servicing the vehicle, refer to the precautions in the beginning of this section.

2. Disconnect negative battery cable.

3. Raise the vehicle.

4. Remove splash shield retaining bolts and splash shield.

5. Remove the structural collar.

6. Remove transmission

7. Remove flexplate attaching bolts, backing plate and flexplate.

8. Remove oil pan.

➥The integrated stamped steel rear crankshaft seal is not interchangeable with the cast aluminum rear seal adapter and seal assembly.

9. Remove seal retainer attaching screws.

10. Remove the crankshaft rear oil seal/adapter.

To install:

➥The integrated rear crankshaft seal is not interchangeable with the cast aluminum rear seal adapter and seal assembly.

11. Clean all sealing surfaces.

12. Install seal assembly using special tool 6926-1.

a. Install seal retaining bolts finger tight.

➥The following steps must be performed to prevent oil leaks at sealing joints.

13. Attach Special Tools 8225 to pan rail using the oil pan fasteners.

➥Make sure that the "2.7L" stamped on the special tool is facing the cylinder block (flat side of tools against pan rail).

14. While applying firm pressure to the seal assembly against Special Tools 8225, tighten seal assembly screws to 105 inch lbs. (12 Nm).

15. Remove special tool 8225.

16. Install oil pan.

17. Install flexplate, backing plate, and attaching bolts.

a. Install transmission.

18. Install lower splash shield retaining bolts and splash shield.

19. Lower vehicle.
20. Fill with oil.

3.6L Engine

See Figure 204.

The rear crankshaft oil seal is incorporated into the seal retainer and cannot be removed from the retainer. The rear crankshaft oil seal and seal retainer are serviced as an assembly.

1. Remove the transmission.
2. Remove the flexplate.
3. Remove the upper oil pan.
4. Remove the eight seal retainer attaching screws.
5. Remove and discard the seal retainer.

To install:

> ❊❊ **WARNING**
>
> **The rear crankshaft oil seal and retainer are an assembly. To avoid damage to the seal lip, DO NOT remove the seal protector from the rear crankshaft oil seal before installation onto the engine.**

> ❊❊ **WARNING**
>
> **Whenever the crankshaft is replaced, the rear crankshaft oil seal must also be replaced. Failure to do so may result in engine fluid leakage.**

6. Inspect the crankshaft to make sure there are no nicks or burrs on the seal surface.
7. Clean the engine block sealing surfaces thoroughly.

➡️ **It is not necessary to lubricate the seal or the crankshaft when installing the seal retainer. Residual oil following**

installation can be mistaken for seal leakage.

8. Carefully position the oil seal retainer assembly, and seal protector on the crankshaft and push firmly into place on the engine block (during this step, the seal protector will be pushed from the rear oil seal assembly as a result of installing the rear oil seal).
9. Verify that the seal lip on the retainer is uniformly curled inward toward the engine on the crankshaft.
10. Install the eight seal retainer bolts and tighten to 9 ft. lbs. (12 Nm).

➡️ **Make sure that the seal retainer flange is flush with the engine block oil pan sealing surface.**

11. Install the upper oil pan.
12. Install the flexplate.
13. Install the transmission.
14. Fill the engine crankcase with the proper oil to the correct level.

5.7L Engine

See Figures 205 and 206.

1. Before servicing the vehicle, refer to the precautions in the beginning of this section.

➡️ **This procedure can be performed in vehicle.**

2. If being performed in vehicle, remove the transmission.
3. Remove the flexplate.

➡️ **The crankshaft oil seal cannot be reused after removal.**

➡️ **The crankshaft rear oil seal remover Special Tool 8506 must be installed deeply into the seal. Continue to tighten the removal tool into the seal**

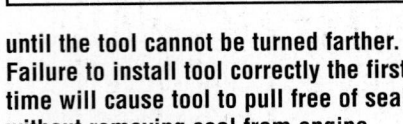

Fig. 206 Rear main seal installation—
5.7L engine

until the tool cannot be turned farther. Failure to install tool correctly the first time will cause tool to pull free of seal without removing seal from engine.

4. Using Special Tool 8506 (1), remove the crankshaft rear oil seal (2).

To install:

> ❊❊ **CAUTION**
>
> **The rear seal must be installed dry for proper operation. Do not lubricate the seal lip or outer edge.**

5. Position the plastic seal guide (2) onto the crankshaft rear face. Then position the crankshaft rear oil seal (3) onto the guide.
6. Using Special Tools 8349 Crankshaft Rear Oil Seal Installer (1) and C-4171 Driver Handle, with a hammer, tap the seal (3) into place. Continue to tap on the driver handle until the seal installer seats against the cylinder block crankshaft bore.
7. Install the flexplate.
8. Install the transmission.

TIMING BELT FRONT COVER

REMOVAL & INSTALLATION

3.5L Engine

See Figures 207 and 208.

1. Before servicing the vehicle, refer to the precautions in the beginning of this section.
2. Disconnect and isolate the negative battery cable.
3. Remove the air cleaner element housing.
4. Partially drain the cooling system.
5. Remove accessory drive belt.
6. Remove accessory drive belt tensioner.

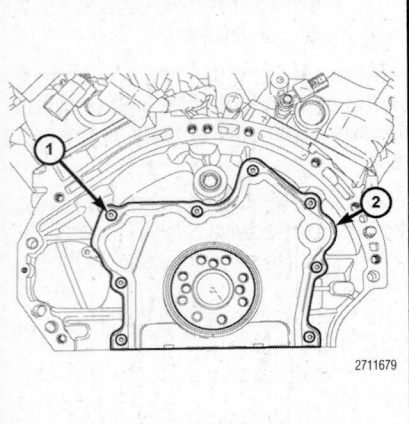

Fig. 204 Removing and installing the rear seal

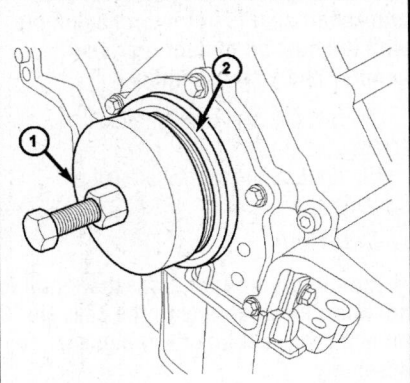

Fig. 205 Rear main seal removal—5.7L engine

7. Remove upper radiator hose.

8. Disconnect cooling fan electrical connector.

9. Remove cooling fan mounting bolts.

10. Remove radiator cooling fan assembly from vehicle.

11. Remove crankshaft damper bolt and remove the damper with a puller.

12. Remove the lower front timing belt cover fasteners.

13. Lower the vehicle.

14. Remove the upper timing belt cover bolts and remove front timing belt cover.

To install:

15. Exchange the accessory drive belt pulley if necessary. Tighten bolt to 45 ft. lbs. (61 Nm).

16. Install upper front timing belt cover.

17. Install lower timing belt front cover.

18. Tighten the timing cover bolts as follows:

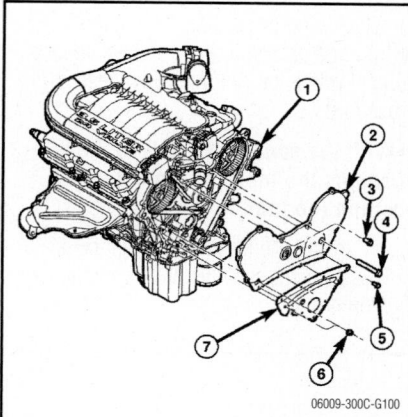

Fig. 207 Front timing belt covers (2, 7)—3.5L engine

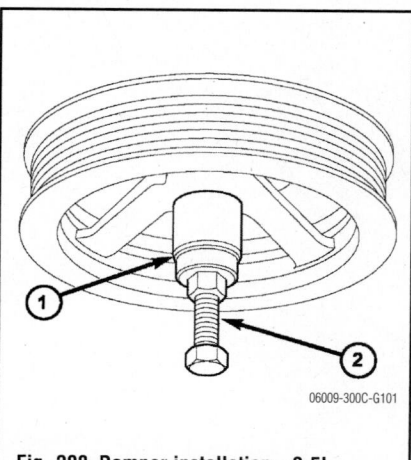

Fig. 208 Damper installation—3.5L engine

- M6 bolts: 105 inch lbs. (12 Nm)
- M8 bolts: 250 inch lbs. (28 Nm)
- M10 bolts: 40 ft. lbs. (54 Nm)

19. Install crankshaft damper using 5.9 inch long Forcing Screw C-4685-C1 with Nut and Thrust Bearing from Crank Sprocket Installer 6792 and tighten to 70 ft. lbs. (95 Nm).

20. Position radiator cooling fan assembly in vehicle.

21. Install cooling fan mounting bolts. Tighten to 50 inch lbs. (6 Nm).

22. Connect cooling fan electrical connector.

23. Install upper radiator hose.

24. Install accessory drive belt tensioner. Torque fastener to 40 ft. lbs. (34 Nm).

25. Install accessory drive belt.

26. Install the air cleaner body.

27. Connect negative battery cable. Tighten nut to 45 inch lbs. (5 Nm).

28. Fill cooling system.

29. Operate engine until it reaches normal operating temperature. Check cooling system for correct fluid level.

TIMING BELT & SPROCKETS

REMOVAL & INSTALLATION

3.5L Engine

See Figures 209 through 213.

1. See all applicable precautions before beginning service procedures.

2. Disconnect and isolate the negative battery cable.

3. Remove the front timing belt cover.

a. Mark belt running direction, if timing belt is to be reused.

✳✳ CAUTION

When aligning timing marks, always rotate engine by turning the crankshaft. Failure to do so will result in valve and/or piston damage.

4. Rotate engine clockwise until crankshaft (10) mark aligns with the TDC mark on oil pump housing (9) and the camshaft sprocket (2, 7) timing marks (1, 8) are aligned with the marks on the rear cover.

5. Raise and support the vehicle.

6. Remove bolt and reposition oil cooler hose.

a. Remove the timing belt tensioner.

7. Lower vehicle.

8. Remove the timing belt.

9. Inspect the tensioner for fluid leakage.

10. Inspect the pivot and bolt for free movement, bearing grease leakage, and smooth rotation. If not rotating freely, replace the arm and pulley assembly.

➡ **When tensioner is removed from the engine it is necessary to compress the plunger into the tensioner body.**

11. Index the tensioner in the vise the same way it is installed on the engine. This ensures proper pin orientation when tensioner is installed on the engine.

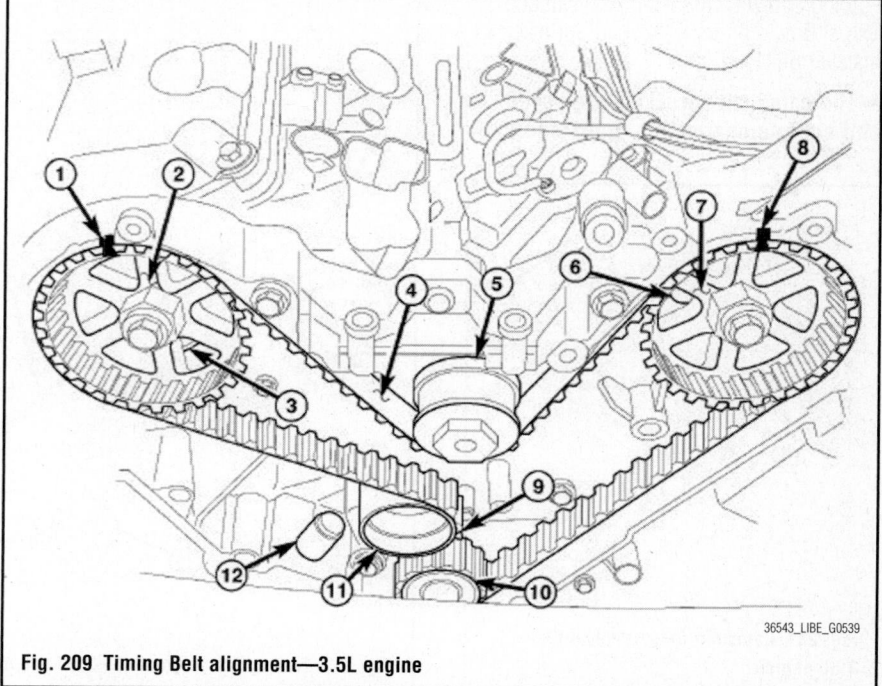

Fig. 209 Timing Belt alignment—3.5L engine

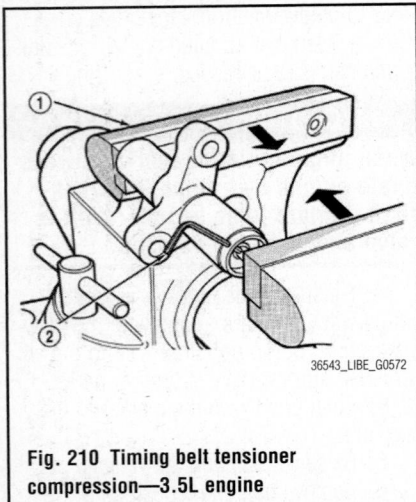

Fig. 210 Timing belt tensioner compression—3.5L engine

a. Place the tensioner into a vise (1) and SLOWLY compress the plunger. Total bleed down of tensioner should take approximately two minutes.

b. When plunger is compressed into the tensioner body install a pin (2) through the body and plunger to retain plunger in place until tensioner is installed.

12. Counter-hold the left cam gear and remove the cam gear retaining bolt.

13. Remove the cam gear.

14. Counter-hold the right cam gear and remove the cam gear retaining bolt.

15. Remove the cam gear.

16. Remove crankshaft sprocket using Gear Puller L-4407-A (1).

To install:

17. Install crankshaft sprocket using Forcing Screw C-4685-C1, with Nut and Thrust Bearing from 6792, and Sprocket Installer 6641.

➡️**The camshaft sprockets are keyed and not interchangeable from side to**

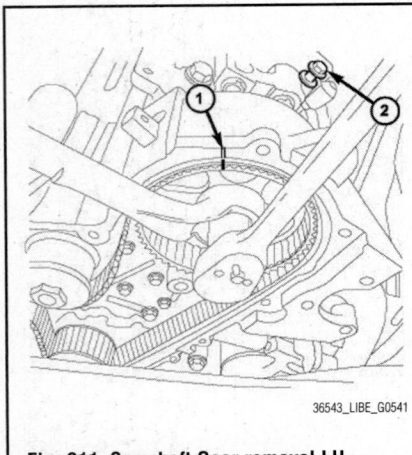

Fig. 211 Camshaft Gear removal LH—3.5L engine

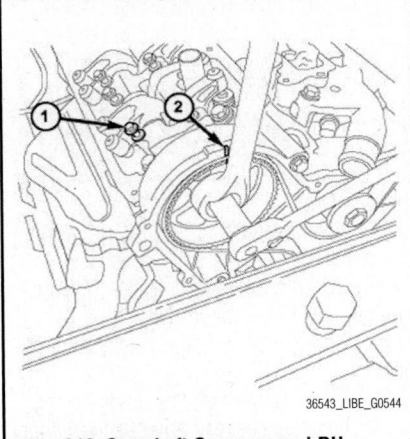

Fig. 212 Camshaft Gear removal RH—3.5L engine

side because of the camshaft position sensor pick-up.

18. Install NEW sprocket attaching bolt into place. The 10 in. (255 mm) bolt is to be installed in the left camshaft and the 8 3/8 in. (213 mm) bolt is to be installed into the right camshaft. Counter-hold the camshaft sprocket and tighten the camshaft sprocket bolt to 75 ft. lbs. (102 Nm) plus a 90° turn.

❊❊ CAUTION

If camshafts have moved from the timing marks, always rotate camshaft towards the direction nearest to the timing marks (DO NOT TURN

CAMSHAFTS A FULL REVOLUTION OR DAMAGE to valves and/or pistons could result).

19. Rotate the right camshaft gear (2) to align its timing mark (1). Verify that the left camshaft gear (7) timing mark (8) and crankshaft gear (10) timing mark (9) are still aligned.

20. Install the timing belt (4) starting at the crankshaft sprocket (10) going in a counterclockwise direction. Install the belt around the last sprocket. Maintain tension on the belt as it is positioned around the tensioner pulley (11).

21. Holding the tensioner pulley (11) against the belt, install the tensioner (12) into the housing and tighten two bolts to 250 inch lbs. (28 Nm) (Each camshaft sprocket mark should remain aligned with the cover marks.

22. When tensioner is in place, pull retaining pin to allow the tensioner to extend to the tensioner pulley bracket.

23. Rotate crankshaft sprocket two revolutions and check the timing marks on the camshafts and crankshaft. The marks should line up within their respective locations. If marks do not line up, repeat procedure.

➡️**With the camshaft gears in these positions the lobes are in a neutral position (no load to the valve).**

24. Install the front timing belt cover.

25. Connect negative battery cable. Tighten nut to 40 inch lbs. (4.5 Nm).

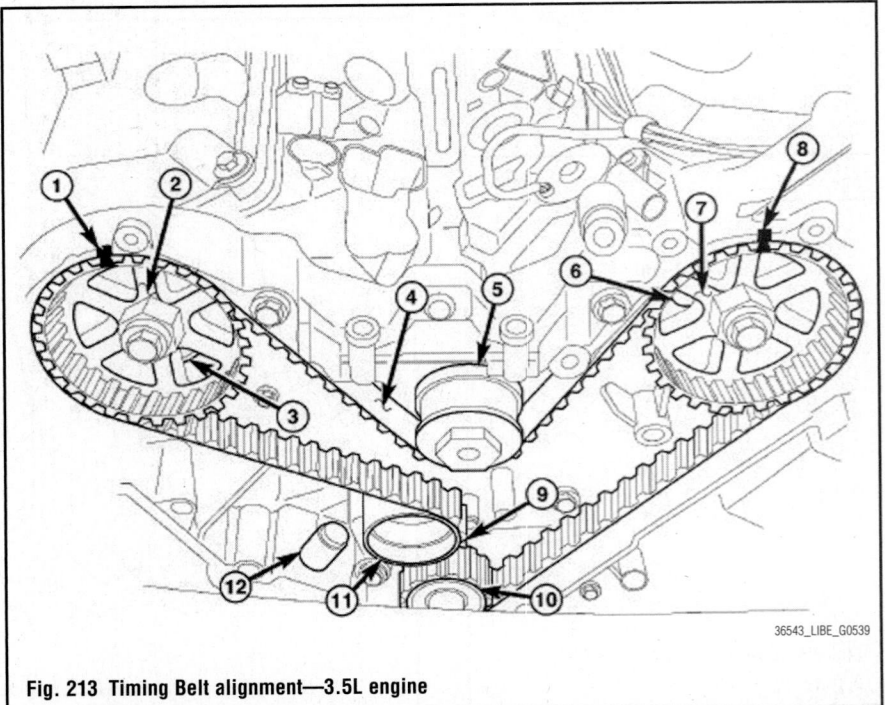

Fig. 213 Timing Belt alignment—3.5L engine

TIMING BELT REAR COVER

REMOVAL & INSTALLATION

3.5L Engine

See Figures 214 and 215.

1. Before servicing the vehicle, refer to the precautions in the beginning of this section.

➡**The rear timing belt cover has O-rings to seal the water pump passages to cylinder block. Do not reuse the O-rings.**

2. Disconnect the negative battery cable.
3. Drain the cooling system.
4. Remove the timing belt.
5. Remove the camshaft sprockets.
6. Remove three power steering pump mounting bolts through access holes in pulley and reposition the power steering pump.
7. Raise and support the vehicle.
   a. Remove the front belly pan.
8. Remove upper most mounting bolt from generator.
9. Remove generator bracket bolt and remove bracket.
10. Remove lower mounting bolts and reposition the generator.

➡**Bottom bolt securing the A/C compressor to the engine cannot be fully removed until the compressor is positioned away from the cylinder block.**

11. Fully loosen the bolt that secures the A/C compressor and automatic transmission cooler line bracket to the cylinder block.

※※ CAUTION

Use care not to deform or damage the automatic transmission cooler lines and retaining bracket when repositioning the A/C compressor.

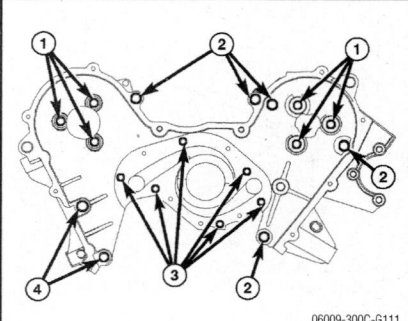

Fig. 214 Rear timing belt cover bolts—3.5L engine

06009-300C-G111

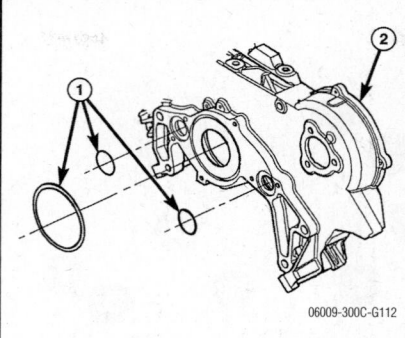

06009-300C-G112

Fig. 215 Rear timing belt cover O-rings—3.5L engine

12. Remove bolts and reposition the A/C compressor.
13. Remove water pump mounting bolts (3).
14. Remove water pump.
15. Remove rear timing belt cover bolts (1, 2) and nuts (4).
16. Remove the rear cover.

To install:

17. Clean rear timing belt cover O-ring sealing surfaces and grooves. Lubricate new O-rings with Mopar® Dielectric Grease, or equivalent, to facilitate assembly.
18. Position NEW O-rings on cover.
19. Install rear timing belt cover. Tighten nuts (4) and bolts (1, 2) to the following specified torque:
   • M10 (2, 4): 40 ft. lbs. (54 Nm)
   • M8 (1): 20 ft. lbs. (28 Nm)
20. Position water pump and new gasket.
21. Install water pump mounting bolts. Tighten to 105 inch lbs. (12 Nm).

➡**Bottom bolt that secures the A/C compressor and transmission cooler line bracket (when equipped) must be installed through the bracket and the lower front mounting hole of the compressor prior to final positioning of the compressor to the cylinder block.**

22. Loosely install the bolt that secures the A/C compressor and automatic transmission cooler line bracket (when equipped) to the compressor and position the compressor, bracket and bolt to the cylinder block.
23. Loosely install the bolts that secure the A/C compressor to the cylinder block.
24. Tighten all three bolts that secure the A/C compressor to the engine in the following order to 19 ft. lbs. (26 Nm):
   a. Upper front bolt.

b. Lower front bolt.
c. Rear bolt.

➡**Position generator, bracket and all bolts to engine compartment. Hand tightening all fasteners. Then torque all fasteners to specifications.**

25. Position generator to engine and loosely install lower mounting bolts.
26. Position generator bracket and loosely install bracket bolt and upper generator mounting bolt.
27. Tighten generator mounting bolts to 48 ft. lbs. (65 Nm) Tighten generator bracket bolt to 40 ft. lbs. (54 Nm).
28. Align pump with mounting holes on engine bracket.
29. Install three pump mounting bolts through access holes in pulley and engine bracket. Tighten bolts to 21 ft. lbs. (28 Nm).
30. Install the camshaft sprockets.
31. Install the timing belt.
32. Install the front timing belt cover.
33. Install the front belly pan.
34. Connect negative battery cable. Tighten nut to 45 inch lbs. (5 Nm).
35. Fill cooling system.
36. Operate engine until it reaches normal operating temperature. Check cooling system for correct fluid level.

TIMING CHAIN FRONT COVER

REMOVAL & INSTALLATION

3.6L Engine

See Figures 216 through 220.

1. Disconnect and isolate the negative battery cable.
2. Drain the cooling system.
3. Remove the upper radiator hose and thermostat housing.
4. Remove the heater core return hose from the water pump housing.
5. Remove the lower radiator hose from the water pump housing.
6. Remove the heater core supply hose from the coolant outlet housing.
7. Remove the bolt and reposition the heater core supply tube.
8. Remove the accessory drive belt.
9. Remove the accessory drive belt tensioner.
10. Remove the accessory idler pulley.
11. Remove the crankshaft vibration damper.
12. Remove the right and left cylinder head covers.
13. Remove the upper and lower oil pans.

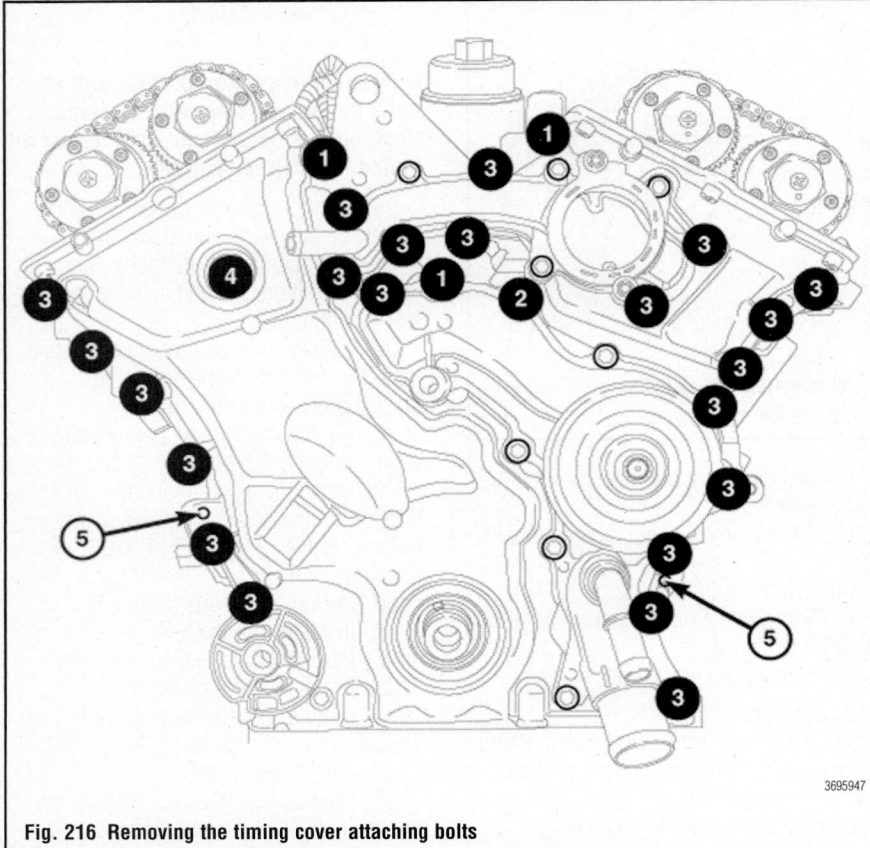

Fig. 216 Removing the timing cover attaching bolts

➡ **It is not necessary to remove the water pump or the coolant outlet housing for engine timing cover removal.**

14. Remove the following timing cover attaching bolts:
  • Three M10 bolts (1)
  • One M8 bolt (2)
  • Twenty-three M6 bolts (3)

15. Using the seven indicated pry points, carefully remove the timing cover.

16. If required, remove the remaining four M6 bolts and the coolant outlet housing from the engine timing cover.

17. If required, remove the remaining four M6 bolts and the water pump from the engine timing cover.

✽✽ WARNING

Do not use oil based liquids, wire brushes, abrasive wheels or metal scrapers to clean the engine gasket surfaces. Use only isopropyl (rubbing) alcohol, along with plastic or wooden scrapers. Improper gasket surface preparation may result in engine fluid leakage.

18. Remove all residual sealant from the timing chain cover, cylinder head and engine block mating surfaces.

19. Remove and discard the coolant outlet housing gasket and the water pump gasket.

To install:

20. If removed, install the coolant outlet housing to the timing cover with a new gasket using only the four bolts shown tightened to 9 ft. lbs. (12 Nm).

21. If removed, install the water pump to the timing cover using only the four bolts shown tightened to 9 ft. lbs. (12 Nm)

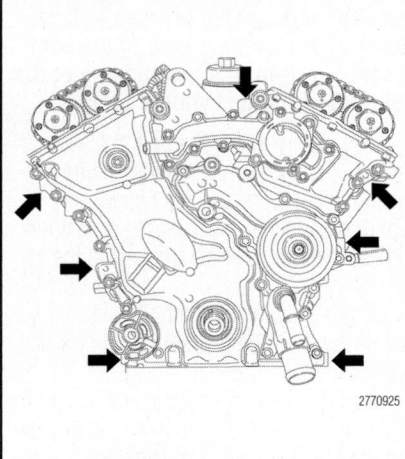

Fig. 217 Identifying the prying points

22. Install the coolant outlet housing gasket and the water pump gasket.

23. Clean the engine timing cover, cylinder head and block mating surfaces with isopropyl alcohol in preparation for sealant application.

✽✽ WARNING

Engine assembly requires the use of a unique sealant that is compatible with engine oil. Using a sealant other than Mopar® Threebond Engine RTV Sealant may result in engine fluid leakage.

✽✽ WARNING

Following the application of Mopar® Threebond Engine RTV Sealant to the gasket surfaces, the components must be assembled within 20 minutes and the attaching fasteners must be tightened to specification within 45 minutes. Prolonged exposure to the air prior to assembly may result in engine fluid leakage.

24. Apply a 2 to 3 mm wide bead of Mopar® Threebond Engine RTV Sealant to the front cover as shown in the following locations:
  • Three cylinder head bosses (1)
  • Right and left flanges (2)
  • Four cylinder head to engine block T-joints (3)
  • Cover to right cam chain tensioner gap (4)

25. Align the locator pins on the engine block to the engine timing cover and install the cover.

26. Install and tighten the timing cover attaching bolts:

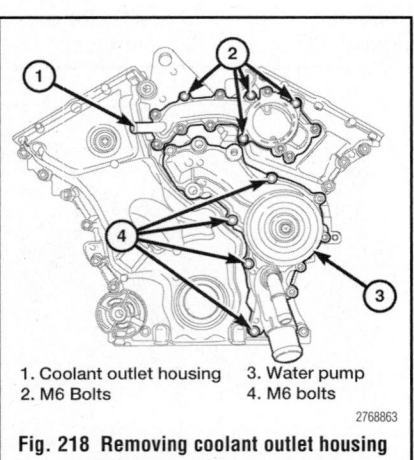

1. Coolant outlet housing 3. Water pump
2. M6 Bolts   4. M6 bolts

Fig. 218 Removing coolant outlet housing and water pump from the engine timing cover

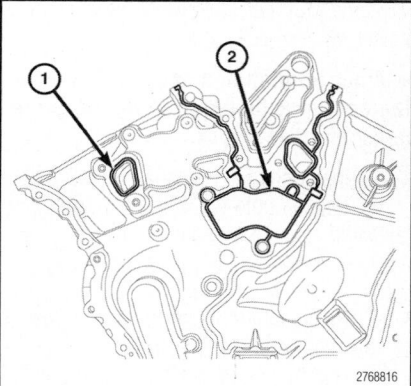

Fig. 219 Removing the coolant outlet housing gasket (1) and water pump gasket (2)

a. Twenty-three M6 bolts to 9 ft. lbs. (12 Nm).

b. One M8 bolt to 18 ft. lbs. (25 Nm).

c. Three M10 bolts to 41 ft. lbs. (55 Nm).

27. Install the upper and lower oil pans.

28. Install the right and left cylinder head covers.

29. Install the crankshaft vibration damper.

30. Install the accessory idler pulley.

31. Install accessory drive belt tensioner.

32. Install the accessory drive belt.

33. Install the heater core supply tube with one bolt tightened to 9 ft. lbs (12 Nm).

34. Install the heater core supply hose to the coolant outlet housing.

35. Install the lower radiator hose to the water pump housing.

36. Install the heater core return hose to the water pump housing.

37. Install the thermostat housing and upper radiator hose.

38. If removed, install the oil filter and fill the engine crankcase with the proper oil to the correct level.

39. Connect the negative battery cable and tighten nut to 45 inch lbs. (5 Nm).

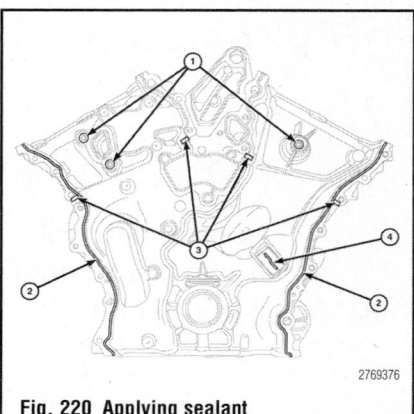

Fig. 220 Applying sealant

40. Fill the cooling system.

41. Run the engine until it reaches normal operating temperature. Check cooling system for correct fluid level.

TIMING CHAIN & SPROCKETS

REMOVAL & INSTALLATION

2.7L Engine

Engine Crankshaft Sprocket

See Figures 221 and 222.

1. Before servicing the vehicle, refer to the precautions in the beginning of this section.

2. Remove primary timing chain.

✳✳ CAUTION

Use care not to turn crankshaft while removing crankshaft sprocket, as damage to valves and or pistons could occur.

3. Remove crankshaft sprocket by first installing the crankshaft damper bolt. Apply grease or equivalent to damper bolt head and position Special Tools 5048-1(3), 5048-6 (2), and 8539 (1) on sprocket and crankshaft nose. Remove sprocket using care not to rotate the crankshaft.

To install:

4. Install crankshaft sprocket using Special Tools 6780-1(1) and 8179 (2) until sprocket bottoms against crankshaft step flange. Use care not to rotate crankshaft.

5. Verify that crankshaft sprocket is installed to proper depth by measuring from sprocket outer face to end of crankshaft. Measurement should read: 39.05 plus or minus 0.50 mm (1.5374 plus or minus 0.020 in.).

6. Install primary timing chain.

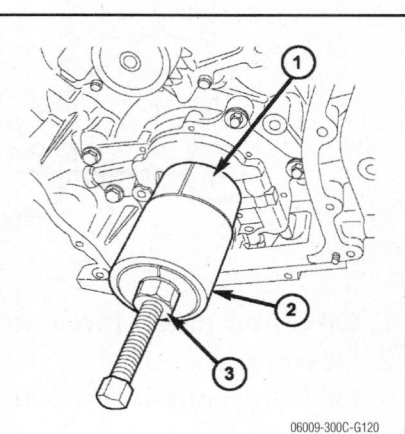

Fig. 221 Crankshaft sprocket removal—2.7L engine

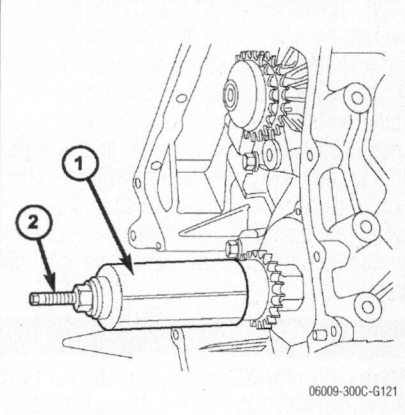

Fig. 222 Crankshaft sprocket installation—2.7L engine

3.6L Engine

See Figures 223 through 225.

✳✳ WARNING

The magnetic timing wheels must not come in contact with magnets (pickup tools, trays, etc.) or any other strong magnetic field. This will destroy the timing wheels ability to correctly relay camshaft position to the camshaft position sensor.

✳✳ WARNING

When the timing chains are removed and the cylinder heads are still installed, DO NOT rotate the camshafts or crankshaft without first locating the proper crankshaft position. Failure to do so will result in valve and/or piston damage.

1. Disconnect and isolate the negative battery cable.

2. Remove the air cleaner housing assembly and upper intake manifold.

3. Remove the cylinder head covers.

4. Remove the spark plugs.

5. Raise and support the vehicle.

6. Drain the cooling system.

7. Remove the oil pan, accessory drive belts, crankshaft vibration damper and engine timing cover.

➡Take this opportunity to measure timing chain wear.

✳✳ WARNING

When aligning timing marks, always rotate engine by turning the crankshaft. Failure to do so will result in valve and/or piston damage.

8. Rotate the crankshaft CW to place the number one piston at TDC on the exhaust stroke by aligning the dimple on the crankshaft with the block/bearing cap junction. The left side cam phaser arrows should point toward each other and be parallel to the valve cover sealing surface. The right side cam phaser arrows should point away from each other and the scribe lines should be parallel to the valve cover sealing surface.

✳✳ WARNING

Always reinstall timing chains so that they maintain the same direction of rotation. Inverting a previously run chain on a previously run sprocket will result in excessive wear to both the chain and sprocket.

9. Mark the direction of rotation on the following timing chains using a paint pen or equivalent to aid in reassembly:
- Left side cam chain
- Right side cam chain
- Oil pump chain
- Primary chain

10. Reset the RH cam chain tensioner by pushing back the tensioner piston and installing Tensioner Pin.

11. Reset the LH cam chain tensioner by lifting the pawl, pushing back the piston and installing tensioner pin.

12. Disengage the oil pump chain tensioner spring from the dowel pin and remove the oil pump chain tensioner.

13. Remove the oil pump sprocket T45 retaining bolt and remove the oil pump sprocket and oil pump chain.

➡ Minor rotation of a camshaft (a few degrees) may be required to install the camshaft phaser lock.

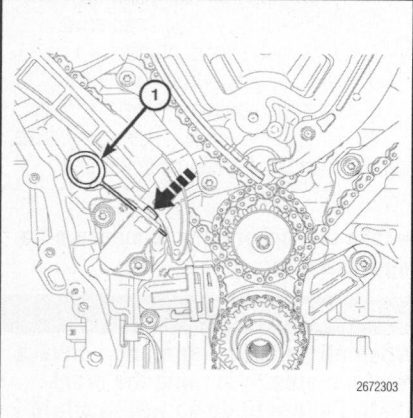

Fig. 223 Resetting the RH cam chain tensioner and installing the tensioner pin

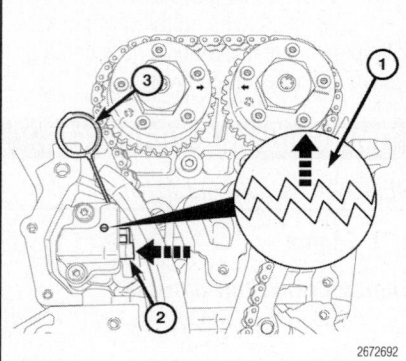

Fig. 224 Reset the LH cam chain tensioner by lifting the pawl (1), pushing back the piston (2) and installing tensioner pin (3)

14. Install the RH Camshaft Phaser Lock.

15. Loosen both the intake oil control valve and exhaust oil control valve.

16. Remove the RH Camshaft Phaser Lock.

17. Remove the oil control valve from the right side intake cam phaser.

18. Pull the right side intake cam phaser off of the camshaft and remove the right side cam chain.

19. If required, remove the oil control valve and pull the right side exhaust cam phaser off of the camshaft.

➡ Minor rotation of a camshaft (a few degrees) may be required to install the camshaft phaser lock.

20. Install the LH Camshaft Phaser Lock.

21. Loosen both the intake oil control valve and exhaust oil control valve.

22. Remove the LH Camshaft Phaser Lock.

23. Remove the oil control valve from the left side exhaust cam phaser.

24. Pull the left side exhaust cam phaser off of the camshaft and remove the left side cam chain.

25. If required, remove the oil control valve and pull the left side intake cam phaser off of the camshaft.

26. Reset the primary chain tensioner by pushing back the tensioner piston and installing Tensioner Pin. Remove two T30 bolts and remove the primary chain tensioner.

27. Remove the T30 bolt and the primary chain guide.

28. Remove the idler sprocket T45 retaining bolt and washer.

29. Remove the primary chain, idler sprocket and crankshaft sprocket as an assembly.

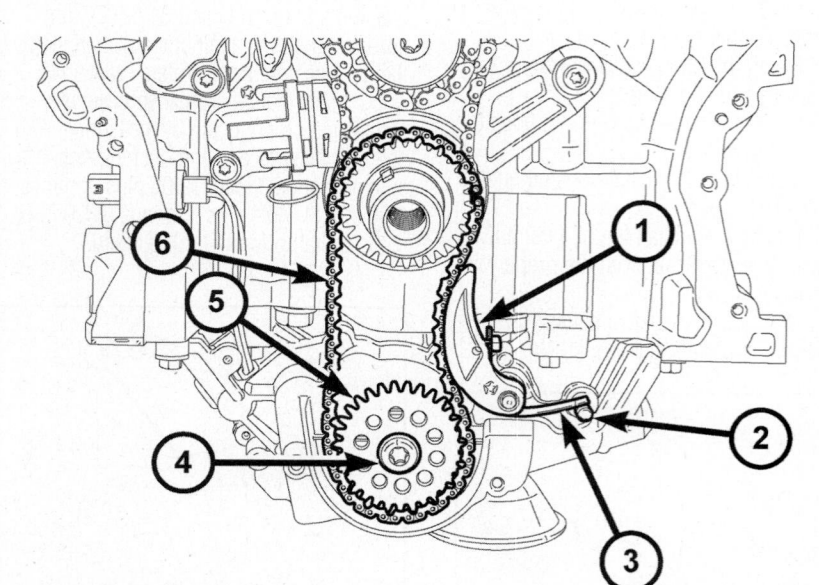

1. Oil pump chain tensioner
2. Dowel pin
3. Oil pump chain tensioner spring
4. T45 retaining bolt
5. Oil pump sprocket
6. Oil pump chain

Fig. 225 Removing the oil pump sprocket and chain

30. If required, remove two T30 bolts and the LH cam chain tensioner.

31. If required, remove two T30 bolts and the LH cam chain guide and tensioner arm.

32. If required, remove two T30 bolts and the RH cam chain tensioner.

33. If required, remove three T30 bolts and the RH cam chain guide and tensioner arm.

34. Inspect all sprockets and chain guides. Replace if damaged.

To install:

> ※ **WARNING**
>
> **The magnetic timing wheels must not come in contact with magnets (pickup tools, trays, etc.) or any other strong magnetic field. This will destroy the timing wheels ability to correctly relay camshaft position to the camshaft position sensor.**

35. Inspect all sprockets and chain guides. Replace if damaged.

36. If removed, install the right side cam chain guide and tensioner arm. Tighten attaching T30 bolts to 9 ft. lbs. (12 Nm).

37. If removed, install the RH cam chain tensioner to the engine block with two bolts. Tighten the T30 bolts to 9 ft. lbs. (12 Nm).

38. Reset the RH cam chain tensioner by pushing back the tensioner piston and installing Tensioner Pin.

39. If removed, install the left side cam chain guide and tensioner arm. Tighten attaching T30 bolts to 9 ft. lbs. (12 Nm).

40. If removed, install the LH cam chain tensioner to the cylinder head with two bolts. Tighten the T30 bolts to 9 ft. lbs. (12 Nm).

41. Reset the LH cam chain tensioner by lifting the pawl, pushing back the piston and installing Tensioner Pin.

42. Verify that the key is installed in the crankshaft.

> ※ **WARNING**
>
> **Do not rotate the crankshaft more than a few degrees independently of the camshafts. Piston to valve contact could occur resulting in possible valve damage. If the crankshaft needs to be rotated more than a few degrees, first remove the camshafts.**

43. Verify that the number one piston is positioned at TDC by aligning the dimple on the crankshaft with the block/bearing cap junction.

> ※ **WARNING**
>
> **Do not rotate the camshafts more than a few degrees independently of the crankshaft. Valve to piston contact could occur resulting in possible valve damage. If the camshafts need to be rotated more than a few degrees, first move the pistons away from the cylinder heads by rotating the crankshaft counterclockwise to a position 30°BTDC. Once the camshafts are positioned at TDC rotate the crankshaft clockwise to return the crankshaft to TDC.**

44. Verify that the camshafts are set at TDC by positioning the alignment holes vertically.

> ※ **WARNING**
>
> **Always reinstall timing chains so that they maintain the same direction of rotation. Inverting a previously run chain on a previously run sprocket will result in excessive wear to both the chain and sprocket.**

45. Place the primary chain onto the crankshaft sprocket so that the arrow is aligned with the plated link on the timing chain.

46. While maintaining this alignment, invert the crankshaft sprocket and timing chain and place the idler sprocket into the timing chain so that the dimple is aligned with the plated link on the timing chain.

47. While maintaining this alignment, lubricate the idler sprocket bushing with clean engine oil and install the sprockets and timing chain on the engine. To verify that the timing is still correct, the timing chain plated link should be located at 12:00 when the dimple on the crankshaft is aligned with the block/bearing cap junction.

48. Install the idler sprocket retaining bolt and washer. Tighten the T45 bolt to 18 ft. lbs. (25 Nm).

49. Install the primary chain guide. Tighten attaching T30 bolt to 9 ft. lbs. (12 Nm).

50. Reset the primary chain tensioner by pushing back the tensioner piston and installing Tensioner Pin.

51. Install the primary chain tensioner to the engine block with two bolts. Tighten the T30 bolts to 9 ft. lbs. (12 Nm) and remove the Tensioner Pin.

52. Press the LH intake cam phaser onto the intake camshaft. Install and hand tighten the oil control valve.

➡ The LH and RH cam chains are identical.

> ※ **WARNING**
>
> **Always reinstall timing chains so that they maintain the same direction of rotation. Inverting a previously run chain on a previously run sprocket will result in excessive wear to both the chain and sprocket.**

53. Drape the left side cam chain over the LH intake cam phaser and onto the idler sprocket so that the arrow is aligned with the plated link on the cam chain.

54. While maintaining this alignment, route the cam chain around the exhaust and intake cam phasers so that the plated links are aligned with the phaser timing marks. Position the left side cam phasers so that the arrows point toward each other and are parallel to the valve cover sealing surface. Press the exhaust cam phaser onto the exhaust cam, install and hand tighten the oil control valve.

➡ Minor rotation of a camshaft (a few degrees) may be required to install the camshaft phaser or phaser lock.

55. Install the LH Camshaft Phaser Lock and tighten the oil control valves to 110 ft. lbs. (150 Nm).

56. Press the RH exhaust cam phaser onto the exhaust camshaft. Install and hand tighten the oil control valve.

> ※ **WARNING**
>
> **Always reinstall timing chains so that they maintain the same direction of rotation. Inverting a previously run chain on a previously run sprocket will result in excessive wear to both the chain and sprocket.**

57. Drape the right side cam chain over the RH exhaust cam phaser and onto the idler sprocket so that the dimple is aligned with the plated link on the cam chain.

58. While maintaining this alignment, route the cam chain around the exhaust and intake cam phasers so that the plated links are aligned with the phaser timing marks. Position the right side cam phasers so that the arrows point away from each other and the scribe lines are parallel to the valve cover sealing surface. Press the intake cam phaser onto the intake cam, install and hand tighten the oil control valve.

➡ Minor rotation of a camshaft (a few degrees) may be required to install the camshaft phaser or phaser lock.

59. Install the RH Camshaft Phaser Lock and tighten the oil control valves to 11 ft. lbs. (110 ft. lbs. (150 Nm).

➡ There are no timing marks on the oil pump gear or chain.

✳✳ WARNING

Always reinstall timing chains so that they maintain the same direction of rotation. Inverting a previously run chain on a previously run sprocket will result in excessive wear to both the chain and sprocket.

60. Place the oil pump sprocket into the oil pump chain. Place the oil pump chain onto the crankshaft sprocket while aligning the oil pump sprocket with the oil pump shaft. Install the oil pump sprocket T45 retaining bolt and tighten to 18 ft. lbs. (25 Nm).

61. Install the oil pump chain tensioner. Insure that the spring is positioned above the dowel pin.

62. Remove the RH and LH Camshaft Phaser Locks.

63. Remove the Tensioner Pins from the RH and LH cam chain tensioners.

64. Rotate the crankshaft CW two complete revolutions stopping when the dimple on the crankshaft is aligned the with the block/bearing cap junction.

65. While maintaining this alignment, verify that the arrows on the left side cam phasers point toward each other and are parallel to the valve cover sealing surface and that the right side cam phaser arrows point away from each other and the scribe lines are parallel to the valve cover sealing surface.

66. There should be 12 chain pins between the exhaust cam phaser triangle marking and the intake cam phaser circle marking.

67. If the engine timing is not correct, repeat this procedure.

68. Install the engine timing cover, crankshaft vibration damper, accessory drive belts and oil pan.

69. Install the spark plugs. Tighten to 13 ft. lbs. (17.5 Nm).

70. Install the cylinder head covers.

71. Install the upper intake manifold and air cleaner housing assembly.

72. Fill the engine crankcase with the proper oil to the correct level.

73. Connect the negative battery cable and tighten nut to 45 inch lbs. (5 Nm).

74. Fill the cooling system.

75. Operate the engine until it reaches normal operating temperature. Check cooling system for correct fluid level.

➡ **The Cam/Crank Variation Relearn procedure must be performed using the scan tool anytime there has been a repair/replacement made to a powertrain system, for example: flywheel, valvetrain, camshaft and/or crankshaft sensors or components.**

5.7L Engine

See Figures 226 and 227.

1. Before servicing the vehicle, refer to the precautions in the beginning of this section.

2. Disconnect negative battery cable.

3. Drain cooling system.

4. Remove timing chain cover.

5. Re-install the vibration damper bolt finger tight. Using a suitable socket and breaker bar, rotate the crankshaft to align timing chain sprockets and keyways as shown.

✳✳ CAUTION

The camshaft pin and the slot in the cam sprocket must be positioned at 12:00 (2). The crankshaft keyway must be positioned at 2:00 (3). The crankshaft sprocket must be installed so that the dots and or paint marking is at 6:00.

6. Retract tensioner shoe until hole in shoe lines up with hole in bracket.

7. Slide a suitable pin into the holes.

8. Remove camshaft sprocket attaching bolt and remove timing chain with crankshaft and camshaft sprockets.

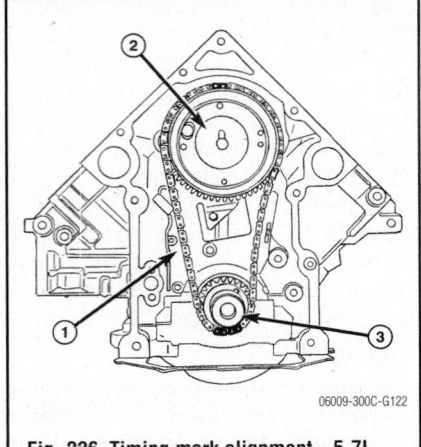

Fig. 226 Timing mark alignment—5.7L engine

9. If tensioner assembly is to be replaced, remove the tensioner to block bolts and remove tensioner assembly.

To install:

10. If tensioner assembly is being replaced, install tensioner and mounting bolts. Torque bolts to 21 ft. lbs. (28 Nm).

11. Retract tensioner if required.

✳✳ CAUTION

The timing chain must be installed with the single plated link aligned with the dot and or paint marking on the camshaft sprocket. The crankshaft sprocket is aligned with the dot and or paint marking on the sprocket between two plated timing chain links.

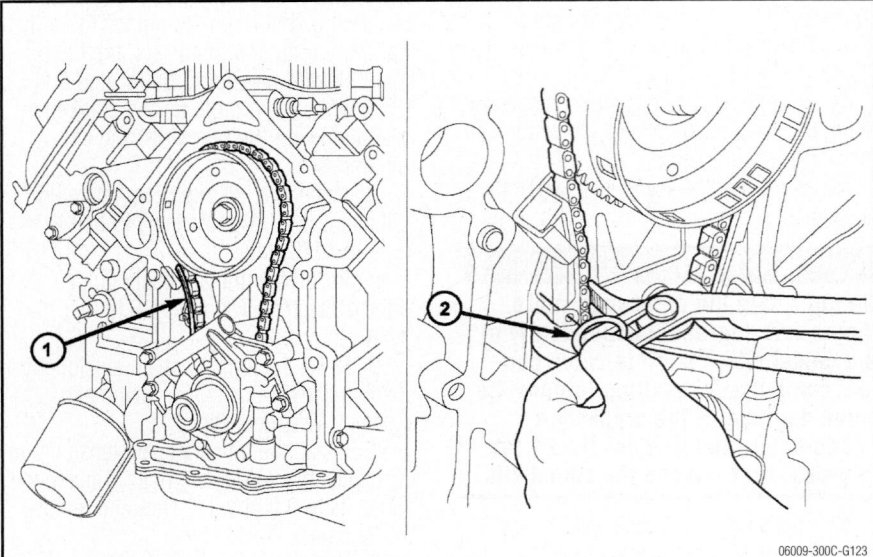

Fig. 227 Retract tensioner shoe (1) until hole in shoe lines up with hole in bracket. Slide a suitable pin (2) into the holes—5.7L engine

✳✳ CAUTION

The camshaft pin and the slot in the cam sprocket must be clocked at 12:00. The crankshaft keyway must be clocked at 2:00. The crankshaft sprocket must be installed so that the dots and or paint marking is at 6:00.

12. Place both camshaft sprocket and crankshaft sprocket on the bench with timing marks on exact imaginary center line through both camshaft and crankshaft bores.

13. Place timing chain around both sprockets.

14. Lift sprockets and chain. Keep sprockets tight against the chain.

15. Slide both sprockets evenly over their respective shafts and check alignment of timing marks.

16. Install the camshaft bolt. Tighten the bolt to 90 ft. lbs. (122 Nm).

17. Remove tensioner pin. Again, verify alignment of timing marks.

18. Install the oil pump.

19. Install the oil pan and pick up.

20. Install the timing chain cover.

21. Refill engine oil.

22. Fill cooling system.

23. Connect negative battery cable.

24. Start engine and check for oil and coolant leaks.

VALVE COVERS

REMOVAL & INSTALLATION

2.7L Engine

Left Side

See Figures 228 and 229.

1. Disconnect negative battery cable located in trunk.

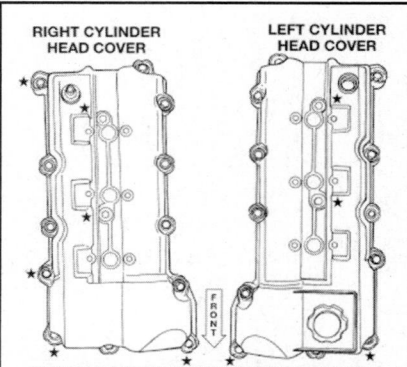

★ INDICATES DOUBLE-ENDED STUD LOCATIONS

36543_300C_G0133

Fig. 228 Double-ended stud locations—2.7L engine

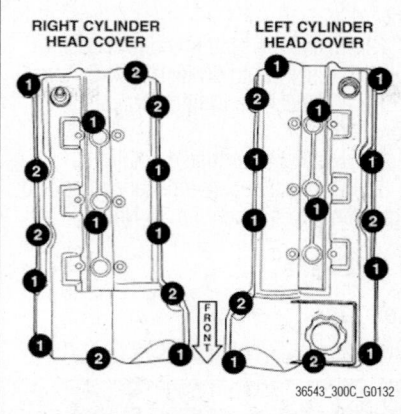

RIGHT CYLINDER HEAD COVER LEFT CYLINDER HEAD COVER

36543_300C_G0132

Fig. 229 Cylinder head cover tightening sequence—2.7L engine

2. Remove the upper intake manifold.

3. Disconnect the electrical connectors from ignition coils.

4. Remove ground strap from cylinder head cover stud and disconnect capacitor connector. Reposition electrical harness.

5. Disconnect electrical harness retaining clips from cylinder head cover studs. Reposition electrical harness.

6. Remove the makeup air hose.

7. Remove the fastener attaching ignition coil capacitor.

8. Remove ignition coils.

9. Loosen all cylinder head cover fasteners.

➡**Cylinder head cover attaching bolts are captured to the cover.**

✳✳ CAUTION

Make certain the double ended studs in the center of the cylinder head cover are loose before attempting to remove cover.

10. Remove cylinder head cover.

To install:

11. Clean cylinder head cover and both sealing surfaces. Inspect and replace gaskets as necessary.

12. Install cylinder head cover and hand start all fasteners. Verify that all double-ended studs are in the correct locations.

13. Tighten cylinder head cover attaching bolts and double-ended studs to 105 inch lbs. (12 Nm).

14. Install ignition coils.

15. Install ignition coil capacitor and fastener.

16. Install ground strap to cylinder head cover stud.

17. Connect all electrical connectors and harness clips.

18. Connect make up air hose.

19. Install upper intake manifold.

20. Connect negative battery cable.

Right Side

See Figures 228 and 229.

1. Disconnect negative battery cable.

2. Remove upper intake manifold.

3. Disconnect electrical connectors from ignition coils.

4. Disconnect capacitor electrical connector.

5. Remove PCV hose from cylinder head cover grommet.

6. Remove ground strap from cylinder head cover stud.

7. Disconnect electrical harness retaining clips from cylinder head cover studs. Reposition electrical harness.

   a. Remove fastener attaching ignition coil capacitor.

   b. Remove ignition coils.

8. Remove foam insulator.

9. Loosen all cylinder head cover fasteners.

➡**Cylinder head cover attaching bolts are captured to the cover.**

✳✳ CAUTION

Make certain the double ended studs in the center of the cylinder head cover are loose before attempting to remove cover.

10. Remove cylinder head cover.

To install:

11. Clean cylinder head cover and both sealing surfaces. Inspect and replace gaskets as necessary.

12. Install cylinder head cover and hand start all fasteners. Verify that all double-ended studs are in the correct locations.

13. Tighten cylinder head cover attaching bolts and double-ended studs to 105 inch lbs. (12 Nm).

14. Install ignition coils.

15. Install ignition coil capacitor and fastener.

16. Connect ground strap to cylinder head cover stud.

17. Connect PCV hose to cylinder head cover grommet.

18. Connect all electrical connectors and harness clips.

19. Install foam insulator on top of cylinder head cover.

20. Install upper intake manifold.

21. Connect negative battery cable.

3.5L Engine

See Figure 230.

> ⁑⁑ **WARNING**
>
> **Do not start or run engine with cylinder head cover removed from the engine. Damage or personal injury may occur.**

1. Disconnect and isolate the negative battery cable.
2. Cover lower intake manifold (4) with a suitable cover during service.
3. Disconnect and remove the three ignition coils (2).
4. Remove the ground strap/resistor retaining bolt from the cylinder head cover.
5. Lift up on the wire harness track (3) retaining tabs.
6. Completely loosen the cylinder head cover retaining bolts and remove the cylinder head cover.

To install:

7. Clean cylinder head and cover mating surfaces. Inspect and replace gasket and seals as necessary.
8. To replace spark plug tube seals:
   a. Using a suitable pry tool, carefully remove tube seals.
   b. Position new seal with the part number on seal facing cylinder head cover.
   c. Install seals using Camshaft Installer MD-998306.
9. Install cylinder head cover and bolts. Tighten bolts to 105 inch lbs. (12 Nm).
10. Position the wiring harness on the cylinder head cover.
11. Re-clip the wire harness track retaining tabs into the cover.
12. Install the ground strap/resistor retaining bolt onto the cylinder head cover.
13. Install the ignition coils. Tighten mounting screws to 60 inch lbs. (6.7 Nm).
14. Connect the ignition coil electrical connectors.
15. Install upper intake manifold.
16. Connect negative battery cable and tighten nut to 45 inch lbs. (5 Nm).

3.6L Engine

Left Side

See Figures 231 through 234.

> ⁑⁑ **WARNING**
>
> **The magnetic timing wheels must not come in contact with magnets (pickup tools, trays, etc.) or any other strong magnetic field. This will destroy the timing wheels ability to correctly relay camshaft position to the camshaft position sensor.**

1. Disconnect and isolate the negative battery cable.
2. Remove the air inlet hose and upper intake manifold.
3. Cover the open intake ports to prevent debris from entering the engine.
4. Remove the insulator from the LH cylinder head cover.
5. Disengage the clips, remove the make-up air tube from the left cylinder head cover and reposition the transmission breather hose.

➡**Mark the variable valve timing solenoid connectors with a paint pen or equivalent so that they may be reinstalled in their original locations.**

6. Disconnect the electrical connectors from the left variable valve timing solenoids.
7. Disengage two starter wire harness retainers from the left cylinder head cover.
8. Mark the variable valve timing solenoids with a paint pen or equivalent so that they may be reinstalled in their original locations.
9. Remove the variable valve timing solenoids.
10. Disengage one main wire harness retainer from the left cylinder head cover.
11. Disconnect the left Camshaft Position (CMP) sensor.
12. Disengage one main wire harness retainer from the cylinder head cover and one main wire harness retainer from the cylinder head cover mounting stud.

➡**Mark the sensors so they can be installed in their original locations.**

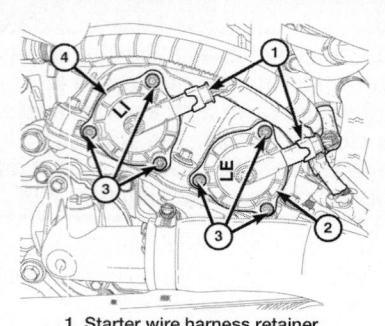

1. Starter wire harness retainer
2. Variable valve timing solenoid
3. Bolt
4. Variable valve timing solenoid

2726797

Fig. 231 Removing the variable valve timing solenoids

13. Remove the camshaft position sensor.
14. Disengage two injection/ignition harness retainers from the left cylinder head cover.
15. Remove the ignition coils.
16. Loosen ten cylinder head cover mounting bolts and two studbolts and remove the cylinder head cover.
17. Remove and discard the cylinder head cover gasket.
18. The spark plug tube seals can be reused if not damaged.

➡**Do not use oil based liquids, wire brushes, abrasive wheels or metal scrapers to clean the engine gasket surfaces. Use only isopropyl (rubbing) alcohol, along with plastic or wooden scrapers. Improper gasket surface preparation may result in engine fluid leakage.**

19. Remove all residual sealant from the cylinder head, timing chain cover and cylinder head cover mating surfaces.

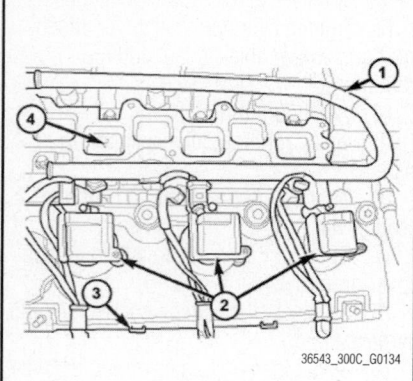

36543_300C_G0134

Fig. 230 Cylinder head cover removal—3.5L engine

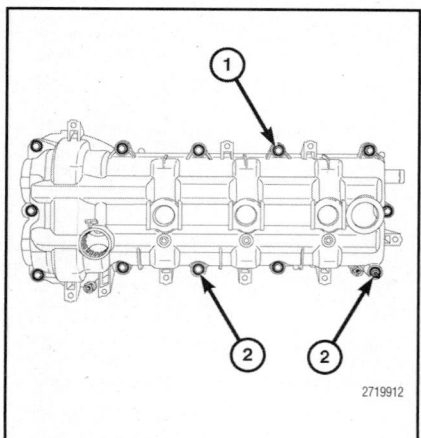

2719912

Fig. 232 Removing the cylinder head cover mounting bolts (1) and stud bolts (2)

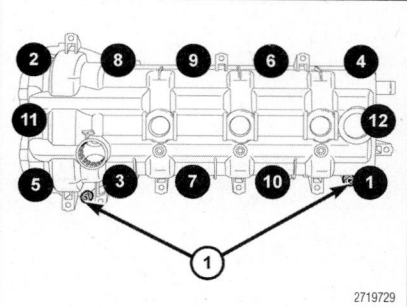

Fig. 233 Identifying the cylinder head bolt installation sequence

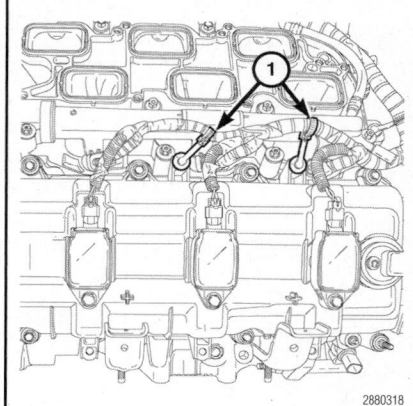

Fig. 234 Engaging the injection/ignition harness retainers

To install:

20. Install the cylinder head cover gasket.

➡ **The spark plug tube seals can be reused if not damaged.**

21. If required, install new spark plug tube seals in the cylinder head cover:

a. Lubricate the spark plug tube seal inner and outer diameters with clean engine oil.

b. Place the spark plug tube seal on the Cam Sensor/Spark Plug Tube Seal Installer.

c. Push the seal into the cylinder head cover until the base of the seal is seated.

d. Remove the tool.

22. Clean the timing engine timing cover, cylinder head and cylinder head cover mating surfaces with isopropyl alcohol in preparation for sealant application.

✳✳ WARNING

Engine assembly requires the use of a unique sealant that is compatible with engine oil. Using a sealant other than Mopar® Threebond Engine RTV

Sealant may result in engine fluid leakage.

✳✳ WARNING

Following the application of Mopar® Threebond Engine RTV Sealant to the gasket surfaces, the components must be assembled within 20 minutes and the attaching fasteners must be tightened to specification within 45 minutes. Prolonged exposure to the air prior to assembly may result in engine fluid leakage.

23. Apply a 2 to 3 mm wide bead of Mopar® Threebond Engine RTV Sealant to the two engine timing cover to cylinder head T-joints.

24. Align the locator pins to the cylinder head and install the cylinder head cover.

25. Tighten the cylinder head cover bolts and double ended studs in the sequence shown to 9 ft. lbs. (12 Nm).

26. If removed, install the spark plugs.

27. Install the ignition coils.

28. Engage two injection/ignition harness retainers to the left cylinder head cover.

29. Refer to the markings made at disassembly and install the variable valve timing solenoids in their original locations.

30. Connect the electrical connectors to the left variable valve timing solenoids.

31. Engage two starter wire harness retainers to the left cylinder head cover.

32. Engage one main wire harness retainer to the left cylinder head cover.

➡ **If both RH and LH CMP sensors where removed, install them into their original locations.**

33. Install the camshaft position sensor.

34. Connect the electrical connector to the left Camshaft Position (CMP) sensor.

35. Engage one main wire harness retainer to the cylinder head cover and one main wire harness retainer to the cylinder head cover mounting stud.

36. Install the make-up air tube to the left cylinder head cover and engage the clips to the transmission breather hose.

37. Install the insulator to the two alignment posts on top of the LH cylinder head cover.

38. Install the upper intake manifold, support brackets and air inlet hose.

39. Connect the negative battery cable and tighten nut to 45 inch lbs. (5 Nm).

➡ **The Cam/Crank Variation Relearn procedure must be performed using the scan tool anytime there has been a**

repair/replacement made to a powertrain system, for example: flywheel, valvetrain, camshaft and/or crankshaft sensors or components.

Right Side

See Figures 235 through 241.

✳✳ WARNING

The magnetic timing wheels must not come in contact with magnets (pickup tools, trays, etc.) or any other strong magnetic field. This will destroy the timing wheels ability to correctly relay camshaft position to the camshaft position sensor.

1. Disconnect and isolate the negative battery cable.

2. Remove the air inlet hose and upper intake manifold.

3. Cover the open intake ports to prevent debris from entering the engine.

➡ **Mark the variable valve timing solenoid connectors with a paint pen or equivalent so that they may be reinstalled in their original locations.**

4. Disconnect the electrical connectors from the variable valve timing solenoids on the right cylinder head.

5. Disengage the starter harness to main harness retainer.

6. Disengage two starter wire harness retainers from the right cylinder head cover.

7. Mark the variable valve timing solenoids with a paint pen or equivalent so that they may be reinstalled in their original locations.

8. Remove the variable valve timing solenoids.

9. Disengage four main wire harness retainers from the right cylinder head cover.

10. Disconnect the electrical connector from the right Camshaft Position (CMP) sensor.

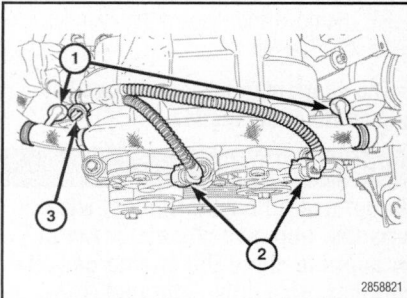

Fig. 235 Disconnecting the electrical connectors (2), starter harness to main harness retainer (3) and starter wire harness retainers

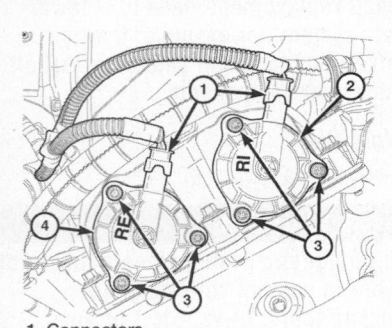

1. Connectors
2. Variable valve timing solenoid (intake)
3. Bolts
4. Variable valve timing solenoid (exhaust)

2731407

Fig. 236 Removing the variable valve timing solenoids

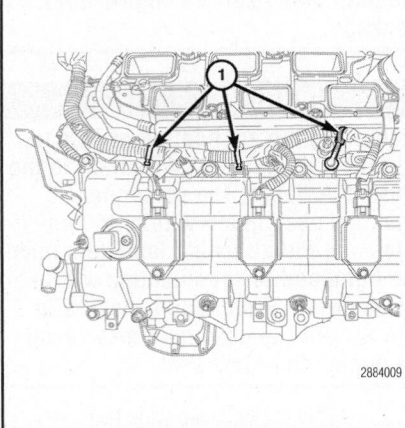

2884009

Fig. 237 Disengaging the injection/ignition harness retainers

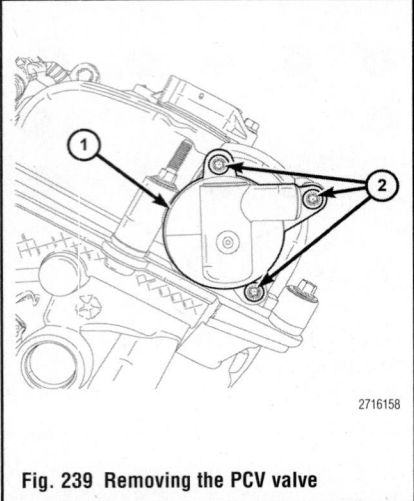

2716158

Fig. 239 Removing the PCV valve

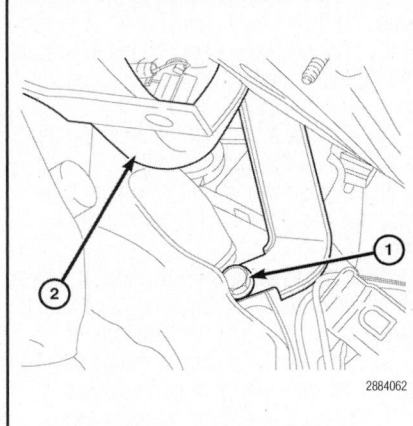

2884062

Fig. 238 Removing the upper transmission to engine bolt (1) and repositioning the transmission oil level indicator tube (2)

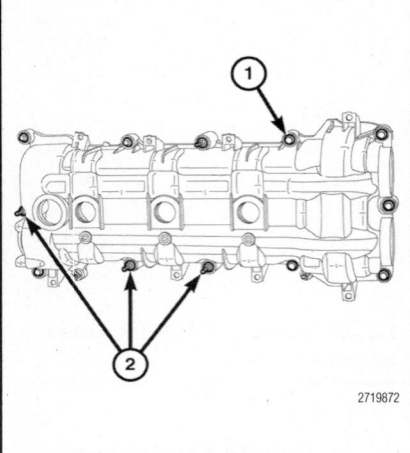

2719872

Fig. 240 Removing the cylinder head cover mounting bolts (1) and studbolts (2)

11. Disengage the main wire harness retainer from the right cylinder head cover mounting stud.

➡ **If removing both RH and LH CMP sensors, mark the sensors so they can be installed in their original locations.**

12. Remove the camshaft position sensor.

13. Disengage three injection/ignition harness retainers from the right cylinder head cover.

➡ **The LH ignition coils are shown, the RH ignition coils are similar.**

14. Remove the ignition coils.
15. Raise and support the vehicle.
16. Loosen the bolt securing the transmission fluid level indicator tube to the transmission housing.
17. Remove the upper transmission to engine bolt and reposition the transmission oil level indicator tube.
18. Lower the vehicle.
19. Remove the PCV valve.
20. Loosen nine cylinder head cover mounting bolts and three studbolts and remove the cylinder head cover.
21. Remove and discard the cylinder head cover gasket.

➡ **The spark plug tube seals can be reused if not damaged.**

✳✳ WARNING

Do not use oil based liquids, wire brushes, abrasive wheels or metal scrapers to clean the engine gasket surfaces. Use only isopropyl (rubbing) alcohol, along with plastic or wooden scrapers. Improper gasket surface preparation may result in engine fluid leakage.

22. Remove all residual sealant from the cylinder head, timing chain cover and cylinder head cover mating surfaces

To install:

23. Install the cylinder head cover gasket.
24. The spark plug tube seals can be reused if not damaged.
25. If required, install new spark plug tube seals in the cylinder head cover:
   a. Lubricate the spark plug tube seal inner and outer diameters with clean engine oil.
   b. Place the spark plug tube seal on the Cam Sensor/Spark Plug Tube Seal Installer.
   c. Push the seal into the cylinder head cover until the base of the seal is seated.
   d. Remove the tool.
26. Clean the timing engine timing cover, cylinder head and cylinder head

cover mating surfaces with isopropyl alcohol in preparation for sealant application.

✳✳ WARNING

Engine assembly requires the use of a unique sealant that is compatible with engine oil. Using a sealant other than Mopar® Threebond Engine RTV Sealant may result in engine fluid leakage.

✳✳ WARNING

Following the application of Mopar® Threebond Engine RTV Sealant to the gasket surfaces, the components must be assembled within 20 minutes and the attaching fasteners must be tightened to specification within 45 minutes. Prolonged exposure to the air prior to assembly may result in engine fluid leakage.

27. Apply a 2 to 3 mm wide bead of Mopar® Threebond Engine RTV Sealant to the two engine timing cover to cylinder head T-joints.

28. Align the locator pins to the cylinder head and install the cylinder head cover.

29. Tighten the cylinder head cover bolts and double ended studs in the sequence shown to 9 ft. lbs. (12 Nm).

30. If removed, install the spark plugs.

31. Install the ignition coils.

32. Engage three injection/ignition harness retainers to the right cylinder head cover.

33. Refer to the markings made at disassembly and install the variable valve timing solenoids in their original locations.

34. Connect the electrical connectors to the variable valve timing solenoids on the right cylinder head.

35. Engage two starter wire harness retainers to the right cylinder head cover.

36. Engage the starter harness to main harness retainer.

37. Engage four main wire harness retainers to the right cylinder head cover.

➡ **If both RH and LH CMP sensors where removed, install them into their original locations.**

38. Install the camshaft position sensor.

39. Connect the electrical connector to the right Camshaft Position (CMP) sensor.

40. Engage the main wire harness retainer to the right cylinder head cover mounting stud.

41. Install the PCV valve.

42. Raise and support the vehicle.

43. Install the transmission oil level indicator tube with the upper transmission to engine bolt tightened to 41 ft. lbs. (55 Nm).

44. Install the bolt securing the transmission fluid level indicator tube to the transmission housing and tighten to 9 ft. lbs. (12 Nm).

45. Lower the vehicle.

46. If removed, install the insulator to the two alignment posts on top of the LH cylinder head cover.

47. Install the upper intake manifold, support brackets and air inlet hose.

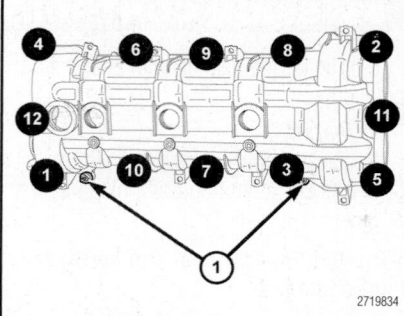

Fig. 241 Identifying the cylinder head cover bolt and double ended stud installation sequence

48. Connect the negative battery cable and tighten nut to 45 inch lbs. (5 Nm.

➡ **The Cam/Crank Variation Relearn procedure must be performed using the scan tool anytime there has been a repair/replacement made to a powertrain system, for example: flywheel, valvetrain, camshaft and/or crankshaft sensors or components.**

5.7L Engine

See Figure 242.

1. Disconnect negative battery cable.
2. Disconnect ignition coil connector.
3. Remove ignition coil retaining bolts.
4. Remove ignition coil.
5. Remove cylinder head cover retaining bolts.
   a. Remove cylinder head cover.

➡ **The gasket may be used again, provided no cuts, tears, or deformation have occurred.**

To install:

⁂ **WARNING**

Do not use harsh cleaners to clean the cylinder head covers. Severe damage to covers may occur. Do not allow other components including the wire harness to rest on or against the

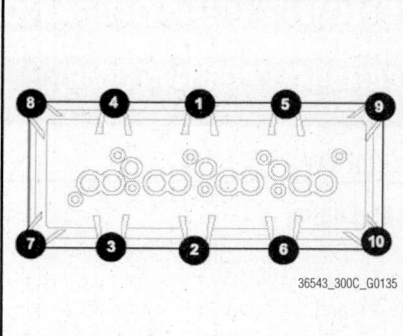

Fig. 242 Cylinder head cover tightening sequence—5.7L engine

engine cylinder head cover. Prolonged contact with other objects may wear a hole in the cylinder head cover.

6. Clean cylinder head cover and both sealing surface. Inspect and replace gasket as necessary.

7. Install cylinder head cover and hand start all fasteners. Verify that all double ended studs are in the correct location.

8. Tighten cylinder head cover bolts and double ended studs to 70 inch lbs. (8 Nm). in the sequence shown.

9. Before installing coil(s), apply dielectric grease to inside of spark plug boots.

10. Install ignition coils.

11. Tighten fasteners to 62 inch lbs. (7 Nm).

12. Connect ignition coil electrical connectors.

13. Install PCV hose.

14. Install the engine cover.

15. Connect the negative battery cable.

VALVE LASH

ADJUSTMENT

These engines use hydraulic lifters to take up the free-play in the valve train system, therefore no lash adjustments are necessary.

ENGINE PERFORMANCE & EMISSION CONTROLS

CAMSHAFT POSITION (CMP) SENSOR

LOCATION

3.6L Engine

The Camshaft Position (CMP) sensors are located at the rear of the cylinder head covers and are bolted to the cylinder head.

REMOVAL & INSTALLATION

3.6L Engine

See Figure 243.

☀ WARNING

The magnetic timing wheels must not come in contact with magnets (pickup tools, trays, etc.) or any other strong magnetic field. This will destroy the timing wheels ability to correctly relay camshaft position to the camshaft position sensor.

1. Disconnect and isolate the negative battery cable.
2. If removing the left CMP sensor, first remove the air inlet hose and upper intake manifold.

➡ **The right CMP sensor is shown, the left CMP sensor is similar. If removing both right and left CMP sensors, mark the sensors so they can be installed in their original locations.**

3. Disconnect the electrical connector from the CMP sensor.
4. Loosen the sensor mounting bolt.
5. Pull the sensor and mounting bolt from the cylinder head cover.

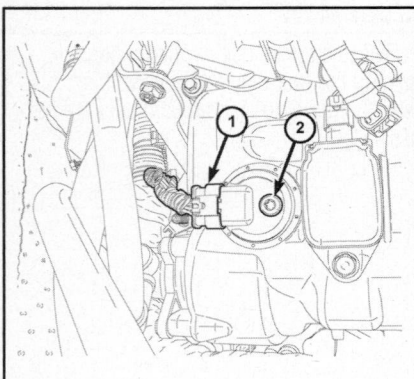

Fig. 243 Disconnecting the CMP electrical connector (1) and loosening the mounting bolt (2)

2726289

6. The O-ring seal can be reused if not damaged.

To install:

7. Clean out the camshaft position (CMP) sensor mounting bolt hole in cylinder head.

➡ **The CMP sensor seal can be reused if not damaged.**

8. If required, install a new CMP sensor seal in the cylinder head cover:
    a. Lubricate the CMP sensor seal inner and outer diameters with clean engine oil.
    b. Place the CMP sensor seal on the Cam Sensor/Spark Plug Tube Seal Installer.
    c. Push the seal into the cylinder head cover until the base of the seal is seated.
    d. Remove the tool.

➡ **A properly installed CMP sensor seal will have a 0.06 - 0.08 inch (1.5 - 2.0 mm) gap between the cylinder head cover and the seal upper flange.**

9. The sensor mounting bolt O-ring can be reused if not damaged.
10. Apply a small amount of engine oil to the sensor mounting bolt O-ring.

➡ **If both right and left CMP sensors where removed, install them into their original locations.**

11. Install the CMP sensor to the cylinder head. Tighten the mounting bolt to 80 inch lbs. (9 Nm).
12. Connect the electrical connector to the sensor.
13. If required, install the upper intake manifold and air inlet hose.
14. Connect the negative battery cable and tighten nut to 45 inch lbs. (5 Nm).

➡ **The Cam/Crank Variation Relearn procedure must be performed using the scan tool anytime there has been a repair/replacement made to a powertrain system, for example: flywheel, valvetrain, camshaft and/or crankshaft sensors or components.**

5.7L Engine

See Figure 244.

1. Disconnect and isolate the negative battery cable.
2. Lift the engine cover retaining grommets off the ball studs and remove the engine cover.

3. Disconnect the electrical connector at the Camshaft Position (CMP) sensor.
4. Remove the CMP sensor retaining bolt.
    a. Using a slight rotating motion, carefully remove the CMP sensor from the timing chain cover.
5. Check the condition of the sensor O-ring, replace if necessary.

To install:

☀ WARNING

Install the camshaft position (CMP) sensor utilizing a slight rotating (side-to-side) motion. Make sure the CMP sensor is fully seated. Do not drive the CMP sensor into the bore with the mounting screw. This may cause the CMP sensor to be incorrectly seated causing a faulty signal or no signal at all.

☀ WARNING

Before tightening the sensor mounting bolt, be sure the sensor is completely flush to the timing chain cover. If the sensor is not flush, damage to sensor mounting tang may result.

➡ **Lubricate the CMP sensor O-ring with clean engine oil to aid in the installation.**

6. Install the CMP sensor into the timing chain cover while using a slight rotating motion.
7. Install the retaining bolt and tighten to 9 ft. lbs. (12 Nm).

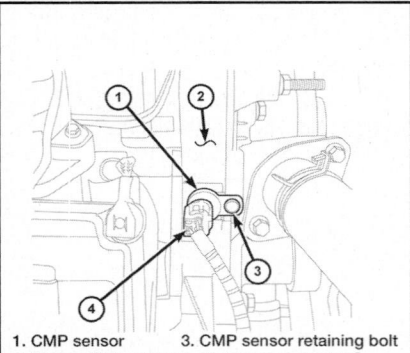

1. CMP sensor   3. CMP sensor retaining bolt
2. Timing chain cover 4. Electrical connector

2999

Fig. 244 Removing the CMP sensor—5.7L engine

8. Connect the CMP sensor electrical connector.

9. Position the engine cover and secure the retaining grommets onto the ball studs.

10. Connect the negative battery cable and tighten nut to 45 inch lbs. (5 Nm).

CRANKSHAFT POSITION (CKP) SENSOR

LOCATION

See Figures 245 and 246.

For the 3.6L engine, the Crankshaft Position (CKP) sensor is mounted into the right rear side of the cylinder block. For the other engines, refer to the accompanying illustrations.

REMOVAL & INSTALLATION

2.7L & 3.5L Engine

See Figure 245.

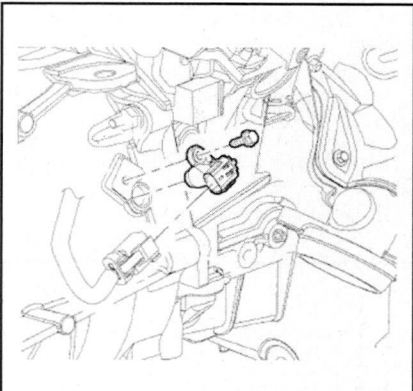

Fig. 245 Crankshaft Position (CKP) sensor location—2.7L and 3.5L engine

36543_300C_G0141

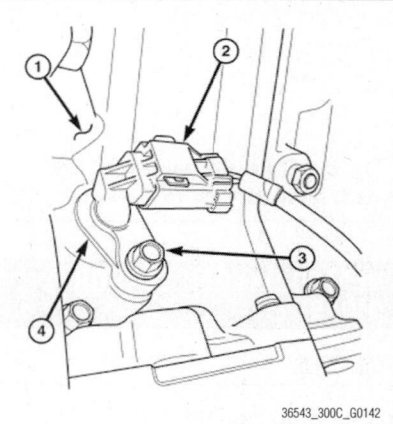

Fig. 246 Crankshaft Position (CKP) sensor location—5.7L engine

36543_300C_G0142

1. Disconnect negative battery cable.
2. Raise vehicle and support.
3. Unlock and disconnect the electrical connector.
4. Remove mounting bolt.
5. Remove sensor.

To install:

6. Install sensor.
7. Install mounting bolt and tighten to 106 inch lbs. (12 Nm).
   a. Connect the electrical connector and lock.
8. Lower vehicle.
9. Connect negative battery cable.

3.6L Engine

See Figures 247 and 248.

1. Disconnect and isolate the negative battery cable.
2. Raise and support the vehicle.
3. Remove the belly pan retainers and remove the belly pan.
4. Push back the heat shield from the crankshaft position (CKP) sensor.
5. Disconnect the electrical connector from the crankshaft position (CKP) sensor.
6. Remove the sensor mounting bolt.
7. Carefully twist the sensor from the cylinder block.
8. The CKP sensor O-ring can be reused if not damaged.

To install:

9. Apply a small amount of engine oil to the sensor O-ring.
10. Clean out the CKP sensor mounting bolt hole in the engine block.
11. Install the sensor into the engine block with a slight rocking and twisting motion.

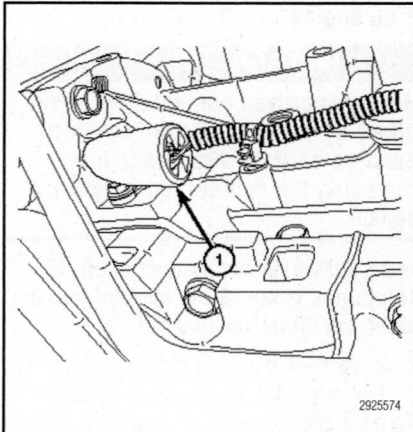

Fig. 247 Identifying the CKP sensor heat shield

2925574

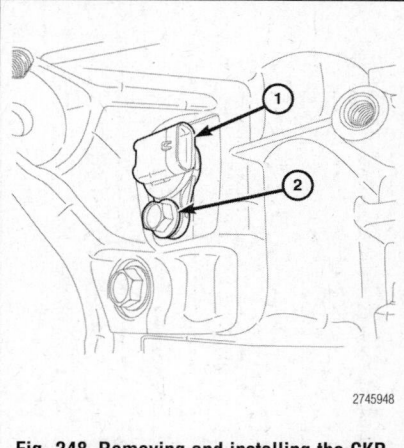

Fig. 248 Removing and installing the CKP sensor

2745948

✳✳ WARNING

Before tightening the CKP sensor mounting bolt, be sure the sensor is completely flush to the cylinder block. If the CKP sensor is not flush, damage to the sensor mounting tang may result.

12. Install the mounting bolt and tighten to 9 ft. lbs. (12 Nm).
13. Connect the CKP sensor electrical connector.
14. Position the heat shield over the CKP sensor.
15. Position the belly pan and install the retainers.
16. Lower the vehicle.
17. Connect the negative battery cable and tighten nut to 45 inch lbs. (5 Nm).

➡The Cam/Crank Variation Relearn procedure must be performed using the scan tool anytime there has been a repair/replacement made to a powertrain system, for example: flywheel, valvetrain, camshaft and/or crankshaft sensors or components.

5.7L Engine

See Figure 249.

1. If equipped with AWD (All Wheel Drive) disconnect and isolate negative battery cable.
2. Raise vehicle.
3. If equipped with AWD (All Wheel Drive) remove starter motor.
4. Disconnect CKP electrical connector at sensor.
5. Remove CKP mounting bolt.
6. Carefully twist sensor from cylinder block.
7. Remove sensor from vehicle.

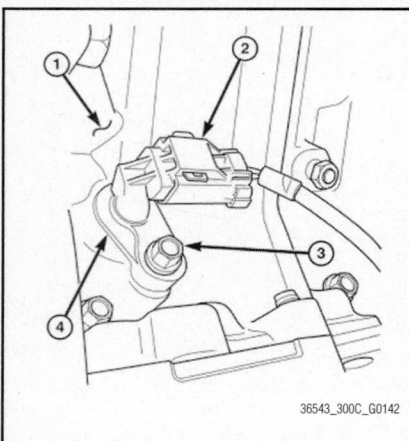

Fig. 249 Crankshaft Position (CKP) sensor location—5.7L engine

8. Check condition of sensor O-ring

To install:

9. Clean out machined hole in engine block.

10. Apply a small amount of engine oil to sensor O-ring.

11. Install sensor into engine block with a slight rocking and twisting action.

➡**Before tightening sensor mounting bolt, be sure sensor is completely flush to cylinder block. If sensor is not flush, damage to sensor mounting tang may result.**

12. Install mounting bolt and tighten to 106 inch lbs. (12 Nm).

13. Connect electrical connector to sensor.

14. Lower vehicle.

ENGINE COOLANT TEMPERATURE (ECT) SENSOR

LOCATION

3.6L Engine

The Engine Coolant Temperature (ECT) sensor on the 3.6L engine is installed into a water jacket at rear of the cylinder head on the left side of the engine.

REMOVAL & INSTALLATION

2.7L & 3.5L Engine

See Figures 250 and 251.

1. Disconnect negative battery cable.
2. Partially drain cooling system.
3. Disconnect the electrical connector.
4. Remove engine coolant sensor.

To install:

5. Apply thread sealant to sensor threads.

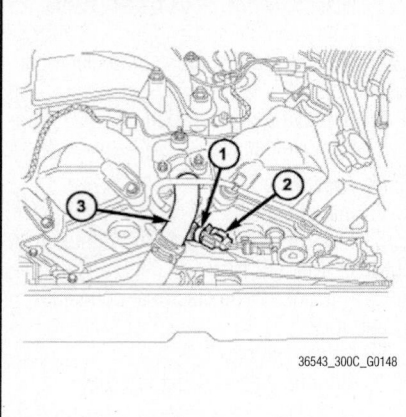

Fig. 250 Engine Coolant Temperature (ECT) sensor location—2.7L engine

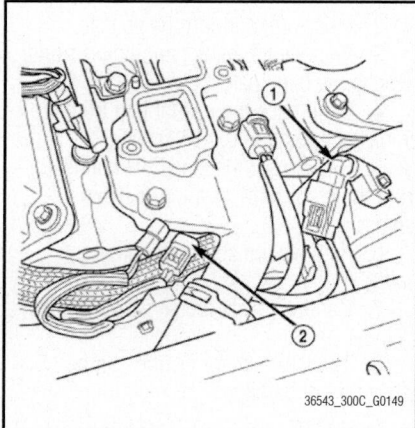

Fig. 251 Engine Coolant Temperature (ECT) sensor location—3.5L engine

6. Install Engine Coolant Temperature (ECT) sensor.

7. Tighten sensor to 20 ft. lbs. (28 Nm).

8. Connect electrical connector to Engine Coolant Temperature (ECT) sensor.

3.6L Engine

❄❄ CAUTION

Hot, pressurized coolant can cause injury by scalding. Cooling system must be partially drained before removing the coolant temperature sensor.

➡**Do not waste reusable coolant. If solution is clean, drain coolant into a clean container for reuse.**

1. Partially drain the cooling system.
2. Disconnect the electrical connector from the sensor.
3. Remove the sensor from the cylinder head.

To install:

4. Apply MOPAR® thread sealant with PFTE part number 04318034 to sensor threads.

5. Install sensor to cylinder head.

6. Tighten sensor to 8 ft. lbs. (11 Nm) torque.

7. Connect electrical connector to sensor.

8. Replace any lost engine coolant

5.7L Engine

See Figure 252.

1. Partially drain the cooling system.
2. Remove accessory drive belt.
3. Carefully unbolt air conditioning compressor from front of engine. Do not disconnect any A/C hoses from compressor. Temporarily support compressor to gain access to ECT sensor.

4. Disconnect electrical connector from sensor.

5. Remove sensor from cylinder block.

To install:

6. Apply thread sealant to sensor threads.

7. Install ECT sensor to engine.

8. Tighten sensor to 98 inch lbs. (11 Nm).

9. Connect electrical connector to ECT sensor.

10. Fill the cooling system.

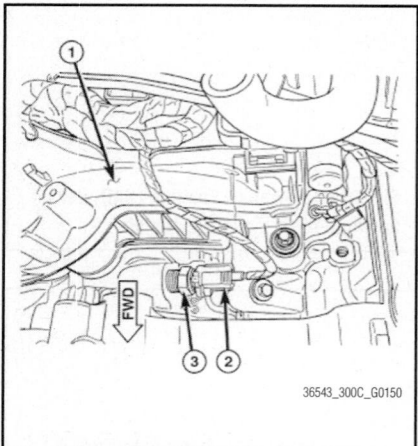

Fig. 252 Engine Coolant Temperature (ECT) sensor location—5.7L engine

HEATED OXYGEN SENSOR (HO2S)

LOCATION

Except 3.6L Engine

See Figure 253.

Refer to the accompanying illustration.

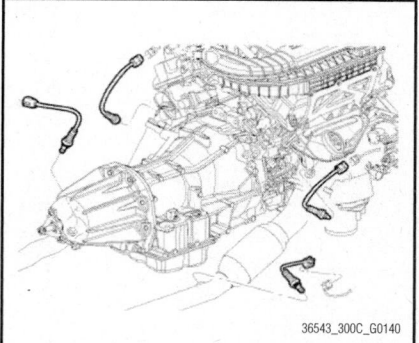

Fig. 253 Heated Oxygen Sensor (HO2S) location

3.6L Engine

See Figure 254.

The engine is equipped with four heated oxygen sensors:
• The right upstream oxygen sensor (1) is referred to as the 1/1 sensor.
• The right downstream oxygen sensor (2) is referred to as the 1/2 sensor.
• The left upstream oxygen sensor (4) is referred to as the 2/1 sensor.
• The left downstream oxygen sensor (3) is referred to as the 2/2 sensor.

✳✳ CAUTION

The exhaust pipes and catalytic converter become very hot during engine operation. Allow the engine to cool before removing the oxygen sensor.

REMOVAL & INSTALLATION

2.7L & 3.5L Engines

See Figure 255.

➡The engines uses two heated oxygen sensors, one in each exhaust manifold.

✳✳ CAUTION

Never apply any type of grease to the oxygen sensor electrical connector, or attempt any soldering of the sensor wiring harness. The exhaust manifold, exhaust pipes and catalytic converter become very hot during engine operation. Allow the engine to cool before removing the oxygen sensor. When disconnecting the sensor electrical connector, do not pull directly on the wire going into sensor.

1. Remove the negative battery cable.
2. Raise vehicle and support.
3. Disconnect the heated oxygen sensor electrical connector.
4. Use a socket such as Snap-On® YA8875 or a crow foot wrench to remove oxygen sensor.

To install:

➡When replacing an O2 Sensor, the PCM RAM memory must be cleared, either by disconnecting the PCM C-1 connector or momentarily disconnecting the Battery negative terminal. The NGC learns the characteristics of each

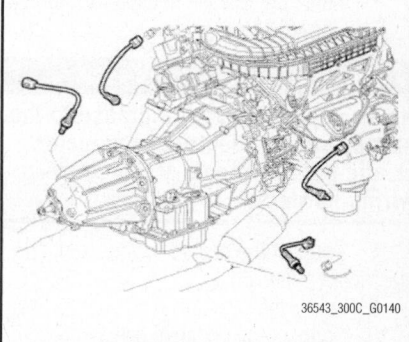

Fig. 255 Heated Oxygen Sensor (HO2S) location

O2 heater element and these old values should be cleared when installing a new O2 sensor. The customer may experience driveability issues if this is not performed.

5. After removing the sensor, the exhaust manifold threads must be cleaned with an 18 mm X 1.5 + 6E tap. If reusing the original sensor, coat the sensor threads with an anti-seize compound such as Loctite 771- 64 or equivalent. New sensors have compound on the threads and do not require an additional coating. Tighten the sensor to 30 ft. lbs. (41 Nm).
6. Connect the heated oxygen sensor electrical connector.
7. Lower vehicle.
8. Install the negative battery cable.

3.6L Engine

1. Disconnect and isolate the negative battery cable.
2. Raise and support the vehicle.

✳✳ WARNING

When disconnecting the oxygen sensor electrical connector, do not pull directly on the wire going into the sensor. The sensor wiring can be damaged resulting in sensor failure.

3. Disconnect the heated oxygen sensor electrical connector.
4. Remove the oxygen sensor.
5. Clean the exhaust pipe threads using an appropriate tap.

To install:

6. If reinstalling the original oxygen sensor, coat the sensor threads with an anti-seize compound such as Loctite® 771- 64 or equivalent. New sensors have compound on the threads and do not require an additional coating. Do Not add any additional anti-seize compound to the threads of a new oxygen sensor.

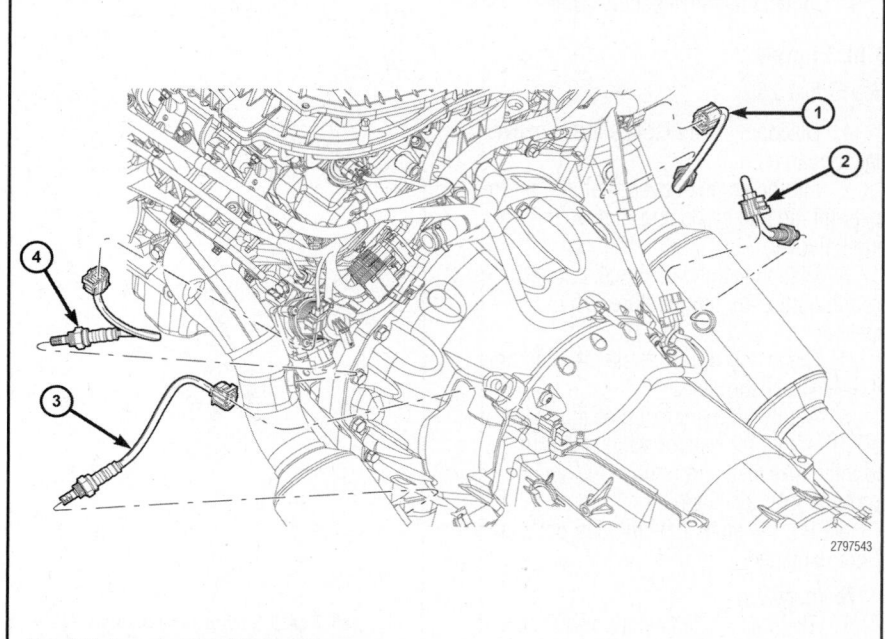

Fig. 254 Locating the Oxygen Sensors

7. Install the oxygen sensor and tighten to 37 ft. lbs. (50 Nm).

❋❋ WARNING

Never apply any type of grease to the oxygen sensor electrical connector, or attempt any repair of the sensor wiring harness.

8. Connect the heated oxygen sensor electrical connector.

9. Lower the vehicle.

10. Connect the negative battery cable and tighten nut to 45 inch lbs. (5 Nm).

INTAKE AIR TEMPERATURE (IAT) SENSOR

LOCATION

See Figures 256 through 258.

Refer to the accompanying illustrations.

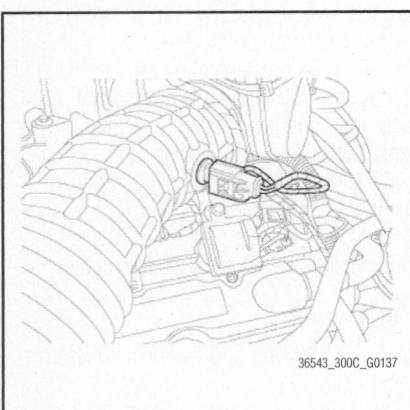

Fig. 256 Intake Air Temperature (IAT) sensor location—2.7L engine

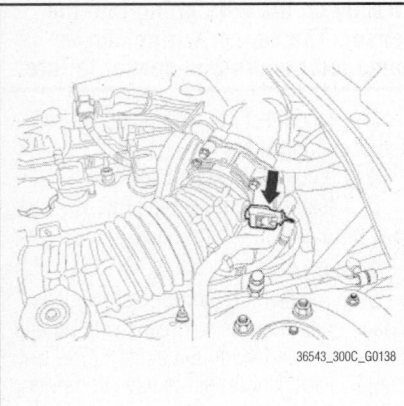

Fig. 257 Intake Air Temperature (IAT) sensor location—3.5L engine

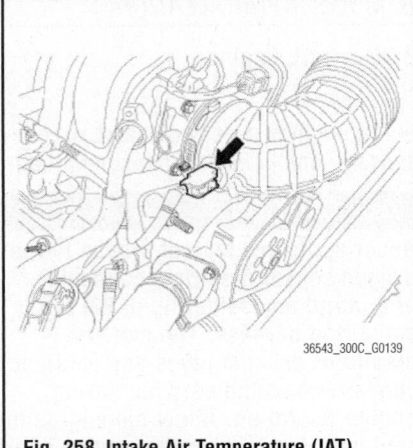

Fig. 258 Intake Air Temperature (IAT) sensor location—5.7L engine

REMOVAL & INSTALLATION

2.7L & 5.7L Engines

See Figures 256 through 258.

1. Disconnect negative battery cable.
2. Unlock the electrical connector.
3. Remove the electrical connector from sensor.
4. Note the orientation of the sensor.
5. Remove the sensor from air inlet hose.

To install:

6. Install the sensor. Rotate for proper orientation.
7. Insure proper orientation of the sensor.
8. Install the electrical connector and lock.
9. Connect negative battery cable.

3.6L Engine

See Figure 259.

1. Disconnect and isolate the negative battery cable.
2. Lift the engine cover retaining grommets off the ball studs and remove the engine cover.
3. Disconnect the electrical connector from the Inlet Air Temperature (IAT) sensor.
4. Clean any dirt from the air inlet tube at the IAT sensor base.
5. Gently lift the small plastic release tab (3), rotate the sensor about 1/4 turn counterclockwise and remove the sensor from the inlet air hose.
6. The IAT sensor O-ring can be reused if not damaged.

To install:

7. The Inlet Air Temperature (IAT) sensor O-ring seal can be reused if not damaged.

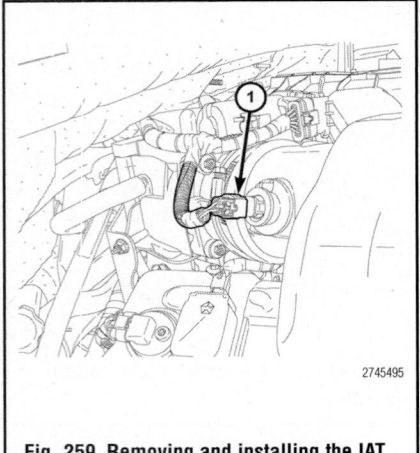

Fig. 259 Removing and installing the IAT sensor

8. Clean the IAT sensor mounting hole in the air inlet hose.
9. Install the IAT sensor into the air inlet hose and rotate clockwise until the release tab engages.
10. Install the electrical connector to the IAT sensor.
11. Position the engine cover and secure the retaining grommets onto the ball studs.
12. Connect the negative battery cable and tighten nut to 45 inch lbs. (5 Nm).

KNOCK SENSOR (KS)

LOCATION

See Figures 260 through 262.

Refer to the accompanying illustrations.

REMOVAL & INSTALLATION

2.7L Engine

See Figure 260.

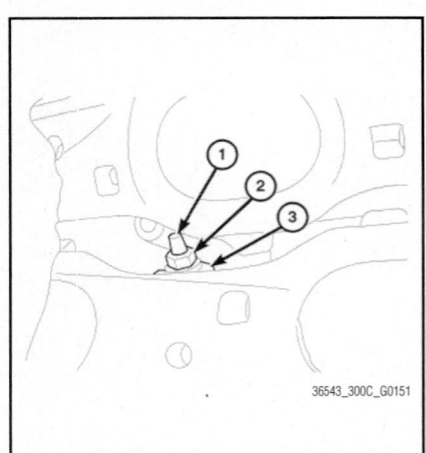

Fig. 260 Knock Sensor (KS) location (1)— 2.7L engine

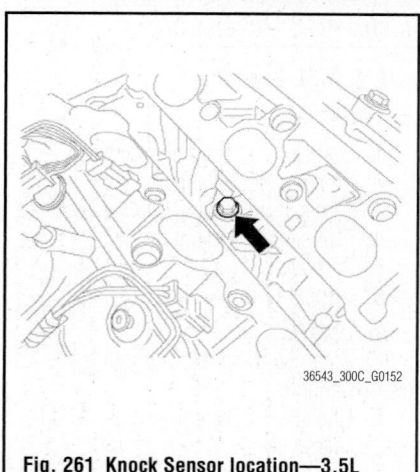

Fig. 261 Knock Sensor location—3.5L engine

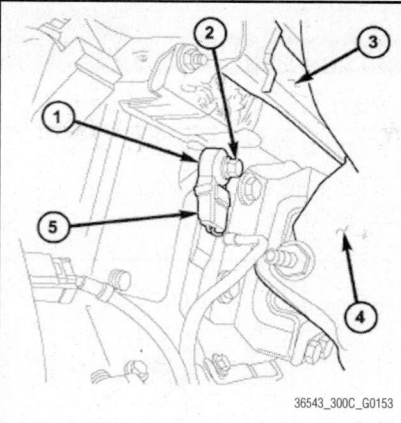

Fig. 262 Knock Sensor (KS) location—5.7L engine

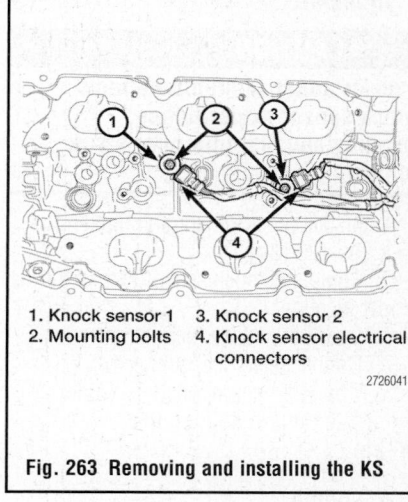

1. Knock sensor 1   3. Knock sensor 2
2. Mounting bolts   4. Knock sensor electrical connectors

Fig. 263 Removing and installing the KS

1. Drain cooling system.
2. Disconnect and isolate the negative battery cable.
3. Remove lower intake manifold.
4. Remove radiator upper hose at water housing outlet tube.
5. Remove heater hose from water housing outlet tube at rear of engine.
6. Disconnect water housing outlet tube from retaining clip at rear of engine.
   a. Disconnect electrical connector from coolant temperature sensor.
7. Remove 4 bolts attaching water housing outlet tube to cylinder heads.
   a. Disconnect electrical connector from knock sensor.
   b. Reposition the water housing outlet tube and remove nut from knock sensor mounting stud.
8. Remove knock sensor from engine block.

To install:

❊❊ CAUTION

Over or under tightening effects knock sensor performance resulting in possible improper spark control.

9. Install knock sensor and nut onto stud.
10. Tighten knock sensor nut to 11 ft. lbs. (15 Nm).
11. Attach electrical connector to knock sensor.
12. Position the water housing outlet tube to the cylinder heads and loosely install four bolts.
13. Attach water housing outlet tube to the retaining clip at rear of engine.
14. Tighten the four bolts to 30 inch lbs. (3 Nm).
15. Connect electrical connector to the coolant temperature sensor.

16. Install heater hose to water housing outlet tube at rear of engine.
17. Install radiator upper hose to water housing outlet tube.
18. Install intake manifold.
19. Connect negative battery cable, tighten nut to 45 inch lbs. (5 Nm).
20. Fill cooling system.
21. Operate engine until it reaches normal operating temperature. Check cooling system for correct fluid levels.

3.6L Engine

See Figure 263.

➡**The forward sensor is known to the powertrain control module (PCM) as knock sensor 1. The rear sensor is known to the PCM as knock sensor 2.**

1. Perform the fuel pressure release procedure.
2. Disconnect and isolate the negative battery cable.
3. Drain the cooling system.
4. Remove the air cleaner housing assembly, upper and lower intake manifolds and the oil filter housing.
5. Remove the knock sensor electrical connector.

➡**There may be a foam strip on the bolt threads. This foam is used only to retain the bolts to the sensors for plant assembly. It is not used as a sealant. Do not apply any adhesive, sealant or thread locking compound to these bolts.**

6. Remove the retaining bolt and knock sensor 1 or knock sensor 2.

To install:

7. The forward sensor is known to the powertrain control module (PCM) as knock sensor 1. The rear sensor is known to the PCM as knock sensor 2.

8. Thoroughly clean the knock sensor mounting holes.

➡**Over or under tightening the sensor mounting bolts will affect knock sensor performance, possibly causing improper spark control. Always use the specified torque when installing the knock sensors. The torque specification for the knock sensor bolt is less than the typical 8 mm bolt.**

➡**There may be a foam strip on the bolt threads. This foam is used only to retain the bolts to the sensors for plant assembly. It is not used as a sealant. Do not apply any adhesive, sealant or thread locking compound to these bolts.**

9. Install knock sensor 1 or knock sensor 2 and retaining bolt. Tighten the retaining bolt to 16 ft. lbs. (22 Nm).
10. Connect the electrical connector.
11. Install the oil filter housing, upper and lower intake manifolds and air cleaner housing assembly.
12. If removed, install the oil filter and fill the engine crankcase with the proper oil to the correct level.
13. Connect the negative battery cable and tighten nut to 45 inch lbs. (5 Nm).
14. Fill the cooling system.
15. Operate the engine until it reaches normal operating temperature. Check cooling system for correct fluid level

3.5L Engine

See Figure 261.

1. Disconnect and isolate the negative battery cable.
2. Remove the upper intake manifold.
3. Disconnect the electrical connector.
   a. Remove the knock sensor.

To install:

❉❉ CAUTION

Over or under tightening effects knock sensor performance, possibly causing improper spark control.

4. Install knock sensor and tighten to 15 ft. lbs. (20 Nm).

5. Route the knock sensor wire in the proper location.

6. Install the intake manifold.

7. Connect electrical connector.

8. Connect negative battery cable and tighten nut to 45 inch lbs. (5 Nm).

5.7L Engine

See Figure 262.

➡**Two knock sensors are used. Each sensor is bolted to the outside of cylinder block below the exhaust manifold.**

1. Disconnect and isolate the negative battery cable.

2. Raise vehicle.

3. Disconnect knock sensor electrical connector.

4. Remove sensor mounting bolt. Note foam strip on bolt threads. This foam is used only to retain the bolts to sensors for plant assembly. It is not used as a sealant. Do not apply any adhesive, sealant or thread locking compound to these bolts.

5. Remove sensor from engine.

To install:

❉❉ CAUTION

Over or under tightening the sensor mounting bolts will affect knock sensor performance, possibly causing improper spark control.

6. .Install knock sensor into cylinder block.

➡**The foam strip used on bolt threads is used only to retain the bolts to sensors for plant assembly. It is not used as a sealant. Do not apply any adhesive, sealant or thread locking compound to these bolts.**

7. Install and tighten mounting bolt to 15 ft. lbs. (20 Nm).

8. Install electrical connector to sensor.

9. Connect negative battery cable and tighten nut to 45 inch lbs. (5 Nm).

MANIFOLD ABSOLUTE PRESSURE (MAP) SENSOR

LOCATION

See Figures 264 through 266.

Refer to the accompanying illustrations.

36543_300C_G0154

Fig. 264 Manifold Absolute Pressure (MAP) sensor location—2.7L engine

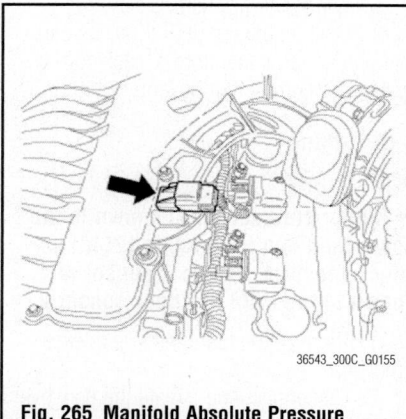

36543_300C_G0155

Fig. 265 Manifold Absolute Pressure (MAP) sensor location—3.5L engine

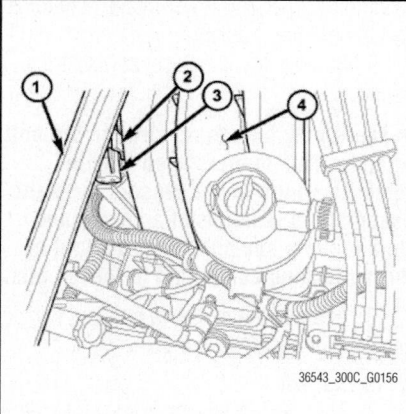

36543_300C_G0156

Fig. 266 Manifold Absolute Pressure (MAP) sensor location—5.7L engine

REMOVAL & INSTALLATION

2.7L & 3.5L Engine

See Figures 264 and 265.

1. Unlock the electrical connector.

2. Remove electrical connector.

3. Turn sensor 1/4 turn counterclockwise.

4. Pull sensor straight up.

5. Remove sensor.

6. Inspect O-ring.

To install:

7. Clean MAP sensor mounting hole at intake manifold.

8. Check MAP sensor O-ring seal for cuts or tears.

9. Position sensor into intake manifold.

10. Rotate sensor 1/4-turn clockwise for installation.

11. Connect electrical connector to sensor.

   a. Lock electrical connector.

   b. Connect negative battery cable.

3.6L Engine

See Figure 267.

1. Disconnect and isolate the negative battery cable.

2. Lift the engine cover retaining grommets off the ball studs and remove the engine cover.

3. Unlock and disconnect the electrical connector from the MAP sensor.

4. Rotate the MAP sensor 1/4 turn counterclockwise and pull the sensor straight up and out of the upper intake manifold.

5. The MAP sensor O-ring can be reused if not damaged.

To install:

6. The manifold air pressure (MAP) sensor O-ring can be reused if not damaged.

7. Apply a small amount of engine oil to the sensor O-ring.

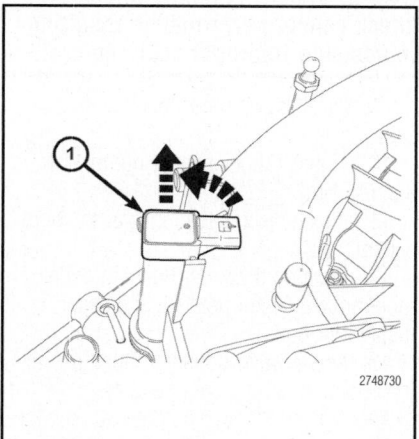

2748730

Fig. 267 Removing and installing the MAP sensor

8. Install the MAP sensor into the upper intake manifold and rotate 1/4 turn clockwise.

9. Connect and lock the electrical connector to the sensor.

10. Position the engine cover and secure the retaining grommets onto the ball studs.

11. Connect the negative battery cable and tighten nut to 45 inch lbs. (5 Nm).

5.7L Engine

See Figure 266.

➡ **The Manifold Absolute Pressure (MAP) sensor is mounted into the top/rear of the intake manifold near the cowl/hood seal.**

1. Disconnect electrical connector at sensor by sliding release lock out. Press down on lock tab for removal.

2. Rotate sensor 1/4-turn counter-clockwise for removal.

3. Check condition of sensor O-ring.

To install:

4. Clean MAP sensor mounting hole at intake manifold.

5. Check MAP sensor O-ring seal for cuts or tears.

6. Position sensor into intake manifold.

7. Rotate sensor 1/4 turn clockwise for installation.

8. Connect electrical connector to sensor.

THROTTLE POSITION SENSOR (TPS)

LOCATION

The Throttle Position Sensor (TPS) is mounted on the throttle body and is connected to the throttle blade.

REMOVAL & INSTALLATION

1. See all applicable precautions before beginning service procedures.

   a. Disconnect Throttle Position Sensor (TPS) electrical connector.

2. Remove TPS mounting screws.

3. Remove TPS.

To install:

4. The throttle shaft end of throttle body slides into a socket in the TPS. The TPS must be installed so that it can be rotated a few degrees. (If sensor will not rotate, install sensor with throttle shaft on other side of socket tangs). The TPS will be under slight tension when rotated.

5. Install TPS and retaining screws.

6. Tighten screws to 60 inch lbs. (7 Nm).

7. Connect TPS electrical connector to TPS.

8. Manually operate throttle (by hand) to check for any TPS binding before starting engine.

VEHICLE SPEED SENSOR (VSS)

LOCATION

The Vehicle Speed Sensor (VSS) is located on the left side of the transmission case.

REMOVAL & INSTALLATION

1. See all applicable precautions before beginning service procedures.

2. Raise and safely support the vehicle.

3. Place a suitable catch pan under the transmission for any fluid.

4. Remove the wiring connector from the output speed sensor.

5. Remove the mounting bolt and remove the speed sensor from the transmission case.

To install:

6. Install the speed sensor into the transmission case and tighten the bolt to 105 inch lbs. (12 Nm).

7. Install the wiring connector to the speed sensor.

8. Verify the proper transmission fluid level and refill as necessary.

9. Lower the vehicle.

FUEL
GASOLINE FUEL INJECTION SYSTEM

FUEL SYSTEM SERVICE PRECAUTIONS

Safety is the most important factor when performing not only fuel system maintenance but any type of maintenance. Failure to conduct maintenance and repairs in a safe manner may result in serious personal injury or death. Maintenance and testing of the vehicle's fuel system components can be accomplished safely and effectively by adhering to the following rules and guidelines.

• To avoid the possibility of fire and personal injury, always disconnect the negative battery cable unless the repair or test procedure requires that battery voltage be applied.

• Always relieve the fuel system pressure prior to disconnecting any fuel system component (injector, fuel rail, pressure regulator, etc.), fitting or fuel line connection. Exercise extreme caution whenever relieving fuel system pressure to avoid exposing skin, face and eyes to fuel spray. Please be advised that fuel under pressure may penetrate the skin or any part of the body that it contacts.

• Always place a shop towel or cloth around the fitting or connection prior to loosening to absorb any excess fuel due to spillage. Ensure that all fuel spillage (should it occur) is quickly removed from engine surfaces. Ensure that all fuel soaked cloths or towels are deposited into a suitable waste container.

• Always keep a dry chemical (Class B) fire extinguisher near the work area.

• Do not allow fuel spray or fuel vapors to come into contact with a spark or open flame.

• Always use a back-up wrench when loosening and tightening fuel line connection fittings. This will prevent unnecessary stress and torsion to fuel line piping.

• Always replace worn fuel fitting O-rings with new Do not substitute fuel hose or equivalent where fuel pipe is installed.

Before servicing the vehicle, make sure to also refer to the precautions in the beginning of this section as well.

RELIEVING FUEL SYSTEM PRESSURE

1. Before servicing the vehicle, refer to the precautions in the beginning of this section.

2. Remove fuel pump relay from Power Distribution Center (PDC). For location of relay, refer to label on underside of PDC cover.

3. Start and run engine until it stalls.

4. Attempt restarting engine until it will no longer run.

5. Turn the ignition key to OFF position.

6. Return fuel pump relay to PDC.

7. One or more Diagnostic Trouble Codes (DTC's) may have been stored in PCM memory due to fuel pump relay removal. A scan tool must be used to erase a DTC.

FUEL FILTER

REMOVAL & INSTALLATION

The fuel filter is replaceable only as part of the fuel pump module. Refer to that procedure for more information.

FUEL INJECTORS

REMOVAL & INSTALLATION

3.6L Engine

See Figures 268 through 270.

✳✳ CAUTION

The fuel system is under constant pressure even with engine off. Before servicing the fuel rail, fuel system pressure must be released.

1. Perform the fuel pressure release procedure.
2. Disconnect and isolate the negative battery cable.
3. Lift the engine cover retaining grommets off the ball studs and remove the engine cover.
4. Disconnect the electrical connector from the Inlet Air Temperature (IAT) sensor.
5. Loosen the clamp at the throttle body.
6. Loosen the clamp at the air cleaner housing.
7. Lift the air inlet hose assembly retaining grommet off the ball stud.
8. Remove the air inlet hose assembly.

✳✳ WARNING

When removing the fuel rail from the lower intake manifold, one or more fuel injectors may remain in the intake manifold resulting in residual fuel spilling onto the engine from the fuel rail.

9. Remove the upper intake manifold and fuel rail.

➡**Number 2 fuel injector removal shown, all other fuel injectors similar.**

10. Remove the fuel injectors from the fuel rail.

➡**Number 2 fuel injector removal shown, all other fuel injectors similar.**

11. Remove the fuel injectors from the lower intake manifold.
12. Remove and discard all fuel injector O-ring seals.

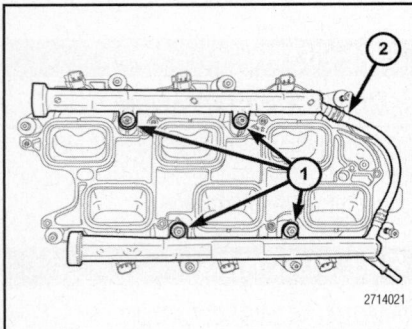

Fig. 268 Removing the upper intake manifold and fuel rail

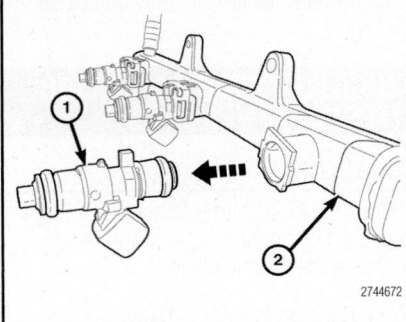

Fig. 269 Removing the fuel injectors from the fuel rail

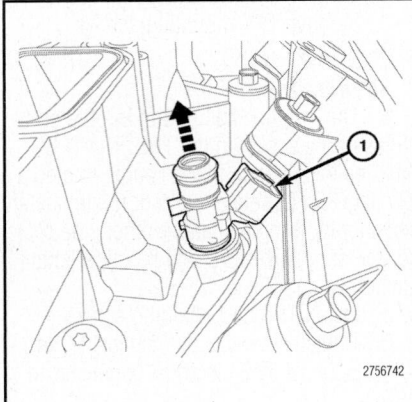

Fig. 270 Removing the fuel injector from the lower intake manifold

To install:

13. Lightly lubricate the new O-ring seals with clean engine oil and position the seals onto the fuel injector.
14. Install the fuel injectors into the fuel rail.
15. Install the fuel rail and upper intake manifold.
16. Position the air inlet hose assembly onto the throttle body and the air cleaner housing.
17. Secure the air inlet hose assembly retaining grommet onto the ball stud.
18. Tighten the clamp at the air cleaner housing to 44 inch lbs. (5 Nm).
19. Tighten the clamp at the throttle body to 44 inch lbs. (5 Nm).
20. Connect the Inlet Air Temperature (IAT) sensor electrical connector.
21. Lift the engine cover retaining grommets off the ball studs and remove the engine cover.
22. Connect the negative battery cable and tighten nut to 45 inch lbs. (5 Nm).
23. Start the engine and check for leaks.

2.7L & 5.7L Engines

See Figure 271.

➡**Right side shown, left side similar.**

✳✳ CAUTION

The fuel system is under constant pressure even with engine off. Before servicing fuel injector(s), fuel system pressure must be released.

➡**To remove one or more fuel injectors, the fuel rail assembly must be removed from engine.**

1. Perform the fuel system pressure release procedure.
2. Remove the fuel rail assembly.
3. Remove the fuel injector retaining clip(s) from the fuel rail.
4. Remove the injector(s) from the fuel rail assembly.

To install:

5. Inspect the fuel injector O-rings and replace if necessary.
6. Apply a small amount of engine oil to each fuel injector O-rings.
7. Install the fuel injector(s) into the fuel rail and install the retaining clip(s).
8. Install the fuel rail assembly.
9. Start the engine and check for leaks.

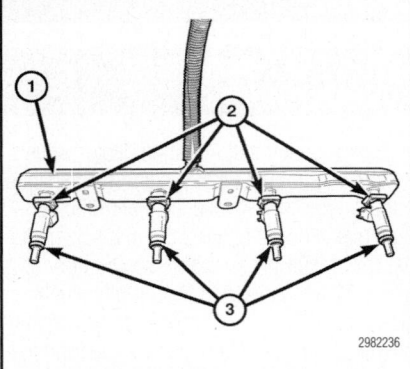

Fig. 271 Remove the fuel injector retaining clips (2) from the fuel rail. Remove the injectors (3) from the fuel rail assembly (1)

FUEL PUMP

REMOVAL & INSTALLATION

See Figures 272 through 275.

1. Before servicing the vehicle, refer to the precautions in the beginning of this section.
2. Release the fuel pressure.
3. Disconnect negative battery cable.

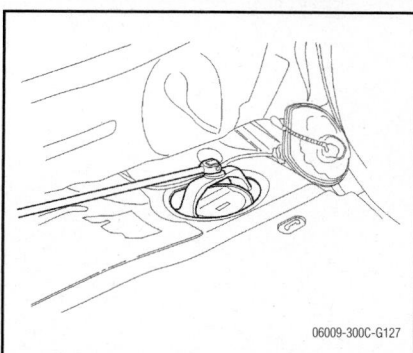

Fig. 272 Use special tool 9340 to remove left side module lock ring

➥The fuel level of the vehicle must be below 5/8 of a tank before you remove the module lock-rings. If it is above that you can spill fuel in the vehicle.

4. Drain partial fuel from fuel tank through the filler tube. Use a hard nylon tube, with a 30°cut on the end, to push the check valve open to drain fuel from tank.
5. Remove the rear lower seat cushion.
6. Push seat back and up to remove seat cushion.
7. Fold back the foam pad covering access cover for modules.
8. Disconnect the electrical connector from left side module.
9. Mark the module orientation.
10. Use special tool 9340 to remove left side module lockring.
11. Drain fuel from left side of fuel tank. Lift module up enough to push hose into tank and drain. Do not spill fuel in interior of vehicle.
12. Disconnect the electrical connectors from the module top.
13. Remove the module top half.

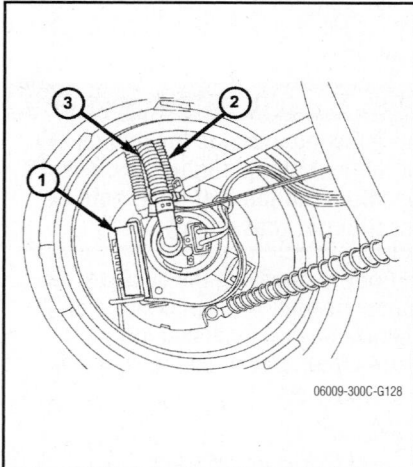

Fig. 273 Fuel level sending card (1), fuel return lines, fuel supply line (3)

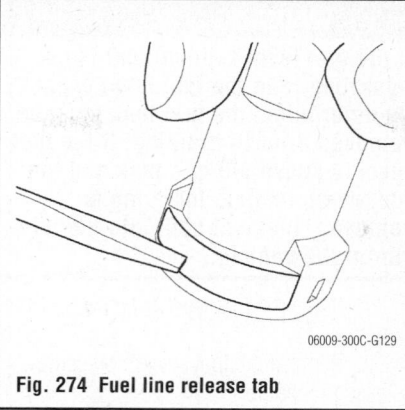

Fig. 274 Fuel line release tab

14. Press in the fuel line release tab and pull up on fuel line.
15. Remove fuel line.
16. Remove fuel return line.
17. Tip module on its side to drain remaining fuel from reservoir and remove module from vehicle.

To install:
18. Install pump module into tank.
19. Connect fuel return lines to module.
20. Lines connected.
21. Connect fuel supply line to module and make sure it is locked in place.
22. Connect electrical connectors to bottom of module top, Install module top to module bottom.
23. Install module and align marks on the module for proper orientation.
24. Install module lockring.
   a. Use special tool 9340 to tighten left side module lock ring.
25. Connect the electrical connector to left side module.
26. Install plastic access cover.
27. Fold the foam pad covering access cover for modules back into place.
28. Install rear lower seat cushion
   a. Fill fuel tank.
29. Connect negative battery cable.

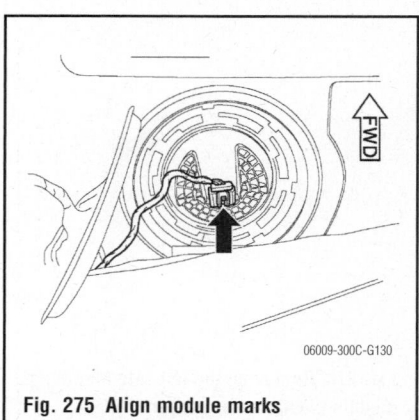

Fig. 275 Align module marks

30. Fill fuel tank. Use the scan tool to pressurize the fuel system. Check for leaks.

FUEL TANK

DRAINING

Conventional Procedure

✳✳ CAUTION

The fuel system is under constant high pressure even with engine off. Until the fuel pressure has been properly released from the system, do not attempt to open the fuel system. Do not smoke or use open flames/sparks when servicing the fuel system. Wear protective clothing and eye protection. Make sure the area in which the vehicle is being serviced is in a well ventilated area and free of flames/sparks. Failure to comply may result in serious or fatal injury.

✳✳ CAUTION

No sparks, open flames or smoking. Risk of poisoning from inhaling and swallowing fuel. Pour fuel only into appropriately marked OSHA approved containers. Wear protective clothing. Risk of injury to eyes and skin from contact with fuel.

➥Due to a one-way check valve installed into the fuel fill fitting at the tank, the tank cannot be drained at the fuel filler tube.

✳✳ WARNING

If the electric fuel pump is not operating, and the fuel level is above 5/8 of a tank, the fuel tank must be removed prior to draining. If the fuel level is above 5/8 of a tank and the fuel pump module lock-ring is removed, fuel will spill into the interior of the vehicle.

✳✳ WARNING

If the fuel level sending unit is not operating, and the fuel level cannot be determined the fuel tank must be removed prior to draining. If the fuel level is above 5/8 of a tank and the fuel pump module lock-ring is removed, fuel will spill into the interior of the vehicle.

1. Perform the fuel system pressure release procedure.

➡Tool number 6539 is used on 5/16" fuel lines while tool number 6631 is used on 3/8" fuel lines.

2. Attach one end of the special test hose at the fuel line quick-connect fitting.

3. Attach the opposite end of the special test hose to the Fuel Chief Gas Caddy 320-FC-P30-A or an OSHA approved gas caddy.

4. Using a diagnostic scan tool, activate the fuel pump until the fuel tank has been evacuated.

Alternative Procedure

See Figures 276 and 277.

❋❋ CAUTION

The fuel system is under constant high pressure even with engine off. Until the fuel pressure has been properly released from the system, do not attempt to open the fuel system. Do not smoke or use open flames/sparks when servicing the fuel system. Wear protective clothing and eye protection. Make sure the area in which the vehicle is being serviced is in a well ventilated area and free of flames/sparks. Failure to comply may result in serious or fatal injury.

❋❋ CAUTION

No sparks, open flames or smoking. Risk of poisoning from inhaling and swallowing fuel. Pour fuel only into appropriately marked OSHA approved containers. Wear protective clothing. Risk of injury to eyes and skin from contact with fuel.

❋❋ WARNING

The fuel level of the vehicle must be below 5/8 of a tank before using the "Alternative Procedure". If the fuel level is above 5/8 of a tank and the fuel pump module lock-ring is removed, fuel will spill into the interior of the vehicle.

❋❋ WARNING

If the electric fuel pump is not operating, and the fuel level is above 5/8 of a tank, the fuel tank must be removed prior to draining. If the fuel level is above 5/8 of a tank and the fuel pump module lock-ring is removed, fuel will spill into the interior of the vehicle.

❋❋ WARNING

If the fuel level sending unit is not operating, and the fuel level cannot be determined the fuel tank must be removed prior to draining. If the fuel level is above 5/8 of a tank and the fuel pump module lock-ring is removed, fuel will spill into the interior of the vehicle.

1. Verify the fuel level is below 5/8 of a tank.

2. Perform the fuel system pressure release procedure.

3. Disconnect the negative battery cable.

4. Push the rear lower seat cushion up and back and remove the seat cushion.

5. Fold back the foam pad covering the fuel pump module plastic access covers.

6. Remove the left side fuel pump module plastic access cover.

7. Disconnect the electrical connector from the fuel pump module.

❋❋ WARNING

An indexing arrow is located on top of the fuel pump module to clock it's position into the fuel tank, note its location for reassembly.

➡Prior to removing the fuel pump module, use compressed air to remove any accumulated dirt and debris from around fuel tank opening.

8. Mark the fuel pump module orientation.

9. Position the lock ring remover/installer (1) into the notches on the outside edge of the lock ring.

10. Install a 1/2 inch drive breaker bar into the lock ring remover/installer 9340 (1).

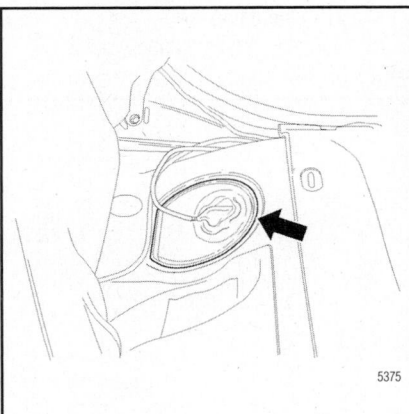

Fig. 276 Removing the left side fuel pump module plastic access cover

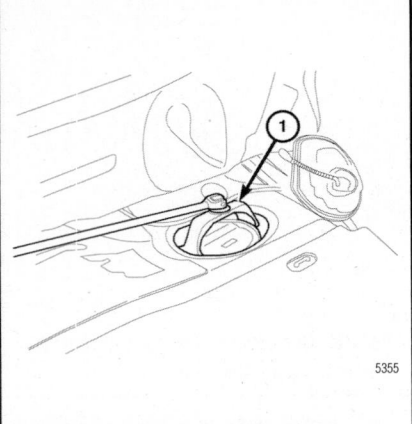

Fig. 277 Disconnecting the electrical connector (1) from the fuel pump module

11. Rotate the breaker bar counterclockwise and remove the lock ring.

❋❋ WARNING

Do not spill fuel into the interior of the vehicle.

❋❋ WARNING

The lower reservoir of the fuel pump module must be drained before removal or fuel can spill into the interior of the vehicle.

12. Lift the fuel pump module up enough to push a 3/8 inch hose into the fuel tank.

13. Attach the opposite end of the hose to the Fuel Chief Gas Caddy 320-FC-P30-A or an OSHA approved gas caddy.

14. Using the Fuel Chief Gas Caddy 320-FC-P30-A or an OSHA approved gas caddy, evacuate the left side of the fuel tank.

15. Remove the right side auxiliary fuel pump module plastic access cover.

16. Disconnect the fuel supply line and the fuel return line at the auxiliary fuel pump module.

❋❋ WARNING

An indexing arrow is located on top of the fuel pump module to clock it's position into the fuel tank, note its location for reassembly.

➡Prior to removing the auxiliary fuel pump module, use compressed air to remove any accumulated dirt and debris from around fuel tank opening.

17. Mark the auxiliary fuel pump module orientation.

18. Position the lock ring remover/installer into the notches on the outside edge of the lock ring.

19. Install a 1/2 inch drive breaker bar into the lock ring remover/installer.

20. Rotate the breaker bar counterclockwise and remove the lock ring.

✷✷ WARNING

Do not spill fuel into the interior of the vehicle.

✷✷ WARNING

The lower reservoir of the fuel pump module must be drained before removal or fuel can spill into the interior of the vehicle.

21. Lift the auxiliary fuel pump module up enough to push a 3/8 inch hose (1) into the fuel tank.

22. Attach the opposite end of the hose to the Fuel Chief Gas Caddy 320-FC-P30-A or an OSHA approved gas caddy.

23. Using the Fuel Chief Gas Caddy 320-FC-P30-A or an OSHA approved gas caddy, evacuate the right side of the fuel tank.

REMOVAL & INSTALLATION

See Figures 278 through 281.

1. Before servicing the vehicle, refer to the precautions in the beginning of this section.

2. Release the fuel pressure, refer to the (Fuel Pressure Release Procedure) in this section.

3. Disconnect negative battery cable.

➡**The fuel level of the vehicle must be below 5/8 of a tank before you remove the module lock-rings. If it is above that you can spill fuel in the vehicle.**

4. Drain the partial fuel from fuel tank through the filler tube. Use a hard nylon

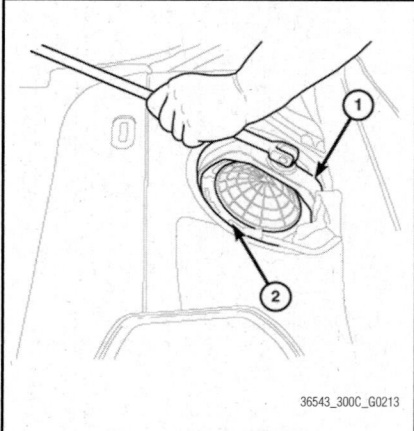

Fig. 278 Use the special tool (1) to remove the lock ring (2)

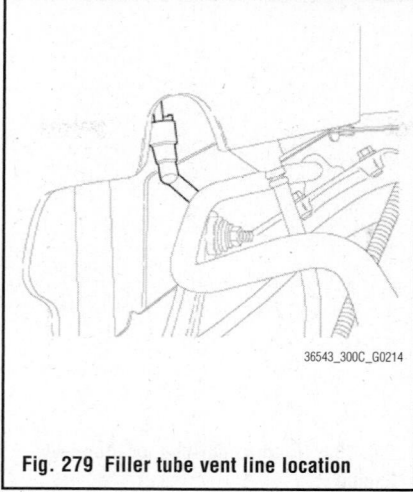

36543_300C_G0214

Fig. 279 Filler tube vent line location

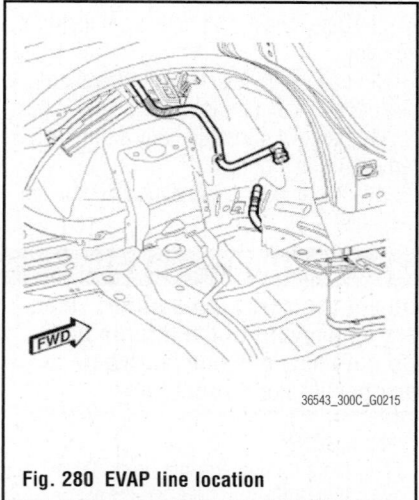

36543_300C_G0215

Fig. 280 EVAP line location

tube, with a 30° cut on the end, to push the check valve open to drain fuel from tank.

5. Remove the rear lower seat cushion.

6. Push seat back and up to remove seat cushion.

7. Fold back the foam pad covering access cover for modules.

8. Remove plastic access covers from floor pan right side.

9. Disconnect the fuel supply line from module.

10. Mark the module orientation.

11. Use the special tool number 9340 to remove right side module lock ring.

12. Drain fuel from right side of fuel tank. Lift module up enough to push hose into tank and drain. Do not spill fuel in interior of vehicle.

13. Disconnect the electrical connector from left side module.

14. Mark the module orientation.

15. Use special tool 9340 to remove left side module lock ring.

16. Drain fuel from left side of fuel tank.

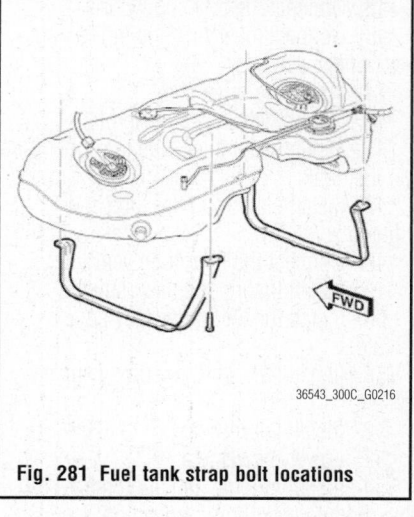

36543_300C_G0216

Fig. 281 Fuel tank strap bolt locations

Lift module up enough to push hose into tank and drain. Do not spill fuel in interior of vehicle.

17. Install both module temporally, hand tighten the lock ring to hold modules in place.

18. Raise and support the vehicle.

19. Remove left rear tire.

   a. Remove the inner splash shield.

20. Disconnect the filler tube vent line.

21. Remove clamp from filler tube.

22. Remove metal filler tube from rubber tube on fuel tank.

23. Remove the exhaust system.

24. Remove the drive shaft.

25. Remove the left underbody splash shield.

26. Remove the right underbody splash shield.

27. Disconnect the EVAP line in the right rear wheel well.

28. Disconnect vapor line.

29. Disconnect the fuel supply line.

30. Support fuel tank with transmission jack.

31. Fuel tank strap bolt locations.

32. Remove bolt for fuel tank strap.

33. Remove bolt for fuel tank strap.

34. Lower tank and pull filler tube vent line through bracket.

35. Lower Fuel tank and remove from vehicle.

36. If fuel tank is being replaced remove modules, control valve and lines.

To install:

37. If fuel tank was replaced install modules, control valve and lines.

38. Support fuel tank with transmission jack.

39. Raise tank and push filler tube vent line through bracket.

40. Install the bolts for fuel tank straps and tighten.

41. Connect vapor line.

42. Connect the fuel supply line.
43. Connect the EVAP line in the right rear wheel well.
44. Install the drive shaft.
45. Install the exhaust system.
46. Install metal filler tube to rubber tube on fuel tank.
47. Install clamp to filler tube and tighten
48. Connect the filler tube vent line.
49. Install the inner splash shield.
50. Install the left underbody splash shield.
51. Install the right underbody splash shield.
52. Install left rear tire.
53. Lower the vehicle.
54. Install module and align marks on the module for proper orientation.
55. Install the module lock-ring.
56. Use the special tool number 9340 to tighten left side module lock ring.
57. Connect the electrical connector to left side module and install plastic access cover.
58. Install module and align marks on the module for proper orientation.
59. Install the module lock-ring.
60. Use then special tool number 9340 to tighten right side module lock ring.
61. Connect the fuel supply line to module.
62. Install plastic access covers to floor pan right side.
63. Fold the foam pad covering access cover for modules back into place.
64. Install rear lower seat cushion
   a. Engage the retainer loops into the cups on the floor kick up.
   b. Push downward on the forward edge of the rear seat cushion to engage the retainer loops to the cups.
65. Fill the fuel tank.
66. Connect negative battery cable.
67. Fill fuel tank. Use the scan tool to pressurize the fuel system. Check for leaks.

IDLE SPEED

ADJUSTMENT

Idle speed is computer controlled and is not adjustable.

THROTTLE BODY

REMOVAL & INSTALLATION

2.7L Engine

See Figure 282.

1. Disconnect the negative battery cable.

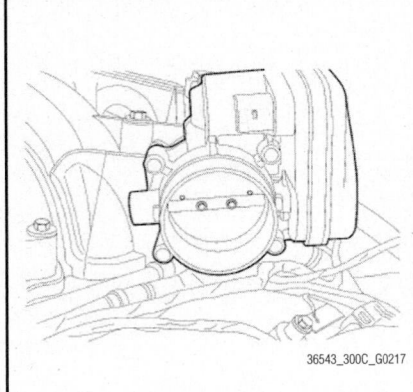

Fig. 282 Throttle body bolt location—V6 Engine

2. Disconnect inlet hose from the throttle body.
3. Label and detach all electrical connectors and vacuum hose(s).
4. Remove 4 throttle body bolts, then remove throttle body.
5. Thoroughly clean the gasket mating surfaces.

✳✳ CAUTION

Do not use spray (carburetor) cleaners on any part of the throttle body. Do not apply silicone lubricants to any part of the throttle body.

To install:

6. Install a new throttle body gasket.
7. Install throttle body and bolts. Torque the bolts to 105 inch lbs. (11.9 Nm).
8. Connect the electrical connectors.
9. Connect vacuum hoses.
10. Install inlet hose and tighten clamp.
11. Connect negative cable to battery.

➡**A Scan Tool may be used to learn electrical parameters. Go to the Miscellaneous menu, and then select ETC Relearn. If the relearn is not preformed, a Diagnostic Trouble Code (DTC) will be set. If necessary, use a scan tool to erase any Diagnostic Trouble Codes (DTC's) from PCM.**

3.6L Engine

See Figure 283.

1. Disconnect and isolate the negative battery cable.
2. Lift the engine cover retaining grommets off the ball studs and remove the engine cover.
3. Disconnect the electrical connector from the Inlet Air Temperature (IAT) sensor.

4. Loosen the clamp at the throttle body.
5. Loosen the clamp at the air cleaner housing.
6. Lift the air inlet hose assembly retaining grommet off the ball stud.
7. Remove the air inlet hose assembly.

✳✳ WARNING

Never have the ignition key in the ON position when checking the throttle body shaft for a binding condition. This may set DTC's.

8. Disconnect the electrical connector from the Electronic Throttle Control (ETC) and unfasten the ETC harness from the clip on the throttle body.
9. Remove four throttle body mounting bolts.
10. Remove the throttle body from the upper intake manifold.
11. Check the condition of the throttle body-to-intake manifold seal. The seal can be reused if not damaged.

To install:

12. Check the condition of the throttle body-to-intake manifold seal. The seal can be reused if not damaged.
13. Clean the mating surfaces of the throttle body and intake manifold.
14. Position the throttle body to the intake manifold.
15. Install the throttle body mounting bolts and tighten in a crisscross pattern sequence to 62 inch lbs. (7 Nm).
16. Connect the electrical connector to the Electronic Throttle Control (ETC) and secure the ETC harness to the clip on the throttle body.
17. Position the air inlet hose assembly

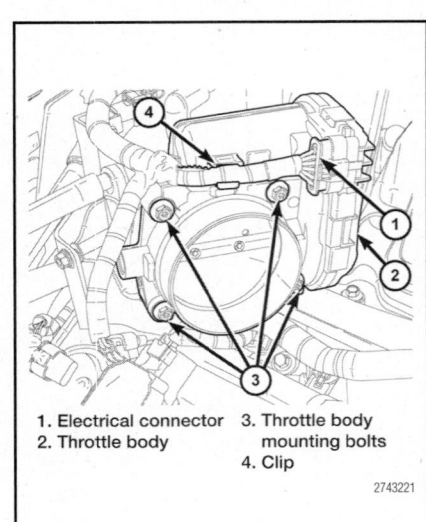

1. Electrical connector
2. Throttle body
3. Throttle body mounting bolts
4. Clip

Fig. 283 Removing and installing the throttle body—3.6L engine

onto the throttle body and the air cleaner housing.

18. Secure the air inlet hose assembly retaining grommet onto the ball stud.

19. Tighten the clamp at the air cleaner housing to 44 inch lbs. (5 Nm).

20. Tighten the clamp at the throttle body to 44 inch lbs. (5 Nm).

21. Connect the Inlet Air Temperature (IAT) sensor electrical connector.

22. Position the engine cover and secure the retaining grommets onto the ball studs.

23. Connect the negative battery cable and tighten nut to 45 inch lbs. (5 Nm).

5.7L Engine

See Figure 284.

> ✳✳ **WARNING**
>
> **Do not use spray (carb) cleaners on any part of the throttle body. Do not apply silicone lubricants to any part of the throttle body.**

1. Remove rubber air duct at front of throttle body.

2. Disconnect electrical connector at throttle body.

3. Remove four throttle body mounting bolts.

4. Remove throttle body from intake manifold.

5. Check condition of throttle body o-ring at front of intake manifold.

To install:

6. Clean and check condition of throttle body-to-intake manifold o-ring.

7. Clean mating surfaces of throttle body and intake manifold.

> ✳✳ **WARNING**
>
> **Do not use spray (carb) cleaners on any part of the throttle body. Do not apply silicone lubricants to any part of the throttle body.**

8. Install throttle body to intake manifold by positioning throttle body to manifold alignment pins.

9. Install and tighten four mounting bolts.

10. Install electrical connector.

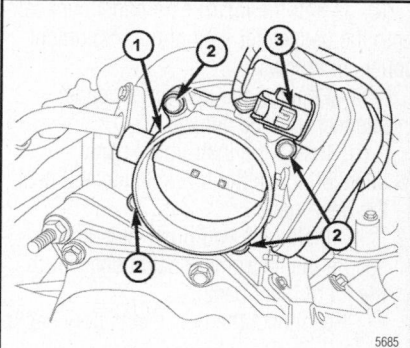

Fig. 284 Detach the electrical connector (3), remove the four mounting bolts (2) and remove the throttle body (1)—5.7L engine

11. Install rubber air hose to throttle body.

12. A Scan Tool may be used to learn electrical parameters. Go to the Miscellaneous menu, and then select ETC Relearn. If the relearn is not preformed, a Diagnostic Trouble Code (DTC) will be set. If necessary, use a scan tool to erase any Diagnostic Trouble Codes (DTC's) from PCM.

HEATING & AIR CONDITIONING SYSTEM

BLOWER MOTOR

REMOVAL & INSTALLATION

See Figures 285 and 286.

> ✳✳ **WARNING**
>
> **On vehicles equipped with airbags, disable the airbag system before attempting any steering wheel, steering column, or instrument panel component diagnosis or service. Disconnect and isolate the negative battery (ground) cable, then wait two minutes for the airbag system capacitor to discharge before performing further diagnosis or service. This is the only sure way to disable the airbag system. Failure to take the proper precautions could result in accidental airbag deployment and possible personal injury or death.**

1. Disconnect and isolate the negative battery cable.

2. Remove the instrument panel silencer from the passenger side of the instrument panel, as follows:

   a. Remove the two push-pins that secure the instrument panel silencer to the instrument panel.

   b. Pull the instrument panel silencer rearward to disengage it from the brackets located near the dash panel.

   c. Remove the instrument panel silencer from the vehicle.

3. Disengage the wire harness connector locking tab and disconnect the wire harness connector and wire harness retainers from the blower motor.

4. Remove the four screws that secure the blower motor to the HVAC housing.

5. Remove the blower motor from HVAC housing.

To install:

6. Position the blower motor into the HVAC housing.

7. Install the four screws that secure the blower motor to the HVAC housing. Tighten the screws to 20 inch lbs. (2.2 Nm).

8. Attach the wire harness connector to the blower motor and engage the wire harness connector locking tab.

9. Install the HVAC wire harness retainers onto the blower motor.

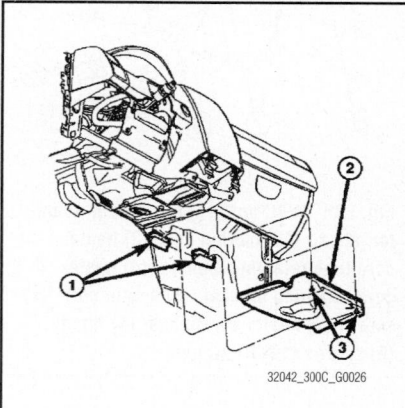

Fig. 285 Instrument panel silencer (2), push pins (3) and brackets (1)

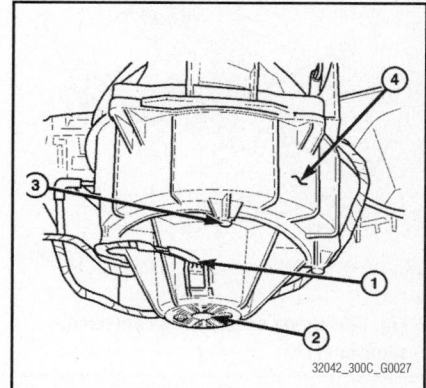

Fig. 286 Blower motor (2), harness connector (1), retaining screws (3) and HVAC housing (4)

10. Install the instrument panel silencer onto the passenger side of the instrument panel, as follows:

a. Position the instrument panel silencer into the vehicle.

b. Install the instrument panel silencer above the brackets located near the dash panel.

c. Install the two push-pins that secure the instrument panel silencer to the instrument panel.

11. Reconnect the negative battery cable.

HEATER CORE

REMOVAL & INSTALLATION

See Figures 287 and 288.

The heater core is mounted into the driver's side of HVAC air distribution housing, located behind the instrument panel.

✳✳ WARNING

On vehicles equipped with airbags, disable the airbag system before attempting any steering wheel, steering column, or instrument panel component diagnosis or service. Disconnect and isolate the negative battery (ground) cable, then wait two minutes for the airbag system capacitor to discharge before performing further diagnosis or service. This is the only sure way to disable the airbag system. Failure to take the proper precautions could result in accidental airbag deployment and possible personal injury or death.

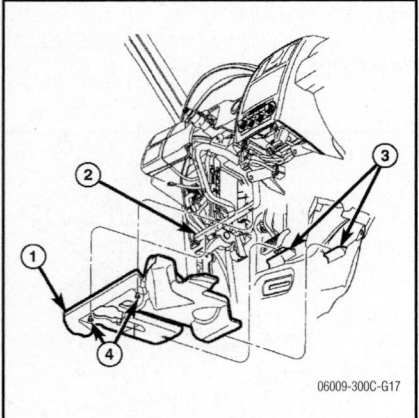

06009-300C-G17

Fig. 287 Driver's side instrument panel silencer (1)

1. Before servicing the vehicle, refer to the precautions in the beginning of this section.

2. Drain the engine cooling system

3. Disconnect and isolate the negative battery cable.

4. Carefully disconnect the heater hoses from the heater core tubes.

5. Remove the two push-pins that secure the instrument panel silencer to the instrument panel bracket.

6. Pull the instrument panel silencer rearward to disengage it from the brackets located near the dash panel.

7. Remove the instrument panel silencer from the vehicle.

8. Remove the blend door actuator from the driver's side of the HVAC air distribution housing.

9. Remove the two screws that secure the flange to the front of the HVAC housing near the dash panel.

10. Remove the flange from the HVAC housing.

➡**Take proper precautions to protect the carpeting from spilled engine coolant. Have absorbent toweling readily available to clean up any spills.**

11. Remove the retaining clamps that secure the heater core tubes to the heater core.

12. Disconnect the heater core tubes from the heater core and remove and discard the O-ring seals.

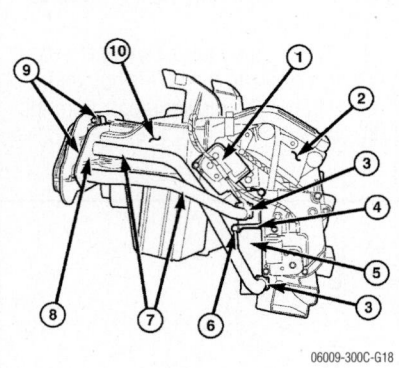

06009-300C-G18

Fig. 288 HVAC unit: (1) blend door actuator, (2) air distribution unit, (3) heater core tube retaining clamps, (4) heater core retaining bracket, (5) heater core, (6) screw, (7) heater core tubes, (8) flange, (9) screws (10) HVAC unit

13. Carefully pull the heater core tubes through the dash panel.

14. Install plugs in, or tape over the opened heater core ports.

15. Remove the screw that secures the heater core retaining bracket to the driver's side of the HVAC air distribution housing.

16. Remove the heater core retaining bracket from the air distribution housing.

17. Carefully pull the heater core out of the air distribution housing.

To install:

18. Carefully install the heater core into the driver's side of the HVAC air distribution housing.

19. Install heater core retaining bracket onto the air distribution housing.

20. Install the screw that secures the heater core retaining bracket onto the air distribution housing. Tighten the screw to 20 inch lbs. (2.2 Nm).

21. Remove the tape or plugs from the heater core ports.

22. Lubricate new rubber O-ring seals with clean engine coolant and install them onto the heater core tube fittings. Use only the specified O-rings as they are made of a special material for the engine cooling system.

23. Install the heater core tubes through the dash panel and onto the heater core.

24. Install the two retaining clamps that secure the heater core tubes to the heater core. Make sure that the clamps are installed correctly and securely.

25. Install the flange over the heater core tubes and onto the HVAC housing near the dash panel.

26. Install the two screws that secure the flange to the HVAC housing. Tighten the screws to 20 inch lbs. (2.2 Nm).

27. Install the blend door actuator to the driver's side of the air distribution housing.

28. Position the instrument panel silencer into the vehicle.

29. Install the instrument panel silencer above the brackets located near the dash panel.

30. Install the two push-pins that secure the instrument panel silencer to the instrument panel bracket.

31. Connect the heater hoses to the heater core tubes.

32. Connect the negative battery cable.

33. If the heater core is being replaced, flush the cooling system.

34. Refill the engine cooling system.

STEERING

POWER STEERING GEAR

REMOVAL & INSTALLATION

AWD Models

See Figures 289 through 292.

1. Before servicing the vehicle, refer to the precautions in the beginning of this section.

2. Disconnect and isolate negative battery cable from battery post.

3. Siphon power steering fluid from pump reservoir.

4. Raise and support vehicle.

5. Remove wheel mounting nuts, then both front tire and wheel assemblies.

❋❋ CAUTION

When loosening jam nut and rotating inner tie rod, use care not to twist bellows at inner tie rod.

6. Remove clamp (2) at inner tie rod (3) and make sure bellows moves freely before rotating inner tie rod.

7. Loosen tie rod jam nut (1) at each outer tie rod (4).

8. Remove outer tie rod end nut at each knuckle.

9. Using Remover, Special Tool 9630, separate outer tie rod from each knuckle.

10. Remove steering coupling pinch bolt at steering gear.

11. Unthread return hose tube nut from steering gear. Remove return hose from steering gear.

12. Unthread pressure hose tube nut from steering gear. Remove pressure hose from steering gear.

13. Remove mounting screws, then heat shield above each inner tie rod bellows.

14. Remove steering gear upper mounting bolt and nut.

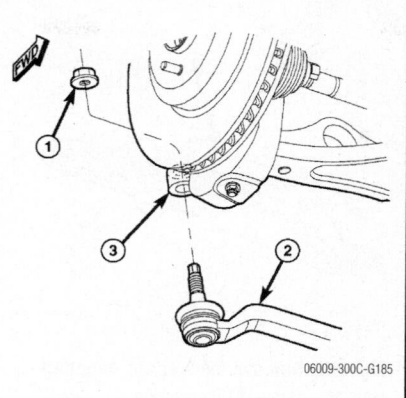

Fig. 290 Outer tie rod end (2) to knuckle (3) connection—AWD models

15. Remove steering gear lower mounting bolts.

16. Remove steering gear.

17. If necessary, remove outer tie rods from gear. Count number of revolutions off for each tie rod for reference upon installation to replacement gear.

To install:

18. If necessary, install outer tie rods from original gear to replacement inner tie rods. Install each outer tie rod same amount of threads as it was installed on original gear. This will get toe setting close, saving some time when toe is set later in this procedure.

19. Lift steering gear into mounted position and install steering gear lower mounting bolts. Install upper mounting bolt and nut. Tighten all bolts to 75 ft. lbs. (102 Nm).

20. Install heat shield above each inner tie rod bellows. Tighten screws to 89 inch lbs. (10 Nm).

➡Always use a NEW O-ring on the ends of the steering hoses.

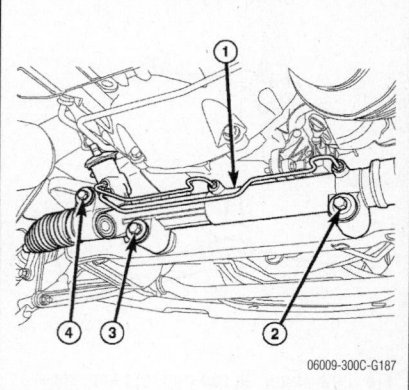

Fig. 292 Steering gear mounting (1) gear, (2, 3) lower mounting bolts, (4) upper mounting bolt—AWD models

21. Lubricate NEW O-ring on end of pressure hose with clean power steering fluid.

22. Install pressure hose to steering gear. Tighten tube nut to 35 ft. lbs. (47 Nm).

23. Lubricate NEW O-ring on end of return hose with clean power steering fluid.

24. Install return hose to steering gear. Tighten tube nut to 35 ft. lbs. (47 Nm).

25. Align splines and install steering coupling to steering gear shaft. Install NEW pinch bolt. Tighten bolt to 40 ft. lbs. (54 Nm).

26. Install each outer tie rod end to its knuckle. Install nut and tighten to 63 ft. lbs. (85 Nm).

27. Install tire and wheel assemblies. Tighten wheel mounting nuts to 110 ft. lbs. (150 Nm).

28. Lower vehicle.

RWD Models

See Figures 293 through 296.

1. Before servicing the vehicle, refer to the precautions in the beginning of this section.

2. Disconnect and isolate negative battery cable from battery post.

3. Siphon power steering fluid from pump reservoir.

4. Raise and support vehicle.

5. Remove wheel mounting nuts, then both front tire and wheel assemblies.

❋❋ CAUTION

When loosening jam nut and rotating inner tie rod, use care not to twist bellows at inner tie rod. Remove clamp at inner tie rod and make sure bellows moves freely before rotating inner tie rod.

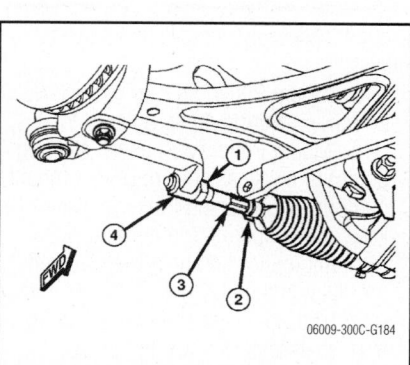

Fig. 289 Inner-to-outer tie rod connection—AWD models

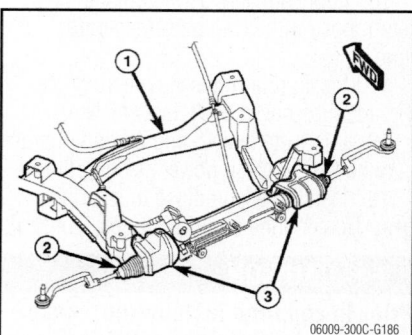

Fig. 291 Steering gear (3) heat shields, (2) boots, (1) crossmember—AWD models

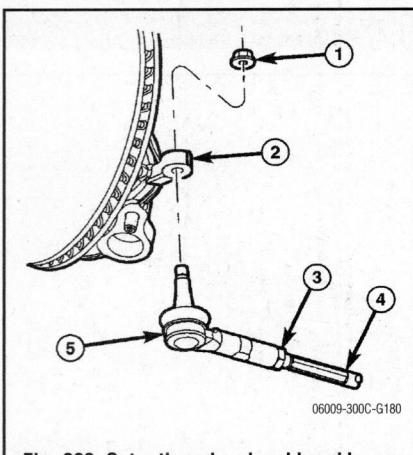

Fig. 293 Outer tie rod end and knuckle—RWD models

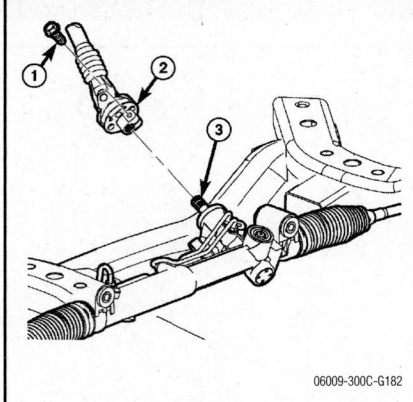

Fig. 295 Remove the steering coupling from the gear—RWD models

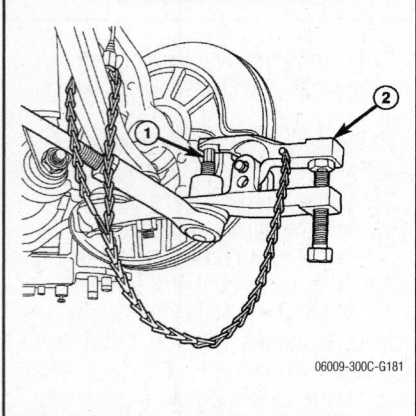

Fig. 294 Removing outer tie rod end from the knuckle with tool 9630

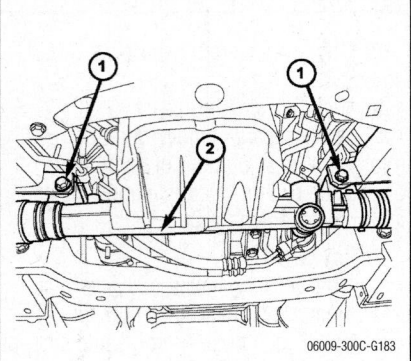

Fig. 296 Steering gear (2) mounting bolts (1)—RWD models

6. Loosen tie rod jam nut (3) at each outer tie rod (5).

7. Remove outer tie rod nut (1) at each knuckle (2).

8. Using Remover (2), Special Tool 9630, separate outer tie rod (1) from each knuckle.

9. Remove steering coupling (2) pinch bolt (1) at steering gear (3).

10. Unthread pressure hose tube nut from steering gear. Remove pressure hose from steering gear.

11. Unthread return hose tube nut from steering gear. Remove return hose from steering gear.

12. Remove steering gear mounting bolts.

13. If necessary, remove outer tie rods from gear. Count number of revolutions off for each tie rod for reference upon installation to replacement gear.

To install:

14. If necessary, install outer tie rods from original gear to replacement inner tie rods. Install each outer tie rod same amount of threads as it was installed on original gear. This will get toe setting close, saving some time when toe is set later in this procedure.

15. Lift steering gear into mounted position and install steering gear mounting bolts. Tighten bolts to 70 ft. lbs. (95 Nm).

➡**Always use a new O-ring on the ends of the steering hoses.**

16. Lubricate new O-ring on end of return hose with clean power steering fluid.

17. Install return hose to steering gear. Tighten tube nut to 35 ft. lbs. (47 Nm).

18. Lubricate new O-ring on end of pressure hose with clean power steering fluid.

19. Install pressure hose to steering gear. Tighten tube nut to 35 ft. lbs. (47 Nm).

✳✳ CAUTION

Prior to coupling installation, make sure gear is centered in its travel to match clockspring centering in steering column.

20. Align coupling with input shaft and install steering coupling. Install new pinch bolt. Tighten bolt to 40 ft. lbs. (54 Nm).

21. Install each outer tie rod end to its knuckle. Install nuts and tighten to 63 ft. lbs. (85 Nm).

22. Install tire and wheel assemblies. Tighten the wheel mounting nuts to 110 ft. lbs. (150 Nm).

23. Lower vehicle.

24. Connect negative battery cable to battery post. It is important that this is performed properly.

25. Fill pump reservoir with fluid and perform pump initial operation procedure.

26. Perform wheel alignment setting toe to specifications.

POWER STEERING PUMP

REMOVAL & INSTALLATION

2.7L & 3.5L Engines

See Figure 297.

1. Disconnect and isolate negative battery cable (2) from battery post.

2. Siphon power steering fluid from pump reservoir.

3. Remove the air cleaner housing and inlet tube to throttle body.

4. Remove the serpentine drive belt.

5. Remove the hose clamp, then the supply hose from pump.

6. Unthread the tube nut, then remove pressure hose from pump.

7. Remove three pump mounting bolts through access holes in pulley.

8. Remove pump from engine bracket.

✳✳ CAUTION

Do not hammer on power steering pump pulley or shaft to remove power steering pump pulley. This will damage pulley and power steering pump.

9. If necessary, remove the pulley as follows:

a. Mount Puller, Special Tool C-4333, on power steering pump pulley.

b. Mount Puller (with power steering pump) in a vise as shown; Do not mount pump in vise. Placing Puller in vise will keep shaft of pump from turning while removing pulley and help keep tension on Puller and pulley hub.

c. Tighten Puller and remove pulley from shaft of power steering pump.

➡**Inspect pulley. Replace if pulley is bent, cracked, or loose.**

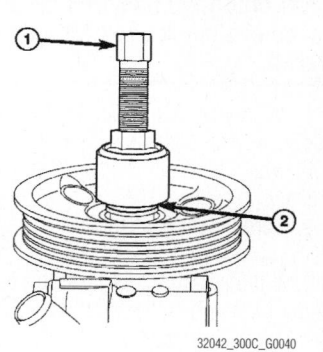

Fig. 297 Remove the mounting bolts (1) through the pulley access holes, then remove the pump (3) from the engine bracket (2)

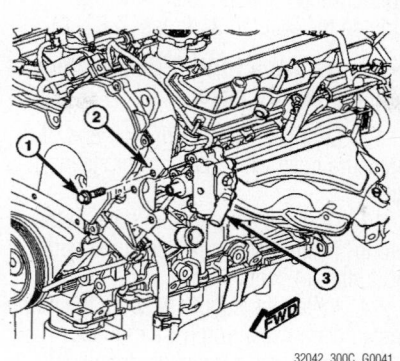

Fig. 298 To remove the power steering pump (1), first remove the mounting bolts (2) through the access holes in the pulley

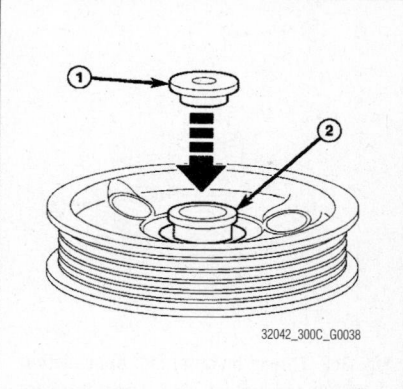

Fig. 300 Place Installation Spacer (1), Special Tool 6936, on top of pump pulley (2)

To install:

10. Align the power steering pump with mounting holes on engine bracket.

11. Install three pump mounting bolts through access holes in pulley and engine bracket. Tighten bolts to 21 ft. lbs. (28 Nm).

➡**Always use a NEW O-ring on the end of the pressure hose.**

12. Lubricate NEW O-ring on end of pressure hose with clean power steering fluid.

13. Connect the pressure hose to pump. Tighten the pressure hose tube nut to 35 ft. lbs. (47 Nm).

14. Install the supply hose on the pump. Install the clamp securing hose in place.

15. Install serpentine drive belt.

16. Install air cleaner housing and inlet tube.

17. Connect negative battery cable to battery post. It is important that this is performed properly.

18. Fill the power steering pump reservoir with fluid and perform pump initial operation procedure.

5.7L Engine

See Figures 298 through 302.

1. Disconnect and isolate the negative battery cable from battery post.

2. Siphon power steering fluid from pump reservoir.

3. Remove the air cleaner housing and inlet tube to throttle body.

4. Remove the serpentine drive belt, as outlined in the Engine Mechanical Section.

5. Remove the hose clamp, then the supply hose from pump.

6. Unthread the tube nut, then remove pressure hose from pump.

7. Remove three pump mounting bolts through access holes in pulley.

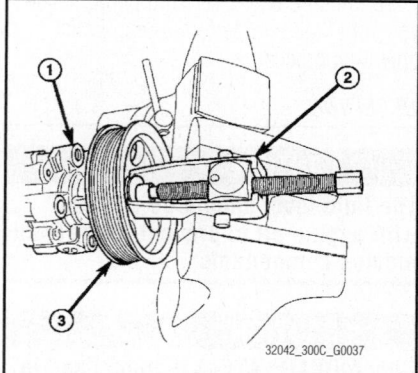

Fig. 299 View of the puller (2) installed on the power steering pump pulley. Mount the puller with the pump (1) in the vise as shown

8. Remove the power steering pump from the engine.

a. Mount Puller, Special Tool C-4333, on power steering pump pulley.

b. Mount Puller (with power steering pump) in a vise as shown; Do not mount pump in vise. Placing Puller in vise will keep shaft of pump from turning while removing pulley and help keep tension on Puller and pulley hub.

c. Tighten Puller and remove pulley from shaft of power steering pump.

➡**Inspect pulley. Replace if pulley is bent, cracked, or loose.**

To install:

✳✳ CAUTION

Do not hammer on power steering pump pulley or pump shaft to install pulley. This action will damage pulley and power steering pump.

9. If the pulley was removed, perform the following:

a. Place power steering pump pulley squarely on end of power steering pump shaft.

b. Place Installation Spacer, Special Tool 6936, on top of pump pulley.

➡**Later build pumps (vehicles built on or after 1/3/05) feature a shaft with internal threads that are not as deep as earlier production, thus requiring a stack of washers, approximately 0.5 in. (13mm) thickness, placed over Spacer 6936, before mounting Installer C-4063C on the pump. To know if a replacement pump requires the stack of washers, measure the depth of the shaft hole. A later build pump will have a depth of 0.78 in. (20mm) while an earlier build pump will have a depth of 1.25 in. (32mm).**

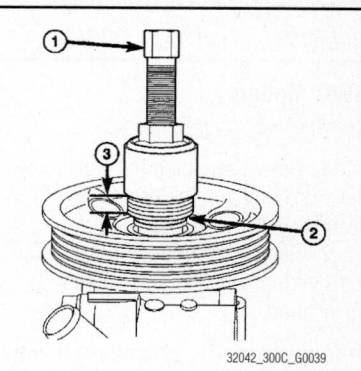

Fig. 301 Later build pumps have a shaft with internal threads that are not as deep as earlier production, thus requiring a stack of washers, approximately 0.5 in. (13mm) thickness (3), placed over Spacer 6936 (2), before mounting Installer C-4063C (1) on the pump

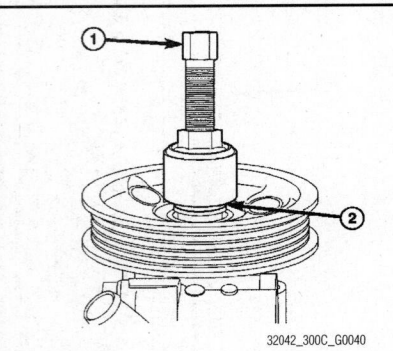

Fig. 302 Thread Installer (1), Special Tool C-4063C, completely into internal threads of power steering pump shaft, then rotate Installer Nut down against Spacer (2) on pump pulley

c. Thread Installer, Special Tool C-4063C, completely into internal threads of power steering pump shaft, then rotate Installer Nut down against Spacer on pump pulley.

d. Ensuring that special tools and pulley remain aligned with pump shaft, tighten Installer Nut, forcing pulley onto power steering pump shaft until Spacer comes in contact with end of pump shaft. When Spacer is against shaft of power steering pump, Installer Nut will no longer rotate.

e. Remove special tools from power steering pump.

10. Align the power steering pump with mounting holes on engine.

11. Install the three pump mounting bolts through access holes in pulley. Tighten the bolts to 21 ft. lbs. (28 Nm).

➡**Always use a NEW O-ring on the end of the pressure hose.**

12. Lubricate NEW O-ring on end of pressure hose with clean power steering fluid.

13. Connect the pressure hose to the pump. Tighten pressure hose tube nut to 35 ft. lbs. (47 Nm).

14. Install the supply hose on the pump. Install clamp securing hose in place.

15. Install the serpentine drive belt.

16. Install the air cleaner housing and inlet tube.

17. Connect negative battery cable to battery post. It is important that this is performed properly.

18. Fill the power steering pump reservoir with fluid and perform pump initial operation procedure

BLEEDING

✳✳ CAUTION

The fluid level should be checked with engine off to prevent injury from moving components.

✳✳ CAUTION

Only MOPAR® ATF+4 is to be used in the power steering system. No other power steering or automatic transmission fluid is to be used in the system. Damage may result to the power steering pump and system if any other fluid is used, and do not overfill.

1. Wipe filler cap clean, then check the fluid level. The dipstick should indicate COLD when the fluid is at normal temperature.

2. Turn steering wheel all the way to the left.

3. Fill the pump fluid reservoir to the proper level and let the fluid settle for at least two (2) minutes.

4. Raise the front wheels off the ground.

5. Slowly turn the steering wheel lock-to-lock 20 times with the engine off while checking the fluid level.

➡**For vehicles with long return lines or oil coolers, you must turn the wheel 40 times.**

6. Start the engine. With the engine idling maintain the fluid level.

7. Lower the front wheels and let the engine idle for two minutes.

8. Turn the steering wheel in both direction and verify power assist and quiet operation of the pump.

9. If the fluid is extremely foamy or milky looking, allow the vehicle to stand a few minutes and repeat the procedure.

✳✳ CAUTION

Do not run a vehicle with foamy fluid for an extended period. This may cause pump damage.

SUSPENSION

LOWER BALL JOINT

REMOVAL & INSTALLATION

RWD Models

See Figures 303 through 306.

1. Before servicing the vehicle, refer to the precautions in the beginning of this section.

2. Remove steering knuckle, refer to the steering knuckle removal and installation.

➡**To perform this procedure it works best to mount press, special tool C4212F, in a vise and hold the component in your hands.**

3. Place Receiver (1), Special Tool 9320-5, into cup area of Press (3), Special Tool C-4212F, as shown and tighten set screw.

4. Place Remover (2), Special Tool 9320-3, onto end of screw-drive of Press (3), Special Tool C-4212F, as shown.

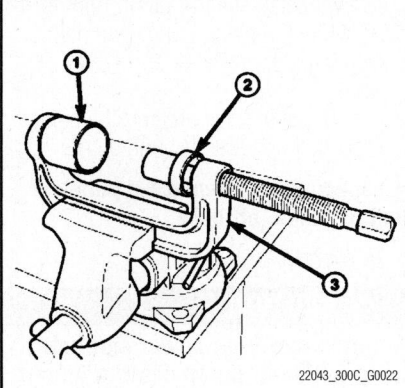

Fig. 303 Special tools and vise shown

FRONT SUSPENSION

5. Using a pair of snap-ring pliers, remove snap-ring from bottom of ball joint.

6. Install halves of Support Clamp (1), Special Tool 9320-1, over ball joint (2) and around knuckle surface (3) as shown. Install and snug Support Clamp (1) screws from underside.

7. Position knuckle (1) over tools guiding top of ball joint inside of Receiver (6), then hand tighten. Press screw-drive (4) until Remover (3) comes into contact with bottom of ball joint (2).

➡**When positioning the knuckle over tools, make sure the Receiver, Special Tool 9320-5, sets into recessed area (4) of Support Clamp, Special Tool 9320-1.**

8. Tighten Press screw-drive (4) forcing ball joint out of knuckle (1) and into Receiver (6).

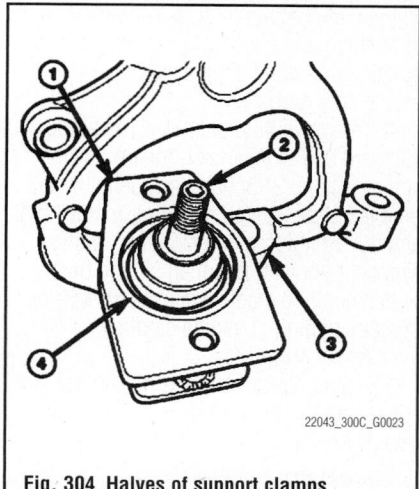

Fig. 304 Halves of support clamps

9. Loosen screw-drive (4) and remove knuckle (1) from Press. Remove ball joint from Receiver (6).

10. Remove Support Clamp (1) from knuckle.

To install:

11. Place Installer (1), Special Tool 9320-4, into cup area of Press (3), Special

Tool C-4212F, as shown and tighten set screw.

12. Place Remover (2), Special Tool 93203, onto end of screw-drive of Press (3), Special Tool C-4212F, as shown.

➡**This is the reverse of how the remover is installed on the screw—drive for removal.**

13. Start new ball joint (1) into bore of knuckle (2).

14. Position knuckle (1) over tools guiding top of ball joint inside of Installer (5) until outside flange of ball joint (4) comes into contact with Installer, then hand tighten Press screw-drive (3) until Remover (2) comes into contact with bottom of knuckle (1).

15. Using hand tools, tighten screw-drive (3), pressing ball joint into knuckle until flange (4) comes to a stop against the knuckle.

16. Loosen screw-drive and remove knuckle from Press.

17. Install the snap ring into groove on bottom of ball joint.

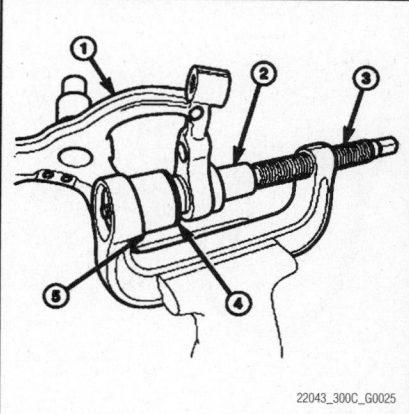

Fig. 306 Lower ball joint installation with special tools

18. Inspect ball joint for proper fit. Make sure seal boot is uniform and wire rings are in place

19. Install knuckle on vehicle, refer to the steering knuckle removal and installation.

LOWER CONTROL ARM

REMOVAL & INSTALLATION

AWD Models

See Figures 307 through 310.

1. Before servicing the vehicle, refer to the precautions in the beginning of this section.

2. Raise and support vehicle.

3. Remove wheel mounting nuts, then tire and wheel assembly.

4. While a helper applies brakes to keep hub from rotating, remove hub nut from the axle halfshaft.

5. Remove belly pan.

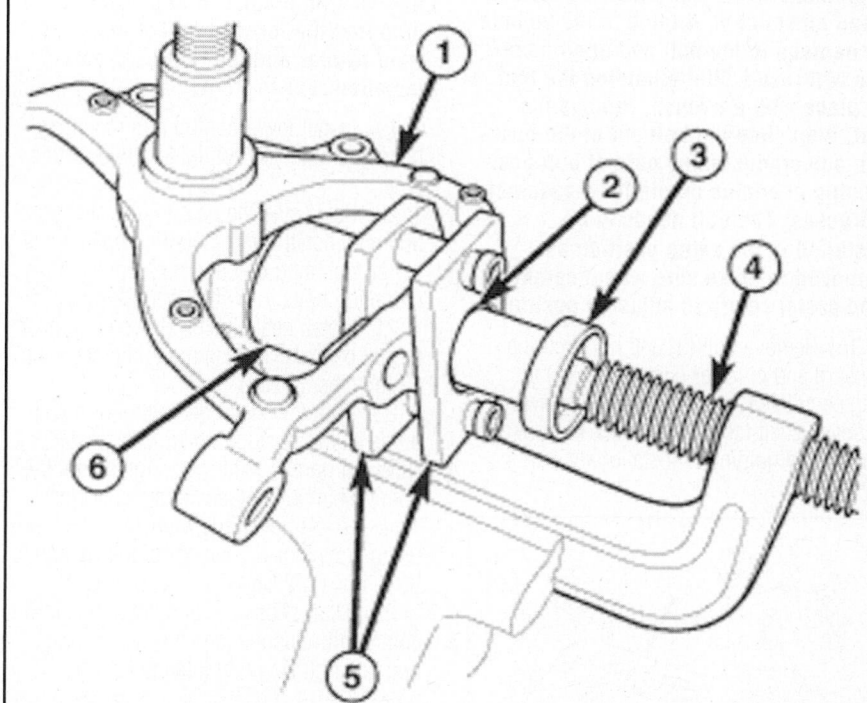

1. **Steering knuckle**
2. **Bottom of ball joint**
3. **Remover**
4. **Screw-drive**
5. **Support clamps**
6. **Receiver**

Fig. 305 Lower ball joint removal with special tools

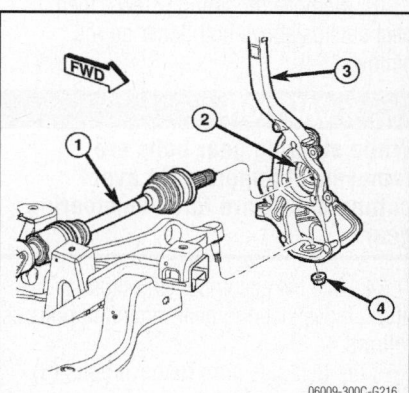

Fig. 307 Knuckle-to-lower control arm attachment. (1) halfshaft, (2) hub/bearing, (3) knuckle, (4) lower control arm stud nut—AWD models

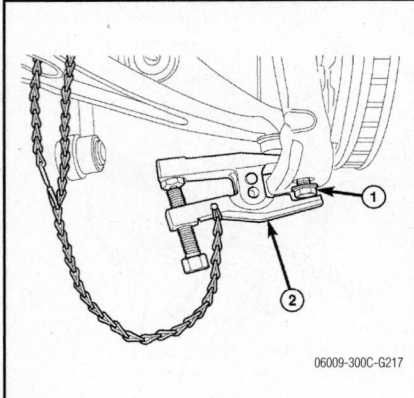

Fig. 308 Separating the lower ball joint from the knuckle with special tool 9360—AWD

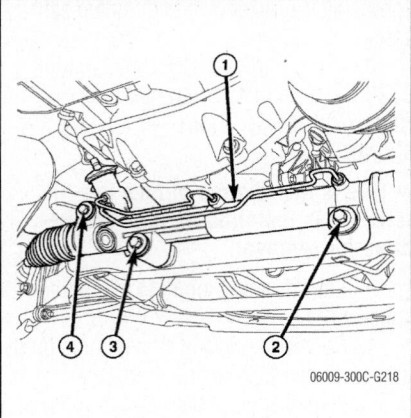

Fig. 309 Steering gear mounting bolt identification—AWD models

6. Loosen nut attaching lower control arm ball joint stud to knuckle. Back nut off until nut is even with end of stud. Keeping nut on at this location will help keep end of stud from distorting while using Puller in next step.

❊❊ CAUTION

In following step, use care not to damage ball joint seal boot.

7. Using Special Tool 9360, separate ball joint stud from knuckle.
8. Remove tool.
9. Remove nut from end of ball joint stud.
10. Back off nut from bolt attaching shock clevis bracket to lower control arm until it is flush with end of bolt.
11. Using a brass drift punch, tap the bolt out of the clevis bracket until bolt serrations clear bracket.
12. Remove nut and bolt for clevis bracket and control arm.
13. Remove mounting screws, then heat shields above both inner tie rod bellows.

❊❊ CAUTION

While steering gear bolts are removed, it important to avoid putting downward force on steering gear.

14. See the accompanying illustration, and remove steering gear mounting bolts as follows:
   a. Left side arm: Remove bolts (3) and (4). Loosen, but do not remove, bolt (2). It is important leave bolt (2) installed to avoid dropping gear too far, putting excessive force on steering coupling.

   b. Right side arm: Remove bolts (2) and (3). Loosen, but do not remove, bolt (4). It is important to leave bolt (4) installed to avoid dropping gear too far, putting excessive force on steering coupling.

➡ **If the lower control arm bolt at the engine cradle has a lengthwise grooved shaft, it is a special wheel alignment adjustment bolt and the bolt head must not be rotated in the vehicle or damage to the bolt and engine cradle will result. While holding the bolt in place with a wrench, remove the nut, then slide the bolt out of the bushing and cradle taking note of bolt positioning in engine cradle for reassembly purposes. The bolt needs to be installed in the same position as removed to make sure wheel camber and caster return to adjusted position.**

15. Remove bolt (3) and nut securing forward end of lower control arm (1) to engine cradle (2). If bolt has a lengthwise grooved shaft (see above note), remove bolt and nut by holding bolt stationary with a

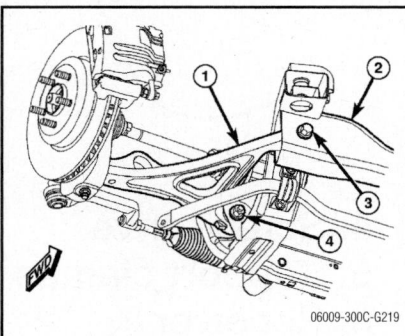

Fig. 310 Lower control arm mounting— AWD models

wrench, removing nut, then sliding bolt out of bushing and cradle while taking note of bolt positioning in engine cradle for reassembly purposes.

16. Remove bolt and nut (4) securing rearward end of lower control arm (1) to engine cradle (2). If bolt has a lengthwise grooved shaft (see above note), remove bolt and nut by holding bolt stationary with a wrench, removing nut, then sliding bolt out of bushing and cradle while taking note of bolt positioning in engine cradle for reassembly purposes.

17. Slide lower control arm (1) from engine cradle (2) and knuckle, and remove from vehicle.

To install:

➡ **If installing a lower control arm engine cradle bolt that is a wheel alignment adjustment bolt (identifying lengthwise grooved shaft), make sure to install it in the same position which it was in upon removal.**

18. Slide lower control arm into position in engine cradle and place ball joint stem into mounting hole in knuckle.

➡ **When installing lower control arm engine cradle bolts, it important to note that the forward bolt is installed front-to-rear and the rearward bolt is installed rear-to-front.**

19. Install lower control arm mounting bolts and nuts. Do not tighten bolts at this time.
20. Raise steering gear to mounted position and install lower mounting bolts. Install upper mounting bolt and nut. Tighten all mounting bolts to 90 ft. lbs. (122 Nm).
21. Install heat shields above both inner tie rod bellows. Tighten mounting screws to 62 inch lbs. (7 Nm).
22. Pull downward on control arm and guide ball joint stud into knuckle. Install NEW nut on ball joint stud. Tighten nut by holding ball joint stud with a hex wrench while turning nut with a wrench. Tighten nut using crow foot wrench on torque wrench to 90 ft. lbs. (122 Nm).
23. Align shock clevis bracket with lower control arm bushing and install mounting bolt and nut. Do not tighten nut at this time.
24. Install hub nut on end of axle half-shaft. While a helper applies brakes to keep hub from turning, tighten hub nut to 157 ft. lbs. (213 Nm).
25. Install tire and wheel assembly. Tighten wheel mounting nuts to 110 ft. lbs. (150 Nm).
26. Lower vehicle.

27. Position vehicle on an alignment rack/drive-on lift.

➡When tightening lower shock clevis mounting bolt, do not attempt rotating bolt. Bolt shaft is serrated. Turn nut only.

28. Tighten lower shock clevis bracket bolt nut to 128 ft. lbs. (174 Nm).
29. Perform wheel alignment.

❉❉ WARNING

If lower control arm engine cradle bolt is a wheel alignment adjustment bolt (lengthwise grooved shaft), be sure to only tighten nut. Do not rotate bolt or damage to cradle will occur.

30. Once camber is found to be within specifications, tighten lower control arm cradle bolt nuts to 130 ft. lbs. (176 Nm) torque while holding the bolts stationary.
31. Install belly pan.

RWD Models

See Figures 311 and 312.

1. Before servicing the vehicle, refer to the precautions in the beginning of this section.
2. Raise and support vehicle.
3. Remove wheel mounting nuts, then tire and wheel assembly.
4. Remove belly pan.
5. Remove screws fastening stabilizer bar heat shield on side of control arm repair.
6. Remove bolts fastening stabilizer bar bushing retainer in place on side of control arm repair.
7. Remove retainer halves from around stabilizer bar bushing.
8. Utilizing slit, remove bushing from stabilizer bar.

➡In the following step, the lower control arm cradle bolt is accessed through the opening created by removal of the bushing from the stabilizer bar.

❉❉ WARNING

If the lower control arm bolt at the engine cradle has a lengthwise grooved shaft, it is a special wheel alignment adjustment bolt and the bolt head must not be rotated in the vehicle or damage to the bolt and engine cradle will result. While holding the bolt in place with a wrench, remove the nut, then slide the bolt out of the bushing and cradle taking note of bolt positioning in engine cra-

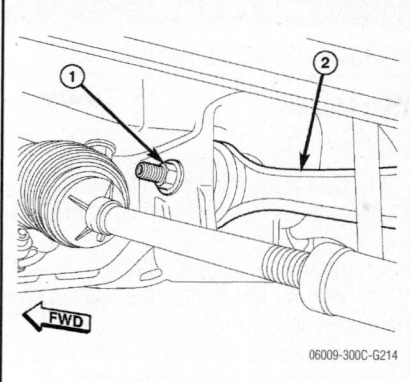

06009-300C-G214

Fig. 311 Remove bolt and nut (1) securing lower control arm (2) to engine cradle— 2WD models

dle for reassembly purposes. The bolt needs to be installed in the same position as removed to make sure wheel camber and caster return to adjusted position.

9. Remove bolt and nut securing lower control arm to engine cradle. If bolt has a lengthwise grooved shaft (see above note), remove bolt and nut by holding the bolt in place with a wrench, removing nut, then sliding bolt out of bushing and cradle while taking note of bolt positioning in lower control arm bushing for reassembly purposes.
10. Remove bolt securing shock assembly to lower control arm.
11. Remove screw fastening wheel speed sensor to knuckle. Pull sensor head out of knuckle.
12. Remove wheel speed sensor cable routing clip from brake flex hose routing bracket.
13. Loosen nut attaching ball joint stud to lower control arm. Back nut off until nut

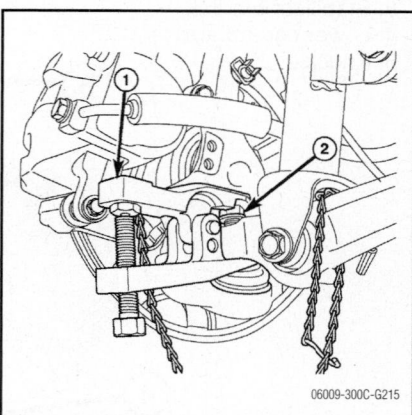

06009-300C-G215

Fig. 312 Using Puller (1), Special Tool 9360, separate ball joint stud (2) from lower control arm—2WD models

is even with end of stud. Keeping nut on at this location will help keep end of stud from distorting while using Puller in next step.

➡In following step, use care not to damage ball joint seal boot.

14. Using Puller, Special Tool 9360, separate ball joint stud from lower control arm.
15. Remove nut from end of ball joint stud attaching lower control arm to knuckle.
16. Pry knuckle downward and slide ball joint stud out of lower control arm. Position knuckle outward, away from lower control arm.
17. Slide lower control arm out of engine cradle and remove from vehicle.

To install:

➡If installing a lower control arm engine cradle bolt that is a wheel alignment adjustment bolt (lengthwise grooved shaft), make sure to install it in the same position which it was in upon removal.

18. Slide lower control arm into position in engine cradle and install mounting bolt from rear.
19. Install nut on lower control arm cradle bolt, but do not tighten at this time.

❉❉ CAUTION

Before installing knuckle to lower control arm, measure height of ball joint seal boot mounted on knuckle. If seal boot height is above 25.5 mm, any air inside seal boot must be expelled. To do so, follow these steps:

a. Tip ball joint stud completely to one side.
b. Using thumb and index finger, gently squeeze seal boot together at center expelling any air. Do not allow grease to be release.
c. Push down very top of seal boot.
d. Return ball joint stud to original "centered" position.
e. Measure ball joint seal boot height making sure it is within specification.
f. Wipe any grease from ball joint stud.

20. Pull knuckle downward and position lower control arm over ball joint stud. Release knuckle, guiding stud into lower control arm. Install NEW nut on ball joint stud attaching lower control arm to knuckle. Tighten nut by holding ball joint stud with a

hex wrench while turning nut with a wrench. Tighten nut using crow foot wrench on torque wrench to 50 ft. lbs. (68 Nm) + 90°.

21. Install wheel speed sensor head into knuckle and install mounting screw. Tighten screw to 95 inch lbs. (11 Nm).

22. Attach wheel speed sensor cable and routing clip to brake flex hose routing bracket.

23. Install lower shock mounting bolt attaching shock assembly to lower control arm. Do not tighten bolt at this time.

24. Install tire and wheel assembly. Tighten wheel mounting nuts to 110 ft. lbs. (150 Nm).

25. Lower vehicle.

❈❈ CAUTION

Because stabilizer bar is disconnected at cradle it is important to use extra care while moving vehicle to alignment rack/drive-on lift.

26. Position vehicle on an alignment rack/drive-on lift.

27. Tighten lower shock mounting bolt to 128 ft. lbs. (174 Nm).

28. Perform wheel alignment.

❈❈ CAUTION

If the control arm engine cradle bolt is a wheel alignment adjustment bolt (lengthwise grooved shaft), be sure to only tighten the nut. Do not rotate the bolt head or damage to the bushing will occur.

29. Once camber is found to be within specifications, using a crowfoot wrench, tighten lower control arm cradle bolt nut to 130 ft. lbs. (176 Nm) torque while holding the bolt stationary.

❈❈ CAUTION

Because of stabilizer bushing outer shape, it is very important to install bushings in position discussed in following step.

30. Utilizing slit in bushing, install stabilizer bar bushing against locating collar on stabilizer. Make sure slit in bushing is positioned toward rear of vehicle.

31. Install stabilizer bar bushing retainer halves around bushing.

32. Install bolts securing stabilizer bar bushing retainer halves to cradle. Tighten bolts to 44 ft. lbs. (60 Nm).

33. Install stabilizer bar heat shield over stabilizer bar bushing retainer. Install mounting screws.

34. Install belly pan.

MACPHERSON STRUT

REMOVAL & INSTALLATION

AWD Models

See Figure 313.

1. Before servicing the vehicle, refer to the precautions in the beginning of this section.

2. Raise and support vehicle.

3. Remove wheel mounting nuts, then tire and wheel assembly.

4. While holding link ball joint stem from rotating, remove nut fastening stabilizer link to strut clevis bracket. Slide link ball joint stem from clevis bracket.

5. Remove nut and pinch bolt fastening clevis bracket to bottom of strut assembly.

6. Remove nut and bolt attaching strut clevis bracket to lower control arm.

7. Pull lower end of clevis bracket outward away from lower control arm bushing, then slide it off strut assembly. It may be necessary to use an appropriate prying tool to spread clamp area of clevis bracket allowing removal from strut assembly.

8. Lower vehicle just enough to access upper strut assembly mounting nuts.

9. If equipped, remove strut tower cap from top of strut assembly.

10. Remove three nuts fastening strut assembly to strut tower.

11. Remove strut assembly from vehicle.

To install:

12. Guide strut assembly up into strut tower and into mounting holes.

13. Install three nuts fastening strut assembly to strut tower. Tighten nuts to 20 ft. lbs. (27 Nm).

14. If equipped, align strut tower cap with strut mounting nuts and snap into place.

15. Raise and support vehicle.

16. Pull lower end of strut assembly outward, then slide clevis bracket onto lower end. Slide clevis bracket onto strut assembly until bracket contacts collar on strut housing.

17. Install pinch bolt and nut fastening clevis bracket to bottom of strut assembly. Install pinch bolt from rear. Do not tighten at this time.

18. Slide clevis bracket over bushing mounted in lower control arm.

19. Install bolt and nut attaching strut clevis bracket to lower control arm. Do not tighten at this time.

20. Tighten pinch bolt attaching clevis bracket to strut assembly to 45 ft. lbs. (61 Nm).

21. Slide stabilizer link ball joint stem into clevis bracket. Install nut fastening link to clevis bracket. Tighten nut by holding ball joint stud while turning nut. Tighten nut using crow foot wrench on torque wrench to 95 ft. lbs. (128 Nm).

22. Install tire and wheel assembly.

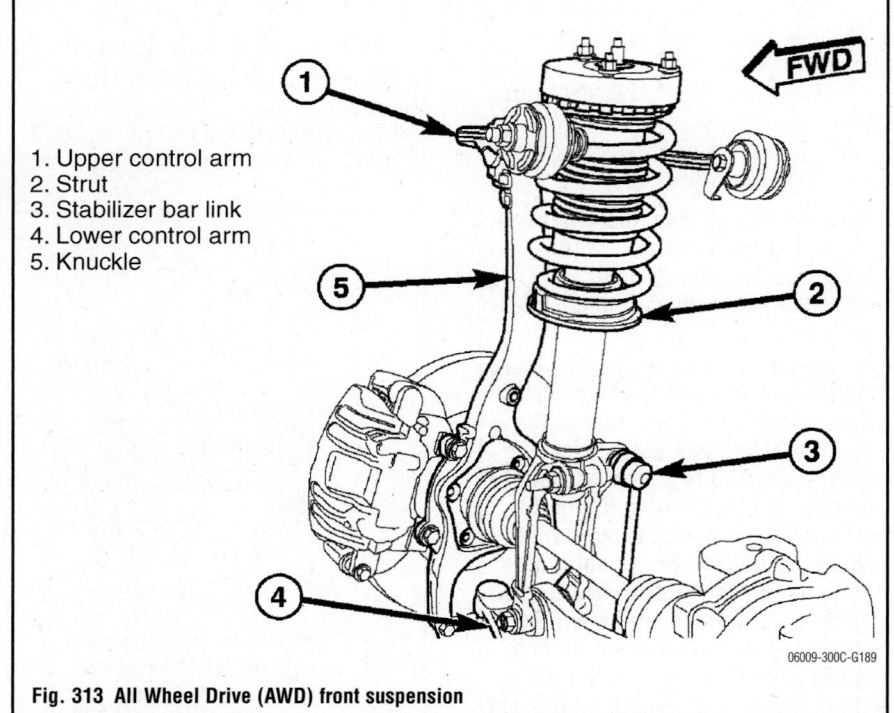

1. Upper control arm
2. Strut
3. Stabilizer bar link
4. Lower control arm
5. Knuckle

06009-300C-G189

Fig. 313 All Wheel Drive (AWD) front suspension

Tighten the wheel mounting nuts to 110 ft. lbs. (150 Nm).

23. Lower vehicle.

➡**When tightening lower strut clevis mounting bolt, do not attempt rotating bolt. Bolt shaft is serrated. Turn nut only.**

24. Tighten the lower strut clevis bracket bolt nut to 128 ft. lbs. (174 Nm).

RWD Models

See Figures 314 through 316.

1. Before servicing the vehicle, refer to the precautions in the beginning of this section.

2. If equipped, remove front strut tower cap from top of strut assembly.

3. Remove three nuts fastening strut assembly to strut tower.

4. Raise and support vehicle.

5. Remove wheel mounting nuts, then tire and wheel assembly.

6. Remove nut (2) fastening stabilizer link (3) to strut assembly (1). Slide link ball joint stem from strut assembly.

7. Remove bolt securing strut assembly to lower control arm.

8. Disconnect wheel speed sensor cable routing clip at brake tube bracket.

9. Loosen nut attaching upper ball joint stud to knuckle. Back nut off until nut is even with end of stud. Keeping nut on at this location will help keep end of stud from distorting while using Puller in next step.

✳✳ CAUTION

In following step, use care not to damage ball joint seal boot while sliding Puller, Special Tool 9360, into place past seal boot.

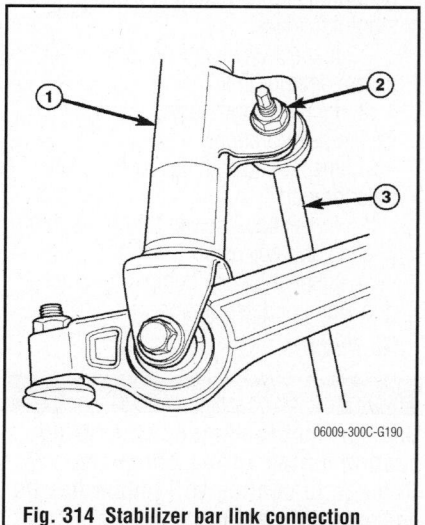

Fig. 314 Stabilizer bar link connection

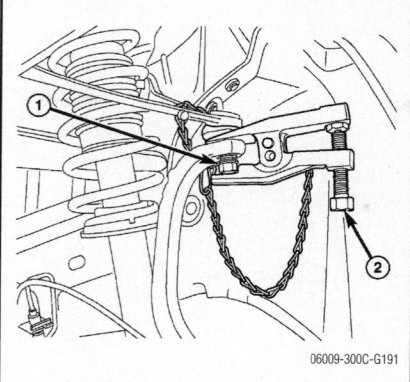

06009-300C-G191

Fig. 315 Separating the upper ball stud from the knuckle

10. Using Puller (2), Special Tool 9360, separate the upper ball joint stud (1) from knuckle.

11. Remove nut from end of upper ball joint stud.

12. Tip top of knuckle outward using care not to overextend bake flex hose.

13. Remove strut assembly from vehicle.

To install:

14. Place strut assembly into front suspension using reverse direction in which it was removed.

✳✳ CAUTION

It is important to tighten nut as described in following step to avoid damaging ball stud joint.

15. Place upper ball joint stud through hole in top of knuckle and install nut. Tighten nut by holding ball joint stud with a hex wrench while turning nut with a wrench. Tighten nut using crow foot wrench on torque wrench to 35 ft. lbs. (47 Nm) + 90°turn torque.

16. Connect wheel speed sensor cable routing clip at brake tube bracket.

17. Install lower strut mounting bolt attaching strut assembly to lower control arm. Do not tighten bolt at this time.

18. Slide stabilizer link ball joint stem into strut assembly from front. Install nut fastening link to strut assembly. Tighten nut by holding ball joint stud while turning nut. Tighten nut using crow foot wrench on torque wrench to 95 ft. lbs. (128 Nm).

19. Install tire and wheel assembly. Tighten wheel mounting nuts to 110 ft. lbs. (150 Nm).

20. Lower vehicle.

21. Install three nuts fastening strut assembly to strut tower. Tighten nuts to 20 ft. lbs. (27 Nm).

1. Strut
2. Upper control arm
3. Knuckle
4. Tension strut
5. Lower control arm
6. Stabilizer bar
7. Stabilizer bar link

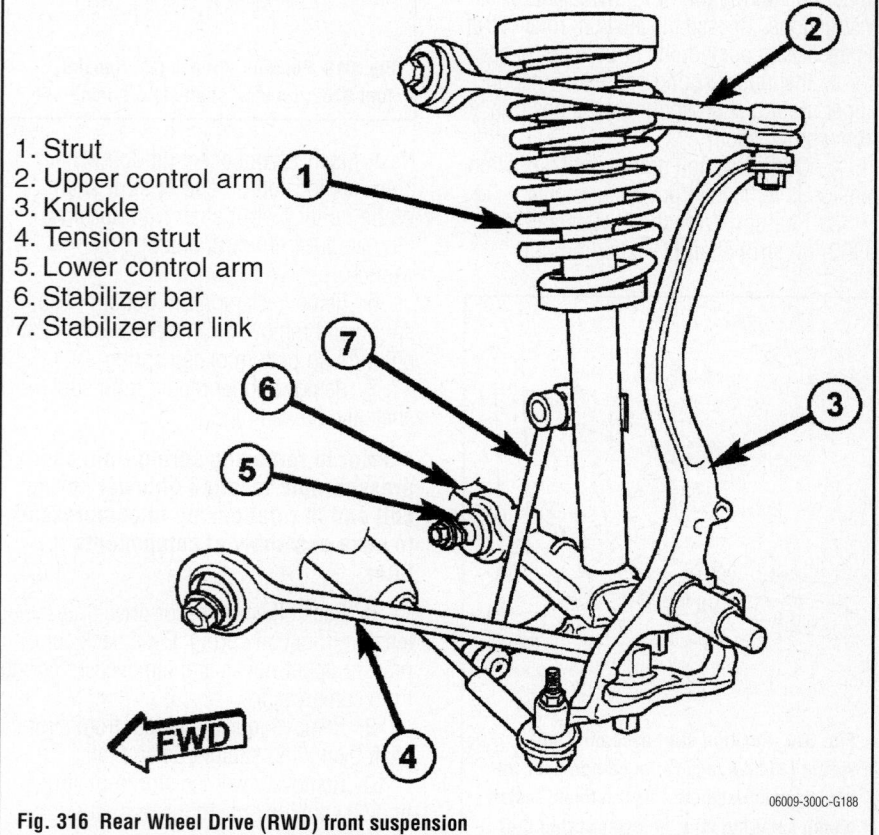

06009-300C-G188

Fig. 316 Rear Wheel Drive (RWD) front suspension

22. If equipped, align strut tower cap with strut mounting nuts and snap into place.

OVERHAUL

See Figures 317 through 323.

1. Before servicing the vehicle, refer to the precautions in the beginning of this section.

The strut assembly must be removed from vehicle for it to be disassembled and assembled. For strut assembly disassembly and assembly, use of strut Spring Compressor, Pentastar® Service Equipment (PSE) tool W-7200, or equivalent, is recommended to compress coil spring. Follow manufacturer's instructions closely.

❊❊ CAUTION

Do not remove strut shaft nut before coil spring is compressed. Coil spring is held under pressure and must be compressed, removing spring tension from upper and lower mounts, before strut removal.

2. Position strut assembly coil spring on hooks of compressor following manufacturer's instructions. Install clamp securing strut to lower spring coil.

3. Position compressor upper hooks on upper coil spring following manufacturer's instructions. To ease installation, rotate strut as necessary positioning strut in compressor so that upper spring coil ends (step in upper mount) at straight outward position from compressor.

4. Compress coil spring until all spring tension is removed from upper mount.

5. Position Wrench (2), Special Tool 9362, on strut shaft (1) retaining nut.

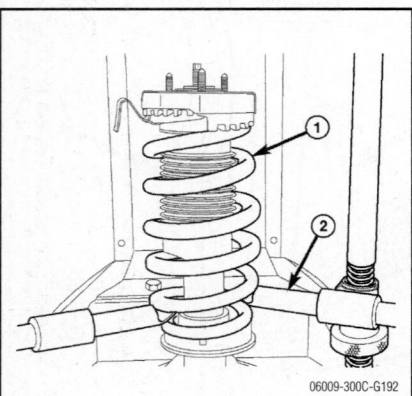

Fig. 317 Position strut assembly coil spring (1) on hooks (2) of compressor following manufacturer's instructions. Install clamp securing strut to lower spring Coil

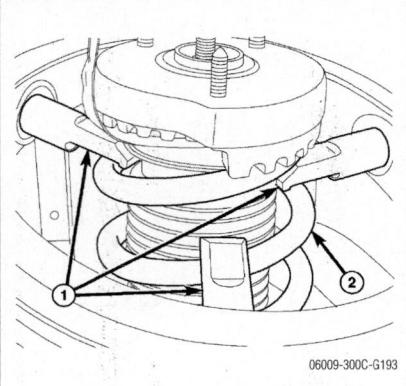

Fig. 318 Position compressor upper hooks (1) on upper coil spring (2) following manufacturer's instructions

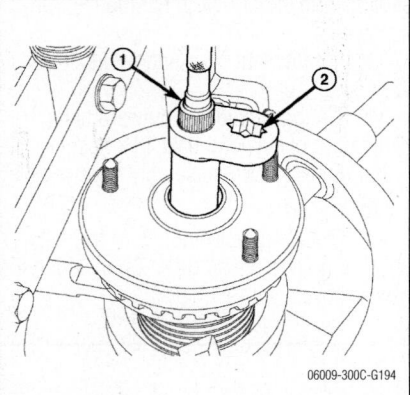

Fig. 319 Position Wrench (2), Special Tool 9362, on strut shaft (1) retaining nut

Next, insert 8mm socket though wrench onto hex located on end of strut shaft. While holding strut shaft from turning, remove nut from strut shaft using wrench.

6. Remove clamp from bottom of coil spring and remove strut and lower isolator out through bottom of coil spring.

7. Remove upper mount from strut shaft and coil spring.

➡**Prior to removing spring from compressor, note location of lower spring coil end in relationship to compressor to ease assembly of components later.**

8. Back off compressor drive, releasing tension from coil spring. Push back compressor upper hooks and remove coil spring from compressor.

9. Remove jounce bumper from strut shaft by pulling straight up and off.

10. Remove lower isolator from strut body by pulling straight up and off strut shaft.

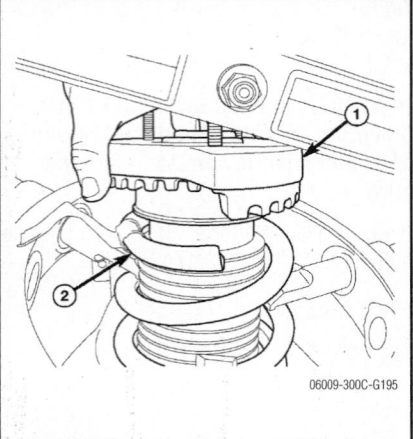

Fig. 320 Remove upper mount (1) from strut shaft and coil spring (2)

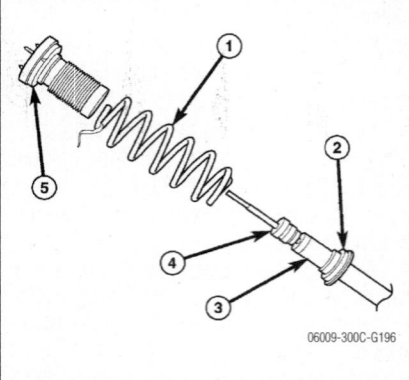

Fig. 321 Strut parts: (1) spring, (2) lower isolator, (3) strut, (4) jounce bumper, (5) upper mount

11. Inspect strut assembly components for following and replace as necessary:

a. Inspect strut for any condition of shaft binding over full stroke of shaft.

b. Inspect upper mount for cracks and distortion and its retaining studs for any sign of damage.

c. Inspect upper spring isolator for severe deterioration.

d. Inspect lower spring isolator for severe deterioration.

e. Inspect dust shield for tears and deterioration.

f. Inspect coil spring for cracks in the coating and corrosion.

g. Inspect jounce bumper for cracks and signs of deterioration.

To install:

❊❊ WARNING

Use care not to damage coil spring coating during spring assembly. Damage to coating will jeopardize its corrosion protection.

➡**Left and right springs must not be interchanged.**

12. Place coil spring (part number tag end upward) in compressor lower hooks following manufacturer's instructions. To ease strut reassembly, rotate coil spring around until upper coil ends at straight outward position from compressor. Proper orientation of spring to upper mount (once installed) is necessary.

13. Position compressor upper hooks over coil spring following manufacturer's instructions.

14. Compress coil spring far enough to allow strut installation.

15. If separated, install upper mount onto coil spring. Match step in upper isolator to end of spring coil.

16. Install lower spring isolator on strut body.

17. Install jounce bumper on strut shaft, small end first.

18. Install strut through bottom of coil spring until lower spring isolator (on strut) contacts lower end of coil spring. Match step built into isolator to lower coil end. Once in this position, stabilizer bar bracket, or clevis key on AWD models, should point straight inward toward compressor body. If not, rotate isolator on strut body until alignment is achieved when isolator is correctly positioned with lower spring coil.

19. Install clamp to hold strut and coil spring together.

20. Install retaining nut on strut shaft as far as possible by hand. Make sure nut is installed far enough for 8mm socket to grasp hex on end of shaft for tightening.

21. Install Wrench (on end of a torque wrench), Special Tool 9362, on strut shaft retaining nut. Next, insert 8mm socket though wrench onto hex located on end of

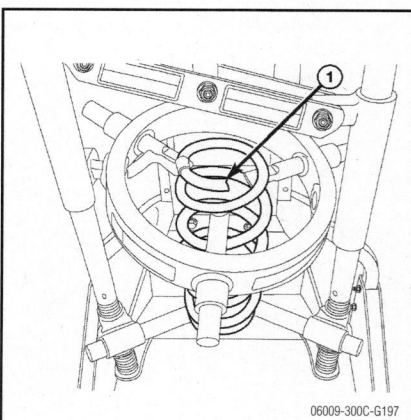

Fig. 322 Coil spring upper end (1) positioning

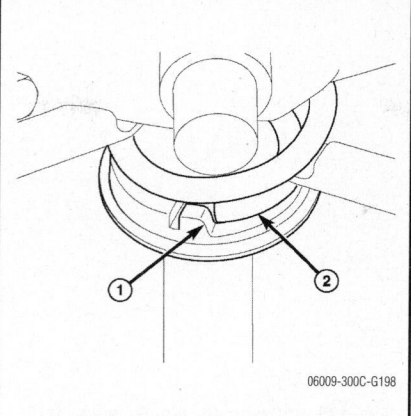

Fig. 323 Match step built into isolator (1) to lower coil end (2)

strut shaft. While holding strut shaft from turning, tighten nut using wrench to 66 ft. lbs. (90 Nm).

22. Slowly release tension from coil spring by backing off compressor drive fully. As tension is relieved, make sure strut components are properly in place.

23. Remove clamp from lower end of coil spring and strut. Push back spring compressor upper and lower hooks, then remove strut assembly from spring compressor.

24. Install strut assembly on vehicle.

STABILIZER BAR (SWAY BAR)

REMOVAL & INSTALLATION

AWD Models

See Figure 324.

1. Before servicing the vehicle, refer to the precautions in the beginning of this section.

2. Raise and support vehicle.

3. Remove belly pan.

4. On each side of vehicle, remove nut fastening stabilizer link to stabilizer bar. Slide link ball joint stem from bar.

5. On each side of vehicle, remove bolts fastening stabilizer bar isolator retainer in place.

6. Remove stabilizer bar with isolators and retainers from vehicle.

7. On each side of bar, remove retainers from around stabilizer bar isolators.

8. Utilizing slit, remove each isolator from stabilizer bar.

To install:

9. Utilizing slit in isolator, install each stabilizer bar isolator on bar. Make sure slit in isolator is positioned toward rear of vehicle once installed on vehicle.

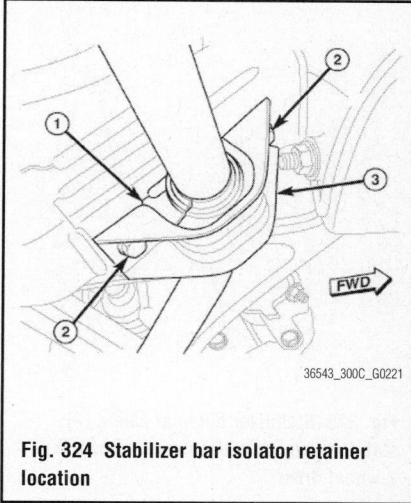

Fig. 324 Stabilizer bar isolator retainer location

10. Install stabilizer bar isolator retainer over each isolator.

➡**When attaching stabilizer link to stabilizer bar, make sure link ball joint stem is pointed inboard toward engine cradle.**

11. Install stabilizer bar ends to each stabilizer link. Slide link ball joint stem through mounting hole in bar. Loosely install nuts at this time.

a. Raise stabilizer bar to engine cradle, placing bushings into mounted position.

12. Install bolts securing each stabilizer bar isolator retainer to cradle. Tighten bolts to 44 ft. lbs. (60 Nm).

13. While holding stem from rotating at hex or flat tighten stabilizer link nuts at each end of stabilizer bar to 95 ft. lbs. (128 Nm).

14. Install belly pan.

15. Lower the vehicle.

RWD Models

See Figures 325 through 329.

1. Before servicing the vehicle, refer to the precautions in the beginning of this section.

2. Raise and support vehicle.

3. Remove belly pan.

4. On each side of vehicle, remove screws fastening stabilizer bar heat shield. Remove heat shield.

5. On each side of vehicle, remove bolts fastening stabilizer bar isolator retainer in place.

6. On each side of vehicle, remove retainer halves from around stabilizer bar isolator.

7. Utilizing slit, remove each isolator from stabilizer bar.

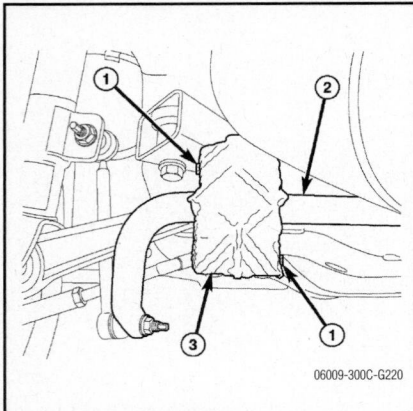

Fig. 325 Stabilizer bat heat shield (3), stabilizer bar (2), heat shield screws (1)—2-wheel drive

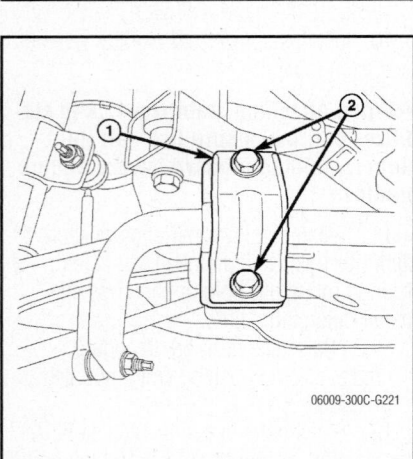

Fig. 326 Isolator retainer (1) and bolts (2)—2-wheel drive

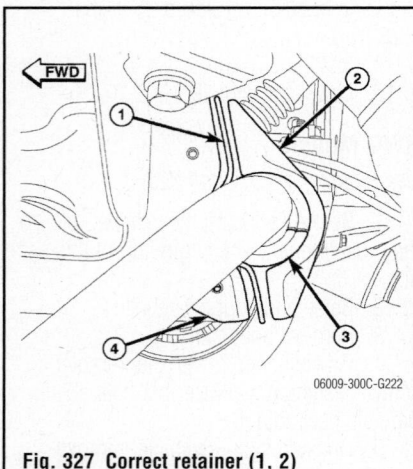

Fig. 327 Correct retainer (1, 2) positioning—2-wheel drive

8. On each side of vehicle, remove nut (5) fastening stabilizer link (3) to stabilizer bar (4). Slide link ball joint stem (1) from bar, then remove bar from vehicle.

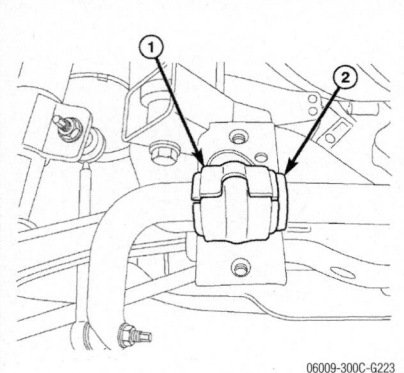

Fig. 328 Utilizing slit, remove each isolator (1) from stabilizer bar (2)—2-wheel drive

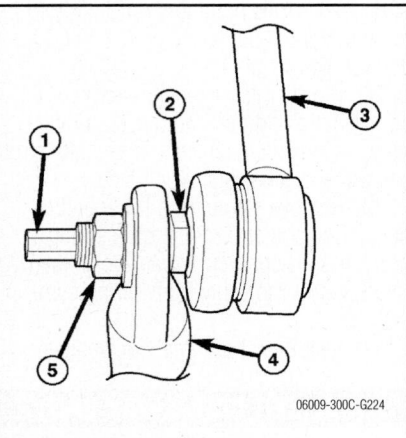

Fig. 329 Stabilizer link-to-bar attachment—2-wheel drive

To install:

➡ When attaching stabilizer link to stabilizer bar, make sure link ball joint stem is pointed inboard toward engine cradle.

9. On each side of vehicle, raise stabilizer bar to stabilizer link and slide link ball joint stem through mounting hole in bar. Loosely install nut at this time.

✷✷ WARNING

Because of stabilizer isolator outer shape, it is very important to install isolators in position discussed in following step.

10. Utilizing slit in isolator, install each stabilizer bar isolator on bar resting against locating collar as shown. Make sure slit in isolator is positioned toward rear of vehicle.

11. On each side of vehicle, install stabilizer bar isolator retainer halves around isolator.

12. On each side of vehicle, install bolts securing stabilizer bar isolator retainer halves to cradle. Tighten bolts to 44 ft. lbs. (60 Nm).

13. On each side of vehicle, install stabilizer bar heat shield over stabilizer bar isolator retainer. Install mounting screws.

14. While holding stem from rotating at hex or flat tighten stabilizer link nuts at each end of stabilizer bar to 95 ft. lbs. (128 Nm).

15. Install belly pan.

16. Lower vehicle.

STEERING KNUCKLE

REMOVAL & INSTALLATION

AWD Models

See Figure 330.

1. Before servicing the vehicle, refer to the precautions in the beginning of this section.

2. Raise and support vehicle.

3. Remove wheel mounting nuts, then tire and wheel assembly.

4. While a helper applies brakes to keep hub from rotating, remove hub nut from axle halfshaft.

5. Remove clip fastening wheel speed sensor to knuckle.

6. Remove screw fastening wheel speed sensor to knuckle. Pull sensor head out of knuckle.

7. Access and remove front brake rotor.

8. Remove nut from outer tie rod end stud.

9. Separate tie rod stud from knuckle.

10. Loosen nut (4) attaching lower control arm ball joint stud to knuckle (3). Back nut off until nut is even with end of stud. Keeping nut on at this location will help

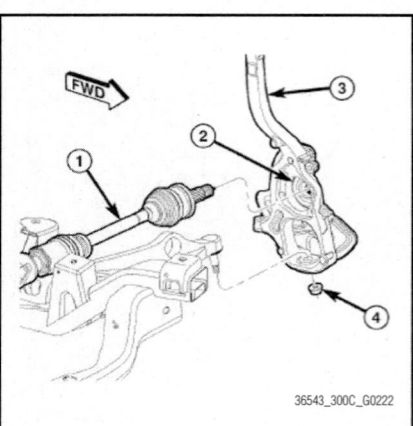

Fig. 330 Lower control arm ball joint stud to knuckle

keep end of stud from distorting while using puller in next step.

> ✳✳ **WARNING**
>
> **In following step, use care not to damage ball joint seal boot.**

11. Separate ball joint stud from knuckle.

    a. Remove tool.

12. Remove nut from end of ball joint stud.

13. Loosen nut attaching upper ball joint stud to knuckle. Back nut off until nut is even with end of stud. Keeping nut on at this location will help keep end of stud from distorting while using Puller in next step.

> ✳✳ **WARNING**
>
> **In following step, use care not to damage ball joint seal boot.**

14. Separate upper ball joint stud from knuckle.

15. Remove tool.

16. Remove nut from end of upper ball joint stud.

17. Slide knuckle off halfshaft and remove from vehicle.

To install:

18. Place knuckle over lower ball joint stud and guide hub and bearing onto axle halfshaft.

19. Start NEW nut on lower ball joint stud. Do not tighten at this time.

> ✳✳ **WARNING**
>
> **It is important to tighten nut as described in following step to avoid damaging ball stud joint.**

20. Place upper ball joint stud through hole in top of knuckle and install nut. Tighten nut by holding ball joint stud with a hex wrench while turning nut with a wrench. Tighten nut using crow foot wrench on torque wrench to 35 ft. lbs. (47 Nm) +90°.

> ✳✳ **WARNING**
>
> **It is important to tighten nut as described in following step to avoid damaging ball stud joint.**

21. Tighten lower ball joint nut by holding ball joint stud with a hex wrench while turning nut with a wrench. Tighten nut using crow foot wrench on torque wrench to 50 ft. lbs. (68 Nm) +90°.

> ✳✳ **WARNING**
>
> **It is important to tighten nut as described in following step to avoid damaging ball stud joint.**

22. Place outer tie rod stud through hole in knuckle and install nut. Tighten nut by holding stud with a wrench while turning nut with another wrench. Tighten nut using crow foot wrench on torque wrench to 63 ft. lbs. (85 Nm).

23. Install brake rotor, then disc brake caliper and adapter assembly.

24. Install hub nut on end of axle halfshaft. While a helper applies brakes to keep hub from turning, tighten hub nut to 157 ft. lbs. (213 Nm).

25. Install wheel speed sensor head into knuckle and install mounting screw. Tighten screw to 95 inch lbs. (11 Nm).

26. Attach wheel speed sensor cable routing clip at knuckle.

27. Install tire and wheel assembly. Tighten wheel mounting nuts to 110 ft. lbs. (150 Nm).

28. Lower vehicle.

29. Pump brake pedal several times to ensure vehicle has a firm brake pedal before moving vehicle.

30. Check and adjust brake fluid level in reservoir as necessary.

31. Perform wheel alignment.

UPPER BALL JOINT

REMOVAL & INSTALLATION

The upper ball joint is not replaceable. If defective, the control arm assembly must be replaced.

UPPER CONTROL ARM

REMOVAL & INSTALLATION

See Figures 331 through 333.

1. Before servicing the vehicle, refer to the precautions in the beginning of this section.

2. If removing left upper control arm, remove and reposition coolant recovery container.

    a. If removing right upper control arm, remove IPM from mount and reposition.

3. If equipped, remove front shock tower cap from top of shock assembly.

4. Remove three nuts fastening shock assembly to shock tower.

5. Remove nuts from upper control arm mounting bolts.

    a. Raise and support vehicle.

    b. Remove wheel mounting nuts, then tire and wheel assembly.

    c. Disconnect the wheel speed sensor cable routing clip at brake tube bracket.

6. Loosen nut attaching upper ball joint stud to knuckle. Back nut off until nut is

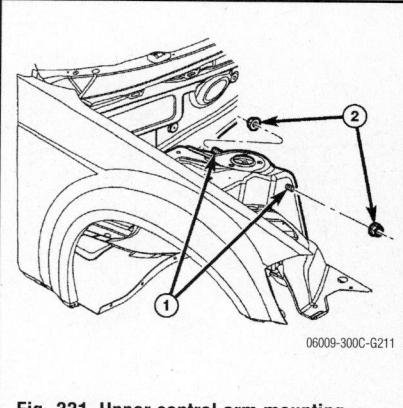

Fig. 331 Upper control arm mounting bolts (1) and nuts (2)

even with end of stud. Keeping nut on at this location will help keep end of stud from distorting while using puller in next step.

> ✳✳ **CAUTION**
>
> **In following step, use care not to damage ball joint seal boot.**

7. Using Puller, Special Tool 9360, separate upper ball joint stud from knuckle.

8. Remove nut from end of upper ball joint stud.

9. Pull shock assembly downward until studs clear shock tower, then pull it outward allowing access to upper control arm mounting bolts.

10. Remove upper control arm mounting (flag) bolts.

11. Remove upper control arm (2) from bracket (3) in shock tower (4).

To install:

➡**Although AWD and RWD upper control arms are similar in appearance, they are not interchangeable.**

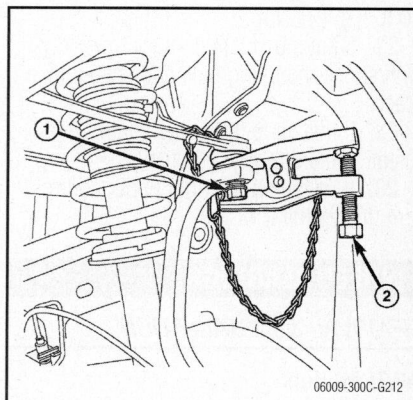

Fig. 332 Using Puller (2), Special Tool 9360, separate upper ball joint stud (1) from knuckle

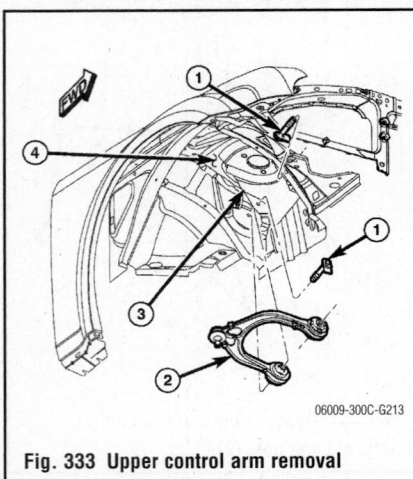

Fig. 333 Upper control arm removal

12. Slide upper control arm into bracket located in shock tower.

13. Install upper control arm mounting (flag) bolts through bracket, arm and tower. Position flags on bolt heads outward, toward wheel opening.

14. Move shock assembly allowing studs to be inserted through shock tower mounting holes.

15. Place upper ball joint stud (1) through hole in top of knuckle and install nut. Tighten nut by holding ball joint stud with a hex wrench while turning nut with a wrench. Tighten nut using crow foot wrench on torque wrench to 35 ft. lbs. (47 Nm) plus 90°.

16. Connect wheel speed sensor cable routing clip at brake tube bracket.

17. Install tire and wheel assembly. Tighten wheel mounting nuts to 110 ft. lbs. (150 Nm).

18. Lower vehicle to curb position.

19. Install nuts on upper control arm body mounting bolts. Tighten nuts to 55 ft. lbs. (75 Nm).

20. Install three nuts fastening shock assembly to shock tower. Tighten nuts to 20 ft. lbs. (27 Nm).

21. If equipped, align shock tower cap with shock mounting nuts and snap into place.

22. If installing left upper control arm, install coolant recovery container.

23. If installing the right upper control arm, install the IPM.

WHEEL BEARINGS

REMOVAL & INSTALLATION

AWD Models

See Figures 334 and 335.

1. Before servicing the vehicle, refer to the precautions in the beginning of this section.

2. Raise and support vehicle.
   a. Remove wheel mounting nuts, then tire and wheel assembly.

3. While a helper applies brakes to keep hub from rotating, remove hub nut from the axle halfshaft.
   a. Access and remove front brake rotor.

4. Remove four bolts fastening hub and bearing to knuckle.

5. Slide hub and bearing off axle halfshaft and knuckle.

To install:

➡**Before installing hub and bearing on end of axle halfshaft, ensure isolation washer is present on end of halfshaft. Inspect washer making sure it is not worn or damaged. Washer can be installed in either direction on shaft.**

6. Slide hub and bearing onto axle halfshaft. Position hub and bearing onto knuckle, lining up mounting bolt holes.

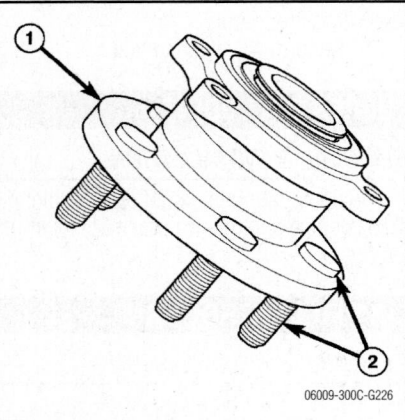

Fig. 334 All Wheel Drive (AWD) front hub/bearing (1), studs (2)

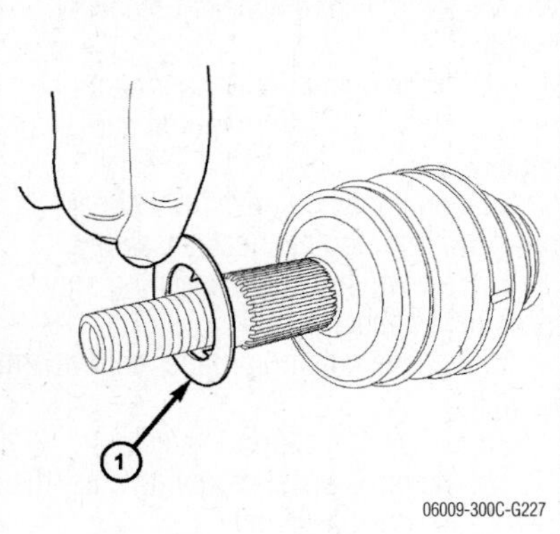

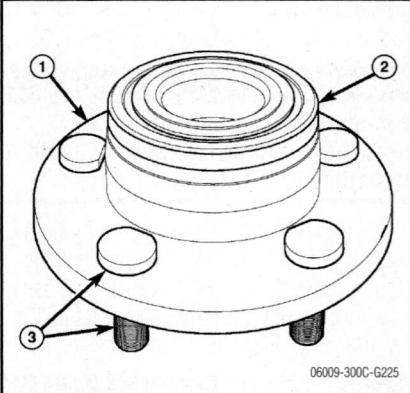

Fig. 335 Isolation washer—All Wheel Drive (AWD) models

7. Install four bolts fastening hub and bearing in place. Tighten mounting bolts to 50 ft. lbs. (68 Nm).

8. Install brake rotor, then disc brake caliper and adapter assembly.

9. Install hub nut on end of axle halfshaft. While a helper applies brakes to keep hub from turning, tighten hub nut to 157 ft. lbs. (213 Nm).

10. Install tire and wheel assembly. Tighten wheel mounting nuts to 110 ft. lbs. (150 Nm).

11. Lower vehicle.

12. Pump brake pedal several times to ensure vehicle has a firm brake pedal before moving vehicle.

13. Check and adjust brake fluid level in reservoir as necessary.

14. Road test vehicle and make several stops to wear off any foreign material on brakes and to seat brake pads.

RWD Models

See Figure 336.

1. Before servicing the vehicle, refer to the precautions in the beginning of this section.

2. Raise and support vehicle.

3. Remove wheel mounting nuts, then tire and wheel assembly.

4. Access and remove front brake rotor.

5. Remove dust cap. When doing this, avoid damaging internal bore of hub to preserve seal integrity.

6. Remove hub nut.

7. Slide hub and bearing off knuckle spindle.

To install:

➡**Prior to installation, inspect magnetic encoder (for wheel speed sensor)**

Fig. 336 2-wheel drive hub/bearing assembly (1), magnetic encoder (2), stud (3)

for any damage and make sure any metal debris sticking to it is removed.

8. Slide hub and bearing onto knuckle spindle.

9. Install hub nut on end of spindle. Tighten hub nut to 184 ft. lbs. (250 Nm).

10. Install brake rotor, then disc brake caliper and adapter assembly.

➡**Install a new dust cap to preserve seal integrity.**

11. Install NEW dust cap on hub and bearing.

12. Install tire and wheel assembly. Tighten wheel mounting nuts to 110 ft. lbs. (150 Nm).

13. Lower vehicle.

14. Pump brake pedal several times to ensure vehicle has a firm brake pedal before moving vehicle.

15. Check and adjust brake fluid level in reservoir as necessary.

16. Road test vehicle and make several stops to wear off any foreign material on brakes and to seat brake pads.

ADJUSTMENT

The front wheel bearing and wheel hub of this vehicle are a one piece sealed unit or hub and bearing unit type assembly. No adjustment is possible.

SUSPENSION

CAMBER LINK

REMOVAL & INSTALLATION

See Figures 337 through 339.

1. Before servicing the vehicle, refer to the precautions in the beginning of this section.

2. Raise and support vehicle.

3. On both sides of vehicle, remove wheel mounting nuts, then rear tire and wheel assembly.

✷✷ CAUTION

Before opening fuel system, review all warnings and cautions under Fuel System.

4. If servicing left side shock absorber, remove fuel filler tube:

a. Disconnect negative battery cable.

b. Drain fuel from tank.

c. Fuel filler tube assembly.

d. Open filler tube door.

e. Remove retaining wire from inside filler tube rubber.

f. Start removing rubber from body sheet metal.

g. Remove retaining wire from inside filler tube rubber.

h. Start removing rubber from body sheet metal.

i. Filler tube and rubber removed from body sheet metal.

j. Remove the left inner splash shield.

k. Disconnect the filler tube vent line.

l. Remove the filler tube mounting bolt.

m. Remove the under body splash shield.

n. Loosen the filler tube hose clamp. Leave the clamp tight on the hose and fuel tank location.

o. Move clamp toward the fuel tank.

p. Remove the filler tube assembly from the vehicle.

5. Position an extra pair of jackstands under and support forward end of engine cradle to help stabilize vehicle during rear suspension removal/installation.

6. Perform following if vehicle is equipped with dual exhaust or are servicing right side on vehicle with single exhaust:

a. Position under-hoist utility jack or stand several inches below exhaust at muffler.

b. Disconnect exhaust isolators at muffler and resonators hangers.

c. Lower exhaust down to rest upon top of jack or stand placed below muffler.

7. Position under-hoist utility jack or transmission jack under center of rear axle differential. Raise jack head to contact differential and secure in place. When securing crossmember to jack, be sure not to secure stabilizer bar.

8. Remove shock absorber upper mounting screws.

9. Remove shock absorber lower mounting bolt and nut.

➡**If equipped with AWD, when removing crossmember mounting bolts in following step, be sure to not to misplace spacers between crossmember mounts and body.**

✷✷ WARNING

When removing crossmember mounting bolts it is important NOT to loosen or remove crossmember mounting bolts on opposite side of vehicle. Doing so will require rear wheel alignment following reinstallation to ensure proper thrust angle.

10. Remove both front and rear crossmember mounting bolts on repair-side of vehicle.

✷✷ WARNING

To avoid damaging other components of vehicle, do not lower crossmem-

REAR SUSPENSION

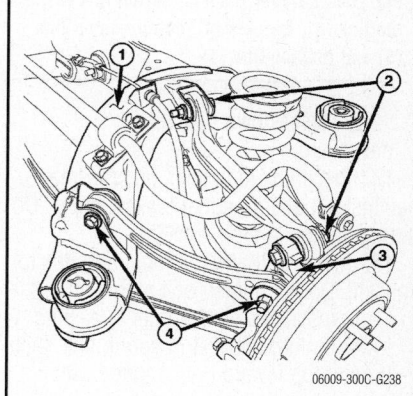

06009-300C-G238

Fig. 337 Camber link attachment points

ber any further than necessary to remove shock absorber.

11. Slowly lower jack allowing repair-side of crossmember to drop. Do not lower jack at a fast rate. Lower jack just enough to allow top of shock absorber to clear body flange.

12. Remove shock absorber by tipping top outward and lifting lower end out of pocket in spring link.

➡**Do not lower side of crossmember any further than necessary to gain access to link mounting bolts at crossmember.**

13. Remove nut (4) and bolt (2) mounting link to knuckle (3).

14. Remove nut (4) and bolt (2) mounting link to crossmember (1).

15. Remove link.

To install:

16. When installing link, note the following:

a. Heavier, thicker end goes toward crossmember.

b. Fore-or-aft bow faces forward (curves around coil spring).

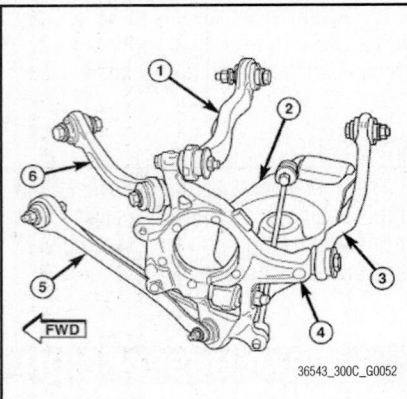

Fig. 338 Camber link (1), spring link (2), toe link (3), knuckle (4), compression link (5) and tension link (6)

c. Up-or-down bow faces downward.

17. Place link in bracket on crossmember. Install bolt and nut at crossmember. Do not tighten bolt at this time.

18. Install bolt and nut mounting link to knuckle. Do not tighten bolt at this time.

a. Install shock absorber by setting lower end into pocket in spring link, then tipping top inward until aligned with upper mounting holes.

19. Install lower shock mounting bolt and nut. Do not tighten at this time.

20. If vehicle is equipped with AWD, make sure spacers on top of crossmember mount bushings on side of repair are in position.

21. Carefully raise jack, guiding coil spring and upper end of shock absorber into mounted positions.

22. Install shock absorber upper mounting screws. Tighten upper mounting screws to 38 ft. lbs. (52 Nm).

➡**Rear crossmember mounting bolts are longer than front mounting bolts. Do not interchange mounting bolts.**

23. Install crossmember mounting bolts. Snug, but do not fully tighten bolts at this time.

24. Measure distance between from tension link to body weld flange directly in front of it, just outboard of front mount bushing. This distance must be at least 12mm to allow proper clearance for suspension movement. If distance is less than 12mm, shift that side of rear crossmember directly rearward until distance is 12mm or greater. To do so, loosen 3 mounting bolts slightly, leaving one on opposite side shifted, snugged to pivot off of. Shift crossmember rearward and snug loosened bolts. Measure opposite side to be sure it also maintains minimum 12mm distance.

25. Tighten all crossmember mounting bolts to 133 ft. lbs. (180 Nm).

26. Remove jack from under rear axle differential.

27. If previously lowered, raise rear exhaust back to mounted position and connect exhaust isolators at muffler and resonators hangers. Remove jack or stand below exhaust muffler.

28. If removed, install fuel filler tube:

a. Insert filler tube into the fuel tank rubber hose.

b. Slide hose clamp into place and tighten.

c. Hose clamp in place and tighten.

d. Install filler tube mounting bolt.

e. Install filler tube vent line.

29. Install the underbody splash shield.

a. Install the left inner splash shield.

30. Lower vehicle until front tires contact floor but rear is still suspended. Place jackstands under each rear suspension spring link. Place an appropriate wooden block between stand and link to avoid damaging spring link, then lower vehicle until full vehicle weight is supported by suspension.

31. Tighten camber link fasteners to:

a. Bolt at crossmember: 63 ft. lbs. (85 Nm).

b. Bolt nut at knuckle: 72 ft. lbs. (98 Nm).

32. Tighten shock absorber lower mounting bolt nut to 53 ft. lbs. (72 Nm).

33. Raise vehicle and remove jackstands.

34. Install tire and wheel assemblies. Tighten wheel mounting nuts to 110 ft. lbs. (150 Nm).

35. Lower vehicle.

36. Perform wheel alignment.

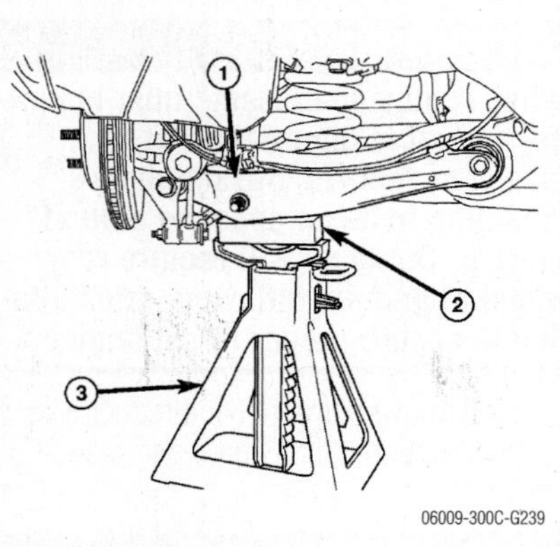

COIL SPRING

REMOVAL & INSTALLATION

See Figures 340 through 345.

1. Raise and support vehicle.

2. On both sides of vehicle, remove wheel mounting nuts, then rear tire and wheel assembly.

3. If servicing left side shock absorber, remove fuel filler tube.

4. Position an extra pair of jack stands under and support forward end of engine cradle to help stabilize vehicle during rear suspension removal/installation.

5. Perform following if vehicle is equipped with dual-exhaust or are servicing right side on vehicle with single exhaust.

a. Position under-hoist utility jack or stand several inches below exhaust at muffler.

b. Disconnect exhaust isolators at muffler and resonators hangers.

c. Lower exhaust down to rest upon top of jack or stand placed below muffler.

6. Position under-hoist utility jack or transmission jack under center of rear axle differential. Raise jack head to contact differential and secure in place. When securing crossmember to jack, be sure not to secure stabilizer bar.

7. Remove shock absorber upper mounting screws.

8. Remove shock absorber (1) lower mounting bolt (2) and nut (4).

➡**If equipped with AWD, when removing crossmember mounting bolts in following step, be sure to not to misplace spacers (1) between crossmember mounts (2) and body.**

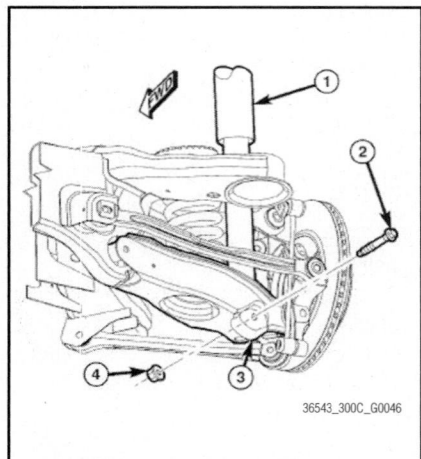

Fig. 339 Jackstand (3) and wood block (2) placement under link (1)

Fig. 340 Rear shock absorber removal

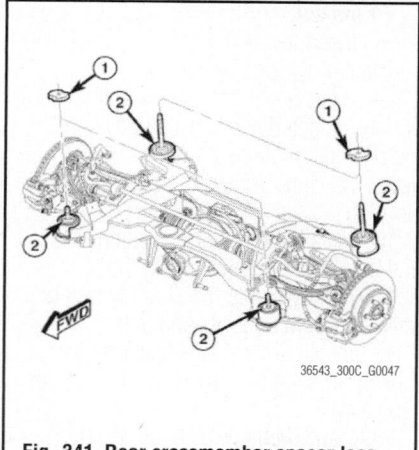

Fig. 341 Rear crossmember spacer locations

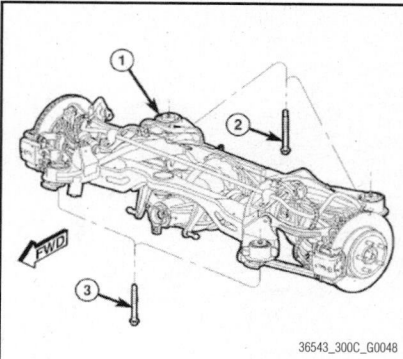

Fig. 342 Removing rear crossmember bolts

⁂ WARNING

When removing crossmember mounting bolts (2 and 3) it is important NOT to loosen or remove crossmember mounting bolts on opposite side of vehicle. Doing so will require rear wheel alignment following reinstallation to ensure proper thrust angle.

9. Remove both front and rear crossmember mounting bolts (2 and 3) on repair-side of vehicle.

⁂ WARNING

To avoid damaging other components of vehicle, do not lower crossmember (1) any further than necessary to remove shock absorber.

10. Slowly lower jack allowing repair-side of crossmember to drop. Do not lower jack at a fast rate. Lower jack just enough to allow top of shock absorber to clear body flange.

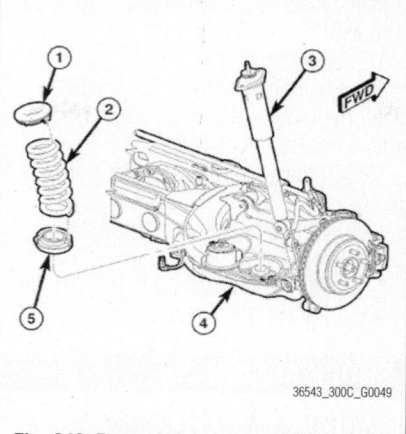

Fig. 343 Removing crossmember components

11. Remove shock absorber (3) by tipping top outward and lifting lower end out of pocket in spring link (4).

12. Disconnect brake hose at bracket mounted to body to allow to avoid overextending hose, damaging it, during following step.

13. Slowly lower jack until crossmember is low enough to remove coil spring. Do not lower jack any further than necessary to remove spring.

14. Remove coil spring and isolators (1, 2 and 5).

To install:

➡**Rear coil springs are interchangeable.**

15. Install upper and lower isolators on coil spring.

➡**Before installing coil spring, make sure isolators are completely installed on ends of spring.**

16. Install coil spring with isolators into spring pocket of spring link fitting lower isolator to shape of pocket, then align top of spring with body mount.

17. Install shock absorber by setting lower end into pocket in spring link, then tipping top inward until aligned with upper mounting holes.

18. Install lower shock mounting bolt and nut. Do not tighten at this time.

19. If vehicle is equipped with AWD, make sure spacers on top of crossmember mount bushings on side of repair are in position.

20. Carefully raise jack, guiding coil spring and upper end of shock absorber (4) into mounted positions.

21. Install shock absorber upper mounting screws (2). Tighten upper mounting screws to 38 ft. lbs. (52 Nm).

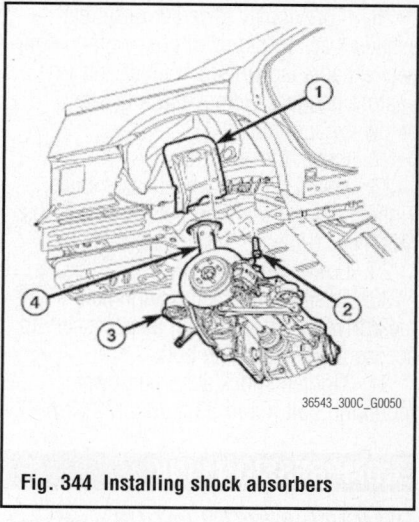

Fig. 344 Installing shock absorbers

➡**Rear crossmember mounting bolts are longer than front mounting bolts. Do not interchange mounting bolts.**

22. Install crossmember mounting bolts. Snug, but do not fully tighten bolts at this time.

23. Measure distance (1) between from tension link (2) to body weld flange (3) directly in front of it, just outboard of front mount bushing (4). This distance must be at least 12 mm to allow proper clearance for suspension movement. If distance is less than 12 mm, shift that side of rear crossmember directly rearward until distance is 12 mm or greater. To do so, loosen 3 mounting bolts slightly, leaving one on opposite side of shift snugged to pivot off of. Shift crossmember rearward and snug loosened bolts. Measure opposite side to be sure it also maintains minimum 12 mm distance.

24. Tighten all crossmember mounting bolts to 133 ft. lbs. (180 Nm).

25. Remove jack from under rear axle differential.

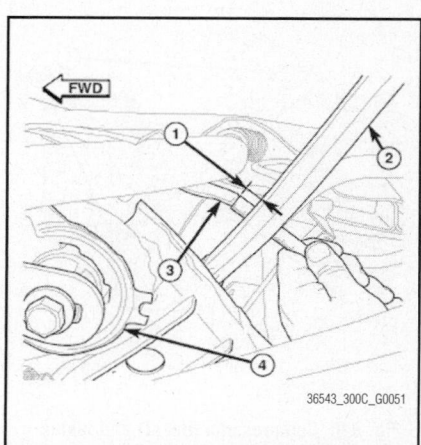

Fig. 345 Measuring suspension clearance

26. If previously lowered, raise rear exhaust back to mounted position and connect exhaust isolators at muffler and resonators hangers. Remove jack or stand below exhaust muffler.

27. Install fuel filler tube.

28. Install tire and wheel assemblies. Tighten wheel mounting nuts to 110 ft. lbs. (150 Nm) (Police - 140 ft. lbs. 190 Nm).

29. Lower vehicle.

30. Position vehicle on alignment rack/drive-on lift. Raise lift as necessary to access lower mounting bolt.

31. Tighten shock absorber lower mounting bolt nut to 53 ft. lbs. (72 Nm).

COMPRESSION LINK

REMOVAL & INSTALLATION

See Figure 346.

1. Before servicing the vehicle, refer to the precautions in the beginning of this section.

2. Raise and support vehicle.

3. Remove wheel mounting nuts, then rear tire and wheel assembly.

4. Remove bolt and nut mounting link at knuckle.

5. Remove bolt and nut mounting link at crossmember.

6. Remove link.

To install:

➡**Although the compression link is different end-to-end, there is no top and bottom.**

7. Position link and install bolt and nut mounting link at crossmember. Do not tighten bolt at this time.

8. Install bolt and nut mounting link at knuckle. Do not tighten bolt at this time.

9. Install tire and wheel assembly.

Tighten wheel mounting nuts to 110 ft. lbs. (150 Nm).

10. Lower vehicle.

11. Position vehicle on alignment rack/drive-on lift. Raise vehicle as necessary to access link fasteners.

12. Tighten compression link fasteners to:

    a. Bolt at crossmember: 63 ft. lbs. (85 Nm).

    b. Bolt at knuckle: 60 ft. lbs. (81 Nm).

13. Perform wheel alignment.

SHOCK ABSORBER

REMOVAL & INSTALLATION

With Load Leveling

See Figures 347 and 348.

1. Before servicing the vehicle, refer to the precautions in the beginning of this section.

2. Raise and support vehicle.

3. Remove wheel mounting nuts, then tire and wheel assembly.

4. Position under-hoist utility jack or jackstand under outer spring link adding just enough support to keep suspension from going into full-rebound when shock absorber mounting bolts are removed.

5. Remove shock absorber lower mounting bolt and nut.

6. Remove shock absorber upper mounting bolts.

7. Remove shock absorber.

To install:

8. Insert lower end of shock absorber into well of spring link.

9. Raise upper end of shock absorber up into mounted position on body and install upper mounting screws. Tighten upper mounting screws to 38 ft. lbs. (52 Nm).

10. Install lower shock mounting bolt and nut. Do not tighten at this time.

11. Remove under-hoist utility jack or jackstand from under spring link.

12. Install tire and wheel assembly. Tighten wheel mounting nuts to 110 ft. lbs. (150 Nm).

13. Lower vehicle.

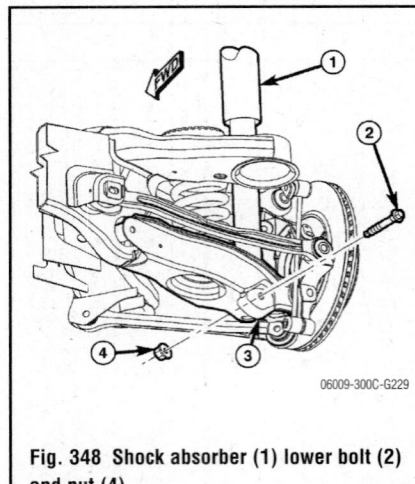

Fig. 348 Shock absorber (1) lower bolt (2) and nut (4)

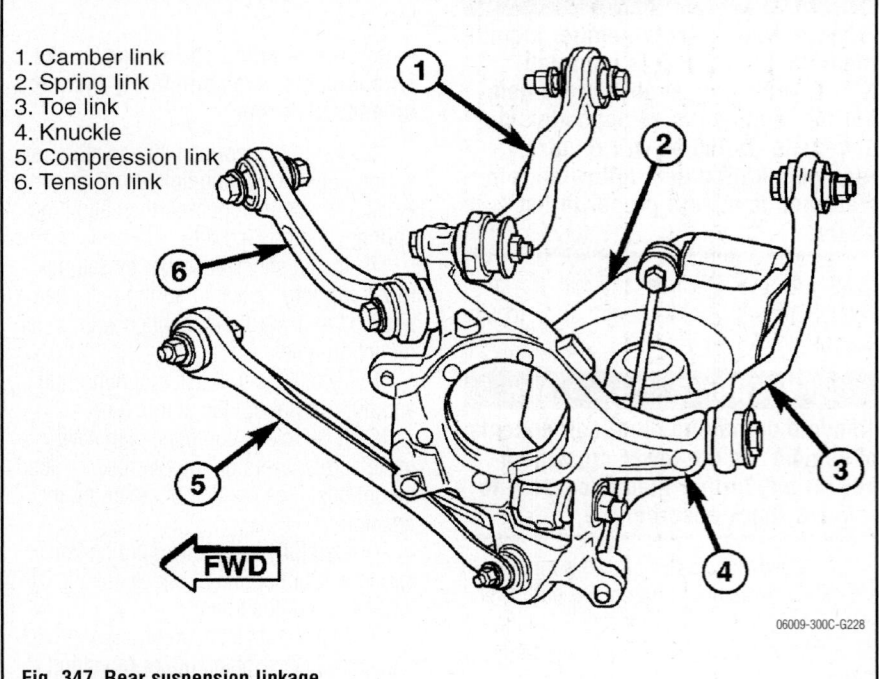

1. Camber link
2. Spring link
3. Toe link
4. Knuckle
5. Compression link
6. Tension link

FWD

Fig. 347 Rear suspension linkage

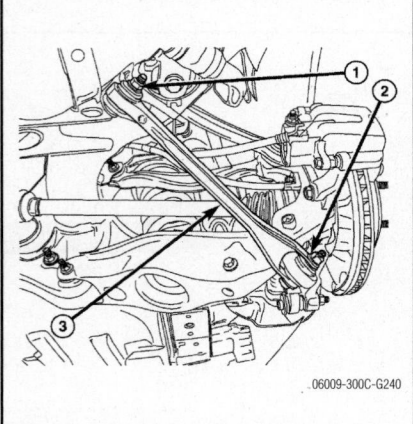

Fig. 346 Compression link (3) and fasteners (1, 2)

14. Position vehicle on alignment rack/drive-on hoist. Raise vehicle as necessary to access lower mounting bolt.

15. Tighten shock absorber lower mounting bolt nut to 53 ft. lbs. (72 Nm).

Without Load Leveling

See Figures 349 through 356.

1. Before servicing the vehicle, refer to the precautions in the beginning of this section.

2. Raise and support vehicle.

3. On both sides of vehicle, remove wheel mounting nuts, then rear tire and wheel assembly.

✳✳ CAUTION

Before opening fuel system, review all warnings and cautions under Fuel System.

4. If servicing left side shock absorber, remove fuel filler tube:

   a. Disconnect negative battery cable.

   b. Drain fuel from tank.

   c. Fuel filler tube assembly.

   d. Open filler tube door.

   e. Remove retaining wire from inside filler tube rubber.

   f. Start removing rubber from body sheet metal.

   g. Remove retaining wire from inside filler tube rubber.

   h. Start removing rubber from body sheet metal.

   i. Filler tube and rubber removed from body sheet metal.

   j. Remove the left inner splash shield.

   k. Disconnect the filler tube vent line.

   l. Remove the filler tube mounting bolt.

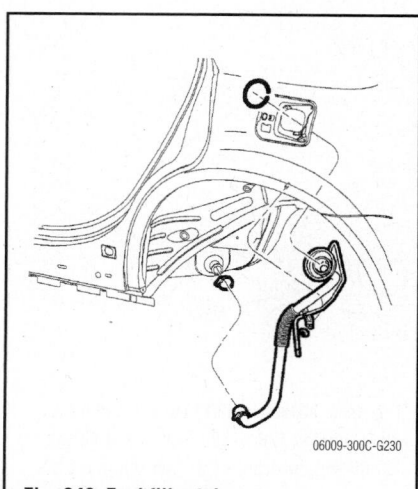

Fig. 349 Fuel filler tube

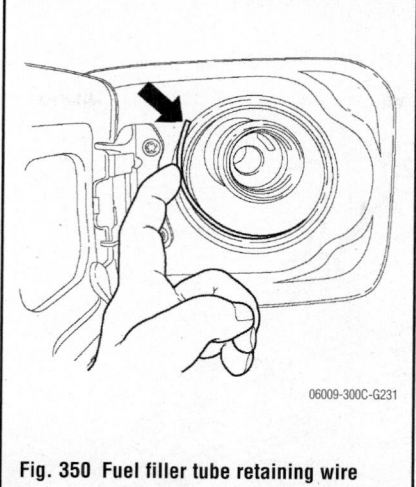

Fig. 350 Fuel filler tube retaining wire

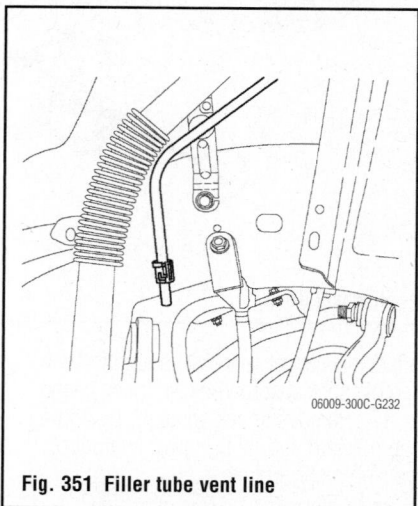
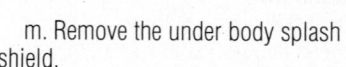

Fig. 351 Filler tube vent line

   m. Remove the under body splash shield.

   n. Loosen the filler tube hose clamp. Leave the clamp tight on the hose and fuel tank location.

   o. Move clamp toward the fuel tank.

   p. Remove the filler tube assembly from the vehicle.

5. Position an extra pair of jackstands under and support forward end of engine cradle to help stabilize vehicle during rear suspension removal/installation.

6. Perform following if vehicle is equipped with dual exhaust or are servicing right side on vehicle with single exhaust:

   a. Position under-hoist utility jack or stand several inches below exhaust at muffler.

   b. Disconnect exhaust isolators at muffler and resonators hangers.

   c. Lower exhaust down to rest upon top of jack or stand placed below muffler.

7. Position under-hoist utility jack or transmission jack (3) under center of rear

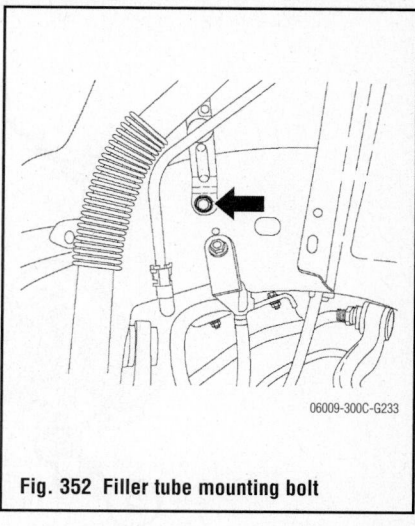

Fig. 352 Filler tube mounting bolt

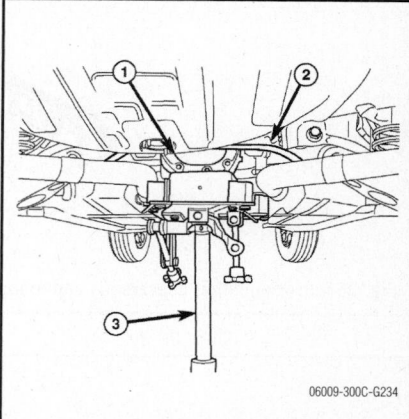

Fig. 353 Utility hoist under the exhaust system

axle differential (1). Raise jack head to contact differential and secure in place. When securing crossmember to jack, be sure not to secure stabilizer bar.

8. Remove shock absorber upper mounting screws.

9. Remove shock absorber lower mounting bolt and nut.

➡ **When removing crossmember mounting bolts in following step, be sure to not to misplace spacers between crossmember mounts and body.**

✳✳ WARNING

If equipped with AWD, when removing crossmember mounting bolts it is important NOT to loosen or remove crossmember mounting bolts on opposite side of vehicle. Doing so will require rear wheel alignment following reinstallation to ensure proper thrust angle.

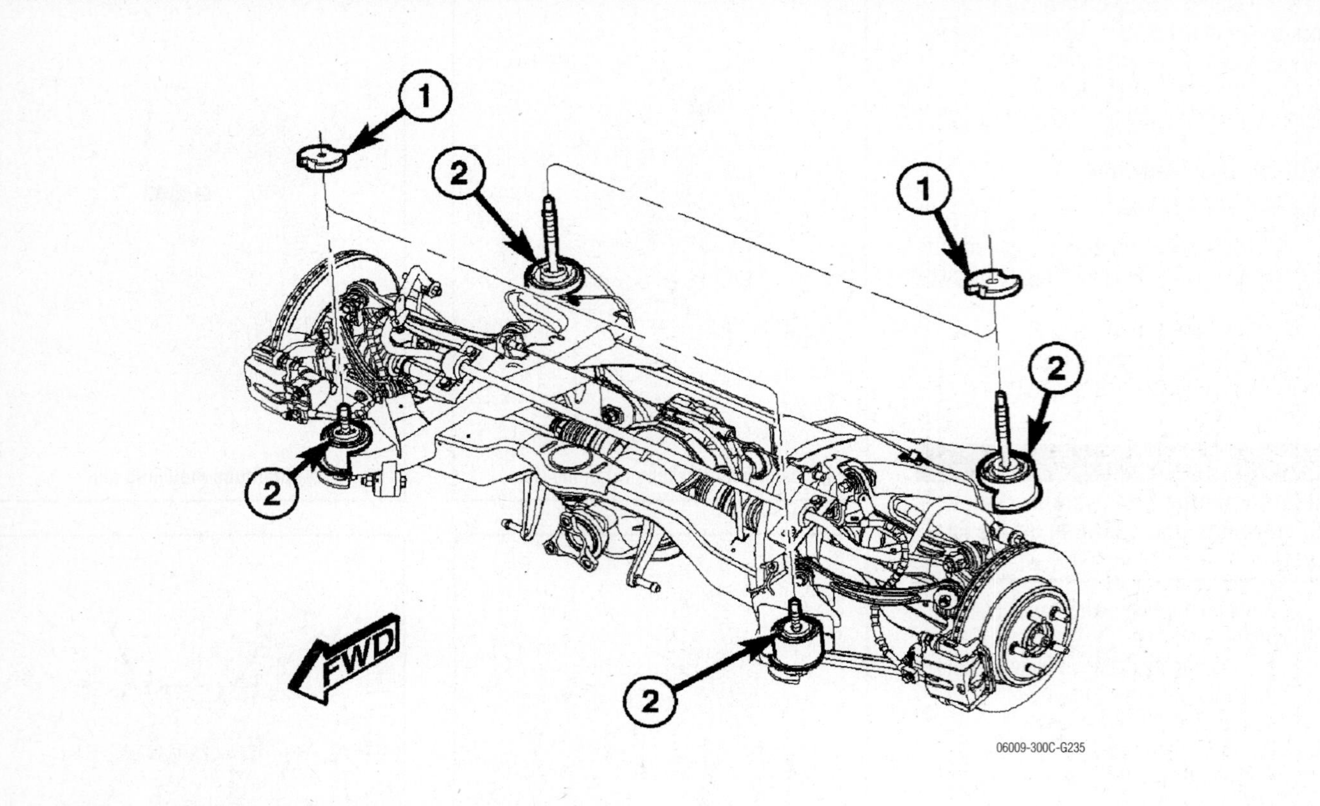

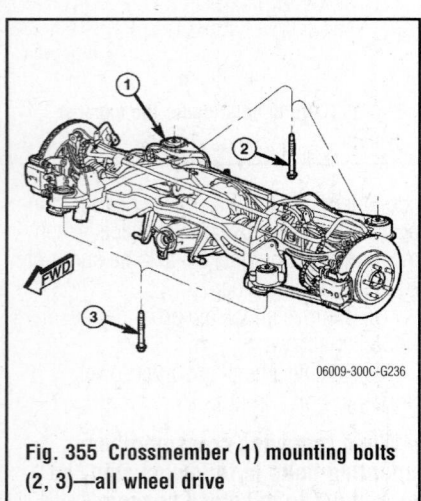

Fig. 354 Crossmember spacers (1) and mounts (2)—all wheel drive

06009-300C-G235

Fig. 355 Crossmember (1) mounting bolts (2, 3)—all wheel drive

06009-300C-G236

10. Remove both front and rear crossmember mounting bolts on side of vehicle being serviced.

❋❋ WARNING

To avoid damaging other components of vehicle, do not lower crossmember any further than necessary to remove shock absorber.

11. Slowly lower jack allowing repair-side of crossmember to drop. Do not lower jack at a fast rate. Lower jack just enough to allow top of shock absorber to clear body flange.

12. Remove shock absorber by tipping top outward and lifting lower end out of pocket in spring link.

To install:

13. Install shock absorber by setting lower end into pocket in spring link, then tipping top inward until aligned with upper mounting holes.

14. Install lower shock mounting bolt and nut. Do not tighten at this time.

15. Make sure spacers on top of crossmember mount bushings on side of repair are in position.

16. Carefully raise jack, guiding coil spring and upper end of shock absorber into mounted positions.

17. Install shock absorber upper mounting bolts. Tighten upper mounting bolts to 38 ft. lbs. (52 Nm).

➡**Rear crossmember mounting bolts are longer than front mounting bolts. Do not interchange mounting bolts.**

18. Install crossmember mounting bolts. Snug, but do not fully tighten bolts at this time.

19. Measure distance between from tension link to body weld flange directly in front of it, just outboard of front mount bushing. This distance must be at least 12mm to allow proper clearance for suspension movement. If distance is less than 12mm, shift that side of rear crossmember directly rearward until distance is 12mm or greater. To do so, loosen 3 mounting bolts slightly, leaving one on opposite side shifted, snugged to pivot off of. Shift crossmember rearward and snug loosened bolts.

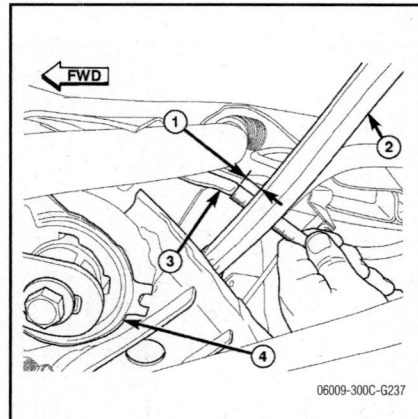

06009-300C-G237

Fig. 356 Measure distance (1) between from tension link (2) to body weld flange (3) directly in front of it, just outboard of front mount bushing (4)

Measure opposite side to be sure it also maintains minimum 12mm distance.

20. Tighten all crossmember mounting bolts to 133 ft. lbs. (180 Nm).

21. Remove jack from under rear axle differential.

22. If previously lowered, raise rear exhaust back to mounted position and connect exhaust isolators at muffler and resonators hangers. Remove jack or stand below exhaust muffler.

23. If removed, install fuel filler tube:

a. Insert filler tube into the fuel tank rubber hose.

b. Slide hose clamp into place and tighten.

c. Hose clamp in place and tighten.

d. Install filler tube mounting bolt.

e. Install Filler tube vent line.

f. Install the underbody splash shield.

g. Install the left inner splash shield.

24. Install tire and wheel assemblies. Tighten wheel mounting nuts to 110 ft. lbs. (150 Nm).

25. Lower vehicle.

26. Position vehicle on alignment rack/drive-on lift. Raise lift as necessary to access lower mounting bolt.

27. Tighten shock absorber lower mounting bolt nut to 53 ft. lbs. (72 Nm).

SPRING LINK

REMOVAL & INSTALLATION

See Figures 357 through 362.

1. Before servicing the vehicle, refer to the precautions in the beginning of this section.

2. Raise and support vehicle.

3. Remove rear spring.

4. Remove spring link-to-knuckle nut and bolt.

✷✷ WARNING

It important to use Guide, Special Tool 9361-2, when tapping sleeve in knuckle to help keep Tap, Special Tool 9361-1, straight during use or damage to Tap may occur.

5. Place Guide 9361-2 against sleeve in knuckle to keep Tap 9361-1 straight. Using Tap with an appropriate handle, cut threads approximately halfway through bushing (or about six complete threads). It is important to back tap out, clean out burrs and lubricate Tap often during process.

➡**Prior to using Special Tool 9361, lubricate bolt threads to provide ease of use and promote tool longevity.**

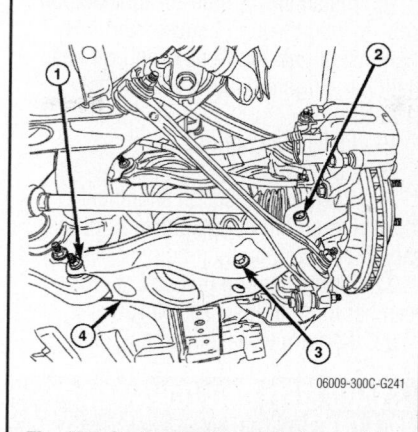

Fig. 357 Spring link (4) and fasteners (1, 2, 3)

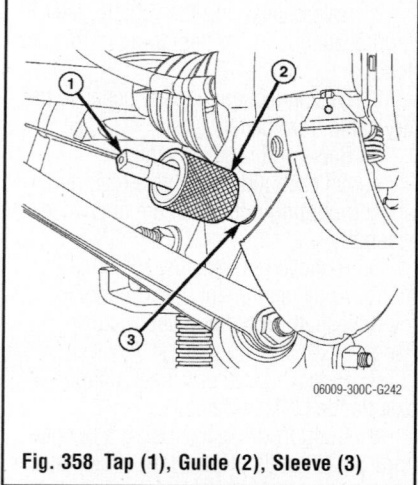

Fig. 358 Tap (1), Guide (2), Sleeve (3)

6. Assemble Remover, Special Tool 9361, as shown.

- 1. Bolt 9361-3
- 2. Nut
- 3. Spherical Washer

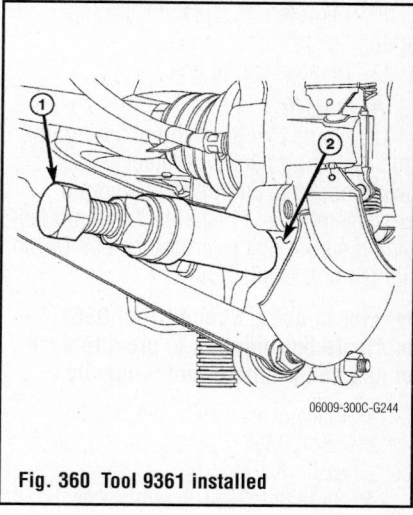

Fig. 360 Tool 9361 installed

- 4. Thrust Bearing
- 5. Sleeve 9361-4 (RWD)
- 5. Sleeve 9361-5 (AWD-Left Side)
- 5. Sleeve 9361-6 (AWD-Right Side)

➡**When installing thrust bearing on remover, be sure to place hardened side against nut.**

➡**It is important to use appropriate Sleeve on Remover to provide proper Tool-to-Knuckle contact. RWD sleeve can be used on either side while AWD knuckles require specific left or right side Sleeves.**

7. Thread Remover Bolt 9361-3 into tapped knuckle sleeve.

8. Rotate nut down, matching sleeve angled end with angled face of knuckle.

9. Continue to rotate Nut until knuckle sleeve is removed from knuckle. Discard knuckle sleeve; replace it with new upon installation.

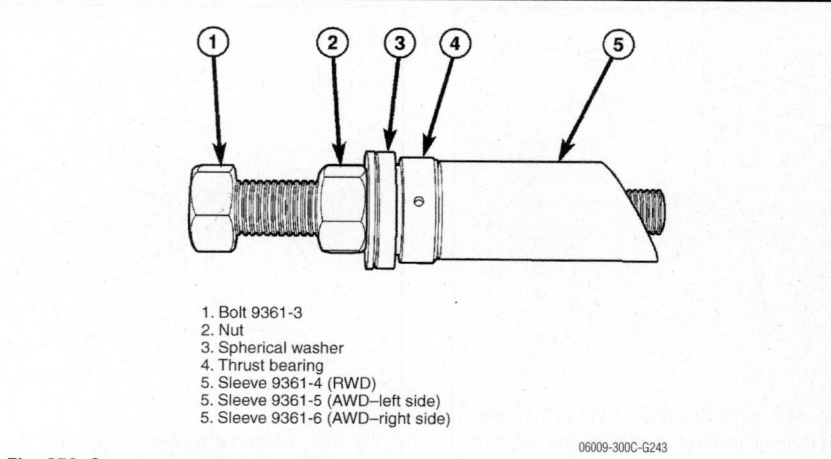

1. Bolt 9361-3
2. Nut
3. Spherical washer
4. Thrust bearing
5. Sleeve 9361-4 (RWD)
5. Sleeve 9361-5 (AWD–left side)
5. Sleeve 9361-6 (AWD–right side)

Fig. 359 Correct assembly of tool 9361

10. Remove bolt and nut fastening spring link to crossmember.

11. Remove spring link.

To install:

12. Guide ball joint end of spring link into mounting pocket of knuckle, then swing opposite end up to bushing in crossmember and install bolt and nut fastening spring link to crossmember. Do not tighten bolt at this time.

➡ **Prior to using Special Tool 9361, lubricate bolt threads to provide ease of use and promote tool longevity.**

13. Place new knuckle sleeve onto Installer Bolt 9361-7, and slide it up to bolt's head.

14. Slide Bolt 9361-7 with sleeve through knuckle and spring link ball joint starting from knuckle forward end.

15. Install thrust bearing and nut on end of bolt.

16. While holding bolt head stationary, rotate nut (using hand tools) installing sleeve in knuckle. Install sleeve until nut stops turning. Do not over tighten nut.

17. Remove special tool.

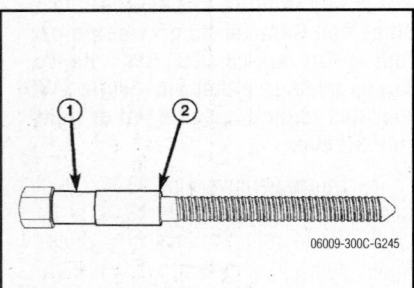

Fig. 361 Place new knuckle sleeve (2) onto Installer Bolt 9361-7 (1), and slide it up to bolt's head

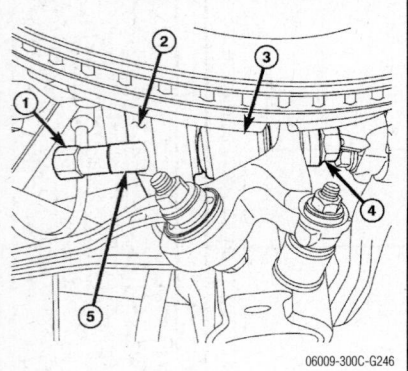

Fig. 362 Slide Bolt 9361-7 (1) with sleeve (5) through knuckle (2) and spring link ball joint (3) starting from knuckle forward end

18. Install spring link-to-knuckle bolt front-to-rear through knuckle and link, then install nut. While holding bolt head stationary, tighten nut to 102 ft. lbs. (138 Nm).

19. Install rear spring.

20. Lower vehicle.

21. Position vehicle on alignment rack/drive-on lift. Raise vehicle as necessary to access mounting bolt.

22. Tighten spring link bolt at crossmember to 80 ft. lbs. (108 Nm).

23. Perform wheel alignment.

STABILIZER BAR (SWAY BAR) & LINKS

REMOVAL & INSTALLATION

See Figures 363 through 365.

1. Before servicing the vehicle, refer to the precautions in the beginning of this section.

2. Disconnect and isolate negative battery cable from battery post.

3. Raise and support vehicle.

4. On each side of vehicle rear, remove wheel mounting nuts, then tire and wheel assembly.

5. Remove rear exhaust system.

6. Apply alignment index marks to the driveshaft rubber coupler and axle flange.

7. Remove three driveshaft coupler-to-axle flange bolts and nuts.

8. Support driveshaft using a bungee cord. Attach ends of cord to fuel tank straps as shown.

➡ **Due to short travel and low spring tension, it is not necessary to lock-out parking brake lever to service parking brake components.**

9. Disconnect front parking brake cable

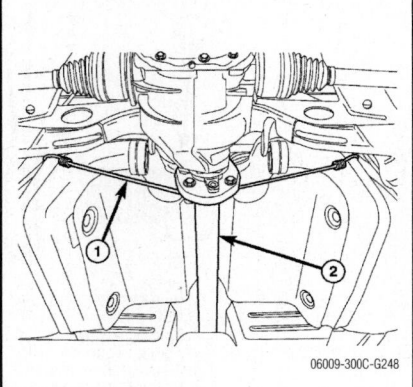

Fig. 363 Support driveshaft (2) using a bungee cord (1)

at connector to right rear parking brake cable.

10. Remove front parking brake cable from equalizer.

11. On each rear disc brake:

a. While holding guide pins from turning, remove disc brake caliper guide pin bolts.

b. Remove brake caliper from brake adapter and pads.

c. Guide brake caliper up through suspension, following brake hose path. Support caliper above rear suspension using with bungee cord or wire to keep caliper from overextending brake hose when crossmember is lowered.

➡ **To remove wheel speed sensor connector from body wiring harness connector, move retaining clip and pull sensor connector outward.**

12. Remove wheel speed sensor connectors from body wiring harness connector located in luggage compartment floor pan.

13. Unclip left wheel speed sensor cable from routing clip near body connector.

14. On each side of vehicle, remove shock absorber lower mounting bolt and nut.

15. Carefully mark location of rear crossmember on body at all four mount (bushing) locations using a marker or crayon. Do not use a scratch awl to mark location.

16. Position an extra pair of jackstands under and support forward end of engine cradle to help stabilize vehicle during rear suspension removal/installation.

17. Position under-hoist utility jack or transmission jack under center of rear axle differential. Raise jack head to contact differential and secure in place. When securing crossmember to jack, be sure not to secure stabilizer bar.

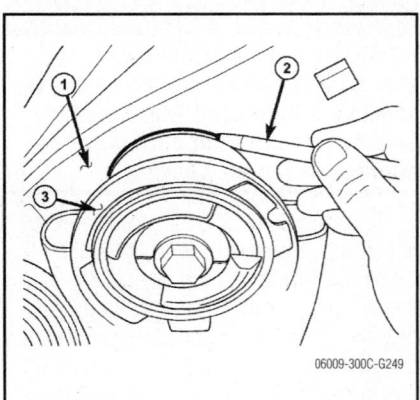

Fig. 364 Carefully mark location of rear crossmember on body at all four mount (bushing) locations using a marker

Before opening fuel system, review all warnings and cautions under Fuel System.

18. Disconnect negative battery cable.
19. Drain fuel from tank.
20. Fuel filler tube assembly.
21. Open filler tube door.
22. Remove retaining wire from inside filler tube rubber.
23. Start removing rubber from body sheet metal.
24. Remove retaining wire from inside filler tube rubber.
25. Start removing rubber from body sheet metal.
26. Filler tube and rubber removed from body sheet metal.
27. Remove the left inner splash shield.
28. Disconnect the filler tube vent line.
29. Remove the filler tube mounting bolt.
30. Remove the under body splash shield.
31. Loosen the filler tube hose clamp. Leave the clamp tight on the hose and fuel tank location.
32. Move clamp toward the fuel tank.
33. Remove the filler tube assembly from the vehicle.

➡ **If equipped with AWD, when removing crossmember mounting bolts in following step, be sure to not to misplace spacers between crossmember mounts and body.**

34. Remove both front and both rear mounting bolts fastening crossmember in place.
35. Slowly lower crossmember using jack. Do not lower jack at a fast rate. Lower just enough to allow driveshaft removal from rear axle differential. Do not lower jack any further than necessary. Slide driveshaft out of rear axle differential and allow bungee cord previously installed to support.
36. Slowly lower crossmember several inches.
37. Remove screw fastening front parking brake cable routing bracket to rear crossmember.
38. Continue to lower jack until crossmember is at a comfortable working level to access stabilizer bar fasteners.
39. On each end, remove bolt (3) and nut fastening stabilizer bar (4) to stabilizer link (2).

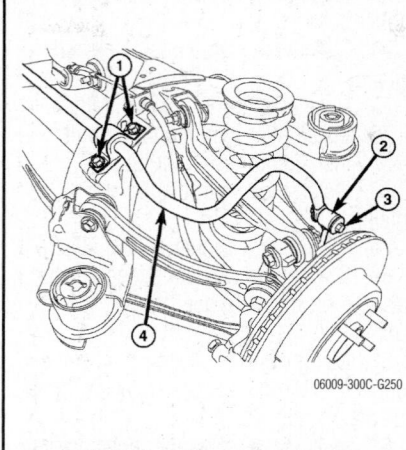

Fig. 365 Rear stabilizer bar and fasteners

06009-300C-G250

40. Remove bolts (1) fastening each stabilizer bar isolator retainer to crossmember.
41. Remove stabilizer bar (4) with isolators and retainers.
42. Remove retainers from isolators.
43. Remove isolators from stabilizer bar utilizing slits in bushings.

To install:

44. Install isolators on stabilizer bar utilizing slits in bushings. Install each isolator so its slit faces forward and flat side is positioned toward crossmember once installed.
45. Install retainers on isolators.
46. Install stabilizer bar with isolators and retainers on crossmember.
47. Install isolator retainer mounting bolts. Do not tighten at this time.
   a. Install bolt and nut fastening stabilizer bar ends to each stabilizer links. Do not tighten at this time.
48. Tighten isolator retainer mounting bolts to 45 ft. lbs. (61 Nm).
49. Remove coil springs with isolators from spring links.
50. Raise crossmember using jack until there is about 10 inches clearance to the body mounting points.
51. Install screw fastening front parking brake cable routing bracket to rear crossmember.
52. Raise crossmember to body mounting points. As crossmember is raised, slide driveshaft onto rear axle differential flange and align shocks with pockets in spring links.

➡ **There are four crossmember mounting bolts. Rear mounting bolts are longer than front mounting bolts. Do not interchange mounting bolts.**

53. Continue to raise crossmember with jack until crossmember mounting bolts can be installed. Install left side crossmember mounting bolts, but not the right side bolts. It is not necessary to tighten bolts at this point.

To avoid damaging other components of vehicle, do not lower crossmember any further than necessary to install coil spring.

54. Slowly lower jack allowing right side of crossmember to drop. Do not lower jack at a fast rate. Lower jack just enough to allow spring Installation. Do not lower jack any further than necessary.

➡ **Before installing coil spring, make sure isolators are completely installed on ends of spring.**

55. Install coil spring with isolators into spring pocket of spring link fitting the lower isolator to the shape of the pocket, then align top of spring with body mount.
56. Carefully raise jack, guiding coil spring and lower end of shock absorber into mounted positions. Once shock absorber lower mounting hole lines up with hole in spring link, stop jacking.
57. Install lower shock mounting bolt and nut. Do not tighten at this time.
58. If vehicle is equipped with AWD, insert spacers on top of right crossmember mount bushings before crossmember is raised into place.

➡ **There are four crossmember mounting bolts. Rear mounting bolts are longer than front mounting bolts. Do not interchange mounting bolts.**

59. Raise right side of crossmember into mounted position. Install right side crossmember mounting bolts. Snug, but do not fully tighten bolts at this time.
60. Remove both front and rear crossmember mounting bolts on left side of vehicle.

To avoid damaging other components of vehicle, do not lower crossmember any further than necessary to install coil spring.

61. Slowly lower jack allowing left side of crossmember to drop. Do not lower jack at a fast rate. Lower jack just enough to allow spring installation. Do not lower jack any further than necessary.

➡**Before installing coil spring, make sure isolators are completely installed on ends of spring.**

62. Install coil spring with isolators into spring pocket of spring link fitting the lower isolator to the shape of the pocket, then align top of spring with body mount.

63. Carefully raise jack, guiding coil spring and lower end of shock absorber into mounted positions. Once shock absorber lower mounting hole lines up with hole in spring link, stop jacking.

64. Install lower shock mounting bolt and nut. Do not tighten at this time.

65. If vehicle is equipped with AWD, insert spacers on top of left crossmember mount bushings before crossmember is raised into place.

➡**There are four crossmember mounting bolts. Rear mounting bolts are longer than front mounting bolts. Do not interchange mounting bolts.**

66. Raise left side of crossmember into mounted position. Install left side crossmember mounting bolts. Snug, but do not fully tighten bolts at this time.

67. Shift crossmember as necessary to line up mounts with location marks drawn on body before removal.

68. Once mounts are lined up with location marks, on both sides of vehicle, measure distance between the tension link and weld flange on body directly in front of it, just outboard of the front mount bushing. This distance must be at least 12mm to allow proper clearance for suspension movement. If distance is less than 12mm on either side of vehicle, shift that side of rear crossmember directly rearward until distance is 12mm or greater. To do so, loosen 3 mounting bolts slightly, leaving one on opposite side of shift snugged to pivot off of. Shift crossmember rearward and snug loosened bolts. Re-measure opposite side to be sure it still maintains minimum 12mm distance.

69. Tighten all four crossmember mounting bolts to 133 ft. lbs. (180 Nm).

70. Remove jack from under rear axle differential.

71. Remove bungee cord supporting driveshaft.

72. Align driveshaft index marks placed upon removal. Install driveshaft rear coupler-to-axle flange bolts and nuts by hand. Tighten driveshaft rear coupler-to-axle flange bolts to 60 ft. lbs. (81 Nm).

73. Insert filler tube into the fuel tank rubber hose.

74. Slide hose clamp into place and tighten.

75. Hose clamp in place and tighten.

76. Install filler tube mounting bolt.

77. Install filler tube vent line.

78. Install the underbody splash shield.

79. Install the left inner splash shield.

80. Clip left rear wheel speed sensor cable to routing clip near body connector.

81. Match left rear wheel speed sensor connector to right sensor connector to make one connector.

82. Insert speed sensor connectors into body wiring harness connector located in luggage compartment floor pan. When installing connector, make sure retaining clip on body connector is properly in place and sensor connector cannot be pulled out.

83. On each rear disc brake:

   a. Push caliper guide pins into caliper adapter to clear caliper mounting bosses when installing.

   b. Guide caliper and brake hose down through rear suspension, then slide caliper over brake pads and onto caliper adapter.

✸✸ WARNING

Extreme caution should be taken not to cross-thread caliper guide pin bolts when they are installed. Align caliper mounting holes with guide pins, then install guide pin bolts. While holding guide pins from turning, tighten bolts to 44 ft. lbs. (60 Nm).

   c. Make sure brake hose is properly routed and will not come in contact with suspension components.

84. Route parking brake cable above rear crossmember, then slide cable through equalizer above rear differential.

➡**Due to short travel and low spring tension, it is not necessary to lock-out parking brake lever to service parking brake components.**

85. Connect front parking brake cable at connector to right rear parking brake cable.

86. Install rear exhaust system.

87. Install tire and wheel assemblies. Tighten wheel mounting nuts to 110 ft. lbs. (150 Nm).

88. Lower vehicle until rear wheels are just above floor level.

89. Apply parking brake lever. Release lever, then reapply.

90. Check to make sure rear wheels will not rotate with lever applied.

91. Lower vehicle.

92. Connect negative battery cable to battery post. It is important that this is performed properly.

93. Pump brake pedal several times to ensure vehicle has a firm brake pedal before moving vehicle.

94. Position vehicle on alignment rack/drive-on hoist. Raise vehicle as necessary to access mounting bolts.

95. Tighten shock absorber lower mounting bolt nuts to 53 ft. lbs. (72 Nm).

96. Tighten stabilizer link fasteners to 45 ft. lbs. (61 Nm).

97. Perform wheel alignment.

STEERING KNUCKLE

REMOVAL & INSTALLATION

See Figures 366 through 371.

1. Before servicing the vehicle, refer to the precautions in the beginning of this section.

2. Raise and support vehicle.

3. Unclip wheel speed sensor cable at rear brake rotor shield.

4. Remove screw fastening sensor head to rear knuckle.

5. Remove wheel speed sensor head from knuckle.

6. Remove rear hub and bearing.

7. Remove parking brake shoes.

8. If not removed, remove parking brake shoe actuator lever from end of cable.

9. Remove shoe support from knuckle.

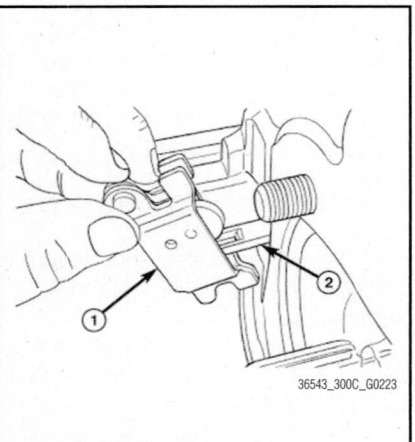

36543_300C_G0223

Fig. 366 Parking brake shoe actuator lever

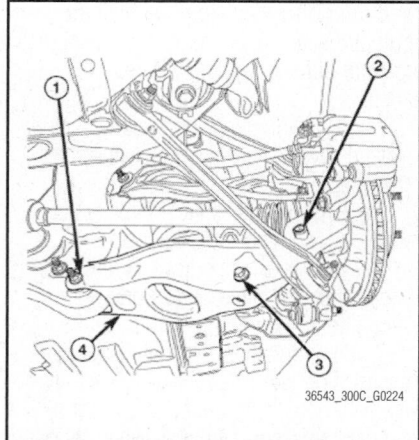

Fig. 367 Spring link-to-knuckle nut and bolt locations

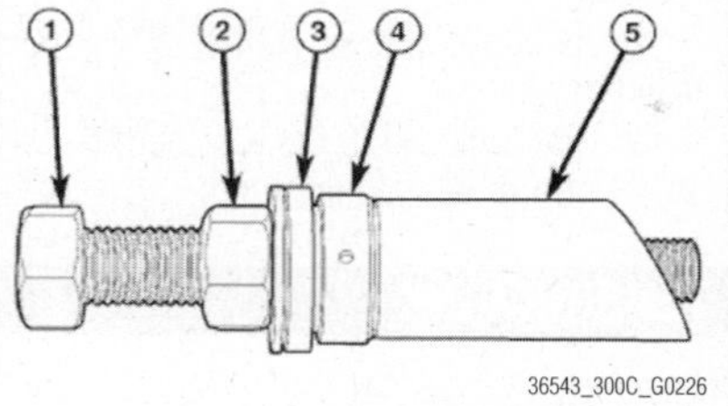

10. Remove parking brake cable screw at knuckle and pull cable out of knuckle.

11. Position under-hoist utility jack or jackstand under spring link. Raise jack head to contact spring link at shock mount secure in place.

12. Remove spring link-to-knuckle nut and bolt.

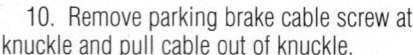

❋❋ WARNING

It important to use Guide, Special Tool 9361-2, when tapping sleeve in knuckle to help keep Tap, Special Tool 9361-1, straight during use or damage to Tap may occur.

13. Place Guide 9361-2 against sleeve in knuckle to keep Tap 9361-1 straight. Using Tap with an appropriate handle, cut threads approximately halfway through bushing (or about six complete threads). It is important to back tap out, clean out burrs and lubricate Tap often during process.

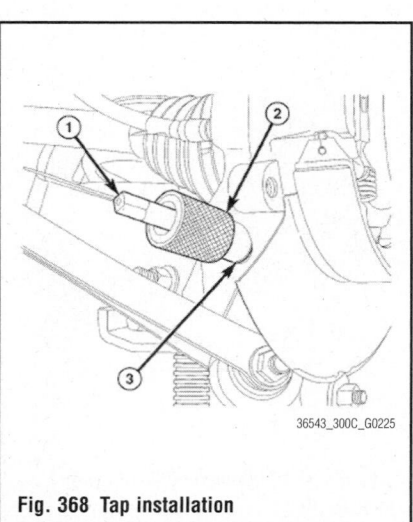

Fig. 368 Tap installation

Fig. 369 Special Tool 9361 assembly

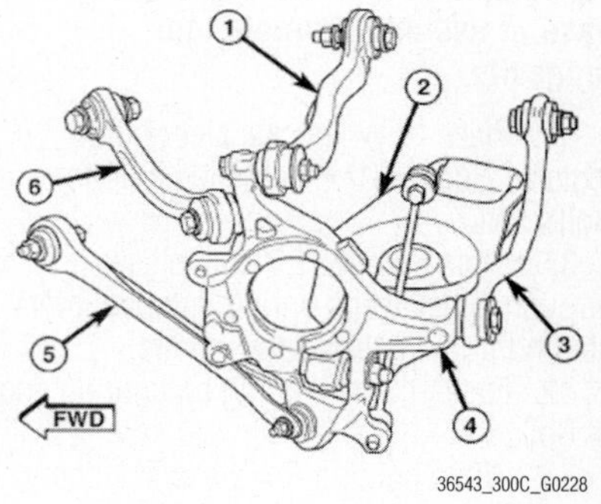

➡Prior to using Special Tool 9361, lubricate Bolt threads to provide ease of use and promote tool longevity. Assemble Remover, Special Tool 9361, as shown.

- (1) Bolt 9361-3
- (2) Nut
- (3) Spherical Washer
- (4) Thrust Bearing
- (5) Sleeve 9361-4 (RWD)
- (5) Sleeve 9361-5 (AWD - Left Side)
- (5) Sleeve 9361-6 (AWD - Right Side)

➡When installing thrust bearing on Remover, be sure to place hardened side against nut.

➡It is important to use appropriate Sleeve on Remover to provide proper Tool-to-Knuckle contact. RWD sleeve can be used on either side while AWD knuckles require specific left or right side Sleeves.

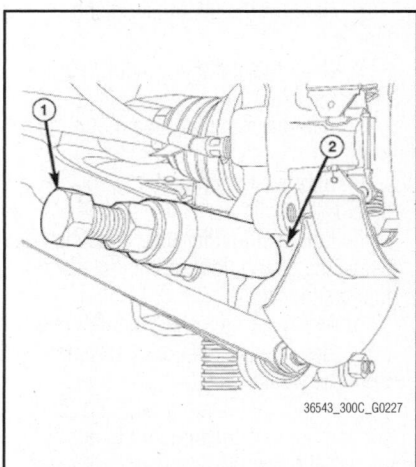

Fig. 370 Special Tool 9361 installation

Fig. 371 Camber link (1), spring link (2), toe link (3), knuckle (4), compression link (5) and tension link (6)

14. Thread Remover Bolt 9361-3 into tapped knuckle sleeve.

15. Rotate Nut down, matching Sleeve angled end with angled face of knuckle.

16. Continue to rotate Nut until knuckle sleeve is removed from knuckle. Discard knuckle sleeve; replace it with new upon installation.

17. Remove bolt and nut fastening compression link (5) to knuckle (4).

18. Remove bolt fastening toe link (3) to knuckle (4).

19. Remove nut and bolt fastening stabilizer link to knuckle (4).

20. Remove nut and bolt fastening tension link (6) to knuckle (4).

21. Remove nut and bolt fastening camber link (1) to knuckle (4).

22. Remove knuckle (4).

23. Remove hub mounting bolts from knuckle.

To install:

24. Install four hub mounting bolts through knuckle from inboard side allowing ends to protrude from opposite side.

25. Position knuckle on vehicle and install bolt and nut fastening camber link to knuckle. Do not tighten bolt at this time.

26. Install bolt and nut fastening tension link to knuckle. Do not tighten bolt at this time.

27. Install bolt and nut fastening stabilizer link to knuckle. Do not tighten bolt at this time.

28. Install bolt fastening toe link to knuckle. Do not tighten bolt at this time.

29. Install bolt and nut fastening compression link to knuckle. Do not tighten bolt at this time.

➡ **Prior to using Special Tool 9361, lubricate bolt threads to provide ease of use and promote tool longevity.**

30. Place NEW knuckle sleeve onto Installer Bolt 9361-7, and slide it up to Bolt's head.

31. Slide Bolt 9361-7 with sleeve through knuckle and spring link ball joint starting from knuckle forward end.

32. Install thrust bearing and nut on end of Bolt.

33. While holding Bolt head stationary, rotate Nut (using hand tools) installing sleeve in knuckle. Install sleeve until Nut stops turning. Do not over tighten Nut.

34. Remove special tool.

35. Install spring link-to-knuckle bolt front-to-rear through knuckle and link, then install nut. While holding bolt head stationary, tighten nut to 102 ft. lbs. (138 Nm).

36. Remove under-hoist utility jack or jackstand from under spring link.

37. Insert end of cable through rear knuckle and install mounting screw. Tighten screw to 71 inch lbs. (8 Nm).

38. Install parking brake shoe support over hub and bearing mounting screws and onto face of knuckle.

39. Install shoe actuator lever on end of parking brake cable. Make sure actuator lever is positioned with word "UP" facing outward.

40. Install parking brake shoes.

➡ **Before installing hub and bearing on end of axle halfshaft, ensure isolation washer is present on end of halfshaft. Inspect washer making sure it is not worn or damaged. Washer can be installed in either direction on shaft.**

41. Install hub and bearing.

42. Insert wheel speed sensor head into mounting hole in rear of knuckle.

43. Install screw fastening sensor head to rear knuckle. Tighten Screw to 97 inch lbs. (11 Nm).

44. Install sensor cable at rear brake rotor shield.

45. Lower vehicle.

46. Adjust parking brake shoes as necessary.

47. Position vehicle on alignment rack/drive-on hoist. Raise vehicle as necessary to access mounting bolts.

48. Tighten fasteners at knuckle (vehicle at curb height) as follows:

　　a. Camber Link: 72 ft. lbs. (98 Nm).

　　b. Compression Link: 60 ft. lbs. (81 Nm).

　　c. Stabilizer Link: 45 ft. lbs. (61 Nm).

　　d. Tension Link: 72 ft. lbs. (98 Nm).

　　e. Toe Link: 60 ft. lbs. (81 Nm).

49. Perform wheel alignment.

TENSION LINK

REMOVAL & INSTALLATION

See Figures 372 through 375.

1. Before servicing the vehicle, refer to the precautions in the beginning of this section.

2. Raise and support vehicle.

3. On both sides of vehicle, remove wheel mounting nuts, then rear tire and wheel assembly.

✳✳ CAUTION

Before opening fuel system, review all warnings and cautions under Fuel System.

4. If servicing left side shock absorber, remove fuel filler tube:

　　a. Disconnect negative battery cable.

　　b. Drain fuel from tank.

　　c. Fuel filler tube assembly.

　　d. Open filler tube door.

　　e. Remove retaining wire from inside filler tube rubber.

　　f. Start removing rubber from body sheet metal.

　　g. Remove retaining wire from inside filler tube rubber.

　　h. Start removing rubber from body sheet metal.

　　i. Filler tube and rubber removed from body sheet metal.

　　j. Remove the left inner splash shield.

　　k. Disconnect the filler tube vent line.

　　l. Remove the filler tube mounting bolt.

　　m. Remove the under body splash shield.

　　n. Loosen the filler tube hose clamp. Leave the clamp tight on the hose and fuel tank location.

　　o. Move clamp toward the fuel tank.

　　p. Remove the filler tube assembly from the vehicle.

5. Position an extra pair of jackstands under and support forward end of engine cradle to help stabilize vehicle during rear suspension removal/installation.

6. Perform following if vehicle is equipped with dual exhaust or are servicing right side on vehicle with single exhaust:

　　a. Position under-hoist utility jack or stand several inches below exhaust at muffler.

　　b. Disconnect exhaust isolators at muffler and resonators hangers.

　　c. Lower exhaust down to rest upon top of jack or stand placed below muffler.

7. Position under-hoist utility jack or transmission jack under center of rear axle differential. Raise jack head to contact differential and secure in place. When securing crossmember to jack, be sure not to secure stabilizer bar.

8. Remove shock absorber upper mounting screws.

9. Remove shock absorber (1) lower mounting bolt (2) and nut (4).

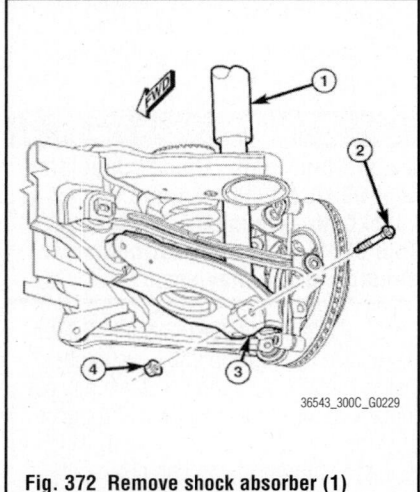

36543_300C_G0229

Fig. 372 Remove shock absorber (1) lower mounting bolt (2) and nut (4)

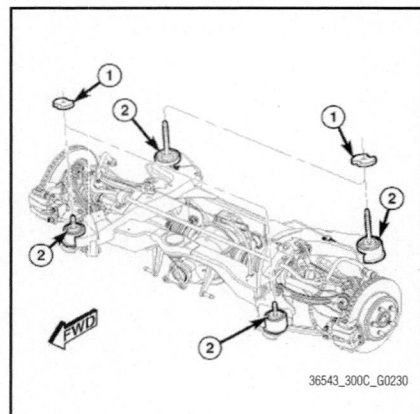

36543_300C_G0230

Fig. 373 Crossmember spacers (1) and mounts (2)

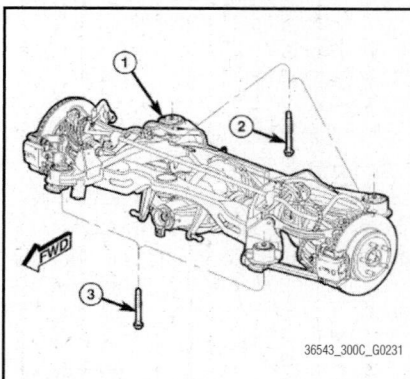

Fig. 374 Crossmember (1) mounting bolt locations (2, 3)

➡**If equipped with AWD, when removing crossmember mounting bolts in following step, be sure to not to misplace spacers between crossmember mounts and body.**

✳✳ CAUTION

When removing crossmember mounting bolts it is important NOT to loosen or remove crossmember mounting bolts on opposite side of vehicle. Doing so will require rear wheel alignment following reinstallation to ensure proper thrust angle.

10. Remove both front and rear crossmember mounting bolts on repair-side of vehicle.

✳✳ WARNING

To avoid damaging other components of vehicle, do not lower crossmember any further than necessary to remove shock absorber.

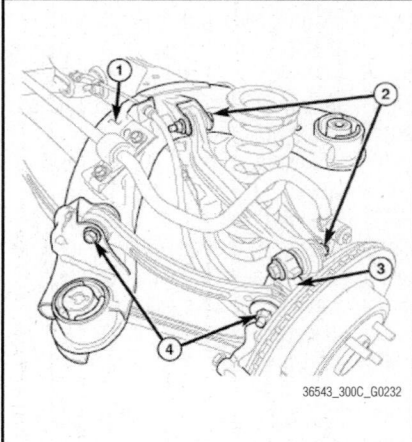

Fig. 375 Tension link bolt locations

11. Slowly lower jack allowing repair-side of crossmember to drop. Do not lower jack at a fast rate. Lower jack just enough to allow top of shock absorber to clear body flange.

12. Remove shock absorber by tipping top outward and lifting lower end out of pocket in spring link.

➡**Do not lower side of crossmember any further than necessary to gain access to link mounting bolts at crossmember.**

13. Remove nut and bolt (4) mounting link to knuckle (3).

14. Remove nut and bolt (4) mounting link to crossmember (1).

15. Remove link.

To install:

➡**When installing tension link, although link is same end-to-end, make sure that center bow is facing downward.**

16. Place link in bracket on crossmember. Install bolt and nut at crossmember. Do not tighten bolt at this time.

17. Install bolt and nut mounting link to knuckle. Do not tighten bolt at this time.

18. Install shock absorber by setting lower end into pocket in spring link, then tipping top inward until aligned with upper mounting holes.

19. Install lower shock mounting bolt and nut. Do not tighten at this time.

20. If vehicle is equipped with AWD, make sure spacers on top of crossmember mount bushings on side of repair are in position.

21. Carefully raise jack, guiding coil spring and upper end of shock absorber into mounted positions.

22. Install shock absorber upper mounting screws. Tighten upper mounting screws to 38 ft. lbs. (52 Nm).

➡**Rear crossmember mounting bolts are longer than front mounting bolts. Do not interchange mounting bolts.**

23. Install crossmember mounting bolts. Snug, but do not fully tighten bolts at this time.

24. Measure distance between from tension link to body weld flange directly in front of it, just outboard of front mount bushing. This distance must be at least 12mm to allow proper clearance for suspension movement. If distance is less than 12mm, shift that side of rear crossmember directly rearward until distance is 12mm or greater. To do so, loosen 3 mounting

bolts slightly, leaving one on opposite side shifted, snugged to pivot off of. Shift crossmember rearward and snug loosened bolts. Measure opposite side to be sure it also maintains minimum 12mm distance.

25. Tighten all crossmember mounting bolts to 133 ft. lbs. (180 Nm).

26. Remove jack from under rear axle differential.

27. If previously lowered, raise rear exhaust back to mounted position and connect exhaust isolators at muffler and resonators hangers. Remove jack or stand below exhaust muffler.

28. If removed, install fuel filler tube:
    a. Insert filler tube into the fuel tank rubber hose.
    b. Slide hose clamp into place and tighten.
    c. Hose clamp in place and tighten.
    d. Install filler tube mounting bolt.
    e. Install Filler tube vent line.
    f. Install the underbody splash shield.

29. Install the left inner splash shield.

30. Lower vehicle until front tires contact floor but rear is still suspended. Place jackstands under each rear suspension spring link. Place an appropriate wooden block between stand and link to avoid damaging spring link, then lower vehicle until full vehicle weight is supported by suspension.

31. Tighten camber link fasteners to:
    a. Bolt at crossmember: 63 ft. lbs. (85 Nm).
    b. Bolt nut at knuckle: 72 ft. lbs. (98 Nm).

32. Tighten shock absorber lower mounting bolt nut to 53 ft. lbs. (72 Nm).
    a. Raise vehicle and remove jackstands.

33. Install tire and wheel assemblies. Tighten wheel mounting nuts to 110 ft. lbs. (150 Nm).

34. Lower vehicle.

35. Perform wheel alignment.

TOE LINK

REMOVAL & INSTALLATION

Left Side

See Figures 376 and 377.

1. Before servicing the vehicle, refer to the precautions in the beginning of this section.

2. Raise and support vehicle.

3. On both sides of vehicle, remove wheel mounting nuts, and then rear tire and wheel assembly.

✳✳ CAUTION

Before opening fuel system, review all warnings and cautions.

4. Disconnect negative battery cable.

5. Drain fuel from tank.

6. Fuel filler tube assembly.

7. Open filler tube door.

8. Remove retaining wire from inside filler tube rubber.

9. Start removing rubber from body sheet metal.

10. Remove retaining wire from inside filler tube rubber.

11. Start removing rubber from body sheet metal.

12. Filler tube and rubber removed from body sheet metal.

13. Remove the left inner splash shield.

14. Disconnect the filler tube vent line.

15. Remove the filler tube mounting bolt.

16. Remove the under body splash shield.

17. Loosen the filler tube hose clamp. Leave the clamp tight on the hose and fuel tank location.

18. Move clamp toward the fuel tank.

19. Remove the filler tube assembly from the vehicle.

20. Position an extra pair of jackstands under and support forward end of engine cradle to help stabilize vehicle during rear suspension removal/installation.

21. Perform following if vehicle is equipped with dual exhaust:

   a. Position under-hoist utility jack or stand several inches below exhaust at muffler.

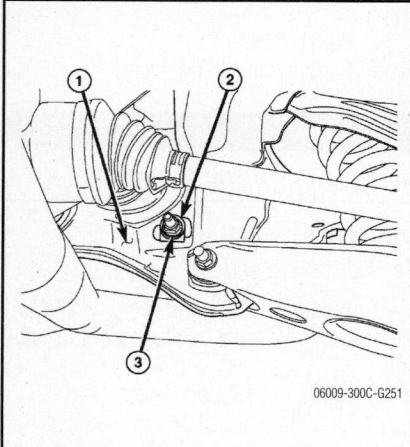

Fig. 376 Toe adjustment cam bolt (3)

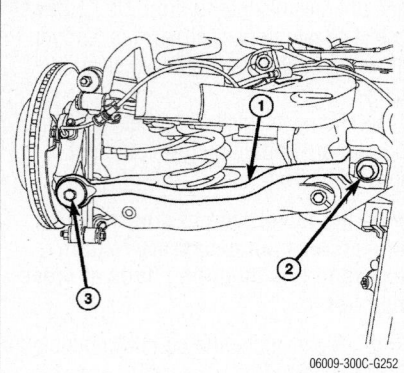

06009-300C-G252

Fig. 377 Cam bolt (2), toe link (1) and mounting bolt (3)

   b. Disconnect exhaust isolators at muffler and resonators hangers.

   c. Lower exhaust down to rest upon top of jack or stand placed below muffler.

22. Position under-hoist utility jack or transmission jack under center of rear axle differential. Raise jack head to contact differential and secure in place.

23. Remove shock absorber lower mounting bolt and nut.

✳✳ CAUTION

When removing crossmember mounting bolts it is important NOT to loosen or remove crossmember mounting bolts on opposite side of vehicle. Doing so will require rear wheel alignment following reinstallation to ensure proper thrust angle.

24. Remove both front and rear crossmember mounting bolts on repair-side of vehicle. If equipped with AWD, be sure to not to misplace spacers between crossmember mounts and body.

✳✳ WARNING

To avoid damaging other components of the vehicle do not lower crossmember any further than necessary to remove shock absorber.

25. Slowly lower jack allowing repair-side of crossmember to drop. Do not lower jack at a fast rate. Lower jack just enough to allow toe link mounting bolt at crossmember.

26. If equipped, remove wheel speed sensor cable from toe link.

27. While holding toe adjustment cam bolt from rotating, remove nut (3) securing toe link at crossmember (1).

28. Slide cam bolt rearward out of crossmember and link.

29. Remove mounting bolt and nut at knuckle.

30. Remove toe link.

To install:

31. Slide crossmember end of toe link into box bracket on crossmember. Slide cam bolt through bracket and link from rear.

32. Install bolt and nut securing link to knuckle. Do not tighten bolt at this time.

33. While holding toe adjustment cam bolt from rotating (cam facing upward), Install cam washer and nut securing toe link at crossmember. Do not tighten nut at this time.

34. If equipped, attach wheel speed sensor cable to toe link.

35. Carefully raise jack, guiding coil spring and lower end of shock absorber into mounted positions.

36. When lower shock mounting bolt holes line up install bolt and nut. Do not tighten at this time.

➡ **Rear crossmember mounting bolts are longer than front mounting bolts. Do not interchange mounting bolts.**

37. Continue to raise crossmember in not already in mounted position, then install crossmember mounting bolts. Snug, but do not fully tighten bolts at this time.

38. Measure distance between from tension link to body weld flange directly in front of it, just outboard of front mount bushing. This distance must be at least 12mm to allow proper clearance for suspension movement. If distance is less than 12mm, shift that side of rear crossmember directly rearward until distance is 12mm or greater. To do so, loosen 3 mounting bolts slightly, leaving one on opposite side of shift snugged to pivot off of. Shift crossmember rearward and snug loosened bolts. Measure opposite side to be sure it also maintains minimum 12mm distance.

39. Tighten all crossmember mounting bolts to 133 ft. lbs. (180 Nm).

40. Remove jack from under rear axle differential.

41. If previously lowered, raise rear exhaust back to mounted position and connect exhaust isolators at muffler and resonators hangers. Remove jack or stand below exhaust muffler.

42. Insert filler tube into the fuel tank rubber hose.

43. Slide hose clamp into place and tighten.

44. Hose clamp in place and tighten.

45. Install filler tube mounting bolt.
46. Install filler tube vent line.
47. Install the underbody splash shield.
48. Install the left inner splash shield.
49. Install tire and wheel assemblies. Tighten wheel mounting nuts to 110 ft. lbs. (150 Nm).
50. Lower vehicle.
51. Position vehicle on alignment rack/drive-on lift. Raise vehicle as necessary to access mounting bolts.
52. Tighten shock absorber lower mounting bolt nut to 53 ft. lbs. (72 Nm).
53. Tighten toe link fasteners to:
   a. Nut at crossmember: 80 ft. lbs. (108 Nm) torque (This nut may be tightened after rear wheel alignment toe is set. Do not tighten from bolt head end.).
   b. Bolt at knuckle: 60 ft. lbs. (81 Nm).
54. Perform wheel alignment.

Right Side

1. Before servicing the vehicle, refer to the precautions in the beginning of this section.
2. Raise and support vehicle.
3. Remove wheel mounting nuts, then rear tire and wheel assembly.
4. If equipped, remove wheel speed sensor cable from toe link.
5. While holding toe adjustment cam bolt from rotating, remove nut securing toe link at crossmember.
6. Slide cam bolt rearward out of crossmember and link.
7. Remove mounting bolt and nut at knuckle.
8. Remove toe link.

To install:

9. Slide crossmember end of toe link into box bracket on crossmember. Slide cam bolt through bracket and link from rear of vehicle.
10. Install bolt and nut securing link to knuckle. Do not tighten bolt at this time.
11. While holding toe adjustment cam bolt from rotating (cam facing upward), Install cam washer and nut securing toe link at crossmember. Do not tighten nut at this time.
12. If equipped, Attach wheel speed sensor cable to toe link.
13. Raise rear exhaust back to mounted position and connect exhaust isolators at muffler and resonators hangers. Remove jack or stand below exhaust muffler.
14. Install tire and wheel assembly. Tighten wheel mounting nuts to 110 ft. lbs. (150 Nm).
15. Lower vehicle.

16. Position vehicle on alignment rack/drive-on lift. Raise vehicle as necessary to access mounting bolts.
17. Tighten toe link fasteners to:
   a. Nut at crossmember: 80 ft. lbs. (108 Nm). (This nut may be tightened after rear wheel alignment toe is set. Do not tighten from bolt head end.).
   b. Bolt at knuckle: 60 ft. lbs. (81 Nm).
   c. Perform wheel alignment.

WHEEL BEARINGS

REMOVAL & INSTALLATION

See Figures 378 and 379.

1. Before servicing the vehicle, refer to the precautions in the beginning of this section.
2. Raise and support vehicle.
3. Remove wheel mounting nuts, then tire and wheel assembly.
4. While a helper applies brakes to keep hub from rotating, remove hub nut from the halfshaft.

➡**In some cases, it may be necessary to retract caliper piston in its bore a small amount in order to provide sufficient clearance between shoes and rotor to easily remove caliper from knuckle. This can usually be accomplished before guide pin bolts are removed, by grasping rear of caliper and pulling outward working with guide pins, thus retracting piston. Never push on piston directly as it may get damaged.**

5. Remove two bolts securing disc brake caliper adapter to knuckle.
6. Remove disc brake caliper and adapter from knuckle as an assembly. Hang

assembly out of way using wire or a bungee cord. Use care not to overextend brake hose when doing this.
7. Remove any clips retaining brake rotor to wheel mounting studs.
8. Slide brake rotor off hub and bearing.
9. Loosen each hub and bearing mounting bolt a turn or two at a time while pulling outward on hub and bearing to avoid bolt contact with halfshaft outer joint. Once removed from threads in hub and bearing (but not knuckle), allow bolts to stay in and protrude through knuckle and brake support plate to keep brake support plate in place when hub and bearing is removed.
10. Slide hub and bearing off knuckle and halfshaft.

To install:

➡**Before installing hub and bearing on end of axle halfshaft, ensure isolation washer is present on end of halfshaft. Inspect washer making sure it is not worn or damaged. Washer can be installed in either direction on shaft.**

11. Position hub and bearing bolts though rear of knuckle and parking brake support just enough to hold support in place as hub and bearing is installed.
12. Slide hub and bearing onto halfshaft. Place hub and bearing through brake support, onto knuckle, lining up mounting bolt holes with bolts.
13. Install four bolts fastening hub and bearing in place. Tighten mounting bolts to 50 ft. lbs. (68 Nm).

➡**Inspect disc brake pads and parking brake shoes before brake rotor installation.**

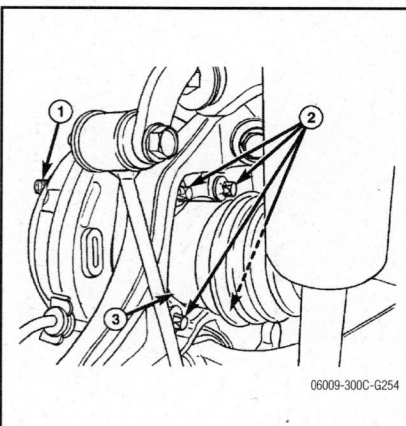

Fig. 378 Rear hub/bearing mounting bolts (2)

06009-300C-G254

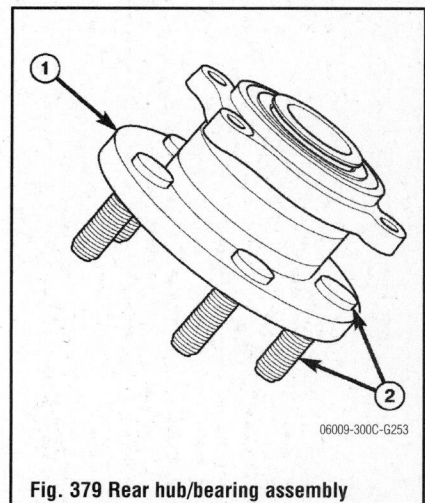

06009-300C-G253

Fig. 379 Rear hub/bearing assembly

14. Install brake rotor over wheel mounting studs and onto hub.

15. Install disc brake caliper and adapter assembly over brake rotor.

16. Install mounting bolts securing caliper adapter to knuckle. Tighten bolts to 70 ft. lbs. (95 Nm).

17. Install hub nut on end of halfshaft. While a helper applies brakes to keep hub from turning, tighten hub nut to 157 ft. lbs. (213 Nm).

18. Verify proper adjustment of the parking brake shoes and adjust as necessary.

19. Install tire and wheel assembly. Tighten wheel mounting nuts to 110 ft. lbs. (150 Nm).

20. Lower vehicle.

21. Pump brake pedal several times to ensure vehicle has a firm brake pedal before moving vehicle.

22. Check and adjust brake fluid level in reservoir as necessary.

23. Road test vehicle and make several stops to wear off any foreign material on brakes and to seat brake pads.

ADJUSTMENT

The rear wheel bearing and wheel hub of this vehicle are a one piece sealed unit or hub and bearing unit type assembly. No adjustments are possible.

The center of the hub and bearing is splined to match the axle halfshaft.

The wheel mounting studs used to mount the tire and wheel to the vehicle are the only replaceable components of the hub and bearing. Otherwise, the hub and bearing is serviced only as a complete assembly.

CHRYSLER AND DODGE

2

200 • Avenger • Sebring

SPECIFICATIONS AND MAINTENANCE CHARTS

ENGINE AND VEHICLE IDENTIFICATION

Engine							Model Year	
Code ①	Liters (cc)	Cu. In.	Cyl.	Fuel Sys.	Engine Type	Eng. Mfg.	Code ②	Year
B	2.4	146.5	4	MFI	DOHC	Chrysler	A	2010
D	2.7	167.0	6	MFI	DOHC	Chrysler	B	2011
V	3.5	214.7	6	MFI	SOHC	Chrysler		
G	3.6	219.7	6	MFI	DOHC	Chrysler		

MFI: Multiport Fuel Injection

DOHC: Double Overhead Camshafts

① 8th position of VIN

② 10th position of VIN

25766_SEBR_C0001

GENERAL ENGINE SPECIFICATIONS

All measurements are given in inches.

Year	Model	Engine Displacement Liters	Engine ID/VIN	Fuel System Type	Net Horsepower @ rpm	Net Torque @ rpm (ft. lbs.)	Bore x Stroke (in.)	Compression Ratio	Oil Pressure @ rpm
2010	Avenger SXT	2.4	B	MFI	173@6,000	166@4,400	3.47 x 3.82	10.5:1	25-80 psi @3,000
	Avenger Express	2.7	D	MFI	189@6,400	191@4,000	3.39 x 3.09	9.7:1	45-105 psi @3,000
	Avenger R/T	3.5	V	MFI	235@6,400	232@4,000	3.78 x 3.19	10.1:1	45-105 psi @3,000
	Sebring Touring/Limited Sedan	2.4	B	MFI	173@6,000	166@4,400	3.47 x 3.82	10.5:1	25-80 psi @3,000
	Sebring LX Convertible	2.4	B	MFI	173@6,000	166@4,400	3.47 x 3.82	10.5:1	25-80 psi @3,000
	Sebring Touring Convertible	2.7	D	MFI	189@6,400	191@4,000	3.39 x 3.09	9.7:1	45-105 psi @3,000
	Sebring Limited Convertible	3.5	V	MFI	235@6,400	232@4,000	3.78 x 3.19	10.1:1	45-105 psi @3,000
2011	Avenger Express/Mainstreet/Lux	2.4	B	MFI	173@6,000	166@4,400	3.47 x 3.82	10.5:1	25-80 psi @3,000
	Avenger Heat	3.6	G	MFI	283@6,400	260@4,400	3.78 x 3.27	10.2:1	30 psi @1,201-3,500
	200 LX/Touring/Limited Sedan	2.4	B	MFI	173@6,000	166@4,400	3.47 x 3.82	10.5:1	25-80 psi @3,000
	200 S Sedan	3.6	G	MFI	283@6,400	260@4,400	3.78 x 3.27	10.2:1	30 psi @1,201-3,500
	200 LX/Touring Convertible	2.4	B	MFI	173@6,000	166@4,400	3.47 x 3.82	10.5:1	25-80 psi @3,000
	200 Limited/S Convertible	3.6	G	MFI	283@6,400	260@4,400	3.78 x 3.27	10.2:1	30 psi @1,201-3,500

25766_SEBR_C0002

ENGINE TUNE-UP SPECIFICATIONS

Year	Engine Displacement Liters	Engine ID/VIN	Spark Plug Gap (in.)	Ignition Timing (deg.) MT	Ignition Timing (deg.) AT	Fuel Pump (psi)	Idle Speed (rpm) MT	Idle Speed (rpm) AT	Valve Clearance Intake	Valve Clearance Exhaust
2010	2.4	B	①	N/A	②	53-63	N/A	③	0.006-0.009	0.010-0.012
	2.7	D	0.050	N/A	②	53-63	N/A	③	HYD	HYD
	3.5	V	0.050	N/A	②	53-63	N/A	③	HYD	HYD
2011	2.4	B	①	N/A	②	53-63	N/A	③	0.006-0.009	0.010-0.012
	3.6	G	0.040	N/A	②	53-63	N/A	③	HYD	HYD

NOTE: The Vehicle Emission Control Information label often reflects specification changes made during production.

The label figures must be used if they differ from those in this chart.

HYD: Hydraulic   N/A: Not Applicable

① Partial Zero Emission Vehicle (PZEV): 0.031 inch

Without PZEV: 0.043 inch

② Ignition timing is controlled by the PCM and is not adjustable

③ Idle speed is controlled by the PCM and is not adjustable

25766_SEBR_C0003

CAPACITIES

Year	Model	Engine Displacement Liters	Engine ID/VIN	Engine Oil with Filter (qts.)	Transaxle (pts.) Auto.	Transaxle (pts.) Manual	Fuel Tank (gal.)	Cooling System (qts.)
2010	Avenger SXT	2.4	B	4.5	①	N/A	16.9	7.7
	Avenger Express	2.7	D	5.5	①	N/A	16.9	9.8
	Avenger R/T	3.5	V	5.5	②	N/A	16.9	11.6
	Sebring Sedan	2.4	B	4.5	①	N/A	16.9	7.7
	Sebring LX Convertible	2.4	B	4.5	①	N/A	16.9	7.7
	Sebring Convertible	2.7	D	5.5	①	N/A	16.9	9.8
	Sebring Convertible	3.5	V	5.5	②	N/A	16.9	11.6
2011	Avenger Express	2.4	B	4.5	①	N/A	16.9	7.7
	Avenger Mainstreet	2.4	B	4.5	②	N/A	18.5	7.7
	Avenger Lux	2.4	B	4.5	②	N/A	16.9	7.7
	Avenger Heat	3.6	G	6.0	②	N/A	16.9	11.4
	200 LX Sedan	2.4	B	4.5	①	N/A	16.9	7.7
	200 Touring Sedan	2.4	B	4.5	②	N/A	18.5	7.7
	200 Limited Sedan	2.4	B	4.5	②	N/A	18.5	7.7
	200 S Sedan	3.6	G	6.0	②	N/A	16.9	11.4
	200 Touring Convertible	2.4	B	4.5	②	N/A	16.9	7.7
	200 Limited Convertible	3.6	G	6.0	②	N/A	16.9	11.4
	200 S Convertible	3.6	G	6.0	②	N/A	16.9	11.4

NOTE: All capacities are approximate. Add fluid gradually and ensure a proper fluid level is obtained.

N/A: Not Applicable

① Drain and refill capacity: 8 pints. Total capacity: 18.4 pints.

② Drain and refill capacity: 11 pints. Total capacity: 18.0 pints.

25766_SEBR_C0004

FLUID SPECIFICATIONS

Year	Model	Engine Disp. Liters	Engine Oil	Manual Trans.	Auto. Trans.	Drive Axle Front	Drive Axle Rear	Transfer Case	Power Steering Fluid	Brake Master Cylinder	Cooling System
2010	Avenger SXT	2.4	5W-20	N/A	①	N/A	N/A	N/A	②	DOT 3	③
	Avenger Express	2.7	5W-20	N/A	①	N/A	N/A	N/A	②	DOT 3	③
	Avenger R/T	3.5	10W-30	N/A	①	N/A	N/A	N/A	②	DOT 3	③
	Sebring Sedan	2.4	5W-20	N/A	①	N/A	N/A	N/A	②	DOT 3	③
	Sebring LX Convertible	2.4	5W-20	N/A	①	N/A	N/A	N/A	②	DOT 3	③
	Sebring Convertible	2.7	5W-20	N/A	①	N/A	N/A	N/A	②	DOT 3	③
	Sebring Convertible	3.5	10W-30	N/A	①	N/A	N/A	N/A	②	DOT 3	③
2011	Avenger Express/Mainstreet/Lux	2.4	5W-20	N/A	①	N/A	N/A	N/A	②	DOT 3	③
	Avenger Heat	3.6	5W-30	N/A	①	N/A	N/A	N/A	②	DOT 3	③
	200 LX/Touring/Limited Sedan	2.4	5W-20	N/A	①	N/A	N/A	N/A	②	DOT 3	③
	200 S Sedan	3.6	5W-30	N/A	①	N/A	N/A	N/A	②	DOT 3	③
	200 Touring Convertible	2.4	5W-20	N/A	①	N/A	N/A	N/A	②	DOT 3	③
	200 Limited/S Convertible	3.6	5W-30	N/A	①	N/A	N/A	N/A	②	DOT 3	③

DOT: Department Of Transportation

N/A: Not Applicable

① MOPAR® ATF+4 Automatic Transmission Fluid

② MOPAR® Power Steering Fluid +4

③ MOPAR® Antifreeze/Coolant 5 Year/100,000 Mile Formula HOAT (Hybrid Organic Additive Technology)

25766_SEBR_C0005

VALVE SPECIFICATIONS

Year	Engine Displacement Liters	Engine ID/VIN	Seat Angle (deg.)	Face Angle (deg.)	Spring Test Pressure (lbs. @ in.)	Spring Free-Length (in.)	Spring Installed Height (in.)	Stem-to-Guide Clearance (in.) Intake	Stem-to-Guide Clearance (in.) Exhaust	Stem Diameter (in.) Intake	Stem Diameter (in.) Exhaust
2010	2.4	B	44.75-45.10	45.25-45.75	78.19-85.83 @1.152	1.850	1.378	0.0008-0.0021	0.0012-0.0024	0.2151-0.2157	0.2148-0.2153
	2.7	D	45.00-45.50	44.50-45.50	56.0-64.0 @1.496	1.797	1.496	0.0009-0.0026	0.0020-0.0037	0.2337-0.2344	0.2326-0.2333
	3.5	V	45.00-45.50	44.50-45.00	①	②	1.496	0.0009-0.0026	0.0020-0.0037	0.2730-0.2737	0.2719-0.2726
2011	2.4	B	44.75-45.10	45.25-45.75	78.19-85.83 @1.152	1.850	1.378	0.0008-0.0021	0.0012-0.0024	0.2151-0.2157	0.2148-0.2153
	3.6	G	44.50-45.00	45.00-45.50	63-69 @1.57	2.067	1.575	0.0009-0.0024	0.0012-0.0027	0.2346-0.2354	0.2343-0.2351

① Intake: 69.5-80.5 lbs. @ 1.4961 inches

Exhaust (Yellow): 70.5-79.5 lbs. @ 1.496 inches

Exhaust (White): 80-90 lbs. @ 1.496 inches

② Intake: 1.7195 inches

Exhaust (Yellow): 1.8543 inches

Exhaust (White): 1.9015 inches

25766_SEBR_C0006

CAMSHAFT SPECIFICATIONS
All measurements in inches unless noted

Year	Engine Displacement Liters	Engine Code/VIN	Journal Diameter	Brg. Oil Clearance	Shaft End-play	Runout	Journal Bore	Lobe Height Intake	Exhaust
2010	2.4	B	①	②	0.0043-0.0098	NS	③	④	⑤
	2.7	D	0.9449-0.9441	0.0020-0.0035	0.0051-0.0110	NS	0.9469-0.0948	0.3543	0.3150
	3.5	V	1.6905-1.6913	0.0031-0.0047	0.0012-0.0014	NS	1.6944-1.6953	0.3367	0.2571
2011	2.4	B	①	②	0.0043-0.0098	NS	③	④	⑤
	3.6	G	⑥	⑦	0.0030-0.0099	NS	⑧	0.4055	0.3937

NS: Not Specified

① Front Intake Cam: 1.1797-1.1803 inches (29.964-29.980 mm)

Front Exhaust Cam: 1.4166-1.4173 inches (35.984-36.000 mm)

Cam Journal Diameter No. 1-4: 0.943-0.944 inch (23.954-23.970 mm)

② Front Intake Journal: 0.0008-0.0022 inch (0.020-0.057 mm)

Front Exhaust Journal: 0.0007-0.0020 inch (0.019-0.051 mm)

All Others: 0.0008-0.0026 inch (0.020-0.067 mm)

③ Front Intake: 1.1810-1.1819 inches (30.000-30.021 mm)

Front Exhaust: 1.5747-1.5756 inches (40.000-40.024 mm)

Cam Bearing Bore No. 1-4: 0.9448-0.9457 inches (24.000-24.021 mm)

④ Max Lift @ 0.007 inch (0.2 mm) lash: 0.362 inch (9.2 mm)

⑤ Max Lift @ 0.011 inch (0.28mm) lash: 0.331 inch (8.42 mm)

⑥ No. 1: 1.2589-1.2596 inches (31.976-31.995 mm)

No. 2, 3, 4: 0.9440-0.9447 inch (23.977-23.996 mm)

⑦ No. 1: 0.00010-0.0026 inch (0.025-0.065 mm)

No. 2, 3, 4: 0.0009-0.0025 inch (0.024-0.064 mm)

⑧ No. 1 Cam Towers: 1.2606-1.2615 inches (32.020-32.041 mm)

No. 2, 3, 4 Cam Towers: 0.9457-0.9465 inch (24.020-24.041 mm)

25766_SEBR_C0007

CRANKSHAFT AND CONNECTING ROD SPECIFICATIONS
All measurements are given in inches.

Year	Engine Displacement Liters	Engine ID/VIN	Crankshaft Main Brg. Journal Dia.	Main Brg. Oil Clearance	Shaft End-play	Thrust on No.	Connecting Rod Journal Diameter	Oil Clearance	Side Clearance
2010	2.4	B	①	0.0011-0.0019	0.0019-0.0098	3	②	0.0012-0.0023	0.0039-0.0098
	2.7	D	2.4996-2.5004	0.0014-0.0021	0.0019-0.0108	3	2.1059-2.1067	0.0009-0.0025	0.0051-0.0150
	3.5	V	2.5192-2.5202	0.0013-0.0024	0.0019-0.0102	3	2.2828-2.2835	0.0009-0.0021	0.0051-0.0153
2011	2.4	B	①	0.0011-0.0019	0.0019-0.0098	3	②	0.0012-0.0023	0.0039-0.0098
	3.6	G	2.8310-2.8380	0.0009-0.0020	0.0020-0.0114	3	2.3193-2.3263	0.0009-0.0025	0.0028-0.0146

① Journal grade

0: 2.0466-2.0467 inches (51.985-51.988 mm)

1: 2.0465-2.0466 inches (51.982-51.985 mm)

2: 2.0464-2.0465 inches (51.979-51.982 mm)

3: 2.0462-2.0464 inches (51.976-51.979 mm)

4: 2.0461-2.0462 inches (51.973-51.976 mm)

② Journal grade

1: 1.8884-1.8887 inches (47.966-47.972 mm)

2: 1.8882-1.8884 inches (47.960-47.966 mm)

3: 1.8880-1.8882 inches (47.954-47.960 mm)

25766_SEBR_C0008

PISTON AND RING SPECIFICATIONS

All measurements are given in inches.

Year	Engine Displacement Liters	Engine ID/VIN	Piston Clearance	Ring Gap			Ring Side Clearance		
				Top Compression	Bottom Compression	Oil Control	Top Compression	Bottom Compression	Oil Control
2010	2.4	B	(-0.0006)- 0.0006	0.0059- 0.0118	0.0118- 0.0177	0.0079- 0.0276	0.0012- 0.0028	0.0012- 0.0028	0.0024- 0.0059
	2.7	D	(-0.0003)- 0.0016	0.0079- 0.0142	0.0146- 0.0249	0.0098- 0.0292	0.0013- 0.0032	0.0016- 0.0031	0.0023- 0.0080
	3.5	V	(-0.0003)- 0.0018	0.0079- 0.0142	0.0079- 0.0157	0.0098- 0.0299	0.0016- 0.0031	0.0016- 0.0031	0.0015- 0.0072
2011	2.4	B	(-0.0006)- 0.0006	0.0059- 0.0118	0.0118- 0.0177	0.0079- 0.0276	0.0012- 0.0028	0.0012- 0.0028	0.0024- 0.0059
	3.6	G	0.0012- 0.0020	0.0098- 0.0157	0.0118- 0.0177	0.0059- 0.0260	0.0010- 0.0033	0.0012- 0.0031	0.0003- 0.0068

25766_SEBR_C0009

TORQUE SPECIFICATIONS

All readings in ft. lbs.

Year	Engine Disp. Liters	Engine ID/VIN	Cylinder Head Bolts	Main Bearing Bolts	Rod Bearing Bolts	Crankshaft Damper Bolts	Flywheel Bolts	Manifold		Spark Plugs	Oil Pan Drain Plug
								Intake	Exhaust		
2010	2.4	B	①	②	③	155	④	18	25	20	30
	2.7	D	⑤	⑥	⑦	125	70	9	17	15	20
	3.5	V	⑧	⑥	⑦	70	70	⑨	17	20	20
2011	2.4	B	①	②	③	155	④	18	25	20	30
	3.6	G	⑩	⑪	③	⑫	70	6	17	13	20

① Short head bolts:
  Step 1: 25 ft. lbs.
  Step 2: 45 ft. lbs.
  Step 3: 45 ft. lbs.
  Step 4: Plus 90 degrees
  Long head bolts:
  Step 1: 25 ft. lbs.
  Step 2: 54 ft. lbs.
  Step 3: 54 ft. lbs.
  Step 4: Plus 90 degrees
② Step 1: 11 ft. lbs.
  Step 2: 20 ft. lbs.
  Step 3: Plus 45 degrees

③ Step 1: 15 ft. lbs.
  Step 2: Plus 90 degrees
④ Step 1: 22 ft. lbs.
  Step 2: Plus 51 degrees
⑤ Step 1: Bolts 1-8: 35 ft. lbs.
  Step 2: Bolts 1-8: 55 ft. lbs.
  Step 3: Bolts 1-8: 55 ft. lbs.
  Step 4: Bolts 1-8: Plus 90 degrees
  Step 5: Bolts 9-11: 21 ft. lbs.
⑥ Tie Bolts: 21 ft. lbs.
  Outer Cap Bolts: 20 ft. lbs., plus 90 degrees
  Inner Cap Bolts: 15 ft. lbs., plus 90 degrees

⑦ Step 1: 20 ft. lbs.
  Step 2: Plus 90 degrees
⑧ Step 1: 45 ft. lbs.
  Step 2: 65 ft. lbs.
  Step 3: 65 ft. lbs.
  Step 4: Plus 90 degrees
⑨ Intake Manifold (Lower): 21 ft. lbs.
  Intake Manifold (Upper): 9 ft. lbs.
⑩ Step 1: 22 ft. lbs.
  Step 2: 33 ft. lbs.
  Step 3: Plus 75 degrees
  Step 4: Plus 50 degrees
  Step 5: Loosen all bolts

  Step 6: 22 ft. lbs.
  Step 7: 33 ft. lbs.
  Step 8: Plus 70 degrees
  Step 9: Plus 70 degrees
⑪ Outer Cap and Windage Tray (M8 Bolts):
  Step 1: 16 ft. lbs.
  Step 2: Plus 90 degrees
  Inner Cap (M11 Bolts):
  Step 1: 15 ft. lbs.
  Step 2: Plus 90 degrees
  Side Cap-Tie Bolt (M8 Bolts): 21 ft. lbs.
⑫ Step 1: 30 ft. lbs.
  Step 2: Plus 105 degrees

25766_SEBR_C0010

WHEEL ALIGNMENT

Year	Model		Caster		Camber		Toe-in (in.)
			Range (+/-Deg.)	Preferred Setting (Deg.)	Range (+/-Deg.)	Preferred Setting (Deg.)	
2010	All Models	F	1.00	+3.00	0.55	0.00	0.10 +/- 0.20
		R	N/A	N/A	0.65	-0.60	0.20 +/- 0.20
2011	All Models	F	1.00	+3.00	0.55	-0.62	0.20 +/- 0.30
		R	N/A	N/A	0.65	-0.78	0.20 +/- 0.30

N/A: Not Applicable

25766_SEBR_C0011

TIRE, WHEEL AND BALL JOINT SPECIFICATIONS

Year	Model	OEM Tires Standard	OEM Tires Optional	Tire Pressures (psi) Front	Tire Pressures (psi) Rear	Wheel Size	Ball Joint Inspection	Lug Nut (ft. lbs.)
2010	Avenger SXT	P215/65TR16	NA	①	①	16 x 6.5	②	100
	Avenger Express	P215/60TR17	NA	①	①	17 x 6.5	②	100
	Avenger R/T	P215/60TR17	NA	①	①	17 x 6.5	②	100
	Sebring Touring Sedan	P215/65TR16	NA	①	①	16 x 6.5	②	100
	Sebring Limited Sedan	P215/60TR17	NA	①	①	17 x 6.5	②	100
	Sebring LX Convertible	P215/65TR16	NA	①	①	16 x 6.5	②	100
	Sebring Limited Convertible	P215/55TR18	NA	①	①	18 x 7	②	100
	Sebring Touring Convertible	P215/60TR17	NA	①	①	17 x 6.5	②	100
2011	Avenger Express	P225/55HR17	NA	①	①	17 x 6.5	②	100
	Avenger Mainstreet	P225/55HR17	NA	①	①	17 x 6.5	②	100
	Avenger Lux	P225/50TR18	NA	①	①	18 x 7	②	100
	Avenger Heat	P225/50TR18	NA	①	①	18 x 7	②	100
	200 LX Sedan	P225/55HR17	NA	①	①	17 x 6.5	②	100
	200 Touring/Limited Sedan	P225/50VR18	NA	①	①	18 x 7	②	100
	200 S Sedan	P225/50TR18	NA	①	①	18 x 7	②	100
	200 Touring Convertible	P225/55HR17	NA	①	①	17 x 6.5	②	100
	200 Limited/S Convertible	P225/50TR18	NA	①	①	18 x 7	②	100

OEM: Original Equipment Manufacturer

PSI: Pounds Per Square Inch

NA: Information not available

① Always refer to the owner's manual and/or vehicle label

② End play is acceptable if no more than 0.039 inch (1.0 mm) of movement is achieved

25766_SEBR_C0012

BRAKE SPECIFICATIONS
All measurements in inches unless noted

Year	Model		Brake Disc Original Thickness	Brake Disc Minimum Thickness	Brake Disc Max. Runout	Brake Drum Diameter Original Inside Diameter	Brake Drum Diameter Max. Wear Limit	Brake Drum Diameter Maximum Machine Diameter	Minimum Pad/Lining Thickness Front	Minimum Pad/Lining Thickness Rear	Brake Caliper Bracket Bolts (ft. lbs.)	Brake Caliper Guide Pin Bolts (ft. lbs.)
2010	All Models	F	1.020-1.028	0.961	0.002	N/A	N/A	N/A	0.039	0.039	80	32
		R	0.386-0.402	0.331	0.002	N/A	N/A	N/A	0.039	0.039	52	32
2011	All Models	F	1.020-1.028	0.961	0.002	N/A	N/A	N/A	0.039	0.039	80	32
		R	0.386-0.402	0.331	0.002	N/A	N/A	N/A	0.039	0.039	52	32

F: Front

R: Rear

N/A: Not Applicable

25766_SEBR_C0013

SCHEDULED MAINTENANCE INTERVALS
2010-2011 Chrysler Sebring, 2011 Chrysler 200 & 2010-2011 Dodge Avenger
2.4L, 2.7L & 3.5L Engines - Normal & Severe (as noted)

TO BE SERVICED	TYPE OF SERVICE	VEHICLE MILEAGE INTERVAL (x1000)												
		6	12	18	24	30	36	42	48	54	60	66	72	78
Engine oil & filter	Replace	✓	✓	✓	✓	✓	✓	✓	✓	✓	✓	✓	✓	✓
Rotate tires, inspect tread wear, measure tread depth and check pressure	Rotate/Inspect	✓	✓	✓	✓	✓	✓	✓	✓	✓	✓	✓	✓	✓
Air conditioner filter	Replace		✓		✓		✓		✓		✓		✓	
Brake system components - Normal	Inspect/Service						✓		✓		✓		✓	
Brake system components - Severe	Inspect/Service		✓		✓		✓		✓		✓		✓	
Exhaust system & heat shields	Inspect		✓		✓		✓		✓		✓		✓	
Inspect the front suspension, tie rod ends and boot seals for cracks or leaks and all parts for damage, wear, improper looseness or end play.	Inspect		✓		✓		✓		✓		✓		✓	
CV Joints	Inspect		✓		✓		✓		✓		✓		✓	
Engine air filter - Normal	Replace					✓					✓			
Engine air filter - Severe	Replace		✓		✓		✓		✓		✓		✓	
Adjust parking brake on vehicles equipped with four-wheel disc brakes.	Adjust					✓					✓			
Engine coolant	Flush/Replace										✓			
Automatic transmisison fluid & filter	Replace	Every 120,000 miles												
Accessory drive belts	Replace	Every 120,000 miles												
Spark plugs (Except PZEV engine)	Replace					✓					✓			
Spark plugs (PZEV engine)	Replace	Every 102,000 miles												
Fluid levels (all)	Top off	✓	✓	✓	✓	✓	✓	✓	✓	✓	✓	✓	✓	✓
Horn, exterior lamps, turn signals and hazard warning light operation	Inspect	✓	✓	✓	✓	✓	✓	✓	✓	✓	✓	✓	✓	✓
Battery	Inspect/Service	✓	✓	✓	✓	✓	✓	✓	✓	✓	✓	✓	✓	✓

25766_SEBR_C0014

SCHEDULED MAINTENANCE INTERVALS
2011 Chrysler Sebring and Dodge Avenger 3.6L Engines - Normal

TO BE SERVICED	TYPE OF SERVICE	VEHICLE MILEAGE INTERVAL (x1000)												
		8	16	24	36	40	48	56	64	72	80	88	96	104
Engine oil & filter	Replace	✓	✓	✓	✓	✓	✓	✓	✓	✓	✓	✓	✓	✓
Rotate tires, inspect tread wear, measure tread depth and check pressure	Rotate/Inspect	✓	✓	✓	✓	✓	✓	✓	✓	✓	✓	✓	✓	✓
Air conditioner filter	Replace		✓			✓			✓		✓		✓	
Brake linings	Inspect/Service						✓		✓		✓		✓	
Exhaust system & heat shields	Inspect			✓			✓			✓			✓	
Inspect the front suspension, tie rod ends and boot seals for cracks or leaks and all parts for damage, wear, improper looseness or end play.	Inspect		✓		✓		✓		✓		✓		✓	
CV Joints	Inspect		✓		✓		✓		✓		✓		✓	
Engine air filter	Replace				✓				✓				✓	
Adjust parking brake on vehicles equipped with four-wheel disc brakes.	Adjust				✓					✓				
Engine coolant	Flush/Replace										✓			
Automatic transaxle fluid & filter	Replace	Every 120,000 miles												
Accessory drive belts	Replace	Every 120,000 miles												
Spark plugs	Replace	Every 96,000 miles												
PVC valve	Replace	Every 96,000 miles												
Fluid levels (all)	Top off	✓	✓	✓	✓	✓	✓	✓	✓	✓	✓	✓	✓	✓
Horn, exterior lamps, turn signals and hazard warning light operation	Inspect	✓	✓	✓	✓	✓	✓	✓	✓	✓	✓	✓	✓	✓
Battery	Inspect/Service	✓	✓	✓	✓	✓	✓	✓	✓	✓	✓	✓	✓	✓

25766_SEBR_C0015

PRECAUTIONS

Before servicing any vehicle, please be sure to read all of the following precautions, which deal with personal safety, prevention of component damage, and important points to take into consideration when servicing a motor vehicle:

• Never open, service or drain the radiator or cooling system when the engine is hot; serious burns can occur from the steam and hot coolant.

• Observe all applicable safety precautions when working around fuel. Whenever servicing the fuel system, always work in a well-ventilated area. Do not allow fuel spray or vapors to come in contact with a spark, open flame, or excessive heat (a hot drop light, for example). Keep a dry chemical fire extinguisher near the work area. Always keep fuel in a container specifically designed for fuel storage; also, always properly seal fuel containers to avoid the possibility of fire or explosion. Refer to the additional fuel system precautions later in this section.

• Fuel injection systems often remain pressurized, even after the engine has been turned **OFF**. The fuel system pressure must be relieved before disconnecting any fuel lines. Failure to do so may result in fire and/or personal injury.

• Brake fluid often contains polyglycol ethers and polyglycols. Avoid contact with the eyes and wash your hands thoroughly after handling brake fluid. If you do get brake fluid in your eyes, flush your eyes with clean, running water for 15 minutes. If eye irritation persists, or if you have taken brake fluid internally, IMMEDIATELY seek medical assistance.

• The EPA warns that prolonged contact with used engine oil may cause a number of skin disorders, including cancer. You should make every effort to minimize your exposure to used engine oil. Protective gloves should be worn when changing oil. Wash your hands and any other exposed skin areas as soon as possible after exposure to used engine oil. Soap and water, or waterless hand cleaner should be used.

• All new vehicles are now equipped with an air bag system, often referred to as a Supplemental Restraint System (SRS) or Supplemental Inflatable Restraint (SIR) system. The system must be disabled before performing service on or around system components, steering column, instrument panel components, wiring and sensors. Failure to follow safety and disabling procedures could result in accidental air bag deployment, possible personal injury and unnecessary system repairs.

• Always wear safety goggles when working with, or around, the air bag system. When carrying a non-deployed air bag, be sure the bag and trim cover are pointed away from your body. When placing a non-deployed air bag on a work surface, always face the bag and trim cover upward, away from the surface. This will reduce the motion of the module if it is accidentally deployed. Refer to the additional air bag system precautions later in this section.

• Clean, high quality brake fluid from a sealed container is essential to the safe and proper operation of the brake system. You should always buy the correct type of brake fluid for your vehicle. If the brake fluid becomes contaminated, completely flush the system with new fluid. Never reuse any brake fluid. Any brake fluid that is removed from the system should be discarded. Also, do not allow any brake fluid to come in contact with a painted surface; it will damage the paint.

• Never operate the engine without the proper amount and type of engine oil; doing so WILL result in severe engine damage.

• Timing belt maintenance is extremely important. Many models utilize an interference-type, non-freewheeling engine. If the timing belt breaks, the valves in the cylinder head may strike the pistons, causing potentially serious (also time-consuming and expensive) engine damage. Refer to the maintenance interval charts for the recommended replacement interval for the timing belt, and to the timing belt section for belt replacement and inspection.

• Disconnecting the negative battery cable on some vehicles may interfere with the functions of the on-board computer system(s) and may require the computer to undergo a relearning process once the negative battery cable is reconnected.

• When servicing drum brakes, only disassemble and assemble one side at a time, leaving the remaining side intact for reference.

• Only an MVAC-trained, EPA-certified automotive technician should service the air conditioning system or its components.

BRAKES

GENERAL INFORMATION

PRECAUTIONS

• Certain components within the ABS system are not intended to be serviced or repaired individually.

• Do not use rubber hoses or other parts not specifically specified for and ABS system. When using repair kits, replace all parts included in the kit. Partial or incorrect repair may lead to functional problems and require the replacement of components.

• Lubricate rubber parts with clean, fresh brake fluid to ease assembly. Do not use shop air to clean parts; damage to rubber components may result.

• Use only DOT 3 brake fluid from an unopened container.

• If any hydraulic component or line is removed or replaced, it may be necessary to bleed the entire system.

• A clean repair area is essential. Always clean the reservoir and cap thoroughly before removing the cap. The slightest amount of dirt in the fluid may plug an orifice and impair the system function. Perform repairs after components have been thoroughly cleaned; use only denatured alcohol to clean components. Do not allow ABS components to come into contact with any substance containing mineral oil; this includes used shop rags.

• The Anti-Lock control unit is a microprocessor similar to other computer units in the vehicle. Ensure that the ignition switch is **OFF** before removing or installing controller harnesses. Avoid static electricity discharge at or near the controller.

ANTI-LOCK BRAKE SYSTEM (ABS)

• If any arc welding is to be done on the vehicle, the control unit should be unplugged before welding operations begin.

SPEED SENSORS

REMOVAL & INSTALLATION

Front Speed Sensor

See Figure 1.

1. Before servicing the vehicle, refer to the Precautions Section.
2. Open the hood.
3. Disconnect the wheel speed sensor cable connector from the wiring harness connector on top of the frame rail from the inside of the strut tower.
4. Raise and safely support the vehicle.
5. Remove the grommet from the hole

in the body and pull the wheel speed sensor cable out of the hole.

6. Remove the speed sensor cable routing clip from the outside frame rail.

7. Remove the screw fastening the cable routing clamp to the outside frame rail.

8. Remove the screw securing the wheel speed sensor routing bracket to the brake flex hose bracket.

9. Remove the mounting screw fastening the wheel speed sensor head to the knuckle. Pull the sensor head out of the knuckle.

➡The routing clip can be easily removed without damaging it by rotating it, with the entire sensor, counterclockwise.

10. Remove the routing clip securing the wheel speed sensor cable to the knuckle. Remove the sensor from the vehicle.

To install:

❋❋ WARNING

Failure to install the speed sensor cables properly may result in contact with moving parts or an over-extension of cables causing an open circuit. Be sure that cables are installed, routed, and clipped properly.

11. Install the wheel speed sensor head into the knuckle. Install the mounting screw and tighten it to 106 inch lbs. (12 Nm).

12. Install the routing clip securing the wheel speed sensor cable to the knuckle.

13. Position the wheel speed sensor routing bracket on the brake flex hose bracket and install the mounting screw. Tighten the mounting screw to 13 ft. lbs. (18 Nm).

14. Position the wheel speed sensor cable routing clamp on the outside frame rail and install the mounting screw. Tighten the mounting screw to 13 ft. lbs. (18 Nm).

15. Install the speed sensor cable routing clip on the outside frame rail.

16. Insert the wheel speed sensor cable through the hole in the body and install the grommet in the hole.

17. Lower the vehicle.

18. Connect the wheel speed sensor cable connector to the wiring harness connector on top of the frame rail.

19. Perform a Diagnostic Verification Test and clear any faults as needed.

Rear Speed Sensor

See Figures 2 and 3.

1. Before servicing the vehicle, refer to the Precautions Section.

2. Move aside the luggage compartment carpet as necessary to access the wheel speed sensor cable connector.

3. Disconnect the wheel speed sensor cable connector at the body wiring harness connector.

4. Raise and safely support the vehicle.

5. Remove the wheel mounting nuts, then the rear tire and wheel assembly.

6. Remove the grommet from the hole in the body and pull the wheel speed sensor cable out through the hole.

7. Remove the speed sensor cable routing clip from the outside frame rail.

8. Remove the screw fastening the cable routing clamp to the rear suspension crossmember.

9. Remove the speed sensor cable routing clips from the trailing link.

10. Remove the screw fastening the cable routing clamp to the trailing link.

11. Remove the screw fastening the wheel speed sensor head in the rear of the hub and bearing.

12. Remove the sensor from the vehicle.

To install:

❋❋ WARNING

Failure to install the speed sensor cables properly may result in contact with moving parts or an over-extension of cables causing an open circuit. Be sure that cables are installed, routed, and clipped properly.

13. Install the wheel speed sensor head into the rear of the hub and bearing.

14. Install the wheel speed sensor head mounting screw. Tighten the screw to 89 inch lbs. (10 Nm).

15. Position the wheel speed sensor on the trailing link and install the screw securing it in place. Tighten the mounting screw to 13 ft. lbs. (18 Nm).

16. Position the wheel speed sensor and install the routing clips fastening the sensor to the trailing link.

17. Position the wheel speed sensor cable routing clamp on the rear suspension crossmember and install the mounting screw. Tighten the mounting screw to 13 ft. lbs. (18 Nm).

18. Install the speed sensor cable routing clip on the outside frame rail.

19. Insert the wheel speed sensor cable through the hole in the body and install the grommet in the hole.

20. Install the front wheel and tire

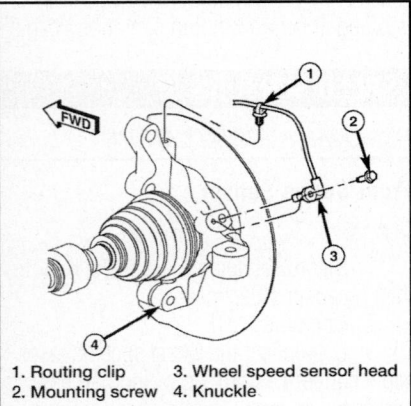

1. Routing clip   3. Wheel speed sensor head
2. Mounting screw   4. Knuckle

247862

Fig. 1 Front wheel speed sensor removal

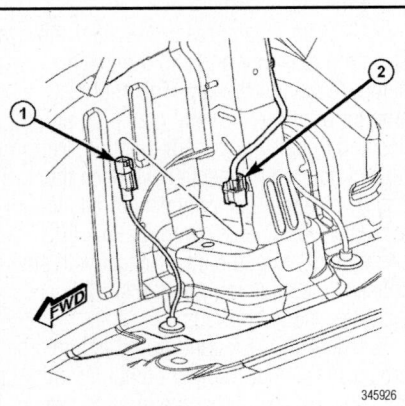

345926

Fig. 2 Disconnect the rear wheel speed sensor cable connector (1) at the body wiring harness connector (2)

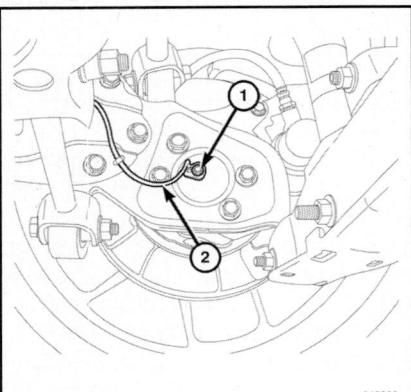

345922

Fig. 3 Remove the screw (1) fastening the wheel speed sensor (2) head in the rear of the hub and bearing

assembly. Tighten the wheel nuts in a star pattern until all nuts are torqued to half the required specification. Then repeat the tightening sequence to the full specified torque of 100 ft. lbs. (135 Nm).

21. Lower the vehicle.
22. Connect the wheel speed sensor cable connector to the body wiring harness connector.

23. Reposition the luggage compartment carpet as necessary.
24. Perform a Diagnostic Verification Test and clear any faults as needed.

BRAKES   BLEEDING THE BRAKE SYSTEM

BLEEDING PROCEDURE

BLEEDING PROCEDURE

For bleeding the Antilock Brake System (ABS) hydraulic system, refer to Bleeding The ABS System procedure.

Before removing the master cylinder cap, wipe it clean to prevent dirt and other foreign matter from dropping into the master cylinder reservoir.

Use only MOPAR® brake fluid, or an equivalent. Brake fluid must conform to DOT 3 specifications.

Do not pump the brake pedal at any time while having a bleeder screw open during the bleeding process. This will only increase the amount of air in the system and make additional bleeding necessary.

Do not allow the master cylinder reservoir to run out of brake fluid while bleeding the system. An empty reservoir will allow additional air into the brake system. Check the fluid level frequently and add fluid as needed.

The following wheel circuit sequence for bleeding the brake hydraulic system should be used to ensure adequate removal of all trapped air from the hydraulic system.
- Left rear wheel
- Right front wheel
- Right rear wheel
- Left front wheel

✳✳ WARNING

Do not use any fluid other than clean brake fluid meeting manufacturer's specification. Additionally, do not use brake fluid that has been previously drained. Following these instructions will help prevent system contamination, brake component damage, and the risk of serious personal injury.

✳✳ CAUTION

Brake fluid contains polyglycol ethers and polyglycols. Avoid contact with the eyes. Wash hands thoroughly after handling. If brake fluid contacts the eyes, flush the eyes for 15 minutes with cold running water. Get medical attention if irritation per-

sists. If taken internally, drink water and induce vomiting. Get medical attention immediately. Failure to follow these instructions may result in personal injury.

✳✳ WARNING

Do not spill brake fluid on painted or plastic surfaces or damage to the surface may occur. If brake fluid is spilled onto a painted or plastic surface, immediately wash the surface with water.

Manual Bleeding

➡**To bleed the brakes manually, the aid of a helper will be required.**

1. Before servicing the vehicle, refer to the Precautions Section.
2. Attach a clear plastic hose to the bleeder screw and feed the hose into a clear jar containing enough fresh brake fluid to submerge the end of the hose.
3. Have a helper pump the brake pedal 3–4 times and hold it in the down position.
4. With the pedal in the down position, open the bleeder screw at least 1 full turn.
5. Once the brake pedal has dropped, close the bleeder screw. After the bleeder screw is closed, release the brake pedal.
6. Repeat the above steps until all trapped air is removed from that wheel circuit (usually 4–5 times).
7. Bleed the remaining wheel circuits in the same manner until all air is removed from the brake system.

➡**Monitor the fluid level in the master cylinder reservoir to make sure it does not go dry.**

8. Check and adjust the brake fluid level to the FULL mark.
9. Check the brake pedal travel. If pedal travel is excessive or has not been improved, some air may still be trapped in the system. Re-bleed the brakes as necessary.
10. If the brake system seems normal, test drive the vehicle to verify the brakes

are operating properly and pedal feel is correct.

Pressure Bleeding

➡**Follow the pressure bleeder manufacturer's instructions for use of pressure bleeding equipment.**

1. Before servicing the vehicle, refer to the Precautions Section.
2. Attach the pressure bleeding equipment to the Master Cylinder.
3. Attach a clear plastic hose to the bleeder screw and feed the hose into a clear jar containing enough fresh brake fluid to submerge the end of the hose.
4. Open the bleeder screw at least 1 full turn or more to obtain a steady stream of brake fluid.
5. After approximately 4–8 ounces (120–240ml) of fluid have been bled through the brake circuit and an air-free flow is maintained in the clear plastic hose and jar, close the bleeder screw.
6. Repeat this procedure at all the remaining bleeder screws.
7. Check and adjust the brake fluid level to the FULL mark on the reservoir.
8. Check the brake pedal travel. If pedal travel is excessive or has not been improved, some air may still be trapped in the system. Re-bleed the brakes as necessary.
9. If the brake system seems normal, test drive the vehicle to verify the brakes are operating properly and pedal feel is correct.

MASTER CYLINDER BLEEDING

Special Tools
- 8358-1: Bleed Tube

✳✳ WARNING

Do not use any fluid other than clean brake fluid meeting manufacturer's specification. Additionally, do not use brake fluid that has been previously drained. Following these instructions will help prevent system contamination, brake component damage, and the risk of serious personal injury.

✳✳ CAUTION

Brake fluid contains polyglycol ethers and polyglycols. Avoid contact with the eyes. Wash hands thoroughly after handling. If brake fluid contacts the eyes, flush the eyes for 15 minutes with cold running water. Get medical attention if irritation persists. If taken internally, drink water and induce vomiting. Get medical attention immediately. Failure to follow these instructions may result in personal injury.

✳✳ WARNING

Do not allow the brake master cylinder to run dry during the bleeding operation. The master cylinder may be damaged if operated without fluid, resulting in degraded braking performance.

✳✳ WARNING

Do not spill brake fluid on painted or plastic surfaces or damage to the surface may occur. If brake fluid is spilled onto a painted or plastic surface, immediately wash the surface with water.

1. Before servicing the vehicle, refer to the Precautions Section.
2. Clamp the master cylinder in a vise with soft-jaw caps.
3. Attach the special tools for bleeding the master cylinder in the following fashion:
   a. Thread a Bleeder Tube, Special Tool 8358-1, into the primary and secondary ports. Tighten the bleeder tube nuts to 15 ft. lbs. (20 Nm).
   b. Flex each Bleeder Tube and place the open ends into the neck of the master cylinder reservoir. Position the open ends of the tubes into the reservoir so their outlets are below the surface of the brake fluid when the reservoir is filled.

➡Make sure the ends of the Bleeder Tubes stay below the surface of the brake fluid in the reservoir at all times during the bleeding procedure.

4. Fill the brake fluid reservoir with fresh MOPAR® Brake Fluid (DOT 3 Motor Vehicle), or equivalent.
5. Using an appropriately sized wooden dowel as a pushrod, slowly press the pistons inward discharging brake fluid through the Bleeder Tubes, then release the pressure, allowing the pistons to return to the

released position. Repeat this several times until all air bubbles are expelled from the master cylinder bore and Bleeder Tubes.

6. Remove the Bleeder Tubes from the master cylinder and plug the master cylinder outlet ports.
7. Install the fill cap on the reservoir.
8. Remove the master cylinder from the vise.
9. Install the master cylinder on the vehicle.

BRAKE LINE BLEEDING

Refer to Bleeding Procedure, Manual Bleeding or Pressure Bleeding.

BLEEDING THE ABS SYSTEM

➡The base brake's hydraulic system must be bled anytime air enters the hydraulic system. The ABS must always be bled anytime it is suspected that the HCU has ingested air.

➡Brake systems with ABS must be bled as two independent braking systems. The non-ABS portion of the brake system with ABS is to be bled the same as any non-ABS system.

➡The ABS portion of the brake system must be bled separately. Use the following procedure to properly bleed the brake hydraulic system including the ABS.

➡During the brake bleeding procedure, be sure the brake fluid level remains close to the FULL level in the master cylinder fluid reservoir. Check the fluid level periodically during the bleeding procedure and add MOPAR® DOT 3 brake fluid as required.

➡When bleeding the ABS system, the following bleeding sequence must be followed to insure complete and adequate bleeding.

1. Before servicing the vehicle, refer to the Precautions Section.
2. Make sure all hydraulic fluid lines are installed and properly torqued.
3. Connect the scan tool to the diagnostic connector. The diagnostic connector is located under the lower steering column cover to the left of the steering column.
4. Using the scan tool, check to make sure the ABS does not have any fault codes stored. If it does, clear them.

✳✳ CAUTION

When bleeding the brake system, wear safety glasses. A clear bleed tube must be attached to the bleeder

screws and submerged in a clear container filled part way with clean brake fluid. Direct the flow of brake fluid away from your body and the painted surfaces of the vehicle. Brake fluid at high pressure may come out of the bleeder screws when opened.

➡Pressure bleeding is recommended to bleed the base brake system to ensure all air is removed from system. Manual bleeding may also be used, but additional time is needed to remove all the air from the system.

5. Bleed the base brake system. Refer to Bleeding Procedure, Manual Bleeding or Pressure Bleeding.
6. Using the scan tool, select ECU VIEW, followed by ABS MISCELLANEOUS FUNCTIONS to access bleeding. Follow the instructions displayed. When finished, disconnect the scan tool and proceed.
7. Bleed the base brake system a second time. Check the brake fluid level in the reservoir periodically to prevent emptying, causing air to enter the hydraulic system.
8. Fill the master cylinder fluid reservoir to the FULL level.
9. If the brake system seems normal, test drive the vehicle to verify the brakes are operating properly and pedal feel is correct.

FLUID FILL PROCEDURE

✳✳ WARNING

Do not use any fluid other than clean brake fluid meeting manufacturer's specification. Additionally, do not use brake fluid that has been previously drained. Following these instructions will help prevent system contamination, brake component damage, and the risk of serious personal injury.

✳✳ CAUTION

Brake fluid contains polyglycol ethers and polyglycols. Avoid contact with the eyes. Wash hands thoroughly after handling. If brake fluid contacts the eyes, flush the eyes for 15 minutes with cold running water. Get medical attention if irritation persists. If taken internally, drink water and induce vomiting. Get medical attention immediately. Failure to follow these instructions may result in personal injury.

✳✳ WARNING

Do not allow the brake master cylinder to run dry during a bleeding operation. The master cylinder may be damaged if operated without fluid, resulting in degraded braking performance.

✳✳ WARNING

Do not spill brake fluid on painted or plastic surfaces or damage to the surface may occur. If brake fluid is spilled onto a painted or plastic surface, immediately wash the surface with water.

1. Before servicing the vehicle, refer to the Precautions Section.

2. Visually inspect the brake fluid level through the brake master cylinder reservoir.

3. If the brake fluid level is at or below the half-full point during routine fluid checks, the brake system should be inspected for wear and possible brake fluid leaks.

4. If the brake fluid level is at or below the half-full point during routine fluid checks, and an inspection of the brake system did not reveal wear or brake fluid leaks, the brake fluid may be topped-off up to the maximum-fill level.

5. If brake system service was just completed, the brake fluid may be topped-off up to the maximum-fill level.

6. If the brake fluid level is above the half-full point, adding brake fluid is not recommended under normal conditions.

7. If brake fluid is to be added to the master cylinder reservoir, clean the outside of the reservoir on and around the reservoir cap prior to removing the cap and diaphragm.

BRAKES

✳✳ CAUTION

Dust and dirt accumulating on brake parts during normal use may contain asbestos fibers from production or aftermarket brake linings. Breathing excessive concentrations of asbestos fibers can cause serious bodily harm. Exercise care when servicing brake parts. Do not sand or grind brake lining unless equipment used is designed to contain the dust residue. Do not clean brake parts with compressed air or by dry brushing. Cleaning should be done by dampening the brake components with a fine mist of water, then wiping the brake components clean with a dampened cloth. Dispose of cloth and all residue containing asbestos fibers in an impermeable container with the appropriate label. Follow practices prescribed by the Occupational Safety and Health Administration (OSHA) and the Environmental Protection Agency (EPA) for the handling, processing, and disposing of dust or debris that may contain asbestos fibers.

BRAKE CALIPER

REMOVAL & INSTALLATION
See Figure 4.

✳✳ WARNING

Do not use any fluid other than clean brake fluid meeting manufacturer's specification. Additionally, do not use brake fluid that has been previously drained. Following these instructions will help prevent system contamination, brake component damage, and the risk of serious personal injury.

✳✳ CAUTION

Brake fluid contains polyglycol ethers and polyglycols. Avoid contact with the eyes. Wash hands thoroughly after handling. If brake fluid contacts the eyes, flush the eyes for 15 minutes with cold running water. Get medical attention if irritation persists. If taken internally, drink water and induce vomiting. Get medical attention immediately. Failure to follow these instructions may result in personal injury.

✳✳ WARNING

Do not spill brake fluid on painted or plastic surfaces or damage to the surface may occur. If brake fluid is spilled onto a painted or plastic surface, immediately wash the surface with water.

✳✳ CAUTION

Use of eye goggles is necessary to prevent personal injury.

1. Before servicing the vehicle, refer to the Precautions Section.

2. Using a brake pedal holding tool, depress the brake pedal past its first 1 inch (25mm) of travel and hold it in this position. This will isolate the master cylinder from the brake hydraulic system and will not allow the brake fluid to drain out of the master cylinder reservoir when the lines are opened.

3. Raise and safely support the vehicle.

4. Remove the wheel mounting nuts, then the tire and wheel assembly.

FRONT DISC BRAKES

5. Remove the banjo bolt connecting the brake flex hose to the brake caliper. There are 2 washers that will come off with the banjo bolt. Discard the washers.

➡When removing the caliper guide pin bolts note that one (upper) has a special sleeve on the end. It is important that this bolt be installed in the upper mounting hole when the caliper is installed.

6. Remove the two brake caliper guide pin bolts.

7. Slide the disc brake caliper from the disc brake adapter bracket and brake pads and remove.

To install:

8. Completely retract the caliper piston back into the bore of the caliper. Use a C-clamp to retract the piston. Place a wood block over the piston before installing the C-clamp to avoid damaging the piston.

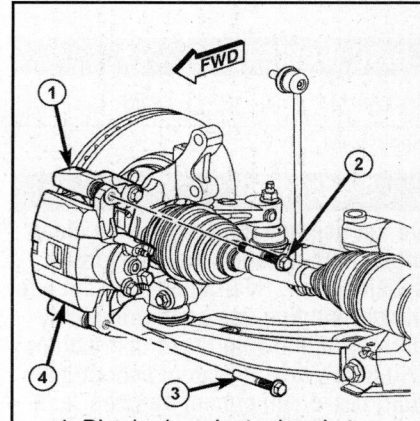

1. Disc brake adapter bracket
2. Brake caliper guide pin bolt
3. Brake caliper guide pin bolt
4. Disc brake caliper

57849

Fig. 4 View of the front brake caliper

✳✳ WARNING

Use care when installing the caliper onto the adapter bracket to avoid damaging the guide pin boots.

9. Install the disc brake caliper over the brake pads on the brake caliper adapter bracket.

➡When installing the caliper guide pin bolts make sure that the one that has a special sleeve on the end is installed in the upper mounting hole.

10. Align the caliper guide pin bolt holes with the adapter bracket. Install the upper (with special sleeve) and lower caliper guide pin bolts. Tighten the guide pin bolts to 32 ft. lbs. (43 Nm).

11. Install the banjo bolt connecting the brake flex hose to the brake caliper. Install NEW washers on each side of the hose fitting as the banjo bolt is guided through the fitting. Thread the banjo bolt into the caliper and tighten it to 26 ft. lbs. (35 Nm).

12. Install the front wheel and tire assembly. Tighten the wheel nuts in a star pattern until all nuts are torqued to half the required specification. Then repeat the tightening sequence to the full specified torque of 100 ft. lbs. (135 Nm).

13. Lower the vehicle.

14. Remove the brake pedal holding tool.

15. Bleed the caliper as necessary. Refer to Bleeding The Brake System, Bleeding Procedure.

16. If the brake system seems normal, test drive the vehicle to verify the brakes are operating properly and pedal feel is correct.

17. Make several stops to wear off any foreign material on the brakes and to seat the brake shoes.

DISC BRAKE PADS

REMOVAL & INSTALLATION

See Figure 5.

✳✳ WARNING

Do not use any fluid other than clean brake fluid meeting manufacturer's specification. Additionally, do not use brake fluid that has been previously drained. Following these instructions will help prevent system contamination, brake component damage, and the risk of serious personal injury.

✳✳ CAUTION

Brake fluid contains polyglycol ethers and polyglycols. Avoid contact with the eyes. Wash hands thoroughly after handling. If brake fluid contacts the eyes, flush the eyes for 15 minutes with cold running water. Get medical attention if irritation persists. If taken internally, drink water and induce vomiting. Get medical attention immediately. Failure to follow these instructions may result in personal injury.

✳✳ WARNING

Do not spill brake fluid on painted or plastic surfaces or damage to the surface may occur. If brake fluid is spilled onto a painted or plastic surface, immediately wash the surface with water.

✳✳ CAUTION

Use of eye goggles is necessary to prevent personal injury.

1. Before servicing the vehicle, refer to the Precautions Section.

2. Raise and safely support the vehicle.

3. Remove the wheel mounting nuts, then the tire and wheel assembly.

➡When removing the caliper guide pin bolts note that one (upper) has a special sleeve on the end. It is important that this bolt be installed in the upper mounting hole when the caliper is installed.

4. Remove the 2 brake caliper guide pin bolts.

5. Remove the disc brake caliper from the disc brake adapter bracket and hang it out of the way using wire or a bungee cord. Use care not to overextend the brake hose when doing this.

6. Remove the brake pads from the caliper adapter bracket.

To install:

➡Make sure that the audible wear indicators (if equipped) are placed toward the top when the inboard brake pads are installed on each side of the vehicle.

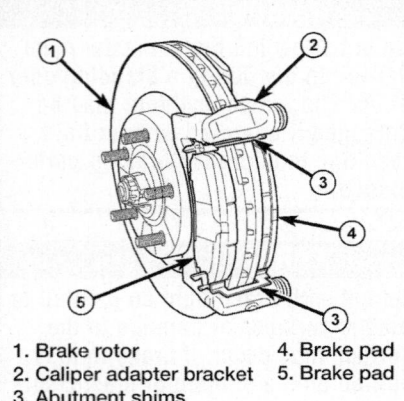

1. Brake rotor
2. Caliper adapter bracket
3. Abutment shims
4. Brake pad
5. Brake pad

57853

Fig. 5 Removing the front brake pads

7. Place the brake pads in the abutment shims clipped into the disc brake caliper adapter bracket. Place the pad with the wear indicator attached on the inboard side.

8. Completely retract the caliper piston back into the bore of the caliper.

✳✳ WARNING

Use care when installing the caliper onto the adapter bracket to avoid damaging the boots.

9. Install the disc brake caliper over the brake pads on the brake caliper adapter bracket.

➡When installing the caliper guide pin bolts make sure that the one that has a special sleeve on the end is installed in the upper mounting hole.

10. Align the caliper guide pin bolt holes with the adapter bracket. Install the upper (with special sleeve) and lower caliper guide pin bolts. Tighten the guide pin bolts to 32 ft. lbs. (43 Nm).

11. Install the tire and wheel assemblies. Tighten the wheel nuts, in a star pattern, to 100 ft. lbs. (135 Nm).

12. Lower the vehicle.

13. Pump the brake pedal several times before moving the vehicle to set the pads to the brake rotor.

14. Check and adjust the brake fluid level in the reservoir as necessary.

15. Road test the vehicle and make several stops to wear off any foreign material on the brakes and to seat the brake pads.

BRAKES

✳✳ CAUTION

Dust and dirt accumulating on brake parts during normal use may contain asbestos fibers from production or aftermarket brake linings. Breathing excessive concentrations of asbestos fibers can cause serious bodily harm. Exercise care when servicing brake parts. Do not sand or grind brake lining unless equipment used is designed to contain the dust residue. Do not clean brake parts with compressed air or by dry brushing. Cleaning should be done by dampening the brake components with a fine mist of water, then wiping the brake components clean with a dampened cloth. Dispose of cloth and all residue containing asbestos fibers in an impermeable container with the appropriate label. Follow practices prescribed by the Occupational Safety and Health Administration (OSHA) and the Environmental Protection Agency (EPA) for the handling, processing, and disposing of dust or debris that may contain asbestos fibers.

BRAKE CALIPER

REMOVAL & INSTALLATION

See Figures 6 and 7.

✳✳ WARNING

Do not use any fluid other than clean brake fluid meeting manufacturer's specification. Additionally, do not use brake fluid that has been previously drained. Following these instructions will help prevent system contamination, brake component damage, and the risk of serious personal injury.

✳✳ CAUTION

Brake fluid contains polyglycol ethers and polyglycols. Avoid contact with the eyes. Wash hands thoroughly after handling. If brake fluid contacts the eyes, flush the eyes for 15 minutes with cold running water. Get medical attention if irritation persists. If taken internally, drink water and induce vomiting. Get medical attention immediately. Failure to follow these instructions may result in personal injury.

✳✳ WARNING

Do not spill brake fluid on painted or plastic surfaces or damage to the surface may occur. If brake fluid is spilled onto a painted or plastic surface, immediately wash the surface with water.

✳✳ CAUTION

Use of eye goggles is necessary to prevent personal injury.

1. Before servicing the vehicle, refer to the Precautions Section.

2. Using a brake pedal holding tool, depress the brake pedal past its first 1 inch (25mm) of travel and hold it in this position. This will isolate the master cylinder from the brake hydraulic system and will not allow the brake fluid to drain out of the master cylinder reservoir while the lines are disconnected.

3. Raise and safely support the vehicle.

4. Remove the wheel mounting nuts, then the rear tire and wheel assembly.

5. Unthread the brake tube nut at the rear flex hose.

6. Remove the clip securing the rear flex hose to the trailing link mounted bracket. Remove the flex hose from the bracket.

7. Unthread and remove the brake flex hose from the brake caliper.

➡When removing the caliper guide pin bolts note that one has a special sleeve on the end. It is important that this bolt be installed in the upper mounting hole when the caliper is installed.

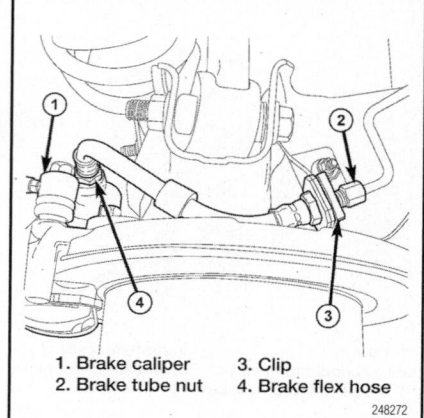

1. Brake caliper   3. Clip
2. Brake tube nut   4. Brake flex hose

248272

Fig. 6 Removing the rear brake flex hose

8. Remove the 2 brake caliper guide pin bolts (2, 3).

9. Slide and remove the disc brake caliper (1) with outboard brake pad attached from the disc brake adapter bracket, inboard brake pad and rotor.

10. Remove the outboard brake pad from the caliper by prying the brake pad retaining clip over the raised area on the caliper. Slide the brake pad off of the brake caliper.

11. Remove the rear brake caliper from the vehicle.

To install:

12. If not already performed, completely retract the caliper piston back into the piston bore of the caliper. Use a C-clamp to retract the piston. Place a wood block over the piston before installing the C-clamp to avoid damaging the piston.

13. Slide the outboard brake pad onto the caliper. Be sure the retaining clip is squarely seated in the depressed areas on the caliper beyond the raised retaining bead.

✳✳ WARNING

Use care when installing the caliper onto the disc brake adapter to avoid damaging the guide pin boots.

14. Install the disc brake caliper with the outboard brake pad attached over the inboard brake pad and rotor, onto the brake caliper adapter bracket.

➡When installing the caliper guide pin bolts make sure that the one that has a special sleeve on the end is installed in the upper mounting hole.

15. Align the caliper guide pin bolt holes with the adapter bracket. Install the lower

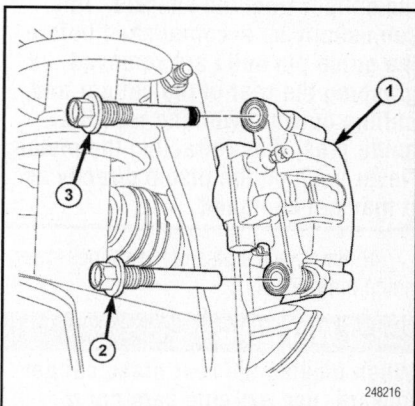

248216

Fig. 7 Removing the rear brake caliper (1), upper guide pin bolt (3), and lower guide pin bolt (2)

and upper (with special sleeve) caliper guide pin bolts. Tighten the guide pin bolts to 32 ft. lbs. (43 Nm).

16. Thread the rear brake flex hose into the brake caliper. Tighten the flex hose fitting at the caliper to 11 ft. lbs. (15 Nm).

17. Route and install the brake flex hose into the trailing link mounted bracket. Install the clip securing the flex hose to the bracket.

18. Thread the brake tube nut into brake flex hose. Tighten the brake tube nut to 15 ft. lbs. (20 Nm).

19. Install the front wheel and tire assembly. Tighten the wheel nuts in a star pattern until all nuts are torqued to half the required specification. Then repeat the tightening sequence to the full specified torque of 100 ft. lbs. (135 Nm).

20. Lower the vehicle.

21. Remove the brake pedal holding tool.

22. Bleed the caliper as necessary. Refer to Bleeding The Brake System, Bleeding Procedure.

23. Road test the vehicle and make several stops to wear off any foreign material on the brakes and to seat the brake shoes.

DISC BRAKE PADS

REMOVAL & INSTALLATION

See Figures 8 through 10.

1. Before servicing the vehicle, refer to the Precautions Section.

2. Raise and safely support the vehicle.

3. Remove the wheel mounting nuts, then the tire and wheel assembly.

❋❋ WARNING

In some cases, it may be necessary to retract the caliper piston in its bore a small amount in order to provide sufficient clearance between the pads and the rotor to easily remove the caliper from the knuckle. This can usually be accomplished before the guide pin bolts are removed, by grasping the rear of the caliper and pulling outward working with the guide pins, thus retracting the piston. Never push on the piston directly as it may get damaged.

4. Remove the disc brake caliper lower guide pin bolt.

❋❋ WARNING

When moving the rear brake caliper upward, use extreme care not to damage or over-extend the flex hose. Damage may occur.

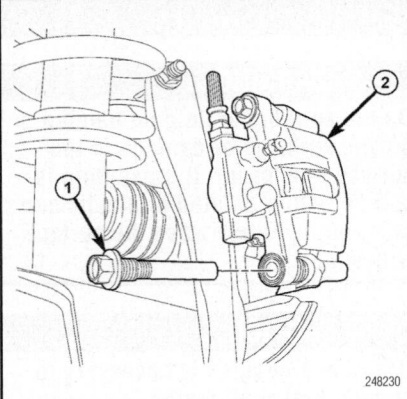

Fig. 8 Remove the disc brake caliper (2) lower guide pin bolt (1)

5. Rotate the caliper upward hinging off the upper guide pin bolt. Rotate the caliper upward just enough to allow for brake pad removal. Hang the caliper assembly in this position using wire or a bungee cord.

6. Remove the inboard brake pad from the caliper adapter bracket.

7. Remove the outboard brake pad from the caliper by prying the brake pad retaining clip over the raised area on the caliper. Slide the brake pad off of the brake caliper.

To install:

8. Completely retract the caliper piston back into the piston bore of the caliper. This is required to gain the necessary pad-to-rotor clearance for the caliper installation.

➡ **Place the brake pad with the audible wear indicator attached on the inboard side. The audible wear indicator should be positioned at the bottom when installed.**

9. Slide the outboard brake pad onto the caliper. Be sure the retaining clip is

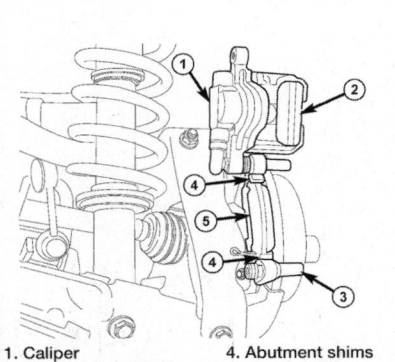

1. Caliper
2. Outboard brake pad
3. Caliper adapter bracket
4. Abutment shims
5. Inboard brake pad

Fig. 9 Removing the rear brake pads

squarely seated in the depressed areas on the caliper beyond the raised retaining bead.

10. Place the inboard brake pad in the abutment shims clipped into the disc brake caliper adapter bracket.

❋❋ WARNING

Use care when installing the caliper onto the adapter bracket to avoid damaging the guide pin boot.

11. Rotate the disc brake caliper downward over the brake rotor and lower part of caliper adapter.

12. Install the disc brake caliper lower guide pin bolt. Tighten the guide pin bolt to 32 ft. lbs. (43 Nm).

➡ **Once the caliper is installed, inspect the outboard brake pad to make sure it is correctly positioned. The retaining clip must be squarely seated in the depressed areas on the caliper fingers. Also, the nubs on the pad's steel backing plate must be fully seated in the depressions formed into the inside of the caliper fingers. There should be no gap between the pad backing plate and the caliper fingers.**

13. Install the front wheel and tire assembly. Tighten the wheel nuts in a star pattern until all nuts are torqued to half the required specification. Then repeat the tightening sequence to the full specified torque of 100 ft. lbs. (135 Nm).

14. Lower the vehicle.

15. Pump the brake pedal several times to ensure the vehicle has a firm brake pedal before moving the vehicle.

16. Road test the vehicle and make several stops to wear off any foreign material on the brakes and to seat the brake pads.

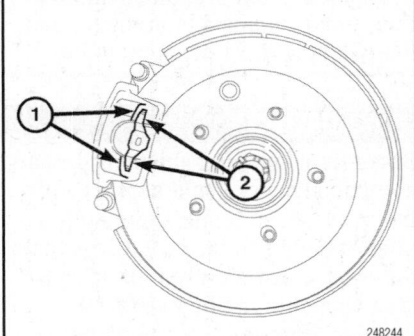

Fig. 10 Inspect the outboard brake pad to make sure it is correctly positioned. The retaining clip (2) must be squarely seated in the depressed areas (1) on the caliper fingers

BRAKES **PARKING BRAKE**

PARKING BRAKE CABLES

ADJUSTMENT

See Figure 11.

1. Before servicing the vehicle, refer to the Precautions Section.

2. Place blocks to the tires and wheel assemblies to prevent vehicle movement.

3. Remove the center console.

➡**Actuating the parking brake lever to its fully applied position 1 time after tightening the adjustment nut will yield (stretch) the bent nail portion of the equalizer approximately ¼ inch (6mm). This process will correctly set the parking brake cable tension.**

4. Adjust parking brake cable tension using the following steps:

   a. Place the parking brake lever in the fully released (down) position.

   b. Tighten the adjusting nut on the parking brake lever output cable until 0.87 inch (22mm) of thread is out past the end of the adjustment nut.

   c. Actuate the parking brake lever to its fully applied position one time, then reposition it to its fully released (down) position.

5. Raise the vehicle to a point where the rear wheels just clear the floor.

6. Check the rear wheels of the vehicle; they should rotate freely without dragging.

7. Apply the parking brake. Check the rear wheels of the vehicle. They should not rotate.

8. Return the parking brake lever to its fully released (down) position and check the rear wheels. They should rotate freely without dragging.

9. Apply the parking brake.
10. Lower the vehicle.
11. Install the center console.
12. Remove the blocks from the tires and wheel assemblies.

PARKING BRAKE SHOES

REMOVAL & INSTALLATION

See Figures 12 through 16.

Special Tools

• C-3919: Gauge, Brake Shoes

1. Before servicing the vehicle, refer to the Precautions Section.

2. Raise and safely support the vehicle.

➡**If removing parking brake shoes on both sides of the vehicle, perform the remaining steps on each side of the vehicle.**

3. Access and remove the rear brake rotor.

4. Turn the brake shoe adjuster wheel until the adjuster is at shortest length.

5. Remove the upper return spring from the anchor pin and the rear brake shoe.

6. Remove the upper return spring from the anchor pin and the front brake shoe.

7. Remove the brake shoe hold-down springs and pins. Rotate the pins 90° to disengage.

8. Remove the parking brake cable from the lever on the rear parking brake shoe.

9. Remove the brake shoes, adjuster and lower return spring as an assembly from the support plate.

10. If necessary, remove the strut.

11. Remove the lower return spring and adjuster from the shoes.

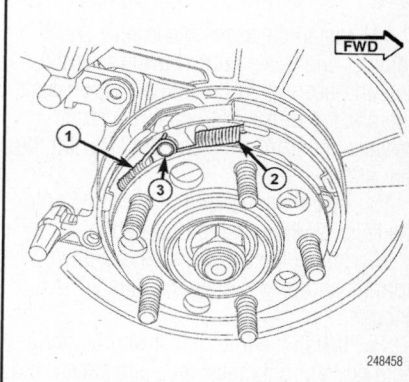

Fig. 13 Remove the upper return spring (1) from the anchor pin (3) and the rear brake shoe. Remove the upper return spring (2) from the anchor pin (3) and the front brake shoe

To install:

➡**If replacing the parking brake shoes on both sides of the vehicle, perform the procedure on one side first.**

➡**The right side shoes are a mirror image of the left except for the adjuster. The threaded portion of the adjuster should always be positioned to the left side in order to maintain consistent side-to-side rotational direction for adjustment purposes.**

12. Install the lower return spring and adjuster between the parking brake shoes. The rear shoe will have the lever mounted on the inside. Make sure the threaded portion of the adjuster is mounted to the left on both right and left side parking brake assemblies.

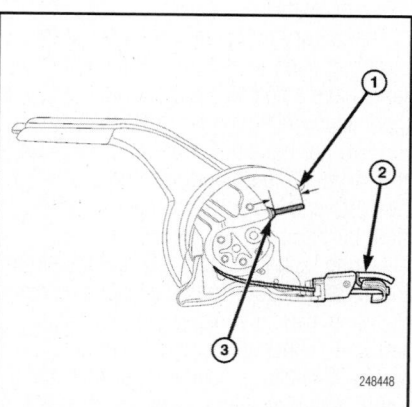

Fig. 11 View of parking brake lever outlet cable thread length (1), equalizer (2), and adjusting nut (3)

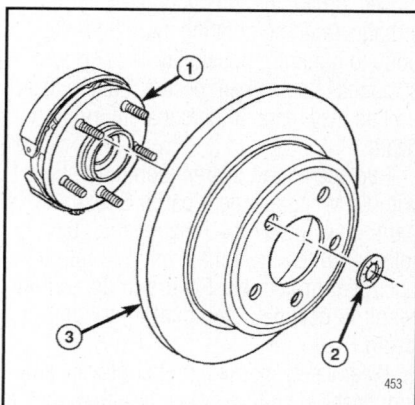

Fig. 12 Remove the disc retaining fastener (2) and rear brake rotor (3) from the hub/bearing assembly (1)

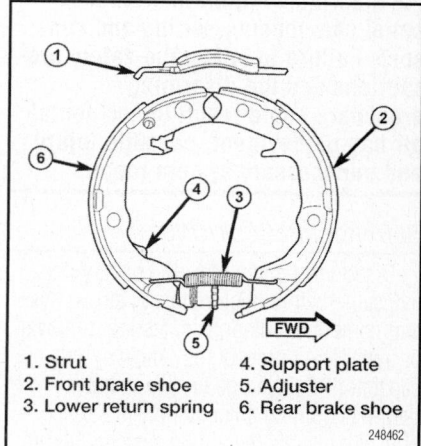

1. Strut
2. Front brake shoe
3. Lower return spring
4. Support plate
5. Adjuster
6. Rear brake shoe

Fig. 14 Parking brake shoe removal

13. If necessary, place the strut above the hub and bearing on the vehicle. Note the curved end of the strut is positioned to the rear.

14. Install the assembled brake shoes, adjuster and lower return spring over the hub and bearing and onto the support plate and anchor. Be sure to install the strut between the front shoe and the lever on the rear shoe.

15. Install the parking brake cable onto the lever on the parking brake shoe.

16. Install the brake shoe hold-down springs and pins. Rotate the pins 90° to engage.

17. Install the front upper return spring holding the front brake shoe and anchor pin.

18. Install the rear upper return spring holding the rear brake shoe and anchor pin.

19. Using Brake Shoe Gauge C-3919, or equivalent, measure the inside diameter of the parking brake drum portion of the rotor. Set the Gauge.

20. Place Gauge over the parking brake shoes at their widest point.

21. Using the adjuster wheel, adjust the parking brake shoes until the linings on both parking brake shoes just touch the jaws on the Gauge.

22. Install the rear brake rotor and install a couple wheel mounting nuts to hold it in place while a final adjustment is made.

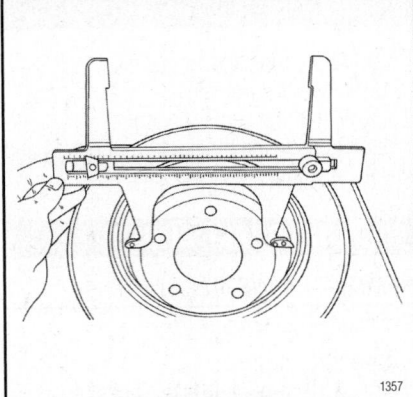

Fig. 15 Using Brake Shoe Gauge C-3919 to measure the inside diameter of parking brake drum portion of the rotor

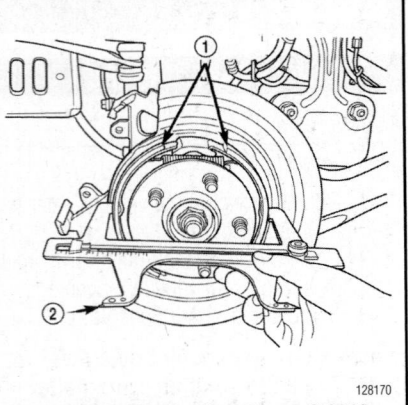

Fig. 16 Using Brake Shoe Gauge C-3919 (2) to adjust the outside diameter of the parking brake shoes (1)

➡To find the adjuster wheel with the drum installed, position the hole in the front of the rotor drum to 7 o'clock for the left side and to 5 o'clock for the right side.

➡When adjusting the parking brake shoes with the drum-in hat rotor installed, rotating the adjuster wheel upward will loosen the adjustment. Rotating the adjuster wheel downward will tighten the adjustment.

23. Remove the rubber plug from the hole in the front of the rotor.

24. Utilizing the hole in the front of the rotor, make a final adjustment of the shoes if necessary.

25. Reinstall the rubber plug.

26. Remove the wheel mounting nuts and finish installing the brake rotor (3) as well as all components removed to access it.

27. Lower the vehicle.

28. Cycle the parking brake lever once, verifying proper operation of the parking brake.

CHASSIS ELECTRICAL   AIR BAG (SUPPLEMENTAL RESTRAINT SYSTEM)

GENERAL INFORMATION

✳✳ CAUTION

These vehicles are equipped with an air bag system. The system must be disarmed before performing service on, or around, system components, the steering column, instrument panel components, wiring and sensors. Failure to follow the safety precautions and the disarming procedure could result in accidental air bag deployment, possible injury and unnecessary system repairs.

SERVICE PRECAUTIONS

Disconnect and isolate the battery negative cable before beginning any airbag system component diagnosis, testing, removal, or installation procedures. Allow system capacitor to discharge for two minutes before beginning any component service. This will disable the airbag system. Failure to disable the airbag system may result in

accidental airbag deployment, personal injury, or death.

Do not place an intact undeployed airbag face down on a solid surface. The airbag will propel into the air if accidentally deployed and may result in personal injury or death.

When carrying or handling an undeployed airbag, the trim side (face) of the airbag should be pointing away from the body to minimize possibility of injury if accidental deployment occurs. Failure to do this may result in personal injury or death.

Replace airbag system components with OEM replacement parts. Substitute parts may appear interchangeable, but internal differences may result in inferior occupant protection. Failure to do so may result in occupant personal injury or death.

Wear safety glasses, rubber gloves, and long sleeved clothing when cleaning powder residue from vehicle after an airbag deployment. Powder residue emitted from a deployed airbag can cause skin irritation.

Flush affected area with cool water if irritation is experienced. If nasal or throat irritation is experienced, exit the vehicle for fresh air until the irritation ceases. If irritation continues, see a physician.

Do not use a replacement airbag that is not in the original packaging. This may result in improper deployment, personal injury, or death.

The factory installed fasteners, screws and bolts used to fasten airbag components have a special coating and are specifically designed for the airbag system. Do not use substitute fasteners. Use only original equipment fasteners listed in the parts catalog when fastener replacement is required.

During, and following, any child restraint anchor service, due to impact event or vehicle repair, carefully inspect all mounting hardware, tether straps, and anchors for proper installation, operation, or damage. If a child restraint anchor is found damaged in any way, the anchor must be replaced. Failure to do this may result in personal injury or death.

Deployed and non-deployed airbags may or may not have live pyrotechnic material within the airbag inflator.

Do not dispose of driver/passenger/curtain airbags or seat belt tensioners unless you are sure of complete deployment. Refer to the Hazardous Substance Control System for proper disposal.

Dispose of deployed airbags and tensioners consistent with state, provincial, local, and federal regulations.

After any airbag component testing or service, do not connect the battery negative cable. Personal injury or death may result if the system test is not performed first.

If the vehicle is equipped with the Occupant Classification System (OCS), do not connect the battery negative cable before performing the OCS Verification Test using the scan tool and the appropriate diagnostic information. Personal injury or death may result if the system test is not performed properly.

Never replace both the Occupant Restraint Controller (ORC) and the Occupant Classification Module (OCM) at the same time. If both require replacement, replace one, then perform the Airbag System test before replacing the other.

Both the ORC and the OCM store Occupant Classification System (OCS) calibration data, which they transfer to one another when one of them is replaced. If both are replaced at the same time, an irreversible fault will be set in both modules and the OCS may malfunction and cause personal injury or death.

If equipped with OCS, the Seat Weight Sensor is a sensitive, calibrated unit and must be handled carefully. Do not drop or handle roughly. If dropped or damaged, replace with another sensor. Failure to do so may result in occupant injury or death.

If equipped with OCS, the front passenger seat must be handled carefully as well. When removing the seat, be careful when setting on floor not to drop. If dropped, the sensor may be inoperative, could result in occupant injury, or possibly death.

If equipped with OCS, when the passenger front seat is on the floor, no one should sit in the front passenger seat. This uneven force may damage the sensing ability of the seat weight sensors. If sat on and damaged, the sensor may be inoperative, could result in occupant injury, or possibly death.

DISARMING THE SYSTEM

1. Before servicing the vehicle, refer to the Precautions Section.

2. Open the hood.

3. Disconnect and isolate the battery negative cable.

4. Wait at least 2 minutes before servicing any airbag components.

✳✳ CAUTION

Wait 2 minutes for the system reserve capacitor to discharge before servicing any airbag components. Failure to do this may result in serious or fatal injury.

ARMING THE SYSTEM

➡**The following procedure should be performed using a diagnostic scan tool to verify proper Supplemental Restraint System (SRS) operation following the service or replacement of any SRS component.**

1. Before servicing the vehicle, refer to the Precautions Section.

2. During the following test, the battery negative cable remains disconnected and isolated, as it was during the Supplemental Restraint System (SRS) component removal and installation procedures.

3. Be certain that the diagnostic scan tool contains the latest version of the proper diagnostic software. Connect the scan tool to the 16-way Data Link Connector (DLC). The DLC is located on the driver side lower edge of the instrument panel, near the steering column opening cover and outboard of the steering column.

4. Turn the ignition switch to the ON position and exit the vehicle with the scan tool.

5. Check to be certain that nobody is in the vehicle, then reconnect the battery negative cable.

6. Using the scan tool, read and record the active (current) Diagnostic Trouble Code (DTC) data.

7. Next, use the scan tool to read and record any stored (historical) DTC data.

8. If any DTC is found, refer to the appropriate diagnostic information.

9. Use the scan tool to erase the stored DTC data. If any problems remain, the stored DTC data will not erase. Refer to the appropriate diagnostic information to diagnose any stored DTC that will not erase.

10. Turn the ignition switch to the OFF position for about 15 seconds, and then back to the ON position. Observe the airbag indicator in the instrument cluster. It should light from 4–6 seconds, and then go out. This indicates that the SRS is functioning normally and that the repairs are complete. If the airbag indicator fails to light, or lights and stays ON, there is still an active SRS fault or malfunction. Refer to the appropriate diagnostic information to diagnose the problem.

CLOCKSPRING CENTERING

See Figure 17.

✳✳ CAUTION

To avoid serious or fatal injury on vehicles equipped with airbags, disable the Supplemental Restraint System (SRS) before attempting any steering wheel, steering column, airbag, seat belt tensioner, impact sensor, or instrument panel component diagnosis or service. Disconnect and isolate the battery negative (ground) cable, then wait 2 minutes for the system capacitor to discharge before performing further diagnosis or service. This is the only sure way to disable the SRS. Failure to take the proper precautions could result in accidental airbag deployment.

➡**A service replacement clockspring is shipped with the clockspring pre-centered and with a molded plastic locking pin installed. This locking pin should NOT be removed until the steering wheel has been installed on the steering column. If the locking pin is removed before the steering wheel is installed, the clockspring centering procedure must be performed.**

➡**The Electronic Stability Control (ESC) may also be referred to as Electronic Stability Program (ESP) depending on the vehicle model year and configuration. Certain components may also reference ESP, ESC, or use the traction control symbol.**

✳✳ WARNING

When a clockspring is installed into a vehicle without properly centering and locking the entire steering system, the Steering Angle Sensor (SAS) data does not agree with the true position of the steering system and causes the ESC system to shut down. This may also damage the clockspring without any immediate malfunction. Unlike some other Chrysler vehicles, this SAS never requires calibration.

➡**Determining if the clockspring/SAS is centered is also possible electrically using the diagnostic scan tool. Steering wheel position is displayed as ANGLE with a range of up to 900°. Refer to the appropriate menu item on the diagnostic scan tool.**

➡**Before starting this procedure, be certain to turn the steering wheel until the front wheels are in the straight-ahead position and that the entire steering system is locked or inhibited from rotation.**

➡**The clockspring may be centered and the rotor may be rotated freely once the steering wheel has been removed.**

1. Before servicing the vehicle, refer to the Precautions Section.
2. Place the front wheels in the straight-ahead position and inhibit the steering column shaft from rotation.

3. Remove the steering wheel from the steering shaft.

4. Rotate the clockspring rotor clockwise to the end of its travel. Do not apply excessive torque.

5. From the end of the clockwise travel, rotate the rotor about 2 ½ turns counterclockwise. Turn the rotor slightly clockwise or counterclockwise as necessary so that the clockspring airbag pigtail wires and connector receptacle are at the top and the dowel pin is at the bottom.

6. The clockspring is now centered. Secure the clockspring rotor to the clockspring case using a locking pin or some similar device to maintain clockspring centering until the steering wheel is reinstalled on the steering column.

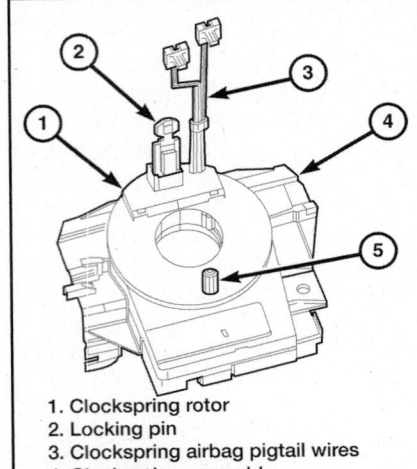

1. Clockspring rotor
2. Locking pin
3. Clockspring airbag pigtail wires
4. Clockspring assembly
5. Dowel pin

97266

Fig. 17 Clockspring assembly illustrated

DRIVE TRAIN

AUTOMATIC TRANSAXLE FLUID

DRAIN AND REFILL

4 Speed Transaxle—40TE/41TE

Fluid and Filter Service (Recommended Procedure)
See Figure 18.

➡**Only fluids of the type labeled MOPAR® ATF+4 (Automatic Transmission Fluid) should be used. A filter change should be made at the time of the transaxle oil change. The magnet (on the inside of the oil pan) should also be cleaned with a clean, dry cloth.**

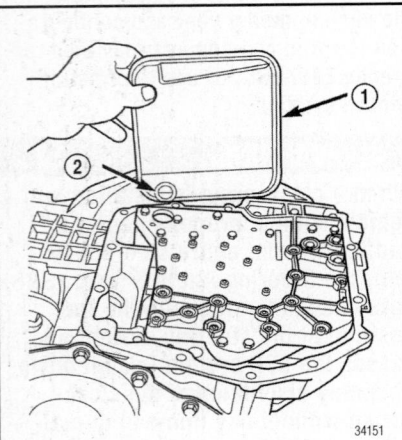

Fig. 18 Install a new filter (1) and O-ring (2) on the bottom of the valve body—4-speed transaxle

➡**If the transaxle is disassembled for any reason, the fluid and filter should be changed.**

1. Before servicing the vehicle, refer to the Precautions Section.
2. Raise and safely secure the vehicle. Place a drain container with a large opening under the transaxle oil pan.
3. Loosen the pan bolts and tap the pan at one corner to break it loose allowing the fluid to drain, then remove the oil pan.
4. Install a new filter and O-ring on the bottom of the valve body.
5. Clean the oil pan and magnet. Reinstall the pan using new MOPAR® Silicone Adhesive sealant. Tighten the oil pan bolts to 14 ft. lbs. (19 Nm).
6. Pour 4 quarts of MOPAR® ATF+4 (Automatic Transmission Fluid) through the dipstick opening.
7. Start the engine and allow it to idle for at least 1 minute. Then, with the parking and service brakes applied, move the selector lever momentarily to each position, ending in the park or neutral position.
8. Check the transaxle fluid level and add an appropriate amount to bring the transaxle fluid level to ⅛ (3mm) below the lowest mark on the dipstick.
9. Recheck the fluid level after the transaxle has reached the normal operating temperature of 180°F (82°C).
10. To prevent dirt from entering the transaxle, make certain that the dipstick is fully seated into the dipstick opening.

Dipstick Tube Filter Suction Method (Alternative Procedure)

1. Before servicing the vehicle, refer to the Precautions Section.
2. When performing the fluid suction method, make sure the transaxle is at full operating temperature of 180°F (82°C).
3. To perform the dipstick tube fluid suction method, use a suitable fluid suction device such as the Vacula®, or equivalent.
4. Insert the fluid suction line into the dipstick tube.

➡**Verify that the suction line is inserted to the lowest point of the transaxle oil pan. This will ensure complete evacuation of the fluid in the pan.**

5. Follow the manufacturers recommended procedure and evacuate the fluid from the transaxle.
6. Remove the suction line from the dipstick tube.
7. Pour 4 quarts of MOPAR® ATF+4 (Automatic Transmission Fluid) through the dipstick opening.
8. Start the engine and allow it to idle for at least 1 minute. Then, with the parking and service brakes applied, move the selector lever momentarily to each position, ending in the park or neutral position.
9. Check the transaxle fluid level and add an appropriate amount to bring the transaxle fluid level to ⅛ inch (3mm) below the lowest mark on the dipstick.
10. Recheck the fluid level after the

transaxle has reached normal operating temperature 180°F (82°C).

11. To prevent dirt from entering the transaxle, make certain that the dipstick is fully seated into the dipstick opening.

6-Speed Transaxle—62TE

➡️**Only fluids of the type labeled MOPAR® ATF+4 should be used. A filter change should be made at the time of the transaxle oil change. The magnet (on the inside of the oil pan) should also be cleaned with a clean, dry cloth.**

➡️**If the transaxle is disassembled for any reason, the fluid and filter should be changed.**

1. Before servicing the vehicle, refer to the Precautions Section.

2. Raise and safely support the vehicle. Place a drain container with a large opening, under the transaxle oil pan.

3. Loosen the pan bolts and tap the pan at one corner to break it loose allowing the fluid to drain, then remove the oil pan.

4. Remove the nuts at the oil filter.

5. Install a new filter and nuts, tighten to 40 inch lbs. (5 Nm).

6. Install the fluid filter oil pan, use a bead of MOPAR® ATF RTV (MS-GF41).

7. Clean the oil pan and magnet. Reinstall the pan using new MOPAR® Silicone Adhesive sealant. Tighten the oil pan bolts to 106 inch lbs. (12 Nm).

8. Pour 4 Quarts of MOPAR® ATF+4 through the dipstick opening.

9. Start the engine and allow to idle for at least 1 minute. Then, with the parking and service brakes applied, move the selector lever momentarily to each position, ending in the park or neutral position.

10. Check the transaxle fluid level and add an appropriate amount to bring the transaxle fluid level to 1/8 inch (3mm) below the lowest mark on the dipstick.

11. Recheck the fluid level after the transaxle has reached normal operating temperature 180°F (82°C).

12. To prevent dirt from entering the transaxle, make certain that the dipstick is fully seated into the dipstick opening.

FILTER REPLACEMENT

4 Speed Transaxle—40TE/41TE

Refer to Drain and Refill, Fluid and Filter Service (Recommended Procedure).

6-Speed Transaxle—62TE

Refer to Drain and Refill procedure.

FRONT HALFSHAFT

REMOVAL & INSTALLATION

Without Intermediate Shaft
See Figures 19 through 21.

✳️✳️ WARNING

Never grasp the halfshaft assembly by the inner or outer boots, doing so may cause damage to the boot.

✳️✳️ WARNING

The inner tripod joints are designed with a retention feature that prevents the tripod rollers from coming out of the inner joint housing up to a specific load. If this feature is overcome and any of the rollers are pulled past the retention feature the joint will "lock-up" and no longer function properly. The entire halfshaft assembly must be replaced if this occurs.

➡️**Some halfshafts use a tuned rubber damper weight. When replacing a halfshaft assembly, be sure the replacement halfshaft has a damper weight.**

1. Before servicing the vehicle, refer to the Precautions Section.

2. Raise and safely support the vehicle.

3. Remove the wheel and tire assembly from the vehicle.

4. Apply the service brakes to keep the hub from turning, then loosen the halfshaft nut.

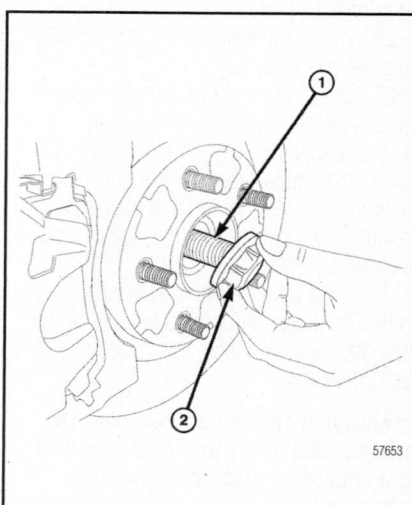

Fig. 19 Remove the nut (2) from the halfshaft (1) and discard it

57653

➡️**Do not re-use the hub nut. The hub nut is a single-use type. A new hub nut is required for reassembly.**

5. Remove the nut from the halfshaft and discard it.

6. Remove the two bolts that secure the front disc brake caliper and adapter to the steering knuckle.

7. Remove the disc brake caliper assembly from the steering knuckle. The caliper assembly is removed by first rotating the top of caliper assembly away from the steering knuckle and then removing the bottom of the assembly out from under the machined abutment on the steering knuckle.

✳️✳️ WARNING

Do not allow the brake caliper assembly to hang by the brake flex hose.

8. Support disc brake caliper assembly by using a wire hanger and suspend it from the strut assembly.

9. Remove the brake rotor from the hub and bearing assembly.

10. Remove the steering knuckle-to-strut attachment bolts from the steering knuckle.

11. Pull the steering knuckle from the strut clevis bracket.

➡️**Due to tight tolerances, the outer C/V joint might have to be forced apart from the bearing hub. To avoid damaging the axle halfshaft threads during removal, install the hub nut so that approximately half the threads are engaged on the shaft, and use a soft faced hammer to tap the shaft out of the hub.**

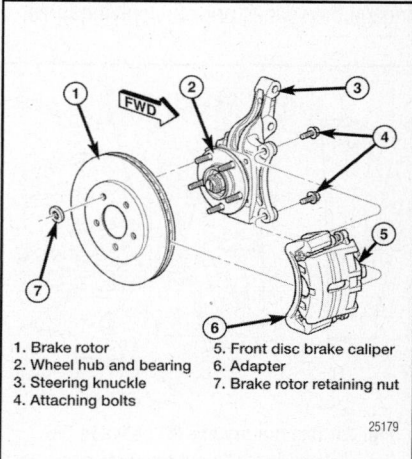

1. Brake rotor
2. Wheel hub and bearing
3. Steering knuckle
4. Attaching bolts
5. Front disc brake caliper
6. Adapter
7. Brake rotor retaining nut

25179

Fig. 20 Remove the bolts that secure the front disc brake caliper and adapter to the steering knuckle

✳✳ WARNING

Care must be taken not to separate the inner C/V joint during this operation. Do not allow the halfshaft to hang by the inner C/V joint after removing the outer C/V Joint from the hub/bearing assembly in the steering knuckle. The end of the halfshaft must be supported.

12. Pull the steering knuckle assembly down and away from the outer C/V joint of the halfshaft assembly while pulling the joint out of the hub bearing.

➡Transaxle fluid might leak when the halfshaft is removed from the transaxle.

13. If equipped, remove the engine belly pan.

14. Support the outer end of the halfshaft assembly. Insert a pry bar between the inner tripod joint and the transaxle case. Pry against the inner tripod joint, until the tripod joint retaining snap-ring is disengaged from the transaxle side gear.

15. Pull the steering knuckle assembly down and away from the outer C/V joint of the halfshaft assembly while pulling the halfshaft out of the transaxle.

16. Remove the halfshaft.

To install:

17. Thoroughly clean the spline and the oil seal sealing surface on the tripod joint. Lightly lubricate the oil seal sealing surface on the tripod joint with fresh clean transaxle lubricant.

18. Holding the halfshaft assembly by the tripod joint and interconnecting shaft, install the tripod joint into the transaxle side gear as far as possible by hand. Be sure to engage the splines prior to applying force.

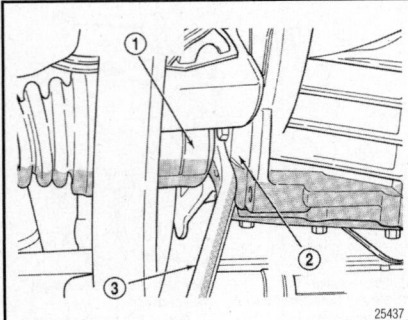

Fig. 21 Insert a pry bar (3) between the inner tripod joint (1) and the transaxle case (2). Pry against the inner tripod joint, until the tripod joint retaining snap-ring is disengaged from the transaxle side gear

➡Attempt to remove the tripod joint by hand to verify that the snap ring is fully engaged. If the snap ring is fully engaged, the tripod joint will not be removable from the transaxle by hand.

19. Forcefully push the tripod joint into the transaxle side gear, until the snap-ring is fully engaged.

20. Clean all debris and moisture out of the steering knuckle, in the area where the outer CV joint will be installed into the steering knuckle.

21. Ensure that the front of the outer CV joint which fits against the face of the hub and bearing is free of debris and moisture before installing the outer CV joint into hub and bearing assembly.

22. Slide the halfshaft back into the front hub and bearing assembly.

✳✳ WARNING

The steering knuckle-to-strut assembly attaching bolts are serrated and must not be turned during installation. Install the nuts while holding the bolts stationary in the steering knuckle.

✳✳ WARNING

If the vehicle being serviced is equipped with an eccentric strut assembly attaching bolts, the eccentric bolt must be installed in the bottom (slotted) hole on the strut clevis bracket.

23. Install the steering knuckle into the clevis bracket. Install the strut damper to the steering knuckle attaching bolts. Tighten both bolts to 65 ft. lbs. (88 Nm), plus an additional ¼ turn.

24. Install the brake disc onto the hub and bearing assembly.

25. Install the front disc brake caliper and adapter to the steering knuckle. The caliper is installed by first sliding the bottom of the caliper assembly under the abutment on the steering knuckle, and then rotating the top of the caliper against the top abutment.

26. Install the 2 bolts that secure the front disc brake caliper and adapter to the steering knuckle. Tighten the bolts to 125 ft. lbs. (169 Nm).

➡Always install a new hub nut. The original hub nut is one-time use only and should be discarded when removed.

27. Clean all foreign matter from the threads of the outer CV joint. Install the

halfshaft to the hub/bearing assembly nut onto the halfshaft.

28. With the brakes applied to keep the hub from turning, tighten the hub nut to 118 ft. lbs. (160 Nm).

29. Install the front wheel and tire assembly. Tighten the wheel nuts in a star pattern until all nuts are torqued to half the required specification. Then repeat the tightening sequence to the full specified torque of 100 ft. lbs. (135 Nm).

30. Lower the vehicle.

31. Check for the correct fluid level in the transaxle assembly.

32. If equipped, install the engine belly pan.

With Intermediate Shaft

See Figures 22 through 25.

✳✳ WARNING

Never grasp the halfshaft assembly by the inner or outer boots. This can cause damage to the boot, which will allow contaminants to enter the C/V joint.

✳✳ WARNING

The inner tripod joints are designed with a retention feature that prevents the tripod rollers from coming out of the inner joint housing up to a specific load. If this feature is overcome and any of the rollers are pulled past the retention feature the joint will "lock-up" and no longer function properly. The entire halfshaft assembly must be replaced if this occurs.

➡Some halfshafts use a tuned rubber damper weight to cancel vibration. When replacing a halfshaft assembly, be sure the replacement halfshaft has a damper.

1. Before servicing the vehicle, refer to the Precautions Section.

2. Raise and safely support the vehicle.

3. Remove the wheel and tire assembly from the vehicle.

4. Apply the service brakes to keep the hub from turning, then loosen the halfshaft nut.

➡Do not re-use the hub nut. The hub nut is a single-use type. A new hub nut is required for reassembly.

5. Remove the nut from the halfshaft and discard it.

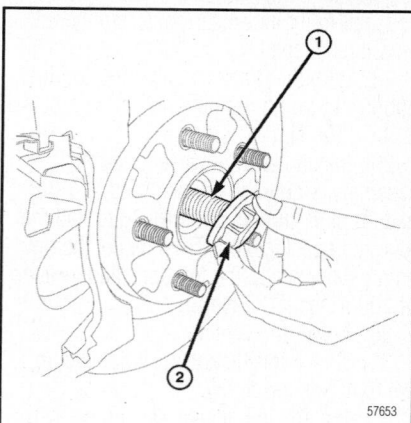

Fig. 22 Remove the nut (2) from the halfshaft (1) and discard it

6. Remove the two bolts that secure the front disc brake caliper and adapter to the steering knuckle.

7. Remove the disc brake caliper assembly from the steering knuckle. The caliper assembly is removed by first rotating the top of the caliper assembly away from the steering knuckle and then removing the bottom of the assembly out from under the machined abutment on the steering knuckle.

✳✳ WARNING

Do not allow the brake caliper assembly to hang by the brake flex hose.

8. Support the disc brake caliper assembly by using a wire hanger and suspend it from the strut assembly.

9. Remove the brake rotor from the hub and bearing assembly.

10. Remove the steering knuckle-to-strut attachment bolts from the steering knuckle.

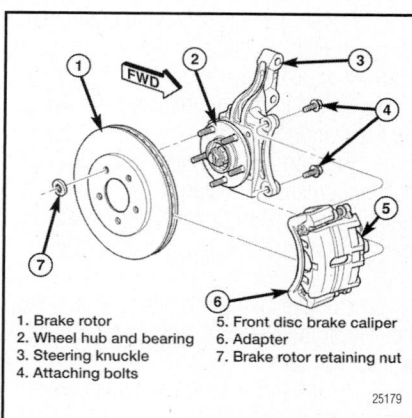

1. Brake rotor
2. Wheel hub and bearing
3. Steering knuckle
4. Attaching bolts
5. Front disc brake caliper
6. Adapter
7. Brake rotor retaining nut

Fig. 23 Remove the bolts that secure the front disc brake caliper and adapter to the steering knuckle

11. Pull the steering knuckle from the strut clevis bracket.

✳✳ WARNING

Due to tight tolerances, the outer C/V joint might have to be forced apart from the bearing hub. To avoid damaging the axle halfshaft threads during removal, install the hub nut so that approximately half the threads are engaged on the shaft, and use a soft faced hammer to tap the shaft out of the hub.

✳✳ WARNING

Care must be taken not to separate the inner C/V joint during this operation. Do not allow the halfshaft to hang by the inner C/V Joint after removing the outer C/V Joint from the hub/bearing assembly in the steering knuckle. The end of the halfshaft must be supported.

12. Pull the steering knuckle assembly down and away from the outer C/V joint of the halfshaft assembly while pulling the joint out of the hub bearing.

➡ **Transaxle fluid might leak when the halfshaft is removed from the transaxle.**

13. If equipped, remove the engine belly pan.

14. Support the outer end of the halfshaft assembly. Insert a pry bar between the inner tripod joint and the intermediate shaft, or the transaxle case if removing the left halfshaft. Pry against the inner tripod joint, until

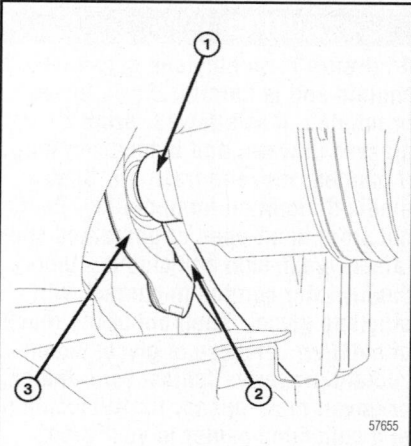

Fig. 24 Insert a pry bar (2) between the inner tripod joint (1) and the intermediate shaft (3), or the transaxle case if removing the left halfshaft

the tripod joint retaining snap-ring is disengaged from the intermediate shaft or the transaxle side gear.

15. Pull the steering knuckle assembly down and away from the outer C/V joint of the halfshaft assembly while pulling the halfshaft out of the transaxle.

16. Remove the halfshaft.

To install:

✳✳ WARNING

Care must be taken not to separate the inner C/V joint during this operation. Do not allow the halfshaft to hang by the inner C/V joint after removing the outer C/V joint from the hub/bearing assembly in the steering knuckle. The end of the halfshaft must be supported.

17. Thoroughly clean the spline and the oil seal sealing surface on the tripod joint. Lightly lubricate the oil seal sealing surface on the tripod joint with fresh clean transaxle lubricant.

18. Holding the halfshaft assembly by the tripod joint and interconnecting shaft, install the tripod joint into the transaxle side gear (left side) or the intermediate shaft (right side) as far as possible by hand. Be sure to engage the splines prior to applying force.

➡ **Attempt to remove the tripod joint by hand to verify that the snap ring is fully engaged. If the snap ring is fully engaged, the tripod joint will not be removable from the transaxle by hand.**

19. Forcefully push the tripod joint into the transaxle side gear, until the snap-ring is fully engaged.

20. Clean all debris and moisture out of

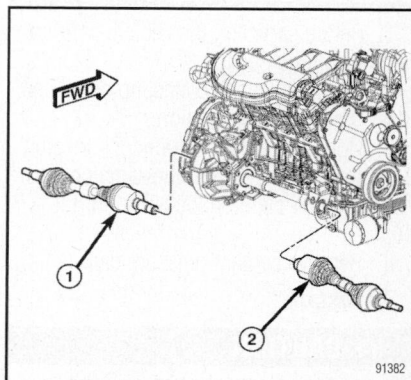

Fig. 25 Removing the left (1) or right (2) halfshaft—3.5L shown, all others equipped with an intermediate shaft are similar

the steering knuckle, in the area where the outer CV joint will be installed into the steering knuckle.

21. Ensure that the front of the outer CV joint which fits against the face of the hub and bearing is free of debris and moisture before installing the outer CV joint into the hub and bearing assembly.

22. Install the steering knuckle to the strut clevis bracket.

23. Install the steering knuckle-to-strut attachment bolts and nuts. While holding the bolts in place, tighten the nuts to 103 ft. lbs. (140 Nm).

24. Install the brake disc onto the hub and bearing assembly.

25. Install the front disc brake caliper

and adapter to the steering knuckle. The caliper is installed by first sliding the bottom of the caliper assembly under the abutment on the steering knuckle, and then rotating the top of the caliper against the top abutment.

26. Install the 2 bolts that secure the front disc brake caliper and adapter to the steering knuckle. Tighten the bolts to 125 ft. lbs. (169 Nm).

➡ Always install a new hub nut. The original hub nut is one-time use only and should be discarded when removed.

27. Clean all foreign matter from the threads of the outer CV joint. Install the

halfshaft to the hub/bearing assembly nut onto the halfshaft.

28. With the brakes applied to keep the hub from turning, tighten the hub nut to 118 ft. lbs. (160 Nm).

29. Install the front wheel and tire assembly. Tighten the wheel nuts in a star pattern until all nuts are torqued to half the required specification. Then repeat the tightening sequence to the full specified torque of 100 ft. lbs. (135 Nm).

30. Lower the vehicle.

31. Check for the correct fluid level in the transaxle assembly.

32. If equipped, install the engine belly pan.

ENGINE COOLING

ENGINE COOLANT

DRAIN & REFILL PROCEDURE

✳✳ WARNING

When servicing the cooling system, it is essential that coolant does not drip onto the accessory drive belts and/or pulleys. Shield the belts with shop towels before working on the cooling system. If coolant contacts the belts or pulleys, flush both with clean water.

✳✳ CAUTION

Make sure the engine cooling system is cool before servicing. Do not remove any clamps or hoses, pressure cap, or open the radiator draincock when the system is hot and under pressure. Serious burns from coolant can occur.

1. Before servicing the vehicle, refer to the Precautions Section.

2. Position a clean collecting container under the draincock location.

3. Open the radiator draincock located at the lower right side of the radiator. Turn the draincock counterclockwise until it stops.

4. Remove coolant pressure cap.

To install:

✳✳ CAUTION

The pressure cap should only be removed if the coolant recovery container is empty.

5. When adding coolant, fill with the

proper type and amount of engine coolant as specified.

6. Bleed the air from the engine coolant system. Refer to Engine Coolant, Bleeding.

BLEEDING

See Figure 26.

Evacuating or purging air from the cooling system involves the use of a pressurized air operated vacuum generator. The vacuum created allows for a quick and complete coolant refilling while removing any airlocks present in the system components.

✳✳ WARNING

To avoid damage to the cooling system, ensure that no component would be susceptible to damage when a vacuum is drawn on the system.

✳✳ CAUTION

Antifreeze is an ethylene glycol based coolant and is harmful if swallowed or inhaled. If swallowed, drink 2 glasses of water and induce vomiting. If inhaled, move to fresh air. Seek medical attention immediately. Do not store in an open or unmarked container. Wash skin and clothing thoroughly after coming in contact with ethylene glycol. Keep out of the reach of children. Dispose of glycol based coolant properly. Contact your dealer or government agency for the location of a collection center in your area.

✳✳ CAUTION

Do not open a cooling system when the engine is at operating tempera-

ture or hot under pressure. Personal injury can result. Avoid the radiator cooling fan when engine compartment related service is performed. Personal injury can result.

✳✳ CAUTION

Wear appropriate eye and hand protection when performing this procedure.

➡ The service area where this procedure is performed should have a minimum shop air requirement of 80 PSI (5.5 bar) and should be equipped with an air dryer system.

➡ For best results, the radiator should be empty. The vehicle's heater control should be set to the heat position (ignition may need to be turned to the on position, but do not start the motor).

Special Tools
• Chrysler Pentastar Service Equipment (Chrysler PSE) Coolant Refiller 85-15-0650, or equivalent

1. Before servicing the vehicle, refer to the Precautions Section.

2. Refer to the Chrysler Pentastar Service Equipment (Chrysler PSE) Coolant Refiller 85-15-0650 or equivalent tool's operating manual for specific assembly steps.

3. Choose an appropriate adapter cone that will fit the vehicle's radiator filler neck or reservoir tank.

4. Attach the adapter cone to the vacuum gauge.

5. Make sure the vacuum generator/venturi ball valve is closed and attach an airline hose (minimum shop air requirement

of 80 PSI (5.5 bar) to the vacuum generator/venturi.

6. Position the adaptor cone/vacuum gauge assembly into the radiator filler neck or reservoir tank. Ensure that the adapter cone is sealed properly.

7. Connect the vacuum generator/venturi to the positioned adaptor cone/vacuum gauge assembly.

8. Open the vacuum generator/venturi ball valve.

➡**Do not bump or move the assembly as it may result in loss of vacuum. Some radiator overflow hoses may need to be clamped off to obtain vacuum.**

9. Let the system run until the vacuum gauge shows a good vacuum through the cooling system. Refer to the tool's operating manual for appropriate pressure readings.

➡**If a strong vacuum is being created in the system, it is normal to see the radiator hoses collapse.**

10. Close the vacuum generator/venturi ball valve.

11. Disconnect the vacuum generator/venturi and airline from the adaptor cone/vacuum gauge assembly.

12. Wait approximately 20 seconds, if the pressure readings do not move, the system has no leaks. If the pressure readings move, a leak could be present in the system and the cooling system should be checked for leaks and the procedure should be repeated.

13. Place the tool's suction hose into the coolant's container.

➡**Ensure there is a sufficient amount of coolant, mixed to the required strength/protection level available for use. For best results and to assist the refilling procedure, place the coolant container at the same height as the radiator filler neck. Always draw more coolant than required. If the coolant level is too low, it will pull air into the cooling system which could result in airlocks in the system.**

14. Connect the tool's suction hose to the adaptor cone/vacuum gauge assembly.

15. Open the suction hose ball valve to begin refilling the cooling system.

16. When the vacuum gauge reads zero, the system is filled.

➡**On some remote pressurized tanks, it is recommended to stop filling when the proper level is reached.**

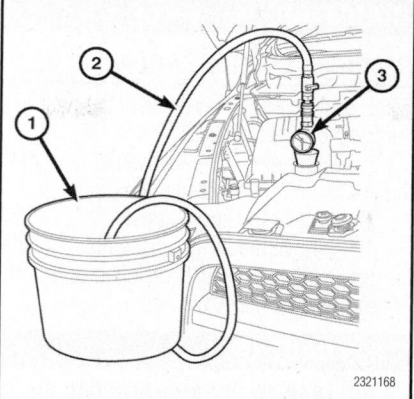

Fig. 26 Adapter cone and vacuum gauge (3), suction hose (2), and mixed coolant container (3) shown installed

17. Close the suction hose ball valve and remove the suction hose from the adaptor cone/vacuum gauge assembly.

18. Remove the adaptor cone/vacuum gauge assembly from the radiator filler neck or reservoir tank.

19. With the heater control unit in the HEAT position, operate the engine with the container cap in place.

20. After the engine has reached the normal operating temperature, shut the engine off and allow it to cool. When the engine is cooling down, coolant will be drawn into the radiator from the pressure container.

21. Add coolant to the recovery bottle/container as necessary. Only add coolant to the container when the engine is cold. Coolant level in a warm engine will be higher due to thermal expansion. Add necessary coolant to raise the container level to the COLD MINIMUM mark after each cool down period.

22. Once the appropriate coolant level is achieved, attach the radiator cap or reservoir tank cap.

FLUSHING

Cleaning

1. Before servicing the vehicle, refer to the Precautions Section.

2. Drain the cooling system and refill with water.

3. Run the engine with the radiator cap installed until the upper radiator hose is hot.

4. Stop the engine and drain the water from system.

5. If the water is dirty, fill the system with water, run the engine and drain the system. Repeat this procedure until the water drains clean.

Reverse Flushing

Reverse flushing of the cooling system is the forcing of water through the cooling system. This is done using air pressure in the opposite direction of normal coolant flow.

This procedure is usually only necessary with very dirty systems with evidence of partial plugging.

Reverse Flushing Radiator

1. Before servicing the vehicle, refer to the Precautions Section.

2. Disconnect the radiator hoses from the radiator inlet and outlet.

3. Attach a section of the radiator hose to the radiator bottom outlet fitting and insert the flushing gun.

4. Connect a water supply hose and air supply hose to the flushing gun.

✳✳ WARNING

Internal radiator pressure must not exceed 20 psi (138 kPa) as damage to the radiator may result.

5. Allow the radiator to fill with water. When the radiator is filled, apply air in short blasts.

6. Allow the radiator to refill between blasts.

7. Continue this reverse flushing until clean water flows out through the rear of the radiator cooling tube passages.

Reverse Flushing Engine

1. Before servicing the vehicle, refer to the Precautions Section.

2. Drain the cooling system.

3. Remove the thermostat housing and thermostat.

4. Install the thermostat housing.

5. Disconnect the radiator upper hose from the radiator and attach the flushing gun to the hose.

6. Disconnect the radiator lower hose from the water pump and attach a lead-away hose to the water pump inlet fitting.

7. Connect the water supply hose and air supply hose to the flushing gun.

8. Allow the engine to fill with water.

9. When the engine is filled, apply air in short blasts, allowing the system to fill between air blasts.

10. Continue until clean water flows through the lead away hose.

11. Remove the lead away hose, flushing gun, water supply hose and air supply hose.

12. Remove the thermostat housing and install the thermostat.

13. Install the thermostat housing with a replacement gasket. Refer to Thermostat, removal & installation.

14. Connect the radiator hoses.

15. Refill the cooling system with the correct antifreeze/water mixture. Refer to Engine Coolant, Drain & Refill Procedure.

Chemical Cleaning

1. Before servicing the vehicle, refer to the Precautions Section.

2. In some instances, use a radiator cleaner (MOPAR® Radiator Kleen, or equivalent) before flushing. This will soften scale and other deposits and aid the flushing operation.

✶✶ WARNING

Follow the manufacturer's instructions when using these products.

ENGINE FAN

REMOVAL & INSTALLATION

1. Before servicing the vehicle, refer to the Precautions Section.

2. Disconnect the negative cable from the auxiliary terminal.

3. Disconnect the radiator fan electrical connector.

4. Remove the screws that secure the wiring harness loom to the upper radiator core support.

5. Partially drain the cooling system.

6. Remove the upper radiator hose at the radiator.

7. Remove the oil indicator tube to help aid in the fan assembly removal.

8. Remove the fasteners and the upper clip attaching fan assembly to the radiator.

9. Remove the radiator fan assembly by lifting it upward.

To install:

10. Position the radiator fan module into the retaining clip.

11. Make sure the clips are fully engaged.

12. Install the wiring harness loom across the upper radiator core support.

13. Connect the radiator fan electrical connector.

14. Install the oil indicator tube.

15. Install the upper radiator hose at the radiator.

16. Fill the cooling system. Refer to Engine Coolant, Drain & Refill Procedure.

RADIATOR

REMOVAL & INSTALLATION

1. Before servicing the vehicle, refer to the Precautions Section.

2. Disconnect the negative cable from the auxiliary jumper terminal.

3. Remove the engine cover.

4. Remove the air box assembly. Refer to Air Cleaner, removal & installation.

5. Recover the A/C system.

✶✶ CAUTION

Do not remove the pressure cap or any hose with the system hot and under pressure as serious burns from coolant can occur.

6. Drain the cooling system. Refer to Engine Coolant, Drain & Refill Procedure.

7. Remove the front bumper fascia.

8. Remove the under belly pan.

9. Remove the front bottom splash shield.

10. Remove the upper and lower radiator hoses at the radiator.

11. Disconnect the radiator fan electrical connector.

12. Remove the cooling fan assembly. Refer to Engine Fan, removal & installation.

13. Disconnect both A/C lines at the condenser/cooler.

14. Remove the transaxle oil cooler tubes support bracket bolt at the left side of the radiator.

✶✶ WARNING

Plastic tanks, while stronger than brass, are subject to damage by impact. Be careful with tools.

15. Remove the 2 Torx® screws located on the upper radiator support that hold the upper radiator mounting brackets.

16. Tilt the top of the radiator rearward so the mounting brackets slide out of the upper core support.

17. Remove radiator/condenser assembly by lifting the assembly out of the vehicle between the engine and the core support.

18. Separate the A/C condenser from the radiator.

To install:

19. Position the A/C condenser onto the radiator.

20. Slide the radiator/condenser assembly into position and seat the radiator assembly lower rubber isolators in the mount holes.

21. Install the mounting brackets to the upper core support using 2 Torx® screws.

22. Install the A/C lines to the condenser/cooler.

23. Install the transaxle oil cooler tubes support bracket to the radiator. Tighten the mounting screws to 45 inch lbs. (5 Nm).

24. Position the radiator cooling fan assembly on the radiator. Refer to Engine Fan, removal & installation.

25. Install the upper and lower radiator hoses at the radiator.

26. Install the front bumper fascia.

27. Install the front bottom splash shield (if equipped).

28. Install the under belly pan (if equipped).

29. Fill the cooling system. Refer to Engine Coolant, Drain & Refill Procedure.

30. Charge the A/C system.

31. Install the air box assembly. Refer to Air Cleaner, removal & installation.

32. Connect the negative battery cable. Refer to Battery, removal & installation.

33. Install the engine cover.

THERMOSTAT

REMOVAL & INSTALLATION

2.4L Engine

Primary Thermostat

See Figure 27.

1. Before servicing the vehicle, refer to the Precautions Section.

2. Partially drain the cooling system. Refer to Engine Coolant, Drain & Refill Procedure.

3. Remove the air filter housing. Refer to Air Cleaner, removal & installation.

4. Disconnect the coolant hose from the inlet housing.

5. Remove the inlet housing bolts.

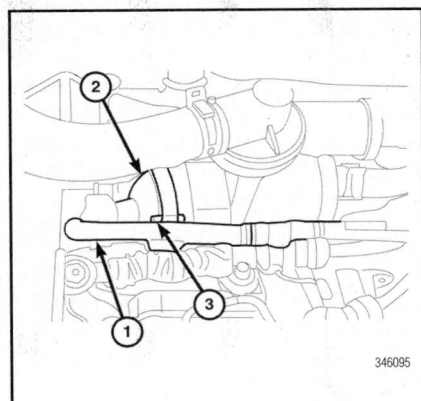

Fig. 27 Disconnect the coolant hose (1) from the inlet housing (2) and remove the inlet housing bolts (3)—2.4L engine

6. Remove thermostat assembly and clean the sealing surfaces.

To install:

7. Position the thermostat into the water plenum, aligning the air bleed with the location notch on the inlet housing.

8. Install the inlet housing onto the coolant adapter. Tighten the bolts to 79 inch lbs. (9 Nm).

9. Connect the coolant hose.

10. Install the air filter housing. Refer to Air Cleaner, removal & installation.

11. Fill the cooling system. Refer to Engine Coolant, Drain & Refill Procedure.

Secondary Thermostat

See Figure 28.

1. Before servicing the vehicle, refer to the Precautions Section.

2. Partially the drain cooling system.

3. Remove air filter housing. Refer to Air Cleaner, removal & installation.

4. Disconnect the coolant hoses from the rear of the coolant adapter.

5. Remove the radiator hose.

6. Remove the radiator hose from the front of the coolant adapter.

7. Remove the coolant adapter mounting bolts.

8. Carefully slide the coolant adapter off the water pump inlet tube and remove the coolant adapter and secondary thermostat.

To install:

9. Position the thermostat into the cylinder head.

10. Inspect the water pump inlet tube O-rings for damage before installing the tube in the coolant adapter. Replace the O-ring as necessary.

11. Lubricate the O-rings with soapy water.

12. Position the coolant adapter on the water pump inlet tube and the cylinder head.

13. Install the coolant adapter mounting bolts. Tighten the bolts to 159 inch lbs. (18 Nm).

14. Connect the front coolant hose.

15. Connect the 2 rear coolant hoses.

16. Connect the radiator hose.

17. Install the air filter housing. Refer to Air Cleaner, removal & installation.

18. Fill the cooling system. Refer to Engine Coolant, Drain & Refill Procedure.

2.7L Engine

See Figures 29 and 30.

1. Before servicing the vehicle, refer to the Precautions Section.

2. Disconnect the negative battery cable.

3. Remove the accessory drive belts. Refer to Accessory Drive Belts, removal & installation.

4. Raise and safely support the vehicle.

5. Remove the left front wheel.

6. Remove the lower engine splash shield.

7. Drain cooling system.

8. Remove the A/C compressor bolts.

9. Position the A/C compressor aside.

10. Remove the nuts that secure the heater line to the thermostat housing and position aside.

11. Remove the upper thermostat housing bolt.

12. Remove the lower thermostat housing studs.

13. Remove thermostat and housing.

14. Remove the hose from the thermostat housing.

To install:

15. Clean the gasket sealing surfaces.

➡ **Install the thermostat with the bleed valve located at the 12 o'clock position.**

16. Install the new seal onto the thermostat housing.

17. Install the thermostat and housing to the cylinder block. Tighten the attaching bolt and studs to 106 inch lbs. (12 Nm).

18. Install the radiator hose to the thermostat housing.

19. Install the heater line to the thermostat housing. Tighten the nuts to 106 inch lbs. (12 Nm).

20. Install the A/C compressor. Tighten the attaching bolt to 37 ft. lbs. (50 Nm) and the front bolts to 19 ft. lbs. (26 Nm).

21. Install the lower engine splash shield.

22. Install the left front wheel.

23. Lower the vehicle.

24. Install accessory drive belt. Refer to Accessory Drive Belts, removal & installation.

25. Reconnect negative battery cable. Refer to Battery, removal & installation.

26. Fill the cooling system. Refer to Engine Coolant, Drain & Refill Procedure.

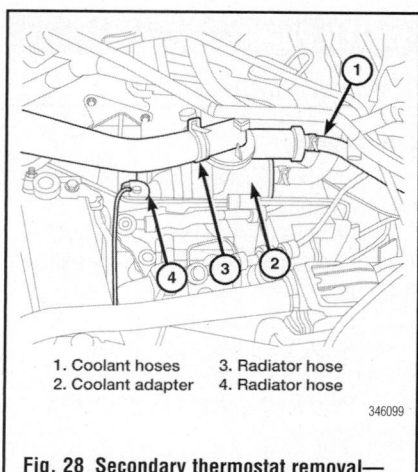

1. Coolant hoses
2. Coolant adapter
3. Radiator hose
4. Radiator hose

346099

Fig. 28 Secondary thermostat removal— 2.4L engine

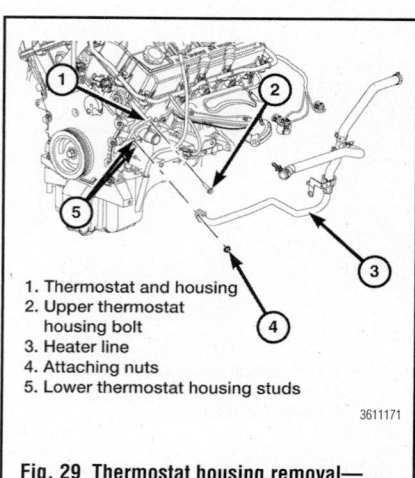

1. Thermostat and housing
2. Upper thermostat housing bolt
3. Heater line
4. Attaching nuts
5. Lower thermostat housing studs

3611171

Fig. 29 Thermostat housing removal— 2.7L engine

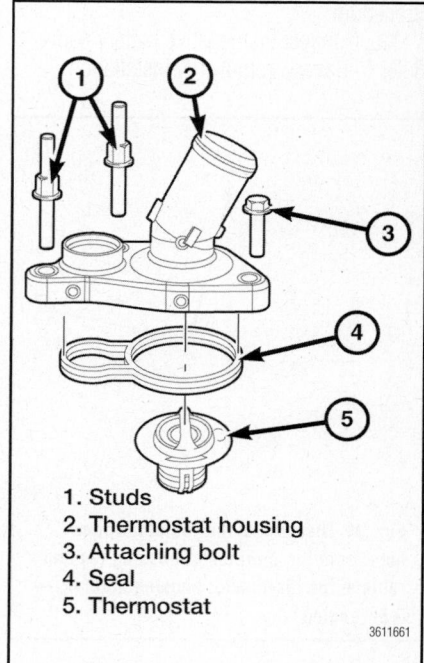

1. Studs
2. Thermostat housing
3. Attaching bolt
4. Seal
5. Thermostat

3611661

Fig. 30 Thermostat housing showing the proper thermostat valve position—2.7L engine

3.5L Engine

See Figure 31.

> **✴✴ CAUTION**
>
> **Do not remove the pressure cap with the system hot and under pressure as serious burns from coolant can occur.**

1. Before servicing the vehicle, refer to the Precautions Section.
2. Disconnect the negative battery cable.
3. Drain the cooling system.
4. Disconnect the radiator upper hose from the thermostat housing.
5. Remove the thermostat housing bolts.
6. Remove the housing, thermostat, and gasket.

To install:

7. Clean the gasket sealing surfaces.
8. Install the thermostat and gasket into the thermostat housing. For ease of installation, install the bolts in the housing for thermostat and gasket retention.
9. Install the thermostat and housing to the intake manifold. Tighten the bolts to 106 inch lbs. (12 Nm).
10. Connect the radiator hoses and install the hose clamp.
11. Fill the cooling system. Refer to Engine Coolant, Drain & Refill Procedure.
12. Connect the negative battery cable. Refer to Battery, removal & installation.

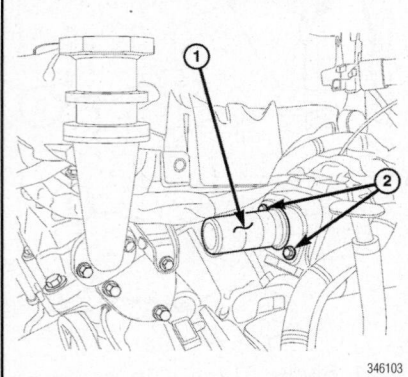

Fig. 31 Disconnect the radiator upper hose from the thermostat housing (1) and remove the thermostat housing bolts (2)— 3.5L engine

3.6L Engine

Thermostat Housing

See Figure 32.

> **✴✴ CAUTION**
>
> **Do not loosen the radiator draincock with the system hot and pressurized. Serious burns from coolant can occur.**

> **✴✴ WARNING**
>
> **The thermostat and housing is serviced as an assembly. Do not remove the thermostat from the housing, damage to the thermostat may occur.**

➡Do not waste reusable coolant. If the solution is clean, drain the coolant into a clean container for reuse.

➡If the thermostat is being replaced, be sure that the replacement is a specified thermostat for the vehicle model and engine type.

1. Before servicing the vehicle, refer to the Precautions Section.
2. Disconnect the negative battery cable at the battery.
3. Drain the cooling system.
4. Remove the coolant recovery bottle and position aside.
5. Remove the upper radiator hose clamp and upper radiator hose at the thermostat housing.
6. Remove the thermostat housing mounting bolts.
7. Remove the thermostat housing from the vehicle and discard the gasket seal.

To install:

8. Clean the mating areas of the timing chain cover and thermostat housing.
9. Install a new gasket seal to the thermostat housing.
10. Position the thermostat housing on the water crossover.

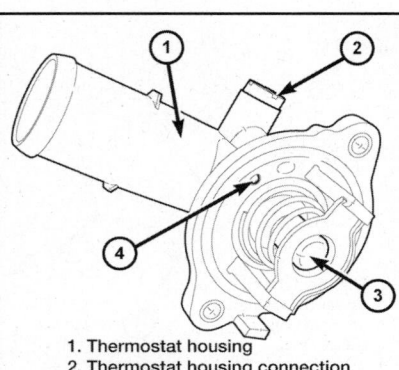

1. Thermostat housing
2. Thermostat housing connection
3. Thermostat
4. Bleed valve location

Fig. 32 View of thermostat housing—3.6L engine

11. Install the 2 thermostat housing bolts. Tighten the bolts to 106 inch lbs. (12 Nm).
12. Install the upper radiator hose on the thermostat housing.
13. Install the coolant recovery bottle. Tighten the bolts to 70 inch lbs. (8 Nm).
14. Fill the cooling system. Refer to Engine Coolant, Drain & Refill Procedure.
15. Connect the negative battery cable to the battery. Refer to Battery, removal & installation.
16. Start and warm the engine. Check for leaks.

Coolant Crossover

1. Before servicing the vehicle, refer to the Precautions Section.
2. Remove the thermostat housing assembly. Refer to Thermostat Housing, removal & installation.
3. Remove the heater supply hose from the coolant crossover.
4. Remove the coolant crossover mounting bolts. Take notice to the 4 bolts that bolt directly to the timing cover.
5. Remove the coolant crossover and discard the gaskets.

To install:

6. Clean the gasket sealing surfaces.
7. Install the new gasket onto the coolant crossover.

➡The shorter M6 mounting bolts, bolt directly to the engine timing cover.

8. Hand tighten the M6 mounting bolts. Tighten the bolts in a crisscross pattern to 106 inch lbs. (12 Nm).
9. Install the heater supply hose to the coolant crossover.
10. Install the thermostat housing. Refer to Thermostat Housing, removal & installation.

WATER PUMP

REMOVAL & INSTALLATION

2.4L Engine

1. Before servicing the vehicle, refer to the Precautions Section.
2. Remove the accessory drive belt. Refer to Accessory Drive Belts, removal & installation.
3. Drain the engine coolant.
4. Raise and safely support the vehicle.
5. Remove the accessory drive belt splash shield.
6. Remove the screws attaching the water pump pulley. Remove the pulley.

7. Remove the water pump mounting bolts.

8. Remove the water pump.

To install:

9. Position the water pump assembly into the water pump housing.

10. Install the mounting bolts. Tighten the bolts to 18 ft. lbs. (24 Nm).

11. Install the water pump pulley. Tighten the bolts to 80 inch lbs. (9 Nm).

12. Install the drive belt splash shield.

13. Lower the vehicle.

14. Install the accessory drive belt. Refer to Accessory Drive Belts, removal & installation.

15. Connect the negative battery terminal. Refer to Battery, removal & installation.

16. Evacuate the air and refill the cooling system. Refer to Engine Coolant, Drain & Refill Procedure.

17. Check the cooling system for leaks.

2.7L Engine

See Figure 33.

1. Before servicing the vehicle, refer to the Precautions Section.

2. Drain the cooling system.

3. Remove the radiator fan assembly. Refer to Engine Fan, removal & installation.

4. Remove accessory drive belt. Refer to Accessory Drive Belts, removal & installation.

5. Remove the timing chain and all chain guides. Refer to Timing Chain & Sprockets, removal & installation.

6. Remove the bolts attaching the water pump to the block.

7. Remove the water pump and gasket.

To install:

8. Clean all the sealing surfaces.

9. Install the water pump and gasket.

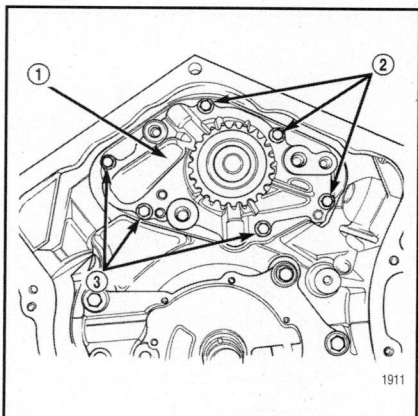

Fig. 33 View of the water pump (1) and bolts (2, 3)—2.7L engine

Tighten the mounting bolts to 106 inch lbs. (12 Nm).

10. Install the timing chain guides and timing chain. Refer to Timing Chain & Sprockets, removal & installation.

11. Install the accessory drive belt. Refer to Accessory Drive Belts, removal & installation.

12. Install the radiator fan assembly. Refer to Engine Fan, removal & installation.

13. Evacuate the air and refill the cooling system. Refer to Engine Coolant, Drain & Refill Procedure.

14. Check the cooling system for leaks.

3.5L Engine

See Figure 34.

➡The water pump can be replaced without discharging the air conditioning system.

✳✳ CAUTION

Do not remove the pressure cap with the system hot and under pressure as serious burns from the coolant can occur.

➡It is normal for the water pump to weep a small amount of coolant from the weep hole (black stain on the water pump body). Do not replace the water pump if this condition exists. Replace the water pump if a heavy deposit or a steady flow of engine coolant is evident on the water pump body from the weep hole (shaft seal failure). Be sure to perform a thorough analysis before replacing water pump.

1. Before servicing the vehicle, refer to the Precautions Section.

2. Drain the cooling system.

➡The water pump is driven by the timing belt.

3. Remove the engine timing belt. Refer to Timing Belt & Sprockets, removal & installation.

4. Remove the water pump mounting bolts. Note the position of the longer bolt for proper installation.

5. Remove the water pump body from the engine.

To install:

6. Clean all O-ring surfaces on the pump and cover.

7. Apply MOPAR® Dielectric Grease or the equivalent silicone grease to the O-ring to facilitate assembly. Install a new O-ring on the water pump.

8. Position the water pump to the engine.

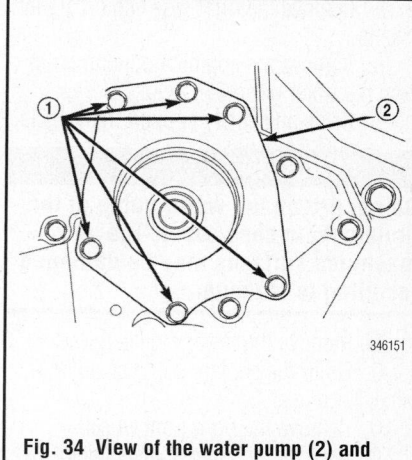

Fig. 34 View of the water pump (2) and bolts (1)—3.5L engine

9. Install the mounting bolts and tighten to 9 ft. lbs. (12 Nm).

10. Install the timing belt. Refer to Timing Belt & Sprockets, removal & installation.

11. Evacuate the air and refill the cooling system. Refer to Engine Coolant, Drain & Refill Procedure.

12. Check the cooling system for leaks.

3.6L Engine

See Figure 35.

➡The water pump on 3.6L engines is bolted directly to the engine timing chain case cover.

1. Before servicing the vehicle, refer to the Precautions Section.

2. Disconnect the negative battery cable from the battery.

✳✳ CAUTION

Constant tension hose clamps are used on most of the cooling system hoses. When removing or installing, use only tools designed for servicing this type of clamp. Always wear safety glasses when servicing constant tension clamps.

✳✳ CAUTION

A number or letter is stamped into the tongue of the constant tension clamps. If replacement is necessary, use only an original equipment clamp with the matching number or letter.

3. Remove the coolant bottle assembly and position aside.

4. Using a suitable jack, support the engine.

5. Remove the right side engine mount assembly.

6. Remove the engine mounting block from the water pump.

7. Raise and safely support the vehicle.

✳✳ WARNING

Do not pry on the water pump at the timing chain case/cover. The machined surfaces may be damaged resulting in leakage.

8. Remove the lower engine cover.

9. Drain the coolant into a clean container for reuse.

10. Remove the right front wheel.

11. Remove the inner splash shield.

12. Remove the accessory drive belt. Refer to Accessory Drive Belts, removal & installation.

13. Remove the accessory drive belt idler pulley.

14. Disconnect the A/C compressor electrical connector.

15. Remove the A/C compressor and position aside.

16. Remove the lower bypass hose and the lower radiator hose from the water pump and position aside.

17. Remove the remaining 10 water pump mounting bolts. Take notice to the 4 water pump bolts that mount directly to the timing chain cover.

18. Remove the water pump and discard the seal.

To install:

19. Clean the mating surfaces.

20. Using a new seal, position the water pump and install the mounting bolts. Note the shorter bolts fasten directly to the timing cover. Loosely tighten the M6 water pump mounting bolts.

21. Spin the water pump to be sure that the pump impeller does not rub against the timing chain case/cover.

22. Install the idler pulley bolt. Tighten the mounting bolt to 18 ft. lbs. (25 Nm).

23. Tighten the M6 water pump mounting bolts to 106 inch lbs. (12 Nm) in sequential order.

✳✳ WARNING

When installing the serpentine accessory drive belt, the belt must be routed correctly. If not, the engine may overheat due to the water pump rotating in the wrong direction.

24. Install the accessory drive belt. Refer to Accessory Drive Belts, removal & installation.

25. Install the lower radiator hose and the bypass hose.

26. Install the right inner splash shield.

27. Install the right front wheel.

28. Lower the vehicle.

29. Position a jack under the engine.

30. Install the engine mounting block onto the front of the water pump. Tighten

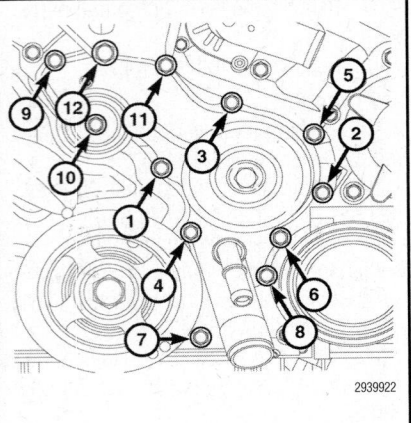

Fig. 35 View of water pump bolt tightening sequence—3.6L engine

the M8 mounting bolt to 18 ft. lbs. (25 Nm). Tighten the M10 mounting bolt to 41 ft. lbs. (55 Nm).

31. Install the engine mount. Tighten the mounting bolt to the engine block to 45 ft. lbs. (61 Nm).

32. Install the coolant bottle.

33. Install the air intake assembly.

34. Evacuate the air and refill the cooling system. Refer to Engine Coolant, Drain & Refill Procedure.

35. Connect the negative battery cable. Refer to Battery, removal & installation.

36. Check the cooling system for leaks.

ENGINE ELECTRICAL

BATTERY

REMOVAL & INSTALLATION
See Figures 36 and 37.

✳✳ CAUTION

To protect the hands from battery acid, a suitable pair of heavy duty rubber gloves should be worn when removing or servicing a battery. Safety glasses also should be worn.

✳✳ CAUTION

Remove metallic jewelry to avoid injury by accidental arcing of battery current.

➡ **The negative battery cable remote terminal must be disconnected and isolated from the remote battery post prior to service of the vehicle electrical systems. The negative battery cable**

remote terminal can be isolated by using the supplied isolation hole in the terminal casing.

1. Before servicing the vehicle, refer to the Precautions Section.

2. Disconnect and isolate the negative battery cable remote terminal from the remote battery post.

3. Remove the left front wheel and tire assembly.

4. Remove the push pins and remove the left front wheelhouse splash shield.

5. Loosen the nut and position the battery hold down bracket out of the way.

6. Loosen the pinch clamp bolts and position aside the battery cable clamps from the battery.

7. Remove the battery from the battery tray.

To install:

8. Install the battery into the battery tray.

9. Install the battery terminal pinch

BATTERY SYSTEM

clamps onto the battery posts. Tighten the pinch clamp nuts to 13 inch lbs. (18 Nm).

10. Position the battery hold down bracket and install the bracket nut. Tighten the pinch clamp nut to 40 ft. lbs. (55 Nm).

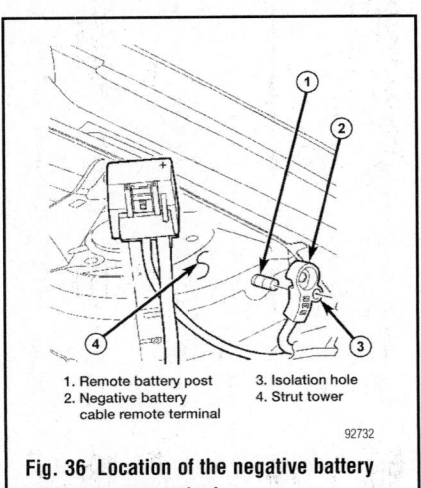

1. Remote battery post
2. Negative battery cable remote terminal
3. Isolation hole
4. Strut tower

Fig. 36 Location of the negative battery cable remote terminal

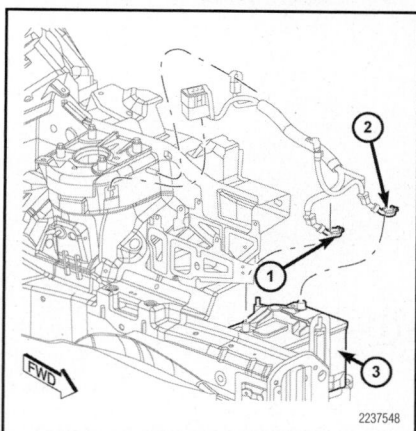

Fig. 37 Loosen the pinch clamp bolts and position aside the battery cable clamps (1, 2) from the battery (3)

11. Install the left front wheelhouse splash shield and push pins.

12. Install the left front wheel and tire assembly. Tighten the wheel nuts in a star

pattern until all nuts are torqued to half the required specification. Then repeat the tightening sequence to the full specified torque of 100 ft. lbs. (135 Nm).

13. Install the negative battery cable remote terminal onto the remote battery post. Tighten the nut to 21 ft. lbs. (28 Nm).

BATTERY RECONNECT/RELEARN PROCEDURE

> ❋❋ **CAUTION**
>
> **Always deplete the backup power supply before repairing or installing any new front or side air bag Supplemental Restraint System (SRS) component and before servicing, removing, installing, adjusting, or striking components near the front or side impact sensors. Nearby components include doors, instrument panel, console, door latches, strikers, seats, and hood latches.**

1. Before servicing the vehicle, refer to the Precautions Section.

2. To deplete the backup power supply energy, disconnect the battery ground cable and wait at least 1 minute. Be sure to disconnect auxiliary batteries and power supplies (if equipped).

> ❋❋ **CAUTION**
>
> **Battery posts, terminals and related accessories contain lead and lead components. Wash hands after handling. Failure to follow these instructions may result in serious personal injury.**

3. When the battery (or PCM) is disconnected and connected, some abnormal drive symptoms may occur while the vehicle relearns its adaptive strategy. The charging system set point may also vary. The vehicle may need to be driven to relearn its strategy.

ENGINE ELECTRICAL

ALTERNATOR

REMOVAL & INSTALLATION

2.4L Engine

See Figures 38 through 40.

1. Before servicing the vehicle, refer to the Precautions Section.

2. Disconnect and isolate the negative battery cable at the battery.

3. Remove the right front wheel.

4. Remove the underbody air dam.

5. Remove the accessory drive splash shield.

6. Remove the serpentine belt. Refer to Accessory Drive Belts, removal & installation.

7. Remove the accessory drive idler pulley.

8. Loosen the lower mounting bolt.

9. Loosen the A/C compressor and relocate, pull down and to the outboard side of the vehicle to make room to remove the alternator.

10. Unplug the field circuit from the alternator.

11. Remove the B+ terminal nut and wire.

12. Remove the upper mounting bolt.

13. Remove the alternator lower mounting bolt.

CHARGING SYSTEM

14. Relocate the battery terminal to the other side of the A/C line for removal of the alternator.

15. Rotate the alternator pulley downward for removal.

16. Slide the alternator down and out of the vehicle.

To install:

17. Move the A/C compressor to the side to install the alternator.

18. Rotate the alternator and set it in place.

19. Make sure the battery terminal is in front of the A/C line.

20. Loosely install the lower mounting bolt.

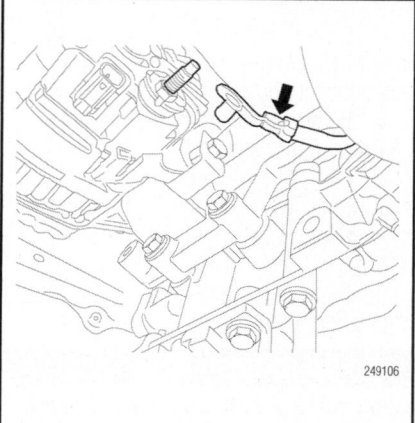

Fig. 38 Remove the B+ terminal nut and wire from the alternator—2.4L engine

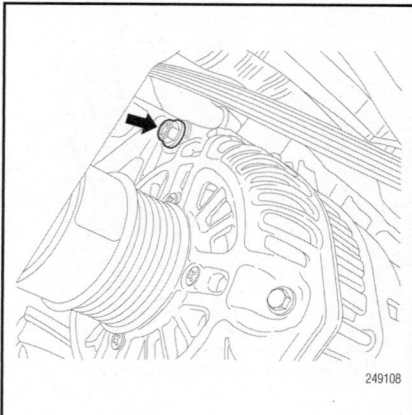

Fig. 39 Remove the upper mounting bolt—2.4L engine

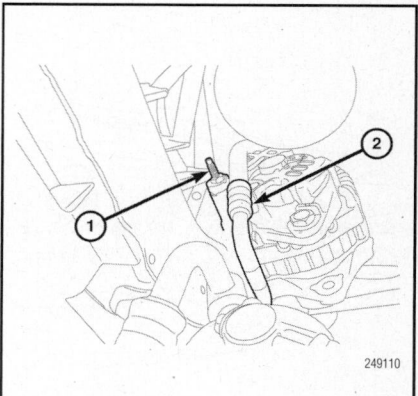

Fig. 40 Relocate the battery terminal (1) to the other side of the A/C line (2) for removal of the alternator—2.4L engine

21. Loosely install the upper mounting bolt.

22. Tighten the alternator mounting bolts to 40 ft. lbs. (54 Nm).

23. Install the B+ terminal nut and wire and tighten to 89 inch lbs. (10 Nm).

24. Plug in the field circuit to the alternator.

25. Install the idler pulley and tighten the bolt.

26. Install the serpentine belt. Refer to Accessory Drive Belts, removal & installation.

27. Install the splash shield.

28. Install the lower air dam.

29. Lower the vehicle.

30. Connect the negative battery cable. Refer to Battery, removal & installation.

2.7L Engine

See Figure 41.

1. Before servicing the vehicle, refer to the Precautions Section.

2. Open the hood.

3. Disconnect and isolate the negative battery cable.

4. Remove the radiator fan. Refer to Engine Fan, removal & installation.

5. Loosen the accessory drive belt, pulling the belt off of the alternator. Refer to Accessory Drive Belts, removal & installation.

6. Remove the lower mounting bolt from the alternator.

7. Remove the B+ terminal and field connection.

8. Remove the 2 upper mounting bolts.

9. Remove the alternator from the vehicle.

To install:

10. Install the alternator to the vehicle.

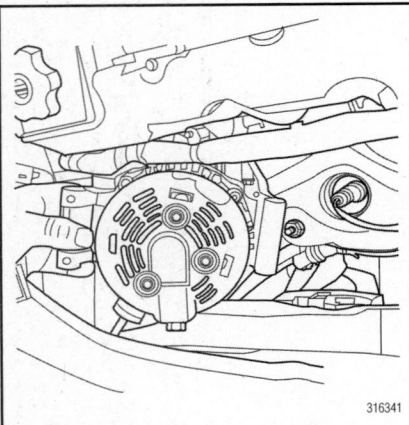

Fig. 41 Removing the alternator from the vehicle—2.7L engine

11. Install the 2 upper bolts, but do not tighten.

12. Connect the B+ terminal and field connectors.

13. Install the lower bolt and tighten to 20 ft. lbs. (27 Nm).

14. Install the accessory drive belt back on the alternator. Refer to Accessory Drive Belts, removal & installation.

15. Tighten the 2 upper mounting bolts to 20 ft. lbs. (27 Nm).

16. Connect the negative battery cable. Refer to Battery, removal & installation.

3.5L Engine

See Figures 42 and 43.

❋❋ WARNING

Never force a belt over a pulley rim using a screwdriver. The synthetic fiber of the belt can be damaged.

1. Before servicing the vehicle, refer to the Precautions Section.

2. Disconnect and isolate the negative battery cable.

3. Remove the alternator drive belt. Refer to Accessory Drive Belts, removal & installation.

4. Unsnap the plastic protective cover from the B+ mounting stud.

5. Remove the B+ terminal mounting nut and the B+ terminal at the top of the alternator.

6. Disconnect the field wire electrical connector by pushing on the connector tab.

7. Remove the short mounting bolt from the alternator.

8. Remove the long mounting bolt from the alternator.

9. Remove the alternator from the engine mounting bracket.

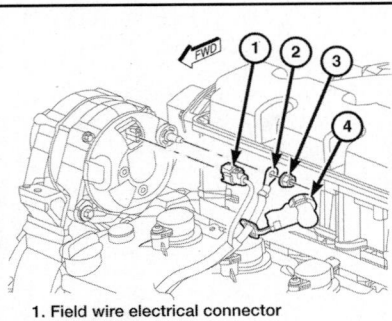

1. Field wire electrical connector
2. B+ terminal
3. B+ terminal mounting nut
4. B+ mounting stud plastic protective cover

Fig. 42 Removing the alternator electrical connections—3.5L engine

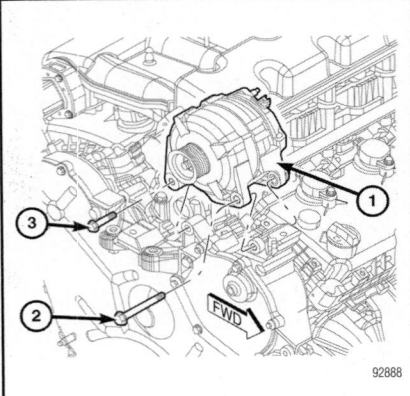

Fig. 43 Removing the alternator (1), long mounting bolt (2), and short mounting bolt (3)—3.5L engine

To install:

10. Install the alternator to the vehicle.

11. Install the mounting bolts and tighten to 19 ft. lbs. (26 Nm).

12. Install the B+ terminal wire. Tighten the nut to 89 inch lbs. (10 Nm).

13. Connect the electrical connector to the alternator.

14. Install the alternator drive belt. Refer to Accessory Drive Belts, removal & installation.

15. Install the negative battery cable remote terminal onto the remote battery post. Tighten the nut to 12 ft. lbs. (17 Nm).

3.6L Engine

See Figures 44 and 45.

➡The negative battery cable remote terminal must be disconnected and isolated from the remote battery post prior to service of the vehicle electrical systems. The negative battery cable remote terminal can be isolated by using the supplied isolation hole in the terminal casing.

1. Disconnect and isolate the negative battery cable remote terminal from the remote battery post.

2. Before servicing the vehicle, refer to the Precautions Section.

3. Remove the air cleaner assembly. Refer to Air Cleaner, removal & installation.

4. Remove the engine oil dipstick tube.

5. Remove the cooling fan. Refer to Engine Fan, removal & installation.

❋❋ WARNING

Never force a belt over a pulley rim using a screwdriver. The synthetic fiber of the belt can be damaged.

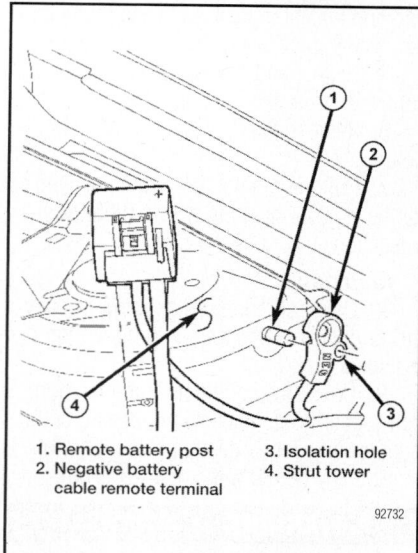

1. Remote battery post
2. Negative battery cable remote terminal
3. Isolation hole
4. Strut tower

92732

Fig. 44 Location of the negative battery cable remote terminal

※※ WARNING

Do not let tensioner arm snap back to the free-arm position, severe damage may occur to the tensioner.

6. Rotate the belt tensioner counterclockwise until it contacts the stop, remove the accessory drive belt and then slowly rotate the tensioner into the free-arm position.

7. Unsnap the plastic insulator cover from the B+ terminal.

8. Remove the B+ terminal retaining nut and remove the B+ terminal.

9. Depress the field wire electrical connector tab and remove the electrical connector from the alternator.

10. Remove the 2 upper mounting bolts from the alternator.

11. Remove the lower mounting bolt from the alternator.

12. Remove the alternator from the engine mounting bracket without damaging the radiator.

To install:

13. Position the alternator onto the engine mounting bracket.

14. Install the 2 upper mounting bolts and the lower mounting bolt to the alternator. Tighten the bolts to 31 ft. lbs. (42 Nm).

15. Connect the field wire connector to the alternator.

16. Install the B+ terminal and nut to the alternator mounting stud. Tighten nut to 89 inch lbs. (10 Nm).

17. Snap the plastic protective cover over the B+ terminal.

18. Install the accessory drive belt. Refer

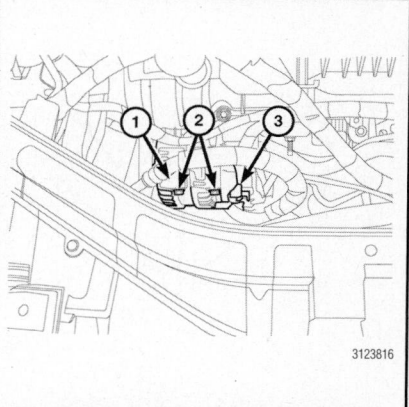

3123816

Fig. 45 Remove the electrical connector (3) from the alternator (1) and the upper mounting bolts (2)

to Accessory Drive Belts, removal & installation.

19. Install the engine cooling fan assembly. Refer to Engine Fan, removal & installation.

20. Install the engine oil dipstick tube.

21. Install the air cleaner body. Refer to Air Cleaner, removal & installation.

22. Connect the negative battery cable. Tighten the nut to 40 inch lbs. (5 Nm).

23. Start the engine and verify the alternator is functioning properly.

ENGINE ELECTRICAL

FIRING ORDER

2.4L engine firing order: 1–3–4–2
2.7L, 3.5L, and 3.6L engine firing order: 1–2–3–4–5–6

IGNITION COIL

REMOVAL & INSTALLATION

2.4L Engine

See Figures 46 and 47.

➡Prior to removing the coil, spray compressed air around the coil top to make sure no dirt drops into the spark plug tube.

➡The electronic ignition coil attaches directly to the valve cover.

1. Before servicing the vehicle, refer to the Precautions Section.

2. Remove the negative battery cable.

3. Disconnect the electrical connector from the ignition coil.

4. Remove the ignition coil mounting bolts.

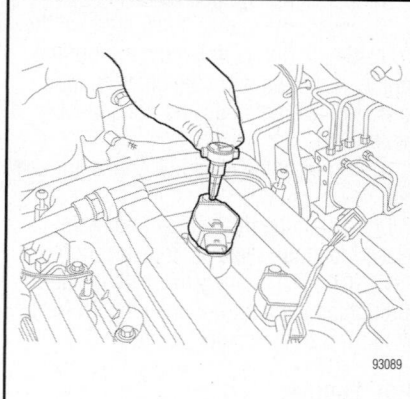

93089

Fig. 46 Removing the ignition coil mounting bolts—2.4L engine

5. Remove the ignition coil.

To install:

6. Install the ignition coil. Tighten the bolt to 80 inch lbs. (9 Nm).

7. Connect the electrical connectors and lock.

8. Install the negative battery cable. Refer to Battery, removal & installation.

IGNITION SYSTEM

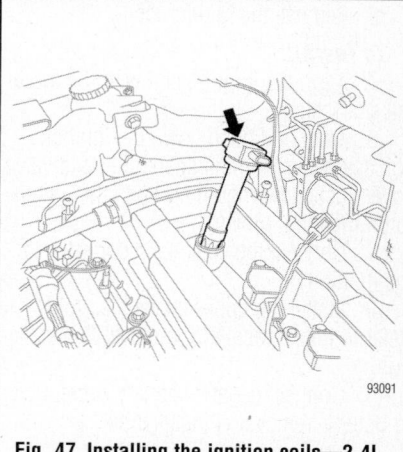

93091

Fig. 47 Installing the ignition coils—2.4L engine

2.7L Engine

See Figure 48.

➡Always remove the ignition coil assembly by turning the assembly ½ turn and pulling up in a steady motion.

1. Before servicing the vehicle, refer to the Precautions Section.

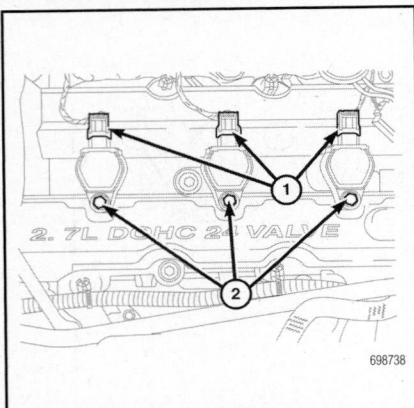

Fig. 48 Removing the ignition coil mounting bolts (2) and electrical connectors (1)—2.7L engine

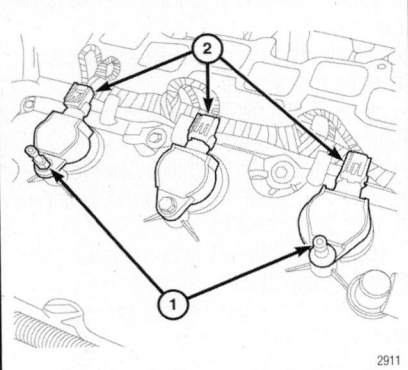

Fig. 49 Removing the ignition coil mounting bolts/studs (1) and electrical connectors (2)—3.5L engine

2. Disconnect the negative battery cable.
3. Remove the upper intake manifold. Refer to Intake Manifold, removal & installation.
4. Disconnect the electrical connector from the ignition coil.
5. Remove the mounting bolt from the ignition coil.

❋❋ WARNING

Prior to removing the ignition coils, spray compressed air around the coils and spark plugs. If dirt and debris enter the engine, this may cause internal engine damage.

6. Remove the ignition coils.

To install:

7. Align the ignition coil with the top of the spark plug.
8. Twist and push down the ignition coil assembly onto the spark plug and valve cover. Install the mounting bolt and tighten to 65 inch lbs. (8 Nm).
9. Connect the electrical connector to the ignition coil.
10. Install the upper intake manifold. Refer to Intake Manifold, removal & installation.
11. Connect negative battery cable. Refer to Battery, removal & installation.

3.5L Engine

See Figure 49.

1. Before servicing the vehicle, refer to the Precautions Section.
2. Remove the engine cover.
3. Disconnect and isolate the negative battery cable.
4. Remove the upper intake manifold. Refer to Intake Manifold, removal & installation.

5. Unlock and disconnect the electrical connector from the ignition coils.
6. Remove the mounting bolts and the engine cover studs.

❋❋ WARNING

Prior to removing the ignition coils, spray compressed air around the coils and spark plugs. If dirt and debris enter the engine, this may cause internal engine damage.

7. Twist, lift, and remove the ignition coils from the engine.

To install:

8. Install the ignition coils.
9. Install the engine cover studs in the 2 outside ignition coils on the front of the engine. Install bolts on the other ignition coils. Tighten the studs and bolts to 71 inch lbs. (8 Nm).
10. Connect the electrical connector and lock.
11. Install the intake manifold. Refer to Intake Manifold, removal & installation.
12. Connect the negative battery cable and tighten the nut to 45 inch lbs. (5 Nm).
13. Install the engine cover.

3.6L Engine

See Figure 50.

1. Before servicing the vehicle, refer to the Precautions Section.
2. Disconnect and isolate the negative battery cable.
3. If removing the ignition coils from cylinders 1 and 3 on the RH side of the engine, first remove the resonator. Refer to Air Cleaner, removal & installation.
4. If removing the ignition coils from cylinders 2, 4 or 6 on the LH side of the engine, first remove the upper intake mani-

fold and insulator. Refer to Intake Manifold, removal & installation.
5. Unlock and disconnect the electrical connector from the ignition coil.
6. Remove the ignition coil mounting bolt.
7. Pull the ignition coil from the cylinder head cover opening with a slight twisting action.

To install:

8. Using compressed air, blow out any dirt or contaminants from around the top of the spark plug.
9. Check the condition of the ignition coil rubber boot. Inspect the opening of the boot for any debris, tears, or rips. Carefully remove any debris with a lint free cloth.

❋❋ WARNING

Do not apply silicone based grease such as MOPAR® Dielectric Grease to the ignition coil rubber boot. The silicone based grease will absorb into the boot causing it to stick and tear.

10. Place a small, 360° bead of Fluostar® 2LF lubricant along the inside opening of the coil boot approximately 0.039–0.079 inch (1–2mm) from the chamfer edge, but not on the chamfered surface.
11. Position the ignition coil into the cylinder head cover opening. Using a twisting action, push the ignition coil onto the spark plug.
12. Install the ignition coil mounting bolt and tighten to 71 inch lbs. (8 Nm).
13. Connect and lock the electrical connector to the ignition coil.
14. If removed, install the insulator, upper intake manifold, and air inlet hose. Refer to Intake Manifold, removal & installation.

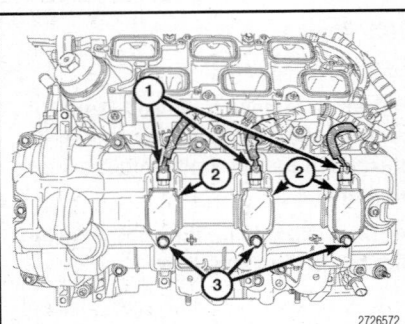

Fig. 50 Unlock and disconnect the electrical connector (1), remove the mounting bolt (3), and pull the ignition coil (2) from the cylinder head cover opening (LH shown, RH ignition coils are similar)—3.6L engine

15. Connect the negative battery cable and tighten the nut to 45 inch lbs. (5 Nm). Refer to Battery, removal & installation.

IGNITION TIMING

ADJUSTMENT

The ignition timing is controlled by the Powertrain Control Module (PCM). No adjustment is necessary.

SPARK PLUGS

REMOVAL & INSTALLATION

2.4L Engine

See Figure 51.

1. Before servicing the vehicle, refer to the Precautions Section.
2. Disconnect the negative battery cable.
3. Remove the ignition coils. Refer to Ignition Coil, removal & installation.

✳✳ WARNING

Prior to loosening the spark plug, use compressed air to blow out any debris that might be in the spark plug tube.

4. Remove the spark plug using a quality socket with a rubber or foam insert.
5. Inspect the spark plug condition.

To install:

✳✳ WARNING

Handle the spark plugs with care. Do not drop or force the spark plugs into the wells, damage to the electrodes and/or porcelain body may occur. Always start each spark plug by hand

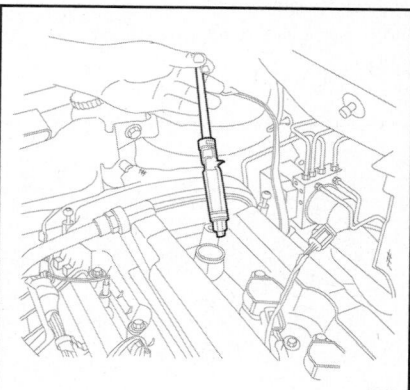

93103

Fig. 51 Using a spark plug socket, remove the spark plugs from the engine—2.4L engine

in order to avoid cross-threading the spark plug in the cylinder head. Always tighten spark plugs to the specified torque. Too much or not enough torque will cause damage to the cylinder head and/or spark plug and may lead to poor engine performance.

6. Install each spark plug to the cylinder head. Tighten the spark plugs to 20 ft. lbs. (27 Nm).
7. Install the ignition coil onto spark plug. Refer to Ignition Coil, removal & installation.
8. Connect the negative battery cable. Refer to Battery, removal & installation.

2.7L Engine

1. Before servicing the vehicle, refer to the Precautions Section.
2. Disconnect the negative battery cable.
3. Remove the ignition coils. Refer to Ignition Coil, removal & installation.

✳✳ WARNING

Prior to removing the ignition coils, spray compressed air around the coils and spark plugs. If dirt and debris enter the engine, this may cause internal engine damage.

4. Using a quality spark plug socket with a rubber or foam insert, remove the spark plugs from the engine.

To install:

✳✳ WARNING

Handle the spark plugs with care. Do not drop or force the spark plugs into the wells, damage to the electrodes and/or porcelain body may occur. Always start each spark plug by hand in order to avoid cross-threading the spark plug in the cylinder head. Always tighten spark plugs to the specified torque. Too much or not enough torque will cause damage to the cylinder head and/or spark plug and may lead to poor engine performance.

5. Install each spark plug to the cylinder head. Tighten the spark plugs to 13 ft. lbs. (17 Nm).
6. Align the ignition coil with top of the spark plug.
7. Install the ignition coils. Refer to Ignition Coil, removal & installation.
8. Connect the negative battery cable. Refer to Battery, removal & installation.

3.5L Engine

1. Before servicing the vehicle, refer to the Precautions Section.
2. Remove the engine cover.
3. Disconnect and isolate the negative battery cable.
4. Remove the ignition coils. Refer to Ignition Coil, removal & installation.

✳✳ WARNING

Prior to removing the spark plugs, use compressed air to remove any accumulated dirt and debris. If dirt and debris enter the engine, this may cause internal engine damage.

5. Remove the spark plugs using a quality socket with a rubber or foam insert.

To install:

✳✳ WARNING

Handle the spark plugs with care. Do not drop or force the spark plugs into the wells, damage to the electrodes and/or porcelain body may occur. Always start each spark plug by hand in order to avoid cross-threading the spark plug in the cylinder head. Always tighten spark plugs to the specified torque. Too much or not enough torque will cause damage to the cylinder head and/or spark plug and may lead to poor engine performance.

6. To avoid cross threading, start the spark plug into the cylinder head by hand.
7. Tighten the spark plugs to 20 ft. lbs. (27 Nm).
8. Install the ignition coils. Refer to Ignition Coils, removal & installation.
9. Reconnect the negative battery cable. Refer to Battery, removal & installation.
10. Install the engine cover.

3.6L Engine

See Figure 52.

1. Before servicing the vehicle, refer to the Precautions Section.
2. Remove the ignition coils. Refer to Ignition Coil, removal & installation.

✳✳ WARNING

Prior to removing the spark plug, spray compressed air into the cylinder head opening. This will help prevent foreign material from entering the combustion chamber.

The spark plug tubes are a thin wall design. Avoid damaging the spark plug tubes. Damage to the spark plug tube can result in oil leaks.

3. Remove the spark plug from the cylinder head using a quality thin wall socket with a rubber or foam insert.

4. Inspect the spark plug condition.

To install:

5. Check and adjust the spark plug gap with a gap gauging tool.

Special care should be taken when installing spark plugs into the cylinder head spark plug wells. Be sure

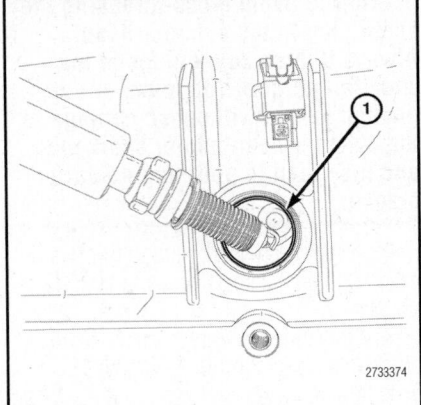

Fig. 52 The spark plug tubes (1) are a thin wall design. Avoid damaging the spark plug tubes

the plugs do not drop into the plug wells as electrodes can be damaged.

6. Start the spark plug into the cylinder head by hand to avoid cross threading.

Spark plug torque is critical and must not exceed the specified value. Overtightening stretches the spark plug shell reducing its heat transfer capability resulting in possible catastrophic engine failure.

7. Tighten the spark plugs to 13 ft. lbs. (18 Nm).

8. Install the ignition coils. Refer to Ignition Coil, removal & installation.

ENGINE ELECTRICAL

STARTER

REMOVAL & INSTALLATION

2.4L Engine

See Figures 53 and 54.

1. Before servicing the vehicle, refer to the Precautions Section.

2. Remove air cleaner box and air tube. Refer to Air Cleaner, removal & installation.

3. Disconnect and isolate the battery negative cable.

4. Remove the starter motor mounting bolt.

5. Disconnect the electrical connector at the throttle body.

6. Remove the throttle body bolts and remove the throttle body.

7. Push the starter under the intake manifold.

8. Tip the starter nose toward the cooling module.

9. Pull the starter up and out.

10. Disconnect the starter motor wiring.

11. Remove the starter motor from the vehicle.

To install:

12. Connect the starter motor wiring. Tighten the battery cable nut to 89 inch lbs. (10 Nm).

13. Install the starter motor into the vehicle lower engine compartment.

14. Loosely install the starter into position.

15. Install the throttle body

16. Install the throttle body bracket.

17. Install the starter motor mounting bolts and tighten to 40 ft. lbs. (54 Nm).

18. Connect the throttle body electrical connector.

STARTING SYSTEM

19. Install the air cleaner box and inlet tube. Refer to Air Cleaner, removal & installation.

20. Connect the battery negative cable. Refer to Battery, removal & installation.

2.7L Engine

See Figures 55 through 59.

1. Before servicing the vehicle, refer to the Precautions Section.

2. Disconnect and isolate the negative battery cable.

3. Remove the front mount through bolt.

4. Remove the lower engine anti-roll mount bolt.

5. Remove the crossmember mounting bolts.

6. Remove the crossmember from the vehicle.

7. Remove the torque reaction bracket transaxle-to-starter bolt.

8. Remove the negative battery cable.

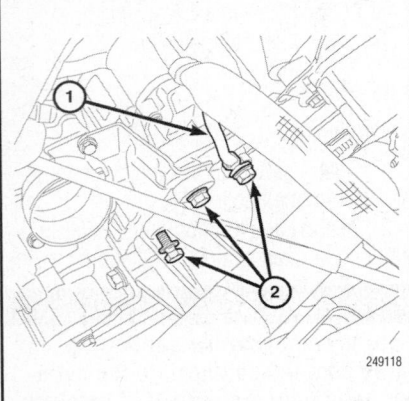

Fig. 53 View of starter (1) and mounting bolts (2)—2.4L engine

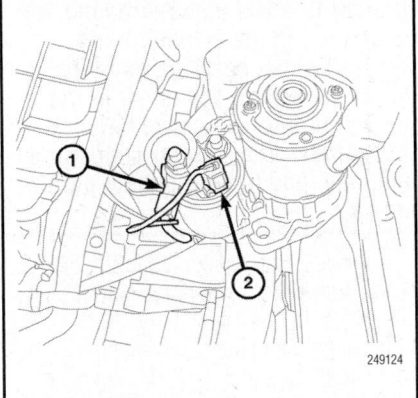

Fig. 54 Disconnect the starter motor wiring (1, 2)—2.4L engine

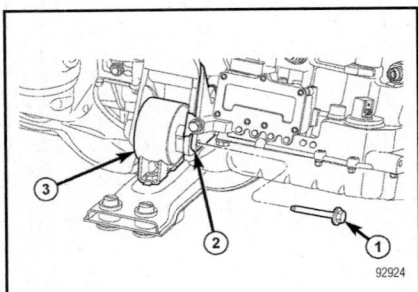

Fig. 55 View of lower engine anti-roll mount (3), front through bolt (1), and lower mount bolt (2)—2.7L engine

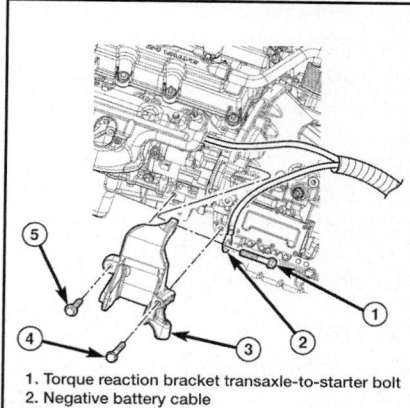

1. Torque reaction bracket transaxle-to-starter bolt
2. Negative battery cable
3. Torque reaction bracket
4. Torque reaction bracket-to-transaxle bolt
5. Torque reaction bracket-to-engine bolt

92930

Fig. 56 Remove the torque reaction bracket from the vehicle—2.7L engine

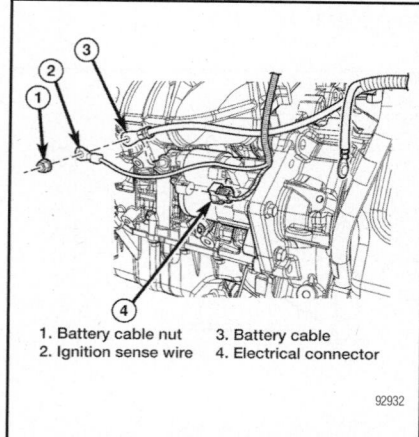

1. Battery cable nut   3. Battery cable
2. Ignition sense wire   4. Electrical connector

92932

Fig. 57 Removing the electrical connections from the starter—2.7L engine

9. Remove the torque reaction bracket-to-transaxle bolt.

10. Remove the torque reaction bracket-to-engine bolt.

11. Remove the torque reaction bracket from the vehicle.

12. Remove the battery cable nut, ignition sense wire, and battery cable from the solenoid stud.

13. Disconnect the electrical connector from the starter solenoid.

14. Remove the starter mounting bolts from the transaxle housing.

15. Remove the starter motor and dust shield from the transaxle housing.

16. Remove the starter motor from the vehicle.

To install:

17. Install the starter motor and dust shield to the transaxle housing.

18. Install the starter mounting bolts to

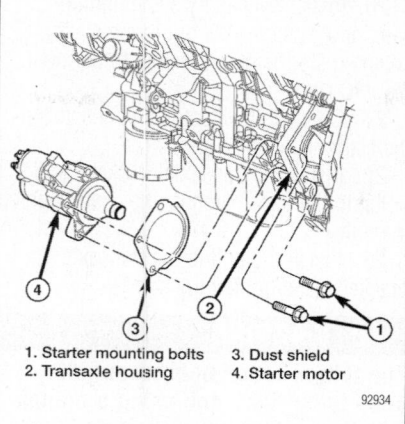

1. Starter mounting bolts   3. Dust shield
2. Transaxle housing   4. Starter motor

92934

Fig. 58 Removing the starter motor from the vehicle—2.7L engine

the transaxle housing. Tighten the bolts to 40 ft. lbs. (54 Nm).

19. Install the battery cable, ignition sense wire, and battery cable nut to the solenoid stud. Tighten the nut to 89 inch lbs. (10 Nm).

20. Connect the electrical connector to the starter solenoid.

21. Install the torque reaction bracket to the vehicle.

22. Install the torque reaction bracket-to-engine bolt. Hand tighten the bolt.

23. Install the torque reaction bracket-to-transaxle bolt. Hand tighten the bolt.

24. Install the negative battery cable.

25. Install the torque reaction bracket transaxle-to-starter bolt. Hand tighten the bolt.

✳✳ WARNING

The torque reaction bracket bolts need to be tightened using a mandatory torque sequence. Failure to tighten the bolts using the mandatory torque sequence provided may result in damage to the fasteners, bracket, and threaded bolt holes for the engine and transaxle.

26. Tighten the bolts in a mandatory torque sequence to 40 ft. lbs. (54 Nm).

27. Install the crossmember to the vehicle. Tighten the bolts to 37 ft. lbs. (50 Nm).

28. Install the lower engine anti-roll mount bolt and tighten the bolt to 35 ft. lbs. (47 Nm).

29. Install the crossmember bolts and tighten the bolts to 41 ft. lbs. (55 Nm).

30. Install the mount through bolt and tighten to 35 ft. lbs. (47 Nm).

31. Connect the negative battery cable, tighten the nut to 40 inch lbs. (5 Nm).

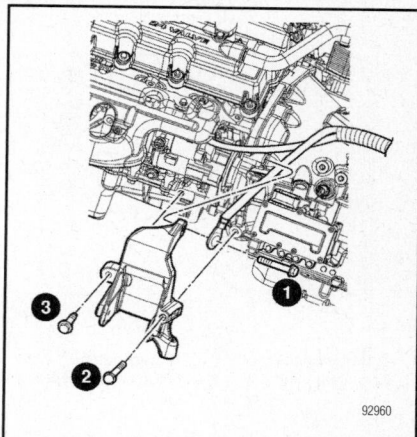

92960

Fig. 59 Torque reaction bracket mandatory torque sequence shown—2.7L engine

3.5L Engine

See Figures 60 through 63.

1. Before servicing the vehicle, refer to the Precautions Section.

2. Disconnect and isolate the negative battery cable at the battery.

3. Remove the heat shield nuts, and position the heat shield aside.

4. Remove the belly pan, if equipped.

5. Remove the front mount through bolt from the transaxle bracket and mount.

6. Remove the rear bolts from the transaxle crossmember.

7. Remove the front bolts from the transaxle crossmember.

8. Remove the transaxle crossmember.

9. Remove the heat shield bolts and remove the heat shield.

10. Remove the oxygen sensor and position aside.

11. Remove the bolt from the transaxle bracket.

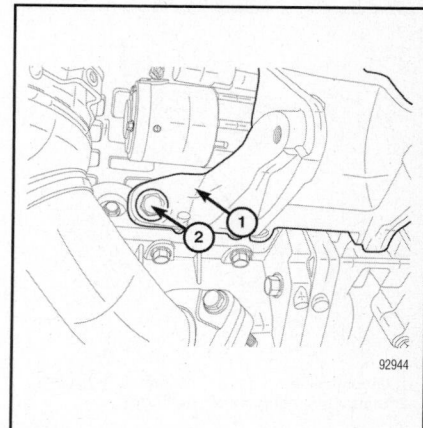

92944

Fig. 60 Remove the bolt (2) from the transaxle bracket (1)—3.5L engine

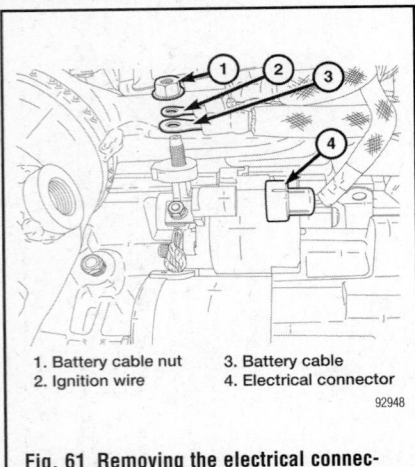

1. Battery cable nut　　3. Battery cable
2. Ignition wire　　　　4. Electrical connector

92948

Fig. 61 Removing the electrical connections from the starter—3.5L engine

12. Remove the bolts, and the transaxle bracket from the transaxle housing.

13. Remove the battery cable nut, ignition wire, and battery cable from the starter solenoid stud.

14. Disconnect the electrical connector from the starter solenoid.

15. Remove the starter mounting bolts and ground wire and remove the starter from the transaxle housing.

16. Remove the starter motor dust shield from the starter.

➡If the flywheel is damaged, the flywheel will require replacement.

17. Rotate and fully inspect the flywheel gears and wields for damage.

To install:

18. Install the starter motor dust shield to the starter.

19. Position the starter into the transaxle housing, install the ground wire and starter mounting bolts. Tighten the bolts to 40 ft. lbs. (54 Nm).

20. Install the battery cable, ignition wire, and battery cable nut to the starter solenoid stud. Tighten the nut to 89 inch lbs. (10 Nm).

21. Connect the electrical connector to the starter solenoid.

22. Install the transaxle bracket and the bolts, to the transaxle housing. Hand tighten the bolts.

23. Install the bolt to the transaxle bracket. Hand tighten the bolt.

✳✳ WARNING

The torque reaction bracket bolts need to be tightened using a mandatory torque sequence. Failure to tighten the bolts using the mandatory torque sequence provided may result in damage to the fasteners, bracket, and threaded bolt holes for the engine and transaxle.

24. Tighten the bolts in a mandatory torque sequence to 37 ft. lbs. (50 Nm).

25. Install the oxygen sensor and tighten to 30 ft. lbs. (41 Nm).

26. Install the heat shield and bolts. Tighten the bolts to 106 inch lbs. (12 Nm).

27. Install the bolts to the transaxle crossmember. Tighten the 2 bolts to 41 ft. lbs. (55 Nm) and the 4 bolts to 37 ft. lbs. (50 Nm).

28. Install the front mount through bolt to the transaxle bracket and mount. Tighten the bolt to 35 ft. lbs. (47 Nm).

29. If equipped, install the belly pan.

➡Make sure the lower heat shield is installed to the lower stud before the upper heat shield is installed. The upper heat shield stacks on top of the lower heat shield, and both shields are held together by the lower nut.

30. Position the heat shield over the studs and install the heat shield nuts,. Tighten the nuts to 106 inch lbs. (12 Nm).

31. Connect the negative battery cable and tighten the nut to 45 inch lbs. (5 Nm). Refer to Battery, removal & installation.

3.6L Engine

See Figures 64 through 66.

1. Before servicing the vehicle, refer to the Precautions Section.

2. Disconnect and isolate the negative battery cable.

3. Remove the catalytic converter. Refer to Catalytic Converter, removal & installation.

4. Remove the front engine mount through bolt.

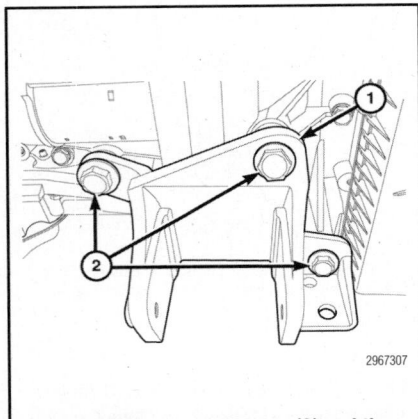

2967307

Fig. 64 Remove the retainers (2) and the front engine mount bracket (1)—3.6L engine

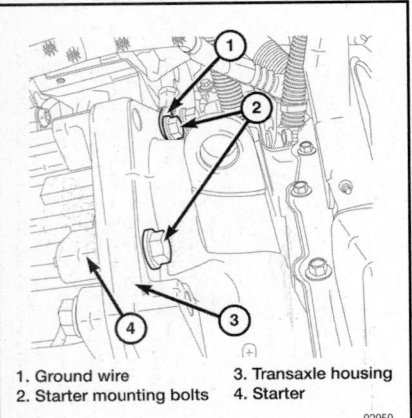

1. Ground wire　　　　3. Transaxle housing
2. Starter mounting bolts　4. Starter

92950

Fig. 62 Starter mounting and bolts shown—3.5L engine

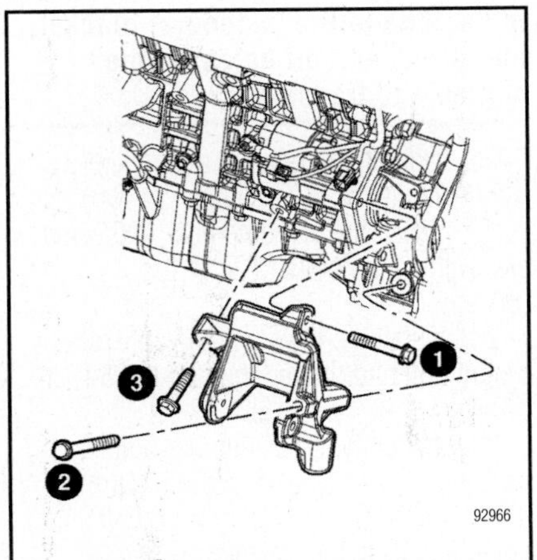

92966

Fig. 63 Torque reaction bracket mandatory torque sequence shown—3.5L engine

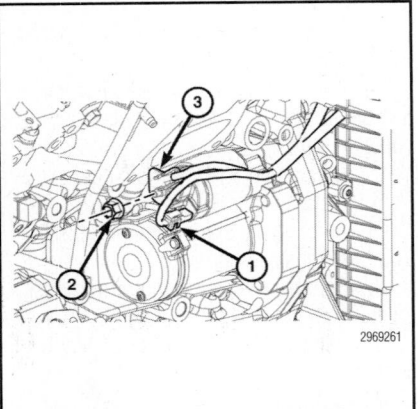

2969261

Fig. 65 View of starter field alternator connector (1), B+ retainer (2), and B+ cable (3)—3.6L engine

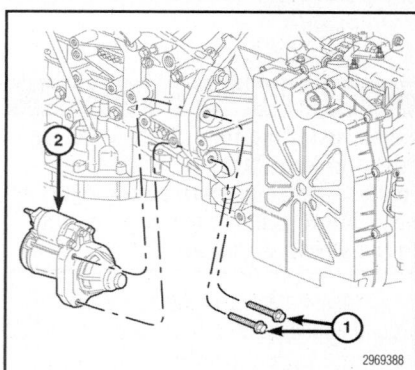

Fig. 66 Remove the starter retainers (1) and remove the starter (2) from the vehicle—3.6L engine

5. Remove the retainers from the front engine mount bracket and remove the bracket.

6. Remove the field alternator connector.

7. Remove the B+ retainer and B+ cable.

8. Remove the starter retainers.

9. Remove the starter from the vehicle.

To install:

10. Install the starter to the vehicle.

11. Install the starter retainers. Tighten to 41 ft. lbs. (55 Nm).

12. Install the B+ cable and retainer. Tighten to 115 inch lbs. (13 Nm).

13. Install the field alternator connector.

14. Install the engine mount bracket.

15. Install the engine mount bracket retainers. Tighten to 41 ft. lbs. (55 Nm).

16. Install the engine mount through bolt. Tighten to 45 ft. lbs. (61 Nm).

17. Install the catalytic converter. Refer to Catalytic Converter, removal & installation.

18. Connect the battery negative cable. Refer to Battery, removal & installation.

ENGINE MECHANICAL

➡**Disconnecting the negative battery cable may interfere with the functions of the on board computer systems and may require the computer to undergo a relearning process, once the negative battery cable is reconnected.**

ACCESSORY DRIVE BELTS

ACCESSORY BELT ROUTING

2.4L Engine
See Figure 67.

2.7L Engine
See Figure 68.

3.5L Engine
See Figure 69.

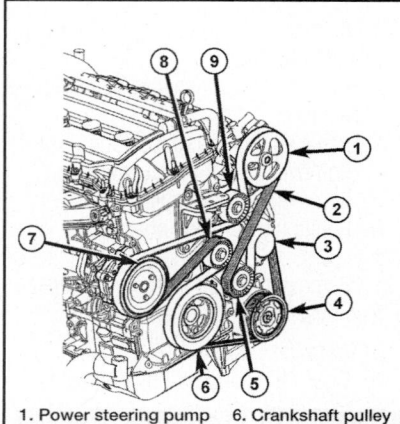

1. Power steering pump
2. Accessory drive belt
3. Alternator
4. A/C pulley
5. Lower idler pulley
6. Crankshaft pulley
7. Water pump pulley
8. Accessory drive belt tensioner
9. Upper idler pulley

248624

Fig. 67 Accessory drive belt routing— 2.4L engine

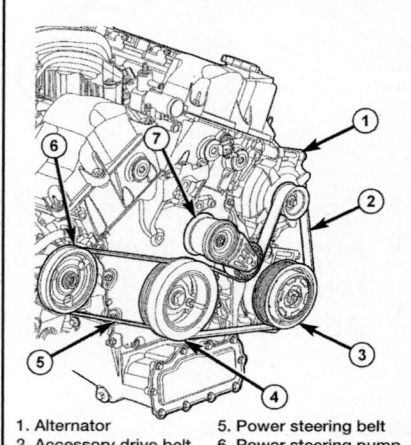

1. Alternator
2. Accessory drive belt
3. A/C pulley
4. Crankshaft pulley
5. Power steering belt
6. Power steering pump
7. Accessory drive belt tensioner

92162

Fig. 68 Accessory drive belt routing— 2.7L engine

3.6L Engine
See Figure 70.

INSPECTION

Inspect the drive belt for signs of glazing or cracking. A glazed belt will be perfectly smooth from slippage, while a good belt will have a slight texture of fabric visible. Cracks will usually start at the inner edge of the belt and run outward. All worn or damaged drive belts should be replaced immediately.

ADJUSTMENT

Accessory belt tension is automatically maintained by a spring-loaded tensioner. No adjustment is necessary.

REMOVAL & INSTALLATION

2.4L Engine

1. Before servicing the vehicle, refer to the Precautions Section.

2. Using a wrench, rotate the accessory drive belt tensioner counterclockwise until the accessory drive belt can be removed from the lower and upper idler pulleys.

3. Remove the accessory drive belt from the vehicle.

To install:

➡**When installing the drive belt on the pulleys, make sure that belt is properly routed and that all V-grooves make proper contact with the pulley grooves.**

4. Install the accessory drive belt around all the pulleys except for the alternator pulley.

5. Using a wrench, rotate the accessory drive belt tensioner counterclockwise until the accessory drive belt can be installed on the alternator pulley. Release the spring tension onto the accessory drive belt.

2.7L Engine

1. Before servicing the vehicle, refer to the Precautions Section.

2. Raise and safely support vehicle.

3. Remove the right front wheel and belt splash shield.

4. Using a suitable tool, rotate the accessory drive belt tensioner counterclockwise.

5. Rotate the tensioner arm counterclockwise to allow enough slack to remove the accessory drive belt.

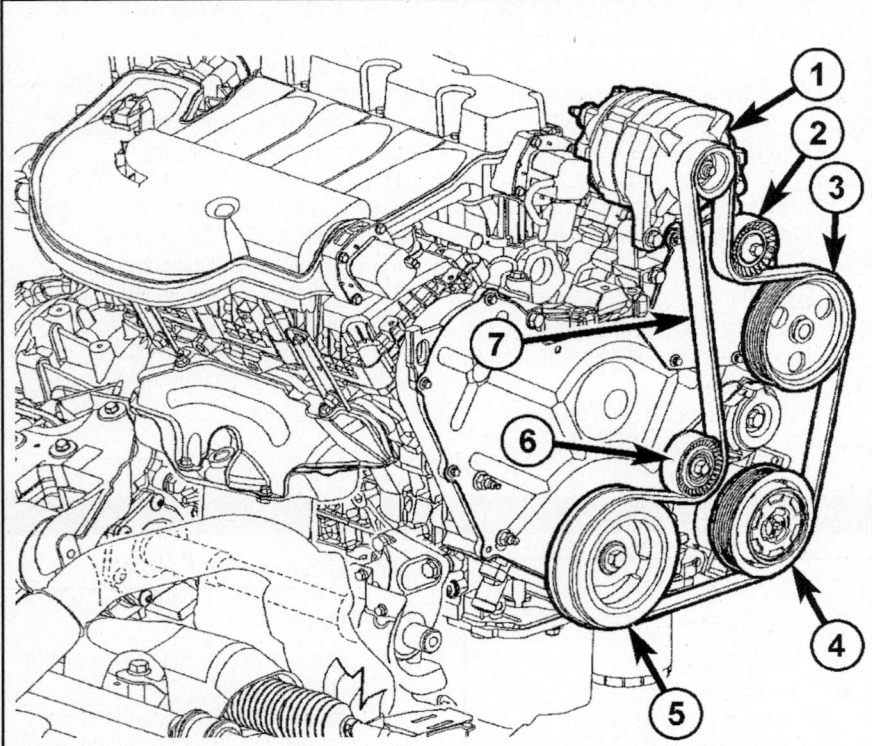

1. Alternator pulley
2. Idler pulley
3. Power steering pump
4. A/C pulley
5. Crankshaft pulley
6. Accessory drive belt tensioner
7. Accessory drive belt

96072

Fig. 69 Accessory drive belt routing—3.5L engine

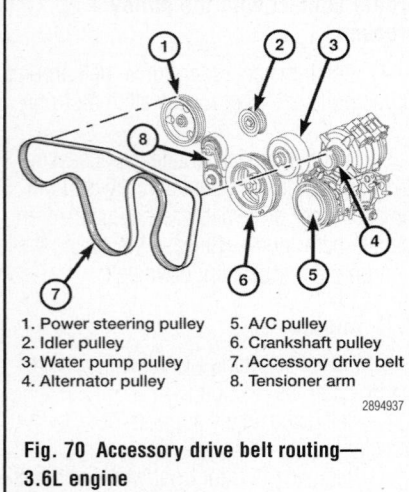

1. Power steering pulley
2. Idler pulley
3. Water pump pulley
4. Alternator pulley
5. A/C pulley
6. Crankshaft pulley
7. Accessory drive belt
8. Tensioner arm

2894937

Fig. 70 Accessory drive belt routing— 3.6L engine

To install:

6. Install the accessory drive belt around all the pulleys except for the alternator pulley.

7. Using a suitable tool, rotate the accessory drive belt tensioner counterclockwise until the accessory drive belt can be installed

on the alternator pulley. Release the spring tension onto the accessory drive belt.

8. Install the belt splash shield and right front wheel.

9. Lower the vehicle.

3.5L Engine

> ✴✴ **WARNING**
>
> **Do not let the tensioner arm snap back to the free-arm position, severe damage may occur to the tensioner.**

➡**Belt tension is not adjustable. The belt adjustment is maintained by an automatic, spring loaded belt tensioner.**

1. Before servicing the vehicle, refer to the Precautions Section.

2. Disconnect the negative battery cable from the battery.

3. Rotate the belt tensioner clockwise until it contacts the stop. Remove the belt, then slowly rotate the tensioner into the free-arm position.

To install:

4. Check the condition of all pulleys.

> ✴✴ **WARNING**
>
> **When installing the accessory drive belt, the belt MUST be routed correctly. If not, the engine may overheat due to the water pump rotating in the wrong direction.**

5. Install a new belt. Route the belt around all the pulleys except the idler pulley. Rotate the tensioner arm until it contacts its stop position. Route the belt around the idler and slowly let the tensioner rotate into the belt. Make sure the belt is seated onto all the pulleys.

➡**The tensioner is equipped with an indexing tang on the back of the tensioner and an indexing stop on the tensioner housing. If a new belt is being installed, the tang must be within approximately 0.24–0.32 inch (6–8mm) of the indexing stop (i.e. the tang is approximately between the two indexing stops). The belt is considered new if it has been used 15 minutes or less.**

6. With the drive belt installed, inspect the belt wear indicator.

7. Connect the negative battery cable. Refer to Battery, removal & installation.

3.6L Engine

> ✴✴ **WARNING**
>
> **Do not let tensioner the arm snap back to the free-arm position, severe damage may occur to the tensioner.**

1. Before servicing the vehicle, refer to the Precautions Section.

2. Disconnect the negative battery cable from the battery.

3. Raise and safely support the vehicle.

4. Remove the right front wheel.

5. Remove the inner splash shield.

6. Rotate the belt tensioner until it contacts its stop.

7. Remove the belt, then slowly rotate the tensioner into the free-arm position.

To install:

8. Check the condition of all pulleys.

> ✴✴ **WARNING**
>
> **When installing the serpentine accessory drive belt, the belt MUST be routed correctly. If not, the engine may overheat due to the water pump rotating in the wrong direction.**

9. Install a new belt. Route the belt around all the pulleys except the idler pulley. Rotate the tensioner arm until it contacts its stop position. Route the belt around the idler and slowly let the tensioner rotate into the belt. Make sure the belt is seated onto all the pulleys.

10. With the drive belt installed, inspect the belt wear indicator. The gap between the tang and the housing stop must not exceed 0.94 inch (24mm).

11. Install the inner splash shield.

12. Install the wheel.

13. Lower the vehicle.

14. Connect the negative battery cable. Refer to Battery, removal & installation.

AIR CLEANER

REMOVAL & INSTALLATION

2.4L Engine

See Figure 71.

1. Before servicing the vehicle, refer to the Precautions Section.

2. Remove the air cleaner housing retaining bolt.

3. Remove the clean air hose from the air cleaner housing.

4. Lift the air cleaner housing upwards and remove.

To install:

5. Position the air cleaner housing in place.

6. Install the retaining bolt.

7. Install the clean air hose.

2.7L Engine

See Figures 72 through 74.

1. Before servicing the vehicle, refer to the Precautions Section.

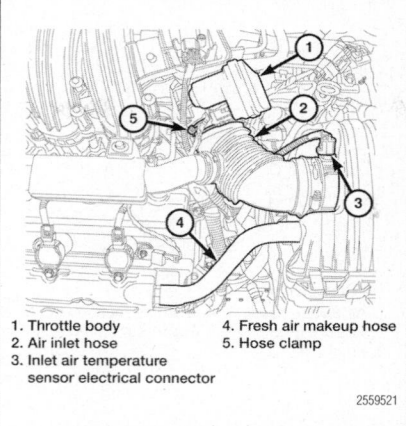

1. Throttle body
2. Air inlet hose
3. Inlet air temperature sensor electrical connector
4. Fresh air makeup hose
5. Hose clamp

2559521

Fig. 72 Removing the air inlet hose—2.7L engine

2. Disconnect and isolate the negative battery cable.

3. Disconnect the inlet air temperature sensor electrical connector.

4. Disconnect the fresh air makeup hose from the air cleaner housing.

5. Loosen the hose clamp at the throttle body. Remove the air inlet hose from the throttle body.

6. Disengage the wire harness connector from the starter cable support bracket.

7. Disengage the starter cable support bracket from the air cleaner housing.

8. Remove the air cleaner housing hold down fastener.

9. Pull the air cleaner housing straight up off of the locating pins.

To install:

10. Install the air cleaner housing straight down on the locating pins.

11. Install the air cleaner housing hold down fastener and tighten to 45 inch lbs. (5 Nm).

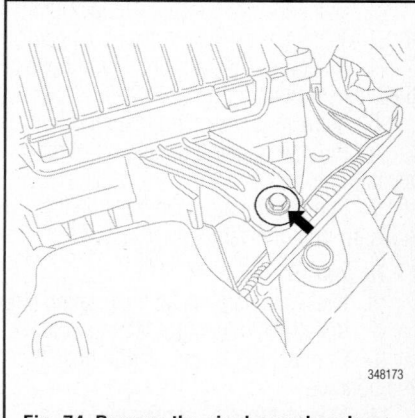

348173

Fig. 74 Remove the air cleaner housing hold down fastener and remove the air cleaner housing—2.7L engine

12. Engage the starter cable support bracket to the air cleaner housing.

13. Engage the wire harness connector to the starter cable support bracket.

14. Install the throttle body air inlet hose to the throttle body. Tighten the hose clamp to 35 inch lbs. (4 Nm).

15. Connect the fresh air makeup hose.

16. Connect the inlet air temperature sensor electrical connector.

17. Connect the negative battery cable and tighten the nut to 45 inch lbs. (5 Nm).

3.5L Engine

See Figure 75.

1. Before servicing the vehicle, refer to the Precautions Section.

2. Remove the air inlet hose at the throttle body.

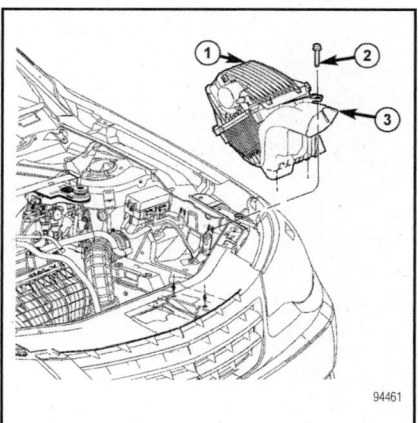

94461

Fig. 71 View of air cleaner housing (1) and retaining bolt (2)—2.4L engine

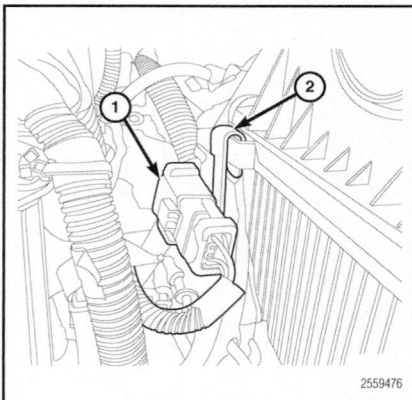

2559476

Fig. 73 Disengage the wire harness connector (1) from the starter cable support bracket (2)—2.7L engine

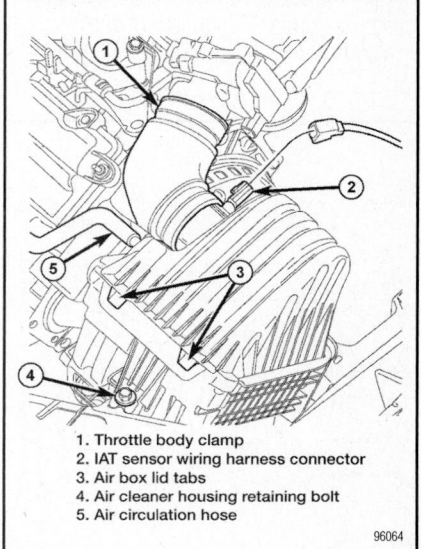

1. Throttle body clamp
2. IAT sensor wiring harness connector
3. Air box lid tabs
4. Air cleaner housing retaining bolt
5. Air circulation hose

96064

Fig. 75 View of the air cleaner housing—3.5L engine

3. Disconnect the Intake Air Temperature (IAT) sensor wiring harness connector.

4. Disconnect the air circulation hose at the element housing.

5. Remove the housing retaining bolt.

6. Pull the housing up and off of the locating pin.

7. Remove the air cleaner element housing from the vehicle.

To install:

8. Install the housing on the locating pin.

9. Install the housing retaining bolt.

10. Connect the air circulation hose to the housing.

11. Connect the IAT sensor wiring harness connector.

12. Connect the air inlet hose to the throttle body and tighten the clamp.

3.6L Engine

See Figures 76 and 77.

1. Before servicing the vehicle, refer to the Precautions Section.

2. Disconnect and isolate the negative battery cable.

3. Remove the engine cover.

4. Disconnect the fresh air makeup hose from the air cleaner body.

5. Remove the push pin.

6. Remove the 2 bolts from the air cleaner body.

7. Loosen the clamp at the resonator and remove the air cleaner body from the vehicle

To install:

8. Engage the air inlet hose to the resonator and install the air cleaner body with the 2 bolts tightened to 80 inch lbs. (9 Nm).

9. Tighten the air inlet hose-to-resonator clamp to 35 inch lbs. (4 Nm).

10. Install the push pin.

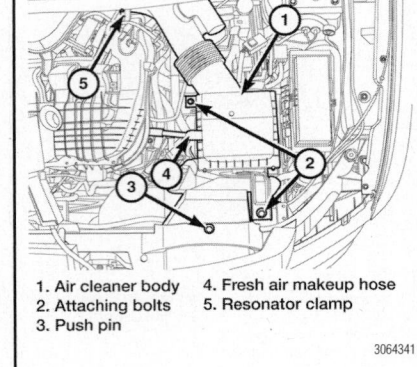

1. Air cleaner body   4. Fresh air makeup hose
2. Attaching bolts   5. Resonator clamp
3. Push pin

3064341

Fig. 77 View of air cleaner body removal—3.6L engine

11. Install the fresh air makeup hose to the air cleaner body.

12. Install the engine cover.

13. Connect the negative battery cable and tighten nut to 45 inch lbs. (5 Nm). Refer to Battery, removal & installation.

FILTER/ELEMENT REPLACEMENT

2.4L Engine

See Figures 78 and 79.

✳✳ WARNING

Do not use an assist tool or excessive force when unlocking the air box lid tabs. Excessive force may break the tabs off of the lid.

1. Before servicing the vehicle, refer to the Precautions Section.

2. Unlock the air box lid tabs and lift the air cleaner housing cover.

3. Pull the cover forward to disengage the rear tabs.

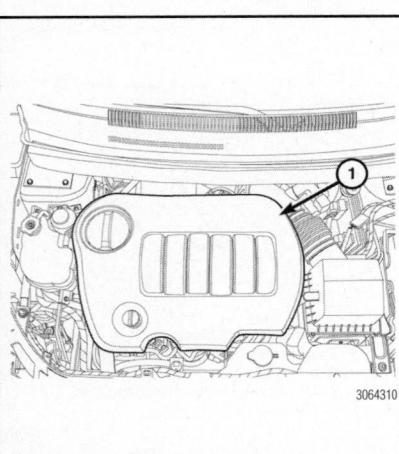

3064310

Fig. 76 Remove the engine cover (1)—3.6L engine

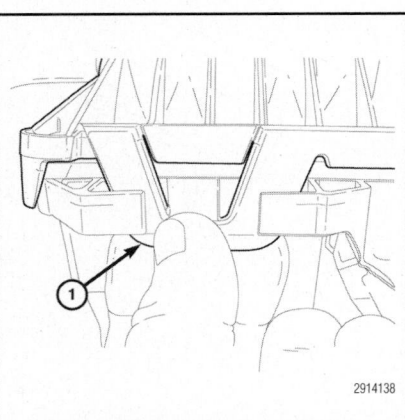

2914138

Fig. 78 Unlock the air box lid tabs and lift the air cleaner housing cover (1)—2.4L engine

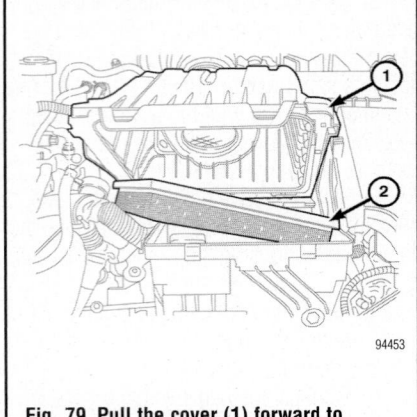

94453

Fig. 79 Pull the cover (1) forward to disengage the rear tabs and remove the air filter element (2)—2.4L engine

4. Remove the air filter element.

To install:

5. Install the air filter element into the air cleaner housing.

6. Install the cover so that the rear tabs insert into the lower air box.

7. Push down on the cover to engage the front locking tabs.

2.7L and 3.5L Engines

See Figure 80.

✳✳ WARNING

Do not use an assist tool or excessive force when unlocking the air box lid tabs. Excessive force may break the tabs off of the lid.

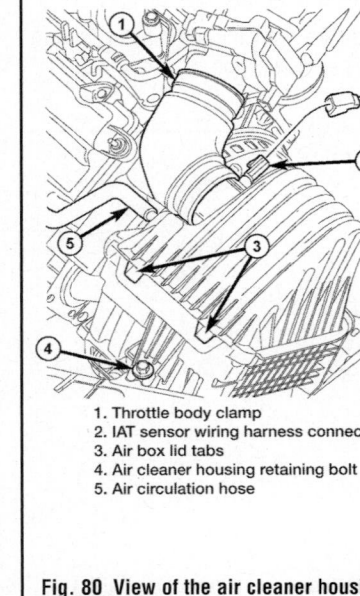

1. Throttle body clamp
2. IAT sensor wiring harness connector
3. Air box lid tabs
4. Air cleaner housing retaining bolt
5. Air circulation hose

96064

Fig. 80 View of the air cleaner housing—3.5L engine

1. Before servicing the vehicle, refer to the Precautions Section.

2. Unlock the air box lid tabs and lift the air cleaner housing cover.

3. Pull the cover forward to disengage the rear tabs.

4. Remove the air filter element.

To install:

5. Install the air filter element into the air cleaner housing.

6. Install the cover so that the rear tabs insert into the lower air box.

7. Push down on the cover to engage the front locking tabs.

3.6L Engine

See Figure 81.

1. Before servicing the vehicle, refer to the Precautions Section.

2. Disconnect the fresh air makeup hose from the air cleaner housing cover.

3. Loosen the 4 screws securing the air cleaner housing cover.

4. Lift the cover and remove the air cleaner element.

> ☀☀ **WARNING**

Do not use compressed air to clean out the air cleaner housing without first covering the air inlet to the throttle body. Dirt or foreign objects could enter the intake manifold causing engine damage.

5. Remove any dirt or debris from the bottom of the air cleaner housing.

To install:

6. Install the air cleaner element into the air cleaner housing.

7. Seat the cover onto the housing and tighten the 4 housing cover screws.

8. Connect the fresh air makeup hose to the air cleaner housing cover.

> **CAMSHAFT AND VALVE LIFTERS**

INSPECTION

1. Before servicing the vehicle, refer to the Precautions Section.

2. Inspect the camshaft bearing journals for damage and binding. If the journals are binding, check the cylinder head for damage. Also check the cylinder head oil holes for clogging.

3. Check the surface of the cam lobes for abnormal wear. Measure and compare the unworn area to the worn area. Replace camshafts that are not within specification.

REMOVAL & INSTALLATION

2.4L Engine

See Figures 82 through 88.

Special Tools
• Locking Wedge 9701

1. Before servicing the vehicle, refer to the Precautions Section.

2. Remove the engine cover by pulling upward.

3. Disconnect and isolate the negative battery cable.

4. Remove the cylinder head cover. Refer to Valve Covers, removal & installation.

5. Raise and safely support the vehicle.

6. Remove the frame cover portion of the right splash shield.

7. Rotate the engine to Top Dead Center (TDC).

8. Make sure the camshaft timing marks are in line with the cylinder head cover sealing surface.

9. Mark the chain link corresponding to the timing marks with a paint marker.

10. Remove the timing tensioner plug from the front cover.

11. Insert a small Allen® wrench through the timing tensioner plug hole and lift the ratchet upward to release the tensioner and push the Allen® wrench inward. Leave the Allen® wrench installed during the remainder of this procedure.

12. Insert Locking Wedge 9701 between the camshaft phasers.

13. Lightly tap Locking Wedge 9701 into place until it will no longer sink down.

➡**The camshaft bearing caps should have been marked during engine manufacturing. For example, number one exhaust camshaft bearing is marked E1.**

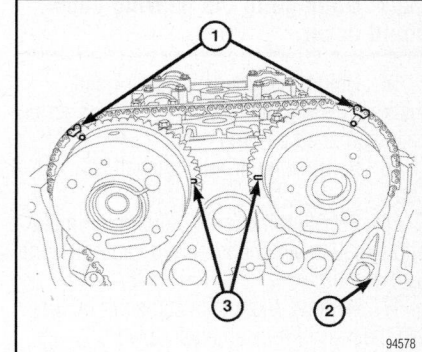

Fig. 83 Make sure the camshaft timing marks (3) are in line with the cylinder head cover sealing surface and mark the chain link corresponding to the timing marks (1). Cylinder head (2) shown—2.4L engine

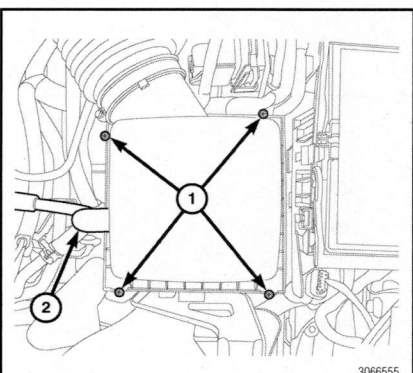

Fig. 81 Disconnect the fresh air makeup hose (2) and loosen the screws (1) securing the air cleaner housing cover—3.6L engine

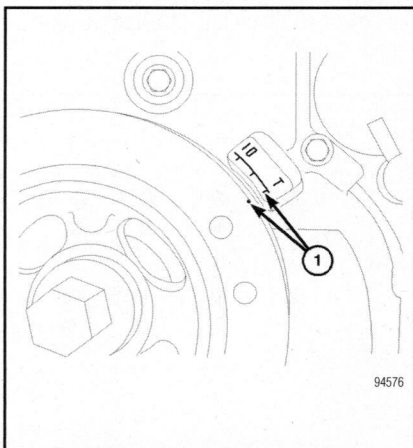

Fig. 82 Rotate the engine to Top Dead Center (TDC) (1)—2.4L engine

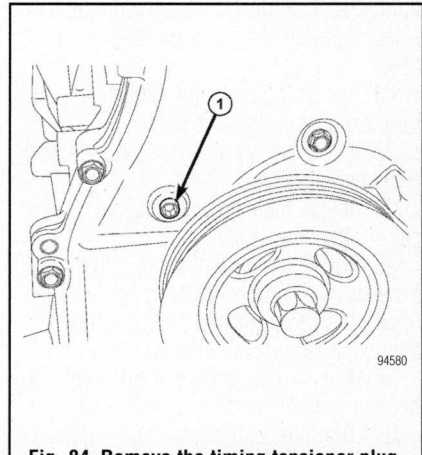

Fig. 84 Remove the timing tensioner plug (1) from the front cover

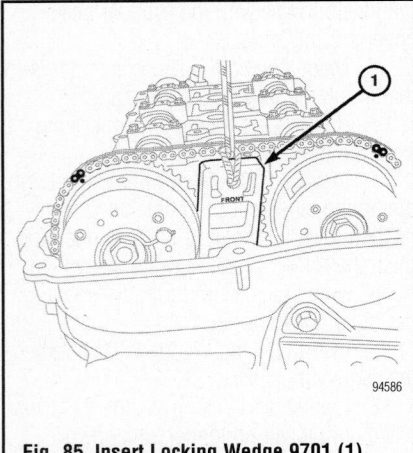

Fig. 85 Insert Locking Wedge 9701 (1) between the camshaft phasers

※※ WARNING

DO NOT use a number stamp or a punch to mark the camshaft bearing caps. Damage to the bearing caps could occur.

14. Using a permanent ink or paint marker, identify the location and position on each camshaft bearing cap.

15. Remove the front camshaft bearing cap.

16. Slowly remove the remaining intake and exhaust camshaft bearing cap bolts one turn at a time.

17. Remove the intake camshaft by lifting the rear of the camshaft upward.

18. Rotate the camshaft while lifting out of the front bearing cradle.

19. Lift the timing chain off the sprocket.

20. Remove the exhaust camshaft.

21. Secure the timing chain with wire so that it does fall into the timing chain cover.

To install:

22. The front camshaft bearing cap is numbered 1, 2, or 3, this corresponds to the select fit front exhaust camshaft bearing to use.

23. Install the corresponding select fit front exhaust camshaft bearing.

24. Oil all of the camshaft journals with clean engine oil.

25. Install the camshaft phasers on the camshafts, if removed.

26. Install the timing chain onto the exhaust cam sprocket making sure that the timing marks on the sprocket and the painted chain link are aligned.

27. Position the exhaust camshaft on the bearing journals in the cylinder head.

28. Align the exhaust cam timing mark so it is in line with the cylinder head cover sealing surface.

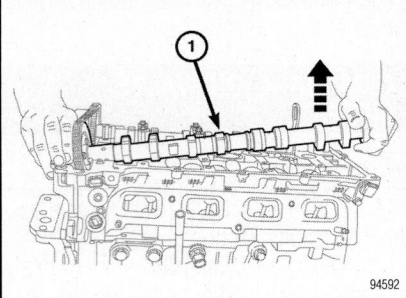

Fig. 86 Remove the intake camshaft (1) by lifting the rear of the camshaft upward

29. Install the intake camshaft by raising the rear of the camshaft upward and roll the sprocket into the chain.

30. Align the timing marks on the intake cam sprocket with the painted chain link.

31. Position the intake camshaft into the bearing journals in the cylinder head.

32. Verify that the timing marks are aligned on both the camshafts and that the timing marks are facing each other and are in line with the cylinder head cover sealing surface.

※※ WARNING

Install the front intake and exhaust camshaft bearing cap last. Ensure that the dowels are seated and follow the torque sequence or damage to the engine could result.

※※ WARNING

If the front camshaft bearing cap is broken, the cylinder head MUST be replaced.

33. Install the intake and exhaust camshaft bearing caps and slowly tighten the bolts to 85 inch lbs. (10 Nm) in the proper sequence.

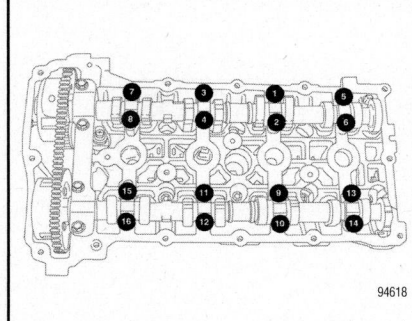

Fig. 87 Camshaft bearing cap bolt tightening sequence—2.4L engine

※※ WARNING

Verify that the exhaust bearing shells are correctly installed, and the dowels are seated in the head, prior to torqueing the bolts.

34. Install the front intake and exhaust bearing cap and tighten the bolts to 18 ft. lbs. (25 Nm) in the proper sequence.

35. Verify that all the timing marks are aligned.

36. Remove the Allen® wrench from the timing chain tensioner.

37. Remove Locking Wedge 9701 by pulling it straight upward on the pull rope.

38. Apply MOPAR® thread sealant to the timing tensioner plug and install.

39. Rotate the crankshaft CLOCKWISE 2 complete revolutions until the crankshaft is repositioned at the TDC position.

40. Verify that the camshaft timing marks are in the proper position and in line with the cylinder head cover sealing surface. If the marks do not line up, the timing chain is not correctly installed.

41. Install the right splash shield.

42. Remove any RTV from the gasket.

43. Inspect the cylinder head cover gaskets for damage. If no damage is present, the gaskets can be re-installed.

44. Install the cylinder head cover. Refer to Valve Covers, removal & installation.

45. Connect the negative battery cable. Refer to Battery, removal & installation.

46. Fill the cooling system. Refer to Engine Coolant, Drain & Refill Procedure.

47. Fill the engine with the proper type and amount of oil.

48. Operate the engine until it reaches the normal operating temperature. Check the oil and cooling systems for correct fluid levels.

49. Install the engine cover.

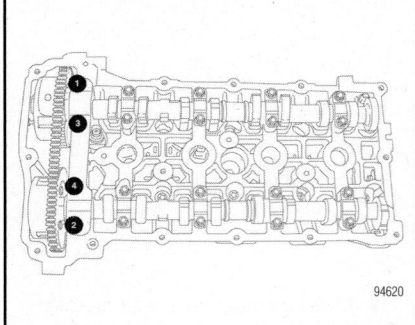

Fig. 88 Front intake and exhaust bearing cap tightening sequence—2.4L engine

2.7L Engine

See Figures 89 through 93.

➡The engine can be equipped with either conventional roller-type (early production) or silent type (late production) secondary timing chains.

1. Before servicing the vehicle, refer to the Precautions Section.
2. Remove the primary timing chain. Refer to Timing Chain & Sprockets, removal & installation.
3. Remove the secondary chain tensioner mounting bolts.

➡The camshaft bearing caps should have been marked during engine manufacturing. For example, number 1 exhaust camshaft bearing is marked 1E>.

4. Slowly loosen the camshaft bearing cap bolts in proper sequence.
5. Remove the camshaft bearing caps.
6. Remove the intake and exhaust camshafts, secondary timing chain, and secondary timing chain tensioner together as an assembly.
7. Remove the secondary timing chain tensioner and secondary timing chain from the camshafts.
8. Inspect the camshafts.

To install:

✳✳ WARNING

When the timing chain is removed and the cylinder heads are installed, DO NOT rotate the camshafts or crankshaft without first locating the proper crankshaft position. Failure to do so may result in valve and/or piston damage.

9. Assemble the camshaft chain on the cams ensuring that the plated links are

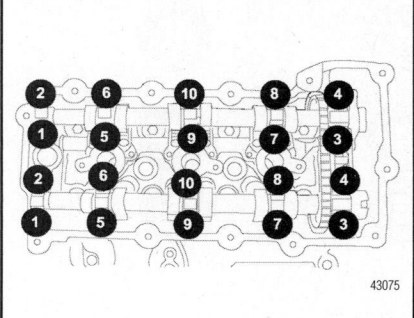

Fig. 89 Camshaft bearing cap bolt loosening sequence—2.7L engine

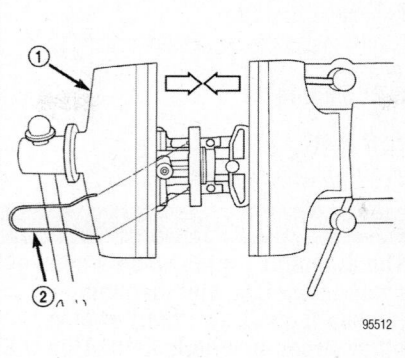

Fig. 90 Compress the tensioner in a soft jaw vise (1) until a lock pin (2) can be inserted—2.7L engine

aligned with the timing dot on the camshaft sprockets.

10. When the camshaft chain tensioner is removed, it is necessary to compress and lock the tensioner using the following procedures:

a. Place the tensioner into a soft jaw vise.

b. SLOWLY compress the tensioner until the fabricated lock pin, or the equivalent, can be inserted into the locking holes.

c. Remove the compressed and locked tensioner from the vise.

11. Insert the compressed and locked camshaft chain tensioner in between the camshafts and chain.

12. For engines equipped with roller chains (early production), rotate the cams so that the plated links and dots are facing the 12 o'clock position.

13. For engines equipped with silent chains (late production), rotate the cams so

Fig. 91 For engines equipped with roller chains (early production), rotate the cams so that the plated links (1) and dots (2) are facing the 12 o'clock position—2.7L engine

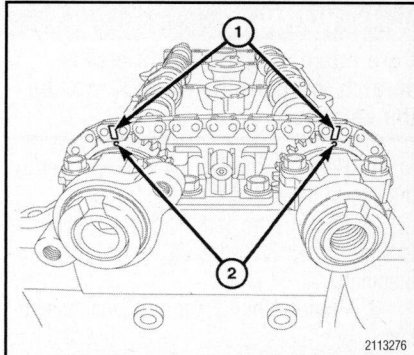

Fig. 92 For engines equipped with silent chains (late production), rotate the cams so that the marked links (1) and dots (2) are facing the 12 o'clock position—2.7L engine

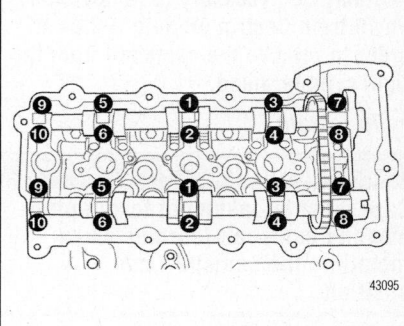

Fig. 93 Camshaft bearing cap bolt tightening sequence—2.7L engine

that the marked links and dots are facing the 12 o'clock position.

14. Install the cams to the cylinder head. Verify that the rocker arms are correctly seated and in proper positions.

15. Install the camshaft bearing caps. Verify that the bearing caps are installed in the same position as removed.

16. Tighten the cam bearing cap bolts gradually, in sequence, to 105 inch lbs. (12 Nm).

17. Install the secondary chain tensioner bolts and tighten to 105 inch lbs. (12 Nm).

18. Remove the locking pin from the secondary tensioners.

19. Verify the end play of the camshafts are within specification.

20. Install the primary timing chain. Refer to Timing Chain & Sprockets, removal & installation.

3.5L Engine

See Figure 94.

➡The camshafts are removed from the rear of the cylinder heads.

✳✳ WARNING

Care must be taken not to nick or scratch the journals when removing the camshaft.

1. Before servicing the vehicle, refer to the Precautions Section.
2. Remove the camshaft sprocket. Refer to Timing Belt & Sprockets, removal & installation.
3. Remove the rocker arm shaft assembly.
4. To remove the right camshaft, remove the EGR Valve assembly.
5. Remove the camshaft thrust plate(s).
6. Carefully remove the camshaft from the rear of the cylinder head.

➡It may be necessary to remove the Powertrain Control Module (PCM) in order to remove the camshaft from the right cylinder head.

To install:

✳✳ WARNING

Care must be taken not to scrape or nick the camshaft journals when installing the camshaft into position.

7. Lubricate the camshaft bearing journals, camshaft lobes, and camshaft seal with clean engine oil and install the camshaft into the cylinder head.
8. Install the camshaft sprocket. Refer to Timing Belt & Sprockets, removal & installation.
9. Install the camshaft thrust plate(s). Clean the mating surfaces and apply the appropriate sealer as necessary. Torque the fasteners to 21 ft. lbs. (28 Nm).

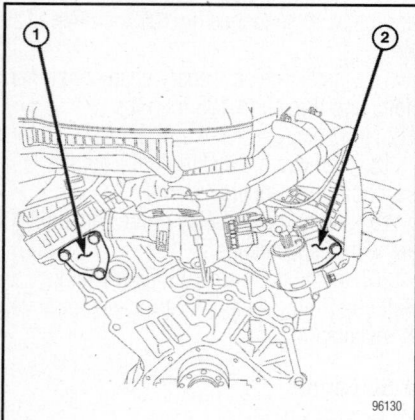

Fig. 94 Remove the camshaft thrust plate (1) or (2)—3.5L engine

10. If necessary, install the EGR Valve assembly and PCM.
11. Install the rocker arm assembly.

3.6L Engine

Left Bank

See Figures 95 through 98.

✳✳ WARNING

The magnetic timing wheels must not come in contact with magnets (pickup tools, trays, etc.) or any other strong magnetic field. This will destroy the timing wheels ability to correctly relay camshaft position to the camshaft position sensor.

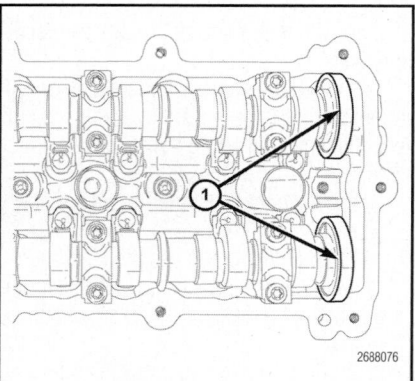

Fig. 95 The magnetic timing wheels (1) must not come in contact with and other magnetic objects (left bank)—3.6L engine

✳✳ WARNING

When the timing chain is removed and the cylinder heads are still installed, DO NOT forcefully rotate the camshafts or crankshaft independently of each other. Severe valve and/or piston damage can occur.

1. Before servicing the vehicle, refer to the Precautions Section.
2. Remove the left cylinder head cover. Refer to Valve Covers, removal & installation.
3. Remove the ignition coils. Refer to Ignition Coil, removal & installation.
4. Remove the spark plugs. Refer to Spark Plugs, removal & installation.
5. Remove the cam phasers.
6. Gently rotate the camshafts counterclockwise approximately 30° until the camshafts are in the neutral position (no valve load).

➡The camshaft bearing caps should have been marked during engine manufacturing. For example, the number 1 exhaust camshaft bearing cap is marked 1E-. The caps should be installed with the notch forward.

7. Slowly loosen the camshaft bearing cap bolts in proper sequence.

✳✳ WARNING

Do not stamp or strike the camshaft bearing caps. Severe damage may occur to the bearing caps.

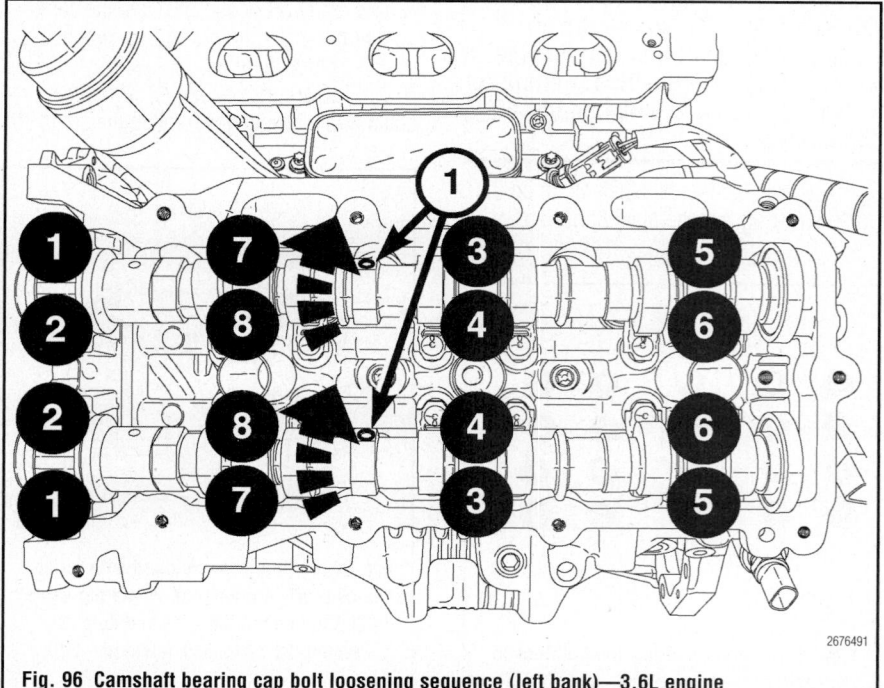

Fig. 96 Camshaft bearing cap bolt loosening sequence (left bank)—3.6L engine

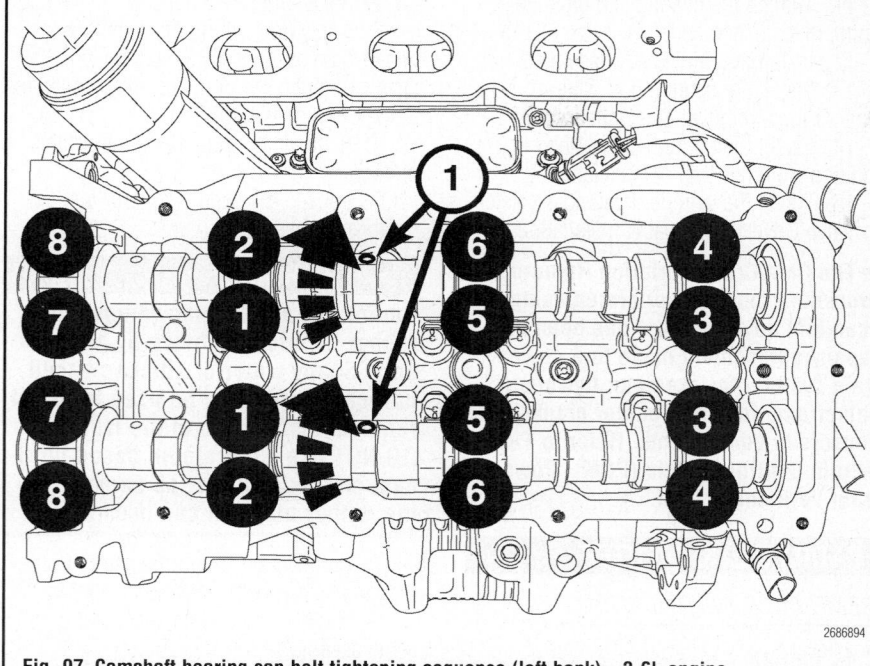

Fig. 97 Camshaft bearing cap bolt tightening sequence (left bank)—3.6L engine

➡When the camshaft is removed, the rocker arms may slide downward, mark the rocker arms before removing the camshaft.

8. Remove the camshaft bearing caps and the camshafts.

To install:

9. Lubricate the camshaft journals with clean engine oil.

10. Install the left side camshaft(s) approximately 30° counterclockwise from the Top Dead Center (TDC) position. This will place the camshafts at the neutral position (no valve load) easing the installation of the camshaft bearing caps.

11. Install the camshaft bearing caps and hand tighten the retaining bolts to 18 inch lbs. (2 Nm).

➡The caps are identified numerically (1–4), Intake or Exhaust (I or E) and should be installed from the front to the rear of the engine. All caps should be installed with the notch forward so that the stamped arrows on the caps point toward the front of the engine.

12. Tighten the bearing cap retaining bolts, in sequence, to 84 inch lbs. (10 Nm).

13. Rotate the camshafts clockwise to TDC by positioning the alignment holes vertically.

14. Install the left cam phasers.

15. Install the spark plugs. Refer to Spark Plugs, removal & installation.

16. Install the ignition coils. Refer to Ignition Coil, removal & installation.

17. Install the cylinder head cover. Refer to Valve Covers, removal & installation.

➡The Cam/Crank Variation Relearn procedure must be performed using the scan tool anytime there has been a repair/replacement made to a powertrain system, for example: flywheel, valvetrain, camshaft and/or crankshaft sensors or components. Refer to Powertrain Control Module (PCM), Powertrain Verification Test.

Right Bank

See Figures 99 through 101.

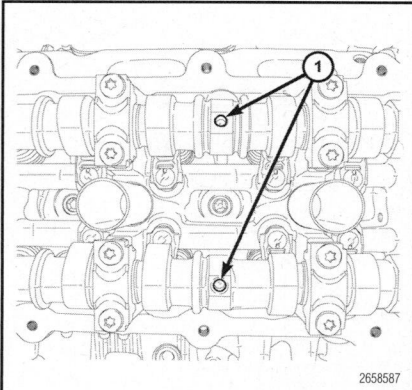

Fig. 98 Rotate the camshafts clockwise to TDC by positioning the alignment holes (1) vertically (left bank)—3.6L engine

The magnetic timing wheels (1) must not come in contact with magnets (pickup tools, trays, etc.) or any other strong magnetic field. This will destroy the timing wheels ability to correctly relay the camshaft position to the camshaft position sensor.

When the timing chain is removed and the cylinder heads are still installed, DO NOT forcefully rotate the camshafts or crankshaft independently of each other. Severe valve and/or piston damage can occur.

1. Before servicing the vehicle, refer to the Precautions Section.

2. Remove the right cylinder head cover. Refer to Valve Covers, removal & installation.

3. Remove the ignition coils. Refer to Ignition Coil, removal & installation.

4. Remove the spark plugs. Refer to Spark Plugs, removal & installation.

5. Remove the cam phasers.

➡The camshaft bearing caps should have been marked during engine manufacturing. For example, the number 1 exhaust camshaft bearing cap is marked 1E->. The caps should be installed with the notch forward.

6. Slowly loosen the camshaft bearing cap bolts in the proper sequence.

Do not stamp or strike the camshaft bearing caps. Severe damage may occur to the bearing caps.

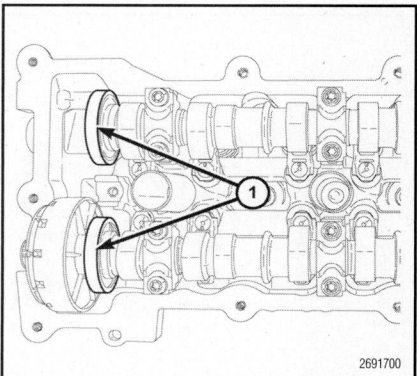

Fig. 99 The magnetic timing wheels (1) must not come in contact with and other magnetic objects (right bank)—3.6L engine

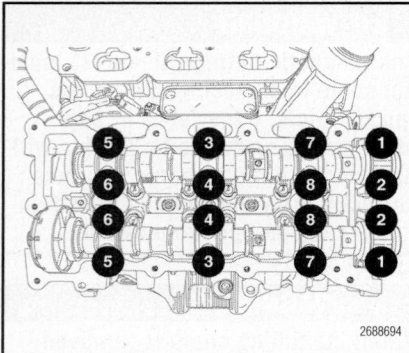

Fig. 100 Camshaft bearing cap bolt loosening sequence (right bank)—3.6L engine

➡When the camshaft is removed, the rocker arms may slide downward. Mark the rocker arms before removing the camshaft.

7. Remove the camshaft bearing caps and the camshafts.

To install:

8. Lubricate camshaft journals with clean engine oil.

9. Install the right side camshaft(s) at Top Dead Center (TDC) by positioning the alignment holes vertically. This will place the camshafts at the neutral position (no valve load) easing the installation of the camshaft bearing caps.

10. Install the camshaft bearing caps, hand tighten the retaining bolts to 18 inch lbs. (2 Nm).

➡The caps are identified numerically (1–4), Intake or Exhaust (I or E) and should be installed from the front to the rear of the engine. All caps should be installed with the notch forward so that the stamped arrows on the caps point toward the front of the engine.

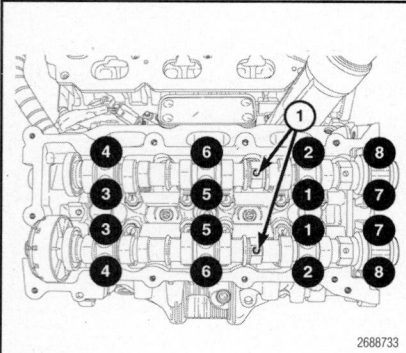

Fig. 101 Camshaft bearing cap bolt tightening sequence showing the vertical alignment holes (1) (right bank)—3.6L engine

11. Tighten the bearing cap retaining bolts, in sequence, to 84 inch lbs. (10 Nm).

12. Install the right cam phasers.

13. Install the spark plugs. Refer to Spark Plugs, removal & installation.

14. Install the ignition coils. Refer to Ignition Coil, removal & installation.

15. Install the cylinder head cover. Refer to Valve Covers, removal & installation.

➡The Cam/Crank Variation Relearn procedure must be performed using the scan tool anytime there has been a repair/replacement made to a powertrain system, for example: flywheel, valvetrain, camshaft and/or crankshaft sensors or components. Refer to Powertrain Control Module (PCM), Powertrain Verification Test.

CATALYTIC CONVERTER

REMOVAL & INSTALLATION

2.4L Engine

See Figures 102 and 103.

✳✳ CAUTION

The normal operating temperature of the exhaust system is very high. Therefore, never work around or attempt to service any part of the exhaust system until it is cooled. Special care should be taken when working near the catalytic converter. The temperature of the converter rises to a high level after a short period of engine operation time.

1. Before servicing the vehicle, refer to the Precautions Section.

2. Raise and safely support the vehicle.

3. Apply penetrating oil to the resonator/pipe assembly band clamp, and the fasteners that connect the catalytic converter to the exhaust manifold.

4. Remove the ground strap from the muffler.

5. Loosen the band clamp for the resonator/pipe assembly.

✳✳ WARNING

Do not use any tools to remove the rubber isolators, remove by hand only. Soapy water or silicone based lubricant spray may be used to assist removal/installation of the isolators. DO NOT use a petroleum based lubricant on the isolators, as damage to the rubber material can occur.

6. Remove the support isolators from the muffler/resonator assembly supports.

7. Remove the muffler/resonator pipe as an assembly.

8. Disconnect the oxygen sensor connector.

9. Remove the flange nuts at the exhaust manifold.

10. Remove the catalytic converter from the vehicle.

11. Remove and discard the gasket.

To install:

➡Always work from the front to rear of exhaust system when aligning and tightening exhaust system components.

12. Clean the manifold-to-converter sealing surfaces.

13. Position a new gasket on the exhaust manifold.

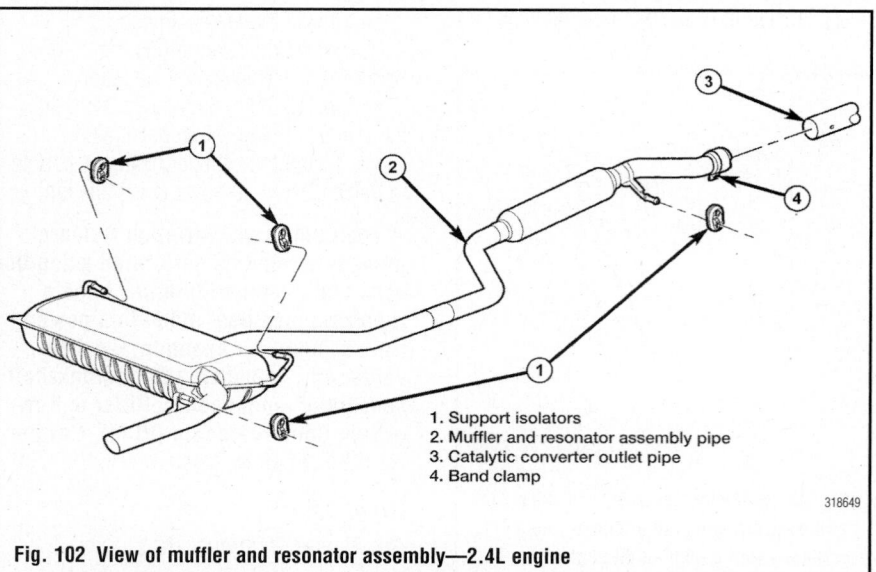

1. Support isolators
2. Muffler and resonator assembly pipe
3. Catalytic converter outlet pipe
4. Band clamp

Fig. 102 View of muffler and resonator assembly—2.4L engine

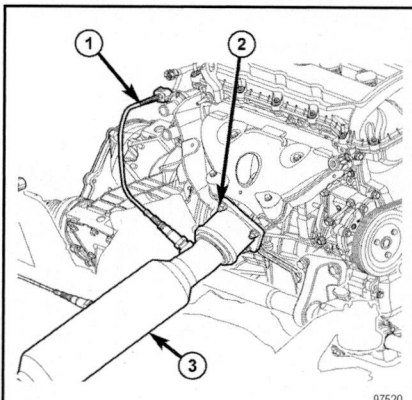

Fig. 103 View of catalytic converter (3), oxygen sensor connector, and exhaust fasteners (2)—2.4L engine

➡**If the catalytic converter is being replaced, transfer the downstream oxygen sensor to the new converter.**

14. Loosely attach the catalytic converter to the exhaust manifold.

15. Loosely install the resonator/pipe and muffler/pipe assembly to the catalytic converter outlet pipe.

16. Install the support isolators to the muffler supports.

17. Align the exhaust system to maintain the position and proper clearance with the underbody parts. All support isolators should have equal load on them. Tighten the fasteners attaching the catalytic converter to the exhaust manifold to 21 ft. lbs. (28 Nm).

18. Tighten the resonator/pipe assembly band clamp to 40 ft. lbs. (54 Nm).

19. Connect the ground strap to the muffler.

20. Lower the vehicle.

21. Start the engine and inspect for exhaust leaks. Repair exhaust leaks as necessary.

22. Check the exhaust system for contact with the body panels. Make the necessary adjustments, if needed.

2.7L Engine

This engine utilizes combined catalytic converter and exhaust manifold assemblies called maniverter assemblies. For service information, refer to Exhaust Manifold, removal & installation.

3.5L Engine

See Figures 104 and 105.

❊❊ **CAUTION**

The normal operating temperature of the exhaust system is very high.

Therefore, never work around or attempt to service any part of the exhaust system until it is cooled. Special care should be taken when working near the catalytic converter. The temperature of the converter rises to a high level after a short period of engine operation time.

1. Before servicing the vehicle, refer to the Precautions Section.

2. Raise and safely support the vehicle.

3. Apply penetrating oil to the resonator/pipe assembly band clamp, and the fasteners that connect the catalytic converter to the exhaust manifold.

4. Remove the ground strap from the muffler.

5. Loosen the band clamp for the resonator/pipe assembly.

❊❊ **WARNING**

Do not use any tools to remove the rubber isolators, remove by hand only. Soapy water or silicone based lubricant spray may be used to assist removal/installation of isolators. DO NOT use a petroleum based lubricant on the isolators, as damage to the rubber material can occur.

6. Remove the support isolators from the muffler/resonator assembly supports.

7. Remove the muffler/resonator pipe as an assembly.

8. Remove the flange nuts at the cross-under pipe.

9. Remove the catalytic converter from the vehicle.

10. Remove and discard the gasket.

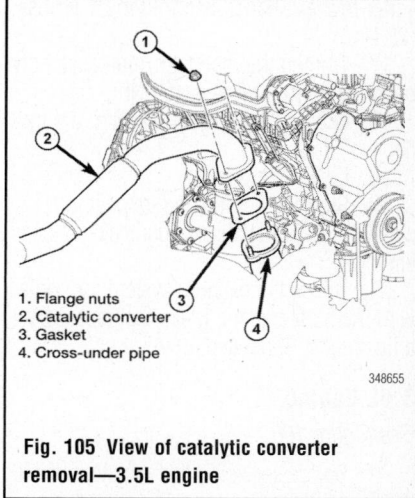

1. Flange nuts
2. Catalytic converter
3. Gasket
4. Cross-under pipe

Fig. 105 View of catalytic converter removal—3.5L engine

To install:

➡**Always work from the front to rear of the exhaust system when aligning and tightening the exhaust system components.**

11. Clean the cross-under to the catalytic converter sealing surfaces.

12. Position a new gasket on the cross-under pipe.

13. Loosely attach the catalytic converter to the cross-under pipe.

14. Loosely install the muffler/resonator assembly to the catalytic converter.

15. Install the support isolators to the muffler supports.

16. Align the exhaust system to maintain the position and proper clearance with the underbody parts. All support isolators should have equal load on them. Tighten the fasteners attaching the catalytic con-

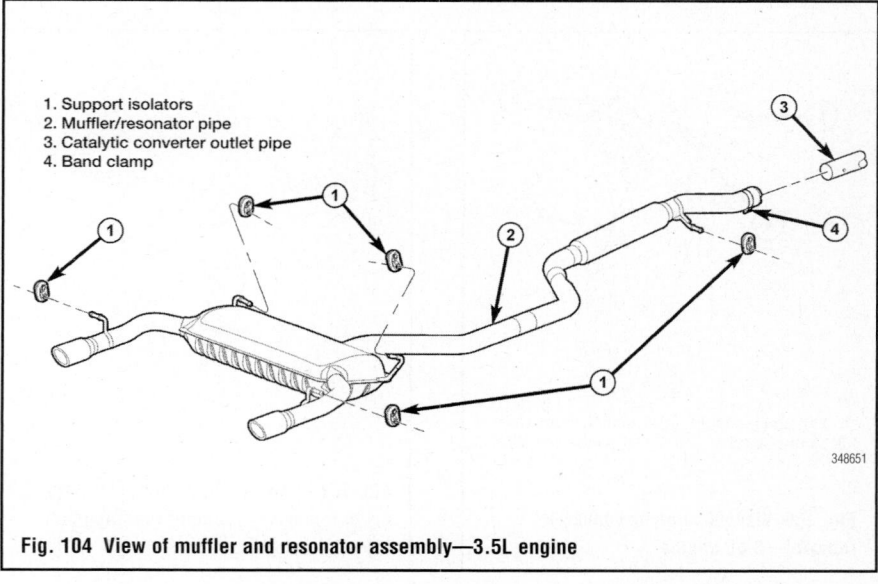

1. Support isolators
2. Muffler/resonator pipe
3. Catalytic converter outlet pipe
4. Band clamp

Fig. 104 View of muffler and resonator assembly—3.5L engine

verter to the exhaust manifold to 21 ft. lbs. (28 Nm).

17. Tighten the resonator/pipe assembly band clamp to 40 ft. lbs. (54 Nm).

18. Connect the ground strap to the muffler.

19. Lower the vehicle.

20. Start the engine and inspect for exhaust leaks. Repair exhaust leaks as necessary.

21. Check the exhaust system for contact with the body panels. Make the necessary adjustments, if needed.

3.6L Engine

See Figure 106.

1. Before servicing the vehicle, refer to the Precautions Section.

2. Remove the cross-under pipe from the vehicle.

➡The lower bolts for the converter flange are used to hold a guide retainer plate. The retainer does not need to be removed. The catalytic converter is held in by the plate and the upper bolts.

3. Disconnect the temperature and oxygen sensor electrical connectors.

4. Remove the catalytic converter to exhaust manifold upper bolts.

5. Remove the catalytic converter by lifting and sliding the flange up and away from the exhaust manifold.

6. Remove the temperature and oxygen sensors.

To install:

7. If gaskets need replacing, position a new gasket onto the manifold flange and install the lower retainer plate. Loosely install all 4 bolts to align the gasket.

Tighten the lower retainer bolts to 27 ft. lbs. (37 Nm).

8. Position the catalytic converter against the exhaust manifold. Position the converter flange to the retainer.

9. Install the upper flange bolts. Tighten the upper bolts to 27 ft. lbs. (37 Nm).

✲✲ WARNING

Be careful not to twist or kink the oxygen sensor wires.

10. Install the temperature and oxygen sensors. Connect the electrical connectors.

11. Install the cross-under pipe.

12. Start the engine and inspect for exhaust leaks. Repair exhaust leaks as necessary.

13. Check the exhaust system for contact with the body panels. Make the necessary adjustments, if needed.

CRANKSHAFT FRONT SEAL

REMOVAL & INSTALLATION

2.4L Engine

See Figures 107 through 109.

1. Before servicing the vehicle, refer to the Precautions Section.

2. Remove the accessory drive belt. Refer to Accessory Drive Belts, removal & installation.

3. Install the damper holder 9707 and remove the damper retaining bolt.

4. Pull the damper off the crankshaft.

5. Remove the front crankshaft oil seal by prying out with a screw driver. Be careful not to damage the cover seal surface.

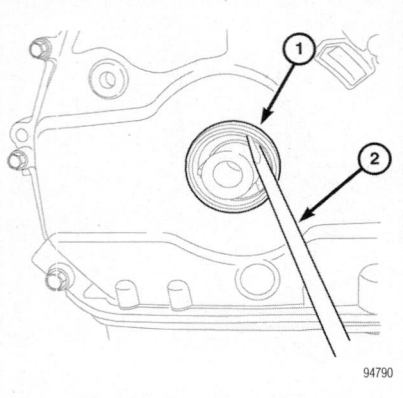

Fig. 108 Removing the front crankshaft oil seal (1) using a screw driver (2)—2.4L engine

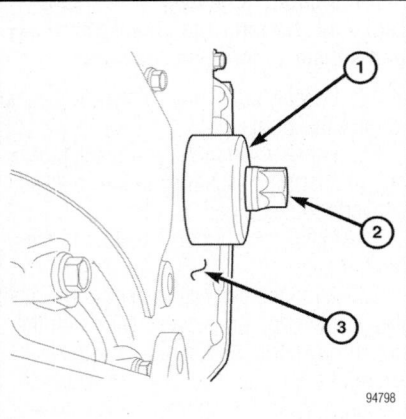

Fig. 109 Using the Seal installer 9506 (1) and the crankshaft damper bolt (2), press the seal until the seal installer seats against the timing chain cover (3)—2.4L engine

To install:

6. Place the seal onto the Seal installer 9506 with the seal spring towards the inside of the engine.

7. Install a new seal by using the Seal installer 9506 and the crankshaft damper bolt.

8. Press the seal into the front cover until the Seal Installer 9506 seats against the timing chain cover.

9. Remove the seal installer 9506.

10. Install the crankshaft vibration damper.

11. Oil the bolt threads and between the bolt head and washer.

12. Install the damper retaining bolt and damper holder 9707. Tighten the bolt to 155 ft. lbs. (210 Nm).

2.7L Engine

See Figures 110 and 111.

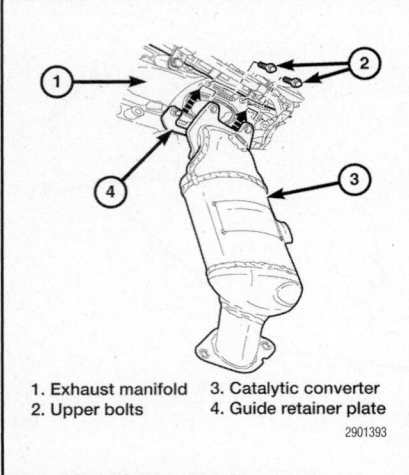

1. Exhaust manifold	3. Catalytic converter
2. Upper bolts	4. Guide retainer plate

Fig. 106 View of catalytic converter removal—3.6L engine

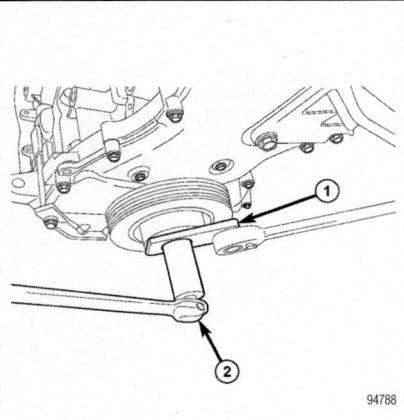

Fig. 107 Using the damper holder 9707 (1) to remove the damper retaining bolt (2)—2.4L engine

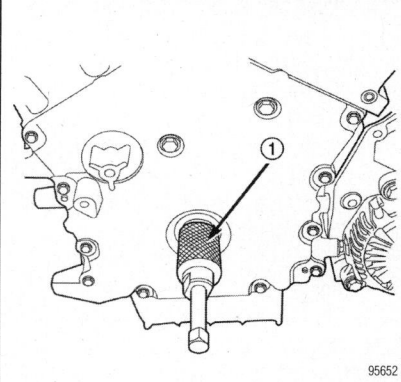

Fig. 110 Remove the crankshaft front seal using Special Tool 6771, Remover (1)— 2.7L engine

1. Before servicing the vehicle, refer to the Precautions Section.
2. Remove the crankshaft vibration damper.
3. Install Special Tool 8194 and insert it into the crankshaft nose.
4. Remove the seal using Special Tool 6771, Remover.

To install:
5. Install a new seal using Special Tools 6780-2 Sleeve, 6780-1 Installer, and 8179 Stud.
6. Install the crankshaft vibration damper.

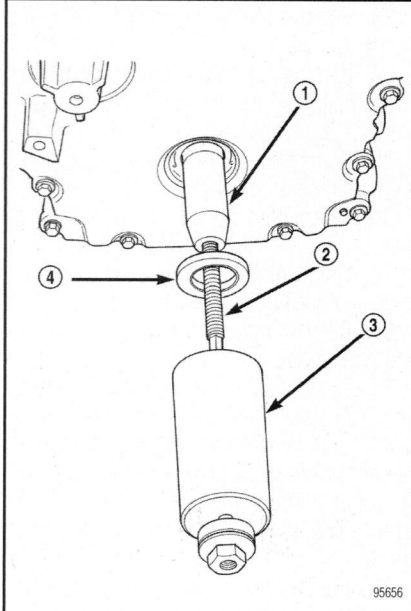

Fig. 111 Installing the crankshaft front seal (4) using Special Tools 6780-2 Sleeve (1), 6780-1 Installer (3), and 8179 Stud (2)—2.7L engine

3.5L Engine
See Figures 112 through 114.

1. Before servicing the vehicle, refer to the Precautions Section.
2. Remove the crankshaft sprocket. Refer to Timing Belt & Sprockets, removal & installation.
3. Tap the dowel pin out of the crankshaft.
4. Remove the crankshaft seal using Special Tool 6341A.

❊❊ WARNING

Do not nick the shaft seal surface or seal bore.

To install:
5. The shaft seal lip surface must be free of varnish, dirt or nicks. Polish with 400 grit paper if necessary.
6. Install the crankshaft seal using Special Tool 6342.

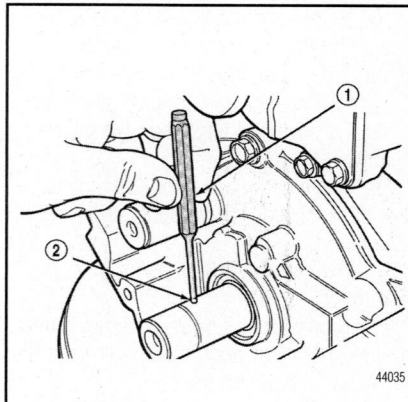

Fig. 112 Tap the dowel pin (2) out of the crankshaft using a punch (1)—3.5L engine

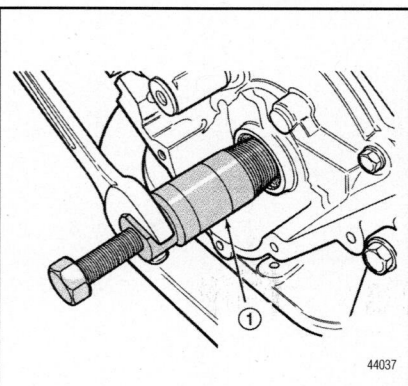

Fig. 113 Using Special Tool 6341A (1) to remove the front crankshaft seal—3.5L engine

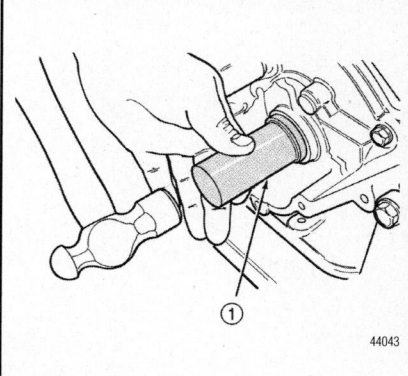

Fig. 114 Using Special Tool 6342 (1) to install the front crankshaft seal—3.5L engine

7. Install the dowel pin into the crankshaft to 0.047 inch (1.2mm) protrusion.
8. Install the crankshaft sprocket. Refer to Timing Belt & Sprockets, removal & installation.

3.6L Engine
See Figures 115 and 116.

1. Before servicing the vehicle, refer to the Precautions Section.
2. Remove the accessory drive belt. Refer to Accessory Drive Belts, removal & installation.
3. Remove the crankshaft vibration damper.
4. Install the sleeve from Seal Remover 8511 around the flywheel key and onto the nose of the crankshaft.
5. Screw the Seal Remover 8511 into the front crankshaft oil seal.
6. Install the extractor screw into the Seal Remover 8511. Hold the seal remover stationary and tighten the extractor screw

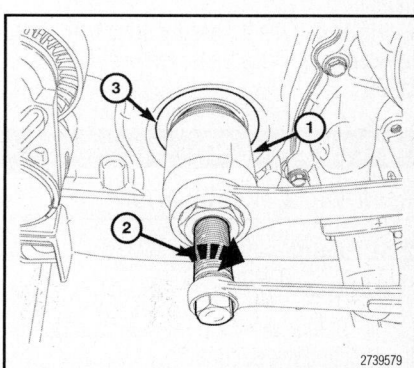

Fig. 115 Install the extractor screw (2) into the Seal Remover 8511 (1) and tighten the extractor screw against the sleeve until the front crankshaft oil seal (3) is removed—3.6L engine

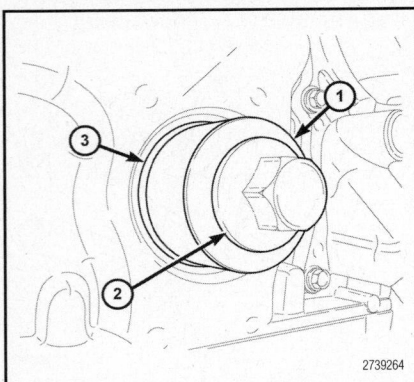

Fig. 116 Using the Front Crankshaft Seal Installer 10199 (1) and crankshaft vibration damper bolt (2) to install the front crankshaft oil seal (3)—3.6L engine

against the sleeve until the front crankshaft oil seal is removed from the engine timing cover.

To install:

7. Position the front crankshaft oil seal (3) into place on the engine timing cover.

8. Align the Front Crankshaft Seal Installer 10199 (1) to the flywheel key on the crankshaft and against the front crankshaft oil seal (3).

✳✳ WARNING

Only tighten the crankshaft vibration damper bolt until the oil seal is seated in the cover. Over-tightening of the bolt can crack the front timing cover.

9. Install and tighten the crankshaft vibration damper bolt (2) until the crankshaft oil seal is seated in the engine timing cover.

10. Install the crankshaft vibration damper.

11. Install the accessory drive belt. Refer to Accessory Drive Belts, removal & installation.

CYLINDER HEAD

REMOVAL & INSTALLATION

2.4L Engine

See Figures 117 through 128.

1. Before servicing the vehicle, refer to the Precautions Section.

2. Remove the engine cover by pulling upward.

3. Release the fuel system pressure. Refer to Relieving Fuel System Pressure.

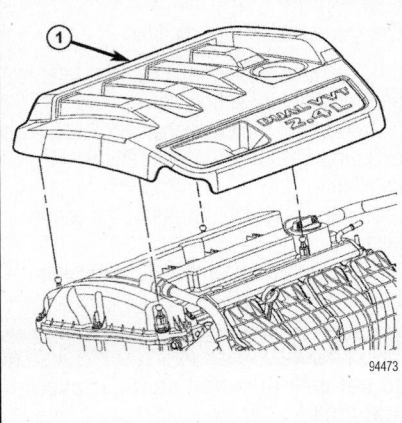

Fig. 117 Remove the engine cover (1) by pulling upward—2.4L engine

4. Disconnect and isolate the negative battery cable.

5. Drain the cooling system. Refer to Engine Cooling, Engine Coolant, Drain & Refill Procedure.

6. Remove the clean air hose and air cleaner housing. Refer to Air Cleaner, removal & installation.

7. Remove the coolant recovery bottle.

8. Remove and reposition the power steering reservoir.

9. Remove the accessory drive belt. Refer to Accessory Drive Belts, removal & installation.

10. Remove the power steering hose hold down.

11. Remove the 3 power steering pump mounting bolts through the openings in the pulley and reposition the pump.

12. Remove the cylinder head cover. Refer to Valve Covers, removal & installation.

13. Remove the ignition coils from the cylinder head cover. Refer to Ignition Coil, removal & installation.

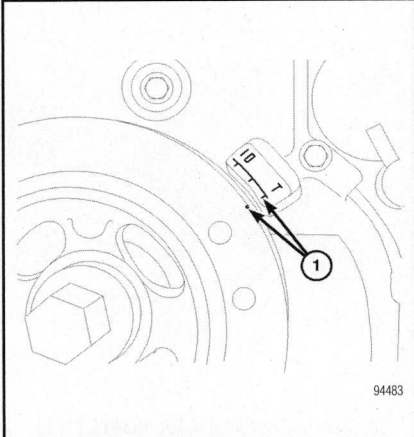

Fig. 118 Engine shown set to Top Dead Center (TDC) (1)—2.4L engine

14. Raise and safely support the vehicle.

15. Remove the frame cover portion of the right splash shield.

16. Set the engine to Top Dead Center (TDC).

17. Remove the lower A/C compressor bolts, if equipped.

18. Remove the lower A/C compressor mount, if equipped.

19. Remove the accessory drive belt lower idler pulley.

20. Remove the crankshaft damper.

21. Remove the 3 bolts and water pump pulley from the water pump.

22. Remove the lower bolt from the right side engine mount bracket.

23. Remove the timing chain cover lower bolts.

24. Remove the exhaust manifold. Refer to Exhaust Manifold, removal & installation.

25. Lower the vehicle.

26. Support the engine with a suitable jack.

27. Remove the right engine mount bracket retaining bolts.

28. Remove the retaining nuts and reposition the mount bracket.

29. Remove the accessory drive upper idler pulley.

30. Remove the right upper engine mount bracket.

31. Remove the accessory drive belt tensioner.

32. Remove the upper timing chain cover retaining bolts.

33. Remove the timing chain cover using the pry points.

34. Remove the tensioner and the timing chain. Refer to Timing Chain & Sprockets, removal & installation.

35. Remove the timing chain guide and the timing chain pivot guide.

36. Disconnect the fuel line from the fuel rail.

37. Unlock and disconnect the electrical connectors from the fuel injectors.

38. Remove the 2 fuel rail retaining bolts and remove the fuel rail.

39. Disconnect the electrical connectors from the coolant temperature sensor, oil temperature sensor, variable valve timing solenoids, camshaft position sensors, MAP sensor, manifold tuning valve, ignition interference suppressor, and electronic throttle control.

40. Remove the wiring harness retainer from the intake manifold and reposition the harness.

41. Remove the throttle body support bracket.

42. Disconnect the vacuum lines at the intake.

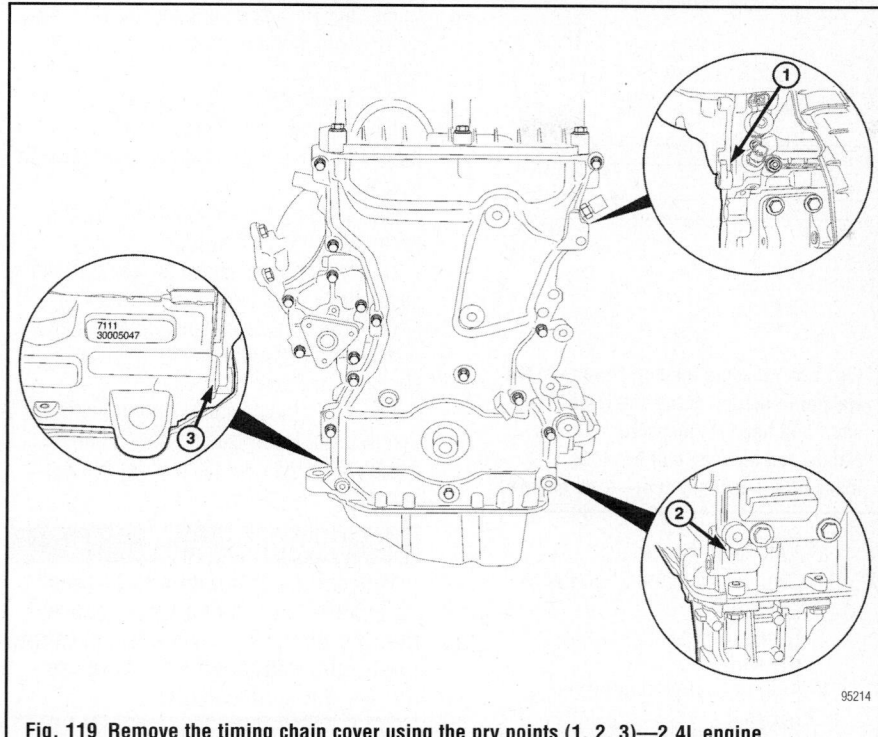

Fig. 119 Remove the timing chain cover using the pry points (1, 2, 3)—2.4L engine

43. Remove the intake manifold retaining bolts and remove the intake manifold. Refer to Intake Manifold, removal & installation.

44. Remove the 4 bolts and reposition the coolant adapter.

45. Remove the ground strap at the right rear of the cylinder head, if equipped.

➡The camshaft bearing caps should have been marked during engine manufacturing. For example, number 1 exhaust camshaft bearing is marked E1.

※ WARNING
DO NOT use a number stamp or a punch to mark the camshaft bearing caps. Damage to the bearing caps could occur.

46. Using a permanent ink or paint marker, identify the location and position on each camshaft bearing cap.

47. Remove the front camshaft bearing cap.

48. Slowly remove the remaining intake and exhaust camshaft bearing cap bolts one turn at a time.

49. Remove the camshafts.

➡All of the cylinder head bolts have captured washers EXCEPT the front two.

50. Remove the cylinder head bolts and the 2 uncaptured washers.

51. Remove the cylinder head from the engine block.

52. Inspect and clean the cylinder head and block sealing surfaces.

➡Ensure the cylinder head bolt holes in the block are clean, dry (free of residual oil or coolant), and the threads are not damaged.

To install:

※ WARNING
The cylinder head bolts are tightened using a torque plus angle procedure. The bolts must be examined BEFORE

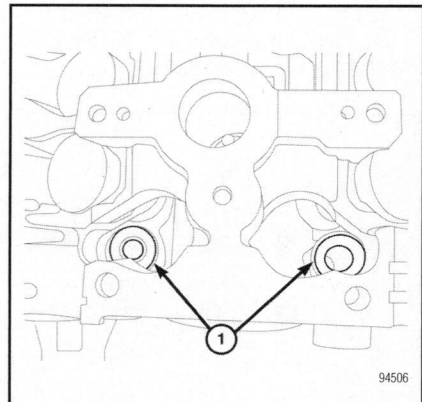

Fig. 120 All of the cylinder head bolts have captured washers EXCEPT the front two (1) shown—2.4L engine

reuse. If the threads are necked down, the bolts must be replaced.

53. Check the cylinder head bolts for necking by holding a scale or straight edge against the threads. If all the threads do not contact the scale, the bolt must be replaced.

※ WARNING
Always replace the variable valve timing filter screen when servicing the head gasket or engine damage could result.

54. Replace the variable valve timing filter screen.

➡When using RTV, the sealing surfaces must be clean and free from grease and oil. The parts should be assembled in 10 minutes and tighten to final torque within 45 minutes.

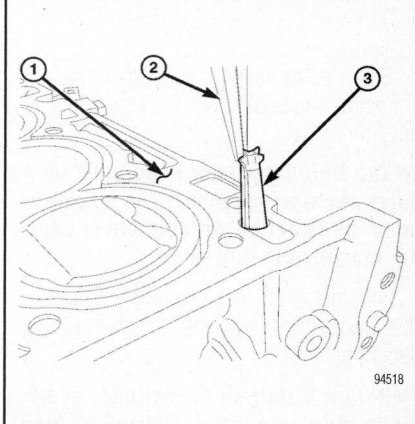

Fig. 121 Replace the variable valve timing filter screen (3) from the block (1) using a needle-nosed pliers (2)–2.4L engine

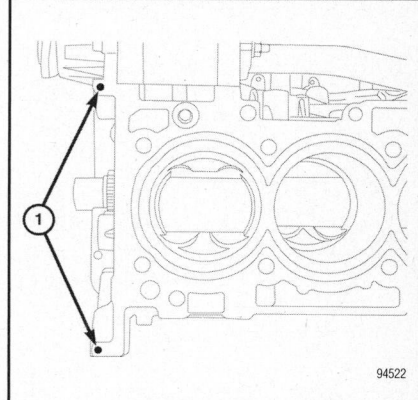

Fig. 122 Place 2 pea size dots of engine sealant RTV (1) on the cylinder block—2.4L engine

55. Place 2 pea size dots of MOPAR® engine sealant RTV, or equivalent, on the cylinder block.

56. Position the new cylinder head gasket on the engine block with the part number facing up. Ensure the gasket is seated over the locating dowels in the block.

57. Place 2 pea size dots of MOPAR® engine sealant RTV, or equivalent, on the cylinder head gasket.

➡️**The head must be installed within 15 minutes before the RTV skins.**

58. Position the cylinder head onto the engine block.

➡️**This engine was built with 2 different style cylinder head bolts. Each style bolt requires a different torque value. The bolts can be identified by the short bolt head and the long bolt head.**

59. Measure the bolt head from the washer to the top of the bolt head. The short bolt head measures ⁵⁄₁₆ inch (8mm) and the long bolt head measures ½ inch (13mm).

60. Identify whether the engine has the short head design or the long head design.

➡️**The front 2 cylinder head bolts do not have captured washers. The washers must be installed with the bevel edge up towards the bolt head.**

61. Install the washers for the front 2 cylinder head bolts with the beveled edge facing up.

➡️**Before installing the cylinder head bolts, lubricate the threads with clean engine oil.**

62. Install the cylinder head bolts and tighten in sequence.

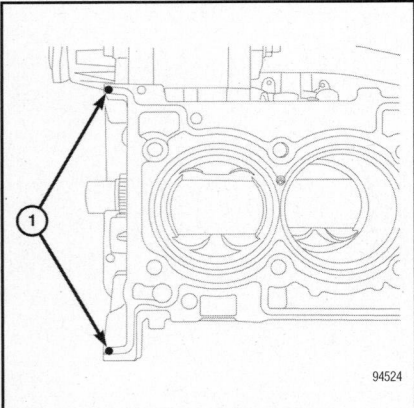

Fig. 123 Place 2 pea size dots of engine sealant RTV (1) on the cylinder head gasket—2.4L engine

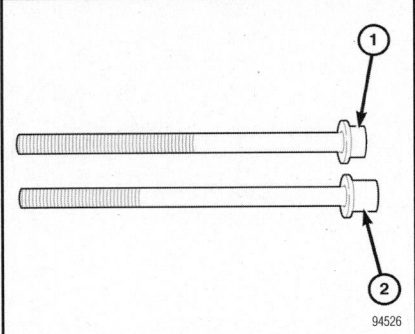

Fig. 124 Measure the bolt head from the washer to the top of the bolt head. The short bolt head (1) measures ⁵⁄₁₆ inch (8mm) and the long bolt head (2) measures ½ inch (13mm)—2.4L engine

a. With short head bolts:
- Step 1: Tighten to 25 ft. lbs. (30 Nm)
- Step 2: Tighten to 45 ft. lbs. (61 Nm)
- Step 3: Tighten to 45 ft. lbs. (61 Nm)
- Step 4: Tighten an additional 90°

✳✳ **WARNING**

Do not use a torque wrench for Step 4.

b. With long head bolts:
- Step 1: Tighten to 25 ft. lbs. (30 Nm)
- Step 2: Tighten to 54 ft. lbs. (73 Nm)
- Step 3: Tighten to 54 ft. lbs. (73 Nm)
- Step 4: Tighten an additional 90°

✳✳ **WARNING**

Do not use a torque wrench for Step 4.

63. Clean the excess RTV from the timing chain cover sealing surface.

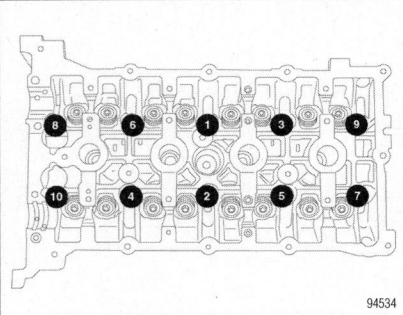

Fig. 125 Cylinder head bolt tightening sequence—2.4L engine

64. Install the coolant adapter with new seals. Tighten the bolts to 13 ft. lbs. (18 Nm).

65. The front camshaft bearing cap is numbered 1, 2, or 3. This corresponds to the select fit front exhaust camshaft bearing to use.

66. Install the corresponding select fit front exhaust camshaft bearing.

67. Oil all of the camshaft journals with clean engine oil.

68. Position the exhaust camshaft and intake camshaft on the bearing journals in the cylinder head.

69. Align the camshaft timing marks so that they are facing each other and are in line with the cylinder head cover sealing surface.

✳✳ **WARNING**

Install the front intake and exhaust camshaft bearing cap last. Ensure that the dowels are seated and follow the torque sequence or damage to the engine could result.

➡️**If the front camshaft bearing cap is broken, the cylinder head MUST be replaced.**

70. Install the intake and exhaust camshaft bearing caps and slowly tighten the bolts to 85 inch lbs. (10 Nm) in sequence.

✳✳ **WARNING**

Verify that the exhaust bearing shells are correctly installed, and the dow-

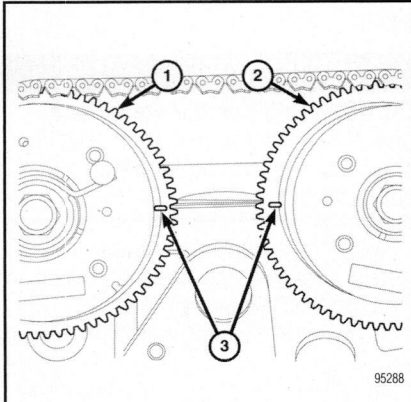

Fig. 126 Position the exhaust camshaft (1) and intake camshaft (2) on the bearing journals in the cylinder head. Align the camshaft timing marks (3) so that they are facing each other and are in line with the cylinder head cover sealing surface—2.4L engine

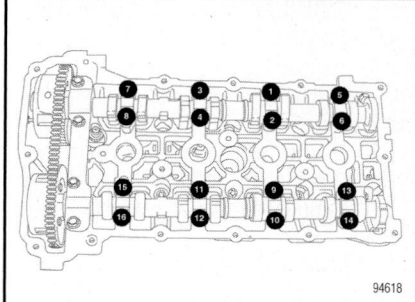

Fig. 127 Camshaft bearing cap bolt tightening sequence—2.4L engine

els are seated in the head, prior to torqueing the bolts.

71. Install the front intake and exhaust bearing cap and tighten the bolts to 18 ft. lbs. (25 Nm) in sequence.

72. Install the timing chain guide and tighten the bolts to 106 inch lbs. (12 Nm).

73. Install the moveable timing chain pivot guide and tighten the bolt to 106 inch lbs. (12 Nm).

74. Install the timing chain and tensioner. Refer to Timing Chain & Sprockets, removal & installation.

75. Install timing chain cover, engine mount, pulleys and accessory drive belt. Refer to Timing Chain Front Cover, removal & installation.

76. Install the cylinder head cover. Refer to Valve Covers, removal & installation.

77. Install the ignition coils. Refer to Ignition Coil, removal & installation.

78. Install the exhaust manifold. Refer to Exhaust Manifold, removal & installation.

79. Install the ground strap at the right rear of the cylinder head, if equipped.

80. Install the intake manifold, vacuum lines and fuel rail. Refer to Intake Manifold, removal & installation.

81. Connect the coil and injector electrical connectors.

82. Connect the electrical connectors to

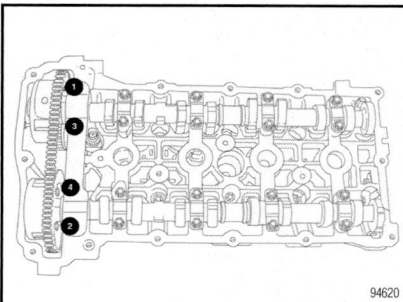

Fig. 128 Front camshaft bearing cap bolt tightening sequence—2.4L engine

the coolant temperature sensor, camshaft position sensors, oil temperature sensor, variable valve timing solenoids, MAP sensor, manifold tuning valve, ignition interference suppressor, and electronic throttle control.

83. Install the power steering pump reservoir. Tighten the mounting screw to 106 inch lbs. (12 Nm).

84. Install the coolant recovery reservoir. Tighten the mounting bolts to 89 inch lbs. (10 Nm).

85. Install the clean air hose and air cleaner housing. Refer to Air Cleaner, removal & installation.

86. Fill the cooling system. Refer to Engine Coolant, Drain & Refill Procedure.

87. Install a new oil filter and fill the engine with the proper type and amount of oil.

88. Connect the negative battery cable to the battery. Refer to Battery, removal & installation.

89. Operate the engine until it reaches the normal operating temperature. Check the oil and cooling systems for leaks and correct fluid levels.

90. Install the engine cover.

2.7L Engine

See Figures 129 and 130.

1. Before servicing the vehicle, refer to the Precautions Section.

2. Release the fuel system pressure. Refer to Relieving Fuel System Pressure.

3. Disconnect the negative cable from the remote jumper terminal.

4. Drain the cooling system. Refer to Engine Cooling, Engine Coolant, Drain & Refill Procedure.

5. Remove the accessory drive belts. Refer to Accessory Drive Belts, removal & installation.

6. Remove the crankshaft vibration damper.

7. Remove the exhaust cross-under pipe.

8. Remove the appropriate catalytic converter. Refer to Catalytic Converter, removal & installation.

9. Remove the oil pressure sensor heat shield. Disconnect the oil pressure sensor connector.

10. Remove upper and lower intake manifolds. Refer to Intake Manifold, removal & installation.

11. Remove cylinder head covers. Refer to Valve Covers, removal & installation.

12. Disconnect the camshaft position sensor and crankshaft position sensor connectors.

13. Reposition the engine wiring harness to the left side of the vehicle.

14. Remove the coolant outlet connector.

15. Remove the timing chain cover. Refer to Timing Chain Front Cover, removal & installation.

16. Rotate the crankshaft until the crankshaft sprocket timing mark aligns with the timing mark on the oil pump housing.

17. Remove the primary timing chain. Refer to Timing Chain & Sprockets, removal & installation.

18. Remove the upper primary timing chain guides.

19. Remove the camshaft bearing caps gradually in REVERSE sequence of installation. Refer to Camshaft and Valve Lifters, removal & installation.

20. Remove the camshafts and valvetrain components from the cylinder head. Note component locations for re-installation in the original locations.

21. For left cylinder head removal:

a. Remove the fastener securing the engine oil dipstick tube to the cylinder head. Remove the engine oil dipstick tube.

b. Remove the alternator. Refer to Alternator, removal & installation.

22. For right cylinder head removal:

a. Remove the cylinder head ground strap.

b. Disconnect the EGR valve electrical connector (if equipped).

❋❋ WARNING

Ensure that all the cylinder head bolts are removed before attempting the removal of cylinder head, as damage to cylinder head and/or block may occur.

23. Remove the cylinder head bolts in reverse sequence of installation.

24. Remove the cylinder head(s).

25. Remove and discard the cylinder head gasket.

26. Clean the cylinder head and block sealing surfaces.

To install:

➡The cylinder head bolts are tightened using a torque plus angle procedure. The bolts must be examined BEFORE reuse. If the threads are necked down, the bolts must be replaced

➡Necking can be checked by holding a straight edge against the threads. If all the threads do not contact the scale, the bolt must be replaced.

⁕⁕ **WARNING**

When cleaning the cylinder head and cylinder block surfaces, DO NOT use a metal scraper as the surfaces could be damaged. Use ONLY a wooden or plastic scraper.

27. Clean the sealing surfaces of the cylinder head and block.

28. Lubricate the bolt threads with clean engine oil.

29. Install a new head gasket over the locating dowels.

30. Install the cylinder head to the block, assuring the head is properly positioned over the locating dowels.

31. Tighten the bolts in sequence, using the following steps:

   a. Step 1: Bolts 1–8 to 35 ft. lbs. (48 Nm).

   b. Step 2: Bolts 1–8 to 55 ft. lbs. (75 Nm).

   c. Step 3: Bolts 1–8 to 55 ft. lbs. (75 Nm).

   d. Step 4: Bolts 1–8 plus 90° (Do not use a torque wrench for this step).

   e. Step 5: Bolts 9–11 to 21 ft. lbs. (28 Nm).

32. For left cylinder head installation:

   a. Install the engine oil dipstick tube.

   b. Install the alternator.

33. For right cylinder head installation:

   a. Install the cylinder head ground strap.

   b. Connect the EGR valve electrical connector (if equipped).

34. Install all valvetrain components and camshafts. Refer to Camshaft and Valve Lifters, removal & installation.

35. Install the primary timing chain, guides, and sprockets. Refer to Timing Chain & Sprockets, removal & installation.

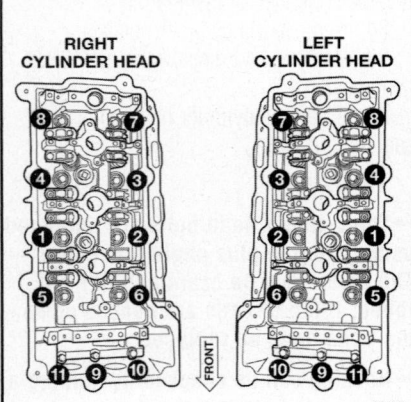

Fig. 129 Cylinder head bolt tightening sequence—2.7L engine

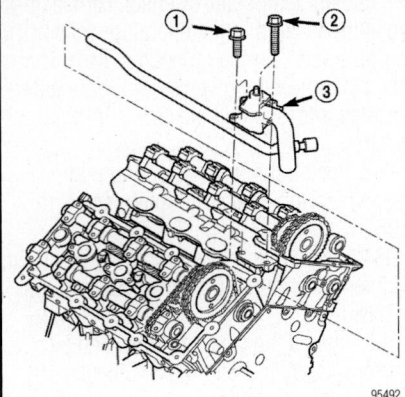

Fig. 130 Install the coolant outlet connector (3) and attaching bolts (1, 2)—2.7L engine

36. Install the coolant outlet connector.

37. Install the cylinder head covers. Refer to Valve Covers, removal & installation.

38. Connect the camshaft position sensor and crankshaft position sensor connectors.

39. Install the timing chain cover. Refer to Timing Chain Front Cover, removal & installation.

40. Install the crankshaft vibration damper.

41. Install the lower and upper intake manifolds. Refer to Intake Manifold, removal & installation.

42. Connect the oil pressure sensor connector. Install the oil pressure sensor heat shield.

43. Install the catalytic converter(s). Refer to Catalytic Converter, removal & installation.

44. Install the exhaust cross-under pipe.

45. Install the accessory drive belts. Refer to Accessory Drive Belts, removal & installation.

46. Fill the cooling system. Refer to Engine Coolant, Drain & Refill Procedure.

47. Connect the negative cable to the remote jumper terminal. Refer to Battery, removal & installation.

3.5L Engine

Left Side

See Figure 131.

1. Before servicing the vehicle, refer to the Precautions Section.

2. Remove the engine cover.

3. Release the fuel system pressure. Refer to Relieving Fuel System Pressure.

4. Disconnect the negative battery cable.

5. Drain the cooling system. Refer to Engine Coolant, Drain & Refill Procedure.

6. Remove the air cleaner element housing. Refer to Air Cleaner, removal & installation.

7. Remove the radiator fan assembly. Refer to Engine Fan, removal & installation.

8. Remove the coolant recovery container.

9. Remove the alternator. Refer to Alternator, removal & installation.

10. Disconnect the fuel line at the fuel rail.

11. Remove the upper intake manifold. Refer to Intake Manifold, removal & installation.

12. Remove the fuel rail.

13. Remove the lower intake manifold. Refer to Intake Manifold, removal & installation.

14. Raise and safely support the vehicle.

15. Remove the left exhaust manifold. Refer to Exhaust Manifold, removal & installation.

16. Remove the right front tire.

17. Remove the right inner splash shield.

18. Remove the crankshaft vibration damper.

19. Remove the lower accessory drive belt idler pulley.

20. Remove the power steering mounting bolts and set the pump aside.

21. Remove the lower outer timing belt cover bolts.

22. Remove the support and lower the vehicle.

23. Remove the upper accessory drive belt idler pulley.

24. Remove the accessory belt tensioner.

25. Support the engine with a block of wood and a floor jack.

26. Remove the upper engine mount.

27. Remove the power steering reservoir bolts and set the reservoir aside.

28. Remove the remaining outer timing belt cover bolts and remove cover.

29. Remove the timing belt. Refer to Timing Belt & Sprockets, removal & installation.

30. Remove the left cylinder head cover-to-cylinder head ground strap.

31. Remove the left cylinder head cover. Refer to Valve Covers, removal & installation.

32. Remove the left rocker arm assembly.

33. Hold the left cam gear and loosen the cam gear retaining bolt.

34. Remove the front timing belt housing-to-cylinder head bolts.

35. Remove the left camshaft thrust plate.

36. Carefully push the camshaft out of the back of the cylinder head approximately 3.5 inches (88.9mm). Remove the camshaft sprocket and bolt.

➡️**It may be necessary to raise the engine slightly in order to remove the camshaft sprocket bolt.**

37. Remove the cylinder head bolts in REVERSE of the tightening sequence.
38. Remove the cylinder head.
39. Clean and inspect all the mating surfaces.

To install:

❄️❄️ **WARNING**

When cleaning the cylinder head and cylinder block surfaces, DO NOT use a metal scraper as the surfaces could be damaged. Use ONLY a wooden or plastic scraper.

40. Clean the sealing surfaces of the cylinder head and block.

➡️**The cylinder head gaskets are not interchangeable between cylinder heads and are clearly marked right or left.**

41. Install the head gasket over the locating dowels. Ensure the gasket is installed on the correct side of the engine.

❄️❄️ **WARNING**

The cylinder head bolts are tightened using a torque plus angle procedure. The bolts must be examined BEFORE reuse. If the threads are necked down, the bolts must be replaced. Failure to replace a damaged bolt may lead to possible engine damage.

42. Inspect the cylinder head bolts for straightness, head damage, thread damage, and necking. Necking can be checked by holding a scale or straight edge against the threads. If all the threads do not contact the scale evenly the bolt must be replaced.
43. Install the cylinder head over the locating dowels.

➡️**Lightly lubricate the threads of the cylinder head bolts with clean engine oil prior to installation.**

44. Install the cylinder head bolts finger tight.
45. Tighten the cylinder head bolts in sequence using the following steps:
   a. Step 1: Tighten to 45 ft. lbs. (61 Nm).
   b. Step 2: Tighten to 65 ft. lbs. (88 Nm).
   c. Step 3: Tighten again to 65 ft. lbs. (88 Nm).
   d. Step 4: Tighten 90°. (Do not use a torque wrench for this step).

➡️**The bolt torque after a 90° turn should be over 90 ft. lbs. (122 Nm) in the tightening direction. If not, replace the bolt.**

46. Install the inner timing cover-to-cylinder head bolts. Tighten the bolts to 40 ft. lbs. (54 Nm).
47. Apply a light coat of clean engine oil to the lip of the camshaft oil seal and Seal Protector Sleeve 6788.

➡️**When installing the camshaft into the cylinder head, first insert the seal protector through the camshaft seal until the camshaft seats, then remove the Seal Protector Sleeve 6788 from the camshaft.**

48. Install the oil seal onto the camshaft using the Seal Protector Sleeve 6788 and install the camshaft into the cylinder head.
49. Install the camshaft sprocket. Hold the camshaft sprocket gear and tighten the camshaft sprocket bolt to 85 ft. lbs. (115 Nm), plus 90°. Refer to Timing Belt & Sprockets, removal & installation.
50. Install the rear camshaft thrust plate.
51. Rotate the left camshaft gear to the alignment mark on the rear timing belt cover. Check the right camshaft gear and crankshaft gear timing alignment marks.
52. Install the timing belt. Refer to Timing Belt & Sprockets, removal & installation.
53. Install the tensioner.
54. Install the timing belt front covers. Refer to Timing Belt Front Cover, removal & installation.
55. Install the power steering reservoir.
56. Install the crankshaft vibration damper.
57. Install the upper engine mount.

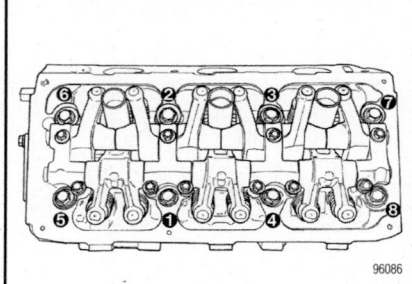

Fig. 131 Cylinder head bolt tightening sequence—3.5L engine

58. Install the accessory drive belt tensioner.
59. Install the lower accessory drive belt idler pulley.
60. Install the left exhaust manifold. Refer to Exhaust Manifold, removal & installation.
61. Install the exhaust cross over pipe.
62. Install the left rocker arm assembly.
63. Install the left cylinder head cover and ground strap. Refer to Valve Covers, removal & installation.
64. Install the lower intake manifold and gasket. Refer to Intake Manifold, removal & installation.
65. Install the fuel rail.
66. Install the upper intake manifold. Refer to Intake Manifold, removal & installation.
67. Connect the fuel line to the fuel rail.
68. Install the radiator cooling fan assembly. Refer to Engine Fan, removal & installation.
69. Install the radiator core support.
70. Install the radiator close out panel.
71. Install the air cleaner housing. Refer to Air Cleaner, removal & installation.
72. Install the engine cover.
73. Fill the cooling system. Refer to Engine Coolant, Drain & Refill Procedure.
74. Connect the negative battery cable. Refer to Battery, removal & installation.

Right Side

See Figure 132.

1. Before servicing the vehicle, refer to the Precautions Section.
2. Remove the engine cover.
3. Release the fuel system pressure. Refer to Relieving Fuel System Pressure.
4. Disconnect the negative battery cable.
5. Drain the cooling system. Refer to Engine Coolant, Drain & Refill Procedure.
6. Remove air cleaner element housing. Refer to Air Cleaner, removal & installation.
7. Remove the coolant recovery container.
8. Remove the alternator. Refer to Alternator, removal & installation.
9. Disconnect the fuel line at the fuel rail.
10. Remove the upper intake manifold. Refer to Intake Manifold, removal & installation.
11. Remove the fuel rail.
12. Remove the lower intake manifold. Refer to Intake Manifold, removal & installation.
13. Raise and safely support the vehicle.
14. Remove the right exhaust manifold.

Refer to Exhaust Manifold, removal & installation.

15. Remove the right front tire.

16. Remove the right inner splash shield.

17. Remove the crankshaft vibration damper.

18. Remove the lower accessory drive belt idler pulley.

19. Remove the lower outer timing belt cover bolts.

20. Remove the supports and lower the vehicle.

21. Remove the upper accessory drive belt idler pulley.

22. Remove the belt tensioner.

23. Support the engine with a block of wood and a floor jack.

24. Remove the upper engine mount.

25. Remove the power steering reservoir bolts and set the reservoir aside.

26. Remove the remaining outer timing belt cover bolts and cover.

27. Remove the timing belt. Refer to Timing Belt & Sprockets, removal & installation.

28. Remove the right valve cover-to-cylinder head ground strap.

29. Remove the EGR valve and tube assembly.

30. Remove the right cylinder head cover. Refer to Valve Covers, removal & installation.

31. Remove the right rocker arm and shaft assembly.

32. Hold the cam gear and loosen the right cam gear retaining bolt.

33. Remove the inner timing cover-to-right cylinder head retaining bolts.

34. Remove the right rear camshaft thrust plate.

35. Carefully push the camshaft out of the back of the cylinder head approximately 3.5 inches (88.9mm). Remove the camshaft sprocket and bolt.

➡️**It may be necessary to raise the engine slightly in order to remove the camshaft sprocket bolt.**

36. Remove the cylinder head bolts in the REVERSE of the tightening sequence.

➡️**Because of clearance restrictions when removing the right cylinder head, the front four cylinder head bolts must be loosened, raised, and supported with rubber bands before the cylinder head can be removed.**

37. Remove the cylinder head.

38. Clean and inspect all mating surfaces.

To install:

❄️❄️ WARNING

When cleaning the cylinder head and cylinder block surfaces, DO NOT use a metal scraper as the surfaces could be damaged. Use ONLY a wooden or plastic scraper.

39. Clean the sealing surfaces of the cylinder head and block.

➡️**The cylinder head gaskets are not interchangeable between the cylinder heads and are clearly marked right or left.**

40. Install the head gasket over the locating dowels. Ensure the gasket is installed on the correct side of the engine.

❄️❄️ WARNING

The cylinder head bolts are tightened using a torque plus angle procedure. The bolts must be examined BEFORE reuse. If the threads are necked down, the bolts must be replaced. Failure to replace a damaged bolt may lead to possible engine damage.

41. Inspect the cylinder head bolts for straightness, head damage, thread damage, and necking. Necking can be checked by holding a scale or straight edge against the threads. If all the threads do not contact the scale evenly the bolt must be replaced.

➡️**Before installing the cylinder head bolts, lubricate the threads with engine oil.**

42. Insert the front 4 cylinder head bolts into the cylinder head. Pull the bolts up to the top of their travel and retain with rubber bands.

43. Install the cylinder head over the locating dowels and finger tighten the head bolts.

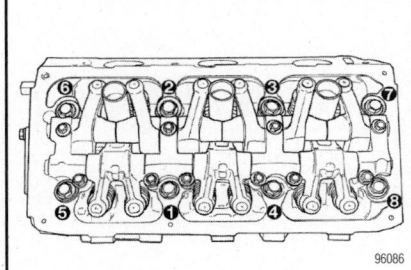

Fig. 132 Cylinder head bolt tightening sequence—3.5L engine

44. Tighten the cylinder head bolts in sequence using the following steps:

a. Step 1: Tighten to 45 ft. lbs. (61 Nm).

b. Step 2: Tighten to 65 ft. lbs. (88 Nm).

c. Step 3: Tighten again to 65 ft. lbs. (88 Nm).

d. Step 4: Tighten 90°. (Do not use a torque wrench for this step).

45. The bolt torque after the 90° turn should be over 90 ft. lbs. (122 Nm) in the tightening direction. If not, replace the bolt.

46. Install the inner timing cover-to-cylinder head bolts. Tighten the bolts to 40 ft. lbs. (54 Nm).

47. Apply a light coat of clean engine oil to the lip of the camshaft oil seal and the Seal Protector Sleeve 6788.

➡️**When installing the camshaft into the cylinder head, first insert the Seal Protector Sleeve 6788 through the camshaft seal until the camshaft seats, then remove the Seal Protector Sleeve 6788 from the camshaft.**

48. Install the camshaft using the Seal Protector Sleeve 6788 into the cylinder head.

49. Install the camshaft sprocket. Hold the camshaft sprocket gear and tighten the camshaft sprocket bolt to 75 ft. lbs. (102 Nm), plus 90°. Refer to Timing Belt & Sprockets, removal & installation.

50. Install the rear camshaft thrust plate.

51. Rotate the camshaft gear to the timing mark and verify the left camshaft gear and crankshaft gear timing marks are aligned.

52. Install the timing belt. Refer to Timing Belt & Sprockets, removal & installation.

53. Install the tensioner.

54. Install the timing belt outer cover. Refer to Timing Belt Front Cover, removal & installation.

55. Install the power steering reservoir.

56. Install the crankshaft vibration damper.

57. Install the upper engine mount.

58. Install the accessory drive belt tensioner.

59. Install the lower accessory drive belt idler pulley.

60. Install the right exhaust manifold. Refer to Exhaust Manifold, removal & installation.

61. Raise and safely support the vehicle.

62. Install the exhaust cross over pipe.

63. Install the catalytic converter and the exhaust system. Refer to Catalytic Converter, removal & installation.

64. Connect both oxygen sensors.

65. Lower the vehicle.

66. Install the right rocker arm assembly.

67. Install the right cylinder head cover and ground strap. Refer to Valve Covers, removal & installation.

68. Install the EGR valve and tube assembly.

69. Install the lower intake manifold and gasket. Refer to Intake Manifold, removal & installation.

70. Install the fuel rail.

71. Install the upper intake manifold. Refer to Intake Manifold, removal & installation.

72. Connect the fuel line to the fuel rail.

73. Install the air cleaner housing. Refer to Air Cleaner, removal & installation.

74. Install the engine cover.

75. Fill the cooling system. Refer to Engine Coolant, Drain & Refill Procedure.

76. Connect the negative battery cable. Refer to Battery, removal & installation.

3.6L Engine

Left Side

See Figures 133 through 136.

> ❊❊ **WARNING**
>
> **The magnetic timing wheels must not come in contact with magnets (pickup tools, trays, etc.) or any other strong magnetic field. This may destroy the timing wheels ability to correctly relay camshaft position to the camshaft position sensor.**

1. Before servicing the vehicle, refer to the Precautions Section.

2. Release the fuel system pressure. Refer to Relieving Fuel System Pressure.

3. Disconnect and isolate the negative battery cable.

4. Raise and safely support the vehicle.

5. Remove the belly pan.

6. Drain the cooling system. Refer to Engine Coolant, Drain & Refill Procedure.

7. Drain the engine oil.

8. Lower the vehicle.

9. Remove the engine cover.

10. Recover the refrigerant from the refrigerant system.

11. Remove the air cleaner body. Refer to Air Cleaner, removal & installation.

12. Remove the resonator.

13. Disconnect the heater core return hose.

14. Disconnect the left upstream oxygen sensor connector from the main wire harness.

15. Disengage the 2 upper wire harness retainers from the intake manifold support brackets.

16. Disengage the 2 lower wire harness retainers from the intake manifold support brackets.

17. Remove the nut, bolt, and the heater core return tube.

18. Remove the bolt and the oil level indicator tube.

19. Remove the upper and lower intake manifolds and insulator. Refer to Intake Manifold, removal & installation.

20. Remove the bolts and remove the LH upper intake manifold support brackets.

21. Remove the accessory drive belt. Refer to Accessory Drive Belts, removal & installation.

22. Remove the alternator. Refer to Alternator, removal & installation.

23. Remove the A/C compressor from the engine compartment.

24. Disconnect the ignition coil capacitor electrical connector.

25. Disconnect the Engine Coolant Temperature (ECT) sensor connector.

26. Disconnect the main harness from the engine injection/ignition harness at the rear of the left cylinder head.

27. Disconnect the main harness from the engine oil pressure/temperature harness at the rear of the left cylinder head.

28. Remove the spark plugs. Refer to Spark Plugs, removal & installation.

29. Remove the cylinder head covers. Refer to Valve Covers, removal & installation.

30. Remove the lower and upper oil pans.

31. Remove the crankshaft vibration damper.

32. Remove the engine timing cover. Refer to Timing Chain Front Cover, removal & installation.

> ❊❊ **WARNING**
>
> **When aligning the timing marks, always rotate the engine by turning the crankshaft. Failure to do so may result in valve and/or piston damage.**

33. Rotate the crankshaft clockwise to place the number 1 piston at Top Dead Center (TDC) on the exhaust stroke by aligning the dimple on the crankshaft with the block/bearing cap junction. The left side cam phaser arrows should point toward each other and be parallel to the valve cover sealing surface. The right side cam phaser arrows should point away from each other and the scribe lines should be parallel to the valve cover sealing surface.

> ❊❊ **WARNING**
>
> **Always reinstall the timing chains so that they maintain the same direction of rotation. Inverting a previously run chain on a previously run sprocket will result in excessive wear to both the chain and sprocket.**

34. Mark the direction of rotation on the timing chain using a paint pen or equivalent to aid in reassembly.

> ❊❊ **WARNING**
>
> **When the timing chains are removed and the cylinder heads are still installed, DO NOT rotate the camshafts or crankshaft without first locating the proper crankshaft position. Failure to do so may result in valve and/or piston damage.**

35. Reset the LH cam chain tensioner by lifting the pawl, pushing back the piston and installing Tensioner Pin 8514.

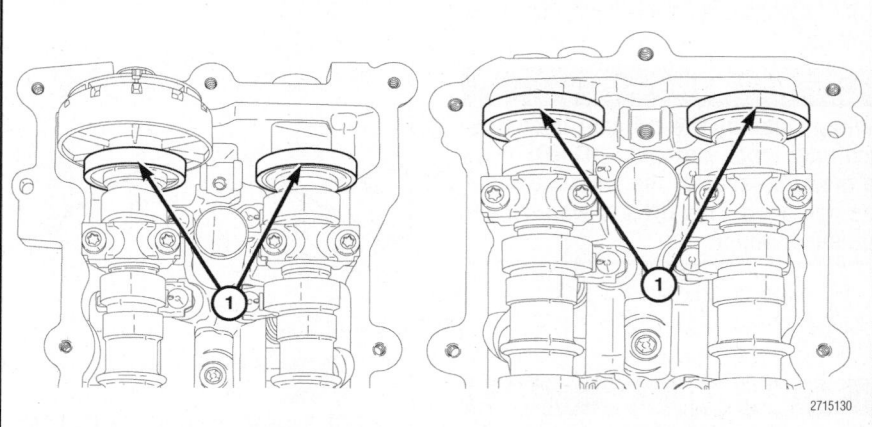

2715130

Fig. 133 The magnetic timing wheels (1) must not come in contact with any other magnetic device—3.6L engine

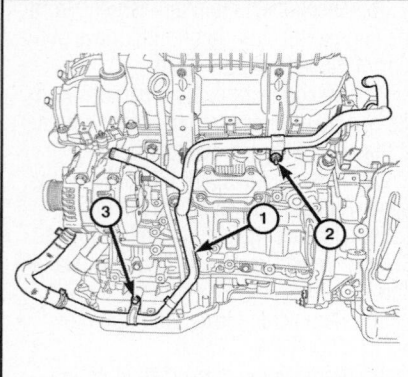

Fig. 134 Remove the nut (2), bolt (3), and the heater core return tube (1)—3.6L engine

➡**A minor rotation of a camshaft (a few degrees) may be required to install the camshaft phaser lock.**

36. Install the LH Camshaft Phaser Lock 10202.

37. Loosen both the intake oil control valve and the exhaust oil control valve.

38. Remove the LH Camshaft Phaser Lock 10202.

39. Remove the oil control valve from the left side exhaust cam phaser and pull the phaser off of the camshaft.

40. Remove the oil control valve from the left side intake cam phaser and pull the phaser off of the camshaft.

41. Remove the LH cam chain tensioner arm.

42. Remove two T30 bolts and the LH cam chain tensioner.

43. Remove two T30 bolts and the LH cam chain guide.

44. Remove the left camshafts. Refer to Camshaft and Lifters, removal & installation.

➡**If the rocker arms are to be reused, identify their positions so that they can be reassembled into their original locations.**

45. Remove the rocker arms.

➡**If the hydraulic lifters are to be reused, identify their positions so that they can be reassembled into their original locations.**

46. If required, remove the hydraulic lifters.

47. Remove the cylinder head retaining bolts in the proper sequence.

✳✳ **CAUTION**

The multi-layered steel head gaskets have very sharp edges that could

cause personal injury if not handled carefully.

➡**The head gasket crimps the locating dowels and the dowels may pull out of the engine block when the head gasket is removed.**

✳✳ **WARNING**

Do not lay the cylinder head on its gasket sealing surface, due to the design of the cylinder head gasket, any distortion to the cylinder head sealing surface may prevent the gasket from properly sealing resulting in leaks.

48. Remove the cylinder head and gasket. Discard the gasket.

49. If required, remove the Engine Coolant Temperature (ECT) sensor.

50. If required, remove the bolt and the ignition coil capacitor.

51. If required, remove the bolt and the engine wire harness retainer bracket.

To install:

52. If removed, install the Engine Coolant Temperature (ECT) sensor and tighten to 97 inch lbs. (11 Nm).

53. If removed, install the ignition coil capacitor with the M6 bolt tightened to 89 inch lbs. (10 Nm).

54. If removed, install the engine wire harness retainer bracket with a T30 bolt tightened to 106 inch lbs. (12 Nm).

➡**The cylinder head bolts are tightened using a torque plus angle procedure. The bolts must be examined BEFORE reuse. If the threads are necked down the bolts must be replaced.**

55. Check the cylinder head bolts for necking by holding a scale or straight edge against the threads. If all the threads do not contact the scale the bolt must be replaced.

✳✳ **WARNING**

When cleaning the cylinder head and cylinder block surfaces, DO NOT use a metal scraper as the surfaces could be damaged. Use ONLY a wooden or plastic scraper.

56. Clean and prepare the gasket sealing surfaces of the cylinder head and block.

✳✳ **WARNING**

Non-compressible debris such as oil, coolant, or RTV sealants that are not removed from bolt holes can cause

the aluminum casting to crack when tightening the bolts.

57. Clean out the cylinder head bolt holes in the engine block.

✳✳ **CAUTION**

The multi-layered steel head gaskets have very sharp edges that could cause personal injury if not handled carefully.

➡**The cylinder head gaskets are not interchangeable between the left and right cylinder heads and are clearly marked with R for Right and L for Left.**

58. Position the new cylinder head gasket on the locating dowels.

59. Position the cylinder head onto the cylinder block. Make sure the cylinder head seats fully over the locating dowels.

➡**Do not apply any additional oil to the bolt threads.**

60. Install the eight head bolts finger tight.

61. Tighten the cylinder head bolts in sequence, using the following steps:

a. Step 1: Tighten to 22 ft. lbs. (30 Nm).

b. Step 2: Tighten to 33 ft. lbs. (45 Nm).

c. Step 3: Tighten 75°. (Do not use a torque wrench for this step).

d. Step 4: Tighten 50°. (Do not use a torque wrench for this step).

e. Step 5: Loosen all the fasteners in reverse of the tightening sequence.

f. Step 6: Tighten to 22 ft. lbs. (30 Nm).

g. Step 7: Tighten to 33 ft. lbs. (45 Nm).

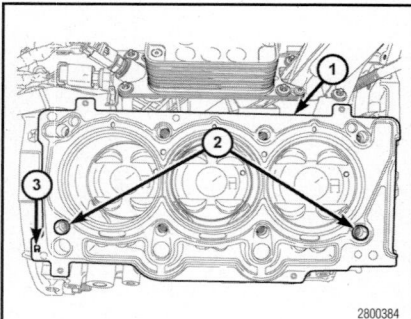

Fig. 135 The cylinder head gaskets are clearly marked with R for Right and L for Left (3). Position the cylinder head gasket (1) on the locating dowels (2)—3.6L engine

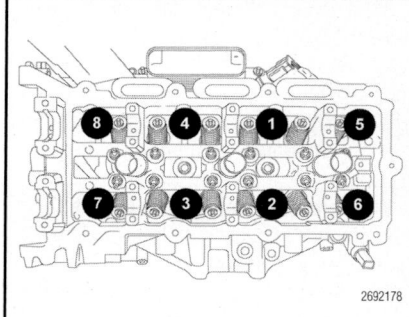

Fig. 136 Cylinder head bolt tightening sequence—3.6L engine

h. Step 8: Tighten 70°. (Do not use a torque wrench for this step).

i. Step 9: Tighten 70°. (Do not use a torque wrench for this step).

➡️**If the hydraulic lifters are being reused, reassemble them into their original locations.**

62. If removed, install the hydraulic lifters.

➡️**If the rocker arms are being reused, reassemble them into their original locations.**

63. Install the rocker arms and camshafts. Refer to Camshaft and Lifters, removal & installation.

64. Rotate the camshafts clockwise to TDC by positioning the alignment holes vertically.

65. Install the LH cam chain guide with two bolts. Tighten the T30 bolts to 106 inch lbs. (12 Nm).

66. Install the LH cam chain tensioner to the cylinder head with two bolts. Tighten the T30 bolts to 106 inch lbs. (12 Nm).

67. Reset the LH cam chain tensioner by lifting the pawl, pushing back the piston, and installing Tensioner Pin 8514.

68. Install the LH tensioner arm.

69. Press the LH intake cam phaser onto the intake camshaft. Install and hand tighten the oil control valve.

✳️ WARNING

Always reinstall the timing chains so that they maintain the same direction of rotation. Inverting a previously run chain on a previously run sprocket will result in excessive wear to both the chain and sprocket.

70. Drape the left side cam chain over the LH intake cam phaser and onto the idler sprocket so that the arrow is aligned with the plated link on the cam chain.

71. While maintaining alignment, route the cam chain around the exhaust and intake cam phasers so that the plated links are aligned with the phaser timing marks. Position the left side cam phasers so that the arrows point toward each other and are parallel to the valve cover sealing surface. Press the exhaust cam phaser onto the exhaust cam, install and hand tighten the oil control valve.

➡️**Minor rotation of a camshaft (a few degrees) may be required to install the camshaft phaser or phaser lock.**

72. Install the LH Camshaft Phaser Lock 10202 and tighten the oil control valves to 110 ft. lbs. (150 Nm).

73. Remove the LH Camshaft Phaser Lock 10202.

74. Remove the Tensioner Pin 8514 from the LH cam chain tensioner.

75. Rotate the crankshaft clockwise 2 complete revolutions stopping when the dimple on the crankshaft is aligned with the block/bearing cap junction.

76. While maintaining this alignment, verify that the arrows on the left side cam phasers point toward each other and are parallel to the valve cover sealing surface and that the right side cam phaser arrows point away from each other and the scribe lines are parallel to the valve cover sealing surface.

77. There should be 12 chain pins between the exhaust cam phaser triangle marking and the intake cam phaser circle marking.

78. If the engine timing is not correct, repeat this procedure.

79. Install the engine timing cover. Refer to Timing Chain Front Cover, removal & installation.

80. Install the crankshaft vibration damper.

81. Install the upper and lower oil pans.

82. Install the cylinder head covers. Refer to Valve Covers, removal & installation.

83. Install the spark plugs. Refer to Spark Plugs, removal & installation.

84. Connect the main harness to the engine oil pressure/temperature harness at the rear of the left cylinder head.

85. Connect the main harness to the engine injection/ignition harness at the rear of the left cylinder head.

86. Connect the Engine Coolant Temperature (ECT) sensor connector.

87. Connect the ignition coil capacitor electrical connector.

88. Install the A/C compressor to the engine compartment.

89. Install the alternator. Refer to Alternator, removal & installation.

90. Install the accessory drive belt. Refer to Accessory Drive Belts, removal & installation.

91. Install the LH upper intake manifold support brackets. Loosely install the studbolts.

92. Install the lower and upper intake manifolds and insulator. Refer to Intake Manifold, removal & installation.

93. Install the oil level indicator tube and the bolt. Tighten the bolt to 106 inch lbs. (12 Nm).

94. Install the heater core return tube, the nut, and bolt. Tighten the nut and bolt to 106 inch lbs. (12 Nm).

95. Engage the 2 lower and 2 upper wire harness retainers to the intake manifold support brackets.

96. Connect the left upstream oxygen sensor connector to the main wire harness.

97. Connect the heater core return hose.

98. Install the resonator and air cleaner body. Refer to Air Cleaner, removal & installation.

99. Evacuate and charge the refrigerant system.

100. Install the engine cover.

101. If removed, install the oil filter and fill the engine crankcase with the proper type and amount of oil.

102. Fill the cooling system. Refer to Engine Coolant, Drain & Refill Procedure.

103. Raise and safely support the vehicle.

104. Install the belly pan.

105. Lower the vehicle.

106. Connect the negative battery cable and tighten the nut to 45 inch lbs. (5 Nm).

107. Run the engine until it reaches the normal operating temperature. Check the cooling system for correct fluid level.

➡️**The Cam/Crank Variation Relearn procedure must be performed using the scan tool anytime there has been a repair/replacement made to a powertrain system, for example: flywheel, valvetrain, camshaft and/or crankshaft sensors or components. Refer to Powertrain Control Module (PCM), Powertrain Verification Test.**

Right Side

See Figures 137 through 139.

✳️ WARNING

The magnetic timing wheels must not come in contact with magnets (pickup tools, trays, etc.) or any other strong magnetic field. This may destroy the timing wheels ability to correctly relay camshaft position to the camshaft position sensor.

1. Before servicing the vehicle, refer to the Precautions Section.

2. Release the fuel system pressure. Refer to Relieving Fuel System Pressure.

3. Disconnect and isolate the negative battery cable.

4. Raise and safely support the vehicle.

5. Remove the belly pan.

6. Drain the cooling system. Refer to Engine Coolant, Drain & Refill Procedure.

7. Drain the engine oil.

8. Lower the vehicle.

9. Remove the engine cover.

10. Recover the refrigerant from the refrigerant system.

11. Remove the air cleaner body. Refer to Air Cleaner, removal & installation.

12. Remove the resonator.

13. Remove the upper and lower intake manifolds and insulator. Refer to Intake Manifold, removal & installation.

14. Remove the accessory drive belt. Refer to Accessory Drive Belts, removal & installation.

15. Remove the 3 bolts and the power steering pump heat shield.

16. Disengage the wire harness retainer from the power steering pump.

17. Remove the 3 bolts and reposition the power steering pump and bracket as an assembly. Do not disconnect the power steering lines from the pump.

18. Remove the 2 bolts and the heater core supply tube.

19. Disconnect the ignition coil capacitor electrical connector.

20. Disengage the wire harness retainer from the intake manifold support bracket.

21. Remove the studbolt and remove the upper intake manifold support bracket.

22. Remove the spark plugs. Refer to Spark Plugs, removal & installation.

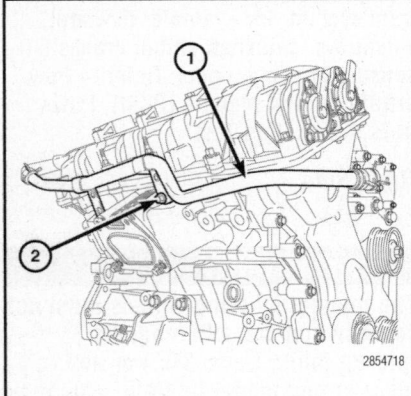

Fig. 137 Remove the 2 bolts (2) and the heater core supply tube (1)—3.6L engine

23. Remove the cylinder head covers. Refer to Valve Covers, removal & installation.

24. Remove the lower and upper oil pans.

25. Remove the crankshaft vibration damper.

26. Remove the engine timing cover. Refer to Timing Chain Front Cover, removal & installation.

✳✳ WARNING

When aligning the timing marks, always rotate the engine by turning the crankshaft. Failure to do so may result in valve and/or piston damage.

27. Rotate the crankshaft clockwise to place the number 1 piston at Top Dead Center (TDC) on the exhaust stroke by aligning the dimple on the crankshaft with the block/bearing cap junction. The left side cam phaser arrows should point toward each other and be parallel to the valve cover sealing surface. The right side cam phaser arrows should point away from each other and the scribe lines should be parallel to the valve cover sealing surface.

✳✳ WARNING

Always reinstall timing chains so that they maintain the same direction of rotation. Inverting a previously run chain on a previously run sprocket will result in excessive wear to both the chain and sprocket.

28. Mark the direction of rotation on the timing chain using a paint pen or equivalent to aid in reassembly.

✳✳ WARNING

When the timing chains are removed and the cylinder heads are still installed, DO NOT rotate the camshafts or crankshaft without first locating the proper crankshaft position. Failure to do so will result in valve and/or piston damage.

29. Reset the RH cam chain tensioner by pushing back the tensioner piston and installing Tensioner Pin 8514.

➡ **Minor rotation of a camshaft (a few degrees) may be required to install the camshaft phaser lock.**

30. Install the RH Camshaft Phaser Lock 10202.

31. Loosen both the intake oil control valve and exhaust oil control valve.

32. Remove the RH Camshaft Phaser Lock 10202.

33. Remove the oil control valve from the right side intake cam phaser and pull the phaser off of the camshaft.

34. Remove the oil control valve from the right side exhaust cam phaser and pull the phaser off of the camshaft.

35. Remove the RH cam chain tensioner arm.

36. Remove the 2 T30 bolts and the RH cam chain tensioner.

37. Remove the 3 T30 bolts and the RH cam chain guide.

38. Remove the right camshafts. Refer to Camshaft and Lifters, removal & installation.

➡ **If the rocker arms are to be reused, identify their positions so that they can be reassembled into their original locations.**

39. Remove the rocker arms.

➡ **If the hydraulic lifters are to be reused, identify their positions so that they can be reassembled into their original locations.**

40. If required, remove the hydraulic lifters.

41. Using the proper sequence, remove the cylinder head retaining bolts.

✳✳ CAUTION

The multi-layered steel head gaskets have very sharp edges that could cause personal injury if not handled carefully.

➡ **The head gasket crimps the locating dowels and the dowels may pull out of the engine block when the head gasket is removed.**

42. Remove the cylinder head and gasket. Discard the gasket.

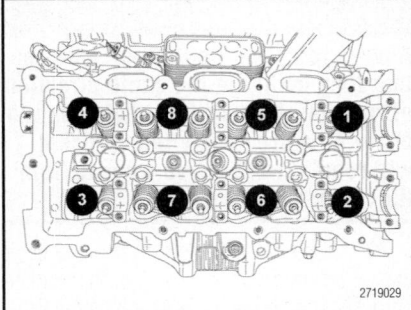

Fig. 138 Cylinder head bolt removal sequence (right side)—3.6L engine

⁕⁕ WARNING

Do not lay the cylinder head on its gasket sealing surface, due to the design of the cylinder head gasket, any distortion to the cylinder head sealing surface may prevent the gasket from properly sealing resulting in leaks.

43. If required, remove the bolt and the ignition coil capacitor.

To install:

44. If removed, install the ignition coil capacitor with the M6 bolt tightened to 89 inch lbs. (10 Nm).

➡The cylinder head bolts are tightened using a torque plus angle procedure. The bolts must be examined BEFORE reuse. If the threads are necked down the bolts must be replaced.

45. Check the cylinder head bolts for necking by holding a scale or straight edge against the threads. If all the threads do not contact the scale, the bolt must be replaced.

⁕⁕ WARNING

When cleaning the cylinder head and cylinder block surfaces, DO NOT use a metal scraper as the surfaces could be damaged. Use ONLY a wooden or plastic scraper.

46. Clean and prepare the gasket sealing surfaces of the cylinder head and block.

⁕⁕ WARNING

Non-compressible debris such as oil, coolant or RTV sealants that are not removed from bolt holes can cause the aluminum casting to crack when tightening the bolts.

47. Clean out the cylinder head bolt holes in the engine block.

➡The cylinder head gaskets are not interchangeable between the left and right cylinder heads and are clearly marked with R for Right and L for Left.

48. Position the new cylinder head gasket on the locating dowels.
49. Position the cylinder head onto the cylinder block. Make sure the cylinder head seats fully over the locating dowels.

➡Do not apply any additional oil to the bolt threads.

50. Install the 8 head bolts finger tight.
51. Tighten the cylinder head bolts in sequence according to the following steps:

a. Step 1: Tighten to 22 ft. lbs. (30 Nm).
b. Step 2: Tighten to 33 ft. lbs. (45 Nm).
c. Step 3: Tighten 75°. (Do not use a torque wrench for this step).
d. Step 4: Tighten 50°. (Do not use a torque wrench for this step).
e. Step 5: Loosen all the fasteners in reverse sequence.
f. Step 6: Tighten to 22 ft. lbs. (30 Nm).
g. Step 7: Tighten to 33 ft. lbs. (45 Nm).
h. Step 8: Tighten 70°. (Do not use a torque wrench for this step).
i. Step 9: Tighten 70°. (Do not use a torque wrench for this step).

➡If the hydraulic lifters are being reused, reassemble them into their original locations.

52. If removed, install the hydraulic lifters.

➡If the rocker arms are being reused, reassemble them into their original locations.

53. Install the rocker arms and camshafts. Refer to Camshaft and Lifters, removal & installation.

⁕⁕ WARNING

Do not rotate the camshafts more than a few degrees independently of the crankshaft. Valve to piston contact could occur resulting in possible valve damage. If the camshafts need to be rotated more than a few degrees, first move the pistons away from the cylinder heads by rotating the crankshaft counterclockwise to a position 30° BTDC. Once the camshafts are positioned at TDC, rotate the crankshaft clockwise to return the crankshaft to TDC.

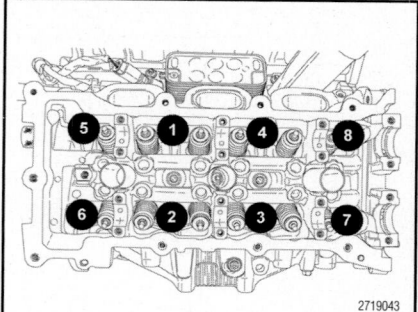

Fig. 139 Cylinder head bolt tightening sequence (right side)—3.6L engine

54. Verify that the camshafts are set at TDC by positioning the alignment holes vertically.
55. Install the RH cam chain guide with the 3 bolts. Tighten the T30 bolts to 106 inch lbs. (12 Nm).
56. Install the RH cam chain tensioner to the engine block with the 2 bolts. Tighten the T30 bolts to 106 inch lbs. (12 Nm).
57. Reset the RH cam chain tensioner by pushing back the tensioner piston and installing Tensioner Pin 8514.
58. Install the RH tensioner arm.
59. Press the RH exhaust cam phaser onto the exhaust camshaft. Install and hand tighten the oil control valve.

⁕⁕ WARNING

Always reinstall timing chains so that they maintain the same direction of rotation. Inverting a previously run chain on a previously run sprocket will result in excessive wear to both the chain and sprocket.

60. Drape the right side cam chain over the RH exhaust cam phaser and onto the idler sprocket so that the dimple is aligned with the plated link on the cam chain.
61. While maintaining this alignment, route the cam chain around the exhaust and intake cam phasers so that the plated links are aligned with the phaser timing marks. Position the right side cam phasers so that the arrows point away from each other and the scribe lines are parallel to the valve cover sealing surface. Press the intake cam phaser onto the intake cam, install and hand tighten the oil control valve.

➡Minor rotation of a camshaft (a few degrees) may be required to install the camshaft phaser or phaser lock.

62. Install the RH Camshaft Phaser Lock 10202 and tighten the oil control valves to 110 ft. lbs. (150 Nm).
63. Remove the RH Camshaft Phaser Lock 10202.
64. Remove the Tensioner Pin 8514 from the RH cam chain tensioner.
65. Rotate the crankshaft clockwise 2 complete revolutions stopping when the dimple on the crankshaft is aligned the with the block/bearing cap junction.
66. While maintaining this alignment, verify that the arrows on the left side cam phasers point toward each other and are parallel to the valve cover sealing surface and that the right side cam phaser arrows point away from each other and the scribe lines are parallel to the valve cover sealing surface.

67. There should be 12 chain pins between the exhaust cam phaser triangle marking and the intake cam phaser circle marking.

68. If the engine timing is not correct, repeat this procedure.

69. Install the engine timing cover, crankshaft vibration damper, upper and lower oil pans and cylinder head covers.

70. Install the spark plugs. Refer to Spark Plugs, removal & installation.

71. Install the upper intake manifold support bracket with the studbolt hand tight.

72. Engage the wire harness retainer from the intake manifold support bracket.

73. Connect the ignition coil capacitor electrical connector.

74. Install the heater core supply tube with 1 bolt tightened to 106 inch lbs. (12 Nm).

75. Reposition the power steering pump and bracket as an assembly and install the 3 bolts. Tighten the bolts to 18 ft. lbs. (25 Nm).

76. Disengage the wire harness retainer from the power steering pump.

77. Install the power steering pump heat shield and the 3 bolts. Tighten the bolts to 18 ft. lbs. (25 Nm).

78. Install the accessory drive belt. Refer to Accessory Drive Belts, removal & installation.

79. Install the upper and lower intake manifolds and insulator. Refer to Intake Manifold, removal & installation.

80. Install the resonator and air cleaner body. Refer to Air Cleaner, removal & installation.

81. Evacuate and charge the refrigerant system.

82. Install the engine cover.

83. If removed, install the oil filter and fill the engine crankcase with the proper type and amount of oil.

84. Fill the cooling system. Refer to Engine Coolant, Drain & Refill Procedure.

85. Raise and safely support the vehicle.

86. Install the belly pan.

87. Lower the vehicle.

88. Connect the negative battery cable and tighten the nut to 45 inch lbs. (5 Nm). Refer to Battery, removal & installation.

89. Run the engine until it reaches the normal operating temperature. Check the cooling system for correct fluid level.

➡**The Cam/Crank Variation Relearn procedure must be performed using the scan tool anytime there has been a repair/replacement made to a powertrain system, for example: flywheel, valvetrain, camshaft and/or crankshaft**

sensors or components. Refer to Powertrain Control Module (PCM), Powertrain Verification Test.

ENGINE OIL & FILTER

REPLACEMENT

2.4L Engine

See Figures 140 and 141.

✳✳ CAUTION

New or used engine oil can be irritating to the skin. Avoid prolonged or repeated skin contact with engine oil. Contaminants in used engine oil, caused by internal combustion, can be hazardous to health. Thoroughly wash exposed skin with soap and water. Do not wash skin with gasoline, diesel fuel, thinner, or solvents as health problems can result. Dispose of used engine oil properly. Contact your dealer or government agency for location of collection center in your area.

➡**Change the engine oil at mileage and time intervals described in the Maintenance Schedule.**

1. Before servicing the vehicle, refer to the Precautions Section.

2. Run the engine until achieving the normal operating temperature.

3. Position the vehicle on a level surface and turn the engine off.

4. Remove the oil fill cap.

5. Raise and safely support the vehicle.

6. Place a suitable oil collecting container under the oil pan drain plug.

7. Remove the oil pan drain plug and allow oil to drain into the collecting con-

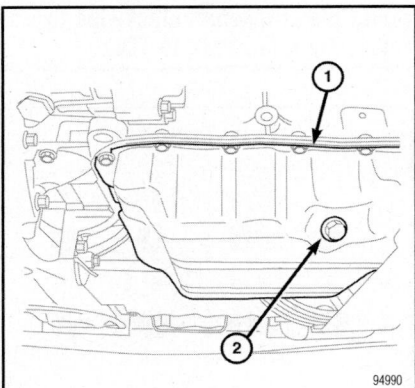

Fig. 140 Oil pan drain plug (2) and oil pan (1) shown—2.4L engine

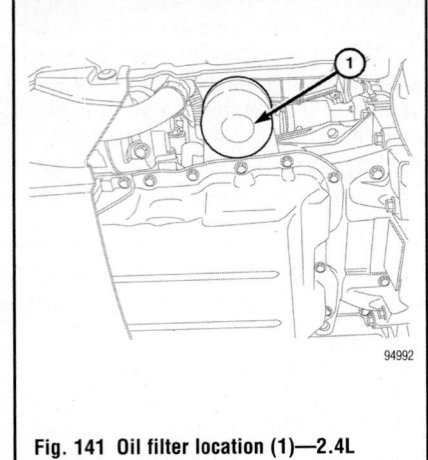

Fig. 141 Oil filter location (1)—2.4L engine

tainer. Inspect the drain plug threads for stretching or other damage. Replace the drain plug and gasket if damaged.

8. Remove the oil filter allowing the oil to drain when loosening before removing.

➡**When servicing the oil filter, avoid deforming the filter. Use a tool band strap.**

To install:

9. Install the oil pan drain plug and tighten the drain plug to 30 ft. lbs. (40 Nm).

10. Wipe the filter base clean, then inspect the gasket sealing surface.

11. Lubricate the gasket of the new filter with clean engine oil.

12. Install a new oil filter and tighten to 10 ft. lbs. (14 Nm) after the gasket contacts the base. Use a filter wrench if necessary.

13. Lower the vehicle and fill the crankcase with the specified type and amount of engine oil.

14. Install the oil fill cap.

15. Start the engine and inspect for leaks.

16. Stop the engine and inspect oil level.

2.7L Engine

See Figure 142.

✳✳ CAUTION

New or used engine oil can be irritating to the skin. Avoid prolonged or repeated skin contact with engine oil. Contaminants in used engine oil, caused by internal combustion, can be hazardous to health. Thoroughly wash exposed skin with soap and water. Do not wash skin with gasoline, diesel fuel, thinner, or solvents as health problems can result. Dispose of used engine oil properly. Contact your dealer or government

agency for location of collection center in your area.

➡ **Change the engine oil at mileage and time intervals described in the Maintenance Schedule.**

1. Before servicing the vehicle, refer to the Precautions Section.
2. Run the engine until achieving the normal operating temperature.
3. Position the vehicle on a level surface and turn the engine off.
4. Raise and safely support the vehicle.
5. Remove the oil fill cap.
6. Place a suitable drain pan under the crankcase drain.
7. Remove the drain plug from the crankcase and allow the oil to drain into the pan. Inspect the drain plug threads for stretching or other damage. Replace the drain plug and gasket if damaged.
8. Position a suitable collecting container under the oil filter location.
9. Remove the oil filter using a suitable oil filter wrench. Dispose of the oil filter following environmental guidelines.

To install:
10. Install the drain plug in the crankcase and tighten to 20 ft. lbs. (40 Nm).
11. Wipe the filter base clean, then inspect the gasket sealing surface.
12. Lubricate the gasket of the new filter with clean engine oil.
13. Install the oil filter and tighten to 12 ft. lbs. (16 Nm) after the gasket contacts the base. Use a filter wrench if necessary.
14. Lower the vehicle and fill the crankcase with the specified type and amount of engine oil.
15. Install the oil fill cap.
16. Start the engine and inspect for leaks.

17. Stop the engine and inspect the oil level.

3.5L Engine
See Figures 143 and 144.

> ❄❄ **CAUTION**
>
> **New or used engine oil can be irritating to the skin. Avoid prolonged or repeated skin contact with engine oil. Contaminants in used engine oil, caused by internal combustion, can be hazardous to health. Thoroughly wash exposed skin with soap and water. Do not wash skin with gasoline, diesel fuel, thinner, or solvents as health problems can result. Dispose of used engine oil properly. Contact your dealer or government agency for location of collection center in your area.**

➡ **Change the engine oil at mileage and time intervals described in the Maintenance Schedule.**

1. Before servicing the vehicle, refer to the Precautions Section.
2. Run the engine until achieving the normal operating temperature.
3. Position the vehicle on a level surface and turn the engine off.
4. Open the hood, remove the engine oil fill cap.
5. Raise and safely support the vehicle.
6. Place a suitable drain pan under the crankcase drain.
7. Remove the oil pan drain plug from the crankcase and allow the oil to drain into the pan. Inspect the drain plug threads for stretching or other damage. Replace the drain plug and gasket if damaged.
8. Remove the oil filter.

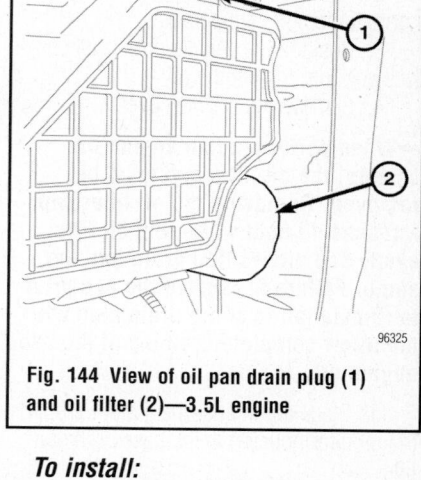

Fig. 144 View of oil pan drain plug (1) and oil filter (2)—3.5L engine

To install:
9. Install the drain plug in the crankcase. Tighten the oil pan drain plug to 20 ft. lbs. (27 Nm).
10. Install a new oil filter.
  a. Wipe the base clean, then inspect the gasket contact surface.
  b. Lubricate the gasket of the new filter with clean engine oil.
  c. Install and tighten the oil filter to 12 ft. lbs. (16 Nm) of torque after the gasket contacts the base. Use a filter wrench if necessary.
11. Lower the vehicle.
12. Fill the crankcase with the specified type and amount of engine oil.
13. Install the oil fill cap.
14. Start the engine and inspect for leaks.
15. Turn the engine off and inspect the oil level.

3.6L Engine
See Figures 145 and 146.

> ❄❄ **CAUTION**
>
> **New or used engine oil can be irritating to the skin. Avoid prolonged or repeated skin contact with engine oil. Contaminants in used engine oil, caused by internal combustion, can be hazardous to health. Thoroughly wash exposed skin with soap and water. Do not wash skin with gasoline, diesel fuel, thinner, or solvents as health problems can result. Dispose of used engine oil properly. Contact your dealer or government agency for location of collection center in your area.**

➡ **Change the engine oil at mileage and time intervals described in the Maintenance Schedule.**

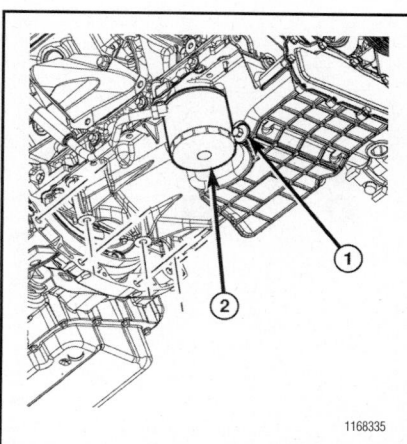

Fig. 142 Oil filter (2) and drain plug (1) location—2.7L engine

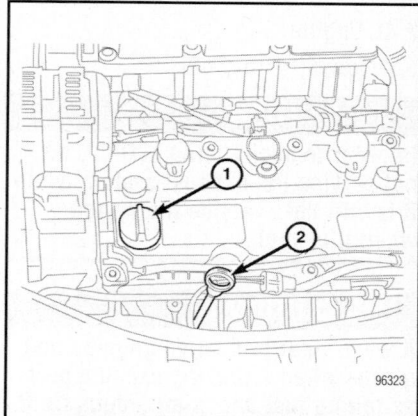

Fig. 143 Location of the engine oil fill cap (1) and engine oil dip stick (2)—3.5L engine

1. Before servicing the vehicle, refer to the Precautions Section.

2. Run the engine until achieving the normal operating temperature.

3. Position the vehicle on a level surface and turn the engine off.

4. Remove the engine cover.

➥When performing an engine oil change, the oil filter cap must be removed. Removing the oil filter cap releases oil held within the oil filter cavity and allows it to drain into the sump. Failure to remove the cap prior to reinstallation of the drain plug will not allow complete draining of the used engine oil.

5. Place an oil absorbent cloth around the oil filter housing at the base of the oil filter cap.

➥The oil filter is attached to the oil filter cap.

6. Rotate the oil filter cap counterclockwise and remove the cap and filter from the oil filter housing.

7. Raise and safely support the vehicle.

8. Place a suitable drain pan under the crankcase drain plug.

9. Remove the drain plug from the oil pan and allow the oil to drain into the pan. Inspect the drain plug threads for stretching or other damage. Replace the drain plug and gasket if damaged.

10. Install the drain plug in the oil pan and tighten to 20 ft. lbs. (27 Nm).

11. Lower the vehicle.

12. Remove the oil filter from the oil filter cap.

13. Remove and discard the O-ring seal.

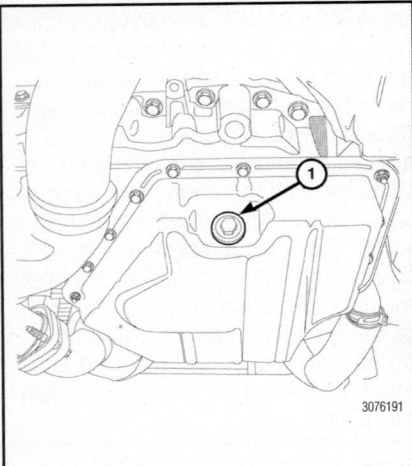

Fig. 145 View of oil pan drain plug (1)—3.6L engine

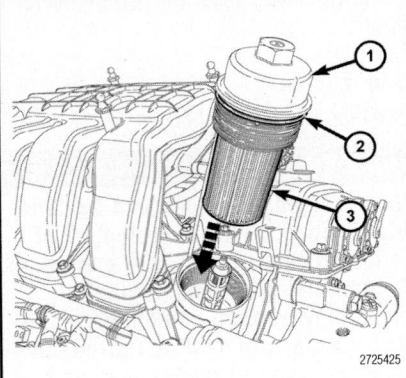

Fig. 146 Oil filter O-ring seal (1), filter cap (2), and oil filter (3) installation—3.6L engine

To install:

➥It is not necessary to pre-oil the oil filter or fill the oil filter housing.

14. Lightly lubricate the new O-ring seal with clean engine oil.

15. Install the O-ring seal on the filter cap.

16. Install the new oil filter into the oil filter cap.

17. Thread the oil filter cap into the oil filter housing and tighten to 18 ft. lbs. (25 Nm).

18. Remove the oil fill cap. Fill the crankcase with the specified type and amount of engine oil.

19. Install the oil fill cap.

20. Start the engine and inspect for leaks.

21. Stop the engine and check the oil level.

22. Install the engine cover.

EXHAUST MANIFOLD

REMOVAL & INSTALLATION

2.4L Engine

See Figures 147 and 148.

❋❋ CAUTION

In order to avoid being burned, do not service the exhaust system while it is still hot. Service the system when it is cool.

❋❋ CAUTION

Always wear protective goggles and gloves when removing exhaust parts as falling rust and sharp edges from worn exhaust components could result in serious personal injury.

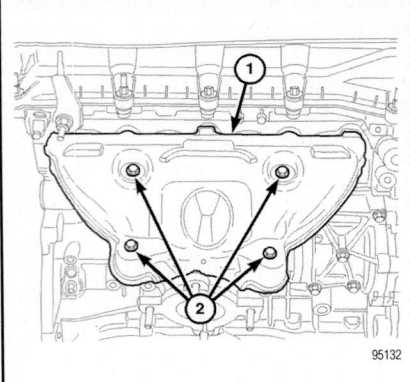

Fig. 147 Remove the bolts (2) attaching the exhaust manifold upper heat shield (1)—2.4L engine

1. Before servicing the vehicle, refer to the Precautions Section.

2. Remove the engine cover.

3. Disconnect the negative cable from the battery.

4. Remove the bolts attaching the upper heat shield.

5. Remove the upper heat shield.

6. Disconnect the exhaust pipe from the manifold.

7. Disconnect the oxygen sensor electrical connector.

8. Remove the manifold support bracket.

9. Remove the lower exhaust manifold heat shield.

10. Remove the exhaust manifold retaining fasteners.

11. Remove and discard the manifold gasket.

To install:

12. Install a new exhaust manifold gasket. Do not apply sealer.

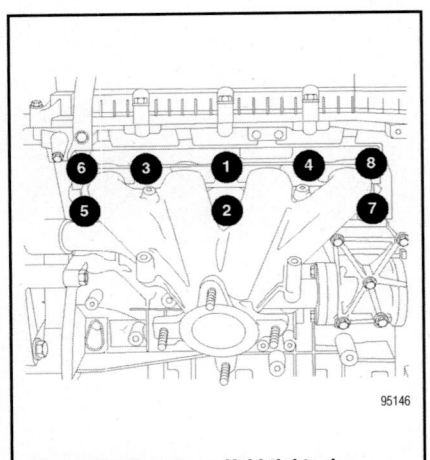

Fig. 148 Exhaust manifold tightening sequence—2.4L engine

13. Position the exhaust manifold in place.

14. Tighten the exhaust manifold bolts to 25 ft. lbs. (34 Nm).

15. Install the exhaust manifold heat shield. Tighten the bolts to 106 inch lbs. (12 Nm).

16. Install the exhaust manifold support bracket.

17. Install a new catalytic converter gasket.

18. Install the exhaust pipe to the manifold. Tighten the fasteners to 21 ft. lbs. (28 Nm).

19. Connect the oxygen sensor electrical connector.

20. Connect the negative battery cable.

21. Install the engine cover.

2.7L Engine

Front Manifold/Converter

See Figures 149 and 150.

> ※ **CAUTION**
>
> **In order to avoid being burned, do not service the exhaust system while it is still hot. Service the system when it is cool.**

> ※ **CAUTION**
>
> **Always wear protective goggles and gloves when removing exhaust parts as falling rust and sharp edges from worn exhaust components could result in serious personal injury.**

1. Before servicing the vehicle, refer to the Precautions Section.

2. Disconnect and isolate the negative battery cable.

3. Remove the engine cover.

4. Disconnect the front upstream oxygen sensor from the engine wiring harness connector.

5. Disconnect the front downstream oxygen sensor from the engine wiring harness connector.

6. Remove the bolt and the engine oil level indicator tube.

7. Remove the front upper maniverter (manifold/converter) heat shield fasteners and remove the heat shield.

8. Remove the upstream and downstream oxygen sensors. Refer to Heated Oxygen (HO2S) Sensor, removal & installation.

9. Raise and safely support the vehicle.

10. Remove the belly pan, if equipped.

11. Remove the front maniverter-to-crossunder fasteners.

12. Lower the vehicle.

13. Remove the front exhaust maniverter attaching bolts, front maniverter, and gasket.

To install:

14. Clean the front maniverter gasket mounting surfaces.

15. Install a new gasket, the front maniverter, and the front exhaust maniverter attaching bolts. Tighten the bolts to 17 ft. lbs. (23 Nm).

16. Raise and safely support the vehicle.

17. Install the front maniverter-to-crossunder fasteners. Tighten the fasteners to 20 ft. lbs. (27 Nm).

18. Install the belly pan, if equipped.

19. Lower the vehicle.

20. Install the upstream and downstream oxygen sensors. Tighten the sensors to 30 ft. lbs. (41 Nm).

21. Install the upper maniverter heat shield and the heat shield fasteners. Tighten the fasteners to 106 inch lbs. (12 Nm).

22. Install the engine oil level indicator tube. Tighten the bolt to 15 ft. lbs. (20 Nm).

23. Connect the front downstream oxygen sensor to the engine wiring harness connector.

24. Connect the front upstream oxygen sensor to the engine wiring harness connector.

25. Connect the negative battery cable and tighten the nut to 45 inch lbs. (5 Nm).

26. Install the engine cover.

Rear Manifold/Converter

See Figures 151 and 152.

> ※ **CAUTION**
>
> **In order to avoid being burned, do not service the exhaust system while it is still hot. Service the system when it is cool.**

> ※ **CAUTION**
>
> **Always wear protective goggles and gloves when removing exhaust parts as falling rust and sharp edges from worn exhaust components could result in serious personal injury.**

1. Before servicing the vehicle, refer to the Precautions Section.

2. Disconnect and isolate the negative battery cable.

3. Remove the engine cover.

4. Raise and safely support the vehicle.

5. Remove the belly pan, if equipped.

6. Remove the exhaust system.

7. Remove the cross-under pipe.

8. Loosen the lower EGR tube flange nut.

9. Lower the vehicle.

10. Remove the lower EGR tube.

11. Raise and safely support the vehicle.

12. Disconnect the rear upstream oxygen sensor from the engine wiring harness connector.

13. Disconnect the rear downstream oxygen sensor from the engine wiring harness connector.

14. Remove the fasteners and the rear maniverter (manifold/converter) heat shield.

15. Remove the upstream and downstream oxygen sensors. Refer to Heated Oxygen (HO2S) Sensor, removal & installation.

16. Remove the rear maniverter fasteners, rear maniverter and rear maniverter gasket.

To install:

17. Clean the rear maniverter gasket mounting surfaces.

18. Install the rear maniverter gasket, rear maniverter, and the rear maniverter

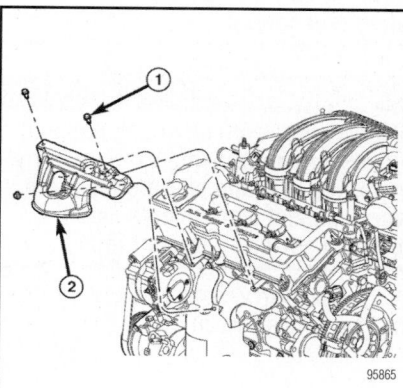

Fig. 149 Remove the front upper maniverter heat shield fasteners (1) and remove the heat shield (2)—2.7L engine

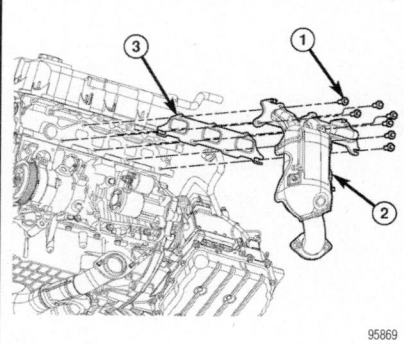

Fig. 150 Remove the front exhaust maniverter attaching bolts (1), front maniverter (2), and gasket (3)—2.7L engine

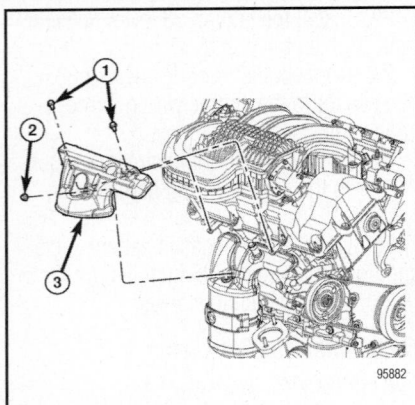

Fig. 151 Remove the fasteners (1, 2) and the rear maniverter heat shield (3)—2.7L engine

fasteners. Tighten the fasteners to 17 ft. lbs. (23 Nm).

19. Install the upstream and downstream oxygen sensors. Tighten the sensors to 30 ft. lbs. (41 Nm).

20. Install the rear maniverter heat shield. Tighten the fasteners to 106 inch lbs. (12 Nm).

21. Connect the rear downstream oxygen sensor to the engine wiring harness connector.

22. Connect the rear upstream oxygen sensor to the engine wiring harness connector.

23. Install the lower EGR tube.

24. Install the crossunder pipe to the rear maniverter with pipe fasteners. Hand tighten the fasteners.

25. Install the exhaust system.

26. Tighten the previously installed rear maniverter-to-cross under pipe fasteners to 21 ft. lbs. (29 Nm).

27. Install the belly pan, if equipped.

28. Connect the negative battery cable

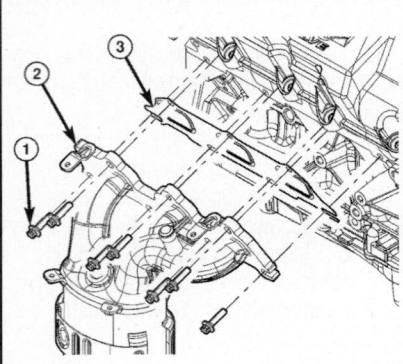

Fig. 152 Remove the rear maniverter fasteners (1), rear maniverter (2) and rear maniverter gasket (3)—2.7L engine

and tighten the nut to 45 inch lbs. (5 Nm).

29. Install the engine cover.

3.5L Engine

Front Manifold/Converter

See Figures 153 and 154.

> **✳✳ CAUTION**
>
> **In order to avoid being burned, do not service the exhaust system while it is still hot. Service the system when it is cool.**

> **✳✳ CAUTION**
>
> **Always wear protective goggles and gloves when removing exhaust parts as falling rust and sharp edges from worn exhaust components could result in serious personal injury.**

1. Before servicing the vehicle, refer to the Precautions Section.

2. Disconnect and isolate the negative battery cable.

3. Remove the 3 fasteners, and remove the upper heat shield.

4. Remove the 12 belly pan fasteners and remove the belly pan.

5. Remove the front crossunder pipe bolts.

6. Disconnect and remove the front lower maniverter oxygen sensor.

7. Loosen the oil level indicator tube retaining bolt and position the dipstick out of the way.

8. Disconnect and remove the front upper maniverter oxygen sensor.

9. Remove the maniverter retaining bolts and maniverter.

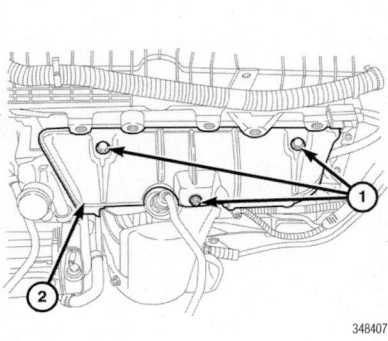

Fig. 153 Remove the 3 fasteners (1) and remove the upper heat shield (2) (front maniverter)—3.5L engine

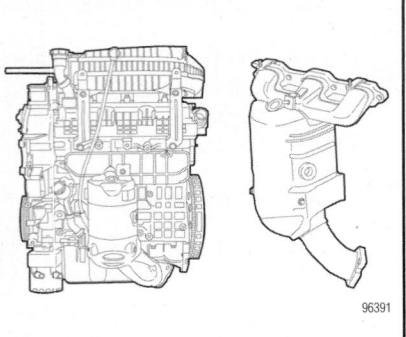

Fig. 154 View of maniverter (front)—3.5L engine

To install:

10. Position the maniverter and gasket. Install the retaining bolts. Tighten the bolts starting at the center working outward to 106 inch lbs. (23 Nm).

11. Install the upper heat shield, and torque the nuts to 106 inch lbs. (12 Nm).

12. Install and connect the front upper maniverter oxygen sensor.

13. Position the oil level indicator tube and install the retaining bolt.

14. Install and connect the front lower maniverter oxygen sensor.

15. Install the maniverter cross under pipe retaining bolts. Tighten the bolts to 23 ft. lbs. (31 Nm).

16. Install the belly pan and the 12 belly pan fasteners.

17. Connect the negative battery cable. Refer to Battery, removal & installation.

Rear Manifold/Converter

> **✳✳ CAUTION**
>
> **In order to avoid being burned, do not service the exhaust system while it is still hot. Service the system when it is cool.**

> **✳✳ CAUTION**
>
> **Always wear protective goggles and gloves when removing exhaust parts as falling rust and sharp edges from worn exhaust components could result in serious personal injury.**

1. Before servicing the vehicle, refer to the Precautions Section.

2. Disconnect the negative battery cable.

3. Raise and safely support the vehicle.

4. Remove the 12 belly pan fasteners and remove the belly pan.

5. Remove the right front halfshaft. Refer to Front Halfshaft, removal & installation.

6. Remove the retainer nuts at the extension pipe.

7. Remove the retainer from the bracket-to-bell housing.

8. Remove the center crossmember.

9. Remove the exhaust maniverter cross under pipe.

10. Remove the front extension pipe.

11. Disconnect and remove rear maniverter lower oxygen sensor.

12. Remove the lower heat shield retainers.

13. Remove the upper heat shield nuts.

14. Disconnect and remove the rear maniverter upper oxygen sensor and heat shields.

15. Remove the rear maniverter retaining bolts the rear maniverter.

To install:

16. Clean the gasket surfaces.

17. Position the maniverter and gasket. Install the retaining bolts. Tighten the bolts starting at the center working outward to 17 ft. lbs. (23 Nm).

18. Install and connect the rear maniverter upper oxygen sensor.

19. Install the rear maniverter upper heat shield.

20. Install the rear maniverter lower heat shield.

21. Install and connect the rear maniverter lower oxygen sensor.

22. Install the front extension pipe.

23. Install the exhaust maniverter cross under pipe.

24. Install the center crossmember.

25. Install the bracket-to-bell housing retainer.

26. Position the extension pipe and install the retainer nuts.

27. Install the right front halfshaft. Refer to Front Halfshaft, removal & installation.

28. Install the belly pan and the 12 belly pan fasteners.

29. Lower the vehicle.

30. Connect the negative battery cable. Refer to Battery, removal & installation.

3.6L Engine

The 3.6L aluminum cylinder heads are a unique design with left and right castings. The exhaust manifolds are integrated into the cylinder heads. If any damage is found to the exhaust manifold portion, the cylinder head must be removed for repair or replacement. Refer to Cylinder Head, removal & installation.

INTAKE MANIFOLD

REMOVAL & INSTALLATION

2.4L Engine

See Figures 155 and 156.

✳✳ CAUTION

Release the fuel system pressure before servicing system components. Service vehicles in well ventilated areas and avoid ignition sources. Never smoke while servicing the vehicle.

1. Before servicing the vehicle, refer to the Precautions Section.

2. Remove the engine cover.

3. Release the fuel system pressure. Refer to Relieving Fuel System Pressure.

4. Remove the air cleaner housing. Refer to Air Cleaner, removal & installation.

5. Disconnect the negative battery cable. Refer to Battery, removal & installation.

6. Disconnect the fuel line at the rail.

7. Remove the fuel injector electrical connectors.

8. Remove the fuel rail retaining bolts and remove the fuel rail.

9. Disconnect the oil temperature sensor.

10. Disconnect the variable valve timing solenoid electrical connector.

11. Disconnect the intake camshaft position sensor electrical connector.

12. Position the harness out of the way.

13. Remove the throttle body support bracket.

14. Disconnect the electronic throttle control electrical connector.

15. Remove the wiring harness retainer from the intake manifold.

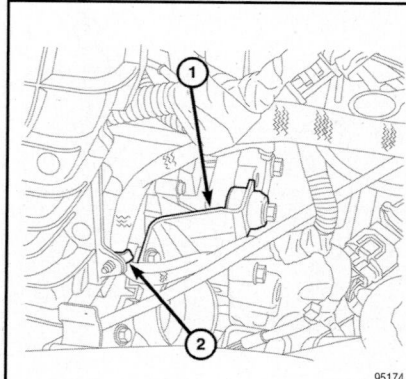

Fig. 155 Location of the throttle body support bracket (1) and wiring harness retainer (2)—2.4L engine

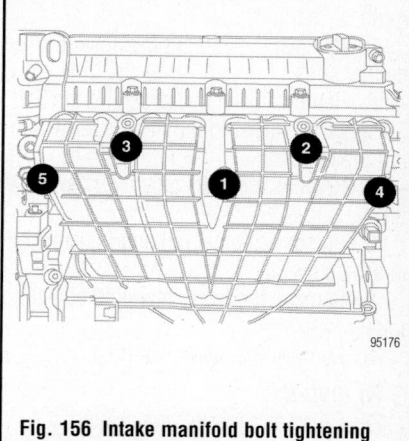

Fig. 156 Intake manifold bolt tightening sequence—2.4L engine

16. Disconnect the MAP sensor electrical connector.

17. Disconnect the vacuum lines at intake.

18. Remove the intake manifold retaining bolts.

19. Remove the intake manifold.

To install:

20. Clean all the gasket surfaces.

21. Replace the intake manifold gasket.

22. Install the intake manifold, tighten the bolts to 18 ft. lbs. (25 Nm).

23. Install the fuel rail assembly to the intake manifold. Tighten the bolts to 17 ft. lbs. (23 Nm).

24. Connect the fuel injector electrical connectors.

25. Inspect the quick connect fittings for damage, replace if necessary.

26. Connect the fuel supply hose to the fuel rail assembly. Check the connection by pulling on the connector to make sure it is locked into position.

27. Install the air cleaner housing. Refer to Air Cleaner, removal & installation.

28. Connect the negative battery cable. Refer to Battery, removal & installation.

29. Fill the cooling system. Refer to Engine Coolant, Drain & Refill Procedure.

30. Start the engine and check for leaks.

31. Install the engine cover.

2.7L Engine

Lower Manifold

See Figure 157.

1. Before servicing the vehicle, refer to the Precautions Section.

2. Release the fuel system pressure. Refer to Relieving Fuel System Pressure.

3. Remove the upper intake manifold. Refer to Upper Manifold, removal & installation.

4. Disconnect the electrical connectors from the fuel injectors.

5. Remove the fuel supply hose from the fuel rail

6. Remove the screw attaching the fuel rail support bracket to the throttle body support bracket.

7. Remove the bolts attaching the fuel rail.

8. Remove the fuel rail and injectors as an assembly.

9. Remove the lower manifold attaching bolts.

10. Remove the lower manifold.

To install:

11. Clean and inspect the sealing surfaces of the cylinder head and manifold. The gaskets can be reused provided they are free of cuts or tears.

12. Position the manifold on the cylinder head surfaces.

➡**For ease of installing the upper intake manifold, install a bolt 2–3 turns to the rearmost attaching hole of the intake. This will properly position the lower manifold.**

13. Install the lower intake manifold attaching bolts and tighten in sequence to 106 inch lbs. (12 Nm). Remove the bolt used for aligning the manifold.

14. Install the fuel rail with the injectors.

15. Connect the fuel injector electrical connectors.

➡**Make sure the fuel injectors are located in the correct location and position, as upper intake manifold interference could occur.**

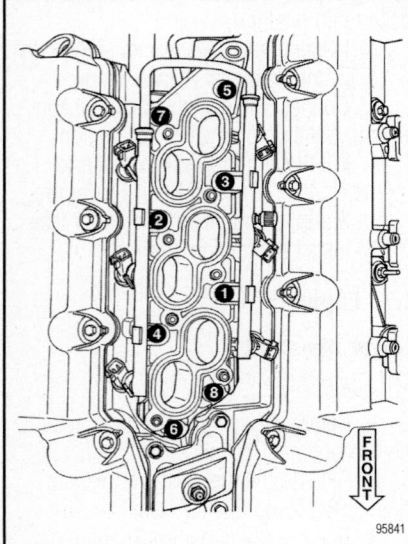

Fig. 157 Lower intake manifold bolt tightening sequence—2.7L engine

16. Install the screw attaching the fuel rail support bracket to the throttle body support bracket.

17. Connect the fuel supply hose to the fuel rail.

18. Install the upper intake manifold. Refer to Upper Manifold, removal & installation.

Upper Manifold

See Figures 158 and 159.

1. Before servicing the vehicle, refer to the Precautions Section.

2. Disconnect and isolate the negative battery cable.

3. Remove the throttle body air inlet hose and the air cleaner housing assembly. Refer to Air Cleaner, removal & installation.

4. Remove the upper EGR tube.

5. Disconnect the brake booster hose and the vapor purge hose from the upper intake manifold.

6. Remove the 2 intake manifold support brackets.

7. Disconnect the electrical connectors from the Manifold Absolute Pressure (MAP) sensor and the Electronic Throttle Control (ETC).

8. Disconnect the Positive Crankcase Ventilation (PCV) hose.

9. Remove the 7 manifold attaching bolts in reverse of the tightening sequence.

10. Remove the upper intake manifold.

To install:

11. Clean and inspect the gasket sealing surfaces. The gaskets can be reused if free of cuts or tears.

➡**Make sure the fuel injectors and wiring harnesses are positioned so that they do not interfere with the upper manifold installation.**

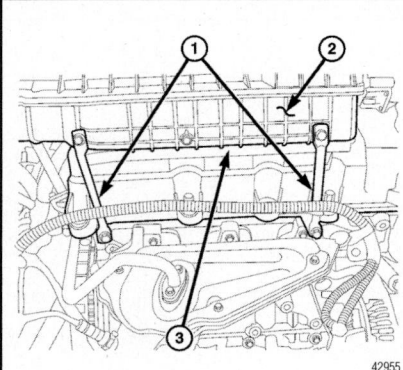

Fig. 158 View of the upper intake manifold support brackets (1), upper intake manifold (2), and lower intake manifold (3)—2.7L engine

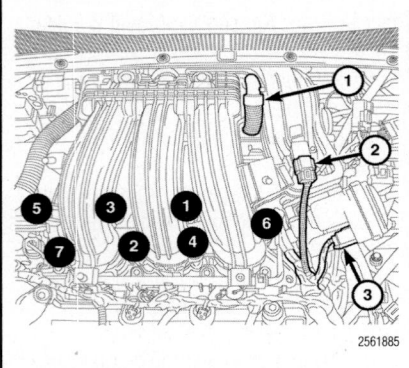

Fig. 159 Upper intake manifold bolt tightening sequence shown along with the PCV hose (1) and electrical connectors to the MAP sensor (2) and the ETC (3)—2.7L engine

12. Position the upper intake manifold onto the lower intake manifold.

13. Install the manifold attaching bolts and tighten in sequence to 106 inch lbs. (12 Nm).

14. Connect the PCV hose.

15. Connect the electrical connectors to the MAP sensor and the ETC.

16. Connect the brake booster hose and the vapor purge hose to the upper intake manifold.

17. Install the upper EGR tube.

18. Install the 2 intake manifold support brackets. Tighten the fasteners to 106 inch lbs. (12 Nm).

19. Install the air cleaner housing assembly and connect the throttle body air inlet hose. Refer to Air Cleaner, removal & installation.

20. Connect the negative battery cable and tighten the nut to 45 inch lbs. (5 Nm). Refer to Battery, removal & installation.

3.5L Engine

Lower Manifold

See Figures 160 and 161.

1. Before servicing the vehicle, refer to the Precautions Section.

2. Disconnect the negative battery cable. Refer to Battery, removal & installation.

3. Release the fuel system pressure. Refer to Relieving Fuel System Pressure.

4. Drain the cooling system. Refer to Engine Cooling, Engine Coolant, Drain & Refill Procedure.

5. Disconnect the upper radiator hose from the thermostat housing.

6. Remove the upper intake manifold. Refer to Upper Manifold, removal & installation.

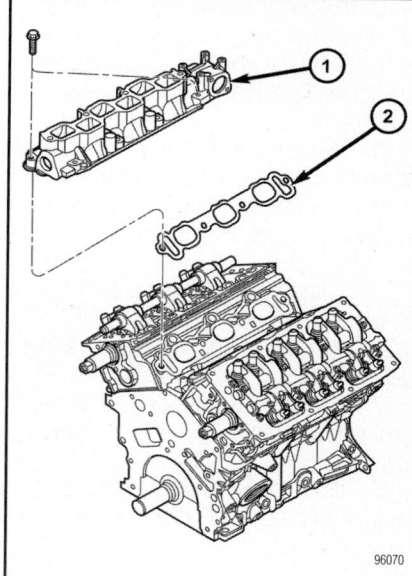

Fig. 160 Lower intake manifold (1) and gasket (2) removal—3.5L engine

7. Disconnect the electrical connectors to the fuel injectors and coolant temperature sensor.

8. Disconnect the heater supply and return hoses from the thermostat housing.

9. Disconnect the fuel line from the fuel rail.

10. Remove the 4 bolts attaching the fuel rail.

11. Remove fuel rail and injectors as an assembly.

12. Remove the lower intake 4 bolts and position the ignition coil capacitor aside.

13. Remove the lower intake manifold.

To install:

14. Clean all the sealing surfaces.

15. Position new gaskets and the intake manifold on the cylinder head surfaces.

16. Position the ignition coil capacitor and install the intake manifold bolts. Gradually tighten, in sequence, until a torque of 21 ft. lbs. (28 Nm) is obtained.

17. Install the fuel rail and injectors as an assembly.

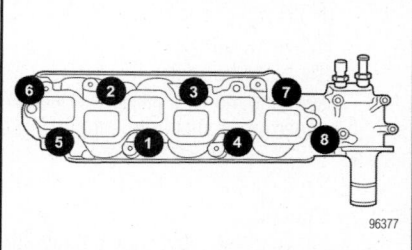

Fig. 161 Lower intake manifold bolt tightening sequence—3.5L engine

18. Connect the fuel supply hose to the fuel rail.

19. Connect the heater supply and return hoses to the intake manifold.

20. Connect the electrical connectors to the fuel injectors and coolant temperature sensor.

21. Install the upper intake manifold. Refer to Upper Manifold, removal & installation.

22. Connect the upper radiator hose to the thermostat housing.

23. Fill the cooling system. Refer to Engine Cooling, Engine Coolant, Drain & Refill Procedure.

24. Connect the negative battery cable. Refer to Battery, removal & installation.

Upper Manifold

See Figures 162 and 163.

1. Before servicing the vehicle, refer to the Precautions Section.

2. Remove the engine cover.

3. Disconnect the negative battery cable. Refer to Battery, removal & installation.

4. Remove the air cleaner housing and inlet hose. Refer to Air Cleaner, removal & installation.

5. Disconnect the EGR tube.

6. Disconnect the following vacuum hoses from the upper intake manifold:

- The Positive Crankcase Ventilation (PCV) Valve
- The EVAP Purge Solenoid
- The EGR Tube
- The Power Brake Booster

7. Disconnect electrical connectors from the following sensors and actuators:

- The Manifold Tuning Valve (MTV)
- The Short Runner Valve

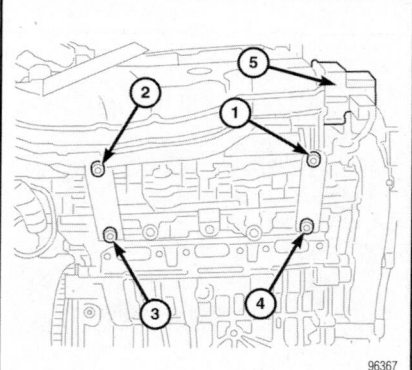

Fig. 162 Remove the Manifold Tuning Valve (5), then remove the 2 nuts (1, 2) from the rear intake manifold brackets. Loosen the lower nuts (3, 4) (upper manifold)—3.5L engine

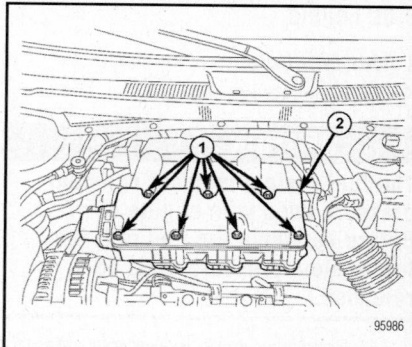

Fig. 163 Remove the upper intake manifold retaining bolts (1) and the upper intake manifold (2)—3.5L engine

- The Throttle Position Sensor (TPS)
- The Manifold Absolute Pressure (MAP)

8. Remove the Manifold Tuning Valve, then remove the 2 nuts from the rear intake manifold brackets.

9. Loosen the 2 bolts and from the rear intake manifold brackets and position the brackets aside.

10. Remove the 7 upper intake manifold retaining bolts and the upper intake manifold.

To install:

11. Clean and inspect all the gasket sealing surfaces.

12. Position a new gasket.

13. Install the throttle body on the upper intake (if required).

14. Install the upper intake manifold and hand start all attaching bolts.

15. Tighten the bolts gradually starting in the center working outward until a torque of 106 inch lbs. (12 Nm) is obtained.

16. Install the rear intake manifold brackets to the head.

17. Install the 2 intake manifold-to-bracket nut retainers.

18. Install the EGR tube.

19. Connect the electrical connectors to the following sensors and actuators:

- The MTV
- The Short Runner Valve
- The TPS
- The MAP

20. Connect the following vacuum hoses to the upper intake manifold:

- The PCV Valve
- The EVAP Purge Solenoid
- The EGR Tube
- The Power Brake Booster

21. Install the air cleaner housing and inlet hose. Refer to Air Cleaner, removal & installation.

22. Connect the negative battery cable. Refer to Battery, removal & installation.

23. Install the engine cover.

3.6L Engine

Lower Manifold

See Figures 164 through 167.

> ✳✳ **CAUTION**
>
> **The fuel system is under constant pressure even with engine off. Before servicing the fuel rail, the fuel system pressure must be released.**

1. Before servicing the vehicle, refer to the Precautions Section.
2. Disconnect the negative battery cable. Refer to Battery, removal & installation.
3. Release the fuel system pressure. Refer to Relieving Fuel System Pressure.
4. Remove the resonator and upper intake manifold. Refer to Upper Manifold, removal & installation.
5. Remove the insulator from the LH cylinder head cover.
6. Disconnect the fuel supply hose from the fuel rail inlet.
7. Disconnect the fuel injector electrical connectors.
8. Disengage the injection/ignition harness retainer from the rear of the lower intake manifold.
9. Disengage the main wire harness retainer from the rear of the lower intake manifold.
10. Remove the 8 lower intake manifold attaching bolts.
11. Remove the lower intake manifold with the fuel injectors and fuel rail.
12. Remove and discard the 6 lower intake manifold-to-cylinder head seals.
13. If required, remove the fuel rail and fuel injectors from the lower intake manifold.

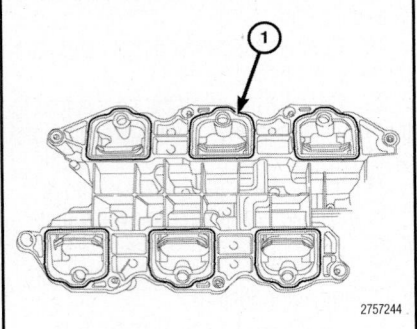

Fig. 165 Install new lower intake manifold-to-cylinder head seals (1)—3.6L engine

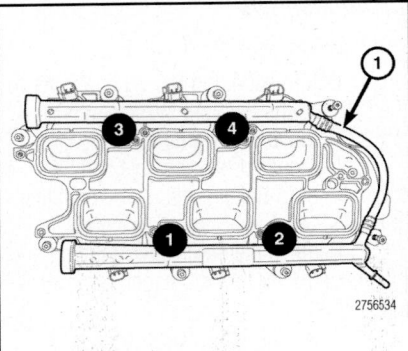

Fig. 166 Fuel rail bolt tightening sequence—3.6L engine

To install:

14. Clean and inspect the sealing surfaces. Install new lower intake manifold-to-cylinder head seals.
15. If removed, install the fuel injectors and the fuel rail to the lower intake manifold. Tighten the 4 bolts, in sequence, to 62 inch lbs. (7 Nm).

16. Position the lower intake manifold on the cylinder head surfaces.
17. Install the manifold attaching bolts and tighten in sequence to 71 inch lbs. (8 Nm).
18. Engage the main wire harness retainer to the rear of the lower intake manifold.
19. Engage the injection/ignition harness retainer to the rear of the lower intake manifold.
20. Connect the fuel injector electrical connectors.
21. Connect the fuel supply hose to the fuel rail inlet.
22. Install the insulator to the 2 alignment posts on top of the LH cylinder head cover.
23. Install the upper intake manifold, support brackets, and resonator. Refer to Upper Manifold, removal & installation.
24. Connect the negative battery cable and tighten the nut to 45 inch lbs. (5 Nm). Refer to Battery, removal & installation.
25. Start the engine and check for leaks.

Upper Manifold

See Figures 168 through 171.

1. Before servicing the vehicle, refer to the Precautions Section.
2. Disconnect and isolate the negative battery cable. Refer to Battery, removal & installation.
3. Remove the engine cover.
4. Remove the resonator. Refer to Air Cleaner, removal & installation.
5. Disconnect the electrical connectors from the Manifold Absolute Pressure (MAP) sensor and the Electronic Throttle Control (ETC).
6. Disengage the ETC harness from the clip on the throttle body. Disengage the wire harness retainers from the upper intake manifold near the MAP sensor and reposition the wire harness.
7. Disconnect the following hoses from the upper intake manifold:
   - The Positive Crankcase Ventilation (PCV)
   - The vapor purge
   - The brake booster
8. Disengage the wire harness retainer from the upper intake manifold support bracket.
9. Disengage the wire harness retainer from the studbolt.
10. Remove 2 nuts, loosen the studbolt, and reposition the upper intake manifold support bracket.

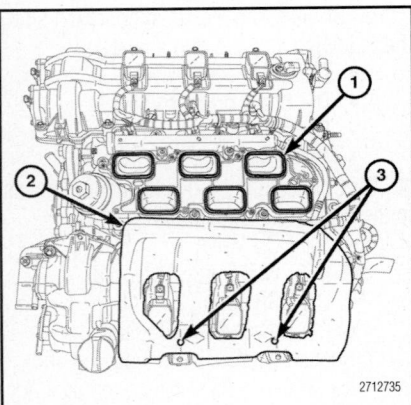

Fig. 164 View of LH cylinder head cover insulator (2), alignment posts (3), and seals (1)—3.6L engine

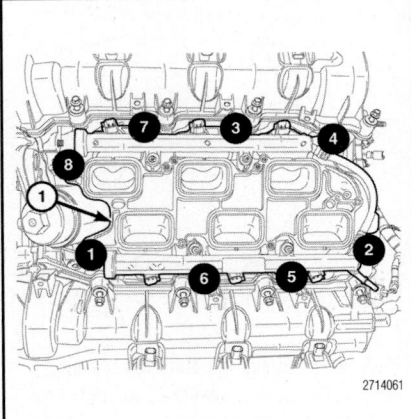

Fig. 167 Lower intake manifold (1) bolt tightening sequence—3.6L engine

11. Remove the nut from the support bracket of the heater core return tube.

12. Remove the 2 nuts, loosen the 2 studbolts, and reposition the 2 upper intake manifold support brackets.

➡The upper intake manifold attaching bolts are captured in the upper intake manifold. Once loosened, the bolts will have to be lifted out of the lower intake manifold and held while removing the upper intake manifold.

➡Exercise care to avoid inadvertently loosening the 2 fuel rail attachment bolts that are in close proximity of the upper intake manifold attaching bolts.

13. Remove the 7 manifold attaching bolts and remove the upper intake manifold.

14. Remove and discard the 6 upper-to-lower intake manifold seals.

15. Cover the open intake ports to prevent debris from entering the engine.

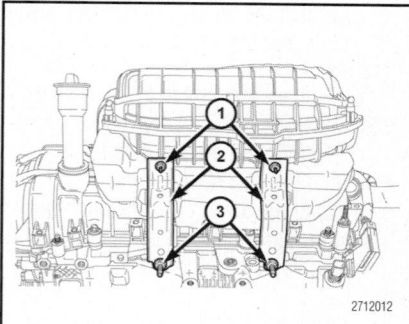

Fig. 168 Remove the nuts (1), loosen the studbolts (3), and reposition the upper intake manifold support brackets (2)—3.6L engine

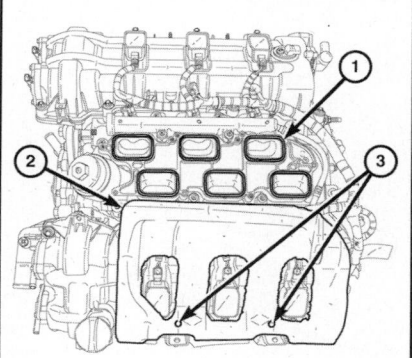

Fig. 169 View of the upper-to-lower intake manifold seals (1) and LH cylinder head cover insulator (2)—3.6L engine

16. If required, remove the insulator from the LH cylinder head cover.

To install:

➡Prior to installing the upper intake manifold, verify that the 4 fuel rail bolts were not inadvertently loosened. The bolts must tightened in sequence to 62 inch lbs. (7 Nm).

17. Clean and inspect the sealing surfaces. Install new upper-to-lower intake manifold seals.

➡Make sure the fuel injectors and wiring harnesses are in the correct position so that they don't interfere with the upper intake manifold installation.

18. If removed, install the insulator to the 2 alignment posts on top of the LH cylinder head cover.

19. Lift and hold the 7 upper intake attaching bolts clear of the mating surface. Back the bolts out slightly or if required, use an elastic band to hold the bolts clear of the mating surface.

20. Position the upper intake manifold onto the lower intake manifold so that the 2 locating posts on the upper intake manifold align with the corresponding holes in the lower intake manifold.

21. Install the 7 upper intake manifold attaching bolts. Tighten the bolts in sequence to 71 inch lbs. (8 Nm).

22. Install the 2 nuts to the upper intake manifold support bracket. Tighten the nuts to 89 inch lbs. (10 Nm) and tighten the studbolt to 15 ft. lbs. (20 Nm).

23. Engage the wire harness retainer to the studbolt.

24. Engage the wire harness retainer

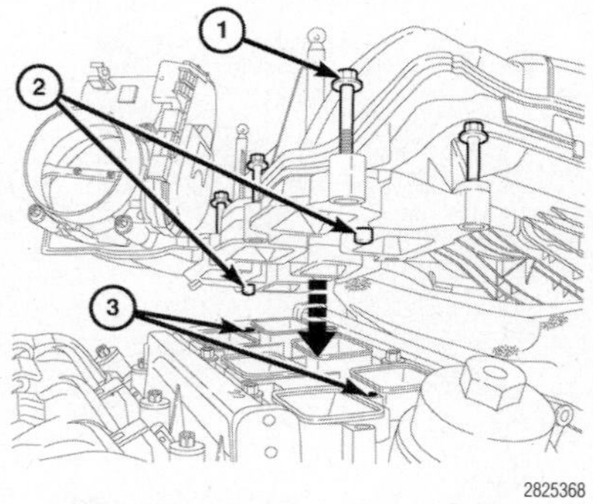

Fig. 170 Exploded view of upper intake attaching bolts (1), locating posts (2) on the upper intake manifold, and alignment holes (3) in the lower intake manifold—3.6L engine

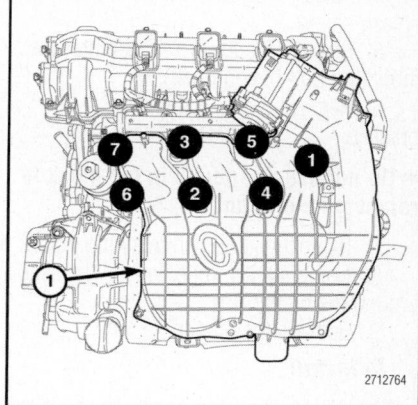

Fig. 171 View of upper intake manifold (1) bolt tightening sequence—3.6L engine

to the upper intake manifold support bracket.

25. Install the 2 upper intake manifold support brackets with the 2 studbolts and 2 nuts. Tighten the studbolts to 15 ft. lbs. (20 Nm) and tighten the nuts to 89 inch lbs. (10 Nm).

26. Install the nut to the support bracket of the heater core return tube and tighten to 106 inch lbs. (12 Nm).

27. Connect the following hoses to the upper intake manifold:
- The PCV
- The vapor purge
- The brake booster

28. Connect the electrical connectors to the MAP sensor and the ETC.

29. Secure the ETC harness to the clip on the throttle body and engage the wire harness retainers to the upper intake manifold near the MAP sensor.

30. Install the resonator. Refer to Air Cleaner, removal & installation.

31. Connect the negative battery cable and tighten the nut to 45 inch lbs. (5 Nm).

32. Start and run the engine until it reaches the normal operating temperature.

33. Install the engine cover.

OIL PAN

REMOVAL & INSTALLATION

2.4L Engine

See Figures 172 and 173.

1. Before servicing the vehicle, refer to the Precautions Section.

2. Raise and safely support the vehicle.

3. Remove the oil drain plug and drain the engine oil.

4. Remove the accessory drive belt splash shield.

5. Remove the lower A/C compressor mounting bolt (if equipped).

6. Remove the A/C mounting bracket.

➡**Do not use pry points in the block to remove the oil pan.**

7. Remove the oil pan retaining bolts.

8. Using a putty knife, loosen the seal around the oil pan.

9. Remove the oil pan.

To install:

➡**The oil pan sealing surfaces must be free of grease or oil.**

➡**Parts must be assembled within 10 minutes of applying RTV.**

10. Apply MOPAR® Engine RTV GEN II at the front cover-to-engine block parting lines.

11. Apply a 0.079 inch (2mm) bead of MOPAR® Engine RTV GEN II around the oil pan.

12. Position the oil pan and install the

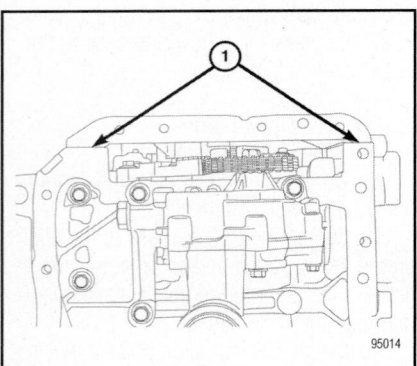

Fig. 172 Apply RTV at the front cover-to-engine block parting lines (1)—2.4L engine

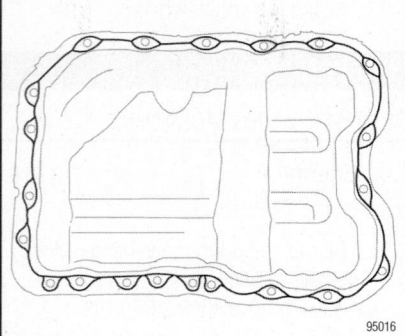

Fig. 173 Apply a bead of RTV sealant around the oil pan as shown—2.4L engine

bolts. Tighten the bolts to 106 inch lbs. (12 Nm).

➡**The 2 long bolts must be tightened to 16 ft. lbs. (22 Nm).**

13. Install the oil drain plug.

14. Lower the vehicle and fill the engine crankcase with the proper oil to the correct level.

15. Start the engine and check for leaks.

2.7L Engine

See Figures 174 and 175.

1. Before servicing the vehicle, refer to the Precautions Section.

2. Disconnect and isolate the negative battery cable. Refer to Battery, removal & installation.

3. Remove the bolt and the engine oil dipstick tube.

4. Raise and safely support the vehicle.

5. Remove the belly pan, if equipped.

6. Remove the right lower splash shield.

7. Drain the engine oil and remove the oil filter. Refer to Engine Oil & Filter, Replacement procedure.

8. Remove the fore/aft cross-member.

9. Remove the structural collar.

10. Remove the exhaust cross-under pipe.

11. Remove the lower bolt attaching the A/C compressor mounting bracket to the oil pan.

✻✻ WARNING

Assure the removal of the 2 bolts attaching the timing cover to the oil pan, as damage to the timing cover and/or oil pan may occur.

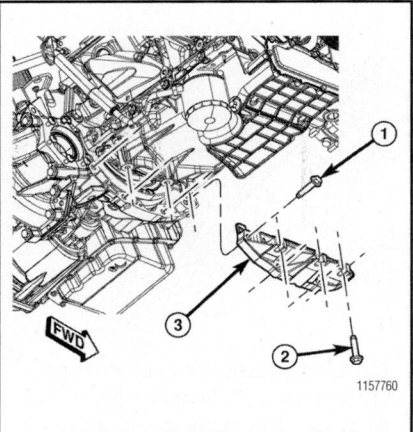

Fig. 174 Remove the bolts (1, 2) and the structural collar (3)—2.7L engine

12. Remove the oil pan attaching fasteners. Remove the oil pan and gasket.

To install:

13. Clean the oil pan and oil pan sealing surfaces. Inspect the oil pan and timing chain cover gaskets. Replace as necessary.

14. Apply a ⅛ inch (3.2mm) bead of MOPAR® Engine RTV GEN II to the front T-joints (oil pan gasket-to-timing cover gasket interface) and the rear T-joints (oil pan gasket-to-crankshaft rear oil seal retainer gasket interface).

15. Install the oil pan gasket to the engine block.

➡**To prevent oil leaks at the oil pan-to-timing chain cover, the following tightening sequence procedure must be performed.**

16. Install the oil pan and fasteners using the following tightening sequence:

a. Install the oil pan bolts and nuts finger tight only—just tight enough to compress the gasket's rubber seal.

b. Install the timing chain cover-to-oil pan bolts and tighten to 106 inch lbs. (12 Nm).

c. Tighten the oil pan bolts to 21 ft. lbs. (28 Nm).

d. Tighten the oil pan nuts to 106 inch lbs. (12 Nm).

17. Install the lower bolt attaching the A/C compressor mounting bracket to the oil pan. Tighten the bolt to 21 ft. lbs. (28 Nm).

18. Install the oil filter and drain plug. Refer to Engine Oil & Filter, Replacement procedure.

19. Install the exhaust cross-under pipe.

20. Install the structural collar.

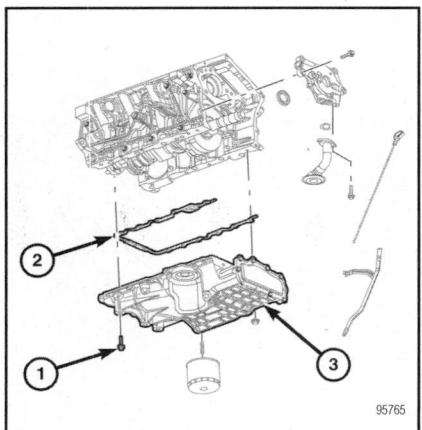

Fig. 175 View of the oil pan (3), attaching fasteners (1), and gasket (2)—2.7L engine

21. Install the fore/aft cross-member.
22. Install the right lower splash shield.
23. Install the belly pan, if equipped.
24. Install the engine oil dipstick and tube. Tighten the bolt to 15 ft. lbs. (20 Nm).
25. Fill the engine crankcase with the proper oil to the correct level. Refer to Engine Oil & Filter, Replacement procedure.
26. Connect the negative battery cable. Refer to Battery, removal & installation.

3.5L Engine

See Figures 176 through 178.

1. Before servicing the vehicle, refer to the Precautions Section.
2. Disconnect the negative battery cable. Refer to Battery, removal & installation.
3. Remove the engine oil indicator.
4. Remove the engine oil indicator tube bolt.
5. Remove the engine oil indicator tube.
6. Raise and safely support the vehicle.
7. Remove the front crossmember.
8. Remove the crossover pipe.
9. Loosen the front exhaust manifold. Refer to Exhaust Manifold, removal & installation.
10. Remove the oil pan bell housing bolts.
11. Drain the engine oil. Refer to Engine Oil & Filter, Replacement procedure.
12. Remove the engine oil filter.
13. Remove the oil pan fasteners. Remove the oil pan.

✳✳ CAUTION

A small amount of oil will remain in the oil pan. Use care when removing the oil pan from the engine.

14. Remove the oil pan gasket.

To install:

15. Clean the oil pan and all gasket surfaces.
16. Apply a ⅛ inch (3.2mm) bead of MOPAR® Engine RTV GEN II at the parting line of the oil pump housing and the rear seal retainer.
17. Install the oil pan gasket to the engine block.
18. Install the oil pan and tighten the oil pan bolts to 21 ft. lbs. (28 Nm).
19. Tighten the oil pan bell housing bolts to 40 ft. lbs. (55 Nm).
20. All engines are equipped with a high quality full-flow, disposable type oil filter. When replacing oil filter, use a MOPAR® filter or equivalent.

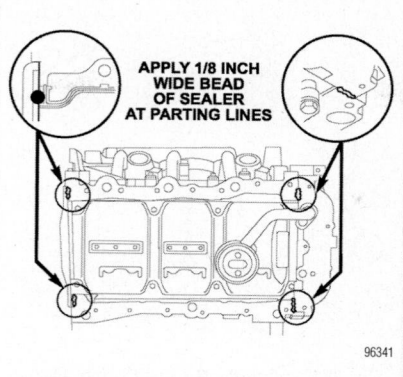

Fig. 176 Apply a bead of RTV sealant at the parting line of the oil pump housing and the rear seal retainer—3.5L engine

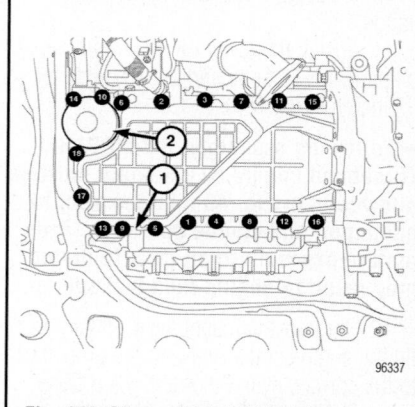

Fig. 177 Oil pan (1) bolt tightening sequence shown along with the engine oil filter (2) location—3.5L engine

21. Wipe the oil filter base clean, then inspect the gasket contact surface.
22. Lubricate the gasket of a new oil filter with clean engine oil.
23. Install and tighten the oil filter to 12 ft. lbs. (16 Nm) of torque after the gasket contacts the base. Use a filter wrench if necessary.
24. Lower the vehicle.
25. Install and tighten the oil pan drain bolt to 20 ft. lbs. (27 Nm).
26. Tighten the front maniverter bolts. Refer to Exhaust Manifold, removal & installation.
27. Install the crossover pipe.
28. Install the front crossmember.
29. Lower the vehicle.
30. Install the oil level indicator tube.
31. Tighten the oil level indicator tube bolt.
32. Install the oil indicator.
33. Fill the engine crankcase with the proper oil to the correct level. Refer to Engine Oil & Filter, Replacement procedure.

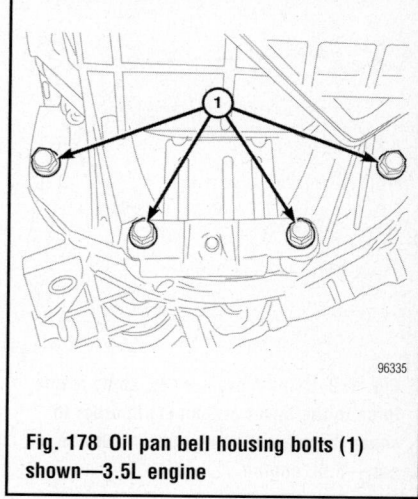

Fig. 178 Oil pan bell housing bolts (1) shown—3.5L engine

34. Connect the negative battery cable. Refer to Battery, removal & installation.

3.6L Engine

On 3.6L engines, there is an upper and lower oil pan. The upper oil pan is cast aluminum and also serves as the lower end structural support. The lower pan is a stamped steel design. Both upper and lower oil pans are sealed using MOPAR® Three-bond Engine RTV Sealant. The lower oil pan must be removed in order to access the upper oil pan attaching bolts.

Lower Oil Pan

See Figures 179 through 181.

1. Before servicing the vehicle, refer to the Precautions Section.
2. Raise and safely support the vehicle.
3. Drain the engine oil. Refer to Engine Oil & Filter, Replacement procedure.
4. Remove the belly pan.
5. Remove the inner splash shield.

➡ **The lower oil pan must be removed to access all of the upper oil pan retaining bolts.**

6. Remove the 15 bolts, 2 nuts, and 2 studs from the flange of the lower oil pan.

✳✳ WARNING

Do not pry on the lower oil pan flange. There are no designated pry points for lower oil pan removal. Prying on only one or a few locations could bend the flange and damage the pan.

7. Using a pry bar, apply a side force to the lower oil pan in order to shear the sealant bond and remove the pan.

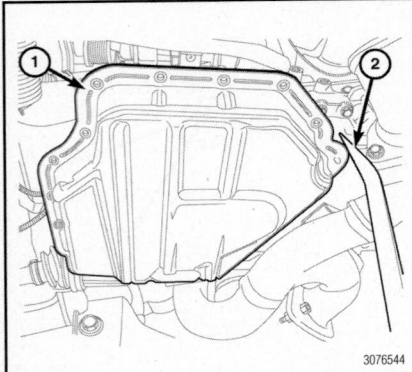

Fig. 179 Using a pry bar (2), apply a side force to the lower oil pan (1) in order to shear the sealant bond and remove the pan—3.6L engine

To install:

8. Clean the upper and lower oil pan mating surfaces with isopropyl alcohol in preparation for sealant application.

➡Engine assembly requires the use of a unique sealant that is compatible with engine oil. Using a sealant other than MOPAR® Threebond Engine RTV Sealant may result in engine fluid leakage.

➡Following the application of MOPAR® Threebond Engine RTV Sealant to the gasket surfaces, the components must be assembled within 20 minutes and the attaching fasteners must be tightened to specification within 45 minutes. Prolonged exposure to the air, prior to assembly, may result in engine fluid leakage.

9. Apply a 0.08–0.12 inch (2–3mm) wide bead of MOPAR® Threebond Engine RTV Sealant (1) to the lower oil pan.

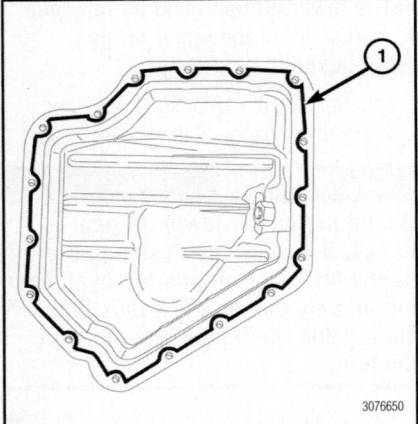

Fig. 180 Apply a bead of RTV sealant (1) to the lower oil pan—3.6L engine

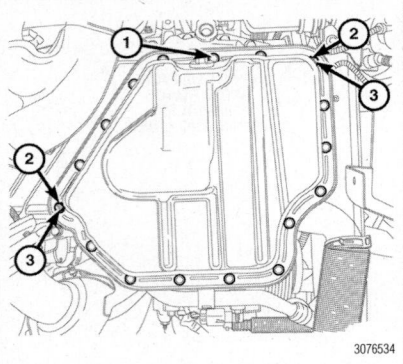

Fig. 181 Install the 2 studs (3) into the upper oil pan flange. Install the lower oil pan to the upper oil pan with 15 bolts (1) and 2 nuts (2)—3.6L engine

10. Install 2 studs into the upper oil pan flange.

11. Install the lower oil pan to the upper oil pan with 15 bolts and 2 nuts tightened to 97 inch lbs. (11 Nm).

➡Following assembly, the MOPAR® Threebond Engine RTV Sealant must be allowed to dry for 45 minutes prior to adding oil and engine operation. Premature exposure to oil prior to drying may result in engine fluid leakage.

12. If removed, install the oil filter and fill the engine crankcase with the proper oil to the correct level. Refer to Engine Oil & Filter, Replacement procedure.

13. Run the engine until it reaches the normal operating temperature.

Upper Oil Pan

See Figures 182 through 187.

1. Before servicing the vehicle, refer to the Precautions Section.

2. Disconnect and isolate the negative battery cable. Refer to Battery, removal & installation.

3. Remove the bolt and the oil level indicator.

4. Raise and safely support the vehicle.

5. Remove the belly pan.

6. Drain the engine oil. Refer to Engine Oil & Filter, Replacement procedure.

7. Remove the right halfshaft assembly from the intermediate shaft. Refer to Front Halfshaft, removal & installation.

➡The lower oil pan must be removed to access all of the upper oil pan retaining bolts.

8. Remove the lower oil pan. Refer to Lower Oil Pan, removal & installation.

9. Remove the crossunder pipe.

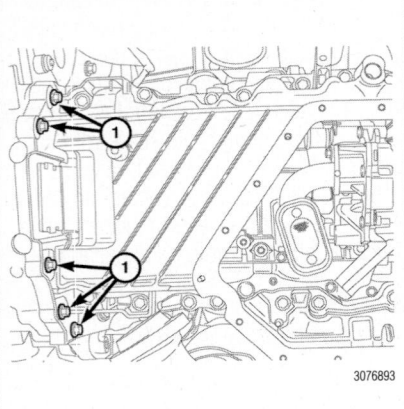

Fig. 182 Remove the 5 oil pan-to-transaxle bolts (1)—3.6L engine

10. Remove the front fore-aft crossmember.

11. Remove the bolt securing the coolant tube to the oil pan.

12. Remove the 5 oil pan-to-transaxle bolts.

13. Remove the torque converter bolt access cover.

14. Remove 2 rubber plugs covering the rear oil seal retainer flange bolts.

✴✴ WARNING

There are 2 hidden M6 bolts that must be removed from the rear of the upper oil pan flange. If these bolts are not removed, the rear oil seal retainer flange will be severely damaged.

15. Remove the 2 M6 bolts from the rear oil seal retainer flange.

16. Remove the 19 M8 oil pan mounting bolts.

17. Using the 4 indicated pry points, carefully remove the upper oil pan.

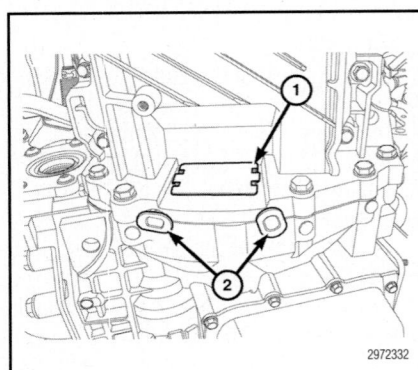

Fig. 183 Remove the torque converter bolt access cover (1) and the rubber plugs (2) covering the rear oil seal retainer flange bolts—3.6L engine

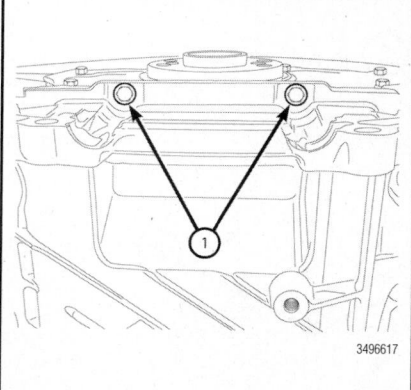

Fig. 184 Remove the 2 M6 bolts (1) from the rear oil seal retainer flange—3.6L engine

To install:

18. Clean the upper and lower oil pans, timing chain cover, rear seal retainer, and engine block mating surfaces with isopropyl alcohol in preparation for sealant application.

➡Engine assembly requires the use of a unique sealant that is compatible with engine oil. Using a sealant other than MOPAR® Threebond Engine RTV Sealant may result in engine fluid leakage.

➡Following the application of MOPAR® Threebond Engine RTV Sealant to the gasket surfaces, the components must be assembled within 20 minutes and the attaching fasteners must be tightened to specification within 45 minutes. Prolonged exposure to the air, prior to assembly, may result in engine fluid leakage.

19. Apply a 0.08–0.12 inch (2–3mm) wide bead of MOPAR® Threebond Engine

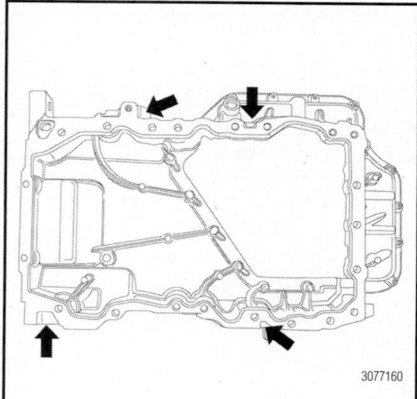

Fig. 185 Using the 4 indicated pry points, carefully remove the upper oil pan—3.6L engine

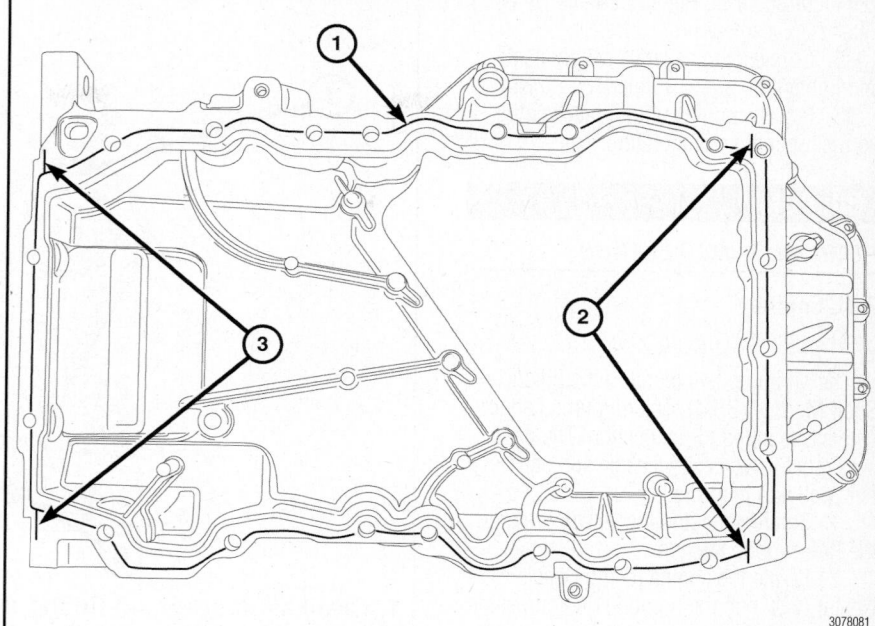

Fig. 186 Apply a bead of RTV sealant to the upper oil pan at the oil pan-to-engine block flange (1), the 2 timing cover-to-engine block T-joints (2), and the 2 rear seal retainer to engine block T-joints (3)

RTV Sealant to the upper oil pan at the oil pan-to-engine block flange, the 2 timing cover-to-engine block T-joints, and the 2 rear seal retainer to engine block T-joints.

❊❊ WARNING

Make sure that the rear face of the oil pan is flush to the transaxle bell housing before tightening any of the oil pan mounting bolts. A gap between the oil pan and the transaxle could crack the oil pan or transaxle casting.

20. Install the oil pan to the engine block so that it is flush to the transaxle bell housing. Secure the oil pan to the engine block with 19 M8 oil pan mounting bolts finger tight.

21. Install the 5 oil pan-to-transaxle bolts and tighten to 41 ft. lbs. (55 Nm).

22. Tighten the 19 previously installed M8 oil pan mounting bolts to 18 ft. lbs. (25 Nm).

23. Install the 2 M6 bolts to the rear oil seal retainer flange and tighten to 106 inch lbs. (12 Nm).

24. Install the torque converter bolt access cover.

25. Install the 2 rubber plugs covering the rear oil seal retainer flange bolts.

26. Install the bolt securing the coolant tube to the oil pan and tighten to 106 inch lbs. (12 Nm).

27. Install the lower oil pan. Refer to Lower Oil Pan, removal & installation.

28. Install the front fore-aft crossmember.

29. Install the crossunder pipe.

30. Install the right halfshaft assembly, steering knuckle, wheel and tire. Refer to Front Halfshaft, removal & installation.

31. Install the belly pan.

32. Lower the vehicle.

33. Install the oil level indicator with the bolt and tightened to 106 inch lbs. (12 Nm).

34. If removed, install the oil filter and fill the engine crankcase with the proper oil

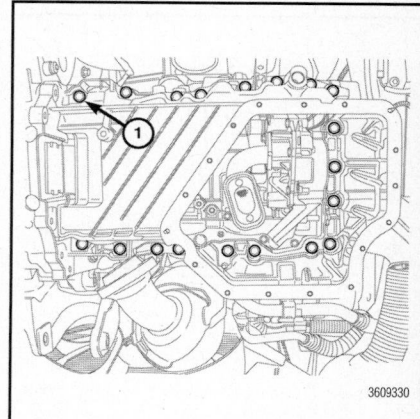

Fig. 187 Tighten the 19 M8 oil pan mounting bolts (1)—3.6L engine

to the correct level. Refer to Engine Oil & Filter, Replacement procedure.

35. Connect the negative battery cable and tighten the nut to 45 inch lbs. (5 Nm).

36. Run the engine until it reaches the normal operating temperature.

OIL PUMP

REMOVAL & INSTALLATION

2.4L Engine

See Figures 188 through 190.

The oil pump is integral to the Balance Shaft Module (BSM). The oil pump cannot be disassembled for inspection. The pressure relief valve is serviceable and can be removed and inspected.

1. Before servicing the vehicle, refer to the Precautions Section.

2. Rotate the engine to Top Dead Center (TDC) on the number 1 compression stroke.

3. Remove the oil pan. Refer to Oil Pan, removal & installation.

4. Mark the chain and the sprocket for reassembly.

5. Push the tensioner piston back into the tensioner body.

6. With the piston held back, insert the tensioner pin 9703 into the tensioner body to hold the piston in the retracted position.

➥Do not remove sprocket from the BSM.

7. Remove the BSM mounting bolts. Discard the 180mm bolts, the 185mm bolts can be reused.

8. Lower the back of the BSM and remove the chain from the sprocket.

9. Remove the BSM from the engine.

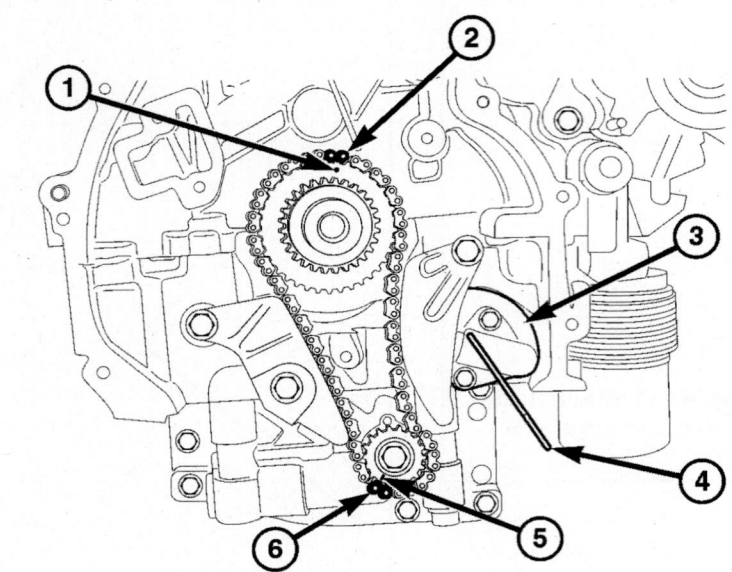

1. Crankshaft sprocket timing mark
2. Chain matchmark
3. Chain tensioner
4. Tensioner pin 9703
5. BSM sprocket timing mark
6. Chain matchmark

95066

Fig. 189 Balance Shaft Module (BSM)/oil pump timing marks shown—2.4L engine

To install:

✳✳ WARNING

There are 2 different BSM-to-engine block bolts used: 180mm bolts with a lock-patch on the threads or 185mm bolts without lock-patch. Do NOT reuse the 180mm bolts. Always discard the 180mm bolts after removing. Failure to replace these bolts can result in engine damage. The 185mm bolts are reusable. Install the same length bolts that were removed and use either 4 new 180mm bolts or 4 185mm bolts.

10. The 7.3 inch (185mm) length bolts must be checked for stretching. Check the bolts with a straight edge for necking. If the bolts are necked down, they must be replaced.

11. Clean the BSM mounting holes with MOPAR® brake parts cleaner.

12. If the chain was removed, align the marks on the crankshaft sprocket and the chain.

13. Align the marks on the oil pump sprocket and the chain.

14. Install the chain on the sprocket.

15. Pivot the BSM assembly upwards and position it on the ladder frame.

16. Start the BSM mounting bolts by hand.

➥Use a 3-step procedure when tightening the BSM mounting bolts.

17. Tighten the new 180mm BSM mounting bolts in sequence as follows:
   a. Step 1: Tighten to 11 ft. lbs. (15 Nm).
   b. Step 2: Tighten to 24 ft. lbs. (33 Nm).
   c. Step 3: Tighten an additional 90°.

18. Tighten the 185mm BSM mounting bolts in sequence as follows:
   a. Step 1: Tighten to 11 ft. lbs. (15 Nm).

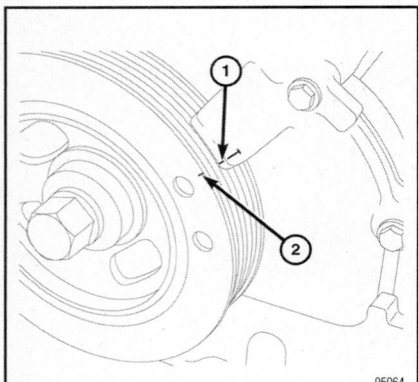

95064

Fig. 188 Rotate the engine to Top Dead Center (TDC) markings (1, 2) on the number 1 compression stroke—2.4L engine

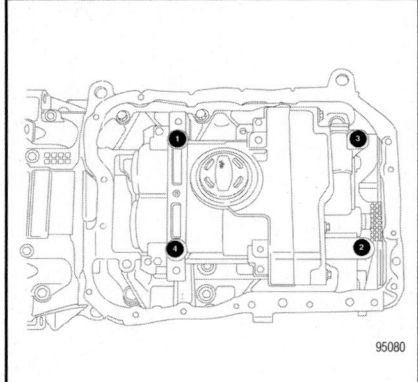

95080

Fig. 190 Balance Shaft Module (BSM)/oil pump bolt tightening sequence—2.4L engine

b. Step 2: Tighten to 22 ft. lbs. (29 Nm).

c. Step 3: Tighten an additional 90°.

19. Remove the tensioner pin 9703.

20. Install the oil pan. Refer to Oil Pan, removal & installation.

21. Fill the engine with the proper type and amount of oil. Refer to Engine Oil & Filter, Replacement procedure.

22. Start the engine and check for leaks.

2.7L Engine

See Figure 191.

➡**The oil pump pressure relief valve can be serviced by removing the oil pan.**

1. Before servicing the vehicle, refer to the Precautions Section.

2. Remove the crankshaft vibration damper.

3. Remove the timing chain cover. Refer to Timing Chain Front Cover, removal & installation.

4. Remove the timing chain and sprockets. Refer to Timing Chain & Sprockets, removal & installation.

5. Remove the oil pan. Refer to Oil Pan, removal & installation.

6. Remove the oil pick-up tube and O-ring.

7. Ensure that the crankshaft is positioned so that the oil pump drive flats are parallel to the oil pan mounting surface. This position will properly locate the oil pump upon installation.

8. Remove the oil pump attaching bolts.

9. Remove the oil pump.

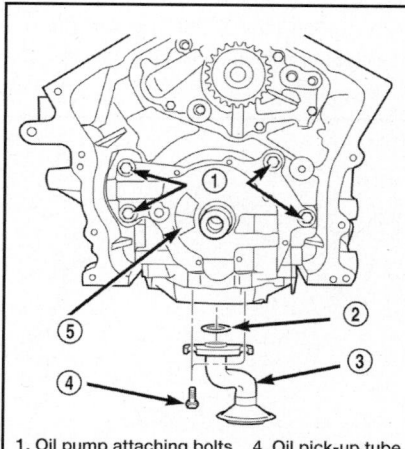

1. Oil pump attaching bolts
2. O-ring
3. Oil pick-up tube
4. Oil pick-up tube attaching bolts
5. Oil pump

95793

Fig. 191 Removing the oil pump—2.7L engine

To install:

⁂ **WARNING**

The crankshaft oil pump drive flats must be parallel to the oil pan mounting surface before installing the oil pump. This position will properly locate the oil pump. If not properly located, severe damage to the oil pump can occur.

10. Prime the oil pump before installation by filling the rotor cavity with engine oil.

11. If the crankshaft has been rotated, it must be repositioned so that the oil pump drive flats are parallel to the oil pan mounting surface prior to oil pump installation.

12. Install the oil pump carefully over the crankshaft and into position.

13. Install the oil pump attaching bolts. Tighten the bolts to 21 ft. lbs. (28 Nm).

14. Install the oil pick-up tube with a new O-ring. Lubricate the O-ring with clean engine oil before installation. Tighten the attaching bolts to 21 ft. lbs. (28 Nm).

15. Install the oil pan. Refer to Oil Pan, removal & installation.

16. Install the timing chain and sprockets. Refer to Timing Chain & Sprockets, removal & installation.

17. Install the timing chain cover. Refer to Timing Chain Front Cover, removal & installation.

18. Install the crankshaft vibration damper.

19. Fill the crankcase with the proper type and amount of engine oil.

3.5L Engine

See Figure 192.

➡**It is necessary to remove the oil pump body to service the oil pump rotors. The oil pump pressure relief valve can be serviced by removing the oil pan.**

1. Before servicing the vehicle, refer to the Precautions Section.

2. Drain the cooling system. Refer to Engine Coolant, Drain & Refill Procedure.

3. Remove the timing belt and crankshaft sprocket. Refer to Timing Belt & Sprockets, removal & installation.

4. Remove the oil pan. Refer to Oil Pan, removal & installation.

5. Remove the oil pickup tube.

6. Remove the oil pump fasteners. Remove the pump and gasket from the engine.

To install:

➡**Thoroughly clean all bolt threads and threaded areas in the engine, removing all oil residue, before assembly.**

7. Prime the oil pump before installation by filling the rotor cavity with clean engine oil.

8. Install the oil pump and gasket carefully over the crankshaft and position the pump onto the block.

➡**DO NOT apply the thread sealant to the underside of the bolt head.**

9. Apply MOPAR® Thread Sealant as directed on the package to the oil pump cover bolts where indicated. The sealant must be applied from the tip to approximately 0.39 inch (10mm) of the thread length. Tighten the oil pump cover bolts to 106 inch lbs. (12 Nm). Tighten the oil pump-to-block bolts to 21 ft. lbs. (28 Nm).

10. Install a new O-ring on the oil pickup tube.

11. Install the oil pickup tube.

12. Install the oil pan. Refer to Oil Pan, removal & installation.

13. Install the crankshaft sprocket and the timing belt. Refer to Timing Belt & Sprockets, removal & installation.

14. Install the timing belt covers. Refer to Timing Belt Front Cover/Timing Belt Rear Cover, removal & installation.

15. Install the crankshaft vibration damper.

16. Install the accessory drive belts. Refer to Accessory Drive Belts, removal & installation.

17. Fill the cooling system. Refer to Engine Coolant, Drain & Refill Procedure.

18. Fill the engine crankcase with proper type and amount of oil.

19. Check for fluid leakage.

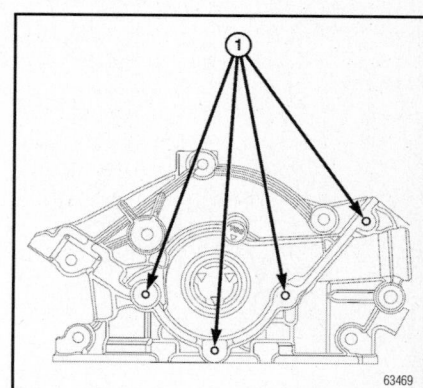

63469

Fig. 192 Apply MOPAR® Thread Sealant as directed on the package to the oil pump cover bolts where indicated (1)—3.5L engine

3.6L Engine

See Figures 193 through 197.

1. Before servicing the vehicle, refer to the Precautions Section.

2. Disconnect and isolate the negative battery cable. Refer to Battery, removal & installation.

3. Remove the upper oil pan. Refer to Oil Pan, removal & installation.

4. Remove the oil pump pick-up.

5. Disconnect the engine wire harness from the oil pump solenoid electrical connector.

6. Depress the connector retention lock tab to disengage the oil pump solenoid electrical connector from the engine block.

7. Remove the bolts and the timing gear splash shield.

8. Push the oil pump solenoid electrical connector into the engine block, rotate the connector slightly clockwise, push it past the primary chain tensioner mounting bolt and into the engine.

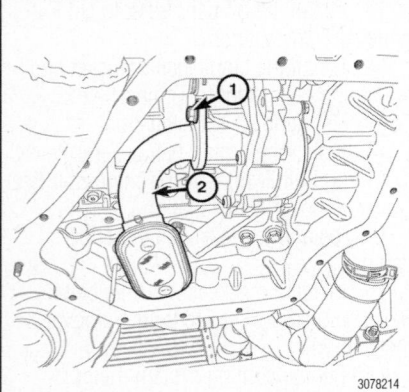

Fig. 193 Remove the oil pump pick-up bolt (1) and oil pump pick-up (2)—3.6L engine

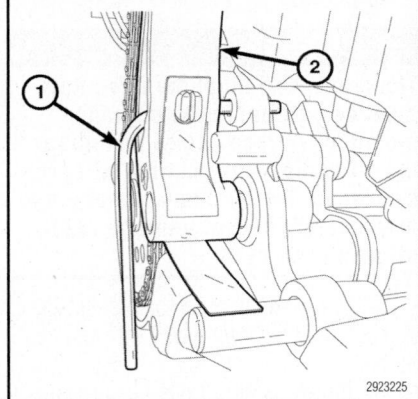

Fig. 195 Push back the oil pump chain tensioner (2) and insert a suitable retaining pin (1)—3.6L engine

9. Push back the oil pump chain tensioner and insert a suitable retaining pin such as a 3mm Allen® wrench.

❊❊ WARNING

Always reinstall timing chains so that they maintain the same direction of rotation. Inverting a previously run chain on a previously run sprocket will result in excessive wear to both the chain and sprocket.

10. Mark the direction of rotation on the oil pump chain and sprocket using a paint pen or equivalent to aid in reassembly.

➥**There are no timing marks on the oil pump gear or chain. Timing of the oil pump is not required.**

11. Remove the oil pump sprocket T45 retaining bolt and remove the oil pump sprocket.

12. Remove the retaining pin and disen-

gage the oil pump chain tensioner spring from the dowel pin.

13. Remove the oil pump chain tensioner from the oil pump.

14. Remove the 4 oil pump bolts and remove the oil pump.

To install:

15. Align the locator pins to the engine block and install the oil pump with 4 bolts. Tighten the bolts to 106 inch lbs. (12 Nm).

16. Install the oil pump chain tensioner on the oil pump.

17. Position the oil pump chain tensioner spring above the dowel pin.

18. Push back the oil pump chain tensioner and insert a suitable retaining pin such as a 3mm Allen® wrench.

19. Place the oil pump sprocket into the oil pump chain. Align the oil pump sprocket with the oil pump shaft and install the sprocket. Install the T45 retaining bolt and tighten to 18 ft. lbs. (25 Nm).

20. Remove the retaining pin. Verify that the oil pump chain is centered on the tensioner and crankshaft sprocket.

21. Rotate the crankshaft clockwise 1 complete revolution to verify proper oil pump chain installation.

22. Position the oil pump solenoid electrical connector into the engine block. Rotate the connector so that it can be pushed past the primary chain tensioner mounting bolt. Then rotate the connector slightly counter clockwise and push it into the engine block until it locks in place.

23. Install the timing gear splash shield. Tighten the bolts to 35 inch lbs. (5 Nm).

24. Verify that the oil pump solenoid electrical connector retention lock tab is engaged to the engine block.

25. Connect the engine wire harness to the oil pump solenoid electrical connector.

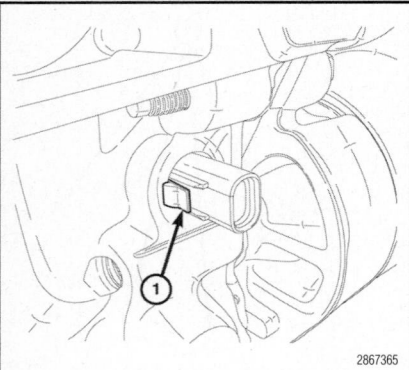

Fig. 194 Depress the connector retention lock tab (1) to disengage the oil pump solenoid electrical connector from the engine block—3.6L engine

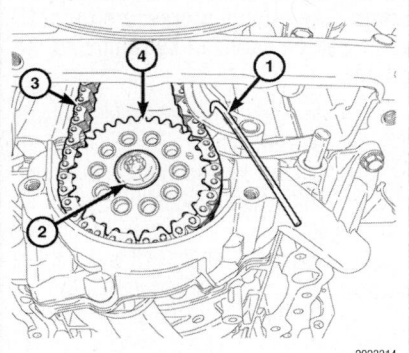

Fig. 196 View of the oil pump sprocket T45 retaining bolt (2), oil pump sprocket (4), tensioner retaining pin (1), and oil pump chain (3)—3.6L engine

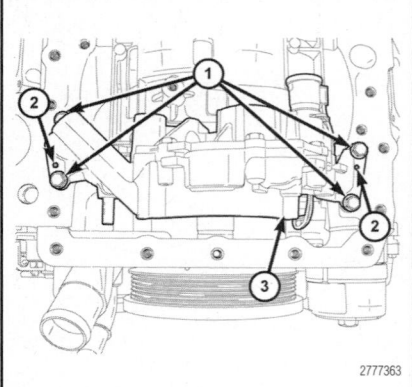

Fig. 197 View of oil pump bolts (1), oil pump (3), and locator pins (2)—3.6L engine

26. Install the oil pump pick-up.
27. Install the oil pan. Refer to Oil Pan, removal & installation.
28. If removed, install the oil filter and fill the engine crankcase with the proper oil to the correct level. Refer to Engine Oil & Filter, Replacement.
29. Connect the negative battery cable and tighten the nut to 45 inch lbs. (5 Nm). Refer to Battery, removal & installation.

✳✳ WARNING

A low oil pressure indicator or Malfunction Indicator Light (MIL) that remains illuminated for more than 2 seconds may indicate low or no engine oil pressure. Stop the engine and investigate the cause of the indication.

30. Start and run the engine until it reaches the normal operating temperature.
31. Check for fluid leakage.

INSPECTION

2.4L Engine

See Figure 198.

1. Before servicing the vehicle, refer to the Precautions Section.
2. Remove the timing chain cover. Refer to Timing Chain Front Cover, removal & installation.
3. Remove the oil pan. Refer to Oil Pan, removal & installation.
4. Measure the distance between the tensioner body and the guide shoe.
5. If the distance is 0.397 inch (10.1mm) or greater, replace the chain.

2.7L Engine

1. Before servicing the vehicle, refer to the Precautions Section.
2. Disassemble the oil pump.
3. Clean all the oil pump components.

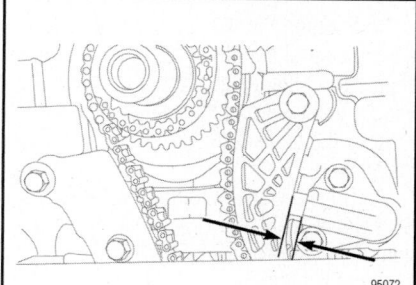

Fig. 198 Measuring the distance between the tensioner body and the guide shoe—2.4L engine

4. Inspect the mating surface of the oil pump housing and cover. Replace the oil pump if it is deeply scratched or grooved (minor surface scratches and polishing is normal).
5. Lay a straightedge across the pump cover surface. If a 0.001 inch (0.025mm) feeler gauge can be inserted between the cover and straight edge, the cover should be replaced.
6. Measure the thickness and diameter of the outer rotor. If the outer rotor thickness measures 0.373 inch (9.474mm) or less, or if the diameter is 3.511 inch (89.174mm) or less, replace the outer rotor.
7. If the inner rotor measures 0.373 inch (9.474mm) or less replace the inner rotor.
8. Slide the outer rotor into the body, press it to one side and measure the clearance between the rotor and the body. If the measurement is 0.015 inch (0.39mm) or more, replace the body only if the outer rotor is within specifications.
9. Install the inner rotor into the body. If the clearance between the inner and the outer rotors is 0.008 inch (0.20mm) or more, replace both rotors.
10. Place a straightedge across the face of the body, between the bolt holes. If a feeler gauge of 0.003 inch (0.077mm) or more can be inserted between the rotors and the straightedge, replace the pump assembly ONLY if the rotors are within specification.
11. Inspect the oil pressure relief valve plunger for scoring and free operation in its bore. Small marks may be removed with 400-grit wet or dry sandpaper.
12. The relief valve spring has a free length of approximately 1.95 inches (49.5mm) it should test between 23–25 lbs. (101–110 N) when compressed to 1.34 inches (34mm). Replace the spring that fails to meet specifications.
13. Assemble the oil pump.

3.5L Engine

1. Before servicing the vehicle, refer to the Precautions Section.
2. Disassemble the oil pump.
3. Clean all the parts thoroughly. The mating surface of the oil pump housing should be smooth. Replace the pump cover if scratched or grooved.
4. Lay a straightedge across the pump cover surface. If a 0.001 inch (0.025mm) feeler gauge blade can be inserted between the cover and the straight edge, the cover should be replaced.
5. Measure the thickness and diameter

of the outer rotor. If the outer rotor thickness measures 0.563 inch (14.299mm) or less, or if the diameter is 3.141 inches (79.78mm) or less, replace the outer rotor.
6. If the inner rotor measures 0.563 inch (14.299mm) or less replace the inner rotor.
7. Slide the outer rotor into the body, press it to one side and measure the clearance between the rotor and the body. If the measurement is 0.015 inch (0.39mm) or more, replace the body only if the outer rotor is within specifications.
8. Install the inner rotor into the body. If the clearance between the inner and the outer rotors is 0.008 inch (0.20mm) or more, replace both rotors.
9. Place a straightedge across the face of the body, between the bolt holes. If a feeler gauge of 0.003 inch (0.077mm) or more can be inserted between the rotors and the straightedge, replace the pump assembly ONLY if the rotors are within specifications.
10. Inspect the oil pressure relief valve plunger for scoring and free operation in its bore. Small marks may be removed with 400-grit wet or dry sandpaper.
11. The relief valve spring has a free length of approximately 1.95 inches (49.5mm). It should test between 23–25 lbs. (101–110 N) when compressed to 1 ^{11}/$_{32}$ inches (34mm). Replace the spring that fails to meet specifications.
12. Assemble the oil pump.

3.6L Engine

See Figure 199.

➡The 3.6L Oil pump is released as an assembly. The assembly includes both the pump and the solenoid. There are no serviceable sub-assembly compo-

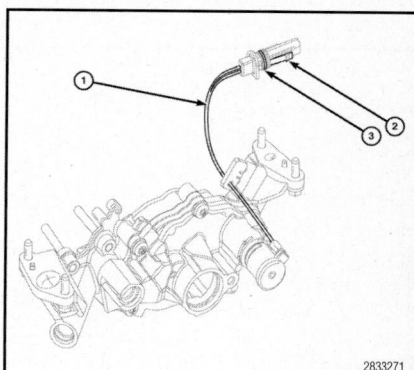

Fig. 199 Inspect the solenoid wires (1) for cuts or chaffing, the condition of the connector O-ring seal (3), and the connector retention lock tab (2) for fatigue or damage—3.6L engine

nents. In the event the oil pump or solenoid are not functioning or out of specification, they must be replaced as an assembly.

1. Before servicing the vehicle, refer to the Precautions Section.
2. Inspect the solenoid wires for cuts or chaffing.
3. Inspect the condition of the connector O-ring seal.
4. Inspect the connector retention lock tab for fatigue or damage.

PISTON AND RING

POSITIONING

2.4L Engine

See Figures 200 and 201.

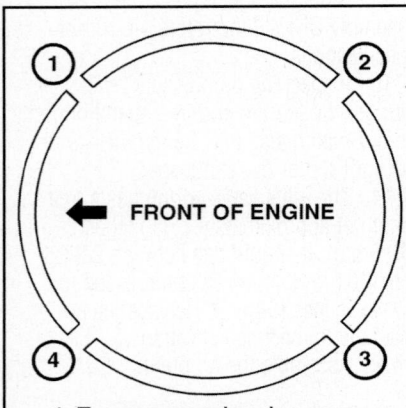

1. Top compression ring gap
2. Oil ring rail gap
3. Second compression ring gap
4. Oil ring rail gap

94844

Fig. 200 Piston ring positioning—2.4L engine

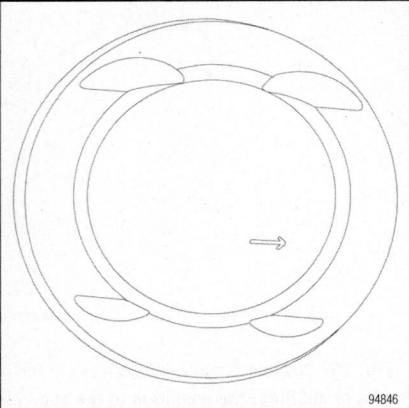

94846

Fig. 201 The directional arrow stamped on the piston should face toward the front of the engine—2.4L engine

2.7L, 3.5L, and 3.6L Engines

See Figure 202.

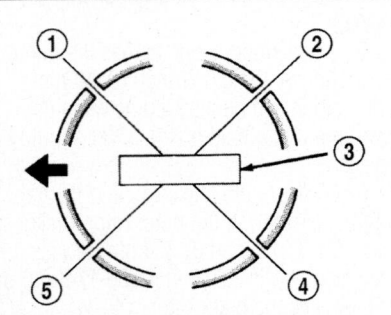

1. Oil ring upper side rail end gap
2. No. 1 (upper) ring end gap
3. Piston pin
4. Oil ring lower side rail end gap
5. No. 2 (intermediate) ring end gap and oil ring expander gap

30343

Fig. 202 Piston ring positioning with arrow pointing toward the front of the engine—2.7L, 3.5L, and 3.6L engines

REAR MAIN SEAL

REMOVAL & INSTALLATION

2.4L Engine

See Figures 203 and 204.

1. Before servicing the vehicle, refer to the Precautions Section.
2. Remove the transaxle and flexplate.
3. Insert a ³⁄₁₆ inch flat-bladed screwdriver between the dust lip and the metal case of the crankshaft seal. Angle the screwdriver through the dust lip against the metal case of the seal. Pry out the seal.

❉❉ WARNING

Do not permit the screwdriver blade to contact the crankshaft seal surface. Contact of the screwdriver blade against the crankshaft edge (chamfer) is permitted.

4. Check to make sure the seals garter spring is not on the crankshaft.

To install:

➡ **If a burr or scratch is present on the crankshaft edge (chamfer), clean it up with 800-grit emery cloth to prevent seal damage during installation of a new seal. If emery cloth is used, the crankshaft must be cleaned off with MOPAR® brake parts cleaner.**

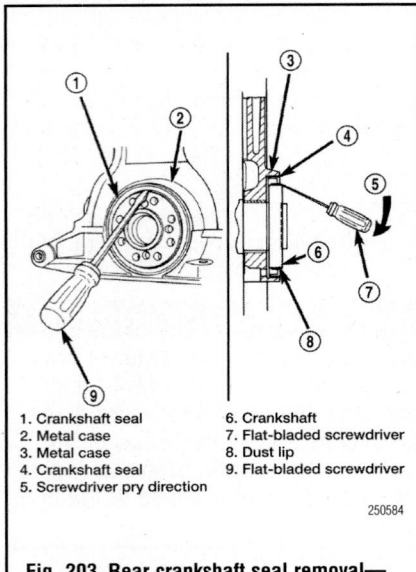

1. Crankshaft seal
2. Metal case
3. Metal case
4. Crankshaft seal
5. Screwdriver pry direction
6. Crankshaft
7. Flat-bladed screwdriver
8. Dust lip
9. Flat-bladed screwdriver

250584

Fig. 203 Rear crankshaft seal removal—2.4L engine

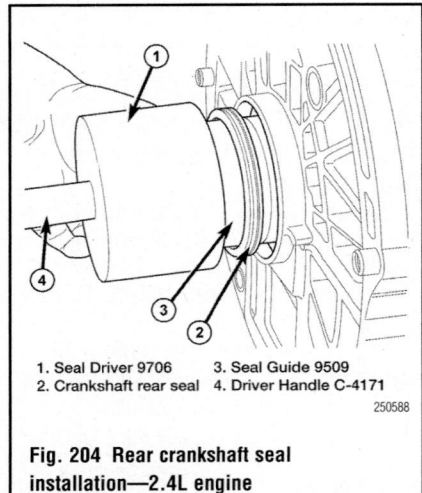

1. Seal Driver 9706
2. Crankshaft rear seal
3. Seal Guide 9509
4. Driver Handle C-4171

250588

Fig. 204 Rear crankshaft seal installation—2.4L engine

➡ **When installing the seal, lubricate the Seal Guide 9509 with clean engine oil.**

5. Place Seal Guide 9509 on the crankshaft.
6. Position the seal over the guide tool. The guide tool should remain on the crankshaft during the installation of the seal. Ensure that the lip of the seal is facing towards the crankcase during installation.
7. Drive the seal into the block using Seal Driver 9706 and Driver Handle C-4171 until the Seal Driver 9706 bottoms out against the block.
8. Install the flexplate and transaxle.

2.7L and 3.5L Engines

See Figures 205 through 208.

1. Before servicing the vehicle, refer to the Precautions Section.

2. Remove the engine oil pan. Refer to Oil Pan, removal & installation.

3. Lower the weight of the engine back onto the engine mounts.

➡**Before separating the transaxle from the engine, use an appropriate support fixture or lifting device to support the weight of the engine.**

4. Remove the transaxle from the vehicle.

5. Remove the flexplate.

6. Remove the rear crankshaft oil seal retainer bolts.

7. Remove the crankshaft oil seal and clean all mating surfaces.

To install:

✴✴ WARNING

If a burr or scratch is present on the crankshaft edge (chamfer), clean the surface using 400-grit sand paper to prevent seal damage during installation. Make sure the rear crankshaft oil seal surface is clean and free of any abrasive materials.

✴✴ WARNING

The rear crankshaft oil seal and retainer are an assembly. DO NOT separate the seal protector from the rear crankshaft oil seal before installation on engine. Damage to the seal lip may occur if the seal protector is removed and installed prior to installation on engine.

8. Apply engine oil to the crankshaft seal surface.

9. If the seal protector is missing or was accidentally dislodged, go to installation step 3. Otherwise, carefully position the

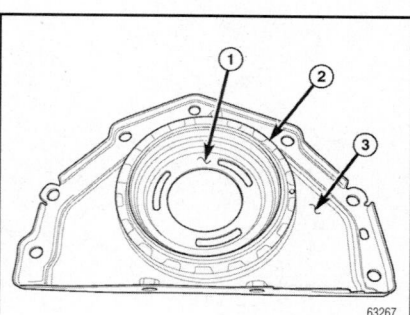

Fig. 205 View of the seal protector (1), oil seal retainer assembly (3), and seal protector (1)—2.7L and 3.5L engines

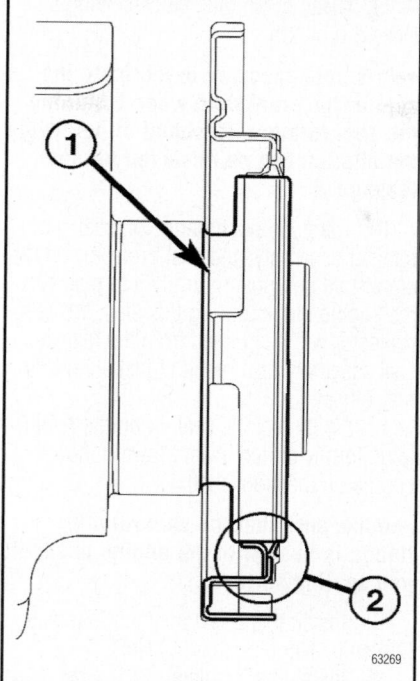

Fig. 206 The seal lip (2) must always uniformly curl inward toward the engine on the crankshaft (1)—2.7L and 3.5L engines

oil seal retainer assembly, and seal protector on crankshaft and push firmly into place on the engine block (during this step, the seal protector will be pushed from the rear oil seal assembly as a result of installing the rear oil seal). Hand tighten the rear oil seal fasteners, and go to installation step 4.

➡**The seal lip must always uniformly curl inward toward the engine on the crankshaft.**

➡**If for any reason the installation sleeve is missing or dislodged from the rear crankshaft oil seal prior to installation, the following procedure must be performed.**

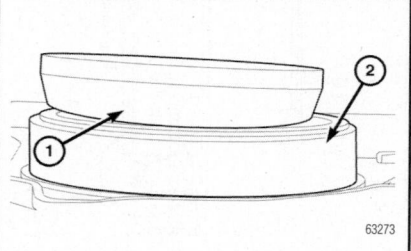

Fig. 207 Using the chamfered seal guide from Special Tool 6926, insert the tapered end (1) into the transaxle side of the rear crankshaft oil seal assembly (2)—2.7L and 3.5L engines

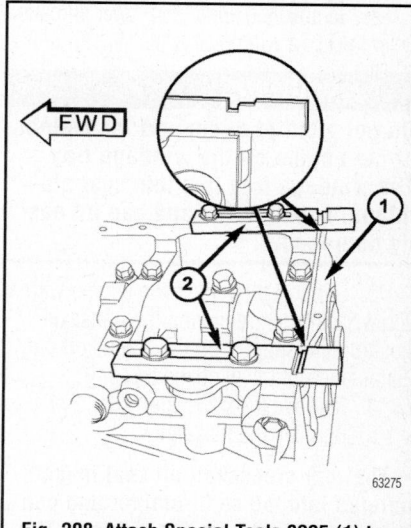

Fig. 208 Attach Special Tools 8225 (1) to the pan rail using the oil pan fasteners (2)—2.7L and 3.5L engines

10. Using the chamfered seal guide from Special Tool 6926, insert the tapered end into the transaxle side of the rear crankshaft oil seal assembly, and push the seal guide through the seal assembly. This will ensure the seal lip is positioned toward the engine when the seal assembly is installed. When the seal lip is correctly positioned, go to installation step 2.

➡**The following steps must be performed to prevent oil leaks at sealing joints.**

11. Attach Special Tools 8225 to the pan rail using the oil pan fasteners.

➡**Special Tools 8225, are used to assist with the fit of the flush mount rear main seal retainer. The notch on the tool should be located away from the seal retainer.**

12. While applying firm pressure to the seal retainer against Special Tools 8225, tighten the seal retainer screws to 106 inch lbs. (12 Nm).

13. Remove Special Tools 8225.

Make sure that the seal flange is flush with the block oil pan sealing surface.

14. Install the oil pan. Tighten the 6mm fasteners to 106 inch lbs. (12 Nm) and the 8mm fasteners to 21 ft. lbs. (28 Nm). Refer to Oil Pan, removal & installation.

15. Install the flexplate and transaxle.

3.6L Engine

See Figures 209 and 210.

1. Before servicing the vehicle, refer to the Precautions Section.

2. Remove the upper and lower oil pans. Refer to Oil Pan, removal & installation.

❋❋ WARNING

Do not attempt to support the weight of the engine on the windage tray. The windage tray is a thin cast aluminum construction and can be easily damaged.

3. Support the rear of the engine with a screw-jack when removing the transaxle. Position the support on the engine oil pan flange and not the windage tray.

4. Remove the transaxle.

5. Remove the flexplate.

➡The rear crankshaft oil seal is incorporated into the seal retainer and cannot be removed from the retainer. The rear crankshaft oil seal and seal retainer are serviced as an assembly.

6. Remove the 8 seal retainer attaching screws.

7. Remove and discard the seal retainer.

To install:

❋❋ WARNING

The rear crankshaft oil seal and retainer are an assembly. To avoid damage to the seal lip, DO NOT remove the seal protector from the rear crankshaft oil seal before installation onto the engine.

➡Whenever the crankshaft is replaced, the rear crankshaft oil seal must also be replaced. Failure to do so may result in engine fluid leakage.

8. Inspect the crankshaft to make sure there are no nicks or burrs on the seal surface.

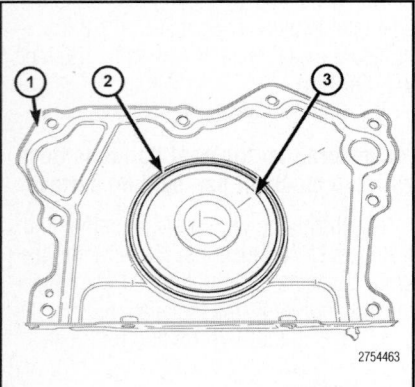

Fig. 209 View of the rear crankshaft oil seal (2), retainer (1), and seal protector (3)—3.6L engine

9. Clean the engine block sealing surfaces thoroughly.

➡It is not necessary to lubricate the seal or the crankshaft when installing the seal retainer. Residual oil following installation can be mistaken for seal leakage.

10. Carefully position the oil seal retainer assembly, and seal protector on the crankshaft and push it firmly into place on the engine block (during this step, the seal protector will be pushed from the rear oil seal assembly as a result of installing the rear oil seal).

11. Verify that the seal lip on the retainer is uniformly curled inward toward the engine on the crankshaft.

➡Make sure that the seal retainer flange is flush with the engine block oil pan sealing surface.

12. Install the 8 seal retainer bolts and tighten to 106 inch lbs. (12 Nm).

13. Install the flexplate.

14. Install the transaxle.

15. Install the upper and lower oil pans. Refer to Oil Pan, removal & installation.

16. Fill the engine crankcase with the proper oil to the correct level. Refer to Engine Oil & Filter, Replacement.

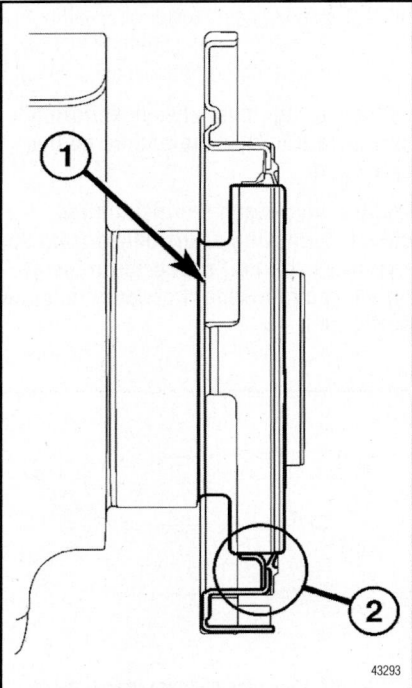

Fig. 210 Verify that the seal lip (2) on the retainer is uniformly curled inward toward the engine on the crankshaft (1)—3.6L engine

TIMING BELT FRONT COVER

REMOVAL & INSTALLATION

3.5L Engine

See Figure 211.

1. Before servicing the vehicle, refer to the Precautions Section.

2. Release the fuel system pressure. Refer to Relieving Fuel System Pressure.

3. Disconnect the negative battery cable. Refer to Battery, removal & installation.

4. Raise and safely support the vehicle.

5. Remove the accessory drive belt. Refer to Accessory Drive Belts, removal & installation.

6. Remove the accessory drive belt tensioner.

7. Remove the bolts for the power steering pump. Reposition the power steering pump aside.

8. Remove the crankshaft damper.

9. Remove the lower front timing belt cover fasteners.

10. Lower the vehicle.

11. Support the engine with a floor jack.

12. Remove the front engine mount.

13. Disconnect the fuel supply line at the fuel rail.

14. Remove the upper timing belt cover bolts and remove the front timing belt cover.

To install:

➡The timing cover bolts and bolt holes to the engine block must be thoroughly cleaned and free of oil residue before assembly. IN ADDITION, add thread sealant to the timing cover bolts that mount to the oil pump.

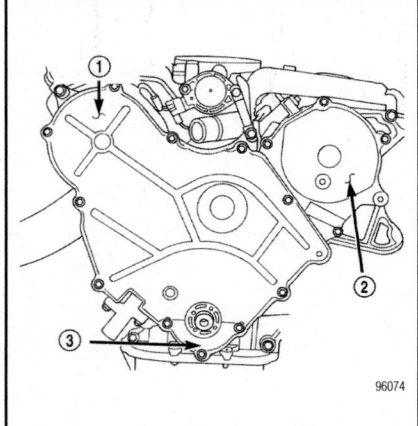

Fig. 211 View of cover bolts (3) and upper timing belt cover (1, 2)—3.5L engine

15. Install the front timing belt cover.

16. Install the upper engine mount.

17. Connect the fuel supply line at the fuel rail.

18. Raise and safely support the vehicle.

19. Install the power steering pump fasteners. Tighten the bolts to 17 ft. lbs. (23 Nm).

20. Install the crankshaft damper.

21. Install the accessory drive belt tensioner. Torque the fastener to 21 ft. lbs. (28 Nm).

22. Install the accessory drive belt. Refer to Accessory Drive Belts, removal & installation.

23. Lower the vehicle.

24. Connect the negative battery cable. Refer to Battery, removal & installation.

TIMING BELT & SPROCKETS

REMOVAL & INSTALLATION

3.5L Engine

Camshaft Sprockets

See Figures 212 and 213.

❋❋ WARNING

The 3.5L engine is NOT a free-wheeling design. Therefore, care should be taken not to rotate the camshafts or crankshaft with the timing belt removed.

➡**The camshaft timing gears are keyed to the camshaft.**

1. Before servicing the vehicle, refer to the Precautions Section.

2. Release the fuel system pressure. Refer to Relieving Fuel System Pressure.

3. Remove the front timing belt cover. Refer to Timing Belt Front Cover, removal & installation.

4. Position the crankshaft sprocket to the Top Dead Center (TDC) mark on the oil pump housing by turning the crankshaft in the clockwise direction.

5. Install a dial indicator in the number 1 cylinder to check TDC of the piston. Rotate the crankshaft until the piston is at exactly TDC.

6. Remove the camshaft retainer/thrust plate from the rear of the right cylinder head.

7. Remove the cylinder head covers. Refer to Valve Covers, removal & installation.

8. Remove rocker arm assemblies.

9. Remove the timing belt tensioner and timing belt. Refer to Timing Belt &

Sprockets, Timing Belt, removal & installation.

10. Loosen and remove the left camshaft gear retaining bolt and washer. The left bolt is 10.0 inches (255mm) long.

11. Hold the left camshaft sprocket with a 1 ⁷⁄₁₆ inch (36mm) box end wrench.

12. Remove the left camshaft sprocket.

❋❋ WARNING

The camshaft must be pushed rearward approximately 3 ½ inches to remove the camshaft gear retaining bolt and gear. Care must be taken not to scratch or nick the camshaft or cylinder head journals when moving the camshaft.

13. Loosen and remove the right camshaft gear retaining bolt and washer. The right bolt is 8 ⅜ inches (213mm) long.

14. Hold the right camshaft sprocket with a 1 ⁷⁄₁₆ inch (36mm) box end wrench and loosen the camshaft bolt.

15. Using a floor jack, raise the right side of the engine enough to allow clearance to remove the right camshaft bolt and washer.

16. Remove the right camshaft sprocket.

To install:

➡**The camshaft sprockets are keyed and not interchangeable from side to side because of the camshaft position sensor pick-up.**

❋❋ WARNING

The camshafts must be pushed back into the cylinder head after the camshaft sprockets and retaining bolts are positioned. Care must be

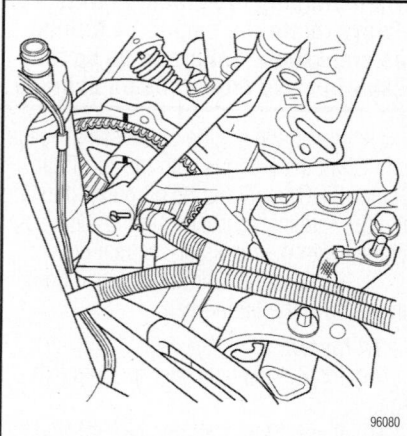

Fig. 212 Hold the camshaft sprocket and loosen the camshaft bolt to remove—3.5L engine

taken not to scratch or nick the camshaft or cylinder head journals when moving the camshafts.

17. Install the camshaft sprockets onto the camshafts. Install NEW sprocket attaching bolts into place. The 10 inch (255mm) bolt is installed in the left camshaft and the 8 ⅜ inch (213mm) bolt is installed into the right camshaft. Do not tighten the bolts at this time, they will be tightened at a later step. The camshaft sprocket timing marks should be aligned with the inner cover timing marks at both sprockets.

18. Install the camshaft thrust plates and seals. Tighten the bolts to 21 ft. lbs. (28 Nm).

19. Install the timing belt starting first at the crankshaft sprocket, then to remaining the sprockets in a counterclockwise direction.

20. Install the belt around the last sprocket. Maintain tension on the belt as it is positioned around the tensioner pulley. The camshaft sprocket timing marks and crankshaft sprocket timing mark should still be aligned with the inner cover marks.

➡**It is necessary to compress the plunger into the tensioner body and install a locking pin prior to reinstalling the tensioner. See the Timing Belt procedure for tensioner compression instructions.**

21. Hold the tensioner pulley against the belt and install the reset (pinned) timing belt tensioner into the housing. Tighten the attaching bolts to 21 ft. lbs. (28 Nm).

22. Remove the tensioner retaining pin to allow the tensioner to extend to the pulley bracket.

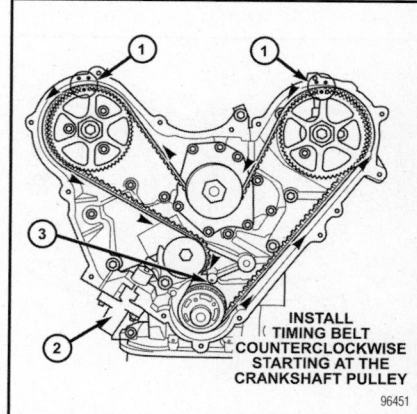

Fig. 213 View of camshaft sprocket timing marks (1), crankshaft sprocket timing mark (3), and timing belt tensioner (2)—3.5L engine

23. Hold the right camshaft sprocket hex with a 1 7/16 inch (36mm) wrench and tighten the right camshaft bolt to 75 ft. lbs. (102 Nm), plus 90°.

24. Hold the left camshaft sprocket hex with a 1 7/16 inch (36mm) wrench and tighten the left camshaft bolts to 75 ft. lbs. (102 Nm), plus 90°.

25. Install the rocker arm assemblies.

26. Install the cylinder head covers. Refer to Valve Covers, removal & installation.

27. Install the front timing belt cover. Refer to Timing Belt Front Cover, removal & installation.

➡The Cam/Crank Variation Relearn procedure must be performed anytime there has been a repair/replacement made to a powertrain system, for example: flywheel, valvetrain, camshaft and/or crankshaft sensors or components. Refer to Powertrain Control Module (PCM), Powertrain Verification Test.

Crankshaft Sprocket

See Figures 214 and 215.

1. Before servicing the vehicle, refer to the Precautions Section.

2. Remove the timing belt. Refer to Timing Belt & Sprockets, Timing Belt, removal & installation.

3. Remove the crankshaft sprocket using Gear Puller L-4407A.

To install:

➡To ensure proper installation depth of the crankshaft sprocket, Sprocket Installer 6641 must be used.

4. Install the crankshaft sprocket using Sprocket Installer 6641 and Forcing Screw C-4685-C1.

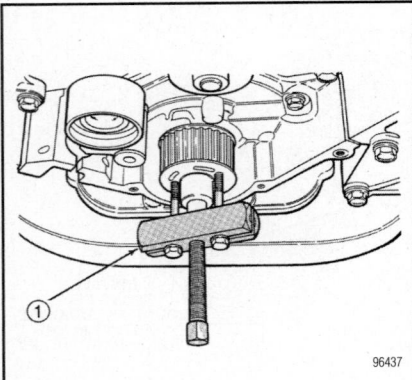

Fig. 214 Removing the crankshaft sprocket using Gear Puller L-4407A (1)— 3.5L engine

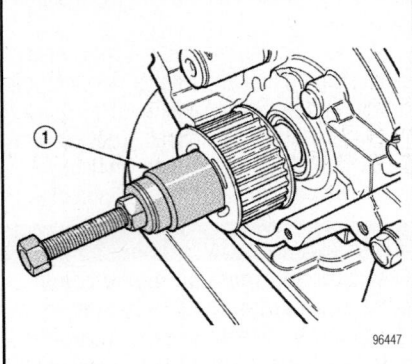

Fig. 215 Installing the crankshaft sprocket using Sprocket Installer 6641 (1) and Forcing Screw C-4685-C1—3.5L engine

5. Install the timing belt. Refer to Timing Belt & Sprockets, Timing Belt, removal & installation.

Timing Belt

See Figures 216 and 217.

1. Before servicing the vehicle, refer to the Precautions Section.

2. Release the fuel system pressure. Refer to Relieving Fuel System Pressure.

3. Disconnect the negative battery cable. Refer to Battery, removal & installation.

4. Remove both cylinder head covers. Refer to Valve Covers, removal & installation.

5. Remove the front timing belt cover. Refer to Timing Belt Front Cover, removal & installation.

6. Mark the belt running direction, if the timing belt is to be reused.

✱✱ WARNING

When aligning the timing marks, always rotate the engine by turning the crankshaft. Failure to do so may result in valve and/or piston damage.

7. Rotate the engine clockwise until the crankshaft mark aligns with the Top Dead Center (TDC) mark on the oil pump housing and the camshaft sprocket timing marks are aligned with the marks on the rear cover.

8. Remove the timing belt tensioner and remove the timing belt.

To install:

9. Inspect the tensioner for fluid leakage.

10. Inspect the pivot and bolt for free movement, bearing grease leakage, and smooth rotation. If not rotating freely, replace the arm and pulley assembly.

11. When the tensioner is removed from the engine, it is necessary to compress the plunger into the tensioner body.

➡Index the tensioner in the vise the same way it is installed on the engine. This ensures proper pin orientation when the tensioner is installed on the engine.

12. Place the tensioner into a vise and SLOWLY compress the plunger. Total bleed down of the tensioner should take about 5 minutes.

13. When the plunger is compressed into the tensioner body, install a pin through the body and the plunger to retain the plunger in place until the tensioner is installed.

✱✱ WARNING

The 3.5L is NOT a freewheeling engine. Therefore, the valve train rocker assemblies must be removed before attempting to rotate either the crankshaft or camshafts independently of each other.

✱✱ WARNING

If the camshafts have moved from the timing marks, always rotate the camshaft towards the direction nearest to the timing marks. DO NOT TURN THE CAMSHAFTS A FULL REVOLUTION OR DAMAGE to the valves and/or pistons could result.

14. Align the crankshaft sprocket with the TDC mark on the oil pump cover.

15. Align the camshaft sprockets timing reference marks with the marks on the rear cover.

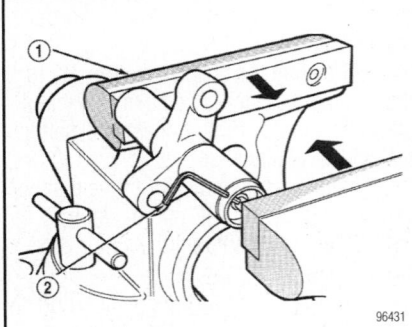

Fig. 216 Timing belt tensioner shown installed to a vise (1). When the plunger is compressed into the tensioner body, install a pin (2) through the body and the plunger to retain the plunger in place— 3.5L engine

16. Install the timing belt starting at the crankshaft sprocket going in a counter-clockwise direction. Install the belt around the last sprocket and maintain tension on the belt as it is positioned around the tensioner pulley.

➡ **It is necessary to compress the plunger into the tensioner body and install a locking pin prior to reinstalling the tensioner.**

17. Hold the tensioner pulley against the belt and install the reset (pinned) timing belt tensioner into the housing. Tighten the attaching bolts to 21 ft. lbs. (28 Nm).

18. When the tensioner is in place, pull the retaining pin to allow the tensioner to extend to the pulley bracket.

19. Rotate the crankshaft sprocket 2 revolutions and check the timing marks on the camshafts and crankshaft. The marks should line up within their respective locations. If the marks do not line up, repeat the procedure.

20. Install the front timing belt cover. Refer to Timing Belt Front Cover, removal & installation.

21. Connect the negative battery cable and tighten the nut to 45 inch lbs. (5 Nm). Refer to Battery, removal & installation.

➡ **The Cam/Crank Variation Relearn procedure must be performed anytime there has been a repair/replacement made to a powertrain system, for example: flywheel, valvetrain, camshaft and/or crankshaft sensors or components. Refer to Powertrain Control Module (PCM), Powertrain Verification Test.**

TIMING BELT REAR COVER

REMOVAL & INSTALLATION

3.5L Engine

See Figure 218.

1. Before servicing the vehicle, refer to the Precautions Section.

2. Release the fuel system pressure. Refer to Relieving Fuel System Pressure.

3. Disconnect the negative battery cable. Refer to Battery, removal & installation.

4. Remove the timing belt and camshaft sprockets. Refer to Timing Belt & Sprockets, removal & installation.

5. Remove the rear timing belt cover bolts.

6. Remove the rear cover.

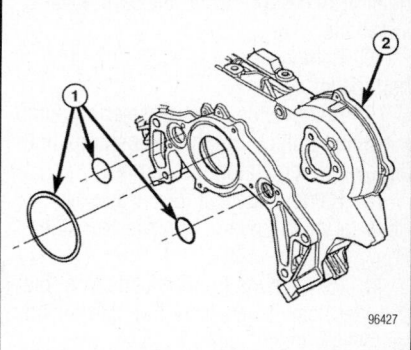

Fig. 218 Position NEW O-rings (1) on the cover timing belt rear cover (2)—3.5L engine

➡ **The rear timing belt cover has O-rings to seal the water pump passages to the cylinder block. Do not reuse the O-rings.**

To install:

7. Clean the rear timing belt cover O-ring sealing surfaces and grooves. Lubricate the new O-rings with MOPAR® Dielectric Grease, or equivalent, to facilitate assembly.

8. Position the NEW O-rings on the cover.

9. Install the rear timing belt cover. Tighten the bolts to the following specified torque:

   a. Tighten the M10 bolts to 40 ft. lbs. (54 Nm).

   b. Tighten the M8 bolts to 20 ft. lbs. (28 Nm).

   c. Tighten the M6 bolts to 106 inch lbs. (12 Nm).

10. Install the camshaft sprockets and the timing belt. Refer to Timing Belt & Sprockets, removal & installation.

TIMING CHAIN FRONT COVER

REMOVAL & INSTALLATION

2.4L Engine

See Figures 219 through 225.

1. Before servicing the vehicle, refer to the Precautions Section.

2. Remove the engine cover by pulling upward.

3. Release the fuel system pressure. Refer to Relieving Fuel System Pressure.

4. Disconnect the negative battery cable. Refer to Battery, removal & installation.

5. Remove the coolant recovery bottle.

6. Remove and reposition the power steering reservoir.

7. Remove the accessory drive belt.

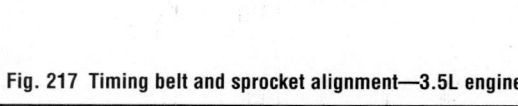

1. Timing reference mark on rear cover
2. Camshaft sprocket
3. Timing belt rear cover
4. Timing belt
5. Idler pulley
6. Timing belt rear cover
7. Camshaft sprocket
8. Timing reference mark on rear cover
9. TDC mark on the oil pump cover
10. Crankshaft sprocket
11. Tensioner pulley
12. Tensioner

Fig. 217 Timing belt and sprocket alignment—3.5L engine

Refer to Accessory Drive Belts, removal &
installation.

    8. Remove the power steering hose
hold down.

    9. Remove the 3 power steering pump
mounting bolts through the openings in the
pulley and reposition the pump.

    10. Remove the cylinder head cover.
Refer to Valve Covers, removal & installation.

    11. Remove the ignition coils from the
cylinder head cover. Refer to Ignition Coil,
removal & installation.

    12. Raise and safely support the
vehicle.

    13. Remove the frame cover portion of
the right splash shield.

    14. Set the engine to Top Dead Center
(TDC).

    15. Remove the lower A/C compressor
bolts if equipped.

    16. Remove the lower A/C compressor
mount if equipped.

    17. Remove the accessory drive belt
lower idler pulley.

    18. Remove the crankshaft damper.

    19. Remove the 3 bolts and the water
pump pulley from the water pump.

    20. Remove the lower bolt from the right
side engine mount bracket.

    21. Remove the timing chain cover lower
bolts.

    22. Lower the vehicle.

    23. Support the engine with a suitable
jack.

    24. Remove the right engine mount
bracket retaining bolts.

    25. Remove the retaining nuts and repo-
sition the mount bracket.

    26. Remove the accessory drive upper
idler pulley.

    27. Remove the right upper engine
mount bracket.

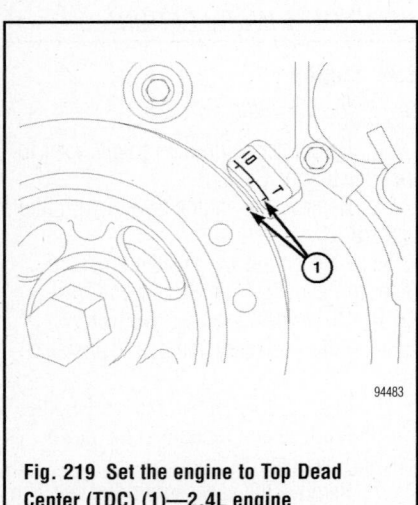

**Fig. 219 Set the engine to Top Dead
Center (TDC) (1)—2.4L engine**

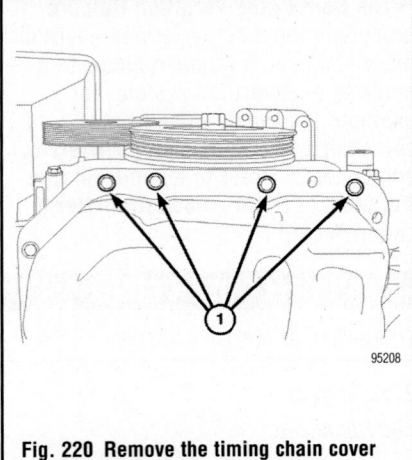

**Fig. 220 Remove the timing chain cover
lower bolts (1)—2.4L engine**

    28. Remove the accessory drive belt ten-
sioner.

    29. Remove the upper timing chain
cover retaining bolts.

    30. Remove the timing chain cover using
the pry points.

    31. Remove the timing chain cover out
through the bottom of the vehicle.

To install:

➡**When using RTV, the sealing surfaces must be clean and free from
grease and oil. The parts should be
assembled in 10 minutes and tighten to
final torque within 45 minutes.**

    32. Clean all sealing surfaces.

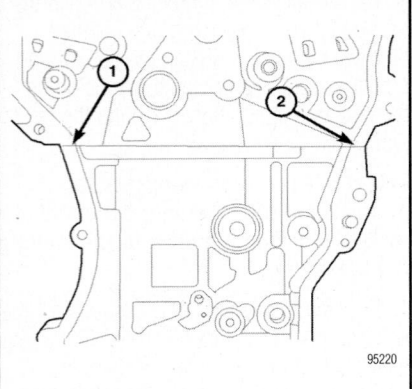

**Fig. 222 Apply engine sealant RTV at the
cylinder head-to-block parting line (1,
2)—2.4L engine**

    33. Apply MOPAR® engine sealant RTV
(or equivalent) at the cylinder head-to-block
parting line.

    34. Apply MOPAR® engine sealant RTV
(or equivalent) at the ladder frame-to-block
parting line.

    35. Apply MOPAR® engine sealant RTV
(or equivalent) in the corner of the oil pan
and block.

    36. Apply a 0.08 inch (2mm) bead of
MOPAR® engine sealant RTV (or equivalent)
to the oil pan.

    37. Apply a 0.08 inch (2mm) bead of
MOPAR® engine sealant RTV (or equivalent)
to the engine block.

    38. Install the timing chain cover
upwards from under the vehicle.

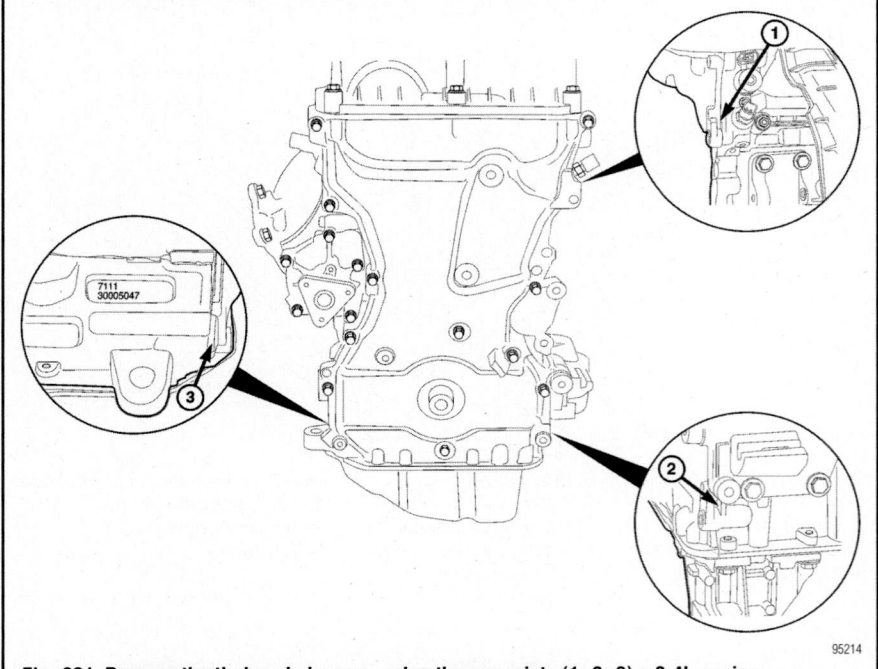

Fig. 221 Remove the timing chain cover using the pry points (1, 2, 3)—2.4L engine

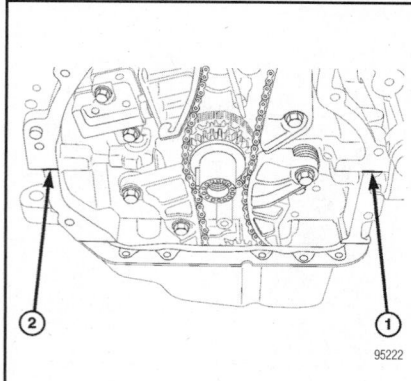

Fig. 223 Apply engine sealant RTV at the ladder frame-to-block parting line (1, 2)— 2.4L engine

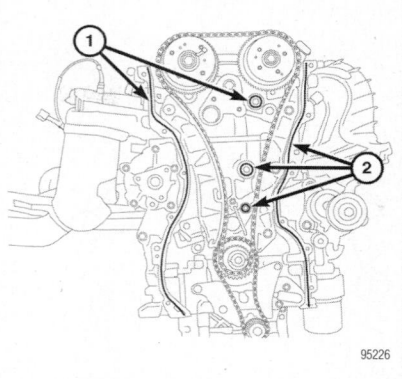

Fig. 225 Apply a bead of engine sealant RTV to the engine block (1, 2) as shown— 2.4L engine

39. Install the timing chain cover upper retaining bolts and tighten the M6 bolts to 80 inch lbs. (9 Nm) and the M8 bolts to 19 ft. lbs. (26 Nm).

40. Install the accessory drive belt tensioner. Tighten the bolt to 18 ft. lbs. (24 Nm).

41. Install the right engine mount bracket. Tighten the bolts to 37 ft. lbs. (50 Nm).

42. Install the accessory drive belt upper idler pulley. Tighten the bolt to 35 ft. lbs. (48 Nm).

43. Position the engine mount adapter and install the bolts.

44. Install the retaining nuts and tighten the nuts to 22 ft. lbs. (30 Nm).

45. Tighten the bolts to 37 ft. lbs. (50 Nm).

46. Remove the jack from under the engine.

47. Raise and safely support the vehicle.

48. Install the oil pan-to-timing chain cover lower retaining bolts and tighten the M6 bolts to 80 inch lbs. (9 Nm).

49. Install the water pump pulley and tighten the 3 bolts to 80 inch lbs. (9 Nm).

50. Install the crankshaft damper.

51. Install the accessory drive belt lower idler pulley. Tighten the bolt to 35 ft. lbs. (48 Nm).

52. Install the lower A/C compressor mounting bracket. Tighten the bolts to 18 ft. lbs. (24 Nm).

53. Install the A/C compressor. Tighten the bolts to 18 ft. lbs. (25 Nm).

54. Install the right lower splash shield.

55. Lower the vehicle.

56. Install the cylinder head cover. Refer to Valve Covers, removal & installation.

57. Install the ignition coils. Refer to Ignition Coil, removal & installation.

58. Place the power steering pump in the mounting position. Install the 3 bolts through the openings in the pulley. Tighten the mounting bolts to 19 ft. lbs. (26 Nm).

59. Install the power steering hose hold down.

60. Install the accessory drive belt. Refer to Accessory Drive Belts, removal & installation.

61. Install the power steering pump reservoir. Tighten the mounting screw to 106 inch lbs. (12 Nm).

62. Install the coolant recovery reservoir. Tighten the mounting bolts to 89 inch lbs. (10 Nm).

63. Install the clean air hose and the air cleaner housing. Refer to Air Cleaner, removal & installation.

64. Connect the negative battery cable. Refer to Battery, removal & installation.

65. Operate the engine until it reaches the normal operating temperature. Check the oil system for leaks and the correct fluid level.

66. Install the engine cover.

2.7L Engine

See Figures 226 and 227.

1. Before servicing the vehicle, refer to the Precautions Section.

2. Disconnect and isolate the negative battery cable. Refer to Battery, removal & installation.

3. Drain the cooling system. Refer to Engine Coolant, Drain & Refill Procedure.

4. Remove the coolant pressure container.

5. Remove the right front wheel and belt splash shield.

6. Remove the accessory drive belts. Refer to Accessory Drive Belts, removal & installation.

7. Remove the crankshaft vibration damper.

8. Remove the AC/Alternator belt tensioner/bracket assembly.

9. Disconnect the heater hose from the tube at the right front frame rail area.

10. Remove the screws securing the heater supply tube to the right frame rail. Reposition the heater supply tube.

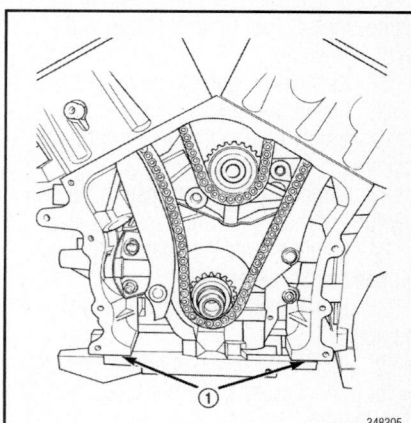

Fig. 226 Apply a bead of RTV sealant to the parting lines (1) between the oil pan and cylinder block—2.7L engine

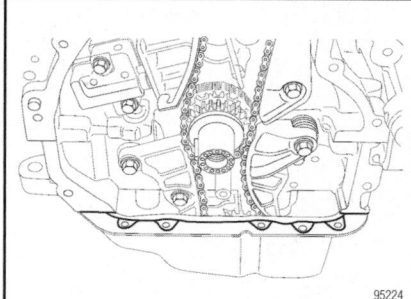

Fig. 224 Apply engine sealant RTV in the corner of the oil pan and block and a bead to the oil pan as shown—2.4L engine

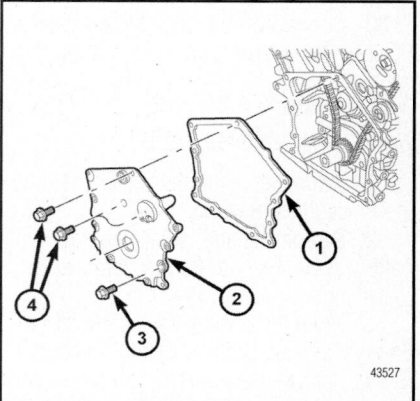

Fig. 227 View of the timing chain cover (2), gasket (1), and attaching bolts (3, 4)—2.7L engine

11. Place a floor jack with a wooden block under the oil pan to support the engine.

12. Remove the right engine mount.

13. Remove the upper timing chain cover bolts.

14. Remove the remaining bolts securing the timing chain cover to the engine.

15. Remove the timing chain cover.

16. Discard the timing chain cover gasket. Remove the front crankshaft oil seal from the cover.

To install:

17. Inspect and clean the timing chain cover sealing surfaces.

18. Before installing the timing cover gasket, apply a ⅛ inch (3.2mm) bead of MOPAR® Engine RTV GEN II to the parting lines between the oil pan and cylinder block.

19. Install the timing cover and gasket. Tighten the M10 cover bolts to 40 ft. lbs. (54 Nm) and the M6 bolts to 106 inch lbs. (12 Nm).

20. Install the front crankshaft oil seal using Special Tool 6780-2 sleeve and 6780-1 installer.

21. Install the right engine mount.

22. Install the screws attaching the heater supply tube to the right front frame rail area.

23. Connect the heater hose to the supply tube at the right front frame rail area.

24. Install the AC/Alternator belt tensioner/bracket assembly.

25. Install the crankshaft vibration damper.

26. Install the accessory drive belts. Refer to Accessory Drive Belts, removal & installation.

27. Install the belt splash shield and the right front wheel.

28. Install the coolant pressure container.

29. Fill the cooling system.

30. Connect the negative battery cable. Refer to Battery, removal & installation.

3.6L Engine

See Figures 228 through 231.

1. Before servicing the vehicle, refer to the Precautions Section.

2. Disconnect and isolate the negative battery cable. Refer to Battery, removal & installation.

3. Drain the cooling system. Refer to Engine Coolant, Drain & Refill Procedure.

4. Remove the upper radiator hose and thermostat housing. Refer to Thermostat, removal & installation.

5. Remove the heater core return hose from the water pump housing.

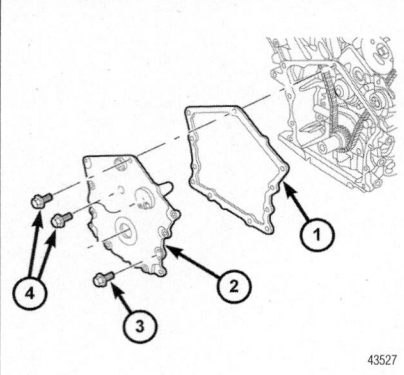

Fig. 228 Remove the right engine mount isolator bolts (2, 3) and bracket (1)—3.6L engine

6. Remove the lower radiator hose from the water pump housing.

7. Remove the heater core supply hose from the coolant outlet housing.

8. Remove the bolt and reposition the heater core supply tube.

9. Remove the accessory drive belt. Refer to Accessory Drive Belts, removal & installation.

10. Remove the accessory drive belt tensioner.

11. Remove the accessory idler pulley.

12. Remove the power steering pump pulley.

13. Remove the crankshaft vibration damper.

14. Remove the right and left cylinder head covers. Refer to Valve Covers, removal & installation.

15. Remove the upper and lower oil pans. Refer to Oil Pan, removal & installation.

16. Temporarily reinstall the front fore and aft crossmember.

17. Remove the right engine mount isolator and bracket.

➡️**It is not necessary to remove the water pump or the coolant outlet housing for engine timing cover removal.**

➡️**One of the timing cover bolts could be an M6 (early production) or an M8 (late production).**

18. Remove the following timing cover attaching bolts:

  a. The 22 M6 bolts.

  b. The 1 M6 (early production) or 1 M8 (late production) bolt.

19. Using the 7 indicated pry points, carefully remove the timing cover.

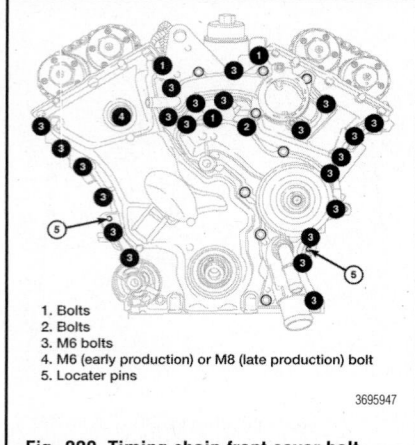

1. Bolts
2. Bolts
3. M6 bolts
4. M6 (early production) or M8 (late production) bolt
5. Locater pins

Fig. 229 Timing chain front cover bolt identifications—3.6L engine

20. If required, remove the remaining 4 M6 bolts and the coolant outlet housing from the engine timing cover.

21. If required, remove the remaining 4 M6 bolts and the water pump from the engine timing cover.

✳✳ WARNING

Do not use oil based liquids, wire brushes, abrasive wheels, or metal scrapers to clean the engine gasket surfaces. Use only isopropyl (rubbing) alcohol, along with plastic or wooden scrapers. Improper gasket surface preparation may result in engine fluid leakage.

22. Remove all residual sealant from the timing chain cover, cylinder head, and engine block mating surfaces.

23. Remove and discard the coolant outlet housing gasket and the water pump gasket.

To install:

24. If removed, install the coolant outlet housing to the timing cover with a new

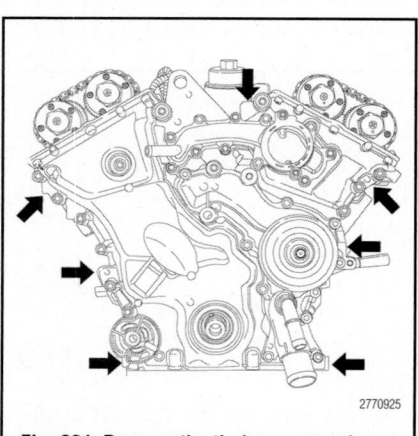

Fig. 231 Remove the timing cover using the 7 indicated pry points—3.6L engine

gasket using only 4 bolts tightened to 106 inch lbs. (12 Nm).

25. If removed, install the water pump to the timing cover using only 4 bolts tightened to 106 inch lbs. (12 Nm).

26. Install the coolant outlet housing gasket and the water pump gasket.

27. Clean the engine timing cover, cylinder head, and block mating surfaces with isopropyl alcohol in preparation for sealant application.

➡️**Engine assembly requires the use of a unique sealant that is compatible with engine oil. Using a sealant other than MOPAR® Threebond Engine RTV Sealant may result in engine fluid leakage.**

➡️**Following the application of MOPAR® Threebond Engine RTV Sealant to the gasket surfaces, the components must be assembled within 20 minutes and the attaching fasteners must be tightened to specification within 45 minutes. Prolonged exposure to the air, prior to assembly, may result in engine fluid leakage.**

28. Apply a 0.08–0.12 inch (2–3mm) wide bead of MOPAR® Threebond Engine RTV Sealant to the front cover in the following locations:

   a. The 3 cylinder head bosses.
   b. The right and left flanges.
   c. The 4 cylinder head-to-engine block T-joints.
   d. The cover-to-right cam chain tensioner gap.

29. Align the locator pins on the engine block to the engine timing cover and install the cover.

30. Install and tighten the timing cover attaching bolts:
   a. Tighten the 22 M6 bolts to 106 inch lbs. (12 Nm).
   b. Tighten the 1 M6 (early production) or 1 M8 (late production) bolt. Tighten the M6 bolt to 106 inch lbs. (12 Nm) or tighten the M8 bolt to 18 ft. lbs. (25 Nm).

31. Install the right engine mount bracket and isolator.

32. Remove the temporarily installed front fore and aft crossmember.

33. Install the upper and lower oil pans. Refer to Oil Pan, removal & installation.

34. Install the front fore-aft crossmember and crossunder pipe.

35. Install the right halfshaft assembly. Refer to Front Halfshaft, removal & installation.

36. Install the right and left cylinder head covers. Refer to Valve Covers, removal & installation.

37. Install the upper intake manifold. Refer to Intake Manifold, removal & installation.

38. Install the crankshaft vibration damper.

39. Install the power steering pump pulley. Refer to Power Steering Pump, removal & installation.

40. Install the accessory idler pulley.

41. Install the accessory drive belt tensioner.

42. Install the accessory drive belt. Refer to Accessory Drive Belts, removal & installation.

43. Install the heater core supply tube with 1 bolt tightened to 106 inch lbs. (12 Nm).

44. Install the heater core supply hose to the coolant outlet housing.

45. Install the lower radiator hose to the water pump housing.

46. Install the heater core return hose to the water pump housing.

47. Install the thermostat housing and upper radiator hose. Refer to Thermostat, removal & installation.

48. Install the electric vacuum pump.

49. If removed, install the oil filter and fill the engine crankcase with the proper oil to the correct level. Refer to Engine Oil & Filter, Replacement.

50. Connect the negative battery cable and tighten the nut to 45 inch lbs. (5 Nm). Refer to Battery, removal & installation.

51. Fill the cooling system. Refer to Engine Coolant, Drain & Refill Procedure.

52. Run the engine until it reaches the normal operating temperature. Check the cooling system for correct fluid level.

TIMING CHAIN & SPROCKETS

REMOVAL & INSTALLATION

2.4L Engine

Camshaft Sprockets

See Figure 232.

➡️**The camshaft phasers and camshaft sprockets are supplied as an assembly, do not attempt to disassemble.**

1. Before servicing the vehicle, refer to the Precautions Section.

2. Remove the camshaft phasers. Refer to Camshaft and Valve Lifters, removal & installation.

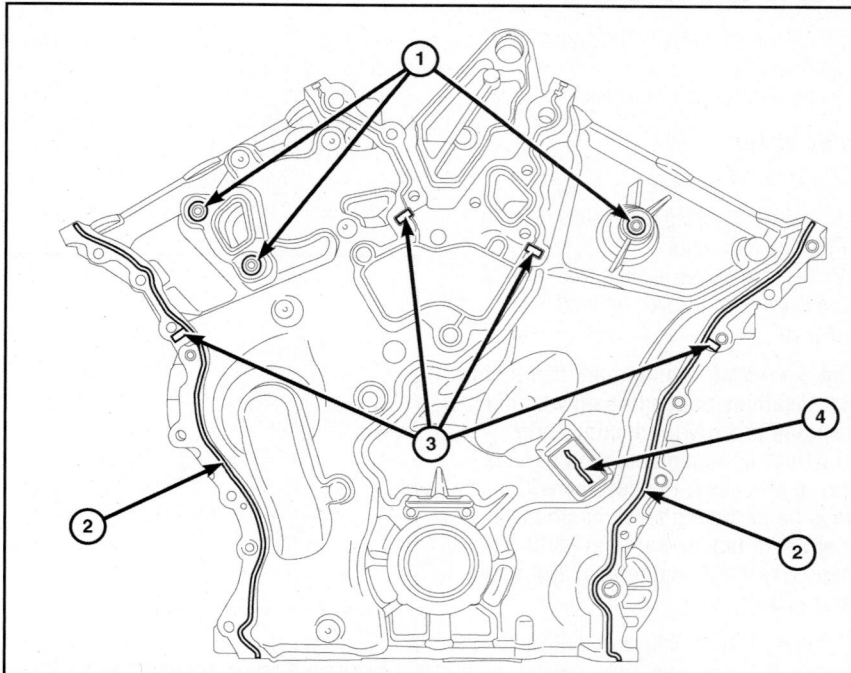

1. Cylinder head bosses   3. Cylinder head-to-engine block T-joints
2. Right and left flanges   4. Cover-to-right cam chain tensioner gap

2769376

Fig. 231 Apply a wide bead of engine RTV sealant to the front cover at the indicated locations—3.6L engine

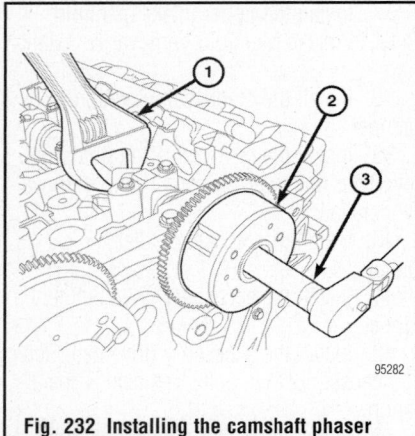

Fig. 232 Installing the camshaft phaser (2) with an adjustable wrench (1) and socket wrench (3)—2.4L engine

To install:

⁂ WARNING

Do not use an impact wrench to tighten the camshaft sprocket bolts. Damage to the camshaft-to-sprocket locating dowel pin and camshaft phaser may occur.

3. Install the camshaft phasers. Refer to Camshaft and Valve Lifters, removal & installation.

Crankshaft Sprocket

See Figure 233.

1. Before servicing the vehicle, refer to the Precautions Section.
2. Remove the timing chain. Refer to Timing Chain & Sprockets, Timing Chain, removal & installation.
3. Remove the oil pan. Refer to Oil Pan, removal & installation.
4. Remove the oil pump drive chain tensioner.
5. Remove the oil pump drive chain.
6. Remove the crankshaft sprocket.

To install:

7. Install the crankshaft sprocket onto the crankshaft.
8. Install the oil pump drive chain. Verify that the oil pump is correctly timed.
9. Reset the oil pump drive chain tensioner by pushing the plunger inward and installing the tensioner pin 8514.
10. Install the oil pump drive chain tensioner and remove the Tensioner Pin 8514.
11. Install the timing chain. Refer to Timing Chain & Sprockets, Timing Chain, removal & installation.
12. Install the oil pan. Refer to Oil Pan, removal & installation.

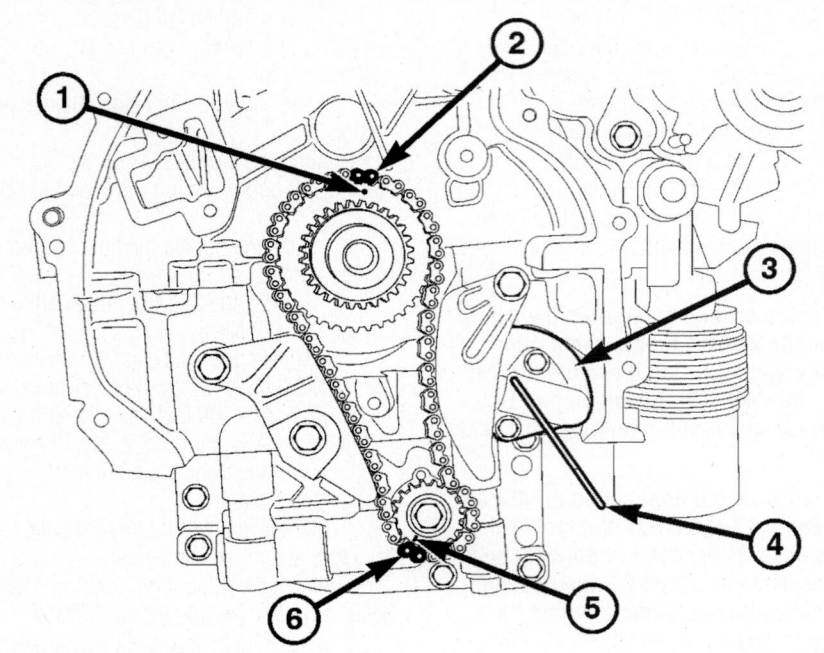

1. Crankshaft sprocket timing mark
2. Chain link timing mark
3. Oil pump chain tensioner
4. Tensioner pin 8514
5. Oil pump sprocket timing mark
6. Chain link timing mark

Fig. 233 Verify oil pump timing alignment—2.4L engine

13. Fill the engine with the proper type and amount of oil.
14. Start the engine and check for leaks.

Timing Chain

See Figures 234 and 235.

1. Before servicing the vehicle, refer to the Precautions Section.
2. Remove timing chain cover. Refer to Timing Chain Front Cover, removal & installation.

➡The crankshaft timing mark can be in 1 of 2 locations depending on whether the engine is early production, late production, or assembled with service parts. In all cases, the keyway will always be in the 9 o'clock position, in line with the ladder frame mounting surface when the engine is at Top Dead Center (TDC).

3. Verify that the engine is still set to TDC.

➡If the timing chain plated links can no longer be seen, the timing chain links corresponding to the timing marks must be marked prior to removal if the chain is to be reused.

4. Mark the chain link corresponding to the crankshaft timing mark.
5. With the engine still set to TDC, verify that the marks on the camshaft sprockets are in line with the cylinder head cover sealing surface. If the marks do not line up, the timing chain is not correctly installed.

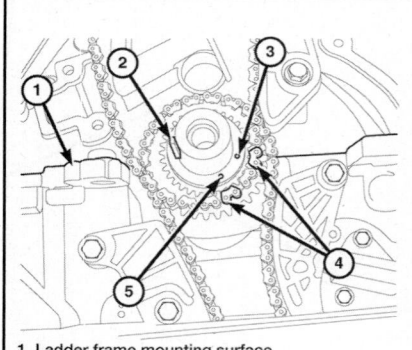

1. Ladder frame mounting surface
2. Keyway
3. Crankshaft timing mark (late production or assembled with service parts)
4. Marked chain links
5. Crankshaft timing mark (early production)

Fig. 234 Crankshaft timing mark alignment based on production—2.4L engine

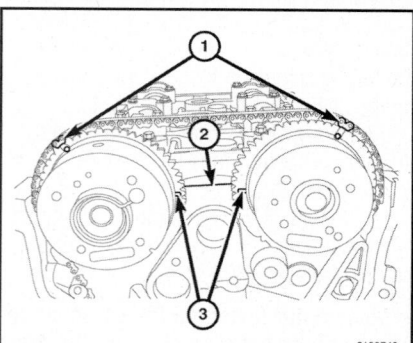

Fig. 235 View of camshaft timing marks: camshaft sprockets in line with cylinder head cover sealing surface and marked chain link corresponding to the camshaft timing mark—2.4L engine

6. Mark the chain link corresponding to the camshaft timing mark.

7. Remove the timing chain tensioner.

8. Remove the timing chain.

To install:

9. Verify that the engine is still set to TDC.

10. Align the camshaft timing marks so they are facing each other and in line with the cylinder head cover sealing surface.

11. Install the timing chain so the plated (or marked) links on the chain align with the timing marks on the camshaft sprockets.

12. Align the timing mark on the crankshaft sprocket with the plated (or marked) link on the timing chain. Position the chain so slack will be on the tensioner side.

➡Keep the slack in the timing chain on the tensioner side.

13. Install the timing chain tensioner.

14. Rotate the crankshaft CLOCKWISE 2 complete revolutions until the crankshaft is repositioned at the TDC position with the key way at the 9 o'clock position.

15. Verify that the camshafts timing marks are in the proper position and in line with the cylinder head cover sealing surface. If the marks do not line up, the timing chain is not correctly installed.

16. Install front timing chain cover. Refer to Timing Chain Front Cover, removal & installation.

17. Connect the negative battery cable. Refer to Battery, removal & installation.

18. Operate the engine until it reaches the normal operating temperature. Check the oil and cooling systems for correct fluid levels. Adjust as needed.

2.7L Engine

Crankshaft Sprocket

See Figures 236 through 238.

1. Before servicing the vehicle, refer to the Precautions Section.

2. Remove the primary timing chain. Refer to Timing Chain and Camshaft Sprockets, removal & installation.

✳✳ WARNING

Use care not to turn the crankshaft while removing the crankshaft sprocket, as damage to valves and or pistons could occur.

3. Remove the crankshaft sprocket by first installing the crankshaft damper bolt. Apply grease, or equivalent, to the damper bolt head and position Special Tools 5048-

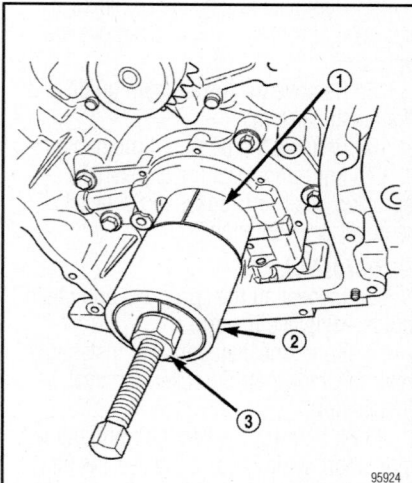

Fig. 236 Using Special Tools 5048-1 (3), 5048-6 (2), and 8539 (1) to remove the crankshaft sprocket—2.7L engine

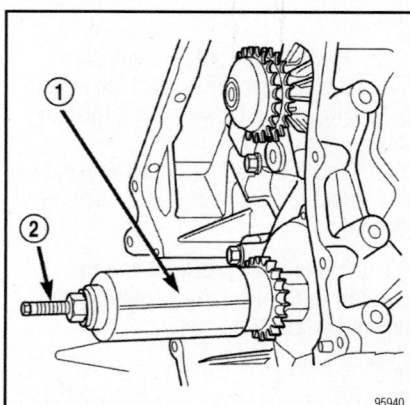

Fig. 237 Using Special Tools 6780-1 (1) and 8179 (2) to install the crankshaft sprocket—2.7L engine

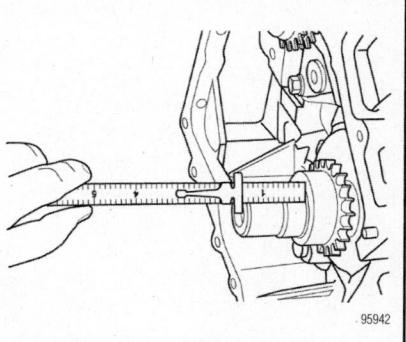

Fig. 238 Measuring the crankshaft sprocket installed depth—2.7L engine

1, 5048-6, and 8539 on the sprocket and crankshaft nose. Remove the sprocket using care not to rotate the crankshaft.

To install:

4. Install the crankshaft sprocket using Special Tools 6780-1 and 8179 until the sprocket bottoms against the crankshaft step flange. Use care not to rotate the crankshaft.

5. Verify that the crankshaft sprocket is installed to the proper depth by measuring from the sprocket outer face to the end of the crankshaft. The measurement should read: 1.52–1.56 inches (38.55–39.55mm).

6. Install the primary timing chain. Refer to Timing Chain and Camshaft Sprockets, removal & installation.

Timing Chain and Camshaft Sprockets

See Figures 239 through 244.

1. Before servicing the vehicle, refer to the Precautions Section.

2. Disconnect the negative battery cable. Refer to Battery, removal & installation.

3. Drain the cooling system. Refer to Engine Coolant, Drain & Refill Procedure.

4. Remove the upper intake manifold. Refer to Intake Manifold, removal & installation.

5. Remove the cylinder head covers. Refer to Valve Covers, removal & installation.

6. Remove the crankshaft vibration damper.

7. Remove the timing chain cover. Refer to Timing Chain Front Cover, removal & installation.

✳✳ WARNING

When aligning the timing marks, always rotate the engine by turning the crankshaft. Failure to do so may result in valve and/or piston damage.

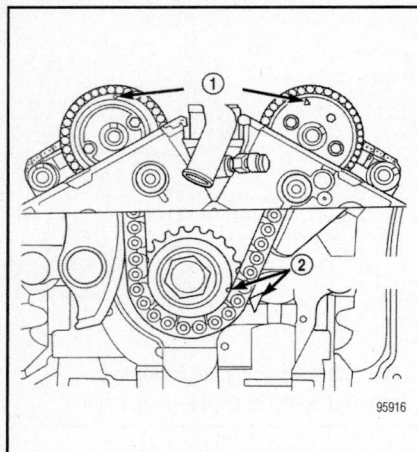

Fig. 239 Align the crankshaft sprocket timing mark to the mark on the oil pump housing (2). The mark on the oil pump housing is 60° ATDC of number 1 cylinder—2.7L engine

8. Align the crankshaft sprocket timing mark to the mark on the oil pump housing. The mark on the oil pump housing is 60° After Top Dead Center (ATDC) of number 1 cylinder.

✳✳ WARNING

When the timing chain is removed and the cylinder heads are still installed, DO NOT rotate the camshafts or crankshaft without first locating the proper crankshaft position. Failure to do so may result in valve and/or piston damage.

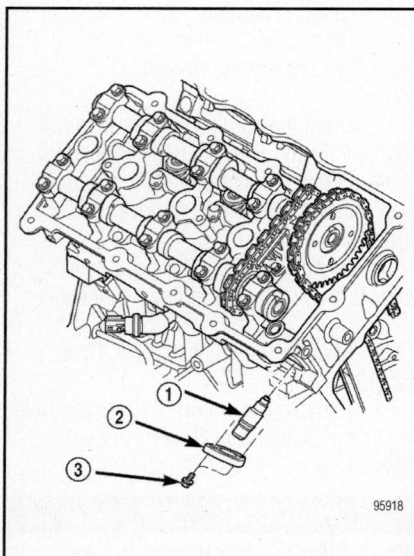

Fig. 240 View of primary timing chain tensioner retainer cap (2), tensioner (1), and attaching bolt (3)—2.7L engine

9. Remove the power steering pump and bracket as an assembly. Do not disconnect the power steering lines from the pump. Reposition the pump and support it with a suitable retaining strap.

10. Remove the primary timing chain tensioner retainer cap and tensioner from the right cylinder head.

11. Disconnect and remove the camshaft position sensor from the left cylinder head.

12. Remove the timing chain guide access plugs from the cylinder heads.

➡**When the camshaft sprocket bolts are removed, the camshafts will rotate in a clockwise direction.**

13. Starting with the right camshaft sprocket, remove the sprocket attaching bolts. Remove the camshaft damper (if equipped) and the sprocket.

14. Remove the left side camshaft sprocket attaching bolts and remove the sprocket.

15. Remove the lower chain guide and the tensioner arm.

16. Remove the primary timing chain.

17. For removal of the crankshaft sprocket, refer to Crankshaft Sprocket, removal & installation.

To install:

18. Inspect all the sprockets and chain guides. Replace if worn.

19. For crankshaft sprocket installation, refer to Crankshaft Sprocket, removal & installation.

20. If removed, install the right and left side short chain guides. Tighten the attaching bolts to 21 ft. lbs. (28 Nm).

21. Align the crankshaft sprocket timing mark to the mark on the oil pump housing.

➡**Lubricate the timing chain and guides with engine oil before installation.**

22. Place the left side primary chain sprocket onto the chain so that the timing mark is located in between the 2 (plated) timing links.

23. Lower the primary chain with the left side sprocket through the left cylinder head opening.

➡**The camshaft sprockets can be allowed to float on the camshaft hub during installation.**

24. Loosely position the left side camshaft sprocket over the camshaft hub.

25. Align the timing (plated) link to the crankshaft sprocket timing mark.

26. Position the primary chain onto the water pump drive sprocket.

27. Align the right camshaft sprocket timing mark to the timing (plated) link on the timing chain and loosely position the timing chain over the camshaft hub.

28. Verify that all chain timing (plated) links are properly aligned to the timing marks on all sprockets.

29. Install the left side lower chain guide and tensioner arm. Tighten the attaching bolts to 21 ft. lbs. (28 Nm).

➡**Inspect the O-ring on the chain guide access plugs before installing. Replace the O-ring as necessary.**

30. Install the chain guide access plugs to the cylinder heads. Tighten the plugs to 15 ft. lbs. (20 Nm).

➡**To reset the primary timing chain tensioner, the engine oil will first need to be purged from the tensioner.**

31. Purge the oil from the timing chain tensioner using the following procedure:

a. Place the check ball end of the tensioner into the shallow end of Chain Tensioner Gauge 8186.

b. Using hand pressure, slowly depress the tensioner until the oil is purged from the tensioner.

32. Reset the timing chain tensioner using the following procedure:

a. Position the cylinder plunger into the deeper end of Chain Tensioner Gauge 8186.

b. Apply a downward force until tensioner is reset.

➡**If oil was not first purged from the**

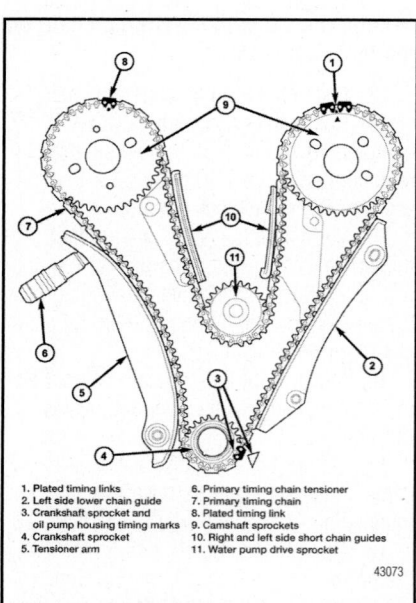

1. Plated timing links
2. Left side lower chain guide
3. Crankshaft sprocket and oil pump housing timing marks
4. Crankshaft sprocket
5. Tensioner arm
6. Primary timing chain tensioner
7. Primary timing chain
8. Plated timing link
9. Camshaft sprockets
10. Right and left side short chain guides
11. Water pump drive sprocket

Fig. 241 View of timing chain and related components—2.7L engine

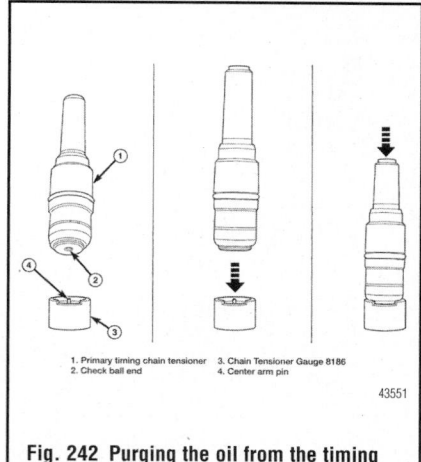

Fig. 242 Purging the oil from the timing chain tensioner—2.7L engine

1. Primary timing chain tensioner
2. Check ball end
3. Chain Tensioner Gauge 8186
4. Center arm pin

43551

tensioner, use slight finger pressure to assist the center arm pin of the Chain Tensioner Gauge 8186 to unseat the tensioner's check ball.

✳✳ WARNING

Ensure the tensioner is properly reset. The tensioner body must bottom against the top edge of Chain Tensioner Gauge 8186. Failure to properly perform the resetting procedure may cause tensioner jamming.

➡ **Inspect the tensioner O-ring for nicks or cuts and make sure the snap ring is correctly installed, replace as necessary.**

33. Install the reset chain tensioner into the right cylinder head.

34. Position the tensioner retaining plate and tighten the bolts to 106 inch lbs. (12 Nm).

35. Starting at the right cylinder bank, position the camshaft damper (if equipped) on the camshaft hub, then insert a ⅜ inch square drive extension with a breaker bar into the intake camshaft drive hub. Rotate the camshaft until the camshaft hub aligns to the camshaft sprocket and the damper attaching holes. Install the sprocket attaching bolts and tighten to 21 ft. lbs. (28 Nm).

36. Insert a ⅜ inch square drive extension with a breaker bar into the intake camshaft drive hub and rotate the camshaft until the sprocket attaching bolts can be installed. Tighten the sprocket bolts to 21 ft. lbs. (28 Nm).

37. Rotate the crankshaft slightly clockwise to remove the timing chain slack, if necessary.

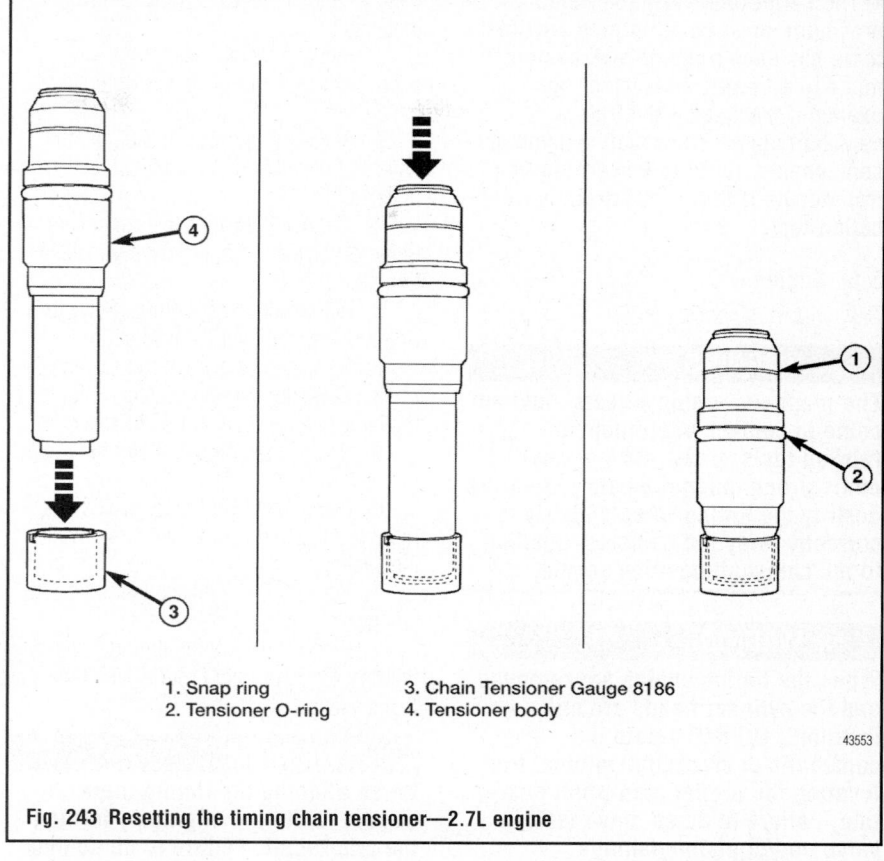

1. Snap ring
2. Tensioner O-ring
3. Chain Tensioner Gauge 8186
4. Tensioner body

43553

Fig. 243 Resetting the timing chain tensioner—2.7L engine

38. Activate the timing chain tensioner using a flat-bladed pry tool to gently pry the tensioner arm towards the tensioner slightly. Then release the tensioner arm. Verify the tensioner is activated (extends).

39. Install the power steering pump and bracket assembly. Refer to Power Steering Pump, removal & installation.

40. Install the camshaft position sensor and connect the electrical connector.

41. Install the timing chain cover. Refer

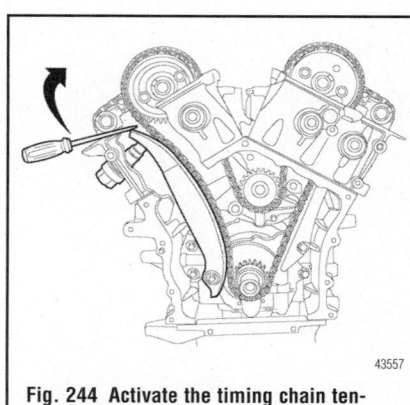

Fig. 244 Activate the timing chain tensioner using a flat-bladed pry tool to gently pry the tensioner arm towards the tensioner, then release the tensioner arm—2.7L engine

to Timing Chain Front Cover, removal & installation.

42. Install the crankshaft vibration damper.

43. Install the accessory drive belts. Refer to Accessory Drive Belts, removal & installation.

44. Install the cylinder head covers. Refer to Valve Covers, removal & installation.

45. Install the upper intake manifold. Refer to Intake Manifold, removal & installation.

46. Install the air cleaner housing assembly. Refer to Air Cleaner, removal & installation.

47. Connect the negative battery cable and tighten the nut to 45 inch lbs. (5 Nm). Refer to Battery, removal & installation.

48. Fill the cooling system. Refer to Engine Coolant, Drain & Refill Procedure.

➡ **After installation of a reset tensioner, some engine noise may occur after the initial start-up. This noise will normally disappear within 5–10 seconds.**

49. Operate the engine until it reaches the normal operating temperature. Check the cooling system for the correct fluid level.

➡The Cam/Crank Variation Relearn procedure must be performed anytime there has been a repair/replacement made to a powertrain system, for example: flywheel, valvetrain, camshaft and/or crankshaft sensors or components. Refer to Powertrain Control Module (PCM), Powertrain Verification Test.

3.6L Engine

See Figures 245 through 255.

❋❋ WARNING

The magnetic timing wheels must not come in contact with magnets (pickup tools, trays, etc.) or any other strong magnetic field. This may destroy the timing wheels ability to correctly relay the camshaft position to the camshaft position sensor.

❋❋ WARNING

When the timing chains are removed and the cylinder heads are still installed, DO NOT rotate the camshafts or crankshaft without first locating the proper crankshaft position. Failure to do so may result in valve and/or piston damage.

➡The Variable Valve Timing (VVT) assemblies (Phasers) and Oil Control Valves (OCVs) can be serviced without removing the engine timing cover.

1. Before servicing the vehicle, refer to the Precautions Section.
2. Disconnect and isolate the negative

battery cable. Refer to Battery, removal & installation.

3. Remove the air cleaner housing assembly. Refer to Air Cleaner, removal & installation.

4. Remove the upper intake manifold. Refer to Intake Manifold, removal & installation.

5. Remove the cylinder head covers. Refer to Valve Covers, removal & installation.

6. Remove the spark plugs. Refer to Spark Plugs, removal & installation.

7. Raise and safely support the vehicle.

8. Drain the cooling system. Refer to Engine Coolant, Drain & Refill Procedure.

9. Remove the oil pan. Refer to Oil Pan, removal & installation.

10. Remove the accessory drive belts. Refer to Accessory Drive Belts, removal & installation.

11. Remove the crankshaft vibration damper.

12. Remove the engine timing cover. Refer to Timing Chain Front Cover, removal & installation.

❋❋ WARNING

When aligning the timing marks, always rotate the engine by turning the crankshaft. Failure to do so may result in valve and/or piston damage.

13. Rotate the crankshaft clockwise to place the number 1 piston at Top Dead Center (TDC) on the exhaust stroke by aligning the dimple on the crankshaft with the block/bearing cap junction. The left side cam phaser arrows should point toward

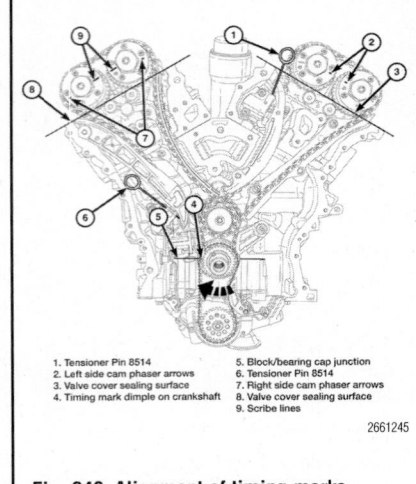

1. Tensioner Pin 8514
2. Left side cam phaser arrows
3. Valve cover sealing surface
4. Timing mark dimple on crankshaft
5. Block/bearing cap junction
6. Tensioner Pin 8514
7. Right side cam phaser arrows
8. Valve cover sealing surface
9. Scribe lines

2661245

Fig. 246 Alignment of timing marks shown at TDC—3.6L engine

each other and be parallel to the valve cover sealing surface. The right side cam phaser arrows should point away from each other and the scribe lines should be parallel to the valve cover sealing surface.

❋❋ WARNING

Always reinstall timing chains so that they maintain the same direction of rotation. Inverting a previously run chain on a previously run sprocket will result in excessive wear to both the chain and sprocket.

14. Mark the direction of rotation on the left side cam chain, right side cam chain, oil pump chain, and the primary chain using a paint pen, or equivalent, to aid in reassembly.

15. Reset the RH cam chain tensioner by pushing back the tensioner piston and installing Tensioner Pin 8514.

16. Reset the LH cam chain tensioner by lifting the pawl, pushing back the piston and installing Tensioner Pin 8514.

17. Remove the bolts and the timing gear splash shield.

18. Disengage the oil pump chain tensioner spring from the dowel pin and remove the oil pump chain tensioner.

19. Remove the oil pump sprocket T45 retaining bolt and remove the oil pump sprocket and oil pump chain.

➡Minor rotation of a camshaft (a few degrees) may be required to install the camshaft phaser lock.

20. Install the RH Camshaft Phaser Lock 10202.

21. Loosen both the intake oil control valve and exhaust oil control valve.

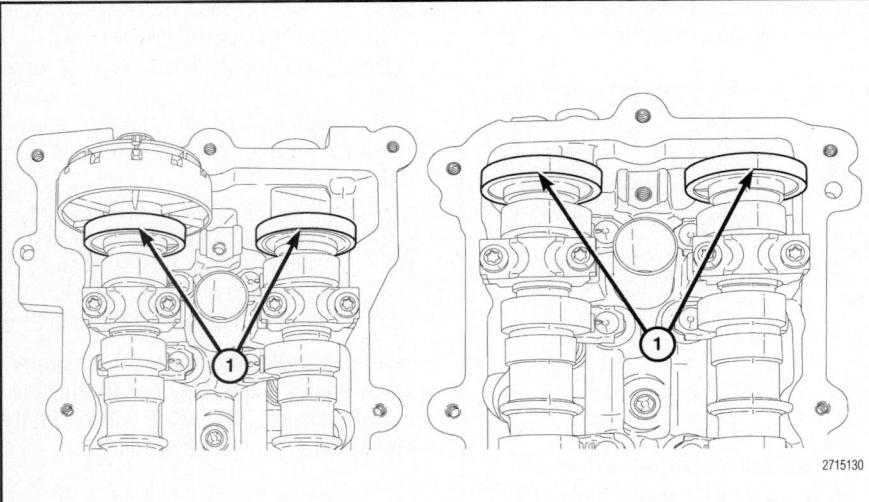

Fig. 245 The magnetic timing wheels (1) must not come in contact with any other magnetic device—3.6L engine

2715130

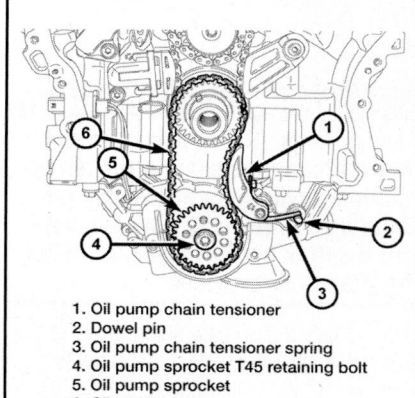

1. Oil pump chain tensioner
2. Dowel pin
3. Oil pump chain tensioner spring
4. Oil pump sprocket T45 retaining bolt
5. Oil pump sprocket
6. Oil pump chain

2682471

Fig. 247 Removing the oil pump sprocket and chain—3.6L engine

22. Remove the RH Camshaft Phaser Lock 10202.

23. Remove the oil control valve from the right side intake cam phaser.

24. Pull the right side intake cam phaser off of the camshaft and remove the right side cam chain.

25. If required, remove the oil control valve and pull the right side exhaust cam phaser off of the camshaft.

26. Install the LH Camshaft Phaser Lock 10202.

27. Loosen both the intake oil control valve and exhaust oil control valve.

28. Remove the LH Camshaft Phaser Lock 10202.

29. Remove the oil control valve from the left side exhaust cam phaser.

30. Pull the left side exhaust cam phaser off of the camshaft and remove the left side cam chain.

31. If required, remove the oil control valve and pull the left side intake cam phaser off of the camshaft.

32. Reset the primary chain tensioner by pushing back the tensioner piston and installing Tensioner Pin 8514. Remove the 2 T30 bolts and remove the primary chain tensioner.

33. Remove the T30 bolt and the primary chain guide.

34. Remove the idler sprocket T45 retaining bolt and washer.

35. Remove the primary chain, idler sprocket, and crankshaft sprocket as an assembly.

36. If required, remove the 2 T30 bolts and the LH cam chain tensioner.

37. If required, remove the 2 T30 bolts and the LH cam chain guide and tensioner arm.

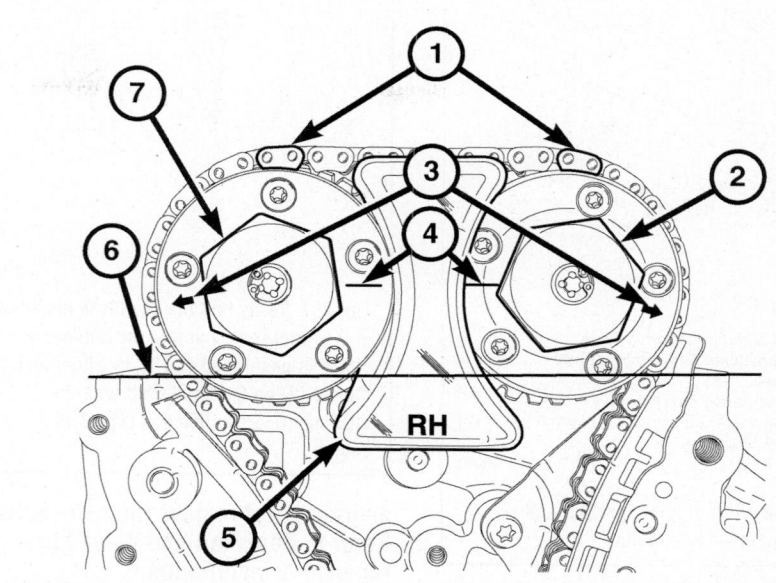

1. Plated chain links
2. Intake oil control valve
3. Cam phaser arrows
4. Scribe lines
5. RH Camshaft Phaser Lock 10202
6. Valve cover sealing surface
7. Exhaust oil control valve

2590445

Fig. 248 Aligning the RH Camshaft Phaser—3.6L engine

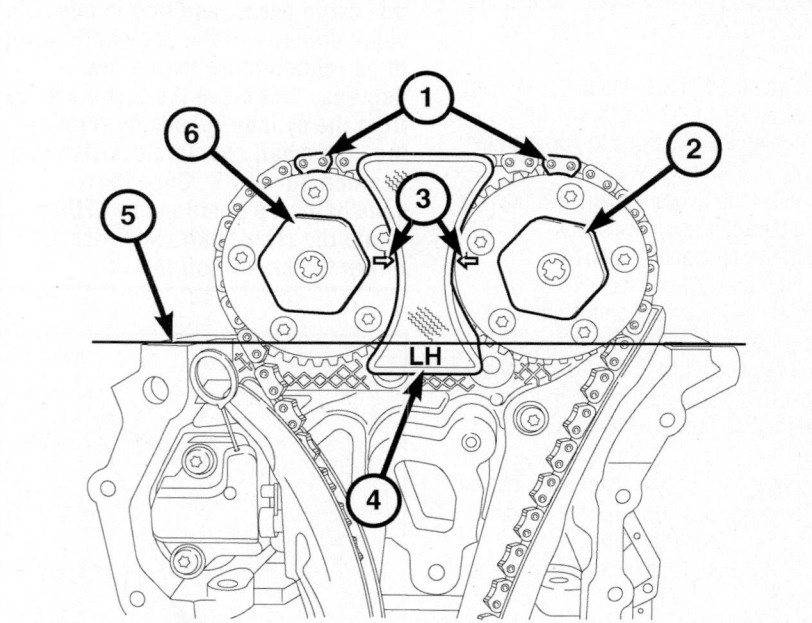

1. Plated chain links
2. Exhaust oil control valve
3. Cam phaser arrows
4. LH Camshaft Phaser Lock 10202
5. Valve cover sealing surface
6. Intake oil control valve

2692045

Fig. 249 Aligning the LH Camshaft Phaser—3.6L engine

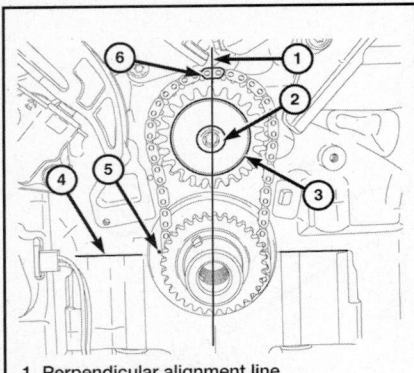

1. Perpendicular alignment line
2. Idler sprocket T45 retaining bolt
3. Washer
4. Block/bearing cap junction
5. Timing mark dimple on crankshaft sprocket
6. Plated chain link

2659817

Fig. 250 View of idler sprocket and components—3.6L engine

38. If required, remove the 2 T30 bolts and the RH cam chain tensioner.

39. If required, remove the 3 T30 bolts and the RH cam chain guide and tensioner arm.

To install:

40. Inspect all sprockets and chain guides. Replace if damaged.

41. If removed, install the right side cam chain guide and tensioner arm. Tighten the attaching T30 bolts to 106 inch lbs. (12 Nm).

42. If removed, install the RH cam chain tensioner to the engine block with the 2 bolts. Tighten the T30 bolts to 106 inch lbs. (12 Nm).

43. Reset the RH cam chain tensioner by pushing back the tensioner piston and installing the Tensioner Pin 8514.

44. If removed, install the left side cam chain guide and tensioner arm. Tighten the attaching T30 bolts to 106 inch lbs. (12 Nm).

45. If removed, install the LH cam chain tensioner to the cylinder head with 2 bolts. Tighten the T30 bolts to 106 inch lbs. (12 Nm).

46. Reset the LH cam chain tensioner by lifting the pawl, pushing back the piston and installing Tensioner Pin 8514.

47. Verify that the key is installed in the crankshaft.

❄❄ WARNING

Do not rotate the crankshaft more than a few degrees independently of the camshafts. Piston to valve contact could occur resulting in possible valve damage. If the crankshaft needs to be rotated more than a few

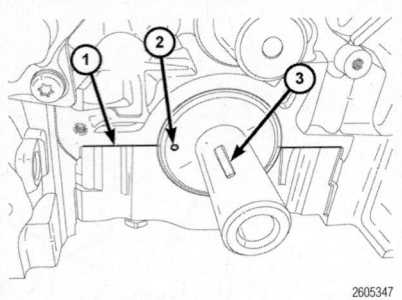

2605347

Fig. 251 Verify that the key (3) is installed in the crankshaft and that the number 1 piston is positioned at TDC by aligning the dimple (2) on the crankshaft with the block/bearing cap junction (1)—3.6L engine

degrees, first remove the camshafts. Refer to Camshaft and Valve Lifters, removal & installation.

48. Verify that the number 1 piston is positioned at TDC by aligning the dimple on the crankshaft with the block/bearing cap junction.

❄❄ WARNING

Do not rotate the camshafts more than a few degrees independently of the crankshaft. Valve to piston contact could occur resulting in possible valve damage. If the camshafts need to be rotated more than a few degrees, first move the pistons away from the cylinder heads by rotating the crankshaft counterclockwise to a position 30° BTDC. Once the camshafts are positioned at TDC rotate the crankshaft clockwise to return the crankshaft to TDC.

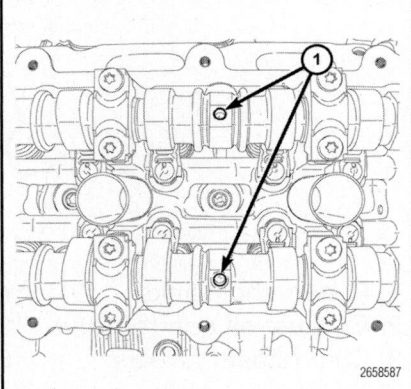

2658587

Fig. 252 Verify that the camshafts are set at TDC by positioning the alignment holes (1) vertically—3.6L engine

49. Verify that the camshafts are set at TDC by positioning the alignment holes vertically.

❄❄ WARNING

Always reinstall timing chains so that they maintain the same direction of rotation. Inverting a previously run chain on a previously run sprocket will result in excessive wear to both the chain and sprocket.

50. Place the primary chain onto the crankshaft sprocket so that the arrow is aligned with the plated link on the timing chain.

51. While maintaining this alignment, invert the crankshaft sprocket and timing chain and place the idler sprocket into the timing chain so that the dimple is aligned with the plated link on the timing chain.

52. While maintaining this alignment, lubricate the idler sprocket bushing with clean engine oil and install the sprockets and timing chain on the engine. To verify that the timing is still correct, the timing chain plated link should be located at 12 o'clock when the dimple on the crankshaft is aligned with the block/bearing cap junction.

53. Install the idler sprocket retaining bolt and washer. Tighten the T45 bolt to 18 ft. lbs. (25 Nm).

54. Install the primary chain guide. Tighten the attaching T30 bolt to 106 inch lbs. (12 Nm).

55. Reset the primary chain tensioner by pushing back the tensioner piston and installing Tensioner Pin 8514.

56. Install the primary chain tensioner to the engine block with 2 bolts. Tighten the T30 bolts to 106 inch lbs. (12 Nm) and remove the Tensioner Pin 8514.

57. Press the LH intake cam phaser onto the intake camshaft. Install and hand tighten the oil control valve.

➡ **The LH and RH cam chains are identical.**

58. Drape the left side cam chain over the LH intake cam phaser and onto the idler sprocket so that the arrow is aligned with the plated link on the cam chain.

59. While maintaining this alignment, route the cam chain around the exhaust and intake cam phasers so that the plated links are aligned with the phaser timing marks. Position the left side cam phasers so that the arrows point toward each other and are parallel to the valve cover sealing surface. Press the exhaust cam phaser onto the exhaust cam, install and hand tighten the oil control valve.

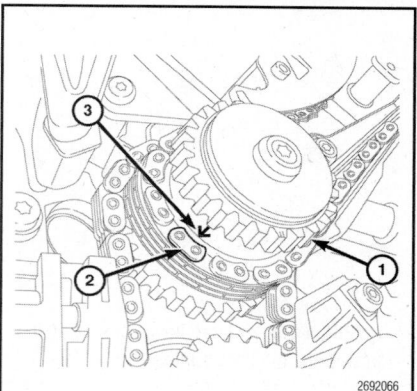

Fig. 253 Drape the left side cam chain over the LH intake cam phaser and onto the idler sprocket (1) so that the arrow (3) is aligned with the plated link (2) on the cam chain—3.6L engine

➡ **Minor rotation of a camshaft (a few degrees) may be required to install the camshaft phaser or phaser lock.**

60. Install the LH Camshaft Phaser Lock 10202 and tighten the oil control valves to 110 ft. lbs. (150 Nm).

61. Press the RH exhaust cam phaser onto the exhaust camshaft. Install and hand tighten the oil control valve.

62. Drape the right side cam chain over the RH exhaust cam phaser and onto the idler sprocket so that the dimple is aligned with the plated link on the cam chain.

63. While maintaining this alignment, route the cam chain around the exhaust and intake cam phasers so that the plated links are aligned with the phaser timing marks. Position the right side cam phasers so that the arrows point away from each other and

the scribe lines are parallel to the valve cover sealing surface. Press the intake cam phaser onto the intake cam, install and hand tighten the oil control valve.

64. Install the RH Camshaft Phaser Lock 10202 and tighten the oil control valves to 110 ft. lbs. (150 Nm).

➡ **There are no timing marks on the oil pump gear or chain.**

65. Place the oil pump sprocket into the oil pump chain. Place the oil pump chain onto the crankshaft sprocket while aligning the oil pump sprocket with the oil pump shaft. Install the oil pump sprocket T45 retaining bolt and tighten to 18 ft. lbs. (25 Nm).

66. Install the oil pump chain tensioner. Insure that the spring is positioned above the dowel pin.

67. Install the timing gear splash shield. Tighten the bolts to 35 inch lbs. (5 Nm).

68. Remove the RH and LH Camshaft Phaser Locks 10202.

69. Remove the Tensioner Pins 8514 from the RH and LH cam chain tensioners.

70. Rotate the crankshaft clockwise 2 complete revolutions stopping when the dimple on the crankshaft is aligned the with the block/bearing cap junction.

71. While maintaining this alignment, verify that the arrows on the left side cam phasers point toward each other and are parallel to the valve cover sealing surface and that the right side cam phaser arrows point away from each other and the scribe lines are parallel to the valve cover sealing surface.

72. There should be 12 chain pins between the exhaust cam phaser triangle marking and the intake cam phaser circle marking.

73. If the engine timing is not correct, repeat this procedure.

74. Install the engine timing cover. Refer to Timing Chain Front Cover, removal & installation.

75. Install the crankshaft vibration damper.

76. Install the accessory drive belts. Refer to Accessory Drive Belts, removal & installation.

77. Install the and oil pan. Refer to Oil Pan, removal & installation.

78. Install the spark plugs. Tighten to 13 ft. lbs. (18 Nm). Refer to Spark Plug, removal & installation.

79. Install the cylinder head covers. Refer to Valve Covers, removal & installation.

80. Install the upper intake manifold. Refer to Intake Manifold, removal & installation.

81. Install the air cleaner housing assembly. Refer to Air Cleaner, removal & installation.

82. Fill the engine crankcase with the proper oil to the correct level. Refer to Engine Oil & Filter, Replacement.

83. Connect the negative battery cable and tighten the nut to 45 inch lbs. (5 Nm). Refer to Battery, removal & installation.

84. Fill the cooling system. Refer to Engine Coolant, Drain & Refill Procedure.

85. Operate the engine until it reaches the normal operating temperature. Check the cooling system for correct fluid level.

➡ **The Cam/Crank Variation Relearn procedure must be performed using the scan tool anytime there has been a repair/replacement made to a powertrain system, for example: flywheel, valvetrain, camshaft and/or crankshaft**

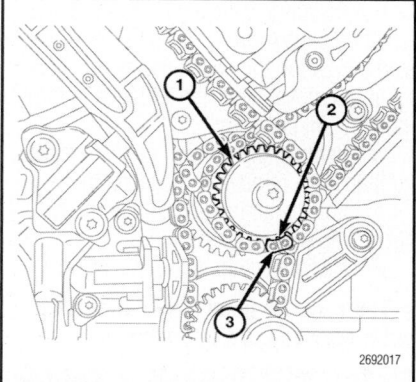

Fig. 254 Drape the right side cam chain over the RH exhaust cam phaser and onto the idler sprocket (1) so that the dimple (2) is aligned with the plated link (3) on the cam chain—3.6L engine

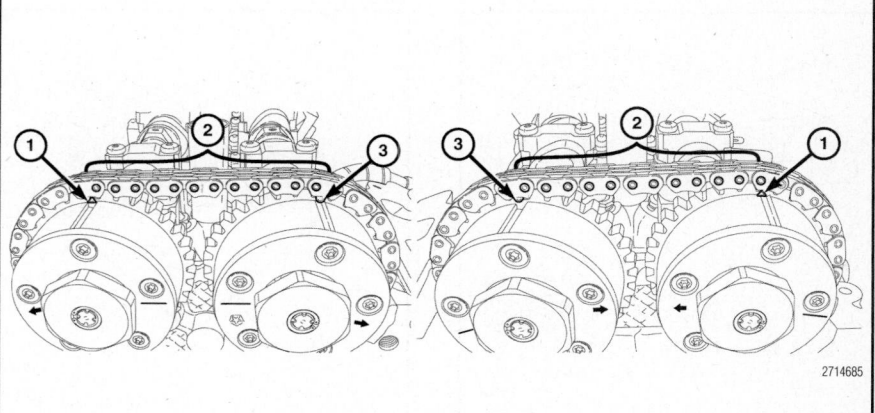

Fig. 255 When properly aligned, there should be 12 chain pins (2) between the exhaust cam phaser triangle marking (1) and the intake cam phaser circle marking (3)—3.6L engine

sensors or components. Refer to Powertrain Control Module (PCM), Powertrain Verification Test.

VALVE COVERS

REMOVAL & INSTALLATION

2.4L Engine

See Figures 256 through 260.

1. Before servicing the vehicle, refer to the Precautions Section.
2. Remove the engine cover by pulling upward.
3. Disconnect and isolate the negative battery cable. Refer to Battery, removal & installation.
4. Remove the makeup air hose.
5. Remove the PCV hose.
6. Disconnect the ignition coil electrical connectors.
7. Use compressed air to blow dirt and debris off the cylinder head cover prior to removal.
8. Remove the cylinder head cover (valve cover) bolts.
9. Remove the cylinder head cover from the cylinder head.

To install:

10. Install new cylinder head cover gaskets.
11. Install the studs in the cover.
12. Clean all RTV from the cylinder head.

➡**When using RTV, the sealing surfaces must be clean and free from grease and oil. The parts should be assembled in 10 minutes and tighten to the final torque within 45 minutes.**

13. Apply a dot of MOPAR® engine sealant RTV, or equivalent, to the cylinder head/front cover T-joint.

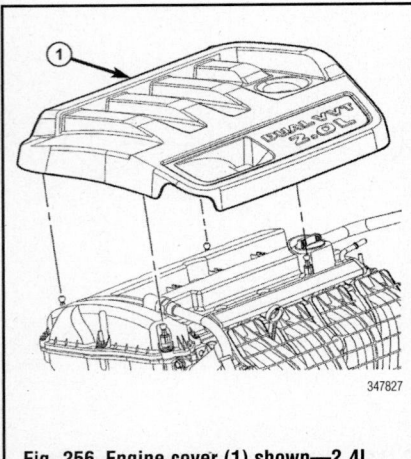

Fig. 256 Engine cover (1) shown—2.4L engine

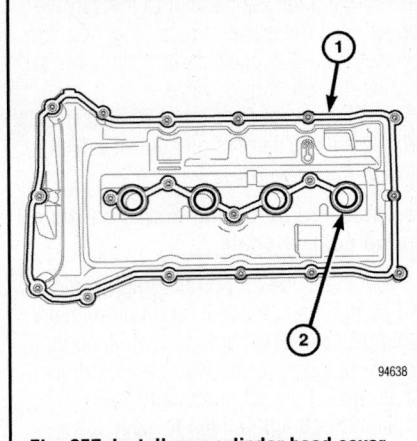

Fig. 257 Install new cylinder head cover gaskets (1, 2)—2.4L engine

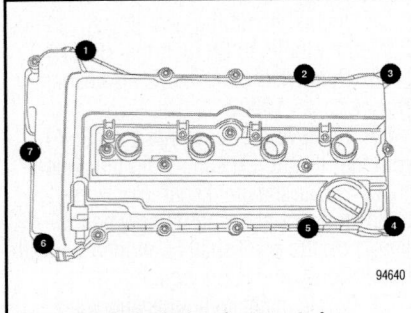

Fig. 258 Cylinder head cover stud locations—2.4L engine

14. Install the cylinder head cover assembly to the cylinder head and install all the bolts/studs.
15. Tighten the cylinder head cover bolts in sequence:
    a. Step 1: Tighten all bolts to 44 inch lbs. (5 Nm).
    b. Step 2: Tighten all bolts to 89 inch lb. (10 Nm).

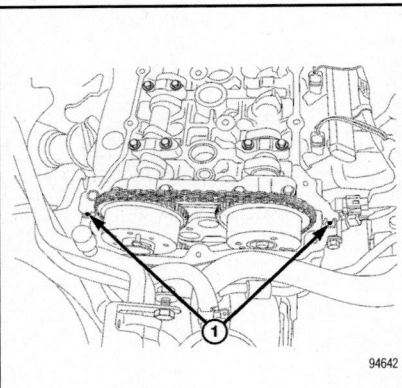

Fig. 259 Apply a dot of engine sealant RTV to the cylinder head/front cover T-joint (1)—2.4L engine

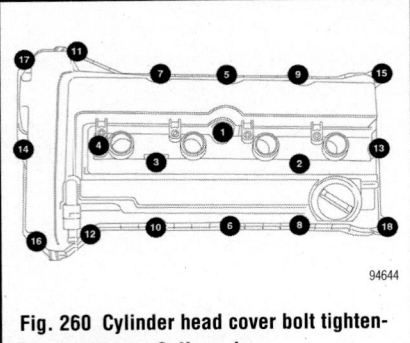

Fig. 260 Cylinder head cover bolt tightening sequence—2.4L engine

16. Install ignition coils. Tighten the fasteners to 70 inch lbs. (8 Nm). Refer to Ignition Coil, removal & installation.
17. If the PCV valve was removed, tighten the PCV valve to 44 inch lbs. (5 Nm).
18. Connect the coil electrical connectors.
19. Connect the PCV hose to the PCV valve.
20. Connect the makeup air hose.
21. Connect the negative battery cable. Refer to Battery, removal & installation.
22. Install the engine cover by pressing the rear of the cover down first.

2.7L Engine

Left Side

See Figures 261 and 262.

1. Before servicing the vehicle, refer to the Precautions Section.
2. Disconnect the negative battery cable. Refer to Battery, removal & installation.
3. Disconnect the electrical connectors from the ignition coils and capacitor. Reposition the electrical harness.
4. Remove the ground strap from the cylinder head cover stud.
5. Disconnect the engine harness retaining clips from the cylinder head cover studs. Position the engine harness aside.
6. Remove the fastener attaching the ignition coil capacitor.
7. Remove the ignition coils. Refer to Ignition Coil, removal & installation.
8. Loosen all the left cylinder head cover (valve cover) fasteners.
9. Disconnect the makeup air hose.

➡**The cylinder head cover attaching bolts are captured to the cover.**

❄❄ WARNING

Make certain the double ended studs in the center of the cylinder head cover are loose before attempting to remove the cover.

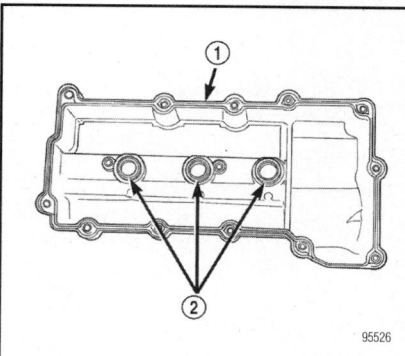

Fig. 261 Left cylinder head cover gaskets shown (1, 2)—2.7L engine

10. Remove the left cylinder head cover.

To install:

11. Clean the cylinder head cover and both sealing surfaces. Inspect and replace gaskets as necessary.

12. Install the cylinder head cover and hand start all of the fasteners. Verify that all the double-ended studs are in the correct locations.

13. Tighten the cylinder head cover attaching bolts and double-ended studs to 106 inch lbs. (12 Nm).

14. Reposition the left engine harness, and install the left engine harness retainers to the double-ended studs.

15. Install the ignition coils. Refer to Ignition Coil, removal & installation.

16. Install the ignition coil capacitor and fastener.

17. Reconnect all the electrical connectors.

18. Install the ground strap to the cylinder head cover stud.

19. Install the makeup air hose.

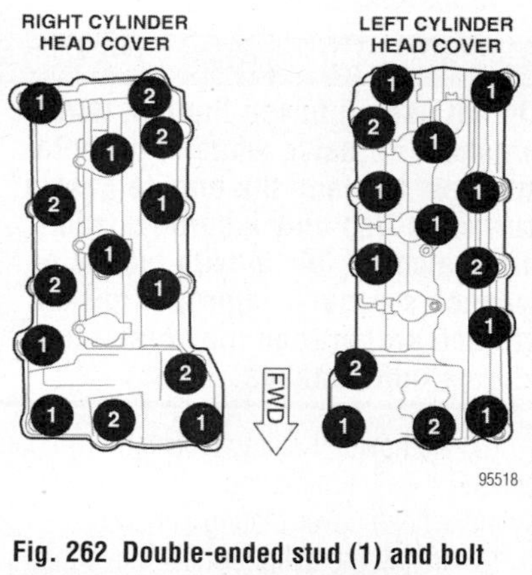

Fig. 262 Double-ended stud (1) and bolt (2) locations for right and left cylinder head covers—2.7L engine

20. Connect the negative battery cable. Refer to Battery, removal & installation.

Right Side

See Figure 262.

1. Before servicing the vehicle, refer to the Precautions Section.

2. Disconnect the negative battery cable. Refer to Battery, removal & installation.

3. Disconnect the electrical connectors from the ignition coils and capacitor.

4. Disconnect the right engine harness retaining clips from the cylinder head cover (valve cover) studs. Position the engine harness aside.

5. Disconnect the PCV hose from the upper intake manifold.

6. Remove the upper intake manifold. Refer to Intake Manifold, removal & installation.

7. Remove the ground strap from the cylinder head cover stud.

8. Disconnect the electrical harness retaining clips from the cylinder head cover studs. Reposition the electrical harness.

9. Remove the fastener attaching the ignition coil capacitor.

10. Remove the ignition coils. Refer to Ignition Coil, removal & installation.

11. Loosen all the cylinder head cover fasteners.

➡ **The cylinder head cover attaching bolts are captured to the cover.**

✳✳ WARNING

Make certain the double-ended studs in the center of the cylinder head cover are loose before attempting to remove the cover.

12. Remove the cylinder head cover.

To install:

13. Clean the cylinder head cover and sealing surfaces. Inspect and replace the gaskets as necessary.

14. Install the cylinder head cover and hand start all the fasteners. Verify that all the double-ended studs are in the correct locations.

15. Tighten the cylinder head cover attaching bolts and double-ended studs to 106 inch lbs. (12 Nm).

16. Install the ignition coils. Refer to Ignition Coil, removal & installation.

17. Install the ignition coil capacitor and fastener.

18. Connect the ground strap to the cylinder head cover stud.

19. Reposition the right engine harness, and install the right engine harness retainers to the double-ended studs.

20. Install the upper intake manifold. Refer to Intake Manifold, removal & installation.

21. Reconnect the PCV to the upper intake manifold.

3.5L Engine

Left Side

See Figure 263.

✳✳ CAUTION

Do not start or run the engine with the cylinder head cover (valve cover) removed. Damage or personal injury may occur.

1. Before servicing the vehicle, refer to the Precautions Section.

2. Disconnect and isolate the negative battery cable. Refer to Battery, removal & installation.

3. Disconnect and remove the ignition coils. Refer to Ignition Coil, removal & installation.

4. Disconnect the engine harness retaining clips from the cylinder head cover studs. Position the engine harness aside.

5. Disconnect the PCV hose from the cylinder head cover (valve cover) assembly (if required).

6. Completely loosen the 8 cylinder head cover retaining bolts and remove the cylinder head cover.

To install:

7. Clean the cylinder head and all the gasket sealing surfaces. Inspect and replace the gasket and seals as necessary.

8. Using a suitable pry tool, carefully remove the spark plug tube seals.

9. Position the new seal with the part number on the seal facing the cylinder head cover.

10. Install the seals using Camshaft Installer MD-998306 (1).

11. Install the cylinder head cover and bolts. Tighten the bolts to 89 inch lbs. (10 Nm).

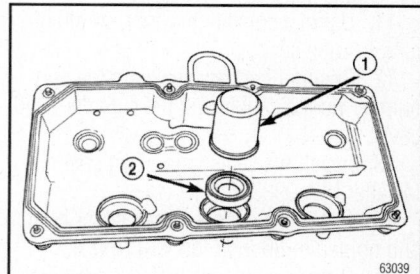

Fig. 263 Using Camshaft Installer MD-998306 (1) to install the cylinder head cover seals (2)—3.5L engine

12. Install the PCV hose (if required).

13. Position the wiring harness on the cylinder head cover.

14. Reinstall the wire harness retainers around the perimeter of the valve cover.

15. Install the ignition coils. Refer to Ignition Coil, removal & installation.

16. Connect the ignition coil electrical connectors.

17. Connect the negative battery cable. Refer to Battery, removal & installation.

Right Side

See Figure 264.

> ✳✳ **CAUTION**
>
> **Do not start or run the engine with the cylinder head cover (valve cover) removed. Damage or personal injury may occur.**

1. Before servicing the vehicle, refer to the Precautions Section.

2. Disconnect and isolate the negative battery cable. Refer to Battery, removal & installation.

3. Remove the upper intake manifold from the engine. Refer to Intake Manifold, removal & installation.

4. Cover the lower intake manifold intake ports with a clean cover to prevent dirt or debris from entering the ports during service.

5. Disconnect the ignition coil harness connectors.

6. Remove the ignition coils. Refer to Ignition Coil, removal & installation.

7. Disconnect the engine wiring harness retainers from the cylinder head cover (valve cover).

8. Disconnect the makeup air hose.

9. Completely loosen the cylinder head cover retaining bolts and remove the cylinder head cover.

To install:

10. Clean the cylinder head and cover mating surfaces. Inspect and replace the gasket and seals as necessary.

11. Using a suitable pry tool, carefully remove tube seals.

12. Position the new seal with the part number on the seal facing the cylinder head cover.

13. Install the seals using Camshaft Installer MD-998306 (1).

14. Install the cylinder head cover bolts and tighten to 89 inch lbs. (10 Nm).

15. Reconnect the wire harness retainers to the cylinder head cover.

16. Install the ignition coils. Refer to Ignition Coil, removal & installation.

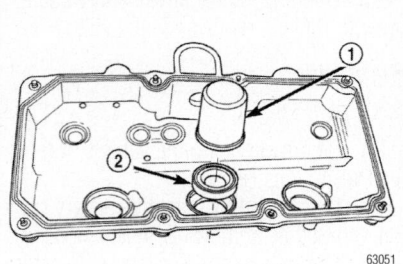

Fig. 264 Using Camshaft Installer MD-998306 (1) to install the cylinder head cover seals (2)—3.5L engine

17. Connect the ignition coil electrical connectors.

18. Reconnect the makeup air hose.

19. Install the upper intake manifold. Refer to Intake Manifold, removal & installation.

20. Connect the negative battery cable. Refer to Battery, removal & installation.

3.6L Engine

Left Side

See Figures 265 through 268.

> ✳✳ **WARNING**
>
> **The magnetic timing wheels must not come in contact with magnets (pickup tools, trays, etc.) or any other strong magnetic field. This may destroy the timing wheels ability to correctly relay the camshaft position to the camshaft position sensor.**

1. Before servicing the vehicle, refer to the Precautions Section.

2. Disconnect and isolate the negative battery cable. Refer to Battery, removal & installation.

3. Remove the air cleaner body, resonator, and upper intake manifold. Refer to Intake Manifold, removal & installation.

4. Cover the open intake ports to prevent debris from entering the engine.

5. Remove the insulator from the LH cylinder head cover (valve cover).

6. Disconnect the electrical connectors from the variable valve timing solenoids on the left cylinder head cover.

7. Disengage the 3 wire harness retainers from the left cylinder head cover.

8. Mark the variable valve timing solenoids with a paint pen or equivalent so that they may be reinstalled in their original locations.

9. Remove the variable valve timing solenoids.

10. Disconnect the left Camshaft Position (CMP) sensor.

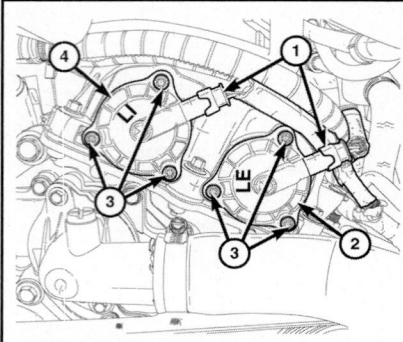

1. Electrical connectors
2. Exhaust variable valve timing solenoid
3. Attaching bolts
4. Intake variable valve timing solenoid

Fig. 265 Variable valve timing solenoids shown marked for reinstallation in original locations—3.6L engine

11. Disengage one main wire harness retainer from the cylinder head cover and one main wire harness retainer from the cylinder head cover mounting stud.

➡**If removing both RH and LH CMP sensors, mark the sensors so they can be installed in their original locations.**

12. Remove the camshaft position sensor. Refer to Camshaft Position (CMP) Sensor, removal & installation.

13. Disengage the 2 injection/ignition harness retainers from the left cylinder head cover.

14. Remove the ignition coils. Refer to Ignition Coil, removal & installation.

15. Loosen the 10 cylinder head cover mounting bolts and the 2 studbolts and remove the cylinder head cover.

16. Remove and discard the cylinder head cover gasket.

17. The spark plug tube seals can be reused if not damaged.

To install:

> ✳✳ **WARNING**
>
> **Do not use oil based liquids, wire brushes, abrasive wheels, or metal scrapers to clean the engine gasket surfaces. Use only isopropyl (rubbing) alcohol, along with plastic or wooden scrapers. Improper gasket surface preparation may result in engine fluid leakage.**

18. Remove all residual sealant from the cylinder head, timing chain cover, and cylinder head cover mating surfaces.

19. Install the cylinder head cover gasket. The spark plug tube seals can be reused if not damaged.

20. If required, install new spark plug tube seals in the cylinder head cover:

a. Lubricate the spark plug tube seal inner and outer diameters with clean engine oil.

b. Place the spark plug tube seal on the Cam Sensor/Spark Plug Tube Seal Installer 10256.

c. Push the seal into the cylinder head cover until the base of the seal is seated.

d. Remove the tool.

21. Clean the engine timing cover, cylinder head, and cylinder head cover mating surfaces with isopropyl alcohol in preparation for sealant application.

→Engine assembly requires the use of a unique sealant that is compatible with engine oil. Using a sealant other than MOPAR® Threebond Engine RTV Sealant may result in engine fluid leakage.

→Following the application of MOPAR® Threebond Engine RTV Sealant to the gasket surfaces, the components must be assembled within 20 minutes and the attaching fasteners must be tightened to specification within 45 minutes. Prolonged exposure to the air, prior to assembly, may result in engine fluid leakage.

22. Apply a 0.08–0.12 inch (2–3mm) wide bead of MOPAR® Threebond Engine RTV Sealant to the 2 engine timing cover-to-cylinder head T-joints.

23. Align the locator pins to the cylinder head and install the cylinder head cover.

24. Tighten the cylinder head cover bolts and double-ended studs in sequence to 106 inch lbs. (12 Nm).

25. If removed, install the spark plugs.

Refer to Spark Plugs, removal & installation.

26. Install the ignition coils. Refer to Ignition Coil, removal & installation.

27. Engage the 2 injection/ignition harness retainers to the left cylinder head cover.

→If both RH and LH CMP sensors were removed, install them into their original locations.

28. Install the camshaft position sensor. Refer to Camshaft Position (CMP) Sensor, removal & installation.

29. Connect the electrical connector to the left CMP sensor.

30. Engage the 1 main wire harness retainer to the cylinder head cover and the 1 main wire harness retainer to the cylinder head cover mounting stud.

31. Refer to the markings made at disassembly and install the variable valve timing solenoids in their original locations.

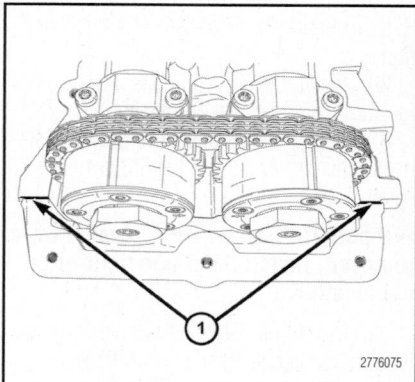

Fig. 267 Apply a wide bead of engine RTV sealant (1) to the 2 engine timing cover-to-cylinder head T-joints—3.6L engine

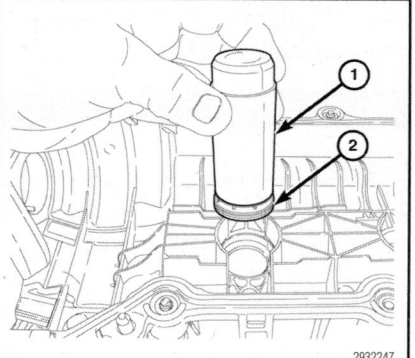

Fig. 266 Using the Cam Sensor/Spark Plug Tube Seal Installer 10256 (1) to install a new spark plug tube seal (2) into the cylinder head cover—3.6L engine

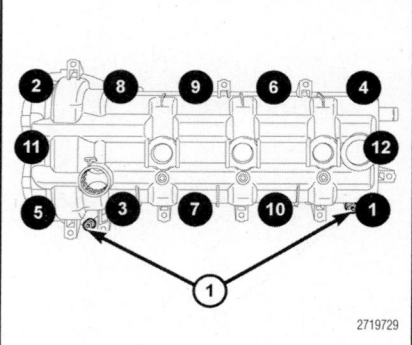

Fig. 268 Cylinder head cover (left side) bolt tightening sequence shown along with the alignment locator pins (1)—3.6L engine

32. Engage the 3 wire harness retainers to the left cylinder head cover.

33. Connect the electrical connectors to the left variable valve timing solenoids.

34. Install the insulator to the 2 alignment posts on top of the LH cylinder head cover.

35. Install the upper intake manifold, support brackets, resonator and air cleaner body. Refer to Intake Manifold, removal & installation.

36. Connect the negative battery cable and tighten the nut to 45 inch lbs. (5 Nm). Refer to Battery, removal & installation.

→The Cam/Crank Variation Relearn procedure must be performed using the scan tool anytime there has been a repair/replacement made to a powertrain system, for example: flywheel, valvetrain, camshaft and/or crankshaft sensors or components. Refer to Powertrain Control Module (PCM), Powertrain Verification Test.

Right Side

See Figures 269 and 270.

✳✳ WARNING

The magnetic timing wheels must not come in contact with magnets (pickup tools, trays, etc.) or any other strong magnetic field. This may destroy the timing wheels ability to correctly relay the camshaft position to the camshaft position sensor.

1. Before servicing the vehicle, refer to the Precautions Section.

2. Disconnect and isolate the negative battery cable. Refer to Battery, removal & installation.

3. Remove the air cleaner body, resonator, and upper intake manifold. Refer to Intake Manifold, removal & installation.

4. Cover the open intake ports to prevent debris from entering the engine.

5. Disconnect the electrical connectors from the variable valve timing solenoids on the right cylinder head.

6. Disengage the 2 wire harness retainers from the right cylinder head cover.

7. Mark the variable valve timing solenoids with a paint pen or equivalent so that they may be reinstalled in their original locations.

8. Remove the variable valve timing solenoids.

9. Disengage the 3 main wire harness retainers from the right cylinder head cover.

10. Disconnect the electrical connector from the right Camshaft Position (CMP) sensor.

➡️If removing both RH and LH CMP sensors, mark the sensors so they can be installed in their original locations.

11. Remove the camshaft position sensor. Refer to Camshaft Position (CMP) Sensor, removal & installation.

12. Disengage the 3 injection/ignition harness retainers from the right cylinder head cover.

13. Remove the ignition coils. Refer to Ignition Coil, removal & installation.

14. Remove the PCV valve.

15. Remove the 2 resonator mounts from the studbolts.

16. Loosen the 9 cylinder head cover mounting bolts and 3 studbolts and remove the cylinder head cover.

17. Remove and discard the cylinder head cover gasket.

18. The spark plug tube seals can be reused if not damaged.

To install:

⁂ WARNING

Do not use oil based liquids, wire brushes, abrasive wheels or metal scrapers to clean the engine gasket surfaces. Use only isopropyl (rubbing) alcohol, along with plastic or wooden scrapers. Improper gasket surface preparation may result in engine fluid leakage.

19. Remove all residual sealant from the cylinder head, timing chain cover, and cylinder head cover mating surfaces.

20. Install the cylinder head cover gasket.

21. The spark plug tube seals can be reused if not damaged.

22. If required, install new spark plug tube seals in the cylinder head cover:

a. Lubricate the spark plug tube seal inner and outer diameters with clean engine oil.

b. Place the spark plug tube seal on the Cam Sensor/Spark Plug Tube Seal Installer 10256.

c. Push the seal into the cylinder head cover until the base of the seal is seated.

d. Remove the tool.

23. Clean the engine timing cover, cylinder head, and cylinder head cover mating surfaces with isopropyl alcohol in preparation for sealant application.

➡️**Engine assembly requires the use of a unique sealant that is compatible with engine oil. Using a sealant other than MOPAR® Threebond Engine RTV**

Sealant may result in engine fluid leakage.

➡️**Following the application of MOPAR® Threebond Engine RTV Sealant to the gasket surfaces, the components must be assembled within 20 minutes and the attaching fasteners must be tightened to specification within 45 minutes. Prolonged exposure to the air, prior to assembly, may result in engine fluid leakage.**

24. Apply a 0.08–0.12 inch (2–3mm) wide bead of MOPAR® Threebond Engine RTV Sealant to the 2 engine timing cover-to-cylinder head T-joints.

25. Align the locator pins to the cylinder head and install the cylinder head cover.

26. Tighten the cylinder head cover bolts and double-ended studs in sequence to 106 inch lbs. (12 Nm).

27. Install the 2 resonator mounts to the studbolts.

28. Install the PCV valve.

29. If removed, install the spark plugs. Refer to Spark Plugs, removal & installation.

30. Install the ignition coils. Refer to Ignition Coil, removal & installation.

31. Engage the 3 injection/ignition harness retainers to the right cylinder head cover.

➡️**If both RH and LH CMP sensors were removed, install them into their original locations.**

32. Install the camshaft position sensor. Refer to Camshaft Position (CMP) Sensor, removal & installation.

33. Connect the electrical connector to the right Camshaft Position (CMP) sensor.

34. Engage the 3 main wire harness retainers to the right cylinder head cover.

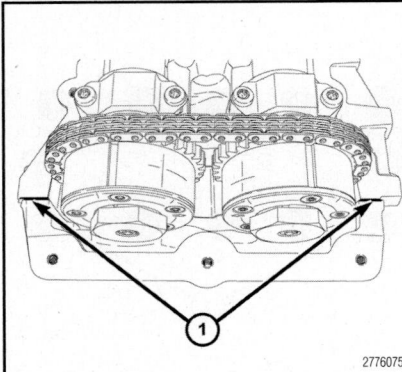

Fig. 269 Apply a wide bead of engine RTV sealant (1) to the 2 engine timing cover-to-cylinder head T-joints—3.6L engine

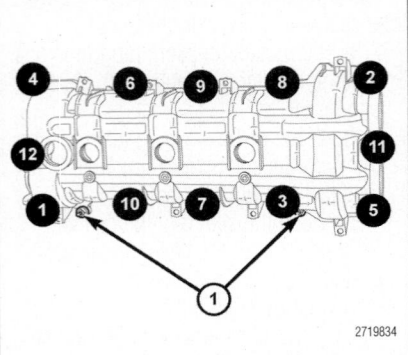

Fig. 270 Cylinder head cover (right side) bolt tightening sequence shown along with the alignment locator pins (1)—3.6L engine

35. Refer to the markings made at disassembly and install the variable valve timing solenoids in their original locations.

36. Connect the electrical connectors to the variable valve timing solenoids on the right cylinder head.

37. Engage the 2 wire harness retainers to the right cylinder head cover.

38. If removed, install the insulator to the 2 alignment posts on top of the LH cylinder head cover.

39. Install the upper intake manifold, support brackets, resonator, and air cleaner body. Refer to Intake Manifold, removal & installation.

40. Connect the negative battery cable and tighten the nut to 45 inch lbs. (5 Nm). Refer to Battery, removal & installation.

➡️**The Cam/Crank Variation Relearn procedure must be performed using the scan tool anytime there has been a repair/replacement made to a powertrain system, for example: flywheel, valvetrain, camshaft and/or crankshaft sensors or components. Refer to Powertrain Control Module (PCM), Powertrain Verification Test.**

VALVE LASH

ADJUSTMENT

2.4L Engine

See Figures 271 and 272.

➡️**The engine must be cold to measure valve lash.**

1. Before servicing the vehicle, refer to the Precautions Section.

2. Remove the engine cover.

3. Remove the cylinder head cover. Refer to Valve Covers, removal & installation.

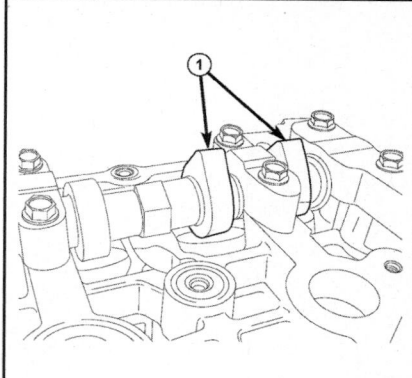

Fig. 271 Rotate the camshaft so the lobes are vertical (1) before measuring the valve lash—2.4L engine

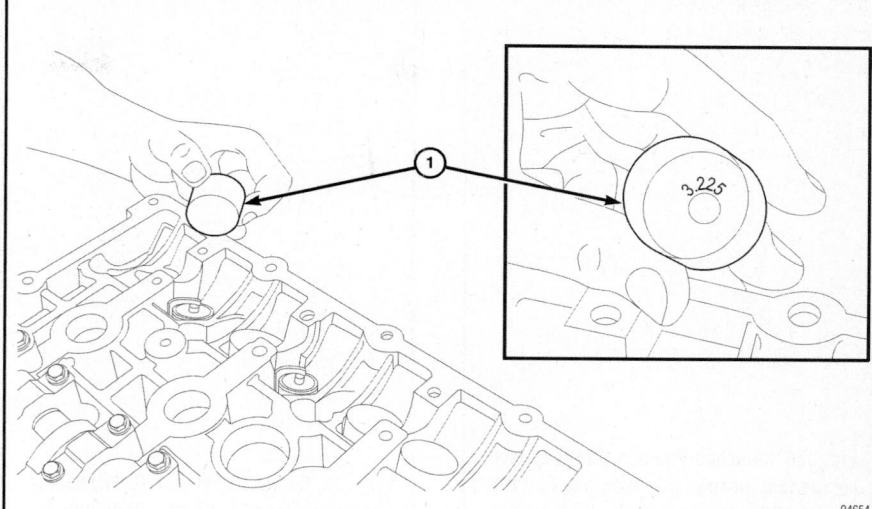

Fig. 272 Increase or decrease the thickness until specifications are met. Tappet thickness is marked on the tappet (1)—2.4L engine

4. Rotate the camshaft so the lobes are vertical.

5. Check the clearance using feeler gauges.

6. Repeat for all the tappets and record the readings.

7. If the clearance is too small:

   a. Remove the camshafts. Refer to Camshaft and Valve Lifters, removal & installation.

   b. Decrease the tappet thickness to match specifications.

   c. Install the camshafts. Refer to Camshaft and Valve Lifters, removal & installation.

   d. Verify that the valve lash is correct.

8. If clearance is too large:

   a. Remove the camshafts. Refer to Camshaft and Valve Lifters, removal & installation.

   b. Increase the tappet thickness to match specifications.

   c. Install the camshafts. Refer to Camshaft and Valve Lifters, removal & installation.

   d. Verify that the valve lash is correct.

2.7L, 3.5L, and 3.6L Engines

These engines utilize hydraulic lash adjusters; no adjustment is necessary.

ENGINE PERFORMANCE & EMISSION CONTROLS

CAMSHAFT POSITION (CMP) SENSOR

LOCATION

2.4L Engine

See Figures 274 and 275.

The Camshaft Position (CMP) sensor is located in the cylinder head near the camshaft, is retained by a single fastener and has an O-ring seal.

2.7L Engine

See Figure 276.

The Camshaft Position (CMP) sensor is mounted in the front of the head.

3.5L Engine

See Figure 277.

The Camshaft Position (CMP) sensor is mounted in the front of the head.

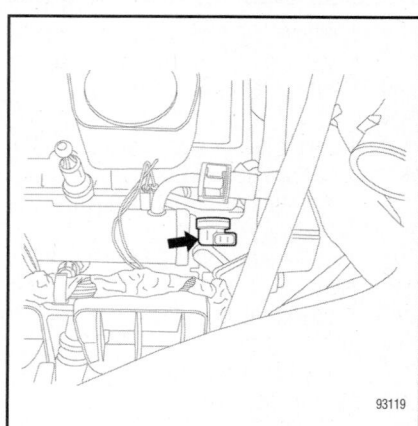

Fig. 273 Camshaft Position (CMP) sensor component location (front)—2.4L engine

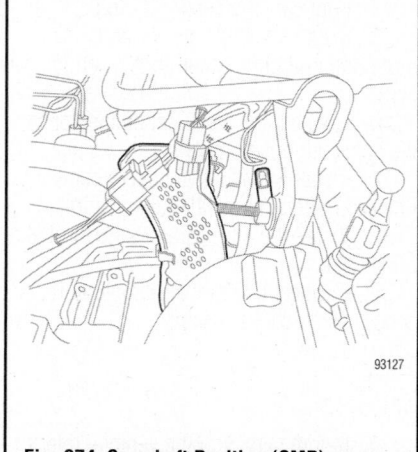

Fig. 274 Camshaft Position (CMP) sensor component location (rear)—2.4L engine

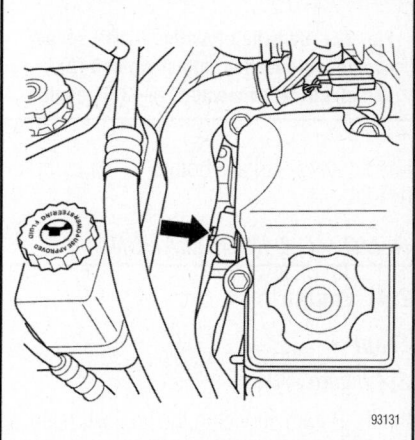

Fig. 275 Camshaft Position (CMP) sensor component location—2.7L engine

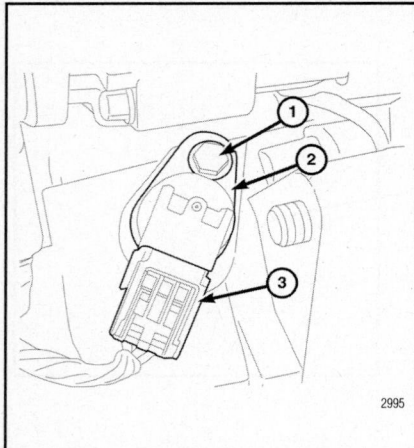

Fig. 276 Camshaft Position (CMP) sensor component location (2), attaching bolt (1), and electrical connector (3)—3.5L engine

3.6L Engine

See Figure 277.

The Camshaft Position (CMP) sensors are located at the rear of the cylinder

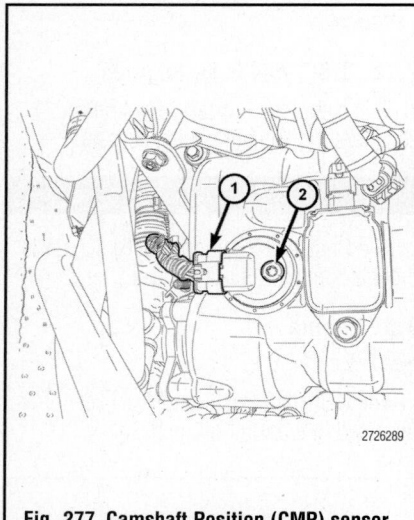

Fig. 277 Camshaft Position (CMP) sensor component location, attaching bolt (2), and electrical connector (1)—3.6L engine

head covers and are bolted to the cylinder head.

REMOVAL & INSTALLATION

2.4L Engine

Front

See Figure 278.

1. Before servicing the vehicle, refer to the Precautions Section.
2. Remove the air cleaner hose from the throttle body.

Fig. 278 Camshaft Position (CMP) sensor component location (front)—2.4L engine

3. Disconnect the inlet air temperature sensor electrical connector.
4. Disconnect the negative battery cable. Refer to Battery, removal & installation.
5. Disconnect the electrical connector from the camshaft position sensor.
6. Remove the camshaft position sensor mounting screws.
7. Remove the sensor.

To install:

❋❋ WARNING

Install the Camshaft Position (CMP) sensor utilizing a twisting motion. Make sure the CMP sensor is fully seated. Do not drive the CMP sensor into the bore with the mounting screw. This may cause the CMP sensor to be incorrectly seated cau sing a faulty signal or no signal at all.

8. Lubricate the sensor O-ring.
9. Install the CMP sensor and mounting bolt and tighten to 80 inch lbs. (9 Nm).
10. Connect the electrical connector to the camshaft position sensor.
11. Install the negative battery cable. Refer to Battery, removal & installation.
12. Install the air cleaner to the throttle body hose.
13. Connect the inlet air temperature sensor electrical connector.

Rear

See Figure 279.

1. Before servicing the vehicle, refer to the Precautions Section.
2. Disconnect the negative battery

Fig. 279 Camshaft Position (CMP) sensor component location (rear)—2.4L engine

cable. Refer to Battery, removal & installation.
3. Disconnect the electrical connector at the sensor.
4. Remove the nut retaining the heat shield.
5. Pull the heat shield out to uncover the sensor.
6. Remove the mounting bolt.
7. Remove the sensor.

To install:

❋❋ WARNING

Install the Camshaft Position (CMP) sensor utilizing a twisting motion. Make sure the CMP sensor is fully seated. Do not drive the CMP sensor into the bore with the mounting screw. This may cause the CMP sensor to be incorrectly seated causing a faulty signal or no signal at all.

8. Lubricate the sensor O-ring.
9. Install the CMP sensor and mounting bolt and tighten to 80 inch lbs. (9 Nm).
10. Connect the electrical connector to the camshaft position sensor.
11. Install the heat shield onto the mounting stud.
12. Install the heat shield retaining nut and tighten.
13. Connect the electrical connector.
14. Connect the negative battery cable. Refer to Battery, removal & installation.

2.7L Engine

See Figure 280.

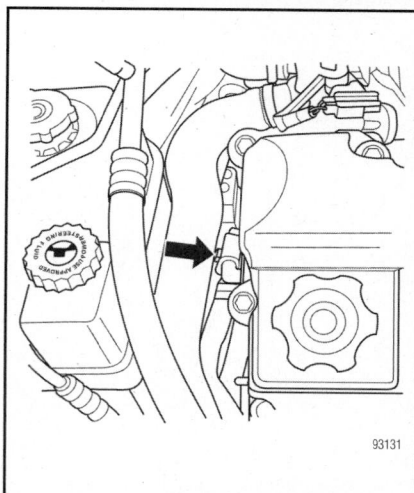

Fig. 280 Camshaft Position (CMP) sensor component location—2.7L engine

➥The camshaft position sensor is mounted in the front of the head.

1. Before servicing the vehicle, refer to the Precautions Section.
2. Disconnect the electrical connector from the sensor.
3. Remove the camshaft position sensor screw.
4. Without pulling on the connector, pull the sensor out of the chain case cover.

To install:

❊❊ WARNING

Install the Camshaft Position (CMP) sensor utilizing a twisting motion. Make sure the CMP sensor is fully seated. Do not drive the CMP sensor into the bore with the mounting screw. This may cause the CMP sensor to be incorrectly seated causing a faulty signal or no signal at all.

➥If reinstalling the sensor, check the sensor O-ring for damage and replace if necessary. Lubricate the O-ring with clean engine oil before installing the sensor.

5. Push the CMP sensor into the chain case cover with a twisting motion until fully seated.
6. While holding the sensor in this position, install and tighten the retaining bolt to 106 inch lbs. (12 Nm).
7. Connect and lock the electrical connector to the CMP sensor.
8. Connect the negative battery cable and tighten the nut to 45 inch lbs. (5 Nm). Refer to Battery, removal & installation.

➥The Cam/Crank Variation Relearn procedure must be performed anytime there has been a repair/replacement made to a powertrain system, for example: flywheel, valvetrain, camshaft and/or crankshaft sensors or components. Refer to Powertrain Control Module (PCM), Powertrain Verification Test.

3.5L Engine

See Figure 276.

1. Before servicing the vehicle, refer to the Precautions Section.
2. Disconnect and isolate the negative battery cable at the battery. Refer to Battery, removal & installation.
3. Disconnect the electrical connector from the Camshaft Position (CMP) sensor.
4. Remove the bolt and the CMP sensor.

To install:

❊❊ WARNING

Install the Camshaft Position (CMP) sensor utilizing a twisting motion. Make sure the CMP sensor is fully seated. Do not drive the CMP sensor into the bore with the mounting screw. This may cause the CMP sensor to be incorrectly seated causing a faulty signal or no signal at all.

➥If reinstalling the sensor, check the sensor O-ring for damage and replace if necessary. Lubricate the O-ring with clean engine oil before installing the sensor.

5. Push the CMP sensor into the timing belt cover with a twisting motion until fully seated.
6. While holding the sensor in this position, install and tighten the retaining bolt to 106 inch lbs. (12 Nm).
7. Connect and lock the electrical connector to the CMP sensor.
8. Connect the negative battery cable and tighten the nut to 45 inch lbs. (5 Nm). Refer to Battery, removal & installation.

➥The Cam/Crank Variation Relearn procedure must be performed anytime there has been a repair/replacement made to a powertrain system, for example: flywheel, valvetrain, camshaft and/or crankshaft sensors or components. Refer to Powertrain Control Module (PCM), Powertrain Verification Test.

3.6L Engine

See Figures 277 and 281.

➥The Camshaft Position (CMP) sensors are located at the rear of the cylinder head covers and are bolted to the cylinder head.

❊❊ WARNING

The magnetic timing wheels must not come in contact with magnets (pickup tools, trays, etc.) or any other strong magnetic field. This may destroy the timing wheels ability to correctly relay the camshaft position to the camshaft position sensor.

1. Before servicing the vehicle, refer to the Precautions Section.
2. Disconnect and isolate the negative battery cable. Refer to Battery, removal & installation.
3. Remove the air cleaner body. Refer to Air Cleaner, removal & installation.
4. If removing the LH CMP sensor, first remove the upper intake manifold. Refer to Intake Manifold, removal & installation.

➥If removing both RH and LH CMP sensors, mark the sensors so they can be installed in their original locations.

5. Disconnect the electrical connector from the CMP sensor.
6. Loosen the sensor mounting bolt.
7. Pull the sensor and mounting bolt from the cylinder head cover.

To install:

8. Clean out the CMP sensor mounting bolt hole in the cylinder head.
9. The CMP sensor seal can be reused if not damaged.
10. If required, install a new CMP sensor seal in the cylinder head cover:
    a. Lubricate the CMP sensor seal inner and outer diameters with clean engine oil.
    b. Place the CMP sensor seal on the Cam Sensor/Spark Plug Tube Seal Installer 10256.
    c. Push the seal into the cylinder head cover until the base of the seal is seated.
    d. Remove the tool.

➥A properly installed CMP sensor seal will have a 0.06–0.08 inch (1.5–2.0mm) gap between the cylinder head cover and the seal upper flange.

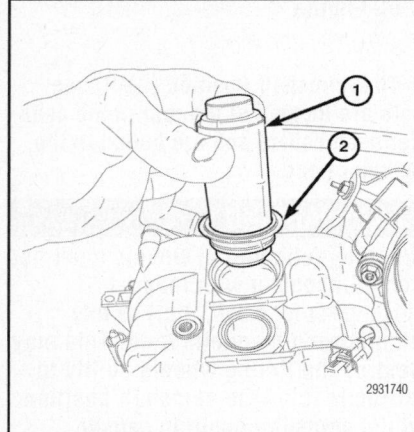

Fig. 281 Using the Cam Sensor/Spark Plug Tube Seal Installer 10256 (1) to install the CMP sensor seal (2) to the cylinder head cover—3.6L engine

11. The sensor mounting bolt O-ring can be reused if not damaged.

12. Apply a small amount of engine oil to the sensor mounting bolt O-ring.

➡**If both RH and LH CMP sensors where removed, install them into their original locations.**

13. Install the CMP sensor to the cylinder head. Tighten the mounting bolt to 80 inch lbs. (9 Nm).

14. Connect the electrical connector to the sensor.

15. Following installation of the LH CMP sensor, install the upper intake manifold. Refer to Intake Manifold, removal & installation.

16. Install the air cleaner body. Refer to Air Cleaner, removal & installation.

17. Connect the negative battery cable and tighten the nut to 45 inch lbs. (5 Nm). Refer to Battery, removal & installation.

➡**The Cam/Crank Variation Relearn procedure must be performed using the scan tool anytime there has been a repair/replacement made to a powertrain system, for example: flywheel, valvetrain, camshaft and/or crankshaft sensors or components. Refer to Powertrain Control Module (PCM), Powertrain Verification Test.**

CRANKSHAFT POSITION (CKP) SENSOR

LOCATION

2.4L Engine

See Figure 282.

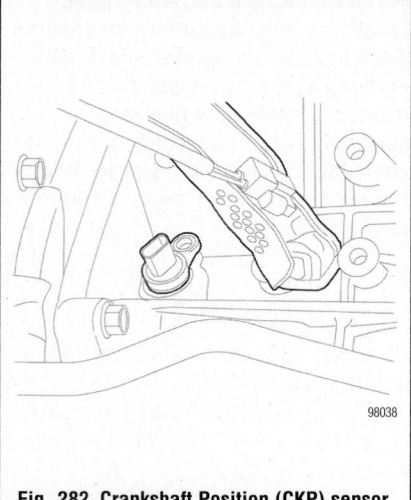

Fig. 282 Crankshaft Position (CKP) sensor component location—2.4L engine

The Crankshaft Position (CKP) sensor is located at the rear of the cylinder block, near the transaxle.

2.7L Engine

See Figure 283.

The Crankshaft Position (CKP) sensor is located on the transaxle housing.

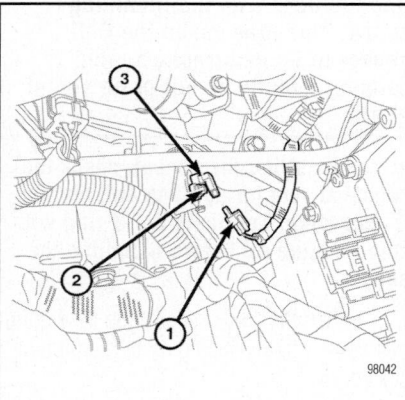

Fig. 283 Crankshaft Position (CKP) sensor component location (3), electrical connector (1), and attaching bolt (2)—2.7L engine

3.5L Engine

See Figure 284.

The Crankshaft Position (CKP) sensor is located on the driver side of the vehicle, above the differential housing. The bottom of the sensor sits above the driveplate.

3.6L Engine

See Figure 285.

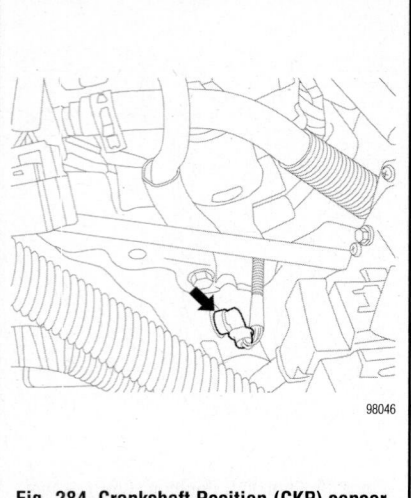

Fig. 284 Crankshaft Position (CKP) sensor component location—3.5L engine

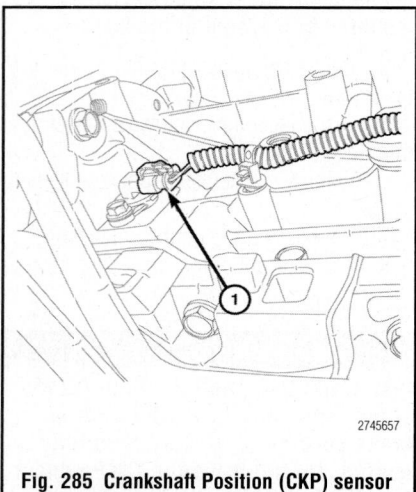

Fig. 285 Crankshaft Position (CKP) sensor component location and electrical connector (1)—3.6L engine

The Crankshaft Position (CKP) sensor is mounted into the right rear side of the cylinder block.

REMOVAL & INSTALLATION

2.4L Engine

See Figure 282.

➡**The Crankshaft Position Sensor is located at the rear of the cylinder block, near the transaxle.**

1. Before servicing the vehicle, refer to the Precautions Section.

2. Disconnect and isolate the negative battery cable. Refer to Battery, removal & installation.

3. Raise and safely support the vehicle.

4. Remove the heat shield retaining bolt.

5. Remove the heat shield.

6. Unlock and disconnect the electrical connector from the crankshaft position sensor.

7. Remove the crankshaft position sensor bolt.

8. Remove the sensor.

To install:

9. Check the O-ring for damage and lubricate the O-ring with engine oil before installing the sensor.

10. Use a twisting motion when installing the sensor.

11. Install and tighten the crankshaft position sensor bolt to 80 inch lbs. (9 Nm).

12. Connect and lock the electrical connector to the crankshaft position sensor.

13. Install the heat shield and retaining bolt.

14. Lower the vehicle.

15. Connect the negative battery cable and tighten the nut to 45 inch lbs. (5 Nm). Refer to Battery, removal & installation.

2.7L Engine

See Figure 283.

➥If the Crankshaft Position (CKP) sensor is difficult to remove, twist side to side during removal.

1. Before servicing the vehicle, refer to the Precautions Section.

2. Disconnect and isolate the negative battery cable. Refer to Batter, removal & installation.

3. Disconnect the electrical connector from the CKP sensor.

4. Remove the bolt and remove the CKP sensor from the transaxle housing.

To install:

➥If reinstalling the sensor, check the sensor O-ring for damage and replace if necessary. Lubricate the O-ring with clean engine oil before installing the sensor.

5. Push the CKP sensor into the transaxle case with a twisting motion until fully seated.

✳✳ WARNING

Before tightening the sensor mounting bolt, be sure the sensor is completely flush to the mounting surface. If the sensor is not flush, damage to the sensor mounting tang may result.

6. While holding the sensor in this position, install and tighten the retaining bolt to 80 inch lbs. (9 Nm).

7. Connect and lock the electrical connector to the CKP sensor.

8. Connect the negative battery cable and tighten the nut to 45 inch lbs. (5 Nm).

➥The Cam/Crank Variation Relearn procedure must be performed anytime there has been a repair/replacement made to a powertrain system, for example: flywheel, valvetrain, camshaft and/or crankshaft sensors or components. Refer to Powertrain Control Module (PCM), Powertrain Verification Test.

3.5L Engine

See Figure 284.

➥The Crankshaft Position (CKP) sensor is located on the driver side of the vehicle, above the differential housing. The bottom of the sensor sits above the driveplate.

1. Before servicing the vehicle, refer to the Precautions Section.

2. Disconnect and isolate the negative battery cable.

3. Unlock and disconnect the electrical connector from the CKP.

4. Remove the CKP sensor mounting screw and the CKP sensor.

To install:

➥If reinstalling the sensor, check the sensor O-ring for damage and replace if necessary. Lubricate the O-ring with clean engine oil before installing the sensor.

5. Push the CKP sensor into the transaxle case with a twisting motion until fully seated.

✳✳ WARNING

Before tightening the sensor mounting bolt, be sure the sensor is completely flush to the mounting surface. If the sensor is not flush, damage to the sensor mounting tang may result.

6. While holding the sensor in this position, install and tighten the retaining bolt to 106 inch lbs. (12 Nm).

7. Connect and lock the electrical connector to the CKP sensor.

8. Connect the negative battery cable and tighten the nut to 45 inch lbs. (5 Nm).

➥The Cam/Crank Variation Relearn procedure must be performed anytime there has been a repair/replacement made to a powertrain system, for example: flywheel, valvetrain, camshaft and/or crankshaft sensors or components. Refer to Powertrain Control Module (PCM), Powertrain Verification Test.

3.6L Engine

See Figure 285.

➥The Crankshaft Position (CKP) sensor is mounted into the right rear side of the cylinder block.

1. Before servicing the vehicle, refer to the Precautions Section.

2. Disconnect and isolate the negative battery cable.

3. Raise and safely support the vehicle.

4. Push back the heat shield from the CKP sensor.

5. Disconnect the electrical connector from the CKP sensor.

6. Remove the sensor mounting bolt.

7. Carefully twist the sensor from the cylinder block.

To install:

8. The CKP sensor O-ring can be reused if not damaged.

9. Apply a small amount of engine oil to the sensor O-ring.

10. Clean out the CKP sensor mounting bolt hole in the engine block.

11. Install the sensor into the engine block with a slight rocking and twisting action.

✳✳ WARNING

Before tightening the CKP sensor mounting bolt, be sure the sensor is completely flush to the cylinder block. If the CKP sensor is not flush, damage to the sensor mounting tang may result.

12. Install the mounting bolt and tighten to 106 inch lbs. (12 Nm).

13. Connect the electrical connector to the sensor.

14. Position the heat shield over the CKP sensor.

15. Lower the vehicle.

16. Connect the negative battery cable and tighten the nut to 45 inch lbs. (5 Nm).

➥The Cam/Crank Variation Relearn procedure must be performed using the scan tool anytime there has been a repair/replacement made to a powertrain system, for example: flywheel, valvetrain, camshaft and/or crankshaft sensors or components. Refer to Powertrain Control Module (PCM), Powertrain Verification Test.

ENGINE COOLANT TEMPERATURE (ECT) SENSOR

LOCATION

2.4L Engine

See Figures 286 and 287.

The Engine Coolant Temperature (ECT) sensor is mounted to the coolant adapter or to the engine block.

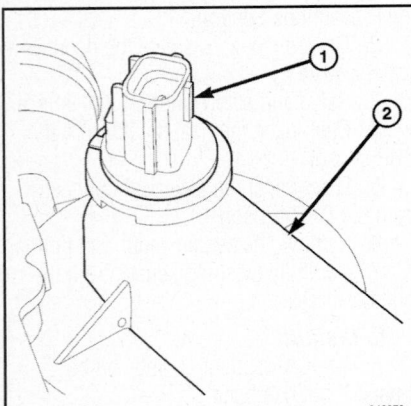

Fig. 286 Engine Coolant Temperature (ECT) sensor component location (1) and coolant adapter (2) shown (coolant adapter mounted)—2.4L engine

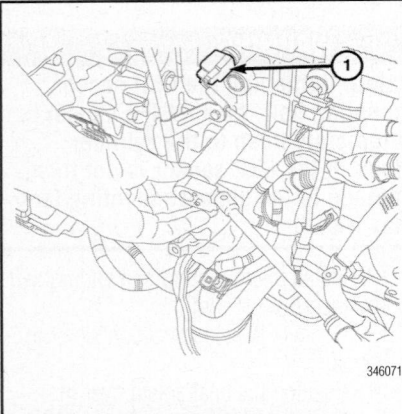

Fig. 287 Engine Coolant Temperature (ECT) sensor component location (1) (engine block mounted)—2.4L engine

2.7L Engine

See Figure 288.

The Engine Coolant Temperature (ECT) sensor is mounted to the coolant outlet tube.

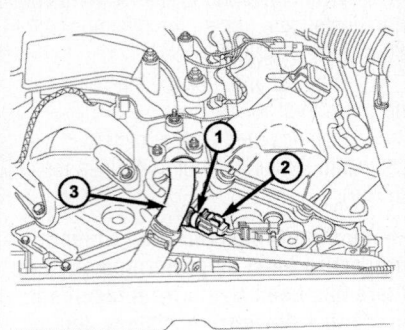

Fig. 288 Engine Coolant Temperature (ECT) sensor component location (1), coolant outlet tube (3), and electrical connector (2) shown—2.7L engine

3.5L Engine

See Figure 289.

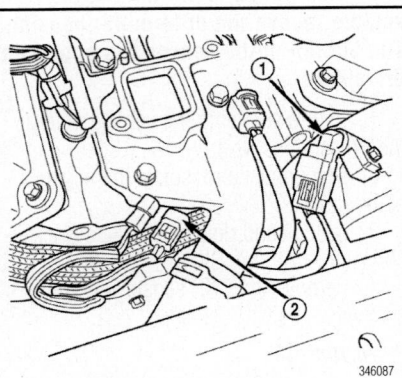

Fig. 289 Engine Coolant Temperature (ECT) sensor component location (2)—3.5L engine

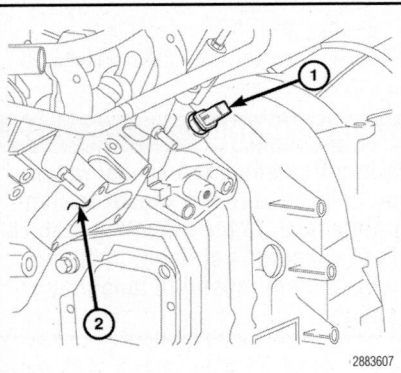

Fig. 290 Engine Coolant Temperature (ECT) sensor component location (1) on left cylinder head (2)—3.6L engine

3.6L Engine

See Figure 290.

➡The Engine Coolant Temperature (ECT) sensor on the 3.6L engine is installed into a water jacket at the rear of the cylinder head on the left side of the engine.

REMOVAL & INSTALLATION

2.4L Engine

Coolant Adapter Mounted

See Figure 286.

1. Before servicing the vehicle, refer to the Precautions Section.
2. Disconnect the negative battery cable. Refer to Battery, removal & installation.
3. Partially drain the cooling system below the level of the Engine Coolant Temperature (ECT) sensor.
4. Disconnect the ECT sensor electrical connector.
5. Remove the ECT sensor by pressing the locking tab and twisting the sensor counter clockwise.

   To install:
6. Install the ECT sensor. Make sure the coolant sensor is locked in place.
7. Connect the ECT sensor electrical connector.
8. Fill the cooling system. Refer to Engine Coolant, Drain & Refill Procedure.
9. Connect the negative battery cable. Refer to Battery, removal & installation.

Engine Block Mounted

See Figure 287.

1. Before servicing the vehicle, refer to the Precautions Section.
2. Disconnect the negative battery cable. Refer to Battery, removal & installation.
3. Partially drain the cooling system below the level of the Engine Coolant Temperature (ECT) sensor.
4. Disconnect the ECT sensor electrical connector.
5. Remove the ECT sensor.

   To install:
6. Install the ECT sensor. Tighten the sensor to 14 ft. lbs. (19 Nm).
7. Connect the ECT sensor electrical connector.
8. Fill the cooling system. Refer to Engine Coolant, Drain & Refill Procedure.
9. Connect the negative battery cable. Refer to Battery, removal & installation.

2.7L Engine

See Figure 288.

1. Before servicing the vehicle, refer to the Precautions Section.

2. Disconnect the negative battery cable. Refer to Battery, removal & installation.

3. Partially drain the cooling system.

4. Disconnect the Engine Coolant Temperature (ECT) sensor electrical connector.

5. Remove the ECT sensor from the coolant outlet tube.

To install:

6. Apply thread sealant to the sensor threads.

7. Install the ECT sensor into the coolant outlet tube.

8. Tighten the ECT sensor to 20 ft. lbs. (28 Nm).

9. Connect the electrical connector to the ECT sensor.

10. Fill the cooling system. Refer to Engine Coolant, Drain & Refill Procedure.

3.5L Engine

See Figure 289.

1. Before servicing the vehicle, refer to the Precautions Section.

2. Disconnect the negative battery cable. Refer to Battery, removal & installation.

3. Partially drain the cooling system.

4. With the engine cold, disconnect the Engine Coolant Temperature (ECT) sensor electrical connector.

5. Remove the ECT sensor.

To install:

6. Install the ECT sensor and tighten to 20 ft. lbs. (28 Nm).

7. Attach the electrical connector to the ECT sensor.

8. Connect the negative battery cable. Refer to Battery, removal & installation.

9. Fill the cooling system. Refer to Engine Coolant, Drain & Refill Procedure.

3.6L Engine

See Figure 290.

➡The Engine Coolant Temperature (ECT) sensor on the 3.6L engine is installed into a water jacket at the rear of the cylinder head on the left side of the engine.

✳✳ CAUTION

Hot, pressurized coolant can cause injury by scalding.

➡Do not waste reusable coolant. If the solution is clean, drain the coolant into a clean container for reuse.

1. Before servicing the vehicle, refer to the Precautions Section.

2. Partially drain the cooling system.

3. Disconnect the electrical connector from the ECT sensor.

4. Remove the ECT sensor from the cylinder head.

To install:

5. Apply MOPAR® thread sealant with PFTE to the ECT sensor threads.

6. Install the ECT sensor to the cylinder head.

7. Tighten the ECT sensor to 97 inch lbs. (11 Nm).

8. Connect the electrical connector to the ECT sensor.

9. Fill the cooling system. Refer to Engine Coolant, Drain & Refill Procedure.

HEATED OXYGEN (HO2S) SENSOR

LOCATION

2.4L Engine

See Figure 291.

2.7L and 3.5L Engines

See Figures 292 and 293.

3.6L Engine

See Figure 294.

REMOVAL & INSTALLATION

2.4L Engine

Upstream Oxygen Sensor (1/1)

See Figure 295.

✳✳ CAUTION

The exhaust manifold, exhaust pipes, and catalytic converter(s) become very hot during engine operation. Allow the engine to cool before

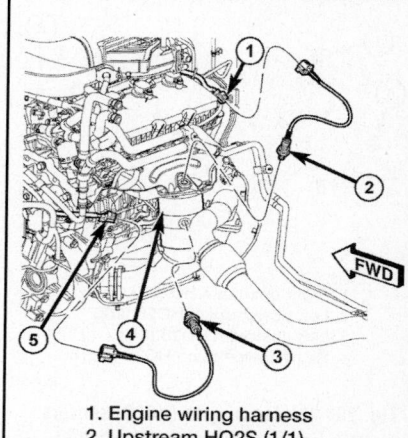

1. Engine wiring harness
2. Upstream HO2S (1/1)
3. Downstream HO2S (1/2)
4. Catalytic converter
5. Engine wiring harness

64907

Fig. 292 Heated Oxygen (HO2S) sensors and related component locations (bank 1)—2.7L and 3.5L engines

removing the oxygen sensor(s). Failure to allow the engine to cool before removal may result in personal injury.

✳✳ WARNING

When disconnecting the sensor electrical connector, do not pull directly on the wires going into the Heated Oxygen (HO2S). Damage to the oxygen sensor may occur.

➡Use an oxygen sensor removal tool for this procedure.

1. Before servicing the vehicle, refer to the Precautions Section.

2. Raise and safely support the vehicle.

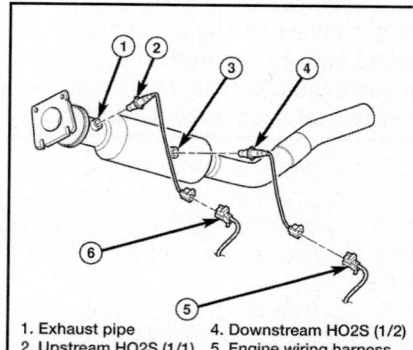

1. Exhaust pipe
2. Upstream HO2S (1/1)
3. Catalytic converter
4. Downstream HO2S (1/2)
5. Engine wiring harness
6. Engine wiring harness

98062

Fig. 291 Heated Oxygen (HO2S) sensor and related component locations—2.4L engine

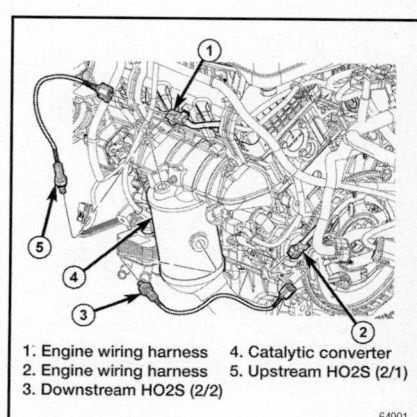

1. Engine wiring harness
2. Engine wiring harness
3. Downstream HO2S (2/2)
4. Catalytic converter
5. Upstream HO2S (2/1)

64901

Fig. 293 Heated Oxygen (HO2S) sensors and related component locations (bank 2)—2.7L and 3.5L engines

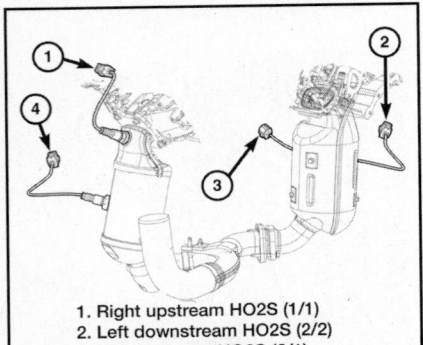

1. Right upstream HO2S (1/1)
2. Left downstream HO2S (2/2)
3. Left upstream HO2S (2/1)
4. Right downstream HO2S (1/2)

3093261

Fig. 294 Heated Oxygen (HO2S) sensors and related component locations—3.6L engine

3. Disconnect the HO2S wire harness mounting clips from the engine or body, if equipped.
4. Disconnect the HO2S pigtail harness from the engine wiring harness.
5. Remove the HO2S from the exhaust pipe.

To install:

✳✳ WARNING

When equipped, the HO2S pigtail harness must be clipped and/or bolted back to the original positions on the engine or body to prevent mechanical damage to the wiring.

6. The threads of new oxygen sensors are factory coated with anti-seize compound to aid in removal. DO NOT add any additional anti-seize compound to threads of a new HO2S.
7. Install the HO2S to the exhaust pipe. Tighten to 30 ft. lbs. (41 Nm).

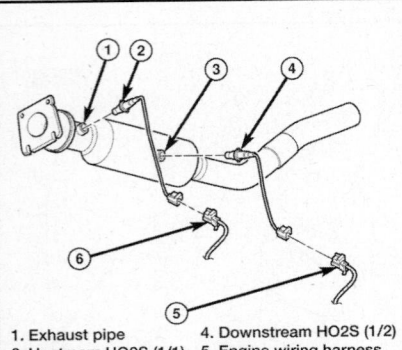

1. Exhaust pipe
2. Upstream HO2S (1/1)
3. Catalytic converter
4. Downstream HO2S (1/2)
5. Engine wiring harness
6. Engine wiring harness

98062

Fig. 295 Heated Oxygen (HO2S) sensor and related component locations—2.4L engine

8. Connect the HO2S pigtail harness to the engine wiring harness.
9. Connect the HO2S wire harness mounting clips to the engine or body, if equipped.

Downstream Oxygen Sensor (1/2)

See Figure 295.

✳✳ CAUTION

The exhaust manifold, exhaust pipes, and catalytic converter(s) become very hot during engine operation. Allow the engine to cool before removing the oxygen sensor(s). Failure to allow the engine to cool before removal may result in personal injury.

✳✳ WARNING

When disconnecting the sensor electrical connector, do not pull directly on the wires going into the Heated Oxygen (HO2S). Damage to the oxygen sensor may occur.

➡ Use an oxygen sensor removal tool for this procedure.

1. Before servicing the vehicle, refer to the Precautions Section.
2. Raise and safely support the vehicle.
3. Disconnect the HO2S wire harness mounting clips from the engine or body, if equipped.
4. Disconnect the HO2S pigtail harness from the engine wiring harness.
5. Remove the HO2S from the catalytic converter.

To install:

✳✳ WARNING

When equipped, the HO2S pigtail harness must be clipped and/or bolted back to the original positions on the engine or body to prevent mechanical damage to the wiring.

6. The threads of new oxygen sensors are factory coated with anti-seize compound to aid in removal. DO NOT add any additional anti-seize compound to threads of a new HO2S.
7. Install the HO2S to the catalytic converter. Tighten to 30 ft. lbs. (41 Nm).
8. Connect the HO2S pigtail harness to the engine wiring harness.
9. Connect the HO2S wire harness mounting clips to the engine or body, if equipped.

2.7L and 3.5L Engines

Downstream Oxygen Sensor (1/2) And Upstream Oxygen Sensor (1/1)

See Figure 296

✳✳ CAUTION

The exhaust manifold, exhaust pipes, and catalytic converter(s) become very hot during engine operation. Allow the engine to cool before removing the oxygen sensor(s). Failure to allow the engine to cool before removal may result in personal injury.

✳✳ WARNING

When disconnecting the sensor electrical connector, do not pull directly on the wires going into the Heated Oxygen (HO2S). Damage to the oxygen sensor may occur.

➡ Use an oxygen sensor removal tool for this procedure.

1. Before servicing the vehicle, refer to the Precautions Section.
2. Raise and safely support the vehicle.
3. Disconnect the HO2S wire harness mounting clips from the engine or body, if equipped.
4. Disconnect the HO2S pigtail harness from the engine wiring harness.
5. Remove the HO2S from the catalytic converter.

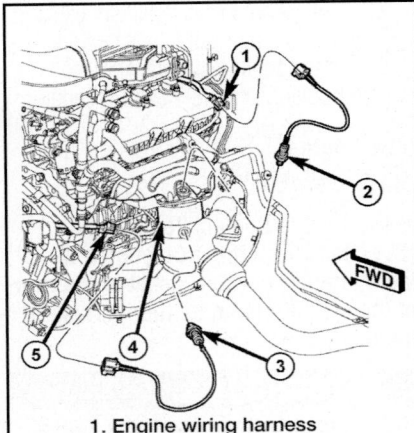

1. Engine wiring harness
2. Upstream HO2S (1/1)
3. Downstream HO2S (1/2)
4. Catalytic converter
5. Engine wiring harness

64907

Fig. 296 Heated Oxygen (HO2S) sensors and related component locations (bank 1)—2.7L and 3.5L engines

6. Disconnect the HO2S pigtail harness from the engine wiring harness.

7. Remove the HO2S from the catalytic converter.

To install:

> ❋❋ **WARNING**
>
> **When equipped, the HO2S pigtail harness must be clipped and/or bolted back to the original positions on the engine or body to prevent mechanical damage to the wiring.**

8. The threads of new oxygen sensors are factory coated with anti-seize compound to aid in removal. DO NOT add any additional anti-seize compound to threads of a new HO2S.

9. Install the HO2S to the catalytic converter.

10. Connect the HO2S pigtail harness to the engine wiring harness.

11. Install the HO2S to the catalytic converter. Tighten to 30 ft. lbs. (41 Nm).

12. Connect the HO2S pigtail harness to the engine wiring harness.

13. Connect the HO2S wire harness mounting clips to the engine or body, if equipped.

Downstream Oxygen Sensor (2/2) And Upstream Oxygen Sensor (2/1)

See Figure 297.

> ❋❋ **CAUTION**
>
> **The exhaust manifold, exhaust pipes, and catalytic converter(s) become very hot during engine operation. Allow the engine to cool before removing the oxygen sensor(s). Failure to allow the engine to cool before removal may result in personal injury.**

> ❋❋ **WARNING**
>
> **When disconnecting the sensor electrical connector, do not pull directly on the wires going into the Heated Oxygen (HO2S). Damage to the oxygen sensor may occur.**

➡Use an oxygen sensor removal tool for this procedure.

1. Before servicing the vehicle, refer to the Precautions Section.

2. Raise and safely support the vehicle.

3. Disconnect the HO2S wire harness mounting clips from the engine or body, if equipped.

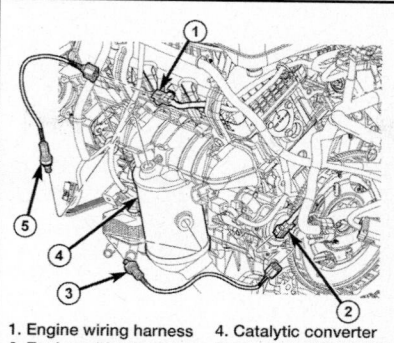

1. Engine wiring harness
2. Engine wiring harness
3. Downstream HO2S (2/2)
4. Catalytic converter
5. Upstream HO2S (2/1)

64901

Fig. 297 Heated Oxygen (HO2S) sensors and related component locations (bank 2)—2.7L and 3.5L engines

4. Disconnect the HO2S pigtail harness from the engine wiring harness.

5. Remove the HO2S from the catalytic converter.

6. Disconnect the HO2S pigtail harness from the engine wiring harness.

7. Remove the HO2S from the catalytic converter.

To install:

> ❋❋ **WARNING**
>
> **When equipped, the HO2S pigtail harness must be clipped and/or bolted back to the original positions on the engine or body to prevent mechanical damage to the wiring.**

8. The threads of new oxygen sensors are factory coated with anti-seize compound to aid in removal. DO NOT add any additional anti-seize compound to threads of a new HO2S.

9. Install the HO2S to the catalytic converter.

10. Connect the HO2S pigtail harness to the engine wiring harness.

11. Install the HO2S to the catalytic converter. Tighten to 30 ft. lbs. (41 Nm).

12. Connect the HO2S pigtail harness to the engine wiring harness.

13. Connect the HO2S wire harness mounting clips to the engine or body, if equipped.

3.6L Engine

See Figure 294.

The engine is equipped with four heated oxygen sensors:

• The right upstream oxygen sensor is referred to as the 1/1 sensor

• The right downstream oxygen sensor is referred to as the 1/2 sensor

• The left upstream oxygen sensor is referred to as the 2/1 sensor

• The left downstream oxygen sensor is referred to as the 2/2 sensor

> ❋❋ **CAUTION**
>
> **The exhaust pipes and catalytic converter become very hot during engine operation. Allow the engine to cool before removing the oxygen sensor.**

1. Before servicing the vehicle, refer to the Precautions Section.

2. Disconnect and isolate the negative battery cable. Refer to Battery, removal & installation.

3. Raise and safely support the vehicle.

> ❋❋ **WARNING**
>
> **When disconnecting the oxygen sensor electrical connector, do not pull directly on the wire going into the sensor. The sensor wiring can be damaged resulting in sensor failure.**

4. Disconnect the heated oxygen sensor electrical connector.

5. Remove the oxygen sensor.

To install:

6. Clean the exhaust pipe threads using an appropriate tap.

7. If reinstalling the original oxygen sensor, coat the sensor threads with an anti-seize compound such as Loctite® 771-64, or equivalent. New sensors have compound on the threads and do not require an additional coating. DO NOT add any additional anti-seize compound to the threads of a new oxygen sensor.

8. Install the oxygen sensor:

  a. Tighten the right upstream oxygen sensor to 32 ft. lbs. (43 Nm).

  b. Tighten the right downstream oxygen sensor to 32 ft. lbs. (43 Nm).

  c. Tighten the left upstream oxygen sensor to 32 ft. lbs. (43 Nm).

  d. Tighten the left downstream oxygen sensor to 33 ft. lbs. (45 Nm).

➡**Never apply any type of grease to the oxygen sensor electrical connector, or attempt any repair of the sensor wiring harness.**

9. Connect the heated oxygen sensor electrical connector.

10. Lower the vehicle.

11. Connect the negative battery cable and tighten the nut to 45 inch lbs. (5 Nm). Refer to Battery, removal & installation.

INTAKE AIR TEMPERATURE (IAT) SENSOR

LOCATION

See Figure 298.

REMOVAL & INSTALLATION

See Figure 298.

1. Before servicing the vehicle, refer to the Precautions Section.

2. Disconnect and isolate the negative battery cable. Refer to Battery, removal & installation.

➡**Clean any dirt or debris from the sensor area prior to removing from the air box.**

3. Disconnect the inlet (intake) air temperature sensor electrical connector.

4. Remove the inlet air temperature sensor from the air box by turning the sensor ¼ turn in the counter clockwise direction.

To install:

5. Install the inlet air temperature sensor to the air box by turning the sensor ¼ turn in the clockwise direction.

6. Connect the inlet air temperature sensor electrical connector.

7. Connect the negative battery cable, tighten the nut to 45 inch lbs. (5 Nm). Refer to Battery, removal & installation.

KNOCK SENSOR (KS)

LOCATION

2.4L Engine

See Figure 299.

2.7L Engine

See Figure 300.

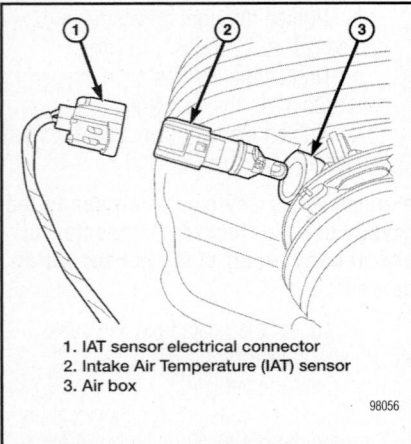

1. IAT sensor electrical connector
2. Intake Air Temperature (IAT) sensor
3. Air box

98056

Fig. 298 Intake Air Temperature (IAT) sensor component location

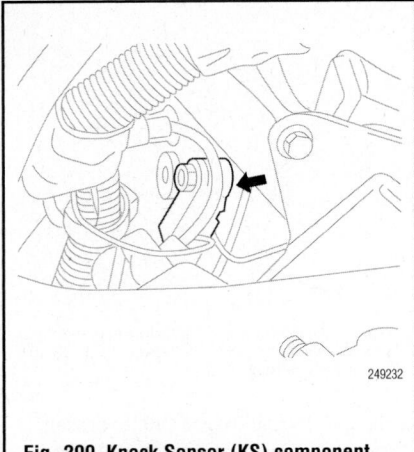

249232

Fig. 299 Knock Sensor (KS) component location—2.4L engine

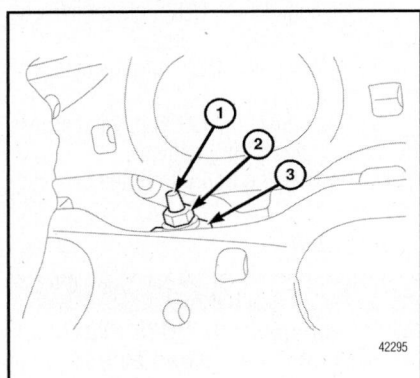

42295

Fig. 300 Knock Sensor (KS) component location (3), nut (2), and mounting stud (1)—2.7L engine

3.5L Engine

See Figure 301.

3.6L Engine

See Figure 302.

93155

Fig. 301 Knock Sensor (KS) wire and component location—3.5L engine

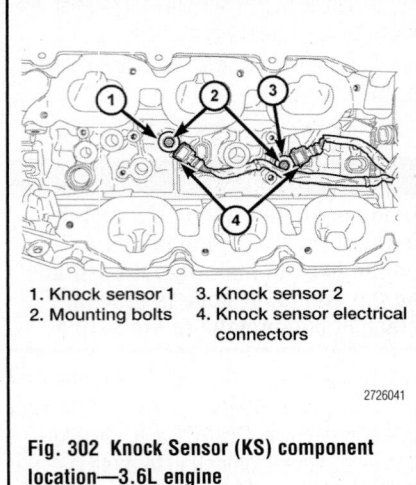

1. Knock sensor 1   3. Knock sensor 2
2. Mounting bolts   4. Knock sensor electrical connectors

2726041

Fig. 302 Knock Sensor (KS) component location—3.6L engine

REMOVAL & INSTALLATION

2.4L Engine

See Figure 299.

➡**The Knock Sensor (KS) bolts into the side of the cylinder block in front of the starter under the intake manifold.**

1. Before servicing the vehicle, refer to the Precautions Section.

2. Disconnect the negative battery cable. Refer to Battery, removal & installation.

3. Remove the bolt holding the KS.

4. Remove the KS with the electrical connector attached.

5. Disconnect the electrical connector from the KS.

6. Remove the KS.

To install:

7. Attach the electrical connector to the KS.

8. Install the KS. Tighten the KS bolt to 16 ft. lbs. (22 Nm).

❊❊ WARNING

Over or under tightening the knock sensor affects performance, possibly causing improper spark control.

9. Connect the negative battery cable. Refer to Battery, removal & installation.

2.7L Engine

See Figure 300.

❊❊ CAUTION

Do not remove the engine coolant pressure cap with the system hot and under pressure as serious burns from coolant can occur.

1. Before servicing the vehicle, refer to the Precautions Section.

2. Drain the cooling system. Refer to Engine Coolant, Drain & Refill Procedure.

3. Disconnect and isolate the negative battery cable. Refer to Battery, removal & installation.

4. Remove the lower intake manifold. Refer to Intake Manifold, removal & installation.

5. Remove the radiator upper hose at the water housing outlet tube.

6. Remove the heater hose from the water housing outlet tube at the rear of the engine.

7. Disconnect the water housing outlet tube from the retaining clip at the rear of the engine.

8. Disconnect the electrical connector from the coolant temperature sensor.

9. Remove the 4 bolts attaching the water housing outlet tube to the cylinder heads.

10. Disconnect the electrical connector from the knock sensor.

11. Reposition the water housing outlet tube and remove the nut from the knock sensor mounting stud.

12. Remove the knock sensor from the engine block.

To install:

✴✴ WARNING

Over or under tightening the knock sensor affects performance resulting in possible improper spark control.

13. Install the knock sensor and the nut onto the stud.

14. Tighten the knock sensor nut to 11 ft. lbs. (15 Nm).

15. Attach the electrical connector to the knock sensor.

16. Position the water housing outlet tube to the cylinder heads and loosely install the 4 bolts.

17. Attach the water housing outlet tube to the retaining clip at the rear of the engine.

18. Tighten the 4 bolts to 30 inch lbs. (3 Nm).

19. Connect the electrical connector to the coolant temperature sensor.

20. Install the heater hose to the water housing outlet tube at the rear of the engine.

21. Install the radiator upper hose to the water housing outlet tube.

22. Install the intake manifold. Refer to Intake Manifold, removal & installation.

23. Connect the negative battery cable, tighten the nut to 45 inch lbs. (5 Nm). Refer to Battery, removal & installation.

24. Fill the cooling system. Refer to Engine Coolant, Drain & Refill Procedure.

25. Operate the engine until it reaches the normal operating temperature. Check the cooling system for correct fluid levels.

3.5L Engine

See Figure 301.

1. Before servicing the vehicle, refer to the Precautions Section.

2. Remove the engine cover.

3. Release the fuel system pressure. Refer to Relieving Fuel System Pressure.

4. Drain the cooling system. Refer to Engine Coolant, Drain & Refill Procedure.

5. Disconnect and isolate the negative battery cable. Refer to Battery, removal & installation.

6. Remove the air cleaner body. Refer to Air Cleaner, removal & installation.

7. Remove the upper and lower intake manifolds. Refer to Intake Manifold, removal & installation.

8. Disconnect the electrical connector from the knock sensor.

9. Remove the knock sensor from the engine block.

To install:

✴✴ WARNING

Always use the specified torque when installing the knock sensor bolt. Over or under tightening the sensor mounting bolt will affect knock sensor performance, possibly causing improper spark control.

10. Install the knock sensor. Tighten the knock sensor to 15 ft. lbs. (20 Nm).

11. Route the knock sensor wire into the proper location.

12. Connect the knock sensor electrical connector.

13. Install the upper and lower intake manifolds. Refer to Intake Manifold, removal & installation.

14. Install the air cleaner body. Refer to Air Cleaner, removal & installation.

15. Connect the negative battery cable, tighten the nut to 45 inch lbs. (5 Nm).

16. Fill the cooling system. Refer to Engine Coolant, Drain & Refill Procedure.

17. Operate the engine until it reaches the normal operating temperature. Check the cooling system for correct fluid levels.

18. Install the engine cover.

3.6L Engine

See Figure 302.

➡**The forward sensor is known to the Powertrain Control Module (PCM) as knock sensor 1. The rear sensor is known to the PCM as knock sensor 2.**

1. Before servicing the vehicle, refer to the Precautions Section.

2. Release the fuel system pressure. Refer to Relieving Fuel System Pressure.

3. Disconnect and isolate the negative battery cable. Refer to Battery, removal & installation.

4. Drain the cooling system. Refer to Engine Coolant, Drain & Refill Procedure.

5. Remove the air cleaner housing assembly and the upper and lower intake manifolds. Refer to Intake Manifold, removal & installation.

6. Remove the oil filter housing.

7. Remove the knock sensor electrical connectors.

➡**There may be a foam strip on the bolt threads. This foam is used only to retain the bolts to the sensors for plant assembly. It is not used as a sealant. Do not apply any adhesive, sealant or thread locking compound to these bolts.**

8. Remove the mounting bolt and knock sensor 1 or knock sensor 2.

To install:

9. Thoroughly clean the knock sensor mounting holes.

✴✴ WARNING

Over or under tightening the sensor mounting bolts will affect knock sensor performance, possibly causing improper spark control. Always use the specified torque when installing the knock sensors. The torque specification for the knock sensor bolt is less than the typical 8mm bolt.

10. Install the knock sensor 1 or knock sensor 2 with the mounting bolt. Tighten the mounting bolt to 16 ft. lbs. (22 Nm).

11. Connect the electrical connector(s) to the knock sensor(s).

12. Install the oil filter housing.

13. Install the upper and lower intake manifolds and air cleaner housing assembly. Refer to Intake Manifold, removal & installation.

14. If removed, install the oil filter and fill the engine crankcase with the proper oil to the correct level. Refer to Engine Oil & Filter, Replacement.

15. Connect the negative battery cable and tighten the nut to 45 inch lbs. (5 Nm). Refer to Battery, removal & installation.

16. Fill the cooling system. Refer to Engine Coolant, Drain & Refill Procedure.

17. Operate the engine until it reaches the normal operating temperature. Check the cooling system for correct fluid levels.

MANIFOLD ABSOLUTE PRESSURE (MAP) SENSOR

LOCATION

2.4L Engine

See Figure 303.

2.7L Engine

See Figure 304.

3.5L Engine

See Figure 305.

3.6L Engine

See Figure 306.

REMOVAL & INSTALLATION

2.4L Engine

See Figure 303.

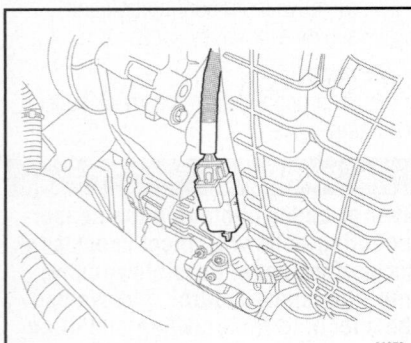

Fig. 303 Manifold Absolute Pressure (MAP) sensor wire and component location—2.4L engine

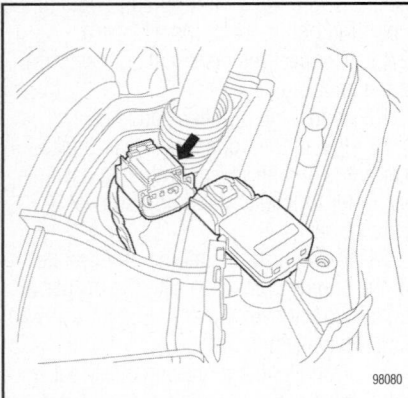

Fig. 304 Manifold Absolute Pressure (MAP) sensor component location with electrical connection shown—2.7L engine

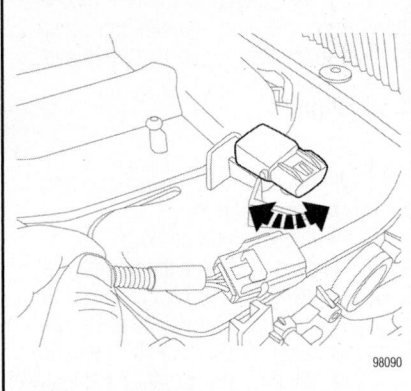

Fig. 305 Manifold Absolute Pressure (MAP) sensor component location—3.5L engine

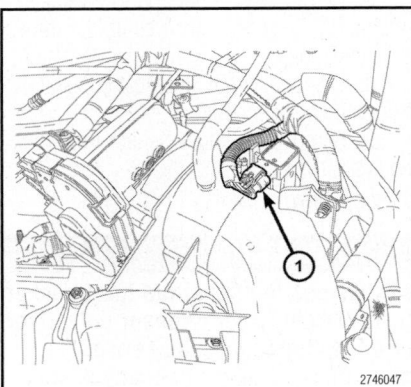

Fig. 306 Manifold Absolute Pressure (MAP) sensor component location and electrical connection (1)—3.6L engine

1. Before servicing the vehicle, refer to the Precautions Section.
2. Disconnect and isolate the negative battery cable. Refer to Battery, removal & installation.
3. Disconnect the electrical connector from the Manifold Absolute Pressure (MAP) sensor.
4. Remove the screw from the MAP sensor.
5. Remove the MAP sensor.

To install:
6. Install the MAP sensor to the intake manifold. Tighten the screw to 40 inch lbs. (5 Nm).
7. Connect the electrical connector to the MAP sensor.
8. Install the negative battery cable and tighten the nut to 45 inch lbs. (5 Nm). Refer to Battery, removal & installation.

2.7L Engine

See Figure 304.

1. Before servicing the vehicle, refer to the Precautions Section.
2. Disconnect and isolate the negative battery cable. Refer to Battery, removal & installation.
3. Disconnect the electrical connector from the MAP sensor.
4. Turn the sensor counterclockwise.
5. Lift the sensor to remove.

To install:
6. Install the sensor to the intake manifold plenum and turn clockwise to tighten.
7. Attach the electrical connector to the MAP sensor.
8. Connect the negative battery cable, tighten the nut to 45 inch lbs. (5 Nm). Refer to Battery, removal & installation.

3.5L Engine

See Figure 305.

1. Before servicing the vehicle, refer to the Precautions Section.
2. Disconnect and isolate the negative battery cable. Refer to Battery, removal & installation.
3. Disconnect the electrical connector from the MAP sensor.
4. Rotate the MAP sensor and lift to remove.

To install:
5. Install the MAP sensor.
6. Rotate the MAP sensor into position.
7. Attach the electrical connector to the MAP sensor.
8. Connect the negative battery cable, tighten the nut to 45 inch lbs. (5 Nm). Refer to Battery, removal & installation.

3.6L Engine

See Figure 306.

1. Before servicing the vehicle, refer to the Precautions Section.
2. Disconnect and isolate the negative battery cable. Refer to Battery, removal & installation.
3. Remove the engine cover.
4. Unlock and disconnect the electrical connector from the MAP sensor.
5. Rotate the MAP sensor ¼ turn counterclockwise and pull the sensor straight up and out of the upper intake manifold.
6. The MAP sensor O-ring can be reused if not damaged.

To install:
7. Apply a small amount of engine oil to the MAP sensor O-ring.
8. Install the MAP sensor into the upper intake manifold and rotate ¼ turn clockwise.

9. Connect and lock the electrical connector to the sensor.

10. Install the engine cover.

11. Connect the negative battery cable and tighten the nut to 45 inch lbs. (5 Nm). Refer to Battery, removal & installation.

MASS AIR FLOW (MAF) SENSOR

LOCATION

See Figure 307.

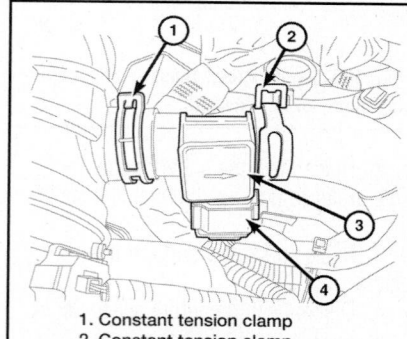

1. Constant tension clamp
2. Constant tension clamp
3. Mass Air Flow (MAF) sensor
4. MAF sensor electrical connector

102039

Fig. 331 Mass Air Flow (MAF) sensor component location

REMOVAL & INSTALLATION

See Figure 307.

1. Before servicing the vehicle, refer to the Precautions Section.

2. Disconnect the Mass Air Flow (MAF) sensor electrical connector.

3. Remove the constant tension clamps, securing the MAF sensor.

4. Remove the MAF sensor from the hoses.

To install:

5. Note the arrow direction on the sensor and correctly position the sensor to the hoses.

6. Install the constant tension clamps, to secure the MAF sensor to the hoses.

7. Connect the MAF sensor electrical connector.

POWERTRAIN CONTROL MODULE (PCM)

LOCATION

See Figure 308.

REMOVAL & INSTALLATION

See Figure 308.

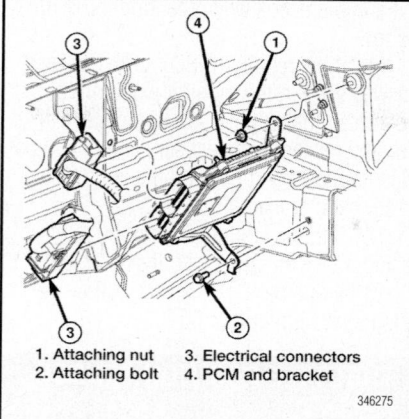

1. Attaching nut   3. Electrical connectors
2. Attaching bolt   4. PCM and bracket

346275

Fig. 308 Powertrain Control Module (PCM) component location

✳✳ WARNING

Do not disconnect the Powertrain Control Module (PCM) electrical connectors before the ignition key is in the OFF position and the battery cable disconnected. If these steps are not performed, damage to the PCM may result from a voltage spike.

➥Note radio programs prior to disconnecting the battery.

1. Before servicing the vehicle, refer to the Precautions Section.

2. Disconnect and isolate the negative battery cable at the battery. Refer to Battery, removal & installation.

3. Remove the air cleaner housing. Refer to Air Cleaner, removal & installation.

4. Disconnect the electrical connectors from the PCM.

5. Remove the nut from the upper shock tower stud.

6. Remove the bolt from the lower shock tower fastener.

7. Remove the PCM and bracket from the vehicle.

8. Remove bolts and separate the PCM from the bracket.

To install:

9. Install the PCM to the bracket. Tighten the bolts to 45 inch lbs. (5 Nm).

10. Install the PCM and bracket to the vehicle.

11. Install the bolt to the lower shock tower fastener and tighten to 80 inch lbs. (9 Nm).

12. Install the nut to the upper shock tower stud and tighten to 80 inch lbs. (9 Nm).

13. Connect the electrical connectors to the PCM.

14. Install the air cleaner housing. Refer to Air Cleaner, removal & installation.

15. Connect the negative battery cable and tighten to 12 ft. lbs. (17 Nm).

16. Reprogram the radio stations and time display.

17. Program the PCM. Refer to PCM Programming.

PCM Programming

The secret key is an ID code that is unique to each WIN. This code is programmed and stored in the WIN, the PCM, and each ignition key transponder chip. When the PCM or WIN is replaced, it is necessary to program the Secret Key Code into the new module using a diagnostic scan tool. Follow the programming steps outlined in the diagnostic scan tool for PCM REPLACED, WIN REPLACED, or TIPM REPLACED under MISCELLANEOUS FUNCTIONS for the WIRELESS CONTROL MODULE menu item as appropriate.

Programming the PCM or WIN is done using a diagnostic scan tool and a PIN to enter secure access mode. If three attempts are made to enter secure access mode using an incorrect PIN, secure access mode will be locked out for one hour. To exit this lockout mode, turn the ignition to the RUN position for one hour and then enter the correct PIN. Be certain that all accessories are turned OFF. Also, monitor the battery state and connect a battery charger if necessary.

Read all notes and cautions for programming procedures.

1. Before servicing the vehicle, refer to the Precautions Section.

2. Connect a battery charger to the vehicle.

3. Connect the scan tool.

4. Have a unique vehicle PIN readily available before running the routine.

5. The ignition key should be in the RUN position.

6. Select "ECU View".

7. Select "WIN Wireless Control".

8. Select "Miscellaneous Functions".

9. Select "PCM Replaced".

10. Enter the PIN when prompted.

11. Verify the correct information.

12. Cycle the ignition key after a successful routine completion.

POWERTRAIN VERIFICATION TEST

The Cam/Crank Variation Relearn must be performed any time there has been a repair or replacement made to a powertrain system. For example: flywheel, valvetrain, camshaft sensors and components, or crankshaft sensors and components.

If the PCM has been replaced and the correct VIN and mileage have not been programmed, a DTC will set in the ABS Module, Airbag Module and the Wireless Control Module (WCM) or Wireless Ignition Node (WIN).

If the vehicle is equipped with a Sentry Key Remote Entry, Secret Key data must be updated. Using the scan tool, program the Secret Key information into the PCM using the PCM replaced function under the WCM menu.

If this vehicle is equipped with an Electronic Throttle Control system and the APP Sensors, PCM or Throttle Body Assembly have been replaced, use the scan tool to perform the ETC RELEARN function.

When replacing an O2 Sensor, the PCM RAM memory must be cleared, either by disconnecting the PCM C1 connector or momentarily disconnecting the Battery negative terminal.

After completing the Powertrain Verification Test, the Transmission Verification Test must be performed.

1. Before servicing the vehicle, refer to the Precautions Section.

2. The PCM learns the characteristics of each O2 heater element and these learned values should be cleared when installing a new O2 sensor. The vehicle may experience drive-ability issues if this is not performed.

3. Inspect the vehicle to make sure that all engine components are properly installed and connected. Reassemble and reconnect components as necessary.

4. Connect the scan tool to the data link connector.

5. Make sure the fuel tank has at least ¼ tank of fuel. Turn off all accessories.

6. If the Catalyst was replaced, with the scan tool select "Catalyst Replaced" under the Miscellaneous Menu Option.

7. If a repair/replacement was made to a powertrain system, with the scan tool select the "Cam Crank Relearn" procedure under PCM Miscellaneous Menu Option.

8. If a Comprehensive Component DTC was repaired, perform steps 10–12. If a Major OBDII Monitor DTC was repaired, skip those steps and continue verification.

9. After the ignition has been off for at least 10 seconds, restart the vehicle and run 2 minutes.

10. Using the scan tool, monitor the appropriate pre-test enabling conditions until all conditions have been met. Once the conditions have been met, switch screen to the appropriate OBDII monitor, (there will

be audible beeps when the monitor is running).

11. If the repaired OBDII DTC has reset or was seen in the monitor while on the road test, the repair is not complete. Check for any related technical service bulletins or flash updates and perform the appropriate diagnostic procedure.

12. If the conditions cannot be duplicated, erase all DTCs with the scan tool.

13. If another DTC has set, follow the path specified for that DTC.

THROTTLE POSITION SENSOR (TPS)

LOCATION

The Throttle Position (TP) sensor is located on the throttle body.

REMOVAL & INSTALLATION

The Throttle Position Sensor (TPS) is integral to the electronic throttle body. Refer to Throttle Body, removal & installation.

VEHICLE SPEED SENSOR (VSS)

LOCATION

40TE and 41TE Transaxles

See Figure 309.

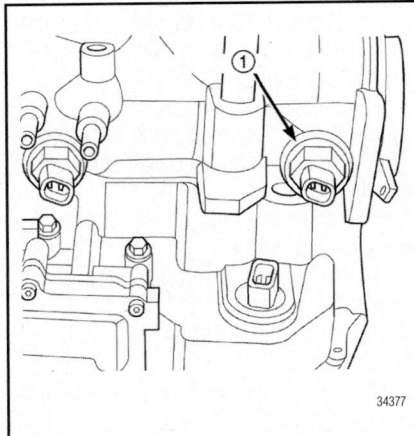

Fig. 309 Output speed sensor component location (1)—40TE and 41TE transaxles

62TE Transaxle

See Figure 310.

REMOVAL & INSTALLATION

40TE and 41TE Transaxles

See Figure 309.

1. Before servicing the vehicle, refer to the Precautions Section.

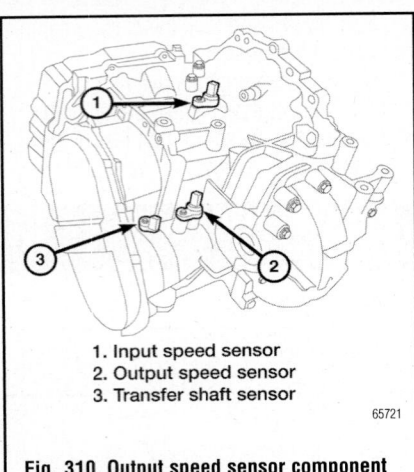

1. Input speed sensor
2. Output speed sensor
3. Transfer shaft sensor

Fig. 310 Output speed sensor component location—62TE transaxle

2. Disconnect the battery negative cable. Refer to Battery, removal & installation.

3. Raise and safely support the vehicle.

4. Disconnect the output speed sensor connector.

5. Unscrew and remove the output speed sensor.

6. Inspect the speed sensor O-ring and replace if necessary.

To install:

7. Verify the O-ring is installed into position.

8. Install and tighten the output speed sensor to 20 ft. lbs. (27 Nm).

9. Connect the output speed sensor connector.

10. Connect the battery negative cable. Refer to Battery, removal & installation.

62TE Transaxle

See Figure 310.

1. Before servicing the vehicle, refer to the Precautions Section.

2. Unplug the electrical connector at the output speed sensor.

3. Remove the bolt at the output speed sensor.

4. Pull up on the output speed sensor to remove.

To install:

5. Install a new O-ring on the output speed sensor.

6. Install the output speed sensor into the case.

7. Install the bolt at the output speed sensor and tighten to 106 inch lbs. (12 Nm).

8. Engage the electrical connector to the output speed sensor.

FUEL   **GASOLINE FUEL INJECTION SYSTEM**

FUEL SYSTEM SERVICE PRECAUTIONS

Safety is the most important factor when performing not only fuel system maintenance but any type of maintenance. Failure to conduct maintenance and repairs in a safe manner may result in serious personal injury or death. Maintenance and testing of the vehicle's fuel system components can be accomplished safely and effectively by adhering to the following rules and guidelines.

• To avoid the possibility of fire and personal injury, always disconnect the negative battery cable unless the repair or test procedure requires that battery voltage be applied.

• Always relieve the fuel system pressure prior to disconnecting any fuel system component (injector, fuel rail, pressure regulator, etc.), fitting or fuel line connection. Exercise extreme caution whenever relieving fuel system pressure to avoid exposing skin, face and eyes to fuel spray. Please be advised that fuel under pressure may penetrate the skin or any part of the body that it contacts.

• Always place a shop towel or cloth around the fitting or connection prior to loosening to absorb any excess fuel due to spillage. Ensure that all fuel spillage (should it occur) is quickly removed from engine surfaces. Ensure that all fuel soaked cloths or towels are deposited into a suitable waste container.

• Always keep a dry chemical (Class B) fire extinguisher near the work area.

• Do not allow fuel spray or fuel vapors to come into contact with a spark or open flame.

• Always use a back-up wrench when loosening and tightening fuel line connection fittings. This will prevent unnecessary stress and torsion to fuel line piping.

• Always replace worn fuel fitting O-rings with new Do not substitute fuel hose or equivalent where fuel pipe is installed.

Before servicing the vehicle, make sure to also refer to the precautions in the beginning of this section as well.

RELIEVING FUEL SYSTEM PRESSURE

✳✳ CAUTION

The fuel system is under constant pressure even with the engine off.

Until the fuel pressure has been properly relieved from the system, do not attempt to open the fuel system. Do not smoke or use open flames/sparks when servicing the fuel system. Wear protective clothing and eye protection. Make sure the area in which the vehicle is being serviced is well-ventilated.

➡**A separate fuel pump relay is no longer used. A circuit within the Totally Integrated Power Module (TIPM) is used to control the electric fuel pump located within the fuel pump module.**

1. Before servicing the vehicle, refer to the Precautions Section.
2. Remove the fuel fill cap.
3. Remove the lower rear seat cushion.
4. Remove the fuel pump module cover.
5. Disconnect the electrical connector from the fuel pump module.
6. Start and run the engine until it stalls.
7. Attempt to restart the engine a few times until the engine will no longer start.
8. Turn the ignition key to the OFF position.
9. Disconnect the negative battery cable. Refer to Battery, removal & installation.
10. Place a shop towel below and disconnect the fuel line quick-connect fitting at the fuel pump module.

➡**After servicing the fuel system, one or more Diagnostic Trouble Codes (DTCs) may have been stored in the Powertrain Control Module (PCM) memory due to disconnecting the fuel pump module circuit.**

FUEL FILTER

REMOVAL & INSTALLATION

A lifetime fuel filter is serviced as part of the fuel pump module. Refer to Fuel Pump Module, removal & installation.

FUEL INJECTORS

REMOVAL & INSTALLATION

2.4L Engine

See Figures 311 and 312.

✳✳ CAUTION

There is a risk of injury to eyes and skin from contact with fuel. Wear

protective clothing and eye protection. There is also a risk of poisoning from inhaling and swallowing fuel. Pour fuel only into appropriately marked and approved containers. Failure to follow these instructions may result in possible serious or fatal injury.

1. Before servicing the vehicle, refer to the Precautions Section.
2. Release the fuel system pressure. Refer to Relieving Fuel System Pressure.
3. Disconnect and isolate the negative battery cable. Refer to Battery, removal & installation.
4. Disconnect the electrical connectors from the fuel injectors.
5. Disconnect the fuel line connection at the fuel rail.
6. Remove the fuel line from the fuel rail.
7. Remove the wire harness from the fuel rail mounting studs.
8. Remove the 2 bolts from the fuel rail at the lower manifold.
9. Remove the fuel rail.
10. Remove the clip holding the fuel injector to the fuel rail.
11. Remove the fuel injector clip and the fuel injector from the fuel rail.

To install:
12. Apply a light coating of clean engine oil to the upper O-ring of the fuel injector.
13. Install the injector into the cup on the fuel rail.
14. Install the retaining clip.
15. Apply a light coating of clean engine oil to the O-ring on the nozzle end of each injector.

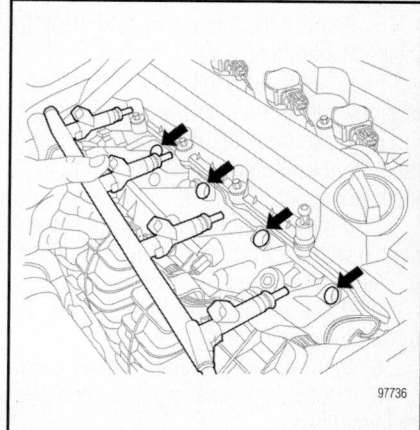

97736

Fig. 311 Removing the fuel rail—2.4L engine

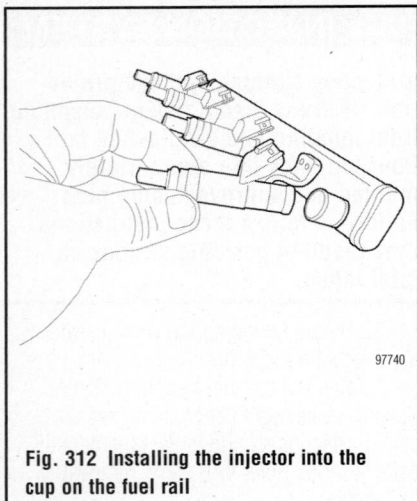

Fig. 312 Installing the injector into the cup on the fuel rail

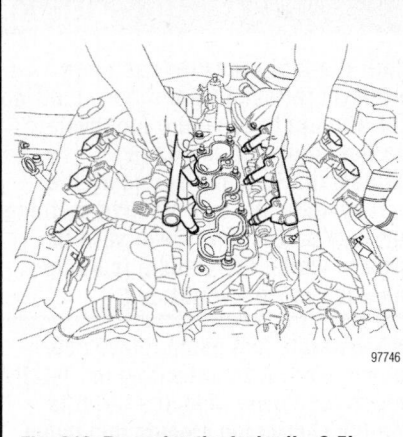

Fig. 313 Removing the fuel rail—3.5L engine

16. Insert the fuel injector nozzles into the openings in the lower intake manifold. Seat the injectors in place.

17. Tighten the fuel rail mounting screws to 20 ft. lbs. (27 Nm).

18. Install the wiring harness clips to the fuel rail mounting studs.

19. Connect the electrical connectors to the fuel injectors.

20. Connect the fuel supply tube to the fuel rail.

21. Connect the negative battery cable and tighten the nut to 45 inch lbs. (5 Nm).

22. Use the scan tool to pressurize the fuel system. Check for leaks.

2.7L Engine

See Figures 312 and 313.

1. Before servicing the vehicle, refer to the Precautions Section.

2. Release the fuel system pressure. Refer to Relieving Fuel System Pressure.

3. Disconnect and isolate the negative battery cable. Refer to Battery, removal & installation.

4. Remove the intake manifold. Refer to Intake Manifold, removal & installation.

5. Cover the intake manifold to prevent foreign material from entering the engine.

6. Disconnect the fuel supply tube quick connect fittings at the rear of the intake manifold.

7. If the injector connectors are not tagged with their cylinder number, tag them to identify the correct cylinder.

8. Remove the electrical connectors from the fuel injectors.

9. Remove the fuel rail mounting bolts.

10. Lift the fuel rail straight up off of the cylinder head.

11. Remove the retaining clips from the fuel injectors at the fuel rail.

12. Remove the fuel injectors.

13. Check the injector O-ring for damage. If the O-ring is damaged, it must be replaced. Replace the injector clip if it is damaged.

To install:

14. Lightly lubricate the fuel injector O-rings with a couple drops of clean engine oil.

15. Install the fuel injectors.

16. Install the retaining clips on the fuel injectors.

17. Push the injectors into the fuel injector rail until the clips are in the correct position.

18. Position the fuel rail over the cylinder head, and push the rail into place. Tighten the fuel rail mounting bolts to 97 inch lbs. (11 Nm).

19. Connect the fuel supply tube quick connect fittings at the rear of intake manifold.

20. Connect the electrical connectors to the fuel injectors.

21. Install the intake manifold. Refer to Intake Manifold, removal & installation.

22. Connect the negative cable to the battery. Refer to Battery, removal & installation.

3.5L Engine

See Figures 314 and 315

> **※※ CAUTION**
>
> **The fuel system is under constant pressure (even with the engine OFF). Before servicing any part on the fuel system, the fuel system pressure must be released.**

1. Before servicing the vehicle, refer to the Precautions Section.

2. Release the fuel system pressure. Refer to Relieving Fuel System Pressure.

3. Disconnect and isolate the negative battery cable. Refer to Battery, removal & installation.

4. Remove the upper intake manifold. Refer to Intake Manifold, removal & installation.

5. Disconnect the quick connect fuel line from the fuel rail.

➡**Mark the fuel injector electrical harness connectors with the correct corresponding cylinder numbers.**

6. Disconnect all the fuel injector electrical connectors from the fuel injectors.

7. Remove the fuel rail mounting bolts from the fuel rail and the lower intake manifold.

➡**Gently rock the fuel rail and injectors back and forth to loosen the seals on the fuel injectors from the cylinder heads.**

> **※※ WARNING**
>
> **Do Not use excessive force or prying tools to remove the fuel rail and injectors. Damage to the fuel rail and injectors may result.**

8. Lift the fuel rail straight up off of cylinder heads.

9. Drain any excess fuel from the fuel rail into an approved fuel storage container.

➡**When replacing individual fuel injectors, each fuel injector must be installed to its original position. Mark or tag each fuel injector to identify the correct cylinder.**

10. Remove the retaining clips from the fuel injectors at the fuel rail.

To install:

➡**Inspect each O-ring seal on all the fuel injectors, replace O-ring seals if any damage is noted. Note the fuel injector O-rings are color coded. The Blue colored O-ring is for the fuel rail side and the Green colored O-ring is for the cylinder head side.**

11. Install and lubricate each of the fuel injector O-rings, with a light drop of clean engine oil.

12. Install all of the fuel injectors to the fuel rail, then install the retaining clip to the fuel rail.

13. Inspect each fuel injector for proper installation. Note how the retaining clip secures the fuel injector to the fuel rail.

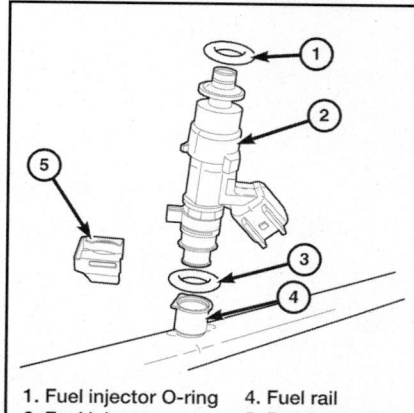

1. Fuel injector O-ring   4. Fuel rail
2. Fuel injector   5. Retaining clip
3. Fuel injector O-ring

97756

Fig. 314 Exploded view of fuel injector—3.5L engine

➡ **The fuel rail bolts are lower intake manifold bolts. These bolts must be torqued in a mandatory torque sequence.**

14. Insert the fuel injector nozzles into the openings in the cylinder heads. Seat the injectors in place. Install the fuel rail bolts and tighten the bolts in a mandatory torque sequence to 21 ft. lbs. (28 Nm).

15. Correctly position and connect the fuel injector electrical harness connectors to the fuel injectors.

✱✱ WARNING

Make sure the fuel line quick connector is connected properly. Failure to connect the fuel line correctly may result in a fuel leak at the rail assembly. Fuel leaked onto a hot engine may ignite resulting in damage to the vehicle.

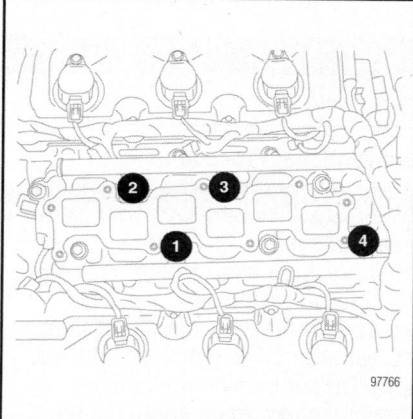

97766

Fig. 315 Fuel rail bolt tightening sequence—3.5L engine

16. Connect the quick connect fuel line to the fuel rail.

17. Connect all of the fuel injector electrical connectors to the fuel injectors.

18. Install the upper intake manifold. Refer to Intake Manifold, removal & installation.

19. Connect the negative battery cable, tighten the nut to 45 inch lbs. (5 Nm). Refer to Battery, removal & installation.

20. Use the scan tool ASD Fuel System Test to pressurize the fuel system. Check for leaks.

3.6L Engine

See Figures 316 and 317.

✱✱ CAUTION

The fuel system is under constant pressure even with engine off. Before servicing the fuel rail, the fuel system pressure must be released.

1. Before servicing the vehicle, refer to the Precautions Section.

2. Release the fuel system pressure. Refer to Relieving Fuel System Pressure.

3. Disconnect and isolate the negative battery cable. Refer to Battery, removal & installation.

✱✱ CAUTION

When removing the fuel rail from the lower intake manifold, one or more fuel injectors may remain in the intake manifold resulting in residual fuel spilling onto the engine from the fuel rail.

4. Remove the air inlet hose.

5. Remove the upper intake manifold. Refer to Intake Manifold, removal & installation.

6. Remove the bolts securing the fuel rail and remove the fuel rail with the fuel injectors.

7. Remove the fuel injectors from the fuel rail.

8. Remove the fuel injectors from the lower intake manifold.

9. Remove and discard all of the fuel injector O-ring seals.

To install:

10. Clean out the fuel injector bores in the lower intake manifold.

11. Lightly lubricate the new O-ring seals with engine oil and install them on the fuel injector.

12. Install the fuel injectors to the fuel rail.

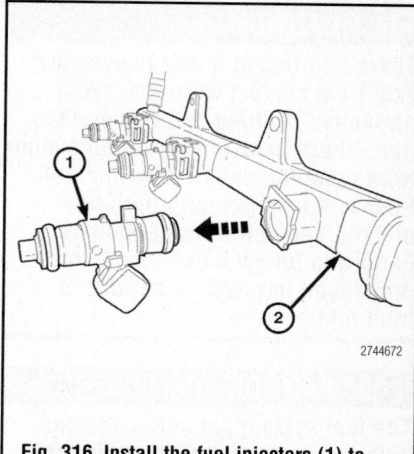

2744672

Fig. 316 Install the fuel injectors (1) to the fuel rail (2)—3.6L engine

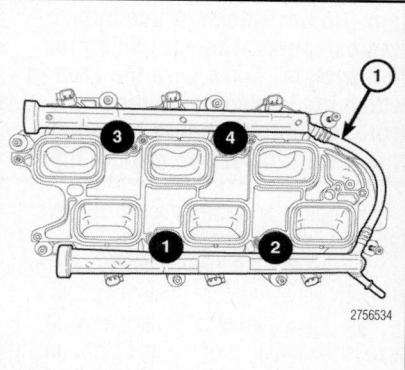

2756534

Fig. 317 Fuel rail (1) bolt tightening sequence—3.6L engine

13. Install the fuel rail to the lower intake manifold with the 4 bolts tightened in sequence to 62 inch lbs. (7 Nm).

14. Connect the fuel injector electrical connectors.

15. Connect the fuel supply hose to the fuel rail.

16. Install the insulator to the 2 alignment posts on the top of the LH cylinder head cover.

17. Install the upper intake manifold. Refer to Intake Manifold, removal & installation.

18. Install the air inlet hose.

19. Connect the negative battery cable and tighten the nut to 45 inch lbs. (5 Nm). Refer to Battery, removal & installation.

20. Start the engine and check for leaks.

FUEL PUMP

REMOVAL & INSTALLATION

See Figures 318 through 320.

✳✳ CAUTION

There is a risk of injury to eyes and skin from contact with fuel. Wear protective clothing and eye protection. There is also a risk of poisoning from inhaling and swallowing fuel. Pour fuel only into appropriately marked and approved containers. Failure to follow these instructions may result in possible serious or fatal injury.

✳✳ CAUTION

The fuel system is under constant high pressure even with engine OFF. Until the fuel pressure has been properly released from the system, do not attempt to open the fuel system. Do not smoke or use open flames/sparks when servicing the fuel system. Make sure the area in which the vehicle is being serviced is well-ventilated. Failure to comply may result in serious or fatal injury.

1. Before servicing the vehicle, refer to the Precautions Section.
2. Release the fuel system pressure. Refer to Relieving Fuel System Pressure.
3. Use a marker and place a mark across the position of the fuel pump module lock-ring, fuel pump module, and the fuel tank prior to removal.
4. Remove the fuel line from the fuel pump module.

➡**Prior to removing the fuel pump module, use compressed air to remove any accumulated dirt and debris from around fuel tank opening.**

5. Position the lock-ring remover/installer 9340 into the notches on the outside edge of the lock-ring.
6. Install a ½ inch drive breaker bar into the lock-ring remover/installer 9340.
7. Rotate the breaker bar counterclockwise and remove the lock-ring.

✳✳ CAUTION

The fuel pump module reservoir does not empty out fully when the tank is drained. The fuel in the reservoir may spill out when the module is removed.

✳✳ WARNING

Do not spill fuel into the interior of the vehicle.

8. Raise the fuel pump module out of

the fuel tank using caution not spill fuel inside the vehicle.
9. Tip the fuel pump module on its side and drain all fuel from the reservoir.
10. Remove the fuel pump module from the fuel tank using caution not to bend the float arm.
11. Remove and discard the rubber O-ring seal.

To install:

➡**Whenever the fuel pump module is serviced, the rubber O-ring seal must be replaced.**

12. Clean the rubber O-ring seal area of the fuel tank and install a new rubber O-ring seal.
13. Lower the fuel pump module into the fuel tank using caution not to bend the float arm.

➡**The fuel pump module has to be properly located in the fuel tank for the fuel level gauge to work properly.**

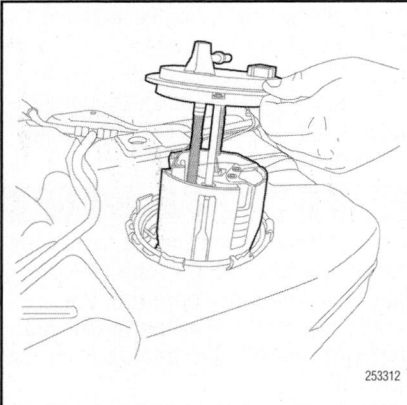

Fig. 318 Removing the fuel pump module from the fuel tank

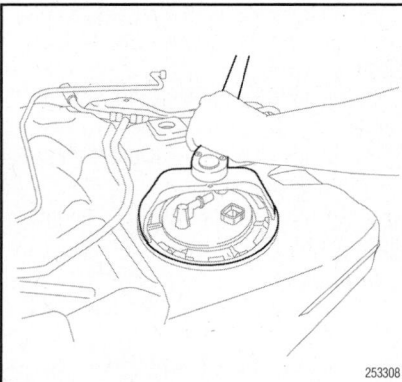

Fig. 319 Using the lock-ring remover/installer 9340 to install the fuel pump module lock-ring

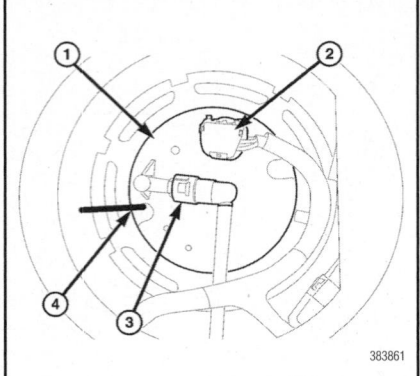

Fig. 320 View of fuel pump module (1) fuel line connection (3), electrical connector (2), and alignment mark (4)

14. Align the rubber O-ring seal and rotate the fuel pump module to the orientation marks noted during removal. This step must be performed for the fuel level gauge to work properly.
15. Position the lock-ring over the top of the fuel pump module.
16. Position the lock-ring remover/installer 9340 into the notches on the outside edge of the lock-ring.
17. Install a ½ inch drive breaker bar into the lock-ring remover/installer 9340.
18. Rotate the breaker bar clockwise until all 7 notches of the lock-ring have engaged.
19. Connect the fuel line to the fuel pump module.
20. Connect the electrical connector to the fuel pump module.
21. Install the fuel pump module access cover.
22. Install the rear seat.
23. Install the negative battery cable. Refer to Battery, removal & installation.
24. Use the Scan Tool to pressurize the system and check for leaks.

FUEL TANK

DRAINING

Conventional Procedure

✳✳ CAUTION

The fuel system is under constant high pressure even with engine OFF. Until the fuel pressure has been properly released from the system, do not attempt to open the fuel system. Do not smoke or use open flames/sparks when servicing the fuel system. Wear protective clothing and eye protection. Make sure the area in which the vehicle is being serviced is well-ventilated and free of flames/sparks. Failure to comply may result in serious or fatal injury.

✳ CAUTION

There is a risk of poisoning from inhaling and swallowing fuel. Pour fuel only into appropriately marked OSHA approved containers. Wear protective clothing. There is also a risk of injury to eyes and skin from contact with fuel.

➡Due to a one-way check valve installed into the fuel fill fitting at the tank, the tank cannot be drained at the fuel fill cap.

1. Before servicing the vehicle, refer to the Precautions Section.
2. Release the fuel system pressure. Refer to Relieving Fuel System Pressure.
3. Disconnect the fuel supply line from the fuel rail.
4. Install the appropriate fuel line adapter fitting from the Decay Tool, Fuel 8978A to the fuel supply line. Route the opposite end of this hose to an OSHA approved fuel storage tank such as the JohnDow Gas Caddy® 320-FC-P30-A, or equivalent.

➡The activation of the fuel pump module may time out and need to be restarted several times to completely drain the fuel tank.

5. Using a diagnostic scan tool, activate the fuel pump module until the fuel tank has been evacuated.

Alternative Procedure

✳ CAUTION

The fuel system is under constant high pressure even with engine OFF. Until the fuel pressure has been properly released from the system, do not attempt to open the fuel system. Do not smoke or use open flames/sparks when servicing the fuel system. Wear protective clothing and eye protection. Make sure the area in which the vehicle is being serviced is well-ventilated and free of flames/sparks. Failure to comply may result in serious or fatal injury.

✳ CAUTION

There is a risk of poisoning from inhaling and swallowing fuel. Pour

fuel only into appropriately marked OSHA approved containers. Wear protective clothing. There is also a risk of injury to eyes and skin from contact with fuel.

➡Due to a one-way check valve installed into the fuel fill fitting at the tank, the tank cannot be drained at the fuel fill cap.

1. Before servicing the vehicle, refer to the Precautions Section.
2. Release the fuel system pressure. Refer to Relieving Fuel System Pressure.

➡If the electric fuel pump is not operating, the fuel tank must be drained through the fuel pump module opening of the fuel tank.

3. Disconnect and isolate the negative battery cable. Refer to Battery, removal & installation.
4. Remove the fuel pump module. Refer to Fuel Pump, removal & installation.
5. Position a ⅜ inch hose into the fuel pump module opening of the fuel tank.
6. Attach the opposite end of this hose to an OSHA approved fuel storage tank such as the JohnDow Gas Caddy® 320-FC-P30-A, or equivalent.
7. Using the gas caddy, evacuate the fuel tank.

REMOVAL & INSTALLATION

See Figures 321 and 322.

✳ CAUTION

The fuel system is under constant pressure even with engine OFF. Until the fuel pressure has been properly relieved from the system, do not attempt to open the fuel system. Do not smoke or use open flames/sparks when servicing the fuel system. Wear protective clothing and eye protection. Make sure the area in which the vehicle is being serviced is well-ventilated.

✳ CAUTION

There is a risk of poisoning from inhaling and swallowing fuel. Pour fuel only into appropriately marked and approved containers. Failure to follow these instructions may result in possible serious or fatal injury.

1. Before servicing the vehicle, refer to the Precautions Section.
2. Remove the fuel filler cap.

3. Remove the fuel pump module. Refer to Fuel Pump, removal & installation.
4. Raise and safely support the vehicle.
5. Remove close-out panels from beneath the vehicle.
6. Remove the exhaust system.
7. On vehicles equipped with a convertible top, remove the 2 front bolts from the cross-braces.
8. Disconnect the quick connect fitting from the fuel tank vapor line.
9. Disconnect the quick connect fitting and remove the fuel tube vent line.
10. Loosen the hose clamp and remove the fuel filler tube from the fuel tank.
11. Disconnect the quick connect fitting from the fuel supply line.

✳ CAUTION

Support the fuel tank with a transmission jack or equivalent. Use straps to secure the fuel tank to the jack. Failure to properly support and secure the fuel tank during removal may cause fuel to spill or the fuel tank to fall from the jack.

12. Using a transmission jack to support the fuel tank, remove the fuel tank strap bolts and straps.
13. Lower the fuel tank from the vehicle.
14. If the fuel tank is to be replaced, remove the fuel line and the heat shield from the fuel tank.

To install:
15. If fuel tank was replaced, install the heat shield to the fuel tank.
16. Install the O-ring seal and the fuel pump module in the marked location. Refer to Fuel Pump, removal & installation.
17. Install the fuel supply line to the fuel tank and connect to the fuel pump module.

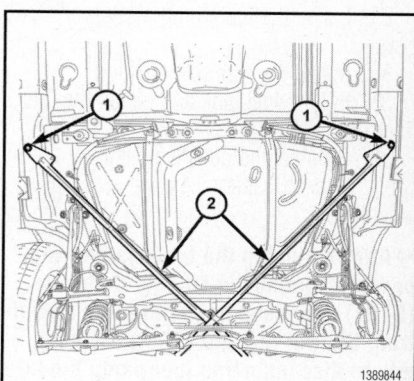

Fig. 321 Remove the 2 front bolts (1) from the cross-braces (2)—convertible top vehicles only

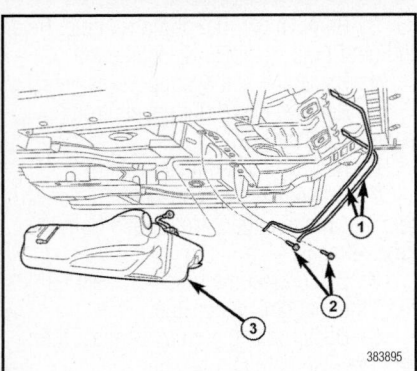

Fig. 322 Using a transmission jack to support the fuel tank (3), remove the fuel tank strap bolts (2) and straps (1)

18. Position fuel tank onto a transmission jack or equivalent and position the fuel tank into the vehicle.

19. Install the straps and the fuel tank strap bolts. Tighten to 35 ft. lbs. (48 Nm).

20. Install the fuel filler tube to the fuel tank. Tighten the hose clamp to 27 inch lbs. (3 Nm).

21. Install the fuel tube vent line to the quick connect fitting.

22. Connect the tank vapor line quick connect fitting.

23. Connect the quick connect fitting to the fuel supply line.

24. On vehicles equipped with a convertible top, install the 2 front bolts to the cross-braces. Tighten the bolts to 35 ft. lbs. (48 Nm).

25. Install the exhaust system.

26. Install the close-out panels underneath the vehicle.

27. Lower the vehicle.

28. Connect the fuel pump/module electrical connector.

29. Install the fuel pump module cover.

30. Install the rear seat cushion.

31. Fill the fuel tank and install the fuel filler cap.

32. Connect the negative battery cable. Refer to Battery, removal & installation.

➡️**After servicing the fuel system, one or more Diagnostic Trouble Codes (DTCs) may have been stored in Powertrain Control Module (PCM) memory due to disconnecting fuel pump module circuit. A diagnostic scan tool may be used to erase the DTCs.**

33. Use the scan tool to pressurize the fuel system. Check for leaks.

IDLE SPEED

ADJUSTMENT

The idle speed is controlled by the Powertrain Control Module (PCM). No adjustment is necessary.

THROTTLE BODY

REMOVAL & INSTALLATION

2.4L Engine

See Figure 323.

✳✳ CAUTION

DO NOT place fingers in or around the throttle body plate. If the throttle body is energized, the throttle plate could move causing personal injury. Always disconnect the negative battery cable prior to servicing the throttle body.

➡️**DO NOT move the throttle plate while power is connected to the throttle body. This may cause fault codes to set.**

1. Before servicing the vehicle, refer to the Precautions Section.

2. Disconnect and isolate the negative battery cable. Refer to Battery, removal & installation.

3. Remove the throttle body air intake hose.

4. Disconnect the throttle body electrical connector from the throttle body.

5. Remove the throttle body support bracket bolt.

6. Remove the 4 bolts, throttle body bracket, and throttle body from the intake manifold.

7. Inspect the 4 j-nuts for damage or excessive wear, remove if necessary.

8. Inspect the intake manifold-to-throttle body gasket for damage, remove if necessary.

To install:

9. Install a new intake manifold-to-throttle body gasket, if replacement was necessary.

10. Install the 4 new j-nuts, if replacement was necessary.

✳✳ WARNING

DO NOT OVER TORQUE. Over tightening can cause damage to the throttle body, gaskets, bolts and/or the intake manifold.

11. Install the throttle body to the intake manifold.

12. Install the throttle body support bracket and bolt and hand tighten.

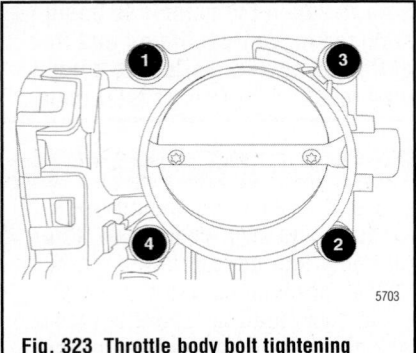

Fig. 323 Throttle body bolt tightening sequence—2.4L engine

13. Install the 4 throttle body bolts and hand tighten.

✳✳ WARNING

The throttle body must be torqued in a mandatory torque sequence.

14. Tighten the bolts in a mandatory torque crisscross pattern sequence to 65 inch lbs. (8 Nm).

15. Tighten the bracket bolt to 18 ft. lbs. (25 Nm).

16. Connect the electrical connector to the throttle body.

17. Install the clean air hose and tighten the clamps to 35 inch lbs. (4 Nm).

18. Install the negative battery cable and tighten the nut to 45 inch lbs. (5 Nm). Refer to Battery, removal & installation.

19. Use a scan tool and clear all fault codes, then perform the ETC RELEARN function.

2.7L Engine

See Figure 324.

✳✳ CAUTION

DO NOT place fingers in or around the throttle body plate. If the throttle body is energized, the throttle plate could move causing personal injury. Always disconnect the negative battery cable prior to servicing the throttle body.

➡️**DO NOT move the throttle plate while power is connected to the throttle body. This may cause fault codes to set.**

1. Before servicing the vehicle, refer to the Precautions Section.

2. Disconnect and isolate the negative battery cable at the battery. Refer to Battery, removal & installation.

3. Loosen the clamp and remove the throttle body air intake hose from the throttle body.

4. Disconnect the electrical connector from the throttle body.

5. Remove the lower throttle body bracket nut.

6. Remove the upper throttle body bracket nut.

7. Remove the throttle body support bracket from the throttle body.

8. Remove the 3 throttle body bolts and one stud.

9. Remove the throttle body from the intake manifold.

To install:

➡Make sure the intake gasket is clean and free of debris. Inspect the intake gasket for damage. Replace as necessary.

✴✴ WARNING

DO NOT OVER TORQUE. Over tightening can cause damage to the throttle body, gaskets, bolts and/or the intake manifold.

10. Install the throttle body, gasket, and bolts to the intake manifold.

✴✴ WARNING

The throttle body must be torqued in a mandatory torque sequence. Tighten in a crisscross pattern to specification.

11. Tighten the 3 bolts and 1 stud in a mandatory torque crisscross pattern sequence to 50 inch lbs. (6 Nm).

12. Install the throttle body support bracket to the throttle body stud and the stud located on the transaxle.

13. Install the lower throttle body bracket nut. Tighten to 21 ft. lbs. (28 Nm).

14. Install the upper throttle body bracket nut. Tighten to 106 inch lbs. (12 Nm).

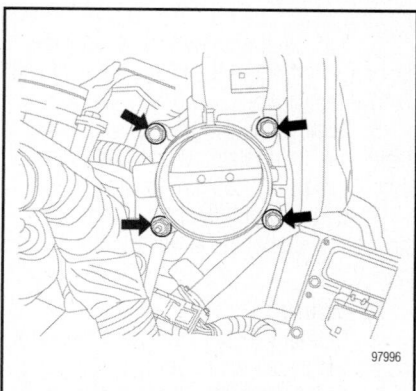

Fig. 324 Throttle body bolts and stud location shown—2.7L engine

15. Connect the electrical connector to the throttle body.

16. Install the throttle body air intake hose and tighten the clamp.

17. Connect the negative battery cable, tighten the nut to 45 inch lbs. (5 Nm). Refer to Batter, removal & installation.

18. Use a scan tool and perform the ETC RELEARN function.

3.5L Engine

See Figure 325.

✴✴ CAUTION

DO NOT place fingers in or around the throttle body plate. If the throttle body is energized, the throttle plate could move causing personal injury. Always disconnect the negative battery cable prior to servicing the throttle body.

➡DO NOT move the throttle plate while power is connected to the throttle body. This may cause fault codes to set.

1. Before servicing the vehicle, refer to the Precautions Section.

2. Disconnect and isolate the negative battery cable at the battery. Refer to Battery, removal & installation.

3. Remove the engine cover.

4. Remove the clean air hose from the throttle body.

5. Disconnect the electrical connector from the throttle body.

6. Remove the nut from the throttle body bracket.

7. Remove the bolt and the throttle body bracket.

8. Remove the bolts, stud, and throttle body from the intake manifold.

To install:

➡Make sure the intake gasket is clean and free of debris. Inspect the intake gasket for damage. Replace as necessary.

✴✴ WARNING

DO NOT OVER TORQUE. Over tightening can cause damage to the throttle body, gaskets, bolts and/or the intake manifold.

9. Install the throttle body, gasket, and bolts to the intake manifold.

10. Install the throttle body and the 3 throttle body bolts, and stud hand tight.

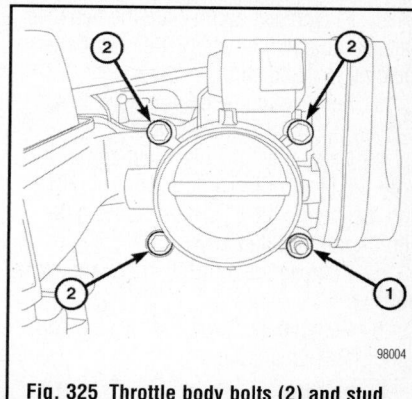

Fig. 325 Throttle body bolts (2) and stud (1) location shown—3.5L engine

✴✴ WARNING

The throttle body must be torqued in a mandatory torque sequence. Tighten in a crisscross pattern to specification.

11. Tighten the 3 bolts and 1 stud in a mandatory torque crisscross pattern sequence to 50 inch lbs. (6 Nm).

12. Install the throttle body bracket, nut, and bolt. Tighten the nut to 106 inch lbs. (12 Nm). Tighten the bolt to 21 ft. lbs. (28 Nm).

13. Connect the electrical connector to the throttle body.

14. Install the clean air hose to the throttle body.

15. Install the engine cover.

16. Connect the negative battery cable, tighten the nut to 45 inch lbs. (5 Nm). Refer to Battery, removal & installation.

17. Use a scan tool and perform the ETC RELEARN function.

3.6L Engine

See Figure 326.

✴✴ CAUTION

DO NOT place fingers in or around the throttle body plate. If the throttle body is energized, the throttle plate could move causing personal injury. Always disconnect the negative battery cable prior to servicing the throttle body.

➡DO NOT move the throttle plate while power is connected to the throttle body. This may cause fault codes to set.

➡Never have the ignition key in the ON position when checking the throttle body shaft for a binding condition. This may set DTCs.

1. Before servicing the vehicle, refer to the Precautions Section.

2. Disconnect and isolate the negative battery cable at the battery. Refer to Battery, removal & installation.

3. Remove the resonator. Refer to Air Cleaner, removal & installation.

4. Disconnect the electrical connector from the Electronic Throttle Control (ETC) and disengage the ETC harness from the clip on the throttle body.

5. Remove the 4 throttle body mounting bolts.

6. Remove the throttle body from the upper intake manifold.

To install:

7. Check the condition of the throttle body-to-intake manifold seal. The seal can be reused if not damaged.

8. Clean the mating surfaces of the throttle body and intake manifold.

9. Position the throttle body to the intake manifold.

10. Install the throttle body mounting bolts and tighten in a crisscross pattern sequence to 62 inch lbs. (7 Nm).

11. Connect the electrical connector to the ETC and secure the ETC harness to the clip on the throttle body.

12. Install the resonator. Refer to Air Cleaner, removal & installation.

13. Connect the negative battery cable and tighten the nut to 45 inch lbs. (5 Nm). Refer to Battery, removal & installation.

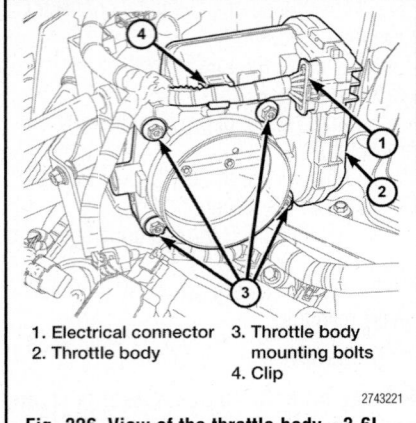

1. Electrical connector
2. Throttle body
3. Throttle body mounting bolts
4. Clip

2743221

Fig. 326 View of the throttle body—3.6L engine

HEATING & AIR CONDITIONING SYSTEM

BLOWER MOTOR

REMOVAL & INSTALLATION

See Figure 327.

➡ **The blower motor is located on the bottom of the passenger side of the HVAC housing. The blower motor can be removed from the vehicle without having to remove the HVAC housing.**

1. Before servicing the vehicle, refer to the Precautions Section.

2. Disconnect and isolate the negative battery cable. Refer to Battery, removal & installation.

3. If equipped, remove the silencer from below the passenger side of the instrument panel.

4. From underneath the instrument panel, disengage the connector lock and disconnect the instrument panel wire harness connector from the blower motor.

5. Remove the 3 screws that secure the blower motor and the wire lead bracket (if equipped) to the bottom of the HVAC housing.

6. Remove the blower motor from the vehicle.

To install:

7. Position the blower motor into the bottom of the HVAC housing.

8. Install the 3 screws that secure the blower motor and the wire lead bracket (if equipped) to the HVAC housing. Tighten the screws to 11 inch lbs. (1 Nm).

9. Connect the instrument panel wire harness connector to the blower motor and engage the connector lock.

10. If equipped, install the silencer below the passenger side of the instrument panel.

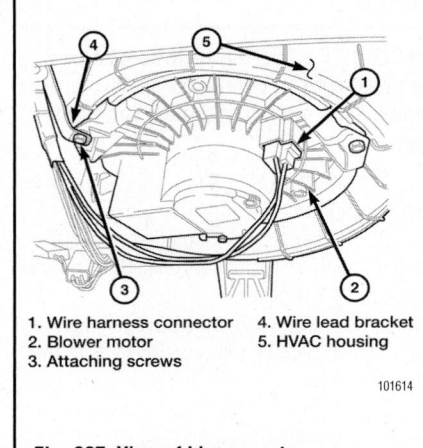

1. Wire harness connector
2. Blower motor
3. Attaching screws
4. Wire lead bracket
5. HVAC housing

101614

Fig. 327 View of blower motor

11. Connect the negative battery cable. Refer to Battery, removal & installation.

HEATER CORE

REMOVAL & INSTALLATION

See Figures 328 and 329.

➡ **The HVAC housing assembly must be removed from the vehicle for service of the heater core.**

1. Before servicing the vehicle, refer to the Precautions Section.

2. Remove the HVAC housing assembly and place it on a workbench. Refer to HVAC Housing, removal & installation.

3. Remove the left side front floor duct:

a. Disconnect the shift interlock cable from the left floor duct and position the cable out of the way.

b. Remove the screw that secures the

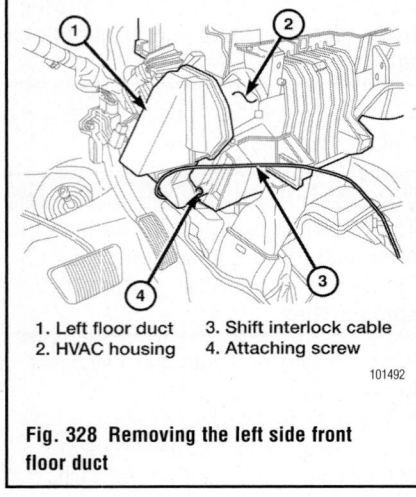

1. Left floor duct
2. HVAC housing
3. Shift interlock cable
4. Attaching screw

101492

Fig. 328 Removing the left side front floor duct

left floor duct to the left side of the HVAC housing.

c. Disconnect the left floor duct from the HVAC housing and remove the duct.

4. Remove the foam seal from the flange located on the front of the HVAC housing.

5. Remove the screw that secures the flange to the front of the HVAC housing and remove the flange.

6. Remove the screws that secure the heater core tube retaining brackets to the side of the air distribution housing.

7. Carefully pull the heater core out of the driver's side of the air distribution housing.

To install:

8. Carefully install the heater core into the side of the air distribution housing.

9. Install the heater core tube brackets and retaining screws. Tighten the screws to 11 inch lbs. (1 Nm).

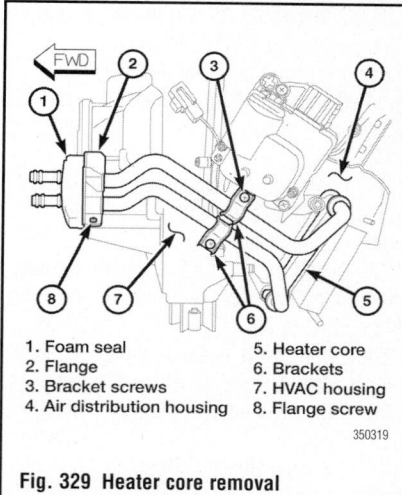

1. Foam seal
2. Flange
3. Bracket screws
4. Air distribution housing
5. Heater core
6. Brackets
7. HVAC housing
8. Flange screw

350319

Fig. 329 Heater core removal

10. Install the flange that secures the heater core tubes to the front of the HVAC housing.

11. Install the screw (80) that secures the flange to the HVAC housing. Tighten the screw to 11 inch lbs. (12 Nm).

➡️**If the foam seal for the flange is deformed or damaged, it must be replaced.**

12. Install the foam seal onto the flange.

13. Install the left side front floor duct:

a. Connect the left floor duct to the left side of the HVAC housing. Make sure the duct is fully engaged to the housing.

b. Install the screw that secures the left floor duct to the HVAC housing. Tighten the screw to 17 inch lbs. (2 Nm).

c. Connect the shift interlock cable to the left floor duct.

➡️**If the heater core is being replaced, flush the cooling system. Refer to Engine Cooling, Engine Coolant, Flushing procedure.**

14. Install the HVAC housing assembly. Refer to HVAC Housing, removal & installation.

HVAC HOUSING

REMOVAL & INSTALLATION

See Figures 330 through 333.

❄️ CAUTION

Disable the airbag system before attempting any steering wheel, steering column, or instrument panel component diagnosis or service. Disconnect and isolate the battery negative (ground) cable, then wait 2 minutes for the airbag system capacitor to discharge before performing

further diagnosis or service. This is the only sure way to disable the airbag system. Failure to take the proper precautions could result in an accidental airbag deployment and possible serious or fatal injury.

➡️**The HVAC housing must be removed from the vehicle and disassembled for service of the heater core, A/C evaporator, air intake housing, and the mode-air and blend-air doors.**

1. Before servicing the vehicle, refer to the Precautions Section.

2. Disconnect and isolate the negative battery cable. Refer to Battery, removal & installation.

3. Recover the refrigerant from the refrigerant system.

4. Partially drain the engine cooling system. Refer to Engine Cooling, Engine Coolant, Drain & Refill Procedure.

5. Remove the top nut that secures the

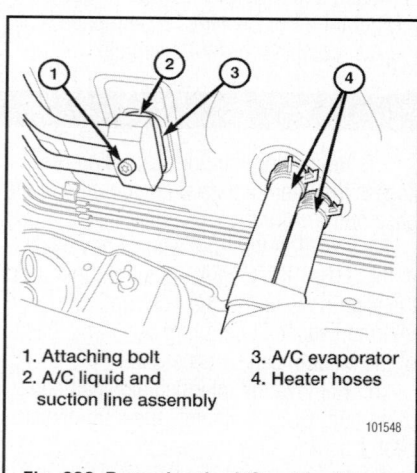

1. Attaching bolt
2. A/C liquid and suction line assembly
3. A/C evaporator
4. Heater hoses

101548

Fig. 330 Removing the A/C and heater lines

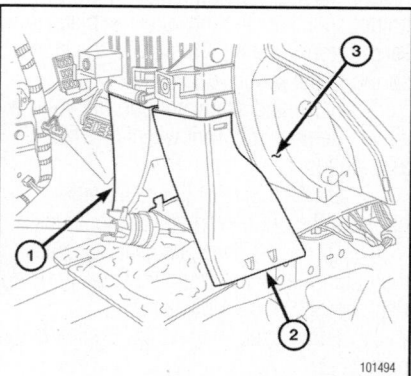

101494

Fig. 331 Disconnect the left rear floor distribution duct (1) and the right rear floor distribution duct (2) from the HVAC housing (3)

heat shield to the stud located on the dash panel.

➡️**Two slots are provided at the bottom of the heat shield to aid in heat shield removal. Complete removal of the 2 bottom heat shield retaining nuts is not required.**

6. Reach behind the engine and remove the two bottom nuts that secure the heat shield to the studs located on the dash panel and remove the heat shield. Rotate and tilt the heat shield as required.

7. Remove the bolt that secures the A/C liquid and suction line assembly to the A/C evaporator.

8. Disconnect the A/C liquid and suction line assembly from the A/C evaporator and remove and discard the dual-plane seals.

9. Install plugs in, or tape over the opened refrigerant line fittings and the evaporator ports.

10. Disconnect the heater hoses from the

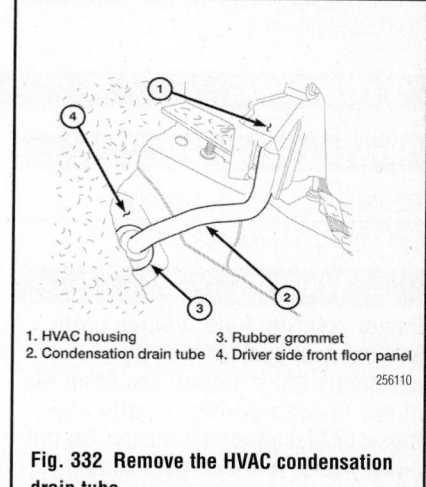

1. HVAC housing
2. Condensation drain tube
3. Rubber grommet
4. Driver side front floor panel

256110

Fig. 332 Remove the HVAC condensation drain tube

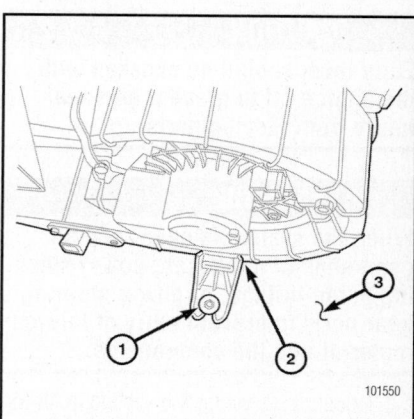

101550

Fig. 333 Remove the nut (1) that secures the passenger side of the HVAC housing (2) to the dash panel (3)

heater core tubes. Install plugs in, or tape over the opened heater core tubes to prevent coolant spillage during housing removal.

➡ **Make sure to remove the 5 bolts that secure the HVAC housing to the instrument panel support prior to removing the instrument panel from the vehicle.**

11. Remove the instrument panel.
12. Remove the rear floor ducts.
13. Remove the condensation drain tube.
14. Remove the nut that secures the passenger side of the HVAC housing to the dash panel.

❉❉ WARNING

Use care to ensure that the interior is covered in case of the loss of residual fluids from the heater and evaporator cores.

15. Pull the HVAC housing rearward and remove the HVAC housing assembly from the passenger compartment.

To install:

16. Position the HVAC housing assembly to the dash panel. Be certain that the passenger side of the HVAC housing is correctly located over the dash panel mounting stud.
17. Install the nut that secures the HVAC housing to the passenger compartment side of dash panel. Tighten the nut to 40 inch lbs. (5 Nm).
18. Install the condensation drain tube.
19. Install the rear floor ducts.
20. Install the instrument panel.
21. Remove the previously installed plugs or caps and connect the heater hoses to the heater core tubes.
22. Remove the tape or plugs from the refrigerant line fittings and the evaporator ports.
23. Lubricate the rubber O-rings on new dual-plane seals with clean refrigerant oil and install the seals onto the liquid and suction line fittings. Use only the specified seals as they are made of special materials compatible to the R-134a system. Use only refrigerant oil of the type recommended for the A/C compressor in the vehicle.

24. Connect the A/C liquid and suction line assembly to the A/C evaporator.
25. Install the bolt that secures the A/C liquid and suction line assembly to the A/C evaporator. Tighten the bolt to 18 ft. lbs. (25 Nm).
26. Position the heat shield onto the 3 studs located on the dash panel in the engine compartment.
27. Install the 3 nuts that secure the heat shield to the dash panel. Tighten the nuts to 10 inch lbs. (1 Nm).
28. Connect the negative battery cable. Refer to Battery, removal & installation.
29. If the heater core is being replaced, flush the cooling system. Refer to Engine Cooling, Engine Coolant, Flushing procedure.
30. Fill the engine cooling system. Refer to Engine Cooling, Engine Coolant, Drain & Refill Procedure.
31. Evacuate and charge the refrigerant system.
32. Initiate the Actuator Calibration function using a scan tool.

STEERING

POWER STEERING GEAR

REMOVAL & INSTALLATION
See Figures 334 through 336.

❉❉ WARNING

Power steering fluid, engine parts and exhaust system may be extremely hot if engine has been running. Do not start engine with any loose or disconnected hoses. Do not allow hoses to touch hot exhaust manifold or catalyst.

❉❉ CAUTION

Fluid level should be checked with the engine off to prevent personal injury from moving parts.

❉❉ WARNING

When the system is open, cap all open ends of the hoses, power steering pump fittings, or power steering gear ports to prevent entry of foreign material into the components.

1. Before servicing the vehicle, refer to the Precautions Section.
2. Siphon out as much power steering fluid as possible from the reservoir.

3. Reposition the floor carpeting to access the intermediate shaft coupling at the base of the column.
4. Position the front wheels of vehicle in the STRAIGHT-AHEAD position, then turn the steering wheel to the right until the intermediate shaft coupling bolt at the base of the column can be accessed.
5. Remove the intermediate shaft coupling bolt. Do not separate the intermediate shaft from the steering gear pinion shaft at this time.
6. Return the front wheels of vehicle (and steering wheel) to the STRAIGHT-AHEAD position. Using a steering wheel holder, lock the steering wheel in place to keep it from rotating. This keeps the clockspring in the proper orientation.
7. Raise and safely support the vehicle.
8. Remove the front wheel and tire assemblies.
9. On each side of the gear, remove the nut from the out tie rod end at the knuckle.
10. On each side of the gear, separate the outer tie rod end from the knuckle using Remover 9360, or equivalent.
11. If equipped, remove the engine belly pan.
12. Remove the rear engine mount.
13. Remove the front engine mount through-bolt.
14. Remove the 2 bolts fastening the

fore/aft crossmember to the lower radiator support.
15. Remove the 4 bolts fastening the fore/aft crossmember to the front crossmember. Remove the fore/aft crossmember.
16. Remove the screws securing the power steering hose routing clamps to the rear of the crossmember.
17. Unscrew the tube nut, then remove the return hose at the steering gear.
18. Unscrew the tube nut, then remove the pressure hose at the steering gear.
19. Remove the screws and push-pins securing the heat shield over the right side of the steering gear. Remove the shield.

➡ **Before removing the front suspension crossmember from the vehicle, the location of the crossmember must be marked on the body of the vehicle. Do this so the crossmember can be relocated, upon reinstallation, against the body of vehicle in the same location as before removal. If the front suspension crossmember is not reinstalled in exactly the same location as before removal, the preset front wheel alignment settings (caster and camber) may be lost.**

20. Mark the location of the front crossmember on the body near each mounting bolt.

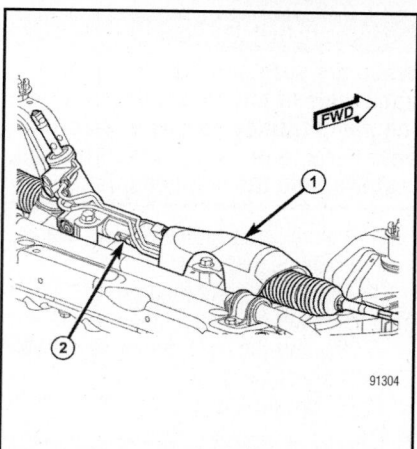

Fig. 334 Remove the heat shield (1) over the right side of the steering gear (2)

21. Support the crossmember with a transmission jack.

22. Remove the 4 mounting bolts securing the front crossmember to the body.

23. If equipped, remove the mounting screws securing the front crossmember reinforcement brackets (one each side of vehicle) to the body. Remove the brackets.

24. If equipped, remove the mounting screws securing the front cross brace/reinforcement bracket to the body. Remove the bracket.

25. Using the jack, slowly lower the crossmember enough to access the intermediate shaft coupling at the steering gear pinion shaft. Slide the coupling off the pinion shaft.

26. Remove the dash seals as necessary.

27. Remove the 2 bolts securing the steering gear to the crossmember.

28. Remove the steering gear from the crossmember.

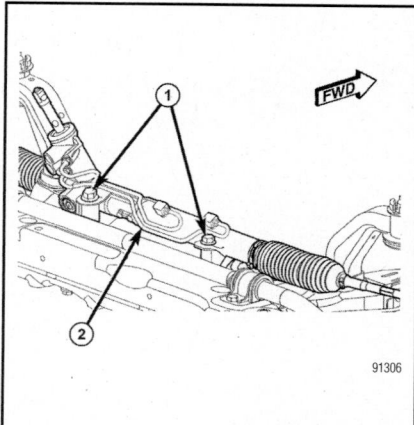

Fig. 335 Remove the bolts (1) securing the steering gear (2) to the crossmember

To install:

29. Install the steering gear on the crossmember.

30. Install the 2 bolts securing the steering gear to the crossmember. Tighten the gear mounting bolts to 74 ft. lbs. (100 Nm).

31. Install the dash seals as necessary.

32. Center the power steering gear rack in its travel as necessary.

➡ **When installing the front suspension crossmember back in the vehicle, it is very important that the crossmember be attached to the body in exactly the same spot as when it was removed. Otherwise, the vehicle wheel alignment settings (caster and camber) will be lost making wheel alignment more difficult.**

➡ **While raising the steering gear into place, it is not necessary to install the intermediate shaft coupling on the steering gear pinion shaft at this time. It can be installed once the vehicle is lowered. Make sure the coupling does not interfere with steering gear/dash seals at this time.**

33. Slowly raise the crossmember into mounted position using the transmission jack matching the crossmember to the marked locations on the body made during removal.

34. Check the positioning of the seals at the dash panel and adjust as necessary.

35. If equipped, position the front crossmember reinforcement brackets (one each side of vehicle) over the crossmember rear mounting bushings and install the mounting screws, but do not tighten at this time.

36. If equipped, position the front cross brace/reinforcement bracket over the crossmember rear mounting bushings and body, then install the mounting screws. Do not tighten screws at this time.

37. Install the 4 mounting bolts securing the front crossmember to the body. Tighten the crossmember mounting bolts to 100 ft. lbs. (135 Nm).

38. If equipped, tighten the crossmember reinforcement bracket mounting screws to 37 ft. lbs. (50 Nm).

39. If equipped, tighten the cross brace/reinforcement bracket mounting screws to 37 ft. lbs. (50 Nm).

40. Remove the transmission jack.

41. Install the heat shield over the steering gear. Install the mounting screws and push-pins. Tighten the screws to 53 inch lbs. (6 Nm).

42. Install the pressure hose tube at the

gear. Tighten the tube nut to 24 ft. lbs. (32 Nm).

43. Install the return hose tube at the gear. Tighten the tube nut to 24 ft. lbs. (32 Nm).

44. Position the power steering hose routing clamps on the crossmember. Install and tighten the screws to 71 inch lbs. (8 Nm).

45. Install the fore/aft crossmember and front engine mount through-bolt.

46. Install the rear engine mount.

47. If equipped, install the engine belly pan.

➡ **Prior to attaching the outer tie rod end to the knuckle, inspect the tie rod seal boot. If the seal boot is damaged, replace the outer tie rod end.**

48. On each side of the gear, install the outer tie rod end into the hole in the knuckle arm. Start a NEW tie rod mounting nut onto the stud. While holding the tie rod end stud with a wrench, tighten the nut with a wrench or crowfoot wrench. Tighten the nut to 63 ft. lbs. (85 Nm).

49. Install the wheel and tire assemblies. Tighten the wheel nuts in a star pattern until all nuts are torqued to half the required specification. Then repeat the tightening sequence to the full specified torque of 100 ft. lbs. (135 Nm).

50. Lower the vehicle.

51. Remove the steering wheel holder.

52. Verify the front wheels of vehicle are in the STRAIGHT-AHEAD position.

53. Center the intermediate shaft over the steering gear pinion shaft, lining up the ends, then slide the intermediate shaft onto the steering gear pinion shaft.

54. From center, rotate the steering wheel to the right until the intermediate shaft coupling bolt can be easily installed.

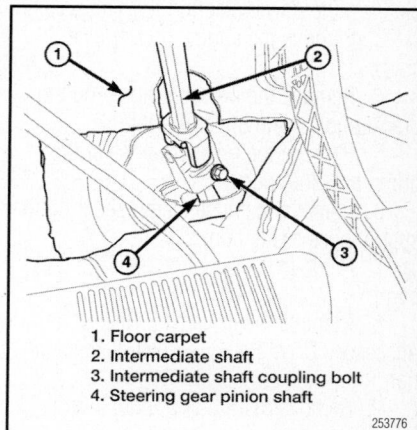

1. Floor carpet
2. Intermediate shaft
3. Intermediate shaft coupling bolt
4. Steering gear pinion shaft

Fig. 336 Connecting the intermediate shaft coupling

55. Install the intermediate shaft coupling bolt. Tighten the bolt to 31 ft. lbs. (42 Nm).

56. Reposition the floor carpet in place.

57. Fill and bleed the power steering system. Refer to Power Steering Pump, Bleeding procedure.

58. Check for fluid leaks.

59. Perform a wheel alignment as necessary.

POWER STEERING PUMP

REMOVAL & INSTALLATION

2.4L Engine

See Figure 337.

✳✳ WARNING

Power steering fluid, engine parts and exhaust system may be extremely hot if engine has been running. Do not start engine with any loose or disconnected hoses. Do not allow hoses to touch hot exhaust manifold or catalyst.

✳✳ CAUTION

Fluid level should be checked with the engine off to prevent personal injury from moving parts.

✳✳ WARNING

When the system is open, cap all open ends of the hoses, power steering pump fittings, or power steering gear ports to prevent entry of foreign material into the components.

1. Before servicing the vehicle, refer to the Precautions Section.

2. Siphon out as much fluid as possible from the power steering fluid reservoir.

3. Remove the engine appearance cover.

4. Remove the pressure hose routing bracket bolt at the upper mount.

5. Remove the pressure hose at the pump pressure port.

6. Remove the hose clamp securing the supply hose at the pump.

7. Remove the supply hose from the pump.

8. Remove the drive belt. Refer to Accessory Drive Belts, removal & installation.

9. Remove the 3 pump mounting bolts through the pulley openings.

10. Remove the power steering pump from the vehicle.

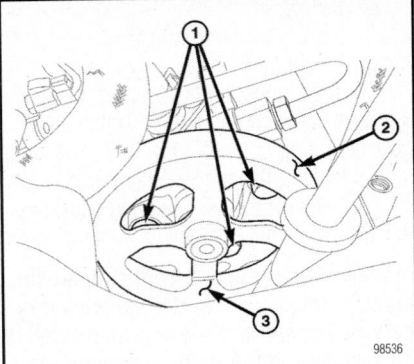

Fig. 337 View of power steering pump mounting bolts (1), pulley (3), and drive belt (2)—2.4L engine

To install:

11. Using a lint free towel, wipe clean the open power steering pressure hose end and the power steering pump port. Replace any used O-rings with new. Lubricate the O-ring with clean power steering fluid.

12. Place the pump in the mounting position. Install the 3 bolts through the pulley openings. Tighten the mounting bolts to 19 ft. lbs. (26 Nm).

13. Install the drive belt. Refer to Accessory Drive Belts, removal & installation.

14. Install the supply hose at the pump.

15. Clamp the hose clamp securing the supply hose to the pump.

16. Install the pressure hose at the pump pressure port. Tighten the tube nut to 24 ft. lbs. (32 Nm).

17. Install the pressure hose routing bracket bolt to the engine mount. Tighten the bolt to 18 ft. lbs. (24 Nm).

18. Fill and bleed the power steering system. Refer to Power Steering Pump, Bleeding procedure.

19. Check for leaks.

20. Install the engine appearance cover.

2.7L Engine

See Figures 338 through 340.

✳✳ WARNING

Power steering fluid, engine parts and exhaust system may be extremely hot if engine has been running. Do not start engine with any loose or disconnected hoses. Do not allow hoses to touch hot exhaust manifold or catalyst.

✳✳ CAUTION

Fluid level should be checked with the engine off to prevent personal injury from moving parts.

✳✳ WARNING

When the system is open, cap all open ends of the hoses, power steering pump fittings, or power steering gear ports to prevent entry of foreign material into the components.

1. Before servicing the vehicle, refer to the Precautions Section.

2. Siphon as much fluid as possible from the power steering fluid reservoir.

3. Remove the hose clamp securing the supply hose at the pump.

4. Remove the supply hose from the pump.

5. Raise and safely support the vehicle.

6. Remove the right tire and wheel assembly.

7. While a helper applies the brakes to keep the hub from rotating, remove the hub nut from the right side axle halfshaft.

8. Remove the drive belt splash shield.

9. Remove the drive belt. Refer to Accessory Drive Belts, removal & installation.

10. Remove the front right halfshaft. Refer to Front Halfshaft, removal & installation.

11. Remove the pressure hose at the pump.

12. Remove the pump mounting bracket bolt near the pump pulley.

13. Remove the pump mounting bracket bolts behind the pump on the back of the engine.

14. Remove the pump with the mounting bracket from the engine. To remove the pump from the engine compartment, rotate the pump so that the pulley is toward the engine, then remove the pump through the opening made by removing the axle halfshaft in an earlier step.

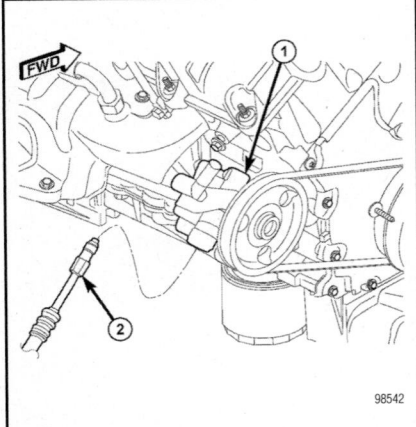

Fig. 338 Remove the pressure hose (2) at the power steering pump (1)—2.7L engine

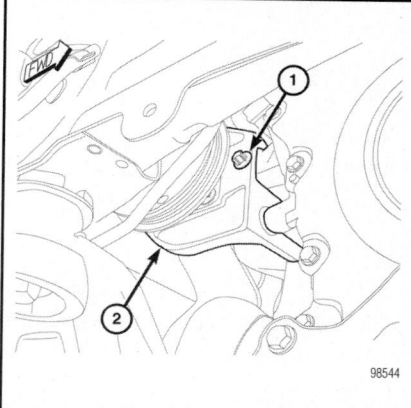

Fig. 339 Remove the pump mounting bracket bolt (1) near the pump pulley—2.7L engine

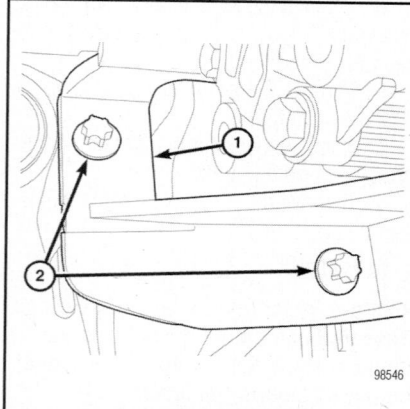

Fig. 340 Remove the pump mounting bracket bolts (2) behind the pump on the back of the engine—2.7L engine

15. Remove the 3 pump mounting bolts through the pulley openings.

16. Remove the power steering pump from the mounting bracket.

To install:

17. Place the pump in the mounting bracket. Install the 3 bolts through the pulley openings. Tighten the mounting bolts to 22 ft. lbs. (30 Nm).

18. Install the pump with the mounting bracket on the engine. To install the pump into the engine compartment, rotate the pump so that the pulley is toward the engine, then insert the pump up through the opening where the axle halfshaft is usually located. Rotate the pump around and into the mounting position.

19. Install the pump mounting bracket bolts behind the pump on the back of the engine. Do not tighten the bolts at this time.

20. Install the pump mounting bracket bolt near the pump pulley.

21. Tighten all 3 pump mounting bracket bolts to 22 ft. lbs. (30 Nm).

22. Using a lint free towel, wipe clean the open power steering pressure hose end and the power steering pump port. Replace any used O-rings with new. Lubricate the O-ring with clean power steering fluid.

23. Install the pressure hose at the pump pressure port. Tighten the tube nut to 24 ft. lbs. (32 Nm).

24. Install the right axle halfshaft.

25. Insert the axle halfshaft into the rear of the hub and bearing hub and bearing. Insert the lower ball joint stud (of the knuckle) into the mounting hole in the lower control arm.

26. Install a NEW ball joint stud nut. Tighten the nut to 70 ft. lbs. (95 Nm).

27. Install the outer tie rod ball stud into the hole in the knuckle arm. Start the tie rod end knuckle nut onto the stud. While holding the tie rod end stud with a wrench, tighten the nut with a wrench or crowfoot wrench to 63 ft. lbs. (85 Nm).

28. Install a NEW power steering pump drive belt. Refer to Accessory Drive Belts, removal & installation.

29. Install the drive belt splash shield.

30. Clean all foreign matter from the threads of the halfshaft outer C/V joint.

31. Install the hub nut on the end of the halfshaft and snug it.

32. While a helper applies the brakes to keep the hub from rotating, tighten the hub nut to 97 ft. lbs. (132 Nm).

33. Install the wheel and tire assembly. Tighten the wheel nuts in a star pattern until all nuts are torqued to half the required specification. Then repeat the tightening sequence to the full specified torque of 100 ft. lbs. (135 Nm).

34. Lower the vehicle.

35. Install the supply hose at the pump.

36. Install the hose clamp securing the supply hose to the pump.

37. Fill and bleed the power steering system. Refer to Power Steering Pump, Bleeding procedure.

38. Check for leaks.

3.5L Engine

See Figures 341 and 342.

❊❊ WARNING

Power steering fluid, engine parts and exhaust system may be extremely hot if engine has been running. Do not start engine with any loose or disconnected hoses. Do not allow hoses to touch hot exhaust manifold or catalyst.

❊❊ CAUTION

Fluid level should be checked with the engine off to prevent personal injury from moving parts.

❊❊ WARNING

When the system is open, cap all open ends of the hoses, power steering pump fittings, or power steering gear ports to prevent entry of foreign material into the components.

1. Before servicing the vehicle, refer to the Precautions Section.

2. Siphon as much fluid as possible from the power steering fluid reservoir.

3. Remove the engine appearance cover.

4. Unscrew the tube nut, then remove the pressure hose at the pump.

5. Remove the pressure hose routing clamp bolt at the engine cylinder head.

6. Remove the clamp securing the supply hose to the power steering pump supply fitting, then remove the hose from the supply fitting.

7. Raise and safely support the vehicle.

8. Remove the right front tire and wheel assembly.

9. Remove the drive belt splash shield.

10. Remove the drive belt. Refer to Accessory Drive Belts, removal & installation.

11. Lower the vehicle.

12. Remove the 2 nuts securing the right engine mount bracket to the mount.

13. Position a floor jack with an appropriate size block of wood below the engine oil pan. Raise the jack until the block of

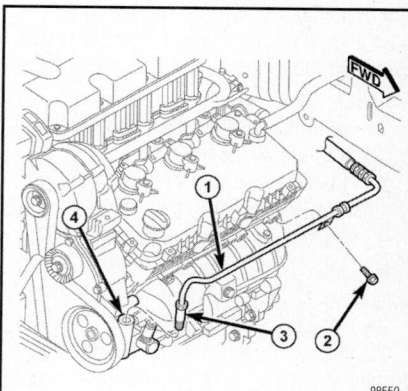

Fig. 341 Unscrew the tube nut (3), remove the pressure hose (1) at the pump (4), and remove the pressure hose routing clamp bolt (2) at the engine cylinder head—3.5L engine

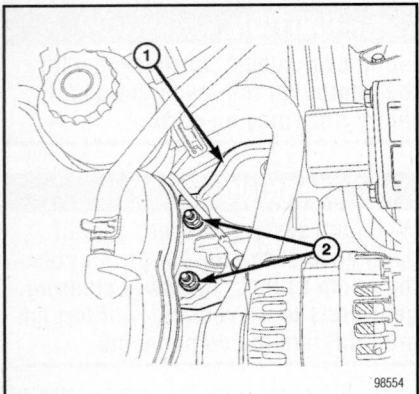

Fig. 342 Remove the nuts (2) securing the right engine mount bracket (1) to the mount—3.5L engine

wood just comes into contact with the bottom of the oil pan, but no further.

14. Slowly raise the right side of the engine using the floor jack while viewing the pump drive pulley. Raise the engine until all 3 power steering pump mounting bolts can be accessed through the openings in the drive pulley.

15. Remove the 3 pump mounting bolts through the pulley openings.

16. Remove the power steering pump.

To install:

17. Using a lint free towel, wipe clean the open power steering pressure hose end and the power steering pump port. Replace any used O-rings with new. Lubricate the O-ring with clean power steering fluid.

18. Place the pump in the mounted position. Install the 3 bolts through the pulley openings. Tighten the mounting bolts to 22 ft. lbs. (30 Nm).

19. Slowly lower the right side of the engine using the floor jack, guiding the right engine mount bracket mounting holes over the mounting studs of the right engine mount.

20. Remove the floor jack and block of wood from below the engine.

21. Install the 2 nuts securing the right engine mount bracket to the mount.

22. Raise and safely support the vehicle.

23. Install the drive belt. Refer to Accessory Drive Belts, removal & installation.

24. Install the drive belt splash shield.

25. Install the wheel and tire assembly. Tighten the wheel nuts in a star pattern until all nuts are torqued to half the required specification. Then repeat the tightening sequence to the full specified torque of 100 ft. lbs. (135 Nm).

26. Lower the vehicle.

27. Place the pump end of the supply

hose onto the pump supply fitting. Expand the hose clamp and slide it over the hose and pump supply fitting. Secure the clamp once it is past the bead formed into the fluid supply fitting.

28. Install the pressure hose at the power steering pump. Tighten the tube nut to 24 ft. lbs. (32 Nm).

29. Position the pressure hose routing clamp at the engine cylinder head. Install and tighten the routing clamp bolt to 16 ft. lbs. (22 Nm).

30. Fill and bleed the power steering system. Refer to Power Steering Pump, Bleeding procedure.

31. Check for leaks.

32. Install the engine appearance cover.

3.6L Engine

See Figures 343 and 344.

> ※※ **WARNING**
>
> **Power steering fluid, engine parts and exhaust system may be extremely hot if engine has been running. Do not start engine with any loose or disconnected hoses. Do not allow hoses to touch hot exhaust manifold or catalyst.**

> ※※ **CAUTION**
>
> **Fluid level should be checked with the engine off to prevent personal injury from moving parts.**

> ※※ **WARNING**
>
> **When the system is open, cap all open ends of the hoses, power steering pump fittings, or power steering gear ports to prevent entry of foreign material into the components.**

1. Before servicing the vehicle, refer to the Precautions Section.

2. Remove the negative (-) battery cable from the battery and isolate the cable. Refer to Battery, removal & installation.

3. Remove the cap from the power steering fluid reservoir.

4. Using a siphon pump, remove as much power steering fluid as possible from the power steering fluid reservoir.

5. Remove the accessory drive belt. Refer to Accessory Drive Belts, removal & installation.

6. Raise and safely support the vehicle.

7. Remove the heat shield mounting bolts and remove the heat shield from the vehicle.

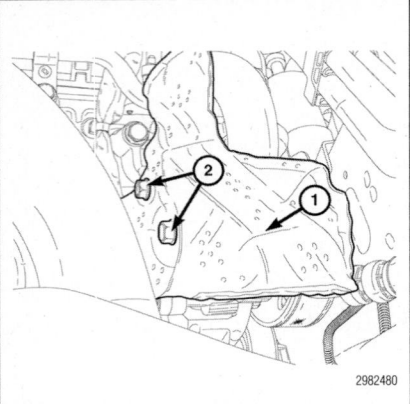

Fig. 343 Remove the heat shield mounting bolts (2) and heat shield (1)—3.6L engine

8. Remove the supply hose clamp and remove the supply hose from the power steering pump fitting.

9. Remove the power steering pump pressure hose fitting.

10. Remove the 3 pump mounting bolts through the pump pulley.

11. Remove the pump (with the pulley) from below.

To install:

➡ **Before installing the power steering pressure hose on the power steering pump, replace the O-ring on the end of the power steering pressure hose. Lubricate the O-ring using clean power steering fluid.**

12. Install the power steering pump onto its mounting bracket.

13. Install the 3 power steering pump mounting bolts through the pulley. Tighten the pump mounting bolts to 22 ft. lbs. (30 Nm).

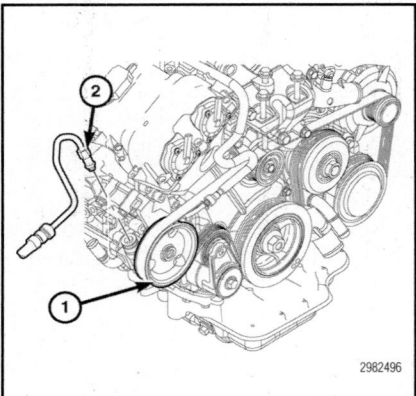

Fig. 344 View of the pressure hose fitting (2) and power steering pump with pulley (1)—3.6L engine

14. Install the power steering pump pressure fitting and tighten it to 14 ft. lbs. (32 Nm).

15. Slide the fluid supply hose onto the pump fitting and install the clamp securing it in place.

16. Install the heat shield and secure it with the 3 mounting bolts. Tighten the bolts to 18 ft. lbs. (25 Nm).

17. Lower the vehicle.

18. Install the accessory drive belt. Refer to Accessory Drive Belts, removal & installation.

19. Connect the negative (-) battery cable on the negative battery post. Refer to Battery, removal & installation.

20. Fill and bleed the power steering system. Refer to Power Steering Pump, Bleeding procedure.

21. Check for leaks.

BLEEDING

See Figure 345.

> ※※ **WARNING**
>
> Power steering fluid, engine parts and exhaust system may be extremely hot if engine has been running. Do not start engine with any loose or disconnected hoses. Do not allow hoses to touch hot exhaust manifold or catalyst.

> ※※ **CAUTION**
>
> Fluid level should be checked with the engine off to prevent personal injury from moving parts.

> ※※ **WARNING**
>
> When the system is open, cap all open ends of the hoses, power steering pump fittings, or power steering gear ports to prevent entry of foreign material into the components.

> ※※ **WARNING**
>
> MOPAR® Power Steering Fluid+4 or MOPAR® ATF+4 Automatic Transmission Fluid is to be used in the power steering system. Both Fluids have the same material standard specifications. No other power steering or automatic transaxle fluid is to be used in the system. Damage may result to the power steering pump and system if another fluid is used. Do not overfill the system.

> ※※ **WARNING**
>
> If the air is not purged from the power steering system correctly, pump failure could result.

➡Be sure the vacuum tool used in the following procedure is clean and free of any fluids.

1. Before servicing the vehicle, refer to the Precautions Section.

2. Check the fluid level. As measured on the side of the reservoir, the level should indicate between MAX and MIN when the fluid is at normal ambient temperature. Adjust the fluid level as necessary.

3. Tightly insert the Power Steering Cap Adapter, Special Tool 9688A, into the mouth of the reservoir.

➡Failure to use a vacuum pump reservoir may allow power steering fluid to be sucked into the hand vacuum pump.

4. Attach Hand Vacuum Pump, Special Tool C-4207-8, or equivalent, with reservoir attached, to the Power Steering Cap Adapter.

> ※※ **WARNING**
>
> Do not run the vehicle while vacuum is applied to the power steering system. Damage to the power steering pump can occur.

➡When performing the following step make sure the vacuum level is maintained during the entire time period.

5. Using the Hand Vacuum Pump, apply 20–25 inches Hg (68–85 kPa) of vacuum to the system for a minimum of 3 minutes.

6. Slowly release the vacuum and remove the special tools.

7. Adjust the fluid level as necessary.

8. Repeat the steps until the fluid no longer drops when vacuum is applied.

9. Start the engine and cycle the steering wheel lock-to-lock 3 times.

➡Do not hold the steering wheel at the stops.

10. Stop the engine and check for leaks at all connections.

11. Check for any signs of air in the reservoir and check the fluid level. If air is present, repeat the procedure as necessary.

FLUID FILL PROCEDURE

See Figure 346.

> ※※ **CAUTION**
>
> The fluid level should be checked with the engine OFF to prevent personal injury from moving parts and to assure an accurate fluid level reading.

> ※※ **WARNING**
>
> MOPAR® Power Steering Fluid+4 or MOPAR® ATF+4 Automatic Transmission Fluid is to be used in the power steering system. Both fluids have the same material standard specifications (MS-9602). No other power steering or automatic transaxle fluid is to be used in the system. Damage may result to the power steering pump and system if another fluid is used. Do not overfill the system.

➡Although not required at specific intervals, the fluid level may be checked periodically. Check the fluid

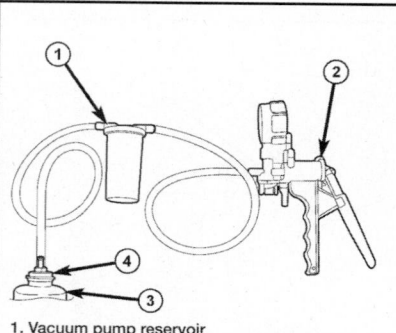

1. Vacuum pump reservoir
2. Special Tool C-4207-8, Hand Vacuum Pump
3. Mouth of the reservoir
4. Special Tool 9688A, Power Steering Cap Adapter

6153

Fig. 345 Special tools for bleeding the power steering system shown

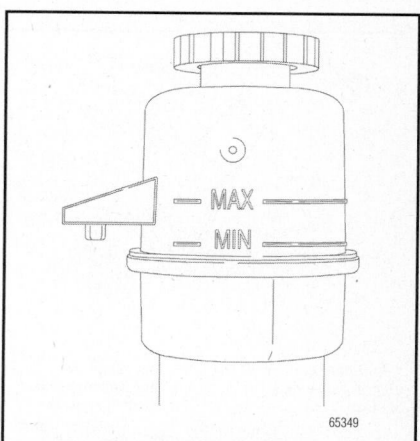

65349

Fig. 346 The fluid level should be maintained between the MIN and MAX markings—power steering reservoir shown

level anytime there is a system noise or fluid leak suspected.

1. Before servicing the vehicle, refer to the Precautions Section.

2. The power steering fluid level can be viewed through the side of the power steering fluid reservoir.

3. Compare the fluid level to the markings on the side of the reservoir. When the fluid is at normal ambient temperature, approximately 70–80° F (21–27° C), the fluid level should read between the MAX and MIN markings. When the fluid is hot, the fluid level is allowed to read up to the MAX line.

4. To add fluid, clean the reservoir cap of any dirt or debris.

5. Remove the power steering reservoir cap.

6. Add specified fluid from a sealed container to the reservoir so that the level is between the MAX and MIN levels marked on the power steering reservoir.

7. Install the power steering reservoir cap.

SUSPENSION

CONTROL LINKS

REMOVAL & INSTALLATION

See Figure 347.

1. Before servicing the vehicle, refer to the Precautions Section.

2. Raise and safely support the vehicle.

3. Remove the front tire and wheel assemblies.

4. While holding the stabilizer bar link stud stationary, remove the nut securing the link to the strut.

5. While holding the stabilizer bar link lower stud stationary, remove the nut securing the link to the stabilizer bar.

6. Remove the stabilizer bar link.

To install:

7. Attach the stabilizer bar link to the stabilizer bar. Install and tighten the nut while holding the stabilizer bar link lower stud stationary. Tighten the nut to 35 ft. lbs. (48 Nm).

8. Attach the stabilizer bar link to the strut. Install and tighten the nut while holding the stabilizer bar link stud stationary. Tighten the nut to 35 ft. lbs. (48 Nm).

9. Install the wheel and tire assemblies. Tighten the wheel nuts in a star pattern until all nuts are torqued to half the required specification. Then repeat the tightening sequence to the full specified torque of 100 ft. lbs. (135 Nm).

10. Lower the vehicle.

LOWER BALL JOINT

REMOVAL & INSTALLATION

See Figures 348 through 350.

1. Before servicing the vehicle, refer to the Precautions Section.

2. Raise and safely support the vehicle.

3. Remove the front tire and wheel assemblies.

4. While a helper applies the brakes to keep the hub from rotating, remove the hub nut from the axle halfshaft.

5. Access and remove the front brake rotor.

6. Remove the routing clip securing the wheel speed sensor cable to the knuckle.

7. Remove the screw fastening the wheel speed sensor head to the knuckle. Pull the sensor head out of the knuckle.

8. Remove the nut attaching the lower ball joint to the lower control arm.

9. Release the lower ball joint from the lower control arm using Remover, Special Tool 9360, or equivalent.

10. Lift the knuckle out of the lower control arm.

FRONT SUSPENSION

✱✱ WARNING

Do not allow the halfshaft to hang by the inner C/V joint; it must be supported to keep the joint from separating during this operation.

11. Pull the knuckle off the axle halfshaft outer C/V joint splines and support the halfshaft.

12. Through the access hole in the knuckle, tap the ends of the snap-ring with a drift punch and remove it from the ball joint.

13. Install Remover, Special Tool 9964-3, and Remover, Special Tool 9964-4 on Remover/Installer, Special Tool 8441-1. Place the tools over the ball joint, then hand tighten the screw-drive.

14. Using hand-tools, tighten the screw-drive forcing the ball joint out of the knuckle.

15. Loosen the screw-drive and remove the tools and the ball joint.

To install:

16. Install Installer, Special Tool 9964-1, and Installer, Special Tool 9964-2 on

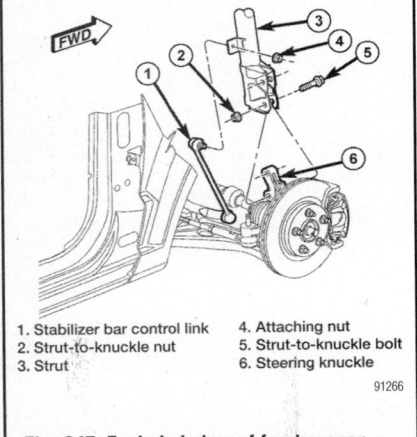

1. Stabilizer bar control link
2. Strut-to-knuckle nut
3. Strut
4. Attaching nut
5. Strut-to-knuckle bolt
6. Steering knuckle

91266

Fig. 347 Exploded view of front suspension components

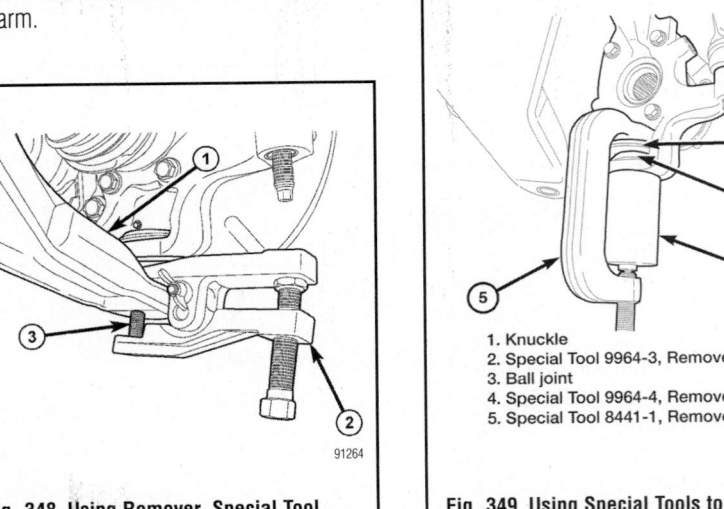

91264

Fig. 348 Using Remover, Special Tool 9360 (2) to release the lower ball joint (3) from the lower control arm (1)

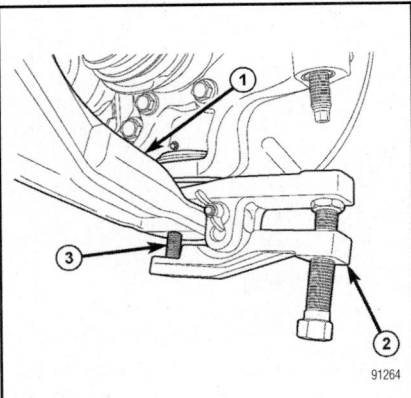

1. Knuckle
2. Special Tool 9964-3, Remover
3. Ball joint
4. Special Tool 9964-4, Remover
5. Special Tool 8441-1, Remover/Installer

91282

Fig. 349 Using Special Tools to remove the lower ball joint from the steering knuckle

Remover/Installer, Special Tool 8441-1. Place a new ball joint (stem down) into Installer 9964-2.

17. Position the assembly onto the knuckle, then hand tighten the screw-drive.

18. Using hand-tools, tighten the screw-drive forcing the ball joint into the knuckle. Continue to install the ball joint until the flange on the ball joint comes to a stop against the bottom of the knuckle.

19. Loosen the screw-drive and remove the tools.

20. Install a NEW snap-ring into the groove in the ball joint using a drift punch.

21. Slide the hub and bearing in the knuckle onto the splines of the halfshaft outer C/V joint.

22. Insert the lower ball joint stud into the mounting hole in the lower control arm.

23. Install a NEW ball joint stud nut. Tighten the nut to 70 ft. lbs. (95 Nm).

24. Install the wheel speed sensor head into the knuckle. Install the mounting screw and tighten it to 106 inch lbs. (12 Nm).

25. Install the routing clip securing the wheel speed sensor cable to the knuckle.

26. Install the brake rotor, disc brake caliper, and adapter.

27. Clean all foreign matter from the threads of the halfshaft outer C/V joint.

28. Install the hub nut on the end of the halfshaft and snug it.

29. While a helper applies the brakes to keep the hub from rotating, tighten the hub nut to 97 ft. lbs. (132 Nm).

30. Install the wheel and tire assemblies. Tighten the wheel nuts in a star pattern until all nuts are torqued to half the required specification. Then repeat the tightening sequence to the full specified torque of 100 ft. lbs. (135 Nm).

31. Lower the vehicle.

32. Perform a wheel alignment as necessary.

LOWER CONTROL ARM

REMOVAL & INSTALLATION

See Figure 351.

1. Before servicing the vehicle, refer to the Precautions Section.

2. Raise and safely support the vehicle.

3. Remove the front tire and wheel assemblies.

4. Remove the nut attaching the lower ball joint to the lower control arm.

5. Release the lower ball joint from the lower control arm using Remover 9360. Do not lift the knuckle out of the lower control arm at this time.

☀☀ WARNING

Upon removing the knuckle from the ball joint stud, do not pull outward on the knuckle. Pulling the knuckle outward at this point can separate the inner C/V joint on the halfshaft thus damaging it.

6. At each end of the stabilizer bar, while holding the stabilizer bar link lower stud stationary, remove the nut securing the link to the stabilizer bar.

7. Rotate the ends of the stabilizer bar upward away from the lower control arm.

8. Remove the front bolt attaching the lower control arm to the front suspension crossmember.

9. Remove the nut on the rear bolt attaching the lower control arm to the front suspension crossmember. Remove the bolt.

10. Remove the lower control arm from the crossmember.

To install:

11. Place the lower control arm into the front suspension crossmember.

12. Insert the rear bolt up through the crossmember and lower control arm. Install the nut on the top-end of the bolt, but do not tighten it at this time.

13. Install, but do not fully tighten, the front bolt attaching the lower control arm to the crossmember.

14. With no weight or obstruction on the lower control arm, tighten the lower control arm front mounting bolt to 129 ft. lbs. (175 Nm).

15. With no weight or obstruction on the lower control arm, tighten the lower control arm rear mounting bolt nut to 107 ft. lbs. (145 Nm).

16. Attach the stabilizer bar link at each end of the stabilizer bar. At each link, install and tighten the nut while holding the stabilizer bar link lower stud stationary. Tighten the nuts to 35 ft. lbs. (48 Nm).

➡️ **If a new or cleaned lower control arm is being installed, it is important to have a film of general purpose grease around the ball joint mounting hole on the lower control arm to avoid any future corrosion issues. Make sure the grease does not get inside the ball joint mounting hole or on the ball joint stud during installation.**

17. Insert the lower ball joint stud into the mounting hole in the lower control arm.

18. Install a NEW ball joint stud nut. Tighten the nut to 70 ft. lbs. (95 Nm).

19. Install the wheel and tire assembly. Tighten the wheel nuts in a star pattern until all nuts are torqued to half the required specification. Then repeat the tightening sequence to the full specified torque of 100 ft. lbs. (135 Nm).

20. Lower the vehicle.

21. Perform a wheel alignment as necessary.

CONTROL ARM BUSHING REPLACEMENT

Inspect the lower control arm for signs of damage from contact with the ground or road debris. If the lower control arm shows any sign of damage, do not attempt to repair or straighten a broken or bent lower control arm. If damaged, the lower control arm is serviced only as a complete component.

Inspect both lower control arm isolator bushings for severe deterioration and replace the lower control arm as required. Refer to Lower Control Arm, removal & installation.

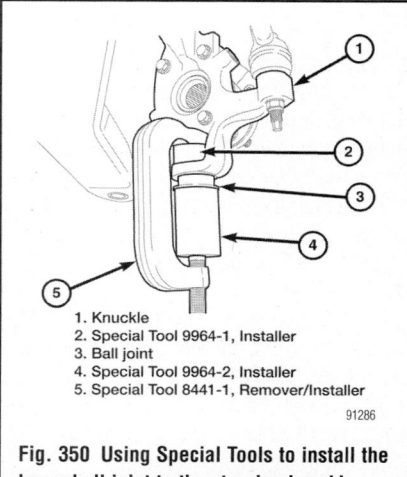

1. Knuckle
2. Special Tool 9964-1, Installer
3. Ball joint
4. Special Tool 9964-2, Installer
5. Special Tool 8441-1, Remover/Installer

91286

Fig. 350 Using Special Tools to install the lower ball joint to the steering knuckle

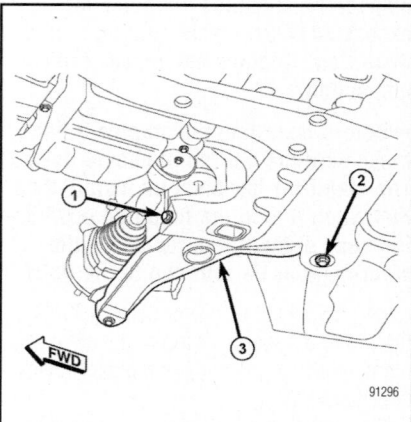

91296

Fig. 351 View of lower control arm (3), control arm front bolt (1), and rear bolt (2)

STABILIZER BAR

REMOVAL & INSTALLATION

See Figure 352.

1. Before servicing the vehicle, refer to the Precautions Section.
2. Raise and safely support the vehicle.
3. If equipped, remove the engine belly pan.
4. Remove the rear engine mount.
5. Remove the front engine mount through-bolt.
6. At each end of the stabilizer bar, while holding the stabilizer bar link lower stud stationary, remove the nut securing the link to the stabilizer bar.
7. Remove the screws securing the power steering hose routing clamps to the rear of the crossmember.
8. Remove the screws and push-pins securing the heat shield over the right side of the steering gear.
9. Remove the 2 bolts securing the steering gear to the crossmember.
10. Support the steering gear using a bungee cord, or equivalent, to keep the steering gear from lowering when the crossmember is lowered.

➡**Before removing the front suspension crossmember from the vehicle, the location of the crossmember must be marked on the body of the vehicle. Do this so the crossmember can be relocated, upon reinstallation, against the body of vehicle in the same location as before removal. If the front suspension crossmember is not reinstalled in exactly the same location as before removal, the preset front wheel alignment settings (caster and camber) may be lost.**

11. Mark the location of the front crossmember on the body near each mounting bolt.
12. Support the crossmember with a transmission jack.
13. Remove the 4 mounting bolts securing the front crossmember to the body.
14. Sedan only—Remove the mounting screws securing the front crossmember reinforcement brackets (one each side of vehicle) to the body. Remove the brackets.
15. Convertible only—Remove the mounting screws securing the front cross brace/reinforcement bracket to the body. Remove the bracket.
16. Slowly lower the crossmember using the jack until there is enough space present to remove the stabilizer bar between the rear of the crossmember and the body. Due to

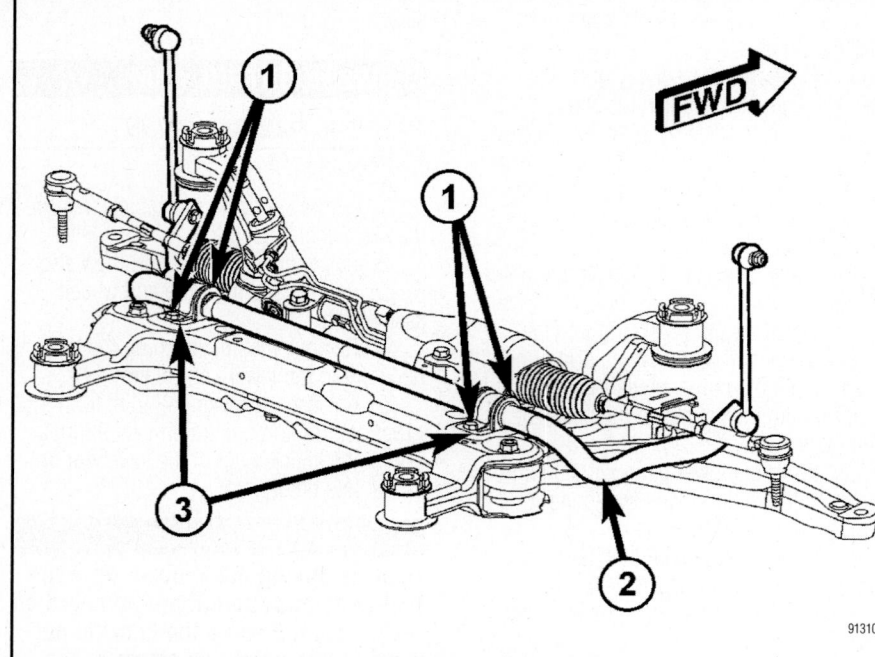

Fig. 352 Remove the screws (1) securing the stabilizer bushing retainers (3) to the crossmember and remove the stabilizer bar (2)

the fact that the fore-and-aft crossmember is still attached, do not lower the crossmember any more than necessary to remove the stabilizer bar.

17. Remove the screws securing the stabilizer bushing retainers to the crossmember.
18. Remove the 2 stabilizer bushing retainers.
19. Utilizing the slit cut into the cushions (bushings), remove the two cushions from the stabilizer bar.
20. Remove the stabilizer bar from the vehicle.

To install:

➡**Before stabilizer bar installation, inspect the cushions and links for excessive wear, cracks, damage, and distortion. Replace any pieces failing inspection.**

➡**Before installing the stabilizer bar, make sure the bar is not upside down. The stabilizer bar must be installed so that when it is in the mounted position, the ends of the bar curve under the steering gear tie rods, up to the links.**

21. Install the stabilizer bar, link ends first, from the rear over top of the crossmember. Curve the ends of the bar under the steering gear.
22. Install the 2 cushions (bushings) on the stabilizer bar utilizing the slit cut into the cushion sides.

23. Install the 2 stabilizer bushing retainers over the cushions.
24. Install the screws securing the stabilizer bushing retainers to the crossmember. Tighten all 4 stabilizer bar cushion retainer screws to 44 ft. lbs. (60 Nm).
25. Slowly raise the crossmember into the mounted position using the transmission jack while matching the crossmember to the marked locations on the body made during removal.
26. Sedan only—Position the front crossmember reinforcement brackets (one each side of vehicle) over the crossmember rear mounting bushings and install the mounting screws, but do not tighten at this time.
27. Convertible only—Position the front cross brace/reinforcement bracket over the crossmember rear mounting bushings and body, then install the mounting screws. Do not tighten screws at this time.
28. Install the 4 mounting bolts securing the front crossmember to the body. Tighten the crossmember mounting bolts to 100 ft. lbs. (135 Nm).
29. Sedan only—Tighten the crossmember reinforcement bracket mounting screws to 37 ft. lbs. (50 Nm).
30. Convertible only—Tighten the cross brace/reinforcement bracket mounting screws to 37 ft. lbs. (50 Nm).
31. Remove the transmission jack.

32. Remove the bungee cord, or equivalent, supporting the steering gear.

33. Install the 2 bolts securing the steering gear to the crossmember. Tighten the steering gear mounting bolts to 74 ft. lbs. (100 Nm).

34. Position the heat shield over the steering gear. Install the mounting screws and push-pins. Tighten the screws to 53 inch lbs. (6 Nm).

35. Position the power steering hose routing clamps on the crossmember. Install and tighten the screws to 71 inch lbs. (8 Nm).

36. Attach the stabilizer bar link at each end of the stabilizer bar. At each link, install and tighten the nut while holding the stabilizer bar link lower stud stationary. Tighten the nuts to 35 ft. lbs. (48 Nm).

37. Install the rear engine mount.

38. Install the front engine mount through-bolt.

39. If equipped, install the engine belly pan.

40. Lower the vehicle.

STEERING KNUCKLE

REMOVAL & INSTALLATION

See Figure 353.

1. Before servicing the vehicle, refer to the Precautions Section.

2. Raise and safely support the vehicle.

3. Remove the front tire and wheel assemblies.

➡**The hub nut is a single use type. A new nut is required for reassembly. Do not reuse the hub nut.**

4. While a helper applies the brakes to keep the hub from rotating, remove the hub nut from the axle halfshaft.

5. Access and remove the front brake rotor.

6. Remove the routing clip securing the wheel speed sensor cable to the knuckle.

7. Remove the screw fastening the wheel speed sensor head to the knuckle. Pull the sensor head out of the knuckle.

8. Remove the nut attaching the outer tie rod to the knuckle. To do this, it might be necessary to hold the tie rod end stud with a wrench while loosening and removing the nut with a standard wrench or crowfoot wrench.

9. Release the outer tie rod end from the knuckle using Remover, Special Tool 9360.

10. Remove the outer tie rod from the knuckle.

11. Remove the nut attaching the lower ball joint to the lower control arm.

12. Release the lower ball joint from the lower control arm using Remover, Special Tool 9360. Do not lift the knuckle out of the lower control arm at this time.

※※ **WARNING**

The strut assembly-to-knuckle attaching bolts are serrated and must not be turned during removal. Proper removal is required. Refer to the following steps for the correct method.

13. While holding the bolt heads stationary, remove the 2 nuts from the bolts attaching the strut to the knuckle.

14. Remove the 2 bolts attaching the strut to the knuckle using a pin punch.

※※ **WARNING**

Do not allow the halfshaft to hang by the inner C/V joint; it must be supported to keep the joint from separating during this operation.

15. Pull the knuckle off the halfshaft outer C/V joint splines and remove the knuckle from the vehicle.

16. If required, remove the 3 screws fastening the shield to the knuckle. Remove the shield.

17. If required, remove the 4 bolts fastening the hub and bearing to the knuckle.

18. If required, slide the hub and bearing out of the knuckle.

To install:

19. If required, install the hub and bearing by sliding it into the knuckle.

20. If installing the hub and bearing, install the 4 bolts fastening the hub and bearing to the knuckle. Tighten the 4 bolts to 60 ft. lbs. (82 Nm).

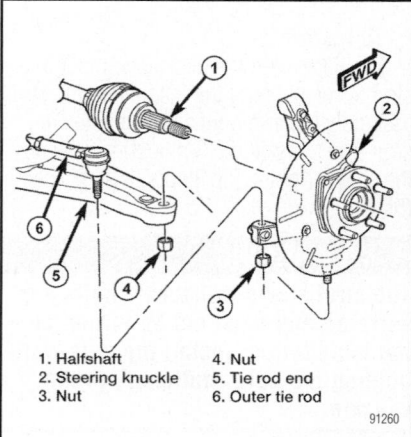

1. Halfshaft
2. Steering knuckle
3. Nut
4. Nut
5. Tie rod end
6. Outer tie rod

91260

Fig. 353 Removing the steering knuckle

21. If required, install the shield on the knuckle. Install and tighten the 3 mounting screws to 89 inch lbs. (10 Nm).

22. Slide the hub and bearing in the knuckle onto the splines of the halfshaft outer C/V joint.

23. Insert the lower ball joint stud into the mounting hole in the lower control arm.

24. Install a NEW ball joint stud nut. Tighten the nut to 70 ft. lbs. (95 Nm).

※※ **WARNING**

The strut clevis-to-knuckle bolts are serrated and must not be turned during installation. Install the nuts while holding the bolts stationary in the steering knuckle. Refer to the following step.

25. Position the lower end of the strut assembly in line with the upper end of the knuckle, aligning the mounting holes. Install the 2 mounting bolts.

26. Install the nuts on the 2 bolts. While holding the bolts in place, tighten the nuts to 103 ft. lbs. (140 Nm).

➡**If a new tie rod end is to be installed, make sure the boot is properly lubricated.**

27. Clean all old grease and debris from the boot with a clean cloth.

28. Apply outer tie rod grease to the tie rod end boot.

29. Install the outer tie rod ball stud into the hole in the knuckle arm. Start the tie rod end-to-knuckle nut onto the stud. While holding the tie rod end stud with a wrench, tighten the nut with a wrench or crowfoot wrench to 63 ft. lbs. (85 Nm).

30. Install the wheel speed sensor head into the knuckle. Install the mounting screw and tighten it to 106 inch lbs. (12 Nm).

31. Install the routing clip securing the wheel speed sensor cable to the knuckle.

32. Install the brake rotor, disc brake caliper, and adapter.

33. Clean all foreign matter from the threads of the halfshaft outer C/V joint.

➡**The hub nut is a single use type. A new nut is required for reassembly. Do not reuse the hub nut.**

34. Install the hub nut on the end of the halfshaft and snug it.

35. While a helper applies the brakes to keep the hub from rotating, tighten the hub nut to 97 ft. lbs. (132 Nm).

36. Install the wheel and tire assemblies. Tighten the wheel nuts in a star pattern until all nuts are torqued to half the required

specification. Then repeat the tightening sequence to the full specified torque of 100 ft. lbs. (135 Nm).

37. Lower the vehicle.

38. Perform a wheel alignment as necessary.

STRUT & SPRING ASSEMBLY

REMOVAL & INSTALLATION

See Figures 354 and 355.

> ❋❋ **WARNING**
>
> **Do not remove the strut rod nut while the strut assembly is installed in the vehicle, or before the coil spring is compressed with a compression tool. The spring is held under high pressure.**

> ❋❋ **WARNING**
>
> **At no time when servicing a vehicle can a sheet metal screw, bolt, or other metal fastener be installed in the shock tower to take the place of an original plastic clip. It may come into contact with the strut or coil spring.**

1. Before servicing the vehicle, refer to the Precautions Section.

2. Raise and safely support the vehicle.

3. Remove the front tire and wheel assemblies.

➡If both strut assemblies are to be removed, mark the strut assemblies right or left and keep the parts separated to avoid mix-up. Not all parts of the strut assembly are interchangeable side-to-side.

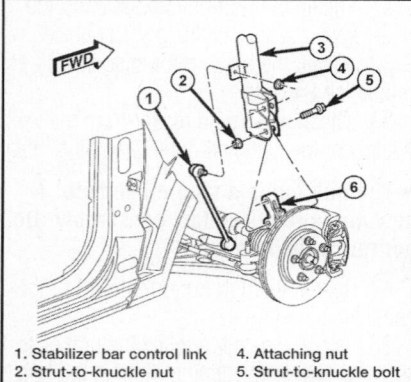

1. Stabilizer bar control link
2. Strut-to-knuckle nut
3. Strut
4. Attaching nut
5. Strut-to-knuckle bolt
6. Steering knuckle

91266

Fig. 354 Exploded view of front suspension components

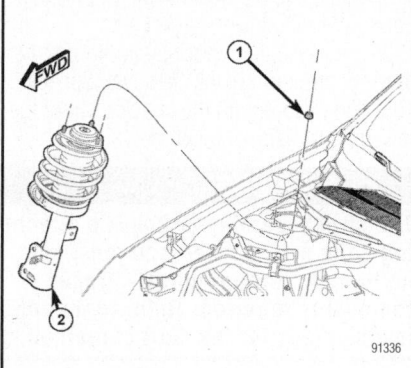

91336

Fig. 355 Remove the nuts (1) attaching the strut assembly (2) upper mount to the strut tower

4. Remove the screw securing the flex hose routing bracket to the strut.

5. While holding the stabilizer bar link stud stationary, remove the nut securing the link to the strut.

> ❋❋ **WARNING**
>
> **The strut assembly-to-knuckle attaching bolts are serrated and must not be turned during removal. Hold the bolts stationary in the knuckle while removing the nuts, then tap the bolts out using a pin punch.**

6. While holding the bolt heads stationary, remove the 2 nuts from the bolts attaching the strut to the knuckle.

7. Remove the 2 bolts attaching the strut to the knuckle using a pin punch.

8. Lower the vehicle just enough to open the hood without allowing the tires to touch the floor.

9. Remove the 3 nuts attaching the strut assembly upper mount to the strut tower.

10. Remove the strut assembly from the vehicle.

To install:

11. Raise the strut assembly into the strut tower, aligning the 3 studs on the strut assembly upper mount with the holes in strut tower. Install the 3 mounting nuts on the studs. Tighten the 3 nuts to 41 ft. lbs. (55 Nm).

> ❋❋ **WARNING**
>
> **The strut clevis-to-knuckle bolts are serrated and must not be turned during installation. Install the nuts while holding the bolts stationary in the knuckle.**

12. Position the lower end of the strut assembly in line with the upper end of the

knuckle, aligning the mounting holes. Install the 2 attaching bolts. Install the nuts. While holding the bolts in place, tighten the nuts to 103 ft. lbs. (140 Nm).

13. Attach the stabilizer bar link to the strut. Install and tighten the nut while holding the stabilizer bar link stud stationary. Tighten the nut to 35 ft. lbs. (48 Nm).

14. Secure the flex hose routing bracket to the strut with the mounting screw. Tighten the mounting screw to 120 inch lbs. (13 Nm).

15. Install the wheel and tire assembly. Tighten the wheel nuts in a star pattern until all nuts are torqued to half the required specification. Then repeat the tightening sequence to the full specified torque of 100 ft. lbs. (135 Nm).

16. Lower the vehicle.

OVERHAUL

See Figures 356 and 357

1. Before servicing the vehicle, refer to the Precautions Section.

➡The strut assembly must be removed from the vehicle for overhaul.

➡For disassembly and assembly of the strut, use a strut spring compressor to compress the coil spring. Follow the manufacturer's instructions closely.

> ❋❋ **CAUTION**
>
> **Do not remove the strut rod nut before the coil spring is properly compressed. The coil spring is held under pressure. The coil spring must be compressed, removing spring tension from the upper mount and bearing, before the strut rod nut is removed.**

2. If both struts are being serviced at the same time, mark both the coil spring and strut assembly according to the side of the vehicle from which the strut is being removed.

3. Position the strut assembly in the strut coil spring compressor following the manufacturer's instructions and set the lower and upper hooks of the compressor on the coil spring. Position the strut clevis bracket straight outward, away from the compressor.

4. Compress the coil spring until all coil spring tension is removed from the upper mount and bearing.

> ❋❋ **WARNING**
>
> **Never use impact or high speed tools to remove the strut rod nut. Damage to the strut internal bearings can occur.**

5. Once the spring is sufficiently compressed, install Strut Nut Wrench, Special Tool 9362, on the strut rod nut. Next, install a deep socket on the end of the strut rod. While holding the strut rod from turning, remove the nut using the strut nut wrench.

6. Remove the clamp (if installed) from the bottom of the coil spring and remove the strut (damper) out through the bottom of the coil spring.

7. Remove the lower spring isolator from the strut seat.

8. Remove the dust shield and jounce bumper.

9. Remove the upper strut mount from the top of the bearing and upper spring seat.

10. Remove the upper spring seat and isolator from the top of the coil spring.

11. Release the tension from the coil spring by backing off the compressor drive completely. Push back the compressor hooks and remove the coil spring.

12. Inspect the strut assembly components for the following and replace as necessary:

  a. Inspect the strut (damper) for shaft binding over the full stroke of the shaft.

  b. Inspect the jounce bumper for cracks and signs of deterioration.

  c. Inspect the dust shield for cracks and tears.

  d. Check the upper mount for cracks and distortion and its retaining studs for any sign of damage.

  e. Check the bearing and upper spring seat for any binding.

  f. Inspect the upper and lower spring isolators (4, 8) for material deterioration and distortion.

  g. Inspect the coil spring for any sign of damage to the coating.

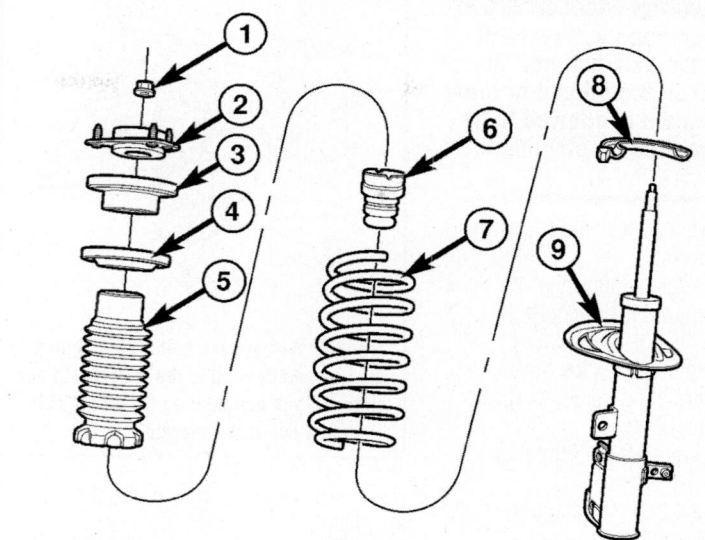

1. Strut rod nut
2. Upper strut mount
3. Upper spring seat
4. Isolator
5. Dust shield
6. Jounce bumper
7. Coil spring
8. Lower spring isolator
9. Strut (damper)

Fig. 357 Exploded view of front strut assembly

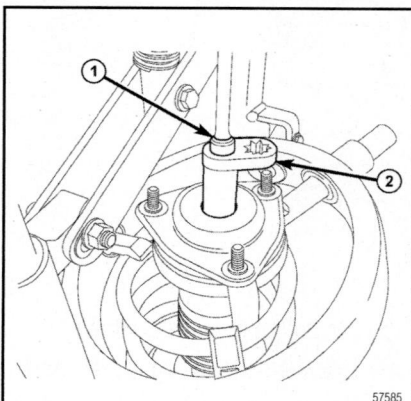

Fig. 356 Install Special Tool 9362, Strut Nut Wrench (2), on the strut rod nut and a deep socket (1) on the end of the strut rod

To assemble:

➡ **To determine the flat coil end of the coil spring for the following step, attempt to stand the coil spring on-end on a flat, level surface. If the coil spring stands on end, the end on the flat surface is the flat coil end. If the coil spring falls over, the end on the flat surface is not the flat coil end. Stand the coil spring on the opposite end to verify.**

13. Place the coil spring flat coil end upward (see above note) in the spring compressor following the manufacturer's instructions. Before compressing the spring, rotate the spring so the end of the bottom coil is at approximately the 9 o'clock position as viewed above (or to where the spring was when removed from the compressor). This action will allow the strut (damper) clevis bracket to be positioned outward, away from the compressor once installed.

14. Slowly compress the coil spring until enough room is available for strut assembly reassembly.

15. Install the bearing and upper spring seat, and isolator on top of the coil spring.

16. Install the upper mount on top of the bearing and upper spring seat.

17. Install the lower spring isolator on the spring seat on the strut (damper).

18. Slide the jounce bumper and dust shield onto the strut rod.

19. Install the strut up through the bottom of the coil spring and upper spring seat, mount, and bearing until the lower spring seat contacts the lower end of the coil spring. Rotate the strut as necessary until the end of the bottom coil comes in contact with the stop built into the lower spring isolator.

20. While holding the strut in position, install the nut on the end of the strut rod.

21. Install Strut Nut Wrench, Special Tool 9362, on the strut rod nut. Next, install a deep socket on the end of the strut rod. While holding the strut rod from turning, tighten the strut rod nut to 44 ft. lbs. (60 Nm) using a torque wrench on the end of Special Tool 9362.

22. Slowly release the tension from the coil spring by backing off the compressor drive completely. As the tension is relieved, make sure the upper mount and bearing align properly. Verify the upper mount does not bind when rotated.

23. Remove the strut assembly from the spring compressor.

24. Install the strut assembly on the vehicle.

WHEEL BEARINGS

REMOVAL & INSTALLATION

See Figure 358.

Wheel bearing damage will result if after loosening the axle hub nut, the vehicle is rolled on the ground or the weight of the vehicle is allowed to be supported by the tires for any length of time.

1. Before servicing the vehicle, refer to the Precautions Section.
2. Raise and safely support the vehicle.
3. Remove the front tire and wheel assemblies.
4. While a helper applies the brakes to keep the hub from rotating, remove the hub nut from the axle halfshaft.
5. Access and remove the front brake rotor.
6. Remove the 4 bolts fastening the hub and bearing to the knuckle.
7. Slide the hub and bearing off the halfshaft and out of the knuckle.

To install:

8. Install the hub and bearing by slid-

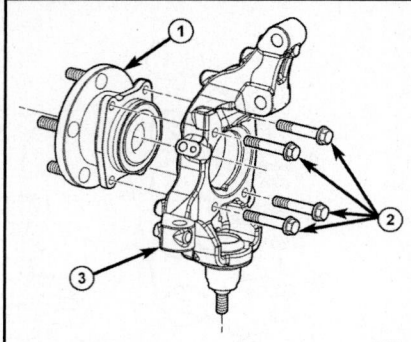

Fig. 358 Remove the bolts (2) fastening the hub and bearing to the knuckle (3) and slide the hub and bearing (1) off the halfshaft and out of the knuckle

ing it over the halfshaft and into the knuckle.

9. Install the 4 bolts fastening the hub and bearing to the knuckle. Tighten the 4 bolts to 60 ft. lbs. (82 Nm).
10. Install the brake rotor, disc brake caliper, and adapter.

➡Always install a new hub nut. The original hub nut is one-time use only and should be discarded when removed.

11. Clean all foreign matter from the threads of the halfshaft outer C/V joint.
12. Install the hub nut on the end of the halfshaft and lightly tighten it.
13. While a helper applies the brakes to keep the hub from rotating, tighten the hub nut to 97 ft. lbs. (132 Nm).
14. Install the wheel and tire assembly. Tighten the wheel nuts in a star pattern until all nuts are torqued to half the required specification. Then repeat the tightening sequence to the full specified torque of 100 ft. lbs. (135 Nm).
15. Lower the vehicle.

ADJUSTMENT

The wheel bearings are sealed at the factory and do not require any adjustment or maintenance.

SUSPENSION

REAR SUSPENSION

LOWER CONTROL ARM

REMOVAL & INSTALLATION

See Figure 359.

1. Before servicing the vehicle, refer to the Precautions Section.
2. Raise and safely support the vehicle.
3. Remove the rear tire and wheel assemblies.
4. If equipped, while holding the stabilizer bar link lower stud stationary, remove the nut securing the link to the lower control arm.
5. Remove the lower shock mounting nut and bolt.
6. Remove the nut and bolt securing the lower control arm to the knuckle.
7. Remove the nut and bolt securing the lower control arm to the rear crossmember.
8. Remove the lower control arm.

To install:

9. Position the lower control arm and install the bolt and nut securing the lower control arm to the crossmember. Do not tighten at this time.
10. Install the bolt and nut securing the lower control arm to the knuckle. Do not tighten at this time.
11. Install the mounting bolt and nut fastening the shock assembly to the lower control arm. Do not tighten at this time.

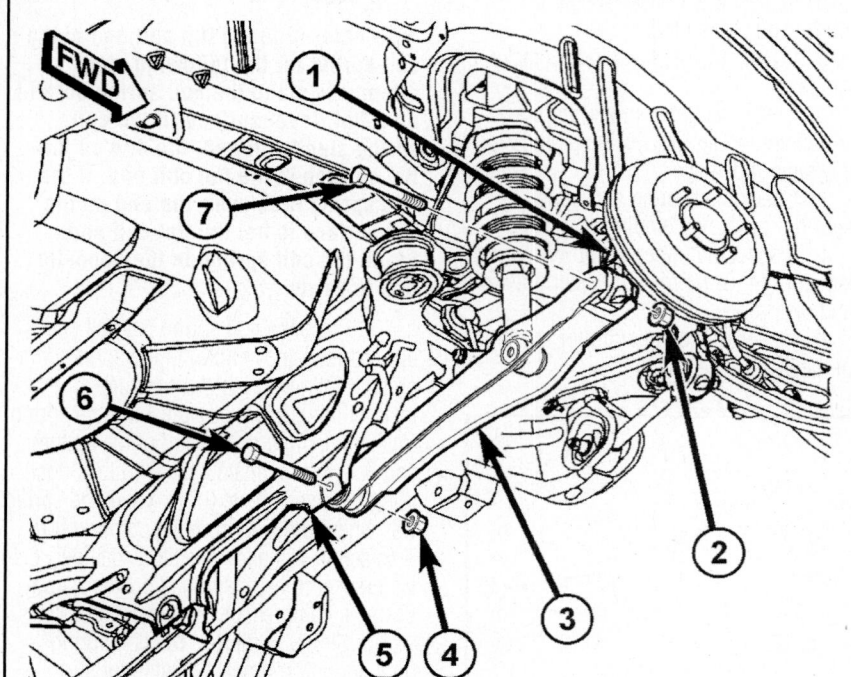

1. Knuckle
2. Lower control arm nut
3. Lower control arm
4. Lower control arm nut
5. Rear crossmember
6. Lower control arm bolt
7. Lower control arm bolt

Fig. 359 View of lower control arm and related components

➥When attaching a stabilizer bar link to the lower control arm it is important that the lower mounting stud be positioned properly. The lower mounting stud on the right side link needs to point toward the front of the vehicle when inserted through the lower control arm mounting flange. The left side link lower stud needs to point toward the rear of the vehicle. Otherwise the suspension geometry will not function properly.

12. If equipped, attach the stabilizer bar link to the lower control arm. Install the nut and while holding the stabilizer bar link lower stud stationary, tighten the nut to 35 ft. lbs. (48 Nm).

13. Install the wheel and tire assembly. Tighten the wheel nuts in a star pattern until all nuts are torqued to half the required specification. Then repeat the tightening sequence to the full specified torque of 100 ft. lbs. (135 Nm).

14. Lower the vehicle.

15. Position the vehicle on an alignment rack/drive-on lift. Raise the vehicle as necessary to access mounting bolts and nuts.

16. Tighten the lower control arm mounting bolt nut at the crossmember to 77 ft. lbs. (105 Nm).

17. Tighten the lower control arm mounting bolt nut at the knuckle to 77 ft. lbs. (105 Nm).

18. Tighten the shock assembly lower mounting bolt nut to 73 ft. lbs. (99 Nm).

19. Perform a wheel alignment as necessary.

STABILIZER BAR

REMOVAL & INSTALLATION

See Figure 360.

❈❈ WARNING

Only frame contact or wheel lift hoisting equipment can be used on this vehicle. It cannot be hoisted using equipment designed to lift a vehicle by the rear axle. If this type of hoisting equipment is used, damage to rear suspension components may occur.

➥If a rear suspension component becomes bent, damaged, or fails, no attempt should be made to straighten or repair it. Always replace it with a new component.

1. Before servicing the vehicle, refer to the Precautions Section.

2. Raise and safely support the vehicle.

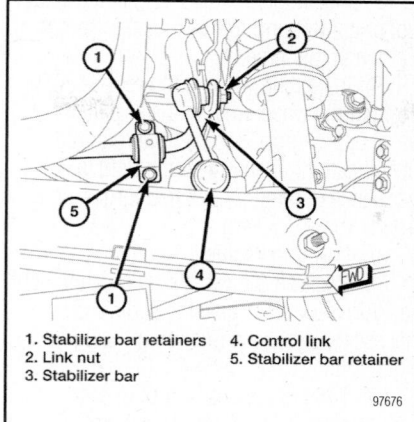

1. Stabilizer bar retainers
2. Link nut
3. Stabilizer bar
4. Control link
5. Stabilizer bar retainer

97676

Fig. 360 Rear stabilizer and related components shown

3. On each side of the vehicle, while holding the stabilizer bar link upper stud stationary, remove the nut securing the link to the stabilizer bar.

4. On each side of the vehicle, remove the screws securing the stabilizer bar retainer to the crossmember.

5. Remove the 2 stabilizer bar retainers.

6. Remove the stabilizer bar from the vehicle.

7. If required, remove the 2 cushions (bushings) from the stabilizer bar utilizing the slit cut into the cushions.

To install:

8. If required, install the 2 cushions (bushings) on the stabilizer bar (one on each side) utilizing the slit cut into the cushions.

9. Position the stabilizer bar on the rear crossmember.

10. Install the 2 retainers over the cushions at the mounting holes and install the retainer screws. Do not tighten the screws at this time.

11. On each side of the vehicle, install the stabilizer link upper stud in the end of the stabilizer bar. Install the nut on the upper stud and while holding the stabilizer link stud stationary, tighten the nut to 35 ft. lbs. (48 Nm).

12. On each side of the vehicle, tighten the stabilizer bar retainer screws to 18 ft. lbs. (25 Nm).

13. Lower the vehicle.

STRUT & SPRING ASSEMBLY

REMOVAL & INSTALLATION

See Figure 361.

❈❈ WARNING

Only frame contact or wheel lift hoisting equipment can be used on

this vehicle. It cannot be hoisted using equipment designed to lift a vehicle by the rear axle. If this type of hoisting equipment is used, damage to rear suspension components may occur.

➥If a rear suspension component becomes bent, damaged, or fails, no attempt should be made to straighten or repair it. Always replace it with a new component.

1. Before servicing the vehicle, refer to the Precautions Section.

2. Move aside the luggage compartment carpet as necessary to access the shock assembly upper mounting nuts.

3. Remove the 2 nuts securing the shock assembly to the body bracket.

4. Raise and safely support the vehicle.

5. Remove the tire and wheel assemblies.

6. Remove the lower shock mounting nut and bolt.

7. Lower the shock assembly out of the body bracket and lift it out over the rear suspension.

To install:

➥When installing the shock assembly into the body bracket in the following step, be sure to position the upper mounting bracket so that the angular formed side (as viewed from above) of the mounting bracket flange is facing outboard of the vehicle (opposite side of bracket is rounded).

8. Insert the lower end of the shock assembly down though the lower control arm from above just enough to clear the body, then lift it up into the body bracket.

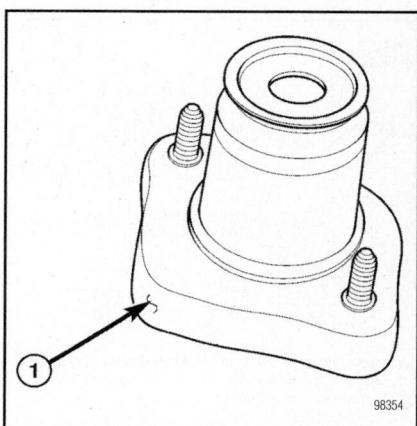

98354

Fig. 361 Position the upper mounting bracket so that the angular formed side (as viewed from above) of the mounting bracket flange (1) is facing outboard of the vehicle

9. Install the mounting bolt and nut fastening the shock assembly to the lower control arm. Do not tighten at this time.

10. Install the wheel and tire assembly. Tighten the wheel nuts in a star pattern until all nuts are torqued to half the required specification. Then repeat the tightening sequence to the full specified torque of 100 ft. lbs. (135 Nm).

11. Lower the vehicle.

12. Install the 2 nuts securing the shock assembly to the body bracket. Tighten the mounting nuts to 41 ft. lbs. (55 Nm).

13. Reposition the luggage compartment carpet as necessary.

14. Position the vehicle on an alignment rack/drive-on lift. Raise the lift as necessary to access the shock mounting bolt and nut.

15. Tighten the shock assembly lower mounting bolt nut to 73 ft. lbs. (99 Nm).

UPPER CONTROL ARM

REMOVAL & INSTALLATION

See Figure 362.

1. Before servicing the vehicle, refer to the Precautions Section.

2. Raise and safely support the vehicle.

3. Remove the tire and wheel assemblies.

4. Remove the nut and bolt securing the upper control arm to the knuckle.

5. Remove the nut and bolt securing the upper control arm to the crossmember.

6. Remove the upper control arm.

To install:

7. Position the upper control arm and install the bolt and nut securing the arm to the crossmember. Do not tighten at this time.

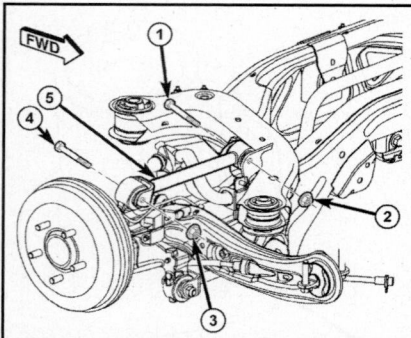

1. Upper control arm bolt
2. Upper control arm nut
3. Upper control arm nut
4. Upper control arm bolt
5. Upper control arm

97682

Fig. 362 Exploded view of upper control arm—rear suspension

8. Install the bolt and nut securing the upper control arm to the knuckle. Do not tighten at this time.

9. Install the wheel and tire assembly. Tighten the wheel nuts in a star pattern until all nuts are torqued to half the required specification. Then repeat the tightening sequence to the full specified torque of 100 ft. lbs. (135 Nm).

10. Lower the vehicle.

11. Position the vehicle on an alignment rack/drive-on lift. Raise the vehicle as necessary to access mounting bolts and nuts.

12. Tighten the upper control arm mounting bolt nut at the crossmember to 77 ft. lbs. (105 Nm).

13. Tighten the upper control arm mounting bolt nut at the knuckle to 77 ft. lbs. (105 Nm).

14. Perform a wheel alignment as necessary.

WHEEL BEARINGS

REMOVAL & INSTALLATION

See Figure 363.

✳✳ WARNING

Only frame contact or wheel lift hoisting equipment can be used on this vehicle. It cannot be hoisted using equipment designed to lift a vehicle by the rear axle. If this type of hoisting equipment is used, damage to rear suspension components may occur.

➡**If a rear suspension component becomes bent, damaged or fails, no attempt should be made to straighten or repair it. Always replace it with a new component.**

1. Before servicing the vehicle, refer to the Precautions Section.

2. Raise and safely support the vehicle.

3. Remove the tire and wheel assemblies.

4. Access and remove the rear brake rotor.

5. Remove the screw fastening the wheel speed sensor head in the rear of the hub and bearing.

6. Remove the 4 bolts securing the hub and bearing to the knuckle.

7. Remove the hub and bearing.

To install:

➡**If equipped, make sure the wheel speed sensor mount on the rear of the**

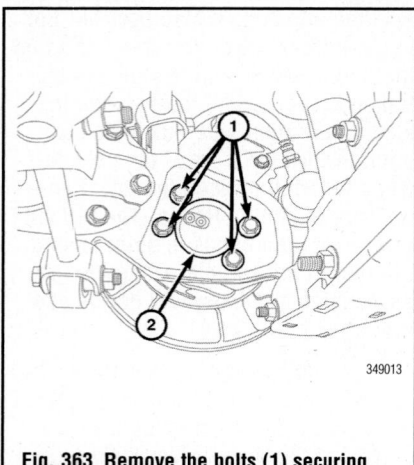

349013

Fig. 363 Remove the bolts (1) securing the hub and bearing (2) to the knuckle

hub and bearing is directed toward the front of the vehicle.

8. Position the hub and bearing on the brake support plate and knuckle.

9. Install the 4 bolts securing the hub and bearing to the knuckle. Tighten the bolts to 77 ft. lbs. (105 Nm).

➡**Before installing the wheel speed sensor head into the rear of the hub and bearing, inspect the O-ring seal to make sure it is not dislodged, split, cut, or damaged in any way. Replace the O-ring as necessary.**

10. If equipped with a wheel speed sensor, install the wheel speed sensor head into the rear of the hub and bearing.

11. If equipped with a wheel speed sensor, install the wheel speed sensor head mounting screw. Tighten the screw to 89 inch lbs. (10 Nm).

12. Install the brake rotor, disc brake caliper, and adapter.

13. Install the wheel and tire assembly. Tighten the wheel nuts in a star pattern until all nuts are torqued to half the required specification. Then repeat the tightening sequence to the full specified torque of 100 ft. lbs. (135 Nm).

14. Lower the vehicle.

15. Pump the brake pedal several times to ensure the vehicle has a firm brake pedal before moving it.

ADJUSTMENT

The rear hub/bearing assembly is a sealed assembly, which requires no periodic maintenance and cannot be serviced. If the hub/bearing assembly becomes worn or damaged, the entire unit must be replaced.

DODGE

Caliber

3

SPECIFICATIONS AND MAINTENANCE CHARTS

ENGINE AND VEHICLE IDENTIFICATION

		Engine					Model Year	
Code ①	Liters	Cu. In.	Cyl.	Fuel Sys. ②	Engine Type	Eng. Mfg.	Code ③	Year
A	2.0	122	4	MPI	DOHC I4 Dual VVT	NS	A	2010
B	2.4	146.5	4	MPI	DOHC I4 Dual VVT	NS	B	2011

NS: Not Specified.

① 8th position of VIN

② Multi-Port Electronic Fuel Injection

③ 10th position of VIN

25766_CALI_C0001

GENERAL ENGINE SPECIFICATIONS

All measurements are given in inches.

Year	Model	Engine Displacement Liters	Engine ID/VIN	Fuel System Type	Net Horsepower @ rpm	Net Torque @ rpm (ft. lbs.)	Bore x Stroke (in.)	Compression Ratio	Oil Pressure @ rpm
2010	Caliber	2.0	A	MPI	158 @ 6400	141 @ 5000	3.386 x 3.386	10.5:1	①
		2.4	B	MPI	172 @ 6000	165 @ 4400	3.465 x 3.819	10.5:1	①
2011	Caliber	2.0	A	MPI	158 @ 6400	141 @ 5000	3.386 x 3.386	10.5:1	①
		2.4	B	MPI	172 @ 6000	165 @ 4400	3.465 x 3.819	10.5:1	①

① 4 psi @ curb idle speed

25-80 psi @ 3000 rpm

25766_CALI_C0002

ENGINE TUNE-UP SPECIFICATIONS

Year	Engine Displacement Liters	Engine ID/VIN	Spark Plug Gap (in.)	Ignition Timing (deg.)		Fuel Pump (psi)	Idle Speed (rpm)		Valve Clearance	
				MT	AT		MT	AT	Intake	Exhaust
2010	2.0	A	0.043	①	①	53-63	①	①	NS	NS
	2.4	B	0.043	①	①	53-63	①	①	NS	NS
2011	2.0	A	0.043	①	①	53-63	①	①	NS	NS
	2.4	B	0.043	①	①	53-63	①	①	NS	NS

NS: Not specified

① Adjusted by Powertrain Control Module (PCM).

25766_CALI_C0003

CAPACITIES

Year	Model	Engine Displacement (Liters)	ID/VIN	Engine Oil (qts.)	Transaxle (pts.) Auto.	Transaxle (pts.) Manual	Drive Axle (pts.) Front	Drive Axle (pts.) Rear	Fuel Tank (gals.)	Cooling System (qts.)
2010	Caliber	2.0	A	4.5	①	2.5-2.8	NA	NA	13.5	7.2 ②
		2.4	B	4.5	①	2.5-2.8	NA	NA	13.5	7.2 ②
2011	Caliber	2.0	A	4.5	①	2.5-2.8	NA	NA	13.5	7.2 ②
		2.4	B	4.5	①	2.5-2.8	NA	NA	13.5	7.2 ②

NOTE: All capacities are approximate. Add fluid gradually and ensure a proper fluid level is obtained.

NA: Not Applicable.

① Drain and Refill: 14.8 pints.

Dry Fill: 17.1 pints (May vary depending on type and size of internal cooler, length and inside diameter of cooler lines, or use of an auxiliary cooler).

② System fill capacity includes heater and coolant recovery bottle filled to MAX level.

25766_CALI_C0004

FLUID SPECIFICATIONS

Year	Model	Engine Disp. Liters	Engine Oil	Manual Trans.	Auto. Trans.	Drive Axle Front	Drive Axle Rear	Power Steering Fluid	Brake Master Cylinder	Cooling System
2010	Caliber	2.0	①	MOPAR® ATF+4	MOPAR® CVT+4	NA	NA	②	③	④
		2.4	①	MOPAR® ATF+4	MOPAR® CVT+4	NA	NA	②	③	④
2011	Caliber	2.0	①	MOPAR® ATF+4	MOPAR® CVT+4	NA	NA	②	③	④
		2.4	①	MOPAR® ATF+4	MOPAR® CVT+4	NA	NA	②	③	④

NA: Not Applicable

① Refer to the engine oil filler cap. Use only Multi-Viscosity oil that meet the requirements of Material Standard MS-6395.

② MOPAR® Power Steering Fluid +4. If unavailable, then MOPAR® ATF +4 Automatic Transmission Fluid (P/N 05166226AA) is acceptable.

③ MOPAR® Brake Fluid DOT 3, SAE J1703. If unavailable, then MOPAR® Brake and Clutch Fluid DOT 4 (P/N 04549625AC) is acceptable.

④ MOPAR® Antifreeze/Coolant 5 Year/100,000 Mile Formula (MS-9769) with hybrid organic corrosion inhibitors HOAT (Hybrid Organic Additive Technology) is recommended.

25766_CALI_C0005

VALVE SPECIFICATIONS

Year	Engine Displacement Liters	Engine ID/VIN	Seat Angle (deg.)	Face Angle (deg.)	Spring Test Pressure (lbs. @ in.)	Spring Free-Length (in.)	Spring Installed Height (in.)	Stem-to-Guide Clearance (in.) Intake	Stem-to-Guide Clearance (in.) Exhaust	Stem Diameter (in.) Intake	Stem Diameter (in.) Exhaust
2010	2.0	A	44.75-45.10	45.25-45.75	①	1.850	1.378	0.0008-0.0030	0.0012-0.0040	0.2151-0.2157	0.2148-0.2153
	2.4	B	44.75-45.10	45.25-45.75	①	1.850	1.378	0.0008-0.0030	0.0012-0.0040	0.2151-0.2157	0.2148-0.2153
2011	2.0	A	44.75-45.10	45.25-45.75	①	1.850	1.378	0.0008-0.0030	0.0012-0.0040	0.2151-0.2157	0.2148-0.2153
	2.4	B	44.75-45.10	45.25-45.75	①	1.850	1.378	0.0008-0.0030	0.0012-0.0040	0.2151-0.2157	0.2148-0.2153

① Nominal force - valve closed: 40.35 lbs. @ 1.38 in.

Nominal force - valve open: 82.01 lbs. +/- 3.82 lbs. @ 1.152 in.

25766_CALI_C0006

CAMSHAFT SPECIFICATIONS
All measurements in inches unless noted

Year	Engine Displacement Liters	Engine Code/VIN	Journal Diameter	Brg. Oil Clearance	Shaft End-play	Runout	Journal Bore	Lobe Height
2010	2.0	A	①	②	0.004-0.009	NS	③	NS
	2.4	B	①	②	0.004-0.009	NS	③	NS
2011	2.0	A	①	②	0.004-0.009	NS	③	NS
	2.4	B	①	②	0.004-0.009	NS	③	NS

NS: Not specified

① Front intake cam: 1.1797-1.1803

  Front exhaust cam: 1.4166-1.4173

  Cam journals No. 1-4: 0.943-0.944

② Front intake journal: 0.0008-0.0022

  Front exhaust journal: 0.0007-0.0020

  All other journals: 0.0008-0.0026

③ Front intake: 1.1810-1.1819

  Front exhaust: 1.5747-1.5756

  Cam bearing bore No. 1-4: 0.9448-0.9457

25766_CALI_C0007

CRANKSHAFT AND CONNECTING ROD SPECIFICATIONS
All measurements are given in inches.

Year	Engine Displacement Liters	Engine ID/VIN	Crankshaft				Connecting Rod		
			Main Brg. Journal Dia.	Main Brg. Oil Clearance	Shaft End-play	Thrust on No.	Journal Diameter	Oil Clearance	Side Clearance
2010	2.0	A	①	0.0011-0.0022	0.0019-0.0098	NS	②	0.001-0.0020	0.0039-0.00098
	2.4	B	①	0.0011-0.0022	0.0019-0.0098	NS	②	0.001-0.0020	0.0039-0.00098
2011	2.0	A	①	0.0011-0.0022	0.0019-0.0098	NS	②	0.001-0.0020	0.0039-0.00098
	2.4	B	①	0.0011-0.0022	0.0019-0.0098	NS	②	0.001-0.0020	0.0039-0.00098

NS: Not Specified.

① Journal Grade 0: 2.0466-2.0467 inches.

  Journal Grade 1: 2.0465-2.0466 inches.

  Journal Grade 2: 2.0446-2.0465 inches.

  Journal Grade 3: 2.0462-2.0464 inches.

  Journal Grade 4: 2.0461-2.0462 inches.

② Journal Grade 1: 1.8884-1.8886 inches.

  Journal Grade 2: 1.8881-1.8884 inches.

  Journal Grade 3: 1.8879-1.8881 inches.

25766_CALI_C0008

PISTON AND RING SPECIFICATIONS

All measurements are given in inches.

Year	Engine Displacement Liters	Engine ID/VIN	Piston Clearance	Ring Gap			Ring Side Clearance		
				Top Compression	Bottom Compression	Oil Control	Top Compression	Bottom Compression	Oil Control
2010	2.0	A	(-0.0006)-0.0006	0.0059-0.0118	0.0118-0.0177	0.0079-0.0276	0.1182-0.0028	0.1182-0.0028	0.0024-0.0059
	2.4	B	(-0.0006)-0.0006	0.0059-0.0118	0.0118-0.0177	0.0079-0.0276	0.1182-0.0028	0.1182-0.0028	0.0024-0.0059
2011	2.0	A	(-0.0006)-0.0006	0.0059-0.0118	0.0118-0.0177	0.0079-0.0276	0.1182-0.0028	0.1182-0.0028	0.0024-0.0059
	2.4	B	(-0.0006)-0.0006	0.0059-0.0118	0.0118-0.0177	0.0079-0.0276	0.1182-0.0028	0.1182-0.0028	0.0024-0.0059

25766_CALI_C0009

TORQUE SPECIFICATIONS

All readings in ft. lbs.

Year	Engine Disp. Liters	Engine ID/VIN	Cylinder Head Bolts	Main Bearing Bolts	Rod Bearing Bolts	Crankshaft Damper Bolts	Flexplate Bolts	Manifold		Spark Plugs	Oil Pan Drain Plug
								Intake	Exhaust		
2010	2.0	A	①	18	②	155	③	18	25	20	30
	2.4	B	①	18	②	155	③	18	25	20	30
2011	2.0	A	①	18	②	155	③	18	25	20	30
	2.4	B	①	18	②	155	③	18	25	20	30

① Short-head bolts:

Step 1: 25 ft. lbs.

Step 2: 45 ft. lbs.

Step 3: Confirm all bolts torqued to 45 ft. lbs.

Step 4: Plus 90 degrees (do not use torque wrench).

Long-head bolts:

Step 1: 25 ft. lbs.

Step 2: 54 ft. lbs.

Step 3: Confirm all bolts torqued to 54 ft. lbs.

Step 4: Plus 90 degrees (do not use torque wrench).

③ Step 1: 15 ft. lbs.

Step 2: Plus 90 degrees.

④ Step 1: 22 ft. lbs.

Step 2: Plus 51 degrees

25766_CALI_C0010

WHEEL ALIGNMENT

Year	Model			Caster ①		Camber		Toe (Deg.)
				Range (+/-Deg.)	Preferred Setting (Deg.)	Range (+/-Deg.)	Preferred Setting (Deg.)	
2010	Caliber	15 Inch Wheels	Front	②	③	④	⑤	⑥ ⑦
			Rear	NA	NA	⑧	⑨	⑥ ⑦
		17 Inch Wheels	Front	②	③	⑪	⑫	⑥ ⑦
			Rear	NA	NA	⑬	⑭	⑥ ⑩
		18 Inch Wheels	Front	②	⑯	⑪	⑫	⑥ ⑦
			Rear	NA	NA	⑪	⑫	⑥ ⑩
2011	Caliber	15 Inch Wheels	Front	②	③	④	⑤	⑥ ⑦
			Rear	NA	NA	⑧	⑨	⑥ ⑦
		17 Inch Wheels	Front	②	③	⑪	⑫	⑥ ⑦
			Rear	NA	NA	⑬	⑭	⑥ ⑩
		18 Inch Wheels	Front	②	⑯	⑪	⑫	⑥ ⑦
			Rear	NA	NA	⑪	⑫	⑥ ⑩

NA: Not Applicable

Note: Positive toe (+) is toe-in and negative toe (−) is toe-out.

① Specifications are for reference only. These are non-adjustable angles.

② Left side: +1.90 to +3.90

Right side: +1.60 to +3.60

Cross caster (maximum side-to-side difference): -0.70 to 1.30

③ Left side: +2.90

Right side: +2.60

Cross caster (maximum side-to-side difference): 0.30

④ Camber: -0.90 to -0.10

Cross camber (maximum side-to-side difference): -0.50 to +0.50

⑤ Camber: -0.50

Cross camber (maximum side-to-side difference): 0.00

⑥ Total Toe: The sum of both left and right wheel toe settings. Total Toe should be equally split between each wheel on the same axle to ensure the steering wheel is centered after setting toe.

⑦ Acceptable range: 0.00 to +0.40

Preferred setting: +0.20

⑧ Camber: -0.80 to 0.00

Cross camber (maximum side-to-side difference): -0.50 to +0.50

⑨ Camber: -0.40

Cross camber (maximum side-to-side difference): 0.00

⑩ Individual toe acceptable range: 0.00 to +0.20

Individual toe preferred setting: +0.10

Total toe acceptable range: 0.00 to +0.40

Total toe preferred setting: +0.20

Thrust angle acceptable range: -0.10 to +0.10

Thrust angle preferred setting: 0.00

⑪ Camber: -0.10 to -0.30

Cross camber (maximum side-to-side difference): -0.50 to +0.50

⑫ Camber: -0.70

Cross camber (maximum side-to-side difference): 0.00

⑬ Camber: -1.00 to -0.20

Cross camber (maximum side-to-side difference): -0.50 to +0.50

⑭ Camber: -0.60

Cross camber (maximum side-to-side difference): 0.00

⑮ Left side: +2.00 to +4.00

Right side: +1.70 to +3.70

Cross caster (maximum side-to-side difference): -0.70 to 1.30

⑯ Left side: +3.00

Right side: +2.70

Cross caster (maximum side-to-side difference): 0.30

TIRE, WHEEL AND BALL JOINT SPECIFICATIONS

| Year | Model | OEM Tires | | Tire Pressures (psi) | | Wheel Size | Ball Joint Inspection | Lug Nut (ft. lbs.) |
		Standard	Optional	Front	Rear			
2010	Caliber	P205/70R15	NA	①	①	15	②	100
		P205/60R17	NA	①	①	17	②	100
		P215/55R18	NA	①	①	18	②	100
2011	Caliber	P205/70R15	NA	①	①	15	②	100
		P205/60R17	NA	①	①	17	②	100
		P215/55R18	NA	①	①	18	②	100

NA: Not Available

OEM: Original Equipment Manufacturer

PSI: Pounds Per Square Inch

① Always refer to the owner's manual and/or vehicle label.

② Replace if any measurable movement is found

25766_CALI_C0012

BRAKE SPECIFICATIONS
All measurements in inches unless noted

| Year | Model | | Brake Disc | | | Brake Drum Diameter | | Minimum Pad/Lining Thickness | | Brake Caliper | |
			Original Thickness	Minimum Thickness	Max. Runout	Original Inside Diameter	Maximum Machine Diameter	Front	Rear	Guide Pin Bolts (ft. lbs.)	Mounting Bolts (ft. lbs.)
2010	Caliber	F	1.020-1.028	0.961	0.004 ①	NA	NA	0.04	0.04	32	100
		R	0.386-0.402	0.331	②	NS	9.079	NS	NS	32	100
2011	Caliber	F	1.020-1.028	0.961	0.004 ①	NA	NA	0.04	0.04	32	100
		R	0.386-0.402	0.331	②	NS	9.079	NS	NS	32	100

F: Front

R: Rear

NA: Not available.

NS: Not specified.

① Total indicator reading (measured on vehicle).

② 0.0024 on 14-inch rotor; 0.0016 on 16-inch rotor.

25766_CALI_C0013

SCHEDULED MAINTENANCE - NORMAL
2010 Dodge Caliber

TO BE SERVICED	TYPE OF SERVICE	VEHICLE MILEAGE INTERVAL (x1000)																
		6	12	18	24	30	36	42	48	54	60	66	72	78	84	90	96	102
Engine oil & filter	Replace	✓	✓	✓	✓	✓	✓	✓	✓	✓	✓	✓	✓	✓	✓	✓	✓	✓
Rotate tires, inspect tread wear, measure tread depth and check pressure	Rotate	✓	✓	✓	✓	✓	✓	✓	✓	✓	✓	✓	✓	✓	✓	✓	✓	✓
Air conditioner filter	Replace		✓		✓		✓		✓		✓		✓		✓		✓	
Brake system components	Inspect/ Service		✓		✓		✓		✓		✓		✓		✓		✓	
Exhaust system & heat shields	Inspect		✓		✓		✓		✓		✓		✓		✓		✓	
Inspect the front suspension, tie rod ends and boot seals for cracks or leaks and all parts for damage, wear, improper looseness or end play.	Inspect		✓		✓		✓		✓		✓		✓		✓		✓	
CV Joints	Inspect		✓		✓		✓		✓		✓		✓		✓		✓	
Engine air filter	Replace					✓					✓					✓		
Adjust parking brake on vehicles equipped with four-wheel disc brakes.	Adjust					✓					✓					✓		
Engine coolant	Replace										✓							✓
Accessory drive belt	Inspect	✓	✓	✓	✓	✓	✓	✓	✓	✓	✓	✓	✓	✓	✓	✓	✓	✓
Automatic trans fluid & filter	Replace	at 120,000 miles																
Accessory drive belt	Replace	at 120,000 miles if not previously serviced																
Spark plugs	Replace					✓					✓					✓		
Fluid levels (all)	Top off	✓	✓	✓	✓	✓	✓	✓	✓	✓	✓	✓	✓	✓	✓	✓	✓	✓
Horn, exterior lamps, turn signals and hazard warning light operation	Inspect	✓	✓	✓	✓	✓	✓	✓	✓	✓	✓	✓	✓	✓	✓	✓	✓	✓
Battery	Inspect/ Service	✓	✓	✓	✓	✓	✓	✓	✓	✓	✓	✓	✓	✓	✓	✓	✓	✓
PCV valve	Replace															✓		

*Oil Change Indicator System

On Electronic Vehicle Information Center (EVIC) equipped vehicles, "Oil Change Required" is displayed in the EVIC and a single chime sounds, indicating that an oil change is necessary. On non-EVIC equipped vehicles, "Change Oil" flashes in the instrument cluster and a single chime sounds indicating that an oil change is necessary. Illumination of the oil change message is based on the operating conditions of the vehicle. When the message is illuminated, the vehicle must be serviced within 500 miles.

The oil change indicator will not monitor the time since the last oil change. Change the oil if it has been more than 6 months since the last oil change, even if the oil change indicator message is not illuminated.

Under no circumstances should oil change intervals exceed 6,000 miles or 6 months, whichever comes first.

To reset the oil change indicator, perform the following procedure:

1. Turn the ignition switch to the ON position. Do not start the engine.
2. Fully press the accelerator pedal 3 times within 10 seconds.
3. Turn the ignition switch to the LOCK position.

If the indicator message illuminates when the vehicle is started, repeat the procedure.

25766_CALI_C0014

SCHEDULED MAINTENANCE - SEVERE
2010 Dodge Caliber

TO BE SERVICED	TYPE OF SERVICE	VEHICLE MILEAGE INTERVAL (x1000)																
		6	12	18	24	30	36	42	48	54	60	66	72	78	84	90	96	102
Engine oil & filter	Replace	✓	✓	✓	✓	✓	✓	✓	✓	✓	✓	✓	✓	✓	✓	✓	✓	✓
Rotate tires, inspect tread wear, measure tread depth and check pressure	Rotate	✓	✓	✓	✓	✓	✓	✓	✓	✓	✓	✓	✓	✓	✓	✓	✓	✓
Air conditioner filter	Replace		✓		✓		✓		✓		✓		✓		✓		✓	
Brake system components	Inspect/ Service		✓		✓		✓		✓		✓		✓		✓		✓	
Exhaust system & heat shields	Inspect		✓		✓		✓		✓		✓		✓		✓		✓	
Inspect the front suspension, tie rod ends and boot seals for cracks or leaks and all parts for damage, wear, improper looseness or end play.	Inspect		✓		✓		✓		✓		✓		✓		✓		✓	
CV Joints	Inspect		✓		✓		✓		✓		✓		✓		✓		✓	
Engine air filter	Inspect/ Service		✓		✓		✓		✓		✓		✓		✓		✓	
Parking brake (vehicles with 4-wheel disc brakes)	Adjust					✓					✓					✓		
Engine coolant	Replace										✓							✓
Spark plugs	Replace					✓					✓					✓		
Automatic trans fluid & filter	Replace										✓							
Manual transmission fluid	Replace								✓								✓	
Accessory drive belt	Inspect	✓	✓	✓	✓	✓	✓	✓	✓	✓	✓	✓	✓	✓	✓	✓	✓	✓
Accessory drive belt	Replace	at 120,000 miles if not previously serviced																
Fluid levels (all)	Top off	✓	✓	✓	✓	✓	✓	✓	✓	✓	✓	✓	✓	✓	✓	✓	✓	✓
Horn, exterior lamps, turn signals and hazard warning light operation	Inspect	✓	✓	✓	✓	✓	✓	✓	✓	✓	✓	✓	✓	✓	✓	✓	✓	✓
Battery	Inspect/ Service	✓	✓	✓	✓	✓	✓	✓	✓	✓	✓	✓	✓	✓	✓	✓	✓	✓
PCV valve	Replace															✓		

*Oil Change Indicator System

On Electronic Vehicle Information Center (EVIC) equipped vehicles, "Oil Change Required" is displayed in the EVIC and a single chime sounds, indicating that an oil change is necessary. On non-EVIC equipped vehicles, "Change Oil" flashes in the instrument cluster and a single chime sounds indicating that an oil change is necessary. Illumination of the oil change message is based on the operating conditions of the vehicle. When the message is illuminated, the vehicle must be serviced within 500 miles.

The oil change indicator will not monitor the time since the last oil change. Change the oil if it has been more than 6 months since the last oil change, even if the oil change indicator message is not illuminated.

Under no circumstances should oil change intervals exceed 6,000 miles or 6 months, whichever comes first.

To reset the oil change indicator, perform the following procedure:

1. Turn the ignition switch to the ON position. Do not start the engine.
2. Fully press the accelerator pedal 3 times within 10 seconds.
3. Turn the ignition switch to the LOCK position.

If the indicator message illuminates when the vehicle is started, repeat the procedure.

25766_CALI_C0015

SCHEDULED MAINTENANCE - NORMAL
2011 Dodge Caliber

TO BE SERVICED	TYPE OF SERVICE	8	16	24	32	40	48	56	64	72	80	88	96	104	112	120	128	136
Engine oil & filter	Replace	✓	✓	✓	✓	✓	✓	✓	✓	✓	✓	✓	✓	✓	✓	✓	✓	✓
Rotate tires, inspect tread wear, measure tread depth and check pressure	Rotate	✓	✓	✓	✓	✓	✓	✓	✓	✓	✓	✓	✓	✓	✓	✓	✓	✓
Air conditioner filter	Replace		✓		✓		✓		✓		✓		✓		✓		✓	
Brake system components	Inspect/ Service		✓		✓		✓		✓		✓		✓		✓		✓	
Exhaust system & heat shields	Inspect			✓			✓			✓			✓	✓				
Inspect the front suspension, tie rod ends and boot seals for cracks or leaks and all parts for damage, wear, improper looseness or end play.	Inspect		✓		✓		✓		✓		✓		✓		✓		✓	
CV Joints	Inspect			✓			✓			✓			✓			✓		
Engine air filter	Replace				✓				✓				✓			✓		
Adjust parking brake on vehicles equipped with four-wheel disc brakes.	Adjust				✓				✓				✓			✓		
Engine coolant	Replace										✓			✓				
Accessory drive belt	Inspect	✓	✓	✓	✓	✓	✓	✓	✓	✓	✓	✓	✓	✓	✓	✓	✓	✓
Automatic trans fluid & filter	Replace															✓		
Accessory drive belt	Replace	at 120,000 miles if not previously serviced																
Spark plugs	Replace				✓				✓				✓			✓		
Fluid levels (all)	Top off	✓	✓	✓	✓	✓	✓	✓	✓	✓	✓	✓	✓	✓	✓	✓	✓	✓
Horn, exterior lamps, turn signals and hazard warning light operation	Inspect	✓	✓	✓	✓	✓	✓	✓	✓	✓	✓	✓	✓	✓	✓	✓	✓	✓
Battery	Inspect/ Service	✓	✓	✓	✓	✓	✓	✓	✓	✓	✓	✓	✓	✓	✓	✓	✓	✓
PCV valve	Replace												✓					

Vehicle mileage interval (x1000)

*Oil Change Indicator System

On Electronic Vehicle Information Center (EVIC) equipped vehicles, "Oil Change Required" is displayed in the EVIC and a single chime sounds, indicating that an oil change is necessary. On non-EVIC equipped vehicles, "Change Oil" flashes in the instrument cluster and a single chime sounds indicating that an oil change is necessary. Illumination of the oil change message is based on the operating conditions of the vehicle. When the message is illuminated, the vehicle must be serviced within 500 miles.

The oil change indicator will not monitor the time since the last oil change. Change the oil if it has been more than 6 months since the last oil change, even if the oil change indicator message is not illuminated.

Under no circumstances should oil change intervals exceed 6,000 miles or 6 months, whichever comes first.

To reset the oil change indicator, perform the following procedure:

1. Turn the ignition switch to the ON position. Do not start the engine.
2. Fully press the accelerator pedal 3 times within 10 seconds.
3. Turn the ignition switch to the LOCK position.

If the indicator message illuminates when the vehicle is started, repeat the procedure.

25766_CALI_C0016

SCHEDULED MAINTENANCE - SEVERE
2011 Dodge Caliber

TO BE SERVICED	TYPE OF SERVICE	VEHICLE MILEAGE INTERVAL (x1000)																
		8	16	24	32	40	48	56	64	72	80	88	96	104	112	120	128	136
Engine oil & filter	Replace	✓	✓	✓	✓	✓	✓	✓	✓	✓	✓	✓	✓	✓	✓	✓	✓	✓
Rotate tires, inspect tread wear, measure tread depth and check pressure	Rotate	✓	✓	✓	✓	✓	✓	✓	✓	✓	✓	✓	✓	✓	✓	✓	✓	✓
Air conditioner filter	Replace		✓		✓		✓		✓		✓		✓		✓		✓	
Brake system components	Inspect/ Service		✓		✓		✓		✓		✓		✓		✓		✓	
Exhaust system & heat shields	Inspect		✓		✓		✓		✓		✓		✓		✓		✓	
Inspect the front suspension, tie rod ends and boot seals for cracks or leaks and all parts for damage, wear, improper looseness or end play.	Inspect		✓		✓		✓		✓		✓		✓		✓		✓	
CV Joints	Inspect			✓			✓			✓			✓			✓		
Engine air filter	Replace		✓		✓		✓		✓		✓		✓		✓		✓	
Adjust parking brake on vehicles equipped with four-wheel disc brakes.	Adjust			✓					✓				✓			✓		
Engine coolant	Replace										✓							
Spark plugs	Replace			✓					✓				✓				✓	
Accessory drive belt	Replace	at 120,000 miles if not previously serviced																
Accessory drive belt	Inspect	✓	✓	✓	✓	✓	✓	✓	✓	✓	✓	✓	✓	✓	✓	✓	✓	✓
Fluid levels (all)	Top off	✓	✓	✓	✓	✓	✓	✓	✓	✓	✓	✓	✓	✓	✓	✓	✓	✓
Horn, exterior lamp, turn signal & hazard warning light operation	Inspect	✓	✓	✓	✓	✓	✓	✓	✓	✓	✓	✓	✓	✓	✓	✓	✓	✓
Battery	Inspect/ Service	✓	✓	✓	✓	✓	✓	✓	✓	✓	✓	✓	✓	✓	✓	✓	✓	✓
Automatic transmisison fluid & filter	Replace					✓							✓					
PCV valve	Replace												✓					
Manual transmission fluid	Replace								✓								✓	

*Oil Change Indicator System

On Electronic Vehicle Information Center (EVIC) equipped vehicles, "Oil Change Required" is displayed in the EVIC and a single chime sounds, indicating that an oil change is necessary. On non-EVIC equipped vehicles, "Change Oil" flashes in the instrument cluster and a single chime sounds indicating that an oil change is necessary. Illumination of the oil change message is based on the operating conditions of the vehicle. When the message is illuminated, the vehicle must be serviced within 500 miles.

The oil change indicator will not monitor the time since the last oil change. Change the oil if it has been more than 6 months since the last oil change, even if the oil change indicator message is not illuminated.

Under no circumstances should oil change intervals exceed 6,000 miles or 6 months, whichever comes first.

To reset the oil change indicator, perform the following procedure:

1. Turn the ignition switch to the ON position. Do not start the engine.
2. Fully press the accelerator pedal 3 times within 10 seconds.
3. Turn the ignition switch to the LOCK position.

If the indicator message illuminates when the vehicle is started, repeat the procedure.

25766_CALI_C0017

PRECAUTIONS

Before servicing any vehicle, please be sure to read all of the following precautions, which deal with personal safety, prevention of component damage, and important points to take into consideration when servicing a motor vehicle:

• Never open, service or drain the radiator or cooling system when the engine is hot; serious burns can occur from the steam and hot coolant.

• Observe all applicable safety precautions when working around fuel. Whenever servicing the fuel system, always work in a well-ventilated area. Do not allow fuel spray or vapors to come in contact with a spark, open flame, or excessive heat (a hot drop light, for example). Keep a dry chemical fire extinguisher near the work area. Always keep fuel in a container specifically designed for fuel storage; also, always properly seal fuel containers to avoid the possibility of fire or explosion. Refer to the additional fuel system precautions later in this section.

• Fuel injection systems often remain pressurized, even after the engine has been turned **OFF**. The fuel system pressure must be relieved before disconnecting any fuel lines. Failure to do so may result in fire and/or personal injury.

• Brake fluid often contains polyglycol ethers and polyglycols. Avoid contact with the eyes and wash your hands thoroughly after handling brake fluid. If you do get brake fluid in your eyes, flush your eyes with clean, running water for 15 minutes. If eye irritation persists, or if you have taken brake fluid internally, IMMEDIATELY seek medical assistance.

• The EPA warns that prolonged contact with used engine oil may cause a number of skin disorders, including cancer. You should make every effort to minimize your exposure to used engine oil. Protective gloves should be worn when changing oil. Wash your hands and any other exposed skin areas as soon as possible after exposure to used engine oil. Soap and water, or waterless hand cleaner should be used.

• All new vehicles are now equipped with an air bag system, often referred to as a Supplemental Restraint System (SRS) or Supplemental Inflatable Restraint (SIR) system. The system must be disabled before performing service on or around system components, steering column, instrument panel components, wiring and sensors. Failure to follow safety and disabling procedures could result in accidental air bag deployment, possible personal injury and unnecessary system repairs.

• Always wear safety goggles when working with, or around, the air bag system. When carrying a non-deployed air bag, be sure the bag and trim cover are pointed away from your body. When placing a non-deployed air bag on a work surface, always face the bag and trim cover upward, away from the surface. This will reduce the motion of the module if it is accidentally deployed. Refer to the additional air bag system precautions later in this section.

• Clean, high quality brake fluid from a sealed container is essential to the safe and proper operation of the brake system. You should always buy the correct type of brake fluid for your vehicle. If the brake fluid becomes contaminated, completely flush the system with new fluid. Never reuse any brake fluid. Any brake fluid that is removed from the system should be discarded. Also, do not allow any brake fluid to come in contact with a painted surface; it will damage the paint.

• Never operate the engine without the proper amount and type of engine oil; doing so WILL result in severe engine damage.

• Timing belt maintenance is extremely important. Many models utilize an interference-type, non-freewheeling engine. If the timing belt breaks, the valves in the cylinder head may strike the pistons, causing potentially serious (also time-consuming and expensive) engine damage. Refer to the maintenance interval charts for the recommended replacement interval for the timing belt, and to the timing belt section for belt replacement and inspection.

• Disconnecting the negative battery cable on some vehicles may interfere with the functions of the on-board computer system(s) and may require the computer to undergo a relearning process once the negative battery cable is reconnected.

• When servicing drum brakes, only disassemble and assemble one side at a time, leaving the remaining side intact for reference.

• Only an MVAC-trained, EPA-certified automotive technician should service the air conditioning system or its components.

BRAKES   ANTI-LOCK BRAKE SYSTEM (ABS)

GENERAL INFORMATION

PRECAUTIONS

• Certain components within the ABS system are not intended to be serviced or repaired individually.

• Do not use rubber hoses or other parts not specifically specified for and ABS system. When using repair kits, replace all parts included in the kit. Partial or incorrect repair may lead to functional problems and require the replacement of components.

• Lubricate rubber parts with clean, fresh brake fluid to ease assembly. Do not use shop air to clean parts; damage to rubber components may result.

• Use only DOT 3 brake fluid from an unopened container.

• If any hydraulic component or line is removed or replaced, it may be necessary to bleed the entire system.

• A clean repair area is essential. Always clean the reservoir and cap thoroughly before removing the cap. The slightest amount of dirt in the fluid may plug an orifice and impair the system function. Perform repairs after components have been thoroughly cleaned; use only denatured alcohol to clean components. Do not allow ABS components to come into contact with any substance containing mineral oil; this includes used shop rags.

• The Anti-Lock control unit is a microprocessor similar to other computer units in the vehicle. Ensure that the ignition switch is **OFF** before removing or installing controller harnesses. Avoid static electricity discharge at or near the controller.

• If any arc welding is to be done on the vehicle, the control unit should be unplugged before welding operations begin.

✳✳ WARNING

The anti-lock brake system uses an electronic control module known as the Anti-lock Brake Module (ABM). This module is designed to withstand normal current draws associated with vehicle operation. Care must be taken to avoid overloading the circuits.

✳✳ WARNING

In testing for open or short circuits, do not ground or apply voltage to any of the circuits unless instructed to do so for a diagnostic procedure.

These circuits should only be tested using a high impedance multi-meter or the designated scan tool as described in this section. Power should never be removed or applied to any control module with the ignition in the ON position. Before removing or connecting battery cables, fuses, or connectors, always turn the ignition to the OFF position.

The ABM 47-way connector should never be connected or disconnected with the ignition switch in the ON position.

This vehicle utilizes active wheel speed sensors. Do not apply voltage to wheel speed sensors at any time.

SPEED SENSORS

REMOVAL & INSTALLATION

Front Speed Sensor

See Figures 1 through 4.

1. Before servicing the vehicle, refer to the Precautions Section.
2. Open the hood.
3. Disconnect the wheel speed sensor cable connector from the wiring harness connector on top of the frame rail to the inside of the strut tower.
4. Raise and support the vehicle.

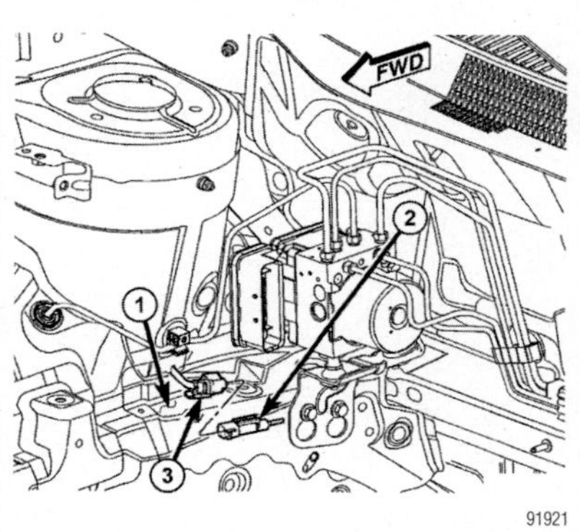

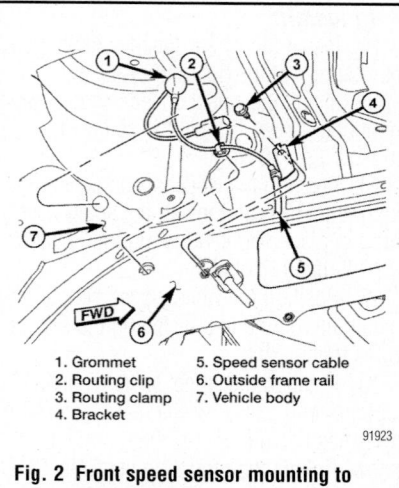

Fig. 1 Disconnect the wheel speed sensor cable connector from the wiring harness connector (3) on top of the frame rail (1) to the inside of the strut tower

91921

5. Remove the grommet from the hole in the body and pull the wheel speed sensor cable out of the hole.
6. Remove the speed sensor cable routing clip from the outside frame rail.
7. Remove the screw fastening the cable routing clamp to the outside frame rail.
8. Remove the screw securing the wheel speed sensor routing bracket to the brake flex hose bracket.
9. Remove the mounting screw fastening the wheel speed sensor head to the knuckle. Pull the sensor head out of the knuckle.

➡ **In the following step, the routing clip can be easily removed without damaging it by rotating it (with entire sensor) counterclockwise.**

10. Remove the routing clip securing wheel speed sensor cable to the knuckle. Remove the sensor from the vehicle.

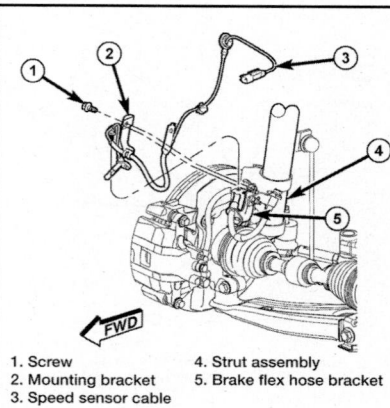

1. Grommet   5. Speed sensor cable
2. Routing clip   6. Outside frame rail
3. Routing clamp   7. Vehicle body
4. Bracket

91923

Fig. 2 Front speed sensor mounting to body—exploded view

1. Screw   4. Strut assembly
2. Mounting bracket   5. Brake flex hose bracket
3. Speed sensor cable

248502

Fig. 3 Front speed sensor mounting to strut—exploded view

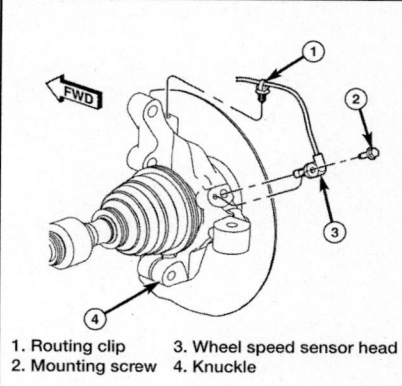

1. Routing clip   3. Wheel speed sensor head
2. Mounting screw   4. Knuckle

247862

Fig. 4 Removing front wheel speed sensor head

To install:

Failure to install speed sensor cables properly may result in contact with moving parts or an over-extension of cables causing an open circuit. Be sure that cables are installed, routed, and clipped properly.

11. Install the wheel speed sensor head into the knuckle. Install the mounting screw and tighten it to 106 inch lbs. (12 Nm).
12. Install the routing clip securing the wheel speed sensor cable to the knuckle.
13. Position the wheel speed sensor routing bracket on the brake flex hose bracket and install the mounting screw. Tighten the mounting screw to 13 ft. lbs. (18 Nm).
14. Position the wheel speed sensor cable routing clamp on the outside frame rail and install the mounting screw. Tighten the mounting screw to 13 ft. lbs. (18 Nm).
15. Install the speed sensor cable routing clip on the outside frame rail.
16. Insert the wheel speed sensor cable through the hole in the body and install the grommet in the hole.
17. Lower the vehicle.
18. Connect the wheel speed sensor cable connector to the wiring harness connector on top of the frame rail.
19. Using scan tool, check for Diagnostic Trouble Codes (DTCs) and repair as necessary.

Rear Speed Sensor

See Figures 5 through 11.

1. Before servicing the vehicle, refer to the Precautions Section.
2. Remove the cargo floor cover.

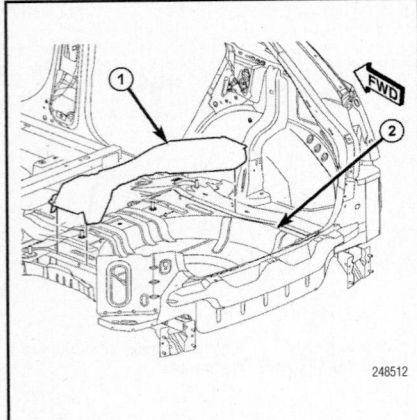

Fig. 5 Remove the rear floor pan silencer (1) from cargo floor (2)

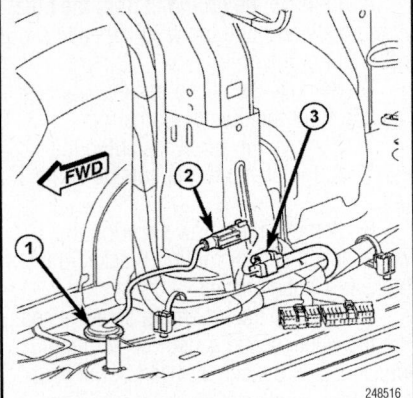

Fig. 7 Disconnect the wheel speed sensor (1) cable connector (2) at the body wiring harness connector (3)

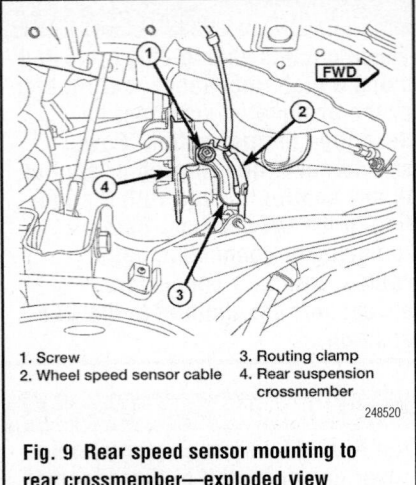

1. Screw
2. Wheel speed sensor cable
3. Routing clamp
4. Rear suspension crossmember

Fig. 9 Rear speed sensor mounting to rear crossmember—exploded view

3. Remove the rear floor pan silencer.

4. If equipped, remove the nuts mounting the satellite receiver or amplifier to the rear floor pan. Move the component aside to allow access to the wheel speed sensor wiring connector through the opening in the bottom of the quarter trim panel.

5. Through the opening in the bottom of the quarter trim panel, disconnect the wheel speed sensor cable connector at the body wiring harness connector.

6. Raise and support the vehicle.

7. Remove the rear tire and wheel assembly.

8. Remove the grommet from the hole in the body, and pull the wheel speed sensor cable out through the hole.

9. Remove the speed sensor cable routing clip from the outside frame rail.

10. Remove the screw fastening the cable routing clamp to the rear suspension crossmember.

11. Remove the speed sensor cable routing clip from the trailing link.

12. Remove the screw fastening the cable routing clamp to the trailing link.

13. Remove the screw fastening the wheel speed sensor head in the rear of the hub and bearing. Remove the sensor from the vehicle.

To install:

14. Install the wheel speed sensor head into the rear of the hub and bearing.

15. Install the wheel speed sensor head mounting screw. Tighten the screw to 89 inch lbs. (10 Nm).

16. Position the wheel speed sensor on the trailing link, and install the screw securing it in place. Tighten the mounting screw to 13 ft. lbs. (18 Nm).

17. Position the wheel speed sensor and install the routing clip fastening the sensor to the trailing link.

18. Position the wheel speed sensor cable routing clamp on the rear suspension crossmember, and install the mounting screw. Tighten the mounting screw to 13 ft. lbs. (18 Nm).

19. Install the speed sensor cable routing clip on the outside frame rail.

➥**When inserting the wheel speed sensor cable through the hole in the body,**

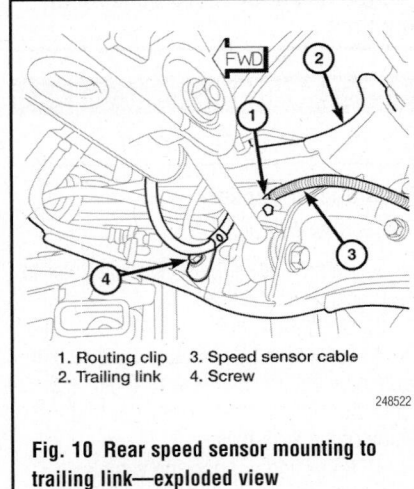

1. Routing clip
2. Trailing link
3. Speed sensor cable
4. Screw

Fig. 10 Rear speed sensor mounting to trailing link—exploded view

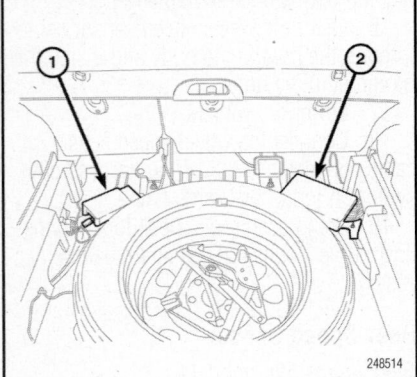

Fig. 6 Remove the nuts mounting the satellite receiver (1) or amplifier (2) to rear floor pan

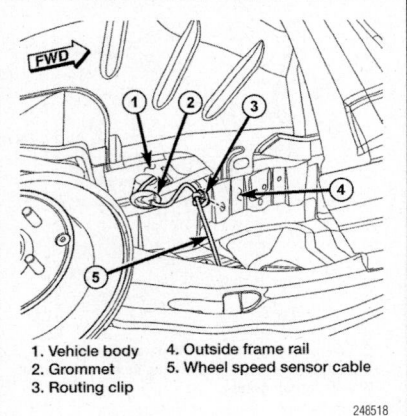

1. Vehicle body
2. Grommet
3. Routing clip
4. Outside frame rail
5. Wheel speed sensor cable

Fig. 8 Rear speed sensor mounting to vehicle body—exploded view

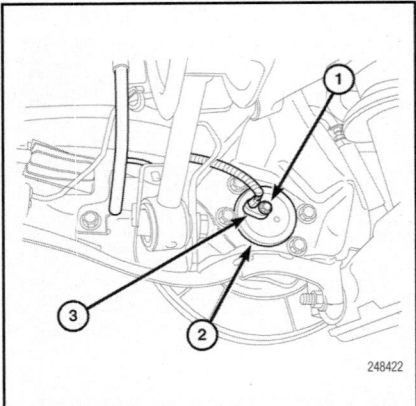

Fig. 11 Remove the screw (1) fastening the wheel speed sensor head (3) in the rear of the hub and bearing (2)

route the cable toward the shock tower to make it easier to grasp the cable to connect it to the body wiring harness connector in a later step.

20. Insert the wheel speed sensor cable through the hole in the body, and install the grommet in the hole.

21. Install tire and wheel assembly. Install and tighten the wheel mounting nuts to 100 ft. lbs. (135 Nm).

22. Lower the vehicle.

23. Through the opening in the bottom of the quarter trim panel, connect the wheel speed sensor cable connector at the body wiring harness connector.

24. If equipped, install the satellite receiver or amplifier to rear floor pan.

25. Install the rear floor pan silencer.

26. Install the cargo floor cover.

27. Using scan tool, check for Diagnostic Trouble Codes (DTCs) and repair as necessary.

BRAKES

BLEEDING THE BRAKE SYSTEM

BLEEDING PROCEDURE

BLEEDING PROCEDURE

Manual Bleeding

⁑ WARNING

Use only Mopar® brake fluid or an equivalent from a fresh, tightly sealed container. Brake fluid must conform to DOT 3 specifications. Do not use petroleum-based fluid, as seal damage in the brake system will result.

⁑ WARNING

Before removing the master cylinder cap, wipe it clean to prevent dirt and other foreign matter from dropping into the master cylinder reservoir.

⁑ WARNING

Do not allow the master cylinder reservoir to run out of brake fluid while bleeding the system. An empty reservoir will allow additional air into the brake system. Check the fluid level frequently and add fluid as needed.

⁑ CAUTION

Brake fluid contains polyglycol ethers and polyglycols. Avoid contact with the eyes and wash your hands thoroughly after handling brake fluid. If you do get brake fluid in your eyes, flush your eyes with clean, running water for 15 minutes. If eye irritation persists, or if you have taken brake fluid internally, IMMEDIATELY seek medical assistance.

⁑ WARNING

When bleeding the brake system, wear safety glasses. A clear bleed tube must be attached to the bleeder screws and submerged in a clear

container filled part way with clean brake fluid. Direct the flow of brake fluid away from yourself and the painted surfaces of the vehicle. Brake fluid at high pressure may come out of the bleeder screws when opened.

→ The following wheel circuit sequence for bleeding the brake hydraulic system should be used to ensure adequate removal of all trapped air from the hydraulic system: Left rear wheel, right front wheel, right rear wheel, left front wheel.

1. Before servicing the vehicle, refer to the Precautions Section.

2. Clean all dirt from around the master cylinder reservoir cap, and remove the filler cap.

3. Fill the brake master cylinder reservoir with clean, specified brake fluid.

4. Attach a clear plastic hose to the left rear wheel bleeder screw and feed the hose into a clear jar containing enough fresh brake fluid to submerge the end of the hose.

5. Have an assistant pump the brake pedal 3–4 times and hold it in the down position.

6. With the pedal in the down position, open the bleeder screw at least one full turn.

→ Do not pump the brake pedal at any time while having a bleeder screw open during the bleeding process. This will only increase the amount of air in the system and make additional bleeding necessary.

7. Once the brake pedal has dropped, close the bleeder screw. After the bleeder screw is closed, release the brake pedal.

8. Repeat the above steps until all trapped air is removed from that wheel circuit (usually 4–5 times).

9. Bleed the right front, right rear and left front wheel circuits in the same manner until all air is removed from the brake system. Monitor the fluid level in the master cylinder reservoir to make sure it does not go dry.

10. Check the brake pedal travel. If pedal travel is excessive or has not been improved, some air may still be trapped in the system. Repeat the bleed procedure as necessary.

11. Test drive the vehicle to verify the brakes are operating properly and pedal feel is correct.

Pressure Bleeding

⁑ WARNING

Use only Mopar® brake fluid or an equivalent from a fresh, tightly sealed container. Brake fluid must conform to DOT 3 specifications. Do not use petroleum-based fluid, as seal damage in the brake system will result.

⁑ WARNING

Before removing the master cylinder cap, wipe it clean to prevent dirt and other foreign matter from dropping into the master cylinder reservoir.

⁑ WARNING

Do not allow the master cylinder reservoir to run out of brake fluid while bleeding the system. An empty reservoir will allow additional air into the brake system. Check the fluid level frequently and add fluid as needed.

⁑ CAUTION

Brake fluid contains polyglycol ethers and polyglycols. Avoid contact with the eyes and wash your hands thoroughly after handling brake fluid. If you do get brake fluid in your eyes, flush your eyes with clean, running water for 15 minutes. If eye irritation persists, or if you have taken brake fluid internally, IMMEDIATELY seek medical assistance.

When bleeding the brake system, wear safety glasses. A clear bleed tube must be attached to the bleeder screws and submerged in a clear container filled part way with clean brake fluid. Direct the flow of brake fluid away from yourself and the painted surfaces of the vehicle. Brake fluid at high pressure may come out of the bleeder screws when opened.

➡ Do not pump the brake pedal at any time while having a bleeder screw open during the bleeding process. This will only increase the amount of air in the system and make additional bleeding necessary.

1. Before servicing the vehicle, refer to the Precautions Section.

2. Clean all dirt from around the master cylinder reservoir cap, and remove the filler cap.

3. Fill the brake master cylinder reservoir with clean, specified brake fluid.

➡ Master cylinder pressure bleeder adapter tools are available from various manufacturers of pressure bleeding equipment. Follow pressure bleeder manufacturer's instructions when installing the adapter.

4. Install the bleeder adapter in place of the filler cap on the master cylinder reservoir, and attach the bleeder tank hose to the fitting on the adapter.

➡ The following wheel circuit sequence for bleeding the brake hydraulic system should be used to ensure adequate removal of all trapped air from the hydraulic system: Left rear wheel, right front wheel, right rear wheel, left front wheel.

5. Attach a clear plastic hose to the left rear wheel bleeder screw and feed the hose into a clear jar containing enough fresh brake fluid to submerge the end of the hose.

6. Open the bleeder screw at least one full turn or more to obtain a steady stream of brake fluid.

7. After approximately 4–8 ounces of fluid have been bled through the brake circuit and an air-free flow is maintained in the clear plastic hose and jar, close the bleeder screw.

8. Repeat this procedure at all the remaining bleeder screws.

9. Check the brake pedal travel. If pedal travel is excessive or has not been

improved, some air may still be trapped in the system. Repeat the bleed procedure as necessary.

10. Test drive the vehicle to verify the brakes are operating properly and pedal feel is correct.

MASTER CYLINDER BLEEDING

See Figure 12.

1. Clamp the master cylinder in a vise with soft-jawed caps.

2. Attach the special tools for bleeding the master cylinder in the following fashion:

   a. Thread bleeder tube adapters (M12 X 1.0) into the primary and secondary outlet ports of the master cylinder. Tighten adapters to 150 inch lbs. (17 Nm).

   b. Thread a bleeder tube into each adapter. Tighten the tube nuts to 150 inch lbs. (17 Nm).

   c. Flex each bleeder tube and place the open ends into the neck of the master cylinder reservoir. Position the open ends of the tubes into the reservoir so their outlets are below the surface of the brake fluid in the reservoir when filled.

➡ Make sure the ends of the bleeder tubes stay below the surface of the brake fluid in the reservoir at all times during the bleeding procedure.

3. Fill the brake fluid reservoir with fresh DOT 3 brake fluid.

4. Using an appropriately-sized wooden dowel as a pushrod, slowly press the pistons inward discharging brake fluid through the bleeder tubes, then release the pressure, allowing the pistons to return to the released position. Repeat this several times until all air bubbles are expelled from the master cylinder bore and bleeder tubes.

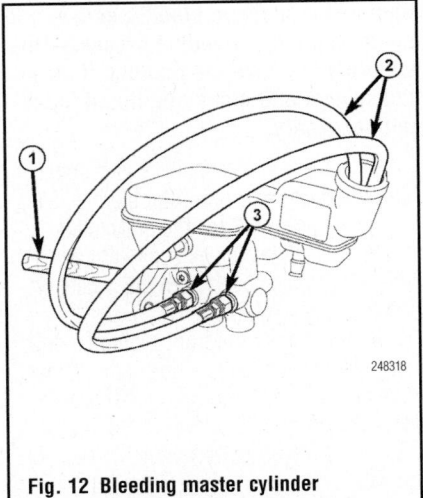

Fig. 12 Bleeding master cylinder

5. Remove the bleeder tubes and adapters from the master cylinder, and plug the master cylinder outlet ports.

6. Install the fill cap on the reservoir.

7. Remove the master cylinder from the vise.

8. Install the master cylinder on the vehicle. Refer to Master Cylinder, removal & installation.

BRAKE LINE BLEEDING

Refer to Bleeding Procedure, Manual Bleeding or Pressure Bleeding.

BLEEDING THE ABS SYSTEM

➡ The base brake's hydraulic system must be bled anytime air enters the hydraulic system. The ABS must always be bled anytime it is suspected that the HCU has ingested air.

➡ Brake systems with ABS must be bled as 2 independent braking systems. The non-ABS portion of the brake system with ABS is to be bled the same as any non-ABS system.

➡ The ABS portion of the brake system must be bled separately. Use the following procedure to properly bleed the brake hydraulic system, including the ABS.

➡ During the brake bleeding procedure, be sure the brake fluid level remains close to the FULL level in the master cylinder fluid reservoir. Check the fluid level periodically during the bleeding procedure and add Mopar® DOT 3 brake fluid as required.

➡ When bleeding the ABS system, the following bleeding sequence must be followed to ensure complete and adequate bleeding.

1. Make sure all hydraulic fluid lines are installed and properly tightened.

2. Connect the scan tool to the diagnostics connector. The diagnostic connector is located under the lower steering column cover to the left of the steering column.

3. Using the scan tool, check to make sure the ABM does not have any fault codes stored. If it does, clear them.

When bleeding the brake system, wear safety glasses. A clear bleed tube must be attached to the bleeder screws and submerged in a clear container filled part way with clean brake fluid. Direct the flow of brake fluid away from yourself and the painted

surfaces of the vehicle. Brake fluid at high pressure may come out of the bleeder screws when opened.

➡Pressure bleeding is recommended to bleed the base brake system to ensure all air is removed from the system. Manual bleeding may also be used, but additional time is needed to remove all the air from the system.

4. Bleed the base brake system. Refer to Bleeding Procedure.

5. Using the scan tool, select ECU VIEW, followed by ABS MISCELLANEOUS FUNCTIONS to access bleeding. Follow the instructions displayed. When finished, disconnect the scan tool and proceed.

6. Bleed the base brake system a second time. Check brake fluid level in the reservoir periodically to prevent emptying, causing air to enter the hydraulic system.

7. Fill the master cylinder fluid reservoir to the FULL level.

8. Test drive the vehicle to be sure the brakes are operating correctly and that the brake pedal does not feel spongy.

FLUID FILL PROCEDURE

➡Brake fluid level should be checked a minimum of twice a year.

✳✳ WARNING

Use only Mopar® brake fluid or an equivalent from a fresh, tightly

sealed container. Brake fluid must conform to DOT 3 specifications. Do not use petroleum-based fluid, as seal damage in the brake system will result.

Master cylinder reservoirs are marked (FULL and ADD), indicating the allowable brake fluid level range in the master cylinder fluid reservoir.

Although there is a range, the preferred level is FULL. As necessary, adjust the brake fluid level to the FULL mark listed on the side of the master cylinder fluid reservoir. Do not overfill the system.

BRAKES

REMOVAL & INSTALLATION

See Figures 13 through 18.

✳✳ WARNING

The vacuum in the power brake booster must be pumped down before removing the master cylinder to prevent the booster from sucking in any contamination. This can be done by pumping the brake pedal while the engine is not running until a firm brake pedal is achieved.

1. Before servicing the vehicle, refer to the Precautions Section.

2. With the engine not running, pump the brake pedal 4–5 strokes until the pedal feel is firm.

3. Disconnect the negative cable from the battery and isolate the cable.

4. Disconnect the wiring harness connector from the brake fluid level switch in the master cylinder brake fluid reservoir.

5. Disconnect the primary and secondary brake tubes at the master cylinder outlet ports. Install plugs at all of the open brake tube outlets on the master cylinder.

6. If equipped with a manual transaxle, remove the clamp and slide the clutch actuator hose off the reservoir port.

7. Clean the area around where the master cylinder attaches to the power brake booster using a suitable brake cleaner.

8. Remove the 2 nuts attaching the master cylinder to the power brake booster.

9. Slide the master cylinder straight out of the power brake booster.

To install:

➡The master cylinder must be bled before installing it on the vehicle.

MASTER CYLINDER

10. Bench bleed the master cylinder. Refer to Master Cylinder Bleeding procedure.

11. Wipe the face of the power brake booster clean where the vacuum seal on the rear of the master cylinder comes in contact when it's installed. Do not get any cleaner or debris inside the booster.

✳✳ WARNING

When installing a master cylinder on the vehicle, a NEW vacuum seal MUST be installed on the master cylinder mounting flange.

12. If the master cylinder does not have a new vacuum seal on the mounting flange, remove it. Install a NEW vacuum seal on the master cylinder mounting flange, making sure the seal fits squarely in its groove.

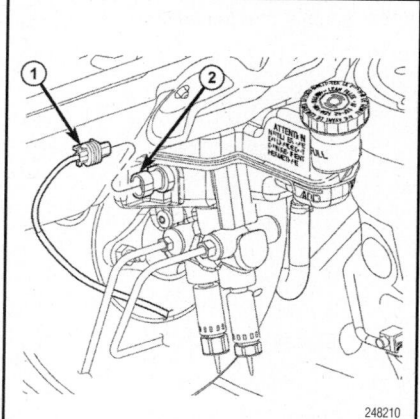

Fig. 13 Disconnect the wiring harness connector (1) from the brake fluid level switch in the master cylinder brake fluid reservoir

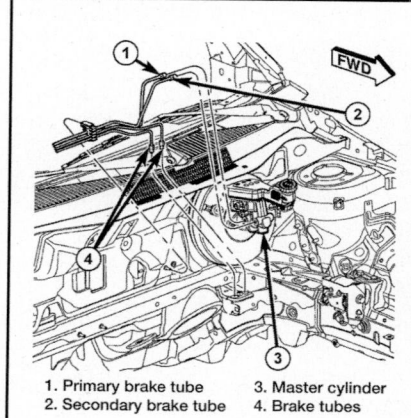

1. Primary brake tube   3. Master cylinder
2. Secondary brake tube 4. Brake tubes

Fig. 14 Locating brake tubes

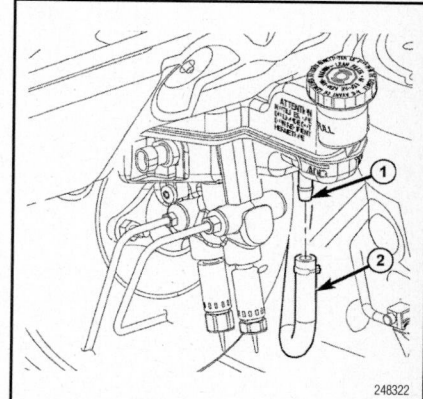

Fig. 15 Remove the clamp and slide the clutch actuator hose off the reservoir port (1)—manual transaxle

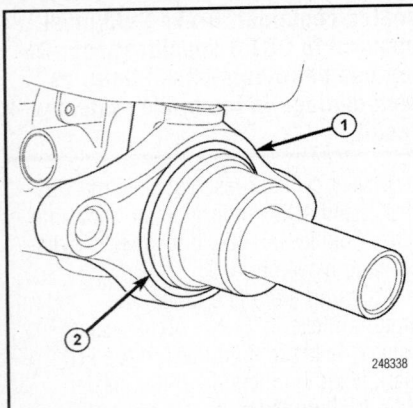

Fig. 16 A NEW vacuum seal MUST be installed on the master cylinder mounting flange (1)

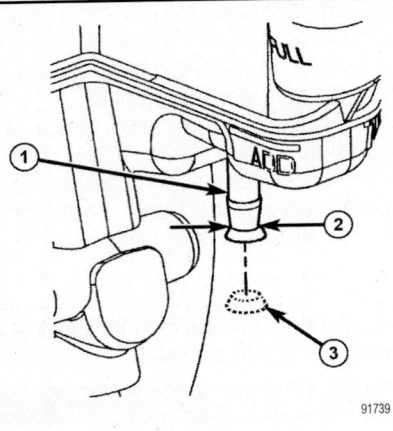

Fig. 17 cut the clutch actuator port at the center of the "V" groove opening the hydraulic clutch port (1). Discard the severed plug (3)—manual transaxle

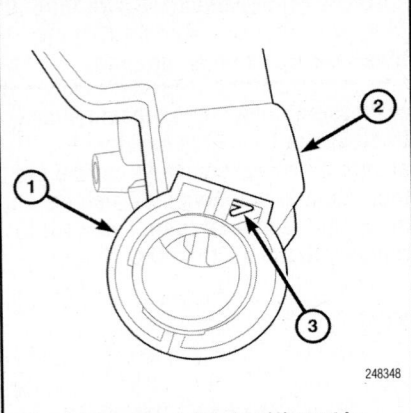

Fig. 18 A reservoir blocker (1) must be installed on the fluid reservoir. The blocker can be removed from the original reservoir by releasing the retaining tab (3) and opening the blocker

※※ WARNING

If resistance is met during master cylinder insertion into power brake booster, the master cylinder push rod may not be lined up with the booster push rod. Remove the master cylinder, realign and insert it again.

13. Line the master cylinder mounting holes up with the mounting studs on the power brake booster. Ensure the master cylinder piston push rod lines up with the booster push rod, then carefully slide the master cylinder into the power brake booster until it contacts the face of the booster.

14. Install two NEW master cylinder mounting nuts. Tighten each nut to 18 ft lbs. (25 Nm).

15. If equipped with a manual transaxle and a new reservoir is being installed, using an appropriate cutting tool, cut the clutch actuator port at the center of the "V" groove opening the hydraulic clutch port. Discard the severed plug.

16. If equipped with a manual transaxle, slide the clutch actuator hose onto the reservoir port. Install the hose clamp just past the upset bead on the port.

17. Connect the primary and secondary brake tubes to the master cylinder outlet ports. Tighten the tube nuts to 150 inch lbs. (17 Nm).

18. Connect the wiring harness connector to the brake fluid level switch.

※※ CAUTION

A reservoir blocker must be installed on the master cylinder brake fluid reservoir. Failure to install the reservoir blocker can result in fire in the event of an accident, resulting in serious or fatal injury.

19. If not present, a reservoir blocker must be installed on the fluid reservoir. The blocker can be removed from the original reservoir by releasing the retaining tab and opening the blocker. To install the blocker, encircle the reservoir neck with the blocker, close the blocker, snapping the retaining tab into place. Make sure the blocker is securely latched.

20. Connect the negative cable on the battery. Refer to Battery Reconnect/Relearn Procedure.

21. Fill the master cylinder reservoir to the proper level.

※※ CAUTION

Be certain a firm brake pedal is achieved prior to attempting to operate the vehicle. If a firm brake pedal cannot be achieved, bleed the brake hydraulic system and check for leaks. Refer to Bleeding Procedure.

22. Road test the vehicle to ensure proper operation of the brakes.

BRAKES

✳ CAUTION

Dust and dirt accumulating on brake parts during normal use may contain asbestos fibers from production or aftermarket brake linings. Breathing excessive concentrations of asbestos fibers can cause serious bodily harm. Exercise care when servicing brake parts. Do not sand or grind brake lining unless equipment used is designed to contain the dust residue. Do not clean brake parts with compressed air or by dry brushing. Cleaning should be done by dampening the brake components with a fine mist of water, then wiping the brake components clean with a dampened cloth. Dispose of cloth and all residue containing asbestos fibers in an impermeable container with the appropriate label. Follow practices prescribed by the Occupational Safety and Health Administration (OSHA) and the Environmental Protection Agency (EPA) for the handling, processing, and disposing of dust or debris that may contain asbestos fibers.

BRAKE CALIPER

PRECAUTIONS

✳ WARNING

Use only Mopar® Brake Fluid DOT 3 Motor Vehicle or equivalent from a tightly sealed container. Do not use petroleum-based fluid because seal damage in the brake system will result.

✳ WARNING

Brake fluid will damage painted surfaces. If brake fluid is spilled on any painted surfaces, wash it off immediately with water.

✳ WARNING

Never use gasoline, kerosene, alcohol, motor oil, Transaxle fluid, or any fluid containing mineral oil to clean system components. These fluids damage rubber cups and seals

✳ WARNING

During service procedures, grease or any other foreign material must be

kept off the caliper assembly, brake linings, brake rotor and external surfaces of the hub.

✳ WARNING

When handling the brake rotor and caliper, be careful to avoid damaging the brake rotor and caliper, and scratching or nicking the brake shoe lining.

✳ CAUTION

Chrysler LLC does not manufacture any vehicles or replacement parts that contain asbestos. Aftermarket products may or may not contain asbestos. Refer to aftermarket product packaging for product information. Whether the product contains asbestos or not, dust and dirt can accumulate on brake parts during normal use. Follow practices prescribed by appropriate regulations for the handling, processing and disposing of dust and debris.

REMOVAL & INSTALLATION
See Figures 19 and 20.

1. Before servicing the vehicle, refer to the Precautions Section.
2. Using a brake pedal holding tool, depress the brake pedal past its first one inch of travel and hold it in this position. This will isolate the master cylinder from the brake hydraulic system, and will not allow the brake fluid to drain out of the master cylinder reservoir when the lines are opened.
3. Raise and support the vehicle.
4. Remove the tire and wheel assembly.
5. Remove the banjo bolt connecting the brake hose to the brake caliper. There are 2 washers (one on each side of the flex hose fitting) that will come off with the banjo bolt. Discard the washers.

➡When removing the caliper guide pin bolts, note that one (upper) has a special sleeve on the end. It is important that this bolt be installed in the upper mounting hole when the caliper is installed.

6. Remove the 2 brake caliper guide pin bolts.
7. Slide the disc brake caliper off the disc brake adapter and pads.

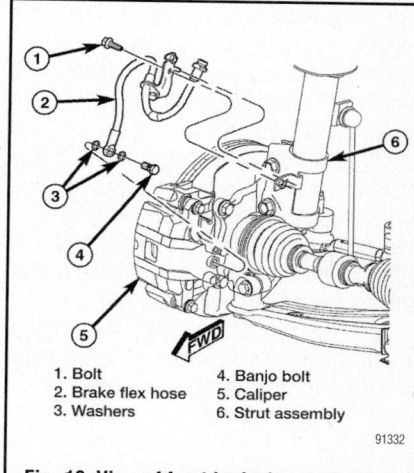

1. Bolt
2. Brake flex hose
3. Washers
4. Banjo bolt
5. Caliper
6. Strut assembly

91332

Fig. 19 View of front brake hose mounting

To install:

8. Completely retract the caliper piston back into the bore of the caliper. Use a C-clamp to retract the piston. Place a wood block over the piston before installing the C-clamp to avoid damaging the piston.

✳ WARNING

Use care when installing the caliper onto the adapter bracket to avoid damaging the guide pin boots.

9. Install the disc brake caliper over the brake pads on the brake caliper adapter bracket.

➡When installing the caliper guide pin bolts, make sure that the one that has

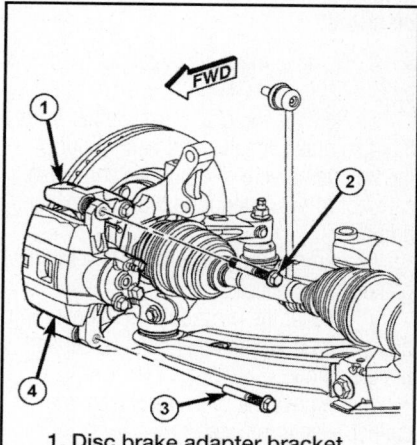

1. Disc brake adapter bracket
2. Brake caliper guide pin bolt
3. Brake caliper guide pin bolt
4. Disc brake caliper

57849

Fig. 20 Removing caliper guide pin bolts

a special sleeve on the end is installed in the upper mounting hole.

10. Align the caliper guide pin bolt holes with the adapter bracket. Install the upper (with special sleeve) and lower caliper guide pin bolts. Tighten the guide pin bolts to 32 ft. lbs. (43 Nm).

11. Install the banjo bolt connecting the brake flex hose to the brake caliper. Install NEW washers on each side of the hose fitting as the banjo bolt is guided through the fitting. Thread the banjo bolt into the caliper and tighten it to 18 ft. lbs. (24 Nm).

12. Install the tire and wheel assembly. Install and tighten the wheel mounting nuts to 100 ft. lbs. (135 Nm).

13. Lower the vehicle.

14. Remove the brake pedal holding tool.

15. Bleed the caliper as necessary. Refer to Bleeding Procedure.

16. Road test the vehicle and make several stops to wear off any foreign material on the brakes and to seat the brake shoes.

DISC BRAKE PADS

REMOVAL & INSTALLATION

See Figure 21.

1. Before servicing the vehicle, refer to the Precautions Section.
2. Raise and support the vehicle.
3. Remove the tire and wheel assembly.

➡When removing the caliper guide pin bolts, note that one (upper) has a special sleeve on the end. It is important that this bolt be installed in the upper mounting hole when the caliper is installed.

4. Remove the 2 brake caliper guide pin bolts.
5. Remove the disc brake caliper from the disc brake adapter, and hang it out of the way using wire or a bungee cord. Use care not to overextend the brake hose when doing this.
6. Remove the brake pads from the disc brake caliper adapter.
7. Repeat the procedure to remove brake pads from the other front wheel and tire assembly.
8. Remove the brake pads from the caliper adapter bracket.

To install:

➡Make sure that the audible wear indicators (if equipped) are placed toward the top when the inboard pads are installed on each side of the vehicle.

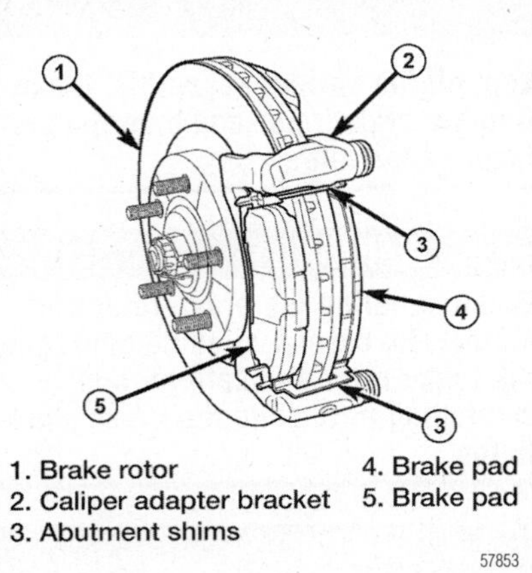
1
2
3
4
5
3
1. Brake rotor
2. Caliper adapter bracket
3. Abutment shims
4. Brake pad
5. Brake pad
57853

Fig. 21 View of front brake pads

9. Place the brake pads in the abutment shims clipped into the disc brake caliper adapter bracket as shown. Place the pad with the wear indicator attached on the inboard side.

10. Completely retract the caliper piston back into the bore of the caliper.

⁂ WARNING

Use care when installing the caliper onto the disc brake adapter bracket to avoid damaging the boots on the caliper guide pins.

11. Install the disc brake caliper over the brake pads on the brake caliper adapter.

➡When installing the caliper guide pin bolts, make sure that the one that has a special sleeve on the end is installed in the upper mounting hole.

12. Align the caliper guide pin bolt holes with the adapter bracket. Install the upper (with special sleeve) and lower caliper guide pin bolts. Tighten the guide pin bolts to 32 ft. lbs. (43 Nm).

13. Install tire and wheel assembly. Install and tighten the wheel mounting nuts to 100 ft. lbs. (135 Nm).

14. Repeat the procedure to install brake pads into other front wheel and tire assembly.

15. Lower the vehicle.

16. Pump the brake pedal several times before moving the vehicle to set the pads to the brake rotor.

17. Check and adjust the brake fluid level as necessary.

18. Road test the vehicle and make several stops to wear off any foreign material on the brakes and to seat the brake pads.

DISC BRAKE ROTOR

REMOVAL & INSTALLATION

See Figure 22.

1. Before servicing the vehicle, refer to the Precautions Section.
2. Raise and support the vehicle.
3. Remove the tire and wheel assembly.

➡In some cases, it may be necessary to retract the caliper piston in its bore a small amount in order to provide sufficient clearance between the pads and the rotor to easily remove the caliper from the knuckle. This can usually be accomplished before the guide pin bolts are removed, by grasping the inboard side of the caliper and pulling outward working with the guide pins, thus retracting the piston. Never push on the piston directly, as it may get damaged.

4. Remove the 2 bolts securing disc brake caliper and adapter bracket to the steering knuckle.
5. Remove the disc brake caliper and adapter bracket from the knuckle and rotor as an assembly. Hang the assembly out of the way using wire or a bungee cord. Use care not to overextend the brake hose when doing this.
6. Remove any clips retaining the brake rotor to the wheel studs.
7. Slide the brake rotor off the hub and bearing.

To install:

➡Inspect disc brake pads before installation.

8. Clean the hub face to remove any dirt or corrosion where the rotor mounts.

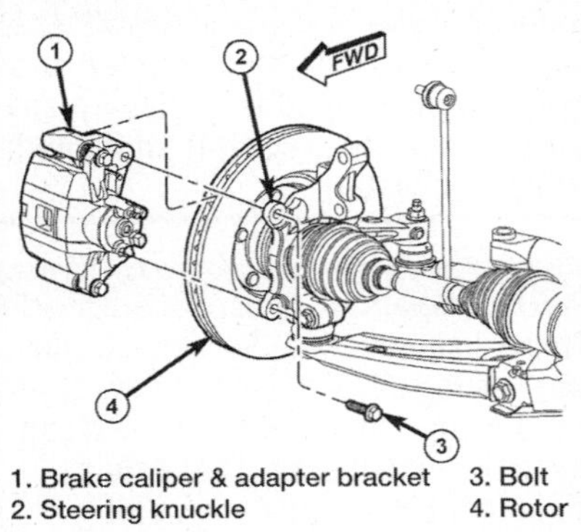
1
2
FWD
4
3
1. Brake caliper & adapter bracket
2. Steering knuckle
3. Bolt
4. Rotor
58089

Fig. 22 View of caliper and adapter mounting

9. Install the brake rotor over the studs on the hub and bearing.

10. Install the disc brake caliper and adapter bracket assembly over the brake rotor and knuckle.

11. Install the mounting bolts securing the caliper adapter bracket to the knuckle. Tighten the bolts to 80 ft. lbs. (108 Nm).

12. Install tire and wheel assembly. Install and tighten the wheel mounting nuts to 100 ft. lbs. (135 Nm).

13. Repeat the procedure to install brake pads into other front wheel and tire assembly.

14. Lower the vehicle.

15. Pump the brake pedal several times before moving the vehicle to set the pads to the brake rotor.

16. Check and adjust the brake fluid level as necessary.

17. Road test the vehicle and make several stops to wear off any foreign material on the brakes and to seat the brake pads.

BRAKES

❋❋ CAUTION

Dust and dirt accumulating on brake parts during normal use may contain asbestos fibers from production or aftermarket brake linings. Breathing excessive concentrations of asbestos fibers can cause serious bodily harm. Exercise care when servicing brake parts. Do not sand or grind brake lining unless equipment used is designed to contain the dust residue. Do not clean brake parts with compressed air or by dry brushing. Cleaning should be done by dampening the brake components with a fine mist of water, then wiping the brake components clean with a dampened cloth. Dispose of cloth and all residue containing asbestos fibers in an impermeable container with the appropriate label. Follow practices prescribed by the Occupational Safety and Health Administration (OSHA) and the Environmental Protection Agency (EPA) for the handling, processing, and disposing of dust or debris that may contain asbestos fibers.

BRAKE CALIPER

REMOVAL & INSTALLATION

See Figures 23 and 24.

1. Before servicing the vehicle, refer to the Precautions Section.

2. Using a brake pedal holding tool, depress the brake pedal past its first one inch of travel and hold it in this position. This will isolate the master cylinder from the brake hydraulic system and will not allow the brake fluid to drain out of the master cylinder reservoir when the lines are opened.

3. Raise and support the vehicle.

4. Remove the tire and wheel assembly.

5. Unthread the brake tube nut at the rear flex hose.

6. Remove the clip securing the rear flex hose to the trailing link mounted

bracket. Remove the flex hose from the bracket.

7. Unthread and remove the brake flex hose from the brake caliper.

➡**When removing the caliper guide pin bolts, note that one bolt has a special sleeve on the tip and the other does not. Depending on the build date (vehicle built before or after 7/27/06), this special sleeve bolt can be located in either the top or bottom location. When installing, make sure the bolts are put back in the same locations as when removed to avoid NVH issues.**

8. Remove the 2 brake caliper guide pin bolts.

9. Slide and remove the disc brake caliper with outboard brake pad attached from the disc brake adapter bracket, inboard brake pad and rotor.

10. Remove the outboard brake pad from the caliper by prying the brake pad retaining clip over the raised area on the caliper. Slide the brake pad off of the brake caliper.

To install:

11. If not already performed, completely retract the caliper piston back into the piston bore of the caliper. Use a C-clamp to retract the piston. Place a wood block over

REAR DISC BRAKES

the piston before installing the C-clamp to avoid damaging the piston.

12. Slide the outboard brake pad onto the caliper. Be sure the retaining clip is squarely seated in the depressed areas on the caliper beyond the raised retaining bead.

❋❋ WARNING

Use care when installing the caliper onto the disc brake adapter to avoid damaging the guide pin boots.

13. Install the disc brake caliper with outboard brake pad attached over the inboard brake pad and rotor, onto the brake caliper adapter bracket.

➡**When removing the caliper guide pin bolts, note that one bolt has a special sleeve on the tip and the other does not. Depending on the build date (vehicle built before or after 7/27/06), this special sleeve bolt can be located in either the top or bottom location. When installing, make sure the bolts are put back in the same locations as when removed to avoid NVH issues.**

14. Align the caliper guide pin bolt holes with the adapter bracket. Install the lower and upper (with special sleeve) caliper guide pin bolts. Tighten the guide pin bolts to 32 ft. lbs. (43 Nm).

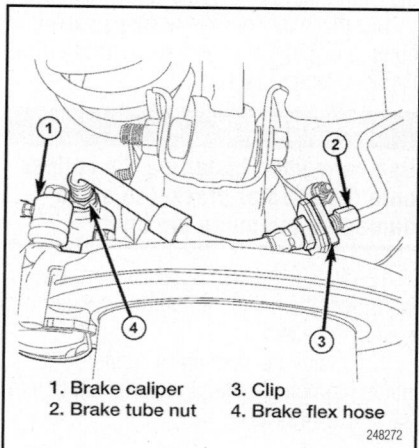

1. Brake caliper　　3. Clip
2. Brake tube nut　　4. Brake flex hose

248272

Fig. 23 Removing rear brake caliper

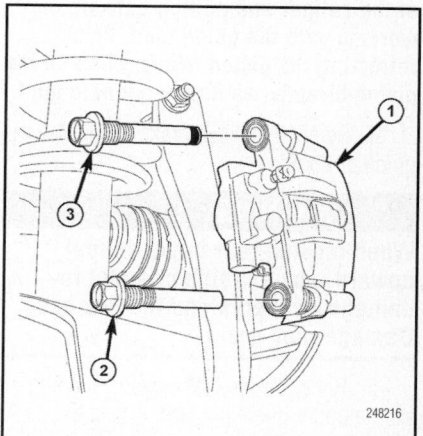

248216

Fig. 24 Remove the 2 brake caliper guide pin bolts (2, 3) and brake caliper (1)

15. Thread the rear brake flex hose into the brake caliper. Tighten the flex hose fitting at the caliper to 133 inch lbs. (15 Nm).

16. Route and install the brake flex hose into the trailing link mounted bracket. Install the clip securing the flex hose to the bracket.

17. Thread the brake tube nut into the brake flex hose. Tighten the brake tube nut to 150 inch lbs. (17 Nm).

18. Install the tire and wheel assembly. Install and tighten the wheel mounting nuts to 100 ft. lbs. (135 Nm).

19. Lower the vehicle.

20. Remove the brake pedal holding tool.

21. Bleed the caliper as necessary. Refer to Bleeding Procedure.

22. Road test the vehicle and make several stops to wear off any foreign material on the brakes and to seat the brake shoes.

DISC BRAKE PADS

REMOVAL & INSTALLATION

See Figures 25 and 26.

➡If the rear brake pads are being replaced due to a howl or moan while driving in reverse, proper diagnosis and correction is essential.

1. Before servicing the vehicle, refer to the Precautions Section.

2. Raise and support the vehicle.

3. Remove the tire and wheel assembly.

➡In some cases, it may be necessary to retract the caliper piston in its bore a small amount in order to provide sufficient clearance between the pads and the rotor to easily remove the caliper from the knuckle. This can usually be accomplished before the guide pin bolts are removed by grasping the rear of the caliper and pulling outward working with the guide pins, thus retracting the piston. Never push on the piston directly, as it may get damaged.

4. Remove the disc brake caliper lower guide pin bolt.

※※ WARNING

When moving rear brake caliper upward, use extreme care not to damage or overextend the flex hose. Damage may occur.

5. Rotate the caliper upward, hinging off the upper guide pin bolt. Rotate the caliper upward just enough to allow brake pad removal. Hang the caliper assembly in this position using wire or a bungee cord.

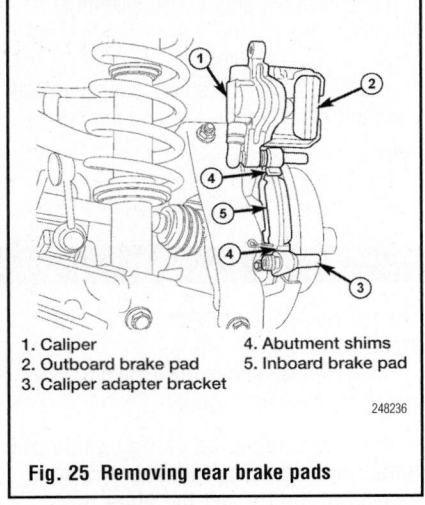

1. Caliper
2. Outboard brake pad
3. Caliper adapter bracket
4. Abutment shims
5. Inboard brake pad

248236

Fig. 25 Removing rear brake pads

6. Remove the inboard brake pad from the caliper adapter bracket.

7. Remove the outboard brake pad from the caliper by prying the brake pad retaining clip over the raised area on the caliper. Slide the brake pad off of the brake caliper.

8. Repeat the procedure to remove brake pads from the other front wheel and tire assembly.

To install:

9. Completely retract the caliper piston back into the piston bore of the caliper. This is required to gain the necessary pad-to-rotor clearance for the caliper installation onto the steering knuckle.

➡Place the brake pad with the audible wear indicator attached on the inboard side. The audible wear indicator should be positioned at the bottom when installed.

10. Slide the outboard brake pad onto the caliper. Be sure the retaining clip is squarely seated in the depressed areas on the caliper beyond the raised retaining bead.

11. Place the inboard brake pad in the abutment shims clipped into the disc brake caliper adapter bracket.

※※ CAUTION

Use care when installing the caliper onto the adapter bracket to avoid damaging the guide pin boot.

12. Rotate the disc brake caliper downward over the brake rotor and lower part of caliper adapter.

13. Install the disc brake caliper lower guide pin bolt. Tighten the guide pin bolt to 32 ft. lbs. (43 Nm).

➡Once the caliper is installed, inspect the outboard brake pad to make sure it

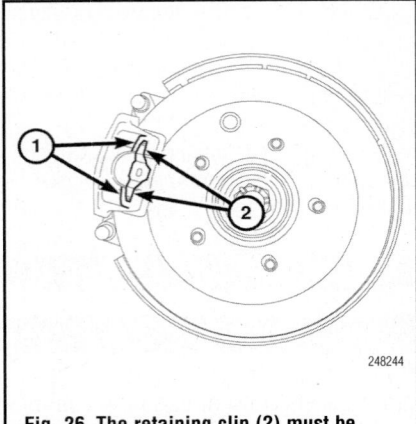

248244

Fig. 26 The retaining clip (2) must be squarely seated in the depressed areas (1) on the caliper fingers

is correctly positioned. The retaining clip must be squarely seated in the depressed areas on the caliper fingers. Also, the nubs on the pad's steel backing plate must be fully seated in the depressions formed into the inside of the caliper fingers. There should be no gap between the pad backing plate and the caliper fingers.

14. Install the tire and wheel assembly. Install and tighten the wheel mounting nuts to 100 ft. lbs. (135 Nm).

15. Lower the vehicle.

16. Pump the brake pedal several times to ensure the vehicle has a firm brake pedal before moving the vehicle.

17. Road test the vehicle and make several stops to wear off any foreign material on the brakes and to seat the brake pads.

DISC BRAKE ROTOR

REMOVAL & INSTALLATION

1. Before servicing the vehicle, refer to the Precautions Section.

2. Raise and support the vehicle.

3. Remove the tire and wheel assembly.

➡In some cases, it may be necessary to retract the caliper piston in its bore a small amount in order to provide sufficient clearance between the pads and the rotor to easily remove the caliper from the knuckle. This can usually be accomplished before the guide pin bolts are removed by grasping the inboard side of the caliper and pulling outward working with the guide pins, thus retracting the piston. Never push on the piston directly, as it may get damaged.

4. Remove the disc brake caliper lower guide pin bolt.

✳✳ WARNING

When moving rear brake caliper upward, use extreme care not to damage or overextend the flex hose. Damage may occur.

5. Rotate the caliper upward hinging off the upper guide pin bolt. Rotate the caliper upward just enough to allow brake rotor removal. Hang the caliper assembly in this position using wire or a bungee cord.

6. Remove any clips retaining the brake rotor to the wheel studs.

7. Slide the brake rotor off the hub and bearing and remove.

To install:

➡Inspect disc brake pads and parking brake shoes before installation.

8. Clean the hub face to remove any dirt or corrosion where the rotor mounts.

9. Install the brake rotor over the studs on the hub and bearing.

✳✳ WARNING

Use care when installing the caliper onto the adapter bracket to avoid damaging the guide pin boot.

10. Rotate the disc brake caliper downward over the brake rotor and lower part of caliper adapter.

11. Install the disc brake caliper lower guide pin bolt. Tighten the guide pin bolt to 32 ft. lbs. (43 Nm).

➡Once the caliper is installed, inspect the outboard brake pad to make sure it is correctly positioned. The retaining

clip must be squarely seated in the depressed areas on the caliper fingers. Also, the nubs on the pad's steel backing plate must be fully seated in the depressions formed into the inside of the caliper fingers. There should be no gap between the pad backing plate and the caliper fingers.

12. Install the tire and wheel assembly. Install and tighten the wheel mounting nuts to 100 ft. lbs. (135 Nm).

13. Lower the vehicle.

14. Pump the brake pedal several times before moving the vehicle to set the pads to the brake rotor.

15. Check and adjust the brake fluid level in the reservoir as necessary.

16. Road test the vehicle and make several stops to seat the brake pads to the rotor.

BRAKES

✳✳ CAUTION

Dust and dirt accumulating on brake parts during normal use may contain asbestos fibers from production or aftermarket brake linings. Breathing excessive concentrations of asbestos fibers can cause serious bodily harm. Exercise care when servicing brake parts. Do not sand or grind brake lining unless equipment used is designed to contain the dust residue. Do not clean brake parts with compressed air or by dry brushing. Cleaning should be done by dampening the brake components with a fine mist of water, then wiping the brake components clean with a dampened cloth. Dispose of cloth and all residue containing asbestos fibers in an impermeable container with the appropriate label. Follow practices prescribed by the Occupational Safety and Health Administration (OSHA) and the Environmental Protection Agency (EPA) for the handling, processing, and disposing of dust or debris that may contain asbestos fibers.

REMOVAL & INSTALLATION

1. Before servicing the vehicle, refer to the Precautions Section.

2. Using a brake pedal holding tool, depress the brake pedal past its first one inch of travel and hold it in this position.

This will isolate the master cylinder from the brake hydraulic system and will not allow the brake fluid to drain out of the master cylinder reservoir when the lines are opened.

3. Raise and support the vehicle.

4. Remove the tire and wheel assembly.

5. Slide the brake drum off the wheel mounting studs of the hub and bearing, and remove it from the vehicle. If the drum does not come off, further brake clearance can be obtained by backing off the brake adjuster screw. To do so, refer to Backing Off Shoe Adjustment procedure.

To install:

➡Before installing drum, inspect brake shoe linings for wear, alignment, and contamination. Repair or replace as necessary.

➡If rust or any foreign material is present on hub, drum or wheel mating surfaces, wet wire brush these areas to remove prior to assembly of parts.

6. Properly remove any buildup formed along outer edge of drum's machined braking surface.

7. Adjust the brake shoes-to-drum diameter using a brake shoe gauge. Refer to Brake Shoes, adjustment procedure.

8. Slide the brake drum onto the wheel mounting studs on the hub and bearing.

9. Install the tire and wheel assembly. Install and tighten the wheel mounting nuts to 100 ft. lbs. (135 Nm).

10. Lower the vehicle.

REAR DRUM BRAKES

11. Road test the vehicle, stopping in both forward and reverse directions. The automatic-adjuster will continue to adjust the brakes as necessary during the road test.

BACKING OFF SHOE ADJUSTMENT
See Figure 27.

1. Remove the plug from the rear of the support plate below the wheel cylinder.

2. Insert a small screwdriver through the access hole in the support plate, under the adjuster, against the lever pawl. The pawl is attached to and pivots from the rear brake shoe.

3. While pushing on the pawl with the screwdriver to disengage it from the

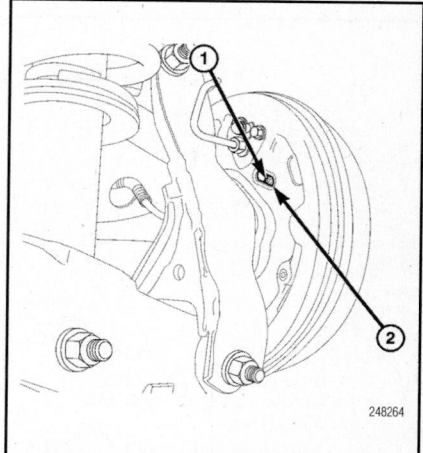

Fig. 27 Locating adjuster wheel (1) through access hole (2)

248264

adjuster wheel teeth, rotate the wheel upward to back off the adjustment using another screwdriver or a brake adjuster tool.

4. Once the adjuster screw is backed off a sufficient amount, slide the drum off the wheel mounting studs.

BRAKE SHOES

REMOVAL & INSTALLATION

See Figures 28 through 30.

1. Before servicing the vehicle, refer to the Precautions Section.

2. Verify the parking brake lever is in the released (down) position.

3. Raise and support the vehicle.

4. Remove the tire and wheel assembly.

5. Remove the brake drum. Refer to Brake Drum, removal & installation.

6. Remove the lower shoe spring.

7. Compress and remove the hold-down spring retaining the rear shoe to the support plate.

8. Pull the rear shoe away from the anchor, allowing better access to the parking brake cable connection at the lever.

9. Compress the cable return spring, then remove the parking brake cable from the parking brake lever.

10. Compress and remove the hold-down spring retaining the front shoe to the support plate.

11. Remove both brake shoes from the wheel cylinder.

12. Remove both shoes and remaining parts as an assembly through the opening between the wheel cylinder and support plate hub and bearing.

13. Place the shoe assembly outboard-side-up on a flat surface.

14. Remove the adjuster spring from the leading shoe and the lever pawl.

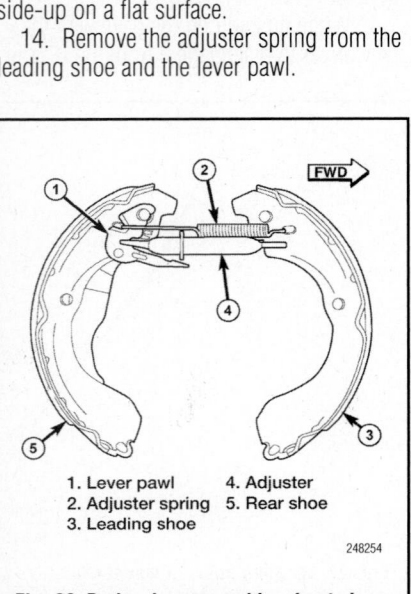

1. Lever pawl   4. Adjuster
2. Adjuster spring   5. Rear shoe
3. Leading shoe

248254

Fig. 28 Brake shoe assembly—front view

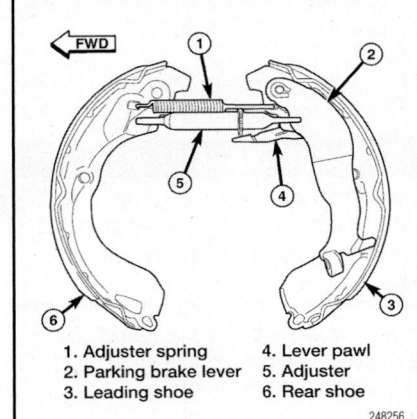

1. Adjuster spring   4. Lever pawl
2. Parking brake lever   5. Adjuster
3. Leading shoe   6. Rear shoe

248256

Fig. 29 Brake shoe assembly—rear view

15. Remove the lever pawl from the pivot on the rear shoe.

16. Flip the shoe assembly over to show the inboard side.

17. Remove the upper shoe adjuster spring.

18. Remove the adjuster from the shoes and parking brake lever.

To install:

19. Lubricate the indicated shoe contact areas on the support plate and anchor using brake lubricant.

20. Lubricate the adjuster screw threads with brake lubricant. Turn adjuster wheel in until it is completely seated.

21. Place one front shoe and one rear shoe inboard-side-up on a flat surface (rear shoe has parking brake lever attached to it).

22. Install the adjuster, adjuster wheel toward the rear, between the 2 brake shoes. Make sure the wide notch in the rear fork aligns with the parking brake lever.

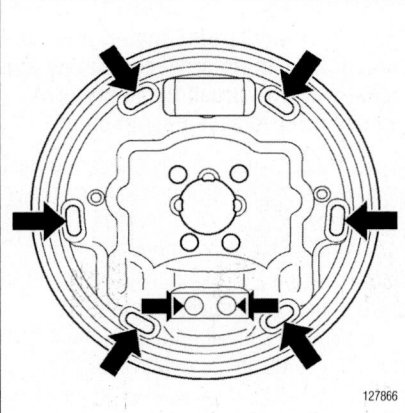

127866

Fig. 30 Lubricate the indicated shoe contact areas on the support plate and anchor

23. Install the upper return spring as shown.

24. Flip the shoe assembly over to show the outboard side.

25. Install the lever pawl onto the pivot located on the rear shoe.

26. Install the adjuster spring between the front shoe and the lever pawl.

27. Install the pre-assembled brake shoe assembly through the opening between the wheel cylinder and support plate hub and bearing.

28. Insert the upper tips of the brake shoes into the grooves of the wheel cylinder pistons.

29. Position the bottom of the front shoe against the anchor pin.

30. Install a shoe hold-down pin from the rear, through the support plate and the front shoe.

31. Compress and install the hold-down spring retaining the front shoe to the support plate.

32. Compress the parking brake cable return spring, then carefully install the cable onto the parking brake lever. Release the spring guiding it beneath the retaining tab on the lever.

33. Position the bottom of the rear shoe against the anchor pin.

34. Install a shoe hold-down pin from the rear, through the support plate and the rear shoe.

35. Compress and install the hold-down spring retaining the rear shoe to the support plate.

36. Install the lower shoe spring.

37. Adjust the brake shoes to the drum diameter using a brake shoe gauge. Refer to Adjustment procedure.

38. Install the brake drum. Refer to Brake Drum, removal & installation.

39. Install the tire and wheel assembly. Install and tighten the wheel mounting nuts to 100 ft. lbs. (135 Nm).

40. Slowly rotate both rear wheels and verify that the brake drums lightly drag on the shoes. Further adjustments may be done using the adjustment procedure as necessary. Refer to Adjustment procedure.

41. Lower the vehicle.

42. Road test vehicle, stopping in both forward and reverse directions. The automatic-adjuster will continue to adjust brakes as necessary during road test.

ADJUSTMENT

See Figures 31 through 33.

1. Before servicing the vehicle, refer to the Precautions Section.

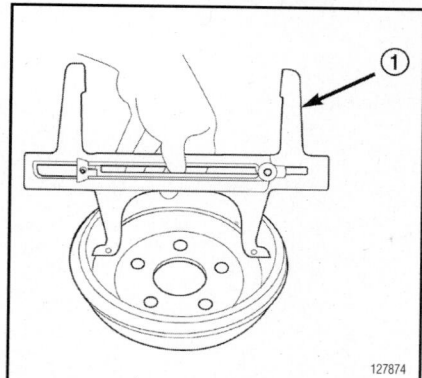

Fig. 31 Using a brake shoe gauge (1), measure the inside diameter of the brake drum at the center of the shoe contact area

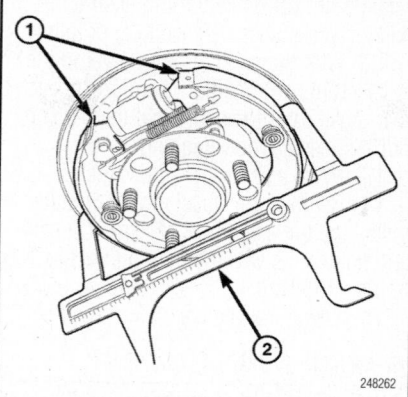
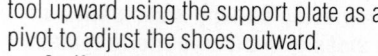

Fig. 32 Place the opposite side of the brake shoe gauge (2) over the brake shoes (1) as shown

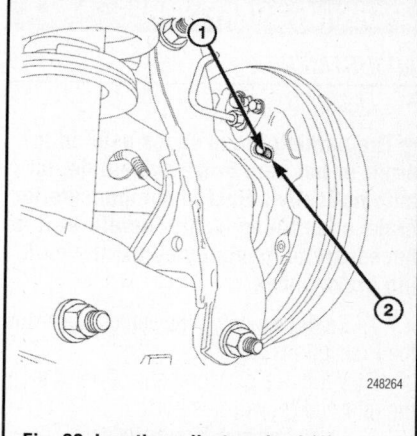

Fig. 33 Locating adjuster wheel (1) through access hole (2)

2. Verify the parking brake lever is in the released (down) position.
3. Raise and support the vehicle.
4. Remove the tire and wheel assembly.
5. Remove the brake drum. Refer to Brake Drum, removal & installation.
6. Using a brake shoe gauge, measure the inside diameter of the brake drum at the center of the shoe contact area. Tighten the gauge setscrew at this measurement.
7. Place the opposite side of the brake shoe gauge over the brake shoes as shown.
8. Adjust the shoe diameter to the setting on the gauge. To adjust the shoe diameter, turn the adjuster wheel using a screwdriver inserted through the adjusting hole in the rear of the shoe support plate. Once the tip of the screwdriver contacts the adjuster wheel teeth, move the handle of

tool upward using the support plate as a pivot to adjust the shoes outward.
9. If at any time the adjustment needs to be backed off, perform the following:
   a. Remove the plug from the rear of the support plate below the wheel cylinder.
   b. Insert a small screwdriver through the access hole in the support plate, under the adjuster, against the lever pawl. The pawl is attached to and pivots from the rear brake shoe.
   c. While pushing on the pawl with the screwdriver to disengage it from the adjuster wheel teeth, rotate the wheel upward to back off the adjustment using another screwdriver or a brake adjuster tool.
10. Once the shoe diameter is set,

remove the tool and install the brake drum. Refer to Brake Drum, removal & installation.
11. Turn the brake drum. A slight drag should be felt while rotating the drum. If not, repeat the above procedure.
12. Install the tire and wheel assembly. Install and tighten the wheel mounting nuts to 100 ft. lbs. (135 Nm).
13. After adjusting both rear drum brakes as necessary, lower the vehicle.
14. Apply and release the parking brake lever one time after the adjustment process is completed, checking parking brake operation.
15. Road test the vehicle, stopping in both forward and reverse directions. The automatic-adjuster will continue to adjust the brakes as necessary during the road test.

BRAKES **PARKING BRAKE**

PARKING BRAKE CABLES

ADJUSTMENT

See Figure 34.

1. Ensure that the parking brake cables are correctly installed on the equalizer and aligned with the cable track on the parking brake lever.

➡**Actuating the parking brake lever to its fully applied position one time after tightening the adjustment nut will yield (stretch) the bent nail portion of the equalizer approximately 1/4 inch. This process will correctly set the parking brake cable tension.**

2. Adjust parking brake cable tension using the following steps:
   a. Place the parking brake lever in the fully released (down) position.

   b. Tighten the adjusting nut on the parking brake lever output cable until 31 millimeters of thread is out past the end of the adjustment nut.
   c. Actuate the parking brake lever to its fully applied position one time, then reposition it to its fully released (down) position.
3. Raise the vehicle to a point where the rear wheels just clear the floor.
4. Check the rear wheels of the vehicle; they should rotate freely without dragging.
5. Apply the parking brake. Check the rear wheels of the vehicle. They should not rotate.
6. Return the parking brake lever to its fully released (down) position and check the rear wheels. They should rotate freely without dragging.
7. Apply the parking brake.
8. Lower the vehicle.

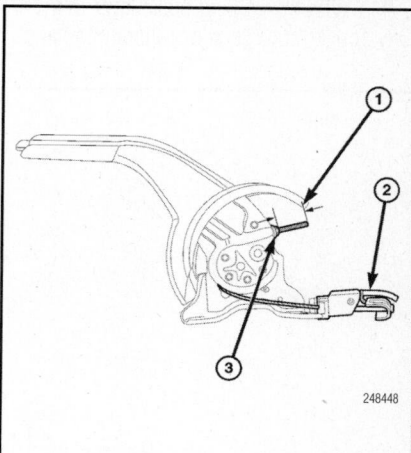

Fig. 34 Tighten the adjusting nut (3) on the parking brake lever (2) output cable until 31 millimeters of thread is out past the end of the adjustment nut (1)

PARKING BRAKE SHOES

ADJUSTMENT

See Figure 35.

➡The parking brake shoes used in the drum-in-hat park brake system do not automatically adjust to compensate for brake shoe lining wear. Therefore, it is necessary to manually adjust the parking brake shoes.

1. Before servicing the vehicle, refer to the Precautions Section.
2. Verify the parking brake lever is in the released (down) position.
3. Raise and support the vehicle.
4. Remove the tire and wheel assembly.
5. Install a couple of wheel mounting nuts to hold the brake rotor in place while adjustment of the brake shoes is made.

➡To find the adjuster wheel with the drum on, position the hole in the front of the rotor drum as follows: Left side at 7 o'clock, right side at 5 o'clock.

➡When adjusting the parking brake shoes with the drum-in hat rotor installed, rotating the adjuster wheel upward will loosen the adjustment. Rotating the adjuster wheel downward will tighten the adjustment.

6. Remove the rubber plug from the hole in the front of the rotor.
7. Utilizing the hole in the front of the rotor, make a fine adjustment of the shoes.
8. Reinstall the rubber plug.
9. Lower the vehicle far enough to access the interior of the vehicle.
10. Reach inside the vehicle and cycle (fully apply and release) the park brakes.
11. With the parking brake lever in the fully applied (up) position, attempt to hand

rotate each rear brake rotor to ensure that the parking brake shoes are working properly.

12. With the parking brake lever in the released (down) position, hand rotate each rear brake rotor to ensure that the parking brake shoes are not dragging.
13. Raise and support the vehicle.
14. Remove the wheel mounting nuts. Install the tire and wheel assembly. Install and tighten the wheel mounting nuts to 100 ft. lbs. (135 Nm).
15. Lower the vehicle.

REMOVAL & INSTALLATION

See Figures 35 through 40.

1. Before servicing the vehicle, refer to the Precautions Section.
2. Raise and support the vehicle.

➡If removing parking brake shoes on both sides of vehicle, perform remaining steps on each side of the vehicle.

3. Access and remove the rear brake rotor. Refer to appropriate Disc Brake Rotor, removal & installation.
4. Turn the brake shoe adjuster wheel until the adjuster is at shortest length.
5. Remove the upper return spring from the anchor pin and the rear brake shoe.
6. Remove the upper return spring from the anchor pin and the front brake shoe.
7. Remove the brake shoe hold-down springs and pins. Rotate the pins 90° to disengage.
8. Remove the parking brake cable from the lever on the rear parking brake shoe.
9. Remove the brake shoes, adjuster and lower return spring as an assembly from the support plate.
10. If necessary, remove the strut.
11. Remove the lower return spring and adjuster from the shoes.

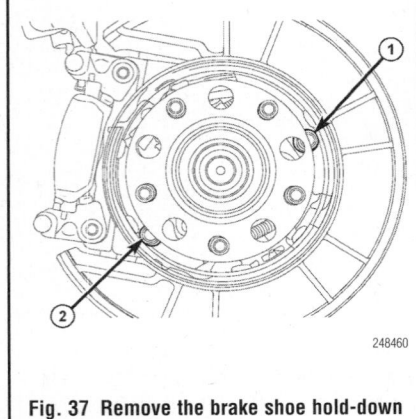

Fig. 37 Remove the brake shoe hold-down springs and pins (1, 2)

➡If removing parking brake shoes on both sides of the vehicle, repeat procedure on other side of the vehicle.

To install:

➡If installing parking brake shoes on both sides of the vehicle, repeat procedure on other side of the vehicle.

➡Left side shoes are shown in the figure. Right side shoes are a mirror image of the left except for the adjuster. The threaded portion of the adjuster should always be positioned to the left side in order to maintain consistent side-to-side rotational direction for adjustment purposes.

12. Install the lower return spring and adjuster between the parking brake shoes. The rear shoe will have the lever mounted on the inside. Make sure the threaded portion of the adjuster is mounted to the left on both right and left side parking brake assemblies.

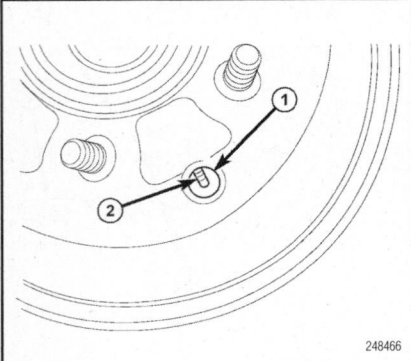

Fig. 35 To find the adjuster wheel with the drum on, position the hole (1) in the front of the rotor drum as follows: Left side at 7 o'clock, right side at 5 o'clock

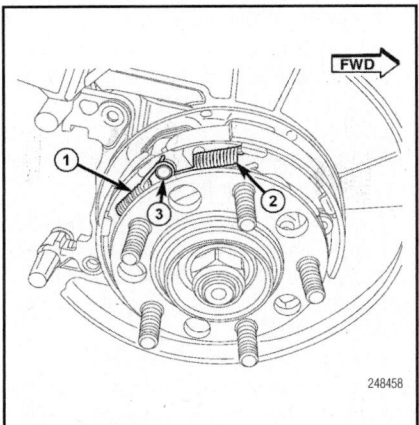

Fig. 36 Remove the return springs (1, 2) from the anchor pin (3) and the brake shoe

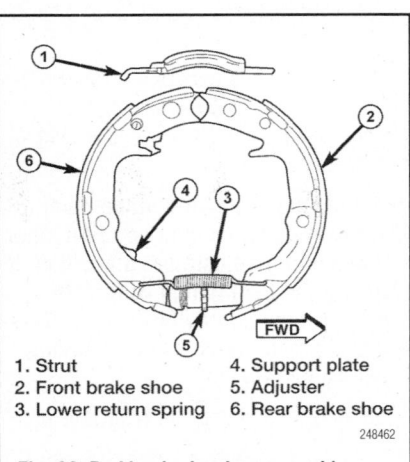

1. Strut
2. Front brake shoe
3. Lower return spring
4. Support plate
5. Adjuster
6. Rear brake shoe

Fig. 38 Parking brake shoe assembly—exploded view

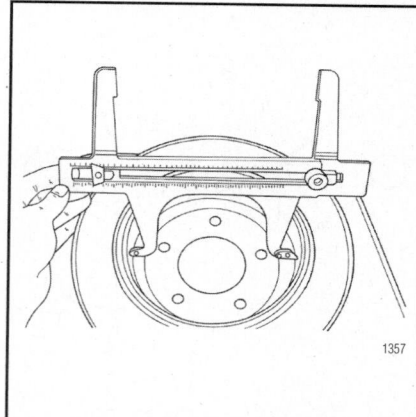

Fig. 39 Using Brake Shoe Gauge, measure the inside diameter of parking brake drum portion of rotor

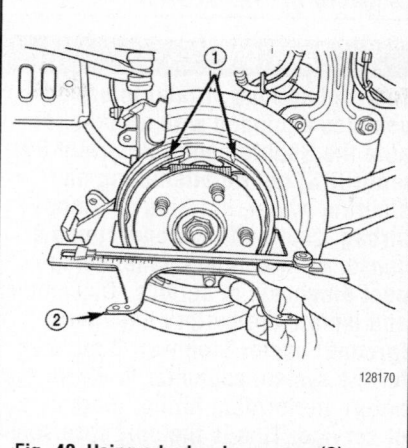

Fig. 40 Using a brake shoe gauge (2), adjust the parking brake shoes (1)

13. If necessary, place the strut above the hub and bearing on the vehicle. Note the curved end of the strut is positioned to the rear.

14. Install the assembled brake shoes, adjuster and lower return spring over the hub and bearing and onto the support plate and anchor. Be sure to install the strut between the front shoe and the lever on the rear shoe.

15. Install the parking brake cable onto the lever on the parking brake shoe.

16. Install the brake shoe hold-down springs and pins. Rotate the pins 90° to engage.

17. Install the front upper return spring holding the front brake shoe and anchor pin.

18. Install the rear upper return spring holding the rear brake shoe and anchor pin.

19. Using a brake shoe gauge, measure the inside diameter of parking brake drum portion of rotor. Set the gauge.

20. Place gauge over the parking brake shoes at their widest point.

21. Using the adjuster wheel, adjust the parking brake shoes until the linings on both parking brake shoes just touch the jaws on the gauge.

22. Install the rear brake rotor, then install a couple wheel mounting nuts to hold it in place while a final adjustment is made.

➡To find the adjuster wheel with the drum on, position the hole in the front of the rotor drum as follows: Left side at 7 o'clock, right side at 5 o'clock.

➡When adjusting the parking brake shoes with the drum-in hat rotor installed, rotating the adjuster wheel upward will loosen the adjustment. Rotating the adjuster wheel downward will tighten the adjustment.

23. Remove the rubber plug from the hole in the front of the rotor.

24. Utilizing the hole in the front of the rotor, make a final adjustment of the shoes if necessary.

25. Reinstall the rubber plug.

26. Remove the wheel mounting nuts and finish installing the brake rotor, as well as all components removed to access it. Refer to appropriate Brake Rotor, removal & installation.

27. Lower the vehicle.

28. Cycle the parking brake lever once, verifying proper operation of the parking brake.

CHASSIS ELECTRICAL

AIR BAG (SUPPLEMENTAL RESTRAINT SYSTEM)

GENERAL INFORMATION

✳✳ CAUTION

These vehicles are equipped with an air bag system. The system must be disarmed before performing service on, or around, system components, the steering column, instrument panel components, wiring and sensors. Failure to follow the safety precautions and the disarming procedure could result in accidental air bag deployment, possible injury and unnecessary system repairs.

SERVICE PRECAUTIONS

Disconnect and isolate the battery negative cable before beginning any airbag system component diagnosis, testing, removal, or installation procedures. Allow system capacitor to discharge for two minutes before beginning any component service. This will disable the airbag system. Failure to disable the airbag system may result in accidental airbag deployment, personal injury, or death.

Do not place an intact undeployed airbag face down on a solid surface. The airbag will propel into the air if accidentally deployed and may result in personal injury or death.

When carrying or handling an undeployed airbag, the trim side (face) of the airbag should be pointing towards the body to minimize possibility of injury if accidental deployment occurs. Failure to do this may result in personal injury or death.

Replace airbag system components with OEM replacement parts. Substitute parts may appear interchangeable, but internal differences may result in inferior occupant protection. Failure to do so may result in occupant personal injury or death.

Wear safety glasses, rubber gloves, and long sleeved clothing when cleaning powder residue from vehicle after an airbag deployment. Powder residue emitted from a deployed airbag can cause skin irritation.

Flush affected area with cool water if irritation is experienced. If nasal or throat irritation is experienced, exit the vehicle for fresh air until the irritation ceases. If irritation continues, see a physician.

Do not use a replacement airbag that is not in the original packaging. This may result in improper deployment, personal injury, or death.

The factory installed fasteners, screws and bolts used to fasten airbag components have a special coating and are specifically designed for the airbag system. Do not use substitute fasteners. Use only original equipment fasteners listed in the parts catalog when fastener replacement is required.

During, and following, any child restraint anchor service, due to impact event or vehicle repair, carefully inspect all mounting hardware, tether straps, and anchors for proper installation, operation, or damage. If a child restraint anchor is found damaged in any way, the anchor must be replaced. Failure to do this may result in personal injury or death.

Deployed and non-deployed airbags may or may not have live pyrotechnic material within the airbag inflator.

Do not dispose of driver/passenger/curtain airbags or seat belt tensioners unless you are sure of complete deployment. Refer to the Hazardous Substance Control System for proper disposal.

Dispose of deployed airbags and tensioners consistent with state, provincial, local, and federal regulations.

After any airbag component testing or service, do not connect the battery negative cable. Personal injury or death may result if the system test is not performed first.

If the vehicle is equipped with the Occupant Classification System (OCS), do not connect the battery negative cable before performing the OCS Verification Test using the scan tool and the appropriate diagnostic information. Personal injury or death may result if the system test is not performed properly.

Never replace both the Occupant Restraint Controller (ORC) and the Occupant Classification Module (OCM) at the same time. If both require replacement, replace one, then perform the Airbag System test before replacing the other.

Both the ORC and the OCM store Occupant Classification System (OCS) calibration data, which they transfer to one another when one of them is replaced. If both are replaced at the same time, an irreversible fault will be set in both modules and the OCS may malfunction and cause personal injury or death.

If equipped with OCS, the Seat Weight Sensor is a sensitive, calibrated unit and must be handled carefully. Do not drop or handle roughly. If dropped or damaged, replace with another sensor. Failure to do so may result in occupant injury or death.

If equipped with OCS, the front passenger seat must be handled carefully as well. When removing the seat, be careful when setting on floor not to drop. If dropped, the sensor may be inoperative, could result in occupant injury, or possibly death.

If equipped with OCS, when the passenger front seat is on the floor, no one should sit in the front passenger seat. This uneven force may damage the sensing ability of the seat weight sensors. If sat on and damaged, the sensor may be inoperative, could result in occupant injury, or possibly death.

DISARMING THE SYSTEM

✷✷ CAUTION

To avoid serious or fatal injury on vehicles equipped with airbags, disable the Supplemental Restraint System (SRS) before attempting any steering wheel, steering column, airbag, seat belt tensioner, impact sensor or instrument panel component diagnosis or service. Disconnect and isolate the battery negative (ground) cable, then wait 2 minutes for the system capacitor to discharge before performing further diagnosis or service. This is the only sure way to disable the SRS. Failure to take the proper precautions could result in accidental airbag deployment.

CLOCKSPRING CENTERING

See Figure 41.

➡ A service replacement clockspring is shipped with the clockspring pre-centered and with a molded plastic locking pin installed. This locking pin should not be removed until the steering wheel has been installed on the steering column. If the locking pin is removed before the steering wheel is installed, the clockspring centering procedure must be performed.

➡ When a clockspring is installed into a vehicle without properly centering and locking the entire steering system, the Steering Angle Sensor (SAS) data does not agree with the true position of the steering system and causes the Electronic Stability Program (ESP) system to shut down. This may also damage the clockspring without any immediate malfunction. Unlike some other Chrysler vehicles, this SAS never requires calibration. However, upon each new ignition ON cycle, the steering wheel must be rotated slightly to initialize the SAS.

➡ Determining if the clockspring/SAS is centered is also possible electrically using the diagnostic scan tool. Steering wheel position is displayed as ANGLE with a range of up to 900 degrees. Refer to the appropriate menu item on the diagnostic scan tool.

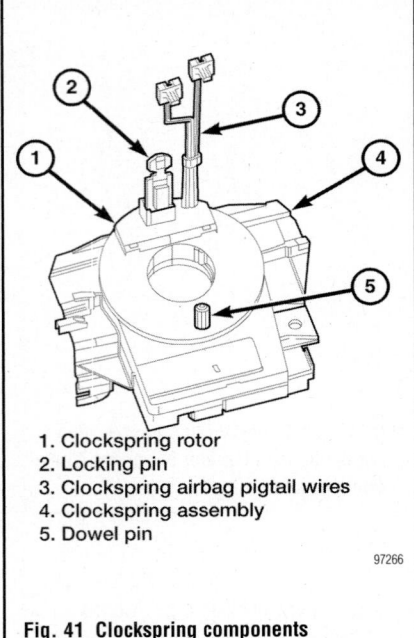

1. Clockspring rotor
2. Locking pin
3. Clockspring airbag pigtail wires
4. Clockspring assembly
5. Dowel pin

97266

Fig. 41 Clockspring components

➡ Before starting this procedure, be certain to turn the steering wheel until the front wheels are in the straight-ahead position and that the entire steering system is locked or inhibited from rotation.

➡ The clockspring may be centered and the rotor may be rotated freely once the steering wheel has been removed.

1. Place the front wheels in the straight-ahead position, and inhibit the steering column shaft from rotation.

2. Remove the steering wheel from the steering shaft.

3. Rotate the clockspring rotor clockwise to the end of its travel. Do not apply excessive torque.

4. From the end of the clockwise travel, rotate the rotor about two and one-half turns counterclockwise. Turn the rotor slightly clockwise or counterclockwise as necessary so that the clockspring airbag pigtail wires and connector receptacle are at the top and the dowel pin is at the bottom.

5. The clockspring is now centered. Secure the clockspring rotor to the clockspring case using a locking pin or some similar device to maintain clockspring centering until the steering wheel is reinstalled on the steering column.

DRIVE TRAIN

AUTOMATIC TRANSAXLE FLUID

CHECKING FLUID LEVEL

See Figure 42.

❋❋ CAUTION

There is a risk of accident from vehicle starting off by itself when engine is running. There is a risk of injury from contusions and burns if you insert your hands into the engine when it is started or when it is running. Secure vehicle to prevent it from moving off by itself. Wear properly fastened and close-fitting work clothes. Do not touch hot or rotating parts.

1. Verify that the vehicle is parked on a level surface.
2. Remove the dipstick tube cap.
3. Actuate the service brake. Start engine and let it run at idle speed in selector lever position "P".
4. Shift through the Transaxle modes several times with the vehicle stationary and the engine idling.
5. Warm up the Transaxle, wait at least 2 minutes and check the oil level with the engine running. Push the oil dipstick into Transaxle fill tube until the dipstick tip contacts the oil pan and pull out again, and read off oil level. Repeat if necessary.

➡**The dipstick will protrude from the fill tube when installed.**

6. Check the Transaxle oil temperature using the appropriate scan tool.
7. The Transaxle oil dipstick has indicator marks every 10 mm. Determine the height of the oil level on the dipstick and using the height, the Transaxle temperature, and the CVT Transaxle Fluid Level Graph, determine if the Transaxle oil level is correct.
8. Add or remove oil as necessary and recheck the oil level.
9. Once the oil level is correct, install the dipstick tube cap.

FLUID AND STRAINER SERVICE

See Figures 43 through 45.

1. Remove the bolts holding the oil pan to the transaxle case.
2. Remove the oil pan from the transaxle case.
3. Remove the oil pan gasket from the transaxle case.

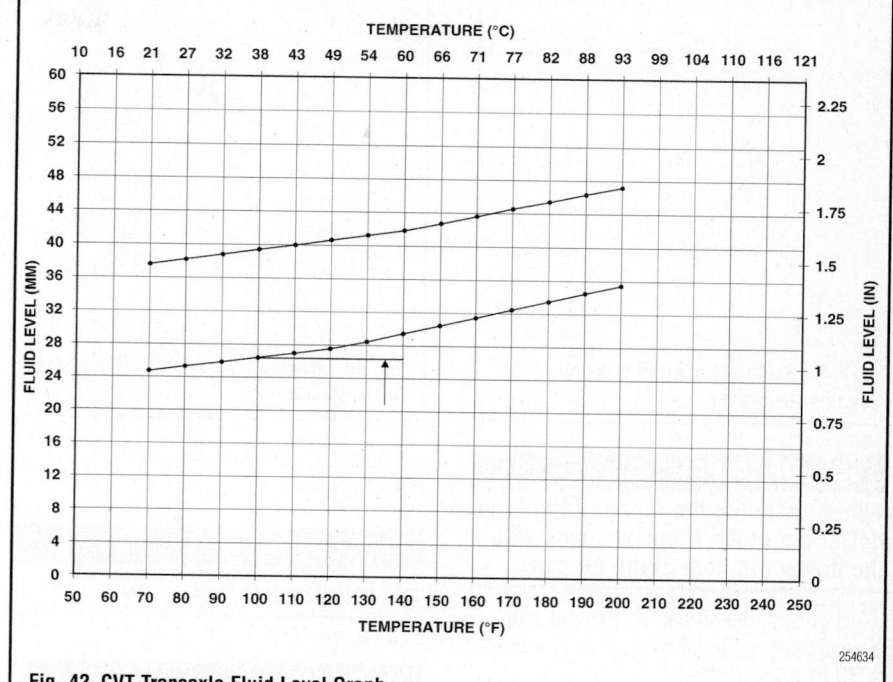

Fig. 42 CVT Transaxle Fluid Level Graph

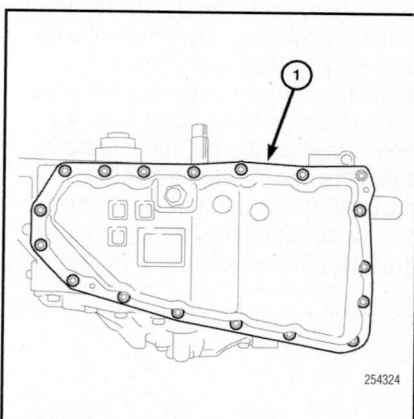

Fig. 43 Remove the bolts holding the oil pan (1) to the transaxle case

4. Remove the bolts holding the oil strainer to the valve body.
5. Remove the oil strainer.
6. Remove and discard the oil strainer O-ring.

❋❋ WARNING

Do not re-use the O-ring. Apply CVT fluid when installing the O-ring.

7. Install the new O-ring onto the new oil strainer.
8. Install the new oil strainer onto the control valve assembly. Install and

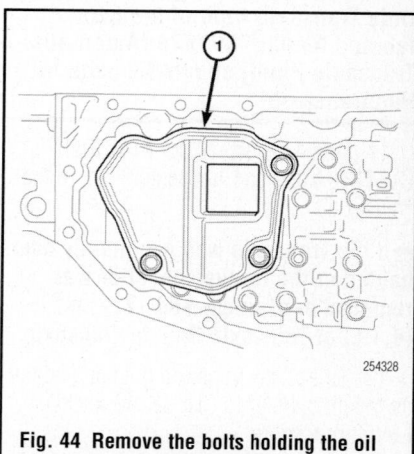

Fig. 44 Remove the bolts holding the oil strainer (1) to the valve body

tighten the mounting bolts to 70 inch lbs. (8 Nm).

❋❋ WARNING

Do not re-use the oil pan gasket. Remove any moisture, oil, and used gasket material from the surface where the new gasket is to be installed. When installing the oil pan gasket, align the dowel pin with the dowel pin hole in the oil pan gasket.

9. Install the oil pan gasket onto the transaxle case.

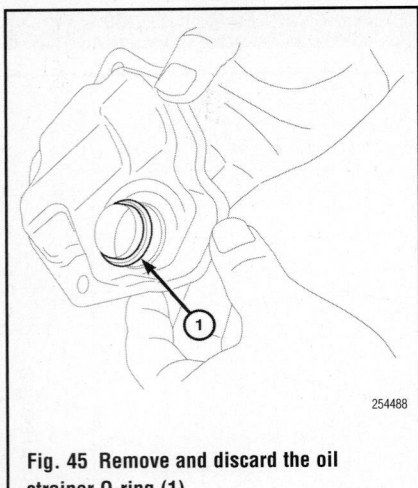

Fig. 45 Remove and discard the oil strainer O-ring (1)

When installing the oil pan, align the dowel pin of the transaxle case with the dowel pin hole of the oil pan.

10. Install the oil pan on the transaxle case. Install and tighten the mounting bolts to 70 inch lbs. (8 Nm)..

❄❄ **WARNING**

Only Transaxle fluid of the type labeled Mopar® CVTF+4 (Automatic Transaxle Fluid) should be used in this transaxle.

11. Add 14.8 pts. (7.0L) of MOPAR® CVTF+4, Automatic Transaxle Fluid, to the Transaxle

➥If the Transaxle was completely overhauled or the torque converter was replaced or drained, add 17.1 pts. (8.1 L) of Transaxle fluid to Transaxle.

12. Check the Transaxle fluid and adjust as required. Refer to CHECKING FLUID LEVEL procedure.

MANUAL TRANSAXLE FLUID

DRAIN AND REFILL
See Figure 46.

➥All T355 manual transaxles require the use of ATF+4 (Automatic Transaxle Fluid).

1. The transaxle fill plug is located on the left side of the transaxle differential area. The fluid level should be within 3/16 inch from the bottom of the transaxle fill hole (vehicle must be level when checking).

2. The transaxle drain plug is located on the lower right side of the transaxle differen-

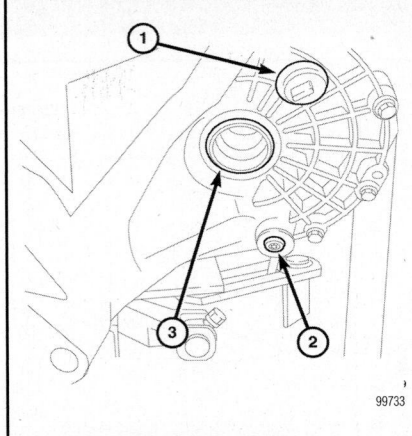

Fig. 46 Locating transaxle (3) fill plug (1) and drain plug (2)

tial housing. Tighten drain plug to 120 inch lbs. (14 Nm).

CLUTCH

REMOVAL & INSTALLATION
See Figure 47.

❄❄ **CAUTION**

Chrysler does not manufacture any vehicles or replacement parts that contain asbestos. Aftermarket products may or may not contain asbestos. Refer to aftermarket product packaging for product information. Whether the product contains asbestos or not, dust and dirt can accumulate on manual clutch parts during normal use. Follow practices prescribed by appropriate regulations

for the handling, processing and disposing of dust and debris

1. Remove the transaxle from the vehicle.
2. Remove the modular clutch assembly from the transaxle input shaft.

To install:
3. Install the clutch module onto the input shaft.
4. Install the transaxle into the vehicle.

BLEEDING

❄❄ **WARNING**

Never use any type of petroleum-based fluid (engine oil, Transaxle oil, power steering fluid, etc.) in the clutch hydraulic system. Use of such fluids will result in master/slave cylinder seal damage, and cause a failure of the hydraulic clutch release system.

➥Under normal operating conditions, the clutch hydraulic system does not require additional fluid for the life of the vehicle. Since the clutch shares the brake reservoir, the fluid level will be maintained whenever the brake system is checked.

➥The fluid required for use in the clutch hydraulic system is brake fluid conforming to DOT 3 specifications and J1703 standards. No other type of fluid is recommended or approved for use in the clutch hydraulic system. Use only MOPAR® brake fluid or equivalent from a tightly sealed container.

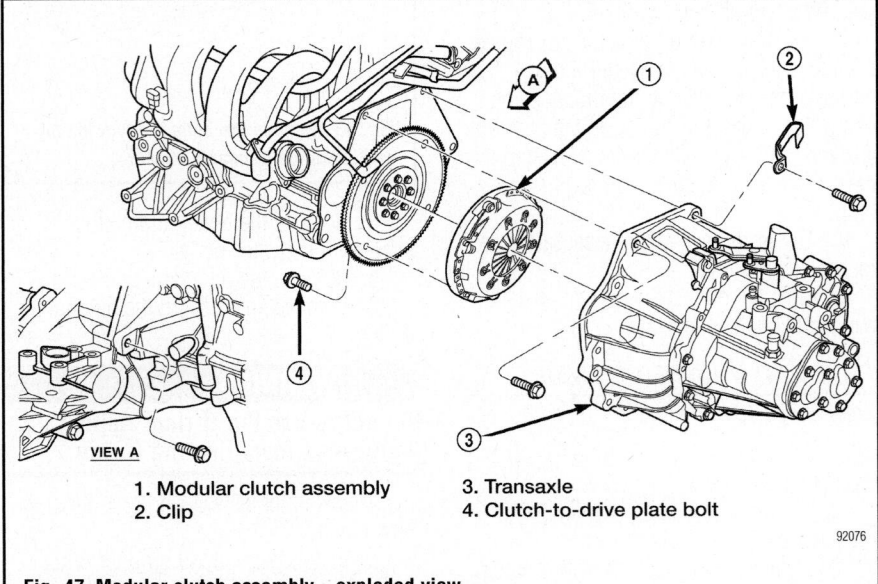

1. Modular clutch assembly
2. Clip
3. Transaxle
4. Clutch-to-drive plate bolt

Fig. 47 Modular clutch assembly—exploded view

Manual Bleeding

➡**An assistant is required to perform this procedure.**

1. Verify fluid level in clutch/brake cylinder. Top off with DOT 3 brake fluid as necessary. Leave cap off.
2. Raise the vehicle on a hoist.

➡**The container must be positioned at a lower level than the bleeder valve on the clutch slave cylinder.**

3. Remove the dust cap from the bleed port on the clutch slave cylinder, and install a suitable size and length of clear hose to monitor and divert fluid into a suitable container.
4. Lower the vehicle, but only enough to gain access to and fill the brake master cylinder.
5. Have the assistant press down and hold the clutch pedal until it reaches the floor.

➡**Do not allow clutch/brake fluid reservoir to run dry while fluid exits bleed port. If the reservoir runs dry during this procedure, it must be refilled and this step must be repeated.**

➡**Ensure the assistant does not release the clutch pedal from the floor while the bleed port on the clutch slave cylinder is open. Otherwise, air will enter the clutch hydraulic circuit.**

6. Open the bleed port on the clutch slave cylinder enough to allow hydraulic fluid to drain. Any air in the system will escape at this time.
7. Close the bleed port on the clutch slave cylinder, and have the assistant release the clutch pedal to the full up position.
8. Repeat the previous 3 steps at least 15 times or until air bubbles are no longer present in the clutch hydraulic fluid.
9. Slowly actuate the clutch pedal 10 times between the full up and pedal stop position.
10. Apply the parking brake. Start the engine and verify clutch operation and pedal feel. If the clutch pedal feels fine and the transaxle can be easily shifted from NEUTRAL to any gear, the clutch is operating correctly. If pedal still feels spongy or clutch does not fully disengage, excessive air is still trapped within the system (most likely at the master cylinder).
11. Disconnect the hose from the bleed port on the clutch master cylinder and install the dust cap.
12. Top off the brake master cylinder fluid level with DOT 3 brake fluid as necessary.

Power Bleeding

1. Remove the reservoir cap, and connect bleeder cap to clutch/brake fluid reservoir.

➡**Use Bleeder Cap/Modified Reservoir Cap Adapter (Snap-on #901-059) or equivalent.**

2. Connect Service Filling/Brake Power Bleeder machine to bleeder cap.
3. Service filling machine should be pressurized between 29–36 psi (2.0–2.5 bar).
4. Remove dust cap from the bleeder valve, and connect the transparent bleeder hose to bleeder valve.

➡**Use bleeder container to capture hydraulic fluid and the transparent bleeder hose to route fluid to the container.**

➡**The container must be at a lower level than the bleeder valve on the clutch slave cylinder.**

5. Place the other end of hose in the bleeder container to capture the used fluid. The end of the hose MUST be submerged in the DOT 3 brake fluid.
6. Turn on the service filling machine.

➡**While bleeding the system, do not allow the clutch fluid reservoir to completely empty out. If this happens, refill the clutch fluid reservoir, and repeat the procedure.**

7. Open the bleeder valve on the clutch slave cylinder enough to allow fluid to flow from the clutch hydraulic system.
8. Allow fluid to flow out of bleed port until no more air bubbles can be seen in the transparent bleeder hose.
9. Once fluid is free of air bubbles, make 15 quick actuations between clutch pedal stop positions.
10. Close the bleeder valve at the clutch slave cylinder. Disconnect the service filling machine.
11. Check clutch pedal to see if vehicle is properly bled.
12. If vehicle is not properly bled, repeat the procedure.
13. Remove the bleeder cap from the clutch fluid reservoir and replace reservoir cap.
14. Disconnect transparent bleeder hose from bleeder valve and replace dust cap.

FLUID FILL PROCEDURE

✳✳ CAUTION

Brake fluid contains polyglycol ethers and polyglycols. Avoid contact with the eyes and wash your hands thoroughly after handling brake fluid. If you do get brake fluid in your eyes, flush your eyes with clean, running water for 15 minutes. If eye irritation persists, or if you have taken brake fluid internally, IMMEDIATELY seek medical assistance.

✳✳ WARNING

Clean, high quality brake fluid is essential to the safe and proper operation of the clutch and brake system. You should always buy the highest quality brake fluid that is available. If the brake fluid becomes contaminated, drain and flush the system. Never reuse any brake fluid. Any brake fluid that is removed from the system should be discarded. Also, do not allow any brake fluid to come in contact with a painted surface; it will damage the paint.

1. Before servicing the vehicle, refer to the Precautions Section.
2. Fill the fluid level so that it is between the MIN and MAX lines marked on the reservoir.

FRONT HALFSHAFT

REMOVAL & INSTALLATION

See Figures 48 through 59.

✳✳ WARNING

Boot sealing is vital to retain special lubricants and to prevent foreign contaminants from entering the CV-joint. Mishandling, such as allowing the assemblies to dangle unsupported, or pulling/pushing the ends can cut boots or damage CV-joints. During removal and installation procedures, always support both ends of the halfshaft to prevent damage.

✳✳ WARNING

The halfshaft, when installed, acts as a bolt and secures the front hub/bearing assembly. If vehicle is to be supported or moved on its wheels with a halfshaft removed, install a PROPER-SIZED BOLT AND NUT through front hub. Tighten bolt and nut to 180 ft. lbs. (244 Nm). This will ensure that the hub bearing cannot loosen.

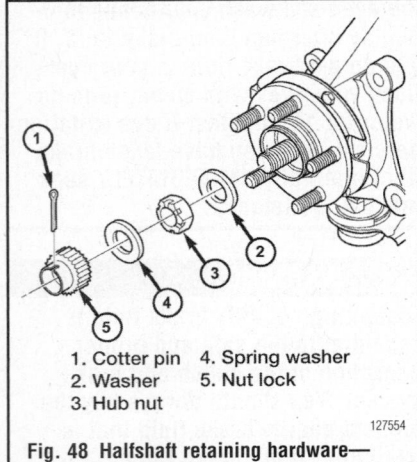

1. Cotter pin   4. Spring washer
2. Washer   5. Nut lock
3. Hub nut
127554

Fig. 48 Halfshaft retaining hardware—exploded view

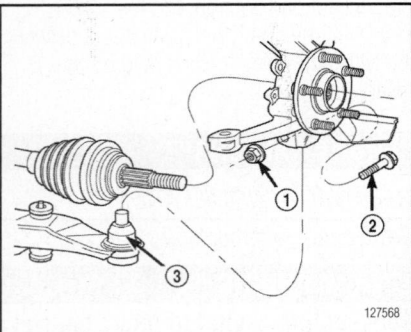

127568

Fig. 49 Remove nut (1) and bolt (2) retaining the ball joint stud (3) into steering knuckle

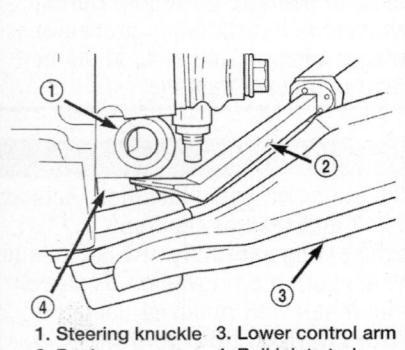

1. Steering knuckle   3. Lower control arm
2. Pry bar   4. Ball joint stud
127570

Fig. 50 Separating lower control arm from steering knuckle

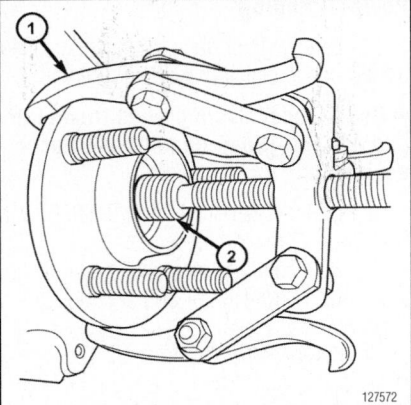

127572

Fig. 51 If difficulty in separating halfshaft (2) from hub is encountered, use puller (1) to separate

1. Disconnect the negative battery cable.

2. Place the transaxle in gated park.

3. Raise the vehicle on a hoist.

4. Remove the wheel and tire assembly.

5. Remove the cotter pin, nut lock, spring washer, and hub nut from the end of the outer CV-joint stub axle.

6. Disconnect the front wheel speed sensor, and secure harness out of the way.

7. Remove nut and bolt retaining the ball joint stud into the steering knuckle.

✳✳ WARNING

Use caution when separating ball joint stud from the steering knuckle, so ball joint seal does not get damaged.

8. Separate ball joint stud from steering knuckle by prying down on lower control arm.

✳✳ WARNING

Care must be taken not to separate the inner CV-joint during this operation. Do not allow the halfshaft to hang by inner CV-joint. Halfshaft must be supported.

9. Remove the halfshaft from the steering knuckle by pulling outward on knuckle while pressing in on halfshaft. Support the outer end of halfshaft assembly. If difficulty in separating halfshaft from hub is encountered, do not strike shaft with hammer; instead, use puller (1026) to separate.

10. Remove the halfshaft bracket from the engine lower mounting bolt.

11. Remove the halfshaft bracket from the engine upper mounting bolts.

12. Support the outer end of the halfshaft assembly.

➡ Removal of the inner tripod joints is made easier if you apply outward pressure on the joint as you strike the punch with a hammer. Do not pull on interconnecting shaft to remove, as the inner joint will become separated.

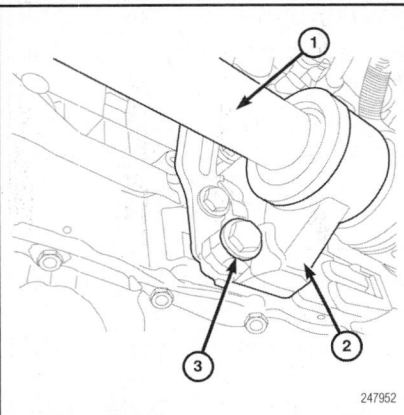

247952

Fig. 52 View of right halfshaft (1), halfshaft bracket (2) and engine lower mounting bolt (3)

13. Remove the inner tripod joints from the side gears of the transaxle using a punch to dislodge the inner tripod joint retaining ring from the transaxle side gear. If removing the right side inner tripod joint, position the punch to the inner tripod joint extraction groove (if equipped). Strike the punch sharply with a hammer to dislodge the right inner joint from the side gear. If removing the left side inner tripod joint, position the punch to the inner tripod joint extraction groove. Strike the punch sharply with a hammer to dislodge the left inner tripod joint from the side gear.

14. Hold inner tripod joint and interconnecting shaft of halfshaft assembly. Remove inner tripod joint from the transaxle by pulling it straight out of transaxle side gear and transaxle oil seal. When removing the tripod joint, do not let spline or snap ring drag across sealing lip of the transaxle-to-tripod joint oil seal. When tripod joint is removed from transaxle, some fluid will leak out.

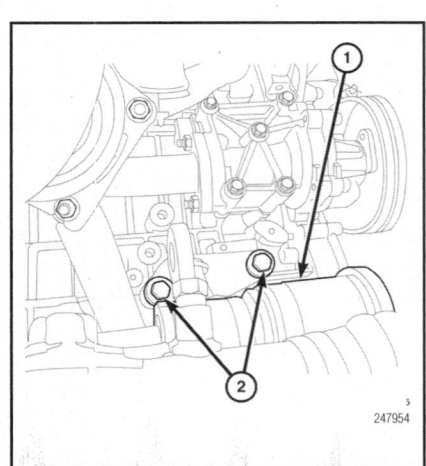

247954

Fig. 53 Remove the halfshaft bracket (1) from the engine upper mounting bolts (2)

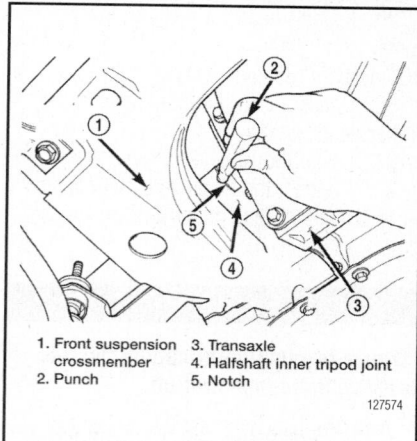

1. Front suspension crossmember
2. Punch
3. Transaxle
4. Halfshaft inner tripod joint
5. Notch

127574

Fig. 54 Disengaging tripod joint from transaxle—left shown

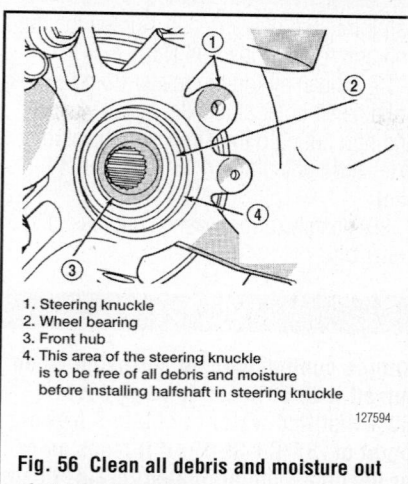

1. Steering knuckle
2. Wheel bearing
3. Front hub
4. This area of the steering knuckle is to be free of all debris and moisture before installing halfshaft in steering knuckle

127594

Fig. 56 Clean all debris and moisture out of steering knuckle

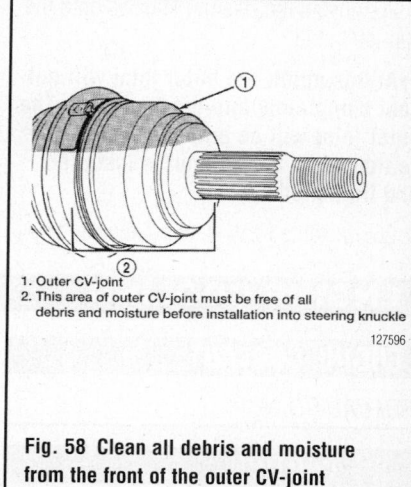

1. Outer CV-joint
2. This area of outer CV-joint must be free of all debris and moisture before installation into steering knuckle

127596

Fig. 58 Clean all debris and moisture from the front of the outer CV-joint

✳✳ WARNING

The halfshaft, when installed, acts as a bolt and secures the front hub/bearing assembly. If vehicle is to be supported or moved on its wheels with a halfshaft removed, install a PROPER-SIZED BOLT AND NUT through front hub. Tighten bolt and nut to 180 ft. lbs. (244 Nm). This will ensure that the hub bearing cannot loosen.

To install:

15. Clean all debris and moisture out of steering knuckle.

✳✳ WARNING

Boot sealing is vital to retain special lubricants and to prevent foreign contaminants from entering the CV-joint. Mishandling (such as allowing the assemblies to dangle unsupported, or pulling or pushing the ends) can cut boots or damage CV-joints. During removal and installation procedures, always support both ends of the halfshaft to prevent damage.

16. Thoroughly clean spline and oil seal sealing surface on tripod joint. Lightly lubricate oil seal sealing surface on tripod joint with fresh clean Transaxle lubricant.

➡**Always use differential output seal protector (9099) when installing the half shaft into the transaxle.**

17. Holding the halfshaft assembly by the tripod joint and interconnecting shaft, install tripod joint into transaxle side gear as far as possible by hand.

18. Carefully align the tripod joint with the transaxle side gears. Then grasp the halfshaft interconnecting shaft, and push tripod joint into transaxle side gear until fully seated. Test that snap ring is fully engaged with side gear by attempting to remove tri-

pod joint from transaxle by hand. If snap ring is fully engaged with side gear, tripod joint will not be removable by hand.

19. Install the halfshaft bracket-to-block lower bolt, and tighten bolt to 55 ft. lbs. 75 Nm).

20. Install the 2 halfshaft bracket-to-block upper mounting bolts, and tighten to 55 ft. lbs. 75 Nm).

21. Ensure that the front of the outer CV-joint which fits into steering knuckle is free of debris and moisture before assembling into the steering knuckle.

22. Apply a light coating of multi-purpose wheel bearing grease around the circumference of the flat surface. Do not apply too much grease, which could spill on to the non-mating surfaces and adversely affect the function of the halfshaft.

23. Wipe the rear of the hub and bearing in the knuckle clean where they contact the CV-joint.

24. Install the halfshaft back into front hub.

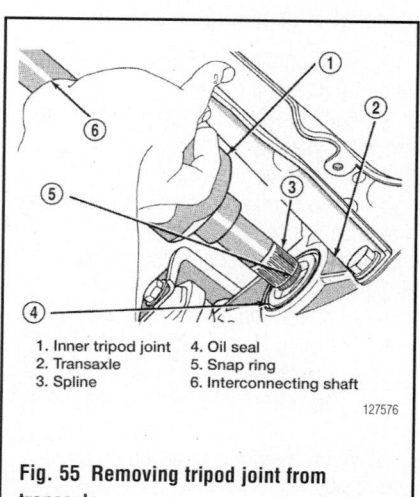

1. Inner tripod joint
2. Transaxle
3. Spline
4. Oil seal
5. Snap ring
6. Interconnecting shaft

127576

Fig. 55 Removing tripod joint from transaxle

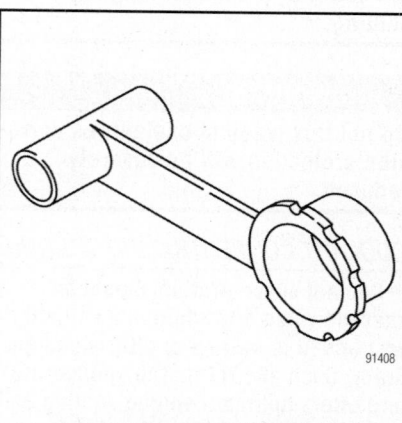

91408

Fig. 57 Always use differential output seal protector (9099) when installing the half-shaft into the transaxle

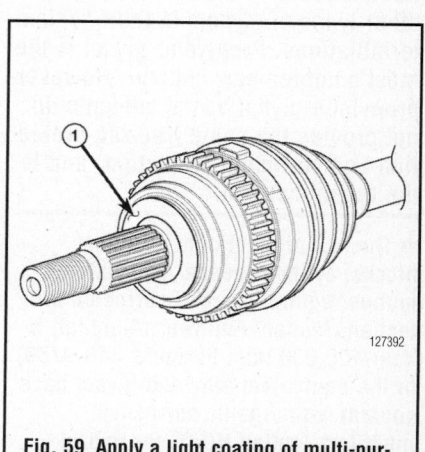

127392

Fig. 59 Apply a light coating of multi-purpose wheel bearing grease around the circumference of the flat surface (1)

25. Install the steering knuckle onto the ball joint stud.

➡**At this point, the outer joint will not seat completely into the front hub. The outer joint will be pulled into hub and seated when the hub nut is installed and tightened.**

26. Install a NEW steering knuckle to ball joint stud bolt and nut. Tighten the nut and bolt to 70 ft. lbs. (95 Nm).

27. Clean all foreign matter from threads of halfshaft outer stub axle. Install washer and hub nut onto the threads of the stub axle, and tighten nut to 180 ft. lbs. (244 Nm).

28. Install spring washer, nut lock, and cotter pin.

29. Install tire and wheel assembly. Install and tighten wheel mounting nuts to 100 ft. lbs. (135 Nm).

30. Check for correct fluid level in the transaxle assembly.

31. Lower the vehicle.

32. Connect the negative battery cable. Refer to Battery Reconnect/Relearn Procedure.

ENGINE COOLING

ENGINE COOLANT

PRECAUTIONS

✳✳ CAUTION

Antifreeze is an ethylene-glycol base coolant and is harmful if swallowed or inhaled. If swallowed, drink two glasses of water and induce vomiting. If inhaled, move to fresh air area. Seek medical attention immediately. Do not store in open or unmarked containers. Wash skin and clothing thoroughly after coming in contact with ethylene-glycol. Keep out of reach of children. Dispose of glycol base coolant properly, contact your dealer or government agency for location of collection center in your area. Do not open a cooling system when the engine is at operating temperature or hot under pressure, as personal injury can result. Avoid radiator cooling fan when engine compartment related service is performed, as personal injury can result.

✳✳ WARNING

Some coolant manufactures use other types of glycols in their coolant formulations. Propylene-glycol is the most common new coolant. However, propylene-glycol based coolants do not provide the same freezing protection and corrosion protection, and is not recommended.

➡The use of aluminum cylinder blocks, cylinder heads, and water pumps requires special corrosion protection. Mopar® Antifreeze/Coolant, 5 Year/100,000 Mile Formula (MS-9769), or the equivalent ethylene-glycol base coolant with organic corrosion inhibitors (called HOAT, for Hybrid Organic Additive Technology) is recommended. This coolant offers the best engine cooling without corrosion when mixed with 50% ethylene-glycol and 50% distilled water to obtain a freeze point of -37°C (-35°F). If it loses color or becomes contaminated, drain, flush, and replace with fresh properly mixed coolant solution.

✳✳ WARNING

Mopar® Antifreeze/Coolant, 5 Year/100,000 Mile Formula (MS-9769) may not be mixed with any other type of antifreeze. Mixing of coolants other than specified (non-HOAT or other HOAT), may result in engine damage that may not be covered under the new vehicle warranty, and decreased corrosion protection.

✳✳ WARNING

Richer antifreeze mixtures cannot be measured with normal field equipment and can cause problems associated with 100 percent ethylene-glycol.

✳✳ WARNING

Do not use coolant additives that are claimed to improve engine cooling.

✳✳ WARNING

Do not mix types of coolant, as corrosion protection will be severely reduced.

COOLANT CONCENTRATION TESTING

➡Coolant concentration should be checked when any additional coolant was added to system or after a coolant drain, flush and refill. The coolant mixture offers optimum engine cooling and protection against corrosion when mixed to a freeze point of -34°F (-37°C) to -50°F (-46°C). The use of a hydrometer or a refractometer can be used to test coolant concentration.

A hydrometer will test the amount of glycol in a mixture by measuring the specific gravity of the mixture. The higher the concentration of ethylene-glycol, the larger the number of balls that will float, and the higher the freeze protection (up to a maximum of 60% by volume glycol).

A refractometer tool will test the amount of glycol in a coolant mixture by measuring the amount a beam of light bends as it passes through the fluid.

DRAIN & REFILL PROCEDURE

✳✳ CAUTION

Do not open the radiator draincock with the system hot and under pressure. Serious burns from coolant can occur.

➡Drain, flush, and fill the cooling system at the mileage or time intervals specified. If the solution is dirty, rusty, or contains a considerable amount of sediment, clean and flush with a reliable cooling system cleaner. Care should be taken in disposing of the used engine coolant from your vehicle. Check governmental regulations for disposal of used engine coolant.

1. Position a clean collecting container under draincock location.

2. Without removing the pressure cap and with system not under pressure, turn draincock counterclockwise to open.

3. Allow coolant reserve bottle to empty first, then remove the pressure cap.

4. If coolant reserve bottle does not empty first:
   - Check condition of the pressure cap and cap seals.
   - Check for kinked or torn overflow hose from filler neck to reserve bottle.

5. Allow the cooling system to drain completely.

BLEEDING

Aeration:

If coolant level drops below a certain point, aeration will occur. This will draw air into the water pump, resulting in the following:

- High reading shown on the temperature gauge.
- Loss of coolant flow through the heater core.
- Corrosion in the cooling system.
- Transaxle oil will become hotter (automatic Transaxle equipped vehicles).
- Water pump seal may run dry, increasing the risk of premature seal failure.
- Combustion gas leaks into the coolant can also cause the above problems.

Deaeration:

As air is removed from the cooling system, it gathers in the coolant recovery container. This pressure is released into the atmosphere through the pressure valve located in the radiator pressure cap when pressure reaches 14–18 psi (96–124 kPa). This air is replaced with coolant from the coolant recovery container.

➡ **Deaeration does not occur at engine idle; higher engine speeds are required. Normal driving will de-aerate cooling system.**

To effectively de-aerate the system, multiple thermal cycles of the system may be required.

NORMAL FLUSHING

In some instances, use a radiator cleaner (Mopar® Radiator Kleen or equivalent) before flushing. This will soften scale and other deposits and aid flushing operation.

✳✳ CAUTION

Follow the manufacturer's instructions when using radiator cleaning products.

1. Drain the cooling system and refill with water.
2. Run the engine with the radiator cap installed until the upper radiator hose is hot.
3. Stop the engine and drain the water from system.
4. If the water is dirty, fill the system with water, run the engine and drain the system. Repeat this procedure until the water drains clean.

REVERSE FLUSHING

Reverse flushing of the cooling system is the forcing of water through the cooling system. This is done using air pressure in the opposite direction of normal coolant flow. It is usually only necessary with very dirty systems with evidence of partial plugging.

Radiator

1. Disconnect the radiator hoses from the radiator inlet and outlet.
2. Attach a section of the radiator hose to the radiator bottom outlet fitting and insert the flushing gun.
3. Connect a water supply hose and air supply hose to the flushing gun.

✳✳ WARNING

Internal radiator pressure must not exceed 20 psi (138 kPa), as damage to the radiator may result.

4. Allow the radiator to fill with water. When the radiator is filled, apply air in short blasts. Allow the radiator to refill between blasts. Continue this reverse flushing until clean water flows out through the rear of the radiator cooling tube passages.

Engine

1. Drain the cooling system.
2. Remove the thermostat housing and thermostat. Install the thermostat housing. Refer to Thermostat, removal & installation.
3. Disconnect the radiator upper hose from the radiator and attach the flushing gun to the hose.
4. Disconnect the radiator lower hose from the water pump, and attach a lead-away hose to the water pump inlet fitting.

✳✳ WARNING

On vehicles equipped with a heater water control valve, be sure the heater control valve is closed (heat off). This will prevent coolant flow with scale and other deposits from entering the heater core.

5. Connect the water supply hose and air supply hose to flushing gun.
6. Allow the engine to fill with water. When the engine is filled, apply air in short blasts, allowing the system to fill between air blasts. Continue until clean water flows through the lead-away hose.
7. Remove the lead-away hose, flushing gun, water supply hose and air supply hose.
8. Remove the thermostat housing and install the thermostat. Install the thermostat housing with a replacement gasket. Refer to Thermostat, removal & installation.
9. Connect the radiator hoses.
10. Refill the cooling system with the correct antifreeze/water mixture. Refer to Drain & Refill procedure.

ENGINE FAN

REMOVAL & INSTALLATION

2010 Models

See Figure 60.

✳✳ CAUTION

Do not open the radiator draincock with the system hot and under pressure, as serious burns from coolant can occur.

1. Disconnect negative cable from battery.
2. Drain the cooling system below upper radiator hose level.
3. Remove the radiator core support.
4. Disconnect the upper radiator hose from radiator.
5. Remove the wiring harness bracket.
6. Disconnect the radiator fan electrical connector.
7. Remove the radiator fan assembly screws.
8. Detach radiator fan assembly from retaining clips.

✳✳ WARNING

Care should be taken not to damage the radiator cooling fins and tubes during fan removal.

9. Remove the radiator fan by lifting up from the engine compartment.

To install:

10. Install the radiator fan assembly into J-clips.
11. Install the radiator fan fasteners.

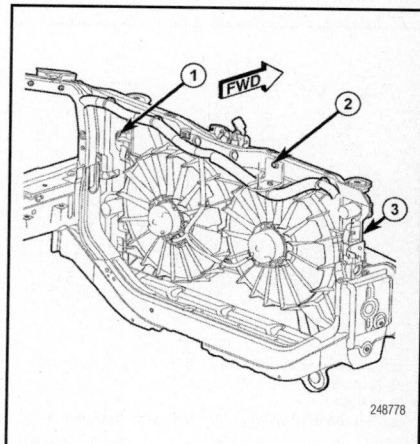

248778

Fig. 60 View of radiator fan electrical connector (1), bracket (2) and radiator (3)

Tighten all radiator fan retaining screws to 55 inch lbs. (6 Nm).

12. Install the radiator crossmember.

13. Install the wiring harness bracket.

14. Connect the radiator fan electrical connector.

15. Install the upper radiator hose.

16. Connect the negative battery cable.

17. Fill the cooling system. Refer to Drain & Refill procedure.

2011 Models

See Figure 61.

> ❊❊ **CAUTION**
>
> **Do not open the radiator draincock with the system hot and under pressure because serious burns from coolant can occur.**

1. Remove the air intake duct.

2. Disconnect negative cable from battery.

3. Drain the coolant just below the upper radiator hose.

4. Remove the upper radiator closure panel.

5. Remove the hood latch cable.

6. Remove the upper core support seal push pins.

7. Remove radiator core support bolts.

8. Remove the upper radiator hose support bracket.

9. Remove the upper radiator hose from the radiator and position aside.

10. Remove the wiring harness from the fan shroud.

11. Disconnect the radiator fan electrical connectors.

12. Remove the radiator fan module by lifting up from the engine compartment.

13. Remove the lower shroud seal.

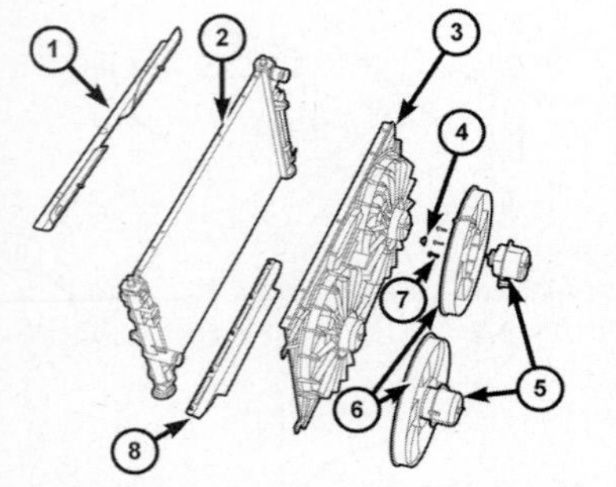

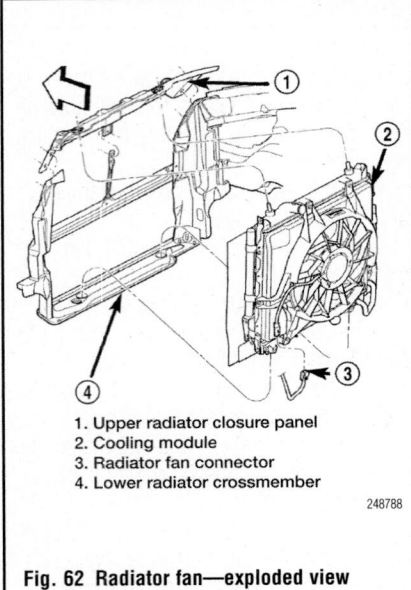

1. Upper core support seal
2. Radiator
3. Bracket
4. Fan blade retaining nut
5. Fan motor assembly
6. Fan
7. Fastener
8. Lower shroud seal

2813566

Fig. 61 Cooling fan—exploded view— 2011 models

14. Remove the fan blade retaining nut from the fan motor.

15. Remove the fan motor assembly from the shroud.

To install:

16. To install, reverse the removal procedure and note the following:

- Install the upper radiator core support. Tighten the outer bolts to 17 ft. lbs. (23 Nm). Tighten the inner support bolts to 6 ft. lbs. (8 Nm).

17. Connect the negative battery cable.

18. Fill the coolant to the proper level. Refer to Drain & Refill procedure.

19. Run vehicle. Check for proper fan operation and coolant level.

20. Install the air intake duct.

RADIATOR

REMOVAL & INSTALLATION

See Figure 62.

> ❊❊ **CAUTION**
>
> **Do not open the radiator draincock with the system hot and under pressure, because serious burns from coolant can occur.**

1. Drain the cooling system. Refer to Drain & Refill procedure.

2. Remove the radiator fan. Refer to Engine Fan, removal & installation.

3. Disconnect the lower radiator hose.

4. Remove the fasteners attaching the A/C condenser to the radiator. Reposition the A/C condenser.

5. Remove the radiator assembly by lifting it up from the engine compartment. Care should be taken not to damage the cooling fins and tubes during removal.

To install:

6. Position the radiator into mounting position.

7. Position the A/C condenser against the radiator. Hand start the fasteners.

8. Install the radiator fan/shroud assembly. Hand start the fasteners.

9. Tighten all condenser fasteners to 70 inch lbs. (8 Nm).

10. Tighten all radiator fan fasteners to 55 inch lbs. (6 Nm).

11. Connect lower radiator hose. Align the hose and position the clamp so it will not interfere with engine components.

12. Install the radiator fan. Refer to Engine Fan, removal & installation.

13. Connect positive battery cable. Connect negative battery cable.

14. Fill the cooling system with coolant. Refer to Drain & Refill procedure.

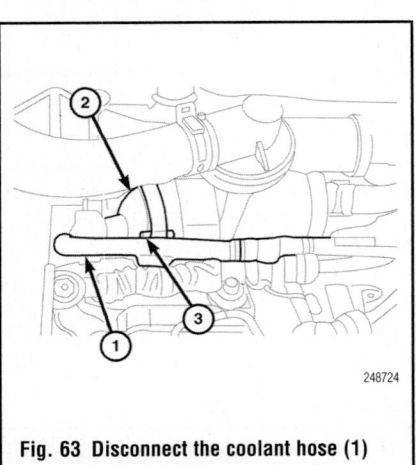

1. Upper radiator closure panel
2. Cooling module
3. Radiator fan connector
4. Lower radiator crossmember

248788

Fig. 62 Radiator fan—exploded view

15. Operate engine until it reaches normal operating temperature. Check cooling system for correct fluid level.

THERMOSTAT

REMOVAL & INSTALLATION

Primary Thermostat

See Figure 63.

1. Partially drain the cooling system. Refer to Drain & Refill procedure.

2. Remove the air filter housing. Refer to Air Cleaner, removal & installation.

3. Disconnect the coolant hose from the inlet housing.

4. Remove the inlet housing bolts.

5. Remove the thermostat assembly, and clean the sealing surfaces.

248724

Fig. 63 Disconnect the coolant hose (1) from the inlet housing. Remove the inlet housing bolts (3)

6. Installation is the reverse of the removal procedure.

Secondary Thermostat

See Figure 64.

1. Partially drain the cooling system. Refer to Drain & Refill procedure.
2. Remove the air filter housing. Refer to Air Cleaner, removal & installation.
3. Disconnect the coolant hoses from the rear of the coolant adapter.
4. Remove the radiator hose.
5. Remove the radiator hose from the front of the coolant adapter.
6. Remove the coolant adapter mounting bolts.
7. Carefully slide the coolant adapter off the water pump inlet tube, and remove the coolant adapter and the secondary thermostat.

To install:

8. Position the thermostat into the cylinder head.
9. Inspect the water pump inlet tube O-rings for damage before installing the tube in the coolant adapter. Replace O-ring(s) as necessary.
10. Lubricate the O-rings with soapy water.
11. Position the coolant adapter on the water pump inlet tube and the cylinder head.
12. Install the coolant adapter mounting bolts. Tighten the bolts to 159 inch lbs. (18 Nm).
13. Connect the front coolant hose.
14. Connect the two rear coolant hoses.
15. Connect the radiator hose.

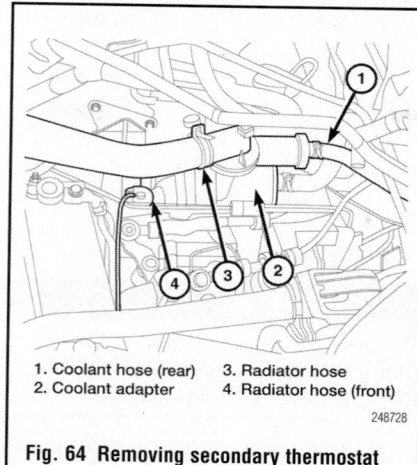

1. Coolant hose (rear) 3. Radiator hose
2. Coolant adapter 4. Radiator hose (front)

248728

Fig. 64 Removing secondary thermostat

16. Install the air filter housing. Refer to Air Cleaner, removal & installation.
17. Fill the cooling system. Refer to Drain & Refill procedure.

WATER PUMP

REMOVAL & INSTALLATION

See Figure 65.

1. Remove the accessory drive belt. Refer to Accessory Drive Belts, removal & installation.
2. Raise the vehicle.
3. Remove the accessory drive belt splash shield.
4. Drain the cooling system. Refer to Drain & Refill procedure.
5. Remove screws attaching the water pump pulley. Remove the pulley.

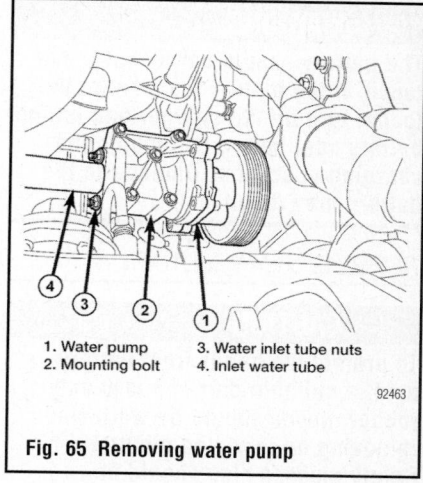

1. Water pump 3. Water inlet tube nuts
2. Mounting bolt 4. Inlet water tube

92463

Fig. 65 Removing water pump

6. Remove the water pump mounting bolts.
7. Remove the water pump.

To install:

8. Position the water pump assembly and gasket onto the cylinder block.
9. Position the water inlet tube and gasket onto the water pump.
10. Install the mounting bolts. Tighten the bolts to 18 ft. lbs. (24 Nm).
11. Install the drive belt splash shield.
12. Lower the vehicle.
13. Install the accessory drive belt. Refer to Accessory Drive Belts, removal & installation.
14. Evacuate air and refill cooling system. Refer to Drain & Refill procedure.
15. Check the cooling system for leaks.

ENGINE ELECTRICAL

BATTERY

PRECAUTIONS

✳✳ CAUTION

If the battery shows signs of freezing, leaking, or loose posts, do not test, assist-boost, or charge. The battery may arc internally and explode. Personal injury and/or vehicle damage may result.

✳✳ CAUTION

Explosive hydrogen gas forms in and around the battery. Do not smoke, use flame, or create sparks near the battery. Personal injury and/or vehicle damage may result.

✳✳ CAUTION

The battery contains sulfuric acid, which is poisonous and caustic. Avoid contact with the skin, eyes, or clothing. In the event of contact, flush with water and call a physician immediately. Keep out of the reach of children.

✳✳ CAUTION

If the battery is equipped with removable cell caps, be certain that each of the cell caps is in place and tight before the battery is returned to service. Personal injury and/or vehicle damage may result from loose or missing cell caps.

BATTERY SYSTEM

✳✳ WARNING

Always disconnect and isolate the battery negative cable before charging a battery. Do not exceed sixteen volts while charging a battery. Damage to the vehicle electrical system components may result.

✳✳ WARNING

Battery electrolyte will bubble inside the battery case during normal battery charging. Electrolyte boiling or being discharged from the battery vents indicates a battery overcharging condition. Immediately reduce the charging rate or turn off the charger to evaluate the battery condition. Damage to the battery may result from overcharging.

✳✳ WARNING

The battery should not be hot to the touch. If the battery feels hot to the touch, turn off the charger and let the battery cool before continuing the charging operation. Damage to the battery may result.

REMOVAL & INSTALLATION

✳✳ CAUTION

To protect the hands from battery acid, a suitable pair of heavy duty rubber gloves should be worn when removing or servicing a battery. Safety glasses also should be worn.

✳✳ CAUTION

Remove metallic jewelry to avoid injury by accidental arcing of battery current.

✳✳ CAUTION

The battery negative and positive cable polarity are different from the gasoline engine equipped vehicles to the diesel engine equipped vehicles. Please note the location of the positive and negative cables prior to service of the battery or related components.

1. Rotate the two retaining clips and remove the air cleaner fresh air duct.

2. Disconnect and isolate the negative battery cable, then the positive cable.

3. Loosen the bolt and retainer that holds the battery down to the tray.

4. Lift battery out of the battery tray and remove from vehicle.

5. Remove thermal guard (if equipped) from battery.

To install:

✳✳ WARNING

When replacing the battery, the thermal guard MUST be transferred to the new battery (if equipped).

6. Install battery in vehicle making sure that the thermal guard (if equipped) is present and battery is properly positioned on battery tray.

7. Install the battery hold down retainer and bolt making sure that it is properly positioned on battery. Tighten the hold down bolt to 62 inch lbs. (7 Nm).

8. Connect the positive battery cable, then the negative cable.

9. Tighten the cable clamp nuts to 45 inch lbs. (5 Nm).

10. Install the air cleaner fresh air duct, and secure in place by rotating the two retaining clips.

11. Verify proper vehicle operation.

BATTERY RECONNECT/RELEARN PROCEDURE

➡**This reconnection procedure is to be performed anytime the battery has been disconnected.**

1. Connect the negative battery cable to the battery post, and tighten the clamp nut.

2. Install the rear compartment floor trim panel.

3. If vehicle is equipped with Electronic Stability Program, refer to Electronic Stability Program (ESP) Recalibration procedure.

ELECTRONIC STABILITY PROGRAM (ESP) RECALIBRATION

✳✳ WARNING

If the vehicle is equipped with ESP, once the battery is reconnected, the Steering Angle Sensor (SAS) in the clockspring needs to be calibrated. The SAS requires calibration any time the battery or an ABS (ESP) component has been disconnected for any length of time. If the SAS is not calibrated following battery reconnection, the ESP/BAS indicator lamp is illuminated following five ignition cycles, indicating the need for calibration.

To calibrate, perform the following:
   a. Start the engine.
   b. Center the steering wheel.
   c. Turn the steering wheel all the way to the left until the internal stop in the steering gear is met, then turn the wheel all the way to the right until the opposite internal stop in the steering gear is met.
   d. Center the steering wheel.
   e. Stop the engine.

ENGINE ELECTRICAL

ALTERNATOR

REMOVAL & INSTALLATION

See Figures 66 through 68.

1. Rotate the 2 retaining clips, and remove the air cleaner fresh air duct.

2. Disconnect and isolate the negative battery cable at the battery.

3. Evacuate the A/C system.

4. Remove the right front wheel.

5. Remove the underbody air dam.

6. Remove the accessory drive splash shield.

7. Position aside the serpentine belt.

8. Remove the accessory drive idler pulley.

9. Remove the A/C compressor.

10. Loosen the lower mounting bolt.

11. Unplug the field circuit from the alternator.

CHARGING SYSTEM

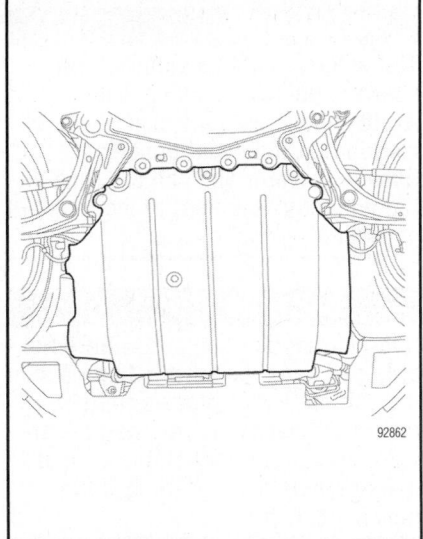

Fig. 66 Remove the underbody air dam

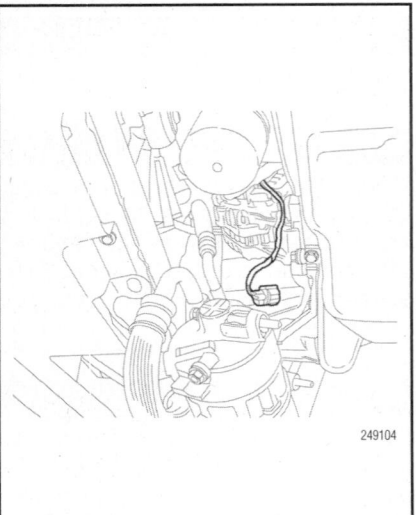

Fig. 67 Unplug the field circuit from the alternator

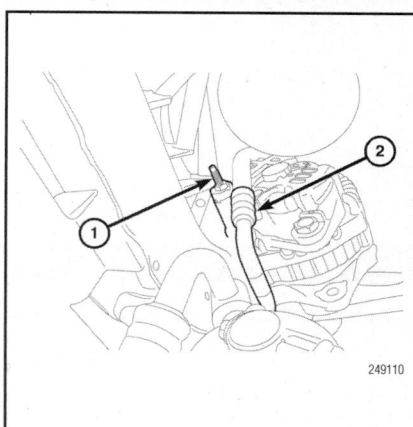

Fig. 68 Make sure the battery terminal (1) is in front of the A/C line (2)

12. Remove the B+ terminal nut and wire.

13. Remove the upper mounting bolt.

14. Remove the alternator lower mounting bolt.

15. Slide the alternator down and out of vehicle.

To install:

16. Install the alternator.

17. Rotate alternator and set in place.

18. Make sure the battery terminal is in front of the A/C line.

19. Install the upper mounting bolt, and tighten to 40 ft. lbs. (54 Nm).

20. Install the B+ terminal nut and wire, and tighten to 88.5 inch lbs. (10 Nm).

21. Plug in the field circuit to the alternator.

22. Install the lower mounting bolt, and tighten to 40 ft. lbs. (54 Nm).

23. Install the A/C compressor.

24. Install the accessory drive idler pulley, and tighten bolt to 35 ft. lbs. (48 Nm).

25. Re-position the serpentine belt. Refer to Accessory Belt Routing.

26. Install the accessory drive splash shield.

27. Install the underbody air dam.

28. Install the right front wheel.

29. Recharge the A/C system.

30. Connect the negative battery cable.

31. Position the air cleaner fresh air duct and rotate the 2 retaining clips to install.

ENGINE ELECTRICAL

FIRING ORDER

See Figure 69.

The 2.0L and 2.4L 4-cylinder engine firing order is 1–3–4–2.

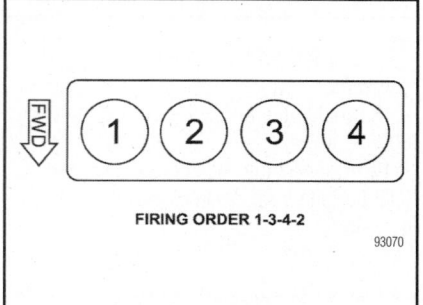

FIRING ORDER 1-3-4-2

93070

Fig. 69 4-cylinder engine firing order

IGNITION COIL

REMOVAL & INSTALLATION

See Figure 70.

➡**The electronic ignition coil attaches directly to the cylinder head cover.**

1. Disconnect the negative battery cable.

2. Disconnect the electrical connector from the ignition coil.

3. Remove the ignition coil mounting bolt.

4. Twist the ignition coil, then pull straight up to remove.

To install:

5. Install the ignition coil.

6. Tighten bolt to 79.5 inch lbs. (9 Nm).

7. Connect the electrical connectors and lock.

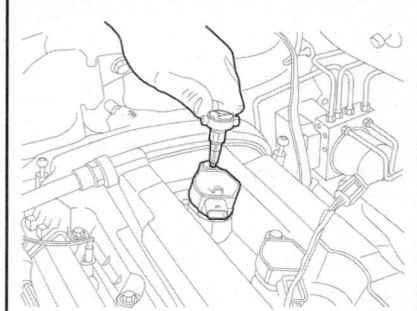

Fig. 70 Remove the ignition coil mounting bolt

8. Reconnect the negative battery cable.

IGNITION TIMING

ADJUSTMENT

The Crankshaft Position (CKP) sensor and Camshaft Position (CMP) sensor are Hall effect devices. The CMP sensor and CKP sensor generate square wave pulses that are inputs to the Powertrain Control Module (PCM). The PCM determines engine position from these sensors. The PCM calculates injector sequence and ignition timing from crankshaft and camshaft position. No adjustment is necessary.

SPARK PLUGS

REMOVAL & INSTALLATION

See Figure 71.

➡**The electronic ignition coil attaches directly to the valve cover.**

1. Disconnect the negative battery cable.

IGNITION SYSTEM

2. Disconnect the electrical connector from the ignition coil.

3. Remove the ignition coil mounting bolt.

4. Twist the ignition coil then pull straight up.

5. Remove the spark plug using a quality socket with a rubber or foam insert.

6. Inspect the spark plug condition.

To install:

✳✳ WARNING

Handle the spark plugs with care. Do not drop or force the spark plugs into the wells, or damage to the electrodes and/or porcelain body may occur. Always start each spark plug by hand in order to avoid cross-threading the spark plug in the cylinder head.

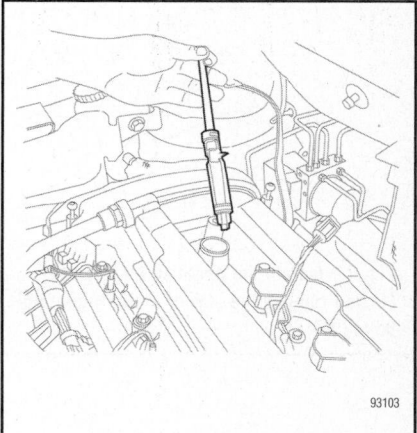

Fig. 71 Remove the spark plug using a quality socket with a rubber or foam insert

7. Install each spark plug to the cylinder head. Tighten spark plugs to 20 ft. lbs.
(27 Nm).

8. Install the ignition coil onto the
spark plug.

9. Install the ignition coil mounting
bolt, and tighten to 79.5 inch lbs. (9 Nm).

10. Connect the ignition coil electrical
connector.

11. Connect the negative battery
cable.

ENGINE ELECTRICAL

STARTING SYSTEM

STARTER

REMOVAL & INSTALLATION

See Figures 72 through 76.

1. Remove the air cleaner box and air
tube.

2. Disconnect and isolate the negative
battery cable.

3. Remove the starter motor mounting
bolts.

4. Disconnect the electrical connector
at the throttle body.

5. Remove bolts, and remove the throttle body.

6. Push the starter under the intake
manifold.

7. Tip the starter nose toward the cooling module.

8. Pull the starter up and out.

9. Disconnect the starter motor wiring.

10. Remove the starter motor from the
vehicle.

To install:

11. Connect the starter motor wiring.
Tighten the battery cable nut to 90 inch lbs.
(10 Nm).

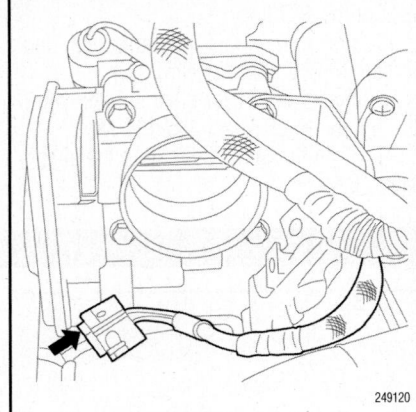

**Fig. 73 Disconnect the electrical connec-
tor at the throttle body**

12. Install the starter motor into the vehicle lower engine compartment.

13. Loosely install the starter into position.

14. Install the throttle body.

15. Install the throttle body bracket.

16. Install the starter motor mounting
bolts, and tighten to 40 ft. lbs. (54 Nm).

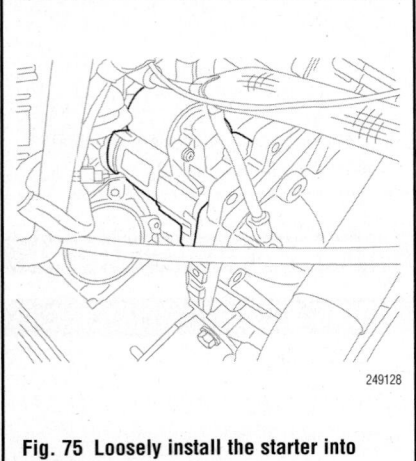

**Fig. 75 Loosely install the starter into
position**

17. Connect the throttle body electrical
connector.

18. Install the air cleaner box and inlet
tube.

19. Connect the negative battery cable.
Refer to Battery Reconnect/Relearn
Procedure.

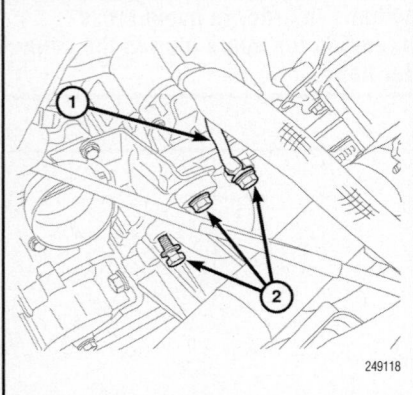

**Fig. 72 Isolate the negative battery cable
(1) and remove the starter motor mounting
bolts (2)**

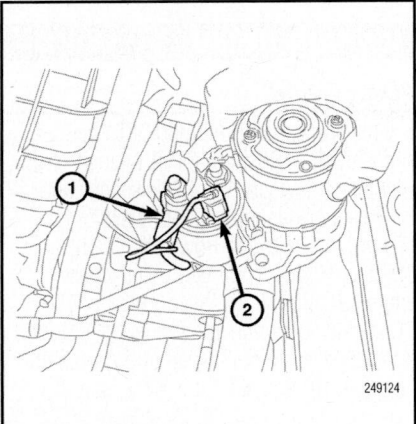

**Fig. 74 Disconnect the starter motor
wiring**

Fig. 76 Install the throttle body bracket

ENGINE MECHANICAL

→Disconnecting the negative battery cable may interfere with the functions of the on board computer systems and may require the computer to undergo a relearning process, once the negative battery cable is reconnected.

ACCESSORY DRIVE BELTS

ACCESSORY BELT ROUTING

See Figure 77.

The accessory drive belt is a serpentine type belt that is driven by the crankshaft pulley.

The belt drives the A/C compressor, generator, power steering pump and water pump. Belt tension is maintained by an automatic belt tensioner.

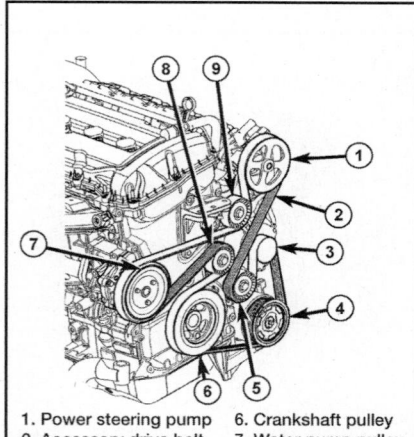

1. Power steering pump	6. Crankshaft pulley
2. Accessory drive belt	7. Water pump pulley
3. Alternator	8. Accessory drive
4. A/C pulley	belt tensioner
5. Lower idler pulley	9. Upper idler pulley

248624

Fig. 77 Accessory drive belt routing

INSPECTION

1. When diagnosing serpentine accessory drive belts, small cracks that run across the ribbed surface of the belt from rib to rib, are considered normal. These are not a reason to replace the belt. However, cracks running along a rib (not across) are not normal. Any belt with cracks running along a rib must be replaced. Also replace the belt if it has excessive wear, frayed cords or severe glazing.

ADJUSTMENT

Accessory belt tension is maintained by an automatic belt tensioner. No adjustment is necessary.

REMOVAL & INSTALLATION

See Figure 77.

1. Using a wrench, rotate the accessory drive belt tensioner counterclockwise until the accessory drive belt can be removed from the pulleys.
2. Remove the accessory drive belt.

To install:

→When installing the drive belt on the pulleys, make sure that the belt is properly routed and all V-grooves make proper contact with pulley grooves.

3. Install the accessory drive belt around all the pulleys except for the generator pulley.
4. Using a wrench, rotate accessory drive belt tensioner counterclockwise until accessory drive belt can be installed on the generator pulley. Release spring tension onto accessory drive belt.

AIR CLEANER

REMOVAL & INSTALLATION

2010 Models

See Figure 78.

1. Remove the fresh air inlet from the air cleaner housing.
2. Remove the intake air temperature sensor electrical connector.
3. Remove the air inlet tube from the housing.
4. Pull the housing upward to remove.

To install:

5. Make sure the rubber grommets for the air cleaner housing lower pins are in place when reinstalling the air cleaner housing. The rubber grommets mount to the

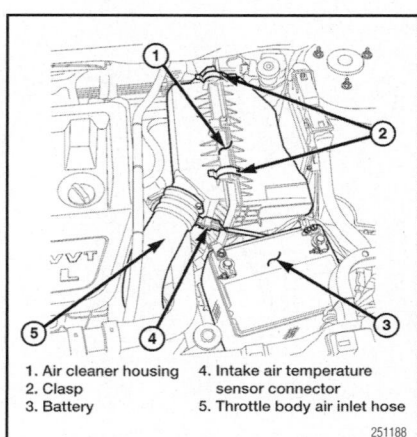

1. Air cleaner housing	4. Intake air temperature
2. Clasp	sensor connector
3. Battery	5. Throttle body air inlet hose

251188

Fig. 78 Removing air cleaner housing—2010 models

Totally Integrated Power Module (TIPM) bracket.

6. Push the air cleaner housing down while aligning pins into the grommets.
7. Connect the throttle body air inlet hose to the air cleaner housing.
8. Connect the intake air temperature sensor connector.
9. Install the fresh air inlet and lock retainers.

2011 Models

See Figures 79 through 81.

1. Unlock the retainers, and remove the fresh air inlet duct from the air cleaner body.
2. Remove the bolts that secure the Powertrain Control Module (PCM) to the air cleaner body cover, and position aside.

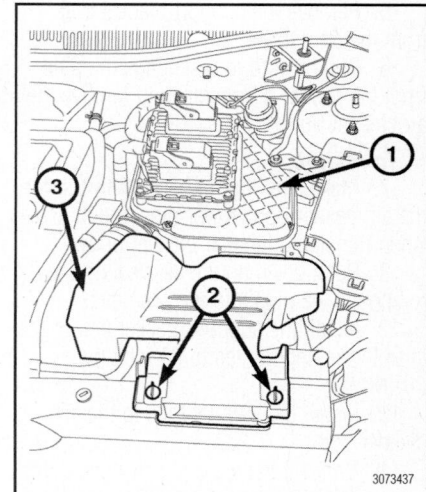

3073437

Fig. 79 Unlock the retainers (2), and remove the fresh air inlet duct (3) from the air cleaner body (1)—2011 models

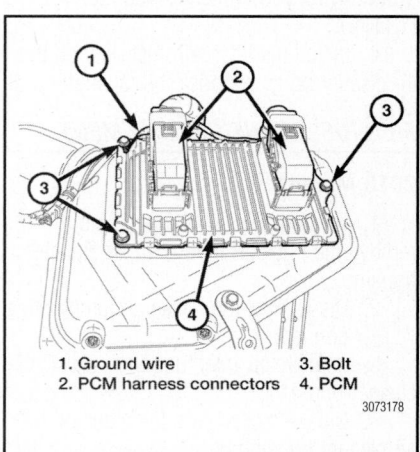

1. Ground wire	3. Bolt
2. PCM harness connectors	4. PCM

3073178

Fig. 80 Powertrain Control Module (PCM) location—2011 models

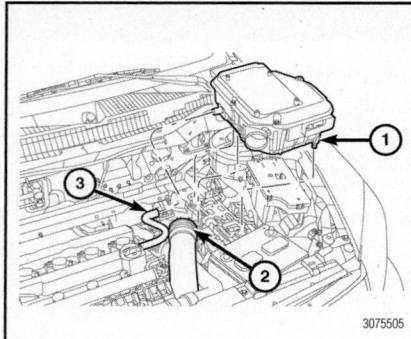

Fig. 81 Remove the air inlet tube (2) from the air cleaner body (1). Disconnect the make-up air hose (3)—2011 models

3. Remove the air inlet tube from the air cleaner body.

4. Disconnect the make-up air hose from the air cleaner body.

5. Remove the support bracket bolt from the strut tower.

6. Pull upward to disengage the pins from the rubber grommets, and remove the air cleaner body.

To install:

7. Make sure the rubber grommets, for the air cleaner body lower pins, are in place when reinstalling the air cleaner body.

8. Push down on the air cleaner body to engage the pins into the grommets.

9. Install the support bracket bolt to the strut tower, and tighten to 89 inch lbs. (10 Nm).

10. Install the air inlet tube to the air cleaner body.

11. Connect the make-up air hose to the air cleaner body.

12. Position the PCM on the air cleaner body cover.

13. Install the 3 mounting bolts with one ground wire, and tighten to 106 inch lbs. (12 Nm).

14. Install the fresh air inlet duct on the air cleaner body, and lock the retainers.

FILTER/ELEMENT REPLACEMENT

2010 Models

1. Turn the 2 lock retainers, and remove the fresh air inlet from air cleaner housing.

2. Disconnect the intake air temperature sensor connector.

3. Remove air inlet tube from air cleaner housing.

4. Unfasten clasps on the sides of the air cleaner housing cover.

5. Pull air cleaner cover aside.

6. Remove the filter element.

7. If necessary, clean the inside of the air cleaner housing.

To install:

8. Install a new filter element.

9. Place the cover over the air cleaner housing. Snap clasps in place.

10. Install the air inlet tube.

11. Connect the intake air temperature sensor connector.

12. Install the fresh air inlet on air cleaner housing, and lock the retainers.

2011 Models

See Figure 82.

1. Unlock the retainers, and remove the fresh air inlet duct from the air cleaner body.

2. Remove the support bracket bolt from the strut tower.

3. Remove the screws that hold the cover on the air cleaner housing.

✳✳ WARNING

Do not unplug the electrical connectors from the Powertrain Control Module (PCM). A possible voltage spike can erase and damage the PCM.

4. Position the air cleaner housing cover aside.

5. Remove the air cleaner element.

6. If necessary, clean the inside of air cleaner housing.

To install:

7. Install the new cleaner element.

8. Place the cover over the air cleaner housing. Hand tighten the cover screws.

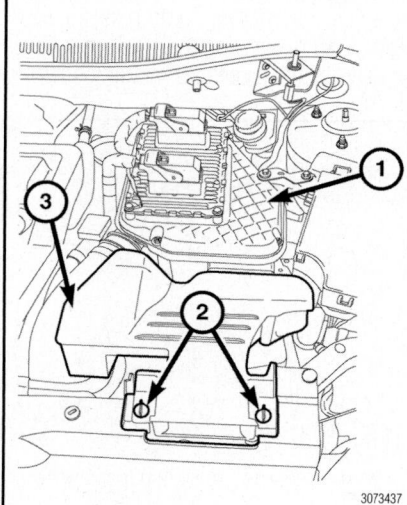

Fig. 82 Unlock the retainers, (2) and remove the fresh air inlet duct (3) from the air cleaner body (1)—2011 models

9. Install the support bracket bolt to the strut tower, and tighten to 89 inch lbs. (10 Nm).

10. Install the fresh air inlet duct on the air cleaner housing and lock the retainers.

CAMSHAFTS

MEASURING END PLAY

See Figure 83.

1. Using a suitable tool, move camshaft as far rearward as it will go.

2. Zero dial indicator.

3. Move camshaft as far forward as it will go.

4. Record the reading on the dial indicator. For end play specification, refer to Camshaft Specifications chart.

5. If end play is excessive, check cylinder head and camshaft for wear. Replace as necessary.

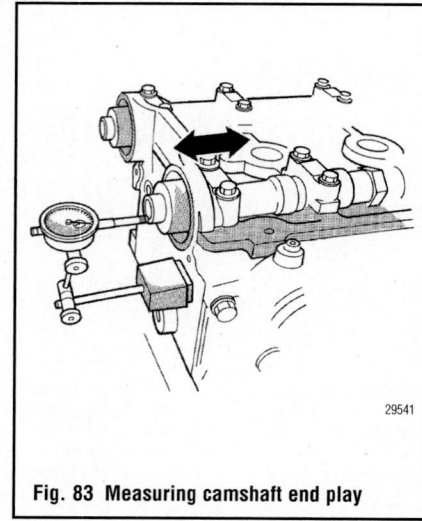

Fig. 83 Measuring camshaft end play

REMOVAL & INSTALLATION

See Figures 84 through 93.

1. Remove engine cover by pulling upward.

2. Disconnect and isolate the negative battery cable.

3. Remove the cylinder head cover. Refer to Cylinder Head Cover, removal & installation.

4. Raise and support the vehicle.

5. Remove the frame cover portion of the right splash shield.

6. Rotate the engine to Top Dead Center (TDC).

7. Make sure the camshaft timing marks are in line with the cylinder head cover sealing surface.

8. Mark the chain link corresponding to timing marks with a paint marker.

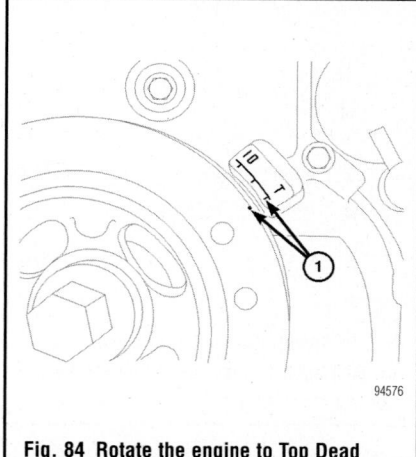

Fig. 84 Rotate the engine to Top Dead Center (TDC) (1)

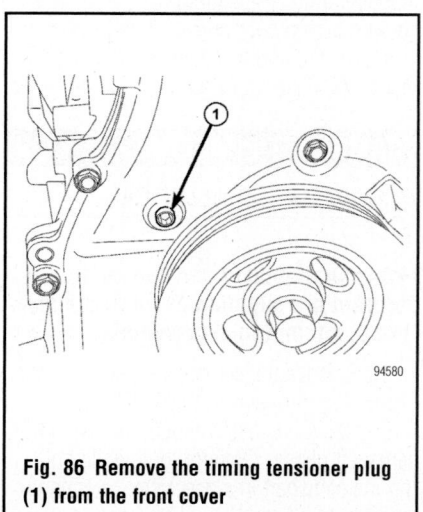

1. Mark the chain link corresponding to timing marks
2. Front cover
3. Camshaft timing marks

Fig. 85 View of timing chain timing marks

9. Remove the timing tensioner plug from the front cover.

10. Insert a small Allen wrench through the timing tensioner plug hole, and lift

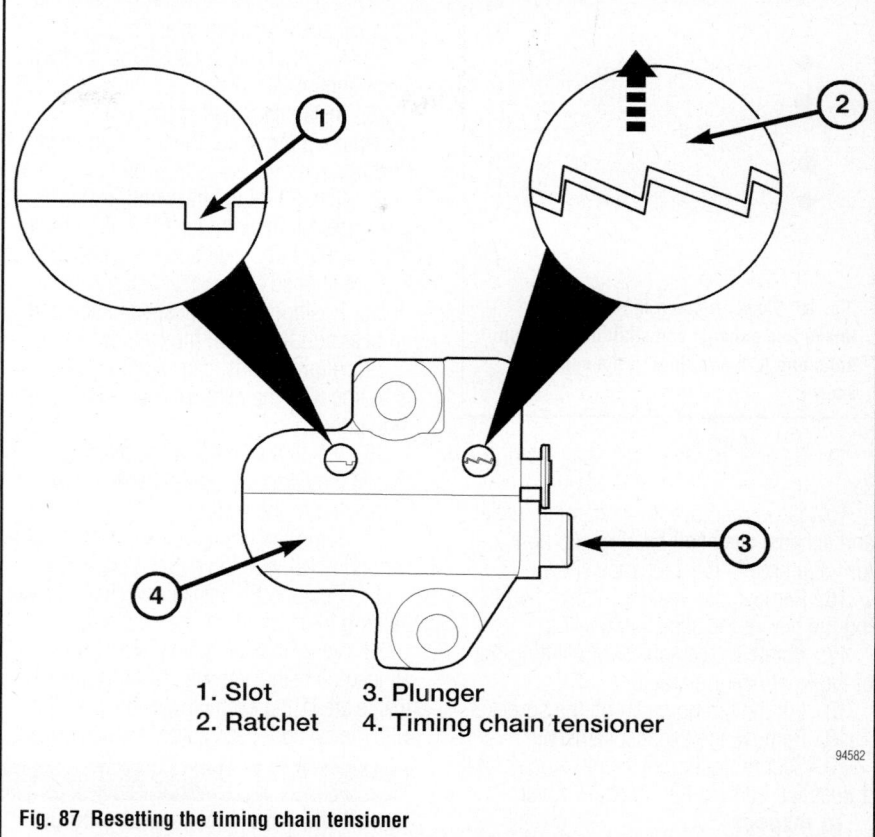

1. Slot
2. Ratchet
3. Plunger
4. Timing chain tensioner

Fig. 87 Resetting the timing chain tensioner

ratchet upward to release the tensioner and push Allen wrench inward. Leave the Allen wrench installed during the remainder of this procedure.

11. Insert a locking wedge (9701) between the camshaft phasers.

12. Lightly tap the locking wedge into place until it will no longer sink down.

➡ Camshaft bearing caps should have been marked during engine manufacturing. For example, number one

exhaust camshaft bearing is marked "E1>".

✲✲ WARNING

DO NOT use a number stamp or a punch to mark camshaft bearing caps. Damage to bearing caps could occur.

13. Using a permanent ink or paint marker, identify the location and position on each camshaft bearing cap.

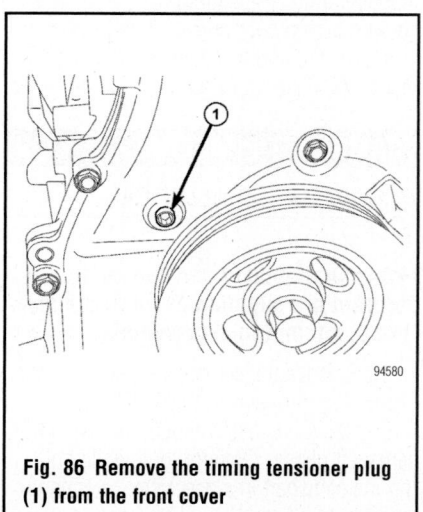

Fig. 86 Remove the timing tensioner plug (1) from the front cover

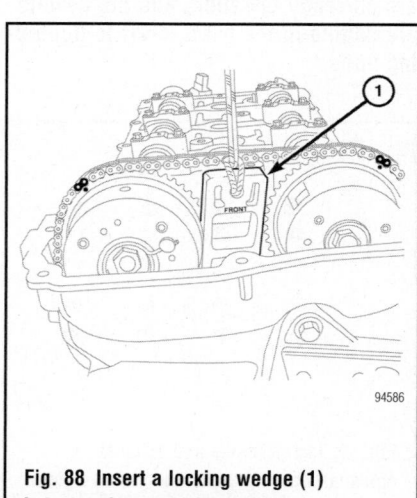

Fig. 88 Insert a locking wedge (1) between the camshaft phasers

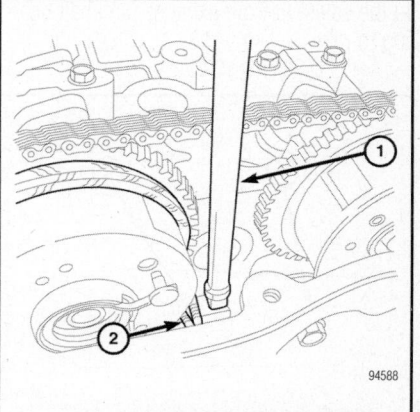

Fig. 89 Lightly tap (1) the Locking Wedge (2) into place until it will no longer sink down.

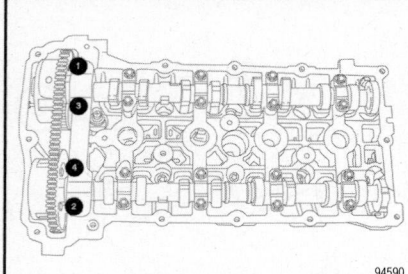

Fig. 90 Slowly remove the remaining intake and exhaust camshaft bearing cap bolts one turn at a time in the sequence shown

14. Remove the front camshaft bearing cap.

15. Slowly remove the remaining intake and exhaust camshaft bearing cap bolts one turn at a time in the sequence shown.

16. Remove the intake camshaft by lifting the rear of the camshaft upward.

17. Rotate the camshaft while lifting out of the front bearing cradle.

18. Lift the timing chain off the sprocket.

19. Remove the exhaust camshaft.

20. Secure timing chain with wire so that it does fall into the timing chain cover.

To inspect:

21. Inspect the camshaft bearing journals for damage. If journals are damaged, check the cylinder head for damage. Also check cylinder head oil holes for clogging.

22. Check the cam lobe and bearing surfaces for abnormal wear and damage. Replace camshaft if defective.

➡**If camshaft is replaced due to lobe wear or damage, always replace the lash buckets.**

To install:

23. The front camshaft bearing cap is numbered either 1, 2, or 3; this corresponds to the select fit front exhaust camshaft bearing to use.

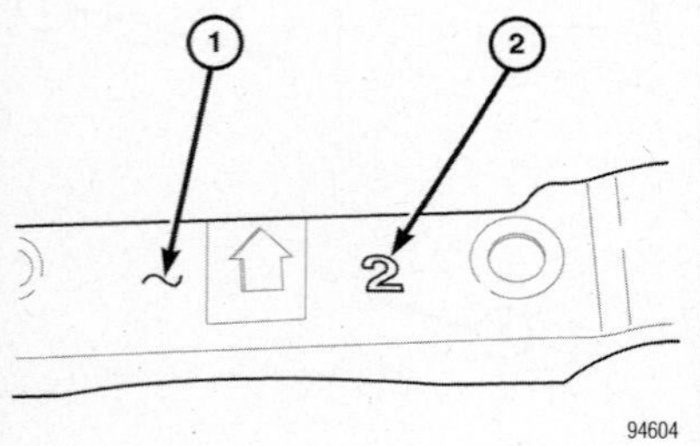

24. Install the corresponding select fit front exhaust camshaft bearing.

25. Oil all of the camshaft journals with clean engine oil.

26. Install camshaft phasers on camshafts if removed. Refer to Camshaft Phasers, removal & installation.

27. Install timing chain onto exhaust cam sprocket, making sure that the timing marks on the sprocket and the painted chain link are aligned.

28. Position the exhaust camshaft and on bearing journals in the cylinder head.

29. Align exhaust cam timing mark so it is in line with the cylinder head cover sealing surface.

30. Install intake camshaft by raising the rear of the camshaft upward and roll the sprocket into the chain.

31. Align the timing marks on the intake cam sprocket with the painted chain link.

32. Position the intake camshaft into the bearing journals in the cylinder head.

33. Verify that the timing marks are aligned on both camshafts and that the timing marks are facing each other and are in line with the cylinder head cover sealing surface.

❊❊ **WARNING**

Install the front intake and exhaust camshaft bearing cap last. Ensure that the dowels are seated and follow torque sequence or damage to engine could result.

➡**If the front camshaft bearing cap is broken, the cylinder head MUST be replaced.**

34. Install intake and exhaust camshaft bearing caps, and slowly tighten bolts to 85 inch lbs. (9.5 Nm) in the sequence shown.

➡**Verify that the exhaust bearing shells are correctly installed, and the dowels are seated in the head, prior to tightening bolts.**

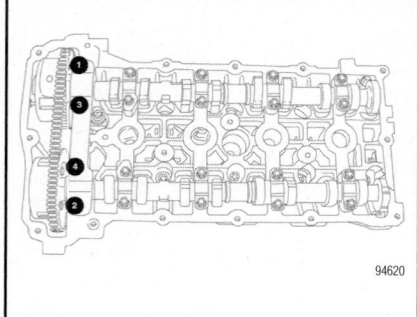

Fig. 93 Install the front intake and exhaust bearing caps, and tighten bolts in the sequence shown

35. Install the front intake and exhaust bearing caps, and tighten bolts to 18 ft. lbs. (25 Nm) in the sequence shown.

36. Verify that all timing marks are aligned.

37. Remove Allen wrench from timing chain tensioner.

38. Remove locking wedge by pulling straight upward on pull rope.

39. Apply MOPAR® thread sealant to timing tensioner plug and install.

40. Rotate the crankshaft CLOCKWISE 2 complete revolutions until the crankshaft is repositioned at the TDC position.

41. Verify that the camshafts timing marks are in the proper position and in line with the cylinder head cover sealing surface. If the marks do not line up, the timing chain is not correctly installed.

42. Install right splash shield.

43. Install the cylinder head cover. Refer to Cylinder Head Cover, removal & installation.

44. Connect the negative battery cable.

45. Fill the cooling system. Refer to Drain & Refill procedure.

46. Fill with oil.

47. Operate engine until it reaches normal operating temperature. Check oil and cooling systems for correct fluid levels.

48. Install engine cover by pressing the rear of the cover down first.

CAMSHAFT PHASERS

REMOVAL & INSTALLATION

See Figure 94.

➡**Camshaft phaser and camshaft sprocket are supplied as an assembly. Do not attempt to disassemble.**

1. Remove the camshafts. Refer to Camshafts, removal & installation.

2. Using a socket wrench, remove the camshaft phaser retaining bolt while holding the camshaft in place with a wrench on the camshaft flats.

Fig. 91 The front camshaft bearing cap (1) is numbered (2) either 1, 2, or 3

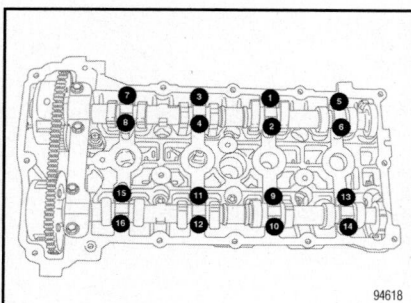

Fig. 92 Install intake and exhaust camshaft bearing caps, and slowly tighten bolts in the sequence shown

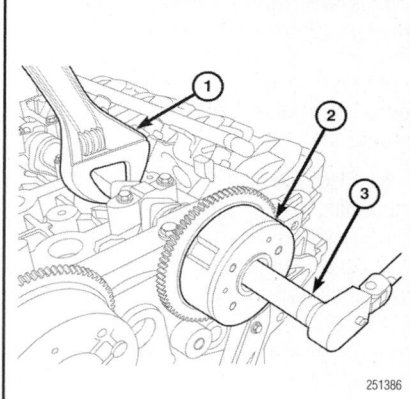

Fig. 94 Using a socket wrench (3), remove the camshaft phaser (2) retaining bolt while holding the camshaft in place with a wrench (1) on the camshaft flats

3. Remove the phaser assembly from the camshaft.

To install:

> ❄❄ **WARNING**
>
> Do not use an impact wrench to tighten camshaft sprocket bolts. Damage to the camshaft-to-sprocket locating dowel pin and camshaft phaser may occur.

4. Install the phaser assembly on the camshaft.

➡**Make sure the dowel is seated in the dowel hole and not in a oil feed hole. The dowel hole is larger than the 4 oil feed holes.**

5. Install the phaser retaining bolt. Hold camshaft in place with a wrench, and tighten bolt to 44 ft. lbs. (59 Nm).

6. Install the camshafts. Refer to Camshafts, removal & installation.

CATALYTIC CONVERTER

REMOVAL & INSTALLATION
See Figure 95.

> ❄❄ **CAUTION**
>
> The normal operating temperature of the exhaust system is very high. Therefore, never attempt to service any part of the exhaust system until it is cooled. Special care should be taken when working near the catalytic converter. The temperature of the converter rises to a high level after a short period of engine operation time.

> ❄❄ **WARNING**
>
> DO NOT remove spark plug wires from plugs or by any other means short out cylinders. Failure of the catalytic converter can occur due to a temperature increase caused by unburned fuel passing through the converter.

> ❄❄ **WARNING**
>
> Unleaded gasoline must be used to avoid contaminating the catalyst core.

➡**The stainless steel catalytic converter body is designed to last the life of the vehicle. Excessive heat can result in bulging or other distortion, but excessive heat will not be the fault of the converter. If unburned fuel enters the converter, overheating may occur. If a converter is heat-damaged, correct the cause of the damage at the same time the converter is replaced. Also, inspect all other components of the exhaust system for heat damage.**

➡**Before replacing a catalytic converter, determine the root cause of failure. Most catalytic converter failures are caused by air, fuel or ignition problems.**

1. Loosen intermediate pipe-to-catalytic converter clamp.

> ❄❄ **WARNING**
>
> Do not use petroleum-based lubricants when removing/installing muffler or exhaust pipe isolators, as it may compromise the life of the part. A suitable substitute is a mixture of liquid dish soap and water.

2. Remove catalytic converter-to-exhaust manifold mounting nuts and gasket. Discard gasket.

3. Remove I-Pipe/Muffler assembly insulators as necessary to slide catalytic converter out of I-Pipe/Muffler.

> ❄❄ **WARNING**
>
> When replacement is required on any component of the exhaust system, original equipment parts (or equivalent) must be used.

To install:
4. Position catalytic converter into I-Pipe/muffler assembly.

5. Using new gasket, position catalytic converter against exhaust manifold.

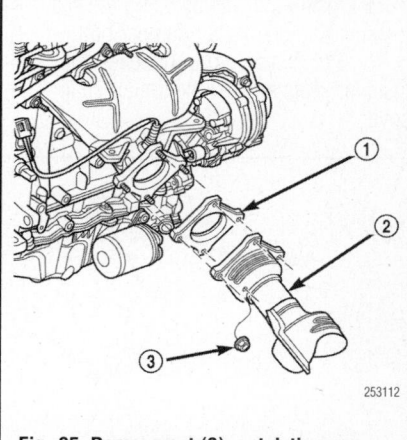

Fig. 95 Remove nut (3), catalytic converter (2) and gasket (1)

6. Install flange nuts. Tighten to 21 ft. lbs. (29 Nm).

7. Working from the front of system; align each component to maintain position and proper clearance with underbody parts.

8. Tighten band clamps to 40 ft. lbs. (55 Nm).

> ❄❄ **WARNING**
>
> Band clamps should never be tightened such that the two sides of the clamps are bottomed out against the center hourglass shaped center block. Once this occurs, the clamp has lost clamping force and must be replaced.

9. Start the engine and inspect for exhaust leaks. Repair exhaust leaks as necessary.

10. Check the exhaust system for contact with the body panels. Make the necessary adjustments, if needed.

CRANKSHAFT FRONT SEAL

REMOVAL & INSTALLATION
See Figures 96 through 98.

1. Remove the accessory drive belt. Refer to Accessory Drive Belt, removal & installation.

2. Remove the crankshaft vibration damper. Refer to Crankshaft Vibration Damper, removal & installation.

3. Remove the front crankshaft oil seal by prying out with a screwdriver. Be careful not to damage the cover seal surface.

To install:
4. Place a new seal onto seal installer with seal spring towards the inside of the engine.

5. Install the seal by using the seal installer and crankshaft damper bolt.

6. Press seal into front cover until seal installer seats against the timing chain cover.

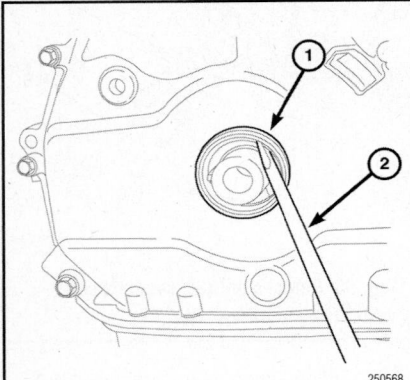

Fig. 96 Remove the front crankshaft oil seal (1) by prying out with a screwdriver (2)

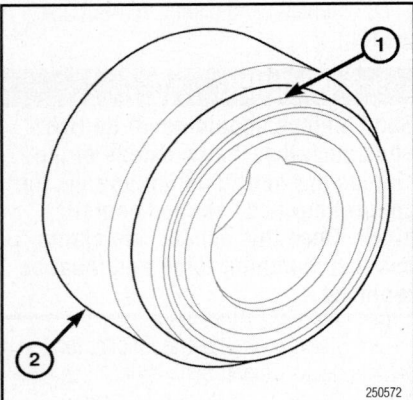

Fig. 97 Place new seal (1) onto seal installer (2) with seal spring towards the inside of engine

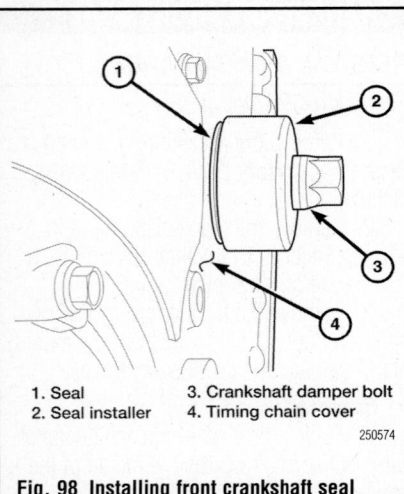

1. Seal   3. Crankshaft damper bolt
2. Seal installer   4. Timing chain cover

Fig. 98 Installing front crankshaft seal

7. Remove the seal installer.

8. Install the crankshaft vibration damper.

9. Oil the bolt threads and between the bolt head and washer.

10. Install the damper retaining bolt and damper holder. Tighten bolt to 37 ft. lbs. + 68° (50 Nm + 68°).

CRANKSHAFT REAR SEAL

REMOVAL & INSTALLATION

See Figures 99 and 100.

1. Remove the transaxle.
2. Remove the flexplate.
3. Insert a 3/16 flat-bladed screwdriver between the dust lip and the metal case of the crankshaft seal. Angle the screwdriver through the dust lip against the metal case of the seal. Pry out seal.

✳ WARNING

Do not permit the screwdriver blade to contact crankshaft seal surface. Contact of the screwdriver blade against crankshaft edge (chamfer) is permitted.

4. Check to make sure the seal's garter spring is not on the crankshaft.

To install:

✳ WARNING

If a burr or scratch is present on the crankshaft edge (chamfer), cleanup with 800 emery cloth to prevent seal damage during installation of the new seal. If emery cloth is used, the

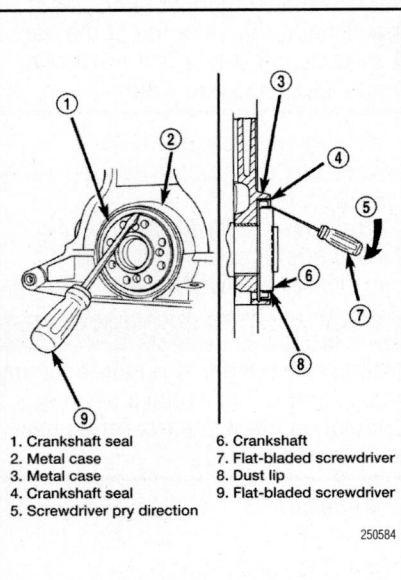

1. Crankshaft seal   6. Crankshaft
2. Metal case   7. Flat-bladed screwdriver
3. Metal case   8. Dust lip
4. Crankshaft seal   9. Flat-bladed screwdriver
5. Screwdriver pry direction

Fig. 99 Removing rear crankshaft oil seal

crankshaft must be cleaned off with Mopar® brake parts cleaner.

➡ **When installing the seal, lubricate the oil seal installer (9509) with clean engine oil.**

5. Place the oil seal installer (9509) on crankshaft.

6. Position the seal over the guide tool. Guide tool should remain on crankshaft during installation of seal. Ensure that the lip of the seal is facing towards the crankcase during installation.

7. Drive the seal into the block using seal driver (9706) and driver handle (C-4171) (4) until the seal driver bottoms out against the block.

8. Install the flexplate and Transaxle.

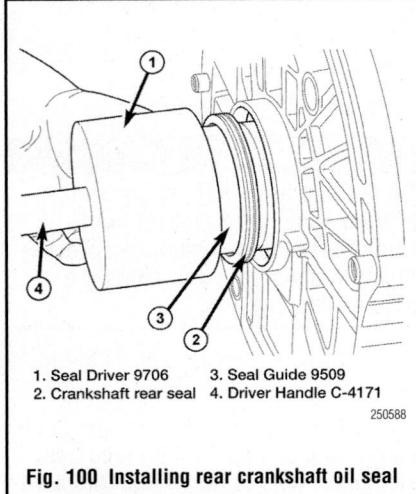

1. Seal Driver 9706   3. Seal Guide 9509
2. Crankshaft rear seal   4. Driver Handle C-4171

Fig. 100 Installing rear crankshaft oil seal

CRANKSHAFT VIBRATION DAMPER

REMOVAL & INSTALLATION

See Figure 101.

1. Remove the accessory drive belt. Refer to Accessory Drive Belts, removal & installation.

2. Install damper holder (9707), and remove the damper retaining bolt.

3. Pull the damper off the crankshaft.

To install:

4. Install the crankshaft damper.

5. Apply clean engine oil to crankshaft damper bolt threads and between bolt head and washer. Tighten bolt to 155 ft. lbs. (210 Nm).

6. Install the accessory drive belt. Refer to Accessory Drive Belts, removal & installation.

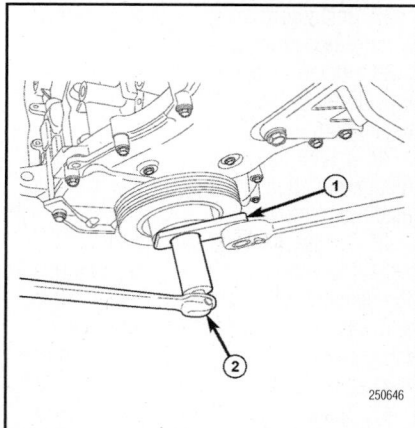

Fig. 101 Install damper holder (1), and remove the damper retaining bolt (2)

CYLINDER HEAD

REMOVAL & INSTALLATION

See Figures 102 through 108.

1. Remove the timing chain cover. Refer to Timing Chain Cover, removal & installation.

2. Remove catalytic converter. Refer to Catalytic Converter, removal & installation.

3. Remove timing chain tensioner. Refer to Timing Chain Tensioner, removal & installation.

4. Remove the timing chain. Refer to Timing Chain, removal & installation.

5. Remove timing chain guide and timing chain pivot guide.

6. Remove fuel rail. Refer to Fuel Injectors, removal & installation.

7. Disconnect electrical connectors from Engine Coolant Temperature (ECT) sensor, oil temperature sensor, variable valve timing solenoids, Camshaft Position (CMP) sensors, Manifold Air Pressure (MAP) sensor, manifold tuning valve, ignition interference suppressor and electronic throttle control.

8. Remove 4 bolts, and reposition the coolant adapter.

9. Remove the intake manifold. Refer to Intake Manifold, removal & installation.

10. Remove ground strap at right rear of cylinder head (if equipped).

11. Remove the camshafts. Refer to Camshafts, removal & installation.

➡ **All of the cylinder head bolts have captured washers EXCEPT the front two.**

12. Remove the cylinder head bolts and 2 uncaptured washers.

13. Remove the cylinder head from the engine block.

To install:

✳ WARNING

The cylinder head bolts are tightened using a torque plus angle procedure. The bolts must be examined BEFORE reuse. If the threads are necked down, the bolts must be replaced.

14. Check cylinder head bolts for necking by holding a scale or straight edge against the threads. If all the threads do not contact the scale the bolt must be replaced.

15. Inspect and clean cylinder head and block sealing surfaces.

➡ **Ensure cylinder head bolt holes in the block are clean, dry (free of residual oil or coolant), and threads are not damaged.**

✳ WARNING

Always replace the variable valve timing filter screen when servicing

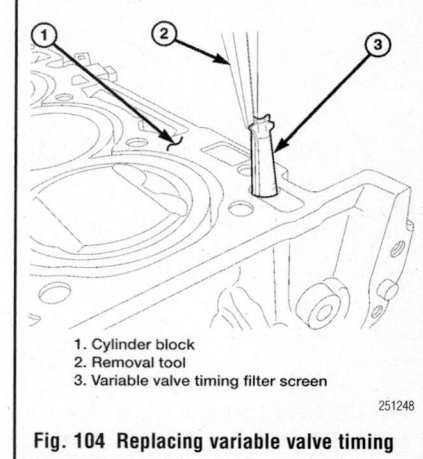

1. Cylinder block
2. Removal tool
3. Variable valve timing filter screen

Fig. 104 Replacing variable valve timing filter screen

the head gasket, or engine damage could result.

16. Replace the variable valve timing filter screen.

➡ **When using RTV, the sealing surfaces must be clean and free from grease and oil.**

➡ **When using RTV, parts should be assembled in 10 minutes and tightened to final torque within 45 minutes.**

17. Place 2 pea-size dots of engine sealant RTV on the cylinder block as shown.

18. Position the new cylinder head gasket on engine block with the part number facing up. Ensure gasket is seated over the locating dowels in block.

19. Place 2 pea-size dots of engine sealant RTV on the cylinder head gasket as shown.

➡ **The head must be installed within 15 minutes before the RTV skins.**

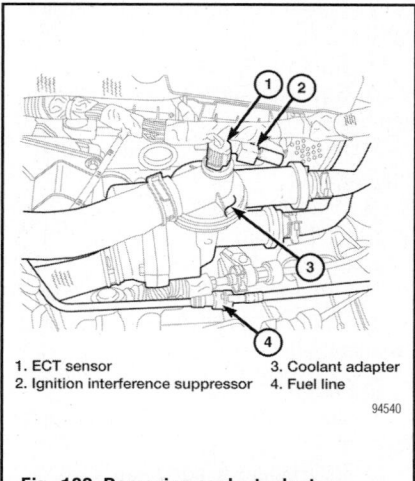

1. ECT sensor
2. Ignition interference suppressor
3. Coolant adapter
4. Fuel line

Fig. 102 Removing coolant adapter

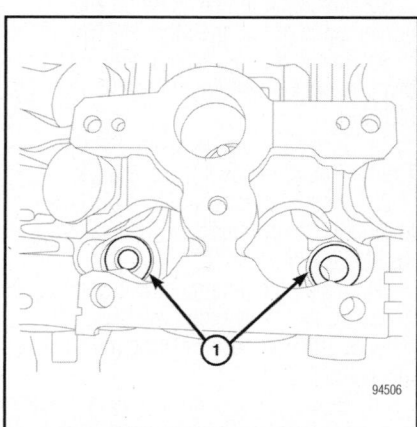

Fig. 103 All of the cylinder head bolts have captured washers EXCEPT the front two (1)

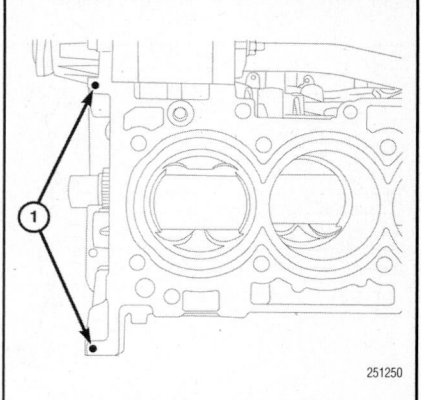

Fig. 105 Place 2 pea-size dots of engine sealant RTV on the cylinder block as shown

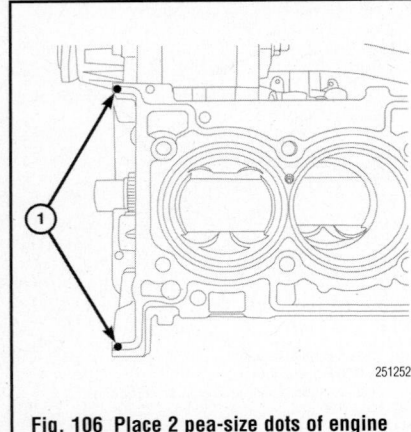

Fig. 106 Place 2 pea-size dots of engine sealant RTV on the cylinder head gasket as shown

20. Position the cylinder head onto the engine block.

❊❊ WARNING

This engine was built with 2 different style cylinder head bolts. Each style bolt requires a different torque value. The bolts can be identified by the short bolt head and the long bolt head.

21. Measure the bolt head from the washer to the top of the bolt head. The short bolt head measures 5/16 inch (8 mm) and the long bolt head measures 1/2 inch (13 mm).

22. Identify whether your engine has the short head design or the long head design.

➡**The front 2 cylinder head bolts do not have captured washers. The washers must be installed with the beveled edge up towards the bolt head.**

23. Install washers for the front 2 cylinder head bolts with the beveled edge facing up.

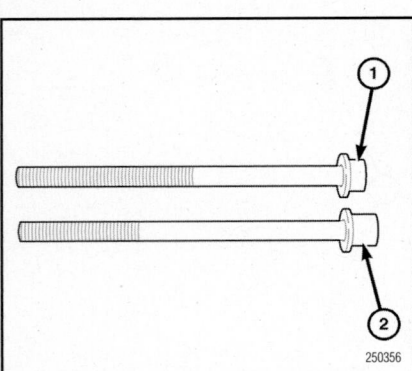

Fig. 107 Bolts can be identified by the short bolt head (1) and the long bolt head (2)

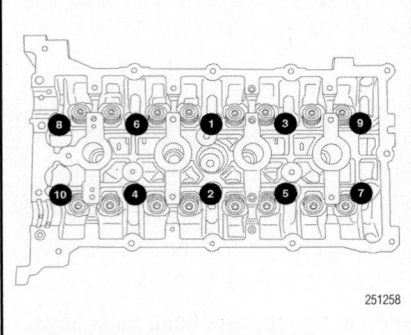

Fig. 108 Install the cylinder head bolts, and tighten in the sequence shown

➡**Before installing the cylinder head bolts, lubricate the threads with clean engine oil.**

24. Install the cylinder head bolts, and tighten in the sequence shown.

25. If your bolt has the short head, use the following torque specifications:
   a. First: All to 25 ft. lbs. (30 Nm).
   b. Second: All to 45 ft. lbs. (61 Nm).
   c. Third: All to 45 ft. lbs. (61 Nm).
   d. Fourth: All an additional 90°. Do not use a torque wrench.

26. If your bolt has the long head, use the following torque specifications:
   a. First: All to 25 ft. lbs. (30 Nm).
   b. Second: All to 54 ft. lbs. (73 Nm).
   c. Third: All to 54 ft. lbs. (73 Nm).
   d. Fourth: All an additional 90°. Do not use a torque wrench.

27. Clean excess RTV from the timing chain cover sealing surface.

28. Install the coolant adapter with new seals. Tighten bolts to 159 inch lbs. (18.1 Nm).

29. Install the camshafts. Refer to Camshafts, removal & installation.

30. Install timing chain guide and tighten bolts to 105 inch lbs. (12 Nm).

31. Install the moveable timing chain pivot guide and tighten bolt to 105 inch lbs. (12 Nm).

32. Install the timing chain. Refer to Timing Chain, removal & installation.

33. Install timing chain tensioner. Refer to Timing Chain Tensioner, removal & installation.

34. Install the timing chain cover, engine mount, pulleys and accessory drive belt. Refer to Timing Chain Cover, removal & installation.

35. Install cylinder head cover and ignition coils. Refer to Cylinder Head Cover, removal & installation.

36. Install exhaust manifold. Refer to Exhaust Manifold, removal & installation.

37. Install ground strap at right rear of cylinder head if equipped.

38. Install intake manifold and vacuum lines. Refer to Intake Manifold, removal & installation.

39. Install fuel rail, and connect coil and injector electrical connectors. Refer to Fuel Injectors, removal & installation.

40. Connect electrical connectors to coolant temperature sensor, camshaft position sensors, oil temperature sensor, variable valve timing solenoids, MAP sensor, manifold tuning valve, ignition interference suppressor and electronic throttle control.

41. Install power steering pump reservoir. Tighten mounting screw to 106 inch lbs. (12 Nm).

42. Install the windshield washer reservoir.

43. Install the coolant recovery reservoir. Tighten mounting bolts to 35 inch lbs. (4 Nm).

44. Install catalytic converter. Refer to Catalytic Converter, removal & installation.

45. Fill the cooling system. Refer to Drain & Refill procedure.

46. Install new oil filter and fill engine with oil. Refer to Engine Oil & Filter, removal & installation.

47. Connect the negative battery cable. Refer to Battery Reconnect/Relearn Procedure.

48. Operate engine until it reaches normal operating temperature. Check oil and cooling systems for leaks and correct fluid levels.

49. Install engine cover by pressing the rear of the cover down first.

CYLINDER HEAD COVER

REMOVAL & INSTALLATION

See Figures 109 through 113.

1. Remove engine cover.
2. Disconnect and isolate the negative battery cable.
3. Remove the makeup air hose.
4. Remove Positive Crankcase Ventilation (PCV) hose.
5. Remove the ignition coil electrical connectors.
6. Use compressed air to blow dirt and debris off the cylinder head cover prior to removal.
7. Remove cylinder head cover bolts.
8. Remove cylinder head cover from cylinder head.

To install:
9. Install new cylinder head cover gaskets.
10. Install studs in cover as shown.
11. Clean all RTV from cylinder head.

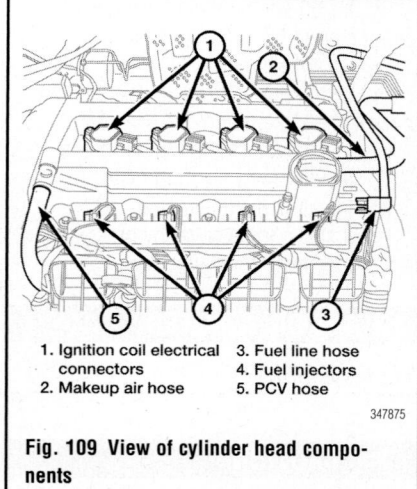

1. Ignition coil electrical   3. Fuel line hose
   connectors   4. Fuel injectors
2. Makeup air hose   5. PCV hose
                                    347875

Fig. 109 View of cylinder head components

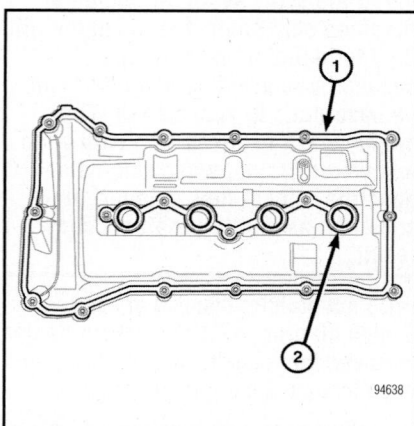

Fig. 110 Install new cylinder head cover gaskets (1, 2)

➡**When using RTV, the sealing surfaces must be clean and free from grease and oil.**

➡**When using RTV, parts should be assembled in 10 minutes and tightened to final torque within 45 minutes.**

12. Apply a dot of engine sealant RTV to cylinder head/front cover T-joint.

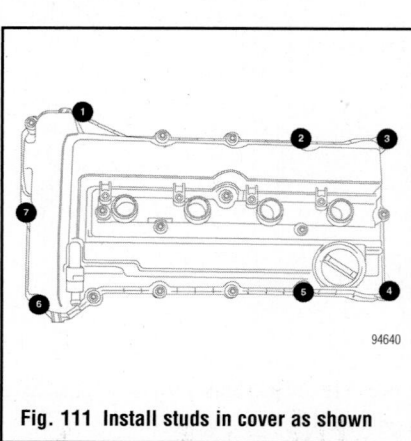

Fig. 111 Install studs in cover as shown

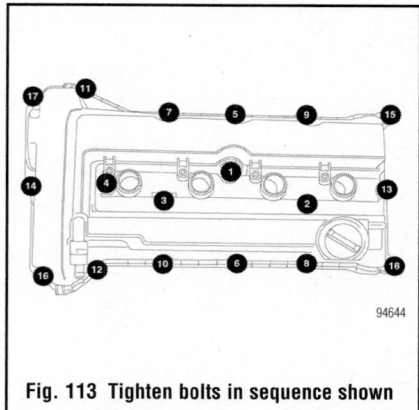

Fig. 112 Apply a dot of engine sealant RTV to cylinder head/front cover T-joint (1)

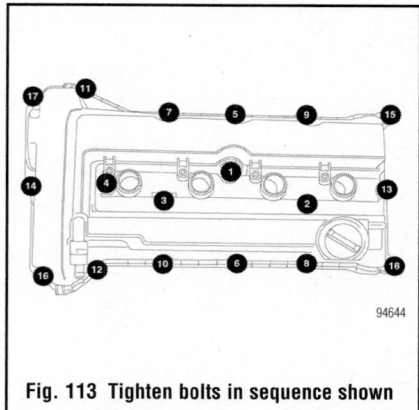

94644

Fig. 113 Tighten bolts in sequence shown

13. Install cylinder head cover assembly to cylinder head and install all bolts, ensuring the studs are located as shown.
14. Tighten bolts in sequence shown using a 2-step torque method as follows:
    a. Tighten all bolts to 44 inch lbs. (5 Nm).
    b. Tighten all bolts to 90 inch lbs. (10 Nm).
15. Install the ignition coil connectors.
16. If the PCV valve was removed, tighten PCV valve to 44 inch lbs. (5 Nm).
17. Connect coil electrical connectors.
18. Connect the PCV hose to PCV valve.
19. Connect the makeup air hose.
20. Reconnect the negative battery cable.
21. Install engine cover by pressing the rear of the cover down first.

ENGINE MOUNTS

REMOVAL & INSTALLATION

Front Engine Mount

See Figure 114.

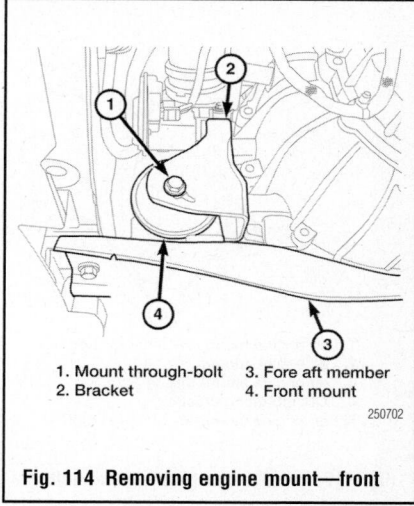

1. Mount through-bolt   3. Fore aft member
2. Bracket   4. Front mount
                                 250702

Fig. 114 Removing engine mount—front

1. Raise the vehicle.
2. Remove fore aft member-to mount bolts.
3. Remove mount through-bolt.
4. Remove fore aft member mounting bolts and remove.
5. Remove the front mount.

To install:

6. Position the front mount, and tighten bolts to 35 ft. lbs. (47 Nm).
7. Install fore aft member, and tighten bolts to 74 ft. lbs. (100 Nm).
8. Install mount through-bolt, and tighten to 35 ft. lbs. (47 Nm).
9. Lower the vehicle.

Left Engine Mount

See Figure 115.

1. Remove air cleaner inlet and air cleaner housing. Refer to Air Cleaner, removal & installation.
2. Remove Powertrain Control Module (PCM).
3. Remove PCM mounting bracket.
4. Disconnect negative cable from the battery.
5. Support the transaxle with a suitable jack.
6. Remove left mount through-bolt.
7. Remove left mount bracket-to-body frame rail fasteners.
8. Remove the left mount.

To install:

9. Position left mount in place.
10. Install left mount-to-frame rail bolts, and tighten to 55 ft. lbs. (75 Nm).
11. Install mount through-bolt, and torque to 74 ft. lbs. (100 Nm).
12. Remove the jack.
13. Install PCM mounting bracket.
14. Install PCM.

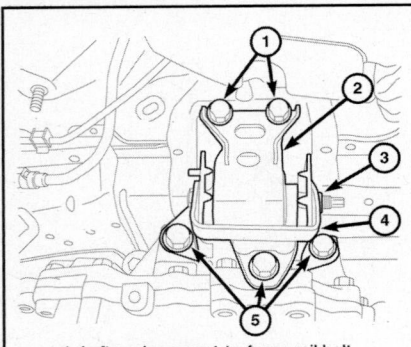

1. Left engine mount-to-frame rail bolt
2. Left engine mount
3. Left engine mount through-bolt
4. PCM mounting bracket
5. Left engine mount-to-frame rail bolt

Fig. 115 Removing engine mount—left

15. Connect the negative battery cable. Refer to Battery Reconnect/Relearn Procedure.

16. Install air cleaner inlet and air cleaner housing. Refer to Air Cleaner, removal & installation.

Rear Engine Mount

See Figure 116.

1. Remove rear mount retaining bolts.
2. Remove rear mount through-bolt.
3. Remove the Heated Oxygen Sensor (HO2S) connector from the mount.
4. Remove the rear mount.

To install:

5. Position the rear mount.
6. Install rear mount retaining bolts, and tighten to 37 ft. lbs. (50 Nm).
7. Install rear mount through-bolt and torque to 35 ft. lbs. (47 Nm).
8. Install the HO2S connector retainer to mount.

Right Engine Mount

See Figures 117 and 118.

1. Remove coolant reservoir and set aside.
2. Remove power steering reservoir and set aside.
3. Remove windshield washer bottle.
4. Remove power steering line support bracket from engine mount.
5. Support transaxle with a block of wood and a suitable jack.
6. Remove engine mount through-bolt.
7. Remove engine mount bracket bolts.
8. Remove engine mount retaining bolts.
9. Remove the right engine mount.

To install:

10. Position right engine mount.
11. Install engine mount retaining bolts, and tighten to 55 ft. lbs. (75 Nm).
12. Install engine mount adapter, and tighten bolts to 50 ft. lbs. (68 Nm).

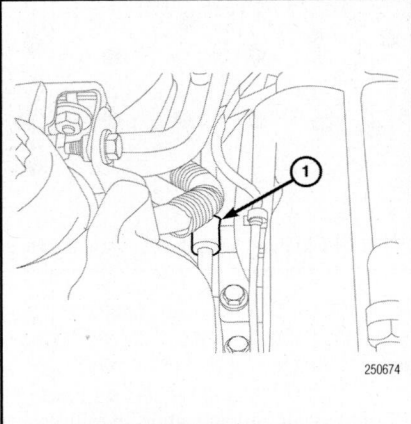

Fig. 117 Remove power steering line support bracket (1) from engine mount

13. Install engine mount through-bolt, and tighten to 65 ft. lbs. (88 Nm).
14. Remove the jack.
15. Install power steering line support bracket at engine mount.
16. Install windshield washer bottle.
17. Install power steering reservoir.
18. Install coolant reservoir.
19. Install engine cover by pressing the rear of the cover down first.

ENGINE OIL & FILTER

REPLACEMENT

See Figures 119 and 120.

✳✳ CAUTION

New or used engine oil can be irritating to the skin. Avoid prolonged or repeated skin contact with engine oil. Contaminants in used engine oil, caused by internal combustion, can be hazardous to your health. Thoroughly wash exposed skin with soap and water. Do not wash skin with gasoline, diesel fuel, thinner, or solvents, as health problems can result.

➡ **Do not pollute; dispose of used engine oil properly. Contact your dealer or government agency for the location of collection centers in your area.**

1. Run engine until achieving normal operating temperature.
2. Position the vehicle on a level surface and turn the engine off.
3. Remove the oil fill cap.
4. Raise the vehicle on a hoist.
5. Place a suitable oil collecting container under the oil pan drain plug.

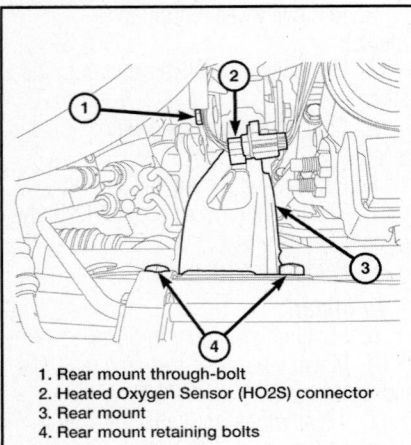

1. Rear mount through-bolt
2. Heated Oxygen Sensor (HO2S) connector
3. Rear mount
4. Rear mount retaining bolts

Fig. 116 Removing engine mount—rear

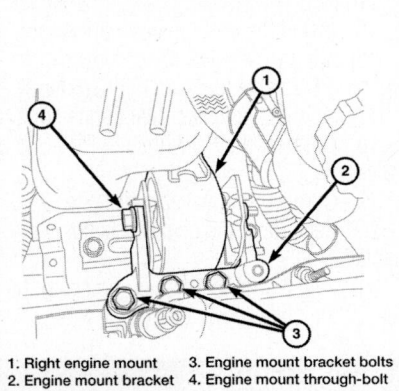

1. Right engine mount
2. Engine mount bracket
3. Engine mount bracket bolts
4. Engine mount through-bolt

Fig. 118 Removing engine mount—right

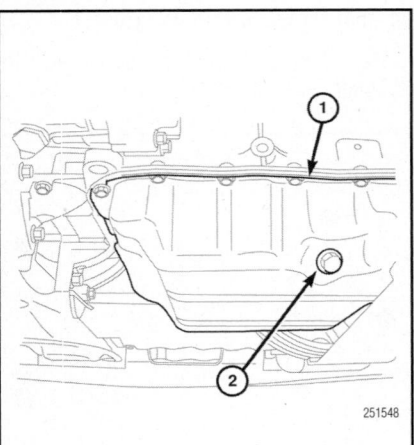

Fig. 119 Oil pan drain plug (2) location on oil pan (1)

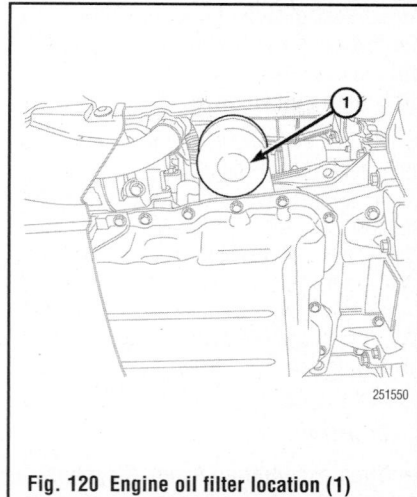

Fig. 120 Engine oil filter location (1)

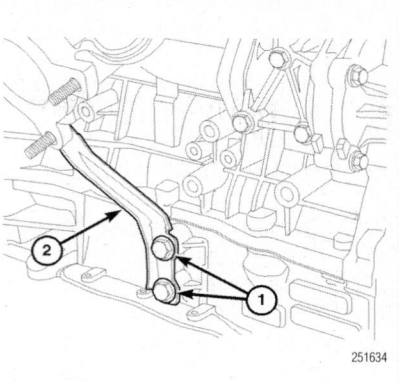

Fig. 121 Remove the 2 bolts (1), and remove the exhaust manifold support bracket (2)

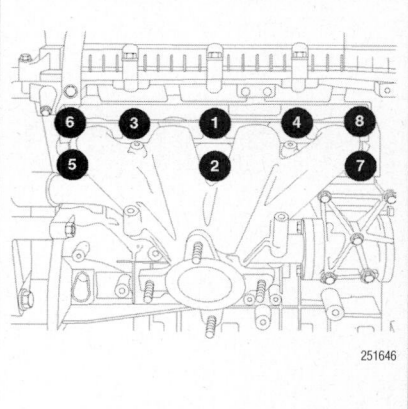

Fig. 123 Install and tighten the exhaust manifold bolts in sequence

6. Remove the oil pan drain plug, and allow the oil to drain into a collecting container. Inspect the drain plug threads for stretching or other damage. Replace drain plug and gasket if damaged.

7. Using a suitable oil filter wrench, remove the oil filter.

To install:

8. Install the oil pan drain plug, and tighten drain plug to 20 ft. lbs. (28 Nm).

9. Clean and check oil filter mounting surface. The surface must be smooth, flat and free of debris or pieces of gasket.

➡ **All engines are equipped with a high quality full-flow, disposable type oil filter. Replace the oil filter with a Mopar® or equivalent.**

10. Lubricate the new oil filter gasket with fresh engine oil.

11. Screw the oil filter on until the gasket contacts base. Tighten to 11 ft. lbs. (14 Nm).

12. Lower the vehicle.

13. Fill crankcase with the specified type and amount of engine oil.

14. Install the oil fill cap.

15. Start engine and inspect for leaks.

16. Stop engine and inspect the oil level.

EXHAUST MANIFOLD

REMOVAL & INSTALLATION

See Figures 121 through 123.

1. Remove engine cover.

2. Disconnect the negative cable from the battery.

3. Remove bolts attaching the upper heat shield.

4. Remove the upper heat shield.

5. Disconnect the exhaust pipe from exhaust manifold.

6. Remove the 2 bolts, and remove the exhaust manifold support bracket.

7. Remove 4 bolts and exhaust manifold heat shield.

8. Disconnect Heated Oxygen Sensor (HO2S) electrical connector.

9. Remove manifold retaining fasteners, and remove the exhaust manifold.

10. Remove and discard manifold gasket.

To install:

11. Install a new exhaust manifold gasket. DO NOT APPLY SEALER.

12. Install and tighten the exhaust manifold bolts in sequence to 25 ft. lbs. (34 Nm).

13. Install the exhaust manifold heat shield. Tighten bolts to 105 inch lbs. (12 Nm).

14. Install exhaust manifold support bracket.

15. Install a new catalytic converter gasket.

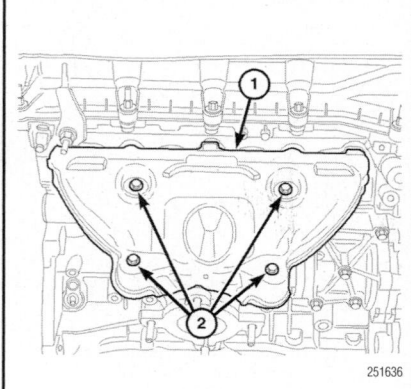

Fig. 122 Remove 4 bolts (2) and exhaust manifold heat shield (1)

16. Install the exhaust pipe to the manifold. Tighten fasteners to 250 inch lbs. (28 Nm).

17. Connect the HO2S electrical connector.

18. Connect the negative battery cable. Refer to Battery Reconnect/Relearn Procedure.

19. Install engine cover by pressing the rear of the cover down first.

INTAKE MANIFOLD

REMOVAL & INSTALLATION

See Figures 124 and 125.

✳✳ CAUTION

Release fuel system pressure before servicing system components. Service vehicles in well-ventilated areas and avoid ignition sources. Never smoke while servicing the vehicle.

1. Remove engine cover.

2. Perform fuel system pressure release procedure before attempting any repairs. Refer to Fuel System Pressure Release procedure.

3. Remove air cleaner housing. Refer to Air Cleaner, removal & installation.

4. Disconnect the negative cable at the battery.

5. Remove fuel injector electrical connectors. Remove fuel rail. Refer to Fuel Injectors, removal & installation.

6. Disconnect the oil temperature sensor.

7. Disconnect the variable valve timing solenoid electrical connector.

8. Disconnect the intake Camshaft Position (CMP) sensor electrical connector.

9. Position harness out of the way.

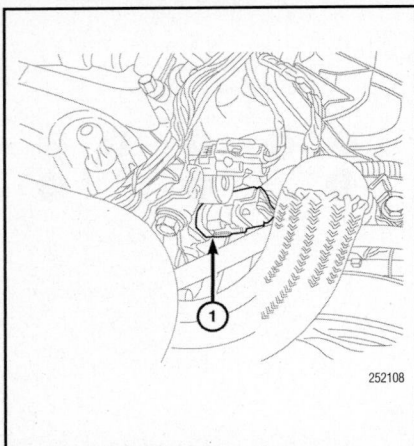

Fig. 124 Disconnect the oil temperature sensor (1)

10. Remove throttle body support bracket.

11. Disconnect the electronic throttle control electrical connector.

12. Remove the wiring harness retainer from the intake manifold.

13. Disconnect the Manifold Air Pressure (MAP) sensor electrical connector.

14. Disconnect vacuum lines at intake.

15. Remove the upper radiator hose retaining bracket.

16. Remove intake manifold retaining bolts.

17. Remove the intake manifold.

To install:

18. Clean all gasket surfaces.

19. Replace the intake manifold gasket.

20. Install the intake manifold, and tighten bolts in sequence to 220 inch lbs. (25 Nm).

21. To complete installation, reverse removal procedure, noting the following:

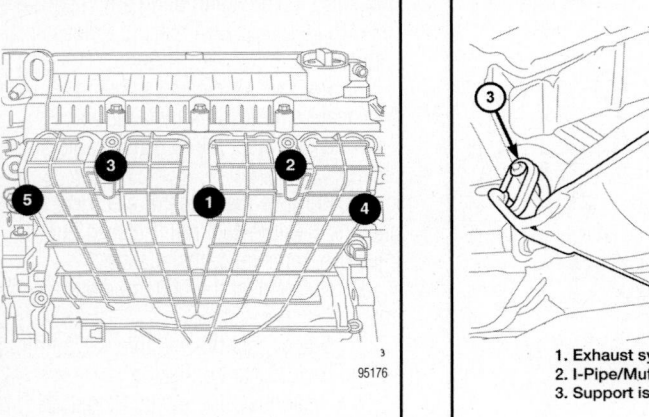

Fig. 125 Install intake manifold, and tighten bolts in sequence

- Inspect the quick-connect fittings for damage, and replace if necessary.
- After connecting the fuel supply hose to the fuel rail assembly, check connection by pulling on connector to ensure it is locked into position.

22. Connect the negative battery cable. Refer to Battery Reconnect/Relearn Procedure.

23. Fill the cooling system. Refer to Drain & Refill procedure.

24. Install the engine cover.

MUFFLER

REMOVAL & INSTALLATION

See Figure 126.

✳ CAUTION

The normal operating temperature of the exhaust system is very high. Therefore, never work around or attempt to service any part of the exhaust system until it is cooled. Special care should be taken when working near the catalytic converter. The temperature of the converter rises to a high level after a short period of engine operating time.

➡When replacement is required on any component of the exhaust system, you must use original equipment parts (or their equivalent).

1. Raise the vehicle on a hoist.

2. Apply penetrating oil to band clamp nut and bolt of the component being removed.

➡Do not use petroleum-based lubricants when removing/installing muffler

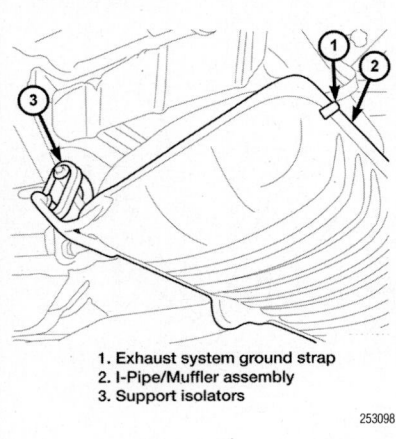

1. Exhaust system ground strap
2. I-Pipe/Muffler assembly
3. Support isolators

Fig. 126 View of I-Pipe/Muffler assembly

or exhaust pipe isolators, as it may compromise the life of the part. A suitable substitute is a mixture of liquid dish soap and water.

3. Remove exhaust system ground strap at the rear of the I-Pipe/Muffler assembly.

4. Loosen band clamp, and remove the support isolators at I-Pipe/Muffler assembly. Remove I-Pipe/Muffler assembly from catalytic converter.

5. Clean ends of pipes and muffler to assure mating of all parts. Discard broken or worn isolators, rusted or overused clamps, supports, and attaching parts.

To install:

➡**When assembling exhaust system, do not tighten clamp until components are aligned and clearances are checked.**

6. Install the I-Pipe/Muffler assembly to catalytic converter and the isolator supports to the underbody.

7. Working from the front of the system, align each component to maintain position and proper clearance with underbody parts. Tighten band clamp to 40 ft. lbs. (55 Nm).

✳ WARNING

Band clamps should never be tightened such that the 2 sides of the clamps are bottomed out against the center hourglass-shaped center block. Once this occurs, the clamp band has been stretched and has lost its clamping force, and must be replaced. To replace the band clamp, remove the nut and peel back the ends of the clamp until the spot weld breaks. File or grind remaining weld material until pipe surface is smooth.

➡Maintain proper clamp orientation when replacing with new clamp.

8. Connect the exhaust system ground strap.

9. Start the engine and inspect for exhaust leaks. Repair leaks as necessary.

10. Check the exhaust system for contact with the body panels. Make the necessary adjustments, if needed.

OIL PAN

REMOVAL & INSTALLATION

See Figures 127 and 128.

1. Raise the vehicle on a hoist.

2. Remove the oil drain plug and drain the engine oil.

3. Remove accessory drive belt splash shield.

4. Remove the lower A/C compressor mounting bolt (if equipped).

5. Remove the A/C mounting bracket.

➡**Do not use pry points in block to remove oil pan.**

6. Remove oil pan retaining bolts.

7. Using a putty knife, loosen the seal around the oil pan.

8. Remove the oil pan.

To install:

➡**Oil pan sealing surfaces must be free of grease or oil.**

➡**Parts must be assembled within 10 minutes of applying RTV.**

9. Apply Mopar® Engine RTV GEN II at the front cover to engine block parting lines.

10. Apply a 2-mm bead of Mopar® Engine RTV GEN II around the oil pan as shown.

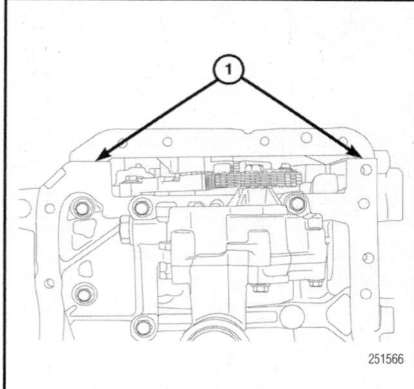

Fig. 127 Apply Mopar® Engine RTV GEN II at the front cover to engine block parting lines (1)

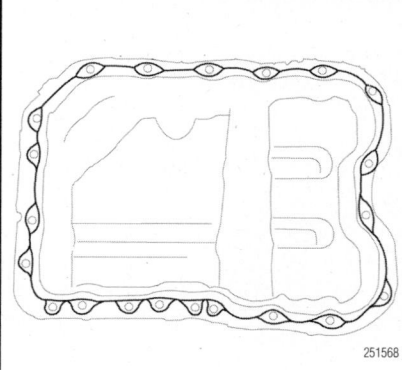

Fig. 128 Apply a 2-mm bead of Mopar® Engine RTV GEN II around the oil pan as shown

11. Position the oil pan and install bolts. Tighten bolts to 105 inch lbs. (12 Nm).

➡**The 2 long bolts must be tightened to 195 inch lbs. (22 Nm).**

12. Install the oil drain plug.

13. Lower the vehicle.

14. Fill engine crankcase with proper oil to the correct level.

15. Start the engine and check for leaks.

OIL PUMP

REMOVAL & INSTALLATION

See Figures 129 through 131.

1. Rotate engine to Top Dead Center (TDC) on #1 compression stroke.

2. Rotate engine to Top Dead Center (TDC) (1, 2) on #1 compression stroke.

3. Remove the oil pan. Refer to Oil Pan, removal & installation.

4. Mark the chain and the sprocket for reassembly.

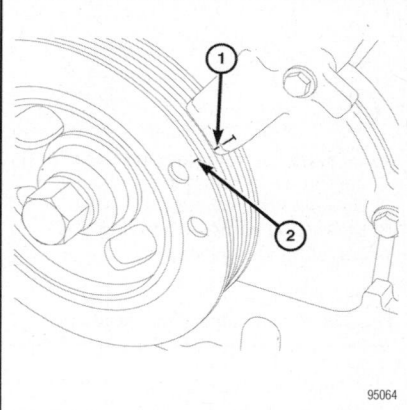

Fig. 129 Rotate engine to Top Dead Center (TDC) (1, 2) on #1 compression stroke.

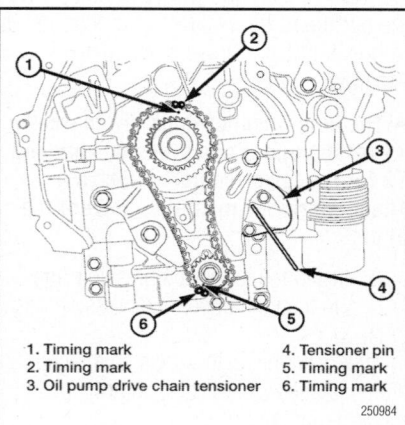

1. Timing mark
2. Timing mark
3. Oil pump drive chain tensioner
4. Tensioner pin
5. Timing mark
6. Timing mark

Fig. 130 View of oil pump drive chain timing marks

5. Push tensioner piston back into the tensioner body.

6. Insert tensioner pin (8514) into slot to hold tensioner plunger in the retracted position.

➡**Do not remove sprocket from the Balance Shaft Module (BSM).**

7. Remove BSM mounting bolts. Discard 180-mm bolts; the 185-mm bolts can be reused.

8. Lower the back of the BSM, and remove the chain from the sprocket.

9. Remove BSM from the engine.

To install:

✲✲ WARNING

There are 2 different BSM-to-engine block bolts used. 180-mm bolts with a lock-patch on the threads or 185-mm bolts without lock-patch. Do not reuse the 180-mm bolts. Always discard 180-mm bolts after removing. Failure to replace these bolts can result in engine damage. The 185-mm bolts are reusable. Install the same length bolts that were removed and use either 4 new 180-mm bolts or 4 185-mm bolts.

10. The 185-mm (7.283 in.) length bolts must be checked for stretching. Check the bolts with a straight edge for necking. If the bolts are necked down, they must be replaced.

11. Clean the BSM mounting holes with brake parts cleaner.

12. If chain was removed, align marks on crankshaft sprocket and chain.

13. Align marks on oil pump sprocket and chain.

14. Install chain on the sprocket.

15. Pivot the BSM assembly upwards, and position on ladder frame.

16. Clean BSM mounting holes with brake parts cleaner.

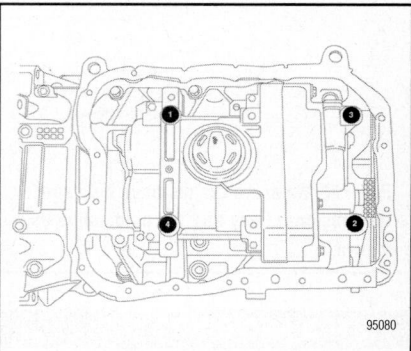

Fig. 131 Tighten BSM mounting bolts in the sequence shown

17. If chain was removed, align marks on crankshaft sprocket and chain.

18. Align marks on oil pump sprocket and chain.

19. Install chain on sprocket.

20. Pivot the BSM assembly upwards, and position on ladder frame.

21. Start BSM mounting bolts by hand.

22. Tighten new 180-mm BSM mounting bolts as follows:

    a. Tighten to 11 ft. lbs. (15 Nm) in the sequence shown.

    b. Tighten to 24 ft. lbs. (33 Nm) in the sequence shown.

    c. Rotate bolts an additional 90° in the sequence shown.

23. Tighten 185-mm BSM mounting bolts as follows:

    a. Tighten to 11 ft. lbs. (15 Nm) in the sequence shown.

    b. Tighten to 22 ft. lbs. (29 Nm) in the sequence shown.

    c. Rotate bolts an additional 90° in the sequence shown.

24. Install the oil pan. Refer to Oil Pan, removal & installation.

25. Fill with oil.

26. Start engine and check for leaks.

INSPECTION

See Figure 132.

1. Remove timing chain cover. Refer to Timing Chain Front Cover, removal & installation.

2. Remove oil pan. Refer to Oil Pan, removal & installation.

3. Measure the distance between the tensioner body and the guide shoe as shown.

4. If the distance is 0.397 inch (10.1 mm) or greater, replace the chain.

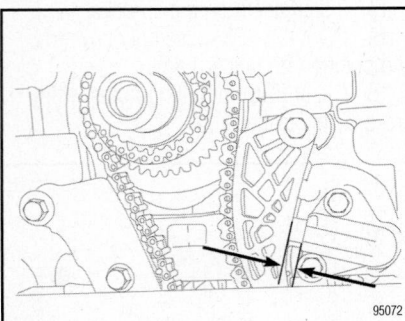

Fig. 132 Measure the distance between the tensioner body and the guide shoe as shown

PISTON AND RING

POSITIONING

See Figures 133 and 134.

Fig. 133 Installing oil ring side rail (1)

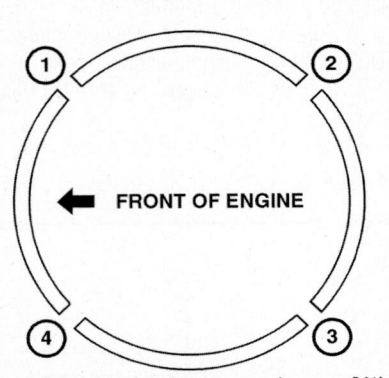

1. Oil expander ring gap and upper (Y1) compression ring gap
2. Upper oil ring rail gap
3. Lower (Y2) compression ring gap
4. Lower oil ring rail gap

Fig. 134 Piston ring end gap positions

1. Install oil ring expander.

2. Install the oil ring upper side rail first, then the lower side rail. Install the side rails by placing one end between the piston ring groove and the oil ring expander. Hold end firmly and press down the portion to be installed until side rail is in position. Do not use a piston ring expander.

➡**The compression rings are marked Y1 for the upper compression ring and Y2 for the lower compression ring. These markings must face toward top of piston..**

3. Install the lower compression ring (Y2), and then the upper compression ring (Y1).

4. Rotate the piston rings so the gaps are positioned as indicated with the piston viewed from the top.

➡**Staggering ring gap is important for oil control.**

REAR MAIN SEAL

REMOVAL & INSTALLATION

Refer to Crankshaft Rear Seal, removal & installation.

TIMING CHAIN FRONT COVER

REMOVAL & INSTALLATION

See Figures 135 through 144.

1. Remove engine cover by pulling upward.

2. Release fuel pressure before attempting any repairs. Refer to Fuel System Pressure Release procedure.

3. Disconnect and isolate the negative battery cable.

4. Drain the cooling system, as necessary. Refer to Drain & Refill procedure.

5. Remove coolant recovery bottle.

6. Remove and reposition the power steering reservoir.

7. Remove the windshield washer bottle.

8. Remove the accessory drive belt. Refer to Accessory Drive Belts, removal & installation.

9. Remove power steering hose hold down.

10. Remove the 3 power steering pump mounting bolts through the openings in the pulley, and reposition the pump.

11. Remove the cylinder head cover and ignition coils. Refer to Cylinder Head Cover, removal & installation.

12. Remove ignition coils from cylinder head cover.

13. Raise and support the vehicle.

14. Remove the right lower splash shield.

15. Set engine to Top Dead Center (TDC).

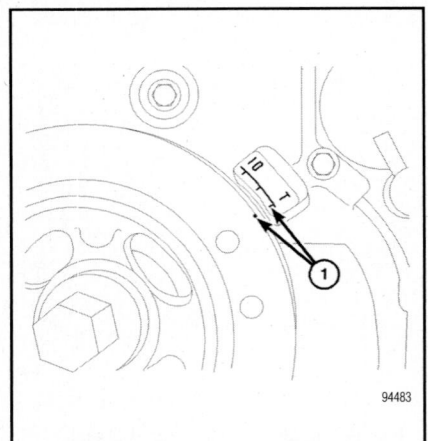

Fig. 135 Set engine to Top Dead Center (TDC) (1)

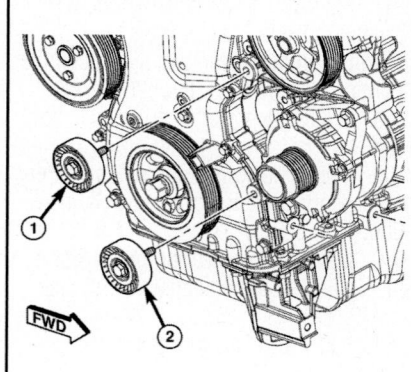

Fig. 136 View of accessory drive belt upper idler pulley (1) and lower idler pulley (2)

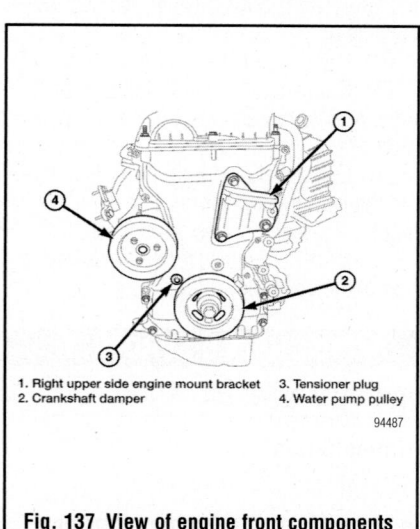

1. Right upper side engine mount bracket
2. Crankshaft damper
3. Tensioner plug
4. Water pump pulley

Fig. 137 View of engine front components

16. Remove lower A/C compressor bolts and compressor mount (if equipped).

17. Remove accessory drive belt lower idler pulley.

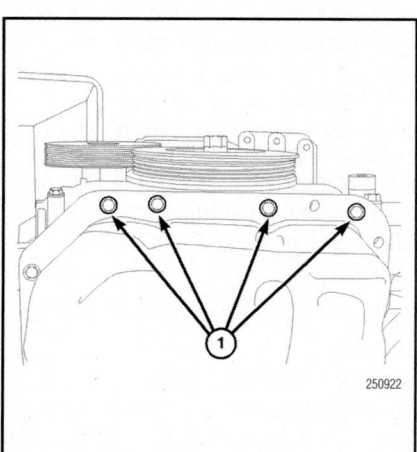

Fig. 138 Remove the 4 timing chain cover lower bolts (1)

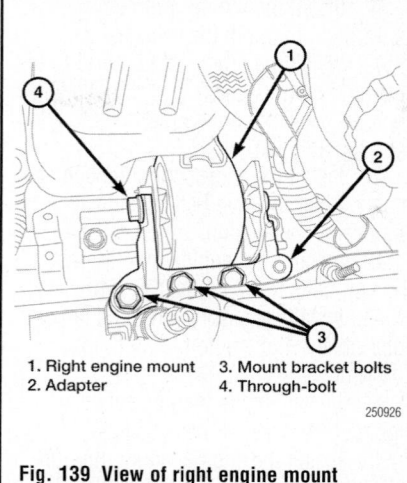

1. Right engine mount
2. Adapter
3. Mount bracket bolts
4. Through-bolt

Fig. 139 View of right engine mount

18. Remove the crankshaft vibration damper. Refer to Crankshaft Vibration Damper, removal & installation.

19. Remove 3 bolts and water pump pulley from water pump.

20. Remove lower bolt from right upper side engine mount bracket.

21. Remove the 4 timing chain cover lower bolts.

22. Lower the vehicle.

23. Support engine with a suitable jack.

24. Remove right engine mount through-bolt.

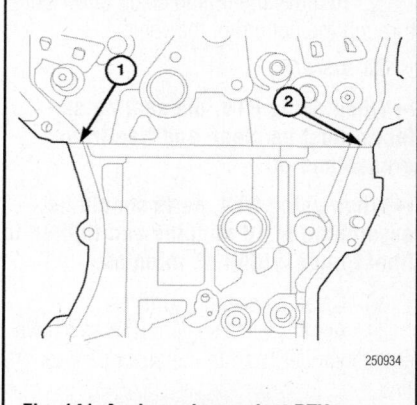

Fig. 141 Apply engine sealant RTV as shown at the cylinder head to the block parting line (1, 2)

25. Remove right engine mount-to-mount bracket bolts.

26. Remove right engine mount adapter.

27. Remove the accessory drive upper idler pulley.

28. Remove right upper engine mount bracket.

29. Remove the accessory drive belt tensioner. Refer to Drive Belt Tensioner, removal & installation.

30. Remove timing chain cover retaining bolts.

31. Remove timing chain cover using the 3 pry points.

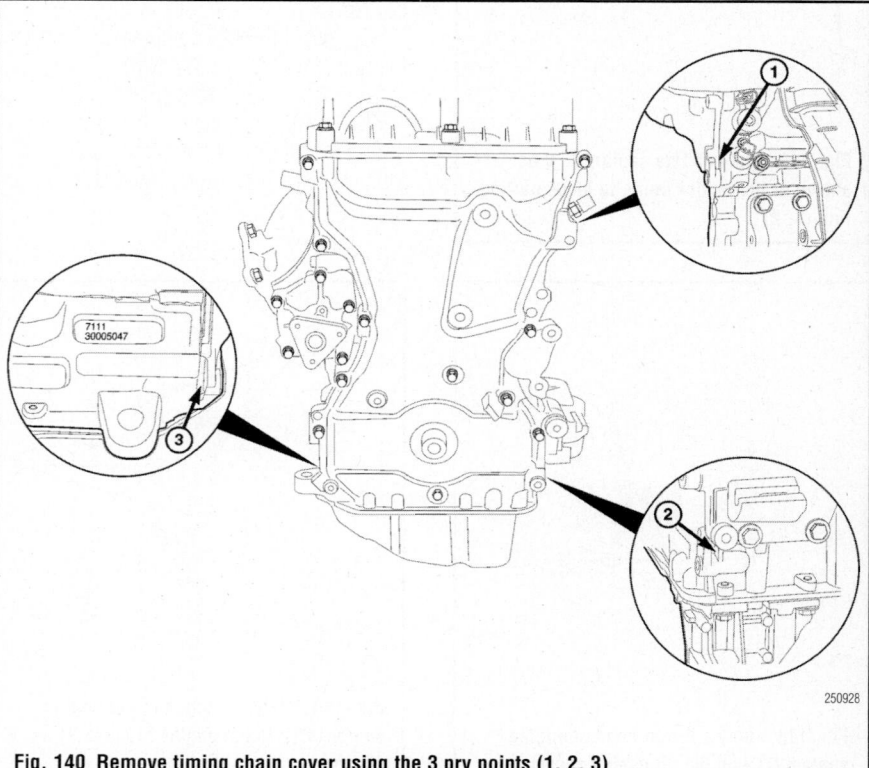

Fig. 140 Remove timing chain cover using the 3 pry points (1, 2, 3)

32. Remove the timing chain cover out through the bottom of the vehicle.

To install:

➡ When using RTV, the sealing surfaces must be clean and free from grease and oil.

➡ When using RTV, parts should be assembled in 10 minutes and tighten to final torque within 45 minutes.

33. Clean all sealing surfaces.

34. Apply engine sealant RTV as shown at the cylinder head to the block parting line.

35. Apply engine sealant RTV as shown at the ladder frame to block parting line.

36. Apply engine sealant RTV as shown in the corner of the oil pan and block.

37. Apply a 2-mm bead of engine sealant RTV on the oil pan as shown.

38. Apply a 2-mm bead of engine sealant RTV to the engine block as shown.

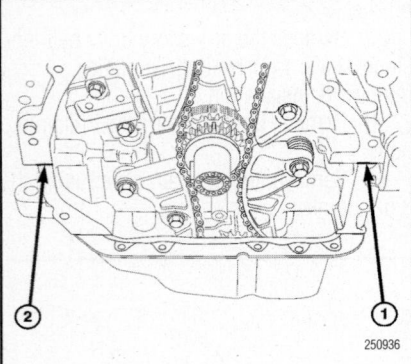

Fig. 142 Apply engine sealant RTV as shown at the ladder frame to block parting line (1, 2)

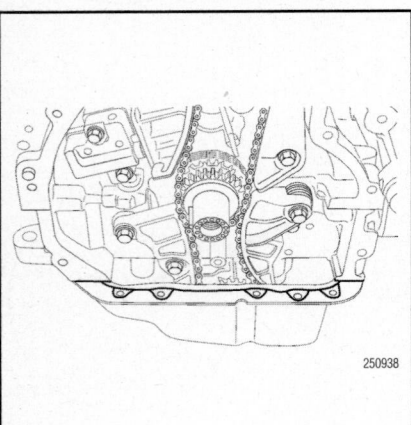

Fig. 143 Apply a 2-mm bead of engine sealant RTV on the oil pan as shown

39. Install the timing chain cover upwards from under the vehicle.

40. Install the timing chain cover upper retaining bolts. Tighten the M6 bolts to 80 inch lbs. (9 Nm) and the M8 bolts to 230 inch lbs. (26 Nm).

41. Install the accessory drive belt tensioner. Refer to Drive Belt Tensioner, removal & installation.

42. Install right engine mount bracket. Tighten bolts to 37 ft. lbs. (50 Nm).

43. Install accessory drive belt upper idler pulley. Tighten bolt to 35 ft. lbs. (48 Nm).

44. Install engine mount adapter, and tighten bolts to 50 ft. lbs. (68 Nm).

45. Install the engine mount through-bolt, and tighten to 65 ft. lbs. (88 Nm).

46. Remove the jack from under the engine.

47. Raise and support the vehicle.

48. Install oil pan-to-timing chain cover lower retaining bolts, and tighten the M6 bolts to 80 inch lbs. (9 Nm).

49. Install the water pump pulley and tighten three bolts to 80 inch lbs. (9 Nm).

50. Install the crankshaft vibration damper. Refer to Crankshaft Vibration Damper, removal & installation.

51. Install accessory drive belt lower idler pulley. Tighten bolt to 35 ft. lbs. (48 Nm).

52. Install lower A/C compressor mounting bracket. Tighten the bolts to 18 ft. lbs. (24 Nm).

53. Install the A/C compressor. Tighten the bolts to 18 ft. lbs. (24 Nm).

54. Install right lower splash shield.

55. Lower the vehicle.

56. Install the cylinder head cover and ignition coils. Refer to Cylinder Head Cover, removal & installation.

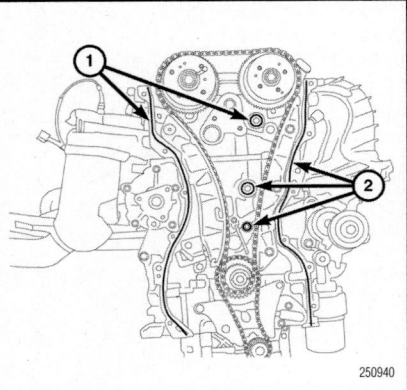

Fig. 144 Apply a 2-mm bead of engine sealant RTV to the engine block (1,2) as shown

57. Place the power steering pump in mounting position. Install the 3 bolts through openings in the pulley. Tighten the mounting bolts to 19 ft. lbs. (26 Nm).

58. Install the power steering hose hold down.

59. Install the accessory drive belt. Refer to Accessory Drive Belts, removal & installation.

60. Install power steering pump reservoir. Tighten mounting screw to 106 inch lbs. (12 Nm).

61. Install windshield washer reservoir.

62. Install the coolant recovery reservoir. Tighten mounting bolts to 35 inch lbs. (4 Nm).

63. Install clean air hose and air cleaner housing. Refer to Air Cleaner, removal & installation.

64. Install air cleaner housing inlet.

65. Connect the negative battery cable. Refer to Battery Reconnect/Relearn Procedure.

66. Operate engine until it reaches normal operating temperature. Check oil system for leaks and correct fluid level.

67. Install engine cover by pressing the rear of the cover down first.

TIMING CHAIN & SPROCKETS

REMOVAL & INSTALLATION

Timing Chain

See Figures 145 through 147.

➡ Inspect timing chain for stretching prior to removal. Refer to Inspection procedure.

1. Remove front timing chain cover. Refer to Front Timing Chain Cover, removal & installation.

➡ The crankshaft timing mark can be in one of 2 locations depending on whether the engine is early production, or if engine is late production or assembled with service parts. In all cases, the keyway will always be in the 9 o'clock position, in-line with the ladder-frame mounting surface when the engine is at Top Dead Center (TDC).

2. Verify that the engine is still set to TDC.

➡ If the timing chain plated links can no longer be seen, the timing chain links corresponding to the timing marks must be marked prior to removal if the chain is to be reused.

3. Mark chain link corresponding to crankshaft timing mark.

4. With the engine still set to TDC, verify that the marks on the camshaft

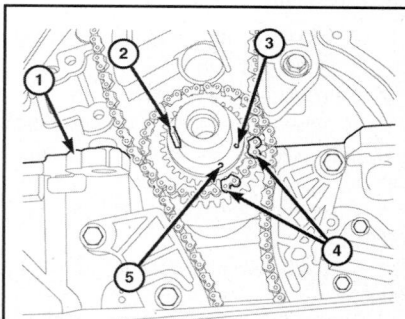

1. Ladder frame mounting surface
2. Keyway
3. Crankshaft timing mark
   (late production or assembled with service parts)
4. Marked chain links
5. Crankshaft timing mark (early production)

Fig. 145 View of crankshaft timing marks

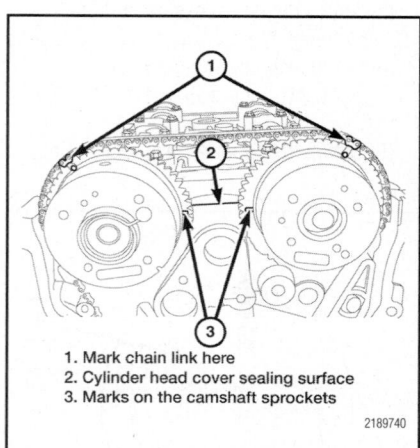

1. Mark chain link here
2. Cylinder head cover sealing surface
3. Marks on the camshaft sprockets

Fig. 146 View of timing chain timing marks

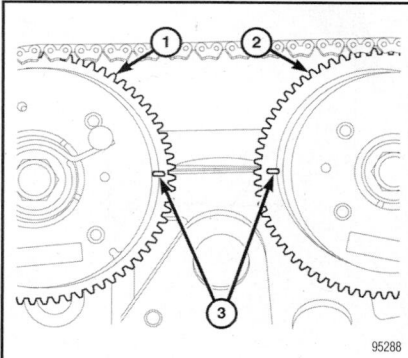

Fig. 147 Verify that the camshafts (1, 2) timing marks (3) are in the proper position and in-line with the cylinder head cover sealing surface

sprockets are in line with the cylinder head cover sealing surface. If the marks do not line up, the timing chain is not correctly installed.

5. Mark chain link corresponding to camshaft timing mark.

6. Remove the timing chain tensioner. Refer to Timing Chain Tensioner, removal & installation.

7. Remove the timing chain.

To install:

8. Verify that the engine is still set to TDC.

9. Align the camshaft timing marks so they are facing each other and in-line with the cylinder head cover sealing surface.

10. Install timing chain so plated (or marked) links on chain align with timing marks on camshaft sprockets.

11. Align timing mark on the crankshaft sprocket with the plated (or marked) link on the timing chain. Position chain so slack will be on the tensioner side.

➡ **Keep the slack in the timing chain on the tensioner side.**

12. Install the timing chain tensioner. Refer to Timing Chain Tensioner, removal & installation.

13. Rotate the crankshaft CLOCKWISE 2 complete revolutions until the crankshaft is repositioned at the TDC position with the key way at the 9 o'clock position.

14. Verify that the camshafts timing marks are in the proper position and in-line with the cylinder head cover sealing surface. If the marks do not line up, the timing chain is not correctly installed.

15. Install front timing chain cover. Refer to Front Timing Chain Cover, removal & installation.

16. Connect the negative battery cable. Refer to Battery Reconnect/Relearn Procedure.

17. Operate engine until it reaches normal operating temperature. Check oil and cooling systems for correct fluid levels.

Camshaft Sprocket

Camshaft phasers and camshaft sprockets are supplied as an assembly. Do not attempt to disassemble.

Refer to Camshaft Phaser, removal & installation.

Crankshaft Sprocket

See Figures 148 and 149.

1. Remove the timing chain. Refer to Timing Chain, removal & installation.

2. Remove oil pan. Refer to Oil Pan, removal & installation.

3. Remove oil pump drive chain tensioner.

4. Remove the oil pump drive chain.

5. Remove the crankshaft sprocket.

To install:

6. Install the crankshaft sprocket onto the crankshaft.

7. Install the oil pump drive chain. Verify that oil pump timing marks are aligned as shown.

8. Reset oil pump drive chain tensioner by pushing plunger inward and installing a tensioner pin (8514).

9. Install oil pump drive chain tensioner, and remove the tensioner pin.

10. Install the timing chain. Refer to Timing Chain, removal & installation.

11. Install oil pan. Refer to Oil Pan, removal & installation.

12. Fill engine with oil.

13. Start engine and check for leaks.

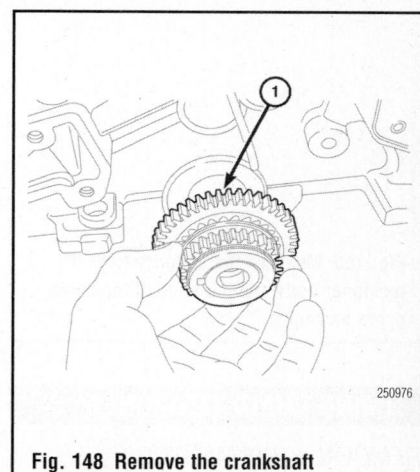

Fig. 148 Remove the crankshaft sprocket (1)

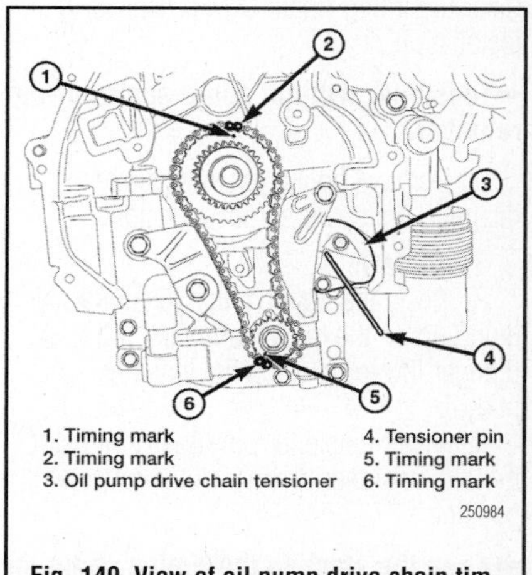

1. Timing mark
2. Timing mark
3. Oil pump drive chain tensioner
4. Tensioner pin
5. Timing mark
6. Timing mark

Fig. 149 View of oil pump drive chain timing marks

INSPECTION

See Figure 150.

➡ **Inspect timing chain for stretching prior to removal.**

1. Rotate the engine while watching the timing chain tensioner plunger. When the plunger reaches its maximum travel, stop rotating engine.

2. Measure the distance from the tensioner body and the edge of the chain guide as shown.

3. If the distance is greater than 0.81 inches (20.5 mm), inspect the guide shoes for excessive wear.

4. If the guides are okay, replace the timing chain.

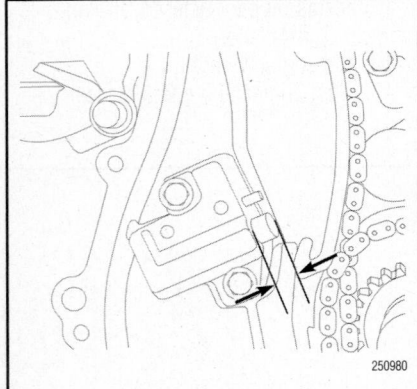

Fig. 150 Measure the distance from the tensioner body and the edge of the chain guide as shown

TIMING CHAIN TENSIONER

REMOVAL & INSTALLATION

See Figures 151 and 152.

1. Remove the engine timing cover. Refer to Timing Chain Cover, removal & installation.

➡ **Tensioner will not come apart during removal.**

2. Remove timing chain tensioner retaining bolts, and remove tensioner.

To install:

3. Reset the timing chain tensioner by lifting up on the ratchet and pushing plunger inward towards the tensioner body.

4. Insert tensioner pin (8514) into slot to hold tensioner plunger in the retracted position.

➡ **Keep the slack in the timing chain on the tensioner side.**

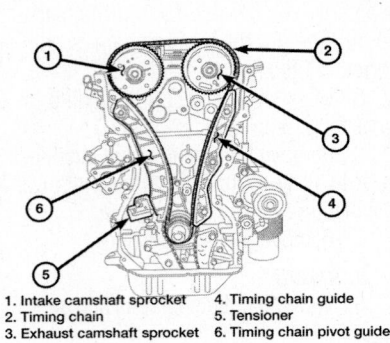

Fig. 151 View of timing chain and components

1. Intake camshaft sprocket
2. Timing chain
3. Exhaust camshaft sprocket
4. Timing chain guide
5. Tensioner
6. Timing chain pivot guide

5. Install timing chain tensioner and tighten bolts to 105 inch lbs. (12 Nm).

6. Remove the timing tensioner pin.

7. Install the engine timing cover. Refer to Timing Chain Cover, removal & installation.

VALVE COVERS

REMOVAL & INSTALLATION

Refer to Cylinder Head Cover, removal & installation.

VALVE LASH

ADJUSTMENT

➡ **The engine must be cold to measure the valve lash.**

1. Before servicing the vehicle, refer to the Precautions Section.

2. Remove the engine cover.

3. Remove the cylinder head cover. Refer to Cylinder Head Cover, removal & installation.

4. Rotate the camshaft so the lobes are vertical.

5. Check the clearance using feeler gauges.

6. Repeat this procedure for all of the valve tappets and record the readings.

7. If the clearance was outside the required specification:

   a. Remove the camshaft. Refer to Camshafts, removal & installation.

   b. If the clearance was too large or too small, increase or decrease the tappet thickness by the necessary amount.

   c. Install the camshafts and verify that the valve lash is correct (intake: 0.006–0.009 inch; exhaust: 0.010–0.012 inch).

8. Install the cylinder head cover. Refer

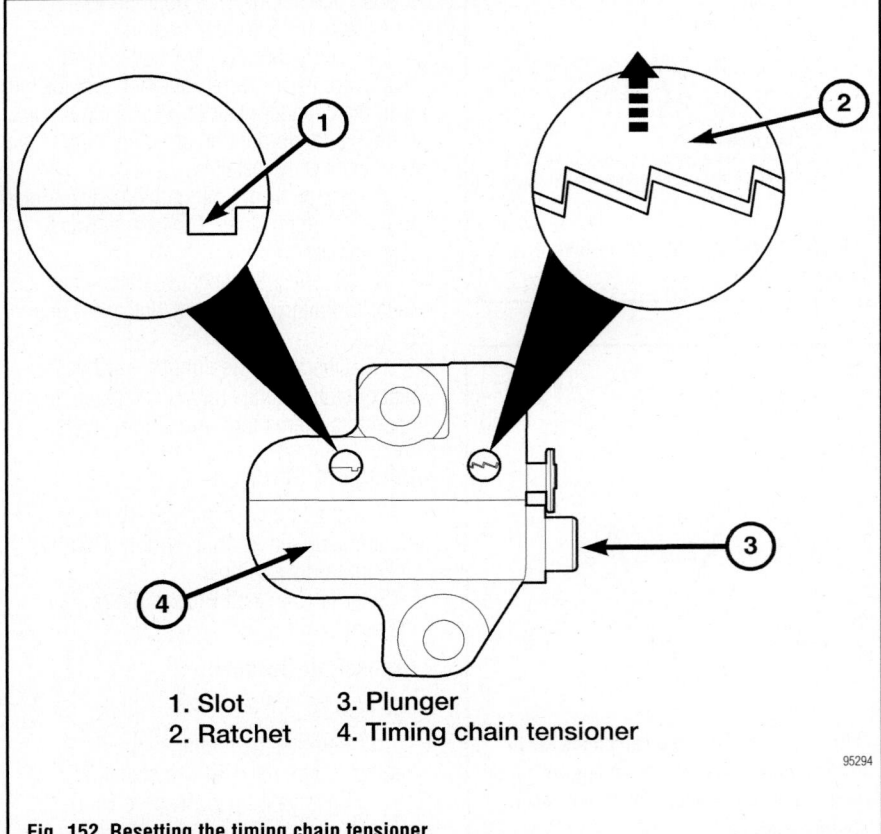

1. Slot
2. Ratchet
3. Plunger
4. Timing chain tensioner

Fig. 152 Resetting the timing chain tensioner

to Cylinder Head Cover, removal & installation.

VALVE SPRINGS

REMOVAL & INSTALLATION

Cylinder Head Off

See Figures 153 through 156.

1. With cylinder head removed from cylinder block, place a ball of rags in the combustion chamber.

❊❊ WARNING

Care must be taken not to damage the tappet bore, or engine damage may result.

2. Mark valve tappet location for assembly.

3. Remove the valve tappets. Refer to Valve Tappet Buckets, removal & installation.

4. Using a metric valve keeper remover (such as Snap-on® GA317), remove valve keepers with a downward push.

5. Remove retainer and springs.

6. Before removing valves, remove any burrs from valve stem lock grooves to prevent damage to the valve guides. Identify valves, locks and retainers to ensure installation in original location.

7. Inspect the valves.

To install:

❊❊ WARNING

Care must be taken not to damage the tappet bore, or engine damage may result.

8. Coat valve stems with clean engine oil, and insert in cylinder head.

9. Install new valve stem seals on all valves using an appropriate-sized socket to seat the seal/spring seat. The valve stem seals should be pushed firmly and squarely over valve guide.

10. Install the valve springs.

11. Install the keepers in the retainer, and place on valve spring.

12. Using a metric valve keeper installer and remover as a handle, push downward to install keepers.

13. Check the valve spring installed height B after refacing the valve and seat. Make sure measurements are taken from top of spring seat to the bottom surface of spring retainer. If height is greater than 1.525 inches (38.75 mm), install a 0.030 inch (0.762 mm) spacer under the valve spring seat to bring spring height back within specification.

14. Install the valve tappets. Refer to Valve Tappet Buckets, removal & installation.

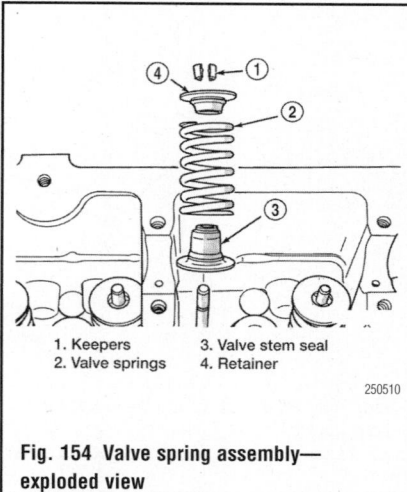

1. Keepers   3. Valve stem seal
2. Valve springs 4. Retainer

Fig. 154 Valve spring assembly—exploded view

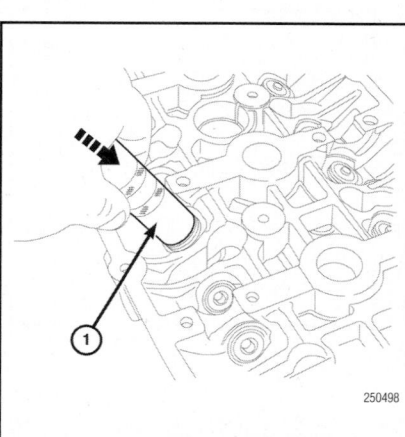

Fig. 153 Using a metric valve keeper remover (1), remove valve keepers with a downward push

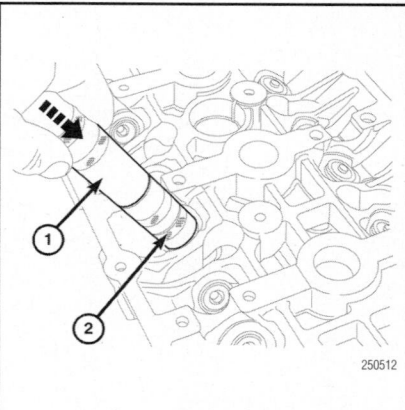

Fig. 155 Using a metric valve keeper installer (2) and remover (1) as a handle, push downward to install keepers

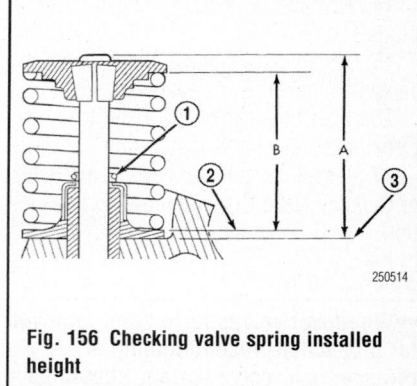

Fig. 156 Checking valve spring installed height

Cylinder Head On

See Figures 153, 157 and 158.

1. Remove the cylinder head cover. Refer to Cylinder Head Cover, removal & installation.

2. Remove the camshafts. Refer to Camshafts, removal & installation.

3. Mark valve tappet location for assembly.

4. Remove valve tappets. Refer to Valve Tappets, removal & installation

5. With air hose attached to an adapter tool installed in spark plug hole, apply 90–120 psi air pressure.

❊❊ WARNING

Care must be taken not to damage the tappet bore, or engine damage may result.

6. Using a metric valve keeper remover (such as Snap-on® GA317), remove valve keepers with a downward push.

7. Remove valve spring(s).

8. Remove valve stem seal(s) by a using valve stem seal tool.

To install:

❊❊ WARNING

Care must be taken not to damage the tappet bore, or engine damage may result.

9. Coat valve stems with clean engine oil, and insert in cylinder head.

10. Install new valve stem seals on all valves using an appropriate-sized socket to seat the seal/spring seat. The valve stem seals should be pushed firmly and squarely over valve guide.

11. Install the valve springs.

12. Install the keepers in the retainer, and place on valve spring.

13. Using a metric valve keeper installer and remover as a handle, push downward to install keepers.

14. Remove air hose and install spark plugs.

15. Install valve tappets. Refer to Valve Tappets, removal & installation

16. Install the camshafts. Refer to Camshafts, removal & installation.

17. Install the cylinder head cover. Refer to Cylinder Head Cover, removal & installation.

INSPECTION

➡Whenever valves have been removed for inspection, reconditioning or replacement, valve springs should be tested for correct load. Discard the springs that do not meet specifications.

1. Inspect each valve spring for correct load. The following specifications apply to both intake and exhaust valves springs:
   - Valve closed nominal load—40.35 lbs. ± 2 lbs.
   - Valve open nominal load—82 lbs. ± 3.8 lbs.

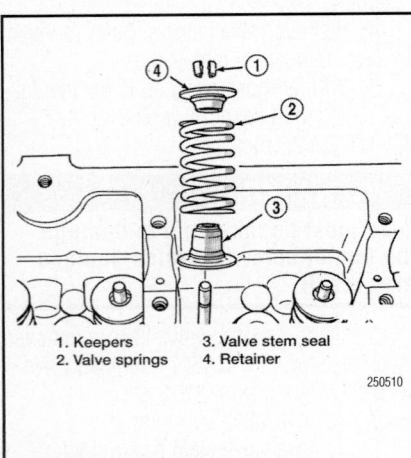

1. Keepers
2. Valve springs
3. Valve stem seal
4. Retainer

250510

Fig. 157 Valve spring assembly— exploded view

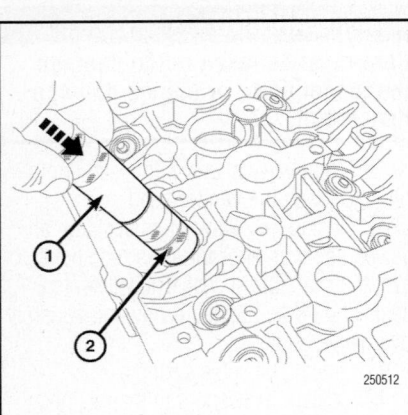

250512

Fig. 158 Using a metric valve keeper installer (2) and remover (1) as a handle, push downward to install keepers

2. Inspect each valve spring for squareness with a steel square and surface plate (test springs from both ends). If the spring is more than 1/16 inch (1.5 mm) out of square, install a new spring.

VALVE TIMING VERIFICATION

See Figures 159 and 160.

☀ WARNING

Painted or colored chain links are used during initial engine assembly and cannot be relied upon for valve timing verification. These markings are in different locations for early production, late production and service parts. Only use TDC marks, cylinder head cover sealing surface and camshaft sprocket marks to verify valve timing, or engine damage may result.

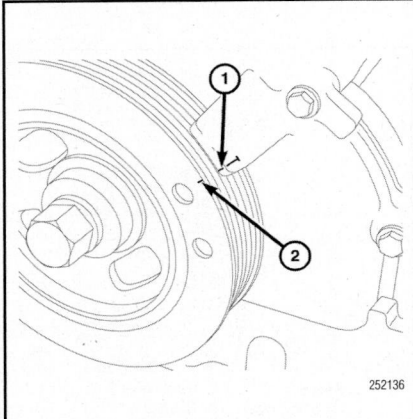

252136

Fig. 159 Set engine to Top Dead Center (TDC) (1, 2)

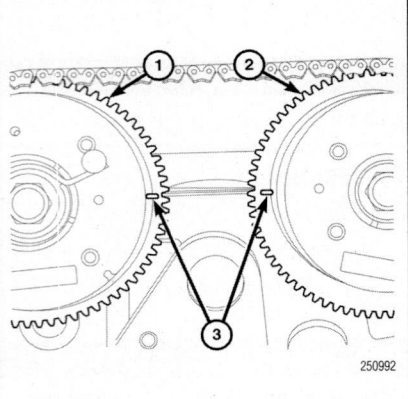

250992

Fig. 160 The marks (3) on the camshaft sprockets (1, 2) should be in line with the cylinder head cover sealing surface

1. Remove engine cover.

2. Remove cylinder head cover. Refer to Cylinder Head Cover, removal & installation.

3. Set engine to Top Dead Center (TDC) (1, 2).

4. The marks on the camshaft sprockets should be in line with the cylinder head cover sealing surface.

5. Install cylinder head cover. Refer to Cylinder Head Cover, removal & installation.

6. Install the engine cover.

VALVE TAPPET BUCKETS

REMOVAL & INSTALLATION

See Figure 161.

➡This procedure is for in-vehicle service with camshafts installed.

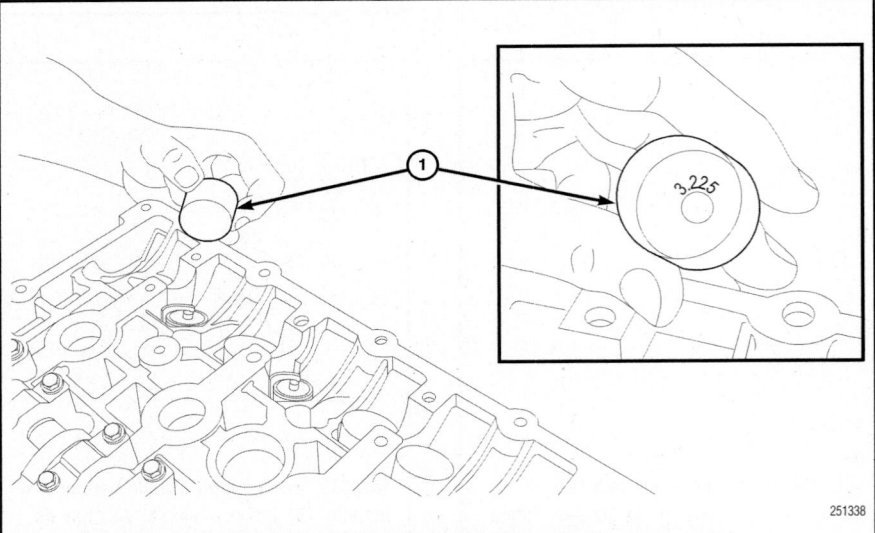

251338

Fig. 161 If reusing, mark each camshaft bucket for reassembly in original position.

➡**Camshaft tappets must be replaced if cylinder head or camshafts are replaced.**

1. Remove cylinder head cover. Refer to Cylinder Head Cover, removal & installation.
2. Remove camshafts. Refer to Camshaft, removal & installation.
3. Remove the camshaft tappets.
4. Repeat removal procedure for each camshaft tappet.
5. If reusing, mark each camshaft bucket for reassembly in original position.

To install

❋❋ WARNING

If reinstalling the original tappets, they must go back in their original location, or engine damage could result.

6. Apply a light coat of clean engine oil to the camshafts tappets prior to assembly.
7. Install the camshaft tappets into the cylinder head.

8. Repeat installation procedure for each camshaft tappet.
9. Install camshafts. Refer to Camshaft, removal & installation.

➡**If installing new tappets, the valve lash procedure must be performed. Refer to Valve Lash, adjustment.**

10. Install cylinder head cover. Refer to Cylinder Head Cover, removal & installation.

ENGINE PERFORMANCE & EMISSION CONTROLS

CAMSHAFT POSITION (CMP) SENSOR

LOCATION

See Figures 162 and 163.

The Camshaft Position (CMP) sensors are mounted to the front and rear of the cylinder head.

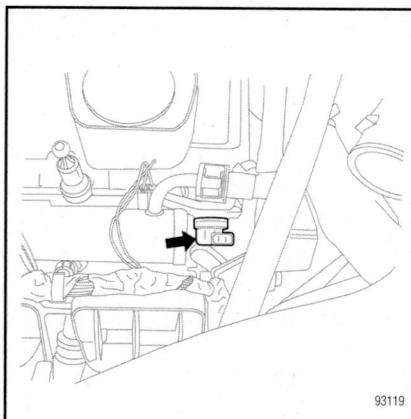

93119

Fig. 162 Camshaft Position (CMP) sensor location—front

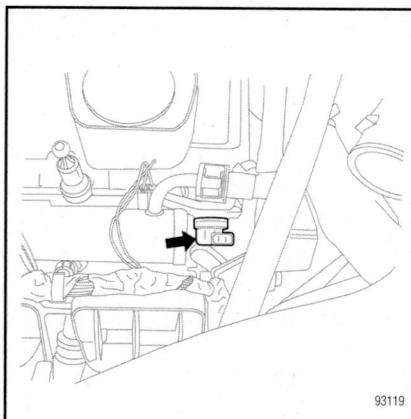

93125

Fig. 163 Camshaft Position (CMP) sensor location—rear (with heat shield installed)

REMOVAL & INSTALLATION

Front

See Figure 162.

1. Remove the air cleaner hose to the throttle body.
2. Disconnect the Inlet Air Temperature (IAT) sensor electrical connector. Refer to Inlet Air Temperature (IAT) Sensor, removal & installation.
3. Disconnect the negative battery cable.
4. Disconnect the electrical connector from the Camshaft Position (CMP) sensor.
5. Remove the CMP sensor mounting bolt.
6. Remove the CMP sensor.

To install:
7. Lubricate the sensor O-ring.
8. Install the sensor utilizing a twisting motion. Make sure the sensor is fully seated.

❋❋ WARNING

Do not drive sensor into the bore by tightening the mounting bolt. This can cause the sensor to be incorrectly seated, causing the engine to fail.

9. Install the sensor mounting bolt, and tighten to 79.5 inch lbs. (9 Nm).
10. Carefully attach the electrical connector to the CMP sensor. Installation at an angle may damage the sensor pins.
11. Connect the negative battery cable. Refer to Battery Reconnect/Relearn Procedure.
12. Install the air cleaner-to-throttle body hose.
13. Connect the IAT sensor electrical connector.

Rear

See Figure 163.

1. Disconnect the negative battery cable.

2. Disconnect the electrical connector from the Camshaft Position (CMP) sensor.
3. Remove the nut retaining the heat shield.
4. Pull the heat shield out to uncover the CMP sensor.
5. Remove the CMP sensor mounting bolt.
6. Remove the CMP sensor.

To install:
7. Lubricate the CMP sensor O-ring.
8. Install the sensor utilizing a twisting motion. Make sure the sensor is fully seated.

❋❋ WARNING

Do not drive sensor into the bore by tightening the mounting bolt. This can cause the sensor to be incorrectly seated, causing engine to fail.

9. Install the sensor mounting bolt, and tighten to 79.5 inch lbs. (9 Nm).
10. Carefully attach the electrical connector to CMP sensor. Feel for positive lock (click). Installation at an angle may damage the sensor pins.
11. Install the heat shield onto the mounting stud.
12. Install the heat shield retaining nut and tighten.
13. Connect the negative battery cable. Refer to Battery Reconnect/Relearn Procedure.

CRANKSHAFT POSITION (CKP) SENSOR

LOCATION

See Figure 164.

The Crankshaft Position (CKP) sensor mounts to the rear of the engine block near the Transaxle.

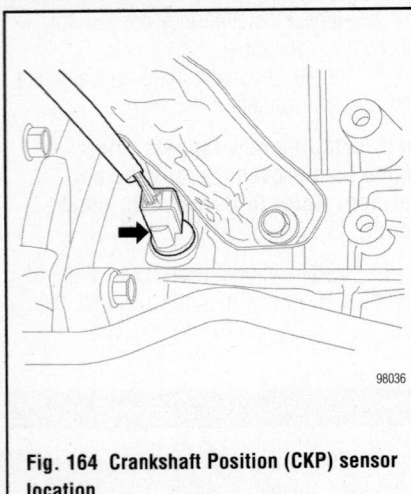

Fig. 164 Crankshaft Position (CKP) sensor location

REMOVAL & INSTALLATION

See Figures 165 and 166.

1. Remove the engine cover.
2. Disconnect and isolate the negative battery cable.
3. Remove the air cleaner body. Refer to Air Cleaner, removal & installation.
4. Disengage the upstream HO2S wire harness retainer and Crankshaft Position (CKP) sensor wire harness retainer from the heat shield.
5. Remove the nut and 2 heat shield retaining bolts.
6. Remove the heat shield.
7. Remove the CKP sensor mounting bolt.
8. Remove sensor with the wire harness attached.
9. Unlock and disconnect the electrical connector from the CKP sensor.

To install:

10. Check O-ring for damage. Lubricate O-ring with engine oil before installing sensor.
11. Using a twisting motion, install the CKP sensor.
12. Install the CKP sensor bolt. Tighten the bolt to 80 inch lbs. (9 Nm).
13. Connect and lock the electrical connector to the CKP sensor.
14. Install the heat shield.
15. Install the upstream HO2S and CKP sensor wire harness retainers to the heat shield.
16. Install the air cleaner body. Refer to Air Cleaner, removal & installation.
17. Connect the negative battery cable. Refer to Battery Reconnect/Relearn Procedure.
18. Install the engine cover.

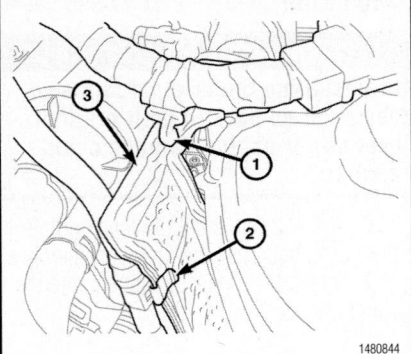

Fig. 165 Disengage the upstream HO2S wire harness retainer (1) and Crankshaft Position (CKP) sensor wire harness retainer (2) from the heat shield (3)

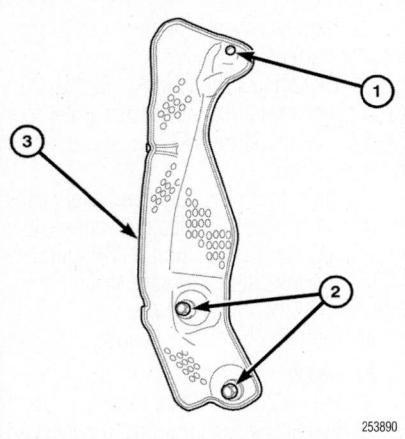

Fig. 166 Remove the nut (1) and 2 heat shield retaining bolts (2). Remove the heat shield (3)

ENGINE COOLANT TEMPERATURE (ECT) SENSOR

LOCATION

See Figures 167 and 168.

There are 2 Engine Coolant Temperature (ECT) sensors. One ETC sensor is located in the coolant adapter, and one ECT sensor threads into the cylinder block. New sensors have sealant applied to the threads.

REMOVAL & INSTALLATION

Coolant Adapter-Mounted ECT Sensor

See Figure 167.

1. Disconnect the negative battery cable.
2. Partially drain the cooling system below the level of the Engine Coolant Temperature (ECT) sensor.
3. Disconnect the ECT sensor electrical connector.

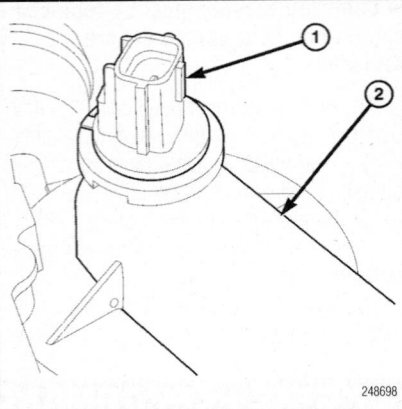

Fig. 167 Engine Coolant Temperature (ECT) sensor (1) and coolant adapter (2) location

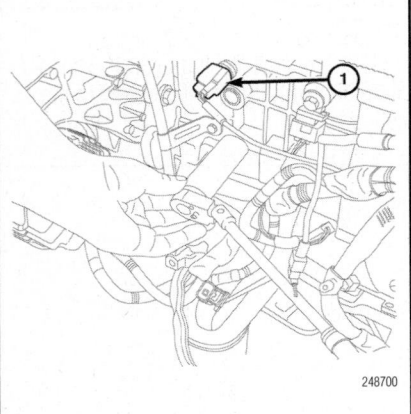

Fig. 168 Cylinder block-mounted Engine Coolant Temperature (ECT) sensor (1) location

4. Remove the ECT sensor.

To install:

5. Lubricate the ECT sensor O-ring with coolant.
   a. Install the ECT sensor. Make sure the coolant sensor is locked in place.
6. Connect the ECT sensor electrical connector.
7. Fill the cooling system. Refer to Drain & Refill procedure.
8. Connect the negative battery cable. Refer to Battery Reconnect/Relearn Procedure.

Cylinder Block-Mounted ECT Sensor

See Figure 168.

1. Disconnect the negative battery cable.
2. Partially drain the cooling system below the level of Engine Coolant Temperature (ECT) sensor.
3. Disconnect the ECT sensor electrical connector.

4. Remove the ECT sensor.

To install:

5. Install the ECT sensor. Tighten the sensor to 168 inch lbs. (19 Nm).

6. Reconnect the ECT sensor electrical connector.

7. Fill the cooling system. Refer to Drain & Refill procedure.

8. Connect the negative battery cable. Refer to Battery Reconnect/Relearn Procedure.

HEATED OXYGEN SENSOR (HO2S)

LOCATION

2.0L Engine

See Figures 169 and 170.

On 2.0L engines, the downstream Heated Oxygen Sensor (HO2S) threads into the catalytic converter. The upstream HO2S threads into the exhaust pipe.

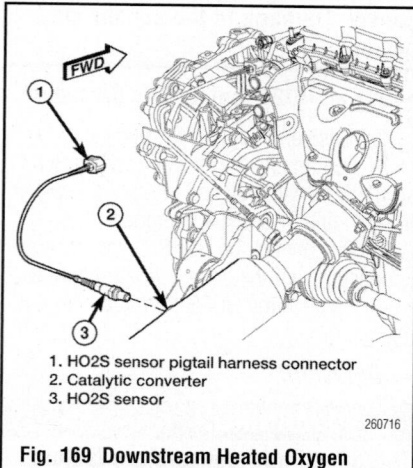

1. HO2S sensor pigtail harness connector
2. Catalytic converter
3. HO2S sensor

260716

Fig. 169 Downstream Heated Oxygen Sensor (HO2S) location—2.0L

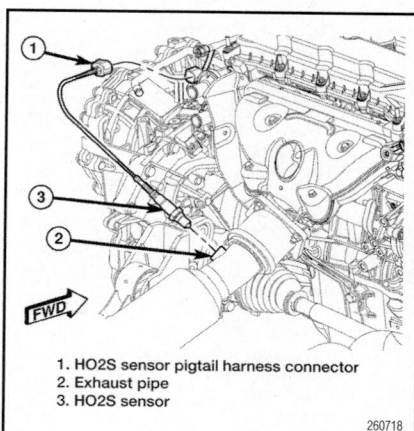

1. HO2S sensor pigtail harness connector
2. Exhaust pipe
3. HO2S sensor

260718

Fig. 170 Upstream Heated Oxygen Sensor (HO2S) location—2.0L

2.4L Engine

See Figures 171 and 172.

On 2.4L engines, the downstream Heated Oxygen Sensor (HO2S) threads into the exhaust pipe. The upstream HO2S threads into the maniverter.

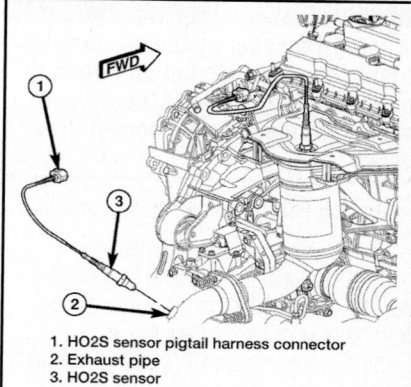

1. HO2S sensor pigtail harness connector
2. Exhaust pipe
3. HO2S sensor

260722

Fig. 171 Downstream Heated Oxygen Sensor (HO2S) location—2.4L

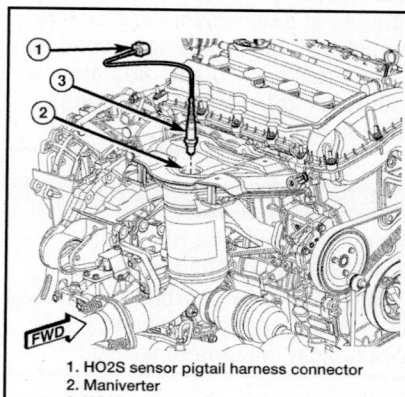

1. HO2S sensor pigtail harness connector
2. Maniverter
3. HO2S sensor

260724

Fig. 172 Upstream Heated Oxygen Sensor (HO2S) location—2.4L

REMOVAL & INSTALLATION

2.0L Engine

Downstream Oxygen Sensor (1/2)
See Figure 169.

✳✳ CAUTION

The exhaust manifold, exhaust pipes and catalytic converter(s) become very hot during engine operation. Allow engine to cool before removing the oxygen sensor(s). Failure to allow engine to cool before removal may result in personal injury caused by burns.

✳✳ WARNING

When disconnecting the sensor electrical connector, do not pull directly on the wires going into the oxygen sensor. Damage to the sensor may occur.

➡ **Use an HO2S tool for this procedure.**

1. Raise and support the vehicle.

2. Disconnect the Heated Oxygen Sensor (HO2S) wire harness mounting clips from engine or body, if equipped.

3. Disconnect the HO2S pigtail harness connector from the engine wiring harness.

4. Remove the HO2S from the catalytic converter.

To install:

✳✳ WARNING

Threads of new sensors are factory coated with anti-seize compound to aid in removal. DO NOT add any additional anti-seize compound to threads of a new sensor.

✳✳ WARNING

When equipped, the HO2S pigtail harness must be clipped and/or bolted back to their original positions on engine or body to prevent mechanical damage to wiring.

5. Install the HO2S sensor to the catalytic converter. Tighten to 30 ft. lbs. (41 Nm).

6. Connect the HO2S sensor pigtail harness connector to the engine wiring harness.

7. Connect the HO2S wire harness mounting clips to engine or body, if equipped.

Upstream Oxygen Sensor (1/1)
See Figure 173.

✳✳ CAUTION

The exhaust manifold, exhaust pipes and catalytic converter(s) become very hot during engine operation. Allow engine to cool before removing the oxygen sensor(s). Failure to allow engine to cool before removal may result in personal injury caused by burns.

✳✳ WARNING

When disconnecting the sensor electrical connector, do not pull directly on the wires going into the oxygen sensor. Damage to the sensor may occur.

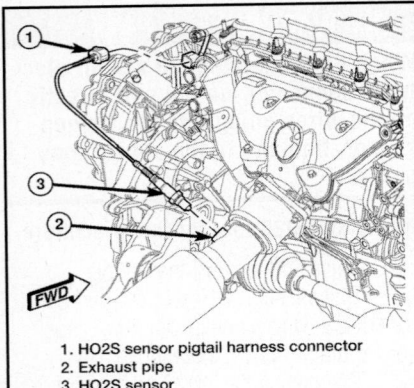

1. HO2S sensor pigtail harness connector
2. Exhaust pipe
3. HO2S sensor

260718

Fig. 173 Upstream Heated Oxygen Sensor (HO2S) location—2.0L

➡ **Use an HO2S tool for this procedure.**

1. Raise and support the vehicle.
2. Disconnect the Heated Oxygen Sensor (HO2S) wire harness mounting clips from engine or body, if equipped.
3. Disconnect the HO2S pigtail harness connector from the engine wiring harness.
4. Remove the HO2S from the exhaust pipe.

To install:

❋❋ **WARNING**

Threads of new sensors are factory coated with anti-seize compound to aid in removal. DO NOT add any additional anti-seize compound to threads of a new sensor.

❋❋ **WARNING**

When equipped, the HO2S pigtail harness must be clipped and/or bolted back to their original positions on engine or body to prevent mechanical damage to wiring.

5. Install the HO2S sensor to the exhaust pipe. Tighten to 30 ft. lbs. (41 Nm).
6. Connect the HO2S sensor pigtail harness connector to the engine wiring harness.
7. Connect the HO2S wire harness mounting clips to engine or body, if equipped.

2.4L Engine

Downstream Oxygen Sensor (1/2)

See Figure 174.

❋❋ **CAUTION**

The exhaust manifold, exhaust pipes and catalytic converter(s) become

very hot during engine operation. Allow engine to cool before removing the oxygen sensor(s). Failure to allow engine to cool before removal may result in personal injury caused by burns.

❋❋ **WARNING**

When disconnecting the sensor electrical connector, do not pull directly on the wires going into the oxygen sensor. Damage to the sensor may occur.

➡ **Use an HO2S tool for this procedure.**

1. Raise and support the vehicle.
2. Disconnect the Heated Oxygen Sensor (HO2S) wire harness mounting clips from engine or body, if equipped.
3. Disconnect the HO2S pigtail harness connector from the engine wiring harness.
4. Remove HO2S from the exhaust pipe.

To install:

❋❋ **WARNING**

Threads of new sensors are factory coated with anti-seize compound to aid in removal. DO NOT add any additional anti-seize compound to threads of a new sensor.

❋❋ **WARNING**

When equipped, the HO2S pigtail harness must be clipped and/or bolted back to their original positions on engine or body to prevent mechanical damage to wiring.

5. Install the HO2S sensor to the exhaust pipe. Tighten to 30 ft. lbs. (41 Nm).

1. HO2S sensor pigtail harness connector
2. Exhaust pipe
3. HO2S sensor

260722

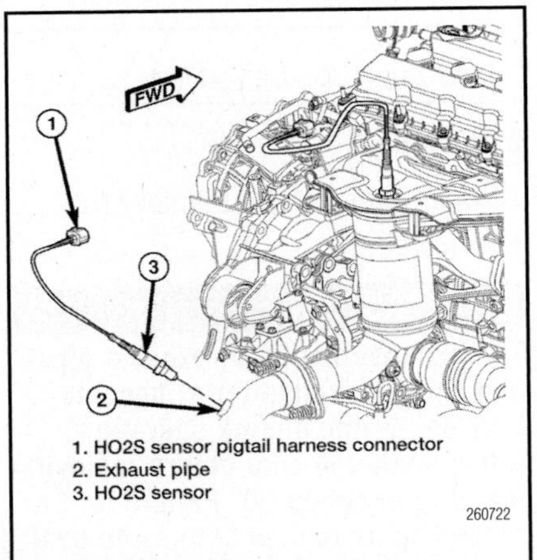

Fig. 174 Downstream Heated Oxygen Sensor (HO2S) location—2.4L

6. Connect the HO2S sensor pigtail harness connector to the engine wiring harness.
7. Connect the HO2S wire harness mounting clips to engine or body, if equipped.

Upstream Oxygen Sensor (1/1)

See Figure 175.

❋❋ **CAUTION**

The exhaust manifold, exhaust pipes and catalytic converter(s) become very hot during engine operation. Allow engine to cool before removing the oxygen sensor(s). Failure to allow engine to cool before removal may result in personal injury caused by burns.

❋❋ **WARNING**

When disconnecting the sensor electrical connector, do not pull directly on the wires going into the oxygen sensor. Damage to the sensor may occur.

➡ **Use an HO2S tool for this procedure.**

1. Raise and support the vehicle.
2. Disconnect the Heated Oxygen Sensor (HO2S) wire harness mounting clips from engine or body, if equipped.
3. Disconnect the HO2S pigtail harness connector from the engine wiring harness.
4. Remove the HO2S from the maniverter.

To install:

❋❋ **WARNING**

Threads of new sensors are factory coated with anti-seize compound to

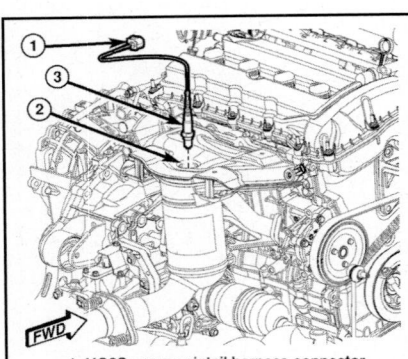

1. HO2S sensor pigtail harness connector
2. Maniverter
3. HO2S sensor

260724

Fig. 175 Upstream Heated Oxygen Sensor (HO2S) location—2.4L

aid in removal. DO NOT add any additional anti-seize compound to threads of a new sensor.

✳✳ WARNING

When equipped, the HO2S pigtail harness must be clipped and/or bolted back to their original positions on engine or body to prevent mechanical damage to wiring.

5. Install the HO2S sensor to the maniverter. Tighten to 30 ft. lbs. (41 Nm).
6. Connect the HO2S sensor pigtail harness connector to the engine wiring harness.
7. Connect the HO2S wire harness mounting clips to engine or body, if equipped.

INLET AIR TEMPERATURE (IAT) SENSOR

LOCATION

See Figure 176.

The Inlet Air Temperature (IAT) sensor is located in the clean air duct.

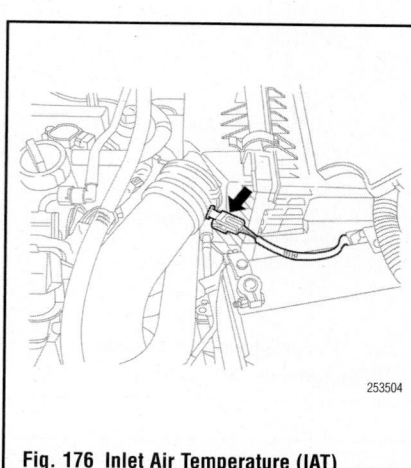

Fig. 176 Inlet Air Temperature (IAT) sensor location

REMOVAL & INSTALLATION

See Figures 176 and 177.

1. Disconnect the negative battery cable.
2. Disconnect the electrical connector from the Inlet Air Temperature (IAT) sensor.
3. Remove the IAT sensor from the clean air duct.

To install:
4. Install the IAT sensor into the clean air duct. The sensor must be installed with the correct orientation.
5. Connect the electrical connector to the IAT sensor.

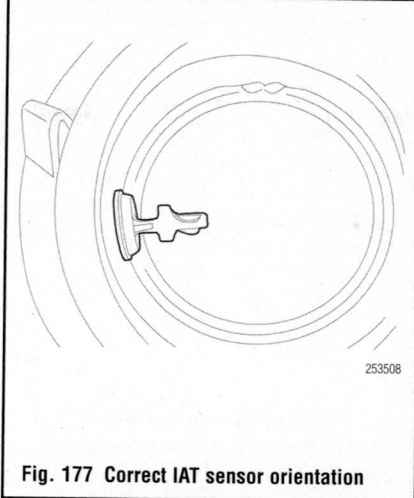

Fig. 177 Correct IAT sensor orientation

6. Connect the negative battery cable. Refer to Battery Reconnect/Relearn Procedure.

KNOCK SENSOR (KS)

LOCATION

The Knock Sensor (KS) is bolted to the engine block in front of the starter, under the intake manifold.

REMOVAL & INSTALLATION

1. Disconnect the negative battery cable.
2. Remove the bolt holding the Knock Sensor (KS).
3. Remove the KS with the electrical connector attached.
4. Disconnect the electrical connector from the KS.
5. Remove the KS.

To install:
6. Attach the electrical connector to the KS.
7. Install the KS into the engine block. Tighten the bolt to 16 ft. lbs. (22 Nm).

✳✳ WARNING

Over- or under-tightening affects the KS performance, possibly causing improper spark control.

8. Connect the negative battery cable. Refer to Battery Reconnect/Relearn Procedure.

MANIFOLD ABSOLUTE PRESSURE (MAP) SENSOR

LOCATION

See Figure 178.

The Manifold Absolute Pressure (MAP) sensor mounts to the intake manifold.

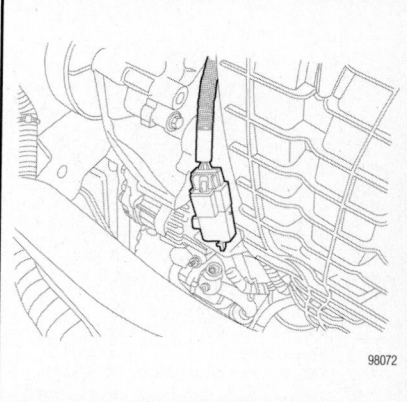

Fig. 178 Manifold Absolute Pressure (MAP) sensor wiring harness connector location

REMOVAL & INSTALLATION

See Figure 178.

1. Disconnect the negative battery cable.
2. Disconnect the electrical connector the from Manifold Absolute Pressure (MAP) sensor.
3. Remove screw from the MAP sensor.
4. Remove the MAP sensor.

To install:
5. Install the MAP sensor to intake manifold.
6. Tighten screw to 40 inch lbs. (4.5 Nm).
7. Connect the electrical connector to the sensor.
8. Connect the negative battery cable. Refer to Battery Reconnect/Relearn Procedure.

POWERTRAIN CONTROL MODULE (PCM)

LOCATION

See Figures 179 and 180.

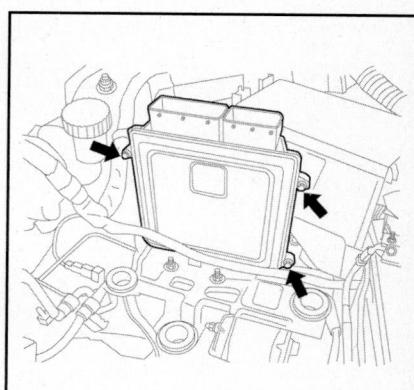

Fig. 179 Powertrain Control Module (PCM) mounting bolt locations—2010 models

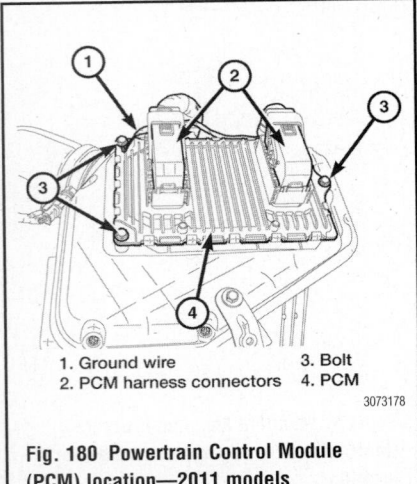

1. Ground wire   3. Bolt
2. PCM harness connectors   4. PCM

3073178

Fig. 180 Powertrain Control Module (PCM) location—2011 models

The Powertrain Control Module (PCM) is located in the left side of the engine compartment, next to or on the air cleaner housing.

REMOVAL & INSTALLATION

2010 Models

See Figures 181 and 182.

※※ WARNING

To avoid possible voltage spike damage to the PCM, the ignition must be OFF, and the negative battery cable must be disconnected before unplugging PCM connectors.

1. Disconnect the negative battery cable.
2. Unlock and disconnect the electrical connectors from the Powertrain Control Module (PCM).
3. Remove the air cleaner box.
4. Remove the 3 mounting bolts.

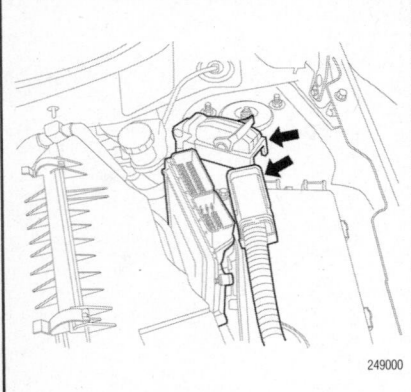

249000

Fig. 181 Powertrain Control Module (PCM) wiring connector locations—2010 models

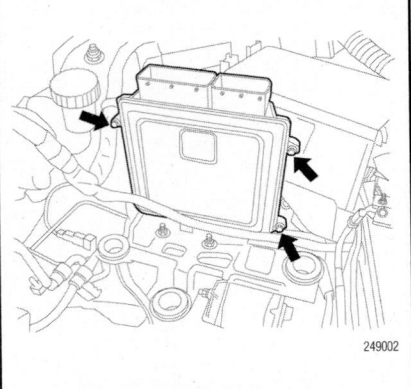

249002

Fig. 182 Powertrain Control Module (PCM) mounting bolt locations—2010 models

5. Tip module out and remove from bracket.

To install:

※※ WARNING

Use the scan tool to reprogram the new PCM with the Vehicles Identification Number (VIN) and the vehicle's mileage. If this step is not done, a Diagnostic Trouble Code (DTC) may be set.

6. Tip the module into the bracket.
7. Install the 3 mounting bolts, and tighten to 80 inch lbs. (9 Nm).
8. Check the pins in the electrical connectors for damage. Repair as necessary.
9. Connect the electrical connectors and lock.
10. Install the air cleaner box.
11. Connect the negative battery cable. Refer to Battery Reconnect/Relearn Procedure.
12. Use the scan tool to reprogram new PCM with Vehicle Identification Number (VIN) and vehicle mileage. If necessary, refer to Pinion Factor Setting.

2011 Models

See Figures 183 through 185.

1. Unlock the retainers, and remove the fresh air inlet duct from the air cleaner body.
2. Disconnect the negative battery cable.
3. Disconnect the Powertrain Control Module (PCM) harness connectors by pressing in the locking tab and lifting the lever.
4. Remove the bolts and the PCM from the air cleaner housing.

To install:

5. Install the PCM onto the air cleaner housing. Hand tighten screws.

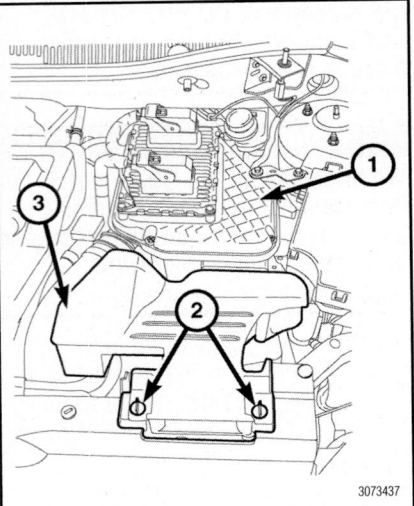

3073437

Fig. 183 Unlock the retainers (2), and remove the fresh air inlet duct (3) from the air cleaner body (1)—2011 models

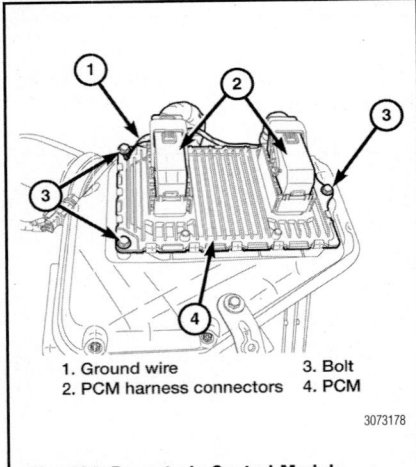

1. Ground wire   3. Bolt
2. PCM harness connectors   4. PCM

3073178

Fig. 184 Powertrain Control Module (PCM) location—2011 models

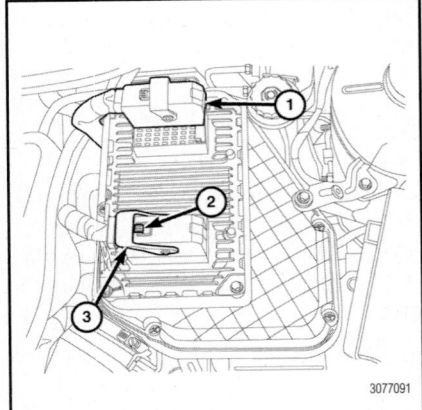

3077091

Fig. 185 Connect both PCM harness connectors (1). Lock the levers (3) into the locking tab (2) —2011 models

6. Connect both PCM harness connectors.

7. Lock the levers into the locking tab.

8. Connect the negative battery cable. Refer to Battery Reconnect/Relearn Procedure.

9. Use the scan tool to reprogram new PCM with Vehicle Identification Number (VIN) and vehicle mileage. If necessary, refer to Pinion Factor Setting.

10. Install the air intake duct.

OBTAINING DIAGNOSTIC TROUBLE CODES (DTCS)

1. Connect the scan tool to the data link (diagnostic) connector. This connector is located in the passenger compartment, at the lower edge of instrument panel, near the steering column.

2. Turn the ignition switch **ON** and access the "Read Fault" screen.

3. Record all the DTCs and "freeze frame" information shown on the scan tool.

4. To erase DTCs, use the "Erase Trouble Code" data screen on the scan tool. Do not erase any DTCs until problems have been investigated and repairs have been performed.

PINION FACTOR SETTING

➥**This procedure must be performed if the PCM has been replaced with a NEW or replacement unit. Failure to perform this procedure will result in an inopera-** tive or improperly calibrated **speedometer.**

The vehicle speed readings for the speedometer are taken from the output speed sensor.

The PCM must be calibrated to the different combinations of equipment (final drive and tires) available.

Pinion Factor allows the technician to set the PCM initial setting so that the speedometer readings will be correct.

To properly read and/or reset the Pinion Factor, it is necessary to use a scan tool.

1. Plug the scan tool into the diagnostic connector located under the instrument panel.

2. Select the Transaxle menu.

3. Select the Miscellaneous menu.

4. Select Pinion Factor, then follow the instructions on the scan tool screen.

THROTTLE POSITION SENSOR (TPS)

LOCATION

The Throttle Position Sensor (TPS) is an integral part of the throttle body.

REMOVAL & INSTALLATION

The Throttle Position Sensor (TPS) is not serviceable as a stand-alone part. The TPS is an integral part of the throttle body. If the TPS requires replacement, replace the throt- tle body assembly. Refer to Throttle Body, removal & installation.

VEHICLE SPEED SENSOR (VSS)

LOCATION

The Vehicle Speed Sensor (VSS) is a Hall effect sensor mounted above the transaxle differential.

REMOVAL & INSTALLATION

1. Remove the air cleaner housing. Refer to Air Cleaner, removal & installation.

2. Disconnect the Vehicle Speed Sensor (VSS) connector.

✳✳ WARNING

Clean the area around the VSS before removing to prevent dirt from entering the transaxle during sensor removal.

3. Remove the VSS retaining bolt.

4. Remove the VSS from the transaxle.

To install:

5. Using a NEW O-ring, install the VSS to the transaxle.

6. Install the bolt, and tighten to 60 inch lbs. (7 Nm).

7. Connect the VSS connector.

8. Install the air cleaner housing. Refer to Air Cleaner, removal & installation.

FUEL

GASOLINE FUEL INJECTION SYSTEM

FUEL SYSTEM SERVICE PRECAUTIONS

Safety is the most important factor when performing not only fuel system maintenance but any type of maintenance. Failure to conduct maintenance and repairs in a safe manner may result in serious personal injury or death. Maintenance and testing of the vehicle's fuel system components can be accomplished safely and effectively by adhering to the following rules and guidelines.

• To avoid the possibility of fire and personal injury, always disconnect the negative battery cable unless the repair or test procedure requires that battery voltage be applied.

• Always relieve the fuel system pressure prior to disconnecting any fuel system component (injector, fuel rail, pressure regulator, etc.), fitting or fuel line connection. Exercise extreme caution whenever relieving fuel system pressure to avoid exposing skin, face and eyes to fuel spray. Please be advised that fuel under pressure may penetrate the skin or any part of the body that it contacts.

• Always place a shop towel or cloth around the fitting or connection prior to loosening to absorb any excess fuel due to spillage. Ensure that all fuel spillage (should it occur) is quickly removed from engine surfaces. Ensure that all fuel soaked cloths or towels are deposited into a suitable waste container.

• Always keep a dry chemical (Class B) fire extinguisher near the work area.

• Do not allow fuel spray or fuel vapors to come into contact with a spark or open flame.

• Always use a back-up wrench when loosening and tightening fuel line connection fittings. This will prevent unnecessary stress and torsion to fuel line piping.

• Always replace worn fuel fitting O-rings with new Do not substitute fuel hose or equivalent where fuel pipe is installed.

Before servicing the vehicle, make sure to also refer to the precautions in the beginning of this section as well.

RELIEVING FUEL SYSTEM PRESSURE

See Figure 186.

1. Remove the lower rear seat cushion.

2. Remove the fuel pump module cover.

3. Disconnect the electrical connector for the fuel pump module.

4. Start and run the engine until it stalls.

5. Attempt restarting the engine until it will no longer run.

6. Turn the ignition key to **OFF** position.

7. Disconnect the negative battery cable.

8. One or more Diagnostic Trouble Codes (DTCs) may have been stored in the Powertrain Control Module (PCM) memory. The scan tool must be used to erase a DTC.

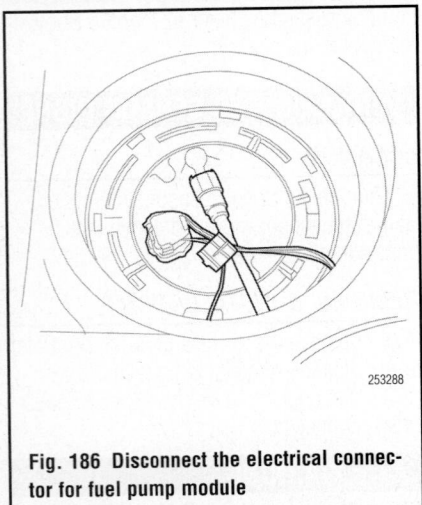

Fig. 186 Disconnect the electrical connector for fuel pump module

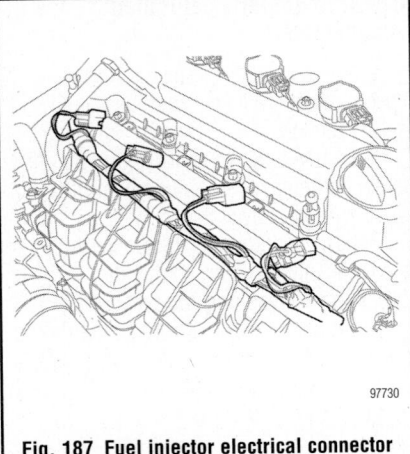

Fig. 187 Fuel injector electrical connector location

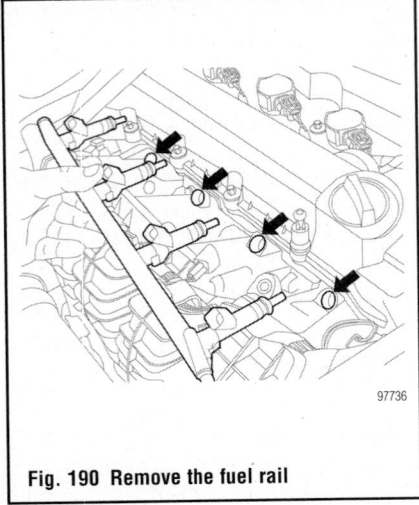

Fig. 190 Remove the fuel rail

FUEL FILTER

REMOVAL & INSTALLATION

Fuel filter is not serviceable. Refer to Fuel Pump Module, removal & installation.

FUEL INJECTORS

REMOVAL & INSTALLATION

See Figures 187 through 190.

❋❋ CAUTION

There is risk of injury to eyes and skin from contact with fuel. Wear protective clothing and eye protection. There is risk of poisoning from inhaling and swallowing fuel. Pour fuel only into appropriately marked and approved containers. Failure to follow these instructions may result in possible serious or fatal injury.

1. Release fuel system pressure. Refer to Relieving Fuel System Pressure procedure.
2. Disconnect the negative battery cable.

➡️**The factory fuel injection wiring harness is numerically tagged (INJ 1, INJ 2, etc.) for injector position identification. If harness is not tagged, make note of wiring location before removal.**

3. Disconnect the electrical connectors from the fuel injectors:
   a. Pull the red-colored slider away from the injector.
   b. While pulling the slider, depress the tab and remove the connector from injector.
4. Remove the fuel line from fuel rail.
5. Remove the wiring harness clips from the fuel rail mounting studs.

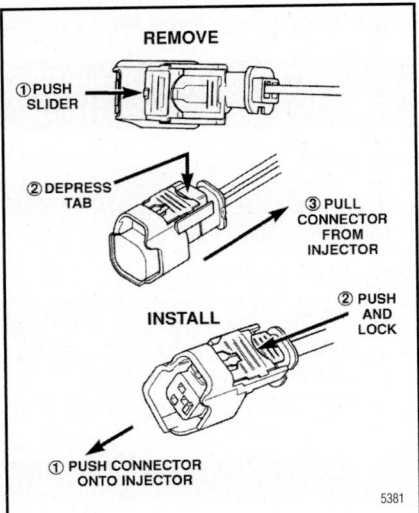

Fig. 188 Fuel injector electrical connector removal/installation

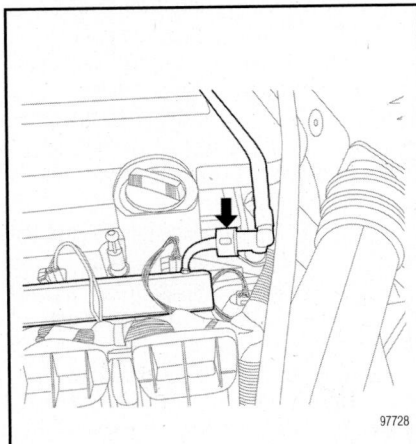

Fig. 189 Remove the fuel line from fuel rail

6. Remove wiring harness from the fuel rail mounting studs.
7. Remove the 2 bolts to the fuel rail at the lower manifold.
8. Remove the fuel rail.
9. Disengage the clip holding the fuel injector to the fuel rail.
10. Remove the fuel injector clip and fuel injector from fuel rail.

To install:

11. Apply a light coating of clean engine oil to the upper O-ring.
12. Install the injector in the cup on the fuel rail.
13. Install the retaining clip.
14. Apply a light coating of clean engine oil to the O-ring on the nozzle end of each injector.
15. Insert fuel injector nozzles into openings in lower intake manifold. Seat the injectors in place.
16. Tighten fuel rail mounting screws to 20 ft. lbs. (27 Nm).
17. Install the wiring harness clips to the fuel rail mounting studs.
18. Connect the electrical connectors to the fuel injectors:
   a. Push the red-colored slider toward the injector until it locks.
   b. Push the connector onto injector.
19. Connect the fuel supply tube to fuel rail.
20. Connect the negative battery cable. Refer to Battery Reconnect/Relearn Procedure.
21. Use scan tool to pressurize the fuel system. Check for leaks.

FUEL PUMP MODULE

REMOVAL & INSTALLATION

See Figures 191 through 193.

❋❋ CAUTION

There is risk of injury to eyes and skin from contact with fuel. Wear protective clothing and eye protection. There is risk of poisoning from inhaling and swallowing fuel. Pour fuel only into appropriately marked and approved containers. Failure to follow these instructions may result in possible serious or fatal injury.

❋❋ CAUTION

The fuel system is under constant high pressure even with the engine off. Until the fuel pressure has been properly released from the system, do not attempt to open the fuel system. Do not smoke or use open flames/sparks when servicing the fuel system. Make sure the area in which the vehicle is being serviced is in a well-ventilated area. Failure to comply may result in serious or fatal injury.

➡The fuel pump module is located on the top left side of the fuel tank.

1. Perform the fuel system pressure release procedure. Refer to Relieving Fuel System Pressure.
2. Disconnect and isolate the negative battery cable.
3. Remove the rear seat.
4. Remove the fuel pump module access cover.
5. Disconnect the electrical connector to the fuel pump module.
6. Disconnect the fuel line to the fuel pump module.

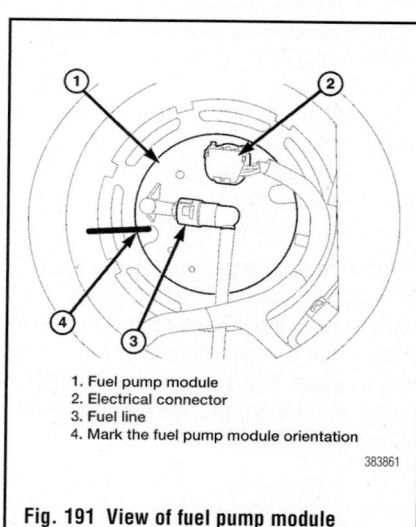

1. Fuel pump module
2. Electrical connector
3. Fuel line
4. Mark the fuel pump module orientation

383861

Fig. 191 View of fuel pump module

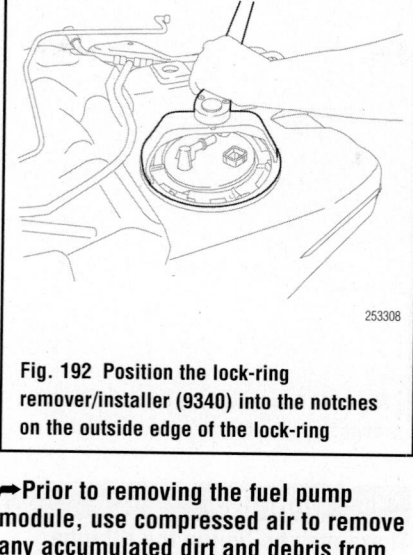

253308

Fig. 192 Position the lock-ring remover/installer (9340) into the notches on the outside edge of the lock-ring

➡Prior to removing the fuel pump module, use compressed air to remove any accumulated dirt and debris from around fuel tank opening.

7. Position the lock-ring remover/installer (9340) into the notches on the outside edge of the lock-ring.
8. Install a 1/2-inch drive breaker bar into the lock-ring remover/installer.
9. Rotate the breaker bar counterclockwise, and remove the lock-ring.

➡The fuel pump module has to be properly located in the tank for the fuel level gauge to work properly.

10. Mark the fuel pump module orientation.

➡Do not spill fuel into the interior of the vehicle.

11. Raise the fuel pump module out of the fuel tank using caution not spill fuel inside the vehicle.

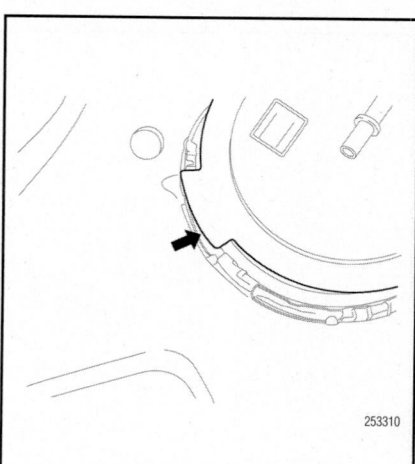

253310

Fig. 193 The fuel pump module has to be properly located in the tank

12. Tip the fuel pump module on its side and drain all fuel from the reservoir.
13. Remove the fuel pump module from the fuel tank, using caution not to bend the float arm.
14. Remove and discard the rubber O-ring seal.

The fuel level sending unit is the only serviceable component of the fuel pump module. If the electric fuel pump, fuel pressure regulator or the fuel filter requires service, the fuel pump module must be replaced as an assembly.

To install:

❋❋ WARNING

Whenever the fuel pump module is serviced, the rubber O-ring seal must be replaced.

15. Clean the O-ring seal area of the fuel tank, and install a new rubber O-ring seal.
16. Lower the fuel pump module into the fuel tank, using caution not to bend the float arm.

➡The fuel pump module must be properly located in the fuel tank for the fuel level gauge to work properly.

17. Align the rubber O-ring seal, and rotate the fuel pump module to the orientation marks noted during removal. This step must be performed for the fuel level gauge to work properly.
18. Position the lock-ring over the top of the fuel pump module.
19. Position the lock-ring remover/installer into the notches on the outside edge of the lock-ring.
20. Install a 1/2-inch drive breaker bar into the lock-ring remover/installer.
21. Rotate the breaker bar clockwise until all 7 notches of the lock-ring have engaged.
22. Connect the fuel line to the fuel pump module.
23. Connect the electrical connector to the fuel pump module.
24. Install the fuel pump module access cover.
25. Install the rear seat.
26. Connect the negative battery cable. Refer to Battery Reconnect/Relearn Procedure.
27. Use scan tool to pressurize the fuel system. Check for leaks.

FUEL TANK

REMOVAL & INSTALLATION

See Figures 194 through 197.

❋ CAUTION

There is risk of injury to eyes and skin from contact with fuel. Wear protective clothing and eye protection. There is risk of poisoning from inhaling and swallowing fuel. Pour fuel only into appropriately marked and approved containers. Failure to follow these instructions may result in possible serious or fatal injury.

❋ CAUTION

The fuel system is under constant high pressure even with the engine off. Until the fuel pressure has been properly released from the system, do not attempt to open the fuel system. Do not smoke or use open flames/sparks when servicing the fuel system. Make sure the area in which the vehicle is being serviced is in a well-ventilated area. Failure to comply may result in serious or fatal injury.

1. Perform the fuel system pressure release procedure. Refer to Relieving Fuel System Pressure.
2. Disconnect and isolate the negative battery cable.
3. Remove the fuel pump module. Refer to Fuel Pump Module, removal & installation.
4. Transfer fuel from the fuel tank into an approved fuel storage container.
5. Raise and support the vehicle.
6. Remove the muffler. Refer to Muffler, removal & installation.
7. Remove the 2 splash shields.
8. Disconnect the vapor canister line.
9. Disconnect the fuel filler tube recirculation vent line and purge line.

Fig. 194 Disconnect the vapor canister line

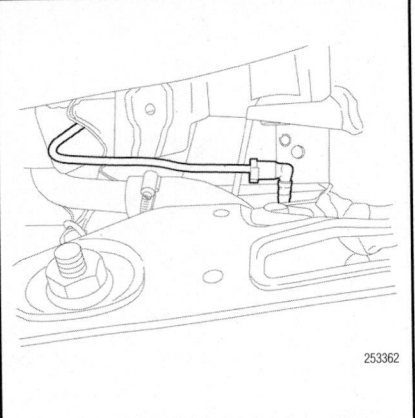

Fig. 195 Disconnect the fuel filler tube recirculation vent line and purge line

❋ WARNING

There may be fuel in the fill tube. Remove hose carefully to reduce fuel splash.

10. Loosen the clamp, and remove the rubber fill hose from the fuel tank.
11. Remove the parking brake cable mounting from the 2 fuel tank straps.

❋ CAUTION

Support the fuel tank with a Transaxle jack or equivalent. Use straps to secure the fuel tank to the jack. Failure to properly support and secure the fuel tank during removal may cause fuel to spill or fuel tank to fall from jack assembly.

12. Position and secure a Transaxle jack to the fuel tank.
13. Remove the bolts from the fuel tank straps.

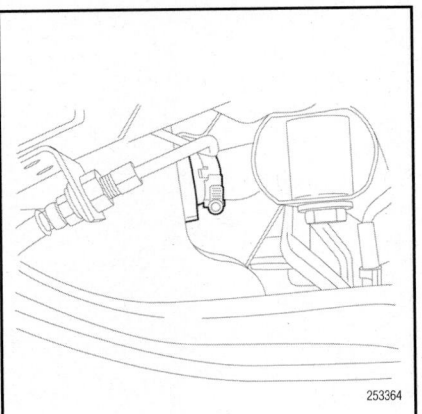

Fig. 196 Loosen the clamp, and remove the rubber fill hose from the fuel tank

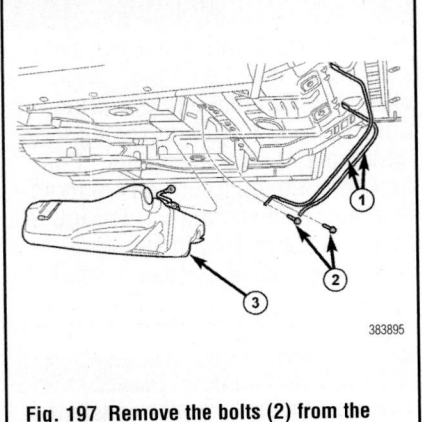

Fig. 197 Remove the bolts (2) from the fuel tank straps (1). Remove the fuel tank (3)

14. Remove the fuel tank from the vehicle.

To install:

15. Install the fuel tank straps to the vehicle.
16. Secure the fuel tank onto a Transaxle jack, and raise the fuel tank into position on the vehicle.
17. Install the straps and fuel tank strap bolts. Tighten the fuel tank strap bolts to 34.5 ft. lbs. (47 Nm). Ensure the fuel tank straps are not twisted or bent.
18. Install the parking brake cable mounting to the 2 fuel tank straps.
19. Connect the fuel fill tube to the fuel tank inlet. Tighten the clamp to 38 inch lbs. (4.1 Nm).
20. Connect the fuel filler tube recirculation vent line and purge line.
21. Connect the vapor canister line.
22. Install the 2 splash shields.
23. Install the muffler. Refer to Muffler, removal & installation.
24. Install the fuel pump module. Refer to Fuel Pump Module, removal & installation.
25. Fill the fuel tank with clean fuel, and install the fuel filler cap.
26. Connect the negative battery cable. Refer to Battery Reconnect/Relearn Procedure.

➡After servicing the fuel system, one or more Diagnostic Trouble Codes (DTC's) may have been stored in the Powertrain Control Module (PCM) memory due to disconnecting the fuel pump module circuit. A scan tool must be used to erase a DTC.

27. Use scan tool to pressurize the fuel system. Check for leaks.

IDLE SPEED

ADJUSTMENT

Idle speed is not manually adjustable. All idle speed functions are controlled by the Powertrain Control Module (PCM).

THROTTLE BODY

REMOVAL & INSTALLATION

See Figures 198 through 201.

✳✳ CAUTION

DO NOT place fingers in or around the throttle body plate. If the throttle body is energized, the throttle plate could move, causing personal injury. Always disconnect the negative battery cable prior to servicing the throttle body.

✳✳ WARNING

DO NOT move the throttle plate while power is connected to the throttle body. This may cause fault codes to set.

1. Disconnect and isolate the negative battery cable.
2. Remove the throttle body air intake hose.
3. Disconnect throttle body electrical connector from the throttle body.

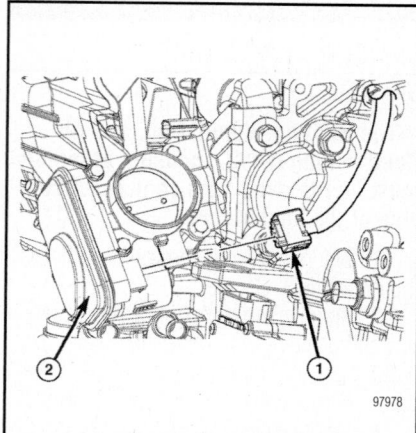

Fig. 198 Disconnect throttle body electrical connector (1) from the throttle body (2)

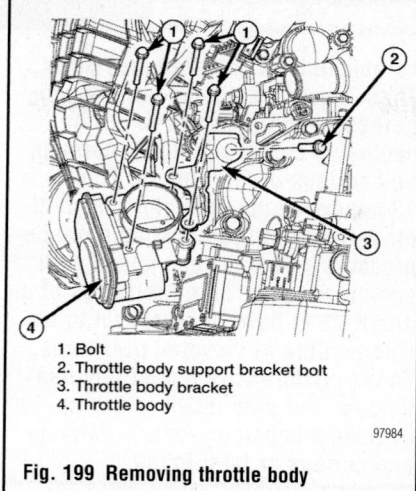

1. Bolt
2. Throttle body support bracket bolt
3. Throttle body bracket
4. Throttle body

Fig. 199 Removing throttle body

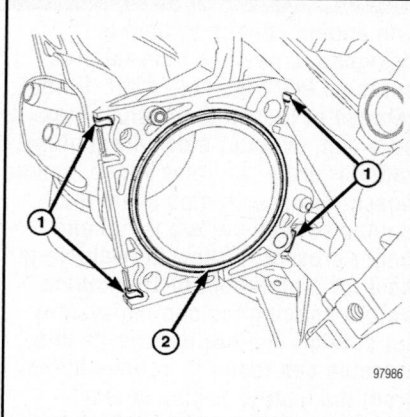

Fig. 200 Inspect the 4 J-nuts (1) and intake manifold-to-throttle body gasket (2)

4. Remove the throttle body support bracket bolt (if equipped).
5. Remove the 4 bolts, throttle body bracket (if equipped), and throttle body from intake manifold.

➥Inspect the intake manifold-to-throttle body gasket for damage. Inspect the J-nuts for damage or excessive wear. Replace as necessary.

6. Inspect the 4 J-nuts for damage or excessive wear, and remove if necessary.
7. Inspect the intake manifold-to-throttle body gasket for damage, and remove if necessary.

To install:

8. Install a new intake manifold to

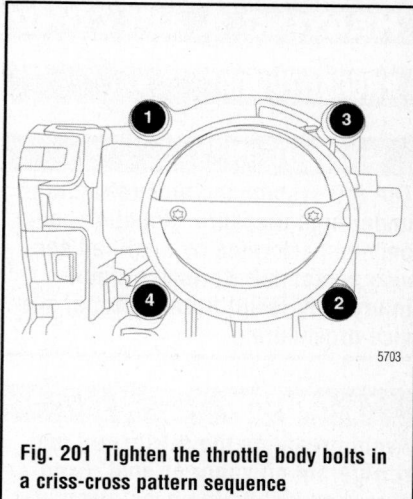

Fig. 201 Tighten the throttle body bolts in a criss-cross pattern sequence

throttle body gasket if replacement was necessary.

9. Install 4 new four J-nuts, if necessary.

✳✳ WARNING

DO NOT OVER-TIGHTEN BOLTS. Over-tightening can cause damage to the throttle body, gaskets, bolts and/or the intake manifold.

10. Install throttle body to the intake manifold.
11. Install the throttle body support bracket and bolt. Tighten the bracket bolt to 18 ft. lbs. (25 Nm).
12. Install the 4 throttle body bolts and hand tighten.

✳✳ WARNING

The throttle body bolts must be tightened in sequence. Tighten in a criss-cross pattern to specification.

13. Tighten the throttle body bolts in a criss-cross pattern sequence to 65 inch lbs. (7.5 Nm).
14. Connect electrical connector to the throttle body.
15. Install the clean air hose, and tighten clamps to 35 inch lbs. (4 Nm).
16. Connect the negative battery cable. Refer to Battery Reconnect/Relearn Procedure.
17. Use a scan tool and clear all fault codes, then perform the ETC RELEARN function.

HEATING & AIR CONDITIONING SYSTEM

PRECAUTIONS

✳✳ CAUTION

The A/C system contains refrigerant under high pressure. Repairs should only be performed by qualified service personnel. Serious or fatal injury may result from improper service procedures.

✳✳ CAUTION

Avoid breathing the refrigerant and refrigerant oil vapor or mist. Exposure may irritate the eyes, nose, and/or throat. Wear eye protection when servicing the A/C refrigerant system. Serious eye injury can result from direct contact with the refrigerant. If eye contact occurs, seek medical attention immediately.

✳✳ CAUTION

Do not expose the refrigerant to open flame. Poisonous gas is created when refrigerant is burned. An electronic leak detector is recommended. Serious or fatal injury may result from improper service procedures.

✳✳ CAUTION

If accidental A/C system discharge occurs, ventilate the work area before resuming service. Large amounts of refrigerant released in a closed work area will displace the oxygen and cause suffocation and serious or fatal injury.

✳✳ CAUTION

The evaporation rate of R-134a refrigerant at average temperature and altitude is extremely high. As a result, anything that comes in contact with the refrigerant will freeze. Always protect the skin or delicate objects from direct contact with the refrigerant.

✳✳ CAUTION

The R-134a service equipment or the vehicle refrigerant system should not be pressure tested or leak tested with compressed air. Some mixtures of air and R-134a have been shown to be

combustible at elevated pressures. These mixtures are potentially dangerous, and may result in fire or explosion causing property damage and serious or fatal injury. The R-134a service equipment or the vehicle refrigerant system should not be pressure tested or leak tested with compressed air. Some mixtures of air and R-134a have been shown to be combustible at elevated pressures. These mixtures are potentially dangerous, and may result in fire or explosion causing property damage and serious or fatal injury.

✳✳ CAUTION

The engine cooling system is designed to develop internal pressures up to 21 psi (145 kPa). Do not remove or loosen the coolant pressure cap, cylinder block drain plugs, radiator drain, radiator hoses, heater hoses, or hose clamps while the engine cooling system is hot and under pressure. Allow the vehicle to cool for a minimum of 15 minutes before opening the cooling system for service. Failure to observe this warning can result in serious burns from the heated engine coolant.

BLOWER MOTOR

REMOVAL & INSTALLATION
See Figure 202.

➡The blower motor is located on the bottom of the passenger side of the Heating, Ventilation, and Air Conditioning (HVAC) housing. The blower motor can be removed from the vehicle without having to remove the HVAC housing.

1. Disconnect and isolate the negative battery cable.
2. If equipped, remove the silencer from below the passenger side of the instrument panel.
3. From underneath the instrument panel, disengage the connector lock and disconnect the instrument panel wiring harness connector from the blower motor.
4. Remove the 3 screws that secure the blower motor and the wire lead bracket (if equipped) to the bottom of the HVAC housing. Remove the blower motor.

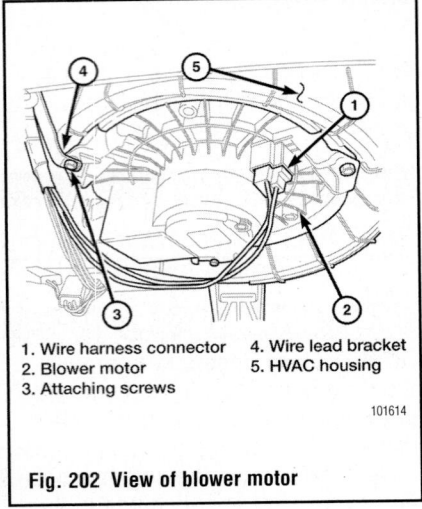

1. Wire harness connector 4. Wire lead bracket
2. Blower motor   5. HVAC housing
3. Attaching screws

101614

Fig. 202 View of blower motor

To install:

5. Position the blower motor into the bottom of the HVAC housing.
6. Install the 3 screws that secure the blower motor and the wire lead bracket (if equipped) to the HVAC housing. Tighten the screws to 10 inch lbs. (1.2 Nm).
7. Connect the instrument panel wire harness connector to the blower motor, and engage the connector lock.
8. If equipped, install the silencer below the passenger side of the instrument panel.
9. Connect the negative battery cable. Refer to Battery Reconnect/Relearn Procedure.

HEATER CORE

REMOVAL & INSTALLATION
See Figure 203.

➡The Heating, Ventilation, and Air Conditioning (HVAC) housing assembly must be removed from vehicle for service of the heater core.

1. Before servicing the vehicle, refer to the Precautions Section.
2. Remove the HVAC housing assembly, and place it on a workbench. Refer to HVAC Housing, removal & installation.
3. Remove the left side front floor duct.
4. Remove the 3 screws that secure the heater core cover to the driver's side of the air distribution housing and the HVAC housing. Remove the cover.
5. Remove the foam seal (1) from the flange (2) located on the front of the HVAC housing (5).
6. Remove the screw (6) that secures the flange to the front of the HVAC housing, and remove the flange.

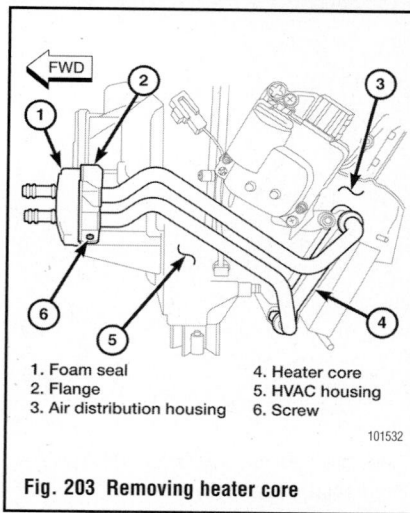

1. Foam seal   4. Heater core
2. Flange   5. HVAC housing
3. Air distribution housing   6. Screw

101532

Fig. 203 Removing heater core

7. Carefully pull the heater core (4) out of the driver side of the air distribution housing (3).

To install:

8. Carefully install the heater core (4) into the side of the air distribution housing (3).

9. Install the flange (2) that secures the heater core tubes to the front of the HVAC housing.

10. Install the screw (6) that secures the flange to the HVAC housing. Tighten the screw to 10 inch lbs. (1.2 Nm).

➡**If the foam seal for the flange is deformed or damaged, it must be replaced.**

11. Install the foam seal (1) onto the flange.

12. Install the left side front floor duct.

➡**If the heater core is being replaced, flush the cooling system. Refer to Normal Flushing procedure.**

13. Install the HVAC housing assembly. Refer to HVAC Housing, removal & installation.

HVAC HOUSING

REMOVAL & INSTALLATION

See Figures 204 and 205.

✳✳ CAUTION

Disable the airbag system before attempting any steering wheel, steering column or instrument panel component diagnosis or service. Disconnect and isolate the negative battery (ground) cable. Wait 2 minutes for the airbag system capacitor to discharge before performing fur-

ther diagnosis or service. This is the only sure way to disable the airbag system. Failure to follow these instructions may result in possible serious or fatal injury.

➡**The Heating, Ventilation, and Air Conditioning (HVAC) housing must be removed from the vehicle and disassembled for service of the heater core, A/C evaporator, air intake housing and the mode-air and blend-air doors.**

1. Before servicing the vehicle, refer to the Precautions Section.

2. Disconnect and isolate the negative battery cable.

3. Recover the refrigerant from the refrigerant system.

4. Partially drain the engine cooling system. Refer to Drain & Refill procedure.

5. Remove the nuts that secure the heat shield to the studs located on the dash panel in the engine compartment, and remove the heat shield.

6. Remove the bolt that secures the A/C liquid and suction line assembly to the A/C expansion valve.

7. Disconnect the A/C liquid and suction line assembly from the A/C expansion valve. Remove and discard the O-ring seals.

8. Install plugs in (or tape over) the opened refrigerant line fittings and the expansion valve ports.

9. Disconnect the heater hoses from the heater core tubes.

10. Install plugs in (or tape over) the opened heater core tubes to prevent coolant spillage during housing removal.

➡**Make sure to remove the 5 bolts that secure the HVAC housing to the instrument panel support prior to removing the instrument panel from the vehicle.**

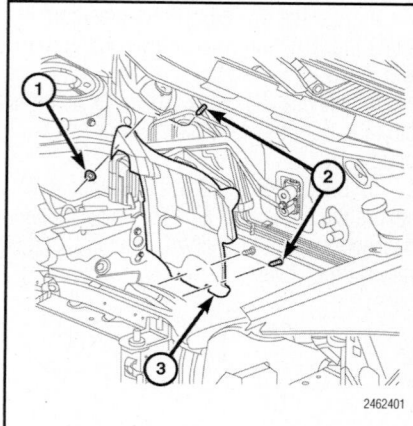

2462401

Fig. 204 Remove the nuts (1) that secure the heat shield (3) to the studs (2)

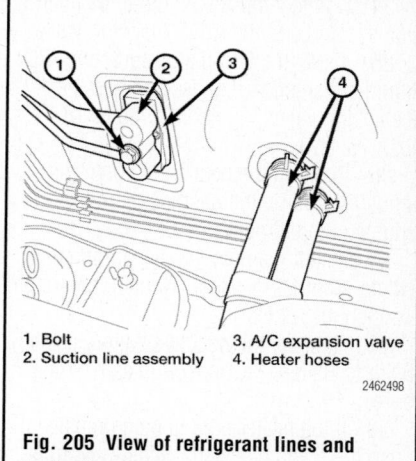

1. Bolt   3. A/C expansion valve
2. Suction line assembly   4. Heater hoses

2462498

Fig. 205 View of refrigerant lines and heater hoses

11. Remove the instrument panel.

12. Remove the rear floor ducts.

13. Remove the condensation drain tube.

14. Remove the nut that secures the passenger side of the HVAC housing to the dash panel.

➡**Use care to ensure that the interior is covered in case of loss of residual fluids from the heater and evaporator cores.**

15. Pull the HVAC housing rearward, and remove the HVAC housing assembly from the passenger compartment.

To install:

16. Position the HVAC housing assembly to the dash panel. Be certain that the passenger side of the HVAC housing is correctly located over the dash panel mounting stud.

17. Install the nut that secures the HVAC housing to the passenger compartment side of dash panel. Tighten the nut to 40 inch lbs. (4.5 Nm).

18. Install the condensation drain tube.

19. Install the rear floor ducts.

20. Install the instrument panel.

21. Remove the previously installed plugs or caps, and connect the heater hoses to the heater core tubes.

22. Remove the tape or plugs from the refrigerant line fittings and the expansion valve ports.

23. Lubricate new rubber O-rings seals with clean refrigerant oil, and install them onto the liquid and suction line fittings. Use only the specified O-ring seals, as they are made of special materials compatible to the R-134a system. Use only refrigerant oil of the type recommended for the A/C compressor in the vehicle.

24. Connect the A/C liquid and suction line assembly to the A/C expansion valve.

25. Install the bolt that secures the A/C liquid and suction line assembly to the A/C expansion valve. Tighten the nut to 18 ft. lbs. (25 Nm).

26. Position the heat shield onto the studs located on the dash panel in the engine compartment.

27. Install the nuts that secure the heat shield to the dash panel. Tighten the nuts to 10 inch lbs. (1 Nm).

28. Connect the negative battery cable. Refer to Battery Reconnect/Relearn Procedure.

29. If the heater core is being replaced, flush the cooling system. Refer to Normal Flushing procedure.

30. Refill the engine cooling system. Refer to Drain & Refill procedure.

31. Evacuate and charge the refrigerant system

PARTICULATE AIR FILTER

REMOVAL & INSTALLATION

See Figures 206 through 208.

✳ CAUTION

Disable the airbag system before attempting any steering wheel, steering column or instrument panel component diagnosis or service. Disconnect and isolate the negative battery (ground) cable, then wait 2 minutes for the airbag system capacitor to discharge before performing further diagnosis or service. This is the only sure way to disable the airbag system. Failure to follow these instructions may result in accidental airbag deployment and possible serious or fatal injury.

✳ CAUTION

Always make sure the A/C-heater system is turned off and that the ignition switch is in the OFF position prior to servicing the particulate air filter. Never place fingers or other objects into the filter opening of the Heating, Ventilation, and Air Conditioning (HVAC) housing. Failure to

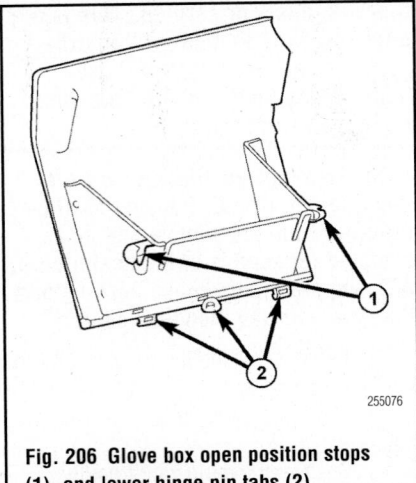

Fig. 206 Glove box open position stops (1), and lower hinge pin tabs (2)

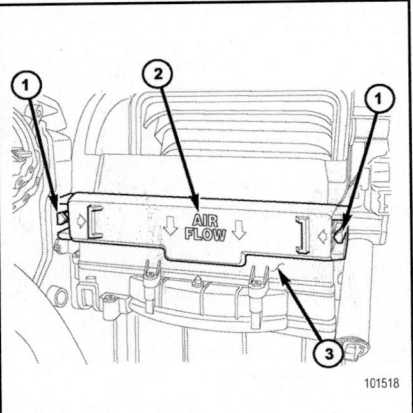

Fig. 207 Particulate air filter cover (2), retaining tabs (1), and HVAC housing (3)

follow this warning may result in serious injury.

1. Open the glove box latch.

2. Unsnap the glove box damper from glove box bin.

3. Flex the glove box open position stops inboard, and rotate glove box outward and down.

4. Unsnap the glove box lower hinge pin tabs from the base panel lower hinge pins.

5. Disengage the 2 retaining tabs that secure the particulate air filter cover to the passenger side of the HVAC housing, and remove the cover.

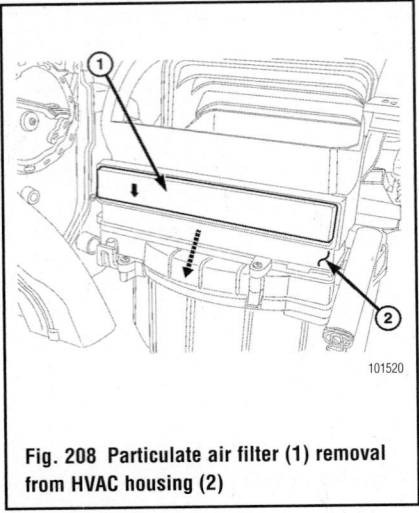

Fig. 208 Particulate air filter (1) removal from HVAC housing (2)

➡**Illustration shown with instrument panel removed for clarity.**

6. Remove the particulate air filter from the HVAC housing by pulling the filter element straight out of the housing.

To install:

➡**The particulate air filter is labeled with an arrow to indicate air flow direction through the filter. Make sure to properly install the particulate air filter. Failure to properly install the filter will result in the need to replace the filter sooner than required by design.**

7. Install the particulate air filter into the filter opening in the HVAC housing. Insert the particulate air filter directly into the housing with the arrow on the filter pointing to the floor.

8. Position the particulate air filter cover to the HVAC housing, and engage the 2 retaining tabs that secure the cover to the housing. Make sure the retaining tabs are fully engaged.

9. Align the glove box door with the glove box opening.

10. Snap the glove box door hinge pin tabs onto the lower base panel hinge pins.

11. Flex the glove box open position stops inboard, and rotate upward and inward past stops.

12. Snap the glove box damper onto glove box bin.

13. Close the glove box.

STEERING

PRECAUTIONS

⁂ CAUTION

Power steering fluid, engine parts and exhaust system may be extremely hot if engine has been running. Do not start engine with any loose or disconnected hoses. Do not allow hoses to touch hot exhaust manifold or catalyst.

⁂ CAUTION

Fluid level should be checked with the engine off to prevent personal injury from moving parts.

⁂ WARNING

When the system is open, cap all open ends of the hoses, power steering pump fittings or power steering gear ports to prevent entry of foreign material into the components.

POWER STEERING GEAR

REMOVAL & INSTALLATION

See Figures 209 through 215.

1. Before servicing the vehicle, refer to the Precautions section.
2. Siphon out as much power steering fluid as possible from the pump.
3. Reposition the floor carpeting to access the intermediate shaft coupling at the base of the column.
4. Position the front wheels of vehicle in the straight-ahead position, then turn the steering wheel to the right until the interme-

diate shaft coupling bolt at the base of the column can be accessed.

5. Remove the intermediate shaft coupling bolt. Do not separate the intermediate shaft from the steering gear pinion shaft at this time.
6. Return the front wheels of vehicle (and steering wheel) to the straight-ahead position. Using a steering wheel holder, lock the steering wheel in place to keep it from rotating. This keeps the clockspring in the proper orientation.
7. Raise and support the vehicle
8. Remove the tire and wheel assembly.
9. On each side of the steering gear, remove the outer tie rod. Refer to Outer Tie Rod, removal & installation.
10. If equipped, remove the engine belly pan.
11. Remove the rear engine mount. Refer to Rear Engine Mount, removal & installation.
12. Remove the front engine mount through-bolt.
13. Remove the 3 screws securing the heat shield to the crossmember. Remove the shield.
14. Remove the return hose and pressure hose at the steering gear.
15. Remove the fasteners securing the power steering hose routing clamps to the crossmember.
16. Remove the screws securing the stabilizer bushing retainers to the crossmember.
17. Remove the 2 stabilizer bushing retainers.

➡**Before removing the front suspension crossmember from the vehicle, the location of the crossmember must be**

marked on the body of the vehicle. Do this so the crossmember can be relocated, upon reinstallation, against the body of vehicle in the same location as before removal. If the front suspension crossmember is not reinstalled in exactly the same location as before removal, the preset front wheel alignment settings (caster and camber) may be lost.

18. Mark the location of the front crossmember on the body near each mounting bolt using a marker or crayon. Do not use a scratch awl or other tool that can penetrate the protective coating on the body.
19. Support the front crossmember with a Transaxle jack.
20. Remove the 4 mounting bolts securing the front crossmember to the body.
21. Lower the crossmember enough to access the intermediate shaft coupling at the

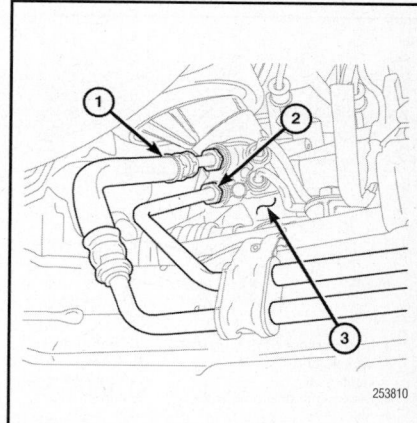

Fig. 211 Remove the return hose (1) and pressure hose (2) at the steering gear (3)

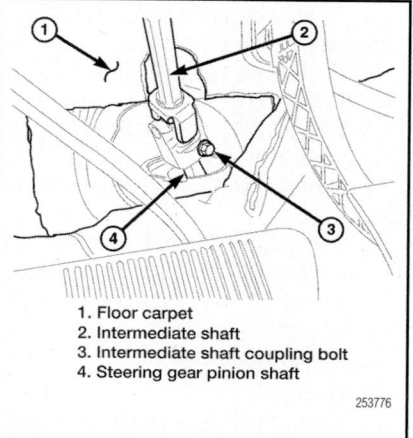

1. Floor carpet
2. Intermediate shaft
3. Intermediate shaft coupling bolt
4. Steering gear pinion shaft

Fig. 209 Removing lower intermediate shaft coupling bolt

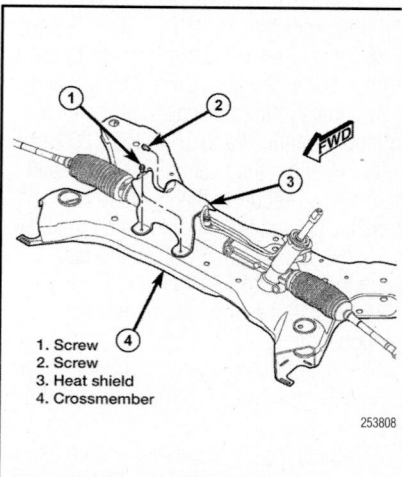

1. Screw
2. Screw
3. Heat shield
4. Crossmember

Fig. 210 Removing heat shield

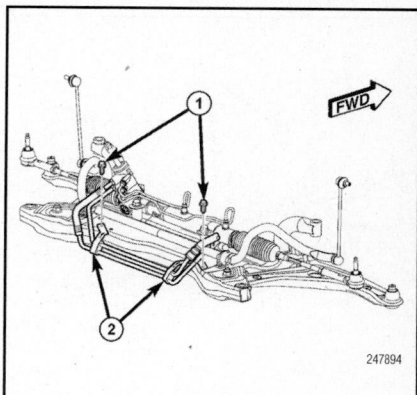

Fig. 212 Remove the fasteners (1) securing the power steering hose routing clamps (2) to the crossmember

steering gear pinion shaft. Slide the coupling off the pinion shaft.

22. Remove the dash seals as necessary.

23. Remove the 2 bolts securing the steering gear to the crossmember.

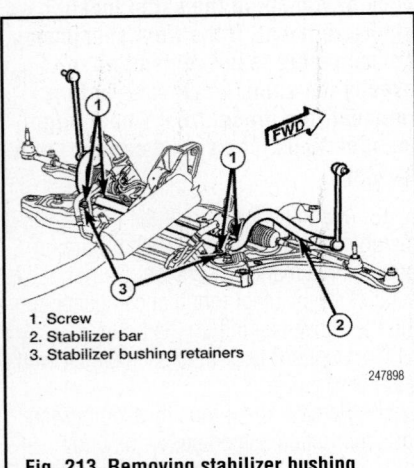

1. Screw
2. Stabilizer bar
3. Stabilizer bushing retainers

247898

Fig. 213 Removing stabilizer bushing retainers

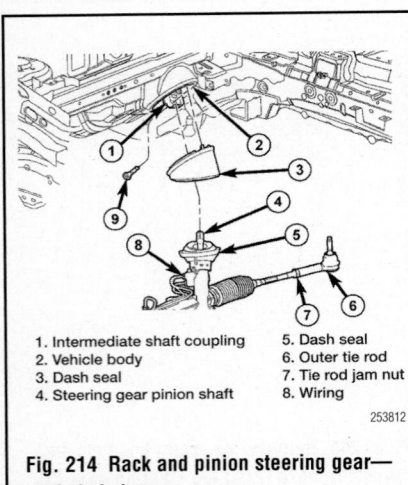

1. Intermediate shaft coupling
2. Vehicle body
3. Dash seal
4. Steering gear pinion shaft
5. Dash seal
6. Outer tie rod
7. Tie rod jam nut
8. Wiring

253812

Fig. 214 Rack and pinion steering gear—exploded view

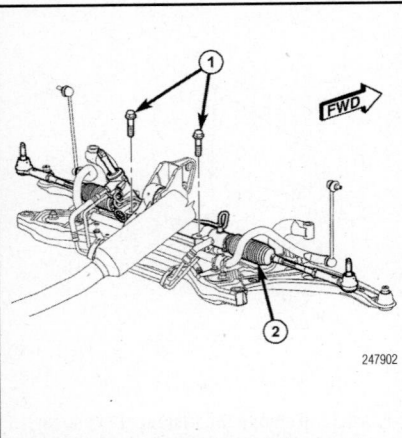

247902

Fig. 215 Remove the 2 bolts (1) securing the steering gear (2) to the crossmember

24. Rotate the stabilizer bar up in order to remove the steering gear from the vehicle.

25. Remove the steering gear from the crossmember.

To install:

26. Rotate the stabilizer bar up and install the steering gear on the crossmember.

27. Install the 2 bolts securing the steering gear to the crossmember. Tighten the steering gear mounting bolts to 52 ft. lbs. (70 Nm).

28. Install the 2 dash seals as necessary.

29. Center the power steering gear rack in its travel as necessary.

➡**When installing the front suspension crossmember back in the vehicle, it is very important that the crossmember be attached to the body in exactly the same spot as when it was removed. Otherwise, the vehicle's wheel alignment settings (caster and camber) will be lost.**

30. Slowly raise the crossmember into mounted position using the Transaxle jack, matching the crossmember to the marked locations on the body made during removal.

31. Check the positioning of the seals at the dash panel, and adjust as necessary.

32. Install the 4 mounting bolts securing the front crossmember to the body. Tighten the crossmember mounting bolts to 111 ft. lbs. (150 Nm).

33. Remove the Transaxle jack.

34. Install the retainers over the stabilizer bar cushions. Install all 4 stabilizer bar cushion retainer screws, and tighten them to 22 ft. lbs. (30 Nm).

35. Install the fasteners securing the power steering hose routing clamps to the crossmember. Use a NEW push clip or install screw (if so equipped) on the left, and tighten screws to 71 inch lbs. (8 Nm).

36. Install the pressure hose at the gear. Tighten the tube nut to 24 ft. lbs. (32 Nm).

37. Install the return hose at the gear. Tighten the tube nut to 15 ft. lbs. (20 Nm).

38. Position the heat shield, and install the 3 screws securing the shield to the crossmember. Tighten the 2 front mounting screws to 35 inch lbs. (4 Nm). Tighten the rear mounting screw to 150 inch lbs. (17 Nm).

39. Install the front engine mount through-bolt.

40. Install the rear engine mount. Refer to Rear Engine Mount, removal & installation.

41. If equipped, install the engine belly pan.

➡**Prior to attaching the outer tie rod end to the knuckle, inspect the tie rod seal boot. If the seal boot is damaged, replace the outer tie rod end.**

42. On each side of the steering gear, install the outer tie rod. Refer to Outer Tie Rod, removal & installation.

43. On each side of the vehicle, install tire and wheel assembly. Install and tighten wheel mounting nuts to 100 ft. lbs. (135 Nm).

44. Lower the vehicle.

45. Remove the steering wheel holder.

46. Verify the front wheels of vehicle are in the straight-ahead position.

47. Center the intermediate shaft over the steering gear pinion shaft, lining up the ends, then slide the intermediate shaft onto the steering gear pinion shaft.

48. From center, rotate the steering wheel to the right approximately 90° or until the intermediate shaft coupling bolt can be easily installed.

49. Install the intermediate shaft coupling bolt. Tighten the bolt to 31 ft. lbs. (42 Nm).

50. Reposition the floor carpet in place.

51. Straighten the steering wheel to straight-ahead position.

52. Fill and bleed the power steering system. Refer to Bleeding procedure.

53. Check for fluid leaks.

54. Adjust front wheel toe as necessary.

POWER STEERING PUMP

REMOVAL & INSTALLATION

See Figure 216.

1. Before servicing the vehicle, refer to the Precautions Section.

2. Siphon as much fluid as possible from the power steering fluid reservoir.

3. Remove the engine cover.

4. Remove the pressure hose routing bracket bolt at the upper mount.

5. Remove the pressure hose at the pump pressure port.

6. Remove the hose clamp securing the supply hose at the pump.

7. Remove the supply hose from the pump.

8. Remove the drive belt. Refer to Accessory Drive Belt, removal & installation.

9. Remove the 3 pump mounting bolts through the pulley openings.

10. Remove the power steering pump.

To install:

11. Using a lint free towel, wipe clean the open power steering pressure hose end and the power steering pump port. Replace

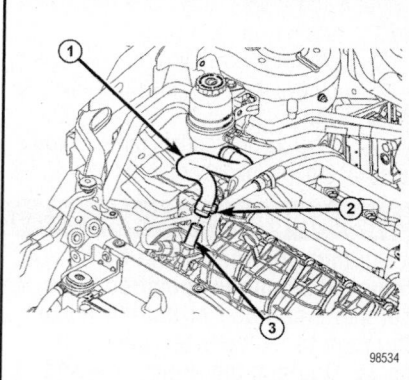

Fig. 216 Remove the hose clamp (2) securing the supply hose (1) at the pump (3)

any used O-rings with new. Lubricate the O-ring with clean power steering fluid.

12. Place the pump in mounting position. Install the 3 bolts through the pulley openings. Tighten the mounting bolts to 19 ft. lbs. (26 Nm).

13. Install the drive belt. Refer to Accessory Drive Belt, removal & installation.

14. Install the supply hose at the pump.

15. Clamp the hose clamp securing the supply hose to the pump.

16. Install the pressure hose at the pump pressure port. Tighten the tube nut to 24 ft. lbs. (32 Nm).

17. Install the pressure hose routing bracket bolt to the upper mount.

18. Fill and bleed the power steering system. Refer to Bleeding procedure.

19. Check for leaks.

20. Install the engine cover.

BLEEDING

See Figure 217.

> ❊❊ **CAUTION**
>
> The fluid level should be checked with the engine off to prevent injury from moving components.

> ❊❊ **WARNING**
>
> Mopar® Power Steering Fluid + 4 or Mopar® ATF+4 Automatic Transaxle Fluid is to be used in the power steering system. Both fluids have the same material standard specifications (MS-9602). No other power steering or automatic Transaxle fluid is to be used in the system. Damage may result to the power steering pump and system if another fluid is used. Do not overfill the system.

> ❊❊ **WARNING**
>
> If the air is not purged from the power steering system correctly, pump failure could result.

➡ Be sure the vacuum tool used in the following procedure is clean and free of any fluids.

1. Check the fluid level. As measured on the side of the reservoir, the level should indicate between MAX and MIN when the fluid is at normal ambient temperature. Adjust the fluid level as necessary.

2. Tightly insert the power steering cap adapter (9688A) into the mouth of the reservoir.

> ❊❊ **WARNING**
>
> Failure to use a vacuum pump reservoir may allow power steering fluid to be sucked into the hand vacuum pump.

3. Attach hand vacuum pump (C-4207-A), with vacuum pump reservoir attached, to the power steering cap adapter.

> ❊❊ **WARNING**
>
> Do not run the vehicle while vacuum is applied to the power steering system. Damage to the power steering pump can occur.

➡ When performing the following step, make sure the vacuum level is maintained during the entire time period.

4. Using the hand vacuum pump, apply 20–25 inches Hg (68–85 kPa) of vacuum to the system for a minimum of 3 minutes.

5. Slowly release the vacuum and remove the special tools.

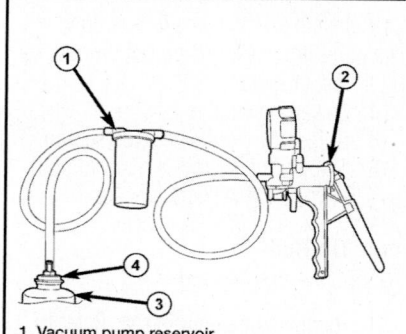

1. Vacuum pump reservoir
2. Special Tool C-4207-8, Hand Vacuum Pump
3. Mouth of the reservoir
4. Special Tool 9688A, Power Steering Cap Adapter

Fig. 217 Bleeding power steering system

6. Adjust the fluid level as necessary.

7. Repeat the procedure until the fluid no longer drops when vacuum is applied.

8. Start the engine and cycle the steering wheel lock-to-lock 3 times.

➡ Do not hold the steering wheel at the stops.

9. Stop the engine and check for leaks at all connections.

10. Check for any signs of air in the reservoir, and check the fluid level.

11. If air is present, repeat the procedure as necessary.

FLUID FILL PROCEDURE

See Figure 218.

> ❊❊ **CAUTION**
>
> Fluid level should be checked with the engine OFF to prevent personal injury from moving parts and to assure an accurate fluid level reading.

> ❊❊ **WARNING**
>
> Only Mopar® Power Steering Fluid + 4 or Mopar® ATF+4 Automatic Transaxle Fluid is to be used in the power steering system. Both fluids have the same material standard specifications (MS-9602). No other power steering or automatic Transaxle fluid is to be used in the system. Damage may result to the power steering pump and system if another fluid is used. Do not overfill the system.

➡ The power steering fluid reservoir is mounted above the engine head cover, and is attached to the backside of the engine.

➡ Although not required at specific intervals, the fluid level may be checked periodically. Check the fluid level any time there is a system noise or fluid leak suspected.

➡ The power steering fluid reservoir is mounted above the right front inner fender well to a bracket.

The power steering fluid level can be viewed through the side of the power steering fluid reservoir. Compare the fluid level to the markings on the side of the reservoir. When the fluid is at normal ambient temperature, approximately 70–80°F (21–27°C), the fluid level should read between the MAX. and MIN. markings. When the fluid is hot, fluid level is allowed to read up to the MAX. line.

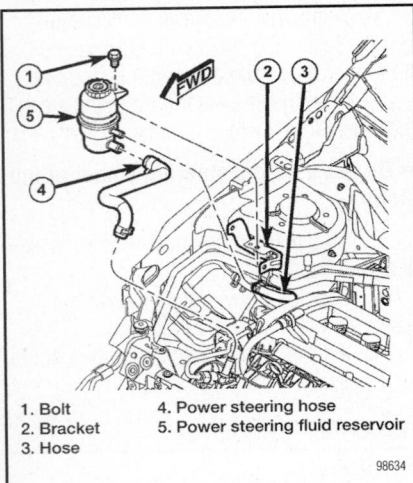

1. Bolt
2. Bracket
3. Hose
4. Power steering hose
5. Power steering fluid reservoir

98634

Fig. 218 Power steering fluid reservoir location

TIE RODS

REMOVAL & INSTALLATION

Outer Tie Rod

See Figures 219 and 220.

1. Before servicing the vehicle, refer to the Precautions section.
2. Raise and support the vehicle.
3. Remove the tire and wheel assembly.
4. Loosen the tie rod jam nut.
5. Remove the nut attaching the outer tie rod to the knuckle. To do this, hold the tie rod end stud with a wrench while loosening and removing the nut with a standard wrench or crowfoot wrench.
6. Release the tie rod end from the knuckle using remover (9360).
7. Remove the outer tie rod from the knuckle.

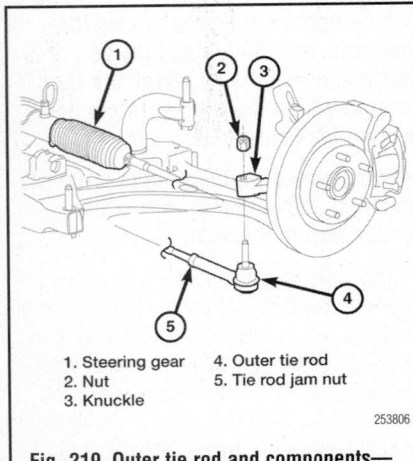

1. Steering gear
2. Nut
3. Knuckle
4. Outer tie rod
5. Tie rod jam nut

253806

Fig. 219 Outer tie rod and components—exploded view

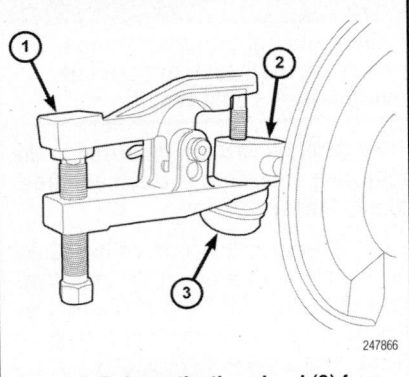

247866

Fig. 220 Release the tie rod end (3) from the knuckle (2) using remover (1)

➡ When unscrewing the outer tie rod from inner, count the number of revolutions to take it off. This action will aid in installation, getting the toe close to where it needs to be when setting the wheel alignment.

8. Remove the outer tie rod from the inner tie rod.

To install:

9. If it is not already installed, install the jam nut on the inner tie rod threads. Thread the nut down the inner tie rod far enough to allow for outer tie rod installation.
10. Thread the outer tie rod onto the inner tie rod approximately the same amount of revolutions as the original was installed.
11. Snug the tie rod jam nut just enough to hold the tie rods in place. Do not tighten the jam nut at this time.
12. Install the outer tie rod ball stud into the hole in the knuckle arm. Start a NEW tie rod mounting nut onto the stud. While holding the tie rod end stud with a wrench, tighten the nut with a wrench or crowfoot wrench. Tighten the nut to 97 ft. lbs. (132 Nm).
13. Install tire and wheel assembly. Install and tighten wheel mounting nuts to 100 ft. lbs. (135 Nm).
14. Lower the vehicle.
15. Adjust the front wheel toe setting.
16. Tighten the tie rod jam nut to 55 ft. lbs. (75 Nm) once wheel toe is set.

Inner Tie Rod

See Figures 221 and 222.

1. Remove the outer tie rod. Refer to Outer Tie Rod procedure.
2. Remove the tie rod jam nut from the inner tie rod.
3. Remove the clamp securing the bellows to the inner tie rod.

4. Remove the clamp securing the bellows to the steering gear body.
5. Remove the bellows.
6. Remove the travel restrictor from the inner tie rod.
7. Install an appropriate inner tie rod removal tool on the inner tie rod hex.

※ WARNING

If the inner tie rod cannot be removed using the specified tools, do not use a hammer or heat to loosen. Damage to the steering gear will occur. Replace the entire steering gear.

8. Unthread and remove the inner tie rod from the steering gear.

To install:

※ WARNING

When installing the travel restrictor, be sure to use the same color and thickness travel restrictor as was removed. This action is necessary to properly set the gear travel for the

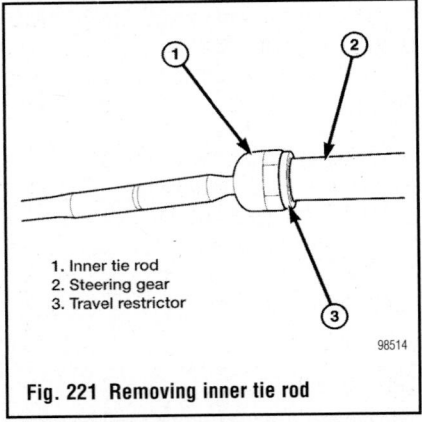

1. Inner tie rod
2. Steering gear
3. Travel restrictor

98514

Fig. 221 Removing inner tie rod

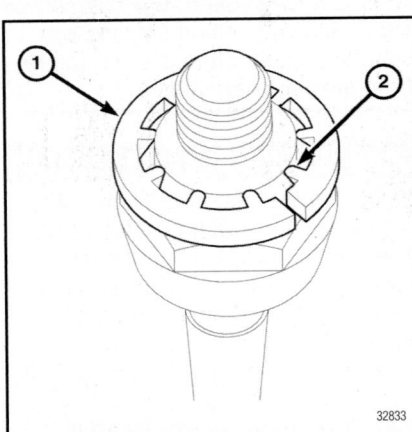

32833

Fig. 222 Install the travel restrictor (1), flat side of teeth (2) facing out, on the inboard end of the inner tie rod ball joint

steering gear being serviced. Travel restrictor thickness can vary side-to-side on the steering gear.

9. Install the travel restrictor, flat side of teeth facing out, on the inboard end of the inner tie rod ball joint.

10. Apply Mopar® Lock AND Seal Adhesive or equivalent medium thread locker adhesive to the inboard end threads of the inner tie rod.

11. Install the inner tie rod onto the gear using an appropriate inner tie rod installation

tool or crowsfoot wrench on the hex. Tighten the inner tie rod to 58 ft. lbs. (78 Nm).

12. Loosely place a NEW clamp over the large end of the NEW bellows.

13. Slide the NEW bellows with clamp over the end of the inner tie rod and onto the gear body.

14. Push the small end of the bellows past the groove machined into the inner tie rod.

15. Apply a small amount of Mopar® Lubriplate or equivalent uniformly to the groove in the inner tie rod shaft. This allows

for toe adjustment without twisting the bellows.

16. Pull the small end of the bellows outward until the ridge inside the bellows engages the groove.

17. Install a NEW clamp over the small end of the bellows.

18. Using crimping pliers, crimp the large clamp securing the bellows to the gear body.

19. Thread the tie rod jam nut onto the inner tie rod far enough to install the outer tie rod.

20. Install the outer tie rod.

SUSPENSION

PRECAUTIONS

✷✷ CAUTION

Chrysler LLC does not manufacture any vehicles or replacement parts that contain asbestos. Aftermarket products may or may not contain asbestos. Refer to aftermarket product packaging for product information.

✷✷ CAUTION

Whether the product contains asbestos or not, dust and dirt can accumulate on brake parts during normal use. Follow practices prescribed by appropriate regulations for the handling, processing and disposing of dust and debris.

✷✷ CAUTION

Do not remove the strut shaft nut while strut assembly is installed in the vehicle or before the coil spring is compressed with a compression tool. The spring is held under high pressure.

✷✷ WARNING

Only frame contact or wheel lift hoisting equipment can be used on this vehicle. It cannot be hoisted using equipment designed to lift a vehicle by the rear axle. If this type of hoisting equipment is used, damage to rear suspension components will occur.

✷✷ WARNING

At no time when servicing a vehicle can a sheet metal screw, bolt, or

other metal fastener be installed in the shock tower to take the place of an original plastic clip. It may come into contact with the strut or coil spring.

✷✷ WARNING

Wheel bearing damage will result if after loosening the hub nut, the vehicle is rolled on the ground or the weight of the vehicle is allowed to be supported by the tires for a length of time.

HUB & BEARING ASSEMBLY

REMOVAL & INSTALLATION

See Figures 223 through 231.

➡The wheel bearing is a Unit 1 type cartridge bearing that is designed to last for the life of the vehicle and requires no type of periodic maintenance. The wheel bearing can be serviced separately from the hub.

✷✷ WARNING

Rotate the wheel hub checking for resistance or roughness. Any roughness or resistance to rotation may indicate dirt intrusion or a failed hub bearing. If the bearing exhibits any of these conditions, the hub bearing will require replacement. Do not attempt to disassemble the bearing for repair. If the wheel bearing is disassembled for any reason, it must be replaced.

✷✷ WARNING

Damaged bearing seals and the resulting excessive grease loss may also require bearing replacement. Moderate grease weeping from the

FRONT SUSPENSION

bearing is considered normal and should not require replacement of the wheel bearing.

➡The removal and installation of the wheel bearing and hub from the knuckle is only to be done with the knuckle removed from the vehicle.

1. Remove the steering knuckle from the vehicle. Refer to Steering Knuckle, removal & installation.

2. Position the knuckle support fixture (9712) as follows:

- For left side knuckles, place the locator block to the left side on the fixture.
- For right side knuckles, place the locator block to the right side on the fixture.
- The side of the locator block with the angle cut goes downward, toward the fixture.
- Install the mounting screws and tighten them to approximately 40 ft. lbs. (54 Nm).

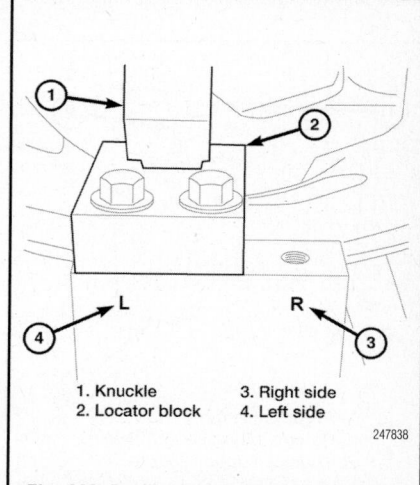

1. Knuckle   3. Right side
2. Locator block   4. Left side

247838

Fig. 223 Positioning knuckle support fixture (9712)

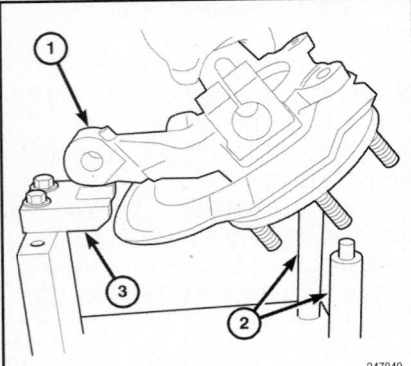

Fig. 224 Install the knuckle in the fixture as shown, guiding the steering arm (1) to rest on the locator block (3) and the brake caliper mounting bosses on the 2 fixture pins (2)

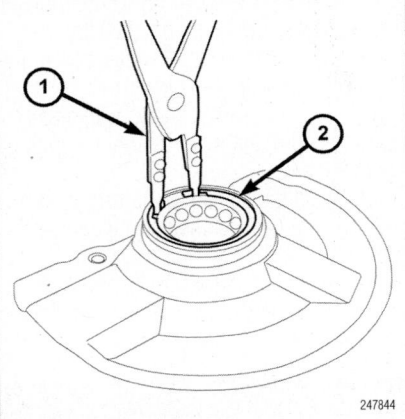

Fig. 226 Remove the snap ring (2) from the knuckle using an appropriate pair of snap ring pliers (1)

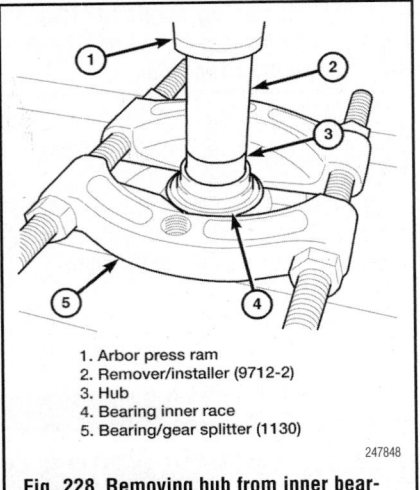

1. Arbor press ram
2. Remover/installer (9712-2)
3. Hub
4. Bearing inner race
5. Bearing/gear splitter (1130)

Fig. 228 Removing hub from inner bearing race

3. Install the knuckle in the fixture as shown, guiding the steering arm to rest on the locator block and the brake caliper mounting bosses on the 2 fixture pins.

4. Place the fixture with knuckle in an arbor press.

5. Position remover/installer (9712-2) in the small end of the hub (NOTE: remover/installer may also be called a press plug). Lower the arbor press ram, and remove the hub from the wheel bearing and knuckle. The bearing race will normally come out of the wheel bearing with the hub as it is pressed out of the bearing.

6. Remove the knuckle from the fixture and turn it over.

7. Remove the snap ring from the knuckle using an appropriate pair of snap ring pliers.

8. Place the knuckle back in the fixture in the arbor press ram.

9. Place seal installer (MD-998334) on the outer race of the wheel bearing. Lower

the arbor press ram, and remove the wheel bearing from the knuckle.

10. Remove the knuckle and tools from the arbor press.

11. If the bearing race is still pressed onto the hub, install the bearing splitter between the hub flange and the bearing inner race.

12. Place the hub, bearing race and bearing splitter in an arbor press. The press support blocks must not obstruct the wheel hub while it is being pressed out of the bearing race.

13. Place remover/installer (9712-2) in the end of the hub. Lower the arbor press ram, and remove the hub from the bearing race.

To install:

✳✳ WARNING

When installing the wheel bearing in the knuckle, it is important to place

the side of bearing with the wheel speed sensor magnetic encoder ring (dark band) in the knuckle first. Otherwise, the wheel speed sensor will not operate correctly.

14. Wipe the bearing bore of the knuckle clean of any grease or dirt with a clean, dry shop towel.

15. Place the knuckle in an arbor press supporting the knuckle from underneath using cup (6310).

16. Place the NEW wheel bearing, magnetic encoder ring side down, into the bore of the knuckle. Be sure the wheel bearing is placed squarely into the bore.

17. Place axle shaft seal receiver (8498), larger inside diameter end down, over the outer race of the wheel bearing.

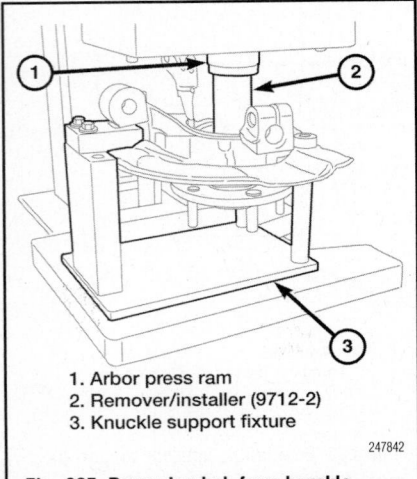

1. Arbor press ram
2. Remover/installer (9712-2)
3. Knuckle support fixture

Fig. 225 Removing hub from knuckle

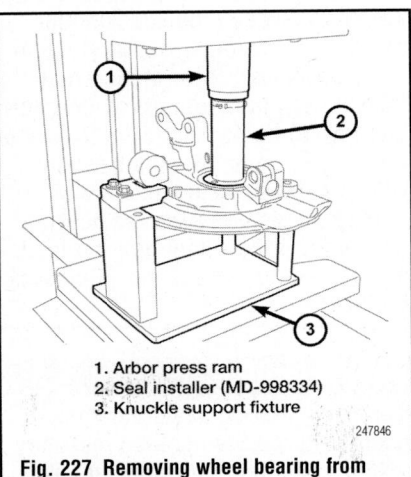

1. Arbor press ram
2. Seal installer (MD-998334)
3. Knuckle support fixture

Fig. 227 Removing wheel bearing from knuckle

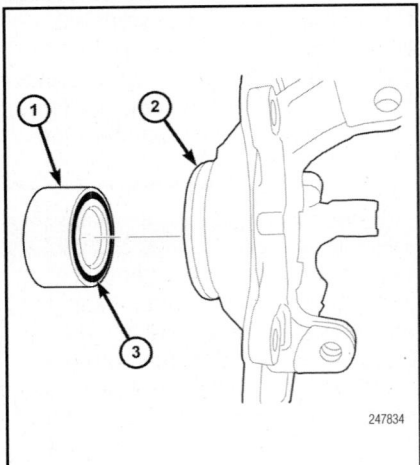

Fig. 229 When installing the wheel bearing (1) in the knuckle, (2) it is important to place the side of bearing with the wheel speed sensor magnetic encoder ring (dark band) (3) in the knuckle first

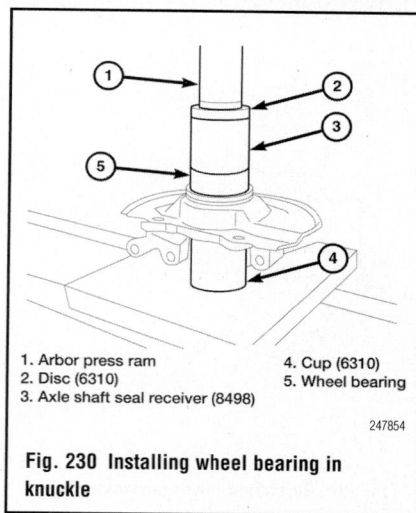

Fig. 230 Installing wheel bearing in knuckle

1. Arbor press ram
2. Disc (6310)
3. Axle shaft seal receiver (8498)
4. Cup (6310)
5. Wheel bearing

247854

18. Place disc (6310) into top of receiver. Lower the arbor press ram, and press the wheel bearing into the knuckle until it is bottomed in the bore of the knuckle.

19. Remove the knuckle and tools from the arbor press.

20. Install a NEW snap ring in the knuckle using an appropriate pair of snap ring pliers. Make sure the snap ring is fully seated.

21. Place the knuckle in an arbor press. Support the knuckle from underneath using remover/installer (MB-990799), smaller end up against the wheel bearing inner race.

22. Place the hub in the wheel bearing, making sure it is square with the bearing inner race.

23. Position remover/installer (9712-2) in the end of the hub. Lower the arbor press

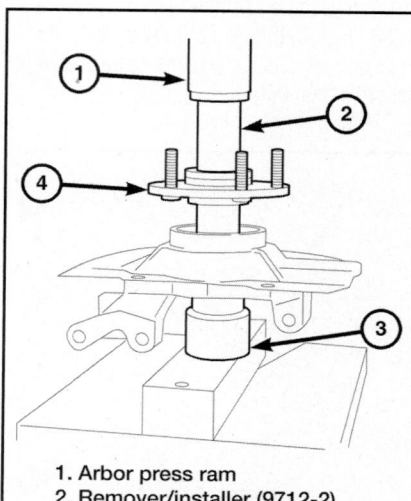

1. Arbor press ram
2. Remover/installer (9712-2)
3. Remover/installer (MB-990799)
4. Hub

247856

Fig. 231 Installing wheel bearing into hub

ram, and press the hub into the wheel bearing until it bottoms.

24. Remove the knuckle and tools from the press.

25. Verify the hub turns smoothly without rubbing or binding.

26. Install the knuckle on the vehicle. Refer to Steering Knuckle, removal & installation.

LOWER BALL JOINT

REMOVAL & INSTALLATION

The lower ball joint is not serviced separately from the control arm on this vehicle. Refer to Diagnosis & Testing procedure and/or appropriate Lower Control Arm, removal & installation.

DIAGNOSIS & TESTING

➡ **If it is determined from this diagnosis and testing procedure that the ball joint is out of specification, the entire lower control arm must be replaced.**

1. Raise the vehicle, allowing the front suspension to hang.

2. Remove the tire and wheel assembly.

3. Using dial indicator set (C-3339A), or equivalent, attach the dial indicator mount to the knuckle and align the dial indicator's plunger with the direction of the stud axis, touching the end of the ball joint stud in the lower control arm.

4. Push up on the lower control arm and zero the dial indicator.

➡ **Use care when applying load to the knuckle to avoid damaging the ball joint seal boot.**

5. From the front of the vehicle, insert a pry bar between the knuckle and lower control arm, resting it on the lower control arm. Use lever principle to push the knuckle up from the lower control arm. Apply the load until the needle of the dial indicator no longer moves.

6. Record the ball joint movement. The end play is acceptable if no more than 0.031 inch (0.8 mm) of end play is achieved back-to-back.

7. Perform this procedure on each side of the vehicle as necessary.

LOWER BALL JOINT SEAL BOOT REPLACEMENT

See Figures 232 and 233.

❊❊ WARNING

This procedure is designed to be used only if a seal boot is damaged during related service procedures. It

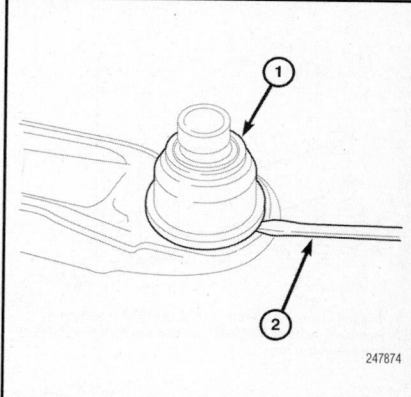

Fig. 232 Using a screwdriver or other suitable tool (2), pry the seal boot (1) off of the ball joint

247874

is not to be used as a repair procedure for a cut seal boot on a vehicle that has been driven and exposed to road and weather conditions.

1. Remove the lower control arm from the vehicle. Refer to appropriate Lower Control Arm, removal & installation.

2. Using a screwdriver or other suitable tool, pry the seal boot off of the ball joint.

To install:

3. Place a liberal dab of Mopar® Multi-Mileage Lube (No more than 10g) or equivalent around the base of the ball joint stud at the socket.

4. Position the ball joint stud straight up.

5. Place the NEW ball joint seal boot over the ball joint stud.

6. By hand, start the seal boot over the sides of the ball joint.

❊❊ WARNING

Prior to installing the sealing boot using remover/installer, make sure there are no burrs on the inside of the tool. Remove any burrs and lubricate with a small amount of Mopar® Multi-Mileage Lube or equivalent.

7. Place remover/installer (6289-4) onto the screw-drive of the ball joint press.

8. Place remover/installer (6289-6) angle-cut end up into the cup of the ball joint press.

9. Before tightening the set, turn the remover/installer (6289-6) so that the tallest point of the angle-cut is away from the body of the control arm when installing the seal boot.

10. Place the control arm ball joint into the remover/installer (6289-6).

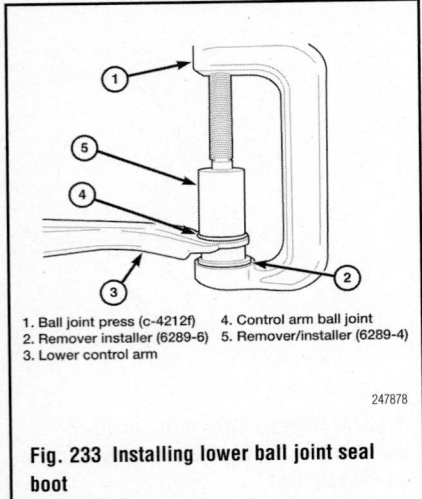

1. Ball joint press (c-4212f)
2. Remover installer (6289-6)
3. Lower control arm
4. Control arm ball joint
5. Remover/installer (6289-4)

247878

Fig. 233 Installing lower ball joint seal boot

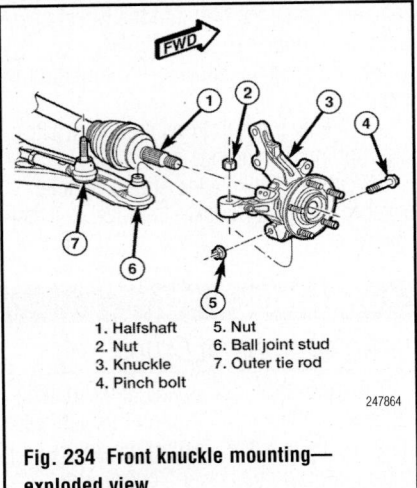

1. Halfshaft
2. Nut
3. Knuckle
4. Pinch bolt
5. Nut
6. Ball joint stud
7. Outer tie rod

247864

Fig. 234 Front knuckle mounting—exploded view

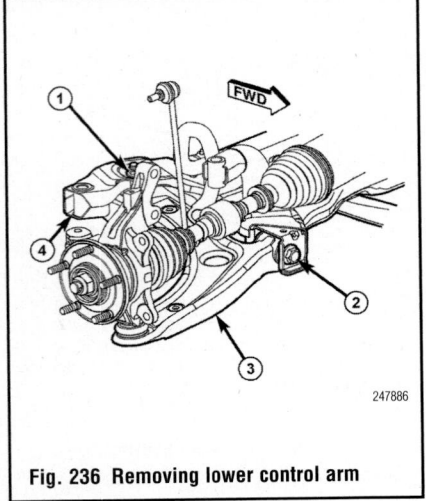

247886

Fig. 236 Removing lower control arm

11. Rotate the arm left or right until the tallest point of the angle cut on the remover/installer (6289-6) is away from the body of the control arm.

12. Lower the remover/installer (6289-4) onto the outer lip of ball joint seal.

13. By hand, tighten the ball joint press screw-drive installing the seal boot. Tighten the screw-drive until the seal boot is seated squarely down against the top surface of the lower control arm. It may be necessary to use a wrench to seat the seal boot, but do not over-tighten.

14. Remove the tools and wipe any grease off the ball joint stud using a clean shop towel with brake parts cleaner applied to it.

15. Install the lower control arm. Refer to appropriate Lower Control Arm, removal & installation.

LOWER CONTROL ARM

REMOVAL & INSTALLATION

See Figures 234 through 237.

➡Inspect the lower control arm for signs of damage from contact with the ground or road debris. If the lower control arm shows any sign of damage, look for distortion. Do not attempt to repair or straighten a broken or bent lower control arm. If damaged, the lower control arm is serviced only as a complete component.

➡Inspect both lower control arm isolator bushings for severe deterioration, and replace the lower control arm as required. Inspect the ball joint, and replace the lower control arm as required.

➡The only serviceable component of the lower control arm is the ball joint

seal boot. It should only be replaced if damaged during service of a chassis component. Otherwise, replace the entire control arm.

1. Before servicing the vehicle, refer to the Precautions section.
2. Raise and support the vehicle.
3. Remove the tire and wheel assembly.
4. Remove the nut and pinch bolt clamping the ball joint stud to the knuckle.

✳✳ WARNING

Upon removing the knuckle from the ball joint stud, do not pull outward on the knuckle. Pulling the knuckle outward at this point can separate the inner CV-joint on the halfshaft, thus damaging it.

✳✳ WARNING

Use care when separating the ball joint stud from the knuckle so the ball joint seal does not get cut.

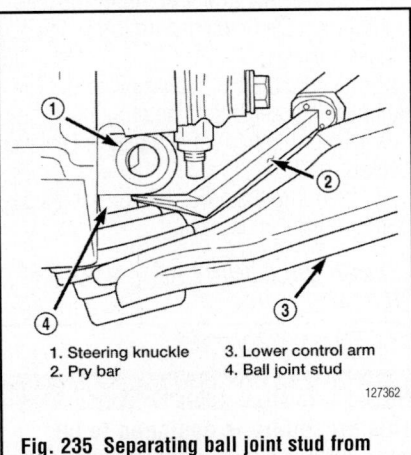

1. Steering knuckle
2. Pry bar
3. Lower control arm
4. Ball joint stud

127362

Fig. 235 Separating ball joint stud from steering knuckle

5. Using an appropriate prying tool, separate the ball joint stud from the knuckle by prying down on lower control arm and up against the ball joint boss on the knuckle.

6. Remove the front bolt attaching the lower control arm to the front suspension crossmember.

7. Remove the nut on the rear bolt attaching the lower control arm to the front suspension crossmember. Remove the bolt.

8. Remove the lower control arm from the crossmember.

To install:

9. Place the lower control arm into the front suspension crossmember.

10. Insert the rear bolt up through the crossmember and lower control arm.

11. Install, but do not fully tighten, the nut on the rear bolt attaching the lower control arm to the crossmember.

12. Install, but do not fully tighten, the front bolt attaching the lower control arm to the crossmember.

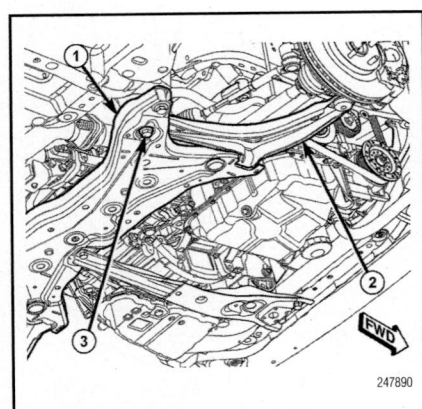

247890

Fig. 237 Insert the rear bolt (3) up through the crossmember (1) and lower control arm (2)

13. With no weight or obstruction on the lower control arm, tighten the lower control arm rear mounting bolt nut to 135 ft. lbs. (183 Nm).

14. With no weight or obstruction on the lower control arm, tighten the lower control arm front pivot bolt to the following:
- 100 ft. lbs. (135 Nm) (Vehicles built up to 8/1/08)
- 118 ft. lbs. (160 Nm) (Vehicles built after 8/1/08)

15. Install the ball joint stud into the knuckle, aligning the bolt hole in the knuckle boss with the groove formed in the side of the ball joint stud.

16. Install a NEW ball joint stud pinch bolt and nut. Tighten the nut to 60 ft. lbs. (82 Nm).

17. Install tire and wheel assembly. Install and tighten wheel mounting nuts to 100 ft. lbs. (135 Nm).

18. Lower the vehicle.

19. Perform wheel alignment as necessary.

MACPHERSON STRUT

INSPECTION
See Figure 238.

1. Inspect the strut assembly for the following conditions:
- Inspect for a damaged or broken coil spring.
- Inspect for a torn or damaged dust shield.
- Lift the dust shield and inspect the strut assembly for evidence of fluid running from the upper end of the strut fluid reservoir. (Actual leakage will be a stream of fluid running down the side and dripping off lower end of unit). A slight amount of seepage between the strut shaft and strut shaft seal is not unusual and does not affect performance of the strut assembly.
- Inspect the jounce bumper for signs of damage or deterioration.
- Inspect the clearance between the shock tower and the coil spring. Make sure no fasteners are protruding through the shock tower possibly contacting the coil spring and strut. Because of the minimum clearance in this area, installation of metal fasteners could damage the coil spring coating and lead to a corrosion failure of the spring.

✳✳ WARNING
At no time when servicing a vehicle can a sheet metal screw, bolt or

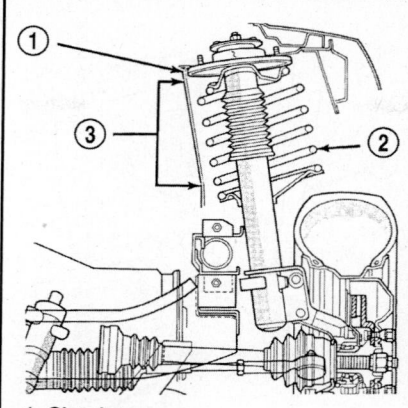

1. Shock tower
2. Coil spring
3. No fasteners are to be installed or holes are to be drilled into shock tower in this area

127488

Fig. 238 Inspect the clearance between the shock tower and the coil spring

other metal fastener be installed into the strut tower to take the place of an original plastic clip. Also, do not drill holes into the front strut tower for the installation of any metal fasteners into the shock tower area indicated.

REMOVAL & INSTALLATION
See Figures 239 through 241.

1. Before servicing the vehicle, refer to the Precautions section.

2. Raise and support the vehicle.

3. Remove the tire and wheel assembly.

➡ **If both strut assemblies are to be removed, mark the strut assemblies right or left and keep the parts separated to avoid mix-up. Not all parts of**

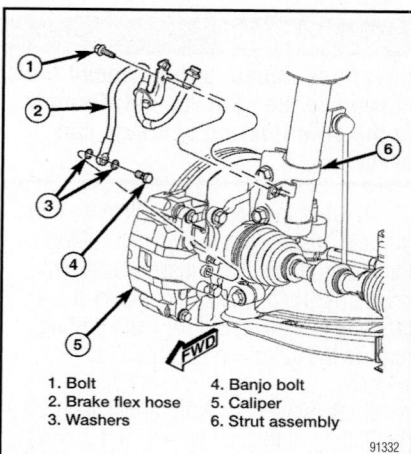

1. Bolt
2. Brake flex hose
3. Washers
4. Banjo bolt
5. Caliper
6. Strut assembly

91332

Fig. 239 View of front brake hose mounting

the strut assembly are interchangeable side-to-side.

4. Remove the screw securing the flex hose routing bracket to the strut.

5. While holding the stabilizer bar link stud stationary, remove the nut securing the link to the strut.

✳✳ WARNING
The strut assembly-to-knuckle attaching bolts are serrated and must not be turned during removal. Hold the bolts stationary in the knuckle while removing the nuts, then tap the bolts out using a pin punch.

6. While holding the bolt heads stationary, remove the 2 nuts from the bolts attaching the strut to the knuckle.

7. Remove the 2 bolts attaching the strut to the knuckle using a pin punch.

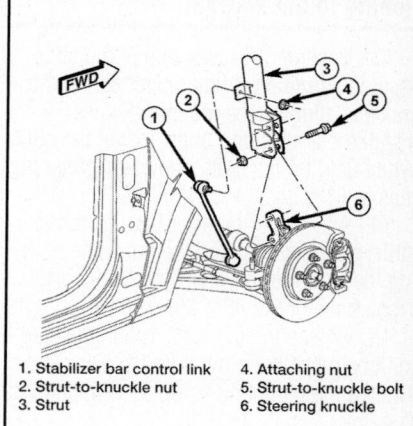

1. Stabilizer bar control link
2. Strut-to-knuckle nut
3. Strut
4. Attaching nut
5. Strut-to-knuckle bolt
6. Steering knuckle

91266

Fig. 240 Strut and knuckle assembly—exploded view

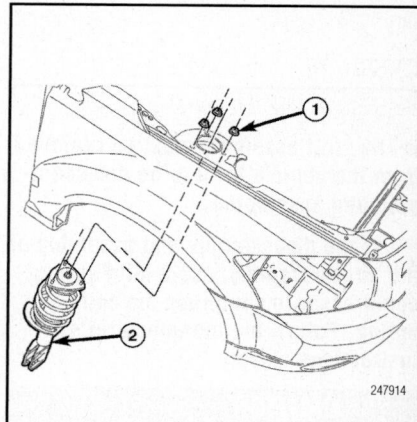

247914

Fig. 241 Remove the 3 nuts (1) attaching the strut assembly (2) upper mount to the strut tower

8. Lower the vehicle just enough to open the hood without allowing the tires to touch the floor.

9. Remove the 3 nuts attaching the strut assembly upper mount to the strut tower.

10. Remove the strut assembly from the vehicle.

11. For disassembly, refer to Overhaul procedure.

To install:

12. Raise the strut assembly into the strut tower, aligning the 3 studs on the strut assembly upper mount with the holes in the strut tower. Install the 3 mounting nuts on the studs. Tighten the 3 nuts to 35 ft. lbs. (48 Nm).

❋❋ WARNING

The strut assembly-to-knuckle attaching bolts are serrated and must not be turned during installation. Install the nuts while holding the bolts stationary in the knuckle.

13. Position the lower end of the strut assembly in line with the upper end of the knuckle, aligning the mounting holes. Install the 2 attaching bolts. Install the nuts. While holding the bolts in place, tighten the nuts to 81 ft. lbs. (110 Nm).

14. Attach the stabilizer bar link to the strut. Install and tighten the nut while holding the stabilizer bar link stud stationary. Tighten the nut to 43 ft. lbs. (58 Nm).

15. Secure the flex hose routing bracket to the strut with the mounting screw. Tighten the mounting screw to 120 inch lbs. (13 Nm).

16. Install tire and wheel assembly. Install and tighten wheel mounting nuts to 100 ft. lbs. (135 Nm).

17. Lower the vehicle.

18. Perform wheel alignment as necessary.

OVERHAUL

See Figures 242 through 245.

➡**The strut assembly must be removed from the vehicle for it to be disassembled and assembled.**

➡**For the disassembly and assembly of the strut assembly, use a strut spring compressor to compress the coil spring. Follow the manufacturer's instructions closely.**

❋❋ CAUTION

Do not remove the strut rod nut before the coil spring is properly compressed. The coil spring is held

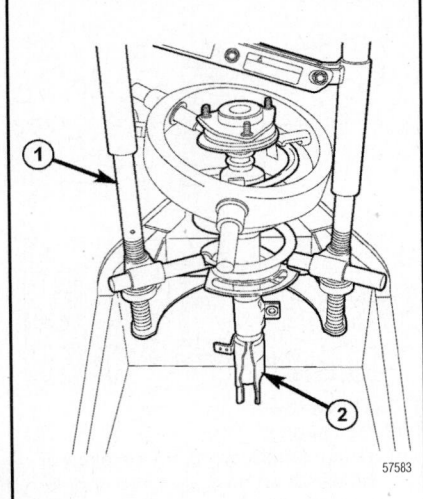

Fig. 242 Position the strut assembly (2) in the strut coil spring compressor (1)

under pressure. The coil spring must be compressed, removing spring tension from the upper mount and bearing, before the strut rod nut is removed.

1. If both struts are being serviced at the same time, mark both the coil spring and strut assembly according to which side of the vehicle the strut is being removed from.

2. Position the strut assembly in the strut coil spring compressor following the manufacturer's instructions, and set the lower and upper hooks of the compressor on the coil spring. Position the strut clevis bracket straight outward, away from the compressor.

3. Compress the coil spring until all coil spring tension is removed from the upper mount and bearing.

❋❋ WARNING

Never use impact or high speed tools to remove the strut rod nut. Damage to the strut internal bearings can occur.

4. Once the spring is sufficiently compressed, install strut nut wrench (9362) on the strut rod nut. Next, install strut shaft socket (9894) on the end of the strut rod. While holding the strut rod from turning, remove the nut using the strut nut wrench.

5. Remove the clamp (if installed) from the bottom of the coil spring, and remove the strut (damper) out through the bottom of the coil spring. The dust shield and jounce bumper will come out with the strut.

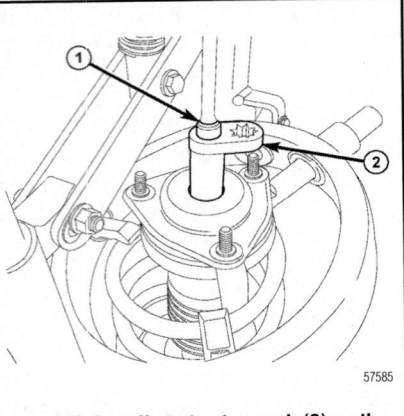

Fig. 243 Install strut nut wrench (2) on the strut rod nut. Next, install strut shaft socket (1) on the end of the strut rod

6. Remove the lower spring isolator from the strut seat.

7. Slide the dust shield and jounce bumper from the strut rod.

8. Remove the upper mount and bearing from the top of the upper spring seat and isolator.

9. Remove the upper spring seat and isolator from the top of the coil spring.

➡**If the coil spring needs to be serviced, perform the following steps.**

10. Release the tension from the coil spring by backing off the compressor drive completely. Push back the compressor hooks and remove the coil spring.

11. Inspect the strut assembly components for the following and replace as necessary:

- Inspect the strut (damper) for shaft binding over the full stroke of the shaft.

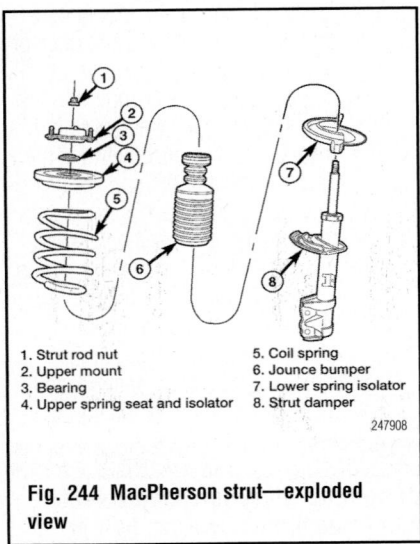

1. Strut rod nut
2. Upper mount
3. Bearing
4. Upper spring seat and isolator
5. Coil spring
6. Jounce bumper
7. Lower spring isolator
8. Strut damper

247908

Fig. 244 MacPherson strut—exploded view

- Inspect the jounce bumper (with dust shield) for cracks and signs of deterioration.
- Check the upper mount for cracks and distortion and its retaining studs for any sign of damage.
- Check the bearing for any binding.
- Check the upper spring seat and isolator for cracks and distortion.
- Inspect the upper and lower spring isolators for material deterioration and distortion.
- Inspect the coil spring for any sign of damage to the coating.

To assemble:

❋❋ WARNING

When installing the coil spring, make sure the end with the ID tag is placed downward, or spring-to-body contact will occur after strut assembly installation.

12. Place the coil spring in the spring compressor following the manufacturer's instructions. Before compressing the spring, rotate the spring so the end of the bottom coil is at approximately the 9 o'clock position as viewed from above (or to where the spring was when removed from the compressor). This action will allow the strut (damper) clevis bracket to be positioned outward, away from the compressor once installed.

13. Slowly compress the coil spring until enough room is available for strut assembly reassembly.

14. Install the upper spring seat and isolator on top of the coil spring.

15. Install the bearing and upper mount on top of the upper spring seat and isolator.

16. Install the lower spring isolator on the spring seat on the strut.

17. Slide the dust shield and jounce bumper onto the strut rod.

18. Install the strut up through the bottom of the coil spring and upper spring seat, mount, and bearing until the lower spring seat contacts the lower end of the coil spring. Rotate the strut as necessary until the end of the bottom coil comes in contact with the stop built into the lower spring isolator.

19. While holding the strut in position, install the nut on the end of the strut rod.

❋❋ WARNING

Never use impact or high speed tools to install the strut shaft nut. Damage

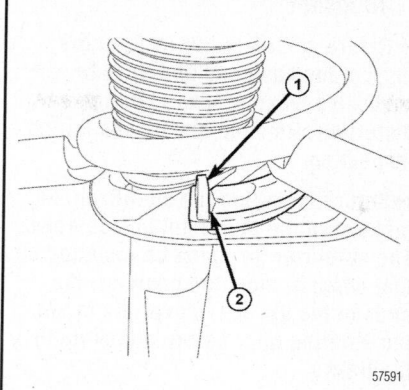

Fig. 245 Rotate the strut as necessary until the end of the bottom coil (2) comes in contact with the stop (1) built into the lower spring isolator

to the strut internal bearings may occur.

20. Install the strut nut wrench on the strut rod nut. Next, install the strut shaft socket on the end of the strut rod. While holding the strut rod from turning, tighten the strut rod nut to 44 ft. lbs. (60 Nm) using a torque wrench on the end of the strut nut wrench.

21. Slowly release the tension from the coil spring by backing off the compressor drive completely. As the tension is relieved, make sure the upper mount and bearing align properly. Verify the upper mount does not bind when rotated.

22. Remove the strut assembly from the spring compressor.

23. Install the strut assembly on the vehicle. Refer to MacPherson Strut, removal & installation.

STABILIZER BAR

REMOVAL & INSTALLATION

See Figures 246 through 249.

1. Before servicing the vehicle, refer to the Precautions section.
2. Raise and support the vehicle.
3. If equipped, remove the engine belly pan.
4. Remove the rear engine mount. Refer to Rear Engine Mount, removal & installation.
5. Remove the front engine mount through-bolt.
6. Remove the fasteners securing the power steering hose routing clamps to the crossmember.
7. At each end of the stabilizer bar, while holding the stabilizer bar link lower

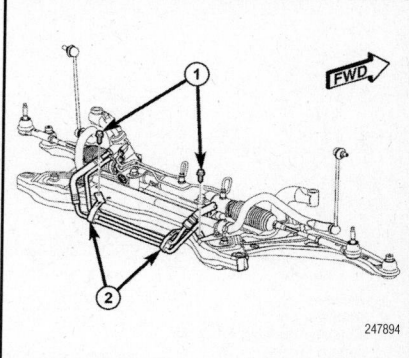

Fig. 246 Remove the fasteners (1) securing the power steering hose routing clamps (2) to the crossmember

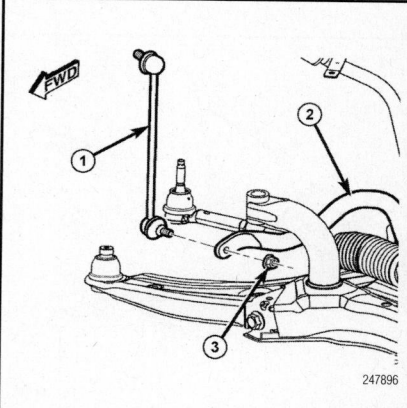

Fig. 247 While holding the stabilizer bar link (1) lower stud stationary, remove the nut (3) securing the link to the stabilizer bar (2)

stud stationary, remove the nut securing the link to the stabilizer bar.

8. Remove the screws securing the stabilizer bushing retainers to the crossmember.

9. Remove the 2 stabilizer bushing retainers.

10. Utilizing the slit cut into the cushions (bushings), remove the 2 cushions from the stabilizer bar.

➡**Before removing the front suspension crossmember from the vehicle, the location of the crossmember must be marked on the body of the vehicle. Do this so the crossmember can be relocated, upon reinstallation, against the body of vehicle in the same location as before removal. If the front suspension crossmember is not reinstalled in exactly the same location as before removal, the preset front wheel alignment settings (caster and camber) may be lost.**

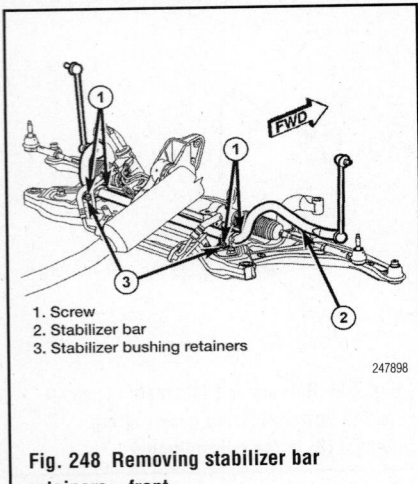

1. Screw
2. Stabilizer bar
3. Stabilizer bushing retainers

247898

Fig. 248 Removing stabilizer bar retainers—front

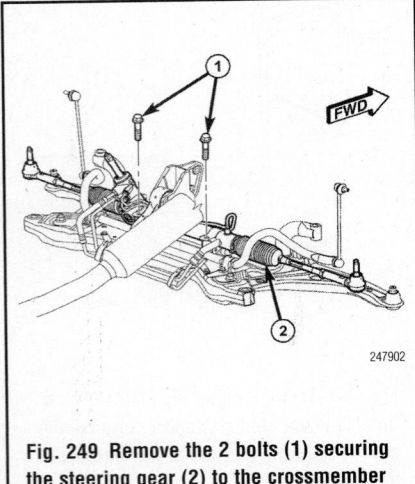

247902

Fig. 249 Remove the 2 bolts (1) securing the steering gear (2) to the crossmember

11. Mark the location of the front cross-member on the body near each mounting bolt.

12. Support the crossmember with a Transaxle jack.

13. Remove the 4 mounting bolts securing the front crossmember to the body.

14. Remove the 2 bolts securing the steering gear to the crossmember.

15. Support the steering gear using a bungee cord or wire to keep the steering gear from lowering when the crossmember is lowered.

16. Slowly lower the crossmember until there is enough space present to remove the stabilizer bar between the rear of the crossmember and the body. Due to the fact that the fore-and-aft crossmember is still attached, do not lower crossmember any more than necessary to remove the stabilizer bar.

17. Remove the stabilizer bar out over rear of crossmember.

To install:

➡Before stabilizer bar installation, inspect the cushions and links for excessive wear, cracks, damage and distortion. Replace any pieces failing inspection.

➡Before installing the stabilizer bar, make sure the bar is not upside down. The stabilizer bar must be installed so that when in mounted position, the ends of the bar curve over the top of the steering gear before attaching to the links.

18. Install the stabilizer bar, link ends first, from the rear over top of the cross-member. Curve the ends of the bar over the steering gear.

19. Slowly raise the crossmember into mounted position using the Transaxle jack, matching the crossmember to the marked locations on the body made during removal.

20. Install the 4 mounting bolts securing the front crossmember to the body. Tighten the crossmember mounting bolts to 140 ft. lbs. (190 Nm).

21. Remove the Transaxle jack.

22. Remove the bungee cord or wire supporting the steering gear.

23. Install the 2 bolts securing the steering gear to the crossmember. Tighten the steering gear mounting bolts to 52 ft. lbs. (70 Nm).

24. Install the 2 cushions (bushings) on the stabilizer bar, utilizing the slit cut into the cushion sides.

25. Install the 2 stabilizer bushing retainers over the cushions.

26. Install the screws securing the stabilizer bushing retainers to the crossmember. Tighten all 4 stabilizer bar cushion retainer screws to 22 ft. lbs. (30 Nm).

27. Attach the stabilizer bar link at each end of the stabilizer bar. At each link, install and tighten the nut while holding the stabilizer bar link lower stud stationary. Tighten the nuts to 43 ft. lbs. (58 Nm).

28. Position the power steering hose routing clamps on the crossmember. Install the fasteners. Tighten the screws to 71 inch lbs. (8 Nm).

29. Install the rear engine mount. Refer to Rear Engine Mount, removal & installation.

30. If equipped, install the engine belly pan.

31. Lower the vehicle.

32. Perform wheel alignment as necessary, paying special attention to front cam-ber and caster. The crossmember may need to be shifted on its mounts slightly to gain the preferred setting.

STEERING KNUCKLE

REMOVAL & INSTALLATION

See Figures 250 through 255.

➡The front suspension knuckle is not a repairable component of the front suspension. It must be replaced if found to be damaged in any way. If it is determined that the knuckle is bent when servicing the vehicle, no attempt is to be made to straighten the knuckle.

1. Before servicing the vehicle, refer to the Precautions section.

2. Raise and support the vehicle.

3. Remove wheel and tire assembly.

4. Remove the cotter pin, lock nut and spring washer from the halfshaft stub shaft.

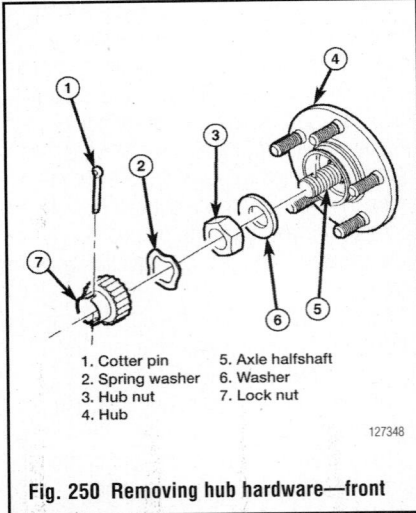

1. Cotter pin
2. Spring washer
3. Hub nut
4. Hub
5. Axle halfshaft
6. Washer
7. Lock nut

127348

Fig. 250 Removing hub hardware—front

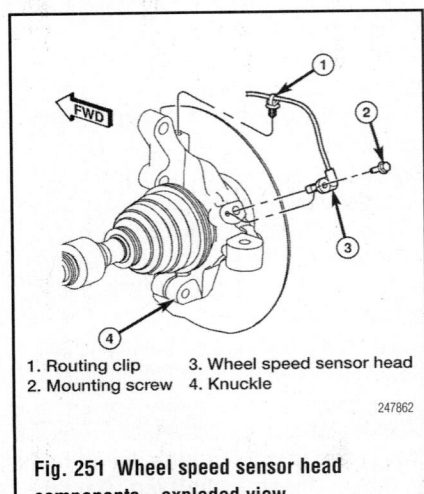

1. Routing clip
2. Mounting screw
3. Wheel speed sensor head
4. Knuckle

247862

Fig. 251 Wheel speed sensor head components—exploded view

5. While a helper applies the brakes to keep the hub from rotating, remove the hub nut and washer from the axle halfshaft.

6. Access and remove the front brake rotor. Refer to appropriate Brake Rotor, removal & installation.

7. Remove the routing clip securing the wheel speed sensor cable to the knuckle.

8. Remove the screw fastening the wheel speed sensor head to the knuckle. Pull the sensor head out of the knuckle.

9. Remove the nut attaching the outer tie rod to the knuckle. To do this, hold the tie rod end stud with a wrench while loosening and removing the nut with a standard wrench or crowfoot wrench.

10. Release the outer tie rod end from the knuckle using remover (9360).

11. Remove the outer tie rod from the knuckle.

12. Remove the nut and pinch bolt clamping the ball joint stud to the knuckle.

✳✳ WARNING

The strut assembly-to-knuckle attaching bolts are serrated and must not be turned during removal. Proper removal is required. Refer to the following steps for the correct method.

13. While holding the bolt heads stationary, remove the 2 nuts from the bolts attaching the strut to the knuckle.

14. Remove the 2 bolts attaching the strut to the knuckle using a pin punch.

✳✳ WARNING

Use care when separating the ball joint stud from the knuckle so the ball joint seal does not get cut.

15. Using an appropriate prying tool, separate the ball joint stud from the knuckle by prying down on lower control arm and up against the ball joint boss on the knuckle.

✳✳ WARNING

Do not allow the halfshaft to hang by the inner CV-joint. It must be supported to keep the joint from separating during this operation.

16. Pull the knuckle off the halfshaft outer CV-joint splines, and remove the knuckle from the vehicle.

To install:

17. Slide the hub of the knuckle onto the splines of the halfshaft outer CV-joint.

18. Install the knuckle onto the ball joint stud aligning the bolt hole in the knuckle boss with the groove formed into the side of the ball joint stud.

19. Install a NEW ball joint stud pinch bolt and nut. Tighten the nut to 60 ft. lbs. (82 Nm).

✳✳ WARNING

The strut assembly-to-knuckle attaching bolts are serrated and must not be turned during installation. Install the nuts while holding the bolts stationary in the steering knuckle.

20. Position the lower end of the strut assembly in line with the upper end of the knuckle, aligning the mounting holes. Install the 2 mounting bolts.

21. Install the nuts on the 2 bolts. While holding the bolts in place, tighten the nuts to 81 ft. lbs. (110 Nm).

22. Install the outer tie rod ball stud into the hole in the knuckle arm. Start the tie rod end-to-knuckle nut onto the stud. While holding the tie rod end stud with a wrench, tighten the nut with a wrench or crowfoot wrench to 97 ft. lbs. (132 Nm).

23. Install the wheel speed sensor head into the knuckle. Install the mounting screw, and tighten it to 106 inch lbs. (12 Nm).

24. Install the routing clip securing the wheel speed sensor cable to the knuckle.

25. Install the brake rotor, disc brake caliper and adapter. Refer to appropriate Brake Rotor, removal & installation.

26. Clean all foreign matter from the threads of the halfshaft stub shaft.

27. Install the washer and hub nut on the end of the halfshaft stub shaft. While a helper applies the brakes to keep the hub from rotating, tighten the hub nut to 180 ft. lbs. (244 Nm).

28. Install the spring washer and hub nut lock over the hub nut and stub shaft. Install a NEW cotter pin, securing nut lock in place, and wrap the cotter pin prongs tightly around the nut lock.

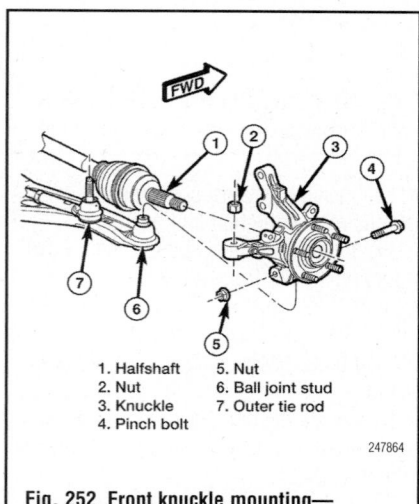

1. Halfshaft
2. Nut
3. Knuckle
4. Pinch bolt
5. Nut
6. Ball joint stud
7. Outer tie rod

Fig. 252 Front knuckle mounting—exploded view

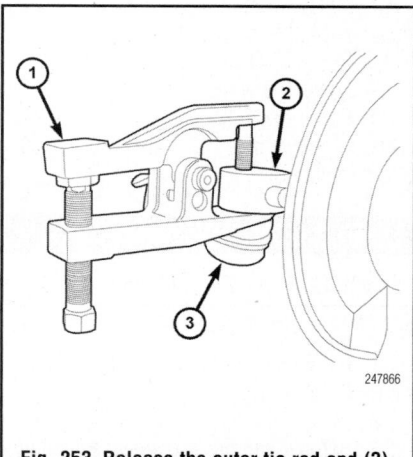

Fig. 253 Release the outer tie rod end (3) from the knuckle (2) using remover (1)

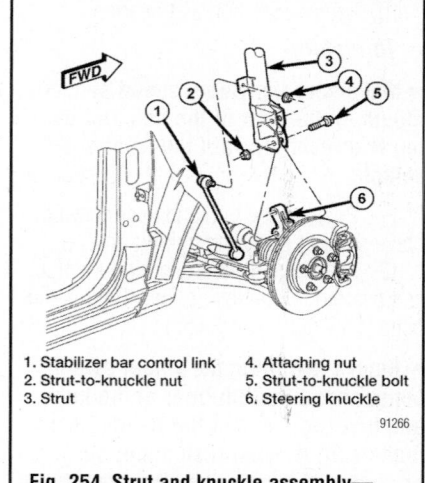

1. Stabilizer bar control link
2. Strut-to-knuckle nut
3. Strut
4. Attaching nut
5. Strut-to-knuckle bolt
6. Steering knuckle

Fig. 254 Strut and knuckle assembly—exploded view

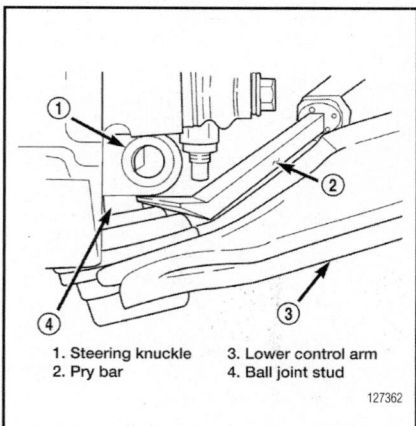

1. Steering knuckle
2. Pry bar
3. Lower control arm
4. Ball joint stud

Fig. 255 Separating ball joint stud from steering knuckle

29. Install tire and wheel assembly. Install and tighten wheel mounting nuts to 100 ft. lbs. (135 Nm).

30. Lower the vehicle.

➡If the original knuckle is being reinstalled, wheel alignment may not be necessary due to Net-Build design.

SUSPENSION

PRECAUTIONS

✳✳ CAUTION

Chrysler LLC does not manufacture any vehicles or replacement parts that contain asbestos. Aftermarket products may or may not contain asbestos. Refer to aftermarket product packaging for product information. Whether the product contains asbestos or not, dust and dirt can accumulate on brake parts during normal use. Follow practices prescribed by appropriate regulations for the handling, processing and disposing of dust and debris.

✳✳ WARNING

Only frame contact or wheel lift hoisting equipment can be used on this vehicle. It cannot be hoisted using equipment designed to lift a vehicle by the rear axle. If this type of hoisting equipment is used, damage to rear suspension components will occur.

✳✳ WARNING

If a rear suspension component becomes bent, damaged or fails, no attempt should be made to straighten or repair it. Always replace it with a new component.

HUB & BEARING ASSEMBLY

REMOVAL & INSTALLATION

See Figures 256 and 257.

➡The following procedure is applicable to models with rear disc brake systems.

1. Before servicing the vehicle, refer to the Precautions section.
2. Raise and support the vehicle.
3. Remove the tire and wheel assembly.
4. Remove the rear brake caliper. Refer to Brake Caliper, removal & installation.

5. Hang the brake caliper from rear strut using wire or cord to prevent the weight of the caliper from damaging the brake hose.

6. Remove any clips retaining the brake rotor to the wheel studs.

7. Slide the brake rotor off the hub and bearing.

8. Remove the screw fastening the wheel speed sensor head in the rear of the hub and bearing.

9. Remove the 4 bolts securing the hub and bearing to the trailing link.

10. Remove the hub and bearing.

To install:

➡**Make sure the wheel speed sensor mount on the rear of the hub and bearing is directed toward the front of the vehicle.**

11. Position the hub and bearing on the brake support plate and trailing link.

12. Install the 4 bolts securing the hub and bearing to the trailing link. Tighten the bolts to 77 ft. lbs. (105 Nm).

➡**Before installing the wheel speed sensor head into the rear of the hub and bearing, inspect the O-ring seal to make sure it is not dislodged, split, cut or damaged in any way. Replace the O-ring as necessary.**

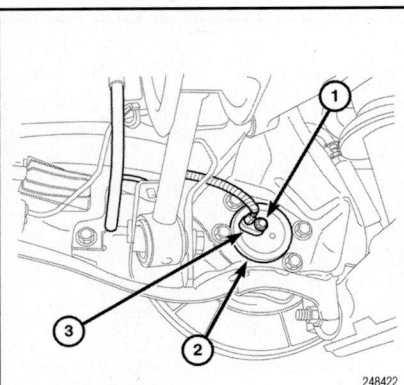

Fig. 256 Remove the screw (1) fastening the wheel speed sensor head (3) in the rear of the hub and bearing (2)

31. Perform wheel alignment as necessary.

WHEEL BEARINGS

REMOVAL & INSTALLATION

The wheel bearing is an integral part of the

hub and bearing assembly. Refer to Hub and Bearing Assembly, removal & installation.

ADJUSTMENT

The wheel bearing is designed to last for the life of the vehicle and requires no type of periodic maintenance.

REAR SUSPENSION

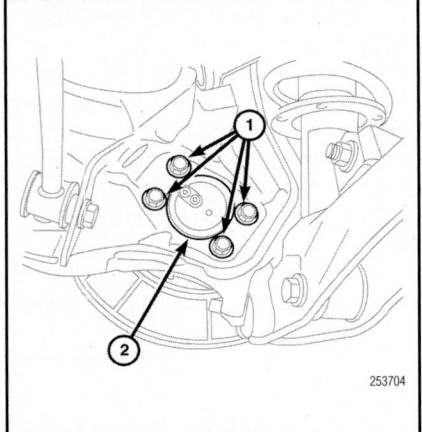

Fig. 257 Remove the 4 bolts (1) securing the hub and bearing (2) to the trailing link

13. Install the wheel speed sensor head into the rear of the hub and bearing.

14. Install the wheel speed sensor head mounting screw. Tighten the screw to 89 inch lbs. (10 Nm).

15. Slide the brake rotor over the parking brake shoes and onto the hub and bearing.

16. Rotate the disc brake caliper downward over the brake rotor and lower part of caliper adapter.

17. Install the disc brake caliper lower guide pin bolt. Tighten the guide pin bolt to 44 ft. lbs. (60 Nm).

18. Install tire and wheel assembly. Install and tighten wheel mounting nuts to 100 ft. lbs. (135 Nm).

19. Lower the vehicle.

20. Pump the brake pedal several times to ensure the vehicle has a firm brake pedal before moving it.

LOWER CONTROL ARM

REMOVAL & INSTALLATION

See Figures 258 through 261.

1. Before servicing the vehicle, refer to the Precautions section.
2. Raise and support the vehicle.
3. Remove the tire and wheel assembly.
4. If equipped, while holding the stabilizer bar link lower stud stationary, remove

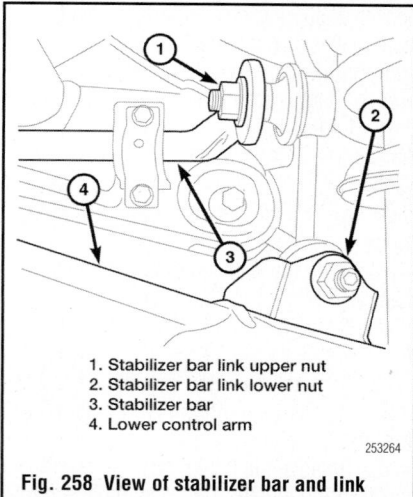

1. Stabilizer bar link upper nut
2. Stabilizer bar link lower nut
3. Stabilizer bar
4. Lower control arm

253264

Fig. 258 View of stabilizer bar and link

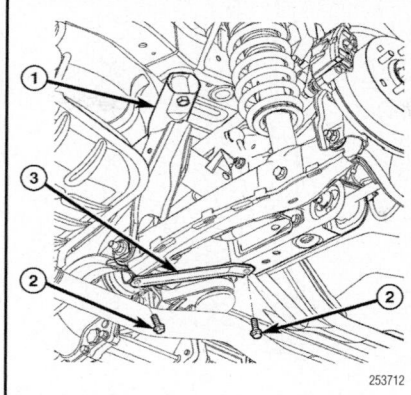

253712

Fig. 260 Remove the stay brace (3) mounting screws (2). Remove the stay brace from the crossmember (1)

the nut securing the link to the lower control arm.

5. Remove the lower shock mounting nut and bolt.

6. Remove the stay brace mounting screws. Remove the stay brace from the crossmember.

7. Remove the nut and bolt securing the lower control arm to the trailing link.

8. Remove the nut and bolt securing the lower control arm to the crossmember.

9. Remove the lower control arm.

To install:

10. Position the lower control arm, and install the bolt and nut securing the lower control arm to the crossmember. Do not tighten at this time.

11. Install the bolt and nut securing the lower control arm to the trailing link. Do not tighten at this time.

12. Install the stay brace on the crossmember. Install and tighten the mounting screws to 18 ft. lbs. (25 Nm).

13. Install the mounting bolt and nut fastening the shock assembly to the lower control arm. Do not tighten at this time.

⁕⁕ WARNING

When attaching the stabilizer bar link to the lower control arm, it is important that the lower mounting stud be positioned properly. The lower mounting stud on the right side link needs to point toward the rear of the vehicle when inserted through the lower control arm mounting flange. The left side link lower stud needs to point toward the front of the vehicle. Otherwise, the suspension geometry will not function properly.

14. If equipped, attach the stabilizer bar link to the lower control arm. Install the nut and, while holding the stabilizer bar link lower stud stationary, tighten the nut to 43 ft. lbs. (58 Nm).

15. Install tire and wheel assembly.

Install and tighten wheel mounting nuts to 100 ft. lbs. (135 Nm).

16. Lower the vehicle.

17. Position the vehicle on an alignment rack/drive-on lift. Raise the vehicle as necessary to access mounting bolts and nuts.

18. Tighten the lower control arm mounting bolt nut at the crossmember to 70 ft. lbs. (95 Nm).

19. Tighten the lower control arm mounting bolt nut at the trailing link to 70 ft. lbs. (95 Nm).

20. Tighten the shock assembly lower mounting bolt nut to 73 ft. lbs. (99 Nm).

21. Perform wheel alignment as necessary.

SHOCK ABSORBER

REMOVAL & INSTALLATION

See Figures 262 and 263.

1. Before servicing the vehicle, refer to the Precautions section.

2. Remove the interior rear quarter trim panel.

3. Remove the 2 nuts securing the shock assembly to the body bracket.

4. Raise and support the vehicle.

5. Remove the tire and wheel assembly.

6. Remove the shock lower mounting nut and bolt.

7. Lower the shock assembly out of the body bracket, and lift out over the rear suspension.

To install:

8. Insert the lower end of the shock assembly down though the lower control arm from above just enough to clear the body, then lift it up into the body bracket.

9. Install the mounting bolt and nut fastening the shock assembly to the lower control arm. Do not tighten at this time.

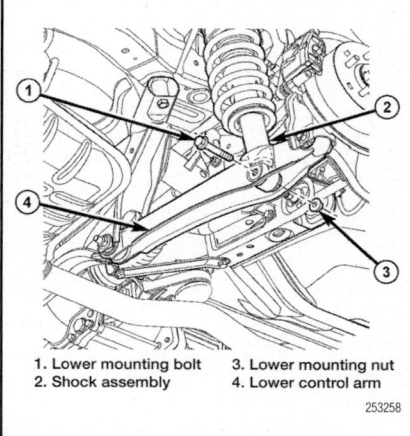

1. Lower mounting bolt   3. Lower mounting nut
2. Shock assembly   4. Lower control arm

253258

Fig. 259 View of rear shock assembly mounting

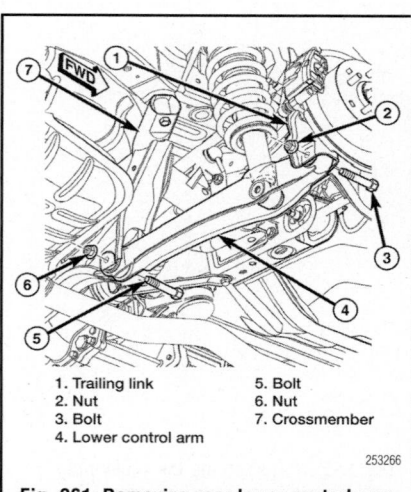

1. Trailing link   5. Bolt
2. Nut   6. Nut
3. Bolt   7. Crossmember
4. Lower control arm

253266

Fig. 261 Removing rear lower control arm

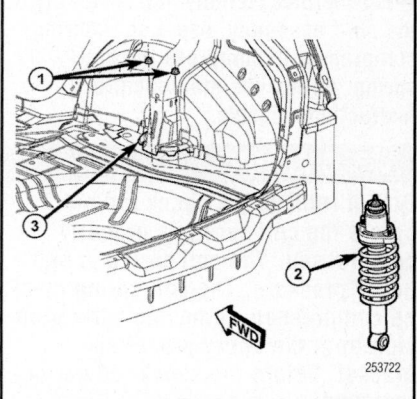

253722

Fig. 262 Remove the 2 nuts (1) securing the shock assembly (2) to the body bracket (3)

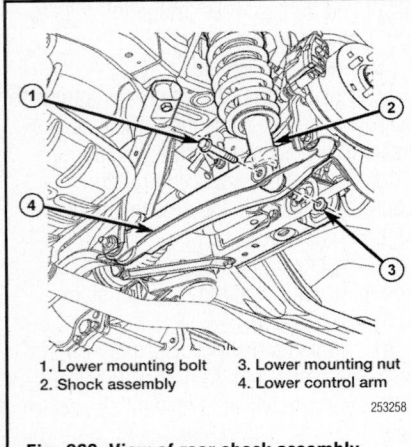

1. Lower mounting bolt
2. Shock assembly
3. Lower mounting nut
4. Lower control arm

253258

Fig. 263 View of rear shock assembly mounting

10. Install tire and wheel assembly. Install and tighten wheel mounting nuts to 100 ft. lbs. (135 Nm).

11. Lower the vehicle.

12. Install the 2 nuts securing the shock assembly to the body bracket. Tighten the mounting nuts to 35 ft. lbs. (48 Nm).

13. Install the interior rear quarter trim panel.

14. Position the vehicle on an alignment rack/drive-on lift. Raise the lift as necessary to access the shock mounting bolt and nut.

15. Tighten the shock assembly lower mounting bolt nut to 73 ft. lbs. (99 Nm).

OVERHAUL

See Figures 264 through 266.

➡The shock assembly must be removed from the vehicle for it to be disassembled and assembled. Refer to Shock Absorber, removal & installation.

➡For the disassembly and assembly of the strut assembly, use a strut spring compressor to compress the coil spring. Follow the manufacturer's instructions closely.

✽✽ CAUTION

Do not remove the shock rod nut before the coil spring is properly compressed. The coil spring is held under pressure. The coil spring must be compressed, removing spring tension from the upper mounting bracket, before the shock rod nut is removed.

1. If both shocks are being serviced at the same time, mark both the coil spring

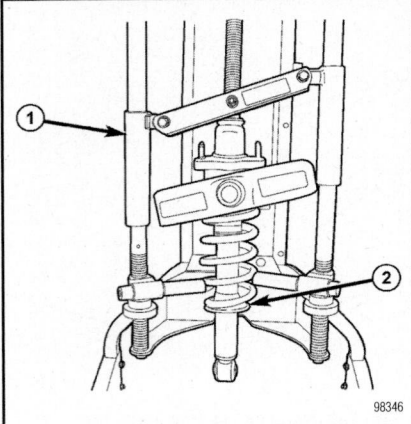

98346

Fig. 264 Position the shock assembly (2) in the strut spring compressor (1)

and shock assembly according to which side of the vehicle the shock is being removed from.

2. If equipped, remove the noise abatement cap from the top of the shock assembly.

3. Position the shock assembly in the strut spring compressor following the manufacturer's instructions, and set the lower and upper hooks of the compressor on the coil spring.

4. Compress the coil spring until all spring tension is removed from the upper mounting bracket and bushings.

✽✽ WARNING

Never use impact or high speed tools to remove the shock rod nut. Damage to the shock internal bearings can occur.

5. Once the spring is sufficiently compressed, install Snap-On® Shock Absorber

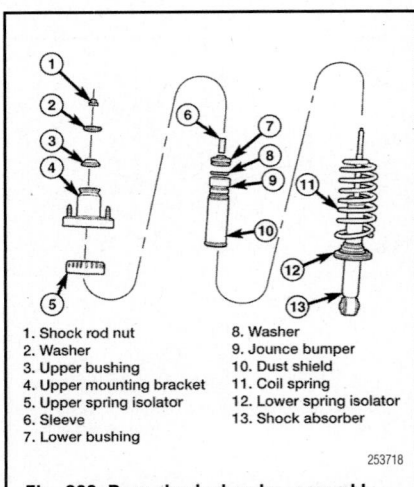

1. Shock rod nut
2. Washer
3. Upper bushing
4. Upper mounting bracket
5. Upper spring isolator
6. Sleeve
7. Lower bushing
8. Washer
9. Jounce bumper
10. Dust shield
11. Coil spring
12. Lower spring isolator
13. Shock absorber

253718

Fig. 266 Rear shock absorber assembly— exploded view

Socket A139, or equivalent, on the end of the shock rod. While holding the shock rod from turning, remove the nut using a wrench. Remove the washer below the nut.

6. Remove the shock absorber out through the bottom of the coil spring. The washer, jounce bumper, dust shield and lower spring isolator will come out with the shock.

7. Slide the washer, jounce bumper, dust shield from the shock rod.

8. Remove the lower spring isolator from the shock spring seat.

9. Remove the upper mounting bracket, bushings, sleeve and upper spring isolator from the top of the spring.

10. Remove the bushings, sleeve and upper spring isolator from the upper mounting bracket.

➡If the coil spring needs to be serviced, perform the following steps.

11. Release the tension from the coil spring by backing off the compressor drive completely. Push back the compressor hooks and remove the coil spring.

12. Inspect the shock assembly components for the following and replace as necessary:

13. Inspect the shock absorber for shaft binding over the full stroke of the shaft.

14. Inspect the jounce bumper for cracks and signs of deterioration.

15. Inspect the dust shield for cracks and tears.

16. Check the upper mounting bracket for cracks and distortion and its retaining studs for any sign of damage.

17. Inspect the upper and lower bushings for material deterioration and signs of deterioration. Inspect the sleeve for wear and distortion.

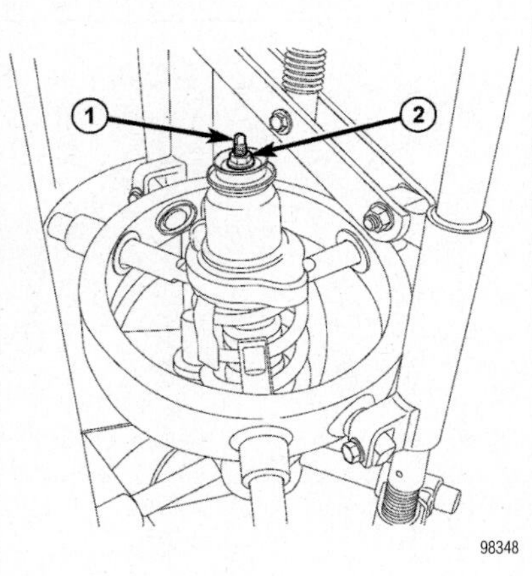

Fig. 265 While holding the shock rod (1) from turning, remove the nut (2)

98348

18. Inspect the upper and lower spring isolators for material deterioration and distortion.

19. Inspect the coil spring for any sign of damage to the coating.

To assemble:

> ☀☀ **WARNING**
>
> **When installing the coil spring, make sure the end with the ID tag is placed upward, or spring-to-body contact will occur after shock assembly installation.**

20. Place the coil spring in the spring compressor following the manufacturer's instructions.

21. Slowly compress the coil spring until enough room is available for shock assembly reassembly.

22. Assemble the bushings and sleeve through the upper mounting bracket.

23. Install the upper spring isolator on the upper mounting bracket.

24. Install the upper mounting bracket on top of the coil spring.

25. Install the lower spring isolator on the spring seat of the shock absorber.

26. Slide the dust shield, jounce bumper and washer onto the shock rod.

27. Install the shock absorber up through the bottom of the coil spring and upper mounting bracket until the lower spring seat contacts the lower end of the coil spring.

28. While holding the shock absorber in position, install the washer and nut on the end of the shock rod.

> ☀☀ **WARNING**
>
> **Never use impact or high speed tools to install the shock rod nut. Damage to the shock internal bearings can occur.**

29. Install Snap-On® Shock Absorber Socket A139, or equivalent, on the end of the shock rod. While holding the shock rod from turning, tighten the nut using a crowfoot wrench and a torque wrench. Tighten the shock rod nut to 18 ft. lbs. (24 Nm).

30. Turn the upper mounting bracket or shock absorber as necessary until the mounting studs on the mounting bracket line up with the lower mounting bolt eyelet at the bottom of the shock absorber.

31. Slowly release the tension from the coil spring by backing off the compressor drive completely.

32. Remove the shock assembly from the spring compressor.

33. If equipped, install the noise abatement cap on top of the shock assembly.

34. Install the shock assembly on the vehicle. Refer to Shock Absorber, removal & installation.

STABILIZER BAR

REMOVAL & INSTALLATION

See Figures 267 and 268.

1. Before servicing the vehicle, refer to the Precautions section.

2. Raise and support the vehicle.

3. On both sides of the vehicle, while holding the stabilizer bar link upper stud stationary, remove the nut securing the link to the stabilizer bar.

4. On both sides of the vehicle, remove the 2 screws securing the stabilizer bushing retainers to the crossmember.

5. Remove the 2 stabilizer bushing retainers.

6. Remove the stabilizer bar from the vehicle.

7. If required, remove the 2 cushions from the stabilizer bar utilizing the slit cut into the cushions (bushings).

To install:

8. If required, install the 2 cushions on the stabilizer bar (one on each side) utilizing the slit cut into the cushions (bushings).

9. Position the stabilizer bar on the rear crossmember.

10. Install the 2 retainers over the cushions at the mounting holes and install the retainer screws. Do not tighten the screws at this time.

11. On each side of the vehicle, install the stabilizer link upper stud in the end of

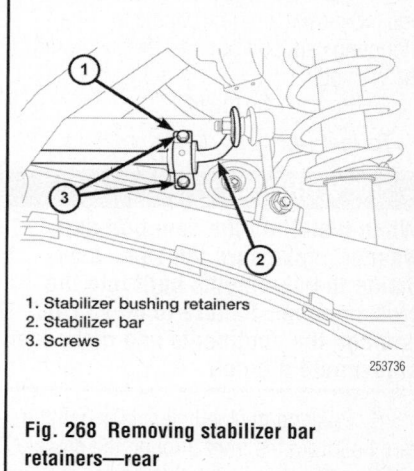

1. Stabilizer bushing retainers
2. Stabilizer bar
3. Screws

253736

Fig. 268 Removing stabilizer bar retainers—rear

the stabilizer bar. Install the nut on each upper stud and, while holding the stabilizer link stud stationary, tighten the nut to 37 ft. lbs. (50 Nm).

12. Tighten the cushion retainer screws to 25 ft. lbs. (34 Nm).

13. Lower the vehicle.

TOE LINK

REMOVAL & INSTALLATION

See Figure 269.

1. Raise and support the vehicle.

2. Remove the bolt securing the toe link to the trailing link.

3. Mark the position of the cam bolt cam on the crossmember using a paint marker or crayon. This mark will be used upon installation to help get the alignment close prior to performing rear wheel alignment. Do not use any type marker that will scratch or damage the surface of the crossmember.

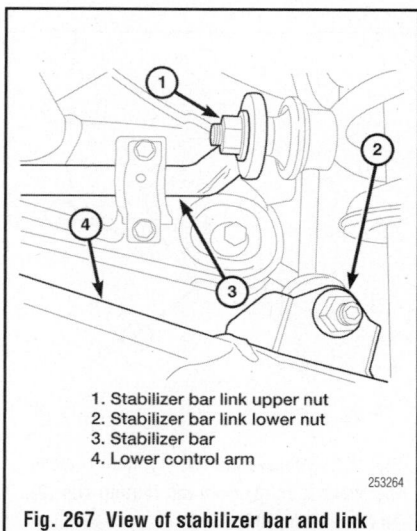

1. Stabilizer bar link upper nut
2. Stabilizer bar link lower nut
3. Stabilizer bar
4. Lower control arm

253264

Fig. 267 View of stabilizer bar and link

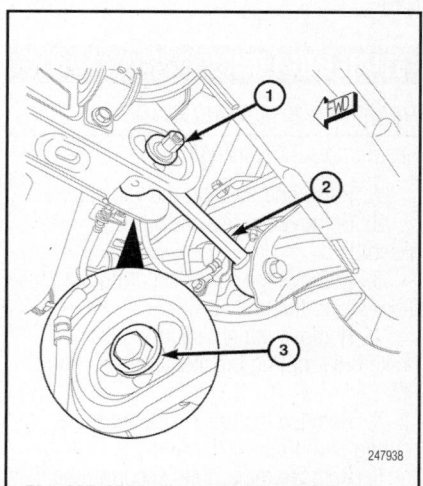

247938

Fig. 269 View of cam bolt head (3), nut (1) and toe link (2)

4. While holding the cam bolt head stationary, loosen and remove the toe link mounting cam bolt nut and washer. Remove the cam bolt.

5. Remove the toe link.

To install:

When installing the cam bolt and washer, make sure the cams stay inside the abutments built into the crossmember. Failure to do so can damage the abutments and make toe adjustment difficult.

6. Position the toe link, and install the cam bolt from the front through the crossmember and link. Match the cam on the bolt to the marks made during removal or position the top of the cam to the 12 o'clock position.

7. Install the cam washer and nut securing the toe link to the crossmember. Do not tighten at this time.

8. Install the bolt securing the link to the trailing link. To install the bolt, it may be necessary to flex the trailing link body mount bushing inward or outward using an appropriate prying tool. Do not tighten at this time.

9. Lower the vehicle.

10. Position the vehicle on an alignment rack/drive-on lift. Raise the vehicle as necessary to access mounting bolts and nuts.

11. Tighten the toe link mounting bolt at the trailing link to 70 ft. lbs. (95 Nm).

12. Perform wheel alignment as necessary.

13. Once rear toe is set, while holding the cam bolt head stationary, tighten the toe link mounting cam bolt nut to 26 ft. lbs. (35 Nm).

TRAILING LINK

REMOVAL & INSTALLATION

See Figures 270 through 277.

1. Raise and support the vehicle.

2. Remove the tire and wheel assembly.

3. Remove the screw securing the brake flex hose to the trailing link.

4. Remove the nut securing the brake tube routing bracket to the trailing link.

5. Remove the brake tube from the routing clip on the trailing link.

6. Remove the 2 bolts securing the disc brake caliper adapter to the brake support plate.

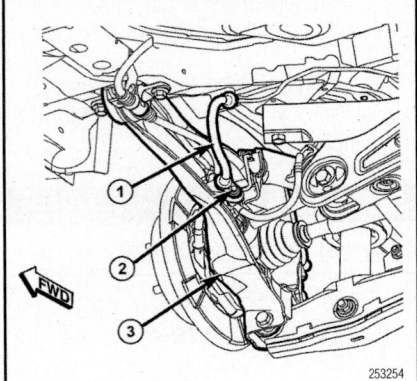

Fig. 270 Remove the screw (2) securing the brake flex hose (1) to the trailing link (3)

7. Remove the disc brake caliper and adapter as an assembly. Hang the assembly out of the way using wire or a bungee cord. Use care not to overextend the brake hose and tubing when doing this.

8. Remove the screw fastening the wheel speed sensor to the trailing link.

9. Remove the routing clip fastening the wheel speed sensor to the trailing link.

10. Remove the brake rotor, then hub and bearing. Refer to appropriate Hub and Bearing Assembly, removal & installation.

11. Remove the parking brake cable from the lever on the parking brake shoe.

12. Remove the hair pin securing the parking brake cable to the brake support plate.

13. Slide the brake support plate with parking brake shoes off the end of the parking brake cable and remove.

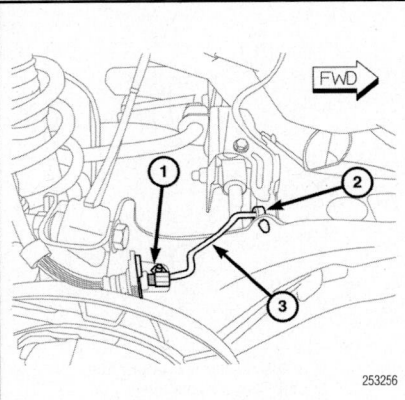

Fig. 271 Remove the nut (1), then remove the brake tube (3) from the routing clip (2) on the trailing link

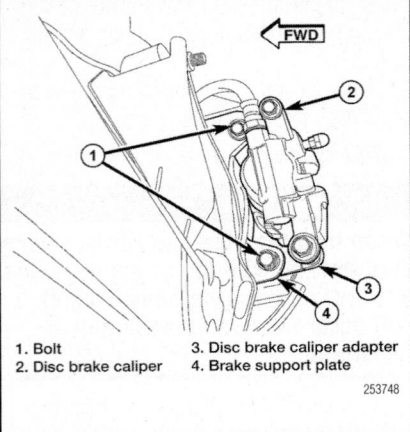

1. Bolt
2. Disc brake caliper
3. Disc brake caliper adapter
4. Brake support plate

Fig. 272 Removing disc brake caliper and adapter assembly

14. Pull the parking brake cable from the trailing link.

15. Remove the bolt securing the toe link to the trailing link.

16. Remove the nut and bolt securing the lower control arm to the trailing link.

17. Remove the nut and bolt securing the upper control arm to the trailing link.

18. Remove the 2 bolts fastening the leading end of the trailing link to the body.

19. Remove the trailing link.

To install:

20. Position the trailing link and install the 2 bolts fastening the leading end of the trailing link to the body. Tighten the 2 mounting bolts to 81 ft. lbs. (110 Nm).

21. Position the upper control arm on the trailing link and install the bolt and nut securing the arm to the link. Tighten the mounting bolt nut to 70 ft. lbs. (95 Nm).

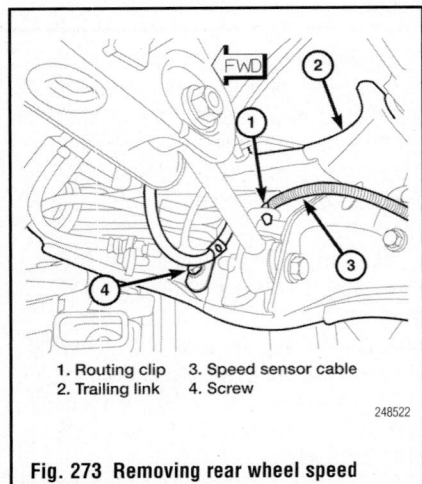

1. Routing clip
2. Trailing link
3. Speed sensor cable
4. Screw

Fig. 273 Removing rear wheel speed sensor

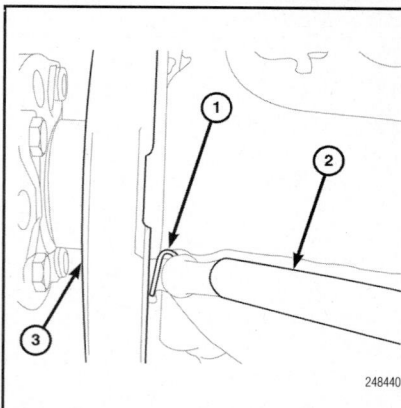

Fig. 274 Remove the hair pin (1) securing the parking brake cable (2) to the brake support plate (3)

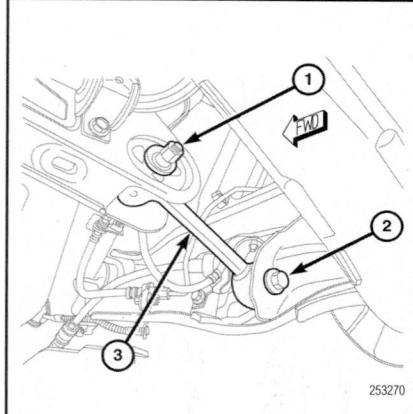

Fig. 275 Remove the bolt (2) securing the toe link (3) to the trailing link

22. Position the lower control arm on the trailing link and install the bolt and nut securing the arm to the link. Tighten the mounting bolt nut to 70 ft. lbs. (95 Nm).

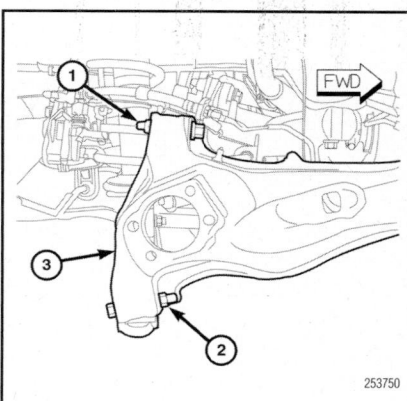

Fig. 276 Remove the nut (1, 2) and bolt securing the control arm to the trailing link (3)

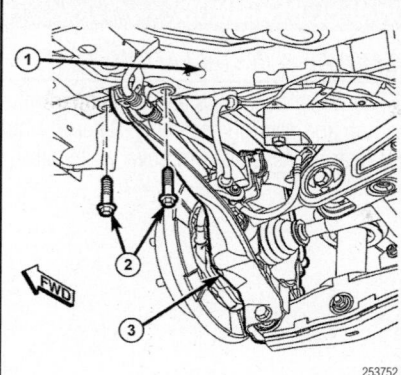

Fig. 277 Remove the 2 bolts (2) fastening the leading end of the trailing link (3) to the body (1)

23. Install the bolt securing the toe link to the trailing link. To install the bolt it may be necessary to flex the trailing link body mount bushing inward or outward using an appropriate prying tool. Tighten the mounting bolt to 70 ft. lbs. (95 Nm).

24. Insert the parking brake cable through the trailing link from the inboard side.

25. Slide the parking brake cable into the brake support plate with the parking brake shoes.

26. Install the hair pin securing the parking brake cable to the brake support plate.

27. Install the parking brake cable onto the lever on the parking brake shoe.

28. Position the wheel speed sensor, and install the screw fastening the sensor to the trailing link. Tighten the mounting screw to 13 ft. lbs. (18 Nm).

29. Position the wheel speed sensor, and install the routing clip fastening the sensor to the trailing link.

30. Install the hub and bearing, then install the brake rotor onto the wheel studs. Refer to appropriate Hub and Bearing Assembly, removal & installation.

31. Slide the disc brake caliper and adapter assembly over the brake rotor and brake support plate.

32. Install the 2 bolts securing the disc brake caliper adapter to the brake support plate. Tighten the mounting bolts to 52 ft. lbs. (71 Nm).

33. Position the brake tube on the trailing link, inserting the tube into the routing clip and routing bracket over the welded stud.

34. Install the nut on the welded stud. Tighten the nut to 11 ft. lbs. (15 Nm).

35. Position the brake flex hose at the trailing link bracket and install the mounting screw. Tighten the screw to 17 ft. lbs. (23 Nm).

36. Install the tire and wheel assembly. Install and tighten the wheel mounting nuts to 100 ft. lbs. (135 Nm).

37. Lower the vehicle.

38. Perform wheel alignment as necessary.

UPPER CONTROL ARM

REMOVAL & INSTALLATION

See Figure 278.

1. Before servicing the vehicle, refer to the Precautions section.

2. Raise and support the vehicle.

3. Remove the tire and wheel assembly.

4. Remove the nut and bolt securing the upper control arm to the trailing link.

5. Remove the bolt securing the upper control arm to the crossmember.

6. Remove the upper control arm.

To install:

7. Position the upper control arm, and install the bolt securing the arm to the crossmember. Do not tighten at this time.

8. Install the bolt and nut securing the upper control arm to the trailing link. Do not tighten at this time.

9. Install tire and wheel assembly. Install and tighten wheel mounting nuts to 100 ft. lbs. (135 Nm).

10. Lower the vehicle.

11. Position the vehicle on an alignment rack/drive-on lift. Raise the vehicle as necessary to access mounting bolts and nuts.

12. Tighten the upper control arm

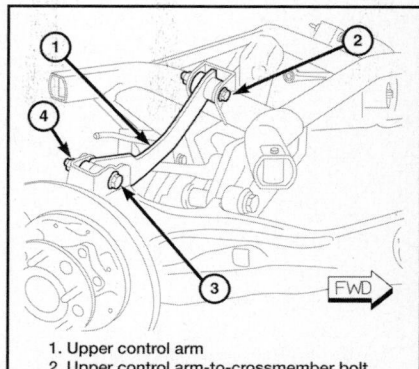

1. Upper control arm
2. Upper control arm-to-crossmember bolt
3. Upper control arm-to-trailing link bolt
4. Upper control arm-to-trailing link nut

Fig. 278 View of upper control arm mounting

mounting bolt at the crossmember to 70 ft. lbs. (95 Nm).

13. Tighten the upper control arm mounting bolt nut at the trailing link to 70 ft. lbs. (95 Nm).

14. Perform wheel alignment as necessary.

WHEEL BEARINGS

REMOVAL & INSTALLATION

The wheel bearing is an integral part of the hub and bearing assembly. Refer to Hub and Bearing Assembly, removal & installation.

ADJUSTMENT

The wheel bearing is designed to last for the life of the vehicle and requires no type of periodic maintenance.

CHRYSLER AND DODGE

Grand Caravan • Town and Country

SPECIFICATIONS AND MAINTENANCE CHARTS

ENGINE AND VEHICLE IDENTIFICATION

Engine							Model Year	
Code ①	Liters (cc)	Cu. In.	Cyl.	Fuel Sys.	Engine Type	Eng. Mfg.	Code ②	Year
E	3.3 (3301)	201	6	FFV	OHV	Chrysler	A	2010
1	3.8 (3778)	230	6	SMFI	OHV	Chrysler	B	2011
X	4.0 (3952)	241	6	SMFI	SOHC	Chrysler		
G	3.6 (3600)	220	6	FFV	DOHC	Chrysler		

① 8th position of VIN

② 10th position of VIN

SMFI: Sequential Multi-port Fuel Injection

25766_CARA_C0001

GENERAL ENGINE SPECIFICATIONS

All measurements are given in inches.

Year	Model	Engine Displacement Liters (cc)	Engine ID/VIN	Fuel System Type	Net Horsepower @ rpm	Net Torque @ rpm (ft. lbs.)	Bore x Stroke (in.)	Compression Ratio	Oil Pressure @ rpm
2010	Grand Caravan &	3.3 (3301)	E	FFV	175@5000	205@4000	3.66X3.43	9.35:1	30@3000
	Town & Country	3.8 (3778)	1	SMFI	197@5200	230@4000	3.78X3.43	9.6:1	30@3000
		4.0 (3952)	X	SMFI	251@6000	259@4100	3.78X3.58	10.2:1	45@3000
2011	Grand Caravan	3.6 (3600)	G	FFV	283@6400	260@4400	3.78X3.27	10.0:1	30@3500
	Town & Country	3.6 (3600)	G	FFV	283@6400	260@4400	3.78X3.27	10.0:1	30@3500

SMFI: Sequential Multi-port Fuel Injection

25766_CARA_C0002

ENGINE TUNE-UP SPECIFICATIONS

Year	Engine Displacement Liters	Engine ID/VIN	Spark Plug Gap (in.)	Ignition Timing (deg.) MT	Ignition Timing (deg.) AT	Fuel Pump (psi)	Idle Speed (rpm) MT	Idle Speed (rpm) AT	Valve Clearance Intake	Valve Clearance Exhaust
2010	3.3	E	0.05	NA	①	58	NA	②	0.001-0.0025	0.002-0.0037
	3.8	1	0.05	NA	①	58	NA	②	0.001-0.0025	0.002-0.0037
	4.0	X	0.051	NA	①	58	NA	②	0.0009-0.0026	0.002-0.0037
2011	3.6	G	0.04	NA	①	58	NA	②	0.0009-0.0024	0.0012-0.0027

NA - Not applicable.

① All engines use a fixed ignition timing system. Basic ignition timing is not adjustable. All spark advance is determined by the Powertrain Control Module (PCM).

② Engine idle speed is adjusted through the idle air control motor.

25766_CARA_C0003

CAPACITIES

Year	Model	Engine Displacement Liters	Engine ID/VIN	Engine Oil with Filter (qts.)	Transmission (pts.) Auto.	Drive Axle (pts.) Front	Rear	Fuel Tank (gal.)	Cooling System (qts.)
2010	Grand Caravan &	3.3	E	5.0	②	N/A	N/A	20.0	13.4
	Town & Country	3.8	1	5.0	②	N/A	N/A	20.0	16.3
		4	X	5.5	②	N/A	N/A	20.0	16.3
2011	Grand Caravan	3.6	G	6.0	①	N/A	N/A	20.0	13.4
	Town & Country	3.6	G	6.0	①	N/A	N/A	20.0	13.4

NOTE: All capacities are approximate. Add fluid gradually and ensure a proper fluid level is obtained.

N/A - Not Available

① Drain and refill: 11 pts.; Overhaul: 18 pts.

② Drain and refill, 4XTE: 8.0 pts.; 62TE: 11 pts; Overhaul, 4XTE: 19.4 pts.; 62TE 18.0 pts.

25766_CARA_C0004

FLUID SPECIFICATIONS

Year	Model	Engine Disp. Liters	Engine Oil	Automatic Trans.	Drive Axle Front	Rear	Power Steering Fluid	Brake Master Cylinder	Cooling System
2010	Grand Caravan &	3.3	5W-30	MOPAR® ATF+4	N/A	N/A	MOPAR® Hydraulic	DOT 3	①
	Town & Country	3.8	5W-30	MOPAR® ATF+4	N/A	N/A	MOPAR® Hydraulic	DOT 3	①
		4.0	5W-30	MOPAR® ATF+4	N/A	N/A	MOPAR® Hydraulic	DOT 3	①
2011	Grand Caravan	3.6	5W-30	MOPAR® ATF+4	N/A	N/A	MOPAR® Hydraulic	DOT 3	①
	Town & Country	3.6	5W-30	MOPAR® ATF+4	N/A	N/A	MOPAR® Hydraulic	DOT 3	①

DOT: Department Of Transpotation

N/A - Not Available

① MOPAR Antifreeze/Coolant

25766_CARA_C0005

VALVE SPECIFICATIONS

Year	Engine Displacement Liters	Engine ID/VIN	Seat Angle (deg.)	Face Angle (deg.)	Spring Test Pressure (lbs. @ in.)	Spring Free-Length (in.)	Spring Installed Height (in.)	Stem-to-Guide Clearance (in.) Intake	Exhaust	Stem Diameter (in.) Intake	Exhaust
2010	3.3	E	44.5	45 ①	84.6-95.4 @ 1.65	2.020	1.61-1.680	0.001-0.0025	0.002-0.0037	0.2732-0.2739	0.2720-0.2728
	3.8	1	44.5	45 ①	84.6-95.4 @ 1.65	2.020	1.61-1.680	0.001-0.0025	0.002-0.0037	0.2732-0.2739	0.2720-0.2728
	4.0	X	45	44.5	③	②	1.496	0.0009-0.0026	0.002-0.0037	0.2730-0.2737	0.2719-0.2726
2011	3.6	G	44.75 ④	45.25 ④	63-69@ 1.57	2.067	1.575	0.0009-0.0024	0.0012-0.0027	0.2346-0.2354	0.2343-0.2351

① Intake & Exhaust

② Intake Free Length (1.7165), Exhaust Free Length (1.8858)

③ Intake (69.5-80.5 @ 1.4964), Exhaust (79.9-90.1@ 1.496)

④ Plus or Minus 0.25 Degrees

25766_CARA_C0006

CAMSHAFT SPECIFICATIONS
All measurements in inches unless noted

Year	Engine Displacement Liters	Engine Code/VIN	Journal Diameter	Brg. Oil Clearance	Shaft End-play	Runout	Journal Bore	Lobe Height Intake	Lobe Height Exhaust
2010	3.3	E	1.997-1.999	0.005	0.010-0.02	N/A	N/A	N/A	N/A
	3.8	1	1.997-1.999	0.005	0.010-0.02	N/A	N/A	N/A	N/A
	4.0	X	1.6905-1.6913	0.0024	0.002-0.02	0.0003	N/A	N/A	N/A
2011	3.6	G	1.2589-1.2596	0.00010-0.0026	0.003-0.01	N/A	N/A	N/A	N/A

N/A - Not Available

25766_CARA_C0007

CRANKSHAFT AND CONNECTING ROD SPECIFICATIONS
All measurements are given in inches.

Year	Engine Displacement Liters	Engine ID/VIN	Crankshaft Main Brg. Journal Dia.	Crankshaft Main Brg. Oil Clearance	Crankshaft Shaft End-play	Thrust on No.	Connecting Rod Journal Diameter	Connecting Rod Oil Clearance	Connecting Rod Side Clearance
2010	3.3	E	2.5192-2.5202	0.0005-0.0022	0.0036-0.0095	2	2.2829-2.2837	0.0007-0.0026	0.0050-0.0160
	3.8	1	2.5192-2.5202	0.0005-0.0022	0.0036-0.0095	2	2.2829-2.2837	0.0007-0.0026	0.0050-0.0160
	4.0	X	2.718-2.7190	0.0013-0.0024	0.002-0.0100	2	2.2828-2.2835	0.0009-0.0021	0.0024
2011	3.6	G	2.8345-2.8380	0.0009-0.0020	0.0020-0.0114	2	2.3228-2.3263	0.0009-0.0025	0.0028-0.0146

25766_CARA_C0008

PISTON AND RING SPECIFICATIONS
All measurements are given in inches.

Year	Engine Displacement Liters	Engine ID/VIN	Piston Clearance	Ring Gap Top Compression	Ring Gap Bottom Compression	Ring Gap Oil Control	Ring Side Clearance Top Compression	Ring Side Clearance Bottom Compression	Ring Side Clearance Oil Control
2010	3.3	E	-0.0002-0.0015	0.007-0.0150	0.011-0.0220	0.009-0.0300	0.0012-0.0031	0.0012-0.0037	0.0015-0.0078
	3.8	1	-0.0002-0.0015	0.007-0.0150	0.011-0.0220	0.009-0.0300	0.0012-0.0027	0.0016-0.0033	0.0015-0.0078
	4.0	X	-0.003 to 0.0018	0.008-0.0140	0.0078-0.0016	0.010-0.0300	0.0016-0.0031	0.0016-0.0031	0.0015-0.0073
2011	3.6	G	0.0001-0.0004	0.010-0.0160	0.012-0.0180	0.006-0.0260	0.0010-0.0033	0.0012-0.0031	0.0003-0.0068

25766_CARA_C0009

TORQUE SPECIFICATIONS
All readings in ft. lbs.

Year	Engine Disp. Liters	Engine ID/VIN	Cylinder Head Bolts	Main Bearing Bolts	Rod Bearing Bolts	Crankshaft Damper Bolts	Flywheel Bolts	Manifold Intake	Manifold Exhaust	Spark Plugs	Oil Pan Drain Plug
2010	3.3	E	①	N/A	N/A	40	70	②	17	12	20
	3.8	1	①	N/A	N/A	40	70	②	17	12	20
	4.0	X	③	N/A	N/A	70	70	②	17	20	20
2011	3.6	G	N/A	N/A	N/A	④	70	⑤	⑥	13	20

N/A - Not Available

① Step 1 (Bolts 1-8): 45 ft. lbs.

  Step 2 (Bolts 1-8): 65 ft. lbs.

  Step 3 (Bolts 1-8): 65 ft. lbs. (again)

  Step 4 (Bolts 1-8): an additional 1/4 turn (do not use a torque wrench)

  After Step 4, the bolt torque should be over 90 ft. lbs.; if not, replace the bolt.

② Lower: 16.6 ft. lbs.; Upper: 8.7 ft. lbs.

③ Step 1 : 45 ft. lbs.

  Step 2: 65 ft. lbs.

  Step 3: 65 ft. lbs. (again)

  Step 4: Plus an additional 90 degrees (do not use a torque wrench)

  After Step 4, the bolt torque should be over 90 ft. lbs.; if not, replace the bolt.

④ 30 ft. lbs., plus an additional 105 degrees

⑤ Both Upper & Lower Intake Manifolds: 5.9 ft. lbs.

⑥ The exhaust manifolds are integrated into the cylinder heads.

25766_CARA_C0010

WHEEL ALIGNMENT

Year	Model		Caster Range (+/-Deg.)	Caster Preferred Setting (Deg.)	Camber Range (+/-Deg.)	Camber Preferred Setting (Deg.)	Toe-in (in.)
2010	Grand Caravan &	F	+1.50 to +3.50	+2.50	①	①	+0.26
	Town & Country	R	NA	NA	-0.46 to +0.34	-0.06	+0.10
2011	Grand Caravan &	F	+1.50 to +3.50	+2.50	①	①	+0.26
	Town & Country	R	NA	NA	-0.46 to +0.34	-0.06	+0.10

NA - Not Applicable

① Left Camber Preferred Setting +0.35; Range -0.05 to +0.75. Right Camber Preferred Setting +0.05; Range -0.35 to +0.45.

25766_CARA_C0011

TIRE, WHEEL AND BALL JOINT SPECIFICATIONS

| Year | Model | OEM Tires | | Tire Pressures (psi) | | Wheel Size | Ball Joint Inspection | Lug Nut (ft. lbs.) |
		Standard	Optional	Front	Rear			
2010	Grand Caravan & Town & Country	①	①	36	36	①	②	100
2011	Grand Caravan & Town & Country	①	①	36	36	①	②	100

OEM: Original Equipment Manufacturer

PSI: Pounds Per Square Inch

NA: Information not available

① P225/65SR16 Standard on the 2011 Grand Caravan C/V model, 2010 Grand Caravan C/V, Express, Mainstreet, & Crew Models; 2010 Town & Country LX, New Touring, & Touring Plus Models

P235/60SR16 Standard on the 2011 Grand Caravan Express, and Mainstreet models; 2011 Town & Country Touring model.

P225/65SR17 Standard on the 2011 Grand Caravan Crew and R/T models, 2010 Grand Caravan Crew model; 2011 Town & Country Touring L and Limited mod 2010 Town & Country Limited and New Limited models.

P225/65SR16 Optional on the 2011 Grand Caravan Express, Mainstreet, and Crew models.

P235/60SR16 Optional on the 2011 Grand Caravan Crew model; 2011 Town & Country Touring L model.

P225/65TR17 Optional on the Town & Country Touring and Touring Plus models.

P225/65SR17 Optional on the 2010 Grand Caravan SXT model.

② If the travel end play exceeds 0.039 inch, replace the ball joint.

25766_CARA_C0012

BRAKE SPECIFICATIONS
All measurements in inches unless noted

| Year | Model | | Brake Disc | | | Minimum Pad/Lining Thickness | | Brake Caliper | |
			Original Thickness	Minimum Thickness	Max. Runout	Front	Rear	Bracket Bolts (ft. lbs.)	Mounting Bolts (ft. lbs.)
2010	Grand Caravan &	F	1.097-1.107	1.040	0.0020	0.040	—	125	—
	Town & Country	R	0.463-0.482	0.409	0.0020	—	0.040	—	74
2011	Grand Caravan &	F	NA	NA	NA	0.040	—	125	—
	Town & Country	R	NA	NA	NA	—	0.040	—	74

F: Front

R: Rear

NA: Information not available

25766_CARA_C0013

SCHEDULED MAINTENANCE - NORMAL
2010 Dodge Grand Caravan, Chrysler Town & Country

TO BE SERVICED	TYPE OF SERVICE	VEHICLE MILEAGE INTERVAL (x1000)																
		6	12	18	24	30	36	42	48	54	60	66	72	78	84	90	96	102
Engine oil & filter	Replace	✔	✔	✔	✔	✔	✔	✔	✔	✔	✔	✔	✔	✔	✔	✔	✔	✔
Rotate tires, inspect tread wear, measure tread depth and check pressure	Rotate	✔	✔	✔	✔	✔	✔	✔	✔	✔	✔	✔	✔	✔	✔	✔	✔	✔
Air conditioner filter	Replace		✔		✔		✔		✔		✔		✔		✔		✔	
Brake system components	Inspect/ Service		✔		✔		✔		✔		✔		✔		✔		✔	
Exhaust system & heat shields	Inspect		✔		✔		✔		✔		✔		✔		✔		✔	
Inspect the front suspension, tie rod ends and boot seals for cracks or leaks and all parts for damage, wear, improper looseness or end play.	Inspect		✔		✔		✔		✔		✔		✔		✔		✔	
CV Joints	Inspect		✔		✔		✔		✔		✔		✔		✔		✔	
Engine air filter	Replace					✔					✔					✔		
Adjust parking brake on vehicles equipped with four-wheel disc brakes.	Adjust					✔					✔					✔		
Engine coolant	Replace										✔							✔
Automatic transmisison fluid & filter	Replace																	
Accessory drive belt	Inspect	✔	✔	✔	✔	✔	✔	✔	✔	✔	✔	✔	✔	✔	✔	✔	✔	✔
Accessory drive belt	Replace	at 120,000 miles if not previously serviced																
Spark plugs & ignition cables	Replace																	✔
Fluid levels (all)	Top off	✔	✔	✔	✔	✔	✔	✔	✔	✔	✔	✔	✔	✔	✔	✔	✔	✔
Horn, exterior lamps, turn signals and hazard warning light operation	Inspect	✔	✔	✔	✔	✔	✔	✔	✔	✔	✔	✔	✔	✔	✔	✔	✔	✔
Battery	Inspect/ Service	✔	✔	✔	✔	✔	✔	✔	✔	✔	✔	✔	✔	✔	✔	✔	✔	✔
PCV valve	Replace															✔		

*Oil Change Indicator System

On Electronic Vehicle Information Center (EVIC) equipped vehicles, "Oil Change Required" is displayed in the EVIC and a single chime sounds, indicating that an oil change is necessary. On non-EVIC equipped vehicles, "Change Oil" flashes in the instrument cluster and a single chime sounds indicating that an oil change is necessary. Illumination of the oil change message is based on the operating conditions of the vehicle. When the message is illuminated, the vehicle must be serviced within 500 miles.

The oil change indicator will not monitor the time since the last oil change. Change the oil if it has been more than 6 months since the last oil change, even if the oil change indicator message is not illuminated.

Under no circumstances should oil change intervals exceed 6,000 miles or 6 months, whichever comes first.

To reset the oil change indicator, perform the following procedure:

1. Turn the ignition switch to the ON position. Do not start the engine.
2. Fully press the accelerator pedal 3 times within 10 seconds.
3. Turn the ignition switch to the LOCK position.

If the indicator message illuminates when the vehicle is started, repeat the procedure.

25766_CARA_C0014

SCHEDULED MAINTENANCE - SEVERE
2010 Dodge Grand Caravan, Chrysler Town & Country

TO BE SERVICED	TYPE OF SERVICE	VEHICLE MILEAGE INTERVAL (x1000)																
		6	12	18	24	30	36	42	48	54	60	66	72	78	84	90	96	102
Engine oil & filter	Replace	✓	✓	✓	✓	✓	✓	✓	✓	✓	✓	✓	✓	✓	✓	✓	✓	✓
Rotate tires, inspect tread wear, measure tread depth and check pressure	Rotate	✓	✓	✓	✓	✓	✓	✓	✓	✓	✓	✓	✓	✓	✓	✓	✓	✓
Air conditioner filter	Replace		✓		✓		✓		✓		✓		✓		✓		✓	
Brake system components	Inspect/Service		✓		✓		✓		✓		✓		✓		✓		✓	
Exhaust system & heat shields	Inspect		✓		✓		✓		✓		✓		✓		✓		✓	
Inspect the front suspension, tie rod ends and boot seals for cracks or leaks and all parts for damage, wear, improper looseness or end play.	Inspect		✓		✓		✓		✓		✓		✓		✓		✓	
CV Joints	Inspect		✓		✓		✓		✓		✓		✓		✓		✓	
Engine air filter	Inspect/Service		✓		✓		✓		✓		✓		✓			✓		
Adjust parking brake on vehicles equipped with four-wheel disc brakes.	Adjust					✓					✓					✓		
Engine coolant	Replace										✓							✓
Automatic transmision fluid & filter	Replace										✓							
Accessory drive belt	Inspect	✓	✓	✓	✓	✓	✓	✓	✓	✓	✓	✓	✓	✓	✓	✓	✓	✓
Accessory drive belt	Replace	at 120,000 miles if not previously serviced																
Spark plugs & ignition cables	Replace																	✓
Fluid levels (all)	Top off	✓	✓	✓	✓	✓	✓	✓	✓	✓	✓	✓	✓	✓	✓	✓	✓	✓
Horn, exterior lamps, turn signals and hazard warning light operation	Inspect	✓	✓	✓	✓	✓	✓	✓	✓	✓	✓	✓	✓	✓	✓	✓	✓	✓
Battery	Inspect/Service	✓	✓	✓	✓	✓	✓	✓	✓	✓	✓	✓	✓	✓	✓	✓	✓	✓
PCV valve	Replace															✓		

*Oil Change Indicator System

On Electronic Vehicle Information Center (EVIC) equipped vehicles, "Oil Change Required" is displayed in the EVIC and a single chime sounds, indicating that an oil change is necessary. On non-EVIC equipped vehicles, "Change Oil" flashes in the instrument cluster and a single chime sounds indicating that an oil change is necessary. Illumination of the oil change message is based on the operating conditions of the vehicle. When the message is illuminated, the vehicle must be serviced within 500 miles.

The oil change indicator will not monitor the time since the last oil change. Change the oil if it has been more than 6 months since the last oil change, even if the oil change indicator message is not illuminated.

Under no circumstances should oil change intervals exceed 6,000 miles or 6 months, whichever comes first.

To reset the oil change indicator, perform the following procedure:

1. Turn the ignition switch to the ON position. Do not start the engine.
2. Fully press the accelerator pedal 3 times within 10 seconds.
3. Turn the ignition switch to the LOCK position.

If the indicator message illuminates when the vehicle is started, repeat the procedure.

25766_CARA_C0015

SCHEDULED MAINTENANCE - NORMAL
2011 Dodge Grand Caravan, Chrysler Town & Country

TO BE SERVICED	TYPE OF SERVICE	VEHICLE MILEAGE INTERVAL (x1000)																
		8	16	24	32	40	48	56	64	72	80	88	96	104	112	120	128	136
Engine oil & filter	Replace	✓	✓	✓	✓	✓	✓	✓	✓	✓	✓	✓	✓	✓	✓	✓	✓	✓
Rotate tires, inspect tread wear, measure tread depth and check pressure	Rotate	✓	✓	✓	✓	✓	✓	✓	✓	✓	✓	✓	✓	✓	✓	✓	✓	✓
Air conditioner filter	Replace		✓		✓		✓		✓		✓		✓		✓		✓	
Brake system components	Inspect/Service		✓		✓		✓		✓		✓		✓		✓		✓	
Exhaust system & heat shields	Inspect			✓			✓			✓			✓			✓		
Inspect the front suspension, tie rod ends and boot seals for cracks or leaks and all parts for damage, wear, improper looseness or end play.	Inspect		✓		✓		✓		✓		✓		✓		✓		✓	
CV Joints	Inspect			✓			✓			✓			✓			✓		
Engine air filter	Replace				✓				✓				✓				✓	
Adjust parking brake on vehicles equipped with four-wheel disc brakes.	Adjust				✓				✓				✓				✓	
Engine coolant	Replace										✓			✓				
Accessory drive belt	Replace	at 120,000 miles if not previously serviced																
Accessory drive belt	Inspect	✓	✓	✓	✓	✓	✓	✓	✓	✓	✓	✓	✓	✓	✓	✓	✓	✓
Spark plugs	Replace												✓					
Fluid levels (all)	Top off	✓	✓	✓	✓	✓	✓	✓	✓	✓	✓	✓	✓	✓	✓	✓	✓	✓
Horn, exterior lamps, turn signals and hazard warning light operation	Inspect	✓	✓	✓	✓	✓	✓	✓	✓	✓	✓	✓	✓	✓	✓	✓	✓	✓
Battery	Inspect/Service	✓	✓	✓	✓	✓	✓	✓	✓	✓	✓	✓	✓	✓	✓	✓	✓	✓
PCV valve	Replace												✓					
Automatic transmision fluid & filter	Replace															✓		

*Oil Change Indicator System

On Electronic Vehicle Information Center (EVIC) equipped vehicles, "Oil Change Required" is displayed in the EVIC and a single chime sounds, indicating that an oil change is necessary. On non-EVIC equipped vehicles, "Change Oil" flashes in the instrument cluster and a single chime sounds indicating that an oil change is necessary. Illumination of the oil change message is based on the operating conditions of the vehicle. When the message is illuminated, the vehicle must be serviced within 500 miles.

The oil change indicator will not monitor the time since the last oil change. Change the oil if it has been more than 6 months since the last oil change, even if the oil change indicator message is not illuminated.

Under no circumstances should oil change intervals exceed 6,000 miles or 6 months, whichever comes first.

To reset the oil change indicator, perform the following procedure:

1. Turn the ignition switch to the ON position. Do not start the engine.
2. Fully press the accelerator pedal 3 times within 10 seconds.
3. Turn the ignition switch to the LOCK position.

If the indicator message illuminates when the vehicle is started, repeat the procedure.

25766_CARA_C0016

SCHEDULED MAINTENANCE - SEVERE
2011 Dodge Grand Caravan, Chrysler Town & Country

TO BE SERVICED	TYPE OF SERVICE	VEHICLE MILEAGE INTERVAL (x1000)																
		8	16	24	32	40	48	56	64	72	80	88	96	104	112	120	128	136
Engine oil & filter	Replace	✓	✓	✓	✓	✓	✓	✓	✓	✓	✓	✓	✓	✓	✓	✓	✓	✓
Rotate tires, inspect tread wear, measure tread depth and check pressure	Rotate	✓	✓	✓	✓	✓	✓	✓	✓	✓	✓	✓	✓	✓	✓	✓	✓	✓
Air conditioner filter	Replace		✓		✓		✓		✓		✓		✓		✓		✓	
Brake system components	Inspect/ Service		✓		✓		✓		✓		✓		✓		✓		✓	
Exhaust system & heat shields	Inspect		✓		✓		✓		✓		✓		✓		✓		✓	
Inspect the front suspension, tie rod ends and boot seals for cracks or leaks and all parts for damage, wear, improper looseness or end play.	Inspect		✓		✓		✓		✓		✓		✓		✓		✓	
CV Joints	Inspect			✓			✓			✓			✓			✓		
Engine air filter	Replace		✓		✓		✓		✓		✓		✓		✓		✓	
Adjust parking brake on vehicles equipped with four-wheel disc brakes.	Adjust				✓				✓				✓				✓	
Engine coolant	Replace										✓							
Spark plugs	Replace												✓					
Accessory drive belt	Replace	at 120,000 miles if not previously serviced																
Accessory drive belt	Inspect	✓	✓	✓	✓	✓	✓	✓	✓	✓	✓	✓	✓	✓	✓	✓	✓	✓
Fluid levels (all)	Top off	✓	✓	✓	✓	✓	✓	✓	✓	✓	✓	✓	✓	✓	✓	✓	✓	✓
Horn, exterior lamps, turn signals and hazard warning light operation	Inspect	✓	✓	✓	✓	✓	✓	✓	✓	✓	✓	✓	✓	✓	✓	✓	✓	✓
Battery	Inspect/ Service	✓	✓	✓	✓	✓	✓	✓	✓	✓	✓	✓	✓	✓	✓	✓	✓	✓
Automatic transmision fluid & filter	Replace						✓						✓					
PCV valve	Replace												✓					

*Oil Change Indicator System

On Electronic Vehicle Information Center (EVIC) equipped vehicles, "Oil Change Required" is displayed in the EVIC and a single chime sounds, indicating that an oil change is necessary. On non-EVIC equipped vehicles, "Change Oil" flashes in the instrument cluster and a single chime sounds indicating that an oil change is necessary. Illumination of the oil change message is based on the operating conditions of the vehicle. When the message is illuminated, the vehicle must be serviced within 500 miles.

The oil change indicator will not monitor the time since the last oil change. Change the oil if it has been more than 6 months since the last oil change, even if the oil change indicator message is not illuminated.

Under no circumstances should oil change intervals exceed 6,000 miles or 6 months, whichever comes first.

To reset the oil change indicator, perform the following procedure:

1. Turn the ignition switch to the ON position. Do not start the engine.
2. Fully press the accelerator pedal 3 times within 10 seconds.
3. Turn the ignition switch to the LOCK position.

If the indicator message illuminates when the vehicle is started, repeat the procedure.

25766_CARA_C0017

PRECAUTIONS

Before servicing any vehicle, please be sure to read all of the following precautions, which deal with personal safety, prevention of component damage, and important points to take into consideration when servicing a motor vehicle:

• Never open, service or drain the radiator or cooling system when the engine is hot; serious burns can occur from the steam and hot coolant.

• Observe all applicable safety precautions when working around fuel. Whenever servicing the fuel system, always work in a well-ventilated area. Do not allow fuel spray or vapors to come in contact with a spark, open flame, or excessive heat (a hot drop light, for example). Keep a dry chemical fire extinguisher near the work area. Always keep fuel in a container specifically designed for fuel storage; also, always properly seal fuel containers to avoid the possibility of fire or explosion. Refer to the additional fuel system precautions later in this section.

• Fuel injection systems often remain pressurized, even after the engine has been turned **OFF**. The fuel system pressure must be relieved before disconnecting any fuel lines. Failure to do so may result in fire and/or personal injury.

• Brake fluid often contains polyglycol ethers and polyglycols. Avoid contact with the eyes and wash your hands thoroughly after handling brake fluid. If you do get brake fluid in your eyes, flush your eyes with clean, running water for 15 minutes. If eye irritation persists, or if you have taken

brake fluid internally, IMMEDIATELY seek medical assistance.

• The EPA warns that prolonged contact with used engine oil may cause a number of skin disorders, including cancer. You should make every effort to minimize your exposure to used engine oil. Protective gloves should be worn when changing oil. Wash your hands and any other exposed skin areas as soon as possible after exposure to used engine oil. Soap and water, or waterless hand cleaner should be used.

• All new vehicles are now equipped with an air bag system, often referred to as a Supplemental Restraint System (SRS) or Supplemental Inflatable Restraint (SIR) system. The system must be disabled before performing service on or around system components, steering column, instrument panel components, wiring and sensors. Failure to follow safety and disabling procedures could result in accidental air bag deployment, possible personal injury and unnecessary system repairs.

• Always wear safety goggles when working with, or around, the air bag system. When carrying a non-deployed air bag, be sure the bag and trim cover are pointed away from your body. When placing a non-deployed air bag on a work surface, always face the bag and trim cover upward, away from the surface. This will reduce the motion of the module if it is accidentally deployed. Refer to the additional air bag system precautions later in this section.

• Clean, high quality brake fluid from a sealed container is essential to the safe and

proper operation of the brake system. You should always buy the correct type of brake fluid for your vehicle. If the brake fluid becomes contaminated, completely flush the system with new fluid. Never reuse any brake fluid. Any brake fluid that is removed from the system should be discarded. Also, do not allow any brake fluid to come in contact with a painted surface; it will damage the paint.

• Never operate the engine without the proper amount and type of engine oil; doing so WILL result in severe engine damage.

• Timing belt maintenance is extremely important. Many models utilize an interference-type, non-freewheeling engine. If the timing belt breaks, the valves in the cylinder head may strike the pistons, causing potentially serious (also time-consuming and expensive) engine damage. Refer to the maintenance interval charts for the recommended replacement interval for the timing belt, and to the timing belt section for belt replacement and inspection.

• Disconnecting the negative battery cable on some vehicles may interfere with the functions of the on-board computer system(s) and may require the computer to undergo a relearning process once the negative battery cable is reconnected.

• When servicing drum brakes, only disassemble and assemble one side at a time, leaving the remaining side intact for reference.

• Only an MVAC-trained, EPA-certified automotive technician should service the air conditioning system or its components.

BRAKES

ANTI-LOCK BRAKE SYSTEM (ABS)

GENERAL INFORMATION

PRECAUTIONS

• Certain components within the ABS system are not intended to be serviced or repaired individually.

• Do not use rubber hoses or other parts not specifically specified for and ABS system. When using repair kits, replace all parts included in the kit. Partial or incorrect repair may lead to functional problems and require the replacement of components.

• Lubricate rubber parts with clean, fresh brake fluid to ease assembly. Do not use shop air to clean parts; damage to rubber components may result.

• Use only DOT 3 brake fluid from an unopened container.

• If any hydraulic component or line is

removed or replaced, it may be necessary to bleed the entire system.

• A clean repair area is essential. Always clean the reservoir and cap thoroughly before removing the cap. The slightest amount of dirt in the fluid may plug an orifice and impair the system function. Perform repairs after components have been thoroughly cleaned; use only denatured alcohol to clean components. Do not allow ABS components to come into contact with any substance containing mineral oil; this includes used shop rags.

• The Anti-Lock control unit is a microprocessor similar to other computer units in the vehicle. Ensure that the ignition switch is **OFF** before removing or installing controller harnesses. Avoid static electricity discharge at or near the controller.

• If any arc welding is to be done on the vehicle, the control unit should be unplugged before welding operations begin.

SPEED SENSORS

REMOVAL & INSTALLATION

Front

See Figures 1 and 2.

1. Access and remove front brake rotor.
2. Remove the brake shield from knuckle.
3. Disconnect the vehicle wiring harness from wheel speed sensor connector.
4. Unclip the wheel speed sensor connector from bracket on frame rail.
5. Remove the wheel speed sensor grommet from flex hose bracket on frame rail.

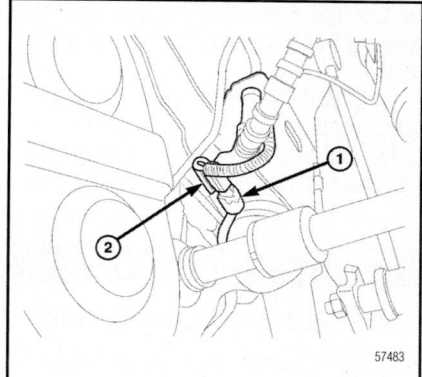

Fig. 1 Disconnect vehicle wiring harness from wheel speed sensor connector (1). Unclip wheel speed sensor connector from bracket on frame rail (2).

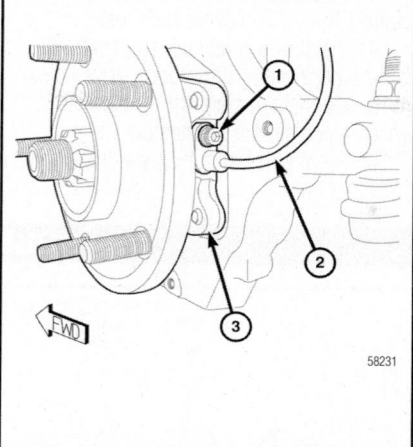

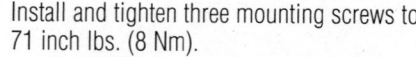

Fig. 2 Remove screw (1) fastening speed sensor (2) head to hub and bearing (3)

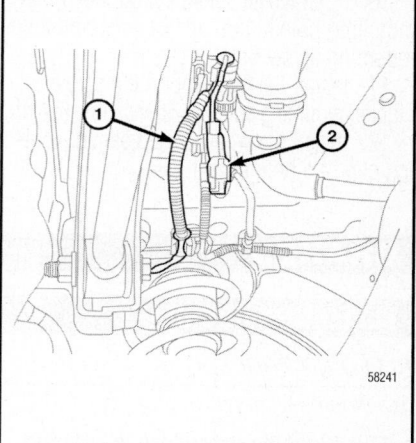

Fig. 3 Disconnect vehicle wiring harness (2) from wheel speed sensor (1) connector

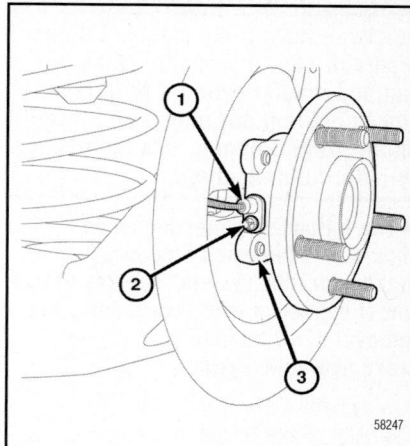

Fig. 4 Wheel speed sensor (1) at rear hub and bearing (3), and align mounting screw hole. Install new screw (2)

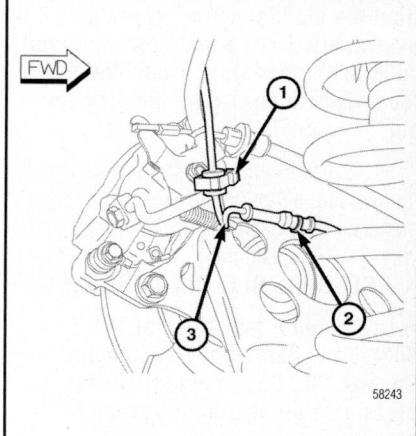

Fig. 5 Install wheel speed sensor routing clip (2) into hole in rear axle. Install wheel speed sensor (3) into routing clips (1) along brake flex hose

6. Remove the screw fastening wheel speed sensor routing bracket to mounting flange on strut.

7. Remove the screw fastening wheel speed sensor routing bracket to knuckle.

➡**Prior to removal, clean the area around sensor head to help prevent contaminants from entering bearing when sensor head is removed.**

8. Remove the screw fastening speed sensor head to hub and bearing.

9. Remove the wheel speed sensor from hub and bearing.

To install:
10. Apply bearing grease (supplied with part) to sensor head shaft and O-ring.

➡**Ensure that sensor mounting surface on bearing is clean before sensor installation.**

11. Push wheel speed sensor head into mounting hole in hub and bearing and align mounting screw hole.

12. Install the NEW mounting screw. Tighten mounting the screw to 55 inch lbs. (6 Nm).

13. Attach wheel speed sensor routing bracket to knuckle. Install and tighten the screw to 71 inch lbs. (8 Nm).

14. Attach wheel speed sensor routing bracket to mounting flange on strut assembly. Install and tighten the screw to 89 inch lbs. (10 Nm).

15. Install the wheel speed sensor grommet into flex hose bracket on frame rail.

16. Clip wheel speed sensor connector and routing clip to bracket on frame rail.

17. Connect vehicle wiring harness to wheel speed sensor connector.

18. Install the brake shield on knuckle.

Install and tighten three mounting screws to 71 inch lbs. (8 Nm).

19. Install the brake rotor as well as all components necessary to access it.

20. Verify that wheel speed sensor cable is properly routed and not coming into contact with rotor or other moving parts.

21. Perform the Diagnostic Verification Test and clear any faults.

Rear
See Figures 3 through 5.

1. Access and remove rear brake rotor.

Right side sensor only
2. Remove the exhaust heat shield above exhaust system covering wheel speed sensor wiring connector.

3. Disconnect vehicle wiring harness from wheel speed sensor connector.

4. Remove the wheel speed sensor from routing clips along underbody of vehicle.

5. Remove the wheel speed sensor from routing clips along brake flex hose.

6. Remove the wheel speed sensor routing clip from rear axle.

➡**Prior to removal, clean area around sensor head to help prevent contaminants from entering bearing when sensor head is removed.**

7. Remove the screw fastening speed sensor head to hub and bearing.

8. Remove the wheel speed sensor from hub and bearing.

To install:
9. Apply bearing grease (supplied with part) to sensor head shaft and O-ring.

➡**Ensure that sensor mounting surface on bearing is clean before sensor installation.**

10. Push wheel speed sensor head into mounting hole in hub and bearing and align mounting screw hole.

11. Install the NEW mounting screw. Tighten mounting screw to 55 inch lbs. (6 Nm).

12. Install the wheel speed sensor routing clip into hole in rear axle.

13. Install the wheel speed sensor into routing clips along brake flex hose.

14. Install the wheel speed sensor into routing clips along underbody of vehicle.

15. Connect vehicle wiring harness to wheel speed sensor connector.

16. Right side sensor only—Install

exhaust heat shield above exhaust system covering wheel speed sensor wiring connector.

17. Install the brake rotor as well as all components necessary to access it.

18. Perform the Diagnostic Verification Test and clear any faults.

BRAKES — BLEEDING THE BRAKE SYSTEM

BLEEDING PROCEDURE

BLEEDING PROCEDURE

See Figures 6 through 8.

➡This bleeding procedure is only for the vehicle's base brakes hydraulic system.

✳✳ WARNING

Before removing the master cylinder reservoir cap, thoroughly clean the cap and master cylinder fluid reservoir to prevent dirt and other foreign matter from dropping into the master cylinder fluid reservoir.

➡The following wheel sequence should be used when bleeding the brake hydraulic system. The use of this wheel sequence will ensure adequate removal of all trapped air from the brake hydraulic system:

- Left Rear Wheel
- Right Front Wheel
- Right Rear Wheel
- Left Front Wheel

➡When bleeding the brake system, some air may be trapped in the brake lines far upstream, as much as ten feet from the bleeder screw. Therefore, it is essential to have a fast flow of a large volume of brake fluid when bleeding the brakes to ensure all the air gets out.

1. Pressure bleeding the brakes is recommended, although the brakes may be manually bled or pressure bled. Refer to the appropriate procedure.

PRESSURE BLEEDING PROCEDURE

➡Use bleeder tank Special Tool C-3496-B or equivalent with Adapter, Special Tool Cap, Master Cylinder, to pressurize the hydraulic system for bleeding.

2. Follow pressure bleeder manufacturer's instructions for use of pressure bleeding equipment.

3. Install the Master Cylinder Pressure

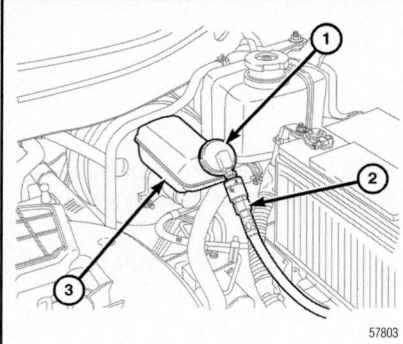

Fig. 6 Install Master Cylinder Pressure Bleed Cap, Special Tool on the master cylinder fluid reservoir. Attach the fluid hose from the pressure bleeder to the fitting on Special Tool

Bleed Cap, Special Tool on the master cylinder fluid reservoir. Attach the fluid hose from the pressure bleeder to the fitting on Special Tool

4. Attach a clear plastic hose to the bleeder screw and feed the hose into a clear jar containing enough fresh brake fluid to submerge the end of the hose.

5. Open the bleeder screw at least one full turn or more to obtain a steady stream of brake fluid.

6. After approximately 4-8 ounces of fluid have been bled through the brake circuit and an air-free flow is maintained in the clear plastic hose and jar, close the bleeder screw.

7. Repeat this procedure at all the remaining bleeder screws.

8. Check and adjust brake fluid level to the FULL mark on the reservoir.

9. Check brake pedal travel and feel. If pedal travel is excessive or if the pedal feels excessively spongy, some air may still be trapped in the system. Re-bleed the brakes as necessary including the IPB Caliper Brake Bleeding Procedure on the rear calipers as listed below.

10. Test drive the vehicle to verify the brakes are operating properly and pedal feel is correct.

MANUAL BLEEDING PROCEDURE

➡To bleed the brakes manually, the aid of a helper will be required.

11. Attach a clear plastic hose to the bleeder screw and feed the hose into a clear jar containing enough fresh brake fluid to submerge the end of the hose.

12. Have a helper pump the brake pedal three or four times and hold it in the down position.

13. With the pedal in the down position, open the bleeder screw at least one full turn.

14. Once the brake pedal has dropped, close the bleeder screw. After the bleeder screw is closed, release the brake pedal.

15. Repeat the above steps until all trapped air is removed from that wheel circuit (usually four or five times).

16. Bleed the remaining wheel circuits in the same manner until all air is removed from the brake system. Monitor the fluid level in the master cylinder reservoir to make sure it does not go dry.

17. Check and adjust brake fluid level to the FULL mark.

18. Check brake pedal travel and feel. If pedal travel is excessive or if the pedal feels excessively spongy, some air may still be trapped in the system. Re-bleed the brakes as necessary including the IPB Caliper Brake Bleeding Procedure on the rear calipers as listed below.

19. Test drive the vehicle to verify the brakes are operating properly and pedal feel is correct.

IPB CALIPER BRAKE BLEEDING PROCEDURE

20. Perform the following procedure on each rear brake caliper as necessary.

21. Raise and support vehicle.

22. Remove the wheel mounting nuts, then the tire and wheel assembly.

23. Remove the brake caliper lower guide pin bolt.

24. Swing the caliper assembly upward, pivoting off the upper guide pin, until clear of the adapter bracket.

25. Remove the outboard pad from the adapter bracket.

26. Return the caliper back down over

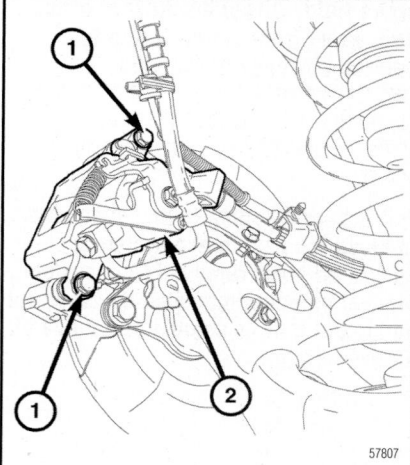

Fig. 7 Remove the brake caliper lower guide pin bolt. Swing the caliper assembly upward, pivoting off the upper guide pin, until clear of the adapter bracket

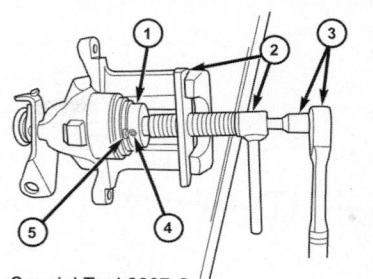

1. Special Tool 8807-2
2. Special Tool 8807-1
3. Drive ratchet handle and an extension
4. Lugs on Special Tool 8807-2
5. Notches in the face of the caliper piston

Fig. 8 Seat (bottom) the caliper piston in the bore

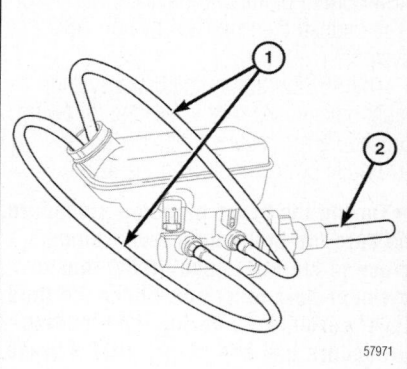

Fig. 9 Thread a Bleeder Tube, Special Tool (1), into each master cylinder outlet port. Using a wooden dowel as a push rod (2), slowly depress master cylinder pistons, then release pressure, allowing pistons to return to released position

the adapter bracket into mounted position and install the lower guide pin bolt finger tight.

27. Slowly pump the brake pedal until the caliper fingers touch the outboard surface of the brake rotor. Release the pedal.

28. Remove the brake caliper lower guide pin bolt.

29. Swing the caliper assembly upward, pivoting off the upper guide pin, until clear of the adapter bracket.

30. Reinstall the outboard pad in the adapter bracket.

31. Open the caliper bleeder screw at least one full turn.

32. Seat (bottom) the caliper piston in the bore as follows:

- Assemble a 3/8 in. drive ratchet handle and an extension.
- Insert the extension through Special Tool.
- Place Special Tool on the end of the extension.
- Insert lugs on Special Tool into notches in face of caliper piston.
- Thread the screw drive on down until it contacts the top of which is against the caliper piston. Do not over tighten the screw-drive. Damage to the piston can occur.
- Turn with the ratchet, rotating the piston in a clockwise direction until fully seated (bottomed) in the bore. It may be necessary to turn with to start the process of piston retraction.

33. Close the bleeder screw.

34. Return the caliper back down over

the adapter bracket into mounted position and install the lower guide pin bolt finger tight.

35. Have a helper pump the brake pedal three or four times and hold it in the down position.

36. With the pedal in the down position, open the bleeder screw at least one full turn and let out fluid and air, if any.

37. Once the brake pedal has dropped, close the bleeder screw. Once the bleeder screw is closed, release the brake pedal.

38. Repeat the previous three steps until all trapped air is removed.

39. Tighten the guide pin bolt to 26 ft. lbs. (35 Nm).

40. Repeat the above procedure on the opposite rear brake caliper as necessary.

41. Check brake pedal travel and feel. If pedal travel is still excessive or if the pedal feels excessively spongy, repeat the entire procedure as necessary.

42. Install the tire and wheel assembly. Install and tighten wheel mounting nuts to 100 ft. lbs. (135 Nm).

43. Lower the vehicle.

44. Test drive the vehicle to verify the brakes are operating properly and pedal feel is correct.

MASTER CYLINDER BLEEDING

See Figure 9.

➡**When clamping master cylinder in vise, only clamp master cylinder by its mounting flange. Do not clamp master cylinder piston rod, reservoir, seal or body.**

1. Clamp master cylinder in a vise.

2. Thread a Bleeder Tube, Special Tool, into each master cylinder outlet port. Tighten each tube to 120 inch lbs. (14 Nm).

Flex bleeder tubes and place open ends into mouth of fluid reservoir as far down as possible to keep them below fluid level while bleeding.

➡**Make sure open ends of bleeder tubes stay below surface of brake fluid once reservoir is filled to proper level.**

3. Fill brake fluid reservoir with Mopar® Brake Fluid DOT 3 Motor Vehicle or equivalent conforming to DOT 3 specifications.

4. Make sure fluid level is above tips of bleeder tubes in reservoir to ensure no air is ingested during bleeding.

5. Using a wooden dowel as a push rod, slowly depress master cylinder pistons, then release pressure, allowing pistons to return to released position. Repeat several times until all air bubbles are expelled. Make sure fluid level stays above tips of bleeder tubes in reservoir while bleeding.

6. Remove the bleeder tubes from master cylinder outlet ports, then plug outlet ports and install fill cap on reservoir.

7. Remove the master cylinder from vise.

8. Install the master cylinder on vehicle.

BLEEDING THE ABS SYSTEM

See Figure 10.

The base brake's hydraulic system must be bled anytime air enters the hydraulic system. The ABS must always be bled anytime it is suspected that the HCU has ingested air.

Brake systems with ABS must be bled as two independent braking systems. The non-

ABS portion of the brake system with ABS is to be bled the same as any non-ABS system.

The ABS portion of the brake system must be bled separately. Use the following procedure to properly bleed the brake hydraulic system including the ABS.

➡ During the brake bleeding procedure, be sure the brake fluid level remains close to the FULL level in the master cylinder fluid reservoir. Check the fluid level periodically during the bleeding procedure and add Mopar®DOT 3 brake fluid as required.

BLEEDING

1. When bleeding the ABS system, the following bleeding sequence must be followed to insure complete and adequate bleeding.

2. Make sure all hydraulic fluid lines are installed and properly torqued.

3. Connect the scan tool to the diagnostics connector. The diagnostic connector is located under the lower steering column cover to the left of the steering column.

4. Using the scan tool, check to make sure the ABM does not have any fault codes stored. If it does, clear them.

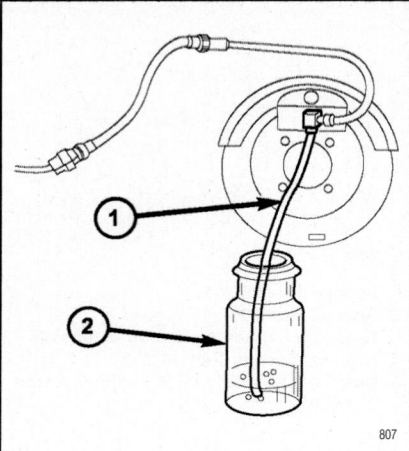

Fig. 10 A clear bleed tube (1) must be attached to the bleeder screws and submerged in a clear container filled part way with clean brake fluid (2)

❊❊ **WARNING**

When bleeding the brake system wear safety glasses. A clear bleed tube must be attached to the bleeder screws and submerged in a clear container filled part way with clean

brake fluid. Direct the flow of brake fluid away from yourself and the painted surfaces of the vehicle.

5. Brake fluid at high pressure may come out of the bleeder screws when opened.

➡ Pressure bleeding is recommended to bleed the base brake system to ensure all air is removed from system. Manual bleeding may also be used, but additional time is needed to remove all air from system.

6. Bleed the base brake system.

7. Using the scan tool, select ECU VIEW, followed by ABS MISCELLANEOUS FUNCTIONS to access bleeding. Follow the instructions displayed. When finished, disconnect the scan tool and proceed.

8. Bleed the base brake system a second time. Check brake fluid level in the reservoir periodically to prevent emptying, causing air to enter the hydraulic system.

9. Fill the master cylinder fluid reservoir to the FULL level.

10. Test drive the vehicle to be sure the brakes are operating correctly and that the brake pedal does not feel spongy.

BRAKES **FRONT DISC BRAKES**

❊❊ **CAUTION**

Dust and dirt accumulating on brake parts during normal use may contain asbestos fibers from production or aftermarket brake linings. Breathing excessive concentrations of asbestos fibers can cause serious bodily harm. Exercise care when servicing brake parts. Do not sand or grind brake lining unless equipment used is designed to contain the dust residue. Do not clean brake parts with compressed air or by dry brushing. Cleaning should be done by dampening the brake components with a fine mist of water, then wiping the brake components clean with a dampened cloth. Dispose of cloth and all residue containing asbestos fibers in an impermeable container with the appropriate label. Follow practices prescribed by the Occupational Safety and Health Administration (OSHA) and the Environmental Protection Agency (EPA) for the handling, processing, and disposing of dust or debris that may contain asbestos fibers.

BRAKE CALIPER

REMOVAL & INSTALLATION

See Figure 11.

1. Using a brake pedal holding tool as shown, depress the brake pedal past its first one inch (25 mm) of travel and hold it in

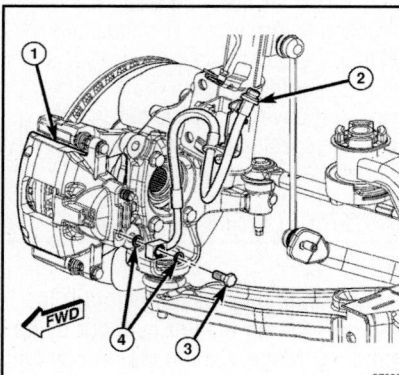

Fig. 11 Remove the banjo bolt (3) connecting the brake flex hose (2) to the brake caliper (1). There are two washers (4) that will come off with the banjo bolt. Discard the washers

this position. This will isolate the master cylinder from the brake hydraulic system and will not allow the brake fluid to drain out of the master cylinder reservoir when the lines are opened.

2. Raise and support the vehicle.

3. Remove the wheel mounting nuts, then the tire and wheel assembly.

4. Remove the banjo bolt connecting the brake flex hose to the brake caliper. There are two washers that will come off with the banjo bolt.

a. Discard the washers.

➡ When removing or installing a caliper guide pin bolt, it is necessary to hold the guide pin stationary while turning the bolt. Hold the guide pin stationary using a wrench placed upon the pin's hex-shaped head.

5. Remove the two brake caliper guide pin bolts.

6. Slide the disc brake caliper from the disc brake adapter bracket and brake pads and remove.

To install:

7. Completely retract the caliper piston back into the bore of the caliper. Use a C-clamp to retract the piston. Place a wood

block over the piston before installing the C-clamp to avoid damaging the piston.

> **⁜ WARNING**
>
> **Use care when installing the caliper onto the adapter bracket to avoid damaging the guide pin boots.**

8. Install the disc brake caliper over the brake pads on the brake caliper adapter bracket.

➡**When removing or installing a caliper guide pin bolt, it is necessary to hold the guide pin stationary while turning the bolt. Hold the guide pin stationary using a wrench placed upon the pin's hex-shaped head.**

9. Align the caliper guide pin bolt holes with the adapter bracket. Install the upper and lower caliper guide pin bolts. Tighten the guide pin bolts to 26 ft. lbs. (35 Nm).

10. Install the banjo bolt connecting the brake flex hose to the brake caliper. Install NEW brake hose washers on each side of the hose fitting as the banjo bolt is guided through the fitting. Thread the banjo bolt into the caliper and tighten it to 18 ft. lbs. (24 Nm).

11. Install the tire and wheel assembly.

12. Install the and tighten the wheel mounting nuts to 100 ft. lbs. (135 Nm).

13. Lower the vehicle.

14. Remove the brake pedal holding tool.

15. Bleed the caliper as necessary.

16. Road test the vehicle and make several stops to wear off any foreign material on the brakes and to seat the brake shoes.

DISC BRAKE PADS

REMOVAL & INSTALLATION

See Figure 12.

1. Raise and support the vehicle.

➡**Perform all steps on each side of the vehicle to complete pad set removal.**

2. Remove the wheel mounting nuts, then the tire and wheel assembly.

➡**When removing or installing a caliper guide pin bolt, it is necessary to hold the guide pin stationary while turning the bolt. Hold the guide pin stationary using a wrench placed upon the pin's hex-shaped head.**

3. Remove the two brake caliper guide pin bolts.

4. Remove the disc brake caliper from the disc brake adapter bracket and hang it out of the way using wire or a bungee cord. Use care not to overextend the brake hose when doing this.

5. Remove the brake pads from the caliper adapter bracket.

To install:

➡**Perform all steps on each side of the vehicle to complete pad set removal.**

➡**Make sure that the audible wear indicator (if equipped) is placed toward the top when the inboard brake pad is installed on each side of the vehicle.**

➡**If the brake pads have a protective paper on the rear face of the brake pad plate, it must be removed before pad installation.**

6. Place the brake pads in the abutment shims clipped into the disc brake caliper adapter bracket. Place the pad with the wear indicator (if equipped) attached on the inboard side.

7. Completely retract the caliper piston back into the bore of the caliper.

➡**Use care when installing the caliper (4) onto the adapter bracket (1) to avoid damaging the boots.**

8. Install the disc brake caliper over the brake pads on the brake caliper adapter bracket.

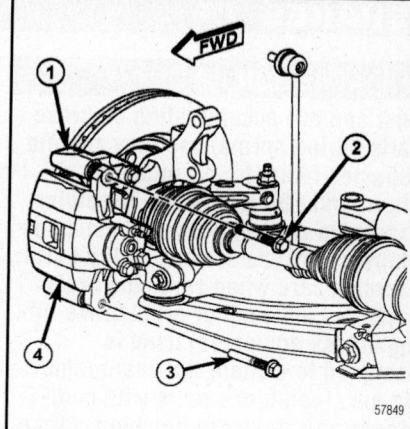

Fig. 12 Remove the two brake caliper guide pin bolts (2, 3). Remove the disc brake caliper (4) from the disc brake adapter bracket (1) and hang it out of the way using wire or a bungee cord.

➡**When removing or installing a caliper guide pin bolt, it is necessary to hold the guide pin stationary while turning the bolt. Hold the guide pin stationary using a wrench placed upon the pin's hex-shaped head.**

9. Align the caliper guide pin bolt holes with the adapter bracket. Install the upper and lower caliper guide pin bolts. Tighten the guide pin bolts to 26 ft. lbs. (35 Nm).

10. Install the tire and wheel assembly.

11. Install the and tighten wheel mounting nuts to 100 ft. lbs. (135 Nm).

12. Lower the vehicle.

13. Pump the brake pedal several times before moving the vehicle to set the pads to the brake rotor.

14. Check and adjust the brake fluid level in the reservoir as necessary.

15. Road test the vehicle and make several stops to wear off any foreign material on the brakes and to seat the brake pads.

BRAKES

✳✳ CAUTION

Dust and dirt accumulating on brake parts during normal use may contain asbestos fibers from production or aftermarket brake linings. Breathing excessive concentrations of asbestos fibers can cause serious bodily harm. Exercise care when servicing brake parts. Do not sand or grind brake lining unless equipment used is designed to contain the dust residue. Do not clean brake parts with compressed air or by dry brushing. Cleaning should be done by dampening the brake components with a fine mist of water, then wiping the brake components clean with a dampened cloth. Dispose of cloth and all residue containing asbestos fibers in an impermeable container with the appropriate label. Follow practices prescribed by the Occupational Safety and Health Administration (OSHA) and the Environmental Protection Agency (EPA) for the handling, processing, and disposing of dust or debris that may contain asbestos fibers.

BRAKE CALIPER

REMOVAL & INSTALLATION

See Figures 13 and 14.

1. Disconnect and isolate battery negative cable from battery post.

2. Using a brake pedal holding tool as shown, depress brake pedal past its first inch of travel and hold it in this position. Holding pedal in this position will isolate master cylinder from hydraulic brake system and will not allow brake fluid to drain out of brake fluid reservoir while brake lines are open.

3. Raise and support vehicle.

4. Remove the wheel mounting nuts, then tire and wheel assembly.

5. Manually release the automatic self-adjusting mechanism tension of the parking brake lever assembly.

Collapse the cable retainer fingers at the end of the cable housing, then pull the cable housing out of the mounting bracket.

6. Slide the cable strand out of the mounting bracket, then pull the parking brake cable strand upward and unhook it from the caliper lever.

7. Remove the banjo bolt connecting the brake flex hose to the brake caliper. There are two washers that will come off with the banjo bolt. Discard the washers. They should not be reused.

➡ When removing or installing a caliper guide pin bolt, it is necessary to hold the guide pin stationary while turning the bolt. Hold the guide pin stationary using a wrench placed upon the pin's hex-shaped head.

8. Remove the two caliper guide pin bolts.

9. Slide the disc brake caliper from the disc brake adapter bracket and brake pads.

To install:

➡ When installing a new brake caliper it is necessary to bleed the brakes using a special procedure which has been integrated to this installation procedure.

10. Remove the outboard pad from the adapter bracket.

➡ Use care when installing the caliper onto the adapter bracket to avoid damaging the guide pin boots.

11. Install the disc brake caliper over the inboard brake pad on the brake caliper adapter bracket and the brake rotor.

➡ When removing or installing a caliper guide pin bolt, it is necessary to hold the guide pin stationary while turning the bolt. Hold the guide pin stationary using a wrench placed upon the pin's hex-shaped head.

12. Align the caliper guide pin bolt holes with the adapter bracket. Install the upper and lower caliper guide pin bolts. Lightly tighten the guide pin bolts at this time.

13. Install the banjo bolt connecting the brake flex hose to the brake caliper. Be sure to install a NEW brake hose washer on each side of the hose fitting as the banjo bolt is guided through the fitting. Thread the banjo bolt into the caliper and tighten it to 18 ft. lbs. (24 Nm).

14. If removed, install the caliper lever return spring between the cable lever and anchor bracket. Do not reconnect cable equalizer at this time.

15. Access the interior of the vehicle, remove the brake pedal holder, then slowly pump the brake pedal until the rear caliper fingers touch the outboard surface of the brake rotor where the brake pad was removed. Release the pedal.

16. Remove the brake caliper lower guide pin bolt.

17. Swing the caliper assembly upward, pivoting off the upper guide pin, until clear of the adapter bracket.

18. Reinstall the outboard pad in the adapter bracket.

19. Open the caliper bleeder screw at least one full turn.

20. Seat (bottom) the caliper piston in the bore as follows:
- Assemble a 3/8 in. drive ratchet handle and an extension.
- Insert the extension through Special Tool.

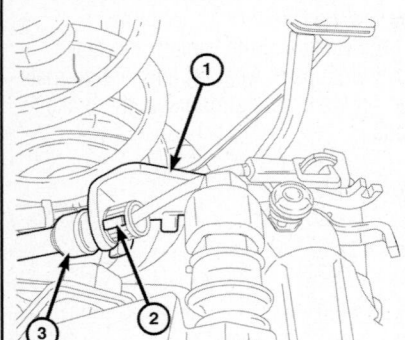

Fig. 13 Collapse the cable retainer fingers (2) at the end of the cable housing (3), then pull the cable housing out of the mounting bracket (1)

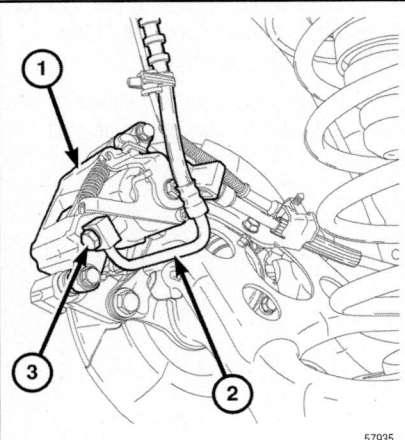

Fig. 14 Remove the banjo bolt (3) connecting the brake flex hose (2) to the brake caliper (1). There are two washers that will come off with the banjo bolt.

21. Place Special Tool on the end of the extension.
- Insert lugs on Special Tool into notches in face of caliper piston.
- Thread the screw drive on down until it contacts the top of which is against the caliper piston.

✳✳ WARNING

Do not over tighten the screw-drive. Damage to the piston can occur.

22. Turn with the ratchet, rotating the piston in a clockwise direction until fully seated (bottomed) in the bore. It may be necessary to turn with to start the process of piston retraction.

23. Close the bleeder screw.

✳✳ WARNING

Use care when installing the caliper onto the adapter bracket to avoid damaging the guide pin boots.

24. Return the brake caliper back down over the adapter bracket into mounted position and install the lower guide pin bolt and lightly tighten.

➡️**While bleeding air from the brake caliper in the following steps, be sure to monitor the fluid level in the master cylinder reservoir making sure it does not go dry. Have a helper pump the brake pedal three or four times and hold it in the down position.**

25. With the pedal in the down position, open the bleeder screw at least one full turn and let out fluid and air, if any.

26. Once the brake pedal has dropped, close the bleeder screw. Once the bleeder screw is closed, release the brake pedal.

27. Repeat the previous three steps as necessary until all trapped air is removed.

28. If necessary, bleed remaining wheel circuits as necessary using normal bleeding procedure.

➡️**When removing or installing a caliper guide pin bolt, it is necessary to hold the guide pin stationary while turning the bolt. Hold the guide pin stationary using a wrench placed upon the pin's hex-shaped head. Tighten both guide pin bolts to 26 ft. lbs. (35 Nm).**

29. Pull the parking brake cable strand outward from the cable housing and hook it onto the caliper lever.

30. Push the excess cable strand back into the cable housing, then insert the cable housing into the mounting bracket until the retainer fingers lock into place. Make sure both fingers are engaged preventing removal of the cable from the bracket.

31. Reconnect the parking brake cable equalizer and reset the automatic self-adjusting mechanism tension of the parking brake lever assembly.

32. Install the tire and wheel assembly.

33. Install the and tighten wheel mounting nuts to 100 ft. lbs. (135 Nm).

34. Lower vehicle.

35. Connect battery negative (-) cable to battery post.

36. Road test vehicle making several stops to wear off any foreign material on brakes and to seat brake pads.

DISC BRAKE PADS

REMOVAL & INSTALLATION

1. Raise and support vehicle.

➡️**Perform all steps on each side of vehicle to complete pad set removal.**

2. Remove the wheel mounting nuts, then tire and wheel assembly.

➡️**When removing or installing a caliper guide pin bolt, it is necessary to hold the guide pin stationary while turning the bolt. Hold the guide pin stationary using a wrench placed upon the pin's hex-shaped head.**

3. Remove the two caliper guide pin bolts.

4. Remove the disc brake caliper from the disc brake adapter bracket and hang it out of the way using wire or a bungee cord. Use care not to overextend the brake hose or parking brake cable when doing this.

5. Prior to pad removal, inspect for freedom of pads to slide on caliper adapter.

6. Remove the brake pads from the caliper adapter bracket.

7. If pads show signs of very uneven wear, and/or pads did not slide easily on adapter, replace adapter bracket. Remove two mounting bolts and remove bracket.

8. If pads did not show signs of very uneven wear, remove and discard old pad shims, and clean abutments (area behind shims) of any debris or corrosion.

To install:

➡️**Perform all steps on each side of vehicle to complete pad set installation.**

✳✳ WARNING

Anytime the brake rotor or brake pads are being replaced, the rear caliper piston must be seated (bottomed) to compensate for the new brake rotor or lining. Because the parking brake self-adjuster mechanism is attached to the piston, a special seating method is required. The only acceptable method is by rotating the piston back into the bore using Retractor, Special Tool Retractor, Rear Caliper Piston, as described below. Any other seating method will damage the self-adjuster mechanism.

9. If necessary, seat (bottom) the caliper piston in the bore as follows:
- Assemble a 3/8 in. drive ratchet handle and an extension.
- Insert the extension through Special.
- Place Special Tool on the end of the extension.
- Insert lugs on Special Tool into notches in face of caliper piston.
- Thread the screw drive on down until it contacts the top of which is against the caliper piston. Do not over tighten the screw-drive. Damage to the piston can occur.
- Turn with the ratchet, rotating the piston in a clockwise direction until fully seated (bottomed) in the bore. It may be necessary to turn with to start the process of piston retraction.

10. If caliper adapter was replaced, install caliper adapter bolts and tighten to 74 ft. lbs. (100 Nm).

➡️**There are two different abutment shims. If installed in wrong orientation, pads will not fit properly.**

➡️**If the brake pads have a protective paper on the rear face of the brake pad plate, it must be removed before pad installation.**

11. Assure adapter abutments are free from debris or corrosion. Apply an even layer of Mopar® Brake Lubricant or equivalent to entire area of four abutments PRIOR to shim installation. Install four new pad shims.

12. Place the brake pads in the abutment shims clipped into the disc brake caliper adapter bracket.

✳✳ WARNING

Use care when installing the caliper onto the adapter bracket to avoid damaging the guide pin boots.

➡️**When removing or installing a caliper guide pin bolt, it is necessary to hold the guide pin stationary while** turning the bolt. Hold the guide pin stationary using a wrench placed upon the pin's hex-shaped head.

13. Install the disc brake caliper over the brake pads on the brake caliper adapter bracket.

14. Align the caliper guide pin bolt holes with the adapter bracket. Install the

upper and lower caliper guide pin bolts. Tighten the guide pin bolts to 26 ft. lbs. (35 Nm).

15. Install the tire and wheel assembly.

16. Install the and tighten wheel mounting nuts to 100 ft. lbs. (135 Nm).

17. Lower vehicle.

18. Pump brake pedal several times to ensure vehicle has a firm brake pedal before moving vehicle.

19. Check and adjust brake fluid level as necessary.

20. Road test vehicle and make several stops to wear off any foreign material on brakes and to seat brake pads.

BRAKES

PARKING BRAKE

PARKING BRAKE CABLES

ADJUSTMENT

The parking brake cables on this vehicle have an automatic self adjuster built into

the park brake pedal mechanism. When the foot operated park brake pedal is in its released (upward most) position, a clockspring automatically adjusts the park brake cables. The park brake cables are

adjusted (tensioned) just enough to remove all the slack from the cables. The automatic adjuster system will not over adjust the cables causing rear brake drag.

CHASSIS ELECTRICAL

AIR BAG (SUPPLEMENTAL RESTRAINT SYSTEM)

GENERAL INFORMATION

✳✳ CAUTION

These vehicles are equipped with an air bag system. The system must be disarmed before performing service on, or around, system components, the steering column, instrument panel components, wiring and sensors. Failure to follow the safety precautions and the disarming procedure could result in accidental air bag deployment, possible injury and unnecessary system repairs.

SERVICE PRECAUTIONS

Disconnect and isolate the battery negative cable before beginning any airbag system component diagnosis, testing, removal, or installation procedures. Allow system capacitor to discharge for two minutes before beginning any component service. This will disable the airbag system. Failure to disable the airbag system may result in accidental airbag deployment, personal injury, or death.

Do not place an intact undeployed airbag face down on a solid surface. The airbag will propel into the air if accidentally deployed and may result in personal injury or death.

When carrying or handling an undeployed airbag, the trim side (face) of the airbag should be pointing towards the body to minimize possibility of injury if accidental deployment occurs. Failure to do this may result in personal injury or death.

Replace airbag system components with

OEM replacement parts. Substitute parts may appear interchangeable, but internal differences may result in inferior occupant protection. Failure to do so may result in occupant personal injury or death.

Wear safety glasses, rubber gloves, and long sleeved clothing when cleaning powder residue from vehicle after an airbag deployment. Powder residue emitted from a deployed airbag can cause skin irritation. Flush affected area with cool water if irritation is experienced. If nasal or throat irritation is experienced, exit the vehicle for fresh air until the irritation ceases. If irritation continues, see a physician.

Do not use a replacement airbag that is not in the original packaging. This may result in improper deployment, personal injury, or death.

The factory installed fasteners, screws and bolts used to fasten airbag components have a special coating and are specifically designed for the airbag system. Do not use substitute fasteners. Use only original equipment fasteners listed in the parts catalog when fastener replacement is required.

During, and following, any child restraint anchor service, due to impact event or vehicle repair, carefully inspect all mounting hardware, tether straps, and anchors for proper installation, operation, or damage. If a child restraint anchor is found damaged in any way, the anchor must be replaced. Failure to do this may result in personal injury or death.

Deployed and non-deployed airbags may or may not have live pyrotechnic material within the airbag inflator.

Do not dispose of driver/passenger/

curtain airbags or seat belt tensioners unless you are sure of complete deployment. Refer to the Hazardous Substance Control System for proper disposal.

Dispose of deployed airbags and tensioners consistent with state, provincial, local, and federal regulations.

After any airbag component testing or service, do not connect the battery negative cable. Personal injury or death may result if the system test is not performed first.

If the vehicle is equipped with the Occupant Classification System (OCS), do not connect the battery negative cable before performing the OCS Verification Test using the scan tool and the appropriate diagnostic information. Personal injury or death may result if the system test is not performed properly.

Never replace both the Occupant Restraint Controller (ORC) and the Occupant Classification Module (OCM) at the same time. If both require replacement, replace one, then perform the Airbag System test before replacing the other.

Both the ORC and the OCM store Occupant Classification System (OCS) calibration data, which they transfer to one another when one of them is replaced. If both are replaced at the same time, an irreversible fault will be set in both modules and the OCS may malfunction and cause personal injury or death.

If equipped with OCS, the Seat Weight Sensor is a sensitive, calibrated unit and must be handled carefully. Do not drop or handle roughly. If dropped or damaged, replace with another sensor. Failure to do so may result in occupant injury or death.

If equipped with OCS, the front passenger seat must be handled carefully as well. When removing the seat, be careful when setting on floor not to drop. If dropped, the sensor may be inoperative, could result in occupant injury, or possibly death.

If equipped with OCS, when the passenger front seat is on the floor, no one should sit in the front passenger seat. This uneven force may damage the sensing ability of the seat weight sensors. If sat on and damaged, the sensor may be inoperative, could result in occupant injury, or possibly death.

DISARMING THE SYSTEM

1. Before servicing the vehicle, refer to the Precautions Section.
2. Turn the ignition switch to **OFF**.
3. Disconnect the negative battery cable and isolate it from accidental reconnection. Insulate the cable end with high-quality electrical tape or a similar non-conductive wrapping.
4. Wait at least 2 minutes for the system capacitor to discharge before performing any service. The airbag system is designed to retain enough voltage to deploy the airbag for a short period of time after the battery has been disconnected.

ARMING THE SYSTEM

1. Before servicing the vehicle, refer to the Precautions Section.
2. Reconnect the negative battery cable.

> **✳✳ CAUTION**
>
> As an added precaution, make sure no one is in the vehicle when reconnecting the negative battery cable.

3. To confirm proper system operation, turn the ignition switch to the **ON** position. The SRS indicator light should light for at least 7 seconds and then go off.

CLOCKSPRING CENTERING

> **✳✳ CAUTION**
>
> To avoid serious or fatal injury on vehicles equipped with airbags, disable the Supplemental Restraint System (SRS) before attempting any steering wheel, steering column, airbag, seat belt tensioner, impact sensor, or instrument panel component diagnosis or service. Disconnect and isolate the battery negative (ground) cable, then wait two minutes for the system capacitor to discharge before performing further diagnosis or service. This is the only sure way to disable the SRS. Failure to take the proper precautions could result in accidental airbag deployment.

➡Always turn the steering wheel until the front wheels are in the straight-ahead position. Then, prior to removing the clockspring from the steering column or disconnecting the steering column from the steering gear, lock the steering wheel to the steering column or securely fasten the clockspring rotor to the clockspring case. If clockspring centering has been compromised for ANY reason, the entire clockspring and Steering Angle Sensor (SAS) unit MUST be replaced with a new unit.

Like the clockspring in a timepiece, the clockspring tape has travel limits and can be damaged by being wound too tightly during full stop-to-stop steering wheel rotation. To prevent this from occurring, the clockspring is centered when it is installed on the steering column. Centering the clockspring indexes the clockspring tape and the SAS integral to the clockspring to the movable steering components so that the tape can operate within its designed travel limits and the SAS can accurately monitor and communicate steering wheel inputs. However, if the clockspring is removed from the steering column or if the steering shaft is disconnected from the steering gear, the clockspring spool and the SAS can change position relative to the movable steering components and relative to each other. The clockspring must be replaced if proper centering has been compromised or the tape may be damaged and Diagnostic Trouble Codes (DTC) or faults may be set within the SAS.

Service replacement clocksprings are shipped pre-centered and with a plastic locking pin installed. This locking pin should not be removed until the clockspring has been installed on the steering column. If the locking pin is removed before the clockspring is installed on a steering column, the clockspring must be replaced with a new unit. Proper clockspring installation must also be confirmed by viewing the SAS Menu Item, Data Display function using a diagnostic scan tool.

DRIVE TRAIN

AUTOMATIC TRANSAXLE FLUID

DRAIN AND REFILL

41TE

See Figure 15.

➡Refer to the maintenance schedules, or the vehicle owner's manual, for the recommended maintenance (fluid/filter change) intervals for this transaxle.

➡Only fluids of the type labeled Mopar®ATF+4 should be used. A filter change should be made at the time of the transmission oil change. The magnet (on the inside of the oil pan) should also be cleaned with a clean, dry cloth.

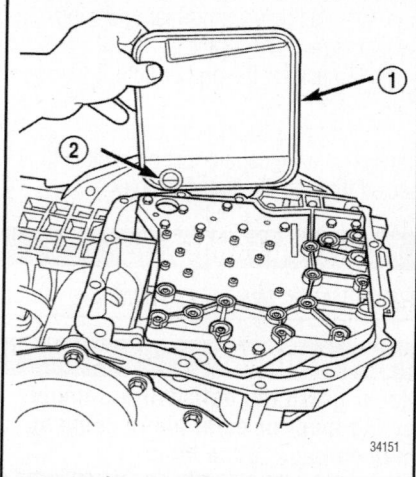

Fig. 15 Transaxle filter (1), and o-ring (2)

34151

➡If the transaxle is disassembled for any reason, the fluid and filter should be changed.

1. Raise vehicle on a hoist. Place a drain container with a large opening, under transaxle oil pan.
2. Remove the both engine mount-to-engine crossmember cradle nuts. Using suitable screw jack and wood block, raise engine and transmission slightly to facilitate transaxle oil pan removal and installation.
3. Loosen pan bolts and tap the pan at one corner to break it loose allowing fluid to drain, then remove the oil pan.
4. Install the a new filter and o-ring on bottom of the valve body.
5. Clean the oil pan and magnet. Reinstall pan using new Mopar Silicone Adhe-

sive sealant. Tighten oil pan bolts to 165 inch lbs. (19 Nm).

6. Pour four Quarts of Mopar®ATF+4 through the dipstick opening.

7. Start engine and allow to idle for at least one minute. Then, with parking and service brakes applied, move selector lever momentarily to each position, ending in the park or neutral position.

8. Check the transaxle fluid level and add an appropriate amount to bring the transaxle fluid level to 3mm (1/8 in.) below the lowest mark on the dipstick.

9. Recheck the fluid level after the transaxle has reached normal operating temperature (180°F.[82°C]). Refer to Fluid Level and Condition

10. Check for the proper fluid fill procedure.

11. To prevent dirt from entering transaxle, make certain that dipstick is fully seated into the dipstick opening.

DIPSTICK TUBE FLUID SUCTION METHOD (ALTERNATIVE)

12. When performing the fluid suction method, make sure the transaxle is at full operating temperature.

13. To perform the dipstick tube fluid suction method, use a suitable fluid suction device (Vacula(tm) or equivalent).

14. Insert the fluid suction line into the dipstick tube.

➡Verify that the suction line is inserted to the lowest point of the transaxle oil pan. This will ensure complete evacuation of the fluid in the pan.

15. Follow the manufacturer's recommended procedure and evacuate the fluid from the transaxle.

16. Remove the suction line from the dipstick tube.

17. Pour four Quarts of Mopar®ATF+4 through the dipstick opening.

18. Start engine and allow to idle for at least one minute. Then, with parking and service brakes applied, move selector lever momentarily to each position, ending in the park or neutral position.

19. Check the transaxle fluid level and add an appropriate amount to bring the transaxle fluid level to 1/8 inch below the lowest mark on the dipstick.

20. Recheck the fluid level after the transaxle has reached normal operating temperature (180°F.[82°C]).

21. To prevent dirt from entering transaxle, make certain that dipstick is fully seated into the dipstick opening.

62TE

➡Refer to the maintenance schedules, or the vehicle owner's manual, for the recommended maintenance (fluid/filter change) intervals for this transaxle.

➡Only fluids of the type labeled MOPAR®ATF+4 should be used. A filter change should be made at the time of the transmission oil change. The magnet (on the inside of the oil pan) should also be cleaned with a clean, dry cloth.

➡If the transaxle is disassembled for any reason, the fluid and filter should be changed.

1. Raise vehicle on a hoist. Place a drain container with a large opening, under transaxle oil pan.

2. Loosen pan bolts and tap the pan at one corner to break it loose allowing fluid to drain, then remove the oil pan.

3. Remove the nuts at the oil filter.

4. Install the a new filter and nuts, tighten to 40 inch lbs. (5 Nm).

5. Install the fluid filter oil pan, use a bead of MOPAR®ATF RTV (MS-GF41).

6. Clean the oil pan and magnet. Reinstall pan using new MOPAR®Silicone Adhesive sealant. Tighten oil pan bolts to 50 inch lbs. (6 Nm).

7. Pour four Quarts of MOPAR®ATF+4 through the dipstick opening.

8. Start engine and allow to idle for at least one minute. Then, with parking and service brakes applied, move selector lever momentarily to each position, ending in the park or neutral position.

9. Check the transaxle fluid level and add an appropriate amount to bring the transaxle fluid level to 3 mm (1/8 in.) below the lowest mark on the dipstick.

10. Recheck the fluid level after the transaxle has reached normal operating temperature 180°F (82°C).

11. Check for the proper fluid fill procedure

12. To prevent dirt from entering transaxle, make certain that dipstick is fully seated into the dipstick opening.

FRONT HALFSHAFT

REMOVAL & INSTALLATION

✳✳ WARNING

Never grasp the halfshaft assembly by the inner or outer boots doing so may damage to the boot.

1. Raise vehicle.

2. Remove the wheel and tire assembly from the vehicle.

3. With the vehicle's brakes applied to keep hub from turning, loosen the halfshaft nut.

4. Remove the nut from the halfshaft.

5. Remove the two front disc brake caliper adapter to steering knuckle attaching bolts.

6. Remove the disc brake caliper assembly from the steering knuckle. Caliper assembly is removed by first rotating top of caliper assembly away from steering knuckle and then removing bottom of assembly out from under machined abutment on steering knuckle.

7. Support disc brake caliper assembly by using a wire hook and suspending it from the strut assembly. Do not allow the brake caliper assembly to hang by the brake flex hose.

8. Remove the brake rotor from the hub and bearing assembly.

9. Remove the steering knuckle-to-strut attachment bolts from the steering knuckle.

10. Pull the steering knuckle from the strut clevis bracket.

➡Care must be taken not to separate the inner C/V joint during this operation. Do not allow halfshaft to hang by inner C/V joint after removing outer C/V Joint from the hub/bearing assembly in steering knuckle, end of halfshaft must be supported.

11. Pull steering knuckle assembly down and away from the outer C/V joint of the half shaft assembly while pulling the joint out of the hub bearing.

12. Support the outer end of the halfshaft assembly. Insert a pry bar between inner tripod joint and transaxle case. Pry against inner tripod joint, until tripod joint retaining snapring is disengaged from transaxle side gear.

13. Pull the steering knuckle from the strut clevis bracket.

14. Pull steering knuckle assembly down and away from the outer C/V joint of the half shaft assembly while pulling the joint out of the intermediate shaft (if equipped) or the transmission.

15. Remove the bolts at the heat shield and remove the heat shield (if equipped).

16. Remove the three bolts holding the mid-shaft bearing to the block.

17. Remove the intermediate shaft.

To install:

18. Install the intermediate shaft into the transaxle.

19. Install the three bolts holding the mid-shaft bearing to the block and tighten to 39ft. lbs. (54 Nm).

20. Install the heat shield and bolts, tighten to 40 inch lbs. (6 Nm) (if equipped).

➡ **A rubber coated washer on the outer CV joint stem us used and should be in place during assembly.**

21. Thoroughly clean spline and oil seal sealing surface, on tripod joint. Lightly lubricate oil seal sealing surface on tripod joint with fresh clean transmission lubricant and install the rubber coated washer.

22. Holding half shaft assembly by tripod joint and interconnecting shaft, install tripod joint into transaxle side gear as far as possible by hand. Be sure to engage splines prior to applying force.

23. Forcefully push the tripod joint onto intermediate shaft, until snap-ring is engaged.

24. Clean all debris and moisture out of steering knuckle, in the area were outer CV joint will be installed into steering knuckle.

25. Ensure that front of outer CV joint which fits against the face of the hub and bearing is free of debris and moisture before installing outer CV joint into hub and bearing assembly.

26. Slide half shaft back into front hub and bearing assembly.

➡ **The steering knuckle to strut assembly attaching bolts are serrated and must not be turned during installation. Install nuts while holding bolts stationary in the steering knuckle.**

➡ **If the vehicle being serviced is equipped with eccentric strut assembly attaching bolts, the eccentric bolt must be installed in the bottom (slotted) hole on the strut clevis bracket.**

27. Install the steering knuckle in clevis bracket of strut damper assembly. Install the strut damper to steering knuckle attaching bolts. Tighten both bolts to a torque of 65 ft. lbs. (88 Nm) plus an additional 1/4 turn.

28. Install the braking disc on hub and bearing assembly.

29. Install the disc brake caliper assembly on steering knuckle. Caliper is installed by first sliding bottom of caliper assembly under abutment on steering knuckle, and then rotating top of caliper against top abutment.

30. Install the disc brake caliper adapter to steering knuckle attaching bolts. Tighten the disc brake caliper adapter attaching bolts to a torque of 125 ft. lbs. (169 Nm).

➡ **Always install a new hub nut. The original hub nut is one-time use only and should be discarded when removed.**

31. Clean all foreign matter from the threads of the outer CV joint. Install the half shaft to hub/bearing assembly nut on half shaft and securely tighten nut.

32. Install the front wheel and tire assembly. Install and tighten the wheel mounting stud nuts in proper sequence until all nuts are torqued to half the required specification. Then repeat the tightening sequence to the full specified torque of 100 ft. lbs. (135 Nm).

33. Lower vehicle.

34. With the vehicle's brakes applied to keep hub from turning, tighten the hub nut to a torque of 118 ft. lbs. (160 Nm).

35. Check for correct fluid level in transaxle assembly.

ENGINE COOLING

ENGINE COOLANT

DRAIN & REFILL PROCEDURE

Draining

See Figure 16.

❋❋ CAUTION

Do not remove or loosen the coolant pressure cap, cylinder block drain plugs, or the draincock when the system is hot and under pressure because serious burns from the coolant can occur.

1. Make sure the system is not pressurized. Without removing radiator pressure cap, use a screwdriver to open the draincock. The draincock is located on the lower left side of radiator.

➡ **DO NOT WASTE reusable coolant. If solution is clean, drain coolant into a clean container for reuse.**

2. After the coolant recovery/reserve container is empty, then remove coolant pressure cap.

3. Remove the cylinder block drain plug(s).

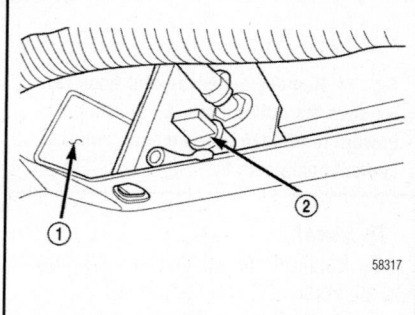

Fig. 16 Left-side frame rail (1), and draincock (2) location

Filling

1. Remove the radiator pressure cap and fill system, using 50/50 mixture of the appropriate fluid and distilled water.

2. Continue filling system until full. Do not spill coolant on drive belts or the generator. For cooling system capacity,

3. Fill coolant recovery/reserve container to at least the MAX mark. It may be necessary to add coolant to the recovery/reserve container after three or four warm up/cool down cycles to maintain coolant level between the MAX and MIN mark. This will allow trapped air to be removed from the system.

CLEANING/REVERSE FLUSHING

CLEANING

1. Drain the cooling system and refill with water. Run the engine with the radiator cap installed until the upper radiator hose is hot. Stop the engine and drain the water from system. If the water is dirty, fill the system with water, run the engine and drain the system. Repeat this procedure until the water drains clean.

REVERSE FLUSHING

2. Reverse flushing of the cooling system is the forcing of water through the cooling system. This is done using air pressure in the opposite direction of normal coolant flow. It is usually only necessary with very dirty systems with evidence of partial plugging.

REVERSE FLUSHING RADIATOR

3. Disconnect the radiator hoses from the radiator inlet and outlet. Attach a section of the radiator hose to the radiator bottom outlet fitting and insert the flushing gun. Connect a water supply hose and air supply hose to the flushing gun.

❋❋ WARNING

Internal radiator pressure must not exceed 20 psi as damage to radiator may result.

4. Allow the radiator to fill with water. When the radiator is filled, apply air in short blasts. Allow the radiator to refill between blasts. Continue this reverse flushing until clean water flows out through the rear of the radiator cooling tube passages.

REVERSE FLUSHING ENGINE

5. Drain the cooling system. Remove the thermostat housing and thermostat. Install the thermostat housing. Disconnect the radiator upper hose from the radiator and attach the flushing gun to the hose. Disconnect the radiator lower hose from the water pump and attach a lead-away hose to the water pump inlet fitting.

➡ **On vehicles equipped with a heater water control valve, be sure the heater control valve is closed (heat off). This will prevent coolant flow with scale and other deposits from entering the heater core.**

6. Connect the water supply hose and air supply hose to flushing gun. Allow the engine to fill with water. When the engine is filled, apply air in short blasts, allowing the system to fill between air blasts. Continue until clean water flows through the lead away hose.

7. Remove the lead away hose, flushing gun, water supply hose and air supply hose. Remove the thermostat housing and install the thermostat. Install the thermostat housing with a replacement gasket. Refer to Thermostat Replacement. Connect the radiator hoses. Refill the cooling system with the correct antifreeze/water mixture.

CHEMICAL CLEANING

8. In some instances, use a radiator cleaner (Mopar® Radiator Kleen or equivalent) before flushing. This will soften scale and other deposits and aid flushing operation.

➡ **Follow manufacturer's instructions when using these products.**

ENGINE FAN

REMOVAL & INSTALLATION

See Figures 17 and 18.

1. Disconnect and isolate negative battery cable.
2. Drain cooling system below upper radiator hose.
3. Remove the coolant recovery container.
4. Disconnect fan motor electrical connection.
5. Remove the upper radiator hose.
6. Remove the radiator fan by lifting upward to release from mounts.

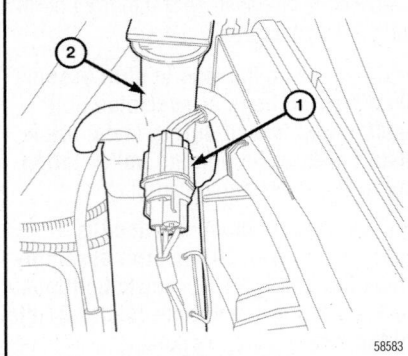

Fig. 17 Remove coolant recovery container (2). Disconnect fan motor electrical connection (1).

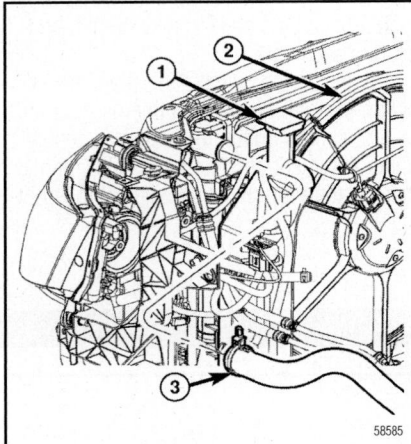

Fig. 18 Remove upper radiator hose (3). Remove the radiator fan (2) by lifting upward to release from mounts, and the coolant container (1).

To install:

7. Position the radiator fan into mounts and attaching clips on the radiator.
8. Connect the radiator fan electrical connectors.
9. Install the upper radiator hose.
10. Install the coolant recovery container.
11. Fill cooling system.

RADIATOR

REMOVAL & INSTALLATION

1. Disconnect negative cable from battery.
2. Drain the cooling system.
3. Remove the coolant recovery container.
4. Remove the radiator fan.
5. Remove the upper and lower radiator hoses.
6. Remove the grill.

7. Remove the upper radiator crossmember and position out of way.
8. Remove the screw that secures the condenser taping block to the radiator located in the right corner of the engine compartment.
9. Disengage the condenser retaining tabs
10. Disengage the radiator retaining tabs.
11. Lift radiator out of vehicle.

To install:

12. Be sure the air seal is in position before radiator is installed. Slide radiator down into position. Seat the radiator with the rubber isolators into the mounting holes provided, with a 10 lbs. force.
13. Position air conditioning condenser onto the radiator lower mounts and engage upper mounting tabs.
14. Install the radiator upper and lower hoses.
15. Connect the coolant recovery hose.
16. Connect the vapor purge solenoid to the mounting bracket.
17. Install the radiator fans.
18. Install the radiator upper crossmember support.
19. Fill the cooling system.
20. Connect negative cable to battery.

THERMOSTAT

REMOVAL & INSTALLATION

3.3L & 3.8L Engines

See Figures 19 and 20.

1. Drain cooling system down below the thermostat level.
2. Remove the radiator upper hose from coolant outlet connector.
3. Remove the coolant outlet connector bolts and connector.
4. Remove the thermostat from outlet connector.

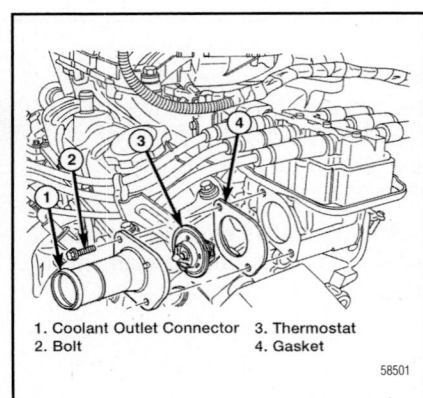

1. Coolant Outlet Connector   3. Thermostat
2. Bolt   4. Gasket

Fig. 19 Thermostat components location

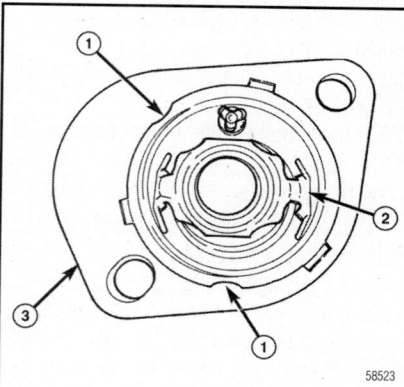

Fig. 20 Position thermostat to coolant outlet connector (3). Align the two locating notches (1) on thermostat (2) to the connector. This position will ensure proper location of the thermostat air bleed

5. Discard gasket and clean both gasket sealing surfaces.

To install:

6. To ensure proper seating of replacement thermostat, carefully remove the bulged metal from the wall of the outlet connector recess that was created during the staking procedure that held the OEM thermostat in place. It is not necessary to restake the replacement thermostat into the connector.

7. Position thermostat to coolant outlet connector. Align the two locating notches on thermostat to the connector. This position will ensure proper location of the thermostat air bleed.

8. Position a new gasket over the thermostat and connector making sure thermostat is in proper position and in the recess provided.

9. Install the thermostat and connector assembly to the intake manifold. Tighten bolts to '105 inch lbs. (12 Nm).

10. Install the radiator upper hose to coolant outlet connector.

11. Refill the cooling system.

3.6L Engine

> **⁜ CAUTION**
>
> **Do not loosen radiator draincock with system hot and pressurized. Serious burns from coolant can occur.**

> **⁜ WARNING**
>
> **The Thermostat and housing is serviced as an assembly. Do not remove the thermostat from the housing, damage to the thermostat may occur.**

Do not waste reusable coolant. If solution is clean, drain coolant into a clean container for reuse.

If thermostat is being replaced, be sure that replacement is specified thermostat for vehicle model and engine type.

1. Disconnect negative battery cable at battery.

2. Remove the air intake assembly.

3. Drain cooling system.

4. Remove the upper radiator hose clamp and upper radiator hose at thermostat housing.

5. Remove the thermostat housing mounting bolts, thermostat housing and thermostat.

To install:

> **⁜ WARNING**
>
> **The Thermostat and housing is serviced as an assembly. Do not remove the thermostat from the housing, damage to the thermostat may occur.**

6. Clean mating areas of timing chain cover and thermostat housing.

7. Install the a new gasket on to the thermostat housing.

8. Position thermostat housing on the water crossover.

9. Install the two thermostat housing bolts. Tighten bolts to 106 inch lbs. (12 Nm).

10. Install the upper radiator hose on thermostat housing.

11. Fill cooling system.

12. Install the air intake system.

13. Connect negative battery cable to battery.

14. Start and warm the engine. Check for leaks.

4.0L Engine

See Figure 21.

> **⁜ CAUTION**
>
> **Do not remove pressure cap with the system hot and under pressure because serious burns from coolant can occur.**

1. Disconnect negative battery cable.

2. Drain cooling system.

3. Disconnect radiator upper hose from thermostat housing.

4. Remove the thermostat housing bolts.

5. Remove the housing, thermostat, and gasket.

To install:

6. Clean gasket sealing surfaces.

7. Install the thermostat and gasket into thermostat housing. For ease of installation,

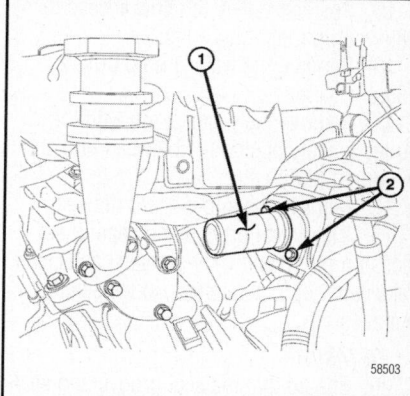

Fig. 21 Disconnect radiator upper hose from thermostat housing (1). Remove thermostat housing bolts (2).

install bolts in housing for thermostat and gasket retention.

8. Install the thermostat and housing to Intake manifold. Tighten the bolts to 105 inch lbs. (12 Nm).

9. Connect radiator hoses and install hose clamp.

10. Refill cooling system.

11. Connect negative battery cable.

WATER PUMP

REMOVAL & INSTALLATION

3.3L & 3.8L Engines

1. Disconnect the negative battery cable.

2. Raise vehicle.

3. Drain the cooling system.

4. Remove the right front wheel and inner shield.

5. Remove the accessory drive belt as outlined in the Engine Mechanical Section.

6. Remove the vibration dampener.

7. Lower vehicle.

8. Remove the air cleaner assembly and the intake duct.

➡ **When using a jack. Use a piece of wood or a thick piece of rubber on the jack so damage will come to the underside of the engine.**

9. Support the engine with a jack.

10. Remove the right side engine mount assembly by removing the frame side bolts and the engine side bolts.

11. Raise the engine.

12. Remove the idler pulley.

13. Remove the water pump pulley bolts.

14. Rotate pulley until openings in pulley align with water pump drive hub spokes. Move pulley inward between pump housing and hub.

15. Position pulley to allow access to water pump mounting bolts.

16. Remove the water pump pulley bolts.

17. Remove the water pump with the pulley loosely positioned between hub and the pump body.

18. Remove the and discard the seal.

19. Clean seal groove and sealing surfaces on pump and timing chain case cover. Take care not to scratch or gouge sealing surfaces.

To install:

20. Ensure that the seal groove and sealing surfaces are clean and free of debris.

21. Install the new seal onto water pump housing groove.

➡**The water pump pulley MUST be positioned loosely between the pump housing and drive hub BEFORE water pump installation.**

22. Position the water pump pulley loosely between pump housing and drive hub.

23. Install the water pump and pulley to the timing chain case cover. Tighten water pump bolts to 108 inch lbs. (12 Nm).

24. Position pulley on water pump hub. Install bolts and tighten to 21 ft. lbs. (28 Nm).

25. Rotate pump by hand to check for freedom of movement.

26. Install the idler pulley. Tighten bolt to 21 ft. lbs. (28 Nm).

27. Lower the engine.

28. Align the engine mount and install the engine side bolts. Tighten bolt to 45 ft. lbs. (61 Nm).

29. Install the frame side bolts. Tighten bolt to 40 ft. lbs. (54 Nm).

30. Install the air intake duct and the air filter housing assembly.

31. Raise vehicle.

32. Install the vibration dampener.

33. Install the accessory drive belt as outlined in the Engine Mechanical Section.

34. Install the drive belt shield.

35. Install the right wheel.

36. Lower vehicle.

37. Evacuate air and refill cooling system.

38. Check cooling system for leaks.

3.6L Engine

See Figure 22.

1. The water pump is bolted directly to the engine timing chain case cover.

2. Disconnect negative battery cable from battery.

✳✳ CAUTION

Constant tension hose clamps are used on most cooling system hoses. When removing or installing, use only tools designed for servicing this type of clamp. Always wear safety glasses when servicing constant tension clamps.

➡**A number or letter is stamped into the tongue of constant tension clamps. If replacement is necessary, use only an original equipment clamp with matching number or letter.**

3. Support the engine with a jack.

4. Remove the air filter housing assembly and intake tube to throttle body.

5. Remove the power steering reservoir and position aside.

6. Remove the right side engine mount assembly.

7. Remove the engine mounting block from the water pump.

8. Raise vehicle.

✳✳ WARNING

Do not pry on the water pump at the timing chain case/cover. The machined surfaces may be damaged resulting in leaks.

9. Remove the accessory drive belt as outlined in the Engine Mechanical Section.

10. Remove the accessory drive belt idler pulley.

11. If equipped, remove the lower engine cover.

12. Drain coolant into clean container for reuse.

13. Remove the right front wheel.

14. Remove the inner splash shield.

15. Remove the lower bypass hose and the lower radiator hose from the water pump and position aside.

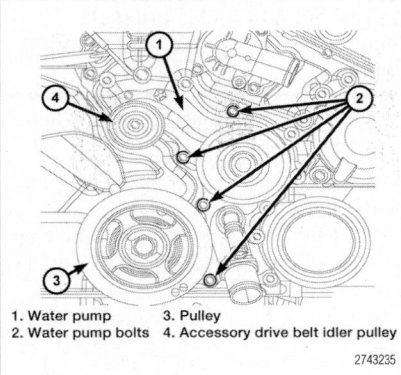

1. Water pump   3. Pulley
2. Water pump bolts   4. Accessory drive belt idler pulley

2743235

Fig. 22 Water pump removal

16. Remove the twelve water pump mounting bolts. Take notice to the four water pump bolts that mount directly to the timing chain cover.

17. Remove the water pump and discard seal.

To install:

The water pump is bolted directly to the engine timing chain case cover.

Clean the mating surfaces.

Using a new seal, position water pump and install mounting bolts. Note the shorter bolts bolt directly to the timing cover. Tighten the M6 water pump mounting bolts to 106 inch lbs. (12 Nm).

Spin water pump to be sure that pump impeller does not rub against timing chain case/cover.

18. Install the lower radiator hose and the bypass hose.

19. Install the idler pulley. Tighten mounting bolt to 18 ft. lbs. (25 Nm).

✳✳ WARNING

When installing the serpentine accessory drive belt, belt must be routed correctly. If not, engine may overheat due to water pump rotating in wrong direction.

20. Install the accessory drive belt as outlined in the Engine Mechanical Section.

21. Install the right inner splash shield.

22. Install the right front wheel.

23. Lower the vehicle.

24. Position jack under engine.

25. Install the engine mount block. Tighten the M8 mounting bolt to 18 ft. lbs. (25 Nm). Tighten the M10 mounting bolt to 41 ft. lbs. (55 Nm).

26. Install the engine mount. Tighten mounting bolt to the engine block to 45 ft. lbs. (61 Nm).

27. Install the air intake assembly.

28. Evacuate air and refill cooling system.

29. Connect negative battery cable.

30. Check the cooling system for leaks.

4.0L Engine

See Figure 23.

1. Drain cooling system.

➡**The water pump is driven by the timing belt.**

2. Remove the engine timing belt as outlined in the Engine Mechanical Section.

3. Remove the water pump mounting

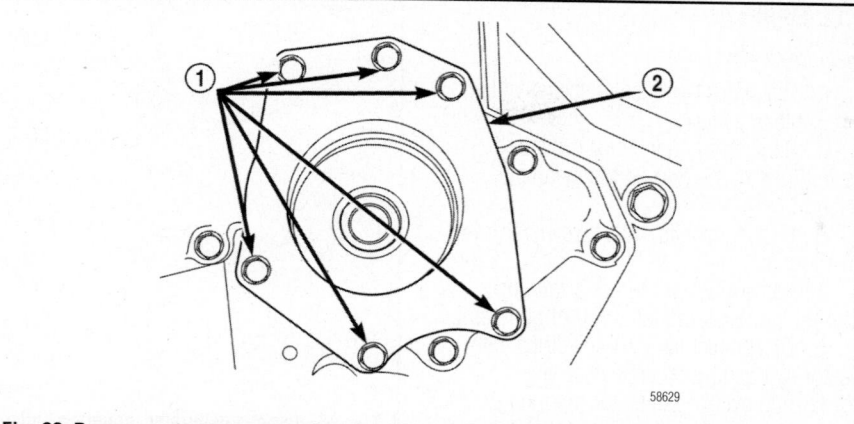

Fig. 23 Remove water pump mounting bolts (1). Note position of the longer bolt for proper re-installation. Remove water pump body (2) from engine

bolts. Note position of the longer bolt for proper re-installation.

4. Remove the water pump body from engine.

To install:

5. Clean all O-ring surfaces on pump and cover.

6. Apply Mopar® Dielectric Grease or the equivalent silicone grease to the O-ring to facilitate assembly. Install new O-ring on water pump.

7. Position water pump to engine.

8. Install the mounting bolts and tighten to 108 inch lbs. (12 Nm).

9. Install the timing belt.

10. Evacuate air and refill cooling system.

11. Check cooling system for leaks.

ENGINE ELECTRICAL

ALTERNATOR

REMOVAL & INSTALLATION

3.3L & 3.8L Engines

See Figures 24 and 25.

1. Disconnect and isolate negative battery cable at battery.

2. Remove the generator drive belt as outlined in the Engine Mechanical Section.

3. Unsnap plastic protective cover from B+ mounting stud.

4. Remove the B+ terminal mounting nut and B+ terminal at top of generator.

5. Disconnect field wire electrical connector by pushing on connector tab.

6. Remove the alternator bracket bolt.

7. Remove the alternator bracket nut and bracket.

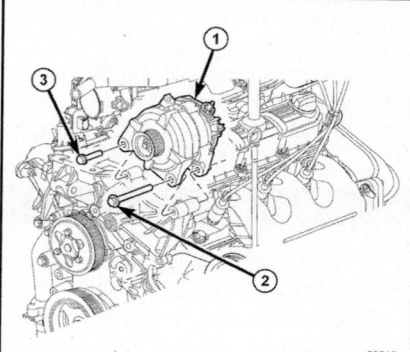

Fig. 25 Remove generator mounting bolts (2) and (3). Remove generator (1) from vehicle.

8. Remove the generator mounting bolts and.

9. Remove the generator from vehicle.

To install:

10. Position generator to engine and install two mounting bolts. Tighten both bolts to 40 ft. lbs. (54 Nm).

11. Install the alternator bracket to the alternator and stud.

12. Install the alternator bracket nut and tighten to 21 ft. lbs. (28 Nm).

13. Install the alternator bracket bolt and tighten to 21 ft. lbs. (28 Nm).

14. Connect field wire connector into generator.

15. Install the B+ terminal and nut to generator mounting stud. Tighten nut to 115 inch lbs. (13 Nm)

16. Snap plastic protective cover to B+ terminal.

17. Install the drive belt as outlined in the Engine Mechanical Section.

CHARGING SYSTEM

18. Connect the negative battery cable, tighten the nut to 45 inch lbs. (5 Nm).

3.6L Engine

See Figures 26 and 27.

1. Disconnect the negative batter cable.

2. Remove the air cleaner body.

3. Remove the cooling fan.

4. Remove the serpentine belt as outlined in the Engine Mechanical Section.

5. Disconnect the generator field electrical connector.

6. Remove the B+ retainer and remove the B+ cable.

7. Remove the generator retainers.

8. Remove the generator.

To install:

9. Place the generator to the engine and install the retainers.

10. Tighten the generator mounting retainers to 18.4 ft. lbs. (25 Nm).

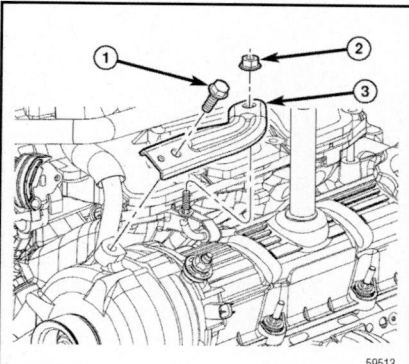

Fig. 24 Remove alternator bracket bolt (1). Remove alternator bracket nut (2) and bracket (3).

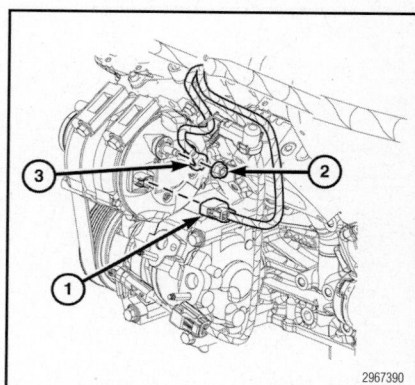

Fig. 26 Disconnect the generator field electrical connector (1). Remove the B+ retainer (2) and remove the B+ cable (3).

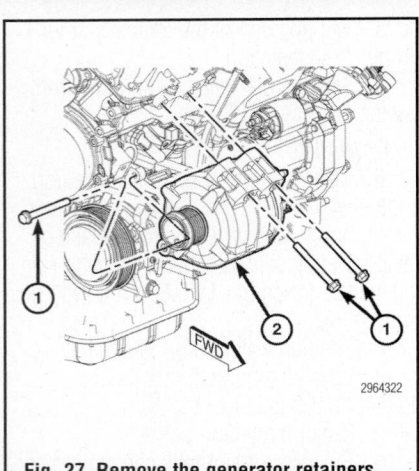

Fig. 27 Remove the generator retainers (1). Remove the generator (2).

11. Install the B+ cable and retainer. Tighten the B+ retainer to 114 inch lbs. (13 Nm).

12. Install the generator field connector.

13. Install the serpentine belt.

14. Install the cooling fan.

15. Install the air cleaner body.

16. Connect the negative battery cable.

4.0L Engine

See Figure 28.

1. Disconnect and isolate negative battery cable at battery.

2. Remove the generator drive belt as outlined in the Engine Mechanical Section.

3. Unsnap plastic protective cover from B+ mounting stud.

4. Remove the B+ terminal mounting nut and B+ terminal at top of generator.

5. Disconnect field wire electrical connector by pushing on connector tab.

6. Remove the generator mounting bolts and.

7. Remove the generator from vehicle.

To install:

8. Position generator to engine and install two mounting bolts. Tighten bolts to 40 ft. lbs. (54 Nm).

9. Connect field wire connector into generator.

10. Install the B+ terminal and nut to generator mounting stud. Tighten nut to 115 inch lbs. (13 Nm)

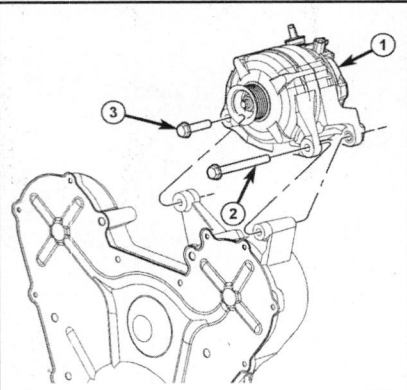

Fig. 28 Remove generator mounting bolts (2) and (3). Remove generator (1) from vehicle.

11. Snap plastic protective cover to B+ terminal.

12. Install the drive belt as outlined in the Engine Mechanical Section.

13. Connect the negative battery cable, tighten the nut to 45 inch lbs. (5 Nm).

ENGINE ELECTRICAL

FIRING ORDER

The firing order is: 1-2-3-4-5-6

IGNITION COIL

REMOVAL & INSTALLATION

3.3L & 3.8L Engines

See Figure 29.

1. Disconnect and isolate the negative battery cable at battery.

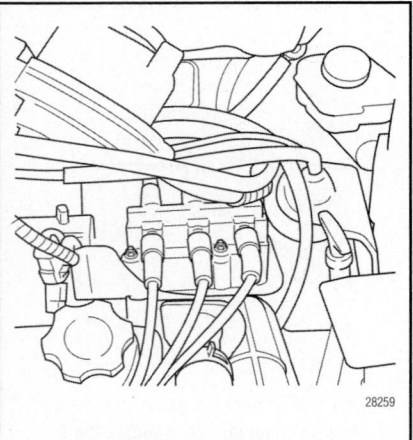

Fig. 29 Ignition coil bracket

2. Remove the 2 bolts from the Power steering reservoir to intake manifold.

3. Loosen the lower nut for the power steering reservoir from stud on ignition coil bracket.

4. Reposition the power steering reservoir.

5. Remove the ignition cables from the ignition coil.

6. Disconnect the electrical connector from the ignition coil.

7. Remove the 2 nuts from the ignition coil studs.

8. Remove the ignition coil from engine.

To install:

9. Install the coil over studs on bracket.

10. Install the 2 nuts to the ignition coil studs and tighten nuts.

11. Connect the electrical connector to the ignition coil.

12. Install the ignition cables to the ignition coil.

13. Reposition the power steering reservoir. Slide bracket over the mounting stud.

14. Install the 2 bolts to the Power steering reservoir to intake manifold.

15. Tighten the lower nut to stud on ignition coil bracket.

16. Connect negative battery cable and tighten nut to 45 inch lbs. (5 Nm).

IGNITION SYSTEM

3.6L Engine

See Figures 30 through 32.

1. Disconnect and isolate the negative battery cable.

2. If removing the ignition coils from cylinders 1 and 3 on the RH side of the engine, first remove the resonator.

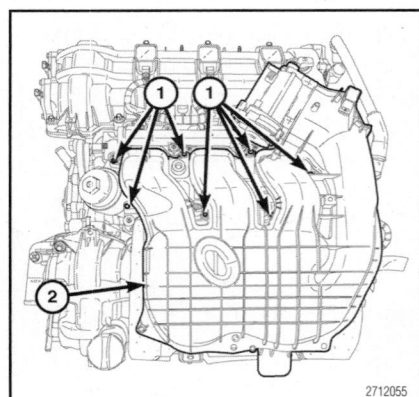

Fig. 30 If removing the ignition coils from cylinders 1 and 3 on the RH side of the engine, first remove the resonator (1). If removing the ignition coils from cylinders 2, 4 or 6 on the LH side of the engine, first remove the upper intake manifold (2) and insulator.

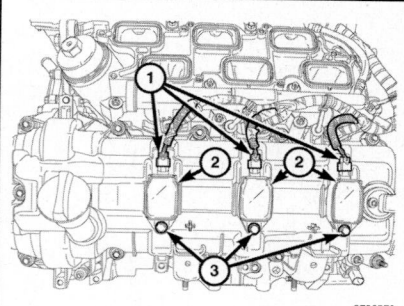

Fig. 31 Unlock and disconnect the electrical connector (1) from the ignition coil. Remove the ignition coil mounting bolt (3). Pull the ignition coil (2) from cylinder head cover opening with a slight twisting action. The LH ignition coils are shown, the RH ignition coils are similar

3. If removing the ignition coils from cylinders 2, 4 or 6 on the LH side of the engine, first remove the upper intake manifold (2) and insulator.

4. Unlock and disconnect the electrical connector from the ignition coil.

5. Remove the ignition coil mounting bolt.

6. Pull the ignition coil from cylinder head cover opening with a slight twisting action.

To install:

7. Using compressed air, blow out any dirt or contaminants from around the top of spark plug.

8. Check the condition of the ignition coil rubber boot. Inspect the opening of the boot for any debris, tears or rips. Carefully remove any debris with a lint free cloth.

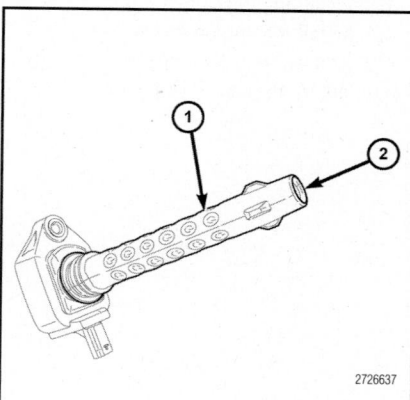

Fig. 32 Check the condition of the ignition coil rubber boot (1). Inspect the opening of the boot (2) for any debris, tears or rips

❊❊ WARNING
Do not apply a silicone based grease such as Mopar®Dielectric Grease to the ignition coil rubber boot. The silicone based grease will absorb into the boot causing it to stick and tear.

9. Place a small, 360°bead of Fluostar 2LF lubricant along the inside opening of the coil boot approximately 1 to 2 mm from the chamfer edge but not on the chamfered surface.

10. Position the ignition coil into the cylinder head cover opening. Using a twisting action, push the ignition coil onto the spark plug.

11. Install the ignition coil mounting bolt and tighten to 71 inch lbs. (8 Nm).

12. Connect and lock the electrical connector to the ignition coil.

13. If removed, install the insulator, upper intake manifold and air inlet hose.

14. Connect the negative battery cable and tighten nut to 45 inch lbs. (5 Nm).

4.0L Engine
See Figure 33.

1. Disconnect and isolate the negative battery cable at battery.

2. Remove the intake manifold as outlined in the Engine Mechanical Section.

➡**Prior to removing coil, spray compressed air around coil top to make sure no dirt drops into the spark plug tube.**

3. Disconnect electrical connector from ignition coils.

4. Remove the mounting bolt.

5. Remove the ignition coil assembly by turning the assembly 1/2 turn and pulling straight up in a steady motion.

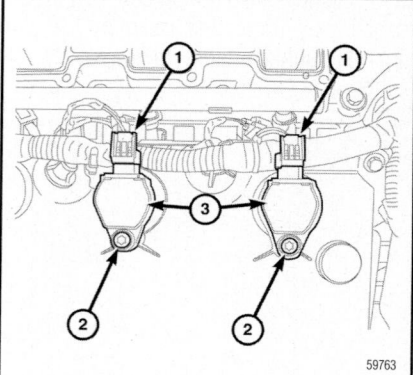

Fig. 33 Disconnect electrical connector (1) from ignition coils (3). Remove mounting bolt (2). Remove the ignition coil assembly (3)

To install:
6. Install the ignition coil and bolt. Tighten bolt to 71 inch lbs. (8 Nm).

7. Connect the electrical connector to ignition coil.

8. Install the intake manifold as outlined in the Engine Mechanical Section.

9. Connect negative battery cable and tighten nut to 45 inch lbs. (5 Nm).

IGNITION TIMING

ADJUSTMENT

The Ignition Timing is adjusted by the Powertrain Control (PCM) Module.

SPARK PLUGS

REMOVAL & INSTALLATION

3.3L & 3.8L Engines

When replacing the spark plugs and spark plug cables, route the cables correctly and secure them in the appropriate retainers. Failure to route the cables properly can cause the radio to reproduce ignition noise, cross ignition of the spark plugs or short circuit the cables to ground. Always remove cables by grasping at the boot, rotating the boot 1/2 turn, and pulling straight back in a steady motion.

1. Prior to removing the spark plug, spray compressed air around the spark plug hole and the area around the spark plug.

2. Remove the spark plug using a quality socket with a foam insert.

3. Inspect the spark plug condition.

To install:

➡**When replacing spark plugs and ignition cables, route cables correctly and secure in appropriate retainers. Failure to route ignition cables properly can cause the radio to reproduce noise, cross ignition of the spark plugs or short circuit the cables to ground.**

➡**Do not over apply anti-seize compound. Only use enough to lightly coat threads on the spark plug.**

4. Apply a small amount of anti-seize to threads of each spark plug.

5. Check and adjust spark plug gap.

➡**Start each spark plug by hand to avoid cross threading and plug damage, use a quality socket with a rubber insert and start each spark plug into the cylinder head by hand.**

6. Install the spark plug and tighten to 13 ft. lbs. (17.5 Nm).

7. Install the ignition cables over spark

plugs. An audible click noise can be heard and felt when the ignition cable is properly attached to spark plug.

3.6L Engine

See Figure 34.

1. Remove the ignition coil.
2. Prior to removing the spark plug, spray compressed air into the cylinder head opening. This will help prevent foreign material from entering combustion chamber.

✵✵ WARNING

The spark plug tubes are a thin wall design. Avoid damaging the spark plug tubes. Damage to the spark plug tube can result in oil leaks.

3. Remove the spark plug from the cylinder head using a quality thin wall socket with a rubber or foam insert.
4. Inspect the spark plug condition.

To install:

5. Check and adjust the spark plug gap with a gap gauging tool.

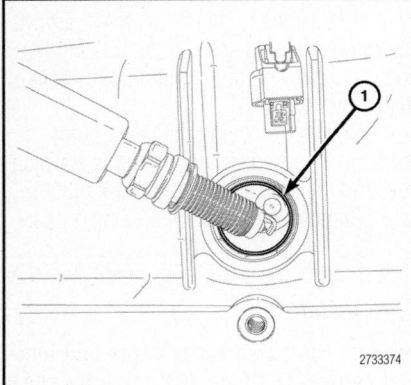

Fig. 34 The spark plug tubes (1) are a thin wall design. Avoid damaging the spark plug tubes. Damage to the spark plug tube can result in oil leaks.

✵✵ WARNING

Special care should be taken when installing spark plugs into the cylinder head spark plug wells. Be sure the plugs do not drop into the plug wells as electrodes can be damaged.

✵✵ WARNING

The spark plug tubes are a thin wall design. Avoid damaging the spark plug tubes. Damage to the spark plug tube can result in oil leaks.

6. Start the spark plug into the cylinder head by hand to avoid cross threading.

✵✵ WARNING

Spark plug torque is critical and must not exceed the specified value. Overtightening stretches the spark plug shell reducing its heat transfer capability resulting in possible catastrophic engine failure. Tighten the spark plugs to 13 ft. lbs. (17.5 Nm).

7. Install the ignition coil.

4.0L Engine

See Figure 35.

1. Disconnect and isolate the negative battery cable.
2. Remove the engine cover.
3. Remove the intake manifold.

➡**Prior to removing coil, spray compressed air around coil top to make sure no debris drops into the spark plug tube.**

4. Disconnect electrical connectors.
5. Remove the mounting bolt.
6. Remove the ignition coil assembly by turning the assembly 1/2 turn and pulling straight up in a steady motion.

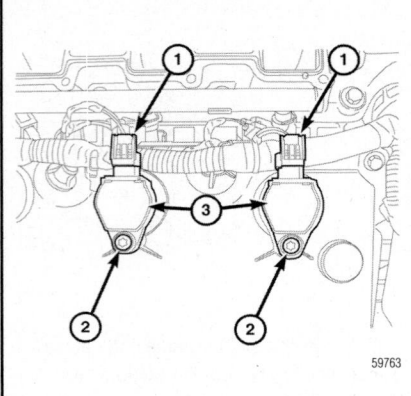

Fig. 35 Disconnect electrical connectors (1), mounting bolt (2), and the ignition coil assembly (3)

➡**Prior to loosening the spark plug, use compressed air to blow out any debris that might be in the spark plug tube.**

7. Remove the spark plug using a quality socket with a foam insert.

To install:

✵✵ WARNING

Start each spark plug by hand to avoid cross threading and plug damage, use a quality socket with a rubber insert and start each spark plug into the cylinder head by hand.

8. Tighten spark plugs to 20 ft. lbs. (27 Nm).
9. Install the ignition coil and bolt. Tighten bolt to 71 inch lbs. (8 Nm).
10. Connect electrical connector to ignition coil.
11. Install the intake manifold.
12. Install the engine cover.
13. Connect negative battery cable and tighten nut to 45 inch (5 Nm).

ENGINE ELECTRICAL   **BATTERY SYSTEM**

BATTERY

REMOVAL & INSTALLATION

See Figure 36.

> ✳✳ **CAUTION**
>
> To protect eyes from battery acid, a suitable pair of industrial grade safety glasses, should be worn when removing or servicing a battery.

> ✳✳ **CAUTION**
>
> To protect the hands from battery acid, a suitable pair of industrial grade heavy duty rubber gloves, should be worn when removing or servicing a battery. Safety glasses also should be worn.

> ✳✳ **CAUTION**
>
> Remove metallic jewelry to avoid injury by accidental arcing of battery current.

1. Disconnect and isolate the battery negative cable.
2. Disconnect and isolate the battery positive cable.
3. Loosen the bolt and retainer that hold the battery down to the tray.

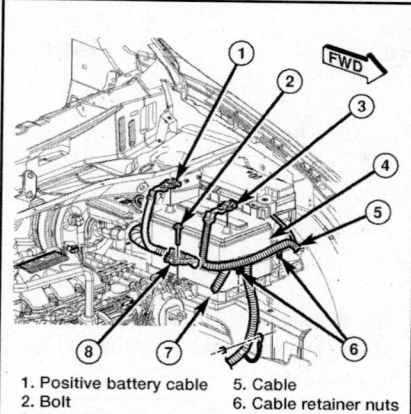

1. Positive battery cable
2. Bolt
3. Negative battery cable
4. Battery
5. Cable
6. Cable retainer nuts
7. Battery tray
8. Hold down retainer

59447

Fig. 36 Battery components

4. Lift the battery out of battery tray and remove from vehicle.
5. Remove the thermal guard (if equipped) from battery.

To install:

> ✳✳ **CAUTION**
>
> To protect eyes from battery acid, a suitable pair of industrial grade safety glasses, should be worn when removing or servicing a battery.

> ✳✳ **CAUTION**
>
> To protect the hands from battery acid, a suitable pair of industrial grade heavy duty rubber gloves, should be worn when removing or servicing a battery. Safety glasses also should be worn.

> ✳✳ **CAUTION**
>
> Remove metallic jewelry to avoid injury by accidental arcing of battery current.

➡ When replacing battery, the thermal guard MUST be transferred to the new battery (if equipped).

6. Install the battery into the vehicle making sure that the thermal guard (if equipped) is present and battery is properly positioned on the battery tray.
7. Install the battery hold-down retainer and bolt making sure that it is properly positioned on battery. Tighten the hold-down bolt to 62 inch lbs. (7 Nm)
8. Connect the battery positive cable. Tighten the cable clamp nut to 45 inch lbs. (5 Nm).
9. Connect the battery negative cable. Tighten the cable clamp nut to 45 inch lbs. (5 Nm).

ENGINE ELECTRICAL   **STARTING SYSTEM**

STARTER

REMOVAL & INSTALLATION

3.3L & 3.8L Engines

See Figures 37 and 38.

1. Install the engine support tool or equivalent.
2. Disconnect and isolate negative battery cable at battery.
3. Remove the battery cable nut and battery cable from solenoid stud.
4. Disconnect electrical connector from starter solenoid.

6 SPD Automatic Transmission

5. Remove the transmission to starter mounting bolt.
6. Remove the two front transmission mount to starter mounting bolts.
7. Remove the starter assembly from transmission.
8. Rotate starter assembly to allow removal from vehicle.

9. Remove the starter motor dust shield.

To install:
10. Install the starter motor dust shield.

11. Rotate starter assembly to allow positioning into transmission.
12. Install the starter assembly to transmission.
13. Install the two front transmission

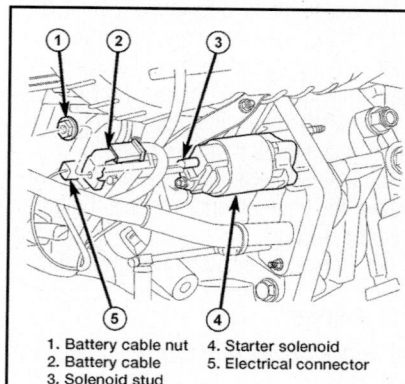

1. Battery cable nut
2. Battery cable
3. Solenoid stud
4. Starter solenoid
5. Electrical connector

59541

Fig. 37 Electrical components of battery and starter solenoid

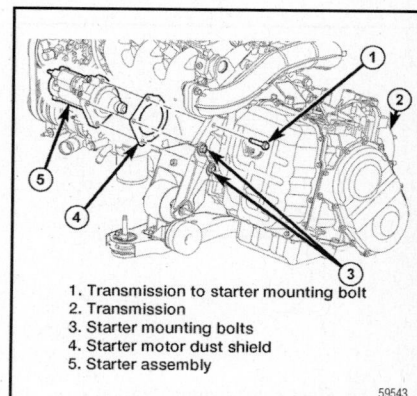

1. Transmission to starter mounting bolt
2. Transmission
3. Starter mounting bolts
4. Starter motor dust shield
5. Starter assembly

59543

Fig. 38 Starter assembly removal. 6 SPD transmission shown, 4 SPD transmission similar

mount to starter mounting bolts and tighten to 35.5 ft. lbs. (47 Nm).

14. If equipped with six speed auto transmission, install transmission to starter mounting bolt and tighten to 35.5 ft. lbs. (47 Nm).

15. Install the starter motor dust shield.

16. Rotate starter assembly to allow positioning into transmission.

17. Install the starter assembly to transmission.

18. Install the two front transmission mount to starter mounting bolts and tighten to 35.5 ft. lbs. (47 Nm).

19. If equipped with four speed auto transmission, install transmission to starter mounting stud and tighten to 35.5 ft. lbs. (47 Nm).

20. Install the battery cable and nut to solenoid stud. Tighten nut to 128 inch lbs. (14.5 Nm).

21. Connect electrical connector to starter solenoid.

22. Remove the engine support tool or equivalent.

23. Connect the negative battery cable, tighten the nut to 45 inch lbs. (5 Nm).

3.6L Engine

See Figures 39 through 41.

1. Disconnect and isolate the negative battery cable.

2. Remove the catalytic converter as outlined in the Engine Performance & Emission Controls Section.

3. Remove the front engine mount through bolt.

4. Remove the retainers from the front engine mount bracket and remove the bracket.

5. Remove the field generator connector.

6. Remove the B+ retainer and B+ cable.

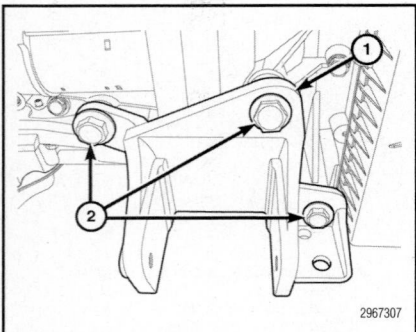

Fig. 39 Front engine mount bracket removal. Remove the retainers (2) from the front engine mount bracket (1) and remove the bracket

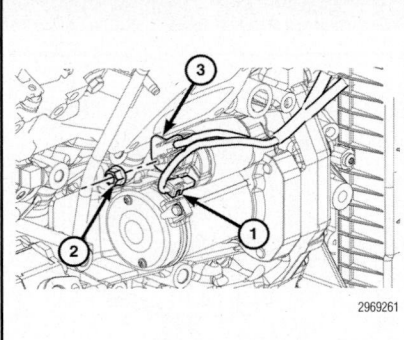

Fig. 40 Remove the field generator connector (1). Remove the B+ retainer (2) and B+ cable (3).

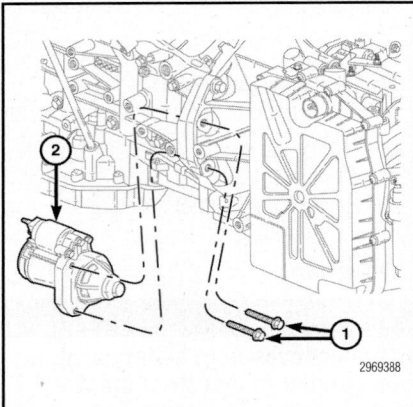

Fig. 41 Remove the starter retainers (1). Remove the starter (2).

7. Remove the starter retainers.

8. Remove the starter.

To install:

9. Install the starter.

10. Install the starter retainers. Tighten to 40.5 ft. lbs. (55 Nm).

11. Install the B+ cable and retainer. Tighten to 115 inch lbs. (13 Nm).

12. Install the field generator connector.

13. Install the engine mount bracket.

14. Install the engine mount bracket retainers. Tighten to 41 ft. lbs. (55 Nm).

15. Install the engine mount through bolt. Tighten to 45 ft. lbs. (61 Nm).

16. Install the catalytic converter as outlined in the Engine Performance & Emission Controls Section.

17. Connect the battery negative cable.

4.0L Engine

See Figures 42 and 43.

1. Install the engine support tool or equivalent.

2. Disconnect and isolate negative battery cable at battery.

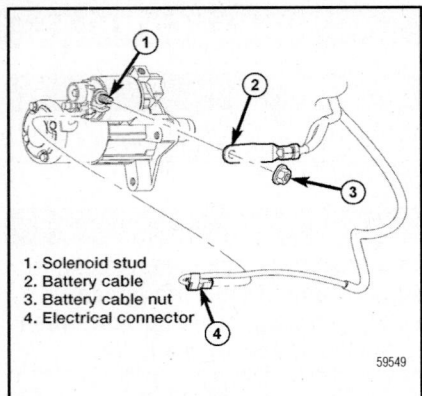

1. Solenoid stud
2. Battery cable
3. Battery cable nut
4. Electrical connector

Fig. 42 Electrical components of battery and starter solenoid

3. Remove the battery cable nut and battery cable from the solenoid stud.

4. Disconnect electrical connector from solenoid.

5. Remove the transmission to starter mounting bolt.

6. Support the engine/transmission assemblies with a jack stand or equivalent.

7. Remove the two front transmission mount to starter mounting bolts.

8. Remove the starter assembly from transmission.

9. Rotate starter assembly to allow removal from vehicle.

10. Remove the starter motor bushing.

11. Remove the starter motor dust shield.

To install:

12. Install the starter motor dust shield.

13. Install the starter motor bushing.

14. Rotate starter assembly to allow positioning into transmission.

15. Install the starter assembly to transmission.

16. Install the two front transmission

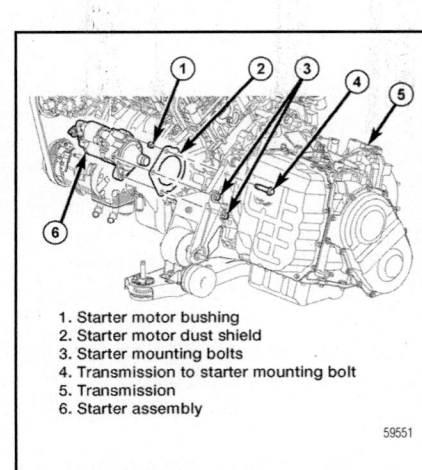

1. Starter motor bushing
2. Starter motor dust shield
3. Starter mounting bolts
4. Transmission to starter mounting bolt
5. Transmission
6. Starter assembly

Fig. 43 Starter assembly removal

mount to starter mounting bolts and tighten to 35.5 ft. lb (47 Nm).

17. Install the transmission to starter mounting bolt and tighten to 35.5 ft. lb (47 Nm).

18. Install the battery cable and nut to the solenoid stud. Tighten to 128 inch lbs. (14.5 Nm).

19. Connect electrical connector to solenoid.

20. Remove the engine support tool or equivalent.

21. Connect the negative battery cable, tighten the nut to 45 inch lbs. (5 Nm).

ENGINE MECHANICAL

➥Disconnecting the negative battery cable may interfere with the functions of the on board computer systems and may require the computer to undergo a relearning process, once the negative battery cable is reconnected.

ACCESSORY DRIVE BELTS

INSPECTION

See Figure 44.

1. Belt replacement under any or all of the following conditions is required:
   - Excessive wear
   - Frayed cords
   - Severe glazing

2. Poly-V Belt system may develop minor cracks across the ribbed side (due to reverse bending). These minor cracks are considered normal and acceptable. Parallel cracks are not.

➥Do not use any type of belt dressing or restorer on Poly-V Belts.

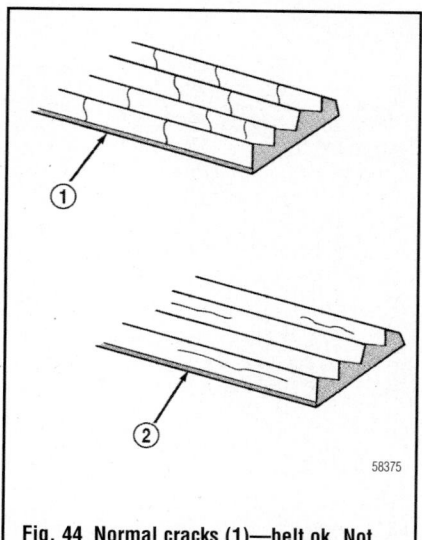

Fig. 44 Normal cracks (1)—belt ok. Not normal cracks (2)—replace belt

REMOVAL & INSTALLATION

3.3L & 3.8L Engines

See Figures 45 and 46.

1. Raise vehicle on hoist.
2. Remove the drive belt shield.

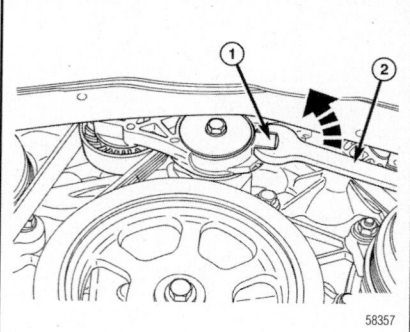

Fig. 45 Position a wrench (2) on the belt tensioner lug. Release belt tension by rotating the tensioner (1) clockwise.

✳✳ CAUTION

Do not allow drive belt tensioner to snap back, as damage to tensioner and/or personal injury could result.

3. Position a wrench on the belt tensioner lug.

4. Release belt tension by rotating the tensioner clockwise.

5. Remove the drive belt.

6. Carefully return tensioner to its relaxed position.

To install:

7. Route and position the drive belt onto all pulleys, except for the crankshaft pulley.

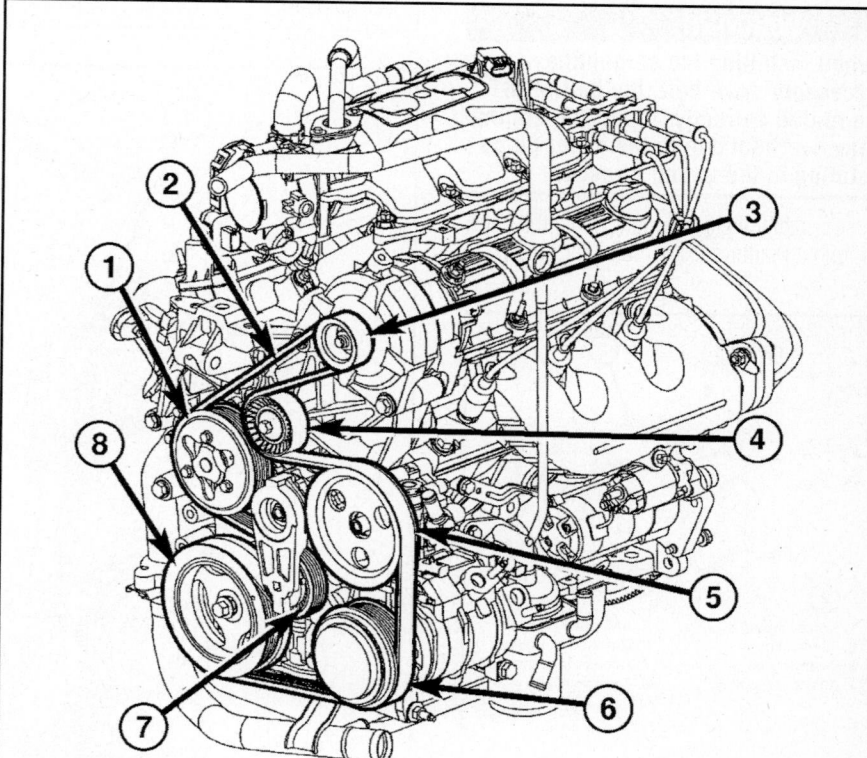

1. Water Pump Pulley
2. Accessory Drive Belt
3. Generator Pulley
4. Idler Pulley
5. P/S Pump
6. A/C Compressor
7. Accessory Drive Belt Tensioner
8. Crankshaft Pulley

Fig. 46 Belt routing

8. Rotate belt tensioner clockwise until belt can be installed onto the crankshaft pulley. Slowly release belt tensioner.

9. Verify belt is properly routed and engaged on all pulleys.

10. Install the drive belt shield and lower vehicle.

3.6L Engine

See Figures 47 and 48.

> ※※ **WARNING**
>
> **Do not let tensioner arm snap back to the freearm position, severe damage may occur to the tensioner.**

1. Disconnect negative battery cable from battery.

2. Raise vehicle.

3. Remove the right front wheel.

4. Remove the inner splash shield.

5. Rotate belt tensioner until it contacts its stop. Remove belt, then slowly rotate the tensioner into the freearm position .

To install:

6. Check condition of all pulleys.

> ※※ **WARNING**
>
> **When installing the serpentine accessory drive belt, the belt MUST be routed correctly. If not, the engine may overheat due to the water pump rotating in the wrong direction.**

7. Install the a new belt. Route the belt around all pulleys except the idler pulley.

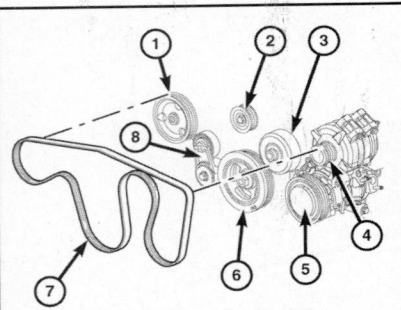

1. Power steering pulley
2. Idler pulley
3. Water pump pulley
4. Alternator pulley
5. A/C pulley
6. Crankshaft pulley
7. Accessory drive belt
8. Tensioner arm

2894937

Fig. 47 Install new belt (7). Route the belt around all pulleys (1, 3, 4, 5, 6) except the idler pulley (2). Rotate the tensioner arm (8) until it contacts its stop position. Route the belt (7) around the idler (2) and slowly let the tensioner (8) rotate into the belt. Make sure the belt (7) is seated onto all pulleys.

Rotate the tensioner arm until it contacts its stop position. Route the belt around the idler and slowly let the tensioner rotate into the belt. Make sure the belt is seated onto all pulleys.

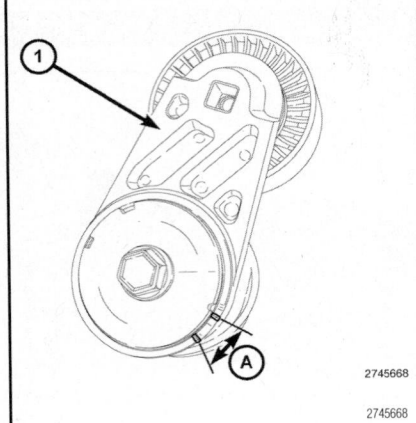

2745668

2745668

Fig. 48 With the drive belt installed, inspect the belt wear indicator. The gap between the tang and the housing stop (measurement A) must not exceed 0.94 inch (24 mm).

8. With the drive belt installed, inspect the belt wear indicator. The gap between the tang and the housing stop must not exceed 0.94 inch (24 mm).

9. Install the inner splash shield.

10. Install the wheel.

11. Lower vehicle.

12. Connect the negative battery.

4.0L Engine

See Figure 49.

1. Raise vehicle on hoist.

2. Remove the drive belt shield.

> ※※ **WARNING**
>
> **Do not allow drive belt tensioner to snap back, as damage to tensioner and/or personal injury could result.**

3. Position a wrench on the belt tensioner lug.

4. Release belt tension by rotating the tensioner clockwise.

5. Remove the drive belt.

6. Carefully return tensioner to its relaxed position.

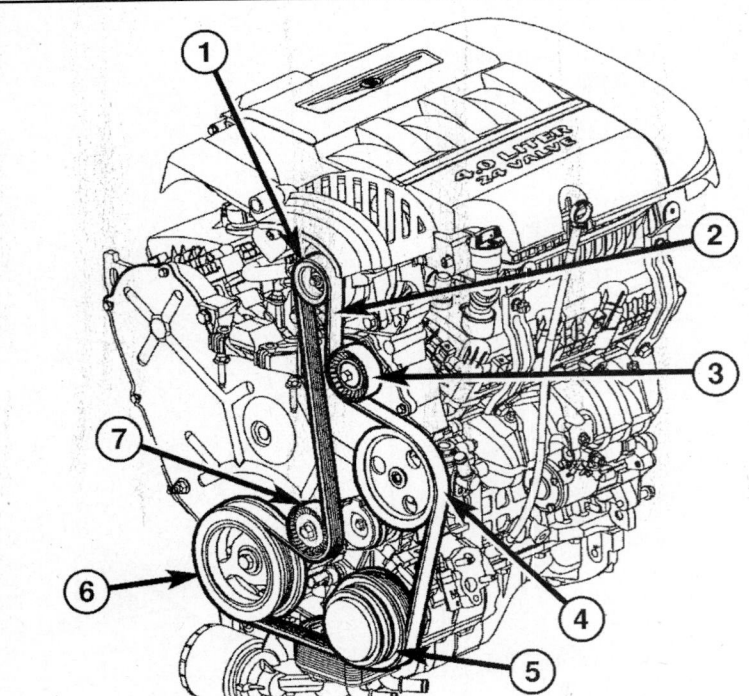

1. Generator
2. Accessory Drive Belt
3. Idler Pulley
4. P/S Pump Pulley
5. A/C Compressor Pulley
6. Crankshaft Pulley
7. Accessory Drive Belt Tensioner

58363

Fig. 49 Accessory drive belt removal and routing

To install:

7. Route and position the drive belt onto all pulleys, except for the crankshaft pulley.

8. Rotate belt tensioner clockwise until belt can be installed onto the crankshaft pulley. Slowly release belt tensioner.

9. Verify belt is properly routed and engaged on all pulleys.

10. Install the drive belt shield

11. Install the drive belt shield and lower vehicle.

AIR CLEANER

REMOVAL & INSTALLATION

See Figure 50.

1. Disengage the two retaining clamps that secure the air cleaner housing cover to air cleaner housing.

2. Lift and pull the air cleaner housing cover toward the engine to disengage the cover from the locating tabs on the air cleaner housing and position the cover out of the way.

3. Remove the air cleaner element from the inside of the air cleaner housing.

To install:

4. Clean any dirt or foreign matter from the inside of the air cleaner housing.

5. Install the air cleaner element into air cleaner housing. Make sure the element is properly seated in the housing.

6. Engage the air cleaner housing cover to the locating tabs on the air cleaner housing. Make sure the cover is properly positioned.

7. Fully install the air cleaner housing cover to the air cleaner housing and engage the two retaining clamps. Make sure the clamps are fully engaged.

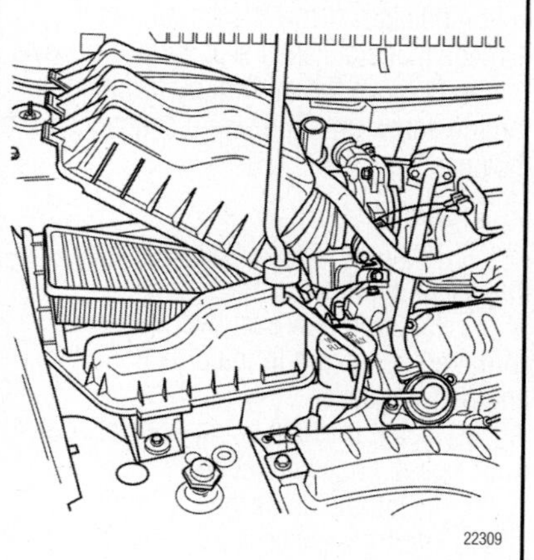

CAMSHAFT AND VALVE LIFTERS

REMOVAL & INSTALLATION

3.3L & 3.8L Engines

See Figures 51 through 54.

1. Remove the radiator and cooling fans from the vehicle.

2. Remove the cylinder heads as outlined in this section.

3. Remove the timing chain and camshaft sprocket as outlined in this section.

4. Remove the yoke retainer.

5. Remove the hydraulic lifters.

6. Identify each tappet for reinstallation in original location.

7. Remove the camshaft thrust plate.

✳✳ WARNING

Slowly remove the camshaft from the engine taking precautions not to damage the camshaft bearings.

8. Install the a long bolt into front of camshaft to facilitate removal of the camshaft.

9. Carefully remove the camshaft.

➡**The camshaft bearings are serviced with the engine block.**

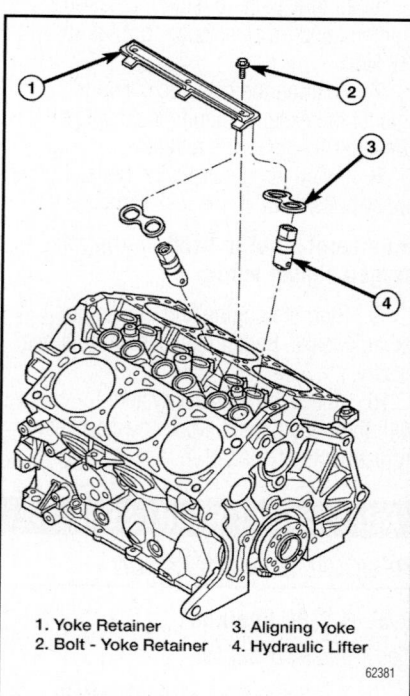

1. Yoke Retainer   3. Aligning Yoke
2. Bolt - Yoke Retainer   4. Hydraulic Lifter

62381

Fig. 51 Hydraulic lifters

62383

Fig. 52 Remove the oil gallery cup plugs (1), and oil feed gallery (3) from the pump. Remove camshaft thrust plate (2).

To install:

10. Lubricate camshaft lobes and camshaft bearing journals with engine oil.

11. Install the a long bolt into the camshaft to assist in the installation of the camshaft.

12. Carefully install the camshaft in engine block.

13. Install the camshaft thrust plate and bolts. Tighten to 105 inch lbs. (12 Nm) torque.

14. Measure the camshaft end play. If not within specifications, replace thrust plate.

15. Install the timing chain and sprockets.

➡**When camshaft is replaced, all of the hydraulic lifters must be replaced.**

16. Install the hydraulic lifters with lubrication hole in the upward position.

17. Install the timing chain cover.

18. Install the cylinder heads as outlined in this section.

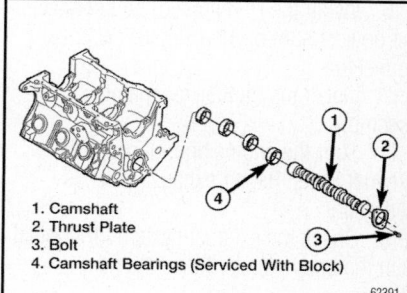

1. Camshaft
2. Thrust Plate
3. Bolt
4. Camshaft Bearings (Serviced With Block)

62391

Fig. 53 Lubricate camshaft lobes (1) and camshaft bearing journals (4) with engine oil. Install a long bolt into the camshaft to assist in the installation of the camshaft. Carefully install the camshaft (1) in engine block. Install camshaft thrust plate (2) and bolts (3).

22309

Fig. 50 Air Cleaner Element and Housing Cover

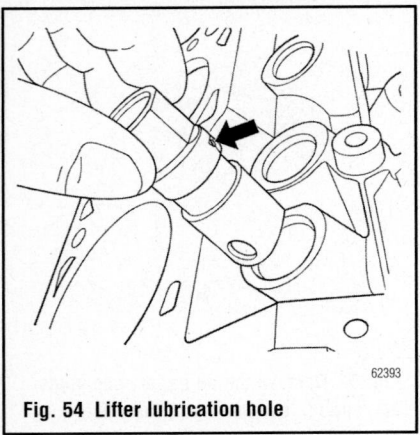

Fig. 54 Lifter lubrication hole

19. Install the cylinder head covers.
20. Install the lower and upper intake manifolds as outlined in this section.
21. Install the radiator and cooling fan.

CATALYTIC CONVERTER

REMOVAL & INSTALLATION

3.3L & 3.8L Engines

1. Loosen clamp and disconnect the muffler and resonator assembly from catalytic converter pipe.
2. Disconnect downstream oxygen sensor electrical connector.
3. Remove the catalytic converter to exhaust manifold attaching bolts.
4. Remove the catalytic converter and gasket.

To install:

5. Position new gasket onto the manifold flange and install catalytic converter. Tighten bolts to 27 ft. lbs. (37 Nm).

➡**Be careful not to twist or kink the oxygen sensor wires.**

6. Install the (if removed) and connect the downstream oxygen sensor electrical connector.
7. Install the muffler/resonator assembly.
8. Start the engine and inspect for exhaust leaks. Repair exhaust leaks as necessary.
9. Check the exhaust system for contact with the body panels. Make the necessary adjustments, if needed.

3.6L Engine

See Figure 55.

➡**The lower bolts for the converter flange are used to hold a guide retainer plate. The retainer does not need to be removed. The catalytic converter is held in by the plate and upper bolts.**

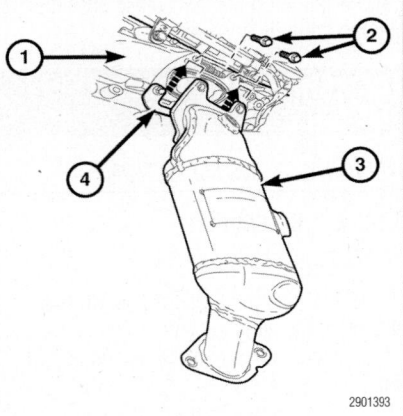

Fig. 55 Removal of the exhaust manifold (1), upper bolts (2), catalytic converter (3), and the guide retainer plate

1. Remove the cross-under pipe from vehicle.
2. Disconnect the temperature and oxygen sensor electrical connectors.
3. Remove the catalytic converter to exhaust manifold upper bolts.
4. Remove the catalytic converter by lifting and sliding the flange up and away from the exhaust manifold.
5. Remove the temperature and oxygen sensors.

To install:

6. If new gaskets need replacing, position new gasket onto the manifold flange and install the lower retainer plate. loosely install all four bolts to align the gasket. Tighten lower retainer bolts to 27 ft. lbs. (37 Nm).
7. Position the catalytic converter against the exhaust manifold. Position the converter flange to the retainer.
8. Install the upper flange bolts. Tighten upper bolts to 27 ft. lbs. (37 Nm).

➡**Be careful not to twist or kink the oxygen sensor wires.**

9. Start the engine and inspect for exhaust leaks. Repair exhaust leaks as necessary.
10. Check the exhaust system for contact with the body panels. Make the necessary adjustments, if needed.

CRANKSHAFT FRONT SEAL

REMOVAL & INSTALLATION

3.3L & 3.8L Engines

See Figures 56 and 57.

1. Disconnect negative cable from battery.

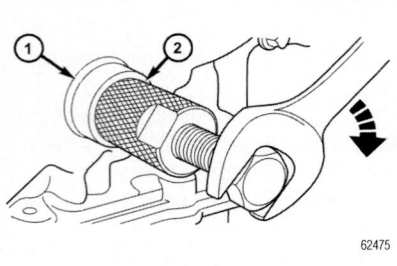

Fig. 56 Position Special Tool (2) on crankshaft nose. Carefully screw the tool into the seal (1) until it engages firmly. Be careful not to damage that crankshaft seal surface of cover.

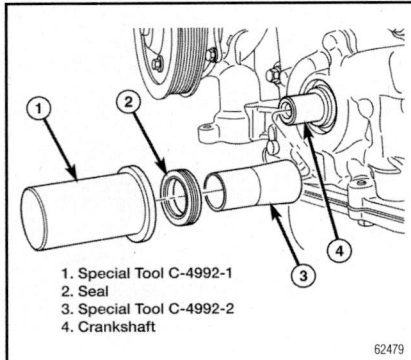

1. Special Tool C-4992-1
2. Seal
3. Special Tool C-4992-2
4. Crankshaft

Fig. 57 Position Special Tool Guide (3), on the crankshaft (4) nose. Position new seal (2) over the guide with the seal spring in the direction of the engine front cover. Install seal using Special Tool (1) until seal is flush with cover.

2. Remove the accessory drive belt as outlined in this section.
3. Remove the crankshaft damper.
4. Position Special Tool on crankshaft nose. Carefully screw the tool into the seal until it engages firmly. Be careful not to damage that crankshaft seal surface of cover.
5. Remove the oil seal by turning the forcing screw until the seal disengages from the cover.

To install:

6. Position Special Tool Guide, on the crankshaft nose.
7. Position new seal over the guide with the seal spring in the direction of the engine front cover.
8. Install the seal using Special Tool until seal is flush with cover.
9. Install the crankshaft damper.
10. Install the accessory drive belt as outlined in this section.
11. Lower vehicle and connect negative cable to battery.

3.6L Engine

See Figure 58.

1. Remove the accessory drive belt and the crankshaft vibration damper.
2. Install the sleeve from Seal Remover around the flywheel key and onto the nose of the crankshaft.
3. Screw Seal Remover into the front crankshaft oil seal.
4. Install the extractor screw into the Seal Remover.
   a. Hold the seal remover stationary and tighten the extractor screw against the sleeve until the front crankshaft oil seal is removed from the engine timing cover.

To install:

5. Position the front crankshaft oil seal into place on the engine timing cover.
6. Align the Front Crankshaft Seal Installer to the flywheel key on the crankshaft and against the front crankshaft oil seal.

✳✳ WARNING

Only tighten the crankshaft vibration damper bolt until the oil seal is seated in the cover. Overtightening of the bolt can crack the front timing cover.

7. Install the and tighten the crankshaft vibration damper bolt until the Crankshaft oil seal is seated in the engine timing cover.
8. Install the crankshaft vibration damper and accessory drive belt.

4.0L Engine

See Figures 59 and 60.

1. Remove the crankshaft sprocket.
2. Tap the dowel pin out of the crankshaft.

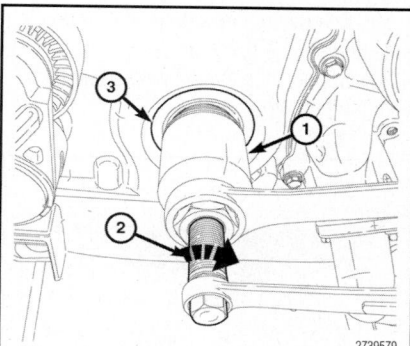

Fig. 58 Install the extractor screw (2) into the Seal Remover (1). Hold the seal remover stationary and tighten the extractor screw against the sleeve until the front crankshaft oil seal (3) is removed from the engine timing cover.

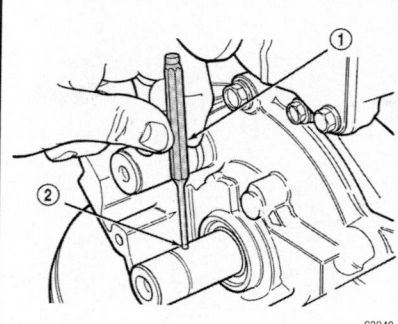

Fig. 59 Remove the crankshaft sprocket. Tap (1) the dowel pin (2) out of the crankshaft.

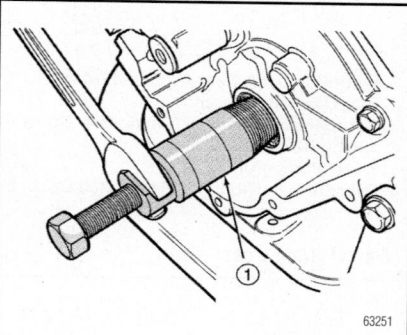

Fig. 60 Crankshaft Oil Seal with Special Tool (1) 6341A

3. Remove the crankshaft seal using Special Tool.

➡**Do not nick shaft seal surface or seal bore.**

4. Shaft seal lip surface must be free of varnish, dirt or nicks. Polish with 400 grit paper if necessary.

To install:

5. Install the crankshaft seal using Special Tool 6342.
6. Install the dowel pin into the crankshaft to 0.047 inch protrusion.
7. Install the crankshaft sprocket.

CYLINDER HEAD

REMOVAL & INSTALLATION

3.3L & 3.8L Engines

See Figures 61 and 62.

1. Drain the cooling system as outlined in the Engine Cooling Section.
2. Disconnect negative cable from battery.
3. Remove the upper and lower intake manifolds.

4. Remove the cylinder head covers.
5. Remove the spark plugs from cylinder head.
6. Remove the dipstick and tube.
7. Remove the exhaust manifold(s).
8. Remove the rocker arm and shaft assemblies.
9. Remove the push rods and mark positions to ensure installation in original locations.
10. Remove the eight head bolts from each cylinder head and remove cylinder heads.

To install:

11. Clean all sealing surfaces of engine block and cylinder heads.
12. Position new gasket on engine block. The left bank gasket is identified with the "L" stamped in the exposed area of the gasket located at front of engine. The right bank gasket is identified with a "R" stamped in the exposed area of the gasket also, but is located at the rear of the engine.
13. The cylinder head bolts should be examined BEFORE reuse. If the threads are necked down, the bolts must be replaced.

Necking can be checked by holding a scale or straight edge against the threads. If all the threads do not contact the scale the bolt should be replaced.

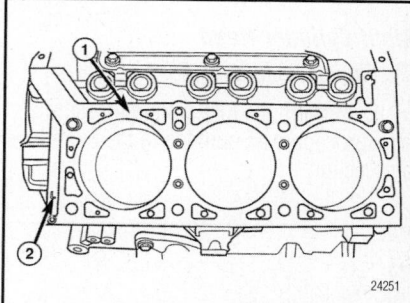

Fig. 61 Position new gasket (1) on engine block. Location of the identification (2) mark

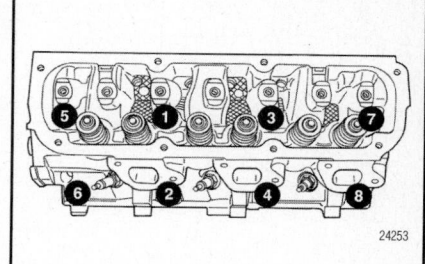

Fig. 62 Cylinder head tightening sequence

14. Tighten the cylinder head bolts 1-8 in the following sequence. Using the 4 step torque turn method, tighten according to the following values:

    a. Step 1: Bolts 1—8 to 45 ft. lbs. (61 Nm)

    b. Step 2: Bolts 1—8 to 65 ft. lbs. (88 Nm)

    c. Step 3: Bolts 1—8 (again) to 65 ft. lbs. (88 Nm)

    d. Step 4: Bolts 1—8 turn an additional 1/4 Turn. (Do not use a torque wrench for this step.)

➡**Bolt torque after 1/4 turn should be over 90 ft. lbs. (122 Nm). If not, replace the bolt.**

15. Inspect push rods and replace worn or bent rods.

16. Install the push rods.

17. Install the rocker arm and shaft assemblies.

18. Install the cylinder head covers.

19. Install the exhaust manifolds.

20. Install the new O-ring on dipstick tube. Install dipstick tube assembly.

21. Install the spark plugs.

22. Install the upper and lower intake manifolds.

23. Fill the cooling system.

24. Connect negative cable to battery.

4.0L Engine

Right Cylinder Head

See Figures 63 through 68.

1. Perform the fuel system pressure relief procedure as outlined in the Fuel System Section.

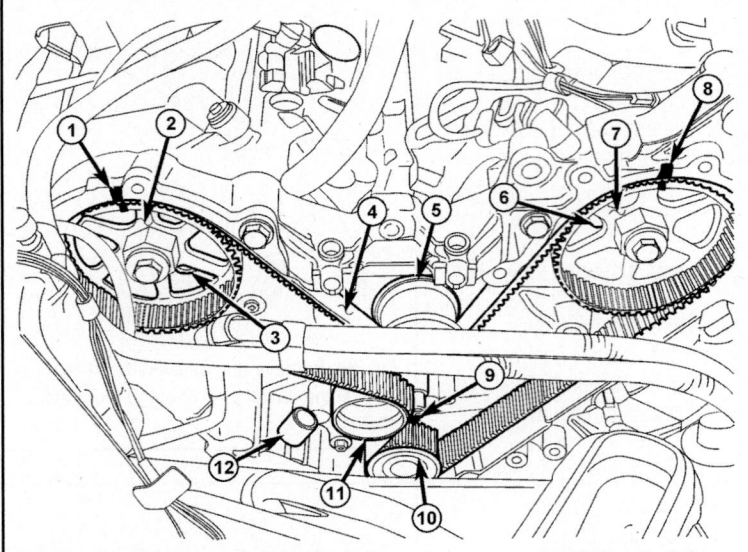

1. Right Camshaft Gear Alignment Mark
2. Right Camshaft Gear
3. Cylinder Head To Inner Timing Belt Cover Bolts – Right
4. Timing Belt
5. Water Pump Pulley
6. Cylinder Head To Inner Timing Belt Cover Bolts - Left
7. Left Camshaft Gear
8. Left Camshaft Gear Alignment Mark
9. Crankshaft Gear Alignment Mark
10. Crankshaft Gear
11. Timing Belt Tensioner Pulley
12. Timing Belt Tensioner

62949

Fig. 64 Timing gear marks

2. Disconnect and isolate the negative battery cable.

3. Drain cooling system as outlined in the Engine Cooling Section.

4. Remove the engine cover.

5. Remove the air cleaner element housing.

6. Remove the upper intake manifold including EGR tube.

7. Remove the fuel rail and lower intake manifold as outlined in this section.

8. Raise the vehicle.

9. Remove the right front tire.

10. Remove the right inner splash shield.

11. Remove the accessory drive belt as outlined in this section.

12. Remove the accessory drive belt tensioner.

13. Remove the crankshaft damper bolt.

14. Using Puller and Crankshaft Insert, remove crankshaft damper.

15. Remove the lower outer timing belt cover bolts.

16. Remove the right exhaust maniverter.

17. Lower vehicle.

18. Remove the accessory drive belt idler pulley.

19. Remove the power steering mounting bolts and set the pump aside.

20. Support the engine with a block of wood and the floor jack.

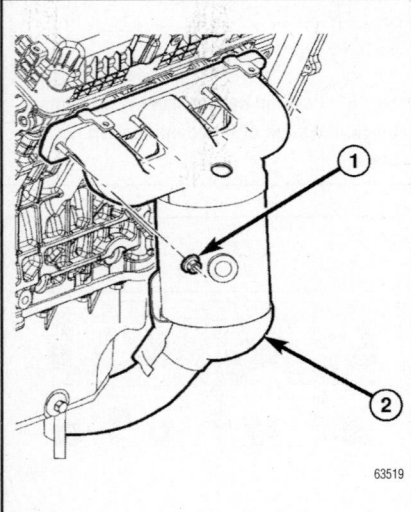

63519

Fig. 63 Remove right exhaust maniverter bolt (1), and exhaust maniverter (2).

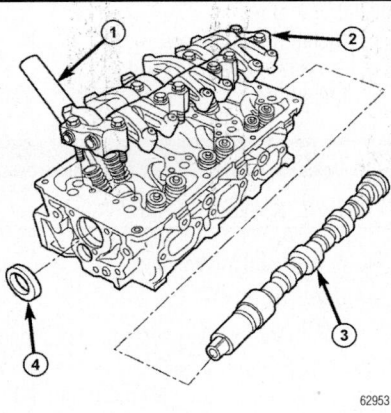

62953

Fig. 65 Camshaft, rocker arm assembly and cylinder head

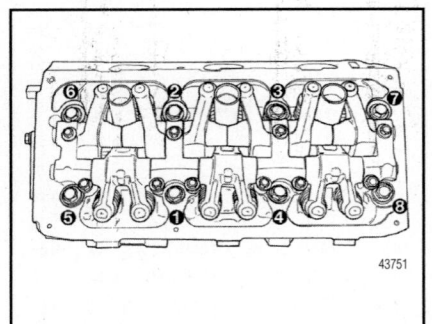

43751

Fig. 66 Right & Left Cylinder Head Bolt Tightening Sequence

21. Remove the upper engine mount.

22. Remove the power steering reservoir bolts and set reservoir aside.

23. Remove the remaining outer timing belt cover bolts and cover.

24. Rotate the engine to TDC and align timing belt marks.

25. Remove the timing belt tensioner and reset the tensioner.

26. Remove the timing belt.

27. Remove the right valve cover to cylinder head ground strap.

28. Remove the EGR valve with two bolts and gasket.

29. Remove the right cylinder head cover.

30. Remove the ten bolts and the right rocker arm assembly.

31. Remove the three bolts and the right rear camshaft thrust plate, and the Cam Thrust Plate Gasket.

32. Counterhold the right cam gear and remove the right cam gear retaining bolt.

33. Push the camshaft out of the back of the cylinder head approximately 3.5 inches and remove the cam gear.

34. Remove the three inner timing cover to right cylinder head retaining bolts.

35. Remove the cylinder head bolts in REVERSE of the tightening sequence.

➡**Because of clearance restrictions when removing the right cylinder head, the front four cylinder head bolts must be loosened, raised and supported with a rubber band before the cylinder head can be removed.**

36. Push the camshaft out of the back of the cylinder head approximately 3.5 inches and remove the cylinder head.

37. Clean and inspect all mating surfaces.

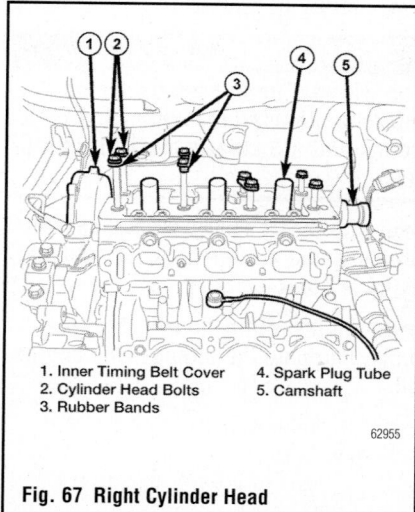

1. Inner Timing Belt Cover
2. Cylinder Head Bolts
3. Rubber Bands
4. Spark Plug Tube
5. Camshaft

62955

Fig. 67 Right Cylinder Head

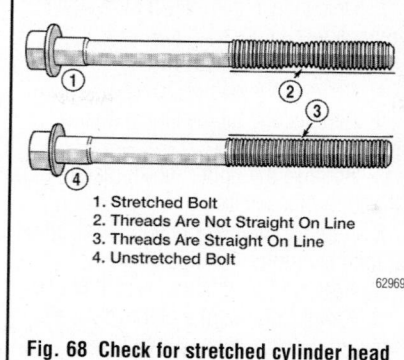

1. Stretched Bolt
2. Threads Are Not Straight On Line
3. Threads Are Straight On Line
4. Unstretched Bolt

62969

Fig. 68 Check for stretched cylinder head bolts

To install:

➡**The cylinder head bolts are tightened using a torque plus angle procedure. The bolts must be examined BEFORE reuse. If the threads are necked down the bolts must be replaced.**

38. Check cylinder head bolts for necking by holding a scale or straight edge against the threads. If all the threads do not contact the scale the bolt must be replaced.

➡**When cleaning cylinder head and cylinder block surfaces, DO NOT use a metal scraper because the surfaces could be cut or ground. Use ONLY a wooden or plastic scraper.**

39. Clean sealing surfaces of cylinder head and block.

40. Install the camshaft in cylinder head.

✳✳ WARNING

The cylinder head gaskets are not interchangeable between cylinder heads and are clearly marked right or left.

➡**Ensure that the correct head gaskets are used and are oriented correctly on cylinder block.**

➡**Before installing the cylinder head bolts, lubricate the threads with engine oil.**

41. Insert the front four cylinder head bolts into the cylinder head. Pull the bolts up to the top of their travel and retain with rubber bands.

42. Push camshaft out of the back of the cylinder head approximately 3.5 inches. Install head gasket and cylinder head over locating dowels.

43. Install the and finger tighten eight head bolts.

44. Tighten the cylinder head bolts in the following sequence, using the 4 step

torque-turn method. Tighten according to the following torque values:

   a. Step 1: All to 45 ft. lbs. (61 Nm)
   b. Step 2: All to 65 ft. lbs. (88 Nm)
   c. Step 3: All (again) to 65 ft. lbs. (88 Nm)
   d. Step 4: + 90° Turn Do not use a torque wrench for this step.

45. Bolt torque after 90° turn should be over 90 ft. lbs. (122 Nm) in the tightening direction. If not, replace the bolt.

46. Install the inner timing cover to cylinder head bolts. Tighten bolts to 40 ft. lbs. (54 Nm).

➡**The camshaft sprockets are keyed and not interchangeable from side to side because of the Camshaft Position (CMP) Sensor pick-up.**

47. Push the camshaft back into the cylinder head and install the camshaft sprocket.

48. Install the NEW sprocket attaching bolt into place. The 10 inch bolt (255 mm) bolt is to be installed in the left camshaft and the 8 3/8 inch (213 mm) bolt is to be installed into the right camshaft. Counterhold the camshaft sprocket and tighten the camshaft sprocket bolt to 75 ft. lbs. (102 Nm) plus a 90°turn.

49. Install the camshaft thrust plate and gasket. Tighten three bolts to 250 inch lbs. (28 Nm).

50. Install the new gasket between EGR solenoid/valve and rear of cylinder head.

51. Position EGR solenoid/valve assembly to rear of cylinder head. Install and tighten two mounting bolts to 80 inch lbs. (8 Nm).

52. Rotate the right camshaft gear to align its timing mark. Verify that the left camshaft gear timing mark and crankshaft gear timing mark are still aligned.

53. Install the timing belt starting at the crankshaft sprocket going in a counter-clockwise direction. Install the belt around the last sprocket. Maintain tension on the belt as it is positioned around the tensioner pulley.

54. Holding the tensioner pulley against the belt, install the tensioner into the housing and tighten two bolts to 250 inch lbs. (28 Nm). Each camshaft sprocket mark should remain aligned with the cover marks.

55. When tensioner is in place pull retaining pin to allow the tensioner to extend to the tensioner pulley bracket.

56. Rotate crankshaft sprocket two revolutions and check the timing marks on the camshafts and crankshaft. The marks should line up within their respective locations. If marks do not line up, repeat procedure.

➡With the camshaft gears in these positions the lobes are in a neutral position (no load to the valve). This will allow the rocker arm shaft assembly to be tightened into position with little or no valve spring load on it.

57. Install the rocker arm and shaft assembly and ten bolts making sure that the identification marks face toward the front of engine for left head and toward the rear of the engine for right head.

58. Tighten the ten rocker arm/shaft assembly bolts in sequence to 275 inch lbs. (31 Nm).

59. Install the right cylinder head cover.

60. Install the right valve cover to cylinder head ground strap.

61. Install the front timing belt outer covers.

62. Tighten the timing cover bolts as follows:
    a. M6 bolts - 105 inch lbs. (12 Nm)
    b. M8 bolts - 250 inch lbs. (28 Nm)
    c. M10 bolts - 40 ft. lbs. (54 Nm)

63. Install the power steering reservoir. Tighten mounting nut to 108 inch lbs. (12 Nm).

64. Install the power steering pump.

65. Install the accessory drive belt idler pulley. Tighten bolt to 250 inch lbs. (28 Nm).

66. Install the upper engine mount.

67. Install the right exhaust maniverter.

68. Install the crankshaft damper using Forcing Screw, with Nut and Thrust Bearing, and Installer.

69. Install the crankshaft damper bolt. Tighten bolt to 70 ft. lbs. (95 Nm) while holding damper with Damper Holding Fixture

70. Install the accessory drive belt tensioner. Tighten bolt to 45 ft. lbs. (61 Nm).

71. Install the accessory drive belt.

72. Install the right inner splash shield.

73. Install the right front tire.

74. Lower the vehicle.

75. Install the lower intake manifold and fuel rail.

76. Install the upper intake manifold (1) including EGR tube.

77. Install the air cleaner element housing.

78. Install the engine cover.

79. Fill the coolant system.

80. Connect the negative battery cable. Tighten nut to 40 inch lbs. (4.5 Nm).

Left Cylinder Head

See Figures 69 and 70.

1. Perform the fuel system pressure relief procedure.

2. Disconnect and isolate the negative battery cable.

3. Drain cooling system.

4. Remove the engine cover.

5. Remove the air cleaner element housing.

6. Remove the upper intake manifold as outlined in this section.

7. Remove the fuel rail and lower intake manifold as outlined in this section.

8. Remove the radiator crossmember.

9. Remove the coolant recovery container and radiator fan assembly.

10. Raise the vehicle.

11. Remove the left front tire.

12. Remove the left inner splash shield.

13. Remove the accessory drive belt as outlined in the Engine Cooling Section.

14. Remove the accessory drive belt tensioner.

15. Remove the crankshaft damper bolt.

16. Using Puller and Crankshaft Insert, remove crankshaft damper.

17. Remove the lower outer timing belt cover bolts.

18. Remove the left exhaust maniverter.

19. Lower vehicle.

20. Remove the accessory drive belt idler pulley.

21. Remove the power steering mounting bolts and set the pump aside.

22. Support the engine with a block of wood and the floor jack.

23. Remove the upper engine mount.

24. Remove the power steering reservoir bolts and set reservoir aside.

25. Remove the remaining outer timing belt cover bolts and cover.

26. Rotate the engine to TDC and align timing belt marks.

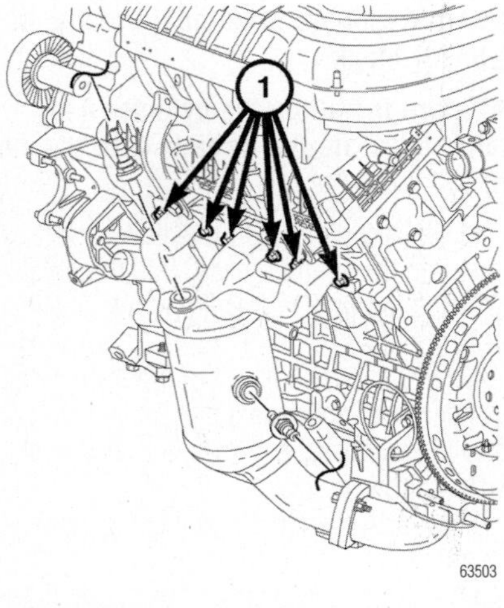

Fig. 69 Front maniverter bolts (1)

27. Remove the timing belt tensioner and reset the tensioner.

28. Remove the timing belt.

29. Remove the left cylinder head cover to cylinder head ground strap.

30. Remove the left cylinder head cover.

31. Remove the ten bolts and left rocker arm assembly.

32. Remove the three bolts and the left camshaft thrust plate.

33. Counterhold the left cam gear and remove the cam gear retaining bolt.

34. Push the camshaft out of the back of the cylinder head approximately 3.5 inches and remove the cam gear.

35. Remove the four inner timing cover to left cylinder head retaining bolts.

36. Remove the cylinder head bolts in REVERSE of the tightening sequence.

37. Push the camshaft out of the back of the cylinder head approximately 3.5 inches and remove the cylinder head.

38. Clean and inspect all mating surfaces.

To install:

➡The cylinder head bolts are tightened using a torque plus angle procedure. The bolts must be examined BEFORE reuse. If the threads are necked down the bolts must be replaced.

39. Check cylinder head bolts for necking by holding a scale or straight edge against the threads. If all the threads do not contact the scale the bolt must be replaced.

➡When cleaning cylinder head and cylinder block surfaces, DO NOT use a metal scraper because the surfaces could be cut or ground. Use ONLY a wooden or plastic scraper.

40. Clean sealing surfaces of cylinder head and block.

41. Install the camshaft in cylinder head.

✳✳ WARNING

The cylinder head gaskets are not interchangeable between cylinder heads and are clearly marked right or left.

➡Ensure that the correct head gaskets are used and are oriented correctly on cylinder block.

➡Before installing the cylinder head bolts, lubricate the threads with engine oil.

42. Insert the front four cylinder head bolts into the cylinder head. Pull the bolts up to the top of their travel and retain with rubber bands.

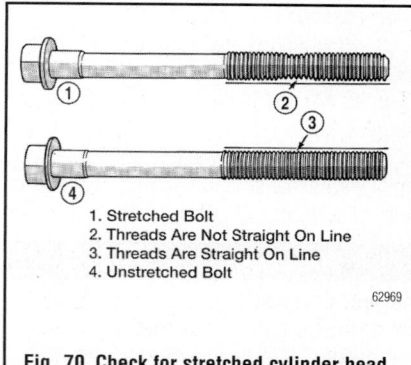

1. Stretched Bolt
2. Threads Are Not Straight On Line
3. Threads Are Straight On Line
4. Unstretched Bolt

62969

Fig. 70 Check for stretched cylinder head bolts

43. Push camshaft out of the back of the cylinder head approximately 3.5 inches. Install head gasket and cylinder head over locating dowels.

44. Install the and finger tighten eight head bolts.

45. Tighten the cylinder head bolts in the following sequence, using the 4 step torque-turn method. Tighten according to the following torque values:

a. Step 1: All to 45 ft. lbs. (61 Nm)

b. Step 2: All to 65 ft. lbs. (88 Nm)

c. Step 3: All (again) to 65 ft. lbs. (88 Nm)

d. Step 4: + 90°Turn Do not use a torque wrench for this step.

46. Bolt torque after 90°turn should be over 90 ft. lbs. (122 Nm) in the tightening direction. If not, replace the bolt.

47. Install the inner timing cover to cylinder head bolts. Tighten bolts to 40 ft. lbs. (54 Nm).

➡**The camshaft sprockets are keyed and not interchangeable from side to side because of the Camshaft Position (CMP) Sensor pick-up.**

48. Push the camshaft back into the cylinder head and install the camshaft sprocket.

49. Install the NEW sprocket attaching bolt into place. The 10 inch bolt (255 mm) bolt is to be installed in the left camshaft and the 8 3/8 inch (213 mm) bolt is to be installed into the left camshaft. Counterhold the camshaft sprocket and tighten the camshaft sprocket bolt to 75 ft. lbs. (102 Nm) plus a 90°turn.

50. Install the camshaft thrust plate and gasket. Tighten three bolts to 250 inch lbs. (28 Nm).

51. Install the new gasket between EGR solenoid/valve and rear of cylinder head.

52. Position EGR solenoid/valve assembly to rear of cylinder head. Install and tighten two mounting bolts to 80 inch lbs. (8 Nm).

53. Rotate the left camshaft gear to align its timing mark. Verify that the left camshaft gear timing mark and crankshaft gear timing mark are still aligned.

54. Install the timing belt starting at the crankshaft sprocket going in a counter-clockwise direction. Install the belt around the last sprocket. Maintain tension on the belt as it is positioned around the tensioner pulley.

55. Holding the tensioner pulley against the belt, install the tensioner into the housing and tighten two bolts to 250 inch lbs. (28 Nm). Each camshaft sprocket mark should remain aligned with the cover marks.

56. When tensioner is in place pull retaining pin to allow the tensioner to extend to the tensioner pulley bracket.

57. Rotate crankshaft sprocket two revolutions and check the timing marks on the camshafts and crankshaft. The marks should line up within their respective locations. If marks do not line up, repeat procedure.

➡**With the camshaft gears in these positions the lobes are in a neutral position (no load to the valve). This will allow the rocker arm shaft assembly to be tightened into position with little or no valve spring load on it.**

58. Install the rocker arm and shaft assembly and ten bolts making sure that the identification marks face toward the front of engine for left head and toward the rear of the engine for left head.

59. Tighten the ten rocker arm/shaft assembly bolts in sequence to 275 inch lbs. (31 Nm).

60. Install the left cylinder head cover.

61. Install the left valve cover to cylinder head ground strap.

62. Install the front timing belt outer covers.

63. Tighten the timing cover bolts as follows:

a. M6 bolts - 105 inch lbs. (12 Nm)

b. M8 bolts - 250 inch lbs. (28 Nm)

c. M10 bolts - 40 ft. lbs. (54 Nm)

64. Install the power steering reservoir. Tighten mounting nut to 108 inch lbs. (12 Nm).

65. Install the power steering pump.

66. Install the accessory drive belt idler pulley. Tighten bolt to 250 inch lbs. (28 Nm).

67. Install the upper engine mount.

68. Install the left exhaust maniverter.

69. Install the crankshaft damper using Forcing Screw, with Nut and Thrust Bearing, and Installer.

70. Install the crankshaft damper bolt.

Tighten bolt to 70 ft. lbs. (95 Nm) while holding damper with Damper Holding Fixture

71. Install the accessory drive belt tensioner. Tighten bolt to45 ft. lbs. (61 Nm).

72. Install the accessory drive belt.

73. Install the left inner splash shield.

74. Install the left front tire.

75. Lower the vehicle.

76. Install the lower intake manifold and fuel rail.

77. Install the upper intake manifold including EGR tube.

78. Install the air cleaner element housing.

79. Install the engine cover.

80. Fill the coolant system.

81. Connect the negative battery cable. Tighten nut to 40 inch lbs. (4.5 Nm).

ENGINE OIL & FILTER

REPLACEMENT

See Figure 71.

✳✳ CAUTION

New or used engine oil can be irritating to the skin. Avoid prolonged or repeated skin contact with engine oil. Contaminants in used engine oil, caused by internal combustion, can be hazardous to your health. Thoroughly wash exposed skin with soap and water. Do not wash skin with gasoline, diesel fuel, thinner, or solvents, health problems can result. Do not pollute, dispose of used engine oil properly. Contact your dealer or government agency for location of collection center in your area.

Change the engine oil and filter at mileage and time intervals described in the Maintenance Schedule.

1. Run the engine until achieving normal operating temperature.

2. Position the vehicle on a level surface and turn the engine off.

3. Remove the engine cover.

✳✳ WARNING

When performing an engine oil change, the oil filter cap must be removed. Removing the oil filter cap releases oil held within the oil filter cavity and allows it to drain into the sump. Failure to remove the cap prior to reinstallation of the drain plug will not allow complete draining of the used engine oil.

4. Place an oil absorbent cloth around the oil filter housing at the base of the oil filter cap.

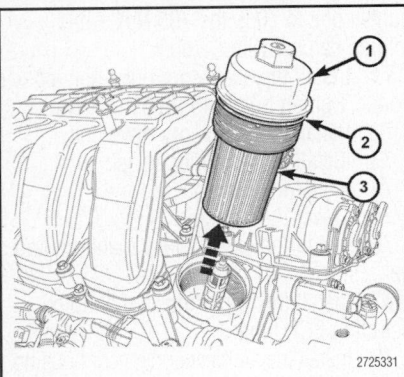

Fig. 71 Rotate the oil filter cap (1) counterclockwise and remove the cap (1), o-ring seal (2) and filter (3) from the oil filter housing.

➡ **The oil filter is attached to the oil filter cap.**

5. Rotate the oil filter cap counterclockwise and remove the cap and filter from the oil filter housing.

6. Raise and support the vehicle.

7. Place a suitable drain pan under the crankcase drain plug.

8. Remove the drain plug from oil pan and allow the oil to drain into the pan. Inspect the drain plug threads for stretching or other damage. Replace the drain plug and gasket if damaged.

9. Install the drain plug in the oil pan and tighten to 20 ft. lbs. (27 Nm).

10. Lower the vehicle.

11. Remove the oil filter from the oil filter cap.

12. Remove the and discard the O-ring seal.

➡ **It is not necessary to pre-oil the oil filter or fill the oil filter housing.**

13. Lightly lubricate the new O-ring seal with clean engine oil.

14. Install the O-ring seal on the filter cap.

15. Install the new oil filter into the oil filter cap.

16. Thread the oil filter cap into the oil filter housing and tighten to 18 ft. lbs. (25 Nm).

17. Remove the oil fill cap. Fill the crankcase with the specified type and amount of engine oil.

18. Install the oil fill cap.

19. Start the engine and inspect for leaks.

20. Stop the engine and check the oil level.

21. Install the engine cover.

Oil Filter Specification

All engines are equipped with a high quality full-flow, disposable type oil filter. When replacing oil filter, use a Mopar® filter or equivalent.

Used Engine Oil Disposal

Care should be exercised when disposing of used engine oil after it has been drained from a vehicle engine.

EXHAUST MANIFOLD

REMOVAL & INSTALLATION

3.3L & 3.8L Engines

Left Exhaust Manifold

See Figures 72 and 73.

1. Disconnect battery negative cable.

2. Remove the bolts attaching crossover pipe to exhaust manifold.

3. Disconnect left cylinder bank spark plug wires.

4. Remove the heat shield attaching bolts.

5. Remove the bolts attaching exhaust manifold to cylinder head.

6. Remove the exhaust manifold.

7. Inspect and clean manifold.

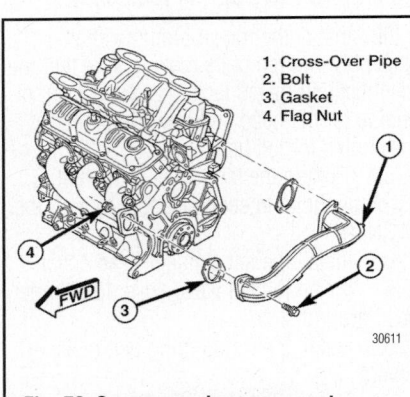

1. Cross-Over Pipe
2. Bolt
3. Gasket
4. Flag Nut

Fig. 72 Cross-over pipe components

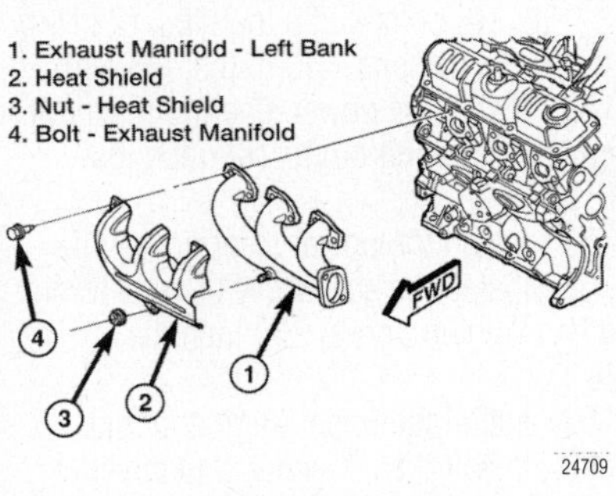

1. Exhaust Manifold - Left Bank
2. Heat Shield
3. Nut - Heat Shield
4. Bolt - Exhaust Manifold

Fig. 73 Remove heat shield attaching bolts. Remove bolts attaching exhaust manifold to cylinder head.

To install:

8. Position exhaust manifold on cylinder head. Install bolts to center runner (cylinder #4) and initial tighten to 25 inch lbs. (2.8 Nm).

9. Using a new gasket, attach crossover pipe (1) to exhaust manifold and tighten bolts to 30 ft. lbs. (41 Nm).

✱✱ WARNING

Inspect crossover pipe fasteners for damage from heat and corrosion. The cross-over bolts are made of a special stainless steel alloy. If replacement is required, OEM bolts are highly recommended.

10. Position heat shield on manifold.

11. Install the remaining manifold attaching bolts. Tighten all bolts to 200 inch lbs. (23 Nm).

12. Install the and tighten heat shield attaching nut to 105 inch lbs. (12 Nm).

13. Connect battery negative cable.

Right Exhaust Manifold

See Figures 74 and 75.

1. Disconnect battery negative cable.

2. Remove the wiper module.

3. Disconnect spark plug wires.

4. Remove the bolts fastening crossover pipe to exhaust manifold.

5. Disconnect and remove the upstream oxygen sensor.

6. Remove the heat shield attaching screws.

7. Remove the upper heat shield.

8. Raise vehicle on hoist and remove drive belt shield.

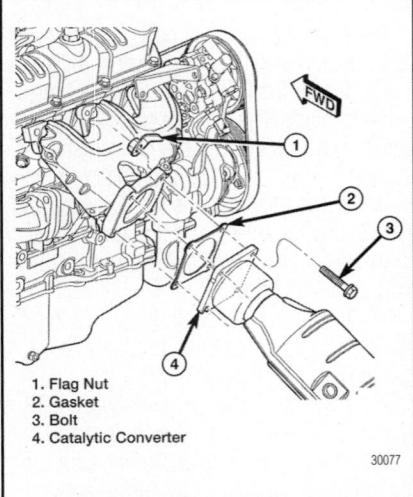

1. Flag Nut
2. Gasket
3. Bolt
4. Catalytic Converter

Fig. 74 Catalytic Converter to Exhaust Manifold

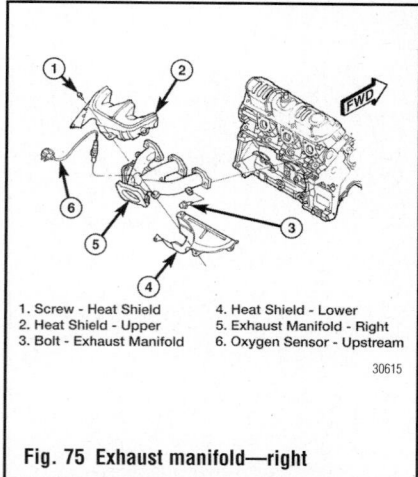

1. Screw - Heat Shield
2. Heat Shield - Upper
3. Bolt - Exhaust Manifold
4. Heat Shield - Lower
5. Exhaust Manifold - Right
6. Oxygen Sensor - Upstream

30615

Fig. 75 Exhaust manifold—right

9. Disconnect downstream oxygen sensor connector.

10. Disconnect catalytic converter pipe from exhaust manifold.

11. Remove the bolts attaching exhaust manifold to cylinder head and remove manifold.

Inspect and clean manifold.

To instill:

12. Position exhaust manifold on cylinder head and install bolts to center runner (cylinder #3) and initial tighten to 25 inch lbs. (2.8 Nm).

13. Using a new gasket, attach crossover pipe to exhaust manifold and tighten bolts to 30 ft. lbs. (41 Nm).

✳✳ WARNING

Inspect crossover pipe fasteners for damage from heat and corrosion. The cross-over bolts are made of a special stainless steel alloy. If replacement is required, OEM bolts are highly recommended.

14. Install the remaining manifold attaching bolts. Tighten all bolts to 200 inch lbs. (23 Nm).

15. Install the heat shield and attaching screws.

16. Install the and connect upstream oxygen sensor.

17. Raise the vehicle.

18. Attach catalytic converter pipe to exhaust manifold using new gasket and tighten bolts to 27 ft. lbs. (37 Nm).

19. Connect downstream oxygen sensor connector.

20. Install the belt splash shield and lower the vehicle.

21. Install the wiper module.

22. Connect battery negative cable.

INTAKE MANIFOLD

REMOVAL & INSTALLATION

3.3L & 3.8L Engines

Lower Intake Manifold

See Figures 76 through 79.

➡ **The fuel system is under constant pressure even with engine off. Before servicing fuel rail, fuel system pressure must be released.**

1. Perform the fuel pressure release procedure.

2. Disconnect and isolate the negative battery cable.

3. Drain the cooling system as outlined in the Engine Cooling Section.

4. Remove the EGR tube and upper intake manifold.

5. Disconnect the fuel supply hose from the fuel rail.

6. Remove the ignition coil and bracket.

7. Disconnect the heater supply hose and the Engine Coolant Temperature (ECT) sensor electrical connector.

8. Disconnect the fuel injector electrical connectors.

➡ **Mark the fuel injector electrical harness connectors with the correct corresponding cylinder numbers.**

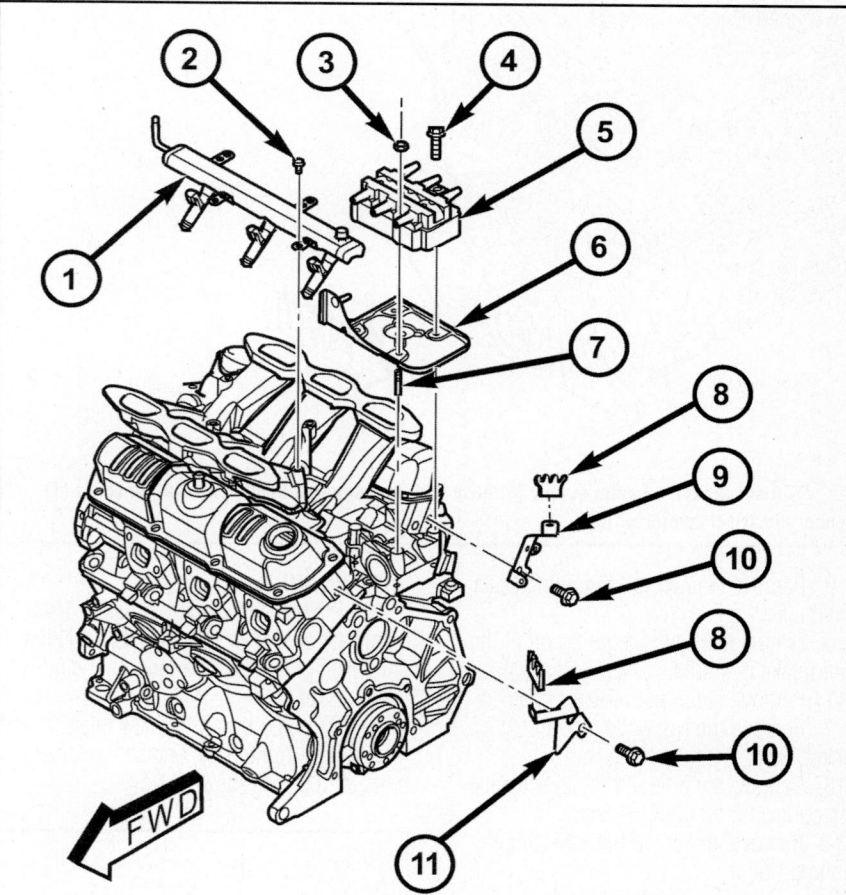

1. Fuel Rail
2. Bolt - Fuel Rail
3. Nut - Ignition Coil
4. Bolt - Ignition Coil
5. Ignition Coil
6. Bracket - Ignition Coil
7. Stud - Ignition Coil
8. Separator - Spark Plug Cable
9. Bracket - Spark Plug Cable Separator
10. Bolt - Separator Bracket
11. Bracket - Spark Plug Cable Separator

62667

Fig. 76 Fuel rail and ignition coil and bracket

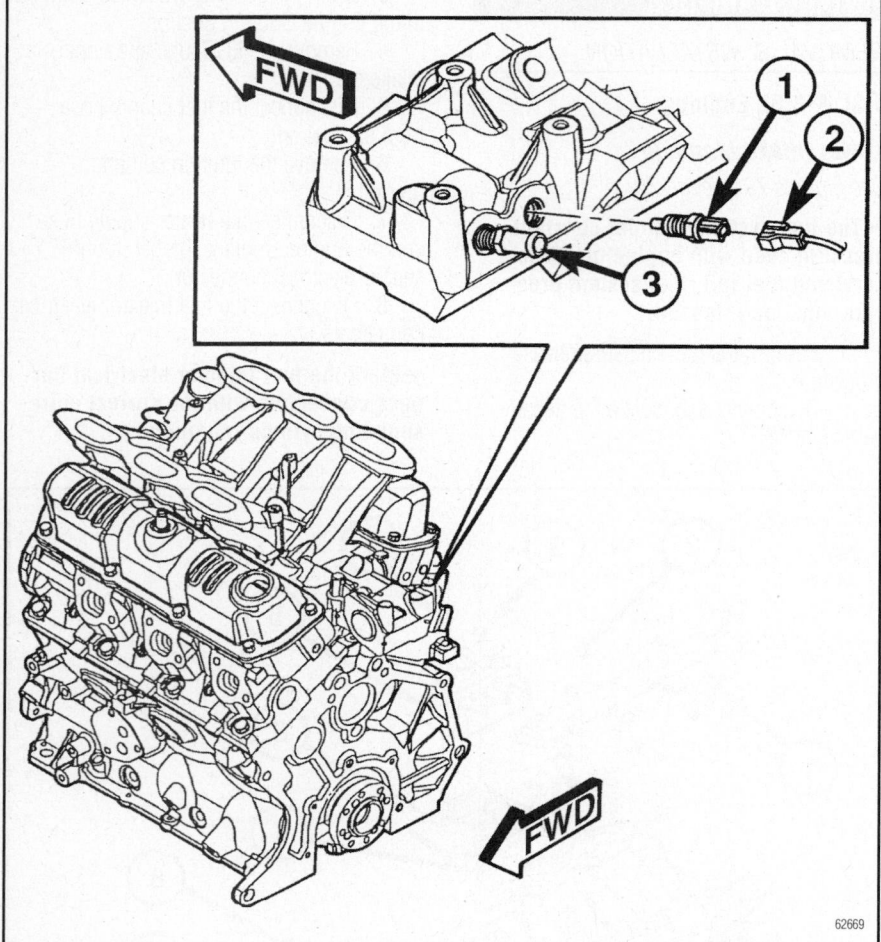

Fig. 77 Disconnect the heater supply (3) hose and the Engine Coolant Temperature (ECT) (1) sensor electrical connector (2)

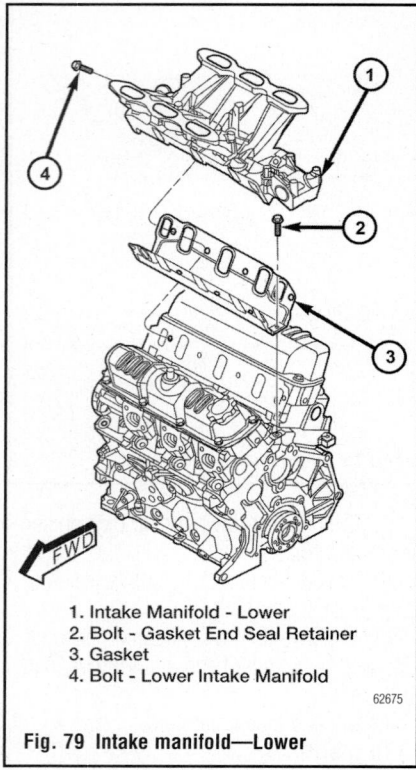

1. Intake Manifold - Lower
2. Bolt - Gasket End Seal Retainer
3. Gasket
4. Bolt - Lower Intake Manifold

Fig. 79 Intake manifold—Lower

9. Remove the fuel rail mounting bolts from the fuel rail.

10. Lift the fuel rail straight up off of the lower intake manifold.

11. Remove the upper radiator hose.

12. Remove the two bolts, nut and bracket.

13. Remove the bolt and the injector harness connector support bracket.

14. Remove the rest of the lower intake manifold bolts.

❋❋ CAUTION

Intake manifold gasket is made of very thin metal and may cause personal injury, handle with care.

15. Remove the lower intake manifold.

16. Remove the intake manifold end seal retainer bolts and remove the intake manifold gasket.

17. Inspect and clean the manifold.

To install:

18. Place a bead (approximately 1/4 in. diameter) of Mopar® Engine RTV GEN II onto each of the four manifold to cylinder head gasket corners.

19. Carefully install the new intake manifold gasket. Tighten the end seal retainer bolts to 105 inch lbs. (12 Nm).

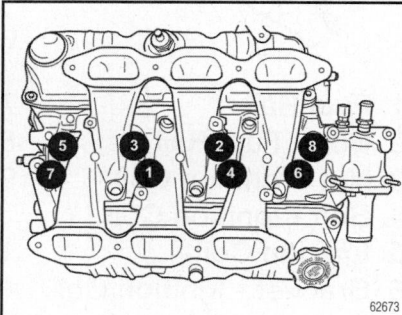

Fig. 78 Lower manifold tightening sequence

20. Install the injector harness connector support bracket and bolt. The bolt will be tightened in the next step.

21. Install the rest of the intake manifold bolts. Initially tighten all bolts to 10 inch lbs. (1 Nm). Finish tightening the bolts in two steps, first to 200 inch lbs. (22 Nm) in the proper sequence, then again to 200 inch lbs. (22 Nm) in the proper sequence. After the intake manifold is in place, inspect to make sure seals are in place.

22. Install the front cover support bracket with two bolts and nut. Tighten the nut to 200 inch lbs. (22 Nm). Tighten the bolts to 18 ft. lbs. (25 Nm).

23. Install the upper radiator hose.

24. Apply a light coating of clean engine oil to the O-ring on the nozzle end of each of the injectors.

25. Insert the fuel injector nozzles into the openings in the lower intake manifold. Seat the injectors in place. Install the fuel rail bolts and tighten bolts to 106 inch lbs. (12 Nm).

26. Correctly position and connect the fuel injector electrical harness connectors to the fuel injectors.

27. Connect the fuel injector electrical harness connectors.

28. Connect the heater supply hose and the Engine Coolant Temperature (ECT) sensor electrical connector. Install the ignition coil and bracket.

29. Connect the fuel supply hose to the fuel rail.

30. Install the upper intake manifold and EGR tube.

31. Fill the cooling system as outlined in the Engine Cooling Section.

32. Connect the negative battery cable and tighten nut to 45 inch lbs. (5 Nm).

33. Use the scan tool ASD Fuel System Test to pressurize the fuel system. Check for leaks.

Upper Intake Manifold

See Figures 80 through 82.

1. Disconnect and isolate the negative battery cable.

2. Disconnect the Inlet Air Temperature (IAT) sensor electrical connector.

3. Remove the air inlet resonator to throttle body hose assembly.

4. Disconnect the EVAP hose at the throttle body.

5. Disconnect the ETC wiring connector from the throttle body.

6. Disconnect the brake booster hose from the intake manifold.

7. Disconnect the Manifold Absolute Pressure (MAP) sensor electrical connector.

8. Disconnect the PCV hose.

9. Remove the EGR tube.

10. Remove the intake manifold bolts and remove the manifold.

11. Cover the lower intake manifold with a suitable cover while the upper manifold is removed.

12. Clean and inspect the upper intake manifold.

To install:

13. Remove the covering from the lower intake manifold and clean the gasket surfaces.

14. Inspect manifold gasket condition. Gaskets can be re-used, if not damaged.

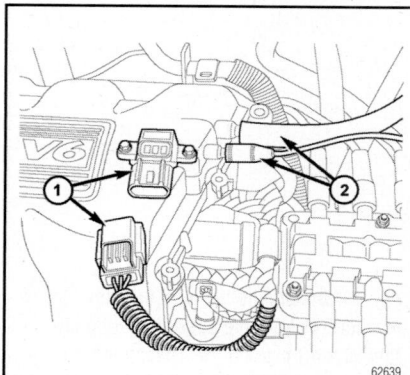

Fig. 80 Disconnect the Manifold Absolute Pressure (MAP) sensor electrical connector (1), and the vacuum lines (2)

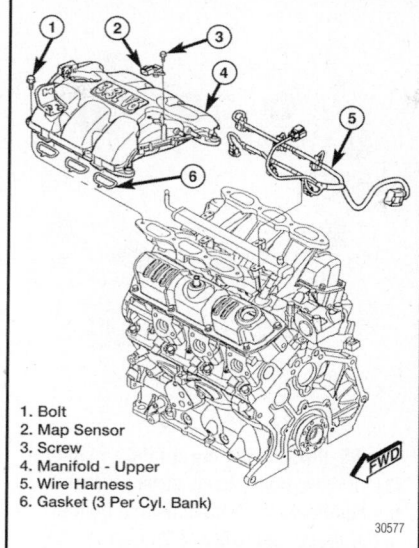

1. Bolt
2. Map Sensor
3. Screw
4. Manifold - Upper
5. Wire Harness
6. Gasket (3 Per Cyl. Bank)

Fig. 81 Upper intake manifold and components

Position gasket (6) in the seal channel and press lightly into place. Repeat procedure for each gasket position.

15. Position the upper manifold on the lower manifold.

16. Apply Mopar®Lock AND Seal Adhesive (Medium Strength Threadlocker) to each upper intake manifold bolt. Install and tighten bolts in the proper sequence to 105 inch lbs. (12 Nm).

✳✳ WARNING

The special screws used for the composite manifold attached components must be installed slowly using hand tools only. This requirement is to prevent the melting of material that causes stripped threads. If threads become stripped, an oversize repair screw is available.

17. Install the Manifold Absolute Pressure (MAP) sensor and torque fasteners to 15 inch lbs. (1.7 Nm).

18. Connect the MAP sensor electrical connector.

19. Connect the brake booster hose to intake manifold .

✳✳ WARNING

The special screws used for attaching the EGR tube to the manifold must be installed slowly using hand tools only. This requirement is to prevent the melting of material that causes stripped threads. If threads become stripped, an oversize repair screw is available.

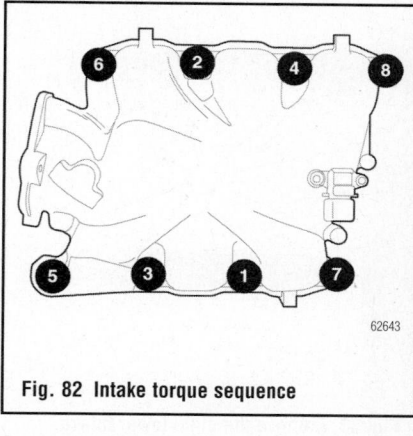

Fig. 82 Intake torque sequence

20. Install the EGR tube.

21. Connect the ETC connector to the throttle body.

22. Connect the EVAP hose to the throttle body.

23. Install the air cleaner and air inlet hose assembly.

24. Connect the Inlet Air Temperature (IAT) sensor electrical connector.

25. Connect the battery negative cable and tighten nut to 45 inch lbs. (5 Nm).

3.6L Engine

Lower Intake Manifold

See Figures 83 through 85.

➡**The fuel system is under constant pressure even with engine off. Before servicing the fuel rail, fuel system pressure must be released.**

1. Release fuel system pressure as outlined in the Fuel System Section.

2. Disconnect and isolate the negative battery cable.

3. Remove the air inlet hose and upper intake manifold.

4. Remove the insulator from the LH cylinder head cover.

5. Disconnect the fuel supply hose from the fuel rail.

6. Disconnect the fuel injector electrical connectors.

7. Disengage the injection/ignition harness retainer form the rear of the lower intake manifold.

8. Disengage the main wire harness retainer form the rear of the lower intake manifold.

9. Remove the eight lower intake manifold attaching bolts.

10. Remove the lower intake manifold with the fuel injectors and fuel rail.

11. Remove the and discard the six lower intake manifold to cylinder head seals.

12. If required, remove the fuel rail and

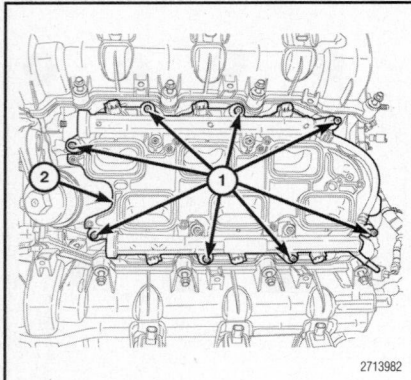

Fig. 83 Remove the eight lower intake manifold attaching bolts (1). Remove the lower intake manifold (2) with the fuel injectors and fuel rail.

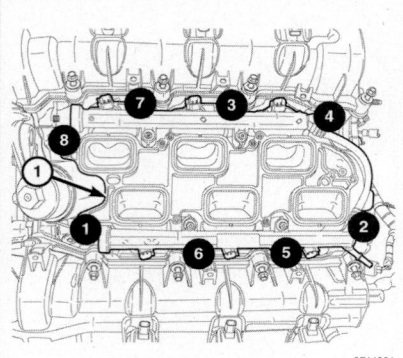

Fig. 85 Position the lower intake manifold (1) on the cylinder head surfaces. Install the manifold attaching bolts and tighten in the proper sequence to 71 inch lbs. (8 Nm).

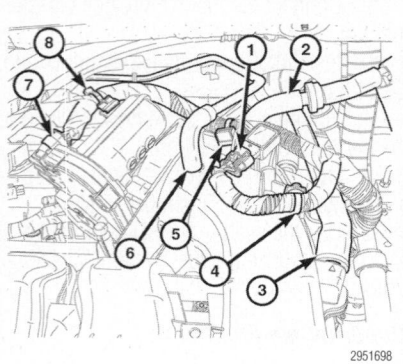

Fig. 86 Disconnect the electrical connectors from the Manifold Absolute Pressure (MAP) sensor (1) and the Electronic Throttle Control (ETC) (7). Disengage the ETC harness from the clip (8) on the throttle body. Disengage the wire harness retainers (4 and 5) from the upper intake manifold near the MAP sensor and reposition the wire harness. Disconnect the following hoses from the upper intake manifold: Positive Crankcase Ventilation (PCV) (3), vapor purge (6), brake booster (2)

fuel injectors from the lower intake manifold as outlined in the Fuel System Section.

To install:

13. Clean and inspect the sealing surfaces. Install new lower intake manifold to cylinder head seals.

14. If removed, install the fuel injectors and the fuel rail to the lower intake manifold. Tighten the four bolts in the proper sequence to 62 inch lbs. (7 Nm)

15. Position the lower intake manifold on the cylinder head surfaces.

16. Install the manifold attaching bolts and tighten in the proper sequence to 71 inch lbs. (8 Nm).

17. Engage the main wire harness retainer to the rear of the lower intake manifold.

18. Engage the injection/ignition harness retainer to the rear of the lower intake manifold.

19. Connect the fuel injector electrical connectors.

20. Connect the fuel supply hose to the fuel rail.

21. Install the insulator to the two align-

ment posts on top of the LH cylinder head cover.

22. Install the upper intake manifold, support brackets and air inlet hose.

23. Connect the negative battery cable and tighten nut to 45 inch lbs. (5 Nm).

24. Start the engine and check for leaks.

Upper Intake Manifold

See Figures 86 through 87.

1. Disconnect and isolate the negative battery cable.

2. Remove the engine cover.

3. Drain the engine cooling system as outlined in the Engine Cooling Section.

4. Disengage the upper radiator hose retainer from the upper intake manifold.

5. Remove the engine cooling fan and shroud assembly as outlined in the Engine Cooling Section.

6. Remove the intake resonator.

7. Disconnect the electrical connectors from the Manifold Absolute Pressure (MAP) sensor and the Electronic Throttle Control (ETC).

8. Disengage the ETC harness from the clip on the throttle body. Disengage the wire harness retainers from the upper intake manifold near the MAP sensor and reposition the wire harness.

9. Disconnect the following hoses from the upper intake manifold:
   • Positive Crankcase Ventilation (PCV).
   • Vapor purge.
   • Brake booster.

10. Disengage the wire harness retainer from the upper intake manifold support bracket.

11. Disengage the wire harness retainer from the studbolt.

12. Remove the two nuts, loosen the studbolt and reposition the upper intake manifold support bracket.

13. Remove the nut from the support bracket of the heater core return tube.

14. Remove the two nuts, loosen two

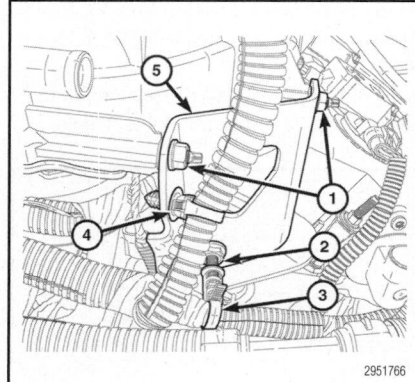

Fig. 87 Disengage the wire harness retainer (4) from the upper intake manifold support bracket (5). Disengage the wire harness retainer (3) from the studbolt (2). Remove two nuts (1), loosen the studbolt (2) and reposition the upper intake manifold support bracket (5).

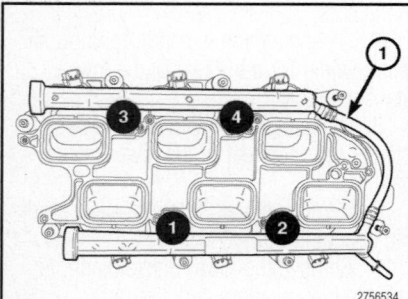

Fig. 84 Fuel rail (1) removal & installation. Tighten the four bolts in the proper sequence

studbolts and reposition the two upper intake manifold support brackets.

➡**The upper intake manifold attaching bolts are captured in the upper intake manifold. Once loosened, the bolts will have to be lifted out of the lower intake manifold and held while removing the upper intake manifold.**

➡**Exercise care not to inadvertently loosen the two fuel rail attachment bolts that are in close proximity of the upper intake manifold attaching bolts.**

15. Remove the seven manifold attaching bolts and remove the upper intake manifold.

16. Remove the and discard the six upper to lower intake manifold seals.

17. Cover the open intake ports to prevent debris from entering the engine.

18. If required, remove the insulator from the LH cylinder head cover.

To install:

19. Clean and inspect the sealing surfaces. Install new upper to lower intake manifold seals.

➡**Make sure the fuel injectors and wiring harnesses are in the correct position so that they don't interfere with the upper intake manifold installation.**

20. If removed, install the insulator to the two alignment posts on top of the LH cylinder head cover.

21. Lift and hold the seven upper intake attaching bolts clear of the mating surface. Back the bolts out slightly or if required, use an elastic band to hold the bolts clear of the mating surface.

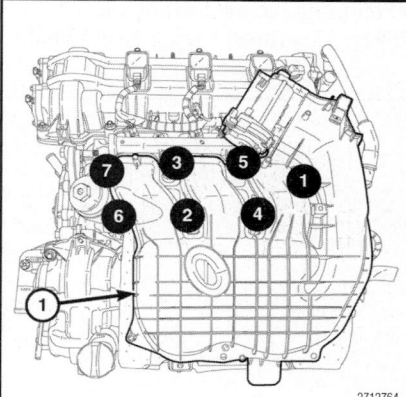

Fig. 88 Install the two nuts to the upper intake manifold support bracket. Tighten the nuts to 89 inch lbs. (10 Nm) and tighten the studbolt to 177 inch lbs. (20 Nm).

22. Position the upper intake manifold onto the lower intake manifold so that the two locating posts on the upper intake manifold align with corresponding holes in the lower intake manifold.

23. Install the seven upper intake manifold attaching bolts. Tighten the bolts in the proper sequence to 80 inch lbs. (9 Nm).

24. Engage the wire harness retainer to the studbolt.

25. Engage the wire harness retainer to the upper intake manifold support bracket.

26. Install the two upper intake manifold support brackets with two studbolts and two nuts. Tighten the studbolts to 177 inch lbs. (20 Nm) and tighten the nuts to 89 inch lbs. (10 Nm).

27. Install the nut to the support bracket of the heater core return tube and tighten to 106 inch lbs. (12 Nm).

28. Connect the following hoses to the upper intake manifold:
- Positive Crankcase Ventilation (PCV).
- Vapor purge.
- Brake booster.

29. Connect the electrical connectors to the Manifold Absolute Pressure (MAP) sensor and the Electronic Throttle Control (ETC).

30. Secure the ETC harness to the clip on the throttle body and engage the wire harness retainers to the upper intake manifold near the MAP sensor.

31. Install the engine cooling fan and shroud assembly as outlined in the Engine Cooling Section.

32. Engage the upper radiator hose retainer to the upper intake manifold.

33. Install the intake resonator.

34. Connect the negative battery cable and tighten nut to 45 inch lbs. (5 Nm).

35. Fill the cooling system as outlined in the Engine Cooling Section.

36. Run the engine until it reaches normal operating temperature. Check cooling system for correct fluid level.

37. Install the engine cover.

OIL PAN

REMOVAL & INSTALLATION

3.3L & 3.8L Engines
See Figure 89.

➡**This engine uses a two-piece oil pan. RTV is used between the upper and lower pans. The lower pan should not be separated from the upper pan unless this junction is leaking.**

1. Disconnect and isolate the negative battery cable.

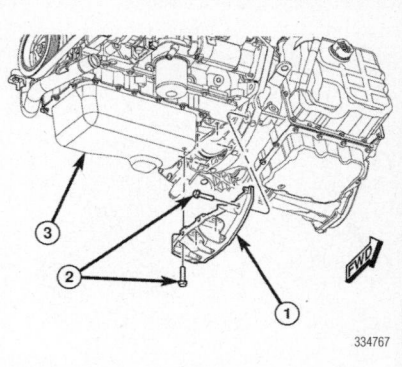

Fig. 89 Install oil pan (3) and tighten bolts. Install structural collar (1) and tighten bolts (2)

2. Remove the engine oil dipstick.

3. Raise and support the vehicle.

4. Drain engine oil.

5. Remove the drive belt splash shield.

6. Remove the seven structural collar bolts and structural collar.

7. Remove the upper oil pan bolts, oil pan and gasket.

To install:

➡**This engine uses a two-piece oil pan. RTV is used between the upper and lower pans. The lower pan should not be separated from the upper pan unless this junction is leaking.**

8. Clean sealing surfaces and apply a 1/8 inch bead of Mopar®Engine RTV GEN II at the parting line of the chain case cover and the rear seal retainer.

9. Position a new pan gasket on oil pan.

10. Install the oil pan and tighten the bolts to 105 inch lbs. (12 Nm).

11. Install the structural collar and tighten the bolts to 55 ft. lbs. (75 Nm).

12. Install the drive belt splash shield.

13. Lower vehicle and install oil dipstick.

14. Connect negative cable to battery.

15. Fill crankcase with oil to proper level.

3.6L Engine

Lower
See Figures 90 and 91.

1. Raise and support the vehicle.
2. Drain the engine oil.
3. Remove the belly pan.
4. Remove the inner splash shield.

➡**The lower oil pan must be removed to access all of the upper oil pan retaining bolts.**

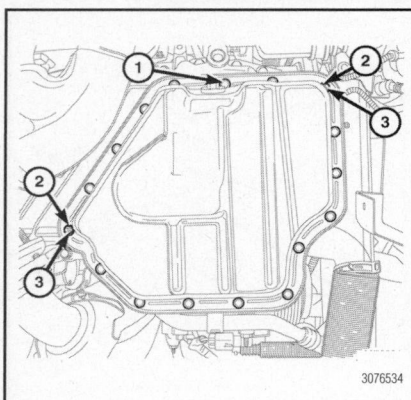

Fig. 90 Remove fifteen bolts (1), two nuts (2) and two studs (3) from the flange of the lower oil pan.

5. Remove the fifteen bolts, two nuts and two studs from the flange of the lower oil pan.

✳✳ WARNING

Do not pry on the lower oil pan flange. There are no designated pry points for lower oil pan removal. Prying on only one or a few locations could bend the flange and damage the pan.

6. Using a pry bar, apply a side force to the lower oil pan in order to shear the sealant bond and remove the pan.

7. Remove the all residual sealant from the upper and lower oil pans.

To install:

8. Clean the upper and lower oil pan mating surfaces with isopropyl alcohol in preparation for sealant application.

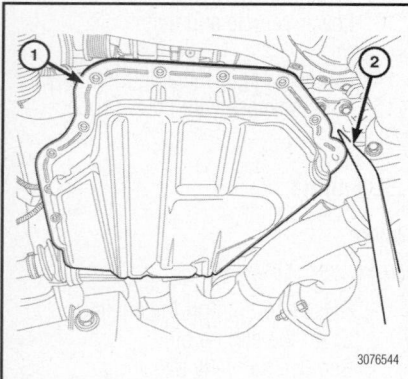

Fig. 91 Using a pry bar (2), apply a side force to the lower oil pan (1) in order to shear the sealant bond and remove the pan.

➡Engine assembly requires the use of a unique sealant that is compatible with engine oil. Using a sealant other than Mopar®Threebond Engine RTV Sealant may result in engine fluid leakage.

✳✳ WARNING

Following the application of Mopar®Threebond Engine RTV Sealant to the gasket surfaces, the components must be assembled within 20 minutes and the attaching fasteners must be tightened to specification within 45 minutes. Prolonged exposure to the air prior to assembly may result in engine fluid leakage.

9. Apply a 2 to 3 mm wide bead of Mopar® Threebond Engine RTV Sealant to the lower oil pan.

10. Install the two studs into the upper oil pan flange.

Install the lower oil pan to the upper oil pan with fifteen bolts and two nuts tightened to 97 inch lbs. (11 Nm).

✳✳ WARNING

Following assembly, the Mopar®Threebond Engine RTV Sealant must be allowed to dry for 45 minutes prior to adding oil and engine operation. Premature exposure to oil prior to drying may result in engine fluid leakage

11. If removed, install the oil filter and fill the engine crankcase with the proper oil to the correct level.

12. Run the engine until it reaches normal operating temperature.

Upper

See Figures 92 through 92.

1. Disconnect and isolate the negative battery cable.

2. Remove the bolt and the oil level indicator.

3. Raise and support the vehicle.

4. Remove the belly pan.

5. Drain the engine oil.

6. Remove the cross-under pipe.

➡The lower oil pan must be removed to access all of the upper oil pan retaining bolts.

7. Remove the lower oil pan.

8. Remove the bolt securing the coolant tube to oil pan.

9. Remove the oil pan to transmission bolts.

10. Remove the two bolts from the rear oil seal retainer flange.

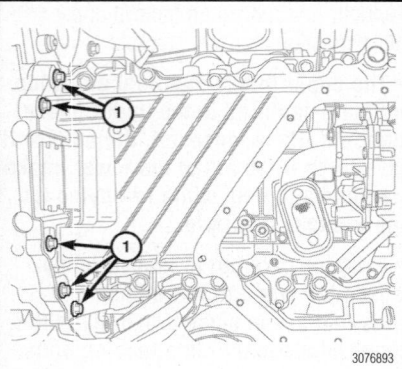

Fig. 92 Remove the oil pan to transmission bolts (1). Remove two bolts (2) from the rear oil seal retainer flange. Remove nineteen oil pan mounting bolts (3)

11. Remove the nineteen oil pan mounting bolts.

12. Using the four indicated pry points, carefully remove the upper oil pan.

13. Remove the all residual sealant from the upper and lower oil pans, timing chain cover, rear seal retainer and engine block mating surfaces.

To install:

14. Clean the upper and lower oil pans, timing chain cover, rear seal retainer and engine block mating surfaces with isopropyl alcohol in preparation for sealant application.

➡Engine assembly requires the use of a unique sealant that is compatible with engine oil. Using a sealant other than Mopar® Threebond Engine RTV Sealant may result in engine fluid leakage.

➡Following the application of Mopar® Threebond Engine RTV Sealant

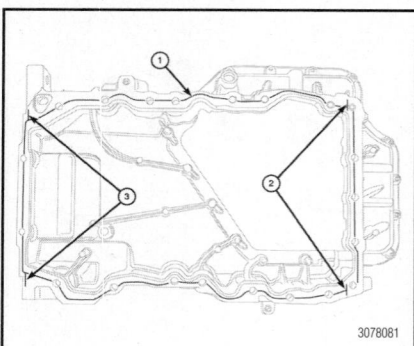

Fig. 93 Oil pan to engine block flange (1). Two timing cover to engine block T-joints (2). Two rear seal retainer to engine block T-joints (3).

to the gasket surfaces, the components must be assembled within 20 minutes and the attaching fasteners must be tightened to specification within 45 minutes. Prolonged exposure to the air prior to assembly may result in engine fluid leakage.

15. Apply a 2 to 3 mm wide bead of Mopar® Threebond Engine RTV Sealant to the upper oil pan in the following locations:

    a. Oil pan to engine block flange.

    b. Two timing cover to engine block T-joints.

    c. Two rear seal retainer to engine block T-joints.

✳✳ WARNING

Make sure that the rear face of the oil pan is flush to the transmission bell housing before tightening any of the oil pan mounting bolts. A gap between the oil pan and the transmission could crack the oil pan or transmission casting.

Install the oil pan to the engine block and flush to the transmission bell housing. Secure the oil pan to the engine block with nineteen oil pan mounting bolts finger tight.

16. Install the two bolts to the rear oil seal retainer flange and tighten finger tight.

17. Install the five oil pan to transmission bolts finger tight.

18. Tighten the nineteen previously installed oil pan mounting bolts to 18 ft. lbs. (25 Nm).

19. Install the two bolts to the rear oil

seal retainer flange and tighten to 106 inch lbs. (12 Nm).

20. Tighten the five transmission to the engine oil pan bolts and tighten to 41 ft. lbs. (55 Nm).

21. Install the bolt securing the coolant tube to oil pan and tighten to 106 inch lbs. (12 Nm).

22. Install the lower oil pan.

23. Install the cross-under pipe.

24. Install the belly pan.

25. Lower the vehicle.

26. Install the oil level indicator with bolt tightened 106 inch lbs. (12 Nm).

27. If removed, install the oil filter and fill the engine crankcase with the proper oil to the correct level.

28. Connect the negative battery cable and tighten nut to 45 inch lbs. (5 Nm).

29. Run the engine until it reaches normal operating temperature.

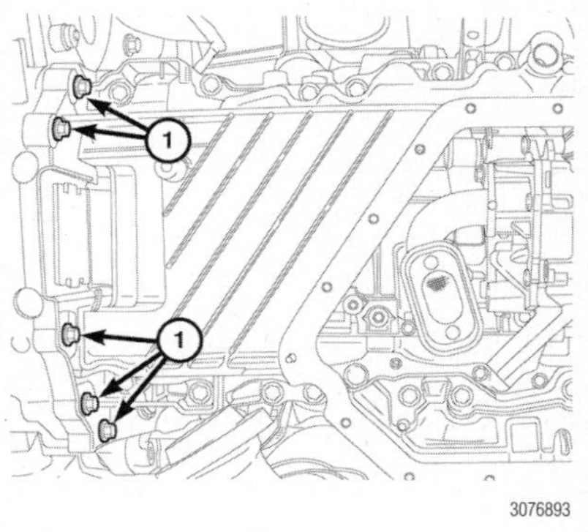

4.0L Engine

See Figures 95 and 96.

1. Disconnect and isolate the negative battery cable.

2. Remove the cross-under pipe.

3. Remove the oil dipstick tube bolt and remove the oil dipstick tube.

4. Remove the front maniverter

5. Raise and support the vehicle.

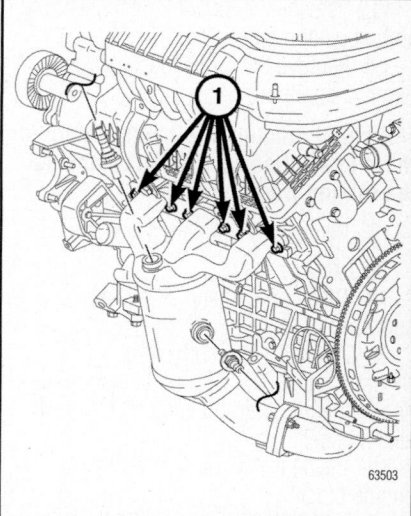

Fig. 95 Remove the front maniverter (1) bolts

6. Remove the cross-under pipe bracket from the bottom of the transaxle bell housing.

7. Remove the bolt and the torque converter access cover.

8. Drain engine oil.

9. Remove the support bolt from the oil filter housing.

10. Remove the bolt from oil filter housing and remove oil filter housing with oil filter from oil cooler.

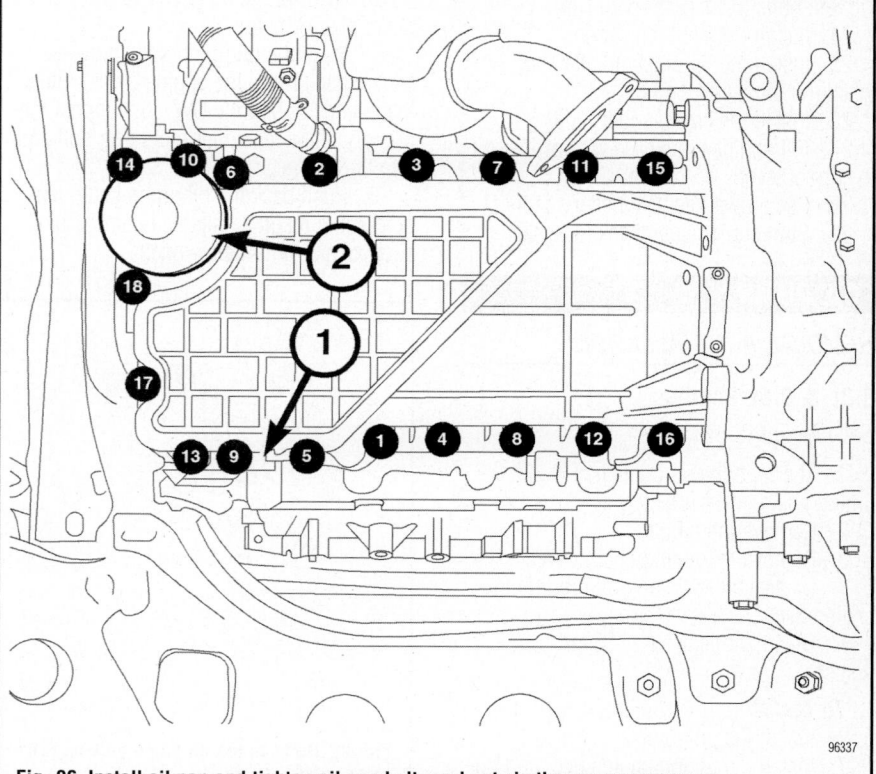

Fig. 94 Secure the oil pan to the engine block with nineteen oil pan mounting bolts (3) finger tight. Install two bolts (2) to the rear oil seal retainer flange and tighten finger tight. Install the five oil pan to transmission bolts (1) finger tight.

Fig. 96 Install oil pan and tighten oil pan bolts and nuts in the proper sequence.

11. Remove the oil cooler connector bolt and reposition oil cooler.

12. Remove the oil pan fasteners. Remove oil pan.

➡**A small amount of oil will remain in the oil pan. Use care when removing the oil pan from the engine.**

13. Remove the oil pan gasket.

To install:

14. Clean oil pan and all gasket surfaces.

15. Apply a 1/8 inch bead of Mopar®Engine RTV GEN II at the parting line of the oil pump housing and the rear seal retainer.

16. Install the oil pan gasket to the engine block.

17. Install the oil pan and tighten oil pan bolts and nuts to 21 ft. lbs. (28 Nm).

18. Position oil cooler to engine block. Install oil cooler connector bolt and tighten to 40 ft. lbs. (54 Nm).

19. Position oil filter adaptor and oil filter to oil cooler..Install bolt finger tight.

20. Install the oil filter housing support bolt and tighten to 70 inch lbs. (8 Nm).

21. Tighten the previously installed oil filter adapter bolt to 40 ft. lbs. (54 Nm).

22. Install the torque converter access cover.

23. Install the cross-under pipe bracket. Tighten bolts to 21 ft. lbs. (28 Nm).

24. Install the front maniverter.

25. Install the oil dipstick tube and install oil dipstick tube bolt.

26. Install the cross-under pipe.

27. Fill engine crankcase with proper oil to correct level.

28. Reconnect negative battery cable.

29. Start engine and check for leaks.

OIL PUMP

REMOVAL & INSTALLATION

3.3L & 3.8L Engines

See Figure 97.

1. The oil pump is contained within the timing chain cover housing.

2. Remove the oil pan.

3. Remove the timing chain cover.

4. Disassemble oil pump from timing chain cover.

5. Clean and Inspect oil pump components.

To install:

6. Install the oil pump.

7. Install the timing chain cover and oil pan.

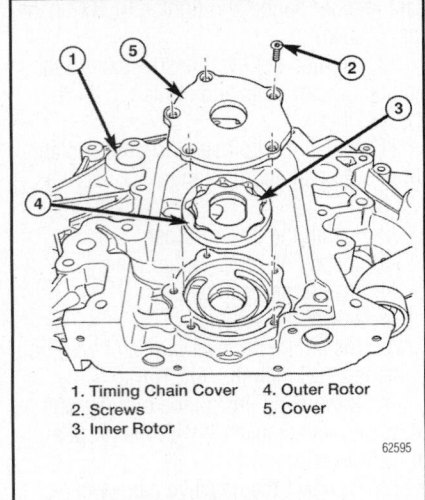

1. Timing Chain Cover   4. Outer Rotor
2. Screws   5. Cover
3. Inner Rotor

62595

Fig. 97 Oil pump and components

3.6L Engine

See Figures 98 through 103.

1. Disconnect and isolate the negative battery cable.

2. Remove the upper oil pan.

3. Remove the oil pump pick-up.

4. Disconnect the engine wire harness from the oil pump solenoid electrical connector.

5. Depress the connector retention lock tab to disengage the oil pump solenoid electrical connector from the engine block.

6. Remove the bolts and the timing gear splash shield.

7. Push the oil pump solenoid electrical connector into the engine block, rotate the connector slightly CW, push it past the primary chain tensioner mounting bolt and into the engine.

8. Push back the oil pump chain tensioner and insert a suitable retaining pin such as a 3 mm Allen wrench.

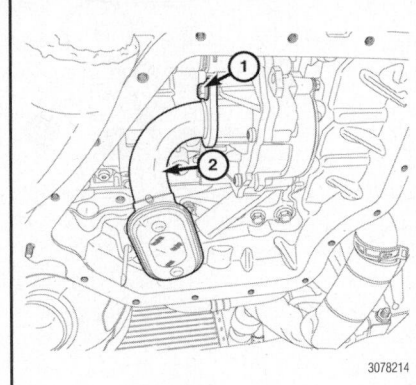

3078214

Fig. 98 Remove the oil pump pick-up (2), and bolt (1)

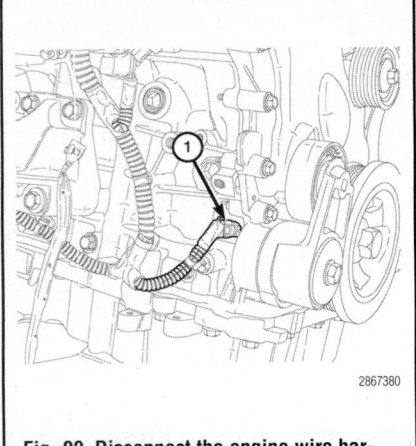

2867380

Fig. 99 Disconnect the engine wire harness from the oil pump solenoid electrical connector (1)

➡**Remove the retaining pin and disengage the oil pump chain tensioner spring from the dowel pin.**

❉❉ WARNING

Always reinstall timing chains so that they maintain the same direction of rotation. Inverting a previously run chain on a previously run sprocket will result in excessive wear to both the chain and sprocket.

9. Mark the direction of rotation on the oil pump chain and sprocket using a paint pen or equivalent to aid in reassembly.

➡**There are no timing marks on the oil pump gear or chain. Timing of the oil pump is not required.**

10. Remove the oil pump sprocket T45 retaining bolt and remove the oil pump sprocket.

11. Remove the retaining pin and disengage the oil pump chain tensioner spring from the dowel pin.

12. Remove the oil pump chain tensioner from the oil pump.

13. Remove the four oil pump bolts and remove the oil pump.

To install:

14. Align the locator pins to the engine block and install the oil pump with four bolts. Tighten the bolts to 106 inch lbs. (12 Nm).

15. Install the oil pump chain tensioner on the oil pump.

16. Position the oil pump chain tensioner spring above the dowel pin.

17. Push back the oil pump chain tensioner and insert a suitable retaining pin such as a 3 mm Allen wrench.

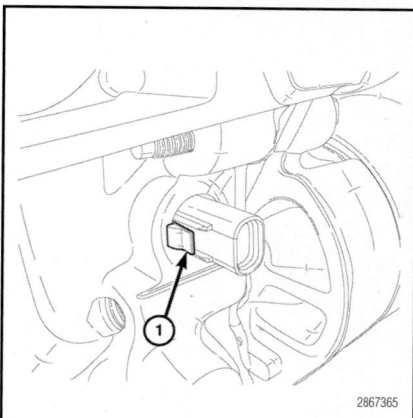

Fig. 100 Depress the connector retention lock tab (1) to disengage the oil pump solenoid electrical connector from the engine block.

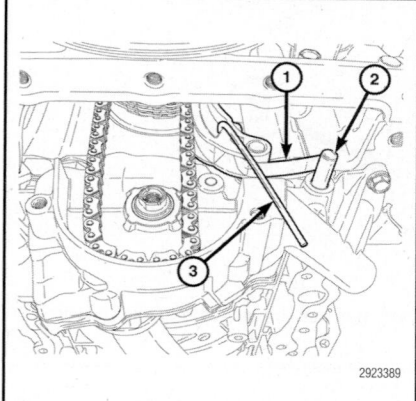

Fig. 101 Remove the retaining pin (3) and disengage the oil pump chain tensioner spring (1) from the dowel pin (2).

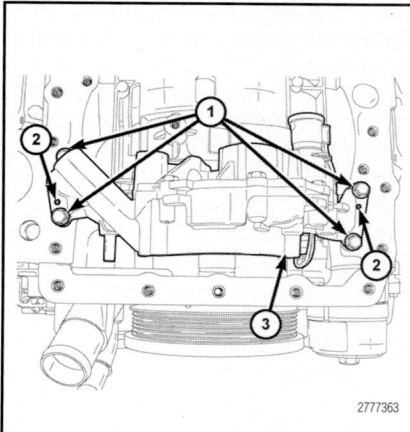

Fig. 102 Align the locator pins (2) to the engine block and install the oil pump (3) with four bolts (1).

➡There are no timing marks on the oil pump gear or chain. Timing of the oil pump is not required.

> ❋❋ **WARNING**
>
> **Always reinstall timing chains so that they maintain the same direction of rotation. Inverting a previously run chain on a previously run sprocket will result in excessive wear to both the chain and sprocket.**

18. Place the oil pump sprocket into the oil pump chain. Align the oil pump sprocket with the oil pump shaft and install the sprocket. Install the T45 retaining bolt and tighten to 18 ft. lbs. (25 Nm).

19. Remove the retaining pin. Verify that the oil pump chain is centered on the tensioner and crankshaft sprocket.

20. Rotate the crankshaft CW one complete revolution to verify proper oil pump chain installation.

21. Position the oil pump solenoid electrical connector into the engine block. Rotate the connector so that it can be pushed past the primary chain tensioner mounting bolt. Then rotate the connector slightly CCW and push it into the engine block until it locks in place.

22. Install the timing gear splash shield. Tighten bolts to 35 inch lbs. (5 Nm).

23. Verify that the oil pump solenoid electrical connector retention lock tab is engaged to the engine block.

24. Connect the engine wire harness to the oil pump solenoid electrical connector.

25. Install the oil pump pick-up.

26. Install the oil pan.

27. If removed, install the oil filter and

fill the engine crankcase with the proper oil to the correct level.

28. Connect the negative battery cable and tighten nut to 45 inch lbs. (5 Nm).

➡A MIL or low oil pressure indicator that remains illuminated for more than 2 seconds may indicate low or no engine oil pressure. Stop the engine and investigate the cause of the indication.

29. Start and run the engine until it reaches normal operating temperature.

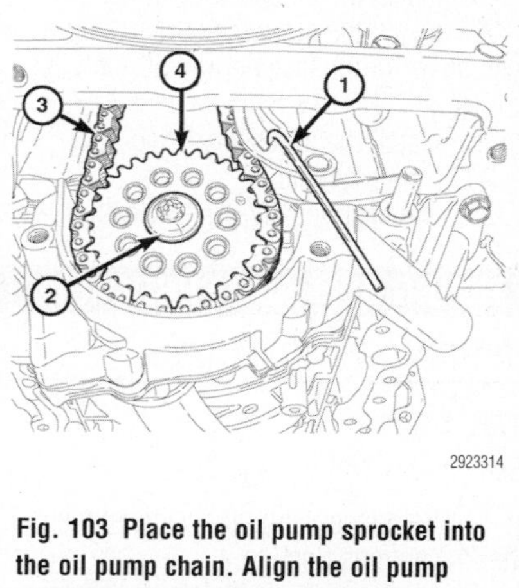

4.0L Engine

See Figure 104.

It is necessary to remove the oil pump body to service the oil pump rotors.

The oil pump pressure relief valve can be serviced by removing the oil pan.

1. Drain the cooling system as outlined in the Engine Cooling Section.

2. Remove the timing belt.

3. Remove the crankshaft sprocket.

4. Remove the oil pan as outlined in this section.

5. Remove the oil pickup tube.

6. Remove the oil pump fasteners.

7. Remove the pump and gasket from engine.

To install:

➡Thoroughly clean all bolt threads and threaded area in the engine, removing all oil residue, before assembly.

8. Prime oil pump before installation by filling rotor cavity with clean engine oil.

9. Install the oil pump and gasket carefully over the crankshaft and position pump onto block.

➡DO NOT apply the thread sealant to the underside of the bolt head.

10. Apply Mopar®Thread Sealant as directed on the package to the oil pump

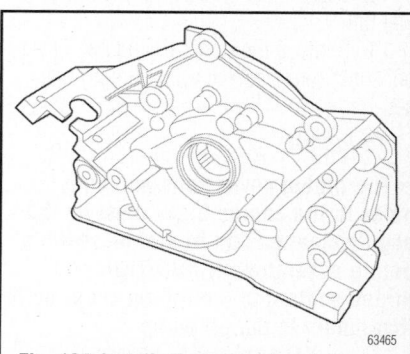

Fig. 103 Place the oil pump sprocket into the oil pump chain. Align the oil pump sprocket with the oil pump shaft and install the sprocket. Install the T45 retaining bolt and remove the retaining pin.

Fig. 104 Install oil pump and gasket carefully over the crankshaft and position pump onto block.

cover bolts where indicated. The sealant must be applied from the tip to approximately 10 mm of the thread length. Tighten the oil pump cover bolts to 105 inch lbs. (12 Nm). Tighten oil pump to block bolts to 250 inch lbs. (28 Nm).

11. Install the new O-ring on oil pickup tube.

12. Install the oil pickup tube.

13. Install the oil pan.

14. Install the crankshaft sprocket.

15. Install the timing belt.

16. Install the timing belt covers.

17. Install the crankshaft vibration damper.

18. Install the accessory drive belts.

19. Fill the cooling system.

20. Fill engine crankcase with proper oil to the correct level.

TIMING BELT FRONT COVER

REMOVAL & INSTALLATION

4.0L Engine

See Figure 105.

1. Perform fuel pressure release procedure as outlined in the Fuel System Section.

2. Disconnect negative battery cable.

3. Raise vehicle on hoist.

4. Remove the accessory drive belt as outlined in this section.

5. Remove the accessory drive belt tensioner.

6. Remove the bolts for power steering pump. Reposition power steering pump aside.

7. Remove the crankshaft damper.

8. Remove the lower front timing belt cover fasteners and the lower timing belt cover.

9. Lower the vehicle.

10. Support the engine with a floor jack.

11. Remove the air cleaner housing.

12. Remove the front engine mount.

13. Disconnect the fuel supply line at the fuel rail.

14. Remove the upper timing belt cover bolts and remove front upper timing belt cover.

To install:

➡**The timing cover bolts and both holes to the engine block must be thoroughly cleaned and free of oil residue before assembly. IN ADDITION add thread sealant to the timing cover bolts that mount to the oil pump.**

15. Install the front timing belt cover .

16. Install the upper engine mount.

17. Connect fuel supply line at fuel rail .

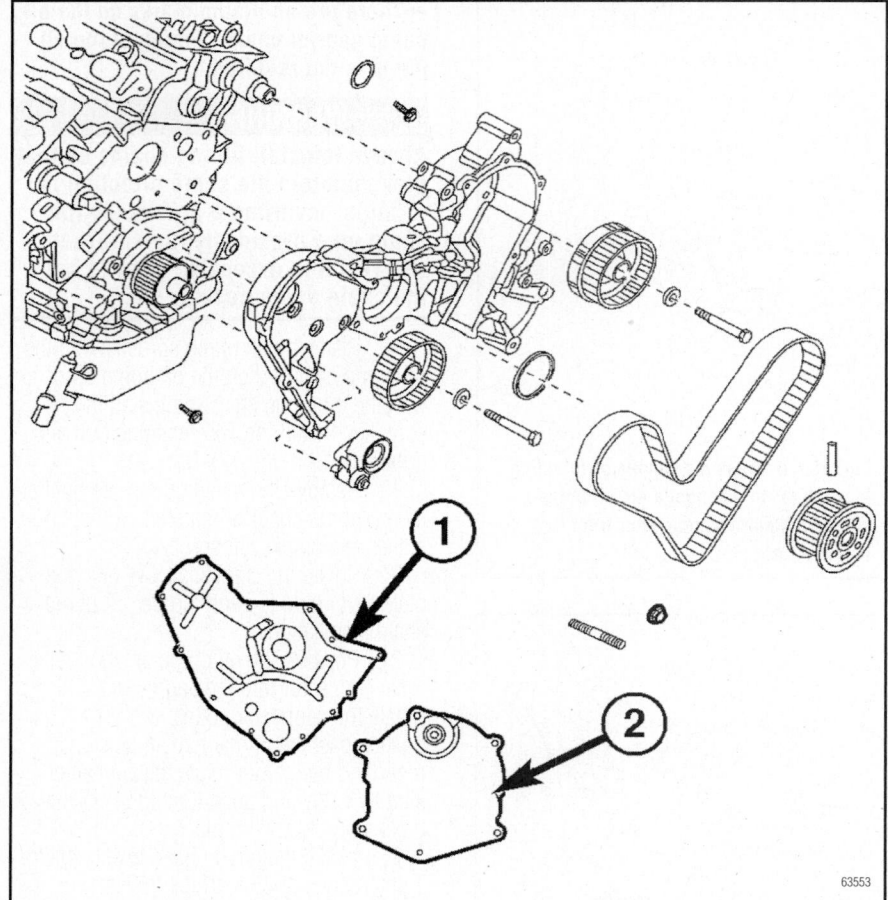

Fig. 105 Remove the lower front timing belt cover fasteners and the lower timing belt cover (1), and upper timing belt cover.

18. Install the air cleaner housing.

19. Remove the floor jack and raise vehicle.

20. Install the power steering pump fasteners. Tighten bolts to 200 inch lbs. (23 Nm).

21. Install the crankshaft damper.

22. Install the accessory drive belt tensioner. Torque fastener to 250 inch lbs. (28 Nm).

23. Install the accessory drive belt.

24. Lower vehicle.

25. Connect negative battery cable.

TIMING BELT AND SPROCKETS

REMOVAL & INSTALLATION

4.0L Engine

See Figures 106 through 109.

1. Before servicing the vehicle, refer to the Precautions Section.

2. Disconnect and isolate the negative battery cable.

3. Remove the front timing belt cover.

Refer to Timing Belt Front Cover, removal & installation.

4. Mark the belt running direction, if the timing belt is to be reused.

✴✴ WARNING

When aligning the timing marks, always rotate the engine by turning the crankshaft. Failure to do so will result in valve and/or piston damage.

5. Rotate the engine clockwise until the crankshaft (10) mark aligns with the TDC mark on the oil pump housing (9) and the camshaft sprocket (2, 7) timing marks (1, 8) are aligned with the marks on the rear cover.

6. Raise and safely support the vehicle.

7. Remove the bolt (2) and reposition the oil cooler hose (1).

8. Remove the timing belt tensioner (12).

9. Lower the vehicle.

10. Remove the timing belt (4).

11. Inspect the tensioner for fluid leakage.

12. Inspect the pivot and bolt for free

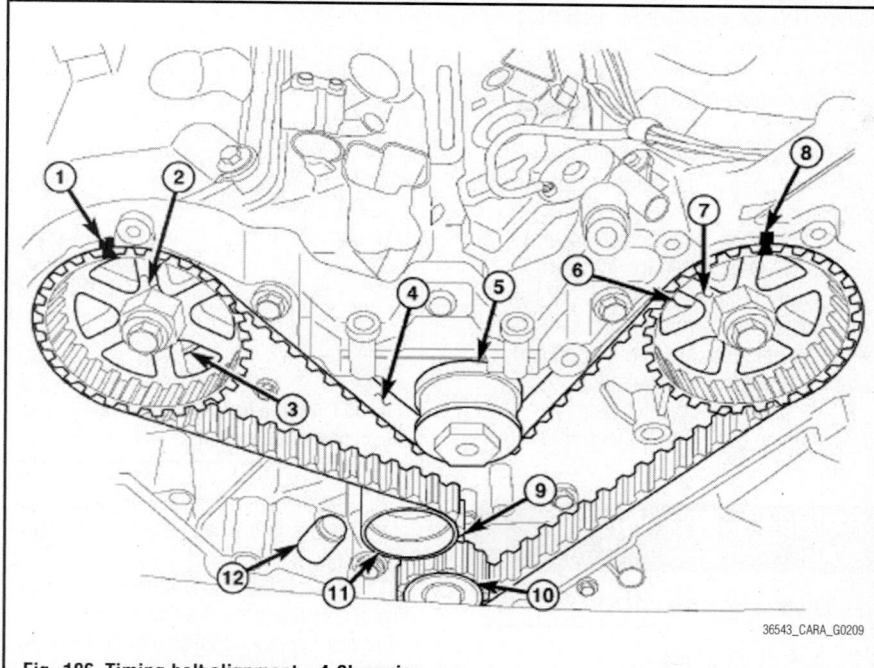

Fig. 106 Timing belt alignment—4.0L engine

movement, bearing grease leakage, and smooth rotation. If it is not rotating freely, replace the arm and pulley assembly.

➡ **When the tensioner is removed from the engine, it is necessary to compress the plunger into the tensioner body.**

13. Index the tensioner in a vise the same way it is installed on the engine. This ensures the proper pin orientation when the tensioner is installed on the engine.

a. Place the tensioner into a vise (1) and SLOWLY compress the plunger. The total bleed down of the tensioner should take approximately 2 minutes.

b. When the plunger is compressed into the tensioner body, install a pin (2) through the body and the plunger to retain the plunger in place until the tensioner is installed.

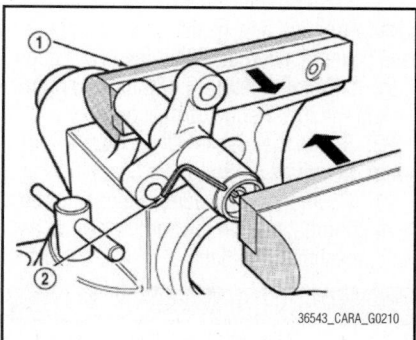

Fig. 107 Timing belt tensioner compression—4.0L engine

14. Counter-hold the left cam gear and remove the cam gear retaining bolt.

15. Remove the cam gear.

16. Counter-hold the right cam gear and remove the cam gear retaining bolt.

17. Remove the cam gear.

18. Remove the crankshaft sprocket using Gear Puller L-4407-A (1).

To install:

19. Install the crankshaft sprocket using Forcing Screw C-4685-C1, with the Nut and Thrust Bearing from 6792, and Sprocket Installer 6641 (1).

➡ **The camshaft sprockets are keyed and are not interchangeable from side to side because of the camshaft position sensor pick-up.**

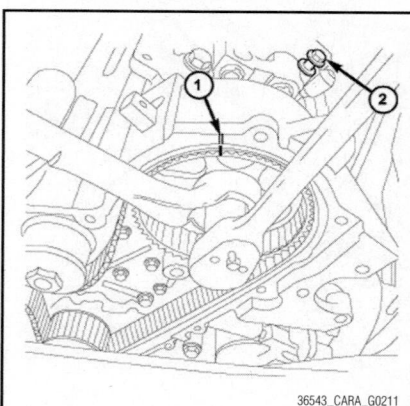

Fig. 108 Camshaft gear removal LH— 4.0L engine

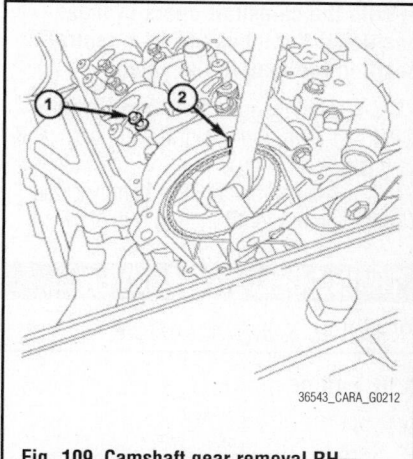

Fig. 109 Camshaft gear removal RH— 4.0L engine

20. Install a NEW sprocket attaching bolt into place. The 10 inch (255mm) bolt is to be installed in the left camshaft and the 8 ⅜inch (213mm) bolt is to be installed into the right camshaft. Counter-hold the camshaft sprocket and tighten the camshaft sprocket bolt to 75 ft. lbs. (102 Nm), plus a 90°turn.

✳✳ WARNING

If the camshafts have moved from the timing marks, always rotate the camshaft towards the direction nearest to the timing marks (DO NOT TURN THE CAMSHAFTS A FULL REVOLUTION OR DAMAGE to the valves and/or pistons could result).

21. Rotate the right camshaft gear (2) to align its timing mark (1). Verify that the left camshaft gear (7) timing mark (8) and the crankshaft gear (10) timing mark (9) are still aligned.

22. Install the timing belt (4) starting at the crankshaft sprocket (10) going in a counterclockwise direction. Install the belt around the last sprocket. Maintain tension on the belt as it is positioned around the tensioner pulley (11).

23. Holding the tensioner pulley (11) against the belt, install the tensioner (12) into the housing and tighten the 2 bolts to 250 inch lbs. (28 Nm). Each camshaft sprocket mark should remain aligned with the cover marks.

24. When the tensioner is in place, pull the retaining pin to allow the tensioner to extend to the tensioner pulley bracket.

25. Rotate the crankshaft sprocket 2 revolutions and check the timing marks on the camshafts and the crankshaft. The marks should line up within their respective locations. If the marks do not line up, repeat the procedure.

➥**With the camshaft gears in these positions, the lobes are in a neutral position (no load to the valve).**

26. Install the front timing belt cover. Refer to Timing Belt Front Cover, removal & installation.

27. Connect the negative battery cable. Tighten the nut to 40 inch lbs. (5 Nm).

TIMING BELT REAR COVER

REMOVAL & INSTALLATION

4.0L Engine

See Figures 110 and 111.

1. Before servicing the vehicle, refer to the Precautions Section.

2. Perform the fuel pressure release procedure.

3. Disconnect the negative battery cable.

4. Remove the timing belt and camshaft sprockets. Refer to Timing Belt and Sprockets, removal & installation.

5. Remove the rear timing belt cover bolts.

6. Remove the rear cover.

➥**The rear timing belt cover has O-rings to seal the water pump passages to the cylinder block . Do not reuse the O-rings.**

To install:

7. Clean the rear timing belt cover O-ring sealing surfaces and grooves. Lubricate

the new O-rings with MOPAR®Dielectric Grease, or equivalent, to facilitate assembly.

8. Position a NEW O-rings on the cover.

9. Install the rear timing belt cover. Tighten the bolts to the following specified torque:
  a. M10 bolts: 40 ft. lbs. (54 Nm).
  b. M8 bolts: 20 ft. lbs. (28 Nm).
  c. M6 bolts: 105 inch lbs. (12 Nm).

10. Install the camshaft sprockets and the timing belt. Refer to Timing Belt and Sprockets, removal & installation.

11. Connect the negative battery cable. Tighten the nut to 40 inch lbs. (5 Nm).

TIMING CHAIN COVER AND SEAL

REMOVAL & INSTALLATION

3.3L & 3.8L Engines

1. Before servicing the vehicle, refer to the Precautions Section.

2. Disconnect negative cable from battery.

3. Drain the cooling system.

4. Raise and safely support the vehicle.

5. Drain the engine oil.

6. Remove the right wheel and inner splash shield.

7. Remove the oil pan. Refer to Oil Pan, removal & installation.

8. Remove the oil pick-up tube.

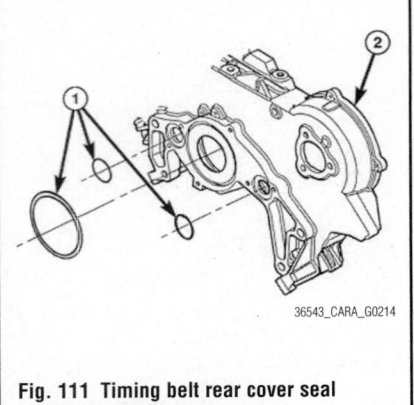

Fig. 111 Timing belt rear cover seal positions—4.0L engine

9. Remove the accessory drive belt. Refer to Accessory Drive Belts, removal & installation.

10. Remove the A/C compressor with the lines attached and set it aside.

11. Remove the crankshaft vibration damper. Refer to Crankshaft Damper, removal & installation.

12. Remove the radiator lower hose.

13. Remove the heater hose from the timing chain cover housing or water pump inlet tube (if equipped with an engine oil cooler).

14. Remove the right side engine mount.

15. Remove the camshaft position sensor from the timing chain cover.

16. Remove the water pump for cover removal clearance.

17. Remove the timing chain cover fasteners. Remove the timing chain cover.

To install:

18. Be sure the mating surfaces of the chain case cover and the cylinder block are clean and free from burrs. The crankshaft oil seal must be removed to insure correct oil pump engagement.

➥**DO NOT USE SEALER ON THE COVER GASKET**

19. Position a new gasket on the timing cover. Adhere a new gasket to the chain case cover, making sure that the lower edge of the gasket is flush to 0.020 inch (0.5mm) passed the lower edge of the cover.

20. Rotate the crankshaft so that the oil pump drive flats are in the vertical position.

21. Position the oil pump inner rotor so the mating flats are in the same position as the crankshaft drive flats.

✳✳ WARNING

Make sure the oil pump is engaged on the crankshaft correctly or severe damage may result.

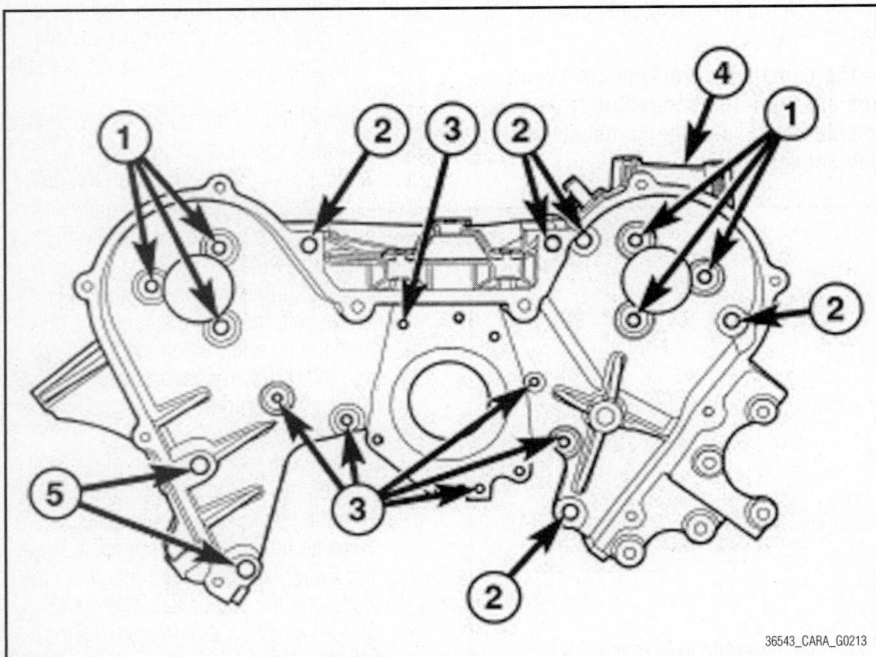

Fig. 110 Timing belt rear cover bolt positions—4.0L engine

22. Install the timing cover.
23. Install the timing chain cover bolts. Tighten the bolts to:
   a. M8 bolts: 20 ft. lbs. (27 Nm).
   b. M10 bolts: 40 ft. lbs. (54 Nm).
24. Install the crankshaft front oil seal. Refer to Crankshaft Front Seal, removal & installation.
25. Install the water pump and pulley. Refer to Water Pump, removal & installation.
26. Install the crankshaft vibration damper. Refer to Crankshaft Damper, removal & installation.
27. Install the right side engine mount.
28. Install the camshaft position sensor.
29. Connect the heater return hose at the rear of the timing chain cover or at the water pump inlet tube (if equipped with an engine oil cooler).
30. Connect the radiator lower hose.
31. Install the A/C compressor. Refer to Heating & Air Condition, Compressor, removal & installation.
32. Install the accessory drive belt. Refer to Accessory Drive Belts, removal & installation.
33. Install the oil pump pick-up tube with a new O-ring. Tighten the attaching bolt to 250 inch lbs. (28 Nm).
34. Install the oil pan. Refer to Oil Pan, removal & installation.
35. Install the inner splash shield and the right front wheel.
36. Fill the crankcase with engine oil to the proper level.
37. Fill the cooling system with the proper type and amount of fluid.
38. Connect the negative battery cable. Tighten the nut to 40 inch lbs. (5 Nm).

TIMING CHAIN AND SPROCKETS

REMOVAL & INSTALLATION

3.3L & 3.8L Engines

See Figures 112 through 114.

1. Before servicing the vehicle, refer to the Precautions Section.
2. Disconnect the negative cable from the battery.
3. Remove the timing chain cover. Refer to Timing Chain Cover and Seal, removal & installation.
4. Rotate the engine by turning the crankshaft until the timing marks are aligned (4).
5. Remove the camshaft sprocket attaching bolt.
6. Remove the timing chain with the camshaft sprocket.

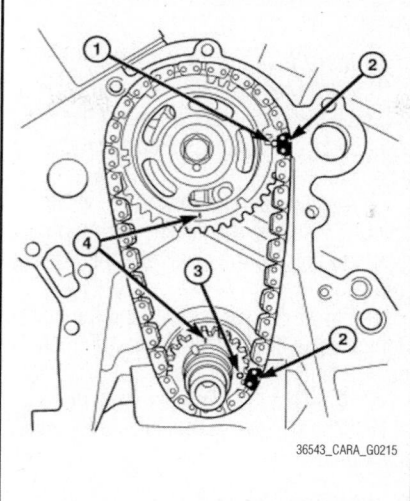

Fig. 112 Timing mark alignment—3.3L and 3.8L engines

7. Using Special Tools 8539, 5048-6, and 5048-1, remove the crankshaft sprocket (4) while holding the crankshaft from turning. Be careful not to damage the crankshaft surfaces.

To install:

8. Position the crankshaft sprocket on the crankshaft (timing mark out) with the timing slot aligned with the timing pin.
9. Install the crankshaft sprocket using Special Tool 8452 (1). Press in the crankshaft sprocket (3) until it fully seats on the crankshaft.

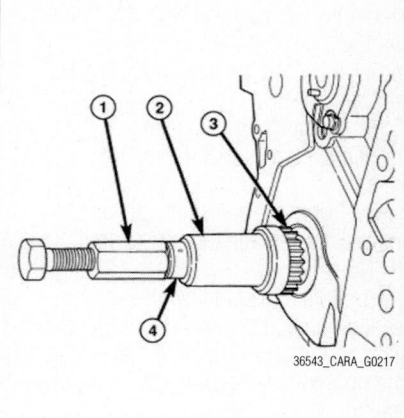

Fig. 114 Using Special Tool 8452, press in the crankshaft sprocket (3) until it fully seats on the crankshaft—3.3L and 3.8L engines

10. Rotate the crankshaft so the timing arrow is to the 12 o'clock position (4).

➡**Lubricate the timing chain and sprockets with clean engine oil before installation.**

11. While holding the camshaft sprocket and the chain in hand, place the timing chain around the sprocket, aligning the plated link with the dot on the sprocket. Position the timing arrow to the 6 o'clock position (4).

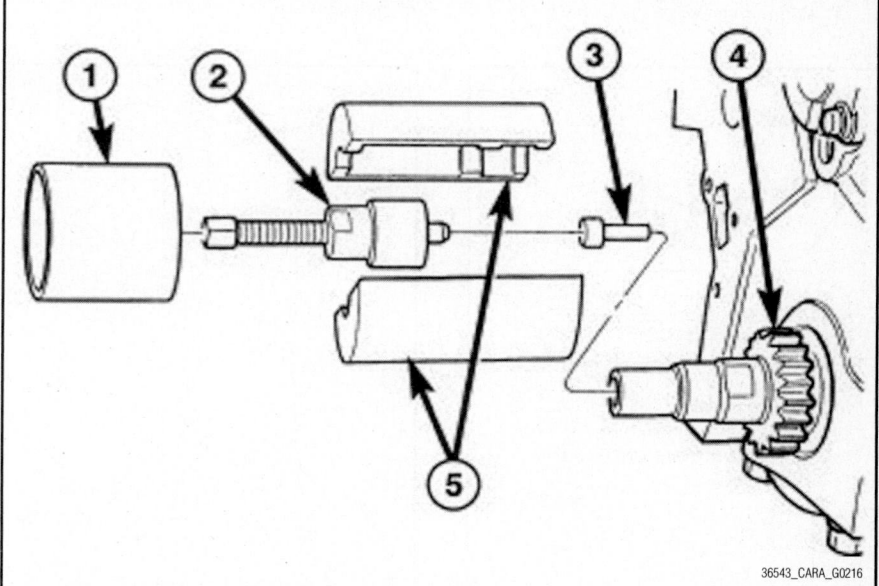

Fig. 113 Using Special Tools 8539, 5048-6, and 5048-1, remove the crankshaft sprocket—3.3L and 3.8L engines

12. Place the timing chain around the crankshaft sprocket with the plated link lined up with the dot on the sprocket. Install the camshaft sprocket into position.

13. Use a straight edge to check the alignment of the timing marks.

14. Install the camshaft sprocket bolt and washer. Tighten the bolt to 40 ft. lbs. (54 Nm).

15. Rotate the crankshaft 2 revolutions and check the timing mark alignment (4). If the timing marks do not line up, remove the camshaft sprocket and realign.

16. Install the timing chain cover. Refer to Timing Chain Cover and Seal, removal & installation.

17. Connect the negative battery cable. Tighten the nut to 40 inch lbs. (5 Nm).

VALVE COVERS

REMOVAL & INSTALLATION

3.3L & 3.8L Engines

Left Valve Cover

See Figure 115.

1. Before servicing the vehicle, refer to the Precautions Section.

2. Disconnect the spark plug wires from the spark plugs.

3. Disconnect the crankcase vent hose from the valve cover (also called the cylinder head cover).

4. Remove the valve cover bolts (2).

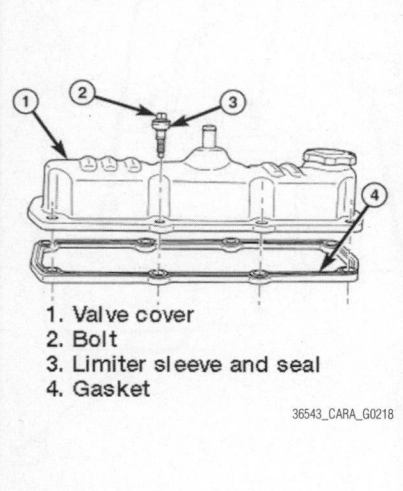

1. Valve cover
2. Bolt
3. Limiter sleeve and seal
4. Gasket

36543_CARA_G0218

Fig. 115 Remove the valve cover bolts—3.3L and 3.8L engines

5. Remove the valve cover and gasket.

To install:

6. Clean the cylinder head and valve cover the mating surfaces. Inspect the valve cover surface for flatness. Replace the gasket as necessary.

7. Assemble the gasket to the valve cover by inserting the fasteners through each bolt hole on the cover and the gasket.

8. Install the valve cover and the bolts. Tighten valve cover bolts (2) to 105 inch lbs. (12 Nm).

9. Connect the crankcase vent hose.

10. Connect the spark plug wires to the spark plugs.

Right Valve Cover

See Figures 115 and 116.

1. Before servicing the vehicle, refer to the Precautions Section.

2. Disconnect the negative cable from the battery.

3. Remove the wiper module.

4. Disconnect the spark plug wires from the plugs.

5. Disconnect the PCV hose from the valve cover (1) (also called the cylinder head cover).

6. Remove the valve cover bolts.

7. Remove the valve cover and the gasket.

To install:

8. Clean the cylinder head and valve cover mating surfaces. Inspect the valve cover surface for flatness. Replace the gasket as necessary.

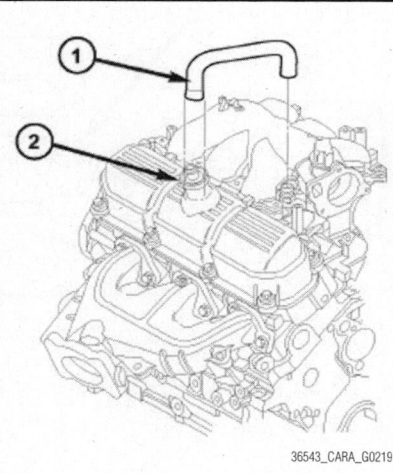

36543_CARA_G0219

Fig. 116 Disconnect the PCV hose (1) from the valve cover (1)—3.3L and 3.8L engines

9. Inspect the PCV valve hose for damage. Replace as necessary.

10. Inspect the seal (3) on the cover bolt for wear or damage. Replace the bolt assembly as necessary.

➡ **The valve cover bolts contain a torque limiter sleeve and a seal (3). The seal and torque sleeve is replaced with the bolt.**

11. Assemble the gasket to the cylinder cover by inserting the bolt assemblies (2) through each bolt hole on the cover and the gasket.

12. Install the valve cover and bolts.

13. Tighten the valve cover bolts (2) to 105 inch lbs. (12 Nm).

➡ **Be sure that the PVC valve is properly seated inside the valve cover protrusion and that the PCV valve hose completely covers the protrusion of the PCV valve housing.**

14. Connect the PCV hose (1) to the valve cover.

15. Connect the spark plug wires to the spark plugs.

16. Install the wiper module.

17. Connect the negative battery cable. Tighten the nut to 40 inch lbs. (5 Nm).

4.0L Engine

Left Valve Cover

See Figures 117 and 118.

✳✳ WARNING

DO NOT START OR RUN THE ENGINE WITH THE VALVE COVER REMOVED FROM THE ENGINE. DAMAGE OR PERSONAL INJURY MAY OCCUR.

1. Before servicing the vehicle, refer to the Precautions Section.

2. Disconnect and isolate the negative battery cable.

3. Remove the upper intake manifold from the engine. Refer to Intake Manifold, removal & installation.

4. Cover the lower intake manifold with a suitable cover during service.

5. Disconnect and remove the 3 ignition coils (3).

6. Remove the upper intake manifold support brackets from the engine.

7. Position the engine wiring harness aside.

8. Completely loosen the valve cover retaining bolts and remove the valve cover.

9. Disconnect the MVA hose from the valve cover assembly, if required.

To install:

10. Clean the cylinder head and valve cover mating surfaces. Inspect and replace the gasket and the seals, as necessary.

11. To replace the spark plug tube seals:

   a. Using a suitable pry tool, carefully remove the tube seals.

   b. Position a new seal with the part number on the seal facing the valve cover.

   c. Install the seals using Special Tool MD-998306.

12. Install the valve cover and the bolts. Tighten to 90 inch lbs. (10 Nm).

13. Connect the MVA hose, if required.

14. Position the wiring harness on the valve cover.

15. Clip the wire harness to the attachment holes around the perimeter of the valve cover.

16. Install the upper intake manifold support brackets onto the front and rear of the engine.

17. Install the ignition coils. Tighten the mounting screws to 60 inch lbs. (7 Nm).

18. Connect the ignition coil electrical connectors.

19. Install the upper intake manifold. Refer to Intake Manifold, removal & installation.

20. Connect the negative battery cable. Tighten the nut to 40 inch lbs. (5 Nm).

Right Valve Cover

See Figures 117 and 118.

> **✳✳ WARNING**
>
> **DO NOT START OR RUN THE ENGINE WITH THE VALVE COVER REMOVED FROM THE ENGINE. DAMAGE OR PERSONAL INJURY MAY OCCUR.**

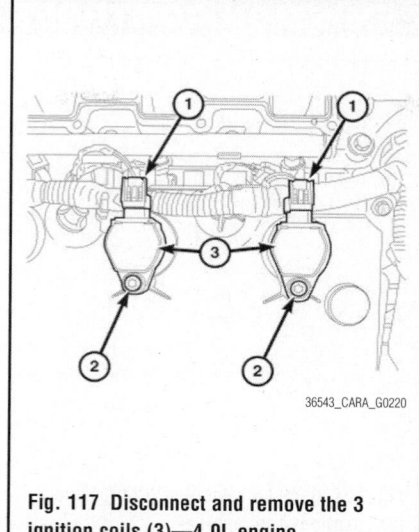

Fig. 117 Disconnect and remove the 3 ignition coils (3)—4.0L engine

1. Before servicing the vehicle, refer to the Precautions Section.

2. Disconnect the negative battery cable.

3. Remove the upper intake manifold from the engine. Refer to Intake Manifold, removal & installation.

4. Cover the lower intake manifold with a suitable cover during service.

5. Disconnect and remove the 3 ignition coils.

6. Unclip the wire harness from the attachment holes around the perimeter of the valve cover.

7. Completely loosen the valve cover retaining bolts and remove the valve cover.

To install:

8. Clean the cylinder head and valve cover mating surfaces. Inspect and replace the gasket and the seals, as necessary.

9. To replace the spark plug tube seals:

   a. Using a suitable pry tool, carefully remove the tube seals.

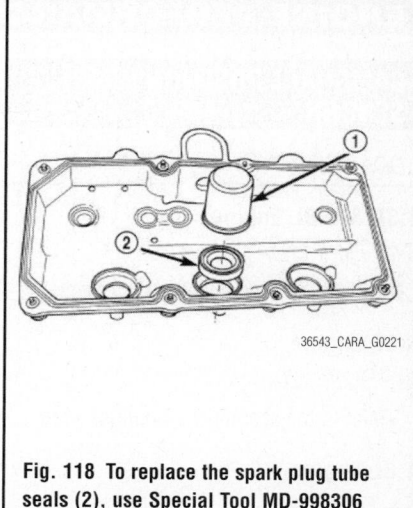

Fig. 118 To replace the spark plug tube seals (2), use Special Tool MD-998306 (1)—4.0L engine

   b. Position a new seal with the part number on the seal facing the valve cover.

   c. Install the seals using Special Tool MD-998306.

10. Install the valve cover bolts and tighten to 90 inch lbs. (10 Nm).

11. Clip the wire harness to the attachment holes around the perimeter of the valve cover.

12. Install the ignition coils. Tighten the mounting screws to 60 inch lbs. (7 Nm).

13. Connect the ignition coil electrical connectors.

14. Install the upper intake manifold. Refer to Intake Manifold, removal & installation.

15. Connect the negative battery cable. Tighten the nut to 40 inch lbs. (5 Nm).

VALVE LASH

ADJUSTMENT

These engines are equipped with hydraulic valve lifters. No valve clearance adjustments are necessary.

ENGINE PERFORMANCE & EMISSION CONTROLS

CAMSHAFT POSITION (CMP) SENSOR

LOCATION

3.3L & 3.8L Engines

See Figure 119.

Refer to the accompanying illustration.

3.6L Engine

See Figure 120.

Refer to the accompanying illustration.

4.0L Engine

See Figure 121.

Refer to the accompanying illustration.

REMOVAL & INSTALLATION

3.3L & 3.8L Engines

See Figure 122.

1. Disconnect and isolate the negative battery cable.

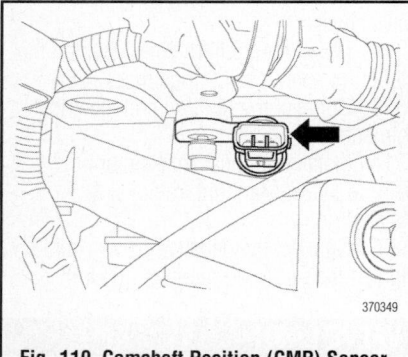

Fig. 119 Camshaft Position (CMP) Sensor Location—3.3L & 3.8L engines

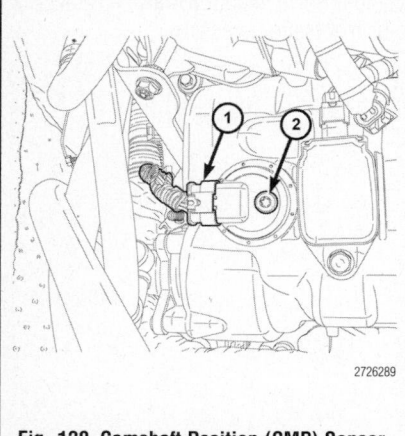

Fig. 120 Camshaft Position (CMP) Sensor Location—3.6L engine

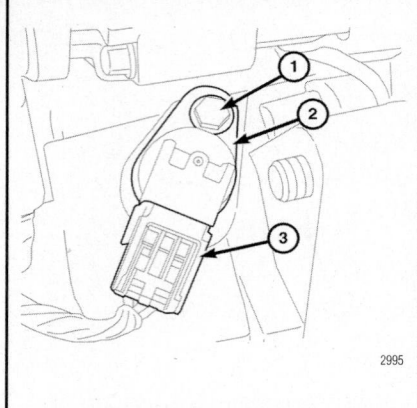

Fig. 121 Camshaft Position (CMP) Sensor (2) Location–4.0L engine

2. Remove the air box cover and inlet tube.

3. Disconnect the electrical connector from the camshaft position (CMP) sensor.

4. Loosen the CMP sensor retaining bolt.

5. Pull the sensor up and out of the chain case cover. Leave the retaining bolt in place.

To install:

✳✳ WARNING

If reinstalling the sensor, check the sensor O-ring for damage and replace if necessary. Lubricate the O-ring with clean engine oil before installing the sensor. Clean off the old spacer on the sensor face. A NEW

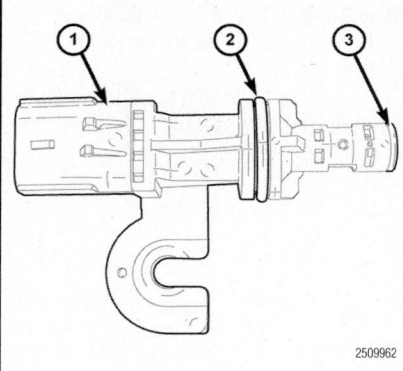

Fig. 122 If reinstalling the sensor (1), check the sensor O-ring (2) for damage and replace if necessary. Lubricate the O-ring with clean engine oil before installing the sensor. Clean off the old spacer (3) on the sensor face.

SPACER must be attached to the face before installation.

✳✳ WARNING

A NEW SPACER must be attached to the face of the sensor before installation. The spacer sets the correct clearance between the sensor and the camshaft gear. An improperly positioned sensor can result in sensor damage, a faulty signal or no signal at all.

6. Install the camshaft position (CMP) sensor in the chain case cover and rotate into position.

7. Push the sensor down until contact is made with the camshaft gear. While holding the sensor in this position, install and tighten the retaining bolt to 125 inch lbs. (14 Nm).

8. Connect and lock the electrical connector to the CMP sensor.

9. Install the air box cover and inlet tube.

10. Connect the negative battery cable and tighten nut to 45 inch lbs. (5 Nm).

➡The Cam/Crank Variation Relearn procedure must be performed anytime there has been a repair/replacement made to a powertrain system, for example: flywheel, valve train, camshaft and/or crankshaft sensors or components.

3.6L Engine

See Figure 123.

✳✳ WARNING

The magnetic timing wheels must not come in contact with magnets (pickup tools, trays, etc.) or any other strong magnetic field. This will destroy the timing wheels ability to correctly relay camshaft position to the Camshaft Position (CMP) Sensor.

1. The Camshaft Position (CMP) sensors are located at the rear of the cylinder head covers and are bolted to the cylinder head.

2. Disconnect and isolate the negative battery cable.

3. Remove the air cleaner body.

4. If removing the LH CMP sensor, first remove the upper intake manifold.

➡If removing both RH and LH CMP sensors, mark the sensors so

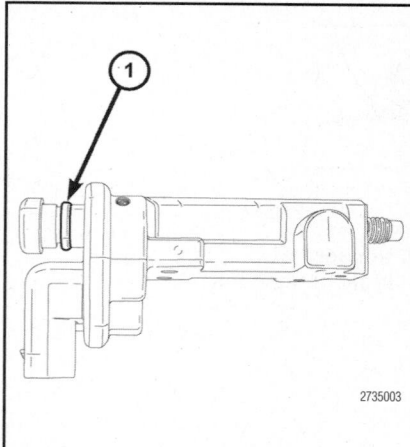

Fig. 123 Pull the sensor and mounting bolt from the cylinder head cover. The O-ring seal (1) can be reused if not damaged

they can be installed in their original locations.

5. Disconnect the electrical connector from the CMP sensor.
6. Loosen the sensor mounting bolt.
7. Pull the sensor and mounting bolt from the cylinder head cover.
8. The O-ring seal can be reused if not damaged.

To install:

✳✳ WARNING

The magnetic timing wheels must not come in contact with magnets (pickup tools, trays, etc.) or any other strong magnetic field. This will destroy the timing wheels ability to correctly relay camshaft position to the Camshaft Position (CMP) Sensor.

9. Clean out the camshaft position (CMP) sensor mounting bolt hole in cylinder head.
10. The CMP sensor seal can be reused if not damaged.
11. If required, install a new CMP sensor seal in the cylinder head cover:
12. Lubricate the CMP sensor seal inner and outer diameters with clean engine oil.
13. Place the CMP sensor seal on the Cam Sensor/Spark Plug Tube Seal Installer.
14. Push the seal into the cylinder head cover until the base of the seal is seated.
15. Remove the tool.

➡**A properly installed CMP sensor seal will have a 0.06—0.08 in. gap between the cylinder head cover and the seal upper flange.**

16. The sensor mounting bolt O-ring can be reused if not damaged.
17. Apply a small amount of engine oil to the sensor mounting bolt O-ring.

➡**The RH CMP sensor is shown, the LH CMP sensor is similar. If both RH and LH CMP sensors where removed, install them into their original locations.**

18. Install the CMP sensor to the cylinder head. Tighten the mounting bolt to 80 inch lbs. (9 Nm).
19. Connect the electrical connector to the sensor.
20. Following installation of the LH CMP sensor, install the upper intake manifold as outlined in the Engine Mechanical Section.
21. Install the air cleaner body.
22. Connect the negative battery cable and tighten nut to 45 inch lbs. (5 Nm).

➡**The Cam/Crank Variation Relearn procedure must be performed using the scan tool anytime there has been a repair/replacement made to a powertrain system, for example: flywheel, valve train, camshaft and/or crankshaft sensors or components.**

4.0L Engine

1. Disconnect and isolate the negative battery cable at battery.
2. Remove the generator mounting bolts, and position the generator aside in order to gain access to the camshaft position (CMP) sensor.
3. Disconnect electrical connector from CMP sensor.
4. Remove the bolt and CMP.

To install:

✳✳ WARNING

Install camshaft position (CMP) sensor utilizing twisting motion. Make sure CMP sensor is fully seated. Do not drive CMP sensor into the bore with mounting screw. This may cause CMP sensor to be incorrectly seated causing a faulty signal or no signal at all.

➡**If reinstalling the sensor, check the sensor O-ring for damage and replace if necessary. Lubricate the O-ring with clean engine oil before installing the sensor.**

5. Push the CMP sensor into the timing belt cover with a twisting motion until fully seated.
6. While holding the sensor in this

position, install and tighten the retaining bolt to 106 inch lbs. (12 Nm).
7. Connect and lock the electrical connector to the CMP sensor.
8. Install the generator.
9. Connect the negative battery cable and tighten nut to 45 inch lbs. (5 Nm).

➡**The Cam/Crank Variation Relearn procedure must be performed anytime there has been a repair/replacement made to a powertrain system, for example: flywheel, valve train, camshaft and/or crankshaft sensors or components.**

CRANKSHAFT POSITION (CKP) SENSOR

LOCATION

3.3L & 3.8L—Flex Fuel And Gas

See Figure 124.

Refer to the accompanying illustration.

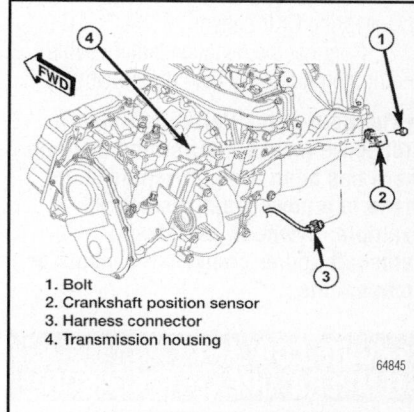

1. Bolt
2. Crankshaft position sensor
3. Harness connector
4. Transmission housing

Fig. 124 Crankshaft Position (CKP) sensor location

REMOVAL & INSTALLATION

3.3L & 3.8L—Flex Fuel And Gas

➡**The normal operating temperature of the exhaust system is very high. Therefore, never work around or attempt to service any part of the exhaust system until it is cooled. Personal injury caused from burns can result from contact made to the exhaust system components.**

✳✳ WARNING

When disconnecting sensor electrical connector, do not pull directly on harness connector wires. Damage to the harness connector and/or wires may occur.

1. Disconnect and isolate negative battery cable at battery.
2. Disconnect harness connector from the crankshaft position sensor.
3. Remove the bolt.
4. Remove the crankshaft position sensor from the transmission housing.

To install:

➥If reinstalling the sensor, check the sensor O-ring for damage and replace if necessary. Lubricate the O-ring with clean engine oil before installing the sensor.

❊❊ WARNING

Before tightening the sensor mounting bolt, be sure the sensor is completely flush to the mounting surface. If the sensor is not flush, damage to the sensor mounting tang may result.

5. While holding the sensor in this position, install and tighten the retaining bolt to 105 inch lbs. (12 Nm).
6. Connect and lock the electrical connector to the CKP sensor.
7. Connect the negative battery cable and tighten nut to 45 inch lbs. (5 Nm).

➥The Cam/Crank Variation Relearn procedure must be performed anytime there has been a repair/replacement made to a powertrain system, for example: flywheel, valvetrain, camshaft and/or crankshaft sensors or components.

ENGINE COOLANT TEMPERATURE (ECT) SENSOR

LOCATION

3.3L and 3.8L Engines

See Figure 125.

Refer to the accompanying illustration for sensor location.

4.0L Engine

See Figure 126.

Refer to the accompanying illustration for sensor location.

REMOVAL & INSTALLATION

3.3L & 3.8L Engines

See Figure 125.

❊❊ CAUTION

Hot, pressurized coolant can cause injury by scalding. The cooling system must be partially drained before

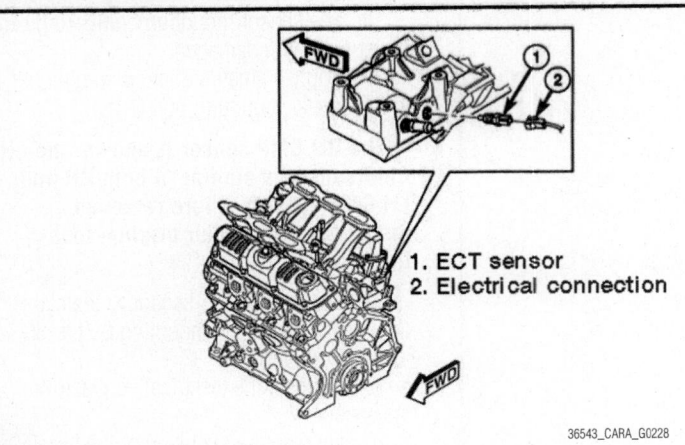

1. ECT sensor
2. Electrical connection

36543_CARA_G0228

Fig. 125 Engine Coolant Temperature (ECT) sensor location (1)—3.3L and 3.8L engines

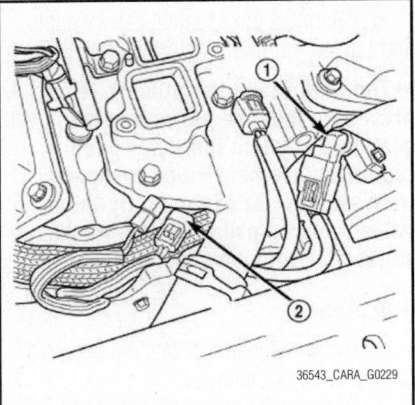

36543_CARA_G0229

Fig. 126 Engine Coolant Temperature (ECT) sensor location (2)—4.0L engine

removing the engine coolant temperature sensor.

1. Before servicing the vehicle, refer to the Precautions Section.
2. Drain the cooling system below the engine coolant temperature sensor level.
3. Disconnect the coolant sensor electrical connector (2).
4. Remove the coolant sensor (1).

To install:

5. Install the engine coolant temperature sensor (1). Tighten the sensor to 60 inch lbs. (7 Nm).
6. Connect the electrical connector (2) to sensor (1).
7. Fill the cooling system with the proper type and amount of fluid.

4.0L Engine

See Figure 126.

❊❊ CAUTION

Hot, pressurized coolant can cause injury by scalding. The cooling

system must be partially drained before removing the engine coolant temperature sensor.

1. Before servicing the vehicle, refer to the Precautions Section.
2. Drain the cooling system below the engine coolant temperature sensor level.
3. Disconnect the coolant sensor electrical connector.
4. Remove the coolant sensor (2).

To install:

5. Install the engine coolant temperature sensor (2). Tighten the sensor to 60 inch lbs. (7 Nm).
6. Connect the electrical connector to the sensor.
7. Fill the cooling system with the proper type and amount of fluid.

EXHAUST GAS RECIRCULATION (EGR) VALVE

LOCATION

3.3L and 3.8L Engines

See Figure 127.

4.0L Engine

See Figure 128.

REMOVAL & INSTALLATION

3.3L & 3.8L Engines

See Figure 127.

❊❊ CAUTION

The normal operating temperature of the Exhaust Gas Recirculation (EGR) valve and tube is very high. Therefore, never work around or attempt to service any engine component until it is completely cooled.

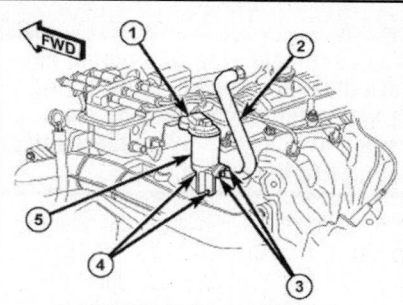

1. Electrical connector
2. EGR tube
3. Bolts
4. Bolts
5. EGR valve

36543_CARA_G0237

Fig. 127 Exhaust Gas Recirculation (EGR) valve location—3.3L and 3.8L engines

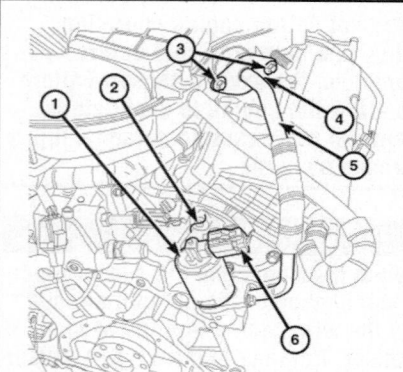

1. EGR valve   4. EGR tube connection
2. Cylinder head   5. EGR tube
3. Bolts   6. Electrical connector

36543_CARA_G0238

Fig. 128 Exhaust Gas Recirculation (EGR) valve location—4.0L engine

➡It is very important to disconnect the battery due to the addresses (cells) within the engine controller that store learned values related to powertrain operation. A malfunctioning EGR system can cause bad values to be stored in these cells that can cause an erroneous fault to occur after the system is repaired. Disconnecting the battery for at least 2 minutes will remove all power from the controller and reset these cells to normal default values.

1. Before servicing the vehicle, refer to the Precautions Section.
2. Disconnect and isolate the negative battery cable at the battery.
3. Disconnect the electrical connector (1) from the Exhaust Gas Recirculation (EGR) valve (5).

4. Remove the bolts (3), gasket, and EGR tube (2) from the EGR valve (5).
5. Remove the bolts (4), gasket, and EGR valve (5) from the cylinder head.

To install:

6. Install a new EGR valve gasket to the EGR valve.
7. Install the EGR valve (5), gasket, and bolts (4) to the cylinder head. Tighten to 22 ft. lbs. (30 Nm).
8. Install the EGR tube (2), gasket, and bolts (3) to the EGR valve (5). Tighten to 11 ft. lbs. (15 Nm).
9. Connect the electrical connector (1) to the EGR valve (5).
10. Connect the negative battery cable, tighten the nut to 45 inch lbs. (5 Nm).

4.0L Engine

See Figure 128.

> ✳✳ **CAUTION**
>
> **The normal operating temperature of the Exhaust Gas Recirculation (EGR) valve and tube is very high. Therefore, never work around or attempt to service any engine component until it is completely cooled.**

➡It is very important to disconnect the battery due to the addresses (cells) within the engine controller that store learned values related to powertrain operation. A malfunctioning EGR system can cause bad values to be stored in these cells that can cause an erroneous fault to occur after the system is repaired. Disconnecting the battery for at least 2 minutes will remove all power from the controller and reset these cells to normal default values.

1. Before servicing the vehicle, refer to the Precautions Section.
2. Disconnect and isolate the negative battery cable at the battery.
3. Remove the EGR tube bolts (3) at the Exhaust Gas Recirculation (EGR) valve (1).
4. Remove the EGR tube (5) from the EGR valve (1).
5. Remove and discard the gasket located between the EGR valve (1) and the EGR tube (5).
6. Disconnect the electrical connector (6) at the EGR valve (1).
7. Remove the EGR valve mounting bolts.
8. Remove the EGR valve from the cylinder head.
9. Remove and discard the gasket located between the EGR valve and the cylinder head.

To install:

10. Install a new EGR valve gasket to the EGR valve.
11. Install the EGR valve (1), gasket, and bolts (3) to the cylinder head (2). Tighten to 22 ft. lbs. (30 Nm).
12. Install a new gasket, EGR tube (5), and bolts (3) to the EGR valve (1). Tighten to 11 ft. lbs. (15 Nm).
13. Connect the electrical connector (6) to the EGR valve (1).
14. Connect the negative battery cable, tighten the nut to 45 inch lbs. (5 Nm).

HEATED OXYGEN SENSOR (HO2S)

LOCATION

3.3L and 3.8L Engines
See Figures 129 and 130.

4.0L Engine
See Figures 131 and 132.

REMOVAL & INSTALLATION

3.3L & 3.8L Engines
See Figures 130 and 133.

> ✳✳ **CAUTION**
>
> **The exhaust manifold, exhaust pipes, and catalytic converter(s) become very hot during engine operation. Allow the engine to cool before removing the oxygen sensor. Failure to allow the engine to cool before removal may result in personal injury caused by burns.**

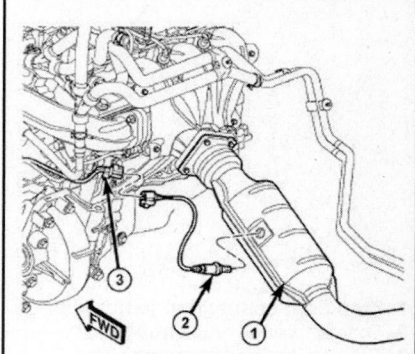

1. Catalytic converter
2. Oxygen sensor
3. Pigtail harness connection

36543_CARA_G0239

Fig. 129 Oxygen (O2S) sensor location (downstream 1/2)—3.3L and 3.8L engines

✴✴ WARNING

When disconnecting the sensor electrical connector, do not pull directly on the wires going into the oxygen sensor. Damage to the oxygen sensor may occur.

➡**Use an oxygen sensor (O2S) removal tool for this procedure.**

1. Before servicing the vehicle, refer to the Precautions Section.
2. Raise and safely support the vehicle.
3. Disconnect the O2S wire harness mounting clips from the engine or body, if equipped.

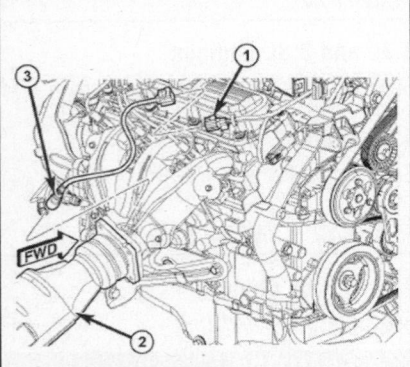

1. Pigtail harness connection
2. Catalytic converter
3. Oxygen sensor

36543_CARA_G0240

Fig. 130 Oxygen (O2S) sensor location (upstream 1/1)—3.3L and 3.8L engines

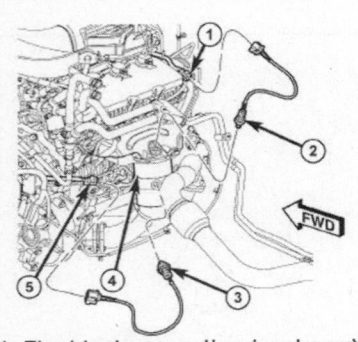

1. Electrical connection (upstream)
2. Oxygen sensor (upstream)
3. Oxygen sensor (downstream)
4. Catalytic converter
5. Electrical connection (downstream)

36543_CARA_G0241

Fig. 131 Oxygen (O2S) sensor location (downstream 1/2, and upstream 1/1)—4.0L engine

4. Disconnect the O2S pigtail harness from the engine wiring harness.
5. Remove the O2S from the catalytic converter.

To install:

➡**Use an O2S removal tool for this procedure.**

➡**Threads of new oxygen sensors are factory coated with anti-seize compound to aid in removal. DO NOT add any additional anti-seize compound to the threads of a new O2S.**

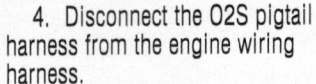

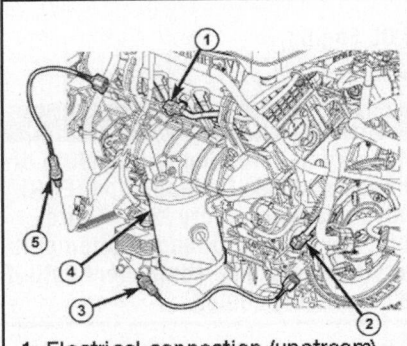

1. Electrical connection (upstream)
2. Electrical connection (downstream)
3. Oxygen sensor (downstream)
4. Catalytic converter
5. Oxygen sensor (upstream)

36543_CARA_G0242

Fig. 132 Oxygen (O2S) sensor location (downstream 2/2, and upstream 2/1)—4.0L engine

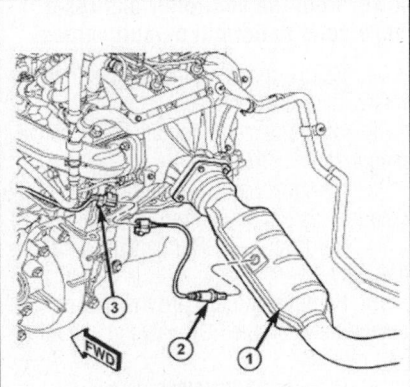

1. Catalytic converter
2. Oxygen sensor
3. Pigtail harness connection

36543_CARA_G0239

Fig. 133 Oxygen (O2S) sensor location (downstream 1/2)—3.3L and 3.8L engines

✴✴ WARNING

When equipped, the O2S pigtail harness must be clipped and/or bolted back to original positions on the engine or body to prevent mechanical damage to the wiring.

6. Install the O2 sensor to the catalytic converter. Tighten to 30 ft. lbs. (41 Nm).
7. Connect the O2 sensor pigtail harness to the engine wiring harness.
8. Connect the O2S wire harness mounting clips to the engine or body, if equipped.

4.0L Engine

See Figures 131 and 132.

✴✴ CAUTION

The exhaust manifold, exhaust pipes, and catalytic converter(s) become very hot during engine operation. Allow the engine to cool before removing the oxygen sensor. Failure to allow the engine to cool before removal may result in personal injury caused by burns.

✴✴ WARNING

When disconnecting the sensor electrical connector, do not pull directly on the wires going into the oxygen sensor. Damage to the oxygen sensor may occur.

➡**Use an oxygen sensor (O2S) removal tool for this procedure.**

1. Before servicing the vehicle, refer to the Precautions Section.
2. Raise and safely support the vehicle.
3. Disconnect the O2S wire harness mounting clips from the engine or body, if equipped.
4. Disconnect the O2S pigtail harness from the engine wiring harness.
5. Remove the O2S from the catalytic converter.
6. Disconnect the O2S pigtail harness from the engine wiring harness.
7. Remove the O2S from the catalytic converter.

To install:

➡**Use an O2S removal tool for this procedure.**

➡**Threads of new oxygen sensors are factory coated with anti-seize compound to aid in removal. DO NOT add any additional anti-seize compound to the threads of a new O2S.**

✳✳ WARNING

When equipped, the O2S pigtail harness must be clipped and/or bolted back to original positions on the engine or body to prevent mechanical damage to the wiring.

8. Install the O2S to the catalytic converter.

9. Connect the O2S pigtail harness to the engine wiring harness.

10. Install the O2S to the catalytic converter. Tighten to 30 ft. lbs. (41 Nm).

11. Connect the O2S pigtail harness to the engine wiring harness.

12. Connect the O2S wire harness mounting clips to the engine or body, if equipped.

INTAKE AIR TEMPERATURE (IAT) SENSOR

LOCATION

See Figure 134.

Refer to the accompanying illustration.

REMOVAL & INSTALLATION

See Figure 134.

1. Before servicing the vehicle, refer to the Precautions Section.

2. Disconnect and isolate the negative battery cable at the battery.

➡ **Clean any dirt from the sensor area prior to removal from the air box.**

3. Disconnect the intake air temperature sensor electrical connector.

4. Remove the intake air temperature sensor (1) from the air box (2) by turning the sensor ¼ turn in the counter-clockwise direction.

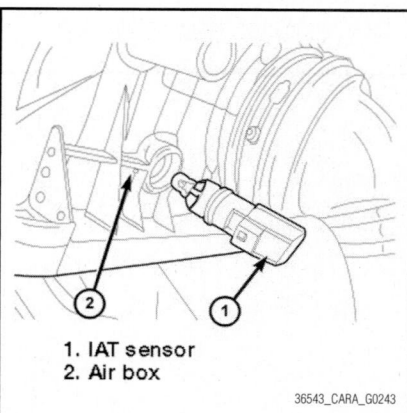

1. IAT sensor
2. Air box

36543_CARA_G0243

Fig. 134 Intake Air Temperature (IAT) sensor location

To install:

5. Install the intake air temperature sensor (1) to the air box (2) by turning the sensor ¼ turn in the clockwise direction.

6. Connect the intake air temperature sensor electrical connector.

7. Connect the negative battery cable, tighten the nut to 45 inch lbs. (5 Nm).

KNOCK SENSOR (KS)

LOCATION

3.3L & 3.8L Engines

See Figure 135.

Refer to the accompanying illustration.

3.6L Engine

See Figure 136.

Refer to the accompanying illustration.

4.0L Engine

See Figure 137.

Refer to the accompanying illustration.

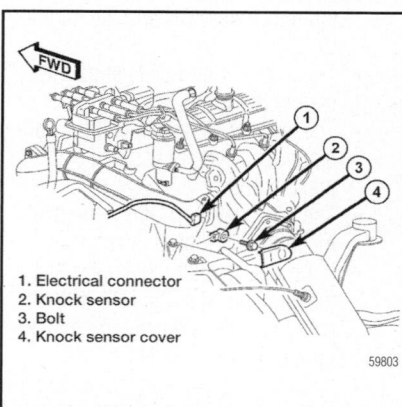

1. Electrical connector
2. Knock sensor
3. Bolt
4. Knock sensor cover

59803

Fig. 135 Knock Sensor location—3.3 & 3.8L engines

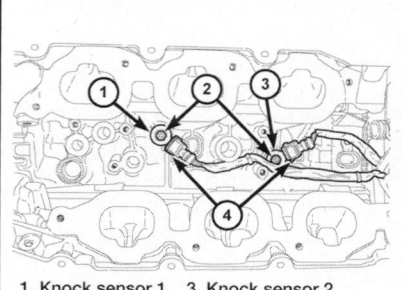

1. Knock sensor 1
2. Mounting bolts
3. Knock sensor 2
4. Knock sensor electrical connectors

2726041

Fig. 136 Knock Sensor location—3.6L engine

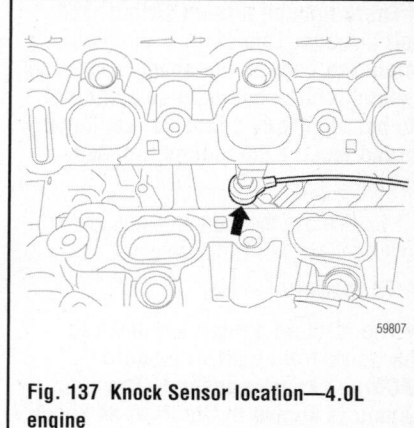

59807

Fig. 137 Knock Sensor location—4.0L engine

REMOVAL & INSTALLATION

3.3L & 3.8L Engines

1. Disconnect and isolate the negative battery cable at battery.

2. Remove the knock sensor cover.

3. Disconnect electrical connector from knock sensor.

4. Remove the bolt and knock sensor from engine.

To install:

✳✳ WARNING

Torque the knock sensor to correct specification. Over or under tightening effects knock sensor performance, possibly causing improper spark control and damage to the sensor.

5. Install the knock sensor and bolt to engine and tighten to 15 ft. lbs. (20 Nm).

6. Connect electrical connector to knock sensor.

7. Install the knock sensor cover.

8. Connect the negative battery cable and tighten nut to 45 inch lbs. (5 Nm).

3.6L Engine

➡ **The forward sensor is known to the powertrain control module (PCM) as knock sensor 1. The rear sensor is known to the PCM as knock sensor 2.**

1. Perform the fuel pressure release procedure.

2. Disconnect and isolate the negative battery cable.

3. Drain the cooling system as outlined in the Engine Cooling Section.

4. Remove the air cleaner housing assembly, upper and lower intake manifolds and the oil filter housing.

5. Remove the electrical connector.

➡There may be a foam strip on the bolt threads. This foam is used only to retain the bolts to the sensors for plant assembly. It is not used as a sealant. Do not apply any adhesive, sealant or thread locking compound to these bolts.

6. Remove the mounting bolt and knock sensor 1 or knock sensor 2.

To install:

➡The forward sensor is known to the powertrain control module (PCM) as knock sensor 1. The rear sensor is known to the PCM as knock sensor 2.

7. Thoroughly clean the knock sensor mounting holes.

➡Over or under tightening the sensor mounting bolts will affect knock sensor performance, possibly causing improper spark control. Always use the specified torque when installing the knock sensors. The torque specification for the knock sensor bolt is less than the typical 8 mm bolt.

➡There may be a foam strip on the bolt threads. This foam is used only to retain the bolts to the sensors for plant assembly. It is not used as a sealant. Do not apply any adhesive, sealant or thread locking compound to these bolts.

8. Install the knock sensor 1 or knock sensor 2 with mounting bolt. Tighten the mounting bolt to 16 ft. lbs. (22 Nm).

9. Connect the electrical connector.

10. Install the oil filter housing, upper and lower intake manifolds and air cleaner housing assembly.

11. If removed, install the oil filter and fill the engine crankcase with the proper oil to the correct level.

12. Connect the negative battery cable and tighten nut to 45 inch lbs. (5 Nm).

13. Fill the cooling system as outlined in the Engine Cooling Section.

14. Operate the engine until it reaches normal operating temperature. Check cooling system for correct fluid level.

4.0L Engine

1. Disconnect and isolate the negative battery cable at battery.
2. Remove the engine cover.
3. Remove the upper intake manifold.
4. Disconnect electrical connector.
5. Remove the knock sensor.

To install:

✳ WARNING

Torque the knock sensor to correct specification. Over or under tightening effects knock sensor performance, possibly causing improper spark control and damage to the sensor.

6. Install the knock sensor and bolt. Tighten bolt to 15 ft. lbs. (20 Nm).

7. Route knock sensor wire in the proper location.

8. Install the upper intake manifold.

9. Connect electrical connector.

10. Connect the negative battery cable and tighten nut to 45 inch lbs. (5 Nm).

MALFUNCTION INDICATOR LIGHT (MIL)

RESET PROCEDURE

1. Proper operation of the Malfunction Indicator Light (MIL):
   - The MIL will illuminate with the ignition switch ON and the engine OFF
   - The MIL will turn OFF when the engine is started
   - The MIL will remain ON if the self-diagnostic system has detected a malfunction
   - The MIL may turn OFF if the malfunction is no longer present
   - If the MIL is illuminated and then the engine stalls, the MIL will remain illuminated as long as the ignition switch is ON
   - If the MIL is not illuminated and the engine stalls, the MIL will not illuminate until the ignition switch is cycled OFF, then ON
2. Resetting the MIL:
   - The control module turns OFF the MIL after 3 consecutive ignition cycles that the diagnostic system runs and does not fail
   - The control module turns OFF the MIL after a current Diagnostic Trouble Code (DTC) clears when the diagnostic cycle runs and passes
   - There may still be a history of DTC's stored in the system. These will clear after 40 consecutive warm-up cycles, if no failures are reported by any other related diagnostic system
   - Manual resetting of the MIL and any DTC stored in the system, requires the use of an OBD-2 scan tool connected to the Data Link

Connector (DLC) for communication with the vehicle. Follow the instructions of the scan tool for both retrieval and resetting of DTC's. The scan tool can be used to command the MIL off.

➡If the error symptoms causing the MIL to illuminate have been corrected, the MIL will return to normal operation.

MANIFOLD ABSOLUTE PRESSURE (MAP) SENSOR

LOCATION

3.3L and 3.8L Engines
See Figure 138.

The Manifold Absolute Pressure (MAP) sensor (1) is located on the intake manifold (3).

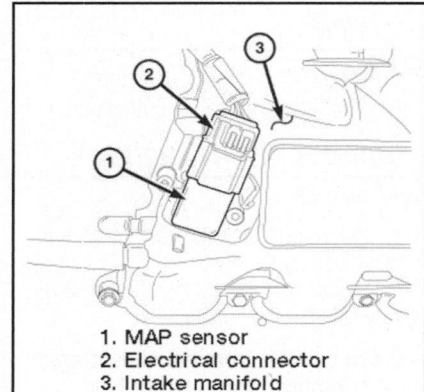

1. MAP sensor
2. Electrical connector
3. Intake manifold

36543_CARA_G0246

Fig. 138 Manifold Absolute Pressure (MAP) sensor location—3.3L and 3.8L engines

4.0L Engine
See Figure 139.

Refer to the accompanying illustration.

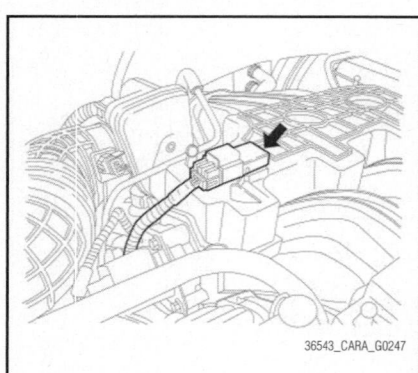

36543_CARA_G0247

Fig. 139 Manifold Absolute Pressure (MAP) sensor location—4.0L engine

REMOVAL & INSTALLATION

3.3L & 3.8L Engines

See Figure 138.

The Manifold Absolute Pressure (MAP) sensor (1) is located on the intake manifold (3).

> ❄❄ **WARNING**
>
> **Before removal, clean the outside area around the sensor to prevent dirt and debris from entering the intake manifold.**

1. Before servicing the vehicle, refer to the Precautions Section.
2. Disconnect and isolate the negative battery cable at the battery.
3. Disconnect the electrical connector (2) from the sensor (1).
4. Remove the MAP sensor (1) from the intake manifold (3) by turning the sensor ¼ turn in the counter-clockwise direction.

To install:

➡**Located on the intake manifold is a tab the prevents the MAP sensor from being incorrectly installed. Seat the sensor by turning the sensor until the sensor contacts the tab on the intake manifold.**

5. Install the MAP sensor (1) to the intake manifold (3) by turning the sensor ¼turn in the clockwise direction.
6. Connect the electrical connector (2) to the sensor (1).
7. Connect the negative battery cable, tighten the nut to 45 inch lbs. (5 Nm).

4.0L Engine

See Figure 139.

The Manifold Absolute Pressure (MAP) sensor is located on the intake manifold.

> ❄❄ **WARNING**
>
> **Before removal, clean the outside area around the sensor to prevent dirt and debris from entering the intake manifold.**

1. Before servicing the vehicle, refer to the Precautions Section.
2. Disconnect and isolate the negative battery cable at the battery.
3. Disconnect the electrical connector from the MAP sensor.
4. Rotate the sensor and lift to remove.

To install:

5. Install the sensor and rotate.
6. Connect the electrical connector to the sensor.
7. Connect the negative battery cable, tighten the nut to 45 inch lbs. (5 Nm).

POSITIVE CRANKCASE VENTILATION (PCV) VALVE

LOCATION

3.3L and 3.8L Engines

See Figure 140.

Refer to the accompanying illustration.

4.0L Engine

See Figure 141.

Refer to the accompanying illustration.

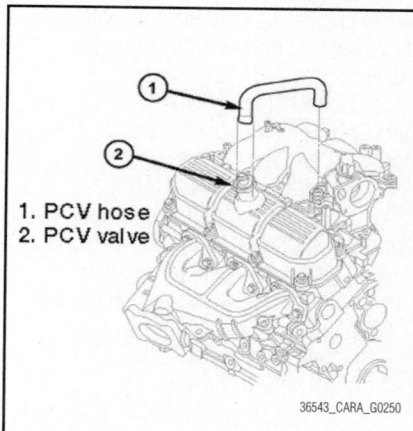

1. PCV hose
2. PCV valve

36543_CARA_G0250

Fig. 140 Positive Crankcase Ventilation (PCV) valve location—3.3L and 3.8L engines

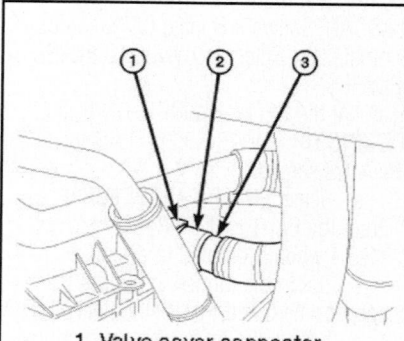

1. Valve cover connector
2. PCV valve
3. PCV hose

36543_CARA_G0251

Fig. 141 Positive Crankcase Ventilation (PCV) valve location—4.0L engine

REMOVAL & INSTALLATION

3.3L & 3.8L Engines

See Figure 140.

1. Before servicing the vehicle, refer to the Precautions Section.
2. Remove the Positive Crankcase Ventilation (PCV) hose (1) from the valve cover.
3. Remove the PCV valve (2) by pulling it out of the valve cover.

To install:

➡**The PCV valve should sit approximately 4.3mm below the top surface of the valve cover nipple. The valve should snap into a molded-in feature at the base of the nipple. Applying a light layer of grease to the PCV valve grommet will aid in assembly. Push the valve into place by applying a load to the top surface of the valve using a socket or the handle of a hammer, if necessary.**

4. Install the PCV valve (2) to the valve cover.
5. Install the PCV hose (1) to the PCV valve (2).

4.0L Engine

See Figure 141.

1. Before servicing the vehicle, refer to the Precautions Section.
2. Remove the Positive Crankcase Ventilation (PCV) hose (3) from the PCV valve (2).
3. Unscrew the PCV valve (2) from the valve cover connector (1).

To install:

4. Install the PCV valve (2) to the valve cover connector (1) and tighten to 35 inch lbs. (4 Nm).
5. Install the PCV hose (3) to the PCV valve (2).

POWERTRAIN CONTROL MODULE (PCM)

LOCATION

See Figure 142.

Refer to the accompanying illustration.

REMOVAL & INSTALLATION

See Figure 142.

1. Before servicing the vehicle, refer to the Precautions Section.
2. Disconnect and isolate the negative battery cable.
3. Remove the left front wheelhouse splash shield.

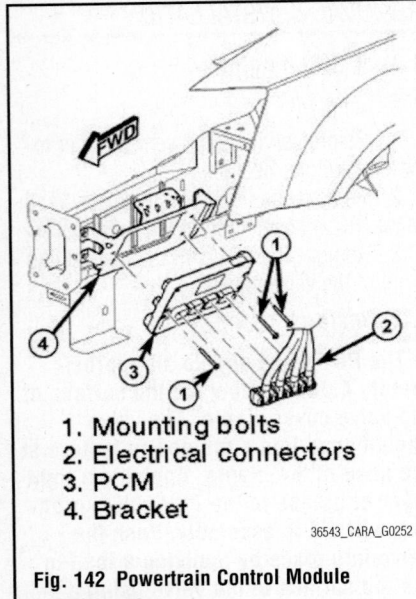

1. Mounting bolts
2. Electrical connectors
3. PCM
4. Bracket

36543_CARA_G0252

Fig. 142 Powertrain Control Module (PCM) location

4. Remove the electrical connectors (2) from the Powertrain Control Module (PCM) (3).

5. Remove the bolts (1) and the PCM (3) from the bracket (4).

To install:

6. Install the PCM (3) and the bolts (1) to the bracket (4). Tighten the bolts to 40 inch lbs. (5 Nm).

7. Install the electrical connectors (2) to the PCM (3).

8. Install the left front wheelhouse splash shield.

9. Connect the negative battery cable, tighten the nut to 45 inch lbs. (5 Nm).

10. Using a scan tool, program all the necessary information into the PCM. Refer to Reset Procedure.

RESET PROCEDURE

Replacement PCM's will require programming utilizing the StarSCAN®, or equivalent. The PCM will not operate the engine until it is programmed. A Diagnostic Trouble Code (DTC) will be set: NOT PROGRAMMED.

❄❄ WARNING

Extreme care must be taken when programming a calibration into a generic PCM. Do not randomly select a calibration. Once a calibration is selected and programmed, the controller cannot be reprogrammed to a different calibration. The module can only be reprogrammed to a more recent version of that calibration.

Special Tools Required (or equivalent):
- NPN: Battery Charger
- CH9401: StarSCAN®Tool
- CH9404: StarSCAN®Vehicle Cable
- CH9409: StarSCAN®Documentation Kit
- CH9410: StarSCAN®Ethernet Cable, 12 ft.
- CH9412: StarSCAN®Software Update Device Kit

➡**If this flash process is interrupted/aborted, the flash should be restarted.**

➡**For detailed information on the operation of the StarSCAN®, refer to the Quick Reference documentation provided in the StarSCAN®documentation kit.**

1. Open the hood, install a battery charger and verify that the charging rate provides approximately 13.5 volts. Set the battery charger timer to maintain the charging voltage for the duration of the flash process.

2. Connect the CH9404 StarSCAN®vehicle cable to the StarSCAN®and the vehicle.

3. Power ON the StarSCAN®.

4. Retrieve the old ECU part number. Using the StarSCAN®at the HOME screen:
   a. Select ECU VIEW.
   b. Touch the screen to highlight the PCM in the list of modules.
   c. Select MORE OPTIONS.
   d. Select ECU FLASH.
   e. Record the part number at the top of the FLASH PCM screen for later reference.

5. Replace the PCM with the appropriate Generic PCM.

6. Insert the StarSCAN®Software Update CD into the PC. The StarSCAN®Software Update CD will start automatically. Select DOWNLOAD FLASH UPDATES.

7. At the SELECT A METHOD FOR LOOKING UP CONTROLLER FLASH UPDATES screen:
   a. Select ENTER PART NUMBER. Enter the PART NUMBER recorded in Step 4 when prompted to do so.
   b. Using the mouse, highlight the appropriate CALIBRATION. Select NEXT.
   c. Follow the on screen instructions.
   d. When completed, proceed to Step 8.

8. With the StarSCAN®powered OFF, connect the USB Key and Gender Changer to the StarSCAN®USB port.

9. Connect the StarSCAN®to the vehicle (if not already connected).

10. Power ON the StarSCAN®.

11. Download the flash file from the USB key to the StarSCAN®. Using the StarSCAN®at the HOME screen:
   a. Select FLASH DOWNLOAD, then select RETRIEVE FILES FROM THE USB STORAGE DEVICE.
   b. Highlight the appropriate calibration. Select DOWNLOAD TO SCAN TOOL.
   c. When the download is complete, select CLOSE and BACK.

12. Reprogram the ECU. Using the StarSCAN®at the HOME screen:
   a. Select ECU VIEW.
   b. Select MORE OPTIONS.
   c. Select ECU FLASH.
   d. Highlight the appropriate calibration.
   e. Select UPDATE CONTROLLER. Follow the on screen instructions.
   f. When the update is complete, select OK.
   g. Verify the part number at the top of the FLASH PCM screen has updated to the new part number.

13. Is WIN-WIRELESS NODE displayed in the ECU OVERVIEW screen list of modules?
   a. If Yes, go to Step 14.
   b. If No, go to Step 15.

14. Program the PCM to the Wireless Ignition Node (WIN). Using the StarSCAN®at the HOME screen:
   a. Select ECU VIEW.
   b. Scroll through the list of controllers and highlight the WIN.
   c. Select MISC. FUNCTION.
   d. Highlight PCM REPLACED.
   e. Select START.
   f. Follow the on screen instructions. Select NEXT after each step. Select FINISH after completing the last step.
   g. When complete, proceed to Step 16.

15. Program the VIN into the PCM.
   a. Scroll through the list of controllers and highlight the PCM.
   b. Select MISC. FUNCTION.
   c. Highlight CHECK PCM VIN.
   d. Select START.
   e. Follow the on screen instructions. Select NEXT after each step. When the window appears with 17 boxes, select SHOW KEYBOARD. Place the cursor to the right of the last box and then backspace to delete the boxes from the window. Enter the VIN. Select FINISH after completing the last step.
   f. Unplug the scan tool from the Data Link Connector (DLC).

g. At the VEHICLE DISCONNECTED screen, press OK.

h. Connect the scan tool to the DLC and verify that the VIN is visible at the top of the HOME screen.

16. Is the vehicle equipped with a 3.7L or 4.7L engine?

a. If Yes, go to Step 18.

b. If No, go to Step 17.

17. Using the StarSCAN® at the HOME screen:

a. Select ECU VIEW.

b. Scroll through the list of controllers and highlight the PCM.

c. Select MISC. FUNCTION.

d. Highlight LEARN ETC.

e. Select START.

f. Follow the on screen instructions. Select NEXT after each step. Select FINISH after completing the last step.

➡ Due to the PCM programming procedure, a DTC may be set in other modules (TCM, BCM, MIC, SKIM, etc.) within the vehicle, if so equipped. Some DTC's may cause the MIL to illuminate. Check all modules using ECU VIEW from the HOME screen, record the DTC's, and erase these DTC's. Erase any DTC's in the PCM only after all other modules have had their DTC's erased.

➡ The following step is required by law.

18. Type the necessary information on the AUTHORIZED MODIFICATION LABEL p/n 04275086AB and attach it near the VECI label.

THROTTLE POSITION SENSOR (TPS)

REMOVAL & INSTALLATION

The throttle body position sensor is not serviceable as a stand-alone part. The throttle body position sensor is an integral part of the throttle body. If the throttle position sensor requires replacement, replace the throttle body assembly.

FUEL   GASOLINE FUEL INJECTION SYSTEM

FUEL SYSTEM SERVICE PRECAUTIONS

Safety is the most important factor when performing not only fuel system maintenance but any type of maintenance. Failure to conduct maintenance and repairs in a safe manner may result in serious personal injury or death. Maintenance and testing of the vehicle's fuel system components can be accomplished safely and effectively by adhering to the following rules and guidelines.

• To avoid the possibility of fire and personal injury, always disconnect the negative battery cable unless the repair or test procedure requires that battery voltage be applied.

• Always relieve the fuel system pressure prior to disconnecting any fuel system component (injector, fuel rail, pressure regulator, etc.), fitting or fuel line connection. Exercise extreme caution whenever relieving fuel system pressure to avoid exposing skin, face and eyes to fuel spray. Please be advised that fuel under pressure may penetrate the skin or any part of the body that it contacts.

• Always place a shop towel or cloth around the fitting or connection prior to loosening to absorb any excess fuel due to spillage. Ensure that all fuel spillage (should it occur) is quickly removed from engine surfaces. Ensure that all fuel soaked cloths or towels are deposited into a suitable waste container.

• Always keep a dry chemical (Class B) fire extinguisher near the work area.

• Do not allow fuel spray or fuel vapors to come into contact with a spark or open flame.

• Always use a back-up wrench when loosening and tightening fuel line connection fittings. This will prevent unnecessary stress and torsion to fuel line piping.

• Always replace worn fuel fitting O-rings with new Do not substitute fuel hose or equivalent where fuel pipe is installed.

Before servicing the vehicle, make sure to also refer to the precautions in the beginning of this section as well.

RELIEVING FUEL SYSTEM PRESSURE

See Figure 143.

❋❋ CAUTION

The fuel system is under constant high pressure even with engine off. Until the fuel pressure has been properly relieved from the system, do not attempt to open the fuel system. Do not smoke or use open flames/sparks when servicing the fuel system. Wear protective clothing and eye protection. Make sure the area in which the vehicle is being serviced is in a well ventilated area and free of flames/sparks.

A separate fuel pump relay is no longer used. A circuit within the Totally Integrated Power Module (TIPM) is used to control the electric fuel pump located within the fuel pump module.

1. Remove the fuel fill cap.

2. Disconnect fuel pump module electrical connector.

3. Start and run engine until it stalls.

4. Attempt restarting engine until it will no longer run.

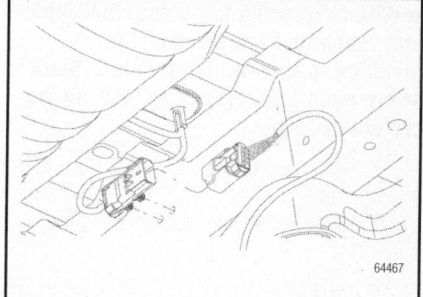

Fig. 143 Body harness electrical connector

5. Turn ignition key to the OFF position.

6. Place a rag or towel below fuel line quick-connect fitting at fuel rail.

7. Disconnect quick-connect fitting at fuel rail.

➡ After servicing the fuel system, one or more Diagnostic Trouble Codes (DTC's) may have been stored in Powertrain Control Module (PCM) memory due to disconnecting fuel pump module circuit. A diagnostic scan tool must be used to erase a DTC.

FUEL INJECTORS

REMOVAL & INSTALLATION

3.3L & 3.8L Engine—Flex Fuel and Gas

See Figure 144.

➡ The fuel system is under a constant pressure (even with the engine off). Before servicing any part on the fuel system, the fuel system pressure must be released.

1. Release the fuel system pressure as outlined in this section.

2. Disconnect and isolate negative battery cable at battery.

3. Remove the clean air hose from throttle body.

4. Use a fuel line release tool to disconnect the quick connect fuel line from the fuel rail.

5. Remove the upper intake manifold as outlined in the Engine Mechanical Section.

➡ **Mark fuel injector electrical harness connectors with correct corresponding cylinder numbers.**

6. Disconnect the fuel injector electrical connectors.

7. Remove the fuel rail mounting bolts from the fuel rail.

8. Lift fuel rail straight up off of the lower intake manifold.

➡ **When replacing individual fuel injectors, each fuel injector must be installed to its original position. Mark or tag each fuel injector to identify the correct cylinder.**

9. Remove the retaining clips from fuel injectors at fuel rail.

10. Remove the fuel injector from fuel rail.

To install:

➡ **Inspect each O-ring seal on all the fuel injectors, replace O-ring seals if any damaged is noted.**

11. Lubricate each fuel injector O-ring with a light drop of clean engine oil.

➡ **If individual fuel injectors are being replaced, return the remaining fuel injectors to the original positions noted during removal.**

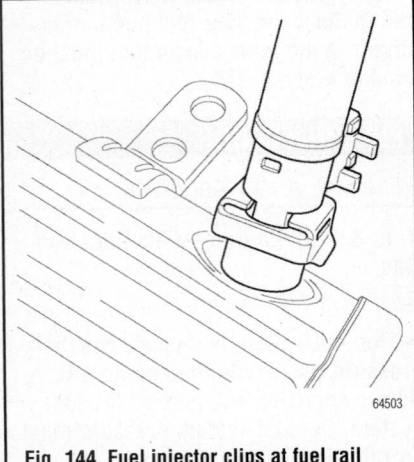

Fig. 144 Fuel injector clips at fuel rail

12. Install the fuel injectors into the fuel rail, attach the retaining clips on the fuel injectors and make sure that each fuel injector is seated properly into the fuel rail.

13. Apply a light coating of clean engine oil to the O-ring on the nozzle end of each of the injectors.

14. Insert fuel injector nozzles into openings in the lower intake manifold. Seat the injectors in place. Install the fuel rail bolts and tighten bolts to 106 inch lbs. (12 Nm).

15. Correctly position and connect the fuel injector electrical harness connectors to the fuel injectors.

16. Install the intake manifold as outlined in the Engine Mechanical Section.

✳✳ WARNING

Make sure the fuel line quick connector is connected properly. Failure to connect the fuel line correctly may result in a fuel leak at the rail assembly. Fuel leaked onto a hot engine may ignite resulting in damage to the vehicle.

17. Connect the quick connect fuel line to the fuel rail.

18. Install the clean air hose to throttle body.

19. Connect the negative battery cable, tighten the nut to 45 inch lbs. (5 Nm).

20. Use the scan tool ASD Fuel System Test to pressurize the fuel system. Check for leaks.

FUEL PUMP

REMOVAL & INSTALLATION

3.3L & 3.8L Engine—Flex Fuel and Gas

See Figure 145.

1. Remove the fuel tank as outlined in this section.

2. Disconnect electrical connector from fuel pump module.

3. Disconnect fuel line quick connect from fuel pump module.

✳✳ WARNING

Clean the area around fuel pump module prior to removal. Make sure this area is free of dirt. Failure to clean fuel pump area prior to removal may cause dirt to get into the fuel system causing damage to the fuel system and/or engine.

4. Clean the area around fuel pump module with suitable cleaner and dry with low pressure filtered compressed air.

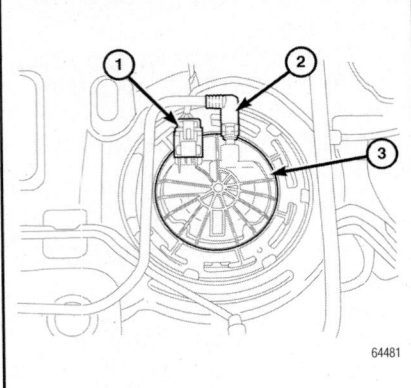

Fig. 145 Disconnect electrical connector (1) from fuel pump module (3). Disconnect fuel line (2) quick connect from fuel pump module.

5. Install the fuel pump module lock ring tool and turn counter-clockwise to remove the fuel pump module lock ring.

6. Remove the fuel pump module as an assembly from the fuel tank.

To install:

7. Install the new fuel pump module O-ring to fuel tank.

✳✳ WARNING

The fuel pump module must be installed correctly to prevent damage to the fuel pump module.

8. Line up the fuel pump module mounting tab to the arrow on the fuel tank.

9. Install the fuel pump module lock ring.

10. Install the fuel pump module lock ring tool and turn clockwise until the fuel pump module lock ring is seated and locked to fuel tank.

11. Connect fuel line quick connect to fuel pump module.

12. Connect electrical connector to fuel pump module.

13. Install the fuel tank as outlined in this section.

FUEL TANK

DRAINING

1. Release fuel system pressure as outlined in this section.

2. Remove the fuel pump module as outlined in this section.

3. Drain fuel from fuel tank with approved siphoning equipment, store fuel in approved fuel storage container.

REMOVAL & INSTALLATION

See Figures 146 through 148.

➡**The fuel system is under constant pressure even with engine off. Before servicing any part of the fuel system, the pressure must be released.**

1. Remove the fuel cap.
2. Release pressure in fuel system.
3. Remove the hose clamp and remove fuel fill hose from fuel tank.
4. Disconnect fuel pump electrical connector from body harness connector.
5. Disconnect fuel line quick connect fittings and evaporator hose.
6. Disconnect electrical connector from evaporative system integrity monitor (ESIM) switch.
7. Disconnect fuel fill vapor hose from fuel tank control valve hose.
8. Disconnect fuel fill vapor hose from ESIM switch.

➡**Support fuel tank with a transmission jack or equivalent. Use straps to secure the fuel tank to the jack. Failure to properly support and secure the fuel**

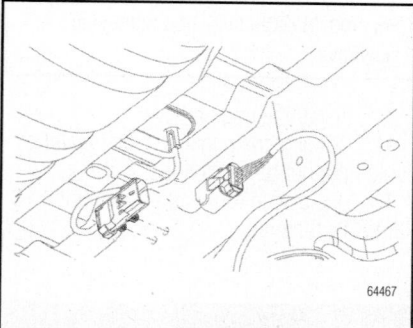

Fig. 146 Body harness electrical connector

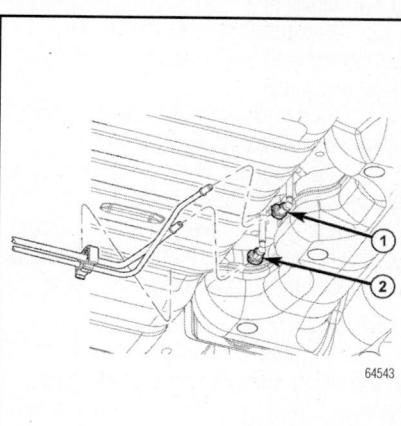

Fig. 147 Disconnect fuel line quick connect fittings (1) and evaporator hose (2).

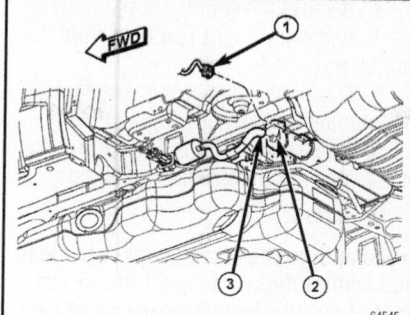

Fig. 148 Disconnect electrical connector (1) from evaporative system integrity monitor (ESIM) switch (2). Disconnect fuel fill vapor hose (3) from fuel tank control valve hose. Disconnect fuel fill vapor hose (3) from ESIM switch (2).

tank during removal may cause fuel to spill or fuel tank to fall from jack assembly.

9. Remove the fuel tank strap bolts and straps.
10. Remove the vapor canister bracket bolt.
11. Lower the fuel tank.
12. Disconnect evaporator quick connector from vapor line.
13. Disconnect evaporator quick connector from fuel tank control valve.
14. Remove the vapor canister filter.
15. Remove the fuel pump module.
16. Remove the all fuel and vapor lines from fuel tank.
17. Transfer fuel into an approved fuel storage container.

THROTTLE BODY

REMOVAL & INSTALLATION

3.3L & 3.8L Engines —Flex Fuel And Gas

See Figures 149 through 151

1. Disconnect and isolate negative battery cable at battery.
2. Remove the throttle body air intake hose.
3. Disconnect throttle body electrical connector.
4. Remove the four bolts.
5. Remove the throttle body from intake manifold.

➡**Inspect intake manifold to throttle body gasket for damage. Inspect the j-nuts for damage or excessive wear. Replace as necessary.**

6. Inspect the four j-nuts for damage or excessive wear, remove if necessary.

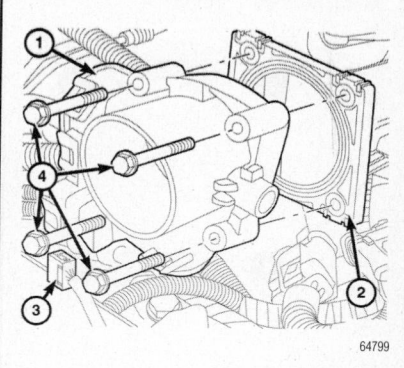

Fig. 149 Disconnect throttle body electrical connector (3). Remove four bolts (4). Remove throttle body (1) from intake manifold (2)

7. Inspect intake manifold to throttle body gasket for damage, remove if necessary.

To install:

8. Install the a new intake manifold to throttle body gasket, if replacement was necessary.
9. Install the four new four j-nuts, if replacement was necessary.

✳✳ WARNING

DO NOT OVER TORQUE. Over tightening can cause damage to the throttle body, gaskets, bolts and/or the intake manifold.

10. Install the throttle body to intake manifold.
11. Install the four bolts and hand tighten.
12. Connect throttle body electrical connector.

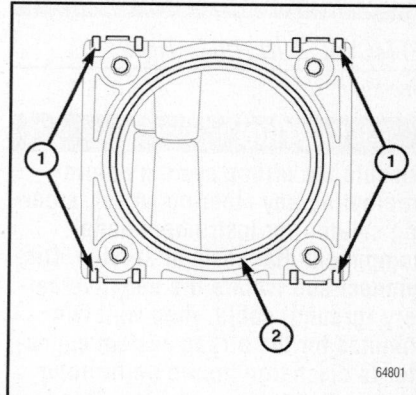

Fig. 150 Inspect the four j-nuts (1) for damage or excessive wear, remove if necessary. Inspect intake manifold to throttle body gasket (2) for damage, remove if necessary

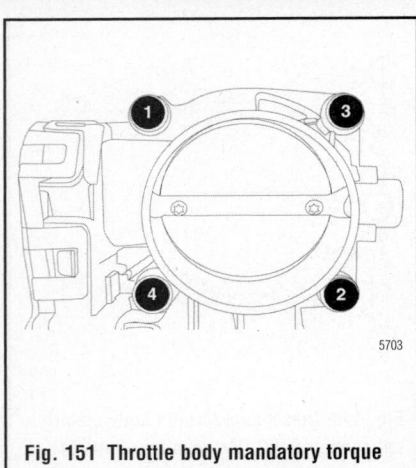

Fig. 151 Throttle body mandatory torque

➡**The throttle body must be torqued in a mandatory torque sequence. Tighten in a criss—cross pattern to specification.**

13. Tighten the bolts in a mandatory torque criss—cross pattern sequence to 65 inch lbs. (7.5 Nm).

14. Install the clean air hose and tighten clamps to 35 inch lbs. (4 Nm).

15. Connect negative battery cable, tighten nut to 45 inch lbs. (5 Nm).

16. Use a scan tool and perform the ETC RELEARN function.

4.0L Engine

See Figures 152 and 153.

1. Before servicing the vehicle, refer to the Precautions Section.

2. Disconnect and isolate the negative battery cable at the battery.

3. Remove the engine cover.

4. Remove the clean air hose from the throttle body.

5. Disconnect the electrical connector (1) from the throttle body (2).

6. Remove the 4 bolts and remove the throttle body from the intake manifold.

To install:

➡**Make sure the intake gasket is clean and free of debris. Inspect the intake gasket for damage. Replace as necessary.**

❋❋ **WARNING**

DO NOT OVER TORQUE. Over-tightening can cause damage to the throttle body, gaskets, bolts, and/or the intake manifold.

7. Install the throttle body, gasket, and bolts to the intake manifold.

❋❋ **WARNING**

The throttle body must be tightened in a mandatory torque sequence. Tighten in a crisscross pattern to specification.

8. Tighten the bolts in a mandatory torque crisscross pattern sequence to 50 inch lbs. (6 Nm).

9. Connect the electrical connector (1) to the throttle body (2).

10. Install the clean air hose to the throttle body.

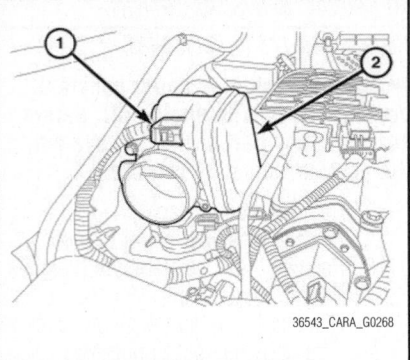

Fig. 152 Disconnect the electrical connector (1) from the throttle body (2)— 4.0L engine

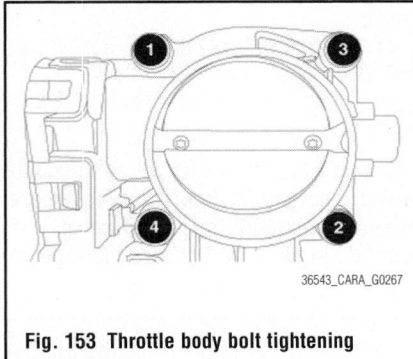

Fig. 153 Throttle body bolt tightening sequence

11. Install the engine cover.

12. Connect the negative battery cable, tighten the nut to 45 inch lbs. (5 Nm).

13. Use a scan tool and perform the ETC RELEARN function.

HEATING & AIR CONDITIONING SYSTEM

BLOWER MOTOR

REMOVAL & INSTALLATION

See Figure 154.

❋❋ **CAUTION**

Disable the airbag system before attempting any steering wheel, steering column, or instrument panel component diagnosis or service. Disconnect and isolate the negative battery (ground) cable, then wait two minutes for the airbag system capacitor to discharge before performing further diagnosis or service. This is the only sure way to disable the airbag system. Failure to take the proper precautions may result in accidental airbag deployment and possible serious or fatal injury.

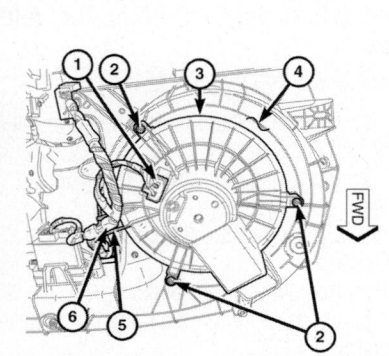

1. Wire harness connector
2. Screws
3. Blower motor
4. Front HVAC housing
5. Mounting bracket
6. HVAC wire harness

Fig. 154 Blower motor components

1. Disconnect and isolate the negative battery cable.

2. If equipped, remove the silencer from underneath the passenger side of the instrument panel.

3. Disconnect the wire harness connector from the blower motor.

4. Disengage the HVAC wire harness from the mounting bracket.

5. Remove the three screws that secure the blower motor to the front HVAC housing and remove the blower motor.

To install:

6. Position the blower motor into the front HVAC housing and install the three retaining screws. Tighten the screws to 10 inch lbs. (1.2 Nm).

7. Engage the wire harness to the mounting bracket.

8. Connect the wire harness connector to the blower motor.

9. If equipped, install the silencer underneath the passenger side of the instrument panel.

10. Reconnect the negative battery cable.

HEATER CORE

REMOVAL & INSTALLATION

2010 Models

See Figures 155 through 160.

✳ CAUTION

Disable the airbag system before attempting any steering wheel, steering column, or instrument panel component diagnosis or service. Disconnect and isolate the negative battery (ground) cable, then wait 2 minutes for the airbag system capacitor to discharge before performing further diagnosis or service. This is the only sure way to disable the airbag system. Failure to take the proper precautions may result in accidental airbag deployment and possible serious or fatal injury.

✳ WARNING

The heater core tubes are not serviced separately from the heater core. The heater core tubes should not be repositioned, loosened, or removed from the heater core. Failure to follow this warning may result in a coolant leak.

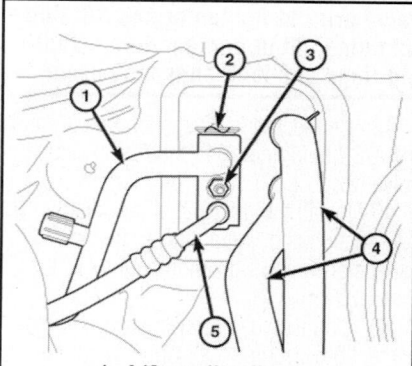

1. A/C suction line
2. A/C expansion valve
3. Mounting nut
4. Heater hoses
5. A/C liquid line

36543_CARA_G0283

Fig. 155 Disconnect the A/C suction and liquid lines from the A/C expansion valve

1. Before servicing the vehicle, refer to the Precautions Section.

2. Disconnect and isolate the negative battery cable.

3. Drain the engine cooling system.

4. Recover the refrigerant from the refrigerant system.

5. Remove the nut (3) that secures the A/C suction line (1) and the A/C liquid line (4) to the A/C expansion valve (2).

6. Disconnect the A/C suction and liquid lines from the A/C expansion valve and remove and discard the washer seals.

7. Remove the 2 bolts (1) that secure the A/C expansion valve (2) to the A/C evaporator.

8. Remove the A/C expansion valve from the A/C evaporator and remove and discard the O-ring seals.

9. Install plugs or tape to seal the opened refrigerant line fittings and the evaporator and expansion valve ports.

10. Loosen the clamps and disconnect the heater hoses (4) from the heater core. Plug the heater core ports.

➥Take the proper precautions to protect the front face of the instrument panel from cosmetic damage during this service procedure.

11. Remove the bolt that secures the HVAC housing to the engine compartment side of the dash panel.

12. Remove the defroster grille from the top of the instrument panel.

13. Remove the bolt (1) that secures the HVAC air inlet housing (3) to the passenger side of the dash panel (2).

➥Illustration shown with instrument panel removed for clarity.

14. Remove the instrument panel and HVAC housing as an assembly and place

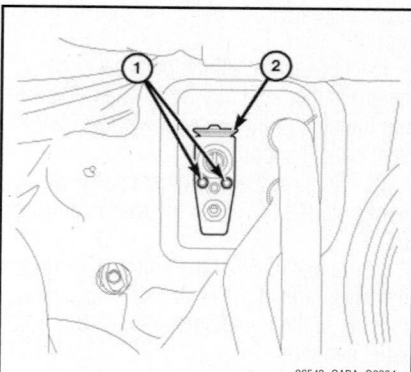

36543_CARA_G0284

Fig. 156 Remove the bolts (1) that secure the A/C expansion valve (2) to the A/C evaporator

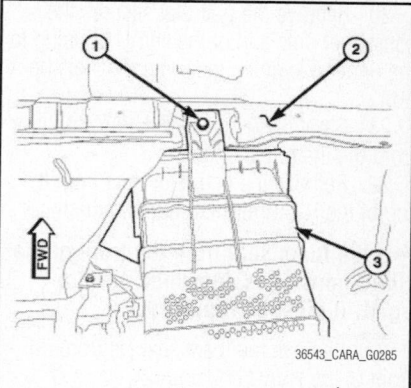

36543_CARA_G0285

Fig. 157 Remove the bolts (1) that secure the A/C expansion valve (2) to the A/C evaporator

them on a workbench. Refer to Instrument Panel, removal & installation.

15. Remove the 2 screws that secure the defroster duct to the top of the instrument panel cover.

16. Remove the bolt that secures the HVAC housing to the front of the instrument panel support, near the lower center of the instrument panel.

17. Remove the bolt (1) that secures the driver side of the HVAC air distribution housing (2) to the underside of the instrument panel support (3).

18. Remove the bolt that secures the passenger side of the HVAC air distribution housing to the underside of the instrument panel support.

19. Disconnect the instrument panel wire harness from the HVAC wire harness connector.

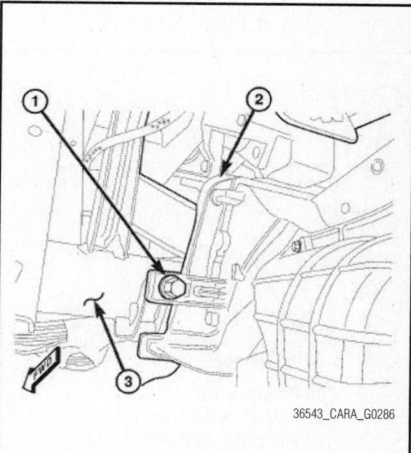

36543_CARA_G0286

Fig. 158 Remove the bolt (1) that secures the driver side of the HVAC air distribution housing (2) to the underside of the instrument panel support (3)

20. Remove the bolt that secures the passenger side end of the HVAC housing to the underside of the instrument panel support.

21. Carefully remove the HVAC housing from the instrument panel.

22. Remove the defroster duct from the top of the HVAC air distribution housing.

➡ **If the foam seal from the front of the HVAC housing is deformed or damaged, it must be replaced.**

23. Remove the foam seal (1) from the front of the HVAC housing (2).

24. Remove the 2 screws (4) that secure the heater core cover (5) to the driver side of the air distribution housing (3).

25. Rotate and tilt the heater core cover as necessary to disengage the retaining tab that secures the front of the cover to the HVAC housing and remove the cover.

26. Carefully pull the heater core (1) out of the driver side of the air distribution housing (2).

To install:

☀☀ **WARNING**

The heater core tubes are not serviced separately from the heater core. The heater core tubes should not be repositioned, loosened, or removed from the heater core. Failure to follow this warning may result in a coolant leak and possible serious injury.

➡ **If the foam seal around the heater core is deformed or damaged, it must be replaced.**

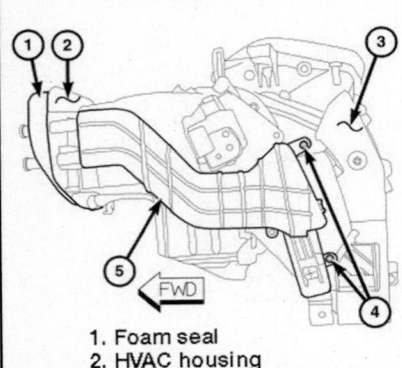

1. Foam seal
2. HVAC housing
3. Air distribution housing
4. Screws
5. Heater core cover

36543_CARA_G0287

Fig. 159 Remove the foam seal from the HVAC housing

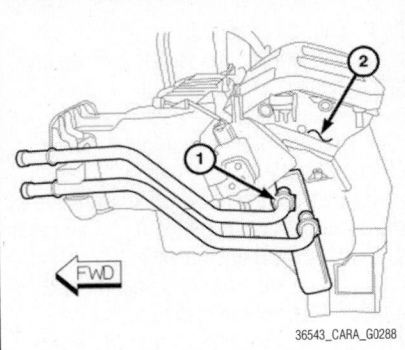

36543_CARA_G0288

Fig. 160 Carefully pull the heater core (1) out of the driver side of the air distribution housing (2)

27. Carefully install the heater core (1) into the driver side of the air distribution housing (2).

28. Position the front of the heater core cover (5) to the front of the HVAC housing (2) and engage the retaining tab that secures the cover to the housing.

29. Install the heater core cover to the driver side of the air distribution housing (3) and install the 2 screws (4). Tighten the screws to 10 inch lbs. (1 Nm).

30. Install the foam seal (1) onto the front of the HVAC housing.

31. Install the A/C expansion valve.

➡ **Replacement of the refrigerant line seals is required anytime a refrigerant line or expansion valve is disconnected or removed. Failure to replace the rubber and metal dual-plane seals may result in a refrigerant system leak.**

32. Install the defroster duct to the top of the HVAC air distribution housing.

33. Position the HVAC housing into the instrument panel support

34. Loosely install the bolt that secures the passenger side end of the HVAC housing to the underside of the instrument panel support.

35. Loosely install the bolt that secures the passenger side of the HVAC air distribution housing to the underside of the instrument panel support.

36. Connect the instrument panel wire harness to the HVAC wire harness connector.

37. Loosely install the bolt that secures the driver side of the HVAC air distribution housing to the underside of the instrument panel support.

38. Loosely install the bolt that secures the HVAC housing to the front of the instrument panel support.

39. Tighten all of the bolts that secure

the HVAC housing to the instrument panel support to 27 inch lbs. (3 Nm).

40. Install the 2 screws that secure the defroster duct to the top of the instrument panel cover. Tighten the screws to 17 inch lbs. (2 Nm).

41. Position the instrument panel and HVAC housing into the vehicle as an assembly. Make sure to align the condensate drain with the drain tube located in the center of the floor panel and to fully engage the floor distribution ducts to the outlets in the bottom of the HVAC housing.

42. Install the instrument panel. Refer to Instrument Panel, removal & installation.

43. Install the bolt that secures the HVAC air inlet housing to the passenger side of the dash panel. Tighten the bolt to 27 inch lbs. (3 Nm).

44. Install the defroster grille onto the top of the instrument panel.

45. Install the bolt that secures the HVAC housing to the engine compartment side of the dash panel. Tighten the bolt to 27 inch lbs. (3 Nm).

46. Remove the tape or plugs from the opened refrigerant line fittings and expansion valve and heater core ports.

47. Lubricate new dual-plane seals with clean refrigerant oil and install them onto the refrigerant line fittings. Use only the specified seals as they are made of a special material for the R-134a system. Use only refrigerant oil of the type recommended for the A/C compressor in the vehicle.

☀☀ **WARNING**

Use care when installing the A/C lines to the A/C expansion valve. Carefully align the tube ends with the valve prior to tightening the A/C line retaining nut or damage to the sealing rings and tube ends may occur.

48. Connect the A/C suction line (1) and the A/C liquid line (5) to the A/C expansion valve (2).

49. Install the nut (3) that secures the A/C suction and liquid lines to the A/C expansion valve. Tighten the nut to 17 ft. lbs. (23 Nm).

50. Connect the heater hoses (4) to the heater core. Tighten the clamps securely.

51. Reconnect the negative battery cable and tighten the nut to 45 inch lbs. (5 Nm).

52. If the heater core is being replaced, flush the cooling system.

53. Refill the engine cooling system with the proper type and amount of fluid.

54. Evacuate the refrigerant system.

55. Charge the refrigerant system.

56. Calibrate the A/C-heater control. Refer to Reset Procedure.

RESET PROCEDURE

➡**The A/C-heater control module must be recalibrated each time an actuator motor or the A/C-heater control is replaced. If the vehicle is so equipped, the calibration procedure also includes the rear HVAC positions for each actuator motor.**

Calibrate the A/C-heater control with the following procedure:

1. Before servicing the vehicle, refer to the Precautions Section.
2. Turn the ignition switch to the ON position.

3. If equipped with the Manual Temperature Control (MTC) system, press and hold the Rear Wipe/Wash and Recirculation buttons for at least 5 seconds.
4. If equipped with the Automatic Temperature Control (ATC) system, simultaneously press and hold the Power and Recirculation buttons on the A/C-heater control for at least 5 seconds.
5. The MTC A/C-heater control Rear Wipe/Wash button Light Emitting Diode (LED) and Recirculation button LED, or the ATC A/C-heater control Delay and Recirculation graphics, will begin to flash when the calibration procedure has begun.
6. The calibration procedure should take less than 2 minutes to complete for the MTC A/C-heater control, and less than 20 seconds for the ATC A/C-heater control. When the LED's or graphics stop flashing, the calibration procedure is complete.
7. If the LED's or graphics continue to flash beyond the 2 minute (manual) or 20 second (ATC) calibration time, this indicates that the A/C-heater control has detected a failure and a Diagnostic Trouble Code (DTC) has been set.

➡**The LED's or graphics will continue to flash even after the ignition switch is cycled OFF and ON, until a successful calibration is completed or until the vehicle has been driven about 8 miles (13 km).**

STEERING

POWER STEERING GEAR

REMOVAL & INSTALLATION

See Figures 161 through 167.

1. Place front wheels of vehicle in STRAIGHT-AHEAD position.
2. Install the steering wheel holder locking steering wheel in STRAIGHT-AHEAD position.
3. Remove the negative (-) battery cable from battery and isolate cable.
4. Remove the cap from power steering fluid reservoir.
5. Using a siphon pump, remove as much power steering fluid as possible from power steering fluid reservoir.
6. Raise and support vehicle.
7. On each side of vehicle, remove wheel mounting nuts, then tire and wheel assembly.
8. At each end of stabilizer bar, while holding stabilizer bar link lower stud stationary (wrench placed on machined flats on stud), remove nut securing link to stabilizer bar.
9. If outer tie rods need to be transferred to new gear, loosen tie rod jam nut on both sides of vehicle.
10. On both sides of vehicle, remove nut attaching outer tie rod to knuckle by holding rod end stud stationary while loosening and removing nut with a wrench.

11. Release each outer tie rod end from knuckle using Remover, Special Tool
12. Remove the front engine mount thru-bolt.
13. Remove the fore-aft crossmember front mounting bolt.
14. Remove the four fore-aft crossmember rear mounting bolts.
15. Remove the fore-aft crossmember.
16. Remove the screws and push-pins securing heat shield over right side of steering gear. Remove heat shield.
17. Remove the rear engine mount.
18. Remove the screws securing power steering pressure hose routing clamp(s) (4.0L engine only uses one) to rear of crossmember.
19. Remove the screws securing the stabilizer bushing retainers to the crossmember.
20. Remove the two stabilizer bushing retainers.

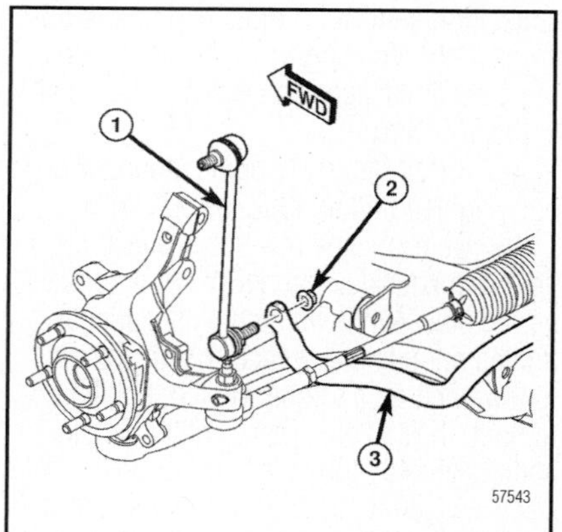

Fig. 161 At each end of stabilizer bar, while holding stabilizer bar link (1) lower stud stationary (wrench placed on machined flats on stud), remove nut (2) securing link to stabilizer bar (3).

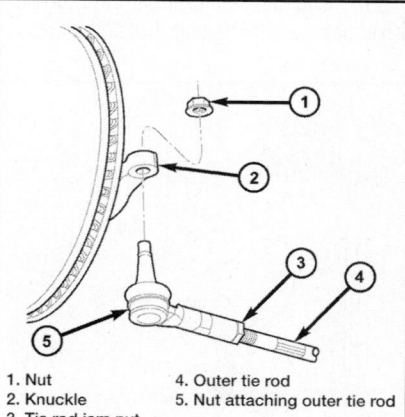

1. Nut
2. Knuckle
3. Tie rod jam nut
4. Outer tie rod
5. Nut attaching outer tie rod

57501

Fig. 162 If outer tie rods need to be transferred to new gear, loosen tie rod jam nut on both sides of vehicle. On both sides of vehicle, remove nut attaching outer tie rod to knuckle by holding rod end stud stationary while loosening and removing nut with a wrench

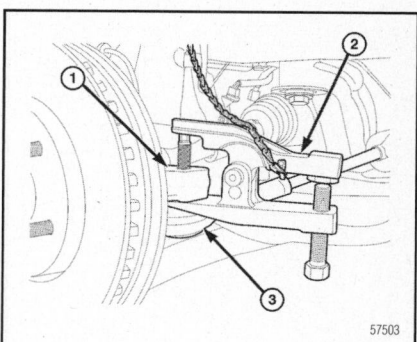

57503

Fig. 163 Release each outer tie rod end (3) from knuckle (1) using Remover (1), Special Tool

21. Utilizing the slit cut into the cushions (bushings), remove the two cushions from the stabilizer bar.

22. Slowly rotate the stabilizer bar as necessary and remove it out through the driver side wheel opening.

23. Remove the tube nut fastening return hose to power steering gear. Remove return hose from gear port.

24. Remove the tube nut fastening pressure hose to power steering gear. Remove pressure hose from gear port.

25. Remove the bolts securing steering gear to crossmember.

26. Slide dust shield upward exposing pinch bolt securing intermediate shaft extension to steering gear shaft.

27. Remove the pinch bolt securing intermediate shaft extension to steering gear shaft.

28. Slide intermediate shaft extension off steering gear shaft.

29. Rotate steering gear to position shown in graphic, then slide steering gear out left wheel opening.

30. If necessary, remove outer tie rods from inner tie rod threads. Count how many rotations it takes to remove each outer tie rod for installation reference.

To install:

31. If necessary, install outer tie rods onto inner tie rod threads. As outer tie rods are installed, count out same number rotations as were counted on tie rod removal. This will get toe setting somewhat close to specification before vehicle is aligned at end of this procedure. Snug tie rod jam nuts on both ends of gear. Do not tighten at this time. Tighten tie rod jam nuts to specification while performing wheel alignment at end of this procedure.

32. Carefully install power steering gear through left wheel opening using the

reverse of how it was removed, then set it up into mounted position.

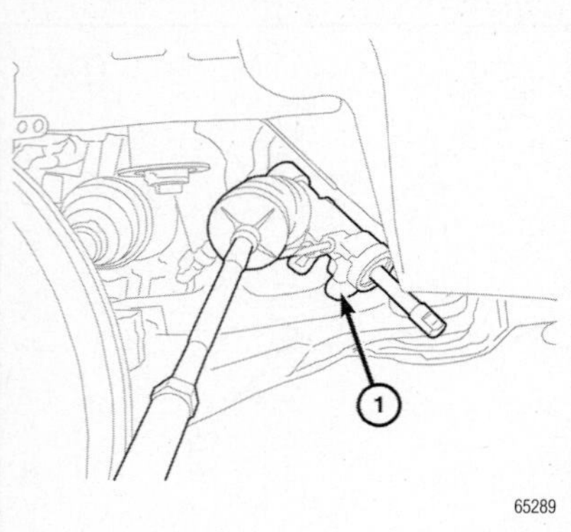

33. Find power steering gear's center of travel, then match intermediate shaft extension with that on steering gear shaft. Slide extension onto steering gear shaft.

34. Install the pinch bolt securing intermediate shaft extension to extension shaft. Tighten pinch bolt to 31 ft. lbs. (42 Nm).

35. Slide dust shield down over pinch bolt and steering gear shaft.

36. Center steering gear mounting bosses over mounting holes in crossmember and install two steering gear mounting bolts. Tighten mounting bolts to 89ft. lbs. (120 Nm).

37. Install the return hose into power steering gear port. Thread return hose tube nut into gear and tighten to 23 ft. lbs. (31 Nm).

38. Install the pressure hose into power steering gear port. Thread pressure hose tube nut into gear and tighten to 23 ft. lbs. (31 Nm).

➡**Before stabilizer bar installation, inspect the cushions and links for excessive wear, cracks, damage and distortion. Replace any pieces failing inspection.**

➡**Before installing the stabilizer bar, make sure the bar is not upside down. The stabilizer bar must be installed so that when in mounted position, the ends of the bar curve under the steering gear tie rods, up to the links.**

39. Install the stabilizer bar through the driver side wheel opening. Rotate the bar as

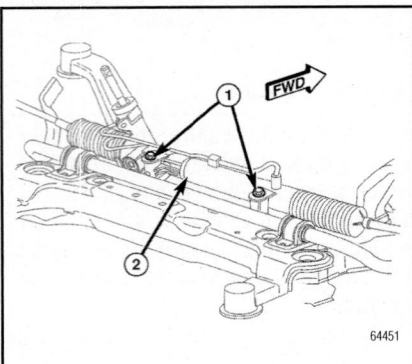

Fig. 166 Center steering gear (2) mounting bosses over mounting holes in crossmember and install two steering gear mounting bolts (1).

necessary until it is centered over the suspension crossmember and the ends curve upward below the steering gear tie rods.

40. Install the two cushions (bushings) on the stabilizer bar utilizing the slit cut into the cushion sides.

41. Install the two stabilizer bushing retainers over the cushions.

42. Install the four screws securing the stabilizer bushing retainers to the crossmember. Tighten screws to 33 ft. lbs. (45 Nm).

43. Position the power steering pressure hose routing clamp(s) (4.0L engine only uses one) on the rear of the crossmember. Install and tighten the screw(s) to 71 inch lbs. (8 Nm).

44. Install the rear engine mount.

45. Position the heat shield over the steering gear. Install the mounting screws and push-pins. Tighten the screws to 71 inch lbs. (8 Nm).

46. Position fore-aft crossmember in engine compartment and install mounting bolts. Tighten forward mounting bolt to 83 ft. lbs. (113 Nm). Tighten rearward mounting bolts at suspension crossmember to 41 ft. lbs. (55 Nm).

47. Install the front engine mount thru-bolt. Tighten bolt to 42 ft. lbs. (57 Nm).

48. On each side of vehicle, attach outer tie rod to knuckle. Start NEW nut onto outer tie rod stud. While holding stud stationary, tighten nut using a wrench. Using a crow-foot wrench on a torque wrench, tighten nut to 55 ft. lb (75 Nm). Then, tighten nut an additional 245° turn after that torque is met.

49. Attach the stabilizer bar link at each end of the stabilizer bar. At each link, install and tighten the nut while holding the stabilizer bar link lower stud stationary. Tighten the nuts to 65 ft. lbs. (88 Nm).

50. On each side of vehicle, install tire and wheel assembly.

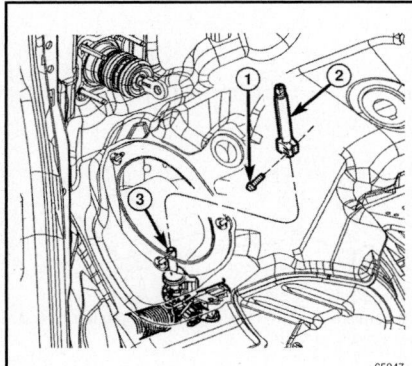

Fig. 165 Find power steering gear's center of travel, then match intermediate shaft extension (2) with that on steering gear shaft (3). Slide extension onto steering gear shaft. Install pinch bolt (1) securing intermediate shaft extension (2) to extension shaft (3)

Fig. 164 Steering gear (1) removal & installation

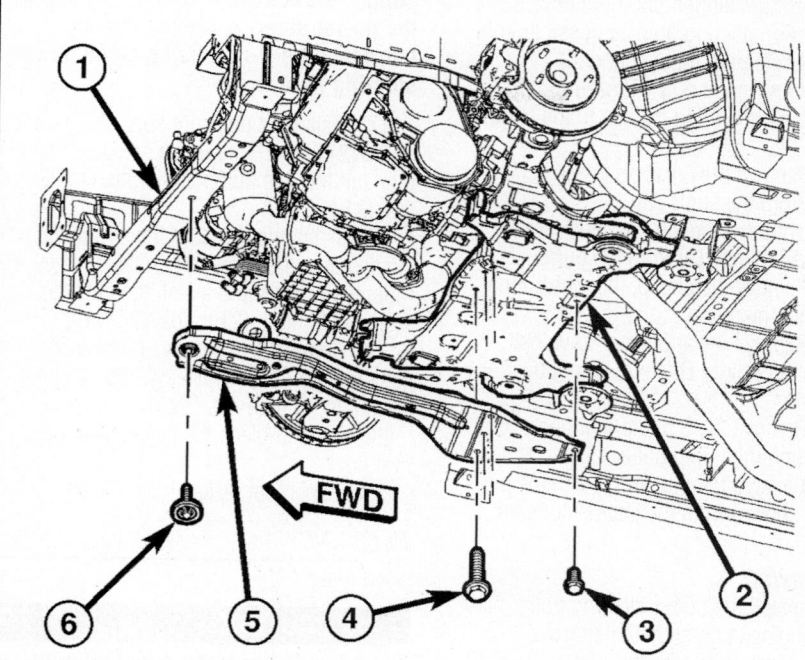

1. Crossmember
2. Suspension crossmember
3. Mounting bolt
4. Mounting bolt
5. Fore-aft crossmember
6. Mounting bolt

57545

Fig. 167 Fore-aft crossmember mounting

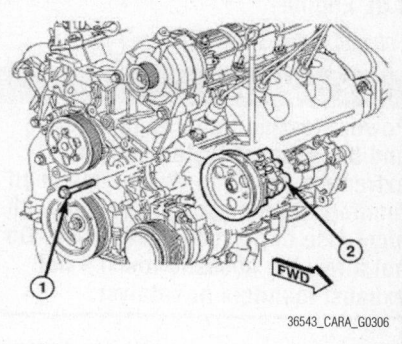

36543_CARA_G0306

Fig. 168 Remove the pump mounting bolts (1) through the pump pulley and remove the pump (2)—3.3L and 3.8L engines

51. Install the and tighten wheel mounting nuts in proper sequence to 100 ft. lbs. (135 Nm).
52. Lower vehicle.
53. Connect negative (-) battery cable on negative battery post.
54. Remove the steering wheel holder.
55. Fill and bleed power steering system.
56. Inspect for leaks.
57. Perform wheel alignment, setting toe to specifications.

POWER STEERING PUMP

REMOVAL & INSTALLATION

3.3L & 3.8L Engines
See Figure 168.

❋❋ **CAUTION**

Power steering fluid, engine parts, and the exhaust system may be extremely hot if the engine has been running. Do not start the engine with any loose or disconnected hoses. Do not allow the hoses to touch a hot exhaust manifold or catalyst.

❋❋ **CAUTION**

The fluid level should be checked with the engine OFF to prevent personal injury from moving parts.

❋❋ **WARNING**

When the system is open, cap all open ends of the hoses, power steering pump fittings, or power steering gear ports to prevent entry of foreign material into the components.

❋❋ **WARNING**

When servicing power steering components, do not pinch off the power steering hoses in any way to stop the fluid flow. Damage to the hoses may result.

1. Before servicing the vehicle, refer to the Precautions Section.
2. Remove the negative (-) battery cable from the battery and isolate the cable.
3. Remove the cap from the power steering fluid reservoir.
4. Using a siphon pump, remove as much power steering fluid as possible from the power steering fluid reservoir.
5. Remove the clamp, then the supply hose from the pump.
6. Unthread the tube nut and remove the pressure hose from the pump.
7. Remove the accessory drive belt. Refer to Accessory Drive Belts, removal & installation.
8. Remove the 3 pump mounting bolts (1) through the pump pulley.
9. Remove the power steering pump (2) from the engine compartment.

To install:
10. Position the power steering pump (2) on the engine.
11. Install the 3 power steering pump mounting bolts (1) using the openings in the pulley. Tighten the pump mounting bolts to 17 ft. lbs. (23 Nm).
12. Install the accessory drive belt. Refer to Accessory Drive Belts, removal & installation.

➡**Before installing the power steering pressure hose on the power steering pump, replace the O-ring on the end of the power steering pressure hose. Lubricate the O-ring using clean power steering fluid.**

13. Install the pressure hose into the pump fitting. Thread the pressure hose tube nut into the pump and tighten to 23 ft. lbs. (31 Nm).
14. Slide the fluid supply hose onto the pump fitting and install the clamp securing it in place.
15. Connect the negative (-) battery cable on the negative battery post. Tighten the nut to 45 inch lbs. (5 Nm).
16. Fill and bleed the power steering system.
17. Inspect for leaks.

4.0L Engine

See Figures 169 and 170.

> ⁂ **CAUTION**
>
> **Power steering fluid, engine parts, and the exhaust system may be extremely hot if the engine has been running. Do not start the engine with any loose or disconnected hoses. Do not allow the hoses to touch a hot exhaust manifold or catalyst.**

> ⁂ **CAUTION**
>
> **The fluid level should be checked with the engine OFF to prevent personal injury from moving parts.**

> ⁂ **WARNING**
>
> **When the system is open, cap all open ends of the hoses, power steering pump fittings, or power steering gear ports to prevent entry of foreign material into the components.**

> ⁂ **WARNING**
>
> **When servicing power steering components, do not pinch off the power steering hoses in any way to stop the fluid flow. Damage to the hoses may result.**

1. Before servicing the vehicle, refer to the Precautions Section.
2. Remove negative (-) battery cable from battery and isolate cable.
3. Remove cap from power steering fluid reservoir.

4. Using a siphon pump, remove as much power steering fluid as possible from the power steering fluid reservoir.
5. Remove the nuts (5) securing the pressure hose routing clamps to the engine (2).
6. Remove the pressure hose routing clamps from the studs (3).
7. Unthread the tube nut and remove the pressure hose (1) from the pump (2).
8. Remove the clamp, then the supply hose from the pump.
9. Remove the accessory drive belt. Refer to Accessory Drive Belts, removal & installation.
10. Remove the 3 pump mounting bolts (3) through the pump pulley.
11. Remove the pump (2) (with the pulley, not shown) from the engine compartment.

To install:

12. Install the power steering pump back in the engine compartment using the reverse order of its removal.
13. Install the power steering pump onto its mounting bracket (1) cast into the engine cover.
14. Install the 3 power steering pump mounting bolts (3) through the pulley. Tighten the pump mounting bolts to 17 ft. lbs. (23 Nm).
15. Install the accessory drive belt. Refer to Accessory Drive Belts, removal & installation.
16. Slide the fluid supply hose onto the pump fitting and install the clamp securing it in place.

➡**Before installing the power steering pressure hose on the power steering**

pump, replace the O-ring on the end of the power steering pressure hose. Lubricate the O-ring using clean power steering fluid.

17. Install the pressure hose (1) into the pump (2) fitting. Thread the pressure hose tube nut into the pump and tighten to 23 ft. lbs. (31 Nm).
18. Install the pressure hose routing clamps over the studs (3) on the engine mounted bracket and install the nuts (5). Tighten the nut to 21 ft. lbs. (28 Nm).
19. Connect the negative (-) battery cable on the negative battery post. Tighten the nut to 45 inch lbs. (5 Nm).
20. Fill and bleed the power steering system.
21. Inspect for leaks.

BLEEDING

See Figure 171.

> ⁂ **CAUTION**
>
> **Fluid level should be checked with the engine OFF to prevent personal injury from moving parts and to assure an accurate fluid level reading.**

> ⁂ **WARNING**
>
> **MOPAR®Power Steering Fluid + 4 or MOPAR®ATF+4 Automatic Transmission Fluid is to be used in the power steering system. Both Fluids have the same material standard specifications (MS-9602). No other power steering or automatic transmission fluid is to be used in the system. Damage may result to the power steering pump and system if another fluid is used. Do not overfill the system.**

> ⁂ **WARNING**
>
> **If the air is not purged from the power steering system correctly, pump failure could result.**

➡**Be sure the vacuum tool used in the following procedure is clean and free of any fluids.**

1. Before servicing the vehicle, refer to the Precautions Section.
2. Check the fluid level.
   a. The power steering fluid level can be viewed through the side of the power steering fluid reservoir.
   b. Compare the fluid level to the markings on the side of the reservoir.

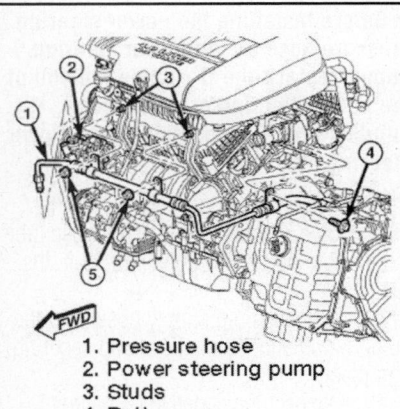

1. Pressure hose
2. Power steering pump
3. Studs
4. Bolt
5. Attaching nuts

36543_CARA_G0307

Fig. 169 Remove the pressure hose from the power steering pump

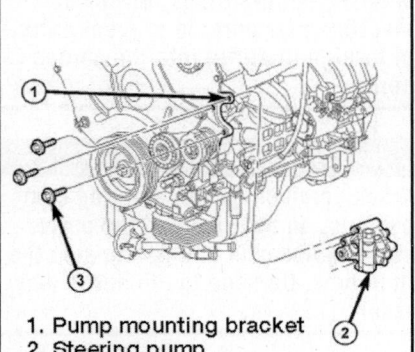

1. Pump mounting bracket
2. Steering pump
3. Mounting bolts

36543_CARA_G0308

Fig. 170 Remove the pressure hose from the power steering pump

When the fluid is at normal ambient temperature, approximately 70–80°F (21–27°C), the fluid level should read between the MAX and MIN markings.

c. When the fluid is hot, the fluid level is allowed to read up to the MAX line.

➡Do not fill fluid beyond the MAX mark. Check the cap seal for damage and replace if needed.

3. Remove the cap from the fluid reservoir and fill the power steering fluid reservoir up to the MAX marking with MOPAR® Power Steering Fluid + 4 or MOPAR®ATF+4 Automatic Transmission Fluid.

4. Tightly insert the Power Steering Cap Adapter (4), Special Tool 9688, into the mouth of the reservoir (3).

➡Failure to use a vacuum pump reservoir (1) may allow power steering fluid to be sucked into the hand vacuum pump.

5. Attach the Hand Vacuum Pump (2), Special Tool C-4207, or equivalent, with reservoir (1) attached, to the Power Steering Cap Adapter (4).

✳✳ WARNING

Do not run the vehicle while vacuum is applied to the power steering system. Damage to the power steering pump can occur.

➡When performing the following step make sure the vacuum level is maintained during the entire time period.

6. Using Hand Vacuum Pump (2), apply 20–25 inches Hg (68–85 kPa) of vacuum to the system for a minimum of 3 minutes.

7. Slowly release the vacuum and remove the Special Tools.

8. Adjust the fluid level as necessary.

9. Repeat above steps until the fluid no longer drops when vacuum is applied.

10. Start the engine and cycle the steering wheel lock-to-lock 3 times.

➡Do not hold the steering wheel at the stops.

11. Stop the engine and check for leaks at all connections.

12. Check for any signs of air in the

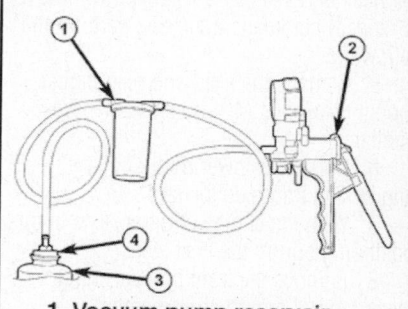

1. Vacuum pump reservoir
2. Hand vacuum pump
3. Reservoir
4. Power steering cap adaptor

36543_DAKO_G0210

Fig. 171 Hand Vacuum Pump, Special Tool C-4207 illustrated

reservoir and check the fluid level. If air is present, repeat the procedure as necessary.

✳✳ WARNING

Do not run a vehicle with foamy fluid for an extended period. This may cause pump damage.

SUSPENSION

PRECAUTIONS

➡Chrysler does not manufacture any vehicles or replacement parts that contain asbestos. Aftermarket products may or may not contain asbestos. Refer to aftermarket product packaging for product information.
Whether the product contains asbestos or not, dust and dirt can accumulate on brake parts during normal use. Follow practices prescribed by appropriate regulations for the handling, processing and disposing of dust and debris.

✳✳ CAUTION

Do not remove the strut rod nut while strut assembly is installed in vehicle, or before the coil spring is compressed with a compression tool. The spring is held under high pressure.

➡At no time when servicing a vehicle can a sheet metal screw, bolt, or other metal fastener be installed in the shock tower to take the place of an original plastic clip. It may come into contact with the strut or coil spring.

✳✳ WARNING

Wheel bearing damage will result if after loosening the axle hub nut, the vehicle is rolled on the ground or the weight of the vehicle is allowed to be supported by the tires for any length of time.

LOWER BALL JOINT

REMOVAL & INSTALLATION

See Figure 172.

1. Raise and support the vehicle.
2. Remove the wheel mounting nuts, then the tire and wheel assembly.
3. Remove the knuckle.
4. Remove the ball joint dust boot.
5. Using Ball Joint Press remover, press the ball joint out of the lower control arm.

To install:

6. Using Ball Joint Press, installer and receiver, press the ball joint into the lower control arm.

7. Install the steering knuckle, brake rotor and caliper.

8. Install the tire and wheel assembly.

9. Install the and tighten wheel mounting nuts to 100 ft. lbs. (135 Nm).

FRONT SUSPENSION

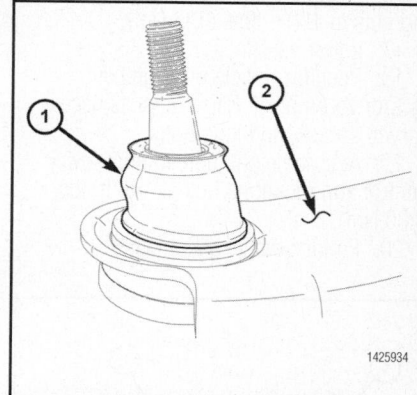

1425934

Fig. 172 Remove the ball joint dust boot (1).

10. Lower the vehicle.
11. Perform wheel alignment.

LOWER CONTROL ARM

REMOVAL & INSTALLATION

See Figure 173.

1. Raise and support vehicle.
2. Remove the wheel mounting nuts, then tire and wheel assembly.
3. Remove the knuckle.
4. If left side lower control arm is being

serviced and vehicle is equipped with 62TE (6-speed) automatic transaxle, perform the following:

5. Remove the front and rear engine mount thru-bolts (4—front shown—rear similar).

6. Rotate the lower portion of the engine and transaxle forward.

7. With the engine and transaxle in this position, perform the next step.

8. Remove the front bolt attaching lower control arm to crossmember.

9. Remove the rear bolt and nut attaching lower control arm to crossmember.

10. Remove the lower control arm.

To install:

11. Position lower control arm into brackets on suspension crossmember.

12. Install the front mounting bolt and rear mounting bolt and nut attaching lower control arm to crossmember. Do not tighten front bolt at this time. Tighten rear mounting bolt nut to 114 ft. lbs. (155 Nm).

13. If left side lower control arm is being serviced and vehicle is equipped with 62TE (6-speed) automatic transaxle, reinstall front and rear engine mount thru-bolts.

14. Install the steering knuckle, brake rotor and caliper.

15. Install the tire and wheel assembly.

16. Install the and tighten wheel mounting nuts to 100 ft. lbs. (135 Nm).

17. Lower vehicle.

18. Position vehicle on alignment rack/drive-on hoist. Raise hoist as necessary to access mounting bolts.

19. At curb height, tighten front lower control arm mounting bolt to 148 ft. lbs. (200 Nm).

20. Perform wheel alignment.

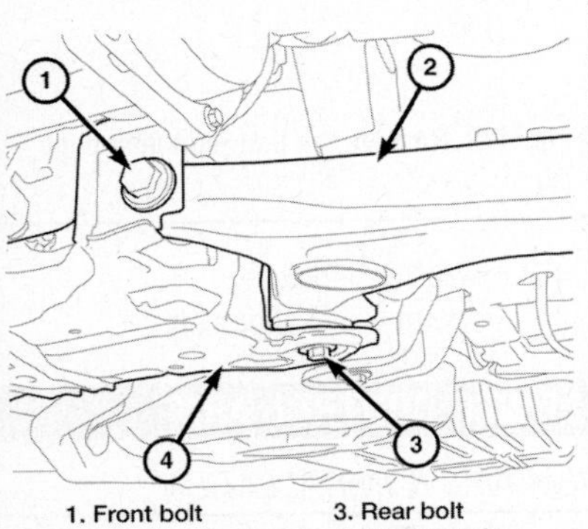

Fig. 173 Lower control arm mounting bolts

1. Front bolt
2. Lower control arm
3. Rear bolt
4. Crossmember

57535

STABILIZER BAR

REMOVAL & INSTALLATION

See Figure 174.

1. Raise and support the vehicle.

2. On each side of vehicle, remove wheel mounting nuts, then tire and wheel assembly.

3. At each end of the stabilizer bar, while holding the stabilizer bar link lower stud stationary (wrench placed on machined flats on stud), remove the nut securing the link to the stabilizer bar.

4. On both sides of vehicle, remove nut attaching outer tie rod to knuckle by holding rod end stud stationary while loosening and removing nut with a wrench.

5. Release each outer tie rod end from knuckle using Remover, Special Tool

6. Remove the front engine mount thru-bolt.

7. Remove the fore-aft crossmember front mounting bolt.

8. Remove the four fore-aft crossmember rear mounting bolts.

9. Remove the fore-aft crossmember.

10. Remove the screws and push-pins securing the heat shield over the right side of the steering gear. Remove heat shield.

11. Remove the rear engine mount.

12. Remove the screws securing the power steering pressure hose routing clamp(s) (4.0L engine only uses one) to the rear of the crossmember.

13. Remove the screws securing the stabilizer bushing retainers to the crossmember.

14. Remove the two stabilizer bushing retainers.

15. Utilizing the slit cut into the cush-

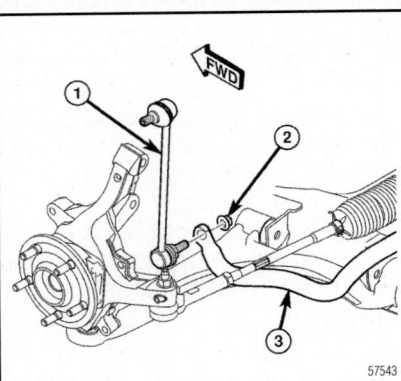

Fig. 174 At each end of the stabilizer bar, while holding the stabilizer bar link (1) lower stud stationary (wrench placed on machined flats on stud), remove the nut (2) securing the link to the stabilizer bar (3)

57543

ions (bushings), remove the two cushions from the stabilizer bar.

16. Slowly rotate the stabilizer bar as necessary and remove it out through the driver side wheel opening.

To install:

➡**Before stabilizer bar installation, inspect the cushions and links for excessive wear, cracks, damage and distortion. Replace any pieces failing inspection.**

➡**Before installing the stabilizer bar, make sure the bar is not upside-down. The stabilizer bar must be installed so that when in mounted position, the ends of the bar curve under the steering gear tie rods, up to the links.**

17. Install the stabilizer bar through the driver side wheel opening. Rotate the bar as necessary until it is centered over the suspension crossmember and the ends curve upward below the steering gear tie rods.

18. Install the two bushings on the stabilizer bar utilizing the slit cut into the bushing sides.

19. Install the two stabilizer bushing retainers over the bushings.

20. Install the four screws securing the stabilizer bushing retainers to the crossmember. Tighten screws to 33 ft. lbs. (45 Nm).

21. Position the power steering pressure hose routing clamp(s) (4.0L engine only uses one) on the rear of the crossmember. Install and tighten the screw(s) to 71 inch lbs. (8 Nm).

22. Install the rear engine mount.

23. Position the heat shield over the steering gear. Install the mounting screws and push-pins. Tighten the screws to 71 inch lbs. (8 Nm).

24. Position the fore-aft crossmember in the engine compartment and install the mounting bolts. Tighten the forward mounting bolt to 83 ft. lbs. (113 Nm). Tighten the rearward mounting bolts at the suspension crossmember to 41 ft. lbs. (55 Nm).

25. Install the front engine mount thru-bolt. Tighten the bolt to 42 ft. lbs. (57 Nm).

26. On each side of vehicle, attach the outer tie rod to the knuckle. Start a NEW nut onto the outer tie rod stud. While holding the stud stationary, tighten the nut using a wrench. Using a crowfoot wrench on a torque wrench, tighten the nut to 55 ft. lbs. (75 Nm).

27. Attach the stabilizer bar link at each end of the stabilizer bar. At each link, install and tighten the nut while holding the stabilizer bar link lower stud stationary. Tighten the nuts to 65 ft. lbs. (88 Nm).

28. On each side of vehicle, install the tire and wheel assembly.

29. Install the and tighten the wheel mounting nuts in proper sequence to 100 ft. lbs. (135 Nm).

30. Lower vehicle.

STEERING KNUCKLE

REMOVAL & INSTALLATION

See Figures 175 through 180.

1. Raise and support vehicle.

2. Remove the wheel mounting nuts, then tire and wheel assembly.

3. With aid of a helper applying brakes to keep front hub from turning, remove hub nut from axle halfshaft stub shaft.

4. Push in on end of halfshaft stub shaft, disengaging its splines from hub splines.

5. Access and remove front brake rotor.

6. Remove the screws fastening brake shield to knuckle, then remove brake shield.

7. Disconnect vehicle wiring harness from wheel speed sensor connector.

8. Unclip wheel speed sensor connector from bracket on frame rail.

9. Remove the screw fastening wheel speed sensor routing bracket to mounting flange on strut.

10. Remove the screw fastening wheel speed sensor routing bracket to knuckle.

11. Remove the nut attaching outer tie rod to steering knuckle by holding outer tie rod stud stationary while loosening and removing nut with a wrench.

12. Remove the outer tie rod stud from steering knuckle using Puller, Special Tool.

➡The strut assembly-to-knuckle attaching bolts are serrated and must not be turned during removal. Proper removal is required. Refer to the following steps for the correct method.

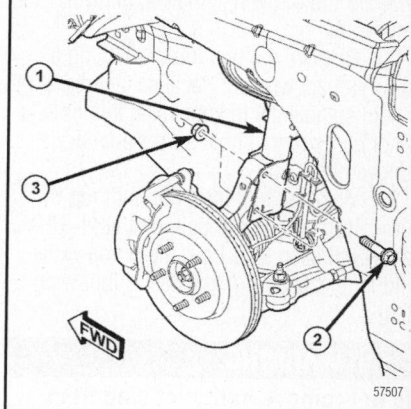

Fig. 179 If servicing the left knuckle: While holding bolt heads stationary, remove two nuts (3) from bolts (2) attaching strut (1) to knuckle. Remove two bolts (2) attaching strut (1) to knuckle using a pin punch.

13. If servicing left knuckle:

14. While holding bolt heads stationary, remove two nuts from bolts attaching strut to knuckle.

15. Remove the two bolts attaching strut to knuckle using a pin punch.

16. If servicing right knuckle:

17. While holding bolt heads stationary, remove two nuts from bolts attaching strut to knuckle.

18. Remove the two bolts attaching strut to knuckle using a pin punch.

19. Tip knuckle outward at top and remove halfshaft stub shaft from hub and bearing. Suspend halfshaft straight outward using a bungee cord or

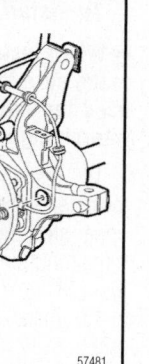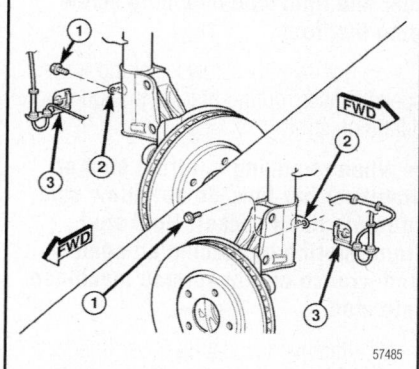

Fig. 175 Remove screws (1) fastening brake shield (3) to knuckle (2), then remove brake shield.

Fig. 177 Remove screw (1) fastening wheel speed sensor routing bracket (3) to mounting flange (2) on strut.

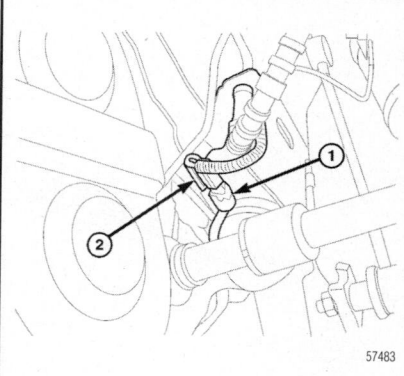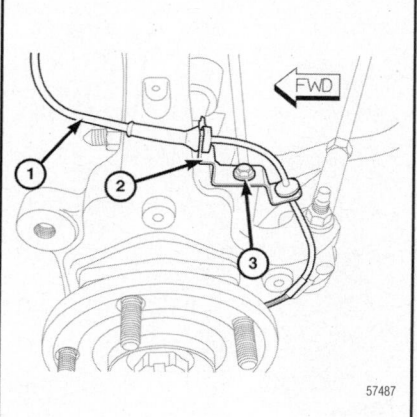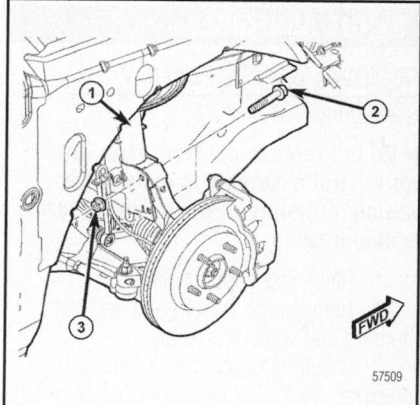

Fig. 176 Disconnect vehicle wiring harness (1) from wheel speed sensor connector. Unclip wheel speed sensor connector from bracket (2) on frame rail.

Fig. 178 Remove screw (3) fastening wheel speed sensor routing bracket (2) to knuckle. Wheel speed sensor cable (1)

Fig. 180 If servicing right knuckle: While holding bolt heads stationary, remove two nuts (3) from bolts (2) attaching strut (1) to knuckle. Remove two bolts (2) attaching strut (1) to knuckle using a pin punch.

wire. Do not allow halfshaft to hang by inner joint.

20. Remove the ball joint nut using a power impact wrench. Because tapered stud is held sufficiently in knuckle at this time, it is not necessary to hold stud stationary to remove nut.

21. Reinstall ball joint nut until top of nut is even with top of ball joint stud. This action will keep stud from distorting while stud is released from knuckle in following step.

❊❊ WARNING

Do not remove ball joint stud from knuckle using a hammer. Damage to ALUMINUM knuckle, ball joint or control arm will result.

22. Using C-4150A To Release Ball Joint.

➡**Lubricate Press, Special Tool Press, Ball Joint, screw-drive threads before use to ease use and promote tool longevity. Place Press, Special Tool over ball joint stud and nut. Release ball joint stud from steering knuckle by tightening tool screw-drive. To ease Remover installation and use, it may help to rotate knuckle around so inside of knuckle faces outward.**

23. Remove the tool and nut from top of ball joint stud.

24. Remove the steering knuckle from vehicle.

25. If hub and bearing needs to be transferred, remove four bolts attaching hub and bearing to knuckle, then remove hub and bearing.

STRUT ASSEMBLY

REMOVAL & INSTALLATION

See Figures 181 and 182.

➡**Do not remove nut from strut rod while strut assembly is installed in vehicle or before strut assembly spring is compressed.**

1. Raise and support vehicle.
2. Remove the wheel mounting nuts, then tire and wheel assembly.
3. If both strut assemblies are to be removed, mark strut assemblies right or left according to which side of vehicle they were removed from to keep from mixing parts.

➡**It is important to note that left and right side wheel speed sensor routing brackets mount opposite each other on the strut making it necessary to install**

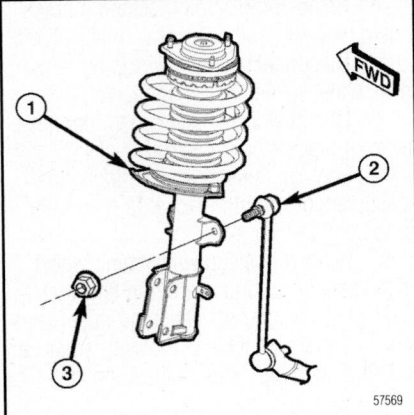

Fig. 181 Remove stabilizer bar link (2) from bracket on strut assembly (1). To do so, place an open-end wrench on flat surface machined into link's mounting stud, then remove nut (3) while holding wrench in place. Push stud out of bracket.

the left side mounting screw from the rear and right side mounting screw from the front.

4. Remove the screw fastening wheel speed sensor routing bracket to mounting flange on strut.

➡**When removing nut from stud of stabilizer bar link, do not allow stud to rotate in its socket. Hold stud from rotating by placing an open-end wrench on flat surface machined into stud.**

5. Remove the stabilizer bar link from bracket on strut assembly. To do so, place an open-end wrench on flat surface machined into link's mounting stud, then

remove nut while holding wrench in place. Push stud out of bracket.

➡**The strut assembly-to-knuckle attaching bolts are serrated and must not be turned during removal. Proper removal is required. Refer to the following steps for the correct method.**

6. If servicing left strut: While holding bolt heads stationary, remove two nuts from bolts attaching strut to knuckle.

7. Remove the two bolts attaching strut to knuckle using a pin punch.

8. If servicing right strut: While holding bolt heads stationary, remove two nuts from bolts attaching strut to knuckle.

9. Remove the two bolts attaching strut to knuckle using a pin punch.

10. Remove the wiper arms and cowl grille from cowl plenum.

11. Remove the three nuts attaching strut assembly upper mount to strut tower, then remove strut assembly from vehicle.

To install:

➡**When installing a strut assembly, make sure the correct coil spring is used for that side of vehicle. Do not interchange the two sides.**

12. Install the strut assembly into strut tower, aligning and inserting three studs on upper strut mount into holes in tower. Install three mounting nuts. Tighten nuts to 21 ft. lbs. (28 Nm).

13. Install the cowl grille and wiper arms.

➡**The strut clevis-to-knuckle bolts are serrated and must not be turned during installation. Install the nuts while hold-**

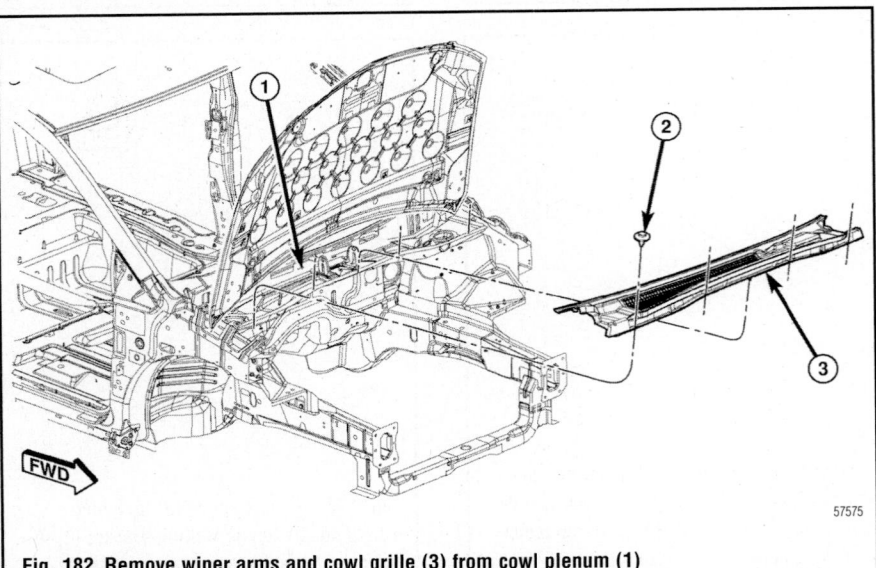

Fig. 182 Remove wiper arms and cowl grille (3) from cowl plenum (1)

ing the bolts stationary in the steering knuckle. Refer to the following steps.

➡ **If vehicle being serviced is equipped with eccentric cam strut attaching bolts, eccentric cam bolt must be installed in bottom (slotted) hole on strut clevis bracket.**

➡ **The strut clevis-to-knuckle bolts are installed differently on each side. Left hand side bolts are to be installed from vehicle rear to front. Right side bolts are to be installed from vehicle front to rear.**

14. If servicing left strut: Position the lower end of the strut assembly in line with the upper end of the knuckle, aligning the mounting holes. Install the two strut clevis-to-knuckle bolts.

15. Install the strut clevis-to-knuckle nuts on the two bolts. While holding the bolts in place, tighten the strut clevis-to-knuckle nuts to 65 ft. lbs. (88 Nm) plus an additional 90°turn after torque is met.

16. If servicing right strut: Position the lower end of the strut assembly in line with the upper end of the knuckle, aligning the mounting holes. Install the two strut clevis-to-knuckle bolts.

17. Install the strut clevis-to-knuckle nuts on the two bolts. While holding the bolts in place, tighten the strut clevis-to-knuckle nuts to 65 ft. lbs. (88 Nm) plus an additional 90° turn after torque is met.

18. Install the stabilizer bar link mounting stud through rearmost hole in bracket on strut assembly.

➡ **When installing nut on mounting stud of stabilizer bar link, do not allow stud to rotate in its socket. Hold stud from rotating by placing an open-end wrench on flat surface machined into stud.**

19. Hand thread nut on end of stabilizer bar link stud. Place an open-end wrench on flat surface machined into link's mounting stud to hold stud from turning while tightening nut. Tighten nut to 65 ft. lbs. (88 Nm).

➡ **It is important to note that left and right side wheel speed sensor routing brackets mount opposite one another on the strut making it necessary to install the left side mounting screw from the rear and right side mounting screw from the front.**

20. Attach wheel speed sensor routing bracket to mounting flange on strut assembly. Install and tighten screw to 89 inch lbs. (10 Nm).

21. Install the tire and wheel assembly.

22. Install the and tighten wheel mounting nuts to 100 ft. lbs. (135 Nm).

23. Lower vehicle.

24. Perform wheel alignment as necessary.

WHEEL HUB & BEARINGS

REMOVAL & INSTALLATION

2010 Models

See Figures 183 through 185.

1. Before servicing the vehicle, refer to the Precautions Section.

2. Raise and safely support the vehicle.

3. Remove the tire and wheel assembly.

4. With the aid of a helper applying the brakes to keep the front hub from turning, remove the hub nut from the axle halfshaft stub shaft.

5. Remove the front brake rotor. Refer to Front Disc Brakes, Rotor, removal & installation.

6. Remove the screws fastening the brake shield to the knuckle, then remove the brake shield.

7. Disconnect the vehicle wiring harness from the wheel speed sensor connector.

8. Unclip the wheel speed sensor connector from the bracket on the frame rail.

9. Remove the screw fastening the wheel speed sensor routing bracket to the mounting flange on the strut.

10. Remove the screw fastening the wheel speed sensor routing bracket to the knuckle.

11. Push in on the end of the halfshaft (3) stub shaft, pushing its splines out of the hub splines.

12. Remove the 4 hub and bearing mounting bolts (2) from the rear of the steering knuckle (1).

13. Remove the hub and bearing with the wheel speed sensor from the steering knuckle.

To install:

➡ **The hub and bearing mounting surfaces on the knuckle and the stub shaft (2) must be smooth and completely free of foreign material or nicks prior to installing the hub and bearing assembly.**

14. Make sure the isolation washer (1) is located on the halfshaft stub shaft (2). The washer is bi-directional, and can be installed in either direction.

15. Install the hub and bearing (3) onto the halfshaft stub shaft (2) and into the knuckle until it is squarely seated on the face of the knuckle. Make sure the wheel speed sensor is positioned toward the rear of the vehicle.

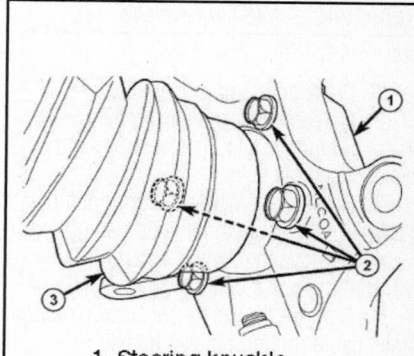

1. Steering knuckle
2. Mounting bolts
3. Halfshaft stub shaft

36543_CARA_G0064

Fig. 184 Remove the hub and bearing with the wheel speed sensor from the steering knuckle

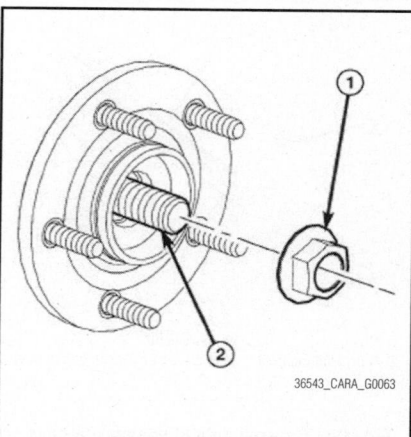

36543_CARA_G0063

Fig. 183 Remove the hub nut (1) from the axle halfshaft stub shaft (2)

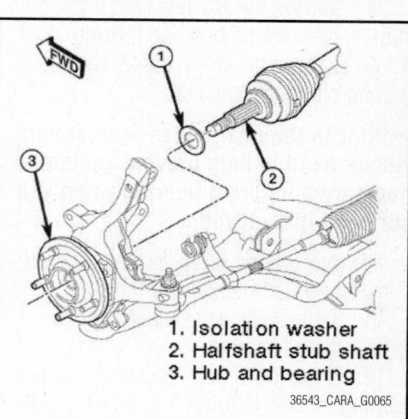

1. Isolation washer
2. Halfshaft stub shaft
3. Hub and bearing

36543_CARA_G0065

Fig. 185 Install the hub and bearing onto the halfshaft stub shaft and into the knuckle

16. Install the 4 hub and bearing mounting bolts (2) from the rear of the knuckle (1). Progressively and equally tighten all 4 mounting bolts using a crisscross pattern. Tighten the mounting bolts to 45 ft. lbs. (65 Nm).

17. Attach the wheel speed sensor routing bracket to the knuckle. Install and tighten the screw to 115 inch lbs. (13 Nm).

18. Attach the wheel speed sensor routing bracket to the mounting flange on the strut assembly. Install and tighten the screw to 89 inch lbs. (10 Nm).

19. Clip the wheel speed sensor connector and routing clip to the bracket on the frame rail.

20. Connect the vehicle wiring harness to the wheel speed sensor connector.

21. Install the brake shield on the knuckle. Install and tighten the 3 mounting screws to 71 inch lbs. (8 Nm).

22. Install the brake rotor, then install the disc brake caliper and adapter assembly. Refer to Front Disc Brakes, Rotor, removal & installation.

23. Verify that the wheel speed sensor is routed properly. Do not allow the cable to come into contact with any moving parts.

24. Install the hub nut on the end of the halfshaft stub shaft. With the aid of a helper applying the brakes to keep the front hub from turning, tighten the hub nut to 118 ft. lbs. (160 Nm).

25. Install the tire and wheel assembly. Tighten the wheel mounting nuts to 100 ft. lbs. (135 Nm).

26. Lower the vehicle.

27. Pump the brake pedal several times to ensure the vehicle has a firm brake pedal before moving the vehicle.

28. Check and adjust the brake fluid level, as necessary.

29. Perform a wheel alignment.

ADJUSTMENT

These models utilize a hub/bearing assembly which is not adjustable.

SUSPENSION

REAR SUSPENSION

AXLE ASSEMBLY

REMOVAL & INSTALLATION

See Figure 186.

1. Raise and support vehicle.
2. On each side of vehicle, remove wheel mounting nuts, then rear tire and wheel assembly.
3. Remove the screw securing left rear parking brake cable to left axle trailing arm.
4. Remove the screws securing right rear parking brake cable to front of axle.
5. Remove the screw securing parking brake cable routing bracket to axle.
6. Remove the two bolts securing disc brake caliper and adapter bracket to axle.
7. Remove the disc brake caliper and adapter bracket from axle and rotor as an assembly. Hang assembly out of way using wire or a bungee cord. Use care not to overextend brake hose when doing this.
8. Remove the any retaining clips, then slide brake rotor off hub and bearing.
9. Remove the wheel speed sensor routing clip from rear axle.

➡**Prior to removal, clean area around sensor head to help prevent contaminants from entering bearing when sensor head is removed.**

10. Remove the screw fastening speed sensor head to hub and bearing.
11. Remove the wheel speed sensor from hub and bearing.
12. Remove the bolts securing hub and bearing to axle. Remove hub and bearing and brake shield.
13. Position transmission jack or equivalent under center of axle raising it enough to support axle.

14. Remove the bolt and nut securing track bar to axle.
15. On each side of vehicle, remove lower mounting bolt and nut securing shock absorber to axle.
16. Lower jack until each coil spring can be removed from axle.
   Remove both coil springs, jounce bumpers and lower isolators.
17. On each side of vehicle, remove nut and thru-bolt fastening axle trailing arm to forward mounting bracket on body.
18. Lower jack and remove axle from vehicle.

To install:

19. Center the axle beam on a transmission jack or equivalent standing at axle removal height.
20. Raise jack as necessary, then swing the axle trailing arms upward aligning bushings with brackets mounted on body.

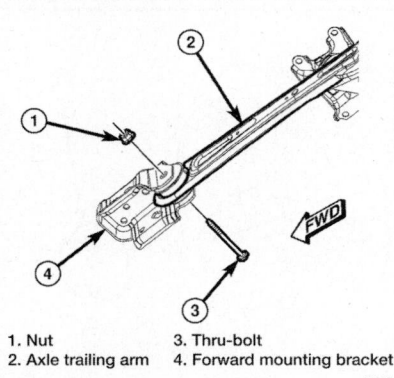

1. Nut
2. Axle trailing arm
3. Thru-bolt
4. Forward mounting bracket

65077

Fig. 186 On each side of vehicle, remove nut and thru-bolt fastening axle trailing arm to forward mounting bracket on body.

21. At each trailing arm, install a thru-bolt through mounting bracket and bushing. Install a nut on end of each thru-bolt. Do not tighten at this time.

➡**Although both ends of the coil spring may appear identical, they are not. Be sure to place the end with the tag upward.**

22. Install the a lower isolator and jounce bumper on end of each coil spring.
23. Place coil spring between body perch and axle at each end of axle. Be sure to place jounce bumper at top.
24. Raise jack guiding the coil springs into mounted position. Continue to raise jack until shock absorber lower mounting bolts can be installed though the axle brackets and shock absorber lower mounting eyes.
25. At each shock absorber, install lower mounting bolt and nut. Do not tighten at this time.
26. Install the bolt and nut securing track bar to axle. Do not tighten at this time.
27. Remove the jack from under axle.
28. Install the hub and bearing and brake shield onto end of axle. Install mounting bolts securing hub and bearing to axle. Tighten the mounting bolts to 41 ft. lbs. (55 Nm).

➡**Ensure that wheel speed sensor mounting surface on bearing is clean before sensor installation.**

29. Push wheel speed sensor head into mounting hole in hub and bearing and align mounting screw hole.
30. Install NEW mounting screw. Tighten mounting screw to 55 inch lbs. (6 Nm).
31. Install the wheel speed sensor routing clip into hole in rear axle.

32. Install the brake rotor over hub and bearing.

33. Install the disc brake caliper and adapter bracket over axle and rotor as an assembly.

34. Install the two bolts securing disc brake caliper and adapter bracket to axle. Tighten mounting bolts to 74 ft. lbs. (100 Nm).

35. Position parking brake cable routing bracket to axle and install screw securing it in place. Tighten screw to 55 inch lbs. (6 Nm).

36. Position right rear parking brake cable in front of axle and install screws securing cable in place. Tighten screws to 55 inch lbs. (6 Nm).

37. Position left rear parking brake cable routing clamp at left axle trailing arm. Tighten screw to 55 inch lbs. (6 Nm).

38. On each side of vehicle, install tire and wheel assembly.

39. Install the and tighten wheel mounting nuts to 100 ft. lbs. (135 Nm).

40. Lower vehicle.

41. Pump the brake pedal several times to ensure the vehicle has a firm brake pedal before moving the vehicle.

42. Position vehicle on alignment rack/drive-on lift. Raise lift as necessary to access the rear suspension while keeping vehicle at curb (riding) height.

43. Tighten both trailing arm mounting bracket pivot thru-bolts to 129 ft. lbs. (175 Nm).

44. Tighten shock absorber lower mounting bolt nut to 55 ft. lbs. (75 Nm).

45. Tighten track bar lower mounting bolt nut to 60 ft. lbs. (81 Nm).

COIL SPRING

REMOVAL & INSTALLATION

See Figure 187.

1. Raise and support vehicle.

2. On each side of vehicle, remove wheel mounting nuts, then rear tire and wheel assembly.

3. Position transmission jack or equivalent under center of axle raising it enough to support axle.

4. Remove the bolt and nut securing track bar to axle.

5. On each side of vehicle, remove lower mounting bolt and nut securing shock absorber to axle.

6. On each side of vehicle, remove screw fastening rear brake flex hose bracket to frame rail. Allow bracket to hang free, but do not bend it downward, overextending flex in brake tubing.

7. Lower jack until each coil spring can be removed from axle.

8. Remove the one side or both coil springs, jounce bumpers and lower isolators.

9. Remove the jounce bumper and lower isolator from spring as necessary.

To install:

➡**Although both ends of the coil spring may appear identical, they are not. Be sure to place the end with the tag upward.**

10. Install the a lower isolator and jounce bumper on end of coil spring as necessary.

11. Place coil spring(s) between body perch and axle at end of axle. Be sure to place jounce bumper end at top.

12. Raise jack guiding the coil springs into mounted position. Continue to raise jack until shock absorber lower mounting bolts can be installed though the axle brackets and shock absorber lower mounting eyes.

13. At each shock absorber, install lower mounting bolt and nut. Do not tighten at this time.

14. Install the bolt and nut securing track bar to axle. Do not tighten at this time.

15. Remove the jack from under axle.

16. On each side of vehicle, fasten rear brake flex hose bracket to frame rail.

17. On each side of vehicle, install tire and wheel assembly.

18. Install the and tighten wheel mounting nuts to 100 ft. lbs. (135 Nm).

19. Lower vehicle.

20. Position vehicle on alignment rack/drive-on lift. Raise lift as necessary to access the rear suspension while keeping vehicle at curb (riding) height.

21. Check for proper vehicle curb height.

22. Tighten shock absorber lower mounting bolt nuts to 55 ft. lbs. (75 Nm).

23. Tighten track bar lower mounting bolt nut to 60 ft. lbs. (81 Nm).

WHEEL HUB & BEARING

REMOVAL & INSTALLATION

See Figures 188 through 190.

1. Raise and support vehicle.

2. Remove the wheel mounting nuts, then rear tire and wheel assembly.

3. Right side only—Remove exhaust

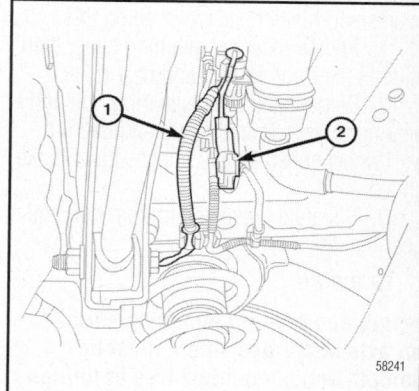

Fig. 188 Disconnect vehicle wiring harness (2) from wheel speed sensor (1) connector. Remove wheel speed sensor (1) from routing clips along underbody of vehicle.

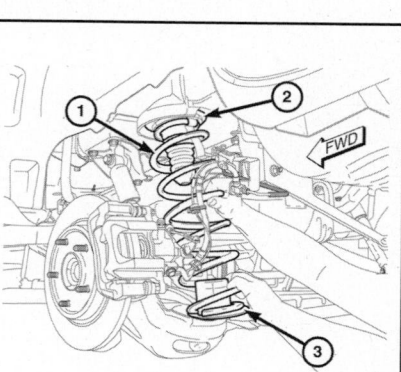

Fig. 187 Lower jack until each coil spring (1) can be removed from axle. Remove one side or both coil springs (1), jounce bumpers (2) and lower isolators (3). Remove jounce bumper (2) and lower isolator (3) from spring as necessary.

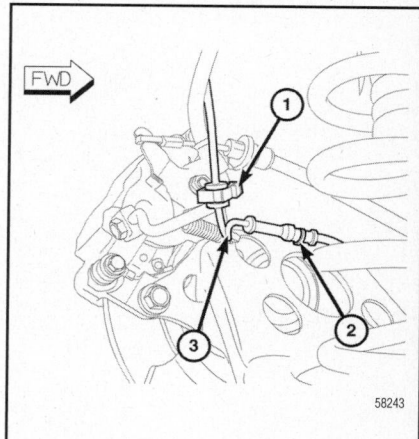

Fig. 189 Remove wheel speed sensor (3) from routing clips (1) along brake flex hose. Remove wheel speed sensor routing clip (2) from rear axle

heat shield above exhaust system covering wheel speed sensor wiring connector.

4. Disconnect vehicle wiring harness from wheel speed sensor (1) connector.

5. Remove the wheel speed sensor from routing clips along underbody of vehicle.

6. Remove the wheel speed sensor from routing clips along brake flex hose.

7. Remove the wheel speed sensor routing clip from rear axle.

8. Remove the screw securing parking brake cable routing bracket to axle.

9. Remove the two bolts securing disc brake caliper and adapter bracket to axle.

10. Remove the disc brake caliper and adapter bracket from axle and rotor as an assembly. Hang assembly out of way using wire or a bungee cord. Use care not to overextend brake hose when doing this.

11. Remove the any retaining clips, then slide brake rotor off hub and bearing.

12. Remove the bolts securing hub and bearing to axle. Remove hub and bearing with wheel speed sensor attached and brake shield.

13. Separate brake shield from hub and bearing.

To install:

➡Hub and bearing mounting surfaces on axle and brake shield must be smooth and completely free of foreign

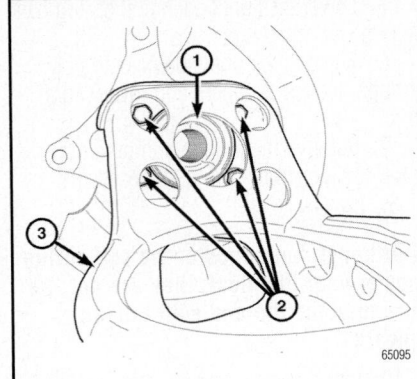

Fig. 190 Remove bolts (2) securing hub and bearing (1) to axle (3). Remove hub and bearing with wheel speed sensor attached and brake shield. Separate brake shield from hub and bearing

material or nicks prior to installing hub and bearing assembly.

14. Position brake shield on wheel speed sensor and route wheel speed sensor cable through access hole in shield.

15. Install the hub and bearing with wheel speed sensor attached and brake shield squarely onto end of axle. Make sure wheel speed sensor is positioned toward rear of vehicle. Install mounting bolts securing hub and bearing to axle.

Tighten the mounting bolts to 41 ft. lbs. (55 Nm).

16. Install the brake rotor over hub and bearing.

17. Install the disc brake caliper and adapter bracket over axle and rotor as an assembly.

18. Install the two bolts securing disc brake caliper and adapter bracket to axle. Tighten mounting bolts to 74 ft. lbs. (100 Nm).

19. Position parking brake cable routing bracket to axle and install screw securing it in place. Tighten screw to 55 inch lbs. (6 Nm).

20. Install the wheel speed sensor routing clip into hole in rear axle.

21. Install the wheel speed sensor into routing clips along brake flex hose.

22. Install the wheel speed sensor into routing clips along underbody of vehicle.

23. Connect vehicle wiring harness to wheel speed sensor connector.

24. Right side only—Install exhaust heat shield above exhaust system covering wheel speed sensor wiring connector.

25. Install the tire and wheel assembly.

26. Install the and tighten wheel mounting nuts to 100 ft. lbs. (135 Nm).

27. Lower vehicle.

28. Pump the brake pedal several times to ensure the vehicle has a firm brake pedal before moving the vehicle.

DODGE

Challenger

SPECIFICATIONS AND MAINTENANCE CHARTS

ENGINE AND VEHICLE IDENTIFICATION

Code ①	Liters	Cu. In.	Cyl.	Fuel Sys.	Engine Type	Eng. Mfg.
V	3.5	214	6	Gas	SFI	Chrysler
G	3.6	220	6	Gas	SFI	Chrysler
T	5.7	345	8	Gas	SFI	Chrysler
W	6.1	370	8	Gas	SFI	Chrysler
J	6.4	392	8	Gas	SFI	Chrysler

Model Year	
Code ②	Year
A	2010
B	2011

① 8th position of VIN

② 10th position of VIN

25766_CHAL_C0001

GENERAL ENGINE SPECIFICATIONS

All measurements are given in inches.

Year	Model	Engine Disp. Liters	Engine ID/VIN	Fuel System Type	Net Horsepower @ rpm	Net Torque @ rpm (ft. lbs.)	Bore x Stroke (in.)	Compression Ratio	Oil Pressure @ rpm
2010	Challenger	3.5	V	SEFI	250 @ 6400	250 @ 3800	3.78x3.19	10.0:1	45-105 @3000
		5.7 (A/T)	T	SEFI	372 @ 5200	400 @ 4400	3.92x3.58	10.5:1	25-110 @3000
		5.7 (M/T)	T	SEFI	376 @ 5150	410 @ 4300	3.92x3.58	10.5:1	25-110 @3000
		6.1	W	SEFI	425 @ 6200	420 @ 4800	4.06x3.58	10.3:1	25-110 @3000
2011	Challenger	3.6	G	SEFI	305 @ 6350	268 @ 4800	3.78x3.27	10.2:1	①
		5.7 (A/T)	T	SEFI	372 @ 5200	400 @ 4400	3.92x3.58	10.5:1	25-110 @3000
		5.7 (M/T)	T	SEFI	376 @ 5150	410 @ 4300	3.92x3.58	10.5:1	25-110 @3000
		6.4	J	SEFI	470 @ 6000	470 @ 4200	4.09x3.72	10.9:1	25-110 @3000

① 30-139 @ 1201-3500

25766_CHAL_C0002

ENGINE TUNE-UP SPECIFICATIONS

Year	Engine Displacement Liters	Engine ID/VIN	Spark Plug Gap (in.)	Ignition Timing (deg.) MT	AT	Fuel Pump (psi)	Idle Speed (rpm) MT	AT	Valve Clearance Intake	Exhaust
2010	3.5	V	0.05	NA	NA	53-64	NA	NA	0.0009-0.0026	0.002-0.0037
	5.7	T	0.04	NA	NA	53-64	NA	NA	0.008-0.0025	0.0009-0.0025
	6.1	W	0.04	NA	NA	53-64	NA	NA	0.0008-0.0025	0.0010-0.0028
2011	3.6	G	0.04	NA	NA	53-64	NA	NA	0.0009-0.0024	0.0012-0.0027
	5.7	T	0.04	NA	NA	53-64	NA	NA	0.008-0.0025	0.0009-0.0025
	6.4	J	0.04	NA	NA	53-64	NA	NA	0.0008-0.0025	0.0010-0.0028

NA: Not Available

25766_CHAL_C0003

CAPACITIES

Year	Model	Engine Displacement Liters	Engine ID/VIN	Engine Oil with Filter	Transmission (pts.)		Drive Axle (pts.)		Transfer Case (pts.)	Fuel Tank (gal.)	Cooling System (qts.)
					Auto.	Manual	Front	Rear			
2010	Challenger	3.5	V	5.7	3.8/8.3	NA	NA	①	NA	18.0	11.1
		5.7	T	6.6	3.8/8.3	NA	NA	①	NA	19.0	14.7
		6.1	W	6.6	3.8/8.3	NA	NA	①	NA	19.0	15.2
2011	Challenger	3.6	G	5.6	5.0/7.7	NA	NA	①	NA	19.0	10.4
		5.7	T	6.6	5.0/7.7	NA	NA	①	NA	19.0	14.7
		6.4	J	6.6	5.0/7.7	NA	NA	①	NA	19.0	15.2

NOTE: All capacities are approximate. Add fluid gradually and ensure a proper fluid level is obtained.

① 198 mm II Rear Axle: 3

   215mm RII Rear Axle: 2.5

   226 mm RII Rear Axle: 2.75

25766_CHAL_C0004

FLUID SPECIFICATIONS

Year	Model	Engine Disp. Liters	Engine Oil	Manual Trans.	Auto. Trans.	Drive Axle		Power Steering Fluid	Brake Master Cylinder	Cooling System
						Front	Rear			
2010	Challenger	3.5	①	ATF+4	ATF+4	NA	75W-140	②	③	④
		5.7	①	ATF+4	ATF+4	NA	75W-140	②	③	④
		6.1	①	ATF+4	ATF+4	NA	75W-140	②	③	④
2011	Challenger	3.6	①	ATF+4	ATF+4	NA	⑤	②	③	④
		5.7	①	ATF+4	ATF+4	NA	⑤	②	③	④
		6.4	①	ATF+4	ATF+4	NA	⑤	②	③	④

DOT: Department Of Transpotation

① 3.5L: MOPAR API Certified SAE 10W-30 Engine Oil

   5.7L: MOPAR API Certified SAE 5W-20 Engine Oil

   6.1L: Full Synthetic Engine Oil

② MOPAR Power Steering Fluid +4

③ MOPAR Brake Fluid DOT 3

④ MOPAR Antifreeze/Coolant 5 Year/100,000 Mile Formula (Hybrid Organic Additive Technology)

⑤ 198 mm: SAE 75W-140

   215mm: SAE 75W-140

   226mm: SAE 75W-90

25766_CHAL_C0005

VALVE SPECIFICATIONS

Year	Engine Displacement Liters	Engine ID/VIN	Seat Angle (deg.)	Face Angle (deg.)	Spring Test Pressure (lbs. @ in.)	Spring Free-Length (in.)	Spring Installed Height (in.)	Stem-to-Guide Clearance (in.)		Stem Diameter (in.)	
								Intake	Exhaust	Intake	Exhaust
2010	3.5	V	45-45.5	44.5-45	①	②	③	0.0009-0.0026	0.002-0.0037	0.2730-0.2737	0.2719-0.2726
	5.7	T	NA	45-45.5	④	2.189	1.810	0.0008-0.0025	0.0009-0.0025	0.312-0.3130	0.312-0.3130
	6.1	W	NA	⑤	⑥	⑦	⑧	0.0008-0.0025	0.0010-0.0028	0.312-0.3130	0.312-0.3130
2011	3.6	G	44.5-45	45.0-45.5	⑨	2.067	1.575	0.0009-0.0024	0.0012-0.0027	0.2346-0.2354	0.2343-0.2351
	5.7	T	NA	45-45.5	④	2.189	1.810	0.0008-0.0025	0.0009-0.0025	0.312-0.3130	0.312-0.3130
	6.4	J	44.5-45	⑤	⑩	2.516	⑪	0.0008-0.0025	0.0010-0.0028	0.312-0.3130	0.312-0.3130

① Intake (Valve Closed): 69.5-80.5 @ 1.4961
  Exhaust Yellow (Valve Closed): 70.5-79.5 @ 1.496
  Exhaust White (Valve Closed): 80-90 @ 1.496
  Intake (Valve Open): 188-204 @ 1.1594
  Exhaust Yellow (Valve Open): 130-144 @ 1.239
  Exhaust White (Valvce Open): 139.5-1554.5 @ 1.239
② Intake: 1.7195
  Exhaust Yellow: 1.8543
  Exhaust White: 1.9015
③ 1.4961 (Spring seat to bottom retainer-intake and exhaust)
④ Valve Closed: 97.8 +/- 5 @ 1.771
  Valve Open: 242 +/- 11 @ 1.283
⑤ Intake:45.5-46.0
  Exhaust: 45.0-45.5
⑥ Intake (Valve Closed): 99.0 +/- 4.0-9.0 @ 1.87
  Exhaust (Valve Closed): 99.0 +/- 4.0-9.0 @ 1.77
  Intake (Valve Open): 325.5 +/- 15.3 @ 1.3
  Exhaust (Valve Open): 325.5 +/- 15.3 @ 1.22

⑦ Intake: 2.133
  Exhaust: 2.023
⑧ Intake: 1.870
  Exhaust: 1.772
⑨ Intake and Exhaust (Valve Closed): 63-69 @ 1.57
  Intake (Valve Open):148-162 @ 0.4055
  Exhaust (Valve Open): 146-158 @ 0.3937
⑩ Valve Closed: 114.7 +/- 5.8 @ 2.051
  Valve Open: 337.2 +/- 15.7 @ 1.48
⑪ Intake: 2.051
  Exhaust: 2.016

25766_CHAL_C0006

CAMSHAFT SPECIFICATIONS

All measurements in inches unless noted

Year	Engine Displacement Liters	Engine Code/VIN	Journal Diameter	Brg. Oil Clearance	Shaft End-play	Runout	Journal Bore	Lobe Height Intake	Lobe Height Exhaust
2010	3.5	V	1.6905-1.6913	0.003-0.0047	0.001-0.014	NA	1.6944-1.6953	NA	NA
	5.7	T	①	②	0.0031-0.0114	NA	NA	NA	NA
	6.1	W	①	②	0.0031-0.0114	NA	NA	NA	NA
2011	3.6	G	③	④	0.003-0.01	NA	⑤	NA	NA
	5.7	T	①	②	0.0031-0.0114	NA	NA	NA	NA
	6.4	J	①	②	0.0031-0.0114	NA	NA	NA	NA

NA: Not Available

① No. 1: 2.29
No. 2: 2.27
No. 3: 2.26
No. 4: 2.24
No. 5: 1.72

② No. 1: 0.0015-0.003
No. 2: 0.0019-0.0035
No. 3: 0.0015-0.003
No. 4: 0.0019-0.0035
No. 5: 0.0015-0.003

③ No. 1: 1.2589-1.2596
No. 2, 3, 4: 0.9440-0.9447

④ No. 1: 0.00010-0.0026
No. 3, 3, 4: 0.0009-0.0025

⑤ No. 1 Cam Tower: 1.2606-1.2615
No. 2, 3, 4 Cam Tower: 0.9457-0.9465

25766_CHAL_C0008

CRANKSHAFT AND CONNECTING ROD SPECIFICATIONS

All measurements are given in inches.

Year	Engine Displacement Liters	Engine ID/VIN	Crankshaft Main Brg. Journal Dia.	Crankshaft Main Brg. Oil Clearance	Crankshaft Shaft End-play	Thrust on No.	Connecting Rod Journal Diameter	Connecting Rod Oil Clearance	Connecting Rod Side Clearance
2010	3.5	V	2.519-2.5200	0.0013-0.0024	0.002-0.0100	NA	2.282-2.2830	0.0014-0.0029	0.0003
	5.7	T	2.5585-2.5595	0.0009-0.0020	0.002-0.0110	NA	2.1260	0.0007-0.0023	0.0002
	6.1	W	2.558-2.5595	0.0009-0.0020	0.0110	NA	2.125-2.1260	0.0007-0.0029	0.0002
2011	3.6		2.5585-2.5595	0.0009-0.0020	0.002-0.0110	NA	2.1260	0.0007-0.0023	0.0002
	5.7	T	2.5585-2.5595	0.0009-0.0020	0.002-0.0110	NA	2.1260	0.0007-0.0023	0.0002
	6.4	J	2.6000	0.0009-0.0020	0.002-0.0110	NA	2.1260	0.0007-0.0029	0.0002

NA: Not Available

25766_CHAL_C0007

PISTON AND RING SPECIFICATIONS

All measurements are given in inches.

Year	Engine Displacement Liters	Engine ID/VIN	Piston Clearance	Ring Gap			Ring Side Clearance		
				Top Compression	Bottom Compression	Oil Control	Top Compression	Bottom Compression	Oil Control
2010	3.5	V	NA	0.008-0.0140	0.0078-0.0157	0.010-0.0300	0.0016-0.0031	0.0016-0.0031	0.0015-0.0073
	5.7	T	①	0.015-0.0210	0.009-0.0200	0.0059-0.0259	0.001-0.0035	0.001-0.0031	0.002-0.008
	6.1	W	②	0.118-0.0157	0.137-0.0236	0.0079-0.0280	0.0007-0.0026	0.0007-0.0022	0.007-0.0091
2011	3.6	G	③	0.010-0.016	0.012-0.018	0.006-0.026	0.0010-0.0033	0.0012-0.0031	0.0003-0.0068
	5.7	T	①	0.015-0.0210	0.009-0.0200	0.0059-0.0259	0.001-0.0035	0.001-0.0031	0.002-0.008
	6.4	J	②	0.0118-0.0157	0.0137-0.0236	0.0079-0.0280	0.0007-0.0026	0.0007-0.0022	0.0007-0.0091

① 0.12-0.023 (measured 1.5 inch below deck)

② 0.00096-0.0020 (measured at 1.5 inch below deck)

③ Clearance at Size Location (Metal to Metal): 0.0012-0.0020

Clearance at Size Location (Meatal to Coating): 0.0004-0.0012

25766_CHAL_C0009

TORQUE SPECIFICATIONS
All readings in ft. lbs.

Year	Engine Disp. Liters	Engine ID/VIN	Cylinder Head Bolts	Main Bearing Bolts	Rod Bearing Bolts	Crankshaft Damper Bolts	Flywheel Bolts	Manifold Intake	Manifold Exhaust	Spark Plugs	Oil Pan Drain Plug
2010	3.5	V	①	②	③	70	70	④	17	NA	20
	5.7	T	⑤	⑥	⑦	129	70	9	18	13	25
	6.1	W	⑤	⑥	⑦	129	70	9	23	NA	20
2011	3.6	G	⑧	⑨	7	⑩	70	6	NA	13	20
	5.7	T	⑤	⑥	⑦	129	70	9	18	13	25
	6.4	J	⑪	⑫	⑦	129	70	9	23	13	20

NA: Not Available

① Step 1: 45
   Step 2: 65
   Step 3: 65
   Step 4: + 1/4 turn

② Inner: 15 + 1/4 turn
   Outer: 20 + 1/4 turn

③ 20 + 1/4 turn

④ Lower: 21
   Upper: 8.75

⑤ Step 1: Tighten bolts 1-10: 25
   Tighten bolts 11-15: 15
   Step 2: Tighten bolts 1-10: 40
   Tighten bolts 11-15 (verify): 15
   Step 3: Rotate bolts 1-10 90 degrees
   Step 4: Tighten bolts 11-15: 25

⑥ M-12 bolts: 21 + 90 degrees
   Crossbolts M-8 Bolts: 16

⑦ 33 + 60 degrees

⑧ Step 1: 22
   Step 2: 33
   Step 3: + 75 degrees
   Step 4: +50 degrees
   Step 5: Loosen all fasteners in reverse of sequence
   Step 6: 22
   Step 7: 33
   Step 8: + 70 degrees
   Step 9: + 70 degrees

⑨ Outer Main Bearing Cap and Windage Tray - M8 Bolts: 16 + 90 degree turn
   Crankshaft Inner Main Bearing Cap - M11 Bolts: 15 + 90 degree turn
   Crankshaft Side Main Bearing Cap (Tie Bolt) - M8 Bolts: 21

⑩ 30 + 105 degrees

⑪ Step 1: Tighten bolts 1-10: 25
   Tighten bolts 11-15: 15
   Step 2: Tighten bolts 1-10: 40
   Verify bolts 11-15 are: 15
   Step 3: Tighten bolts 1-10: 45
   Step 4: Rotate bolts 1-10 an additional 90 degrees
   Step 5: Tighten bolts 11-15: 25

⑫ M-12 bolts: 21 + 90 degrees
   M-8 bolts (Crossbolts): 23

25766_CHAL_C0010

WHEEL ALIGNMENT

Year	Model		Caster Range (+/-Deg.)	Caster Preferred Setting (Deg.)	Camber Range (+/-Deg.)	Camber Preferred Setting (Deg.)	Toe-in (in.)
2010	Challenger Base	LF	7.00-9.00	8.00	-0.50-0.80	-0.50-0.80	NA
		RF	8.00-10.00	9.00	-0.90-0.40	-0.90-0.40	NA
		LR	NA	NA	-1.20 - -0.10	-0.55	NA
		RR	NA	NA	-1.20 - -0.10	-0.55	NA
	Challenger SRT8	LF	7.30-9.30	8.30	-0.50-0.50	-0.05	NA
		RF	8.30-10.30	9.30	-0.90-0.10	-0.35	NA
		LR	NA	NA	-1.25 - -0.15	-0.75	NA
		RR	NA	NA	-1.25 - -0.15	-0.75	NA
2011	Challenger Base	LF	7.00-9.00	8.00	-1.40 - -0.30	-0.85	NA
		RF	7.70-9.70	8.70	-1.80 - -0.70	-1.25	NA
		LR	NA	NA	-2.30 - -1.20	-1.75	NA
		RR	NA	NA	-2.30 - -1.20	-1.75	NA
	Challenger SRT8	LF	7.30-9.30	8.30	-1.60 - -0.50	-1.05	NA
		RF	8.00-10.00	9.00	-1.90 - -0.80	-1.35	NA
		LR	NA	NA	-1.40 - -0.10	-0.75	NA
		RR	NA	NA	-1.40 - -0.10	-0.75	NA

25766_CHAL_C0011

TIRE, WHEEL AND BALL JOINT SPECIFICATIONS

Year	Model	OEM Tires Standard	Optional	Tire Pressures (psi) Front	Rear	Wheel Size	Ball Joint Inspection	Lug Nut (ft. lbs.)
2010	Challenger Base	P215/65R17	NA	NA	NA	16	0.59	110
	Challenger SRT8	P245/45ZR20	NA	NA	NA	20	0.59	110
2011	Challenger Base	P215/65R17	NA	NA	NA	16	0.59	110
	Challenger SRT8	P245/45ZR20	NA	NA	NA	20	0.59	110

OEM: Original Equipment Manufacturer

PSI: Pounds Per Square Inch

NA: Information not available

25766_CHAL_C0012

BRAKE SPECIFICATIONS

All measurements in inches unless noted

| Year | Model | | Brake Disc | | | Minimum Pad/Lining Thickness | | Brake Caliper | |
			Original Thickness	Minimum Thickness	Max. Runout	Front	Rear	Bracket Bolts (ft. lbs.)	Mounting Bolts (ft. lbs.)
2010	Challenger	F	1.097-1.107	1.040	0.0014	0.040	NA	NA	NA
	Base	R	0.389-0.399	0.355	0.0014	0.040	NA	NA	NA
	Challenger	F	1.097-1.107	1.040	0.0014	0.040	NA	NA	NA
	Premium	R	0.861-0.871	0.807	0.0014	0.040	NA	NA	NA
	Challenger	F	1.256-1.264	1.181	0.0012	0.040	NA	NA	140
	SRT8	R	1.098-1.106	1.024	0.0012	0.040	NA	NA	96
2011	Challenger	F	1.097-1.107	1.040	0.0014	0.040	NA	NA	NA
	Base	R	0.389-0.399	0.355	0.0014	0.040	NA	NA	NA
	Challenger	F	1.097-1.107	1.040	0.0014	0.040	NA	NA	NA
	Premium	R	0.861-0.871	0.807	0.0014	0.040	NA	NA	NA
	Challenger	F	1.256-1.264	1.181	0.0012	0.040	NA	NA	140
	SRT8	R	1.098-1.106	1.024	0.0012	0.040	NA	NA	96

F: Front

R: Rear

NA: Information not available

25766_CHAL_C0013

SCHEDULED MAINTENANCE - NORMAL
2010 Dodge Challenger

TO BE SERVICED	TYPE OF SERVICE	6	12	18	24	30	36	42	48	54	60	66	72	78	84	90	96	102
		VEHICLE MILEAGE INTERVAL (x1000)																
Engine oil & filter	Replace	✓	✓	✓	✓	✓	✓	✓	✓	✓	✓	✓	✓	✓	✓	✓	✓	✓
Rotate tires, inspect tread wear, measure tread depth and check pressure	Rotate	✓	✓	✓	✓	✓	✓	✓	✓	✓	✓	✓	✓	✓	✓	✓	✓	✓
Air conditioner filter	Replace		✓		✓		✓		✓		✓		✓		✓		✓	
Brake system components	Inspect/ Service		✓		✓		✓		✓		✓		✓		✓		✓	
Exhaust system & heat shields	Inspect		✓		✓		✓		✓		✓		✓		✓		✓	
Inspect front suspension, tie rod ends and boot seals for cracks or leaks and all parts for damage, wear, improper looseness or end play.	Inspect		✓			✓			✓			✓			✓		✓	
CV Joints	Inspect		✓		✓		✓		✓		✓		✓		✓		✓	
Rear/front axle fluid level	Inspect			✓			✓			✓	✓		✓			✓		
Engine air filter	Replace					✓					✓					✓		
Adjust parking brake on vehicles with four-wheel disc brakes	Adjust					✓					✓					✓		
Engine coolant	Replace										✓							✓
Spark plugs	Replace																	✓
Spark plugs (5.7L only)	Replace					✓					✓					✓		
PCV valve	Inspect/ Service															✓		
Transmisison fluid (& filter)	Replace																	✓
Accessory drive belt	Inspect	✓	✓	✓	✓	✓	✓	✓	✓	✓	✓	✓	✓	✓	✓	✓	✓	✓
Accessory drive belt	Replace	at 120,000 miles if not previously serviced																
Rear axle fluid	Replace								✓								✓	
Timing belt (3.5L)	Replace																	✓
Transfer case fluid	Replace															✓		
Battery	Inspect/ Service	✓	✓	✓	✓	✓	✓	✓	✓	✓	✓	✓	✓	✓	✓	✓	✓	✓
Fluid levels (all)	Top off	✓	✓	✓	✓	✓	✓	✓	✓	✓	✓	✓	✓	✓	✓	✓	✓	✓
Horn, exterior lamps, turn signals and hazard warning light operation	Inspect	✓	✓	✓	✓	✓	✓	✓	✓	✓	✓	✓	✓	✓	✓	✓	✓	✓

*Oil Change Indicator System

On Electronic Vehicle Information Center (EVIC) equipped vehicles, "Oil Change Required" is displayed in the EVIC and a single chime sounds, indicating that an oil change is necessary. On non-EVIC equipped vehicles, "Change Oil" flashes in the instrument cluster and a single chime sounds indicating that an oil change is necessary. Illumination of the oil change message is based on the operating conditions of the vehicle. When the message is illuminated, the vehicle must be serviced within 500 miles.

The oil change indicator will not monitor the time since the last oil change. Change the oil if it has been more than 6 months since the last oil change, even if the oil change indicator message is not illuminated.

Under no circumstances should oil change intervals exceed 6,000 miles or 6 months, whichever comes first.

To reset the oil change indicator, perform the following procedure:

1. Turn the ignition switch to the ON position. Do not start the engine.
2. Fully press the accelerator pedal 3 times within 10 seconds.
3. Turn the ignition switch to the LOCK position.

If the indicator message illuminates when the vehicle is started, repeat the procedure.

SCHEDULED MAINTENANCE - SEVERE
2010 Dodge Challenger

TO BE SERVICED	TYPE OF SERVICE	6	12	18	24	30	36	42	48	54	60	66	72	78	84	90	96	102
		VEHICLE MILEAGE INTERVAL (x1000)																
Engine oil & filter	Replace	✓	✓	✓	✓	✓	✓	✓	✓	✓	✓	✓	✓	✓	✓	✓	✓	✓
Rotate tires, inspect tread wear, measure tread depth, check pressure	Rotate	✓	✓	✓	✓	✓	✓	✓	✓	✓	✓	✓	✓	✓	✓	✓	✓	✓
Air conditioner filter	Replace		✓		✓		✓		✓		✓		✓		✓		✓	
Brake system components	Inspect/Service						✓		✓		✓		✓		✓		✓	
Exhaust system & heat shields	Inspect		✓		✓		✓		✓		✓		✓		✓		✓	
Inspect front suspension, tie rod ends & boot seals for cracks or leaks & all parts for damage, wear, improper looseness or end play.	Inspect		✓		✓		✓		✓		✓		✓		✓		✓	
CV Joints	Inspect		✓		✓		✓		✓		✓		✓		✓		✓	
Front axle fluid	Replace								✓								✓	
Rear/front axle fluid level	Inspect			✓			✓			✓			✓			✓		
Engine air filter	Inspect/Service		✓		✓		✓		✓		✓		✓		✓		✓	
Adjust parking brake on vehicles with four-wheel disc brakes	Adjust					✓					✓					✓		
Engine coolant	Replace										✓							✓
Spark plugs	Replace																	✓
Spark plugs (5.7L only)	Replace					✓					✓					✓		
PCV valve	Inspect/Service															✓		
Transmisison fluid (& filter)	Replace										✓							
Accessory drive belt	Inspect	✓	✓	✓	✓	✓	✓	✓	✓	✓	✓	✓	✓	✓	✓	✓	✓	✓
Accessory drive belt	Replace	at 120,000 miles if not previously serviced																
Rear axle fluid	Replace								✓								✓	
Timing belt (3.5L)	Replace																	✓
Transfer case fluid	Replace										✓							
Battery	Inspect/Service	✓	✓	✓	✓	✓	✓	✓	✓	✓	✓	✓	✓	✓	✓	✓	✓	✓
Fluid levels (all)	Top off	✓	✓	✓	✓	✓	✓	✓	✓	✓	✓	✓	✓	✓	✓	✓	✓	✓
Horn, exterior lamps, turn signals and hazard warning light operation	Inspect	✓	✓	✓	✓	✓	✓	✓	✓	✓	✓	✓	✓	✓	✓	✓	✓	✓

*Oil Change Indicator System

On Electronic Vehicle Information Center (EVIC) equipped vehicles, "Oil Change Required" is displayed in the EVIC and a single chime sounds, indicating that an oil change is necessary. On non-EVIC equipped vehicles, "Change Oil" flashes in the instrument cluster and a single chime sounds indicating that an oil change is necessary. Illumination of the oil change message is based on the operating conditions of the vehicle. When the message is illuminated, the vehicle must be serviced within 500 miles.

The oil change indicator will not monitor the time since the last oil change. Change the oil if it has been more than 6 months since the last oil change, even if the oil change indicator message is not illuminated.

Under no circumstances should oil change intervals exceed 6,000 miles or 6 months, whichever comes first.

To reset the oil change indicator, perform the following procedure:

1. Turn the ignition switch to the ON position. Do not start the engine.
2. Fully press the accelerator pedal 3 times within 10 seconds.
3. Turn the ignition switch to the LOCK position.

If the indicator message illuminates when the vehicle is started, repeat the procedure.

SCHEDULED MAINTENANCE - NORMAL
2011 Dodge Challenger

TO BE SERVICED	TYPE OF SERVICE	VEHICLE MILEAGE INTERVAL (x1000)																
		8	16	24	32	40	48	56	64	72	80	88	96	104	112	120	128	136
Engine oil & filter	Replace	✓	✓	✓	✓	✓	✓	✓	✓	✓	✓	✓	✓	✓	✓	✓	✓	✓
Rotate tires, inspect tread wear, measure tread depth and check pressure	Rotate		✓		✓		✓		✓		✓		✓		✓		✓	
Brake system components	Inspect/ Service		✓		✓		✓		✓		✓		✓		✓		✓	
Exhaust system & heat shields	Inspect		✓		✓		✓		✓		✓		✓		✓		✓	
Inspect the front suspension, tie rod ends and boot seals for cracks or leaks and all parts for damage, wear, improper looseness or end play.	Inspect		✓		✓		✓		✓		✓		✓		✓		✓	
CV Joints	Inspect	✓	✓	✓	✓	✓	✓	✓	✓	✓	✓	✓	✓	✓	✓	✓	✓	✓
Engine air filter	Replace			✓					✓					✓			✓	
Adjust parking brake on vehicles equipped with four-wheel disc brakes.	Adjust			✓					✓					✓			✓	
Engine coolant	Replace										✓							
Spark plugs (3.6L)	Replace												✓					
Spark plugs (5.7L)	Replace			✓					✓				✓				✓	
PCV valve	Inspect/ Service												✓					
Auto transmission fluid & filter	Replace															✓		
Accessory drive belt	Inspect	✓	✓	✓	✓	✓	✓	✓	✓	✓	✓	✓	✓	✓	✓	✓	✓	✓
Accessory drive belt	Replace	at 120,000 miles if not previously serviced																
Horn, exterior lamps, turn signals and hazard warning light operation	Inspect	✓	✓	✓	✓	✓	✓	✓	✓	✓	✓	✓	✓	✓	✓	✓	✓	✓
Fluid levels (all)	Top off	✓	✓	✓	✓	✓	✓	✓	✓	✓	✓	✓	✓	✓	✓	✓	✓	✓
Air conditioner filter	Replace		✓		✓		✓		✓		✓		✓		✓		✓	
Front & rear axle fluid	Inspect/ Add			✓				✓					✓			✓		
Transfer case fluid	Inspect/ Add				✓				✓				✓				✓	

*Oil Change Indicator System

On Electronic Vehicle Information Center (EVIC) equipped vehicles, "Oil Change Required" is displayed in the EVIC and a single chime sounds, indicating that an oil change is necessary. On non-EVIC equipped vehicles, "Change Oil" flashes in the instrument cluster and a single chime sounds indicating that an oil change is necessary. Illumination of the oil change message is based on the operating conditions of the vehicle. When the message is illuminated, the vehicle must be serviced within 500 miles.

The oil change indicator will not monitor the time since the last oil change. Change the oil if it has been more than 6 months since the last oil change, even if the oil change indicator message is not illuminated.

Under no circumstances should oil change intervals exceed 6,000 miles or 6 months, whichever comes first.

To reset the oil change indicator, perform the following procedure:

1. Turn the ignition switch to the ON position. Do not start the engine.
2. Fully press the accelerator pedal 3 times within 10 seconds.
3. Turn the ignition switch to the LOCK position.

If the indicator message illuminates when the vehicle is started, repeat the procedure.

25766_CHAL_C0016

SCHEDULED MAINTENANCE - SEVERE
2011 Dodge Challenger

TO BE SERVICED	TYPE OF SERVICE	8	16	24	32	40	48	56	64	72	80	88	96	104	112	120	128	136
Engine oil & filter	Replace	✓	✓	✓	✓	✓	✓	✓	✓	✓	✓	✓	✓	✓	✓	✓	✓	✓
Rotate tires, inspect tread wear, measure tread depth and check pressure	Rotate	✓	✓	✓	✓	✓	✓	✓	✓	✓	✓	✓	✓	✓	✓	✓	✓	✓
Brake system components	Inspect/ Service		✓		✓		✓		✓		✓		✓		✓		✓	
Exhaust system & heat shields	Inspect		✓		✓		✓		✓		✓		✓		✓		✓	
Inspect front suspension, tie rod ends & boot seals for cracks or leaks & all parts for damage, wear, improper looseness or end play.	Inspect		✓		✓		✓		✓		✓		✓		✓		✓	
CV Joints	Inspect			✓			✓			✓			✓			✓		
Engine air filter	Inspect/ Service		✓		✓		✓		✓		✓		✓		✓		✓	
Engine coolant	Replace										✓							
Spark plugs (3.6L)	Replace												✓					
Spark plugs (5.7L)	Replace			✓					✓				✓				✓	
PCV valve	Inspect/ Service												✓					
Auto transmission fluid & filter	Replace								✓								✓	
Accessory drive belt	Inspect	✓	✓	✓	✓	✓	✓	✓	✓	✓	✓	✓	✓	✓	✓	✓	✓	✓
Accessory drive belt	Replace	at 120,000 miles if not previously serviced																
Battery	Inspect/ Service	✓	✓	✓	✓	✓	✓	✓	✓	✓	✓	✓	✓	✓	✓	✓	✓	✓
Fluid levels (all)	Top off	✓	✓	✓	✓	✓	✓	✓	✓	✓	✓	✓	✓	✓	✓	✓	✓	✓
Horn, exterior lamps, turn signals and hazard warning light operation	Inspect	✓	✓	✓	✓	✓	✓	✓	✓	✓	✓	✓	✓	✓	✓	✓	✓	✓
Pass. compartment air filter	Replace		✓		✓		✓		✓		✓		✓		✓		✓	
Rear axle fluid	Inspect/ Add		✓		✓		✓		✓		✓		✓		✓		✓	
Transfer case fluid	Replace															✓		
Front & rear axle fluid	Inspect/ Add		✓		✓		✓		✓		✓		✓		✓		✓	

VEHICLE MILEAGE INTERVAL (x1000)

*Oil Change Indicator System

On Electronic Vehicle Information Center (EVIC) equipped vehicles, "Oil Change Required" is displayed in the EVIC and a single chime sounds, indicating that an oil change is necessary. On non-EVIC equipped vehicles, "Change Oil" flashes in the instrument cluster and a single chime sounds indicating that an oil change is necessary. Illumination of the oil change message is based on the operating conditions of the vehicle. When the message is illuminated, the vehicle must be serviced within 500 miles.

The oil change indicator will not monitor the time since the last oil change. Change the oil if it has been more than 6 months since the last oil change, even if the oil change indicator message is not illuminated.

Under no circumstances should oil change intervals exceed 6,000 miles or 6 months, whichever comes first.

To reset the oil change indicator, perform the following procedure:

1. Turn the ignition switch to the ON position. Do not start the engine.
2. Fully press the accelerator pedal 3 times within 10 seconds.
3. Turn the ignition switch to the LOCK position.

If the indicator message illuminates when the vehicle is started, repeat the procedure.

PRECAUTIONS

Before servicing any vehicle, please be sure to read all of the following precautions, which deal with personal safety, prevention of component damage, and important points to take into consideration when servicing a motor vehicle:

• Never open, service or drain the radiator or cooling system when the engine is hot; serious burns can occur from the steam and hot coolant.

• Observe all applicable safety precautions when working around fuel. Whenever servicing the fuel system, always work in a well-ventilated area. Do not allow fuel spray or vapors to come in contact with a spark, open flame, or excessive heat (a hot drop light, for example). Keep a dry chemical fire extinguisher near the work area. Always keep fuel in a container specifically designed for fuel storage; also, always properly seal fuel containers to avoid the possibility of fire or explosion. Refer to the additional fuel system precautions later in this section.

• Fuel injection systems often remain pressurized, even after the engine has been turned **OFF**. The fuel system pressure must be relieved before disconnecting any fuel lines. Failure to do so may result in fire and/or personal injury.

• Brake fluid often contains polyglycol ethers and polyglycols. Avoid contact with the eyes and wash your hands thoroughly after handling brake fluid. If you do get brake fluid in your eyes, flush your eyes with clean, running water for 15 minutes. If eye irritation persists, or if you have taken

brake fluid internally, IMMEDIATELY seek medical assistance.

• The EPA warns that prolonged contact with used engine oil may cause a number of skin disorders, including cancer. You should make every effort to minimize your exposure to used engine oil. Protective gloves should be worn when changing oil. Wash your hands and any other exposed skin areas as soon as possible after exposure to used engine oil. Soap and water, or waterless hand cleaner should be used.

• All new vehicles are now equipped with an air bag system, often referred to as a Supplemental Restraint System (SRS) or Supplemental Inflatable Restraint (SIR) system. The system must be disabled before performing service on or around system components, steering column, instrument panel components, wiring and sensors. Failure to follow safety and disabling procedures could result in accidental air bag deployment, possible personal injury and unnecessary system repairs.

• Always wear safety goggles when working with, or around, the air bag system. When carrying a non-deployed air bag, be sure the bag and trim cover are pointed away from your body. When placing a non-deployed air bag on a work surface, always face the bag and trim cover upward, away from the surface. This will reduce the motion of the module if it is accidentally deployed. Refer to the additional air bag system precautions later in this section.

• Clean, high quality brake fluid from a sealed container is essential to the safe and

proper operation of the brake system. You should always buy the correct type of brake fluid for your vehicle. If the brake fluid becomes contaminated, completely flush the system with new fluid. Never reuse any brake fluid. Any brake fluid that is removed from the system should be discarded. Also, do not allow any brake fluid to come in contact with a painted surface; it will damage the paint.

• Never operate the engine without the proper amount and type of engine oil; doing so WILL result in severe engine damage.

• Timing belt maintenance is extremely important. Many models utilize an interference-type, non-freewheeling engine. If the timing belt breaks, the valves in the cylinder head may strike the pistons, causing potentially serious (also time-consuming and expensive) engine damage. Refer to the maintenance interval charts for the recommended replacement interval for the timing belt, and to the timing belt section for belt replacement and inspection.

• Disconnecting the negative battery cable on some vehicles may interfere with the functions of the on-board computer system(s) and may require the computer to undergo a relearning process once the negative battery cable is reconnected.

• When servicing drum brakes, only disassemble and assemble one side at a time, leaving the remaining side intact for reference.

• Only an MVAC-trained, EPA-certified automotive technician should service the air conditioning system or its components.

BRAKES

ANTI-LOCK BRAKE SYSTEM (ABS)

GENERAL INFORMATION

PRECAUTIONS

• Certain components within the ABS system are not intended to be serviced or repaired individually.

• Do not use rubber hoses or other parts not specifically specified for and ABS system. When using repair kits, replace all parts included in the kit. Partial or incorrect repair may lead to functional problems and require the replacement of components.

• Lubricate rubber parts with clean, fresh brake fluid to ease assembly. Do not use shop air to clean parts; damage to rubber components may result.

• Use only DOT 3 brake fluid from an unopened container.

• If any hydraulic component or line is removed or replaced, it may be necessary to bleed the entire system.

• A clean repair area is essential. Always clean the reservoir and cap thoroughly before removing the cap. The slightest amount of dirt in the fluid may plug an orifice and impair the system function. Perform repairs after components have been thoroughly cleaned; use only denatured alcohol to clean components. Do not allow ABS components to come into contact with any substance containing mineral oil; this includes used shop rags.

• The Anti-Lock control unit is a microprocessor similar to other computer units in the vehicle. Ensure that the ignition switch is **OFF** before removing or installing controller harnesses. Avoid static

electricity discharge at or near the controller.

• If any arc welding is to be done on the vehicle, the control unit should be unplugged before welding operations begin.

SPEED SENSORS

REMOVAL & INSTALLATION

Front

See Figures 1 and 2.

1. Raise and support the vehicle.
2. Remove the sensor cable routing clip from the brake hose bracket.

➡**In the following step, to release the sensor connector (3) from the body wiring harness, move the retaining clip**

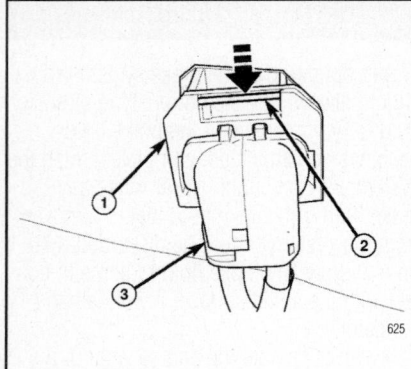

Fig. 1 Removing the sensor cable routing clip (2) and releasing the wheel speed sensor connector (3) from the body wiring harness (1)

as shown , then pull the sensor connector outward.

3. Remove the sensor connector from the body wiring harness connector.

4. Remove the screw fastening the wheel speed sensor to knuckle.

5. Pull the sensor head out of the knuckle.

6. Remove the wheel speed sensor cable routing clip from the brake hose routing bracket.

To install:

7. Install the wheel speed sensor head into knuckle and install mounting screw. Tighten screw to 8 ft. lbs. (11 Nm).

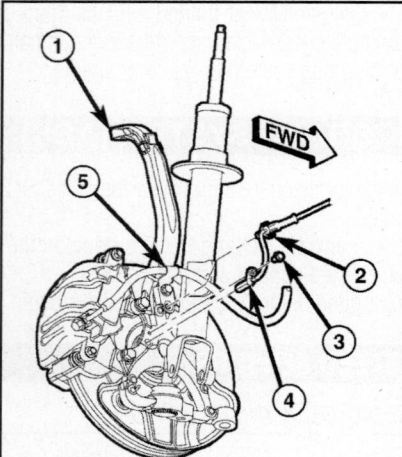

1. Knuckle
2. Wheel speed sensor cable routing clip
3. Screw
4. Sensor head
5. Brake hose routing bracket

Fig. 2 Wheel speed sensor at front knuckle

8. Attach wheel speed sensor cable and routing clip to brake hose routing bracket.

9. Attach sensor cable routing clip to brake hose bracket.

10. Connect sensor connector to body wiring harness connector. When installing connector, make sure retaining clip on body connector is properly in place and sensor connector cannot be pulled out.

11. Carefully lower the vehicle.

12. Perform Verification Test and clear any faults.

Rear

See Figures 3 through 6.

1. Raise and safely support the vehicle.

➡**To release sensor connector from body wiring harness connector in following step, move retaining clip as indicated here, then pull sensor connector outward.**

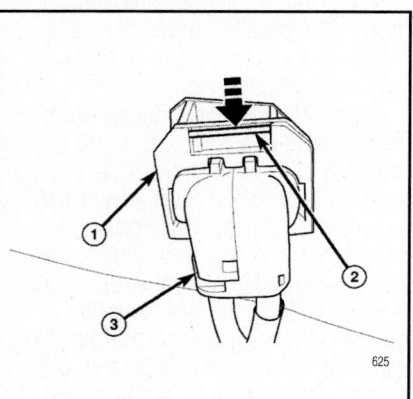

Fig. 3 Releasing the wheel speed sensor connector

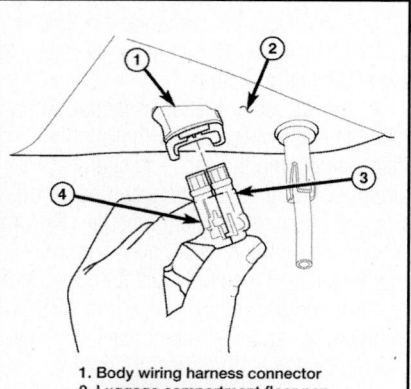

1. Body wiring harness connector
2. Luggage compartment floor pan
3. Right sensor connector
4. Left sensor connector

Fig. 4 Sensor connection to body connector

2. Remove the sensor connectors from body wiring harness connector located in luggage compartment floor pan.

3. Separate left sensor connector from right sensor connector.

4. If removing left sensor, unclip sensor cable from routing clip near body connector.

5. If removing left sensor, unclip sensor cable from routing clips along rear of crossmember near rear differential.

6. If removing left sensor, unclip sensor cable from routing clip above toe link mount on rear crossmember.

7. Unclip sensor cable from routing clips along toe link.

8. Unclip sensor cable at rear brake rotor shield.

9. Remove the screw fastening sensor head to rear knuckle.

10. Remove the wheel speed sensor.

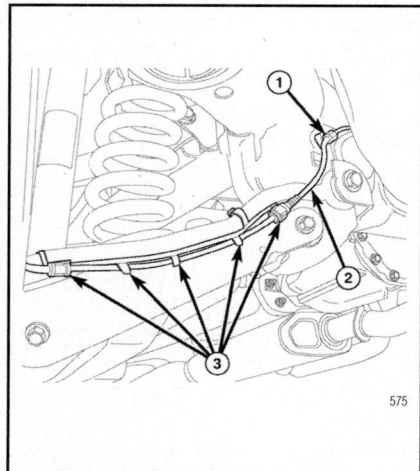

Fig. 5 WSS routing along left toe link

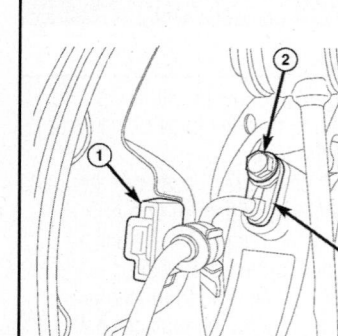

Fig. 6 Unclip cable at rear brake rotor shield (1), remove the screw (2) fastening the sensor head (3)

To install:

11. Insert wheel speed sensor head into mounting hole in rear of knuckle.

12. Install the screw fastening sensor head to rear knuckle. Tighten the screw to 8 ft. lbs. (11 Nm).

13. Install the sensor cable at rear brake rotor shield.

14. Clip sensor cable to routing clips along toe link.

15. If installing left sensor, clip sensor cable to routing clip above toe link mount on rear crossmember.

16. If installing left sensor, clip sensor cable to routing clips along rear of cross-member near rear differential.

17. If installing left sensor, clip sensor cable to routing clip near body connector.

18. Match left sensor connector to right sensor connector to make one connector.

19. Insert sensor connectors into body wiring harness connector located in luggage compartment floor pan. When installing connector, make sure retaining clip on body connector is properly in place and sensor connector cannot be pulled out.

20. Carefully lower the vehicle.

21. Perform Verification Test and clear any faults.

BRAKES — BLEEDING THE BRAKE SYSTEM

BLEEDING PROCEDURE

BLEEDING PROCEDURE

> ✳✳ **WARNING**
>
> **Before removing the master cylinder cover, wipe it clean to prevent dirt and other foreign matter from dropping into the master cylinder.**

> ✳✳ **WARNING**
>
> **Use only Mopar®brake fluid or an equivalent from a fresh, tightly sealed container. Brake fluid must conform to DOT 3 specifications.**

➡**Do not pump the brake pedal at any time while having a bleeder screw open during the bleeding process. This will only increase the amount of air in the system and make additional bleeding necessary.**

➡**Do not allow the master cylinder reservoir to run out of brake fluid while bleeding the system. An empty reservoir will allow additional air into the brake system. Check the fluid level frequently and add fluid as needed.**

The following wheel circuit sequence for bleeding the brake hydraulic system should be used to ensure adequate removal of all trapped air from the brake hydraulic system:

- Right rear wheel
- Left rear wheel
- Right front wheel
- Left front wheel

➡**Pressure bleeding is highly recommended to bleed this brake system to ensure all air is removed from system. Manual bleeding may also be used, but additional time is needed to remove all air from system.**

The base brake system can be bled using the pressure method or the manual method. Both methods are presented in this text.

Base

Pressure Bleeding Method

See Figures 7 and 8.

1. Remove the filler cap from the top of fluid reservoir on master cylinder.

2. Install the Special Tool, in the caps place on the reservoir (2).

3. Attach Bleeder Tank, or equivalent, to Adapter Cap, Master Cylinder.

   a. Pressurize the system following the pressure bleeder manufacturer's instructions.

➡**To ensure all air is bled from the ICU or junction block in a timely manner, it is recommended to raise the rear of the vehicle approximately 5°higher than the front or approximately 10-12 inches as measured at the rear bumper.**

4. Raise and support vehicle placing rear of vehicle approximately 5°higher than the front or if measured at the rear bumper, approximately 10-12 inches above level. It will be necessary to add extra support stands under vehicle to support this angle.

5. If installed, remove rubber dust caps from all four bleeder screws on calipers.

6. Starting at the first wheel circuit as listed earlier, attach a clear hose to the bleeder screw at that wheels brake caliper and feed the other end of hose into a clear jar containing enough fresh brake fluid to submerge the end of the hose.

> ✳✳ **WARNING**
>
> **Open the bleeder screw at least one full turn when instructed. Some air may be trapped in the brake lines or valves far upstream, as far as ten feet or more from the bleeder screw. If the bleeder screw is not opened sufficiently, fluid flow is restricted causing a slow, weak fluid discharge. This will NOT get all the air out. Therefore, it is essential to open the bleeder screw at least one full turn to allow a fast, large volume discharge of brake fluid.**

7. Open bleeder screw at least one full turn or more to obtain an adequate flow of brake fluid.

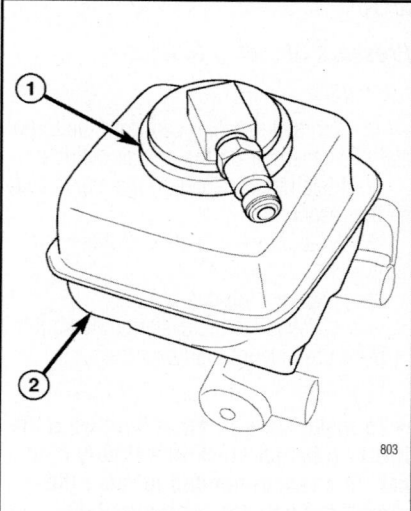

Fig. 7 Installing the special tool (1) on the reservoir (2)

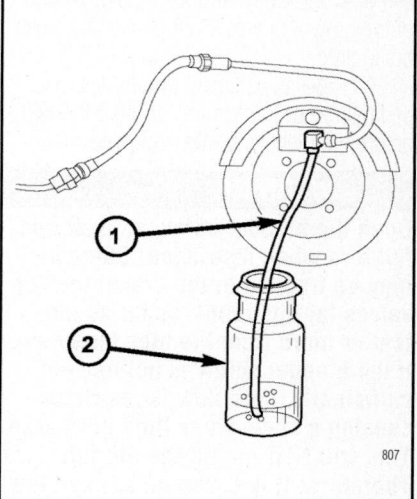

Fig. 8 Bleed hose set up with clear jar (2) and clear hose (1)

8. After 4 to 8 ounces of brake fluid has been bled through the brake hydraulic circuit, and an air-free flow (no bubbles) is maintained in the clear plastic hose and jar, close the bleeder screw.

9. Bleed the remaining wheel circuits in the same manner until all air is removed from the brake hydraulic system.

10. Check brake pedal travel. If pedal travel is excessive or has not improved, some air may still be trapped in the hydraulic system. Rebleed the brake system as necessary.

11. If equipped with antilock brakes, the hydraulic control unit may need to be bled, then rebleed base brakes.

12. Reinstall all 4 bleeder screw dust caps.

13. Test drive vehicle to ensure brakes are operating properly and pedal feel is correct.

Manual Bleeding Method

➡To bleed the base brake system manually, an assistants help is required.

➡To ensure all air is bled from the ICU or junction block in a timely manner, it is recommended to raise the rear of the vehicle approximately 5°higher than the front or approximately 10-12 inches as measured at the rear bumper.

1. Raise and support vehicle placing rear of vehicle approximately 5°higher than the front or if measured at the rear bumper, approximately 10-12 inches above level. It will be necessary to add extra support stands under vehicle to support this angle.

2. Remove the rubber duct caps from all 4 bleeder screws.

3. Attach a clear hose to the bleeder screw at one wheel and feed the other end of the hose into a clear jar containing fresh brake fluid.

4. Have an assistant pump the brake pedal three or four times and hold it down before the bleeder screw is opened.

✳✳ WARNING

Open the bleeder screw at least one full turn when instructed. Some air may be trapped in the brake lines or valves far upstream, as far as ten feet or more from the bleeder screw. If the bleeder screw is not opened sufficiently, fluid flow is restricted causing a slow, weak fluid discharge. This will NOT get all the air out. Therefore, it is essential to open the bleeder screw at least one full turn to allow a fast, large volume discharge of brake fluid.

5. While the pedal is being held down, open the bleeder screw at least 1 full turn. When the bleeder screw opens the brake pedal will drop all the way to the floor. Continue to hold the pedal all the way down.

6. Once the brake pedal has dropped, close the bleeder screw. The pedal can then be released.

7. Repeat steps One through Five until all trapped air is removed from that wheel circuit (usually four or five times). This should pass a sufficient amount of fluid to expel all the trapped air from the brakes hydraulic system. Be sure to monitor brake fluid level in master cylinder fluid reservoir making sure it stays at a proper level. This will ensure air does not reenter brake hydraulic system through master cylinder.

➡**Monitor the brake fluid level in the fluid reservoir periodically to make sure it does not go too low. This will ensure that air does not reenter the brake hydraulic system.**

8. Bleed the remaining wheel circuits in the same manner until all air is removed from the brake hydraulic system.

9. Check brake pedal travel. If pedal travel is excessive or has not improved, some air may still be trapped in the hydraulic system. Rebleed the brake system as necessary.

10. If equipped with antilock brakes, the hydraulic control unit may need to be bled, then rebleed base brakes.

11. Reinstall all 4 bleeder screw dust caps.

12. Test drive vehicle to ensure brakes are operating properly and pedal feel is correct.

SRT8

Pressure Bleeding Method
See Figure 9.

1. Remove the filler cap from the top of the fluid reservoir on the master cylinder.

2. Install the Adapter, in the caps place on the reservoir.

3. Attach Bleeder Tank C-3496-B, or equivalent, to Adapter Cap, Master Cylinder.

   a. Pressurize the system following the pressure bleeder manufacturer's instructions.

➡**To make sure all air is bled from the ICU or junction block in a timely manner, it is recommended to raise the rear of the vehicle approximately 5°higher than the front or approximately 254-305 mm(10-12 inches) as measured at the rear bumper.**

4. Raise and support vehicle placing rear of vehicle approximately 5°higher than the front or if measured at the rear bumper, approximately 10-12 inches above level. It will be necessary to add extra support stands under vehicle to support this angle.

5. Use the following wheel circuit sequence for bleeding the brake hydraulic system to adequately remove all trapped air from the brake hydraulic system.

- Right rear wheel
- Left rear wheel
- Right front wheel
- Left front wheel

Rear Brakes

6. If installed, remove the rubber dust caps from both bleeder screws on each caliper.

7. Start at the first wheel circuit that needs to be bled. Attach a clear hose to the inboard bleeder screw at the wheels brake caliper and feed the other end of hose into a clear jar containing enough fresh brake fluid to submerge the end of the hose.

✳✳ WARNING

Open the bleeder screw at least one full turn when instructed. Some air may be trapped in the brake lines or valves far upstream, as far as ten feet or more from the bleeder screw. If the bleeder screw is not opened sufficiently, fluid flow is restricted causing a slow, weak fluid discharge. This will NOT get all the air out. Therefore, it is essential to open the bleeder screw at least one full turn to allow a fast, large volume discharge of brake fluid.

8. Open the inboard bleeder screw one full turn to obtain an adequate flow of brake fluid.

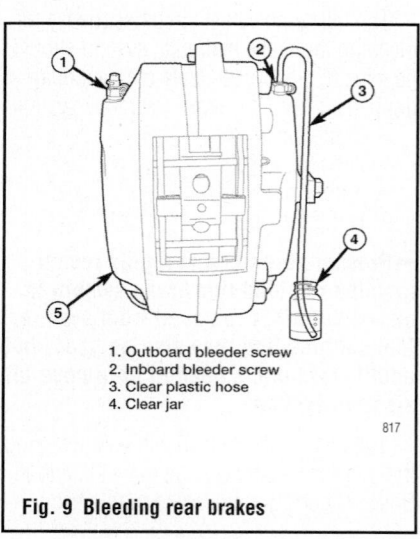

1. Outboard bleeder screw
2. Inboard bleeder screw
3. Clear plastic hose
4. Clear jar

817

Fig. 9 Bleeding rear brakes

9. After bleeding 118-237 ml. (4-8 oz.) of brake fluid through the brake hydraulic circuit, and maintain an air-free flow (no bubbles) is in the clear plastic hose and jar, close the bleeder screw.

10. Remove the clear hose and install the bleeder screw dust cap.

Front Brakes

11. If installed, remove the rubber dust cap from bleeder screw on each front brake caliper.

12. Start at the first wheel circuit that needs to be bled, attach a clear hose to the bleeder screw at that wheels brake caliper and feed the other end of hose into a clear jar containing enough fresh brake fluid to submerge the end of the hose.

✳✳ WARNING

Open the bleeder screw at least one full turn when instructed. Some air may be trapped in the brake lines or valves far upstream, as far as ten feet or more from the bleeder screw. If the bleeder screw is not opened sufficiently, fluid flow is restricted causing a slow, weak fluid discharge. This will NOT get all the air out. Therefore, it is essential to open the bleeder screw at least one full turn to allow a fast, large volume discharge of brake fluid.

13. Open bleeder screw one full turn to obtain an adequate flow of brake fluid.

14. After bleeding 118-237 ml. (4-8 oz.) of brake fluid through the brake hydraulic circuit, and maintaining an air-free flow (no bubbles) is in the clear plastic hose and jar, close the bleeder screw.

15. Install the bleeder screw dust cap.

16. Bleed the opposite front brake wheel circuit as necessary in the same manner until all air is removed from the brake hydraulic system.

17. If equipped with anti-lock brakes, and the hydraulic control unit needs to be bled, then rebleed the base brakes.

18. Once all brakes are bled, check brake pedal travel. If pedal travel is excessive or has not improved, some air may still be trapped in the brake hydraulic system. Rebleed the brake system as necessary.

19. Test drive vehicle to make sure the brakes are operating properly and pedal feel is correct.

Manual Bleeding Procedure

See Figure 10.

➡**To bleed the base brake system manually, an assistant's help is required.**

➡**To make sure all air is bled from the ICU or junction block in a timely manner, it is recommended to raise the rear of the vehicle approximately 5°higher than the front or approximately 254-305 mm (10-12 inches) as measured at the rear bumper.**

1. Raise and support vehicle placing rear of vehicle approximately 5°higher than the front or if measured at the rear bumper, approximately 10-12 inches above level. It will be necessary to add extra support stands under vehicle to support this angle.

➡**Use the following wheel circuit sequence for bleeding the brake hydraulic system to adequately remove all trapped air from the brake hydraulic system.**

- Right rear wheel
- Left rear wheel
- Right front wheel
- Left front wheel

Rear Brakes

2. If installed, remove the rubber dust caps from both bleeder screws on each caliper.

3. Start at the first wheel circuit that needs to be bled, attach a clear hose to the inboard bleeder screw at that the brake caliper and feed the other end of hose into a clear jar containing enough fresh brake fluid to submerge the end of the hose.

4. Have an assistant pump the brake pedal three or four times, then hold it down before the bleeder screw is opened.

✳✳ WARNING

Open the bleeder screw at least one full turn when instructed. Some air may be trapped in the brake lines or valves far upstream, as far as ten feet or more from the bleeder screw. If the bleeder screw is not opened sufficiently, fluid flow is restricted causing a slow, weak fluid discharge. This will NOT get all the air out. Therefore, it is essential to open the bleeder screw at least one full turn to allow a fast, large volume discharge of brake fluid.

5. While holding down the brake pedal, open the inboard bleeder screw at least one full turn. When the bleeder screw opens the brake pedal will drops all the way to the floor. Continue holding the pedal all the way down.

6. Once the brake pedal drops, close the bleeder screw. Release the pedal.

7. Repeat the previous three steps until all trapped air is removed from that wheel circuit (usually four or five times). This should pass a sufficient amount of fluid to expel all the trapped air from the brake hydraulic system. Be sure to monitor brake fluid level in master cylinder fluid reservoir making sure it stays at a proper level. This will ensure air does not reenter brake hydraulic system through master cylinder.

➡**Monitor the brake fluid level in the fluid reservoir periodically to make sure it does not go too low. This makes sure that air does not reenter the brake hydraulic system.**

8. Remove the clear hose and install the bleeder screw dust cap.

9. Attach a clear hose to the outboard bleeder screw at the brake caliper and feed the other end of hose into a clear jar containing enough fresh brake fluid to submerge the end of the hose.

10. Have an assistant pump the brake pedal three or four times, then hold it down before the bleeder screw is opened.

✳✳ WARNING

Open the bleeder screw at least one full turn when instructed. Some air may be trapped in the brake lines or valves far upstream, as far as ten feet or more from the bleeder screw. If the bleeder screw is not opened sufficiently, fluid flow is restricted causing a slow, weak fluid discharge. This will NOT get all the air out. Therefore, it is essential to open the bleeder screw at least one full turn to allow a fast, large volume discharge of brake fluid.

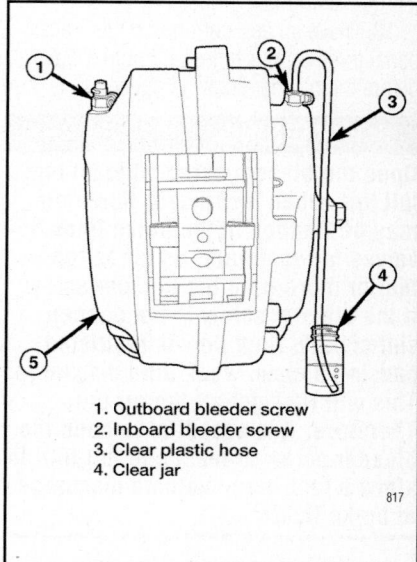

1. Outboard bleeder screw
2. Inboard bleeder screw
3. Clear plastic hose
4. Clear jar

817

Fig. 10 Bleeding caliper inboard half

11. While holding down the brake pedal, open the outboard bleeder screw at least one full turn. When the bleeder screw opens the brake pedal drops all the way to the floor. Continue holding the pedal all the way down.

12. Once the brake pedal drops, close the bleeder screw. Release the pedal.

13. Repeat the previous three steps until all trapped air is removed from that wheel circuit (usually four or five times). This passes a sufficient amount of fluid to expel all the trapped air from the brake hydraulic system. Be sure to monitor brake fluid level in master cylinder fluid reservoir making sure it stays at a proper level. This will ensure air does not reenter brake hydraulic system through master cylinder.

➡**Monitor the brake fluid level in the fluid reservoir periodically to make sure it does not go too low. This will ensure that air does not reenter the brake hydraulic system.**

14. Remove the clear hose and install the bleeder screw dust cap.

15. Bleed the opposite rear brake wheel circuits as necessary in the same manner until all air is removed from the brake hydraulic system, then proceed to the front brakes.

Front Brakes

16. If installed, remove the rubber dust cap from the bleeder screw on each front brake caliper.

17. Start at the first wheel circuit that needs to be bled, attach a clear hose to the bleeder screw at that the brake caliper and feed the other end of hose into a clear jar containing enough fresh brake fluid to submerge the end of the hose.

18. Have an assistant pump the brake pedal three or four times and hold it down before the bleeder screw is opened.

✳✳ WARNING

Open the bleeder screw at least one full turn when instructed. Some air may be trapped in the brake lines or valves far upstream, as far as ten feet or more from the bleeder screw. If the bleeder screw is not opened sufficiently, fluid flow is restricted causing a slow, weak fluid discharge. This will NOT get all the air out. Therefore, it is essential to open the bleeder screw at least one full turn to allow a fast, large volume discharge of brake fluid.

19. While holding down the brake pedal open the bleeder screw at least one full turn.

When the bleeder screw opens the brake pedal drops all the way to the floor. Continue holding the pedal all the way down.

20. Once the brake pedal drops, close the bleeder screw. Release the pedal.

21. Repeat the previous five steps until all trapped air is removed from that wheel circuit (usually four or five times). This passes a sufficient amount of fluid to expel all the trapped air from the brake hydraulic system. Be sure to monitor brake fluid level in master cylinder fluid reservoir making sure it stays at a proper level. This will ensure air does not reenter brake hydraulic system through master cylinder.

➡**Monitor the brake fluid level in the fluid reservoir periodically to make sure it does not go too low. This makes sure that air does not reenter the brake hydraulic system.**

22. Install the bleeder screw dust cap.

23. Bleed the opposite front brake wheel circuit as necessary in the same manner until all air is removed from the brake hydraulic system.

24. If equipped with anti-lock brakes, and the hydraulic control unit needs to be bled, then rebleed the base brakes.

25. Once all brakes are bled, check brake pedal travel. If pedal travel is excessive or has not improved, some air may still be trapped in the brake hydraulic system. Rebleed the brake system as necessary.

26. Test drive the vehicle to make sure the brakes are operating properly and pedal feel is correct.

MASTER CYLINDER BLEEDING

See Figure 11.

✳✳ WARNING

When clamping master cylinder in vise, only clamp master cylinder by its mounting flange. Do not clamp master cylinder piston rod, reservoir, seal or body.

1. Clamp master cylinder in a vise.

✳✳ WARNING

When installing Adapters in master cylinder, do not overtighten. Damage to master cylinder could occur.

➡**Bleeder Adapters Adapter, Bleeder and Adapter, Bleeder are not interchangeable. To avoid mix-up, Bleeder Adapter, is silver while Bleeder Adapter, is black.**

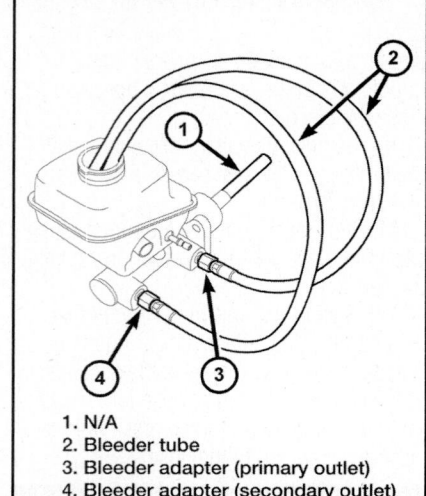

1. N/A
2. Bleeder tube
3. Bleeder adapter (primary outlet)
4. Bleeder adapter (secondary outlet)

1095751

Fig. 11 Bleeder tube (2), bleeder adapter primary outlet (3) and second outlet (4) on master cylinder - MK25E

2. Attach special tools for bleeding master cylinder in following fashion:
into primary outlet port. Tighten to 10 ft. lbs. (14 Nm).

3. Thread Bleeder Adapter, Bleeder (4), into secondary outlet port. Tighten to 10 ft. lbs. (14 Nm).

4. Thread a Bleeder Tube Bleed Tube (2), into each Adapter. Tighten each tube to 10 ft. lbs. (14 Nm). Flex each bleeder tube and place open end into mouth of fluid reservoir as far down as possible.

➡**Make sure open ends of bleeder tubes stay below surface of brake fluid once reservoir is filled to proper level.**

5. Fill brake fluid reservoir to the MAX level with Mopar® brake fluid or equivalent conforming to DOT 3 specifications. Make sure fluid level is above tips of bleeder tubes in reservoir to ensure no air is ingested during bleeding.

6. Using a wooden dowel as a pushrod, slowly depress master cylinder pistons, then release pressure, allowing pistons to return to released position. Repeat several times until all air bubbles are expelled. Make sure fluid level stays above tips of bleeder tubes in reservoir while bleeding.

7. Remove the bleeder tubes and adapters from master cylinder outlet ports, then plug outlet ports and install fill cap on reservoir.

8. Remove the master cylinder from vise.

9. Install the master cylinder on vehicle

BLEEDING THE ABS SYSTEM

1. When bleeding the ABS system, the following bleeding sequence must be followed to insure complete and adequate bleeding.

2. Make sure all hydraulic fluid lines are installed and properly torqued.

3. Connect the scan tool to the diagnostics connector. The diagnostic connector is located under the lower steering column cover to the left of the steering column.

4. Using the scan tool, check to make sure the ABM does not have any fault codes stored. If it does, clear them.

✳✳ CAUTION

When bleeding the brake system wear safety glasses. A clear bleed tube must be attached to the bleeder screws and submerged in a clear container filled part way with clean brake fluid. Direct the flow of brake fluid away from yourself and the painted surfaces of the vehicle. Brake fluid at high pressure may come out of the bleeder screws when opened.

➡**Pressure bleeding is recommended to bleed the base brake system to ensure all air is removed from system. Manual bleeding may also be used, but** additional time is needed to remove all air from system.

5. Bleed the base brake system.

6. Using the scan tool, select ECU VIEW, followed by ABS MISCELLANEOUS FUNCTIONS to access bleeding. Follow the instructions displayed. When finished, disconnect the scan tool and proceed.

7. Bleed the base brake system a second time. Check brake fluid level in the reservoir periodically to prevent emptying, causing air to enter the hydraulic system.

8. Fill the master cylinder fluid reservoir to the MAX level.

9. Test drive the vehicle to be sure the brakes are operating correctly and that the brake pedal does not feel spongy.

BRAKES

✳✳ WARNING

Dust and dirt accumulating on brake parts during normal use may contain asbestos fibers from production or aftermarket brake linings. Breathing excessive concentrations of asbestos fibers can cause serious bodily harm. Exercise care when servicing brake parts. Do not sand or grind brake lining unless equipment used is designed to contain the dust residue. Do not clean brake parts with compressed air or by dry brushing. Cleaning should be done by dampening the brake components with a fine mist of water, then wiping the brake components clean with a dampened cloth. Dispose of cloth and all residue containing asbestos fibers in an impermeable container with the appropriate label. Follow practices prescribed by the Occupational Safety and Health Administration (OSHA) and the Environmental Protection Agency (EPA) for the handling, processing, and disposing of dust or debris that may contain asbestos fibers.

BRAKE CALIPER

REMOVAL & INSTALLATION

SRT8

See Figures 12 and 13.

1. Disconnect and isolate battery negative cable from battery post.

2. Using a brake pedal holding tool, depress brake pedal past its first inch of travel and hold it in this position. Holding pedal in this position will isolate master cylinder from hydraulic brake system and will not allow brake fluid to drain out of brake fluid reservoir while brake lines are open.

3. Raise and safely support the vehicle.

4. Remove the wheel mounting nuts, then tire and wheel assembly.

5. Remove the banjo bolt connecting flexible brake hose to caliper. There are two sealing washers (one one each side of hose fitting) that will come off when bolt is removed. Discard these washers; use NEW washers upon installation.

✳✳ WARNING

When pushing pistons back into caliper bores, use only a trim stick as shown or other suitable soft tool. Never use a screwdriver or other

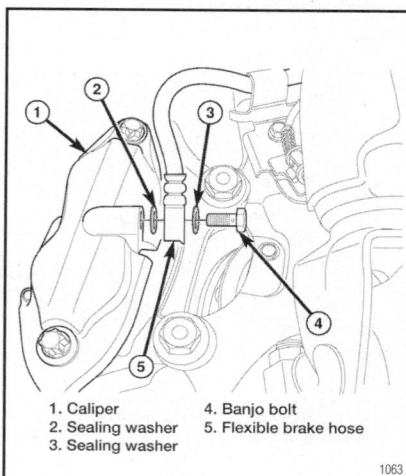

1. Caliper
2. Sealing washer
3. Sealing washer
4. Banjo bolt
5. Flexible brake hose

1063

Fig. 12 Flex hose connection at caliper- SRT8

FRONT DISC BRAKES

metal pry bar due to potential damage to braking surface of rotor, caliper, pistons or dust boots.

6. Place trim stick between brake pad and outer edge of rotor.

7. Using trim stick, slowly apply pressure against brake pad until both pistons (on that side of caliper) are completely bottomed in bores of caliper half.

➡**Repeat above procedure to opposite brake pad and pistons as necessary.**

8. Remove the caliper mounting bolts.

9. Remove the brake caliper with pads from knuckle and brake rotor.

➡**If brake pads need to be removed from caliper. These calipers are not serviceable. Do not attempt disassembly.**

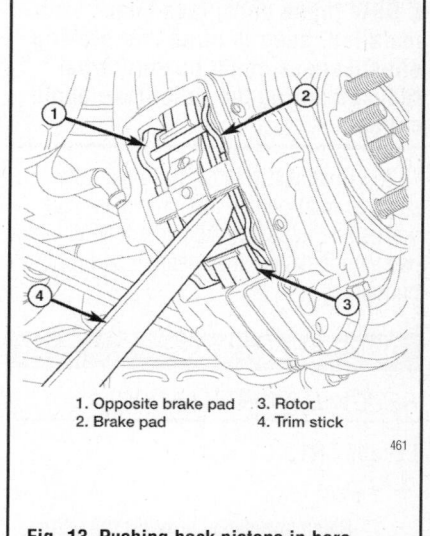

1. Opposite brake pad
2. Brake pad
3. Rotor
4. Trim stick

461

Fig. 13 Pushing back pistons in bore

To install:

> ✳✳ **WARNING**
>
> **Always inspect brake pads before installing disc brake caliper and replace as necessary.**

10. Completely retract caliper pistons back into bores of caliper. Use hand pressure or a C-clamp may also be used to retract pistons, first placing a wood block or used brake pad (not to be reused) over pistons before installing C-clamp to avoid damaging piston.

11. If brake pads need to be installed in caliper before installation.

12. Slide caliper with pads over brake rotor and align with knuckle.

13. Install the caliper mounting bolts. Tighten bolts to 140 ft. lbs. (190 Nm) torque.

14. Install the banjo bolt attaching brake hose to caliper. Install NEW washers on each side of hose fitting as banjo bolt is placed through banjo fitting. Thread banjo bolt into caliper and tighten to 24 ft. lbs. (33 Nm) torque.

15. Install the tire and wheel assembly. Titan wheel mounting nuts to 110 ft. lbs. (150 Nm) torque.

16. Carefully lower the vehicle.

17. Remove the brake pedal holding tool.

18. Connect battery negative cable to battery post. It is important that this is performed properly.

19. Bleed the area of repair for the brake system. If a proper pedal is not felt during bleeding an area of repair then a base bleed system must be performed.

> ✳✳ **WARNING**
>
> **If NEW brake pads have been installed, keep in mind that braking effectiveness might be somewhat reduced during the first brake applications.**

20. Road test vehicle making several stops to wear off any foreign material on brakes and to seat brake pads. If NEW brake pads are installed, they need to be properly burnished.

DISC BRAKE PADS

REMOVAL & INSTALLATION

Except SRT8

See Figure 14.

1. Raise and safely support the vehicle.

➡**Perform steps 2 through 6 on each side of the vehicle.**

2. Remove the wheel mounting nuts, then tire and wheel assembly.

➡**In some cases, it may be necessary to retract caliper piston in its bore a small amount in order to provide sufficient clearance between shoes and rotor to easily remove caliper from knuckle. This can usually be accomplished before guide pin bolts are removed by grasping rear of caliper and pulling outward working with guide pins, thus retracting piston. Never push on piston directly as it may get damaged.**

3. Remove the lower caliper guide pin bolt. To do so, hold the guide pin stationary while turning bolt.

4. Rotate caliper upward, exposing brake pads. Use care not to overextend brake hose when doing this or damage may occur.

5. Remove the inboard and outboard brake pads from caliper adapter.

6. If necessary, remove anti-rattle clips from upper and lower abutments of adapter.

To install:

➡**Perform steps 1 through 7 on each side of the vehicle.**

7. Completely retract caliper piston(s) back into bore(s) of caliper. To do so:

   a. Remove fluid reservoir cap.

   b. Use hand pressure or a C-clamp may be used to retract piston, first placing a wood block over piston(s) before installing C-clamp to avoid damaging piston(s).

   c. Install fluid reservoir cap.

8. If removed, attach anti-rattle clips to upper and lower abutments of adapter.

9. If equipped, remove the film from the brake pad double sticky isolator.

10. Install the NEW inboard and outboard brake pads on caliper adapter. NEW inboard and outboard pads are interchangeable.

11. Push caliper guide pins into caliper adapter to clear caliper mounting bosses when installing.

12. Rotate caliper downward, aligning upper mounting boss with lower guide pin.

13. Install the Upper caliper guide pin bolt. While holding guide pin stationary tighten bolt to 44 ft. lbs. (60 Nm).

14. Install the tire and wheel assembly. Tighten wheel mounting nuts to 110 ft. lbs. (150 Nm).

15. Carefully lower the vehicle.

16. Pump brake pedal several times to set pads to caliper and brake rotor.

> ✳✳ **WARNING**
>
> **When NEW brake pads have been installed, keep in mind that braking effectiveness might be somewhat reduced during the first brake applications following installation.**

17. Check and adjust brake fluid level in reservoir.

18. Road test vehicle making several stops to wear off any foreign material on brakes and to seat brake shoes.

SRT8

See Figures 15 through 19.

1. Raise and safely support the vehicle.

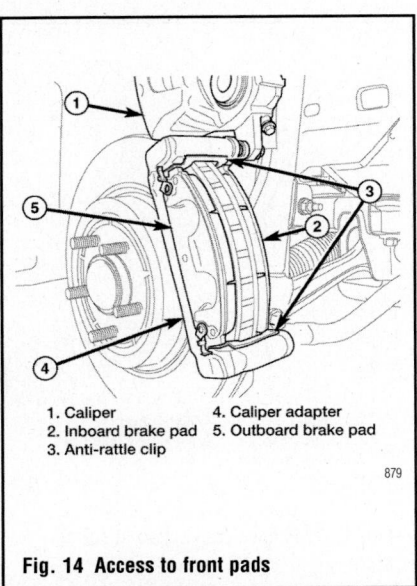

1. Caliper
2. Inboard brake pad
3. Anti-rattle clip
4. Caliper adapter
5. Outboard brake pad

879

Fig. 14 Access to front pads

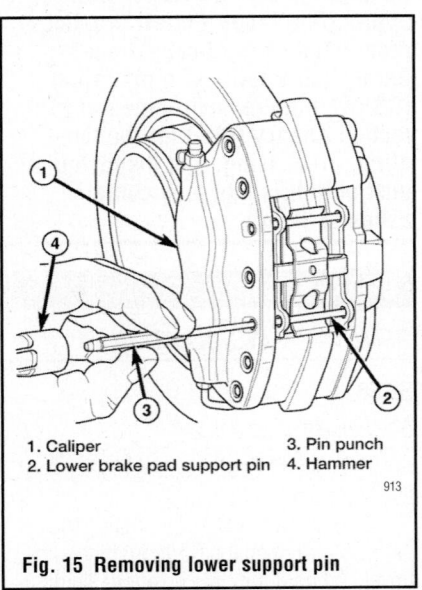

1. Caliper
2. Lower brake pad support pin
3. Pin punch
4. Hammer

913

Fig. 15 Removing lower support pin

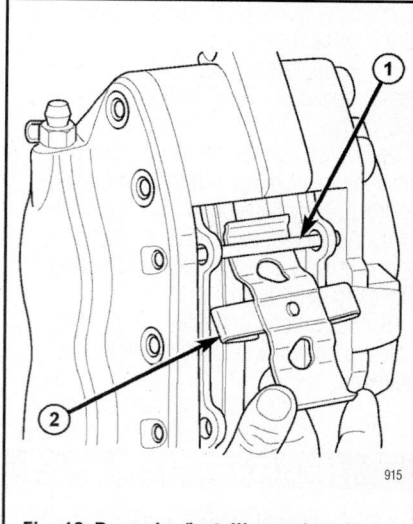

Fig. 16 Removing/installing spring clip (2) from upper support pin (1)

➡ **Perform steps 1 through 7 on each side of vehicle to complete pad set removal.**

2. Remove the wheel mounting nuts, then tire and wheel assembly.

3. Using hammer and pin punch on outboard end, tap lower brake pad support pin out of caliper.

4. Remove the brake pad spring clip out from under the upper support pin still in caliper.

5. Using pin punch and hammer, remove upper brake pad support pin in same manner used on lower support pin.

✳✳ WARNING

When pushing pistons back into caliper bores, if hand pressure is not sufficient, use only a trim stick as shown or other suitable soft tool to

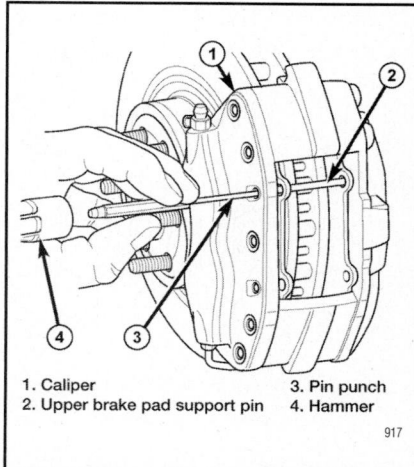

1. Caliper   3. Pin punch
2. Upper brake pad support pin   4. Hammer

Fig. 17 Removing upper support pin (2) with a pin punch (3) and a hammer (4)

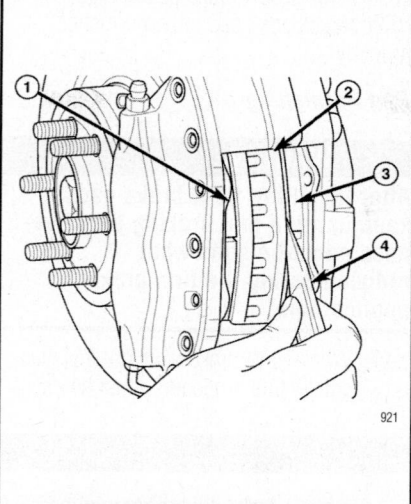

Fig. 18 Placing a trim stick (3) between the brake pad and rotor (1)

do so. Never use a screwdriver or other metal pry bar due to potential damage to braking surface of rotor or pads.

6. Using hand pressure, pull pads back to seat caliper pistons into bores if possible. If not possible, perform the following to do this correctly without damaging the caliper, pistons, dust boots or brake rotor disc.

a. Place trim stick between inboard brake pad and outer edge of rotor.

b. Using trim stick, apply pressure against the inboard brake pad until both pistons are completely bottomed in bores of inboard caliper half. Leave trim stick in place to hold pistons in place.

c. Place second trim stick between outboard brake pad and rotor, then repeat above step on outboard pad and pistons.

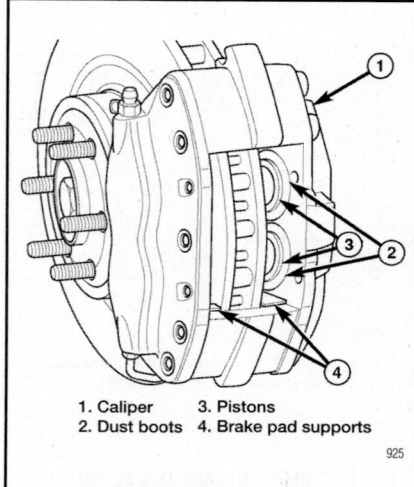

1. Caliper   3. Pistons
2. Dust boots   4. Brake pad supports

Fig. 19 Piston and seal inspection

7. Remove the inboard brake pad through opening in caliper. Remove outboard brake pad in same manner.

8. Once brake pads are removed from caliper, inspect all four caliper pistons and dust boots for evidence of brake fluid leakage. Also inspect dust boots on all caliper pistons for any cuts, tears or heat cracks and brake pad supports (if equipped) for excess wear or damage. If caliper fails inspection, it should be replaced.

To install:

9. Make sure all caliper pistons are fully seated (bottomed) in bores.

10. If equipped, remove the film from the brake pad double sticky isolator.

11. Slide NEW inboard and outboard brake pads into opening in disc brake caliper. If installing rear brake pads, make sure beveled end of each pad lining is directed against the direction the rotor is rotating in when vehicle is moving forward, in other words, the rear pads need to have beveled end facing upward.

12. From inboard side, slide upper brake pad support pin through caliper and upper holes in both brake pads. Ensure that small end of support pin is in hole in outboard half of caliper.

13. Install the upper end of brake pad spring clip under upper brake pad support pin.

14. Press on lower end of spring clip until it touches brake rotor.

15. Slide lower brake pad support pin through caliper and lower holes in both brake pads in the same manner the upper pin was installed. Ensure small end of support pin is in hole in outboard half of caliper.

16. Release the spring clip allowing it to engage lower support pin.

17. From inboard side, seat upper and lower support pins into caliper using pin punch and hammer. Support pins must be driven into caliper until support pin retaining rings are locked into place.

18. Once support pins are fully installed into caliper, inspect assembled caliper to make sure spring clip is centered in opening of caliper, correctly engaging upper and lower support pins, and is resting against both brake pads.

19. Install the tire and wheel assembly. Tighten wheel mounting nuts to 110 ft. lbs. (150 Nm) torque.

20. Carefully lower the vehicle.

21. Pump brake pedal several times to set pads to caliper and brake rotor.

22. Check and adjust brake fluid level in reservoir.

✳✳ WARNING

When NEW brake pads have been installed, keep in mind that braking effectiveness might be somewhat reduced during the first brake applications following installation.

➡ When NEW brake pads are installed, they must be burnished (seated) to the rotor. This must be done to ensure the proper performance of the replacement brake pads.

23. Road test vehicle making several stops to wear off any foreign material on brakes and to seat brake pad linings. NEW brake pads need to be burnished properly.

Pad Burnishing

✳✳ WARNING

After installing NEW brake pads, keep in mind that braking effectiveness might be somewhat reduced during the first brake applications.

1. When NEW brake pads are installed on a vehicle, this procedure must be used to correctly burnish (seat) the brake linings to the brake rotor discs.

2. Accelerate the vehicle to a steady speed of about 40 mph (65 km/h).

3. Using light brake pedal pressure, slow the vehicle from 40 mph to 0 mph in approximately 6 seconds.

4. Accelerate back up to 40 mph for approximately one minute to allow the brakes to cool down.

5. Repeat this procedure 15 to 20 times to correctly seat the brake lining material.

BRAKES

✳✳ WARNING

Dust and dirt accumulating on brake parts during normal use may contain asbestos fibers from production or aftermarket brake linings. Breathing excessive concentrations of asbestos fibers can cause serious bodily harm. Exercise care when servicing brake parts. Do not sand or grind brake lining unless equipment used is designed to contain the dust residue. Do not clean brake parts with compressed air or by dry brushing. Cleaning should be done by dampening the brake components with a fine mist of water, then wiping the brake components clean with a dampened cloth. Dispose of cloth and all residue containing asbestos fibers in an impermeable container with the appropriate label. Follow practices prescribed by the Occupational Safety and Health Administration (OSHA) and the Environmental Protection Agency (EPA) for the handling, processing, and disposing of dust or debris that may contain asbestos fibers.

BRAKE CALIPER

REMOVAL & INSTALLATION

Except SRT8

See Figures 20 and 21.

1. Disconnect and isolate battery negative cable from battery post.

2. Using a brake pedal holding tool, depress brake pedal past its first inch of travel and hold it in this position. Holding pedal in this position will isolate master cylinder from hydraulic brake system and will not allow brake fluid to drain out of brake fluid reservoir while brake lines are open.

3. Raise and safely support the vehicle.

4. Remove the wheel mounting nuts, then tire and wheel assembly.

5. Remove the banjo bolt connecting flexible brake hose to caliper. There are two sealing washers (one one each side of hose fitting) that will come off when bolt is removed. Discard these washers; install NEW washers on installation.

6. While holding guide pins from turning, remove caliper guide pin bolts.

7. Remove the brake caliper from brake adapter and pads.

To install:

✳✳ WARNING

Always inspect brake pads before installing disc brake caliper and replace as necessary.

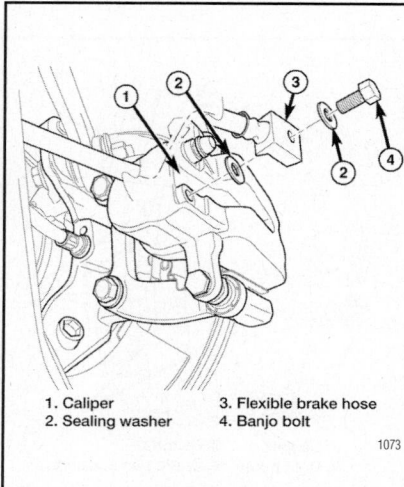

1. Caliper
2. Sealing washer
3. Flexible brake hose
4. Banjo bolt

1073

Fig. 20 Flex hose connection at rear caliper

REAR DISC BRAKES

8. Completely retract caliper piston back into bore of caliper. Use hand pressure or a C-clamp may be used to retract piston, first placing a wood block over piston before installing C-clamp to avoid damaging piston.

✳✳ WARNING

Use care when installing caliper onto disc brake adapter to avoid damaging boots on caliper guide pins.

9. Push caliper guide pins into caliper adapter to clear caliper mounting bosses when installing.

10. Slide caliper over brake pads and onto caliper adapter.

✳✳ WARNING

Extreme caution should be taken not to crossthread caliper guide pin bolts when they are installed.

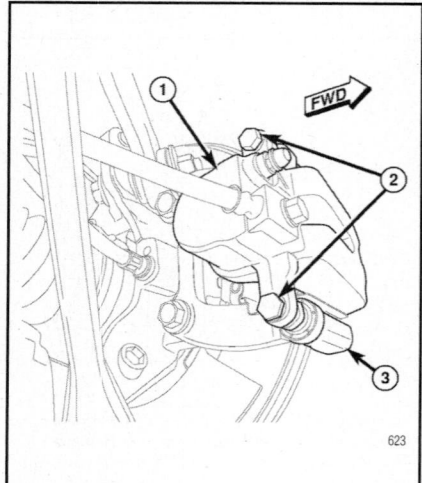

623

Fig. 21 Removing the caliper (1) and guide pin bolts (2) from the adapter (3)

➡**Before installing caliper guide pin bolts, clean guide pin bolt threads and apply Mopar®Lock AND Seal Adhesive or equivalent.**

11. Align caliper mounting holes with guide pins, then install guide pin bolts. While holding guide pins from turning, tighten bolts to 23 ft. lbs. (31 Nm).

12. Install the banjo bolt attaching brake hose to caliper. Install NEW washers on each side of hose fitting as banjo bolt is placed through fitting. Thread banjo bolt into caliper and tighten to 37 ft. lbs. (50 Nm).

13. Install the tire and wheel assembly. Tighten wheel mounting nuts to 110 ft. lbs. (150 Nm) (Police - 140 ft. lbs. (190 Nm)).

14. Carefully lower the vehicle.

15. Remove the brake pedal holding tool.

16. Connect battery negative cable to battery post. It is important that this is performed properly.

17. Bleed the area of repair for the brake system. If a proper pedal is not felt during bleeding an area of repair then a base bleed system must be performed.

18. Road test vehicle making several stops to wear off any foreign material on brakes and to seat brake shoes.

SRT8

See Figures 22 through 25.

1. Disconnect and isolate battery negative cable from battery post.

2. Using a brake pedal holding tool, depress brake pedal past its first inch of travel and hold it in this position. Holding pedal in this position will isolate master

cylinder from hydraulic brake system and will not allow brake fluid to drain out of brake fluid reservoir while brake lines are open.

3. Raise and safely support the vehicle.

4. Remove the wheel mounting nuts, then tire and wheel assembly.

5. Remove the banjo bolt connecting flexible brake hose to caliper. There are two sealing washers (one one each side of hose fitting) that will come off when bolt is removed. Discard these washers; install NEW washers on installation.

❊❊ WARNING

When pushing pistons back into caliper bores, use only a trim stick as shown or other suitable soft tool. Never use a screwdriver or other metal pry bar due to potential damage to braking surface of rotor, caliper, pistons or dust boots.

6. Place trim stick between brake pad and outer edge of rotor.

7. Using trim stick, slowly apply pressure against brake pad until both pistons (on that side of caliper) are completely bottomed in bores of caliper half.

➡**Repeat above procedure to opposite brake pad and pistons as necessary.**

8. Support spring link using a transmission jack or other appropriate jack. Raise spring link just enough to access brake caliper lower mounting bolt from above compression link.

9. Remove the lower and upper caliper mounting bolts.

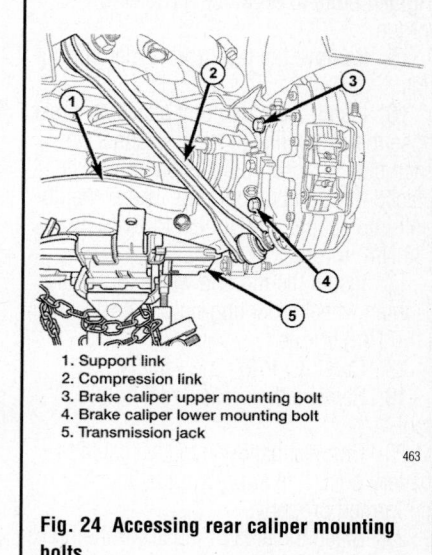

1. Support link
2. Compression link
3. Brake caliper upper mounting bolt
4. Brake caliper lower mounting bolt
5. Transmission jack

Fig. 24 Accessing rear caliper mounting bolts

10. Remove the brake caliper with pads from knuckle and brake rotor.

➡**If brake pads need to be removed from caliper, these calipers are not serviceable. Do not attempt disassembly.**

To install:

11. Completely retract caliper pistons back into bores of caliper. Use hand pressure or a C-clamp may also be used to retract pistons, first placing a wood block or used brake pad (not to be reused) over piston before installing C-clamp to avoid damaging piston.

12. If brake pads need to be installed in caliper before installation.

13. Slide caliper with pads over brake rotor and align with knuckle.

14. Install the caliper mounting bolts.

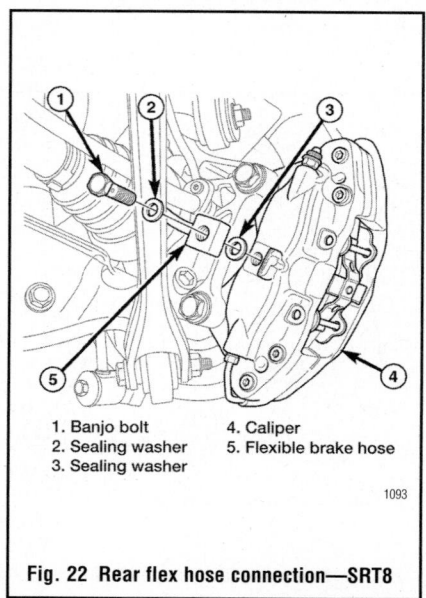

1. Banjo bolt
2. Sealing washer
3. Sealing washer
4. Caliper
5. Flexible brake hose

Fig. 22 Rear flex hose connection—SRT8

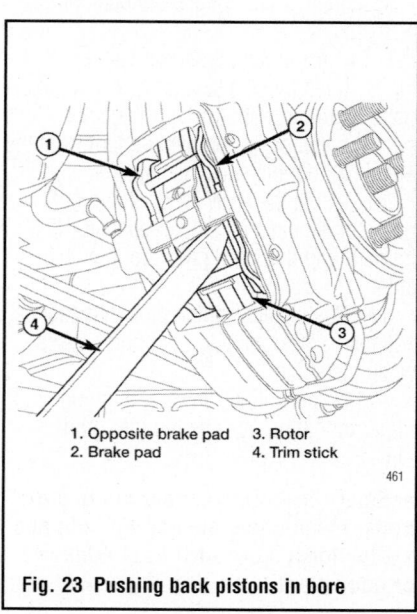

1. Opposite brake pad
2. Brake pad
3. Rotor
4. Trim stick

Fig. 23 Pushing back pistons in bore

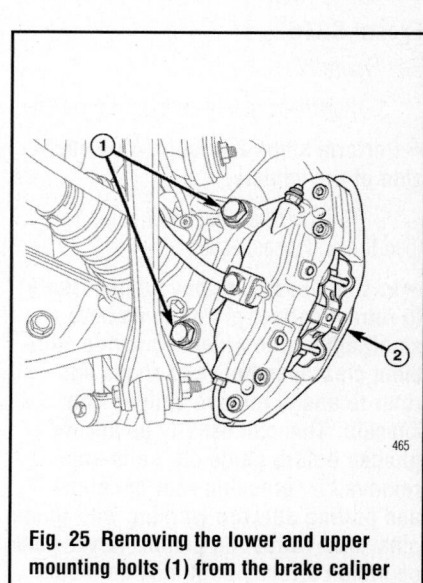

Fig. 25 Removing the lower and upper mounting bolts (1) from the brake caliper (2)

Tighten bolts to 96 ft. lbs. (130 Nm) torque.

15. Remove the jack from under spring link.

16. Install the banjo bolt attaching brake hose to caliper. Install NEW washers on each side of hose fitting as banjo bolt is placed through banjo fitting. Thread banjo bolt into caliper and tighten to 24 ft. lbs. (33 Nm) torque.

17. Install the tire and wheel assembly. Tighten wheel mounting nuts to 110 ft. lbs. (150 Nm) torque.

18. Carefully lower the vehicle.

19. Remove the brake pedal holding tool.

20. Connect battery negative cable to battery post. It is important that this is performed properly.

21. Bleed the area of repair for the brake system. If a proper pedal is not felt during bleeding an area of repair then a base bleed system must be performed.

✷✷ WARNING

If NEW brake pads have been installed, keep in mind that braking effectiveness might be somewhat reduced during the first brake applications.

22. Road test vehicle making several stops to wear off any foreign material on brakes and to seat brake pads. If NEW brake pads are installed, they need to be properly burnished.

DISC BRAKE PADS

REMOVAL & INSTALLATION

Except SRT8

See Figure 26.

1. Raise and safely support the vehicle.

➡**Perform steps 2 through 6 on each side of the vehicle.**

2. Remove the wheel mounting nuts, then tire and wheel assembly.

➡**In some cases, it may be necessary to retract caliper piston in its bore a small amount in order to provide sufficient clearance between shoes and rotor to easily remove caliper from knuckle. This can usually be accomplished before guide pin bolts are removed by grasping rear of caliper and pulling outward working with guide pins, thus retracting piston. Never push on piston directly as it may get damaged.**

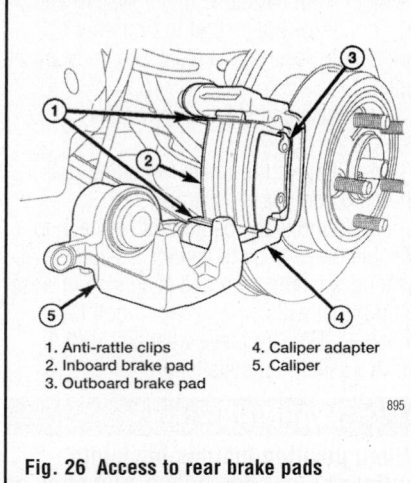

1. Anti-rattle clips
2. Inboard brake pad
3. Outboard brake pad
4. Caliper adapter
5. Caliper

895

Fig. 26 Access to rear brake pads

3. Remove the Upper caliper guide pin bolt. To do so, hold the guide pin stationary while turning bolt.

4. Rotate caliper downward, exposing brake pads. Use care not to overextend brake hose when doing this or damage may occur.

5. Remove the inboard and outboard brake pads from caliper adapter.

6. If necessary, remove anti-rattle clips from upper and lower abutments of adapter.

To install:

➡**Perform steps 2 through 6 on each side of the vehicle.**

7. Completely retract caliper piston back into bore of caliper. To do so:

a. Remove fluid reservoir cap.

b. Use hand pressure or a C-clamp may be used to retract piston, first placing a wood block over piston before installing C-clamp to avoid damaging piston.

c. Install fluid reservoir cap.

8. If removed, attach anti-rattle clips to upper and lower abutments of adapter.

9. If equipped, remove the film from the brake pad double sticky isolator.

10. Install the NEW inboard and outboard brake pads on caliper adapter. NEW Inboard and outboard pads are interchangeable.

11. Push caliper guide pins into caliper adapter to clear caliper mounting bosses when installing.

12. Rotate caliper upward, aligning upper mounting boss with upper guide pin.

➡**Before installing caliper guide pin bolts, clean guide pin bolt threads and apply Mopar®Lock AND Seal Adhesive or equivalent.**

13. Install the upper caliper guide pin bolt. While holding guide pin stationary tighten bolt to 23 ft. lbs. (31 Nm).

14. Install the tire and wheel assembly. Tighten wheel mounting nuts to 110 ft. lbs. (150 Nm).

15. Carefully lower the vehicle.

16. Pump brake pedal several times to set pads to caliper and brake rotor.

✷✷ WARNING

When NEW brake pads have been installed, keep in mind that braking effectiveness might be somewhat reduced during the first brake applications following installation.

17. Check and adjust brake fluid level in reservoir.

18. Road test vehicle making several stops to wear off any foreign material on brakes and to seat brake shoes.

SRT8

See Figures 27 through 31.

1. Raise and safely support the vehicle.

➡**Perform 2 through 6 on each side of vehicle to complete pad set removal.**

2. Remove the wheel mounting nuts, then tire and wheel assembly.

3. Using hammer and pin punch on outboard end, tap lower brake pad support pin out of caliper.

4. Remove the brake pad spring clip out from under the upper support pin still in caliper.

5. Using pin punch and hammer, remove upper brake pad support pin in same manner used on lower support pin.

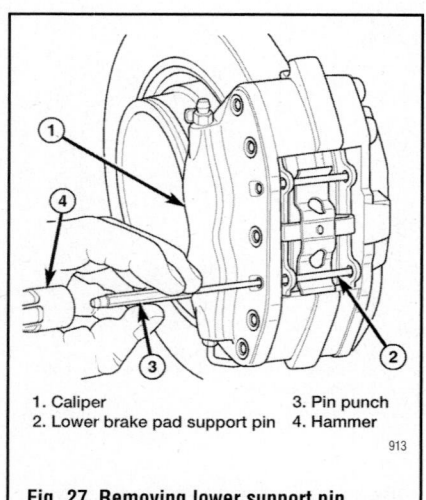

1. Caliper
2. Lower brake pad support pin
3. Pin punch
4. Hammer

913

Fig. 27 Removing lower support pin

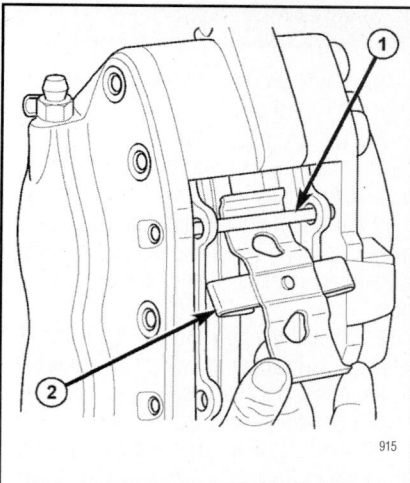

Fig. 28 Removing/installing spring clip (2) from upper support pin (1)

⁕⁕ **WARNING**

When pushing pistons back into caliper bores, if hand pressure is not sufficient, use only a trim stick as shown or other suitable soft tool to do so. Never use a screwdriver or other metal pry bar due to potential damage to braking surface of rotor or pads.

6. Using hand pressure, pull pads back to seat caliper pistons into bores if possible. If not possible, perform the following to do this correctly without damaging the caliper, pistons, dust boots or brake rotor disc.

7. Place trim stick between inboard brake pad and outer edge of rotor.

8. Using trim stick, apply pressure against the inboard brake pad until both pistons are completely bottomed in bores of inboard caliper half. Leave trim stick in place to hold pistons in place.

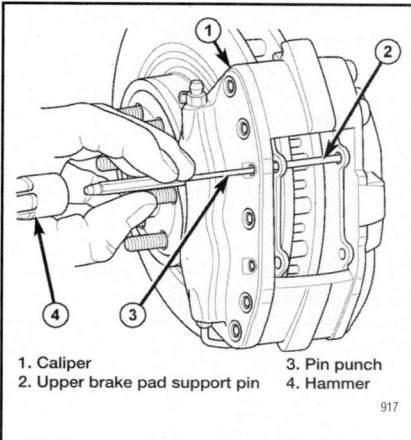

1. Caliper
2. Upper brake pad support pin
3. Pin punch
4. Hammer

Fig. 29 Removing upper support pin (2) with a pin punch (3) and a hammer (4)

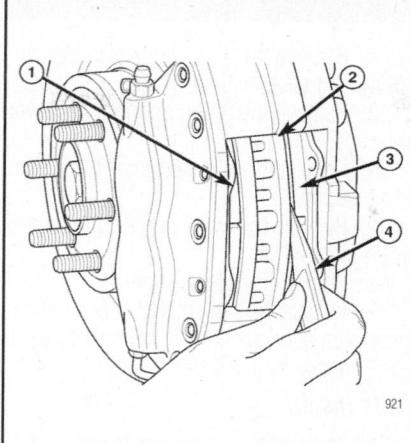

Fig. 30 Placing the trim stick (3) between the brake pad and rotor (1)

9. Place second trim stick between outboard brake pad and rotor, then repeat above step on outboard pad and pistons.

10. Remove the inboard brake pad through opening in caliper. Remove outboard brake pad in same manner.

11. Once brake pads are removed from caliper, inspect all four caliper pistons and dust boots for evidence of brake fluid leakage. Also inspect dust boots on all caliper pistons for any cuts, tears or heat cracks and brake pad supports (if equipped) for excess wear or damage. If caliper fails inspection, it should be replaced.

To install:

12. Make sure all caliper pistons are fully seated (bottomed) in bores.

13. If equipped, remove the film from the brake pad double sticky isolator.

14. Slide NEW inboard and outboard brake pads into opening in disc brake

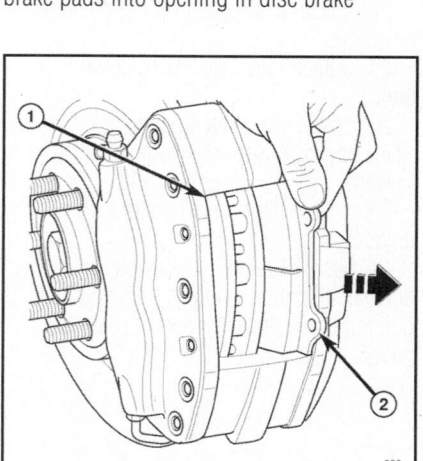

Fig. 31 Removing the brake pad through the opening in the caliper (1)

caliper. If installing rear brake pads, make sure beveled end of each pad lining is directed against the direction the rotor is rotating in when vehicle is moving forward, in other words, the rear pads need to have beveled end facing upward.

15. From inboard side, slide upper brake pad support pin through caliper and upper holes in both brake pads. Ensure that small end of support pin is in hole in outboard half of caliper.

16. Install the upper end of brake pad spring clip under upper brake pad support pin.

17. Press on lower end of spring clip until it touches brake rotor.

18. Slide lower brake pad support pin through caliper and lower holes in both brake pads in the same manner the upper pin was installed. Ensure small end of support pin is in hole in outboard half of caliper.

19. Release the spring clip allowing it to engage lower support pin.

20. From inboard side, seat upper and lower support pins into caliper using pin punch and hammer. Support pins must be driven into caliper until support pin retaining rings are locked into place.

21. Once support pins are fully installed into caliper, inspect assembled caliper to make sure spring clip is centered in opening of caliper, correctly engaging upper and lower support pins, and is resting against both brake pads.

22. Install the tire and wheel assembly. Tighten wheel mounting nuts to 110 ft. lbs. (150 Nm) torque.

23. Carefully lower the vehicle.

24. Pump brake pedal several times to set pads to caliper and brake rotor.

25. Check and adjust brake fluid level in reservoir.

⁕⁕ **WARNING**

When NEW brake pads have been installed, keep in mind that braking effectiveness might be somewhat reduced during the first brake applications following installation.

➡When NEW brake pads are installed, they must be burnished (seated) to the rotor. This must be done to ensure the proper performance of the replacement brake pads.

26. Road test vehicle making several stops to wear off any foreign material on brakes and to seat brake pad linings. NEW brake pads need to be burnished properly.

PARKING BRAKE SHOES

REMOVAL & INSTALLATION

See Figures 32 through 35.

1. Raise and safely support the vehicle.
2. Access and remove rear hub and bearing.
3. Completely back off parking brake shoe adjustment.
4. Remove the parking brake shoe adjuster spring.
5. Remove the shoe adjuster.
6. Remove the upper brake shoe hold-down clip and pin.

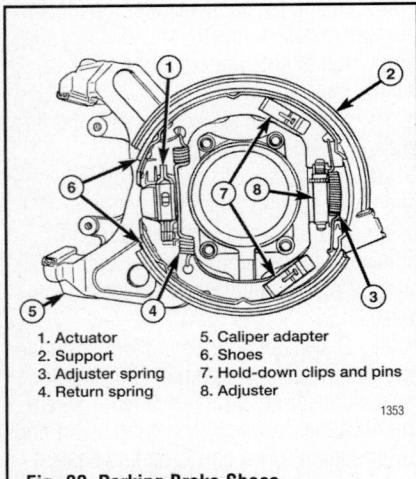

1. Actuator   5. Caliper adapter
2. Support   6. Shoes
3. Adjuster spring   7. Hold-down clips and pins
4. Return spring   8. Adjuster

1353

Fig. 32 Parking Brake Shoes

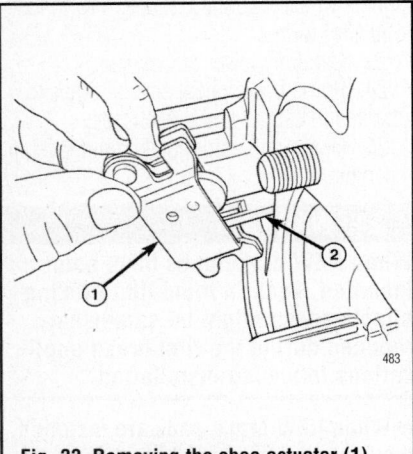

483

Fig. 33 Removing the shoe actuator (1) from the cable end (2)

7. Remove the upper shoe from return spring and shoe actuator lever.
8. Remove the return spring from lower shoe.
9. Remove the shoe actuator lever from end of cable.
10. Remove the lower brake shoe hold-down clip and pin.
11. Remove the lower shoe.
12. Inspect springs, adjuster, lever and aluminum shoe anchor pin for wear or damage. Replace as necessary.

To install:

➡**The following procedure may be used to install shoes on either side of the vehicle.**

➡**Inspect springs, adjuster, lever and aluminum shoe anchor pin for wear or damage prior to installation. Replace as necessary.**

13. Install the lower brake shoe hold-down pin through rear of support.
14. Install the lower shoe against support plate.
15. Install the lower brake shoe hold-down clip.
16. Install the shoe actuator lever on end of parking brake cable (2). Make sure actuator lever is positioned with word "UP" facing outward.
17. Install the return spring to lower shoe.
18. Install the upper shoe against support plate and onto shoe actuator lever.
19. Install the upper brake shoe hold-down pin through rear of support and upper shoe.
20. Install the upper brake shoe hold-down clip.
21. Attach return spring to upper shoe.
22. Install the shoe adjuster. Place end of adjuster with star wheel upward.
23. Install the parking brake shoe adjuster spring.
24. Using Brake Shoe Gauge, or equivalent, measure inside diameter of parking brake drum portion of rotor. Set gauge.

25. Place Gauge over parking brake shoes at widest point.
26. Using adjuster star wheel, adjust parking brake shoes until linings on both park brake shoes just touch jaws on gauge. This will give a good preliminary adjustment of parking brake shoes, before a final adjustment is made at end of this procedure.
27. Install the hub and bearing with wheel speed sensor as well as all components necessary to access it.
28. Carefully lower the vehicle.
29. Perform final adjustment of parking brake shoes.

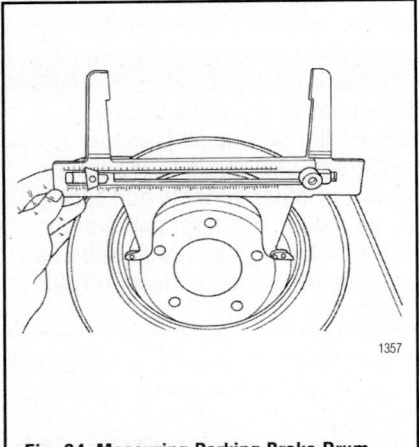

1357

Fig. 34 Measuring Parking Brake Drum Diameter

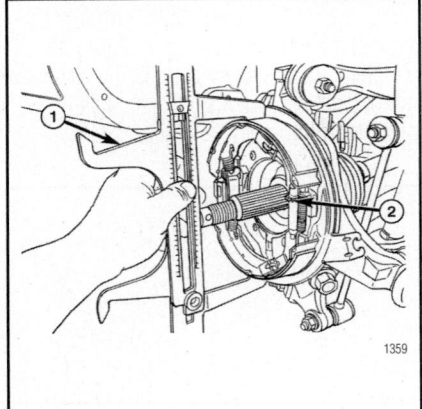

1359

Fig. 35 Using the brake shoe gauge (1) and adjuster star wheel (2)

GENERAL INFORMATION

※※ WARNING

These vehicles are equipped with an air bag system. The system must be disarmed before performing service on, or around, system components, the steering column, instrument panel components, wiring and sensors. Failure to follow the safety precautions and the disarming procedure could result in accidental air bag deployment, possible injury and unnecessary system repairs.

SERVICE PRECAUTIONS

Disconnect and isolate the battery negative cable before beginning any airbag system component diagnosis, testing, removal, or installation procedures. Allow system capacitor to discharge for two minutes before beginning any component service. This will disable the airbag system. Failure to disable the airbag system may result in accidental airbag deployment, personal injury, or death.

Do not place an intact undeployed airbag face down on a solid surface. The airbag will propel into the air if accidentally deployed and may result in personal injury or death.

When carrying or handling an undeployed airbag, the trim side (face) of the airbag should be pointing towards the body to minimize possibility of injury if accidental deployment occurs. Failure to do this may result in personal injury or death.

Replace airbag system components with OEM replacement parts. Substitute parts may appear interchangeable, but internal differences may result in inferior occupant protection. Failure to do so may result in occupant personal injury or death.

Wear safety glasses, rubber gloves, and long sleeved clothing when cleaning powder residue from vehicle after an airbag deployment. Powder residue emitted from a deployed airbag can cause skin irritation. Flush affected area with cool water if irritation is experienced. If nasal or throat irritation is experienced, exit the vehicle for fresh air until the irritation ceases. If irritation continues, see a physician.

Do not use a replacement airbag that is not in the original packaging. This may result in improper deployment, personal injury, or death.

The factory installed fasteners, screws and bolts used to fasten airbag components have a special coating and are specifically designed for the airbag system. Do not use substitute fasteners. Use only original equipment fasteners listed in the parts catalog when fastener replacement is required.

During, and following, any child restraint anchor service, due to impact event or vehicle repair, carefully inspect all mounting hardware, tether straps, and anchors for proper installation, operation, or damage. If a child restraint anchor is found damaged in any way, the anchor must be replaced. Failure to do this may result in personal injury or death.

Deployed and non-deployed airbags may or may not have live pyrotechnic material within the airbag inflator.

Do not dispose of driver/passenger/curtain airbags or seat belt tensioners unless you are sure of complete deployment. Refer to the Hazardous Substance Control System for proper disposal.

Dispose of deployed airbags and tensioners consistent with state, provincial, local, and federal regulations.

After any airbag component testing or service, do not connect the battery negative cable. Personal injury or death may result if the system test is not performed first.

If the vehicle is equipped with the Occupant Classification System (OCS), do not connect the battery negative cable before performing the OCS Verification Test using the scan tool and the appropriate diagnostic information. Personal injury or death may result if the system test is not performed properly.

Never replace both the Occupant Restraint Controller (ORC) and the Occupant Classification Module (OCM) at the same time. If both require replacement, replace one, then perform the Airbag System test before replacing the other.

Both the ORC and the OCM store Occupant Classification System (OCS) calibration data, which they transfer to one another when one of them is replaced. If both are replaced at the same time, an irreversible fault will be set in both modules and the OCS may malfunction and cause personal injury or death.

If equipped with OCS, the Seat Weight Sensor is a sensitive, calibrated unit and must be handled carefully. Do not drop or handle roughly. If dropped or damaged, replace with another sensor. Failure to do so may result in occupant injury or death.

If equipped with OCS, the front passenger seat must be handled carefully as well. When removing the seat, be careful when setting on floor not to drop. If dropped, the sensor may be inoperative, could result in occupant injury, or possibly death.

If equipped with OCS, when the passenger front seat is on the floor, no one should sit in the front passenger seat. This uneven force may damage the sensing ability of the seat weight sensors. If sat on and damaged, the sensor may be inoperative, could result in occupant injury, or possibly death.

DISARMING THE SYSTEM

Disconnect and isolate the negative battery cable. Wait 2 minutes for the system capacitor to discharge before performing any service.

ARMING THE SYSTEM

To arm the system, connect the negative battery cable.

SRS VERFICATION TEST

※※ CAUTION

The following procedure should be performed using a diagnostic scan tool to verify proper Supplemental Restraint System (SRS) operation following the service or replacement of any SRS component. In addition, if the vehicle is equipped with the Occupant Classification System (OCS) and one of the passenger front seat SRS components has been replaced, following successful completion of the SRS Verification Test procedure, perform the OCS Verification Test using a diagnostic scan tool. Refer to the appropriate diagnostic procedures.

1. During the following test, the negative battery cable remains disconnected and isolated, as it was during the Supplemental Restraint System (SRS) component removal and installation procedures.

2. Be certain that the diagnostic scan tool contains the latest version of the proper diagnostic software. Connect the scan tool to the 16-way Data Link Connector (DLC). The DLC is located on the driver side lower edge of the instrument panel, inboard of the steering column.

3. Turn the ignition switch to the ON position and exit the vehicle with the scan tool.

4. Check to be certain that nobody is in the vehicle, then reconnect the negative battery cable.

5. Using the scan tool, read and record the active (current) Diagnostic Trouble Code (DTC) data.

6. Next, use the scan tool to read and record any stored (historical) DTC data.

7. If any DTC is found in Step No. 5 or Step No. 6, refer to the appropriate diagnostic information.

8. Use the scan tool to erase the stored DTC data. If any problems remain, the stored DTC data will not erase. Refer to the appropriate diagnostic information to diagnose any stored DTC that will not erase. If the stored DTC information is successfully erased, go to Step No. 9.

9. Turn the ignition switch to the OFF position for about 15 seconds, and then back to the ON position. Observe the airbag indicator in the instrument cluster. It should light for six to eight seconds, and then go out. This indicates that the SRS is functioning normally and that the repairs are complete. If the airbag indicator fails to light, or lights and stays ON, there is still an active SRS fault or malfunction. Refer to the appropriate diagnostic information to diagnose the problem.

CLOCKSPRING CENTERING

✳✳ CAUTION

To service any component of the Steering Column Control Module (SCCM), the entire assembly must be removed from the column. This must be done due to the clockspring passing through the assembly and into the self docking connector. Failure to remove the assembly could damage the pins of the clockspring and prevent the airbag system from operating properly Failure to follow these instructions may result in possible serious or fatal injury.

If the rotating tape (wire coil) in the clockspring is not positioned properly with the steering wheel and the front wheels, the clockspring may fail. The following procedure must be used to center the clockspring if it is not known to be properly positioned, or if the front wheels were moved from the straight ahead position.

➡**Before starting this procedure, be certain to turn the steering wheel until the front wheels are in the straight ahead position.**

1. Position the steering wheel and front wheels straight ahead.

2. Remove the Steering Column Control Module (SCCM).

3. Remove the clockspring.

4. The clockspring can rotate approximately 5 3/4 turns from lock-to-lock. To be properly centered, rotate the clockspring rotor clockwise until the rotor stops. Do not apply excessive force.

5. From the end of travel, slowly rotate the rotor counterclockwise until the arrow points to the 12 o'clock position. Then continue two rotations returning to the 12 o'clock position. Temporarily secure the rotor to prevent inadvertent rotation, until the SCCM assembly is reinstalled in the vehicle.

6. Install the SCCM (Refer to Steering/Column/MODULE, Steering Column Control - Installation).

7. Install the wire pigtail routing clip over the lower left airbag stud, and remove temporary aid used to secure clockspring.

✳✳ CAUTION

Do not connect the battery negative cable. If the system test is not performed first it may result in serious or fatal injury.

DRIVE TRAIN

AUTOMATIC TRANSMISSION FLUID

DRAIN AND REFILL

Fill

To avoid overfilling transmission after a fluid change or overhaul, perform the following procedure:

1. Remove the dipstick and insert clean funnel in transmission fill tube.

2. Add following initial quantity of Mopar®ATF +4, Automatic Transmission Fluid, to transmission:

   a. If only fluid and filter were changed, add 3 pints (1-1/2 quarts) of ATF +4 to transmission.

   b. If transmission was completely overhauled, or torque converter was replaced or drained, add 12 pints (6 quarts) of ATF +4 to transmission.

3. Apply parking brakes.

4. Start and run engine at normal curb idle speed.

5. Apply service brakes, shift transmission through all gear ranges then back to NEUTRAL, set parking brake,

and leave engine running at curb idle speed.

6. Remove the funnel, insert dipstick and check fluid level. If level is low, add fluid to bring level to MIN mark on dipstick. Check to see if the oil level is equal on both sides of the dipstick. If one side is noticeably higher than the other, the dipstick has picked up some oil from the dipstick tube. Allow the oil to drain down the dipstick tube and re-check.

7. Drive vehicle until transmission fluid is at normal operating temperature.

8. With the engine running at curb idle speed, the gear selector in NEUTRAL, and the parking brake applied, check the transmission fluid level.

✳✳ WARNING

Do not overfill transmission, fluid foaming and shifting problems can result.

9. Add fluid to bring level up to MAX arrow mark.

When fluid level is correct, shut engine off, release park brake, remove funnel, and install dipstick in fill tube.

FILTER REPLACEMENT

See Figure 36.

➡**Only fluids of the type labeled Mopar®ATF+4, Automatic Transmission Fluid, should be used in the transmission sump. A filter change should be made at the time of the transmission oil change. The magnet (on the inside of the oil pan) should also be cleaned with a clean, dry cloth.**

➡**If the transmission is disassembled for any reason, the fluid and filter should be changed.**

1. Raise vehicle on a hoist. Place a drain container with a large opening, under transmission oil pan.

➡**One of the oil pan bolts has a sealing patch applied from the factory. Separate this bolt for reuse.**

2. Loosen pan bolts and tap the pan at one corner to break it loose allowing fluid to drain, then remove the oil pan.

3. Install the a new filter and O-ring on bottom of the valve body and tighten retaining screws to 3.75 ft. lbs. (5 Nm).

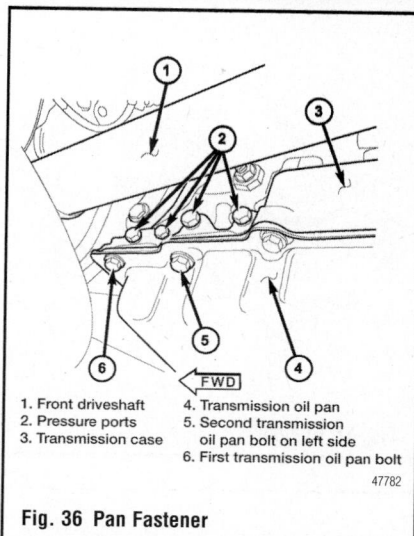

1. Front driveshaft
2. Pressure ports
3. Transmission case
4. Transmission oil pan
5. Second transmission oil pan bolt on left side
6. First transmission oil pan bolt

47782

Fig. 36 Pan Fastener

➡️**Before installing the oil pan bolt in the bolt hole located between the torque converter clutch on and U/D clutch pressure tap circuits, it will be necessary to replenish the sealing patch on the bolt using Mopar®Lock AND Seal Adhesive.**

4. Clean the oil pan and magnet. Reinstall pan using new Mopar® Silicone Adhesive sealant. Tighten oil pan bolts to 14.5 ft. lbs. (20 Nm).

5. Pour four quarts of Mopar®ATF+4, Automatic Transmission Fluid, through the dipstick opening.

6. Start engine and allow to idle for at least one minute. Then, with parking and service brakes applied, move selector lever momentarily to each position, ending in the park or neutral position.

7. Check the transmission fluid level and add an appropriate amount to bring the transmission fluid level to 1/8 inch (3mm) below the lowest mark on the dipstick.

8. Recheck the fluid level after the transmission has reached normal operating temperature, 180°F (82°C).

9. To prevent dirt from entering transmission, make certain that dipstick is fully seated into the dipstick opening.

MANUAL TRANSMISSION FLUID

DRAIN AND REFILL

See Figure 37.

✱✱ WARNING

Hypoid gear lube must not be used in this transmission. Use of hypoid gear lube will cause hard shifting effort/transmission failure.

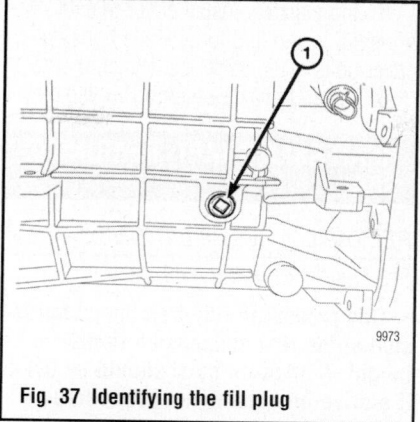

9973

Fig. 37 Identifying the fill plug

1. With vehicle in neutral, position vehicle on hoist.

2. Remove the belly pan.

3. Remove the drain plug located on the right side of the transmission tail housing.

4. Remove the transmission fill plug located on the left side of the transmission case.

5. Install the drain plug into tail housing and tighten to 20 ft. lbs. (27 Nm).

6. Fill transmission with Mopar®ATF + 4. The transmission is full when the fluid level is even with the bottom of the fill hole.

7. Install the transmission fill plug and tighten to 20 ft. lbs. (27 Nm).

8. Install the belly pan.

CLUTCH

REMOVAL & INSTALLATION

See Figure 38.

1. Remove the transmission.

2. Mark pressure plate and flywheel for installation reference.

3. Insert Clutch Tool through the clutch discs into the pilot bearing.

4. Loosen pressure plate bolts evenly in a crisscross pattern. This will release

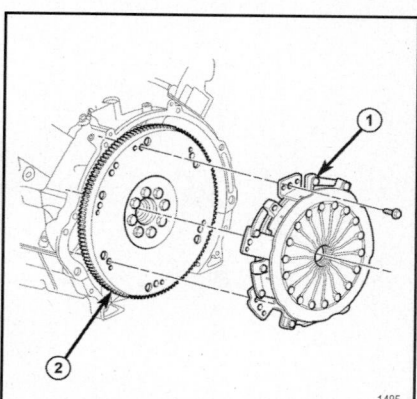

1485

Fig. 38 Pressure plate (1) and flywheel (2)

spring pressure evenly and avoid pressure plate damage.

5. Remove the pressure plate assembly and independent disc from flywheel.

To install:

➡️**If flywheel is replaced or removed apply thread sealer to the flywheel retaining bolts. This will prevent engine oil from leaking onto the clutch.**

6. Insert Clutch Tool into pilot bearing.

7. Install the independent clutch disc over the clutch tool up against flywheel.

8. Install the pressure plate assembly over clutch tool up against flywheel and onto the dowel pins.

9. If new clutch or flywheel is installed, align cover balance spot as close as possible to flywheel balance orange spot.

10. Tighten new pressure plate bolts a few turns at a time in a star pattern until bolts are seated. Then tighten bolts in star pattern to 55 ft. lbs. (75 Nm). Remove clutch disc alignment tool.

11. Install the transmission

BLEEDING

➡️**Be certain the clutch pedal returns to the upper most position while bleeding the clutch system.**

➡️**It may take as many as two hundred strokes of the clutch pedal to properly bleed the clutch system.**

1. Check the fluid level in the brake master cylinder reservoir. If the brake fluid level is not up to the step in the reservoir, add DOT 4 brake fluid.

2. Slowly depress the clutch pedal.

3. If pedal feels hard in a short distance, air is present in the clutch slave cylinder.

4. If pedal feels spongy, air is present in the clutch master cylinder.

5. Continue checking the fluid level while depressing and releasing the clutch pedal. Depress and release the clutch pedal until an appropriate clutch pedal response and feel is achieved.

REAR AXLE FLUID

DRAIN & REFILL

See Figure 39.

➡️**The fluid required for use in this axle is Mopar®Synthetic Gear and Axle Lubricant 75W-140.**

1. Drive the vehicle until the differential lubricant is at the normal operating temperature.

2. With vehicle in neutral, position and raise vehicle on hoist.

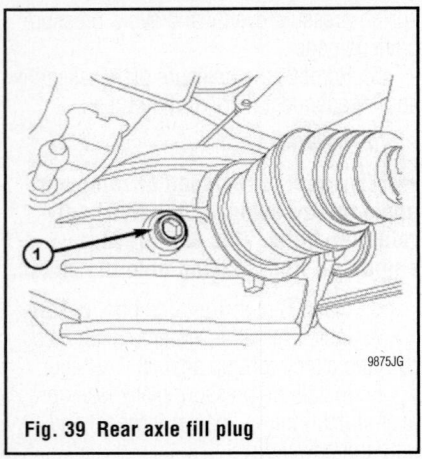

Fig. 39 Rear axle fill plug

3. Remove the rear axle drain plug and drain lubricant completely from the axle.

4. Install the drain plug and tighten to 44 ft. lbs. (60 Nm).

5. Remove the fill plug and fill rear axle with 1.4 L (1.5 qts.) Mopar®Synthetic Gear AND Axle Lubricant 75W-140 and insure axle is filled to the bottom of the fill hole.

6. Install the fill plug and tighten to 44 ft. lbs. (60 Nm).

REAR AXLE HOUSING

REMOVAL & INSTALLATION

See Figure 40.

1. Remove the axle assembly from vehicle.

2. Remove the axle housing cover bolts.

3. Using suitable screwdriver, remove axle housing cover.

To install:

4. After thoroughly cleaning axle housing cover, apply a 4 mm (0.157 in.) bead of Mopar®Axle RTV.

5. Immediately install cover to axle housing. Install and torque axle housing cover bolts (1) to 22 ft. lbs. (30 Nm) + 45°.

6. Install the axle assembly to vehicle.

REAR AXLE SHAFT, BEARING & SEAL

REMOVAL & INSTALLATION

See Figures 41 through 49.

➡This procedure requires the compression of the rear suspension to ride height. A drive-on hoist should be used. If a drive-on hoist is not used, screw-style under-hoist jack stands are required to compress the rear suspension, facilitating rear halfshaft removal.

➡Halfshaft inner and outer boots are not serviceable separately. Boot replacement requires entire shaft assembly replacement.

✳✳ WARNING

Unequal-length halfshafts are used. The right halfshaft is shorter than the left, and it is necessary to identify and tag halfshafts upon removal to ensure proper installation.

✳✳ WARNING

Never grasp halfshaft assembly by the inner or outer boots. Doing so may cause the boot to pucker or crease, reducing the service life of the boot and joint. Avoid over angulating or stroking the C/V joints when handling the halfshaft.

1. With vehicle in neutral, position and raise vehicle on hoist.

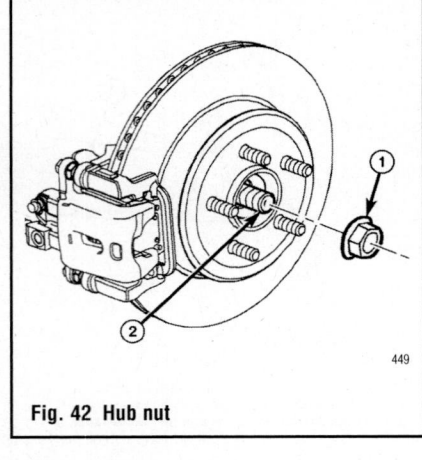

Fig. 42 Hub nut

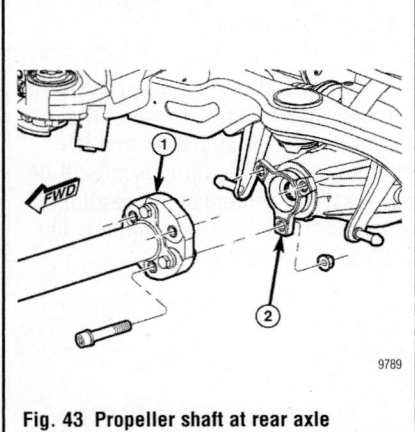

Fig. 43 Propeller shaft at rear axle

2. Using 14mm hex, remove axle drain plug and drain rear axle fluid into container suitable for fluid reuse.

3. Install the drain plug and torque to 37 ft. lbs. (50 Nm)

4. Remove the rear exhaust system.

5. Remove the wheel/tire assembly from sides that shaft is to be removed.

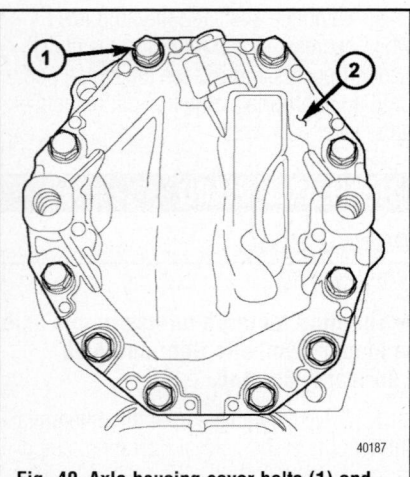

Fig. 40 Axle housing cover bolts (1) and cover (2)

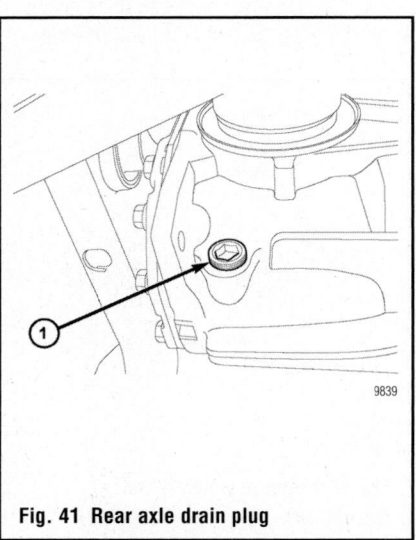

Fig. 41 Rear axle drain plug

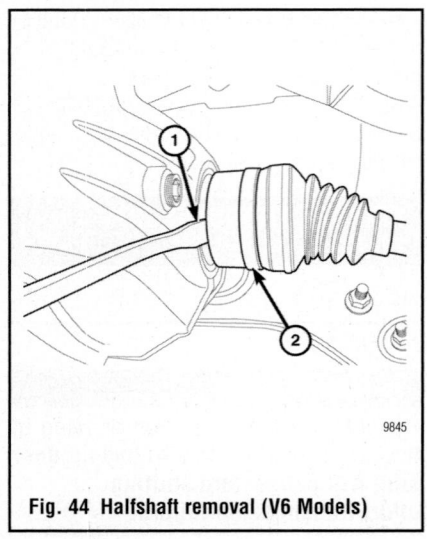

Fig. 44 Halfshaft removal (V6 Models)

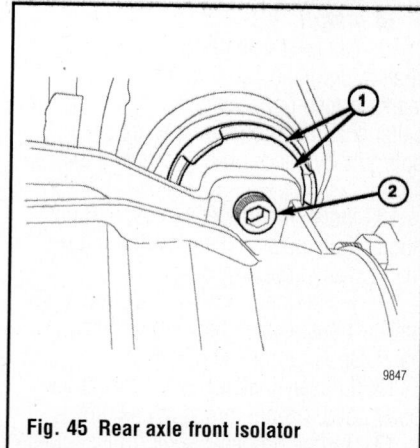

Fig. 45 Rear axle front isolator

6. Remove the wheel hub nut and discard.

7. Apply alignment index marks to the propeller shaft rubber coupler and axle flange.

8. Remove the three propeller shaft coupler-to-axle flange bolt/nuts.

9. Using suitable screwdriver, partially disengage halfshaft(s) from axle assembly.

10. If a drive-on hoist is used, position transmission jack (1) to rear axle assembly. If a drive-on hoist is not used, compress rear suspension using screw-style under-hoist jack stands, then position transmission jack to rear axle assembly.

11. Remove the rear axle forward mount isolator bolt/nut.

✳✳ WARNING

Access to rear axle-to-crossmember bolts is best achieved by use of short socket and a flexible-head ratchet.

12. Remove the two rear axle-to-crossmember bolts.

13. Carefully lower rear axle. While lowering axle, separate propeller shaft from axle and support with suitable rope or wire.

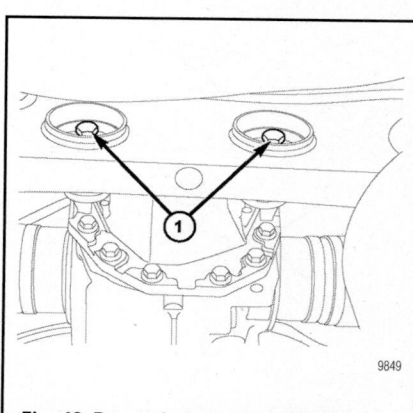

Fig. 46 Rear axle-to-crossmember bolts

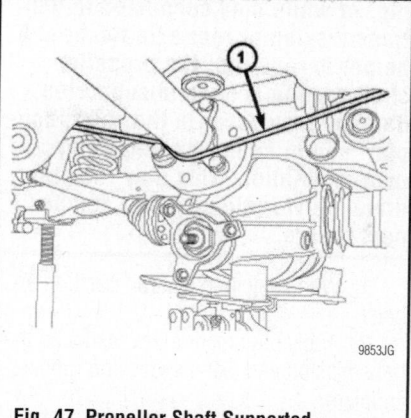

Fig. 47 Propeller Shaft Supported

✳✳ WARNING

Unequal-length halfshafts are used. The right halfshaft is shorter than the left, and it is necessary to identify and tag halfshafts upon removal to ensure proper installation.

14. Lower axle just enough to remove halfshafts one at a time. Shift axle assembly in one direction, compressing one halfshaft while removing the other. Use caution to protect axle seal and journal.

✳✳ WARNING

Never grasp halfshaft assembly by the inner or outer boots. Doing so may cause the boot to pucker or crease, reducing the service life of the boot and joint. Avoid over angulating or stroking the C/V joints when handling the halfshaft.

✳✳ WARNING

Use care while handling/storing halfshaft assembly. Damage to the slinger can result from improper handling. If slinger gets bent or

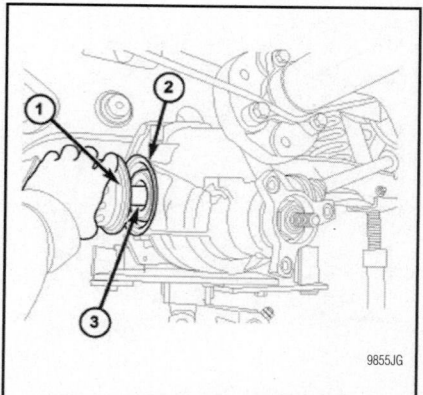

Fig. 48 Halfshaft removal/installation

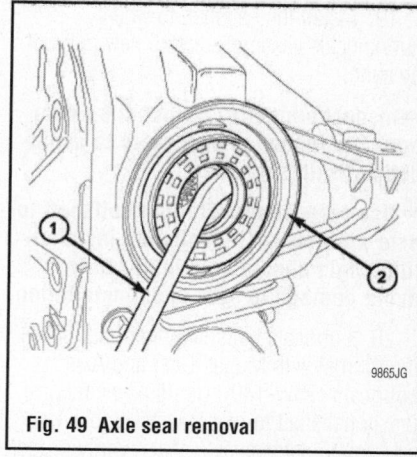

Fig. 49 Axle seal removal

damaged, straighten slinger to avoid contact with axle seal assembly.

15. Remove the halfshaft from hub. Remove and inspect rubber isolation washer (1). Discard washer if rubber surfaces are worn away. Repeat on other side if necessary.

16. Remove the axle seals using suitable screwdriver.

To install:

✳✳ WARNING

Halfshaft inner and outer boots are not serviceable separately. Boot replacement requires entire shaft assembly replacement.

✳✳ WARNING

Unequal-length halfshafts are used. The right halfshaft is shorter than the left, and it is necessary to identify and tag halfshafts upon removal to ensure proper installation.

✳✳ WARNING

Never grasp halfshaft assembly by the inner or outer boots. Doing so may cause the boot to pucker or crease, reducing the service life of the boot and joint. Avoid over angulating or stroking the C/V joints when handling the halfshaft.

17. Install the new axle seals using Installer Drift.

18. Install the halfshaft isolation washer. Washer is bi-directional, and can be installed in either direction.

➥**Always install a new hub nut. The original hub nut is one-time use only and should be discarded when removed.**

19. Install the halfshaft to wheel hub/knuckle assembly. Install new hub nut by hand.

➡ **Inspect slinger(s) for handling damage. Straighten as necessary to avoid contact with axle seal.**

➡ **Use care when installing halfshaft to axle assembly. The halfshaft installation angle should be minimized to avoid damage to seal upon installation.**

20. Lubricate halfshaft inner joint bearing journal with Mopar®Gear and Axle Lubricant (75W-140). Using new circlip(s), install halfshaft to rear axle assembly. Use care not to damage axle seals. Verify proper installation by pulling outward on joint by hand.

21. Raise rear axle assembly into position. Align propeller shaft index marks and start propeller shaft coupler-to-axle bolt/nuts by hand.

22. Install the two rear axle-to-crossmember bolts and torque to 162 ft. lbs. (220 Nm).

23. Install the rear axle front mount isolator and torque bolt/nut to 48 ft. lbs. (65 Nm).

24. Again verify halfshaft inner joints are fully engaged to axle assembly.

25. Remove the transmission jack.

26. If used, remove screw-type under-hoist jack stands.

27. Torque the propeller shaft coupler-to-axle flange bolt/nuts to 43 ft. lbs. (58 Nm).

28. Using a 14mm hex, remove rear axle fill plug. Fill the axle with Mopar®with 1.2L (1.3 qts) of 75W-140 Synthetic Gear AND Axle Lubricant.

29. Install the and torque fill plug and torque to 37 ft. lbs. (50 Nm)

30. Install the exhaust system.

31. Lower the vehicle. Torque the halfshaft hub nut to 157 ft. lbs. (213 Nm). Install wheel center cap.

32. Install the wheel/tire assembly and torque lug nuts to 110 ft. lbs. (150 Nm).

33. Lower the vehicle.

REAR DRIVESHAFT

REMOVAL & INSTALLATION

Automatic Non SRT8

See Figures 50 through 53.

✳✳ WARNING

Propeller shaft removal is a two-man operation. Never allow propeller shaft to hang from the center bear- ing, or while only connected to the transmission or rear axle flanges. A helper is required. If a propeller shaft section is hung unsupported, damage may occur to the shaft, coupler, and/or center bearing from over-angulation. This may result in driveline vibrations and/or component failure.

1. With vehicle in neutral, position on hoist.

2. Apply alignment index marks on the transmission and axle flanges and rubber couplers.

3. Remove the rear exhaust system.

4. Remove the heat shield retainers and remove the heat shield.

5. Remove the propeller shaft front coupler-to-flange bolts.

6. Remove the propeller shaft rear coupler-to-flange bolts.

7. Remove the center bearing mounting bolts.

8. With the aid of a helper, remove propeller shaft assembly.

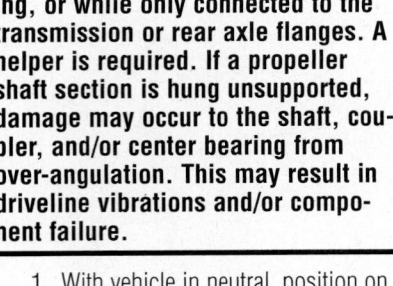

Fig. 50 Identifying the rubber couplers (1), axle flanges (2) and alignment index marks (3)

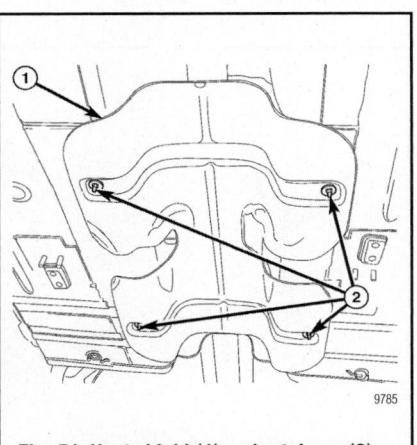

Fig. 51 Heat shield (1) and retainers (2)

To install:

9. Obtain a helper and install propeller shaft into position at axle. Align index marks placed upon removal. Install propeller shaft rear coupler-to-axle flange bolt/nuts by hand. Do not torque at this time.

10. Install the propeller shaft into position at transmission flange. Align index marks placed upon removal.

11. Install the propeller shaft front coupler-to-transmission flange bolt/nuts by hand. Do not torque at this time.

12. Loosely install center bearing-to-body bolts. Do not torque at this time.

13. Torque propeller shaft front coupler-to-transmission flange bolt/nuts to 50 ft. lbs. (68 Nm).

14. Torque propeller shaft rear coupler-to-axle flange bolt/nuts to 50 ft. lbs. (68 Nm)

➡ **It is necessary to compress rear suspension to ride height before securing center bearing to body. Failure to compress suspension may result in**

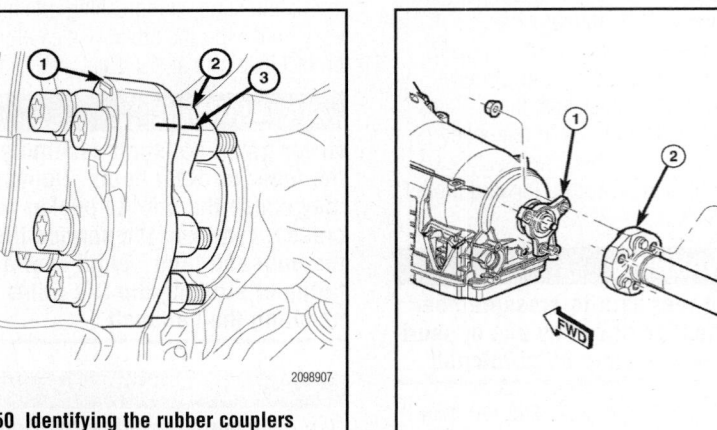

Fig. 52 Propeller shaft at transmission

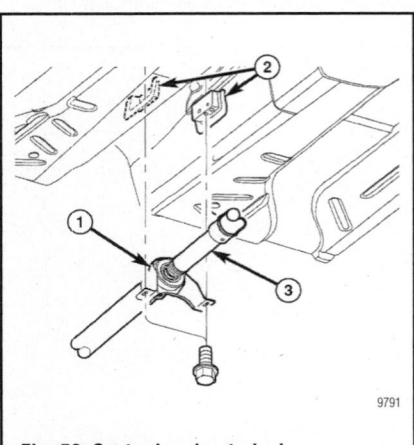

Fig. 53 Center bearing-to-body

objectionable noise and premature bearing wear.

15. Compress rear suspension with suitable jack stands.

16. Torque center bearing-to-body bolts to 20 ft. lbs. (27 Nm).

17. Install the heat shield.

18. Install the rear exhaust system.

Automatic SRT8

See Figures 51, 52, 54 and 55.

1. With vehicle in neutral, position on hoist.

2. Apply alignment index marks on the transmission and axle flanges and rubber couplers.

3. Remove the rear exhaust system.

4. Remove the heat shield retainers and remove the heat shield.

5. Remove the propeller shaft front coupler-to-flange bolts.

6. Remove the propeller shaft rear coupler-to-flange bolts.

7. Remove the three coupler-to-propeller shaft bolt/nuts. Note orientation and direction of components during disassembly. To avoid driveline vibration or damage, it is critical that all components are reinstalled in their original orientations

8. Separate coupler and damper (if equipped) from propeller shaft. Note orientation and direction of components during disassembly. To avoid driveline vibration or damage, it is critical that all components are reinstalled in their original orientations.

To install:

✳✳ WARNING

Propeller shaft installation is a two-man operation. Never allow propeller shaft to hang from the center bearing, or while only connected to the

transmission or rear axle flanges. A helper is required. If a propeller shaft section is hung unsupported, damage may occur to the shaft, coupler, and/or center bearing from over-angulation. This may result in driveline vibrations and/or component failure.

9. Install the coupler and damper (if equipped) in the same orientation noted before disassembly. To avoid driveline vibration or damage, it is critical that all components are reinstalled in their original orientations.

10. Install the three coupler-to-propeller shaft bolt/nuts in the same orientation noted before disassembly. To avoid driveline vibration or damage, it is critical that all components are reinstalled in their original orientations. Do not tighten at this time.

11. Obtain a helper and install propeller shaft into position at axle. Align index marks placed upon removal. Install propeller shaft rear coupler-to-axle flange bolt/nuts by hand. Do not tighten at this time.

12. Install the propeller shaft into position at transmission flange. Align index marks placed upon removal. Install propeller shaft front coupler-to-transmission flange bolt/nuts by hand. Do not tighten at this time.

13. Loosely install center bearing-to-body bolts. Do not torque at this time.

14. Torque propeller shaft front coupler-to-transmission flange bolt/nuts to 50 ft. lbs. (68 Nm).

15. Torque propeller shaft rear coupler-to-axle flange bolt/nuts to 89 ft. lbs. (122 Nm).

➡It is necessary to compress rear suspension to ride height before securing center bearing to body. Failure to

compress suspension may result in objectionable noise and premature bearing wear.

16. Compress rear suspension with suitable jack stands.

17. Torque center bearing-to-body bolts to 20 ft. lbs. (27 Nm).

18. Install the heat shield.

19. Install the rear exhaust system.

Manual Transmission

See Figures 51, 56 through 58.

✳✳ WARNING

Propeller shaft removal is a two-man operation. Never allow propeller shaft to hang from the center bearing, or while only connected to the transmission or rear axle flanges. A helper is required. If a propeller shaft section is hung unsupported, damage may occur to the shaft, coupler, and/or center bearing from over-angulation. This may result in driveline vibrations and/or component failure.

1. With vehicle in neutral, position on hoist.

2. Apply alignment index marks on the transmission and axle flanges and rubber couplers.

3. Remove the rear exhaust system.

4. Remove the heat shield retainers and remove the heat shield.

5. Remove the propeller shaft front coupler-to-flange bolts.

6. Remove the propeller shaft rear coupler-to-flange bolts.

7. Remove the center bearing mounting bolts.

8. With the aid of a helper, remove propeller shaft assembly.

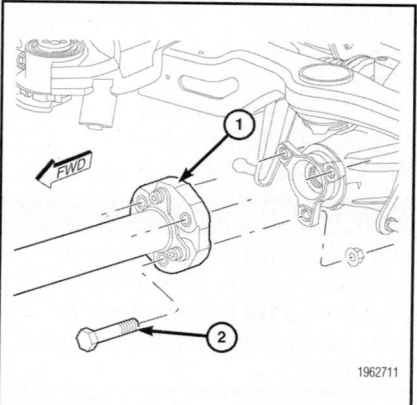

Fig. 54 Removing the propeller shaft rear coupler to flange bolts

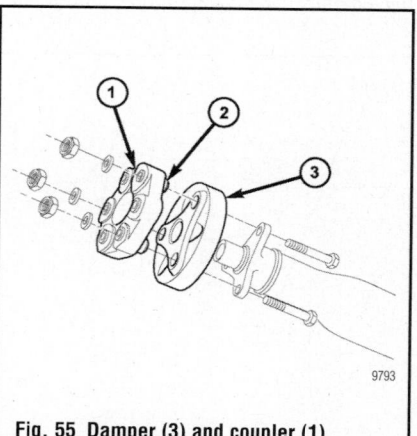

Fig. 55 Damper (3) and coupler (1) removal/installation

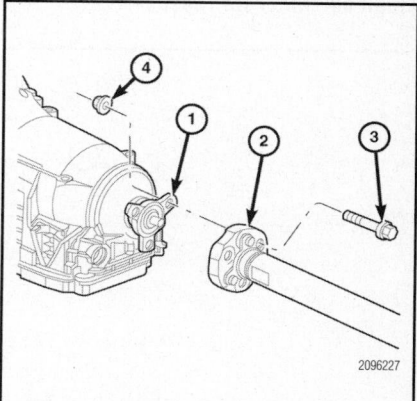

Fig. 56 Removing the propeller shaft front coupler to flange bolts

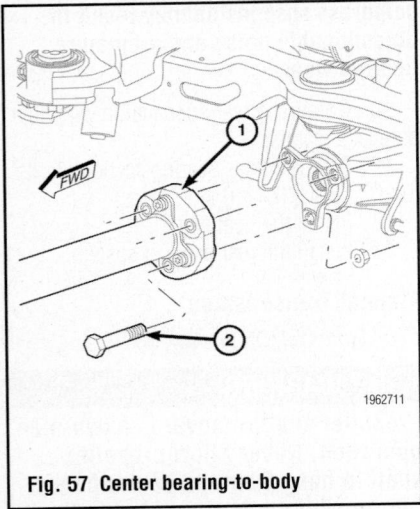

Fig. 57 Center bearing-to-body

To install:

9. Obtain a helper and install propeller shaft into position at axle. Align index marks placed upon removal. Install propeller shaft rear coupler-to-axle flange

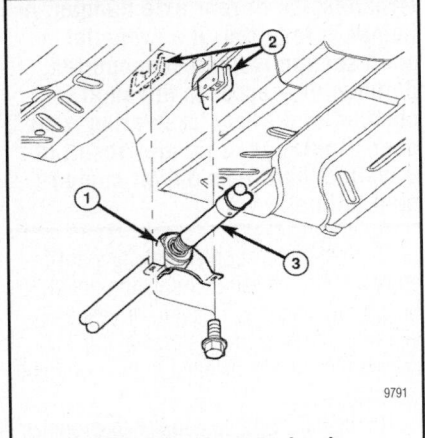

Fig. 58 Removing the center bearing mounting bolts

bolt/nuts by hand. Do not torque at this time.

10. Install the propeller shaft into position at transmission flange. Align index marks placed upon removal.

11. Install the propeller shaft front coupler-to-transmission flange bolt/nuts by hand. Do not torque at this time.

12. Loosely install center bearing-to-body bolts. Do not torque at this time.

13. Torque propeller shaft front coupler-to-transmission flange bolt/nuts to 67 ft. lbs. (91 Nm).

14. Torque propeller shaft rear coupler-to-axle flange bolt/nuts to 89 ft. lbs. (122 Nm).

➡It is necessary to compress rear suspension to ride height before securing center bearing to body. Failure to compress suspension may result in objectionable noise and premature bearing wear.

15. Compress rear suspension with suitable jack stands.

16. Torque center bearing-to-body bolts to 20 ft. lbs. (27 Nm).

17. Install the heat shield.

18. Install the rear exhaust system.

ENGINE COOLING

ENGINE COOLANT

DRAIN & REFILL PROCEDURE

Draining

See Figures 59 and 60.

> ✳✳ **CAUTION**
>
> **Do not remove cylinder block drain plugs or loosen radiator draincock with system hot and under pressure. Serious burns from coolant can occur.**

➡**Typical drain plug shown.**

➡**DO NOT WASTE reusable coolant. If solution is clean, drain coolant into a clean container for reuse.**

1. Remove the radiator pressure cap.

2. Raise and secure vehicle.

3. If equipped, remove the underbody splash shield.

4. Loosen radiator petcock.

5. Drain coolant into a clean container.

6. If necessary, to perform a complete coolant drain of the engine, remove the drain plug from the engine block.

Filling

The use of aluminum cylinder blocks, cylinder heads and water pumps requires special corrosion protection. In order to maintain the required protection for these components and cooling system performance, only use the appropriate fluid when servicing the vehicle. This coolant offers the best engine cooling without corrosion when mixed with 50% distilled water to obtain a freeze point of -35°F (-37°C). If it loses color or becomes contaminated, drain, flush, and replace with fresh properly mixed coolant solution.

> ✳✳ **CAUTION**
>
> **Make sure engine cooling system is cool before removing pressure cap or any hose. Severe personal injury may result from escaping hot coolant. The cooling system is pressurized when hot.**

➡**Cooling system fill procedure is critical to overall cooling system performance.**

1. Close radiator draincock. Hand tighten only.

2. Install the engine block drain plugs, if removed. Coat the threads with Mopar®Thread Sealant with Teflon.

> ✳✳ **CAUTION**
>
> **When installing drain hose to air bleed valve, route hose away from accessory drive belts, accessory drive pulleys, and electric cooling fan motors.**

➡**It may be necessary to install a bleed fitting on the 5.7L engine.**

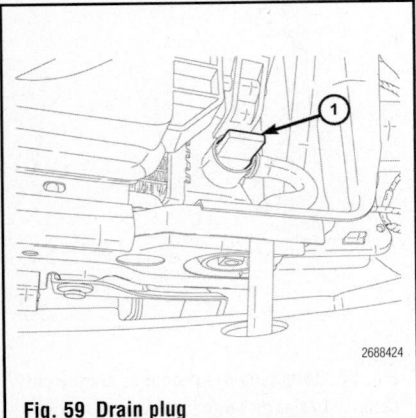

Fig. 59 Drain plug

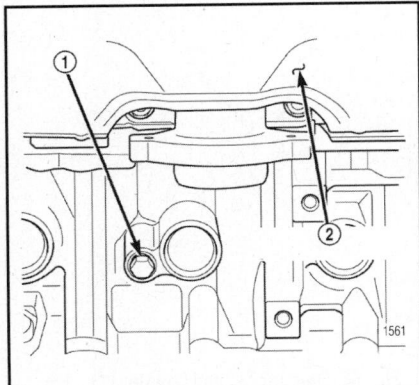

Fig. 60 Drain plug on the engine block

3. Attach a 4—6 ft. (1.5 - 2 m) long 1/4 inch. (6.35 mm) ID clear hose to bleeder fitting

    a. Bleed Valve Location (2.7L): Located on the water outlet connector at the front of engine .

    b. Bleed Valve Location (3.5L): Located on the lower intake manifold, left of center and below the upper intake plenum.

    c. Plug Location (5.7L/6.1L): Located on the front of the water outlet housing at the front of engine.

4. Route hose away from the accessory drive belt, drive pulleys and electric cooling fan. Place the other end of hose into a clean container. The hose will prevent coolant from contacting the accessory drive belt when bleeding the system during the refilling operation.

➡**It is imperative that the cooling system air bleed valve be opened before any coolant is added to the cooling system. Failure to open the bleed valve first will result in an incomplete fill of the system.**

5. 5.7L/6.1L ENGINE - Install a threaded and barbed fitting (1/4 - 18 npt) into water pump housing.

6. Attach tool funnel, filling aid funnel to pressure bottle filler neck.

7. Using hose pinch-off pliers, pinch overflow hose that connects between the two chambers of the coolant bottle.

8. Open bleed fitting.

✳✳ WARNING

Do not mix coolants. If coolant is used other than specified, a reduction in corrosion protection will occur.

9. Pour the antifreeze mixture into the larger section of Filling Aid Funnel (the smaller section of funnel is to allow air to escape).

10. Slowly fill the cooling system until a steady stream of coolant flows from the hose attached to the bleed valve.

11. Close the bleed valve and continue filling system to the top of the tool funnel, filling aid funnel.

12. Remove the pinch-off pliers from overflow hose.

13. Allow the coolant in Filling Funnel to drain into overflow chamber of the pressure bottle.

14. Remove the tool funnel, filling aid funnel. Install cap on coolant pressure bottle.

15. Remove the hose from bleed valve.

16. 5.7L/6.1L ENGINE - Install fitting into thermostat housing. Coat the threads with Mopar®Thread Sealant with Teflon.

17. Start engine and run at 1500—2000 RPM for 30 minutes.

➡**The engine cooling system will push any remaining air into the coolant bottle within about an hour of normal driving. As a result, a drop in coolant level in the pressure bottle may occur. If the engine cooling system overheats and pushes coolant into the overflow side of the coolant bottle, this coolant will be sucked back into the cooling system ONLY IF THE PRESSURE CAP IS LEFT ON THE BOTTLE. Removing the pressure cap breaks the vacuum path between the two bottle sections and the coolant will not return to cooling system.**

18. Shut off engine allow it to cool down for 30 minutes. This permits coolant to be drawn into the pressure chamber.

19. With engine COLD, observe coolant level in pressure chamber. Coolant level should be within MIN and MAX marks. Adjust coolant level as necessary.

➡**The coolant bottle has two chambers. Coolant will normally only be in the inboard of the two. The outboard chamber is only to recover coolant in the event of an overheat or after a recent service fill.**

BLEEDING

Refer to FILLING.

FLUSHING

REVERSE FLUSHING

Reverse flushing of cooling system is the forcing of water through the cooling system. This is done using air pressure in the opposite direction of normal coolant flow. It is usually only necessary with very dirty systems with evidence of partial plugging.

REVERSE FLUSHING RADIATOR

Disconnect radiator hoses from radiator inlet and outlet. Attach a section of radiator hose to radiator bottom outlet fitting and insert flushing gun. Connect a water supply hose and air supply hose to flushing gun.

✳✳ WARNING

Internal radiator pressure must not exceed 20 psi (138 kPa) as damage to radiator may result.

Allow radiator to fill with water. When radiator is filled, apply air in short blasts. Allow radiator to refill between blasts. Continue this reverse flushing until clean water flows out through rear of radiator cooling tube passages. Have radiator cleaned more extensively by a radiator repair shop.

REVERSE FLUSHING ENGINE

Drain cooling system. Remove thermostat housing and thermostat. Install thermostat housing. Disconnect radiator upper hose from radiator and attach flushing gun to hose. Disconnect radiator lower hose from water pump and attach a lead-away hose to water pump inlet fitting.

✳✳ WARNING

On vehicles equipped with a heater water control valve, be sure heater control valve is closed (heat off). This will prevent coolant flow with scale and other deposits from entering heater core.

Connect water supply hose and air supply hose to flushing gun. Allow engine to fill with water. When engine is filled, apply air in short blasts, allowing system to fill between air blasts. Continue until clean water flows through the lead away hose.

Remove lead away hose, flushing gun, water supply hose and air supply hose. Remove thermostat housing and install thermostat. Install thermostat housing with a replacement gasket. Connect radiator hoses. Refill cooling system with correct antifreeze/water mixture.

ENGINE FAN

REMOVAL & INSTALLATION

See Figure 61.

1. Disconnect negative battery cable.
2. Partially drain cooling system.
3. Remove the air filter housing assembly.

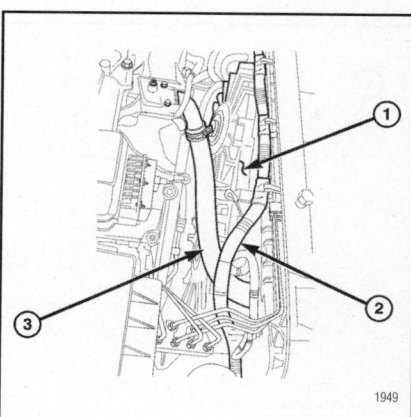

1949

Fig. 61 Radiator fan assembly (1), electrical connector (2) and upper radiator hose (3)

4. Remove the upper radiator hose.

5. Disconnect the cooling fan electrical connector.

6. Remove the cooling fan mounting bolts.

7. Remove the radiator cooling fan assembly from vehicle.

8. Remove the fan blade from the fan motor.

9. Remove the fan motor from cooling fan shroud.

To install:

10. Position fan motor on radiator fan shroud.

11. Install the mounting bolts. Tighten to 89 inch lbs. (10 Nm).

12. Position fan blade on motor and install retaining nut. Tighten nut to 18.5 ft. lbs. (25 Nm).

13. Position radiator cooling fan assembly in vehicle.

14. Install the cooling fan mounting bolts. Tighten to 50 inch lbs. (6 Nm).

15. Connect cooling fan electrical connector.

16. Install the upper radiator hose.

17. Install the air filter housing.

18. Fill the cooling system.

19. Operate engine until it reaches normal operating temperature. Check cooling system and automatic transmission for correct fluid levels.

RADIATOR

REMOVAL & INSTALLATION

See Figures 62 and 63.

1. Disconnect negative battery cable.

2. Drain cooling system.

3. Remove the upper radiator hose.

4. Remove the upper radiator closure panels.

5. Remove the radiator fan assembly.

6. Raise vehicle.

7. Remove the lower splash shield.

8. Remove the lower radiator hose.

9. Remove the lower condenser mount bolts.

10. Carefully lower the vehicle.

11. Remove the upper radiator hose.

> **✳✳ WARNING**
>
> **Bolts are installed with threadlocker. Use hand tools to remove the upper radiator mounting bolts.**

12. Remove the upper radiator mounting brackets and bolts.

13. Remove the upper condenser mounting bolts.

14. Separate condenser assembly from radiator.

15. Tilt radiator toward engine and remove radiator from vehicle.

To install:

16. Position the radiator into engine compartment. Seat the radiator assembly lower rubber isolators into the mounting holes in radiator lower support.

17. Install the radiator mounting bracket and bolts. Tighten to 9 ft. lbs. (12 Nm).

18. Position the condenser on radiator and install upper mounting bolts. Tighten bolts to 50 inch lbs. (6 Nm).

19. Raise the vehicle.

20. Install the lower condenser mounting bolts. Tighten bolts to 88 inch lbs. (10 Nm).

21. Install the lower radiator hose and clamp.

22. Lower the vehicle.

23. Install the radiator fan.

24. Install the upper radiator upper hose. Align hose so it does not interfere with the accessory drive belt or engine. Position

hose clamp so it will not interfere with the hood.

25. Install the upper radiator closure panels.

26. Connect the negative cable.

27. Fill the cooling system with coolant.

28. Operate the engine until it reaches normal operating temperature. Check the cooling system and automatic transmission for the correct fluid levels.

THERMOSTAT

REMOVAL & INSTALLATION

3.5L Engine

See Figure 64.

1. Disconnect negative battery cable.

2. Raise vehicle on hoist.

3. Remove the belly pan.

4. Drain cooling system.

5. Lower vehicle on hoist.

6. Remove the air box assembly.

7. Disconnect lower radiator hose from thermostat housing.

8. Remove the thermostat housing bolts.

9. Remove the thermostat housing, thermostat, and gasket.

➡**The OEM thermostat is staked in place at the factory. To ensure proper seating of replacement thermostat, carefully remove the bulged metal from the thermostat housing using a suitable hand held grinder. It is not necessary to restake the replacement thermostat into the thermostat housing.**

10. Clean gasket surfaces.

To install:

11. Position gasket on thermostat and housing.

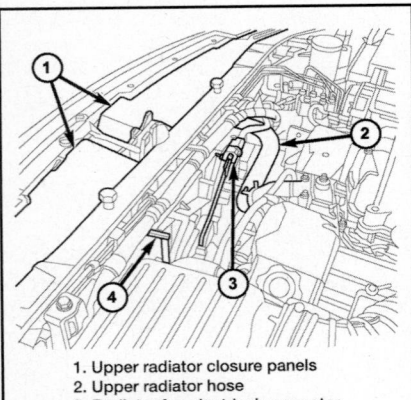

1. Upper radiator closure panels
2. Upper radiator hose
3. Radiator fan electrical connector
4. Radiator fan assembly

1867

Fig. 62 Radiator fan assembly

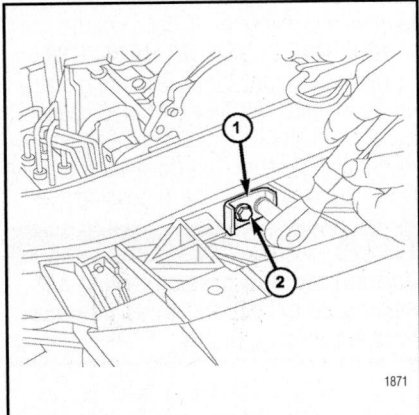

1871

Fig. 63 Radiator mounting bracket (1) and bolts (2)

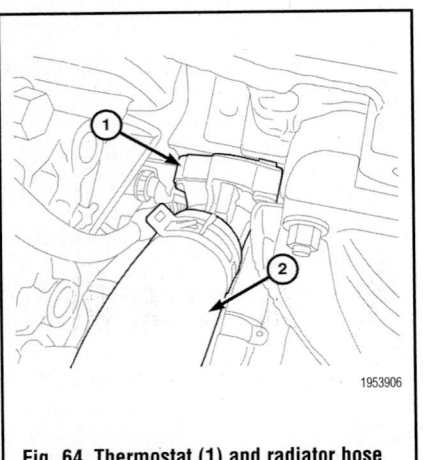

1953906

Fig. 64 Thermostat (1) and radiator hose (2) 3.5L engine

12. Install the thermostat housing, gasket and mounting bolts onto block. Tighten attaching bolts to 9 ft. lbs. (12 Nm).

13. Install the radiator hose.

14. Install the air box assembly.

15. Fill cooling system.

16. Raise vehicle on hoist.

17. Install the belly pan.

18. Connect negative battery cable.

5.7L Engine

See Figure 65.

1. Disconnect the negative battery cable.

2. Drain the cooling system until the coolant level is below the thermostat.

3. Remove the radiator hose from the thermostat housing.

4. Remove the thermostat housing mounting bolts, thermostat housing, and thermostat.

To install:

5. Clean the mating areas of the intake manifold and thermostat housing.

6. Install the thermostat into the recessed machined groove on the front cover.

7. Install the housing-to-front cover bolts. Tighten the bolts to 17 ft. lbs. (23 Nm).

8. Install the radiator upper hose to the thermostat housing.

9. Fill the cooling system.

10. Connect the negative battery cable.

11. Start and warm the engine. Check for leaks.

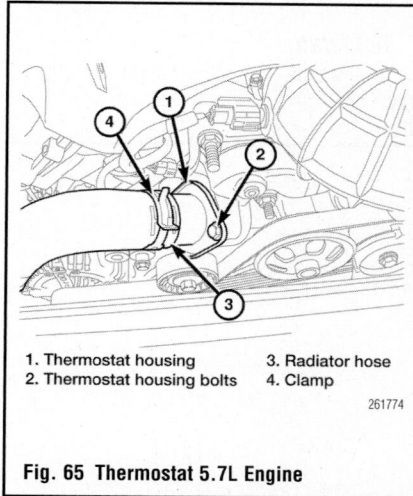

1. Thermostat housing   3. Radiator hose
2. Thermostat housing bolts   4. Clamp

261774

Fig. 65 Thermostat 5.7L Engine

6.1L Engine

See Figure 66.

1. Disconnect negative battery cable at battery.

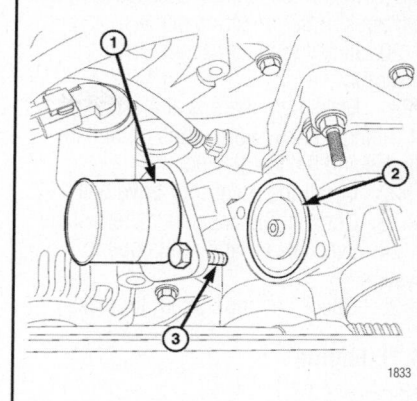

Fig. 66 Thermostat (2), housing (1) and bolt (3)—6.1L Engine

2. Drain cooling system.

3. Remove the radiator hose at thermostat housing.

➡️**Thermostat O-ring is part of thermostat and is not serviced separately.**

4. Remove the thermostat housing mounting bolts, thermostat housing and thermostat.

To install:

5. Clean mating areas of timing chain cover and thermostat housing.

➡️**Install thermostat with the bleed valve located at the 12 o'clock position.**

6. Install the thermostat (spring side down) into recessed machined groove on timing chain cover with bleed valve located at the 12 o'clock position.

7. Position thermostat housing on timing chain cover.

❄️ WARNING

Thermostat housing must be tightened evenly and thermostat must be centered into recessed groove in timing chain cover. If not, it may result in a cracked thermostat housing, damaged timing chain cover threads or coolant leaks.

8. Install the two housing-to-timing chain cover bolts. Tighten bolts to 9 ft. lbs. (13 Nm) torque.

9. Install the lower radiator hose on thermostat housing.

10. Carefully lower the vehicle.

11. Fill cooling system.

12. Connect negative battery cable to battery.

13. Start and warm the engine. Check for leaks.

WATER PUMP

REMOVAL & INSTALLATION

3.5L Engine

The water pump on all models can be replaced without discharging the air conditioning system.

1. Drain cooling system.

2. Remove the accessory drive belts.

3. Remove the engine timing belt.

4. Remove the water pump mounting bolts. Note position of longer bolts for proper re-installation.

5. Remove the water pump body from engine.

To install:

6. Clean all O-ring surfaces on front cover.

7. Position water pump and O-ring to engine.

8. Install the mounting bolts. Tighten to 9 ft. lbs. (12 Nm).

9. Install the timing belt.

10. Install the accessory drive belts.

11. Evacuate air and refill cooling system.

12. Check cooling system for leaks.

5.7L Engine

See Figure 67.

1. Disconnect the negative battery cable.

2. Drain the cooling system.

3. Remove the fan/viscous fan drive assembly from the water pump. Do not attempt to remove the fan/viscous fan drive assembly from vehicle at this time.

4. If the water pump is being replaced, do not unbolt the fan blade assembly from the thermal viscous fan drive.

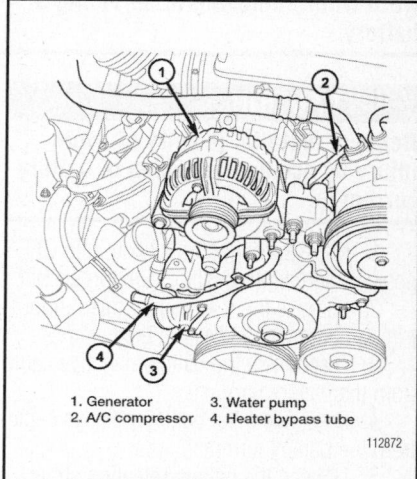

1. Generator   3. Water pump
2. A/C compressor   4. Heater bypass tube

112872

Fig. 67 Water pump—5.7L Engine

5. Remove the two fan shroud-to-radiator screws. Disconnect the coolant overflow hose, windshield washer fluid hose and washer pump electrical connector.

6. Remove the fan shroud and the fan blade/viscous fan drive assembly from the vehicle.

7. Remove the A/C compressor and generator brace.

8. Remove the idler pulleys.

9. Remove the belt tensioner assembly.

10. Remove the upper and lower radiator hoses.

11. Remove the heater hoses.

12. Remove the water pump mounting bolts and remove the pump.

To install:

13. Install the water pump and the mounting bolts. Tighten mounting bolts to 18 ft. lbs. (24 Nm).

14. Install the heater hoses.

15. Install the upper and lower radiator hoses.

16. Install the accessory drive belt tensioner assembly.

17. Install the idler pulleys and mounting bolts. Tighten the bolts to 40 ft. lbs. (54 Nm).

18. Install the A/C compressor and the alternator brace. Tighten bolt and nuts to 21 ft. lbs. (28 Nm).

19. Install the fan shroud assembly and two fan shroud mounting screws.

20. Install the fan/viscous drive assembly.

21. Make sure there is at least 25 mm (1.0 inches) between the tips of the fan blades and the fan shroud.

22. Install the accessory drive belt.

23. Connect the negative battery cable.

24. Evacuate air and refill cooling system.

25. Check cooling system for leaks.

6.1L Engine

See Figure 68.

1. Disconnect negative battery cable.

2. Drain cooling system.

3. Remove the radiator fan assembly.

4. Remove the accessory drive belt.

5. Remove the thermostat.

➡**The water pump mounting bolts are different lengths. Note the location of the water pump mounting bolts.**

6. Remove the water pump mounting bolts and remove water pump.

To install:

7. Install the water pump and mounting bolts. Tighten mounting bolts to 20 ft. lbs. (28 Nm).

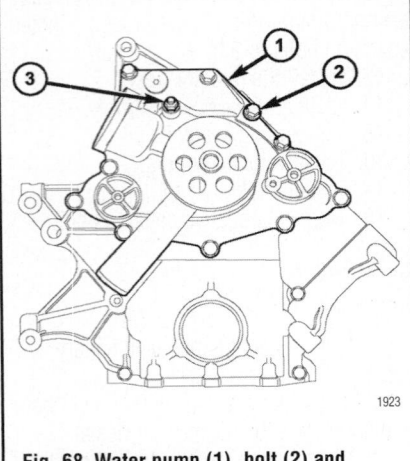

Fig. 68 Water pump (1), bolt (2) and double ended bolt (3)—6.1L Engine

8. Make sure double ended bolt is in the proper location. Tighten double ended bolt to 20 ft. lbs. (28 Nm).

9. Install the thermostat.

10. Install the accessory drive belt.

11. Install the radiator fan assembly.

12. Connect negative battery cable.

13. Evacuate air and refill cooling system.

14. Check cooling system for leaks.

ENGINE ELECTRICAL

BATTERY

REMOVAL & INSTALLATION

See Figures 69 and 70.

✳✳ CAUTION

A suitable pair of heavy duty rubber gloves and safety glasses should be worn when removing or servicing a battery.

✳✳ CAUTION

Remove metallic jewelry to avoid injury by accidental arcing of battery current.

1. Make sure ignition switch is in OFF position and all accessories are turned OFF.

2. Remove the rear compartment floor, trim panel to gain access to the battery.

3. Disconnect the battery negative cable from the battery terminal.

4. Disconnect the battery positive cable from the battery terminal.

5. Unlatch the battery retention strap.

✳✳ WARNING

Use care when disconnecting the battery vent tube from the battery. The vent tube nipple is made of plastic and is easily damaged if not disconnected properly.

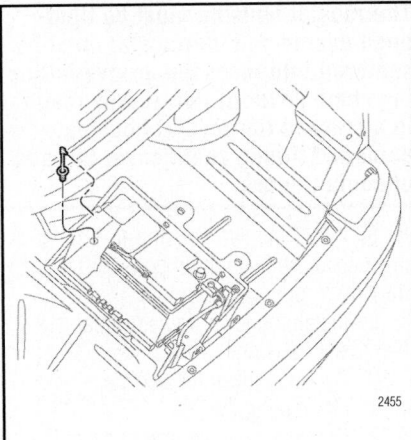

Fig. 69 Disconnecting the battery vent tube

BATTERY SYSTEM

6. Gently disconnect the battery vent tube from the battery nipple.

7. Remove the battery hold down clamp and remove the battery from the vehicle.

To install:

8. Position the battery in the battery tray.

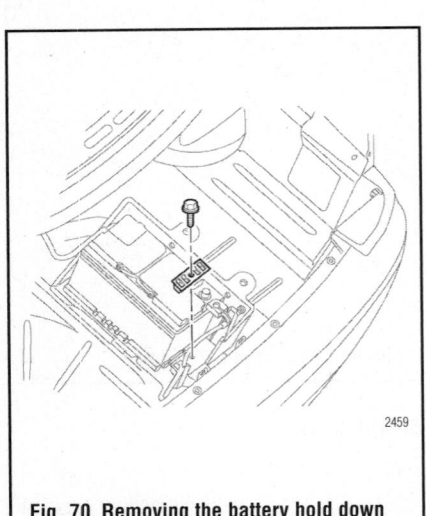

Fig. 70 Removing the battery hold down clamp

9. Install the battery hold down clamp and bolt. Torque the bolt to 35 inch lbs. (4 Nm).

✳✳ WARNING

Use care when connecting the battery vent tube to the battery. The vent tube nipple is made of plastic and is easily damaged if not connected properly.

10. Gently connect the battery vent tube to the battery nipple.
11. Latch the battery retention strap.
12. Connect the battery positive cable.
13. Connect the battery negative cable. Follow the battery reconnection procedure.
14. Install the rear compartment floor trim panel.

BATTERY RECONNECT/RELEARN PROCEDURE

➡ **This reconnection procedure is to be performed anytime the battery has been disconnected.**

1. Connect the battery negative cable to the battery post and tighten the clamp nut.
2. Install the rear compartment floor trim panel.

✳✳ WARNING

Once the battery has been connected, review and perform the following information as applicable.

AUTO UP FRONT WINDOW

If the vehicle is equipped with the auto-up front window feature, once the battery is reconnected the door module needs to be calibrated. The door module requires calibration anytime the battery or door module has been disconnected for any length of time. To calibrate, perform the following:

3. Turn the Ignition to the Run position.
4. Regardless of current window position, move the driver side front window upward until the window stalls in the full up position. Allow the window motor to stall for at least 2 seconds before releasing the switch.
5. Move the driver side front window downward until the window stalls in the full down position. Allow the window motor to stall for at least 2 seconds before releasing the switch.
6. Move the driver side front window upward until the window stalls in the full up position. Allow the window motor to stall for at least 2 second before releasing the switch.
7. Repeat steps 2, 3 and 4 for the passenger side front window.

8. Verify the windows are properly calibrated by operating the express down and up features on the windows. Repeat this procedure if the calibration failed. If unable to properly calibrate after the second attempt, check the Driver's Door Module (DDM) and Passenger's Door Module (PDM) for Diagnostic Trouble Codes (DTCs) and correct as required.

ELECTRONIC STABILITY PROGRAM (ESP)

If the vehicle is equipped with ESP, once the battery is reconnected, the Steering Angle Sensor (SAS) within the Antilock Brake Module (ABM) needs to be calibrated. The SAS requires calibration (initialization) using the scan tool anytime the battery or an ABS (ESP) component has been disconnected for any length of time. If the SAS is not calibrated following battery reconnection, the ESP/BAS indicator lamp will flash continuously with no DTCs.

9. To calibrate (initialize), perform the following:
   a. Position the front wheels straight ahead and center the steering wheel.
   b. Connect the scan tool to the vehicle.
   c. Follow the directions on the scan tool.

ENGINE ELECTRICAL

ALTERNATOR

REMOVAL & INSTALLATION

3.5L Engine

See Figures 71 through 74.

✳✳ CAUTION

Disconnect negative cable from battery before removing battery output wire (b+ wire) from generator. Failure to do so can result in injury or damage to electrical system.

1. Disconnect and isolate negative battery cable at battery.
2. Remove the generator drive belt.
3. Remove the upper most mounting bolt from generator.
4. Remove the generator bracket bolt and remove bracket.
5. Unsnap plastic protective cover from B+ mounting stud.
6. Remove the B+ terminal mounting nut and B+ terminal at rear of generator.

7. Disconnect field wire electrical connector by pushing on connector tab.
8. Raise and safely support the vehicle.
9. Remove the middle splash shield.

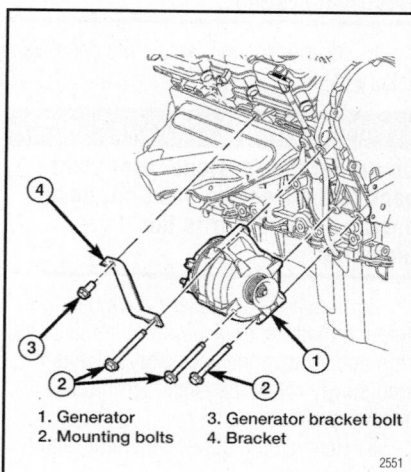

1. Generator
2. Mounting bolts
3. Generator bracket bolt
4. Bracket

2551

Fig. 71 Removing the generator (1) bracket and lower mounting bolts (2)

CHARGING SYSTEM

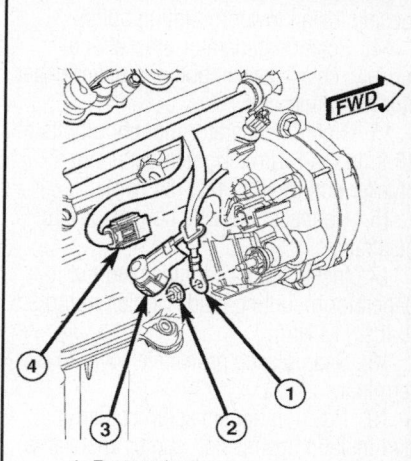

1. B+ terminal
2. B+ terminal mounting nut
3. Plastic protective cover
4. Field wire electrical connector

2543

Fig. 72 Disconnecting the alternator electrical connectors

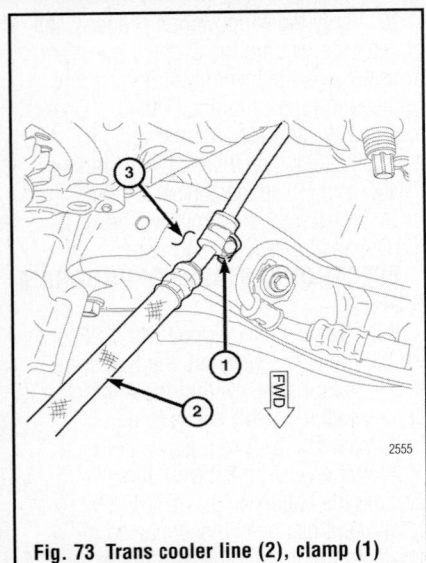

Fig. 73 Trans cooler line (2), clamp (1) and crossmember (3)

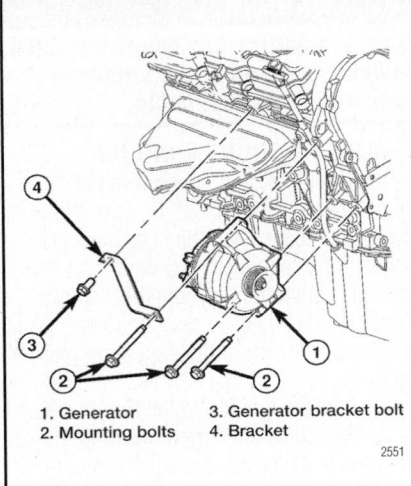

1. Generator
2. Mounting bolts
3. Generator bracket bolt
4. Bracket

Fig. 74 Removing the generator (1) bracket and lower mounting bolts (2)

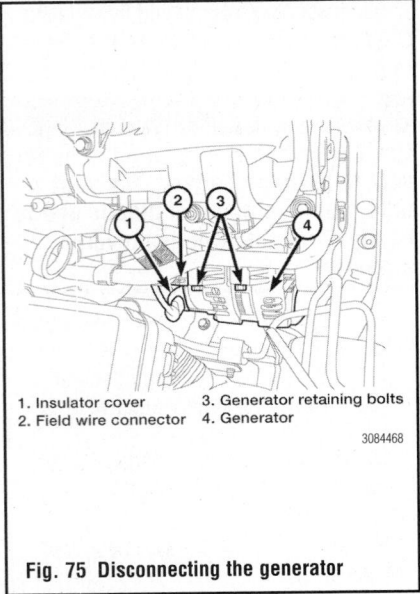

1. Insulator cover
2. Field wire connector
3. Generator retaining bolts
4. Generator

Fig. 75 Disconnecting the generator

10. Remove the bolt from transmission cooler line clamp at right crossmember and reposition transmission cooler line.

11. Remove the lower mounting bolts from generator.

12. Remove the generator from engine compartment.

To install:

➡ **Position generator, bracket and all bolts to engine compartment. Hand tightening all fasteners. Then torque all fasteners to specifications.**

13. Position generator to engine and loosely install lower mounting bolts.

14. Position generator bracket and loosely install bracket bolt and upper generator mounting bolt.

15. Tighten generator mounting bolts to 48 ft. lbs. (65 Nm). Tighten generator bracket bolt to 40 ft. lbs. (54 Nm).

16. Connect field wire connector into generator.

17. Install the B+ terminal and nut to generator mounting stud. Tighten nut to 9.5 ft. lbs. (13 Nm).

18. Snap plastic protective cover to B+ terminal.

19. Position transmission cooler line and install transmission cooler line clamp bolt to right crossmember.

20. Install the middle splash shield.

21. Carefully lower the vehicle.

✴✴ WARNING

When installing a serpentine accessory drive belt, the belt MUST be routed correctly. **The water pump will be rotating in the wrong direction if the belt is installed incorrectly, causing the engine to overheat.**

22. Install the drive belt.

23. Connect the negative battery cable and tighten nut to 45 inch lbs. (5 Nm).

3.6L Engine

See Figure 75 and 76.

✴✴ CAUTION

Disconnect the negative battery cable before removing the battery output wire (B+ wire) from the generator. Failure to do so can result in injury or damage the electrical system.

1. Disconnect and isolate the negative battery cable.

✴✴ WARNING

Do not let the tensioner arm snap back to the freearm position, sever damage may occur to the tensioner.

2. Rotate the accessory drive belt tensioner counterclockwise until it contacts it's stop and remove the accessory drive belt, then slowly rotate the tensioner into the freearm position.

3. Remove the upper generator retaining bolts.

4. Remove the insulator cover from the B+ output terminal at the rear of the generator.

5. Remove the B+ terminal retaining nut at the rear of the generator and remove the B+ terminal.

6. Depress the field wire connector tab at the rear of the generator and disconnect the field wire connector.

7. Raise and support the vehicle.

8. Remove the belly pan retainers and remove the belly pan.

9. Remove the lower generator retaining bolt.

10. Remove the generator from below the engine compartment.

To install:

➡ **Position the generator, install all bolts to engine finger tight, then tighten fasteners to specification.**

11. Position the generator to the engine and install the lower retaining bolt finger tight.

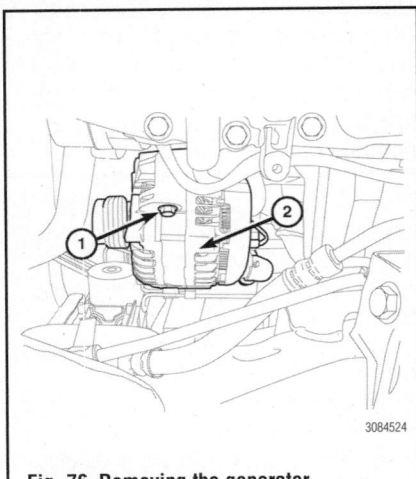

Fig. 76 Removing the generator

12. Lower the vehicle.

13. Install the upper generator retaining bolts and tighten to 18 ft. lbs. (25 Nm).

14. Snap the field wire connector into the rear of the generator.

15. Position the generator B+ terminal eyelet to the generator output stud, install the retaining nut and tighten to 10 ft. lbs. (13 Nm).

16. Install the insulator cover onto the B+ output terminal.

17. Raise and support the vehicle.

18. Tighten the lower generator retaining bolt to 18 ft. lbs. (25 Nm).

19. Position the belly pan and install the belly pan retainers.

20. Lower the vehicle.

✳✳ WARNING

When installing a serpentine accessory drive belt, the belt MUST be routed correctly. The water pump will be rotating in the wrong direction if the belt is installed incorrectly, causing the engine to overheat.

✳✳ WARNING

Do not let the tensioner arm snap back to the freearm position, sever damage may occur to the tensioner.

21. Rotate the accessory drive belt tensioner counterclockwise until it contacts the stop and install the accessory drive belt onto the pulleys and slowly release the tensioner.

22. Connect the negative battery cable and tighten nut to 45 inch lbs. (5 Nm).

5.7L Engine

See Figures 73, 77 and 78.

✳✳ CAUTION

Disconnect the negative battery cable before removing the battery output wire (B+ wire) from the generator. Failure to do so can result in injury or damage the electrical system.

1. Disconnect and isolate negative battery cable at battery.

2. Remove the generator drive belt.

3. Remove the upper generator mounting bolt.

4. Raise and safely support the vehicle.

5. Remove the lower splash shield.

6. Remove the bolt from transmission cooler line clamp at right crossmember and reposition transmission cooler line.

7. Remove the generator support bracket nut and bolt. Remove support bracket.

8. Unsnap plastic insulator cap from B+ output terminal.

9. Remove the B+ terminal mounting nut at rear of generator. Disconnect terminal from generator.

10. Disconnect field wire connector at rear of generator by pushing on connector tab.

11. Remove the lower generator mounting bolt.

12. Remove the generator from vehicle.

To install:

13. Position generator to engine and loosely install 2 mounting bolts.

14. Position support bracket to generator and loosely install bolt and nut.

15. Tighten generator mounting bolts to 48 ft. lbs. (65 Nm).

16. Tighten bracket nut to 20.5 ft. lbs. (28 Nm).

17. Snap field wire connector into rear of generator.

18. Install the B+ terminal eyelet to generator output stud. Tighten nut to 9.5 ft. lbs. (13 Nm).

19. Position transmission cooler line and install transmission cooler line clamp bolt to right crossmember.

20. Install the lower splash shield.

21. Carefully lower the vehicle.

✳✳ WARNING

When installing a serpentine accessory drive belt, the belt MUST be routed correctly. The water pump may be rotating in the wrong direction if the belt is installed incorrectly, causing the engine to overheat.

22. Install the generator drive belt.

23. Connect the negative battery cable and tighten nut to 48 inch lbs. (5 Nm).

6.1L Engine

See Figures 73, 77, 79 and 80.

✳✳ CAUTION

Disconnect negative cable from battery before removing battery output wire (b+ wire) from generator. Failure to do so can result in injury or damage to electrical system.

1. Disconnect and isolate the negative battery cable at battery.

2. Remove the generator drive belt.

3. Remove the upper generator mounting bolt.

4. Raise and support the vehicle.

5. Remove the lower splash shield.

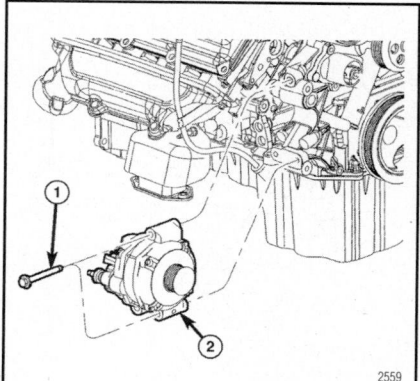

Fig. 77 Identifying the generator mounting bolts

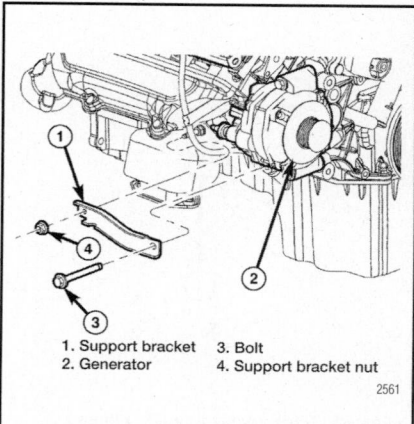

1. Support bracket
2. Generator
3. Bolt
4. Support bracket nut

Fig. 78 Generator support bracket

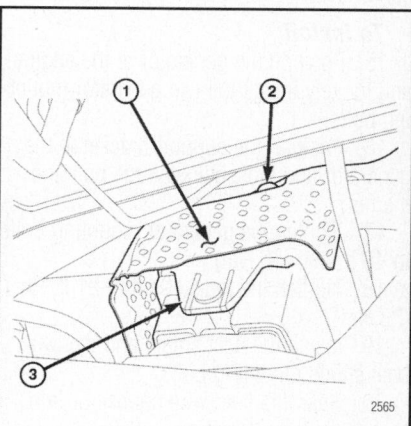

Fig. 79 Heat shield (1), heat shield mounting bolts (2) and right engine mount (3)

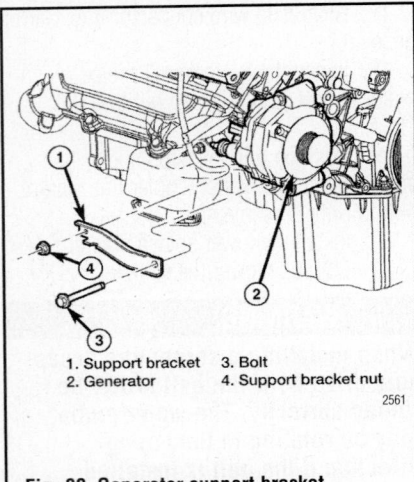

1. Support bracket 3. Bolt
2. Generator 4. Support bracket nut

Fig. 80 Generator support bracket

6. Remove the bolt from transmission cooler line clamp at right the crossmember and reposition the transmission cooler line.

7. A heat shield is used over the right engine mount. The heat shield must be removed to gain access to the generator support bracket nut. Remove the two heat shield mounting bolts.

8. Loosen, but do not remove the generator support bracket nut.

9. Remove the bolt.

10. Unsnap the plastic insulator cap from the B+ output terminal.

11. Remove the B+ terminal mounting nut at the rear of the generator. Disconnect the terminal from the generator.

12. Disconnect the field wire connector at the rear of the generator by pushing on the connector tab.

13. Remove the lower generator mounting bolt.

14. Remove the generator from the vehicle.

To install:

15. Position the generator to the engine and loosely install the two generator mounting bolts.

16. Position the support bracket to the generator and loosely install the bolt and the nut.

17. Tighten the generator mounting bolts to 48 ft. lbs. (65 Nm).

18. Tighten the bracket nut to 21 ft. lbs. (28 Nm).

19. Install the heat shield and the two heat shield mounting bolts.

20. Snap the field wire connector into the rear of the generator.

21. Install the generator B+ terminal eyelet to the generator output stud. Tighten to 9.5 ft. lbs. (13 Nm).

22. Position the transmission cooler line and install the transmission cooler line bracket bolt to the right crossmember.

23. Install the lower splash shield.

24. Lower the vehicle.

✳✳ WARNING

When installing a serpentine accessory drive belt, the belt MUST be routed correctly. The water pump may be rotating in the wrong direction if the belt is installed incorrectly, causing the engine to overheat.

25. Install the generator drive belt.

26. Connect the negative battery cable. Follow the battery reconnection procedure.

6.4L Engine

See Figures 81 through 84.

✳✳ CAUTION

Disconnect the negative battery cable before removing the battery output wire (B+ wire) from the generator. Failure to do so can result in injury or damage the electrical system.

1. Disconnect and isolate the negative battery cable.

2. Rotate the accessory drive belt tensioner clockwise until it contacts it's stop and remove the accessory drive belt, then slowly rotate the tensioner into the freearm position.

3. Raise and support the vehicle.

4. Remove the belly pan retainers and remove the belly pan.

5. Remove the transmission cooler line retaining clamp (1) at the right crossmember and position the transmission cooler line aside.

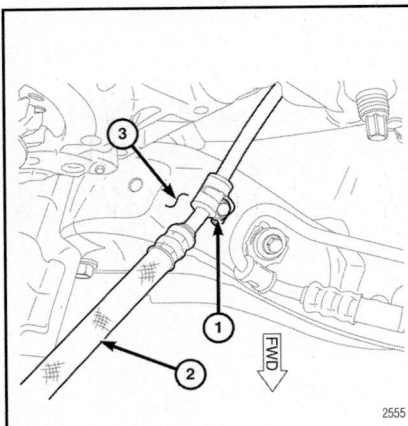

Fig. 81 Trans cooler line (2), clamp (1) and crossmember (3)

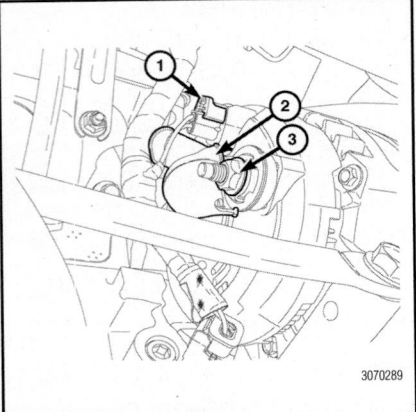

Fig. 82 Generator field wire connector tabs (1), insulator cover (2) and retaining nut (3)

6. Depress the field wire connector tab at the rear of the generator and disconnect the field wire connector.

7. Remove the insulator cover from B+ output terminal at the rear of the generator.

8. Remove the B+ terminal retaining nut at the rear of the generator and remove the B+ terminal.

9. Remove the generator support bracket to engine mount retaining nut.

10. Remove the generator support bracket retaining bolt and remove the support bracket.

11. Unsnap the plastic insulator cap from B+ output terminal at the rear of the generator.

12. Remove the B+ terminal retaining nut at the rear of the generator and remove the B+ terminal.

13. Depress the field wire connector tab at the rear of the generator and disconnect the field wire connector.

14. Remove the remaining lower generator retaining bolt.

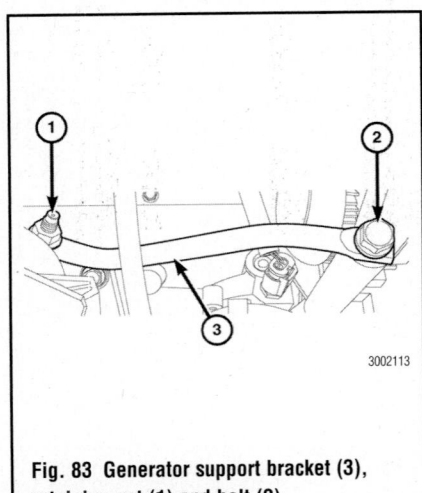

Fig. 83 Generator support bracket (3), retaining nut (1) and bolt (2)

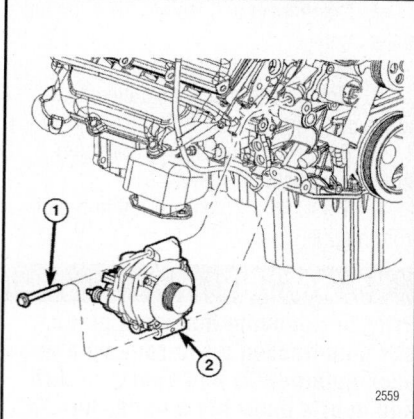

Fig. 84 Generator removal and installation

15. Lower the vehicle.
16. Remove the upper generator retaining bolt and remove the generator (2) from the vehicle.

To install:

17. Position the generator and install the upper generator mounting bolt finger tight.

18. Raise and support the vehicle.
19. Position the generator B+ terminal eyelet to the generator output stud, install the retaining nut and tighten to 10 ft. lbs. (13 Nm).
20. Install the insulator cover onto the B+ output terminal.
21. Snap the field wire connector into the rear of the generator.
22. Position the generator support bracket to the engine mount, install the retaining nut finger tight.
23. Position the generator support bracket to the generator and install the retaining bolt finger tight.
24. Install the remaining generator retaining bolt and tighten both lower retaining bolts to 48 ft. lbs. (65 Nm).
25. Tighten the generator support bracket to engine mount retaining nut to 21 ft. lbs. (28 Nm).
26. Position transmission cooler line and install the transmission cooler line retainer clamp to the right crossmember.
27. Position the belly pan and install the belly pan retainers.

28. Lower the vehicle.
29. Tighten the generator upper retaining bolt to 48 ft. lbs. (65 Nm).

✻✻ WARNING

When installing a serpentine accessory drive belt, the belt MUST be routed correctly. The water pump may be rotating in the wrong direction if the belt is installed incorrectly, causing the engine to overheat.

✻✻ WARNING

Do not let the tensioner arm snap back to the freearm position, sever damage may occur to the tensioner.

30. Rotate the accessory drive belt tensioner clockwise until it contacts the stop, install the accessory drive belt onto the pulleys and slowly release the tensioner.
31. Connect the negative battery cable and tighten the nut to 45 inch lbs. (5 Nm).

ENGINE ELECTRICAL

FIRING ORDER

3.5L & 3.6L Engines

The firing order is 1-2-3-4-5-6.

6.1L & 6.4L Engines

The firing order is 1-8-4-3-6-5-7-2.

IGNITION COIL

REMOVAL & INSTALLATION

3.5L Engine

See Figure 85.

1. Disconnect and isolate the negative battery cable.
2. Remove the upper intake manifold.
3. Unlock and disconnect electrical connector from ignition coils.
4. Remove the ignition coil mounting bolts.

✻✻ WARNING

Prior to removing the ignition coils, spray compressed air around the coils and spark plugs. If dirt and debris enter the engine, this may cause internal engine damage.

5. Twist, lift and remove ignition coil from engine.

To install:

6. Install the ignition coil. Tighten bolts to 71 inch lbs. (8 Nm).
7. Connect electrical connector and lock.
8. Install the intake manifold.
9. Connect negative battery cable and tighten nut to 45 inch lbs. (5 Nm).

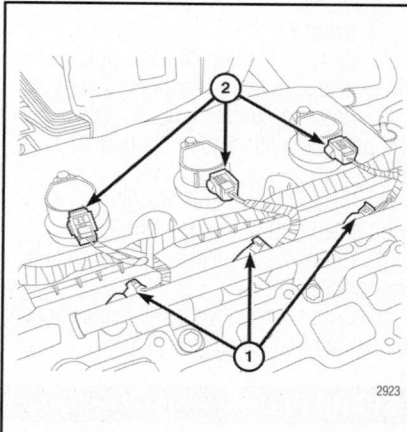

Fig. 85 Disconnecting the ignition coil electrical connectors

IGNITION SYSTEM

3.6L Engine

See Figure 86.

1. Disconnect and isolate the negative battery cable.
2. Lift the engine cover retaining grommets off the ball studs and remove the engine cover.
3. If removing the ignition coils from cylinders 1, 3 or 5 on the right side of the engine, first remove the air inlet hose.

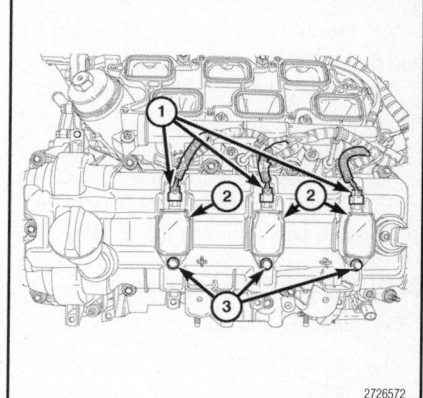

Fig. 86 Ignition coil (2), electrical connector (1) and retaining bolt (3)

4. If removing the ignition coils from cylinders 2, 4 or 6 on the left side of the engine, first remove the air inlet hose, upper intake manifold and insulator.

➡ **The left side ignition coils are shown, the right side ignition coils are similar.**

5. Unlock and disconnect the electrical connector from the ignition coil.

6. Remove the ignition coil retaining bolt.

7. Pull the ignition coil from cylinder head cover opening with a slight twisting action.

To install:

8. Using compressed air, blow out any dirt or contaminants from around the top of spark plug.

9. Check the condition of the ignition coil rubber boot. Inspect the opening of the boot for any debris, tears or rips. Carefully remove any debris with a lint free cloth.

✳✳ WARNING

Do not apply a silicone based grease such as Mopar®Dielectric Grease to the ignition coil rubber boot. The silicone based grease will absorb into the boot causing it to stick and tear.

10. Place a small, 360°bead of Fluostar 2LF lubricant (1) along the inside opening of the coil boot approximately 1 to 2 mm from the chamfer edge but not on the chamfered surface.

➡ **The LH ignition coils are shown, the RH ignition coils are similar.**

11. Position the ignition coil into the cylinder head cover opening. Using a twisting action, push the ignition coil onto the spark plug.

12. Install the ignition coil mounting bolt and tighten to 71 inch lbs. (8 Nm).

13. Connect and lock the electrical connector to the ignition coil.

14. If removed, install the insulator, upper intake manifold and air inlet hose.

15. Connect the negative battery cable and tighten nut to 45 inch lbs. (5 Nm).

5.7L, 6.1L & 6.4L Engines

See Figures 87 and 88.

1. Disconnect and isolate the negative battery cable.

2. Unlock electrical connector by pressing on tab while pulling electrical connector from coil.

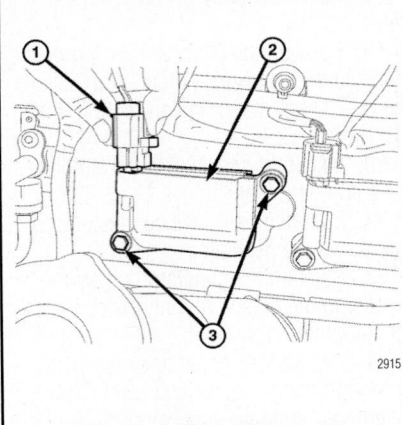

Fig. 87 Ignition coil mounting bolts (3), ignition coil (2) and connector (1)

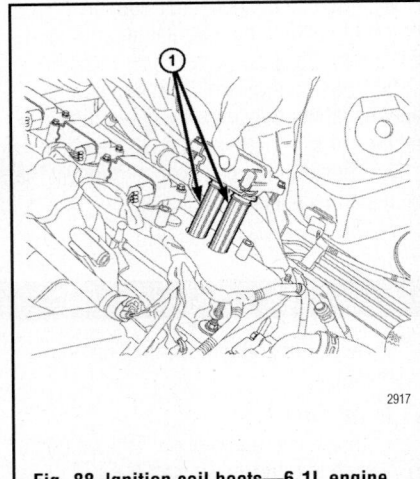

Fig. 88 Ignition coil boots—6.1L engine

3. Remove the two coil mounting bolts.

4. Carefully pull up coil from cylinder head opening with a slight twisting action. Twisting will help break loose boots from spark plugs.

To install:

5. Before installing coil(s), apply dielectric grease to inside of spark plug boots.

6. Position ignition coil into valve cover and push both spark plug boots onto each spark plug.

7. Install the two coil mounting bolts and tighten to 8 ft. lbs. (12 Nm).

8. Connect electrical connector to coil and lock connector.

9. Connect negative battery cable and tighten nut to 45 inch lbs. (5 Nm).

SPARK PLUGS

REMOVAL & INSTALLATION

1. Remove the engine cover.

2. Disconnect and isolate the negative battery cable.

3. Remove the intake manifold.

4. Unlock and disconnect electrical connector from ignition coils.

5. Remove the mounting bolts and engine cover studs.

6. Twist, lift and remove ignition coil from engine.

✳✳ WARNING

Prior to removing the spark plugs, use compressed air to remove any accumulated dirt and debris. If dirt and debris enter the engine, this may cause internal engine damage.

7. Remove the spark plug using a quality socket with a rubber or foam insert.

To install:

✳✳ WARNING

Handle the spark plugs with care. Do not drop or force the spark plugs into the wells, damage to the electrodes and/or porcelain body may occur. Always start each spark plug by hand in order to avoid cross-threading the spark plug in the cylinder head.

✳✳ WARNING

Always tighten spark plugs to the specified torque. Too much or not enough torque will cause damage to the cylinder head and/or spark plug and may lead to poor engine performance.

8. To avoid cross threading, start the spark plug into the cylinder head by hand.

9. Tighten spark plugs to 20 ft. lbs. (27 Nm).

10. Install the ignition coil.

11. Install the engine cover studs in the two outside ignition coils on the front of the engine. Install bolts on the other ignition coils.

12. Tighten studs and bolts to 71 inch lbs. (8 Nm).

13. Connect electrical connector and lock.

14. Install the intake manifold.

15. Reconnect the negative battery cable.

16. Install the engine cover.

STARTER

REMOVAL & INSTALLATION

3.5L Engine

See Figures 89 and 90.

➡**All Wheel Drive procedure shown. Rear Wheel Drive Similar.**

1. Disconnect and isolate negative battery cable at battery.
2. Remove the left side catalytic converter.
3. Remove the battery cable nut and battery cable from solenoid stud.
4. Disconnect the electrical connector from the starter solenoid terminal.
5. Remove the starter mounting bolts, the electrical harness mounting bracket should remain in position.
6. Rotate and remove starter assembly from transmission.

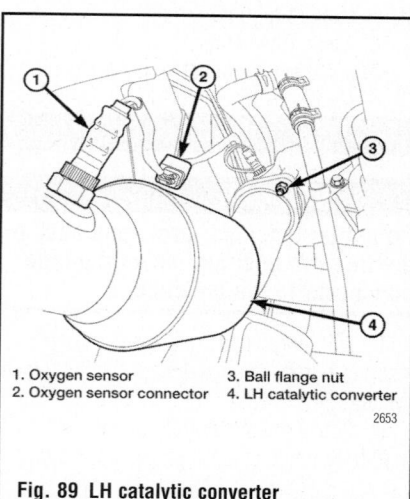

1. Oxygen sensor
2. Oxygen sensor connector
3. Ball flange nut
4. LH catalytic converter

2653

Fig. 89 LH catalytic converter

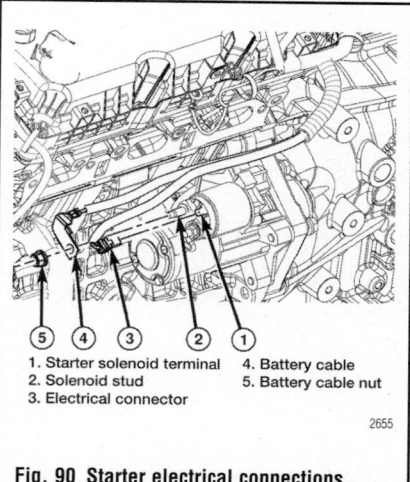

1. Starter solenoid terminal
2. Solenoid stud
3. Electrical connector
4. Battery cable
5. Battery cable nut

2655

Fig. 90 Starter electrical connections

7. Remove the starter motor dust shield.

To install:

8. Install the starter motor dust shield.
9. Rotate and install starter assembly to transmission.
10. Install the starter mounting bolts, and electrical harness mounting bracket. Tighten bolts to 40 ft. lbs. (54 Nm).
11. Connect electrical connector to starter solenoid terminal.
12. Install the battery cable and nut to solenoid stud. Tighten nut to 97 inch lbs. (11 Nm).
13. Install the left side catalytic converter.
14. Connect negative battery cable, tighten nut to 45 inch lbs. (5 Nm).

3.6L Engine

See Figure 91.

1. Disconnect and isolate the negative battery cable at the battery.
2. Secure the steering wheel.
3. Remove the steering gear intermediate shaft.
4. Remove the starter solenoid heat shield.
5. Disconnect the starter solenoid electrical connector from starter solenoid terminal.
6. Remove the battery cable nut and battery cable from solenoid stud.
7. Remove the starter mounting bolts, the electrical harness mounting bracket should remain in position.
8. Rotate and remove starter assembly from transmission.

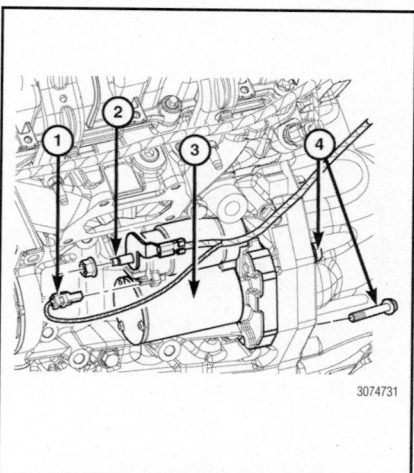
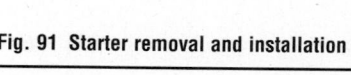

3074731

Fig. 91 Starter removal and installation

To install:

9. Position the starter inside the transmission.
10. Install the starter mounting bolts to the starter.
11. Tighten the bolts to 40 ft. lbs. (55 Nm).
12. Connect the starter solenoid electrical connector to starter solenoid terminal.
13. Install the battery cable and nut to the solenoid stud. Tighten the nut to 97 inch lbs. (11 Nm).
14. Install the starter solenoid heat shield.
15. Install the steering gear lower intermediate shaft.
16. Remove the steering wheel holder.
17. Connect the negative battery cable.

5.7L Engine

See Figure 92.

1. Disconnect and isolate negative battery cable.
2. Raise and safely support the vehicle.
3. Remove the three starter mounting bolts.
4. Move starter motor towards front of vehicle far enough for nose of starter to clear. Always support starter motor during this process. Do not let starter motor hang from wire harness.
5. Remove the battery cable-to-solenoid nut.
6. Remove the solenoid wire from solenoid stud.
7. Remove the starter motor.

To install:

8. Position starter into transmission but do not install bolts.

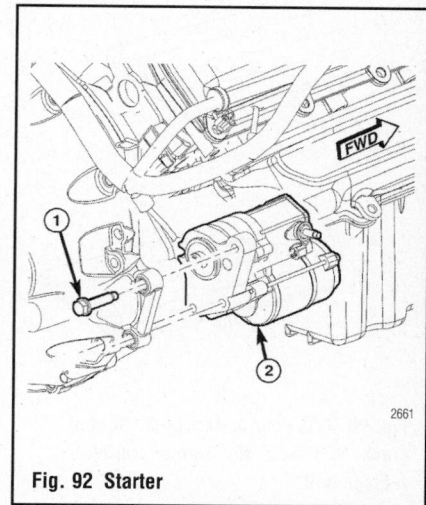

2661

Fig. 92 Starter

9. Connect solenoid wire to starter motor (snaps on).

10. Position battery cable to solenoid stud. Install and tighten battery cable eyelet nut. Do not allow starter motor to hang from wire harness.

11. Install the and tighten three mounting bolts.

12. Carefully lower the vehicle.

13. Connect negative battery cable.

6.1L & 6.4L Engines

See Figures 93 and 94.

1. Disconnect and isolate the negative battery cable.

2. Raise and support the vehicle.

3. Remove the two heat shield nuts and remove the heat shield.

4. Remove the three starter mounting bolts.

5. Move the starter motor towards the front of vehicle far enough for the nose of starter to clear. Always support the starter motor during this process. Do not let the starter motor hang from the wire harness.

6. Remove the battery cable-to-solenoid nut.

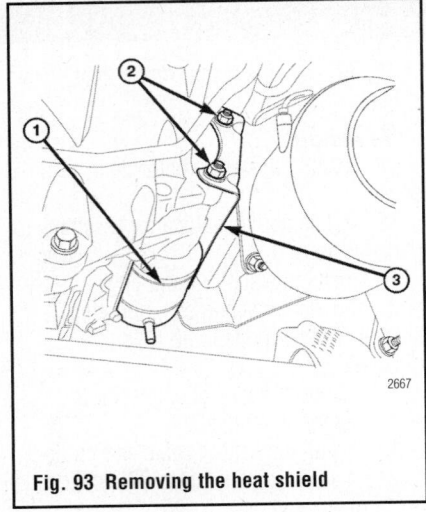

Fig. 93 Removing the heat shield

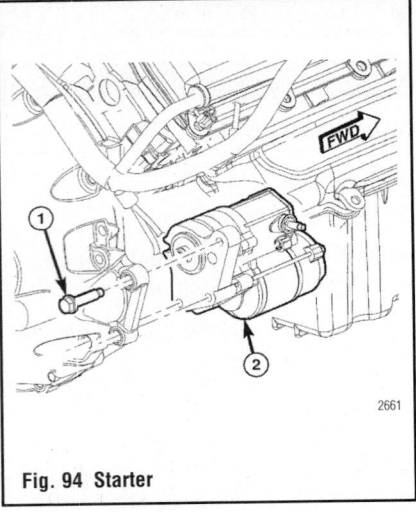

Fig. 94 Starter

7. Remove the solenoid wire from the solenoid stud.

8. Remove the starter motor.

To install:

9. Position the starter into the transmission but do not install bolts.

10. Connect the solenoid wire to the starter motor (snaps on).

11. Position the battery cable to the solenoid stud. Install the battery cable eyelet nut. Tighten to 8 ft. lbs. (11 Nm).

12. Install the three mounting bolts. Tighten to 40 ft. lbs. (54 Nm).

13. Position the heat shield and install the two shield mounting nuts.

14. Lower the vehicle.

15. Connect the negative battery cable.

ENGINE MECHANICAL

➡Disconnecting the negative battery cable may interfere with the functions of the on board computer systems and may require the computer to undergo a relearning process, once the negative battery cable is reconnected.

ACCESSORY DRIVE BELTS

INSPECTION

See Figure 95.

Any belt with bumps, surface coming apart, or any other uneven indications along the flat surface of the belt must be remove and inspected and replaced if necessary.

REMOVAL & INSTALLATION

3.5L & 3.6L Engine

See Figures 96 through 98.

❊➤ WARNING

Do not let tensioner arm snap back to the freearm position, sever damage may occur to the tensioner.

1. 3.6L engine with electronic power steering pump, remove the air cleaner intake system.

2. Rotate belt tensioner counterclockwise until it contacts it's stop. Remove belt

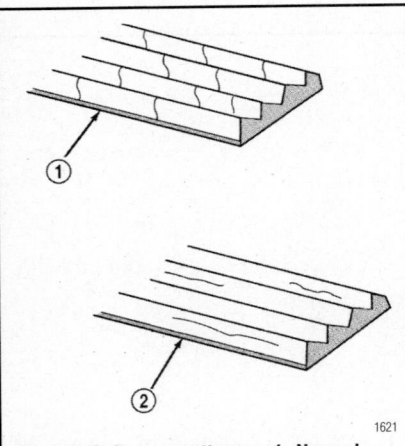

Fig. 95 Belt wear patterns—1. Normal cracks belt ok, 2. Not normal cracks, replace belt

1. Idler pulley	4. Crankshaft
2. P/S pump	5. Tensioner
3. A/C compressor	6. Generator

Fig. 96 Accessory drive belt—3.5L engine

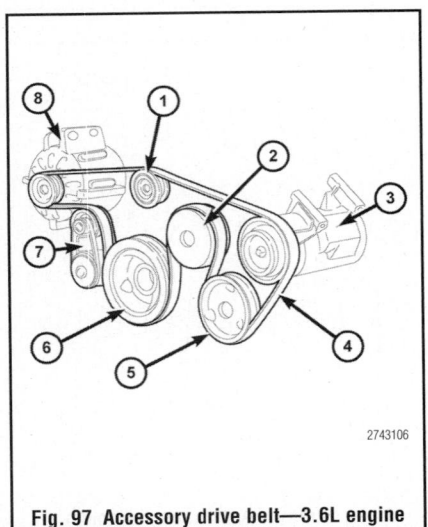

Fig. 97 Accessory drive belt—3.6L engine

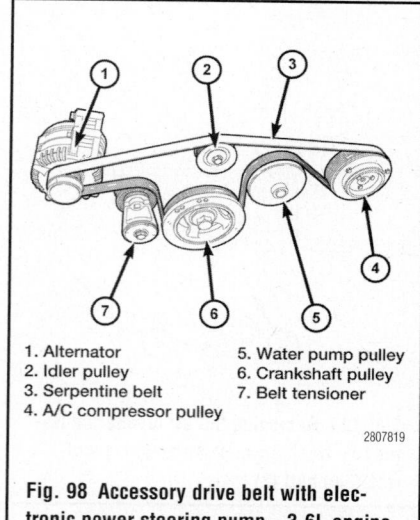

1. Alternator
2. Idler pulley
3. Serpentine belt
4. A/C compressor pulley
5. Water pump pulley
6. Crankshaft pulley
7. Belt tensioner

2807819

Fig. 98 Accessory drive belt with electronic power steering pump—3.6L engine

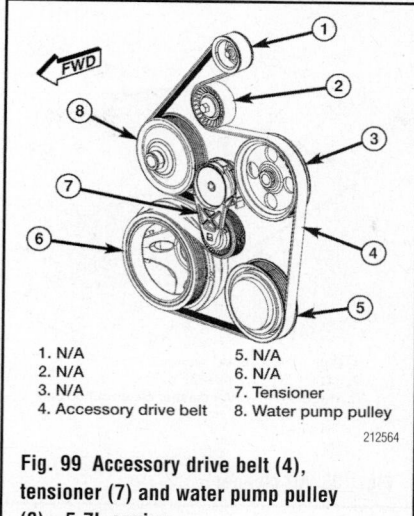

1. N/A
2. N/A
3. N/A
4. Accessory drive belt
5. N/A
6. N/A
7. Tensioner
8. Water pump pulley

212564

Fig. 99 Accessory drive belt (4), tensioner (7) and water pump pulley (8)—5.7L engine

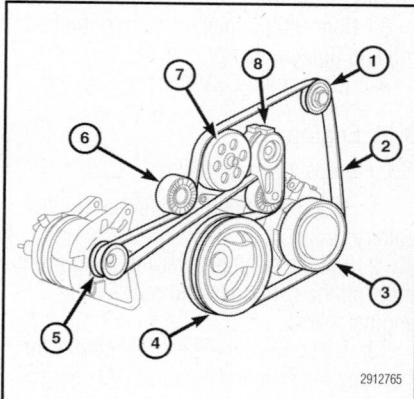

2912765

Fig. 100 Accessory drive belt with electronic power steering pump—5.7L engine

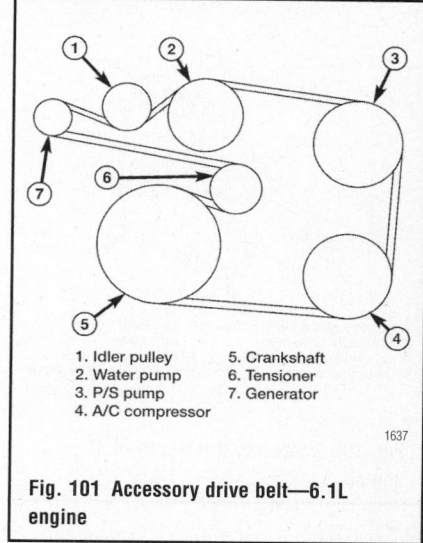

1. Idler pulley
2. Water pump
3. P/S pump
4. A/C compressor
5. Crankshaft
6. Tensioner
7. Generator

1637

Fig. 101 Accessory drive belt—6.1L engine

(3), then slowly rotate the tensioner (7) into the freearm position.

To install:

3. Check condition of all pulleys.

⁜ **WARNING**

When installing the serpentine accessory drive belt, the belt MUST be routed correctly. If not, the engine may overheat due to the water pump rotating in the wrong direction.

4. Position accessory drive belt around all pulleys except the idler pulley. Rotate the tensioner arm until it contacts it's stop position. Route the accessory drive belt around the idler and slowly let the tensioner rotate into the belt. Make sure the belt is seated onto all pulleys.

➡**ON all engines, the tensioner is equipped with an indexing tang on back of tensioner and an indexing stop on tensioner housing. If a new belt is being installed, tang must be within approximately 6 - 8mm (0.24 - 0.32 in.) of indexing stop (i.e. tang is approximately between the two indexing stops). Belt is considered new if it has been used 15 minutes or less.**

5. With the drive belt installed, inspect the belt wear indicator.

5.7L Engine

See Figures 99 and 100.

1. Remove the air intake tube between the intake manifold and the air filter assembly.
2. Insert a suitable square drive ratchet into the square hole on the belt tensioner arm.
3. Release the belt tension by rotating the tensioner (8) clockwise. Rotate the belt

tensioner until the accessory drive belt (2) can be removed from the pulleys.

4. Remove the accessory drive belt.
5. Gently release the tensioner.

To install:

6. Position the accessory drive belt over all pulleys except for the water pump pulley.
7. Rotate the tensioner clockwise and slip the accessory drive belt over the water pump pulley.
8. Gently release the tensioner.
9. Install the air intake tube between the intake manifold and air filter assembly.

6.1L Engine

See Figure 101.

⁜ **WARNING**

Do not let the tensioner arm snap back to the freearm position, sever damage may occur to the tensioner.

1. Disconnect negative battery cable from battery.
2. Rotate accessory drive belt tensioner counterclockwise until it contacts it's stop. Remove accessory drive belt, then slowly rotate the tensioner into the freearm position.

To install:

3. Check condition of all pulleys.

⁜ **WARNING**

When installing the serpentine accessory drive belt, the belt MUST be routed correctly. If not, the engine may overheat due to the water pump rotating in the wrong direction.

4. Position accessory drive belt around all pulleys except the idler pulley. Rotate the tensioner arm until it contacts it's stop position. Route the accessory drive belt around the idler and slowly let the tensioner rotate into the belt. Make sure the belt is seated onto all pulleys.

➡**ON all engines, the tensioner is equipped with an indexing tang on back of tensioner and an indexing stop on tensioner housing. If a new belt is being installed, tang must be within approximately 6 - 8mm (0.24 - 0.32 in.) of indexing stop (i.e. tang is approximately between the two indexing stops). Belt is considered new if it has been used 15 minutes or less.**

5. With the accessory drive belt installed, inspect the belt wear indicator.

6.4L Engine

See Figure 102.

1. Using a suitable square drive tool, release the belt tension by rotating the

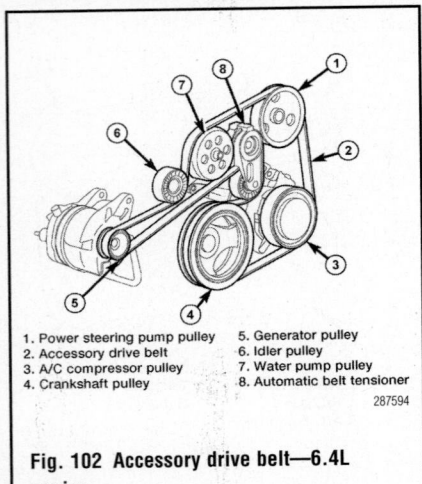

Fig. 102 Accessory drive belt—6.4L engine

1. Power steering pump pulley
2. Accessory drive belt
3. A/C compressor pulley
4. Crankshaft pulley
5. Generator pulley
6. Idler pulley
7. Water pump pulley
8. Automatic belt tensioner

287594

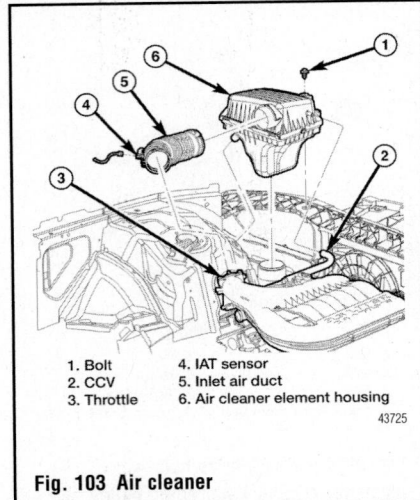

Fig. 103 Air cleaner

1. Bolt
2. CCV
3. Throttle
4. IAT sensor
5. Inlet air duct
6. Air cleaner element housing

43725

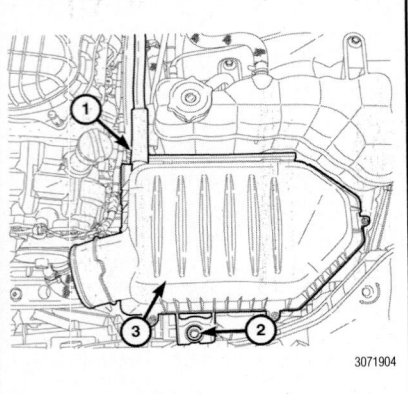

Fig. 105 Removing the air cleaner housing (3), fresh air makeup hose (1) and retaining bolt (2)

3071904

tensioner clockwise. Rotate belt tensioner until belt can be removed from pulleys.

2. Remove the belt.

3. Gently release tensioner.

To install:

❄❄ WARNING

Do not let tensioner arm snap back to the freearm position, sever damage may occur to the tensioner.

➤When installing accessory drive belt onto pulleys, make sure that belt is properly routed and all V-grooves make proper contact with pulleys.

4. Position the drive belt over all pulleys except for the water pump pulley.

5. Rotate tensioner clockwise and slip the belt over the water pump pulley.

6. Gently release tensioner.

AIR CLEANER

REMOVAL & INSTALLATION

3.5L Engine

See Figure 103.

1. Separate the air inlet duct at the element housing.

2. Disconnect the CCV hose at the element housing.

3. Remove the housing retaining bolt.

4. Pull housing up and off of the locating pin.

5. Remove the element housing from vehicle.

To install:

6. Align the housing with the lower air inlet duct and alignment grommet in the wheel housing.

7. Properly fit the housing and install housing retaining bolt.

8. Connect the inlet air duct to the housing and tighten clamp.

9. Connect the CCV hose to housing.

3.6L Engine

See Figures 104 and 105.

1. Disconnect and isolate the negative battery cable.

2. Lift the engine cover retaining grommets off the ball studs and remove the engine cover.

3. Disconnect the electrical connector from the Inlet Air Temperature (IAT) sensor.

4. Loosen the clamp at the throttle body.

5. Loosen the clamp at the air cleaner housing.

6. Lift the air inlet hose assembly retaining grommet off the ball stud.

7. Remove the air inlet hose assembly.

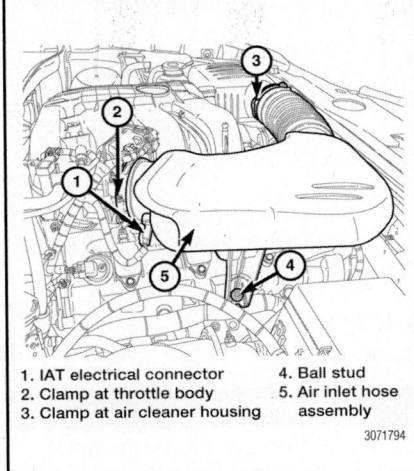

1. IAT electrical connector
2. Clamp at throttle body
3. Clamp at air cleaner housing
4. Ball stud
5. Air inlet hose assembly

3071794

Fig. 104 Removing the air inlet hose assembly

8. Disconnect the fresh air makeup hose from the air cleaner housing.

9. Remove the air cleaner housing retaining bolt.

10. Remove the air cleaner housing.

To install:

11. Position the air cleaner housing into the vehicle.

12. Install the air cleaner housing retaining bolt and tighten to 35 inch lbs. (4 Nm).

13. Connect the fresh air makeup hose onto the air cleaner housing.

14. Position the air inlet hose assembly, connect the air inlet hose to the throttle body and the air cleaner housing.

15. Secure the air inlet hose assembly retaining grommet onto the ball stud.

16. Tighten the clamp at the air cleaner housing to 35 inch lbs. (4 Nm.

17. Tighten the clamp at the throttle body to 35 inch lbs. (4 Nm).

18. Connect the electrical connector to the Inlet Air Temperature (IAT) sensor.

19. Position the engine cover and secure the retaining grommets to the ball studs.

20. Connect the negative battery cable and tighten nut to 45 inch lbs. (5 Nm).

5.7L Engine

See Figure 106.

1. Lift the engine cover retaining grommets off the ball studs and remove the engine cover.

2. Disconnect the intake air temperature (IAT) sensor electrical connector.

3. Loosen the air duct retaining clamps at the throttle body and the air cleaner housing and remove the air duct.

4. Disconnect the makeup air hose (MUA).

5. Remove the air cleaner housing retaining bolt.

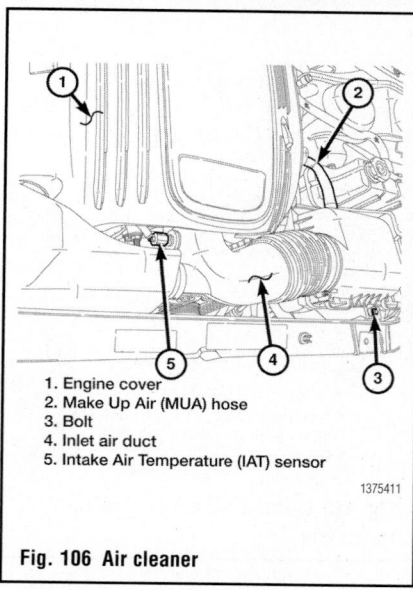

1. Engine cover
2. Make Up Air (MUA) hose
3. Bolt
4. Inlet air duct
5. Intake Air Temperature (IAT) sensor

1375411

Fig. 106 Air cleaner

6. Remove the air cleaner housing from the vehicle.

To install:

7. Position the air cleaner housing into the engine compartment.

8. Install the air cleaner housing retaining bolt and tighten to 44 inch lbs. (5 Nm).

9. Connect the air duct to the throttle body and the air cleaner housing and tighten clamps to 30 inch lbs. (3 Nm).

10. Connect the Make Up Air hose (MUA).

11. Connect the Intake Air Temperature (IAT) sensor electrical connector.

12. Position the engine cover and secure the retaining grommets onto the ball studs.

6.1L & 6.4L Engines

See Figure 107.

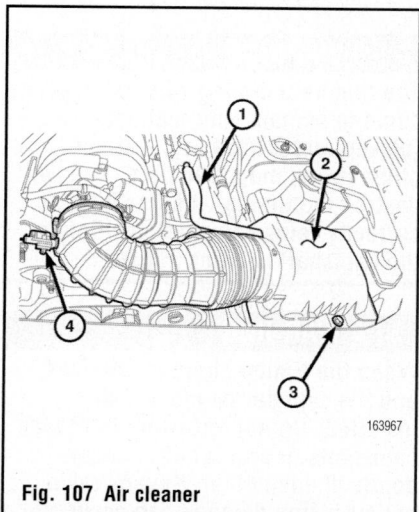

163967

Fig. 107 Air cleaner

1. Loosen clamp and disconnect air duct at throttle body.

2. Disconnect intake air temperature sensor electrical connector.

3. Remove the makeup air hose.

4. Remove the air cleaner housing retaining bolt and remove air cleaner housing.

To install:

5. Install the air filter housing into locating pin.

6. Install the hold down bolt into the air filter housing.

7. Install the air duct to air cleaner cover and tighten hose clamp to 30 inch lbs. (3 Nm).

8. If any other hose clamps were removed from air intake system, tighten them to 30 inch lbs. (3.4 Nm).

FILTER/ELEMENT REPLACEMENT

3.5L Engine

See Figure 108.

1. Disconnect the CCV hose at the housing cover.

2. Release the housing cover tabs.

3. Lift the cover and pull toward the front of the vehicle to release the rear cover to housing alignment tabs.

4. Remove the element.

To install:

5. Install the air filter element into air box.

6. Position the cover so that the rear locking tabs insert into the lower housing.

7. Seat cover onto element housing and assure that the front locking tabs engage.

8. Reconnect the CCV hose.

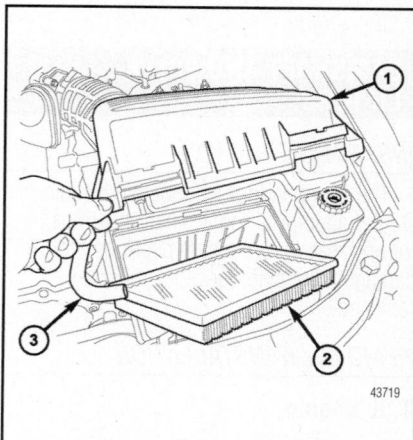

43719

Fig. 108 Air cleaner element (2), air cleaner cover (1) and CCV hose (3)

3.6L Engine

See Figure 109.

1. Remove the fresh air makeup hose at the air cleaner housing.

2. Remove the air cleaner housing cover retaining bolts.

✳✳ WARNING

Do not use compressed air to clean out the air cleaner housing without first covering the air inlet to the throttle body. Dirt or foreign objects could enter the intake manifold causing engine damage.

3. Lift the air cleaner housing cover off the housing and position aside.

4. Remove the air cleaner element.

5. Remove the any dirt or debris from the bottom of the air cleaner housing.

To install:

6. Install the a new air cleaner element into the air cleaner housing.

7. Position the air cleaner housing cover so that the alignment tabs insert into the lower housing.

8. Seat the cover onto the housing and install the retaining bolts and tighten to 35 inch lbs. (4 Nm).

9. Connect the fresh air makeup hose onto the air cleaner housing.

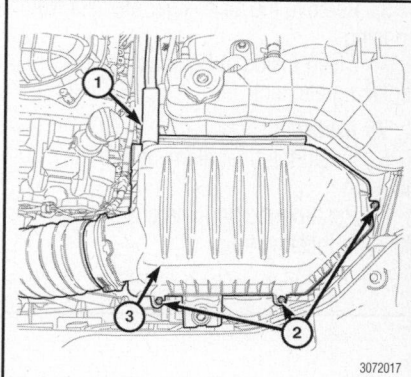

3072017

Fig. 109 Removing the air cleaner housing (3), fresh air makeup hose (1) and retaining bolts (2)

5.7L Engine

See Figure 110.

1. Disengage the two retaining clamps and lift the cover upwards.

2. Remove the air cleaner element from the inside of the air cleaner housing.

To install:

3. Clean any dirt or foreign matter from the inside of the air cleaner housing.

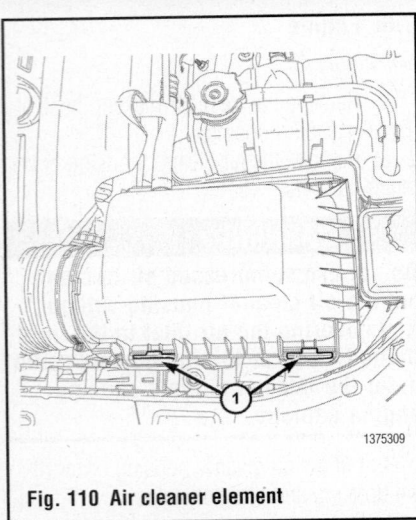

Fig. 110 Air cleaner element

➡️**The air cleaner element must be properly seated for the air cleaner housing cover to fit correctly.**

4. Install the air cleaner element into the air cleaner housing.

5. Position the air cleaner housing cover in place and secure the two retainer clips.

6.1L Engine

See Figure 111.

1. Release tabs from housing cover.
2. Reposition cover.
3. Remove the air cleaner element from housing.
4. Clean inside of housing before replacing element.

To install:

5. Install the filter element into the housing.
6. Position the housing cover into the housing locating tabs.

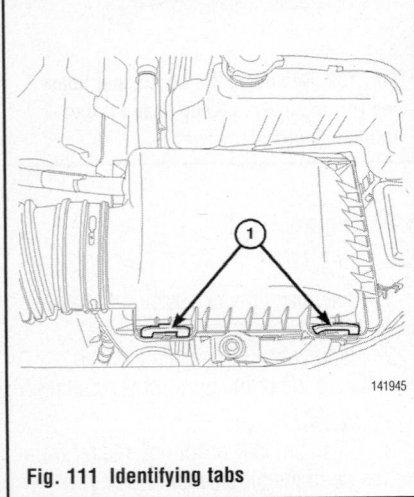

Fig. 111 Identifying tabs

7. Push the cover in place and verify that the retaining clips are fully seated.

6.4L Engine

See Figure 112.

1. Remove the air cleaner housing cover retaining screws.

2. Lift the air cleaner housing cover while separating the locating tabs from the housing.

3. Remove the air cleaner element from the housing.

4. Clean the inside of air cleaner housing before replacing element.

To install:

5. Install the air cleaner element into the housing.

6. Align the air cleaner housing cover locating tabs into the housing while lowering the cover into position.

7. Install the air cleaner housing cover retaining screws and tighten to 30 inch lbs. (3 Nm).

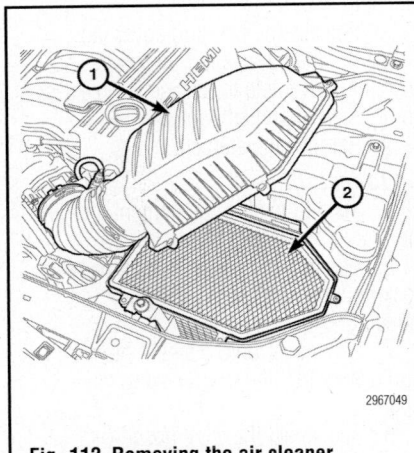

Fig. 112 Removing the air cleaner element (2) and housing cover (1)

CAMSHAFT AND VALVE LIFTERS

INSPECTION

The cam bearings are not serviceable. Do not attempt to replace cam bearings for any reason. If the cam bearings are damaged, the cylinder block must be replaced.

REMOVAL & INSTALLATION

3.5L Engine

See Figure 113.

➡️**Camshafts are removed from the rear of each cylinder head.**

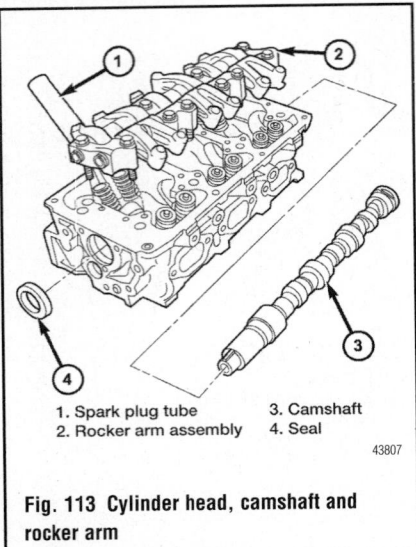

1. Spark plug tube   3. Camshaft
2. Rocker arm assembly 4. Seal

Fig. 113 Cylinder head, camshaft and rocker arm

1. Remove the cylinder head.

✳️ WARNING

Care must be taken not to nick or scratch the journals when removing the camshaft.

2. Carefully remove the camshaft from the rear of the cylinder head.

To install:

➡️**Care must be taken not to scrape or nick the camshaft journals when installing the camshaft into position.**

3. Lubricate camshaft bearing journals, camshaft lobes and camshaft seal with clean engine oil and install camshaft into cylinder head.

4. Install the cylinder head

3.6L Engine

Left Side

See Figures 114 through 116.

✳️ WARNING

The magnetic timing wheels must not come in contact with magnets (pickup tools, trays, etc.) or any other strong magnetic field. This will destroy the timing wheels ability to correctly relay camshaft position to the camshaft position sensor.

✳️ WARNING

When the timing chain is removed and the cylinder heads are still installed, Do not forcefully rotate the camshafts or crankshaft independently of each other. Severe valve and/or piston damage can occur.

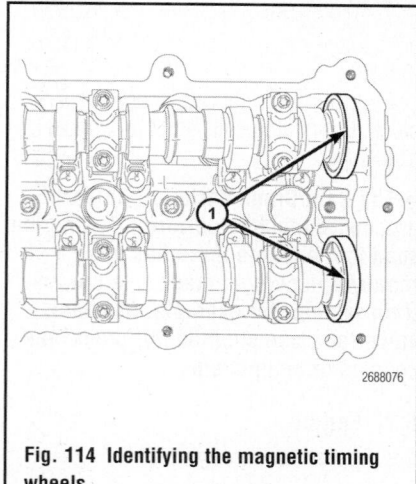

Fig. 114 Identifying the magnetic timing wheels

1. Remove the Left cylinder head cover, RH ignition coils, spark plugs and left cam phasers.

2. Gently rotate the camshafts CCW approximately 30°until the camshafts are in the neutral position (no valve load).

➡️**Camshaft bearing caps should have been marked during engine manufacturing. For example, the number one exhaust camshaft bearing cap is marked "1E->". The caps should be installed with the notch forward.**

3. Slowly loosen the camshaft bearing cap bolts in the sequence shown.

❄❄ WARNING

DO NOT STAMP OR STRIKE THE CAMSHAFT BEARING CAPS. SEVERE DAMAGE WILL OCCUR TO THE BEARING CAPS.

➡️**When the camshaft is removed the rocker arms may slide downward, mark the rocker arms before removing the camshaft.**

4. Remove the camshaft bearing caps and the camshafts.

To install:

5. Lubricate the camshaft journals with clean engine oil.

6. Install the left side camshaft(s) approximately 30°CCW from the TDC position. This will place the camshafts at the neutral position (no valve load) easing the installation of the camshaft bearing caps.

7. Install the camshaft bearing caps and hand tighten the retaining bolts to 18 inch lbs. (2 Nm.

➡️**Caps are identified numerically (1 through 4), intake or exhaust (I or E) and should be installed from the front**

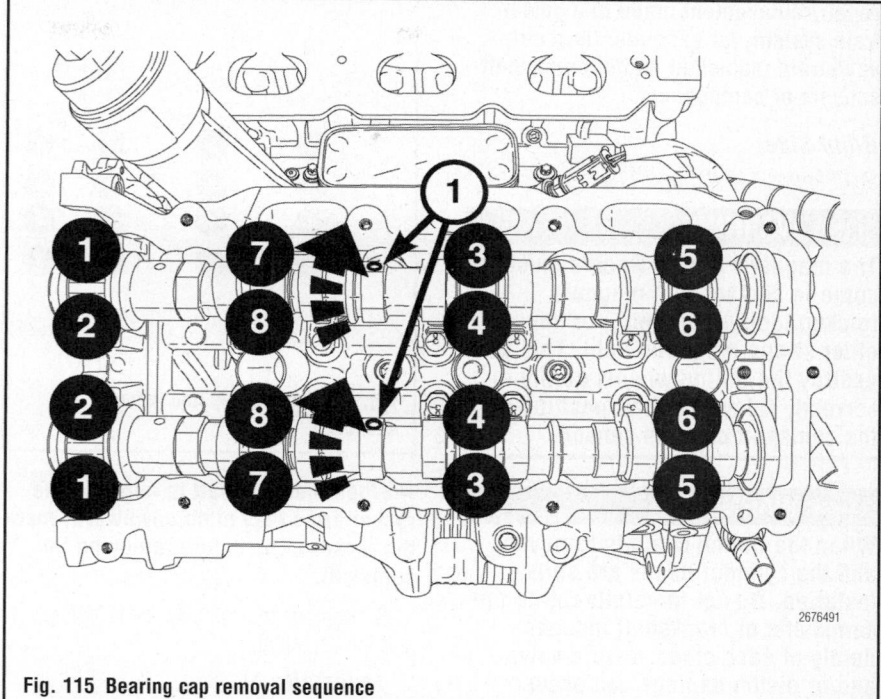

Fig. 115 Bearing cap removal sequence

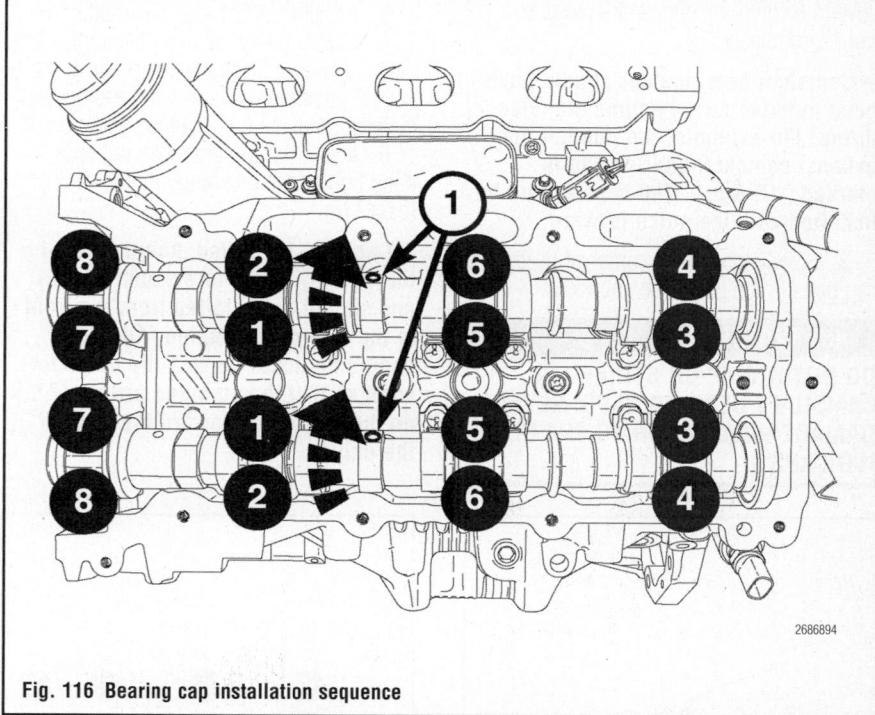

Fig. 116 Bearing cap installation sequence

to the rear of the engine. All caps should be installed with the notch forward so that the stamped arrows (<) on the caps point toward the front of the engine.

8. Tighten the bearing cap retaining bolts in the sequence shown to 84 inch lbs. (9.5 Nm).

9. Rotate the camshafts CW to TDC by positioning the alignment holes vertically.

10. Install the left cam phasers, spark plugs, RH ignition coils and the cylinder head cover.

➡️**The Cam/Crank Variation Relearn procedure must be performed using the scan tool anytime there has been a** repair/replacement made to a power-train system, for example: flywheel, valvetrain, camshaft and/or crankshaft sensors or components

Right Side

See Figures 117 through 119.

> ※※ **WARNING**
>
> **The magnetic timing wheels must not come in contact with magnets (pickup tools, trays, etc.) or any other strong magnetic field. This will destroy the timing wheels ability to correctly relay camshaft position to the camshaft position sensor.**

> ※※ **WARNING**
>
> **When the timing chain is removed and the cylinder heads are still installed, Do not forcefully rotate the camshafts or crankshaft independently of each other. Severe valve and/or piston damage can occur.**

1. Remove the Right cylinder head cover, LH ignition coils, spark plugs and right cam phasers.

➡ **Camshaft bearing caps should have been marked during engine manufacturing. For example, the number one exhaust camshaft bearing cap is marked "1E->". The caps should be installed with the notch forward.**

2. Slowly loosen the camshaft bearing cap bolts in the sequence shown.

> ※※ **WARNING**
>
> **DO NOT STAMP OR STRIKE THE CAMSHAFT BEARING CAPS. SEVERE DAMAGE WILL OCCUR TO THE BEARING CAPS.**

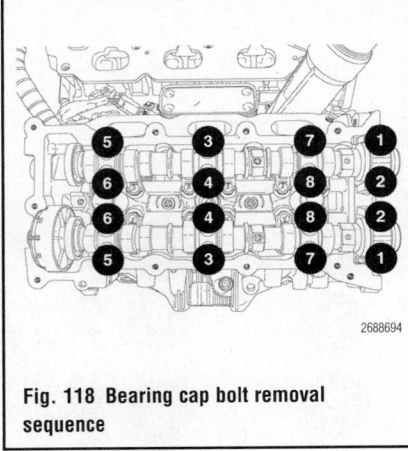

Fig. 118 Bearing cap bolt removal sequence

➡ **When the camshaft is removed the rocker arms may slide downward, mark the rocker arms before removing the camshaft.**

3. Remove the camshaft bearing caps and the camshafts.

To install:

4. Lubricate camshaft journals with clean engine oil.

5. Install the right side camshaft(s) at TDC by positioning the alignment holes vertically. This will place the camshafts at the neutral position (no valve load) easing the installation of the camshaft bearing caps.

6. Install the camshaft bearing caps, hand tighten the retaining bolts to 18 inch lbs. (2 Nm).

➡ **Caps are identified numerically (1 through 4), intake or exhaust (I or E) and should be installed from the front to the rear of the engine. All caps should be installed with the notch forward so that the stamped arrows (<) on the caps point toward the front of the engine.**

7. Tighten the bearing cap retaining bolts in the sequence shown to 84 inch lbs. (9.5 Nm).

8. Install the right cam phasers, spark plugs, LH ignition coils and the cylinder head cover.

➡ **The Cam/Crank Variation Relearn procedure must be performed using the scan tool anytime there has been a repair/replacement made to a power-train system, for example: flywheel, valvetrain, camshaft and/or crankshaft sensors or components.**

5.7L Engine

See Figures 120 through 123.

1. Remove the battery negative cable.
2. Remove the air cleaner assembly.
3. Drain coolant.
4. Remove the accessory drive belt.
5. Remove the left and right cylinder heads.
6. Remove the radiator.
7. Remove the oil pan.
8. Remove the timing case cover.

➡ **Identify lifters to ensure installation in original location.**

9. Remove the tappets and retainer assembly.
10. Remove the oil pick up tube.
11. Remove the oil pump retaining bolts and remove the oil pump.
12. Remove the timing chain.
13. Remove the camshaft thrust plate.

➡ **Slowly rotate the camshaft while pulling camshaft out.**

14. Install the a long bolt into front of camshaft to aid in removal of the camshaft. Remove camshaft, being careful not to damage cam bearings with the cam lobes.

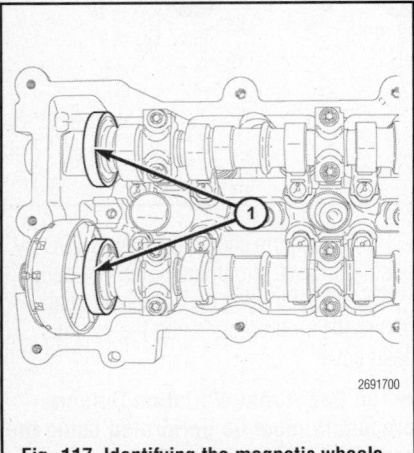

Fig. 117 Identifying the magnetic wheels

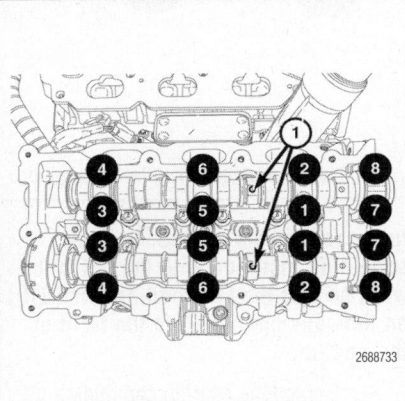

Fig. 119 Bearing cap installation sequence

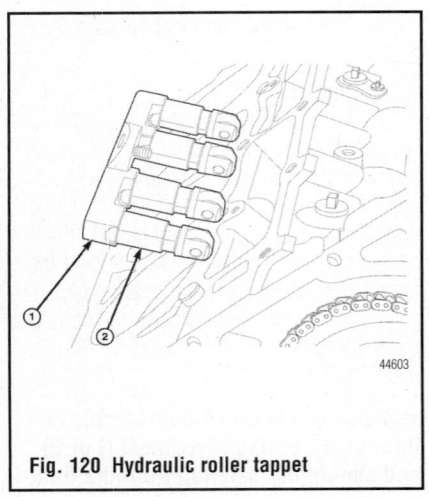

Fig. 120 Hydraulic roller tappet

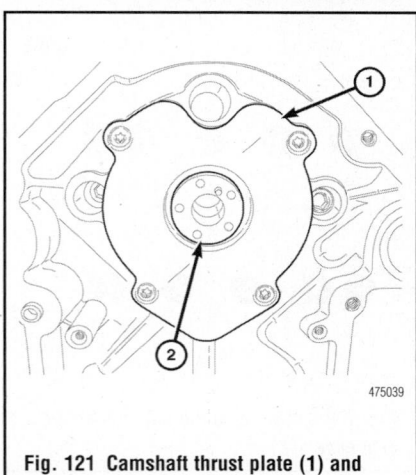

Fig. 121 Camshaft thrust plate (1) and camshaft (2)

To install:

15. Lubricate camshaft lobes and camshaft bearing journals and insert the camshaft.

16. Install the camshaft thrust plate.

    a. Tighten the bolts to 21 ft. lbs. (28 Nm) in the sequence shown.

17. Measure camshaft end play. If not within limits install a new thrust plate.

18. Install the timing chain and sprockets.

19. Install the timing chain tensioner and guide.

20. Install the oil pump and tighten bolts to 21 ft. lbs. (28 Nm).

21. Inspect oil pick up tube O-rings and replace as necessary.

22. Install the oil pick up tube and tighten fasteners to 21 ft. lbs. (28 Nm).

23. Install the timing chain cover.

24. Install the oil pan.

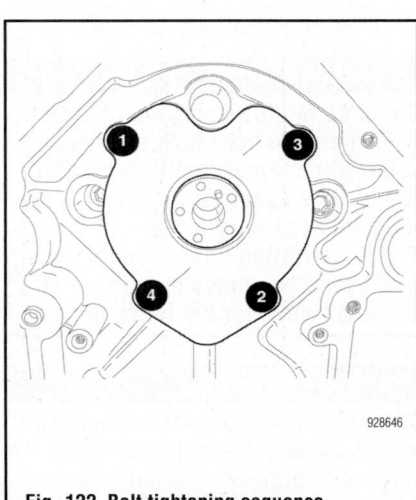

Fig. 122 Bolt tightening sequence

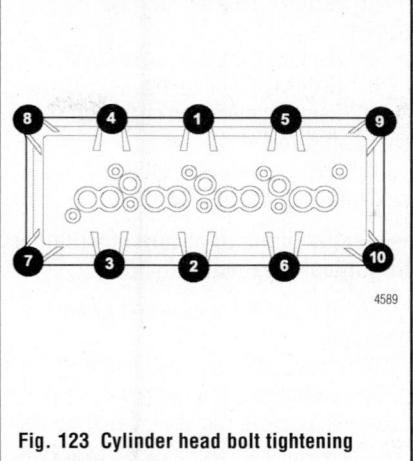

Fig. 123 Cylinder head bolt tightening sequence

> ✳✳ **WARNING**
>
> **Engines equipped with MDS use both standard roller lifters and deactivating roller lifters. The deactivating roller lifters must be used in cylinders 1,4,6,7. The deactivating lifters can be identified by the two holes in the side of the lifter body, for the latching pins.**

➡ **Each tappet reused must be installed in the same position from which it was removed. When camshaft is replaced, all of the tappets must be replaced.**

25. Install the rear MDS lifter assembly and tighten bolt to 9 ft. lbs. (12 Nm).

26. Install the front MDS lifter assembly and tighten bolt to 9 ft. lbs. (12 Nm).

27. Install the both left and right cylinder heads.

28. Install the pushrods.

29. Install the rocker arms.

30. Install the cylinder head covers.

31. Install the intake manifold.

32. Install the generator.

33. Install the power steering pump.

34. Install the accessory drive belt.

35. Install the radiator.

36. Install the air cleaner assembly.

37. Install the battery negative cable.

38. Refill coolant.

39. Refill engine oil.

40. Start engine and check for leaks.

6.1L Engine

See Figures 124 through 128.

1. Remove the engine covers, they snap off of the fuel rail.

2. Disconnect the manifold absolute pressure (MAP) sensor harness connector, located at the back of the Intake Manifold.

3. Disconnect the short runner valve (SRV), located at the back of the intake manifold.

4. Disconnect the intake air temperature (IAT) sensor harness connector.

5. Remove the air cleaner housing and clean air tube.

6. Disconnect the electronic throttle body harness connector.

7. Disconnect the brake booster vacuum hose (it may be easier to disconnect the vacuum hose at the booster).

8. Disconnect the evaporative purge vacuum hose, and the make-up air (MUA) hose from the intake manifold.

9. Perform the fuel system pressure release procedure.

10. Disconnect the fuel injector harness connectors.

11. Disconnect the fuel supply line.

12. Remove the negative battery cable.

> ✳✳ **CAUTION**
>
> **Do not remove the cylinder block drain plugs or loosen the radiator draincock with the system hot and under pressure. Serious burns from the coolant can occur.**

13. Drain the cooling system.

> ✳✳ **WARNING**
>
> **Do not let the tensioner arm snap back to the freearm position, sever damage may occur to the tensioner.**

14. Rotate the accessory drive belt tensioner counterclockwise until it contacts it's stop. Remove the accessory drive belt, then slowly rotate the tensioner into the freearm position.

➡ **It is not necessary to disconnect the power steering pump hoses from the**

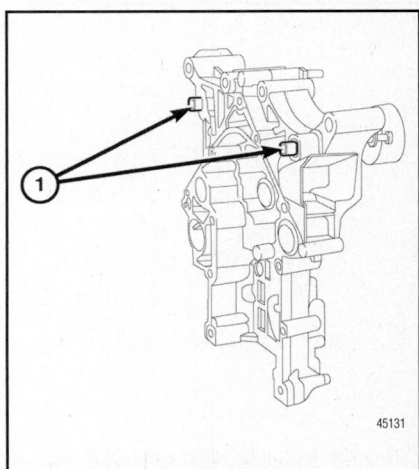

Fig. 124 Front cover slide bushings

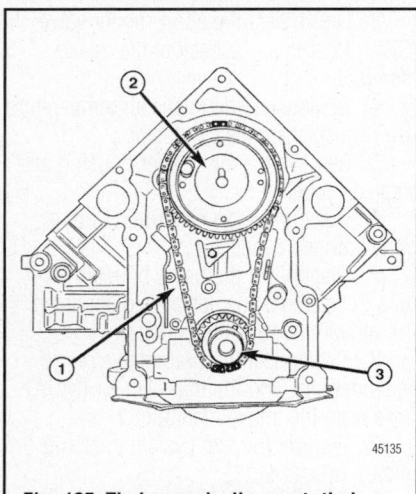

Fig. 125 Timing mark alignment, timing chain (1) and camshaft sprocket (2)

pump, for power steering pump removal.

15. Remove the three power steering pump mounting bolts through the access holes in the pulley.

16. Remove the power steering pump and secure out of the way.

17. Disconnect the ignition coil electrical connectors.

18. Remove the ignition coil mounting bolts.

19. Remove the ignition coils.

20. Remove the generator.

21. Remove the A/C compressor, and set aside.

22. Remove the radiator.

23. Remove the intake manifold.

24. Remove the cylinder head covers

25. Remove the both left and right cylinder heads.

26. Remove the oil pan.

27. Remove the oil pick up tube.

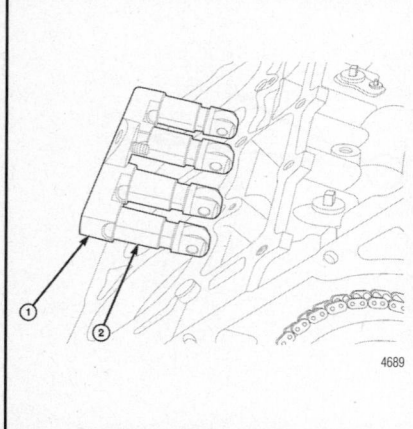

Fig. 126 Hydraulic roller and tappet (2) and retainer (1)

28. Remove the windage tray/oil pan gasket.

29. Remove the timing case cover.

30. Remove the oil pump.

31. Remove the timing chain and camshaft sprocket.

32. Remove the camshaft tensioner/thrust plate assembly.

→Identify lifters to ensure installation in original location.

33. Remove the tappets and retainer assembly.

34. Install the a long bolt into the front of the camshaft to aid in removal of the camshaft. Remove camshaft, being careful not to damage cam bearings with the cam lobes.

To install:

35. Lubricate the camshaft lobes and camshaft bearing journals and carefully insert the camshaft.

36. Install the camshaft tensioner plate assembly and tighten the bolts to 21 ft. lbs. (28 Nm).

37. Install the timing chain and sprockets.

38. Measure camshaft end play. If not within limits install a new thrust plate.

39. Install the oil pump.

→Each tappet must be installed in the same position from which it was removed.

→When the camshaft is replaced, all of the tappets must be replaced.

40. Install the tappets and retainer assembly.

41. Install the both left and right cylinder heads.

42. Install the pushrods in the same position from which they were removed.

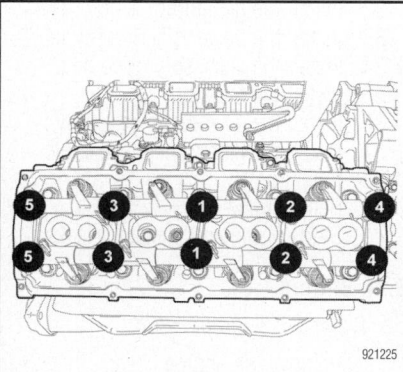

Fig. 127 Rocker arm and shaft installation sequence

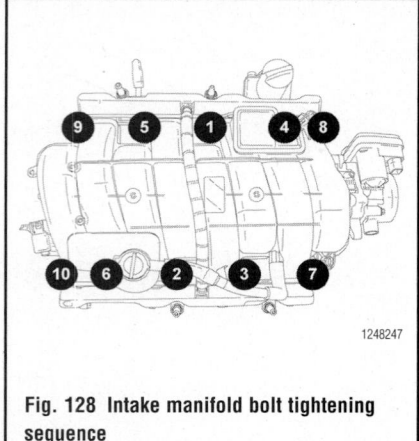

Fig. 128 Intake manifold bolt tightening sequence

43. Install the rocker arms and shaft assembly.

44. Using the sequence shown, install the rocker arm shaft bolts and tighten to 16 ft. lbs. (22 Nm).

45. Install the timing chain cover.

46. Install the oil pick up tube.

47. Install the oil pan.

48. Using the sequence shown, install the intake manifold and tighten the bolts to 9 ft. lbs. (12 Nm).

49. Install the cylinder head covers.

50. Install the A/C compressor.

51. Install the generator.

52. Install the accessory drive belt.

53. Install the radiator.

54. Install the air cleaner housing and clean air tube.

55. Install the negative battery cable.

56. Fill the cooling system.

57. Fill the engine with oil.

58. Install the engine covers.

59. Start engine and check for leaks.

6.4L Engine

See Figures 129 through 134

1. Remove the both cylinder heads.

✳✳ WARNING

The 6.4L Multi Displacement System (MDS) engine uses both standard roller lifters and deactivating roller lifters. The deactivating roller lifters must be used in cylinders 1,4,6,7. The deactivating lifters can be identified by the two holes in the side of the lifter body, for the latching pins.

✳✳ WARNING

Whenever the camshaft is replaced, all lifters must be replaced. If the lifter and retainer assemblies are to be reused, identify the lifters to

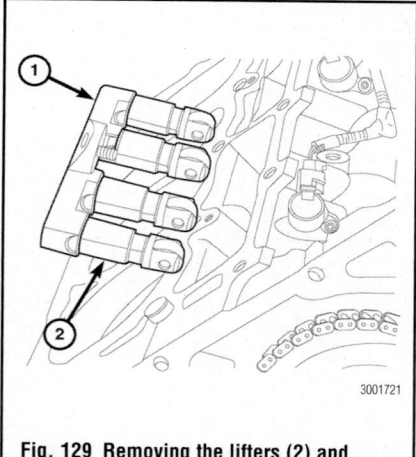

Fig. 129 Removing the lifters (2) and retainer (1)

ensure installation in their original location or engine damage could result.

The lifter and retainer assembly must be installed as a unit.

2. Remove the lifters and retainer as an assembly.
3. Remove the generator.
4. Remove the A/C compressor.
5. Remove the radiator.
6. Remove the A/C condenser.
7. Raise and safely support the vehicle.
8. Remove the oil pan and oil pump pickup tube.

➡It is not necessary to remove the water pump for timing cover removal.

9. Remove the engine timing cover.

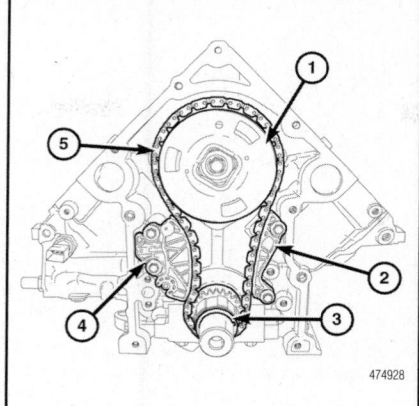

Fig. 131 Removing the timing chain (5)and camshaft phaser (1)

10. Remove the oil pump.
11. Remove the timing chain (5) and camshaft phaser (1).
12. Remove the camshaft thrust plate.

Use care when removing the camshaft, do not damage the camshaft bearings with the camshaft lobes.

13. Install the a long bolt into the front of the camshaft to aid in removal.
14. Remove the camshaft using care not to damage the camshaft bearings with the camshaft lobes.

To install:

15. Lubricate the camshaft lobes and the camshaft bearing journals with clean engine oil.
16. Install the a long bolt into the front of the camshaft to aid in the installation,

carefully install the camshaft into the engine block.

17. Install the camshaft thrust plate and tighten retaining bolts to 21 ft. lbs. (28 Nm).
18. Install the timing chain and camshaft phaser.
19. Using a suitable dial indicator, measure the camshaft end play. If not within specification, install a new thrust plate.
20. Install the oil pump.
21. Install the engine timing cover.
22. Raise and safely support the vehicle.
23. Install the oil pump pickup tube and oil pan.
24. Install the A/C condenser.
25. Install the radiator.
26. Install the A/C compressor.
27. Install the generator.

The 6.4L Multi Displacement System (MDS) engine uses both standard roller lifters and deactivating roller lifters. The deactivating roller lifters must be used in cylinders 1,4,6,7. The deactivating lifters can be identified by the two holes in the side of the lifter body, for the latching pins.

Whenever the camshaft is replaced, all lifters must be replaced. If the lifter and retainer assemblies are to be reused, identify the lifters to ensure installation in their original location or engine damage could result.

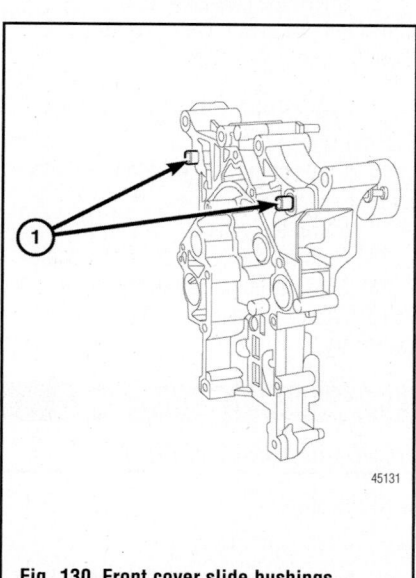

Fig. 130 Front cover slide bushings

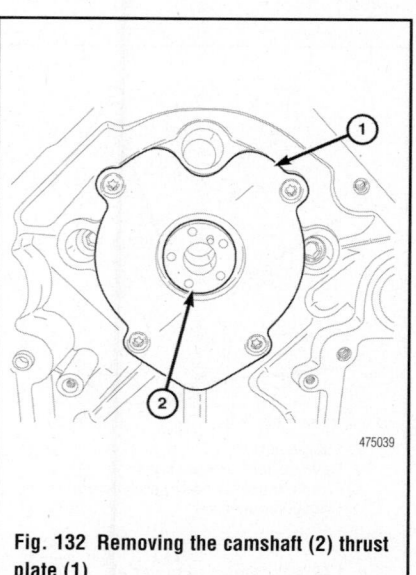

Fig. 132 Removing the camshaft (2) thrust plate (1)

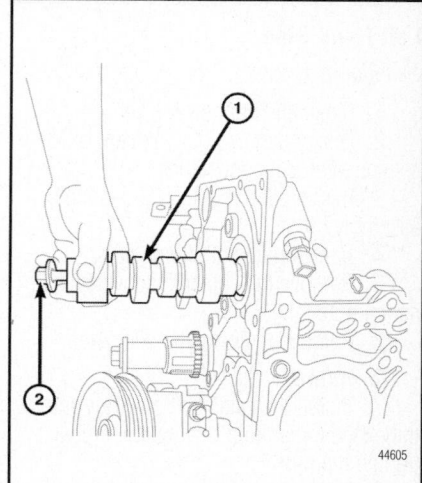

Fig. 133 Identifying the camshaft lobes (1) and long bolt (2)

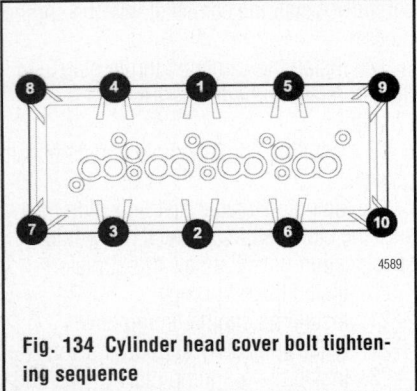

Fig. 134 Cylinder head cover bolt tightening sequence

> ## ☀☀ WARNING
>
> **The lifter and retainer assembly must be installed as a unit.**

28. Install the lifters and retainer as an assembly into their original location.
29. Install the both cylinder heads.
30. Install the pushrods in the same location as removed.
31. Install the rocker arms.
32. Install the cylinder head covers.
33. Install the accessory drive belt.
34. Install the air cleaner housing and clean air tube.
35. Install the negative battery cable.
36. Fill the cooling system with the specified type and amount of engine coolant.
37. Fill the crankcase with the specified type and amount of engine oil.
38. Install the engine covers.
39. Start the engine and check for leaks.

CATALYTIC CONVERTER

REMOVAL & INSTALLATION

Left Hand Side

See Figure 135.

1. Raise and support the vehicle.
2. Disconnect the downstream oxygen sensor electrical connectors.
3. Remove the muffler and resonator assembly.
4. Remove the ball flange nuts.
5. Remove the catalytic converter ball flange nuts.
6. Remove the catalytic converter.

To install:

7. Install the catalytic converter onto the exhaust manifold ball flange. Finger tighten the nuts.
8. Install the muffler and resonator assembly.
9. Install the bolts and the cross brace. Tighten the bolts to 40 ft. lbs. (55 Nm).

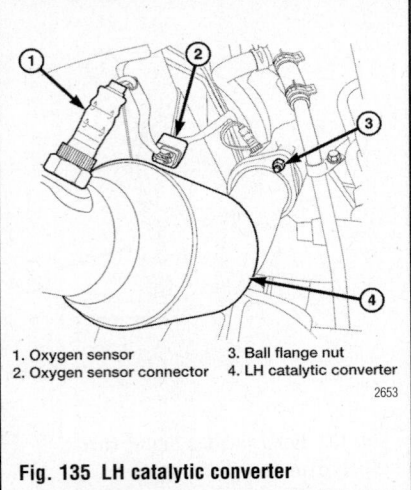

1. Oxygen sensor
2. Oxygen sensor connector
3. Ball flange nut
4. LH catalytic converter

Fig. 135 LH catalytic converter

10. Tighten the manifold ball flange nut to 9 ft. lbs. (12 Nm).
11. Check the clearance between exhaust module and fuel tank. Clearance is 14mm (.55 in.).
12. Check the clearance at the rear tunnel reinforcement. Clearance is 15 - 20mm (.59 - .78 in.).
13. Adjust the clearance as necessary.
14. Tighten the ball flange nuts to 25 ft. lbs. (34 Nm).
15. Lower the vehicle.
16. Connect the negative battery cable.
17. Start the engine and inspect for exhaust leaks. Repair exhaust leaks as necessary.

Right Hand Side

See Figures 136 and 137.

1. Disconnect the negative battery cable.

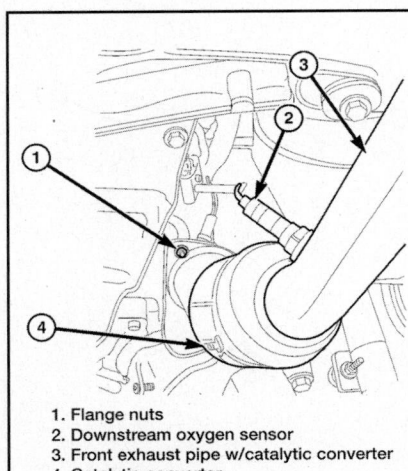

1. Flange nuts
2. Downstream oxygen sensor
3. Front exhaust pipe w/catalytic converter
4. Catalytic converter

Fig. 136 RH catalytic converter

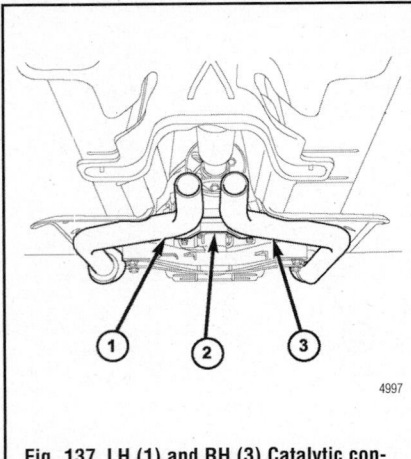

Fig. 137 LH (1) and RH (3) Catalytic converter brace (2)

2. Raise and support the vehicle.
3. Disconnect the downstream oxygen sensor electrical connectors.
4. Remove the muffler and resonator.
5. Remove the catalytic converter-to-ball flange nuts.
6. Remove the RH catalytic converter.

To install:

7. Install the catalytic converter onto the exhaust manifold ball flange. Finger tighten the nuts at this time.
8. Install the muffler and resonator assembly.
9. Install the bolts and cross brace. Tighten the bolts to 40 ft. lbs. (55 Nm).
10. Tighten the manifold ball flange nut to 9 ft. lbs. (12 Nm).
11. Check the clearance between the exhaust module and the fuel tank. Clearance is 14mm (.55 in.).
12. Check the clearance at the rear tunnel reinforcement. Clearance is 0.59–0.78 in. (15—20mm).
13. Adjust clearance as necessary.
14. Tighten the ball flange nuts to 25 ft. lbs. (34 Nm).
15. Connect the oxygen sensor connectors.
16. Lower the vehicle.
17. Connect the negative battery cable.
18. Start the engine and inspect for exhaust leaks. Repair exhaust leaks as necessary.

CRANKSHAFT FRONT SEAL

REMOVAL & INSTALLATION

3.5L Engine

See Figures 138 through 140.

1. Remove the crankshaft sprocket.

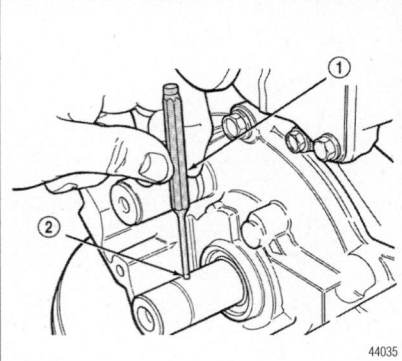

Fig. 138 Crankshaft sprocket dowel pin removal and installation using a pin punch (1) and dowel (2)

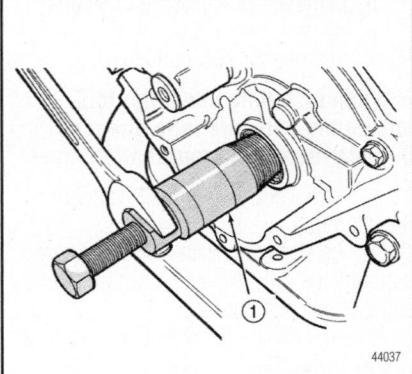

Fig. 139 Crankshaft Oil Seal with Special Tool 6341A

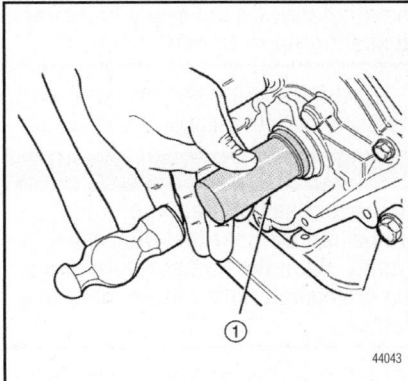

Fig. 140 Crankshaft Oil Seal with Special Tool 6342

2. Tap the dowel pin out of the crankshaft.

3. Remove the crankshaft seal using the special tool.

✳✳ WARNING

Do not nick shaft seal surface or seal bore.

4. Shaft seal lip surface must be free of varnish, dirt or nicks. Polish with 400 grit paper if necessary.

To install:

5. Install the crankshaft seal using the special tool.

6. Install the dowel pin into the crankshaft to 1.2 mm (0.047 in.) protrusion.

7. Install the crankshaft sprocket.

3.6L Engine

See Figure 141.

1. Remove the accessory drive belt and the crankshaft vibration damper.

2. Install the sleeve from the Seal Remover around the flywheel key and onto the nose of the crankshaft.

3. Screw the Seal Remover into the front crankshaft oil seal.

4. Install the extractor screw into the Seal Remover.

5. Hold the seal remover stationary and tighten the extractor screw against the sleeve until the front crankshaft oil seal is removed from the engine timing cover.

To install:

6. Position the front crankshaft oil seal into place on the engine timing cover.

7. Align the Front Crankshaft Seal Installer to the flywheel key on the crankshaft and against the front crankshaft oil seal.

✳✳ WARNING

Only tighten the crankshaft vibration damper bolt until the oil seal is

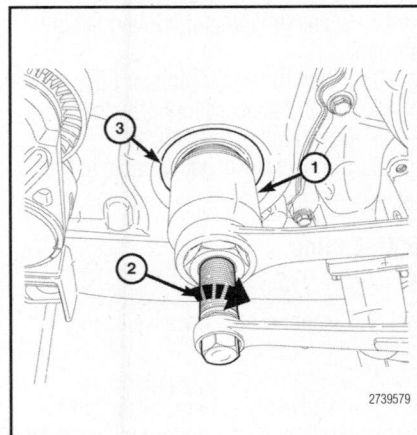

Fig. 141 Seal remover (1), extractor screw (2) and oil seal (3)

seated in the cover. Overtightening of the bolt can crack the front timing cover.

8. Install the and tighten the crankshaft vibration damper bolt until the Crankshaft oil seal is seated in the engine timing cover.

9. Install the crankshaft vibration damper and accessory drive belt

5.7L Engine

See Figures 142 and 143.

1. Disconnect the negative cable from the battery.

2. Remove the accessory drive belt.

3. Drain cooling system.

4. Remove the upper radiator hose.

5. Remove the radiator shroud attaching fasteners.

6. Remove the radiator cooling fan and shroud.

7. Remove the crankshaft damper bolt.

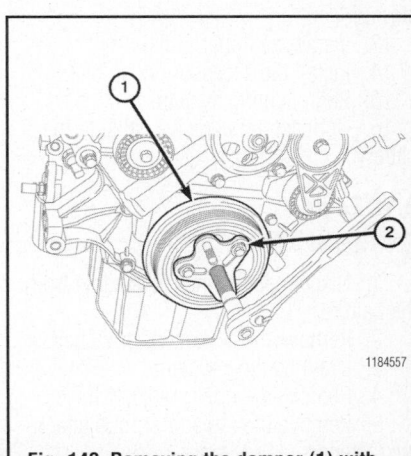

Fig. 142 Removing the damper (1) with bolt grip type puller (2)

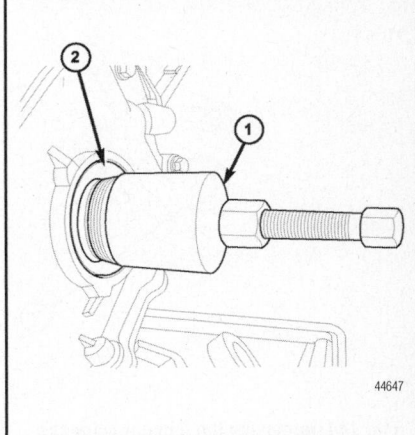

Fig. 143 Removing the crankshaft front seal (2) with the seal remover (1)

8. Remove the damper using bolt grip type puller.

9. Using Seal Remover, remove crankshaft front seal.

To install:

> ✳✳ **WARNING**
>
> **The front crankshaft seal must be installed dry. Do not apply lubricant to the sealing lip or the outer edge.**

10. Using crankshaft front oil seal installer and damper installer, install crankshaft front seal.

> ✳✳ **WARNING**
>
> **To prevent severe damage to the crankshaft or damper, thoroughly clean the damper bore and the crankshaft nose before installing damper.**

11. Install the vibration damper.

12. Install the radiator cooling fan and shroud.

13. Install the upper radiator hose.

14. Install the accessory drive belt.

15. Refill cooling system.

16. Connect the negative cable to the battery.

6.1L Engine

See Figures 144 and 145.

1. Disconnect the negative cable from the battery.

2. Remove the accessory drive belt.

3. Drain cooling system.

4. Remove the upper radiator hose.

5. Remove the radiator shroud attaching fasteners.

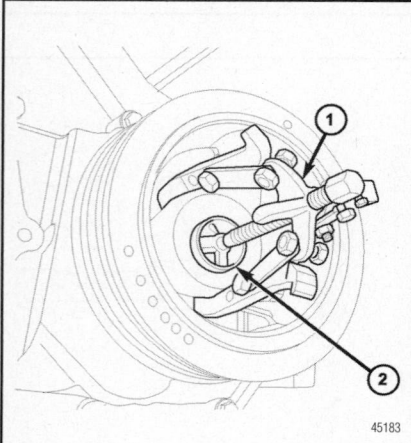

Fig. 144 Removing the damper using the crankshaft insert (1) and Three Jaw Puller (2)

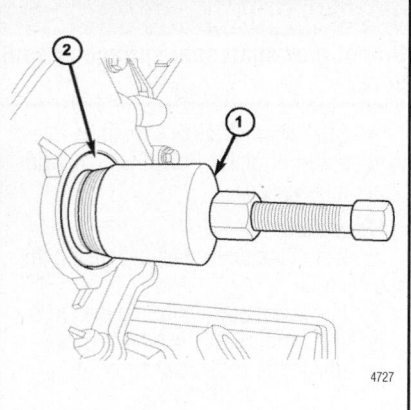

Fig. 145 Removing the front crankshaft seal (2) using the seal remover (1)

6. Remove the radiator cooling fan and shroud.

7. Remove the crankshaft damper bolt.

8. Remove the damper using the Crankshaft Insert and the Three Jaw Puller.

9. Use Seal Remover to remove the crankshaft front seal (2).

To install:

> ✳✳ **WARNING**
>
> **The front crankshaft seal must be installed dry. Do not apply lubricant to sealing lip or to outer edge.**

10. Use seal installer and damper installer to install the crankshaft front oil seal.

> ✳✳ **WARNING**
>
> **To prevent severe damage to the Crankshaft or Damper, thoroughly clean the damper bore and the crankshaft nose before installing Damper.**

11. Install the vibration damper.

12. Install the radiator cooling fan and shroud.

13. Install the upper radiator hose.

14. Install the accessory drive belt.

15. Refill cooling system.

16. Connect the negative cable to the battery.

6.4L Engine

See Figure 146.

1. Disconnect the negative battery cable.

2. Drain the cooling system.

3. Remove the upper radiator hose clamp and remove the upper radiator hose.

4. Remove the oil cooler hose clamp and remove oil cooler hose.

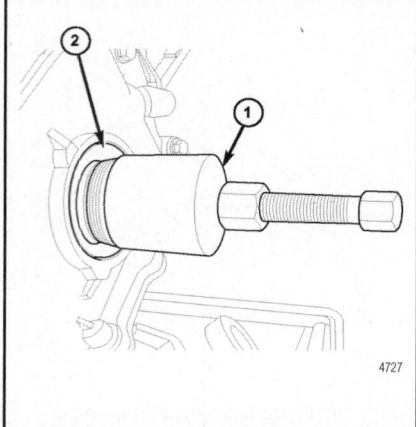

Fig. 146 Removing the crankshaft front oil seal

5. Remove the accessory drive belt.

6. Remove the radiator.

7. Remove the A/C condenser.

➡ **When installing the puller tool, ensure the bolts are fully threaded through the entire crankshaft damper.**

8. Remove the crankshaft damper retaining bolt.

9. Install the puller tool making sure the bolts are fully threaded through the entire crankshaft damper.

10. Remove the crankshaft damper.

11. Using Seal Remover, remove the crankshaft front seal.

To install:

> ✳✳ **WARNING**
>
> **The front crankshaft seal must be installed dry. Do not apply lubricant to sealing lip or to outer edge.**

12. Using Seal Installer and Damper Installer, install the crankshaft front oil seal.

> ✳✳ **WARNING**
>
> **To prevent severe damage to the crankshaft Damper Installer, thoroughly clean the damper bore and the crankshaft nose before installing damper.**

13. Position the damper on the crankshaft.

> ✳✳ **WARNING**
>
> **The Damper Installer is assembled in a specific sequence. Failure to assemble this tool in this sequence may result in tool failure and severe damage to either the tool or the crankshaft.**

14. Assemble the damper installer as follows:

a. Install the nut onto the threaded shaft.

b. Install the roller bearing onto the threaded shaft making sure the hardened bearing surface is facing the nut.

c. Install the pressing cup from the A/C Hub Installer onto the threaded shaft.

d. Coat the threaded shaft with MOPAR®Nickel Anti-Seize or equivalent.

15. Using the Damper Installer and the pressing cup from A/C Hub Installer, press the damper onto the crankshaft.

16. Install the vibration damper bolt and tighten to 129 ft. lbs. (176 Nm).

17. Install the accessory drive belt.

18. Install the A/C condenser.

19. Install the radiator.

20. Install the oil cooler hose and clamp.

21. Install the upper radiator hose and clamp.

22. Refill the cooling system.

23. Connect the negative battery cable.

CYLINDER HEAD

REMOVAL & INSTALLATION

3.5L Engine

See Figures 147 through 151.

1. Perform the fuel system pressure relief procedure.

2. Disconnect and isolate the negative battery cable.

3. Drain the cooling system.

4. Remove the air cleaner element housing.

5. Remove the upper intake manifold including the wiper module, strut tower support and EGR tube.

6. Remove the fuel rail and lower intake manifold.

7. Remove the accessory drive belt.

8. Remove the accessory drive belt idler pulley.

9. Remove the accessory drive belt tensioner.

10. Remove the three power steering pump mounting bolts through the access holes in the pulley and reposition the power steering pump.

11. Remove the upper radiator hose.

12. Disconnect the cooling fan electrical connector.

13. Remove the cooling fan mounting bolts.

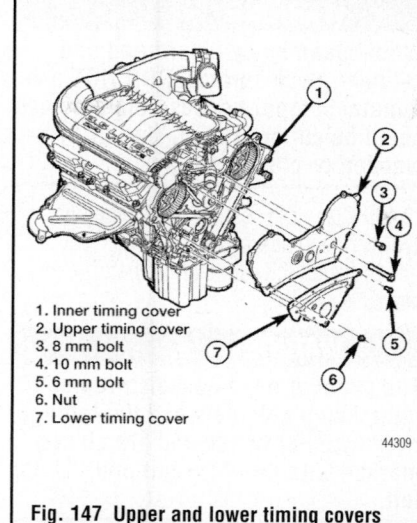

1. Inner timing cover
2. Upper timing cover
3. 8 mm bolt
4. 10 mm bolt
5. 6 mm bolt
6. Nut
7. Lower timing cover

44309

Fig. 147 Upper and lower timing covers

14. Remove the radiator cooling fan assembly from the vehicle.

15. Remove the crankshaft damper bolt.

16. Remove the crankshaft damper using Puller and Crankshaft Insert.

17. Remove the upper timing belt cover fasteners and remove the front upper timing belt cover.

18. Remove the lower timing belt cover fasteners and remove the front lower timing belt cover.

19. Raise and support the vehicle on a hoist.

20. Disconnect both upstream and downstream oxygen sensor harness connectors.

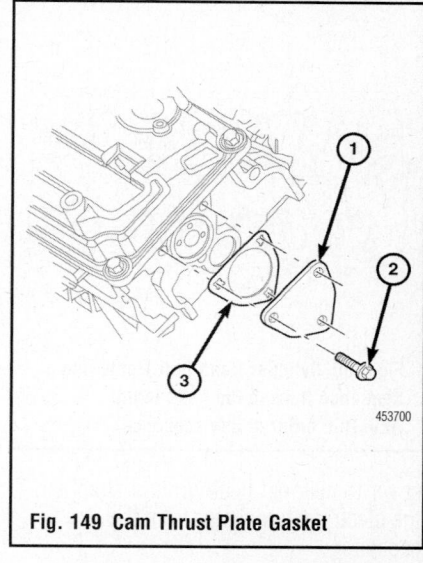

453700

Fig. 149 Cam Thrust Plate Gasket

21. Remove the front exhaust pipe to exhaust manifold mounting nuts.

22. Lower the vehicle.

23. Rotate the engine to TDC and align timing belt marks (1,8,9).

24. Remove the timing belt tensioner (12) and reset the tensioner.

25. Remove the timing belt.

26. Unlock and disconnect the electrical connector from the EGR valve.

27. Remove the EGR valve mounting bolts and remove the EGR valve.

28. Disconnect and remove the three ignition coils.

29. Lift up on the wire harness track retaining tabs.

30. Remove the right cylinder head

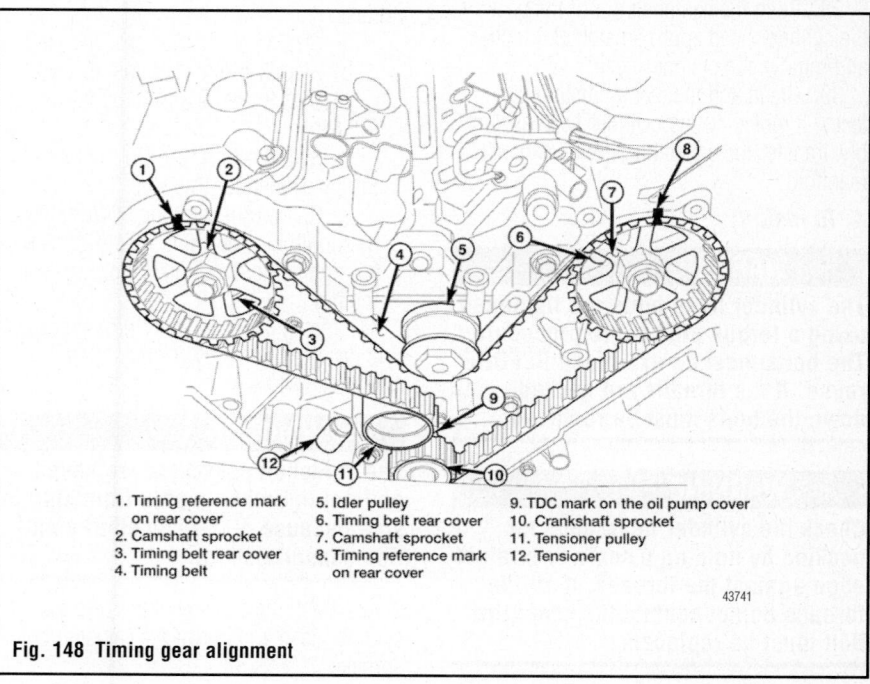

1. Timing reference mark on rear cover
2. Camshaft sprocket
3. Timing belt rear cover
4. Timing belt
5. Idler pulley
6. Timing belt rear cover
7. Camshaft sprocket
8. Timing reference mark on rear cover
9. TDC mark on the oil pump cover
10. Crankshaft sprocket
11. Tensioner pulley
12. Tensioner

43741

Fig. 148 Timing gear alignment

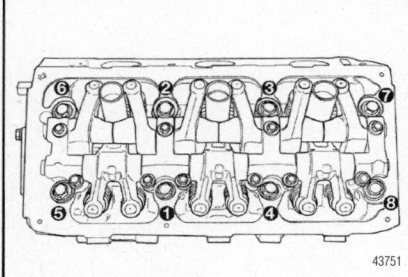

43751

Fig. 150 Cylinder Head Bolt Tightening Sequence (loosen the bolts in the REVERSE order of this sequence)

cover to cylinder head ground strap and the electrical connector from the capacitor.

31. Completely loosen the cylinder head cover retaining bolts and remove the cylinder head cover.

32. Remove the rocker arm assembly bolts and remove the right rocker arm assembly.

33. Remove the three bolts and the right rear camshaft thrust plate.

34. Counterhold the cam gear and remove the right cam gear retaining bolt.

35. Push the camshaft out of the back of the cylinder head approximately 3.5 inches and remove the cam gear.

36. Remove the three inner timing cover to right cylinder head retaining bolts.

37. Remove the cylinder head bolts in REVERSE of the tightening sequence shown.

38. Push the camshaft out of the back of the cylinder head approximately 3.5 inches and remove the cylinder head.

39. Clean and inspect all mating surfaces. If replacing the cylinder head assembly, transfer the capacitor and the exhaust manifold.

To install:

✳✳ WARNING

The cylinder head bolts are tightened using a torque plus angle procedure. The bolts must be examined BEFORE reuse. If the threads are necked down the bolts must be replaced.

✳✳ WARNING

Check the cylinder head bolts for necking by holding a scale or straight edge against the threads. If all the threads do not contact the scale the bolt must be replaced.

✳✳ WARNING

When cleaning cylinder head and cylinder block surfaces, DO NOT use a metal scraper because the surfaces could be cut or ground. Use ONLY a wooden or plastic scraper.

40. Clean the sealing surfaces of the cylinder head and block.

41. Install the camshaft in the cylinder head.

✳✳ WARNING

The cylinder head gaskets are not interchangeable between the left and right cylinder heads and are clearly marked with "R" for right and "L" for left.

✳✳ WARNING

Ensure that the correct head gaskets are used and are oriented correctly on cylinder block.

42. Push the camshaft out of the back of the cylinder head approximately 3.5 inches. Install the head gasket and cylinder head over the locating dowels.

➡ Before installing the cylinder head bolts, lubricate the threads with clean engine oil.

43. Install the and finger tighten eight head bolts.

44. Tighten the cylinder head bolts in the sequence shown, using the 4 step torque-turn method to the following torque values:

    a. Step 1: All to 45 ft. lbs. (61 Nm)

    b. Step 2: All to 65 ft. lbs. (88 Nm)

    c. Step 3: All (again) to 65 ft. lbs. (88 Nm)

    d. Step 4: + 90°Turn Do not use a torque wrench for this step.

    e. Bolt torque after the 90°turn (Step 4) should be over 90 ft. lbs. (122 Nm) in the tightening direction. If not, replace the bolt.

45. Install the three inner timing cover to cylinder head bolts (1). Tighten the bolts to 40 ft. lbs. (54 Nm).

✳✳ WARNING

The camshaft sprockets are keyed and not interchangeable from side to side because of the camshaft position sensor pick-up.

46. Push the camshaft back into the cylinder head and install the camshaft sprocket.

47. Install the a NEW sprocket attaching bolt into place. The 255 mm (10 in.) bolt is to be installed in the left camshaft and the 213 mm (8 3/8 in.) bolt is to be installed into the right camshaft. Counterhold the camshaft sprocket and tighten the camshaft sprocket bolt to 75 ft. lbs. (102 Nm) plus a 90°turn.

48. Install the camshaft thrust plate and gasket. Tighten three bolts to 21 ft. lbs. (28 Nm).

49. Install the a new gasket between the EGR solenoid/valve and the rear of the cylinder head.

50. Position the EGR solenoid/valve assembly to the rear of the cylinder head. Install and tighten two mounting bolts to 80 inch lbs. (8 Nm).

51. Rotate the right camshaft gear (2) to align its timing mark (1). Verify that the left camshaft gear (7) timing mark (8) and crankshaft gear (10) timing mark (9) are still aligned.

52. Install the timing belt (4) starting at the crankshaft sprocket (10) going in a counterclockwise direction. Install the belt around the last sprocket. Maintain tension on the belt as it is positioned around the tensioner pulley (11).

53. Holding the tensioner pulley (11) against the belt, install the tensioner (12) into the housing and tighten two bolts to 21 ft. lbs. (28 Nm). Each camshaft sprocket mark should remain aligned with the cover marks.

54. When the tensioner is in place, pull the retaining pin to allow the tensioner to extend to the tensioner pulley bracket.

55. Rotate the crankshaft sprocket two revolutions and check the timing marks on the camshafts and crankshaft. The marks should line up within their respective locations. If the marks do not line up, repeat the procedure.

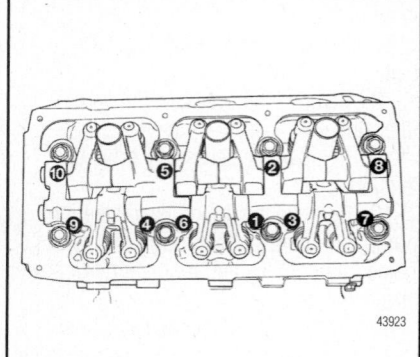

43923

Fig. 151 Rocker arm/shaft assembly bolt tightening sequence

➡️**With the camshaft gears in these positions the lobes are in a neutral position (no load to the valve). This will allow the rocker arm shaft assembly to be tightened into position with little or no valve spring load on it.**

56. Install the rocker arm and shaft assembly and ten bolts making sure that the identification marks face toward the front of engine for the left head and toward the rear of the engine for the right head.

57. Tighten the ten rocker arm/shaft assembly bolts in the sequence shown to 23 ft. lbs. (31 Nm).

58. Clean the cylinder head and cover mating surfaces. Inspect and replace the gasket and seals as necessary.

59. Install the cylinder head cover and eight bolts. Tighten bolts to 9 ft. lbs. (12 Nm).

60. Install the spark plugs. Tighten to 20 ft. lbs. (28 Nm).

61. Install the ignition coils into the cylinder head.

62. Install the and tighten the coil mounting bolts to 71 inch lbs. (8 Nm).

63. Reposition the engine wire harness and install the wire harness track retaining tabs. Connect and lock electrical connectors to the ignition coils, capacitor and EGR valve.

64. Install the front timing belt outer covers with 14 bolts.

65. Tighten the timing cover bolts as follows:
    a. M6 bolts - 9 ft. lbs. (12 Nm)
    b. M8 bolts - 21 ft. lbs. (28 Nm)
    c. M10 bolts - 40 ft. lbs. (54 Nm)

66. Install the crankshaft damper using Forcing Screw, with Nut and Thrust Bearing from Installer, Crank Sprocket, and Cup Installer.

67. Install the crankshaft damper bolt. Tighten the bolt to 70 ft. lbs. (95 Nm) while holding the damper with Damper Holding Fixture.

68. Align the power steering pump to the mounting holes on the engine bracket and install three pump mounting bolts through the access holes in the pulley. Tighten the bolts to 21 ft. lbs. (28 Nm).

69. Install the accessory drive belt tensioner. Tighten the bolt to 40 ft. lbs. (34 Nm).

70. Install the accessory drive belt idler pulley. Tighten the bolt to 21 ft. lbs. (28 Nm).

71. Install the accessory drive belt.

72. Install the radiator cooling fan assembly into the vehicle.

73. Install the cooling fan mounting bolts and tighten to 50 inch lbs. (6 Nm).

74. Connect the cooling fan electrical connector.

75. Install the upper radiator hose.

76. Raise and support the vehicle.

77. Install the front exhaust pipe. Tighten the ball flange nuts to 25 ft. lbs. (34 Nm).

78. Connect both upstream and downstream oxygen sensor harness connectors.

79. Lower the vehicle.

80. Install the fuel rail and lower intake manifold.

81. Install the upper intake manifold including the wiper module, strut tower support and EGR tube.

82. Install the air cleaner element housing.

83. Connect the negative battery cable. Tighten nut to 45 inch lbs. (5 Nm).

84. Fill and level check the coolant system.

85. Check for Stretched Bolts

3.6L Engine

Left Side

See Figures 152 through 159.

1. The magnetic timing wheels must not come in contact with magnets (pickup tools, trays, etc.) or any other strong magnetic field. This will destroy the timing wheels ability to correctly relay camshaft position to the camshaft position sensor.

2. Perform the fuel pressure release procedure.

3. Disconnect and isolate the negative battery cable.

4. Lift the engine cover retaining grommets off the ball studs and remove the engine cover.

5. Disconnect the electrical connector from the Inlet Air Temperature (IAT) sensor.

6. Loosen the clamp at the throttle body.

7. Loosen the clamp at the air cleaner housing.

8. Lift the air inlet hose assembly retaining grommet off the ball stud.

9. Remove the air inlet hose assembly.

10. Disconnect the fresh air makeup hose from the air cleaner housing.

11. Remove the air cleaner housing retaining bolt.

12. Remove the air cleaner housing.

13. Remove the fresh air makeup hose from the rear of the intake manifold.

14. Rotate the accessory drive belt tensioner counterclockwise until it contacts the stop and remove the accessory drive belt, then slowly rotate the tensioner into the freearm position.

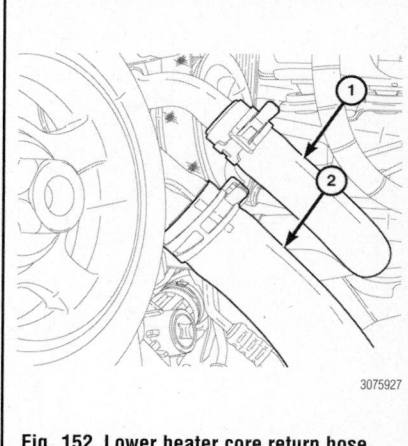

Fig. 152 Lower heater core return hose (1)

15. Raise and support the vehicle.

16. Remove the belly pan retainers and remove the belly pan.

17. Drain the cooling system.

18. Drain the engine oil.

19. Remove the lower heater core return hose from the engine coolant pump housing.

20. Remove the heater core return tube lower support bracket retaining nut.

21. Disconnect the A/C compressor electrical connector and disengage the wire harness retainer from the A/C compressor discharge line.

22. Remove the A/C compressor lower retaining studs.

23. Lower the vehicle.

24. Remove the A/C compressor upper retaining bolts and reposition the A/C compressor aside.

25. Remove the coolant bottle return hose.

26. Remove the heater core purge hose from the coolant bottle.

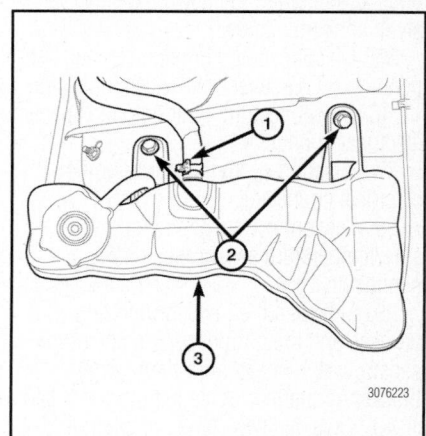

Fig. 153 Removing the coolant bottle (3), purge hose (1) and retaining bolts (3)

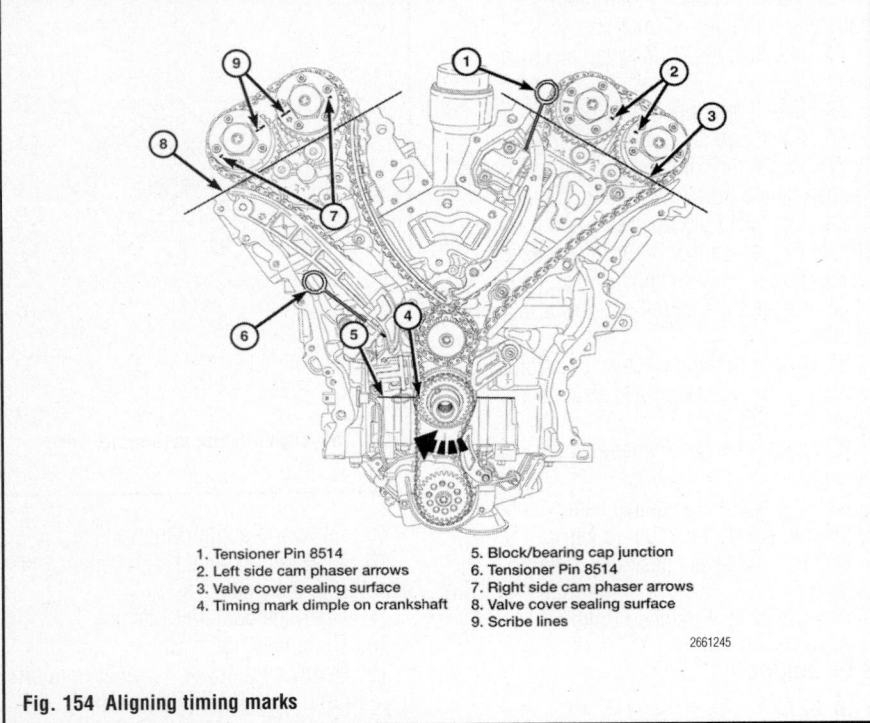

1. Tensioner Pin 8514
2. Left side cam phaser arrows
3. Valve cover sealing surface
4. Timing mark dimple on crankshaft
5. Block/bearing cap junction
6. Tensioner Pin 8514
7. Right side cam phaser arrows
8. Valve cover sealing surface
9. Scribe lines

2661245

Fig. 154 Aligning timing marks

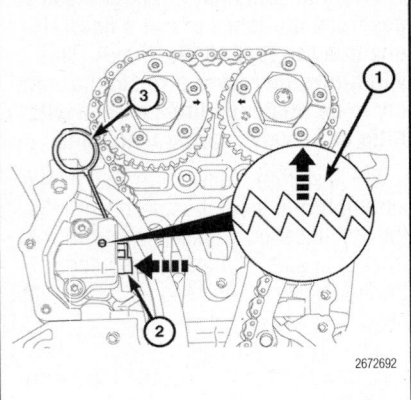

2672692

Fig. 155 Identifying the pawl (1), piston (2) and tensioner pin (3)

27. Remove the coolant bottle retaining bolts.

28. Remove the coolant bottle.

29. Disconnect the heater core return hose.

30. Remove the heater core return tube upper support bracket retaining nut and remove the tube.

31. Remove the upper and lower intake manifolds and insulator.

32. Disconnect the left upstream oxygen sensor electrical connector from the main wire harness.

33. Loosen the lower down pipe flange bolts.

34. Remove the upper down pipe flange bolts and position the down pipe and catalytic converter aside.

35. Disconnect the Engine Coolant Temperature (ECT) sensor electrical connector.

36. Disconnect the ignition coil capacitor electrical connector.

37. Disconnect the injection/ignition electrical connector.

38. Disconnect the engine oil pressure/temperature sensor electrical connector.

39. Unfasten the injection/ignition wire harness and the oil pressure/temperature sensor wire harness from the retainer bracket on the rear of the left cylinder head.

40. Unfasten two starter wire harness retainers from the upper intake manifold support brackets.

41. Unfasten one main wire harness retainer from the left cylinder head cover and two retainers from the upper intake manifold support brackets.

42. Remove the bolts and remove the left upper intake manifold support brackets.

43. Remove the ignition coils.

44. Remove the cylinder head covers, lower and upper oil pans, crankshaft vibration damper and engine timing cover.

➡ **Take this opportunity to measure timing chain wear.**

✳✳ WARNING

When aligning timing marks, always rotate engine by turning the crankshaft. Failure to do so will result in valve and/or piston damage.

45. Rotate the crankshaft clockwise to place the number one piston at TDC on the exhaust stroke by aligning the dimple on the crankshaft with the block/bearing cap junction. The left side cam phaser arrows should point toward each other and be parallel to the valve cover sealing surface. The right side cam phaser arrows should point away from each other and the scribe lines should be parallel to the valve cover sealing surface.

✳✳ WARNING

Always reinstall timing chains so that they maintain the same direction of

rotation. Inverting a previously run chain on a previously run sprocket will result in excessive wear to both the chain and sprocket.

46. Mark the direction of rotation on the timing chain using a paint pen or equivalent to aid in reassembly.

✳✳ WARNING

When the timing chains are removed and the cylinder heads are still installed, DO NOT rotate the camshafts or crankshaft without first locating the proper crankshaft position. Failure to do so will result in valve and/or piston damage.

47. Reset the left cam chain tensioner by lifting the pawl, pushing back the piston and installing Tensioner Pin.

➡ **Minor rotation of a camshaft (a few degrees) may be required to install the camshaft phaser lock.**

48. Install the LH Camshaft Phaser Lock.

49. Loosen both the intake oil control valve and exhaust oil control valve.

50. Remove the LH Camshaft Phaser Lock.

51. Remove the oil control valve from the left side exhaust cam phaser and pull the phaser off of the camshaft.

52. Remove the oil control valve from the left side intake cam phaser and pull the phaser off of the camshaft.

53. Remove the left cam chain tensioner arm.

54. Remove the two T30 bolts and the left cam chain tensioner.

55. Remove the two T30 bolts and the left cam chain guide.

56. Remove the left camshafts.

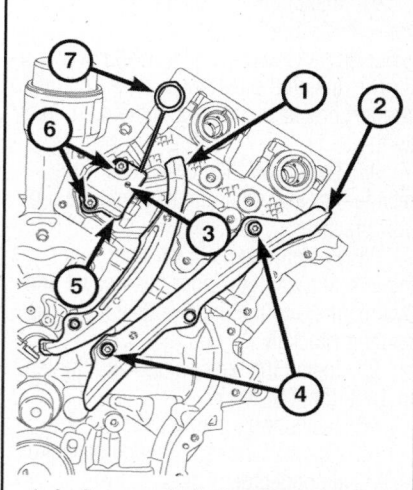

1. Left cam chain tensioner arm
2. Left cam chain guide
3. Pin
4. T30 bolts
5. Left cam chain tensioner
6. T30 bolts

2659731

Fig. 156 Removing the cam chain tensioner

➡️If the rocker arms are to be reused, identify their positions so that they can be reassembled into their original locations.

57. Remove the rocker arms.

➡️If the hydraulic lifters are to be reused, identify their positions so that they can be reassembled into their original locations.

58. If required, remove the hydraulic lifters.

59. Using the sequence shown, remove the cylinder head retaining bolts.

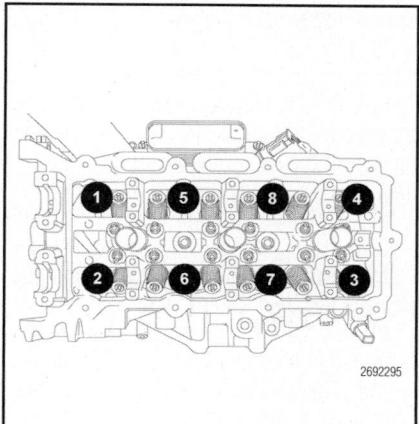

2692295

Fig. 157 Cylinder head retaining bolt removal sequence

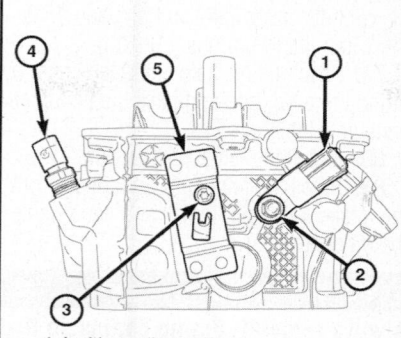

1. Ignition coil capacitor
2. Bolt
3. Bolt
4. ECT sensor
5. Engine wire harness retainer bracket

2876978

Fig. 158 Removing the ECT, ignition coil capacitor and engine wire harness retainer bracket

✳✳ CAUTION
The multi-layered steel head gaskets have very sharp edges that could cause personal injury if not handled carefully.

✳✳ WARNING
Do not lay the cylinder head on its gasket sealing surface, due to the design of the cylinder head gasket, any distortion to the cylinder head sealing surface may prevent the gasket from properly sealing resulting in leaks.

➡️The head gasket crimps the locating dowels and the dowels may pull out of the engine block when the head gasket is removed.

60. Remove the cylinder head and gasket and discard the gasket.

61. If required, remove the Engine Coolant Temperature (ECT) sensor.

62. If required, remove the bolt and the ignition coil capacitor.

63. If required, remove the bolt and the engine wire harness retainer bracket.

To install:
64. If removed, install the Engine Coolant Temperature (ECT) sensor and tighten to 97 inch lbs. (11 Nm).

65. If removed, install the ignition coil capacitor with a M6 bolt and tightened to 89 inch lbs. (10 Nm).

66. If removed, install the engine wire harness retainer bracket with a T30 bolt and tightened to 9 ft. lbs. (12 Nm).

✳✳ WARNING
The cylinder head bolts are tightened using a torque plus angle procedure. The bolts must be examined BEFORE reuse. If the threads are necked down the bolts must be replaced.

67. Check cylinder head bolts for necking by holding a scale or straight edge against the threads. If all the threads do not contact the scale the bolt must be replaced.

✳✳ WARNING
When cleaning cylinder head and cylinder block surfaces, DO NOT use a metal scraper because the surfaces could be cut or ground. Use ONLY a wooden or plastic scraper.

68. Clean and prepare the gasket sealing surfaces of the cylinder head and block.

✳✳ WARNING
Non-compressible debris such as oil, coolant or RTV sealants that are not removed from bolt holes can cause the aluminum casting to crack when tightening the bolts.

69. Clean out the cylinder head bolt holes in the engine block.

✳✳ CAUTION
The multi-layered steel head gaskets have very sharp edges that could cause personal injury if not handled carefully.

✳✳ WARNING
The cylinder head gaskets are not interchangeable between the left and right cylinder heads and are clearly marked with "R" for right and "L" for left.

70. Position the new cylinder head gasket onto the locating dowels.

71. Position the cylinder head onto the cylinder block. Make sure the cylinder head seats fully over the locating dowels.

➡️Do not apply any additional oil to the bolt threads.

72. Install the eight cylinder head bolts finger tight.

73. Tighten the cylinder head bolts in the sequence shown, following this 9 step torque plus angle method. Tighten according to the following torque values:
   a. Step 1: All to 22 ft. lbs. (30 Nm)
   b. Step 2: All to 33 ft. lbs. (45 Nm)

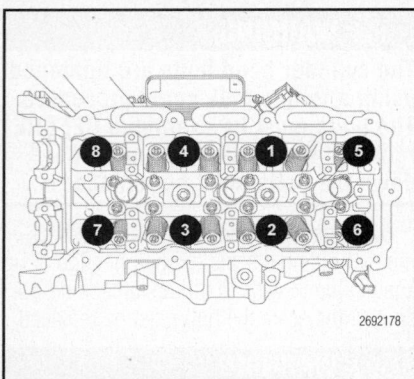

Fig. 159 Cylinder head bolt tightening sequence

c. Step 3: All + 75°Turn Do not use a torque wrench for this step.

d. Step 4: All + 50°Turn Do not use a torque wrench for this step.

e. Step 5: Loosen all fasteners in reverse of sequence shown

f. Step 6: All to 22 ft. lbs. (30 Nm)

g. Step 7: All to 33 ft. lbs. (45 Nm)

h. Step 8: All + 70°Turn Do not use a torque wrench for this step.

i. Step 9: All + 70°Turn Do not use a torque wrench for this step.

✳✳ WARNING

Do not rotate the camshafts more than a few degrees independently of the crankshaft. Valve to piston contact could occur resulting in possible valve damage. If the camshafts need to be rotated more than a few degrees, first move the pistons away from the cylinder heads by rotating the crankshaft counterclockwise to a position 30°BTDC. Once the camshafts are positioned at TDC rotate the crankshaft clockwise to return the crankshaft to TDC.

➡**If the hydraulic lifters are being reused, reassemble them into their original locations.**

74. If removed, install the hydraulic lifters.

➡**If the rocker arms are being reused, reassemble them into their original locations.**

75. Install the rocker arms and camshafts.

76. Rotate the camshafts clockwise to TDC by positioning the alignment holes vertically.

77. Install the left cam chain guide with two bolts and tighten the T30 bolts to 9 ft. lbs. (12 Nm).

78. Install the left cam chain tensioner to the cylinder head with two bolts and tighten the T30 bolts to 9 ft. lbs. (12 Nm).

79. Reset the left cam chain tensioner by lifting the pawl, pushing back the piston and installing Tensioner Pin.

80. Install the left tensioner arm.

81. Press the left intake cam phaser onto the intake camshaft, install and hand tighten the oil control valve.

✳✳ WARNING

Always reinstall timing chains so that they maintain the same direction of rotation. Inverting a previously run chain on a previously run sprocket will result in excessive wear to both the chain and sprocket.

82. Drape the left side cam chain over the left intake cam phaser and onto the idler sprocket so that the arrow is aligned with the plated link on the cam chain.

83. While maintaining this alignment, route the cam chain around the exhaust and intake cam phasers so that the plated links are aligned with the phaser timing marks. Position the left side cam phasers so that the arrows point toward each other and are parallel to the valve cover sealing surface. Press the exhaust cam phaser onto the exhaust cam, install and hand tighten the oil control valve.

➡**Minor rotation of a camshaft (a few degrees) may be required to install the camshaft phaser or phaser lock.**

84. Install the LH Camshaft Phaser Lock and tighten the oil control valves to 110 ft. lbs. (150 Nm).

85. Remove the LH Camshaft Phaser Lock.

86. Remove the Tensioner Pin from the left cam chain tensioner.

87. Rotate the crankshaft clockwise two complete revolutions stopping when the dimple on the crankshaft is aligned the with the block/bearing cap junction.

88. While maintaining this alignment, verify that the arrows on the left side cam phasers point toward each other and are parallel to the valve cover sealing surface and that the right side cam phaser arrows point away from each other and the scribe lines are parallel to the valve cover sealing surface.

89. There should be 12 chain pins between the exhaust cam phaser triangle marking and the intake cam phaser circle marking.

90. If the engine timing is not correct, repeat this procedure.

91. Install the engine timing cover, crankshaft vibration damper, upper and lower oil pans and cylinder head covers.

92. Install the left upper intake manifold support brackets and tighten the stud finger tight.

93. Fasten two starter wire harness retainers to the upper intake manifold support brackets.

94. Fasten one main wire harness retainer to the left cylinder head cover and two retainers to the upper intake manifold support brackets.

95. Install the spark plugs and tighten to 13 ft. lbs. (18 Nm).

96. Install the ignition coils.

97. Connect the ignition coil capacitor electrical connector.

98. Connect the injection/ignition electrical connector.

99. Connect the engine oil pressure/temperature sensor electrical connector.

100. Fasten the injection/ignition wire harness and the oil pressure/temperature sensor wire harness from the retainer bracket on the rear of the left cylinder head.

101. Connect the Engine Coolant Temperature (ECT) sensor electrical connector.

102. Install the upper and lower intake manifolds.

103. Position the heater core return tube onto the upper support bracket, install the retaining nut and tighten to 9 ft. lbs. (12 Nm).

104. Connect the heater core return hose.

105. Position the A/C compressor, install the upper bolts finger tight.

106. Install the lower A/C compressor retaining studs finger tight

107. Tightened the A/C compressor upper bolts to 18 ft. lbs. (25 Nm).

108. Raise and support the vehicle.

109. Position the heater core return tube lower support bracket onto the A/C compressor lower retaining stud, install the nut and tighten both A/C compressor lower retaining nuts to 18 ft. lbs. (25 Nm).

110. Connect the A/C compressor electrical connector and fasten the wire harness retainer to the A/C compressor discharge line.

111. Connect the lower heater core return hose to the engine coolant pump housing.

112. Position the left down pipe onto the partially installed lower flange bolts.

113. Install the upper down pipe flange bolts and tighten to 17 ft. lbs. (23 Nm).

114. Tighten the lower down pipe flange bolts to 17 ft. lbs. (23 Nm).

115. Connect the left upstream oxygen sensor electrical connector to the main wire harness.

116. If removed, install the oil filter.

117. Position the belly pan and install the retainers.

118. Lower the vehicle.

119. Rotate the accessory drive belt tensioner counterclockwise until it contacts the stop and install the accessory drive belt, then slowly rotate the tensioner into position.

120. Connect the fresh air makeup hose to the rear of the intake manifold.

121. Position the coolant bottle into the engine compartment.

122. Install the coolant bottle retaining bolts and tighten to 9 ft. lbs. (12 Nm).

123. Connect the heater core purge hose to the coolant bottle.

124. Connect the coolant bottle return hose.

125. Position the air cleaner housing into the vehicle.

126. Install the air cleaner housing retaining bolt and tighten to 9 ft. lbs. (12 Nm).

127. Connect the fresh air makeup hose to the air cleaner housing.

128. Position the air inlet hose assembly onto the throttle body and the air cleaner housing.

129. Secure the air inlet hose assembly retaining grommet onto the ball stud.

130. Tighten the clamp at the air cleaner housing to 44 inch lbs. (5 Nm).

131. Tighten the clamp at the throttle body to 44 inch lbs. (5 Nm).

132. Connect the Inlet Air Temperature (IAT) sensor electrical connector.

133. Fill the crankcase with the specified type and amount of engine oil.

134. Fill the cooling system with the specified type and amount of engine coolant.

135. Position the engine cover and secure the retaining grommets onto the ball studs.

136. Connect the negative battery cable and tighten nut to 45 inch lbs. (5 Nm).

137. Run the engine until it reaches normal operating temperature and check for leaks.

➡**The Cam/Crank Variation Relearn procedure must be performed using the scan tool anytime there has been a repair/replacement made to a powertrain system, for example: flywheel, valvetrain, camshaft and/or crankshaft sensors or components.**

Right Side

See Figures 160 through 163.

1. The magnetic timing wheels must not come in contact with magnets (pickup tools, trays, etc.) or any other strong mag-

netic field. This will destroy the timing wheels ability to correctly relay camshaft position to the camshaft position sensor.

2. Perform the fuel pressure release procedure.

3. Disconnect and isolate the negative battery cable.

4. Lift the engine cover retaining grommets off the ball studs and remove the engine cover.

5. Disconnect the electrical connector from the Inlet Air Temperature (IAT) sensor.

6. Loosen the clamp at the throttle body.

7. Loosen the clamp at the air cleaner housing.

8. Lift the air inlet hose assembly retaining grommet off the ball stud.

9. Remove the air inlet hose assembly.

10. Disconnect the fresh air makeup hose from the air cleaner housing.

11. Remove the air cleaner housing retaining bolt.

12. Remove the air cleaner housing.

13. Rotate the accessory drive belt tensioner counterclockwise until it contacts the stop and remove the accessory drive belt, then slowly rotate the tensioner into the freearm position.

14. Remove the generator.

15. Disconnect the vacuum line at the EVAP purge solenoid.

16. Disconnect the EVAP purge solenoid vacuum line at the intake manifold and remove the vacuum line.

17. Disconnect the PCV hose from the PCV valve and the intake manifold and remove hose.

18. Disconnect the brake booster vacuum hose and position aside.

19. Disconnect the electrical connector at the Manifold Absolute Pressure (MAP) Sensor.

20. Disconnect the electrical connector at the Electronic Throttle Control (ETC).

21. Disconnect the electrical connector at the Camshaft Position Sensor (CMP) and position harness aside.

22. Remove the upper and lower intake manifolds and insulator.

23. Raise and support the vehicle.

24. Remove the belly pan retainers and remove the belly pan.

25. Drain the cooling system.

26. Drain the engine oil.

27. Disconnect the right upstream oxygen electrical sensor connector from the main wire harness.

28. Loosen the lower down pipe flange bolts.

29. Remove the upper down pipe flange bolts and position the down pipe and catalytic converter aside.

30. Remove the oil level indicator retaining bolt and remove the oil level indicator.

31. Remove the heater core supply tube support bracket retaining bolt and remove the heater core supply tube.

32. Disconnect the ignition coil capacitor electrical connector.

33. Remove the stud and remove the upper intake manifold support bracket.

34. Remove the cylinder head covers, lower and upper oil pans, crankshaft vibration damper and engine timing cover.

➡**Take this opportunity to measure timing chain wear.**

35. Lower the vehicle.

36. Remove the ignition coils.

✳✳ WARNING

When aligning timing marks, always rotate engine by turning the crankshaft. Failure to do so will result in valve and/or piston damage.

✳✳ WARNING

Always reinstall timing chains so that they maintain the same direction of rotation. Inverting a previously run chain on a previously run sprocket will result in excessive wear to both the chain and sprocket.

37. Rotate the crankshaft clockwise to place the number one piston at TDC on the exhaust stroke by aligning the dimple on the crankshaft with the block/bearing cap junction. The left side cam phaser arrows should point toward each other and be parallel to the valve cover sealing surface. The

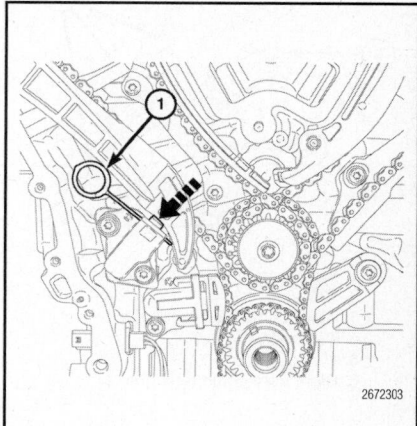

Fig. 160 Resetting the right cam chain tensioner

right side cam phaser arrows should point away from each other and the scribe lines should be parallel to the valve cover sealing surface.

38. Mark the direction of rotation on the timing chain using a paint pen or equivalent to aid in reassembly.

✳✳ WARNING

When the timing chains are removed and the cylinder heads are still installed, DO NOT rotate the camshafts or crankshaft without first locating the proper crankshaft position. Failure to do so will result in valve and/or piston damage.

39. Reset the right cam chain tensioner by pushing back the tensioner piston and installing Tensioner Pin.

➡**Minor rotation of a camshaft (a few degrees) may be required to install the camshaft phaser lock.**

40. Install the RH Camshaft Phaser Lock.
41. Loosen both the intake oil control valve and exhaust oil control valve.
42. Remove the RH Camshaft Phaser Lock.
43. Remove the oil control valve from the right side intake cam phaser and pull the phaser off of the camshaft.
44. Remove the oil control valve from the right side exhaust cam phaser and pull the phaser off of the camshaft.
45. Remove the right cam chain tensioner arm.
46. Remove the two T30 bolts and the right cam chain tensioner.

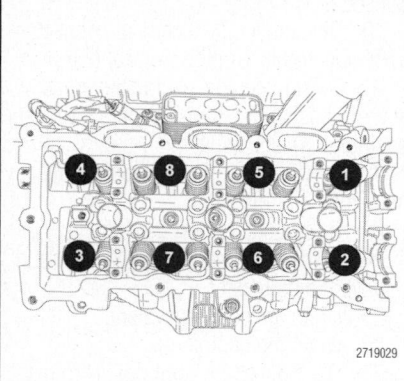

1. Right cam chain guide
2. T30 bolts
3. Right cam chain tensioner
4. T30 bolts
5. –
6. Right cam chain tensioner arm

2659678

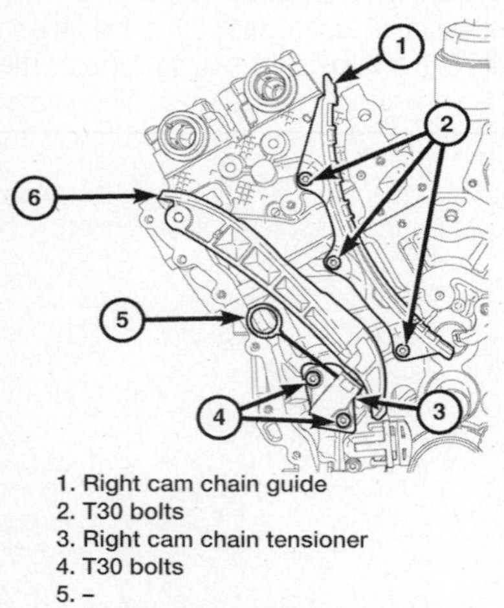

Fig. 161 Removing the right cam chain tensioner

47. Remove the three T30 bolts and the right cam chain guide.
48. Remove the right camshafts.

➡**If the rocker arms are to be reused, identify their positions so that they can be reassembled into their original locations.**

49. Remove the rocker arms.

➡**If the hydraulic lifters are to be reused, identify their positions so that they can be reassembled into their original locations.**

50. If required, remove the hydraulic lifters.
51. Using the sequence shown, remove the cylinder head retaining bolts.

✳✳ CAUTION

The multi-layered steel head gaskets have very sharp edges that could cause personal injury if not handled carefully.

✳✳ WARNING

Do not lay the cylinder head on its gasket sealing surface, due to the design of the cylinder head gasket, any distortion to the cylinder head sealing surface may prevent the gasket from properly sealing resulting in leaks.

➡**The head gasket crimps the locating dowels and the dowels may pull out of the engine block when the head gasket is removed.**

52. Remove the cylinder head and gasket. Discard the gasket.
53. If required, remove the bolt and the ignition coil capacitor.

2719029

Fig. 162 Cylinder head retaining bolt removal sequence

To install:

54. If removed, install the ignition coil capacitor with an M6 bolt tightened to 89 inch lbs. (10 Nm).

✳✳ WARNING

The cylinder head bolts are tightened using a torque plus angle procedure. The bolts must be examined BEFORE reuse. If the threads are necked down the bolts must be replaced.

55. Check the cylinder head bolts for necking by holding a scale or straight edge against the threads. If all the threads do not contact the scale the bolt must be replaced.

✳✳ WARNING

When cleaning cylinder head and cylinder block surfaces, DO NOT use a metal scraper because the surfaces could be cut or ground. Use ONLY a wooden or plastic scraper.

56. Clean and prepare the gasket sealing surfaces of the cylinder head and block.

✳✳ WARNING

Non-compressible debris such as oil, coolant or RTV sealants that are not removed from bolt holes can cause the aluminum casting to crack when tightening the bolts.

57. Clean out the cylinder head bolt holes in the engine block.

✳✳ CAUTION

The multi-layered steel head gaskets have very sharp edges that could cause personal injury if not handled carefully.

✳✳ WARNING

The cylinder head gaskets are not interchangeable between the left and right cylinder heads and are clearly marked with "R" for right and "L" for left.

58. Position the new cylinder head gasket on the locating dowels.
59. Position the cylinder head onto the cylinder block. Make sure the cylinder head seats fully over the locating dowels.

➡**Do not apply any additional oil to the bolt threads.**

60. Install the eight cylinder head bolts finger tight.

61. Tighten the cylinder head bolts in the sequence shown, following this 9 step torque plus angle method. Tighten according to the following torque values:

   a. Step 1: All to 22 ft. lbs. (30 Nm)

   b. Step 2: All to 33 ft lbs. (45 Nm)

   c. Step 3: All + 75°Turn Do not use a torque wrench for this step.

   d. Step 4: All + 50°Turn Do not use a torque wrench for this step.

   e. Step 5: Loosen all fasteners in reverse of sequence shown

   f. Step 6: All to 22 ft. lbs. (30 Nm)

   g. Step 7: All to 33 ft. lbs. (45 Nm)

   h. Step 8: All + 70°Turn Do not use a torque wrench for this step.

   i. Step 9: All + 70°Turn Do not use a torque wrench for this step.

➡**If the hydraulic lifters are being reused, reassemble them into their original locations.**

62. If removed, install the hydraulic lifters.

➡**If the rocker arms are being reused, reassemble them into their original locations.**

63. Install the rocker arms and camshafts.

✳✳ WARNING

Do not rotate the camshafts more than a few degrees independently of the crankshaft. Valve to piston contact could occur resulting in possible valve damage. If the camshafts need to be rotated more than a few degrees, first move the pistons away from the cylinder heads by rotating the crankshaft counterclockwise to a position 30° BTDC. Once the camshafts are positioned at TDC

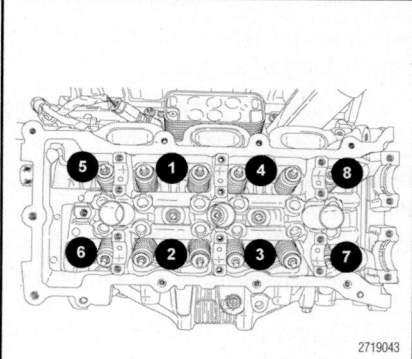

2719043

Fig. 163 Cylinder head bolt tightening sequence

rotate the crankshaft clockwise to return the crankshaft to TDC.

64. Verify that the camshafts are set at TDC by positioning the alignment holes vertically.

65. Install the right cam chain guide with three bolts. Tighten the T30 bolts to 9 ft. lbs. (12 Nm).

66. Install the right cam chain tensioner to the engine block with two bolts. Tighten the T30 bolts to 9 ft. lbs. (12 Nm).

67. Reset the right cam chain tensioner by pushing back the tensioner piston and installing Tensioner Pin.

68. Install the right tensioner arm.

✳✳ WARNING

Always reinstall timing chains so that they maintain the same direction of rotation. Inverting a previously run chain on a previously run sprocket will result in excessive wear to both the chain and sprocket.

69. Press the right exhaust cam phaser onto the exhaust camshaft. Install and hand tighten the oil control valve.

70. Drape the right side cam chain over the right exhaust cam phaser and onto the idler sprocket so that the dimple is aligned with the plated link on the cam chain.

71. While maintaining this alignment, route the cam chain around the exhaust and intake cam phasers so that the plated links are aligned with the phaser timing marks. Position the right side cam phasers so that the arrows point away from each other and the scribe lines are parallel to the valve cover sealing surface. Press the intake cam phaser onto the intake cam, install and hand tighten the oil control valve.

➡**Minor rotation of a camshaft (a few degrees) may be required to install the camshaft phaser or phaser lock.**

72. Install the RH Camshaft Phaser Lock and tighten the oil control valves to 110 ft. lbs. (150 Nm).

73. Remove the RH Camshaft Phaser Lock.

74. Remove the Tensioner Pin from the RH cam chain tensioner.

75. Rotate the crankshaft clockwise two complete revolutions stopping when the dimple on the crankshaft is aligned the with the block/bearing cap junction.

76. While maintaining this alignment, verify that the arrows on the left side cam

phasers point toward each other and are parallel to the valve cover sealing surface and that the right side cam phaser arrows point away from each other and the scribe lines are parallel to the valve cover sealing surface.

77. There should be 12 chain pins between the exhaust cam phaser triangle marking and the intake cam phaser circle marking.

78. If the engine timing is not correct, repeat this procedure.

79. Install the engine timing cover, crankshaft vibration damper, upper and lower oil pans and cylinder head covers.

80. Install the spark plugs and tighten to 13 ft. lbs. (18 Nm).

81. Install the ignition coils.

82. Position the upper intake manifold support bracket and install the retaining stud finger tight.

83. Install the heater core supply tube with one bolt tightened to 9 ft. lbs. (12 Nm).

84. Position the oil level indicator, install the retaining bolt and tighten to 9 ft. lbs. (12 Nm).

85. Install the generator.

86. Rotate the accessory drive belt tensioner counterclockwise until it contacts the stop and install the accessory drive belt, then slowly rotate the tensioner into position.

87. Install the right down pipe onto the partially installed lower flange bolts.

88. Install the upper down pipe flange bolts and tighten all M8 bolts to 17 ft. lbs. (23 Nm).

89. Connect the right upstream oxygen sensor connectors to the main wire harness.

90. Install the upper and lower intake manifolds.

91. Connect the electrical connector at the Camshaft Position Sensor (CMP).

92. Connect the electrical connector at the Electronic Throttle Control (ETC).

93. Connect the electrical connector at the Manifold Absolute Pressure (MAP) Sensor.

94. Connect the brake booster vacuum hose.

95. Connect the PCV hose to the PCV valve and to the intake manifold.

96. Connect the EVAP purge solenoid vacuum line to the intake manifold.

97. Connect the vacuum line to the EVAP purge solenoid.

98. Raise and support the vehicle.

99. If removed, install the oil filter.

100. Position the belly pan and install the retainers.

101. Lower the vehicle.

102. Position the air cleaner housing into the vehicle.

103. Install the air cleaner housing retaining bolt and tighten to 9 ft. lbs. (12 Nm).

104. Connect the fresh air makeup hose to the air cleaner housing.

105. Position the air inlet hose assembly onto the throttle body and the air cleaner housing.

106. Secure the air inlet hose assembly retaining grommet onto the ball stud.

107. Tighten the clamp at the air cleaner housing to 44 inch lbs. (5 Nm).

108. Tighten the clamp at the throttle body to 44 inch lbs. (5 Nm).

109. Connect the Inlet Air Temperature (IAT) sensor electrical connector.

110. Fill the crankcase with the specified type and amount of engine oil.

111. Fill the cooling system with the specified type and amount of engine coolant.

112. Position the engine cover and secure the retaining grommets onto the ball studs.

113. Connect the negative battery cable and tighten nut to 45 inch lbs. (5 Nm).

114. Run the engine until it reaches normal operating temperature and check for leaks.

➡ **The Cam/Crank Variation Relearn procedure must be performed using the scan tool anytime there has been a repair/replacement made to a powertrain system, for example: flywheel, valvetrain, camshaft and/or crankshaft sensors or components.**

5.7L Engine

See Figures 164 through 172.

❊❊ **CAUTION**

The fuel system is under a constant pressure (even with engine off). Before servicing any fuel system hose, fitting or line, fuel system pressure must be released.

1. Perform the fuel system pressure release procedure.

❊❊ **WARNING**

Before separating a quick-connect fitting, pay attention to what type of fitting is being used. This will prevent unnecessary fitting or fitting latch breakage.

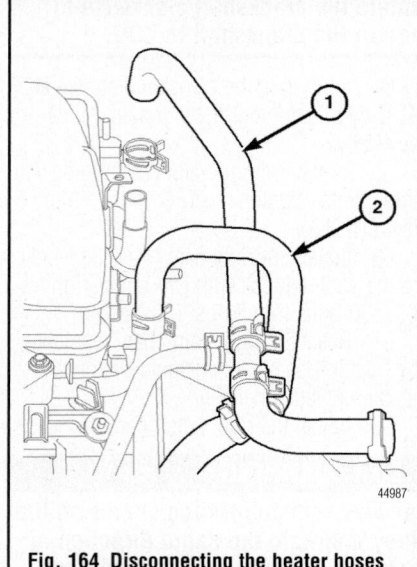

Fig. 164 Disconnecting the heater hoses

2. Disconnect the fuel supply line.

3. Disconnect the negative battery cable.

❊❊ **CAUTION**

Do not remove cylinder block drain plugs or loosen radiator draincock with system hot and under pressure. Serious burns from coolant can occur.

4. Drain the cooling system.

5. Disconnect the Intake Air Temperature (IAT) sensor electrical connector.

6. Remove the air cleaner resonator and duct work as an assembly.

❊❊ **WARNING**

When servicing or replacing exhaust system components, disconnect the oxygen sensor connector(s). Allowing the exhaust to hang by the oxygen sensor wires will damage the harness and/or sensor.

7. Saturate all exhaust bolts and nuts with Mopar®Rust Penetrant. Allow 5 minutes for penetration.

8. Remove the exhaust pipe to manifold bolts.

9. Disconnect the evaporation control system.

10. Disconnect the heater hoses.

11. Insert a suitable square drive ratchet into the square hole on the belt tensioner arm.

12. Release the belt tension by rotating the tensioner clockwise. Rotate the belt tensioner and remove the accessory drive belt from the pulleys.

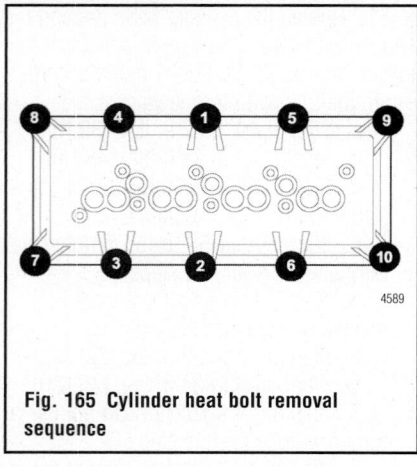

Fig. 165 Cylinder heat bolt removal sequence

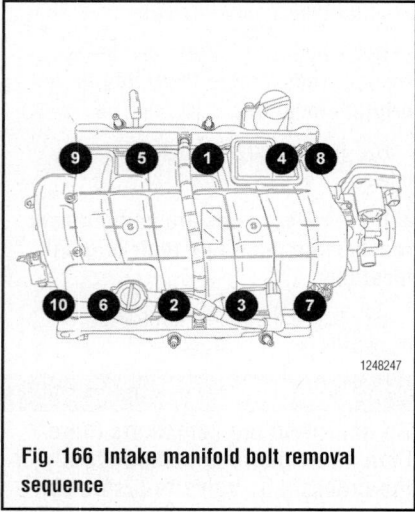

Fig. 166 Intake manifold bolt removal sequence

➡ **It is not necessary to disconnect the P/S hoses from the pump, for P/S pump removal.**

13. Remove the three power steering pump mounting bolts through access holes in pulley.

14. Remove the cylinder head covers and gaskets, using the sequence shown.

➡ **Remove the intake manifold and throttle body as an assembly.**

15. Remove the intake manifold retaining fasteners in the sequence shown.

➡ **Make sure to identify the original location of the rocker arms and push rods for correct assembly.**

16. Remove the rocker arm assemblies using the sequence shown.

17. Remove the push rods.

18. Remove the head bolts from each cylinder head using the sequence shown.

19. Remove the cylinder head and discard the cylinder head gasket(s).

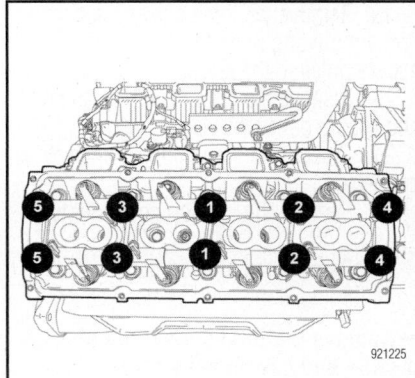

Fig. 167 Rocker arm assembly removal sequence

To install:

⁂ WARNING

The cylinder head gaskets are not interchangeable between the left and right sides. They are marked with an "L" and "R" to indicate the left or right side and they are marked "TOP" to indicate which side goes up.

⁂ WARNING

The head gaskets are marked "TOP" to indicate which side goes up.

20. Clean all surfaces of the cylinder block and cylinder heads.

21. Clean the cylinder block front and the rear gasket surfaces using a suitable solvent.

22. Position the new cylinder head gaskets onto the cylinder block.

23. Position the cylinder heads onto the head gaskets and the cylinder block.

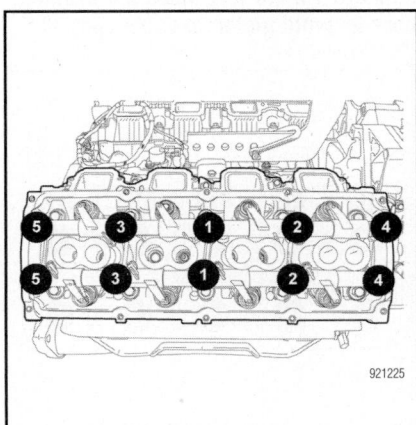

Fig. 168 Cylinder head bolt removal sequence

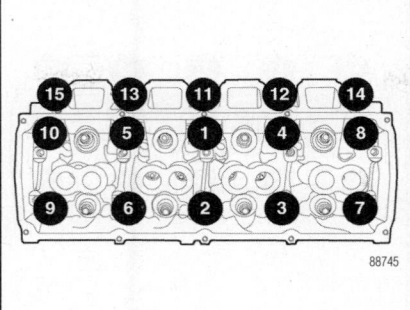

Fig. 169 Cylinder head bolt tightening sequence

24. Tighten the cylinder head bolts 1 through 10 to 25 ft. lbs. (34 Nm) using the sequence shown.

25. Tighten the cylinder head bolts 11 through 15 to 15 ft. lbs. (20 Nm) using the sequence shown.

26. Tighten the cylinder head bolts 1 through 10 to 40 ft. lbs. (54 Nm) using the sequence shown.

27. Tighten the cylinder head bolts 11 through 15 to 15 ft. lbs. (20 Nm) using the sequence shown.

28. Rotate the cylinder head bolts 1 through 10 90° using the sequence shown.

29. Tighten the cylinder head bolts 11 through 15 to 25 ft. lbs. (34 Nm) using the sequence shown.

30. Install the push rods and rocker arm assemblies in their original position, using Pushrod Retainer
Retainer.

31. Install the intake manifold seals.

32. Position the intake manifold in place.

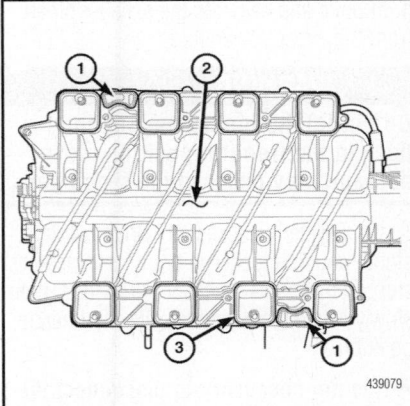

Fig. 170 Installing intake manifold seals (1, 3) and intake manifold (2)

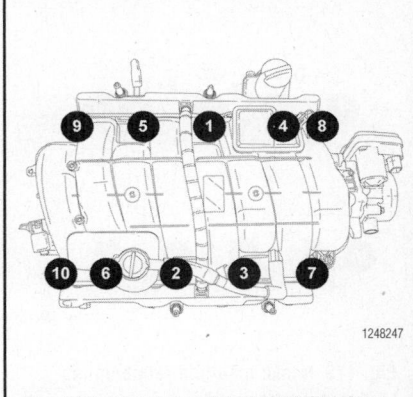

Fig. 171 Intake manifold bolt tightening sequence

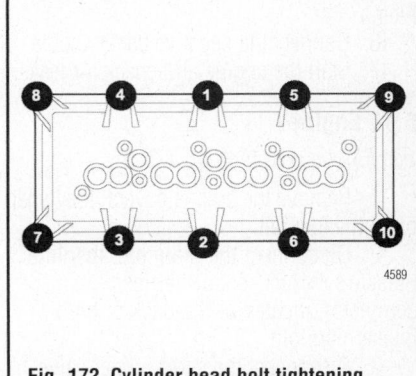

Fig. 172 Cylinder head bolt tightening sequence

33. Install the new intake manifold bolts (with thread lock patch) and tighten to 9 ft. lbs. (12 Nm) in the sequence shown.

34. Connect the heater hoses.

35. Connect the fuel supply line.

36. Install the three power steering pump mounting bolts through access holes in pulley. Tighten bolts to 21 ft. lbs. (28 Nm).

37. Position the accessory drive belt over all pulleys except for the water pump pulley.

38. Insert a suitable square drive ratchet into the square hole on the belt tensioner arm.

39. Rotate the tensioner clockwise and slip the accessory drive belt over the water pump pulley.

40. Install the cylinder head covers and tighten retainers in the sequence shown.

41. Connect the evaporation control system.

42. Install the air cleaner resonator and duct work as an assembly.

43. Connect the Intake Air Temperature (IAT) sensor electrical connector.

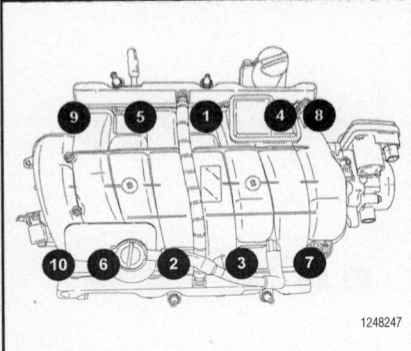

Fig. 173 Intake manifold retaining fastener removal sequence

44. Fill the cooling system.
45. Change the engine oil and engine oil filter.
46. Connect the negative battery cable.
47. Start the engine and check for leaks.

6.1L Engine

See Figures 173 through 175.

1. Remove the engine covers, they snap off of the fuel rail.
2. Disconnect the manifold absolute pressure (MAP) sensor harness connector, located at the back of the intake manifold.
3. Disconnect the short runner valve (SRV), located at the back of the intake manifold.
4. Disconnect the intake air temperature (IAT) sensor harness connector.
5. Remove the air cleaner housing and clean air tube.
6. Disconnect the electronic throttle body harness connector.
7. Disconnect the brake booster vacuum hose (it may be easier to disconnect the vacuum hose at the booster).

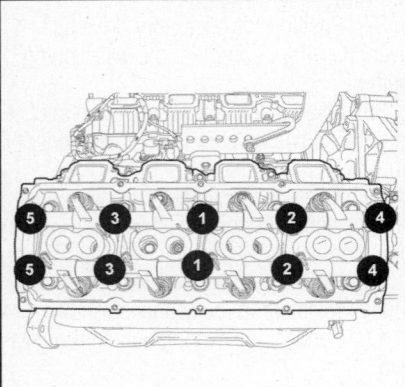

Fig. 174 Rocker arm assembly removal sequence

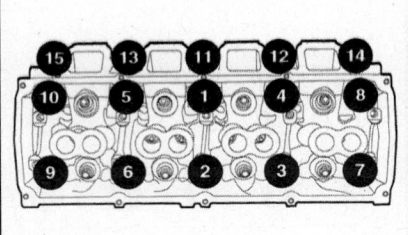

Fig. 175 Cylinder head bolt removal sequence

8. Disconnect the evaporative purge vacuum hose, and the make-up air (MUA) hose from the intake manifold.
9. Perform the fuel system pressure release procedure.
10. Disconnect the fuel injector harness connectors.
11. Disconnect the fuel supply line.
12. Disconnect the negative battery cable.
13. Drain the cooling system.
14. Disconnect the heater hoses.

✳✳ WARNING

When separating the catalytic converters from the manifolds, disconnect the oxygen sensor connectors. Allowing the catalytic converters hanging from the oxygen sensor wires damages the harness and/or sensors.

15. Disconnect the oxygen sensor electrical connectors.
16. Saturate all exhaust bolts and nuts with Mopar®Rust Penetrant. Allow five minutes for penetration.
17. Remove the exhaust pipe to the manifold bolts and separate the exhaust pipes from the exhaust manifolds.

✳✳ WARNING

Do not let the tensioner arm snap back to the freearm position, sever damage may occur to the tensioner.

18. Rotate the accessory drive belt tensioner counterclockwise until it contacts it's stop. Remove the accessory drive belt, then slowly rotate the tensioner into the freearm position.

➡It is not necessary to disconnect the power steering pump hoses from the pump, for power steering pump removal.

19. Remove the three power steering pump mounting bolts (2) through the access holes in the pulley.
20. Remove the power steering pump and secure out of the way.
21. Disconnect the ignition coil electrical connectors.
22. Remove the ignition coil mounting bolts.
23. Remove the ignition coils.
24. Remove the cylinder head cover.

➡Remove the intake manifold and throttle body as an assembly.

25. Using the sequence shown, remove the intake manifold retaining fasteners
26. Remove the intake manifold and throttle body as an assembly.

➡Make sure to identify the original location of the rocker arms and push rods for correct assembly.

27. Using the sequence shown, remove the rocker arm assemblies.
28. Remove the push rods.
29. Using the sequence shown, remove the head bolts from each cylinder head and remove the cylinder heads. Discard the cylinder head gaskets.

To install:
See Figure 176.

30. Clean all surfaces of cylinder block and cylinder heads.
31. Clean cylinder block front and rear gasket surfaces using a suitable solvent.

✳✳ WARNING

The head gaskets are interchangeable between left and right sides. They are marked "UP" to indicate direction to face up.

➡Rotate crankshaft 45°, so that all pistons are 1/2 the way down the cylinder bore to avoid piston to valve contact.

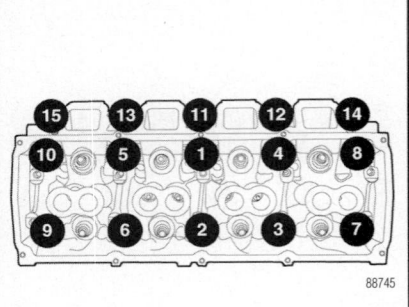

Fig. 176 Cylinder head bolt tightening sequence

32. Position new cylinder head gaskets onto the cylinder block.

33. Position cylinder heads in place.

34. Install the head bolts.

35. Tighten the cylinder head bolts in four steps using the sequence shown:

a. Step 1 - Tighten bolts 1-10 to 25 ft. lbs. (34 Nm) and bolts 11-15 to 15 ft. lbs. (20 Nm) in the sequence shown.

b. Step 2 - Tighten bolts 1-1 0 to 40 ft. lbs. (54 Nm) and verify bolts 11-15 are 15 ft. lbs. (20 Nm) in the sequence shown.

c. Step 3 - Rotate bolts 1-10 an additional 90 degrees in the sequence shown.

d. Step 4 - Tighten bolts 11-15 to 25 ft. lbs. (34 Nm) in the sequence shown.

✳✳ WARNING

Pushrods and rocker arm assemblies must be installed in their original locations or engine damage could result.

36. Install the Pushrod retainer on cylinder head.

37. Install the intake pushrods in their original position and snap push rods into pushrod retainer.

38. Install the intake rocker shaft and remove pushrod retainer.

39. Install the exhaust pushrods and rocker shaft.

40. Install the intake manifold and throttle body assembly.

41. Install the spark plugs.

42. Connect the heater hoses.

43. Install the fuel supply line.

44. Install the power steering pump.

45. Install the accessory drive belt.

46. Install the cylinder head covers.

47. Install the ignition coils.

48. Connect the ignition coil electrical connectors and injector electrical connectors.

49. Connect the evaporation control system.

50. Install the air cleaner housing and connect to throttle body.

51. Connect make-up air hose, and vacuum lines.

52. Connect intake air temperature sensor electrical connector.

53. Fill cooling system.

54. Connect the negative cable to the battery.

55. Install the engine covers.

56. Start engine check for leaks.

6.4L Engine

See Figures 177 through 182.

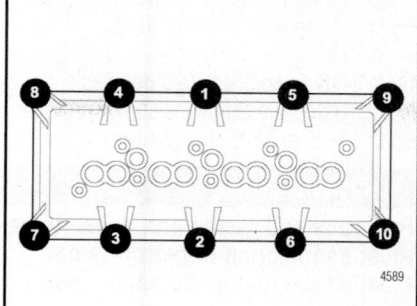

Fig. 177 Cylinder head cover bolt removal sequence

1. Perform the fuel system pressure release procedure.

2. Disconnect the negative battery cable.

3. Remove the engine covers.

4. Remove the intake manifold.

5. Drain the cooling system.

6. Disconnect the heater hoses.

7. Remove the catalytic converters.

8. Lower the vehicle.

✳✳ WARNING

Do not let the tensioner arm snap back to the freearm position, sever damage may occur to the tensioner.

9. Rotate the accessory drive belt tensioner clockwise until it contacts it's stop. Remove the accessory drive belt, then slowly rotate the tensioner into the freearm position.

➡**It is not necessary to disconnect the power steering pump hoses from the pump, for power steering pump removal.**

10. Remove the three power steering pump retaining bolts through the access holes in the pulley.

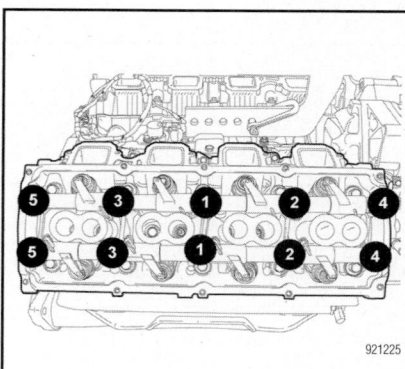

Fig. 178 Rocker arm and pushrod removal sequence

11. Remove the power steering pump and secure out of the way.

12. Using the sequence shown, remove the cylinder head cover retaining bolts and remove cover.

13. If removing the right cylinder head, remove the engine oil dip stick tube retaining nut at the exhaust manifold and remove the oil dip stick tube.

✳✳ WARNING

Pushrods and rocker arm assemblies must be installed in their original locations or engine damage could result.

➡**Make sure to identify the original location of the rocker arms and push rods for correct assembly.**

14. Remove the rocker arms and pushrods.

➡**Left side shown, right side similar.**

➡**It is not necessary to remove the exhaust manifolds to remove the cylinder heads.**

15. Using the sequence shown, remove the cylinder head bolts and remove the cylinder head(s).

➡**Left side shown, right side similar.**

16. Discard the cylinder head gasket.

17. Inspect and clean the cylinder head mating surface.

18. If necessary, using the sequence shown, remove the exhaust manifold bolts and remove the manifold.

To install:

➡**Left side shown, right side similar.**

19. If removed, using a new exhaust manifold gasket, position the exhaust mani-

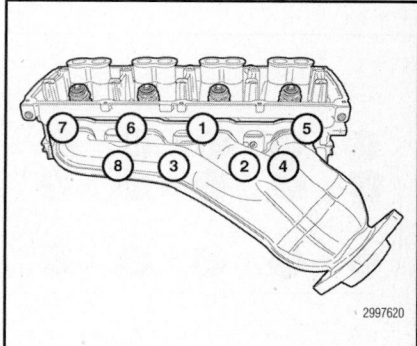

Fig. 179 Exhaust manifold bolt tightening sequence (remove the bolts in the REVERSE of this sequence)

fold and install the retaining bolts finger tight.

20. Using the sequence shown, tighten the retaining bolts to 23 ft. lbs. (31 Nm).

> ✴ **WARNING**
>
> **The cylinder head gaskets are not interchangeable between left and right sides. They are marked "UP" to indicate direction to face up and "L" or "R" to indicate left side or right side of engine block.**

21. Clean all sealing surfaces of the engine block and the cylinder head(s).

➡ **Rotate crankshaft 45°so that all pistons are 1/2 the way down the cylinder bore to avoid piston to valve contact.**

22. Position the new cylinder head gasket(s) onto the engine block.
23. Position the cylinder head(s) onto the engine block.
24. Install the cylinder head bolts finger tight.

> ✴ **WARNING**
>
> **The 6.4L engine uses a unique 4 layer steel head gasket that must be compressed evenly and completely across the deck surface for proper sealing. The tightening sequence must be followed to ensure all layers are compressed before applying the additional 90 degree turn.**

25. Using the sequence below, tighten the retaining bolts.
26. Using the sequence shown, tighten bolts 1-10 to 25 ft. lbs. (34 Nm).
27. Using the sequence shown, tighten bolts 11-15 to 15 ft. lbs. (20 Nm).
28. Using the sequence shown, tighten bolts 1-10 to 40 ft. lbs. (54 Nm).
29. Using the sequence shown, verify bolts 11-15 are 15 ft. lbs. (20 Nm).

30. Using the sequence shown, tighten bolts 1-10 to 45 ft. lbs. (61 Nm).
31. Using the sequence shown, rotate bolts 1-10 an additional 90 degrees.
32. Using the sequence shown, tighten bolts 11-15 to 25 ft. lbs. (34 Nm).

> ✴ **WARNING**
>
> **Pushrods and rocker arm assemblies must be installed in their original locations or engine damage could result.**

33. Install the pushrods and rocker arms.
34. If removed, install the oil dip stick tube and tighten the retaining nut at the exhaust manifold.
35. Position the cylinder head covers, using the sequence shown, tighten the cylinder head cover bolts to 70 inch lbs. (8 Nm).
36. Install the power steering pump.

> ✴ **WARNING**
>
> **Do not let the tensioner arm snap back to the freearm position, sever damage may occur to the tensioner.**

37. Rotate the accessory drive belt tensioner clockwise until it contacts it's stop, install the accessory drive belt, then slowly release the tensioner into position.
38. Raise and support the vehicle.
39. Install the catalytic converters.
40. Lower the vehicle.
41. Connect the heater hoses.
42. Install the intake manifold and throttle body as an assembly.
43. Connect the fuel supply line.
44. Install the engine covers.
45. Fill cooling system.
46. Connect the negative battery cable.
47. Start engine check for leaks.

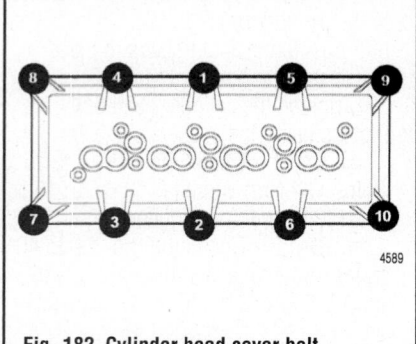

Fig. 182 Cylinder head cover bolt tightening sequence

ENGINE OIL & FILTER

REPLACEMENT

3.5L Engine

See Figure 183.

➡ **When servicing the oil filter, avoid deforming the filter can. Install the remove/install tool band strap against the base lock seam. The lock seam joining the can to the base is reinforced by the base plate.**

1. Using a suitable oil filter wrench, unscrew filter from base and discard.

To install:

2. Wipe base clean, then inspect gasket contact surface.
3. Lubricate gasket of new filter with clean engine oil.
4. Install the and tighten filter to 9 ft. lbs. (12 Nm) of torque after gasket contacts base. Use filter wrench if necessary.
5. Start engine and check for leaks.

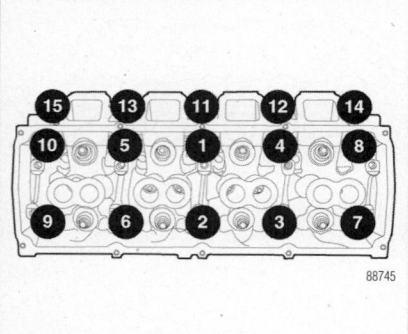

Fig. 180 Retaining bolt tightening sequence

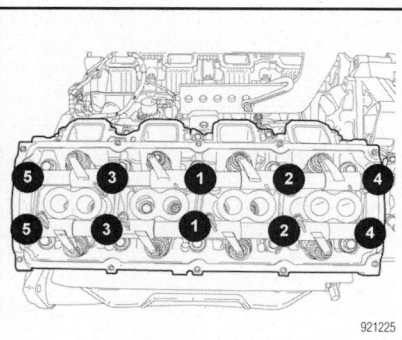

Fig. 181 Pushrod and rocker arm installation sequence

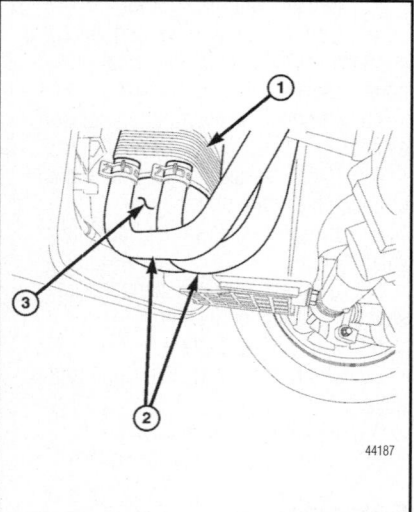

Fig. 183 Removing the oil filter (3), lines (2) and cooler (1)

3.6L Engine

See Figures 184 through 186.

✳✳ CAUTION

New or used engine oil can be irritating to the skin. Avoid prolonged or repeated skin contact with engine oil. Contaminants in used engine oil, caused by internal combustion, can be hazardous to your health. Thoroughly wash exposed skin with soap and water. Do not wash skin with gasoline, diesel fuel, thinner, or solvents, health problems can result. Do not pollute, dispose of used engine oil properly. Contact your dealer or government agency for location of collection center in your area.

1. Run the engine until achieving normal operating temperature.
2. Position the vehicle on a level surface and turn the engine off.
3. Remove the oil filter access cover.

✳✳ WARNING

When performing an engine oil change, the oil filter cap must be removed. Removing the oil filter cap releases oil held within the oil filter cavity and allows it to drain into the sump. Failure to remove the cap prior to reinstallation of the drain plug will not allow complete draining of the used engine oil.

4. Place an oil absorbent cloth around the oil filter housing at the base of the oil filter cap.

➡**The oil filter is attached to the oil filter cap.**

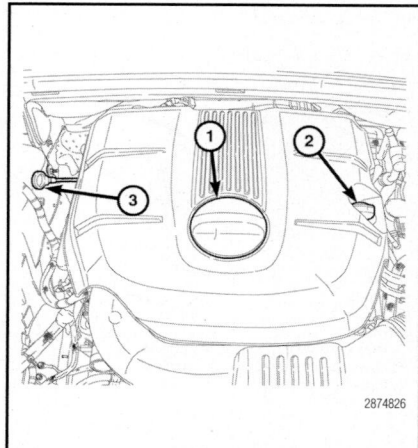

Fig. 184 Removing the oil filter access cover (1)

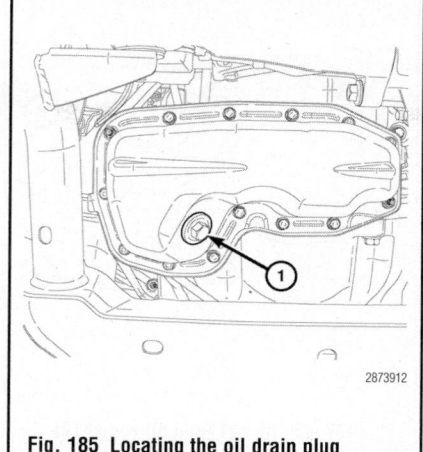

Fig. 185 Locating the oil drain plug

5. Rotate the oil filter cap counterclockwise and remove the cap and filter from the oil filter housing.
6. Raise and support the vehicle.
7. Place a suitable drain pan under the crankcase drain plug.
8. Remove the drain plug from oil pan and allow the oil to drain into the pan. Inspect the drain plug threads for stretching or other damage. Replace the drain plug and gasket if damaged.
9. Install the drain plug in the oil pan and tighten to 20 ft. lbs. (27 Nm).
10. Lower the vehicle.
11. Remove the oil filter from the oil filter cap.
12. Remove the and discard the O-ring seal.

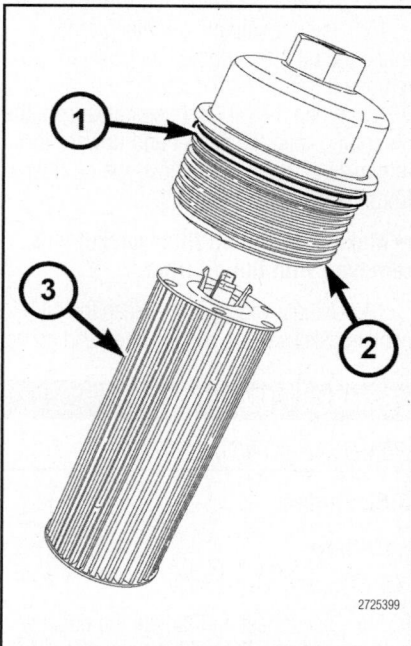

Fig. 186 Removing the oil filter (3), O-ring seal (1) and oil filter cap (2)

➡**It is not necessary to pre-oil the oil filter or fill the oil filter housing.**

13. Lightly lubricate the new O-ring seal with clean engine oil.
14. Install the O-ring seal on the filter cap.
15. Install the new oil filter into the oil filter cap.
16. Thread the oil filter cap into the oil filter housing and tighten to 18 ft. lbs. (25 Nm).
17. Remove the oil fill cap. Fill the crankcase with the specified type and amount of engine oil.
18. Install the oil fill cap.
19. Start the engine and inspect for leaks.
20. Stop the engine and check the oil level.

5.7L Engine

All engines are equipped with a high quality full-flow, disposable type oil filter. Chrysler Corporation recommends a Mopar®or equivalent oil filter be used.

1. Position a drain pan under the oil filter.
2. Using a suitable oil filter wrench loosen filter.
3. Rotate the oil filter counterclockwise to remove it from the cylinder block oil filter boss.
4. When filter separates from cylinder block oil filter boss, tip gasket end upward to minimize oil spill. Remove filter from vehicle.

➡**Make sure filter gasket was removed with filter.**

5. With a wiping cloth, clean the gasket sealing surface of oil and grime.

To install:

6. Lightly lubricate oil filter gasket with engine oil.
7. Thread filter onto adapter nipple. When gasket makes contact with sealing surface, hand tighten filter one half turn, or 180°. Do not over tighten.
8. Add oil, verify crankcase oil level and start engine. Inspect for oil leaks.

6.1L Engine

All engines are equipped with a high quality full-flow, disposable type oil filter.

1. Remove the belly pan.
2. Position a drain pan under the oil filter.
3. Using a suitable oil filter wrench loosen the oil filter.
4. Rotate the oil filter counterclockwise to remove it from the cylinder block oil filter boss.

5. When the oil filter separates from the cylinder block oil filter boss, tip the gasket end upward to minimize oil spill. Remove the oil filter from vehicle.

➡**Make sure the oil filter gasket was removed with the oil filter.**

6. With a wiping cloth, clean the gasket sealing surface of oil and grime.

To install:

7. Lightly lubricate the oil filter gasket with clean engine oil.

➡**Do not over tighten the oil filter.**

8. Thread the oil filter onto the cylinder block oil filter boss. When the gasket makes contact with the sealing surface, hand tighten the oil filter one half turn, or 180°.

9. Install the belly pan.

10. Lower the vehicle and fill the crankcase with the specified type and amount of engine oil as described in this section.

11. Install the oil fill cap.

12. Start the engine and check for leaks.

13. Turn the engine off and check the oil level.

6.4L Engine

See Figure 187.

Oil

On the 6.4L engine, the oil level indicator is located on the right side of the engine.

⚠️ **WARNING**

Do not overfill crankcase with engine oil, pressure loss or oil foaming can result.

Inspect the engine oil level approximately every 500 miles (800 kilometers). Unless the engine has exhibited loss of oil pressure, run the engine for about ten minutes before checking the oil level. Checking the engine oil level on a cold engine is not accurate.

To ensure proper lubrication of an engine, the engine oil must be maintained at an acceptable level. The acceptable levels are indicated between the ADD and SAFE marks on the engine oil level indicator.

Run the engine until it reaches normal operating temperature.

1. Remove the oil fill cap.

2. Raise and support the vehicle.

3. Remove the belly pan.

4. Place a suitable drain pan under the oil pan drain.

5. Remove the drain plug from the oil pan and allow the oil to drain.

6. Inspect the drain plug threads for stretching or other damage and replace if necessary.

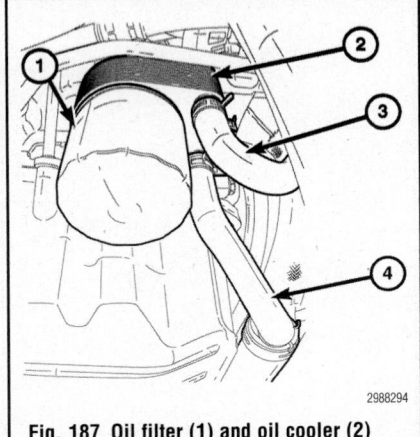

Fig. 187 Oil filter (1) and oil cooler (2)

7. Install the drain plug and tighten to 20 ft. lbs. (27 Nm).

8. Install the belly pan.

9. Lower the vehicle and fill the crankcase with the specified type and amount of engine oil.

10. Install the oil fill cap.

11. Start the engine and check for leaks.

12. Stop the engine and check the oil level.

➡**Care should be exercised when disposing of used engine oil.**

Filter

All engines are equipped with a high quality full-flow, disposable type oil filter.

13. Raise and support the vehicle.

14. Remove the belly pan retainers and remove the belly pan.

15. Position a drain pan under the oil filter.

16. Using a suitable oil filter wrench, rotate the oil filter counterclockwise to remove it from the oil cooler.

17. When the oil filter separates from the oil cooler, keep the gasket end upward to minimize oil spill and remove the oil filter from vehicle.

➡**Make sure the oil filter gasket was removed with the oil filter.**

18. Using a wiping cloth, clean the oil cooler gasket sealing surface of oil and grime.

EXHAUST MANIFOLD

REMOVAL & INSTALLATION

3.5L Engine

Left Side

See Figures 188 and 189.

1. Disconnect and isolate the negative battery cable.

2. Disconnect the upstream oxygen sensor electrical connector.

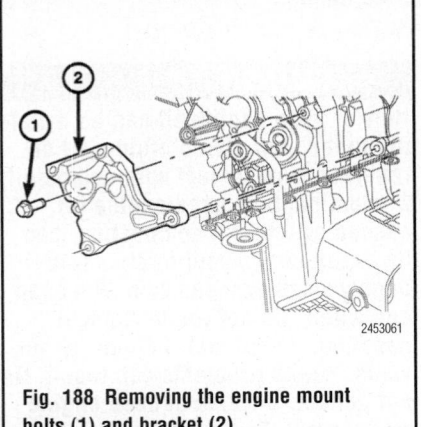

Fig. 188 Removing the engine mount bolts (1) and bracket (2)

3. Remove the upper two nuts from the exhaust manifold heat shields.

4. Raise and secure the vehicle on a hoist.

5. Use a socket such as Snap-On YA Disconnect, Transmission Cooler Line or a crow foot wrench to remove the upstream oxygen sensor from the exhaust manifold.

6. Support the engine and remove the engine mount.

7. Remove the three bolts and the engine mount bracket.

8. Remove the catalytic converter ball flange nuts.

9. Remove the two bolts and the upper and lower exhaust manifold heat shields.

10. Remove the exhaust manifold and gasket.

To install:

11. Clean the gasket surfaces.

➡**If replacing the exhaust manifold, tighten the exhaust outlet studs to 29 ft. lbs. (39 Nm).**

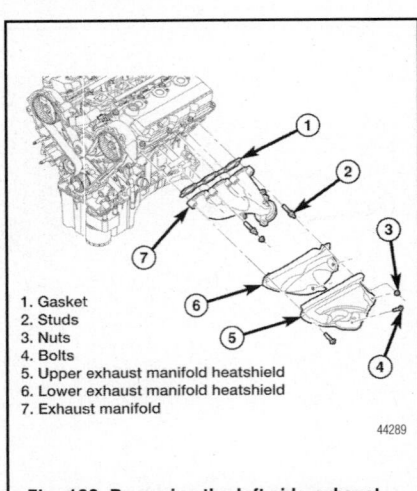

1. Gasket
2. Studs
3. Nuts
4. Bolts
5. Upper exhaust manifold heatshield
6. Lower exhaust manifold heatshield
7. Exhaust manifold

Fig. 189 Removing the left side exhaust manifold

12. Position the exhaust manifold and gasket. Install the retaining bolts. Tighten the bolts starting at the center working outward to 17 ft. lbs. (23 Nm).

13. Connect the catalytic converter to the exhaust manifold. Tighten the ball flange nuts to 25 ft. lbs. (34 Nm).

14. Install the upper and lower exhaust manifold heat shields with two bolts. Tighten the bolts to 9 ft. lbs. (12 Nm).

15. Install the engine mount bracket with three bolts. Tighten the bolts to 52 ft. lbs. (70 Nm).

16. Install the engine mount.

17. Install the upstream oxygen sensor.

18. Install the upper two exhaust manifold heat shield nuts. Tighten nuts to 73 inch lbs. (8 Nm).

19. Connect the negative battery cable.

Right Side

See Figures 190 and 191.

1. Disconnect and isolate the negative battery cable.

2. Disconnect the upstream oxygen sensor electrical connector.

3. Remove the upper two nuts from the exhaust manifold heat shields.

4. Raise and secure the vehicle on a hoist.

5. Use a socket such as Snap-On YA Disconnect, Transmission Cooler Line or a crow foot wrench to remove the upstream oxygen sensor from the exhaust manifold.

6. Support the engine and remove the engine mount.

7. Remove the three bolts and the engine mount bracket.

8. Remove the catalytic converter ball flange nuts.

9. Remove the two bolts and the upper and lower exhaust manifold heat shields.

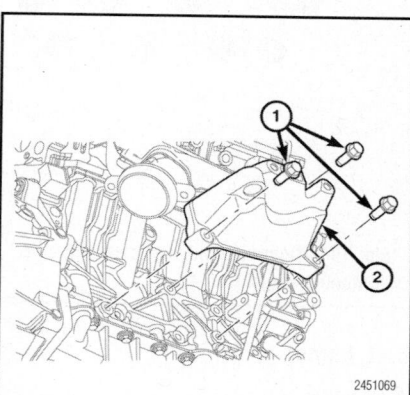

2451069

Fig. 190 Removing the bolts (1) and engine mount bracket (2)

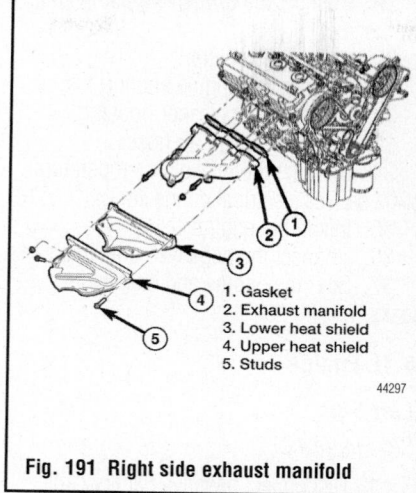

1. Gasket
2. Exhaust manifold
3. Lower heat shield
4. Upper heat shield
5. Studs

44297

Fig. 191 Right side exhaust manifold

10. Remove the exhaust manifold and gasket.

To install:

11. Clean the gasket surfaces.

➡If replacing the exhaust manifold, tighten the exhaust outlet studs to 29 ft. lbs. (39 Nm).

12. Position the exhaust manifold and gasket. Install the retaining bolts. Tighten the bolts starting at the center working outward to 17 ft. lbs. (23 Nm).

13. Connect the catalytic converter to the exhaust manifold. Tighten the ball flange nuts to 25 ft. lbs. (34 Nm).

14. Install the upper and lower exhaust manifold heat shields with two bolts. Tighten the bolts to 9 ft. lbs. (12 Nm).

15. Install the engine mount bracket with three bolts. Tighten the bolts to 52 ft. lbs. (70 Nm).

16. Install the engine mount.

17. Install the upstream oxygen sensor.

18. Install the upper two exhaust manifold heat shield nuts. Tighten nuts to 73 inch lbs. (8 Nm).

19. Connect the negative battery cable.

3.6L Engine

The 3.6L aluminum cylinder heads are a unique design with left and right castings. The exhaust manifolds are integrated into the cylinder heads. If any damaged is found to the exhaust manifold portion, the cylinder head must be removed for repair or replacement

5.7L Engine

See Figures 192 through 194.

1. Disconnect the intake air temperature (IAT) sensor electrical connector.

2. Remove the clean air hose.

3. Remove the air cleaner housing.
4. Remove the engine cover.
5. Disconnect the negative battery cable.

6. Install the engine support fixture.
7. Raise and support the vehicle.

❄ WARNING

When servicing or replacing exhaust system components, disconnect the oxygen sensor connector(s). Allowing the exhaust to hang by the oxygen sensor wires will damage the harness and/or sensor.

8. Disconnect the oxygen sensor electrical connectors.

9. Saturate the front exhaust pipe/catalytic converter retaining bolts and nuts with Mopar®Rust Penetrant or equivalent and allow 5 minutes for penetration.

10. Remove the right and left exhaust pipe/catalytic converter assembly.

11. Remove the right and left engine mount through bolts.

12. Lower the vehicle.

❄ WARNING

Do not damage engine harness while raising the engine.

13. Raise the engine enough to gain access to the exhaust manifold retaining bolts.

14. Remove the exhaust manifold heat shield.

15. Right Side: Using the sequence shown, remove the exhaust manifold retaining bolts.

16. Left Side: Using the sequence shown, remove the exhaust manifold retaining bolts.

17. Remove the exhaust manifold and gasket.

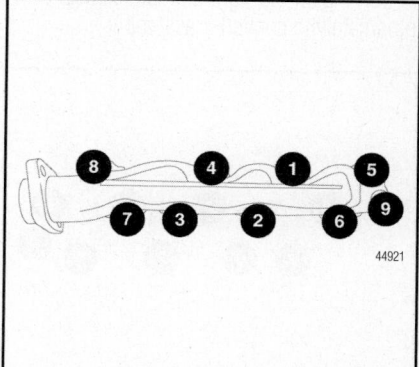

44921

Fig. 192 Right side exhaust manifold retaining bolt removal and installation sequence

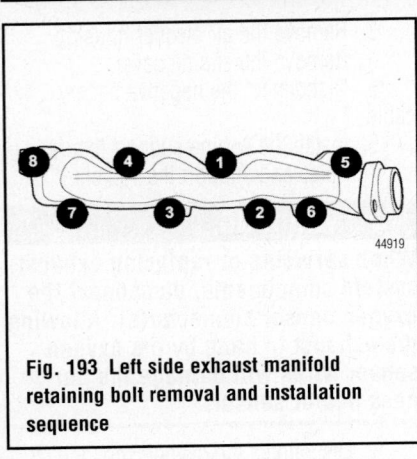

Fig. 193 Left side exhaust manifold retaining bolt removal and installation sequence

18. Inspect the exhaust manifold for any damage.

19. Clean the mating surfaces.

To install:

20. Prior to installation, make sure all gasket mating surfaces are clean and free of any debris.

21. Position the exhaust manifold gasket and manifold.

22. Left Side: Using the sequence shown, Install the exhaust manifold retaining bolts and tighten to 18 ft. lbs. (25 Nm).

23. Right Side: Using the sequence shown, install the exhaust manifold retaining bolts and tighten to 18 ft. lbs. (25 Nm).

24. Install the heat shield and tighten nuts to 70 inch lbs. (8 Nm).

❊❊ WARNING

Do not damage engine harness while lowering the engine.

25. Using the engine support fixture, lower the engine into position.

26. Raise and support the vehicle.

27. Install the right and left engine mount through bolts and tighten to 74 ft. lbs. (100 Nm).

28. Install the right and left exhaust pipe/catalytic converter assembly.

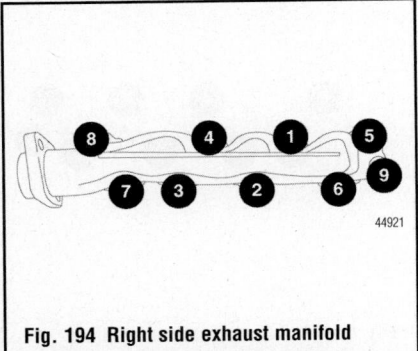

Fig. 194 Right side exhaust manifold retaining bolt removal and installation sequence

29. Connect the oxygen sensor electrical connectors.

30. Lower the vehicle.

31. Remove the engine support fixture.

32. Install the air cleaner housing.

33. Install the clean air hose.

34. Connect the intake air temperature (IAT) sensor electrical connector.

35. Install the engine cover.

36. Connect the negative battery cable.

37. Start the engine and check for leaks.

6.1L Engine

Left Side

See Figure 195.

1. Disconnect negative battery cable.

2. Remove the air cleaner housing.

3. Remove the coolant bottle, and set aside without removing hoses.

4. Remove the top row of bolts from manifold from under the hood.

5. Support and raise the vehicle on a hoist.

6. Remove the lower splash shield.

7. Remove the exhaust pipe as an assembly.

8. Remove the knock sensor.

9. Remove the bottom row of bolts from manifold from under vehicle.

10. Remove the manifold from under vehicle.

To install:

11. Install the exhaust manifold gasket and the exhaust manifold.

12. Using the sequence shown, install the exhaust manifold bolts and tighten to 23 ft. lbs. (31 Nm).

13. Install the coolant bottle.

14. Install the air cleaner housing.

15. Install the knock sensor.

16. Install the exhaust pipe to manifold bolts.

17. Connect negative battery cable.

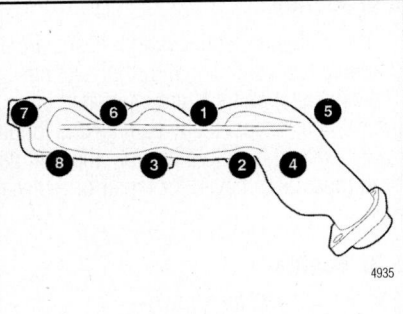

Fig. 195 Left side exhaust manifold bolt tightening sequence

Right Side

See Figure 196.

1. Disconnect negative battery cable.

2. Remove the power distribution box.

3. Loosen the power distribution box mounting bracket.

4. Unfasten, and relocate the wire harness mounted on the right hand inner fender panel.

5. Remove the bottom row of bolts from manifold from under vehicle.

6. Support and raise the vehicle on a hoist.

7. Remove the exhaust pipe as an assembly.

8. Remove the lower splash shield.

9. Remove the starter and heat shield.

10. Remove the knock sensor.

11. Remove the top row of bolts from manifold from under the hood.

12. Remove the manifold from under vehicle.

To install:

13. Install the exhaust manifold gasket and the exhaust manifold.

14. Using the sequence shown, install the exhaust manifold bolts and tighten to 23 ft. lbs. (31 Nm).

15. Connect the wire harness mounted on the right hand inner fender panel.

16. Install the power distribution box mounting bracket.

17. Install the power distribution box.

18. Install the starter and heat shield.

19. Install the knock sensor.

20. Install the exhaust pipe to manifold bolts.

21. Connect the negative battery cable.

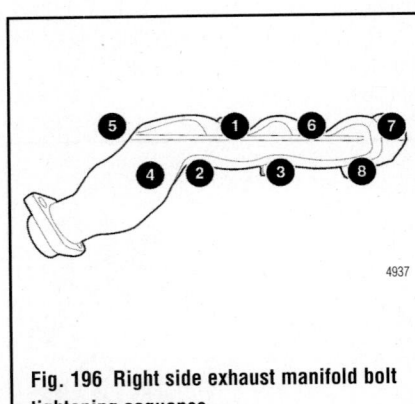

Fig. 196 Right side exhaust manifold bolt tightening sequence

6.4L Engine

Left Side

See Figures 197 and 198.

1. Disconnect the negative battery cable.

2. Remove the both front engine mounts and mounting brackets.

✳✳ WARNING

When separating the catalytic converters from the manifolds, disconnect the oxygen sensor connectors. Allowing the catalytic converters hanging from the oxygen sensor wires damages the harness and/or sensors.

3. Remove the both catalytic converters.
4. Remove the heat shield from the knock sensor (shield snaps onto sensor).
5. Disconnect the knock sensor electrical connector.

➡**Note the foam strip on the knock sensor retaining bolt threads. This foam is only used to retain the bolts to the knock sensors for plant assembly. It is not used as a sealant. Do not apply any adhesive, sealant or thread locking compound to these bolts.**

6. Remove the knock sensor retaining bolt and remove the knock sensor.
7. Lower the vehicle.

➡**It is not necessary to remove the hoses from the coolant bottle for coolant bottle removal.**

8. Remove the coolant bottle retaining bolts and position aside.
9. Remove the exhaust manifold top row of bolts.

➡**The left exhaust manifold is removed from below the engine and out through the rear of the engine compartment.**

10. Raise and support the vehicle.
11. Remove the exhaust manifold heat shield.

12. Remove the exhaust manifold bottom row of bolts.
13. Remove the exhaust manifold out through the rear of the engine compartment.

To Install:

➡**Install the left exhaust manifold and gasket from below the engine and through the rear of the engine compartment. Make sure the gasket is properly seated before installing the manifold bolts.**

14. Clean the sealing surfaces of the exhaust manifold and cylinder head.
15. Using a new exhaust manifold gasket, position the exhaust manifold.
16. Install the exhaust manifold bottom row of bolts finger tight.
17. Lower the vehicle.
18. Install the exhaust manifold top row of bolts and tighten to 23 ft. lbs. (31 Nm).
19. Position the coolant bottle and install the retaining bolts.
20. Raise and support the vehicle.
21. Tighten the exhaust manifold bottom row of bolts to 23 ft. lbs. (31 Nm).
22. Install the exhaust manifold heat shield.

✳✳ WARNING

Over or under tightening the knock sensor mounting bolts will affect knock sensor performance, possibly causing improper spark control.

➡**The foam strip used on bolt threads is used only to retain the bolts to the sensors for plant assembly. It is not used as a sealant. Do not apply any adhesive, sealant or thread locking compound to these bolts.**

23. Position the knock sensor onto the engine block.
24. Install the retaining bolt and tighten to 15 ft. lbs. (20 Nm).
25. Connect the electrical connector to the knock sensor.
26. Snap the heat shield onto the knock sensor.
27. Install the both catalytic converters.
28. Install the both front engine mount mounting brackets and engine mounts.
29. Connect the negative battery cable.
30. Start the engine and check for leaks.

Right Side

See Figures 199 through 203.

1. Disconnect negative battery cable.
2. Remove the both front engine mounts and mounting brackets.

✳✳ WARNING

When separating the catalytic converters from the manifolds, disconnect the oxygen sensor connectors. Allowing the catalytic converters hanging from the oxygen sensor wires damages the harness and/or sensors.

3. Remove the both catalytic converters.
4. Remove the starter motor and heat shield.
5. Remove the heat shield from the knock sensor (shield snaps onto sensor).
6. Disconnect the knock sensor electrical connector.

➡**Note the foam strip on the knock sensor retaining bolt threads. This foam is only used to retain the bolts to the knock sensors for plant assembly. It is not used as a sealant. Do not apply any**

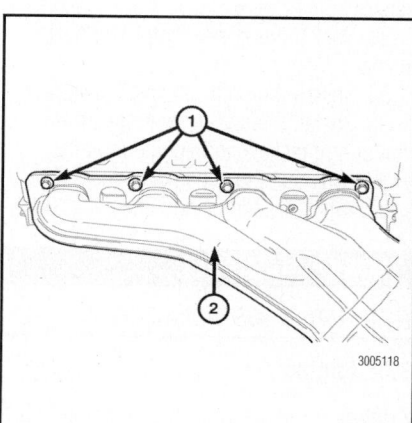

Fig. 197 Removing the exhaust manifold (2) top row of bolts (1)

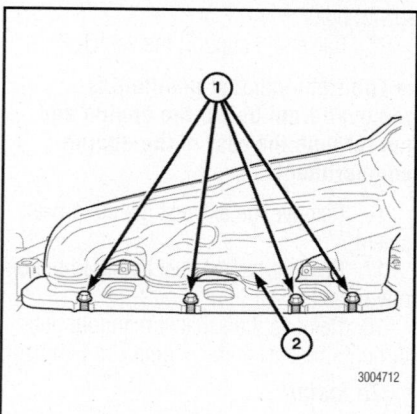

Fig. 198 Removing the exhaust manifold (2) bottom row of bolts (1)

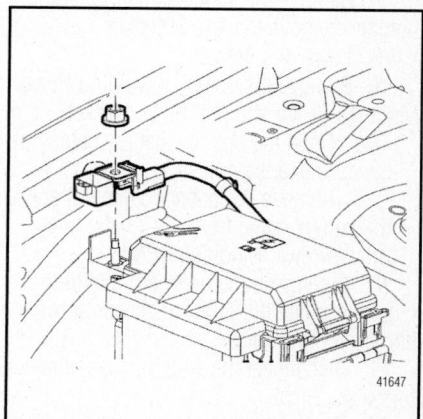

Fig. 199 Removing the positive battery cable nut

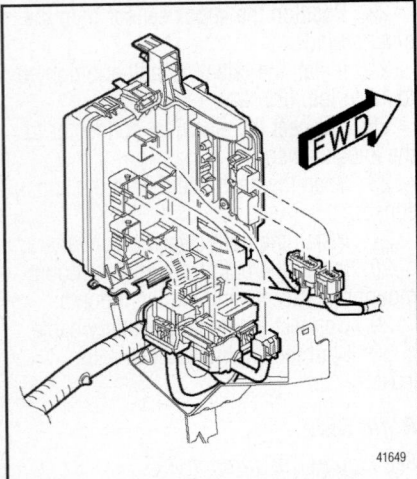

Fig. 200 Disconnecting the wiring harness connectors and retaining clips

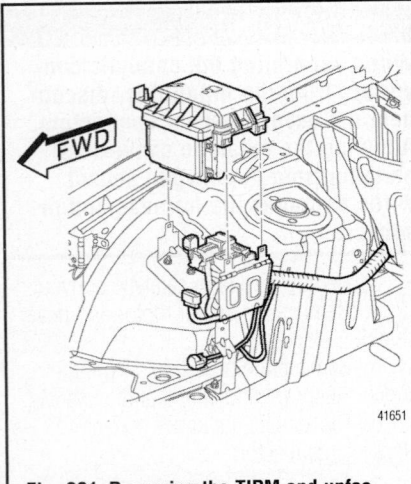

Fig. 201 Removing the TIPM and unfastening the wiring harness

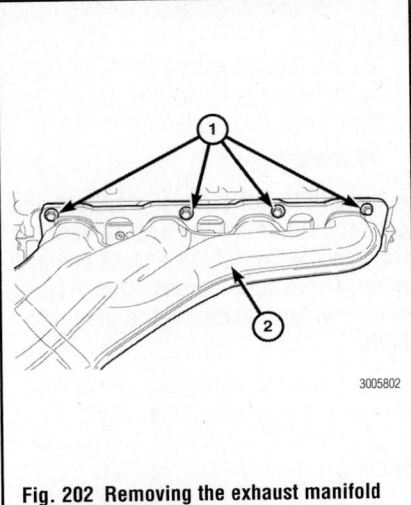

Fig. 202 Removing the exhaust manifold (2) top row of bolts

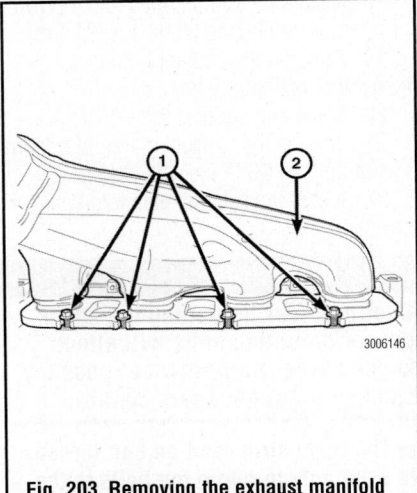

Fig. 203 Removing the exhaust manifold (2) bottom row of bolts (1)

adhesive, sealant or thread locking compound to these bolts.

7. Remove the knock sensor retaining bolt and remove the knock sensor.

8. Lower the vehicle.

9. Remove the Totally Integrated Power Module (TIPM) and mounting bracket.

a. Open the positive battery cable nut cover to expose nut.

b. Remove the battery cable nut and the battery cable from the Totally Integrated Power Module (TIPM).

10. Disengage the outboard retaining clip, and rotate the TIPM to access wire harness connectors.

11. Disconnect the wire harness connectors from TIPM.

12. Disengage the two inboard retaining clips.

a. Remove the TIPM from vehicle.

13. Unfasten the wire harness mounted

on the right hand inner fender panel and position aside.

14. Remove the exhaust manifold top row of bolts.

15. Raise and support the vehicle.

➡**The right exhaust manifold is removed from below the engine and out through the rear of the engine compartment.**

16. Remove the exhaust manifold heat shield.

17. Remove the exhaust manifold bottom row of bolts.

18. Remove the exhaust manifold out through the rear of the engine compartment.

To install:

➡**Install the right exhaust manifold and gasket from below the engine and through the rear of the engine compart-**

ment. Make sure the gasket is properly seated before installing the manifold bolts.

19. Clean the sealing surfaces of the exhaust manifold and cylinder head.

20. Using a new exhaust manifold gasket, position the exhaust manifold.

21. Install the exhaust manifold bottom row of bolts finger tight.

22. Lower the vehicle.

23. Install the exhaust manifold top row of bolts and tighten to 23 ft. lbs. (31 Nm).

24. Position the wire harness mounted onto the right hand inner fender panel and secure fasteners.

25. Install the Totally Integrated Power Module (TIPM) and mounting bracket.

26. Raise and support the vehicle.

27. Tighten the exhaust manifold bottom row of bolts to 23 ft. lbs. (31 Nm).

28. Install the exhaust manifold heat shield.

✹✹ WARNING
Over or under tightening the knock sensor mounting bolts will affect knock sensor performance, possibly causing improper spark control.

29. Position the knock sensor onto the engine block.

➡**The foam strip used on bolt threads is used only to retain the bolts to the sensors for plant assembly. It is not used as a sealant. Do not apply any adhesive, sealant or thread locking compound to these bolts.**

30. Install the retaining bolt and tighten to 15 ft. lbs. (20 Nm).

31. Connect the electrical connector to the knock sensor.

32. Snap the heat shield onto the knock sensor.

33. Install the starter motor and heat shield.

34. Install the both catalytic converters.

35. Install the both front engine mount mounting brackets and engine mounts.

36. Connect the negative battery cable.

37. Start the engine and check for leaks.

INTAKE MANIFOLD

REMOVAL & INSTALLATION

3.5L Engine

Lower

See Figures 204 and 205.

1. Disconnect and isolate the negative battery cable.

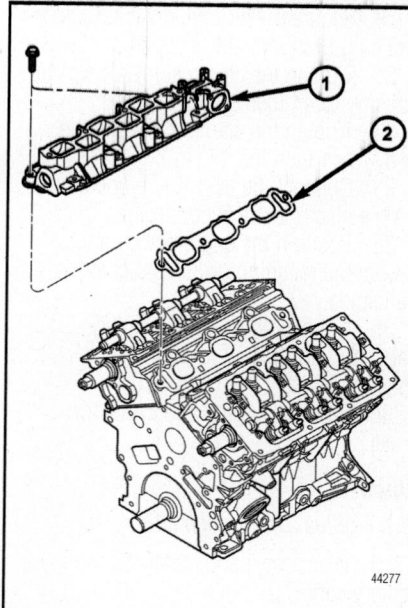

Fig. 204 Removing the lower intake manifold

2. Perform the fuel pressure release procedure.

3. Drain the cooling system.

4. Disconnect the upper radiator hose from the thermostat housing.

5. Remove the upper intake manifold.

6. Disconnect the heater hose from the coolant pipe.

7. Disconnect the coolant container hose from the coolant pipe.

8. Disconnect the electrical connectors from the fuel injectors and the coolant temperature sensor.

9. Disconnect the fuel supply hose from the fuel rail.

10. Remove the bolts attaching the fuel rail.

11. Remove the fuel rail and injectors as an assembly.

12. Remove the bolts attaching the lower intake manifold and remove the intake manifold.

To install:

13. Clean all sealing surfaces.

14. Position new gaskets and the intake manifold on the cylinder heads.

15. Install the intake manifold bolts and gradually tighten in the sequence shown to 21 ft. lbs. (28 Nm).

16. Install the fuel rail and injectors as an assembly.

17. Connect the fuel supply hose to the fuel rail.

18. Connect the electrical connectors to the fuel injectors and the coolant temperature sensor.

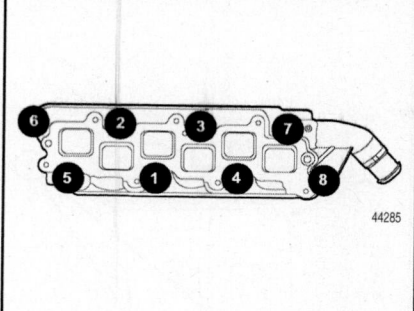

Fig. 205 Lower intake manifold bolt tightening sequence

19. Connect the heater hose to the coolant pipe.

20. Connect the coolant container hose to the coolant pipe.

21. Install the upper intake manifold.

22. Connect the upper radiator hose to the thermostat housing.

23. Fill the cooling system.

24. Connect the negative battery cable and tighten nut to 45 inch lbs. (5 Nm).

Upper

See Figure 206.

1. Disconnect and isolate the negative battery cable.

2. Disconnect the Inlet Air Temperature (IAT) sensor electrical connector.

3. Remove the air inlet hose from the throttle body.

4. Disconnect the Manifold Absolute Pressure (MAP) sensor electrical connector.

5. Disconnect the PCV hose, purge hose and power brake booster hose from the upper intake manifold.

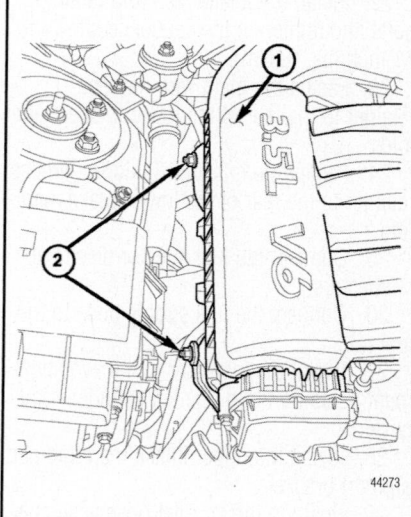

Fig. 206 Removing the intake manifold

6. Disconnect the electrical connector from the electronic throttle control.

7. Remove the fasteners from the throttle body and cylinder head and remove the throttle bracket.

8. Remove the wiper module, strut tower support and EGR tube.

9. Remove the fasteners from the intake manifold support brackets.

10. Remove the upper intake manifold retaining bolts, insulation foam pad and manifold. Clean all gasket sealing surfaces.

To install:

11. Clean and inspect the gasket sealing surfaces.

12. Position the new gasket.

13. Install the upper intake manifold insulator foam.

14. Install the upper intake manifold. Tighten the bolts to 9 ft. lbs. (12 Nm) starting in the center working outward in a cross sequence pattern.

15. Install the right manifold support brackets. Tighten fasteners to 9 ft. lbs. (12 Nm).

16. Install the throttle bracket. Tighten fasteners to 9 ft. lbs. (12 Nm) at the throttle body and 25 ft. lbs. (28 Nm) at the cylinder head.

17. Connect the harness connector to the electronic throttle control.

18. Connect the PCV hose, purge hose and power brake booster vacuum hose to the intake manifold.

19. Install the EGR tube, strut tower support, wiper module and cowl panel.

20. Connect the Manifold Absolute Pressure (MAP) sensor harness connector.

21. Install the inlet hose and connect the Inlet Air Temperature (IAT) sensor harness connector.

22. Connect the negative battery cable and tighten nut to 45 inch lbs. (5 Nm).

3.6L Engine

Lower

See Figures 207 through 209.

1. Perform the fuel pressure release procedure.

2. Disconnect and isolate the negative battery cable.

3. Lift the engine cover retaining grommets off the ball studs and remove the engine cover.

4. Disconnect the electrical connector from the Inlet Air Temperature (IAT) sensor.

5. Loosen the clamp at the throttle body.

6. Loosen the clamp at the air cleaner housing.

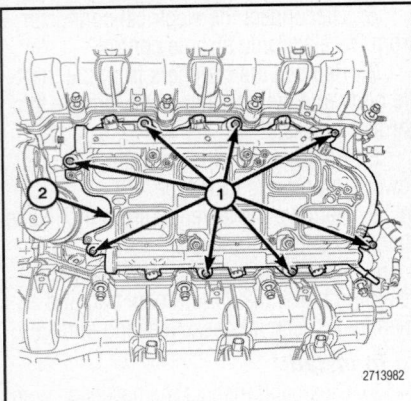

Fig. 207 Removing the lower intake attaching bolts (1) and lower intake manifold (2)

7. Lift the air inlet hose assembly retaining grommet off the ball stud.

8. Remove the air inlet hose assembly.

✳✳ CAUTION

The fuel system is under constant pressure even with engine off. Before servicing the fuel rail, fuel system pressure must be released.

9. Remove the upper intake manifold and support brackets.

10. Remove the insulator from the left cylinder head cover.

11. Disconnect the fuel supply hose from the fuel rail.

12. Disconnect the fuel injector electrical connectors.

13. Unfasten the injection/ignition harness retainer from the rear of the lower intake manifold.

14. Disengage the main wire harness

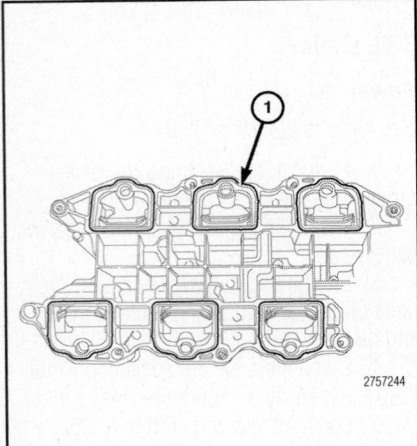

Fig. 208 Identifying the lower intake manifold to cylinder head seals

retainer form the rear of the lower intake manifold.

15. Remove the eight lower intake manifold attaching bolts.

16. Remove the lower intake manifold with the fuel injectors and fuel rail as an assembly.

17. Remove the and discard the six lower intake manifold to cylinder head seals.

18. If required, remove the fuel rail and fuel injectors from the lower intake manifold.

To install:

19. Clean and inspect the sealing surfaces. Install new lower intake manifold to cylinder head seals.

20. If removed, install the fuel injectors and the fuel rail to the lower intake manifold. Tighten the four bolts in the sequence shown to 62 inch lbs. (7 Nm).

21. Position the lower intake manifold onto the cylinder head surfaces.

22. Install the intake manifold retaining bolts and tighten in the sequence shown to 71 inch lbs. (8 Nm).

23. Fasten the main wire harness retainer to the rear of the lower intake manifold.

24. Fasten the injection/ignition harness retainer to the rear of the lower intake manifold.

25. Connect the fuel injector electrical connectors.

26. Connect the fuel supply hose to the fuel rail.

27. Install the insulator to the two alignment posts on top of the left cylinder head cover.

28. Install the upper intake manifold and support brackets.

29. Position the air inlet hose assembly onto the throttle body and the air cleaner housing.

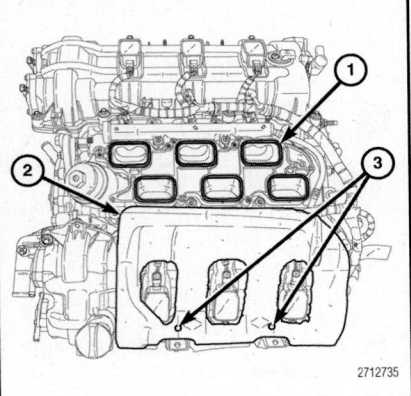

Fig. 209 Seal (1), insulator (2) and alignment posts (3)

30. Secure the air inlet hose assembly retaining grommet onto the ball stud.

31. Tighten the clamp at the air cleaner housing to 44 inch lbs. (5 Nm).

32. Tighten the clamp at the throttle body to 44 inch lbs. (5 Nm).

33. Connect the Inlet Air Temperature (IAT) sensor electrical connector.

34. Position the engine cover and secure the retaining grommets onto the ball studs.

35. Connect the negative battery cable and tighten nut to 45 inch lbs. (5 Nm).

36. Start the engine and check for leaks.

Upper

See Figures 210 through 218.

1. Disconnect and isolate the negative battery cable.

2. Lift the engine cover retaining grommets off the ball studs and remove the engine cover.

3. Disconnect the electrical connector from the Inlet Air Temperature (IAT) sensor.

4. Loosen the clamp at the throttle body.

5. Loosen the clamp at the air cleaner housing.

6. Lift the air inlet hose assembly retaining grommet off the ball stud.

7. Remove the air inlet hose assembly.

8. Disengage the brake booster hose retainer from the upper intake manifold.

9. Disconnect the electrical connectors from the Manifold Absolute Pressure (MAP) sensor and the Electronic Throttle Control (ETC).

10. Disengage the ETC harness from the clip on the throttle body and unfasten the wire harness retainer from the upper intake

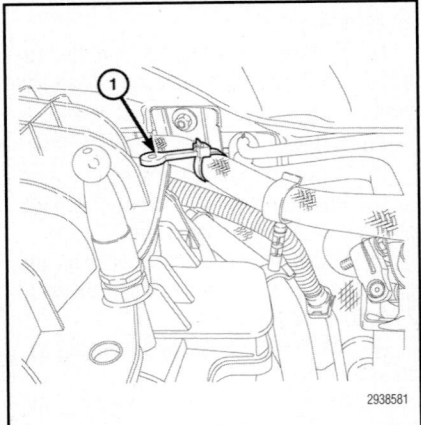

Fig. 210 Disengaging the brake booster hose retainer from the upper intake manifold

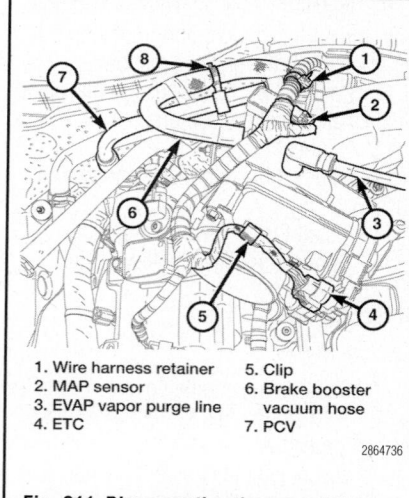

1. Wire harness retainer
2. MAP sensor
3. EVAP vapor purge line
4. ETC
5. Clip
6. Brake booster vacuum hose
7. PCV

2864736

Fig. 211 Disconnecting the upper intake manifold (1 of 2)

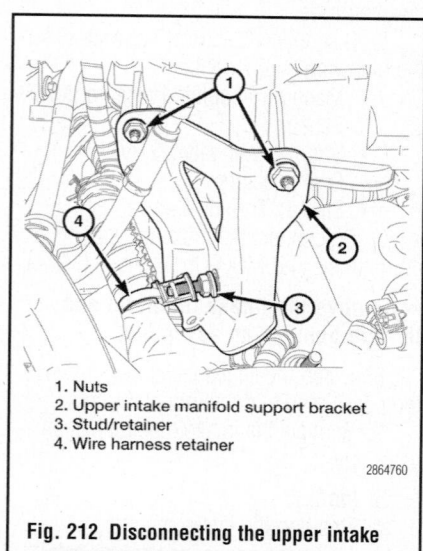

1. Nuts
2. Upper intake manifold support bracket
3. Stud/retainer
4. Wire harness retainer

2864760

Fig. 212 Disconnecting the upper intake manifold (2 of 2)

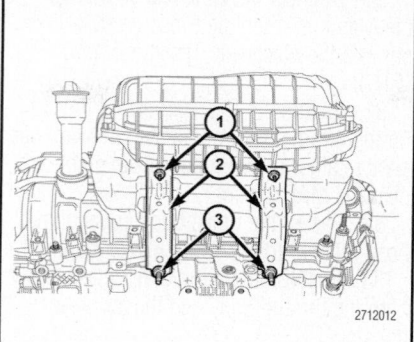

2712012

Fig. 213 Removing the upper intake manifold support brackets (2), nuts (1) and stud retainers (3)

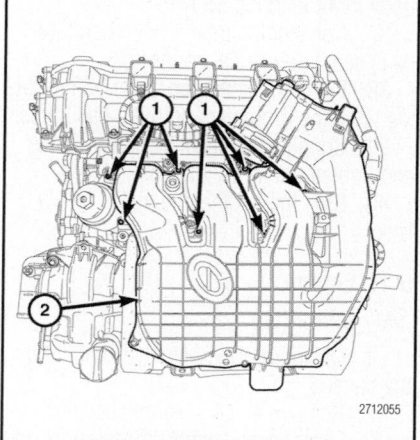

2712055

Fig. 214 Removing the upper intake manifold (2) and attaching bolts (1)

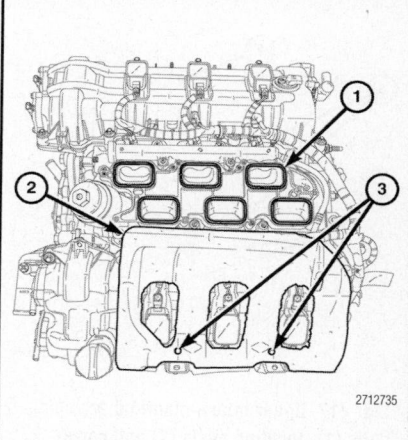

2712735

Fig. 215 Identifying the upper to lower intake manifold seals (1) and the left cylinder head insulator (2)

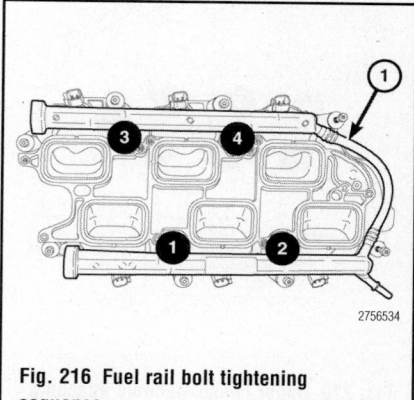

2756534

Fig. 216 Fuel rail bolt tightening sequence

manifold near the MAP sensor and reposition the wire harness.

11. Disconnect the following hoses from the upper intake manifold:
   - Positive Crankcase Ventilation (PCV)
   - Brake booster vacuum hose
   - EVAP vapor purge line

12. Unfasten the wire harness retainer from the upper intake manifold support bracket stud retainer.

13. Remove the two nuts, loosen the stud and reposition the upper intake manifold support bracket.

14. Remove the heater core return tube upper support bracket retaining nut and reposition tube.

15. Remove the two nuts, loosen two stud retainers and reposition the two upper intake manifold support brackets.

➡The upper intake manifold attaching bolts are captured in the upper intake manifold. Once loosened, the bolts will have to be lifted out of the lower intake manifold and held while removing the upper intake manifold.

➡Exercise care not to inadvertently loosen the two fuel rail attachment bolts that are in close proximity of the upper intake manifold attaching bolts.

16. Remove the seven manifold attaching bolts and remove the upper intake manifold.

17. Remove the and discard the six upper to lower intake manifold seals.

18. Cover the open intake ports to prevent debris from entering the engine.

19. If required, remove the insulator from the left cylinder head cover.

To install:

➡Prior to installing the upper intake manifold, verify that the four fuel rail bolts were not inadvertently loosened. The bolts must tightened in the

sequence shown to 62 inch lbs. (7 Nm).

20. Clean and inspect the sealing surfaces. Install new upper to lower intake manifold seals.

➡Make sure the fuel injectors and wiring harnesses are in the correct position so that they don't interfere with the upper intake manifold installation.

21. If removed, position the insulator onto the two alignment posts on top of the left cylinder head cover.

22. Lift and hold the seven upper intake attaching bolts clear of the mating surface. Back the bolts out slightly or if required, use an elastic band to hold the bolts clear of the mating surface.

23. Position the upper intake manifold onto the lower intake manifold so that the two locating posts on the upper intake manifold align with corresponding holes (3) in the lower intake manifold.

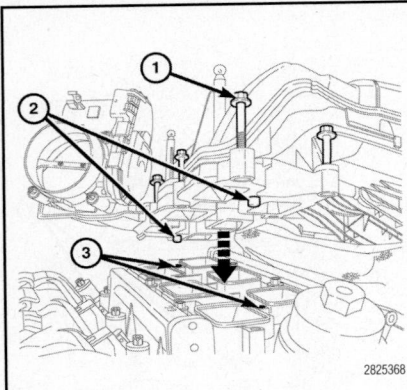

Fig. 217 Upper intake manifold attaching bolts (1), locating posts (2) and corresponding holes (3)

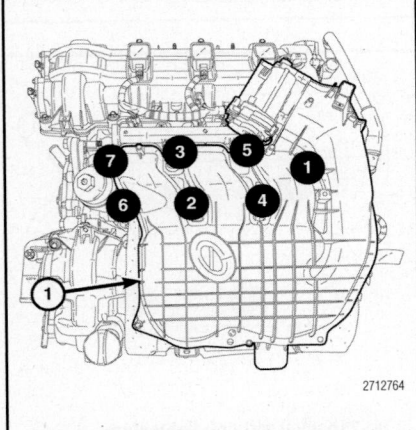

Fig. 218 Upper intake manifold attaching bolt tightening sequence

24. Install the seven upper intake manifold attaching bolts. Tighten the bolts in the sequence shown to 71 inch lbs. (8 Nm).

25. Install the two nuts to the upper intake manifold support bracket. Tighten the nuts to 89 inch lbs. (10 Nm) and tighten the stud to 15 ft. lbs. (20 Nm).

26. Engage the wire harness retainer to the stud.

27. Install the two upper intake manifold support brackets with two stud retainers and two nuts. Tighten the stud retainers to 15 ft. lbs. (20 Nm) and tighten the nuts to 89 inch lbs. (10 Nm).

28. Position the heater core return tube, install the retaining nut and tighten to 9 ft. lbs. (12 Nm).

29. Connect the following hoses to the upper intake manifold:
- Positive Crankcase Ventilation (PCV)
- Brake booster vacuum hose
- EVAP vapor purge line

30. Connect the electrical connectors to the Manifold Absolute Pressure (MAP) sensor and the Electronic Throttle Control (ETC).

31. Secure the ETC harness to the clip on the throttle body and fasten the wire harness retainer to the upper intake manifold near the MAP sensor.

32. Fasten the brake booster vacuum hose retainer to the upper intake manifold.

33. Position the air inlet hose assembly onto the throttle body and the air cleaner housing.

34. Secure the air inlet hose assembly retaining grommet onto the ball stud.

35. Tighten the clamp at the air cleaner housing to 44 inch lbs. (5 Nm).

36. Tighten the clamp at the throttle body to 44 inch lbs. (5 Nm).

37. Connect the Inlet Air Temperature (IAT) sensor electrical connector.

38. Position the engine cover and secure the retaining grommets onto the ball studs.

39. Connect the negative battery cable and tighten nut to 45 inch lbs. (5 Nm).

40. Start the engine and check for leaks.

5.7L Engine

See Figure 219.

1. Disconnect the negative cable from the battery.

2. Remove the air cleaner assembly.

3. Disconnect electrical connectors and reposition harness.

4. Disconnect vacuum lines.

5. Perform fuel pressure release procedure.

6. Remove the intake manifold retaining fasteners.

7. Remove the intake manifold.

To install:

8. Install the intake manifold seals.

9. Position intake manifold in place.

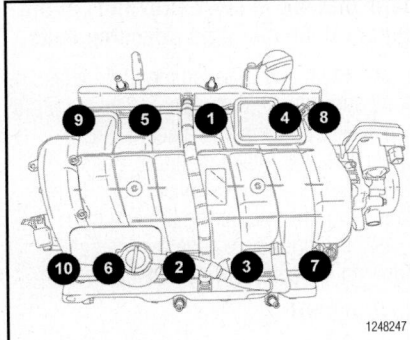

Fig. 219 Intake manifold bolt removal and installation sequence

10. Install the new intake manifold bolts (with thread lock patch) and tighten to 9 ft. lbs (12 Nm) in the sequence shown.

11. Position wiring harness in place and connect electrical connectors.

12. Connect fuel line.

13. Connect brake booster and vacuum hoses.

14. Install the air cleaner assembly.

15. Connect negative battery cable.

6.1L Engine

See Figure 219.

1. Remove the engine covers.

2. Perform the fuel system pressure release procedure.

3. Disconnect the fuel supply line.

4. Disconnect the negative battery cable.

5. Remove the air cleaner housing and clean air tube.

6. Disconnect electrical connectors for the following components:
- Manifold Absolute Pressure (MAP) Sensor
- Short runner valve (SRV)
- Fuel Injectors
- Electric Throttle Control (ETC)

7. Disconnect the brake booster hose, purge hose, and Make Up Air Hose (MUA).

➡**Remove the intake manifold and throttle body as an assembly.**

8. Using the sequence shown, remove the intake manifold retaining fasteners

9. Remove the intake manifold as an assembly.

To install:

10. Position the intake manifold.

11. Using the sequence shown, install the intake manifold retaining bolts and tighten the fasteners to 9 ft. lbs. (12 Nm).

12. Connect the electrical connectors for the following components:
- Manifold Absolute Pressure (MAP) Sensor
- Short runner valve (SRV)
- Fuel Injector electrical connectors
- ETC (Electronic Throttle Control)

13. Connect the brake booster hose, purge hose, and make-up air hose (MUA).

14. Install the air cleaner housing and clean air tube.

15. Connect the negative battery cable.

16. Position the engine covers and snap onto the fuel rails.

6.4L Engine

See Figure 220.

1. Perform the fuel system pressure release procedure.

2. Disconnect the negative battery cable.

3. Remove the engine covers.

4. Disconnect the fuel supply line.

5. Remove the air cleaner housing.

6. Disconnect the brake booster hose and the EVAP purge hose.

7. Disconnect the electrical connectors from the following components:

- Manifold Absolute Pressure (MAP) Sensor
- Short Runner Valve (SRV)
- Fuel Injectors
- Electronic Throttle Control (ETC)

➡️**Remove the intake manifold and throttle body as an assembly.**

8. Using the sequence shown, remove the intake manifold retaining bolts.

9. Remove the intake manifold and throttle body as an assembly from the vehicle.

To install:

➡️**The intake manifold seals may be used again, provided no cuts, tears, or deformation have occurred.**

10. Inspect the intake manifold seals and replace if necessary.

➡️**If reinstalling the original manifold, apply Mopar®Lock & Seal Adhesive to the intake manifold bolts. Not required when installing a new manifold.**

11. If required, apply Mopar®Lock & Seal Adhesive to the intake manifold bolts.

12. Position the intake manifold.

13. Using the sequence shown, install the intake manifold retaining bolts and tighten to 9 ft. lbs. (12 Nm).

14. Connect the fuel supply line.

15. Connect the brake booster hose and the EVAP purge hose.

16. Connect the electrical connectors to the following components:

- Manifold Absolute Pressure (MAP) Sensor
- Short Runner Valve (SRV)
- Fuel Injectors
- Electronic Throttle Control (ETC)

17. While sliding the air duct onto the throttle body, lower the air cleaner housing into position and align the locating pin on the bottom of the housing.

18. Install the air cleaner housing retaining bolt and tighten to 44 inch lbs. (5 Nm).

19. Install the makeup air hose at the air cleaner housing.

20. Connect the intake air temperature sensor electrical connector.

21. Position the air duct retaining clamp at the throttle body and tighten to 30 inch lbs. (3 Nm).

22. Install the engine covers on to the ball studs.

23. Connect the negative battery cable.

OIL PAN

REMOVAL & INSTALLATION

3.5L Engine

See Figures 221 through 224.

1. Disconnect and isolate the negative battery cable.

2. Lock the steering wheel in the center position.

3. Remove the generator bracket bolt.

4. Loosen the upper most generator mounting bolt and reposition the generator bracket.

5. Remove the engine oil level indicator tube retaining bolt and remove the indicator tube.

6. Raise and support the vehicle.

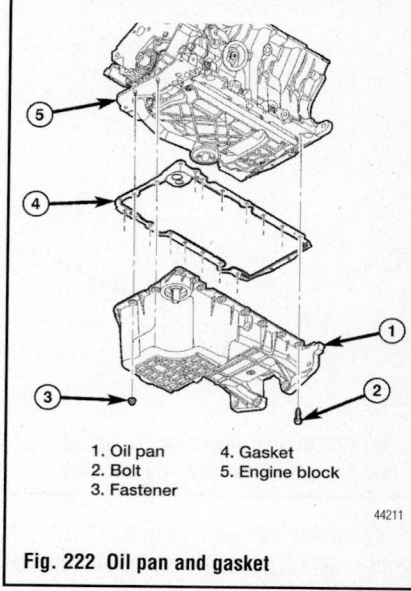

1. Oil pan   4. Gasket
2. Bolt   5. Engine block
3. Fastener

44211

Fig. 222 Oil pan and gasket

7. Remove the belly pan.

8. Drain the engine oil and remove the oil filter.

9. Remove the oil cooler mounting stud and relocate the oil cooler.

10. Remove the pinch bolt and separate the steering column coupler from the steering gear.

11. Remove the steering gear to cradle mounting bolts and relocate the steering gear.

12. Remove the transmission to oil pan bolts.

13. Remove the four bolts that secure the oil pan to the transmission.

14. Remove the flex plate access cover.

15. Remove the two rear oil pan bolts.

16. Remove the remaining oil pan bolts and nuts.

➡️**A small amount of oil will remain in the oil pan. Use care when removing the oil pan from the engine.**

17. Remove the oil pan.

18. Clean all mating surfaces.

To install:

19. Clean the oil pan and all gasket surfaces.

20. Apply a 1/8 inch bead of Mopar®Engine RTV GEN II at the parting line of the oil pump housing and the rear seal retainer.

21. Install the oil pan gasket to the engine block.

22. Install the oil pan and attaching fasteners finger tight.

➡️**Assure that the rear face of the oil pan is flush to the transmission bell housing when installing the oil pan.**

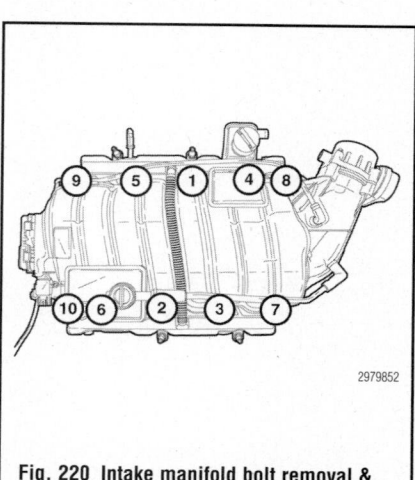

2979852

Fig. 220 Intake manifold bolt removal & installation sequence

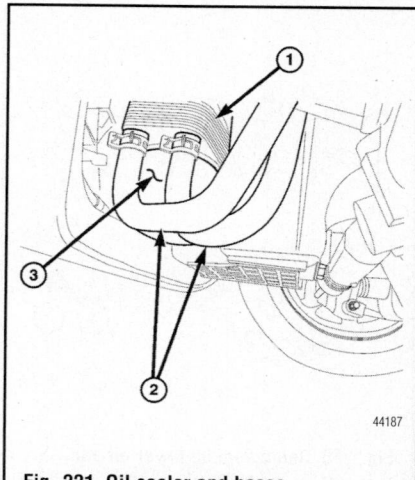

44187

Fig. 221 Oil cooler and hoses

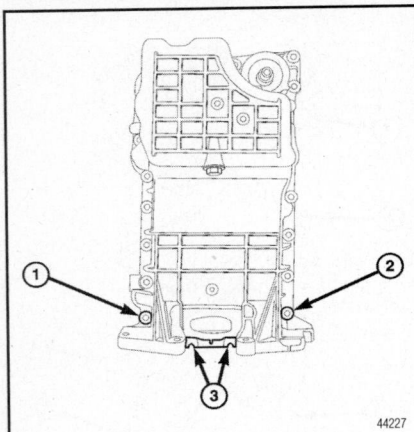

Fig. 223 Oil pan alignment (1. Tighten first 2. Tighten second 3. Tighten last)

23. Install and pre-tighten four M10 horizontal rear oil pan to transmission bolts to 12 inch lbs. (1.4 Nm).

24. First tighten the M8 oil pan alignment bolt to 21 inch lbs. (28 Nm).

25. Tighten the remaining M8 bolts and M8 nuts to 21 inch lbs. (28 Nm).

26. Tighten the four previously installed horizontal M10 oil pan to transmission bolts to 40 ft. lbs. (55 Nm).

27. Install the flex plate inspection cover and tighten the fastener to 97 inch lbs. (11 Nm).

28. Install the steering gear to cradle bolts and tighten the fasteners to 70 ft. lbs. (95 Nm).

⁑ **WARNING**

Prior to coupling installation, make sure gear is centered in its travel to match clockspring centering in steering column.

29. Align the coupling with the input

shaft and install the steering coupling. Install a new pinch bolt. Tighten the bolt to 40 ft. lbs. (54 Nm).

30. Install the oil cooler and attaching fastener (if equipped) and tighten to 45 ft. lbs. (61 Nm).

31. Install the engine oil filter. Tighten filter to 9 ft. lbs. (12 Nm).

32. Install the belly pan.

33. Lower the vehicle.

34. Install the engine oil level indicator tube and tighten the retaining bolt to 9 ft. lbs. (12 Nm).

35. Position the generator bracket and install the bracket bolt. Tighten the generator mounting bolt to 48 ft. lbs. (65 Nm) and tighten the generator bracket bolt to 40 ft. lbs. (54 Nm).

36. Fill the engine crankcase with the proper oil to the correct level.

37. Reconnect the negative battery cable.

3.6L Engine

Lower

See Figures 225 and 226.

1. Disconnect and isolate the negative battery cable.

2. Raise and support the vehicle.

3. Remove the belly pan retainers and remove the belly pan.

4. Drain the engine oil.

➡ **The lower oil pan must be removed to access all of the upper oil pan retaining bolts.**

5. Remove the twelve bolts, two studs and two nuts from the lower oil pan flange.

⁑ **WARNING**

Do not pry on the lower oil pan flange. There are no designated pry

points for lower oil pan removal. Prying on only one or a few locations could bend the flange and damage the pan.

6. Using a pry bar, apply side force to the lower oil pan in order to sever the sealant bond and remove the pan.

7. Remove the all residual sealant from the upper and lower oil pans

To install:

⁑ **WARNING**

Engine assembly requires the use of a unique sealant that is compatible with engine oil. Using a sealant other than Mopar®Threebond Engine RTV Sealant may result in engine fluid leakage.

⁑ **WARNING**

Following the application of Mopar®Threebond Engine RTV Sealant to the gasket surfaces, the components must be assembled within 20 minutes and the attaching fasteners must be tightened to specification within 45 minutes. Prolonged exposure to the air prior to assembly may result in engine fluid leakage.

8. Clean the upper and lower oil pan mating surfaces with isopropyl alcohol in preparation for sealant application.

9. Apply a 2 to 3 mm wide bead of Mopar®Threebond Engine RTV Sealant to the lower oil pan.

⁑ **WARNING**

Following assembly, the Mopar®Threebond Engine RTV

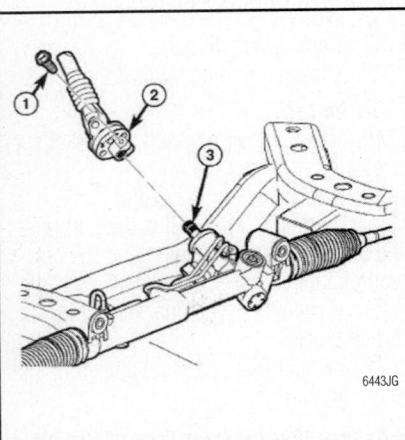

Fig. 224 Steering coupling (2), pinch bolt (1) and input shaft (3)

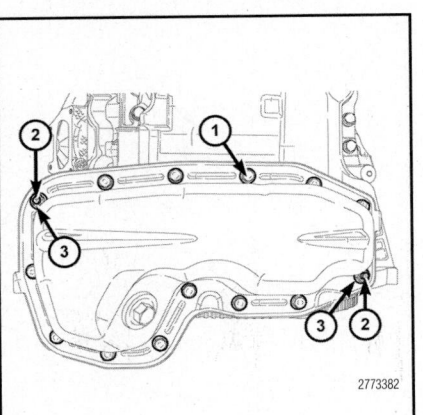

Fig. 225 Removing the lower oil pan, bolts (1), studs (2) and nuts (3)

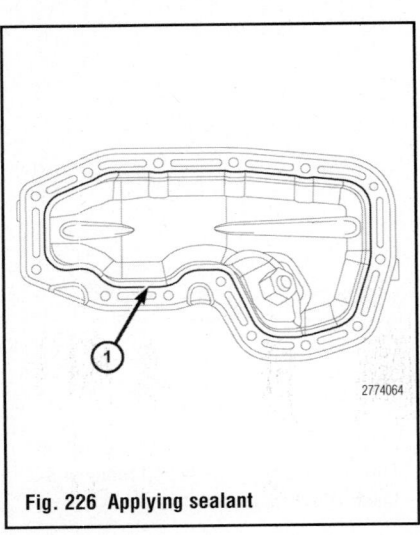

Fig. 226 Applying sealant

Sealant must be allowed to dry for 45 minutes prior to adding oil and engine operation. Premature exposure to oil prior to drying may result in engine fluid leakage.

10. Install the two studs into the upper oil pan flange.

11. Install the lower oil pan to the upper oil pan with twelve bolts and two nuts tightened to 8 ft. lbs. (11 Nm).

12. Fill the crankcase with the specified type and amount of engine oil.

13. Run the engine until it reaches normal operating temperature and check for leaks.

Upper

See Figures 227 through 232.

1. Disconnect and isolate the negative battery cable.

2. Lift the engine cover retaining grommets off the ball studs and remove the engine cover.

3. Disconnect the electrical connector from the Inlet Air Temperature (IAT) sensor.

4. Loosen the clamp at the throttle body.

5. Loosen the clamp at the air cleaner housing.

6. Lift the air inlet hose assembly retaining grommet off the ball stud.

7. Remove the air inlet hose assembly.

8. Remove the bolt and remove the oil level indicator.

9. Raise and support the vehicle.

10. Remove the belly pan retainers and remove the belly pan.

11. Drain the engine oil.

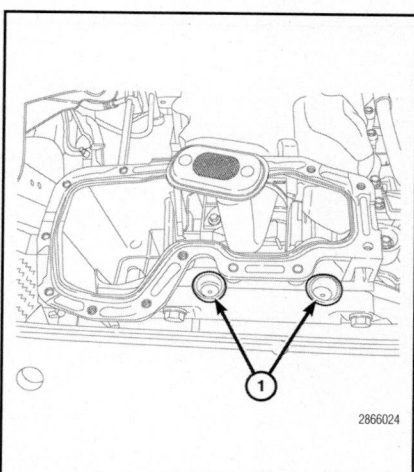

Fig. 227 Removing the rubber plugs

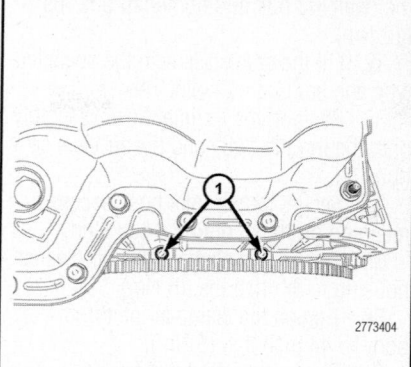

Fig. 228 Removing the bolts from the rear oil seal retainer flange

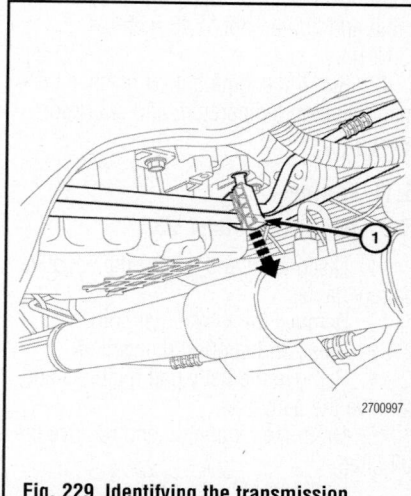

Fig. 229 Identifying the transmission cooler line retainer

➡**The lower oil pan must be removed to access all of the upper oil pan retaining bolts.**

12. Remove the lower oil pan.

13. Remove the two rubber plugs covering the rear oil seal retainer flange bolts.

14. Remove the two bolts from the rear oil seal retainer flange.

15. Unfasten the transmission cooler line retainer from the oil pan flange.

16. Remove the four transmission to the engine oil pan bolts.

17. Remove the nineteen oil pan mounting bolts.

18. Using the four indicated pry points, carefully remove the upper oil pan.

19. Remove the all residual sealant from the upper and lower oil pans, timing chain cover, rear seal retainer and engine block mating surfaces.

To install:

❋❋ WARNING

Engine assembly requires the use of a unique sealant that is compatible with engine oil. Using a sealant other than Mopar®Threebond Engine RTV Sealant may result in engine fluid leakage.

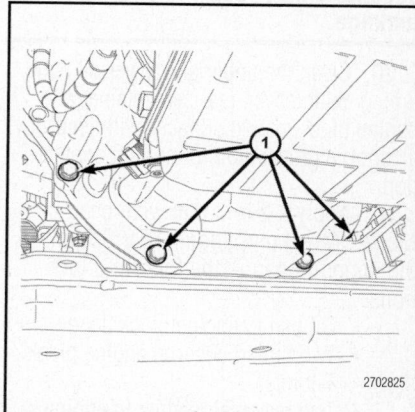

Fig. 230 Identifying the transmission to engine oil pan bolts

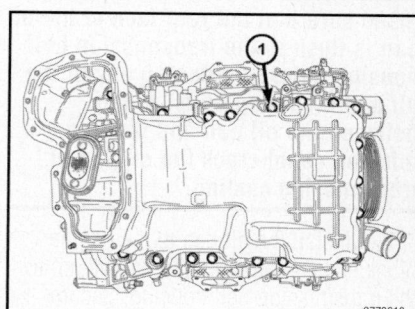

Fig. 231 Identifying the oil pan mounting bolts

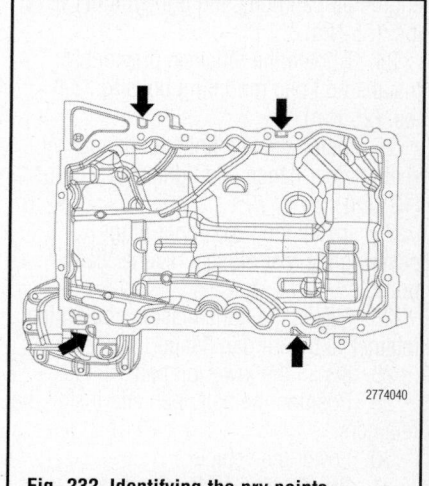

Fig. 232 Identifying the pry points

> **⁑ WARNING**
>
> Following the application of Mopar®Threebond Engine RTV Sealant to the gasket surfaces, the components must be assembled within 20 minutes and the attaching fasteners must be tightened to specification within 45 minutes. Prolonged exposure to the air prior to assembly may result in engine fluid leakage.

20. Clean the upper and lower oil pans, timing chain cover, rear seal retainer and engine block mating surfaces with isopropyl alcohol in preparation for sealant application.

21. Apply a 2 to 3 mm wide bead of Mopar®Threebond Engine RTV Sealant to the upper oil pan in the following locations:
- Oil pan to engine block flange
- Two timing cover to engine block T-joints
- Two rear seal retainer to engine block T-joints

> **⁑ WARNING**
>
> Make sure that the rear face of the oil pan is flush to the transmission bell housing before tightening any of the oil pan mounting bolts. A gap between the oil pan and the transmission could crack the oil pan or transmission casting.

22. Install the oil pan to the engine block making sure the oil pan is flush to the transmission bell housing. Secure the oil pan to the engine block with nineteen oil pan mounting bolts finger tight.

23. Install the four transmission to the engine oil pan bolts and tighten to 41 ft. lbs. (55 Nm).

24. Tighten the nineteen previously installed oil pan mounting bolts to 18 ft. lbs. (25 Nm).

25. Install the two bolts to the rear oil seal retainer flange and tighten to 9 ft. lbs. (12 Nm).

26. Install the two rubber plugs covering the rear oil seal retainer flange bolts.

27. Fasten the transmission cooler line retainer to the oil pan flange.

28. Install the lower oil pan.

29. Position the belly pan and install the retainers.

30. Lower the vehicle.

31. Position the oil level indicator, install

the retaining bolt and tighten to 9 ft. lbs. (12 Nm).

32. Fill the crankcase with the specified type and amount of engine oil.

33. Position the air inlet hose assembly onto the throttle body and the air cleaner housing.

34. Secure the air inlet hose assembly retaining grommet onto the ball stud.

35. Tighten the clamp at the air cleaner housing to 44 inch lbs. (5 Nm).

36. Tighten the clamp at the throttle body to 44 inch lbs. (5 Nm).

37. Connect the Inlet Air Temperature (IAT) sensor electrical connector.

38. Position the engine cover and secure the retaining grommets onto the ball studs.

39. Connect the negative battery cable and tighten nut to 45 inch lbs. (5 Nm).

40. Run the engine until it reaches normal operating temperature and check for leaks.

5.7L Engine

See Figures 233 through 235.

1. Disconnect and isolate the negative battery cable.

2. Remove the intake manifold.

3. Raise and support the vehicle.

4. Remove the belly pan retainers and remove the belly pan.

5. Drain the engine oil and remove the oil filter.

> ➡ **Do not remove P/S hoses, tie rod ends or disconnect steering column coupler.**

6. Remove the steering gear mounting bolts and lower the steering gear to provide clearance to remove the oil pan.

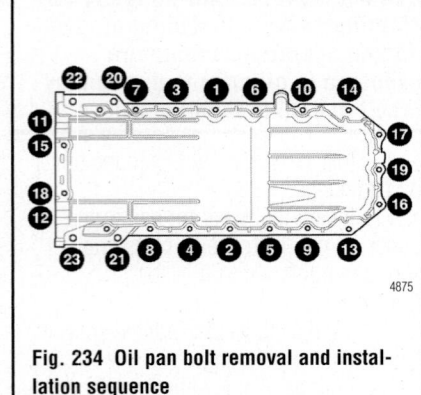

Fig. 234 Oil pan bolt removal and installation sequence

7. Remove the both left/right front engine mount heat shield retaining nuts and remove the heat shields.

8. Remove the both left/right front engine mount lower retaining bolts.

9. Lower the vehicle.

> ➡ **Do not use air tools to install engine lift fixture.**

10. Install the Engine Lift Fixture and the Engine Support Fixture.

11. Raise the engine to provide clearance to remove the oil pan.

> ➡ **Do not pry on the oil pan or oil pan gasket. The oil pan gasket is integral to the engine windage tray and does not come out with the oil pan.**

> ➡ **The horizontal M10 retaining bolts (11, 12, 15, 18) are 5 mm longer in length then the vertical M10 retaining bolts (20, 21, 22, 23) and must be reinstalled in their original locations.**

12. Raise and support the vehicle.

13. Remove the M10 retaining bolts (horizontal 11, 12, 15, 18 and vertical 20,

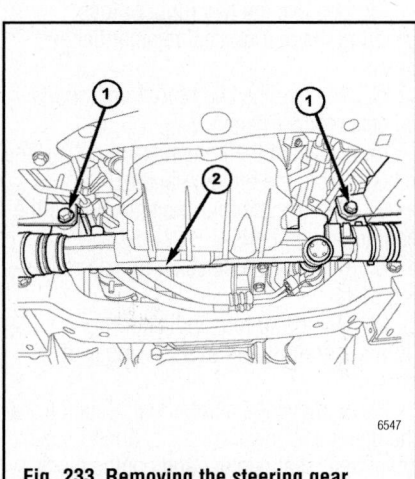

Fig. 233 Removing the steering gear mounting bolts (1) and gear (2)

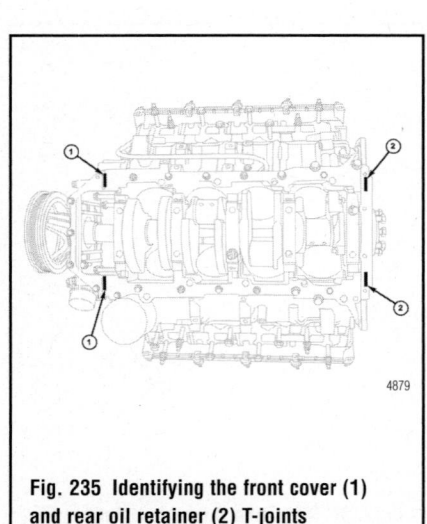

Fig. 235 Identifying the front cover (1) and rear oil retainer (2) T-joints

21, 22, 23) from the rear of the oil pan to the transmission.

14. Remove the M6 retaining bolts and remove the oil pan.

➡When the oil pan is removed, a new oil pan gasket and the integral windage tray assembly must be installed, the old gasket cannot be reused.

15. Remove the oil pump pickup tube retaining bolt and nut and remove the pickup tube.

16. Remove the and discard the oil pan gasket/windage tray.

To install:

➡Mopar®Engine RTV must be applied to the 4 T-joints, the area where the front cover, rear retainer and oil pan gasket meet. The bead of RTV should cover the bottom of the gasket. This area is approximately 4.5 mm x 25 mm in each of the 4 T-joint locations.

17. Clean the oil pan gasket mating surface of the engine block and oil pan.

18. Apply Mopar®Engine RTV at the 4 T- joints.

➡When the oil pan is removed a new oil pan gasket and the integral windage tray assembly must be installed, the old gasket cannot be reused.

19. Install the a new oil pan gasket/windage tray.

20. Using a new O-ring, position the oil pump pickup tube into the oil pump.

21. Install the oil pump pickup tube retaining bolt and nut and tighten to 21 ft. lbs. (28 Nm).

➡The horizontal M10 retaining bolts (11, 12, 15, 18) are 5 mm longer in length then the vertical M10 retaining bolts (20, 21, 22, 23) and must be reinstalled in their original locations.

➡New M6 retaining bolts must be used when reinstalling the oil pan. Do not reuse the old M6 retaining bolts.

22. Align the rear of the oil pan with the rear face of the engine block and install the M10 and M6 retaining bolts finger tight.

23. Using the sequence shown, tighten the M6 retaining bolts to 44 inch lbs. (5 Nm).

24. Using the sequence shown, tighten the M10 retaining bolts to 40 ft. lbs. (54 Nm).

25. Using the sequence shown, tighten the M6 retaining bolts to 9 ft. lbs. (12 Nm).

26. Lower the vehicle.

27. Using the Engine Lift Fixture, Engine Lift Adapter and the Engine Support Fixture

Support Fixture, lower the engine into position and remove.

28. Install the engine oil dipstick tube and dipstick.

29. Raise and support the vehicle.

30. Install the both engine mount lower retaining bolts and tighten to 45 ft. lbs. (61 Nm).

31. Position both engine mount heat shields and install retaining nuts.

32. Position the steering gear, install mounting bolts and tighten to 70 ft. lbs. (95 Nm).

33. Lightly lubricate the oil filter gasket with clean engine oil.

➡Do not over tighten the oil filter.

34. Install the oil filter.

35. Position the belly pan to the underside of vehicle and install belly pan retainers.

36. Lower the vehicle.

37. Install the intake manifold.

38. Fill the crankcase with the specified type and amount of engine oil.

39. Connect the negative battery cable.

40. Start engine and check for leaks.

6.4L Engine

See Figures 234, 236 through 238.

1. Disconnect the negative battery cable.

2. Remove the intake manifold.

3. Remove the engine oil dipstick and tube from the oil pan.

4. Raise and support the vehicle.

5. Remove the belly pan retainers and remove the belly pan.

6. Drain the engine oil and remove the oil filter.

➡Do not remove P/S hoses, tie rod ends or disconnect the steering column coupler.

7. Remove the steering gear mounting bolts and lower the steering gear to provide clearance to remove the oil pan.

8. Remove the both left/right front engine mount heat shield retaining nuts and remove the heat shields.

9. Remove the both left/right front engine mount lower retaining bolts.

10. Lower the vehicle.

➡Do not use air tools to install engine lift fixture.

11. Install the Engine Lift Fixture, Engine Lift Adapter, Engine Lift and the Engine Support Fixture

Support Fixture.

12. Raise the engine to provide clearance to remove the oil pan.

➡Do not pry on the oil pan or oil pan gasket. The oil pan gasket is integral to the engine windage tray and does not come out with the oil pan.

➡The horizontal M10 retaining bolts (11, 12, 15, 18) are 5 mm longer in length then the vertical M10 retaining bolts (20, 21, 22, 23) and must be reinstalled in their original locations.

13. Raise and support the vehicle.

14. Remove the M10 retaining bolts (horizontal 11, 12, 15, 18 and vertical 20, 21, 22, 23) from the rear of the oil pan to the transmission.

15. Remove the M6 retaining bolts and remove the oil pan.

➡When the oil pan is removed, a new oil pan gasket and the integral windage tray assembly must be installed, the old gasket cannot be reused.

16. Remove the oil pump pickup tube retaining bolt and nut.

17. Remove the oil pump pickup tube.

18. Remove the and discard the oil pan gasket/windage tray.

To install:

➡Mopar®Engine RTV must be applied to the 4 T-joints, the area where the front cover, rear retainer and oil pan gasket meet. The bead of RTV should cover the bottom of the gasket. This area is approximately 4.5 mm x 25 mm in each of the 4 T-joint locations.

19. Clean the oil pan gasket mating surface of the engine block and oil pan.

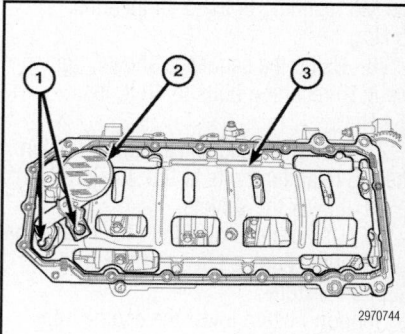

Fig. 236 Removing the oil pump tube (2) bolt and nut (1) and oil pan gasket/windage tray (3)

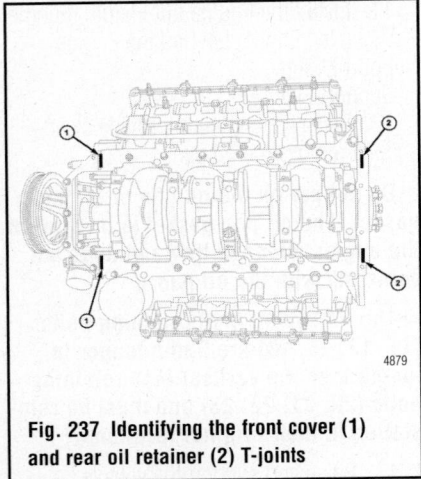

Fig. 237 Identifying the front cover (1) and rear oil retainer (2) T-joints

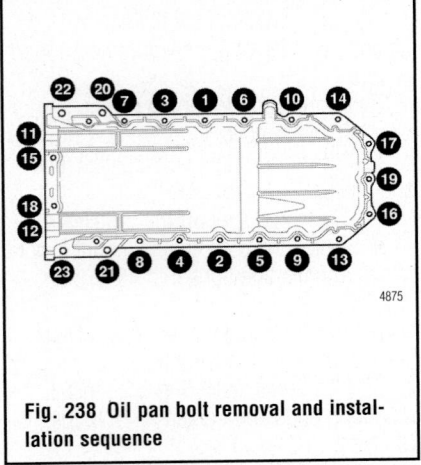

Fig. 238 Oil pan bolt removal and installation sequence

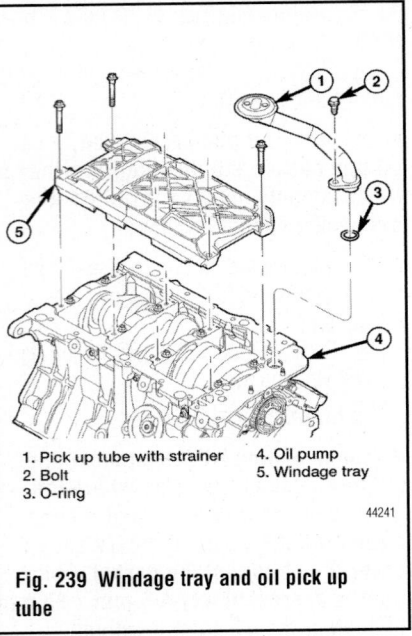

1. Pick up tube with strainer
2. Bolt
3. O-ring
4. Oil pump
5. Windage tray

Fig. 239 Windage tray and oil pick up tube

20. Apply Mopar®Engine RTV at the 4 T- joints.

➡When the oil pan is removed a new oil pan gasket and the integral windage tray assembly must be installed, the old gasket cannot be reused.

21. Install the a new oil pan gasket/windage tray.
22. Using a new O-ring, position the oil pump pickup tube into the oil pump.
23. Install the oil pump pickup tube retaining bolt and nut and tighten to 21 ft. lbs. (28 Nm).

➡The horizontal M10 retaining bolts (11, 12, 15, 18) are 5 mm longer in length then the vertical M10 retaining bolts (20, 21, 22, 23) and must be reinstalled in their original locations.

➡New M6 retaining bolts must be used when reinstalling the oil pan. Do not reuse the old M6 retaining bolts.

24. Align the rear of the oil pan with the rear face of the engine block and install the M10 and M6 retaining bolts finger tight.
25. Using the sequence shown, tighten the M6 retaining bolts to 44 inch lbs. (5 Nm).
26. Using the sequence shown, tighten the M10 retaining bolts to 40 ft. lbs. (54 Nm).
27. Using the sequence shown, tighten the M6 retaining bolts to 9 ft. lbs. (12 Nm).
28. Lower the vehicle.
29. Using the Engine Lift Fixture, Engine Lift Adapter, Engine Lift and the Engine Support Fixture
Support Fixture lower the engine into position and remove.
30. Install the engine oil dipstick tube and dipstick.
31. Raise and support the vehicle.

32. Install the both engine mount lower retaining bolts and tighten to 45 ft. lbs. (61 Nm).
33. Position both engine mount heat shields and install retaining nuts.
34. Position the steering gear, install mounting bolts and tighten to 70 ft. lbs. (95 Nm).
35. Lightly lubricate the oil filter gasket with clean engine oil.

➡Do not over tighten the oil filter.

36. Thread the oil filter onto the oil cooler oil filter boss.
37. When the oil filter gasket makes contact with the oil cooler sealing surface, hand tighten the oil filter one half turn, or 180°.
38. Position the belly pan to the underside of vehicle and install belly pan retainers.
39. Lower the vehicle.
40. Install the intake manifold.
41. Fill the engine with oil.
42. Connect the negative battery cable.
43. Start the engine and check for leaks.

OIL PUMP

REMOVAL & INSTALLATION

3.5L Engine

See Figures 239 through 241.

1. Center and secure the steering wheel.
2. Disconnect and isolate the negative battery cable.
3. Drain the cooling system.
4. Remove the timing belt.
5. Remove the crankshaft sprocket.
6. Drive the dowel pin into the center of the crankshaft nose and retrieve the pin with a magnet.
7. Remove the engine oil pan.

8. Remove the bolt and the oil pickup tube.

➡The bolt securing the A/C compressor to the engine cannot be fully removed until the compressor is positioned away from the cylinder block.

9. Fully loosen the bolt that secures the A/C compressor (5) and automatic transmission cooler line bracket (if equipped) to the cylinder block.

✳✳ WARNING

Use care not to deform or damage the automatic transmission cooler lines and retaining bracket when repositioning the A/C compressor.

10. Support the A/C compressor and remove the bolts and that secure the

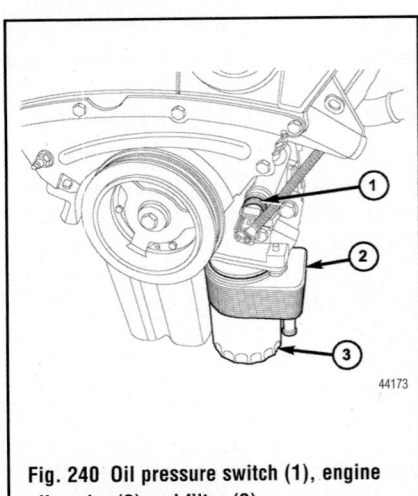

Fig. 240 Oil pressure switch (1), engine oil cooler (2) and filter (3)

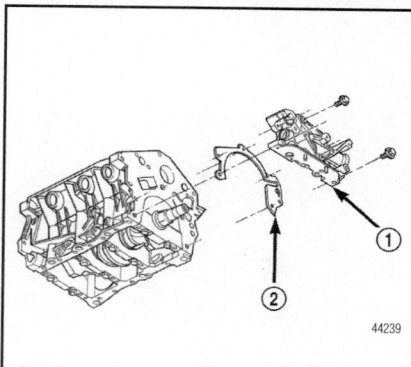

Fig. 241 Removing the oil pump (1) and gasket (2)

compressor to the cylinder block and reposition the A/C compressor.

11. Remove the oil pressure switch.

12. Remove the oil pump fasteners. Remove the oil pump and gasket from the engine.

To install:

13. Prime the oil pump before installation by filling the rotor cavity with clean engine oil.

14. Install the oil pump and gasket carefully over the crankshaft. Position the pump onto the block and tighten the bolts to 21 ft. lbs. (28 Nm).

15. Install the oil pressure switch.

✳✳ WARNING

When equipped, use care not to deform or damage the automatic transmission cooler lines and retaining bracket when repositioning the A/C compressor.

➡**The bolt that secures the A/C compressor and transmission cooler line bracket (when equipped) must be installed through the bracket and the lower front mounting hole of the compressor prior to final positioning of the compressor to the cylinder block.**

16. Loosely install the bolt that secures the A/C compressor and automatic transmission cooler line bracket (when equipped) to the compressor and position the compressor, bracket and bolt to the cylinder block.

17. Loosely install the bolts that secure the A/C compressor to the cylinder block.

18. Tighten all three bolts that secure the A/C compressor to the engine in the following order to 19 ft. lbs. (26 Nm):

   a. Upper front bolt.
   b. Lower front bolt.
   c. Rear bolt.

19. Install a new O-ring on the oil pickup tube.

20. Install the oil pickup tube. Tighten the bolt to 9 ft. lbs. (12 Nm).

21. Install the engine oil pan.

22. Install the dowel pin into the crankshaft until 0.047 inch (1.2 mm) of the dowel pin remains protruding above the crankshaft surface.

23. Install the crankshaft sprocket.

24. Install the timing belt.

25. Install the timing belt covers.

26. Install the crankshaft vibration damper.

27. Install the accessory drive belt.

28. Fill the cooling system to the proper level using the appropriate coolant.

29. Fill the engine crankcase with the proper oil to the correct level.

30. Connect the negative battery cable and tighten nut to 45 inch lbs. (5 Nm).

3.6L Engine

See Figures 242 through 245.

1. Disconnect and isolate the negative battery cable.

2. Remove the upper oil pan.

3. Remove the oil pump pick-up.

4. Disconnect the engine wire harness from the oil pump solenoid electrical connector.

5. Depress the connector retention lock tab to disengage the oil pump solenoid electrical connector from the engine block.

6. Push the oil pump solenoid electrical connector into the engine block, rotate the connector slightly CW, push it past the primary chain tensioner mounting bolt (1) and into the engine.

7. Push back the oil pump chain tensioner and insert a suitable retaining pin such as a 3 mm Allen wrench.

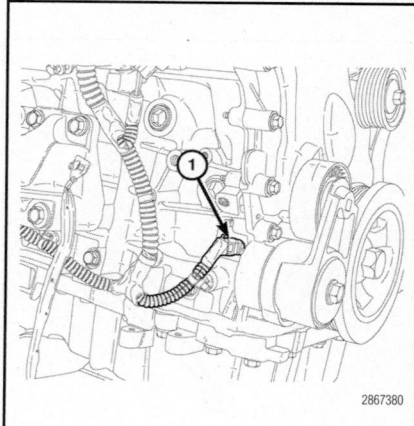

Fig. 242 Disconnecting the oil pump electrical connector

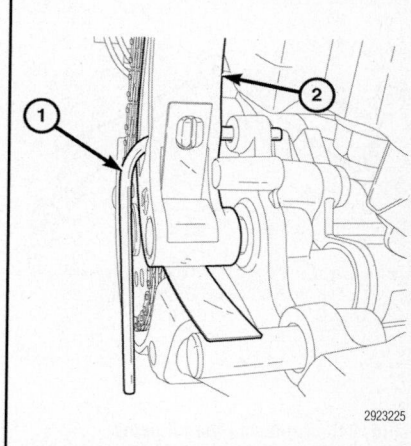

Fig. 243 Pushing back the oil pump chain tensioner (2) and inserting a retaining pin (1)

✳✳ WARNING

Always reinstall timing chains so that they maintain the same direction of rotation. Inverting a previously run chain on a previously run sprocket will result in excessive wear to both the chain and sprocket.

8. Mark the direction of rotation on the oil pump chain (3) and sprocket using a paint pen or equivalent to aid in reassembly.

➡**There are no timing marks on the oil pump gear or chain. Timing of the oil pump is not required.**

9. Remove the oil pump sprocket T45 retaining bolt and remove the oil pump sprocket.

10. Remove the retaining pin and disengage the oil pump chain tensioner spring from the dowel pin.

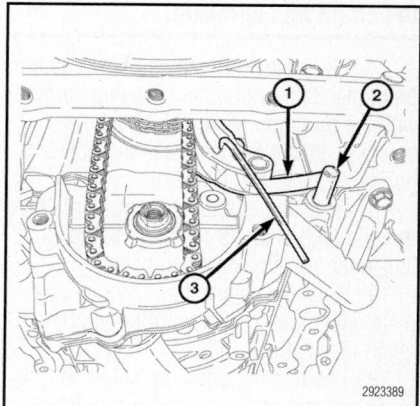

Fig. 244 Removing the retaining pin (3) and disengaging the oil pump chain tensioner spring (1) from the dowel pin (2)

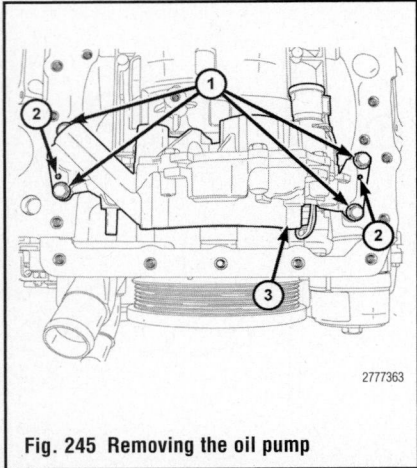

Fig. 245 Removing the oil pump

11. Remove the oil pump chain tensioner from the oil pump.

12. Remove the four oil pump bolts and remove the oil pump.

To install:

13. Align the locator pins to the engine block and install the oil pump with four bolts. Tighten the bolts to 9 ft. lbs. (12 Nm).

14. Install the oil pump chain tensioner on the oil pump.

15. Position the oil pump chain tensioner spring above the dowel pin.

16. Push back the oil pump chain tensioner and insert a suitable retaining pin such as a 3 mm Allen wrench.

➡There are no timing marks on the oil pump gear or chain. Timing of the oil pump is not required.

❋❋ WARNING

Always reinstall timing chains so that they maintain the same direction of rotation. Inverting a previously run chain on a previously run sprocket will result in excessive wear to both the chain and sprocket.

17. Place the oil pump sprocket into the oil pump chain. Align the oil pump sprocket with the oil pump shaft and install the sprocket. Install the T45 retaining bolt and tighten to 18 ft. lbs. (25 Nm).

18. Remove the retaining pin. Verify that the oil pump chain is centered on the tensioner and crankshaft sprocket.

19. Rotate the crankshaft CW one complete revolution to verify proper oil pump chain installation.

20. Position the oil pump solenoid electrical connector into the engine block. Rotate the connector so that it can be pushed past the primary chain tensioner mounting bolt. Then rotate the connector

slightly CCW and push it into the engine block until it locks in place.

21. Verify that the oil pump solenoid electrical connector retention lock tab is engaged to the engine block.

22. Connect the engine wire harness to the oil pump solenoid electrical connector.

23. Install the oil pump pick-up.

24. Install the oil pan.

25. If removed, install the oil filter and fill the engine crankcase with the proper oil to the correct level.

26. Connect the negative battery cable and tighten nut to 45 inch lbs. (5 Nm).

❋❋ WARNING

A MIL or low oil pressure indicator that remains illuminated for more than 2 seconds may indicate low or no engine oil pressure. Stop the engine and investigate the cause of the indication.

27. Start and run the engine until it reaches normal operating temperature.

5.7L Engine

See Figures 246 and 247.

1. Remove the oil pan.

2. Remove the timing cover.

3. Remove the four bolts and the oil pump.

To install:

4. Position the oil pump on the crankshaft and install the oil pump retaining bolts finger tight.

5. Using the sequence shown, tighten the oil pump retaining bolts to 21 ft. lbs. (28 Nm).

6. Install the timing cover.

7. Install the oil pan

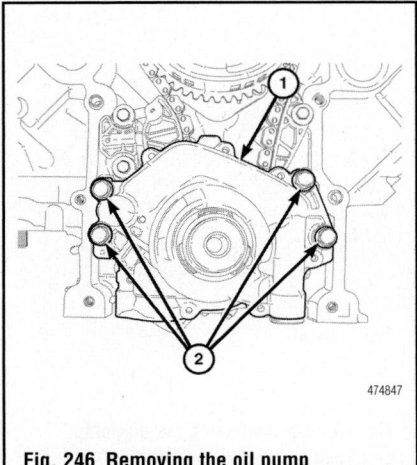

Fig. 246 Removing the oil pump

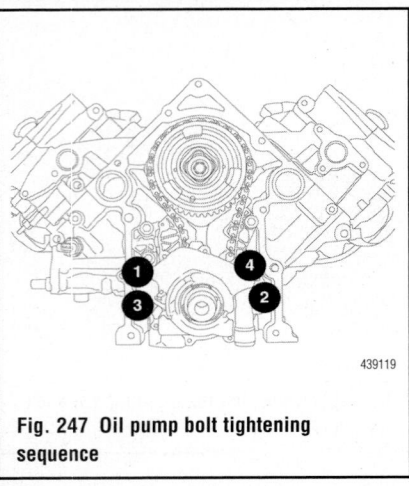

Fig. 247 Oil pump bolt tightening sequence

6.1L Engine

See Figure 248.

1. Remove the oil pan and pick-up tube.

2. Remove the timing chain cover.

3. Remove the four bolts, and the oil pump.

To install:

4. Position the oil pump onto the crankshaft and install the 4 oil pump retaining bolts.

5. Tighten the oil pump retaining bolts to 21 ft. lbs. (28 Nm).

6. Install the timing chain cover.

7. Install the pick-up tube and oil pan.

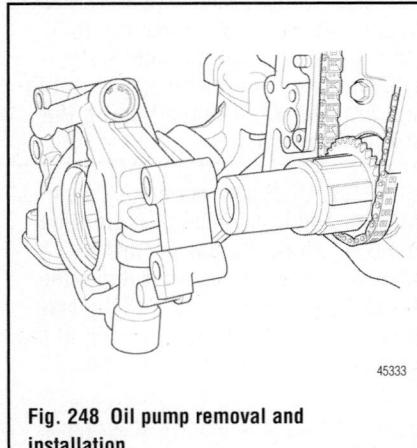

Fig. 248 Oil pump removal and installation

6.4L Engine

See Figure 246.

➡It is not necessary to remove water pump for timing cover removal.

1. Remove the engine timing cover.

➡When the oil pan is removed, a new oil pan gasket and the integral windage tray assembly must be installed, the old gasket cannot be reused.

2. Remove the oil pan and oil pump pickup tube.

3. Remove the oil pump retaining bolts and remove the oil pump.

To install:

4. Position the oil pump onto the crankshaft, install the retaining bolts and tighten to 21 ft. lbs. (28 Nm).

5. Install the timing chain cover.

6. Install the oil pump pickup tube and oil pan.

INSPECTION

3.5L Engine

See Figures 249 through 254.

➡**DO NOT** inspect the oil relief valve assembly. If the oil relief valve is suspect, replace the oil pump.

1. Disassemble oil pump.

2. Clean all parts thoroughly. Mating surface of the oil pump housing should be smooth. Replace pump cover if scratched or grooved.

3. Lay a straightedge across the pump cover surface. If a 0.001 inch (0.025 mm) feeler gauge can be inserted between cover and straight edge, cover should be replaced.

4. Measure thickness and diameter of outer rotor. If outer rotor thickness measures 0.563 inch (14.299 mm) or less , or if the diameter is 3.141 inches (79.78 mm) or less, replace outer rotor.

5. If inner rotor measures 0.563 inch (14.299 mm) or less replace inner rotor.

6. Slide outer rotor into body, press to one side with fingers and measure clearance between rotor and body. If measurement is 0.015 inch. (0.39 mm) or more, replace body only if outer rotor is in specifications.

7. Install the inner rotor into body. If

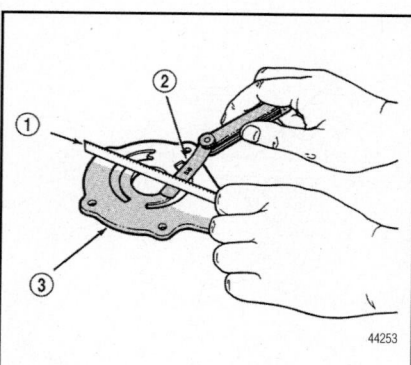

Fig. 249 Checking Oil Pump Cover (3) flatness with a straight edge (1) and feeler gauge (2)

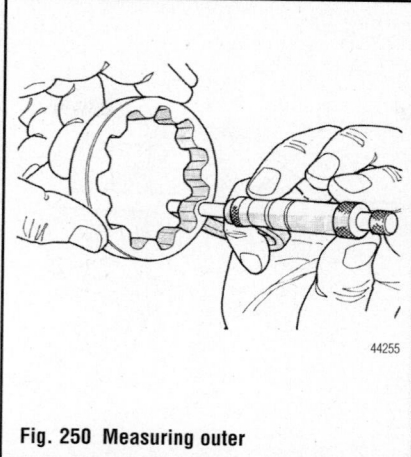

Fig. 250 Measuring outer

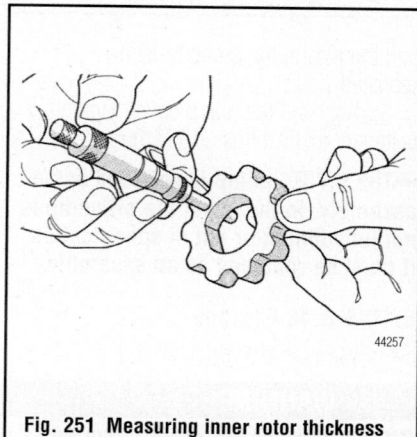

Fig. 251 Measuring inner rotor thickness

clearance between inner and outer rotors is 0.008 inch (0.20 mm) or more, replace both rotors.

8. Place a straightedge across the face of the body, between bolt holes. If a feeler gauge of 0.003 inch (0.077 mm) or more can be inserted between rotors and the straightedge, replace pump assembly ONLY if rotors are in specs.

9. Assemble oil pump.

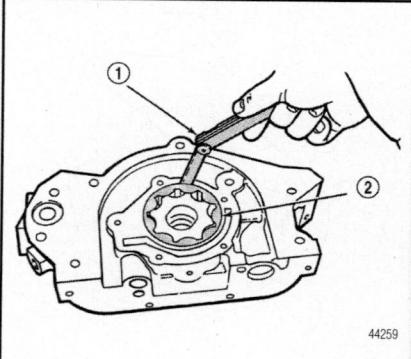

Fig. 252 Measuring outer rotor (2) clearance in housing with a feeler gauge (1)

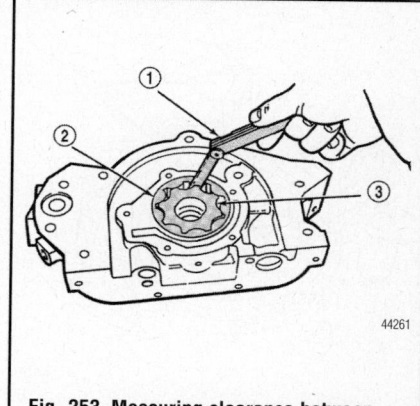

Fig. 253 Measuring clearance between rotors

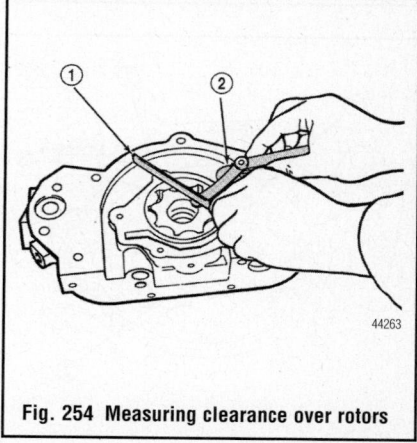

Fig. 254 Measuring clearance over rotors

3.6L Engine

➡**The 3.6L oil pump is serviced as an assembly. The assembly includes both the pump and the solenoid. There are no serviceable sub-assembly components. In the event the oil pump or solenoid are not functioning or out of specification they must be replaced as an assembly.**

1. Inspect the solenoid wires for cuts or chaffing.

2. Inspect the condition of the connector O-ring seal.

3. Inspect the connector retention lock tab for fatigue or damage.

5.7L Engine

See Figures 255 through 257.

✳✳ WARNING

The oil pump pressure relief valve and spring should not be removed from the oil pump. If these components are disassembled and or removed from the pump the entire oil pump assembly must be replaced.

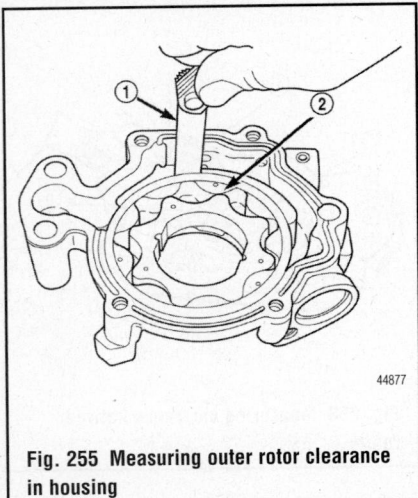

Fig. 255 Measuring outer rotor clearance in housing

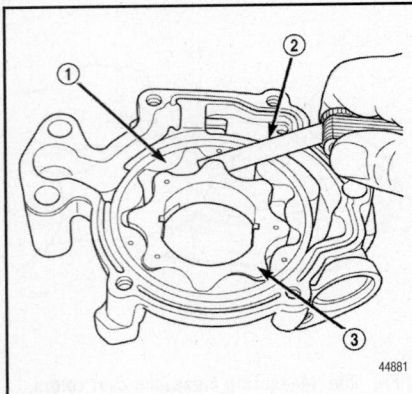

Fig. 256 Using the measuring tool (2) to measure clearance between inner (3) and outer (1) rotors

1. Remove the pump cover.
2. Clean all parts thoroughly. Mating surface of the oil pump housing should be smooth. If the pump cover is scratched or grooved the oil pump assembly should be replaced.
3. Slide outer rotor into the body of the oil pump. Press the outer rotor to one side of the oil pump body and measure clearance between the outer rotor and the body. If the measurement is 0.009 inch (0.235mm) or more the oil pump assembly must be replaced.
4. Install the inner rotor into the oil pump body. Measure the clearance between the inner and outer rotors. If the clearance between the rotors is 0.006 inch (0.150 mm) or more the oil pump assembly must be replaced.
5. Place a straight edge across the body of the oil pump (between the bolt holes), if a feeler gauge of 0.0038 inch (0.095 mm) or greater can be inserted between the straightedge

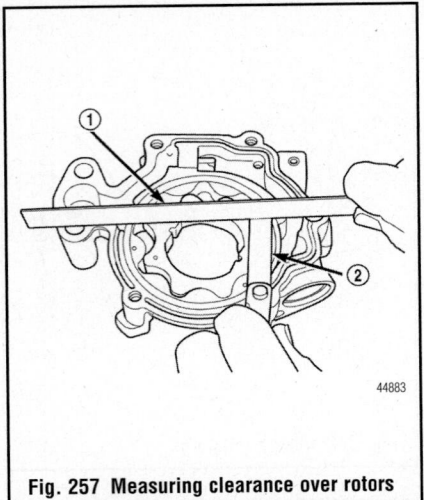

Fig. 257 Measuring clearance over rotors

and the rotors, the pump must be replaced.
6. Reinstall the pump cover. Tighten fasteners to 11 ft. lbs. (15 Nm).

➡ **The 5.7 Oil pump is serviced as an assembly. In the event the oil pump is not functioning or out of specification, it must be replaced as an assembly.**

6.1L & 6.4L Engines

See Figures 258 through 260.

❖❖ **WARNING**

Oil pump pressure relief valve and spring should not be removed from the oil pump. If these components are disassembled and or removed from the pump the entire oil pump assembly must be replaced.

1. Remove the pump cover.
2. Clean all parts thoroughly. The mating surface of the oil pump housing should be smooth. If the oil pump cover is

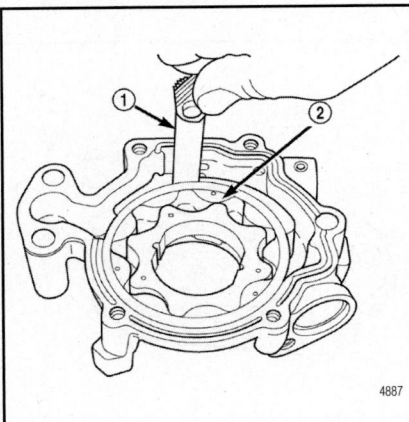

Fig. 258 Measuring outer rotor (2) clearance in housing using the feeler gauge (1)

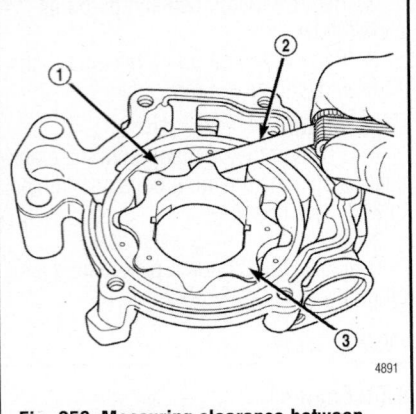

Fig. 259 Measuring clearance between the inner (3) and outer (1) rotors with the feeler gauge (2)

scratched or grooved the oil pump assembly should be replaced.
3. Slide the outer rotor into the body of the oil pump. Press the outer rotor to one side of the oil pump body and measure the clearance between the outer rotor and the body. If the measurement is 0.009 inch (0.235 mm) or greater the oil pump assembly must be replaced.
4. Install the inner rotor into the oil pump body. Measure the clearance between the inner and outer rotors. If the clearance between the rotors is 0.006 inch (.150 mm) or greater the oil pump assembly must be replaced.
5. Place a straight edge across the body of the oil pump (between the bolt holes), using a feeler gauge, measure the clearance between the straightedge and the rotors. If the clearance is 0.0038 inch (.095 mm) or greater the oil pump must be replaced.
6. Install the pump cover and tighten retainers to 11 ft. lbs. (15 Nm)

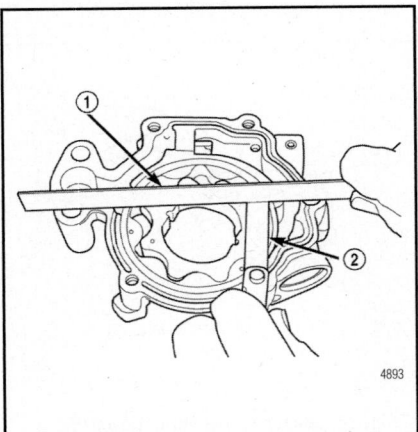

Fig. 260 Measuring clearance over rotor with straight edge (1) and feeler gauge (2)

➥The 6.4L oil pump is serviced as an assembly. There are no Chrysler part numbers for sub-assembly components. In the event the oil pump is not functioning or out of specification it must be replaced as an assembly.

REAR MAIN SEAL

REMOVAL & INSTALLATION

3.5L Engine

See Figure 261.

1. Remove the engine oil pan.
2. Lower the weight of the engine back onto the engine mounts.
3. Remove the transmission from vehicle.
4. Remove the flex plate.
5. Remove the rear crankshaft oil seal retainer bolts.
6. Remove the crankshaft oil seal and clean all mating surfaces.

To install:
To install, reverse the removal procedure.

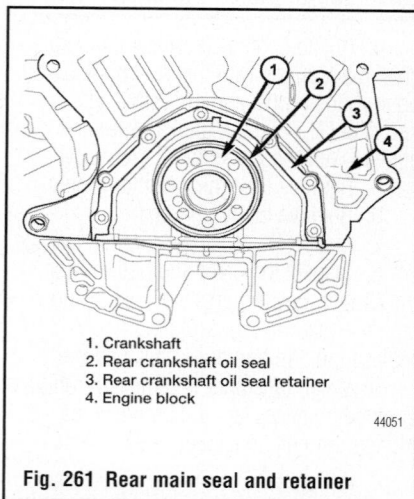

1. Crankshaft
2. Rear crankshaft oil seal
3. Rear crankshaft oil seal retainer
4. Engine block

44051

Fig. 261 Rear main seal and retainer

3.6L Engine

See Figure 262.

The rear crankshaft oil seal is incorporated into the seal retainer and cannot be removed from the retainer. The rear crankshaft oil seal and seal retainer are serviced as an assembly.

1. Remove the transmission.
2. Remove the flexplate.
3. Remove the oil pan.
4. Remove the eight seal retainer attaching screws.
5. Remove the and discard the seal retainer.

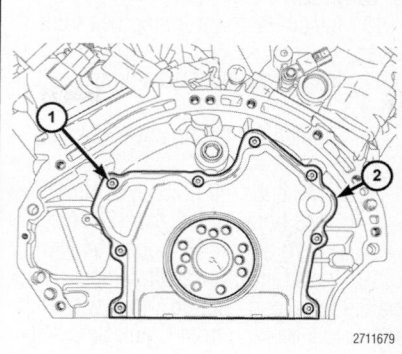

2711679

Fig. 262 Removing the rear main seal, seal retainer (2) and retainer attaching screw (1)

To install:

✸✸ WARNING

The rear crankshaft oil seal and retainer are an assembly. To avoid damage to the seal lip, DO NOT remove the seal protector from the rear crankshaft oil seal before installation onto the engine.

✸✸ WARNING

Whenever the crankshaft is replaced, the rear crankshaft oil seal must also be replaced. Failure to do so may result in engine fluid leakage.

6. Inspect the crankshaft to make sure there are no nicks or burrs on the seal surface.
7. Clean the engine block sealing surfaces thoroughly.

➥It is not necessary to lubricate the seal or the crankshaft when installing the seal retainer. Residual oil following installation can be mistaken for seal leakage.

8. Carefully position the oil seal retainer assembly, and seal protector on the crankshaft and push firmly into place on the engine block (during this step, the seal protector will be pushed from the rear oil seal assembly as a result of installing the rear oil seal).
9. Verify that the seal lip on the retainer is uniformly curled inward toward the engine on the crankshaft.
10. Install the eight seal retainer bolts and tighten to 9 ft. lbs. (12 Nm).

➥Make sure that the seal retainer flange is flush with the engine block oil pan sealing surface.

11. Install the oil pan.
12. Install the flexplate.
13. Install the transmission.
14. Fill the engine crankcase with the proper oil to the correct level.

5.7L Engine

See Figures 263.

The crankshaft rear oil seal is integral to the crankshaft rear oil seal retainer.

➥The crankshaft rear oil seal is integral to the crankshaft rear oil seal retainer and must be replaced as an assembly.

➥The crankshaft rear oil seal retainer cannot be reused after removal.

➥This procedure can be performed in vehicle.

1. Disconnect the negative battery cable.
2. Remove the transmission.
3. Remove the flexplate.
4. Remove the oil pan.
5. Using the sequence shown, remove the rear oil seal retainer mounting bolts.
6. Carefully remove the retainer from the engine block.

To install:
7. Thoroughly clean all gasket residue from the engine block.
8. Position the gasket onto the new crankshaft rear oil seal retainer.
9. Position the crankshaft rear oil seal retainer onto the engine block.
10. Using the sequence shown, install the crankshaft rear oil seal retainer mounting bolts and tighten to 11 ft. lbs. (15 Nm).
11. Install the oil pan.
12. Install the flexplate.
13. Install the transmission.

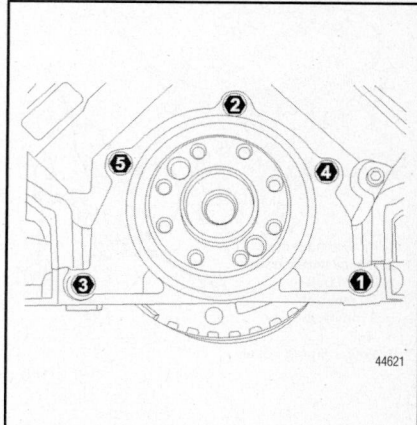

44621

Fig. 263 Removing and installing the rear oil seal retainer

14. Fill the engine with oil.

15. Start the engine and check for leaks.

TIMING BELT FRONT COVER

REMOVAL & INSTALLATION

3.5L Engine

See Figure 264.

1. Disconnect and isolate the negative battery cable.

2. Remove the air cleaner element housing.

3. Partially drain the cooling system.

4. Remove the accessory drive belt.

5. Remove the accessory drive belt idler pulley.

6. Remove the accessory drive belt tensioner.

7. Remove the three power steering pump mounting bolts through the access holes in the pulley and reposition the power steering pump.

8. Remove the upper radiator hose.

9. Disconnect the cooling fan electrical connector.

10. Remove the cooling fan mounting bolts.

11. Remove the radiator cooling fan assembly from the vehicle.

12. Remove the crankshaft damper bolt.

13. Remove the crankshaft damper using Puller and Crankshaft Insert.

14. Remove the upper timing belt cover fasteners and remove the front upper timing belt cover.

15. Remove the lower timing belt cover fasteners and remove the front lower timing belt cover.

To install:

16. Install the lower timing belt front cover.

17. Install the upper front timing belt cover.

18. Tighten the timing cover bolts as follows:

    a. M6 bolts - 9 ft. lbs. (12 Nm)

    b. M8 bolts - 21 ft. lbs. (28 Nm)

    c. M10 bolts - 40 ft. lbs. (54 Nm)

19. Install the crankshaft damper using the 5.9 inch long Forcing Screw with Nut and Thrust Bearing from Crank Sprocket Installer Cup.

20. Install the crankshaft damper bolt. Tighten the bolt to 70 ft. lbs. (95 Nm) while holding the damper with Damper Holding Fixture.

21. Align the power steering pump to the mounting holes on the engine bracket and install three pump mounting bolts through the access holes in the pulley. Tighten the bolts to 21 ft. lbs. (28 Nm).

22. Install the accessory drive belt tensioner. Tighten the bolt to 40 ft. lbs. (34 Nm).

23. Install the accessory drive belt idler pulley. Tighten the bolt to 21 ft. lbs. (28 Nm).

24. Install the accessory drive belt.

25. Install the radiator cooling fan assembly into the vehicle.

26. Install the cooling fan mounting bolts and tighten to 50 inch lbs. (6 Nm).

27. Connect the cooling fan electrical connector.

28. Install the upper radiator hose.

29. Install the air cleaner body.

30. Connect the negative battery cable and tighten nut to 45 inch lbs. (5 Nm).

31. Fill the cooling system.

32. Operate the engine until it reaches normal operating temperature. Check the cooling system for correct fluid level

TIMING BELT & SPROCKETS

REMOVAL & INSTALLATION

3.5L Engine

Timing Belt

See Figures 265 and 266.

✱✱ WARNING

The 3.5L is NOT a freewheeling engine. Therefore, the valve train rocker assemblies must be removed before attempting to rotate either crankshaft or camshafts independently of each other.

1. Disconnect and isolate the negative battery cable.

2. Remove the front timing belt cover.

3. Mark belt running direction, if timing belt is to be reused.

✱✱ WARNING

When aligning timing marks, always rotate engine by turning the crankshaft. Failure to do so will result in valve and/or piston damage.

4. Rotate engine clockwise until crankshaft mark aligns with the TDC mark on oil pump housing (9) and the camshaft sprocket (2, 7) timing marks (1, 8) are aligned with the marks on the rear cover.

5. Remove the timing belt tensioner.

6. Remove the timing belt.

7. Inspect the tensioner for fluid leakage.

8. Inspect the pivot and bolt for free movement, bearing grease leakage, and smooth rotation. If not rotating freely, replace the arm and pulley assembly.

9. When tensioner is removed from the engine it is necessary to compress the plunger into the tensioner body.

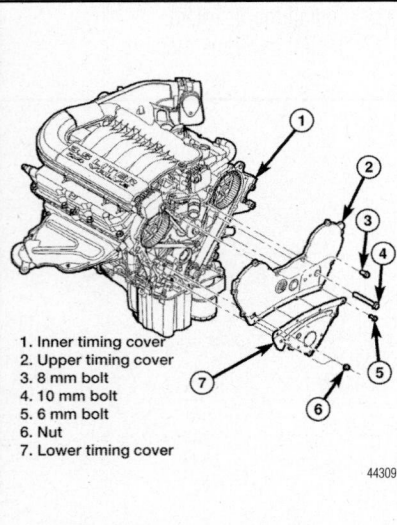

1. Inner timing cover
2. Upper timing cover
3. 8 mm bolt
4. 10 mm bolt
5. 6 mm bolt
6. Nut
7. Lower timing cover

44309

Fig. 264 Removing the upper and lower timing belt covers

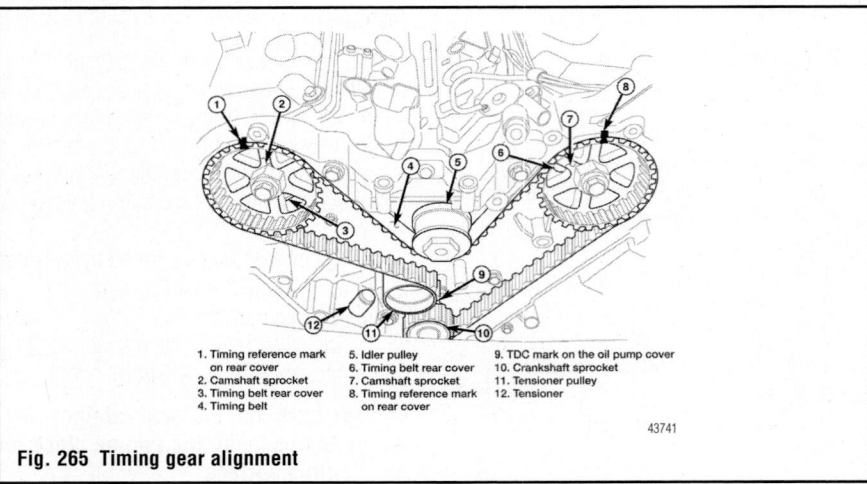

1. Timing reference mark on rear cover
2. Camshaft sprocket
3. Timing belt rear cover
4. Timing belt
5. Idler pulley
6. Timing belt rear cover
7. Camshaft sprocket
8. Timing reference mark on rear cover
9. TDC mark on the oil pump cover
10. Crankshaft sprocket
11. Tensioner pulley
12. Tensioner

43741

Fig. 265 Timing gear alignment

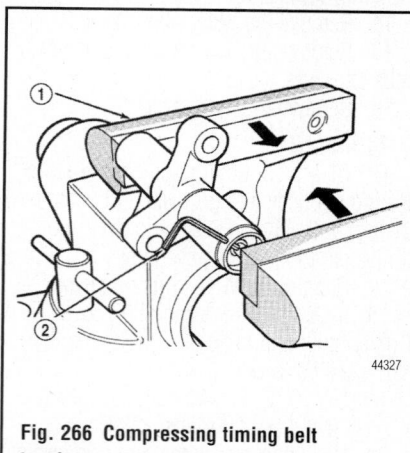

Fig. 266 Compressing timing belt
tensioner

✻✻ WARNING

**Index the tensioner in the vise the
same way it is installed on the
engine. This ensures proper pin orientation when tensioner is installed
on the engine.**

10. Place the tensioner into a vise and
SLOWLY compress the plunger. Total bleed
down of tensioner should take approximately two minutes.

11. When plunger is compressed into
the tensioner body install a pin through the
body and plunger to retain plunger in place
until tensioner is installed.

To install:

12. Align the crankshaft sprocket with
the TDC mark on the oil pump cover.

13. Align the camshaft sprockets (2, 7)
timing reference marks (1, 8) with the marks
on the rear cover.

14. Install the timing belt starting at the
crankshaft sprocket (10) going in a counterclockwise direction. Install the belt around
the last sprocket and maintain tension on
the belt as it is positioned around the tensioner pulley.

➡**It is necessary to compress the
plunger into the tensioner body and
install a locking pin prior to reinstalling
the tensioner.**

15. Hold the tensioner pulley against the
belt and install the reset (pinned) timing belt
tensioner into the housing. Tighten attaching bolts to 21 ft. lbs. (28 Nm).

16. When tensioner is in place, pull the
retaining pin to allow the tensioner to
extend to the pulley bracket.

17. Rotate the crankshaft sprocket two
revolutions and check the timing marks on
the camshafts and crankshaft. The marks
should line up within their respective loca-

tions. If the marks do not line up, repeat the
procedure.

18. Install the front timing belt cover.

19. Connect the negative battery cable
and tighten nut to 45 inch lbs. (5 Nm).

20. Fill the cooling system.

21. Operate the engine until it reaches
normal operating temperature. Check cooling system for correct fluid level.

➡**The Cam/Crank Variation Relearn
procedure must be performed anytime
there has been a repair/replacement
made to a powertrain system, for
example: flywheel, valvetrain,
camshaft and/or crankshaft sensors or
components.**

Camshaft Sprocket

See Figures 267 and 268.

✻✻ WARNING

**The 3.5L engine is NOT a free-wheel-
ing design. Therefore, care should be
taken not to rotate the camshafts or
crankshaft with the timing belt
removed.**

➡**The camshaft timing gears are keyed
to the camshaft.**

1. Remove the timing belt.

2. Hold the right camshaft sprocket
with a 1⁷⁄₁₆(36 mm) box end wrench so that
the timing mark does not move while
removing the retaining bolt.

3. Loosen and remove the camshaft
gear retaining bolt and washer. The right
bolt is 213 mm (8 3/8 in.) long.

➡**The camshaft timing gears are keyed
to the camshaft.**

4. Remove the right camshaft sprocket.

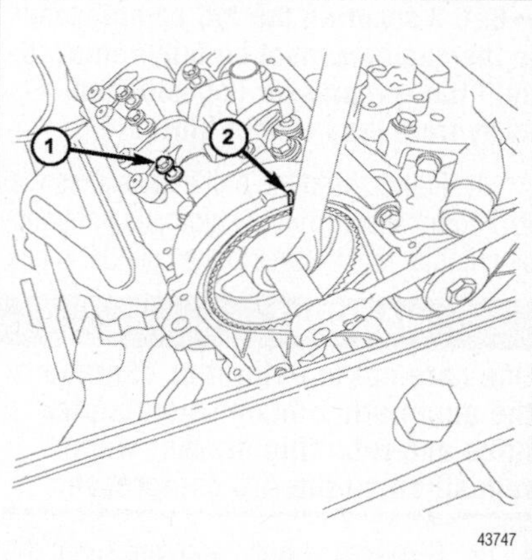

Fig. 267 Right camshaft sprocket, loosened rocker assembly (1) and right
camshaft TDC (2)

5. Hold the left camshaft sprocket with
a 1⁷⁄₁₆(36 mm) box end wrench so that the
timing mark does not move while removing
the retaining bolt.

6. Loosen the left camshaft gear retaining bolt.

7. Remove the grill closure panels.

8. Loosen the upper radiator mounting
bolts.

9. Reposition the radiator/condenser
forward and remove the left camshaft gear
retaining bolt and washer. The left bolt is
10.0 inches (255 mm) long.

➡**The camshaft timing gears are keyed
to the camshaft.**

10. Remove the left camshaft
sprocket.

To install:

11. Install the right camshaft sprocket
onto the camshaft.

12. Install the a NEW sprocket attaching
bolt into place. The 8³⁄₈inch (213 mm) bolt
is to be installed into the right camshaft and
the 10 inch (255 mm) bolt is to be installed
into the left camshaft.

13. Hold the right camshaft sprocket
with a 1⁷⁄₁₆inch (36 mm) box end wrench
so that the timing mark does not move
while tightening the retaining bolt. Tighten
the bolt to 75 ft. lbs. (102 Nm) +90°turn.

14. Install the left camshaft sprocket
onto the camshaft.

15. Install the a NEW sprocket attaching
bolt into place. The 10 inch (255 mm) bolt
is to be installed into the left camshaft and
the 8³⁄₈inch (213 mm) bolt is to be installed
into the right camshaft.

16. Hold the left camshaft sprocket with
a 1⁷⁄₁₆inch (36 mm) box end wrench so
that the timing mark does not move while

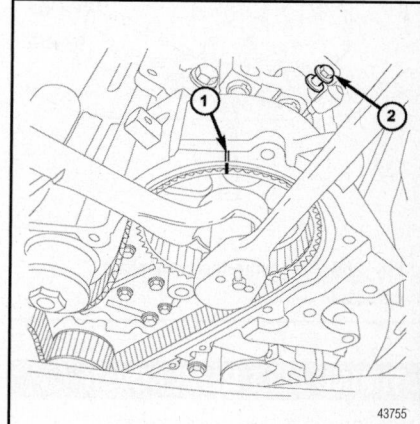

Fig. 268 Left camshaft sprocket, loosened
rocker assembly (2) and left camshaft TDC
(1)

tightening the retaining bolt. Tighten the bolt to 75 ft. lbs. (102 Nm) +90°turn.

17. Tighten the upper radiator mounting bolts to 9 ft. lbs. (12 Nm).

18. Install the grill closure panels.

19. Install the timing belt and tensioner.

20. Install the front timing belt cover.

21. Connect the negative battery cable and tighten nut to 45 inch lbs. (5 Nm).

22. Fill cooling system.

23. Operate engine until it reaches normal operating temperature. Check cooling system for correct fluid level.

➡**The Cam/Crank Variation Relearn procedure must be performed anytime there has been a repair/replacement made to a powertrain system, for example: flywheel, valvetrain, camshaft and/or crankshaft sensors or components.**

Crankshaft Sprocket

See Figure 269.

1. Remove the timing belt.

2. Remove the crankshaft sprocket using the gear puller.

To install:

✳✳ WARNING

To ensure proper installation depth of crankshaft sprocket, Sprocket Installer, Sprocket must be used.

3. Install the crankshaft sprocket using the Sprocket Installer and Forcing Screw.

4. Install the timing belt

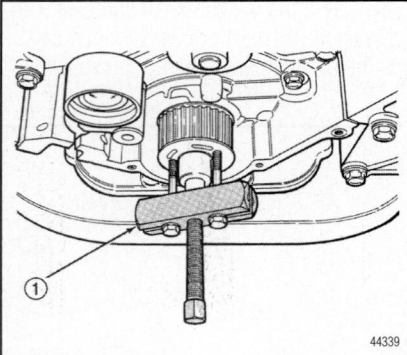

Fig. 269 Removing the crankshaft sprocket

TIMING BELT REAR COVER

REMOVAL & INSTALLATION

3.5L Engine

See Figures 270 and 271.

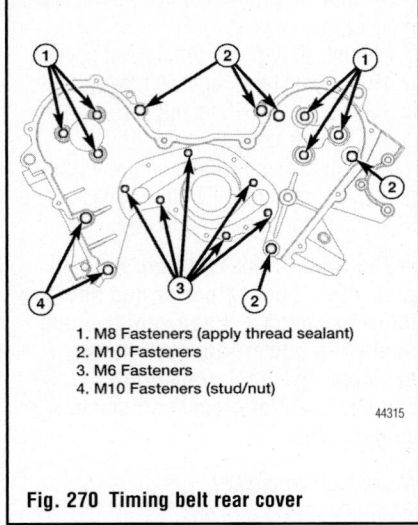

1. M8 Fasteners (apply thread sealant)
2. M10 Fasteners
3. M6 Fasteners
4. M10 Fasteners (stud/nut)

44315

Fig. 270 Timing belt rear cover

➡**The rear timing belt cover has O-rings to seal the water pump passages to cylinder block. Do not reuse the O-rings.**

1. Disconnect and isolate the negative battery cable.

2. Drain the cooling system.

3. Remove the timing belt.

4. Remove the right and left camshaft sprockets.

5. Remove the three power steering pump mounting bolts through access holes in pulley and reposition the power steering pump.

6. Raise and support the vehicle.

7. Remove the front belly pan.

8. Remove the upper most mounting bolt from generator.

9. Remove the generator bracket bolt and remove bracket.

10. Remove the lower mounting bolts and reposition the generator.

➡**Bolt 3 securing the A/C compressor to the engine cannot be fully removed until the compressor is positioned away from the cylinder block.**

11. Fully loosen the bolt that secures the A/C compressor (5) and automatic transmission cooler line bracket to the cylinder block.

✳✳ WARNING

Use care not to deform or damage the automatic transmission cooler lines and retaining bracket when repositioning the A/C compressor.

12. Remove the bolts and reposition the A/C compressor.

13. Remove the water pump mounting bolts.

14. Remove the water pump.

15. Remove the rear timing belt cover bolts and nuts.

16. Remove the rear cover.

To install:

17. Clean rear timing belt cover O-ring sealing surfaces and grooves. Lubricate new O-rings with Mopar®Dielectric Grease or equivalent to facilitate assembly.

18. Position NEW O-rings on cover.

19. Install the rear timing belt cover. Tighten nuts and bolts (1, 2) to the following specified torque:

   a. M10 (2, 4) - 40 ft. lbs. (54 Nm)

   b. M8 (1) - 20 ft. lbs. (28 Nm)

20. Position water pump and new gasket.

21. Install the water pump mounting bolts. Tighten to 9 ft. lbs. (12 Nm).

✳✳ WARNING

When equipped, use care not to deform or damage the automatic transmission cooler lines and retaining bracket when repositioning the A/C compressor.

➡**Bolt 3 that secures the A/C compressor and transmission cooler line bracket (when equipped) must be installed through the bracket and the lower front mounting hole of the compressor prior to final positioning of the compressor to the cylinder block.**

22. Loosely install the bolt that secures the A/C compressor and automatic transmission cooler line bracket (when equipped) to the compressor and position the compressor, bracket and bolt to the cylinder block.

23. Loosely install the bolts that secure the A/C compressor to the cylinder block.

24. Tighten all three bolts that secure the A/C compressor to the engine in the following order to 19 ft. lbs. (26 Nm):

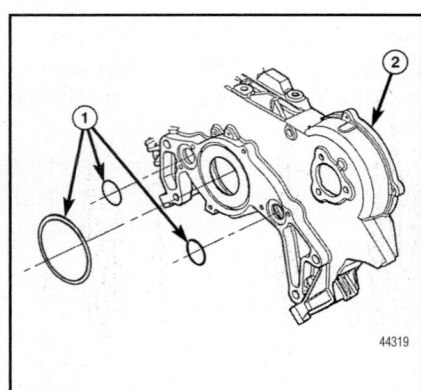

44319

Fig. 271 Rear timing belt cover seals (1) and cover (2)

a. Upper front bolt.
b. Lower front bolt.
c. Rear bolt.

➡**Position generator, bracket and all bolts to engine compartment. Hand tightening all fasteners. Then torque all fasteners to specifications.**

25. Position generator to engine and loosely install lower mounting bolts.
26. Position generator bracket and loosely install bracket bolt and upper generator mounting bolt.
27. Tighten generator mounting bolts to 48 ft. lbs. (65 Nm). Tighten generator bracket bolt to 40 ft. lbs. (54 Nm).
28. Align pump with mounting holes on engine bracket.
29. Install the three pump mounting bolts through access holes in pulley and engine bracket. Tighten bolts to 21 ft. lbs. (28 Nm) torque.
30. Install the camshaft sprockets.
31. Install the timing belt.
32. Install the front timing belt cover.
33. Install the front belly pan.
34. Connect negative battery cable. Tighten nut to 45 inch lbs. (5 Nm).
35. Fill cooling system.
36. Operate engine until it reaches normal operating temperature. Check cooling system for correct fluid level.

TIMING CHAIN FRONT COVER

REMOVAL & INSTALLATION

3.6L Engine

See Figures 272 through 274.

1. Disconnect and isolate the negative battery cable.
2. Drain the cooling system.
3. Remove the upper radiator hose and thermostat housing.
4. Remove the heater core return hose from the water pump housing.
5. Remove the lower radiator hose from the water pump housing.
6. Remove the heater core supply hose from the coolant outlet housing.
7. Remove the bolt and reposition the heater core supply tube.
8. Remove the accessory drive belt.
9. Remove the accessory drive belt tensioner.
10. Remove the accessory idler pulley.
11. Remove the crankshaft vibration damper.
12. Remove the right and left cylinder head covers.
13. Remove the upper and lower oil pans.

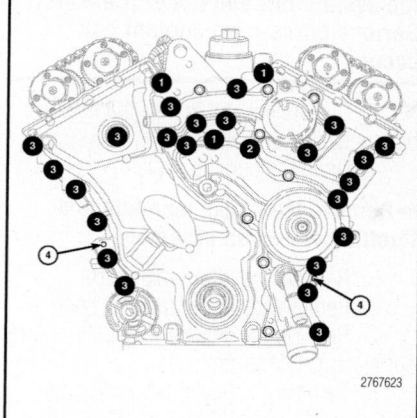

Fig. 272 Removing the timing cover M10 (1), M8 (2) and M6 (3) attaching bolts

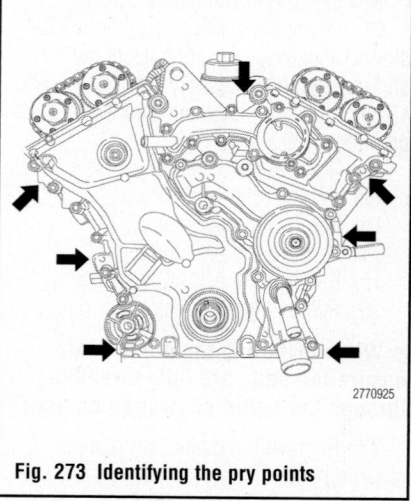

Fig. 273 Identifying the pry points

➡**It is not necessary to remove the water pump or the coolant outlet housing for engine timing cover removal.**

14. Remove the following timing cover attaching bolts:
   • Three M10 bolts
   • One M8 bolt
   • Twenty-three M6 bolts
15. Using the seven indicated pry points, carefully remove the timing cover.
16. If required, remove the remaining four M6 bolts and the coolant outlet housing from the engine timing cover.
17. If required, remove the remaining four M6 bolts and the water pump from the engine timing cover.

❈❈ WARNING

Do not use oil based liquids, wire brushes, abrasive wheels or metal scrapers to clean the engine gasket surfaces. Use only isopropyl (rubbing) alcohol, along with plastic or

wooden scrapers. Improper gasket surface preparation may result in engine fluid leakage.

18. Remove the all residual sealant from the timing chain cover, cylinder head and engine block mating surfaces.
19. Remove the and discard the coolant outlet housing gasket and the water pump gasket.

To install:

20. If removed, install the coolant outlet housing to the timing cover with a new gasket using only the four bolts shown tightened to 9 ft. lbs. (12 Nm).
21. If removed, install the water pump to the timing cover using only the four bolts shown tightened to 9 ft. lbs. (12 Nm).
22. Install the coolant outlet housing gasket and the water pump gasket.
23. Clean the engine timing cover, cylinder head and block mating surfaces with isopropyl alcohol in preparation for sealant application.

❈❈ WARNING

Engine assembly requires the use of a unique sealant that is compatible with engine oil. Using a sealant other than Mopar®Threebond Engine RTV Sealant may result in engine fluid leakage.

❈❈ WARNING

Following the application of Mopar®Threebond Engine RTV Sealant to the gasket surfaces, the components must be assembled within 20 minutes and the attaching fasteners must be tightened to specification within 45 minutes. Prolonged exposure to the air prior to assembly may result in engine fluid leakage.

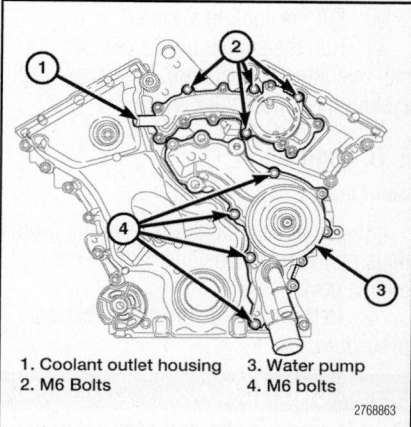

1. Coolant outlet housing   3. Water pump
2. M6 Bolts   4. M6 bolts

Fig. 274 Installing the coolant outlet housing/water pump to the timing cover

24. Apply a 2 to 3 mm wide bead of Mopar®Threebond Engine RTV Sealant to the front cover as shown in the following locations:
- Three cylinder head bosses
- Right and left flanges
- Four cylinder head to engine block T-joints
- Cover to right cam chain tensioner gap

25. Align the locator pins on the engine block to the engine timing cover and install the cover.

26. Install the and tighten the timing cover attaching bolts:

   a. Twenty-three M6 bolts to 9 ft. lbs. (12 Nm).

   b. One M8 bolt to 18 ft. lbs. (25 Nm).

   c. Three M10 bolts to 41 ft. lbs. (55 Nm)

27. Install the upper and lower oil pans.

28. Install the right and left cylinder head covers.

29. Install the crankshaft vibration damper.

30. Install the accessory idler pulley.

31. Install the accessory drive belt tensioner.

32. Install the accessory drive belt.

33. Install the heater core supply tube with one bolt tightened to 9 ft. lbs. (12 Nm).

34. Install the heater core supply hose to the coolant outlet housing.

35. Install the lower radiator hose to the water pump housing.

36. Install the heater core return hose to the water pump housing.

37. Install the thermostat housing and upper radiator hose.

38. If removed, install the oil filter and fill the engine crankcase with the proper oil to the correct level.

39. Connect the negative battery cable and tighten nut to 45 inch lbs. (5 Nm).

40. Fill the cooling system.

41. Run the engine until it reaches normal operating temperature. Check cooling system for correct fluid level

5.7L Engine

See Figure 275.

1. Lift the engine cover retaining grommets off the ball studs and remove the engine cover.

2. Perform the fuel pressure release procedure.

※※ CAUTION

Do not remove the radiator pressure cap, cylinder block drain plugs or loosen the radiator draincock with the system hot and under pressure. Serious burns from coolant can occur.

3. Disconnect and isolate the negative battery cable.

4. Drain the cooling system.

➡**Remove the intake manifold and throttle body as an assembly.**

5. Remove the intake manifold.

6. Remove the upper radiator hose.

7. Remove the coolant temperature sensor electrical connector.

8. Remove the heater tube retaining bolt.

9. Lift the heater tube out of the water pump.

10. Disconnect the camshaft position (CMP) sensor electrical connector.

11. Rotate the accessory drive belt tensioner clockwise until it contacts the stop and remove the accessory drive belt, then slowly rotate the tensioner into the freearm position.

12. Remove the accessory drive belt tensioner and the idler pulley.

13. Remove the radiator.

14. Remove the A/C condenser.

15. Remove the A/C compressor.

16. Remove the generator.

➡**When installing the puller tool, ensure the bolts are fully threaded through the entire crankshaft damper.**

17. Remove the crankshaft damper retaining bolt.

18. Install the puller tool making sure the bolts are fully threaded through the entire crankshaft damper and remove the crankshaft damper.

19. Raise and support the vehicle

20. Remove the belly pan retainers and remove the belly pan.

21. Remove the lower radiator hose clamp and remove the lower radiator hose.

22. Drain the engine oil.

➡**When the oil pan is removed, a new oil pan gasket and the integral windage tray assembly must be installed, the old gasket cannot be reused.**

23. Remove the oil pan.

24. Remove the oil pump pickup tube retaining bolt and nut.

25. Remove the oil pump pickup tube.

26. Remove the and discard the oil pan gasket/windage tray.

➡**It is not necessary to remove water pump for timing cover removal.**

27. Lower the vehicle.

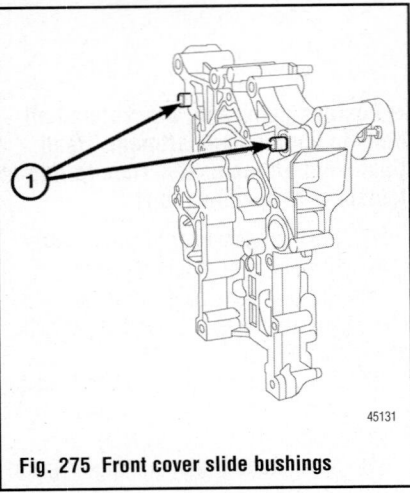

Fig. 275 Front cover slide bushings

28. Remove the engine timing cover retaining bolts and remove the engine timing cover.

29. Verify that the engine timing cover slide bushings remain located in the engine timing cover.

To install:

30. Clean the engine timing cover and engine block surface.

➡**Always install a new gasket when servicing the engine timing cover.**

31. Verify that the engine timing cover slide bushings remain located in the engine timing cover.

32. Using a new gasket, install the engine timing cover and tighten the retaining bolts to 21 ft. lbs. (28 Nm).

➡**The large lifting stud is torqued to 40 ft. lbs. (55 Nm).**

33. Tighten the large lifting stud to 40 ft. lbs. (55 Nm).

34. Raise and support the vehicle.

35. Install the oil pump pickup tube and the oil pan.

36. Install the lower radiator hose and clamp.

※※ WARNING

The Damper Installer is assembled in a specific sequence. Failure to assemble this tool in this sequence may result in tool failure and severe damage to either the tool or the crankshaft.

37. Assemble the Damper Installer as follows:

   a. Install the nut onto the threaded shaft.

   b. Install the roller bearing onto the threaded shaft making sure the hardened bearing surface is facing the nut.

c. Install the pressing cup from the A/C Hub Installer
Installer, A/C Hub onto the threaded shaft.

d. Coat the threaded shaft with MOPAR®Nickel Anti-Seize or equivalent.

✳✳ WARNING

To prevent severe damage to the crankshaft Damper Installer, Damper, thoroughly clean the damper bore and the crankshaft nose before installing damper.

38. Position the crankshaft damper onto the crankshaft.

39. Using the crankshaft Damper Installer and the pressing cup from A/C Hub Installer, press the crankshaft damper onto the crankshaft.

40. Install the crankshaft damper bolt and tighten to 129 ft. lbs. (176 Nm).

41. Position the belly pan and install the belly pan retainers.

42. Lower the vehicle.

43. Install the generator.

44. Install the A/C compressor.

45. Install the A/C condenser.

46. Install the radiator.

47. Install the accessory drive belt tensioner assembly and idler pulley.

48. Rotate the accessory drive belt tensioner clockwise until it contacts the stop and remove the accessory drive belt, then slowly rotate the tensioner into the freearm position.

49. Install the oil dipstick tube and retaining nut.

50. Connect the camshaft position (CMP) sensor electrical connector.

51. Install the heater tube into of the water pump.

52. Install the heater tube retaining bolt and tighten to 9 ft. lbs. (12 Nm).

53. Connect the coolant temperature sensor electrical connector.

54. Install the upper radiator hose and clamp.

55. Install the intake manifold.

56. Fill the cooling system with the specified type and amount of engine coolant.

57. Fill the crankcase with the specified type and amount of engine oil.

58. Position the engine cover and secure the retaining grommets onto the ball studs.

59. Connect the negative battery cable and tighten nut to 45 inch lbs. (5 Nm).

60. Perform the Refrigerant System Charge procedure.

61. Start the engine and check for leaks.

6.1L Engine
See Figure 276.

1. Remove the engine covers.

2. Disconnect the battery negative cable from battery.

3. Remove the clean air hose from throttle body.

4. Remove the retaining bolt and remove air cleaner housing.

5. Drain the cooling system.

6. Remove the accessory drive belt.

7. Remove the cooling fan.

8. Remove the fan shroud.

➡**It is not necessary to disconnect A/C lines or discharge Freon.**

9. Remove the A/C compressor and set aside.

10. Remove the generator.

11. Remove the upper radiator hose.

12. Disconnect both heater hoses at the timing cover.

13. Disconnect the lower radiator hose at engine.

14. Remove the accessory drive belt tensioner and both idler pulleys.

15. Remove the crankshaft damper.

➡**Do not remove the hoses from the power steering pump.**

16. Remove the power steering pump and set aside.

17. Remove the dipstick support bolt.

18. Drain the engine oil.

19. Remove the oil pan and pick up tube.

➡**It is not necessary to remove water pump for timing cover removal.**

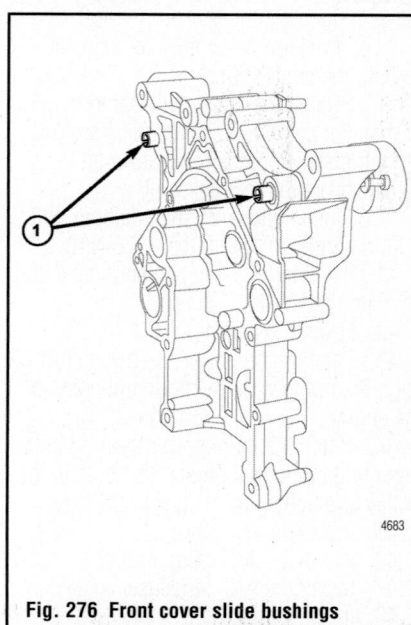

Fig. 276 Front cover slide bushings

20. Remove the timing cover bolts and remove cover.

21. Verify that the timing cover slide bushings are located in timing cover.

To install:

22. Clean timing chain cover and block surface.

➡**Always install a new gasket on timing cover.**

23. Verify that the slide bushings are installed in timing cover.

24. Install the cover and new gasket. Tighten fasteners to 21 ft. lbs. (28 Nm).

➡**The large lifting stud is torqued to 40 ft. lbs. (55 Nm).**

25. Install the oil pan and pick up tube.

26. Install the A/C compressor.

27. Install the generator.

28. Install the power steering pump.

29. Install the dipstick support bolt.

30. Install the thermostat housing.

31. Install the crankshaft damper.

32. Install the accessory drive belt tensioner assembly and both idler pulleys.

33. Install the radiator lower hose.

34. Install the both heater hoses at the timing cover.

35. Install the radiator fan shroud.

36. Install the cooling fan.

37. Install the accessory drive belt.

38. Install the coolant bottle and washer bottle.

39. Install the upper radiator hose.

40. Install the air cleaner assembly.

41. Fill cooling system.

42. Refill engine oil.

43. Connect the battery negative cable.

44. Install the engine covers.

6.4L Engine
See Figure 275.

1. Remove the engine covers.

2. Perform the fuel pressure release procedure.

3. Disconnect the negative battery cable.

4. Drain the cooling system.

5. Remove the intake manifold.

6. Remove the upper radiator hose clamp and remove the upper radiator hose.

7. Remove the oil cooler hose clamp and remove oil cooler hose.

8. Remove the coolant temperature sensor electrical connector.

9. Remove the heater tube retaining bolt.

10. Lift the heater tube out of the water pump.

11. Disconnect the camshaft position sensor electrical connector.

12. Remove the accessory drive belt.

13. Remove the accessory drive belt tensioner and the idler pulley.

14. Remove the radiator.

15. Remove the A/C condenser.

16. Remove the A/C compressor.

17. Remove the generator.

➡**It is not necessary to remove the power steering pump hoses for power steering pump removal.**

18. Remove the three power steering pump mounting bolts through the access holes in the pulley.

19. Remove the power steering pump from the engine and position aside.

➡**When installing the puller tool, ensure the bolts are fully threaded through the entire crankshaft damper.**

20. Remove the crankshaft damper retaining bolt.

21. Install the puller tool making sure the bolts are fully threaded through the entire crankshaft damper and remove the crankshaft damper.

22. Raise and support the vehicle.

23. Remove the belly pan retainers and remove the belly pan.

24. Remove the lower radiator hose clamp and remove the lower radiator hose.

25. Drain the engine oil.

➡**When the oil pan is removed, a new oil pan gasket and the integral windage tray assembly must be installed, the old gasket cannot be reused.**

26. Remove the oil pan.

27. Remove the oil pump pickup tube retaining bolt and nut.

28. Remove the oil pump pickup tube.

29. Remove the and discard the oil pan gasket/windage tray.

➡**It is not necessary to remove water pump for timing cover removal.**

30. Lower the vehicle.

31. Remove the engine timing cover retaining bolts and remove the engine timing cover.

32. Verify that the engine timing cover slide bushings remain located in the engine timing cover.

To install:

33. Clean the engine timing cover and engine block surface.

➡**Always install a new gasket when servicing the engine timing cover.**

34. Verify that the engine timing cover slide bushings remain located in the engine timing cover.

35. Using a new gasket, install the engine timing cover and tighten the retaining bolts to 21 ft. lbs. (28 Nm).

➡**The large lifting stud is torqued to 40 ft. lbs. (55 Nm).**

36. Tighten the large lifting stud to 40 ft. lbs. (55 Nm).

37. Raise and support the vehicle.

38. Install the oil pump pickup tube and the oil pan.

39. Install the lower radiator hose and clamp.

> ✳✳ **WARNING**
>
> **The Damper Installer, is assembled in a specific sequence. Failure to assemble this tool in this sequence may result in tool failure and severe damage to either the tool or the crankshaft.**

40. Assemble the Damper Installer as follows:

a. Install the nut onto the threaded shaft.

b. Install the roller bearing onto the threaded shaft making sure the hardened bearing surface is facing the nut.

c. Install the pressing cup from the A/C Hub Installer onto the threaded shaft.

d. Coat the threaded shaft with MOPAR®Nickel Anti-Seize or equivalent.

> ✳✳ **WARNING**
>
> **To prevent severe damage to the crankshaft Damper Installer, thoroughly clean the damper bore and the crankshaft nose before installing damper.**

e. Position the crankshaft damper onto the crankshaft.

f. Using the crankshaft Damper Installer and the pressing cup from A/C Hub Installer, press the crankshaft damper onto the crankshaft.

g. Install the crankshaft damper bolt and tighten to 129 ft. lbs. (176 Nm).

41. Position the belly pan and install the belly pan retainers.

42. Lower the vehicle.

43. Position the power steering pump, align the pump with the mounting holes on the engine.

44. Install the three power steering pump mounting bolts through access holes in the pulley and tighten to 21 ft. lbs. (28 Nm).

45. Install the generator.

46. Install the A/C compressor.

47. Install the A/C condenser.

48. Install the radiator.

49. Install the accessory drive belt tensioner assembly and idler pulley.

50. Install the accessory drive belt.

51. Install the oil dipstick tube and retaining nut.

52. Connect the camshaft position sensor electrical connector.

53. Install the heater tube into of the water pump.

54. Install the heater tube retaining bolt and tighten to 9 ft. lbs. (12 Nm).

55. Connect the coolant temperature sensor electrical connector.

56. Install the oil cooler hose and clamp.

57. Install the upper radiator hose and clamp.

58. Install the intake manifold.

59. Fill the cooling system with the specified type and amount of engine coolant.

60. Fill the crankcase with the specified type and amount of engine oil.

61. Connect the negative battery cable.

62. Install the engine covers.

63. Perform the Refrigerant System Charge procedure.

64. Start the engine and check for leaks.

TIMING CHAIN & SPROCKETS

REMOVAL & INSTALLATION

3.6L Engine
See Figures 277 through 281.

> ✳✳ **WARNING**
>
> **The magnetic timing wheels must not come in contact with magnets (pickup tools, trays, etc.) or any other strong magnetic field. This will destroy the timing wheels ability to correctly relay camshaft position to the camshaft position sensor.**

> ✳✳ **WARNING**
>
> **When the timing chains are removed and the cylinder heads are still**

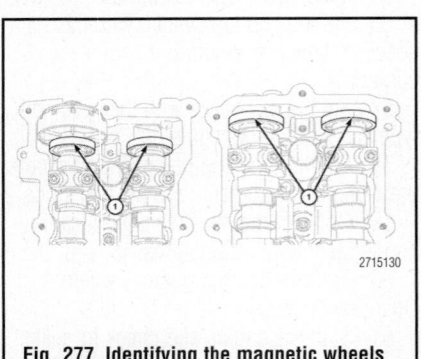

2715130

Fig. 277 Identifying the magnetic wheels

installed, DO NOT rotate the camshafts or crankshaft without first locating the proper crankshaft position. Failure to do so will result in valve and/or piston damage.

1. Disconnect and isolate the negative battery cable.
2. Remove the air cleaner housing assembly and upper intake manifold.
3. Remove the cylinder head covers.
4. Remove the spark plugs.
5. Raise and support the vehicle.
6. Drain the cooling system.
7. Remove the oil pan, accessory drive belts, crankshaft vibration damper and engine timing cover.

➡Take this opportunity to measure timing chain wear.

❋❋ WARNING

When aligning timing marks, always rotate engine by turning the crankshaft. Failure to do so will result in valve and/or piston damage.

8. Rotate the crankshaft CW to place the number one piston at TDC on the exhaust stroke by aligning the dimple on the crankshaft with the block/bearing cap junction. The left side cam phaser arrows should point toward each other and be parallel to the valve cover sealing surface. The right side cam phaser arrows should point away from each other and the scribe lines should be parallel to the valve cover sealing surface.

❋❋ WARNING

Always reinstall timing chains so that they maintain the same direction of rotation. Inverting a previously run chain on a previously run sprocket will result in excessive wear to both the chain and sprocket.

9. Mark the direction of rotation on the following timing chains using a paint pen or equivalent to aid in reassembly:
  • Left side cam chain
  • Right side cam chain
  • Oil pump chain
  • Primary chain
10. Reset the RH cam chain tensioner by pushing back the tensioner piston and installing Tensioner Pin.
11. Reset the LH cam chain tensioner by lifting the pawl (1), pushing back the piston and installing Tensioner Pin.
12. Disengage the oil pump chain tensioner spring from the dowel pin and remove the oil pump chain tensioner.

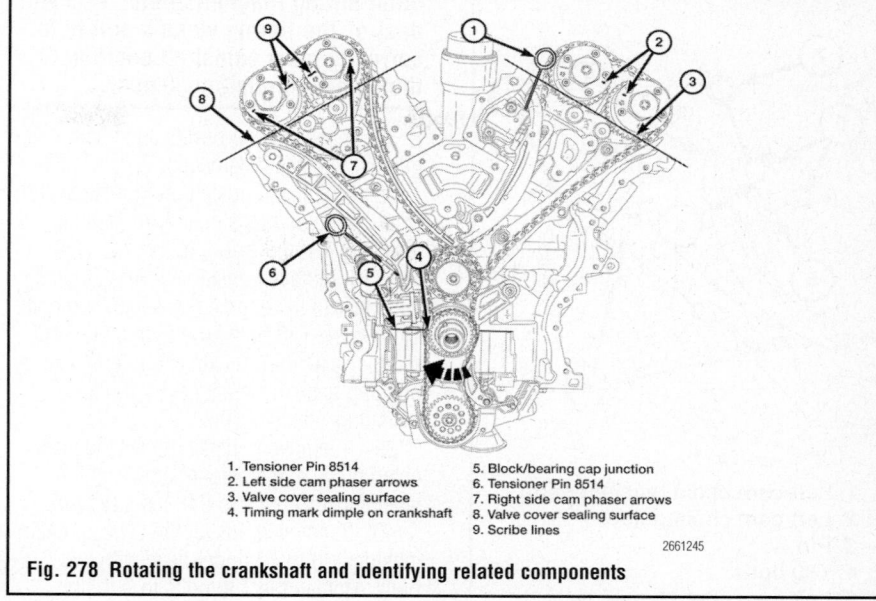

1. Tensioner Pin 8514
2. Left side cam phaser arrows
3. Valve cover sealing surface
4. Timing mark dimple on crankshaft
5. Block/bearing cap junction
6. Tensioner Pin 8514
7. Right side cam phaser arrows
8. Valve cover sealing surface
9. Scribe lines

2661245

Fig. 278 Rotating the crankshaft and identifying related components

13. Remove the oil pump sprocket T45 retaining bolt and remove the oil pump sprocket and oil pump chain.

➡Minor rotation of a camshaft (a few degrees) may be required to install the camshaft phaser lock.

14. Install the RH Camshaft Phaser Lock.
15. Loosen both the intake oil control valve and exhaust oil control valve.
16. Remove the RH Camshaft Phaser Lock.
17. Remove the oil control valve from the right side intake cam phaser.
18. Pull the right side intake cam phaser off of the camshaft and remove the right side cam chain.

19. If required, remove the oil control valve and pull the right side exhaust cam phaser off of the camshaft.

➡Minor rotation of a camshaft (a few degrees) may be required to install the camshaft phaser lock.

20. Install the LH Camshaft Phaser Lock.
21. Loosen both the intake oil control valve and exhaust oil control valve.
22. Remove the LH Camshaft Phaser Lock.
23. Remove the oil control valve from the left side exhaust cam phaser.
24. Pull the left side exhaust cam phaser off of the camshaft and remove the left side cam chain.

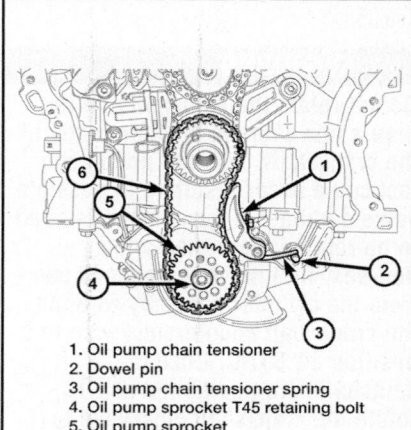

1. Oil pump chain tensioner
2. Dowel pin
3. Oil pump chain tensioner spring
4. Oil pump sprocket T45 retaining bolt
5. Oil pump sprocket
6. Oil pump chain

2682471

Fig. 279 Removing the oil pump and sprocket

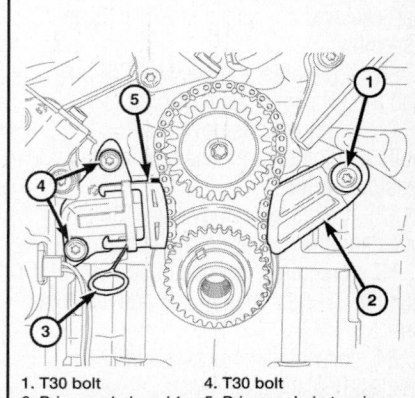

1. T30 bolt
2. Primary chain guide
3. Tensioner pin
4. T30 bolt
5. Primary chain tensioner

2679970

Fig. 280 Removing the primary chain tensioner and guide

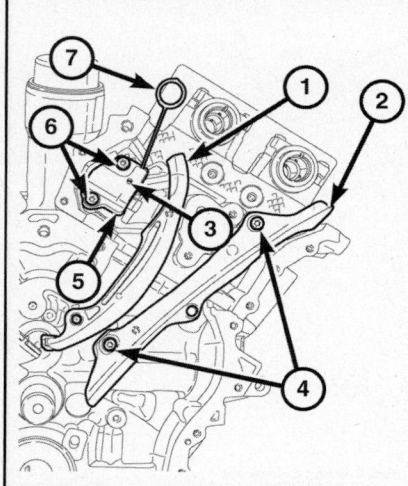

1. Left cam chain tensioner arm
2. Left cam chain guide
3. Pin
4. T30 bolts
5. Left cam chain tensioner
6. T30 bolts

2659731

Fig. 281 Removing the LH cam chain guide, tensioner arm and tensioner

25. If required, remove the oil control valve and pull the left side intake cam phaser off of the camshaft.

26. Reset the primary chain tensioner by pushing back the tensioner piston and installing Tensioner Pin. Remove two T30 bolts and remove the primary chain tensioner.

27. Remove the T30 bolt and the primary chain guide.

28. Remove the idler sprocket T45 retaining bolt and washer.

29. Remove the primary chain, idler sprocket and crankshaft sprocket as an assembly.

30. If required, remove two T30 bolts and the LH cam chain tensioner.

31. If required, remove two T30 bolts and the LH cam chain guide and tensioner arm.

32. If required, remove two T30 bolts and the RH cam chain tensioner.

33. If required, remove three T30 bolts and the RH cam chain guide and tensioner arm.

34. Inspect all sprockets and chain guides. Replace if damaged.

To install:

✳✳ WARNING

The magnetic timing wheels must not come in contact with magnets (pickup tools, trays, etc.) or any

other strong magnetic field. This will destroy the timing wheels ability to correctly relay camshaft position to the camshaft position sensor.

35. Inspect all sprockets and chain guides. Replace if damaged.

36. If removed, install the right side cam chain guide and tensioner arm. Tighten attaching T30 bolts to 9 ft. lbs. (12 Nm).

37. If removed, install the RH cam chain tensioner to the engine block with two bolts. Tighten the T30 bolts to 9 ft. lbs. (12 Nm).

38. Reset the RH cam chain tensioner by pushing back the tensioner piston and installing Tensioner Pin.

39. If removed, install the left side cam chain guide and tensioner arm. Tighten attaching T30 bolts to 9 ft. lbs. (12 Nm).

40. If removed, install the LH cam chain tensioner to the cylinder head with two bolts. Tighten the T30 bolts to 9 ft. lbs. (12 Nm).

41. Reset the LH cam chain tensioner by lifting the pawl, pushing back the piston and installing Tensioner Pin.

42. Verify that the key is installed in the crankshaft.

✳✳ WARNING

Do not rotate the crankshaft more than a few degrees independently of the camshafts. Piston to valve contact could occur resulting in possible valve damage. If the crankshaft needs to be rotated more than a few degrees, first remove the camshafts.

43. Verify that the number one piston is positioned at TDC by aligning the dimple on the crankshaft with the block/bearing cap junction.

✳✳ WARNING

Do not rotate the camshafts more than a few degrees independently of the crankshaft. Valve to piston contact could occur resulting in possible valve damage. If the camshafts need to be rotated more than a few degrees, first move the pistons away from the cylinder heads by rotating the crankshaft counterclockwise to a position 30°BTDC. Once the camshafts are positioned at TDC rotate the crankshaft clockwise to return the crankshaft to TDC.

44. Verify that the camshafts are set at TDC by positioning the alignment holes vertically.

✳✳ WARNING

Always reinstall timing chains so that they maintain the same direction of rotation. Inverting a previously run chain on a previously run sprocket will result in excessive wear to both the chain and sprocket.

45. Place the primary chain onto the crankshaft sprocket so that the arrow is aligned with the plated link on the timing chain.

a. While maintaining this alignment, invert the crankshaft sprocket and timing chain and place the idler sprocket into the timing chain so that the dimple is aligned with the plated link on the timing chain.

b. While maintaining this alignment, lubricate the idler sprocket bushing with clean engine oil and install the sprockets and timing chain on the engine. To verify that the timing is still correct, the timing chain plated link should be located at 12:00 when the dimple on the crankshaft is aligned with the block/bearing cap junction.

46. Install the idler sprocket retaining bolt and washer. Tighten the T45 bolt to 18 ft. lbs. (25 Nm).

47. Install the primary chain guide. Tighten attaching T30 bolt to 9 ft. lbs. (12 Nm).

48. Reset the primary chain tensioner by pushing back the tensioner piston and installing Tensioner Pin.

49. Install the primary chain tensioner to the engine block with two bolts. Tighten the T30 bolts to 9 ft. lbs. (12 Nm) and remove the Tensioner Pin.

50. Press the LH intake cam phaser onto the intake camshaft. Install and hand tighten the oil control valve.

➡ **The LH and RH cam chains are identical.**

✳✳ WARNING

Always reinstall timing chains so that they maintain the same direction of rotation. Inverting a previously run chain on a previously run sprocket will result in excessive wear to both the chain and sprocket.

51. Drape the left side cam chain over the LH intake cam phaser and onto the idler sprocket so that the arrow is aligned with the plated link on the cam chain.

52. While maintaining this alignment, route the cam chain around the exhaust and intake cam phasers so that the plated links

are aligned with the phaser timing marks. Position the left side cam phasers so that the arrows point toward each other and are parallel to the valve cover sealing surface. Press the exhaust cam phaser onto the exhaust cam, install and hand tighten the oil control valve.

➥**Minor rotation of a camshaft (a few degrees) may be required to install the camshaft phaser or phaser lock.**

53. Install the LH Camshaft Phaser Lock and tighten the oil control valves to 110 ft. lbs. (150 Nm).

54. Press the RH exhaust cam phaser onto the exhaust camshaft. Install and hand tighten the oil control valve.

✷✷ WARNING

Always reinstall timing chains so that they maintain the same direction of rotation. Inverting a previously run chain on a previously run sprocket will result in excessive wear to both the chain and sprocket.

55. Drape the right side cam chain over the RH exhaust cam phaser and onto the idler sprocket so that the dimple is aligned with the plated link on the cam chain.

56. While maintaining this alignment, route the cam chain around the exhaust and intake cam phasers so that the plated links are aligned with the phaser timing marks. Position the right side cam phasers so that the arrows point away from each other and the scribe lines are parallel to the valve cover sealing surface. Press the intake cam phaser onto the intake cam, install and hand tighten the oil control valve.

➥**Minor rotation of a camshaft (a few degrees) may be required to install the camshaft phaser or phaser lock.**

57. Install the RH Camshaft Phaser Lock and tighten the oil control valves to 110 ft. lbs. (150 Nm).

➥**There are no timing marks on the oil pump gear or chain.**

✷✷ WARNING

Always reinstall timing chains so that they maintain the same direction of rotation. Inverting a previously run chain on a previously run sprocket will result in excessive wear to both the chain and sprocket.

58. Place the oil pump sprocket into the oil pump chain. Place the oil pump chain onto the crankshaft sprocket while aligning the oil pump sprocket with the oil pump

shaft. Install the oil pump sprocket T45 retaining bolt and tighten to 18 ft. lbs. (25 Nm).

59. Install the oil pump chain tensioner. Insure that the spring is positioned above the dowel pin.

60. Remove the RH and LH Camshaft Phaser Locks.

61. Remove the Tensioner Pins and from the RH and LH cam chain tensioners.

62. Rotate the crankshaft CW two complete revolutions stopping when the dimple on the crankshaft is aligned the with the block/bearing cap junction.

63. While maintaining this alignment, verify that the arrows on the left side cam phasers point toward each other and are parallel to the valve cover sealing surface and that the right side cam phaser arrows point away from each other and the scribe lines are parallel to the valve cover sealing surface.

64. There should be 12 chain pins between the exhaust cam phaser triangle marking and the intake cam phaser circle marking.

65. If the engine timing is not correct, repeat this procedure.

66. Install the engine timing cover, crankshaft vibration damper, accessory drive belts and oil pan.

67. Install the spark plugs. Tighten to 13 ft. lbs. (17.5 Nm).

68. Install the cylinder head covers.

69. Install the upper intake manifold and air cleaner housing assembly.

70. Fill the engine crankcase with the proper oil to the correct level.

71. Connect the negative battery cable and tighten nut to 45 inch lbs. (5 Nm).

72. Fill the cooling system.

73. Operate the engine until it reaches normal operating temperature. Check cooling system for correct fluid level.

➥**The Cam/Crank Variation Relearn procedure must be performed using the scan tool anytime there has been a repair/replacement made to a powertrain system, for example: flywheel, valvetrain, camshaft and/or crankshaft sensors or components.**

5.7L Engine

See Figures 282 through 284.

1. Disconnect the negative battery cable.

2. Drain the cooling system.

➥**It is not necessary to remove water pump for timing chain cover removal.**

3. Remove the timing chain cover.

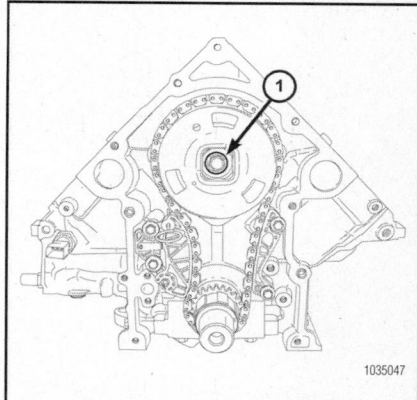

Fig. 282 Identifying the camshaft phaser retaining bolt

4. Verify the slide bushings remain installed in the timing chain cover during removal.

5. Remove the oil pump retaining bolts and remove the oil pump.

6. Install the vibration damper bolt finger tight. Using a suitable socket and breaker bar, rotate the crankshaft to align the timing marks with the timing chain sprockets.

7. Retract the chain tensioner arm until the hole in the arm lines up with the hole in the bracket.

8. Install the Tensioner Pin into the chain tensioner holes.

✷✷ WARNING

Never attempt to disassemble the camshaft phaser, severe engine damage could result.

9. Remove the camshaft phaser retaining bolt and remove the timing chain with the camshaft phaser and crankshaft sprocket.

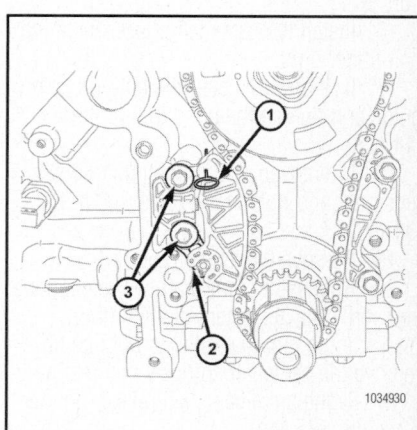

Fig. 283 Removing the retaining bolts (3) and timing chain tensioner (2)

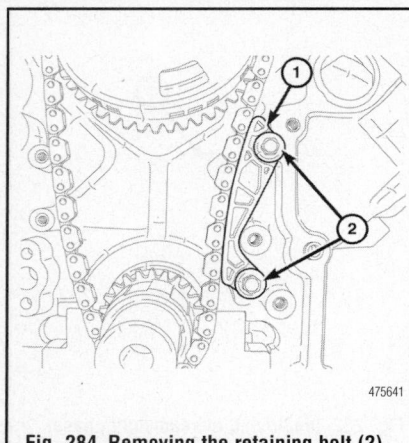

Fig. 284 Removing the retaining bolt (2) and timing chain guide

→Inspect the timing chain tensioner and timing chain guide shoes for wear and replace as necessary.

10. If the timing chain tensioner is being replaced, remove the retaining bolts and remove the timing chain tensioner.

11. If the timing chain guide is being replaced, remove the retaining bolts and remove the timing chain guide.

To install:

12. Install the crankshaft sprocket and position halfway onto the crankshaft.

13. While holding the camshaft phaser in hand, position the timing chain on the camshaft phaser and align the timing marks as shown.

14. While holding the camshaft phaser and timing chain in hand, position the timing chain on the crankshaft sprocket and align the timing mark as shown.

15. Align the slot in the camshaft phaser with the dowel on the camshaft and position the camshaft phaser on the camshaft while sliding the crankshaft sprocket into position.

16. Install the camshaft phaser retaining bolt finger tight.

17. If removed, install the timing chain guide and tighten the bolts to 8 ft. lbs. (11 Nm).

18. If removed, install the timing chain tensioner and tighten the bolts to 8 ft. lbs. (11 Nm).

19. Remove the tensioner pin.

20. Rotate the crankshaft two revolutions and verify the alignment of the timing marks. If the timing marks do not line up, remove the camshaft sprocket and realign.

21. Tighten the camshaft phaser bolt to 63 ft. lbs. (85 Nm).

22. Position the oil pump onto the crankshaft and install the oil pump retaining bolts finger tight.

23. Using the sequence shown, tighten the oil pump retaining bolts to 21 ft. lbs. (28 Nm).

24. Verify the slide bushings are installed in the timing chain cover.

25. Install the timing chain cover.

26. Fill the engine with oil.

27. Fill the cooling system.

28. Connect the negative battery cable.

29. Start the engine and check for leaks.

6.1L Engine

See Figure 285.

1. Disconnect the negative battery cable.

2. Drain the cooling system.

3. Remove the timing chain cover.

4. Verify the slide bushings remain installed in the timing chain cover during removal.

5. Install the vibration damper bolt finger tight. Using a suitable socket and breaker bar, rotate the crankshaft to align timing chain plated links with the timing marks on the sprockets.

✳✳ WARNING

The camshaft pin and the slot in the cam sprocket must be clocked at 12:00. The crankshaft keyway must be clocked at 2:00. The crankshaft sprocket must be installed so that the dots and or paint marking is at 6:00.

6. Remove the oil pump.

7. Retract the chain tensioner arm until the hole in the arm lines up with the hole in the bracket.

8. Install the Tensioner Pin into the holes in the chain tensioner.

9. Remove the camshaft sprocket retaining bolt and remove the timing chain with the camshaft and crankshaft sprockets (2, 3).

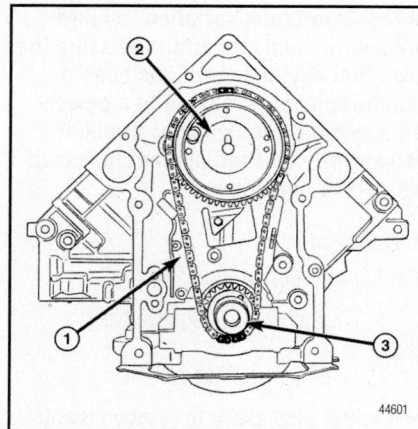

Fig. 285 Timing mark alignment, cam sprocket (2) and crankshaft keyway (3)

→Inspect the timing chain tensioner and timing chain guide shoes for wear and replace as necessary.

10. If the timing chain tensioner is being replaced, remove the retaining bolts and remove the chain tensioner.

11. If the timing chain guide is being replaced, remove the retaining bolts and remove the timing chain guide.

To install:

12. If removed, install the timing chain guide and tighten bolts to 21 ft. lbs. (28 Nm).

13. If removed, install the timing chain tensioner and tighten bolts to 21 ft. lbs. (28 Nm).

14. If required, retract the chain tensioner arm and install the Tensioner Pin into the holes of the chain tensioner.

✳✳ WARNING

The timing chain must be installed with the single plated link aligned with the dot and or paint marking on the camshaft sprocket. The crankshaft sprocket is aligned with the dot and or paint marking on the sprocket between two plated timing chain links.

✳✳ WARNING

The camshaft pin and the slot in the cam sprocket must be clocked at 12:00. The crankshaft keyway must be clocked at 2:00. The crankshaft sprocket must be installed so that the dots and or paint marking is at 6:00.

15. Place both camshaft sprocket and crankshaft sprocket on the bench with timing marks on exact imaginary center line through both camshaft and crankshaft bores.

16. Place timing chain around both sprockets with timing marks aligned with the plated links.

17. Lift the sprockets and chain keeping sprockets tight against the chain in the position as shown).

18. Position both sprockets (2, 3) onto their respective shafts and verify alignment of timing marks.

19. Install the camshaft sprocket retaining bolt and tighten to 90 ft. lbs. (122 Nm).

20. Remove the Tensioner Pin.

21. Rotate the crankshaft two revolutions and verify the alignment of the timing marks. If the timing marks do not line up, remove the camshaft sprocket and realign.

22. Install the oil pump.

23. Verify the slide bushings are installed in the timing chain cover.

24. Install the timing chain cover.

25. Fill the engine with oil.

26. Fill the cooling system.

27. Connect the negative battery cable.

28. Start the engine and check for leaks.

6.4L Engine

See Figures 286 through 289.

1. Disconnect the negative battery cable.

2. Raise and support the vehicle.

3. Drain the cooling system.

4. Remove the oil pan and oil pump pick up tube.

5. Remove the engine timing cover.

6. Verify the slide bushings remain located in the engine timing cover during removal.

7. Remove the oil pump retaining bolts and remove the oil pump.

8. Install the vibration damper bolt finger tight. Using a suitable socket and breaker bar, rotate the crankshaft to align the timing marks with the timing chain sprockets.

9. Retract the chain tensioner arm until the hole in the arm lines up with the hole in the bracket.

10. Install the Tensioner Pin into the chain tensioner holes.

✳✳ WARNING

Never attempt to disassemble the camshaft phaser, severe engine damage could result.

11. Remove the camshaft phaser retaining bolt and remove the timing chain with the camshaft phaser and crankshaft sprocket.

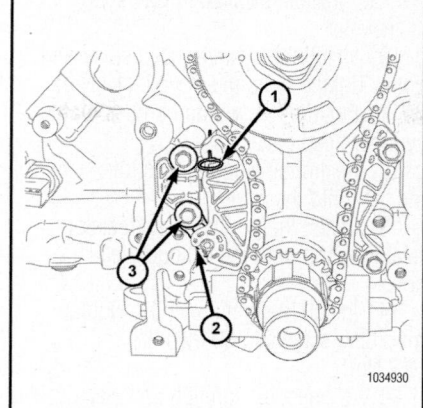

Fig. 287 Removing the timing chain tensioner

➡**Inspect the timing chain tensioner and timing chain guide shoes for wear and replace as necessary.**

12. If the timing chain tensioner is to be replaced, remove the retaining bolts and remove the timing chain tensioner.

13. If the timing chain guide is to be replaced, remove the retaining bolts and remove the timing chain guide.

To install:

14. Install the crankshaft sprocket and position halfway onto the crankshaft.

15. While holding the camshaft phaser in hand, position the timing chain on the camshaft phaser and align the timing marks.

16. While holding the camshaft phaser and timing chain in hand, position the timing chain on the crankshaft sprocket and align the timing mark.

17. Align the slot in the camshaft phaser with the dowel on the camshaft and position the camshaft phaser on the camshaft while sliding the crankshaft sprocket into position.

18. Install the camshaft phaser retaining bolt finger tight.

19. If removed, install the timing chain guide and tighten the bolts to 8 ft. lbs. (11 Nm).

20. If removed, install the timing chain tensioner and tighten the bolts to 8 ft. lbs. (11 Nm).

21. If required, retract the chain tensioner arm and install the Tensioner Pin into the holes of the chain tensioner arm.

22. Rotate the crankshaft two revolutions and verify the alignment of the timing marks. If the timing marks do not line up, remove the camshaft sprocket and realign.

23. Tighten the camshaft phaser bolt to 63 ft. lbs. (85 Nm).

24. Position the oil pump onto the crankshaft and install the oil pump retaining bolts finger tight.

25. Using the sequence shown, tighten the oil pump retaining bolts to 21 ft. lbs. (28 Nm).

26. Verify the slide bushings remain located in the engine timing cover.

27. Using a new gasket, install the engine timing cover and tighten the retaining bolts to 21 ft. lbs. (28 Nm).

➡**The large lifting stud is torqued to 40 ft. lbs. (55 Nm).**

28. Tighten the large lifting stud to 40 ft. lbs. (55 Nm).

29. Raise and support the vehicle.

30. Install the oil pump pickup tube and the oil pan.

31. Install the negative battery cable.

32. Fill the cooling system with the specified type and amount of engine coolant.

33. Fill the crankcase with the specified type and amount of engine oil.

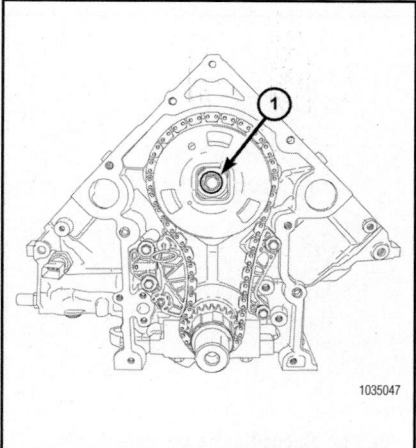

Fig. 286 Removing the camshaft phaser retaining bolt

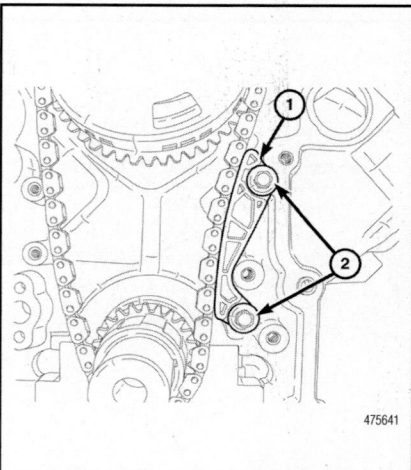

Fig. 288 Removing the timing chain guide

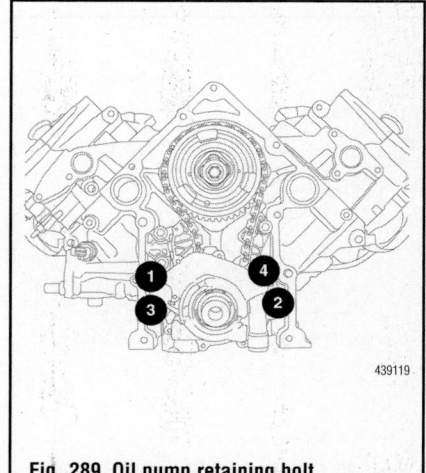

Fig. 289 Oil pump retaining bolt tightening sequence

34. Install the engine covers.
35. Start the engine and check for leaks.

VALVE COVERS

REMOVAL & INSTALLATION

3.5L Engine

Left Side

See Figure 290.

> ✳✳ **CAUTION**
>
> **Do not start or run engine with cylinder head cover removed from the engine. Damage or personal injury may occur.**

1. Disconnect and isolate the negative battery cable.
2. Remove the upper intake manifold from the engine.
3. Cover lower intake manifold with a suitable cover during service.
4. Disconnect and remove the three ignition coils.
5. Remove the ground strap/resistor retaining bolt from the cylinder head cover.
6. Lift up on the wire harness track retaining tabs.
7. Completely loosen the cylinder head cover retaining bolts and remove the cylinder head cover.

To install:

8. Clean cylinder head and cover mating surfaces. Inspect and replace gasket and seals as necessary.
9. To replace spark plug tube seals:
   a. Using a suitable pry tool, carefully remove tube seals.
   b. Position new seal with the part number on seal facing cylinder head cover.
   c. Install seals using Camshaft Installer.
10. Install the cylinder head cover and bolts. Tighten bolts to 9 ft. lbs. (12 Nm).
11. Position the wiring harness on the cylinder head cover.
12. Reclip the wire harness track retaining tabs into the cover.
13. Install the ground strap/resistor retaining bolt onto the cylinder head cover.
14. Install the ignition coils. Tighten mounting screws to 60 inch lbs. (6.7 Nm).
15. Connect the ignition coil electrical connectors.
16. Install the upper intake manifold.
17. Connect negative battery cable and tighten nut to 45 inch lbs. (5 Nm).

Right Side

See Figure 291.

> ✳✳ **CAUTION**
>
> **Do not start or run engine with cylinder head cover removed from the engine. Damage or personal injury may occur.**

1. Disconnect and isolate the negative battery cable.
2. Remove the upper intake manifold.
3. Cover lower intake manifold openings during service.
4. Disconnect and remove the three ignition coils.
5. Lift up on the wire harness track retaining tabs.
6. Remove the ground strap retaining bolt from the cylinder head cover.
7. Completely loosen the cylinder head cover retaining bolts and remove the cylinder head cover.

To install:

8. Clean cylinder head and cover mating surfaces. Inspect and replace gasket and seals as necessary.
9. To replace spark plug tube seals:
   a. Using a suitable pry tool, carefully remove tube seals.
   b. Position new seal with the part number on seal facing cylinder head cover.
   c. Install seals using Camshaft Installer.
10. Install the cylinder head cover and bolts. Tighten bolts to 9 ft. lbs. (12 Nm).
11. Install the ground strap retaining bolt to the cylinder head cover.
12. Install the wire harness track.
13. Install the ignition coils. Tighten mounting screws to 60 inch lbs. (6.7 Nm).
14. Connect the ignition coil electrical connectors.
15. Install the upper intake manifold.
16. Connect negative battery cable and tighten nut to 45 inch lbs. (5 Nm).

3.6L Engine

Left Side

See Figures 292 through 298.

1. The magnetic timing wheels must not come in contact with magnets (pickup tools, trays, etc.) or any other strong magnetic field. This will destroy the timing wheels ability to correctly relay camshaft position to the camshaft position sensor.
2. Disconnect and isolate the negative battery cable.
3. Remove the air inlet hose and upper intake manifold.
4. Cover the open intake ports to prevent debris from entering the engine.

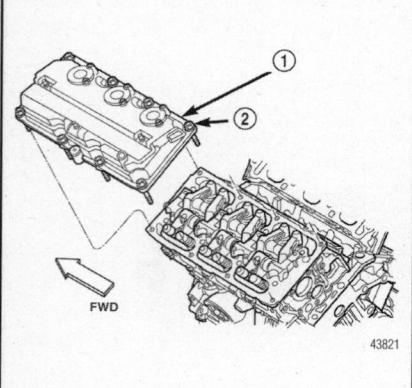

Fig. 290 Cylinder head cover left side (1) and bolts (2)

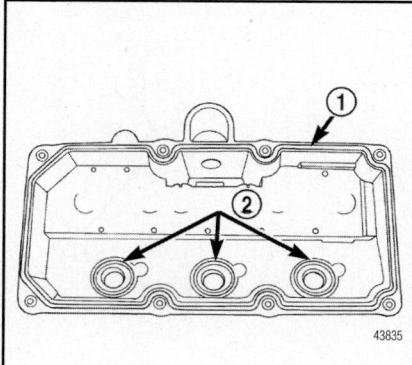

Fig. 291 Cylinder head cover gasket (1) and spark plug tube seal (2)

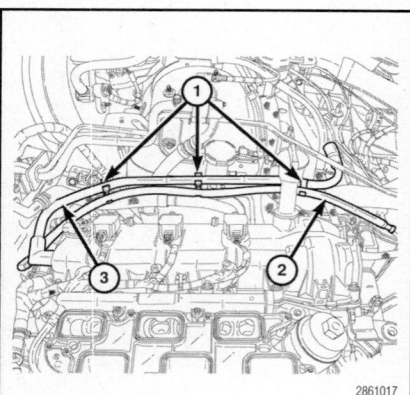

Fig. 292 Repositioning the transmission breather hose (2), make up air tube (3) and clips (1)

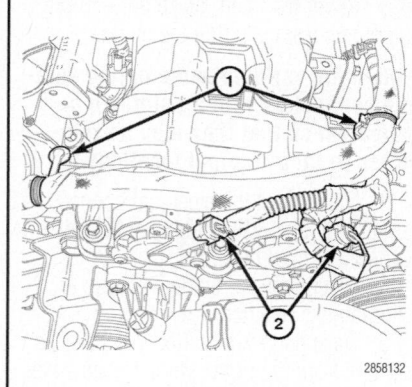

Fig. 293 Disconnecting the valve timing solenoids and starter wire retainers (1) and electrical connector (2)

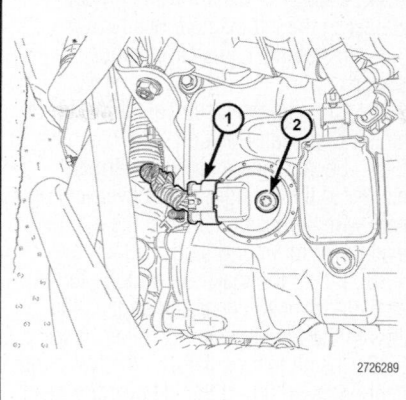

Fig. 295 Removing the CMP sensor, electrical connector (1) and mounting bolts (2)

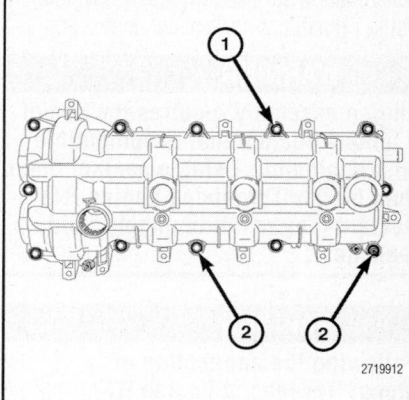

Fig. 297 Removing the cylinder head cover mounting bolts (1) and studbolts (2)

5. Remove the insulator from the LH cylinder head cover.

6. Disengage the clips, remove the make-up air tube from the left cylinder head cover and reposition the transmission breather hose.

➡**Mark the variable valve timing solenoid connectors with a paint pen or equivalent so that they may be reinstalled in their original locations.**

7. Disconnect the electrical connectors from the left variable valve timing solenoids.

8. Disengage two starter wire harness retainers from the left cylinder head cover.

9. Mark the variable valve timing solenoids (2 and 4) with a paint pen or equivalent so that they may be reinstalled in their original locations.

10. Remove the variable valve timing solenoids.

11. Disengage one main wire harness retainer from the left cylinder head cover.

12. Disconnect the left Camshaft Position (CMP) sensor.

13. Disengage one main wire harness retainer from the cylinder head cover and one main wire harness retainer from the cylinder head cover mounting stud.

➡**The RH CMP sensor is shown, the LH CMP sensor is similar. If removing both RH and LH CMP sensors, mark the sensors so they can be installed in their original locations.**

14. Remove the camshaft position sensor.

15. Disengage two injection/ignition harness retainers from the left cylinder head cover.

16. Remove the ignition coils.

17. Loosen ten cylinder head cover mounting bolts and two studbolts and remove the cylinder head cover.

18. Remove the and discard the cylinder head cover gasket.

19. The spark plug tube seals can be reused if not damaged.

✳✳ WARNING

Do not use oil based liquids, wire brushes, abrasive wheels or metal scrapers to clean the engine gasket surfaces. Use only isopropyl (rubbing) alcohol, along with plastic or wooden scrapers. Improper gasket surface preparation may result in engine fluid leakage.

20. Remove the all residual sealant from the cylinder head, timing chain cover and cylinder head cover mating surfaces

To install:
21. Install the cylinder head cover gasket.

22. The spark plug tube seals can be reused if not damaged.

23. If required, install new spark plug tube seals in the cylinder head cover:

a. Lubricate the spark plug tube seal inner and outer diameters with clean engine oil.

b. Place the spark plug tube seal on the Cam Sensor/Spark Plug Tube Seal Installer

Installer, Cam Installer, Cam Sensor/Spark Plug Tube Seal.

c. Push the seal into the cylinder head cover until the base of the seal is seated.

d. Remove the tool.

24. Clean the timing engine timing cover, cylinder head and cylinder head

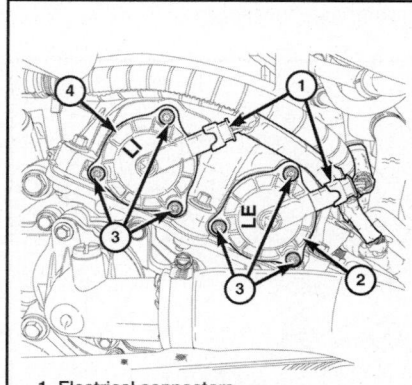

1. Electrical connectors
2. Exhaust variable valve timing solenoid
3. Attaching bolts
4. Intake variable valve timing solenoid

Fig. 294 Removing the variable valve timing solenoids

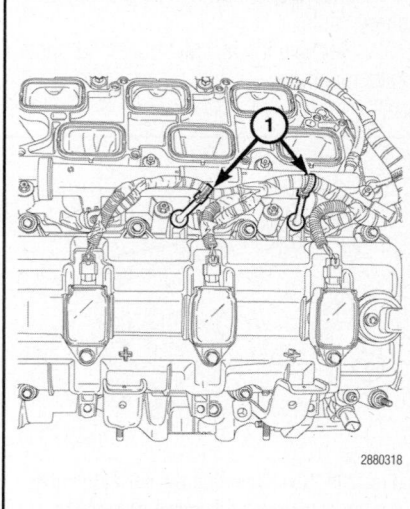

Fig. 296 Disengaging the 2 injection/ignition harness retainers

cover mating surfaces with isopropyl alcohol in preparation for sealant application.

※ **WARNING**

Engine assembly requires the use of a unique sealant that is compatible with engine oil. Using a sealant other than Mopar®Threebond Engine RTV Sealant may result in engine fluid leakage.

※ **WARNING**

Following the application of Mopar®Threebond Engine RTV Sealant to the gasket surfaces, the components must be assembled within 20 minutes and the attaching fasteners must be tightened to specification within 45 minutes. Prolonged exposure to the air prior to assembly may result in engine fluid leakage.

25. Apply a 2 to 3 mm wide bead of Mopar®Threebond Engine RTV Sealant to the two engine timing cover to cylinder head T-joints.

26. Align the locator pins to the cylinder head and install the cylinder head cover.

27. Tighten the cylinder head cover bolts and double ended studs in the sequence shown to 9 ft. lbs. (12 Nm).

28. If removed, install the spark plugs.

29. Install the ignition coils.

30. Engage two injection/ignition harness retainers to the left cylinder head cover.

31. Refer to the markings made at disassembly and install the variable valve timing solenoids (2 and 4).

32. Connect the electrical connectors to the left variable valve timing solenoids.

33. Engage two starter wire harness retainers to the left cylinder head cover.

34. Engage one main wire harness retainer to the left cylinder head cover.

35. Install the camshaft position sensor.

36. Connect the electrical connector to the left Camshaft Position (CMP) sensor.

37. Engage one main wire harness retainer to the cylinder head cover and one main wire harness retainer to the cylinder head cover mounting stud.

38. Install the make-up air tube to the left cylinder head cover and engage the clips to the transmission breather hose.

39. Install the insulator to the two alignment posts on top of the LH cylinder head cover.

40. Install the upper intake manifold, support brackets and air inlet hose.

41. Connect the negative battery cable and tighten nut to 45 inch lbs. (5 Nm).

➡The Cam/Crank Variation Relearn procedure must be performed using the scan tool anytime there has been a repair/replacement made to a powertrain system, for example: flywheel, valvetrain, camshaft and/or crankshaft sensors or components.

Right Side

See Figures 299 through 302.

※ **WARNING**

The magnetic timing wheels must not come in contact with magnets (pickup tools, trays, etc.) or any other strong magnetic field. This will destroy the timing wheels ability to correctly relay camshaft position to the camshaft position sensor.

1. Disconnect and isolate the negative battery cable.

2. Remove the air inlet hose and upper intake manifold.

3. Cover the open intake ports to prevent debris from entering the engine.

➡Mark the variable valve timing solenoid connectors with a paint pen or equivalent so that they may be reinstalled in their original locations.

4. Disconnect the electrical connectors from the variable valve timing solenoids on the right cylinder head.

5. Disengage the starter harness to main harness retainer.

6. Disengage two starter wire harness retainers from the right cylinder head cover.

7. Mark the variable valve timing solenoids (2 and 4) with a paint pen or equivalent so that they may be reinstalled in their original locations.

8. Remove the variable valve timing solenoids.

9. Disengage four main wire harness retainers from the right cylinder head cover.

10. Disconnect the electrical connector from the right Camshaft Position (CMP) sensor.

11. Disengage the main wire harness retainer from the right cylinder head cover mounting stud.

➡If removing both RH and LH CMP sensors, mark the sensors so they can be installed in their original locations.

12. Remove the camshaft position sensor.

13. Disengage three injection/ignition harness retainers from the right cylinder head cover.

14. Remove the ignition coils.

15. Raise and support the vehicle.

16. Loosen the bolt securing the transmission fluid level indicator tube to the transmission housing.

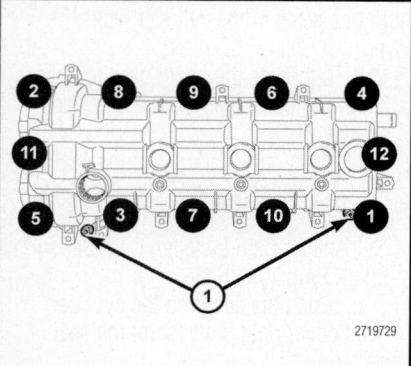

Fig. 298 Cylinder head cover bolt tightening sequence

Fig. 299 Disconnecting the variable valve timing solenoids and starter harness to main harness retainer (3), right cylinder head cover (1), electrical connectors (2)

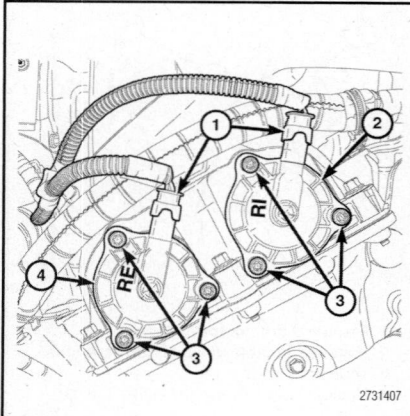

Fig. 300 Removing the variable valve timing solenoids (2), electrical connectors (1) and bolt (3)

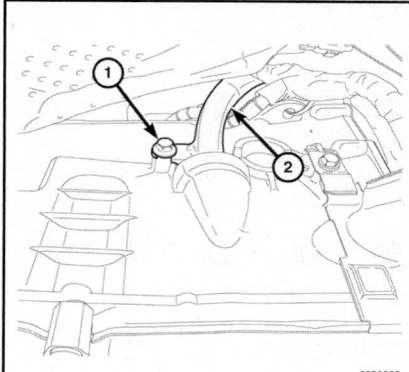

Fig. 301 Loosening the bolt (1) securing the transmission fluid level indicator tube (2)

17. Remove the upper transmission to engine bolt and reposition the transmission oil level indicator tube.

18. Lower the vehicle.

19. Remove the PCV valve.

20. Loosen nine cylinder head cover mounting bolts and three studbolts and remove the cylinder head cover.

➡**The LH cylinder head cover is shown, the RH cylinder head cover is similar.**

21. Remove the and discard the cylinder head cover gasket.

22. The spark plug tube seals can be reused if not damaged.

➡**The LH cylinder head cover T-joints are shown, the RH cylinder head cover T-joints are similar.**

✳✳ WARNING

Do not use oil based liquids, wire brushes, abrasive wheels or metal scrapers to clean the engine gasket

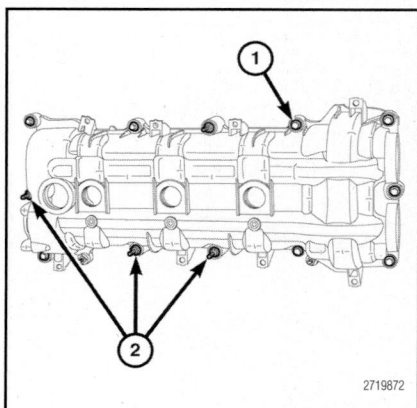

Fig. 302 Removing the cylinder head cover mounting bolts (1) and studbolts (2)

surfaces. Use only isopropyl (rubbing) alcohol, along with plastic or wooden scrapers. Improper gasket surface preparation may result in engine fluid leakage.

23. Remove the all residual sealant from the cylinder head, timing chain cover and cylinder head cover mating surfaces

To install:

24. Install the cylinder head cover gasket.

25. The spark plug tube seals can be reused if not damaged.

26. If required, install new spark plug tube seals in the cylinder head cover:

   a. Lubricate the spark plug tube seal inner and outer diameters with clean engine oil.

   b. Place the spark plug tube seal on the Cam Sensor/Spark Plug Tube Seal Installer

   Installer, Cam Installer, Cam Sensor/Spark Plug Tube Seal.

   c. Push the seal into the cylinder head cover until the base of the seal is seated.

   d. Remove the tool.

27. Clean the timing engine timing cover, cylinder head and cylinder head cover mating surfaces with isopropyl alcohol in preparation for sealant application.

✳✳ WARNING

Engine assembly requires the use of a unique sealant that is compatible with engine oil. Using a sealant other than Mopar®Threebond Engine RTV Sealant may result in engine fluid leakage.

✳✳ WARNING

Following the application of Mopar®Threebond Engine RTV Sealant to the gasket surfaces, the components must be assembled within 20 minutes and the attaching fasteners must be tightened to specification within 45 minutes. Prolonged exposure to the air prior to assembly may result in engine fluid leakage.

28. Apply a 2 to 3 mm wide bead of Mopar®Threebond Engine RTV Sealant to the two engine timing cover to cylinder head T-joints.

29. Align the locator pins to the cylinder head and install the cylinder head cover.

30. Tighten the cylinder head cover bolts and double ended studs in the sequence shown to 9 ft. lbs. (12 Nm).

31. If removed, install the spark plugs.

32. Install the ignition coils.

33. Engage three injection/ignition harness retainers to the right cylinder head cover.

34. Refer to the markings made at disassembly and install the variable valve timing solenoids (2 and 4) in their original locations.

35. Connect the electrical connectors to the variable valve timing solenoids on the right cylinder head.

36. Engage two starter wire harness retainers to the right cylinder head cover.

37. Engage the starter harness to main harness retainer.

38. Engage four main wire harness retainers to the right cylinder head cover.

➡**If both RH and LH CMP sensors where removed, install them into their original locations.**

39. Install the camshaft position sensor.

40. Connect the electrical connector to the right Camshaft Position (CMP) sensor.

41. Engage the main wire harness retainer to the right cylinder head cover mounting stud.

42. Install the PCV valve.

43. Raise and support the vehicle.

44. Install the transmission oil level indicator tube with the upper transmission to engine bolt tightened to 41 ft. lbs. (55 Nm).

45. Install the bolt securing the transmission fluid level indicator tube to the transmission housing and tighten to 9 ft. lbs. (12 Nm).

46. Lower the vehicle.

47. If removed, install the insulator to the two alignment posts on top of the LH cylinder head cover.

48. Install the upper intake manifold, support brackets and air inlet hose.

49. Connect the negative battery cable and tighten nut to 45 inch lbs. (5 Nm).

➡**The Cam/Crank Variation Relearn procedure must be performed using the scan tool anytime there has been a repair/replacement made to a powertrain system, for example: flywheel, valvetrain, camshaft and/or crankshaft sensors or components.**

5.7L, 6.1L & 6.4L Engines

See Figures 303 and 304.

1. Disconnect the negative battery cable.

2. Remove the engine cover.

3. Disconnect the ignition coil electrical connectors.

4. Position the electrical harness aside.

5. Remove the ignition coil retaining bolts and remove the ignition coils.

6. Using the sequence shown, remove the cylinder head cover retaining bolts.

✴✴ WARNING

Do not use harsh cleaners to clean the cylinder head covers. Severe damage to covers may occur.

7. Remove the cylinder head cover.

8. Clean the sealing surface of the cylinder head and cover.

➡ **The cylinder head cover gasket may be used again, provided no cuts, tears, or deformation have occurred.**

To install:

9. Clean the cylinder head cover and the sealing surface of the cylinder head. Inspect and replace gasket if necessary.

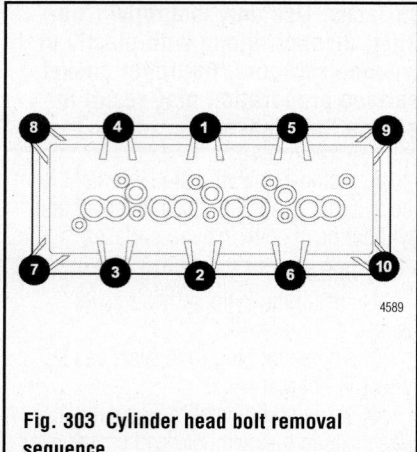

Fig. 303 Cylinder head bolt removal sequence

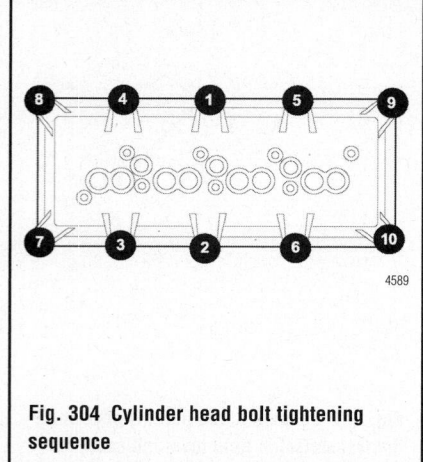

Fig. 304 Cylinder head bolt tightening sequence

10. Install the cylinder head cover and hand start all fasteners.

11. Using the sequence shown, tighten the cylinder head cover bolts to 70 inch lbs. (8 Nm).

12. Before installing the ignition coils, apply dielectric grease to the inside of the spark plug boots.

13. Install the ignition coils.

14. Tighten the ignition coil retaining bolts to 62 inch lbs. (7 Nm).

15. Position the electrical harness.

16. Connect the ignition coil electrical connectors.

17. Install the engine cover.

18. Connect the negative battery cable.

ENGINE PERFORMANCE & EMISSION CONTROLS

CAMSHAFT POSITION (CMP) SENSOR

REMOVAL & INSTALLATION

3.5L Engine

See Figure 305.

1. Disconnect and isolate the negative battery cable at battery.

2. Disconnect the electrical connector from the camshaft position (CMP) sensor.

3. Remove the bolt and CMP sensor.

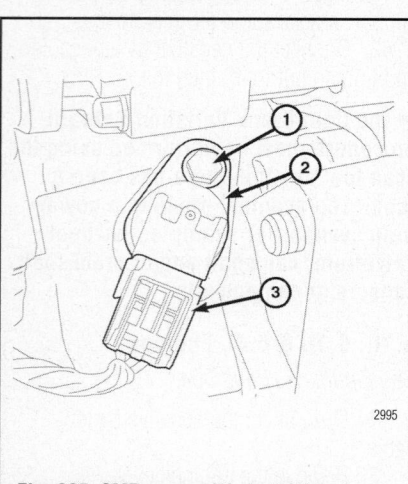

Fig. 305 CMP sensor (2), bolt (1) and electrical connector (3)—3.5L engine

To install:

✴✴ WARNING

Install camshaft position (CMP) sensor utilizing twisting motion. Make sure CMP sensor is fully seated. Do not drive CMP sensor into the bore with mounting screw. This may cause CMP sensor to be incorrectly seated causing a faulty signal or no signal at all.

➡ **If reinstalling the sensor, check the sensor O-ring for damage and replace if necessary. Lubricate the O-ring with clean engine oil before installing the sensor.**

4. Push the CMP sensor into the timing belt cover with a twisting motion until fully seated.

5. While holding the sensor in this position, install and tighten the retaining bolt to 9 ft. lbs. (12 Nm).

6. Connect and lock the electrical connector to the CMP sensor.

7. Connect the negative battery cable and tighten nut to 45 inch lbs. (5 Nm).

➡ **The Cam/Crank Variation Relearn procedure must be performed anytime there has been a repair/replacement made to a powertrain system, for example: flywheel, valvetrain,** camshaft and/or crankshaft sensors or components

3.6L Engine

See Figures 306 and 307.

✴✴ WARNING

The magnetic timing wheels must not come in contact with magnets (pickup tools, trays, etc.) or any other strong magnetic field. This will destroy the timing wheels ability to

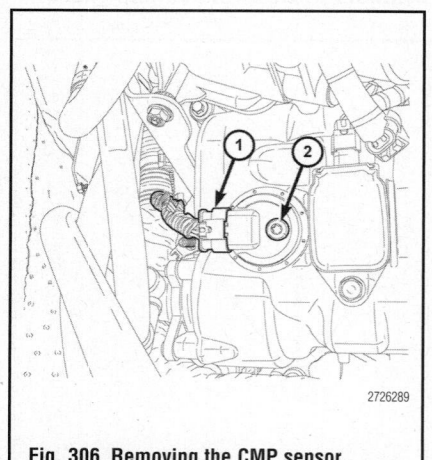

Fig. 306 Removing the CMP sensor, electrical connector (1) and mounting bolts (2)—3.6L engine

correctly relay camshaft position to the camshaft position sensor.

The Camshaft Position (CMP) sensors are located at the rear of the cylinder head covers and are bolted to the cylinder head.

1. Disconnect and isolate the negative battery cable.

2. If removing the left CMP sensor, first remove the air inlet hose and upper intake manifold.

➡The right CMP sensor is shown, the left CMP sensor is similar. If removing both right and left CMP sensors, mark the sensors so they can be installed in their original locations.

3. Disconnect the electrical connector from the CMP sensor.

4. Loosen the sensor mounting bolt.

5. Pull the sensor and mounting bolt from the cylinder head cover.

6. The O-ring seal can be reused if not damaged.

To install:

7. Clean out the camshaft position (CMP) sensor mounting bolt hole in cylinder head.

8. The CMP sensor seal can be reused if not damaged.

9. If required, install a new CMP sensor seal in the cylinder head cover:

   a. Lubricate the CMP sensor seal inner and outer diameters with clean engine oil.

   b. Place the CMP sensor seal on the Cam Sensor/Spark Plug Tube Seal Installer .

   c. Push the seal into the cylinder head cover until the base of the seal is seated.

   d. Remove the tool.

➡A properly installed CMP sensor seal will have a 0.06–0.08 inch (1.5–2.0 mm) gap between the cylinder head cover and the seal upper flange.

10. The sensor mounting bolt O-ring can be reused if not damaged.

11. Apply a small amount of engine oil to the sensor mounting bolt O-ring.

➡Install the CMP sensor to the cylinder head. Tighten the mounting bolt to 80 inch lbs. (9 Nm).

12. Connect the electrical connector to the sensor.

13. If required, install the upper intake manifold and air inlet hose.

14. Connect the negative battery cable and tighten nut to 48 inch lbs. (5 Nm).

➡The Cam/Crank Variation Relearn procedure must be performed using the scan tool anytime there has been a repair/replacement made to a powertrain system, for example: flywheel, valvetrain, camshaft and/or crankshaft sensors or components.

5.7L, 6.1L & 6.4L Engines
See Figure 308.

1. Disconnect and isolate the negative battery cable.

2. Disconnect the electrical connector at the Camshaft Position (CMP) sensor.

3. Remove the CMP sensor mounting bolt.

4. Using a slight rotating motion, carefully remove the CMP sensor from the timing chain cover.

5. Check the condition of the sensor O-ring.

To install:

> ✳✳ **WARNING**

Install the Camshaft Position (CMP) sensor using a slight rotating motion (side to side). Make sure the CMP sensor is fully seated. Do not drive the CMP sensor into the bore with the mounting screw. This may cause the CMP sensor to be incorrectly seated causing a faulty signal or no signal at all.

6. Using a rotating motion, carefully install the CMP sensor into the timing chain cover.

> ✳✳ **WARNING**

Before tightening the sensor mounting bolt, be sure the sensor is completely flush to the timing cover. If the sensor is not flush, damage to the sensor mounting tang may result.

7. Install the CMP mounting bolt and tighten to 9 ft. lbs. (12 Nm).

8. Connect the electrical connector to the CMP sensor.

9. Connect the negative battery cable and tighten nut to 45 inch lbs. (5 Nm).

CRANKSHAFT POSITION (CKP) SENSOR

LOCATION
See Figure 309.

Refer to the accompanying illustration.

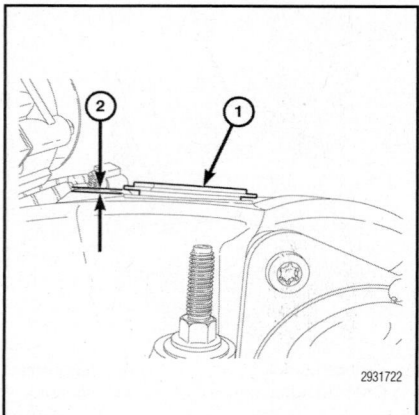

Fig. 307 Installing a new CMP sensor seal (1) and identifying the gap (2)—3.6L engine

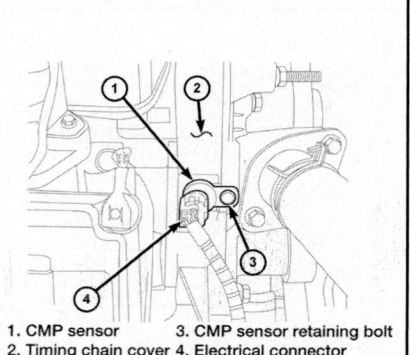

1. CMP sensor   3. CMP sensor retaining bolt
2. Timing chain cover 4. Electrical connector

Fig. 308 CMP sensor—5.7L, 6.1L & 6.4L engines

Fig. 309 CKP sensor—3.5L engine

REMOVAL & INSTALLATION

3.5L Engine

See Figure 310.

1. Disconnect negative battery cable.
2. Raise and safely support the vehicle.
3. Unlock and disconnect the electrical connector.
4. Remove the mounting bolt.
5. Remove the sensor.

To install:

➡**If reinstalling the sensor, check the sensor O-ring for damage and replace if necessary. Lubricate the O-ring with clean engine oil before installing the sensor.**

6. Push the crankshaft position (CKP) sensor into the transmission case with a twisting motion until fully seated.

> ❋❋ **WARNING**
>
> **Before tightening the sensor mounting bolt, be sure the sensor is completely flush to the mounting surface. If the sensor is not flush, damage to the sensor mounting tang may result.**

7. While holding the sensor in this position, install and tighten the retaining bolt to 9 ft. lbs. (12 Nm).
8. Connect and lock the electrical connector to the CKP sensor.
9. Connect the negative battery cable and tighten nut to 45 inch lbs. (5 Nm).

➡**The Cam/Crank Variation Relearn procedure must be performed anytime there has been a repair/replacement made to a powertrain system, for example: flywheel, valvetrain, camshaft and/or crankshaft sensors or components.**

3.6L Engine

See Figures 311 and 312.

1. Disconnect and isolate the negative battery cable.
2. Raise and support the vehicle.
3. Remove the belly pan retainers and remove the belly pan.

The crankshaft position (CKP) sensor is mounted into the right rear side of the cylinder block.

4. Push back the heat shield from the crankshaft position (CKP) sensor.
5. Disconnect the electrical connector from the crankshaft position (CKP) sensor.
6. Remove the sensor mounting bolt.
7. Carefully twist the sensor from the cylinder block.
8. The CKP sensor O-ring can be reused if not damaged.

To install:

9. Apply a small amount of engine oil to the sensor O-ring.
10. Clean out the CKP sensor mounting bolt hole in the engine block.
11. Install the sensor into the engine block with a slight rocking and twisting motion.

> ❋❋ **WARNING**
>
> **Before tightening the CKP sensor mounting bolt, be sure the sensor is completely flush to the cylinder block. If the CKP sensor is not flush, damage to the sensor mounting tang may result.**

12. Install the mounting bolt and tighten to 9 ft. lbs. (12 Nm).
13. Connect the CKP sensor electrical connector.
14. Position the heat shield over the CKP sensor.

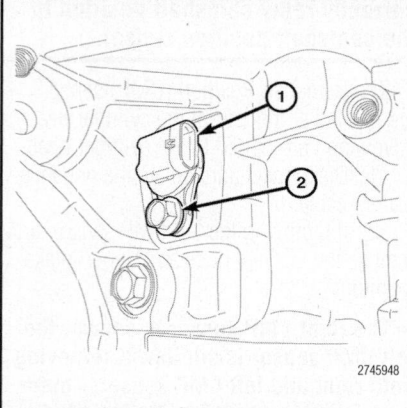

Fig. 312 Removing and installing the mounting bolt (2) and CKP sensor(1)— 3.6L engine

2745948

15. Position the belly pan and install the retainers.
16. Lower the vehicle.
17. Connect the negative battery cable and tighten nut to 45 inch lbs. (5 Nm).

➡**The Cam/Crank Variation Relearn procedure must be performed using the scan tool anytime there has been a repair/replacement made to a powertrain system, for example: flywheel, valvetrain, camshaft and/or crankshaft sensors or components.**

5.7L & 6.4L Engines

See Figure 313.

The Crankshaft Position (CKP) sensor is located at the right-rear side of the engine cylinder block. It is positioned and bolted into a machined hole in the engine block.

1. Raise vehicle.

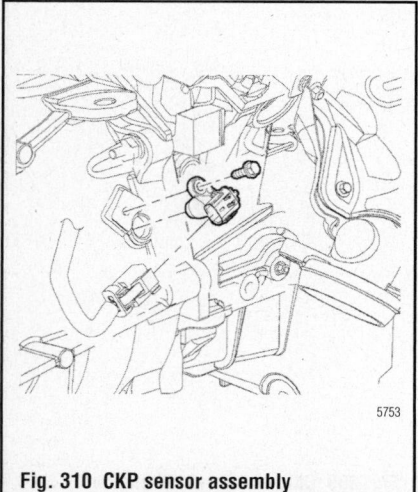

Fig. 310 CKP sensor assembly

5753

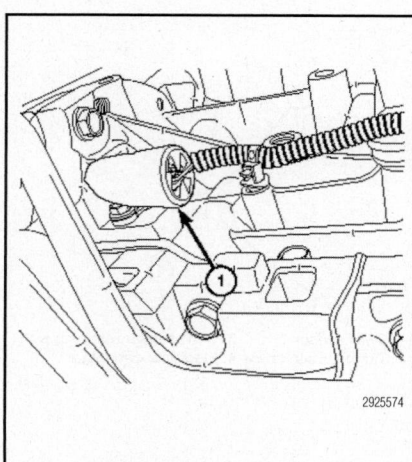

Fig. 311 Identifying the CKP heat shield

2925574

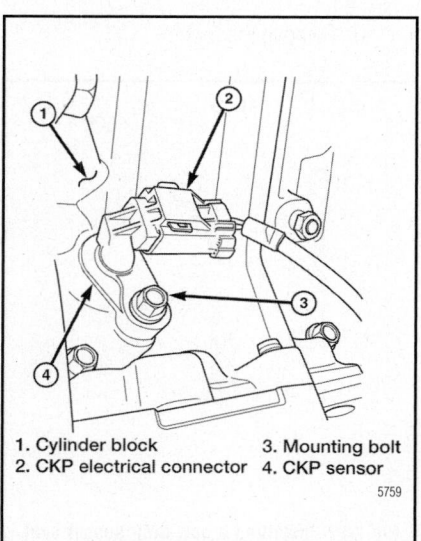

1. Cylinder block	3. Mounting bolt
2. CKP electrical connector	4. CKP sensor

5759

Fig. 313 CKP sensor removal and installation

2. Disconnect CKP electrical connector at sensor.

3. Remove the CKP mounting bolt.

4. Carefully twist sensor from cylinder block.

5. Remove the sensor from vehicle.

6. Check condition of sensor O-ring.

To install:

7. Clean out machined hole in engine block.

8. Apply a small amount of engine oil to sensor O-ring.

9. Install the sensor into engine block with a slight rocking and twisting action.

✳✳ WARNING

Before tightening sensor mounting bolt, be sure sensor is completely flush to cylinder block. If sensor is not flush, damage to sensor mounting tang may result.

10. Install the mounting bolt and tighten to 9 ft. lbs. (12 Nm) torque.

11. Connect electrical connector to sensor.

12. Lower vehicle

6.1L Engine

See Figures 314 through 316.

The Crankshaft Position (CKP) sensor is located at the right-rear side of the engine block (1). It is positioned and bolted into a machined hole in the engine block.

1. Disconnect and isolate the negative battery cable.

2. Raise and support the vehicle.

3. Remove the starter motor.

4. Disconnect the CKP sensor electrical connector.

5. Remove the CKP sensor mounting bolt.

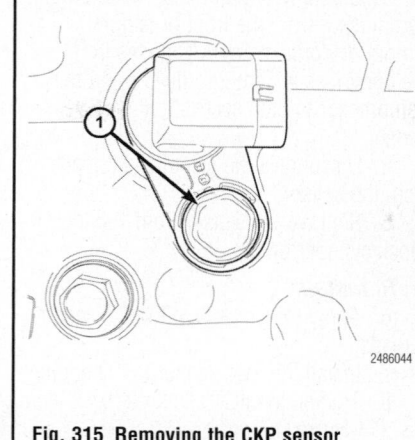

Fig. 315 Removing the CKP sensor mounting bolt

6. Using a slight twisting motion, remove the CKP sensor from the engine block.

7. Check the condition of the sensor O-ring and replace if necessary.

To install:

➡**Before installing the Crankshaft Position (CKP) sensor, check the condition of the sensor O-ring and replace if necessary.**

8. Clean the machined hole in the engine block.

9. Apply a small amount of engine oil to the CKP sensor O-ring.

10. Install the CKP sensor into the engine block with a slight twisting motion.

✳✳ WARNING

Before tightening the CKP sensor mounting bolt, be sure the sensor is completely flush to the cylinder block. If sensor is not flush, damage to the sensor mounting tang may result.

11. Install the CKP sensor mounting bolt and tighten to 9 ft. lbs. (12 Nm).

12. Connect the CKP sensor electrical connector.

13. Install the starter motor.

14. Lower the vehicle.

15. Install the negative battery cable.

ENGINE COOLANT TEMPERATURE (ECT) SENSOR

REMOVAL & INSTALLATION

3.5L Engine

See Figure 317.

1. Disconnect negative battery cable.

2. Partially drain cooling system.

3. With the engine cold, disconnect coolant sensor electrical connector.

4. Remove the sensor.

To install:

5. Install the engine coolant temperature sensor. Tighten sensor to 20 ft. lbs. (28 Nm).

6. Attach electrical connector to sensor.

7. Connect negative battery cable.

3.6L Engine

See Figure 318.

The Engine Coolant Temperature (ECT) sensor on the 3.6L engine is installed into a water jacket at rear of the cylinder head on the left side of the engine.

✳✳ CAUTION

Hot, pressurized coolant can cause injury by scalding. Cooling system must be partially drained before removing the coolant temperature sensor.

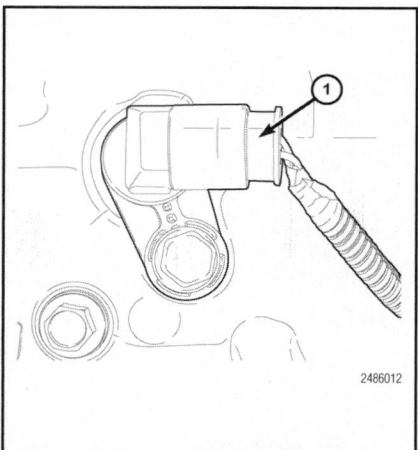

Fig. 314 Disconnecting the CKP sensor electrical connector

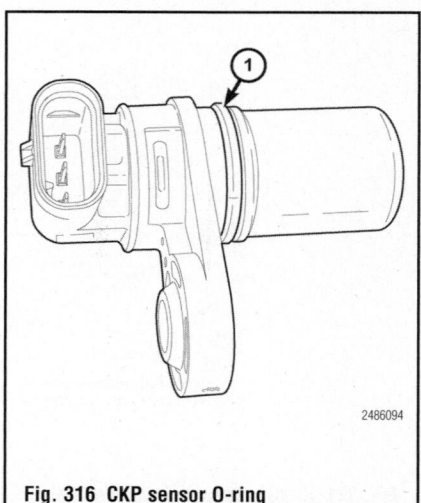

Fig. 316 CKP sensor O-ring

Fig. 317 ECT sensor (2) and CMP sensor (1)

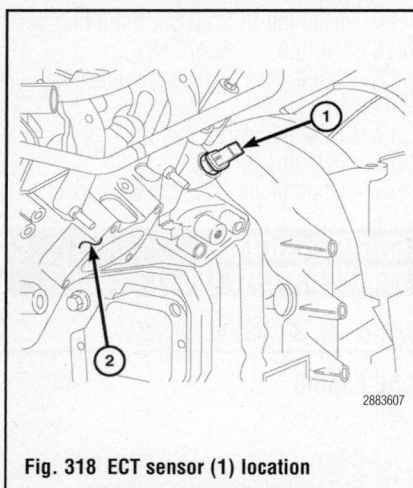

Fig. 318 ECT sensor (1) location

➡**Do not waste reusable coolant. If solution is clean, drain coolant into a clean container for reuse.**

1. Partially drain the cooling system.
2. Disconnect the electrical connector from the sensor.
3. Remove the sensor from the cylinder head.

To install:

4. Apply MOPAR®thread sealant with PFTE part number 04318034 to sensor threads.
5. Install the sensor to cylinder head.
6. Tighten sensor to 8 ft. lbs. (11 Nm) torque.
7. Connect electrical connector to sensor.
8. Replace any lost engine coolant.

5.7L & 6.4L Engines

See Figure 319.

1. Partially drain the cooling system.
2. Remove the accessory drive belt.

3. Carefully unbolt the air conditioning compressor from the front of engine. Do not disconnect any A/C hoses from the compressor. Temporarily support the compressor to gain access to the ECT sensor.
4. Disconnect the electrical connector from the sensor.
5. Remove the sensor from cylinder block cylinder block.

To install:

6. Apply thread sealant to ECT sensor threads.
7. Install the ECT sensor to the engine.
8. Tighten the ECT sensor to 97.3 inch lbs. (11 Nm).
9. Connect the electrical connector.
10. Fill the cooling system.

6.1L Engine

See Figure 320.

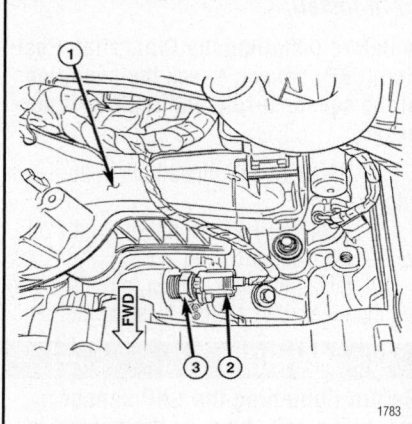

Fig. 320 Removing and installing the ECT sensor (2) and electrical connector (2)

1. Partially drain the cooling system.
2. Remove the accessory drive belt.
3. Carefully unbolt air conditioning compressor from front of engine. Do not disconnect any A/C hoses from compressor. Temporarily support compressor to gain access to ECT sensor.
4. Disconnect the electrical connector from the sensor.
5. Remove the sensor from cylinder block.

To install:

6. Apply thread sealant to sensor threads.
7. Install the ECT sensor to engine.
8. Tighten sensor to 98 inch lbs. (11 Nm).
9. Connect electrical connector to ECT sensor.
10. Fill the cooling system.

HEATED OXYGEN SENSOR (HO2S)

LOCATION

See Figure 321.

Refer to the accompanying illustration.

REMOVAL & INSTALLATION

3.5L Engine

See Figure 322.

The engines uses two heated oxygen sensors, one in each exhaust manifold.

✳✳ WARNING

Never apply any type of grease to the oxygen sensor electrical connector, or attempt any soldering of the sensor wiring harness.

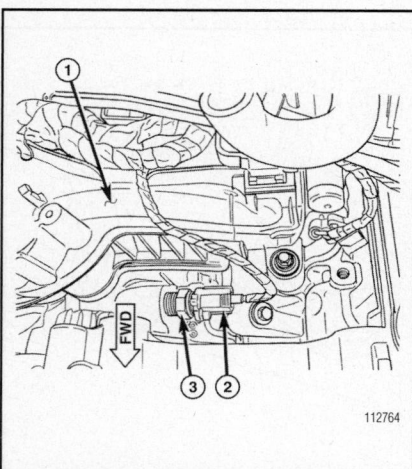

Fig. 319 ECT sensor (3) and electrical connector (2) removal and installation

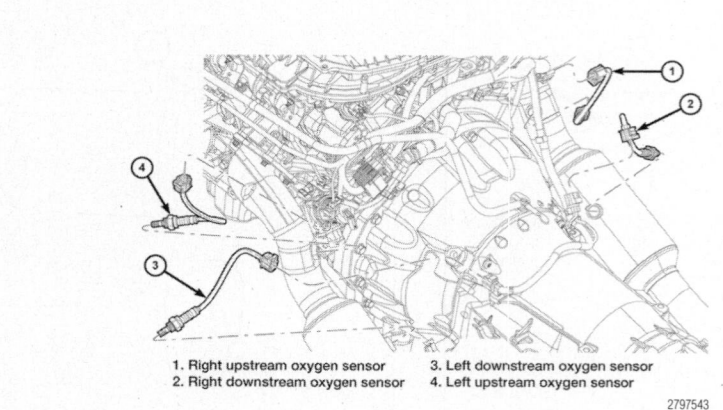

1. Right upstream oxygen sensor
2. Right downstream oxygen sensor
3. Left downstream oxygen sensor
4. Left upstream oxygen sensor

Fig. 321 HO2S locations—3.6L Engine

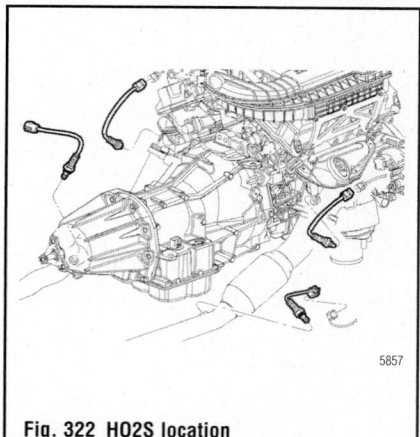

Fig. 322 HO2S location

> ❋❋ **CAUTION**
>
> **The exhaust manifold, exhaust pipes and catalytic converter become very hot during engine operation. Allow engine to cool before removing oxygen sensor.**

> ❋❋ **WARNING**
>
> **When disconnecting sensor electrical connector, do not pull directly on wire going into sensor.**

1. Remove the negative battery cable.
2. Raise and safely support the vehicle.
3. Disconnect the heated oxygen sensor electrical connector.
4. Use a socket such as Snap-On YA Disconnect, Transmission Cooler Line or a crow foot wrench to remove oxygen sensor.

To install:

➡ **When replacing an O2 Sensor, the PCM RAM memory must be cleared, either by disconnecting the PCM C-1 connector or momentarily disconnecting the Battery negative terminal. The NGC learns the characteristics of each O2 heater element and these old values should be cleared when installing a new O2 sensor. The customer may experience driveability issues if this is not performed.**

> ❋❋ **WARNING**
>
> **Never apply any type of grease to the oxygen sensor electrical connector, or attempt any soldering of the sensor wiring harness.**

The engines uses two heated oxygen sensors, one in each exhaust manifold.
5. After removing the sensor, the exhaust manifold threads must be cleaned with an 18 mm X 1.5 + 6E tap. If reusing the

original sensor, coat the sensor threads with an anti-seize compound such as Loctite 771- 64 or equivalent. New sensors have compound on the threads and do not require an additional coating. Tighten the sensor to 30 ft. lbs. (41 Nm) torque.
6. Connect the heated oxygen sensor electrical connector.
7. Carefully lower the vehicle.
8. Install the negative battery cable.

3.6L Engine

The engine is equipped with four heated oxygen sensors:
• The left upstream oxygen sensor (4) is referred to as the 1/1 sensor.
• The left downstream oxygen sensor (3) is referred to as the 1/2 sensor.
• The right upstream oxygen sensor (1) is referred to as the 2/1 sensor.
• The right downstream oxygen sensor (2) is referred to as the 2/2 sensor.

> ❋❋ **CAUTION**
>
> **The exhaust pipes and catalytic converter become very hot during engine operation. Allow the engine to cool before removing the oxygen sensor.**

1. Disconnect and isolate the negative battery cable.
2. Raise and support the vehicle.

> ❋❋ **WARNING**
>
> **When disconnecting the oxygen sensor electrical connector, do not pull directly on the wire going into the sensor. The sensor wiring can be damaged resulting in sensor failure.**

3. Disconnect the heated oxygen sensor electrical connector.
4. Remove the oxygen sensor.
5. Clean the exhaust pipe threads using an appropriate tap.

5.7L & 6.4L Engines
See Figure 323.

Refer to graphic for typical O2S (oxygen sensor) locations if equipped with four oxygen sensors.

> ❋❋ **WARNING**
>
> **Never apply any type of grease to the O2S sensor electrical connector or attempt any soldering of wiring harness.**

> ❋❋ **CAUTION**
>
> **The exhaust manifold, exhaust pipes and catalytic converter become very**

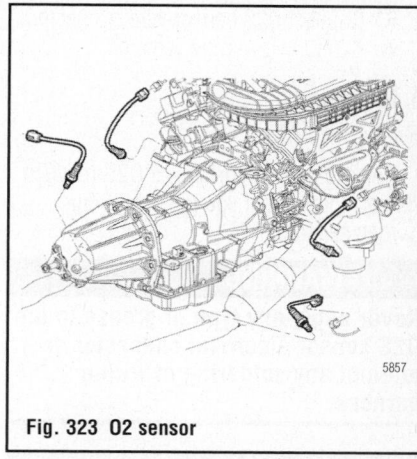

Fig. 323 O2 sensor

hot during engine operation. Allow the engine to cool before removing O2S sensors.

1. Raise and safely support the vehicle.
2. Disconnect wire connector from O2S sensor.

> ❋❋ **WARNING**
>
> **When disconnecting the O2S sensor electrical connector, do not pull directly on O2S sensor wiring harness.**

3. Remove the O2S sensor with an oxygen sensor removal and installation tool.
4. Clean threads in exhaust pipe using appropriate tap.

To install:

➡ **When replacing an O2 Sensor, the PCM's RAM memory must be cleared. This can be done by either by disconnecting the PCM's C-1 connector, or by momentarily disconnecting the negative battery cable. The PCM learns the characteristics of each O2 heater element, and these old values should be cleared when installing a new O2 sensor. Driveability problems may be experienced if this step is not performed.**

> ❋❋ **WARNING**
>
> **Never apply any type of grease to the O2S sensor electrical connector or attempt any soldering of the sensor wiring harness.**

Threads of new oxygen sensors are factory coated with anti-seize compound to aid in removal. DO NOT add any additional anti-seize compound to threads of a new oxygen sensor.
5. Install the O2S sensor. Tighten to 30 ft. lbs. (41 Nm) torque.

6. Connect O2S sensor wire connector.

7. Carefully lower the vehicle.

6.1L Engine

See Figure 322.

Refer to graphic for typical O2S (oxygen sensor) locations if equipped with four oxygen sensors.

❋❋ WARNING

Never apply any type of grease to the O2S sensor electrical connector or attempt any soldering of wiring harness.

❋❋ CAUTION

The exhaust manifold, exhaust pipes and catalytic converter become very hot during engine operation. Allow the engine to cool before removing O2S sensors.

1. Raise and safely support the vehicle.

2. Disconnect wire connector from O2S sensor.

❋❋ WARNING

When disconnecting the O2S sensor electrical connector, do not pull directly on O2S sensor wiring harness.

3. Remove the O2S sensor with an oxygen sensor removal and installation tool.

4. Clean threads in exhaust pipe using appropriate tap.

To install:

➥When replacing an O2 Sensor, the PCM's RAM memory must be cleared. This can be done by either by disconnecting the PCM's C-1 connector, or by momentarily disconnecting the negative battery cable. The PCM learns the characteristics of each O2 heater element, and these old values should be cleared when installing a new O2 sensor. Driveability problems may be experienced if this step is not performed.

❋❋ WARNING

Never apply any type of grease to the O2S sensor electrical connector or attempt any soldering of the sensor wiring harness.

Threads of new oxygen sensors are factory coated with anti-seize compound to aid in removal. DO NOT add any additional

anti-seize compound to threads of a new oxygen sensor.

5. Install the O2S sensor. Tighten to 30 ft. lbs. (41 Nm).

6. Connect O2S sensor wire connector.

7. Carefully lower the vehicle.

INTAKE AIR TEMPERATURE (IAT) SENSOR

LOCATION

See Figures 324 through 326.

Refer to the accompanying illustrations.

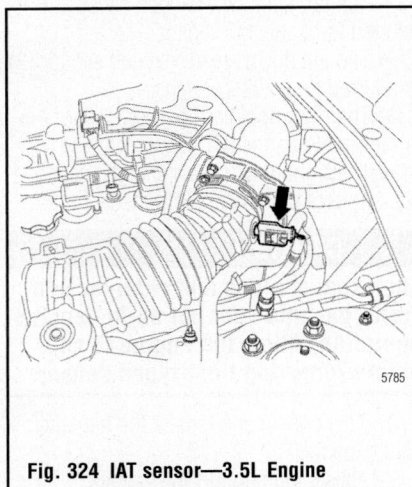

Fig. 324 IAT sensor—3.5L Engine

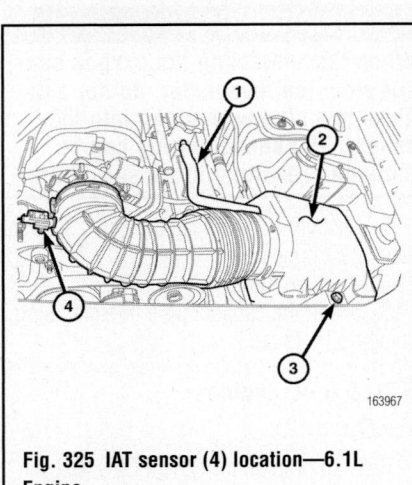

Fig. 325 IAT sensor (4) location—6.1L Engine

REMOVAL & INSTALLATION

3.5L Engine

See Figures 327 through 329.

1. Disconnect negative battery cable.

2. Unlock the electrical connector.

3. Remove the electrical connector from sensor.

4. Note sensor orientation.

5. Remove the sensor.

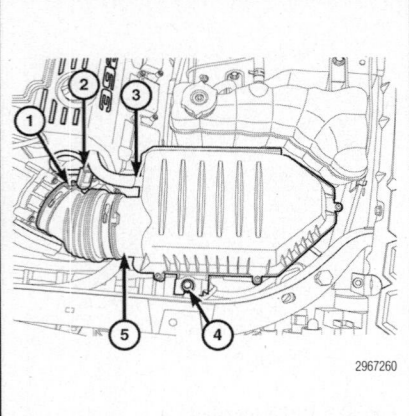

Fig. 326 IAT sensor (2) location—6.4L engine

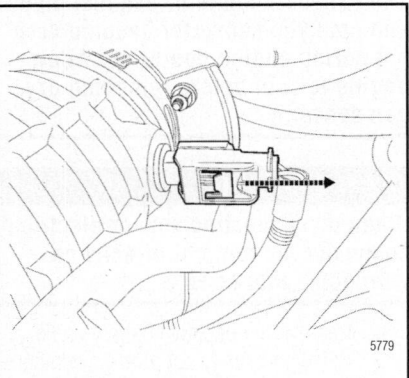

Fig. 327 Unlocking the electrical connector

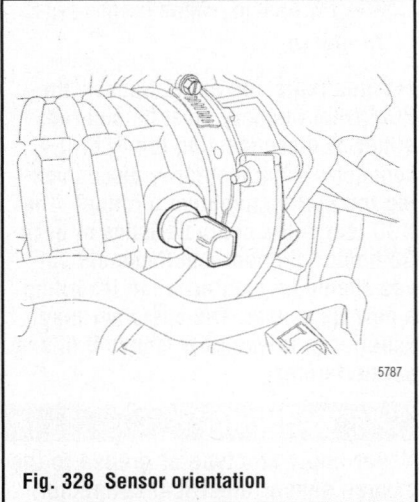

Fig. 328 Sensor orientation

To install:

6. Install the sensor. Rotate for proper orientation

7. Proper orientation of sensor.

8. Install the electrical connector and lock.

9. Connect negative battery cable.

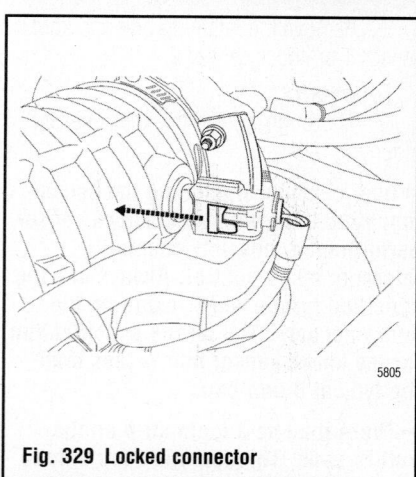

Fig. 329 Locked connector

3.6L Engine

See Figure 330.

1. Disconnect and isolate the negative battery cable.

2. Lift the engine cover retaining grommets off the ball studs and remove the engine cover.

3. Disconnect the electrical connector from the Inlet Air Temperature (IAT) sensor.

4. Clean any dirt from the air inlet tube at the IAT sensor base.

5. Gently lift the small plastic release tab, rotate the sensor about 1/4 turn counterclockwise and remove the sensor from the inlet air hose.

6. The IAT sensor O-ring can be reused if not damaged.

To install:

7. The Inlet Air Temperature (IAT) sensor O-ring seal can be reused if not damaged.

8. Clean the IAT sensor mounting hole in the air inlet hose.

9. Install the IAT sensor into the air inlet hose and rotate clockwise until the release tab engages.

10. Install the electrical connector to the IAT sensor.

11. Position the engine cover and secure the retaining grommets onto the ball studs.

12. Connect the negative battery cable and tighten nut to 45 inch lbs. (5 Nm).

5.7L Engine

See Figures 331 and 332.

The Inlet Manifold Air Temperature (IAT) sensor is installed into the rubber air intake hose near front of throttle body.

1. Disconnect the electrical connector from the IAT sensor.

2. Clean dirt from sensor base.

3. Pull sensor from rubber hose.

To install:

4. Press sensor into rubber air hose.

5. Rotate sensor into position as shown. For proper system operation, sensor must be positioned as shown.

6. Connect electrical connector to sensor.

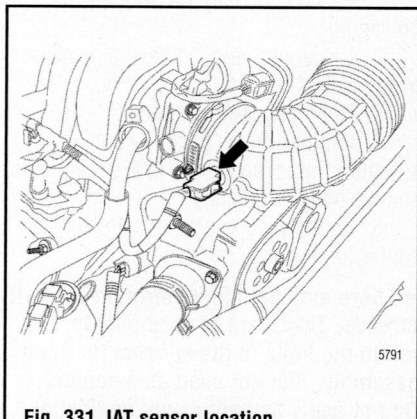

Fig. 331 IAT sensor location

6.1L Engine

See Figure 333.

The Inlet Manifold Air Temperature (IAT) sensor is installed into the rubber air intake hose near front of throttle body.

1. Pull sensor from rubber hose.

2. Disconnect the electrical connector from the IAT sensor.

3. Check sensor probe for damage.

4. Clean dirt from sensor base.

To install:

5. Connect electrical connector to sensor.

6. Press sensor into rubber air hose. Mate the notches. Be careful not to bend or damage probe.

6.4L Engine

See Figure 333.

The Intake Air Temperature (IAT) sensor is installed into the rubber air intake hose near the front of the throttle body.

1. Disconnect the electrical connector from IAT sensor.

2. Turn the IAT sensor 1/4 turn counterclockwise and remove the IAT sensor from the rubber air intake hose.

3. Inspect the sensor probe for any damage.

4. Clean any dirt or debris from sensor base.

To install:

5. Use care not to bend or damage the IAT sensor probe while installing.

6. Install the IAT sensor into the rubber air intake hose, turn the IAT sensor 1/4 turn clockwise and lock into position.

7. Connect the electrical connector to the IAT sensor.

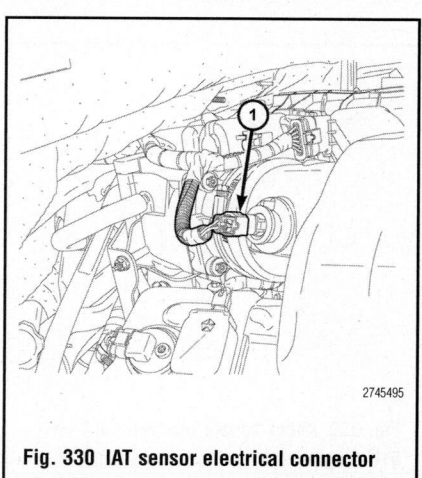

Fig. 330 IAT sensor electrical connector

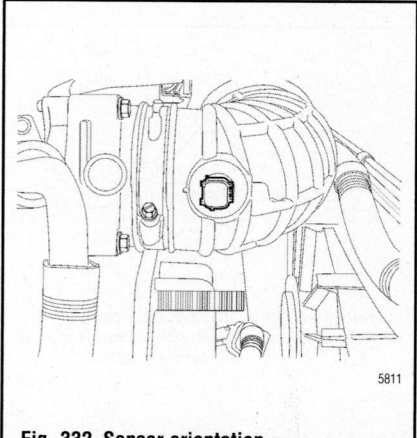

Fig. 332 Sensor orientation

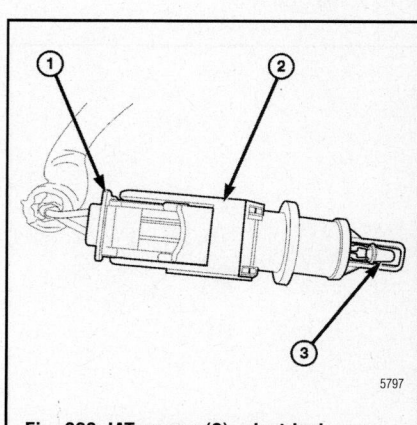

Fig. 333 IAT sensor (2), electrical connector (1) and probe (3)

KNOCK SENSOR (KS)

LOCATION

See Figure 334.

Refer to the accompanying illustration.

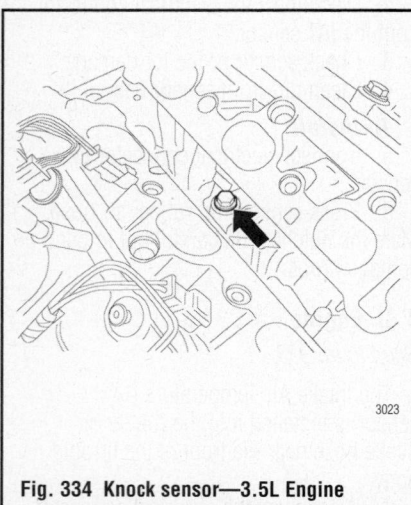

Fig. 334 Knock sensor—3.5L Engine

REMOVAL & INSTALLATION

3.5L Engine

See Figures 335 and 336.

1. Disconnect and isolate the negative battery cable.
2. Remove the upper intake manifold.
3. Disconnect the electrical connector.
4. Remove the knock sensor.

To install:

✳✳ WARNING

Over or under tightening effects knock sensor performance, possibly causing improper spark control.

5. Install the knock sensor and tighten to 15 ft. lbs. (20 Nm).

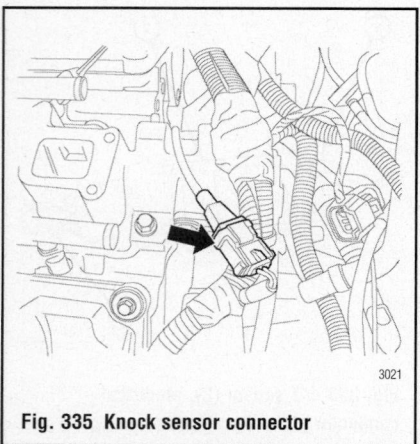

Fig. 335 Knock sensor connector

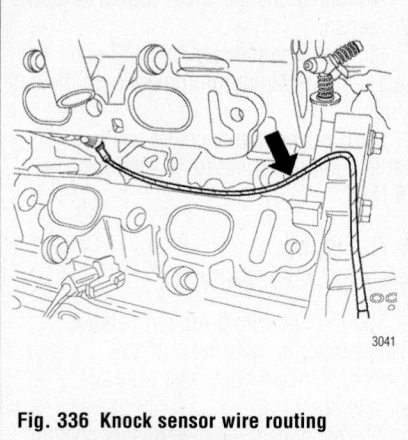

Fig. 336 Knock sensor wire routing

6. Route the knock sensor wire in the proper location.
7. Install the intake manifold,

3.6L Engine

See Figure 337.

➡**The forward sensor is known to the powertrain control module (PCM) as knock sensor 1. The rear sensor is known to the PCM as knock sensor 2.**

1. Perform the fuel pressure release procedure.
2. Disconnect and isolate the negative battery cable.
3. Drain the cooling system.
4. Remove the air cleaner housing assembly, upper and lower intake manifolds and the oil filter housing.
5. Remove the knock sensor electrical connector.

➡**There may be a foam strip on the bolt threads. This foam is used only to retain the bolts to the sensors for plant assembly. It is not used as a sealant. Do not apply any adhesive, sealant or thread locking compound to these bolts.**

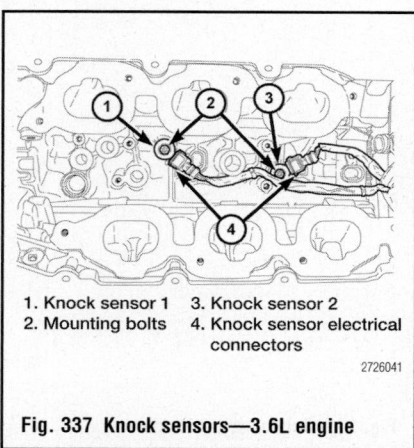

1. Knock sensor 1	3. Knock sensor 2
2. Mounting bolts	4. Knock sensor electrical connectors

Fig. 337 Knock sensors—3.6L engine

6. Remove the retaining bolt and knock sensor 1 or knock sensor 2.

To install:

7. Thoroughly clean the knock sensor mounting holes.

➡**Over or under tightening the sensor mounting bolts will affect knock sensor performance, possibly causing improper spark control. Always use the specified torque when installing the knock sensors. The torque specification for the knock sensor bolt is less than the typical 8 mm bolt.**

➡**There may be a foam strip on the bolt threads. This foam is used only to retain the bolts to the sensors for plant assembly. It is not used as a sealant. Do not apply any adhesive, sealant or thread locking compound to these bolts.**

8. Install the knock sensor 1 or knock sensor 2 and retaining bolt (2). Tighten the retaining bolt to 16 ft. lbs. (22 Nm).
9. Connect the electrical connector.
10. Install the oil filter housing, upper and lower intake manifolds and air cleaner housing assembly.
11. If removed, install the oil filter and fill the engine crankcase with the proper oil to the correct level.
12. Connect the negative battery cable and tighten nut to 45 inch lbs. (5 Nm).
13. Fill the cooling system.
14. Operate the engine until it reaches normal operating temperature. Check cooling system for correct fluid level

5.7L, 6.1L & 6.4L Engine

See Figures 338 and 339.

Two knock sensors are used. Each sensor is bolted to the outside of cylinder block below the exhaust manifold.

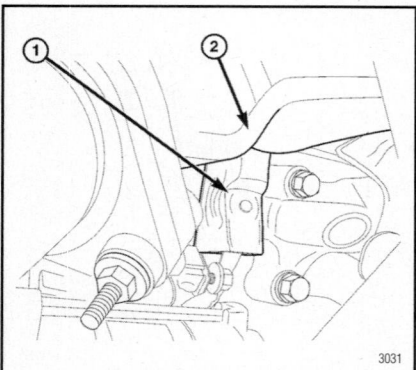

Fig. 338 Knock sensor heat shield(1)—6.1L Engine

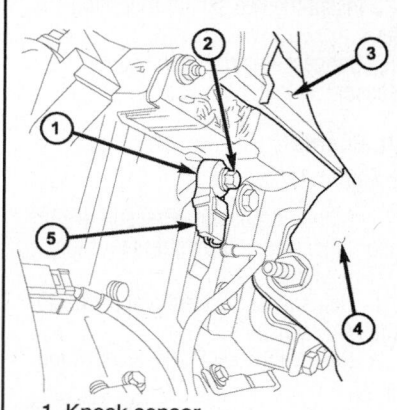

1. Knock sensor
2. Mounting bolt
3. N/A
4. N/A
5. Knock sensor electrical connector

3027

Fig. 339 Knock sensor (1), connector (5) and mounting bolt (2)—5.7L and 6.1L engine

1. Disconnect and isolate the negative battery cable.
2. Raise vehicle.
3. Remove the heat shield from knock sensor. Shield snaps to sensor.
4. Disconnect knock sensor electrical connector.
5. Remove the sensor mounting bolt. Note foam strip on bolt threads. This foam is used only to retain the bolts to sensors for plant assembly. It is not used as a sealant. Do not apply any adhesive, sealant or thread locking compound to these bolts.
6. Remove the sensor from engine.

To install:

❊❊ WARNING

Over or under tightening the knock sensor mounting bolts will affect knock sensor performance, possibly causing improper spark control.

7. Install the knock sensor onto cylinder block.

➡**The foam strip used on bolt threads is used only to retain the bolts to sensors for plant assembly. It is not used as a sealant. Do not apply any adhesive, sealant or thread locking compound to these bolts.**

8. Install the mounting bolt and tighten to 15 ft. lbs. (20 Nm).
9. Connect electrical connector to sensor.
10. Install the heat shield to sensor.
11. Connect negative battery cable and tighten nut to 45 inch lbs. (5 Nm).

MANIFOLD ABSOLUTE PRESSURE (MAP) SENSOR

LOCATION

See Figures 340 through 342.

Refer to the accompanying illustrations.

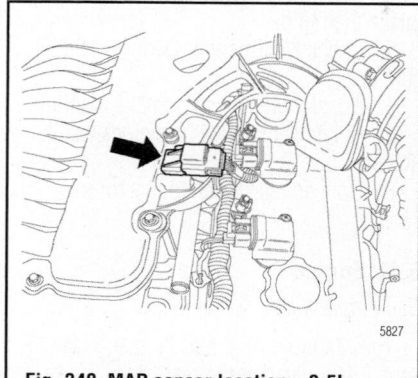

5827

Fig. 340 MAP sensor location—3.5L engine

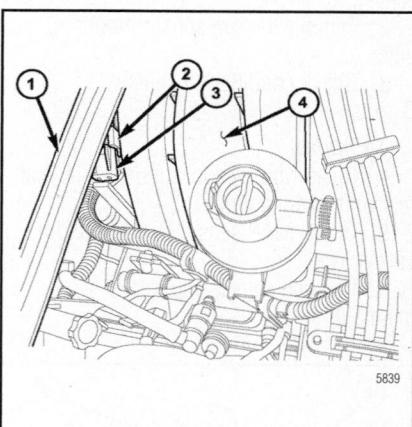

5839

Fig. 341 MAP sensor (3), cowl/hood seal (1) and intake manifold (4)—5.7L engine

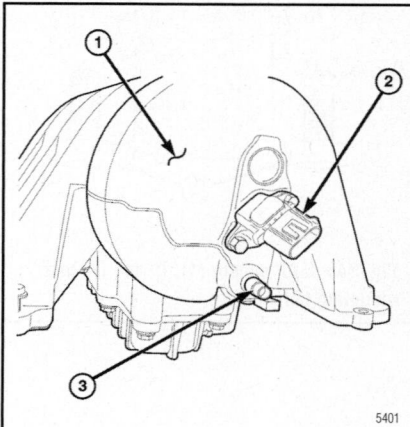

5401

Fig. 342 MAP sensor (2) and intake manifold (1)—6.1L engine

REMOVAL & INSTALLATION

3.5L Engine
See Figure 343.

1. Disconnect negative battery cable.
2. Unlock the electrical connector.
3. Disconnect the electrical connector.
4. Rotate sensor 1/4 turn clockwise.
5. Pull up on sensor.
6. Remove the sensor.

To install:

7. Clean MAP sensor mounting hole at intake manifold.
8. Check MAP sensor O-ring seal for cuts or tears.
9. Position sensor into intake manifold.
10. Rotate sensor 1/4 turn clockwise for installation.
11. Connect electrical connector to sensor.
12. Lock electrical connector.
13. Connect negative battery cable.

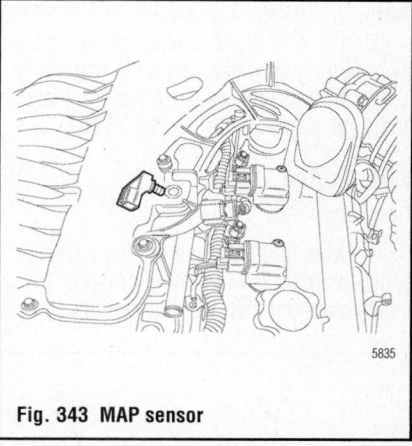

5835

Fig. 343 MAP sensor

3.6L Engine
See Figure 344.

1. Disconnect and isolate the negative battery cable.
2. Lift the engine cover retaining grommets off the ball studs and remove the engine cover.
3. Unlock and disconnect the electrical connector from the MAP sensor.
4. Rotate the MAP sensor 1/4 turn counterclockwise and pull the sensor straight up and out of the upper intake manifold.
5. The MAP sensor O-ring can be reused if not damaged.

To install:

6. The manifold air pressure (MAP) sensor O-ring can be reused if not damaged.

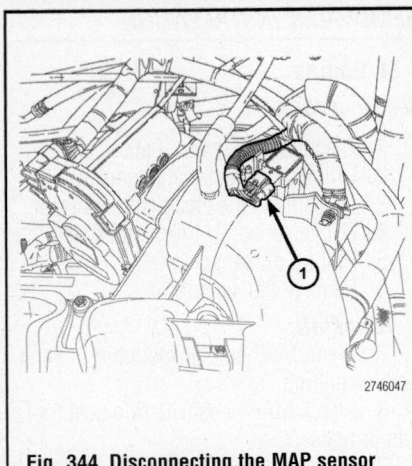

Fig. 344 Disconnecting the MAP sensor electrical connector

7. Apply a small amount of engine oil to the sensor O-ring.

8. Install the MAP sensor into the upper intake manifold and rotate 1/4 turn clockwise.

9. Connect and lock the electrical connector to the sensor.

10. Position the engine cover and secure the retaining grommets onto the ball studs.

11. Connect the negative battery cable and tighten nut to 45 inch lbs. (5 Nm).

5.7L Engine

See Figure 345.

The Manifold Absolute Pressure (MAP) sensor is mounted into the top/rear of the intake manifold near the cowl/hood seal.

1. Disconnect electrical connector at sensor by sliding release lock out (1). Press down on lock tab (2) for removal.

2. Rotate sensor 1/4 turn counter-clockwise for removal.

3. Check condition of sensor O-ring.

To install:

4. Clean MAP sensor mounting hole at intake manifold.

5. Check MAP sensor O-ring seal for cuts or tears.

6. Position sensor into intake manifold.

7. Rotate sensor 1/4 turn clockwise for installation.

8. Connect electrical connector to sensor.

6.1L Engine

See Figure 346.

The Manifold Absolute Pressure (MAP) sensor is located at the rear of the intake manifold.

1. Disconnect electrical connector at sensor.

2. Remove the two sensor mounting bolts.

3. Check condition of sensor O-ring.

To install:

4. Clean MAP sensor mounting hole at rear of intake manifold.

5. Check MAP sensor O-ring seal for cuts or tears.

6. Position sensor into intake manifold.

7. Install the two sensor mounting bolts.

8. Connect electrical connector to sensor.

6.4L Engine

See Figure 347.

The Manifold Absolute Pressure (MAP) sensor is located at the right rear of the intake manifold.

1. Disconnect the electrical connector at the MAP sensor.

2. Remove the MAP sensor retaining bolt.

3. Rotate the MAP sensor 1/4 turn counterclockwise for removal.

4. Check the condition of the MAP sensor O-ring and replace if necessary.

To install:

5. Clean the Manifold Absolute Pressure (MAP) sensor mounting hole at rear of intake manifold.

6. Check the condition of the MAP sensor O-ring seal and replace if necessary.

7. Position the MAP sensor into intake manifold.

8. Rotate the MAP sensor 1/4 turn clockwise for installation.

9. Install the MAP sensor retaining bolt and tighten to 25 inch lbs. (3 Nm).

10. Connect the electrical connector to the MAP sensor.

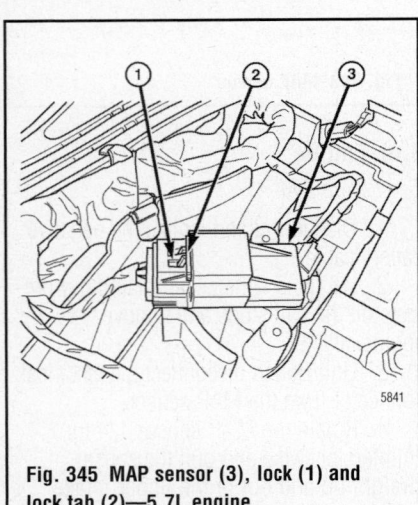

Fig. 345 MAP sensor (3), lock (1) and lock tab (2)—5.7L engine

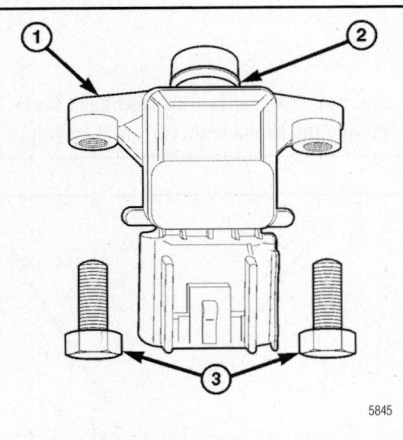

Fig. 346 MAP sensor (1), O-ring (2) and mounting bolts (3)

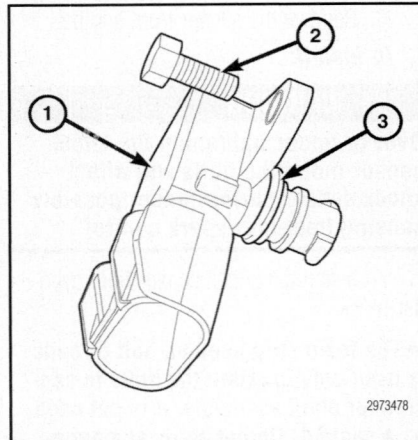

Fig. 347 Removing the MAP sensor (1) retaining bolt (2)

FUEL

FUEL SYSTEM SERVICE PRECAUTIONS

Safety is the most important factor when performing not only fuel system maintenance but any type of maintenance. Failure to conduct maintenance and repairs in a safe manner may result in serious personal injury or death. Maintenance and testing of the vehicle's fuel system components can be accomplished safely and effectively by adhering to the following rules and guidelines.

• To avoid the possibility of fire and personal injury, always disconnect the negative battery cable unless the repair or test procedure requires that battery voltage be applied.

• Always relieve the fuel system pressure prior to disconnecting any fuel system component (injector, fuel rail, pressure regulator, etc.), fitting or fuel line connection. Exercise extreme caution whenever relieving fuel system pressure to avoid exposing skin, face and eyes to fuel spray. Please be advised that fuel under pressure may penetrate the skin or any part of the body that it contacts.

• Always place a shop towel or cloth around the fitting or connection prior to loosening to absorb any excess fuel due to spillage. Ensure that all fuel spillage (should it occur) is quickly removed from engine surfaces. Ensure that all fuel soaked cloths or towels are deposited into a suitable waste container.

• Always keep a dry chemical (Class B) fire extinguisher near the work area.

• Do not allow fuel spray or fuel vapors to come into contact with a spark or open flame.

• Always use a back-up wrench when loosening and tightening fuel line connection fittings. This will prevent unnecessary stress and torsion to fuel line piping.

• Always replace worn fuel fitting O-rings with new Do not substitute fuel hose or equivalent where fuel pipe is installed.

Before servicing the vehicle, make sure to also refer to the precautions in the beginning of this section as well.

RELIEVING FUEL SYSTEM PRESSURE

✳✳ CAUTION

The fuel system is under constant high pressure even with engine off. Until the fuel pressure has been properly released from the system, do not attempt to open the fuel system. Do not smoke or use open flames/sparks when servicing the fuel system. Wear protective clothing and eye protection. Make sure the area in which the vehicle is being serviced is in a well ventilated area and free of flames/sparks. Failure to comply may result in serious or fatal injury.

1. Remove the fuel pump relay from the Power Distribution Center (PDC). A relay location label can also be found on the underside of the PDC cover.
2. Start and run the engine until it stalls.
3. Attempt restarting engine until it will no longer run.
4. Turn ignition key to the OFF position.
5. Return fuel pump relay to the Power Distribution Center (PDC).

➡**After servicing the fuel system, one or more Diagnostic Trouble Codes (DTC's) may have been stored in the Powertrain Control Module (PCM) memory due to disconnecting the fuel pump module circuit. A diagnostic scan tool must be used to erase a DTC.**

FUEL INJECTORS

REMOVAL & INSTALLATION

3.5L Engine

See Figure 348.

✳✳ CAUTION

The fuel system is under constant pressure even with engine off. Before servicing fuel injector(s), fuel system pressure must be released.

1. To remove one or more fuel injectors, the fuel rail assembly must be removed from engine.
2. Release fuel system pressure.
3. Disconnect negative cable to battery.
4. Remove the intake manifold plenum.
5. Cover intake manifold to prevent foreign material from entering engine.
6. Disconnect fuel supply tube quick connect fittings at the rear of intake manifold.
7. If the injector connectors are not tagged with their cylinder number, tag them to identify the correct cylinder
8. Remove the electrical connectors from the fuel injectors.

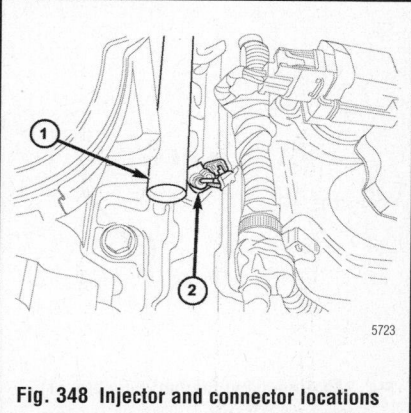

Fig. 348 Injector and connector locations

9. Remove the fuel rail mounting bolts.
10. Lift fuel rail straight up off of the cylinder head.
11. Remove the retaining clips from fuel injectors at fuel rail.
12. Remove the fuel injectors.
13. Repeat for remaining injectors.
14. Check injector O-ring for damage. If O-ring is damaged, it must be replaced. Replace the injector clip if it is damaged.

To install:

15. Lightly lubricate the fuel injector O-rings with a couple drops of clean engine oil.
16. Install the retaining clips on fuel injectors.
17. Push injectors into fuel injector rail until clips are in the correct position.
18. Position fuel rail over cylinder head, and push rail into place. Tighten fuel rail mounting bolts to 100 inch lbs. (11 Nm) torque.
19. Connect fuel supply tube quick connect fittings at the rear of intake manifold.
20. Connect electrical connectors to fuel injectors.
21. Install the intake manifold plenum.
22. Connect the negative cable to the battery.
23. Use the scan tool to pressurize the fuel system. Check for leaks

3.6L Engine

See Figures 349 and 350.

✳✳ CAUTION

The fuel system is under constant pressure even with engine off. Before servicing the fuel rail, fuel system pressure must be released.

1. Perform the fuel pressure release procedure.

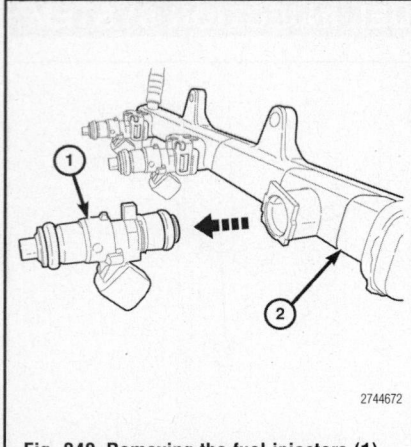

Fig. 349 Removing the fuel injectors (1) from the fuel rail (2)

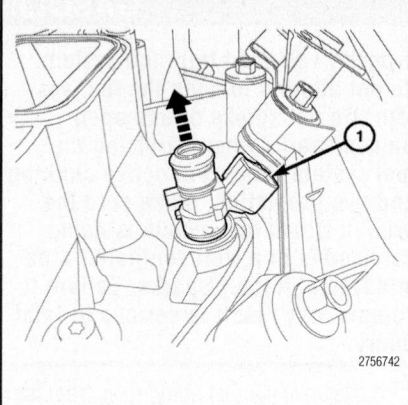

Fig. 350 Removing the fuel injectors from the lower intake manifold

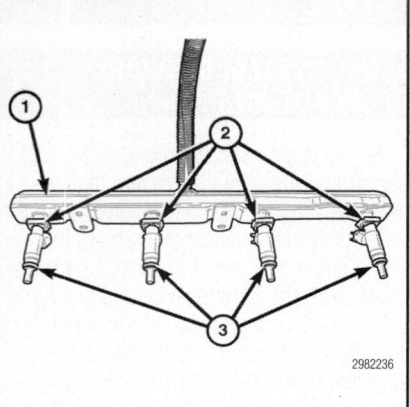

Fig. 351 Removing the fuel injectors (3), retaining clips (2) and fuel rail (1)

2. Disconnect and isolate the negative battery cable.

3. Lift the engine cover retaining grommets off the ball studs and remove the engine cover.

4. Disconnect the electrical connector from the Inlet Air Temperature (IAT) sensor.

5. Loosen the clamp at the throttle body.

6. Loosen the clamp at the air cleaner housing.

7. Lift the air inlet hose assembly retaining grommet off the ball stud.

8. Remove the air inlet hose assembly.

✳✳ WARNING

When removing the fuel rail from the lower intake manifold, one or more fuel injectors may remain in the intake manifold resulting in residual fuel spilling onto the engine from the fuel rail.

9. Remove the upper intake manifold and fuel rail.

➡**Number 2 fuel injector removal shown, all other fuel injectors similar.**

10. Remove the fuel injectors from the fuel rail.

➡**Number 2 fuel injector removal shown, all other fuel injectors similar.**

11. Remove the fuel injectors (1) from the lower intake manifold.

12. Remove the and discard all fuel injector O-ring seals.

To install:

13. Lightly lubricate the new O-ring seals with clean engine oil and position the seals onto the fuel injector.

14. Install the fuel injectors into the fuel rail.

15. Install the fuel rail and upper intake manifold.

16. Position the air inlet hose assembly onto the throttle body and the air cleaner housing.

17. Secure the air inlet hose assembly retaining grommet onto the ball stud.

18. Tighten the clamp at the air cleaner housing to 44 inch lbs. (5 Nm).

19. Tighten the clamp at the throttle body to 44 inch lbs. (5 Nm).

20. Connect the Inlet Air Temperature (IAT) sensor electrical connector.

21. Lift the engine cover retaining grommets off the ball studs and remove the engine cover.

22. Connect the negative battery cable and tighten nut to 45 inch lbs. (5 Nm).

23. Start the engine and check for leaks.

5.7L & 6.4L Engines
See Figure 351.

✳✳ CAUTION

The fuel system is under constant pressure even with engine off. Before servicing fuel injector(s), fuel system pressure must be released.

➡**To remove one or more fuel injectors, the fuel rail assembly must be removed from engine.**

1. Perform the fuel system pressure release procedure.

2. Remove the fuel rail assembly.

3. Remove the fuel injector retaining clip(s) from the fuel rail.

4. Remove the injector(s) from the fuel rail assembly.

To install:

➡**The fuel injector O-rings may be used again, provided no cuts, tears, or deformation have occurred.**

5. Inspect the fuel injector O-rings and replace if necessary.

6. Apply a small amount of engine oil to each fuel injector O-rings.

7. Install the fuel injector(s) into the fuel rail and install the retaining clip(s).

8. Install the fuel rail assembly.

9. Start the engine and check for leaks.

6.1L Engine
See Figure 352.

✳✳ CAUTION

The fuel system is under constant pressure even with engine off. Before servicing fuel injector(s), fuel system pressure must be released.

➡**To remove one or more fuel injectors, the fuel rail assembly must be removed from engine.**

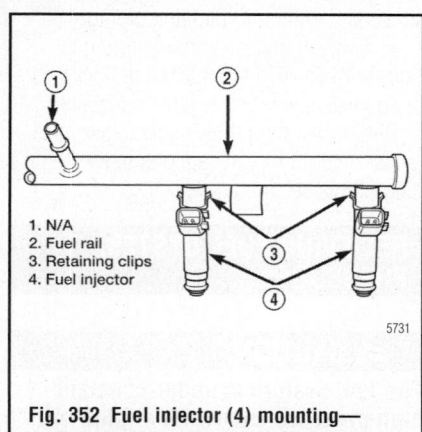

1. N/A
2. Fuel rail
3. Retaining clips
4. Fuel injector

Fig. 352 Fuel injector (4) mounting—typical, fuel rail (2), retaining clips (3)

1. Perform the fuel system pressure release procedure.

2. Remove the fuel rail assembly.

3. Remove the fuel injector retaining clip(s) from the fuel rail.

4. Remove the injector(s) from the fuel rail assembly.

To install:

5. Apply a small amount of engine oil to each fuel injector O-ring. This will help with the fuel rail installation.

6. Install the fuel injector(s) into the fuel rail and install the retainer clip(s).

7. Install the fuel rail assembly.

8. Start the engine and check for leaks.

FUEL PUMP

REMOVAL & INSTALLATION

See Figures 353 through 358.

✳✳ CAUTION

The fuel system is under constant high pressure even with engine off. Until the fuel pressure has been properly released from the system, do not attempt to open the fuel system. Do not smoke or use open flames/sparks when servicing the fuel system. Wear protective clothing and eye protection. Make sure the area in which the vehicle is being serviced is in a well ventilated area and free of flames/sparks. Failure to comply may result in serious or fatal injury.

✳✳ CAUTION

No sparks, open flames or smoking. Risk of poisoning from inhaling and swallowing fuel. Pour fuel only into appropriately marked OSHA approved containers. Wear protective clothing. Risk of injury to eyes and skin from contact with fuel.

✳✳ WARNING

If the electric fuel pump module is not operating or the fuel level sending unit is not operating and the fuel level cannot be determined, the fuel tank must be removed prior to draining. If the fuel level is above 5/8 of a tank and the fuel pump module lockring is removed, fuel will spill into the interior of the vehicle.

1. Verify the fuel level is below 5/8 of a tank.

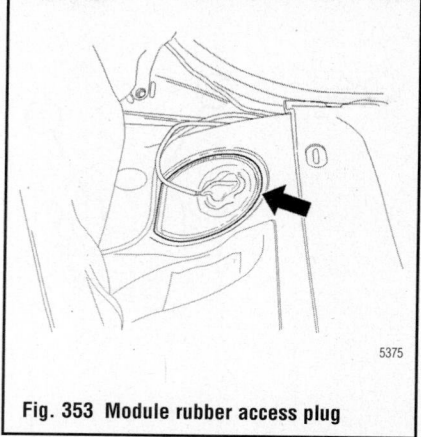

Fig. 353 Module rubber access plug

2. Perform the fuel pressure release procedure.

3. If required, perform the draining fuel tank procedure.

4. Disconnect the negative battery cable.

5. Push the rear lower seat cushion up and back and remove the seat cushion.

6. Fold back the foam pad covering the fuel pump module plastic access covers.

7. Remove the left side main fuel pump module plastic access cover.

8. Disconnect the electrical connector from the main fuel pump module.

✳✳ WARNING

An indexing arrow is located on top of the fuel pump module to clock it's position into the fuel tank, note its location for reassembly.

➡**Prior to removing the fuel pump module, use compressed air to remove any accumulated dirt and debris from around fuel tank opening.**

9. Mark the main fuel pump module orientation.

10. Position the SAE Fuel Pump Lock

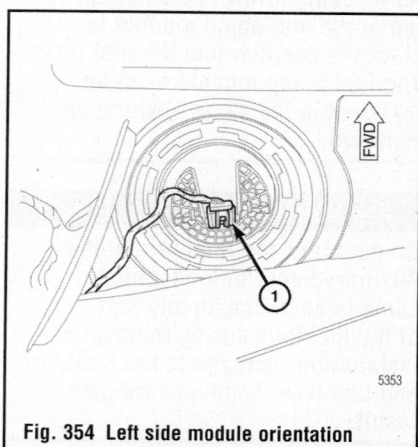

Fig. 354 Left side module orientation

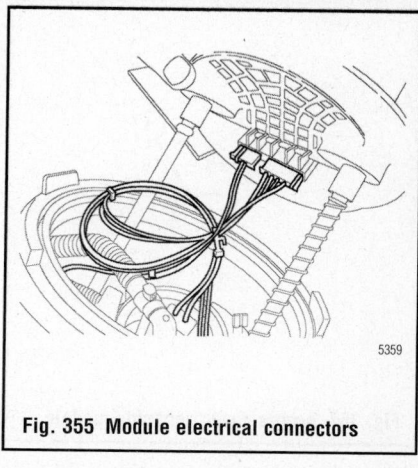

Fig. 355 Module electrical connectors

Ring Wrench into the notches on the outside edge of the lock ring.

11. Install the a 1/2 inch drive breaker bar into the SAE Fuel Pump Lock Ring Wrench.

➡**The main fuel pump module will spring up slightly when the lock ring is removed.**

12. Rotate the breaker bar counterclockwise and remove the lock ring.

✳✳ WARNING

Do not allow the float arm of the Main Fuel Pump Module to come in contact with any part of the fuel tank during removal or installation, damage to the float arm and fuel level sending card may result.

13. Raise and separate the top section from the bottom section of the main fuel pump module.

14. Disconnect the electrical connectors from under the top section of the main fuel pump module.

15. Remove the top section of the main fuel pump module from the vehicle.

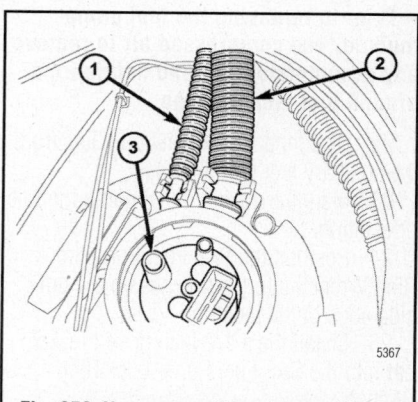

Fig. 356 Hose connections drivers side (1, 2)

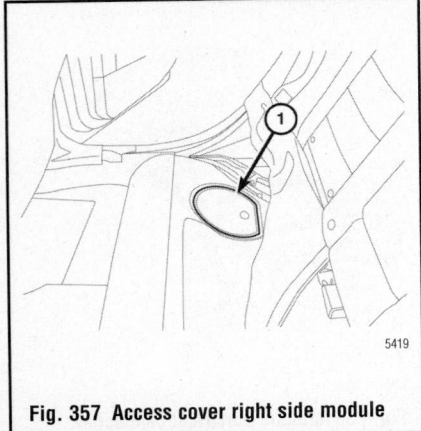

Fig. 357 Access cover right side module

16. Press the quick connect release tab and remove the fuel supply line from the main fuel pump module.

17. Disconnect the fuel return lines from the main fuel pump module.

➡**Do not spill fuel into the interior of the vehicle.**

18. Carefully lift the bottom section of the main fuel pump module out of the fuel tank, tip the bottom section on its side and drain the remaining fuel from the bottom reservoir into the fuel tank and remove from vehicle.

➡**Whenever a fuel pump module is serviced, the rubber O-ring seal must be replaced.**

19. Remove the and discard the rubber O-ring seal.

Auxiliary Fuel Pump Module

➡**The Main Fuel Pump Module must be removed for Auxiliary Fuel Pump Module removal.**

20. Remove the main fuel pump module.

21. Remove the auxiliary fuel pump module plastic access cover from the floor pan.

➡**Prior to removing the fuel pump module, use compressed air to remove any accumulated dirt and debris from around fuel tank opening.**

22. Disconnect the fuel supply line from the auxiliary fuel pump module.

23. Mark the auxiliary fuel pump module orientation.

24. Position the SAE Fuel Pump Lock Ring Wrench into the notches on the outside edge of the lock ring.

25. Install the a 1/2 inch drive breaker bar into the SAE Fuel Pump Lock Ring Wrench.

26. Rotate the breaker bar counterclockwise and remove the lock ring.

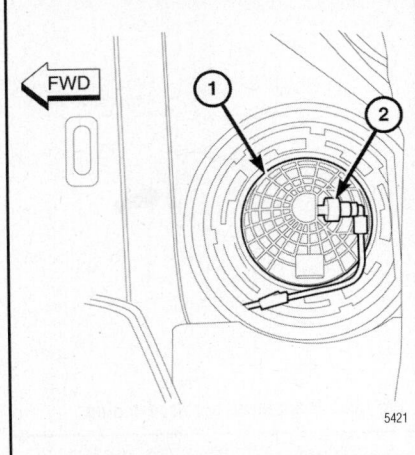

Fig. 358 Right side module orientation (1) and fuel supply line (2)

> ❋❋ **WARNING**
>
> **Do not allow the float arm of the Auxiliary Fuel Pump Module to come in contact with any part of the fuel tank during removal or installation, damage to the float arm and fuel level sending card may result.**

27. Lift the auxiliary fuel pump module up and out of fuel tank while guiding the fuel supply and return lines out from the left side of the fuel tank.

➡**Whenever a fuel pump module is serviced, the rubber O-ring seal must be replaced.**

28. Remove the and discard the rubber O-ring seal.

To install:

➡**The Auxiliary Fuel Pump Module must be installed before the Main Fuel Pump Module.**

> ❋❋ **WARNING**
>
> **An indexing arrow is located on top of the fuel pump module to clock it's position into the fuel tank. The fuel pump module must be installed in the same position as removed.**

> ❋❋ **WARNING**
>
> **Do not allow the float arm of the Auxiliary Fuel Pump Module to come in contact with any part of the fuel tank during removal or installation, damage to the float arm and fuel level sending card may result.**

➡**Whenever the fuel pump module is serviced, the rubber O-ring seal must be replaced.**

29. Install the a new rubber O-ring seal.

30. Using caution not to bend the float arm, lower the auxiliary fuel pump module into the fuel tank while guiding the fuel return lines, fuel supply line and electrical connector over to the left side of the fuel tank.

31. Align the rubber O-ring seal and lower the auxiliary fuel pump module into position as noted during removal.

32. Position the lock ring over top of the auxiliary fuel pump module.

33. Verify the auxiliary fuel pump module is in the same position as noted during removal. This step must be performed to prevent the float from contacting the side of the fuel tank.

34. Position the SAE Fuel Pump Lock Ring Wrench into the notches on the outside edge of the lock ring.

35. Install the a 1/2 inch drive breaker bar into the SAE Fuel Pump Lock Ring Wrench.

36. Rotate the breaker bar clockwise until all seven notches of the lock ring have engaged.

37. Connect the fuel supply line to auxiliary fuel pump module.

38. Install the auxiliary fuel pump module plastic access cover.

39. Install the main fuel pump module.

➡**Whenever the fuel pump module is serviced, the rubber O-ring seal must be replaced.**

40. Install the a new rubber O-ring seal.

41. Using caution not to bend the float arm, lower the bottom section of the main fuel pump module into the fuel tank.

42. Connect the fuel return lines (1,2) to the main fuel pump module.

43. Connect the fuel supply line (1) to the main fuel pump module.

44. Connect the electrical connectors at the top section of the main fuel pump module.

45. Join the upper section and lower section of the main fuel pump module together.

46. Position the main fuel pump module as noted during removal.

> ❋❋ **WARNING**
>
> **Verify the electrical wires are tucked away into the fuel tank so they don't**

get pinched between the top of the
fuel pump module and the rubber
O-ring seal.

✳✳ WARNING

An indexing arrow is located on top
of the fuel pump module to clock it's
position into the fuel tank. The fuel
pump module must be installed in
the same position as removed.

47. Align the rubber O-ring seal and
lower the main fuel pump module into position.

48. Verify the main fuel pump module is
in the same position as noted during
removal. This step must be performed to
prevent the float from contacting the side of
the fuel tank.

49. Position the lock ring over top of the
main fuel pump module.

50. Position the SAE Fuel Pump Lock
Ring Wrench into the notches on the outside edge of the lock ring.

51. Install the a 1/2 inch drive breaker
bar into the SAE Fuel Pump Lock Ring
Wrench.

52. Rotate the breaker bar clockwise
until all seven notches of the lock ring have
engaged.

53. Connect the electrical connector to
the main fuel pump module.

54. Fill the fuel tank and check for leaks
around the rubber O-ring seal.

55. Install the main fuel pump module
plastic access cover.

56. Lower the foam pad covering back
into place.

57. Push the rear lower seat cushion
back and down and install the seat
cushion.

58. Connect the negative battery
cable.

✳✳ WARNING

An indexing arrow is located on top
of the fuel pump module to clock it's
position into the fuel tank. The fuel
pump module must be installed in
the same position as removed.

✳✳ WARNING

Do not allow the float arm of the
Auxiliary Fuel Pump Module to
come in contact with any part of
the fuel tank during removal or
installation, damage to the float
arm and fuel level sending card may
result.

FUEL TANK

DRAINING

Conventional Procedure

✳✳ CAUTION

The fuel system is under constant
high pressure even with engine off.
Until the fuel pressure has been
properly released from the system,
do not attempt to open the fuel system. Do not smoke or use open
flames/sparks when servicing the
fuel system. Wear protective clothing
and eye protection. Make sure the
area in which the vehicle is being
serviced is in a well ventilated area
and free of flames/sparks. Failure to
comply may result in serious or fatal
injury.

✳✳ CAUTION

No sparks, open flames or smoking.
Risk of poisoning from inhaling and
swallowing fuel. Pour fuel only into
appropriately marked OSHA approved
containers. Wear protective clothing.
Risk of injury to eyes and skin from
contact with fuel.

✳✳ WARNING

If the electric fuel pump is not operating, and the fuel level is above 5/8
of a tank, the fuel tank must be
removed prior to draining. If the fuel
level is above 5/8 of a tank and the
fuel pump module lock-ring is
removed, fuel will spill into the interior of the vehicle.

✳✳ WARNING

If the fuel level sending unit is not
operating, and the fuel level cannot
be determined the fuel tank must be
removed prior to draining. If the fuel
level is above 5/8 of a tank and the
fuel pump module lock-ring is
removed, fuel will spill into the interior of the vehicle.

1. Perform the fuel system pressure
release procedure.

➥Due to a one-way check valve
installed into the fuel fill fitting at the
tank, the tank cannot be drained at the
fuel filler tube.

2. Attach one end of Adapter included

with the Fuel Decay Tool to the fuel supply
line quick-connect fitting.

3. Attach the opposite end of Adapter to
the Fuel Chief Gas Caddy 320-FC-P30-A or
an OSHA approved gas caddy.

➥Due to a built in time out feature of
the diagnostic scan tool, the fuel pump
may need to be reactivated several
times before the fuel tank evacuation is
complete.

4. Using a diagnostic scan tool, activate
the fuel pump until the fuel tank has been
evacuated.

Alternative Procedure

✳✳ CAUTION

The fuel system is under constant
high pressure even with engine off.
Until the fuel pressure has been properly released from the system, do not
attempt to open the fuel system. Do
not smoke or use open flames/sparks
when servicing the fuel system. Wear
protective clothing and eye protection. Make sure the area in which the
vehicle is being serviced is in a well
ventilated area and free of
flames/sparks. Failure to comply may
result in serious or fatal injury.

✳✳ CAUTION

No sparks, open flames or smoking.
Risk of poisoning from inhaling and
swallowing fuel. Pour fuel only into
appropriately marked OSHA approved
containers. Wear protective clothing.
Risk of injury to eyes and skin from
contact with fuel.

✳✳ WARNING

The fuel level of the vehicle must be
below 5/8 of a tank before using the
"Alternative Procedure". If the fuel
level is above 5/8 of a tank and the
fuel pump module lock-ring is
removed, fuel will spill into the
interior of the vehicle.

✳✳ WARNING

If the electric fuel pump is not operating, and the fuel level is above 5/8
of a tank, the fuel tank must be
removed prior to draining. If the fuel
level is above 5/8 of a tank and the
fuel pump module lock-ring is
removed, fuel will spill into the interior of the vehicle.

✳✳ WARNING

If the fuel level sending unit is not operating, and the fuel level cannot be determined the fuel tank must be removed prior to draining. If the fuel level is above 5/8 of a tank and the fuel pump module lock-ring is removed, fuel will spill into the interior of the vehicle.

1. Verify the fuel level is below 5/8 of a tank.

2. Perform the fuel system pressure release procedure.

3. Disconnect the negative battery cable.

4. Push the rear lower seat cushion up and back and remove the seat cushion.

5. Fold back the foam pad covering the fuel pump module plastic access covers.

6. Remove the left side fuel pump module plastic access cover.

7. Disconnect the electrical connector from the fuel pump module.

✳✳ WARNING

An indexing arrow is located on top of the fuel pump module to clock it's position into the fuel tank, note its location for reassembly.

➡ **Prior to removing the fuel pump module, use compressed air to remove any accumulated dirt and debris from around fuel tank opening.**

8. Mark the fuel pump module orientation.

9. Position the SAE Fuel Pump Lock Ring Wrench into the notches on the outside edge of the lock ring.

10. Install the a 1/2 inch drive breaker bar into the SAE Fuel Pump Lock Ring Wrench.

11. Rotate the breaker bar counterclockwise and remove the lock ring.

✳✳ WARNING

Do not spill fuel into the interior of the vehicle.

✳✳ WARNING

The lower reservoir of the fuel pump module must be drained before removal or fuel can spill into the interior of the vehicle.

12. Lift the fuel pump module up enough to push a 3/8 inch hose into the fuel tank.

13. Attach the opposite end of the hose to the Fuel Chief Gas Caddy 320-FC-P30-A or an OSHA approved gas caddy.

14. Using the Fuel Chief Gas Caddy 320-FC-P30-A or an OSHA approved gas caddy, evacuate the left side of the fuel tank.

15. Remove the right side auxiliary fuel pump module plastic access cover.

16. Disconnect the fuel supply line at the auxiliary fuel pump module.

✳✳ WARNING

An indexing arrow is located on top of the fuel pump module to clock it's position into the fuel tank, note its location for reassembly.

➡ **Prior to removing the auxiliary fuel pump module, use compressed air to remove any accumulated dirt and debris from around fuel tank opening.**

17. Mark the auxiliary fuel pump module orientation.

18. Position the SAE Fuel Pump Lock Ring Wrench into the notches on the outside edge of the lock ring.

19. Install the a 1/2 inch drive breaker bar into the SAE Fuel Pump Lock Ring Wrench.

20. Rotate the breaker bar counterclockwise and remove the lock ring.

21. Lift the auxiliary fuel pump module up enough to push a 3/8 inch hose into the fuel tank.

22. Attach the opposite end of the hose to the Fuel Chief Gas Caddy 320-FC-P30-A or an OSHA approved gas caddy.

23. Using the Fuel Chief Gas Caddy 320-FC-P30-A or an OSHA approved gas caddy, evacuate the right side of the fuel tank.

REMOVAL & INSTALLATION
See Figures 359 through 365.

✳✳ CAUTION

The fuel system is under constant high pressure even with engine off. Until the fuel pressure has been properly released from the system, do not attempt to open the fuel system. Do not smoke or use open flames/sparks when servicing the fuel system. Wear protective clothing and eye protection. Make sure the area in which the vehicle is being serviced is in a well ventilated area and free of flames/sparks. Failure to comply may result in serious or fatal injury.

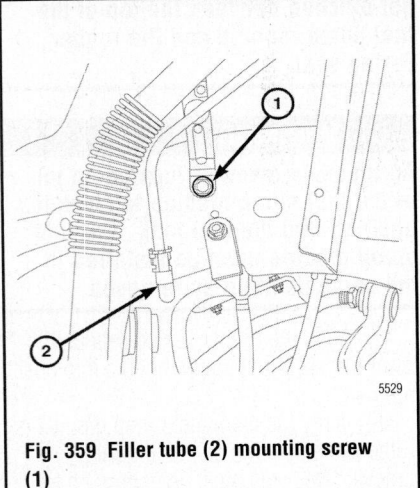

Fig. 359 Filler tube (2) mounting screw (1)

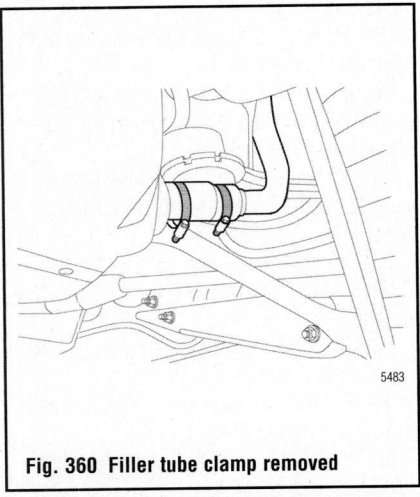

Fig. 360 Filler tube clamp removed

✳✳ CAUTION

No sparks, open flames or smoking. Risk of poisoning from inhaling and swallowing fuel. Pour fuel only into appropriately marked OSHA approved containers. Wear protective clothing. Risk of injury to eyes and skin from contact with fuel.

1. Perform the fuel pressure release procedure.

2. Perform the draining fuel tank procedure.

3. Disconnect the negative battery cable.

4. Raise and support the vehicle.

5. Remove the left rear tire.

6. Remove the push-pins that secure the rear wheelhouse shield to the body.

7. Remove the left rear wheelhouse splash shield.

8. Disconnect the fuel filler tube ORVR vent line.

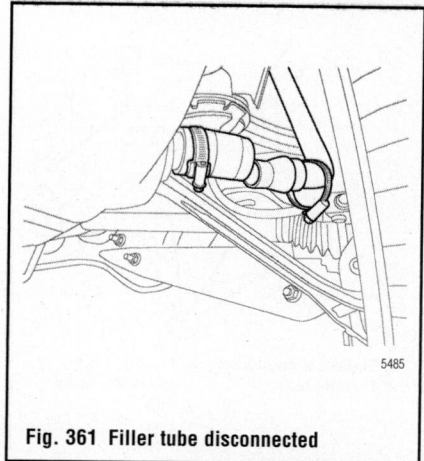

Fig. 361 Filler tube disconnected

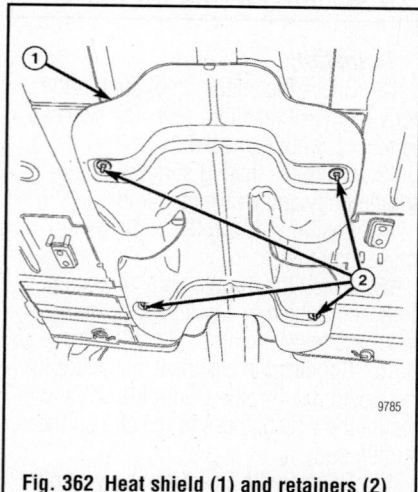

Fig. 362 Heat shield (1) and retainers (2)

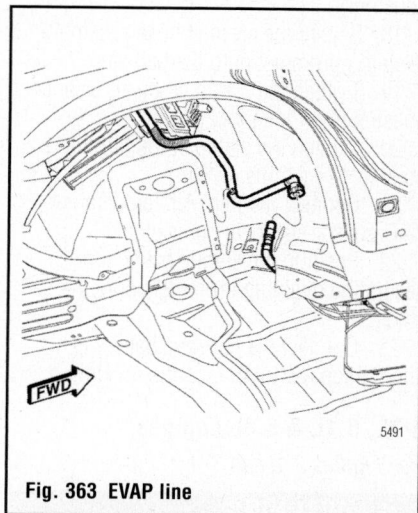

Fig. 363 EVAP line

9. Remove the fuel filler tube retaining bolt.

10. Remove the under body splash shield.

11. Remove the hose clamp from the fuel filler tube.

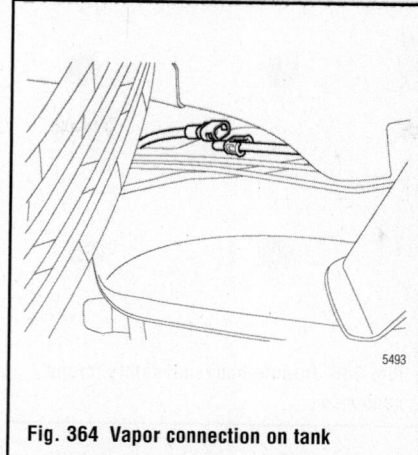

Fig. 364 Vapor connection on tank

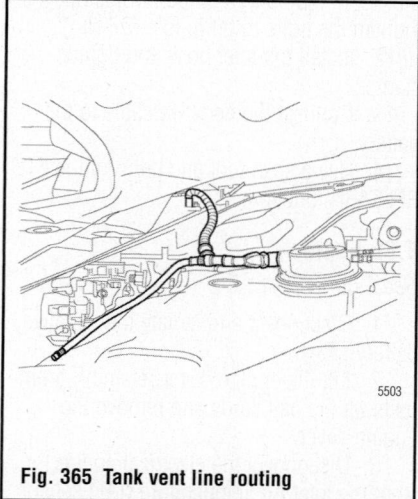

Fig. 365 Tank vent line routing

12. Remove the fuel filler tube from the rubber hose on the fuel tank and position aside.

13. Remove the muffler and tailpipe assembly.

14. Remove the propeller shaft.

15. Remove the heat shield retainers and remove the heat shield.

16. Remove the right underbody splash shield.

17. Disconnect the EVAP line in the right rear wheel well.

18. Disconnect the vapor line.

19. Disconnect the fuel supply line.

20. Using a suitable hydraulic jack with a fuel tank adapter, support the fuel tank.

21. Remove the fuel tank support strap retaining bolts.

22. Remove the fuel tank support straps.

23. Carefully lower the fuel tank and pull the ORVR vent line through bracket.

24. Lower and remove the fuel tank from the vehicle.

To install:

> ❊❊❊ **CAUTION**
>
> **No sparks, open flames or smoking. Risk of poisoning from inhaling and swallowing fuel. Pour fuel only into appropriately marked OSHA approved containers. Wear protective clothing. Risk of injury to eyes and skin from contact with fuel.**

25. If removed, install the fuel pump modules.

26. Using a suitable hydraulic jack with a fuel tank adapter, support the fuel tank.

27. Carefully raise the fuel tank into position while guiding the ORVR vent line through bracket.

28. Position the fuel tank support straps.

29. Install the fuel tank support strap retaining bolts and tighten to 20 ft. lbs. (27 Nm).

30. Connect the fuel supply line.

31. Connect the vapor line.

32. Connect the EVAP line in the right rear wheel well.

33. Position the heat shield and install the heat shield retainers.

34. Install the propeller shaft.

35. Install the muffler and tailpipe assembly.

36. Connect the fuel filler tube to the rubber hose on the fuel tank.

37. Install the hose clamp to the rubber hose connecting the fuel filler tube to the fuel tank and tighten the clamp to 35 inch lbs. (4 Nm).

38. Connect the ORVR vent line.

39. Install the fuel filler tube retaining bolt and tighten to 62 inch lbs. (7 Nm).

40. Position the left rear wheelhouse splash shield.

41. Install the push-pins that secure the rear wheelhouse shield to the body.

42. Install the left rear tire.

43. Install the left underbody splash shield.

44. Install the right underbody splash shield.

45. Lower the vehicle.

46. Fill the fuel tank.

47. Connect the negative battery cable.

48. Use the scan tool to pressurize the fuel system and check for leaks.

THROTTLE BODY

REMOVAL & INSTALLATION

3.5L Engine

See Figures 366 through 368.

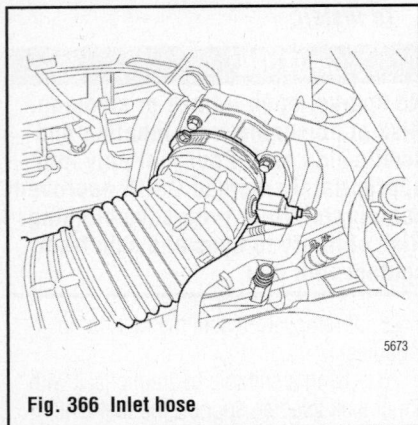

Fig. 366 Inlet hose

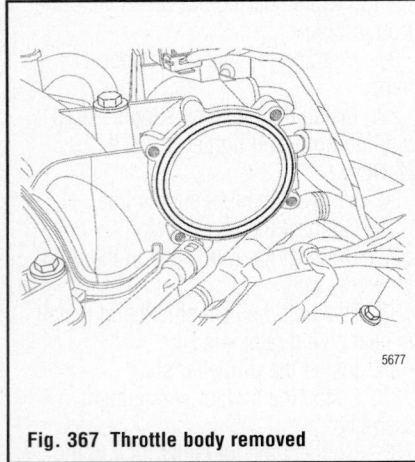

Fig. 367 Throttle body removed

1. Disconnect the negative cable from the battery
2. Remove the inlet hose from throttle body.
3. Disconnect electrical connectors.
4. Disconnect vacuum hose.
5. Remove the throttle body support bracket.
6. Remove the throttle body bolts.
7. Clean mating surfaces.

To install:

✳✳ WARNING

Do not apply silicone lubricants to any part of the throttle body.

8. Install the throttle gasket.
9. Install the throttle body and bolts.

✳✳ WARNING

The throttle body must be torqued in a mandatory torque sequence. Tighten in a criss - cross pattern to specification.

10. Tighten the bolts in a mandatory torque criss - cross pattern sequence to 50 inch lbs. (5.5 Nm).

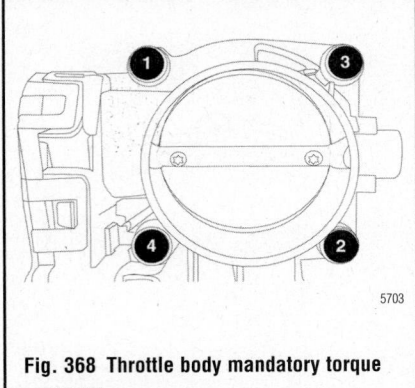

Fig. 368 Throttle body mandatory torque sequence

11. Install the throttle body support bracket to the bottom of the throttle body. Tighten the bolts to 20 ft. lbs. (27 Nm).
12. Install the inlet hose and tighten clamp.
13. Connect the negative cable to the battery.
14. Use a scan tool and perform the ETC RELEARN function.

3.6L Engine

See Figure 369.

1. Disconnect and isolate the negative battery cable.
2. Lift the engine cover retaining grommets off the ball studs and remove the engine cover.
3. Disconnect the electrical connector from the Inlet Air Temperature (IAT) sensor.
4. Loosen the clamp at the throttle body.
5. Loosen the clamp at the air cleaner housing.
6. Lift the air inlet hose assembly retaining grommet off the ball stud.
7. Remove the air inlet hose assembly.

✳✳ WARNING

Never have the ignition key in the ON position when checking the throttle body shaft for a binding condition. This may set DTC's.

8. Disconnect the electrical connector from the Electronic Throttle Control (ETC) and unfasten the ETC harness from the clip on the throttle body.
9. Remove the four throttle body mounting bolts.
10. Remove the throttle body from the upper intake manifold.
11. Check the condition of the throttle body-to-intake manifold seal. The seal can be reused if not damaged.

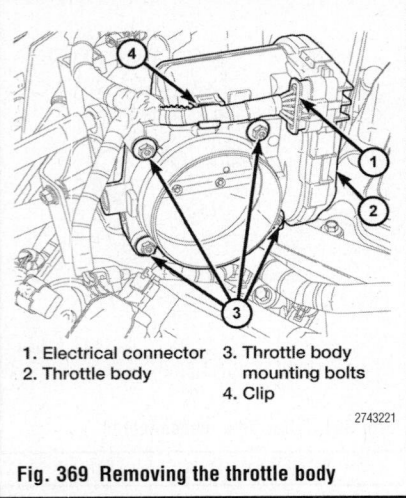

1. Electrical connector
2. Throttle body
3. Throttle body mounting bolts
4. Clip

Fig. 369 Removing the throttle body

To install:

12. Check the condition of the throttle body-to-intake manifold seal. The seal can be reused if not damaged.
13. Clean the mating surfaces of the throttle body and intake manifold.
14. Position the throttle body to the intake manifold.
15. Install the throttle body mounting bolts and tighten in a crisscross pattern sequence to 62 inch lbs. (7 Nm).
16. Connect the electrical connector to the Electronic Throttle Control (ETC) and secure the ETC harness to the clip on the throttle body.
17. Position the air inlet hose assembly onto the throttle body and the air cleaner housing.
18. Secure the air inlet hose assembly retaining grommet onto the ball stud.
19. Tighten the clamp at the air cleaner housing to 44 inch lbs. (5 Nm).
20. Tighten the clamp at the throttle body to 44 inch lbs. (5 Nm).
21. Connect the Inlet Air Temperature (IAT) sensor electrical connector.
22. Position the engine cover and secure the retaining grommets onto the ball studs.
23. Connect the negative battery cable and tighten nut to 45 inch lbs. (5 Nm).

5.7L, 6.1L & 6.4L Engines

See Figures 370 and 371.

✳✳ WARNING

Do not use spray (crab) cleaners on any part of the throttle body. Do not apply silicone lubricants to any part of the throttle body.

1. Remove the rubber air duct at front of throttle body.

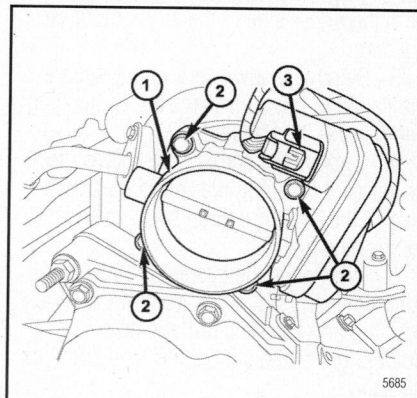

Fig. 370 Throttle body (1), mounting bolts (2) and electrical connector (3)

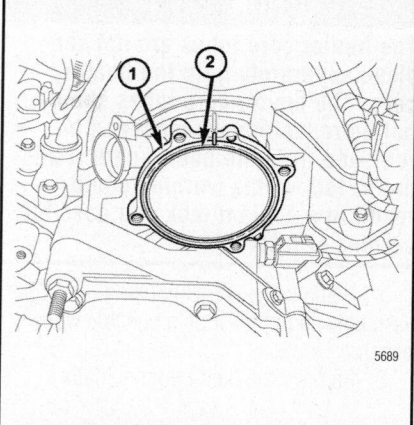

Fig. 371 Throttle body O-ring (2), intake manifold (1)

2. Disconnect electrical connector at throttle body.

3. Remove the four throttle body mounting bolts.

4. Remove the throttle body from intake manifold.

5. Check condition of throttle body O-ring at front of intake manifold.

To install:

6. Clean and check condition of throttle body-to-intake manifold O-ring.

7. Clean mating surfaces of throttle body and intake manifold.

✳✳ WARNING

Do not use spray (carb) cleaners on any part of the throttle body. Do not apply silicone lubricants to any part of the throttle body.

8. Install the throttle body to intake manifold by positioning throttle body to manifold alignment pins.

9. Install and tighten the four mounting bolts.

10. Install the electrical connector.

11. Install the rubber air hose to throttle body.

12. A Scan Tool may be used to learn electrical parameters. Go to the Miscellaneous menu, and then select ETC Relearn. If the relearn is not preformed, a Diagnostic Trouble Code (DTC) will be set. If necessary, use a scan tool to erase any Diagnostic Trouble Codes (DTC's) from PCM.

HEATING & AIR CONDITIONING SYSTEM

BLOWER MOTOR

REMOVAL & INSTALLATION
See Figure 372.

✳✳ CAUTION

Disable the airbag system before attempting any steering wheel, steering column, or instrument panel component diagnosis or service. Disconnect and isolate the negative battery (ground) cable, then wait two minutes for the airbag system capacitor to discharge before performing further diagnosis or service. This is the only sure way to disable the airbag system. Failure to take the proper precautions could result in accidental airbag deployment and possible serious or fatal injury.

1. Disconnect and isolate the negative battery cable.

2. Remove the instrument panel silencer from the passenger side of the instrument panel.

3. Disengage the wire harness connector locking tab and disconnect the wire harness connector from the blower motor.

4. Disengage the wire harness from the two wire harness retainers.

5. Remove the three screws that secure the blower motor to the HVAC housing.

6. Remove the blower motor from the HVAC housing.

To install:

7. Position the blower motor into the HVAC housing.

8. Install the three screws that secure the blower motor to the HVAC housing. Tighten the screws to 20 inch lbs. (2.2 Nm).

9. Connect the wire harness connector to the blower motor and engage the wire harness connector locking tab.

10. Engage the HVAC wire harness onto the two wire harness retainers.

11. Install the instrument panel silencer onto the passenger side of the instrument panel.

12. Reconnect the negative battery cable.

HEATER CORE

REMOVAL & INSTALLATION
See Figure 373.

✳✳ CAUTION

Disable the airbag system before attempting any steering wheel, steering column or instrument panel component diagnosis or service. Disconnect and isolate the negative battery (ground) cable and wait two minutes for the airbag system capacitor to discharge before performing further diagnosis or service. This is the only sure way to disable the airbag system. Failure to follow these instructions may result in accidental airbag deployment and possible serious or fatal injury.

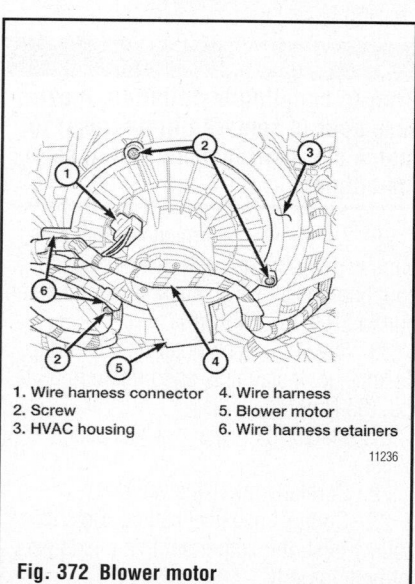

1. Wire harness connector
2. Screw
3. HVAC housing
4. Wire harness
5. Blower motor
6. Wire harness retainers

Fig. 372 Blower motor

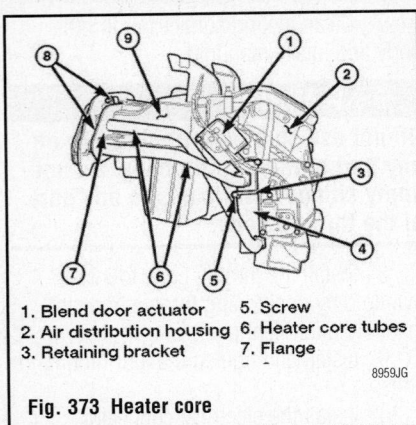

1. Blend door actuator
2. Air distribution housing
3. Retaining bracket
5. Screw
6. Heater core tubes
7. Flange

Fig. 373 Heater core

8959JG

✳✳ CAUTION

The heater core tubes are not serviced separately from the heater core. The heater core tubes should not be repositioned, loosened or removed from the heater core. Failure to follow this warning could result in a coolant leak and possible serious or fatal injury.

1. Remove the HVAC housing assembly and place it on a suitable workbench.
2. Remove the blend door actuator

from the driver side of the air distribution housing.

3. Remove the two screws that secure the flange to the front of the HVAC housing and remove the flange.
4. Remove the screw that secures the heater core retaining bracket to the driver side of the air distribution housing and remove the bracket.
5. Disengage the heater core tubes from the foam seal at the front of the HVAC housing and carefully pull the heater core straight out of the side of the air distribution housing.

STEERING

POWER STEERING GEAR

REMOVAL & INSTALLATION

See Figures 374 and 375.

1. Disconnect and isolate negative battery cable from battery post.
2. Siphon power steering fluid from pump reservoir.
3. Raise and safely support the vehicle.
4. Remove the wheel mounting nuts, then both front tire and wheel assemblies.

✳✳ WARNING

When loosening jam nut and rotating inner tie rod, use care not to twist bellows at inner tie rod. Remove clamp at inner tie rod and make sure bellows moves freely before rotating inner tie rod.

5. Loosen tie rod jam nut at each outer tie rod.

6. Remove the outer tie rod nut at each knuckle.
7. Using Remover, separate outer tie rod from each knuckle.
8. Remove the lower intermediate shaft steering coupling pinch bolt at steering gear shaft. Separate lower intermediate shaft from steering gear.
9. Unthread pressure hose tube nut from steering gear. Remove pressure hose from steering gear.
10. Unthread return hose tube nut from steering gear. Remove return hose from steering gear.
11. Remove the steering gear mounting bolts.
12. If necessary, remove outer tie rods from gear. Count number of revolutions off for each tie rod for reference upon installation to replacement gear.

To install:

13. If necessary, install outer tie rods from original gear to replacement inner tie

rods. Install each outer tie rod same amount of threads as it was installed on original gear. This will get toe setting close, saving some time when toe is set later in this procedure.

14. Lift steering gear into mounted position and install steering gear mounting bolts. Tighten bolts to 70 ft. lbs. (95 Nm).

➡**Always use a NEW O-ring on the ends of the steering hoses.**

15. Lubricate new O-ring on end of return hose with clean power steering fluid.
16. Install the return hose to steering gear. Tighten tube nut to 35 ft. lbs. (47 Nm).
17. Lubricate new O-ring on end of pressure hose with clean power steering fluid.
18. Install the pressure hose to steering gear. Tighten tube nut to 35 ft. lbs. (47 Nm).

✳✳ WARNING

Prior to coupling installation, make sure gear is centered in its travel to match clockspring centering in steering column.

19. Align lower intermediate shaft coupling with input shaft and install steering coupling. Install NEW pinch bolt and tighten bolt to 33 ft. lbs. (45 Nm).
20. Install the each outer tie rod end to its knuckle. Install nuts and tighten to 63 ft. lbs. (85 Nm).
21. Install the tire and wheel assemblies.
22. Carefully lower the vehicle.
23. Connect negative battery cable to battery post. It is important that this is performed properly .

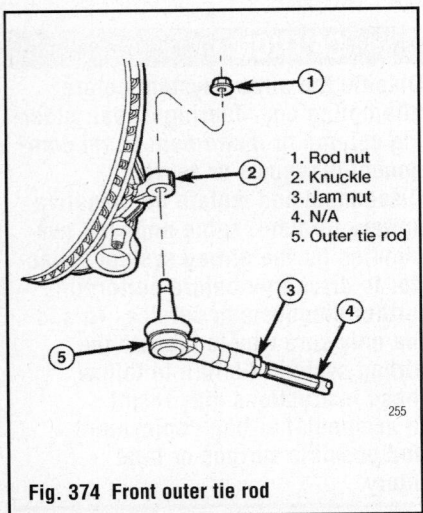

1. Rod nut
2. Knuckle
3. Jam nut
4. N/A
5. Outer tie rod

255

Fig. 374 Front outer tie rod

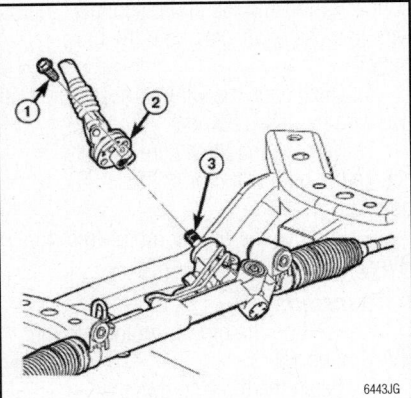

6443JG

Fig. 375 Steering gear (3), pinch bolt (1) and lower intermediate shaft (2)

24. Fill and bleed power steering system.

25. Perform wheel alignment setting toe to specifications.

26. Tighten both tie rod jam nuts to 55 ft. lbs. (75 Nm).

POWER STEERING PUMP

REMOVAL & INSTALLATION

Non SRT

See Figures 376 and 377.

1. Disconnect and isolate battery negative cable from battery post.

2. Raise and safely support the vehicle.

3. Remove the right front wheel mounting nuts, then tire and wheel assembly.

4. Remove the right front wheelhouse splash shield.

5. Siphon power steering fluid from pump reservoir.

6. Disconnect electrical connectors from Electro Hydraulic Power Steering (EHPS) pump body.

7. Remove the power steering pressure line bolt and position the pressure line away from the EHPS pump.

8. Remove the EHPS pump bracket mounting bolts.

9. Remove the EHPS pump bracket retaining nut and remove the EHPS pump from the vehicle.

To install:

10. If Electro Hydraulic Power Steering (EHPS) pump bracket has been removed, install the bracket to the vehicle and tighten fasteners to 9 ft. lbs. (12 Nm).

11. Install the EHPS pump into vehicle and install EHPS bracket retaining nut. Tighten retaining nut to 9 ft. lbs. (12 Nm).

12. Install the EHPS pump bracket

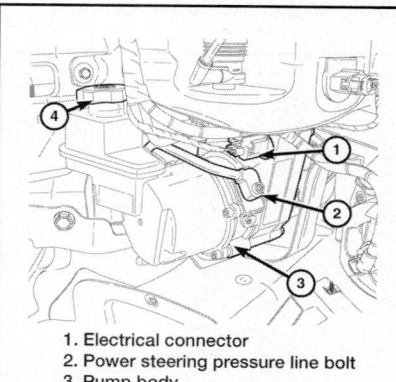

1. Electrical connector
2. Power steering pressure line bolt
3. Pump body
4. Pump reservoir

2946671

Fig. 376 Power steering pump

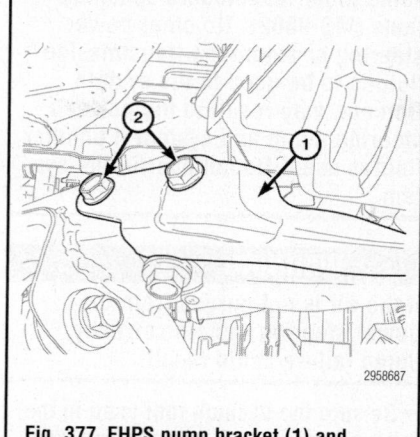

2958687

Fig. 377 EHPS pump bracket (1) and mounting bolts (2)

mounting bolts and tighten to 37 ft. lbs. (50 Nm).

➡**Always use a new O-ring on the end of the pressure line.**

13. Lubricate the new O-ring on the end of the pressure line with clean power steering fluid.

14. Install the power steering pressure line to EHPS Pump.

15. Install the pressure line retaining bolt and tighten to 89 inch lbs. (10 Nm).

16. Install the EHPS pump electrical connectors.

17. Fill and bleed power steering system.

18. Install the right front wheelhouse splash shield.

19. Carefully lower the vehicle.

20. Connect battery negative cable to battery post. It is important that this is performed properly.

SRT

See Figures 378 and 379.

1. Disconnect and isolate battery negative cable from battery post.

2. Siphon power steering fluid from pump reservoir.

3. Loosen the air duct retaining clamp at the throttle body.

4. Disconnect the intake air temperature sensor electrical connector.

5. Remove the makeup air hose at the air cleaner housing.

6. Remove the air cleaner housing retaining bolt.

7. While lifting up the air cleaner housing, slide the air duct off the throttle body and remove the air cleaner housing from the vehicle.

8. Remove the serpentine drive belt.

9. Remove the hose clamp, then supply hose from pump.

10. Unthread tube nut, then remove pressure hose from pump.

11. Remove the three pump mounting bolts through access holes in pulley.

12. Remove the pump from engine.

To install:

13. Align pump with mounting holes on engine.

14. Install the three pump mounting bolts through access holes in pulley. Tighten bolts to 21 ft. lbs. (28 Nm).

➡**Always use a NEW O-ring on the end of the pressure hose.**

15. Lubricate NEW O-ring on end of pressure hose with clean power steering fluid.

16. Install the pressure hose to pump. Tighten pressure hose tube nut to 35 ft. lbs. (47 Nm).

17. Install the return hose to power steering pump and install clamp securing hose in place.

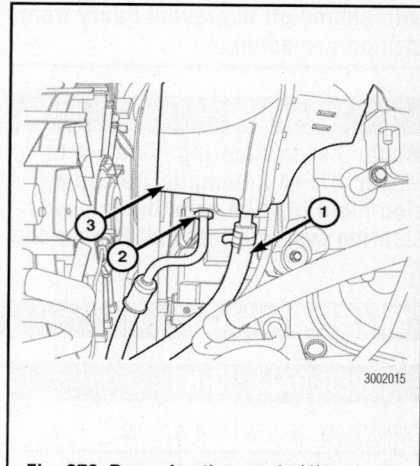

3002015

Fig. 378 Removing the supply (1) and pressure (2) hoses from the pump (3)

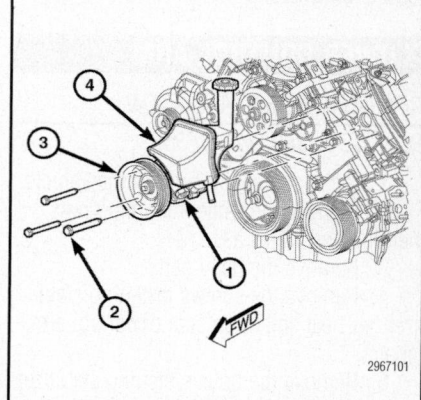

2967101

Fig. 379 Removing the power steering pump (1), mounting bolts (2) and pulley (3)

18. Install the serpentine drive belt.
19. While sliding the air duct onto the throttle body, lower the air cleaner housing into position and align the locating pin on the bottom of the housing.
20. Install the air cleaner housing retaining bolt and tighten to 44 inch lbs. (5 Nm).
21. Install the makeup air hose at the air cleaner housing.
22. Connect the intake air temperature sensor electrical connector.
23. Position the air duct retaining clamp at the throttle body and tighten to 30 inch lbs. (3 Nm).
24. Connect battery negative cable to battery post. It is important that this is performed properly.
25. Fill and bleed power steering system.

BLEEDING

✳✳ CAUTION

The fluid level should be checked with engine off to prevent injury from moving components.

✳✳ WARNING

Mopar®Power Steering Fluid + 4 or Mopar®ATF+4 Automatic Transmission Fluid is to be used in the power steering system. Both Fluids have the same material standard specifications (MS-9602). No other power steering or automatic transmission fluid is to be used in the system. Damage may result to the power steering pump and system if another fluid is used. Do not overfill the system.

✳✳ WARNING

If the air is not purged from the power steering system correctly, pump failure could result.

➡Be sure the vacuum tool used in the following procedure is clean and free of any fluids.

1. Check the fluid level. As measured on the side of the reservoir, the level should indicate between ADD and FULL COLD when the fluid is at normal ambient temperature. Adjust the fluid level as necessary.
2. Tightly insert Power Steering Cap Adapter, Special Tool
Cap Adapter, Power Steering Pump, into the mouth of the reservoir.

✳✳ WARNING

Failure to use a vacuum pump reservoir may allow power steering fluid to be sucked into the hand vacuum pump.

3. Attach Hand Vacuum Pump or equivalent, with reservoir attached, to the Power Steering Cap Adapter.

✳✳ WARNING

Do not run the vehicle while vacuum is applied to the power steering system. Damage to the power steering pump can occur.

➡When performing the following step make sure the vacuum level is maintained during the entire time period.

4. Using Hand Vacuum Pump, apply 20-25 in. Hg (68-85 kPa) of vacuum to the system for a minimum of three minutes.
5. Slowly release the vacuum and remove the special tools.
6. Adjust the fluid level as necessary.
7. Repeat until the fluid no longer drops when vacuum is applied.
8. Start the engine and cycle the steering wheel lock-to-lock three times.

➡Do not hold the steering wheel at the stops.

9. Stop the engine and check for leaks at all connections.
10. Check for any signs of air in the reservoir and check the fluid level. If air is present, repeat the procedure as necessary.

SUSPENSION

LOWER BALL JOINT

REMOVAL & INSTALLATION

To service the lower ball joint or the lower control arm, the knuckle must be removed from the vehicle, then the ball joint can be removed.

LOWER CONTROL ARM

REMOVAL & INSTALLATION

See Figures 380 through 388.

1. Raise and safely support the vehicle.
2. Remove the wheel mounting nuts, then tire and wheel assembly.
3. Remove the belly pan.
4. Remove the screws fastening stabilizer bar heat shield on side of control arm repair.
5. Remove the bolts fastening stabilizer bar bushing retainer (1) in place on side of control arm repair.
6. Remove the retainer halves from around stabilizer bar bushing.

7. Utilizing slit, remove bushing from stabilizer bar.

➡In the following step, the lower control arm cradle bolt is accessed through the opening created by removal of the bushing from the stabilizer bar.

FRONT SUSPENSION

✳✳ WARNING

If the lower control arm bolt at the engine cradle has a lengthwise grooved shaft, it is a special wheel alignment adjustment bolt and the bolt head must not be rotated in the vehicle or damage to the bolt and

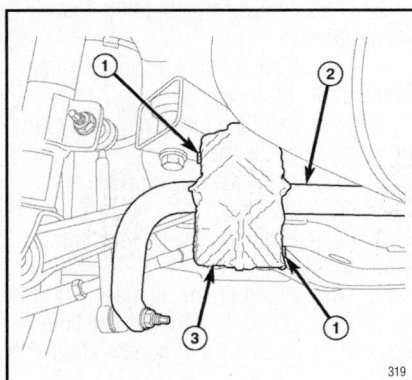

Fig. 380 Front stabilizer bar heat shield (3) and screw (1)

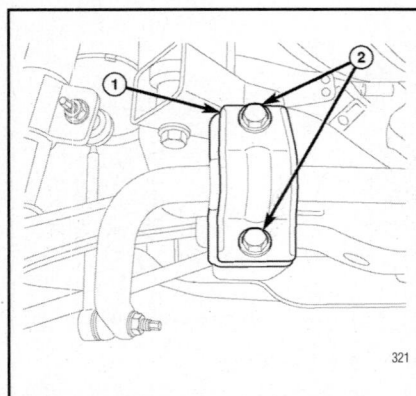

Fig. 381 Front stabilizer bar bushing retainer bolts

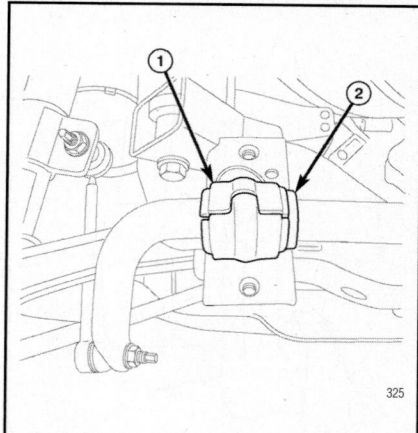

Fig. 382 Front stabilizer bar bushing (1) on bar (2)

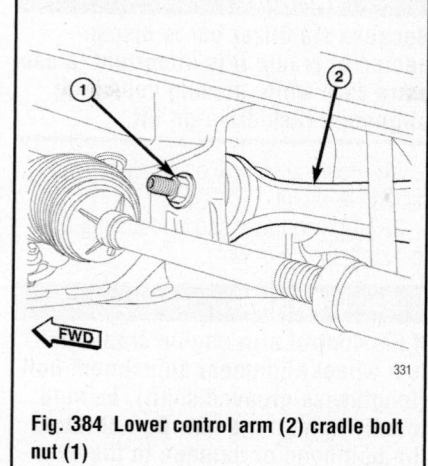

Fig. 384 Lower control arm (2) cradle bolt nut (1)

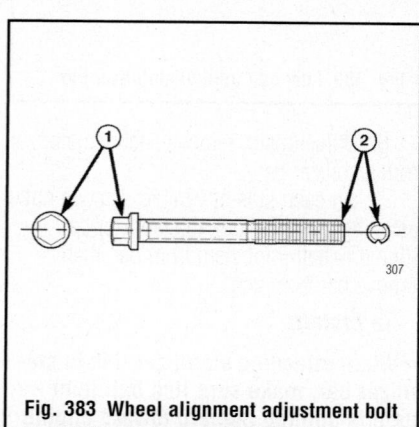

Fig. 383 Wheel alignment adjustment bolt head (1) and grooved shaft (2)

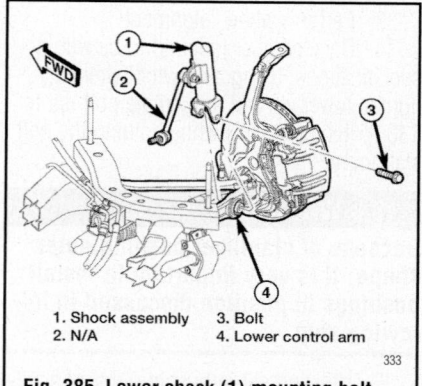

1. Shock assembly
2. N/A
3. Bolt
4. Lower control arm

Fig. 385 Lower shock (1) mounting bolt (3) and lower control arm (4)

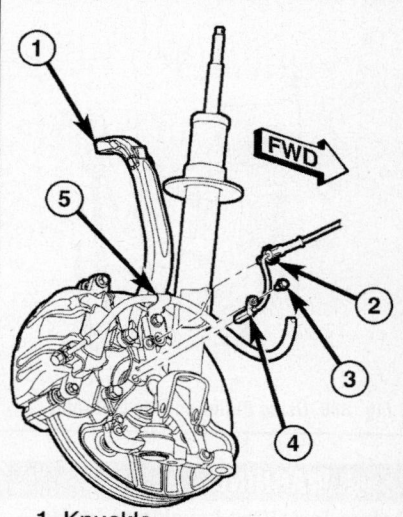

1. Knuckle
2. Wheel speed sensor cable routing clip
3. Screw
4. Sensor head
5. Brake hose routing bracket

Fig. 386 Wheel speed sensor at front knuckle

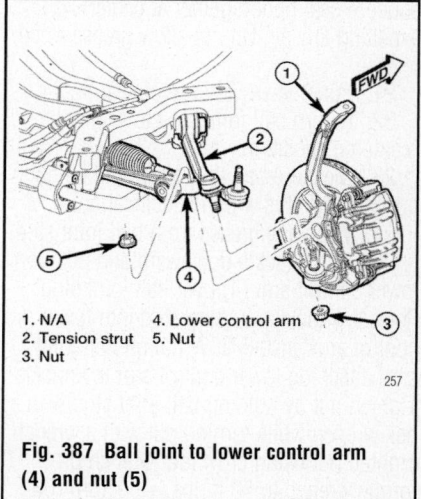

1. N/A
2. Tension strut
3. Nut
4. Lower control arm
5. Nut

Fig. 387 Ball joint to lower control arm (4) and nut (5)

engine cradle will result. While holding the bolt in place with a wrench, remove the nut, then slide the bolt out of the bushing and cradle taking note of bolt positioning in engine cradle for reassembly purposes. The bolt needs to be installed in the same position as removed to make sure wheel camber and caster return to adjusted position.

8. Remove the bolt and nut securing lower control arm to engine cradle. If bolt has a lengthwise grooved shaft (see above note), remove bolt and nut by holding the bolt in place with a wrench, removing nut, then sliding bolt out of bushing and cradle while taking note of bolt positioning in lower control arm bushing for reassembly purposes.

9. Remove the bolt securing shock assembly (1) to lower control arm (4).

10. Remove the screw fastening wheel speed sensor to knuckle. Pull sensor head out of knuckle.

11. Remove the wheel speed sensor cable routing clip from brake flex hose routing bracket.

12. Loosen nut attaching ball joint stud to lower control arm. Back nut off until nut is even with end of stud. Keeping nut on at this location will help keep end of stud from distorting while using Puller in next step.

✳✳ WARNING

In following step, use care not to damage ball joint seal boot while sliding Ball Joint Remover, into place past seal boot.

13. Using Ball Joint Remover, separate ball joint stud from lower control arm.

14. Remove the nut from end of ball joint stud attaching lower control arm to knuckle.

15. Pry knuckle downward and slide ball joint stud out of lower control arm. Position knuckle outward, away from lower control arm.

16. Slide lower control arm out of engine cradle and remove from vehicle.

To install:

➡ **If installing a lower control arm engine cradle bolt that is a wheel alignment adjustment bolt (lengthwise grooved shaft), make sure to install it in the same position which it was in upon removal.**

17. Slide lower control arm into position in engine cradle and install mounting bolt from rear.

18. Install the nut on lower control arm cradle bolt, but do not tighten at this time.

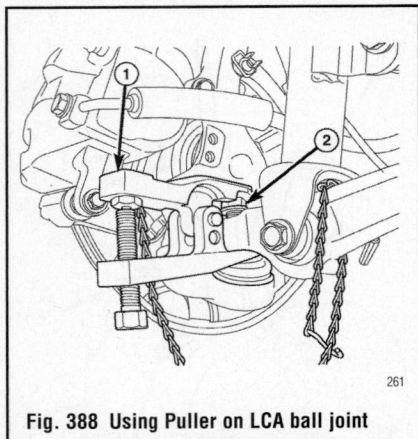

Fig. 388 Using Puller on LCA ball joint

✷✷ WARNING

Before installing knuckle to lower control arm, measure height of ball joint seal boot mounted on knuckle. If seal boot height is above 25.5 mm, any air inside seal boot must be expelled. To do so, follow these steps.

19. Tip ball joint stud completely to one side.

20. Using thumb and index finger, gently squeeze seal boot together at center expelling any air. Do not allow grease to be release.

21. Push down very top of seal boot.

22. Return ball joint stud to original "centered" position.

23. Measure ball joint seal boot height making sure it is within specification.

24. Wipe any grease from ball joint stud.

25. Pull knuckle downward and position lower control arm (4) over ball joint stud. Release knuckle, guiding stud into lower control arm. Install NEW nut on ball joint stud attaching lower control arm to knuckle. Tighten nut by holding ball joint stud with a hex wrench while turning nut with a wrench. Tighten nut using crow foot wrench on torque wrench to 50 ft. lbs. + 90°turn (68 Nm + 90°turn).

26. Install the wheel speed sensor head into knuckle and install mounting screw. Tighten screw to 95 inch lbs. (11 Nm).

27. Attach wheel speed sensor cable and routing clip to brake flex hose routing bracket.

28. Install the lower shock mounting bolt attaching shock assembly to lower control arm. Do not tighten bolt at this time.

29. Install the tire and wheel assembly. Tighten wheel mounting nuts to 110 ft. lbs. (150 Nm).

30. Carefully lower the vehicle.

✷✷ WARNING

Because stabilizer bar is disconnected at cradle it is important to use extra care while moving vehicle to alignment rack/drive-on lift.

31. Position vehicle on an alignment rack/drive-on lift.

32. Tighten lower shock mounting bolt to 128 ft. lbs. (174 Nm).

✷✷ WARNING

If the control arm engine cradle bolt is a wheel alignment adjustment bolt (lengthwise grooved shaft), be sure to only tighten the nut. Do not rotate the bolt head or damage to the bushing will occur.

33. Perform wheel alignment.

34. Once camber is found to be within specifications, using a crowfoot wrench, tighten lower control arm cradle bolt nut to 130 ft. lbs. (176 Nm) while holding the bolt stationary.

✷✷ WARNING

Because of stabilizer bushing outer shape, it is very important to install bushings in position discussed in following step.

35. Utilizing slit in bushing, install stabilizer bar bushing against locating collar on stabilizer bar. Make sure slit in bushing is positioned toward rear of vehicle.

36. Install the stabilizer bar bushing retainer halves around bushing.

37. Install the bolts securing stabilizer bar bushing retainer halves to cradle. Tighten bolts to 44 ft. lbs. (60 Nm).

38. Install the stabilizer bar heat shield over stabilizer bar bushing retainer. Install mounting screws.

39. Install the belly pan.

STABILIZER BAR

REMOVAL & INSTALLATION

See Figure 389.

1. Raise and safely support the vehicle.

2. Remove the belly pan.

3. On each side of vehicle, remove screws fastening stabilizer bar heat shield. Remove heat shield.

4. On each side of vehicle, remove bolts fastening stabilizer bar isolator retainer in place.

5. On each side of vehicle, remove retainer halves from around stabilizer bar isolator.

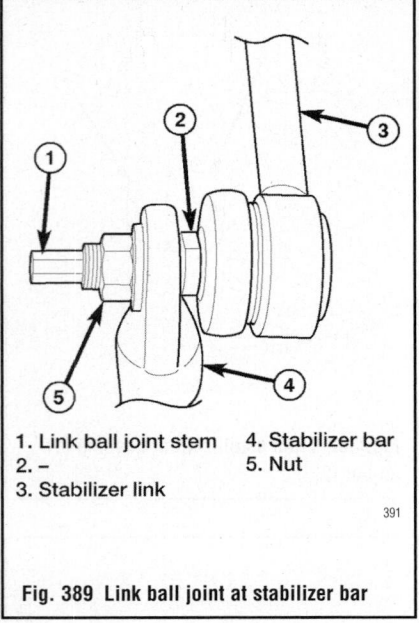

1. Link ball joint stem   4. Stabilizer bar
2. –
3. Stabilizer link   5. Nut

Fig. 389 Link ball joint at stabilizer bar

6. Utilizing slit, remove each isolator from stabilizer bar.

7. On each side of vehicle, remove nut fastening stabilizer link to stabilizer bar. Slide link ball joint stem from bar, then remove bar from vehicle.

To install:

➡ **When attaching stabilizer link to stabilizer bar, make sure link ball joint stem is pointed inboard toward engine cradle.**

8. On each side of vehicle, raise stabilizer bar to stabilizer link and slide link ball joint stem through mounting hole in bar. Loosely install nut at this time.

✷✷ WARNING

Because of stabilizer isolator outer shape, it is very important to install isolators in position discussed in following step.

9. Utilizing slit in isolator, install each stabilizer bar isolator on bar resting against locating collar. Make sure slit in isolator is positioned toward rear of vehicle.

10. On each side of vehicle, install stabilizer bar isolator retainer halves around isolator.

11. On each side of vehicle, install bolts securing stabilizer bar isolator retainer halves to cradle. Tighten bolts to 44 ft. lbs. (60 Nm).

12. On each side of vehicle, install stabilizer bar heat shield over stabilizer bar isolator retainer. Install mounting screws.

13. While holding stem from rotating at hex or flat tighten stabilizer link nuts at

each end of stabilizer bar to 95 ft. lbs.
(128 Nm).

14. Install the belly pan.

15. Carefully lower the vehicle.

STEERING KNUCKLE

REMOVAL & INSTALLATION

See Figure 390.

1. Raise and safely support the vehicle.

2. Remove the wheel mounting nuts,
then tire and wheel assembly.

3. Remove the screw fastening wheel
speed sensor to knuckle. Pull sensor head
out of knuckle.

4. Remove the wheel speed sensor
cable routing clip from brake flex hose routing bracket.

5. Remove the screw fastening brake
flex hose routing bracket to knuckle.

6. Access and remove front brake rotor.

7. Remove the nut from outer tie rod
end stud.

8. Using Ball Joint Remover, separate
tie rod stud from knuckle.

9. Loosen nut attaching upper ball joint
stud to knuckle. Back nut off until nut is
even with end of stud. Keeping nut on at
this location will help keep end of stud from
distorting while using Puller in next step.

> ✳✳ **WARNING**
>
> **In following step, use care not to
> damage ball joint seal boot while
> sliding Ball Joint Remover, into place
> past seal boot.**

10. Using Ball Joint Remover, separate
upper ball joint stud from knuckle.

11. Remove the nut from end of upper
ball joint stud.

12. Loosen nut attaching tension strut
ball joint stud to knuckle. Back nut off until
nut is even with end of stud. Keeping nut on
at this location will help keep end of stud
from distorting while using Puller in next
step.

> ✳✳ **WARNING**
>
> **In following step, use care not to
> damage ball joint seal boot while
> sliding Ball Joint Remover, into place
> past seal boot.**

13. Using Ball Joint Remover, separate
tension strut ball joint stud from knuckle.

14. Remove the nut from end of tension
strut ball joint stud.

15. Loosen nut attaching ball joint stud to
lower control arm (4). Back nut off until nut
is even with end of stud. Keeping nut on at

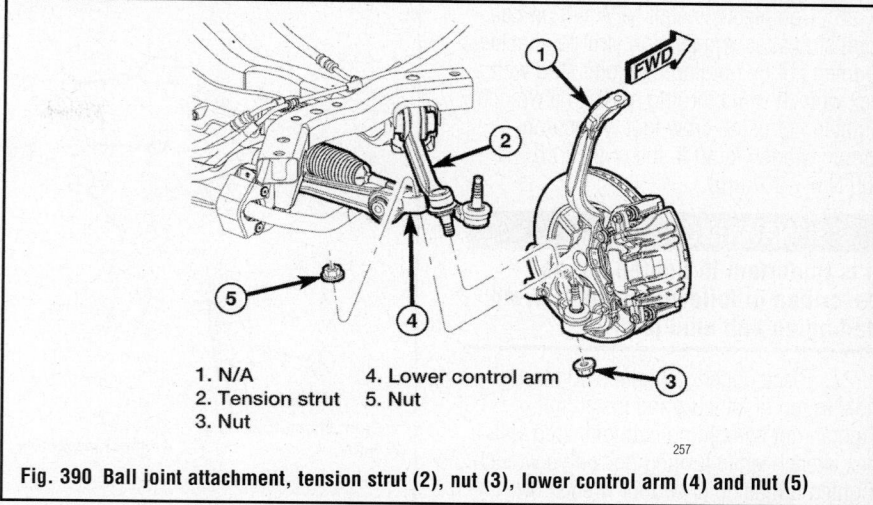

1. N/A
2. Tension strut
3. Nut
4. Lower control arm
5. Nut

Fig. 390 Ball joint attachment, tension strut (2), nut (3), lower control arm (4) and nut (5)

this location will help keep end of stud from
distorting while using Puller in next step.

> ✳✳ **WARNING**
>
> **In following step, use care not to
> damage ball joint seal boot while
> sliding Ball Joint Remover, into place
> past seal boot.**

16. Using Ball Joint Remover, separate
ball joint stud from lower control arm.

17. Remove the nut from end of ball
joint stud attaching lower control arm to
knuckle.

18. Remove the knuckle from vehicle.

19. If hub and bearing needs to be
removed, perform the following:

   a. Remove dust cap. When doing
   this, avoid damaging internal bore of hub
   to preserve seal integrity.

   b. Remove hub nut.

   c. Slide hub and bearing off knuckle
   spindle.

20. If shield needs to be removed from
knuckle, remove 3 mounting screws, then
shield.

21. If lower control arm ball joint needs
to be removed from knuckle.

To install:

➡ **Always install a new hub nut. The
original hub nut is one-time use only
and should be discarded when
removed.**

➡ **Install a new dust cap to preserve
seal integrity.**

22. If shield needs to be installed on
knuckle, place shield in place and attach to
knuckle using 3 screws. Tighten screws to
89 inch lbs. (10 Nm).

23. If hub and bearing needs to be
installed on knuckle, perform the following:

   a. Slide hub and bearing onto knuckle
   spindle.

   b. Install hub nut on end of spindle.
   Tighten hub nut to 184 ft. lbs. (250 Nm).

   c. Install NEW dust cap.

> ✳✳ **WARNING**
>
> **Before installing knuckle on lower
> control arm, measure height of ball
> joint seal boot (1) mounted on
> knuckle. If seal boot height is above
> 25.5 mm, any air inside seal boot
> must be expelled. To do so, follow
> these steps.**

   d. Tip ball joint stud completely to
   one side.

   e. Using thumb and index finger, gently squeeze seal boot together at center
   expelling any air. Do not allow grease to
   be release.

   f. Push down very top of seal boot.

   g. Return ball joint stud to original
   "centered" position.

   h. Measure ball joint seal boot height
   making sure it is within specification.

   i. Wipe any grease from ball joint stud.

> ✳✳ **WARNING**
>
> **It is important to tighten nuts as
> described in following steps to avoid
> damaging ball stud joints.**

24. Place knuckle over lower ball joint
studs on vehicle and loosely install NEW
nuts by hand.

25. Completely install NEW nut on ball
joint stud attaching lower control arm to
knuckle. Tighten nut by holding ball joint
stud with a hex wrench while turning nut
with a wrench. Tighten nut using crow foot
wrench on torque wrench to 50 ft. lbs. +
90°turn (68 Nm + 90°turn).

26. Completely install NEW nut on ball joint stud attaching tension strut to knuckle. Tighten nut by holding ball joint stud with a hex wrench while turning nut with a wrench. Tighten nut using crow foot wrench on torque wrench to 50 ft. lbs. + 90°turn (68 Nm + 90°turn).

✴✴ WARNING

It is important to tighten nut as described in following step to avoid damaging ball stud joint.

27. Place upper ball joint stud through hole in top of knuckle and install nut. Tighten nut by holding ball joint stud with a hex wrench while turning nut with a wrench. Tighten nut using crow foot wrench on torque wrench to 35 ft. lbs. + 90°turn (47 Nm + 90°turn).

✴✴ WARNING

It is important to tighten nut as described in following step to avoid damaging ball stud joint.

28. Place outer tie rod stud through hole in knuckle and install nut. Tighten nut by holding stud with a wrench while turning nut with another wrench. Tighten nut using crow foot wrench on torque wrench to 63 ft. lbs. (85 Nm).

29. Install the brake rotor, then disc brake caliper and adapter assembly.

30. Install the screw fastening brake flex hose routing bracket (2) to knuckle. Tighten screw to 9 ft. lbs. (12 Nm).

31. Install the wheel speed sensor head into knuckle and install mounting screw. Tighten screw to 95 inch lbs. (11 Nm).

32. Attach wheel speed sensor cable and routing clip to brake flex hose routing bracket.

33. Install the tire and wheel assembly. Tighten wheel mounting nuts to 110 ft. lbs. (150 Nm).

34. Carefully lower the vehicle.

35. Pump brake pedal several times to ensure vehicle has a firm brake pedal before moving vehicle.

36. Check and adjust brake fluid level in reservoir as necessary.

37. Perform wheel alignment.

STRUT & SPRING ASSEMBLY (COIL-OVER)

REMOVAL & INSTALLATION

See Figures 391 through 393.

1. If equipped, remove front shock tower cap from top of shock assembly.

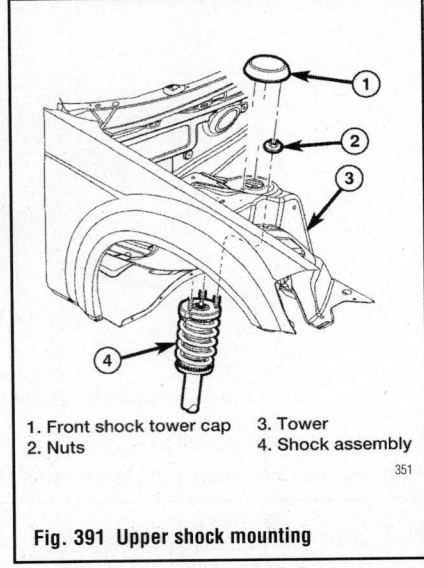

1. Front shock tower cap   3. Tower
2. Nuts   4. Shock assembly

351

Fig. 391 Upper shock mounting

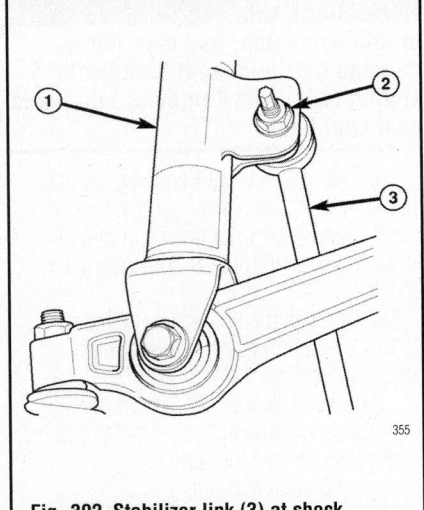

355

Fig. 392 Stabilizer link (3) at shock assembly (1) with nut (2)

2. Remove the three nuts fastening shock assembly to shock tower.

3. Raise and safely support the vehicle.

4. Remove the wheel mounting nuts, then tire and wheel assembly.

5. Remove the nut fastening stabilizer link to shock assembly. Slide link ball joint stem from shock assembly.

6. Remove the bolt securing shock assembly to lower control arm.

7. Disconnect wheel speed sensor cable routing clip at brake tube bracket.

8. Loosen nut attaching upper ball joint stud to knuckle. Back nut off until nut is even with end of stud. Keeping nut on at this location will help keep end of stud from distorting while using Puller in next step.

✴✴ WARNING

In following step, use care not to damage ball joint seal boot while sliding Ball Joint Remover, into place past seal boot.

9. Using Ball Joint Remover, separate upper ball joint stud from knuckle.

10. Remove the nut from end of upper ball joint stud.

11. Tip top of knuckle outward using care not to overextend brake flex hose.

12. Remove the shock assembly from vehicle.

UPPER CONTROL ARM

REMOVAL & INSTALLATION

See Figures 394 and 395.

1. If removing left upper control arm, remove and reposition coolant recovery container.

2. If removing right upper control arm,

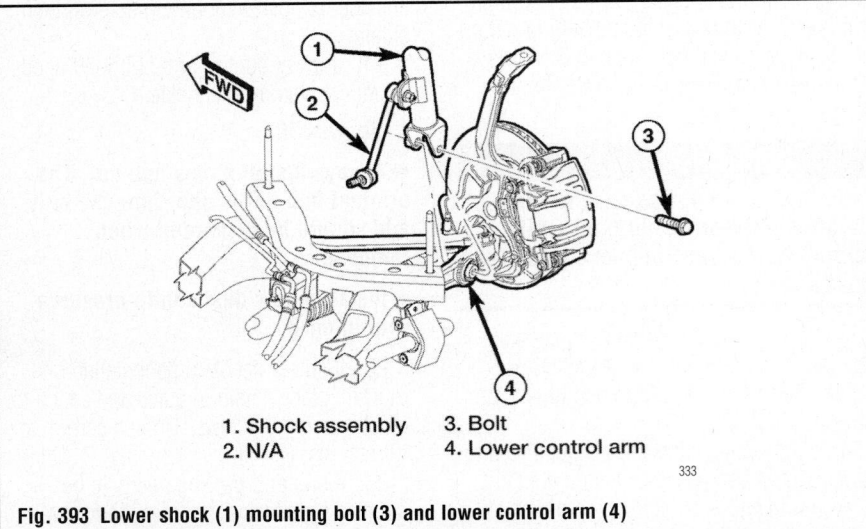

1. Shock assembly   3. Bolt
2. N/A   4. Lower control arm

333

Fig. 393 Lower shock (1) mounting bolt (3) and lower control arm (4)

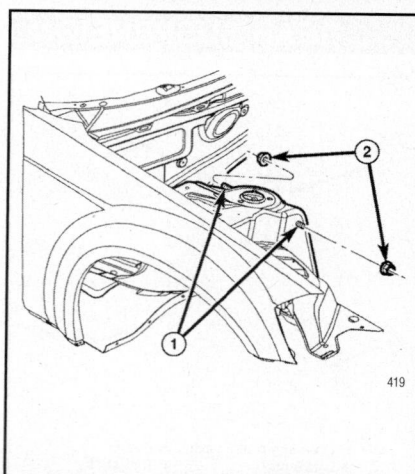

Fig. 394 Upper control arm mounting nuts (2) and bolts (1)

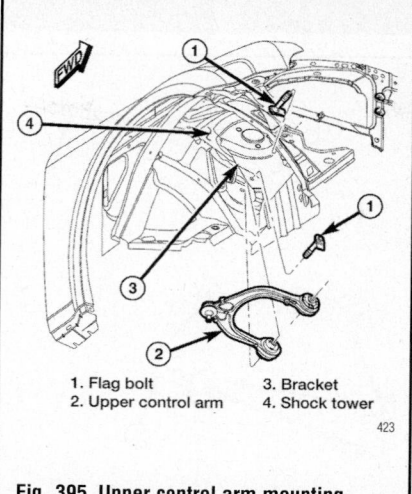

1. Flag bolt
2. Upper control arm
3. Bracket
4. Shock tower

Fig. 395 Upper control arm mounting

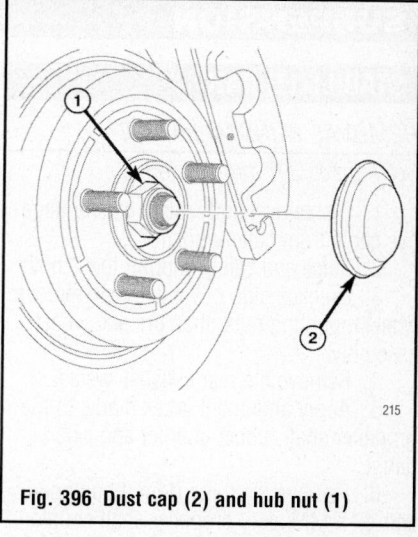

Fig. 396 Dust cap (2) and hub nut (1)

remove the totally integrated power module (TIPM) from mount and reposition.

3. If equipped, remove front shock tower cap from top of shock assembly.

4. Remove the three nuts fastening shock assembly to shock tower.

5. Remove the nuts from upper control arm mounting bolts.

6. Raise and safely support the vehicle.

7. Remove the wheel mounting nuts, then tire and wheel assembly.

8. Disconnect wheel speed sensor cable routing clip at brake tube bracket.

9. Loosen nut attaching upper ball joint stud to knuckle. Back nut off until nut is even with end of stud. Keeping nut on at this location will help keep end of stud from distorting while using Puller in next step.

✷✷ WARNING

In following step, use care not to damage ball joint seal boot while sliding Ball Joint Remover, into place past seal boot.

10. Using Puller, separate upper ball joint stud from knuckle.

11. Remove the nut from end of upper ball joint stud.

12. Pull shock assembly downward until studs clear shock tower, then pull it outward allowing access to upper control arm mounting bolts.

13. Remove the upper control arm mounting (flag) bolts.

14. Remove the upper control arm from bracket in shock tower.

To install:

15. Slide upper control arm into bracket located in shock tower.

16. Install the upper control arm mount-

ing (flag) bolts through bracket, arm and tower. Position flags on bolt heads outward, toward wheel opening.

17. Move shock assembly allowing studs to be inserted through shock tower mounting holes.

18. Place upper ball joint stud through hole in top of knuckle and install nut. Tighten nut by holding ball joint stud with a hex wrench while turning nut with a wrench. Tighten nut using crow-foot wrench on torque wrench to 35 ft. lbs. + 90°turn (47 Nm + 90°turn).

19. Connect wheel speed sensor cable routing clip at brake tube bracket.

20. Install the tire and wheel assembly. Tighten wheel mounting nuts to 110 ft. lbs. (150 Nm).

21. Lower vehicle to curb position.

22. Install the nuts on upper control arm body mounting bolts. Tighten nuts to 55 ft. lbs. (75 Nm).

23. Install the three nuts fastening shock assembly to shock tower. Tighten nuts to 20 ft. lbs. (27 Nm).

24. If equipped, align shock tower cap with shock mounting nuts and snap into place.

25. If installing left upper control arm, install coolant recovery container.

26. If installing right upper control arm, install the totally integrated power module (TIPM).

WHEEL BEARINGS

REMOVAL & INSTALLATION

See Figure 396.

1. Raise and safely support the vehicle.

2. Remove the wheel mounting nuts, then tire and wheel assembly.

3. Access and remove front brake rotor.

4. Remove the dust cap. When doing this, avoid damaging internal bore of hub to preserve seal integrity.

5. Remove the hub nut.

6. Slide hub and bearing off knuckle spindle.

To install:

➡Prior to installation, inspect magnetic encoder (for wheel speed sensor) for any damage and make sure any metal debris sticking to it is removed.

7. Slide hub and bearing onto knuckle spindle.

➡Always install a new hub nut. The original hub nut is one-time use only and should be discarded when removed.

8. Install the hub nut on end of spindle. Tighten hub nut to 187 ft. lbs. (250 Nm) torque.

9. Install the brake rotor, then disc brake caliper and adapter assembly.

➡Install a new dust cap to preserve seal integrity.

10. Install the new dust cap on hub and bearing.

11. Install the tire and wheel assembly. Tighten wheel mounting nuts to 110 ft. lbs. (150 Nm) torque.

12. Carefully lower the vehicle.

13. Pump brake pedal several times to ensure vehicle has a firm brake pedal before moving vehicle.

14. Check and adjust brake fluid level in reservoir as necessary.

15. Road test vehicle and make several stops to wear off any foreign material on brakes and to seat brake pads.

SUSPENSION

STABILIZER BAR

REMOVAL & INSTALLATION

See Figures 397 through 403.

1. Disconnect and isolate battery negative cable from battery post.

2. Raise and safely support the vehicle.

3. On each side of vehicle rear, remove wheel mounting nuts, then tire and wheel assembly.

4. Remove the rear exhaust system.

5. Apply alignment index marks to the propeller shaft rubber coupler and axle flange.

6. Remove the three (four if equipped with 215 MM axle) propeller shaft coupler-to-axle flange bolts and nuts.

7. Support propeller shaft using a bungee cord. Attach ends of cord to fuel tank straps.

➡**Due to short travel and low spring tension, it is not necessary to lock-out parking brake lever to service parking brake components.**

8. Disconnect front parking brake cable at connector to right rear parking brake cable.

9. Remove the front parking brake cable from equalizer.

10. Remove the screw fastening front parking brake cable routing bracket to rear crossmember front flange.

11. If equipped with standard or premium disc brakes, on each rear disc brake:

   a. While holding guide pins from turning, remove disc brake caliper guide pin bolts.

   b. Remove brake caliper from brake adapter and pads.

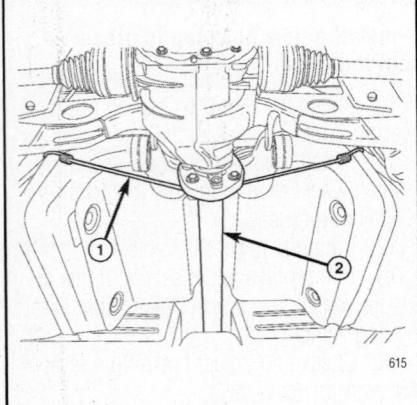

Fig. 397 Prop shaft (2) supported by bungee (1)

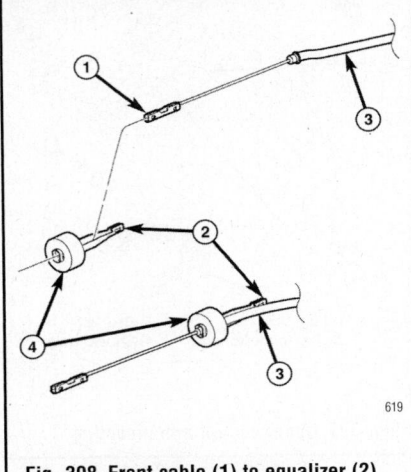

Fig. 398 Front cable (1) to equalizer (2)

c. Guide brake caliper up through suspension, following brake hose path. Support caliper above rear suspension using with bungee cord or wire to keep caliper from overextending brake hose when crossmember is lowered.

✳✳ WARNING

When pushing pistons back into caliper bores, use only a trim stick or other suitable soft tool. Never use a screwdriver or other metal pry bar due to potential damage to braking surface of rotor, caliper, pistons or dust boots.

12. If equipped with SRT8 disc brakes, on each rear disc brake, place trim stick between brake pad and outer edge of rotor.

13. If equipped with SRT8 disc brakes, on each rear disc brake, using trim stick, slowly apply pressure against brake pad until both pistons (on that side of caliper) are completely bottomed in bores of caliper half.

➡**Repeat above procedure to opposite brake pad and pistons as necessary.**

14. If equipped with SRT8 disc brakes, on each rear disc brake, support spring link using a transmission jack or other appropriate jack. Raise spring link just enough to access brake caliper lower mounting bolt from above compression link.

15. If equipped with SRT8 disc brakes, on each rear disc brake, remove the lower and upper caliper mounting bolts.

16. If equipped with SRT8 disc brakes, on each rear disc brake, remove brake caliper with pads from knuckle and brake rotor. Hang assembly out of way using wire

REAR SUSPENSION

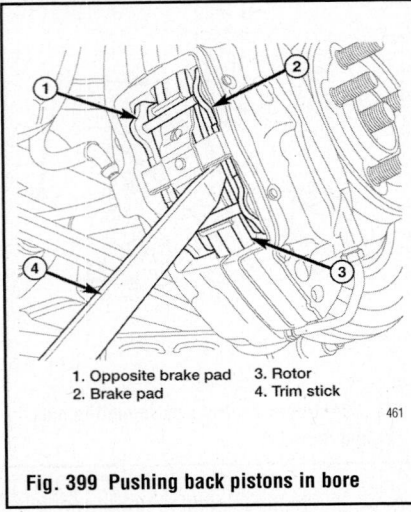

1. Opposite brake pad   3. Rotor
2. Brake pad   4. Trim stick

Fig. 399 Pushing back pistons in bore

or a bungee cord. Use care not to overextend brake hose when doing this.

17. If equipped with SRT8 disc brakes, remove jack from under spring link.

➡**To remove wheel speed sensor connector from body wiring harness connector, move retaining clip and pull sensor connector outward.**

18. Remove the wheel speed sensor connectors from body wiring harness connector located in luggage compartment floor pan.

19. Unclip left wheel speed sensor cable from routing clip near body connector.

20. On each side of vehicle, remove shock absorber lower mounting bolt and nut.

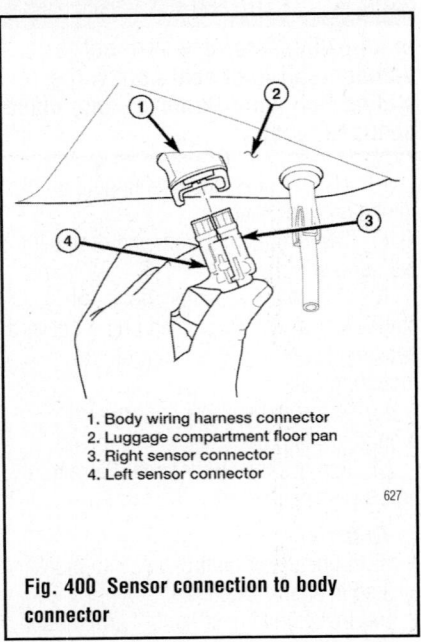

1. Body wiring harness connector
2. Luggage compartment floor pan
3. Right sensor connector
4. Left sensor connector

Fig. 400 Sensor connection to body connector

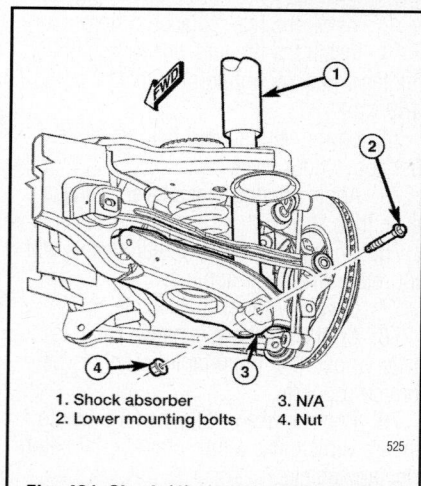

1. Shock absorber
2. Lower mounting bolts
3. N/A
4. Nut

525

Fig. 401 Shock (1) mounting—lower bolts (2) and nut (4)

21. Carefully mark location of rear crossmember on body at all four mount (bushing) locations using a marker or crayon. Do not use a scratch awl to mark location.

22. Position an extra pair of jack stands under and support forward end of engine cradle to help stabilize vehicle during rear suspension removal/installation.

23. Position under-hoist utility jack or transmission jack under center of rear axle differential. Raise jack head to contact differential and secure in place. When securing crossmember to jack, be sure not to secure stabilizer bar.

❊❊ CAUTION

Before opening fuel system, review all Warnings and Cautions.

24. Remove the fuel filler tube.
25. Remove the both front and both rear mounting bolts fastening crossmember in place.

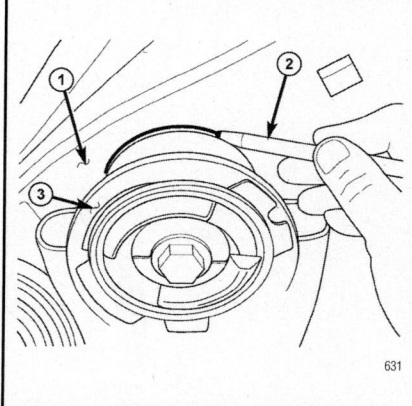

631

Fig. 402 Marking (2) location of crossmember bushing flange to body (1)

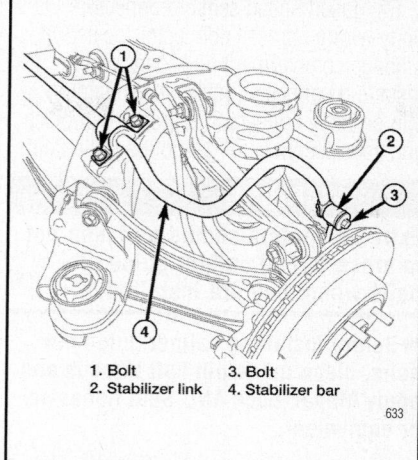

1. Bolt
2. Stabilizer link
3. Bolt
4. Stabilizer bar

633

Fig. 403 Rear stabilizer (2, 4) mounting bolt (1, 3)

26. Slowly lower crossmember using jack. Do not lower jack at a fast rate. Lower just enough to allow propeller shaft removal from rear axle differential. Do not lower jack any further than necessary. Slide propeller shaft out of rear axle differential and allow bungee cord previously installed to support.

27. Continue to lower jack until crossmember is at a comfortable working level to access stabilizer bar fasteners.

28. On each end, remove bolt and nut fastening stabilizer bar to stabilizer link.

29. Remove the bolts fastening each stabilizer bar isolator retainer to crossmember.

30. Remove the stabilizer bar with isolators and retainers.

31. Remove the retainers from isolators.

32. Remove the isolators from stabilizer bar utilizing slits in bushings.

To install:

33. Install the isolators on stabilizer bar utilizing slits in bushings. Install each isolator so its slit faces forward and flat side is positioned toward crossmember once installed.

34. Install the retainers on isolators.

35. Install the stabilizer bar with isolators and retainers on crossmember.

36. Install the isolator retainer mounting bolts. Do not tighten at this time.

37. Install the bolt and nut fastening stabilizer bar ends to each stabilizer links. Do not tighten at this time.

38. Tighten isolator retainer mounting bolts to 45 ft. lbs. (61 Nm).

39. Remove the coil springs with isolators from spring links.

40. Raise crossmember to body mounting points. As crossmember is raised, slide propeller shaft onto rear axle differential flange and align shocks with pockets in spring links.

➡ **There are four crossmember mounting bolts. Rear mounting bolts are longer than front mounting bolts. Do not interchange mounting bolts.**

41. Continue to raise crossmember with jack until crossmember mounting bolts can be installed. Install left side crossmember mounting bolts, but not the right side bolts. It is not necessary to tighten bolts at this point.

❊❊ WARNING

To avoid damaging other components of vehicle, do not lower crossmember any further than necessary to install coil spring.

42. Slowly lower jack allowing right side of crossmember to drop. Do not lower jack at a fast rate. Lower jack just enough to allow spring installation. Do not lower jack any further than necessary.

➡ **Before installing coil spring, make sure isolators are completely installed on ends of spring.**

43. Install the coil spring with isolators into spring pocket of spring link fitting the lower isolator to the shape of the pocket, then align top of spring with body mount.

44. Carefully raise jack, guiding coil spring and lower end of shock absorber into mounted positions. Once shock absorber lower mounting hole lines up with hole in spring link, stop jacking.

45. Install the lower shock mounting bolt and nut. Do not tighten at this time.

➡ **There are four crossmember mounting bolts. Rear mounting bolts are longer than front mounting bolts. Do not interchange mounting bolts.**

46. Raise right side of crossmember into mounted position. Install right side crossmember mounting bolts. Snug, but do not fully tighten bolts at this time.

47. Remove the both front and rear crossmember mounting bolts on left side of vehicle.

❊❊ WARNING

To avoid damaging other components of vehicle, do not lower crossmember any further than necessary to install coil spring.

48. Slowly lower jack allowing left side of crossmember to drop. Do not lower jack at a fast rate. Lower jack just enough to

allow spring installation. Do not lower jack any further than necessary.

➡**Before installing coil spring, make sure isolators are completely installed on ends of spring.**

49. Install the coil spring with isolators into spring pocket of spring link fitting the lower isolator to the shape of the pocket, then align top of spring with body mount.

50. Carefully raise jack, guiding coil spring and lower end of shock absorber into mounted positions. Once shock absorber lower mounting hole lines up with hole in spring link, stop jacking.

51. Install the lower shock mounting bolt and nut. Do not tighten at this time.

➡**There are four crossmember mounting bolts. Rear mounting bolts are longer than front mounting bolts. Do not interchange mounting bolts.**

52. Raise left side of crossmember into mounted position. Install left side crossmember mounting bolts. Snug, but do not fully tighten bolts at this time.

53. Shift crossmember as necessary to line up mounts with location marks drawn on body before removal.

54. Once mounts are lined up with location marks, on both sides of vehicle, measure distance between the tension link and weld flange on body directly in front of it, just outboard of the front mount bushing. This distance must be at least 12 mm to allow proper clearance for suspension movement. If distance is less than 12 mm on either side of vehicle, shift that side of rear crossmember directly rearward until distance is 12 mm or greater. To do so, loosen 3 mounting bolts slightly, leaving one on opposite side of shift snugged to pivot off of. Shift crossmember rearward and snug loosened bolts. Re-measure opposite side to be sure it still maintains minimum 12 mm distance.

55. Tighten all four crossmember mounting bolts to 133 ft. lbs. (180 Nm).

56. Remove the jack from under rear axle differential.

57. Remove the bungee cord supporting propeller shaft.

58. Align propeller shaft index marks placed upon removal. Install propeller shaft rear coupler-to-axle flange bolts and nuts by hand. Tighten propeller shaft rear coupler-to-axle flange bolts to 60 ft. lbs. (81 Nm).

59. Install the fuel filler tube.

60. Clip left rear wheel speed sensor cable to routing clip near body connector.

61. Match left rear wheel speed sensor connector to right sensor connector to make one connector.

62. Insert speed sensor connectors into body wiring harness connector located in luggage compartment floor pan. When installing connector, make sure retaining clip on body connector is properly in place and sensor connector cannot be pulled out.

⁕⁕ **WARNING**

Extreme caution should be taken not to cross-thread caliper guide pin bolts when they are installed.

➡**Before installing caliper guide pin bolts, clean guide pin bolt threads and apply Mopar®Lock AND Seal Adhesive or equivalent.**

63. If equipped with standard or premium disc brakes, on each rear disc brake:
   a. Push caliper guide pins into caliper adapter to clear caliper mounting bosses when installing.
   b. Guide caliper and brake hose down through rear suspension, then slide caliper over brake pads and onto caliper adapter.
   c. Align caliper mounting holes with guide pins, then install guide pin bolts. While holding guide pins from turning, tighten bolts to 23 ft. lbs. (31 Nm).

64. Make sure brake hose is properly routed and will not come in contact with suspension components.

65. If equipped with SRT8 disc brakes, at each rear disc brake, support spring link using a transmission jack or other appropriate jack as indicated in removal procedure.

66. If equipped with SRT8 disc brakes, on each rear disc brake, slide caliper with pads over brake rotor and align with knuckle.

67. If equipped with SRT8 disc brakes, on each rear disc brake, install caliper mounting bolts. Tighten bolts to 96 ft. lbs. (130 Nm).

68. If equipped with SRT8 disc brakes, on each rear disc brake, remove jack from under spring link.

69. Insert routing front parking brake cable bracket locating pin in front flange of crossmember, then install screw fastening cable routing bracket to rear crossmember.

70. Route parking brake cable above rear crossmember, then slide cable through equalizer above rear axle differential.

➡**Due to short travel and low spring tension, it is not necessary to lock-out parking brake lever to service parking brake components.**

71. Connect front parking brake cable at connector to right rear parking brake cable.

72. Install the rear exhaust system.

73. Install the tire and wheel assemblies. Tighten wheel mounting nuts to 110 ft. lbs. (150 Nm).

74. Lower vehicle until rear wheels are just above floor level.

75. Apply parking brake lever. Release lever, then reapply.

76. Check to make sure rear wheels will not rotate with lever applied.

77. Carefully lower the vehicle.

78. Connect battery negative cable to battery post. It is important that this is performed properly.

79. Pump brake pedal several times to ensure vehicle has a firm brake pedal before moving vehicle.

80. Position vehicle on alignment rack/drive-on hoist. Raise vehicle as necessary to access mounting bolts.

81. Tighten shock absorber lower mounting bolt nuts to 53 ft. lbs. (72 Nm).

82. Tighten stabilizer link fasteners to 45 ft. lbs. (61 Nm).

83. Perform wheel alignment, paying special attention to thrust angle. If rear crossmember needs to be shifted to align thrust angle, try to avoid compromising tension link clearance

STRUT & SPRING ASSEMBLY

REMOVAL & INSTALLATION
See Figures 404 through 409.

1. Raise and safely support the vehicle.
2. On both sides of vehicle, remove wheel mounting nuts, then rear tire and wheel assembly.

⁕⁕ **CAUTION**

Before opening fuel system, review all Warnings and Cautions.

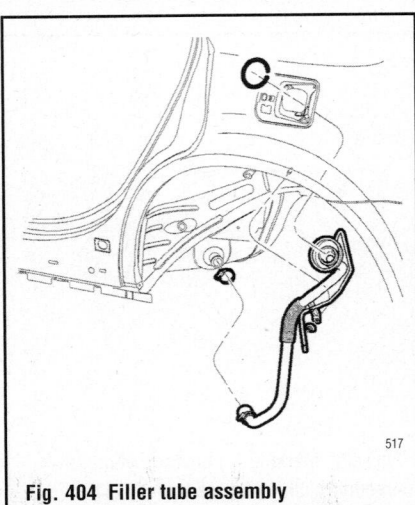

Fig. 404 Filler tube assembly

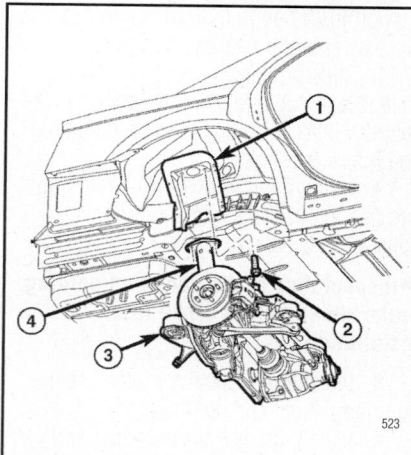

Fig. 405 Shock (1) mounting—upper screws (2)

3. If servicing left side shock absorber, remove fuel filler tube.

4. Position an extra pair of jack stands under and support forward end of engine cradle to help stabilize vehicle during rear suspension removal/installation.

5. Perform following if vehicle is equipped with dual exhaust or if servicing right side on vehicle with single exhaust:

    a. Position under-hoist utility jack or stand several inches below exhaust at muffler.

    b. Disconnect exhaust isolators at muffler and resonators hangers.

    c. Lower exhaust down to rest upon top of jack or stand placed below muffler.

6. Position under-hoist utility jack or transmission jack under center of rear axle differential. Raise jack head to contact differential and secure in place. When securing crossmember to jack, be sure not to secure stabilizer bar.

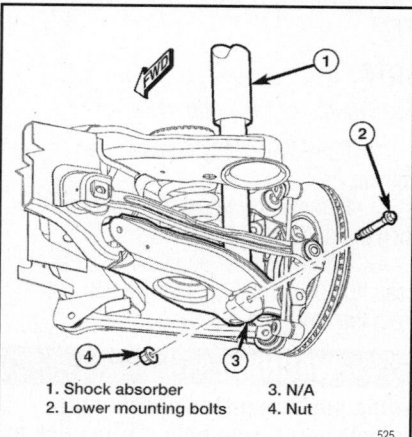

| 1. Shock absorber | 3. N/A |
| 2. Lower mounting bolts | 4. Nut |

Fig. 406 Shock (1) mounting—lower bolt (2) and nut (4)

7. Remove the shock absorber upper mounting screws.

    a. Remove shock absorber lower mounting bolt and nut.

✳✳ WARNING

When removing crossmember mounting bolts (2 and 3) it is important NOT to loosen or remove crossmember mounting bolts on opposite side of vehicle. Doing so will require rear wheel alignment following reinstallation to ensure proper thrust angle.

8. Remove the both front and rear crossmember mounting bolts (2 and 3) on repair-side of vehicle.

✳✳ WARNING

To avoid damaging other components of vehicle, do not lower crossmember any further than necessary to remove shock absorber.

9. Slowly lower jack allowing repair-side of crossmember to drop. Lower jack just enough to allow top of shock absorber to clear body flange.

10. Remove the shock absorber by tipping top outward and lifting lower end out of pocket in spring link.

11. Disconnect brake hose at bracket mounted to body to allow to avoid overextending hose, damaging it, during following step.

12. Slowly lower jack until crossmember is low enough to remove coil spring. Do not lower jack any further than necessary to remove spring.

13. Remove the coil spring and isolators.

To install:

➡**Rear coil springs are interchangeable.**

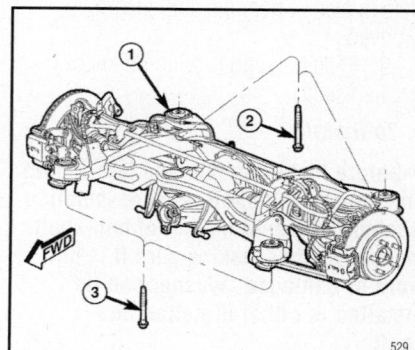

Fig. 407 Rear crossmember (1) mounting bolts (2, 3)

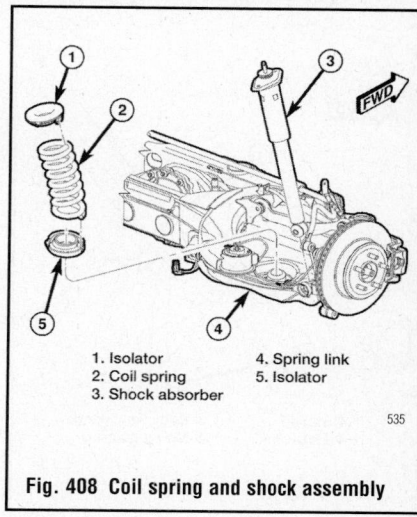

1. Isolator	4. Spring link
2. Coil spring	5. Isolator
3. Shock absorber	

Fig. 408 Coil spring and shock assembly

14. Install the upper and lower isolators on coil spring.

➡**Before installing coil spring, make sure isolators are completely installed on ends of spring.**

15. Install the coil spring with isolators into spring pocket of spring link fitting lower isolator to shape of pocket, then align top of spring with body mount.

16. Install the shock absorber by setting lower end into pocket in spring link, then tipping top inward until aligned with upper mounting holes.

17. Install the lower shock mounting bolt and nut. Do not tighten at this time.

18. Carefully raise jack, guiding coil spring and upper end of shock absorber into mounted positions.

19. Install the shock absorber upper mounting screws. Tighten upper mounting screws to 38 ft. lbs. (52 Nm).

➡**Rear crossmember mounting bolts are longer than front mounting bolts. Do not interchange mounting bolts.**

20. Install the crossmember mounting bolts. Snug, but do not fully tighten bolts at this time.

21. Measure distance between from tension link to body weld flange directly in front of it, just outboard of front mount bushing. This distance must be at least 12 mm to allow proper clearance for suspension movement. If distance is less than 12 mm, shift that side of rear crossmember directly rearward until distance is 12 mm or greater. To do so, loosen 3 mounting bolts slightly, leaving one on opposite side of shift snugged to pivot off of. Shift crossmember rearward and snug loosened bolts. Measure opposite side to be sure it also maintains minimum 12 mm distance.

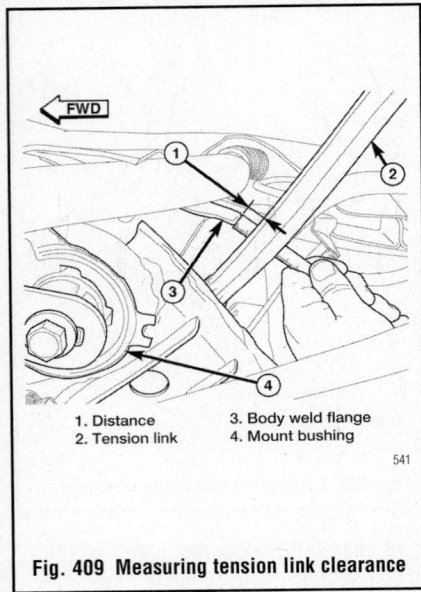

1. Distance
2. Tension link
3. Body weld flange
4. Mount bushing

541

Fig. 409 Measuring tension link clearance

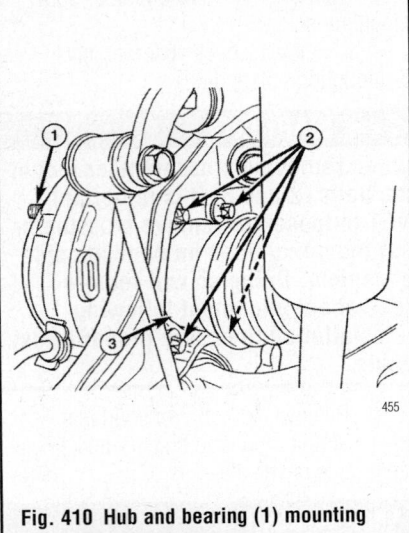

455

Fig. 410 Hub and bearing (1) mounting bolts (2) and half shaft (3)

22. Tighten all crossmember mounting bolts to 133 ft. lbs. (180 Nm).

23. Remove the jack from under rear axle differential.

24. If previously lowered, raise rear exhaust back to mounted position and connect exhaust isolators at muffler and resonators hangers. Remove jack or stand below exhaust muffler.

25. Install the fuel filler tube.

26. Install the tire and wheel assemblies. Tighten wheel mounting nuts to 110 ft. lbs. (150 Nm).

27. Carefully lower the vehicle.

28. Position vehicle on alignment rack/drive-on lift. Raise lift as necessary to access lower mounting bolt.

29. Tighten shock absorber lower mounting bolt nut to 53 ft. lbs. (72 Nm).

WHEEL BEARINGS

REMOVAL & INSTALLATION

Non SRT8

See Figure 410.

1. Raise and safely support the vehicle.

2. Remove the wheel mounting nuts, then tire and wheel assembly.

3. While a helper applies brakes to keep hub from rotating, remove hub nut from the half shaft.

➡**In some cases, it may be necessary to retract caliper piston in its bore a small amount in order to provide sufficient clearance between shoes and rotor to easily remove caliper from knuckle. This can usually be accomplished before guide pin bolts are removed, by grasping rear of caliper and pulling outward working with guide pins, thus retracting piston. Never push on piston directly as it may get damaged.**

4. Remove the two bolts securing disc brake caliper adapter to knuckle.

5. Remove the disc brake caliper and adapter from knuckle as an assembly. Hang assembly out of way using wire or a bungee cord. Use care not to overextend brake hose when doing this.

6. Remove the any clips retaining brake rotor to wheel mounting studs.

7. Slide brake rotor off hub and bearing.

8. Loosen each hub and bearing mounting bolt a turn or two at a time while pulling outward on hub and bearing to avoid bolt contact with half shaft outer joint. Once removed from threads in hub and bearing (but not knuckle), allow bolts to stay in and protrude through knuckle and brake support plate to keep brake support plate in place when hub and bearing is removed.

9. Slide hub and bearing off knuckle and half shaft.

To install:

➡**Before installing hub and bearing on end of axle half shaft, ensure isolation washer is present on end of half shaft. Inspect washer making sure it is not worn or damaged. Washer can be installed in either direction on shaft.**

10. Position hub and bearing bolts though rear of knuckle and parking brake

support just enough to hold support in place as hub and bearing is installed.

11. Slide hub and bearing onto half shaft. Place hub and bearing through brake support, onto knuckle, lining up mounting bolt holes with bolts.

12. Install the four bolts fastening hub and bearing in place. Tighten mounting bolts to 50 ft. lbs. (68 Nm).

➡**Inspect disc brake pads and parking brake shoes before brake rotor installation.**

13. Install the brake rotor over wheel mounting studs and onto hub.

14. Install the disc brake caliper and adapter assembly over brake rotor.

15. Install the mounting bolts securing caliper adapter to knuckle. Tighten bolts to 85 ft. lbs. (115 Nm).

➡**Always install a new hub nut. The original hub nut is one-time use only and should be discarded when removed.**

16. Install the hub nut on end of half shaft. While a helper applies brakes to keep hub from turning, tighten hub nut to 157 ft. lbs. (213 Nm).

17. Verify proper adjustment of the parking brake shoes and adjust as necessary.

18. Install the tire and wheel assembly. Tighten wheel mounting nuts to 110 ft. lbs. (150 Nm).

19. Carefully lower the vehicle.

20. Pump brake pedal several times to ensure vehicle has a firm brake pedal before moving vehicle.

21. Check and adjust brake fluid level in reservoir as necessary.

22. Road test vehicle and make several stops to wear off any foreign material on brakes and to seat brake pads.

SRT8

See Figures 411 through 413.

1. Raise and safely support the vehicle.

2. Remove the wheel mounting nuts, then tire and wheel assembly.

3. While a helper applies brakes to keep hub from rotating, remove hub nut from the half shaft.

✳✳ WARNING

When pushing pistons back into caliper bores, use only a trim stick as shown or other suitable soft tool. Never use a screwdriver or other

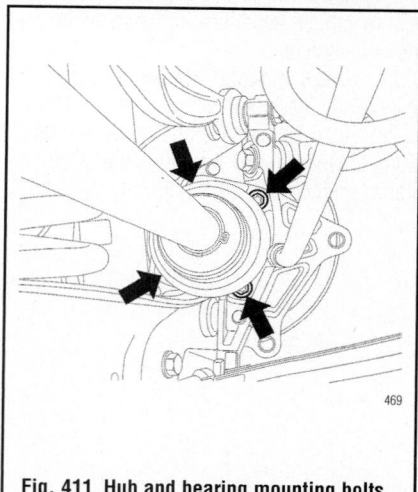

Fig. 411 Hub and bearing mounting bolts

metal pry bar due to potential damage to braking surface of rotor, caliper, pistons or dust boots.

4. Place trim stick between brake pad and outer edge of rotor.

5. Using trim stick, slowly apply pressure against brake pad until both pistons (on that side of caliper) are completely bottomed in bores of caliper half.

➡Repeat above procedure to opposite brake pad and pistons as necessary.

6. Support spring link using a transmission jack or other appropriate jack. Raise spring link just enough to access brake caliper lower mounting bolt from above compression link.

7. Remove the lower and upper caliper mounting bolts.

8. Remove the brake caliper with pads from knuckle and brake rotor. Hang assembly out of way using wire or a bungee cord. Use care not to overextend brake hose when doing this.

9. Remove the any clips retaining brake rotor to wheel mounting studs.

10. Slide brake rotor off hub and bearing.

11. Push inward on end of half shaft until C/V joints bottom. This is necessary to give as much access to hub and bearing mounting bolts as possible.

➡It is important to keep suspension jacked up as requested to ease access to lower hub and bearing mounting bolts.

➡Use a 3/8 inch drive wobble extension along with a Torx®socket to access and remove two top and lower front mounting bolt. Use a standard 3/8 inch drive universal joint along with a

Torx®socket to access and remove lower rear mounting bolt.

12. Loosen each (of the four) hub and bearing mounting bolt a turn or two at a time while pulling outward on hub and bearing to avoid bolt contact with half shaft outer joint. Once removed from threads in hub and bearing (but not knuckle), allow bolts to stay in and protrude through knuckle and parking brake adapter to keep brake adapter in place while hub and bearing is off vehicle.

13. Slide hub and bearing out of knuckle and off half shaft.

To install:

➡Before installing hub and bearing on end of axle half shaft, ensure isolation washer is present on end of half shaft. Inspect washer making sure it is not worn or damaged. Washer can be installed in either direction on shaft.

➡To help upon installation, make sure that hub and bearing mounting bolts extend through knuckle and parking brake adapter to hold adapter in place during hub and bearing installation.

14. Position hub and bearing mounting bolts though rear of knuckle and parking brake adapter just enough to hold adapter in place.

➡Hub and bearing mounting bolt holes are not evenly spaced. Upper mounting holes are not as far apart as lower mounting holes. Make note of this before installing hub and bearing.

15. Slide hub and bearing onto half shaft. Insert hub and bearing through parking brake adapter and knuckle, lining up mounting bolt holes with bolts.

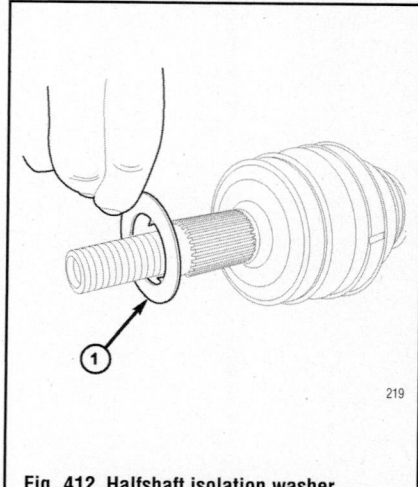

Fig. 412 Halfshaft isolation washer

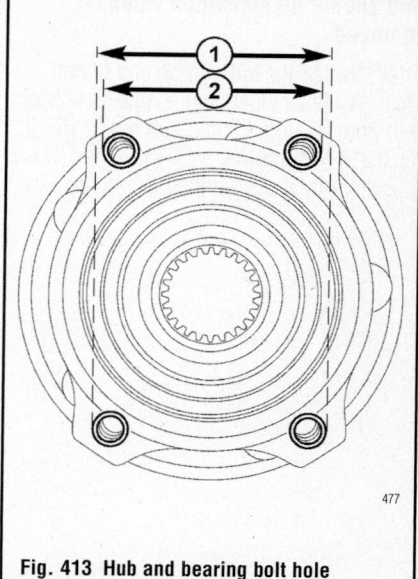

Fig. 413 Hub and bearing bolt hole pattern—Upper (1), Lower (2)

➡Make sure suspension is jacked up as requested during removal to ease access to lower hub and bearing mounting bolts.

➡Use a 3/8 inch drive wobble extension along with a Torx®socket to slip past half shaft outer C/V joint and install two top and lower front mounting bolts. Use a standard 3/8 inch drive universal joint along with a Torx®socket to install lower rear mounting bolt.

16. Carefully start all four mounting bolts into hub and bearing. Using a cross pattern, tighten each hub and bearing mounting bolt a turn or two at a time, slowly drawing hub and bearing into mounted position. Periodically, push in on end of half shaft to give as much room as possible for tools on mounting bolts. Tighten mounting bolts to 50 ft. lbs. (68 Nm) torque.

➡Inspect disc brake pads and parking brake shoes before brake rotor installation.

17. Clean hub face to remove any dirt or corrosion where rotor mounts.

18. Install the brake rotor over studs on hub and bearing.

19. Slide caliper with pads over brake rotor and align with knuckle.

20. Install the caliper mounting bolts. Tighten bolts to 96 ft. lbs. (130 Nm) torque.

21. Remove the jack from under spring link.

➡Always install a new hub nut. The original hub nut is one-time use only

and should be discarded when removed.

22. Install the hub nut on end of half shaft. While a helper applies brakes to keep hub from turning, tighten hub nut to 157 ft. lbs. (213 Nm) torque.

23. Verify proper adjustment of the parking brake shoes and adjust as necessary.

24. Install the tire and wheel assembly. Tighten wheel mounting nuts to 110 ft. lbs. (150 Nm) torque.

25. Carefully lower the vehicle.

26. Pump brake pedal several times to ensure vehicle has a firm brake pedal before moving vehicle.

27. Check and adjust brake fluid level in reservoir as necessary.

28. Road test vehicle and make several stops to wear off any foreign material on brakes and to seat brake pads.

JEEP

Commander

6

SPECIFICATIONS AND MAINTENANCE CHARTS

ENGINE AND VEHICLE IDENTIFICATION

		Engine						Model Year	
Code ①	Liters (cc)	Cu. In.	Cyl.	Fuel Sys.	Engine Type	Eng. Mfg.		Code ②	Year
N-08; P-09	4.7 (4701)	287	8	MFI	SOHC	Chrysler		A	2010
2-08; T-09	5.7 (5654)	345	8	MFI	OHV	Chrysler			

MFI: Multi-port Fuel Injection

OHV: Over Head Valve

SOHC: Single Overhead Camshaft

① 8th position of VIN

② 10th position of VIN

25766_COMM_C0001

GENERAL ENGINE SPECIFICATIONS

Year	Model	Engine Displ. Liters	Engine VIN	Net Horsepower @ rpm	Net Torque @ rpm (ft. lbs.)	Bore x Stroke (in.)	Comp. Ratio	Oil Pressure @ rpm
2010	Commander	3.7	K	211@5200	236@4000	3.66x3.40	9.6:1	25-110@3000
		4.7	P	303@5650	330@3950	3.66x3.40	9.6:1	35-105@3000
		5.7	T	335@5200	370@4200	3.92x3.58	10.5:1	25-110@3000

25766_COMM_C0002

GASOLINE ENGINE TUNE-UP SPECIFICATIONS

Year	Engine Displ. Liters	Engine VIN	Spark Plug Gap (in.)	Ignition Timing (deg.)	Fuel Pump (psi)	Idle Speed (rpm)	Valve Clearance	
							Intake	Exhaust
2010	3.7	K	0.043	①	56-60	①	HYD	HYD
	4.7	P	0.040/0.050 B	①	56-60	①	HYD	HYD
	5.7	T	0.040	①	56-60	①	HYD	HYD

Note: The information on the Vehicle Emission Control label must be used, if different from the figures in this chart.

HYD: Hydraulic

① Ignition timing and idle speed are controlled by the PCM. No adjustment is necessary.

② Intake (upper row)/Exhaust (lower row)

25766_COMM_C0003

CAPACITIES

Year	Model	Engine Displ. Liters	Engine VIN	Engine Oil with Filter	Transmission (pts.) Man.	Transmission (pts.) Auto.**	Transfer Case (pts.)	Drive Axle Front (pts.)	Drive Axle Rear* (pts.)	Fuel Tank (gal.)	Cooling System (qts.)
2010	Commander	3.7	K	5.0	—	16.3	1.4	3.6	4.4	21.0	9.0
		4.7	P	6.0	—	28.0	3.8	3.6	4.4	21.0	14.5
		5.7	T	7.0	—	28.0	3.8	3.6	4.4	21.0	14.5

* When equipped with Trac Lok, add 4 oz. of limited slip additive

**Overhaul

25766_COMM_C0004

FLUID SPECIFICATIONS

Year	Model	Engine Displacement Liters (VIN)	Engine Oil	Auto. Trans.	Front & Rear Axle	Power Steering Fluid	Brake Master Cylinder
2010	Commander	3.7 (K)	5W-20	Mopar® ATF +4	Mopar® Synthetic Gear Lube 75W-140	Mopar® Hydraulic System/Power Steering Fluid (MS-10838)	DOT 3
		4.7 (N)	5W-20	Mopar® ATF +4	Mopar® Synthetic Gear Lube 75W-140	Mopar® Hydraulic System/Power Steering Fluid (MS-10838)	DOT 3
		5.7 (2)	5W-20	Mopar® ATF +4	Mopar® Synthetic Gear Lube 75W-140	Mopar® Hydraulic System/Power Steering Fluid (MS-10838)	DOT 3

DOT: Department Of Transpotation

25766_COMM_C0005

VALVE SPECIFICATIONS

Year	Engine Displ. Liters	Engine VIN	Seat Angle (deg.)	Face Angle (deg.)	Spring Test Pressure (lbs. @ in.)	Spring Installed Height (in.)	Stem-to-Guide Clearance (in.) Intake	Stem-to-Guide Clearance (in.) Exhaust	Stem Diameter (in.) Intake	Stem Diameter (in.) Exhaust
2010	3.7	K	44.5-45	45-45.5	213-234@ 1.107	1.579	0.0008-0.0028	0.0019-0.0039	0.2729-0.2739	0.2717-0.2728
	4.7	P	44.5-45	45-45.5	174.5-195.6 @1.137	1.579	0.0008-0.0028	0.0019-0.0039	0.2729-0.2739	0.2717-0.2728
	5.7	T	44.5-45	45-45.5	231-253@ 1.283	1.81	0.0008-0.0025	0.0009-0.0025	0.3120-0.3130	0.3120-0.3130

25766_COMM_C0006

CAMSHAFT AND BEARING SPECIFICATIONS CHART

All measurements are given in inches.

Year	Engine Displacement Liters	Engine VIN	Journal Diameter	Brg. Oil Clearance	Shaft End-play	Runout	Journal Bore	Lobe Lift	
								Intake	Exhaust
2010	3.7	K	1.0227-1.0235	0.0010-0.0026	0.0030-0.0079	NA	1.0245-1.0252	0.2950-0.3150	0.2950-0.3150
	4.7	P	1.0227-1.0235	0.0010-0.0026	0.0039-0.0079	NA	1.0245-1.0252	0.2769-0.2953	0.2683-0.2861
	5.7	T	①	②	0.0031-0.0114	NA	NA	0.2950-0.3147	0.2875-0.3067

NA: Not Available

① No. 1: 2.29 in.
   No. 2: 2.28 in.
   No. 3: 2.26 in.
   No. 4: 2.24 in.
   No. 5: 1.72 in.

② No. 1: 0.0015-0.0030 in.
   No. 2: 0.0019-0.0035 in.
   No. 3: 0.0015-0.0030 in.
   No. 4: 0.0019-0.0035 in.
   No. 5: 0.0015-0.0030 in.

25766_COMM_C0007

CRANKSHAFT AND CONNECTING ROD SPECIFICATIONS

All measurements are given in inches.

Year	Engine Displ. Liters	Engine VIN	Crankshaft				Connecting Rod		
			Main Brg. Journal Dia.	Main Brg. Oil Clearance	Shaft End-play	Thrust on No.	Journal Diameter	Oil Clearance	Side Clearance
2010	3.7	K	2.4996-2.5005	0.0008-0.0018	0.0021-0.0112	2	2.2792-2.2798	0.0002-0.0011	0.0040-0.0138
	4.7	P	2.4996-2.5005	0.0002-0.0013	0.0021-0.0112	2	2.0076-2.0082	0.0004-0.0019	0.0040-0.0138
	5.7	T	2.5585-2.5595	0.0009-0.0020	0.0020-0.0110	3	2.1260	0.0007-0.0023	0.0030-0.0137

25766_COMM_C0008

PISTON AND RING SPECIFICATIONS

All measurements are given in inches.

Year	Engine Displ. Liters	Engine VIN	Piston Clearance	Ring Gap			Ring Side Clearance		
				Top Compression	Bottom Compression	Oil Control	Top Compression	Bottom Compression	Oil Control
2010	3.7	K	0.0011-0.0017	0.0079-0.0142	0.0146-0.0249	0.0099-0.0300	0.0020-0.0037	0.0016-0.0031	0.0007-0.0091
	4.7	P	0.0011-0.0017	0.0079-0.0142	0.0146-0.0249	0.0099-0.0300	0.0020-0.0037	0.0016-0.0031	0.0007-0.0091
	5.7	T	0.0012-0.0023	0.0150-0.0210	0.0090-0.0200	0.0059-0.0259	0.0010-0.0035	0.0010-0.0031	0.0020-0.0080

25766_COMM_C0009

TORQUE SPECIFICATIONS

All readings in ft. lbs.

Year	Engine Displ. Liters	Engine VIN	Cylinder Head Bolts	Main Bearing Bolts	Rod Bearing Bolts	Crankshaft Damper Bolts	Flywheel Bolts	Manifold		Spark Plugs	Oil Pan Drain Plug
								Intake	Exhaust		
2010	3.7	K	①	②	③	130	70	9	18	20	25
	4.7	P	④	⑤	③	130	45	9	18	20/16⑥	25
	5.7	T	⑦	⑧	⑨	130	55	9	18	13	20

① Refer to procedure for illustration
  Step 1: Tighten bolts 1-8 to 20 ft. lbs. (27 Nm)
  Step 2: Verify bolts 1-8 at 20 ft. lbs. (27 Nm)
  Step 3: Tighten bolts 9-12 to 10 ft. lbs. (14 Nm)
  Step 4: Tighten bolts 1-8 an addt'l 90 degrees
  Step 5: Tighten bolts 1-8 another 90 degrees
  Step 6: Tighten bolts 9-12 to 19 ft. lbs. (26 Nm)

② Bed plate bolt sequence. Refer to illustration
  Step 1: Tighten bolts 1D,1G, 1F until bedplate contacts block
  Step 2: Tighten bolts 1A - 1J to 40 ft. lbs. (54 Nm)
  Step 3: Tighten bolts 1 - 8 to 5 ft. lbs. (7 Nm)
  Step 4: Turn bolts 1 - 8 an additional 90°.
  Step 5: Tighten bolts A - E to 20 ft. lbs. (27 Nm)

③ 20 ft. lbs. + 90 degrees

④ Refer to procedure for illustration
  Step 1: Tighten bolts 1-10 to 20 ft. lbs. (27 Nm)
  Step 2: Verify bolts 1-10 at 20 ft. lbs. (27 Nm)
  Step 3: Tighten bolts 11-14 to 10 ft. lbs. (14 Nm)
  Step 4: Tighten bolts 1-10 an addt'l 90 degrees
  Step 5: Tighten bolts 1-10 another 90 degrees
  Step 6: Tighten bolts 11-14 to 19 ft. lbs. (26 Nm)

⑤ Bed plate bolt sequence. Refer to illustrations
  Step 1: Bolts 1-22 to 26 inch lbs.
  Step 2: Bolts 1-12 40 ft. lbs.
  Step 3: Bolts 1-10 plus 90 degrees
  Step 4: Side Bolts 1-6 20 ft. lbs.

⑥ Upper/Lower

⑦ Refer to procedure for illustration
  Step 1: Tighten M12 bolts to 25 ft. lbs. (34 Nm)
  Step 2: Tighten M8 bolts 1-10 at 15 ft. lbs. (20 Nm)
  Step 3: Tighten M12 bolts to 40 ft. lbs. (54 Nm)
  Step 4: Tighten M8 bolts to 25 ft. lbs. (34 Nm)
  Step 5: Tighten M12 bolts an addt'l 90 degrees

⑧ Step 1: Tighten bolts to 20 ft. lbs. (27 Nm)
  Step 2: Tighten bolts an addt'l 90 degrees
  Step 3: Tighten crossbolts to 21 ft. lbs. (28 Nm)
  Step 4: Tighten crossbolts again to 21 ft. lbs. (28 Nm)

⑨ 15 ft. lbs., plus 90 degrees

25766_COMM_C0010

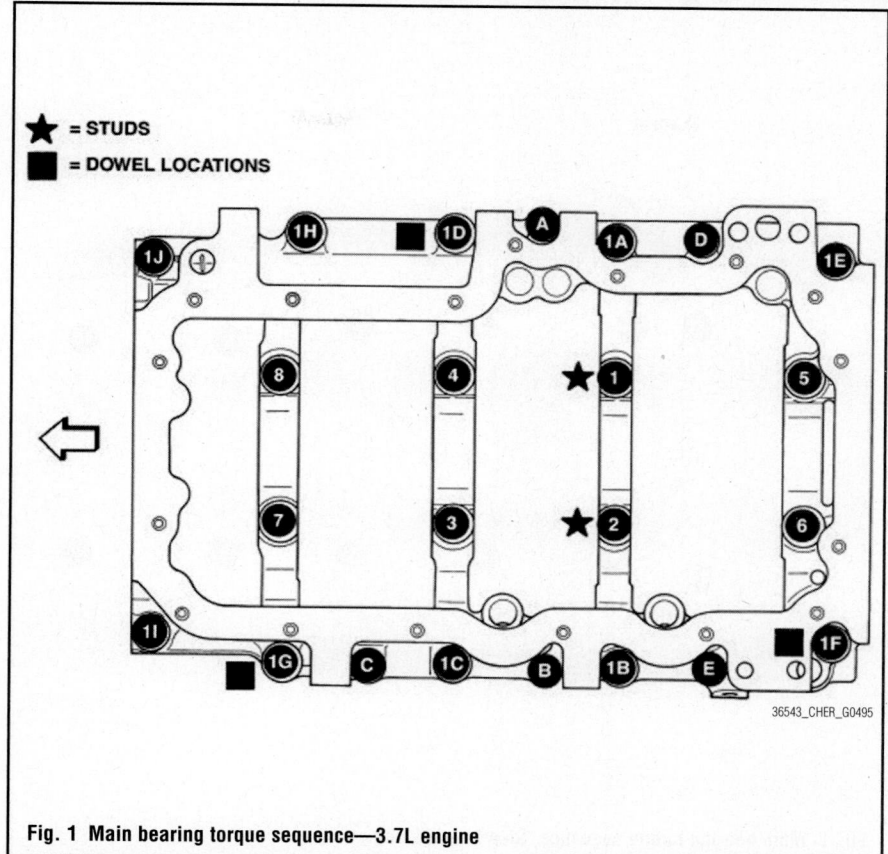

Fig. 1 Main bearing torque sequence—3.7L engine

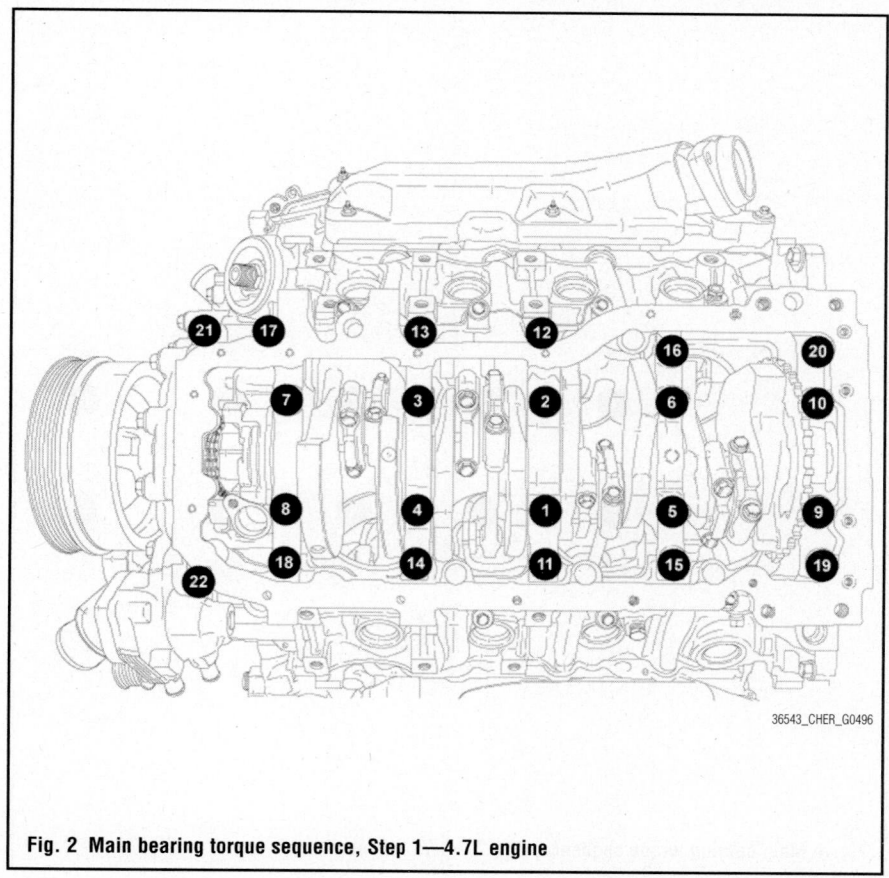

Fig. 2 Main bearing torque sequence, Step 1—4.7L engine

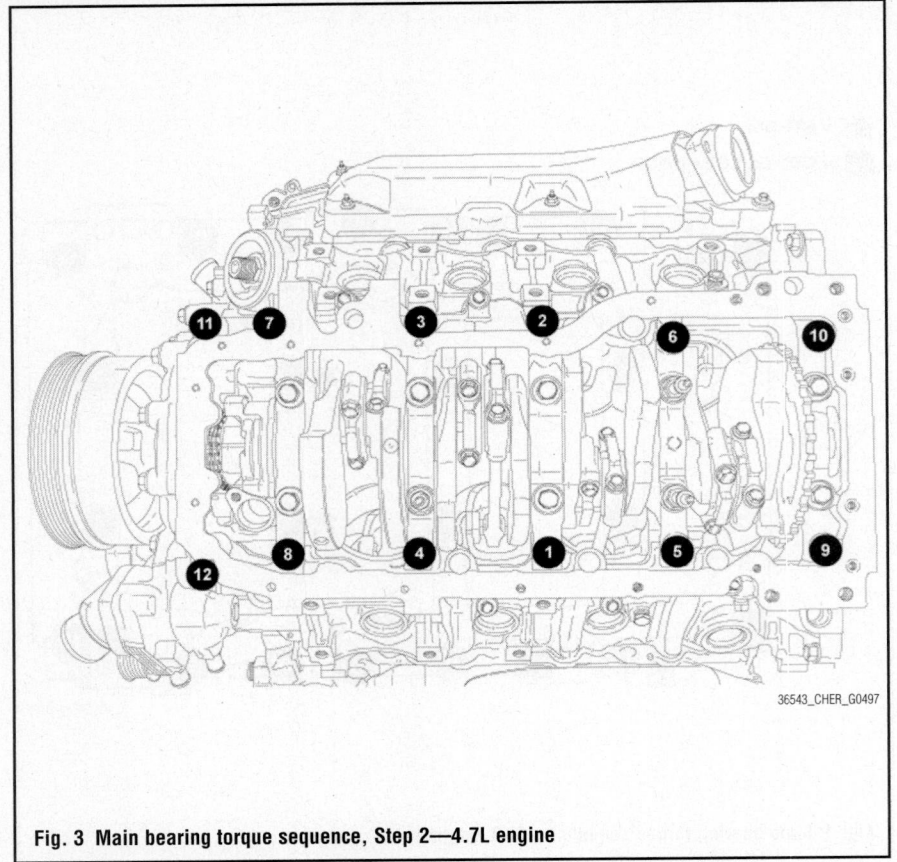

Fig. 3 Main bearing torque sequence, Step 2—4.7L engine

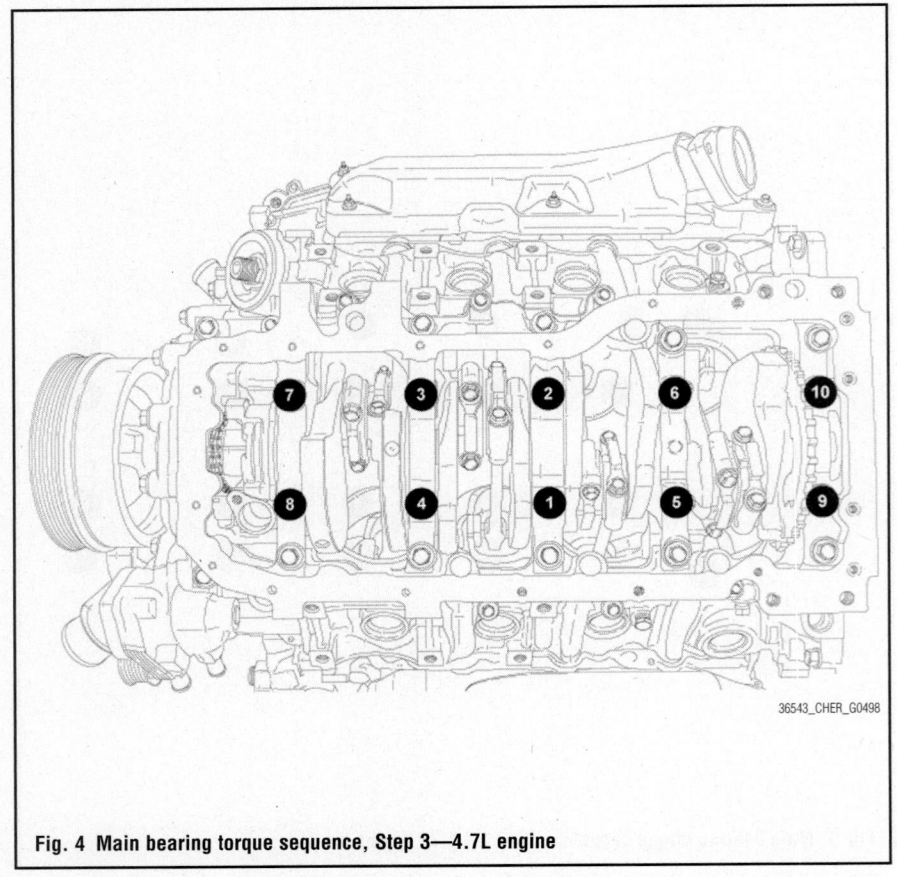

Fig. 4 Main bearing torque sequence, Step 3—4.7L engine

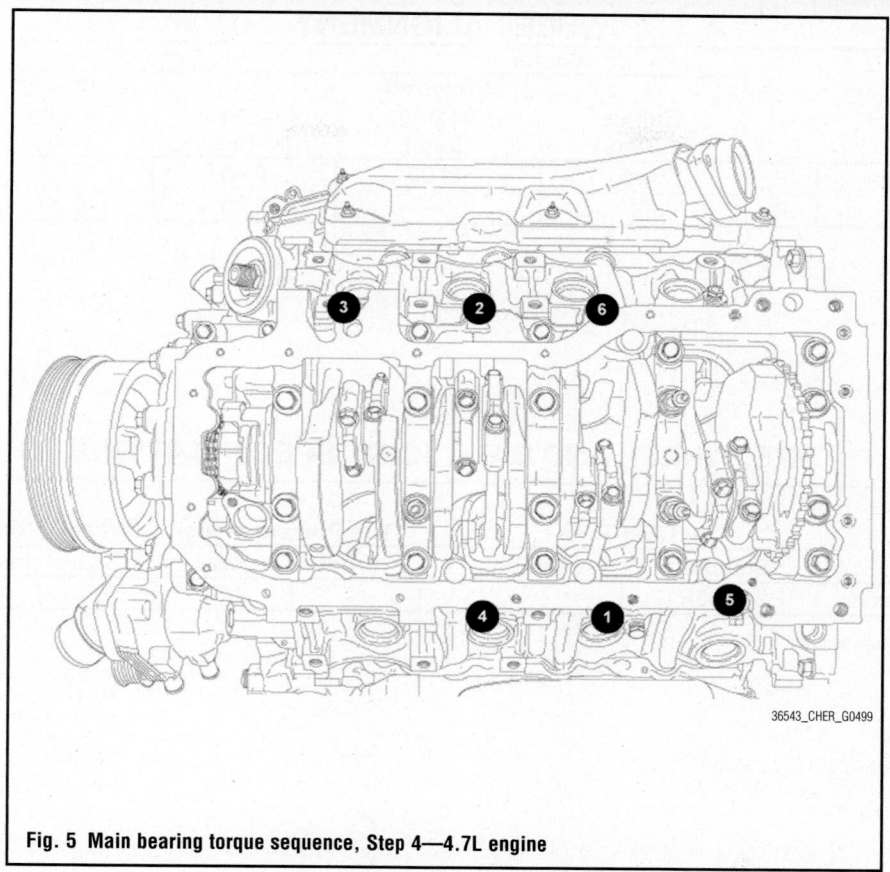

Fig. 5 Main bearing torque sequence, Step 4—4.7L engine

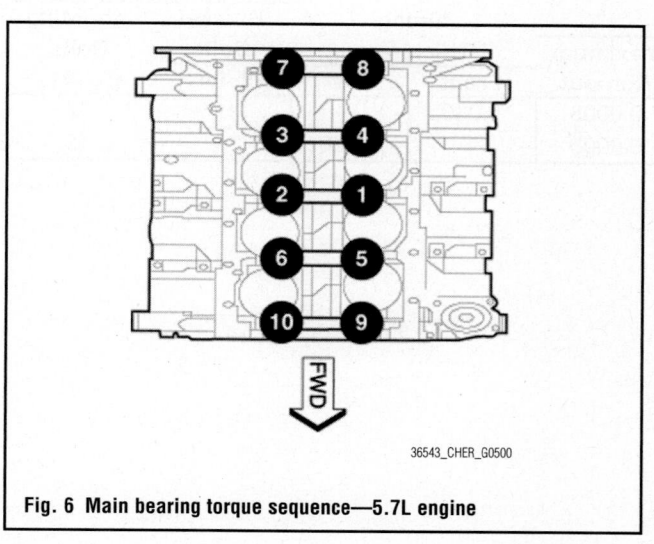

Fig. 6 Main bearing torque sequence—5.7L engine

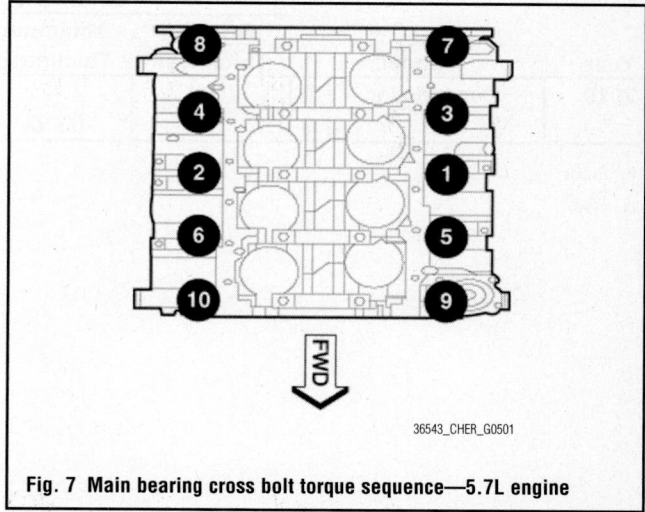

Fig. 7 Main bearing cross bolt torque sequence—5.7L engine

WHEEL ALIGNMENT

Year	Model		Caster Range (+/-Deg.)	Caster Preferred Setting (Deg.)	Camber Range (+/-Deg.)	Camber Preferred Setting (Deg.)	Toe-in (deg.)
2010	Commander	F	0.45	+4.00	0.45	-0.25	0.25+/-0.25
		R	—	—	0.25	-0.25	0.25+/-0.25

25766_COMM_C0011

TIRE, WHEEL AND BALL JOINT SPECIFICATIONS

Year	Model	OEM Tires Standard	OEM Tires Optional	Tire Pressures (psi) Front	Tire Pressures (psi) Rear	Wheel Size	Ball Joint Inspection	Lug Nut Torque (ft. lbs.)
2010	Commander	P245/65R17	—	①	①	①	②	85-115

OEM: Original Equipment Manufacturer

STD: Standard

OPT: Optional

① See placard on vehicle

② Replace if travel exceeds 0.020 in. (0.5 mm)

25766_COMM_C0012

BRAKE SPECIFICATIONS

All measurements in inches unless noted

Year	Model		Brake Disc Original Thickness	Brake Disc Minimum Thickness	Brake Disc Maximum Run-out	Minimum Lining Thickness Front	Minimum Lining Thickness Rear	Brake Caliper Bracket Bolts (ft. lbs.)	Brake Caliper Mounting Bolts (ft. lbs.)
2010	Commander	F	NA	1.122	0.0008	0.030	—	125	32
		R	NA	0.492	0.0008	—	0.030	—	18

F - Front

R - Rear

25766_COMM_C0013

SCHEDULED MAINTENANCE INTERVALS
Jeep Commander

TO BE SERVICED	TYPE OF SERVICE	VEHICLE MILEAGE INTERVAL (x1000)												
		3	6	9	12	15	18	21	24	27	30	33	36	39
Engine oil & filter ①	R	✓	✓	✓	✓	✓	✓	✓	✓	✓	✓	✓	✓	✓
Tires	Rotate		✓		✓		✓		✓		✓		✓	
Brake hoses & linings	S/I				✓				✓				✓	
Lubricate steering and suspension ball joints	C/L		✓		✓		✓		✓		✓		✓	
Brake caliper pins	C/L				✓				✓				✓	
Air filter	I/R					✓					✓			
Spark plugs	R										✓			
Drive axle lubricant	R					✓			✓				✓	
Transfer case fluid	R	Every 60,000 miles												
PCV valve	I/R										✓			
Accessory drive belt	S/I	Every 60,000 miles												
Spark plug cables (5.7L)	I/R	Every 60,000 miles												
Automatic trans. fluid and filter (4.7L and 5.7L)	R	Every 60,000 miles												
Engine coolant	R	Every 60,000 miles												

R: Replace   S/I: Service or Inspect   C/L: Clean and lubricate   I/R: Inspect and rerplace if necessary

The above schedule is to be used if you drive under any of the following conditions:

Driving in temperatures under 32 degrees F

Stop and go traffic

Extensive engine idling

Driving in dusty conditions

Frequent trips under 10 miles

More than 50 % of your driving is in hot weather (90 deg. F) above 50 miles per hour

Trailer towing

Taxi, police or delivery service

Off-road driving

The vehicle is equipped for and operated with E85 (ethonol) fuel

If none of these conditions is met, double the maintenance intervals

① ENGINE OIL CHANGE RESET PROCEDURE:

The vehicle is equipped with an engine oil change indicator system. The "Oil Change Required" message flashes in the Electronic Vehicle Information Center (EVIC) display for approximately 10 seconds after a single chime has sounded, to indicate the next scheduled oil change interval. The engine oil change indicator system is duty cycle based, which means the engine oil change interval may fluctuate depening on driving habits. Unless reset, this message continues to display each time the ignition switch is turned to the ON/RUN position. To turn off the message temporarily, press and release the Menu button.

To reset the oil change indicator system (after performing the scheduled maintenance), perform the following procedure:

1. Turn the ignition switch to the "ON" position. Do not start the engine.
2. Fully press the accelerator pedal slowly 3 times within 10 seconds.
3. Turn the ignition switch to the "LOCK" position.

NOTE: If indicator message illuminates when starting the vehicle, the oil change indicator system did not reset. Repeat above procedure.

25766_COMM_C0014

PRECAUTIONS

Before servicing any vehicle, please be sure to read all of the following precautions, which deal with personal safety, prevention of component damage, and important points to take into consideration when servicing a motor vehicle:

• Never open, service or drain the radiator or cooling system when the engine is hot; serious burns can occur from the steam and hot coolant.

• Observe all applicable safety precautions when working around fuel. Whenever servicing the fuel system, always work in a well-ventilated area. Do not allow fuel spray or vapors to come in contact with a spark, open flame, or excessive heat (a hot drop light, for example). Keep a dry chemical fire extinguisher near the work area. Always keep fuel in a container specifically designed for fuel storage; also, always properly seal fuel containers to avoid the possibility of fire or explosion. Refer to the additional fuel system precautions later in this section.

• Fuel injection systems often remain pressurized, even after the engine has been turned **OFF**. The fuel system pressure must be relieved before disconnecting any fuel lines. Failure to do so may result in fire and/or personal injury.

• Brake fluid often contains polyglycol ethers and polyglycols. Avoid contact with the eyes and wash your hands thoroughly after handling brake fluid. If you do get brake fluid in your eyes, flush your eyes with clean, running water for 15 minutes. If eye irritation persists, or if you have taken brake fluid internally, IMMEDIATELY seek medical assistance.

• The EPA warns that prolonged contact with used engine oil may cause a number of skin disorders, including cancer. You should make every effort to minimize your exposure to used engine oil. Protective gloves should be worn when changing oil. Wash your hands and any other exposed skin areas as soon as possible after exposure to used engine oil. Soap and water, or waterless hand cleaner should be used.

• All new vehicles are now equipped with an air bag system, often referred to as a Supplemental Restraint System (SRS) or Supplemental Inflatable Restraint (SIR) system. The system must be disabled before performing service on or around system components, steering column, instrument panel components, wiring and sensors. Failure to follow safety and disabling procedures could result in accidental air bag deployment, possible personal injury and unnecessary system repairs.

• Always wear safety goggles when working with, or around, the air bag system. When carrying a non-deployed air bag, be sure the bag and trim cover are pointed away from your body. When placing a non-deployed air bag on a work surface, always face the bag and trim cover upward, away from the surface. This will reduce the motion of the module if it is accidentally deployed. Refer to the additional air bag system precautions later in this section.

• Clean, high quality brake fluid from a sealed container is essential to the safe and proper operation of the brake system. You should always buy the correct type of brake fluid for your vehicle. If the brake fluid becomes contaminated, completely flush the system with new fluid. Never reuse any brake fluid. Any brake fluid that is removed from the system should be discarded. Also, do not allow any brake fluid to come in contact with a painted surface; it will damage the paint.

• Never operate the engine without the proper amount and type of engine oil; doing so WILL result in severe engine damage.

• Timing belt maintenance is extremely important. Many models utilize an interference-type, non-freewheeling engine. If the timing belt breaks, the valves in the cylinder head may strike the pistons, causing potentially serious (also time-consuming and expensive) engine damage. Refer to the maintenance interval charts for the recommended replacement interval for the timing belt, and to the timing belt section for belt replacement and inspection.

• Disconnecting the negative battery cable on some vehicles may interfere with the functions of the on-board computer system(s) and may require the computer to undergo a relearning process once the negative battery cable is reconnected.

• When servicing drum brakes, only disassemble and assemble one side at a time, leaving the remaining side intact for reference.

• Only an MVAC-trained, EPA-certified automotive technician should service the air conditioning system or its components.

BRAKES

GENERAL INFORMATION

PRECAUTIONS

• Certain components within the ABS system are not intended to be serviced or repaired individually.

• Do not use rubber hoses or other parts not specifically specified for and ABS system. When using repair kits, replace all parts included in the kit. Partial or incorrect repair may lead to functional problems and require the replacement of components.

• Lubricate rubber parts with clean, fresh brake fluid to ease assembly. Do not use shop air to clean parts; damage to rubber components may result.

• Use only DOT 3 brake fluid from an unopened container.

• If any hydraulic component or line is removed or replaced, it may be necessary to bleed the entire system.

• A clean repair area is essential. Always clean the reservoir and cap thoroughly before removing the cap. The slightest amount of dirt in the fluid may plug an orifice and impair the system function. Perform repairs after components have been thoroughly cleaned; use only denatured alcohol to clean components. Do not allow ABS components to come into contact with any substance containing mineral oil; this includes used shop rags.

• The Anti-Lock control unit is a microprocessor similar to other computer units in the vehicle. Ensure that the ignition switch is **OFF** before removing or installing controller harnesses. Avoid static electricity discharge at or near the controller.

ANTI-LOCK BRAKE SYSTEM (ABS)

• If any arc welding is to be done on the vehicle, the control unit should be unplugged before welding operations begin.

SPEED SENSORS

REMOVAL & INSTALLATION

Front

See Figures 8 and 9.

1. Raise and support the vehicle.
2. Remove the tire and wheel assembly.
3. Remove the caliper adaptor bolts. Support the caliper and adaptor assembly.

➡**Do Not let assembly hang by the hose.**

4. Remove the disc brake rotor.

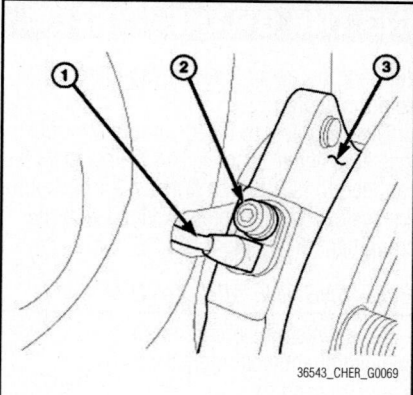

Fig. 8 Remove the front wheel sensor mounting nut (2) to the hub (3)

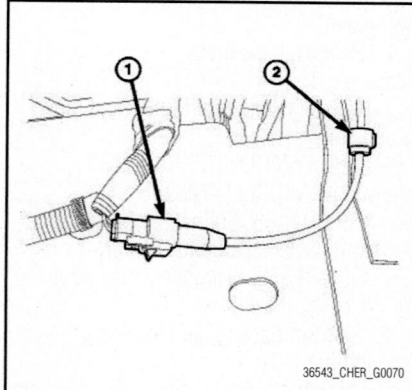

Fig. 9 Disconnect the wire sensor routing clips (2)

5. Remove the front wheel sensor mounting nut (2) to the hub (3).

6. Remove the wheel speed sensor (1) from the hub (3).

7. Disconnect the wire sensor routing clips (2).

8. Disconnect the wheel speed sensor wire connector (1).

9. Remove the sensor and wire.

To install:

10. Reconnect the wheel speed sensor wire connector.

11. Reroute and connect the wheel speed sensor wire to the routing clips.

12. Install the wheel speed sensor into the hub and then install the mounting bolt. Tighten the nut to 106–124 inch lbs. (12–14 Nm).

13. Check the sensor wire routing. Be sure the wire is clear of all chassis components and is not twisted or kinked at any spot.

14. Install the disc brake rotor.

15. Install the caliper adaptor over the rotor.

16. Install the caliper adaptor bolts and tighten to 66–85 ft. lbs. (90–115 Nm).

17. Install the tire and wheel assembly.

18. Remove the support and lower vehicle.

Rear

See Figures 10 and 11.

1. Raise and support the vehicle.

2. Remove the wheel speed sensor mounting bolt (2) from the rear support plate (1).

3. Remove the wheel speed sensor (3) from the support plate.

4. Disconnect the wheel speed sensor electrical connector (3).

To install:

5. Insert the wheel speed sensor through the support plate.

6. Tighten the wheel speed sensor bolt to 106–124 inch lbs. (12–14 Nm).

7. Secure the wheel speed sensor wire to the routing clips. Verify that the sensor

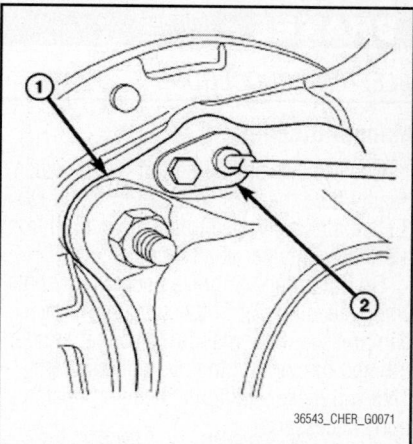

Fig. 10 Remove the wheel speed sensor mounting bolt (2)

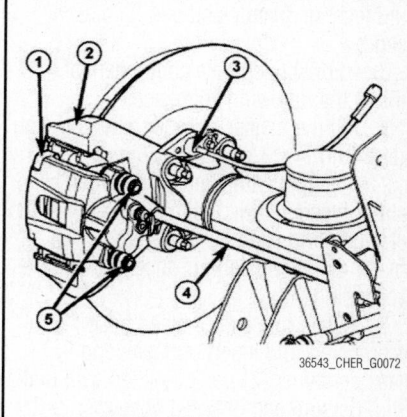

Fig. 11 Remove the wheel speed sensor (3) from the support plate

wire is secure and clear of the rotating components.

8. Reconnect the wheel speed sensor electrical connector.

9. Lower the vehicle.

BLEEDING PROCEDURE

Manual Bleeding

Use Mopar® brake fluid, or an equivalent quality fluid meeting SAE J1703-F and DOT 3 standards only. Use fresh, clean fluid from a sealed container at all times.

Do not pump the brake pedal at any time while bleeding. Air in the system will be compressed into small bubbles that are distributed throughout the hydraulic system. This will make additional bleeding operations necessary.

Do not allow the master cylinder to run out of fluid during bleed operations. An empty cylinder will allow additional air to be drawn into the system. Check the cylinder fluid level frequently and add fluid as needed.

Bleed only one brake component at a time in the following sequence:

1. Fill the master cylinder reservoir with brake fluid.
2. If calipers are overhauled, open all caliper bleed screws. Then close each bleed screw as fluid starts to drip from it. Top off master cylinder reservoir once more before proceeding.
3. Attach one end of bleed hose (1) to bleed screw and insert opposite end in glass container (2) partially filled with brake fluid. Be sure end of bleed hose is immersed in fluid.

4. Open up bleeder, then have a helper press down the brake pedal. Once the pedal is down close the bleeder. Repeat bleeding until fluid stream is clear and free of bubbles. Then move to the next wheel.

Pressure Bleeding

Use Mopar brake fluid, or an equivalent quality fluid meeting SAE J1703-F and DOT 3 standards only. Use fresh, clean fluid from a sealed container at all times.

Do not pump the brake pedal at any time while bleeding. Air in the system will be compressed into small bubbles that are distributed throughout the hydraulic system. This will make additional bleeding operations necessary.

Do not allow the master cylinder to run out of fluid during bleed operations. An empty cylinder will allow additional air to be drawn into the system. Check the cylinder fluid level frequently and add fluid as needed.

Bleed only one brake component at a time.

Follow the manufacturer's instructions carefully when using pressure equipment. Do not exceed the tank manufacturer's pressure recommendations. Generally, a tank pressure of 51-67 kPa (15-20 psi) is sufficient for bleeding.

Fill the bleeder tank with recommended

fluid and purge air from the tank lines before bleeding.

Do not pressure bleed without a proper master cylinder adapter. The wrong adapter can lead to leakage, or drawing air back into the system. Use adapter provided with the equipment or Adapter 6921.

BLEEDING THE ABS SYSTEM

ABS system bleeding requires conventional bleeding methods plus use of a scan tool. The procedure involves performing a base brake bleeding, followed by use of the scan tool to cycle and bleed the HCU pump and solenoids. A second base brake bleeding procedure is then required to remove any air remaining in the system.

1. Perform base brake bleeding.
2. Connect scan tool to the Data Link Connector.
3. Select ANTILOCK BRAKES, followed by MISCELLANEOUS, then ABS BRAKES. Follow the instructions displayed. When scan tool displays TEST COMPLETE, disconnect scan tool and proceed.
4. Perform base brake bleeding a second time.
5. Top off master cylinder fluid level and verify proper brake operation before moving vehicle.

✳✳ CAUTION

Dust and dirt accumulating on brake parts during normal use may contain asbestos fibers from production or aftermarket brake linings. Breathing excessive concentrations of asbestos fibers can cause serious bodily harm. Exercise care when servicing brake parts. Do not sand or grind brake lining unless equipment used is designed to contain the dust residue. Do not clean brake parts with compressed air or by dry brushing. Cleaning should be done by dampening the brake components with a fine mist of water, then wiping the brake components clean with a dampened cloth. Dispose of cloth and all residue containing asbestos fibers in an impermeable container with the appropriate label. Follow practices prescribed by the Occupational Safety and Health Administration

(OSHA) and the Environmental Protection Agency (EPA) for the handling, processing, and disposing of dust or debris that may contain asbestos fibers.

BRAKE CALIPER

REMOVAL & INSTALLATION

See Figure 12.

1. Install prop rod on the brake pedal to keep pressure on the brake system, Holding pedal in this position will isolate master cylinder from hydraulic brake system and will not allow brake fluid to drain out of brake fluid reservoir while brake lines are open. This will allow you to bleed out the area of repair instead of the entire system.
2. Raise and support vehicle.
3. Remove front wheel and tire assembly.

4. Drain small amount of fluid from master cylinder brake reservoir with clean suction gun.
5. Bottom caliper pistons into the caliper by prying the caliper over.

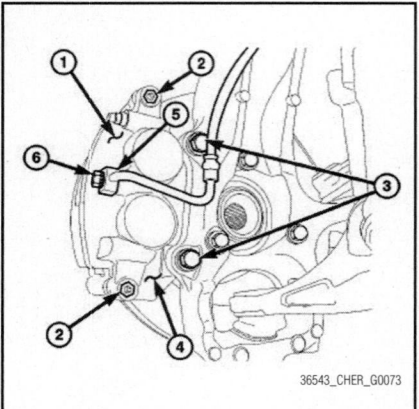

36543_CHER_G0073

Fig. 12 Remove brake hose banjo bolt and gasket washers (6)

6. Remove brake hose banjo bolt and gasket washers (6). Discard gasket washers.

7. Remove the caliper slide bolts (2).

8. Remove the caliper (1) from the adapter (4).

To install:

9. Install the caliper on the adapter.

10. Caliper slide pins should be free from debris and lightly lubricated.

11. Install the caliper slide pin bolts and tighten to 32 ft. lbs. (44 Nm).

12. Gently lift one end of the slide pin boot to equalize air pressure, then release the boot and verify that the boot is fully covering the slide pin.

✳✳ CAUTION

Verify brake hose is not twisted or kinked before tightening banjo bolt.

13. Install brake hose to caliper with new copper washers. Tighten banjo bolt to 23 ft. lbs. (31 Nm).

14. Remove the prop rod from the brake pedal.

15. Bleed the area of repair for the brake system. If a proper pedal is not felt during bleeding an area of repair then a base bleed system must be performed.

16. Install wheel and tire assemblies.

17. Remove supports and lower vehicle.

18. Verify brake fluid level.

DISC BRAKE PADS

REMOVAL & INSTALLATION

See Figures 12 through 13.

1. Raise and support vehicle.

2. Remove wheel and tire assembly.

3. Drain small amount of fluid from master cylinder brake reservoir with clean suction gun.

4. Remove the 2 caliper mounting bolts (2).

5. Compress the caliper and remove from the adaptor (4).

6. Secure caliper (1) to nearby suspension part with wire. Do not allow brake hose to support caliper weight.

7. Remove the inboard and outboard brake pads (4) from the caliper adapter (2).

8. Remove the anti-rattle clips (3) from the brake caliper adapter (2).

To install:

9. Remove and clean all rust and debris from the anti-rattle clip mounting surfaces on the brake caliper adapter.

10. Install new anti-rattle clips into the caliper adapter.

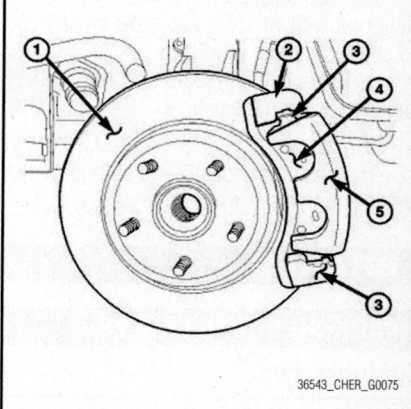

Fig. 13 Remove the inboard and outboard brake pads (4) from the caliper adapter (2)

11. Install the inboard and outboard brake pads onto the caliper adapter.

12. Install caliper on the caliper adapter.

13. Install the caliper slide pin bolts and tighten to 32 ft. lbs. (44 Nm).

14. Install wheel and tire assembly.

15. Remove support and lower vehicle.

16. Pump brake pedal until caliper pistons and brake pads are seated and a firm brake pedal is obtained.

17. Fill brake fluid.

BRAKES

BRAKE CALIPER

REMOVAL & INSTALLATION

See Figure 14.

1. Install prop rod on the brake pedal to keep pressure on the brake system, Holding pedal in this position will isolate master cylinder from hydraulic brake system and will not allow brake fluid to drain out of brake fluid reservoir while brake lines are open. This will allow you to bleed out the area of repair instead of the entire system.

2. Raise and support vehicle.

3. Remove rear wheel and tire assembly.

4. Drain small amount of fluid from master cylinder brake reservoir with a clean suction gun.

5. Bottom caliper pistons into the caliper by prying the caliper over.

6. Remove brake hose (3) banjo bolt (5) and discard gasket washers.

7. Remove the caliper slide pins (4).

8. Remove caliper from the anchor.

To install:

9. Lubricate the slide pins and slide pin bushings with caliper slide grease or the grease provided with the caliper.

10. Install the caliper on the anchor.

11. Install the caliper slide pin bolts and tighten to 18 ft. lbs. (25 Nm).

✳✳ CAUTION

Verify that the brake hose is not twisted or kinked before tightening the fitting bolt.

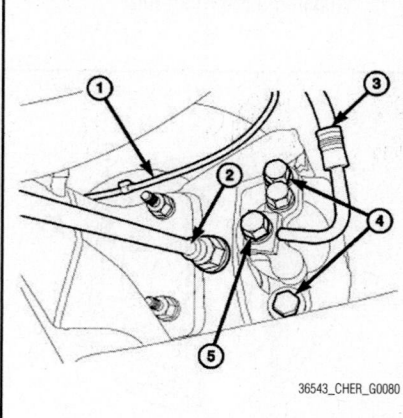

Fig. 14 View of the brake hose (3) banjo bolt (5), and caliper slide pins (4)

REAR DISC BRAKES

12. Install brake hose to caliper with new gasket washers and tighten banjo bolt to 23 ft. lbs. (31 Nm).

13. Remove the prop rod from the brake pedal.

14. Bleed the area of repair for the brake system, If a proper pedal is not felt during bleeding an area of repair then a base bleed system must be performed.

15. Install wheel and tire assemblies.

16. Remove supports and lower vehicle.

DISC BRAKE PADS

REMOVAL & INSTALLATION

See Figure 14.

1. Raise and support vehicle.

2. Remove rear wheel and tire assembly.

3. Drain small amount of fluid from master cylinder brake reservoir with a clean suction gun.

4. Bottom caliper pistons into the caliper by prying the caliper over.

5. Remove the caliper slide pins (4).

6. Remove caliper (1) from the anchor.

7. Secure caliper (1) to nearby suspension part with wire. Do not allow brake hose to support caliper weight.

8. Remove the inboard and outboard brake pads from the caliper.

To install:

9. Install the inboard and outboard brake pads onto the caliper.

10. Lubricate the slide pins and slide pin bushings with caliper slide grease or the grease provided with the brake pads.

11. Install caliper on the anchor.

12. Install the caliper slide pin bolts and tighten to 18 ft. lbs. (25 Nm).

13. Install wheel and tire assembly.

14. Remove support and lower vehicle.

15. Pump brake pedal until caliper piston and brake pads are seated and a firm brake pedal is obtained.

16. Fill brake fluid level if necessary.

BRAKES

PARKING BRAKE CABLES

ADJUSTMENT

The parking brakes are operated by an automatic tensioner mechanism built into the hand lever and cable system. The front cable is connected to the hand lever and the equalizer. The rear cables are attached to the equalizer and the parking brake shoe actuator.

A set of drum type brake shoes are used for parking brakes. The shoes are mounted to the rear disc brake adaptor. The parking brake drum is integrated into the rear disc brake rotor.

Parking brake cable adjustment is controlled by an automatic tensioner mechanism. The only adjustment if necessary is to the park brake shoes if the linings are worn.

PARKING BRAKE SHOES

REMOVAL & INSTALLATION

See Figures 14, 15 and 16.

1. Raise and safely support the vehicle.

2. Remove the rear wheel and tire assembly.

3. Remove the 2 caliper bolts (4) then remove the caliper. Support the caliper. Do not let the caliper hang by the brake hose.

4. Remove the rubber access plug (1) from the back of rear disc brake support plate (3).

5. If necessary, retract the parking brake shoes with a brake adjuster tool (2). Position the tool at the top of star wheel and rotate the wheel.

6. Remove the rotor from the axle hub flange.

7. Remove the four axle flange nuts.

8. Remove the axle shaft from the rear differential.

9. Remove the shoe to shoe return spring (6) with needle nose pliers and then remove the adjuster (5).

10. Remove the shoe to shoe return spring (3) with brake pliers.

11. Remove the shoe hold-down clips (4) and pins. The clip is held in place by a pin which fits into the clip notch. To remove the clip, first push the clip ends together and slide the clip until the head of pin clears the narrow part of the notch. Then remove clip (4) and pin.

12. Remove the shoes (1) off the actuator lever (2) for the parking brake then remove the shoes (1).

To install:

13. Install the park brake shoes onto the actuator lever.

14. Install shoes on support plate with hold down clips and pins. Be sure shoes are properly engaged in the park brake actuator lever.

15. Install the return spring.

PARKING BRAKE

16. Lubricate and install adjuster screw assembly. Be sure notched ends of screw assembly are properly seated on shoes and that star wheel is aligned with access hole in the support plate.

17. Install shoe to shoe adjuster spring. Needle nose pliers can be used to connect spring to each shoe.

18. Install the axle shaft to the rear differential.

19. Install and tighten the axle flange nuts.

20. Install rotor to the axle hub.

21. Install the caliper and the 2 mounting bolts to 32 ft. lbs. (44 Nm).

22. Adjust the parking brake shoes.

23. Install wheel and tire assembly.

24. Lower vehicle and verify correct parking brake operation.

ADJUSTMENT

Adjustment can be made with a standard brake gauge or with adjusting tool. Adjustment is performed with the complete brake assembly installed on the backing plate.

1. Be sure parking brake lever is fully released.

2. Raise vehicle so rear wheels can be rotated freely.

3. Remove plug from each access hole in brake support plates.

4. Loosen parking brake cable adjustment nut until there is slack in front cable.

5. Insert adjusting tool through support plate access hole and engage tool in teeth of adjusting screw star wheel.

6. Rotate adjuster screw star wheel (move tool handle upward) until slight drag can be felt when wheel is rotated.

7. Push and hold adjuster lever away from star wheel with thin screwdriver.

8. Back off adjuster screw star wheel until brake drag is eliminated.

9. Repeat adjustment at opposite wheel. Be sure adjustment is equal at both wheels.

10. Install support plate access hole plugs.

11. Adjust parking brake cable and lower vehicle.

12. Depress park brake lever and make sure park brakes hold the vehicle stationary.

13. Release park brake lever.

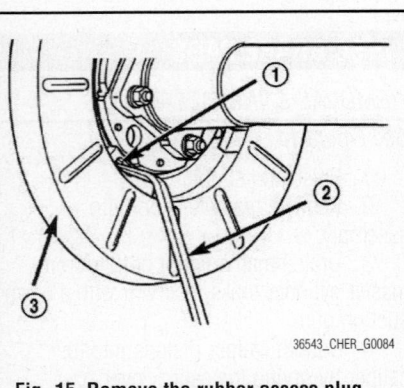

Fig. 15 Remove the rubber access plug (1) from the back of rear disc brake support plate (3)

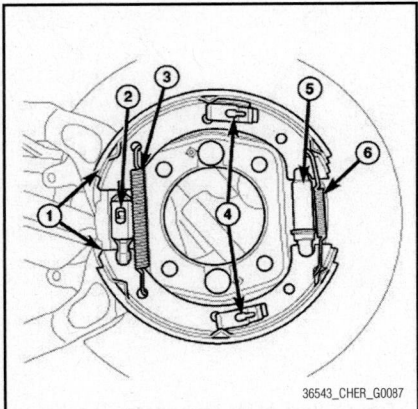

36543_CHER_G0087

Fig. 16 Parking brake assembly

CHASSIS ELECTRICAL — AIR BAG (SUPPLEMENTAL RESTRAINT SYSTEM)

GENERAL INFORMATION

※ CAUTION

These vehicles are equipped with an air bag system. The system must be disarmed before performing service on, or around, system components, the steering column, instrument panel components, wiring and sensors. Failure to follow the safety precautions and the disarming procedure could result in accidental air bag deployment, possible injury and unnecessary system repairs.

SERVICE PRECAUTIONS

※ WARNING

To avoid serious or fatal injury on vehicles equipped with the Supplemental Restraint System (SRS), never attempt to repair the electrically conductive circuits or wiring components related to the SRS. Such repairs can compromise the conductivity and current carrying capacity of those critical electrical circuits, which may cause the SRS components not to deploy when required, or to deploy when not required. Any wire harness containing broken, cut, burned or otherwise damaged electrically conductive SRS wiring, terminals or connector components must be removed and replaced with an entire new wire harness. Only minor cuts or abrasions of wire and terminal insulation where the conductive material has not been damaged, or connector insulators where the integrity of the latching and locking mechanisms have not been compromised may be repaired using appropriate methods. Failure to follow these instructions may result in possible serious or fatal injury.

※ WARNING

To avoid serious or fatal injury during and following any seat belt or child restraint anchor service, carefully inspect all seat belts, buckles, mounting hardware, retractors, tether straps, and anchors for proper installation, operation, or damage. Replace any belt that is cut, frayed, or torn. Straighten any belt that is twisted. Tighten any loose fasteners. Replace any belt that has a damaged or ineffective buckle or retractor. Replace any belt that has a bent or damaged latch plate or anchor plate. Replace any child restraint anchor or the unit to which the anchor is integral that has been bent or damaged. Never attempt to repair a seat belt or child restraint component. Always replace damaged or ineffective seat belt and child restraint components with the correct, new and unused replacement parts listed in the Chrysler Mopar® Parts Catalog.

※ WARNING

To avoid serious or fatal injury on vehicles equipped with side curtain airbags, disable the Supplemental Restraint System (SRS) before attempting any Occupant Restraint Controller (ORC) diagnosis or service. The ORC contains a rollover sensor, which enables the system to deploy the side curtains in the event of a vehicle rollover event. If an ORC is accidentally rolled during service while still connected to battery power, the side curtain airbags will deploy. Disconnect and isolate the battery negative (ground) cable, then wait two minutes for the system capacitor to discharge before performing further diagnosis or service. This is the only sure way to disable the SRS. Failure to take the proper precautions could result in accidental airbag deployment.

※ WARNING

To avoid serious or fatal injury on vehicles equipped with airbags, disable the Supplemental Restraint System (SRS) before attempting any steering wheel, steering column, airbag, seat belt tensioner, impact sensor, or instrument panel component diagnosis or service. Disconnect and isolate the battery negative (ground) cable, then wait two minutes for the system capacitor to discharge before performing further diagnosis or service. This is the only sure way to disable the SRS. Failure to take the proper precautions could result in accidental airbag deployment.

※ WARNING

To avoid serious or fatal injury on vehicles equipped with airbags, before performing any welding operations disconnect and isolate the battery negative (ground) cable and disconnect all wire harness connectors from the Occupant Restraint Controller (ORC). Failure to take the proper precautions could result in accidental airbag deployment and other possible damage to the Supplemental Restraint System (SRS) circuits and components.

※ WARNING

To avoid serious or fatal injury, do not attempt to dismantle an airbag unit or tamper with its inflator. Do not puncture, incinerate or bring into contact with electricity. Do not store at temperatures exceeding 200°F (93°C). An airbag inflator unit may contain sodium azide and potassium nitrate. These materials are poisonous and extremely flammable. Contact with acid, water, or heavy metals may produce harmful and irritating gases (sodium hydroxide is formed in the presence of moisture) or combustible compounds. An airbag inflator unit may also contain a gas canister pressurized to over 2500 psi (17.24 kPa). Failure to follow these instructions may result in possible serious or fatal injury.

※ WARNING

To avoid serious or fatal injury when handling a seat belt tensioner retractor, proper care should be exercised to keep fingers out from under the retractor cover or buckle scabbard and away from the seat belt webbing where it exits from the retractor cover or buckle cable where it exits from the scabbard.

※ WARNING

To avoid serious or fatal injury, replace all Supplemental Restraint System (SRS) components only with parts specified in the Chrysler Mopar® Parts Catalog. Substitute parts may appear interchangeable, but internal differences may result in inferior occupant protection.

To avoid serious or fatal injury, the fasteners, screws, and bolts originally used for the Supplemental Restraint System (SRS) components must never be replaced with any substitutes. These fasteners have special coatings and are specifically designed for the SRS. Any time a new fastener is needed, replace it with the correct fasteners provided in the service package or specified in the Chrysler Mopar® Parts Catalog.

To avoid serious or fatal injury when a steering column has an airbag unit attached, never place the column on the floor or any other surface with the steering wheel or airbag unit face down. Failure to follow these instructions may result in possible serious or fatal injury.

DISARMING THE SYSTEM

To avoid serious or fatal injury on vehicles equipped with airbags, disable the Supplemental Restraint System (SRS) before attempting any steering wheel, steering column, airbag, seat belt tensioner, impact sensor, or instrument panel component diagnosis or service.

Disconnect and isolate the battery negative (ground) cable, then wait two minutes for the system capacitor to discharge before performing further diagnosis or service. This is the only sure way to disable the SRS. Failure to take the proper precautions could result in accidental airbag deployment.

ARMING THE SYSTEM

1. During the following test, the battery negative cable remains disconnected and isolated, as it was during the Supplemental Restraint System (SRS) component removal and installation procedures.

2. Be certain that the diagnostic scan tool contains the latest version of the proper diagnostic software. Connect the scan tool to the 16-way Data Link Connector (DLC) (1). The DLC is located on the driver side lower edge of the instrument panel (2), outboard of the steering column.

3. Turn the ignition switch to the ON position and exit the vehicle with the scan tool.

4. Check to be certain that nobody is in the vehicle, then reconnect the battery negative cable.

5. Using the scan tool, read and record the active (current) Diagnostic Trouble Code (DTC) data.

6. Next, use the scan tool to read and record any stored (historical) DTC data.

7. If any DTC is found, refer to the appropriate diagnostic information.

8. Use the scan tool to erase the stored DTC data. If any problems remain, the stored DTC data will not erase. Refer to the appropriate diagnostic information to diagnose any stored DTC that will not erase. If the stored DTC information is successfully erased, go to the next step.

9. Turn the ignition switch to the OFF position for about 15 seconds, and then back to the ON position. Observe the airbag indicator in the instrument cluster. It should light for six to eight seconds, and then go out. This indicates that the SRS is functioning normally and that the repairs are complete. If the airbag indicator fails to light, or lights and stays ON, there is still an active SRS fault or malfunction. Refer to the appropriate diagnostic information to diagnose the problem.

CLOCKSPRING CENTERING
See Figure 17.

To avoid serious or fatal injury on vehicles equipped with airbags, disable the Supplemental Restraint System (SRS) before attempting any steering wheel, steering column, airbag, seat belt tensioner, impact sensor, or instrument panel component diagnosis or service. Disconnect and isolate the battery negative (ground) cable, then wait two minutes for the system capacitor to discharge before performing further diagnosis or service. This is the only sure way to disable the SRS. Failure to take the proper precautions could result in accidental airbag deployment.

➡A service replacement clockspring is shipped with the clockspring pre-centered and with a molded plastic locking pin installed. This locking pin should not be removed until the steering wheel has been installed on the steering column. If the locking pin is removed before the steering wheel is installed, the clockspring centering procedure must be performed.

➡When a clockspring is installed into a vehicle without properly centering and locking the entire steering system, the Steering Angle Sensor (SAS) data does not agree with the true position of the steering system and causes the Electronic Stability Program (ESP) system to shut down. This may also damage the clockspring without any immediate malfunction. Unlike some other Chrysler vehicles, this SAS never requires calibration. However, upon each new ignition ON cycle, the steering wheel must be rotated slightly to initialize the SAS.

➡Determining if the clockspring/SAS is centered is also possible electrically using the diagnostic scan tool. Steering wheel position is displayed as ANGLE with a range of up to 900 degrees. Refer to the appropriate menu item on the diagnostic scan tool.

➡Before starting this procedure, be certain to turn the steering wheel until the front wheels are in the straight-ahead position and that the entire steering system is locked or inhibited from rotation.

➡The clockspring may be centered and the rotor may be rotated freely once the steering wheel has been removed.

1. Place the front wheels in the straight-ahead position and inhibit the steering column shaft from rotation.

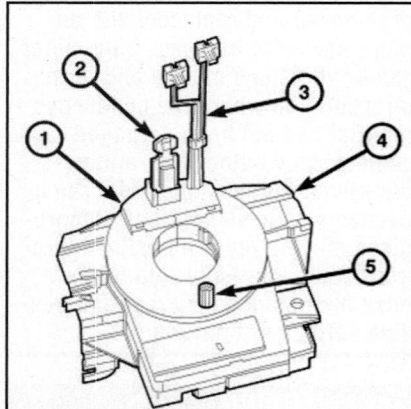

1. Clockspring rotor
2. Locking pin
3. Clockspring airbag pigtail wires
4. Clockspring housing
5. Dowel or drive pin

36543_CHER_G0089

Fig. 17 Rotate the clockspring rotor (1) clockwise

2. Remove the steering wheel from the steering shaft.

3. Rotate the clockspring rotor (1) clockwise to the end of its travel. Do not apply excessive torque.

4. From the end of the clockwise travel, rotate the rotor about two and one-half turns counterclockwise. Turn the rotor slightly clockwise or counterclockwise as necessary so that the clockspring airbag pigtail wires (3) and connector receptacle are at the top and the dowel or drive pin (5) is at the bottom.

5. The clockspring is now centered. Secure the clockspring rotor to the clockspring case using a locking pin (2) or some similar device to maintain clockspring centering until the steering wheel is reinstalled on the steering column.

DRIVE TRAIN

TRANSFER CASE ASSEMBLY

REMOVAL & INSTALLATION

NV140 Transfer Case

See Figure 18.

1. Raise vehicle.

> ※ **CAUTION**
>
> **Do not allow propeller shafts to hang at attached end. Damage to joint can result.**

2. Remove the front and rear propeller shafts.

3. Support transmission with jack stand.

4. Remove rear crossmember and skid plate, if equipped.

5. Disconnect transfer case vent hose (4).

6. Disconnect the wiring connector from the shift motor, if necessary.

7. Support transfer case with transmission jack and secure with chains.

8. Remove nuts (2) attaching transfer case (1) to transmission (3).

9. Pull transfer case and jack rearward to disengage transfer case.

10. Remove transfer case from under vehicle.

To install:

11. Mount transfer case on a transmission jack.

12. Secure transfer case to jack with chains.

13. Position transfer case under vehicle.

14. Align transfer case and transmission shafts and install transfer case onto the transmission.

15. Install and tighten transfer case attaching nuts to 26 ft. lbs. (35 Nm).

16. Connect the transfer case vent hose.

17. Connect front propeller shaft and install rear propeller shaft.

18. Fill transfer case with correct fluid. Correct as necessary.

19. Install the transfer case fill plug. Tighten the plug to 15–25 ft. lbs. (20–34 Nm).

20. Install rear crossmember and skid plate, if equipped. Tighten crossmember bolts to 30 ft. lbs. (41 Nm).

21. Remove transmission jack and support stand.

22. Lower vehicle and verify transfer case shift operation.

NV245 Transfer Case

See Figures 19 and 20.

1. Shift transfer case into NEUTRAL.
2. Raise vehicle.
3. Remove transfer case drain plug (2) and drain transfer case lubricant.

4. Support transmission (3) with jack stand.

5. Remove rear crossmember and skid plate, if equipped.

6. Disconnect front propeller shaft from transfer case at companion flange. Remove rear propeller shaft from vehicle.

> ※ **CAUTION**
>
> **Do not allow propeller shafts to hang at attached end. Damage to joint can result.**

7. Disconnect the transfer case shift motor and mode sensor connector.

8. Disconnect transfer case vent hose (4).

9. Support transfer case (1) with transmission jack.

10. Secure transfer case to jack with chains.

11. Remove nuts (2) attaching transfer case to transmission.

12. Pull transfer case and jack rearward to disengage transfer case.

13. Remove transfer case from under vehicle.

To install:

14. Mount transfer case on a transmission jack.

15. Secure transfer case to jack with chains.

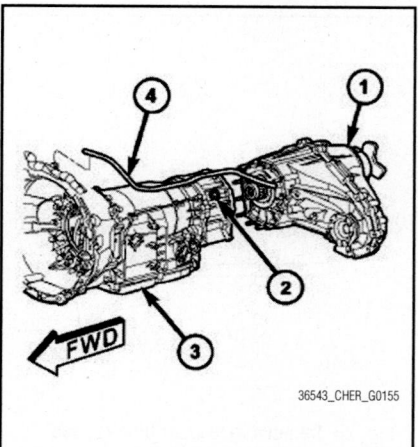

Fig. 18 NV140 transfer case assembly

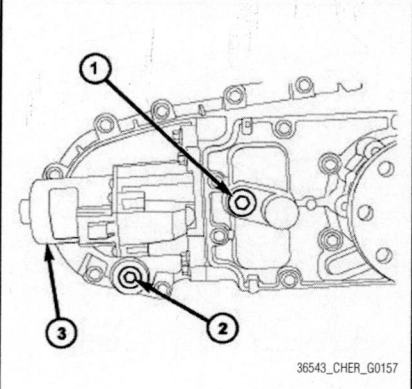

Fig. 19 Remove transfer case drain plug (2) and drain transfer case lubricant

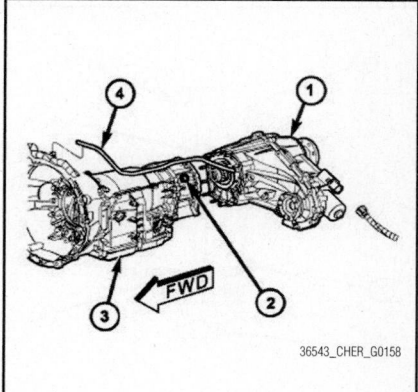

Fig. 20 Support transfer case (1) with transmission jack

16. Position transfer case under vehicle.

17. Align transfer case and transmission shafts and install transfer case onto transmission.

18. Install and tighten transfer case attaching nuts to 26 ft. lbs. (35 Nm).

19. Connect the transfer case vent hose to the transfer case.

20. Install rear crossmember and skid plate, if equipped.

21. Remove transmission jack and support stand.

22. Connect front propeller shaft and install rear propeller shaft.

23. Fill transfer case with correct fluid. Check transmission fluid level. Correct as necessary.

24. Install the transfer case fill plug. Tighten the plug to 15–25 ft. lbs. (20–34 Nm).

25. Connect the shift motor and mode sensor wiring connector.

26. Lower vehicle and verify transfer case shift operation.

FRONT AXLE SHAFT, BEARING & SEAL

REMOVAL & INSTALLATION

Axle Shaft

See Figures 21 through 24.

1. With vehicle in neutral, position vehicle on hoist.

2. Remove half shaft hub/bearing nut.

3. Remove wheel speed sensor nut from hub/bearing and remove sensor.

4. Remove brake calipers bolts and remove calipers from caliper adapters.

5. Remove lower stabilizer link (3) bolt (6) from control arm.

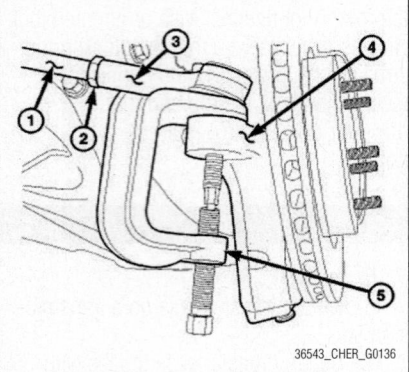

Fig. 22 Remove outer tie rod end nuts and separate tie rods (3) from knuckles (4) with Remover 8677 (5)

6. Remove outer tie rod end nuts and separate tie rods (3) from knuckles (4) with Remover 8677 (5).

7. Remove upper ball joint nuts (4) and separate ball joints (2) from knuckles (3) with Remover 8677.

8. Remove shock clevis (3) bolt and nut (4) from lower control arm.

9. Lean the knuckle out and push half shaft out of the hub/bearing.

10. Pry half shafts from axle/axle tube with pry bar.

To install:

11. Install half shaft on the axle and through the hub/bearing. Verify half shaft has engaged.

12. Install shock clevis on lower control arm and tighten nut.

13. Install upper control arm on knuckle and tighten ball joint nut.

14. Install tie rod end on knuckle and tighten.

15. Install stabilizer link on lower control arm and tighten.

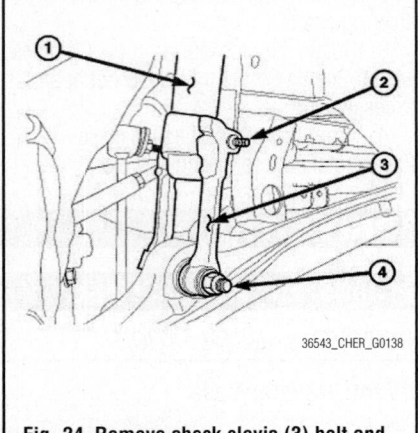

Fig. 24 Remove shock clevis (3) bolt and nut (4) from lower control arm

16. Install caliper on caliper adapter and tighten.

17. Install wheel speed sensor on the hub/bearing.

18. Install half shaft hub/bearing nut and tighten to 100 ft. lbs. (135 Nm).

Bearing

See Figures 25 through 28.

1. Remove axle shaft.

2. Remove axle shaft tube (1) seal with seal Remover 7794-A (2) and slide hammer.

3. Install axle bearing remover C-4660-A (1) into the axle bearing (2) in the axle tube (3) and tighten remover nut (4).

4. Install bearing receiver C-4660-A (1) washer and nut (2) on remover. Tighten nut (2) and draw bearing into receiver (1).

➡Do not re-use bearing.

To install:

5. Install axle bushing (1) with Installer 5063 (2) and Handle C-4171.

6. Install axle shaft and seal.

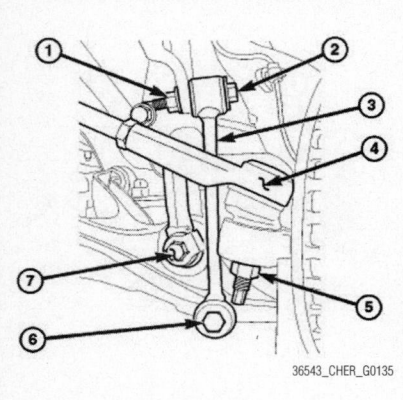

Fig. 21 Remove lower stabilizer link (3) bolt (6) from control arm

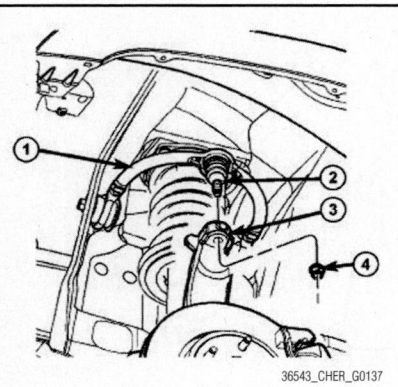

Fig. 23 Remove upper ball joint nuts (4) and separate ball joints (2) from knuckles (3) with Remover 8677

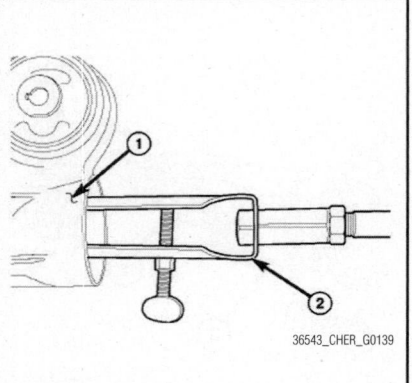

Fig. 25 Remove axle shaft tube (1) seal with seal Remover 7794-A (2) and slide hammer

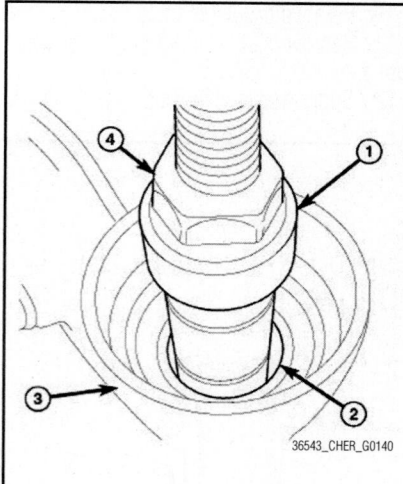

Fig. 26 Install axle bearing remover C-4660-A (1) into the axle bearing (2) in the axle tube (3)

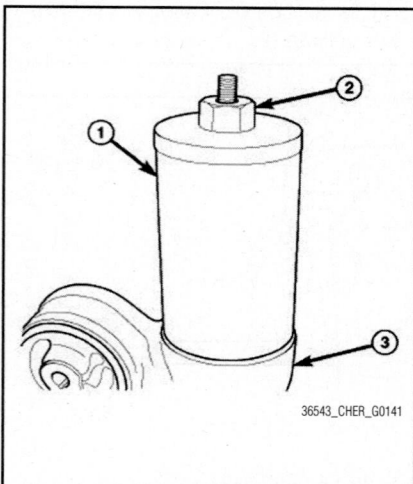

Fig. 27 Install bearing receiver C-4660-A (1) washer and nut (2) on remover

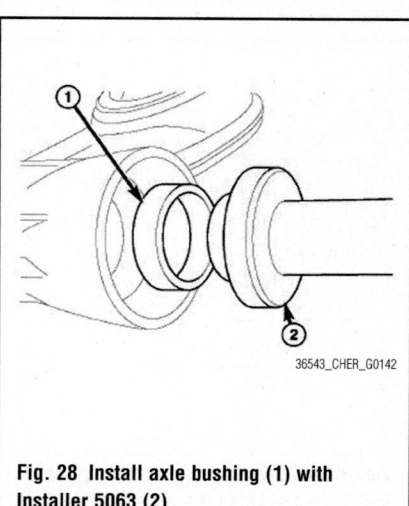

Fig. 28 Install axle bushing (1) with Installer 5063 (2)

Seal

1. Remove half shaft from axle.
2. Pry seal out with a seal pick.

To install:

3. Install differential seal with seal Install 9504 and Handle C-4171.
4. Install half shaft.

FRONT PINION SEAL

REMOVAL & INSTALLATION

See Figures 29 through 32.

1. Remove wheels.
2. Push back brake pads and release hand brake.
3. Remove propeller shaft.
4. Rotate pinion with inch pound torque and record torque to rotate.
5. Mark installation position of collared nut with respect to drive pinion.
6. Bend pinion nut lock back with a punch and hammer.
7. Hold pinion flange (1) with flange Wrench C-3281(2) and remove pinion nut.

8. Mark a line across the pinion shaft and flange for installation reference.
9. Remove pinion flange (1) with Puller C-452 (2).
10. Remove pinion seal with a seal pick.

To install:

11. Install pinion seal with seal Installer C-3972A and Handle C-4171.
12. Position pinion flange on pinion shaft with reference mark aligned.
13. Install pinion flange (1) on pinion with flange Installer 9616 (2). Tap flange on pinion, then thread installer center bolt on pinion shaft and draw flange onto the pinion.
14. Install new pinion collared nut and carefully tighten nut in stages holding flange with flange Wrench C-3281. Check torque to rotate after each stage, until previously value of torque to rotate is exceeded by 4.4 inch lbs. (0.5 Nm).
15. Cut the pinion nut collar.
16. Bend nut collar so it touches the wall of the slot in the pinion shaft.

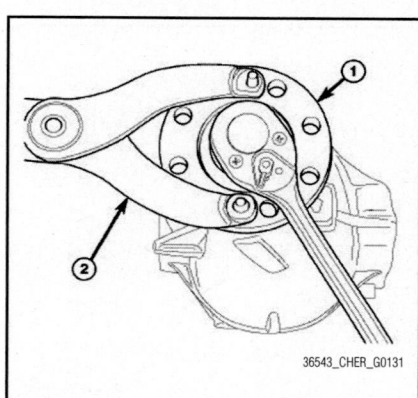

Fig. 29 Hold pinion flange (1) with flange Wrench C-3281(2)

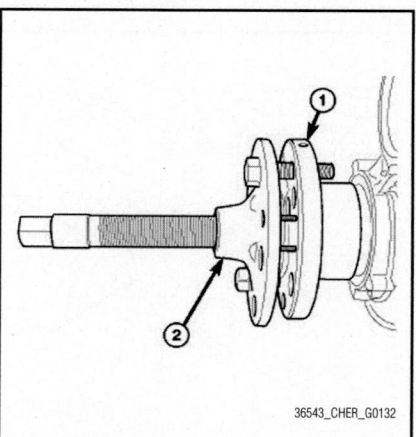

Fig. 30 Remove pinion flange (1) with Puller C-452 (2)

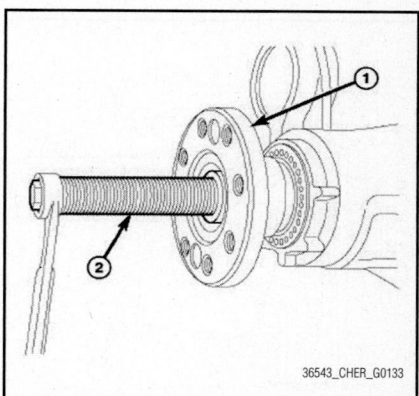

Fig. 31 Install pinion flange (1) on pinion with flange Installer 9616 (2)

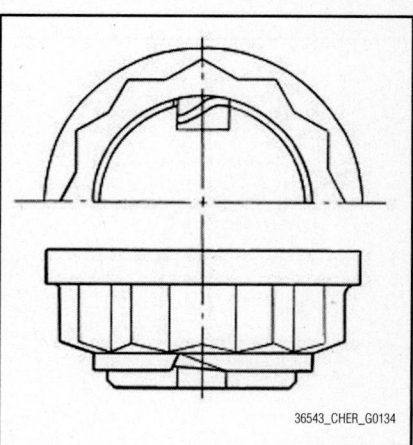

Fig. 32 Bend nut collar so it touches the wall of the slot in the pinion shaft

17. Connect propeller shaft to pinion flange.

18. Install wheel and tires.

19. Operate brake pedal several times until brake pads contact brake discs (brake pressure built up).

REAR AXLE HOUSING

REMOVAL & INSTALLATION

See Figures 33 through 40.

1. With vehicle in neutral, position on hoist.

2. Remove differential cover and drain fluid.

3. Remove calipers and rotors.

4. Remove speed sensors from axle tube flange.

5. Remove axle flange nuts (1) from axle (2).

6. Pull axle shaft and backing plate out of axle tube until axle bearing (1) is exposed.

7. Remove O-ring (2) from the axle bearing.

8. Remove axle shaft (1) from axle tube and backing plate.

9. Remove axle vent hose (1) from axle vent (2) and cover bracket.

10. Remove propeller shaft.

11. Remove stabilizer bar (1) clamp (2) from axle.

12. Support axle with jack.

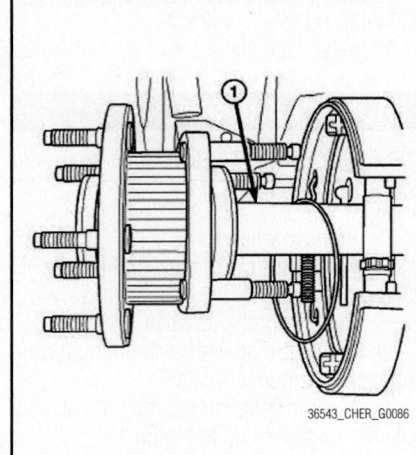

Fig. 35 Remove axle shaft (1) from axle tube and backing plate

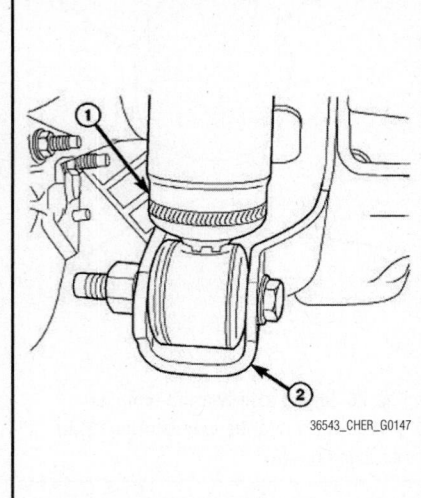

Fig. 38 Remove shock absorbers (1) from axle brackets (2)

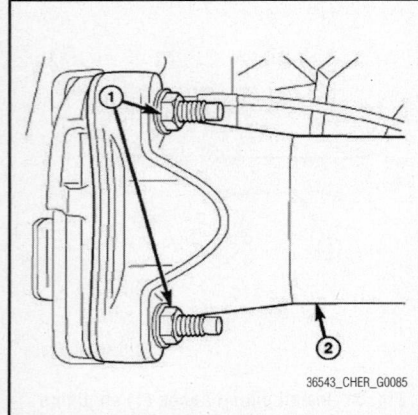

Fig. 33 Remove axle flange nuts (1) from axle (2)

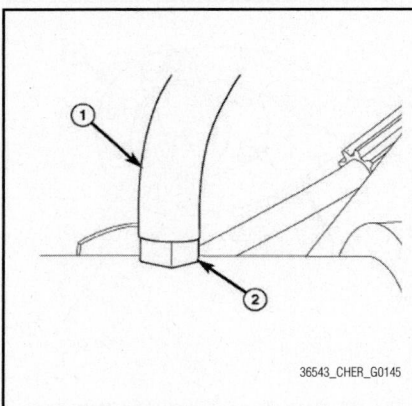

Fig. 36 Remove axle vent hose (1) from axle vent (2) and cover bracket

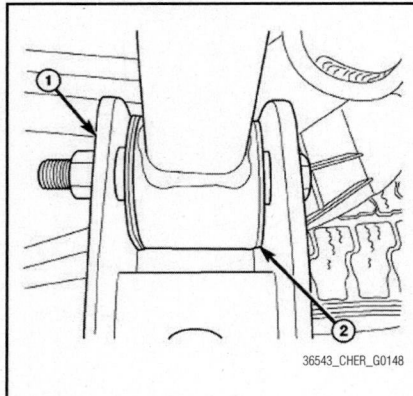

Fig. 39 Remove upper control arms (2) from axle brackets (1)

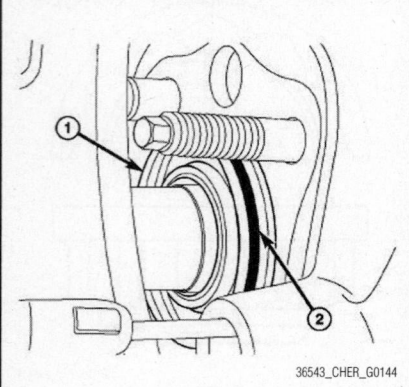

Fig. 34 Remove O-ring (2) from the axle bearing

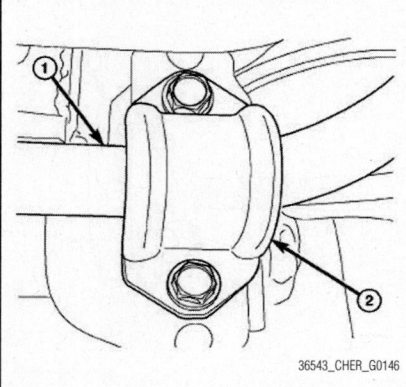

Fig. 37 Remove stabilizer bar (1) clamp (2) from axle

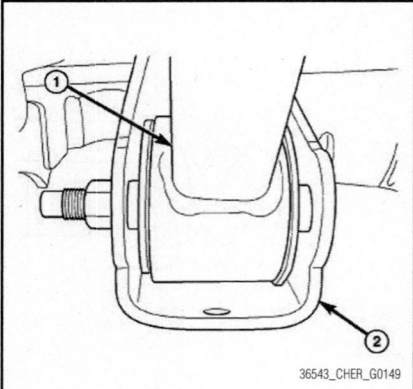

Fig. 40 Remove lower control arms (1) from axle brackets (2)

13. Remove track bar from axle.

14. Remove shock absorbers (1) from axle brackets (2).

15. Remove upper control arms (2) from axle brackets (1).

16. Remove lower control arms (1) from axle brackets (2).

17. Lower axle from vehicle and remove coil springs and insulators.

To install:

18. Install coil springs and insulators. Raise axle into place.

19. Install lower control arms to axle brackets.

20. Install upper control arms to axle brackets.

21. Install shock absorbers to axle brackets.

22. Install stabilizer bar and clamps to axle.

23. Install propeller shaft.

24. Install axle vent hose to axle vent and cover bracket.

➡**If a bearing flange stud is loose or has backed out tighten stud to 20 ft. lbs. (27 Nm).**

25. Install axle shaft into axle tube and backing plate with new O-ring on axle.

26. Slip O-ring through backing plate, then push axle through backing plate until bearing is exposed.

27. Install O-ring axle bearing.

28. Push axle into axle tube.

29. Install axle flange nuts and tighten to 88 ft. lbs. (119 Nm).

30. Install speed sensors in axle tube flange.

31. Install calipers and rotors.

32. Install differential cover, fill differential and install fill plug.

REAR AXLE SHAFT, BEARING & SEAL

REMOVAL & INSTALLATION

See Figures 10, 33 through 35 and 41.

1. With vehicle in neutral, position on hoist.

2. Remove calipers and rotors.

3. Tap axle end plug (1) loose from the axle flange (2) with a hammer and punch. Pull plug (1) out of axle flange (2).

4. Remove speed sensors (2) from axle tube (1) flange.

5. Remove axle flange nuts (1) from axle (2).

6. Pull axle shaft and backing plate out of axle tube until axle bearing (1) is exposed.

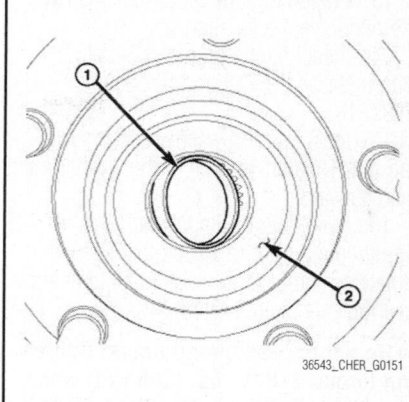

Fig. 41 Tap axle end plug (1) loose from the axle flange (2)

7. Remove O-ring (2) from the axle bearing.

8. Slide axle shaft (1) from axle tube and backing plate.

9. Tap axle shaft out of the bearing and axle flange through the plug hole with a hammer and brass drift.

To install:

➡**If a bearing flange stud is loose or has backed out tighten stud to 20 ft. lbs. (27 Nm).**

10. Tap axle shaft into axle bearing and axle flange.

11. Install axle shaft into axle tube and backing plate with new O-ring on axle.

12. Slip O-ring through backing plate, then push axle through backing plate until bearing is exposed.

13. Install O-ring axle bearing.

14. Push axle into axle tube.

15. Install axle flange nuts and tighten to 88 ft. lbs. (119 Nm).

16. Install speed sensors in axle tube flange.

17. Coat new axle flange plug with Mopar® Stud N' Bearing Mount Adhesive or equivalent and install plug with freeze plug installer.

18. Install calipers and rotors.

REAR PINION SEAL

REMOVAL & INSTALLATION

See Figures 42 through 44.

1. With vehicle in neutral, position vehicle on hoist.

2. Mark a reference line across the axle flange (3) and propeller shaft flange (4).

3. Remove propeller shaft

4. Remove brake calipers and rotors to prevent any drag.

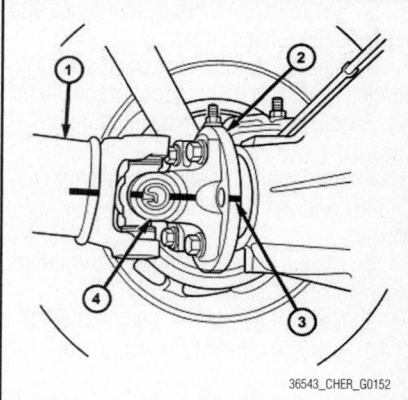

Fig. 42 Mark a reference line across the axle flange (3) and propeller shaft flange (4)

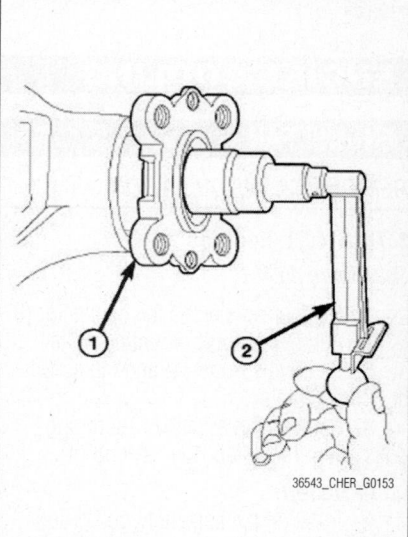

Fig. 43 Measure torque to rotating pinion flange (1) with an inch pound torque wrench (2)

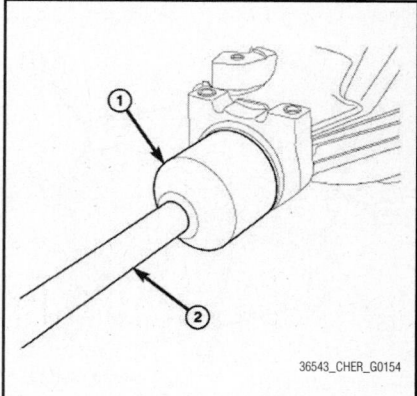

Fig. 44 Install new pinion seal with Installer C-3972A (1) and Handle C-4171 (2)

5. Rotate flange three or four times and verify flange rotates smoothly.

6. Measure torque to rotating pinion flange (1) with an inch pound torque wrench (2). Record reading for installation reference.

7. Hold pinion flange with Wrench C-3281 and remove pinion nut and washer.

8. Mark line on pinion shaft and flange for installation reference.

9. Remove flange with two jaw puller.

10. Remove pinion seal with a seal puller.

To install:

11. Apply a light coating of gear lubricant on the lip of pinion seal.

12. Install new pinion seal with Installer C-3972A (1) and Handle C-4171 (2).

13. Position flange on pinion shaft with the reference marks aligned.

14. Install flange on pinion shaft with Installer C-3718 and Wrench C-3281.

15. Install pinion washer and a new pinion nut. The convex side of the washer must face outward.

16. Hold flange with Wrench C-3281and tighten pinion nut to 210 ft. lbs. (285 Nm). Rotate pinion several revolutions to ensure bearing rollers are seated.

➡**Do not exceed the minimum tightening torque 210 ft. lbs. (285 Nm) when installing the companion flange retaining nut at this point.**

17. Rotate pinion several times to ensure bearings are seated.

18. Measure pinion torque to rotate with

an inch pound torque wrench. Pinion torque to rotate should be equal to recorded reading plus additional 5 inch lbs. (0.56 Nm).

➡**If pinion torque to rotate is low, tighten pinion nut in 5 ft. lbs (6.8 Nm) increments until pinion torque to rotate is achieved.**

✳✳ CAUTION

Never loosen pinion nut to decrease pinion bearing rotating torque. If pinion torque to rotate is exceeded, a new collapsible spacer must be installed. Failure to follow these instructions will result in damage to the axle.

19. Install propeller shaft.
20. Install rear brake components.

ENGINE COOLING

ENGINE FAN

REMOVAL & INSTALLATION

3.7L & 4.7L Engines

See Figure 45.

1. Disconnect electric fan connector (3).
2. Remove shroud mounting bolts.
3. Remove shroud (4) and fan assembly from vehicle.
4. Remove fan assembly mounting bolts and remove fan from shroud (4).

To install:

5. Position fan assembly on shroud.
6. Install fan to fan shroud mounting nuts.
7. Position fan and shroud assembly in vehicle.

8. Install shroud mounting bolts.
9. Connect electric fan electrical connector.
10. Start engine and check fan operation.

5.7L Engine

See Figures 46 through 48.

1. Raise vehicle on hoist.
2. Drain cooling system.

➡**The hydraulic fan drive is driven by the power steering pump. When removing lines or hoses from fan drive assembly use a drain pan to catch any power steering fluid that may exit the fan drive or the lines and hoses.**

➡**Whenever the high pressure line fittings are removed from the hydraulic fan drive the O-rings must be replaced.**

3. Disconnect two high pressure lines at hydraulic fan drive.
4. Remove and discard O-rings from line fittings.
5. Disconnect low pressure return hose at hydraulic fan drive.

➡**The lower mounting bolts can only be accessed from under vehicle.**

6. Remove two lower mounting bolts from the shroud.
7. Lower vehicle.
8. Disconnect the electrical connector for the fan control solenoid.
9. Disconnect the upper radiator hose at the radiator and position out of the way.
10. Disconnect the power steering gear outlet hose and fluid return hose at the cooler.

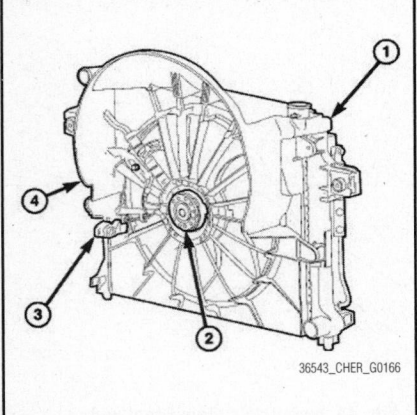

36543_CHER_G0166

Fig. 45 Disconnect electric fan connector (3)

36543_CHER_G0167

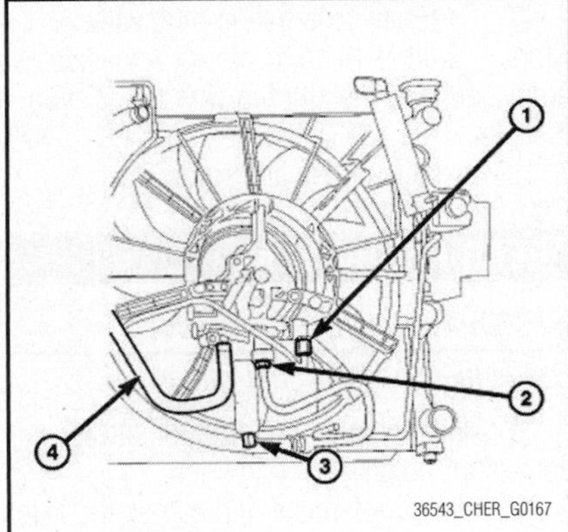

Fig. 46 Disconnect two high pressure lines at hydraulic fan drive

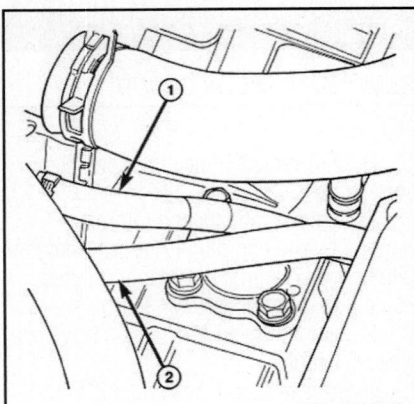

36543_CHER_G0168

Fig. 47 Disconnect the power steering gear outlet hose and fluid return hose at the cooler

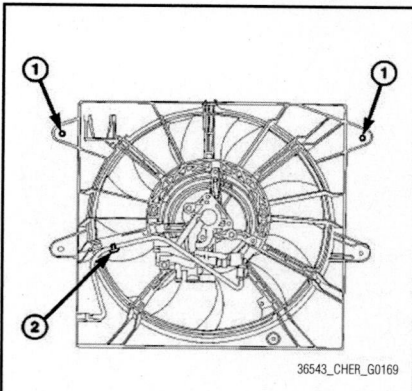

Fig. 48 Remove two upper mounting bolts from the shroud

11. Remove two upper mounting bolts from the shroud.

12. Remove the shroud and fan drive from vehicle.

To install:

> ✸✸ CAUTION
>
> **There is an external ground wire connected to the hydraulic fan drive located at the electrical connector on the fan assembly. This ground MUST remain connected at all times. Failure to ensure ground wire is connected when engine is operating can cause severe damage to the JTEC module.**

13. Position the fan drive and shroud in the vehicle.

14. Install the fan shroud upper mounting bolts. Do not tighten at this time.

15. Install the upper radiator hose onto the radiator.

16. Connect the power steering cooler hoses.

17. Raise the vehicle on a hoist.

18. Install the fan shroud lower mounting bolts.

➡**Whenever the high pressure line fittings are removed from the hydraulic fan drive the O-rings located on the fittings must be replaced.**

19. Lubricate the O-rings on the fittings with power steering fluid then connect the inlet and outlet high pressure lines to fan drive. Tighten the inlet line to 36 ft. lbs. (49 Nm). Tighten the outlet line to 22 ft. lbs. (29 Nm).

20. Connect the low pressure return hose to the fan drive.

21. Lower the vehicle.

22. Install the upper radiator hose.

23. Connect the electrical connector for the hydraulic fan control solenoid.

24. Tighten the fan shroud upper mounting bolts.

25. Refill the cooling system.

> ✸✸ CAUTION
>
> **Do not run engine with the power steering fluid below the full mark in the reservoir. Severe damage to the hydraulic cooling fan or the engine can occur.**

26. Refill the power steering fluid reservoir and bleed air from the steering system.

27. Run the engine and check for leaks.

RADIATOR

REMOVAL & INSTALLATION

> ✸✸ WARNING
>
> **Do not remove the cylinder block drain plugs or loosen the radiator draincock with the system hot and under pressure. Serious burns from coolant can occur. Refer to cooling system draining.**

Do not waste reusable coolant. If the solution is clean, drain the coolant into a clean container for reuse.

> ✸✸ CAUTION
>
> **When removing the radiator or A/C condenser for any reason, note the location of all radiator-to-body and radiator-to-A/C condenser rubber air seals. These are used at the top, bottom and sides of the radiator and A/C condenser. To prevent overheating, these seals must be installed to their original positions.**

1. Disconnect the negative battery cable at battery.

2. Drain coolant from radiator.

3. Remove the front grille.
   a. Remove the 6 upper push pins.
   b. Tip grill forward and remove grill.

4. Remove two radiator mounting bolts.

5. Disconnect both transmission cooler lines from radiator.

6. Disconnect electrical connector for the fan control solenoid.

7. Disconnect the power steering cooler line from cooler and filter.

8. Disconnect the radiator upper and lower hoses.

9. Disconnect the overflow hose from radiator.

10. Remove the air inlet duct at the grille.

11. The lower part of radiator is equipped with two alignment dowel pins. They are located on the bottom of radiator tank and fit into rubber grommets. These rubber grommets are pressed into the radiator lower crossmember.

> ✸✸ WARNING
>
> **The air conditioning system (if equipped) is under a constant pressure even with the engine off. Refer to refrigerant warnings in, heating and air conditioning before handling any air conditioning component.**

➡**The radiator and radiator cooling fan can be removed as an assembly. It is not necessary to remove the cooling fan before removing or installing the radiator.**

12. Disconnect the two high pressure fluid lines at the hydraulic fan drive.

13. Disconnect the low pressure return hose at the hydraulic fan drive.

14. Gently lift up and remove radiator from vehicle. Be careful not to scrape the radiator fins against any other component. Also be careful not to disturb the air conditioning condenser (if equipped).

To install:

> ✸✸ CAUTION
>
> **Before installing the radiator or A/C condenser, be sure the radiator-to-body and radiator-to-A/C condenser rubber air seals are properly fastened to their original positions. These are used at the top, bottom and sides of the radiator and A/C condenser. To prevent overheating, these seals must be installed to their original positions.**

15. Equipped with air conditioning: Gently lower the radiator and fan shroud into the vehicle. Guide the two radiator alignment dowels through the holes in the rubber air seals first and then through the A/C support brackets. Continue to guide the alignment dowels into the rubber grommets located in lower radiator crossmember. The holes in the L-shaped brackets (located on bottom of A/C condenser) must be positioned between bottom of rubber air seals and top of rubber grommets.

16. Connect the radiator upper and lower hoses and hose clamps to radiator.

> ✳✳ **CAUTION**
>
> **The tangs on the hose clamps must be positioned straight down.**

17. Install coolant reserve/overflow tank hose at radiator.

18. Connect both transmission cooler lines at the radiator.

19. Install both radiator mounting bolts.

20. Install air inlet duct at grille.

21. Attach electric connector for hydraulic fan control solenoid.

22. Install the grille.

23. Connect the two high pressure lines to the hydraulic fan drive. Tighten ½ inch pressure line fitting to 36 ft. lb. (49 Nm). and the ⅜ inch pressure line fitting to 21 ft. lbs. (29 Nm).

24. Connect the low pressure hose to the hydraulic fan drive. Position the spring clamp.

25. Connect the power steering filter hoses to the filter. Install new hose clamps.

26. Rotate the fan blades (by hand) and check for interference at fan shroud.

27. Refill cooling system.

28. Refill the power steering reservoir and bleed air from system.

29. Connect battery cable at battery.

30. Start and warm engine. Check for leaks.

THERMOSTAT

REMOVAL & INSTALLATION

3.7L & 4.7L Engines

See Figure 49.

> ✳✳ **WARNING**
>
> **Do not loosen the radiator draincock with the system hot and pressurized. Serious burns from the coolant can occur.**

Do not waste the reusable coolant. If the solution is clean, drain the coolant into a clean container for reuse.

If the thermostat is being replaced, be sure that the replacement is the specified thermostat for the vehicle model and engine type.

1. Disconnect the negative battery cable.

2. Drain the cooling system.

3. Raise the vehicle on a hoist.

4. Remove the splash shield.

5. Remove the lower radiator hose clamp and the lower radiator hose at the thermostat housing (1).

6. Remove the thermostat housing

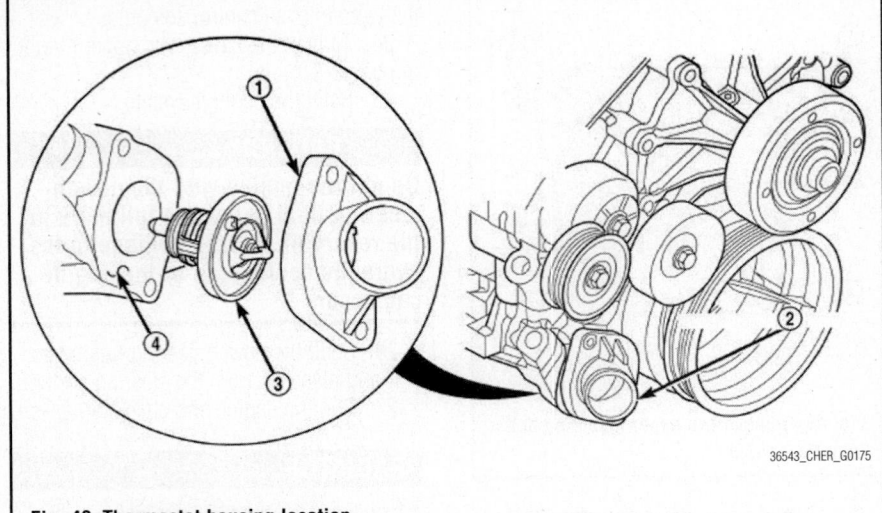

Fig. 49 Thermostat housing location

mounting bolts, the thermostat housing (1) and the thermostat (3).

To install:

7. Clean the mating areas of the timing chain cover and thermostat housing.

8. Install the thermostat with the spring side down into the recessed machined groove on the timing chain cover.

9. Position the thermostat housing on the timing chain cover.

10. Install the two housing-to-timing chain cover bolts. Tighten the bolts to 115 inch lbs. (13 Nm).

> ✳✳ **CAUTION**
>
> **Housing must be tightened evenly and the thermostat must be centered into the recessed groove in the timing chain cover. If not, it may result in a cracked housing, damaged timing chain cover threads or coolant leaks.**

11. Install the lower radiator hose on the thermostat housing.

12. Install the splash shield.

13. Lower vehicle.

14. Fill the cooling system.

15. Connect the negative battery cable to battery.

16. Start and warm the engine. Check for leaks.

5.7L Engine

See Figures 50 and 51.

> ✳✳ **WARNING**
>
> **Do not loosen the radiator draincock with the cooling system hot and pressurized. Serious burns from the coolant can occur.**

Do not waste reusable coolant. If the solution is clean, drain the coolant into a clean container for reuse.

If the thermostat is being replaced, be sure that the replacement is the specified thermostat for the vehicle model and engine type.

1. Disconnect the negative battery cable.

2. Drain the cooling system

3. Remove the radiator hose clamp and radiator hose at the thermostat housing (1).

4. Remove the thermostat housing mounting bolts (2), thermostat housing (1) and thermostat.

To install:

5. Position the thermostat and housing (2) on the front cover.

6. Install thermostat housing bolts (1). Tighten the bolts (1) to 115 inch lbs. (13 Nm).

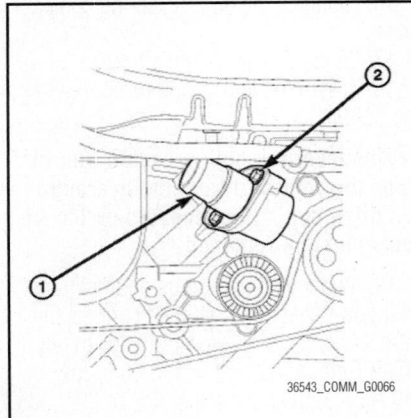

Fig. 50 Remove the radiator hose clamp and radiator hose at the thermostat housing (1)

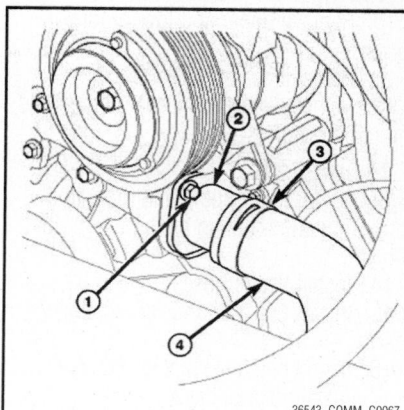

Fig. 51 Position the thermostat and housing (2) on the front cover

7. Install the radiator hose (4) onto the thermostat housing (2).
8. Fill the cooling system.
9. Connect negative battery cable.
10. Start and warm the engine.
11. Check for leaks.

WATER PUMP

REMOVAL & INSTALLATION

3.7L & 4.7L Engine

See Figures 52 and 53.

The water pump on 3.7L engines is bolted directly to the engine timing chain case cover (2).

1. Disconnect negative battery cable from battery.
2. Drain cooling system.

✳✳ WARNING

Constant tension hose clamps are used on most cooling system hoses. When removing or installing, use
only tools designed for servicing this type of clamp. Always wear safety glasses when servicing constant tension clamps.

✳✳ CAUTION

A number or letter is stamped into the tongue of constant tension clamps. If replacement is necessary, use only an original equipment clamp with matching number or letter.

3. Remove two fan shroud-to-radiator screws.
4. Remove viscous fan (if equipped).
5. Remove accessory drive belt.
6. Remove accessory drive belt tensioner.
7. Remove seven water pump mounting bolts and one stud bolt.

✳✳ CAUTION

Do not pry on the water pump at the timing chain case/cover. The machined surfaces may be damaged resulting in leaks.

8. Remove water pump (1) and gasket. Discard gasket.

To install:

9. Clean gasket mating surfaces.
10. Using a new gasket, position water pump and install mounting bolts and stud. Tighten water pump mounting bolts to 43 ft. lbs. (58 Nm).
11. Spin water pump to be sure that pump impeller does not rub against timing chain case/cover.
12. Install accessory drive belt tensioner.
13. Install accessory drive belt.

✳✳ CAUTION

When installing the serpentine accessory drive belt, belt must be routed correctly. If not, engine may overheat due to water pump rotating in wrong direction.

14. Be sure the upper and lower portions of the fan shroud are firmly connected. All air must flow through the radiator.
15. Install two fan shroud-to-radiator screws.
16. Install viscous fan (if originally equipped).
17. Be sure there is clearance of at least 1.0 inches (25 mm) between tips of fan blades and fan shroud.
18. Evacuate air and refill cooling system.
19. Connect negative battery cable.
20. Check the cooling system for leaks.

5.7L Engine

See Figures 54 and 55.

1. Disconnect negative battery cable.
2. Drain coolant.
3. Remove serpentine belt.
   a. Remove the air intake tube between intake manifold and air filter assembly.
   b. Using a suitable square drive tool, release the belt tension by rotating the tensioner clockwise. Rotate belt tensioner until belt can be removed from pulleys.
   c. Remove belt.
   d. Gently release tensioner.
4. Remove fan clutch assembly.

➡ **The thermal viscous fan drive/fan blade assembly is attached (threaded) to water pump hub shaft.**

   a. Remove fan blade/viscous fan drive assembly (2) from water pump using

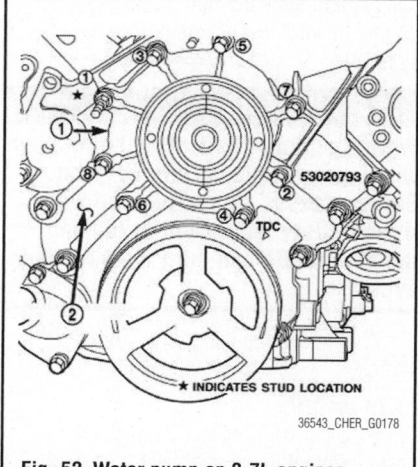

Fig. 52 Water pump on 3.7L engines

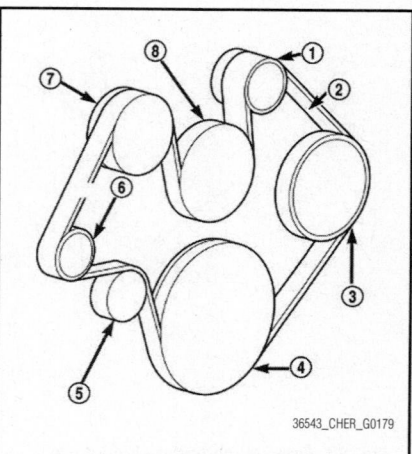

Fig. 53 Install accessory drive belt

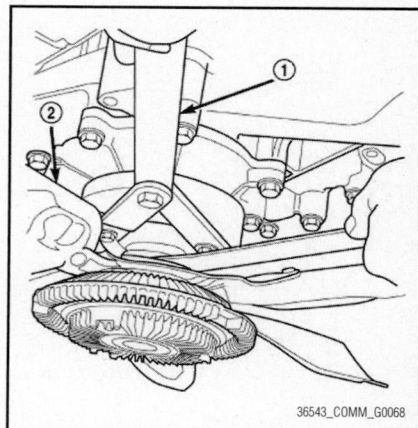

Fig. 54 Remove fan blade/viscous fan drive assembly (2) from water pump

special tool 6958 spanner wrench and 8346 adapters (1), by turning mounting nut counterclockwise as viewed from front. Threads on viscous fan drive are RIGHT HAND.

   b. Do not attempt to remove fan/viscous fan drive assembly (2) from vehicle at this time.

   c. Do not unbolt fan blade assembly from viscous fan drive at this time.

   d. Remove fan shroud to radiator bolts.

   e. Remove fan shroud and fan blade/viscous fan drive assembly as a complete unit from vehicle.

   f. After removing fan blade/viscous fan drive assembly, DO NOT place viscous fan drive in horizontal position. If stored horizontally, silicone fluid in the viscous fan drive could drain into its bearing assembly and contaminate lubricant.

✳✳ CAUTION

Do not remove water pump pulley-to-water pump bolts. This pulley is under belt tension.

   g. Remove four bolts securing fan blade assembly to viscous fan drive.

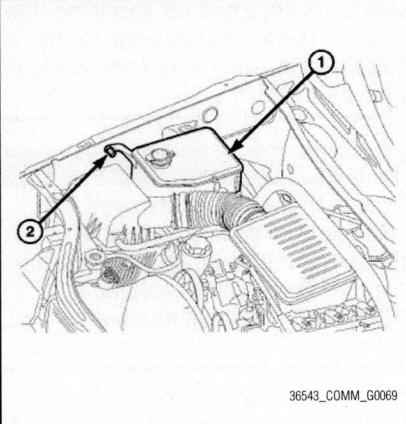

Fig. 55 Disconnect the coolant overflow hose (2)

  5. Remove coolant fill bottle.
   a. Disconnect the coolant overflow hose (2).
   b. Remove two mounting bolts.
   c. Remove the coolant reservoir/overflow tank (1).
  6. Remove fan shroud assembly.
  7. Remove A/C compressor, alternator brace and alternator.
  8. Remove idler pulleys.
  9. Remove belt tensioner assembly.

  10. Remove upper and lower radiator hoses.
  11. Remove heater hoses.
  12. Remove water pump mounting bolts and remove pump.

  To install:
  13. Install water pump and mounting bolts. Tighten mounting bolts to 18 ft. lbs. (24 Nm).
  14. Install heater hoses.
  15. Install upper and lower radiator hoses.
  16. Install belt tensioner assembly.
  17. Install idler pulleys.
  18. Install A/C compressor, alternator and alternator brace. Tighten bolt and nuts to 21 ft. lbs. (28 Nm).
  19. Install fan shroud assembly.
  20. Connect washer bottle wiring and hose.
  21. Install coolant fill bottle.
  22. Install fan clutch assembly.
  23. Install serpentine belt.
  24. Connect negative battery cable.
  25. Evacuate air and refill cooling system.
  26. Check cooling system for leaks.

ENGINE ELECTRICAL

BATTERY

REMOVAL & INSTALLATION

See Figures 56 and 57.

➡**It may be necessary to use a battery terminal puller (2) if the battery cable terminal clamps are seized on to the battery posts.**

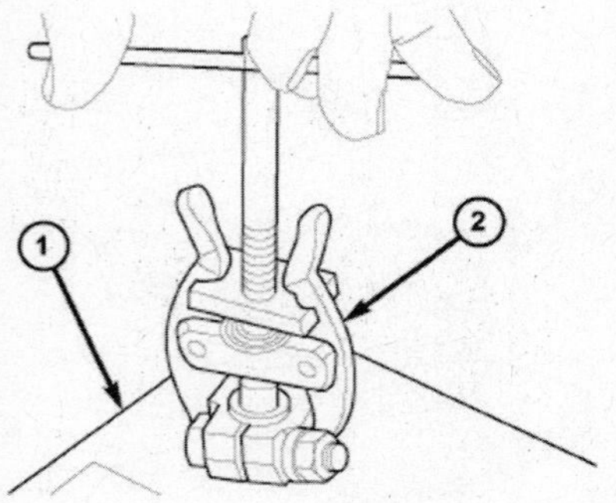

  1. Turn the ignition switch to the Off position. Be certain that all electrical accessories are turned off.
  2. Loosen the battery negative cable terminal clamp pinch-bolt hex nut (4).
  3. Disconnect the battery negative cable terminal clamp from the battery negative terminal post. If necessary, use a battery terminal puller to remove the terminal clamp from the battery post.
  4. Loosen the battery positive cable terminal clamp pinch-bolt hex nut (8).
  5. Disconnect the battery positive cable terminal clamp from the battery positive terminal post. If necessary, use a battery terminal puller to remove the terminal clamp from the battery post.
  6. Remove the battery hold down bolt (2) and slide the hold down (4) up and forward in the battery tray slots (3).

BATTERY SYSTEM

✳✳ WARNING

Wear a suitable pair of rubber gloves when removing a battery by hand. Safety glasses should also be worn. If the battery is cracked or leaking, the electrolyte can burn the skin and eyes.

  7. Remove the battery (1) from the vehicle.

  To install:
  8. Clean and inspect the battery case, terminal posts and battery cable clamps.

Fig. 56 Battery terminal puller

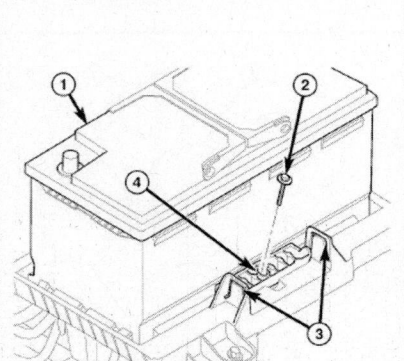

Fig. 57 Remove the battery hold down bolt (2)

9. Position the battery into the vehicle. Ensure that the battery positive and negative terminal posts are correctly positioned. The battery cable terminal clamps must reach the correct battery terminal post without stretching the cables.

10. Install the battery hold down by sliding it back and downward in the battery tray slots. Install the battery hold down bolt.

✳✳ CAUTION

Be certain that the battery cable terminal clamps are connected to the correct battery terminal posts. Reverse battery polarity may damage electrical components of the vehicle.

11. Connect the battery positive cable

terminal clamp to the battery positive terminal post.

12. Connect the battery negative cable terminal clamp to the battery negative terminal post.

13. Apply a thin coating of petroleum jelly or chassis grease to the exposed surfaces of the battery cable terminal clamps and the battery terminal posts.

ENGINE ELECTRICAL

ALTERNATOR

REMOVAL & INSTALLATION

3.7L & 4.7L Engines

See Figures 58 and 59.

✳✳ WARNING

Disconnect negative cable from battery before removing battery output wire (B+ wire) from alternator. Failure to do so can result in injury or damage to electrical system.

1. Disconnect negative battery cable at battery.

2. Remove alternator drive belt.

3. Unsnap plastic insulator cap (3) from B+ output terminal.

4. Remove B+ terminal mounting nut (2) at rear of alternator. Disconnect terminal from alternator.

5. Disconnect field wire connector (4) at rear of alternator by pushing on connector tab.

To install:

6. Position alternator (3) to engine and install 2 horizontal bolts (1) and 1 vertical bolt (2).

7. Tighten all 3 bolts to 40 ft. lbs. (55 Nm).

8. Snap field wire connector into rear of alternator.

9. Install B+ terminal eyelet to alternator output stud. Tighten mounting nut to 108 inch lbs. (12 Nm).

✳✳ CAUTION

Never force a belt over a pulley rim using a screwdriver. The synthetic fiber of the belt can be damaged.

✳✳ CAUTION

When installing a serpentine accessory drive belt, the belt must be routed correctly. The water pump may be rotating in the wrong direction if the belt is installed incorrectly, causing the engine to overheat.

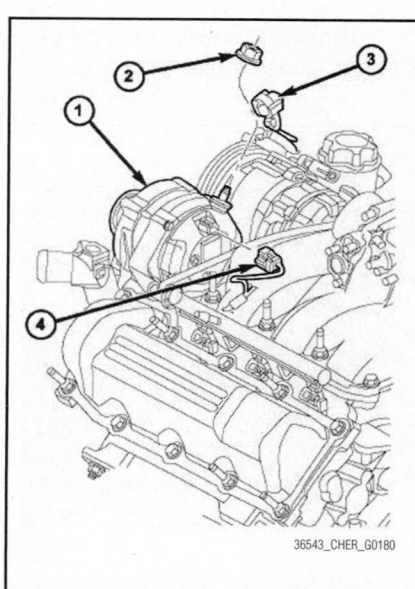

36543_CHER_G0180

Fig. 58 Unsnap plastic insulator cap (3) from B+ output terminal

---

CHARGING SYSTEM

10. Install alternator drive belt.

11. Install negative battery cable to battery.

5.7L Engine

See Figure 60.

✳✳ WARNING

Disconnect negative cable from battery before removing battery output wire (B+ wire) from alternator. Failure to do so can result in injury or damage to electrical system.

1. Disconnect negative battery cable at battery.

2. Remove alternator drive belt.

3. Unsnap plastic insulator cap from B+ output terminal.

4. Remove B+ terminal mounting nut at rear of alternator. Disconnect terminal from alternator.

5. Disconnect field wire connector (3) at rear of alternator by pushing on connector tab.

6. Remove 2 alternator mounting bolts (1).

7. Remove alternator (2) from vehicle.

36543_CHER_G0183

Fig. 60 Disconnect field wire connector (3) at rear of alternator by pushing on connector tab

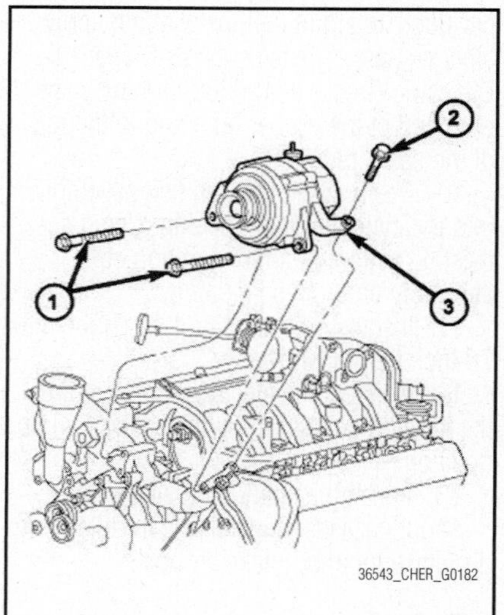

Fig. 59 Position alternator (3) to engine and install 2 horizontal bolts (1) and 1 vertical bolt (2)

36543_CHER_G0182

To install:

8. Position alternator to engine and install 2 mounting bolts.

9. Torque bolts to 30 ft. lbs. (41 Nm).

10. Snap field wire connector into rear of alternator.

11. Install B+ terminal eyelet to alternator output stud. Tighten mounting nut to 108 inch lbs. (12 Nm).

> ⁂ **CAUTION**
>
> **Never force a belt over a pulley rim using a screwdriver. The synthetic fiber of the belt can be damaged.**

> ⁂ **CAUTION**
>
> **When installing a serpentine accessory drive belt, the belt must be**

routed correctly. The water pump may be rotating in the wrong direction if the belt is installed incorrectly, causing the engine to overheat.

12. Install alternator drive belt.

13. Install negative battery cable to battery.

ENGINE ELECTRICAL

FIRING ORDERS

The firing order for the 3.7L engine is 1–6–5–4–3–2.

The firing order for the 4.7L and 5.7 L V8 engines is 1–8–4–3–6–5–7–2.

IGNITION COIL

REMOVAL & INSTALLATION

3.7L Engine

See Figure 61.

➡An ignition coil (2) with a spark plug wire (1) attached is used for two cylinders. The three coils fits into machined holes in the cylinder head for cylinders 1, 3, and 5. A mounting stud/nut secures each coil to the top of the intake manifold. The bottom of the coil is equipped with a rubber boot (4) to seal the spark plug (5) to the coil. Inside each rubber boot is a spring. The spring is used for a mechanical contact between the coil and the top of

the spark plug. These rubber boots and springs are a permanent part of the coil and are not serviced separately. An O-ring is used to seal the coil at the opening into the cylinder head.

1. Depending on which coil is being removed, the throttle body air intake tube or intake box may need to be removed to gain access to coil.

2. Disconnect electrical connector from coil by pushing downward on release lock on top of connector and pull connector from coil.

3. Disconnect spark plug wire from coil (1).

4. Clean area at base of coil with compressed air before removal.

5. Remove coil mounting bolt.

6. Carefully pull up coil from cylinder head opening with a slight twisting action.

7. Remove coil from vehicle.

To install:

8. Using compressed air, blow out any dirt or contaminants from around top of spark plug.

9. Check the condition of the coil rubber boot. To aid in coil installation, apply silicone based grease such as Mopar® Dielectric Grease J8126688 into the spark plug end of the rubber boot and to the top of the spark plug.

10. Position the ignition coil assembly into the cylinder head opening. Using a twisting action, push the ignition coil assembly onto the spark plug.

11. Install coil mounting bolt. Tighten to 70 inch lbs. (8 Nm).

12. Connect the electrical connector to the ignition coil assembly by snapping into position.

13. Install the spark plug wires.

14. If necessary, install the throttle body air intake tube, or intake air box.

4.7L Engine

See Figures 61 through 62.

An individual ignition coil (1) is used for each pair of spark plugs. Each coil attaches

IGNITION SYSTEM

directly to the top of the eight upper bank of spark plugs. Secondary cables (3) connect each coil to the eight lower bank of spark plugs. The coils themselves fit into machined holes in the cylinder head. Each coil also has its own individual electrical connector (2).

➡The bolt used to mount the ignition coil assembly is the same bolt used to mount the intake manifold. If replacing either one or all eight coils, check and re-torque all eight bolts.

A mounting bolt (3) secures each coil assembly to the top of the intake manifold. The bottom of the coil assembly is equipped with a rubber boot (4) to seal the spark plug (5) to the coil. Inside each rubber boot is a spring. The spring is used for a mechanical contact between the coil and the top of the upper bank of spark plugs. These rubber boots and springs are a permanent part of the coil assembly and are not serviced separately. The rubber boot (4) is also used to seal the coil at the opening into the cylinder head.

1. Depending on which coil assembly is being removed, the throttle body air

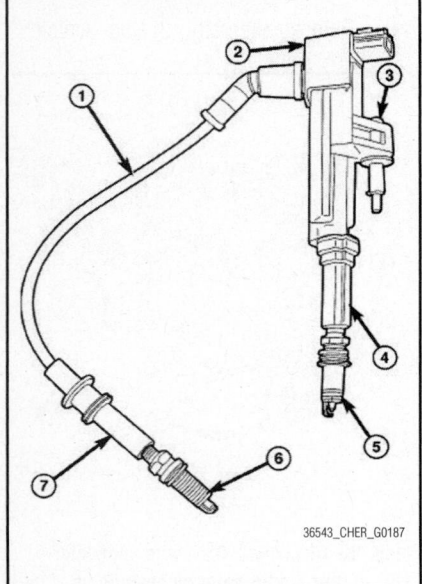

36543_CHER_G0187

Fig. 61 Ignition coil assembly

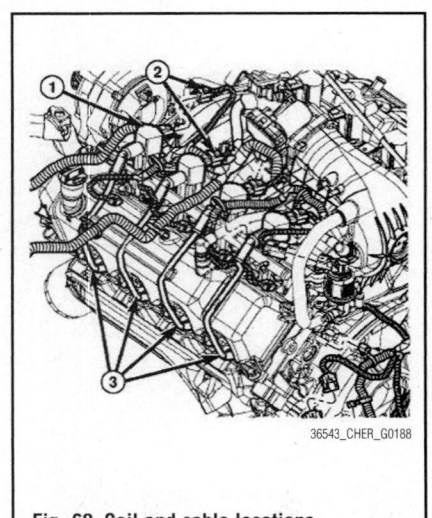

36543_CHER_G0188

Fig. 62 Coil and cable locations

intake tube or intake box may need to be removed, to gain access to the coil.

2. Disconnect the electrical connector (2) from the coil assembly by pushing downward on the release lock on the top of the connector and pull connector from the coil.

3. Disconnect the secondary cable (3) at the coil assembly.

4. Clean the area at the base of the coil assembly with compressed air before removal.

5. Remove the coil assembly mounting bolt (3).

6. Carefully pull up the coil assembly (2) from the cylinder head opening with a slight twisting action. This helps to disengage the rubber boot (4) from the spark plug (5).

7. Remove the coil assembly from the engine.

To install:

8. Using compressed air, blow out any dirt or contaminants from around the top of the spark plug.

9. Check the condition of the coil rubber boot. To aid in coil installation, apply silicone based grease such as Mopar® Dielectric Grease J8126688 into the spark plug end of the rubber boot and to the top of the spark plug.

10. Position the ignition coil assembly into the cylinder head opening. Using a twisting action, push the ignition coil assembly onto the spark plug.

➡**The bolt used to mount the ignition coil assembly is also the same bolt used to mount the intake manifold. If replacing either one or all eight coils, check and re-torque all eight bolts.**

11. Tighten the coil assembly mounting bolt to 9 ft. lbs. (12 Nm).

12. Connect the electrical connector to the coil assembly by snapping into position.

13. Connect the secondary cable to the coil assembly.

14. If necessary, install the throttle body air intake tube or intake air box to the top of the engine.

5.7L Engine

See Figures 63 and 64.

1. Disconnect the electrical connector (1) from the coil (3).

2. Clean the area at the base of the coil with compressed air before removal.

➡**The ignition coil mounting bolts are retained in the ignition coil.**

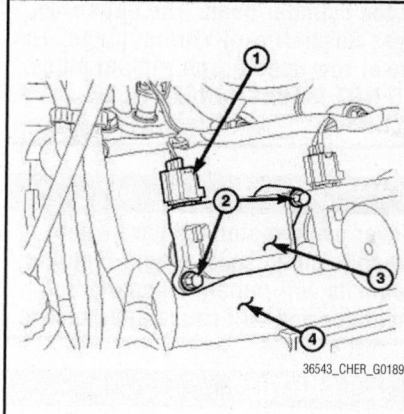

Fig. 63 Disconnect the electrical connector (1) from the coil (3)

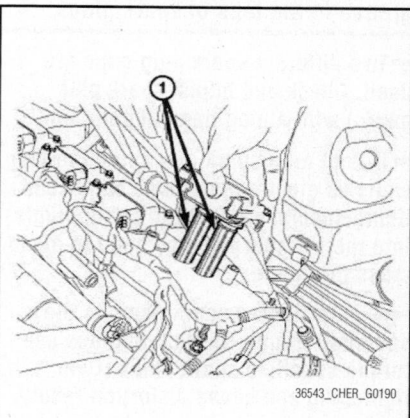

Fig. 64 Pull up the ignition coil (1) from the valve cover

3. Remove the two ignition coil mounting bolts (2).

4. Carefully pull up the ignition coil (1) from the valve cover.

5. Remove ignition coil (1) from vehicle.

To install:

6. Using compressed air, blow out any dirt or contaminants from around top of spark plug.

➡**Use dielectric grease on each of the spark plug boots before installing the coil.**

7. Position ignition coil into valve cover and push onto spark plugs.

8. Install 2 ignition coil mounting bolts. Tighten to 62 inch lbs. (7 Nm).

9. Connect electrical connector to the ignition coil by snapping into position.

IGNITION TIMING

ADJUSTMENT

Ignition timing is not adjustable on any of the available engines.

SPARK PLUGS

REMOVAL & INSTALLATION

3.7L Engine

1. Remove the necessary air filter tubing and air intake components at the top of the engine at the throttle body.

➡**The three spark plugs located on the left bank of the engine are under three individual ignition coils. Each individual ignition coil must be removed to gain access to each spark plug located on the left bank of the engine.**

2. Prior to removing the ignition coil, spray compressed air around the coil base at the cylinder head.

3. Remove the ignition coil.

4. Check the condition of ignition coil O-ring and replace as necessary.

5. Prior to removing the spark plug, spray compressed air into the cylinder head opening. This will help prevent foreign material from entering combustion chamber.

6. Remove the spark plug from the cylinder head using a quality thin wall socket with a rubber or foam insert.

7. Inspect the spark plug condition.

To install:

8. Check and adjust the spark plug gap with a gap gauging tool.

✱✱ CAUTION

Special care should be taken when installing spark plugs into the cylinder head spark plug wells. Be sure the plugs do not drop into the plug wells as electrodes can be damaged.

9. Start the spark plug into the cylinder head by hand to avoid cross threading.

10. Tighten the spark plugs to 20 ft. lbs. (27 Nm).

11. Before installing the ignition coil, check the condition of the coil O-ring and replace as necessary. Apply silicone based grease such as Mopar® Dielectric Grease J8126688 into the spark plug end of the rubber boot, coil O-rings and to the top of spark plugs.

12. Install the ignition coil.

13. Install the necessary air filter tubing and air intake components at the top of the engine at the throttle body.

4.7L Engine

> ✳✳ **CAUTION**
>
> This engine uses TWO DIFFERENT types of spark plugs. A total of 16 plugs are used. The plugs are mounted in two rows (banks). The upper row is used on the intake valve side of the cylinder head. The lower row is used on the exhaust valve side of the cylinder head. The upper row uses Bosch Nickel Yttrium plugs. The lower row uses Bosch Iridium plugs. DO NOT INTERCHANGE THESE PLUGS.

1. Remove necessary air filter tubing and air intake components at top of engine and at throttle body.

➡ To remove the upper row of spark plugs, each individual ignition coil must be removed first.

2. Remove the ignition coil(s).
3. Prior to removing the spark plug(s), spray compressed air into cylinder head opening. This will help prevent foreign material from entering combustion chamber.

> ✳✳ **CAUTION**
>
> Due to tight clearances between UPPER row of plugs and cylinder head, a conventional deep, thick-wall spark plug socket will not fit. Use a deep, THIN-WALL ⅝ inches spark plug socket for plug removal and installation.

> ✳✳ **CAUTION**
>
> Do not attempt to clean any of the spark plugs. Replace only.

4. Remove the spark plug(s) and inspect their condition.

To install:

> ✳✳ **CAUTION**
>
> This engine uses TWO DIFFERENT types of spark plugs. A total of 16 plugs are used. The plugs are mounted in two rows (banks). The upper row is used on the intake valve side of the cylinder head. The lower row is used on the exhaust valve side of the cylinder head. The upper row uses Bosch Nickel Yttrium plugs. The lower row uses Bosch Iridium plugs. DO NOT INTERCHANGE THESE PLUGS.

> ✳✳ **CAUTION**
>
> Never use a motorized wire wheel brush to clean spark plugs. Metallic deposits will remain on spark plug insulator and will cause plug misfire.

> ✳✳ **CAUTION**
>
> To aid in coil installation, apply silicone based grease such as Mopar® Dielectric Grease into spark plug end of rubber boots. Also apply this grease to the tops of spark plugs.

➡ Two different spark plug gaps are used. Check and adjust spark plug gap(s) with a plug gap gauging tool.

➡ Do not drop spark plugs into the plug wells as electrode damage can occur. Using special care install spark plug(s) into the cylinder head by hand to avoid cross threading.

➡ Always tighten spark plugs to the specified torque. Certain engines use torque sensitive spark plugs. Over tightening can cause distortion resulting in a change to the spark plug gap, or a cracked porcelain insulator. s

> ✳✳ **CAUTION**
>
> Due to tight clearances between upper row of plugs and cylinder head, a conventional deep, thick-wall spark plug socket will not fit. Use a deep, THIN-WALL ⅝ inches spark plug socket for plug removal and installation.

5. Tighten spark plug(s) to the specified torque.
6. Install ignition coil(s).
7. Install necessary air filter tubing and air intake components to top of engine and to throttle body.

5.7L Engine

1. Remove the necessary air filter tubing and air intake components at the top of the engine and at the throttle body.
2. Prior to removing the ignition coil, spray compressed air around coil base at the cylinder head.
3. Remove the ignition coil.
4. Prior to removing the spark plug, spray compressed air into the cylinder head opening.
5. Remove the spark plug from the cylinder head using a quality socket with a rubber or foam insert.
6. Inspect spark plug condition.

To install:

> ✳✳ **CAUTION**
>
> Never use a motorized wire wheel brush to clean spark plugs. Metallic deposits will remain on spark plug insulator and will cause plug misfire.

> ✳✳ **CAUTION**
>
> Do not attempt to clean any of the spark plugs. Replace only.

7. To aid in the coil installation, apply silicone based grease such as Mopar® Dielectric Grease into the spark plug end of the ignition coil rubber boots. Also apply this grease to the tops of spark plugs.
8. Check and adjust the spark plug gap with a gap gauging tool.
9. Start the spark plug into the cylinder head by hand to avoid cross threading. Special care should be taken when installing spark plugs into the cylinder head spark plug wells. Be sure the plugs do not drop into the plug wells as electrodes can be damaged.

➡ Always tighten spark plugs to the specified torque. Certain engines use torque sensitive spark plugs. It is a good practice to always tighten spark plugs to a specific torque. Over tightening can cause distortion resulting in a change in the spark plug gap, or a cracked porcelain insulator.

10. Install the ignition coil.
11. Install necessary air filter tubing and air intake components to the top of the engine and to the throttle body.

STARTER

REMOVAL & INSTALLATION

3.7L & 4.7L Engines

See Figure 65.

1. Disconnect and isolate negative battery cable.
2. Raise and support vehicle.
3. If equipped with 4WD, remove front drive shaft.
4. If equipped with 4WD and certain transmissions, a support bracket is used between front axle and side of transmission. Remove 2 support bracket bolts at transmission. Pry support bracket slightly to gain access to lower starter mounting bolt.
5. Remove two bolts (3).
6. Move starter motor (4) towards front of vehicle far enough for nose of starter pinion housing to clear housing. Always support starter motor during this process, do not let starter motor hang from wire harness.
7. Tilt nose downwards and lower starter motor far enough to access and remove nut (2) that secures battery positive cable wire harness connector eyelet (1) to solenoid battery terminal stud. Do not let starter motor hang from wire harness.
8. Remove battery positive cable wire harness connector eyelet (5) from solenoid battery terminal stud.
9. Disconnect battery positive cable wire harness connector from solenoid terminal connector receptacle.
10. Remove starter motor.

To install:

11. Connect solenoid wire to starter motor (snaps on).
12. Position battery cable to solenoid stud. Install and tighten battery cable eyelet nut. Torque nut to 19 ft. lbs. (25 Nm). Do not allow starter motor to hang from wire harness.
13. Position starter motor to transmission.

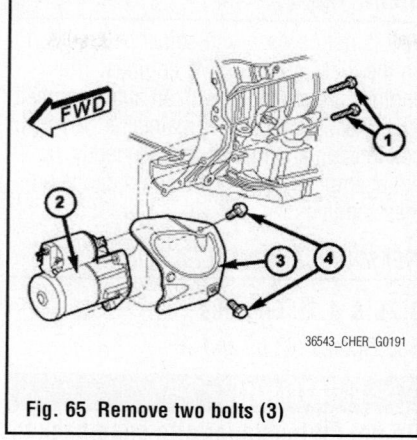

Fig. 65 Remove two bolts (3)

14. Slide the automatic transmission cooler tube bracket into position.
15. Install and tighten both bolts. Torque bolts to 50 ft. lbs. (68 Nm).
16. If equipped with 4WD and certain transmissions, a support bracket is used between front axle and side of transmission. Install 2 support bracket bolts at transmission.
17. If equipped with 4WD, install front drive shaft.
18. Lower vehicle.
19. Connect negative battery cable.

5.7L Engine

See Figure 66.

1. Disconnect and isolate negative battery cable.
2. Raise and support vehicle.
3. If equipped with 4WD and certain transmissions, a support bracket is used between front axle and side of transmission. Remove 2 support bracket bolts at transmission. Pry support bracket slightly to gain access to lower starter mounting bolt.
4. Remove two mounting bolts (2).
5. Move starter motor towards front of vehicle far enough for nose of starter pinion housing to clear housing. Always support starter motor (1) during this process,

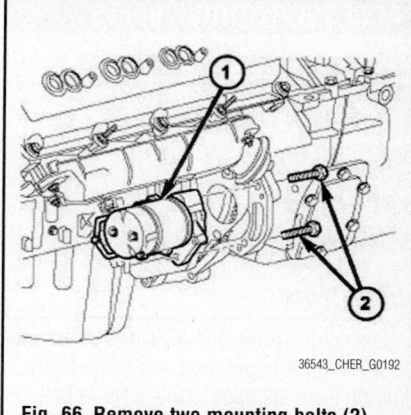

Fig. 66 Remove two mounting bolts (2)

do not let starter motor hang from wire harness.

6. Tilt nose downwards and lower starter motor far enough to access and remove nut that secures battery positive cable wire harness connector eyelet to solenoid battery terminal stud. Do not let starter motor hang from wire harness.
7. Remove battery positive cable wire harness connector eyelet from solenoid battery terminal stud.
8. Disconnect battery positive cable wire harness connector from solenoid terminal connector receptacle.
9. Remove starter motor.

To install:

10. Connect solenoid wire to starter motor (snaps on).
11. Position battery cable to solenoid stud. Install and tighten battery cable eyelet nut. Torque nut to 19 ft. lbs. (25 Nm). Do not allow starter motor to hang from wire harness.
12. Position starter motor to engine.
13. Slide the automatic transmission cooler tube bracket into position.
14. Install and tighten both mounting bolts. Torque bolts to 50 ft. lbs. (68 Nm).
15. Lower vehicle.
16. Connect negative battery cable.

ENGINE MECHANICAL

ACCESSORY DRIVE BELTS

ACCESSORY BELT ROUTING

3.7L & 4.7L Engines
See Figure 67.

5.7L Engine
See Figure 68.

INSPECTION

Inspect the drive belt for signs of glazing or cracking. A glazed belt will be perfectly smooth from slippage, while a good belt will have a slight texture of fabric visible. Cracks will usually start at the inner edge of the belt and run outward. All worn or damaged drive belts should be replaced immediately.

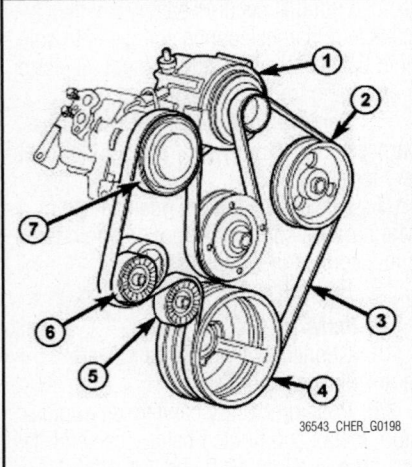

Fig. 67 Serpentine belt routing for 3.7L/4.7L engines

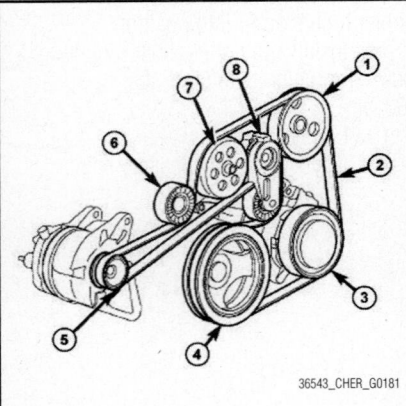

Fig. 68 Serpentine belt routing for 5.7L engine

ADJUSTMENT

It is not necessary to adjust belt tension on the 3.7L, 4.7L, or 5.7L engines. These engines are equipped with an automatic belt tensioner. The tensioner maintains correct belt tension at all times; consequently, do not attempt to use a belt tension gauge on these engines.

REMOVAL & INSTALLATION

3.7L & 4.7L Engines
See Figures 67, 69 and 70.

✳✳ CAUTION

Do not let tensioner arm snap back to the freearm position, severe damage may occur to the tensioner.

1. Disconnect negative battery cable from battery.
2. Rotate belt tensioner (6) until it contacts its stop. Remove belt (3), then slowly rotate the tensioner (6) into the freearm position.

To install:
3. Check condition of all pulleys.

✳✳ CAUTION

When installing the serpentine accessory drive belt, the belt MUST be routed correctly. If not, the engine may overheat due to the water pump rotating in the wrong direction.

4. Install new belt (2). Route the belt (2) around all pulleys except the idler pulley (5). Rotate the tensioner arm (6) until it contacts its stop position. Route the belt (2) around the idler (5) and slowly let the ten-

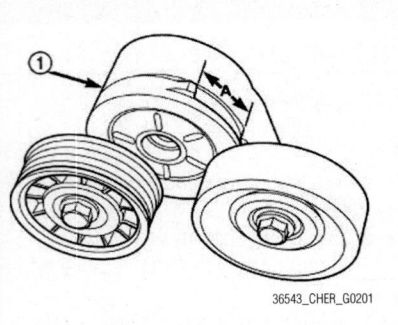

Fig. 70 The gap between the tang and the housing stop (measurement A) must not exceed .94 inches (4 mm)

sioner (6) rotate into the belt. Make sure the belt (2) is seated onto all pulleys.

5. With the drive belt (2) installed, inspect the belt wear indicator. The gap between the tang and the housing stop (measurement A) must not exceed .94 inches (4 mm).

5.7L Engine
See Figure 68.

1. Remove the air intake tube between intake manifold and air filter assembly.
2. Using a suitable square drive tool, release the belt tension by rotating the tensioner (8) clockwise. Rotate belt tensioner (8) until belt (2) can be removed from pulleys .
3. Remove belt (2).
4. Gently release tensioner (8).

To install:

➡**When installing accessory drive belt onto pulleys, make sure that belt is properly routed and all V-grooves make proper contact with pulleys.**

5. Position the drive belt over all pulleys except for the water pump pulley.
6. Rotate tensioner (8) clockwise and slip the belt over the water pump pulley.
7. Gently release tensioner (8).
8. Install the air intake tube between intake manifold and air filter assembly.

CAMSHAFT AND VALVE LIFTERS

REMOVAL & INSTALLATION

3.7L Engine

Left Side
See Figures 71 through 74.

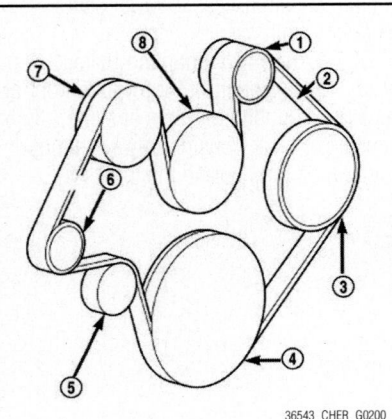

Fig. 69 Proper sequence for installing serpentine belt

※ **CAUTION**

When the timing chain is removed and the cylinder heads are still installed, DO NOT forcefully rotate the camshafts or crankshaft independently of each other. Severe valve and/or piston damage can occur.

※ **CAUTION**

When removing the cam sprocket, timing chains or camshaft, Failure to use Wedge Locking Tool 8379 will result in hydraulic tensioner ratchet over extension, requiring timing chain cover removal to reset the tensioner ratchet.

1. Remove cylinder head cover.
2. Set engine to TDC cylinder No. 1, camshaft sprocket V6 marks (1) at the 12 o'clock position.
3. Mark one link on the secondary timing chain on both sides of the V6 mark on the camshaft sprocket to aid in installation.

※ **CAUTION**

Do not hold or pry on the camshaft target wheel (Located on the right side camshaft sprocket) for any reason, Severe damage will occur to the target wheel resulting in a vehicle no start condition.

4. Loosen but DO NOT remove the camshaft sprocket retaining bolt. Leave the bolt snug against the sprocket.

➡The timing chain tensioners must be secured prior to removing the camshaft sprockets. Failure to secure tensioners will allow the tensioners to extend,

requiring timing chain cover removal in order to reset tensioners.

※ **CAUTION**

Do not force the wedge past the narrowest point between the chain strands. Damage to the tensioners may occur.

5. Position Wedge Locking Tool 8379 (1) between the timing chain strands, tap the tool to securely wedge the timing chain against the tensioner arm and guide.
6. Hold the camshaft with the Spanner Wrench 6958 and Adapter Pins 8346 while removing the camshaft sprocket bolt.
7. Using Camshaft Holder 8428 (2), remove the sprocket and gently allow the camshaft to rotate 5° clockwise until the camshaft is in the neutral position (no valve load).
8. Starting at the outside working inward, loosen the camshaft bearing cap

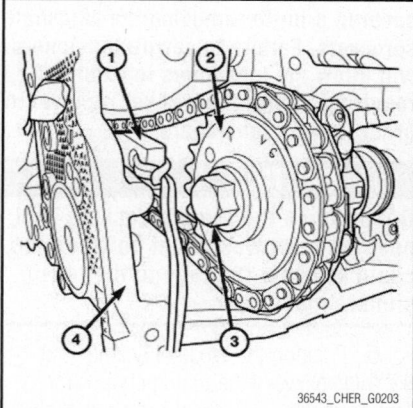

36543_CHER_G0203

Fig. 72 Position Wedge Locking Tool 8379 (1) between the timing chain strands

retaining bolts 1/2 turn at a time. Repeat until all load is off the bearing caps.

※ **CAUTION**

Do not stamp or strike the camshaft bearing caps. Severe damage will occur to the bearing caps.

➡When the camshaft is removed the rocker arms may slide downward, mark the rocker arms before removing camshaft.

9. Remove the camshaft bearing caps and the camshaft.

To install:
10. Lubricate the camshaft journals with clean engine oil.

➡Position the left side camshaft so that the camshaft sprocket dowel is near the 1 o'clock position, This will place the camshaft at the neutral position easing the installation of the camshaft bearing caps.

11. Position the camshaft into the cylinder head.
12. Install the camshaft bearing caps, hand tighten the retaining bolts.

➡Caps should be installed so that the stamped numbers on the caps are in numerical order, (1 through 4) from the front to the rear of the engine. All caps should be installed so that the stamped arrows on the caps point toward the front of the engine.

13. Working in ½ turn increments, tighten the bearing cap retaining bolts starting with the middle cap working outward.
14. Tighten the camshaft bearing cap retaining bolts to 100 inch lbs. (11 Nm).

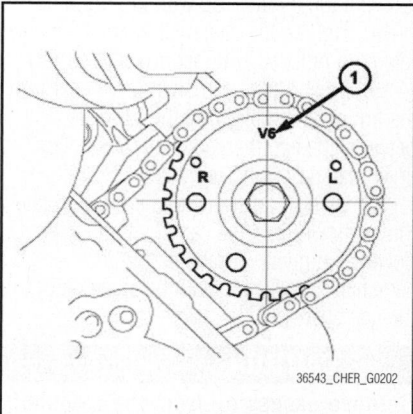

36543_CHER_G0202

Fig. 71 Set engine to TDC cylinder No. 1, camshaft sprocket V6 marks (1) at the 12 o'clock position

36543_CHER_G0204

Fig. 73 Using Camshaft Holder 8428 (2)

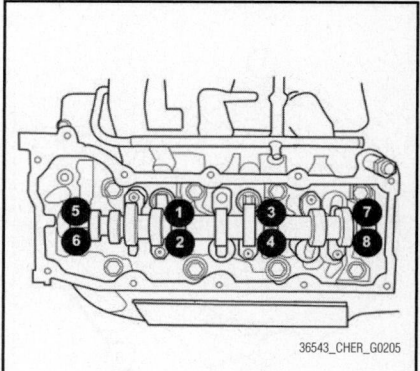

36543_CHER_G0205

Fig. 74 Tighten the bearing cap retaining bolts starting with the middle cap working outward

15. Position the camshaft drive gear into the timing chain aligning the V6 mark between the two marked chain links (Two links marked during removal).

16. Using the Camshaft Holder 8428A, rotate the camshaft until the camshaft sprocket dowel is aligned with the slot in the camshaft sprocket. Install the sprocket onto the camshaft.

✳✳ CAUTION

Remove excess oil from the camshaft sprocket bolt. Failure to do so can cause bolt over-torque resulting in bolt failure.

17. Remove excess oil from bolt, then install the camshaft sprocket retaining bolt and hand tighten.

18. Remove the Wedge Locking Tool 8379.

19. Using Spanner Wrench 6958 with adapter pins 8346, tighten the camshaft sprocket retaining bolt to 90 ft. lbs. (122 Nm).

20. Install the cylinder head cover.

Right Side

See Figures 72 through 75.

✳✳ CAUTION

When the timing chain is removed and the cylinder heads are still installed, DO NOT forcefully rotate the camshafts or crankshaft independently of each other. Severe valve and/or piston damage can occur.

✳✳ CAUTION

When removing the cam sprocket, timing chains or camshaft, failure to use special tool 8379 will result in

hydraulic tensioner ratchet over extension, requiring timing chain cover removal to re-set the tensioner ratchet.

1. Remove the cylinder head cover.
2. Set engine to TDC cylinder No. 1, camshaft sprocket V6 marks at the 12 o'clock position (1).
3. Mark one link on the secondary timing chain on both sides of the V6 mark on the camshaft sprocket to aid in installation.

✳✳ CAUTION

Do not hold or pry on the camshaft target wheel for any reason, Severe damage will occur to the target wheel. A damaged target wheel could cause a vehicle no start condition.

4. Loosen but DO NOT remove the camshaft sprocket retaining bolt. Leave bolt snug against sprocket.

➡ **The timing chain tensioners must be secured prior to removing the camshaft sprockets. Failure to secure tensioners will allow the tensioners to extend, requiring timing chain cover removal in order to reset tensioners.**

✳✳ CAUTION

Do not force the Wedge Locking Tool past the narrowest point between the chain strands. Damage to the tensioners may occur.

5. Position the Wedge Locking Tool 8379 (1) between the timing chain strands. Tap the tool to securely wedge the timing chain against the tensioner arm and guide.

6. Remove the camshaft position sensor.

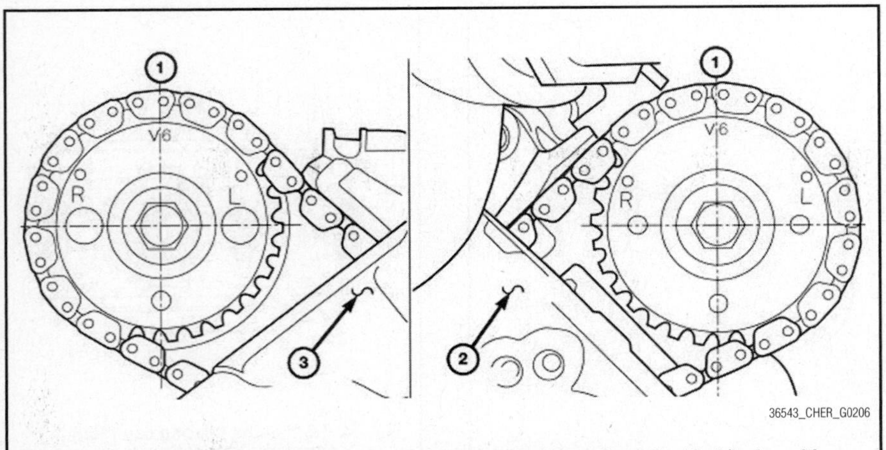

7. Hold the camshaft with Spanner Wrench 8428 (2), while removing the camshaft sprocket bolt and sprocket.

8. Starting at the outside working inward, loosen the camshaft bearing cap retaining bolts ½ turn at a time. Repeat until all load is off the bearing caps.

✳✳ CAUTION

Do not stamp or strike the camshaft bearing caps. Severe damage will occur to the bearing caps.

➡ **When the camshaft is removed the rocker arms may slide downward, mark the rocker arms before removing camshaft.**

9. Remove the camshaft bearing caps and the camshaft.

To install:

10. Lubricate camshaft journals with clean engine oil.

➡ **Position the right side camshaft so that the camshaft sprocket dowel is near the 10 o'clock position, This will place the camshaft at the neutral position easing the installation of the camshaft bearing caps.**

11. Position the camshaft into the cylinder head.

12. Install the camshaft bearing caps, hand tighten the retaining bolts.

➡ **Caps should be installed so that the stamped numbers on the caps are in numerical order (1 through 4) from the front to the rear of the engine. All caps should be installed so that the stamped arrows on the caps point toward the front of the engine.**

13. Working in ½ turn increments, tighten the bearing cap retaining bolts starting with the middle cap working outward.

14. Tighten the camshaft bearing cap retaining bolts to 100 inch lbs. (11 Nm).

15. Position the camshaft drive gear into the timing chain aligning the V6 mark between the two marked chain links (Two links marked during removal).

16. Using Camshaft Holder 8428, rotate the camshaft until the camshaft sprocket dowel is aligned with the slot in the camshaft sprocket. Install the sprocket onto the camshaft.

✳✳ CAUTION

Remove excess oil from the camshaft sprocket bolt. Failure to do so can cause bolt over-torque resulting in bolt failure.

36543_CHER_G0206

Fig. 75 Set engine to TDC cylinder No. 1, camshaft sprocket V6 marks at the 12 o'clock position (1)

17. Remove excess oil from camshaft sprocket bolt, then install the camshaft sprocket retaining bolt and hand tighten.

18. Remove the Wedge Locking Tool 8379.

19. Using Spanner Wrench 6958 with adapter pins 8346, tighten the camshaft sprocket retaining bolt to 90 ft. lbs. (122 Nm).

20. Install the camshaft position sensor.

21. Install the cylinder head cover.

4.7L Engine

Left Side

See Figures 76 through 81.

1. Remove cylinder head cover.

> ❋ **CAUTION**
>
> **When the timing chain is removed and the cylinder heads are still installed, DO NOT forcefully rotate the camshafts or crankshaft independently of each other. Severe valve and/or piston damage can occur.**

> ❋ **CAUTION**
>
> **When removing the cam sprocket, timing chains or camshaft, Failure to use Locking Wedge 9867 will result in hydraulic tensioner ratchet over extension, requiring timing chain cover removal to reset the tensioner ratchet.**

2. Set engine to TDC cylinder 1, camshaft sprocket V8 marks at the 12 o'clock position.

3. Mark one link on the secondary timing chain on both sides of the V8 mark on the camshaft sprocket to aid in installation.

> ❋ **CAUTION**
>
> **Do not hold or pry on the camshaft target wheel (Located on the right side camshaft sprocket) for any reason, Severe damage will occur to the target wheel resulting in a vehicle no start condition.**

4. Loosen but DO NOT remove the camshaft sprocket retaining bolt. Leave the bolt snug against the sprocket.

➡ **The timing chain tensioners must be secured prior to removing the camshaft sprockets. Failure to secure tensioners will allow the tensioners to extend, requiring timing chain cover removal in order to reset tensioners.**

> ❋ **CAUTION**
>
> **Do not force wedge past the narrowest point between the chain strands. Damage to the tensioners may occur.**

5. Position Locking Wedge Tool 9867 (4) timing chain wedge between the timing chain strands, tap the tool to securely wedge the timing chain against the tensioner arm and guide.

➡ **When gripping the camshaft, place the pliers on the tube portion of the camshaft only. Do not grip the lobes or the sprocket areas.**

6. Hold the camshaft (3) with adjustable pliers (2) while removing the camshaft sprocket bolt and sprocket (1).

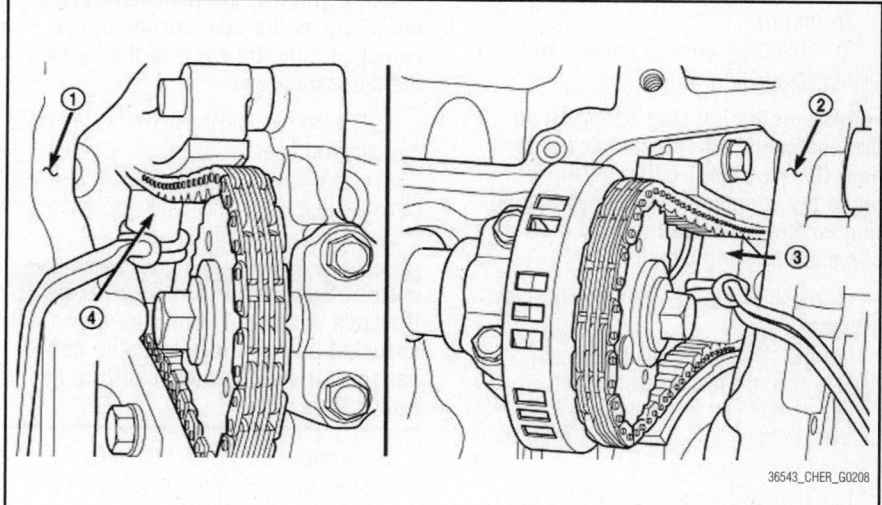

36543_CHER_G0208

Fig. 77 Position Locking Wedge Tool 9867 (4) timing chain wedge between the timing chain strands

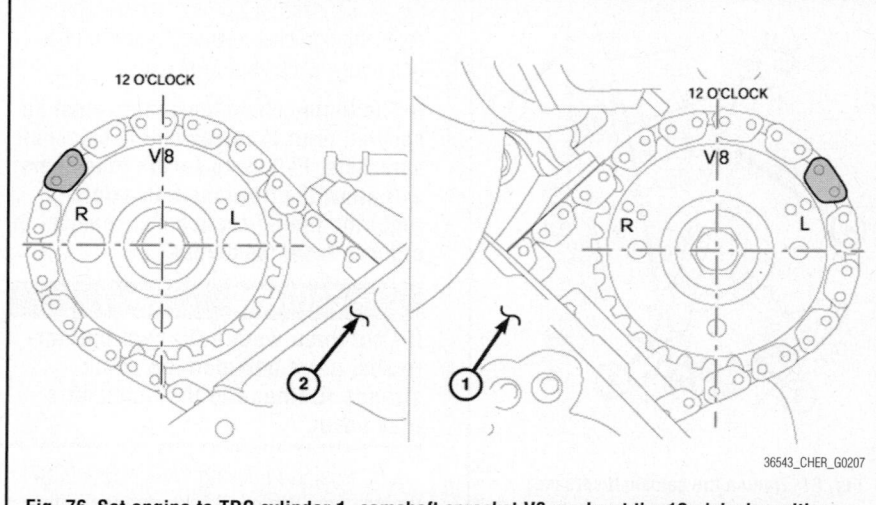

36543_CHER_G0207

Fig. 76 Set engine to TDC cylinder 1, camshaft sprocket V8 marks at the 12 o'clock position

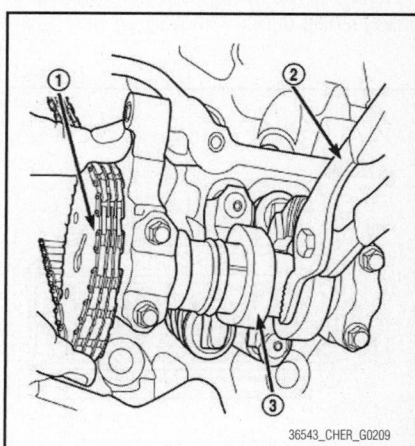

36543_CHER_G0209

Fig. 78 Hold the camshaft (3) with adjustable pliers (2) while removing the camshaft sprocket bolt and sprocket (1)

7. Using the pliers, gently allow the camshaft to rotate 15° clockwise until the camshaft is in the neutral position (no valve load).

8. Starting at the outside working inward, loosen the camshaft bearing cap retaining bolts ½ turn at a time. Repeat until all load is off the bearing caps.

> ✷✷ **CAUTION**
>
> **Do not stamp or strike the camshaft bearing caps. Severe damage will occur to the bearing caps.**

➡ **When the camshaft is removed the rocker arms may slide downward, mark the rocker arms before removing camshaft.**

9. Remove the camshaft bearing caps and the camshaft.

To install:

10. Lubricate camshaft journals with clean engine oil.

➡ **Position the left side camshaft so that the camshaft sprocket dowel is near the 1 o'clock position, This will place the camshaft at the neutral position easing the installation of the camshaft bearing caps.**

11. Position the camshaft into the cylinder head.

12. Install the camshaft bearing caps, hand tighten the retaining bolts.

13. Working in ½ turn increments, tighten the bearing cap retaining bolts following the torque sequence.

14. Tighten the camshaft bearing cap retaining bolts to 100 inch lbs. (11 Nm).

15. Position the camshaft drive gear into the timing chain aligning the V8 mark between the two marked chain links (Two links marked during removal).

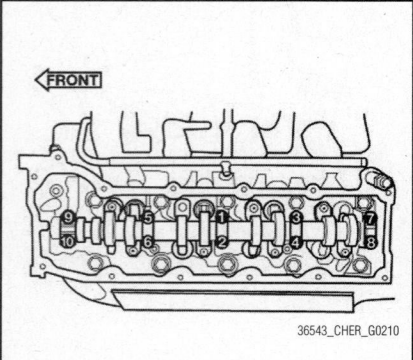

Fig. 79 Tighten the bearing cap retaining bolts following the torque sequence

Fig. 80 Rotate the camshaft until the camshaft sprocket dowel is aligned with the slot in the camshaft sprocket

➡ **When gripping the camshaft, place the pliers on the tube portion of the camshaft only. Do not grip the lobes or the sprocket areas.**

16. Using the adjustable pliers (1), rotate the camshaft until the camshaft sprocket dowel (2) is aligned with the slot in the camshaft sprocket. Install the sprocket onto the camshaft.

> ✷✷ **CAUTION**
>
> **Remove excess oil from the camshaft sprocket bolt. Failure to do so can cause bolt over-torque resulting in bolt failure.**

17. Remove excess oil from bolt, then install the camshaft sprocket retaining bolt and hand tighten.

18. Remove Locking Wedge Tool 9867 timing chain wedge.

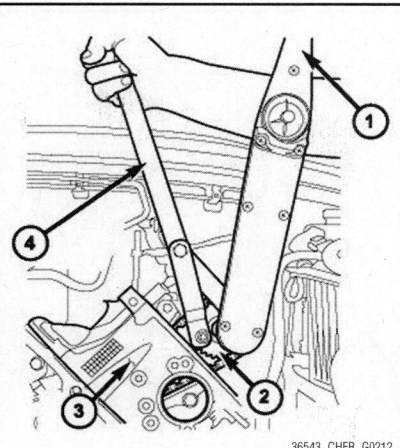

Fig. 81 Tighten the camshaft sprocket retaining bolt

19. Using Spanner Wrench 6958 (4) with adapter pins 8346, tighten the camshaft sprocket retaining bolt (2) to 90 ft. lbs. (122 Nm).

20. Install the cylinder head cover.

Right Side

See Figures 76, 77, 79, 80, 82 and 83.

1. Remove the cylinder head.

> ✷✷ **CAUTION**
>
> **When the timing chain is removed and the cylinder heads are still installed, DO NOT forcefully rotate the camshafts or crankshaft independently of each other. Severe valve and/or piston damage can occur.**

> ✷✷ **CAUTION**
>
> **When removing the cam sprocket, timing chains or camshaft, Failure to use locking wedge tool 9867 will result in hydraulic tensioner ratchet over extension, Requiring timing chain cover removal to re-set the tensioner ratchet.**

2. Set engine to TDC cylinder 1, camshaft sprocket V8 marks at the 12 o'clock position.

3. Mark one link on the secondary timing chain on both sides of the V8 mark on the camshaft sprocket to aid in installation.

> ✷✷ **CAUTION**
>
> **Do not hold or pry on the camshaft target wheel for any reason, Severe damage will occur to the target wheel. A damaged target wheel could cause a vehicle no start condition.**

4. Loosen but DO NOT remove the camshaft sprocket retaining bolt (2). Leave bolt snug against sprocket (3).

➡ **The timing chain tensioners must be secured prior to removing the camshaft sprockets. Failure to secure tensioners will allow the tensioners to extend, requiring timing chain cover removal in order to reset tensioners.**

> ✷✷ **CAUTION**
>
> **Do not force wedge (3) past the narrowest point between the chain strands. Damage to the tensioners may occur.**

5. Position Locking Wedge Tool 9867 timing chain wedge (3) between the timing

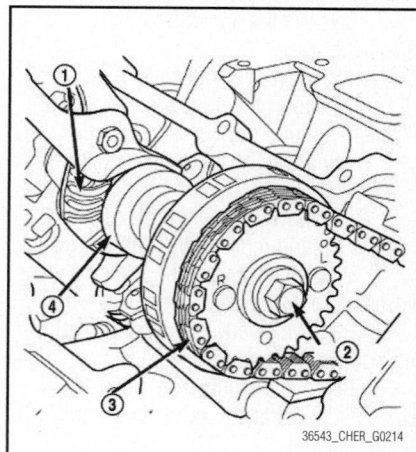

Fig. 82 Hold the camshaft with adjustable pliers (1) while removing the camshaft sprocket bolt (2) and sprocket (3)

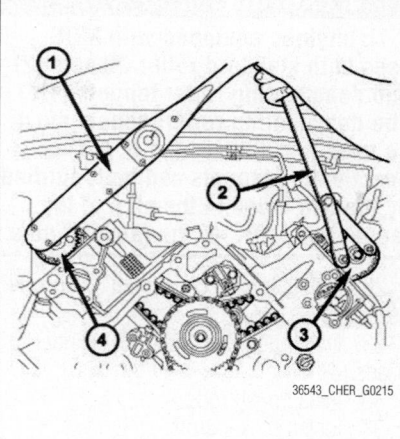

Fig. 83 Using spanner wrench 6958 with adapter pins 8346 (2)

chain strands. Tap the tool to securely wedge the timing chain against the tensioner arm and guide.

6. Remove the camshaft position sensor.

➡**When gripping the camshaft, place the pliers (1) on the tube portion of the camshaft only. Do not grip the lobes or the sprocket areas.**

7. Hold the camshaft with adjustable pliers (1) while removing the camshaft sprocket bolt (2) and sprocket (3).

8. Using the pliers (1), gently allow the camshaft to rotate 45° counter-clockwise until the camshaft is in the neutral position (no valve load).

9. Starting at the outside working inward, loosen the camshaft bearing cap retaining bolts ½ turn at a time. Repeat until all load is off the bearing caps.

✳✳ CAUTION

Do not stamp or strike the camshaft bearing caps. Severe damage will occur to the bearing caps.

➡**When the camshaft is removed the rocker arms may slide downward, mark the rocker arms before removing camshaft.**

10. Remove the camshaft bearing caps and the camshaft.

To install:

11. Lubricate camshaft journals with clean engine oil.

➡**Position the right side camshaft so that the camshaft sprocket dowel is near the 10 o'clock position, This will place the camshaft at the neutral posi-**

tion easing the installation of the camshaft bearing caps.

12. Position the camshaft into the cylinder head.

13. Install the camshaft bearing caps, hand tighten the retaining bolts.

14. Working in ½ turn increments, tighten the bearing cap retaining bolts starting with the middle cap working outward.

15. Torque the camshaft bearing cap retaining bolts to 100 inch lbs. (11 Nm).

16. Position the camshaft drive gear into the timing chain aligning the V8 mark between the two marked chain links (Two links marked during removal).

➡**When gripping the camshaft, place the pliers on the tube portion of the camshaft only. Do not grip the lobes or the sprocket areas.**

17. Using the adjustable pliers, rotate the camshaft until the camshaft sprocket dowel is aligned with the slot in the camshaft sprocket. Install the sprocket onto the camshaft.

✳✳ CAUTION

Remove excess oil from the camshaft sprocket bolt. Failure to do so can cause bolt over-torque resulting in bolt failure.

18. Remove excess oil from camshaft sprocket bolt, then install the camshaft sprocket retaining bolt and hand tighten.

19. Remove locking wedge tool 9867.

20. Using spanner wrench 6958 with adapter pins 8346 (2), tighten the camshaft sprocket retaining bolt (4) to 90 ft. lbs. (122 Nm).

21. Install the camshaft position sensor.

22. Install the cylinder head cover.

5.7L Engine

See Figures 84 through 86.

1. Remove the battery negative cable.
2. Remove the air cleaner assembly.
3. Drain the coolant.
4. Remove the accessory drive belt.
5. Remove the alternator.
6. Remove the A/C compressor, and set aside.
7. Remove the radiator.
8. Remove intake manifold.
9. Remove cylinder head covers.
10. Remove both left and right cylinder heads.
11. Remove the rocker arms.
12. Remove the push rods.
13. Remove timing case cover.
14. Remove the oil pan.
15. Remove the oil pick up tube.
16. Remove the oil pump.

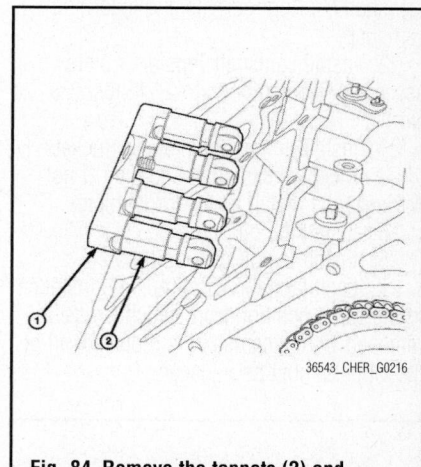

Fig. 84 Remove the tappets (2) and retainer (1) assembly

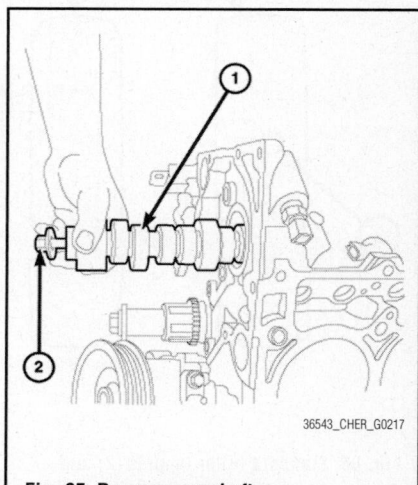

Fig. 85 Remove camshaft

17. Remove timing chain.

18. Remove camshaft tensioner/thrust plate assembly.

➡ **Identify lifters to ensure installation in original location.**

19. Remove the tappets (2) and retainer (1) assembly.

20. Install a long bolt into front of camshaft to aid in removal of the camshaft. Remove camshaft, being careful not to damage cam bearings with the cam lobes.

To install:

✷✷ CAUTION

5.7L engines equipped with MDS uses a unique camshaft for use with the Multi Displacement System. When installing a new camshaft, the replacement camshaft must be compatible with the Multi Displacement System.

21. Lubricate camshaft lobes and camshaft bearing journals and insert the camshaft.

22. Install camshaft Tensioner plate assembly. Tighten bolts to 21 ft. lbs. (28 Nm).

23. Install timing chain and sprockets.

24. Measure camshaft end play. If not within limits install a new thrust plate.

25. Install the oil pump.

26. Install the oil pick up tube.

27. Each tappet reused must be installed in the same position from which it was removed. When camshaft is replaced, all of the tappets must be replaced.

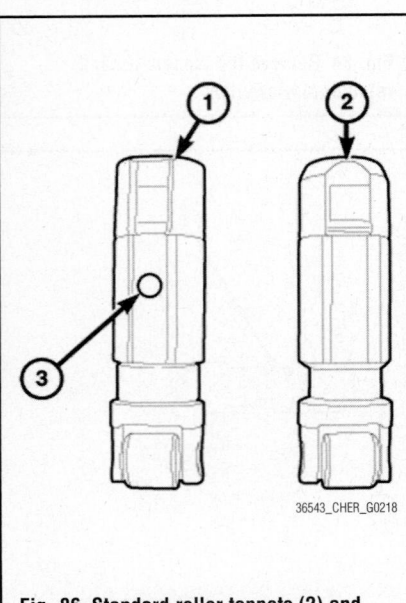

Fig. 86 Standard roller tappets (2) and deactivating roller tappets (1)

36543_CHER_G0218

✷✷ CAUTION

5.7L engines equipped with MDS uses both standard roller tappets (2) and deactivating roller tappets (1). The deactivating roller tappets must be used in cylinders 1,4,6,7. The deactivating tappets can be identified by the two holes in the side of the tappet body (3), for the latching pins.

28. Install tappets (2) and retaining yoke assembly (1).

29. Install both left and right cylinder heads (4).

30. Install push rods.

31. Install rocker arms.

32. Install timing case cover.

33. Install the oil pan.

34. Install cylinder head covers.

35. Install intake manifold.

36. Install the A/C compressor (2).

37. Install the alternator (2).

38. Install the accessory drive belt.

39. Install the radiator.

40. Install the air cleaner assembly.

41. Install the battery negative cable.

42. Refill coolant.

43. Refill engine oil.

44. Start engine and check for leaks.

CATALYTIC CONVERTER

REMOVAL & INSTALLATION

3.7L Engine

See Figures 87 through 89.

1. Raise and support the vehicle.

2. Saturate the bolts and nuts with heat valve lubricant. Allow 5 minutes for penetration.

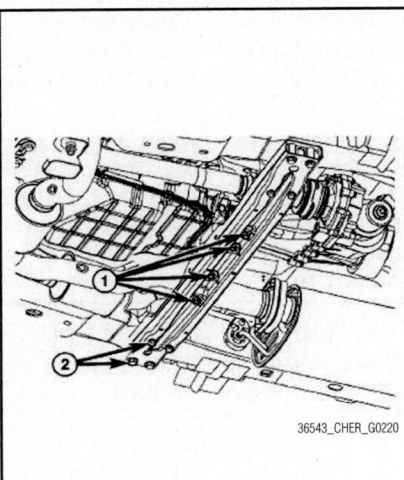

Fig. 87 Remove the transmission crossmember

36543_CHER_G0220

3. Remove the transmission crossmember.

   a. Remove the skid plate.

   b. Support the transmission with a suitable lifting device.

   c. Remove the four transmission mount bolts (1).

   d. Remove the eight crossmember bolts (2) and remove the crossmember.

4. Disconnect and mark oxygen sensor electrical connectors.

5. Remove steady rest bracket mounting bolt (5) from transmission.

6. Remove the nuts from the front exhaust pipe/catalytic converter assembly to muffler flange.

7. Remove bolts (2) and flanged nuts (1) at the exhaust manifold.

8. Remove the front exhaust pipe/catalytic converter assembly (3) from the vehicle.

9. Remove steady rest bracket (4) from front exhaust pipe/catalytic converter assembly (3).

To install:

10. Position steady rest bracket onto the front exhaust pipe/catalytic converter assembly.

11. Position the front exhaust pipe/catalytic converter assembly into vehicle.

12. Install the bolts and nuts at the front exhaust pipe/catalytic converter assembly to exhaust manifold flange. Do not tighten.

13. Install the nuts at the front exhaust pipe/catalytic converter assembly to muffler flange. Do not tighten.

14. Position the exhaust pipe for proper clearance with the frame and underbody parts. A minimum clearance of 1.0 inches (25.4 mm) is required.

15. Tighten front exhaust pipe/catalytic converter assembly to exhaust manifold bolts.

16. Tighten the front exhaust pipe and catalytic converter assembly to muffler flange nuts to 35 ft. lbs. (47 Nm).

17. Install steady rest bracket bolts. Tighten bolts to 35 ft. lbs. (47 Nm).

18. Connect oxygen sensor electrical connectors.

19. Install transmission crossmember.

20. Lower vehicle.

21. Start the vehicle and inspect for exhaust leaks.

22. Repair exhaust leaks as necessary.

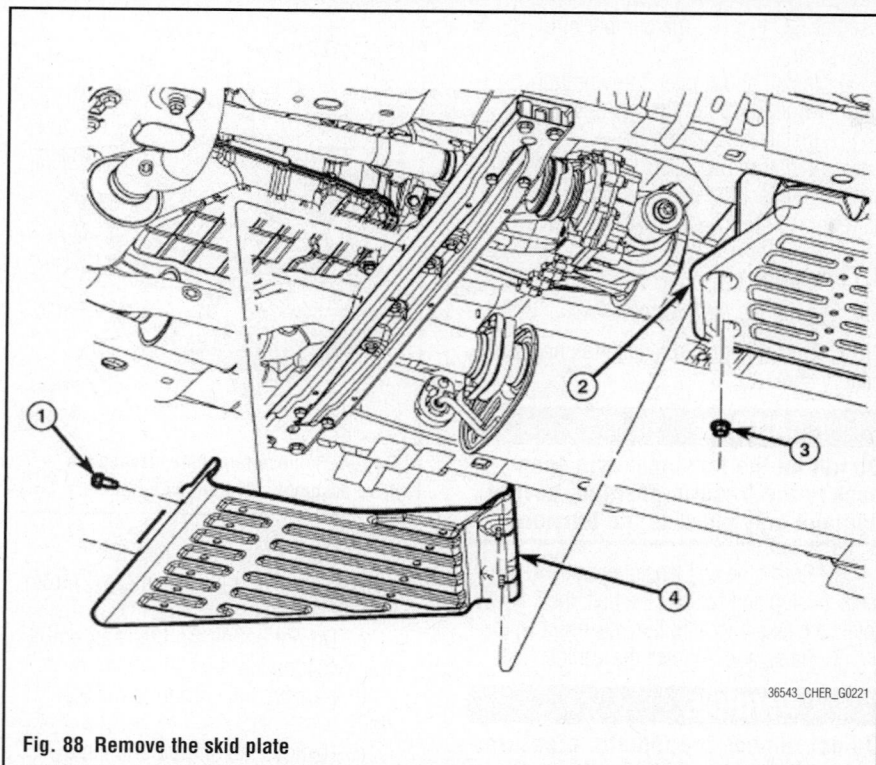

Fig. 88 Remove the skid plate

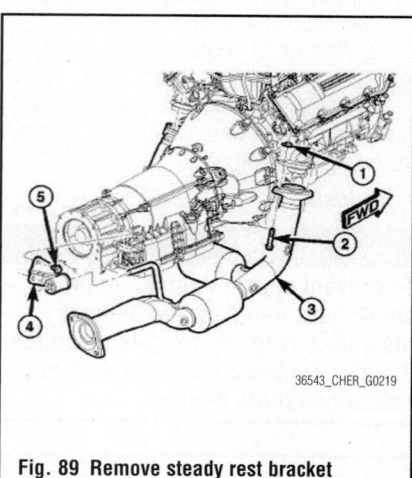

Fig. 89 Remove steady rest bracket mounting bolt (5) from transmission

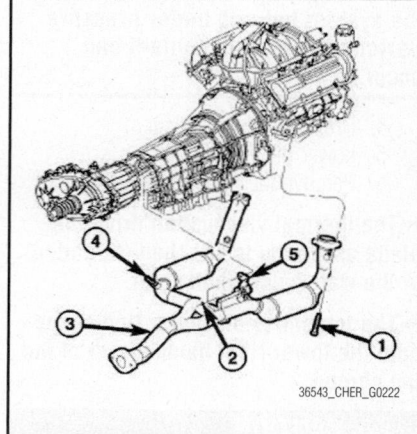

Fig. 90 Remove steady rest bracket mounting bolt (5) from transmission

4.7L & 5.7L Engines

See Figures 87, 88 and 90.

1. Raise and support the vehicle.
2. Saturate the bolts and nuts with heat valve lubricant. Allow 5 minutes for penetration.
3. Remove transmission crossmember.
   a. Remove the skid plate.
   b. Support the transmission with a suitable lifting device.
   c. Remove the four transmission mount bolts (1).
   d. Remove the eight crossmember bolts (2) and remove the crossmember.

4. Disconnect and mark oxygen sensor electrical connectors.
5. Remove steady rest bracket mounting bolt (5) from transmission.
6. Remove the nuts from the front exhaust pipe/catalytic converter assembly to muffler flange.
7. Remove bolts (2) and flanged nuts (1) at the exhaust manifold.
8. Remove the front exhaust pipe/catalytic converter assembly (3) from the vehicle.
9. Remove steady rest bracket (4) from front exhaust pipe/catalytic converter assembly (3).

To install:

10. Position steady rest bracket onto the front exhaust pipe/catalytic converter assembly.
11. Position the front exhaust pipe/catalytic converter assembly into vehicle.
12. Install the bolts and nuts at the front exhaust pipe/catalytic converter assembly to exhaust manifold flange. Do not tighten.
13. Install the nuts at the front exhaust pipe/catalytic converter assembly to muffler flange. Do not tighten.
14. Position the exhaust pipe for proper clearance with the frame and underbody parts. A minimum clearance of 1.0 inches (25.4 mm) is required.
15. Tighten front exhaust pipe/catalytic converter assembly to exhaust manifold bolts.
16. Tighten the front exhaust pipe and catalytic converter assembly to muffler flange nuts to 35 ft. lbs. (47 Nm).
17. Install steady rest bracket bolts. Tighten bolts to 35 ft. lbs. (47 Nm).
18. Connect oxygen sensor electrical connectors.
19. Install transmission crossmember.
20. Lower vehicle.
21. Start the vehicle and inspect for exhaust leaks.
22. Repair exhaust leaks as necessary.

CRANKSHAFT DAMPER

REMOVAL & INSTALLATION

3.7L Engine

See Figures 91 through 93.

1. Disconnect the negative cable from battery.

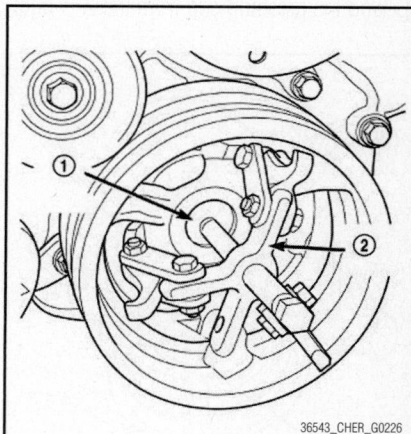

Fig. 91 Remove damper using the Crankshaft Insert 8513A (1) and Three Jaw Puller 1026 (2)

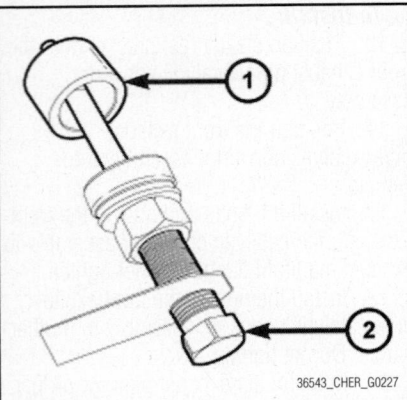

Fig. 92 Assemble the damper installer 8512A (2) , and the pressing cup (1) from A/C hub installer 6871

2. Remove the radiator fan.
3. Remove accessory drive belt.
4. Remove the vibration damper bolt.
5. Remove damper using the Crank-shaft Insert 8513A (1) and Three Jaw Puller 1026 (2).

To install:

> ✳✳ **CAUTION**
>
> **To prevent severe damage to the Crankshaft, Damper or Damper Installer 8512A, thoroughly clean the damper bore and the crankshaft nose before installing Damper.**

6. Position the damper onto crankshaft.
7. Assemble the damper installer 8512A (2) , and the pressing cup (1) from A/C hub installer 6871.
8. Coat the threads of damper installer 8512A with Mopar® Nickel Anti-Seize or equivalent.
9. Using the damper installer 8512A (1), and the pressing cup from the A/C hub

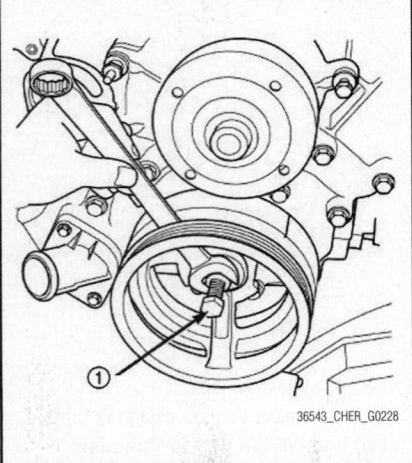

Fig. 93 Press the damper onto crankshaft

installer 6871, press the damper onto crankshaft.
10. Install and tighten the vibration damper bolt to 130 ft. lbs. (175 Nm).
11. Install the cooling fan.
12. Install the accessory drive belt.
13. Connect the negative cable to battery.

4.7L Engine

See Figures 92, 94 through 96.

1. Disconnect and isolate the negative battery cable.

> ✳✳ **CAUTION**
>
> **Do not let the tensioner arm snap back to the freearm position, severe damage may occur to the tensioner.**

2. Rotate the belt tensioner until it contacts its stop and remove the belt, then slowly rotate the tensioner into the freearm position.
3. Raise and support the vehicle.

> ✳✳ **WARNING**
>
> **Do not remove the radiator pressure cap, cylinder block drain plugs or loosen the radiator draincock with the system hot and under pressure. Serious burns from coolant can occur.**

4. Drain the cooling system.
5. Lower the vehicle.
6. Remove the upper radiator hose.

➡ **The thermal viscous fan drive/fan blade assembly is attached (threaded) to the water pump hub shaft.**

➡ **The transmission cooler line snaps onto the lower right hand corner of the fan shroud.**

> ✳✳ **CAUTION**
>
> **After removing fan blade/viscous fan drive assembly, do not place viscous fan drive in horizontal position. If stored horizontally, silicone fluid in the viscous fan drive could drain into the bearing assembly and contaminate the bearing lubricant.**

7. Remove the fan shroud and fan blade/viscous fan drive assembly as a complete unit from the vehicle.
   a. Remove fan blade/viscous fan drive assembly (2) from water pump using special tool 6958 spanner wrench and 8346 adapters (1), by turning mounting nut counterclockwise as viewed from front. Threads on viscous fan drive are RIGHT HAND.

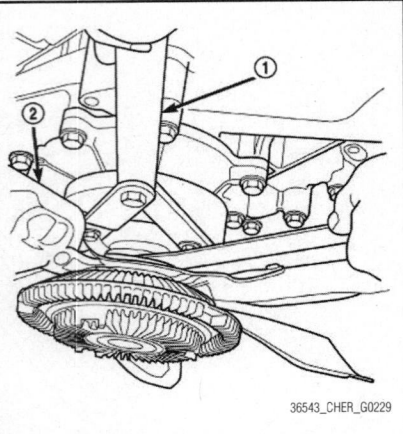

Fig. 94 Remove fan blade/viscous fan drive assembly (2) from water pump

   b. Do not attempt to remove fan/viscous fan drive assembly (2) from vehicle at this time.
   c. Do not unbolt fan blade assembly from viscous fan drive at this time.
   d. Remove fan shroud to radiator bolts.
   e. Remove fan shroud and fan blade/viscous fan drive assembly as a complete unit from vehicle.
8. Remove the vibration damper retaining bolt.
9. Using the crankshaft insert 8513A (1) and the three jaw puller 8454 (2) remove the crankshaft damper.

To install:

> ✳✳ **CAUTION**
>
> **To prevent severe damage to the crankshaft, damper, and damper installer 8512A, thoroughly clean the damper bore and the crankshaft nose before installing damper.**

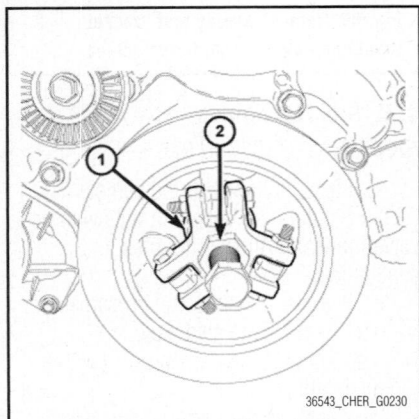

Fig. 95 Use the crankshaft insert (1) and suitable puller (2) to remove the crankshaft damper

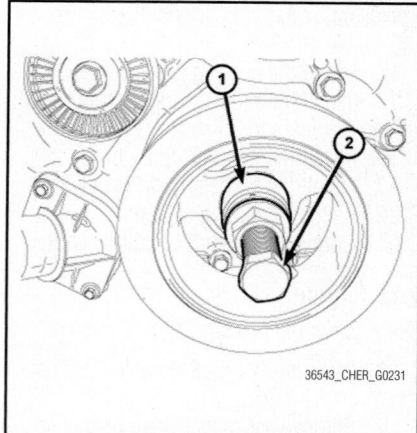

Fig. 96 Press the damper onto the crankshaft using the special tools (1, 2)

10. Position the damper onto the crankshaft.

11. Assemble the damper installer 8512A (2) and the A/C hub installer cup 6871 (1).

12. Using the damper installer 8512A (2) and the A/C hub installer cup 6871 (1), press the damper onto the crankshaft.

13. Coat the vibration damper bolt threads with Mopar® Nickel Anti-Seize or equivalent, install and tighten the bolt to 130 ft. lbs. (175 Nm).

14. Install the cooling fan assembly.

15. Install the radiator upper shroud and tighten fasteners to 95 inch lbs. (11 Nm).

16. Install the radiator upper hose.

17. Install the accessory drive belt.

18. Refill the cooling system

19. Connect the negative battery cable.

5.7L Engine

See Figures 97 and 98.

1. Disconnect negative cable from battery.

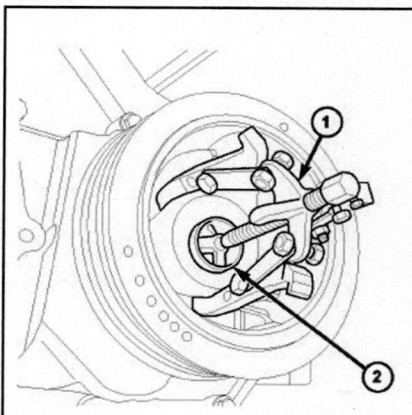

Fig. 97 Remove damper using Crankshaft Insert 8513A (1) and Three Jaw Puller 1023 (2)

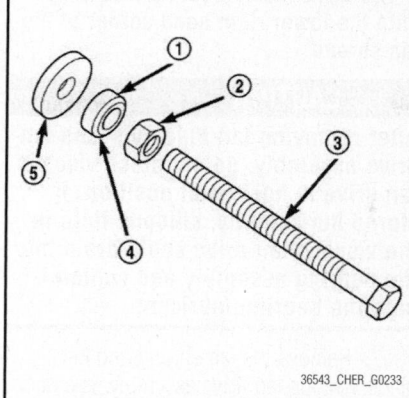

Fig. 98 Special Tool 8512-A, is assembled in a specific sequence

2. Remove accessory drive belt.

3. Drain cooling system.

4. Remove radiator upper hose.

5. Remove fan shroud.

6. Remove crankshaft damper bolt.

7. Remove damper using Crankshaft Insert 8513A and Three Jaw Puller 1023.

To install:

> ✳✳ **CAUTION**
>
> **To prevent severe damage to the Crankshaft, Damper or Damper Installer 8512A, thoroughly clean the damper bore and the crankshaft nose before installing Damper.**

8. Slide damper onto crankshaft slightly.

> ✳✳ **CAUTION**
>
> **Special Tool 8512-A, is assembled in a specific sequence. Failure to assemble this tool in this sequence can result in tool failure and severe damage to either the tool or the crankshaft.**

9. Assemble Damper Installer 8512-A as follows, thread nut (2) onto the bolt (3) then install the roller bearing (1) followed by the hardened washer (5) slides onto the threaded rod (3). Once assembled coat the threaded rod's threads with Mopar® Nickel Anti-Seize (or equivalent).

10. Using Damper Installer 8512-A, press damper onto crankshaft.

11. Install then tighten crankshaft damper bolt to 130 ft. lbs. (175 Nm).

12. Install radiator upper hose.

13. Install accessory drive belt.

14. Refill cooling system.

15. Connect negative cable to battery.

CRANKSHAFT FRONT SEAL

REMOVAL & INSTALLATION

3.7L Engine

See Figures 91 through 93, 99 and 100.

1. Disconnect the negative cable from battery.

2. Remove the radiator fan.

3. Remove accessory drive belt.

4. Remove the vibration damper bolt.

5. Remove damper using the Crankshaft Insert 8513A (1) and Three Jaw Puller 1026 (2).

6. Using the Seal Remover 8511 (1), remove crankshaft front seal.

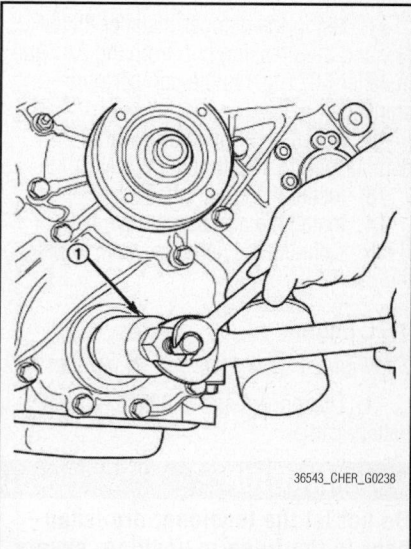

Fig. 99 Using the Seal Remover 8511 (1), remove crankshaft front seal

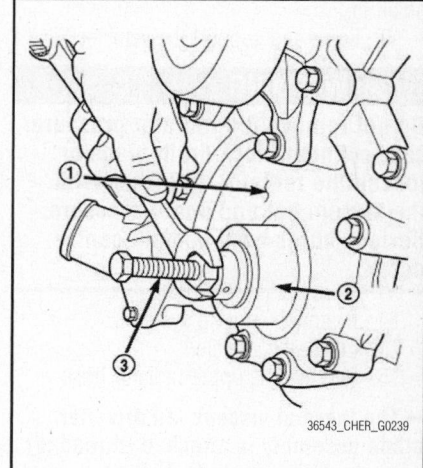

Fig. 100 Install the crankshaft front seal

To install:

> ※ **CAUTION**
>
> To prevent severe damage to the Crankshaft, Damper or Damper Installer 8512A, thoroughly clean the damper bore and the crankshaft nose before installing Damper.

7. Using the Seal Installer 8348 (2) and Damper Installer 8512A (3), install the crankshaft front seal.

8. Position the damper onto crankshaft.

9. Assemble the damper installer 8512A (2), and the pressing cup (1) from A/C hub installer 6871.

10. Coat the threads of damper installer 8512A with Mopar® Nickel Anti-Seize or equivalent.

11. Using the damper installer 8512A (1), and the pressing cup from the A/C hub installer 6871, press the damper onto crankshaft.

12. Install and tighten the vibration damper bolt to 130 ft. lbs. (175 Nm).

13. Install the cooling fan.

14. Install the accessory drive belt.

15. Connect the negative cable to battery.

4.7L Engine

See Figures 92, 94 through 96, 99 and 100.

1. Disconnect and isolate the negative battery cable.

> ※ **CAUTION**
>
> Do not let the tensioner arm snap back to the freearm position, severe damage may occur to the tensioner.

2. Rotate the belt tensioner (6) until it contacts its stop and remove the belt, then slowly rotate the tensioner into the freearm position.

3. Raise and support the vehicle.

> ※ **WARNING**
>
> Do not remove the radiator pressure cap, cylinder block drain plugs or loosen the radiator draincock with the system hot and under pressure. Serious burns from coolant can occur.

4. Drain the cooling system.

5. Lower the vehicle.

6. Remove the upper radiator hose.

➡The thermal viscous fan drive/fan blade assembly is attached (threaded) to the water pump hub shaft.

➡The transmission cooler line snaps onto the lower right hand corner of the fan shroud.

> ※ **CAUTION**
>
> After removing fan blade/viscous fan drive assembly, do not place viscous fan drive in horizontal position. If stored horizontally, silicone fluid in the viscous fan drive could drain into the bearing assembly and contaminate the bearing lubricant.

7. Remove the fan shroud and fan blade/viscous fan drive assembly as a complete unit from the vehicle.

   a. Remove fan blade/viscous fan drive assembly (2) from water pump using special tool 6958 spanner wrench and 8346 adapters (1), by turning mounting nut counterclockwise as viewed from front. Threads on viscous fan drive are RIGHT HAND.

   b. Do not attempt to remove fan/viscous fan drive assembly (2) from vehicle at this time.

   c. Do not unbolt fan blade assembly from viscous fan drive at this time.

   d. Remove fan shroud to radiator bolts.

   e. Remove fan shroud and fan blade/viscous fan drive assembly as a complete unit from vehicle.

8. Remove the vibration damper retaining bolt.

9. Using the crankshaft insert 8513A (1) and the three jaw puller 8454 (2) remove the crankshaft damper.

10. Using the Seal Remover 8511 (1), remove crankshaft front seal.

To install:

> ※ **CAUTION**
>
> To prevent severe damage to the crankshaft, damper, and damper installer 8512A, thoroughly clean the damper bore and the crankshaft nose before installing damper.

11. Using the Seal Installer 8348 (2) and Damper Installer 8512A (3), install the crankshaft front seal.

12. Position the damper onto the crankshaft.

13. Assemble the damper installer 8512A (2) and the A/C hub installer cup 6871 (1).

14. Using the damper installer 8512A (2) and the A/C hub installer cup 6871 (1), press the damper onto the crankshaft.

15. Coat the vibration damper bolt threads with Mopar® Nickel Anti-Seize or

equivalent, install and tighten the bolt to 130 ft. lbs. (175 Nm).

16. Install the cooling fan assembly.

17. Install the radiator upper shroud and tighten fasteners to 95 inch lbs. (11 Nm).

18. Install the radiator upper hose.

19. Install the accessory drive belt

20. Refill the cooling system

21. Connect the negative battery cable.

5.7L Engine

See Figures 97 through 98, 101 and 102.

1. Disconnect negative cable from battery.

2. Remove accessory drive belt.

3. Drain cooling system.

4. Remove radiator upper hose.

5. Remove fan shroud.

6. Remove crankshaft damper bolt.

7. Remove damper using Crankshaft Insert 8513A and Three Jaw Puller 1023.

8. Using Crankshaft Front Seal Remover 9071 (1), remove crankshaft front seal (2).

To install:

> ※ **CAUTION**
>
> The front crankshaft seal must be installed dry. Do not apply lubricant to the sealing lip or the outer edge.

9. Using Crankshaft Front Oil Seal Installer 9072 (2) and Damper Installer 8512A (1), install crankshaft front seal.

> ※ **CAUTION**
>
> To prevent severe damage to the Crankshaft, Damper or Damper Installer 8512A, thoroughly clean the damper bore and the crankshaft nose before installing Damper.

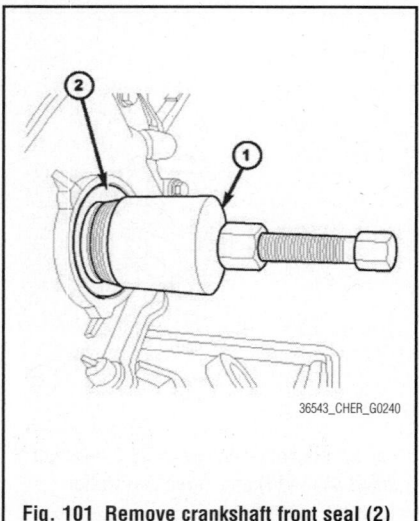

36543_CHER_G0240

Fig. 101 Remove crankshaft front seal (2)

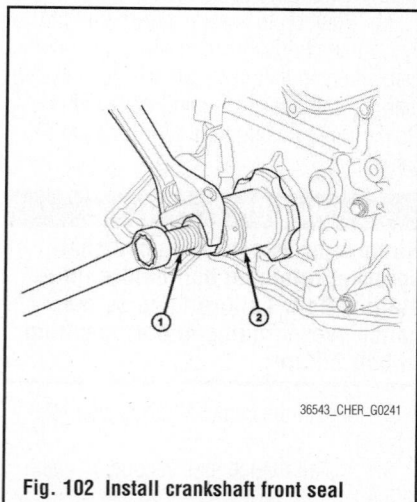

Fig. 102 Install crankshaft front seal

10. Slide damper onto crankshaft slightly.

> ✳✳ **CAUTION**
>
> **Special Tool 8512-A, is assembled in a specific sequence. Failure to assemble this tool in this sequence can result in tool failure and severe damage to either the tool or the crankshaft.**

11. Assemble Damper Installer 8512-A as follows, thread nut (2) onto the bolt (3) then install the roller bearing (1) followed by the hardened washer (5) slides onto the threaded rod (3). Once assembled coat the threaded rod's threads with Mopar® Nickel Anti-Seize (or equivalent).

12. Using Damper Installer 8512-A, press damper onto crankshaft.

13. Install then tighten crankshaft damper bolt to 130 ft. lbs. (175 Nm).

14. Install radiator upper hose.
15. Install accessory drive belt.
16. Refill cooling system.
17. Connect negative cable to battery.

CYLINDER HEAD

REMOVAL & INSTALLATION

3.7L Engine

See Figures 103 through 107.

1. Disconnect the negative cable from the battery.
2. Raise the vehicle on a hoist.
3. Disconnect the exhaust pipe at the left side exhaust manifold.
4. Drain the engine coolant.
5. Lower the vehicle.
6. Remove the intake manifold.
7. Remove the master cylinder and booster assembly.

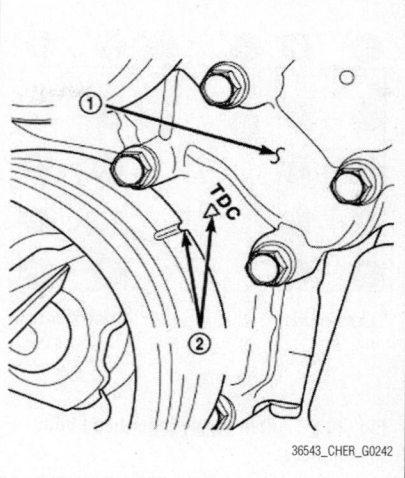

Fig. 103 Rotate the crankshaft until the damper timing mark is aligned with TDC indicator mark (2)

8. Remove the cylinder head cover.
9. Remove the fan shroud and fan blade assembly.
10. Remove the accessory drive belt.
11. Remove the power steering pump and set aside.
12. Rotate the crankshaft until the damper timing mark is aligned with TDC indicator mark (2).
13. Verify the V6 mark (1) on the camshaft sprocket is at the 12 o'clock position, with the No. 1 cylinder at TDC on the exhaust stroke. Rotate the crankshaft one turn if necessary.
14. Remove the vibration damper.
15. Remove the timing chain cover.
16. Lock the secondary timing chains (2) to the idler sprocket using Secondary Camshaft Chain Holder 8429 (1).

➡ **Mark the secondary timing chain prior to removal to aid in installation.**

17. Mark the secondary timing chain (2), one link on each side of the V6 mark on the camshaft drive gear.
18. Remove the left side secondary chain tensioner.
19. Remove the cylinder head access plug (1) and (2).
20. Remove the left side secondary chain guide..
21. Remove the retaining bolt and the camshaft drive gear.

> ✳✳ **CAUTION**
>
> **Do not allow the engine to rotate. Severe damage to the valve train can occur.**

> ✳✳ **CAUTION**
>
> **Do not overlook the four smaller bolts at the front of the cylinder head. Do not attempt to remove the cylinder head without removing these four bolts.**

➡ **The cylinder head is attached to the cylinder block with twelve bolts.**

22. Remove the cylinder head retaining bolts.
23. Remove the cylinder head and gasket. Discard the gasket.

> ✳✳ **CAUTION**
>
> **Do not lay the cylinder head on its gasket sealing surface, due to the design of the cylinder head gasket any distortion to the cylinder head sealing surface may prevent the gasket from properly sealing resulting in leaks.**

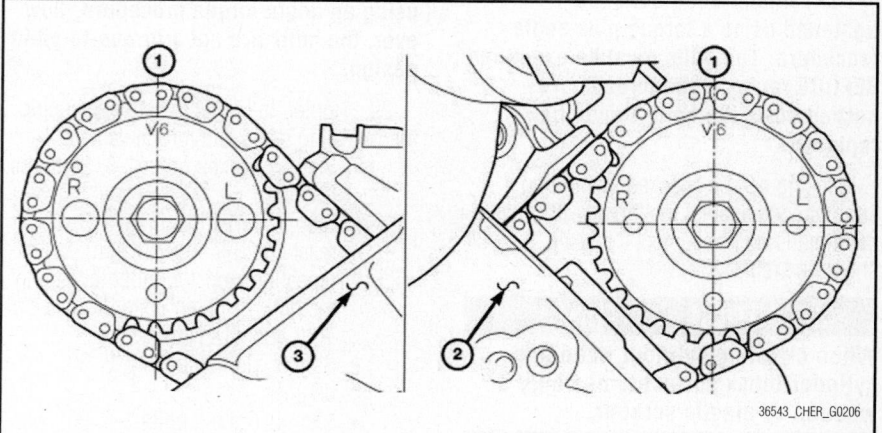

Fig. 104 Verify the V6 mark (1) on the camshaft sprocket is at the 12 o'clock position

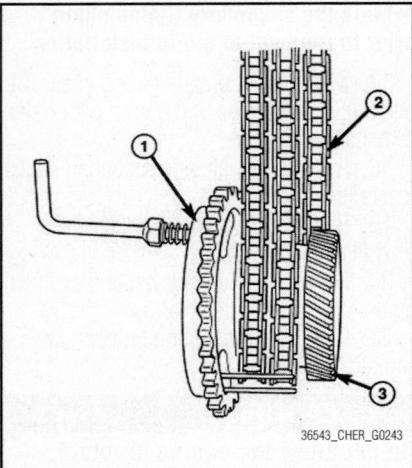

Fig. 105 Lock the secondary timing chains (2) to the idler sprocket using Secondary Camshaft Chain Holder 8429 (1)

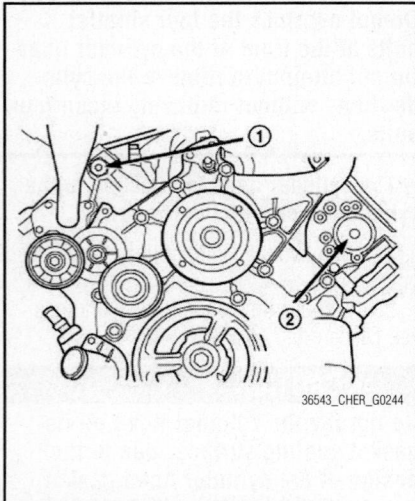

Fig. 106 Remove the cylinder head access plug (1) and (2)

To install:

➡The cylinder head bolts are tightened using a torque plus angle procedure. The bolts must be examined BEFORE reuse. If the threads are necked down the bolts should be replaced.

Necking can be checked by holding a straight edge against the threads (2). If all the threads do not contact the scale, the bolt should be replaced.

✳✳ CAUTION

When cleaning cylinder head and cylinder block surfaces, use only a wooden or plastic scraper.

24. Clean the cylinder head and cylinder block mating surfaces.

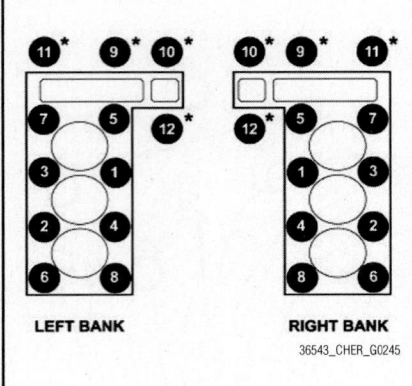

Fig. 107 Tighten the cylinder head bolts in sequence

25. Position the new cylinder head gasket on the locating dowels.

✳✳ CAUTION

When installing cylinder head, use care not damage the tensioner arm or the guide arm.

26. Position the cylinder head onto the cylinder block. Make sure the cylinder head seats fully over the locating dowels.

➡The four smaller cylinder head mounting bolts require sealant to be added to them before installing. Failure to do so may cause leaks. The locations are identified with an *.

27. Lubricate the cylinder head bolt threads with clean engine oil and install the eight M11 bolts.

28. Coat the four M8 cylinder head bolts with Mopar® Lock and Seal Adhesive then install the bolts.

➡The cylinder head bolts are tightened using an angle torque procedure, however, the bolts are not a torque-to-yield design.

29. Tighten the bolts in sequence using the following steps and torque values:
- Step 1: Tighten bolts 1-8, 20 ft. lbs. (27 Nm).
- Step 2: Verify that bolts 1-8, all reached 20 ft. lbs. (27 Nm), by repeating step 1 without loosening the bolts. Tighten bolts 9 thru 12 to 10 ft. lbs. (14 Nm).
- Step 3: Tighten bolts 1-8, 90 degrees.
- Step 4: Tighten bolts 1-8, 90 degrees, again. Tighten bolts 9-12, 19 ft. lbs. (26 Nm)

30. Position the secondary chain onto the camshaft drive gear, making sure one marked chain link is on either side of the V6 mark on the gear then using Camshaft Holder 8428 position the gear onto the camshaft.

✳✳ CAUTION

Remove excess oil from camshaft sprocket retaining bolt before reinstalling bolt. Failure to do so may cause over-torquing of bolt resulting in bolt failure.

31. Install the camshaft drive gear retaining bolt.
32. Install the left side secondary chain guide.
33. Install the cylinder head access plug.
34. Re-set and install the left side secondary chain tensioner.
35. Remove Secondary Camshaft Chain Holder 8429.
36. Install the timing chain cover.
37. Install the crankshaft damper. Tighten damper bolt 130 ft. lbs. (175 Nm).
38. Install the power steering pump.
39. Install the fan blade assembly and fan shroud.
40. Install the cylinder head cover.
41. Install the master cylinder and booster assembly.
42. Install the intake manifold.
43. Refill the cooling system.
44. Raise the vehicle.
45. Install the exhaust pipe onto the left exhaust manifold.
46. Lower the vehicle.
47. Connect the negative cable to the battery.
48. Start the engine and check for leaks.

4.7L Engine

See Figures 103, 105, 106, 108 through 110.

1. Disconnect the negative cable from the battery.
2. Raise the vehicle on a hoist.
3. Disconnect the exhaust pipe at the exhaust manifold.
4. Drain the engine coolant.
5. Lower the vehicle.
6. Remove the intake manifold.
7. Remove the master cylinder and booster assembly, if removing the left cylinder head..
8. Remove the cylinder head cover.
9. Remove the fan shroud and fan blade assembly.
10. Remove the oil fill housing from right cylinder head.

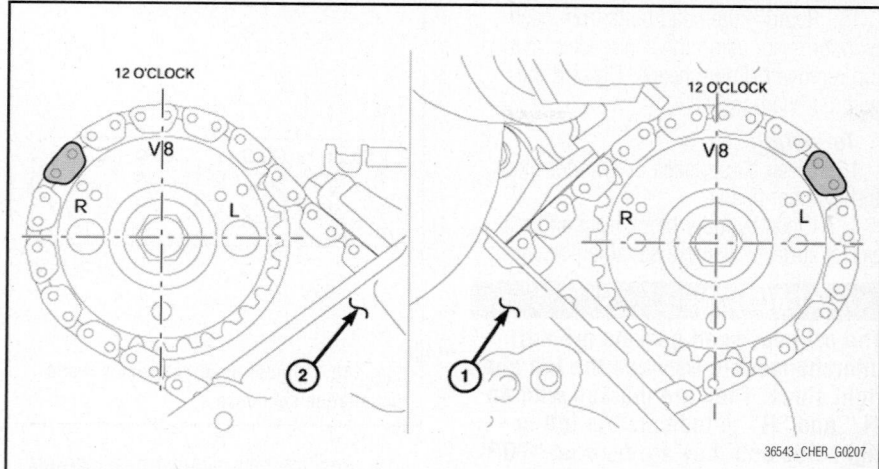

Fig. 108 Verify the V8 mark on the camshaft sprocket is at the 12 o'clock position

11. Remove accessory drive belt.
12. Remove the power steering pump and set aside.
13. Rotate the crankshaft until the damper timing marks are aligned (2).
14. Verify the V8 mark on the camshaft sprocket is at the 12 o'clock position. Rotate the crankshaft one turn if necessary.
15. Remove the crankshaft damper.
16. Remove the timing chain cover.
17. Lock the secondary timing chains to the idler sprocket using secondary camshaft chain holder 8429 (6).

➡**Mark the secondary timing chain prior to removal to aid in installation.**

18. Mark the secondary timing chain, one link on each side of the V8 mark on the camshaft drive gear.
19. Remove the secondary chain tensioner.

❊❊ **CAUTION**

Do not allow the engine to rotate. Severe damage to the valve train can occur.

20. Remove the cylinder head access plug (2).
21. Remove the secondary chain guide.
22. Remove the retaining bolt and the camshaft drive gear.

❊❊ **CAUTION**

Do not overlook the four smaller bolts at the front of the cylinder head. Do not attempt to remove the cylinder head without removing these four bolts.

➡**The cylinder head is attached to the cylinder block with fourteen bolts.**

23. Remove the cylinder head retaining bolts in sequence.

❊❊ **CAUTION**

Do not lay the cylinder head on its gasket sealing surface, due to the design of the cylinder head gasket any distortion to the cylinder head sealing surface may prevent the gasket from properly sealing resulting in leaks.

24. Remove the cylinder head and gasket. Discard the gasket.

To install:

➡**The cylinder head bolts are tightened using a torque plus angle procedure. The bolts must be examined BEFORE reuse. If the threads are necked down (2) the bolts should be replaced.**

Necking can be checked by holding a straight edge against the threads. If all the threads do not contact the scale, the bolt should be replaced.

❊❊ **CAUTION**

When cleaning cylinder head and cylinder block surfaces, use only a wooden or plastic scraper.

25. Clean the cylinder head and cylinder block mating surfaces.
26. Position the new cylinder head gasket on the locating dowels.

❊❊ **CAUTION**

When installing cylinder head, use care not damage the tensioner arm or the guide arm.

27. Position the cylinder head onto the cylinder block. Make sure the cylinder head seats fully over the locating dowels.

➡**The four M8 cylinder head mounting bolts (11–14) require sealant to be added to them before installing. Failure to do so may cause leaks.**

28. Lubricate the cylinder head bolt threads with clean engine oil and install the ten M11 bolts.
29. Coat the four M8 cylinder head bolts with Mopar® Thread Sealant with PTFE then install the bolts.

➡**The cylinder head bolts are tightened using an torque angle procedure.**

30. Tighten the bolts in sequence using the following steps and torque values:
- Tighten bolts 1–10 to 20 ft. lbs. (27 Nm).
- Verify that bolts 1–10 have all reached 20 ft. lbs. (27 Nm), by repeating step 1 without loosening the bolts.
- Tighten bolts 11–14 to 89 inch lbs. (14 Nm).
- Rotate bolts 1–10 an additional 90°.
- Rotate bolts 1–10 an additional 90° again.

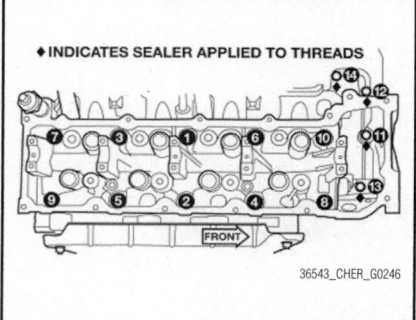

Fig. 109 Cylinder head bolt removal and installation sequence

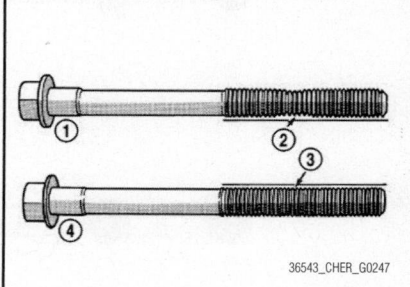

Fig. 110 If the threads are necked down (2) the bolts should be replaced

- Tighten bolts 11–14 to 19 ft. lbs. (26 Nm).

31. Position the secondary chain onto the camshaft drive gear, making sure one marked chain link is on either side of the V8 mark on the gear and position the gear onto the camshaft.

32. Install the camshaft drive gear retaining bolt.

33. Install the left side secondary chain guide.

34. Install the cylinder head access plug.

35. Re-set and Install the left side secondary chain tensioner.

36. Remove Secondary Camshaft Chain Holder 8429.

37. Install the timing chain cover.

38. Install the crankshaft damper.

39. Install the power steering pump.

40. Install the fan blade assembly and fan shroud.

41. Install the cylinder head cover.

42. Reinstall the master cylinder and booster assembly.

43. Install the intake manifold.

44. Fill the cooling system.

45. Raise the vehicle.

46. Install the exhaust pipe onto the left exhaust manifold.

47. Lower the vehicle.

48. Fill with oil.

49. Connect the negative cable to the battery.

50. Start the engine and check for leaks.

5.7L Engine

See Figures 111 through 115.

1. Perform the Fuel System Pressure Release procedure.

2. Disconnect the fuel supply line.

3. Disconnect the battery negative cable.

4. Drain cooling system.

5. Remove the air cleaner resonator and duct work.

6. Remove closed crankcase ventilation system.

7. Disconnect the exhaust at the exhaust manifolds.

8. Disconnect the evaporation control system.

9. Disconnect heater hoses.

10. Remove the power steering pump.

11. Remove cylinder head cover bolts in sequence.

12. Remove cylinder head covers and gaskets.

13. Remove intake manifold and throttle body as an assembly.

14. Remove rocker arm assemblies and push rods. Identify to ensure installation in original locations.

15. Remove the head bolts from each cylinder head, using the sequence provided, and remove cylinder heads. Discard the cylinder head gasket.

To install:

16. Clean all surfaces of cylinder block and cylinder heads.

17. Clean cylinder block front and rear gasket surfaces using a suitable solvent.

❋❋ CAUTION

The cylinder head gaskets are not interchangeable between the left and right sides. They are marked with an "L" and "R" to indicate the left or right side and they are marked "TOP" to indicate which side goes up.

❋❋ CAUTION

The head gaskets are marked "TOP" to indicate which side goes up.

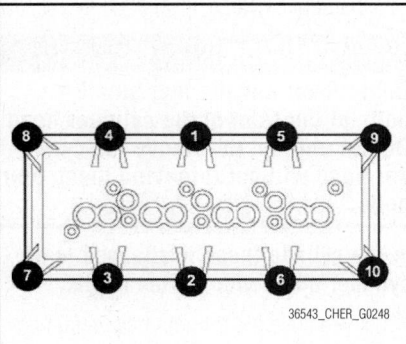

Fig. 111 The cylinder head cover bolts must be removed and installed in the proper sequence

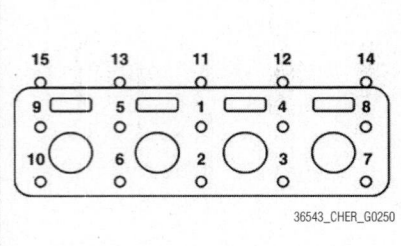

Fig. 113 Cylinder head bolt removal and installation sequence

18. Position new cylinder head gaskets (5) onto the cylinder block.

19. Position cylinder heads (4) onto head gaskets (5) and cylinder block.

20. Tighten the cylinder head bolts in three steps using the sequence provided:

- Step 1: Snug tighten M12 cylinder head bolts, in sequence, to 25 ft. lbs. (34 Nm) and M8 bolts to 15 ft. lbs. (20 Nm).
- Step 2: Tighten M12 cylinder head bolts, in sequence, to 40 ft. lbs. (54 Nm) and verify M8 bolts to 15 ft. lbs. (20 Nm).
- Step 3: Turn M12 cylinder head bolts, in sequence, 90 degrees and tighten M8 bolts to 25 ft. lbs. (34 Nm).

21. Install push rods and rocker arm assemblies in their original position, using push rod retainer 9070 (1).

22. Install the intake manifold and throttle body assembly.

23. If required, adjust spark plugs to specifications. Install the plugs.

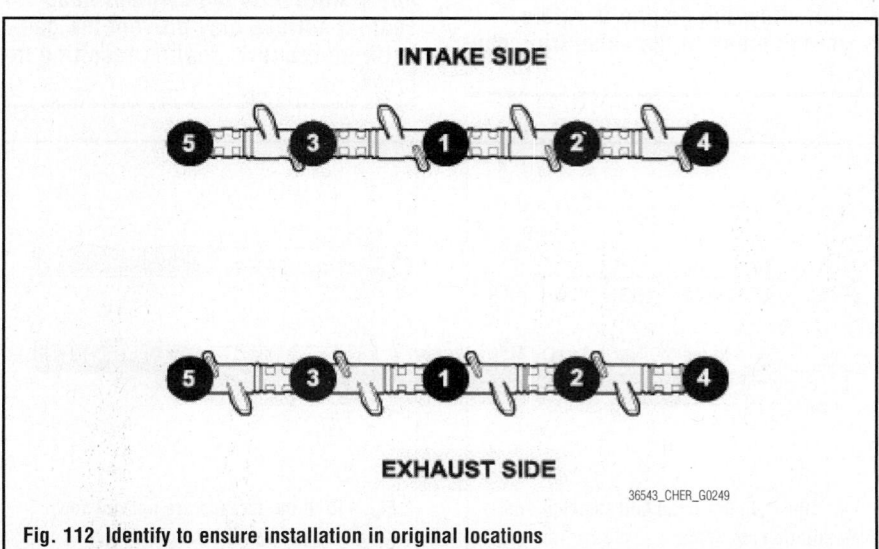

Fig. 112 Identify to ensure installation in original locations

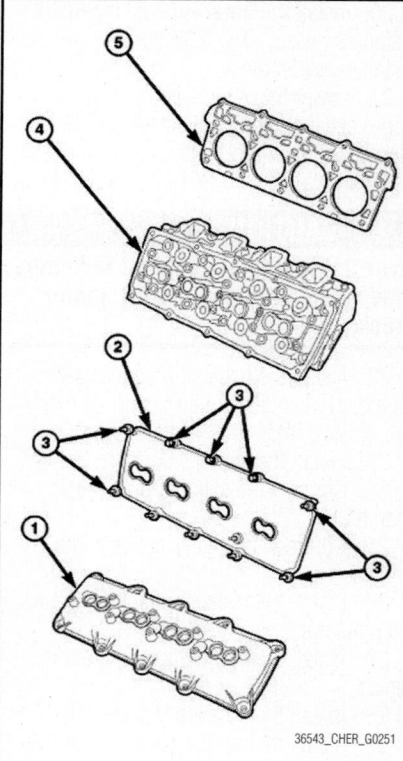

Fig. 114 Position new cylinder head gaskets (5) onto the cylinder block

24. Connect the heater hoses.
25. Install the fuel supply line.
26. Install the power steering pump.
27. Install the drive belt.
28. Install cylinder head covers.
29. Connect the evaporation control system.
30. Install the air cleaner.
31. Fill cooling system.
32. Connect the negative cable to the battery.
33. Start engine check for leaks.

EXHAUST MANIFOLD

REMOVAL & INSTALLATION

3.7L Engine

Right Exhaust Manifold

See Figure 116.

1. Disconnect the negative cable from the battery.
2. Raise and support the vehicle.
3. Remove the bolts and nuts attaching the exhaust pipe to the engine exhaust manifold.
4. Lower the vehicle.
5. Remove the exhaust heat shield (1).
6. Remove bolts, nuts (2) and washers attaching manifold to cylinder head.
7. Remove manifold and gasket from the cylinder head.

To install:

✳✳ CAUTION

If the studs came out with the nuts when removing the engine exhaust manifold, install new studs. Apply sealer on the coarse thread ends. Water leaks may develop at the studs if this precaution is not taken.

8. Position the engine exhaust manifold and gasket on the two studs located on the cylinder head. Install conical washers and nuts on these studs.
9. Install remaining conical washers. Starting at the center arm and working outward, tighten the bolts and nuts to 18 ft. lbs. (25 Nm).
10. Install the exhaust heat shields.
11. Raise and support the vehicle.

✳✳ CAUTION

Over tightening heat shield fasteners, may cause shield to distort and/or crack.

12. Assemble exhaust pipe to manifold and secure with bolts, nuts and retainers. Tighten the bolts and nuts to 25 ft. lbs. (34 Nm).

Left Exhaust Manifold

See Figure 117.

1. Disconnect the negative cable from the battery.
2. Raise and support the vehicle.
3. Remove the bolts and nuts attaching the exhaust pipe to the engine exhaust manifold.
4. Lower the vehicle.
5. Remove the exhaust heat shields (1).
6. Remove bolts, nuts (2) and washers attaching manifold to cylinder head.
7. Remove manifold and gasket from the cylinder head.

To install:

✳✳ CAUTION

If the studs came out with the nuts when removing the engine exhaust manifold, install new studs. Apply sealer on the coarse thread ends. Water leaks may develop at the studs if this precaution is not taken.

8. Position the engine exhaust manifold and gasket on the two studs located on the cylinder head. Install conical washers and nuts on these studs.
9. Install remaining conical washers. Starting at the center arm and working outward, tighten the bolts and nuts to 18 ft. lbs. (25 Nm).

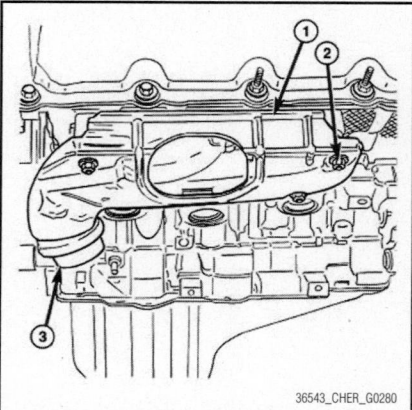

Fig. 116 Remove the exhaust heat shield (1)

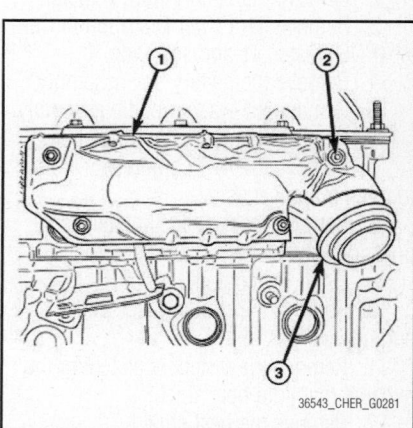

Fig. 117 Remove the exhaust heat shields (1)

Fig. 115 Install push rods and rocker arm assemblies in their original position, using push rod retainer 9070 (1)

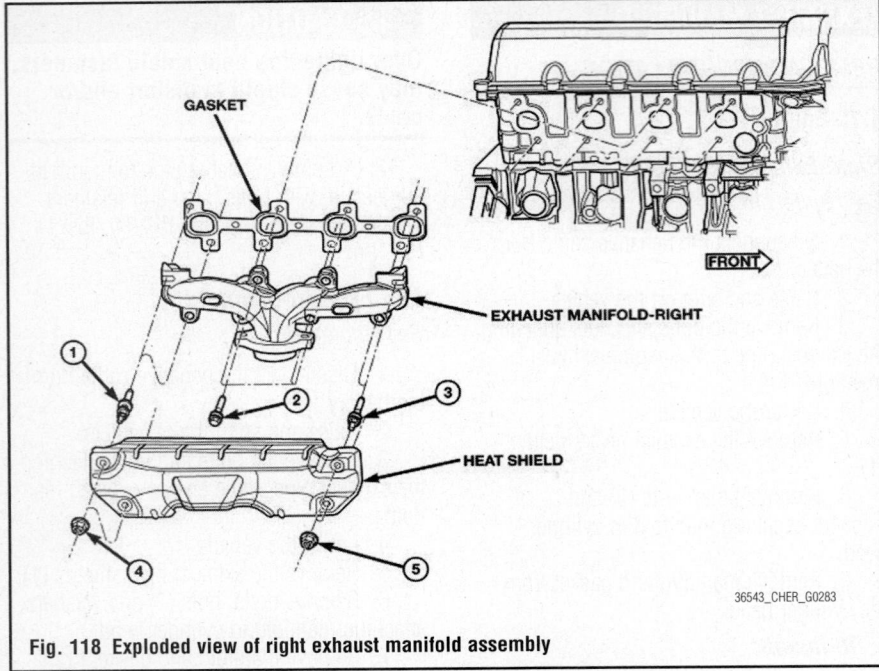

Fig. 118 Exploded view of right exhaust manifold assembly

10. Install the exhaust heat shields.

11. Raise and support the vehicle.

✳✳ CAUTION

Over tightening heat shield fasteners, may cause shield to distort and/or crack.

12. Assemble exhaust pipe to manifold and secure with bolts, nuts and retainers. Tighten the bolts and nuts to 25 ft. lbs. (34 Nm).

4.7L Engine

Right Exhaust Manifold

See Figure 118.

1. Disconnect the negative cable from the battery.

2. Remove the battery from vehicle.

3. Remove the Power Distribution Center (PDC) fasteners and set aside.

4. Remove the battery tray assembly.

5. Remove the washer bottle assembly.

6. Remove the accessory drive belt.

7. Remove the A/C compressor from mounting and set aside.

8. Remove the A/C accumulator support bracket fastener.

9. Drain the coolant.

10. Remove the heater hoses at the engine.

11. Remove the fasteners attaching the exhaust manifold heat shield.

12. Remove the heat shield.

13. Remove the upper exhaust manifold attaching fasteners.

14. Raise the vehicle on a hoist.

15. Disconnect the exhaust pipe from the manifold.

16. Remove the bolts attaching the starter. Move the starter aside.

17. Remove the lower exhaust manifold attaching fasteners.

18. Remove the exhaust manifold and gasket. The manifold is removed from below the engine compartment.

To install:

19. Install the exhaust manifold and gasket from below the engine compartment.

20. Install the lower exhaust manifold fasteners (1,2,3,). DO NOT tighten until all fasteners are in place.

21. Lower the vehicle and install the upper exhaust manifold fasteners (1,2,3,). Tighten all manifold bolts starting at center and working outward to 18 ft. lbs. (25 Nm).

✳✳ CAUTION

Over tightening heat shield fasteners, may cause shield to distort and/or crack.

22. Install the exhaust manifold heat shield. Tighten fasteners (4,5) to 72 inch lbs. (8 Nm), then loosen 45 degrees.

23. Install the starter.

24. Connect the exhaust pipe to the manifold.

25. Connect the heater hoses at the engine.

26. Install the fastener attaching the A/C accumulator.

27. Install the A/C compressor and fasteners.

28. Install the accessory drive belt.

29. Install the washer bottle and battery tray assembly.

30. Install the PDC.

31. Install the battery and connect the cables.

32. Fill the cooling system.

Left Exhaust Manifold

See Figure 119.

1. Disconnect the negative battery cable.

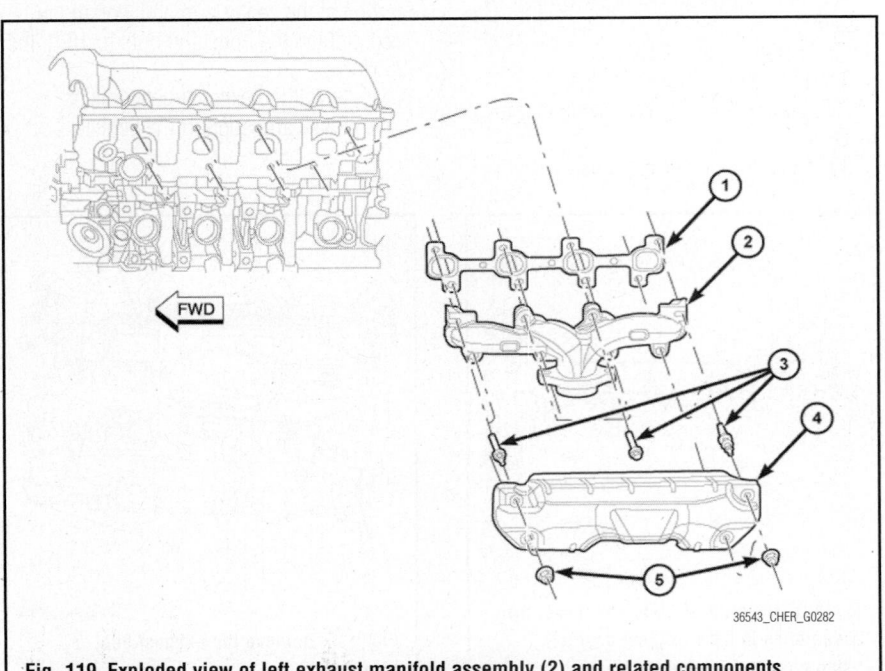

Fig. 119 Exploded view of left exhaust manifold assembly (2) and related components

2. Remove the air cleaner housing and clean air tube.

3. Remove the front two exhaust manifold heat shield retaining nuts (5).

4. Raise and support the vehicle.

5. Disconnect the exhaust pipe at the exhaust manifold.

6. Remove the rear two exhaust manifold heat shield retaining nuts (5) and remove the heat shield (4).

7. Remove the lower exhaust manifold retaining bolts (3).

8. Lower the vehicle.

9. Remove the upper exhaust manifold retaining bolts (3).

➡**The Exhaust manifold is removed from below the engine compartment.**

10. Raise and support the vehicle.

11. Remove the exhaust manifold (2) and gasket (1).

To install:

12. Position the exhaust manifold (2) and gasket (1) from below the engine compartment.

13. Install the lower exhaust manifold retaining bolts (3) hand tight.

14. Lower the vehicle.

15. Install the upper exhaust manifold retaining bolts (3) and tighten all manifold bolts starting at center and working outward to 18 ft. lbs. (25 Nm).

✳✳ CAUTION

Over tightening heat shield fasteners, may cause shield to distort and/or crack.

16. Position the exhaust manifold heat shield (4) and install the front two heat shield retaining nuts hand tight.

17. Raise and support the vehicle.

18. Install the back two exhaust manifold heat shield retaining nuts (5) and tighten to 72 inch lbs. (8 Nm), then loosen 45 degrees.

19. Connect the exhaust pipe to the exhaust manifold.

20. Lower the vehicle.

21. Tighten the front two exhaust manifold heat shield retaining nuts (5) to 72 inch lbs. (8 Nm), then loosen 45 degrees.

22. Install the air cleaner housing and clean air tube.

23. Connect the negative battery cable.

5.7L Engine

Right Exhaust Manifold

See Figure 120.

1. Partially drain the engine coolant.

2. Remove the engine cover.

3. Disconnect the negative battery terminal.

4. Remove the air box assembly.

5. Remove the coolant recovery bottle.

6. Disconnect and re-position the upper right side engine harness.

✳✳ CAUTION

Use caution when connecting, disconnecting or repositioning any wiring harness. Damage could occur to the wiring harness due to vehicle mileage, vehicle age and environmental conditions.

7. If required, disconnect and re-position the heater hoses from the heater core tubes in the engine compartment.

8. Raise and secure the vehicle.

9. Remove any skid plates (if equipped).

10. Saturate the front exhaust pipe/catalytic converter assembly bolts and nuts with heat valve lubricant. Allow 5 minutes for penetration.

11. Disconnect and remove the upstream O2 sensor from the exhaust pipe/catalytic converter assembly.

12. Remove the bolts from the front right exhaust pipe/catalytic converter assembly.

13. Loosen the bolts from the front left exhaust pipe/catalytic converter assembly. Do not remove the bolts.

14. Remove the front right tire and wheel assembly.

15. Remove the front right side wheelhouse splash shield.

16. Lower the vehicle.

17. Remove the right side exhaust manifold heat shield.

18. Remove the eight bolts/studs from the exhaust manifold using the sequence provided.

19. Remove the exhaust manifold and gasket from the front of the vehicle.

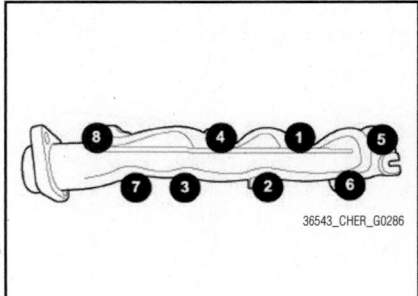

Fig. 120 Remove the eight bolts/studs from the exhaust manifold

36543_CHER_G0286

20. Inspect the exhaust manifold for any damage.

21. Clean the mating surfaces.

To install:

22. Prior to installation, make sure all gasket mating surfaces are clean and free of any debris.

23. Inspect the exhaust manifold for any damage.

24. Install manifold gasket and manifold through the front of the vehicle.

➡**Make sure gasket is properly seated before tightening the manifold stud/bolts.**

25. Install the eight manifold studs/bolts using the sequence provided. Tighten the studs/bolts to 18 ft. lbs. (25 Nm).

26. Install the exhaust manifold heat shield. Tighten the nuts to 71 inch lbs. (8 Nm).

27. Raise and secure the vehicle.

28. Install the bolts and nuts at the right front exhaust pipe/catalytic converter assembly to exhaust manifold flange. Do not tighten.

29. Position the exhaust pipe for proper clearance with the frame and underbody parts. A minimum clearance of 1.0 inches (25.4 mm) is required.

30. Once properly aligned, tighten the right front exhaust pipe/catalytic converter assembly to exhaust manifold bolts to 19 ft. lbs. (26 Nm).

31. Tighten the left front exhaust pipe/catalytic converter assembly to the exhaust manifold bolts to 19 ft. lbs. (26 Nm).

32. Connect and install the upstream O2 sensor to the exhaust pipe/catalytic converter assembly.

33. Install the front right side wheelhouse splash shield.

34. Install any skid plates (if equipped).

35. Install the front tire and wheel.

36. Lower the vehicle.

37. If required, connect and position the heater hoses from the heater core tubes in the engine compartment.

✳✳ CAUTION

Use caution when connecting, disconnecting or repositioning any wiring harness. Damage could occur to the wiring harness due to vehicle mileage, vehicle age and environmental conditions.

38. Connect and position the upper right side engine harness.

39. Install the coolant recovery bottle.
40. Install the air box assembly.
41. Fill the engine coolant.
42. Connect the negative battery terminal.
43. Install the engine cover.
44. Start the engine and check for any leaks.

Left Exhaust Manifold

See Figures 121 through 125.

1. Lock the steering wheel in the center position.

> ※※ **CAUTION**
>
> **Steering column module is centered to the vehicle's steering system. Failure to keep the system and steering column module centered and locked/inhibited from rotating can result in steering column module damage.**

2. Remove the engine cover.
3. Disconnect the battery terminals.
4. Remove the battery and battery tray.

> ※※ **CAUTION**
>
> **Use caution when connecting, disconnecting or repositioning any wiring harness. Damage could occur to the wiring harness due to vehicle mileage, vehicle age and environmental conditions.**

5. Disconnect the bulk connector (4).
6. Disconnect the tail lamp harness.
7. Remove the nut from the bulk connector retaining bracket (3) and reposition the bracket.
8. Disconnect the power steering switch (1) and reposition the harness.
9. Disconnect power distribution center (PDC) connector and reposition harness.

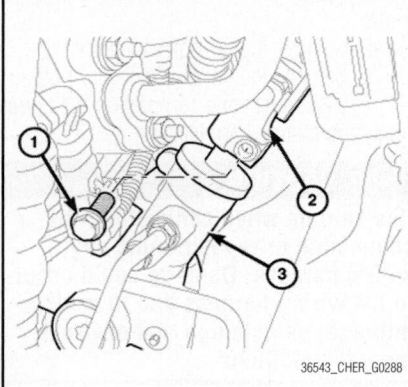

Fig. 122 Remove the lower coupling pinch bolt (1) from the intermediate steering shaft (2) at the rack and pinion assembly (3)

10. Remove the lower coupling pinch bolt (1) from the intermediate steering shaft (2) at the rack and pinion assembly (3).
11. Remove upper mounting bolt from dipstick tube.
12. Remove the two left front exhaust manifold heat shield nuts.
13. Lift and secure the vehicle.
14. Remove any skid plates (if equipped).
15. Remove the front propeller shaft (4 X 4 equipped vehicles).
16. Remove the front left side tire and wheel.
17. Remove the front left side wheelhouse splash shield.
18. Reposition any harnesses as needed.
19. Remove the two bolts and two nuts from the intermediate steering shaft support bracket (2).
20. Remove the intermediate steering shaft support bracket (2).

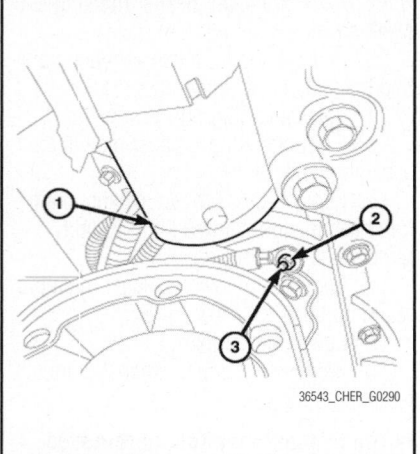

Fig. 124 Remove the nut (2) from the battery ground harness, located in front of the starter (1)

21. Remove the nut (2) from the battery ground harness, located in front of the starter (1).
22. Remove the battery ground harness.
23. Remove the lower stud/bolt from the dipstick tube.
24. Remove the two left rear exhaust manifold heat shield nuts.
25. Saturate the front exhaust pipe/catalytic converter assembly bolts and nuts with heat valve lubricant. Allow 5 minutes for penetration.
26. Remove the bolts from the front left exhaust pipe/catalytic converter assembly.
27. Loosen the bolts from the front right exhaust pipe/catalytic converter assembly. Do not remove the bolts.
28. Lower the vehicle.
29. Remove the eight bolts/studs from the exhaust manifold using the sequence provided.

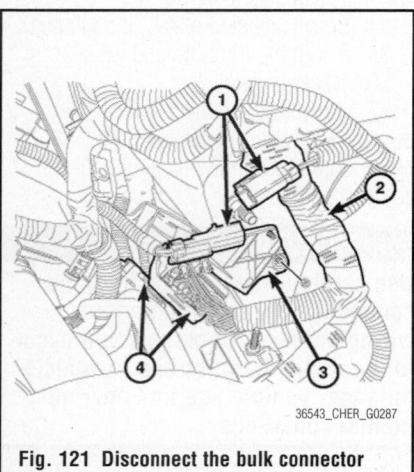

Fig. 121 Disconnect the bulk connector (4)

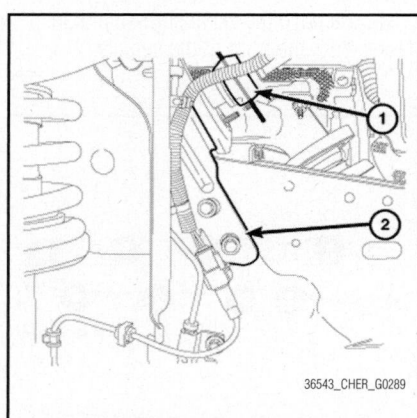

Fig. 123 Remove the two bolts and two nuts from the intermediate steering shaft support bracket (2)

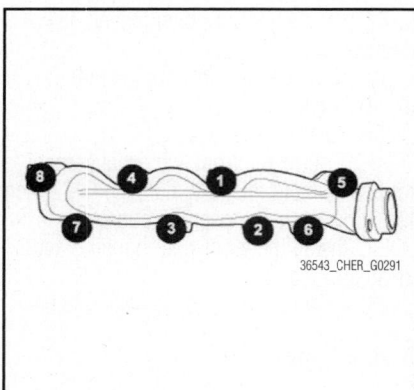

Fig. 125 Remove the eight bolts/studs from the exhaust manifold using the sequence provided

30. Remove the exhaust manifold (2) and gasket from the front of the vehicle.

To install:

31. Prior to installation, make sure all gasket mating surfaces are clean and free of any debris.

32. Inspect the exhaust manifold for any damage.

33. Install manifold gasket and manifold through the front of the vehicle.

➡ **Make sure gasket is properly seated before tightening the manifold stud/bolts.**

34. Install the exhaust manifold heat shield. Tighten the nuts to 71 inch lbs. (8 Nm).

35. Install the dipstick tube upper mounting bolt. Tighten the bolt to 9 ft. lbs. (12 Nm).

36. Raise and secure the vehicle.

37. Install the bolts and nuts at the left front exhaust pipe/catalytic converter assembly to exhaust manifold flange. Do not tighten.

38. Position the exhaust pipe for proper clearance with the frame and underbody parts. A minimum clearance of 1.0 inches (25.4 mm) is required.

39. Once properly aligned, tighten the left front exhaust pipe/catalytic converter assembly to exhaust manifold bolts.

40. Tighten the right front exhaust pipe/catalytic converter assembly to the exhaust manifold bolts.

41. Install the lower dipstick stud/bolt located in front of the starter. Tighten the stud/bolt to 9 ft. lbs. (12 Nm).

42. Install the battery ground harness to the lower dipstick stud/bolt. Tighten the nut to 8 ft. lbs. (11 Nm).

43. Install the front propeller shaft (4WD equipped vehicles).

44. Install the two bolts and two nuts from the intermediate steering shaft support bracket to the frame. Tighten the bolts to 9 ft. lbs. (12 Nm).

45. Install the front left side wheelhouse splash shield.

46. Install any skid plates (if equipped).

47. Install the front tire and wheel.

48. Lower the vehicle.

49. Install the lower coupling pinch bolt through the intermediate steering shaft to the rack and pinion assembly. Tighten the bolt to 36 ft. lbs. (49 Nm).

✳✳ CAUTION

Use caution when connecting, disconnecting or repositioning any wiring harness. Damage could occur to the wiring harness due to vehicle mileage, vehicle age and environmental conditions.

50. Connect the Power Distribution Center (PDC) connector and position the harness.

51. Connect the power steering switch and position the harness.

52. Position the bulk connector retaining bracket and install the nut.

53. Connect the tail lamp harness.

54. Connect the bulk connector.

55. Install the battery tray.

56. Install the battery.

57. Install the engine cover.

58. Start the engine and check for any leaks.

FLEXPLATE

REMOVAL & INSTALLATION

See Figure 126.

1. Remove the transmission.

2. Remove the bolts using the sequence provided.

3. Remove the flexplate.

To install:

4. Position the flexplate onto the crankshaft and install the bolts hand tight.

5. For 3.7L/5.7L engines, tighten the flexplate retaining bolts to 70 ft. lbs. (95 Nm) in the sequence shown.

6. For 4.7L engines, tighten the flexplate retaining bolts to 45 ft. lbs. (70 Nm) in the sequence shown.

7. Install the transmission.

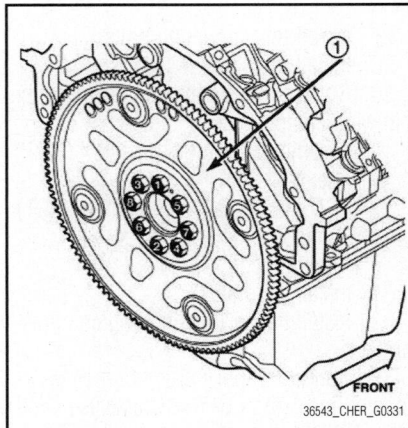

36543_CHER_G0331

Fig. 126 Flexplate bolt removal and installation sequence

INTAKE MANIFOLD

REMOVAL & INSTALLATION

3.7L Engine

See Figures 127 through 131.

1. Perform the Fuel System Pressure Release procedure.

2. Disconnect negative cable from battery.

3. Remove resonator assembly and air inlet hose.

4. Disconnect electrical connectors for the following components:
   - Manifold Absolute Pressure (MAP) sensor (2)
   - Engine Coolant Temperature (ECT) sensor (3)
   - Ignition coil towers

5. Disconnect vapor purge hose, brake booster hose, Positive Crankcase Ventilation (PCV) hose.

6. Remove the alternator.

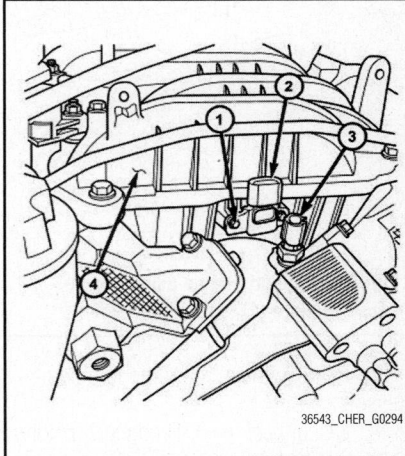

36543_CHER_G0294

Fig. 127 Disconnect electrical connectors

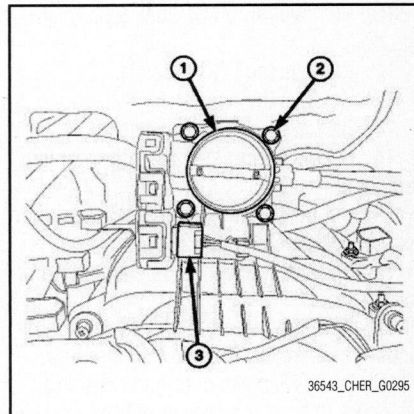

36543_CHER_G0295

Fig. 128 Disconnect the ETC connector from the throttle body (3)

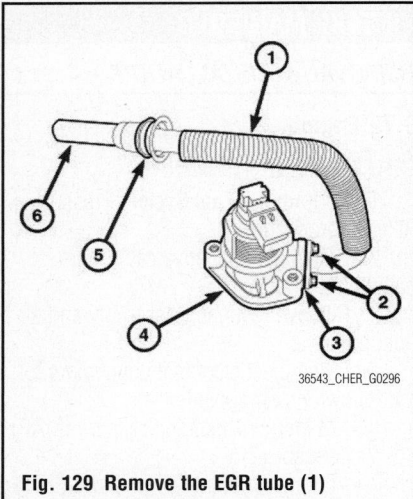

Fig. 129 Remove the EGR tube (1)

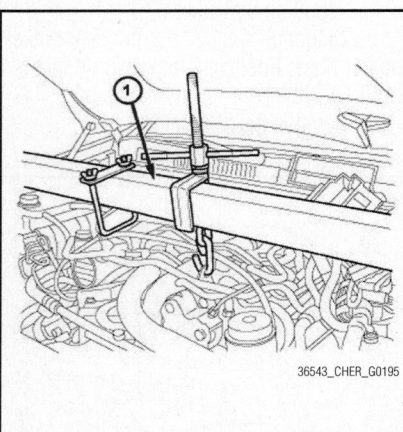

Fig. 130 Support engine using engine support fixture (1), special tool 8534

7. Remove the air conditioning compressor.

8. Disconnect the ETC connector from the throttle body (3).

9. Disconnect and remove ignition coil towers.

10. Remove top oil dipstick tube retaining bolt.

11. Remove the EGR tube (1).

12. Remove the fuel rail.

13. Remove throttle body assembly.

14. Drain cooling system below coolant temperature level.

15. Support engine using engine support fixture (1), special tool 8534.

16. Remove the right side engine mount to frame bolt.

17. With the bolt removed, lower engine until engine mount rests in frame mount.

18. Remove intake manifold retaining fasteners in reverse order of tightening sequence.

19. Remove intake manifold.

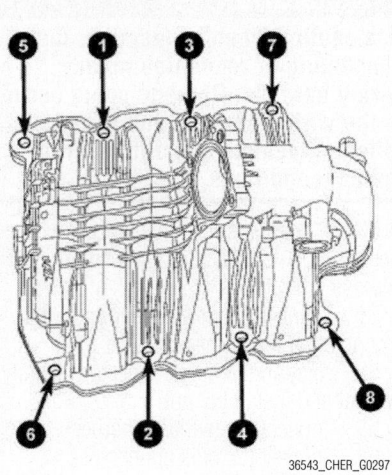

Fig. 131 Remove intake manifold retaining fasteners in reverse order

To install:

20. Install intake manifold gaskets.

21. Install intake manifold.

22. Install intake manifold retaining bolts and tighten in sequence shown to 105 inch lbs. (12 Nm).

23. Install fuel rail.

24. Install the EGR tube.

25. Install top oil dipstick tube retaining bolt.

❊❊ CAUTION

Proper torque of the throttle body is critical to normal operation. If the throttle body is over-torqued, damage to the throttle body can occur resulting in throttle plate malfunction.

26. Install throttle body-to-intake manifold O-ring.

27. Install throttle body to intake manifold.

28. Install four mounting bolts.

29. Install ignition coil towers.

30. Connect electrical connectors for the following components:
  • Manifold Absolute Pressure (MAP) sensor
  • Engine Coolant Temperature (ECT) sensor
  • Ignition coil towers

31. Install alternator.

32. Install the air conditioning compressor.

33. Connect Vapor purge hose, Brake booster hose, and Positive Crankcase Ventilation (PCV) hose.

34. Connect the ETC connector to the throttle body).

35. Fill cooling system.

36. Raise engine using engine support fixture, special tool 8534.

37. Install the right side engine mount to frame bolt.

38. Remove engine support fixture, special tool 8534.

39. Install resonator assembly and air inlet hose.

40. Connect negative cable to battery.

41. Using the scan tool, perform the ETC Relearn function.

4.7L Engine

See Figure 132.

1. Perform the Fuel System Pressure Release procedure.

2. Disconnect negative cable from battery.

3. Remove air cleaner housing and throttle body resonator.

4. Disconnect throttle and speed control cables.

5. Disconnect electrical connectors for the following components:
  • Manifold Absolute Pressure (MAP) sensor
  • Electronic Throttle Control (ETC)
  • Intake Air Temperature (IAT) sensor
  • Engine Coolant Temperature (ECT) sensor
  • Ignition coils
  • Fuel injectors

6. Disconnect vapor purge hose, brake booster hose, speed control servo hose, positive crankcase ventilation (PCV) hose.

7. Remove accessory drive belt.

8. Disconnect alternator electrical connections.

9. Unbolt the alternator and move it away from the intake manifold for clearance.

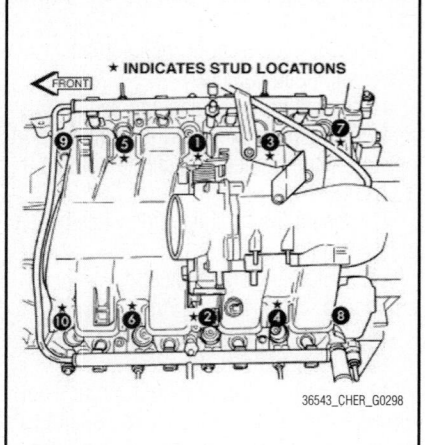

Fig. 132 Remove intake manifold retaining fasteners, in reverse order

10. Disconnect air conditioning compressor electrical connections.

11. Unbolt the air conditioning compressor and move it away from the intake manifold for clearance.

12. Disconnect left and right radio suppressor straps.

13. Disconnect and remove ignition coil towers.

14. Remove top oil dipstick tube retaining bolt and ground strap.

15. Remove fuel rail.

16. Remove throttle body assembly and mounting bracket.

17. Drain cooling system.

18. Remove intake manifold retaining fasteners, in reverse order of tightening sequence.

➡**Intake must be lifted upward and level in the front and rear to clear the cowl. Interference with the cowl will occur during removal.**

19. Remove intake manifold.

To install:

20. Install intake manifold gaskets.

21. Install intake manifold.

22. Install intake manifold retaining bolts and tighten in sequence shown in to 105 inch lbs. (12 Nm).

23. Install left and right radio suppressor straps.

24. Install throttle body assembly.

25. Install fuel rail.

26. Install ignition coils.

27. Install coolant temperature sensor.

28. Connect electrical connectors for the following components:
- Manifold Absolute Pressure (MAP) sensor
- Electronic Throttle Control (ETC)
- Intake Air Temperature (IAT) sensor
- Engine Coolant Temperature (ECT) sensor
- Ignition coils
- Fuel injectors

29. Install top oil dipstick tube retaining bolt and ground strap.

30. Install alternator including electrical connections.

31. Connect Vapor purge hose, Brake booster hose, and Positive Crankcase Ventilation (PCV) hose.

32. Install air conditioning compressor including electrical connections.

33. Fill cooling system.

34. Install accessory drive belt.

35. Install air cleaner housing and throttle body resonator.

36. Connect negative cable to battery.

5.7L Engine

1. Remove engine cover.

2. Bleed fuel system.

3. Disconnect negative cable from battery.

4. Remove air inlet hose.

5. Remove ignition wires from on top of intake manifold.

6. Disconnect electrical connectors for the following components:
- Manifold Absolute Pressure (MAP) Sensor
- Fuel Injectors
- Electric Throttle Control (ETC)

7. Remove wire harness from intake manifold.

8. Disconnect brake booster hose, purge hose, and Make Up Air (MUA) hose.

9. Remove EGR tube from intake manifold.

10. Remove intake manifold retaining fasteners in a crisscross pattern starting from the outside bolts and ending at the middle bolts.

11. Remove intake manifold as an assembly.

To install:

12. Position intake manifold.

13. Install intake manifold retaining bolts, and tighten in sequence from the middle bolts towards the outside in a crisscross pattern. Torque fasteners to 105 inch lbs. (12 Nm).

14. Install EGR tube.

15. Install wire harness on intake manifold.

16. Connect electrical connectors for the following components:
- Manifold Absolute Pressure (MAP) sensor
- Fuel Injectors
- Electronic Throttle Control (ETC)

17. Install ignition wires.

18. Connect Brake booster hose, purge hose, and MUA hose (Make Up Air hose).

19. Install air inlet hose.

20. Connect negative cable to battery.

21. Install engine cover.

OIL PAN

REMOVAL & INSTALLATION

3.7L Engine

See Figures 130, 133 and 134.

1. Disconnect negative battery cable.

2. Remove the radiator fan.

3. Remove the intake manifold.

4. Install Special Tool 8534. Do not raise engine at this time.

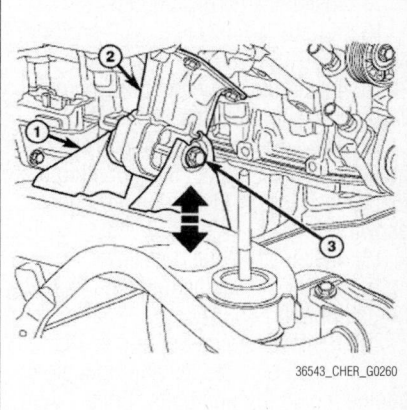

36543_CHER_G0260

Fig. 133 Remove both left and right side engine mount through bolts (3)

5. Remove the structural cover.

6. Remove both left and right side engine mount through bolts (3).

7. Raise engine using Engine Support 8534, to provide clearance to remove oil pan.

8. Drain engine oil and remove oil filter.

➡**Do not pry on oil pan or oil pan gasket. Gasket is mounted to engine and does not come out with oil pan.**

9. Remove the oil pan mounting bolts and oil pan.

10. Unbolt oil pump pickup tube and remove tube and oil pan gasket from engine.

To install:

11. Clean the oil pan gasket mating surface of the bedplate and oil pan.

12. Inspect integrated oil pan gasket, and replace as necessary.

13. Position the integrated oil pan gasket/windage tray assembly.

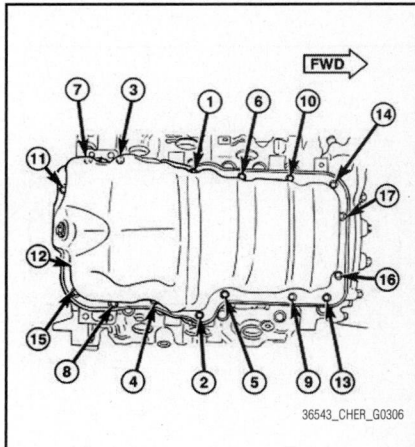

36543_CHER_G0306

Fig. 134 Install stud at position No. 9

14. Install the oil pickup tube.

15. If removed, install stud at position No. 9.

16. Install the mounting bolt and nuts. Tighten nuts to 20 ft. lbs. (28 Nm).

17. Position the oil pan and install the mounting bolts. Tighten the mounting bolts to 140 inch lbs. (16 Nm) in the sequence shown.

18. Install structural dust cover.

19. Lower the engine into mounts using Engine Support 8534.

20. Remove Engine Support 8534.

21. Install both the left and right side engine mount through bolts. Tighten the nuts to 50 ft. lbs. (68 Nm).

22. Install the intake manifold.

23. Fill engine oil.

24. Reconnect the negative battery cable.

25. Start engine and check for leaks.

4.7L Engine

See Figures 130, 133 and 135.

1. Disconnect the negative battery cable.

2. Install engine support fixture (1) special tool 8534. Do not raise engine at this time.

3. Loosen both left and right side engine mount through bolts (3). Do not remove bolts.

4. Remove the structural dust cover.

5. Drain engine oil.

✳✳ CAUTION

Only raise the engine enough to provide clearance for oil pan removal. Check for proper clearance at fan shroud to fan and cowl to intake manifold.

6. Raise engine using special tool 8534 to provide clearance to remove oil pan.

7. Remove the front axle.

➡ **Do not pry on oil pan or oil pan gasket. Gasket is integral to engine windage tray and does not come out with oil pan.**

8. Remove the oil pan mounting bolts and oil pan.

9. Unbolt oil pump pickup tube and remove tube.

10. Inspect the integral windage tray and gasket and replace as needed.

To install:

11. Clean the oil pan gasket mating surface of the bedplate and oil pan.

12. Position the oil pan gasket and pickup tube with new O-ring. Install the mounting bolt and nuts. Tighten bolt and nuts to 20 ft. lbs. (28 Nm).

13. Position the oil pan and install the mounting bolts. Tighten the mounting bolts to 11 ft. lbs. (15 Nm) in the sequence shown.

14. Lower the engine into mounts using special tool 8534.

15. Install both the left and right side engine mount through bolts Tighten the nuts to 50 ft. lbs. (68 Nm).

16. Remove special tool 8534.

17. Install structural dust cover.

18. Install the front axle.

19. Fill engine oil.

20. Reconnect the negative battery cable.

21. Start engine and check for leaks.

5.7L Engine

See Figures 133, 130, 136 through 137.

1. Disconnect the negative battery cable.

2. Remove the engine cover.

3. Raise vehicle.

4. Remove both left and right side engine mount to frame bolts (3).

5. Drain engine oil and remove the oil filter.

6. Remove the engine oil dipstick and tube from the oil pan.

7. Lower the vehicle.

8. Install Engine Support Fixture 8534 (1). Do not use the third leg.

9. Raise engine using Engine Support Fixture 8534 to provide clearance to remove oil pan.

10. Raise the vehicle.

11. Remove the front axle.

12. Remove the structural dust cover.

➡ **Do not pry on oil pan or oil pan gasket. Gasket is integral to engine windage tray and does not come out with oil pan.**

➡ **The horizontal M10 fasteners are 5 mm longer in length, and must be reinstalled in original locations.**

13. Remove the M10 fasteners (1) (vertical and horizontal) from the rear of the oil pan to the transmission and engine.

14. Remove the oil pan mounting bolts using the sequence provided, and oil pan.

➡ **When the oil pan is removed, a new oil pan gasket/windage tray assembly must be installed. The old gasket cannot be reused.**

15. Discard the integral windage tray and gasket and replace.

To install:

16. Clean the oil pan gasket mating surface of the block and oil pan.

➡ **Mopar® Engine RTV must be applied to the 4 T-joints, (area where front cover, rear retainer, block, and oil pan gasket meet). The bead of RTV should cover the bottom of the gasket. This area is approximately 4.5 mm x 25 mm in each of the 4 T-joint locations.**

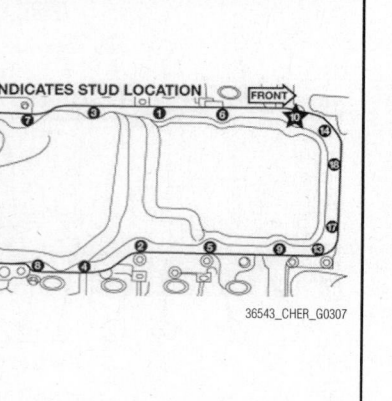

36543_CHER_G0307

Fig. 135 Position the oil pan and install the mounting bolts

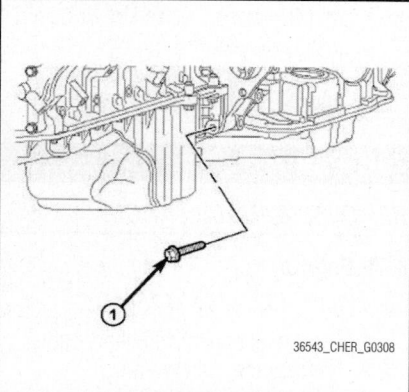

36543_CHER_G0308

Fig. 136 Remove the M10 fasteners (1) (vertical and horizontal) from the rear of the oil pan

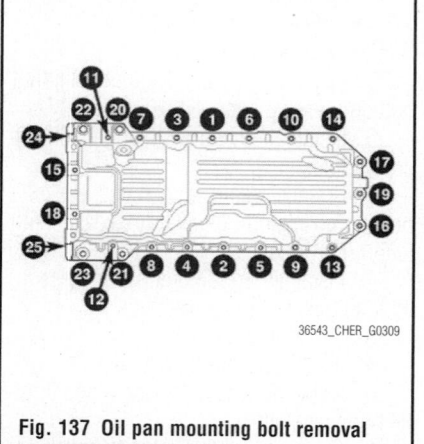

36543_CHER_G0309

Fig. 137 Oil pan mounting bolt removal and installation sequence

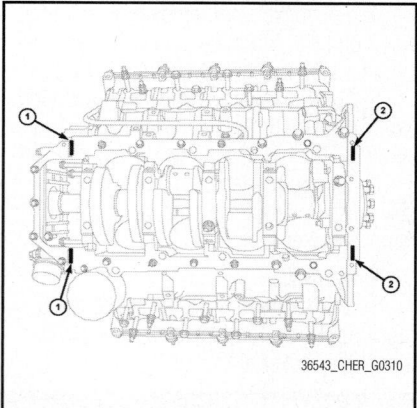

Fig. 138 Apply Mopar® Engine RTV at the 4 T- joints

17. Apply Mopar® Engine RTV at the 4 T- joints.

➡**When the oil pan is removed, a new oil pan gasket/windage tray assembly must be installed. The old gasket cannot be reused.**

18. Install a new oil pan gasket/windage tray assembly.

19. If removed, reinstall the oil pump pickup tube with new O-ring. Tighten tube to pump fasteners to 21 ft. lbs. (28 Nm).

➡**The horizontal M10 fasteners are 5 mm longer in length, and must be reinstalled in original locations.**

➡**New M6 fasteners must be used when reinstalling the oil pan. Do not reuse the old M6 fasteners.**

20. Align the rear of the oil pan with the rear face of the engine block, and install the M10 and M6 oil pan fasteners finger tight. Using the following torque sequence, torque the M6 mounting bolts to 44 inch lbs. (5 Nm).

21. Using the following torque sequence, tighten the M10 oil pan fasteners to 39 ft. lbs. (54 Nm).

22. Using the following torque sequence, tighten the M6 oil pan fasteners to 106 inch lbs. (12 Nm).

23. Install both the left and right side oil pan to transmission bolts. Tighten the bolts to 39 ft. lbs. (54 Nm).

24. Lower the engine into mounts using Engine Support Fixture 8534.

25. Install both the left and right side engine mount bolts and nuts. Tighten the studs and nuts to 39 ft. lbs. (54 Nm).

26. Install the engine oil dipstick and tube.

27. Remove Engine Support Fixture 8534.

28. Install the front axle.
29. Install the engine cover.
30. Fill engine oil.
31. Install oil filter, if removed.
32. Connect the negative battery cable.
33. Start engine and check for leaks.

OIL PUMP

REMOVAL & INSTALLATION

3.7L & 4.7L Engines
See Figure 139.

1. Remove the oil pan and pick-up tube.
2. Remove the timing chain cover.
3. Remove the timing chains and tensioners.
4. Remove the four bolts, primary timing chain tensioner and the oil pump.

To install:

5. Position the oil pump onto the crankshaft and install one oil pump retaining bolt.

6. Position the primary timing chain tensioner and install three retaining bolts.

7. Tighten the oil pump and primary timing chain tensioner retaining bolts to 21 ft. lbs. (28 Nm) in the sequence shown.

8. Install the secondary timing chain tensioners and timing chains.

9. Install the timing chain cover.
10. Install the pick-up tube and oil pan.

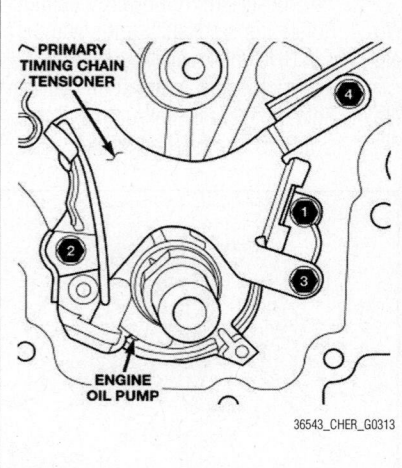

Fig. 139 Engine oil pump tightening sequence

5.7L Engine
See Figures 140 and 141.

1. Remove the oil pan and pick-up tube.
2. Remove the timing chain cover.

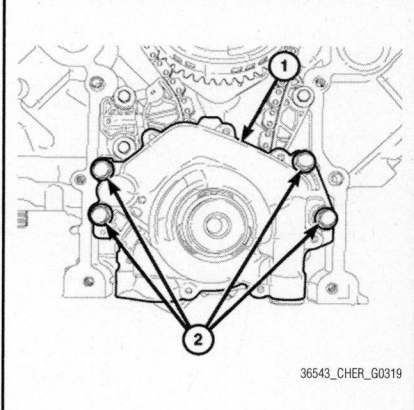

Fig. 140 Remove the four bolts (2) and the oil pump (1)

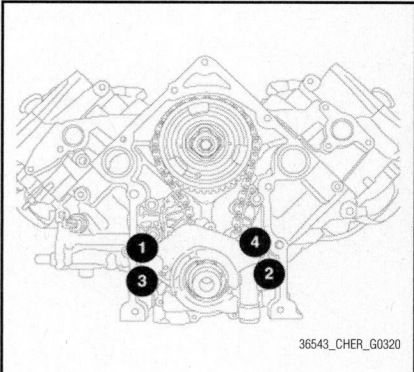

Fig. 141 Tighten the oil pump retaining bolts to 21 ft. lbs. (28 Nm) in the sequence shown

3. Remove the four bolts (2) and the oil pump (1).

To install:

4. Position the oil pump onto the crankshaft and install the 4 oil pump retaining bolts.

5. Tighten the oil pump retaining bolts to 21 ft. lbs. (28 Nm) in the sequence shown.

6. Install the timing chain cover.
7. Install the pick-up tube and oil pan.

REAR MAIN SEAL

REMOVAL & INSTALLATION

See Figures 142 through 144.

➡**This procedure can be performed in vehicle.**

1. If being performed in vehicle, remove the transmission.
2. Remove the flexplate.

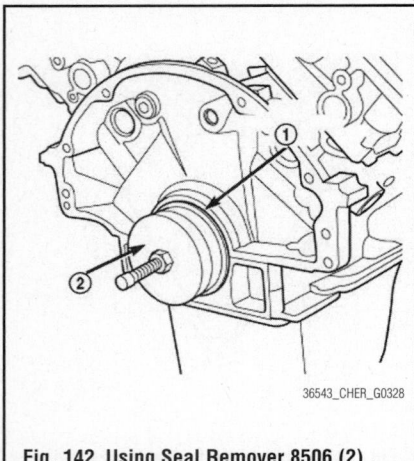

Fig. 142 Using Seal Remover 8506 (2) , remove the crankshaft rear oil seal (1)

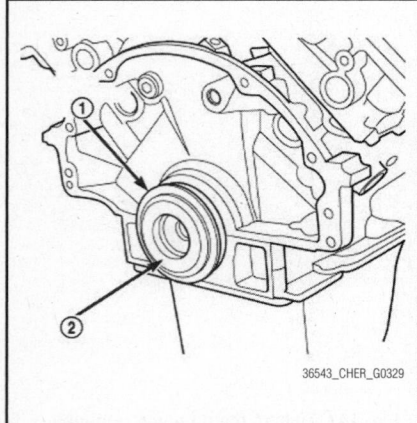

Fig. 143 Position the Seal Installer 8349-2 (2) onto the crankshaft rear face

➡The crankshaft oil seal (1) CANNOT be reused after removal.

➡The Seal Remover 8506 (2) must be installed deeply into the seal. Continue to tighten the removal tool into the seal until the tool cannot be turned farther. Failure to install tool correctly the first time will cause tool to pull free of seal without removing seal from engine.

3. Using Seal Remover 8506 (2) , remove the crankshaft rear oil seal (1).

To install:

4. Lubricate the crankshaft flange with engine oil.

5. Position the Seal Installer 8349-2 (2) onto the crankshaft rear face. Then position the crankshaft rear oil seal (1) onto the guide.

6. Using the Seal Installer 8349 (2) and Universal Drive Handle C-4171 (3), with a hammer, tap the seal (1) into place. Continue to tap on the driver handle until the

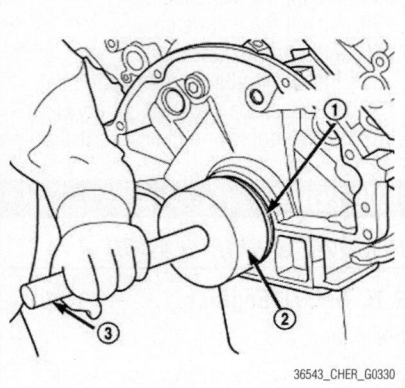

Fig. 144 Using the Seal Installer 8349 (2) and Universal Drive Handle C-4171 (3)

seal installer seats against the cylinder block crankshaft bore.

7. Install the flexplate.
8. Install the transmission.

ROCKER ARMS/SHAFTS

REMOVAL & INSTALLATION

3.7L Engine

See Figure 145.

➡Disconnect the battery negative cable to prevent accidental starter engagement.

1. Remove the cylinder head cover.
2. For rocker arm removal on cylinder No. 4, Rotate the crankshaft until cylinder No. 1 is at BDC intake stroke.
3. For rocker arm removal on cylinder No. 1, Rotate the crankshaft until cylinder No. 1 is at BDC combustion stroke.

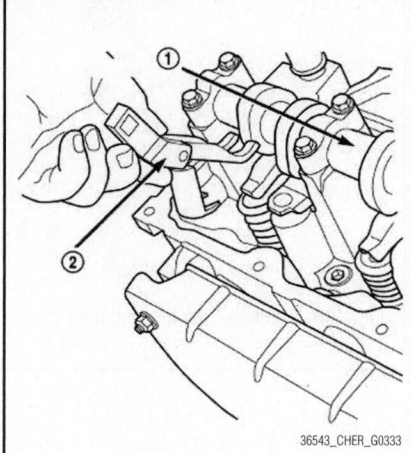

Fig. 145 Using the Remover/Installer 8516 (2), press downward on the valve spring, remove rocker arm

4. For rocker arm removal on cylinders No. 3 and No. 5, Rotate the crankshaft until cylinder No. 1 is at TDC exhaust stroke.
5. For rocker arm removal on cylinders No. 2 and No. 6, Rotate the crankshaft until cylinder No. 1 is at TDC ignition stroke.
6. Using the Remover/Installer 8516 (2), press downward on the valve spring, remove rocker arm.

To install:

7. Using the Remover/Installer 8516 press downward on the valve spring and install the rocker arm.

✳✳ CAUTION

Make sure the rocker arms are installed with the concave pocket over the lash adjusters. Failure to do so may cause severe damage to the rocker arms and/or lash adjusters.

➡Coat the rocker arms with clean engine oil prior to installation.

8. For rocker arm installation on cylinders No. 4, Rotate the crankshaft until cylinder No. 1 is at BDC intake stroke.
9. For rocker arm installation on cylinder No. 1, Rotate the crankshaft until cylinder No. 1 is at BDC combustion stroke.
10. For rocker arm installation on cylinders No. 3 and No. 5, Rotate the crankshaft until cylinder No. 1 is at TDC exhaust stroke.
11. For rocker arm installation on cylinders No. 2 and No. 6, Rotate the crankshaft until cylinder No. 1 is at TDC ignition stroke.
12. Install the cylinder head cover.

4.7L Engine

See Figure 145.

➡Disconnect the battery negative cable to prevent accidental starter engagement.

1. Remove the cylinder head cover.
2. For rocker arm removal on cylinders 3 and 5 Rotate the crankshaft until cylinder 1 is at TDC exhaust stroke.
3. For rocker arm removal on cylinders 2 and 8 Rotate the crankshaft until cylinder 1 is at TDC compression stroke.
4. For rocker arm removal on cylinders 4 and 6 Rotate the crankshaft until cylinder 3 is at TDC compression stroke.
5. For rocker arm removal on cylinders 1 and 7 Rotate the crankshaft until cylinder 2 is at TDC compression stroke.
6. Using special tool 8516 Rocker Arm Remover (2), press downward on the valve spring, remove rocker arm.

To install:

➡Coat the rocker arms with clean engine oil prior to installation.

7. For rocker arm installation on cylinders 3 and 5 Rotate the crankshaft until cylinder 1 is at TDC exhaust stroke.

8. For rocker arm installation on cylinders 2 and 8 Rotate the crankshaft until cylinder 1 is at TDC compression stroke.

9. For rocker arm installation on cylinders 4 and 6 Rotate the crankshaft until cylinder 3 is at TDC compression stroke.

10. For rocker arm installation on cylinders 1 and 7 Rotate the crankshaft until cylinder 2 is at TDC compression stroke.

11. Using valve spring compressor 10102 press downward on the valve spring, install rocker arm.

12. Install the cylinder head cover.

5.7L Engine

See Figures 146 through 150.

1. Disconnect the negative battery cable.
2. Remove the engine cover.
3. Remove the ignition coils.
4. Using the sequence shown, remove the cylinder head cover.
5. Install the pushrod retainer 9070 (1).
6. Using the sequence shown, loosen the rocker shafts retaining bolts.

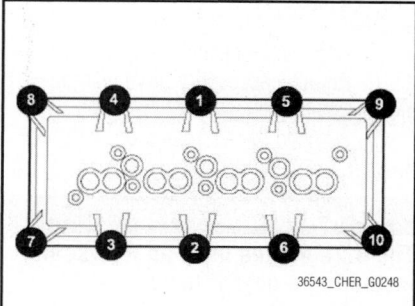

Fig. 146 Using the sequence shown, remove the cylinder head cover

rocker arms (1) are marked with the letter "I" (2).

7. Remove the rocker shaft (3). Note the rocker shaft location during removal.

8. Remove the pushrods. Note the pushrod location during removal.

To install:

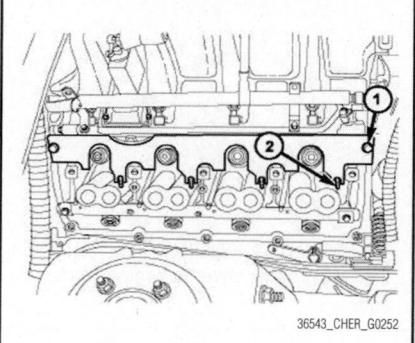

Fig. 147 Install the pushrod retainer 9070 (1)

9. Install the pushrods in the same order as removed.

10. Install the pushrod retainer 9070.

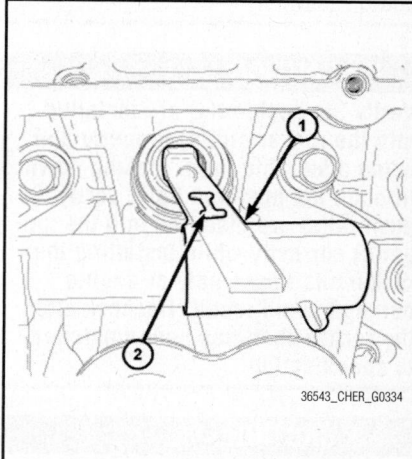

Fig. 149 The intake rocker arms (1) are marked with the letter "I" (2)

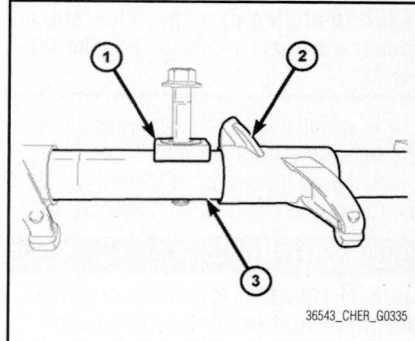

Fig. 150 Do not remove the retainers (1) from the rocker shaft (3)

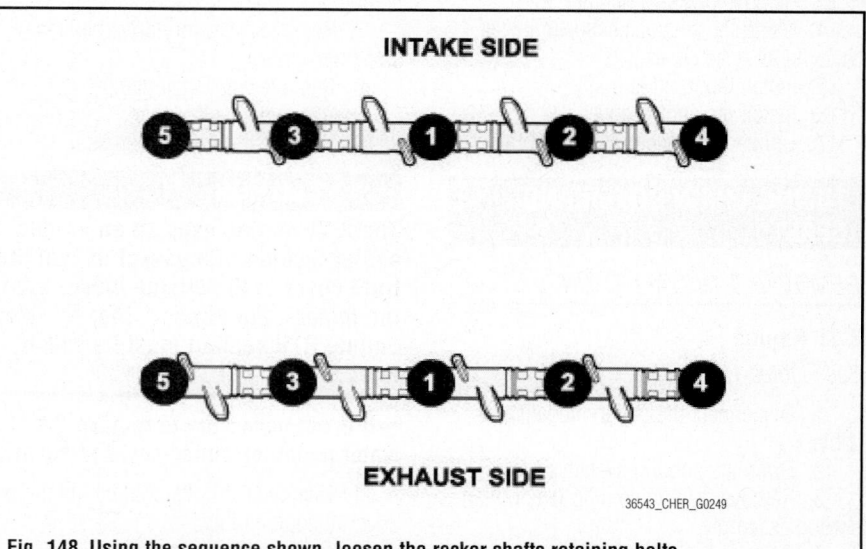

INTAKE SIDE

EXHAUST SIDE

Fig. 148 Using the sequence shown, loosen the rocker shafts retaining bolts

> ✳✳ **CAUTION**
>
> Make sure that the retainers and the rocker arms are not overlapped when tightening bolts or engine damage could result.

> ✳✳ **CAUTION**
>
> Verify the pushrod(s) are installed into the rocker arm(s) properly and using a suitable light, looking down through the push rod hole, verify the pushrod(s) are installed into the tappet(s) correctly while installing the rocker shaft assembly or engine damage could result. Recheck after the rocker shaft has been tightened to specification.

> ✳✳ **CAUTION**
>
> The rocker shaft assemblies are not interchangeable between the intake and the exhaust, failure to install them in the correct location could result in engine damage. The intake rocker arms are marked with the letter "I".

11. Install the rocker shaft assemblies in the same order as removed.

12. Using the sequence shown, tighten the rocker shaft bolts to 16 ft. lbs. (22 Nm).

> ✳✳ **CAUTION**
>
> Do NOT rotate or crank the engine during or immediately after rocker arm installation. Allow the hydraulic roller tappets adequate time to bleed down (about five minutes).

13. Remove pushrod retainer 9070.

14. Using the sequence shown, install the cylinder head cover.

15. Install the ignition coils.

16. Install the engine cover.

17. Connect the negative battery cable.

TIMING CHAIN COVER AND SEAL

REMOVAL & INSTALLATION

3.7L Engine

See Figures 151 and 152.

1. Disconnect the battery negative cable.

2. Drain the cooling system.

3. Remove electric cooling fan and fan shroud assembly.

4. Remove the radiator fan.

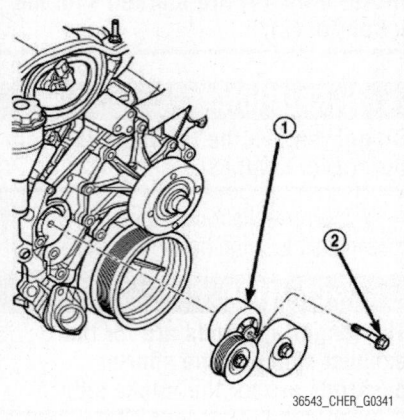

Fig. 151 Remove accessory drive belt tensioner assembly (1)

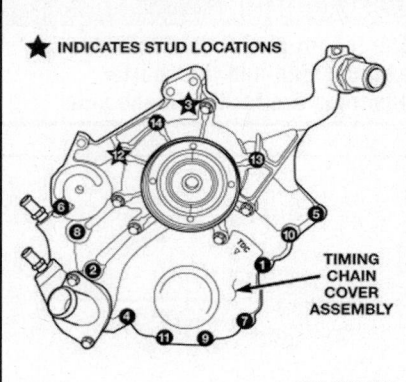

Fig. 152 Timing cover to engine block bolts

5. Disconnect both heater hoses at timing cover.

6. Disconnect lower radiator hose at engine.

7. Remove accessory drive belt tensioner assembly.

8. Remove crankshaft damper.

9. Remove the alternator.

10. Remove the A/C compressor.

> ✳✳ **CAUTION**
>
> The 3.7L engine uses an anaerobic sealer instead of a gasket to seal the front cover to the engine block, from the factory. For service, Mopar® Grey Engine RTV sealant must be substituted.

➥ It is not necessary to remove the water pump for timing cover removal.

11. Remove the bolts holding the timing cover to engine block.

12. Remove the timing cover.

To install:

> ✳✳ **CAUTION**
>
> Do not use oil based liquids to clean timing cover or block surfaces. Use only rubbing alcohol, along with plastic or wooden scrapers. Use no wire brushes or abrasive wheels or metal scrapers, or damage to surfaces could result.

13. Clean timing chain cover and block surface using rubbing alcohol.

> ✳✳ **CAUTION**
>
> The 3.7L uses a special anaerobic sealer instead of a gasket to seal the timing cover to the engine block, from the factory. For service repairs, Mopar® Engine RTV must be used as a substitute.

14. Inspect the water passage O-rings for any damage, and replace as necessary.

15. Apply Mopar® Engine RTV sealer to front cover using a 3 to 4 mm thick bead.

16. Install cover. Tighten fasteners in sequence to 43 ft. lbs. (58 Nm).

17. Install crankshaft damper.

18. Install the A/C compressor.

19. Install the alternator.

20. Install accessory drive belt tensioner.

21. Install radiator upper and lower hoses.

22. Install both heater hoses.

23. Install the radiator fan.

24. Fill the cooling system.

25. Connect the battery negative cable.

4.7L Engine

See Figures 151 through 152.

1. Disconnect the battery negative cable.

2. Drain cooling system.

3. Disconnect both heater hoses at timing cover.

4. Disconnect lower radiator hose at engine.

5. Remove crankshaft damper.

6. Remove accessory drive belt tensioner assembly.

7. Remove the alternator and A/C compressor.

> ✳✳ **CAUTION**
>
> The 4.7L engine uses an RTV sealer instead of a gasket to seal the front cover to the engine block, from the factory. For service, Mopar® Grey Engine RTV sealant must be substituted.

➡It is not necessary to remove the water pump for timing cover removal.

8. Remove the bolts holding the timing cover to engine block.

9. Remove cover.

To install:

✳✳ CAUTION

Do not use oil based liquids to clean timing cover or block surfaces. Use only rubbing alcohol, along with plastic or wooden scrapers. Use no wire brushes or abrasive wheels or metal scrapers, or damage to surfaces could result.

10. Clean timing chain cover and block surface using rubbing alcohol.

✳✳ CAUTION

The 4.7L can use a special RTV sealer instead of a carrier gasket to seal the timing cover to the engine block, from the factory. For service repairs, Mopar® Grey Engine RTV must be used as a substitute, if RTV is present. If the front cover being used has no provisions for the water passage O-rings, then Mopar® Grey Engine RTV must be applied around the water passages.

11. Inspect the water passage O-rings, if equipped for any damage, and replace as necessary.

12. Apply Mopar® Grey Engine RTV sealer to the front cover following the path above, using a 3 to 4mm thick bead.

13. Install cover. Tighten flange head fasteners in sequence to 43 ft. lbs. (58 Nm).

14. Install the A/C compressor and alternator.

15. Install crankshaft damper.

16. Install accessory drive belt tensioner assembly. Tighten fastener to 40 ft. lbs. (54 Nm).

17. Install lower radiator hose.

18. Install both heater hoses.

19. Fill cooling system.

20. Connect the battery negative cable.

5.7L Engine

See Figure 153.

1. Disconnect the battery negative cable.

2. Remove the engine cover.

3. Remove air cleaner assembly.

4. Drain cooling system.

5. Remove accessory drive belt.

6. Remove the cooling fan.

7. Remove coolant bottle and washer bottle.

8. Remove fan shroud.

➡It is not necessary to disconnect A/C lines or discharge Freon.

9. Remove A/C compressor and set aside.

10. Remove the alternator.

11. Remove upper radiator hose.

12. Disconnect both heater hoses at timing cover.

13. Disconnect lower radiator hose at engine.

14. Remove accessory drive belt tensioner and both idler pulleys.

15. Remove crankshaft damper.

➡Do not remove the hoses from the power steering pump.

16. Remove power steering pump and set aside.

17. Remove the dipstick support bolt.

18. Drain the engine oil.

19. Remove the oil pan and pick up tube.

➡It is not necessary to remove water pump for timing cover removal.

20. Remove timing cover bolts and remove cover.

21. Verify that timing cover slide bushings are located in timing cover.

To install:

22. Clean timing chain cover and block surface.

➡Always install a new gasket on timing cover.

23. Verify that the slide bushings are installed in timing cover.

24. Install cover and new gasket. Tighten fasteners to 21 ft. lbs. (28 Nm).

➡The large lifting stud is torqued to 40 ft. lbs. (55 Nm).

25. Install the oil pan and pick up tube.

26. Install the A/C compressor.

27. Install the alternator.

28. Install power steering pump.

29. Install the dipstick support bolt.

30. Install the thermostat housing.

31. Install crankshaft damper.

32. Install accessory drive belt tensioner assembly and both idler pulleys.

33. Install radiator lower hose.

34. Install both heater hoses.

35. Install radiator fan shroud.

36. Install the cooling fan.

37. Install the accessory drive belt.

38. Install the coolant bottle and washer bottle.

39. Install the upper radiator hose.

40. Install the air cleaner assembly.

41. Fill cooling system.

42. Refill engine oil.

43. Connect the battery negative cable.

44. Install the engine cover.

TIMING CHAIN AND SPROCKETS

REMOVAL & INSTALLATION

3.7L Engine

See Figures 154 through 163.

1. Disconnect negative cable from battery.

2. Drain cooling system.

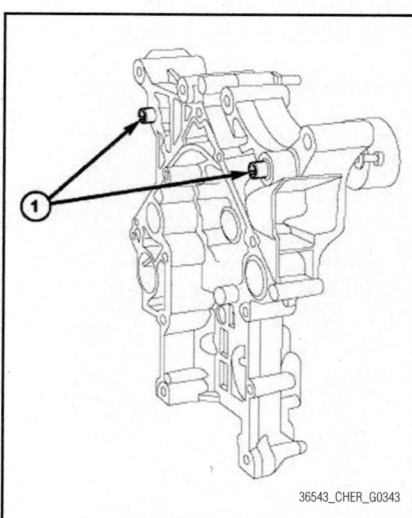

Fig. 153 Verify that timing cover slide bushings (1) are located in timing cover

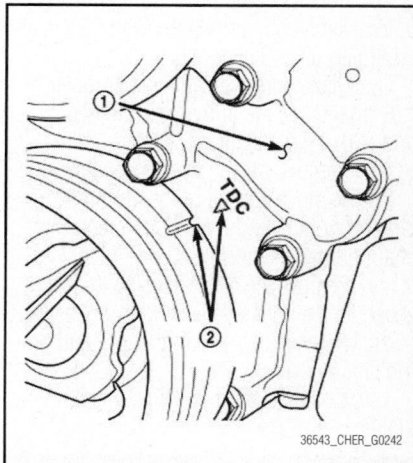

Fig. 154 Rotate engine until timing mark (2) on crankshaft damper aligns with TDC mark on timing chain cover (1)

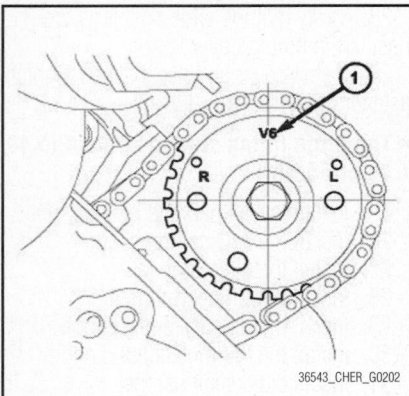

Fig. 155 Make sure the camshaft sprocket "V6" marks (1) are at the 12 o'clock position

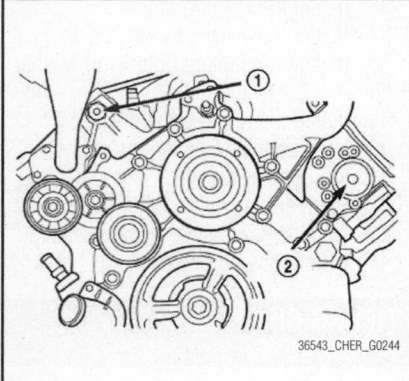

Fig. 156 Remove access plugs (1 and 2) from left and right cylinder heads for access to chain guide fasteners

3. Remove right and left cylinder head covers.

4. Remove radiator fan.

5. Rotate engine until timing mark (2) on crankshaft damper aligns with TDC mark on timing chain cover (1).

6. Make sure the camshaft sprocket "V6" marks (1) are at the 12 o'clock position (No. 1 TDC exhaust stroke).

7. Remove power steering pump.

8. Remove access plugs (1 and 2) from left and right cylinder heads for access to chain guide fasteners.

9. Remove the oil fill housing to gain access to the right side tensioner arm fastener.

10. Remove crankshaft damper and timing chain cover.

11. Collapse and pin primary chain tensioner.

⁂ CAUTION

Plate behind left secondary chain tensioner could fall into oil pan. Therefore, cover pan opening.

12. Remove secondary chain tensioners.

13. Remove Camshaft Position (CMP) sensor.

⁂ CAUTION

Care should be taken not to damage the camshaft target wheel. Do not hold the target wheel while loosening or tightening the camshaft sprocket. Do not place the target wheel near a magnetic source of any kind. A damaged or magnetized target wheel could cause a vehicle no start condition.

⁂ CAUTION

Do not forcefully rotate the camshafts or crankshaft independently of each other. Damaging intake valve to piston contact will occur. Ensure the negative battery cable is disconnected and isolated to guard against accidental starter engagement.

14. Remove left and right camshaft sprocket bolts.

15. While holding the left camshaft steel tube Camshaft Holder 8428A (2), remove the left camshaft sprocket. Slowly rotate the camshaft approximately 5 degrees clockwise to a neutral position.

16. While holding the right camshaft steel tube with Camshaft Holder 8428A (2), remove the right camshaft sprocket.

17. Remove idler sprocket assembly bolt.

18. Slide the idler sprocket assembly and crank sprocket forward simultaneously to remove the primary and secondary chains.

19. Remove both pivoting tensioner arms and chain guides.

20. Remove primary chain tensioner.

Fig. 157 Using Camshaft Holder 8428 (2)

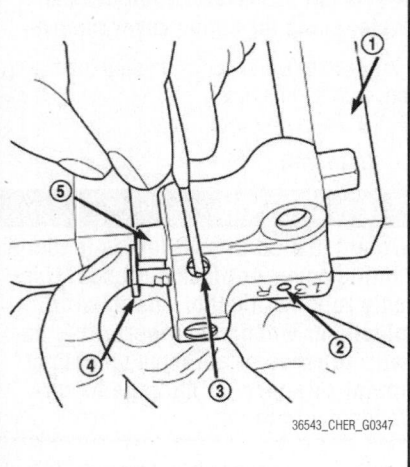

Fig. 158 Using a vise, lightly compress the secondary chain tensioner piston until the piston step (5) is flush with the tensioner body

To install:

21. Using a vise, lightly compress the secondary chain tensioner piston until the piston step (5) is flush with the tensioner body. Using a pin or suitable tool, release ratchet pawl (4) by pulling pawl back against spring force through access hole on side of tensioner. While continuing to hold pawl back, Push ratchet device to approximately 2 mm from the tensioner body. Install Tensioner Pins 8514 (2) into hole on front of tensioner. Slowly open vise to transfer piston spring force to lock pin.

22. Position primary chain tensioner over oil pump and insert bolts into lower two holes on tensioner bracket. Tighten bolts to 21 ft. lbs. (28 Nm).

23. Install right side chain tensioner arm. Install Torx® bolt. Tighten Torx® bolt to 21 ft. lbs. (28 Nm).

⁂ CAUTION

The silver bolts retain the guides to the cylinder heads and the black bolts retain the guides to the engine block.

24. Install the left side chain guide. Tighten the bolts to 21 ft. lbs. (28 Nm).

25. Install left side chain tensioner arm, and Torx® bolt. Tighten Torx® bolt to 21 ft. lbs. (28 Nm).

26. Install the right side chain guide. Tighten the bolts to 21 ft. lbs. (28 Nm).

27. Install both secondary chains onto the idler sprocket (2). Align two plated links on the secondary chains to be visible through the two lower openings on the idler sprocket (4 o'clock and 8 o'clock). Once the

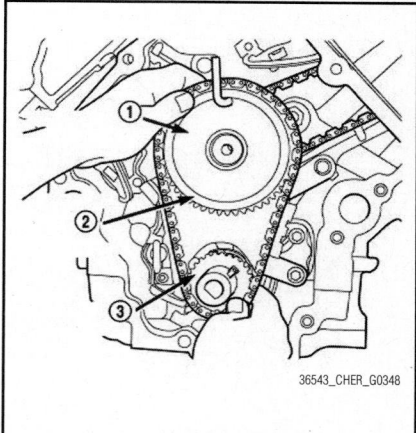

Fig. 159 Install both secondary chains onto the idler sprocket (2)

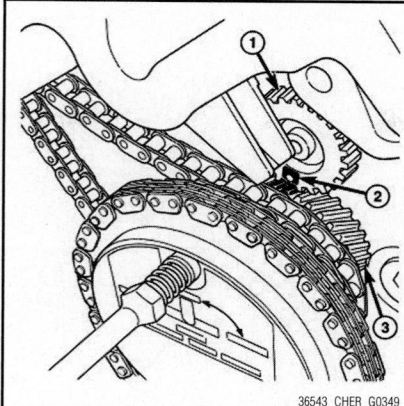

Fig. 160 Install all chains, crankshaft sprocket, and idler sprocket as an assembly

Fig. 162 Using Spanner Wrench 6958, with Adaptor Pins 8346 (2)

secondary timing chains are installed, Secondary Camshaft Chain Holder 8429 (1) to hold chains in place for installation.

28. Align primary chain double plated links with the timing mark at 12 o'clock on the idler sprocket. Align the primary chain single plated link with the timing mark at 6 o'clock on the crankshaft sprocket.

29. Lubricate idler shaft and bushings with clean engine oil.

➡The idler sprocket must be timed to the counterbalance shaft drive gear before the idler sprocket is fully seated.

30. Install all chains, crankshaft sprocket, and idler sprocket as an assembly. After guiding both secondary chains through the block and cylinder head openings, affix chains with a elastic strap or equivalent. This will maintain tension on chains to aid in installation. Align the timing mark (2) on the idler sprocket gear (3) to the timing mark on the counterbalance shaft drive gear (1), then seat idler sprocket fully. Before installing idler sprocket bolt, lubricate washer with oil, and tighten idler sprocket assembly retaining bolt to 25 ft. lbs. (34 Nm).

➡It will be necessary to slightly rotate camshafts for sprocket installation.

31. Align left camshaft sprocket "L" dot to plated link on chain.

32. Align right camshaft sprocket "R" dot to plated link on chain.

❊❊ CAUTION

Remove excess oil from the camshaft sprocket bolt. Failure to do so can result in over-torque of bolt resulting in bolt failure.

33. Remove Secondary Camshaft Chain Holder 8429, then attach both sprockets to camshafts. Remove excess oil from bolts, then Install sprocket bolts, but do not tighten at this time.

34. Verify that all plated links are aligned with the marks on all sprockets and the "V6" marks on camshaft sprockets are at the 12 o'clock position.

❊❊ CAUTION

Ensure the plate between the left secondary chain tensioner and block is correctly installed.

35. Install both secondary chain tensioners. Tighten bolts to 21 ft. lbs. (28 Nm).

➡Left and right secondary chain tensioners are not common.

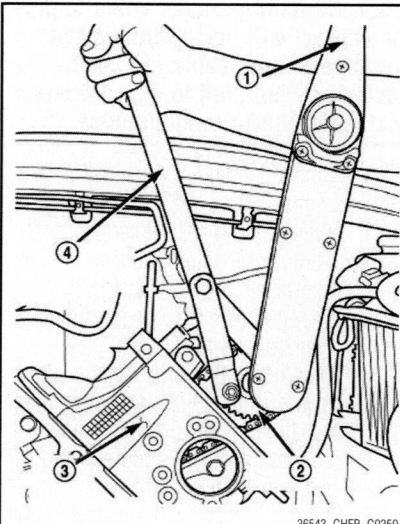

Fig. 161 Using Spanner Wrench 6958, with Adaptor Pins 8346 (4)

36. Remove all locking pins from tensioners.

❊❊ CAUTION

After pulling locking pins out of each tensioner, DO NOT manually extend the tensioner(s) ratchet. Doing so will over tension the chains, resulting in noise and/or high timing chain loads.

37. Using Spanner Wrench 6958, with Adaptor Pins 8346 (4), tighten left camshaft sprocket bolts to 90 ft. lbs. (122 Nm).

38. Using Spanner Wrench 6958, with Adaptor Pins 8346 (2), tighten right camshaft sprocket bolts to 90 ft. lbs. (122 Nm).

39. Rotate engine two full revolutions. Verify timing marks are at the follow locations:

- primary chain idler sprocket dot is at 12 o'clock
- primary chain crankshaft sprocket dot is at 6 o'clock
- secondary chain camshaft sprockets "V6" marks are at 12 o'clock
- balance shaft drive gear dot is aligned to the idler sprocket gear dot

40. Lubricate all three chains with engine oil.

41. After installing all chains, it is recommended that the idler gear end play be checked. The end play must be within 0.004–0.010 inches (0.10–0.25 mm). If not within specification, the idler gear (1) must be replaced.

42. Install timing chain cover and crankshaft damper.

43. Install cylinder head covers.

➡Before installing threaded plug in right cylinder head, the plug must be coated with sealant to prevent leaks.

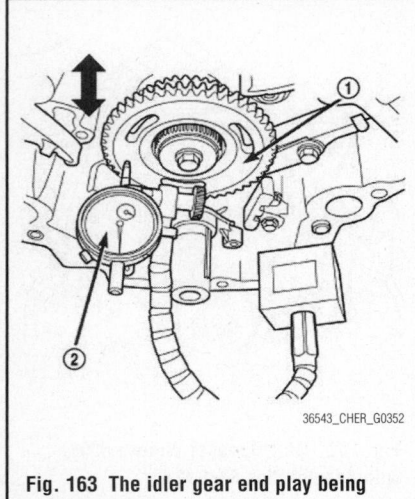

Fig. 163 The idler gear end play being checked

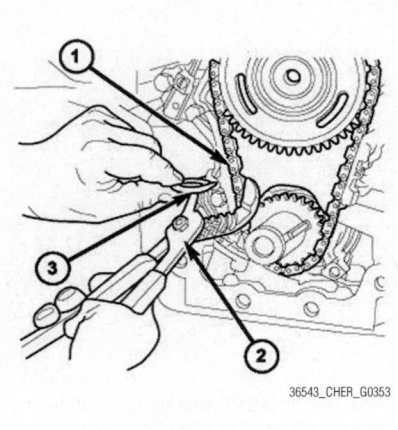

Fig. 164 Collapse and pin primary chain tensioner

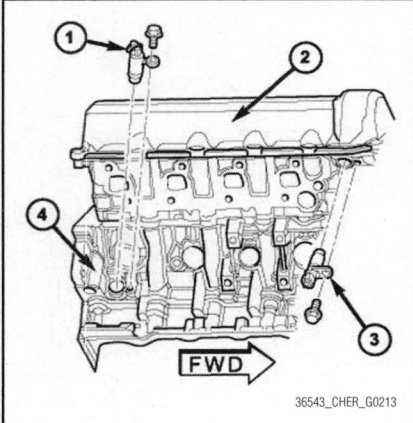

Fig. 165 Remove Camshaft Position (CMP) sensor from right cylinder head

44. Coat the large threaded access plug with Mopar® Thread Sealant with Teflon, then install into the right cylinder head and tighten to 60 ft. lbs. (81 Nm).

45. Install the oil fill housing.

46. Install access plug in left cylinder head.

47. Install power steering pump.

48. Fill cooling system.

49. Connect negative cable to battery.

4.7L Engine

See Figures 76, 103, 106, 158, 161, 163 through 166.

1. Disconnect negative cable from battery.

2. Drain cooling system.

3. Remove right and left cylinder head covers.

4. Remove radiator fan.

5. Rotate engine until timing mark on crankshaft damper aligns with TDC mark on timing chain cover (1 cylinder exhaust stroke).

6. Align the camshaft sprocket, so the "V8" marks are at the 12 o'clock position.

7. Remove power steering pump.

8. Remove access plugs (2) from left and right cylinder heads for access to chain guide fasteners.

9. Remove the oil fill housing to gain access to the right side tensioner arm fastener.

10. Remove crankshaft damper and timing chain cover.

11. Collapse and pin primary chain tensioner.

✳✳ CAUTION

Plate behind left secondary chain tensioner could fall into oil pan. Therefore, cover pan opening.

12. Remove secondary chain tensioners.

13. Remove Camshaft Position (CMP) sensor from right cylinder head.

✳✳ CAUTION

Care should be taken not to damage the camshaft target wheel. Do not hold the target wheel while loosening or tightening the camshaft sprocket. Do not place the target wheel near a magnetic source of any kind. A damaged or magnetized target wheel could cause a vehicle no start condition.

✳✳ CAUTION

Do not forcefully rotate the camshafts or crankshaft independently of each other. Damaging intake valve to piston contact will occur. Ensure the negative battery cable is disconnected and isolated to guard against accidental starter engagement.

14. Remove left and right camshaft sprocket bolts.

15. While holding the left camshaft steel tube with adjustable pliers, remove the left camshaft sprocket. Slowly rotate the camshaft approximately 15 degrees clockwise to a neutral position.

16. While holding the right camshaft steel tube with adjustable pliers, remove the right camshaft sprocket. Slowly rotate the camshaft approximately 45 degrees counterclockwise to a neutral position.

17. Remove idler sprocket assembly bolt.

18. Slide the idler sprocket assembly and crank sprocket forward simultaneously to remove the primary and secondary chains.

19. Remove both pivoting tensioner arms and chain guides.

20. Remove chain tensioner.

To install:

21. Using a vise, lightly compress the secondary chain tensioner piston until the piston step is flush with the tensioner body. Using a pin or suitable tool, release ratchet pawl by pulling pawl back against spring force through access hole on side of tensioner. While continuing to hold pawl back, Push ratchet device to approximately 2 mm from the tensioner body. Install Special Tool 8514 lock pin into hole on front of tensioner. Slowly open vise to transfer piston spring force to lock pin.

22. Position primary chain tensioner over oil pump and insert bolts into lower two holes on tensioner bracket. Tighten bolts to 21 ft. lbs. (28 Nm).

23. Install right side chain tensioner arm. Apply Mopar® Lock N, Seal to Torx® bolt, tighten bolt to 21 ft. lbs. (28 Nm).

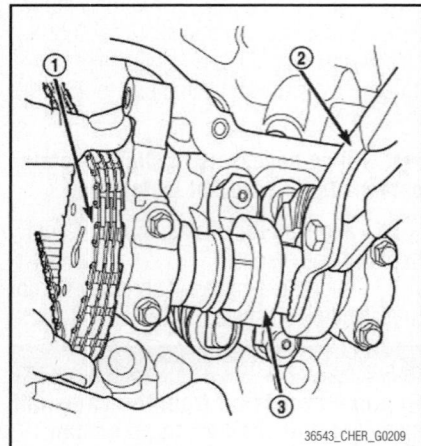

Fig. 166 Remove the left camshaft sprocket

➡The silver bolts retain the guides to the cylinder heads and the black bolts retain the guides to the engine block.

24. Install the left side chain guide. Tighten the bolts to 21 ft. lbs. (28 Nm).

❉❉ **CAUTION**

Over-tightening the tensioner arm Torx® bolt can cause severe damage to the cylinder head. Tighten Torx® bolt to specified torque only.

25. Install left side chain tensioner arm. Apply Mopar® Lock N, Seal to Torx® bolt, tighten bolt to 21 ft. lbs. (28 Nm).
26. Install the right side chain guide. Tighten the bolts to 21 ft. lbs. (28 Nm).
27. Install both secondary chains onto the idler sprocket. Align two plated links on the secondary chains to be visible through the two lower openings on the idler sprocket (4 o'clock and 8 o'clock). Once the secondary timing chains are installed, position special tool 8429 to hold chains in place for installation.
28. Align primary chain double plated links with the timing mark at 12 o'clock on the idler sprocket. Align the primary chain single plated link with the timing mark at 6 o'clock on the crankshaft sprocket.
29. Lubricate idler shaft and bushings with clean engine oil.
30. Install all chains, crankshaft sprocket, and idler sprocket as an assembly . After guiding both secondary chains through the block and cylinder head openings, affix chains with a elastic strap or the equivalent, This will maintain tension on chains to aid in installation.

➡It will be necessary to slightly rotate camshafts for sprocket installation.

31. Align left camshaft sprocket "L" dot to plated link on chain.
32. Align right camshaft sprocket "R" dot to plated link on chain.

❉❉ **CAUTION**

Remove excess oil from the camshaft sprocket bolt. Failure to do so can result in over-torque of bolt resulting in bolt failure.

33. Remove Special Tool 8429, then attach both sprockets to camshafts. Remove excess oil from bolts, then Install sprocket bolts, but do not tighten at this time.
34. Verify that all plated links are aligned with the marks on all sprockets and the "V8" marks on camshaft sprockets are at the 12 o'clock position.

❉❉ **CAUTION**

Ensure the plate between the left secondary chain tensioner and block is correctly installed.

35. Install both secondary chain tensioners. Tighten bolts to 21 ft. lbs. (28 Nm).

➡Left and right secondary chain tensioners are not common.

36. Before installing idler sprocket bolt, lubricate washer with oil, and tighten idler sprocket assembly retaining bolt to 25 ft. lbs. (34 Nm).
37. Remove all 3 locking pins from tensioners.

❉❉ **CAUTION**

After pulling locking pins out of each tensioner, DO NOT manually extend the tensioner(s) ratchet. Doing so will over tension the chains, resulting in noise and/or high timing chain loads.

38. Using Special Tool 6958, Spanner with Adaptor Pins 8346, tighten left and right camshaft sprocket bolts to 90 ft. lbs. (122 Nm).
39. Rotate engine two full revolutions. Verify timing marks are at the following locations:
- primary chain idler sprocket dot is at 12 o'clock.
- primary chain crankshaft sprocket dot is at 6 o'clock.

- secondary chain camshaft sprockets "V8" marks are at 12 o'clock.
40. Lubricate all three chains with engine oil.
41. After installing all chains, it is recommended that the idler gear end play be checked . The end play must be within 0.004–0.010 inches (0.10–0.25 mm). If not within specification, the idler gear and idler shaft must be replaced.
42. Install timing chain cover and crankshaft damper.
43. Install cylinder head covers.

➡Before installing threaded plug in right cylinder head, the plug must be coated with sealant to prevent leaks.

44. Coat the large threaded access plug with Mopar® Thread Sealant with Teflon, then install into the right cylinder head and tighten to 60 ft. lbs. (81 Nm).
45. Install the oil fill housing.
46. Install access plug in left cylinder head.
47. Install power steering pump.
48. Install radiator fan.
49. Fill cooling system.
50. Connect negative cable to battery.

5.7L Engine

See Figures 167 through 174.

1. Disconnect the negative battery cable.
2. Drain the cooling system.
3. Remove the timing chain cover.

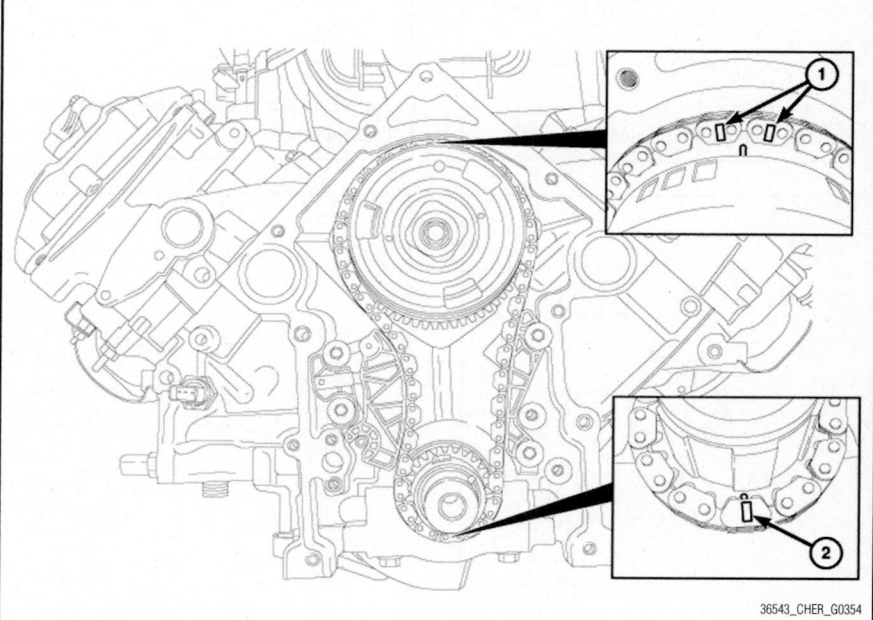

36543_CHER_G0354

Fig. 167 Rotate the crankshaft to align the timing chain sprockets and keyways

4. Remove the oil pump retaining bolts (2) and pump (1).

5. Install the vibration damper bolt finger tight. Using a suitable socket and breaker bar, rotate the crankshaft to align the timing chain sprockets and keyways as shown.

6. Retract the tensioner shoe (1) until the hole in the shoe lines up with the hole in the bracket.

7. Install the tensioner pin 8514 (1) into the holes.

8. Remove the camshaft sprocket attaching bolt (1).

9. Remove the timing chain with the camshaft and crankshaft sprockets.

To install:

10. Slide crankshaft sprocket (1) on crankshaft.

11. Align camshaft timing marks and install sprocket on camshaft.

12. Install camshaft retaining bolt finger tight.

13. Align crankshaft timing marks.

14. Install timing chain guide (1) and tighten bolts (2) to 106 inch lbs. (12 Nm).

15. Verify timing marks (1,2).

16. Remove Tensioner Pin 8514.

17. Tighten camshaft sprocket bolt to 90 ft. lbs. (122 Nm).

18. Install the oil pump.

19. Install the timing chain cover.

20. Fill engine with oil.

21. Fill cooling system.

22. Connect negative battery cable.

23. Start engine and check for leaks.

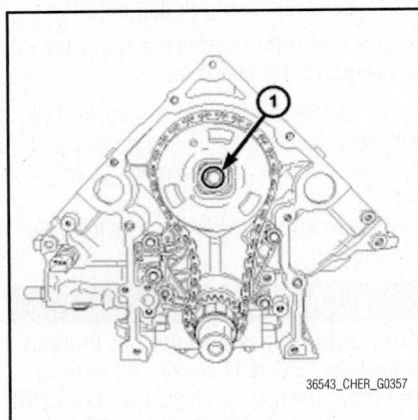

Fig. 170 Remove the camshaft sprocket attaching bolt (1)

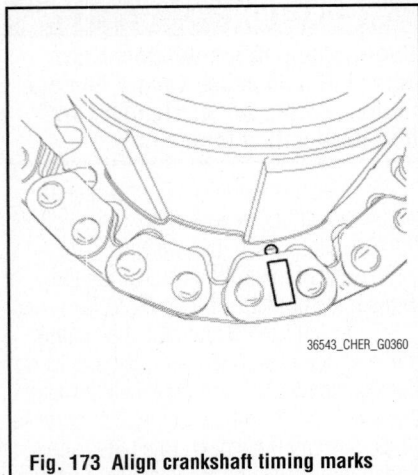

Fig. 173 Align crankshaft timing marks

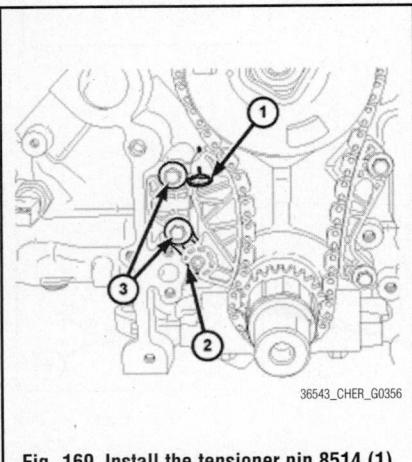

Fig. 168 Retract the tensioner shoe (1)

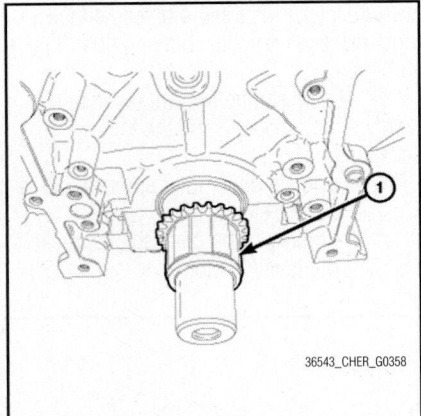

Fig. 171 Slide crankshaft sprocket (1) on the crankshaft

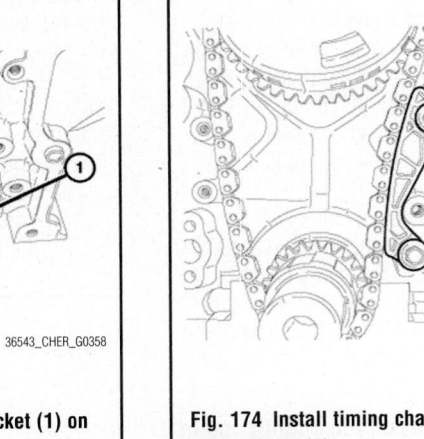

Fig. 174 Install timing chain guide (1) and tighten bolts (2)

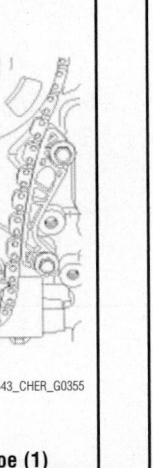

Fig. 169 Install the tensioner pin 8514 (1) into the holes

Fig. 172 Align camshaft timing marks and install sprocket on camshaft

CYLINDER HEAD COVERS

REMOVAL & INSTALLATION

3.7L Engine

See Figure 175.

➡The gasket may be used again, providing no cuts, tears, or deformation has occurred.

1. Disconnect negative cable from battery.

2. Remove the resonator assemble and air inlet hose.

3. Disconnect injector connectors and un-clip the injector harness.

4. Route injector harness in front of cylinder head cover (2).

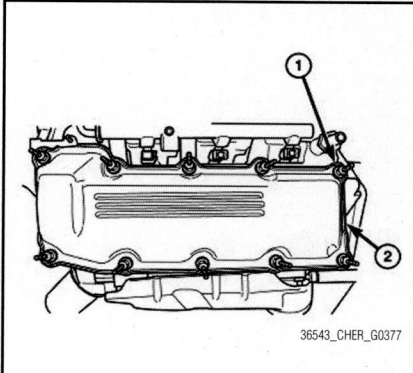

Fig. 175 Route injector harness in front of cylinder head cover (2)

5. Disconnect the left side breather tube and remove the breather tube.

6. Remove the cylinder head cover mounting bolts (1).

7. Remove cylinder head cover and gasket.

To install:

❋❋ CAUTION

Do not use harsh cleaners to clean the cylinder head covers. Severe damage to covers may occur.

➡**The gasket may be used again, provided no cuts, tears, or deformation has occurred.**

8. Clean cylinder head cover and both sealing surfaces. Inspect and replace gasket as necessary.

9. Tighten cylinder head cover bolts and double ended studs to 105 inch lbs. (12 Nm).

10. Install left side breather and connect breather tube.

11. Connect injector electrical connectors and injector harness retaining clips.

12. Install the resonator and air inlet hose.

13. Connect negative cable to battery.

4.7L Engine

Left Side

See Figure 176.

1. Disconnect negative cable from battery.

2. Remove the resonator assemble and air inlet hose.

3. Remove the spark plug wires (3).

4. Route injector harness in front of cylinder head cover.

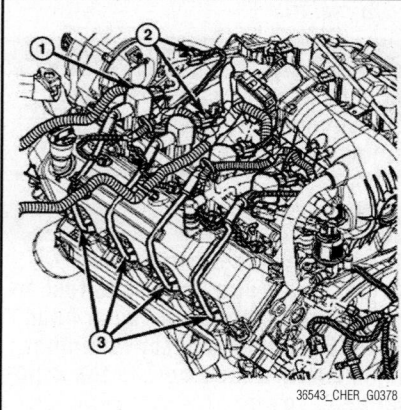

Fig. 176 Remove the spark plug wires (3)

5. Disconnect the left side breather tube and remove the breather tube.

6. Remove the cylinder head cover mounting bolts.

7. Remove cylinder head cover and gasket.

➡**The gasket may be used again, provided no cuts, tears, or deformation has occurred.**

To install:

❋❋ CAUTION

Do not use harsh cleaners to clean the cylinder head covers. Severe damage to covers may occur.

8. Clean cylinder head cover and both sealing surfaces. Inspect and replace gasket as necessary.

9. Install cylinder head cover and hand start all fasteners. Verify that all studs are in the correct location.

10. Tighten cylinder head cover bolts and double ended studs to 105 inch lbs. (12 Nm).

11. Install left side breather and connect breather tube.

12. Install the spark plug wires.

13. Install the resonator and air inlet hose.

14. Connect negative cable to battery.

Right Side

1. Disconnect battery negative cable.

2. Disconnect battery positive cable.

3. Remove the battery tray.

4. Drain cooling system.

5. Remove accessory drive belt.

6. Remove air conditioning compressor retaining bolts and move compressor to the left.

7. Remove heater hoses.

8. Disconnect injector and ignition coil connectors.

9. Disconnect and remove positive crankcase ventilation (PCV) hose.

10. Remove oil fill tube.

11. Un-clip injector and ignition coil harness and move away from cylinder head cover.

12. Remove right rear breather tube and filter assembly.

13. Remove cylinder head cover retaining bolts.

14. Remove cylinder head cover.

➡**The gasket may be used again, provided no cuts, tears, or deformation has occurred.**

To install:

❋❋ CAUTION

Do not use harsh cleaners to clean the cylinder head covers. Severe damage to covers may occur.

15. Clean cylinder head cover and both sealing surfaces. Inspect and replace gasket as necessary.

16. Install cylinder head cover and hand start all fasteners.

17. Tighten cylinder head cover bolts and double ended studs to 105 inch lbs. (12 Nm).

18. Install right rear breather tube and filter assembly.

19. Install spark plug wires.

20. Install the oil fill tube.

21. Install PCV hose.

22. Install heater hoses.

23. Install air conditioning compressor retaining bolts.

24. Install accessory drive belt.

25. Fill Cooling system.

26. Install air cleaner assembly, resonator assembly and air inlet hose.

27. Connect battery negative cable.

5.7L Engine

See Figures 177 and 178.

1. Disconnect negative battery cable.

2. Disconnect ignition coil connector.

3. Remove ignition coil retaining bolts.

4. Remove ignition coil.

5. Remove cylinder head cover retaining bolts.

6. Remove cylinder head cover (1).

➡**The gasket (2) may be used again, provided no cuts, tears, or deformation have occurred.**

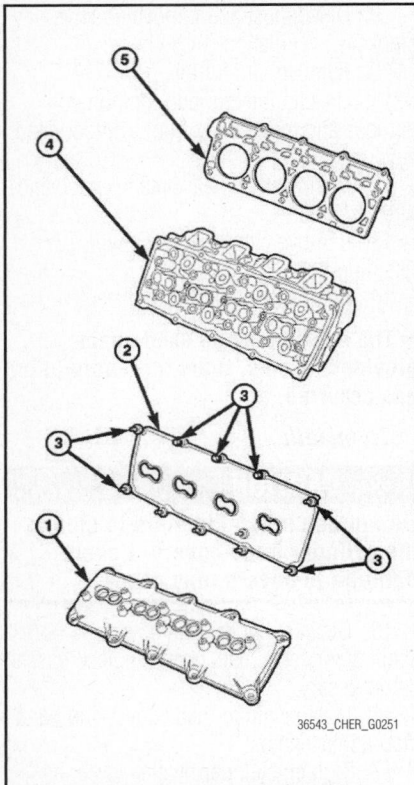

Fig. 177 Remove cylinder head cover (1)

To install:

> ☀☀ **CAUTION**
>
> **Do not use harsh cleaners to clean the cylinder head covers. Severe damage to covers may occur.**

> ☀☀ **CAUTION**
>
> **Do not allow other components including the wire harness to rest on or against the engine cylinder head cover. Prolonged contact with other objects may wear a hole in the cylinder head cover.**

7. Clean cylinder head cover and both sealing surface.

8. Inspect and replace gasket as necessary.

9. Install cylinder head cover and hand start all fasteners. Verify that all double ended studs are in the correct location.

10. Tighten cylinder head cover bolts and double ended studs to 70 inch lbs. (8 Nm) in the sequence shown.

11. Before installing coil(s), apply dielectric grease to inside of spark plug boots.

12. Install ignition coils.

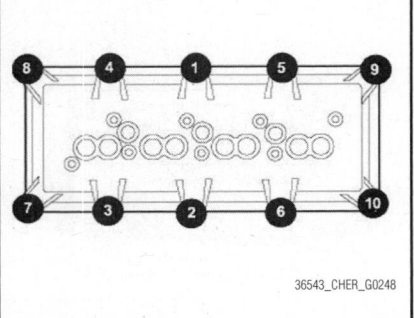

Fig. 178 Tighten cylinder head cover bolts and double ended studs in sequence

13. Connect ignition coil electrical connectors.

14. Install PCV hose.

15. Install the engine cover.

16. Connect the negative battery cable.

VALVE LASH

ADJUSTMENT

The 3.7L and 4.7L engines use hydraulic valve lash adjusters. No adjustment is possible. If the hydraulic lash adjuster is not operating properly it must be replaced.

ENGINE PERFORMANCE & EMISSION CONTROLS

ACCELERATOR PEDAL POSITION (APP) SENSOR

LOCATION

The Accelerator Pedal Position (APP) Sensor is attached to the accelerator pedal assembly under the instrument panel.

The APP sensor is used only with the 5.7L V-8 engines. The 5.7L engines do not use a mechanical throttle cable.

REMOVAL & INSTALLATION

See Figure 179.

The accelerator pedal is serviced as a complete assembly including the bracket.

1. Disconnect electrical connector (3) at APP sensor(6).

2. Remove two accelerator pedal mounting bracket nuts (4). Remove accelerator pedal assembly.

3. Remove three sensor-to-pedal nuts (5). Remove APP sensor from accelerator pedal assembly.

To install:

4. Install APP sensor to pedal assembly and install three nuts.

5. Place accelerator pedal assembly over two mounting studs.

6. Install and tighten two mounting nuts.

7. Install electrical connector to APP sensor.

8. Use a scan tool may to learn electrical parameters. Go to the Miscellaneous menu, and then select ETC Learn.

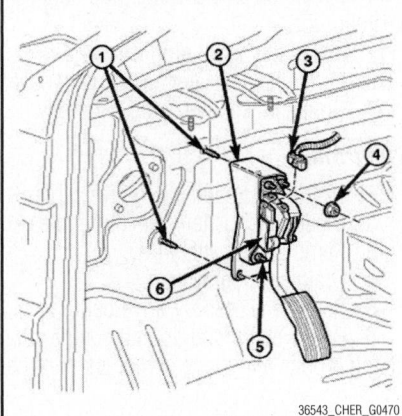

Fig. 179 Disconnect electrical connector (3) at APP sensor(6)

9. If the previous step is not performed, a Diagnostic Trouble Code (DTC) will be set.

10. If necessary, also use a scan tool to erase any Diagnostic Trouble Codes (DTC's) from PCM.

11. Before starting engine, operate accelerator pedal to check for any binding.

CAMSHAFT POSITION (CMP) SENSOR

LOCATION

The Camshaft Position (CMP) sensor is bolted to the right-front side of the right cylinder head on 3.7L and 4.7L engines. On 5.7L engines, it is located below the alternator on the timing chain cover.

REMOVAL & INSTALLATION

1. Raise and safely support the vehicle.

2. Disconnect the CMP electrical connector.

3. Remove the CMP sensor mounting bolts.

4. Carefully twist the sensor from the cylinder.

To install:

5. Check the condition of the sensor O-ring.

6. Clean out the machined hole in the cylinder head.

7. Apply a small amount of clean engine oil to the sensor O-ring.

8. Install the CMP sensor into the cylinder head with a slight rocking and twisting action.

9. Install the mounting bolt and tighten to 106 inch lbs. (12 Nm).

10. Connect the electrical connector.

11. Lower the vehicle.

CRANKSHAFT POSITION (CKP) SENSOR

LOCATION

The Crankshaft Position (CKP) sensor is mounted into the right rear side of the cylinder block. It is positioned and bolted into a machined hole.

REMOVAL & INSTALLATION

3.7L Engine

See Figure 180.

1. Raise vehicle.

2. Disconnect sensor electrical connector.

3. Remove sensor mounting bolt (1).

4. Carefully twist sensor from cylinder block.

5. Check condition of sensor O-ring (3).

To install:

6. Clean out machined hole in engine block.

7. Apply a small amount of engine oil to sensor O-ring.

8. Install sensor into engine block with a slight rocking and twisting action.

> ❊❊ **CAUTION**
>
> **Before tightening the sensor mounting bolt, be sure the sensor is completely flush to the cylinder block. If the sensor is not flush, damage to the sensor mounting tang may result.**

9. Install mounting bolt tighten to 21 ft. lbs. (28 Nm) torque.

10. Connect electrical connector to sensor.

11. Lower vehicle.

4.7L Engine

See Figure 181.

1. Raise vehicle.

2. Disconnect CKP electrical connector at sensor.

3. Remove CKP mounting bolt (2).

4. Carefully twist sensor from cylinder block.

5. Remove sensor from vehicle.

6. Check condition of sensor O-ring.

To install:

7. Clean out machined hole in engine block.

8. Apply a small amount of engine oil to sensor O-ring.

9. Install sensor into engine block with a slight rocking and twisting action.

> ❊❊ **CAUTION**
>
> **Before tightening the sensor mounting bolt, be sure the sensor is completely flush to the cylinder block. If the sensor is not flush, damage to**

the sensor mounting tang may result.

10. Install mounting bolt tighten to 21 ft. lbs. (28 Nm) torque.

11. Connect electrical connector to sensor.

12. Lower vehicle.

5.7L Engine

See Figure 182.

1. Raise vehicle.

2. Disconnect CKP electrical connector (2) at sensor.

3. Remove CKP mounting bolt (3).

4. Carefully twist sensor from cylinder block.

5. Remove sensor from vehicle.

6. Check condition of sensor O-ring.

To install:

7. Clean out machined hole in engine block.

8. Apply a small amount of engine oil to sensor O-ring.

9. Install sensor into engine block with a slight rocking and twisting action.

> ❊❊ **CAUTION**
>
> **Before tightening the sensor mounting bolt, be sure the sensor is completely flush to the cylinder block. If the sensor is not flush, damage to the sensor mounting tang may result.**

10. Install mounting bolt tighten to 21 ft. lbs. (28 Nm) torque.

11. Connect electrical connector to sensor.

12. Lower vehicle.

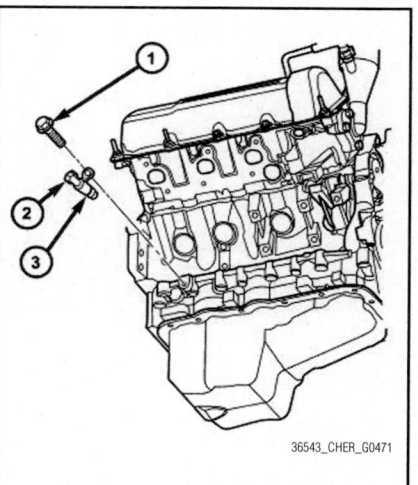

36543_CHER_G0471

Fig. 180 Remove sensor mounting bolt (1)

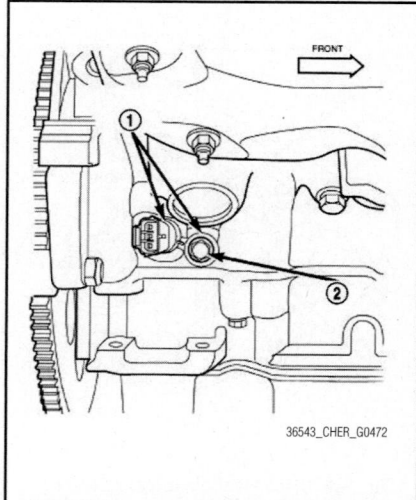

36543_CHER_G0472

Fig. 181 Remove CKP mounting bolt (2)

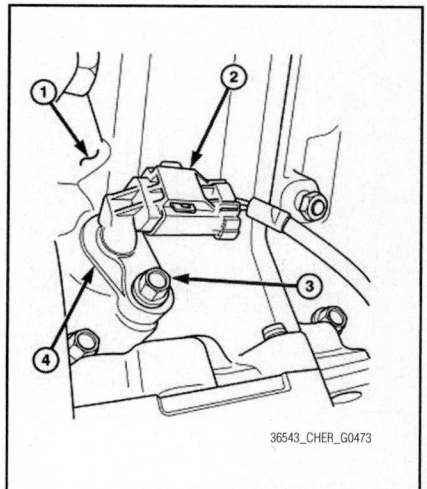

36543_CHER_G0473

Fig. 182 Remove CKP mounting bolt (3)

ENGINE COOLANT TEMPERATURE (ECT) SENSOR

LOCATION

The Engine Coolant Temperature (ECT) sensor is used to sense engine coolant temperature. The sensor protrudes into an engine water jacket.

The Engine Coolant Temperature (ECT) sensor on the 3.7L engine is installed into a water jacket at front of intake manifold near rear of alternator.

On the 4.7L engine, the ECT sensor is located near the front of the intake manifold.

The Engine Coolant Temperature (ECT) sensor on the 5.7L engine is located under the air conditioning compressor. It is installed into a water jacket at the front of the cylinder block.

REMOVAL & INSTALLATION

3.7L Engine

See Figure 183.

> ❄❄ **WARNING**
>
> **Hot, pressurized coolant can cause injury by scalding. Cooling system must be partially drained before removing the Engine Coolant Temperature (ECT) sensor.**

➡ **Do not waste reusable coolant. If solution is clean, drain coolant into a clean container for reuse.**

1. Partially drain the cooling system.
2. Disconnect the electrical connector from the sensor (3).
3. Remove the sensor (3) from the intake manifold (4).

To install:

4. Apply MOPAR® thread sealant with PFTE part number 04318034 to sensor threads.
5. Install sensor to engine.
6. Tighten sensor to 8 ft. lbs. (11 Nm) torque.
7. Connect electrical connector to sensor.
8. Replace any lost engine coolant.

4.7L Engine

See Figure 184.

> ❄❄ **WARNING**
>
> **Hot, pressurized coolant can cause injury by scalding. Cooling system must be partially drained before removing the Engine Coolant Temperature (ECT) sensor.**

➡ **Do not waste reusable coolant. If solution is clean, drain coolant into a clean container for reuse.**

1. Partially drain cooling system.
2. Disconnect electrical connector from ECT sensor (1).
3. Remove sensor (1) from intake manifold.

To install:

4. Apply MOPAR® thread sealant with PFTE part number 04318034 to sensor threads.
5. Install sensor to engine.
6. Tighten sensor to 8 ft. lbs. (11 Nm) torque.
7. Connect electrical connector to sensor.
8. Replace any lost engine coolant.

5.7L Engine

See Figure 185.

> ❄❄ **WARNING**
>
> **Hot, pressurized coolant can cause injury by scalding. Cooling system must be partially drained before removing the coolant temperature sensor.**

➡ **Do not waste reusable coolant. If solution is clean, drain coolant into a clean container for reuse.**

1. Partially drain the cooling system.
2. Remove accessory drive belt.
3. Carefully unbolt air conditioning compressor from front of engine. Do not disconnect any A/C hoses from compressor. Temporarily support compressor to gain access to ECT sensor (3).
4. Disconnect electrical connector (2) from sensor (3).
5. Remove sensor (3) from engine cylinder block (1).

To install:

6. Apply MOPAR® thread sealant with PFTE part number 04318034 to sensor threads.
7. Install sensor to the engine block.
8. Tighten sensor to 8 ft. lbs. (11 Nm) torque.
9. Connect electrical connector to sensor.
10. Carefully bolt air conditioning compressor onto the front of engine.
11. Install accessory drive belt.
12. Replace any lost engine coolant.

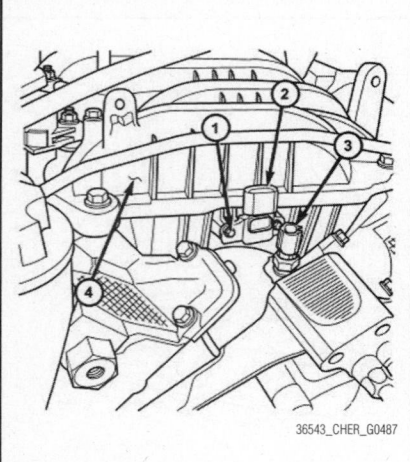

36543_CHER_G0487

Fig. 183 Disconnect the electrical connector from the sensor (3)

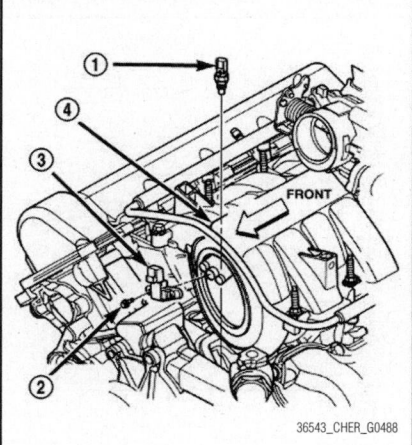

36543_CHER_G0488

Fig. 184 Disconnect electrical connector from ECT sensor (1)

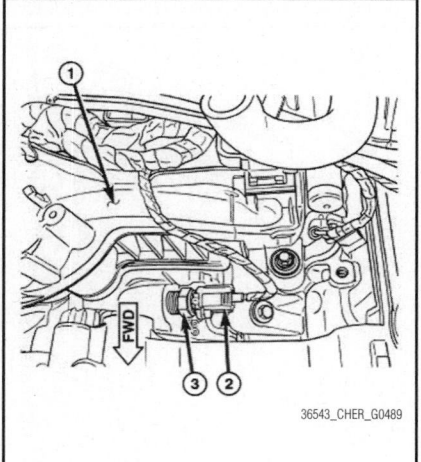

36543_CHER_G0489

Fig. 185 Disconnect electrical connector (2) from sensor (3)

EVAPORATIVE EMISSIONS (EVAP) CANISTER

LOCATION

The Evaporative System Vapor Canister is located in the left-rear quarter-panel behind the left-rear tire.

REMOVAL & INSTALLATION

See Figures 186 through 189.

The Natural Vacuum Leak Detection (NVLD) pump (2) is attached to the Evaporative System Vapor Canister (3). This assembly is located in the left-rear quarter-panel behind the left-rear tire.

1. Raise and support vehicle.
2. Remove left-rear tire.
3. To access EVAP canister or NVLD pump, remove plastic splash shield at rear of left-rear tire.
4. Disconnect electrical connector (4) at pump.
5. Carefully remove vapor/vacuum hoses (1) and (6) at pump.
6. Remove three canister bracket-to-body nuts (1) and (2).
7. Separate canister from mounting bracket by removing two canister-to-bracket nuts at front of canister (4). The opposite end of canister is equipped with two alignment pins. Remove canister from support bracket by pulling these two pins from the two rubber grommets
8. To Separate NVLD Pump from EVAP canister:

  a. Pry outward on tab (3) and rotate pump clockwise about 70 degrees for removal.

  b. Remove NVLD pump O-ring (2) from EVAP canister (1).

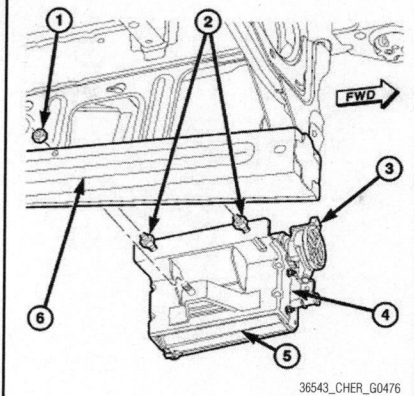

Fig. 187 Remove three canister bracket-to-body nuts (1) and (2)

To install:

9. Install new NVLD pump O-ring to EVAP canister.
10. Position NVLD pump into EVAP canister.
11. Rotate pump until tab aligns with notch in EVAP canister.
12. Position canister into mounting bracket. Install and tighten two canister-to-mounting bracket nuts.
13. Position canister/pump assembly to body. Install and tighten three mounting bracket-to-body nuts.
14. Carefully install vapor/vacuum lines and to NVLD pump and EVAP canister. The vapor/vacuum lines and hoses must be firmly connected. Check the vapor/vacuum lines at the NVLD pump, filter and EVAP canister purge solenoid for damage or leaks. If a leak is present, a Diagnostic Trouble Code (DTC) may be set.

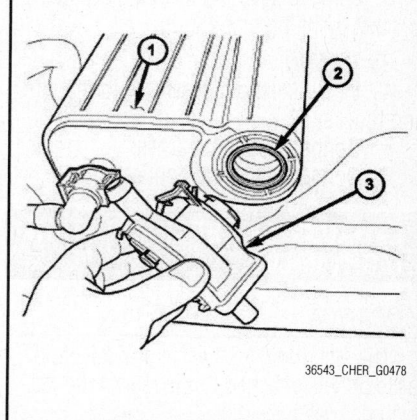

Fig. 189 Remove NVLD pump O-ring (2) from EVAP canister (1)

15. Connect electrical connector to pump.
16. Install plastic splash shield at rear of left-rear tire.
17. Install left-rear tire.

EVAPORATIVE EMISSIONS (EVAP) PURGE CONTROL SOLENOID

LOCATION

See Figure 190.

The duty cycle EVAP canister purge solenoid (2) is located in the engine compartment attached to a bracket.

REMOVAL & INSTALLATION

1. Disconnect electrical wiring connector at solenoid.
2. Disconnect vacuum lines at solenoid.

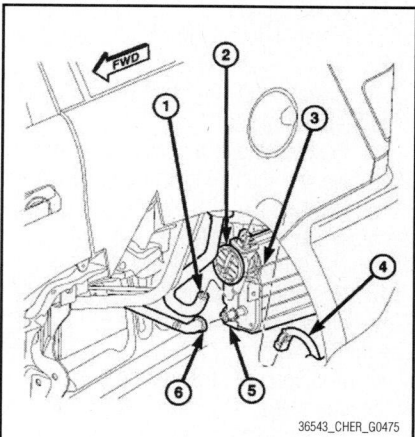

Fig. 186 The Natural Vacuum Leak Detection (NVLD) pump (2) is attached to the Evaporative System Vapor Canister (3)

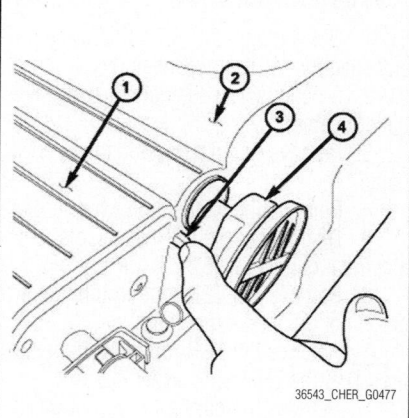

Fig. 188 Pry outward on tab (3) and rotate pump clockwise about 70 degrees for removal

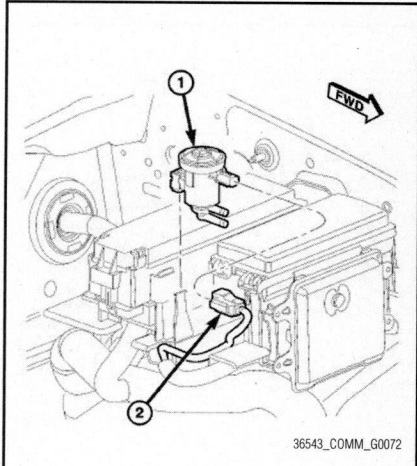

Fig. 190 EVAP canister purge solenoid (2) location

3. Remove solenoid from mounting bracket by lifting straight up.

To install:

4. Install solenoid assembly to mounting bracket.

5. Connect vacuum harness.

6. Connect electrical connector.

EXHAUST GAS RECIRCULATION (EGR) VALVE

LOCATION

The electronic EGR valve and solenoid assembly is attached to the rear of the left cylinder head.

REMOVAL & INSTALLATION

3.7L Engine

See Figures 191 and 192.

1. Use a diagnostic scan tool to record any Diagnostic Trouble Codes (DTC).

2. Disconnect and isolate the negative battery cable.

➡**An exhaust gas routing tube (1) connects the EGR valve (4) to the intake manifold.**

3. Remove two tube mounting bolts (2).

4. Remove tube (1) from solenoid (4). Slip opposite end of tube (6) from intake manifold.

5. Remove gasket (3) located between EGR valve solenoid and tube flange.

6. Disconnect electrical connector (3) at solenoid (1).

7. Remove two EGR valve solenoid mounting bolts (2).

8. Remove solenoid (1) from engine.

9. Remove and discard gasket located under EGR solenoid.

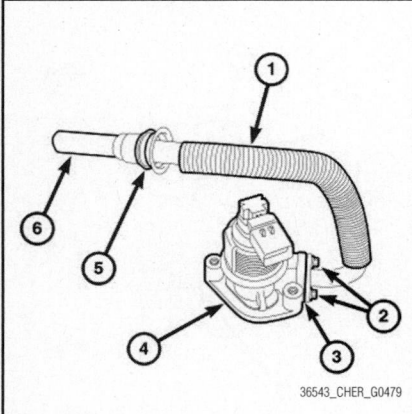

Fig. 191 An exhaust gas routing tube (1) connects the EGR valve (4) to the intake manifold

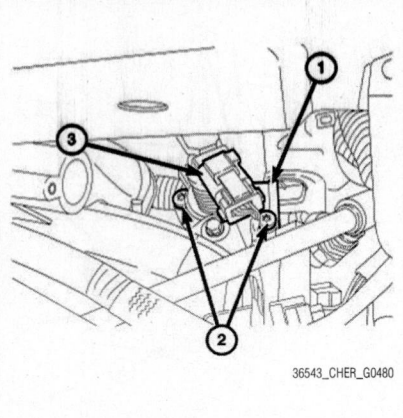

Fig. 192 Disconnect electrical connector (3) at solenoid (1)

To install:

10. Clean gasket area at rear of left cylinder head where it joins base of EGR valve.

11. Clean EGR tube where it joins EGR valve.

12. Position new gasket between EGR valve and cylinder head.

13. Position EGR valve to cylinder head. Install and tighten two bolts. Torque to 80 inch lbs. (9 Nm).

14. Position new gasket between EGR tube flange and EGR valve assembly.

15. Position EGR tube to side of EGR valve. Position end of tube into intake manifold. Install two bolts. Torque to 9 ft. lbs. (11 Nm).

16. Connect electrical connector to top of EGR valve solenoid.

17. Connect negative battery cable.

18. Using a diagnostic scan tool, erase any previously recorded DTCs.

4.7L Engine

See Figures 193 and 194.

1. Use a diagnostic scan tool to record any Diagnostic Trouble Codes (DTC).

2. Disconnect and isolate the negative battery cable.

3. Remove the plastic windshield cowl panel.

4. Remove the windshield wiper motor.

5. Disconnect the EGR valve solenoid electrical connector (5).

6. Remove the EGR routing tube retainers (1) at the intake manifold.

7. Remove the EGR routing tube retainers (4) at the EGR valve assembly.

8. Remove the gasket located between EGR routing tube flange and the EGR valve assembly.

9. Remove the EGR valve assembly retainers (5).

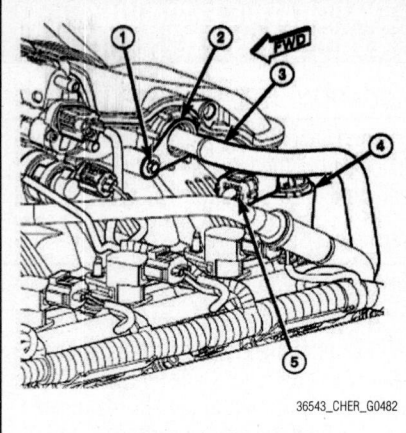

Fig. 193 Disconnect the EGR valve solenoid electrical connector (5)

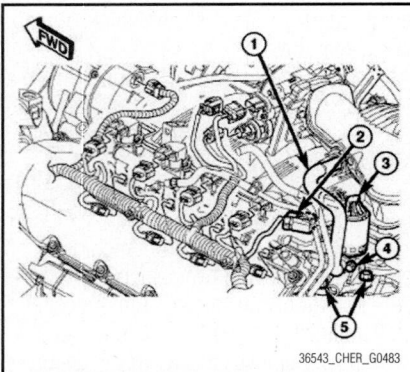

Fig. 194 Remove the EGR routing tube retainers (4) at the EGR valve assembly

10. Remove the EGR valve assembly (3) from the engine.

11. Remove and discard the metal gasket located between the cylinder head and the EGR valve assembly.

To install:

12. Clean the area at the rear of the left cylinder head where it joins the base of the EGR valve.

13. Clean the EGR routing tube where it joins the EGR valve.

14. Position the new gasket between the EGR valve and the cylinder head.

15. Position the EGR valve to the cylinder head and install the retainers and tighten to 80 inch lbs. (9 Nm).

16. Position a new gasket between the EGR routing tube flange and the EGR valve assembly.

17. Position the EGR routing tube to the side of the EGR valve and into the intake manifold and install the retainers hand tight.

18. Install the EGR routing tube flange retainers at the intake manifold and tighten to 9 ft. lbs. (11 Nm).

19. Connect the electrical connector to the EGR valve solenoid.

20. Tighten the EGR routing tube retainers to 9 ft. lbs. (11 Nm).

21. Install the windshield wiper motor.

22. Install the plastic windshield cowl panel.

23. Connect the negative battery cable.

24. Using a diagnostic scan tool, erase any previously recorded DTCs.

5.7L Engine

See Figures 195 and 196.

1. Use a diagnostic scan tool to record any Diagnostic Trouble Codes (DTC).

2. Disconnect and isolate the negative battery cable.

3. Remove air resonator box above EGR valve/solenoid.

4. Remove accessory serpentine drive belt.

5. Remove alternator mounting bolts.

6. Reposition alternator to gain access to EGR valve-to-cylinder head mounting bolts. No need to remove alternator wiring from alternator.

7. Disconnect electrical connector (1) from EGR solenoid (2).

8. Remove two bolts (3) connecting EGR tube (4) to valve assembly.

9. Remove gasket located between EGR tube flange and EGR valve assembly.

10. Remove two mounting bolts (2).

11. Separate valve assembly (3) from cylinder head (1).

12. Remove and discard metal gasket located between cylinder head and valve assembly.

To install:

13. Position a new metal gasket between cylinder head and valve assembly.

14. Install two mounting bolts and tighten to 20 ft. lbs. (27 Nm).

15. Clean EGR tube where it joins EGR valve.

16. Position new gasket between EGR tube flange and EGR valve assembly.

17. Install two bolts connecting EGR tube to valve assembly. Tighten bolts to 20 ft. lbs. (27 Nm).

18. Connect electrical connector to EGR solenoid.

19. Position alternator to alternator mounting bracket.

20. Install alternator mounting bolts. Tighten alternator mounting bolts to 30 ft. lbs. (41 Nm).

> ✳✳ **CAUTION**
>
> **Never force a belt over a pulley rim using a screwdriver. The synthetic fiber of the belt can be damaged.**

> ✳✳ **CAUTION**
>
> **When installing a serpentine accessory drive belt, the belt must be routed correctly. The water pump may be rotating in the wrong direction if the belt is installed incorrectly, causing the engine to overheat.**

21. Install accessory serpentine drive belt.

22. Install air resonator box above EGR valve/solenoid.

23. Connect negative battery cable to battery.

24. Using a diagnostic scan tool, erase any previously recorded DTCs.

HEATED OXYGEN (HO2S) SENSOR

LOCATION

See Figure 197.

If equipped with a Federal Emission Package, two sensors are used: upstream (referred to as 1/1) and downstream (referred to as 1/2). With this emission package, the upstream sensor (1/1) is located just before the main catalytic converter. The downstream sensor (1/2) is located just after the main catalytic converter.

If equipped with a California Emission Package, 4 sensors are used: 2 upstream (referred to as 1/1 and 2/1) and 2 downstream (referred to as 1/2 and 2/2). With this emission package, the right upstream sensor (2/1) is located in the right exhaust downpipe just before the mini-catalytic converter. The left upstream sensor (1/1) is located in the left exhaust downpipe just before the mini-catalytic converter. The right downstream sensor (2/2) is located in the right exhaust downpipe just after the mini-catalytic converter, and before the main catalytic converter. The left downstream sensor (1/2) is located in the left exhaust downpipe just after the mini-catalytic converter, and before the main catalytic converter.

REMOVAL & INSTALLATION

1. Raise and safely support the vehicle.

2. Disconnect the wire connector from oxygen sensor.

> ✳✳ **WARNING**
>
> **When disconnecting sensor electrical connector, do not pull directly on wire going into sensor.**

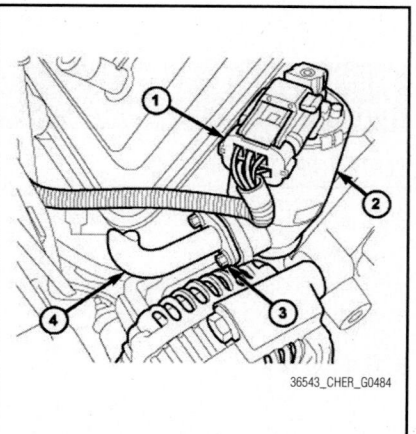

Fig. 195 Disconnect electrical connector (1) from EGR solenoid (2)

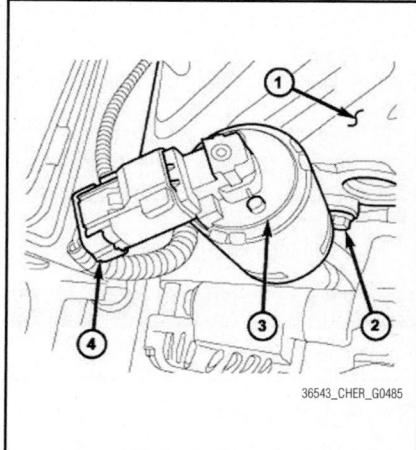

Fig. 196 Remove two mounting bolts (2)

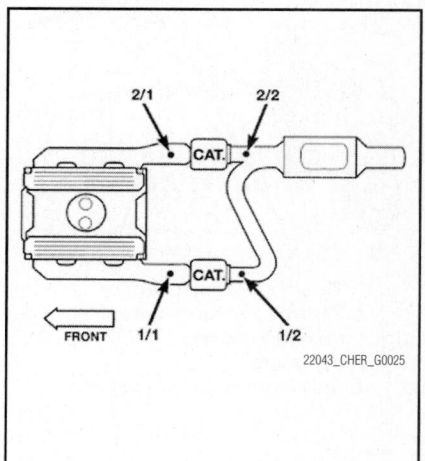

Fig. 197 Oxygen sensor mounting points

3. Remove the sensor with an oxygen sensor removal and installation tool.

4. Clean threads in exhaust pipe using appropriate tap.

To install:

➡Threads of new oxygen sensors are factory coated with anti-seize compound.

✳✳ WARNING

Do not add any additional anti-seize compound to the threads of a new oxygen sensor.

5. Install the oxygen sensor and tighten to 22 ft. lbs. (30 Nm).
6. Connect the electrical connector.
7. Lower the vehicle.

IDLE AIR CONTROL (IAC) VALVE

LOCATION

➡**An IAC valve/motor is not used with the 5.7L engine.**

The IAC motor is mounted to the throttle body.

REMOVAL & INSTALLATION

See Figure 198.

1. Remove air resonator box at throttle body.
2. Disconnect electrical connector from IAC motor.
3. Remove two mounting bolts (screws).
4. Remove IAC motor from throttle body.

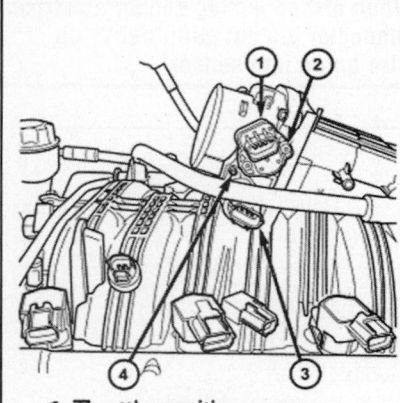

1. Throttle position sensor
2. Throttle position sensor mounting screw
3. IAC motor
4.: IAC motor mounting screw

22043_CHER_G0023

Fig. 198 IAC motor mounting

To install:

5. Install IAC motor to throttle body.
6. Install and tighten two mounting bolts (screws) to 60 inch lbs. (7 Nm).
7. Install electrical connector.
8. Install air resonator to throttle body.

INTAKE AIR TEMPERATURE (IAT) SENSOR

LOCATION

The Intake Air Temperature (IAT) sensor is installed in the air inlet tube.

REMOVAL & INSTALLATION

See Figure 199.

1. Disconnect the electrical connector form the Intake Air Temperature (IAT) sensor.
2. Clean any dirt from the air inlet tube at the sensor base.
3. Gently lift the small plastic release tab and rotate the sensor about ¼ turn counterclockwise to remove.

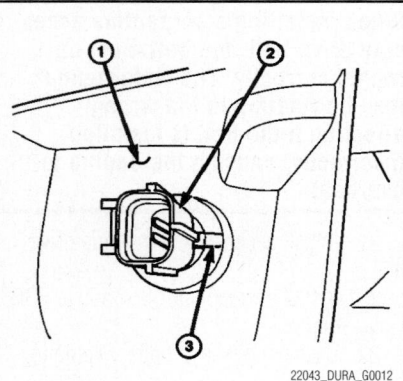

22043_DURA_G0012

Fig. 199 The IAT sensor (2) is located in the air inlet (1). Lift the tab (3) to remove it

To install:

4. Check the condition of the sensor O-ring.
5. Clean the sensor mounting hole.
6. Position the sensor into the intake air tube and rotate clockwise until the release tab clicks into place.
7. Install the electrical connector.

KNOCK SENSOR (KS)

LOCATION

3.7L & 4.7L Engines

Two Knock Sensors (KS) are bolted into the engine block under the intake manifold.

5.7L Engine

Two Knock Sensors (KS) are bolted into each side of the engine block under the exhaust manifolds.

REMOVAL & INSTALLATION

3.7L & 4.7L Engines

1. Disconnect the knock sensor dual pigtail harness from engine wiring harness. This connection is made near rear of engine.
2. Remove the intake manifold
3. Remove the Knock Sensor (KS) mounting bolts.
4. Remove the sensors from engine.

To install:

5. Thoroughly clean the KS mounting holes.
6. Install the sensors into the engine block. Tighten the mounting bolts to 15 ft. lbs. (20 Nm).
7. Install the intake manifold.
8. Connect the KS wiring harness to the engine wiring harness at the rear of the engine.

5.7L Engine

1. Raise and safely support the vehicle.
2. Disconnect the Knock Sensor (KS) electrical connector.
3. Remove the KS mounting bolt.
4. Remove the sensor from the engine.

To install:

5. Thoroughly clean the KS mounting holes.
6. Install the sensors into the engine block. Tighten the mounting bolts to 15 ft. lbs. (20 Nm).
7. Connect the KS electrical connectors.
8. Lower the vehicle.

MANIFOLD ABSOLUTE PRESSURE (MAP) SENSOR

LOCATION

3.7L & 4.7L Engines

The Manifold Absolute Pressure (MAP) sensor is mounted to the front of the intake manifold with two bolts.

5.7L Engine

The Manifold Absolute Pressure (MAP) sensor is mounted to the back of the intake manifold by a quarter turn fastener.

REMOVAL & INSTALLATION

3.7L & 4.7L Engines

See Figure 200.

1. Disconnect the sensor electrical connector.
2. Clean the area around the Manifold Absolute Pressure (MAP) sensor.
3. Remove the two mounting screws.
4. Remove the MAP sensor from the intake manifold.

To install:

5. Inspect the condition of the sensor O-ring and replace if necessary.
6. Position the MAP sensor into the manifold and install the two mounting screws.
7. Connect the electrical connector.

5.7L Engine

1. Disconnect the electrical connector at the Manifold Absolute Pressure (MAP) sensor by sliding the release lock out. Then press down on the lock tab.
2. Rotate the MAP sensor ¼ turn counter-clockwise to remove.

To install:

3. Inspect the condition of the sensor O-ring and replace if necessary.
4. Position the MAP sensor into the intake manifold and rotate ¼ turn clockwise.
5. Connect the electrical connector to the MAP sensor until it clicks into place.

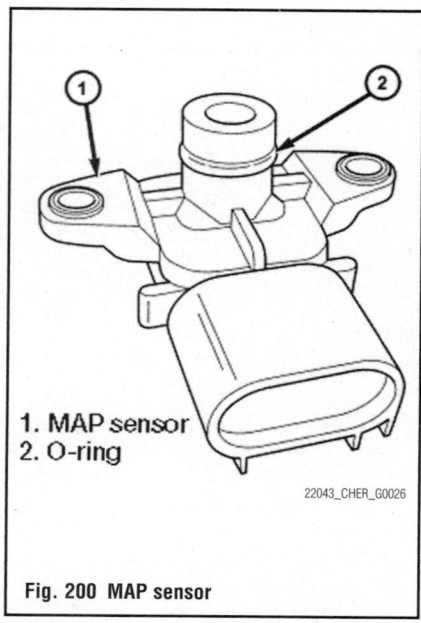

1. MAP sensor
2. O-ring

22043_CHER_G0026

Fig. 200 MAP sensor

OUTPUT SHAFT SPEED (OSS) SENSOR

LOCATION

NAG1 Transmission

The speed sensors, N2 and N3 are fixed to the shell of the electro-hydraulic control unit's lead frame via contact blades. The speed sensors are pressed against the transmission housing by a spring which is held against the valve housing of the shift plate. This ensures a defined distance between the speed sensors and the exciter ring.

45RFE/545RFE Transmission

The Input and Output Speed Sensors are two-wire magnetic pickup devices that generate AC signals as rotation occurs. They are mounted in the left side of the transmission case and are considered primary inputs to the Transmission Control Module (TCM).

REMOVAL & INSTALLATION

45RFE/545RFE Transmission

See Figure 201.

1. Raise vehicle.
2. Place a suitable fluid catch pan under the transmission.
3. Remove the wiring connector from the output speed sensor (1).
4. Remove the bolt holding the output speed sensor (1) to the transmission case.
5. Remove the output speed sensor (1) from the transmission case.

To install:

6. Install the output speed sensor into the transmission case.

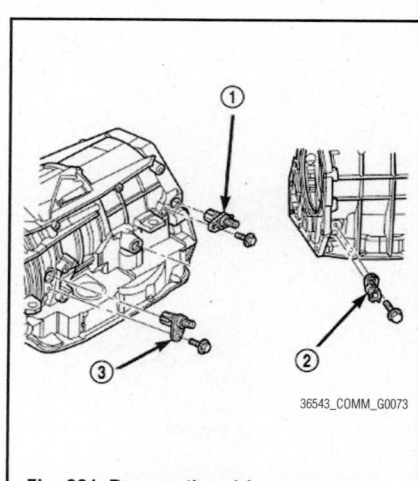

36543_COMM_G0073

Fig. 201 Remove the wiring connector from the output speed sensor (1)

7. Install the bolt to hold the output speed sensor into the transmission case. Tighten the bolt to 105 inch lbs. (12 Nm).
8. Install the wiring connector onto the output speed sensor.
9. Verify the transmission fluid level. Add fluid as necessary.
10. Lower vehicle.

POSITIVE CRANKCASE VENTILATION (PCV) VALVE

LOCATION

3.7L Engine

The PCV valve is located at the rear of the left cylinder head.

4.7L Engine

The PCV valve is mounted into the top/rear of the left valve cover.

5.7L Engine

The PCV valve is mounted into the top of the intake manifold. This is located to the right / rear of the throttle body.

REMOVAL & INSTALLATION

3.7L Engine

See Figures 202 and 203.

1. Remove the line (1) and rubber connector hose from the PCV valve.
2. Unthread the PCV valve (3) from the metal fitting (2).

To install:

3. Check the condition of PCV valve rubber O-ring.
4. Clean the fitting.
5. Install the PCV valve into fitting.

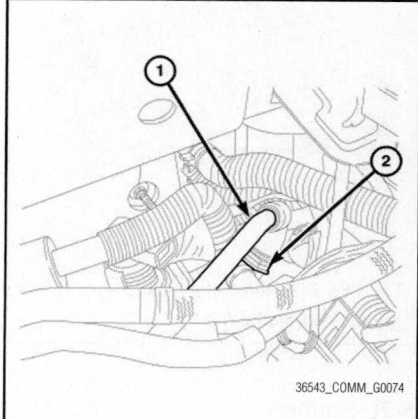

36543_COMM_G0074

Fig. 202 Remove the line (1) and rubber connector hose from the PCV valve

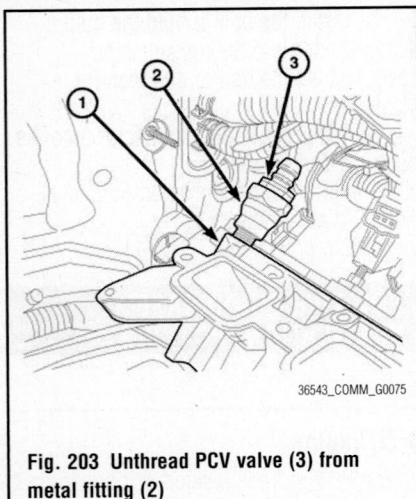

Fig. 203 Unthread PCV valve (3) from metal fitting (2)

6. Install the PCV line and rubber connector to valve.

4.7L Engine

See Figure 204.

1. Disconnect the plastic line (1) from end of the PCV valve (2).
2. Use a small screwdriver to disengage PCV valve from valve cover.

To install:

3. Clean out PCV valve opening at valve cover.
4. Check condition of PCV valve O-ring.
5. Apply engine oil to O-ring.
6. Place PCV valve into valve cover.
7. Attach plastic line to PCV valve.

Fig. 204 Disconnect the plastic line (1) from end of the PCV valve (2)

5.7L Engine

See Figure 205.

1. The PCV valve is sealed to the intake manifold with 2 O-rings (2).

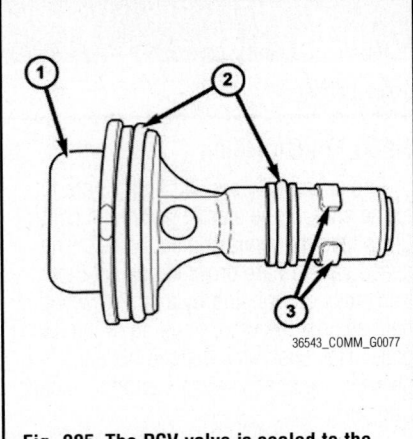

Fig. 205 The PCV valve is sealed to the intake manifold with 2 O-rings (2)

2. Remove PCV valve by rotating counter-clockwise 90 degrees until locating tabs (3) have been freed. After tabs have cleared, pull valve straight up from intake manifold.
3. After valve is removed, check condition of 2 valve O-rings (2).

To install:

4. Clean out intake manifold opening.
5. Check condition of two O-rings on PCV valve.
6. Apply engine oil to two O-rings.
7. Place PCV valve into intake manifold and rotate 90 degrees clockwise for installation.

POWERTRAIN CONTROL MODULE (PCM)

LOCATION

See Figure 206.

The PCM is attached to the right-front inner fender located in the engine compartment.

REMOVAL & INSTALLATION

See Figures 207 and 208.

➡ To avoid possible voltage spike damage to the PCM, ignition key must be off, and negative battery cable must be disconnected before unplugging PCM connectors.

1. Disconnect and isolate negative battery cable.
2. Carefully unplug the 38-way connectors (2) from PCM.
3. A locating pin (5) is used in place of one of the PCM mounting bolts. Pry clip (4) from pin (5).
4. Remove two PCM mounting bolts (2), and remove PCM from vehicle.
5. Position ground strap (3) to the side.

To install:

❄ CAUTION

Certain ABS systems rely on having the Powertrain Control Module (PCM) broadcast the Vehicle Identification Number (VIN) over the bus network. To prevent problems of DTCs and other items related to the VIN broadcast, it is recommend that you disconnect the ABS CAB (controller) temporarily when replacing the PCM. Once the PCM is replaced, write the VIN to the PCM using a diagnostic scan tool. This is done from the engine main menu. Arrow over to the second page to "1. Miscellaneous". Select "Check VIN" from the choices.

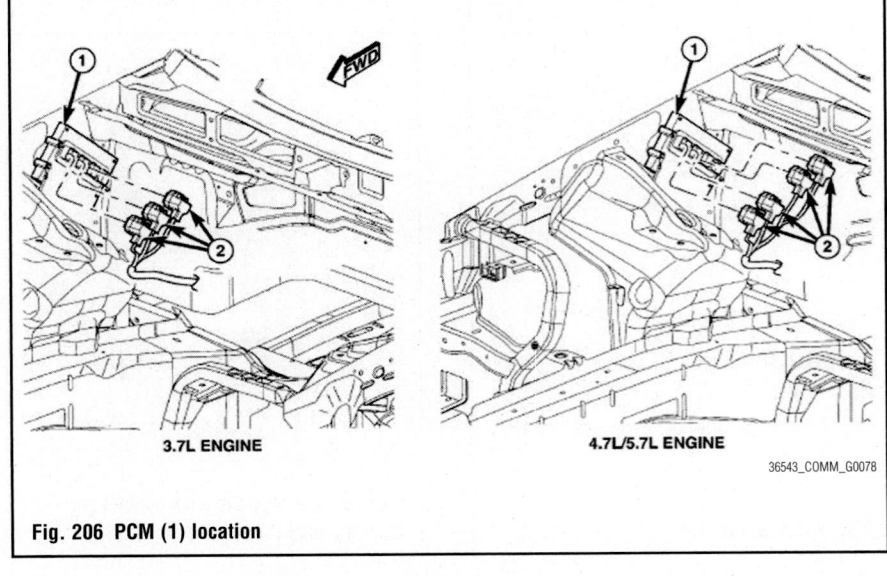

3.7L ENGINE

4.7L/5.7L ENGINE

Fig. 206 PCM (1) location

Make sure it has the correct VIN entered before continuing. When the VIN is complete, turn off the ignition key and reconnect the ABS module connector. This will prevent the setting of DTCs and other items associated with the lack of a VIN detected when you turn the key ON after replacing the PCM.

✳✳ CAUTION

Use a diagnostic scan tool to reprogram the new PCM with the vehicles original identification number (VIN)

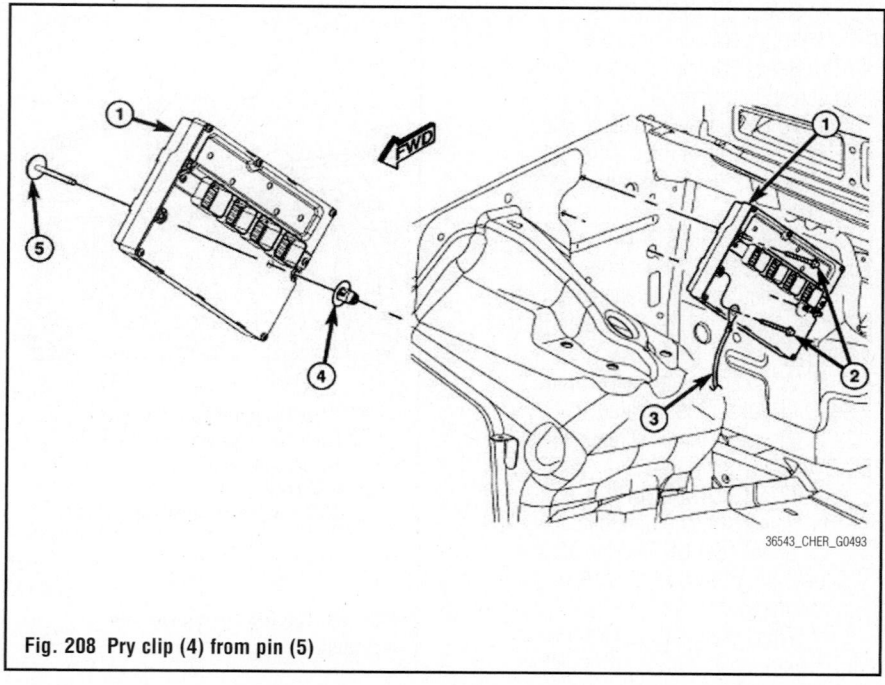

3.7L ENGINE

4.7L/5.7L ENGINE

36543_CHER_G0492

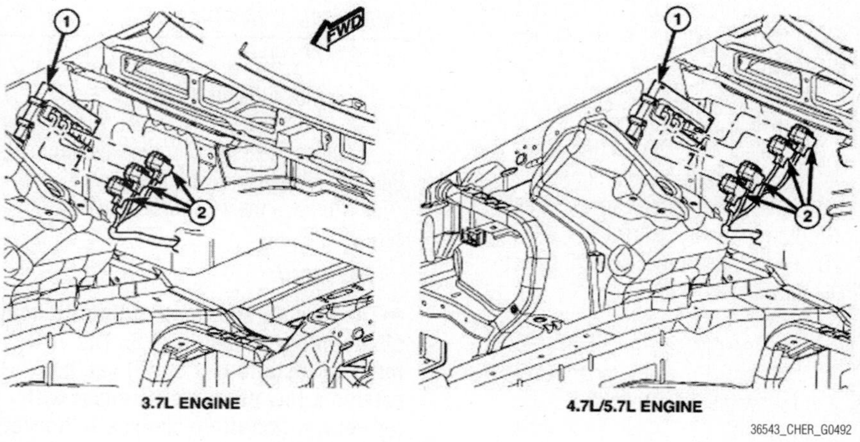

Fig. 207 Unplug the 38-way connectors (2) from PCM

Fig. 208 Pry clip (4) from pin (5)

36543_CHER_G0493

and the vehicles original mileage. If this step is not done, a Diagnostic Trouble Code (DTC) may be set.

6. Install clip to pin.

7. Position PCM to body and install two bolts. Be sure to position ground strap before installing bolt.

8. Check pin connectors in PCM. Also check the 38-way connectors for corrosion or damage. Repair as necessary.

9. Carefully plug the 38-way connectors into PCM.

10. Connect negative battery cable.

11. Use a diagnostic scan tool to reprogram new PCM with vehicles original identification number (VIN) and original vehicle mileage. If this step is not done, a Diagnostic Trouble Code (DTC) may be set.

Reset Procedure

This procedure will need to be done when one or more of the following situations are true:

1. A vehicle's Powertrain Control Module/Engine Control Module (PCM/ECM) has been replaced.

2. A diagnostic trouble code (DTC) is set P1602 - PCM/ECM Not Programmed.

3. An updated calibration or software release is available for either the PCM/ECM or TCM ECUs.

Check PCM/ECM VIN

4. From the "Home" screen, select "ECU View"

   a. Select "PCM/ECM"

   b. Select "Misc. Functions"

   c. Select "Check PCM/ECM VIN" and follow the on screen instructions.

   d. When complete, select "Finish"

Diesel Particulate Filter (Used) Learning

5. From the "Home" screen, select "ECU View"

   a. Select "PCM/ECM"

   b. Select "Misc. Functions"

   c. Select "Diesel Particulate Filter (Used) Learning" and follow the on screen instructions.

   d. When complete, select "Finish"

ECU Replacement with Value Transfer

6. From the "Home" screen, select "ECU View"

   a. Select "PCM/ECM"

   b. Select "Misc. Functions"

   c. Select "ECU Replacement with Value Transfer" and follow the on screen instructions.

   d. When complete, select "Finish"

ECU Replacement without Value Transfer

7. From the "Home" screen, select "ECU View"

   a. Select "PCM/ECM"

   b. Select "Misc. Functions"

   c. Select "ECU Replacement without Value Transfer" and follow the on screen instructions.

   d. When complete, select "Finish"

Enable / Disable Vehicle Features

8. From the "Home" screen, select "ECU View"

   a. Select "PCM/ECM"

b. Select "Misc. Functions"

c. Select "Enable / Disable Vehicle Features" and follow the on screen instructions.

d. When complete, select "Finish"

Exhaust Throttle Plate Adaptive Learn Position

9. From the "Home" screen, select "ECU View"

a. Select "PCM/ECM"

b. Select "Misc. Functions"

c. Select "Exhaust Throttle Plate Adaptive Learn Position" and follow the on screen instructions.

d. When complete, select "Finish"

Fuel Mean Value Adaptation Initialization

10. From the "Home" screen, select "ECU View"

a. Select "PCM/ECM"

b. Select "Misc. Functions"

c. Select "Fuel Mean Value Adaptation Initialization" and follow the on screen instructions.

d. When complete, select "Finish"

IMA Rapid Calibration

11. From the "Home" screen, select "ECU View"

a. Select "PCM/ECM"

b. Select "Misc. Functions"

c. Select "IMA Rapid Calibration Test" and follow the on screen instructions.

d. When complete, select "Finish"

Initialize EGS

12. From the "Home" screen, select "ECU View"

a. Select "PCM/ECM"

b. Select "Misc. Functions"

c. Select "Initialize EGS" and follow the on screen instructions.

d. When complete, select "Finish"

Injector Quantity Adjustment

13. From the "Home" screen, select "ECU View"

a. Select "PCM/ECM"

b. Select "Misc. Functions"

c. Select "Injector Quantity Adjustment" and follow the on screen instructions.

d. When complete, select "Finish"

Mobile DeSoot - NO Minimum Required Soot Load

14. From the "Home" screen, select "ECU View"

a. Select "PCM/ECM"

b. Select "Misc. Functions"

c. Select "Mobile DeSoot - NO Minimum Required Soot Load" and follow the on screen instructions.

d. When complete, select "Finish" NOx Catalyst (New) Initialization

15. From the "Home" screen, select "ECU View"

a. Select "PCM/ECM"

b. Select "Misc. Functions"

c. Select "NOx Catalyst (New) Initialization" and follow the on screen instructions.

d. When complete, select "Finish"

PCM/ECM Replaced

The vehicle pin (Personal Identification Number) will be required to complete the routine. This information may be obtained in three ways:

16. The original selling invoice

17. Dealer CONNECT> Parts> Key Codes

18. Contacting the District Manager.

19. From the "Home" screen, select "ECU View"

a. Select "WIN"

b. Select "Misc. Functions"

c. Select "PCM/ECM Replaced" and follow the on screen instructions.

d. When complete, select "Finish"

Program Variant Code

20. From the "Home" screen, select "ECU View"

a. Select "PCM/ECM"

b. Select "Misc. Functions"

c. Select "Program Variant Code" and follow the on screen instructions.

d. When complete, select "Finish"

Quicklearn

21. From the "Home" screen, select "ECU View"

a. Select "PCM/ECM"

b. Select "Misc. Functions"

c. Select "Quicklearn" and follow the on screen instructions.

d. When complete, select "Finish"

Reset Regenerative Filter Timers

22. From the "Home" screen, select "ECU View"

a. Select "PCM/ECM"

b. Select "Misc. Functions"

c. Select "Reset Regenerative Filter Times" and follow the on screen instructions.

d. When complete, select "Finish"

Set Oil Dilution Mass Value

23. From the "Home" screen, select "ECU View"

a. Select "PCM/ECM"

b. Select "Misc. Functions"

c. Select "Set Oil Dilution Mass Value" and follow the on screen instructions.

d. When complete, select "Finish"

THROTTLE POSITION SENSOR (TPS)

LOCATION

3.7L & 4.7L Engines

The Throttle Position Sensor (TPS) is mounted on the throttle body and connected to the throttle blade shaft.

5.7L Engine

The 5.7L engine does not use a separate Throttle Position Sensor (TPS) on the throttle body. If it is determined, that the TPS signal is bad, the throttle body assembly must be replaced.

REMOVAL & INSTALLATION

See Figure 209.

1. Remove the air intake tube.

2. Disconnect the Throttle Position Sensor (TPS) electrical connector.

3. Remove the TPS mounting screws.

To install:

➡**The throttle shaft end of throttle body slides into a socket in TPS. The TPS must be installed so that it can be rotated a few degrees. If sensor will not rotate, install the sensor with throttle shaft on other side of socket tangs. The TPS will be under slight tension when rotated.**

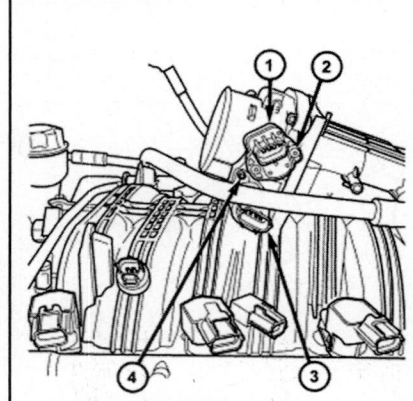

1. Throttle position sensor
2. Throttle position sensor mounting screw
3. IAC motor
4.: IAC motor mounting screw

22043_CHER_G0023

Fig. 209 Throttle position sensor mounting

5. Install the TPS and tighten the mounting screws to 60 inch lbs. (7 Nm).

6. Connect the TPS electrical connector.

7. Manually operate the throttle by hand to check for any TPS binding before starting the engine.

8. Install the air intake tube.

VEHICLE SPEED SENSOR (VSS)

REMOVAL & INSTALLATION

1. Raise and safely support the vehicle.

2. Place a suitable catch pan under the transmission for any fluid.

3. Remove the wiring connector from the output speed sensor.

4. Remove the mounting bolt and remove the speed sensor from the transmission case.

To install:

5. Install the speed sensor into the transmission case and tighten the bolt to 105 inch lbs. (12 Nm).

6. Install the wiring connector to the speed sensor.

7. Verify the proper transmission fluid level and refill as necessary.

8. Lower the vehicle.

FUEL   GASOLINE FUEL INJECTION SYSTEM

FUEL SYSTEM SERVICE PRECAUTIONS

✳✳ WARNING

High-pressure fuel lines deliver fuel under extreme pressure from the injection pump to the injectors. This may be as high as 19,580 psi (1350 bar). Use extreme caution when inspecting for high-pressure fuel leaks. Inspect high-pressure fuel leaks with a sheet of cardboard. Wear safety goggles and adequate protective clothing when servicing fuel system. Fuel under this amount of pressure can penetrate skin causing serious or fatal injury.

Safety is the most important factor when performing not only fuel system maintenance but any type of maintenance. Failure to conduct maintenance and repairs in a safe manner may result in serious personal injury or death. Maintenance and testing of the vehicle's fuel system components can be accomplished safely and effectively by adhering to the following rules and guidelines.

• To avoid the possibility of fire and personal injury, always disconnect the negative battery cable unless the repair or test procedure requires that battery voltage be applied.

• Always relieve the fuel system pressure prior to disconnecting any fuel system component (injector, fuel rail, pressure regulator, etc.), fitting or fuel line connection. Exercise extreme caution whenever relieving fuel system pressure to avoid exposing skin, face and eyes to fuel spray. Please be advised that fuel under pressure may penetrate the skin or any part of the body that it contacts.

• Always place a shop towel or cloth around the fitting or connection prior to loosening to absorb any excess fuel due to spillage. Ensure that all fuel spillage (should it occur) is quickly removed from

engine surfaces. Ensure that all fuel soaked cloths or towels are deposited into a suitable waste container.

• Always keep a dry chemical (Class B) fire extinguisher near the work area.

• Do not allow fuel spray or fuel vapors to come into contact with a spark or open flame.

• Always use a back-up wrench when loosening and tightening fuel line connection fittings. This will prevent unnecessary stress and torsion to fuel line piping.

• Always replace worn fuel fitting O-rings with new. Do not substitute fuel hose or equivalent where fuel pipe is installed.

RELIEVING FUEL SYSTEM PRESSURE

Use following procedure if the fuel injector rail is, or is not equipped with a fuel pressure test port.

1. Remove fuel fill cap.

2. Remove fuel pump relay from Power Distribution Center (PDC). For location of relay, refer to label on underside of PDC cover.

3. Start and run engine until it stalls.

4. Attempt restarting engine until it will no longer run.

5. Turn ignition key to OFF position.

✳✳ CAUTION

Steps 1, 2, 3, and 4 must be performed to relieve high pressure fuel from within fuel rail. Do not attempt to use following steps to relieve this pressure as excessive fuel will be forced into a cylinder chamber.

6. Unplug connector from any fuel injector.

7. Attach one end of a jumper wire with alligator clips (18 gauge or smaller) to either injector terminal.

8. Connect other end of jumper wire to positive side of battery.

9. Connect one end of a second jumper wire to remaining injector terminal.

✳✳ CAUTION

Powering an injector for more than a few seconds will permanently damage the injector.

10. Momentarily touch other end of jumper wire to negative terminal of battery for no more than a few seconds.

11. Place a rag or towel below fuel line quick-connect fitting at fuel rail.

12. Disconnect quick-connect fitting at fuel rail.

13. Return fuel pump relay to PDC.

14. One or more Diagnostic Trouble Codes (DTC's) may have been stored in Powertrain Control Module (PCM) memory due to fuel pump relay removal. A diagnostic scan tool must be used to erase a DTC.

FUEL FILTER

REMOVAL & INSTALLATION

Two fuel filters are used. One is located at the bottom of the fuel pump module. The other is located inside the module. A separate frame mounted fuel filter is not used with any engine.

Both fuel filters are designed for extended service. They do not require normal scheduled maintenance. Filters should only be replaced if a diagnostic procedure indicates to do so.

FUEL PUMP MODULE

REMOVAL & INSTALLATION

See Figure 210.

✳✳ WARNING

The fuel system is under a constant pressure, even with the engine off. Before servicing the fuel system, the fuel pressure must be released.

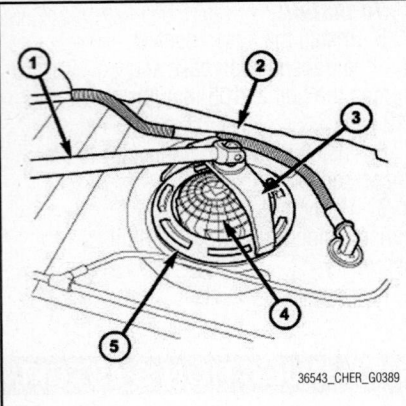

Fig. 210 Position SAE Fuel Pump Lock Ring Wrench 9340 (3)

1. Perform the fuel pressure release procedure.
2. Disconnect the negative battery cable.
3. Drain and remove fuel tank.
4. Note rotational position of module before attempting removal. An indexing arrow is located on top of module for this purpose.
5. Position SAE Fuel Pump Lock Ring Wrench 9340 (3) into notches on outside edge of lockring (5).
6. Install ½ inch drive breaker bar (1) to SAE Fuel Pump Lock Ring Wrench 9340 (3).
7. Rotate breaker bar counter-clockwise to remove lockring.
8. Remove lockring. The module will spring up slightly when lockring is removed.
9. Remove module from fuel tank. Be careful not to bend float arm while removing.

To install:

➡ **Whenever the fuel pump module is serviced, the module seal must be replaced.**

10. Using a new seal, position fuel pump module into opening in fuel tank.
11. Position lockring over top of fuel pump module.
12. Rotate module until embossed alignment arrow points to center alignment mark. This step must be performed to prevent float from contacting side of fuel tank. Also be sure fuel fitting on top of pump module is pointed to driver's side of vehicle.
13. Install SAE Fuel Pump Lock Ring Wrench 9340 to lockring.
14. Tighten lockring until all seven notches have engaged.
15. Install fuel tank.

FUEL RAIL & INJECTORS

REMOVAL & INSTALLATION

3.7L Engine
See Figures 211 and 212.

❄❄ WARNING

The fuel system is under constant pressure even with engine off. Before servicing the fuel rail, fuel system pressure must be released.

❄❄ CAUTION

The left and right fuel rails are replaced as an assembly. Do not attempt to separate rail halves at connector tubes. Due to design of tubes, it does not use any clamps. Never attempt to install a clamping device of any kind to tubes. When removing fuel rail assembly for any reason, be careful not to bend or kink tubes.

1. Remove fuel tank filler tube cap.
2. Perform Fuel System Pressure Release Procedure.
3. Remove negative battery cable at battery.
4. Remove air duct at throttle body air box.
5. Remove air box at throttle body.
6. Remove air resonator mounting bracket at front of throttle body (2 bolts).
7. Disconnect fuel line latch clip and fuel line at fuel rail. A tool, Snap-On number FIH 9055-1 or equivalent, will be necessary for fuel line disconnection.
8. Remove necessary vacuum lines at throttle body.

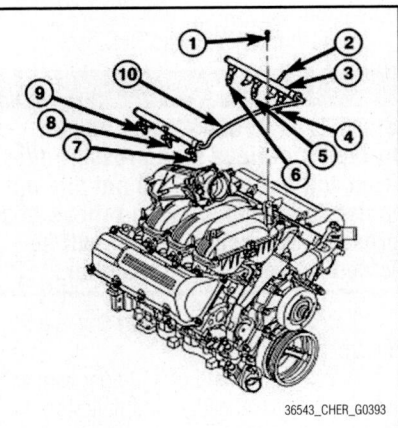

Fig. 211 Remove four fuel rail mounting bolts (1)

9. Disconnect electrical connectors at all 6 fuel injectors. Push red colored slider away from injector. While pushing slider, depress tab and remove connector from injector. The factory fuel injection wiring harness is numerically tagged (INJ 1, INJ 2, etc.) for injector position identification. If harness is not tagged, note wiring location before removal.
10. Disconnect electrical connectors at all throttle body sensors.
11. Remove 6 ignition coils.
12. Remove four fuel rail mounting bolts (1).
13. Gently rock and pull left side of fuel rail until fuel injectors just start to clear machined holes in cylinder head. Gently rock and pull right side of rail until injectors just start to clear cylinder head holes. Repeat this procedure (left/right) until all injectors have cleared cylinder head holes.
14. Remove fuel rail (with injectors attached) from engine.
15. Using suitable pliers, remove the fuel injector retaining clip (2).
16. Remove the fuel injector (3) from the fuel rail (4) using a side to side motion while pulling the injector out of the fuel rail assembly.

To install:

➡ **If the same fuel injector is to be rein-stalled, install new O-rings.**

➡ **Apply a small amount of clean engine oil to each injector O-ring. This will aid in the installation.**

17. Install the fuel injector into the fuel rail using a side to side motion while pushing injector into the fuel rail assembly.
18. Using suitable pliers, install the fuel injector retaining clip.

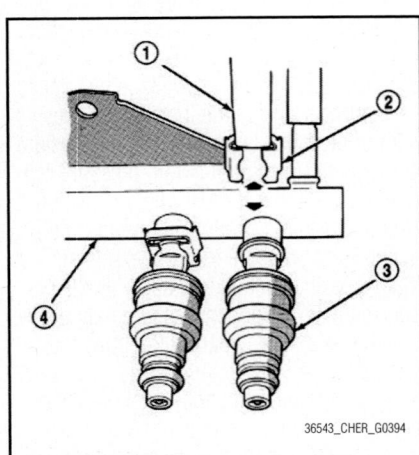

Fig. 212 Remove the fuel injector retaining clip (2)

19. Clean out fuel injector machined bores in intake manifold.

20. Apply a small amount of engine oil to each fuel injector O-ring. This will help in fuel rail installation.

21. Position fuel rail/fuel injector assembly to machined injector openings in cylinder head.

22. Guide each injector into cylinder head. Be careful not to tear injector O-rings.

23. Push right side of fuel rail down until fuel injectors have bottomed on cylinder head shoulder. Push left fuel rail down until injectors have bottomed on cylinder head shoulder.

24. Install 4 fuel rail mounting bolts and tighten. Tighten to 100 inch lbs. (11 Nm).

25. Install 6 ignition coils.

26. Connect electrical connectors to throttle body.

27. Connect electrical connectors at all fuel injectors. Push connector onto injector and then push and lock red colored slider. Verify connector is locked to injector by lightly tugging on connector.

28. Connect necessary vacuum lines to throttle body.

29. Install air resonator mounting bracket near front of throttle body (2 bolts).

30. Connect fuel line latch clip and fuel line to fuel rail.

31. Install air box to throttle body.

32. Install air duct to air box.

33. Connect battery cable to battery.

34. Start engine and check for leaks.

4.7L Engine

See Figures 212 and 213.

✳✳ WARNING

The fuel system is under constant pressure even with engine off. Before servicing the fuel rail, fuel system pressure must be released.

✳✳ CAUTION

The left and right fuel rails are replaced as an assembly. Do not attempt to separate rail halves at connector tubes. Due to design of tubes, it does not use any clamps. Never attempt to install a clamping device of any kind to tubes. When removing fuel rail assembly for any reason, be careful not to bend or kink tubes.

1. Remove fuel tank filler tube cap.
2. Perform Fuel System Pressure Release Procedure.

3. Remove negative battery cable at battery.

4. Remove air duct at throttle body air box.

5. Remove air box at throttle body.

6. Remove air resonator mounting bracket at front of throttle body (2 bolts).

7. Disconnect fuel line latch clip and fuel line at fuel rail . A tool will be necessary for fuel line disconnection.

8. Remove necessary vacuum lines at throttle body.

9. Disconnect electrical connectors at all 8 fuel injectors. Push red colored slider away from injector. While pushing slider, depress tab and remove connector from injector. The factory fuel injection wiring harness is numerically tagged (INJ 1, INJ 2, etc.) for injector position identification. If harness is not tagged, note wiring location before removal.

10. Disconnect electrical connectors at all throttle body sensors.

11. Remove 8 ignition coils.

12. Remove 4 fuel rail mounting bolts.

13. Gently rock and pull left side of fuel rail until fuel injectors just start to clear machined holes in cylinder head. Gently rock and pull right side of rail until injectors just start to clear cylinder head holes. Repeat this procedure (left/right) until all injectors have cleared cylinder head holes.

14. Remove fuel rail (with injectors attached) from engine.

15. Using suitable pliers, remove the fuel injector retaining clip.

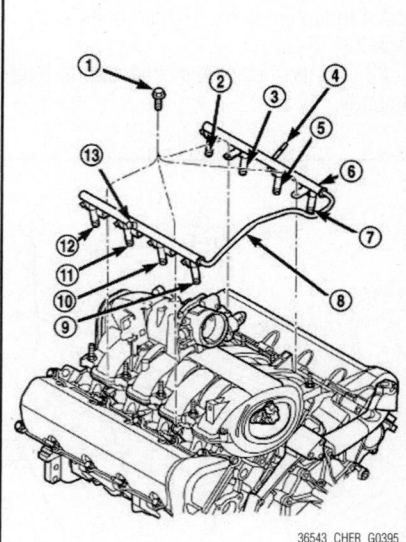

Fig. 213 Remove 4 fuel rail mounting bolts (1)

16. Remove the fuel injector (3) from the fuel rail (4) using a side to side motion while pulling the injector out of the fuel rail assembly.

To install:

➡ If the same fuel injector is to be reinstalled, install new O-rings.

➡ Apply a small amount of clean engine oil to each injector O-ring. This will aid in the installation.

17. Install the fuel injector into the fuel rail using a side to side motion while pushing injector into the fuel rail assembly.

18. Using suitable pliers, install the fuel injector retaining clip.

19. Clean out fuel injector machined bores in intake manifold.

20. Apply a small amount of engine oil to each fuel injector O-ring. This will help in fuel rail installation.

21. Position fuel rail/fuel injector assembly to machined injector openings in cylinder head.

22. Guide each injector into cylinder head. Be careful not to tear injector O-rings.

23. Push right side of fuel rail down until fuel injectors have bottomed on cylinder head shoulder. Push left fuel rail down until injectors have bottomed on cylinder head shoulder.

24. Install 4 fuel rail mounting bolts and tighten. Tighten to 100 inch lbs. (11 Nm).

25. Install 8 ignition coils.

26. Connect electrical connectors to throttle body.

27. Connect electrical connectors at fuel injectors. Push connector onto injector and then push and lock red colored slider. Verify connector is locked to injector by lightly tugging on connector.

28. Connect necessary vacuum lines to throttle body.

29. Install air resonator mounting bracket near front of throttle body (2 bolts).

30. Connect fuel line latch clip and fuel line to fuel rail.

31. Install air box to throttle body.

32. Install air duct to air box.

33. Connect battery cable to battery.

34. Start engine and check for leaks.

5.7L Engine

See Figures 212 and 214.

✳✳ WARNING

The fuel system is under constant pressure even with engine off. Before servicing the fuel rail, fuel system pressure must be released.

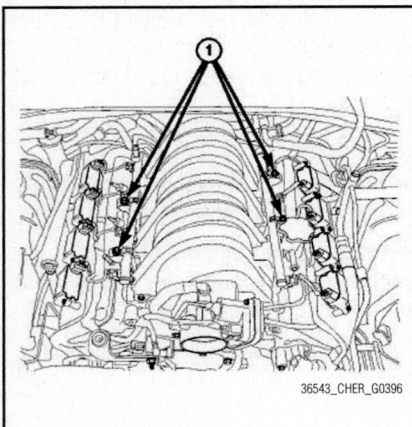

Fig. 214 Remove four fuel rail mounting bolts (1) and hold-down clamps

✳✳ CAUTION

The left and right fuel rails are replaced as an assembly. Do not attempt to separate rail halves at connector tube. Due to design of tube, it does not use any clamps. Never attempt to install a clamping device of any kind to tube. When removing fuel rail assembly for any reason, be careful not to bend or kink tube.

1. Remove fuel tank filler tube cap.
2. Perform fuel system pressure release procedure.
3. Remove negative battery cable at battery.
4. Remove flex tube (air cleaner housing to engine).
5. Remove air resonator box at throttle body.
6. Disconnect electrical connectors at all 8 fuel injectors. Push red colored slider away from injector. While pushing slider, depress tab and remove connector from injector. The factory fuel injection wiring harness is numerically tagged (INJ 1, INJ 2, etc.) for injector position identification. If harness is not tagged, note wiring location before removal.
7. Disconnect electrical connectors at all throttle body sensors.
8. Disconnect fuel supply tube quick connect fitting at the fuel rail.
9. Remove four fuel rail mounting bolts and hold-down clamps.
10. Gently rock and pull left side of fuel rail until fuel injectors just start to clear machined holes in intake manifold. Gently rock and pull right side of rail until injectors just start to clear intake manifold head holes. Repeat this procedure (left/right) until

all injectors have cleared machined holes.
11. Remove fuel rail (with injectors attached) from engine.
12. Using suitable pliers, remove the fuel injector retaining clip.
13. Remove the fuel injector (3) from the fuel rail (4) using a side to side motion while pulling the injector out of the fuel rail assembly.

To install:

➡If the same fuel injector is to be reinstalled, install new O-rings.

➡Apply a small amount of clean engine oil to each injector O-ring. This will aid in the installation.

14. Install the fuel injector into the fuel rail using a side to side motion while pushing injector into the fuel rail assembly.
15. Using suitable pliers, install the fuel injector retaining clip.
16. Clean out fuel injector machined bores in intake manifold.
17. Apply a small amount of engine oil to each fuel injector O-ring. This will help in fuel rail installation.
18. Position fuel rail/fuel injector assembly to machined injector openings in intake manifold.
19. Guide each injector into intake manifold. Be careful not to tear injector O-rings.
20. Push right side of fuel rail down until fuel injectors have bottomed on shoulders. Push left fuel rail down until injectors have bottomed on shoulders.
21. Install 4 fuel rail hold-down clamps and 4 mounting bolts. Tighten bolts to 71 inch lbs. (8 Nm).
22. Connect electrical connector to throttle body.

23. Connect electrical connectors at all fuel injectors. Push connector onto injector and then push and lock red colored slider. Verify connector is locked to injector by lightly tugging on connector.
24. Connect fuel line latch clip and fuel line to fuel rail.
25. Install air resonator to throttle body (2 bolts).
26. Install flexible air duct to air box.
27. Connect battery cable to battery.
28. Start engine and check for leaks.

FUEL TANK

REMOVAL & INSTALLATION

See Figures 215 through 217.

1. Release fuel system pressure.
2. Drain fuel tank.
3. Loosen clamp (9) and disconnect rubber fill hose (3) at tank fitting (7).
4. At rear of tank, disconnect fuel pump module electrical jumper connector (5) from body connector (6).
5. At rear of tank, disconnect EVAP lines (2) and (3) from lines (1) and (4).
6. At front of tank, disconnect fuel and EVAP lines (9) and (10) from lines (11) and (12).
7. Support tank with a hydraulic jack.
8. Remove bolts (1) and (2) at right side of fuel tank.
9. Remove bolts (3) at left side of fuel tank.
10. Lower tank for removal.
11. If fuel tank is to be replaced, remove fuel pump module from tank.

To install:

12. Position fuel tank to hydraulic jack.
13. Raise tank until positioned to body.

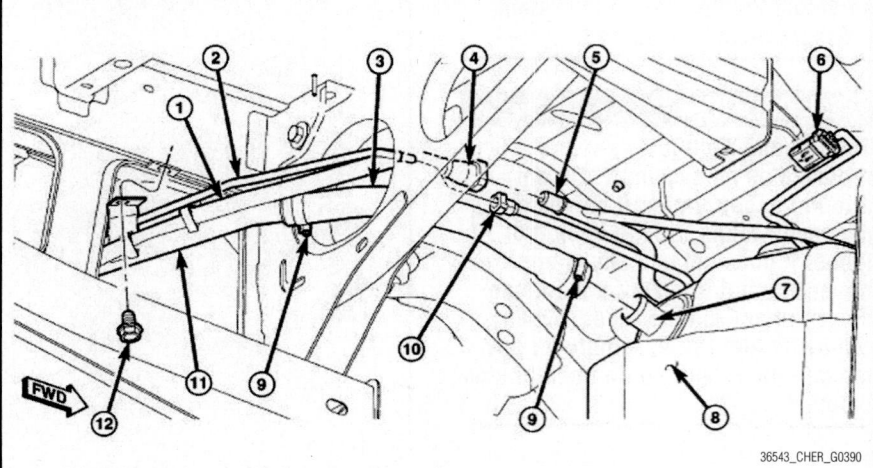

Fig. 215 Loosen clamp (9) and disconnect rubber fill hose (3) at tank fitting (7)

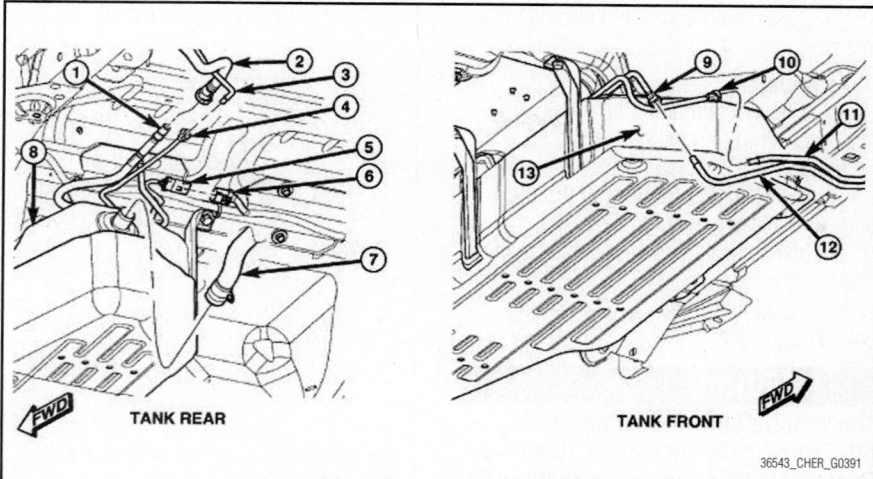

Fig. 216 Disconnect fuel pump module electrical jumper connector (5) from body connector (6)

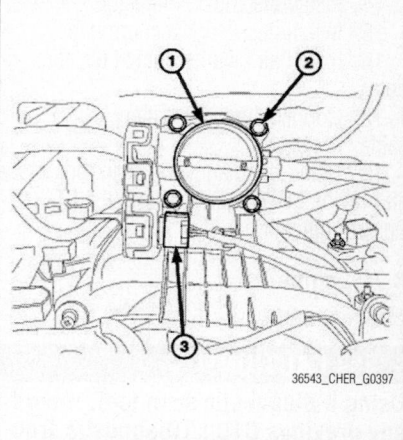

Fig. 218 Remove air intake tube at throttle body flange (1)

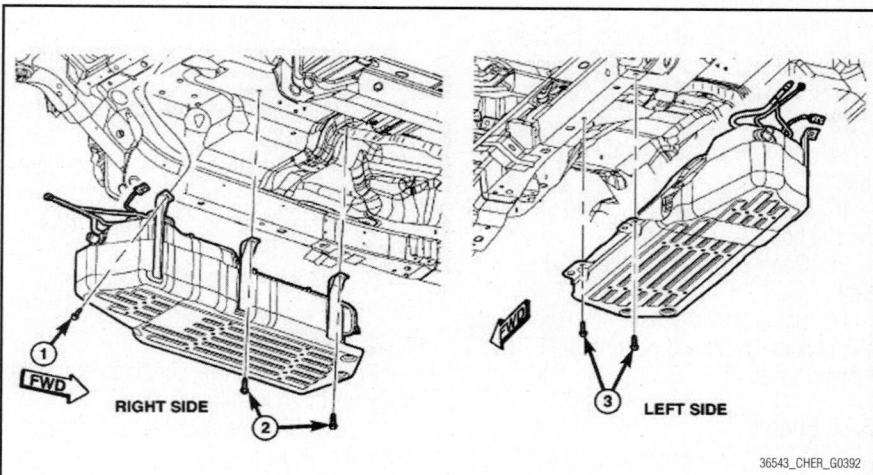

Fig. 217 Remove bolts (1) and (2) at right side of fuel tank

14. Install fuel tank mounting bolts and tighten to 50 ft. lbs. (68 Nm).

15. Remove hydraulic jack.

16. Connect EVAP, ORVR, fuel and NVLD lines at front and rear of tank.

17. Connect fuel pump module electrical jumper connector to body connector.

18. Connect rubber fill hose to tank fitting and tighten clamp.

19. Lower vehicle.

20. Fill fuel tank with fuel.

21. Start engine and check for fuel leaks near top of module.

IDLE SPEED

ADJUSTMENT

Idle speed is controlled by the Powertrain Control Module (PCM). No adjustment is necessary or possible. If idle speed is not within proper range, the PCM should be replaced.

THROTTLE BODY

REMOVAL & INSTALLATION

3.7L Engine

See Figure 218.

✷✷ CAUTION

Using a diagnostic scan tool, record any previous DTC's (Diagnostic Trouble Codes).

✷✷ CAUTION

Never have the ignition key in the ON position when checking the throttle body shaft for a binding condition. This may set DTC's.

A (factory adjusted) set screw is used to mechanically limit the position of the throttle body throttle plate. Never attempt to

adjust the engine idle speed using this screw. All idle speed functions are controlled by the Powertrain Control Module (PCM).

1. Disconnect and isolate negative battery cable at battery.

2. Remove air intake tube at throttle body flange (1).

3. Disconnect throttle body electrical connector (3).

4. Disconnect necessary vacuum lines at throttle body.

5. Remove four throttle body mounting bolts (2).

6. Remove throttle body from intake manifold.

7. Check condition of old throttle body-to-intake manifold O-ring.

To install:

8. Check condition of throttle body-to-intake manifold O-ring. Replace as necessary.

9. Clean mating surfaces of throttle body and intake manifold.

10. Install O-ring between throttle body and intake manifold.

11. Position throttle body to intake manifold.

12. Install all throttle body mounting bolts finger tight.

✷✷ CAUTION

The throttle body mounting bolts MUST be tightened to specifications. Over tightening can cause damage to the throttle body or the intake manifold.

13. Tighten mounting bolts in a mandatory torque criss-cross pattern sequence to 65 inch lbs. (7.5 Nm).

14. Install electrical connector.
15. Install necessary vacuum lines.
16. Install air cleaner duct at throttle body.
17. Connect negative battery cable.
18. Using the diagnostic scan tool, erase all previous DTC's and perform the ETC Relearn function.

4.7L Engine

See Figure 219.

> ※※ **CAUTION**
>
> **Using a diagnostic scan tool, record any previous DTC's (Diagnostic Trouble Codes).**

> ※※ **CAUTION**
>
> **Never have the ignition key in the ON position when checking the throttle body shaft for a binding condition. This may set DTC's.**

1. Disconnect and isolate negative battery cable at battery.
2. Remove air duct and air resonator box at throttle body (3).
3. Disconnect throttle body electrical connector (2).
4. Disconnect necessary vacuum lines at throttle body.
5. Remove four throttle body mounting bolts (1).
6. Remove throttle body from intake manifold.

Fig. 219 Remove air duct and air resonator box at throttle body (3)

7. Check condition of old throttle body-to-intake manifold O-ring.

To install:

8. Check condition of throttle body-to-intake manifold O-ring. Replace as necessary.
9. Clean mating surfaces of throttle body and intake manifold.
10. Install throttle body-to-intake manifold O-ring.
11. Install all throttle body mounting bolts finger tight.

> ※※ **CAUTION**
>
> **The throttle body mounting bolts MUST be tightened to specifications. Over tightening can cause damage to the throttle body or the intake manifold.**

12. Tighten mounting bolts in a mandatory torque criss-cross pattern sequence to 65 inch lbs. (7.5 Nm).
13. Install electrical connector.
14. Install necessary vacuum lines.
15. Install air cleaner duct and plenum at throttle body.
16. Connect negative battery cable.
17. Using the diagnostic scan tool, erase all previous DTC's and perform the ETC Relearn function.

5.7L Engine

See Figures 220 and 221.

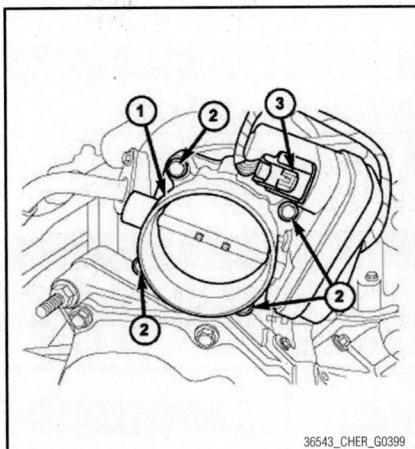

Fig. 220 Disconnect electrical connector at throttle body (3)

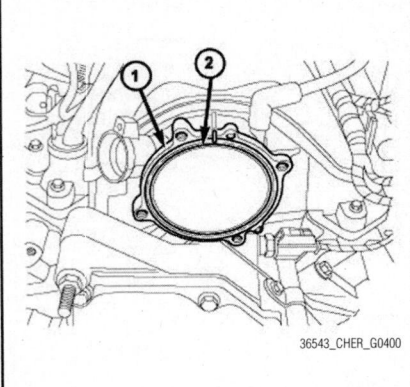

Fig. 221 Check condition of throttle body O-ring (2)

1. Disconnect and isolate negative battery cable from battery.
2. Remove air duct and air resonator box at throttle body.
3. Disconnect electrical connector at throttle body (3).
4. Remove four throttle body mounting bolts (2).
5. Remove throttle body from intake manifold.
6. Check condition of throttle body O-ring (2).

To install:

7. Clean and check condition of throttle body-to-intake manifold O-ring.
8. Clean mating surfaces of throttle body and intake manifold.
9. Install throttle body to intake manifold by positioning throttle body to manifold alignment pins.
10. Install all throttle body mounting bolts finger tight.

> ※※ **CAUTION**
>
> **The throttle body mounting bolts MUST be tightened to specifications. Over tightening can cause damage to the throttle body or the intake manifold.**

11. Tighten mounting bolts in a mandatory torque criss-cross pattern sequence to 50 inch lbs. (5.6 Nm).
12. Install electrical connector.
13. Install air plenum to flange.
14. Connect negative battery cable.
15. Using the diagnostic scan tool, perform the ETC Relearn function.

HEATING & AIR CONDITIONING SYSTEM

BLOWER MOTOR

REMOVAL & INSTALLATION

See Figure 222.

1. Disconnect and isolate the negative battery cable.
2. If equipped, remove the instrument panel silencer from the passenger side of the instrument panel.
3. Remove the glove box from the instrument panel.
4. Disconnect the blower motor wire harness connector (1) from the blower motor power module or resistor (2), depending on how equipped.
5. Remove the three screws (3) that secure the blower motor (4) to the HVAC housing (5).
6. Remove the blower motor from the HVAC housing.

To install:

7. Position the blower motor into the HVAC housing.
8. Install the three screws that secure the blower motor to the HVAC housing.
9. Connect the wire harness connector to the blower motor power module or resistor, depending on how equipped.
10. Install the glove box into the instrument panel.
11. If equipped, install the instrument panel silencer onto the passenger side of the instrument panel.
12. Reconnect the negative battery cable.

HEATER CORE

REMOVAL & INSTALLATION

See Figures 223 and 224.

> **✳✳ WARNING**
>
> **Refer to the applicable warnings and cautions for this system before performing the following operation. Failure to follow these instructions may result in possible serious or fatal injury.**

> **✳✳ WARNING**
>
> **Disable the airbag system before attempting any steering wheel, steering column or instrument panel component diagnosis or service. Disconnect and isolate the negative battery (ground) cable, then wait two minutes for the airbag system capacitor to discharge before performing further diagnosis or service. This is the only sure way to disable the airbag system. Failure to follow these instructions may result in accidental airbag deployment and possible serious or fatal injury.**

➡ **Take the proper precautions to protect the front face of the instrument panel from cosmetic damage while performing this procedure.**

1. Drain the engine cooling system.
2. Disconnect and isolate the negative battery cable.
3. If required, disconnect the heater hoses from the heater core tubes in the engine compartment.

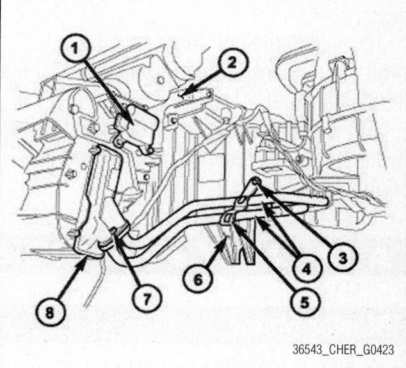

Fig. 224 Remove the blend door actuator (1) from the passenger side of the HVAC air distribution housing (2)

4. Remove the instrument panel.
5. Remove the five screws (1) that secure the heater core and tube cover (2) to the HVAC housing (3).
6. Remove the heater core and tube cover from the HVAC housing.
7. If equipped with dual zone heating-A/C, remove the blend door actuator (1) from the passenger side of the HVAC air distribution housing (2).
8. Remove the screw (3) that secure the heater core tubes (4) and retaining bracket (5) to the HVAC housing (6).

➡ **Take proper precautions to protect the carpeting from engine coolant. Have absorbent toweling readily available to clean up any spills.**

9. Remove the bolt (7) that secures the heater tubes to the heater core (8).
10. Disconnect the heater core tubes from the heater core and remove and discard the O-ring seals.
11. Install plugs in, or tape over the opened heater core ports.
12. Carefully pull the heater core out of the HVAC air distribution housing.
13. If required, remove the heater core tubes from the vehicle.

To install:

14. Carefully install the heater core into the passenger side of the HVAC air distribution housing.
15. Remove the tape or plugs from the heater core ports.
16. If removed, position the heater core tubes into the vehicle.
17. Lubricate new rubber O-ring seals with clean engine coolant and install them onto the heater core tubes. Use only the specified O-ring as they are made of a

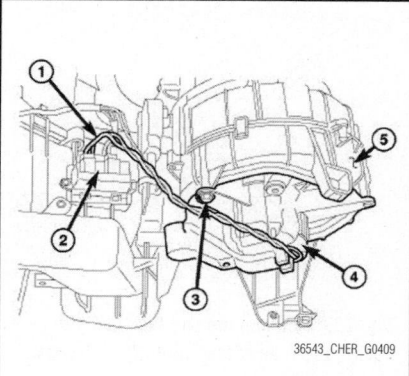

Fig. 222 Disconnect the blower motor wire harness connector (1) from the blower motor power module or resistor (2)

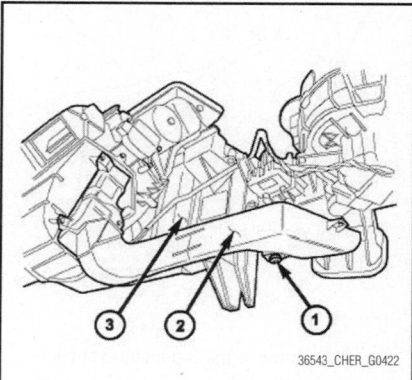

Fig. 223 Remove the five screws (1) that secure the heater core and tube cover (2) to the HVAC housing (3)

special material for the engine cooling system.

18. Connect the heater core tubes to the heater core.

19. Install the bolt that secures the heater core tubes to the heater core. Tighten the bolt securely.

20. Install the screw that secures the heater core tube retaining bracket to the HVAC housing.

21. If equipped with dual zone heating-A/C, install the blend door actuator onto the passenger side of the HVAC air distribution housing.

22. Install the heater core and tube cover onto the HVAC housing.

23. Install the five screws that secure the heater core and tube cover to the HVAC housing.

24. Install the instrument panel.

25. If disconnected, connect the heater hoses to the heater core tubes in the engine compartment.

26. Connect the negative battery cable.

27. If the heater core is being replaced, flush the cooling system.

28. Refill the engine cooling system.

AUXILIARY HEATING & AIR CONDITIONING SYSTEM

Blower Motor

REMOVAL & INSTALLATION

See Figure 225.

1. Remove the rear HVAC housing (1) and place it on a workbench.

2. Disconnect the rear HVAC wire harness connector (4) from the rear blower motor (2).

3. Remove the three screws (3) that secure the rear blower motor to the rear HVAC housing and remove the blower motor.

To install:

4. Install the three screws that secure the rear blower motor to the rear HVAC housing.

5. Connect the rear HVAC wire harness connector to the rear blower motor.

6. Install the rear HVAC housing unit in the vehicle.

7. Check for proper operation.

HEATER CORE

REMOVAL & INSTALLATION

See Figures 226 and 227.

1. Remove the rear HVAC housing and place it on a workbench.

2. Carefully remove the foam seal (1) from the flange (2) located at the bottom of the rear HVAC housing (3). If the seal is deformed or damaged, it must be replaced.

3. Partially bend the inner half of the flange downward and remove the heater core tubes (4) from the flange.

4. Release the two tabs (1) that secure the rear heater core (2) in the rear HVAC housing (3).

5. Carefully pull the rear heater core out of the end of the rear HVAC housing. If the foam seals on the heater core are deformed or damaged, they must be replaced.

6. If required, remove the heater core tubes from the rear heater core and remove and discard the O-ring seals.

To install:

7. Install the rear heater core into the end of the rear HVAC housing. Make sure that the foam seals are properly installed and that the two retaining tabs are fully engaged.

8. If the rear heater core tubes where removed from the heater core, lubricate new rubber O-ring seals with clean engine coolant and install them onto the heater core tubes. Use only the specified O-ring as they are made of a special material for the engine cooling system. Connect the heater core tubes to the heater core and install two retaining clamps securely.

9. Partially bend the inner half of the flange located at the bottom of the rear HVAC housing downward and install the heater core tubes into the flange.

10. Install the foam seal onto the flange. If the seal is deformed or damaged, it must be replaced.

➡ **If the heater core is being replaced, flush the cooling system.**

11. Install the rear HVAC housing.

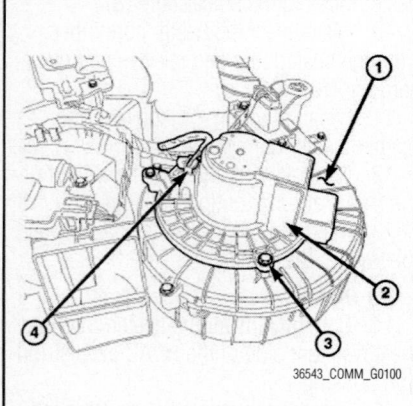

Fig. 225 Disconnect the rear HVAC wire harness connector (4) from the rear blower motor (2)

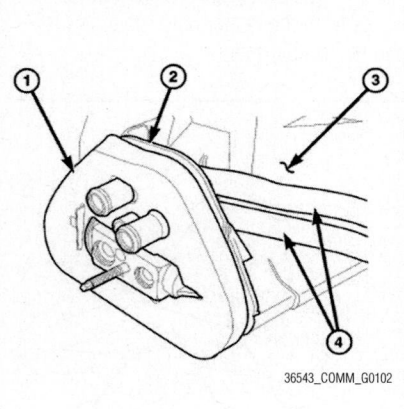

Fig. 226 Remove the foam seal (1) from the flange (2)

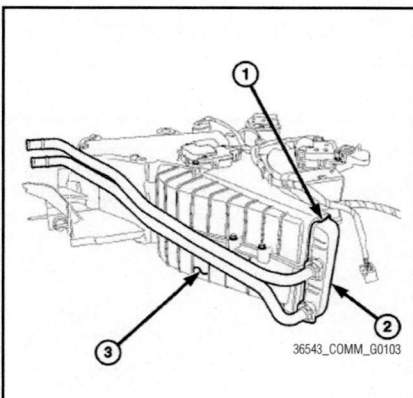

Fig. 227 Release the two tabs (1) that secure the rear heater core (2) in the rear HVAC housing (3)

STEERING

POWER RACK & PINION STEERING GEAR

REMOVAL & INSTALLATION
See Figures 228 through 234.

✳✳ CAUTION

Steering column module is centered to the vehicles steering system. Failure to keep the system and steering column module centered and locked/inhibited from rotating can result in steering column module damage.

1. Place the front wheels in the straight ahead position with the steering wheel centered and locked with a steering wheel lock.
2. Drain or siphon the power steering system.

3. Remove the column coupler shaft bolt (2) and remove the shaft from the gear (3).

➡**The power steering lines on the 8 cylinder engines are removed from below the vehicle.**

4. 6 Cylinder engine only—Remove the pressure line (2), and the return line (3) at the gear (1).
5. Raise and support the vehicle,.
6. Remove the front tires.
7. Loosen the tie rod end jam nuts (3).
8. Remove the oil drip tray (1), if equipped.
9. Remove the outer tie rod end nut and separate the tie rod (3) from the knuckle (4) using Ball Joint Remover 8677 (5).
10. Remove the front skid plate, (if equipped).

11. Remove the front splash shield (if equipped).
12. 4WD Only—Remove the front axle.
13. 8 Cylinder engine only—Remove the pressure line (2), and the return line (3) at the gear (1).
14. Remove the two steering gear mounting bolts (2).

➡**The tie rods would move to the right when turning the steering gear to the left.**

15. Move the steering gear to the right side of the vehicle, then turn the steering gear to the full left position to allow clearance from the control arms (2) and remove the gear by lowering the left side first.
16. Remove the outer tie rod ends from the steering gear (if needed).

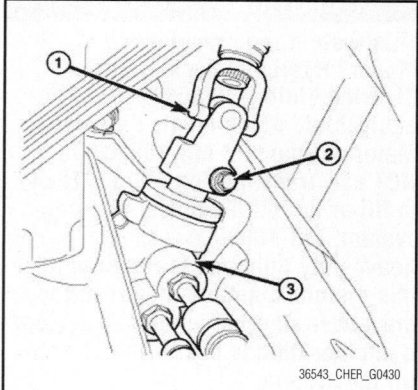

36543_CHER_G0430

Fig. 228 Remove the column coupler shaft bolt (2) and remove the shaft from the gear (3)

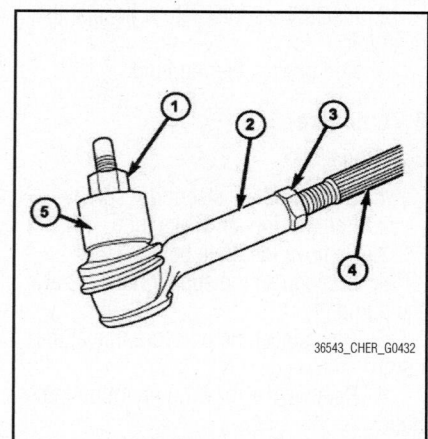

36543_CHER_G0432

Fig. 230 Loosen the tie rod end jam nuts (3)

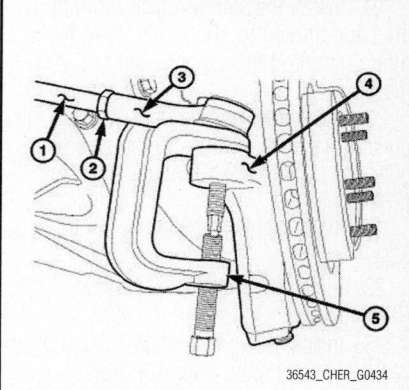

36543_CHER_G0434

Fig. 232 Remove the outer tie rod end nut and separate the tie rod (3) from the knuckle (4)

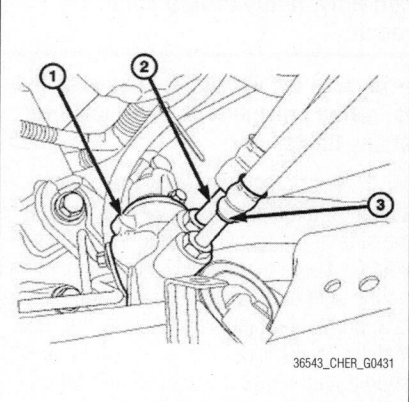

36543_CHER_G0431

Fig. 229 Remove the pressure line (2), and the return line (3) at the gear (1)

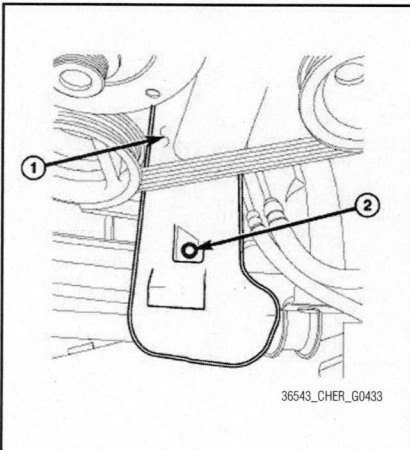

36543_CHER_G0433

Fig. 231 Remove the oil drip tray (1)

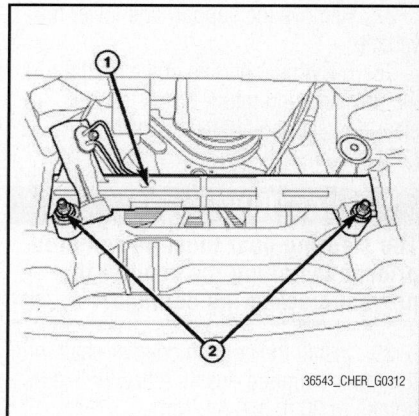

36543_CHER_G0312

Fig. 233 Remove the two steering gear mounting bolts (2)

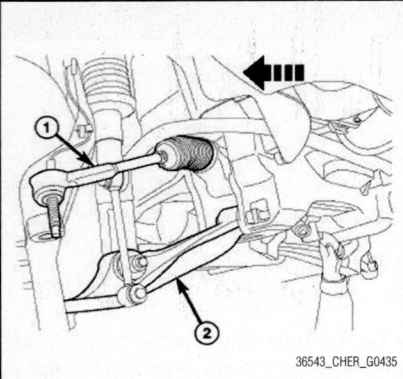

Fig. 234 Turn the steering gear to the full left position to allow clearance from the control arms (2)

To install:

17. Install the outer tie rod ends. (if removed).

18. Position the steering gear back into the vehicle the same way it was removed.

19. Install the steering gear mounting nuts and tighten to 180 ft. lbs. (244 Nm). After tightening the nuts, re-center the steering gear.

20. 8 Cylinder engine only—Install the pressure and return lines to the steering gear and tighten to 21 ft. lbs. (28 Nm).

21. 4WD ONLY—Install the front axle.

22. Install the front splash shield (if removed).

23. Install the front skid plate (if removed).

24. Install the oil filter drip tray.

25. Install the outer tie rod ends to the knuckles and tighten the tie rod end nuts to 70 ft. lbs. (95 Nm).

26. Install the wheel and tire assembly.

27. Remove the support and lower the vehicle.

28. 6 Cylinder engine only—Install the pressure and return hoses to the steering gear and tighten to 21 ft. lbs. (28 Nm).

✳✳ CAUTION

The steering gear must be centered prior to installing the coupler to prevent clockspring damage.

29. Install the column coupler shaft into the lower coupling, install a new bolt, and tighten to 36 ft. lbs. (49 Nm).

30. Remove the steering wheel lock.

31. Fill the power steering pump.

POWER STEERING PUMP

REMOVAL & INSTALLATION

3.7L & 4.7L Engines

1. Siphon power steering reservoir.

2. Remove the cooler return hose at the reservoir.

3. Disconnect the pressure hose nut at the pump.

4. Remove the pressure hose at the pump.

5. Remove serpentine drive belt.

6. Remove 3 pump mounting bolts.

7. Remove pulley from pump if necessary.

To install:

8. Install pulley on pump if removed.

9. Install 3 pump mounting bolts and tighten to 21 ft. lbs. (28 Nm).

10. Install the drive belt.

11. Install the pressure hose on the pump and tighten the nut to 21 ft. lbs. (28 Nm).

12. Install the cooler return hose at the reservoir.

13. Add power steering fluid.

5.7L Engine

See Figure 235.

1. Siphon power steering reservoir.

2. Remove the air intake tube.

3. Remove the drive belt.

4. Disconnect the supply hose (2) at the pump (1).

5. Disconnect the pressure line at the pump.

6. Remove the three pump mounting bolts.

To install:

7. Install pulley on pump if removed.

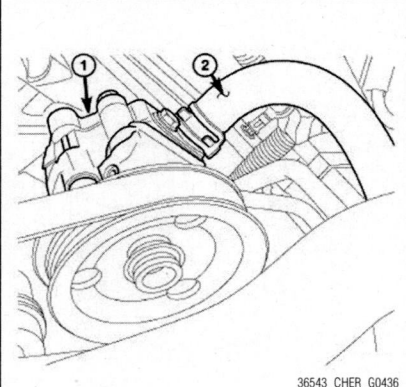

Fig. 235 Disconnect the supply hose (2) at the pump (1)

8. Install 3 pump mounting bolts and tighten to 21 ft. lbs. (28 Nm).

9. Install the pressure hose on the pump and tighten the nut to 35 ft. lbs. (47 Nm).

10. Reconnect the supply hose at the pump.

11. Install the drive belt.

12. Install the air intake tube.

13. Fill the system with power steering fluid.

14. Bleed the hydraulic fan system using a scan tool.

BLEEDING

See Figure 236.

✳✳ WARNING

Fluid level should be checked with the engine OFF to prevent personal injury from moving parts and to assure an accurate fluid level reading.

✳✳ CAUTION

This system requires the use of Mopar® Hydraulic System Power Steering Fluid (P/N 05142893AA) or equivalent, which meets Chrysler Material Standard MS-10838. Do NOT use Transmission Fluid (ATF+4) to fill or top-off the power steering system. MS-10838 is a special heavy-duty fluid and is required for this system. Damage may result to the power steering pump and system if another fluid is used. Do not over-fill the system.

✳✳ CAUTION

If the air is not purged from the power steering system correctly, pump failure could result.

➡Be sure the vacuum tool used in the following procedure is clean and free of any fluids.

1. Check the fluid level. The power steering fluid level can be viewed through the side of the power steering fluid reservoir. Compare the fluid level to the markings on the side of the reservoir. When the fluid is at normal ambient temperature, approximately 70–80°F (21–27°C), the fluid level should read between the MAX and MIN markings. When the fluid is hot, fluid level is allowed to read up to the MAX line.

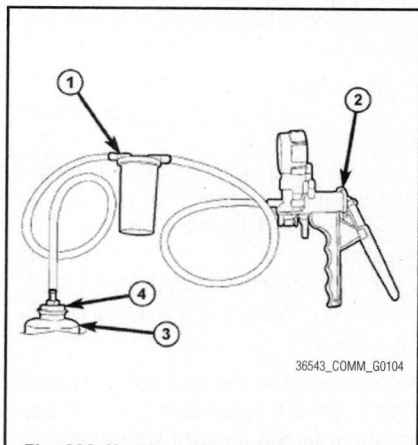

Fig. 236 Vacuum pump, reservoir and adapter

✳✳ CAUTION

Do not fill fluid beyond the MAX mark. Check cap seal for damage and replace if needed.

2. Remove the cap from the fluid reservoir and fill the power steering fluid reservoir up to the MAX marking with Mopar® Hydraulic System Power Steering Fluid (P/N 05142893AA) or equivalent, which meets Chrysler Material Standard MS-10838.

3. Tightly insert Power Steering Cap Adapter (4), Special Tool 9688, into the mouth of the reservoir (3).

✳✳ CAUTION

Failure to use a vacuum pump reservoir (1) may allow power steering fluid to be sucked into the hand vacuum pump.

4. Attach Hand Vacuum Pump (2), Special Tool C-4207 or equivalent, with reservoir (1) attached, to the Power Steering Cap Adapter (4).

✳✳ CAUTION

Do not run the vehicle while vacuum is applied to the power steering system. Damage to the power steering pump can occur.

➡ **When performing the following step make sure the vacuum level is maintained during the entire time period.**

5. Using Hand Vacuum Pump (2), apply 20–25 inches Hg (68–85 kPa) of vacuum to the system for a minimum of three minutes.

6. Slowly release the vacuum and remove the special tools.

7. Adjust the fluid level as necessary.

8. Repeat Steps 1 through 7 until the fluid no longer drops when vacuum is applied.

9. Start the engine and cycle the steering wheel lock-to-lock three times.

➡ **Do not hold the steering wheel at the stops.**

10. Stop the engine and check for leaks at all connections.

11. Check for any signs of air in the reservoir and check the fluid level. If air is present, repeat the procedure as necessary.

SUSPENSION

LOWER BALL JOINT

REMOVAL & INSTALLATION

See Figures 237 through 241.

1. Remove the tire and wheel assembly.
2. Remove the brake caliper and rotor.
3. Disconnect the tie rod (2) from the steering knuckle (4) using special tool C-3894-A (1).
4. Separate the upper ball joint (2) from the knuckle (3) using special tool 8677 (1).

5. Separate the lower ball joint (3) from the steering knuckle (1) using special tool 8677 (2).

6. Remove the steering knuckle.

7. 4WD only: Remove the clevis bracket and move the halfshaft to the side and support the halfshaft out of the way.

a. Remove the clevis bolt (2) at the shock (1).

b. Remove the lower clevis bolt/nut (4) at the lower control arm.

FRONT SUSPENSION

➡ **Extreme pressure lubrication must be used on the threaded portions of the tool. This will increase the longevity of the tool and insure proper operation during the removal and installation process.**

8. Press the ball joint from the lower control arm (3) using special tools C-4212-F (Press) (1), C-4212-3 (Driver) (2) and 9654-3 (Receiver) (4).

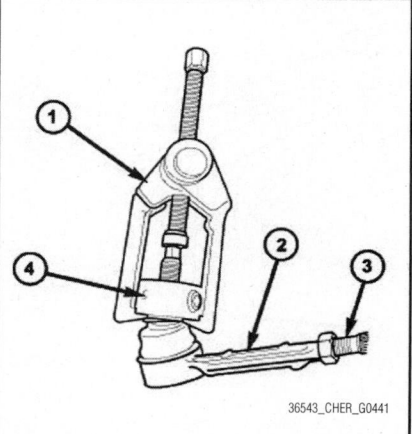

Fig. 237 Disconnect the tie rod (2) from the steering knuckle (4)

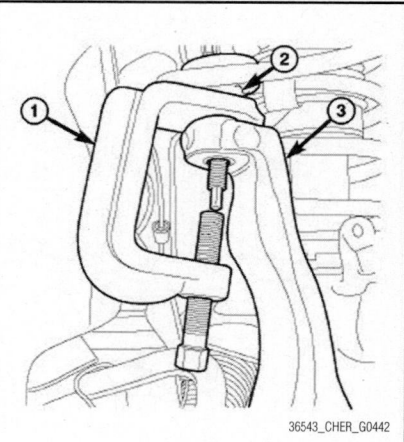

Fig. 238 Separate the upper ball joint (2) from the knuckle (3)

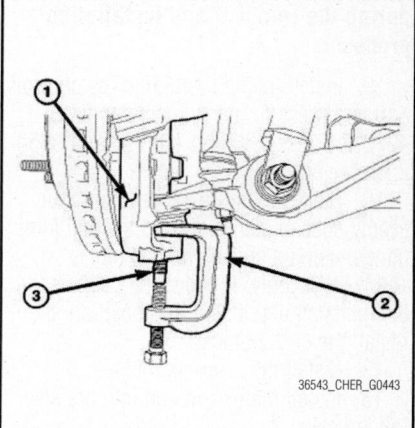

Fig. 239 Separate the lower ball joint (3) from the steering knuckle (1)

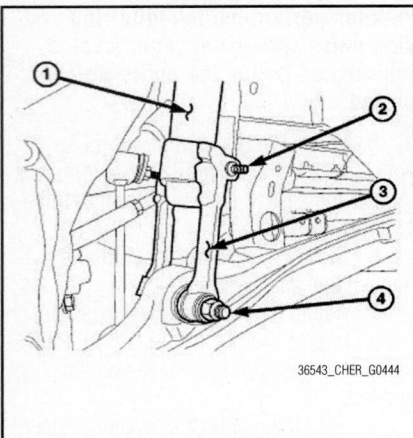

Fig. 240 Remove the clevis bolt (2) at the shock (1)

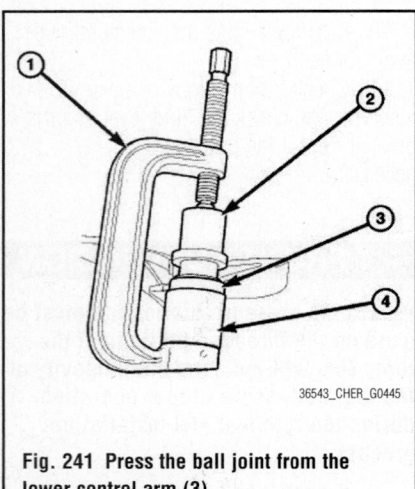

Fig. 241 Press the ball joint from the lower control arm (3)

To install:

➡**Extreme pressure lubrication must be used on the threaded portions of the tool. This will increase the longevity of the tool and insure proper operation during the removal and installation process.**

9. Install the ball joint into the control arm and press in using special tools C-4212-F (Press), 9654-1 (Driver) and 9654-2 (Receiver).

10. Stake the ball joint flange in four evenly spaced places around the ball joint flange, using a chisel and hammer.

11. 4WD only: Remove the support for the halfshaft and install into position, then install the clevis bracket.

12. Install the steering knuckle.

13. Install the tie rod end into the steering knuckle.

14. Install and tighten the halfshaft nut to 185 ft. lbs. (251 Nm). (If equipped).

15. Install the brake caliper and rotor.

16. Install the tire and wheel assembly.

17. Check the vehicle ride height.

18. Perform a wheel alignment.

LOWER CONTROL ARM

REMOVAL & INSTALLATION

See Figures 242 through 245.

1. Raise and support the vehicle.

2. Remove the tire and wheel assembly.

3. Remove the steering knuckle (3).

4. Remove the shock clevis bracket (3) from the lower control arm.

5. Remove the stabilizer link (2) at the lower control arm.

6. Remove the nut and bolt from the front of the lower control arm.

7. Remove the rear bolts (2) and flag nuts (3) from the lower control arm (1).

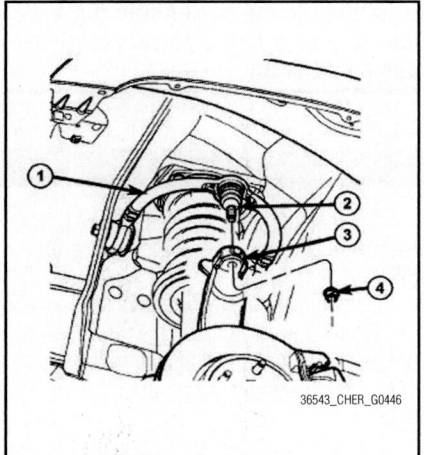

Fig. 242 Remove the steering knuckle (3)

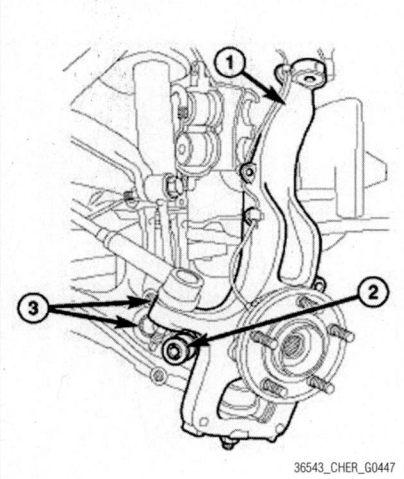

Fig. 243 Remove the shock clevis bracket (3) from the lower control arm

8. Remove the lower control arm from the vehicle.

To install:

9. Position the lower suspension arm into the cradle.

10. Install the rear bolts and flag nuts to secure the lower control arm to the frame, Tighten the bolts to 65 ft. lbs. (88 Nm).

11. Install the nut and bolt for the front of the lower control arm Tighten to 125 ft. lbs. (169 Nm).

➡**Orientation of the flag bolt is critical. Flag and head of the bolt (7) must be installed on the forward side of the lower control arm.**

12. Install the lower clevis bolt at the lower control arm and tighten to 125 ft. lbs. (169 Nm).

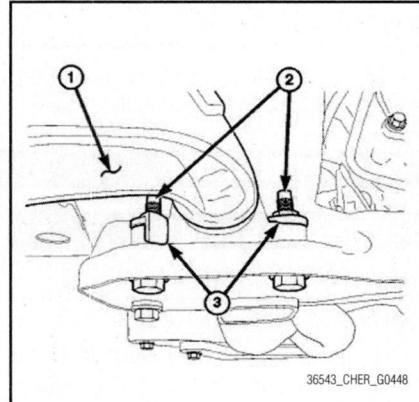

Fig. 244 Remove the rear bolts (2) and flag nuts (3) from the lower control arm (1)

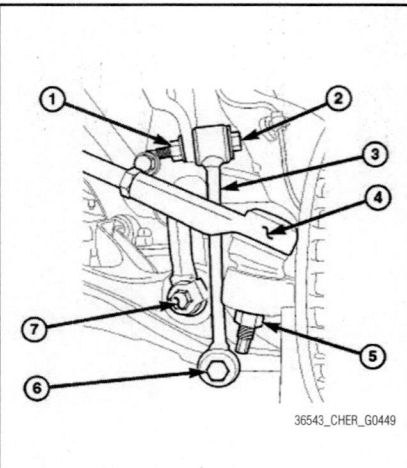

Fig. 245 Flag and head of the bolt (7) must be installed on the forward side of the lower control arm

13. Install the stabilizer link (6) at the lower control arm and tighten to 85 ft. lbs. (115 Nm).

14. Install the steering knuckle to the upper ball joint and tighten the nut to 70 ft. lbs. (95 Nm).

15. Install the tire and wheel assembly.

16. Lower the vehicle.

17. Perform wheel alignment.

STABILIZER BAR

REMOVAL & INSTALLATION

See Figures 246 and 247.

1. Raise and support the vehicle.

2. Remove the front splash shield.

3. Remove the stabilizer bar link upper nut (1) and bolt (2).

4. Remove the two stabilizer bushing clamp (2) bolts.

5. Remove the stabilizer bar (1).

> *To install:*

6. Install the stabilizer bar to the vehicle.

7. Install the stabilizer bushing clamp and tighten the bolts to 95 ft. lbs. (129 Nm).

8. Install the upper stabilizer link and tighten nut and bolt to 80 ft. lbs. (108 Nm).

9. Install the front splash shield.

10. Lower the vehicle.

STABILIZER BAR CONTROL LINKS

REMOVAL & INSTALLATION

See Figure 248.

1. Raise and support the vehicle.

2. Remove the tire and wheel assembly.

3. Remove the upper link bolt and nut (1 and 2).

4. Remove the lower link bolt (6).

5. Remove the stabilizer link (3).

> *To install:*

6. Install the stabilizer link to the vehicle.

7. Install the lower link bolt and tighten to 85 ft. lbs. (115 Nm).

a suitable support to hang the caliper securely.

3. Remove the brake caliper.

4. Remove the caliper adapter.

5. Remove the O-ring (2) and discard then remove disc brake rotor (1).

6. Remove the wheel speed sensor bolt and disconnect the wire from the retaining clips from the knuckle.

7. Remove the axle shaft nut. (if equipped with 4WD)

8. Remove the hub/bearing.

9. Remove the outer tie rod end retaining nut.

10. Separate the outer tie rod end (3) from the steering knuckle using special tool 8677 (5).

11. Remove the lower ball joint nut.

12. Separate the lower ball joint from the knuckle (1) using tool C-4150A (2).

13. Remove the upper ball joint nut.

14. Separate the upper ball joint (2) from the knuckle (3) using tool 8677 (1).

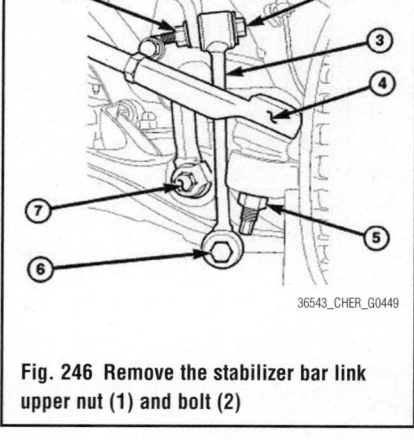

Fig. 246 Remove the stabilizer bar link upper nut (1) and bolt (2)

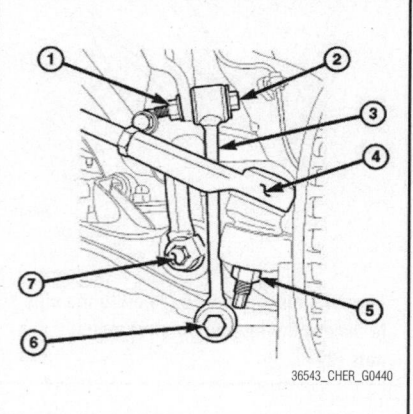

Fig. 248 Remove the upper link bolt and nut (1 and 2)

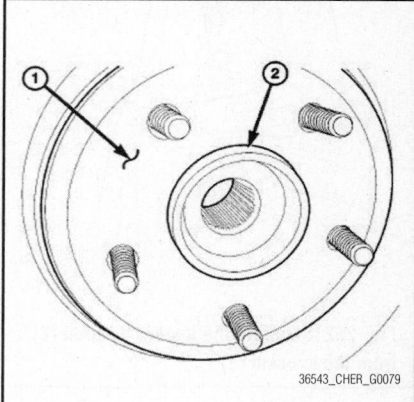

Fig. 249 Remove the O-ring (2) and discard then remove disc brake rotor (1)

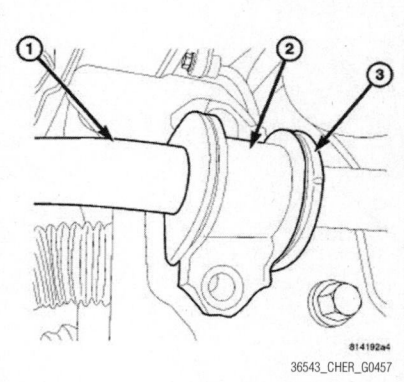

Fig. 247 Remove the two stabilizer bushing clamp (2) bolts

8. Install the upper link bolt and nut and tighten to 80 ft. lbs. (108 Nm).

9. Install the tire and wheel assembly.

10. lower the vehicle.

STEERING KNUCKLE

REMOVAL & INSTALLATION

See Figures 242 through 243, 249 through 252.

1. Raise and support the vehicle.

2. Remove the tire and wheel assembly.

✱✱ CAUTION

Never allow the disc brake caliper to hang from the brake hose. Damage to the brake hose will result. Provide

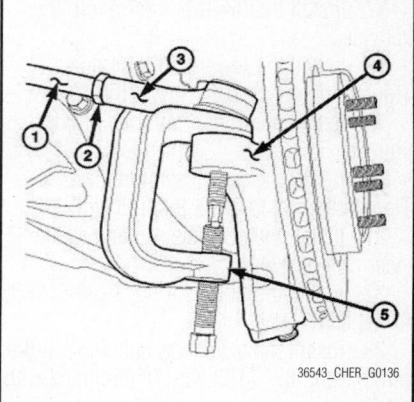

Fig. 250 Separate the outer tie rod end (3) from the steering knuckle

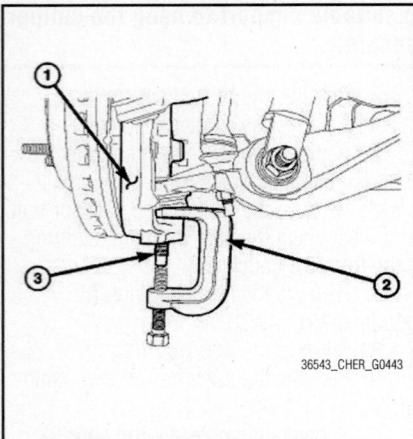

Fig. 251 Separate the lower ball joint from the knuckle (1)

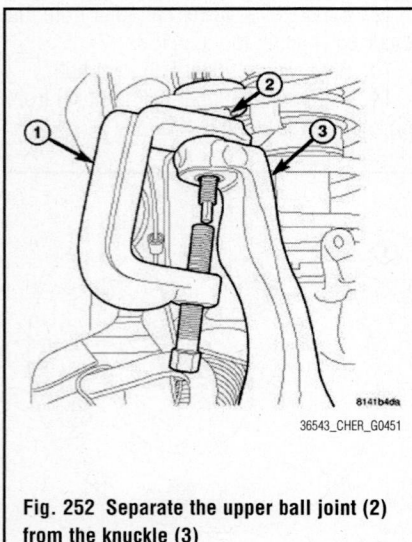

Fig. 252 Separate the upper ball joint (2) from the knuckle (3)

15. Remove the knuckle (3) from the vehicle.

To install:

16. Install the knuckle (1) to the vehicle.
17. Install the lower ball joint into the knuckle.
18. Install the lower ball joint nut. Tighten the nut to 70 ft. lbs. (95 Nm).
19. Install the upper ball joint into the knuckle.
20. Install the upper ball joint nut. Tighten the nut to 70 ft. lbs. (95 Nm).
21. Install the outer tie rod end to the steering knuckle.
22. Install the hub/bearing. Tighten to 85 ft. lbs. (115 Nm).
23. Install the axle shaft nut. Tighten the nut to 96 ft. lbs. (135 Nm).(if equipped with 4WD).

➡**Check the sensor wire routing. Be sure the wire is clear of all chassis**

components and is not twisted or kinked at any spot.

24. Install the wheel speed sensor into the hub and then install the mounting bolt and tighten to 106–124 inch lbs. (12–14 Nm).
25. Install the disc brake rotor.
26. Install the caliper adapter.
27. Install the tire and wheel assembly.
28. Perform wheel alignment.

STRUT

REMOVAL & INSTALLATION

Left Front

See Figures 243, 253 and 254.

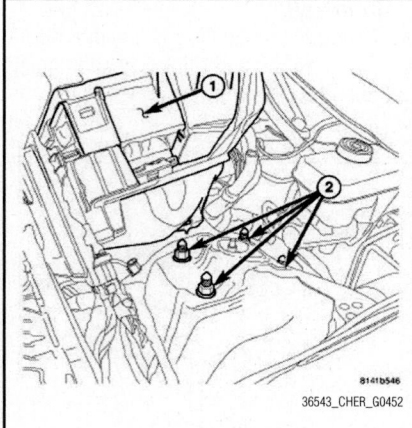

Fig. 253 Move the PDC (1) off to the side to access the four upper strut mount nuts (2)

1. Remove the air box cover and air intake hose.
2. Remove the 3 Power Distribution Center (PDC) bracket nuts.
3. Move the PDC (1) off to the side to access the four upper strut mount nuts (2).
4. Remove the four upper strut mount nuts.
5. Raise and support the vehicle.
6. Remove the tire.
7. Remove the two brake caliper adapter bolts.
8. Support the brake caliper adaptor and caliper. Do not allow the caliper to hang by the brake hose.
9. Remove the disc brake rotor.
10. Remove the upper ball joint nut.
11. Separate the upper ball joint from the knuckle using special tool 8677.
12. Remove the lower clevis bolt (3) at the lower control arm.
13. Remove the lower stabilizer bolt (2) at the lower control arm.
14. Remove the strut (3) from the vehicle.

To install:

15. Install the strut assembly to the vehicle.
16. Install the four upper strut nuts. Tighten to 70 ft. lbs. (95 Nm).
17. Install the 3 PDC bracket nuts.
18. Raise the vehicle up.
19. Install the lower stabilizer bolt at the lower control arm and tighten to 85 ft. lbs. (115 Nm).
20. Install the lower clevis bolt at the lower control arm and tighten to 125 ft. lbs. (169 Nm).

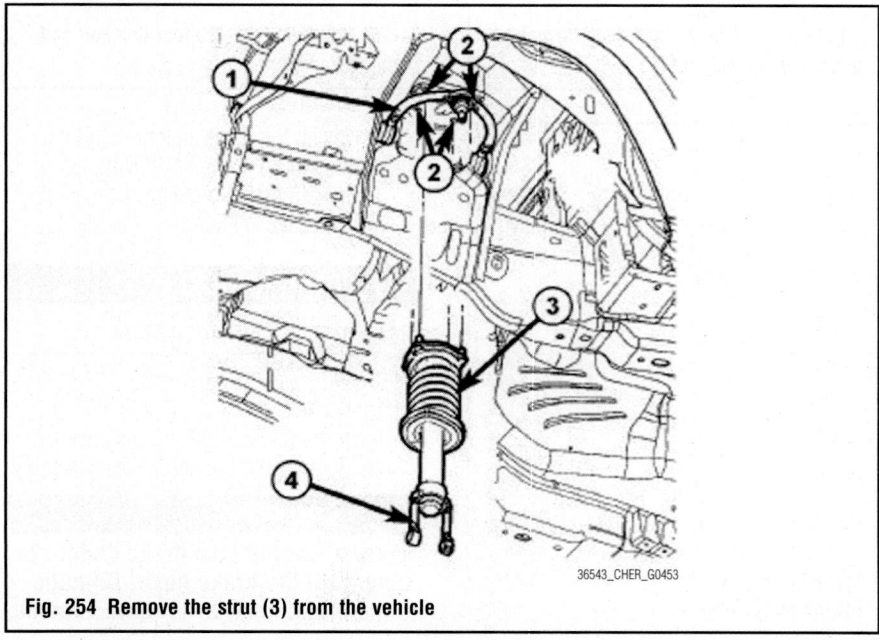

Fig. 254 Remove the strut (3) from the vehicle

21. Install the upper ball joint into the knuckle and tighten the nut to 55 ft. lbs. (75 Nm).

22. Install the disc brake rotor.

23. Install the caliper adaptor mounting bolts to 130 ft. lbs. (176 Nm).

24. Install the tire and wheel assembly.

25. Lower the vehicle.

Right Front

See Figures 243, 254 and 255.

1. Remove the air box cover and air intake hose.

2. Disconnect the cruise control servo electrical connector.

3. Remove the coolant reservoir mounting bolt and move the coolant reservoir off to the side.

4. Remove the four upper strut mounting nuts (1).

5. Raise and support the vehicle.

6. Remove the tire.

7. Remove the two brake caliper adapter bolts.

8. Support the brake caliper adaptor and caliper. Do not allow the caliper to hang by the brake hose.

9. Remove the disc brake rotor.

10. Remove the upper ball joint nut.

11. Separate the upper ball joint (2) from the knuckle (3) using special tool 8677(1).

12. Remove the lower clevis bolt (3) at the lower control arm.

13. Remove the lower stabilizer bolt (2) at the lower control arm.

14. Remove the strut (3) from the vehicle.

To install:

15. Install the strut assembly to the vehicle.

16. Install the four upper strut nuts. Tighten to 70 ft. lbs. (95 Nm).

17. Install the coolant reservoir bolt.

18. Reconnect the cruise control servo wiring connector.

19. Install the air box cover and air intake hose.

20. Raise the vehicle up.

21. Install the lower stabilizer bolt at the lower control arm.

22. Install the lower clevis bolt at the lower control arm and tighten to 125 ft. lbs. (169 Nm).

23. Install the upper ball joint into the knuckle and tighten the nut to 55 ft. lbs. (75 Nm).

24. Install the disc brake rotor.

25. Install the caliper adaptor mounting bolts to 130 ft. lbs. (176 Nm).

26. Install the tire and wheel assembly.

27. Lower the vehicle.

UPPER BALL JOINT

REMOVAL & INSTALLATION

See Figures 252 and 256.

1. Raise vehicle and support the axle.

2. Remove the tire and wheel.

3. Remove the upper ball joint retaining nut.

4. Separate the upper ball joint (2) from the knuckle (3) using special tool 8677 (1).

5. Move the knuckle (3) out of the way to allow ball joint removal tool access.

➡**When installing a new ball joint, Do not remove the rubber grease boot on the new ball joint during installation.**

6. Remove the rubber grease boot from the ball joint in the control arm. This will allow better fit of the ball joint tool when removing.

➡**Extreme pressure lubrication must be used on the threaded portions of the**

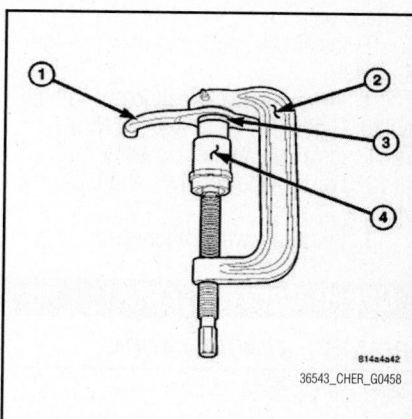

Fig. 256 Press the ball joint (3) from the upper control arm (1)

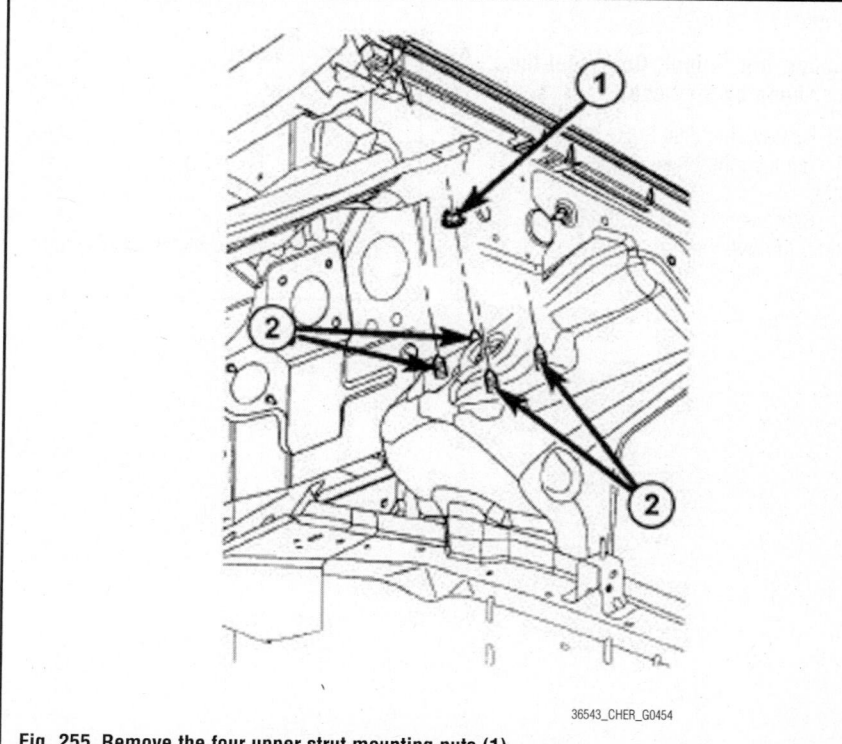

Fig. 255 Remove the four upper strut mounting nuts (1)

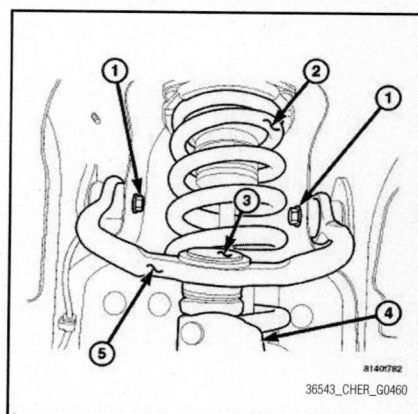

Fig. 257 Remove the nut and bolt (1) securing the upper control arm (5) to the body

tool. This will increase the longevity of the tool and insure proper operation during the removal and installation process.

7. Press the ball joint (3) from the upper control arm (1) using special tools C-4212-F (Press) (2) and 9652 (Driver) (4).

To install:

➡Do not remove the grease boot from the new ball joint. When installing the new ball joint the grease boot should not be removed.

➡Extreme pressure lubrication must be used on the threaded portions of the tool. This will increase the longevity of the tool and insure proper operation during the removal and installation process.

8. Install the ball joint into the upper control arm and press in using special tools C-4212-F (Press), 9652 (Driver) and 8975-2 (Receiver).

9. Install the upper ball joint into the knuckle.

10. Install the upper ball joint retaining nut and tighten to 70 ft. lbs. (95 Nm).

11. Install the tire and wheel.

12. Remove the supports and lower the vehicle.

13. Perform a wheel alignment.

UPPER CONTROL ARM

REMOVAL & INSTALLATION

See Figures 252 and 258.

1. Raise vehicle and support the axle.

2. Remove the tire and wheel.

3. Remove the inner fender well.

4. Remove the upper ball joint retaining nut.

5. Separate the upper ball joint (2) from the knuckle (3) using special tool 8677 (1).

6. Remove the nut and bolt (1) securing the upper control arm (5) to the body.

7. Remove the upper control arm (5) from the vehicle.

To install:

8. Install the upper control arm to the vehicle.

9. Install the nut and bolt securing the upper control arm to the body and tighten to 80 ft. lbs. (108 Nm.

10. Install the upper ball joint into the knuckle.

11. Install the upper ball joint retaining nut and tighten the nut to 70 ft. lbs. (95 Nm).

12. Install the inner fender well.

13. Install the tire and wheel.

14. Remove the supports and lower the vehicle.

15. Perform a wheel alignment.

WHEEL HUB & BEARING

REMOVAL & INSTALLATION

See Figure 258.

1. Raise and support the vehicle.

2. Remove the wheel and tire assembly.

➡Support the caliper, Do not let the caliper hang by the hose.

3. Remove the disc brake caliper.

4. Remove the brake caliper adaptor.

5. Remove and discard the O-ring and then remove the disc brake rotor.

6. Remove the wheel speed sensor nut (2).

7. Remove the wheel speed sensor.

8. Remove the 3 hub bearing mounting bolts from the back of the steering knuckle.

9. Remove hub bearing from the steering knuckle.

To install:

10. Install the hub bearing to the knuckle then tighten the 3 bolts to 85 ft. lbs. (115 Nm).

11. Install the wheel speed sensor into the hub. Install the mounting bolt and tighten to 106–124 inch lbs. (12–14 Nm).

12. Install the brake rotor.

13. Install the brake caliper adaptor.

14. Install the caliper.

15. Install the wheel and tire assembly.

16. Remove the support and lower the vehicle.

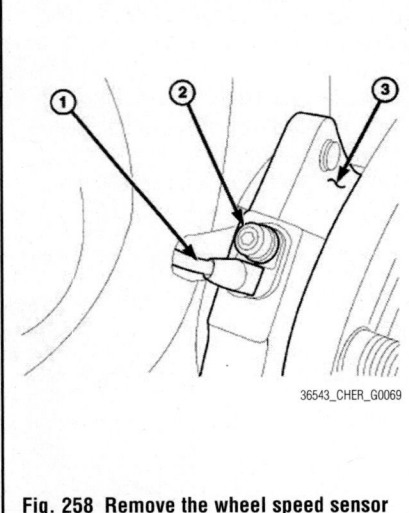

36543_CHER_G0069

Fig. 258 Remove the wheel speed sensor nut (2)

SUSPENSION   **REAR SUSPENSION**

COIL SPRING

REMOVAL & INSTALLATION

See Figures 259 and 260.

1. Raise and support the vehicle. Position a hydraulic jack under the axle to support the axle.
2. Remove the wheel and tire assembly on the side of the repair.
3. Remove the lower shock bolt (3) from the axle bracket.
4. If the left spring is being serviced, remove the left rear bolt securing the fuel tank skid plate in place. This will allow clearance for the suspension when the spring is removed.
5. Remove the stabilizer bar link from the body rail.
6. Lower the hydraulic jack and tilt the axle.
7. Pull down on the axle as necessary and remove the coil spring (4) by lifting it up and off the lower perch first.
8. Remove and inspect the spring isolators.

To install:

9. Install the upper isolator on the spring seat on body.
10. Install the lower isolator (3) on the axle bracket.
11. Pull down on the axle and position the coil spring (1), ID tag end up, over the upper perch, then lower it onto the lower perch.
12. Raise the axle with the hydraulic jack.
13. Install the shock absorber to the axle bracket and tighten the bolt to 85 ft. lbs. (115 Nm).

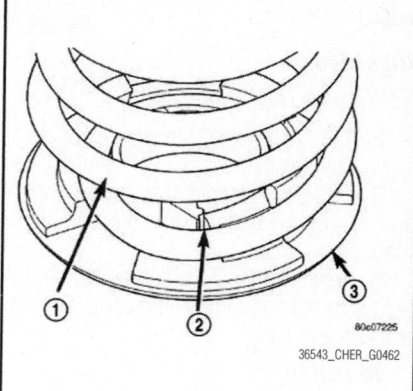

Fig. 260 Install the lower isolator (3) on the axle bracket

14. If the left spring is being serviced, install the previously removed fuel tank skid plate bolt and tighten to 50ft. lbs. (68 Nm).
15. Install the stabilizer bar link to the body rail and tighten the bolt to 75 ft. lbs. (102 Nm).
16. Install the wheel and tire assembly.
17. Remove the supports and lower the vehicle.

CONTROL ARMS/LINKS

REMOVAL & INSTALLATION

Lower Control Arm

Left Side

See Figures 261 and 262.

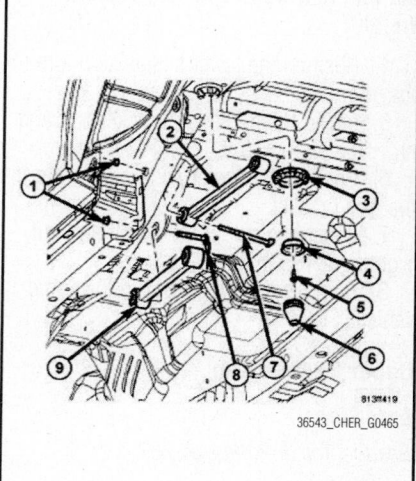

Fig. 262 Remove the nut (1) and bolt (8) from the frame rail and remove the lower suspension arm (9)

1. Raise the vehicle and support the rear axle.
2. Remove the fuel tank.
3. Remove the lower suspension arm nut (2) and bolt (1) from the axle bracket.
4. Remove the nut (1) and bolt (8) from the frame rail and remove the lower suspension arm (9).

To install:

➡️**All torques should be done with vehicle on the ground with full vehicle weight.**

5. Position the lower suspension arm in the frame rail.
6. Install the frame rail bracket bolt and nut. Tighten to 130 ft. lbs. (176 Nm).
7. Position the lower suspension arm in the axle bracket.
8. Install the axle bracket bolt and nut. Tighten to 155 ft. lbs. (210 Nm).
9. Install the fuel tank.
10. Remove the supports and lower the vehicle.

Right Side

See Figures 261 through 262.

1. Raise the vehicle and support the rear axle.
2. Remove the lower suspension arm nut (2) and bolt (1) from the axle bracket.
3. Remove the nut (1) and bolt (8) from the frame rail and remove the lower suspension arm (9).

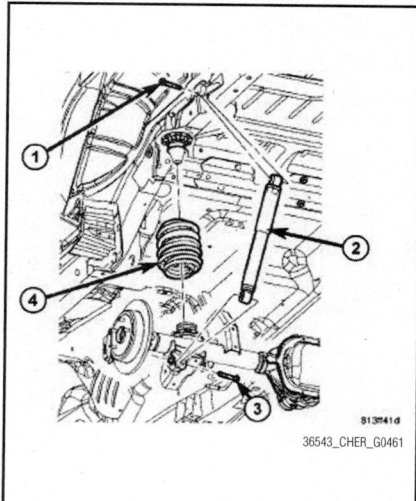

Fig. 259 Remove the lower shock bolt (3) from the axle bracket

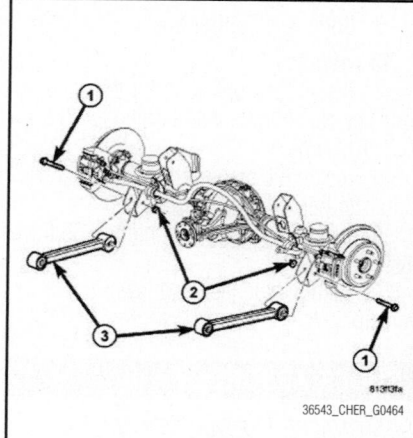

Fig. 261 Remove the lower suspension arm nut (2) and bolt (1) from the axle bracket

To install:

➡ **All torques should be done with vehicle on the ground with full vehicle weight.**

4. Position the lower suspension arm in the frame rail.
5. Install the frame rail bracket bolt and nut. Tighten to 130 ft. lbs. (176 Nm).
6. Position the lower suspension arm in the axle bracket.
7. Install the axle bracket bolt and nut. Tighten to 155 ft. lbs. (210 Nm).
8. Remove the supports and lower the vehicle.

Upper Control Arm

Left Side

See Figures 262 through 263.

1. Raise and support the vehicle.
2. Support the rear axle.
3. Lower the fuel tank in order to gain access to the bolt.
4. Remove the upper suspension arm nut (2) and bolt (3) from the axle bracket.
5. Remove the nut (1) and bolt (7) from the frame rail and remove the upper suspension arm (2).

To install:

➡ **All torques should be done with vehicle on the ground with full vehicle weight.**

6. Position the upper suspension arm in the frame rail bracket.
7. Install the mounting bolt and nut tighten to 95 ft. lbs. (129 Nm).
8. Position the upper suspension arm in the axle bracket.
9. Install the mounting bolt and nut tighten to 100 ft. lbs. (136 Nm).

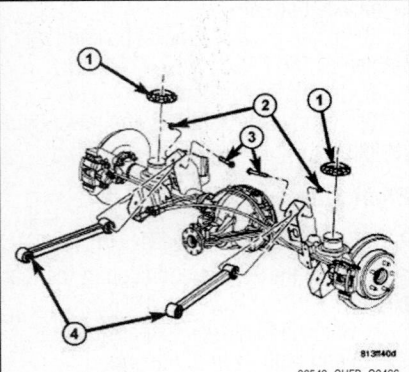

Fig. 263 Remove the upper suspension arm nut (2) and bolt (3) from the axle bracket

10. Raise the fuel tank back into place and secure.
11. Remove the supports and lower the vehicle.

Right Side

See Figures 262 through 263.

1. Raise and support the vehicle.
2. Support the rear axle.
3. Remove the upper suspension arm nut (2) and bolt (3) from the axle bracket.
4. Remove the nut (1) and bolt (7) from the frame rail and remove the upper suspension arm (2).

To install:

➡ **All torques should be done with vehicle on the ground with full vehicle weight.**

5. Position the upper suspension arm in the frame rail bracket.
6. Install the mounting bolt and nut tighten to 95 ft. lbs. (129 Nm).
7. Position the upper suspension arm in the axle bracket.
8. Install the mounting bolt and nut tighten to 100 ft. lbs. (136 Nm).
9. Remove the supports and lower the vehicle.

Stabilizer Bar Link

1. Raise and support the vehicle.
2. Remove the rear tire.
3. Support the rear axle with a jack.
4. Remove the upper link bolt at the frame.
5. Remove the lower link nut at the stabilizer bar.
6. Remove stabilizer link.

To install:

7. Install the upper bolt for the stabilizer link to the frame and tighten to 75 ft. lbs. (102 Nm).
8. Install the stabilizer link to the stabilizer bar.
9. Install the nut and tighten to 65 ft. lbs. (88 Nm).
10. Remove the jack and lower the vehicle.

SHOCK ABSORBER

REMOVAL & INSTALLATION

See Figures 259 and 264.

1. Raise and support the vehicle. Position a hydraulic jack under the axle to support the axle.

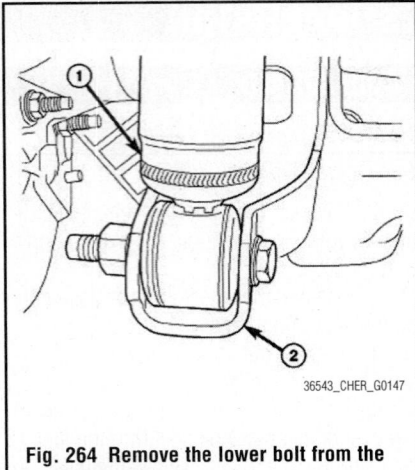

Fig. 264 Remove the lower bolt from the axle bracket (2)

2. Remove the upper bolt (1) from the frame bracket.
3. Remove the lower bolt from the axle bracket (2).
4. Remove the shock absorber (1).

To install:

5. Install the shock absorber in the frame bracket and install the bolt.
6. Install the shock absorber in the axle bracket and install the bolt.
7. Tighten the upper mounting bolt and nut to 70 ft. lbs. (95 Nm).
8. Tighten the lower mounting bolt and nut to 85 ft. lbs. (115 Nm).
9. Remove the supports and lower the vehicle.

TRACK BAR

REMOVAL & INSTALLATION

See Figures 265 and 266.

1. Raise and support the vehicle. Position a hydraulic jack under the axle to support the axle.

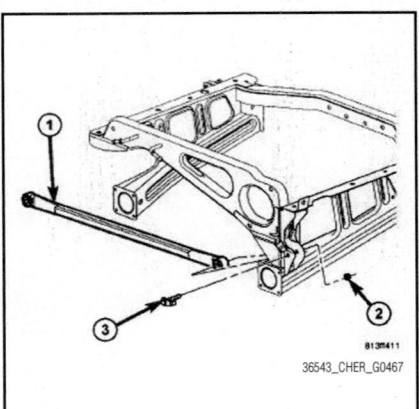

Fig. 265 Remove the track bar bolt (3) and nut (2) from the frame bracket

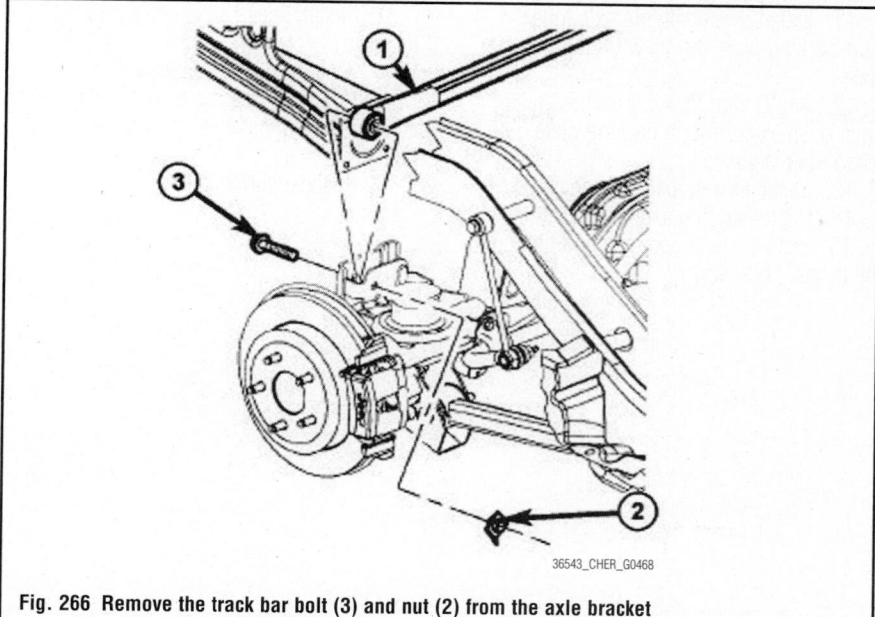

Fig. 266 Remove the track bar bolt (3) and nut (2) from the axle bracket

2. Remove the track bar bolt (3) and nut (2) from the frame bracket.

3. Remove the left lower shock bolt at the axle.

4. Pry in between the coil springs to remove track bar bolt.

5. Remove the track bar bolt (3) and nut (2) from the axle bracket.

To install:

6. Install the track bar to the vehicle.

7. Pry in between the coil springs to install track bar bolt.

8. Install the track bar bolt and nut in the frame bracket.

9. Install the track bar into the axle bracket.

10. Install the track bar bolt and nut in the axle bracket.

11. Install the left lower shock bolt to the axle Tighten to 85 ft. lbs. (115 Nm).

12. Remove the supports and lower the vehicle.

➡**Torques should be done with vehicle on the ground with full vehicle weight.**

13. Tighten the upper mounting bolt/nut to 140 ft. lbs. (190 Nm).

14. Tighten the lower mounting bolt/nut to 140 ft. lbs. (190 Nm).

WHEEL HUB & BEARING

REMOVAL & INSTALLATION

See Figures 267 through 270.

1. With vehicle in neutral, position on hoist.

2. Remove calipers and rotors.

3. Tap axle end plug (1) loose from the axle flange (2) with a hammer and punch. Pull plug (1) out of axle flange (2).

4. Remove speed sensors from axle tube flange.

5. Remove axle flange nuts (1) from axle (2).

6. Pull axle shaft and backing plate out of axle tube until axle bearing (1) is exposed.

7. Remove O-ring (2) from the axle bearing.

8. Slide axle shaft (1) from axle tube and backing plate.

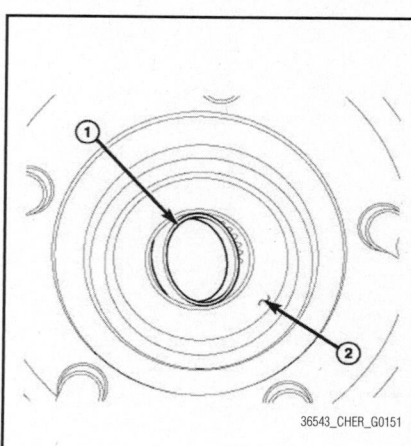

Fig. 267 Tap axle end plug (1) loose from the axle flange (2)

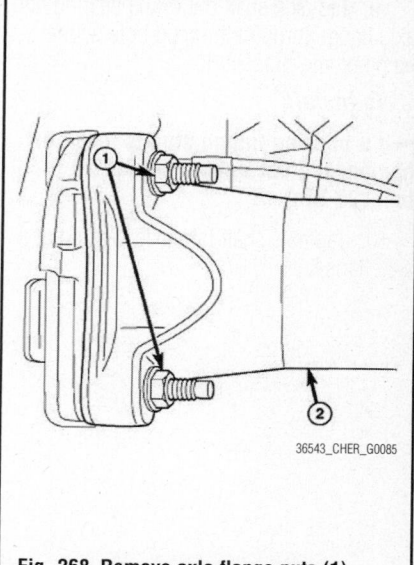
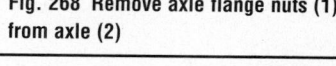

Fig. 268 Remove axle flange nuts (1) from axle (2)

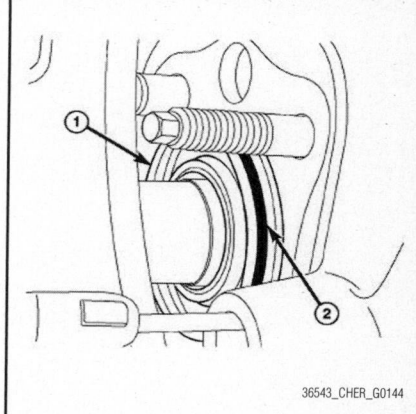

Fig. 269 Remove O-ring (2) from the axle bearing

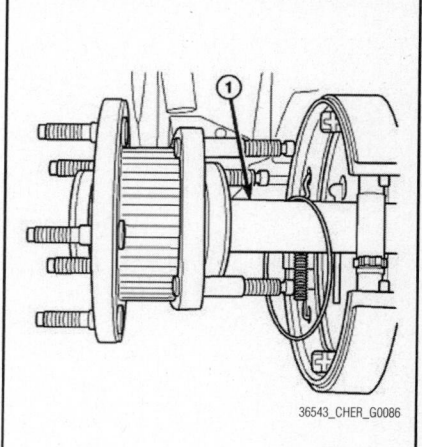

Fig. 270 Slide axle shaft (1) from axle tube and backing plate

9. Tap axle shaft out of the bearing and axle flange through the plug hole with a hammer and brass drift.

To install:

➡**If a bearing flange stud is loose or has backed out tighten stud to 20 ft. lbs. (27 Nm).**

10. Tap axle shaft into axle bearing and axle flange.

11. Install axle shaft into axle tube and backing plate with new O-ring on axle.

12. Slip O-ring through backing plate, then push axle through backing plate until bearing is exposed.

13. Install O-ring axle bearing.

14. Push axle into axle tube.

15. Install axle flange nuts and tighten to 88 ft. lbs. (119 Nm).

16. Install speed sensors in axle tube flange.

17. Coat new axle flange plug with Mopar® Stud N' Bearing Mount Adhesive or equivalent and install plug with freeze plug installer.

18. Install calipers and rotors.

SPECIFICATIONS AND MAINTENANCE CHARTS

ENGINE AND VEHICLE IDENTIFICATION

	Engine							Model Year	
Code ①	Liters (cc)	Cu. In.	Cyl.	Fuel Sys.	Engine Type	Eng. Mfg.		Code ②	Year
A	2.0 (1998)	122	4	Gas	DOHC	GEMA		A	2010
B	2.4 (2360)	144	4	Gas	DOHC	GEMA		B	2011

① 8th position of VIN

② 10th position of VIN

25766_COMP_C0001

GENERAL ENGINE SPECIFICATIONS

All measurements are given in inches.

Year	Model	Engine Disp. Liters (cc)	Engine ID/VIN	Fuel System Type	Net Horsepower @ rpm	Net Torque @ rpm (ft. lbs.)	Bore x Stroke (in.)	Compression Ratio	Oil Pressure @ rpm
2010	Compass/ Patriot	2.0 (1998)	A	MPI	158 @ 6400	141 @ 5000	3.386 x 3.386	10.5:1	25-80 @ 3000
		2.4 (2360)	B	MPI	172 @ 6000	165 @ 4400	3.465 X 3.819	10.5:1	25-80 @ 3000
2011	Compass/ Patriot	2.0 (1998)	A	MPI	158 @ 6400	141 @ 5000	3.386 x 3.386	10.5:1	25-80 @ 3000
		2.4 (2360)	B	MPI	172 @ 6000	165 @ 4400	3.465 X 3.819	10.5:1	25-80 @ 3000

MPI Sequential Multi-Port Electronic Fuel Injection system

25766_COMP_C0002

ENGINE TUNE-UP SPECIFICATIONS

Year	Engine Displacement Liters	Engine ID/VIN	Spark Plug Gap (in.)	Ignition Timing (deg.) MT	Ignition Timing (deg.) AT	Fuel Pump (psi)	Idle Speed (rpm) MT	Idle Speed (rpm) AT	Valve Lash Clearance Intake	Valve Lash Clearance Exhaust
2010	2.0	A	0.043	①	①	59 ± 5	②	②	0.006 - 0.009	0.010 - 0.012
	2.4	B	0.043	①	①	59 ± 5	②	②	0.006 - 0.009	0.010 - 0.012
2011	2.0	A	0.043	①	①	59 ± 5	②	②	0.006 - 0.009	0.010 - 0.012
	2.4	B	0.043	①	①	59 ± 5	②	②	0.006 - 0.009	0.010 - 0.012

NOTE: The Vehicle Emission Control Information label reflects specification changes made during production. Follow the figures on the label if they differ from those in this chart.

① All engines use a fixed ignition timing system. Basic ignition timing is not adjustable. All spark advance is determined by the Powertrain Control Module (PCM).

② Idle speed is controlled by the PCM and is not adjustable.

25766_COMP_C0003

CAPACITIES

Year	Model	Engine Displacement Liters	Engine ID/VIN	Engine Oil with Filter	Transaxle (pts.) Auto.	Transaxle (pts.) Manual	Drive Axle (pts.) Front	Drive Axle (pts.) Rear	Transfer Case (pts.)	Fuel Tank (gal.)	Cooling System (qts.)
2010	Compass/	2.0	A	4.5	14.8 ①	5.0-5.6	NA	1.0-1.1	1.1	13.5	7.2
	Patriot	2.4	B	4.5	14.8 ①	5.0-5.6	NA	1.0-1.1	1.1	13.5	7.2
2011	Compass/	2.0	A	4.5	14.8 ①	5.0-5.6	NA	1.0-1.1	1.1	13.5	7.2
	Patriot	2.4	B	4.5	14.8 ①	5.0-5.6	NA	1.0-1.1	1.1	13.5	7.2

NOTE: All capacities are approximate. Add fluid gradually and ensure a proper fluid level is obtained.

NA: Not Applicable

① If the transmission was completely overhauled or the torque converter was replaced or drained, add 17.1 pts. of fluid to the transmission. This is the dry fill capacity. Depending on type and size of internal cooler, length and inside diameter of cooler lines, or use of an auxiliary cooler, these figures may vary. Refer to the appropriate service information for the correct procedures.

25766_COMP_C0004

FLUID SPECIFICATIONS

Year	Model	Engine Disp. Liters	Engine Oil	Manual Trans.	Auto. Trans.	Drive Axle Rear	Transfer Case	Power Steering Fluid	Brake Master Cylinder	Cooling System
2010	Compass/	2.0	5W-20	MOPAR® ATF+4	MOPAR® CVTF+4	①	①	②	DOT 3 ③	④
	Patriot	2.4	5W-20	MOPAR® ATF+4	MOPAR® CVTF+4	①	①	②	DOT 3 ③	④
2011	Compass/	2.0	5W-20	MOPAR® ATF+4	MOPAR® CVTF+4	①	①	②	DOT 3 ③	④
	Patriot	2.4	5W-20	MOPAR® ATF+4	MOPAR® CVTF+4	①	①	②	DOT 3 ③	④

DOT: Department Of Transpotation

NA: Not Applicable

① MOPAR® MS 9020 SAE 80W90 Gear Lube.

② If MOPAR® Power Steering Fluid +4 (P/N 05013457AA) is not available, then MOPAR® ATF +4 Automatic Transmission Fluid (P/N 05166226AA), is acceptable

③ If MOPAR® Brake Fluid DOT 3 (P/N 04318080AB - 12 oz bottle or 04318081AB - 32 oz bottle) is not available, then MOPAR® Brake and Clutch Fluid DOT 4 (P/N 04549625AC), is acceptable.

④ MOPAR® Antifreeze/Coolant 5 Year/100,000 Mile Formula HOAT (Hybrid Organic Additive Technology)

25766_COMP_C0005

VALVE SPECIFICATIONS

Year	Engine Displacement Liters	Engine ID/VIN	Seat Angle (deg.)	Face Angle (deg.)	Nominal Force-- Valve Open (lbs. @ in.)	Spring Free- Length (in.)	Spring Installed Height (in.)	Stem-to-Guide Clearance (in.) Intake	Stem-to-Guide Clearance (in.) Exhaust	Stem Diameter (in.) Intake	Stem Diameter (in.) Exhaust
2010	2.0	A	44.75-45.10	45.25-45.75	82.01 ± 3.82 @ 1.152	1.850	1.378	0.0008-0.0021	0.0012-0.0024	0.2151-0.2157	0.2148-0.2153
	2.4	B	44.75-45.10	45.25-45.75	82.01 ± 3.82 @ 1.152	1.850	1.378	0.0008-0.0021	0.0012-0.0024	0.2151-0.2157	0.2148-0.2153
2011	2.0	A	44.75-45.10	45.25-45.75	82.01 ± 3.82 @ 1.152	1.850	1.378	0.0008-0.0021	0.0012-0.0024	0.2151-0.2157	0.2148-0.2153
	2.4	B	44.75-45.10	45.25-45.75	82.01 ± 3.82 @ 1.152	1.850	1.378	0.0008-0.0021	0.0012-0.0024	0.2151-0.2157	0.2148-0.2153

25766_COMP_C0006

CAMSHAFT SPECIFICATIONS
All measurements in inches unless noted

Year	Engine Displacement Liters	Engine Code/VIN	Journal Diameter	Bearing Clearance Diametrical	Shaft End-play	Runout	Journal Bore	Maximum Lift @ lash	
								Intake	Exhaust
2010	2.0	A	①	②	0.004-0.009	NS	③	0.362 @ 0.007	0.331 @ 0.011
	2.4	B	①	②	0.004-0.009	NS	③	0.362 @ 0.007	0.331 @ 0.011
2011	2.0	A	①	②	0.004-0.009	NS	③	0.362 @ 0.007	0.331 @ 0.011
	2.4	B	①	②	0.004-0.009	NS	③	0.362 @ 0.007	0.331 @ 0.011

NS: Not specified by Chrysler/Jeep

① Front Intake Cam: 1.1797-1.1803 inches; Front Exhaust Cam: 1.4166-1.4173 inches; Cam Journal No. 1-4: 0.943- 0.944 inch

② Front Intake Journal: 0.0008-0.0022 inch; Front Exhaust Journal: 0.0007-0.0020 inch; All Others: 0.0011-0.0026 inch

③ Cylinder head camshaft bearing bore diameter: Front Intake: 1.1810-1.1819 inches, Front Exhaust: 1.5747-1.5756 inches, Cam Bearing Bore Numbers 1-4: 0.9448-0.9457 inch

25766_COMP_C0007

CRANKSHAFT AND CONNECTING ROD SPECIFICATIONS
All measurements are given in inches.

Year	Engine Displacement Liters	Engine ID/VIN	Crankshaft			Connecting Rod		
			Main Brg. Journal Dia.	Main Brg. Oil Clearance	Shaft End-play	Journal Diameter	Bearing Clearance	Side Clearance
2010	2.0	A	①	0.0011-0.0018	0.0019-0.0098	②	0.001-0.002	0.0039-0.0098
	2.4	B	①	0.0011-0.0018	0.0019-0.0098	②	0.001-0.002	0.0039-0.0098
2011	2.0	A	①	0.0011-0.0018	0.0019-0.0098	②	0.001-0.002	0.0039-0.0098
	2.4	B	①	0.0011-0.0018	0.0019-0.0098	②	0.001-0.002	0.0039-0.0098

① Journal grade: main bearing journal diameter. 0: 2.0466-2.0467 inches, 1: 2.0465-2.0466 inches, 2: 2.0464-2.0465 inches, 3: 2.0462-2.0464 inches, 4: 2.0461-2.0462 inches

② Journal grade: connecting rod journal diameter: 1: 1.8884-1.8886 inches, 2: 1.8884-1.8881 inches, 3: 1.8879-1.8881 inches

25766_COMP_C0008

PISTON AND RING SPECIFICATIONS
All measurements are given in inches.

Year	Engine Displacement Liters	Engine ID/VIN	Piston Clearance	Ring Gap			Ring Side Clearance		
				Top Compression	Bottom Compression	Oil Control	Top Compression	Bottom Compression	Oil Control
2010	2.0	A	(-0.0006)-0.0006	0.0059-0.0118	0.0118-0.0177	0.0059-0.0118	0.0059-0.0118	0.0059-0.0118	0.0059-0.0118
	2.4	B	(-0.0006)-0.0006	0.0059-0.0118	0.0118-0.0177	0.0059-0.0118	0.0059-0.0118	0.0059-0.0118	0.0059-0.0118
2011	2.0	A	(-0.0006)-0.0006	0.0059-0.0118	0.0118-0.0177	0.0059-0.0118	0.0059-0.0118	0.0059-0.0118	0.0059-0.0118
	2.4	B	(-0.0006)-0.0006	0.0059-0.0118	0.0118-0.0177	0.0059-0.0118	0.0059-0.0118	0.0059-0.0118	0.0059-0.0118

25766_COMP_C0009

TORQUE SPECIFICATIONS
All readings in ft. lbs.

Year	Engine Disp. Liters	Engine ID/VIN	Cylinder Head Bolts	Main Bearing Bolts	Rod Bearing Bolts	Crankshaft Damper Bolts	Flexplate to Crankshaft Bolts	Manifold Intake	Manifold Exhaust	Spark Plugs	Oil Pan Drain Plug
2010	2.0	A	①	②	③	155	④	18	25	20	30
	2.4	B	①	②	③	155	④	18	25	20	30
2011	2.0	A	①	②	③	155	④	18	25	20	30
	2.4	B	①	②	③	155	④	18	25	20	30

① Refer to procedure for torque sequence illustration and bolt identification. Lubricate head bolts with clean engine oil.

Step 1: Tighten to 25 ft. lbs.

Step 2: Tighten short bolts to: 45 ft. lbs.; Tighten long bolts to 54 ft. lbs.

Step 3: Verify all short bolts are 45 ft. lbs. and long bolts are 54 ft. lbs.

Step 4: Tighten the bolts an additional 90 degrees (do NOT use a torque wrench for this step)

② Refer to the procedure for torque sequence illustration and bolt identification. There are different sets of main bolts supplied with this engine.

Each bolt set has a different torque value and engine damage could result if bolts are not torqued correctly. The bolts are not interchangeable.

Step 1: Tighten to 11 ft. lbs.

Step 2: Tighten to 20 ft. lbs. or 33 ft. lbs.

Step 3: Tighten all bolts an additional 45 degrees.

③ Step 1: Tighten to 15 ft. lbs.

Step 2: Tighten bolts an addtitional 90 degrees

④ Step 1: Tighten bolts to 22 ft. lbs.

Step 2: Tighten bolts an additional 51 degrees

25766_COMP_C0010

WHEEL ALIGNMENT

Year	Model		Cross Caster * Range (+/-Deg.)	Cross Caster * Preferred Setting (Deg.)	Camber Range (+/-Deg.)	Camber Preferred Setting (Deg.)	Total Toe Range (+/-Deg.)	Total Toe Preferred Setting (Deg.)
2010	Compass/Patriot	F	-0.70 to +1.30	0.30	-1.20 to -0.40	-0.80	0.00 to +0.40	+0.20
	16-inch wheels	R	NS	NS	-1.10 to -0.30	-0.70	0.00 to +0.40	+0.20
	Compass/Patriot	F	-0.70 to +1.30	0.30	-1.10 to -0.30	-0.70	0.00 to +0.40	+0.20
	17-inch wheels w/ AWL	R	NS	NS	-1.00 to -0.20	-0.60	0.00 to +0.40	+0.20
	Compass/Patriot	F	-0.70 to +1.30	0.30	-1.30 to -0.50	-0.90	0.00 to +0.40	+0.20
	17-inch wheels w/out AWL	R	NS	NS	-1.20 to -0.40	-0.80	0.00 to +0.40	+0.20
	Compass/Patriot	F	-0.70 to +1.30	0.30	-1.10 to -0.30	-0.70	0.00 to +0.40	+0.20
	18-inch wheels	R	NS	NS	-1.10 to -0.30	-0.70	0.00 to +0.40	+0.20
2011	Compass/Patriot	F	-0.70 to +1.30	0.30	-1.26 to -0.16	0.71	0.00 to +0.40	+0.20
	4X4 with AWL	R	NS	NS	-1.45 to -0.15	-0.80	-0.05 to +0.45	+0.20
	Compass/Patriot	F	-0.70 to +1.30	0.30	-1.19 to -0.09	-0.64	0.00 to +0.40	+0.20
	4X2 or 4X4 without AWL	R	NS	NS	-1.26 to -0.04	-0.61	-0.05 to +0.45	+0.20

Cross Caster: Maximum Side-To-Side Difference

AWL: Off road group

NS: Not specified by Jeep/Chrysler

25766_COMP_C0011

TIRE, WHEEL AND BALL JOINT SPECIFICATIONS

Year	Model	OEM Tires Standard	OEM Tires Optional	Tire Pressures (psi) Front	Tire Pressures (psi) Rear	Wheel Size (inches)	Ball Joint Inspection	Lug Nut (ft. lbs.)
2010	Compass Sport	P215/60R17	NA	①	①	6.5 x 17	②	100
	Compass Limited	P225/55R18	NA	①	①	7.0 x 18	②	100
	Patriot Sport	P205/70R16	P215/65R17	①	①	6.5 x 16 6.5 x 17	②	100
	Patriot Limited	P215/60R17	P215/65R17	①	①	6.5 x 17	②	100
2011	Compass Sport	P215/60R17	NA	①	①	6.5 x 17	②	100
	Compass Limited	P225/55R18	NA	①	①	7.0 x 18	②	100
	Patriot Sport	P205/70R16	P215/65R17	①	①	6.5 x 16 6.5 x 17	②	100
	Patriot Limited	P215/60R17	P215/65R17	①	①	6.5 x 17	②	100

OEM: Original Equipment Manufacturer

PSI: Pounds Per Square Inch

NA: Information not available

① See the tire placard on the vehicle.

② If the travel end play exceeds 0.031 inch (0.8mm), replace the ball joint.

25766_COMP_C0012

BRAKE SPECIFICATIONS
All measurements in inches unless noted

Year	Model		Brake Disc Original Thickness	Brake Disc Minimum Thickness	Brake Disc Maximum Runout	Brake Drum Diameter Original Inside Diameter	Brake Drum Diameter Max. Wear Limit	Brake Drum Diameter Maximum Machine Diameter	Minimum Lining Thickness	Brake Caliper Bracket Bolts (ft. lbs.)	Brake Caliper Guide Pin Bolts (ft. lbs.)
2010	Compass	F	1.020-1.028	0.961	0.0020	NA	NA	NA	0.040	80	32
		R	0.386-0.402	0.331	0.0024	NS	9.079	①	0.040	52	32
	Patriot	F	1.020-1.028	0.961	0.0020	NA	NA	NA	0.040	80	32
		R	0.386-0.402	0.331	0.0024	NS	9.079	①	0.040	52	32
2011	Compass	F	1.020-1.028	0.961	0.0020	NA	NA	NA	0.040	80	32
		R	0.386-0.402	0.331	0.0024	NS	9.079	①	0.040	52	32
	Patriot	F	1.020-1.028	0.961	0.0020	NA	NA	NA	0.040	80	32
		R	0.386-0.402	0.331	0.0024	NS	9.079	①	0.040	52	32

F: Front

R: Rear

NA: Not Applicable

NS: Not Specified

① All brake drums are marked on the inside with the maximum allowable brake drum diameter.

② Rear drum brake shoe lining thickness is not specified; rear disc brake pad minimum thickness is 0.040 inch (1mm).

25766_COMP_C0013

SCHEDULED MAINTENANCE INTERVALS
2010 JEEP COMPASS & PATRIOT

TO BE SERVICED	TYPE OF SERVIC	6	12	18	24	30	36	42	48	54	60	66	72	78	84	90	96	102	108	114	120
Accessory drive belts	R																				✓
Air cleaner element ①	R					✓					✓					✓					✓
Air conditioner system	S/I	Inspect system operation annually																			
Automatic transaxle fluid	S/I	Once a month																			
Automatic transaxle fluid and filter	R																				✓
Battery (clean/tighten terminals)	S/I	Once a month																			
Brake fluid level	S/I	Once a month																			
Brake hoses/lines (incl.	S/I	✓	✓	✓	✓	✓	✓	✓	✓	✓	✓	✓	✓	✓	✓	✓	✓	✓	✓	✓	✓
Cabin air filter	R		✓		✓		✓		✓		✓		✓		✓		✓		✓		✓
CV joints	S/I		✓		✓				✓				✓				✓				✓
Engine coolant	R	60 months or 102,000 miles																			
Engine oil and filter ②	R	✓	✓	✓	✓	✓	✓	✓	✓	✓	✓	✓	✓	✓	✓	✓	✓	✓	✓	✓	✓
Engine oil and coolant	I	Inspect at each fuel stop																			
Exhaust system	S/I		✓		✓				✓				✓				✓				✓
Front and rear brake linings	S/I		✓		✓		✓		✓		✓		✓		✓		✓		✓		✓
Lights	S/I	Once a month																			
Manual transaxle fluid	S/I	✓	✓	✓	✓	✓	✓	✓	✓	✓	✓	✓	✓	✓	✓	✓	✓	✓	✓	✓	✓
Parking brake adjust (4-wheel disc)	S/I					✓					✓					✓					✓
PCV valve	S/I																✓				
Power steering fluid level	S/I	Once a month																			
Power Transfer Unit (PTU) fluid	R										✓										✓
Rear Drive Assembly (RDA) fluid	R										✓										✓
Rotate and inspect tires	S/I	✓	✓	✓	✓	✓	✓	✓	✓	✓	✓	✓	✓	✓	✓	✓	✓	✓	✓	✓	✓
Spark plugs (except 2.4L PZ	R					✓					✓					✓					✓
Spark plugs (2.4L PZEV)																		✓			
Suspension components	S/I				✓				✓				✓				✓				✓
Tire inflation and condition	S/I	Once a month																			
Windshield washer solvent level	I	Inspect at each fuel stop																			

R: Replace   S/I: Service or Inspect

25766_COMP_C0014

SCHEDULED MAINTENANCE INTERVALS
2010 JEEP COMPASS & PATRIOT

FREQUENT OPERATION MAINTENANCE (SEVERE SERVICE)

If a vehicle is operated under any of the following conditions it is considered severe service:

- Extremely dusty areas.

- 50% or more of the vehicle operation is in 90°F (32°C) or higher temperatures, or constant operation in temperatures below 32°F (0°C).

- Prolonged idling (vehicle operation in stop and go traffic).

- Frequent short running periods (engine does not warm to normal operating temperatures).

- Police, taxi, delivery usage, or trailer towing usage.

Air cleaner element (engine) replace every 12,000 miles, if necessary

Automatic transmission fluid replace every 60,000 miles

Manual transmission replace every 48,000 miles

① Inspect every 12,000 miles

② **ENGINE OIL CHANGE RESET PROCEDURE**

The vehicle is equipped with an engine oil change indicator system. The "Oil Change Required" message flashes in the Electronic Vehicle Information Center (EVIC) display for approximately 10 seconds after a single chime has sounded to indicate the next scheduled oil change interval. The engine oil change indicator sytem is duty cycle based, which means the engine oil change interval may fluctuate depending upon driving habits.

Have the vehicle serviced as soon as possible within the next 500 miles (805 km)

Unless reset, this message continues to display each time the ignition switch is turned to the ON/RUN position. To turn off the message temporarily, press and release the Menu button.

To reset the oil change indicator system (after performing the scheduled maintenance), perform the following procedure:

1. Turn the ignition switch to the "ON" position. Do not start the engine.
2. Fully press the accelerator pedal slowly 3 times within 10 seconds.
3. Turn the ignition switch to the "LOCK" position.

NOTE: If the indicator message illuminates when starting the vehicle, the oil change indicator system did not reset. If necessary, repeat the above proce

25766_COMP_C0015

SCHEDULED MAINTENANCE - NORMAL
2011 Jeep Compass & Patriot

TO BE SERVICED	TYPE OF SERVICE	VEHICLE MILEAGE INTERVAL (x1000)																
		8	16	24	32	40	48	56	64	72	80	88	96	104	112	120	128	136
Engine oil & filter	Replace	✓	✓	✓	✓	✓	✓	✓	✓	✓	✓	✓	✓	✓	✓	✓	✓	✓
Rotate tires, inspect tread wear, measure tread depth and check pressure	Rotate/ Inspect		✓		✓		✓		✓		✓		✓		✓		✓	
Brake system components	Inspect/ Service		✓		✓		✓		✓		✓		✓		✓		✓	
Exhaust system & heat shields	Inspect		✓		✓		✓		✓		✓		✓		✓		✓	
Inspect front suspension, tie rod ends and boot seals for cracks or leaks and all parts for damage, wear, improper looseness or end play.	Inspect		✓		✓		✓		✓		✓		✓		✓		✓	
CV Joints	Inspect			✓			✓			✓			✓			✓		
Engine air filter	Replace				✓				✓				✓				✓	
Adjust parking brake on vehicles equipped with four-wheel disc brakes.	Adjust				✓				✓				✓				✓	
Engine coolant	Flush/ Replace										✓							
Spark plugs	Replace				✓				✓				✓				✓	
PCV valve	Inspect/ Service												✓				✓	
Automatic transmisison fluid	Replace								✓								✓	
Accessory drive belt	Replace															✓		
Battery	Inspect/ Service	✓	✓	✓	✓	✓	✓	✓	✓	✓	✓	✓	✓	✓	✓	✓	✓	✓
Horn, exterior lamps, turn signals and hazard warning light operation	Inspect	✓	✓	✓	✓	✓	✓	✓	✓	✓	✓	✓	✓	✓	✓	✓	✓	✓
Fluid levels (all)	Top off	✓	✓	✓	✓	✓	✓	✓	✓	✓	✓	✓	✓	✓	✓	✓	✓	✓
Passenger compartment air filter	Replace		✓		✓		✓		✓		✓		✓		✓		✓	
Rear axle fluid	Replace								✓								✓	
Transfer case fluid	Replace								✓								✓	

*Oil Change Indicator System

The oil change indicator system will remind you that it is time to take your vehicle in for scheduled maintenance.

On Electronic Vehicle Information Center (EVIC) equipped vehicles, "Oil Change Required" will be displayed in the EVIC and a single chime will sound, indicating that an oil change is necessary.

On Non-EVIC equipped vehicles, "Change Oil" will flash in the instrument cluster odometer and a single chime will sound, indicating that an oil change is necessary.

Based on engine operation conditions, the oil change indicator message will illuminate. This means that service is required for your vehicle. Have your vehicle serviced as soon as possible, within the next 500 miles (805 km).

The oil change indicator message will not monitor the time since the last oil change. Change your vehicle's oil if it has been six months since your last oil change, even if the oil change indicator message is NOT illuminated.

Change your engine oil more often if you drive your vehicle off-road for an extended period of time.

Under no circumstances should oil change intervals eaxceed 8,000 miles (13 000 km) or six months, whichever comes first.

To reset the oil change indicator, perform the following procedure:

1. Turn the ignition switch to the ON position. Do not start the engine.

2. Fully press the accelerator pedal 3 times within 10 seconds.

3. Turn the ignition switch to the LOCK position.

If the indicator message illuminates when the vehicle is started, repeat the procedure.

25766_COMP_C0016

SCHEDULED MAINTENANCE - SEVERE
2011 Jeep Compass & Patriot

TO BE SERVICED	TYPE OF SERVICE	VEHICLE MILEAGE INTERVAL (x1000)																
		8	16	24	32	40	48	56	64	72	80	88	96	104	112	120	128	136
Engine oil & filter	Replace	✓	✓	✓	✓	✓	✓	✓	✓	✓	✓	✓	✓	✓	✓	✓	✓	✓
Brake system components	Inspect/		✓		✓		✓		✓		✓		✓		✓		✓	
Exhaust system & heat shields	Inspect		✓		✓		✓		✓		✓		✓		✓		✓	
Inspect the front suspension, tie rod ends and boot seals for cracks or leaks and all parts for damage, wear, improper looseness or end play.	Inspect		✓		✓		✓		✓		✓		✓		✓		✓	
CV Joints	Inspect			✓			✓			✓			✓			✓		
Engine air filter	Replace		✓		✓		✓		✓		✓		✓		✓		✓	
Adjust parking brake on vehicles equipped with four-wheel disc brakes.	Adjust				✓				✓				✓				✓	
Engine coolant	Flush/ Replace										✓							
Spark plugs	Replace			✓					✓				✓				✓	
PCV valve	Inspect/ Service												✓					
Manual trans. fluid	Replace							✓					✓					
Accessory drive belt	Replace															✓		
Battery	Inspect/	✓	✓	✓	✓	✓	✓	✓	✓	✓	✓	✓	✓	✓	✓	✓	✓	✓
Fluid levels (all)	Inspect/ Service	✓	✓	✓	✓	✓	✓	✓	✓	✓	✓	✓	✓	✓	✓	✓	✓	✓
Horn, exterior lamps, turn signals and hazard warning light operation	Inspect	✓	✓	✓	✓	✓	✓	✓	✓	✓	✓	✓	✓	✓	✓	✓	✓	✓
Passenger compartment air filter	Replace		✓		✓		✓		✓		✓		✓		✓		✓	
Rear axle fluid	Replace								✓							✓		
Transfer case fluid	Replace								✓							✓		

*Oil Change Indicator System

The oil change indicator system will remind you that it is time to take your vehicle in for scheduled maintenance.

On Electronic Vehicle Information Center (EVIC) equipped vehicles, "Oil Change Required" will be displayed in the EVIC and a single chime will sound, indicating that an oil change is necessary.

On Non-EVIC equipped vehicles, "Change Oil" will flash in the instrument cluster odometer and a single chime will sound, indicating that an oil change is necessary.

Based on engine operation conditions, the oil change indicator message will illuminate. This means that service is required for your vehicle. Have your vehicle serviced as soon as possible, within the next 500 miles (805 km).

The oil change indicator message will not monitor the time since the last oil change. Change your vehicle's oil if it has been six months since your last oil change, even if the oil change indicator message is NOT illuminated.

Change your engine oil more often if you drive your vehicle off-road for an extended period of time.

Under no circumstances should oil change intervals eaxceed 8,000 miles (13 000 km) or six months, whichever comes first.

To reset the oil change indicator, perform the following procedure:

1. Turn the ignition switch to the ON position. Do not start the engine.

2. Fully press the accelerator pedal 3 times within 10 seconds.

3. Turn the ignition switch to the LOCK position.

If the indicator message illuminates when the vehicle is started, repeat the procedure.

PRECAUTIONS

Before servicing any vehicle, please be sure to read all of the following precautions, which deal with personal safety, prevention of component damage, and important points to take into consideration when servicing a motor vehicle:

• Never open, service or drain the radiator or cooling system when the engine is hot; serious burns can occur from the steam and hot coolant.

• Observe all applicable safety precautions when working around fuel. Whenever servicing the fuel system, always work in a well-ventilated area. Do not allow fuel spray or vapors to come in contact with a spark, open flame, or excessive heat (a hot drop light, for example). Keep a dry chemical fire extinguisher near the work area. Always keep fuel in a container specifically designed for fuel storage; also, always properly seal fuel containers to avoid the possibility of fire or explosion. Refer to the additional fuel system precautions later in this section.

• Fuel injection systems often remain pressurized, even after the engine has been turned **OFF**. The fuel system pressure must be relieved before disconnecting any fuel lines. Failure to do so may result in fire and/or personal injury.

• Brake fluid often contains polyglycol ethers and polyglycols. Avoid contact with the eyes and wash your hands thoroughly after handling brake fluid. If you do get brake fluid in your eyes, flush your eyes with clean, running water for 15 minutes. If eye irritation persists, or if you have taken brake fluid internally, IMMEDIATELY seek medical assistance.

• The EPA warns that prolonged contact with used engine oil may cause a number of skin disorders, including cancer. You should make every effort to minimize your exposure to used engine oil. Protective gloves should be worn when changing oil. Wash your hands and any other exposed skin areas as soon as possible after exposure to used engine oil. Soap and water, or waterless hand cleaner should be used.

• All new vehicles are now equipped with an air bag system, often referred to as a Supplemental Restraint System (SRS) or Supplemental Inflatable Restraint (SIR) system. The system must be disabled before performing service on or around system components, steering column, instrument panel components, wiring and sensors. Failure to follow safety and disabling procedures could result in accidental air bag deployment, possible personal injury and unnecessary system repairs.

• Always wear safety goggles when working with, or around, the air bag system. When carrying a non-deployed air bag, be sure the bag and trim cover are pointed away from your body. When placing a non-deployed air bag on a work surface, always face the bag and trim cover upward, away from the surface. This will reduce the motion of the module if it is accidentally deployed. Refer to the additional air bag system precautions later in this section.

• Clean, high quality brake fluid from a sealed container is essential to the safe and proper operation of the brake system. You should always buy the correct type of brake fluid for your vehicle. If the brake fluid becomes contaminated, completely flush the system with new fluid. Never reuse any brake fluid. Any brake fluid that is removed from the system should be discarded. Also, do not allow any brake fluid to come in contact with a painted surface; it will damage the paint.

• Never operate the engine without the proper amount and type of engine oil; doing so WILL result in severe engine damage.

• Timing belt maintenance is extremely important. Many models utilize an interference-type, non-freewheeling engine. If the timing belt breaks, the valves in the cylinder head may strike the pistons, causing potentially serious (also time-consuming and expensive) engine damage. Refer to the maintenance interval charts for the recommended replacement interval for the timing belt, and to the timing belt section for belt replacement and inspection.

• Disconnecting the negative battery cable on some vehicles may interfere with the functions of the on-board computer system(s) and may require the computer to undergo a relearning process once the negative battery cable is reconnected.

• When servicing drum brakes, only disassemble and assemble one side at a time, leaving the remaining side intact for reference.

• Only an MVAC-trained, EPA-certified automotive technician should service the air conditioning system or its components.

HOISTING—STANDARD PROCEDURE

See Figure 1.

✳✳ CAUTION

The hoisting and jack lifting points provided are for a complete vehicle. When the engine or rear suspension is removed from a vehicle, the center of gravity is altered making some hoisting conditions unstable. Properly support or secure vehicle to hoisting device when these conditions exist.

✳✳ WARNING

Do not position hoisting device on suspension components, damage to vehicle can result. Do not attempt to raise one entire side of the vehicle by placing a floor jack midway between the front and rear wheels. This practice may result in permanent damage to the body.

When properly positioned, a floor jack can be used to lift the vehicle and support the raised vehicle with jack stands.

A floor jack, or any lifting device, must never be used on any part of the underbody other then the described areas.

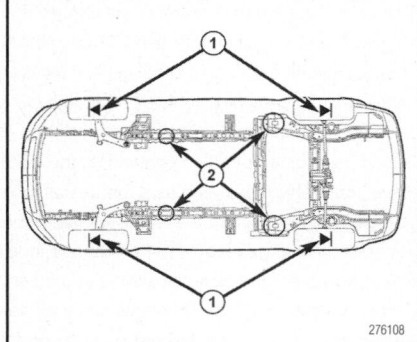

276108

Fig. 1 Standard procedure—hoisting for drive on lift (1) and single-post or frame contact lift (2), dual-post or chassis lift (2), dual-lift or outboard lift (2), and floor jack (2)

GENERAL INFORMATION

PRECAUTIONS

- Certain components within the ABS system are not intended to be serviced or repaired individually.

- The Anti-Lock control unit is a microprocessor similar to other computer units in the vehicle. Ensure that the ignition switch is **OFF** before removing or installing controller harnesses. Avoid static electricity discharge at or near the controller.

- The antilock brake system uses an electronic control module known as the Antilock Brake Module (ABM). This module is designed to withstand normal current draws associated with vehicle operation. Care must be taken to avoid overloading the circuits.

- In testing for open or short circuits, do not ground or apply voltage to any of the circuits unless instructed to do so for a diagnostic procedure.

- These circuits should only be tested using a high impedance multimeter or the designated scan tool as described in the procedure. Never remove or apply power to any control module with the ignition in the ON position. Before removing or connecting battery cables, fuses, or connectors, always turn the ignition to the OFF position.

- Never connect or disconnect the ABM 47-way with the ignition switch in the ON position.

- This vehicle uses active wheel speed sensors. Do not apply voltage to wheel speed sensors at any time.

- Use only factory wiring harnesses. Do not cut or splice wiring to the brake circuits. Adding aftermarket electrical equipment (such as, car phone, radar detector, citizen band radio, trailer lighting, trailer brakes, etc.) on a vehicle equipped with antilock brakes may affect the function of the antilock brake system.

- When performing any service procedure on a vehicle equipped with ABS, do not apply a 12-volt power source to the ground circuit of the pump motor in the HCU (Hydraulic Control Unit). Doing this will damage the pump motor and will require replacement of the entire HCU.

- An attempt to remove or disconnect certain system components may result in improper system operation.

- If welding work is to be performed on the vehicle using an electric arc welder, disconnect the ABM (Antilock Brake Module) connector.

- Many components of the ABS are not serviceable and must be replaced as an assembly. Do not disassemble any component which is not designed to be serviced.

- Use only the recommended jacking or hoisting positions for this vehicle whenever it is necessary to lift a vehicle. Refer to Hoisting Standard Procedure in Precautions.

- Do not use rubber hoses or other parts not specifically specified for an ABS system. When using repair kits, replace all parts included in the kit. Partial or incorrect repair may lead to functional problems and require the replacement of components.

- Brake fluid will damage painted surfaces. If brake fluid is spilled on any painted surfaces, wash it off immediately with water.

- Never use gasoline, kerosene, alcohol, motor oil, transmission fluid, or any fluid containing mineral oil to clean system components. These fluids damage rubber cups and seals.

- During service procedures, grease or any other foreign material must be kept off the caliper assembly, brake linings, brake rotor and external surfaces of the hub.

- Lubricate rubber parts with clean, fresh brake fluid to ease assembly. Do not use shop air to clean parts; damage to rubber components may result.

- Use only Mopar® Brake Fluid DOT 3 Motor Vehicle or its equivalent from a tightly sealed container. Do not use petroleum-based fluid because seal damage in the brake system will result.

- If any hydraulic component or line is removed or replaced, it may be necessary to bleed the entire system.

- A clean repair area is essential. Always clean the reservoir and cap thoroughly before removing the cap. The slightest amount of dirt in the fluid may plug an orifice and impair the system function. Perform repairs after components have been thoroughly cleaned; use only denatured alcohol to clean components. Do not allow ABS components to come into contact with any substance containing mineral oil; this includes used shop rags.

- Chrysler LLC does not manufacture any vehicles or replacement parts that contain asbestos. Aftermarket products may or may not contain asbestos. Refer to aftermarket product packaging for product information.

Whether the product contains asbestos or not, dust and dirt can accumulate on brake parts during normal use. Follow practices prescribed by appropriate regulations for the handling, processing and disposing of dust and debris.

- When handling the brake rotor and caliper, be careful to avoid damaging the brake rotor and caliper, and to avoid scratching or nicking the brake shoe lining.

ABS DIAGNOSIS & TESTING— INSPECTION & ROAD TEST

1. Visually inspect the ABS for damaged or disconnected components and connectors.

2. Verify the brake lamps are operational. If they are not, repair them prior to continuing.

3. Connect a scan tool to the Data Link Connector located under the instrument panel to the left of the steering column. If the scan tool does not power-up, check the power and ground supplies to the connector.

4. Turn the ignition key to the ON position.

5. Using the scan tool, read and record any Diagnostic Trouble Codes (DTCs). If any DTCs are present, refer to the appropriate diagnostic information.

If no problems are observed, it will be necessary to road test the vehicle.

Many ABS conditions judged to be a problem by the driver may be normal operating conditions.

✳✳ CAUTION

Conditions that result in turning on the red brake warning indicator lamp may indicate reduced braking ability.

Before road testing a brake complaint vehicle, note whether the red BRAKE warning indicator lamp, amber ABS warning indicator lamp, or both are turned on. If it is the red BRAKE warning indicator, there is a brake hydraulic problem that must be corrected before driving the vehicle.

If the amber ABS warning indicator is on, road test the vehicle as described below. While only the amber ABS warning indicator is on, the ABS is not functional. The ability to stop the car using the base brake system should not be affected.

6. Turn the key to the OFF position and then back to the ON position. Note whether the amber ABS warning indicator lamp continues to stay on.

7. If the amber ABS warning indicator lamp stays on, shift into gear and drive the car to a speed of approximately 15 mph (25 km/h) to complete the ABS Start-Up and Drive-Off Cycles. If at this time the amber

ABS warning indicator lamp stays on, refer to the appropriate diagnostic information.

8. If the amber ABS warning indicator lamp goes out at any time, drive the vehicle a short distance. Accelerate the vehicle to a speed of at least 40 mph (64 km/h). Bring the vehicle to a complete stop, braking hard enough to cause the ABS to cycle. Repeat this action several times. Using the scan tool read and record any Diagnostic Trouble Codes (DTCs). If any DTCs are present, refer to the appropriate diagnostic information.

WHEEL SPEED SENSORS

REMOVAL & INSTALLATION

Front

See Figures 2 through 5.

1. Refer to Brake System precautions.
2. Open the hood.
3. Disconnect the wheel speed sensor cable connector (2) from the wiring harness connector (3) on top of the frame rail (1) to the inside of the strut tower.
4. Raise and support the vehicle. (Refer to Hoisting—Standard Procedure).
5. Remove the grommet (1) from the hole in the body (7) and pull the wheel speed sensor cable out of the hole.
6. Remove the speed sensor cable routing clip (2) from the outside frame rail (6).
7. Remove the screw fastening the cable routing clamp (3) to the outside frame rail (6).
8. Remove the screw (1) securing the wheel speed sensor routing bracket (2) to the brake flex hose bracket (5).
9. Remove the mounting screw (2) fastening the wheel speed sensor head (3) to the knuckle (4). Pull the sensor head out of the knuckle.

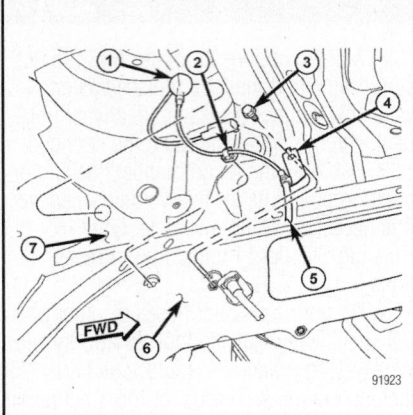

Fig. 3 Remove the grommet (1) from the hole in the body (7) and pull the wheel speed sensor cable out of the hole

➡ **In the following step, the routing clip can be easily removed without damaging it by rotating it (with entire sensor) counterclockwise.**

10. Remove the routing clip (1) securing wheel speed sensor cable to the knuckle (4). Remove the sensor from the vehicle.

To install:

※※ WARNING

Failure to install speed sensor cables properly may result in contact with moving parts or an over extension of cables causing an open circuit. Be sure that cables are installed, routed, and clipped properly.

11. Install the wheel speed sensor head into the knuckle. Install the mounting screw and tighten it to 106 inch lbs. (12 Nm).

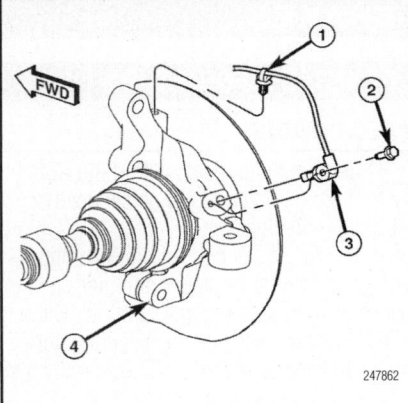

Fig. 5 Remove the mounting screw (2) fastening the wheel speed sensor head (3) to the knuckle (4). Pull the sensor head out of the knuckle

12. Install the routing clip, securing the wheel speed sensor cable to the knuckle.
13. Position the wheel speed sensor routing bracket on the brake flex hose bracket and install the mounting screw. Tighten the mounting screw to 13 ft. lbs. (18 Nm).
14. Position the wheel speed sensor cable routing clamp on the outside frame rail and install the mounting screw. Tighten the mounting screw to 13 ft. lbs. (18 Nm).
15. Install the speed sensor cable routing clip on the outside frame rail.
16. Insert the wheel speed sensor cable through the hole in the body and install the grommet in the hole.
17. Lower the vehicle.
18. Connect the wheel speed sensor cable connector to the wiring harness connector on top of the frame rail.
19. Verify the repair and clear any faults.

Rear

See Figures 6 through 12.

1. Refer to Brake System precautions.
2. Raise the cargo floor cover.
3. Through the opening in the bottom of the quarter trim panel, disconnect the wheel speed sensor cable connector (2) at the body wiring harness connector (3).
4. Raise and support the vehicle. (Refer to Hoisting—Standard Procedure).
5. Remove the wheel mounting nuts (3), then the rear tire and wheel assembly (1).
6. Remove the grommet (2) from the hole in the body (1) and pull the wheel speed sensor cable out through the hole.
7. Remove the speed sensor cable routing clip (3) from the outside frame rail (4).
8. Remove the screw (1) fastening the

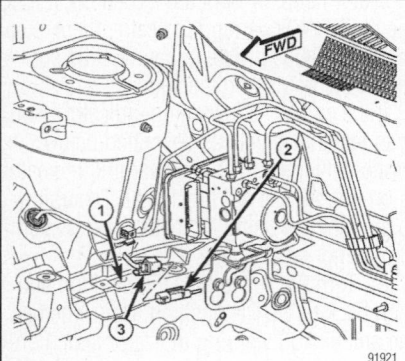

Fig. 2 Disconnect the wheel speed sensor cable connector (2) from the wiring harness connector (3) on top of the frame rail (1) to the inside of the strut tower

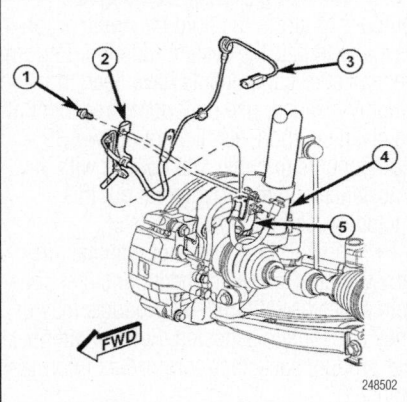

Fig. 4 Remove the screw (1) securing the wheel speed sensor routing bracket (2) to the brake flex hose bracket (5)

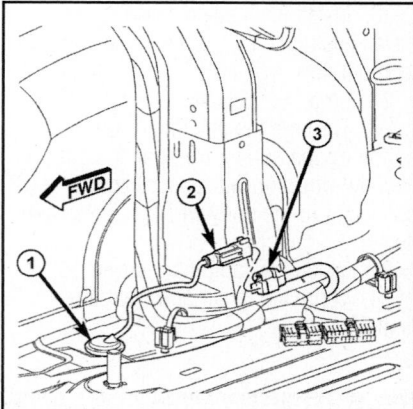

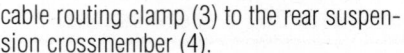

Fig. 6 Through the opening in the bottom of the quarter trim panel, disconnect the wheel speed sensor cable connector (2) at the body wiring harness connector (3)

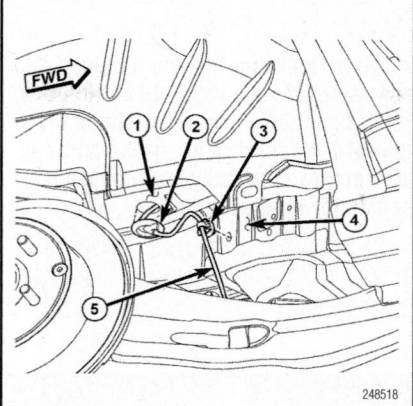

Fig. 8 Remove the grommet (2) from the hole in the body (1) and pull the wheel speed sensor cable out through the hole

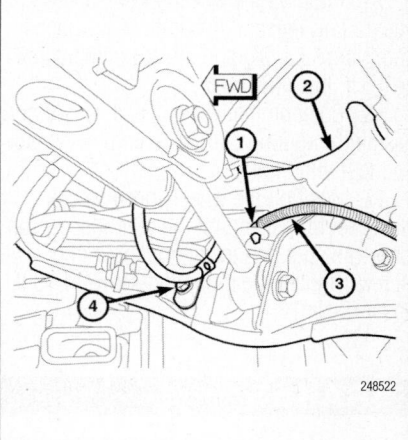

Fig. 10 Remove the speed sensor cable routing clip (1) from the trailing link (2)

cable routing clamp (3) to the rear suspension crossmember (4).

9. Remove the speed sensor cable routing clip (1) from the trailing link (2).

10. Remove the screw (4) fastening the cable routing clamp to the trailing link.

11. For AWD only: Unclip the wheel speed sensor head (1) from the spring-loaded retainer on the rear of the hub and bearing (2). Remove the sensor from the vehicle.

12. For FWD only: Remove the screw (1) fastening the wheel speed sensor head (3) in the rear of the hub and bearing (2). Remove the sensor from the vehicle.

To install:

❋❋ WARNING

Failure to install speed sensor cables properly may result in contact with moving parts or an over extension of cables causing an open circuit. Be

sure that cables are installed, routed, and clipped properly.

➡When installing the sensor head to the spring-loaded retainer on the hub and bearing, make sure the head is held snug in the retainer. If there is any play, the clip is deformed and the hub and bearing must be replaced. The retainer is not serviced separately.

13. For AWD vehicles:

a. Clip the wheel speed sensor head (flat side to bearing rear face) into the spring-loaded retainer on the rear of the hub and bearing.

14. For FWD vehicles:

a. Install the wheel speed sensor head into the rear of the hub and bearing.

b. Install the wheel speed sensor head mounting screw. Tighten the screw to 89 inch lbs. (10 Nm).

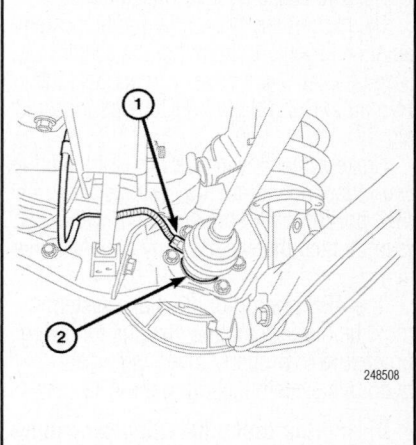

Fig. 11 Unclip the wheel speed sensor head (1) from the spring-loaded retainer on the rear of the hub and bearing (2)— AWD only.

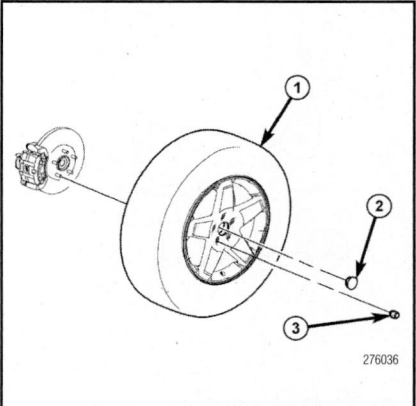

Fig. 7 Remove the wheel mounting nuts (3), then the rear tire and wheel assembly (1)

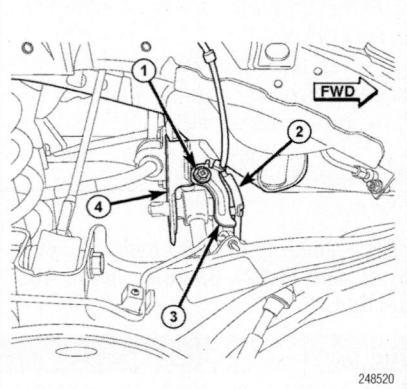

Fig. 9 Remove the screw (1) fastening the cable routing clamp (3) to the rear suspension crossmember (4)

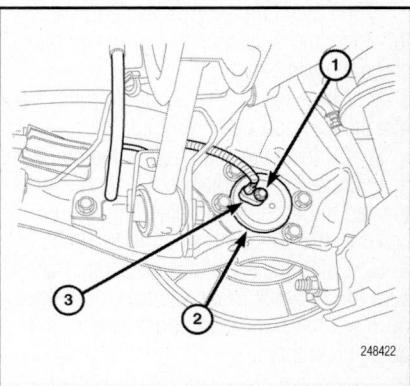

Fig. 12 Remove the screw (1) fastening the wheel speed sensor head (3) in the rear of the hub and bearing (2)—FWD only. Remove the sensor from the vehicle

15. Position the wheel speed sensor on the trailing link and install the screw securing it in place. Tighten the mounting screw to 13 ft. lbs. (18 Nm).

16. Position the wheel speed sensor and install the routing clip, fastening the sensor to the trailing link.

17. Position the wheel speed sensor cable routing clamp on the rear suspension crossmember and install the mounting screw. Tighten the mounting screw to 13 ft. lbs. (18 Nm).

18. Install the speed sensor cable routing clip on the outside frame rail.

➡ When inserting the wheel speed sensor cable through the hole in the body, route the cable toward the shock tower to make it easier to grasp the cable to connect it to the body wiring harness connector in a later step.

19. Insert the wheel speed sensor cable through the hole in the body and install the grommet in the hole.

20. Install the tire and wheel assembly. Install and tighten the wheel mounting nuts to 100 ft. lbs. (135 Nm).

21. Lower the vehicle.

22. Through the opening in the bottom of the quarter trim panel, connect the wheel speed sensor cable connector to the body wiring harness connector.

23. Install the cargo floor cover.

24. Verify the repair and clear any faults.

BRAKES   BLEEDING THE BRAKE SYSTEM

BLEEDING PROCEDURE

ANTILOCK BRAKE SYSTEM (ABS) BLEEDING

Refer to Brake System precautions.

Bleed the base brake's hydraulic system anytime air enters the hydraulic system. Bleed the ABS whenever you suspect the Hydraulic Control Unit (HCU) has ingested air.

Brake systems with ABS must be bled as two independent braking systems. The non-ABS portion of the brake system with ABS is to be bled the same as any non-ABS system.

The ABS portion of the brake system must be bled separately. Use the following procedure to properly bleed the brake hydraulic system including the ABS.

➡ During the brake bleeding procedure, be sure the brake fluid level remains close to the FULL level in the master cylinder fluid reservoir. Check the fluid level periodically during the bleeding procedure and add Mopar® DOT 3 brake fluid as required.

When bleeding the ABS system, follow this bleeding sequence to insure complete and adequate bleeding.

1. Make sure all hydraulic fluid lines are installed and properly torqued.

2. Connect the scan tool to the diagnostics connector. The diagnostic connector is located under the lower steering column cover to the left of the steering column.

3. Using the scan tool, check to make sure the Antilock Brake Module, or ABM, does not have any fault codes stored. If it does, clear them.

✳✳ CAUTION

When bleeding the brake system wear safety glasses. A clear bleed tube (see figure for Manual Bleeding)

must be attached to the bleeder screws and submerged in a clear container filled part way with clean brake fluid. Direct the flow of brake fluid away from yourself and the painted surfaces of the vehicle. Brake fluid at high pressure may come out of the bleeder screws when they are opened.

➡ Pressure bleeding is recommended to bleed the base brake system to ensure all air is removed from system. Manual bleeding may also be used, but additional time is needed to remove all air from system.

➡ Bleed the base brake system. (Refer to Bleeding the Brake System.)

4. Using the scan tool, select ECU VIEW, followed by ABS MISCELLANEOUS FUNCTIONS to access bleeding. Follow the instructions displayed. When finished, disconnect the scan tool and proceed.

5. Bleed the base brake system a second time. Check brake fluid level in the reservoir periodically to prevent emptying, causing air to enter the hydraulic system.

6. Fill the master cylinder fluid reservoir to the FULL level.

7. Test drive the vehicle to be sure the brakes are operating correctly and that the brake pedal does not feel spongy.

MANUAL BLEEDING

See Figure 13.

➡ For bleeding the ABS hydraulic system, refer to ABS Bleeding in the ABS section.

✳✳ WARNING

Before removing the master cylinder cap, wipe it clean to prevent dirt and other foreign matter from dropping into the master cylinder reservoir.

✳✳ WARNING

Use only Mopar® brake fluid or an equivalent from a fresh, tightly sealed container. Brake fluid must conform to DOT 3 specifications.

Do not pump the brake pedal at any time while having a bleeder screw open during the bleeding process. This will only increase the amount of air in the system and make additional bleeding necessary.

Do not allow the master cylinder reservoir to run out of brake fluid while bleeding the system. An empty reservoir will allow additional air into the brake system. Check the fluid level frequently and add fluid as needed.

Use the following wheel circuit sequence for bleeding the brake hydraulic system to ensure adequate removal of all trapped air from the hydraulic system:

- Left rear wheel
- Right front wheel

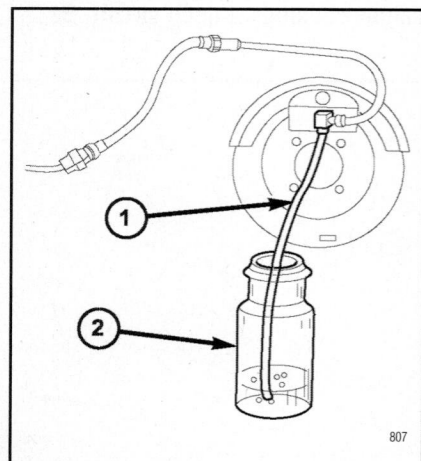

807

Fig. 13 Attach a clear plastic hose (1) to the bleeder screw and feed the hose into a clear jar (2) containing enough fresh brake fluid to submerge the end of the hose

- Right rear wheel
- Left front wheel

Manual Bleeding Procedure

➡️**You will need a helper to bleed the brakes manually.**

1. Attach a clear plastic hose (1) to the bleeder screw and feed the hose into a clear jar (2) containing enough fresh brake fluid to submerge the end of the hose.

2. Have a helper pump the brake pedal three or four times and hold it in the down position.

3. With the pedal in the down position, open the bleeder screw at least one full turn.

4. Once the brake pedal has dropped, close the bleeder screw. After the bleeder screw is closed, release the brake pedal.

5. Repeat the above steps until all trapped air is removed from that wheel circuit (usually four or five times).

6. Bleed the remaining wheel circuits in the same manner until all air is removed from the brake system.

7. Monitor the fluid level in the master cylinder reservoir to make sure it does not go dry.

8. Check and adjust brake fluid level to the FULL mark.

9. Check the brake pedal travel. If pedal travel is excessive or has not been improved, some air may still

10. Test drive the vehicle to verify the brakes are operating properly and pedal feel is correct.

MASTER CYLINDER BLEEDING

See Figure 14.

➡️**On vehicles without ABS this procedure is designed to be performed with the proportioning valves installed in the master cylinder.**

1. Clamp the master cylinder in a vise with soft-jaw caps.

2. Attach the special tools for bleeding the master cylinder in the following fashion:

   a. Thread the bleeder tube adapters (3), Special Tool 8822-2, into the primary and secondary outlet ports of the master cylinder. Tighten the adapters to 150 inch lbs. (17 Nm).

   b. Thread a bleeder tube (2), Special Tool 8358-1, into each adapter. Tighten the tube nuts to 150 inch lbs. (17 Nm).

   c. Flex each bleeder tube and place the open ends into the neck of the master cylinder reservoir. Position the open ends of the tubes into the reservoir so their outlets are below the surface of the brake fluid in the reservoir when filled.

➡️**Make sure the ends of the bleeder tubes stay below the surface of the brake fluid in the reservoir at all times during the bleeding procedure.**

3. Fill the brake fluid reservoir with fresh Mopar® Brake Fluid DOT 3 Motor Vehicle, or an equivalent. Refer to Brake Specifications.

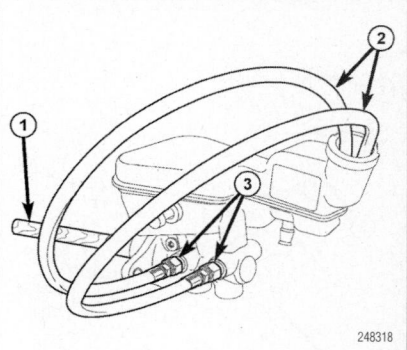

Fig. 14 Thread bleeder tube adapters (3), Special Tool 8822-2, into the primary and secondary outlet ports of the master cylinder

4. Using an appropriately sized wooden dowel as a pushrod, slowly press the pistons inward discharging brake fluid through the bleeder tubes, then release the pressure, allowing the pistons to return to the released position. Repeat this several times until all air bubbles are expelled from the master cylinder bore and bleeder tubes.

5. Remove the bleeder tubes and adapters from the master cylinder and plug the master cylinder outlet ports.

6. Remove the master cylinder from the vise.

7. Install the master cylinder on the vehicle.

BRAKES
FRONT DISC BRAKES

❊❊ WARNING

Dust and dirt accumulating on brake parts during normal use may contain asbestos fibers from production or aftermarket brake linings. Breathing excessive concentrations of asbestos fibers can cause serious bodily harm. Exercise care when servicing brake parts. Do not sand or grind brake lining unless equipment used is designed to contain the dust residue. Do not clean brake parts with compressed air or by dry brushing. Cleaning should be done by dampening the brake components with a fine mist of water, then wiping the brake components clean with a dampened cloth. Dispose of cloth and all residue containing asbestos fibers in an impermeable container with the appropriate label. Follow practices prescribed by the Occupational

Safety and Health Administration (OSHA) and the Environmental Protection Agency (EPA) for the handling, processing, and disposing of dust or debris that may contain asbestos fibers.

BRAKE CALIPER

REMOVAL & INSTALLATION

See Figures 15 through 17.

1. Refer to Brake System precautions.

2. Using a brake pedal holding tool as shown, depress the brake pedal past its first inch (25 mm) of travel and hold it in this position. This will isolate the master cylinder from the brake hydraulic system and will not allow the brake fluid to drain out of the master cylinder reservoir when the lines are opened.

3. Raise and support the vehicle. (Refer to Hoisting—Standard Procedure).

4. Remove the wheel mounting nuts, then the tire and wheel assembly. (Refer to second image in Rear Wheel Sensor Removal procedure).

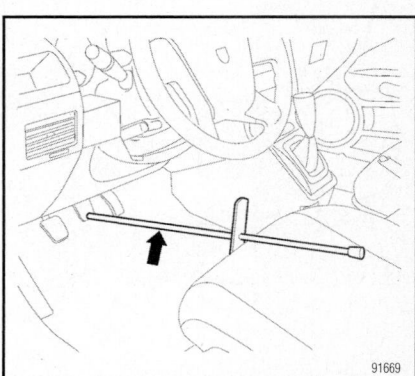

Fig. 15 Using a brake pedal holding tool as shown, depress the brake pedal past its first inch (25 mm) of travel and hold it in this position

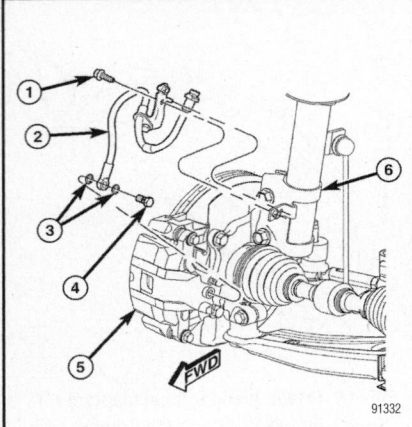

Fig. 16 Remove the banjo bolt (4) connecting the brake flex hose (2) to the brake caliper (5). There are two washers (3) that will come off with the banjo bolt. Discard the washers

5. Remove the banjo bolt (4) connecting the brake flex hose (2) to the brake caliper (5). There are two washers (3) that will come off with the banjo bolt. Discard the washers.

➡When removing the caliper guide pin bolts (2, 3) note that one (upper) has a special sleeve on the end. Install this bolt in the upper mounting hole when the caliper is installed.

6. Remove the two brake caliper guide pin bolts (2, 3).

7. Slide the disc brake caliper (4) from the disc brake adapter bracket (1) and brake pads and remove.

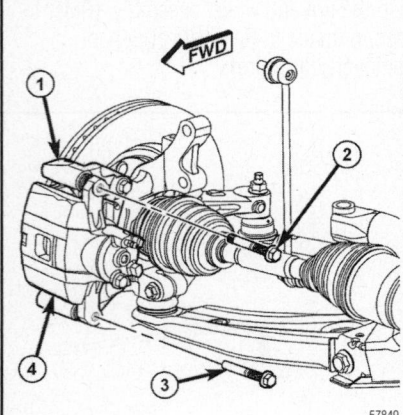

Fig. 17 When removing the caliper guide pin bolts (2, 3) note that one bolt (upper) has a special sleeve on the end. Install this bolt in the upper mounting hole when the caliper is installed

8. Verify the repair and clear any faults.

To install:

9. Completely retract the caliper piston back into the bore of the caliper. Use a C-clamp to retract the piston. Place a wood block over the piston before installing the C-clamp to avoid damaging the piston.

✳✳ WARNING

Use care when installing the caliper onto the adapter bracket to avoid damaging the guide pin boots.

10. Install the disc brake caliper over the brake pads on the brake caliper adapter bracket.

➡When installing the caliper guide pin bolts make sure that the one that has a special sleeve on the end is installed in the upper mounting hole.

11. Align the caliper guide pin bolt holes with the adapter bracket. Install the upper (with special sleeve) and lower caliper guide pin bolts. Tighten the guide pin bolts to 32 ft. lbs. (43 Nm).

12. Install the banjo bolt connecting the brake flex hose to the brake caliper. Install NEW washers on each side of the hose fitting as the banjo bolt is guided through the fitting. Thread the banjo bolt into the caliper and tighten it to 18 ft. lbs. (24 Nm).

13. Install the tire and wheel assembly. Install and tighten the wheel mounting nuts to 100 ft. lbs. (135 Nm).

14. Lower the vehicle.

15. Remove the brake pedal holding tool.

16. Bleed the caliper as necessary.

17. Road test the vehicle and make several stops to wear off any foreign material on the brakes and to seat the brake shoes.

DISC BRAKE PADS

REMOVAL & INSTALLATION

See Figure 18.

1. Refer to Brake System precautions.

2. Raise and support the vehicle. (Refer to Hoisting—Standard Procedure).

➡Perform Step #2 through Step #5 on each side of the vehicle to complete the pad set removal.

3. Remove the wheel mounting nuts, then the tire and wheel assembly. (Refer to second image in Rear Wheel Sensor Removal procedure).

➡When removing the caliper guide pin bolts (refer to image for Front Caliper

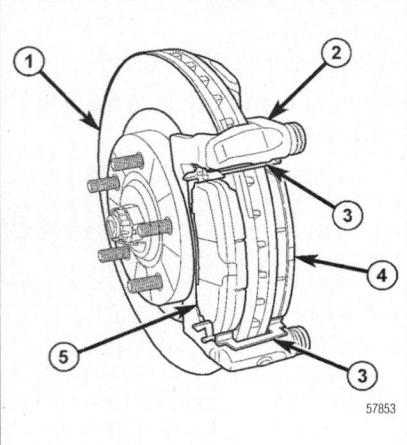

Fig. 18 Remove the disc brake caliper (4) from the disc brake adapter bracket (1) and hang it out of the way using wire or a bungee cord. Use care not to overextend the brake hose when doing this

Removal) note that one (upper) has a special sleeve on the end. It important to install this bolt in the upper mounting hole when installing the caliper.

4. Remove the two brake caliper guide pin bolts.

5. Remove the disc brake caliper (4) from the disc brake adapter bracket (1) and hang it out of the way using wire or a bungee cord. Use care not to overextend the brake hose when doing this.

6. Remove the brake pads (4, 5) from the caliper adapter bracket (2).

To install:

➡Perform Step #1 through Step #5 on each side of the vehicle to complete pad set installation, then proceed to Step #6.

➡Make sure that the audible wear indicators (if equipped) are placed toward the top when the inboard brake pads are installed on each side of the vehicle.

7. Place the brake pads in the abutment shims clipped into the disc brake caliper adapter bracket as shown. Place the pad with the wear indicator attached on the inboard side.

8. Completely retract the caliper piston back into the bore of the caliper.

✳✳ WARNING

Use care when installing the caliper onto the adapter bracket to avoid damaging the boots.

9. Install the disc brake caliper over the

brake pads on the brake caliper adapter bracket.

➥**When installing the caliper guide pin bolts make sure that the one that has a special sleeve on the end is installed in the upper mounting hole.**

10. Align the caliper guide pin bolt holes with the adapter bracket. Install the upper (with special sleeve) and lower caliper guide pin bolts. Tighten the guide pin bolts to 32 ft. lbs. (43 Nm).

11. Install the tire and wheel assembly. Install and tighten the wheel mounting nuts to 100 ft. lbs. (135 Nm).

12. Lower the vehicle.

13. Pump the brake pedal several times before moving the vehicle to set the pads to the brake rotor.

14. Check and adjust the brake fluid level in the reservoir as necessary.

15. Road test the vehicle and make several stops to wear off any foreign material on the brakes and to seat the brake pads.

BRAKES

REAR DISC BRAKES

✳✳ WARNING

Dust and dirt accumulating on brake parts during normal use may contain asbestos fibers from production or aftermarket brake linings. Breathing excessive concentrations of asbestos fibers can cause serious bodily harm. Exercise care when servicing brake parts. Do not sand or grind brake lining unless equipment used is designed to contain the dust residue. Do not clean brake parts with compressed air or by dry brushing. Cleaning should be done by dampening the brake components with a fine mist of water, then wiping the brake components clean with a dampened cloth. Dispose of cloth and all residue containing asbestos fibers in an impermeable container with the appropriate label. Follow practices prescribed by the Occupational Safety and Health Administration (OSHA) and the Environmental Protection Agency (EPA) for the handling, processing, and disposing of dust or debris that may contain asbestos fibers.

BRAKE CALIPER

REMOVAL & INSTALLATION

See Figures 19 through 21.

1. Refer to Brake System precautions.
2. Using a brake pedal holding tool as shown, depress the brake pedal past its first inch (25 mm) of travel and hold it in this position. This will isolate the master cylinder from the brake hydraulic system and will not allow the brake fluid to drain out of the master cylinder reservoir while the lines are disconnected.
3. Raise and support the vehicle. (Refer to Hoisting—Standard Procedure).
4. Remove the wheel mounting nuts, then the tire and wheel assembly. (Refer to second image in Rear Wheel Sensor Removal procedure).

5. Unthread the brake tube nut (2) at the rear flex hose.
6. Remove the clip (3) securing the rear flex hose to the trailing link mounted bracket. Remove the flex hose from the bracket.
7. Unthread and remove the brake flex hose (4) from the brake caliper (1).

➥**When removing the caliper guide pin bolts (2, 3), note that one bolt has a special sleeve on the tip and the other**

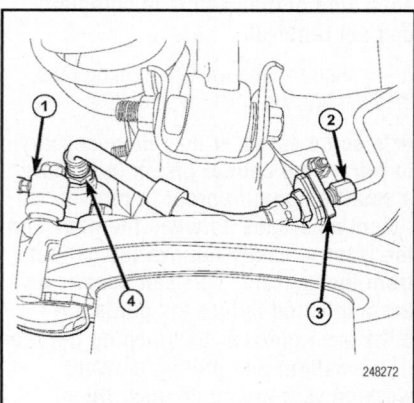

Fig. 19 Unthread the brake tube nut (2) at the rear flex hose

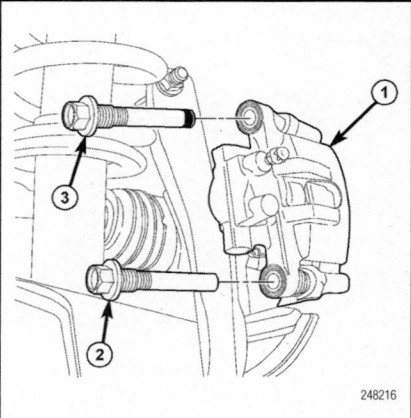

Fig. 20 Two brake caliper guide pin bolts (2, 3)

does not. Depending on the build date, this special sleeve bolt (3) can be located in either the top or bottom location. When installing, make sure the bolts are put back in the same locations as when removed to avoid NVH (Noise, Vibration and Harshness) issues.

8. Remove the two brake caliper guide pin bolts (2, 3).
9. Slide and remove the disc brake caliper (1) with outboard brake pad attached from the disc brake adapter bracket, inboard brake pad and rotor.
10. Remove the outboard brake pad from the caliper by prying the brake pad retaining clip over the raised area on the caliper. Slide the brake pad off of the brake caliper.

To install:

11. If not already performed, completely retract the caliper piston back into the piston bore of the caliper. Use a C-clamp to retract the piston. Place a wood block over the piston before installing the C-clamp to avoid damaging the piston.
12. Slide the outboard brake pad onto the caliper. Be sure the retaining clip is squarely seated in the depressed areas on the caliper beyond the raised retaining bead.

✳✳ WARNING

Use care when installing the caliper onto the disc brake adapter to avoid damaging the guide pin boots.

13. Install the disc brake caliper with outboard brake pad attached over the inboard brake pad and rotor, onto the brake caliper adapter bracket.

➥**When installing the caliper guide pin bolts, make sure the bolts are put back in the same locations as when removed to avoid NVH issues. Depending on the build date and services performed, the location of the bolt with the special sleeve on the tip can vary.**

14. Align the caliper guide pin bolt holes with the adapter bracket. Install the lower

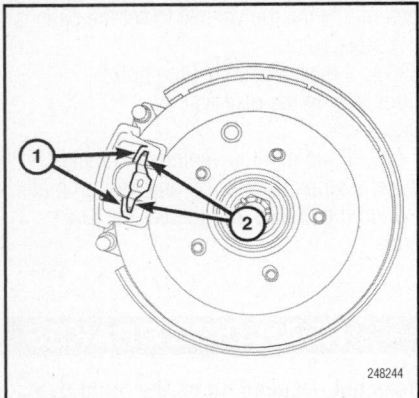

Fig. 21 The retaining clip (2) must be squarely seated in the depressed areas (1) on the caliper fingers

(with the special sleeve) and upper caliper guide pin bolts. Tighten the guide pin bolts to 32 ft. lbs. (43 Nm).

➡ Once the caliper is installed, inspect the outboard brake pad to make sure it is correctly positioned. The retaining clip (2) must be squarely seated in the depressed areas (1) on the caliper fingers. Also, the nubs on the pad's steel backing plate must be fully seated in the depressions formed into the inside of the caliper fingers. There should be no gap between the pad backing plate and the caliper fingers.

15. Thread the rear brake flex hose into the brake caliper. Tighten the flex hose fitting at the caliper to 133 inch lbs. (15 Nm).

16. Route and install the brake flex hose into the trailing link mounted bracket. Install the clip securing the flex hose to the bracket.

17. Thread the brake tube nut into the brake flex hose. Tighten the brake tube nut to 150 inch lbs. (17 Nm).

18. Install the tire and wheel assembly. Install and tighten the wheel mounting nuts to 100 ft. lbs. (135 Nm).

19. Lower the vehicle.

20. Remove the brake pedal holding tool.

21. Bleed the caliper as necessary.

22. Road test the vehicle and make several stops to wear off any foreign material on the brakes and to seat the brake shoes.

DISC BRAKE PADS

REMOVAL & INSTALLATION

See Figures 22 through 24.

1. Refer to Brake System precautions.

➡ If the rear brake pads are being replaced due to a howl or moan while

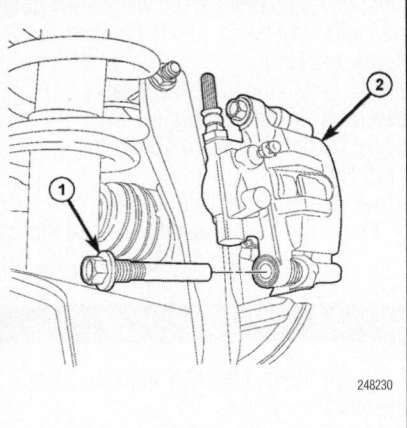

Fig. 22 Remove the disc brake caliper (2) lower guide pin bolt (1)

driving in reverse, proper diagnosis and correction is essential.

2. Raise and support the vehicle. (Refer to Hoisting—Standard Procedure).

➡ Perform Step #2 through Step #6 on each side of the vehicle to complete pad set removal.

3. Remove the wheel mounting nuts, then the tire and wheel assembly.

➡ In some cases, it may be necessary to retract the caliper piston in its bore a small amount in order to provide sufficient clearance between the pads and the rotor to easily remove the caliper from the knuckle. This can usually be accomplished before the guide pin bolts are removed, by grasping the rear of the caliper and pulling outward working with the guide pins, thus retracting the piston. Never push on the piston directly as it may get damaged.

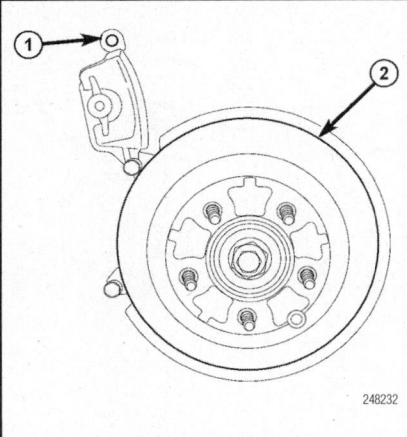

Fig. 23 Rotate the caliper (1) upward hinging off the upper guide pin bolt

4. Remove the disc brake caliper (2) lower guide pin bolt (1).

✳ WARNING

When moving rear brake caliper upward, use extreme care not to damage or overextend the flex hose. Damage may occur.

5. Rotate the caliper (1) upward hinging off the upper guide pin bolt. Rotate the caliper upward just enough to allow brake pad removal. Hang the caliper assembly in this position using wire or a bungee cord.

6. Remove the inboard brake pad (5) from the caliper adapter bracket (3).

To install:

➡ If the rear brake pads are being replaced due to a howl or moan while driving in reverse, proper diagnosis and correction is essential.

➡ Perform Step #1 through Step #6 on each side of the vehicle to complete pad set installation, then proceed to Step #7.

7. Completely retract the caliper piston back into the piston bore of the caliper. This is required to gain the necessary pad-to-rotor clearance for the caliper installation onto the steering knuckle.

➡ Place the brake pad with the audible wear indicator attached on the inboard side. The audible wear indicator should be positioned at the bottom when installed.

8. Slide the outboard brake pad onto the caliper. Be sure the retaining clip is squarely seated in the depressed areas on the caliper beyond the raised retaining bead.

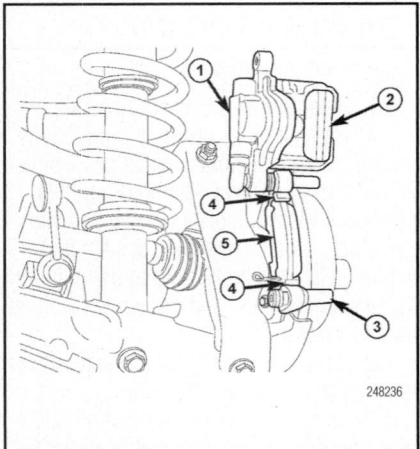

Fig. 24 Remove the inboard brake pad (5) from the caliper adapter bracket (3)

9. Place the inboard brake pad in the abutment shims clipped into the disc brake caliper adapter bracket as shown (see preceding note).

✳✳ WARNING

Use care when installing the caliper onto the adapter bracket to avoid damaging the guide pin boot. Rotate the disc brake caliper downward over the brake rotor and lower part of caliper adapter.

10. Install the disc brake caliper lower guide pin bolt. Tighten the guide pin bolt to 32 ft. lbs. (43 Nm).

➡**Once the caliper is installed, inspect the outboard brake pad to make sure it is correctly positioned. The retaining clip (refer to image for the Front Brake Caliper Installation) must be squarely seated in the depressed areas (1) on the caliper fingers. Also, the nubs on the pad's steel backing plate must be fully seated in the depressions formed into the inside of the caliper fingers.**

There should be no gap between the pad backing plate and the caliper fingers.

11. Install the tire and wheel assembly. Install and tighten the wheel mounting nuts to 100 ft. lbs. (135 Nm).
12. Lower the vehicle.
13. Pump the brake pedal several times to ensure the vehicle has a firm brake pedal before moving the vehicle.
14. Road test the vehicle and make several stops to wear off any foreign material on the brakes and to seat the brake pads.

BRAKES | REAR DRUM BRAKES

✳✳ WARNING

Dust and dirt accumulating on brake parts during normal use may contain asbestos fibers from production or aftermarket brake linings. Breathing excessive concentrations of asbestos fibers can cause serious bodily harm. Exercise care when servicing brake parts. Do not sand or grind brake lining unless equipment used is designed to contain the dust residue. Do not clean brake parts with compressed air or by dry brushing. Cleaning should be done by dampening the brake components with a fine mist of water, then wiping the brake components clean with a dampened cloth. Dispose of cloth and all residue containing asbestos fibers in an impermeable container with the appropriate label. Follow practices prescribed by the Occupational Safety and Health Administration (OSHA) and the Environmental Protection Agency (EPA) for the handling, processing, and disposing of dust or debris that may contain asbestos fibers.

BRAKE DRUM

REMOVAL & INSTALLATION

See Figures 25 and 26.

1. Refer to Brake System precautions.
2. Raise and support the vehicle. (Refer to Hoisting—Standard Procedure).
3. Remove the wheel mounting nuts (3), then the tire and wheel assembly.
4. Slide the brake drum (4) off the wheel mounting studs of the hub and bearing (5) and remove it from the vehicle. If the drum does not come off, further brake clearance can be obtained by backing off the brake adjuster screw.

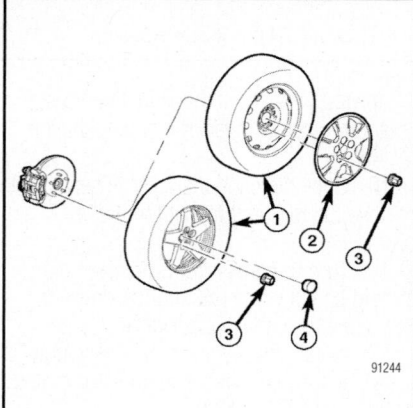

Fig. 25 Remove the wheel mounting nuts (3), then the tire and wheel assembly

To install:

➡**Before installing the drum, inspect the brake shoe linings for wear, alignment, and contamination. Repair or replace as necessary.**

➡**If rust or any foreign material is present on hub, drum or wheel mating surfaces, wet wire brush these areas to remove prior to assembly of parts.**

5. Properly remove any buildup formed along outer edge of drum's machined braking surface.
6. Adjust the brake shoes-to-drum diameter using a brake shoe gauge.
7. Slide the brake drum onto the wheel mounting studs on the hub and bearing.
8. Install the tire and wheel assembly. Install and tighten the wheel mounting nuts to 100 ft. lbs. (135 Nm).
9. Lower the vehicle.
10. Road test the vehicle, stopping in both forward and reverse directions. The automatic-adjuster will continue to adjust the brakes as necessary during the road test.

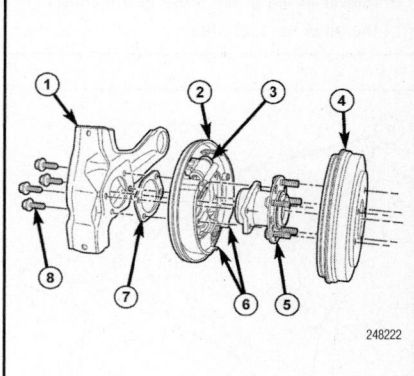

Fig. 26 Slide the brake drum (4) off the wheel mounting studs of the hub and bearing (5)

BRAKE SHOES

ADJUSTMENT

See Figures 27 through 29.

1. Refer to Brake System precautions.
2. Verify the parking brake lever is in the fully released position.
3. Raise and support the vehicle. (Refer to Hoisting—Standard Procedure).

➡**Perform the following steps on each rear drum brake assembly as necessary.**

4. Remove the wheel mounting nuts, then the tire and wheel assembly. (Refer to second image in Rear Wheel Sensor Removal procedure).
5. Remove the brake drum.
6. Using a brake shoe gauge C-3919 (1) or an equivalent, measure the inside diameter of the brake drum at the center of the shoe contact area. Tighten the gauge setscrew at this measurement.
7. Place the opposite side of the brake shoe gauge (2) over the brake shoes (1) as shown.

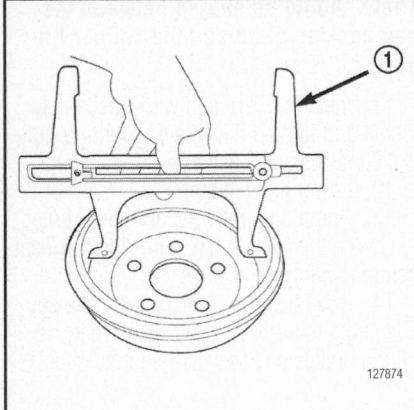

Fig. 27 Using a brake shoe gauge C-3919 (1) or an equivalent, measure the inside diameter of the brake drum at the center of the shoe contact area

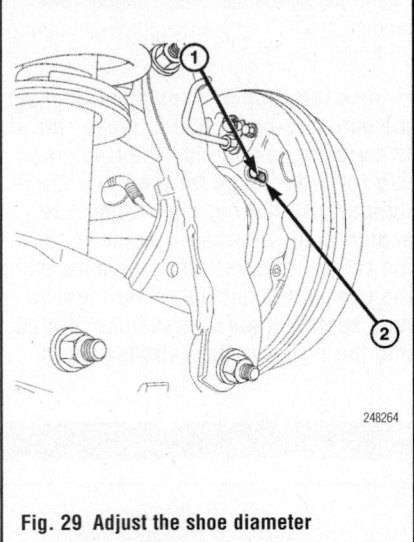

Fig. 29 Adjust the shoe diameter

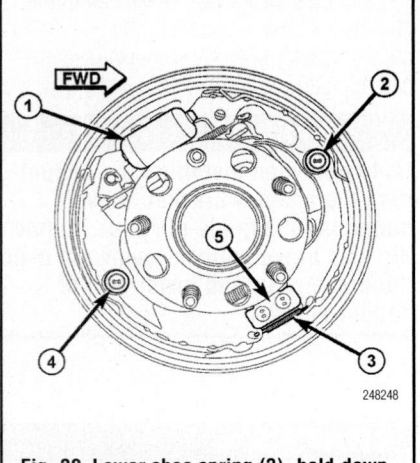

Fig. 30 Lower shoe spring (3), hold-down spring (4) and hold-down spring retaining the front shoe to the support plate (2)

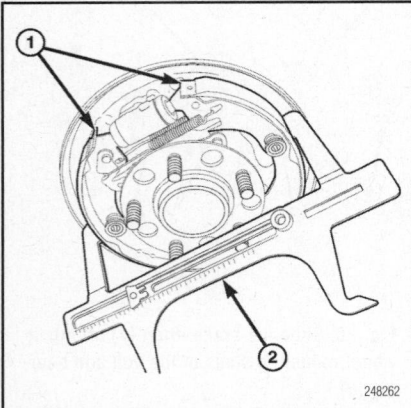

Fig. 28 Place the opposite side of the brake shoe gauge (2) over the brake shoes (1) as shown

8. Adjust the shoe diameter to the setting on the gauge. To adjust the shoe diameter, turn the adjuster wheel using a screwdriver inserted through the adjusting hole in the rear of the shoe support plate. Once the tip of the screwdriver contacts the adjuster wheel teeth, move the handle of tool upward using the support plate as a pivot to adjust the shoes outward.

9. If at any time the adjustment needs to be backed off, perform the following:

a. Remove the plug from the rear of the support plate below the wheel cylinder.

b. Insert a small screwdriver through the access hole (2) in the support plate, under the adjuster, against the lever pawl. The pawl is attached to and pivots from the rear brake shoe.

c. While pushing on the pawl with the screwdriver to disengage it from the adjuster wheel teeth, rotate the wheel (1)

upward to back off the adjustment using another screwdriver or a brake adjuster tool.

10. Once the shoe diameter is set, remove the tool and install the brake drum.

11. Turn the brake drum. A slight drag should be felt while rotating the drum. If not, repeat the above procedure.

12. Install the tire and wheel assembly. Install and tighten the wheel mounting nuts to 100 ft. lbs. (135 Nm).

13. After adjusting both rear drum brakes as necessary, lower the vehicle.

14. Apply and release the parking brake lever one time after the adjustment process is completed checking parking brake operation.

15. Road test vehicle, stopping in both forward and reverse directions. The automatic-adjuster will continue to adjust the brakes as necessary during the road test.

REMOVAL & INSTALLATION

See Figures 30 through 35.

1. Refer to Brake System precautions.

➡**Make sure parking brake is in "released" position before raising vehicle.**

2. Raise and support the vehicle. (Refer to Hoisting—Standard Procedure).

➡**Perform Step #2 through Step #17 on each side of the vehicle to complete shoe set removal. It may be easier to install the new components on the first side of the vehicle before disassembling the opposite side so it may be used as a reference guide for proper installation.**

3. Remove the wheel mounting nuts (refer to image in Brake Drum Removal), then the tire and wheel assembly.

4. Remove the brake drum (4). Refer to the image in Brake Drum Removal.

5. Remove the lower shoe spring (3).

6. Compress and remove the hold-down spring (4) retaining the rear shoe to the support plate.

7. Pull the rear shoe (4) away from the anchor (3) allowing better access to the parking brake cable (2) connection at the lever (1).

8. Compress the cable return spring, then remove the parking brake cable from the parking brake lever.

9. Compress and remove the hold-down spring (2) retaining the front shoe to the support plate. (See first image for Brake Shoe Removal.)

10. Remove both brake shoes from the wheel cylinder.

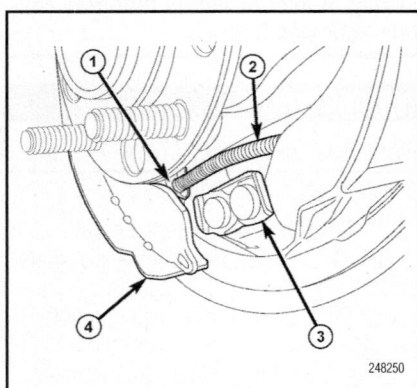

Fig. 31 Pull the rear shoe (4) away from the anchor (3) allowing better access to the parking brake cable (2) connection at the lever (1)

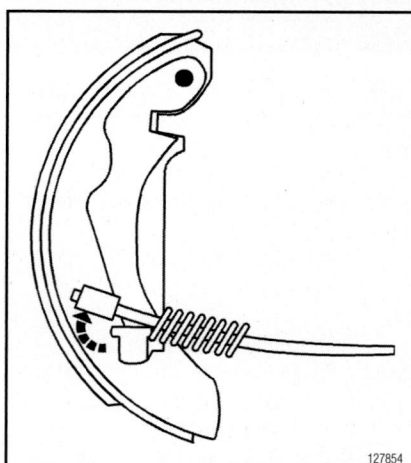

Fig. 32 Compress the cable return spring, and then remove the parking brake cable from the parking brake lever

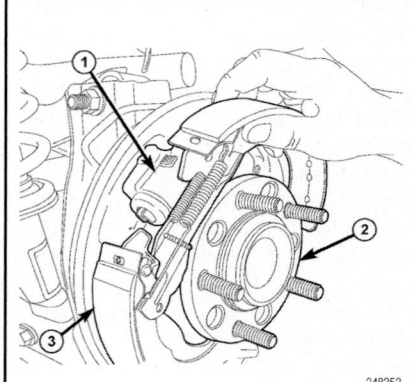

Fig. 33 Remove both shoes and remaining parts as an assembly (3) through the opening between the wheel cylinder (1) and support plate hub and bearing

11. Remove both shoes and remaining parts as an assembly (3) through the opening between the wheel cylinder (1) and support plate hub and bearing.

12. Place the shoe assembly outboard-side-up on a flat surface.

13. Remove the adjuster spring (2) from the leading shoe (3) and the lever pawl (1).

14. Remove the lever pawl (1) from the pivot on the rear shoe (5).

15. Flip the shoe assembly over to show the inboard side.

16. Remove the upper shoe return spring (1).

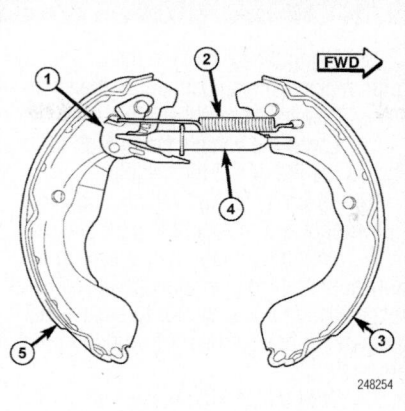

Fig. 34 Remove the adjuster spring (2) from the leading shoe (3) and the lever pawl (1)

17. Remove the adjuster (5) from the shoes and parking brake lever (2).

To install:

➡**Perform Step #18 through Step #38 on each side of vehicle to complete the shoe set installation, then proceed to Step #22.**

18. Lubricate shoe contact areas on support plate and anchor using Mopar® Brake Lubricant or equivalent.

19. Place one front shoe and one rear shoe inboard-side-up on a flat surface. (The rear shoe has the parking brake lever attached to it.)

20. Install the adjuster, adjuster wheel toward the rear, between the two brake shoes. Make sure the wide notch in the rear fork aligns with the parking brake lever.

21. Install the upper return spring as shown in the image for Brake Shoe Removal.

22. Flip the shoe assembly over to show the outboard side.

23. Install the lever pawl onto the pivot located on the rear shoe.

24. Install the adjuster spring between the front shoe and the lever pawl.

25. Install the pre-assembled brake shoe assembly through the opening between the wheel cylinder and support plate hub and bearing.

26. Insert the upper tips of the brake shoes into the grooves of the wheel cylinder pistons.

27. Position the bottom of the front shoe against the anchor pin.

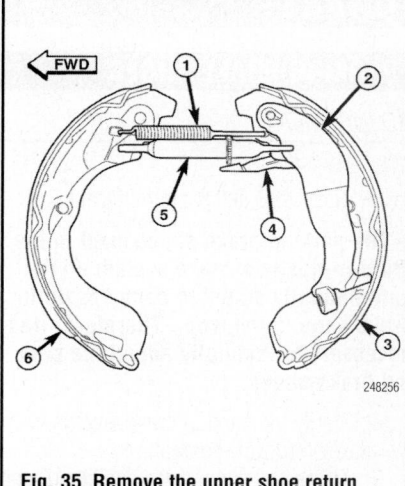

Fig. 35 Remove the upper shoe return spring (1)

28. Install a shoe hold-down pin from the rear, through the support plate and the front shoe.

29. Compress and install the hold-down spring retaining the front shoe to the support plate.

30. Compress the parking brake cable return spring, then carefully install the cable onto the parking brake lever. Release the spring guiding it beneath the retaining tab on the lever.

31. Position the bottom of the rear shoe against the anchor pin.

32. Install a shoe hold-down pin from the rear, through the support plate and the rear shoe.

33. Compress and install the hold-down spring retaining the rear shoe to the support plate.

34. Install the lower shoe spring.

35. Adjust the brake shoes to the drum diameter using a brake shoe gauge.

36. Install the brake drum.

37. Install the tire and wheel assembly. Install and tighten the wheel mounting nuts to 100 ft. lbs. (135 Nm).

38. Slowly rotate both rear wheels and verify that the brake drums **lightly** drag on the shoes. Use the adjustment procedure as necessary.

39. Lower the vehicle.

40. Road test vehicle, stopping in both forward and reverse directions. The automatic-adjuster will continue to adjust the brakes as necessary during the road test.

PARKING BRAKE SHOES

ADJUSTMENT

See Figure 36.

1. Refer to Brake System precautions.

➡ **The parking brake shoes used in the drum-in-hat park brake system do not automatically adjust to compensate for brake shoe lining wear. Therefore, it is necessary to manually adjust the parking brake shoes.**

2. Verify the parking brake lever is in the released (down) position.

3. Raise and support the vehicle. (Refer to Hoisting—Standard Procedure).

4. Remove the wheel mounting nuts, then the tire and wheel assembly. (Refer to second image in Rear Wheel Sensor Removal procedure).

5. Install a couple of wheel mounting nuts to hold the brake rotor in place while you adjust the brake shoes.

➡ **To find the adjuster wheel with the drum on, position the hole (1) in the front of the rotor drum as follows:**

- Left side: 7 o'clock.
- Right side: 5 o'clock.

➡ **When adjusting the parking brake shoes with the drum-in hat rotor installed, rotating the adjuster wheel (2) upward will loosen the adjustment. Rotating the adjuster wheel (2) downward will tighten the adjustment.**

6. Remove the rubber plug from the hole (1) in the front of the rotor.

7. Using the hole (1) in the front of the rotor, make a fine adjustment of the shoes.

8. Reinstall the rubber plug.

9. Lower the vehicle far enough to access the interior of the vehicle.

10. Reach inside the vehicle and cycle (fully apply and release) the park brakes.

11. With the parking brake lever in the fully applied (up) position, attempt to hand rotate each rear brake rotor to ensure that the parking brake shoes are working properly.

12. With the parking brake lever in the released (down) position, hand rotate each rear brake rotor to ensure that the parking brake shoes are not dragging.

13. Raise and support the vehicle. (Refer to Hoisting—Standard Procedure).

14. Remove the wheel mounting nuts and install the tire and wheel assembly. (Refer to second image in Rear Wheel Sensor Removal procedure).

15. Lower the vehicle.

REMOVAL & INSTALLATION

See Figures 37 through 40.

1. Refer to Brake System precautions.

2. Raise and support the vehicle. (Refer to Hoisting—Standard Procedure).

➡ **If removing parking brake shoes on both sides of vehicle, perform remaining steps on each side of the vehicle.**

3. Access and remove the rear brake rotor.

4. Turn the brake shoe adjuster wheel until the adjuster is at shortest length.

5. Remove the upper return spring (1) from the anchor pin (3) and the rear brake shoe.

6. Remove the upper return spring (2) from the anchor pin (3) and the front brake shoe.

7. Remove the brake shoe hold-down springs and pins (1, 2). Rotate the pins 90° to disengage.

8. Remove the parking brake cable from the lever on the rear parking brake shoe.

9. Remove the brake shoes (2, 6), adjuster (5) and lower return spring (3) as an assembly from the support plate.

10. If necessary, remove the strut (1).

11. Remove the lower return spring (3) and adjuster (5) from the shoes (2, 6).

To install:

12. If replacing parking brake shoes on both sides of vehicle, perform Step #1 through Step #15 on each side of the vehicle to complete shoe set installation, then proceed to Step #16.

13. Left side shoes are shown in the Brake Shoe Removal figure. The right side shoes are a mirror image of the left except for the adjuster. Always position the threaded portion of the adjuster to the left side in order to maintain consistent side-to-side rotational direction for adjustment purposes.

14. Install the lower return spring and adjuster between the parking brake shoes. The rear shoe will have the lever mounted on the inside. Make sure the threaded portion of the adjuster is mounted to the left on both right and left side parking brake assemblies (see preceding note).

15. If necessary, place the strut above the hub and bearing on the vehicle. Note the curved end of the strut is positioned to the rear.

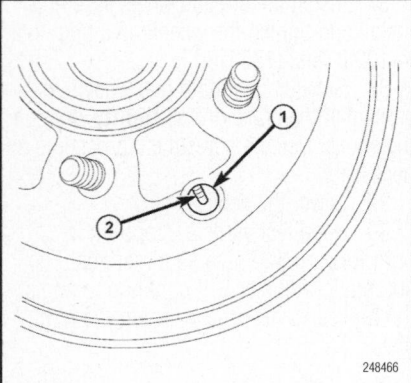

Fig. 36 To find the adjuster wheel with the drum on, position the hole (1) in the front of the rotor

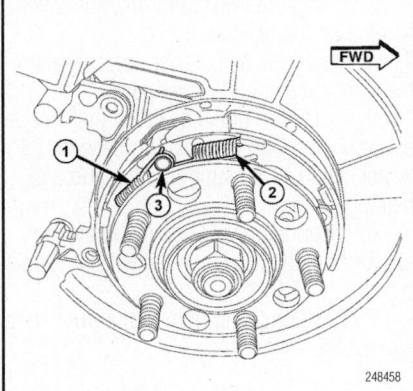

Fig. 37 Remove the upper return spring (1) from the anchor pin (3) and the rear brake shoe

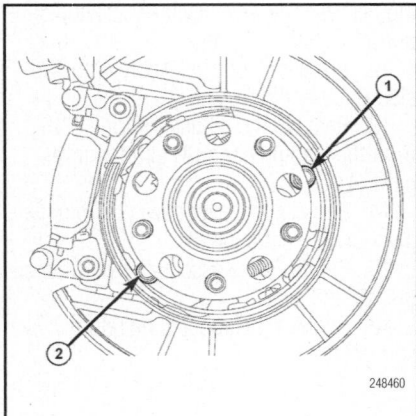

Fig. 38 Brake shoe hold-down springs and pins (1, 2)

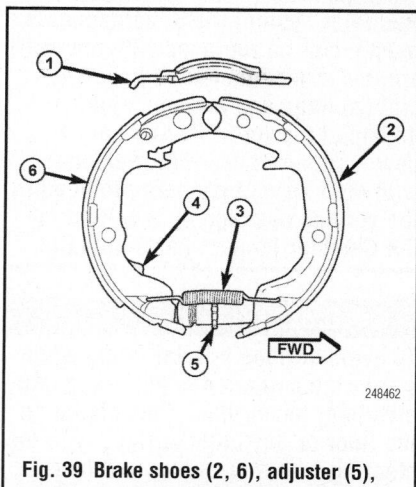

Fig. 39 Brake shoes (2, 6), adjuster (5), lower return spring (3) and strut (1)

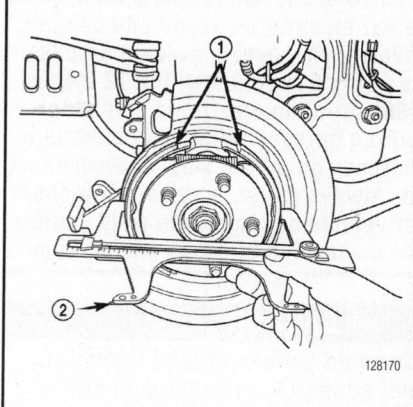

Fig. 40 Place the gauge (2) over the parking brake shoes (1) at their widest point

16. Install the assembled brake shoes, adjuster and lower return spring over the hub and bearing and onto the support plate and anchor. Be sure to install the strut between the front shoe and the lever on the rear shoe.

17. Install the parking brake cable onto the lever on the parking brake shoe.

18. Install the brake shoe hold-down springs and pins. Rotate the pins 90° to engage.

19. Install the front upper return spring holding the front brake shoe and anchor pin.

20. Install the rear upper return spring holding the rear brake shoe and anchor pin.

21. Using brake shoe gauge C-3919, or an equivalent, measure the inside diameter of parking brake drum portion of rotor. Set the gauge.

22. Place the gauge (2) over the parking brake shoes (1) at their widest point.

23. Using the adjuster wheel, adjust the parking brake shoes until the linings on both parking brake shoes just touch the jaws on the gauge.

24. Install the rear brake rotor and install a couple of wheel mounting nuts to hold it in place while a final adjustment is made.

➡To find the adjuster wheel with the drum on, position the hole (refer to image for Brake Shoe Adjustment) in the front of the rotor drum as follows:

- Left side—7 o'clock.
- Right side—5 o'clock.

➡When adjusting the parking brake shoes with the drum-in hat rotor installed, rotating the adjuster wheel (2) upward will loosen the adjustment. Rotating the adjuster wheel (2) downward will tighten the adjustment.

25. Remove the rubber plug from the hole (1) in the front of the rotor.

26. Using the hole in the front of the rotor, make a final adjustment of the shoes if necessary.

27. Reinstall the rubber plug.

28. Remove the wheel mounting nuts and finish installing the brake rotor as well as all components you removed to access it.

29. Lower the vehicle.

30. Cycle the parking brake lever once, verifying proper operation of the parking brake.

CHASSIS ELECTRICAL AIR BAG (SUPPLEMENTAL RESTRAINT SYSTEM; SRS)

GENERAL INFORMATION

❊❊ WARNING

These vehicles are equipped with an air bag system. The system must be disarmed before performing service on, or around, system components, the steering column, instrument panel components, wiring and sensors. Failure to follow the safety precautions and the disarming procedure could result in accidental air bag deployment, possible injury and unnecessary system repairs.

SERVICE PRECAUTIONS

❊❊ CAUTION

To avoid serious or fatal injury on vehicles equipped with the Supplemental Restraint System (SRS), never attempt to repair the electrically conductive circuits or wiring

components related to the SRS for which there is no MOPAR wiring repair kit. It is important to use ONLY the recommended splicing kit and procedure. For applicable and available MOPAR wiring repair kits, please visit the MOPAR Connector Web Site at the following address on the internet: (http://dto.vftis.com/mopar/disclaimer.asp). Inappropriate repairs can compromise the conductivity and current carrying capacity of those critical electrical circuits, which may cause SRS components not to deploy when required, or to deploy when not required. Only minor cuts or abrasions of wire and terminal insulation where the conductive material has not been damaged, or connector insulators where the integrity of the latching and locking mechanisms have not been compromised may be repaired using appropriate methods.

❊❊ CAUTION

To avoid serious or fatal injury during and following any seat belt or child restraint anchor service, carefully inspect all seat belts, buckles, mounting hardware, retractors, tether straps, and anchors for proper installation, operation, or damage. Replace any belt that is cut, frayed, or torn. Straighten any belt that is twisted. Tighten any loose fasteners. Replace any belt that has a damaged or ineffective buckle or retractor. Replace any belt that has a bent or damaged latch plate or anchor plate. Replace any child restraint anchor or the unit to which the anchor is integral that has been bent or damaged. Never attempt to repair a seat belt or child restraint component. Always replace damaged or ineffective seat belt and child restraint components with the correct, new and unused replacement parts listed in the Chrysler Mopar® Parts Catalog.

> ❋❋ CAUTION
>
> To avoid serious or fatal injury on vehicles equipped with side curtain airbags, disable the Supplemental Restraint System (SRS) before attempting any Occupant Restraint Controller (ORC) diagnosis or service. The ORC contains a rollover sensor, which enables the system to deploy the side curtains and seat airbags in the event of a vehicle rollover event. If an ORC is accidentally rolled during service while still connected to battery power, the side curtain and seat airbags will deploy. Disconnect and isolate the battery negative (ground) cable, then wait two minutes for the system capacitor to discharge before performing further diagnosis or service. This is the only sure way to disable the SRS. Failure to take the proper precautions could result in accidental airbag deployment.

> ❋❋ CAUTION
>
> To avoid serious or fatal injury on vehicles equipped with airbags, disable the Supplemental Restraint System (SRS) before attempting any steering wheel, steering column, airbag, seat belt tensioner, impact sensor or instrument panel component diagnosis or service. Disconnect and isolate the battery negative (ground) cable, then wait two minutes for the system capacitor to discharge before performing further diagnosis or service. This is the only sure way to disable the SRS. Failure to take the proper precautions could result in accidental airbag deployment.

> ❋❋ CAUTION
>
> To avoid potential physical injury or damage to sensitive electronic circuits and systems, always disconnect and isolate the battery negative (ground) cable and the positive cable, then ground the positive cable to discharge the Occupant Restraint Controller (ORC) capacitor before performing any welding operations on the vehicle. Failure to take the proper precautions could result in accidental airbag deployment, possible damage to the Supplemental Restraint System (SRS) circuits and

components, and possible damage to other electronic circuits and components. Whenever a welding process is being performed within 12 inches (30 cm) of an electronic module or wiring harness, move that module or harness out of the way, or disconnect it. Always protect against component or vehicle damage from weld spatter by using weld blankets and screens.

> ❋❋ CAUTION
>
> To avoid serious or fatal injury, do not attempt to dismantle an airbag unit or tamper with its inflator. Do not puncture, incinerate or bring into contact with electricity. Do not store at temperatures exceeding 200°F (93°C). An airbag inflator unit may contain sodium azide and potassium nitrate. These materials are poisonous and extremely flammable. Contact with acid, water, or heavy metals may produce harmful and irritating gases (sodium hydroxide is formed in the presence of moisture) or combustible compounds. An airbag inflator unit may also contain a gas canister pressurized to over 2500 psi (17.24 kPa). Failure to follow these instructions may result in possible serious or fatal injury.

> ❋❋ CAUTION
>
> To avoid serious or fatal injury when handling a seat belt tensioner retractor. Exercise proper care to keep fingers out from under the retractor cover and away from the seat belt webbing where it exits from the retractor cover. Failure to follow these instructions may result in possible serious or fatal injury.

> ❋❋ CAUTION
>
> To avoid serious or fatal injury, replace all Supplemental Restraint System (SRS) components only with parts specified in the Chrysler Mopar® Parts Catalog. Substitute parts may appear interchangeable, but internal differences may result in inferior occupant protection.

> ❋❋ CAUTION
>
> To avoid serious or fatal injury, the fasteners, screws, and bolts originally used for the Supplemental

Restraint System (SRS) components must never be replaced with any substitutes. These fasteners have special coatings and are specifically designed for the SRS. Any time a new fastener is needed, replace it with the correct fasteners provided in the service package or specified in the Chrysler Mopar® Parts Catalog.

> ❋❋ CAUTION
>
> To avoid serious or fatal injury when a steering column has an airbag unit attached, never place the column on the floor or any other surface with the steering wheel or airbag unit face down. Failure to follow these instructions may result in possible serious or fatal injury.

DISARMING THE SYSTEM

> ❋❋ CAUTION
>
> To avoid serious or fatal injury on vehicles equipped with airbags, disable the Supplemental Restraint System (SRS) before attempting any steering wheel, steering column, airbag, seat belt tensioner, impact sensor or instrument panel component diagnosis or service. Disconnect and isolate the battery negative (ground) cable, then wait two minutes for the system capacitor to discharge before performing further diagnosis or service. This is the only sure way to disable the SRS. Failure to take the proper precautions could result in accidental airbag deployment.

1. Before servicing the vehicle, refer to the Precautions.

2. Turn the ignition switch to OFF.

3. Disconnect the negative battery cable and isolate it from accidental reconnection. Insulate the cable end with high-quality electrical tape or a similar non-conductive wrapping.

4. Wait at least two minutes for the system capacitor to discharge before performing any service. The airbag system is designed to retain enough voltage to deploy the airbag for a short period of time after the battery has been disconnected.

*ARMING THE SYSTEM:
SUPPLEMENTAL RESTRAINTS
VERIFICATION TEST*

➡Perform the following procedure using a diagnostic scan tool to verify proper Supplemental Restraint System (SRS) operation following the service or replacement of any SRS component. Refer to the appropriate diagnostic procedures.

✳✳ CAUTION

To avoid serious or fatal injury on vehicles equipped with airbags, disable the Supplemental Restraint System (SRS) before attempting any steering wheel, steering column, airbag, seat belt tensioner, impact sensor or instrument panel component diagnosis or service. Disconnect and isolate the battery negative (ground) cable, then wait two minutes for the system capacitor to discharge before performing further diagnosis or service. This is the only sure way to disable the SRS. Failure to take the proper precautions could result in accidental airbag deployment.

1. During the following test, the battery negative cable remains disconnected and isolated, as it was during the Supplemental Restraint System (SRS) component removal and installation procedures.

2. Be certain that the diagnostic scan tool contains the latest version of the proper diagnostic software. Connect the scan tool to the 16-way Data Link Connector (DLC). The DLC is located on the driver side lower edge of the instrument panel, near the cowl side inner panel.

3. Turn the ignition switch to the ON position and exit the vehicle with the scan tool.

4. Check to be certain that no one is in the vehicle, then reconnect the battery negative cable.

5. Using the scan tool, read and record the active (current) Diagnostic Trouble Code (DTC) data.

6. Next, use the scan tool to read and record any stored (historical) DTC data.

7. If any DTC is found in Step #5 or Step #6, refer to the appropriate diagnostic information.

8. Use the scan tool to erase the stored DTC data. If any problems remain, the stored DTC data will not erase. Refer to the appropriate diagnostic information to diagnose any stored DTC that will not erase. If the stored DTC information is successfully erased, go to Step #9.

9. Turn the ignition switch to the OFF

position for about 15 seconds, and then back to the ON position. Observe the airbag indicator in the instrument cluster. It should light for six to eight seconds, and then go out. This indicates that the SRS is functioning normally and that the repairs are complete. If the airbag indicator fails to light, or lights and stays ON, there is still an active SRS fault or malfunction. Refer to the appropriate diagnostic information to diagnose the problem.

CLOCKSPRING CENTERING

See Figure 41.

✳✳ CAUTION

To avoid serious or fatal injury on vehicles equipped with airbags, disable the Supplemental Restraint System (SRS) before attempting any steering wheel, steering column, airbag, seat belt tensioner, impact sensor or instrument panel component diagnosis or service. Disconnect and isolate the battery negative (ground) cable, then wait two minutes for the system capacitor to discharge before performing further diagnosis or service. This is the only sure way to disable the SRS. Failure to take the proper precautions could result in accidental airbag deployment.

➡️ A service replacement clockspring is shipped with the clockspring pre-centered and with a molded plastic locking pin installed. This locking pin should not be removed until the steering wheel has been installed on the steering column. If the locking pin is removed before the steering wheel is installed, the clockspring centering procedure must be performed.

➡️ When a clockspring is installed into a vehicle without properly centering and locking the entire steering system, the Steering Angle Sensor (SAS) data does not agree with the true position of the steering system and causes the Electronic Stability Program (ESP) system to shut down. This may also damage the clockspring without any immediate malfunction. Unlike some other Chrysler vehicles, this SAS never requires calibration. However, upon each new ignition ON cycle, the steering wheel must be rotated slightly to initialize the SAS.

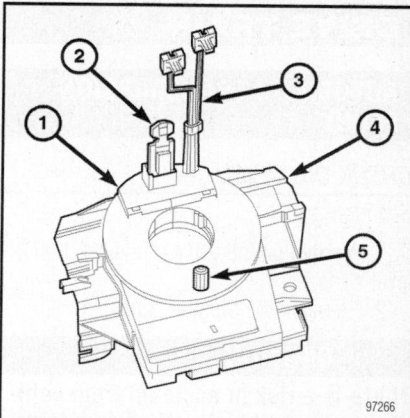

Fig. 41 Rotate the clockspring rotor (1) clockwise to the end of its travel. Do not apply excessive torque

➡️ Determining if the clockspring/SAS is centered is also possible electrically using the diagnostic scan tool. Steering wheel position is displayed as ANGLE with a range of up to 900 degrees. Refer to the appropriate menu item on the diagnostic scan tool.

➡️ Before starting this procedure, be certain to turn the steering wheel until the front wheels are in the straight-ahead position and that the entire steering system is locked or inhibited from rotation.

➡️ The clockspring may be centered and the rotor may be rotated freely once the steering wheel has been removed.

1. Place the front wheels in the straight-ahead position and inhibit the steering column shaft from rotation.

2. Remove the steering wheel from the steering shaft.

3. Rotate the clockspring rotor (1) clockwise to the end of its travel. Do not apply excessive torque.

4. From the end of the clockwise travel, rotate the rotor about two and one-half turns counterclockwise.

5. Turn the rotor slightly clockwise or counterclockwise as necessary so that the clockspring airbag pigtail wires (3) and connector receptacle are at the top and the dowel or drive pin (5) is at the bottom.

6. The clockspring is now centered. Secure the clockspring rotor to the clockspring case using a locking pin (2) or some similar device to maintain clockspring centering until the steering wheel is reinstalled on the steering column.

DRIVE TRAIN

AUTOMATIC TRANSMISSION FLUID

CHECK OIL LEVEL

See Figure 42.

1. Verify that the vehicle is parked on a level surface.
2. Remove the dipstick tube cap.

✳✳ CAUTION

There is a risk of accident from vehicle starting off by itself when engine is running. There is a risk of injury from contusions and burns if you insert your hands into the engine when it is started or when it is running. Secure the vehicle to prevent it from moving off by itself. Wear properly fastened and close-fitting work clothes. Do not touch hot or rotating parts.

3. Actuate the service brake. Start engine and let it run at idle speed in selector lever position "P".
4. Shift through the transmission modes several times with the vehicle stationary and the engine idling.
5. Warm up the transmission, wait at least 2 minutes and check the oil level with the engine running. Push the Oil Dipstick 9336A into transmission fill tube until the dipstick tip contacts the oil pan and pull out again, read off oil level, repeat if necessary.

➡ **The dipstick will protrude from the fill tube when installed.**

6. Check the transmission oil temperature using the appropriate scan tool.
7. The transmission Oil Dipstick 9336A has indicator marks every 0.39 inches (10 mm). Determine the height of the oil level on the dipstick and using the height, the transmission temperature, and the Transmission Fluid Graph, determine if the transmission oil level is correct.
8. Add or remove oil as necessary and recheck the oil level.
9. Once the oil level is correct, install the dipstick tube cap.

FLUID AND STRAINER SERVICE

See Figures 43 through 46.

1. Remove the bolts holding the oil pan (1) to the transaxle case.
2. Remove the oil pan from the transaxle case.
3. Remove the oil pan gasket (1) from the transaxle case.
4. Remove the bolts holding the oil strainer (1) to the valve body.

5. Remove the oil strainer.
6. Remove and discard the oil strainer o-ring.

✳✳ WARNING

Do not re-use the O-ring. Apply CVT fluid when installing the O-ring.

7. Install the new o-ring (1) onto the new oil strainer.
8. Install the new oil strainer onto the control valve assembly. Install and tighten the mounting bolts to 70 inch lbs. (8 Nm).

✳✳ WARNING

Do not re-use the oil pan gasket. Remove any moisture, oil, and used gasket material from the surface where the new gasket is to be installed. When installing the oil

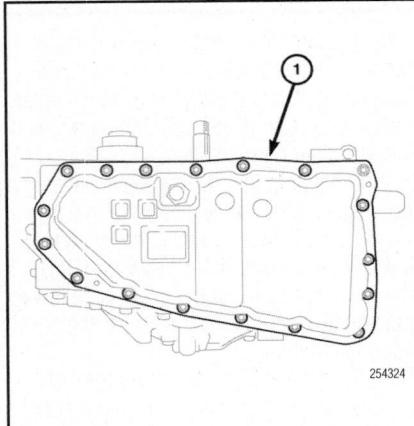

Fig. 43 Remove the bolts holding the oil pan (1) to the transaxle case

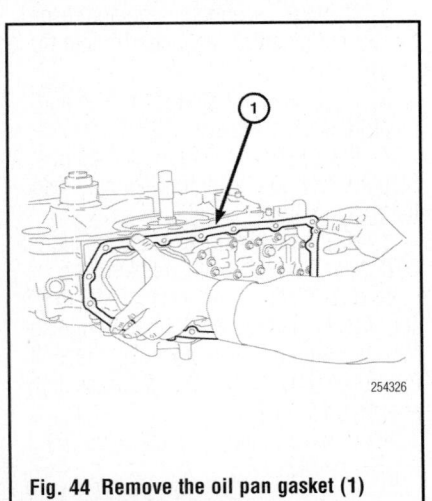

Fig. 44 Remove the oil pan gasket (1) from the transaxle case

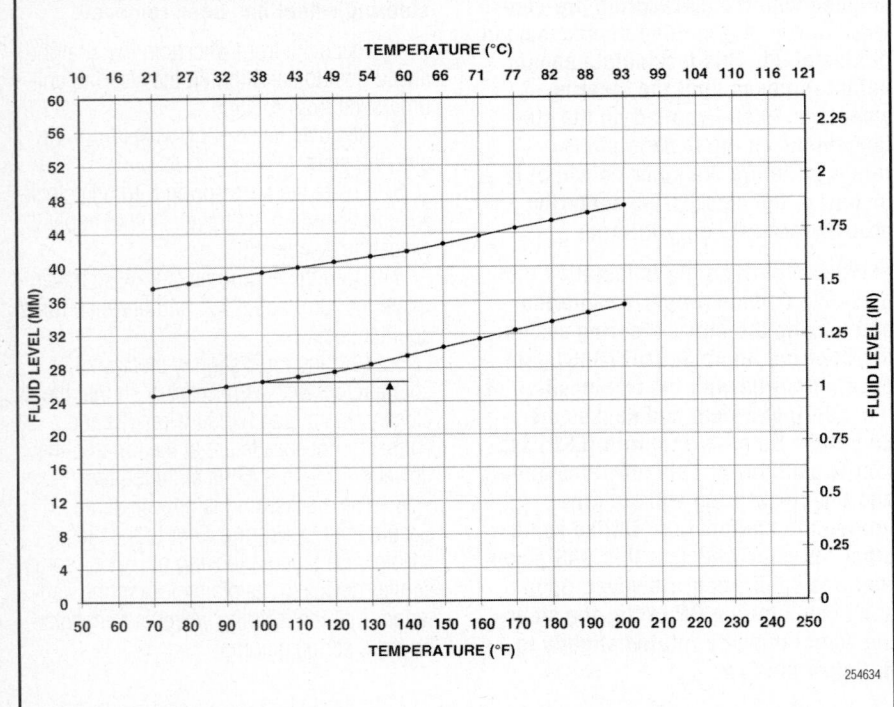

Fig. 42 CVT transmission fill graph

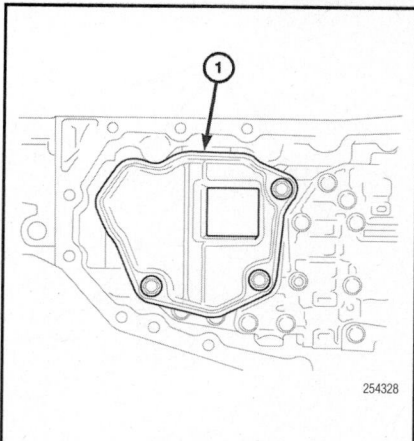

Fig. 45 Remove the bolts holding the oil strainer (1) to the valve body

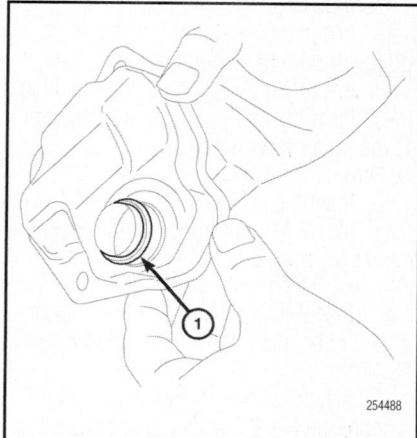

Fig. 46 Install the new o-ring (1) onto the new oil strainer

pan gasket, align the dowel pin with the dowel pin hole in the oil pan gasket.

9. Install the oil pan gasket onto the transaxle case.

✳✳ WARNING

When installing the oil pan, align the dowel pin of the transaxle case with the dowel pin hole of the oil pan.

10. Install the oil pan on the transaxle case. Install and tighten the mounting bolts to 70 inch lbs. (8 Nm).

➡**Only transmission fluid of the type labeled Mopar® CVTF+4 (Automatic Transmission Fluid) should be used in this transaxle.**

11. Check the oil level.

TRANSMISSION FILL

To avoid overfilling the transmission after a fluid change or overhaul, perform the following procedure:

1. Verify that the vehicle is parked on a level surface.
2. Remove the dipstick tube cap.
3. Add the following initial quantity of MOPAR® CVTF+4, Automatic Transmission Fluid, to the transmission:

   a. If only fluid and filter were changed, add 14.8 pts. (7.0 L) of transmission fluid to the transmission.

   b. If the transmission was completely overhauled or the torque converter was replaced or drained, add 17.1 pts. (8.1 L) of transmission fluid to the transmission.

4. Check the transmission fluid and adjust as required.

MANUAL TRANSAXLE ASSEMBLY

REMOVAL & INSTALLATION

See Figures 47 through 54.

1. Raise the hood.
2. Remove the resonator.
3. Remove engine cover.
4. Remove air cleaner assembly.
5. Disconnect negative battery cable.
6. Unplug the speed sensor connector (if equipped).
7. Disconnect the back-up lamp switch connector (2).
8. Remove the shift cable-to-bracket clips (1).
9. Disconnect the shift selector and crossover cable (1) from levers. Remove the cables and secure them out of the way.
10. Remove the slave cylinder hose at the bracket.
11. Remove the air inlet tube by loosening the screw at the throttle body.
12. Remove the throttle body support bracket bolts.
13. Remove the throttle body support bracket.
14. Remove the upper bell housing bolts.
15. Remove the starter bolts and slide the starter back. (Refer to Starter Removal.)
16. Support the transmission and loosen the left/upper transmission mount through bolt (1).
17. Remove the transmission mount bolts (2).
18. Raise the vehicle on a hoist. Refer to Hoisting Standard Procedure in Precautions.
19. Remove the splash shields.

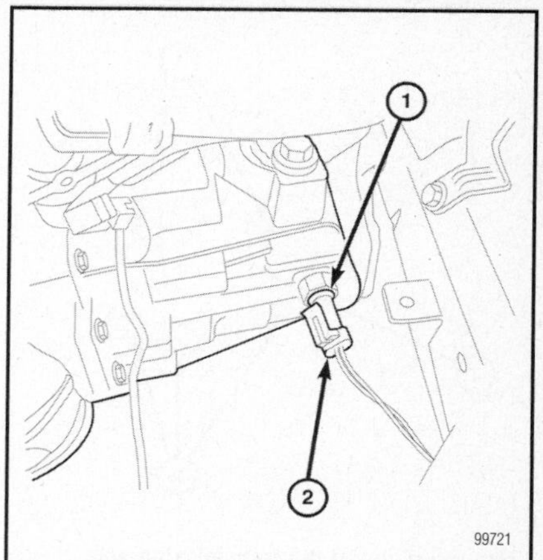

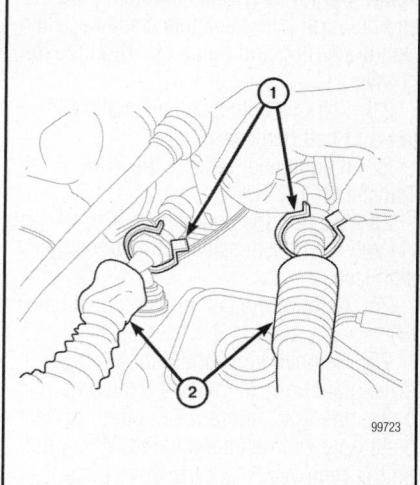

Fig. 47 Back-up lamp switch connector (2)

Fig. 48 Remove the shift cable-to-bracket clips (1)

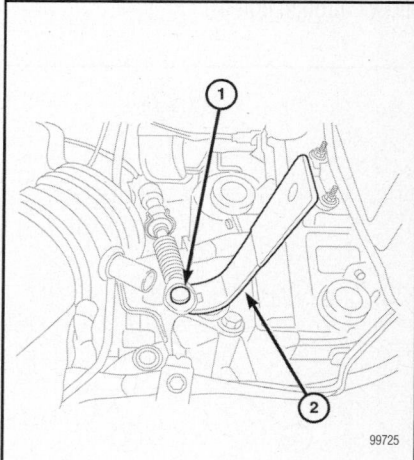

Fig. 49 Disconnect the shift selector and crossover cable (1) from levers. Remove the cables and secure them out of the way

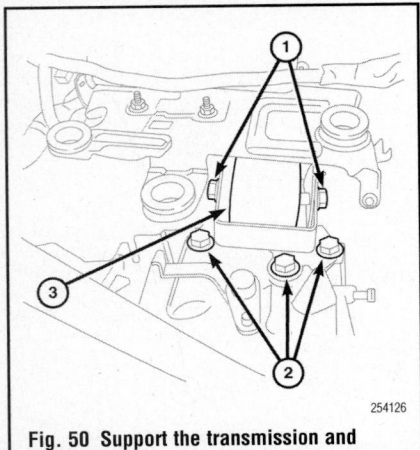

Fig. 50 Support the transmission and loosen the left/upper transmission mount through bolt (1)

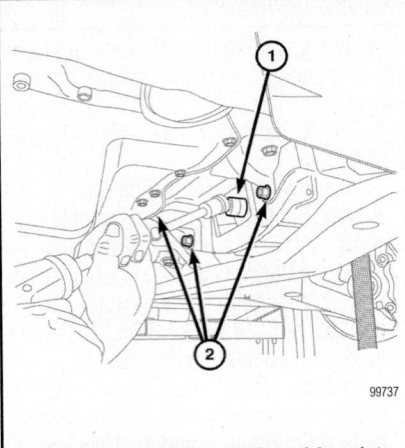

Fig. 52 Four modular clutch-to-drive plate bolts (1)

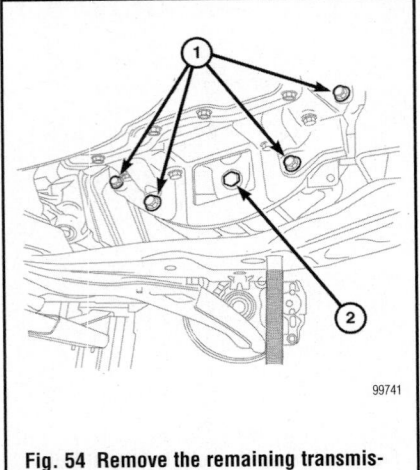

Fig. 54 Remove the remaining transmission bell housing bolts (1)

20. Remove transaxle oil drain plug (2) and drain oil into a suitable container. Reinstall drain plug and tighten to 120 inch lbs. (14 Nm).

21. Remove both axle half shafts (Refer to Half Shaft Removal).

22. If equipped, remove the Power Transfer Unit (PTU).

23. Support the engine with a screw jack (1) and the transmission with a transmission jack.

24. Remove the bell housing dust cover (3).

25. Remove four modular clutch-to-drive plate bolts (1). While removing bolts, one tight-tolerance (slotted) drive plate hole will be encountered. When this bolt is removed, mark the drive plate and modular clutch assembly at this location. Be sure to align the marks upon reassembly.

26. Remove the front transmission mount through bolt (4).

27. Remove the transmission crossmember mounting bolts (2, 3).

28. Remove the transmission crossmember (1).

29. Remove the rear transmission through bolt.

30. Remove the rear transmission mount bolts and mount from the frame.

31. Remove the rear transmission mount bracket bolts and bracket from transmission.

32. Remove the remaining transmission bell housing bolts (1).

33. Carefully lower the engine and transaxle on the screw jack and transmission jack until proper removal clearance is obtained.

34. Obtain a helper to assist in holding the transaxle while removing transaxle-to-engine mounting bolts.

35. Remove the transaxle from the vehicle.

36. Remove the clutch module from the transaxle input shaft (1).

To install:

37. Install the clutch module (1) (if equipped) onto the input shaft.

38. Install the transaxle (1) into position.

39. Install the transaxle-to-engine lower (1) mounting bolts and tighten to 35 ft. lbs. (48 Nm).

40. If equipped, install the PTU.

41. Install the rear transmission mount bracket (2) and bolts and tighten them to 50 ft. lbs. (68 Nm).

42. Install the rear transmission mount (1) and bolts and tighten them to 50 ft. lbs. (68 Nm).

43. Install the rear transmission mount through bolt (4) at this time and tighten it to 50 ft. lbs. (68 Nm).

44. Install the front mount bracket to the transmission and tighten to 50 ft. lbs. (68 Nm).

45. Install the transmission crossmember and tighten to 50 ft. lbs. (68 Nm).

46. Lower the vehicle on the hoist.

47. Raise the engine and transaxle until the upper mount bracket aligns with upper mount. Install mount bolts (2) and tighten them to 50 ft. lbs. (68 Nm).

48. Tighten the through bolt to 50 ft. lbs. (68 Nm).

49. Remove the jack.

50. Raise the vehicle on the hoist. Refer to Hoisting Standard Procedure in Precautions.

51. Install four modular clutch-to-drive-plate bolts. Align the drive plate and modular clutch alignment marks placed upon disassembly. Start with the tight-tolerance (slotted) hole, install and torque the bolts to 65 ft. lbs. (88 Nm).

52. Install the starter motor; make sure to fasten the ground cable to the upper starter bolt. (Refer to Starter Installation.)

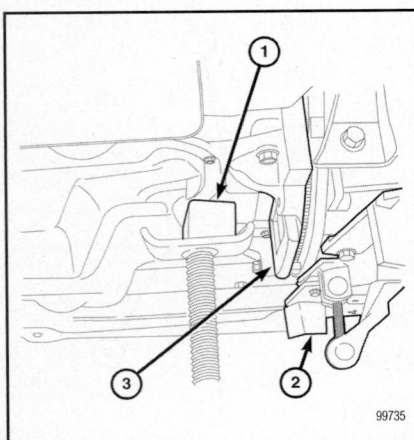

Fig. 51 Screw jack (1) and bell housing dust cover (3)

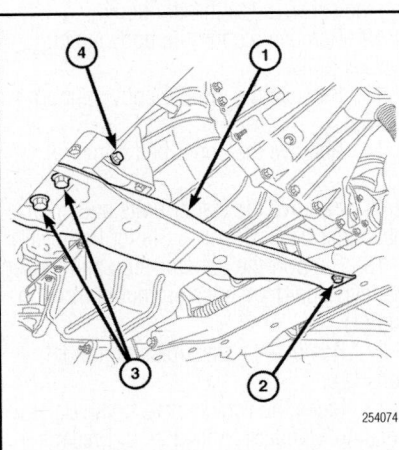

Fig. 53 Remove the front transmission mount through bolt (4)

53. Install the bell housing dust cover.

54. Install both front axle driveshafts (Refer to Half Shaft Installation).

55. Fill the transaxle with a suitable amount of fluid (approximately 2.85 quarts or 2.7 liters).

56. Install the splash shields.

57. Lower the vehicle.

58. Install the remaining top bell housing bolts and tighten them to 35 ft. lbs. (48 Nm).

59. Connect the hydraulic clutch slave cylinder (1). An audible click should be heard. Verify the connection by pushing and pulling the quick connect.

60. Connect the shift and selector cables to the shift lever. Install the cables to the bracket.

61. Connect the back-up lamp switch connector (1).

62. Connect the vehicle speed sensor connector if equipped.

63. Install battery and battery tray.

64. Install the air cleaner assembly.

65. Connect the battery cables.

66. Road test vehicle and inspect for leaks.

MANUAL TRANSAXLE FLUID

DRAIN AND FILL

See Figure 55.

➡**All T355 Manual Transaxles require the use of ATF+4 (Automatic Transmission Fluid).**

The transaxle fill plug (1) is located on the left side of the transaxle differential area. The fluid level should be within 3/16 inch from the bottom of the transaxle fill hole (the vehicle must be level when checking).

The transaxle drain plug (2) is located on the lower right side of the transaxle differential housing. Tighten the drain plug to 120 inch lbs. (14 Nm).

CLUTCH ASSEMBLY—MODULAR

REMOVAL & INSTALLATION

See Figures 56 and 57.

✳✳ CAUTION

Chrysler LLC does not manufacture any vehicles or replacement parts that contain asbestos. Aftermarket products may or may not contain asbestos. Refer to aftermarket product packaging for product information. Whether the product contains asbestos or not, dust and dirt can accumulate on manual clutch parts during normal use. Follow practices prescribed by appropriate regulations for the handling, processing and disposing of dust and debris.

1. Remove the transaxle (3) from the vehicle. (Refer to Manual Transaxle Removal.)

2. Remove the modular clutch assembly (1) from the transaxle input shaft.

To install:

3. Install the clutch module onto the input shaft.

4. Install the transaxle into the vehicle. (Refer to Manual Transaxle Installation.)

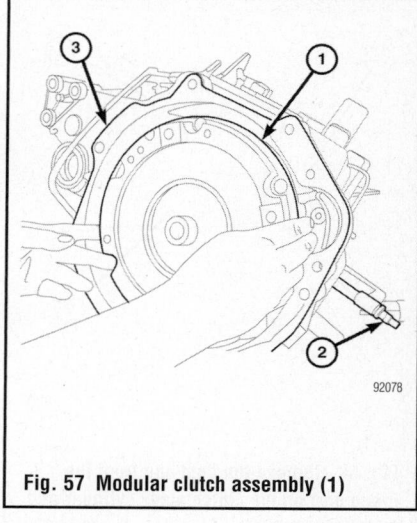

Fig. 57 Modular clutch assembly (1)

BLEEDING

See Figure 58.

➡**An assistant is required to perform this procedure.**

1. Verify the fluid level in the clutch/brake cylinder. Top off with DOT 3 brake fluid as necessary. Leave the cap off.

2. Raise the vehicle on a hoist. Refer to Hoisting Standard Procedure in Precautions.

➡**Position the container at a lower level than the bleeder valve on the clutch slave cylinder.**

3. Remove the dust cap from the bleed port on the clutch slave cylinder and install

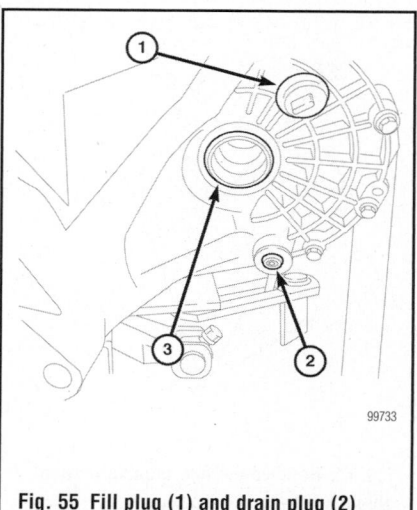

Fig. 55 Fill plug (1) and drain plug (2)

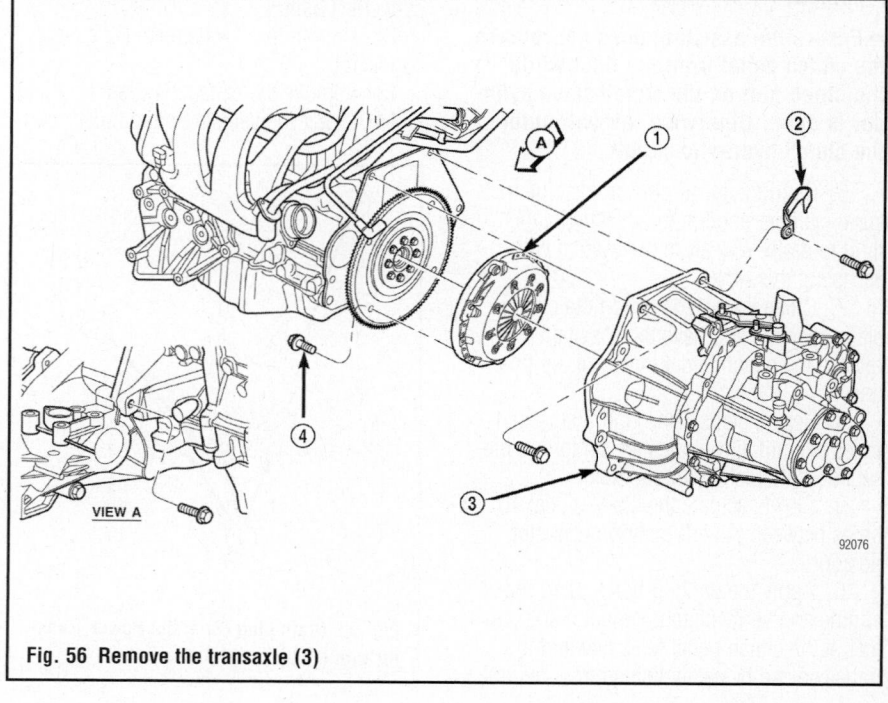

Fig. 56 Remove the transaxle (3)

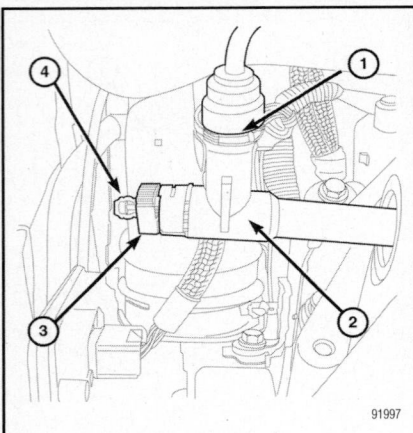

Fig. 58 Remove the dust cap from the bleed port on the clutch slave cylinder and install a suitable size and length of clear hose (4) to monitor and divert fluid into a suitable container

a suitable size and length of clear hose (4) to monitor and divert fluid into a suitable container.

4. Lower the vehicle, but only enough to gain access to and fill the brake master cylinder.

5. Have the assistant press down and hold the clutch pedal until it reaches the floor.

➡ **Do not allow the clutch/brake fluid reservoir to run dry while fluid exits bleed port. If the reservoir runs dry during this procedure, it must be refilled, and this step must be repeated.**

➡ **Ensure the assistant does not release the clutch pedal from the floor while the bleed port on the clutch slave cylinder is open. Otherwise, air will enter the clutch hydraulic circuit.**

6. Open the bleed port on the clutch slave cylinder enough to allow hydraulic fluid to drain. Any air in the system will escape at this time.

7. Close the bleed port on the clutch slave cylinder, and have the assistant release the clutch pedal to the full up position.

8. Repeat steps 5 through 7 at least 15 times or until air bubbles are no longer present in the clutch hydraulic fluid.

9. Slowly actuate the clutch pedal 10 times between the full up and pedal stop position.

10. Apply the parking brake. Start the engine and verify clutch operation and pedal feel. If the clutch pedal feels fine and the transaxle can be easily shifted from neutral

to any gear, the clutch is operating correctly. If the pedal still feels spongy or clutch does not fully disengage, excessive air is still trapped within the system, most likely at the master cylinder.

11. Disconnect the hose from the bleed port on the clutch master cylinder and install the dust cap.

12. Top off the brake master cylinder fluid level with DOT 3 brake fluid as needed.

POWER TRANSFER UNIT (PTU)

REMOVAL & INSTALLATION

See Figures 59 through 64.

1. Disconnect the negative battery cable (2).
2. Remove the engine trim cover.
3. Remove the air cleaner assembly (refer to Engine Air Cleaner).
4. Remove the Power Distribution Center (PDC) from the bracket.
5. Raise the vehicle on a hoist. Refer to Hoisting Standard Procedure in Precautions.
6. Remove the front half shafts (Refer to Half Shaft Removal).
7. Remove drain plug (2) at the Power Transfer Unit (PTU) and allow fluid to drain.
8. Reinstall the drain plug.
9. Mark the prop shaft (2) and differential (3) for proper installation.
10. Remove the rear prop shaft (Refer to Propeller Shaft Removal).
11. Remove the two exhaust to maniverter (exhaust manifold with catalytic converter) bolts.
12. Unplug the downstream O2 sensor connector.
13. Remove the exhaust system.
14. Lower the vehicle on the hoist.

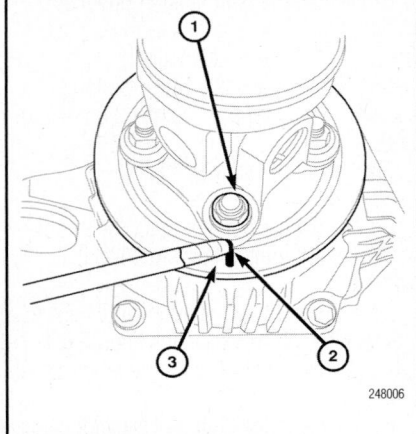

Fig. 60 Mark the prop shaft (2) and differential (3) for proper installation

15. Unplug the upstream O2 sensor connector.
16. Remove the upstream O2 sensor from the maniverter using the Oxygen Sensor Remover/Installer 8439.
17. Remove the four maniverter heat shield bolts (1).
18. Remove the two retaining bolts and one nut from the maniverter side heat shield.
19. Remove the seven maniverter to head retaining bolts.
20. Slide the maniverter up and to the right; support the maniverter (1) with the help of a bungee cord.
21. Raise the vehicle on the hoist. Refer to Hoisting Standard Procedure in Precautions.
22. Remove the four (1) engine to maniverter bracket bolts.
23. Remove the rear engine mount through bolt (2).
24. Remove the three front engine mount to frame bolts and the mount through bolt.

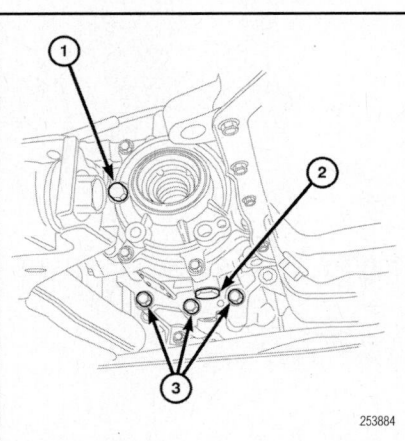

Fig. 59 Drain plug (2) at the Power Transfer Unit (PTU)

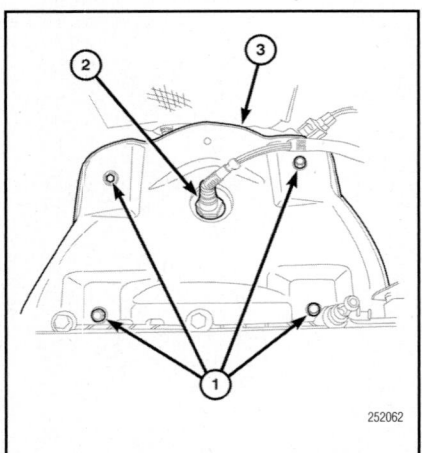

Fig. 61 Remove the four maniverter heat shield bolts (1)

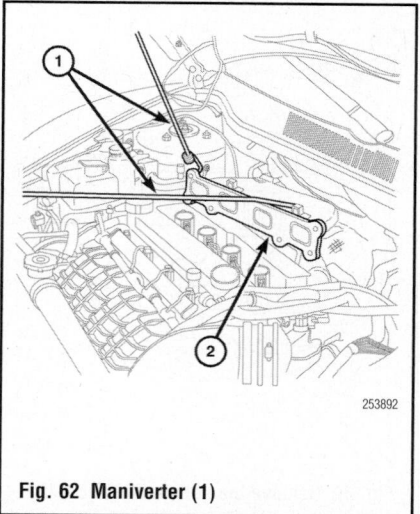

Fig. 62 Maniverter (1)

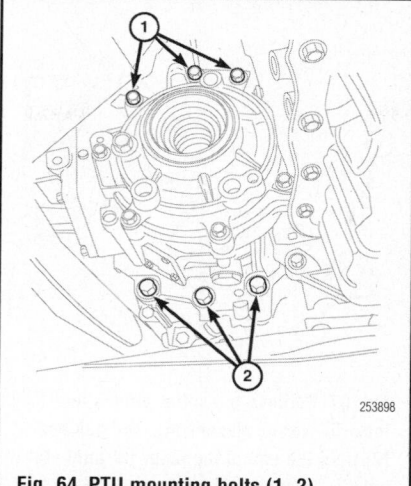

Fig. 64 PTU mounting bolts (1, 2)

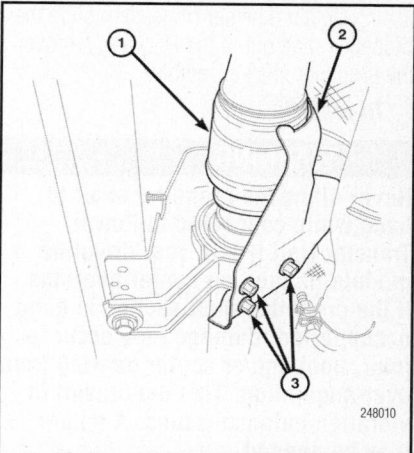

Fig. 65 Remove the three bolts (3) from the center support heat shield (2)

25. Remove the PTU mounting bolts (1, 2).

26. Install a screw jack on the front engine mount bracket.

27. Raise the front of the engine until the rear mount drops (1, 2).

28. Separate the PTU from the transaxle.

29. Remove and discard the old O-ring between the transmission and the PTU.

30. Roll the PTU forward and down to remove.

To install:

31. Roll the PTU in, moving from front to back.

32. Rest the PTU on the frame while you raise the engine and transaxle back into position.

33. Lower the screw jack until the rear mount through bolt can be installed.

34. Install rear mount through bolt and tighten the bolt to 55 ft. lbs. (75 Nm).

35. Install the transmission crossmem-

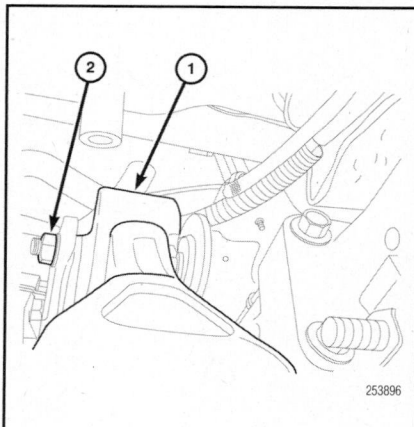

Fig. 63 Rear engine mount through bolt (2)

ber and bolts and tighten them to 55 ft. lbs. (75 Nm).

36. Install the through bolt at the front transmission mount and tighten it to 55 ft. lbs. (75 Nm).

➡**LUBRICATING THE O-RING WITH VASELINE OR TRANS ASSEMBLY GREASE IS RECOMMENDED.**

37. Insure that the O-ring between the PTU and transaxle is in place.

38. Slide the PTU into place.

39. Install and tighten the PTU mounting bolts (1, 2) to 43 ft. lbs. (58 Nm).

40. Lower the hoist.

41. Install the maniverter. (Refer to Engine Catalytic Converter Installation).

42. Install the air cleaner assembly.

43. Install engine trim cover.

44. Raise the vehicle on the hoist. Refer to Hoisting Standard Procedure in Precautions.

45. Install the exhaust system.

46. Install the Prop shaft. (Refer to Propeller Shaft Installation).

47. Install the axle shafts. (Refer to Half Shaft Installation).

48. Fill the PTU. (Refer to Transfer Case/Power Transfer Unit).

49. Lower the hoist.

50. Connect the battery cables.

51. Top off the fluids (refer to Fluid Specifications.)

PROPELLER SHAFT

REMOVAL & INSTALLATION

2.4L Engine

See Figures 65 and 66.

1. Raise the vehicle on the hoist. Refer to Hoisting Standard Procedure in Precautions.

2. Mark the propeller shaft and differential for proper installation (view the image in Transfer Case/PTU Removal).

3. Remove four rear propeller shaft to rear axle retaining nuts.

4. Remove the three bolts (3) from the center support heat shield (2).

5. Remove the heat shield (2).

✳✳ WARNING

Propeller shaft removal: Never allow propeller shaft to hang while connected to Power Transfer Unit (PTU), rear driveline module flanges or center bearings. If propeller shaft section is hung unsupported, damage may occur to joint, boot and/or center bearing from over-angulation. This may result in vibration/balance issues. A helper may be needed.

6. Remove the two center support mounting bolts (3).

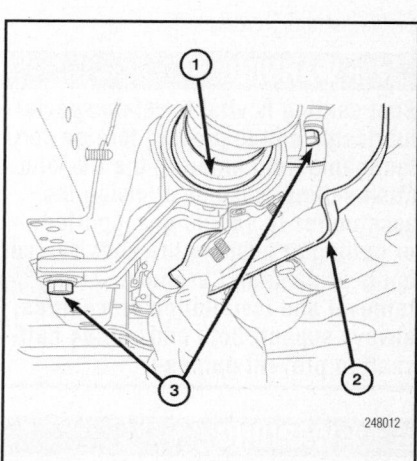

Fig. 66 Remove the two center support mounting bolts (3)

7. Obtain a helper (if needed) slide the propeller shaft out of the PTU and remove the propeller shaft assembly.

To install:

☀ WARNING

Never allow the propeller shaft to hang while connected to Power Transfer Unit (PTU), rear driveline module flanges, or center bearings. If the propeller shaft section is hung unsupported, damage may occur to joint, boot and/or center bearing from over-angulation. This may result in vibration/balance issues. A helper may be needed.

8. Make sure the transaxle is in Neutral (N) position.

9. Obtain a helper (if needed) and lift the propeller shaft assembly into position. Install the propeller shaft spline into the PTU.

10. Align the marks on the propeller shaft with the marks on the rear axle flange. Slide the propeller shaft over the studs on the rear axle flange.

11. Install the four retaining nuts.

12. Raise the center support into position.

13. Install the center support bolts and tighten them to 30 ft. lbs. (41 Nm).

14. Install the propeller shaft nuts and tighten them to 43 ft. lbs. (58 Nm).

15. Install the heat shield nuts and tighten them to 15 ft. lbs. (21 Nm).

16. Check the fluid levels, starting with the PTU.

FRONT HALFSHAFT

REMOVAL & INSTALLATION

2.0L & 2.4L Engines

See Figures 67 through 76.

☀ WARNING

Boot sealing is vital to retain special lubricants and to prevent foreign contaminants from entering the CV-joint. Mishandling, such as allowing the assemblies to dangle unsupported, or pulling or pushing the ends can cut boots or damage CV-joints. During removal and installation procedures, always support both ends of the halfshaft to prevent damage.

☀ WARNING

The halfshaft, when installed, acts as a bolt and secures the front

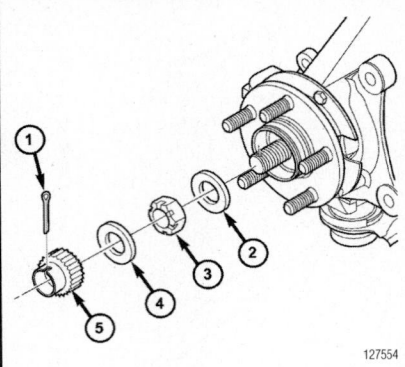

Fig. 67 Remove the cotter pin (1), nut lock (5), spring washer (4), and hub nut (3) from the end of the outer CV-joint stub axle

hub/bearing assembly. If the vehicle is to be supported or moved on its wheels with a halfshaft removed, install a PROPER-SIZED BOLT AND NUT through front hub. Tighten bolt and nut to 180 ft. lbs. (244 Nm). This will ensure that the hub bearing cannot loosen.**

1. Disconnect the battery negative cable.

2. Place the transaxle in gated park.

3. Raise the vehicle on a hoist. Refer to Hoisting Standard Procedure in Precautions.

4. Remove the wheel and tire assembly.

5. Remove the cotter pin (1), nut lock (5), spring washer (4), and hub nut (3) from the end of the outer CV-joint stub axle.

6. For the SRT 4: Remove the hub nut (1).

7. If equipped with ABS, disconnect the front wheel speed sensor and secure the harness out of the way.

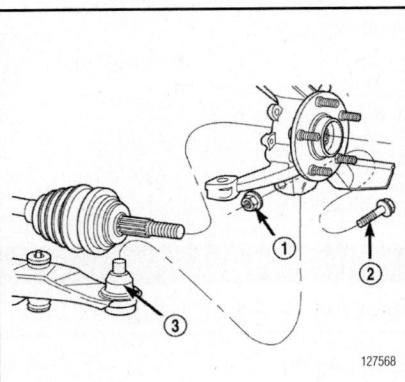

Fig. 68 Remove nut and bolt (1 and 2) retaining ball joint stud (3) into steering knuckle

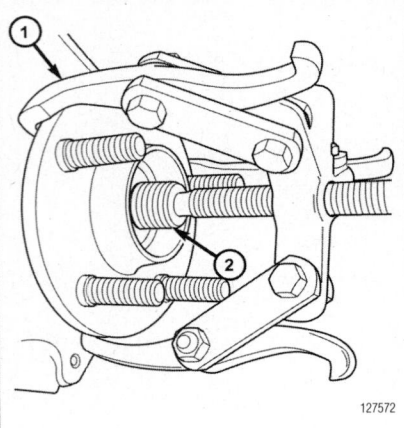

Fig. 69 Remove the halfshaft (2) from the steering knuckle by pulling outward on the knuckle while pressing in on the halfshaft. Support the outer end of the halfshaft assembly. If difficulty in separating the halfshaft from the hub is encountered, do not strike the shaft with a hammer, instead use Puller 1026 (1) to separate

8. Remove the nut and bolt (1, 2) retaining the ball joint stud (3) into the steering knuckle.

➡ **Use caution when separating the ball joint stud from the steering knuckle, so the ball joint seal does not get damaged.**

9. Separate the ball joint stud from the steering knuckle by prying down on the lower control arm.

➡ **Care must be taken not to separate the inner CV-joint during this operation. Do not allow the halfshaft to hang by inner the CV-joint, the halfshaft must be supported.**

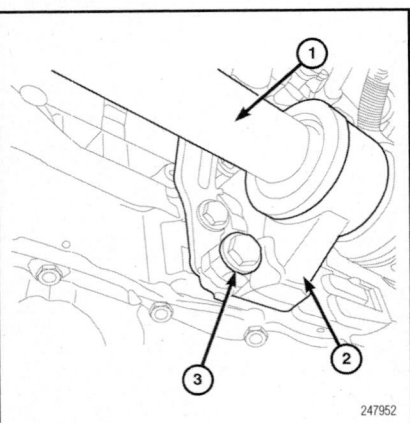

Fig. 70 For two wheel drive vehicles, remove the halfshaft bracket (2) from the engine lower mounting bolt (3)

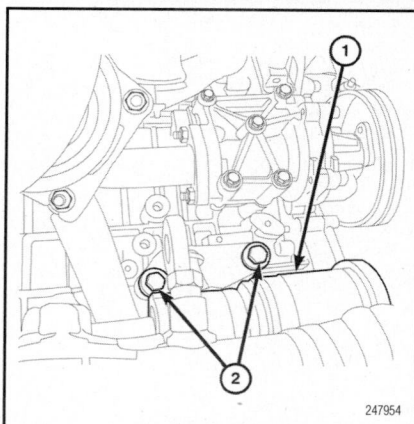

Fig. 71 For two wheel drive vehicles, remove the halfshaft bracket from the engine upper mounting bolts (2)

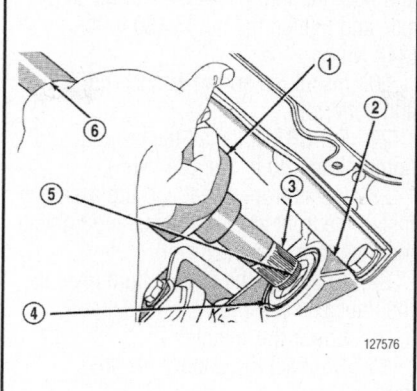

Fig. 73 Tripod joint (1), interconnecting shaft (6), and transaxle oil seal (4)

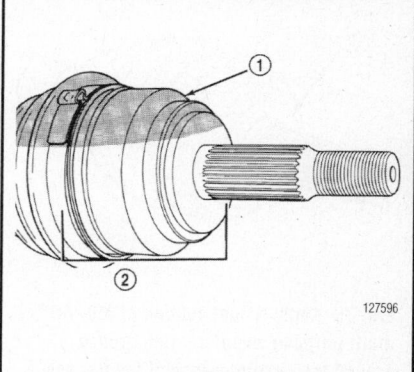

Fig. 75 Ensure that front of the outer CV-joint (2) which fits into steering knuckle, is free of debris and moisture before assembling into steering knuckle

10. Remove the halfshaft (2) from the steering knuckle by pulling outward on the knuckle while pressing in on the halfshaft. Support the outer end of the halfshaft assembly. If difficulty in separating the half-shaft from the hub is encountered, do not strike the shaft with a hammer, instead use Puller 1026 (1) to separate.

11. For two wheel drive vehicles, remove the halfshaft bracket (2) from the engine lower mounting bolt (3).

12. For two wheel drive vehicles, remove the halfshaft bracket from the engine upper mounting bolts (2).

13. Support the outer end of the halfshaft assembly.

➡**Removal of the inner tripod joints is made easier if you apply outward pressure on the joint as you strike the punch with a hammer. Do not pull on interconnecting shaft to remove, as the inner joint will become separated.**

14. Remove the inner tripod joints (4) from the side gears of the transaxle using a punch (2) to dislodge the inner tripod joint retaining ring from the transaxle side gear. If removing the right side inner tripod joint, position the punch to the inner tripod joint extraction groove (5; if equipped). Strike the punch sharply with a hammer to dislodge the right inner joint from the side gear. If removing the left side inner tripod joint, position the punch to the inner tripod joint extraction groove. Strike the punch sharply with a hammer to dislodge the left inner tri-pod joint from the side gear.

Hold inner tripod joint (1) and interconnecting shaft (6) of halfshaft assembly. Remove inner tripod joint from transaxle by pulling it straight out of transaxle side gear and transaxle oil seal (4). When removing tripod joint, do not let spline or snap ring drag across sealing lip of the transaxle to tripod joint oil seal. When tripod joint is removed from transaxle, some fluid will leak out.

⚹⚹ **WARNING**

The halfshaft, when installed, acts as a bolt and secures the front hub/bearing assembly. If vehicle is to be supported or moved on its wheels with a halfshaft removed, install a PROPER-SIZED BOLT AND NUT through front hub. Tighten bolt and nut to 180 ft. lbs. (244 Nm). This will ensure that the hub bearing cannot loosen.

To install:

15. Clean all debris and moisture out of the steering knuckle (4).

⚹⚹ **WARNING**

Boot sealing is vital to retain special lubricants and to prevent foreign con-taminants from entering the CV-joint. Mishandling, such as allowing the assemblies to dangle unsupported, or pulling or pushing the ends can cut boots or damage CV-joints. During removal and installation procedures, always support both ends of the half-shaft to prevent damage.

16. Thoroughly clean the spline and oil seal sealing surface on the tripod joint. Lightly lubricate the oil seal sealing surface on the tripod joint with fresh clean trans-mission lubricant.

➡**Always use Seal Protector 9099 when installing half shaft into the transaxle.**

17. Holding the halfshaft assembly by the tripod joint and interconnecting shaft, install the tripod joint into the transaxle side gear as far as possible by hand.

18. Carefully align the tripod joint with

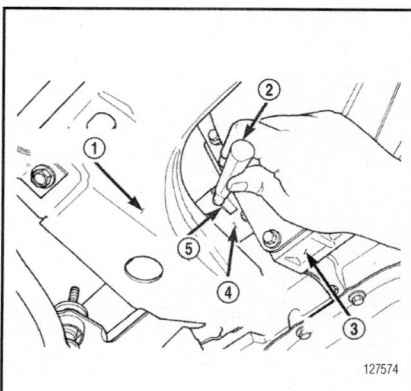

Fig. 72 Inner tripod joints (4), punch (2) and inner tripod joint extraction groove (5; if equipped)

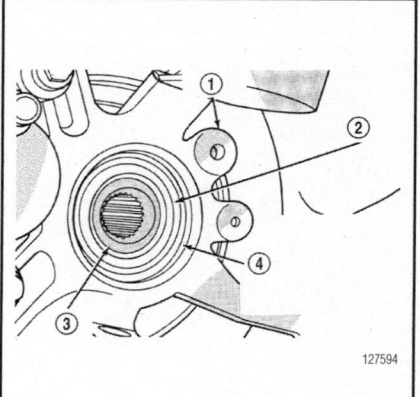

Fig. 74 Clean all debris and moisture out of the steering knuckle (4)

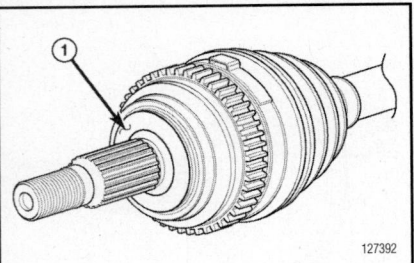

**Fig. 76 Apply a light coating of MOPAR®
multi-purpose wheel bearing grease
around the circumference of the flat surface (1). Do not apply too much grease,
which could spill onto the non-mating and
adversely affect the function of the halfshaft**

the transaxle side gears. Then grasp the
halfshaft interconnecting shaft and push the
tripod joint into the transaxle side gear until
it seats fully. Test that the snap ring is fully
engaged with side gear by attempting to
remove the tripod joint from the transaxle
by hand. If the snap ring is fully engaged
with the side gear, the tripod joint will not
be removable by hand.

19. For two wheel drive vehicles, install
the intermediate shaft bracket-to-block and
tighten the bolt to 55 ft. lbs. (75 Nm).

20. For two wheel drive vehicles, install
the intermediate shaft bracket- to-block
upper mounting bolts and tighten them to
55 ft. lbs. (75 Nm).

21. Ensure that front of the outer CV-
joint (2) which fits into steering knuckle, is
free of debris and moisture before assembling into the steering knuckle.

22. Apply a light coating of MOPAR®
multi-purpose wheel bearing grease around
the circumference of the flat surface (1). Do
not apply too much grease, which could
spill onto the non-mating and adversely
affect the function of the halfshaft.

23. Wipe the rear of the hub and bearing
in the knuckle clean where they contact the
CV-joint.

24. Install the halfshaft back into the
front hub.

➡ **At this point, the outer joint will not
seat completely into the front hub. The
outer joint will be pulled into the hub
and seated when the hub nut is
installed and tightened to specification.**

➡ **Install a NEW steering knuckle to
ball joint stud bolt and nut. Tighten the
nut and bolt to 70 ft. lbs. (95 Nm).**

25. Clean all foreign matter from threads
of halfshaft outer stub axle. Install a washer

and hub nut onto the threads of the stub
axle and tighten the nut to 180 ft. lbs.
(244 Nm).

26. Install the spring washer, nut lock,
and cotter pin.

27. For SRT 4, install the hub nut and
tighten it to 180 ft. lbs. (244 Nm).

28. Install front wheel and tire assembly.
Install the front wheel lug nuts and tighten
them to 95 ft. lbs. (128 Nm).

29. Check for the correct fluid level in
the transaxle assembly.

30. Lower the vehicle.

31. Connect the battery negative
cable.

REAR HALFSHAFT

REMOVAL & INSTALLATION

See Figures 77 through 83.

1. Raise the vehicle on a hoist. Refer to
Hoisting Standard Procedure in Precautions.

2. Remove the rear tires.

3. Drain the fluid from the rear driveline
module.

4. Remove the rear propeller shaft.
(Refer to Propeller Shaft Removal).

5. Remove the right side sway bar nut
(1; if equipped).

6. Remove left side sway bar nut
(if equipped).

7. Roll the sway bar (2; if equipped)
down and out of the way.

8. Remove the left side stay bracket
bolts (1).

9. Remove the right side stay bracket
bolts.

10. Remove the exhaust system up to the
catalytic converter.

11. Support the rear driveline module
with a transmission jack.

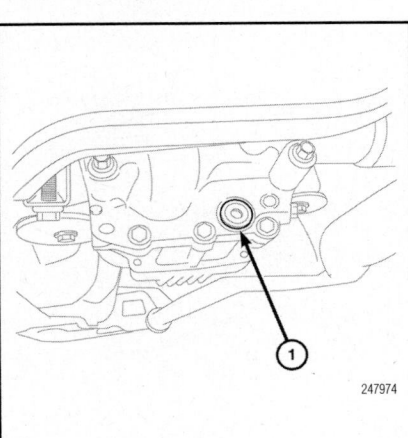

**Fig. 77 Drain the fluid from the rear drive-
line module**

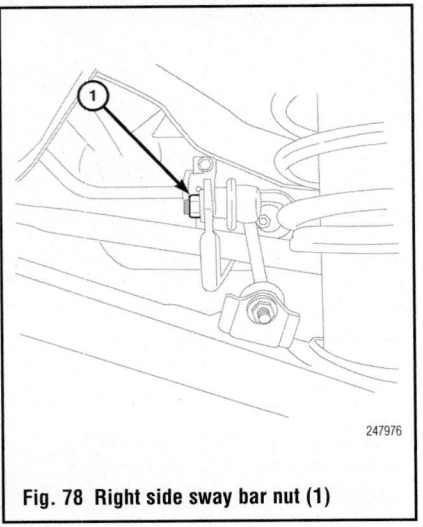

Fig. 78 Right side sway bar nut (1)

12. Remove the rear bolt at the driveline
module.

13. Remove the two side bolts (1) at the
driveline module (3).

14. Lower the driveline module enough
to gain access to the electrical connector
and bracket.

15. Remove the routing bracket bolt.

16. Remove the breather hose from
the Electronically Controlled Clutch
(ECC).

17. Unplug the electrical connector (1).

18. Lower the driveline module (1).

19. Disengage the axle shaft (2).

20. Remove the nut and washer from the
halfshaft to the left rear hub.

21. Remove the halfshaft from the rear
hub. If it is hard to remove or sticking, use
a punch and hammer to tap it out.

To install:

22. Lift the driveline module with a
transmission jack while installing the halfshaft.

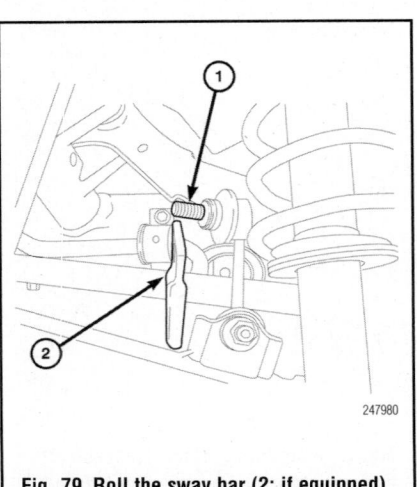

**Fig. 79 Roll the sway bar (2; if equipped)
down and out of the way**

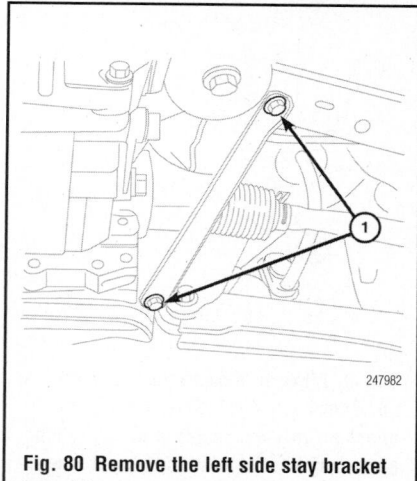

Fig. 80 Remove the left side stay bracket bolts (1)

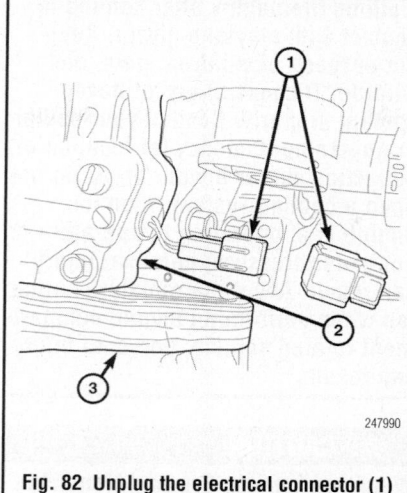

Fig. 82 Unplug the electrical connector (1)

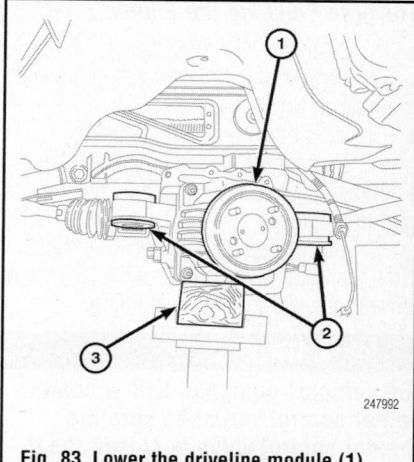

Fig. 83 Lower the driveline module (1) and disengage the axle shaft (2)

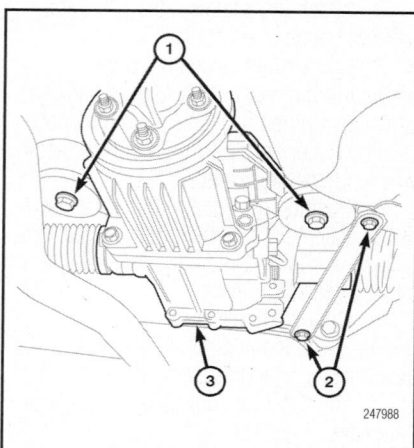

Fig. 81 Remove the two side bolts (1) at the driveline module (3)

23. Install the nut and washer halfshaft to the left rear hub and tighten them to 180 ft. lbs. (244 Nm).

24. Left rear halfshaft:
   a. Connect the breather hose to the ECC.
   b. Connect the electrical connector.

25. Right rear halfshaft:
   a. Connect the electrical connector.
   b. Connect the breather hose to the ECC.

26. Install the wire harness bracket and two mounting bolt and tighten them to 89 inch lbs. (10 Nm).

27. Lift the driveline module into place.

28. Install the two driveline module side mounting bolts and tighten them to 75 ft. lbs. (102 Nm).

29. Install the rear driveline module mounting bolt and tighten it to 75 ft. lbs. (102 Nm).

30. Install the right side stay bracket and bolts tighten them to 45 ft. lbs. (61 Nm).

31. Install the left side stay bracket and bolts and tighten them to 45 ft. lbs. (61 Nm).

32. Install the propeller shaft (refer to Propeller Shaft Installation).

33. Fill the rear axle with fluid.

34. Roll the sway bar (if equipped) into place.

35. Install left side sway bar nut (if equipped) and tighten it to 45 ft. lbs. (61 Nm).

36. Install right side sway bar nut (if equipped) and tighten it to 45 ft. lbs. (61 Nm).

37. Install the exhaust.

38. Install the wheels.

ENGINE COOLING

ENGINE COOLANT

CLEANING/REVERSE FLUSHING

Cleaning

1. Drain the cooling system and refill with water.

2. Run the engine with the radiator cap installed until the upper radiator hose is hot.

3. Stop the engine and drain the water from system.

4. If the water is dirty, fill the system with water, run the engine and drain the system.

5. Repeat this procedure until the water drains clean.

➡**Chemical Cleaning: In some instances, use a radiator cleaner (Mopar® Radiator Kleen or an equivalent) before flushing. This will soften** scale and other deposits and aid in the flushing operation.

❊❊ WARNING

Follow the manufacturer's instructions when using chemical cleaning products.

Reverse Flushing

Reverse flushing of the cooling system is the forcing of water through the cooling system. This is done using air pressure in the opposite direction of normal coolant flow. It is usually only necessary with very dirty systems with evidence of partial plugging.

Reverse Flushing the Radiator

1. Disconnect the radiator hoses from the radiator inlet and outlet.

2. Attach a section of the radiator hose to the radiator bottom outlet fitting and insert the flushing gun.

3. Connect a water supply hose and air supply hose to the flushing gun.

❊❊ WARNING

The internal radiator pressure must not exceed 20 psi (138 kPa) as damage to the radiator may result.

4. Allow the radiator to fill with water.

5. When the radiator is filled, apply air in short blasts.

6. Allow the radiator to refill between blasts.

7. Continue this reverse flushing until clean water flows out through the rear of the radiator cooling tube passages.

Reverse Flushing the Engine

1. Drain the cooling system.
2. Remove the thermostat housing and thermostat.
3. Install the thermostat housing.
4. Disconnect the radiator upper hose from the radiator and attach the flushing gun to the hose.
5. Disconnect the radiator lower hose from the water pump and attach a lead-away hose to the water pump inlet fitting.

✳✳ WARNING

On vehicles equipped with a heater water control valve, be sure the heater control valve is closed (heat off). This will prevent coolant flow with scale and other deposits from entering the heater core.

6. Connect the water supply hose and air supply hose to flushing gun.
7. Allow the engine to fill with water.
8. When the engine is filled, apply air in short blasts, allowing the system to fill between air blasts.
9. Continue until clean water flows through the lead away hose.
10. Remove the lead away hose, flushing gun, water supply hose and air supply hose.
11. Remove the thermostat housing and install the thermostat.
12. Install the thermostat housing with a replacement gasket. Refer to Thermostat replacement.
13. Connect the radiator hoses.
14. Refill the cooling system with the correct antifreeze/water mixture.

COOLANT AIR EVACUATION

See Figures 84 through 86.

Evacuating or purging air from the cooling system involves the use of a pressurized air operated vacuum generator. The vacuum created allows for a quick and complete coolant refilling while removing any airlocks present in the system components.

➡ **To avoid damage to the cooling system, ensure that no component would be susceptible to damage when a vacuum is drawn on the system.**

✳✳ CAUTION

Antifreeze is an ethylene glycol base coolant and is harmful if swallowed or inhaled. If swallowed, drink two glasses of water and induce vomiting. If inhaled, move to fresh air area. Seek medical attention immediately. Do not store in open or unmarked containers. Wash skin and clothing thoroughly after coming in contact with ethylene glycol. Keep out of reach of children, pets, and wildlife. Dispose of glycol-based coolant properly. Contact your dealer or government agency for location of collection center in your area. Do not open a cooling system when the engine is at operating temperature or hot under pressure; personal injury can result. Avoid the radiator cooling fan when performing engine compartment related service; personal injury can result.

✳✳ CAUTION

Wear Appropriate Eye And Hand Protection When Performing This Procedure.

➡ **The service area where this procedure is performed should have a minimum shop air requirement of 80 psi (5.5 bar) and should be equipped with an air dryer system.**

➡ **For best results, empty the radiator. Set the vehicle's heater control to the heat position (the ignition may need to be turned to the on position but do not start the motor).**

1. Refer to the Chrysler Pentastar Service Equipment Coolant Refiller #85-15-0650 or an equivalent tool's operating manual for specific assembly steps.
2. Choose an appropriate adapter cone that will fit the vehicle's radiator filler neck or reservoir tank.

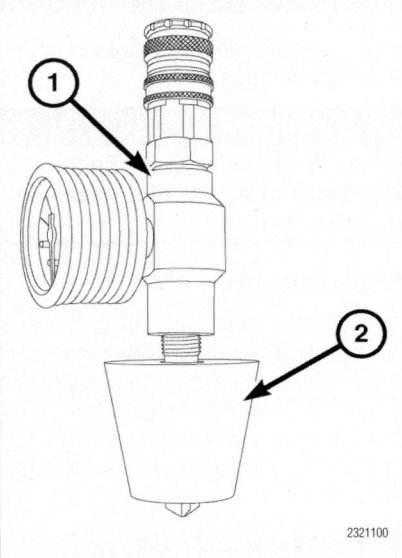

Fig. 84 Attach the adapter cone (2) to the vacuum gauge (1)

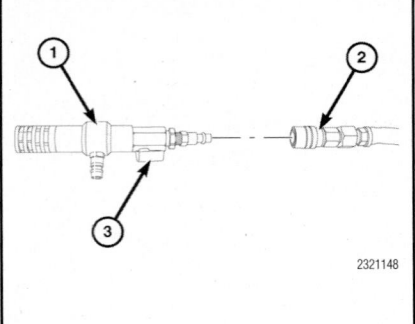

Fig. 85 Make sure the vacuum generator/venturi ball valve (3) is closed and attach an airline hose (2) (minimum shop air requirement of 80 PSI/5.5 bar) to the vacuum generator/venturi (1)

3. Attach the adapter cone (2) to the vacuum gauge (1).
4. Make sure the vacuum generator/venturi ball valve (3) is closed and attach an airline hose (2) (minimum shop air requirement of 80 PSI/5.5 bar) to the vacuum generator/venturi (1).
5. Position the adaptor cone/vacuum gauge assembly into the radiator filler neck or reservoir tank. Ensure that the adapter cone is sealed properly.
6. Connect the vacuum generator/venturi to the positioned adaptor cone/vacuum gauge assembly.
7. Open the vacuum generator/venturi ball valve.

➡ **Do not bump or move the assembly as it may result in loss of vacuum. Some radiator overflow hoses may need to be clamped off to obtain vacuum.**

8. Let the system run until the vacuum gauge shows a good vacuum through the cooling system. Refer to the tool's operating manual for appropriate pressure readings.

➡ **If a strong vacuum is being created in the system, it is normal to see the radiator hoses collapse.**

9. Close the vacuum generator/venturi ball valve.
10. Disconnect the vacuum generator/venturi and airline from the adaptor cone/vacuum gauge assembly.
11. Wait approximately 20 seconds, if the pressure readings do not move, the system has no leaks. If the pressure readings move, a leak could be present in the system. You should check the cooling system for leaks and repeat the procedure.
12. Place the tool's suction hose into the coolant's container.

➡️**Ensure there is a sufficient amount of coolant, mixed to the required strength/protection level available for use. For best results and to assist the refilling procedure, place the coolant container at the same height as the radiator filler neck. Always draw more coolant than required. If the coolant level is too low, it will pull air into the cooling system which could result in airlocks in the system.**

13. Connect the tool's suction hose to the adaptor cone/vacuum gauge assembly.

14. Open the suction hose's ball valve to begin refilling the cooling system.

15. When the vacuum gauge reads zero, the system is filled.

➡️**On some remote pressurized tanks, it is recommended to stop filling when the proper level is reached.**

16. Close the suction hose's ball valve and remove the suction hose from the adaptor cone/vacuum gauge assembly.

17. Remove the adaptor cone/vacuum gauge assembly from the radiator filler neck or reservoir tank.

18. With the heater control unit in the HEAT position, operate the engine with the container cap in place.

19. After the engine has reached normal operating temperature, shut the engine off and allow it to cool. When the engine is cooling down, coolant will be drawn into the radiator from the pressure container.

20. Add coolant to the recovery bottle/container as necessary. Only add coolant to the container when the engine is cold. Coolant level in a warm engine will be higher due to thermal expansion. Add necessary coolant to raise container level to the COLD MINIMUM mark after each cool down period.

21. Once the appropriate coolant level is achieved, attach the radiator cap or reservoir tank cap.

COOLANT LEVEL CHECK

See Figure 87.

➡️**Do not remove pressure cap for routine coolant level inspections.**

The coolant recovery/reserve system provides a quick visual method for determining the coolant level without removing the pressure cap. Simply observe, with the engine idling and warmed up to normal operating temperature, that the level of the coolant in the recovery/reserve bottle is between the FULL HOT and ADD marks.

COOLING SYSTEM DRAINING

✳✳ CAUTION

Do not open the radiator draincock when the system is hot and under pressure. Serious burns from coolant can occur.

Drain, flush, and fill the cooling system at the mileage or time intervals specified in the Maintenance Schedule. If the solution is dirty, rusty, or contains a considerable amount of sediment; clean and flush with a reliable cooling system cleaner. Use care when disposing of the used engine coolant from your vehicle. Coolant is extremely toxic to humans, pets, and wildlife. Check governmental regulations for disposal of used engine coolant.

1. Position a clean collecting container under the draincock location.

2. Without removing the pressure cap and when the system is not under pressure, turn the draincock counterclockwise to open.

3. The coolant reserve bottle should empty first, and then remove the pressure cap.

4. If the coolant reserve bottle does not empty first:

   a. Check condition of the pressure cap and cap seals.

   b. Check for a kinked or torn overflow hose from the filler neck to the reserve bottle.

5. Allow the cooling system to drain completely.

<$Editors: Add any other pertinent coolant heads>$

ENGINE FAN

REMOVAL & INSTALLATION

2010 Models

See Figure 88.

✳✳ CAUTION

Do not open the radiator draincock when the system is hot and under pressure because serious burns from coolant can occur.

1. Disconnect the negative cable from the battery.

2. Drain the cooling system below the upper radiator hose level.

3. Remove the radiator core support.

4. Disconnect the upper radiator hose from the radiator.

5. Remove the wiring harness bracket (2).

6. Disconnect the radiator fan electrical connector (1).

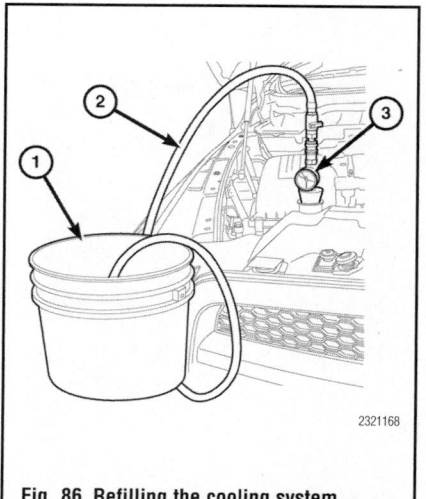

Fig. 86 Refilling the cooling system

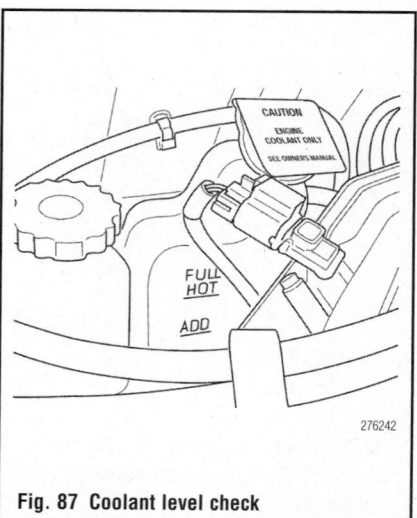

Fig. 87 Coolant level check

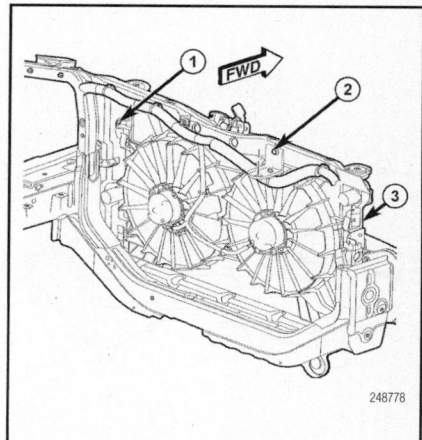

Fig. 88 Remove the wiring harness bracket (2)

7. Remove the radiator fan assembly screws.

8. Detach the radiator fan assembly from the retaining clips.

✳✳ WARNING

Work with care so as not to damage the radiator cooling fins and tubes during fan removal.

9. Remove the radiator fan by lifting up from the engine compartment.

To install:

10. Install the radiator fan assembly into the J-clips.

11. Install the radiator fan fasteners. Tighten all radiator fan retaining screws to 55 inch lbs. (6 Nm).

12. Install the radiator crossmember.

13. Install the wiring harness bracket.

14. Connect the radiator fan electrical connector.

15. Install the upper radiator hose.

16. Connect the negative battery cable.

17. Fill the cooling system

2011 Models

See Figures 89 and 91.

✳✳ CAUTION

Do not open the radiator draincock when the system is hot and under pressure because serious burns from coolant can occur.

1. Remove the air intake duct.

2. Disconnect negative cable from battery.

3. Drain the coolant just below the upper radiator hose.

4. Remove the upper radiator closure panel (2).

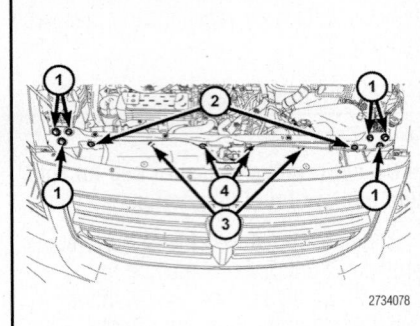

Fig. 90 Upper core support seal push pins (3) and radiator core support bolts (1)

5. Remove the hood latch cable.

6. Remove the upper core support seal push pins (3).

7. Remove the radiator core support bolts (1).

8. Remove the upper radiator hose support bracket (2; refer to image for 2010).

9. Remove the upper radiator hose from the radiator and position it aside.

10. Disconnect the radiator fan electrical connectors.

11. Remove the radiator fan module (1; refer to image for 2010) by lifting up from the engine compartment.

12. Remove the lower (8) shroud seal.

13. Remove the fan blade retaining nut (4) from the fan motor.

14. Remove the fan motor (5) assembly from the shroud.

To install:

15. Install the fan motor onto the shroud.

16. Install the fan onto the motor.

17. Install the lower shroud seal.

18. Install the radiator fan module.

19. Connect the electrical connectors.

20. Install the wiring harness mounting retainers into the fan shroud.

21. Install the upper radiator hose support bracket.

22. Install the upper radiator hose to the radiator.

23. Install the upper radiator core support. Tighten the outer bolts to 17 ft. lbs. (23 Nm). Tighten the inner support bolts to 6 ft. lbs. (8 Nm).

24. Install the hood latch cable.

25. Install the core support seal.

26. Install the radiator closure panel (2).

27. Connect the negative battery cable.

28. Fill the coolant to the proper level.

29. Run the vehicle. Check for proper fan operation and coolant level.

30. Install the air intake duct.

RADIATOR

REMOVAL & INSTALLATION

See Figure 92.

✳✳ CAUTION

Do not open the radiator draincock when the system is hot and under pressure because serious burns from coolant can occur.

1. Drain the cooling system.

2. Remove the radiator fan (Refer to Engine Fan Removal.)

3. Disconnect the lower radiator hose.

4. Remove the fasteners attaching the A/C condenser to the radiator. Reposition the A/C condenser.

5. Remove the radiator assembly by lifting it up from the engine compartment.

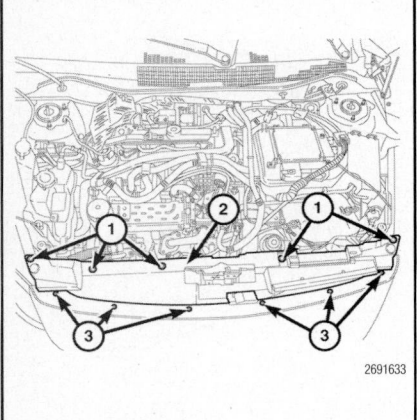

Fig. 89 Remove the upper radiator closure panel (2)

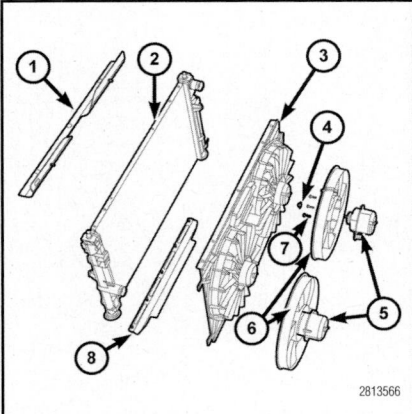

Fig. 91 Lower (8) shroud seal, fan blade retaining nut (4), fan motor assembly (5), and fan (6)

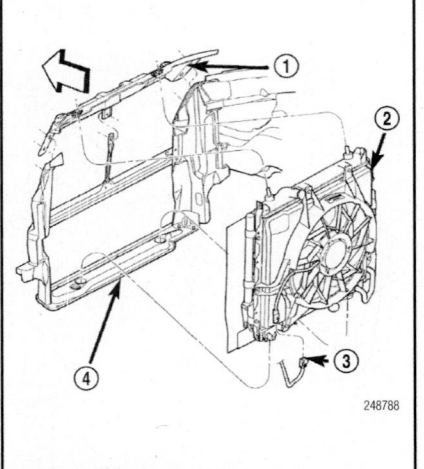

Fig. 92 Radiator replacement

Care should be taken not to damage the cooling fins and tubes during removal.

✳✳ WARNING

Work with care so as not to damage the radiator cooling fins and tubes during fan removal.

To install:

6. Install the lower air seal to the radiator.

7. Position the radiator into the mounting position.

8. Position the A/C condenser against the radiator. Hand start the fasteners.

9. Install the radiator fan/shroud assembly. Hand start the fasteners.

10. Tighten all condenser fasteners to 70 inch lbs. (8 Nm).

11. Tighten all the radiator fan fasteners to 55 inch lbs. (6 Nm).

12. Install the fasteners attaching the transmission oil cooler to the radiator. Tighten the fasteners to 70 inch lbs. (8 Nm).

13. Raise the vehicle on a hoist.

14. Connect the lower air seal to the side air seals.

15. Connect the lower radiator hose. Align the hose and position the clamp so it will not interfere with engine components.

16. Connect the radiator fan electrical connector.

17. Connect the power steering hoses.

18. Close the radiator draincock.

19. Lower the vehicle.

20. Connect the upper radiator hose. Align the hose and position the clamp to prevent interference with the engine or hood.

21. Install the upper radiator closure panel and center brace.

22. Install the grille.

23. Install the battery tray and battery.

24. Connect the positive battery cable. Connect the negative battery cable.

25. Install the air cleaner housing assembly.

26. Fill the cooling system with coolant.

27. Operate the engine until it reaches normal operating temperature. Check cooling system for correct fluid level.

THERMOSTAT

REMOVAL & INSTALLATION

Primary

See Figure 93.

1. Partially drain the cooling system.

2. Remove the air filter housing.

3. Disconnect the coolant hose (1) from the inlet housing (2).

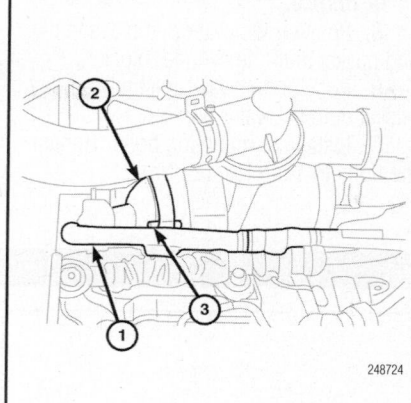

Fig. 93 Coolant hose (1), inlet housing (2), and inlet housing bolts (3)

4. Remove the inlet housing bolts (3).

5. Remove the thermostat assembly, and clean the sealing surfaces.

To install:

6. Position the thermostat into the water plenum, aligning the air bleed with the location notch on the inlet housing.

7. Install the inlet housing onto the coolant adapter. Tighten the bolts to 79 inch lbs. (9 Nm).

8. Connect the coolant hose.

9. Install the air filter housing.

10. Fill the cooling system.

Secondary

See Figure 94.

1. Partially drain the cooling system.

2. Remove the air filter housing.

3. Disconnect the coolant hoses (1) from the rear of the coolant adapter (2).

4. Remove the radiator hose (3).

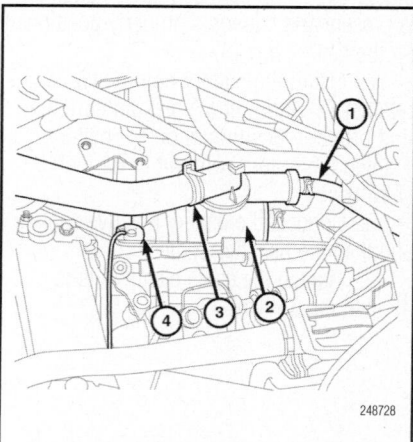

Fig. 94 Disconnect coolant hoses (1) from rear of the coolant adapter (2)

5. Remove the radiator hose (4) from the front of the coolant adapter (2).

6. Remove the coolant adapter mounting bolts.

7. Carefully slide the coolant adapter off the water pump inlet tube and remove the coolant adapter (2) and the secondary thermostat.

To install:

8. Position the thermostat into the cylinder head.

9. Inspect the water pump inlet tube O-rings for damage before installing the tube in the coolant adapter. Replace the O-ring as necessary.

10. Lubricate the O-rings with soapy water.

11. Position the coolant adapter on the water pump inlet tube and the cylinder head.

12. Install the coolant adapter mounting bolts. Tighten the bolts to 159 inch lbs. (18 Nm).

13. Connect the front coolant hose.

14. Connect the two rear coolant hoses.

15. Connect the radiator hose.

16. Install the air filter housing (Refer to Engine Air Cleaner Installation).

17. Fill the cooling system.

WATER PUMP

REMOVAL & INSTALLATION

See Figure 95.

1. Remove the accessory drive belt (Refer to Engine Accessory Drive Belt Installation).

2. Raise the vehicle. (Refer to Hoisting Standard Procedure in Precautions.)

3. Remove the accessory drive belt splash shield.

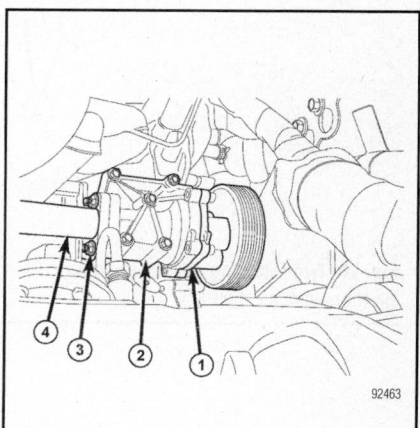

Fig. 95 Water pump pulley (1), mounting bolts (2), and pump (3)

4. Drain the cooling system.
5. Remove screws attaching water pump pulley (1). Remove the pulley (1).
6. Remove the water pump mounting bolts (2).
7. Remove the water pump (3).

To install:

8. Position the water pump assembly and gasket onto the cylinder block.
9. Position the water inlet tube and gasket onto the water pump.
10. Install the mounting bolts. Tighten the bolts to 18 ft. lbs. (24 Nm).

11. Install the drive belt splash shield.
12. Lower the vehicle.
13. Install the accessory drive belt (Refer to Engine Accessory Drive Belt Installation).
14. Evacuate the air and refill the cooling system.
15. Check the cooling system for leaks.

ENGINE ELECTRICAL

BATTERY

REMOVAL & INSTALLATION

See Figures 96 and 97.

> ❊❊ **CAUTION**
>
> **To protect your hands from battery acid, wear a suitable pair of heavy duty rubber gloves when removing or servicing a battery. Wear safety glasses also.**

> ❊❊ **CAUTION**
>
> **Remove metallic jewelry. You can be injured by accidental arcing of battery current.**

1. Rotate the two retaining clips (3) and remove the air cleaner fresh air duct (2).
2. Disconnect and isolate the battery negative cable then the positive cable.

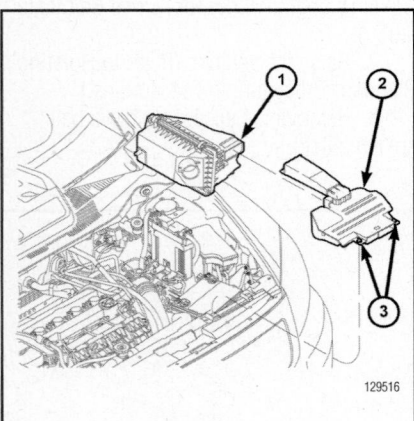

Fig. 96 Two retaining clips (3) and air cleaner fresh air duct (2)

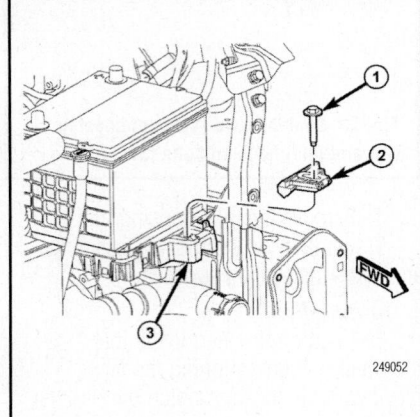

Fig. 97 Battery tray (3), battery hold down retainer (2) and bolt (1)

3. Loosen the bolt and the retainer that hold the battery to the tray.
4. Lift the battery out of battery tray and remove it from the vehicle.
5. Remove the thermal guard (if equipped) from the battery.

To install:

➡**When replacing the battery, the thermal guard MUST be transferred to the new battery (if equipped).**

6. Install the battery in the vehicle making sure that the thermal guard (if equipped) is present and battery is properly positioned on the battery tray (3).
7. Install the battery hold down retainer (2) and bolt (1) making sure that it is properly positioned on the battery. Tighten the hold down bolt to 62 inch lbs. (7 Nm).
8. Connect the battery positive cable and then the negative cable.
9. Tighten the cable clamp nuts to 45 inch lbs. (5 Nm).

BATTERY SYSTEM

10. Install the air cleaner fresh air duct and secure it in place by rotating the two retaining clips.
11. Verify proper vehicle operation.

STANDARD PROCEDURE—BATTERY RECONNECTION

2010 Models

➡**Perform this reconnection procedure anytime the battery has been disconnected.**

1. Connect the battery negative cable to the battery post and tighten the clamp nut.
2. Install the rear compartment floor trim panel.

> ❊❊ **WARNING**
>
> **Once the battery has been connected, review and perform the following information as applicable.**

If the vehicle is equipped with ESP, once the battery is reconnected, the Steering Angle Sensor (SAS) in the clockspring needs to be calibrated. The SAS requires calibration anytime the battery or an ABS (ESP) component has been disconnected for any length of time. **If the SAS is not calibrated following battery reconnection, the ESP/BAS indicator lamp is illuminated following five ignition cycles indicating the need for calibration.**

To calibrate, perform the following:
3. Start the engine.
4. Center the steering wheel.
5. Turn the steering wheel all the way to the left until the internal stop in the steering gear is met, then turn the wheel all the way to the right until the opposite internal stop in the steering gear is met.
6. Center the steering wheel.
7. Stop the engine.

ENGINE ELECTRICAL

GENERATOR (ALTERNATOR)

REMOVAL & INSTALLATION

See Figures 98 through 104.

1. Rotate the two retaining clips and remove the air cleaner fresh air duct. Refer to battery removal instructions.
2. Disconnect and isolate the negative battery cable at the battery.
3. Evacuate the A/C system.
4. Remove the right front wheel.
5. Remove the underbody air dam.
6. Remove the accessory drive splash shield.
7. Position aside the serpentine belt (Refer to Engine Accessory Drive Belt Removal).
8. Remove the accessory drive idler pulley.
9. Remove the A/C compressor.

10. Loosen the lower mounting bolt.
11. Unplug the field circuit from the generator.
12. Remove the B+ terminal nut and wire.
13. Remove the upper mounting bolt.
14. Remove the generator lower mounting bolt.
15. Slide the generator down and out of the vehicle.

To install:

16. Install the generator.
17. Rotate the generator and set it in place.
18. Make sure the battery terminal (1) is in front of the A/C line (2).
19. Install the upper mounting bolt. Tighten the bolts to 40 ft. lbs. (54 Nm).
20. Install the B+ terminal nut and wire and tighten them to 88.5 inch lbs. (10 Nm).

Fig. 102 Unplug the field circuit from the generator

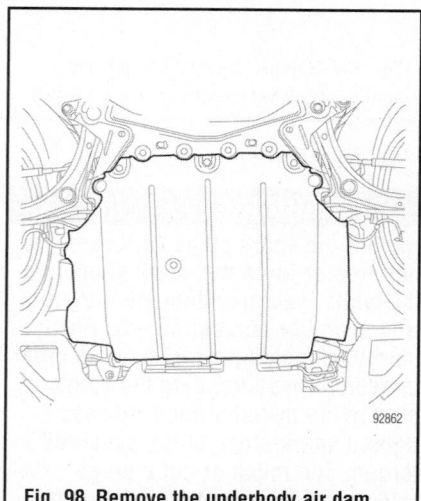

Fig. 98 Remove the underbody air dam

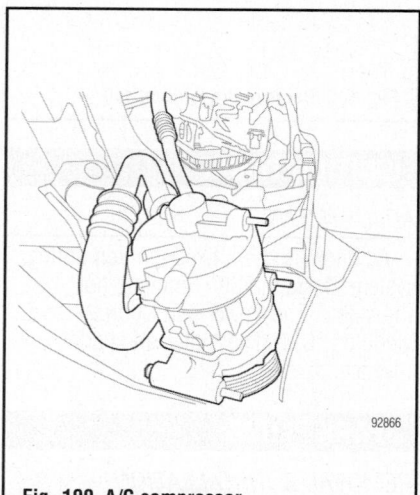

Fig. 100 A/C compressor

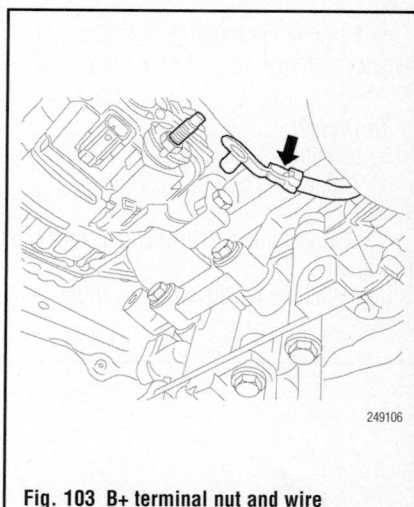

Fig. 103 B+ terminal nut and wire

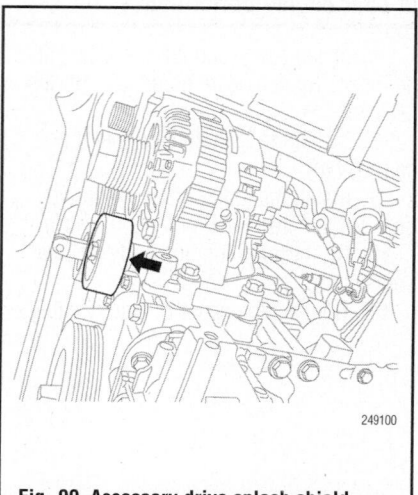

Fig. 99 Accessory drive splash shield

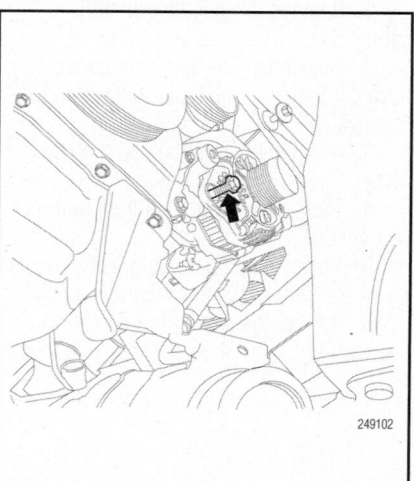
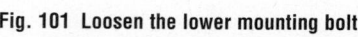

Fig. 101 Loosen the lower mounting bolt

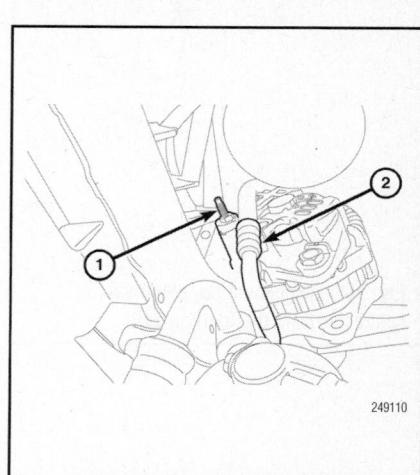

Fig. 104 Make sure the battery terminal (1) is in front of the A/C line (2)

21. Plug in the field circuit to the generator.

22. Install the lower mounting bolt. Tighten the bolts to 40 ft. lbs. (54 Nm).

23. Install the A/C compressor.

24. Install the accessory drive idler pulley. Tighten the bolt to 35 ft. lbs. (48 Nm).

25. Position back the serpentine belt.

26. Install the accessory drive splash shield.

27. Install underbody air dam.

28. Install the right front wheel.

29. Recharge the A/C system.

30. Connect the negative battery cable.

31. Install the air cleaner fresh air duct and rotate the two retaining clips to install.

ENGINE ELECTRICAL

FIRING ORDER

The firing order for the 2.0L & 2.4L engines is: 1–3–4–2.

IGNITION COIL

REMOVAL & INSTALLATION

See Figures 105 and 106.

1. Remove the negative battery cable.

2. Disconnect the electrical connector from the ignition coil.

3. Remove the ignition coil mounting bolts.

4. Remove the ignition coil. (See also coil removal tip in Spark Plug Removal).

To install:

5. Install the ignition coil.

6. Tighten the bolt to 79.5 inch lbs. (9 Nm).

7. Connect the electrical connectors and lock them.

8. Install the negative battery cable.

Fig. 105 Disconnect the electrical connector from the ignition coil

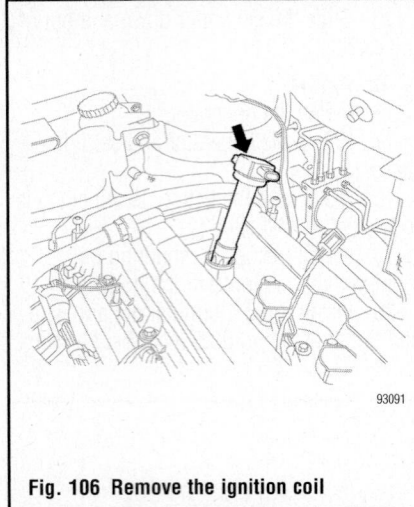

Fig. 106 Remove the ignition coil

IGNITION TIMING

ADJUSTMENT

All engines use a fixed ignition timing system. Basic ignition timing is not adjustable. The Powertrain Control Module (PCM) determines all spark advance.

SPARK PLUGS

REMOVAL & INSTALLATION

See Figure 107.

1. Remove the negative battery cable.

2. Disconnect the electrical connector from the ignition coil. Refer to Ignition Coil Removal.

3. Remove the ignition coil mounting bolts.

4. Twist the ignition coil then pull straight up.

5. Remove the spark plug using a quality socket with a rubber or foam insert.

6. Inspect the spark plug condition.

IGNITION SYSTEM

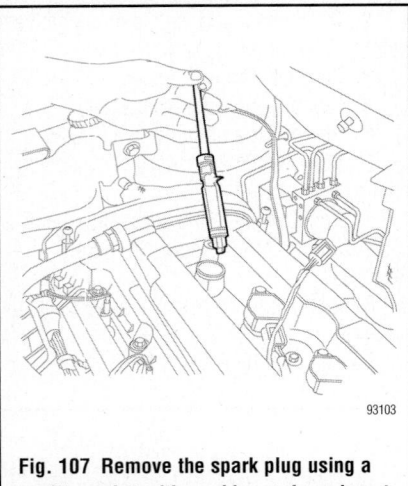

Fig. 107 Remove the spark plug using a quality socket with a rubber or foam insert

To install:

✣✣ WARNING

Handle the spark plugs with care. Do not drop or force the spark plugs into the wells, you may damage the electrodes and/or porcelain body. Always start each spark plug by hand in order to avoid cross-threading the spark plug in the cylinder head. Always tighten spark plugs to the specified torque. Too much or not enough torque will damage to the cylinder head and/or spark plug and may lead to poor engine performance.

7. Install each spark plug to the cylinder head. Tighten spark plugs to 20 ft. lbs. (27 Nm).

8. Install the ignition coil onto the spark plug.

9. Install the ignition coil mounting bolt. Tighten it to 79.5 inch lbs. (9 Nm).

10. Connect the ignition coil electrical connectors.

11. Connect the negative battery cable.

ENGINE ELECTRICAL | STARTING SYSTEM

STARTER

REMOVAL & INSTALLATION

See Figures 108 through 110.

1. Remove the air cleaner box and the air tube.
2. Disconnect and isolate the battery negative cable
3. Remove the starter motor mounting bolts.
4. Disconnect the electrical connector at throttle body.
5. Remove the throttle body

bolts and then remove the throttle body.

6. Push the starter under the intake manifold.
7. Tip the starter nose toward the cooling module.
8. Pull the starter up and out.
9. Disconnect the starter motor wiring.
10. Remove the starter motor from the vehicle.

To install:

11. Connect the starter motor wiring. Tighten the battery cable nut to 90 inch lbs. (10 Nm).

12. Install the starter motor into the vehicle's lower engine compartment.
13. Loosely install the starter into position.
14. Install the throttle body
15. Install the throttle body bracket.
16. Install starter motor mounting bolts and tighten them to 40 ft. lbs. (54 Nm).
17. Connect the throttle body electrical connector.
18. Install the air cleaner box and the inlet tube.
19. Connect the battery negative cable.

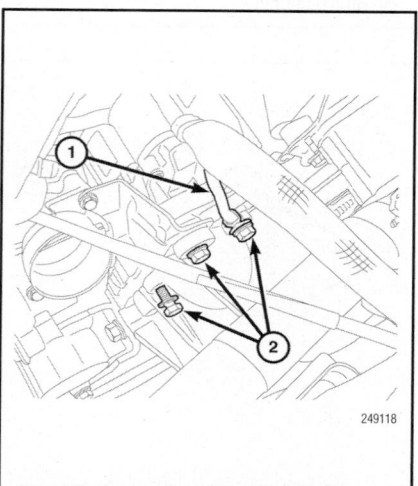

Fig. 108 Starter motor mounting bolts

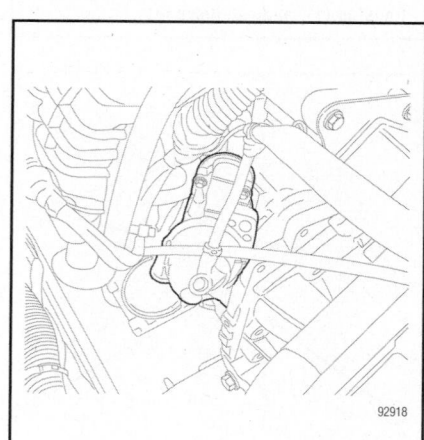

Fig. 109 Push the starter under the intake manifold

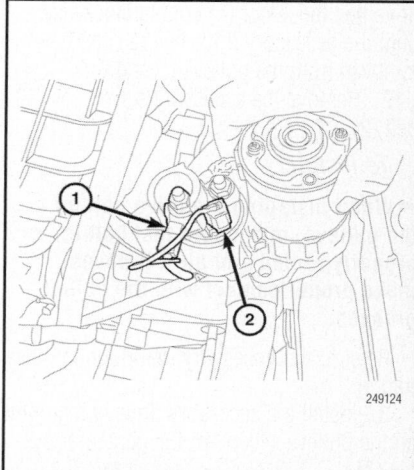

Fig. 110 Starter motor wiring and starter

ENGINE MECHANICAL

➡ Disconnecting the negative battery cable may interfere with the functions of the on board computer systems and may require the computer to undergo a relearning process, once the negative battery cable is reconnected.

ACCESSORY DRIVE BELTS

ACCESSORY BELT ROUTING

See Figure 111.

Refer to the accompanying illustration

INSPECTION

See Figure 112.

When diagnosing serpentine accessory drive belts, small cracks that run across the ribbed surface of the belt from rib to rib (1), are considered normal. These are not a reason to replace the belt. However, cracks running along a rib (not across; 2) are not normal.

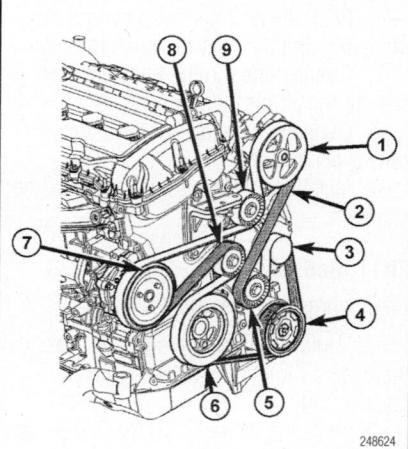

Fig. 111 View of the accessory drive belt (2), crankshaft pulley (6), A/C compressor, generator (3), power steering pump (1), water pump (7) and tensioner (8)

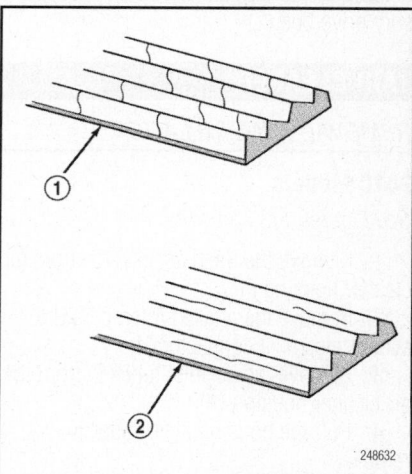

Fig. 112 Small cracks that run across the ribbed surface of the belt from rib to rib (1) are considered normal. However, cracks running along a rib (not across; 2) are not normal

Replace any belt with cracks running along a rib. Also replace the belt if it has excessive wear, frayed cords or severe glazing.

Noises generated by the accessory drive belt are most noticeable at idle. Before replacing a belt to resolve a noise condition, inspect all of the accessory drive pulleys for contamination, alignment, glazing, and excessive end play.

ADJUSTMENT

The automatic belt tensioner maintains proper tension on the accessory drive belt.

REMOVAL & INSTALLATION

See Figure 111.

1. Using a wrench, rotate the accessory drive belt tensioner (8) counterclockwise until the accessory drive belt (2) can be removed from the pulleys (5 and 9).

2. Remove the accessory drive belt (2).

To install:

➡ **When installing the drive belt on the pulleys, make sure that belt is properly routed and all V-grooves make proper contact with the pulley grooves.**

Refer to the Accessory Belt Routing illustration.

3. Install the accessory drive belt around all the pulleys except for the generator pulley (3).

4. Using a wrench, rotate the accessory drive belt tensioner (8) counterclockwise until the accessory drive belt (2) can be installed on the generator pulley (3). Release the spring tension onto the accessory drive belt (2).

AIR CLEANER

REMOVAL & INSTALLATION

2010 Models

See Figures 113 and 114.

1. Remove the fresh air inlet (2) from air cleaner housing (1).

2. Remove the intake air temperature sensor electrical connector (4).

3. Remove the air inlet tube (5) from the air cleaner housing (1).

4. Pull the housing (1) upward to remove.

To install:

5. Make sure the rubber grommets for the air cleaner housing lower pins, are in place when reinstalling the air cleaner housing. The rubber grommets mount to the

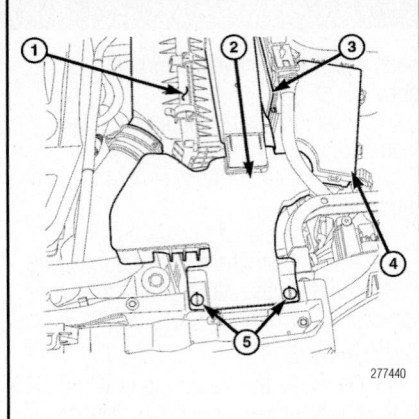

Fig. 113 Fresh air inlet (2), air cleaner housing (1), and retainers (3)

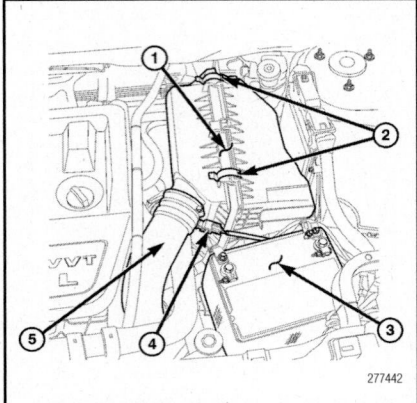

Fig. 114 Intake air temperature sensor electrical connector (4), air inlet tube (5), and housing (1)

Totally Integrated Power Module (TIPM) bracket.

6. Push the air cleaner housing down while aligning the pins into the grommets.

7. Connect the throttle body air inlet hose to the air cleaner housing.

8. Connect the intake air temperature sensor connector.

9. Install the fresh air inlet and lock the retainers.

2011 Models

See Figures 115 through 117.

1. Unlock the retainers (2) and remove the fresh air inlet duct (3) from the air cleaner body (1).

2. Remove the bolts (3) that secure the PCM (4) to the air cleaner body cover and position them aside.

3. Remove the air inlet tube (2) from the air cleaner body (1).

4. Disconnect the make-up air hose (3) from the air cleaner body.

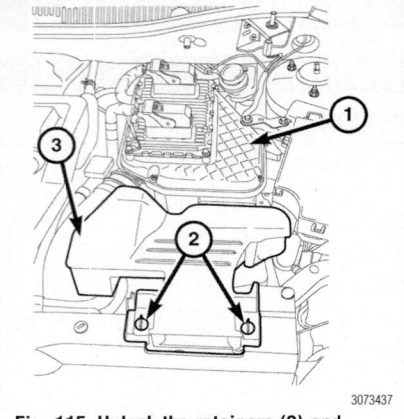

Fig. 115 Unlock the retainers (2) and remove the fresh air inlet duct (3) from air cleaner body (1)

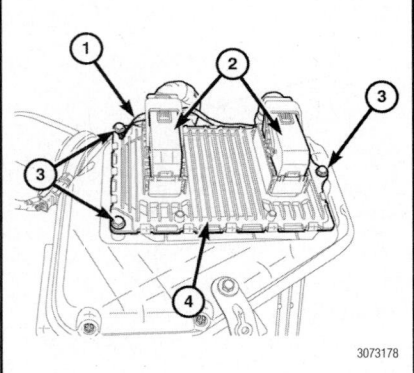

Fig. 116 The three mounting bolts (3) that secure the PCM (4) and one ground wire (1)

5. Remove the support bracket bolt from the strut tower.

6. Pull upward to disengage the pins from the rubber grommets and remove the air cleaner body (1).

To install:

7. Make sure the rubber grommets, for the air cleaner body lower pins, are in place when reinstalling the air cleaner body.

8. Push down on the air cleaner body to engage the pins into the grommets.

9. Install the support bracket bolt to the strut tower and tighten it to 89 inch lbs. (10 Nm).

10. Install the air inlet tube to the air cleaner body.

11. Connect the make-up air hose to the air cleaner body.

12. Position the PCM on the air cleaner body cover.

13. Install three mounting bolts with one ground wire (1; see image in Removal) and tighten them to 89 inch lbs. (10 Nm).

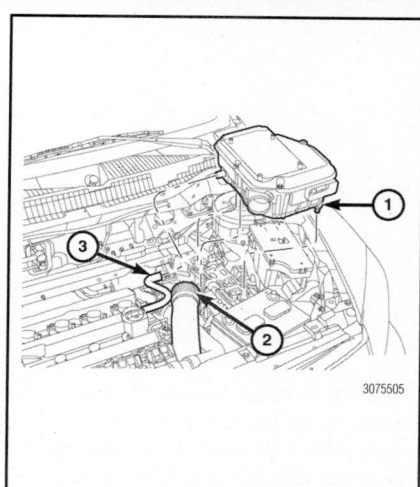

Fig. 117 Air inlet tube (2), make-up air hose (3), and air cleaner body (1)

14. Install the fresh air inlet duct on the air cleaner body and lock the retainers.

FILTER ELEMENT REPLACEMENT

2010 Models

See Figures 118 through 121.

1. Turn the lock retainers (5) and remove the fresh air inlet (2) from the air cleaner housing (1).

2. Disconnect the intake air temperature sensor connector (4).

3. Remove the air inlet tube (5) from the air cleaner housing (1).

4. Unfasten the clasps (2) on the sides of the air cleaner housing cover.

5. Pull the air cleaner cover (1) aside.

6. Remove the filter element (3).

7. If necessary, clean the inside of the air cleaner housing (2).

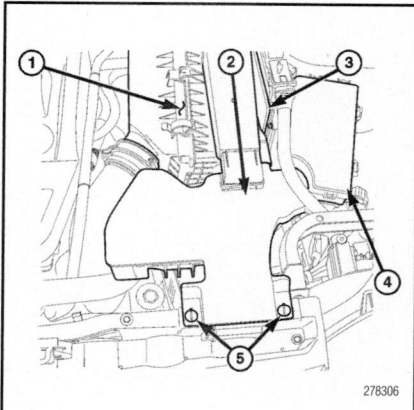

Fig. 118 Lock retainers (5), fresh air inlet (2), and air cleaner housing (1)

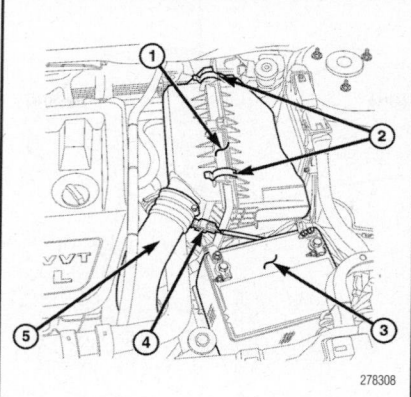

Fig. 119 Intake air temperature sensor connector (4), air inlet tube (5), air cleaner housing (1), and air cleaner housing cover clasps (2)

To install:

8. Install a new filter element.

9. Place the cover over the air cleaner housing. Snap clasps (2) in place.

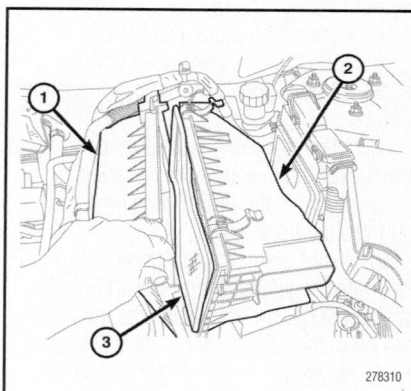

Fig. 120 Air cleaner cover (1), filter element (3), and air cleaner housing (2)

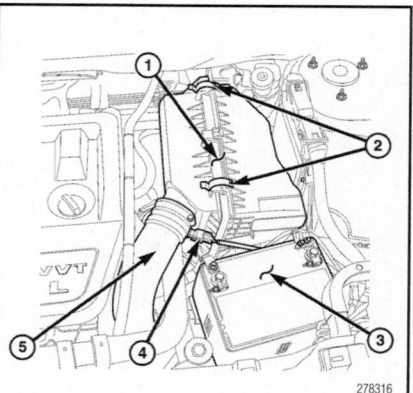

Fig. 121 Air cleaner housing clasps (2), air inlet tube (5), and intake air temperature sensor connector (4)

10. Install the air inlet tube (5).

11. Connect the intake air temperature sensor connector (4).

12. Install the fresh air inlet on the air cleaner housing and lock the retainers.

2011 Models

See Figures 122 and 123.

1. Unlock the retainers and remove the fresh air inlet duct from air cleaner housing. Refer to the image for Air Cleaner Removal.

2. Remove the support bracket bolt from the strut tower.

3. Remove the screws that hold the cover on the air cleaner housing.

✳✳ WARNING

Do Not unplug the electrical connectors from the Powertrain Control Module (PCM). A possible voltage spike can erase and damage the PCM.

4. Position the air cleaner housing cover aside.

5. Remove the air cleaner element (1).

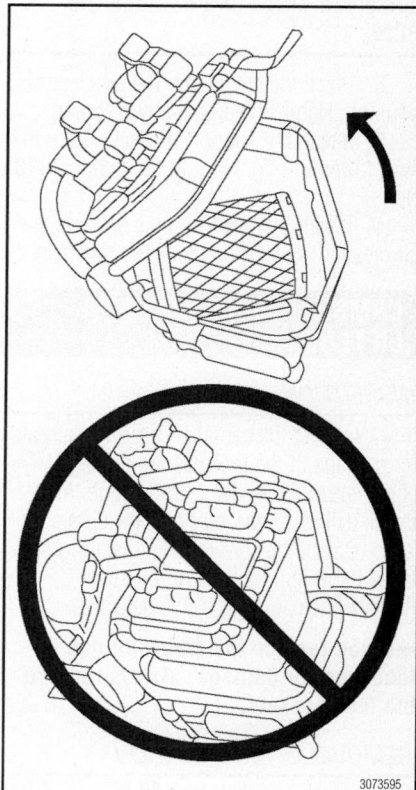

Fig. 122 Do not unplug the electrical connectors from the Powertrain Control Module (PCM). A possible voltage spike can erase and damage the PCM

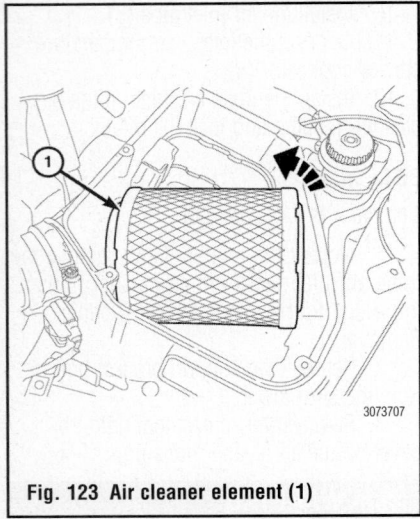

Fig. 123 Air cleaner element (1)

6. If necessary, clean the inside of the air cleaner housing.

To install:

7. Install the new cleaner element.

❊❊ WARNING

Do NOT unplug the electrical connectors from the Powertrain Control Module (PCM). A possible voltage spike can erase and damage the PCM.

8. Place the cover over the air cleaner housing. Hand-tighten the cover screws.

9. Install the support bracket bolt to the strut tower and tighten it to 89 inch lbs. (10 Nm).

10. Install the fresh air inlet duct on the air cleaner housing and lock the retainers.

CAMSHAFT AND VALVE LIFTERS

INSPECTION

1. Inspect the camshaft bearing journals for damage. If the journals are damaged, check the cylinder head for damage. Also check cylinder head oil holes for clogging.

2. Check the cam lobe and bearing surfaces for abnormal wear and damage. Replace the camshaft if it is defective.

➡️**If you replace the camshaft due to lobe wear or damage, always replace the lash buckets.**

REMOVAL & INSTALLATION

See Figures 124 through 138.

1. Remove the engine cover (1) by pulling upward.

2. Disconnect and isolate the negative battery cable.

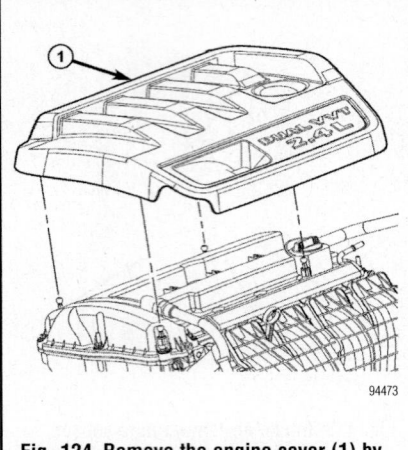

Fig. 124 Remove the engine cover (1) by pulling upward

3. Remove the cylinder head cover. Refer to Valve Covers/Cylinder Head Covers Removal.

4. Raise and support the vehicle. (Refer to Hoisting—Standard Procedure).

5. Remove the frame cover portion of the right splash shield.

6. Rotate the engine to TDC (1).

7. Make sure the camshaft timing marks (3) are in line with the cover sealing surface.

8. Mark the chain link corresponding to timing marks (1) with a paint marker.

9. Remove the timing tensioner plug (1) from the front cover.

10. Insert a small Allen wrench through the timing tensioner plug hole and lift the ratchet (2) upward to release the tensioner and push the Allen wrench inward. Leave the Allen wrench installed during the remainder of this procedure.

11. Insert the Locking Wedge 9701 (1) between the camshaft phasers.

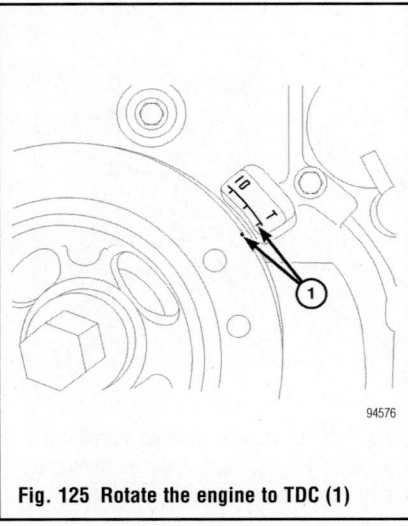

Fig. 125 Rotate the engine to TDC (1)

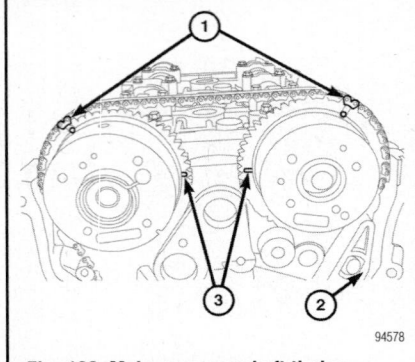

Fig. 126 Make sure camshaft timing marks (3) are in line with the cylinder head cover sealing surface and mark the chain link corresponding to timing marks (1) with a paint marker

12. Lightly tap Locking Wedge 9701 (2) into place until it will no longer sink down.

➡️**The camshaft bearing caps should have been marked during engine manufacturing. For example, number one exhaust camshaft bearing is marked "E1>".**

❊❊ WARNING

DO NOT use a number stamp or a punch to mark camshaft bearing caps. Damage to bearing caps could occur.

13. Using a permanent ink or paint marker, identify the location and position on each camshaft bearing cap.

14. Remove the front camshaft bearing cap.

15. Slowly remove the remaining intake and exhaust camshaft bearing cap bolts one turn at a time.

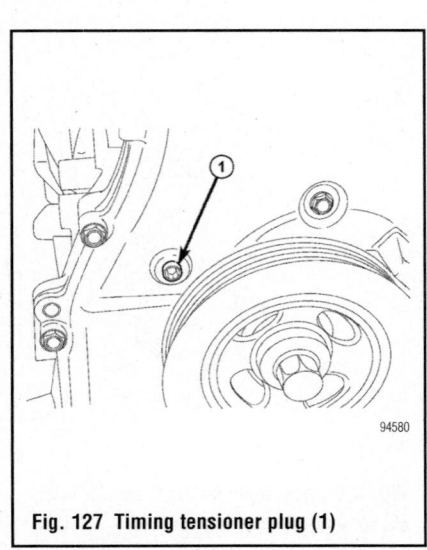

Fig. 127 Timing tensioner plug (1)

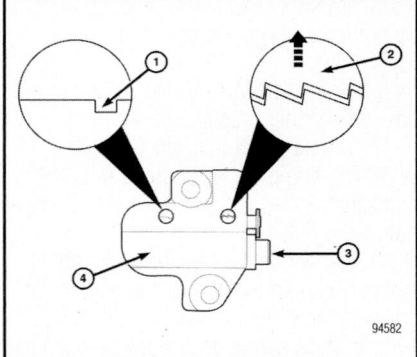

Fig. 128 Insert a small Allen wrench through the timing tensioner plug hole and lift the ratchet (2) upward to release the tensioner and push the Allen wrench inward

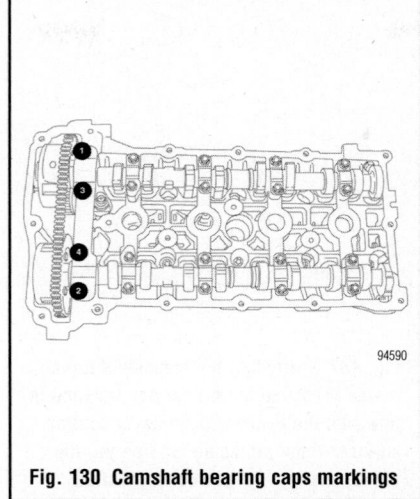

Fig. 130 Camshaft bearing caps markings

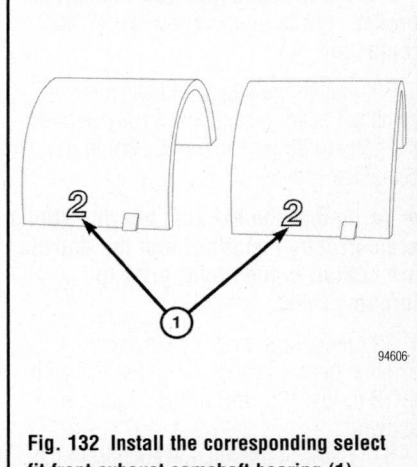

Fig. 132 Install the corresponding select fit front exhaust camshaft bearing (1)

16. Remove the intake camshaft by lifting the rear of the camshaft upward.

17. Rotate the camshaft while lifting it out of the front bearing cradle.

18. Lift the timing chain off the sprocket.

19. Remove the exhaust camshaft.

20. Secure the timing chain with wire so that it does fall into the timing chain cover.

To install:

21. The front camshaft bearing cap (1) is labeled (2) with a one, two, or three, this corresponds to the select fit front exhaust camshaft bearing to use.

22. Install the corresponding select fit front exhaust camshaft bearing (1).

23. Oil all of the camshaft journals with clean engine oil.

24. Install the camshaft phasers on the camshafts if they were removed.

25. Install the timing chain onto the exhaust cam sprocket making sure that the timing marks (1) on the sprocket and the painted chain link are aligned.

26. Position the exhaust camshaft and bearing journals in the cylinder head.

27. Align the exhaust cam timing mark (3) so it is in line with the cylinder head cover sealing surface (2).

28. Install the intake camshaft by raising the rear of the camshaft upward and roll the sprocket into the chain.

29. Align the timing marks (1) on the intake cam sprocket with the painted chain link.

30. Position the intake camshaft into the bearing journals in the cylinder head.

31. Verify that the timing marks (1) are aligned on both camshafts and that the timing marks (3) are facing each other and are in line with the cylinder head cover sealing surface (2).

❋❋ WARNING

Install the front intake and exhaust camshaft bearing cap last. Ensure

that you fully seat the dowels and follow the torque sequence or damage to engine could result.

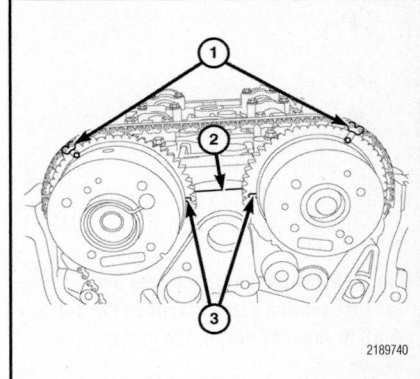

Fig. 133 Install the timing chain onto the exhaust cam sprocket making sure that the timing marks (1) on the sprocket and the painted chain link are aligned

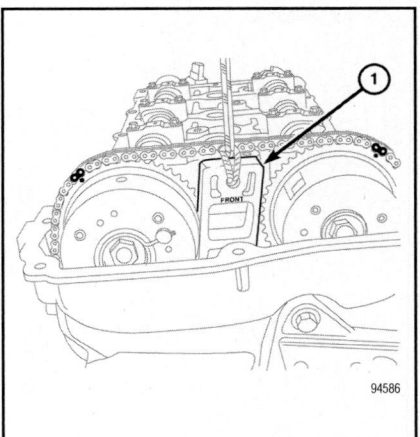

Fig. 129 Locking Wedge 9701 (1) between the camshaft phasers

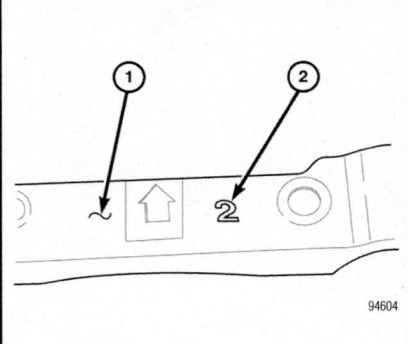

Fig. 131 The front camshaft bearing cap (1) is labeled (2) with a one, two, or three, this corresponds to the select fit front exhaust camshaft bearing to use

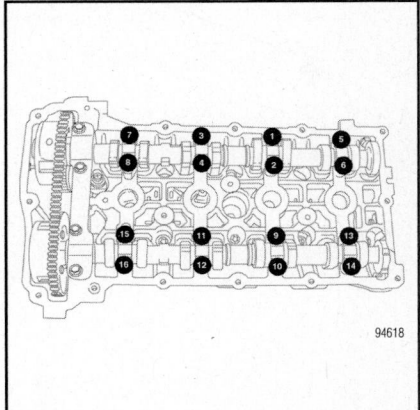

Fig. 134 Intake and exhaust camshaft bearing caps installation sequence

➡**If the front camshaft bearing cap is broken, the cylinder head MUST be replaced.**

32. Install the intake and exhaust camshaft bearing caps and slowly tighten the bolts to 85 inch lbs. (9.5 Nm) in the sequence shown.

➡**Verify that the exhaust bearing shells are correctly installed, and the dowels are seated in the head, prior to torquing bolts.**

33. Install the front intake and exhaust bearing cap and tighten the bolts to 18 ft. lbs. (25 Nm) in the sequence shown.

34. Remove the Allen wrench from the timing chain tensioner.

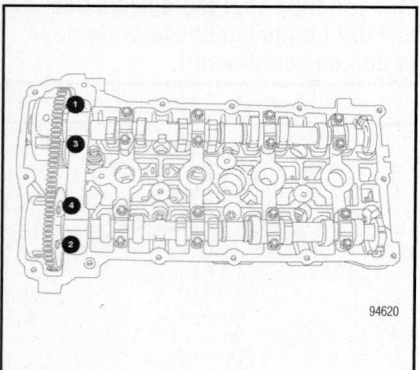

Fig. 135 Install the front intake and exhaust bearing cap and tighten the bolts to 18 ft. lbs. (25 Nm) in the sequence shown

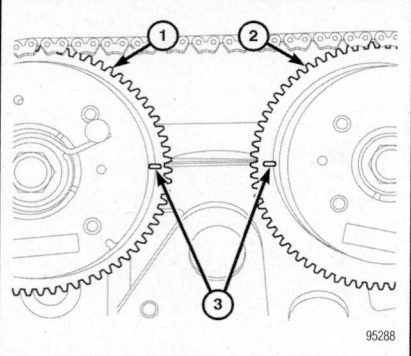

Fig. 137 Verify that the camshafts timing marks (3) are in the proper position and in line with the cylinder head cover sealing surface. If the marks do not line up, the timing chain is not correctly installed

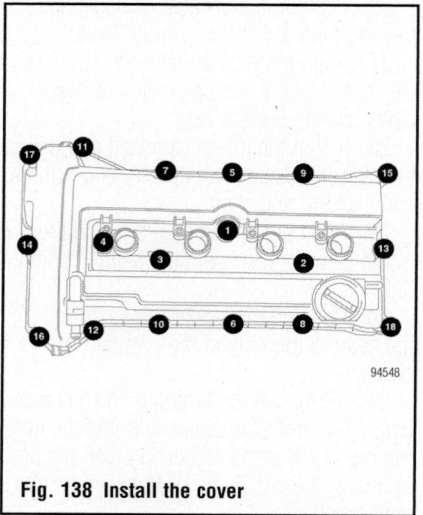

Fig. 138 Install the cover

35. Remove the Locking Wedge 9701 by pulling straight upward on the pull rope.

36. Apply MOPAR® thread sealant to the timing tensioner plug and install it.

37. Rotate the crankshaft CLOCKWISE two complete revolutions until the crankshaft is repositioned at the TDC position.

38. Verify that the camshafts timing marks (3) are in the proper position and in line with the cylinder head cover sealing surface. If the marks do not line up, the timing chain is not correctly installed.

39. Install the right splash shield

40. Remove the RTV from the gasket.

41. Inspect the cylinder head cover gaskets for damage. If no damage is present, the gaskets can be re-installed.

42. Install the cylinder head cover. Refer to Valve Covers/Cylinder Head Covers Installation.

43. Connect the negative battery cable.

44. Fill the cooling system (Refer to Engine Cooling).

45. Fill with oil.

46. Operate the engine until it reaches normal operating temperature. Check the oil and cooling systems for correct fluid levels.

47. Install the engine cover.

CATALYTIC CONVERTER

REMOVAL & INSTALLATION

FWD Vehicles

See Figure 139.

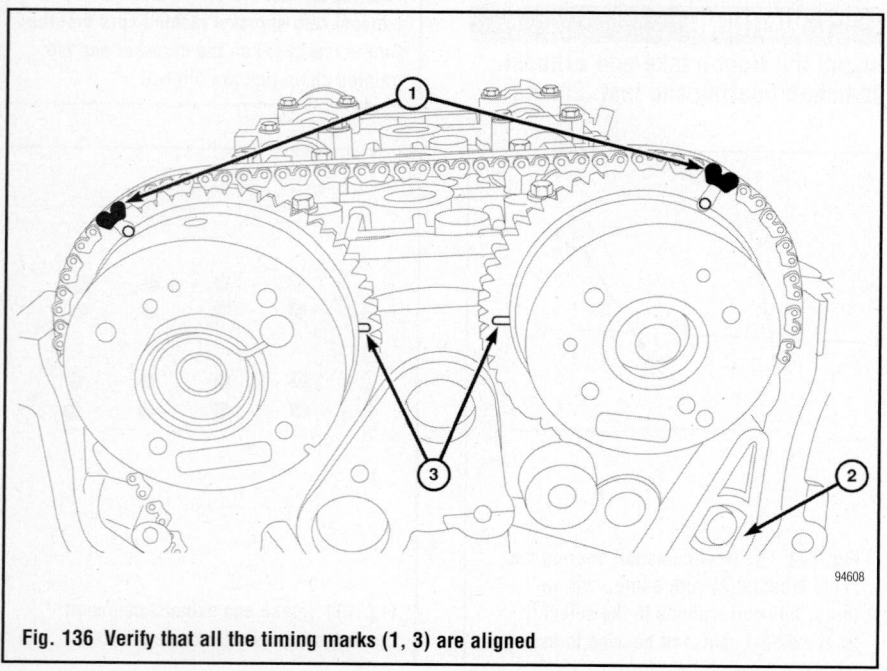

Fig. 136 Verify that all the timing marks (1, 3) are aligned

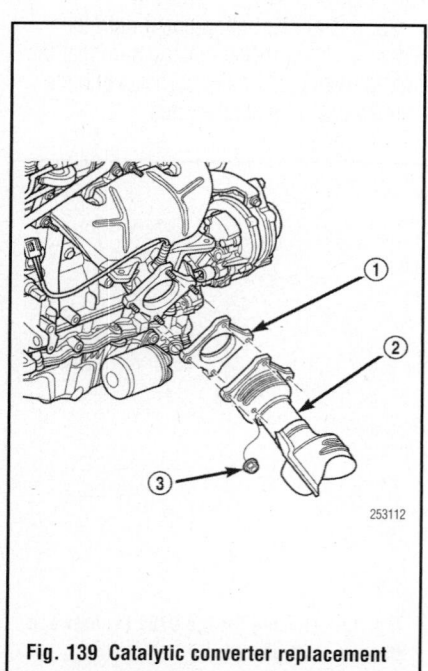

Fig. 139 Catalytic converter replacement

✳✳ CAUTION

The normal operating temperature of the exhaust system is very high. Therefore, never attempt to service any part of the exhaust system until it is cooled. Special care should be taken when working near the catalytic converter. The temperature of the converter rises to a high level after a short period of engine operation time.

  1. Loosen the intermediate pipe-to-catalytic converter clamp.

➡**Do not use petroleum-based lubricants when removing/installing the muffler or exhaust pipe isolators as it may compromise the life of the part. A suitable substitute is a mixture of liquid dish soap and water.**

  2. Remove the catalytic converter to exhaust manifold mounting nuts and gasket Discard the gasket.
  3. Remove the I-Pipe/Muffler assembly insulators as necessary to slide the catalytic converter out of the I-Pipe/Muffler.

➡**When replacement is required on any component of the exhaust system, original equipment parts (or equivalent) must be used.**

  To install:
  4. Position the catalytic converter into the I-Pipe/muffler assembly.
  5. Using a new gasket, position the catalytic converter against the exhaust manifold.
  6. Install the flange nuts. Tighten them to 21 ft. lbs. (29 Nm).
  7. Working from the front of system; align each component to maintain position and proper clearance with the underbody parts.
  8. Tighten the band clamps to 40 ft. lbs. (55 Nm).

✳✳ WARNING

Band clamps should never be tightened such that the two sides of the clamps are bottomed out against the center hourglass shaped center block. Once this occurs, the clamp has lost clamping force and must be replaced.

  9. Start the engine and inspect for exhaust leaks. Repair exhaust leaks as necessary.
  10. Check the exhaust system for contact with the body panels. Make the necessary adjustments, if needed.

Under Floor Catalytic Converter— 2.4L AWD Vehicles
See Figure 140.

✳✳ CAUTION

The normal operating temperature of the exhaust system is very high. Therefore, never work around or attempt to service any part of the exhaust system until it is cooled. Special care should be taken when working near the catalytic converter. The temperature of the converter rises to a high level after a short period of engine operating time.

  1. Raise the vehicle on hoist and apply penetrating oil to band clamp fastener of component being removed.

➡**Do not use petroleum-based lubricants when removing/installing muffler or exhaust pipe isolators as it may compromise the life of the part. A suitable substitute is a mixture of liquid dish soap and water.**

  2. Remove the I-Pipe/Muffler assembly.
  3. Disconnect the oxygen sensor electrical connectors.

➡**If a spherical gasket is to be reused, mark the orientation.**

  4. Remove the flange bolts (3), springs, and spherical gasket.
  5. Remove the under floor catalytic converter (4) from the maniverter or catalytic converter assembly (1).
  6. Clean the ends of the pipes to assure mating of all parts. Discard broken or worn isolators, rusted or overused clamps, supports, and attaching parts.

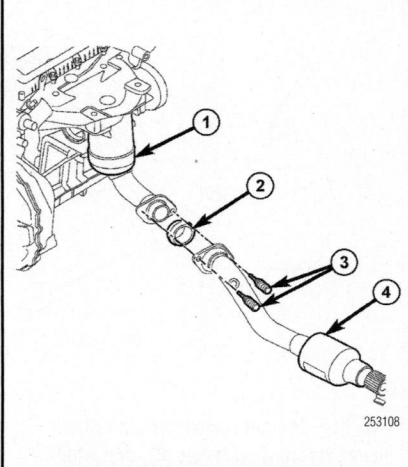

Fig. 140 I-Pipe/Muffler assembly

➡**When replacement is required on any component of the exhaust system, you must use original equipment parts (or their equivalent).**

  To install:
  When you are assembling the exhaust system, do not tighten the clamps until you align the components and check the clearances.
  7. Install the under floor catalytic converter and the isolator supports to the underbody.
  8. Position the spherical gasket with the white side facing the rear of vehicle, install the springs, and bolts. Tighten the bolts to 24 ft. lbs. (33 Nm).
  9. Install the I-Pipe/muffler assembly.
  10. Working from the front of system; align each component to maintain position and proper clearance with underbody parts.
  11. Tighten the band clamps to 40 ft. lbs. (55 Nm).

✳✳ WARNING

Band clamps should never be tightened such that the two sides of the clamps are bottomed out against the center hourglass shaped center block. Once this occurs, the clamp band has been stretched and has lost its clamping force and must be replaced.

➡**Maintain proper clamp orientation when you replace with a new clamp.**

  12. Start the engine and inspect for exhaust leaks. Repair exhaust leaks as necessary.
  13. Check the exhaust system for contact with the body panels. Make the necessary adjustments, if needed.

CRANKSHAFT FRONT OIL SEAL

REMOVAL & INSTALLATION
See Figures 141 through 143.

  1. Remove the accessory drive belt.
  2. Install the Damper Holder 9707 (1) and remove the damper retaining bolt.
  3. Pull the damper off the crankshaft.
  4. Remove the front crankshaft oil seal by prying out with a screw driver. Be careful not to damage the cover seal surface.

  To install:
  5. Place the seal (1) onto the Front Crankshaft Seal Installer 9506 (2) with the seal spring towards the inside of the engine.
  6. Install the new seal (1) by using Front Crankshaft Seal Installer 9506 (2) and crankshaft damper bolt (3).

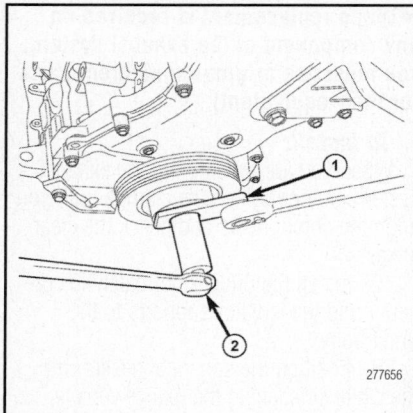

Fig. 141 Install the Damper Holder 9707 (1) and remove the damper retaining bolt

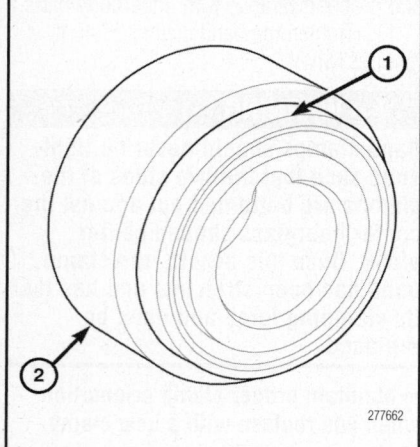

Fig. 142 Place the seal (1) onto the Front Crankshaft Seal Installer 9506 (2) with the seal spring towards the inside of the engine

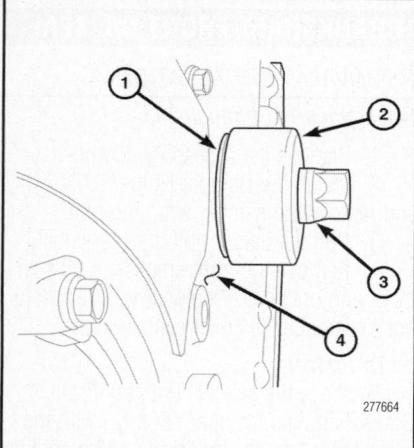

Fig. 143 Install the new seal (1) by using Front Crankshaft Seal Installer 9506 (2) and crankshaft damper bolt (3)

7. Press the seal into the front cover until the Front Crankshaft Seal Installer 9506 seats against the timing chain cover.

8. Remove the Front Crankshaft Seal Installer 9506.

9. Install the crankshaft vibration damper.

10. Oil the bolt threads and between the bolt head and washer.

11. Install the damper retaining bolt and Damper Holder 9707. Tighten the bolt to 155 ft. lbs. (210 Nm).

CYLINDER HEAD

REMOVAL & INSTALLATION

See Figures 144 through 162.

1. Remove the engine cover by pulling upward (see image in Camshaft and Valve Lifters Removal).

2. Perform the fuel system pressure release procedure (Refer to Fuel System Pressure Release—Standard Procedure).

3. Disconnect and isolate the negative battery cable.

4. For 2011 models: Remove the air cleaner (Refer to Air Cleaner Removal):

5. Drain the cooling system. Refer to Engine Cooling.

6. For 2010 models: Remove the clean air hose and air cleaner housing. Refer to Air Cleaner.

7. Remove the coolant recovery bottle (3).

8. Remove and reposition the power steering reservoir (2).

9. Remove the windshield washer bottle (1).

10. Remove the accessory drive belt (Refer to Accessory Drive Belt Removal).

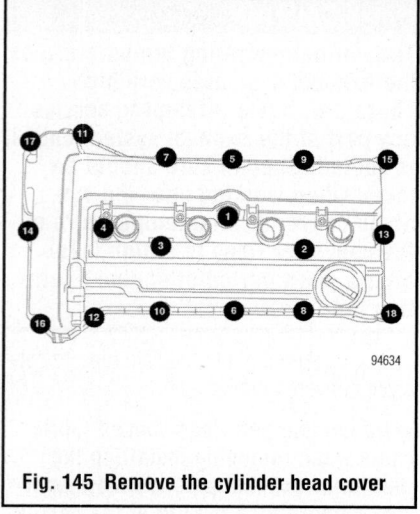

Fig. 145 Remove the cylinder head cover

11. Remove the power steering hose hold down (Refer to Steering section for the Power Steering Pump Removal).

12. Remove the three power steering pump mounting bolts through the openings in the pulley and reposition the pump.

13. Remove the cylinder head cover. Refer to Valve Covers/Cylinder Head Covers Installation.

14. Remove the ignition coils from the cylinder head cover.

15. Raise and support the vehicle. (Refer to Hoisting—Standard Procedure).

16. Remove the right splash shield.

17. Set the engine to TDC (1).

18. Remove the lower A/C compressor bolts if equipped.

19. Remove the lower A/C compressor mount (2) if equipped.

20. Remove the accessory drive belt lower idler pulley (2).

21. Remove the crankshaft damper (2).

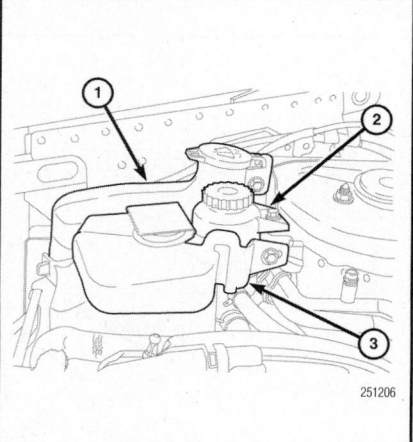

Fig. 144 Coolant recovery bottle (3), power steering reservoir (2), and windshield washer bottle (1)

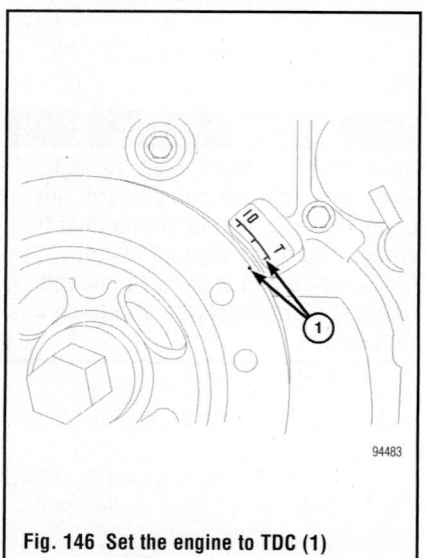

Fig. 146 Set the engine to TDC (1)

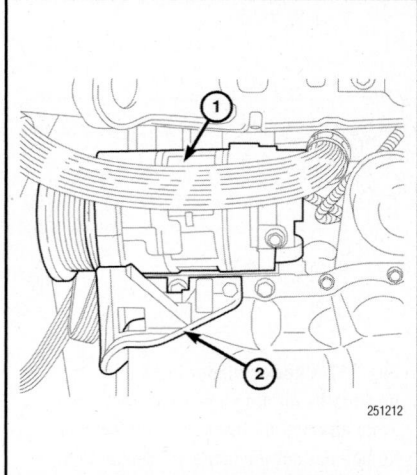

Fig. 147 Lower A/C compressor mount (2)

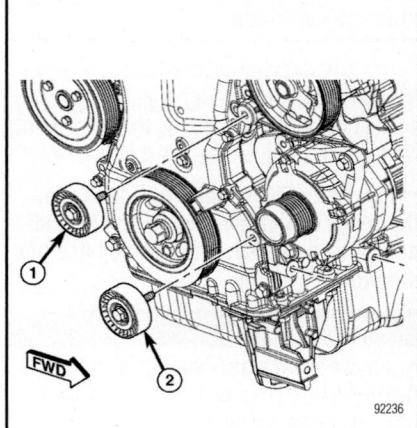

Fig. 148 Accessory drive belt lower idler pulley (2) and accessory drive upper idler pulley (1)

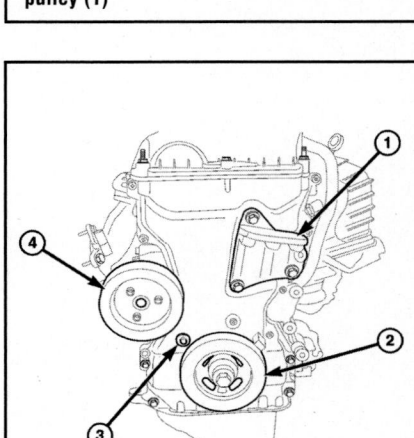

Fig. 149 Crankshaft damper (2), water pump pulley (4) and right side engine mount bracket (1)

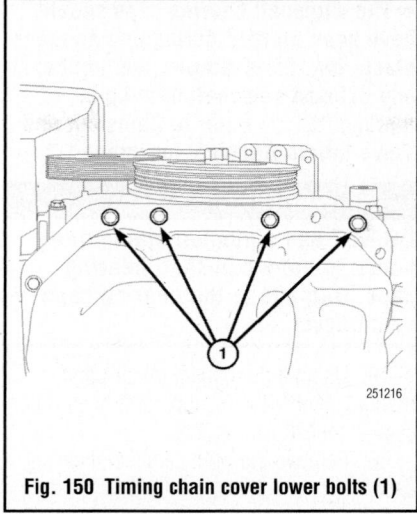

Fig. 150 Timing chain cover lower bolts (1)

22. Remove the three bolts and water pump pulley (4) from the water pump.

23. Remove the lower bolt from the right side engine mount bracket (1).

24. Remove the timing chain cover lower bolts (1).

25. For 2011 models: Remove the under floor catalytic converter (Refer to Catalytic Converter Removal).

26. Lower the vehicle.

27. Support the engine with a suitable jack.

28. Remove the right engine mount through bolt (4).

29. Remove right engine mount to mount bracket bolts (3).

30. Remove right engine mount adapter (1).

31. Remove accessory drive upper idler pulley (1; refer to image for accessory drive lower and upper idler pulleys).

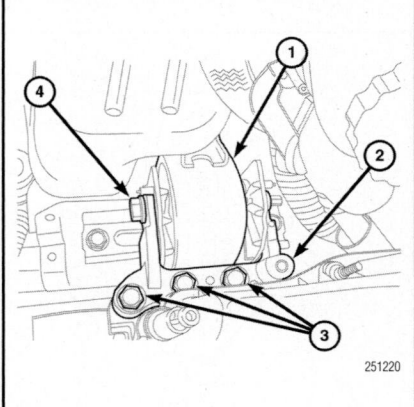

Fig. 151 Right engine mount through bolt (4), right engine mount to mount bracket bolts (3), and the right engine mount adapter (1)

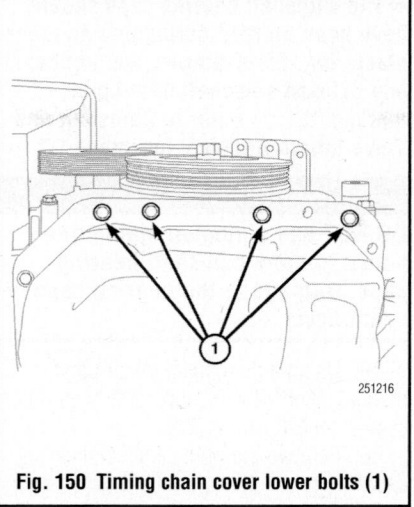

Fig. 152 Remove the timing chain cover using the pry points (1, 2, and 3)

32. Remove right upper engine mount bracket.

33. Remove the accessory drive belt tensioner.

34. Remove the upper timing chain cover retaining bolts.

35. Remove the timing chain cover using the pry points (1, 2, and 3).

36. Remove the tensioner (5) and timing chain (2) (Refer to Valve Timing/Chain and Sprockets Removal).

37. Remove the timing chain guide (4) and the timing chain pivot guide (6).

38. Disconnect the fuel line from the fuel rail.

39. Unlock and disconnect the electrical connectors from the fuel injectors.

40. Remove the two fuel rail retaining bolts and remove the fuel rail.

41. Disconnect the electrical connectors from the coolant temperature sensor (1), oil temperature sensor, variable valve timing

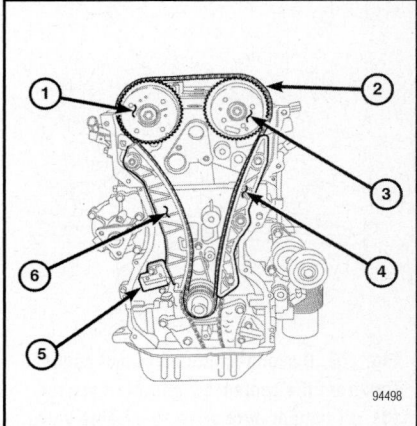

Fig. 153 Tensioner (5), timing chain (2), timing chain guide (4), and timing chain pivot guide (6)

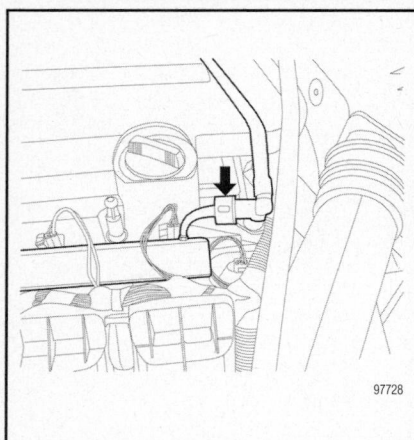

Fig. 154 Disconnect the fuel line from the fuel rail

solenoids, Camshaft Position (CMP) sensors, MAP sensor, manifold tuning valve, ignition interference suppressor (2) and electronic throttle control.

42. Remove the wiring harness retainer from the intake manifold and reposition the harness.

43. Remove the throttle body support bracket.

44. Disconnect the vacuum lines at intake.

45. Remove the upper radiator hose retaining bolt.

46. Remove the intake manifold retaining bolts and remove the intake manifold.

47. Remove the four bolts and reposition the coolant adapter (3; Refer to previous image with the electrical connectors).

48. Remove the ground strap (1) at the right rear of the cylinder head if equipped.

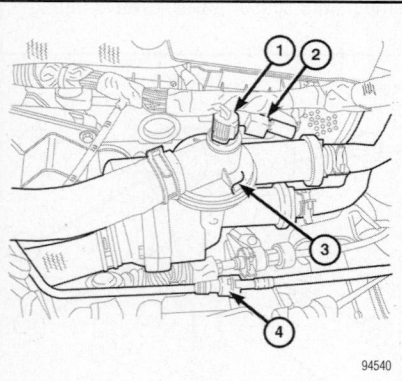

Fig. 155 Disconnect the electrical connectors from the coolant temperature sensor (1), oil temperature sensor, variable valve timing solenoids, Camshaft Position (CMP) sensors, MAP sensor, manifold tuning valve, ignition interference suppressor (2) and electronic throttle control.

➡ The camshaft bearing caps should have been marked during engine manufacturing. For example, the number one exhaust camshaft bearing is marked "E1>". Refer to Camshaft and Valve Lifters Removal for image.

✳✳ WARNING

DO NOT use a number stamp or a punch to mark camshaft bearing caps. Damage to the bearing caps could occur.

49. Using a permanent ink or paint marker, identify the location and position on each camshaft bearing cap.

50. Remove the front camshaft bearing cap.

51. Slowly remove the remaining intake and exhaust camshaft bearing cap bolts one turn at a time.

52. Remove the camshafts.

53. All of the cylinder head bolts have captured washers EXCEPT the front two (1).

54. Remove the cylinder head bolts and two uncaptured washers.

55. Remove the cylinder head from the engine block.

56. Inspect and clean the cylinder head and block sealing surfaces.

➡ Ensure the cylinder head bolt holes in the block are clean, dry (free of residual oil or coolant), and that the threads are not damaged.

To install:

✳✳ WARNING

Tighten the cylinder head bolts using a torque plus angle procedure. Examine the bolts BEFORE reuse. If the

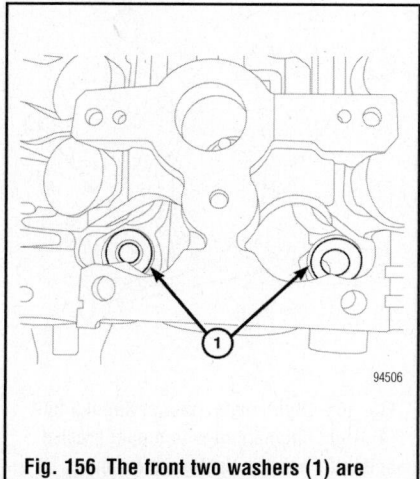

Fig. 156 The front two washers (1) are uncaptured

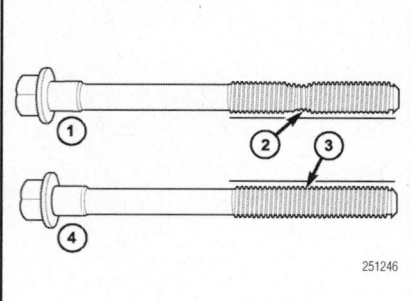

Fig. 157 Check cylinder head bolts for necking by holding a scale or straight edge against the threads. If all the threads do not contact the scale (2) replace the bolt

threads are necked down the bolts must be replaced.

57. Check cylinder head bolts for necking by holding a scale or straight edge against the threads. If all the threads do not contact the scale (2) replace the bolt.

➡ Ensure cylinder head bolt holes in the block are clean, dry (free of residual oil or coolant), and threads are not damaged.

✳✳ WARNING

Always replace the variable valve timing filter screen (3) when servicing the head gasket or engine damage could result.

58. Replace the variable valve timing filter screen (3).

59. When using RTV, the sealing surfaces must be clean and free from grease and oil.

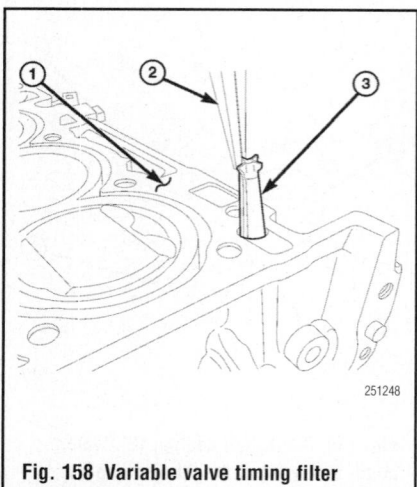

Fig. 158 Variable valve timing filter screen (3)

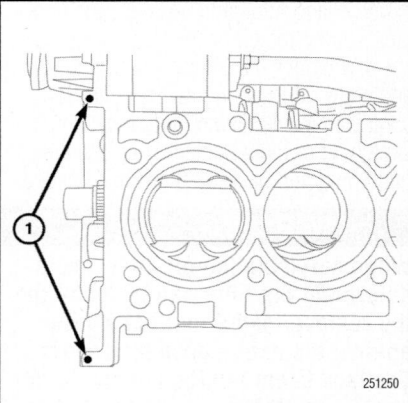

Fig. 159 Place two pea size dots of Mopar® engine sealant RTV or an equivalent (1) on the cylinder block as shown

60. When using RTV, assemble the parts within 10 minutes and tighten to final torque within 45 minutes.

61. Place two pea size dots of Mopar® engine sealant RTV or an equivalent (1) on the cylinder block as shown.

62. Position the new cylinder head gasket on the engine block with the part number facing up. Ensure that the gasket is seated over the locating dowels in the block.

63. Place two pea size dots of Mopar® engine sealant RTV or an equivalent (1) on the cylinder head gasket as shown in the preceding image.

➡**Install the head within 15 minutes before the RTV skins.**

64. Position the cylinder head onto the engine block.

✸✸ WARNING

This engine was built with 2 different style cylinder head bolts. Each style

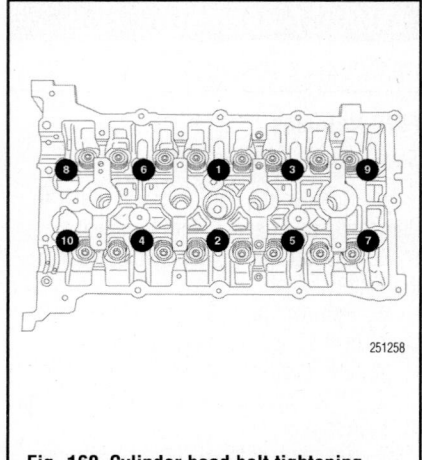

Fig. 160 Cylinder head bolt tightening sequence

bolt requires a different torque value. The bolts can be identified by the short bolt head and the long bolt head.

65. Measure the bolt head from the washer to the top of the bolt head. The short bolt head measures 5/16" (8 mm) and the long bolt head measures ½" (13 mm).

66. Identify whether your engine has the short head design or the long head design.

➡**The front two cylinder head bolts do not have captured washers. Install the washers with the bevel edge up towards the bolt head.**

67. Install the washers for the front two cylinder head bolts with the beveled edge facing up.

➡**Before installing the cylinder head bolts, lubricate the threads with clean engine oil.**

68. Install the cylinder head bolts and tighten them in the sequence shown.

69. If your bolt has the short head (1), use the following torque specifications:
- First: All to 25 ft. lbs. (30 Nm)
- Second: All to 45 ft. lbs. (61 Nm)
- Third: All to 45 ft. lbs. (61 Nm)
- Fourth: All an additional 90° **CAUTION:** Do not use a torque wrench for the Fourth step.

70. If your bolt has the long head (2), use the following torque specifications:
- First: All to 25 ft. lbs. (30 Nm)
- Second: All to 54 ft. lbs. (73 Nm)
- Third: All to 54 ft. lbs. (73 Nm)
- Fourth: All an additional 90° **CAUTION:** Do not use a torque wrench for the Fourth step.

71. Clean excess RTV from the timing chain cover sealing surface.

72. Install the coolant adapter with new seals. Tighten the bolts to 159 inch lbs. (18.1 Nm).

73. The front camshaft bearing cap (1) is numbered (2) either one, two, or three, this corresponds to the select fit front exhaust camshaft bearing to use. Refer to Camshaft and Valve Lifters Installation for Steps 16– 22.

74. Install the corresponding select fit front exhaust camshaft bearing.

75. Oil all of the camshaft journals with clean engine oil.

76. Position the exhaust camshaft and intake camshaft on the bearing journals in the cylinder head.

77. Align the camshaft timing marks so that they are facing each other and are in line with the cylinder head cover sealing surface.

✸✸ WARNING

Install the front intake and exhaust camshaft bearing cap last. Ensure that the dowels are seated and follow torque sequence or damage to engine could result.

➡**If the front camshaft bearing cap is broken, the cylinder head MUST be replaced.**

78. Install intake and exhaust camshaft bearing caps and slowly tighten bolts to 85 inch lbs. (9.5 Nm). in the sequence shown.

79. Verify that the exhaust bearing shells are correctly installed, and the dowels are seated in the head, prior to torquing the bolts.

80. Install the front intake and exhaust bearing cap and tighten the bolts to 18 ft. lbs. (25 Nm) in the sequence shown.

81. Install the timing chain guide (4) and tighten the bolts to 105 inch lbs. (12 Nm).

82. Install the moveable timing chain pivot guide (6) and tighten the bolt to 105 inch lbs. (12 Nm).

83. Install the timing chain (2) and tensioner (5). Refer to Valve Timing Chain & Sprockets Installation).

84. Install the timing chain cover, engine mount, pulleys and the accessory drive belt.

85. Install the cylinder head cover and ignition coils.

86. Install the exhaust manifold. (Refer to Exhaust Manifold Installation).

87. Install the ground strap at the right rear of the cylinder head if equipped.

88. Install the intake manifold, vacuum lines and fuel rail. (Refer to Intake Manifold Installation).

89. Install the upper radiator hose retaining bracket bolt.

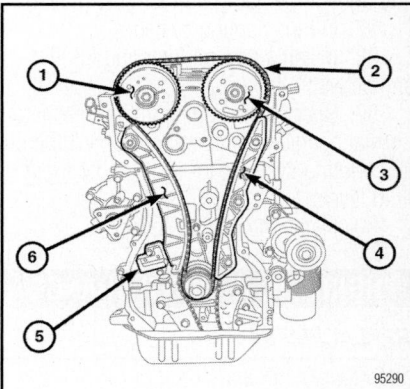

Fig. 161 Timing chain guide (4), moveable timing chain pivot guide (6), timing chain (2), and tensioner (5)

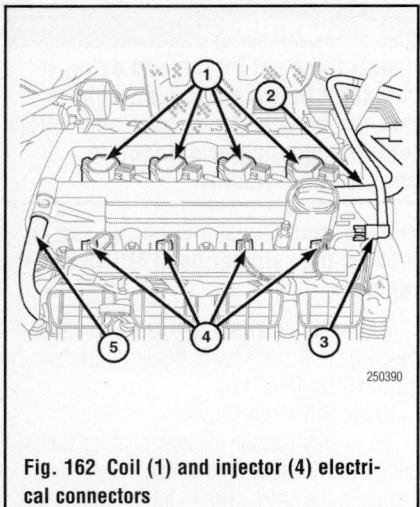

Fig. 162 Coil (1) and injector (4) electrical connectors

90. Connect the coil (1) and injector (4) electrical connectors.

91. Connect electrical connectors to the coolant temperature sensor, Camshaft Position (CMP) sensors, oil temperature sensor, variable valve timing solenoids, MAP sensor, manifold tuning valve, ignition interference suppressor and electronic throttle control.

92. Install the power steering pump reservoir. Tighten the mounting screw to 106 inch lbs. (12 Nm).

93. Install the windshield washer reservoir.

94. Install the coolant recovery reservoir. Tighten the mounting bolts to 35 inch lbs. (4 Nm).

95. Install the air cleaner (refer to Air Cleaner Installation):

    a. For 2011 models: Install the air cleaner.

    b. For 2010 models: Install the clean air hose and air cleaner housing.

96. Connect the negative battery cable and tighten the nut to 45 inch lbs. (5 Nm).

97. Fill the cooling system.

98. Install a new oil filter and fill the engine with oil.

99. Operate the engine until it reaches normal operating temperature. Check the oil and cooling systems for leaks and correct fluid levels.

100. Install the engine cover.

ENGINE OIL & FILTER CHANGE

REPLACEMENT

See Figures 163 and 164.

❋❋ CAUTION

New or used engine oil can be irritating to the skin. Avoid prolonged or

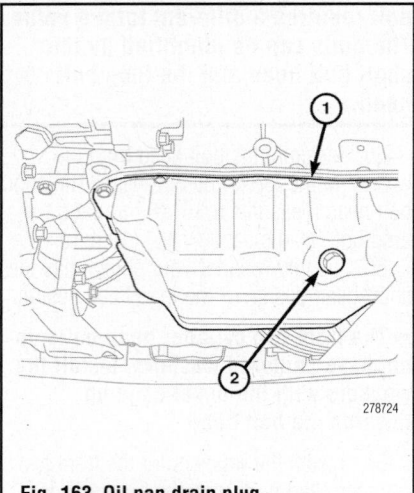

Fig. 163 Oil pan drain plug

repeated skin contact with engine oil. Contaminants in used engine oil, caused by internal combustion, can be hazardous to your health. Thoroughly wash exposed skin with soap and water. Do not wash skin with gasoline, diesel fuel, thinner, or solvents, health problems can result. Do not pollute: dispose of used engine oil properly. Contact your dealer or government agency for the location of a collection center in your area. Change engine oil at mileage and time intervals described in the Maintenance Schedule for the vehicle.

1. Run the engine until it reaches normal operating temperature.

2. Position the vehicle on a level surface and turn the engine off.

3. Remove the oil fill cap.

4. Raise the vehicle on a hoist.

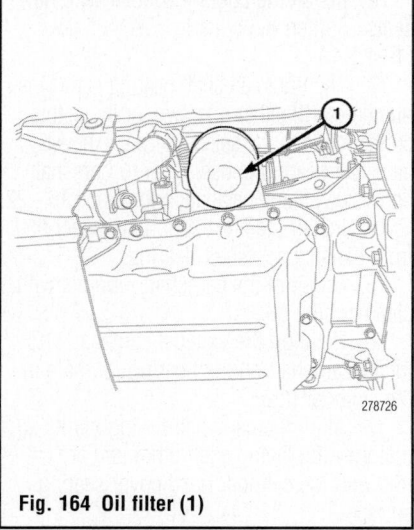

Fig. 164 Oil filter (1)

5. Place a suitable oil collecting container under the oil pan drain plug (2).

6. Remove the oil pan drain plug (2) and allow oil to drain into the collecting container. Inspect drain plug threads for stretching or other damage. Replace the drain plug and gasket if they are damaged.

❋❋ WARNING

When servicing the oil filter, avoid deforming the filter can by installing the remove/install tool band strap against the can to base lock seam. The lock seam joining the can to the base is reinforced by the base plate.

7. Remove the oil filter (1):

    a. Using a suitable filter wrench, turn the oil filter (1) counterclockwise to remove.

8. Install the oil pan drain plug and tighten the drain plug to 30 ft. lbs. (40 Nm).

9. Clean and check filter mounting surface. The surface must be smooth, flat and free of debris or pieces of gasket.

10. Lubricate the new oil filter gasket.

11. Screw on the oil filter (1) until the gasket contacts the base and tighten it to 10 ft. lbs. (14 Nm).

12. Lower the vehicle and fill the crankcase with 4.5 quarts of MOPAR® API Certified SAE 5W-20 engine oil, meeting the requirements of Chrysler Material Standard MS-6395.

13. Install the oil fill cap.

14. Start the engine and inspect for leaks.

15. Stop the engine and inspect the oil level.

OIL FILTER SPECIFICATION: All engines are equipped with a high quality full-flow, disposable oil filter. Replace the oil filter with a Mopar® or the equivalent.

EXHAUST MANIFOLD

REMOVAL & INSTALLATION

FWD Vehicles

See Figures 165 through 168.

1. Remove the engine cover. (Refer to Camshafts and Valve Lifters Removal.)

2. Disconnect the negative cable from the battery.

3. Remove the bolts (2) attaching the upper heat shield.

4. Remove the upper heat shield (1).

5. Disconnect the exhaust pipe (1) from the manifold.

6. Disconnect the oxygen sensor electrical connector (3).

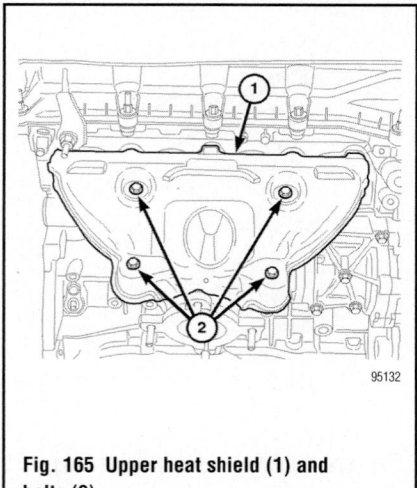

Fig. 165 Upper heat shield (1) and bolts (2)

Fig. 167 Manifold support bracket (2)

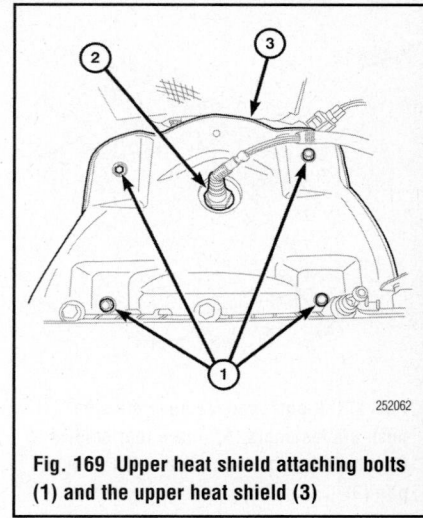

Fig. 169 Upper heat shield attaching bolts (1) and the upper heat shield (3)

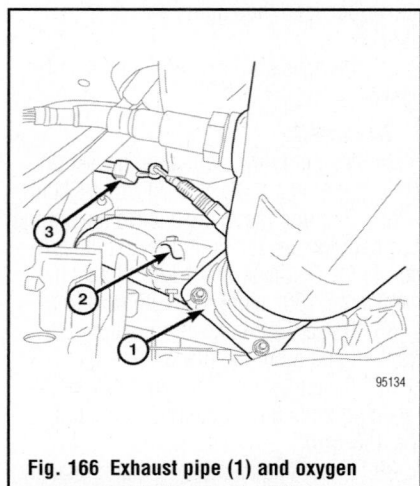

Fig. 166 Exhaust pipe (1) and oxygen sensor electrical connector (3)

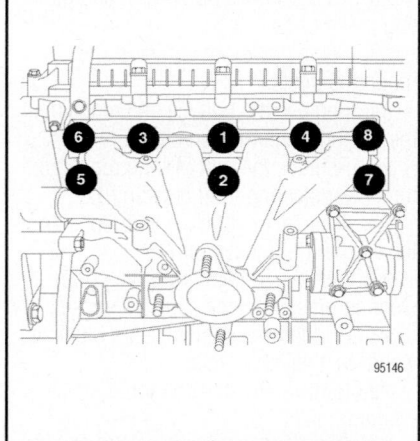
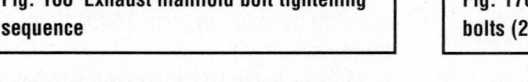

Fig. 168 Exhaust manifold bolt tightening sequence

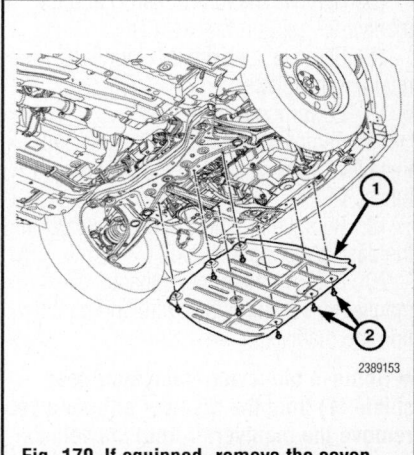

Fig. 170 If equipped, remove the seven bolts (2) and the front skid plate (1)

7. Remove the manifold support bracket (2).

8. Remove the lower exhaust manifold heat shield.

9. Remove the exhaust manifold retaining fasteners. (See image in Installation.)

10. Remove and discard the manifold gasket.

To install:

11. Install a new exhaust manifold gasket. **DO NOT APPLY SEALER.**

12. Position the exhaust manifold in place.

13. Tighten the exhaust manifold bolts to 25 ft. lbs. (34 Nm).

14. Install the exhaust manifold heat shields. Tighten the bolts to 105 inch lbs. (12 Nm).

15. Install the exhaust manifold support bracket.

16. Install a new catalytic converter gasket.

17. Install the exhaust pipe to the manifold. Tighten the fasteners to 250 inch lbs. (28 Nm).

18. Connect the oxygen sensor electrical connector.

19. Connect the negative battery cable.

20. Install the engine cover.

AWD Vehicles—Maniverter

See Figures 169 through 183.

1. Remove the engine cover by pulling upward (see image in Camshaft and Valve Lifters Removal).

2. For 2010 models: Loosen the retainers and remove the air cleaner inlet. Refer to Air Cleaner Removal.

3. For 2011 models: Unlock the retainers and remove the fresh air inlet duct from the air cleaner body. Refer to Air Cleaner Removal.

4. Disconnect and isolate the negative battery cable.

5. Remove the upstream oxygen sensor.

Refer to the Engine Performance Section for Oxygen Sensor Removal).

6. Remove the upper heat shield attaching bolts (1) and the upper heat shield (3).

7. Raise and support the vehicle. (Refer to Hoisting—Standard Procedure).

8. If equipped, remove the seven bolts (2) and the front skid plate (1).

9. If equipped, remove the side push pin fasteners (1), three rear screws (2), three front screws (4) and the belly pan (3).

10. Partially drain the cooling system. (Refer to Engine Cooling—Cooling System Draining).

11. Disconnect the wire harness connector from the downstream oxygen sensor (2).

12. Remove the exhaust pipe to maniverter bolts (1) and reposition the exhaust pipe.

13. Remove three bolts (1) and the steering gear heat shield (3).

14. Remove the front engine mount bolt (2) and the front fore and aft crossmember (4).

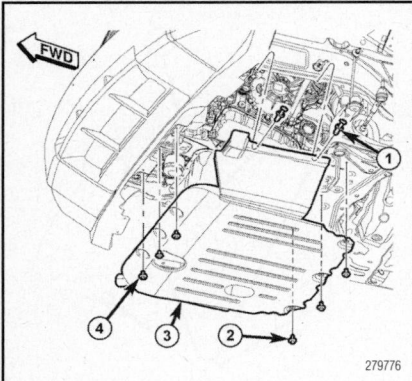

Fig. 171 If equipped, remove the side push pin fasteners (1), three rear screws (2), three front screws (4) and the belly pan (3)

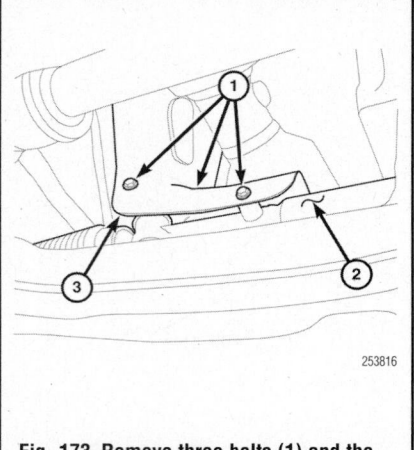

Fig. 173 Remove three bolts (1) and the steering gear heat shield (3)

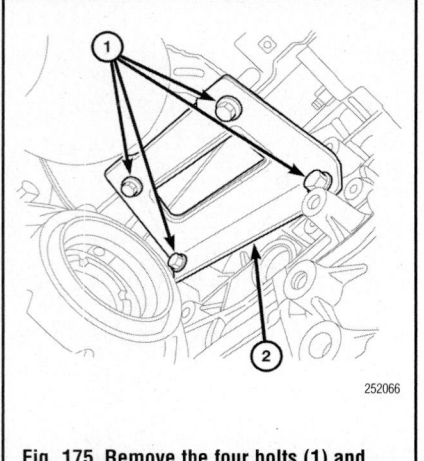

Fig. 175 Remove the four bolts (1) and the maniverter support bracket (2)

15. Remove the four bolts (1) and the maniverter support bracket (2).

16. Remove the exhaust maniverter lower retaining fasteners.

17. Lower the vehicle.

18. Remove the heater hoses (4) and installed plugs or caps to the heater core tubes.

19. Remove the three speed-nuts (2) and the dash panel heat shield (1).

20. Remove the upper exhaust maniverter retaining fasteners and reposition the maniverter.

➡**Remove the lower maniverter heat shield (1) from the maniverter before you remove the maniverter from the vehicle.**

20. Remove the lower heat shield (1) from the maniverter.

21. Remove the nut (4) and reposition the heat shield (1).

22. Remove the stud bolt (3) and the engine lift bracket (2).

23. Remove the two engine cover mounting posts (1).

24. Remove the bolt (5) and reposition the engine coolant reservoir (6).

25. Remove the bolt (4) and reposition the power steering fluid reservoir (2).

26. Remove the bolt (3) and reposition the washer fluid reservoir (1).

27. Remove the bolt from the power steering pressure hose support bracket.

28. Support the engine with a block of wood on a suitable jack.

29. Remove the engine mount isolator retaining bolts (3).

30. Remove the engine mount bracket retaining bolts (1) and remove the right engine mount (4).

31. Adjust the jack to lower the engine.

32. Rotate the maniverter (1) counterclockwise 180° and remove it from

above/between the engine and dash panel.

33. Remove and discard the maniverter gasket.

To install:

34. Install a new maniverter gasket on the cylinder head. DO NOT APPLY SEALER.

35. Position the maniverter in the engine compartment as shown in the last illustration in the Removal procedure. Rotate the maniverter 180° clockwise into position.

36. Raise the engine and position the right engine mount in place.

37. Install the engine mount bracket retaining bolts and tighten them to 50 ft. lbs. (68 Nm).

38. Install engine mount isolator retaining bolts and tighten them to 55 ft. lbs. (75 Nm).

39. If removed, install the engine mount through bolt and tighten it to 65 ft. lbs. (88 Nm).

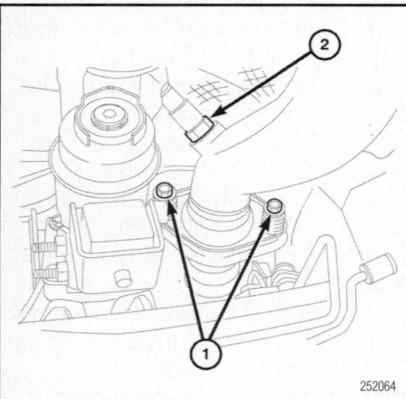

Fig. 172 Disconnect the wire harness connector from the downstream oxygen sensor (2) and remove the exhaust pipe to maniverter bolts (1) and reposition the exhaust pipe

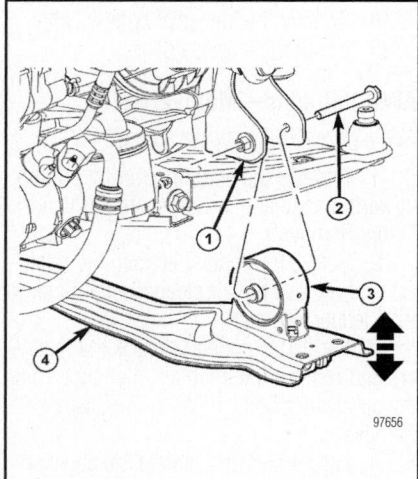

Fig. 174 Front engine mount bolt (2) and the front fore and aft crossmember (4)

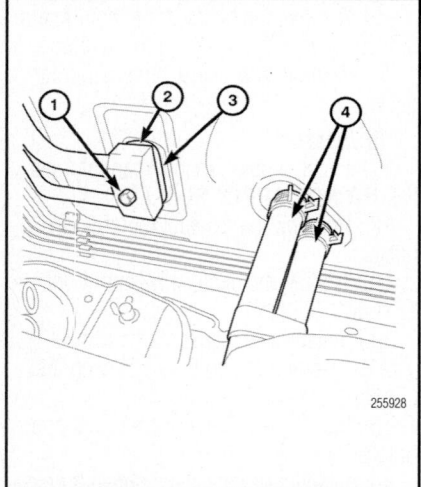

Fig. 176 Heater hoses (4) and installed plugs or caps to the heater core tubes

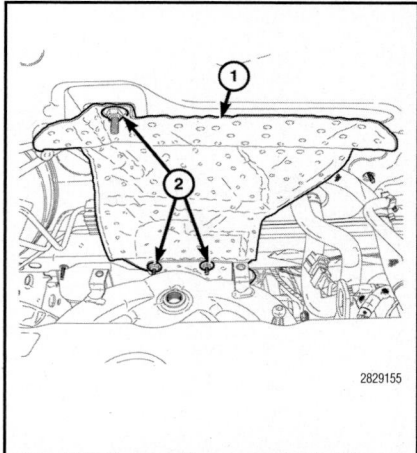

Fig. 177 Remove three speed-nuts (2) and the dash panel heat shield (1)

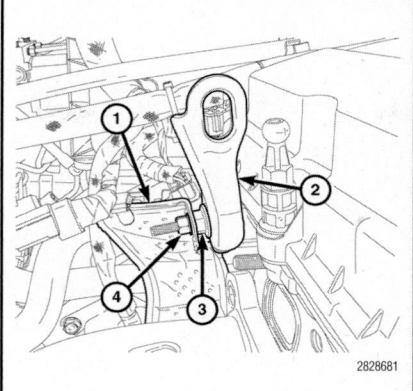

Fig. 179 Heat shield nut (4), heat shield (1), stud bolt (3), and engine lift bracket (2)

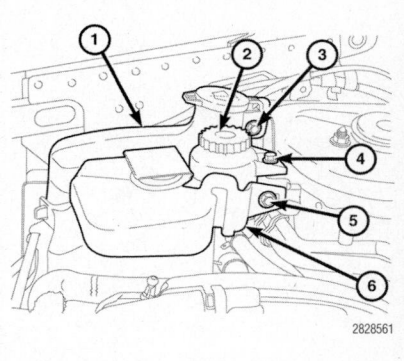

Fig. 181 Engine coolant reservoir (6) and bolt (5); power steering fluid reservoir (2) and bolt (4); washer fluid reservoir (1) and bolt (3)

40. Install the power steering pressure hose support bracket to the engine mount bracket (8) and tighten the bolt to 14 ft. lbs. (18 Nm).

41. Install the washer fluid reservoir and tighten the bolt to 79 inch lbs. (9 Nm).

42. Install the power steering fluid reservoir and tighten the bolt 106 inch lbs. (12 Nm).

43. Install the engine coolant reservoir and tighten the bolt to 35 inch lbs. (4 Nm).

44. Install the two engine cover mounting posts and tighten to 35 inch lbs. (4 Nm).

45. Install the engine lift bracket and tighten the stud bolt to 18 ft. lbs. (25 Nm).

46. Install the repositioned heat shield to the stud bolt and tighten the nut to 79 inch lbs. (9 Nm).

➡**Place the lower maniverter heat shield in position before the maniverter is installed to the cylinder head.**

47. Position the lower heat shield in its installed position on the maniverter.

48. Install the dash panel heat shield with three speed-nuts tightened to 10 inch lbs. (1 Nm).

49. Remove the previously installed plugs or caps and connect the heater hoses to the heater core tubes.

50. Raise and support the vehicle. (Refer to Hoisting—Standard Procedure).

51. Tighten the maniverter to cylinder head fasteners, starting at the center and progressing outward in both directions to 300 inch lbs. (34 Nm). Raise and lower the vehicle for fastener access as necessary.

52. Install the maniverter support bracket with four bolts tightened to 18 ft. lbs. (25 Nm).

53. Install the front fore and aft crossmember and front engine mount bolt.

54. Install the steering gear heat shield with three bolts tightened to 71 inch lbs. (8 Nm).

55. Install the exhaust pipe to maniverter bolts and tighten them to 250 inch lbs. (28 Nm).

56. Connect the wire harness connector to the downstream oxygen sensor.

57. If removed, install the belly pan with three front screws, three rear screws, and side push pin fasteners.

58. If removed, install the front skid plate with seven bolts tightened to 22 ft. lbs. (30 Nm).

59. Lower the vehicle.

60. Install the maniverter heat shields with four bolts tightened to 106 inch lbs. (12 Nm).

61. Install the upstream oxygen sensor and connect the electrical connector. (Refer to the Engine Performance section for Oxygen Sensor Installation).

62. Install the engine cover.

63. Connect the negative battery cable and tighten the nut to 45 inch lbs. (5 Nm).

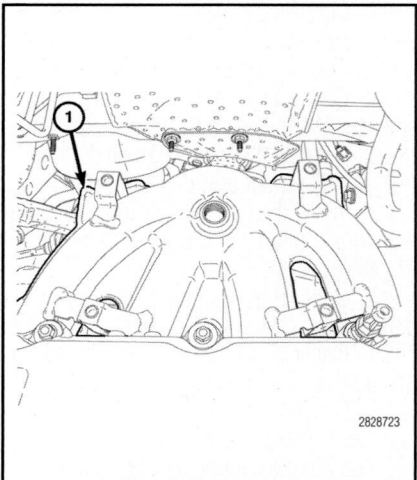

Fig. 178 Maniverter lower heat shield (1)

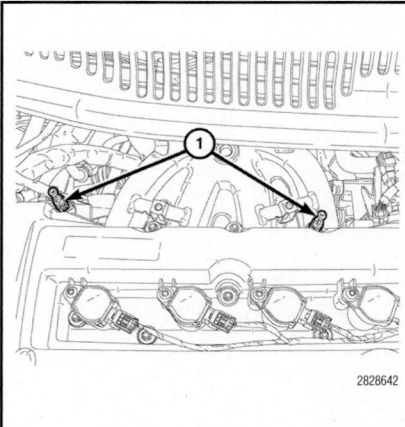

Fig. 180 Two engine cover mounting posts (1)

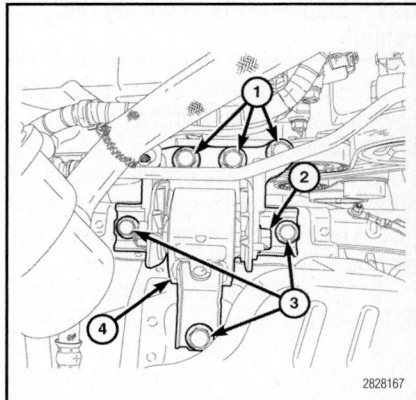

Fig. 182 Engine mount isolator retaining bolts (3), bracket retaining bolts (1), and right engine mount (4)

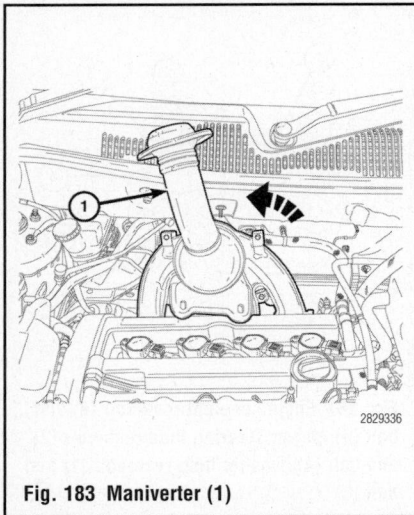

Fig. 183 Maniverter (1)

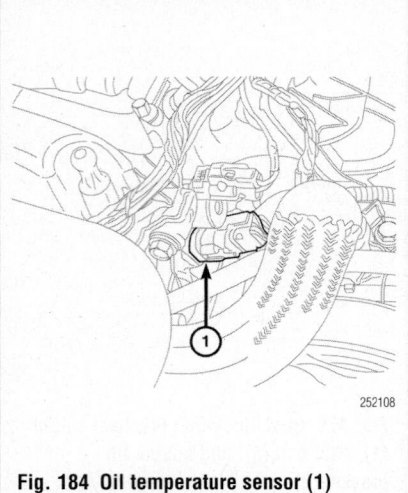

Fig. 184 Oil temperature sensor (1)

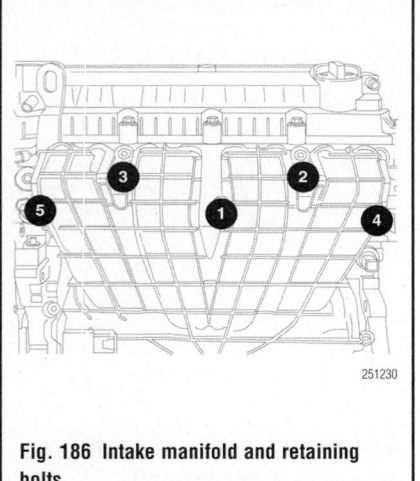

Fig. 186 Intake manifold and retaining bolts

64. For 2010 models: Install the air cleaner inlet and tighten the retainers. Refer to Air Cleaner Installation.

65. For 2011 models: Install the fresh air inlet duct on the air cleaner body and lock the retainers. Refer to Air Cleaner Installation.

66. Fill the cooling system. (Refer to Engine Cooling).

67. Run the engine until it reaches normal operating temperature. Check the cooling system for correct fluid level. (Refer to Engine Cooling).

INTAKE MANIFOLD

REMOVAL & INSTALLATION

See Figures 184 through 186.

✳✳ CAUTION

Release the fuel system pressure before servicing system components. Service vehicles in well-ventilated areas and avoid ignition sources. Never smoke while servicing the vehicle.

1. Remove the engine cover by pulling upward (see image in Camshaft and Valve Lifters Removal).

2. Perform the fuel system pressure release procedure before attempting any repairs (Refer to Fuel System Pressure Release—Standard Procedure).

3. Disconnect and isolate the negative battery cable.

4. For 2010 models:

 a. Remove the clean air hose from the air cleaner housing. Refer to Air Cleaner Removal.

 b. Drain the cooling system. Refer to Engine Cooling.

5. For 2011 models: Remove the air cleaner. Refer to Air Cleaner Removal

6. Disconnect the fuel line from the fuel rail. (Refer to Cylinder Head Removal for this image.)

7. Remove the fuel injector electrical connectors.

8. Remove the two fuel rail retaining bolts and remove the fuel rail.

9. Disconnect the oil temperature sensor (1).

10. Disconnect the variable valve timing solenoid electrical connector.

11. Disconnect the intake Camshaft Position (CMP) sensor electrical connector.

12. Position the harness out of the way.

13. Remove the throttle body support bracket (1).

14. Disconnect the electronic throttle control electrical connector.

15. Remove the wiring harness retainer from the intake manifold.

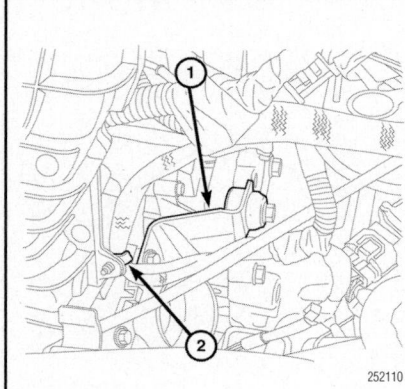

Fig. 185 Throttle body support bracket (1) and intake manifold wiring harness retainer (2)

16. Disconnect the MAP sensor electrical connector.

17. Disconnect the vacuum lines from the intake manifold.

18. Remove the upper radiator hose retaining bracket.

19. Remove the intake manifold retaining bolts.

20. Remove the intake manifold.

To install:

21. Clean all gasket surfaces.

22. Replace the intake manifold gasket.

23. Install the intake manifold and tighten bolts to 220 inch lbs. (25 Nm).

24. Install the upper radiator hose retaining bracket.

25. Install the throttle body support bracket.

26. Connect the electronic throttle control electrical connector.

27. Install the wiring harness retainer to the intake manifold.

28. Connect the MAP sensor electrical connector.

29. Connect the vacuum lines to the intake manifold.

30. Connect the oil temperature sensor.

31. Connect the variable valve timing solenoid electrical connector.

32. Connect the intake Camshaft Position (CMP) sensor electrical connector.

33. Install the fuel rail assembly to intake manifold. Tighten the bolts to 220 inch lbs. (25 Nm).

34. Connect the fuel injector electrical connectors.

35. Inspect the quick connect fittings for damage and replace them if necessary.

36. For 2010 models:

 a. Connect the fuel line.

 b. Fill the cooling system. (Refer to Engine Cooling).

c. Install the air cleaner housing and clean air hose. (Refer to Air Cleaner Installation.)

37. For 2011 models: Connect the fuel supply hose to fuel rail assembly. Check the connection by pulling on the connector to ensure it is locked into position.

38. Install the Air Cleaner. (Refer to Air Cleaner Installation.)

39. Connect the negative battery cable and tighten the nut to 45 inch lbs. (5 Nm).

40. Start the engine and check for leaks.

41. Install the engine cover.

OIL PAN

REMOVAL & INSTALLATION

See Figures 187 through 189.

1. Raise the vehicle on a hoist.
2. Remove the oil drain plug and drain the engine oil.
3. Remove the accessory drive belt splash shield.
4. Remove the lower A/C compressor mounting bolt (if equipped).
5. Remove the A/C mounting bracket (2).

➡**Do not use pry points in block to remove oil pan.**

6. Remove oil pan retaining bolts.
7. Using a putty knife (1), loosen seal around oil pan (2).
8. Remove the oil pan (2).

To install:

➡**The oil pan sealing surfaces must be free of grease or oil.**

➡**Parts must be assembled within 10 minutes of applying RTV.**

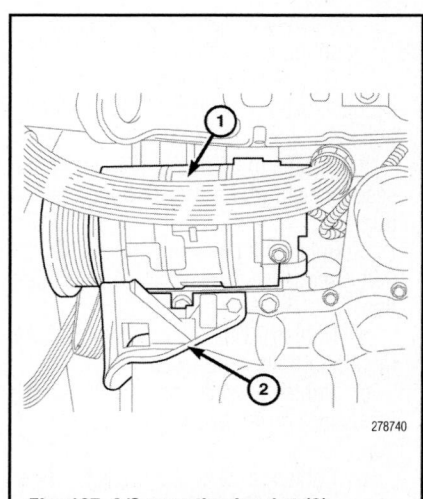

Fig. 187 A/C mounting bracket (2)

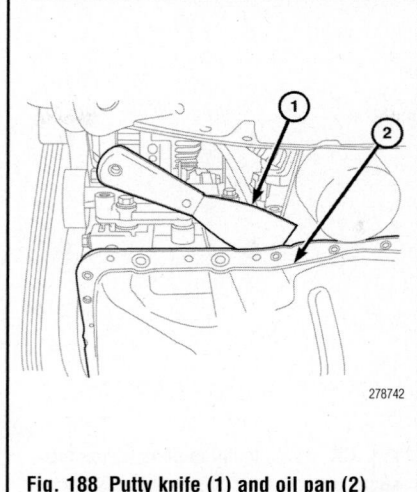

Fig. 188 Putty knife (1) and oil pan (2)

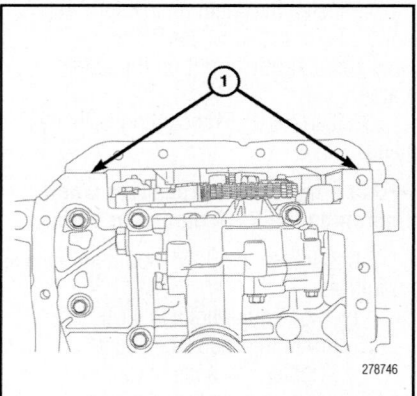

Fig. 189 Apply Mopar® Engine RTV GEN II at the front cover to the engine block parting lines (1)

9. Apply Mopar® Engine RTV GEN II at the front cover to the engine block parting lines (1).

10. Apply a 0.078 inch (2 mm)) bead of Mopar® Engine RTV GEN II around the oil pan as shown.

11. Position the oil pan and install the bolts. Tighten the bolts to 105 inch lbs. (12 Nm).

➡**The 2 long bolts must be tightened to 195 inch lbs. (22 Nm).**

12. Install the oil drain plug.
13. Lower the vehicle and fill the engine crankcase with proper oil to the correct level.
14. Start the engine and check for leaks.

OIL PUMP

REMOVAL

See Figures 190 through 192.

➡**The oil pump is integral to the balance shaft module (BSM; 2). The oil**

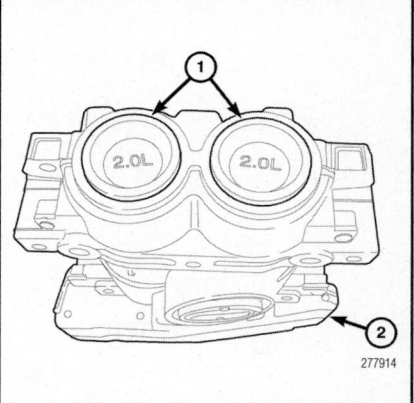

Fig. 190 Balance shaft module with integral oil pump (2) and plastic end caps (1)—2.0L shown.

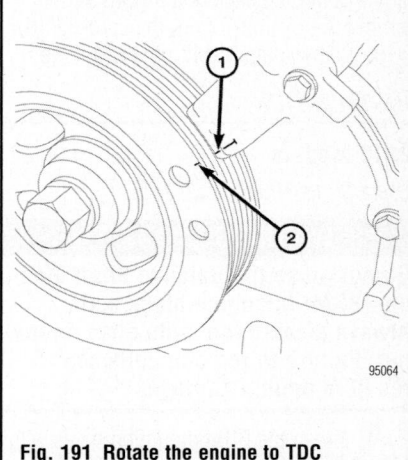

Fig. 191 Rotate the engine to TDC (1 and 2) on the #1 compression stroke

pump cannot be disassembled for inspection. The pressure relief valve is serviceable and can be removed and inspected. The BSM can be identified by the plastic end caps (1).

1. Rotate the engine to TDC (1 and 2) on the #1 compression stroke.
2. Remove the oil pan. (Refer Oil Pan Removal).
3. Mark the chain (6) and the sprocket (5) for reassembly.
4. Push the tensioner piston back into the tensioner body.
5. With the piston held back, insert the tensioner pin 9703 (4) into the tensioner body to hold the piston in the retracted position.

➡**Do not remove the sprocket from the BSM.**

6. Remove the BSM mounting bolts. Discard the 7.283 inch (180 mm) bolts; the 7.087 inch (7.087 inch (185 mm)) bolts can be reused.

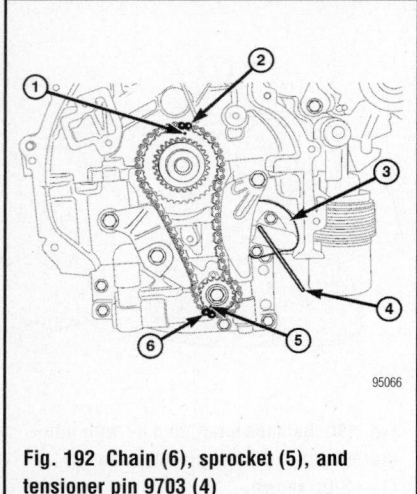

Fig. 192 Chain (6), sprocket (5), and tensioner pin 9703 (4)

7. Lower the back of the BSM and remove the chain (6) from the sprocket (5).

8. Remove the BSM from the engine.

INSTALLATION

2010 Models

See Figures 193 through 195.

✷✷ WARNING

Do not reuse the Balance Shaft Module (BSM) to engine block bolts. Always discard the bolts after removing. Failure to replace bolts can result in engine damage.

1. Clean the BSM mounting holes with Mopar® brake parts cleaner.

2. If the chain was removed, align the marks on the crankshaft sprocket (2) and chain (1).

3. Align the marks on the oil pump sprocket (5) and chain (4).

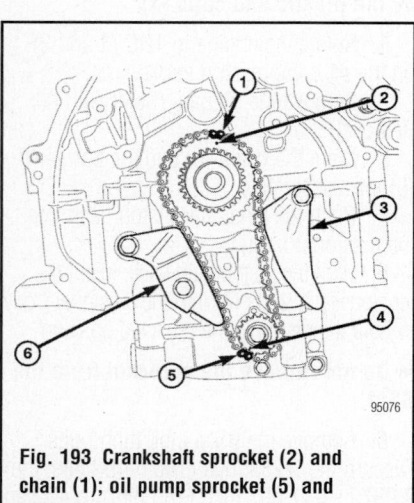

Fig. 193 Crankshaft sprocket (2) and chain (1); oil pump sprocket (5) and chain (4)

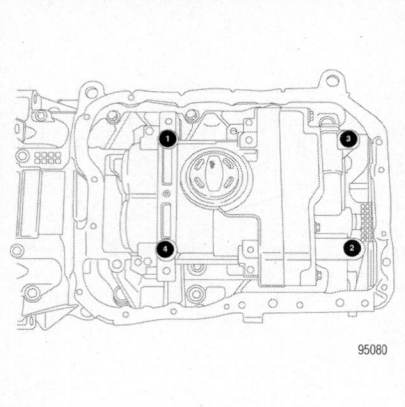

Fig. 194 BSM mounting bolts tightening sequence

4. Install the chain on the sprocket.

5. Pivot the BSM assembly upwards and position it on the ladder frame.

6. Start the BSM mounting bolts by hand.

➡️**Use a three-step procedure when tightening the BSM mounting bolts.**

a. Tighten the BSM mounting bolts as follows:

b. Tighten the bolts to 11 ft. lbs. (15 Nm) in the sequence shown.

c. Tighten the bolts to 22 ft. lbs. (29 Nm) in the sequence shown.

d. Rotate the bolts an additional 90° in the sequence shown.

7. Remove the tensioner pin 9703 (4).

8. Install the oil pan. (Refer to Oil Pan Installation).

9. Fill with oil.

10. Start the engine and check for leaks.

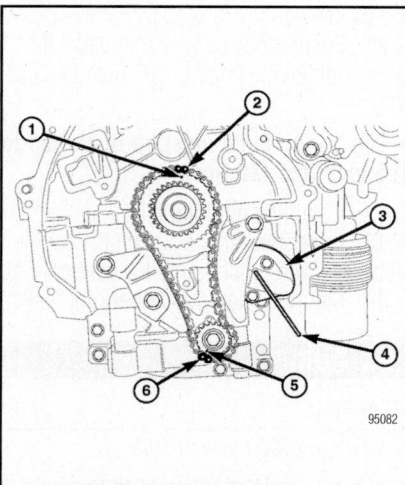

Fig. 195 Tensioner pin 9703 (4)

2011 Models

See Figures 193 through 195.

➡️**Refer to 2010 for illustrations.**

✷✷ WARNING

There are two different Balance Shaft Module (BSM) to engine block bolts used. 7.283 inch (180 mm) bolts with a lock-patch on the threads or 7.087 inch (185 mm) bolts without lock-patch. Do not reuse the 7.283 inch (180 mm). Always discard 7.283 inch (180 mm) bolts after removing them. Failure to replace these bolts can result in engine damage. The 7.087 inch (185 mm) bolts are reusable. Install the same length bolts that were removed and use either four new 7.283 inch (180 mm) or four 7.087 inch (185 mm) bolts.

1. Check the 7.087 inch (185 mm) length bolts for stretching. Check the bolts with a straight edge for necking (refer to Cylinder Head Installation). If the bolts are necked down, they must be replaced.

2. Clean the BSM mounting holes with Mopar® brake parts cleaner.

3. If the chain was removed, align the marks on the crankshaft sprocket and chain.

4. Align the marks on the oil pump sprocket and chain.

5. Install the chain on the sprocket.

6. Pivot the BSM assembly upwards and position it on the ladder frame.

7. Start the BSM mounting bolts by hand.

➡️**Use a three-step procedure when tightening the BSM mounting bolts. For new 7.283 inch (180 mm) bolts, go to step 8. For 7.087 inch (185 mm) bolts, go to step 9.**

8. Tighten new 7.283 inch (180 mm) BSM mounting bolts as follows:

a. Tighten to 11 ft. lbs. (15 Nm) in the sequence shown for the 2010 Installation.

b. Tighten to 24 ft. lbs. (33 Nm) in the sequence shown for the 2010 Installation.

c. Rotate the bolts an additional 90° in the sequence shown for 2010 Installation.

d. Tighten 7.087 inch (185 mm) BSM mounting bolts as follows:

e. Tighten to 11 ft. lbs. (15 Nm) in the sequence shown for the 2010 Installation.

f. Tighten to 22 ft. lbs. (29 Nm) in the sequence shown for the 2010 Installation.

g. Rotate the bolts an additional 90° in the sequence shown for 2010 Installation.

9. Remove the tensioner pin 9703 (see 2010 Installation image).

10. Install the oil pan (Refer to Oil Pan Installation).

11. Fill with oil.

12. Start the engine and check for leaks.

INSPECTION

See Figure 196.

1. Remove the timing chain cover. (Refer to Valve Timing Cover Removal).

2. Remove the oil pan. (Refer to Oil Pan Removal).

3. Measure the distance between the tensioner body and the guide shoe as shown.

4. If the distance is 0.397 inch (10.1 mm) or greater, replace the chain.

PISTON AND RING

POSITIONING

See Figures 197 through 199.

➡**The identification mark on the face of the upper and intermediate piston rings must point toward the top of the piston.**

REAR MAIN SEAL/REAR CRANKSHAFT OIL SEAL

REMOVAL & INSTALLATION

See Figures 200 and 201.

1. Remove the transmission and flex-plate.

2. Insert a ³⁄₁₆ flat bladed screwdriver (7) between the dust lip (8) and the metal case (4) of the crankshaft seal (1).

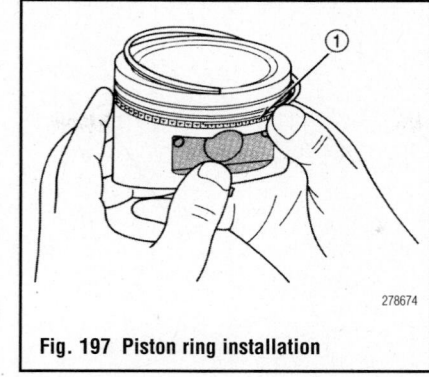

Fig. 197 Piston ring installation

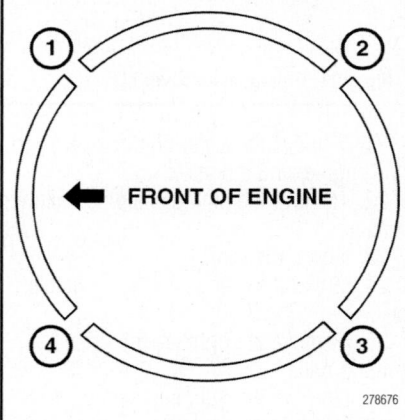

Fig. 198 Position the piston ring end gaps as shown

Angle the screwdriver through the dust lip against metal case of the seal. Pry out the seal.

✳✳ WARNING

Do not permit the screwdriver blade to contact the crankshaft seal surface. Contact of the screwdriver blade against

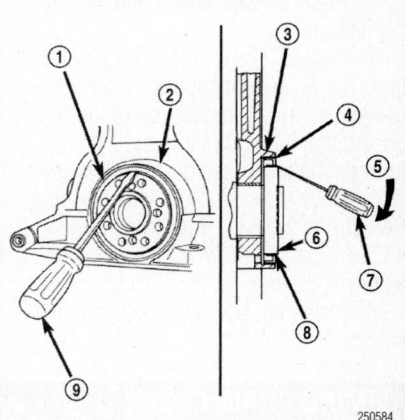

Fig. 200 Insert a ³⁄₁₆ flat bladed screwdriver (7) between the dust lip (8) and the metal case (4) of the crankshaft seal (1). Angle the screwdriver through the dust lip against metal case of the seal. Pry out the seal

crankshaft edge (chamfer) is permitted.

3. Check to make sure the seals garter spring is not on the crankshaft.

To install:

✳✳ WARNING

If a burr or scratch is present on the crankshaft edge (chamfer), cleanup with 800 emery cloth to prevent seal damage during installation of the new seal. If emery cloth is used, the crankshaft must be cleaned off with Mopar® brake parts cleaner.

➡**When installing the seal, lubricate the Seal Guide 9509 with clean engine oil.**

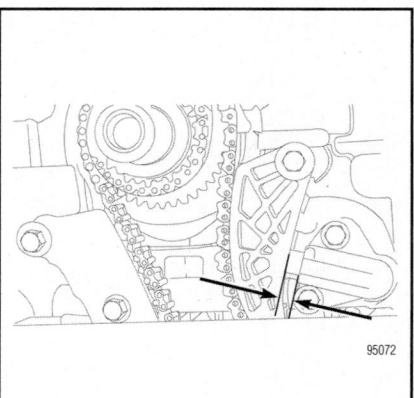

Fig. 196 Measure the distance between the tensioner body and the guide shoe as shown

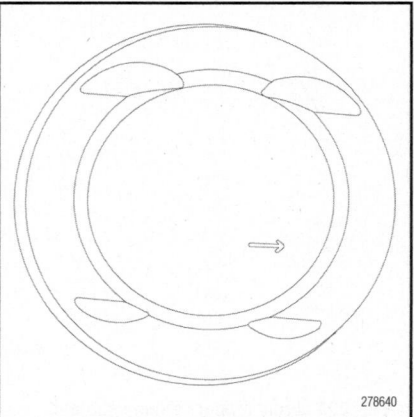

Fig. 199 The directional arrow stamped on the piston should face toward the front of the engine—2.4L

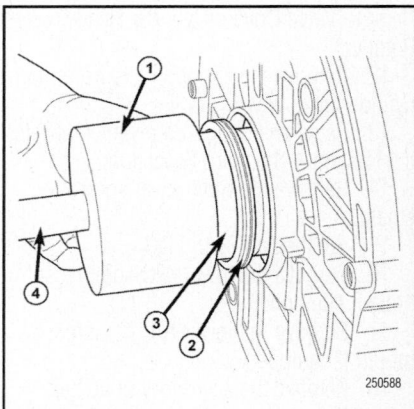

Fig. 201 Seal Guide 9509 (3), seal (2), Seal Driver 9706 (1), and Driver Handle C-4171 (4)

4. Place the Seal Guide 9509 (3) on the crankshaft.

5. Position the seal (2) over the guide tool. The guide tool should remain on crankshaft during installation of the seal. Ensure that the lip of the seal is facing towards the crankcase during installation.

6. Drive the seal into the block using Seal Driver 9706 (1) and Driver Handle C-4171 (4) until Seal Driver 9706 bottoms out against the block.

7. Install the flexplate and the transmission.

TIMING CHAIN COVER

REMOVAL & INSTALLATION

See Figures 202 through 206.

Refer to Cylinder Head Removal and Installation for many of the illustrations.

1. Remove the engine cover by pulling upward (see image in Camshaft and Valve Lifters Removal).

2. Perform the fuel system pressure release procedure (Refer to Fuel System Pressure Release—Standard Procedure).

3. Disconnect and isolate the negative battery cable.

4. Remove air cleaner components as needed.

5. Remove the coolant recovery bottle.

6. Remove and reposition the power steering reservoir.

7. Remove the windshield washer bottle.

8. Remove the accessory drive belt. Refer to Accessory Drive Belt Removal.

9. Remove the power steering hose hold down.

10. Remove the three power steering pump mounting bolts through the openings in the pulley and reposition the pump.

11. Remove the cylinder head cover. Refer to Valve Covers/Cylinder Head Covers Removal.

12. Remove the ignition coils from the cylinder head cover.

13. Raise and support the vehicle. (Refer to Hoisting—Standard Procedure).

14. Remove the right lower splash shield.

15. Set the engine to TDC.

16. Remove the lower A/C compressor bolts if equipped.

17. Remove the lower A/C compressor mount if equipped.

18. Remove the accessory drive belt lower idler pulley.

19. Remove the crankshaft damper.

20. Remove the three bolts and the water pump pulley from the water pump.

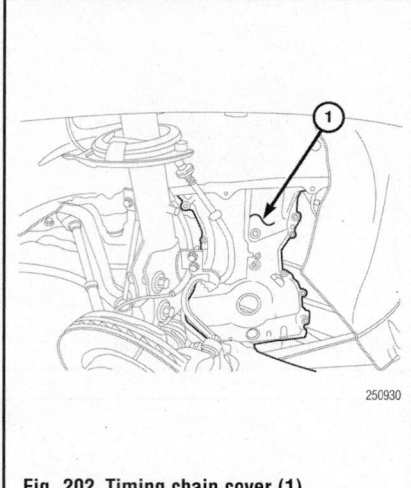

Fig. 202 Timing chain cover (1)

21. Remove the lower bolt from the right side engine mount bracket.

22. Remove the timing chain cover lower bolts.

23. Lower the vehicle.

24. Support the engine with a suitable jack.

25. Remove the right engine mount through bolt.

26. Remove the right engine mount to mount bracket bolts.

27. Remove the right engine mount adapter.

28. Remove the accessory drive upper idler pulley.

29. Remove the right upper engine mount bracket.

30. Remove the accessory drive belt tensioner.

31. Remove the timing chain cover retaining bolts.

32. Remove the timing chain cover using pry points (1, 2, and 3).

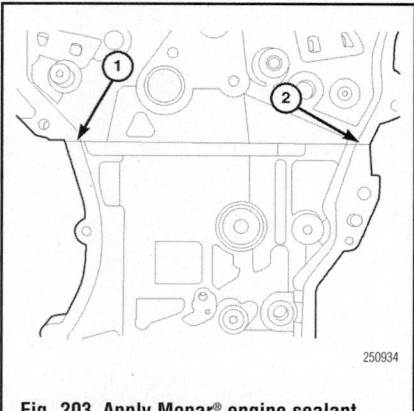

Fig. 203 Apply Mopar® engine sealant RTV (or an equivalent) as shown at the cylinder head to the block parting line (1, 2)

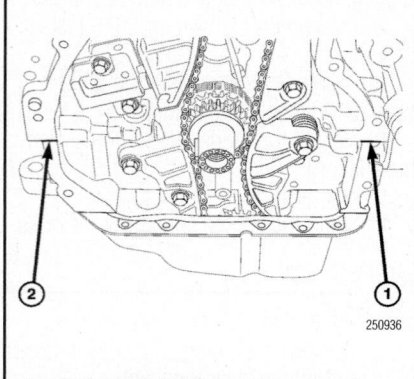

Fig. 204 Apply Mopar® engine sealant RTV (or an equivalent) as shown at the ladder frame to the block parting line (1, 2)

33. Remove the timing chain cover (1) out through the bottom of the vehicle.

To install:

➡ **When using RTV, the sealing surfaces must be clean and free from grease and oil. Also, parts should be assembled in 10 minutes and tightened to final torque within 45 minutes.**

34. Clean all sealing surfaces.

35. Apply Mopar® engine sealant RTV (or an equivalent) as shown at the cylinder head to block parting line (1, 2).

36. Apply Mopar® engine sealant RTV (or an equivalent) as shown at the ladder frame to the block parting line (1, 2).

37. Apply Mopar® engine sealant RTV (or an equivalent) as shown in the corner of the oil pan and block.

38. Apply 0.078 inch (2 mm) bead of Mopar® engine sealant RTV (or equivalent) to the oil pan as shown.

39. Apply 0.078 inch (2 mm) bead of

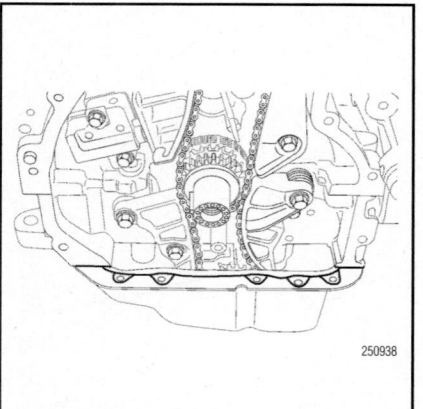

Fig. 205 Apply Mopar® engine sealant RTV (or an equivalent) as shown in the corner of the oil pan and block

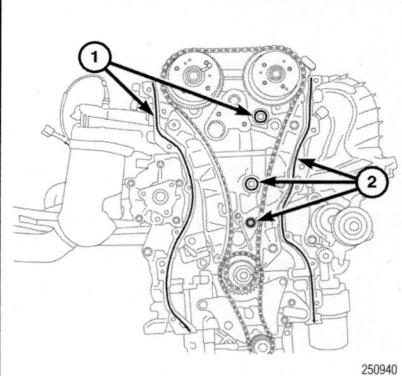

Fig. 206 Apply 0.078 inch (2 mm) bead of Mopar® engine sealant RTV (or equivalent) to the engine block (1, 2) as shown

Mopar® engine sealant RTV (or equivalent) to the engine block (1, 2) as shown.

40. Install the timing chain cover upwards from under the vehicle.

41. Install the timing chain cover upper retaining bolts and tighten M6 bolts to 80 inch lbs. (9 Nm) and M8 bolts to 230 inch lbs. (26 Nm).

42. Install the accessory drive belt tensioner. Tighten the bolt to 212 inch lbs. (24 Nm).

43. Install the right engine mount bracket. Tighten the bolts to 37 ft. lbs. (50 Nm).

44. Install accessory drive belt upper idler pulley. Tighten bolt to 35 ft. lbs. (48 Nm).

45. Install engine mount adapter and tighten the bolts to 50 ft. lbs. (68 Nm).

46. Install engine mount through bolt and tighten it to 65 ft. lbs. (88 Nm).

47. Remove the jack from under the engine.

48. Raise and support the vehicle. (Refer to Hoisting—Standard Procedure).

49. Install the oil pan to the timing chain cover lower retaining bolts and tighten the M6 bolts to 80 inch lbs. (9 Nm).

50. Install the water pump pulley and tighten the three bolts to 80 inch lbs. (9 Nm).

51. Install the crankshaft damper.

52. Install the accessory drive belt lower idler pulley. Tighten the bolt to 35 ft. lbs. (48 Nm).

53. Install the lower A/C compressor mounting bracket. Tighten the bolts to 18 ft. lbs. (24 Nm).

54. Install the A/C compressor. Tighten the bolts to 18 ft. lbs. (25 Nm).

55. Install the right lower splash shield.

56. Lower the vehicle.

57. Install the cylinder head cover and ignition coils.

58. Place the power steering pump in mounting position. Install the three bolts through the openings in the pulley. Tighten the mounting bolts to 19 ft. lbs. (26 Nm).

59. Install the power steering hose hold down.

60. Install the accessory drive belt. (Refer to Accessory Drive Belt Installation).

61. Install the power steering pump reservoir. Tighten the mounting screw to 106 inch lbs. (12 Nm).

62. Install the windshield washer reservoir.

63. Install the coolant recovery reservoir. Tighten the mounting bolts to 35 inch lbs. (4 Nm).

64. Install the clean air hose and air cleaner housing. Refer to Air Cleaner Installation.

65. Install the air cleaner housing inlet.

66. Connect the negative battery cable.

67. Operate the engine until it reaches normal operating temperature. Check the oil system for leaks and correct fluid level.

68. Install the engine cover (1).

TIMING CHAIN & SPROCKETS

REMOVAL & INSTALLATION

Camshaft Sprocket(s)

See Figure 207.

➡ **Camshaft phasers and camshaft sprockets are supplied as an assembly; do not attempt to disassemble them. Refer to camshaft phaser removal and installation in the Camshaft and Valve Lifters Removal & Installation procedure.**

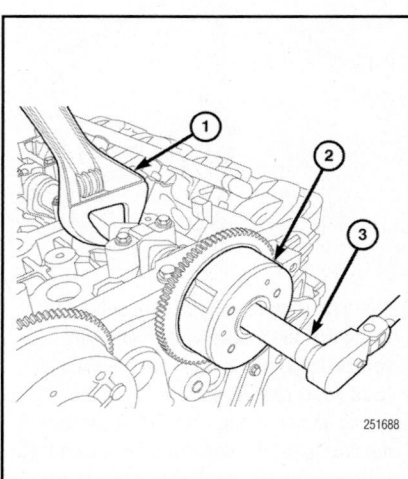

Fig. 207 Camshaft phaser (2)

⁕⁕ **WARNING**

Do not use an impact wrench to tighten camshaft sprocket bolts. Damage to the camshaft-to-sprocket locating dowel pin and camshaft phaser may occur.

Crankshaft Sprocket

See Figures 208 through 210.

1. Remove the timing chain. (Refer to Timing Chain and Sprockets for Timing Chain Removal).

2. Remove the oil pan (Refer to Oil Pan Removal).

3. Remove the oil pump drive chain tensioner.

4. Remove the oil pump drive chain.

5. Remove the crankshaft sprocket (1).

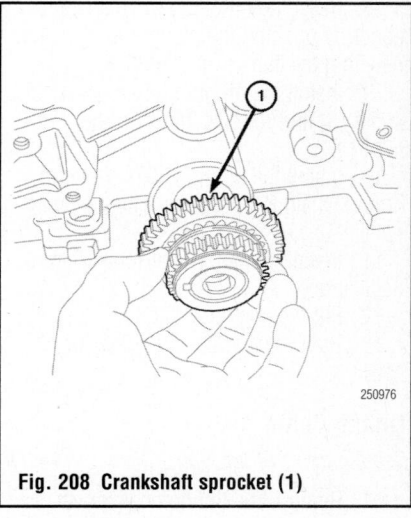

Fig. 208 Crankshaft sprocket (1)

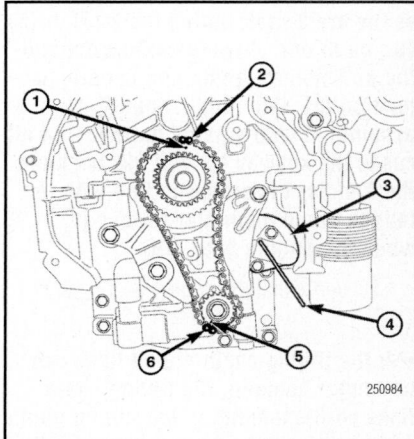

Fig. 209 Install the oil pump drive chain. Verify that the oil pump is correctly timed (1, 2, 5, and 6). Oil pump drive chain tensioner (3) and Tensioner Pin 8514 (4)

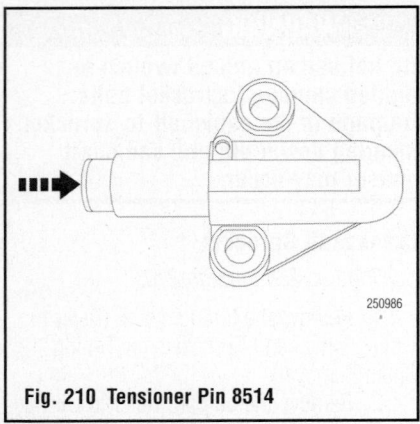

Fig. 210 Tensioner Pin 8514

To install:

6. Install the crankshaft sprocket onto the crankshaft.

7. Install the oil pump drive chain. Verify that the oil pump is correctly timed (1, 2, 5, and 6).

8. Reset the oil pump drive chain tensioner by pushing the plunger inward and installing the Tensioner Pin 8514.

9. Install the oil pump drive chain tensioner (3) and remove the Tensioner Pin 8514 (4).

10. Install the timing chain. (Refer to Timing Chain & Sprockets, Timing Chain Installation).

11. Install oil pan. (Refer to Oil Pan Installation).

12. Fill the engine with oil.

13. Start the engine and check for leaks.

Timing Chain

See Figures 211 through 214.

1. Remove the timing chain cover, as outlined in this section.

➡**The crankshaft timing mark (3) or (5) can be in one of two locations depending on whether the engine is early production (5), late production (3) or assembled with service parts (3). In all cases the keyway (2) will always be in the 9 o'clock position, in line with the ladder frame mounting surface (1) when the engine is at TDC.**

2. Verify that the engine is still set to TDC.

➡**If the timing chain plated links can no longer be seen, the timing chain links corresponding to the timing marks must be marked prior to removal if the chain is to be reused.**

3. Mark the chain link (4) corresponding to the crankshaft timing mark (3) or (5).

4. With the engine still set to TDC, ver-

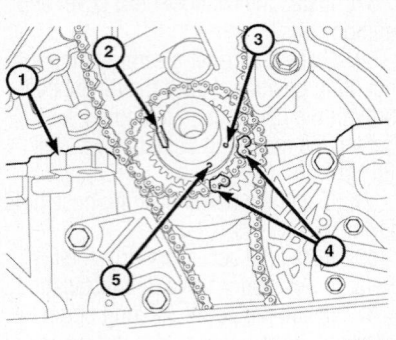

Fig. 211 The crankshaft timing mark (3) or (5) can be in one of two locations depending on whether the engine is early production (5), late production (3) or assembled with service parts (3). In all cases the keyway (2) will always be in the 9 o'clock position, in line with the ladder frame mounting surface (1) when the engine is at TDC

ify that the marks on the camshaft sprockets (3) are in line with the cylinder head cover sealing surface (2). If the marks do not line up, the timing chain is not correctly installed.

5. Mark the chain link (1) corresponding to the camshaft timing mark.

6. Remove the timing chain tensioner (5). Refer to Timing Chain Tensioner Removal.

7. Remove the timing chain (2).

To install:

➡**The crankshaft timing mark (3) or (5) can be in one of two locations depend-**

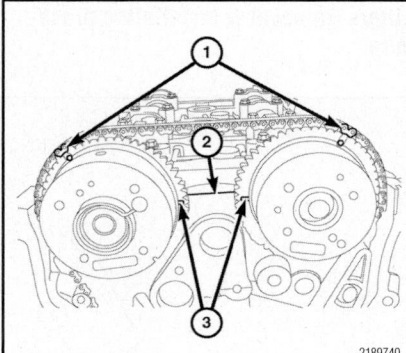

Fig. 212 With the engine still set to TDC, verify that the marks on the camshaft sprockets (3) are in line with the cylinder head cover sealing surface (2). If the marks do not line up, the timing chain is not correctly installed. Mark the chain link (1) corresponding to the camshaft timing mark

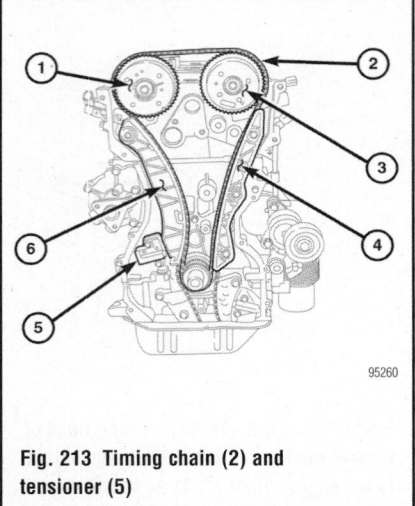

Fig. 213 Timing chain (2) and tensioner (5)

ing on whether the engine is early production (5), late production (3) or assembled with service parts (3). In all cases the keyway (2) will always be in the 9 o'clock position, in line with the ladder frame mounting surface (1) when the engine is at TDC.

8. Verify that the engine is still set to TDC.

9. Align the camshaft timing marks (3) so they are facing each other and in line with the cylinder head cover sealing surface (2).

10. Install the timing chain so plated (or marked) links on chain align with the timing marks on the camshaft sprockets (1).

11. Align the timing mark on the crankshaft sprocket (3) or (5) with the plated (or marked) link (4) on the timing chain. Position the chain so slack will be on the tensioner side.

➡**Keep the slack in the timing chain on the tensioner side.**

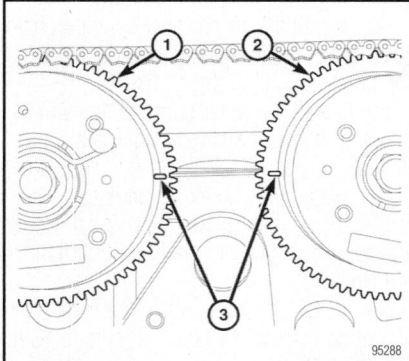

Fig. 214 Verify that the camshaft's timing marks (3) are in the proper position and in line with the cylinder head cover sealing surface. If the marks do not line up, the timing chain is not correctly installed

12. Install the timing chain tensioner. Refer to Timing Chain Tensioner Installation.

13. Rotate the crankshaft CLOCKWISE two complete revolutions until the crankshaft is repositioned at the TDC position with the keyway at the 9 o'clock position.

14. Verify that the camshaft's timing marks (3) are in the proper position and in line with the cylinder head cover sealing surface. If the marks do not line up, the timing chain is not correctly installed.

15. Install the front timing chain cover. (Refer to Timing Chain Cover Installation).

16. Connect the negative battery cable.

17. Operate the engine until it reaches normal operating temperature. Check the oil and cooling systems for correct fluid levels.

TIMING CHAIN TENSIONER

REMOVAL & INSTALLATION

See Figures 215 and 216.

1. Remove the engine timing cover. (Refer to Timing Chain Cover Removal).

➡**The tensioner will not come apart during removal.**

2. Remove the timing chain tensioner retaining bolts and remove the tensioner. (Refer to Timing Chain & Sprockets, Timing Chain, for illustration.)

To install:

3. Reset the timing chain tensioner (4) by lifting up on the ratchet (2) and pushing the plunger (3) inward towards the tensioner body (4). Insert Tensioner Pin 8514 into the slot (1) to hold the tensioner plunger in the retracted position.

➡**Keep the slack in the timing chain on the tensioner side.**

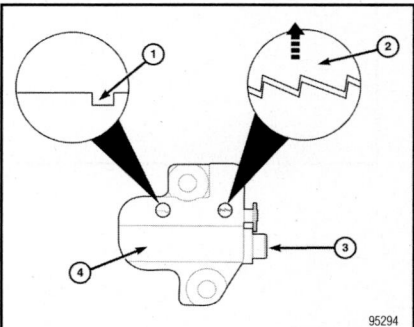

Fig. 215 Reset the timing chain tensioner (4) by lifting up on the ratchet (2) and pushing the plunger (3) inward towards the tensioner body (4). Insert Tensioner Pin 8514 into the slot (1) to hold the tensioner plunger in the retracted position

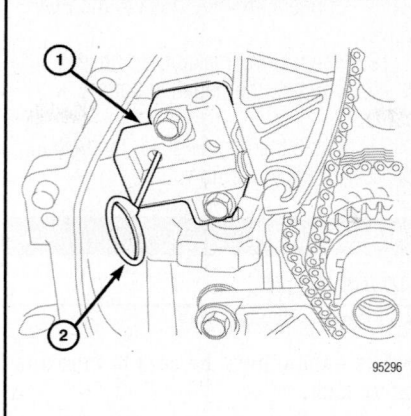

Fig. 216 Timing chain tensioner (1) and Tensioner Pin 8514 (2)

4. Install the timing chain tensioner (1) and tighten the bolts to 105 inch lbs. (12 Nm).

5. Remove the timing Tensioner Pin 8514 (2).

6. Install the engine timing cover. (Refer to Timing Chain Cover Installation).

VALVE COVERS/CYLINDER HEAD COVERS

REMOVAL & INSTALLATION

See Figures 217 through 221.

1. Remove the engine cover by pulling upward (see image in Camshaft and Valve Lifters Removal).

2. Disconnect and isolate the negative battery cable.

3. Remove the makeup air hose (2).

4. Remove PCV hose (5).

5. Disconnect the ignition coil electrical connectors (1).

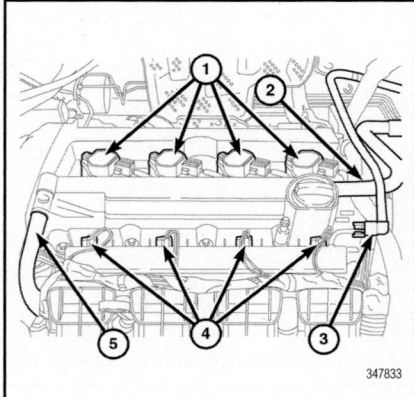

Fig. 217 Make up air hose (2), PCV hose (5), and ignition coil electrical connectors (1)

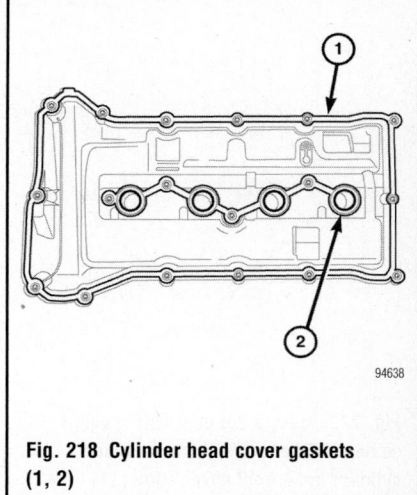

Fig. 218 Cylinder head cover gaskets (1, 2)

6. Use compressed air to blow dirt and debris off the cylinder head cover prior to removal.

7. Remove the cylinder head cover bolts.

8. Remove the cylinder head cover from the cylinder head.

To install:

9. Install new cylinder head cover gaskets (1, 2).

10. Install the studs in cover as shown.

11. Clean all RTV from the cylinder head.

➡**When using RTV, the sealing surfaces must be clean and free from grease and oil.**

➡**When using RTV, parts should be assembled in 10 minutes and tighten to final torque within 45 minutes.**

12. Apply a dot of Mopar® engine sealant RTV or an equivalent to the cylinder head/front cover T-joint (1).

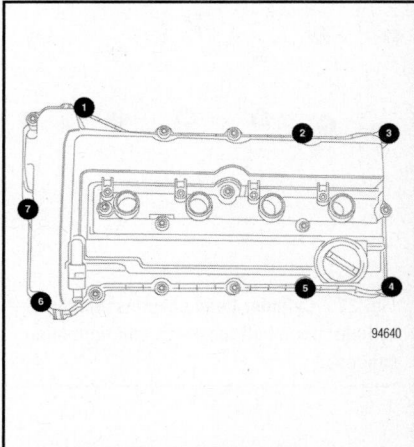

Fig. 219 Install the studs in cover as shown

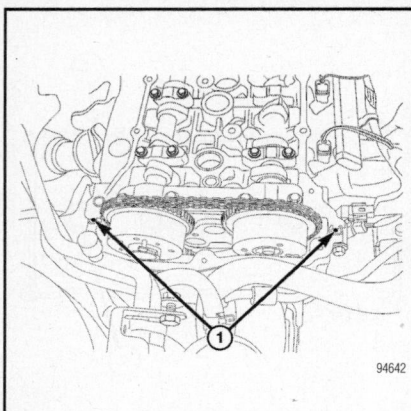

Fig. 220 Apply a dot of Mopar® engine sealant RTV or an equivalent to the cylinder head/front cover T-joint (1)

13. Install the cylinder head cover assembly to cylinder head and install all bolts, ensuring the studs are located as shown.

14. Tighten the bolts in sequence shown using a 2 step torque method as follows:

   a. Tighten all bolts to 44 inch lbs. (5 Nm).

   b. Tighten all bolts to 90 inch lbs. (10 Nm).

15. Install the ignition coils. Tighten fasteners to 70 inch lbs. (8 Nm).

16. If the PCV valve was removed, tighten the PCV valve to 44 inch lbs. (5 Nm).

17. Connect the coil electrical connectors.

18. Connect the PCV hose to the PCV valve.

19. Connect the makeup air hose.

20. Connect the negative battery cable.

21. Install the engine cover by pressing the rear of the cover down first.

VALVE LASH

ADJUSTMENT

See Figures 222 and 223.

➡**The engine must be cold to measure valve lash.**

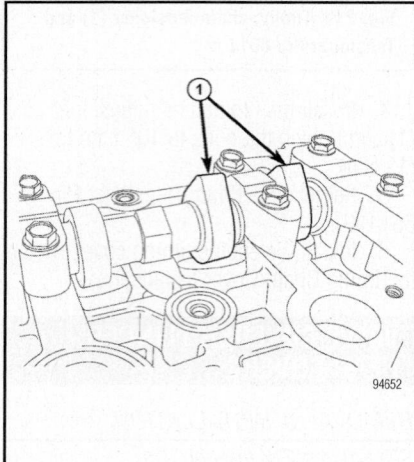

Fig. 222 Rotate the camshaft so the lobes are vertical (1)

1. Remove the engine cover by pulling upward (see image in Camshaft and Valve Lifters Removal).

2. Remove the cylinder head cover. Refer to Valve Covers/Cylinder Head Covers Removal.

3. Rotate the camshaft so the lobes are vertical (1).

4. Check the clearance using feeler gauges.

5. Repeat for all tappets and record the readings.

6. If clearance was too small, refer to the Clearance Too Small procedure.

7. If clearance was too large, refer to the Clearance Too Large procedure.

  Clearance Too Small

8. Remove the camshafts. (Refer to Camshaft and Valve Lifters Removal).

9. Specification - clearance = change.

10. Decrease the tappet thickness by the change figure.

11. Install the camshafts. (Refer to Camshaft and Valve Lifters Installation).

12. Verify that the valve lash is correct.

  Clearance Too Large

13. Remove the camshafts. (Refer to Camshaft and Valve Lifters Removal).

14. Clearance - specification = change.

15. Increase the tappet thickness by the change figure.

16. Install the camshafts. (Refer to Camshaft and Valve Lifters Installation).

17. Verify that the valve lash is correct.

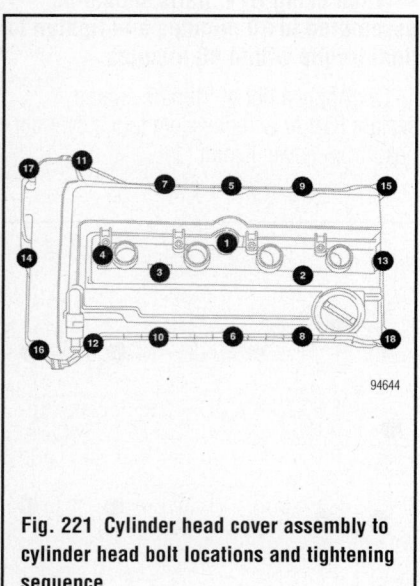

Fig. 221 Cylinder head cover assembly to cylinder head bolt locations and tightening sequence

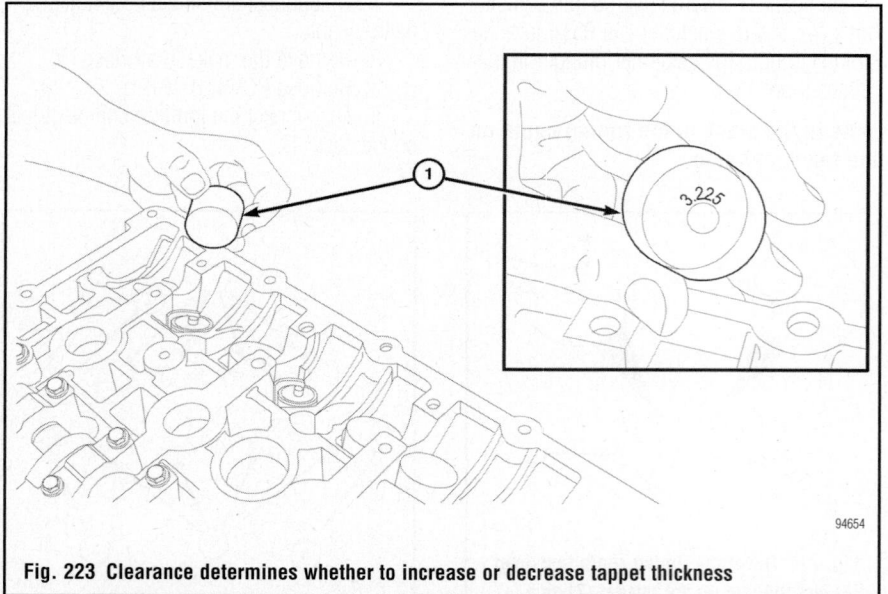

Fig. 223 Clearance determines whether to increase or decrease tappet thickness

ENGINE PERFORMANCE & EMISSION CONTROLS

COMPONENT LOCATIONS

See Figures 224 through 228.

AIR TEMPERATURE INLET/ INTAKE AIR TEMPERATURE (IAT) SENSOR

LOCATION

In the clean air duct of the intake manifold.

REMOVAL & INSTALLATION

See Figures 229 and 230.

1. Disconnect the negative battery cable.
2. Disconnect the electrical connector from the sensor.
3. Remove the sensor from the clean air duct.

To install:

4. Install the inlet air temperature sensor into the clean air duct.

5. Connect the electrical connector to the sensor.
6. Connect the negative battery cable.

CAMSHAFT POSITION (CMP) SENSOR

LOCATION

The Camshaft Position (CMP) sensors mount to the front and rear of the cylinder head.

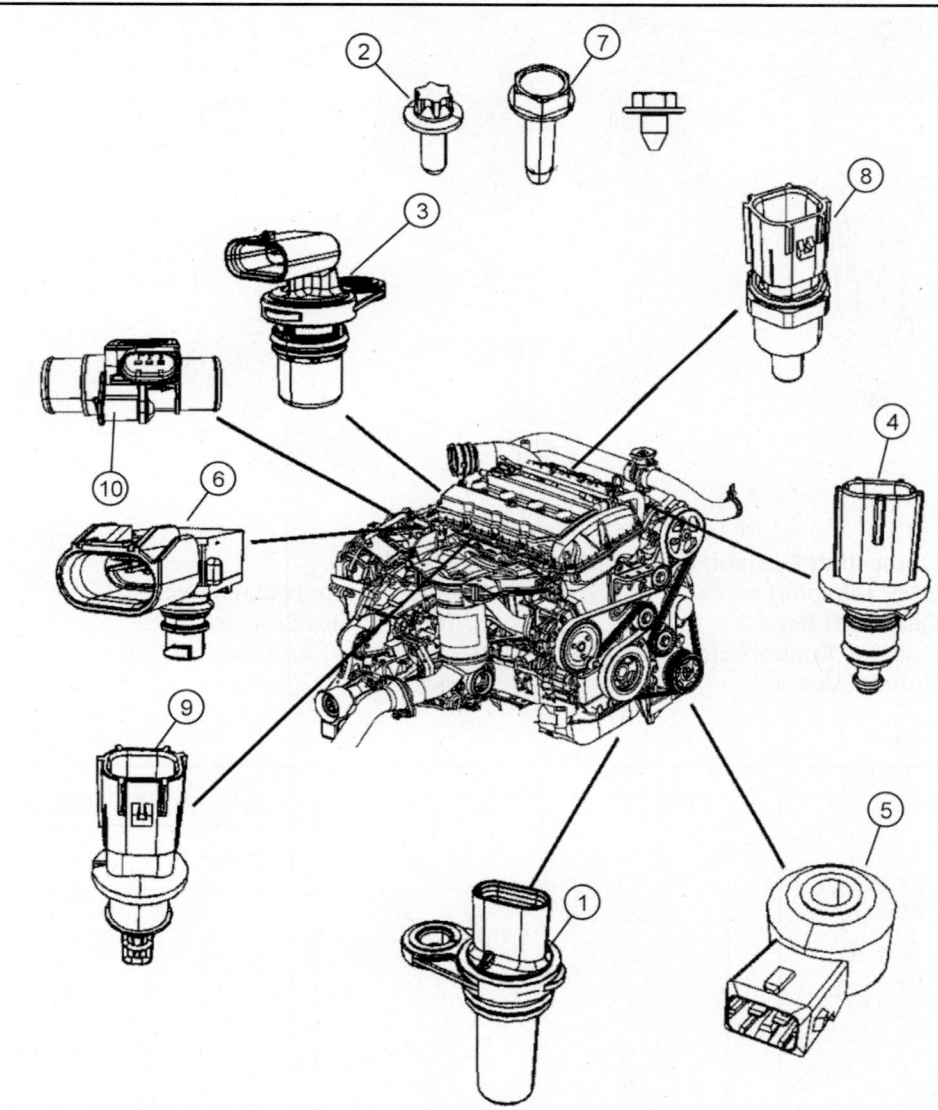

1. Crankshaft position sensor
2. Hex flange head screw, M6x1.00x20.00
3. Camshaft sensor
4. Coolant temperature sensor
5. Knock sensor
6. MAP sensor
7. Tapping hex head screw, M4.2X1.70X16.00
8. Temperature sensor
9. Charge air temperature sensor
10. Mass airflow sensor

I2243714

Fig. 224 Sensor locations—2010

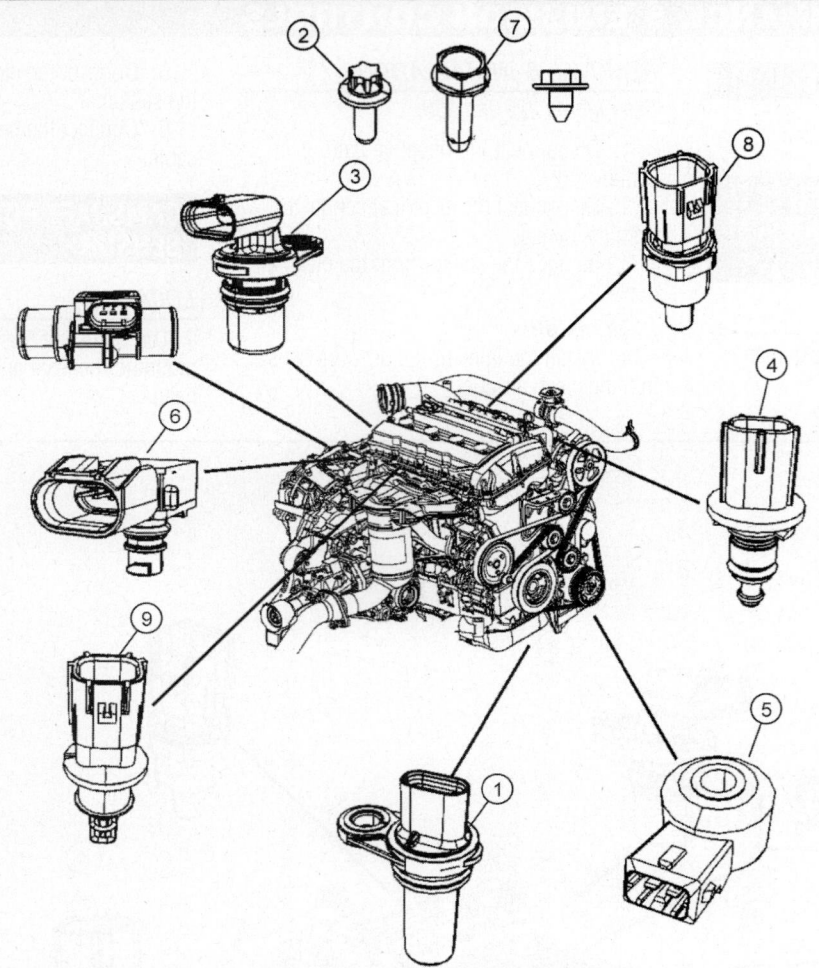

1. Crankshaft Position Sensor (CMP)
2. CMP retaining screw
3. Camshaft Sensor
4. Coolant Temperature Sensor
5. Knock Sensor
6. MAP Sensor
7. MAP Sensor retaining screw
8. Temperature Sensor
9. Charge Air Temperature Sensor

I2261835

Fig. 225 Sensor locations—2011

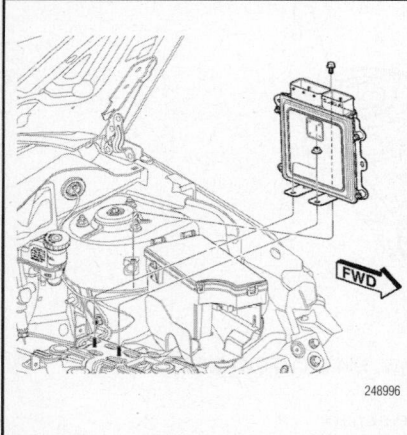

Fig. 226 Powertrain control module location—2010

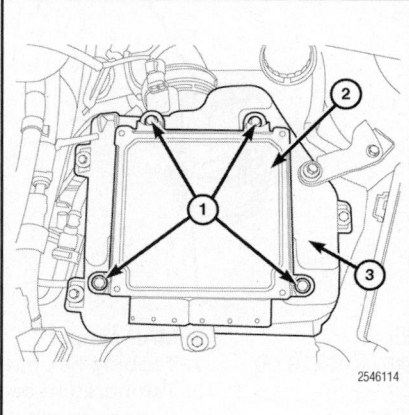

Fig. 227 Powertrain control module location—2011

REMOVAL & INSTALLATION

Front

See Figures 231 and 232.

1. Remove the air cleaner hose to throttle body.

2. Disconnect the inlet air temperature sensor electrical connector.

3. Disconnect the negative battery cable.

4. Disconnect the electrical connector from the Camshaft Position (CMP) sensor.

5. Remove the Camshaft Position (CMP) sensor mounting screws.

6. Remove the Camshaft Position (CMP) sensor.

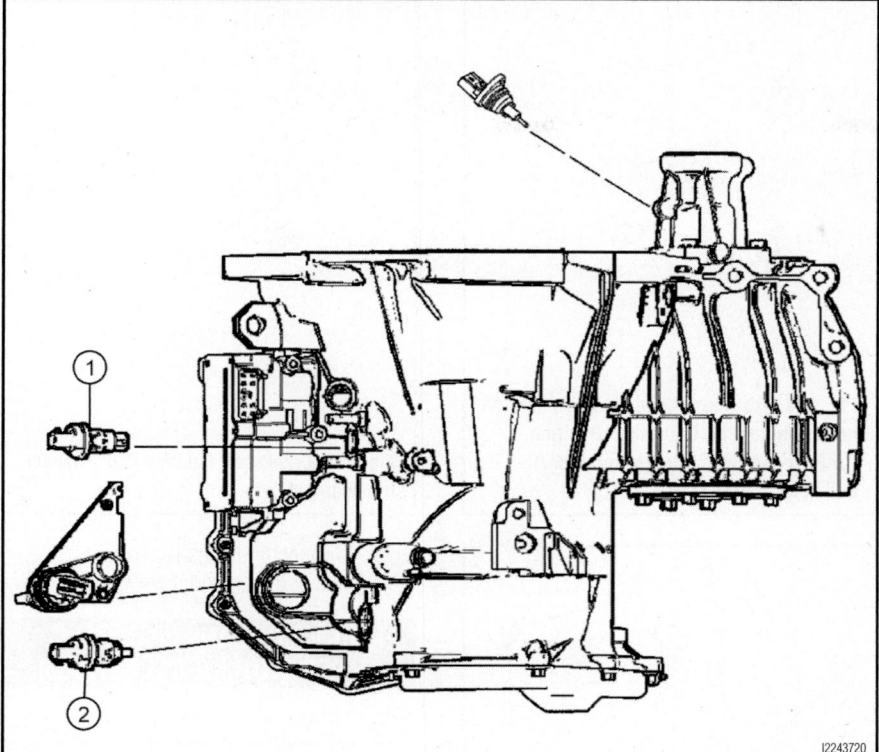

Fig. 228 Vehicle speed sensors: Primary revolution (1) and (2) secondary revolution—Manual transaxle

Rear

See Figure 233.

1. Disconnect the negative battery cable.
2. Disconnect the electrical connector at the sensor.
3. Remove the nut retaining the heat shield.
4. Pull the heat shield out to uncover the sensor.
5. Remove the mounting bolt.
6. Remove the sensor. (Refer to illustration of Front Camshaft Position (CMP) sensor.)

To install:
7. Lubricate the sensor o-ring.
8. Install the sensor using a twisting motion. Make sure the sensor is fully seated. Do not drive the sensor into the bore with a screw. This can cause the sensor to be incorrectly seated causing engine to fail.

Fig. 231 Camshaft Position (CMP) sensor replacement

To install:
7. Lubricate the sensor O-ring.
8. Install the Camshaft Position (CMP) sensor using a twisting motion. Make sure the sensor is fully seated. Do not drive the sensor into the bore with a screw. This can cause the sensor to be incorrectly seated causing the engine to fail. Tighten the sensor mounting screws to 79.5 inch lbs. (9 Nm).

9. Carefully attach the electrical connector to the Camshaft Position (CMP) sensor. Installation at an angle may damage the sensor pins.
10. Install the negative battery cable.
11. Install the air cleaner to the throttle body hose.
12. Connect the inlet air temperature sensor electrical connector.

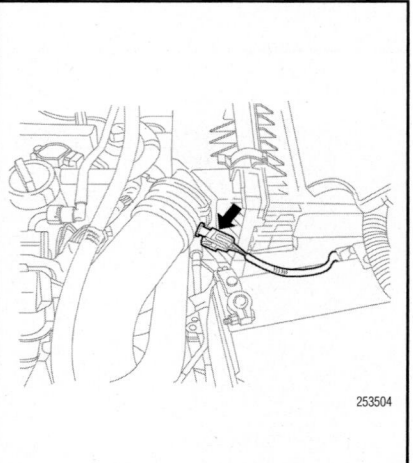

Fig. 229 Air temperature inlet sensor replacement

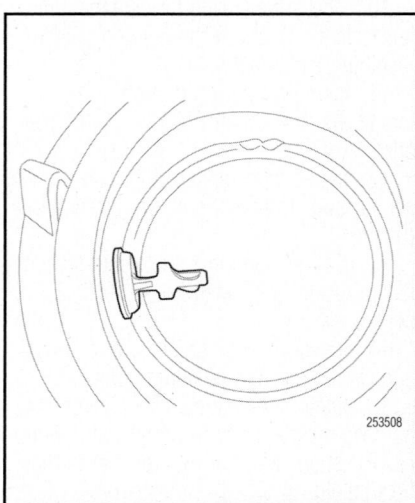

Fig. 230 Install the inlet air temperature sensor into the clean air duct

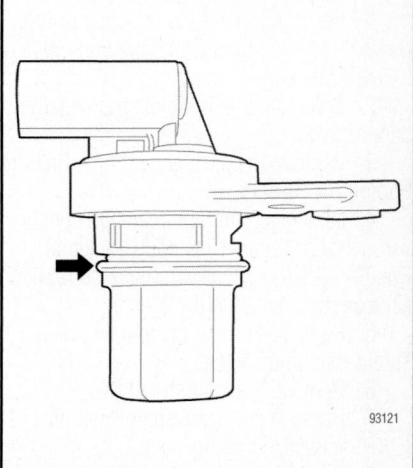

Fig. 232 Lubricate the camshaft sensor O-ring

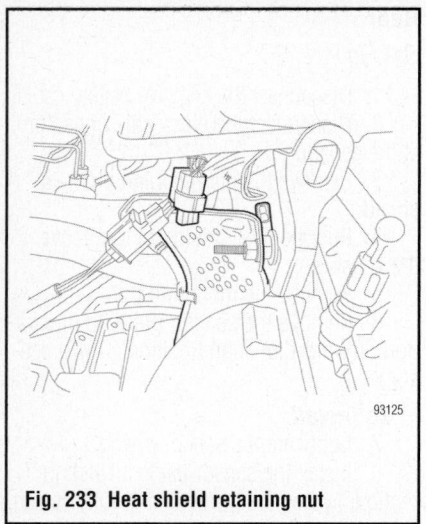

Fig. 233 Heat shield retaining nut

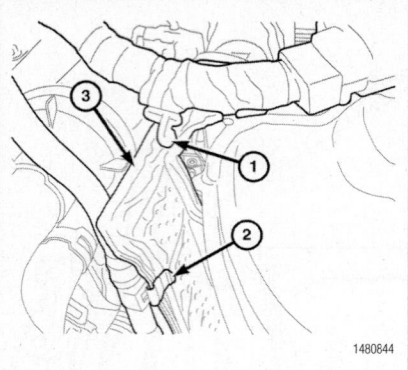

Fig. 234 Upstream O2 sensor wire harness retainer (1), Crankshaft Position (CKP) sensor wire harness retainer (2), and heat shield (3)

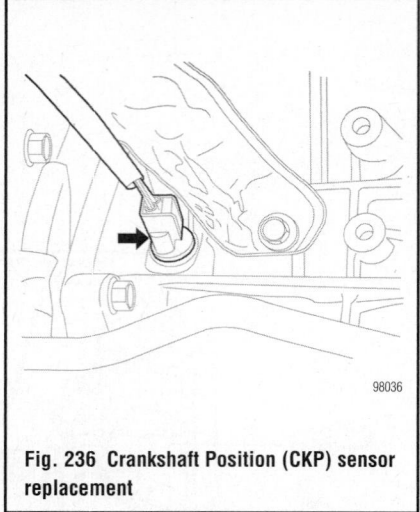

Fig. 236 Crankshaft Position (CKP) sensor replacement

9. Install the mounting bolt and tighten to 79.5 inch lbs. (9 Nm).

10. Carefully attach the electrical connector to the Camshaft Position (CMP) sensor. Feel for positive lock (click). Installation at an angle may damage the sensor pins.

11. Install the heat shield onto the mounting stud.

12. Install the heat shield retaining nut and tighten it.

13. Connect the negative battery cable.

CRANKSHAFT POSITION (CKP) SENSOR

LOCATION

The Crankshaft Position (CKP) sensor mounts to the rear of the engine block near the transmission.

REMOVAL & INSTALLATION

See Figures 234 through 236.

1. Remove the engine cover by pulling upward (see image in Camshaft and Valve Lifters Removal).

2. Disconnect and isolate the negative battery cable.

3. Remove the air cleaner body. Refer to Engine Air Cleaner.

4. Disengage the upstream O2 sensor wire harness retainer (1) and Crankshaft Position (CKP) sensor wire harness retainer (2) from the heat shield (3).

5. Remove one nut (1) and two heat shield retaining bolts (2).

6. Remove the heat shield (3).

7. Remove the Crankshaft Position (CKP) sensor mounting bolt.

8. Remove the sensor with the wire harness attached.

9. Unlock and disconnect the electrical

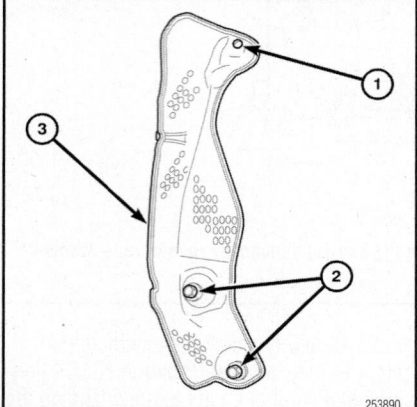

Fig. 235 Heat shield nut (1), two heat shield retaining bolts (2), and heat shield (3)

connector from the Crankshaft Position (CKP) sensor.

To install:

10. Check the O-ring for damage and lubricate the O-ring with engine oil before installing the sensor.

11. Using a twisting motion, install the Crankshaft Position (CKP) sensor.

12. Install the Crankshaft Position (CKP) sensor bolt. Tighten the bolt to 80 inch lbs. (9 Nm).

13. Connect and lock the electrical connector to the Crankshaft Position (CKP) sensor.

14. Install the heat shield with one nut and two heat shield retaining bolts.

15. Install the upstream O2 sensor wire harness retainer and the Crankshaft Position (CKP) sensor wire harness retainer to the heat shield (3).

16. Install the air cleaner body. Refer to Engine Air Cleaner Installation.

17. Connect the negative battery cable.

18. Install the engine cover.

ENGINE COOLANT TEMPERATURE (ECT) SENSOR

LOCATION

There are two Engine Coolant Temperature sensors (ETC). One ETC is located in the coolant adapter and one threads into the cylinder block.

REMOVAL & INSTALLATION

Cylinder Block Mounted

See Figure 237.

1. Disconnect the negative battery cable.

2. Partially drain the cooling system below the level of the ECT sensor.

3. Disconnect the ECT sensor electrical connector.

4. Remove the ECT sensor.

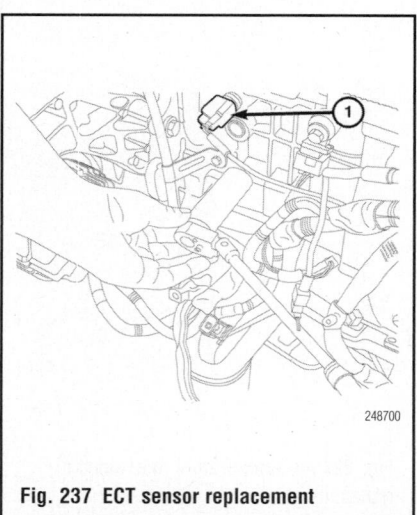

Fig. 237 ECT sensor replacement

To install:

➡ **New sensors have sealant applied to the threads.**

5. Install the ECT sensor. Tighten the sensor to 168 inch lbs. (19 Nm).
6. Reconnect the ECT sensor electrical connector.
7. Fill the cooling system (Refer to the Engine Cooling section).
8. Connect the negative battery cable.

Coolant Adapter Mounted

See Figure 238.

1. Disconnect the negative battery cable.
2. Partially drain the cooling system below the level of the ECT sensor.
3. Disconnect the ECT sensor electrical connector.
4. Remove the ECT sensor (1). 2011 model instructions: Remove the ECT sensor by pressing the locking tab down and turning the sensor counterclockwise.

To install:

New sensors have sealant applied to the threads.

5. Install the ECT sensor. Make sure the coolant sensor is locked in place.
6. Reconnect the ECT sensor electrical connector.
7. Fill the cooling system (Refer to the Engine Cooling section).
8. Connect the negative battery cable.

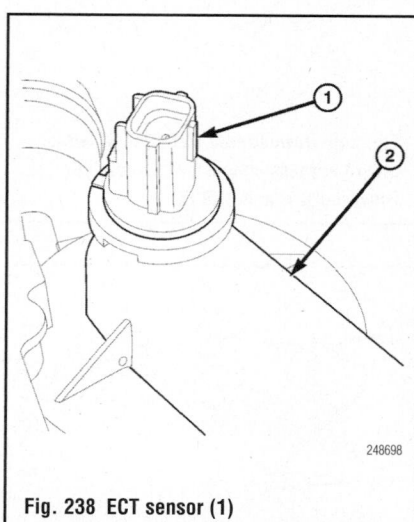

Fig. 238 ECT sensor (1)

KNOCK SENSOR (KS)

LOCATION

See Figure 239.

The knock sensor bolts into the side of the cylinder block in front of the starter under the intake manifold.

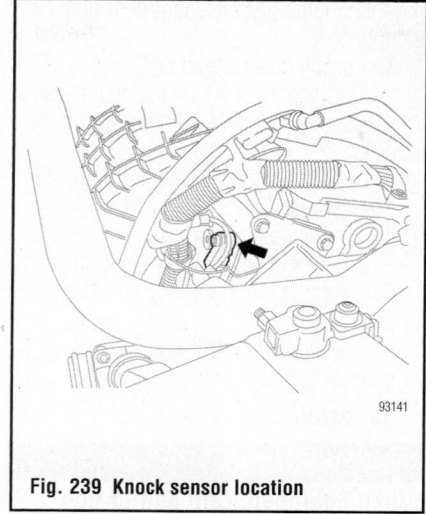

Fig. 239 Knock sensor location

REMOVAL & INSTALLATION

See Figure 240.

1. Disconnect the negative battery cable.
2. Remove the bolt holding the knock sensor.
3. Remove the sensor with the electrical connector attached.
4. Disconnect the electrical connector from the knock sensor.
5. Remove the knock sensor.

To install:

6. Attach the electrical connector to the knock sensor.
7. Install the knock sensor. Tighten the knock sensor bolt to 195 inch lbs. (22 Nm). Over or under tightening affects knock sensor performance, possibly causing improper spark control.
8. Connect the negative battery cable.

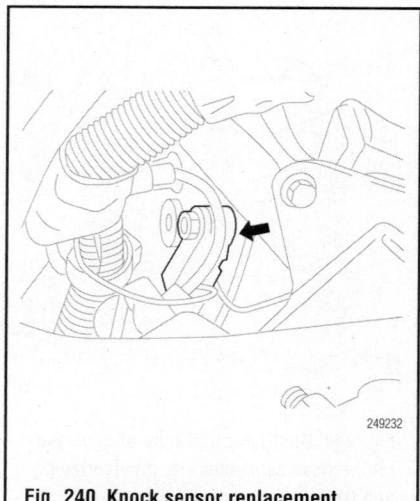

Fig. 240 Knock sensor replacement

MANIFOLD ABSOLUTE PRESSURE (MAP) SENSOR

LOCATION

The MAP sensor mounts to the intake manifold.

REMOVAL & INSTALLATION

See Figures 241 and 242.

1. Disconnect the negative battery cable.
2. Disconnect the electrical connector from the manifold absolute pressure (MAP) sensor.
3. Remove the screw from the MAP sensor.
4. Remove the MAP sensor.

To install:

5. Install the manifold absolute pressure (MAP) sensor to the intake manifold.
6. Tighten the screw to 40 inch lbs. (4.5 Nm).

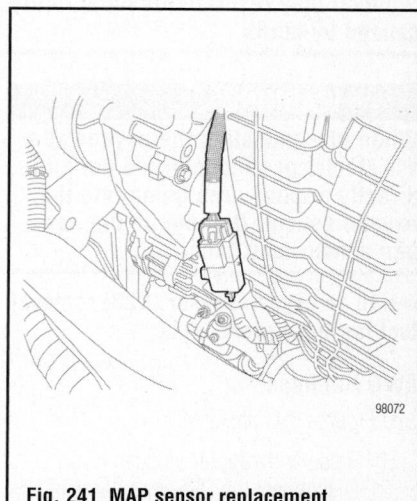

Fig. 241 MAP sensor replacement

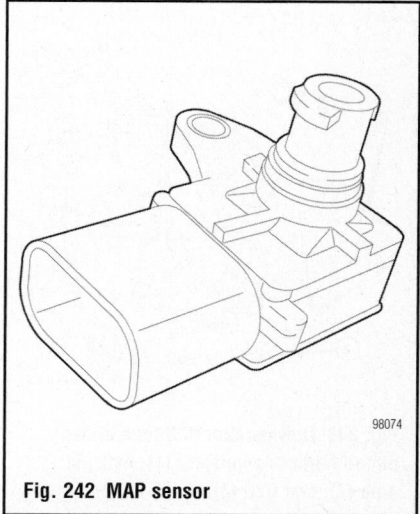

Fig. 242 MAP sensor

7. Connect the electrical connector to the sensor.

8. Connect the negative battery cable.

OXYGEN SENSOR (O2S)

LOCATION

The upstream oxygen sensor threads into the outlet flange of the exhaust manifold. The downstream heated oxygen sensor threads into the emission system depending on the emission package.

REMOVAL & INSTALLATION

> ⁂ **CAUTION**
>
> **The exhaust manifold, exhaust pipes, and catalytic converter(s) become very hot during engine operation. Allow the engine to cool before removing the oxygen sensor. Failure to allow the engine to cool before removal may result in personal injury caused by burns.**

> ⁂ **WARNING**
>
> **When disconnecting the oxygen sensor electrical connector, do not pull directly on the wires going into the oxygen sensor. Damage to the oxygen sensor may occur.**

➡ **Use an oxygen sensor (O2S) removal tool for these procedures.**

AWD Vehicles

See Figures 243 and 244.

1. Raise and support vehicle.
2. Disconnect the O2S wire harness mounting clips from the engine or body, if equipped.

3. For the downstream O2S:
   a. Disconnect the O2S pigtail harness connector (1) from the engine wiring harness.
   b. Remove the O2S (3) from the exhaust pipe (2).
4. For the upstream O2S:
   a. Disconnect the O2S pigtail harness connector (1) from the engine wiring harness.
   b. Remove the O2S (3) from the maniverter (2).

To install:

> ⁂ **WARNING**
>
> **When Equipped: Clip and/or bolt back the oxygen sensor (O2S) pigtail harnesses to their original positions on the engine or body to prevent mechanical damage to the wiring.**

➡ **The threads of new oxygen sensors are factory coated with anti-seize compound to aid in removal. DO NOT add any additional anti-seize compound to the threads of a new O2S.**

5. For the downstream O2S: Install the O2 sensor to the exhaust pipe. Tighten to 30 ft. lbs. (41 Nm).
6. For the upstream O2S: Install the O2 sensor to the maniverter. Tighten to 30 ft. lbs. (41 Nm).
7. Connect the O2 sensor pigtail harness connector to the engine wiring harness.
8. Connect the O2S wire harness mounting clips to the engine or body, if equipped.

FWD Vehicles

See Figures 245 and 246.

1. Raise and support vehicle.
2. Disconnect the O2S wire harness mounting clips from the engine or body, if equipped.
3. Disconnect the O2S pigtail harness connector (1) from the engine wiring harness.
4. Remove the O2S (3) from the catalytic converter (2).

To install:

> ⁂ **WARNING**
>
> **When Equipped: Clip and/or bolt back the oxygen sensor (O2S) pigtail harnesses to their original positions on the engine or body to prevent mechanical damage to the wiring.**

➡ **The threads of new oxygen sensors are factory coated with anti-seize com-**

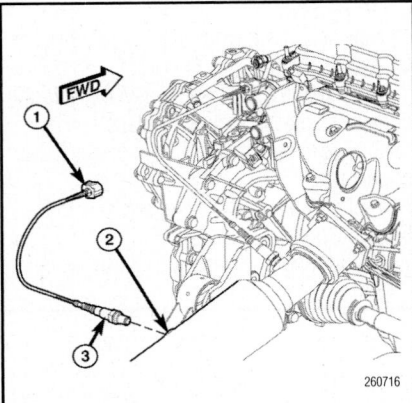

Fig. 245 Downstream O2S (one of two): pigtail harness connector (1), catalytic converter (2), and O2S (3)

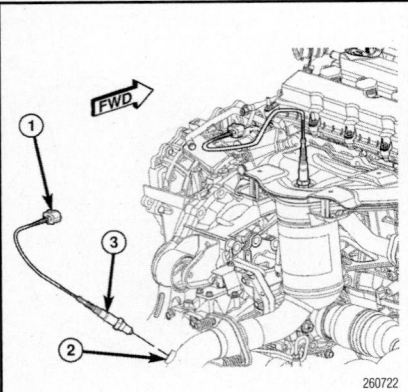

Fig. 243 Downstream O2S (one of two): pigtail harness connector (1), exhaust pipe (2), and O2S (3)

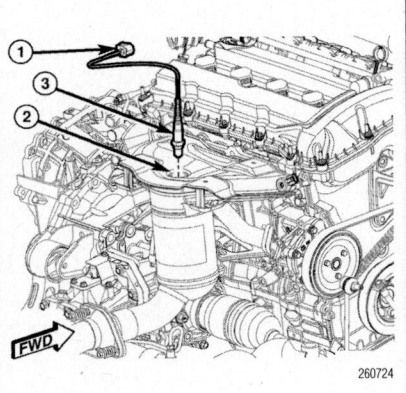

Fig. 244 Upstream O2S (one of one): pigtail harness connector (1), maniverter (2), and O2S (3)

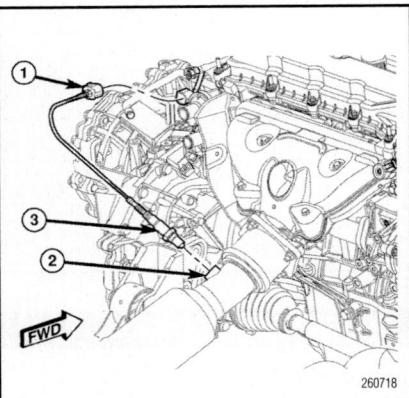

Fig. 246 Upstream O2S (one of one): pigtail harness connector (1), exhaust pipe (2), and O2S (3)

pound to aid in removal. **DO NOT add any additional anti-seize compound to the threads of a new O2S.**

5. For the downstream O2S: Install the O2 sensor to the catalytic converter. Tighten to 30 ft. lbs. (41 Nm).

6. For the upstream O2S: Install the O2 sensor to the exhaust pipe. Tighten to 30 ft. lbs. (41 Nm).

7. Connect the O2 sensor pigtail harness connector to the engine wiring harness.

8. Connect the O2S wire harness mounting clips to the engine or body, if equipped.

POWERTRAIN CONTROL MODULE (PCM)

LOCATION

For 2010 models: In the engine compartment near the air cleaner (see Engine Performance Component Locations).

For 2011 models: In the left side of engine compartment, attached to the top of the air cleaner housing (see Engine Performance Component Locations).

REMOVAL & INSTALLATION

2010 Models

See Figures 247 through 249.

➡ **The appropriate scan tool is required for PCM replacement.**

To avoid a possible voltage spike damage to PCM, turn the ignition key off, and disconnect the negative battery cable before unplugging PCM connectors.

1. Disconnect the negative battery cable.

2. Unlock and disconnect the electrical connectors from the PCM.

3. Remove the air cleaner box.
4. Remove the three mounting bolts.
5. Tip the module out and remove it from the bracket.

To install:

➡ **Use the scan tool to reprogram the new powertrain control module (PCM) with the vehicle's original identification number (VIN) and the vehicle's original mileage. If this step is not done, a diagnostic trouble code (DTC) may be set.**

6. Tip the module into the bracket.
7. Install the three mounting bolts and tighten them to 80 inch lbs. (9 Nm) torque.
8. Check the pins in the electrical connectors for damage. Repair as necessary.
9. Connect the electrical connectors and lock them.
10. Install the air cleaner box.
11. Connect the negative battery cable.

Fig. 248 Remove the three mounting bolts

12. Use the scan tool to reprogram the new PCM with the vehicle's original Identification Number (VIN) and original vehicle mileage.

2011 Models

See Figure 250.

To avoid a possible voltage spike damage to PCM, turn the ignition key off, and disconnect the negative battery cable before unplugging PCM connectors.

1. Disconnect and isolate the negative battery cable.
2. Unlock and disconnect the electrical connectors (2) from the PCM (4).
3. Remove the three mounting bolts (3) and ground wire (1).
4. Remove the PCM (4) from the air cleaner body cover.

To install:

➡ **Use the scan tool to reprogram the new powertrain control module (PCM) with the vehicle's original identification number (VIN) and the vehicle's original mileage. If this step is not done, a diagnostic trouble code (DTC) may be set.**

5. Position the PCM on the air cleaner body cover.
6. Install the three mounting bolts with the ground wire and tighten them to 89 inch lbs. (10 Nm).
7. Check the pins in the electrical connectors for damage. Repair as necessary.
8. Connect and lock the electrical connectors.
9. Connect the negative battery cable and tighten the nut to 45 inch lbs. (5 Nm).
10. Use the scan tool to reprogram the new PCM with the vehicle's original Identifi-

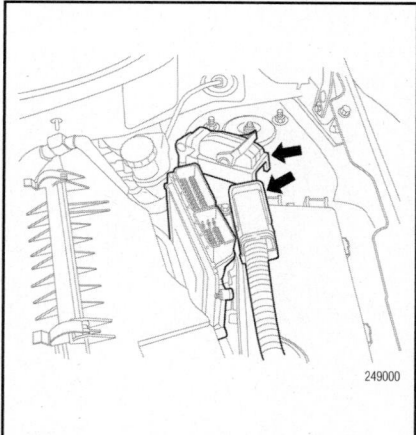

Fig. 247 Unlock and disconnect the electrical connectors from the PCM

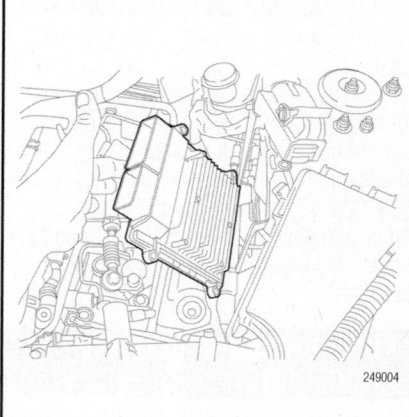

Fig. 249 Tip the module out and remove it from the bracket

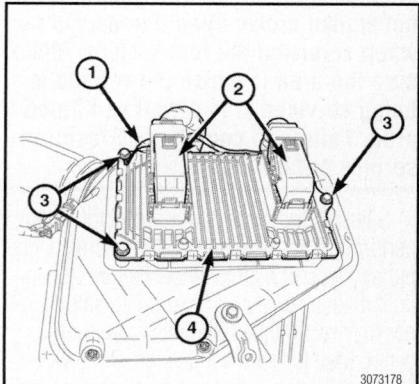

Fig. 250 Electrical connectors (2), PCM (4), the three mounting bolts (3), and the ground wire (1)

cation Number (VIN) and original vehicle mileage.

THROTTLE POSITION SENSOR (TPS)

LOCATION

The throttle body mounts to the intake manifold. The throttle position sensor and throttle actuating DC motor are integral to the throttle body.

The Throttle Position Sensor (TPS) is not serviceable as a standalone part. The TPS is an integral part of the throttle body. If the TPS requires replacement, replace the throttle body assembly. Refer to Fuel Systems for Throttle Body replacement.

VEHICLE SPEED SENSOR (VSS)

LOCATION

The Vehicle Speed Sensor (VSS) is a Hall Effect sensor mounted above the transaxle differential.

REMOVAL & INSTALLATION

1. Open the hood.
2. Remove the air cleaner housing. (Refer Engine Air Cleaner Removal).
3. Disconnect the speed sensor connector.

✳✳ WARNING

Clean the area around the speed sensor before removing it to prevent dirt from entering the transaxle during speed sensor removal.

4. Remove the speed sensor retaining bolt.
5. Remove the speed sensor from the transaxle.

To install:

6. Using a NEW O-ring, install the speed sensor to the transaxle.
7. Install the bolt and tighten it to 60 inch lbs. (7 Nm).
8. Connect the speed sensor connector.
9. Install the air cleaner housing.

FUEL
GASOLINE FUEL INJECTION SYSTEM

FUEL SYSTEM SERVICE PRECAUTIONS

✳✳ CAUTION

There is a risk of injury to eyes and skin from contact with fuel. Wear protective clothing and eye protection. There is a risk of poisoning from inhaling and swallowing fuel. Pour fuel only into appropriately marked and approved containers. Failure to follow these instructions may result in possible serious or fatal injury.

✳✳ CAUTION

The fuel system is under constant high pressure even with the engine OFF. Until the fuel pressure has been properly released from the system, do not attempt to open the fuel system. Do not smoke or use open flames/sparks when servicing the fuel system. Make sure the area in which the vehicle is being serviced is in a well ventilated area. Failure to comply may result in serious or fatal injury.

Safety is the most important factor when performing not only fuel system maintenance but any type of maintenance. Failure to conduct maintenance and repairs in a safe manner may result in serious personal injury or death. Maintenance and testing of the vehicle's fuel system components can be accomplished safely and effectively by adhering to the following rules and guidelines.

• To avoid the possibility of fire and personal injury, always disconnect the negative battery cable unless the repair or test procedure requires that battery voltage be applied.

• Always relieve the fuel system pressure prior to disconnecting any fuel system component (injector, fuel rail, pressure regulator, etc.), fitting or fuel line connection. Exercise extreme caution whenever relieving fuel system pressure to avoid exposing skin, face and eyes to fuel spray. Please be advised that fuel under pressure may penetrate the skin or any part of the body that it contacts.

• Always place a shop towel or cloth around the fitting or connection prior to loosening to absorb any excess fuel due to spillage. Ensure that all fuel spillage (should it occur) is quickly removed from engine surfaces. Ensure that all fuel soaked cloths or towels are deposited into a suitable waste container.

• Always keep a dry chemical (Class B) fire extinguisher near the work area.

• Do not allow fuel spray or fuel vapors to come into contact with a spark or open flame.

• Always use a back-up wrench when loosening and tightening fuel line connection fittings. This will prevent unnecessary stress and torsion to fuel line piping.

• Always replace worn fuel fitting O-rings with new ones. Do not substitute fuel hose or an equivalent where fuel pipe is installed.

FUEL PRESSURE RELEASE PROCEDURE

See Figures 251 through 253.

1. Remove the lower rear seat cushion.
2. Remove the fuel pump module cover.

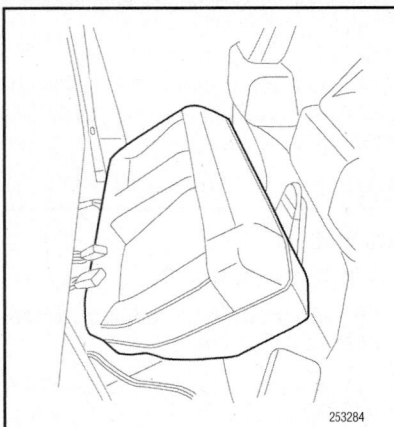

Fig. 251 Remove the lower rear seat cushion

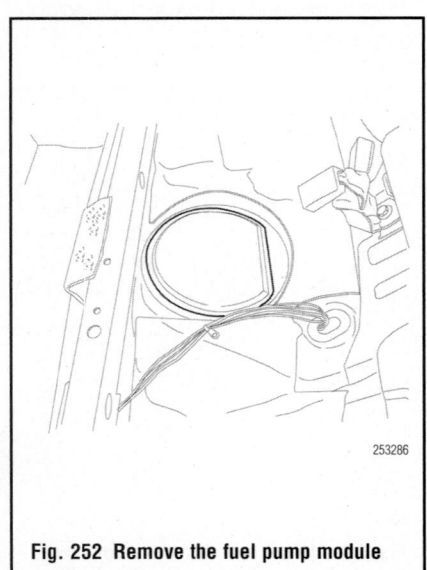

Fig. 252 Remove the fuel pump module cover

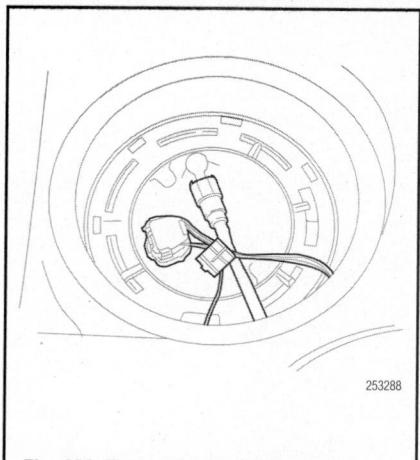

Fig. 253 Fuel pump module electrical connector

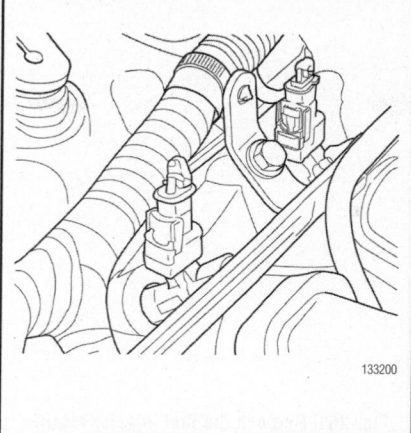

Fig. 254 Fuel injector electrical connectors

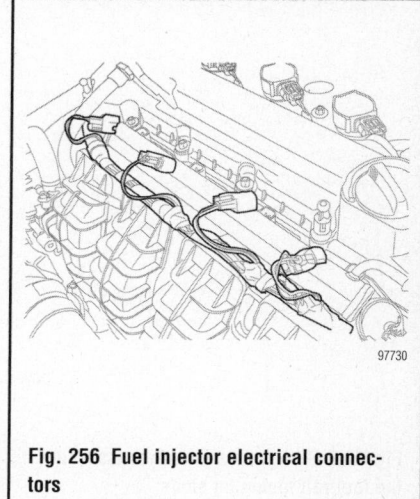

Fig. 256 Fuel injector electrical connectors

3. Disconnect the electrical connector for the fuel pump module.

4. Start and run engine until it stalls.

5. Attempt restarting engine until it will no longer run.

6. Turn the ignition key to the OFF position.

7. Disconnect the negative battery cable.

8. One or more Diagnostic Trouble Codes (DTCs) may have been stored in PCM memory. Use a scan tool to erase a DTC.

FUEL FILTER

REMOVAL & INSTALLATION

A fuel filter is integral to the main fuel pump module located in the fuel tank. If the electric fuel pump, fuel pressure regulator or fuel filter require service, the fuel pump module must be replaced as an assembly.

AWD vehicles are also equipped with a second fuel pump module. This auxiliary fuel pump module does not contain a fuel filter. If any component of the auxiliary fuel pump module requires service, the auxiliary fuel pump module must be replaced as an assembly.

Refer to Fuel Pump Module.

FUEL INJECTORS

CONNECTOR PROCEDURE

See Figures 254 and 255.

1. Disconnect the electrical connectors at the fuel injectors.

2. To remove the connector pull the red colored slider away from the injector (1). While pulling the slider, depress the tab (2) and remove the connector (3) from the injector. The factory fuel injection wiring harness is numerically tagged (INJ 1, INJ 2,

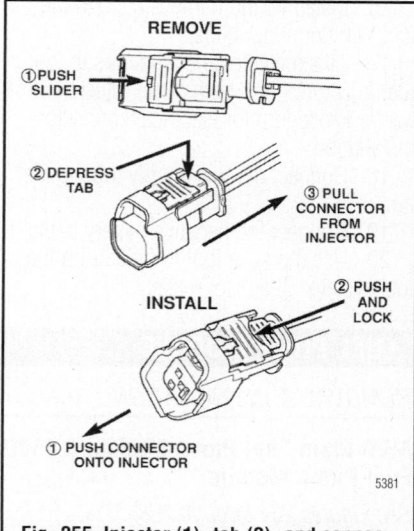

Fig. 255 Injector (1), tab (2), and connector (3)

etc.) for injector position identification. If the harness is not tagged, make note of the wiring location before removal.

REMOVAL & INSTALLATION

See Figures 256 through 261.

❊❊ CAUTION

Refer to Fuel System Service Precautions.

1. Release the fuel pressure, refer to the Fuel Pressure Release Procedure.

2. Disconnect the negative battery cable.

3. Disconnect the electrical connectors from the fuel injectors.

4. Remove the fuel line from the fuel rail.

5. Remove the wire harness from the fuel rail mounting studs.

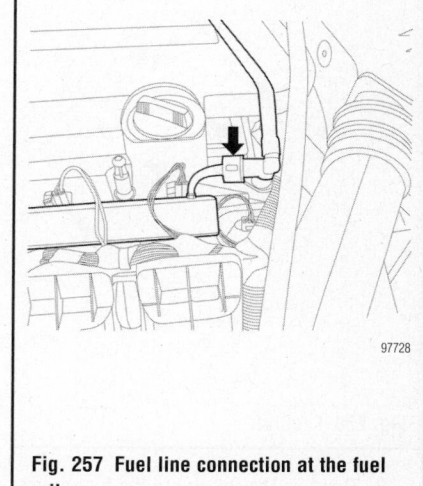

Fig. 257 Fuel line connection at the fuel rail.

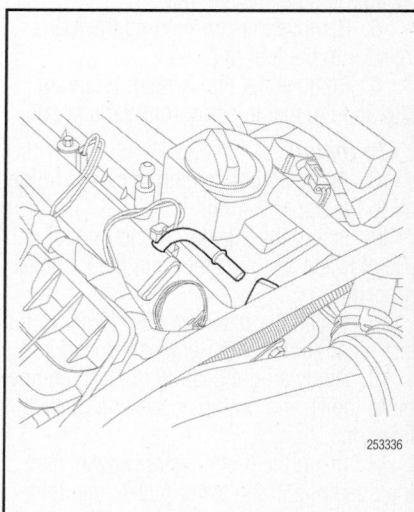

Fig. 258 Remove the fuel line from the fuel rail

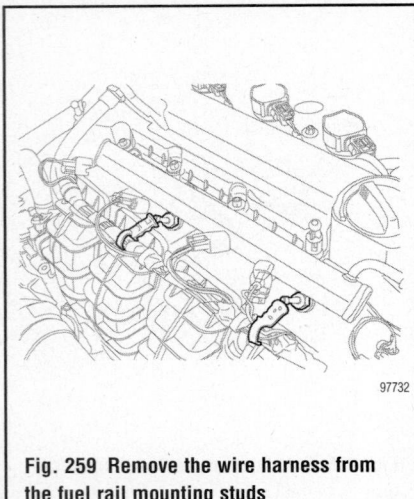

Fig. 259 Remove the wire harness from the fuel rail mounting studs

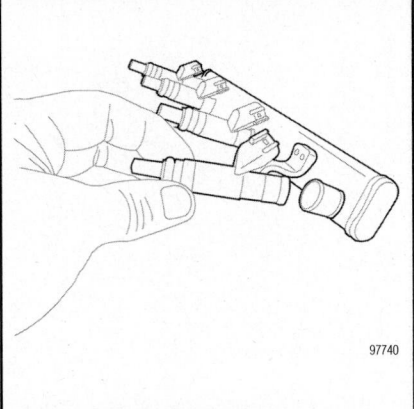

Fig. 261 Remove the fuel injector retaining clip and the fuel injector from the fuel rail

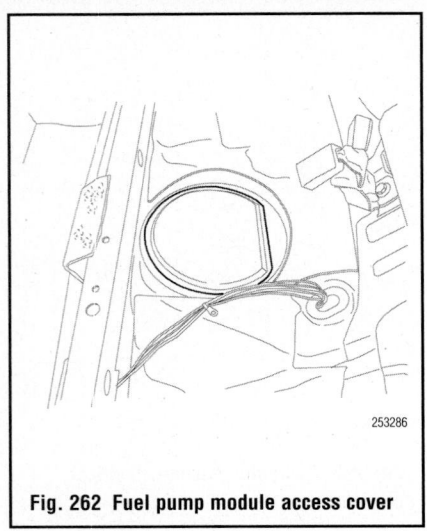

Fig. 262 Fuel pump module access cover

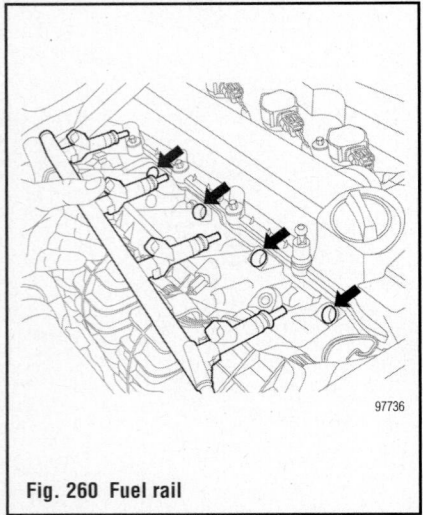

Fig. 260 Fuel rail

6. Remove the 2 bolts to the fuel rail at the lower manifold.

7. Remove the fuel rail.

8. Remove the clip holding the fuel injector to the fuel rail.

9. Remove the fuel injector retaining clip and the fuel injector from the fuel rail.

To install:

10. Apply a light coating of clean engine oil to the upper O-ring.

11. Install the injector in cup on fuel rail. (Refer to the last illustration in the Removal procedure.)

12. Install the retaining clip. (Refer to the last illustration in the Removal procedure.)

13. Apply a light coating of clean engine oil to the O-ring on the nozzle end of each injector.

14. Insert the fuel injector nozzles into the openings in the lower intake manifold. Seat the injectors in place.

15. Tighten the fuel rail mounting screws to 20 ft. lbs. (27 Nm).

16. Install wiring harness clips to the fuel rail mounting studs.

17. Attach electrical connectors to the fuel injectors, refer to the Fuel Injector Connector Procedure for electrical connector installation.

18. Connect the fuel supply tube to the fuel rail.

19. Connect the negative battery cable.

20. Use the scan tool to pressurize the fuel system. Check for leaks.

FUEL PUMP MODULE

REMOVAL & INSTALLATION

AWD Main Fuel Pump Module & FWD Fuel Pump Module

See Figures 262 through 268.

> ✻✻ **CAUTION**
>
> **Refer to Fuel System Service Precautions.**

1. Perform the fuel system pressure release procedure. (Refer to Fuel System Pressure Release Procedure.)

2. Remove the negative battery cable.

3. Remove the rear seat.

4. Remove the fuel pump module access cover.

5. Disconnect the electrical connector (2) from the fuel pump module (1).

6. Disconnect the fuel line (3) to the fuel pump module.

➡**Prior to removing the fuel pump module, use compressed air to remove any accumulated dirt and debris from around the fuel tank opening.**

7. Position the lock-ring remover/installer 9340 into the notches on the outside edge of the lock-ring.

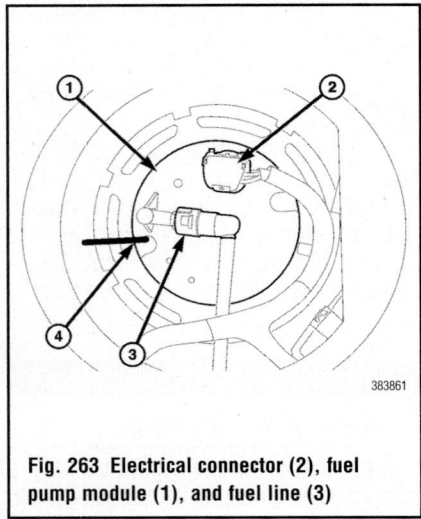

Fig. 263 Electrical connector (2), fuel pump module (1), and fuel line (3)

8. Install a ½ inch drive breaker bar into the lock-ring remover/installer 9340.

9. Rotate the breaker bar counterclockwise and remove the lock-ring.

➡**The fuel pump module has to be properly located in the fuel tank for the fuel level gauge to work properly.**

10. Mark the fuel pump module orientation.

> ✻✻ **CAUTION**
>
> **The fuel pump module reservoir does not empty out when the tank is drained. The fuel in the reservoir will spill out when the module is removed.**

➡**Do not spill fuel into the interior of the vehicle.**

11. Raise the fuel pump module out of the fuel tank using caution not to spill fuel inside the vehicle.

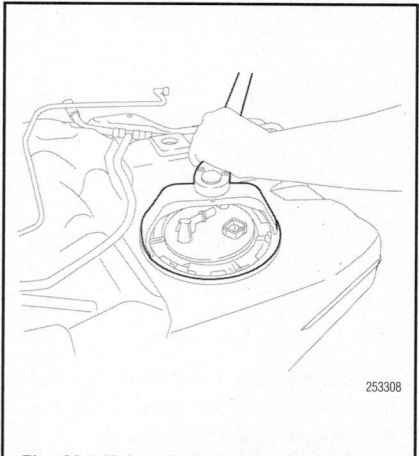

Fig. 264 Using the lock-ring remover/installer 9340

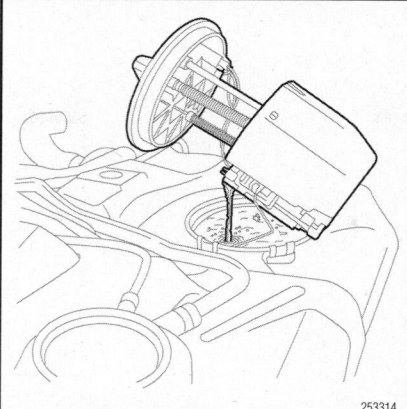

Fig. 266 Drain fuel from the fuel pump module without spilling fuel into the interior of the vehicle

Fig. 268 Remove the fuel pump module from the fuel tank using caution not to bend the float arm

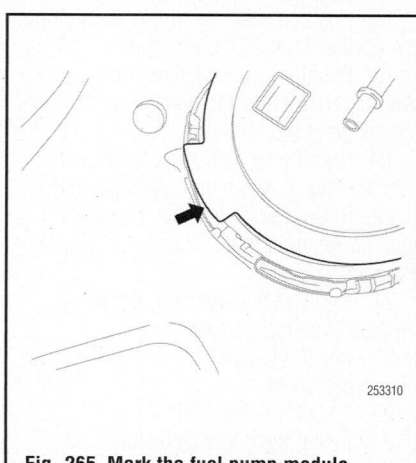

Fig. 265 Mark the fuel pump module orientation

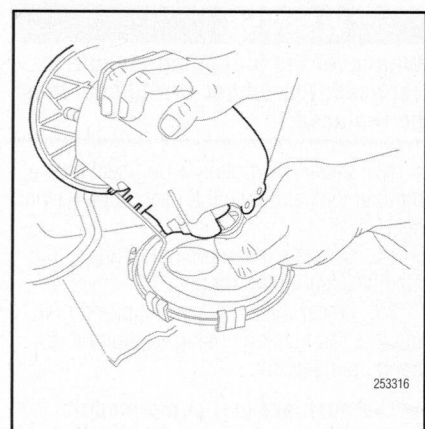

Fig. 267 Disconnect the internal fuel line from the fuel pump module—AWD models

12. AWD models: Tip the main fuel pump module and drain enough fuel from the main fuel pump module reservoir to gain access to the internal fuel line without spilling fuel into the interior of the vehicle.

13. FWD models: Tip the fuel pump module on its side and drain all fuel from the reservoir.

14. AWD only: Disconnect the internal fuel line from the fuel pump module.

15. Remove the fuel pump module from the fuel tank using caution not to bend the float arm.

16. AWD only: Tip the main fuel pump module on its side to drain all remaining fuel from the reservoir.

17. Remove and discard the rubber O-ring seal.

To install:

⁂ CAUTION

Refer to Fuel System Service Precautions.

⁂ WARNING

Whenever the fuel pump module is serviced, the rubber O-ring seal must be replaced.

18. Clean the rubber O-ring seal area of the fuel tank and install a new rubber O-ring seal.

19. AWD models: Connect the internal fuel line to the main fuel pump module.

20. Lower the fuel pump module into the fuel tank using caution not to bend the float arm.

21. The fuel pump module must be properly located in the fuel tank for the fuel level gauge to work properly.

22. Align the rubber O-ring seal and rotate the fuel pump module to the orientation marks noted during removal. This step must be performed for the fuel level gauge to work properly.

23. Position the lock-ring over top of the fuel pump module.

24. Position the lock-ring remover/installer 9340 into the notches on the outside edge of the lock-ring.

25. Install a ½ inch drive breaker bar into the lock-ring remover/installer 9340.

26. Rotate the breaker bar clockwise until all seven notches of the lock-ring have engaged.

27. Connect the fuel line to the fuel pump module.

28. Connect the electrical connector to the fuel pump module.

29. Install the fuel pump module access cover.

30. Install the rear seat.

31. Install the negative battery cable.

32. Use a scan tool to pressurize the system and check for leaks.

AWD Auxiliary Fuel Pump Module

See Figures 269 through 273.

⁂ CAUTION

Refer to Fuel System Service Precautions.

1. Perform the fuel system pressure release procedure. (Refer to Fuel System Pressure Release Procedure.)

2. Remove the negative battery cable.

3. Remove the rear seat.

4. Remove the auxiliary fuel pump module access cover. (Refer to illustration for the main fuel pump module.)

5. Disconnect the electrical connector (2) from the auxiliary fuel pump module.

➡**The auxiliary fuel pump module has to be properly located in the fuel tank for the fuel level gauge to work properly.**

6. Mark the auxiliary fuel pump module orientation (1).

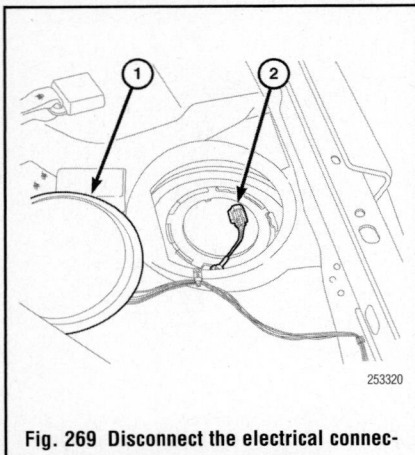

Fig. 269 Disconnect the electrical connector (2) from the auxiliary fuel pump module

➡**Prior to removing the auxiliary fuel pump module, use compressed air to remove any accumulated dirt and debris from around the fuel tank opening.**

7. Position the Fuel Tank Module Wrench 10189 into the notches on the outside edge of the lock-ring.

8. Install a ½ inch drive breaker bar into the Fuel Tank Module Wrench 10189.

9. Rotate the breaker bar counterclockwise and remove the lock-ring.

10. Raise the auxiliary fuel pump module and disconnect the internal fuel line.

11. Remove the auxiliary fuel pump module from the fuel tank.

12. Remove and discard the rubber O-ring seal.

To install:

✳✳ **CAUTION**

Refer to Fuel System Service Precautions.

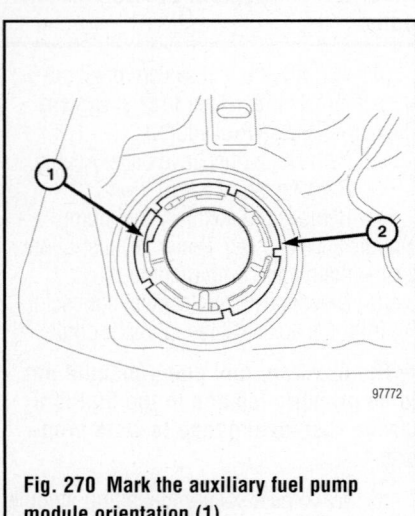

Fig. 270 Mark the auxiliary fuel pump module orientation (1)

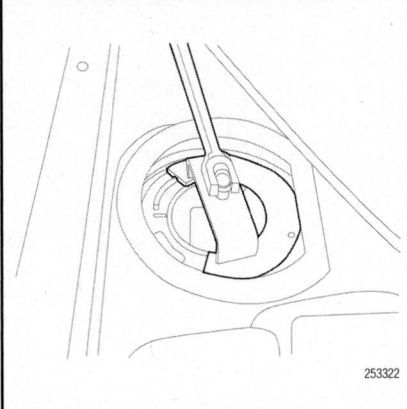

Fig. 271 Position the Fuel Tank Module Wrench 10189 into the notches on the outside edge of the lock-ring

✳✳ **WARNING**

Whenever the fuel pump module is serviced, the rubber O-ring seal must be replaced.

13. Clean the rubber O-ring seal area of the fuel tank and install a new rubber O-ring seal.

14. Connect the internal fuel line to the auxiliary fuel pump module.

15. Lower the auxiliary fuel pump module into the fuel tank using caution not to bend the float arm.

➡**The auxiliary fuel pump module must be properly located in the fuel tank for the fuel level gauge to work properly.**

16. Align the rubber O-ring seal and rotate the auxiliary fuel pump module to the orientation marks noted during removal. This step must be performed for the fuel level gauge to work properly.

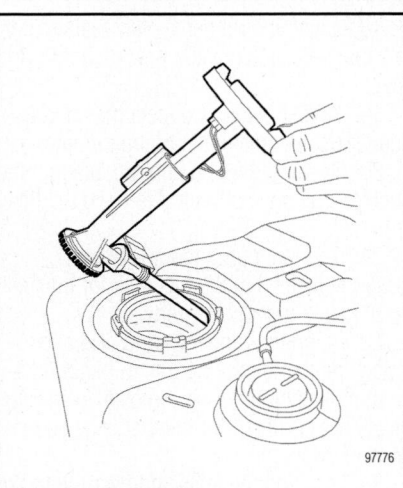

Fig. 272 Auxiliary fuel pump

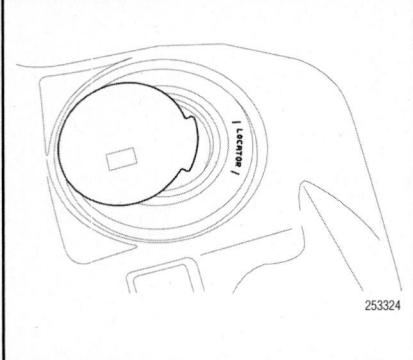

Fig. 273 Align the rubber O-ring seal and rotate the auxiliary fuel pump module to the orientation marks noted during removal. This step must be performed for the fuel level gauge to work properly

17. Position the lock-ring over the top of the auxiliary fuel pump module.

18. Position the Fuel Tank Module Wrench 10189 into the notches on the outside edge of the lock-ring.

19. Install a ½ inch drive breaker bar into the Fuel Tank Module Wrench 10189.

20. Rotate the breaker bar clockwise until all seven notches of the lock-ring have engaged.

21. Connect the auxiliary fuel pump module electrical connector.

22. Install the auxiliary fuel pump module access cover.

23. Install the rear seat.

24. Install the negative battery cable.

25. Use a scan tool to pressurize the system and check for leaks.

FUEL TANK

REMOVAL & INSTALLATION

See Figures 274 through 284.

✳✳ **CAUTION**

Refer to Fuel System Service Precautions.

1. Perform the fuel system pressure release procedure. (Refer to Fuel System Pressure Release Procedure.)

2. Remove the air cleaner lid; disconnect the inlet air temperature sensor and the makeup air hose. Refer to Engine Air Cleaner Removal.

3. Disconnect and isolate the negative battery cable.

4. Remove the rear seat cushion.

5. Remove the plastic cover. (See fuel pump module cover illustration in Fuel Pump Module—AWD Main and FWD replacement procedure.)

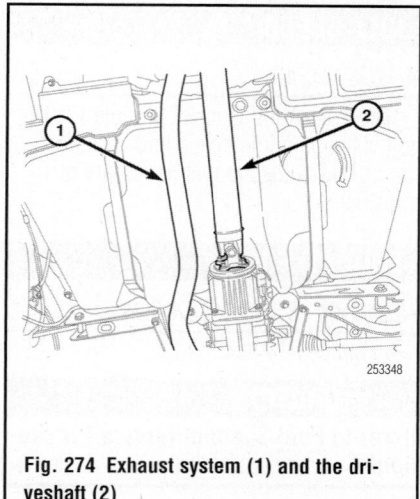

Fig. 274 Exhaust system (1) and the driveshaft (2)

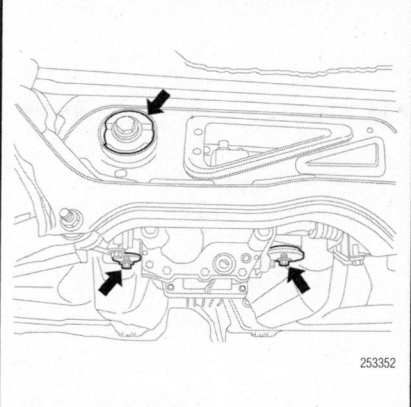

Fig. 276 Remove the 3 mounting bolts and the lower rear drive line module from the suspension crossmember

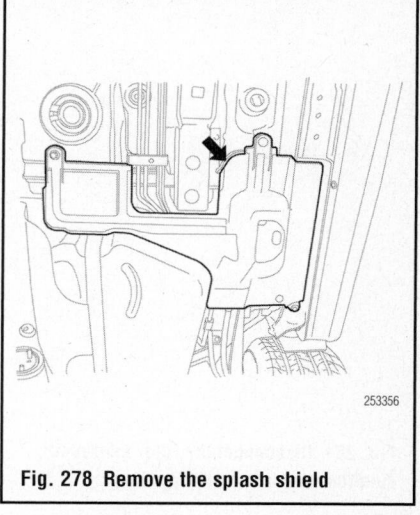

Fig. 278 Remove the splash shield

6. Clean the top of tank to remove loose dirt and debris.

7. Use the Fuel Pump Lock Ring Wrench 9340 or an equivalent to remove the left side fuel pump module lock ring. (Refer to illustration in Fuel Pump Module—AWD Main and FWD replacement procedure.)

➡**Wrap shop towels around hoses to catch any gasoline spillage.**

8. Disconnect the electrical and fuel lines from the module.

9. Drain fuel from the tank.

10. Raise and support the vehicle.

11. Remove the fuel tank skid plates, if equipped.

12. Remove the exhaust system (1).

13. For All Wheel Drive vehicles, remove the driveshaft (2).

14. Remove the stay bars.

15. For All Wheel Drive vehicles the rear driveline module must be lowered to remove the fuel tank assembly.

16. Tie the rear driveline module to the suspension crossmember.

17. Support the rear driveline module.

18. Remove the 3 mounting bolts and the lower rear drive line module from the suspension crossmember.

19. Remove the splash shield.

20. Remove the other splash shield.

21. Disconnect the vapor canister line.

22. Disconnect the filler tube recirculation vent line and purge line.

✳✳ WARNING

There may be fuel in the fill tube. Remove the hose carefully to reduce fuel splash.

23. Disconnect the fuel tank from the rubber fill hose.

24. Remove the parking brake cable mounting from the fuel tank strap.

25. Remove the parking brake cable mounting from the fuel tank strap.

26. Support the fuel tank.

27. Remove the bolts from the fuel tank straps.

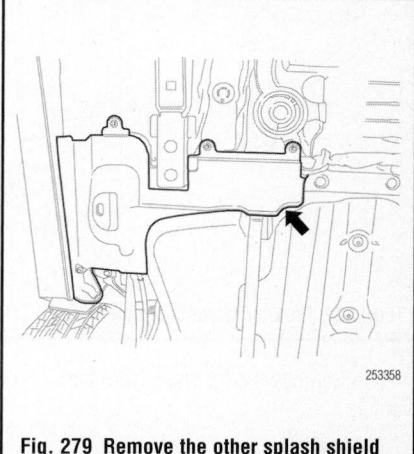

Fig. 279 Remove the other splash shield

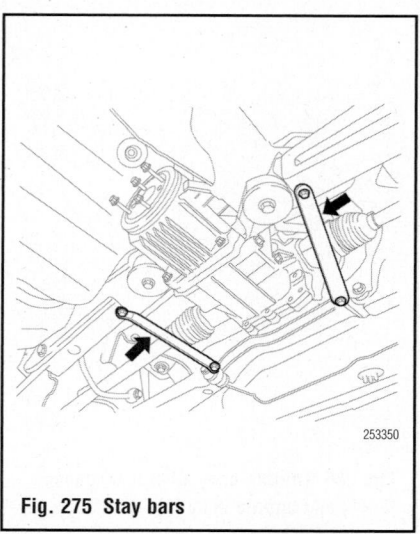

Fig. 275 Stay bars

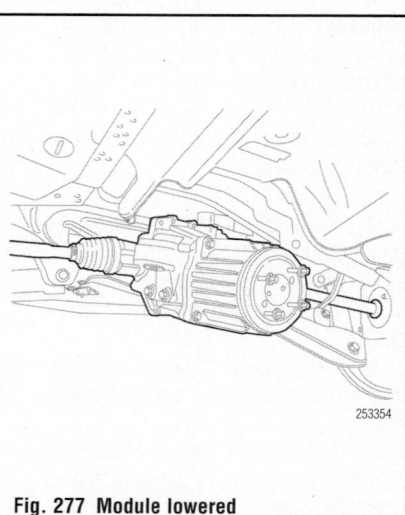

Fig. 277 Module lowered

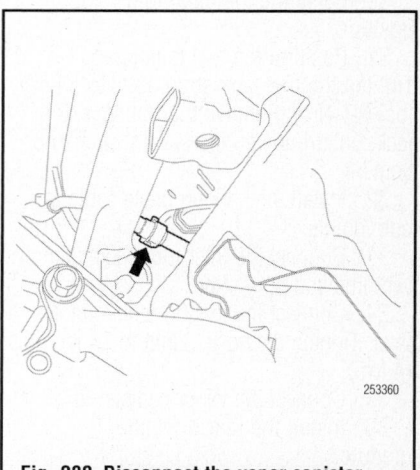

Fig. 280 Disconnect the vapor canister line

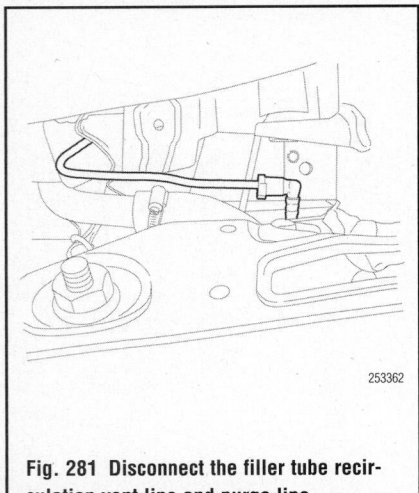

Fig. 281 Disconnect the filler tube recirculation vent line and purge line

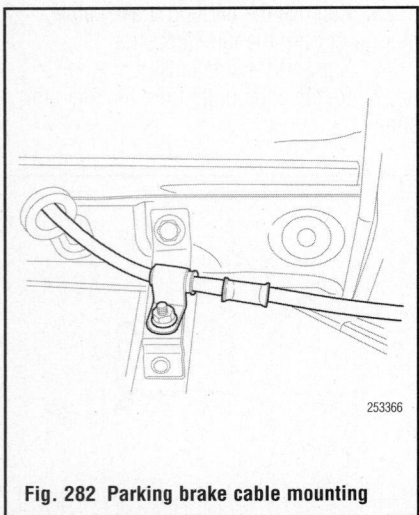

Fig. 282 Parking brake cable mounting

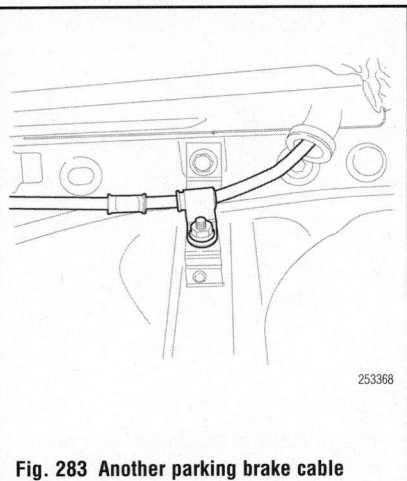

Fig. 283 Another parking brake cable mounting

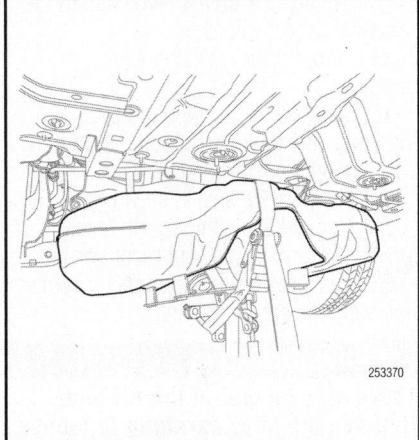

Fig. 284 Remove the fuel tank from the vehicle

28. Remove the fuel tank from the vehicle.

To install:
29. Install the fuel tank straps.
30. Raise the fuel tank into position.
31. Position the fuel tank straps. Tighten the fuel tank strap bolts to 34.5 ft. lbs. (47 Nm). Remove the transmission jack. Ensure the straps are not twisted or bent.
32. Install the parking brake cable at both points.
33. Connect the filler tube recirculation vent line and purge line.
34. Connect the fuel fill tube to tank inlet. Tighten the hose clamp to 35 inch lbs. (4 Nm).
35. Connect the vapor canister line.
36. Install the rear driveline module.
37. Install the stay bars.
38. Install both splash shields.

39. Install the exhaust system.
40. Install the driveshaft.
41. Install the fuel tank skid plates, if equipped.
42. While holding the pump module in position, install lock ring and use Fuel Pump Lock Ring Wrench 9340 or an equivalent to tighten the lock ring.
43. Connect the electrical connector and lock the connector.
44. Connect the fuel line.
45. Install the plastic cover on the fuel pump module.
46. Install rear seat cushion.
47. Reconnect the negative battery cable.
48. Install the air cleaner lid; connect the inlet air temperature sensor, and makeup air hose.
49. Fill fuel tank with clean fuel. Use a scan tool to pressurize the system and check for leaks.

IDLE SPEED

ADJUSTMENT

The Powertrain Control Module (PCM adjusts engine idle speed and ignition timing. No adjustment is necessary or possible.

THROTTLE BODY

REMOVAL & INSTALLATION
See Figures 285 through 288.

✳✳ CAUTION
Refer to Fuel System Service Precautions.

✳✳ CAUTION
DO NOT place fingers in or around the throttle body plate. If the throttle body is energized, the throttle plate could move causing personal injury. Always disconnect the negative battery cable prior to servicing the throttle body.

✳✳ WARNING
DO NOT move the throttle plate while power is connected to the throttle body. This may cause fault codes to set.

1. Disconnect and isolate the negative battery cable at the battery.
2. Remove the throttle body air intake hose.
3. Disconnect the throttle body electrical connector (1) from the throttle body (2).

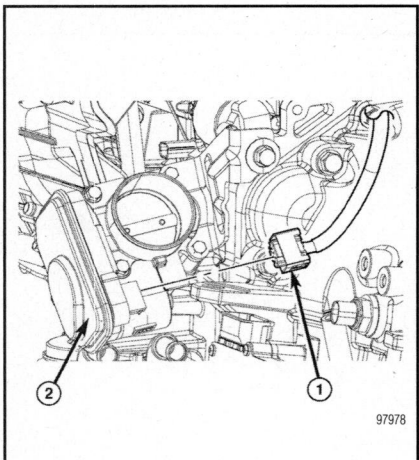

Fig. 285 Throttle body electrical connector (1) and throttle body (2)

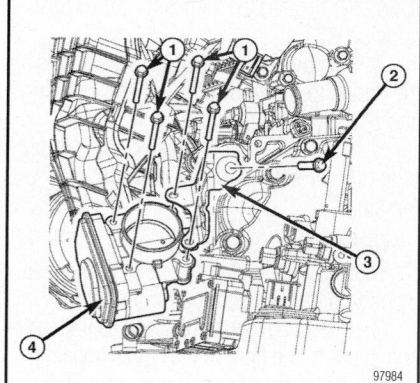

Fig. 286 Throttle body support bracket bolt (2), four bolts, throttle body bracket (3), and throttle body (4)

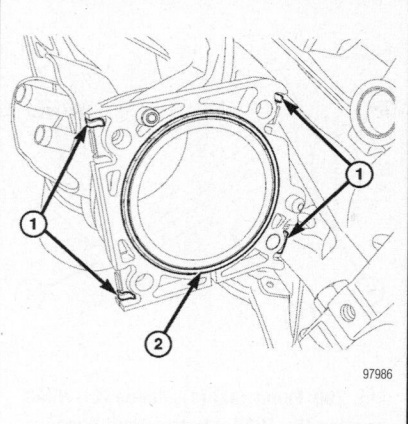

Fig. 287 Throttle body gasket (2) and four j-nuts (1)

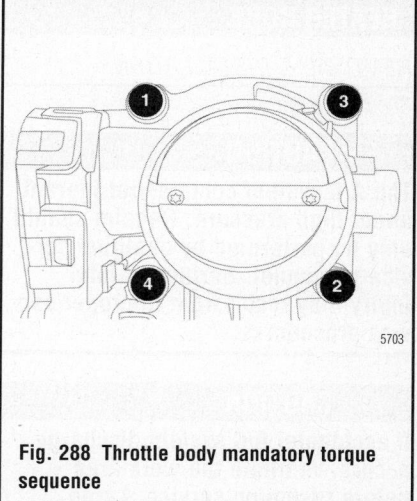

Fig. 288 Throttle body mandatory torque sequence

4. Remove throttle body support bracket bolt (2).

5. Remove the four bolts (1), the throttle body bracket (3) and the throttle body (4) from the intake manifold.

➡**Inspect the intake manifold to throttle body gasket (2) for damage. Inspect the j-nuts for damage or excessive wear. Replace as necessary.**

6. Inspect the four j-nuts (1) for damage or excessive wear; remove if necessary.

7. Inspect the intake manifold to throttle body gasket (2) for damage; remove if necessary.

To install:

8. Install a new intake manifold to the throttle body gasket, if replacement was necessary.

9. Install four new four j-nuts, if replacement was necessary.

✳✳ WARNING

DO NOT OVER TORQUE. Over tightening can damage the throttle body, gaskets, bolts and/or the intake manifold.

10. Install the throttle body to the intake manifold.

11. Install the throttle body support bracket and bolt and tighten the bracket bolt to 18 ft. lbs. (25 Nm).

12. Install the four bolts (1) and Hand-tighten.

✳✳ WARNING

The throttle body must be torqued in a mandatory torque sequence. Tighten in a criss-cross pattern to specification.

13. Tighten the bolts in a mandatory torque criss - cross pattern sequence to 65 inch lbs. (7.5 Nm).

14. Connect the electrical connector to the throttle body.

15. Install the clean air hose and tighten the clamps to 35 inch lbs. (4 Nm).

16. Connect the negative battery cable and tighten the nut to 45 inch lbs. (5 Nm).

17. Use a scan tool and clear all fault codes then perform the ETC RELEARN function.

HEATING & AIR CONDITIONING SYSTEM

BLOWER MOTOR

REMOVAL & INSTALLATION

See Figure 289.

➡**The blower motor is located on the bottom of the passenger side of the HVAC housing. The blower motor can be removed from the vehicle without having to remove the HVAC housing.**

1. Disconnect and isolate the negative battery cable.

2. If equipped, remove the silencer from below the passenger side of the instrument panel.

3. From underneath the instrument panel, disengage the connector lock and disconnect the instrument panel wire harness connector (1) from the blower motor (2).

4. Remove the three screws (3) that secure the blower motor and the wire lead bracket (4) (if equipped) to the bottom of the HVAC housing (5) and remove the blower motor.

To install:

5. Position the blower motor into the bottom of the HVAC housing.

6. Install the three screws that secure the blower motor and the wire lead bracket (if equipped) to the HVAC housing. Tighten the screws to 10 inch lbs. (1.2 Nm).

7. Connect the instrument panel wire harness connector to the blower motor and engage the connector lock.

8. If equipped, install the silencer below the passenger side of the instrument panel.

9. Reconnect the negative battery cable.

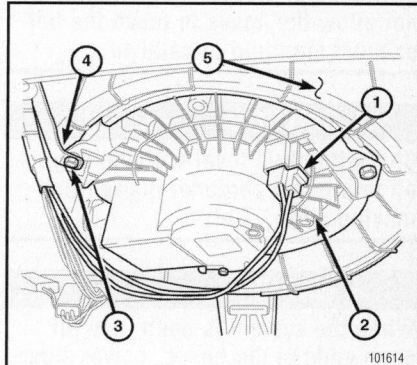

Fig. 289 Instrument panel wire harness connector (1), blower motor (2), three screws (3) that secure the blower motor, the wire lead bracket (4; if equipped), and the HVAC housing (5)

HEATER CORE

REMOVAL & INSTALLATION

See Figure 290.

> ※※ **CAUTION**
>
> The A/C system contains refrigerant under high pressure. Repairs should only be performed by qualified service personnel. Serious or fatal injury may result from improper service procedures.

> ※※ **CAUTION**
>
> If accidental A/C system discharge occurs, ventilate the work area before resuming service. Large amounts of refrigerant released in a closed work area will displace the oxygen and cause suffocation and serious or fatal injury.

➡ The HVAC housing assembly must be removed from vehicle for service of the heater core.

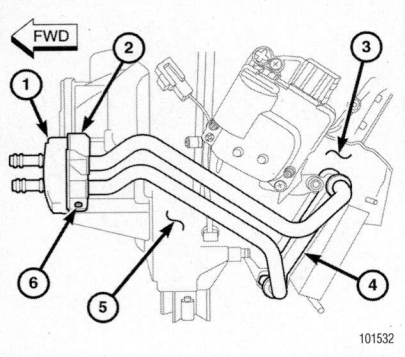

Fig. 290 Foam seal (1), flange (2), HVAC housing (5), HVAC housing front flange screw (6), heater core (4), and air distribution housing (3)

1. Remove the HVAC housing assembly and place it on a workbench.
2. Remove the left side front floor duct.

➡ If the foam seal for the flange is deformed or damaged, it must be replaced.

3. Remove the foam seal (1) from the flange (2) located on the front of the HVAC housing (5).
4. Remove the screw (6) that secures the flange to the front of the HVAC housing and remove the flange.
5. Carefully pull the heater core (4) out of the driver side of the air distribution housing (3).

To install:

6. Carefully install the heater core into the side of the air distribution housing.
7. Install the flange that secures the heater core tubes to the front of the HVAC housing.
8. Install the screw that secures the flange to the HVAC housing. Tighten the screw to 10 inch lbs. (1.2 Nm).

➡ If the foam seal for the flange is deformed or damaged, it must be replaced.

9. Install the foam seal onto the flange.
10. Install the left side front floor duct.

➡ If the heater core is being replaced, flush the cooling system (Refer to Engine Cooling.)

11. Install the HVAC housing assembly.

STEERING

POWER STEERING GEAR

REMOVAL & INSTALLATION

See Figures 291 through 299.

> ※※ **CAUTION**
>
> Power steering fluid, engine parts, and the exhaust system may be extremely hot if the engine has been running. Do not start the engine with any loose or disconnected hoses. Do not allow the hoses to touch the hot exhaust manifold or catalyst.

> ※※ **CAUTION**
>
> Check the fluid level with the engine off to prevent personal injury from moving parts.

> ※※ **WARNING**
>
> When the system is open, cap all open ends of the hoses, power steering pump fittings or power steering gear ports to prevent entry of foreign material into the components.

1. Siphon out as much power steering fluid as possible from the pump.
2. Reposition the floor carpeting to access the intermediate shaft coupling at the base of the column.
3. Position the front wheels of vehicle in the STRAIGHT-AHEAD position, then turn the steering wheel to the right until you can access the intermediate shaft coupling bolt (3) at the base of the column.
4. Remove the intermediate shaft coupling bolt (3). Do not separate the intermediate shaft (2) from the steering gear pinion shaft (4) at this time.
5. Return the front wheels of vehicle (and steering wheel) to the STRAIGHT-AHEAD position. Using a steering wheel holder, lock the steering wheel in place to keep it from rotating. This keeps the clockspring in the proper orientation.
6. Raise and support the vehicle.
7. Remove the wheel mounting nuts, then the tire and wheel assembly.
8. On each side of the gear, remove the

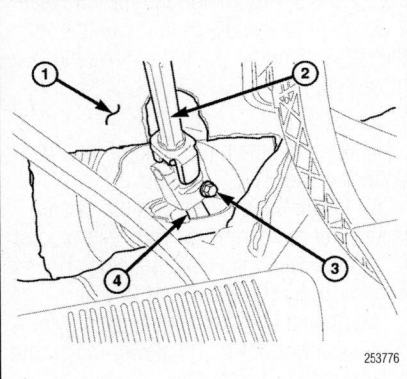

Fig. 291 Intermediate shaft coupling bolt (3), intermediate shaft (2), and steering gear pinion shaft (4)

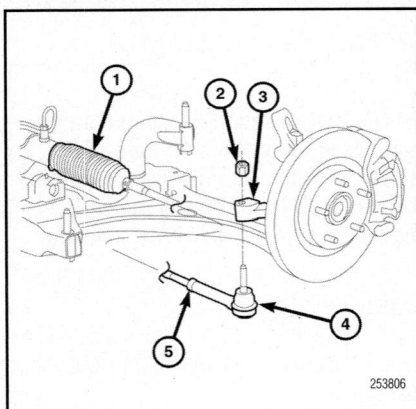

Fig. 292 On each side of the gear, remove the nut (2) from the outer tie rod end (4) at the knuckle (3)

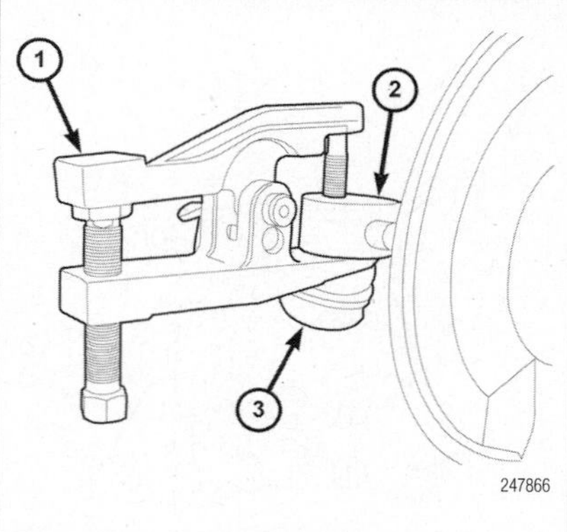

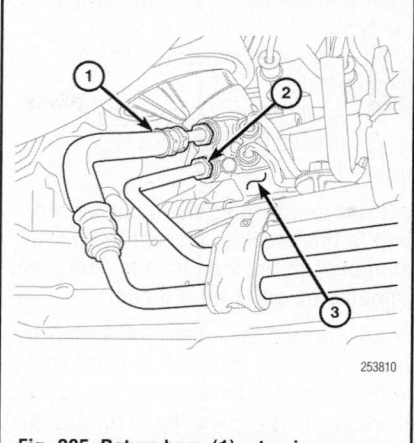

Fig. 293 On each side of the steering gear, separate the tie rod end (3) from the knuckle (2) using Ball Joint Remover 9360 (1) or an equivalent

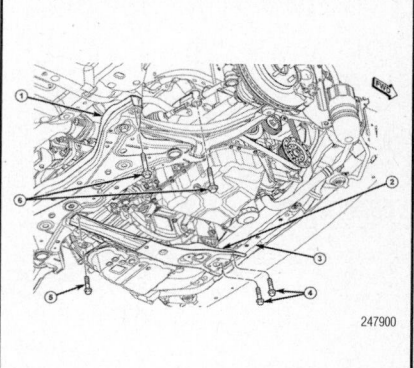

Fig. 295 Return hose (1), steering gear (3), and pressure hose (2)

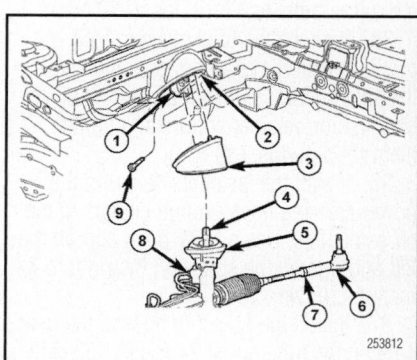

Fig. 297 Remove the four mounting bolts (two each side; 6) securing the front crossmember (1) to the body

nut (2) from the outer tie rod end (4) at the knuckle (3).

9. On each side of the steering gear, separate the tie rod end (3) from the knuckle (2) using a Ball Joint Remover 9360 (1) or an equivalent.

10. If equipped, remove the engine belly pan.

11. Remove the rear engine mount.

12. Remove the front engine mount through-bolt.

13. Remove the three screws (1, 2) securing the heat shield (3) to the crossmember (4). Remove the shield.

14. Remove the return hose (1) at the steering gear (3).

15. Remove the pressure hose (2) at the steering gear.

16. Remove the fasteners securing the power steering hose routing clamps to the crossmember.

17. Remove the screws (1) securing the

stabilizer bushing retainers (3) to the crossmember.

18. Remove the two stabilizer bushing retainers.

➡ Before removing the front suspension crossmember from the vehicle, mark the location of the crossmember on the body of the vehicle. Do this so the crossmember can be relocated, upon reinstallation, against the body of vehicle in the same location as before removal. If the front suspension crossmember is not reinstalled in exactly the same location as before removal, the preset front wheel alignment settings (caster and camber) may be lost.

19. Mark the location of the front crossmember on the body near each mounting bolt using a marker or crayon. Do not use a scratch awl or other tool that can penetrate the protective coating on the body.

20. Support the front crossmember with a transmission jack.

21. Remove the four mounting bolts (two each side; 6) securing the front crossmember (1) to the body.

22. Lower the crossmember enough to access the intermediate shaft coupling (1) at the steering gear pinion shaft (4). Slide the coupling off the pinion shaft.

23. Remove the dash seals (3 and 5) as necessary.

24. Remove the two bolts (1) securing the steering gear (2) to the crossmember.

25. Rotate the stabilizer bar up in order to remove the steering gear from the vehicle.

26. Remove the steering gear from the crossmember.

To install:

27. Rotate the stabilizer bar up and install the steering gear on the crossmember.

28. Install the two bolts (1) securing the steering gear (2) to the crossmember.

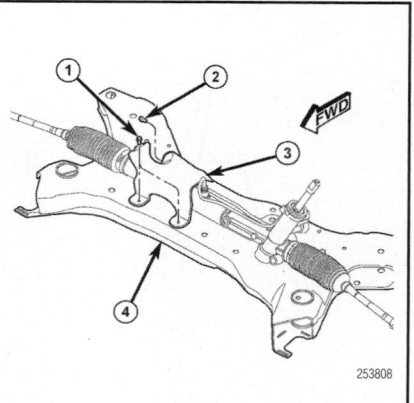

Fig. 294 Remove the three screws (1, 2) securing the heat shield (3) to the crossmember (4). Remove the shield

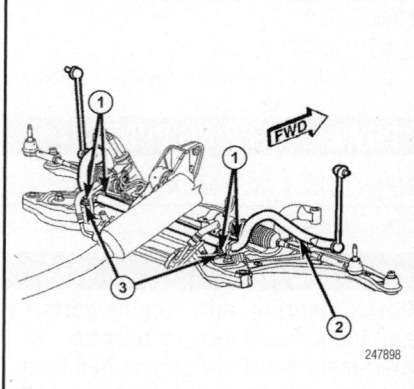

Fig. 296 Remove the screws (1) securing the stabilizer bushing retainers (3) to the crossmember

Fig. 298 Intermediate shaft coupling (1), steering gear pinion shaft (4), dash seals (3 and 5), the two steering gear-to-crossmember bolts (1), and the steering gear (2)

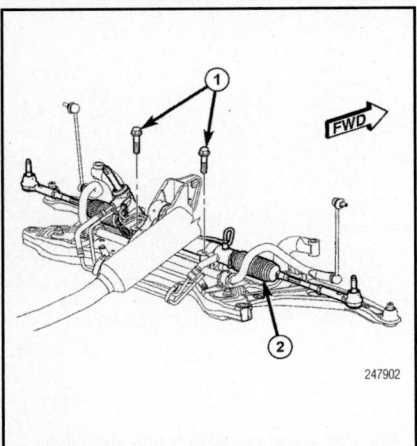

Fig. 299 The two steering gear-to-crossmember bolts (1) and the steering gear (2)

Tighten the steering gear mounting bolts to 70 Nm (52 ft. lbs.).

29. Install the dash seals as necessary.

30. Center the power steering gear rack in its travel as necessary.

➡When installing the front suspension crossmember back in the vehicle, it is very important that the crossmember be attached to the body in exactly the same spot as when it was removed. Otherwise, the vehicle's wheel alignment settings (caster and camber) will be lost.

31. Slowly raise the crossmember into the mounted position using the transmission jack matching the crossmember to the marked locations on the body made during removal.

32. Check the positioning of the seals at the dash panel and adjust as necessary.

33. Install the four mounting bolts (two on each side) securing the front crossmember to the body. Tighten the crossmember mounting bolts to 111 ft. lbs. (150 Nm).

34. Remove the transmission jack.

35. Install the retainers over the stabilizer bar cushions. Install all four stabilizer bar cushion retainer screws and tighten them to 22 ft. lbs. (30 Nm).

36. Install the fasteners securing the power steering hose routing clamps to the crossmember. Use a NEW push clip on the left and tighten the screw on the right to 71 inch lbs. (8 Nm).

37. Install the pressure hose at the gear. Tighten the tube nut to 24 ft. lbs. (32 Nm).

38. Install the return hose at the gear. Tighten the tube nut to 15 ft. lbs. (20 Nm).

39. Position the heat shield and install the three screws securing the shield to the crossmember. Tighten the two front mounting screws to 35 inch lbs. (4 Nm). Tighten

the rear mounting screw to 150 inch lbs. (17 Nm).

40. Install the front engine mount through-bolt.

41. Install the rear engine mount.

42. If equipped, install the engine belly pan.

➡Prior to attaching the outer tie rod end to the knuckle, inspect the tie rod seal boot. If the seal boot is damaged, replace the outer tie rod end.

43. On each side of the gear, install the outer tie rod end into the hole in the knuckle arm. Start a NEW tie rod mounting nut onto the stud. While holding the tie rod end stud with a wrench, tighten the nut with a wrench or crowfoot wrench. Tighten the nut to 97 ft. lbs. (132 Nm).

44. On each side of the vehicle, install the tire and wheel assembly. Install and tighten the wheel mounting nuts to 100 ft. lbs. (135 Nm).

45. Lower the vehicle.

46. Remove the steering wheel holder.

47. Verify the front wheels of vehicle are in the STRAIGHT-AHEAD position.

48. Center the intermediate shaft over the steering gear pinion shaft, lining up the ends, then slide the intermediate shaft onto the steering gear pinion shaft.

49. From center, rotate the steering wheel to the right approximately 90° or until the intermediate shaft coupling bolt can be easily installed.

50. Install the intermediate shaft coupling bolt. Tighten the bolt to 31 ft. lbs. (42 Nm).

51. Reposition the floor carpet in place.

52. Straighten the steering wheel to STRAIGHT-AHEAD position.

53. Fill and bleed the power steering system. (Refer to Power Steering System Bleeding).

54. Check for fluid leaks.

55. Adjust front wheel toe as necessary.

POWER STEERING PUMP

REMOVAL & INSTALLATION

See Figures 300 and 301.

> ❋❋ CAUTION
>
> **Power steering fluid, engine parts, and the exhaust system may be extremely hot if the engine has been running. Do not start the engine with any loose or disconnected hoses. Do not allow the hoses to touch the hot exhaust manifold or catalyst.**

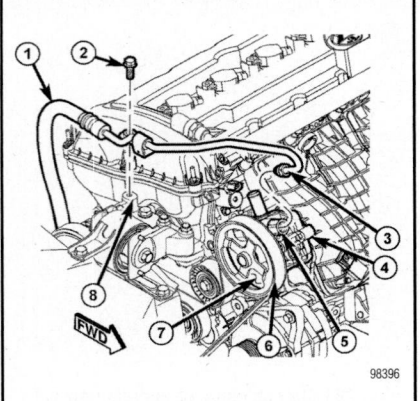

Fig. 300 Pressure hose routing bracket bolt (2), upper mount (8), pressure hose (3), and pump pressure port (5)

> ❋❋ CAUTION
>
> **Check the fluid level with the engine off to prevent personal injury from moving parts.**

> ❋❋ WARNING
>
> **When the system is open, cap all open ends of the hoses, power steering pump fittings or power steering gear ports to prevent entry of foreign material into the components.**

1. Siphon as much fluid as possible from the power steering fluid reservoir.

2. Remove the engine appearance cover.

3. Remove the pressure hose routing bracket bolt (2) at the upper mount (8).

4. Remove the pressure hose (3) at the pump pressure port (5).

5. Remove the hose clamp securing the supply hose at the pump.

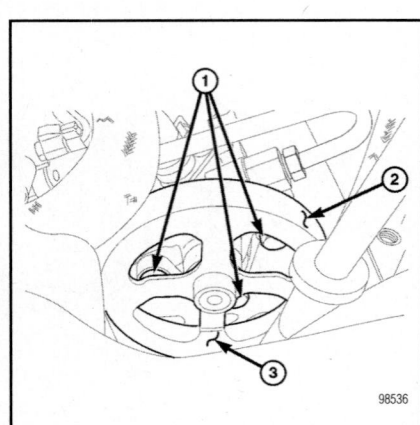

Fig. 301 Remove the drive belt (2) and remove the three pump mounting bolts (1) through the pulley (3) openings

6. Remove the supply hose from the pump.

7. Remove the drive belt (2; Refer to Engine Accessory Drive Belt Removal).

8. Remove the three pump mounting bolts (1) through the pulley (3) openings.

9. Remove the power steering pump.

To install:

10. Using a lint free towel, wipe clean the open power steering pressure hose end and the power steering pump port. Replace any used O-rings with new. Lubricate the O-ring with clean power steering fluid.

11. Place the pump in mounting position. Install the three bolts through the pulley openings. Tighten the mounting bolts to 19 ft. lbs. (26 Nm).

12. Install the drive belt. (Refer to Engine Accessory Drive Belt Installation).

13. Install the supply hose at the pump.

14. Clamp the hose clamp securing the supply hose to the pump.

15. Install the pressure hose at the pump pressure port. Tighten the tube nut to 24 ft. lbs. (32 Nm).

16. Install the pressure hose routing bracket bolt to the upper mount.

17. Fill and bleed the power steering system. (Refer to Power Steering System Bleeding.)

18. Check for leaks.

19. Install the engine appearance cover.

POWER STEERING SYSTEM

BLEEDING

See Figure 302.

✳✳ CAUTION

Check the fluid level with the engine off to prevent injury from moving components.

✳✳ WARNING

Use Mopar® Power Steering Fluid + 4 or Mopar® ATF+4 Automatic Transmission Fluid in the power steering system. Both Fluids have the same material standard specifications (MS-9602). No other power steering or automatic transmission fluid is to be used in the system. Damage may result to the power steering pump and system if another fluid is used. Do not overfill the system.

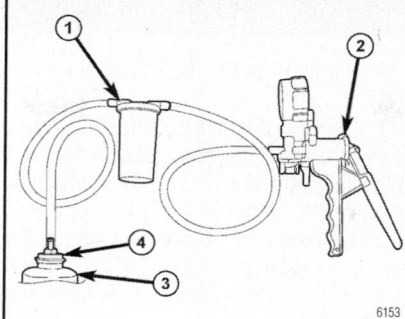

Fig. 302 Special Tool 9688A Power Steering Cap Adapter (4), reservoir mouth (3), vacuum pump reservoir (1), and Hand Vacuum Pump (2), Special Tool C-4207-8

✳✳ WARNING

If the air is not purged from the power steering system correctly, pump failure could result.

➡Be sure the vacuum tool used in the following procedure is clean and free of any fluids.

1. Check the fluid level. As measured on the side of the reservoir, the level should indicate between MAX and MIN when the fluid is at normal ambient temperature. Adjust the fluid level as necessary. (Refer to Fluid Level Checking Procedure).

2. Tightly insert the Power Steering Cap Adapter (4), Special Tool 9688A, into the mouth of the reservoir (3).

3. Failure to use a vacuum pump reservoir (1) may allow power steering fluid to be sucked into the hand vacuum pump.

4. Attach Hand Vacuum Pump (2), Special Tool C-4207-8 or equivalent, with reservoir (1) attached, to the Power Steering Cap Adapter (4).

✳✳ WARNING

Do not run the vehicle while vacuum is applied to the power steering system. Damage to the power steering pump can occur.

➡When performing the following step make sure the vacuum level is maintained during the entire time period.

5. Using a Hand Vacuum Pump (2), apply 68-85 kPa (20-25 in. Hg) of vacuum

to the system for a minimum of three minutes.

6. Slowly release the vacuum and remove the special tools.

7. Adjust the fluid level as necessary. Refer to Step #1.

8. Repeat Step #1 through Step #6 until the fluid no longer drops when vacuum is applied.

9. Start the engine and cycle the steering wheel lock-to-lock three times.

➡**Do not hold the steering wheel at the stops.**

10. Stop the engine and check for leaks at all connections.

11. Check for any signs of air in the reservoir and check the fluid level. If air is present, repeat the procedure as necessary.

FLUID LEVEL CHECKING

✳✳ CAUTION

Check the fluid level with the engine off to prevent injury from moving components.

✳✳ WARNING

Use Mopar® Power Steering Fluid + 4 or Mopar® ATF+4 Automatic Transmission Fluid in the power steering system. Both Fluids have the same material standard specifications (MS-9602). No other power steering or automatic transmission fluid is to be used in the system. Damage may result to the power steering pump and system if another fluid is used. Do not overfill the system.

➡Although not required at specific intervals, the fluid level may be checked periodically. Check the fluid level anytime there is a system noise or fluid leak suspected.

View the power steering fluid level through the side of the power steering fluid reservoir. Compare the fluid level to the markings on the side of the reservoir. When the fluid is at normal ambient temperature, approximately 70°F to 80°F (21°C to 27°C), the fluid level should read between the MAX. and MIN. markings. When the fluid is hot, fluid level is allowed to read up to the MAX. line.

✳✳ CAUTION

Chrysler LLC does not manufacture any vehicles or replacement parts that contain asbestos. Aftermarket products may or may not contain asbestos. Refer to aftermarket product packaging for product information.

Whether the product contains asbestos or not, dust and dirt can accumulate on brake parts during normal use. Follow practices prescribed by appropriate regulations for the handling, processing and disposing of dust and debris.

✳✳ CAUTION

Do not remove the strut shaft nut while the strut assembly is installed in the vehicle or before the coil spring is compressed with a compression tool. The spring is held under high pressure.

✳✳ WARNING

Only frame contact hoisting equipment can be used on this vehicle. It cannot be hoisted using equipment designed to lift a vehicle by the rear axle. If this type of hoisting equipment is used, damage to rear suspension components will occur.

✳✳ WARNING

At no time when servicing a vehicle can a sheet metal screw, bolt, or other metal fastener be installed in the shock tower to take the place of an original plastic clip. It may come into contact with the strut or coil spring.

✳✳ WARNING

Wheel bearing damage will result if after loosening the hub nut, the vehicle is rolled on the ground or the weight of the vehicle is allowed to be supported by the tires for a length of time.

BALL JOINT

DIAGNOSIS & TESTING

1. Raise the vehicle allowing the front suspension to hang.

2. Remove the tire and wheel assembly.

3. Using Dial Indicator C-3339A, or an equivalent, attach the dial indicator mount to the knuckle and align the dial indicator's plunger with the direction of the stud axis, touching the end of the ball joint stud in the lower control arm.

4. Push up on the lower control arm and zero the dial indicator.

➡ Use care when applying a load to the knuckle to avoid damaging the ball joint seal boot.

5. From the front of the vehicle, insert a pry bar between the knuckle and lower control arm, resting it on the lower control arm. Use lever principle to push the knuckle up from the lower control arm. Apply the load until the needle of the dial indicator no longer moves.

6. Record the ball joint movement. The end play is acceptable if no more than 0.031 inches (0.8 mm) of end play is achieved back-to-back.

7. Perform this procedure on each side of the vehicle as necessary.

LOWER BALL JOINT

REMOVAL & INSTALLATION

The lower ball joint is not serviced separately from the control arm on this vehicle. If you determine from the Diagnosis and Testing procedure that the ball joint is out of specification, replace the entire lower control arm. Refer to Lower Control Arm.

LOWER BALL JOINT SEAL BOOT

REMOVAL & INSTALLATION
See Figures 303 and 304.

✳✳ WARNING

This procedure is designed to be used only if a seal boot is damaged during related service procedures. It is not to be used as a repair procedure for a cut seal boot on a vehicle that has been driven and exposed to road and weather conditions.

1. Remove the lower control arm from the vehicle. Refer to Lower Control Arm.

2. Using a screwdriver or other suitable tool (2), pry the seal boot (1) off of the ball joint.

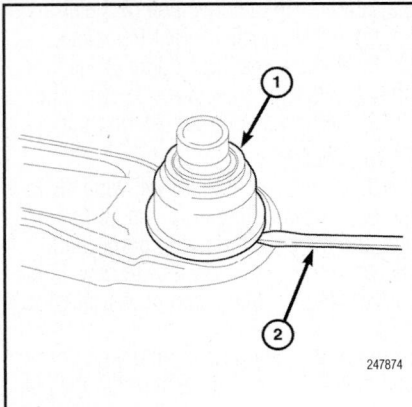

Fig. 303 Using a screwdriver or other suitable tool (2), pry the seal boot (1) off of the ball joint

To install:

✳✳ WARNING

This procedure is designed to be used only if a seal boot is damaged during related service procedures. It is not to be used as a repair procedure for a cut seal boot on a vehicle that has been driven and exposed to road and weather conditions.

3. Place a liberal dab of Mopar® Multi-Mileage Lube (no more than 0.35 ounces [10g]) or an equivalent around the base of the ball joint stud at the socket.

4. Position the ball joint stud straight up.

5. Place the NEW ball joint seal boot over the ball joint stud.

6. By hand, start the seal boot over the sides of the ball joint.

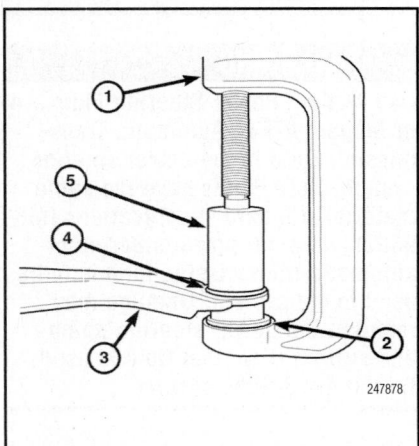

Fig. 304 Lower ball joint seal boot installation

Prior to installing the sealing boot using Remover/Installer 6289-4, make sure there are no burrs on the inside of the tool. Remove any burrs and lubricate with a small amount of Mopar® Multi-Mileage Lube or an equivalent.

7. Place Remover/Installer 6289-4 onto the screw-drive of Ball Joint Press C-4212F.

8. Place the Remover/Installer 6289-6 with the angle-cut end up into the cup of Ball Joint Press C-4212F. Before tightening the set, turn the Remover/Installer so that the tallest point of the angle-cut is away from the body of the control arm when installing the seal boot.

9. Place the control arm ball joint into Remover/Installer 6289-6. Rotate the arm left or right until the tallest point of the angle cut on the Remover/Installer is away from the body of the control arm.

10. Lower Remover/Installer 6289-4 onto the outer lip of ball joint seal.

11. By hand, tighten the Ball Joint Press screw-drive installing the seal boot. Tighten the screw-drive until the seal boot is seated squarely down against the top surface of the lower control arm. It may be necessary to use a wrench to seat the seal boot, but do not over-tighten.

12. Remove the tools and wipe any grease off the ball joint stud using a clean shop towel with Mopar® Brake Parts Cleaner applied to it.

13. Install the lower control arm.

LOWER CONTROL ARM

REMOVAL & INSTALLATION

See Figures 305 through 307.

1. Raise and support the vehicle. (Refer to Hoisting—Standard Procedure).

2. Remove the wheel mounting nuts, then the tire and wheel assembly.

3. Remove the nut (5) and pinch bolt (4) clamping the ball joint (6) stud to the knuckle (3).

❄❄ **WARNING**

Upon removing the knuckle from the ball joint stud, do not pull outward on the knuckle. Pulling the knuckle outward at this point can separate the inner CV-joint on the halfshaft thus damaging it.

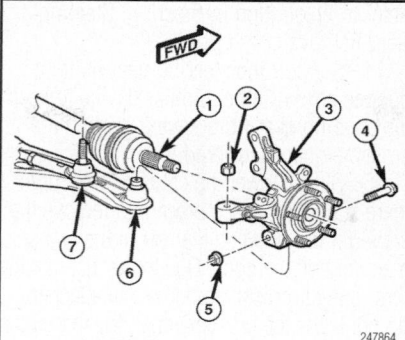

Fig. 305 Remove the nut (5) and pinch bolt (4) clamping the ball joint (6) stud to the knuckle (3). Also shown are the following parts: the nut (2) attaching the outer tie rod (7) to the knuckle (3).

❄❄ **WARNING**

Use care when separating the ball joint stud (4) from the knuckle (1), so the ball joint seal does not get cut.

4. Using an appropriate prying tool (2), separate the ball joint stud (4) from the knuckle (1) by prying down on lower control arm (3) and up against the ball joint boss on the knuckle.

5. Remove the front bolt (2) attaching the lower control arm (3) to the front suspension crossmember (4).

6. Remove the nut (1) on the rear bolt attaching the lower control arm (3) to the front suspension crossmember (4). Remove the bolt.

7. Remove the lower control arm (3) from the crossmember (4).

To install:

8. Place the lower control arm into the front suspension crossmember.

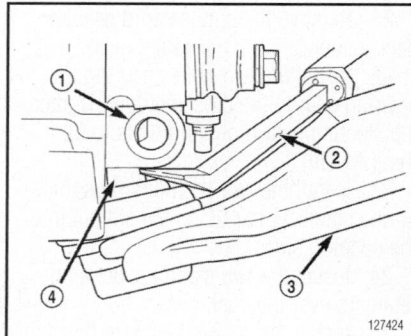

Fig. 306 Using an appropriate prying tool (2), separate the ball joint stud (4) from the knuckle (1) by prying down on lower control arm (3) and up against the ball joint boss on the knuckle

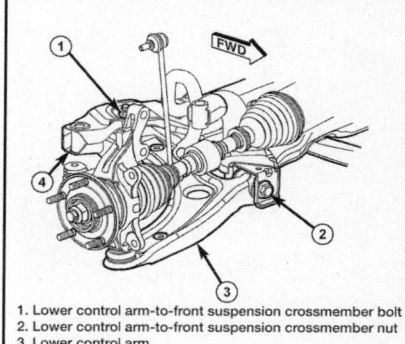

1. Lower control arm-to-front suspension crossmember bolt
2. Lower control arm-to-front suspension crossmember nut
3. Lower control arm
4. Crossmember

Fig. 307 Removing the lower control arm from the crossmember (Removal steps 5–7 and Installation steps 3–6)

9. Insert the rear bolt up through the crossmember and lower control arm.

10. Install, but do not fully tighten, the nut on the rear bolt attaching the lower control arm to the crossmember.

11. Install, but do not fully tighten, the front bolt attaching the lower control arm to the crossmember.

12. With no weight or obstruction on the lower control arm, tighten the lower control arm rear mounting bolt nut (1) to 135 ft. lbs. (183 Nm).

13. With no weight or obstruction on the lower control arm, tighten the lower control arm front pivot bolt to the following:
- 100 ft. lbs. (135 Nm) on vehicles built up to 8/1/08
- 118 ft. lbs. (160 Nm) on vehicles built after 8/1/08

14. Install the ball joint stud into the knuckle, aligning the bolt hole in the knuckle boss with the groove formed in the side of the ball joint stud.

15. Install a NEW ball joint stud pinch bolt and nut. Tighten the nut to 60 ft. lbs. (82 Nm).

16. Install the tire and wheel assembly. Install and tighten the wheel mounting nuts to 100 ft. lbs. (135 Nm).

17. Lower the vehicle.

18. Perform wheel alignment as necessary.

STABILIZER BAR

REMOVAL & INSTALLATION

See Figure 308.

1. Raise and support the vehicle. (Refer to Hoisting—Standard Procedure).

2. If equipped, remove the engine belly pan.

3. Remove the rear engine mount.

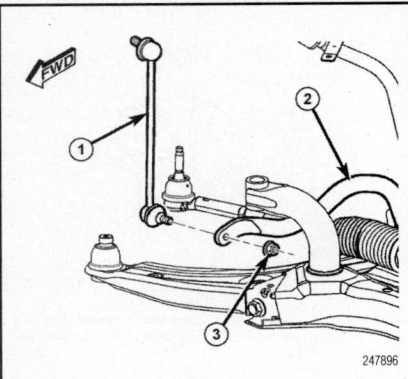

Fig. 308 At each end of the stabilizer bar, while holding the stabilizer bar link (1) lower stud stationary, remove the nut (3) securing the link to the stabilizer bar (2)

4. Remove the front engine mount through-bolt.

5. Remove the fasteners securing the power steering hose routing clamps to the crossmember.

6. At each end of the stabilizer bar, while holding the stabilizer bar link (1) lower stud stationary, remove the nut (3) securing the link to the stabilizer bar (2).

7. Remove the screws (1) securing the stabilizer bushing retainers (3) to the crossmember. Refer to illustration in Steering, Steering Gear Removal.

8. Remove the two stabilizer bushing retainers.

9. Using the slit cut into the cushions (bushings), remove the two cushions from the stabilizer bar.

➡**Before removing the front suspension crossmember from the vehicle, the location of the crossmember must be marked on the body of the vehicle. Do this so the crossmember can be relocated, upon reinstallation, against the body of vehicle in the same location as before removal. If the front suspension crossmember is not reinstalled in exactly the same location as before removal, the preset front wheel alignment settings (caster and camber) may be lost.**

10. Mark the location of the front crossmember on the body near each mounting bolt.

11. Support the crossmember with a transmission jack.

12. Remove the four mounting bolts (6) securing the front crossmember (1) to the body. Refer to illustration in Steering, Steering Gear Removal.

13. Remove the two bolts (1) securing the steering gear (2) to the crossmember.

Refer to illustration in Steering, Steering Gear Removal.

14. Support the steering gear using a bungee cord or other similar device to keep the steering gear from lowering when the crossmember is lowered.

15. Slowly lower the crossmember until there is enough space present to remove the stabilizer bar between the rear of the crossmember and the body. Due to the fact that the fore- and aft-crossmember is still attached, do not lower the crossmember any more than necessary to remove the stabilizer bar.

16. Remove the stabilizer bar out over the rear of the crossmember.

To install:

➡**Before installing the stabilizer bar, inspect the cushions and links for excessive wear, cracks, damage, and distortion. Replace any pieces failing inspection.**

➡**Before installing the stabilizer bar, make sure the bar is not upside down. The stabilizer bar must be installed so that when in mounted position, the ends of the bar curve over the top of the steering gear before attaching to the links.**

17. Install the stabilizer bar, link ends first, from the rear over top of the crossmember. Curve the ends of the bar over the steering gear.

18. Slowly raise the crossmember into mounted position using the transmission jack, matching the crossmember to the marked locations on the body made during removal.

19. Install the four mounting bolts securing the front crossmember to the body. Tighten the crossmember mounting bolts to 140 ft. lbs. (190 Nm).

20. Remove the transmission jack.

21. Remove the bungee cord or other device supporting the steering gear.

22. Install the two bolts securing the steering gear to the crossmember. Tighten the steering gear mounting bolts to 52 ft. lbs. (70 Nm).

23. Install the two cushions (bushings) on the stabilizer bar using the slit cut into the cushion sides.

24. Install the two stabilizer bushing retainers over the cushions.

25. Install the screws securing the stabilizer bushing retainers to the crossmember. Tighten all four stabilizer bar cushion retainer screws to 22 ft. lbs. (30 Nm).

26. Attach the stabilizer bar link at each end of the stabilizer bar. At each link, install and tighten the nut while holding the stabi-

lizer bar link lower stud stationary. Tighten the nuts to 43 ft. lbs. (58 Nm).

27. Position the power steering hose routing clamps on the crossmember. Install the fasteners. Tighten the screw to 71 inch lbs (8 Nm).

28. Install the rear engine mount.

29. If equipped, install the engine belly pan.

30. Lower the vehicle.

31. Perform wheel alignment as necessary, paying special attention to front camber and caster. The crossmember may need to be shifted on its mounts slightly to gain preferred setting

STEERING KNUCKLE

REMOVAL & INSTALLATION

See Figures 309 through 312.

1. Raise and support the vehicle. (Refer to Hoisting—Standard Procedure).

2. Remove the wheel mounting nuts, then the tire and wheel assembly.

3. Remove the cotter pin (1), lock (7) and spring washer (2) from halfshaft stub shaft (5).

4. While a helper applies the brakes to keep the hub (1) from rotating, remove the hub nut (3) and washer (6).

5. Access and remove the front brake rotor. (Refer to Brakes, Front Brake Rotor Removal.)

6. Remove the routing clip (1) securing wheel speed sensor cable to the knuckle (4).

7. Remove the screw (2) fastening the wheel speed sensor head (3) to the knuckle (4). Pull the sensor head out of the knuckle.

8. Remove the nut (2) attaching the outer tie rod (7) to the knuckle (3). To do this, hold the tie rod end stud with a wrench while loosening and removing the nut with a

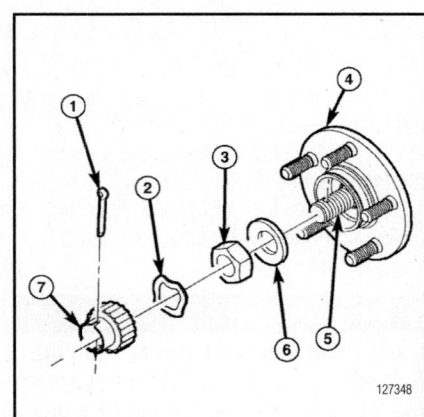

Fig. 309 Cotter pin and hub (1), lock (7), spring washer (2), halfshaft stub shaft (5), hub nut (3) and washer (6)

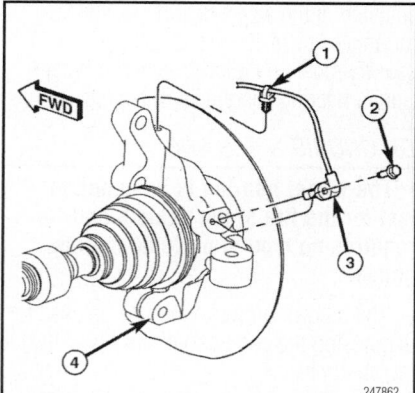

Fig. 310 Routing clip (1) and the screw (2) fastening the wheel speed sensor head (3) to the knuckle (4)

standard wrench or crowfoot wrench. Refer to the first illustration in Lower Control Arm Removal procedure.

9. Release the outer tie rod end (3) from the knuckle (2) using Remover (1), Special Tool 9360.

10. Remove the outer tie rod from the knuckle.

11. Remove the nut (5) and pinch bolt (4) clamping the ball joint stud (6) to the knuckle (3). Refer to the first illustration in Lower Control Arm Removal procedure.

✳✳ WARNING

The strut assembly-to-knuckle attaching bolts (5) are serrated and must not be turned during removal. Proper removal is required. Refer to the following steps for the correct method.

12. While holding the bolt heads stationary, remove the two nuts (2) from the bolts (5) attaching the strut (3) to the knuckle (6).

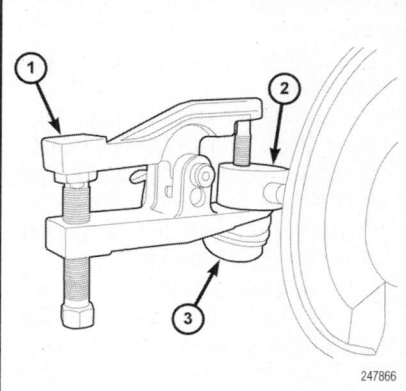

Fig. 311 Release the outer tie rod end (3) from the knuckle (2) using Remover (1), Special Tool 9360

13. Remove the two bolts (5) attaching the strut (3) to the knuckle (6) using a pin punch.

✳✳ WARNING

Use care when separating the ball joint stud (4) from the knuckle (1), so that the ball joint seal does not get cut.

14. Using an appropriate prying tool (2), separate the ball joint stud (4) from the knuckle (1) by prying down on lower control arm (3) and up against the ball joint boss on the knuckle. Refer to illustration in Lower Control Arm Removal.

15. Do not allow the half shaft (1) to hang by the inner CV-joint; it must be supported to keep the joint from separating during this operation. Refer to the first illustration in Lower Control Arm Removal procedure.

16. Pull the knuckle (3) off the half shaft (1) outer CV-joint splines and remove the knuckle from the vehicle. Refer to the first illustration in Lower Control Arm Removal procedure.

To install:

17. Slide the hub of the knuckle onto the splines of the halfshaft outer CV-joint.

18. Install the knuckle onto the ball joint stud aligning the bolt hole in the knuckle boss with the groove formed into the side of the ball joint stud.

19. Install a NEW ball joint stud pinch bolt and nut. Tighten the nut to 60 ft. lbs. (82 Nm).

✳✳ WARNING

The strut assembly-to-knuckle attaching bolts are serrated and must not be turned during installation. Install the nuts while holding the bolts stationary in the steering knuckle. Refer to the following step.

20. Position the lower end of the strut assembly in line with the upper end of the knuckle, aligning the mounting holes. Install the two mounting bolts.

21. Install the nuts on the two bolts. While holding the bolts in place, tighten the nuts to 81 ft. lbs. (110 Nm).

➡**If a new tie rod end is to be installed, make sure the boot is properly lubricated.**

22. Clean all old grease and debris from the boot with a clean cloth.

23. Apply outer tie rod grease P/N 68088623AA to the tie rod end boot.

24. Install the outer tie rod ball stud into

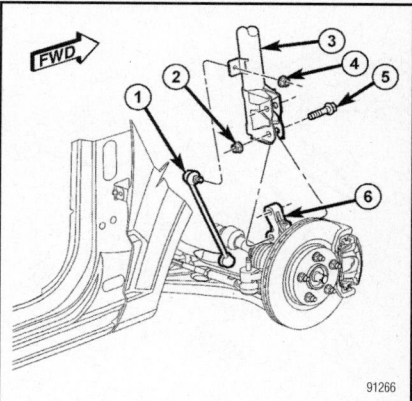

Fig. 312 While holding the bolt heads stationary, remove the two nuts (2) from the bolts (5) attaching the strut (3) to the knuckle (6). Also shown are the stabilizer bar link (1) and the nut (4) securing the link to the strut (3).

the hole in the knuckle arm. Start the tie rod end-to-knuckle nut onto the stud. While holding the tie rod end stud with a wrench, tighten the nut with a wrench or crowfoot wrench to 97 ft. lbs. (132 Nm).

25. Install the wheel speed sensor head into the knuckle. Install the mounting screw and tighten it to 106 inch lbs. (12 Nm).

26. Install the routing clip securing the wheel speed sensor cable to the knuckle.

27. Install the brake rotor, disc brake caliper and adapter. (Refer to Brakes.)

28. Clean all foreign matter from the threads of the halfshaft stub shaft.

29. Install the washer and hub nut on end of halfshaft stub shaft. While a helper applies the brakes to keep the hub from rotating, tighten the hub nut to 180 ft. lbs. (244 Nm).

30. Install the spring washer and hub nut lock over the hub nut and stub shaft. Install a NEW cotter pin securing nut lock in place and wrap the cotter pin prongs tightly around the nut lock.

31. Install the tire and wheel assembly. Install and tighten the wheel mounting nuts to 100 ft. lbs. (135 Nm).

32. Lower the vehicle.

➡**If the original knuckle is being reinstalled, wheel alignment may not be necessary due to Net-Build design.**

33. Perform wheel alignment as necessary

STRUT ASSEMBLY

REMOVAL & INSTALLATION

See Figures 313 and 314.

1. Raise and support the vehicle. (Refer to Hoisting—Standard Procedure).

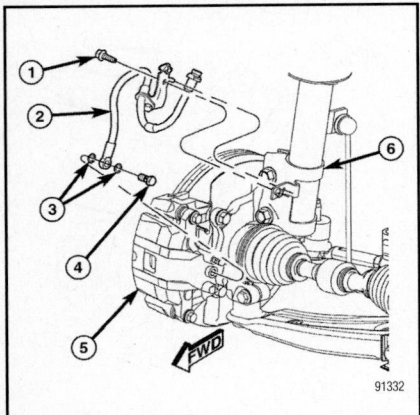

Fig. 313 Remove the screw (1) securing the flex hose (2) routing bracket to the strut (6)

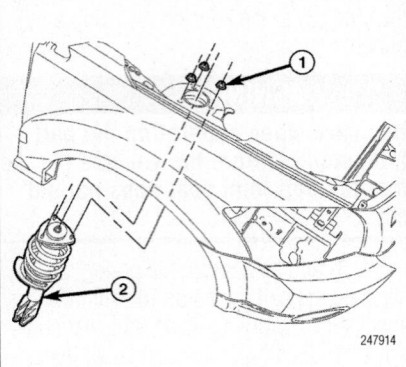

Fig. 314 Remove the three nuts (1) attaching the strut assembly (2) upper mount to the strut tower

2. Remove the wheel mounting nuts, then the tire and wheel assembly.

➡ **If you plan to remove both strut assemblies, mark the strut assemblies right or left and keep the parts separated to avoid mix-up. Not all parts of the strut assembly are interchangeable side-to-side.**

3. Remove the screw (1) securing the flex hose (2) routing bracket to the strut (6).

4. While holding the stabilizer bar link (1) stud stationary, remove the nut (4) securing the link to the strut (3). Refer to the last illustration for the Steering Knuckle Removal.

❊❊ WARNING

The strut assembly-to-knuckle attaching bolts (5) are serrated and must not be turned during removal. Hold the bolts stationary in the knuckle while removing the nuts, and then tap the bolts out using a pin punch. Refer to the last illustration for the Steering Knuckle Removal.

5. While holding the bolt heads stationary, remove the two nuts (2) from the bolts (5) attaching the strut (3) to the knuckle (6). Refer to the last illustration for the Steering Knuckle Removal.

6. Remove the two bolts (5) attaching the strut (3) to the knuckle (6) using a pin punch. Refer to the last illustration for the Steering Knuckle Removal.

7. Lower the vehicle just enough to open the hood without allowing the tires to touch the floor.

8. Remove the three nuts (1) attaching the strut assembly (2) upper mount to the strut tower.

9. Remove the strut assembly (2) from the vehicle.

To install:

10. Raise the strut assembly into the strut tower, aligning the three studs on the strut assembly upper mount with the holes in strut tower. Install the three mounting nuts on the studs. Tighten the three nuts to 35 ft. lbs. (48 Nm).

❊❊ WARNING

The strut assembly-to-knuckle attaching bolts are serrated and must not be turned during installation. Install the nuts while holding the bolts stationary in the knuckle.

11. Position the lower end of the strut assembly in line with the upper end of the knuckle, aligning the mounting holes. Install the two attaching bolts. Install the nuts. While holding the bolts in place, tighten the nuts to 81 ft. lbs. (110 Nm).

12. Attach the stabilizer bar link to the strut. Install and tighten the nut while holding the stabilizer bar link stud stationary. Tighten the nut to 43 ft. lbs. (58 Nm).

13. Secure the flex hose routing bracket to the strut with the mounting screw. Tighten the mounting screw to 120 inch lbs. (13 Nm).

14. Install the tire and wheel assembly. Install and tighten the wheel mounting nuts (3) to 100 ft. lbs. (135 Nm).

15. Lower the vehicle.

16. Perform wheel alignment as necessary. If the original strut is being reinstalled, wheel alignment is not necessary.

WHEEL HUB & BEARING

ADJUSTMENT

The wheel bearing is designed to last for the life of the vehicle and is unable to be adjusted. If the wheel bearing exhibits any roughness or resistance to rotation, the bearing must be replaced. Refer to Wheel Hub & Bearing Diagnosis & Testing.

DIAGNOSIS & TESTING

➡ **The wheel bearing is designed to last for the life of the vehicle and requires no type of periodic maintenance.**

The following procedure may be used for diagnosing the condition of the wheel bearing and hub:

1. Remove the wheel and tire assembly, disc brake caliper and brake rotor. (Refer to Brakes.)

2. Rotate the wheel hub checking for resistance or roughness.

Any roughness or resistance to rotation may indicate dirt intrusion or a failed hub bearing. If the bearing exhibits any of these conditions, the hub bearing will require replacement. Do not attempt to disassemble the bearing for repair. If the wheel bearing is disassembled for any reason, it must be replaced.

Damaged bearing seals and the resulting excessive grease loss may also require bearing replacement. Moderate grease weeping from the bearing is considered normal and should not require replacement of the wheel bearing.

To diagnose a bent hub, measure hub runout.

REMOVAL & INSTALLATION

See Figures 315 through 322.

➡ **The removal and installation of the wheel bearing and hub from the knuckle is only to be done with the knuckle removed from the vehicle.**

1. Remove the steering knuckle from the vehicle. (Refer to Steering Knuckle Removal).

2. Position the knuckle support fixture 9712 as follows:

a. For left side knuckles, place the locator block (2) to the left side (4) on the Fixture. The side of the locator block with the angle cut goes downward, toward the Fixture. Install the mounting screws and tighten them to approximately 40 ft. lbs. (54 Nm).

b. For right side knuckles, place the locator block (2) to the right side (3) on the Fixture. The side of the locator block with the angle cut goes downward, toward the Fixture. Install the mounting screws and tighten them to approximately 40 ft. lbs. (54 Nm).

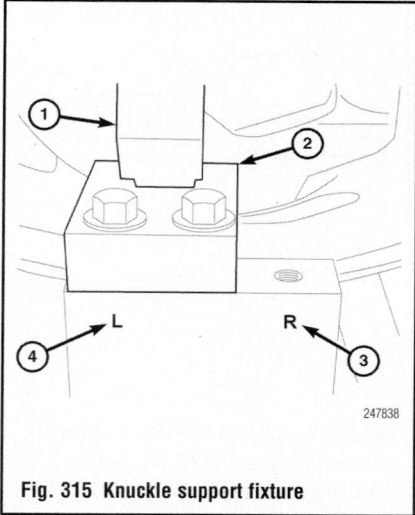

Fig. 315 Knuckle support fixture

3. Install the knuckle in the Fixture as shown, guiding the steering arm (1) to rest on the locator block (3) and the brake caliper mounting bosses on the two Fixture pins (2).

4. Place the Fixture (3) with the knuckle in an arbor press.

5. Position the Remover/Installer 9712-2 (2), in the small end of the hub. Lower the arbor press ram (1) and remove the hub from the wheel bearing and knuckle. The bearing race will normally come out of the wheel bearing with the hub as it is pressed out of the bearing.

6. Remove the knuckle from the Fixture and turn it over.

7. Remove the snap ring from the knuckle using an appropriate pair of snap ring pliers.

8. Place the knuckle back in the Fixture (3) in the arbor press ram.

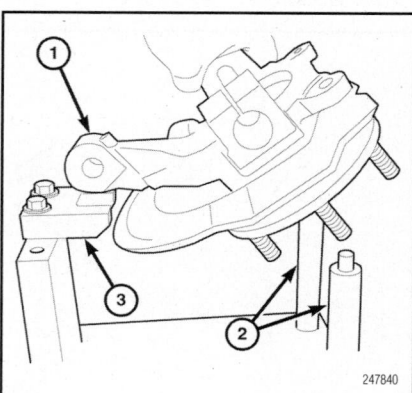

Fig. 316 Install the knuckle in the Fixture (3) as shown, guiding the steering arm (1) to rest on the locator block (3) and the brake caliper mounting bosses on the two Fixture pins (2)

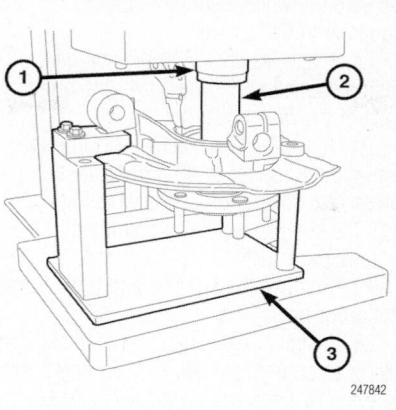

Fig. 317 Position the Remover/Installer 9712-2 (2), in the small end of the hub. Lower the arbor press ram (1) and remove the hub from the wheel bearing and knuckle. The bearing race will normally come out of the wheel bearing with the hub as it is pressed out of the bearing

9. Place the Installer (2) MD-998334, on the outer race of the wheel bearing. Lower the arbor press ram (1) and remove the wheel bearing from the knuckle.

10. Remove the knuckle and tools from the arbor press.

11. If the bearing race is still pressed onto the hub, install the Bearing Splitter (5), Special Tool 1130, between the hub flange and the bearing inner race (4).

12. Place the hub, bearing race and Bearing Splitter in an arbor press. The press support blocks must not obstruct the wheel

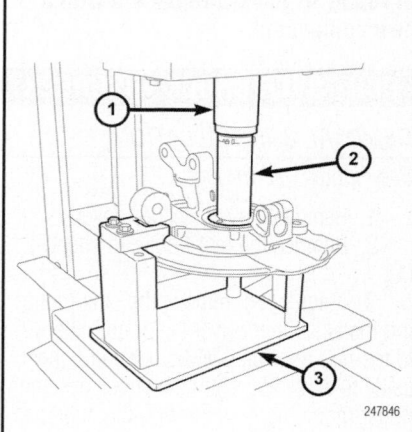

Fig. 318 Place the knuckle back in the Fixture (3) in the arbor press ram. Then place the Installer (2) MD-998334, on the outer race of the wheel bearing. Lower the arbor press ram (1) and remove the wheel bearing from the knuckle

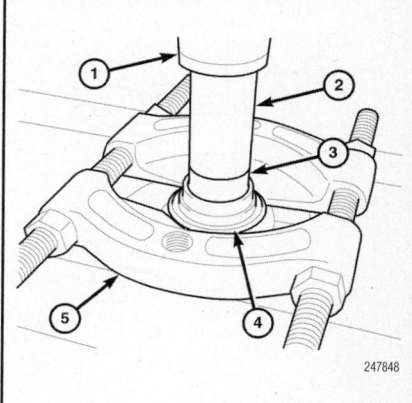

Fig. 319 Bearing Splitter (5), Special Tool 1130, bearing inner race (4), Remover/Installer 9712-2 (2), end of the hub (3) and the arbor press ram (1)

hub while it is being pressed out of the bearing race.

13. Place the Remover/Installer 9712-2 (2) in the end of the hub (3). Lower the arbor press ram (1) and remove the hub from the bearing race.

To install:

※※ WARNING

When installing the wheel bearing (1) in the knuckle (2) it is important to place the side of the bearing with the wheel speed sensor magnetic encoder ring (dark band; 3) in the knuckle first. Otherwise, the wheel speed sensor will not operate correctly.

14. Wipe the bearing bore of the knuckle clean of any grease or dirt with a clean, dry shop towel.

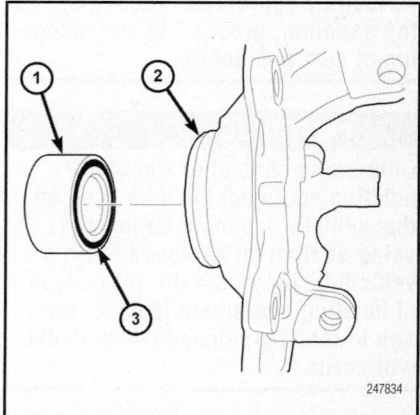

Fig. 320 Wheel bearing (1), knuckle (2), and wheel speed sensor magnetic encoder ring (dark band; 3)

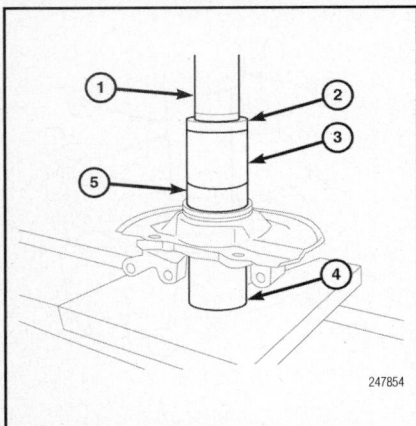

Fig. 321 Cup 6310-1 (4), wheel bearing (5), Receiver 8498 (3), Disc 6310-2 (2), and the arbor press ram (1)

15. Place the knuckle in an arbor press supporting the knuckle from underneath using Cup 6310-1 (4).

16. Place the NEW wheel bearing (5) magnetic encoder ring side down (see above Caution) into the bore of the knuckle.

Be sure the wheel bearing is placed squarely into the bore.

17. Place Receiver 8498 (3), larger inside diameter end down over the outer race of the wheel bearing.

18. Place the Disc 6310-2 (2) into the top of the Receiver 8498. Lower the arbor press ram (1) and press the wheel bearing into the knuckle until it is bottomed in the bore of the knuckle.

19. Remove the knuckle and tools from the arbor press.

20. Install a NEW snap ring in the knuckle using an appropriate pair of snap ring pliers. Make sure the snap ring is fully seated.

21. Place the knuckle in an arbor press. Support the knuckle from underneath using Remover/Installer MB-990799 (3), smaller end up against the wheel bearing inner race.

22. Place the hub (4) in the wheel bearing making sure it is square with the bearing inner race.

23. Position the Remover/Installer 9712-2 (2) in the end of the hub. Lower the arbor press ram (1) and press the hub into the wheel bearing until it bottoms.

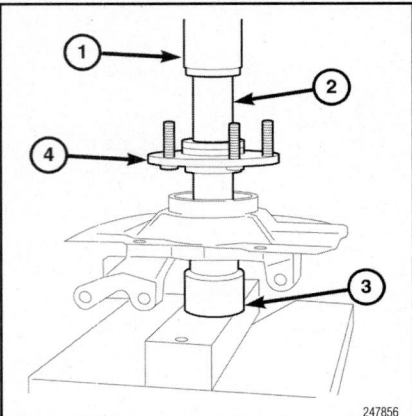

Fig. 322 Installer MB-990799 (3), hub (4), Remover/Installer 9712-2 (2), and the arbor press ram (1)

24. Remove the knuckle and tools from the press.

25. Verify the hub turns smoothly without rubbing or binding.

26. Install the knuckle on the vehicle.

SUSPENSION

✳✳ CAUTION

Chrysler LLC does not manufacture any vehicles or replacement parts that contain asbestos. Aftermarket products may or may not contain asbestos. Refer to aftermarket product packaging for product information.

Whether the product contains asbestos or not, dust and dirt can accumulate on brake parts during normal use. Follow practices prescribed by appropriate regulations for the handling, processing and disposing of dust and debris.

✳✳ WARNING

Only frame contact or wheel lift hoisting equipment can be used on this vehicle. It cannot be hoisted using equipment designed to lift a vehicle by the rear axle. If this type of hoisting equipment is used, damage to rear suspension components will occur.

✳✳ WARNING

All-Wheel-Drive only—Wheel bearing damage will result if after loosening the hub nut, the vehicle is rolled on the ground or the weight of the vehicle is allowed to be supported by the tires for a length of time.

➡If a rear suspension component becomes bent, damaged or fails, no attempt should be made to straighten or repair it. Always replace it with a new component.

COIL-OVER SHOCK ABSORBER

REMOVAL & INSTALLATION

See Figures 323 through 327.

1. Remove the cargo floor cover.
2. Remove the rear floor pan silencer (1).
3. If equipped, remove the nuts mounting the satellite receiver (1) or amplifier (2) to the rear floor pan. Move the component aside to allow access to the shock assembly upper mounting nuts through the opening in the bottom of the quarter trim panel.
4. Remove the spare tire.
5. Fold the shock assembly upper mounting nut access door (2) upward. Use this opening and the one (1) created when the rear floor pan silencer was removed to access the upper mounting nuts in the following step.

REAR SUSPENSION

6. Remove the two nuts (1) securing the shock assembly (2) to the body bracket (3).
7. Raise and support the vehicle. (Refer to Hoisting—Standard Procedure).
8. Remove the wheel mounting nuts, then the rear tire and wheel assembly.
9. Remove the shock lower mounting nut and bolt.
10. Lower the shock assembly (2) out of the body bracket (1) and lift it out over the rear suspension.

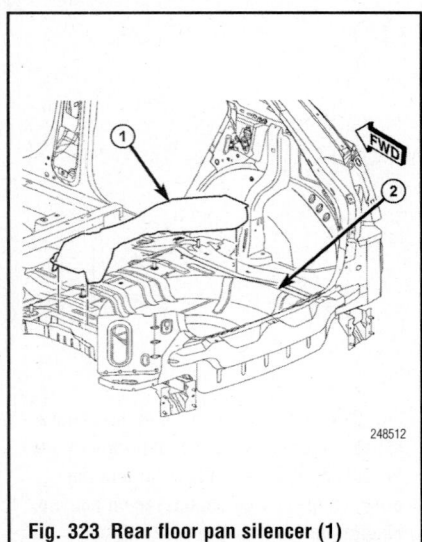

Fig. 323 Rear floor pan silencer (1)

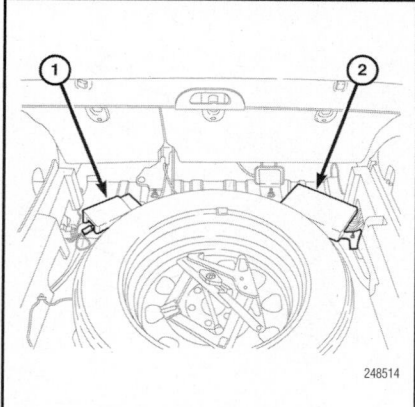

Fig. 324 If equipped, remove the nuts mounting the satellite receiver (1) or amplifier (2) to the rear floor pan

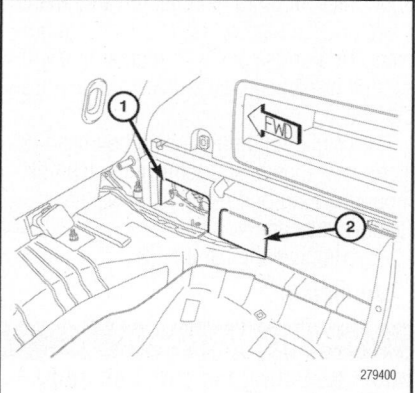

Fig. 325 Fold the shock assembly upper mounting nut access door (2) upward. Use this opening and the one (1) created when the rear floor pan silencer was removed to access the upper mounting nuts in the following step

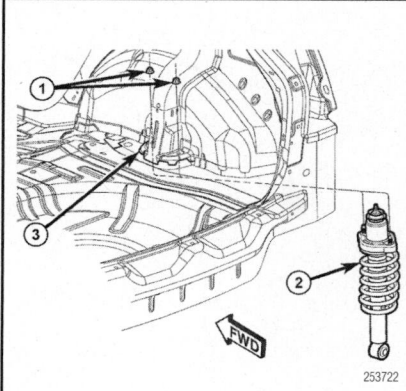

Fig. 326 Remove the two nuts (1) securing the shock assembly (2) to the body bracket (3)

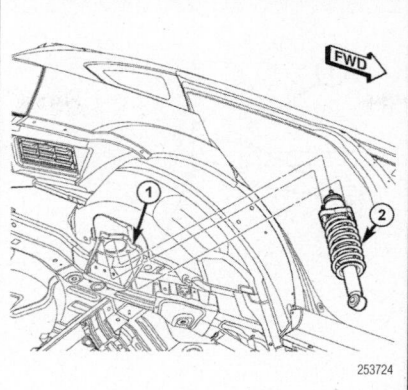

Fig. 327 Lower the shock assembly (2) out of the body bracket (1) and lift it out over the rear suspension

To install:

11. Insert the lower end of the shock assembly down though the lower control arm from above just enough to clear the body, and then lift it up into the body bracket.

12. Install the mounting bolt and nut fastening the shock assembly to the lower control arm. Do not tighten them at this time.

13. Install the tire and wheel assembly. Install and tighten the wheel mounting nuts to 100 ft. lbs. (135 Nm).

14. Lower the vehicle.

➡Use the openings in the interior rear quarter trim panel when installing the upper mounting nuts in the following step.

15. Install the two nuts securing the shock assembly to the body bracket. Tighten the mounting nuts to 35 ft. lbs. (48 Nm).

16. Fold the shock assembly upper mounting nut access door down, closing off the opening.

17. If equipped, install the satellite receiver or amplifier to the rear floor pan.

18. Install the rear floor pan silencer.

19. Install the cargo floor cover.

20. Position the vehicle on an alignment rack/drive-on lift. Raise the lift as necessary to access the shock mounting bolt and nut.

21. Tighten the shock assembly lower mounting bolt nut to 73 ft. lbs. (99 Nm).

LOWER CONTROL ARM

REMOVAL & INSTALLATION

See Figures 328 and 329.

1. Raise and support the vehicle. (Refer to Hoisting—Standard Procedure).

2. Remove the wheel mounting nuts, then the tire and wheel assembly.

3. If equipped, while holding the stabi-

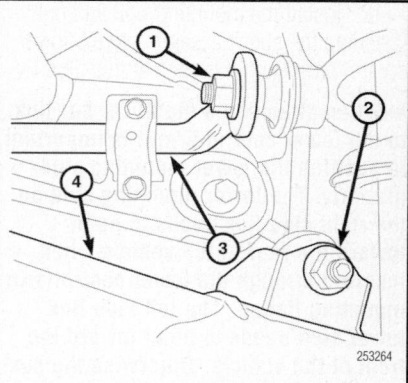

Fig. 328 Remove the nut (2) securing the link to the lower control arm (4). Also shown: the nut (1) securing the link to the stabilizer bar (3)

lizer bar link lower stud stationary, remove the nut (2) securing the link to the lower control arm (4).

4. Remove the lower shock mounting nut and bolt.

5. Remove the stay brace (3) mounting screws (2). Remove the stay brace.

6. Remove the nut and bolt securing the lower control arm to the trailing link.

7. Remove the nut and bolt securing the lower control arm to the crossmember.

8. Remove the lower control arm.

To install:

9. Position the lower control arm and install the bolt and nut securing the lower control arm to the crossmember. Do not tighten at this time.

10. Install the bolt and nut securing the lower control arm to the trailing link. Do not tighten at this time.

11. Install the stay brace on the crossmember. Install and tighten the mounting screws to 18 ft. lbs. (25 Nm).

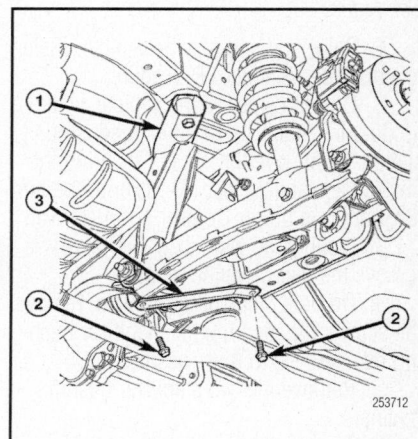

Fig. 329 The stay brace (3) and its mounting screws (2)

12. Install the mounting bolt and nut, fastening the shock assembly to the lower control arm. Do not tighten at this time.

➥**When attaching a stabilizer bar link to the lower control arm it is important to position the lower mounting stud properly. The lower mounting stud on the right side link needs to point toward the rear of the vehicle when inserted through the lower control arm mounting flange. The left side link lower stud needs to point toward the front of the vehicle. Otherwise the suspension geometry will not function properly.**

13. If equipped, attach the stabilizer bar link to the lower control arm. Install the nut and while holding the stabilizer bar link lower stud stationary, tighten the nut to 43 ft. lbs. (58 Nm).

14. Install the tire and wheel assembly. Install and tighten the wheel mounting nuts to 100 ft. lbs. (135 Nm).

15. Lower the vehicle.

16. Position the vehicle on an alignment rack/drive-on lift. Raise the vehicle as necessary to access the mounting bolts and nuts.

17. Tighten the lower control arm mounting bolt nut at the crossmember to 70 ft. lbs. (95 Nm).

18. Tighten the lower control arm mounting bolt nut at the trailing link to 70 ft. lbs. (95 Nm).

19. Tighten the shock assembly lower mounting bolt nut to 73 ft. lbs. (99 Nm).

20. Perform wheel alignment as necessary.

STABILIZER BAR

REMOVAL & INSTALLATION

See Figure 330.

1. Raise and support the vehicle. (Refer to Hoisting—Standard Procedure).

2. On both sides of the vehicle, while holding the stabilizer bar link upper stud stationary, remove the nut (1) securing the link to the stabilizer bar (3). Refer to the first illustration in Lower Control Arm Removal.

3. If equipped with all-wheel-drive, remove the rear driveline module.

4. On both sides of the vehicle, remove the screws (3) securing the stabilizer bushing retainers (1) to the crossmember.

5. Remove the two stabilizer bushing retainers.

6. Remove the stabilizer bar (2) from the vehicle.

7. If required, remove the two cushions

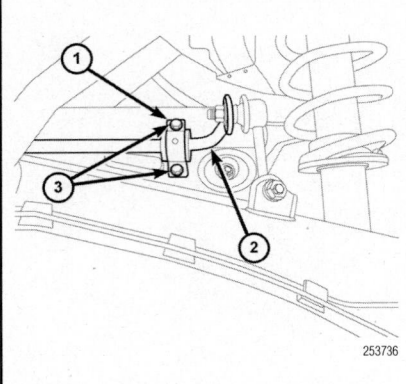

Fig. 330 The screws (3) securing the stabilizer bushing retainers (1) and the stabilizer bar (2)

from the stabilizer bar utilizing the slit cut into the cushions (bushings).

To install:

8. If required, install the two cushions on the stabilizer bar (one on each side) utilizing the slit cut into the cushions (bushings).

9. When installing the stabilizer bar on a vehicle with all-wheel-drive, position the bar so that the bar loops under the axle half shafts once installed, not over the axle half shafts.

10. Position the stabilizer bar on the rear crossmember.

11. Install the two retainers over the cushions at the mounting holes and install the retainer screws. Do not tighten the screws at this time.

12. If equipped with all-wheel-drive, install the rear driveline module.

13. On each side of the vehicle, install the stabilizer link upper stud in the end of the stabilizer bar. Install the nut on each upper stud and while holding the stabilizer link stud stationary, tighten the nut to 37 ft. lbs. (50 Nm).

14. Tighten the cushion retainer screws to 25 ft. lbs. (34 Nm).

15. Lower the vehicle.

TOE LINK

REMOVAL & INSTALLATION

See Figures 331 and 332.

1. Raise and support the vehicle. (Refer to Hoisting—Standard Procedure).

2. Remove the bolt (2) securing the toe link (3) to the trailing link.

3. Mark the position of the cam bolt cam on the crossmember using a paint marker or crayon. This mark will be used

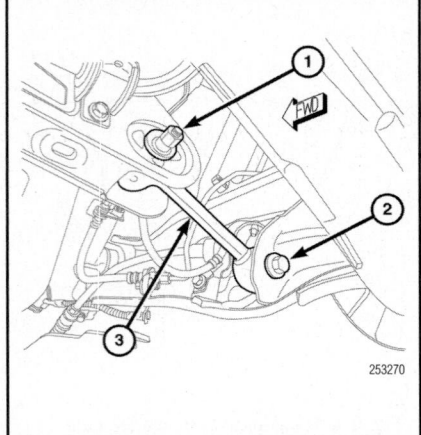

Fig. 331 Remove the bolt (2) securing the toe link (3) to the trailing link

upon installation to help get the alignment close prior to performing rear wheel alignment. Do not use any type marker that will scratch or damage the surface of the crossmember.

4. While holding the cam bolt head (3) stationary, loosen and remove the toe link mounting cam bolt nut (1) and washer. Remove the cam bolt.

5. Remove the toe link (2).

To install:

✳✳ WARNING

When installing the cam bolt and washer make sure the cams stay inside the abutments built into the crossmember. Failure to do so can damage the abutments and make toe adjustment difficult.

6. Position the toe link and install the cam bolt from the front through the crossmember and link. Match the cam on the bolt

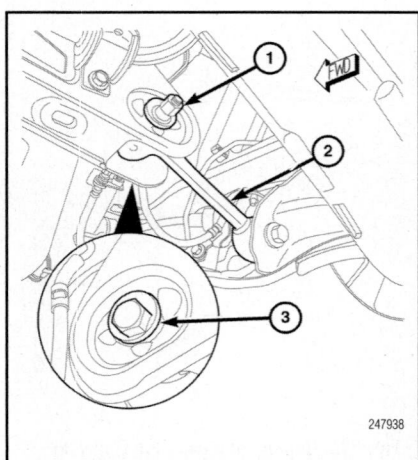

Fig. 332 Cam bolt head (3), toe link mounting cam bolt nut (1), and toe link (2)

to the marks made during removal or position the top of the cam to the 12 o'clock position.

7. Install the cam washer and nut securing the toe link to the crossmember. Do not tighten them at this time.

8. Install the bolt securing the link to the trailing link. To install the bolt it may be necessary to flex the trailing link body mount bushing inward or outward using an appropriate prying tool. Do not tighten it at this time.

9. Lower the vehicle.

10. Position the vehicle on an alignment rack/drive-on lift. Raise the vehicle as necessary to access the mounting bolts and nuts.

11. Tighten the toe link mounting bolt at the trailing link to 70 ft. lbs. (95 Nm).

12. Perform wheel alignment as necessary.

13. Once rear toe is set, while holding the cam bolt head stationary, tighten the toe link mounting cam bolt nut to 26 ft. lbs. (35 Nm).

TRAILING LINK

REMOVAL & INSTALLATION

See Figures 333 through 339.

1. Raise and support the vehicle. (Refer to Hoisting—Standard Procedure).

2. Remove the wheel mounting nuts, then the tire and wheel assembly.

3. Remove the screw (2) securing the brake flex hose (1) to the trailing link (3).

4. Remove the nut (1) securing the brake tube routing bracket to the trailing link.

5. Remove the brake tube (3) from the routing clip (2) on the trailing link.

6. Remove the two bolts (1) securing

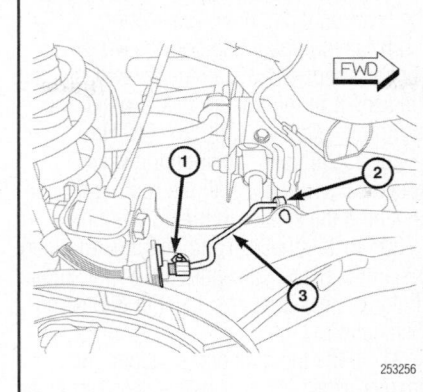

Fig. 334 The nut (1) securing the brake tube routing bracket to the trailing link, the brake tube (3), and the trailing link routing clip (2)

disc brake caliper adapter (3) to the brake support plate (4).

7. Remove the disc brake caliper (2) and adapter (3) as an assembly. Hang the assembly out of the way using wire or a bungee cord. Use care not to overextend the brake hose and tubing when doing this.

8. If equipped, remove the screw (4) fastening the wheel speed sensor (3) to the trailing link (2).

9. If equipped, remove the routing clip (1) fastening the wheel speed sensor (3) to the trailing link (2).

10. Remove the brake rotor, then the hub and bearing. (Refer to Rear Suspension Wheel Hub & Bearing Removal.)

11. Remove the parking brake cable from the lever on the parking brake shoe.

12. Remove the hair pin (1) securing the parking brake cable (2) to the brake support plate (3).

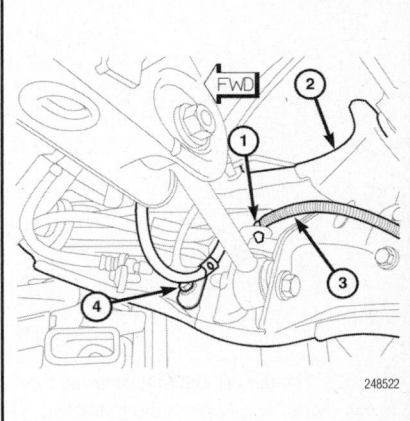

Fig. 336 The screw (4) and the routing clip (1) fastening the wheel speed sensor (3) to the trailing link (2)

13. Slide the brake support plate (3) with parking brake shoes off the end of the parking brake cable (2) and remove.

14. Pull the parking brake cable from the trailing link.

15. Remove the bolt securing the toe link to the trailing link. Refer to the first illustration for Toe Link Removal.

16. Remove the nut (2) and bolt securing the lower control arm to the trailing link (3).

17. Remove the nut (1) and bolt securing the upper control arm to the trailing link (3).

18. Remove the two bolts (2) fastening the leading end of the trailing link (3) to the body (1).

19. Remove the trailing link.

To install:

20. Position the trailing link and install the two bolts fastening the leading end of the trailing link to the body. Tighten the two mounting bolts to 81 ft. lbs. (110 Nm).

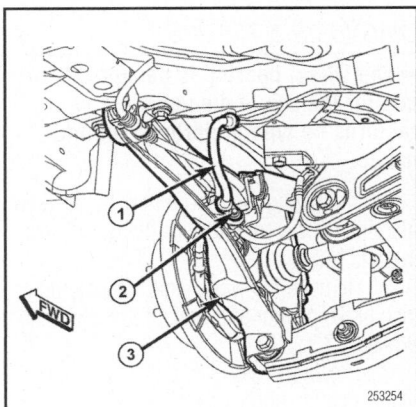

Fig. 333 Remove the screw (2) securing the brake flex hose (1) to the trailing link (3)

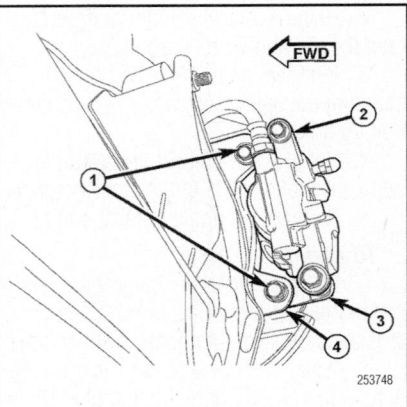

Fig. 335 The two bolts (1) securing disc brake caliper adapter (3) to the brake support plate (4), and the disc brake caliper (2)

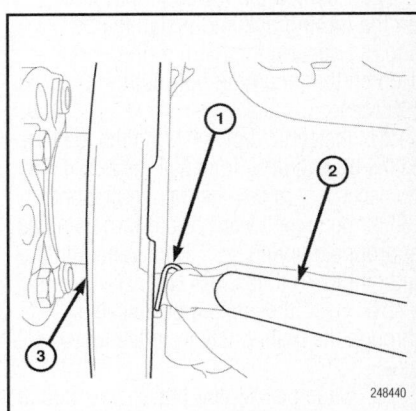

Fig. 337 Hair pin (1) securing the parking brake cable (2) to the brake support plate (3)

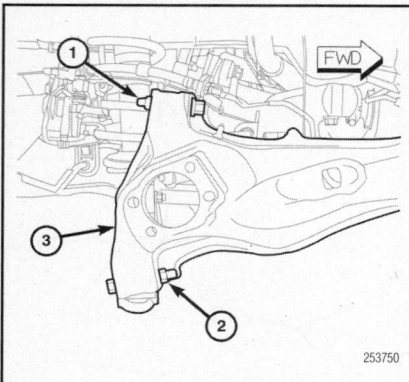

Fig. 338 The nut (2) and bolt securing the lower control arm to the trailing link (3), and the nut (1) securing the upper control arm to the trailing link

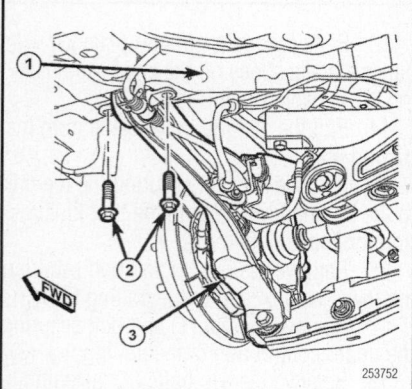

Fig. 339 The two bolts (2) fastening the leading end of the trailing link (3) to the body (1)

21. Position the upper control arm on the trailing link and install the bolt and nut securing the arm to the link. Tighten the mounting bolt nut to 70 ft. lbs. (95 Nm).

22. Position the lower control arm on the trailing link and install the bolt and nut securing the arm to the link. Tighten the mounting bolt nut to 70 ft. lbs. (95 Nm).

23. Install the bolt securing the toe link to the trailing link. To install the bolt it may be necessary to flex the trailing link body mount bushing inward or outward using an appropriate prying tool. Tighten the mounting bolt to 70 ft. lbs. (95 Nm).

24. Insert the parking brake cable through the trailing link from the inboard side.

25. Slide the parking brake cable into the brake support plate with parking brake shoes.

26. Install the hair pin securing the parking brake cable to the brake support plate.

27. Install the parking brake cable onto the lever on the parking brake shoe.

28. If equipped, position the wheel speed sensor and install the screw fastening the sensor to the trailing link. Tighten the mounting screw to 13 ft. lbs. (18 Nm).

29. If equipped, position the wheel speed sensor and install the routing clip, fastening the sensor to the trailing link.

30. Install the hub and bearing, and then install the brake rotor onto the wheel studs. (Refer to Rear Suspension, Hub & Bearing Installation.)

31. Slide the disc brake caliper and adapter assembly over brake rotor and brake support plate.

32. Install the two bolts securing disc brake caliper adapter to the brake support plate. Tighten the mounting bolts to 52 ft. lbs. (71 Nm).

33. Position the brake tube on the trailing link inserting the tube into the routing clip and position the routing bracket over the welded stud.

34. Install the nut on the welded stud. Tighten the nut to 11 ft. lbs. (15 Nm).

35. Position the brake flex hose at the trailing link bracket and install the mounting screw. Tighten the screw to 17 ft. lbs. (23 Nm).

36. Install the tire and wheel assembly. Install and tighten the wheel mounting nuts to 100 ft. lbs. (135 Nm).

37. Lower the vehicle.

38. Perform wheel alignment as necessary.

UPPER CONTROL ARM

REMOVAL & INSTALLATION
See Figure 340.

1. Raise and support the vehicle. (Refer to Hoisting—Standard Procedure).

2. Remove the wheel mounting nuts, then the tire and wheel assembly.

3. Remove the nut (4) and bolt (3) securing the upper control arm (1) to the trailing link.

4. Remove the bolt (2) securing the upper control arm (1) to the crossmember.

5. Remove the upper control arm (1).

To install:

6. Position the upper control arm and install the bolt securing the arm to the crossmember. Do not tighten it at this time.

7. Install the bolt and nut securing the upper control arm to the trailing link. Do not tighten at this time.

8. Install the tire and wheel assembly. Install and tighten the wheel mounting nuts to 100 ft. lbs. (135 Nm).

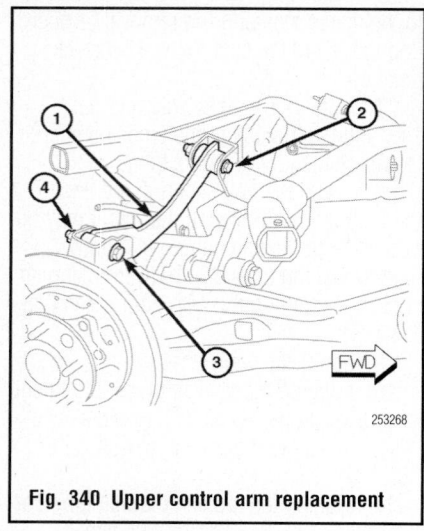

Fig. 340 Upper control arm replacement

9. Lower the vehicle.

10. Position the vehicle on an alignment rack/drive-on lift. Raise the vehicle as necessary to access the mounting bolts and nuts.

11. Tighten the upper control arm mounting bolt at the crossmember to 70 ft. lbs. (95 Nm).

12. Tighten the upper control arm mounting bolt nut at the trailing link to 70 ft. lbs. (95 Nm).

13. Perform wheel alignment as necessary.

WHEEL HUB & BEARING

ADJUSTMENT

The wheel bearing is designed to last for the life of the vehicle and is unable to be adjusted. If the wheel bearing exhibits any roughness or resistance to rotation, the bearing must be replaced. Refer to Wheel Hub & Bearing Diagnosis & Testing.

DIAGNOSIS & TESTING

➡**The wheel bearing is designed to last for the life of the vehicle and requires no type of periodic maintenance.**

The following procedure may be used for diagnosing the condition of the wheel bearing and hub.

1. Remove the wheel and tire assembly, disc brake caliper and brake rotor. (Refer to Brakes.)

2. Rotate the wheel hub checking for resistance or roughness.

Any roughness or resistance to rotation may indicate dirt intrusion or a failed hub bearing. If the bearing exhibits any of these conditions, the hub bearing will require replacement. Do not attempt to disassemble the bearing for repair. If the wheel bearing is disassembled for any reason, it must be replaced.

Damaged bearing seals and the resulting excessive grease loss may also require bearing replacement. Moderate grease weeping from the bearing is considered normal and should not require replacement of the wheel bearing.

To diagnose a bent hub, measure hub runout.

REMOVAL & INSTALLATION

AWD Vehicles

See Figures 341 through 343.

1. Raise and support the vehicle. (Refer to Hoisting—Standard Procedure).

2. Remove the wheel mounting nuts, then the tire and wheel assembly.

3. Remove the cotter pin from the hub nut on the end of the axle half shaft.

4. While a helper applies the brakes to keep the hub from rotating, remove the hub nut and washer from the axle half shaft.

5. Tap the end of the half shaft inward, loosening it from the hub and bearing.

6. Remove the disc brake caliper lower guide pin bolt.

> **✳✳ WARNING**
>
> **When moving the rear brake caliper upward, use extreme care not to damage or overextend the flex hose. Damage may occur.**

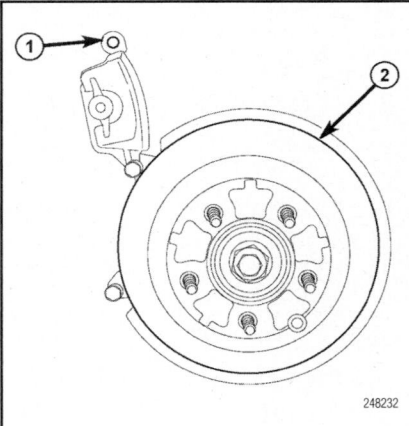

Fig. 341 Rotate the caliper upward hinging off the upper guide pin bolt. Rotate the caliper upward just enough to allow brake rotor removal. Hang the caliper assembly in this position using wire or a bungee cord

7. Rotate the caliper upward hinging off the upper guide pin bolt. Rotate the caliper upward just enough to allow brake rotor removal. Hang the caliper assembly in this position using wire or a bungee cord.

8. Remove any clips retaining the brake rotor to the wheel mounting studs.

9. Slide the brake rotor off the hub and bearing.

10. Unclip the wheel speed sensor head (1) from the retainer on the rear of the hub and bearing (2).

11. Remove the four bolts (1) securing the hub and bearing (2) to the trailing link.

12. Remove the hub and bearing.

To install:

13. Slide the hub and bearing over the axle half shaft and position it on the brake support plate and trailing link.

14. Install the four bolts (1) securing the hub and bearing (2) to the trailing link. Tighten the bolts to 77 ft. lbs. (105 Nm).

15. Clip the wheel speed sensor head (flat side to bearing rear) into the retainer on the rear of the hub and bearing.

16. Slide the brake rotor over the parking brake shoes and onto the hub and bearing.

17. Rotate the disc brake caliper downward over the brake rotor and lower part of caliper adapter.

18. Install the disc brake caliper lower guide pin bolt. Tighten the guide pin bolt to 44 ft. lbs. (60 Nm).

19. Clean all foreign matter from the threads of the half shaft outer CV-joint.

20. Install the washer and hub nut on the end of the half shaft and snug it.

21. While a helper applies the brakes to

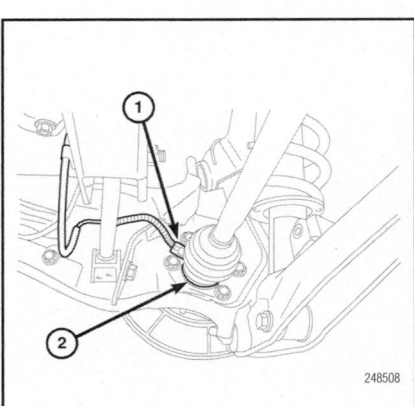

Fig. 342 Unclip the wheel speed sensor head (1) from the retainer on the rear of the hub and bearing (2)

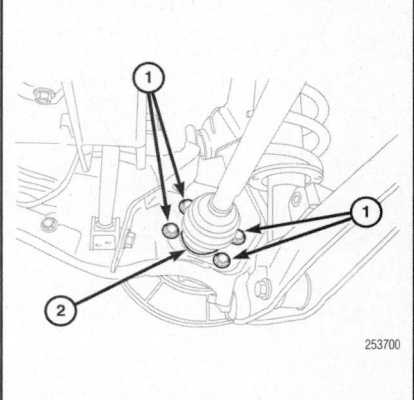

Fig. 343 Remove the four bolts (1) securing the hub and bearing (2) to the trailing link

keep the hub from rotating, tighten the hub nut to 181 ft. lbs. (245 Nm).

22. Insert the cotter pin through the notches in the nut and the hole in half shaft. If the notches in the nut do not line up with the hole in the half shaft, continue to tighten the nut until they do. Do not loosen the nut.

23. Wrap the cotter pin ends tightly around the lock nut.

24. Install the tire and wheel assembly. Install and tighten the wheel mounting nuts to 100 ft. lbs. (135 Nm).

25. Lower the vehicle.

26. Pump the brake pedal several times to ensure the vehicle has a firm brake pedal before moving it.

FWD Vehicles

See Figures 344 and 345.

➡**Before proceeding, (Refer Rear Suspension Warnings).**

1. Raise and support the vehicle. (Refer to Hoisting—Standard Procedure).

2. Remove the wheel mounting nuts, then the tire and wheel assembly.

3. Remove the disc brake caliper lower guide pin bolt.

> **✳✳ WARNING**
>
> **When moving rear brake caliper upward, use extreme care not to damage or overextend the flex hose. Damage may occur.**

4. Rotate the caliper upward hinging off the upper guide pin bolt. Rotate the caliper upward just enough to allow brake rotor removal. Hang the caliper assembly in this position using wire or a bungee cord. Refer to illustration for AWD Wheel Hub & Bearing Removal.

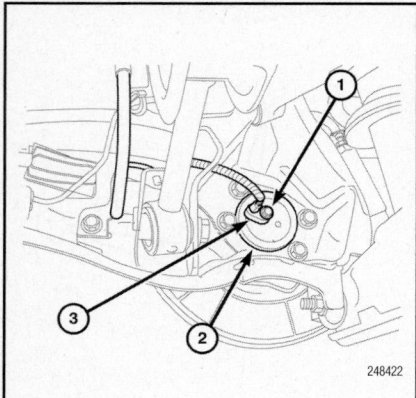

Fig. 344 Remove the screw (1) fastening the wheel speed sensor head (3) in the rear of the hub and bearing (2)

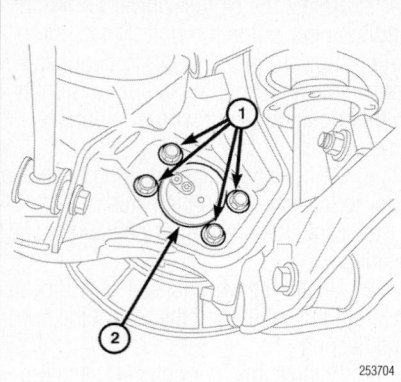

Fig. 345 Remove the four bolts (1) securing the hub and bearing (2) to the trailing link

5. Remove any clips retaining the brake rotor to the wheel mounting studs.

6. Slide the brake rotor off the hub and bearing.

7. Remove the screw (1) fastening the wheel speed sensor head (3) in the rear of the hub and bearing (2).

8. Remove the four bolts (1) securing the hub and bearing (2) to the trailing link.

9. Remove the hub and bearing.

To install:

➡ If equipped, make sure the wheel speed sensor mount on the rear of the hub and bearing is directed toward the front of the vehicle.

10. Position the hub and bearing on the brake support plate and trailing link.

11. Install the four bolts securing the hub and bearing to the trailing link. Tighten the bolts to 77 ft. lbs. (105 Nm).

➡ Before installing the wheel speed sensor head into the rear of the hub and bearing, inspect the O-ring seal to make sure it is not dislodged, split, cut or damaged in any way. Replace the O-ring as necessary.

12. If equipped with a wheel speed sensor, install the wheel speed sensor head (3) into the rear of the hub and bearing.

13. If equipped with a wheel speed sensor, install the wheel speed sensor head mounting screw. Tighten the screw to 89 inch lbs. (10 Nm).

14. Slide the brake rotor over the parking brake shoes and onto the hub and bearing.

Rotate the disc brake caliper downward over the brake rotor and lower part of caliper adapter.

7. Install the disc brake caliper lower guide pin bolt. Tighten the guide pin bolt to 44 ft. lbs. (60 Nm).

15. Install the tire and wheel assembly. Install and tighten the wheel mounting nuts to 100 ft. lbs. (135 Nm).

16. Lower the vehicle.

17. Pump the brake pedal several times to ensure the vehicle has a firm brake pedal before moving it.

DODGE

Dakota

SPECIFICATIONS AND MAINTENANCE CHARTS

ENGINE AND VEHICLE IDENTIFICATION

Engine							Model Year	
Code ①	Liters (cc)	Cu. In.	Cyl.	Fuel Sys.	Engine Type	Eng. Mfg.	Code ②	Year
K	3.7		6	SFI	SOHC	Chrysler	A	10
P	4.7		8	SFI	OHC	Chrysler	B	11

① 8th position of VIN

② 10th position of VIN

25742_DAKO_C0001

GENERAL ENGINE SPECIFICATIONS

All measurements are given in inches.

Year	Model	Engine Displacement Liters (cc)	Engine ID/VIN	Fuel System Type	Net Horsepower @ rpm	Net Torque @ rpm (ft. lbs.)	Bore x Stroke (in.)	Com-pression Ratio	Oil Pressure @ rpm
2010	Dakota	3.7	K	SFI	210 @ 5200	235 @ 4000	3.66x3.57	9.7:1	25-110 @ 3000
		4.7	P	SFI	302 @ 5650	329 @ 3950	3.66x3.40	9:01	35-105 @ 3000
2011	Dakota	3.7	K	SFI	210 @ 5200	235 @ 4000	3.66x3.57	9.7:1	25-110 @ 3000
		4.7	P	SFI	302 @ 5650	329 @ 3950	3.66x3.40	9:01	35-105 @ 3000

25742_DAKO_C0002

ENGINE TUNE-UP SPECIFICATIONS

Year	Engine Displacement Liters	Engine ID/VIN	Spark Plug Gap (in.)	Ignition Timing (deg.) MT	AT	Fuel Pump (psi)	Idle Speed (rpm) MT	AT	Valve Clearance Intake	Exhaust
2010	3.7	K	0.043	②	②	58 psi +/- 2 psi	NA	NA	0.0028	0.0039
	4.7	P	0.040 ①	②	②	58 psi +/- 2 psi	NA	NA	0.0028	0.0039
2011	3.7	K	0.043	②	②	58 psi +/- 2 psi	NA	NA	0.0028	0.0039
	4.7	P	0.040 ①	②	②	58 psi +/- 2 psi	NA	NA	0.0028	0.0039

NA: Not Avaialble

①: Iridium tip: 0.50 inches

②: Ignition timing is not adjustable on any engine

25742_DAKO_C0003

CAPACITIES

Year	Model	Engine Displacement Liters	Engine ID/VIN	Engine Oil with Filter	Transmission/axle (pts.)		Drive Axle (pts.)		Transfer Case (pts.)	Fuel Tank (gal.)	Cooling System (qts.)
					Auto.	Manual	Front	Rear			
2010	Dakota	3.7	K	5	①	②	3.4	4	2.5-3.4	22	13.3
		4.7	P	6	①	②	3.4	4	NA	22	13.3
2011	Dakota	3.7	K	5	①	②	3.4	4	2.5-3.4	22	13.3
		4.7	P	6	①	②	3.4	4	NA	22	13.3

NOTE: All capacities are approximate. Add fluid gradually and ensure a proper fluid level is obtained.

NA: Not Available

①: 42RLE - Service Fill: 4 quarts
   45RFE/545RFE - Service Fill: 4x2: 5.5 quarts. 4x4: 6.5 quarts

②: GETRAG 238: 2.8 quarts

25742_DAKO_C0004

FLUID SPECIFICATIONS

Year	Model	Engine Disp. Liters	Engine Oil	Manual Trans.	Auto. Trans.	Drive Axle		Transfer Case	Power Steering Fluid	Brake Master Cylinder	Cooling System
						Front	Rear				
2010	Dakota	3.7	5W-20	ATF+4	ATF+4	75W-90	75W-140	ATF+4	ATF+4	DOT 3	Antifreeze
		4.7	5W-20	ATF+4	ATF+4	75W-90	75W-140	ATF+4	ATF+4	DOT 3	Antifreeze
2011	Dakota	3.7	5W-20	ATF+4	ATF+4	75W-90	75W-140	ATF+4	ATF+4	DOT 3	Antifreeze
		4.7	5W-20	ATF+4	ATF+4	75W-90	75W-140	ATF+4	ATF+4	DOT 3	Antifreeze

DOT: Department Of Transpotation

25742_DAKO_C0005

VALVE SPECIFICATIONS

Year	Engine Displacement Liters	Engine ID/VIN	Seat Angle (deg.)	Face Angle (deg.)	Spring Test Pressure (lbs. @ in.)	Spring Free-Length (in.)	Spring Installed Height (in.)	Stem-to-Guide Clearance (in.)		Stem Diameter (in.)	
								Intake	Exhaust	Intake	Exhaust
2010	3.7	K	44.5-45	45-45.5	NA	①	1.579	0.0008 - 0.0028	0.0019 - 0.0039	0.2729 - 0.2739	0.2717 - 0.2728
	4.7	P	44.5-45	45-45.5	NA	1.9291	1.579	0.0008 - 0.0028	0.0019 - 0.0039	0.2729 - 0.2739	0.2717 - 0.2728
2011	3.7	K	44.5-45	45-45.5	NA	①	1.579	0.0008 - 0.0028	0.0019 - 0.0039	0.2729 - 0.2739	0.2717 - 0.2728
	4.7	P	44.5-45	45-45.5	NA	1.9291	1.579	0.0008 - 0.0028	0.0019 - 0.0039	0.2729 - 0.2739	0.2717 - 0.2728

NA: Not Available

①: Intake: 1.896 inches
   Exhaust: 1.973

25742_DAKO_C0006

CAMSHAFT SPECIFICATIONS

All measurements in inches unless noted

Year	Engine Displacement Liters	Engine Code/VIN	Journal Diameter	Brg. Oil Clearance	Shaft End-play	Runout	Journal Bore	Lobe Height	
								Intake	Exhaust
2010	3.7	K	1.0227 - 1.0235	0.001 - 0.0026	0.003 - 0.0079	NA	1.0245 - 1.0252	NA	NA
	4.7	P	1.0227 - 1.0235	0.001 - 0.0026	0.003 - 0.0079	NA	1.0245 - 1.0252	NA	NA
2011	3.7	K	1.0227 - 1.0235	0.001 - 0.0026	0.003 - 0.0079	NA	1.0245 - 1.0252	NA	NA
	4.7	P	1.0227 - 1.0235	0.001 - 0.0026	0.003 - 0.0079	NA	1.0245 - 1.0252	NA	NA

NA: Not Available

25742_DAKO_C0007

CRANKSHAFT AND CONNECTING ROD SPECIFICATIONS

All measurements are given in inches.

Year	Engine Displacement Liters	Engine ID/VIN	Crankshaft				Connecting Rod		
			Main Brg. Journal Dia.	Main Brg. Oi Clearance	Shaft End-play	Thrust on No.	Journal Diameter	Oil Clearance	Side Clearance
2010	3.7	K	2.4996 - 2.5005	0.00008 - 0.0018	0.0021 - 0.0112	NA	2.2798 - 2.2792	0.0002 - 0.0017	0.004 - 0.0138
	4.7	P	2.4996 - 2.5005	0.0002 - 0.0013	0.0021 - 0.0112	NA	2.0076 - 2.0082	0.0006 - 0.0022	0.004 - 0.0138
2011	3.7	K	2.4996 - 2.5005	0.00008 - 0.0018	0.0021 - 0.0112	NA	2.2798 - 2.2792	0.0002 - 0.0017	0.004 - 0.0138
	4.7	P	2.4996 - 2.5005	0.0002 - 0.0013	0.0021 - 0.0112	NA	2.0076 - 2.0082	0.0006 - 0.0022	0.004 - 0.0138

25742_DAKO_C0008

PISTON AND RING SPECIFICATIONS

All measurements are given in inches.

Year	Engine Displacement Liters	Engine ID/VIN	Piston Clearance	Ring Gap			Ring Side Clearance		
				Top Compression	Bottom Compression	Oil Control	Top Compression	Bottom Compression	Oil Control
2010	3.7	K	NA	0.0079 - 0.0142	0.0146 - 0.0249	0.0099 - 0.3	0.0020 - 0.0037	0.0016 - 0.0031	0.0007 - 0.0091
	4.7	P	NA	0.0079 - 0.0142	0.0146 - 0.0249	0.0099 - 0.3	0.0020 - 0.0037	0.0016 - 0.0031	0.0007 - 0.0091
2011	3.7	K	NA	0.0079 - 0.0142	0.0146 - 0.0249	0.0099 - 0.3	0.0020 - 0.0037	0.0016 - 0.0031	0.0007 - 0.0091
	4.7	P	NA	0.0079 - 0.0142	0.0146 - 0.0249	0.0099 - 0.3	0.0020 - 0.0037	0.0016 - 0.0031	0.0007 - 0.0091

25742_DAKO_C0009

TORQUE SPECIFICATIONS
All readings in ft. lbs.

Year	Engine Disp. Liters	Engine ID/VIN	Cylinder Head Bolts	Main Bearing Bolts	Rod Bearing Bolts	Crankshaft Damper Bolts	Flywheel Bolts	Manifold Intake	Manifold Exhaust	Spark Plugs	Oil Pan Drain Plug
2010	3.7	K	①	NA	②	130	70	9	18	20	25
	4.7	P	③	NA	②	130	45	9	18	20	25
2011	3.7	K	①	NA	②	130	70	9	18	20	25
	4.7	P	③	NA	②	130	45	9	18	20	25

①: Step 1: Tighten bolts 1-8 to 20 ft. lbs.

Step 2: . Tighten bolts 9 thru 12 to 10 ft. lbs.

Step 3: Tighten bolts 1-8 to 90 degrees

Step 4: Tighten bolts 1-8 to 90 degrees, again. Tighten bolts 9-12 to 19 ft. lbs.

* Refer to illustration for number references and tightening sequence.

②: Tighten NEW bolts to 20 ft. lbs. plus 90 degrees.

③: Step 1: Tighten bolts 1 - 10 to 20 ft. lbs.

Step 2: Verify that bolts 1 - 10 have all reached 20 ft. lbs. by repeating step 1 without loosening the bolts.

Step 3: Tighten bolts 11 - 14 to 89 in. lbs.

Step 4: Rotate bolts 1 - 10 an additional 90 degrees.

Step 5: Rotate bolts 1 - 10 an additional 90 degrees again.

Step 6: Tighten bolts 11 - 14 to 19 ft. lbs.

* Refer to illustration for number references and tightening sequence.

25742_DAKO_C0010

WHEEL ALIGNMENT

Year	Model		Caster Range (+/-Deg.)	Caster Preferred Setting (Deg.)	Camber Range (+/-Deg.)	Camber Preferred Setting (Deg.)	Toe-in (in.)
2010	Dakota	L	+3.00° to +4.00°	+3.50°	-0.40° to +0.60°	0.10°	+0.20°
	Front	R	+3.30° to +4.30°	+3.80°	-0.60° to +0.40°	-0.10°	+0.20°
	Rear	L	NA	NA	-0.45° to +0.25°	-0.10°	-0.00° to +0.60°
		R	NA	NA	-0.45° to +0.25°	-0.10°	-0.00° to +0.60°
2011	Dakota	L	+3.00° to +4.00°	+3.50°	-0.40° to +0.60°	0.10°	+0.20°
	Front	R	+3.30° to +4.30°	+3.80°	-0.60° to +0.40°	-0.10°	+0.20°
	Rear	L	NA	NA	-0.45° to +0.25°	-0.10°	-0.00° to +0.60°
		R	NA	NA	-0.45° to +0.25°	-0.10°	-0.00° to +0.60°

NA: Not Available

25742_DAKO_C0011

TIRE, WHEEL AND BALL JOINT SPECIFICATIONS

Year	Model	OEM Tires Standard	OEM Tires Optional	Tire Pressures (psi) Front	Tire Pressures (psi) Rear	Wheel Size	Ball Joint Inspection	Lug Nut (ft. lbs.)
2010	Dakota	P245/70R16	NA	35	35	16	NA	135 ± 10
		P265/70R16	NA	35	35	16	NA	135 ± 10
		P265/60R18	NA	35	35	18	NA	135 ± 10
2011	Dakota	P245/70R16	NA	35	35	16	NA	135 ± 10
		P265/70R16	NA	35	35	16	NA	135 ± 10
		P265/60R18	NA	35	35	18	NA	135 ± 10

OEM: Original Equipment Manufacturer

PSI: Pounds Per Square Inch

NA: Information not available

25742_DAKO_C0012

BRAKE SPECIFICATIONS

All measurements in inches unless noted

Year	Model		Brake Disc Original Thickness	Brake Disc Minimum Thickness	Brake Disc Max. Runout	Brake Drum Diameter Original Inside Diameter	Max. Wear Limit	Maximum Machine Diamter	Minimum Pad/Lining Thickness Front	Minimum Pad/Lining Thickness Rear	Brake Caliper Bracket Bolts (ft. lbs.)	Brake Caliper Mounting Bolts (ft. lbs.)
2010	Dakota	F	NA	1.039	0.001	NA	NA	NA	NA	NA	26	55
		R	NA	NA	NA	11.5x2.36	0.0024	NA	NA	NA	NA	NA
2011	Dakota	F	NA	1.039	0.001	NA	NA	NA	NA	NA	26	55
		R	NA	NA	NA	11.5x2.36	0.0024	NA	NA	NA	NA	NA

F: Front

R: Rear

NA: Information not available

25742_DAKO_C0013

SCHEDULED MAINTENANCE INTERVALS
2010-2011 Dodge Dakota 3.7L Engine - Normal & Severe (as noted)

TO BE SERVICED	TYPE OF SERVICE	VEHICLE MILEAGE INTERVAL (x1000)												
		6	12	18	24	30	36	42	48	54	60	66	72	78
Engine oil & filter	Replace	✓	✓	✓	✓	✓	✓	✓	✓	✓	✓	✓	✓	✓
Rotate tires, inspect tread wear, measure tread depth and check pressure	Rotate/Inspect	✓	✓	✓	✓	✓	✓	✓	✓	✓	✓	✓	✓	✓
Brake system components	Inspect/Service		✓		✓		✓		✓		✓		✓	
Exhaust system & heat shields	Inspect		✓		✓		✓		✓		✓		✓	
Inspect the front suspension, tie rod ends and boot seals for cracks or leaks and all parts for damage, wear, improper looseness or end play.	Inspect		✓		✓		✓		✓		✓		✓	
Engine air filter - Normal	Replace					✓					✓			
Engine air filter - Severe	Replace		✓		✓		✓		✓		✓		✓	
Engine coolant	Flush/Replace										✓			
Spark plugs	Replace					✓					✓			
PCV valve	Inspect/Service	Every 90,000 miles												
Automatic transmission fluid and filter - Normal	Inspect	Every 120,000 miles												
Automatic transmission fluid and filter - Severe	Inspect	Every 60,000 miles												
Accessory drive belt	Replace	Every 120,000 miles												
Battery	Inspect/Service	✓	✓	✓	✓	✓	✓	✓	✓	✓	✓	✓	✓	✓
Horn, exterior lamps, turn signals and hazard warning light operation	Inspect	✓	✓	✓	✓	✓	✓	✓	✓	✓	✓	✓	✓	✓
Fluid levels (all)	Inspect/Service	✓	✓	✓	✓	✓	✓	✓	✓	✓	✓	✓	✓	✓
Rear axle fluid - Severe	Replace			✓			✓			✓			✓	
Ignition cables	Replace										✓			

25742_DAKO_C0014

SCHEDULED MAINTENANCE INTERVALS
2010-2011 Dodge Dakota 4.7L Engine - Normal & Severe (as noted)

TO BE SERVICED	TYPE OF SERVICE	VEHICLE MILEAGE INTERVAL (x1000)												
		6	12	18	24	30	36	42	48	54	60	66	72	78
Engine oil & filter	Replace	✓	✓	✓	✓	✓	✓	✓	✓	✓	✓	✓	✓	✓
Rotate tires, inspect tread wear, measure tread depth and check pressure	Rotate/Inspect	✓	✓	✓	✓	✓	✓	✓	✓	✓	✓	✓	✓	✓
Brake system components - Normal	Inspect/Service						✓		✓		✓		✓	
Brake system components - Severe	Inspect/Service		✓		✓		✓		✓		✓		✓	
Exhaust system & heat shields	Inspect		✓		✓		✓		✓		✓		✓	
Inspect the front suspension, tie rod ends and boot seals for cracks or leaks and all parts for damage, wear, improper looseness or end play.	Inspect		✓		✓		✓		✓		✓		✓	
CV Joints - Severe	Inspect		✓		✓		✓		✓		✓		✓	
Engine air filter - Normal	Replace					✓					✓			
Engine air filter - Severe	Replace		✓		✓		✓		✓		✓		✓	
Adjust parking brake on vehicles equipped with four-wheel disc brakes	Adjust					✓					✓			
Engine coolant	Flush/Replace										✓			
Spark plugs - (top row only) - Normal	Replace								✓					
Spark plugs - (side row only) - Normal	Replace	Every 96,000 miles												
PCV valve	Inspect/Service	Every 90,000 miles												
Automatic transmission fluid and filter - Normal	Inspect	Every 120,000 miles												
Automatic transmission fluid and filter - Severe	Inspect	Every 60,000 miles												
Accessory drive belt	Replace	Every 120,000 miles												
Battery	Inspect/Service	✓	✓	✓	✓	✓	✓	✓	✓	✓	✓	✓	✓	✓
Horn, exterior lamps, turn signals and hazard warning light operation	Inspect	✓	✓	✓	✓	✓	✓	✓	✓	✓	✓	✓	✓	✓
Fluid levels (all)	Inspect/Service	✓	✓	✓	✓	✓	✓	✓	✓	✓	✓	✓	✓	✓
Passenger compartment air filter - Normal	Replace				✓				✓				✓	
Ignition cables	Replace	Every 96,000 miles												

25742_DAKO_C0015

PRECAUTIONS

Before servicing any vehicle, please be sure to read all of the following precautions, which deal with personal safety, prevention of component damage, and important points to take into consideration when servicing a motor vehicle:

• Never open, service or drain the radiator or cooling system when the engine is hot; serious burns can occur from the steam and hot coolant.

• Observe all applicable safety precautions when working around fuel. Whenever servicing the fuel system, always work in a well-ventilated area. Do not allow fuel spray or vapors to come in contact with a spark, open flame, or excessive heat (a hot drop light, for example). Keep a dry chemical fire extinguisher near the work area. Always keep fuel in a container specifically designed for fuel storage; also, always properly seal fuel containers to avoid the possibility of fire or explosion. Refer to the additional fuel system precautions later in this section.

• Fuel injection systems often remain pressurized, even after the engine has been turned **OFF**. The fuel system pressure must be relieved before disconnecting any fuel lines. Failure to do so may result in fire and/or personal injury.

• Brake fluid often contains polyglycol ethers and polyglycols. Avoid contact with the eyes and wash your hands thoroughly after handling brake fluid. If you do get brake fluid in your eyes, flush your eyes with clean, running water for 15 minutes. If eye irritation persists, or if you have taken

brake fluid internally, IMMEDIATELY seek medical assistance.

• The EPA warns that prolonged contact with used engine oil may cause a number of skin disorders, including cancer. You should make every effort to minimize your exposure to used engine oil. Protective gloves should be worn when changing oil. Wash your hands and any other exposed skin areas as soon as possible after exposure to used engine oil. Soap and water, or waterless hand cleaner should be used.

• All new vehicles are now equipped with an air bag system, often referred to as a Supplemental Restraint System (SRS) or Supplemental Inflatable Restraint (SIR) system. The system must be disabled before performing service on or around system components, steering column, instrument panel components, wiring and sensors. Failure to follow safety and disabling procedures could result in accidental air bag deployment, possible personal injury and unnecessary system repairs.

• Always wear safety goggles when working with, or around, the air bag system. When carrying a non-deployed air bag, be sure the bag and trim cover are pointed away from your body. When placing a non-deployed air bag on a work surface, always face the bag and trim cover upward, away from the surface. This will reduce the motion of the module if it is accidentally deployed. Refer to the additional air bag system precautions later in this section.

• Clean, high quality brake fluid from a sealed container is essential to the safe and

proper operation of the brake system. You should always buy the correct type of brake fluid for your vehicle. If the brake fluid becomes contaminated, completely flush the system with new fluid. Never reuse any brake fluid. Any brake fluid that is removed from the system should be discarded. Also, do not allow any brake fluid to come in contact with a painted surface; it will damage the paint.

• Never operate the engine without the proper amount and type of engine oil; doing so WILL result in severe engine damage.

• Timing belt maintenance is extremely important. Many models utilize an interference-type, non-freewheeling engine. If the timing belt breaks, the valves in the cylinder head may strike the pistons, causing potentially serious (also time-consuming and expensive) engine damage. Refer to the maintenance interval charts for the recommended replacement interval for the timing belt, and to the timing belt section for belt replacement and inspection.

• Disconnecting the negative battery cable on some vehicles may interfere with the functions of the on-board computer system(s) and may require the computer to undergo a relearning process once the negative battery cable is reconnected.

• When servicing drum brakes, only disassemble and assemble one side at a time, leaving the remaining side intact for reference.

• Only an MVAC-trained, EPA-certified automotive technician should service the air conditioning system or its components.

BRAKES

GENERAL INFORMATION

PRECAUTIONS

• Certain components within the ABS system are not intended to be serviced or repaired individually.

• Do not use rubber hoses or other parts not specifically specified for and ABS system. When using repair kits, replace all parts included in the kit. Partial or incorrect repair may lead to functional problems and require the replacement of components.

• Lubricate rubber parts with clean, fresh brake fluid to ease assembly. Do not use shop air to clean parts; damage to rubber components may result.

• Use only DOT 3 brake fluid from an unopened container.

• If any hydraulic component or line is

removed or replaced, it may be necessary to bleed the entire system.

• A clean repair area is essential. Always clean the reservoir and cap thoroughly before removing the cap. The slightest amount of dirt in the fluid may plug an orifice and impair the system function. Perform repairs after components have been thoroughly cleaned; use only denatured alcohol to clean components. Do not allow ABS components to come into contact with any substance containing mineral oil; this includes used shop rags.

• The Anti-Lock control unit is a microprocessor similar to other computer units in the vehicle. Ensure that the ignition switch is **OFF** before removing or installing controller harnesses. Avoid static electricity discharge at or near the controller.

ANTI-LOCK BRAKE SYSTEM (ABS)

• If any arc welding is to be done on the vehicle, the control unit should be unplugged before welding operations begin.

SPEED SENSORS

REMOVAL & INSTALLATION

Front

See Figure 1.

1. Raise and support the vehicle.
2. Remove the front rotor and caliper adapter.
3. Remove the wheel speed sensor mounting bolt from the hub.
4. Remove the wheel speed sensor from the hub.
5. Remove the wiring from the clips and disconnect the electrical connector.

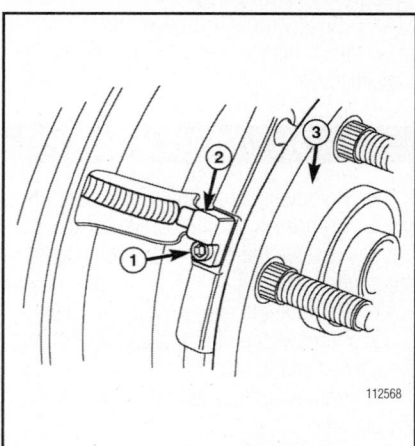

Fig. 1 Remove the sensor mounting bolt (1) and sensor (2) from the hub (3)

6. To install, reverse the removal procedure.

Rear

See Figure 2.

1. Raise the vehicle on hoist.
2. Remove brake line mounting nut and remove the brake line from the sensor stud.
3. Remove the park brake cable and bracket from the sensor stud.
4. Disconnect the electrical connector.
5. Remove the mounting stud from the sensor.
6. Remove the sensor from differential housing.
7. To install, reverse the removal procedure.

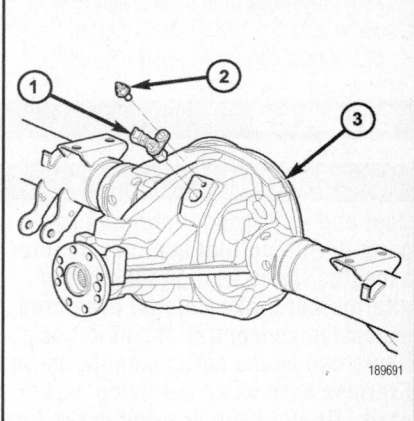

Fig. 2 Removing the sensor (1) and stud (2) from the housing (3)

BRAKES

BLEEDING THE BRAKE SYSTEM

BLEEDING PROCEDURE

BLEEDING PROCEDURE

Manual Bleeding

➡Use Mopar brake fluid, or an equivalent quality fluid meeting SAE J1703-F and DOT 3 standards only. Use fresh, clean fluid from a sealed container at all times.

1. Remove reservoir filler caps and fill reservoir.
2. If calipers were overhauled, open all caliper bleed screws. Then close each bleed screw as fluid starts to drip from it. Top off master cylinder reservoir once more before proceeding.
3. Attach one end of bleed hose to bleed screw and insert opposite end in glass container partially filled with brake fluid. Be sure end of bleed hose is immersed in fluid.

➡Bleed procedure should be in this order, Right rear, Left rear, Right front and Left front.

4. Open up bleeder, then have a helper press down the brake pedal. Once the pedal is down, hold the pedal down while closing the bleeder. Repeat bleeding until fluid stream is clear and free of bubbles. Then move to the next wheel.
5. Top off the brake fluid and install the reservoir cap.

Pressure Bleeding

1. Use Mopar brake fluid, or an equivalent quality fluid meeting SAE J1703-F and DOT 3 standards only. Use fresh, clean fluid from a sealed container at all times.

2. Follow the manufacturer's instructions carefully when using pressure equipment. Do not exceed the tank manufacturer's pressure recommendations. Generally, a tank pressure of 15-20 psi is sufficient for bleeding.
3. Fill the bleeder tank with recommended fluid and purge air from the tank lines before bleeding.
4. Do not pressure bleed without a proper master cylinder adapter. The wrong adapter can lead to leakage, or drawing air back into the system.

BLEEDING THE ABS SYSTEM

> ✳✳ **WARNING**
>
> **Do not use any fluid other than clean brake fluid meeting manufacturer's specification. Additionally, do not use brake fluid that has been previously drained. Following these instructions will help prevent system contamination, brake component damage and the risk of serious personal injury.**

> ✳✳ **CAUTION**
>
> **Brake fluid contains polyglycol ethers and polyglycols. Avoid contact with the eyes and wash your hands thoroughly after handling brake fluid. If you do get brake fluid in your eyes, flush your eyes with clean, running water for 15 minutes. If eye irritation persists, or if you have taken brake fluid internally, IMMEDIATELY seek medical assistance.**

1. Perform the bleeding procedure.
2. Connect scan tool to the Data Link Connector.
3. Select ANTILOCK BRAKES, followed by MISCELLANEOUS, then ABS BRAKES. Follow the instructions displayed. When scan tool displays TEST COMPLETE, disconnect scan tool and proceed.
4. Perform the bleeding procedure again.
5. Top off master cylinder fluid level and verify proper brake operation before moving vehicle.

FLUID FILL PROCEDURE

> ✳✳ **WARNING**
>
> **Do not use any fluid other than clean brake fluid meeting manufacturer's specification. Additionally, do not use brake fluid that has been previously drained. Following these instructions will help prevent system contamination, brake component damage and the risk of serious personal injury.**

> ✳✳ **CAUTION**
>
> **Brake fluid contains polyglycol ethers and polyglycols. Avoid contact with the eyes and wash your hands thoroughly after handling brake fluid. If you do get brake fluid in your eyes, flush your eyes with clean, running water for 15 minutes. If eye irritation persists, or if you have taken brake fluid internally, IMMEDIATELY seek medical assistance.**

1. Always clean the master cylinder reservoir and cap before checking fluid level. If not cleaned, dirt could enter the fluid.

2. The fluid fill level is indicated on the side of the master cylinder reservoir.

3. The correct fluid level is to the

MAX indicator on the side of the reservoir. If necessary, add fluid to the proper level.

BRAKES

❊❊ CAUTION

Dust and dirt accumulating on brake parts during normal use may contain asbestos fibers from production or aftermarket brake linings. Breathing excessive concentrations of asbestos fibers can cause serious bodily harm. Exercise care when servicing brake parts. Do not sand or grind brake lining unless equipment used is designed to contain the dust residue. Do not clean brake parts with compressed air or by dry brushing. Cleaning should be done by dampening the brake components with a fine mist of water, then wiping the brake components clean with a dampened cloth. Dispose of cloth and all residue containing asbestos fibers in an impermeable container with the appropriate label. Follow practices prescribed by the Occupational Safety and Health Administration (OSHA) and the Environmental Protection Agency (EPA) for the handling, processing, and disposing of dust or debris that may contain asbestos fibers.

BRAKE CALIPER

REMOVAL & INSTALLATION
See Figure 3.

❊❊ WARNING

Do not use any fluid other than clean brake fluid meeting manufacturer's specification. Additionally, do not use brake fluid that has been previously drained. Following these instructions will help prevent system contamination, brake component

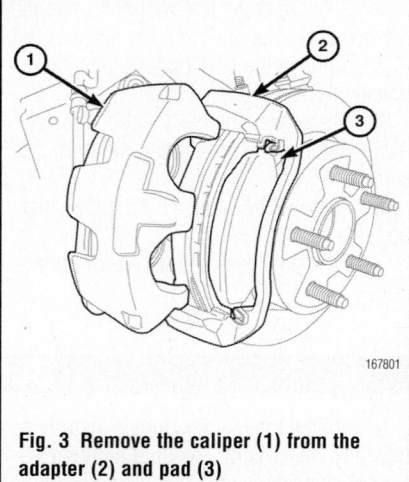

Fig. 3 Remove the caliper (1) from the adapter (2) and pad (3)

damage and the risk of serious personal injury.

❊❊ CAUTION

Brake fluid contains polyglycol ethers and polyglycols. Avoid contact with the eyes and wash your hands thoroughly after handling brake fluid. If you do get brake fluid in your eyes, flush your eyes with clean, running water for 15 minutes. If eye irritation persists, or if you have taken brake fluid internally, IMMEDIATELY seek medical assistance.

1. Install prop rod on the brake pedal to keep pressure on the brake system, Holding pedal in this position will isolate master cylinder from hydraulic brake system and will not allow brake fluid to drain out of brake fluid reservoir while brake lines are open. This will allow you to bleed out the area of repair instead of the entire system.

2. Raise and support the vehicle.

FRONT DISC BRAKES

3. Remove the tire and wheel assembly.
4. Compress the disc brake caliper.
5. Remove the banjo bolt and discard the copper washers.
6. Remove the caliper slide pin bolts.
7. Remove the disc brake caliper from the caliper adapter.
8. Remove the caliper slide pins from the adapter.

To install:

➡ **Petroleum based grease should not be used on any of the rubber components of the caliper, Use only Non-Petroleum based grease.**

9. Thoroughly coat the new slide pins on all working surfaces.
10. Install the boot onto the slide pin and then insert into the adapter.
11. Push the pin all the way into the adapter and carefully expel the trapped air by gently pushing on the boot near the slide pin head.
12. Install the disc brake caliper to the brake caliper adapter.
13. Install the banjo bolt with new copper washers to the caliper. Tighten to 21 ft. lbs. (28 Nm).
14. Install the caliper slide pin bolts. Tighten to 24 ft. lbs. (32 Nm)
15. Remove the prop rod from the brake pedal.
16. Bleed the area of repair for the brake system, If a proper pedal is not felt during bleeding an area of repair then a base bleed system must be performed..
17. Install the tire and wheel assembly.
18. Lower the vehicle.

DISC BRAKE PADS

REMOVAL & INSTALLATION

Refer to Brake Caliper.

❊ CAUTION

Dust and dirt accumulating on brake parts during normal use may contain asbestos fibers from production or aftermarket brake linings. Breathing excessive concentrations of asbestos fibers can cause serious bodily harm. Exercise care when servicing brake parts. Do not sand or grind brake lining unless equipment used is designed to contain the dust residue. Do not clean brake parts with compressed air or by dry brushing. Cleaning should be done by dampening the brake components with a fine mist of water, then wiping the brake components clean with a dampened cloth. Dispose of cloth and all residue containing asbestos fibers in an impermeable container with the appropriate label. Follow practices prescribed by the Occupational Safety and Health Administration (OSHA) and the Environmental Protection Agency (EPA) for the handling, processing, and disposing of dust or debris that may contain asbestos fibers.

BRAKE SHOES

REMOVAL & INSTALLATION

See Figure 4.

1. Raise and support vehicle.
2. Remove wheel and tire assembly.
3. Remove clip nuts securing brake drum to wheel studs.
4. Remove drum. If drum is difficult to remove, remove rear plug from access hole in support plate.
5. Back-off self adjusting by inserting a thin screwdriver into access hole and push lever away from adjuster star wheel. Then insert an adjuster tool into brake adjusting hole rotate adjuster star wheel to retract brake shoes.
6. Vacuum brake components to remove brake lining dust.
7. Remove shoe return spring with brake spring plier tool.
8. Remove the adjuster spring and level. Disengage lever from spring by sliding lever forward to clear pivot and work lever out from under spring.
9. Disengage and remove shoe return spring from brake shoes.
10. Remove brake shoe hold down clips.

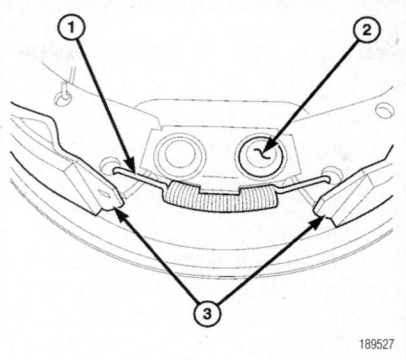

Fig. 4 Disengage and remove shoe return spring (1) from brake shoes (3)

11. Remove rear brake shoe from support plate.
12. Remove front brake shoe from support plate.
13. Remove park brake lever from the brake shoe.

To install:

14. Clean and inspect individual brake components.
15. Lubricate where the brake shoe contacts the support plate with high temperature grease or Lubriplate.
16. Lubricate adjuster screw socket, nut, button and screw thread surfaces with grease or Lubriplate.
17. Install parking brake lever to the rear shoe and install the hold down clip.
18. Install the adjuster strut onto the shoes and park brake lever.
19. Install the front shoe on support plate, and install the hold down clip.
20. Install the adjuster spring and lever in the slot in the adjuster strut.
21. Install the lower return spring to the shoes.
22. Verify adjuster operation. Pull both shoes outward to move the adjuster lever (4) to rotate the star wheel. Be sure adjuster lever properly engages star wheel teeth.
23. Adjust brake shoes to drum with brake gauge.
24. Install wheel and tire assembly.

ADJUSTMENT

The rear drum brakes are equipped with a self-adjusting mechanism. Under normal circumstances, the only time adjustment is required is when the shoes are replaced, removed for access to other parts, or when one or both drums are replaced.

Adjustment can be made with a standard brake gauge or with adjusting tool. Adjust-

ment is performed with the complete brake assembly installed on the backing plate.

ADJUSTMENT WITH BRAKE GAUGE

1. Be sure parking brakes are fully released.
2. Raise rear of vehicle and remove wheels and brake drums.
3. Verify that left and right automatic adjuster levers and cables are properly connected.
4. Insert brake gauge in drum. Expand gauge until gauge inner legs contact drum braking surface. Then lock gauge in position.
5. Reverse gauge and install it on brake shoes. Position gauge legs at shoe centers as shown. If gauge does not fit (too loose/too tight), adjust shoes.
6. Pull shoe adjuster lever away from adjuster screw star wheel.
7. Turn adjuster screw star wheel (by hand) to expand or retract brake shoes. Continue adjustment until gauge outside legs are light drag-fit on shoes.
8. Install brake drums and wheels and lower vehicle.
9. Drive vehicle and make 8-10 forward stops to operate automatic adjusters and equalize adjustment.

ADJUSTMENT WITH ADJUSTING TOOL

10. Be sure parking brake lever is fully released.
11. Raise vehicle so rear wheels can be rotated freely.
12. Remove plug from each access hole in brake support plates.
13. Loosen parking brake cable adjustment nut until there is slack in front cable.
14. Insert adjusting tool through support plate access hole and engage tool in teeth of adjusting screw star wheel.
15. Rotate adjuster screw star wheel (move tool handle upward) until slight drag can be felt when wheel is rotated.
16. Push and hold adjuster lever away from star wheel with thin screwdriver.
17. Back off adjuster screw star wheel until brake drag is eliminated.
18. Repeat adjustment at opposite wheel. Be sure adjustment is equal at both wheels.
19. Install support plate access hole plugs.
20. Adjust parking brake cable and lower vehicle.
21. Drive vehicle and make 8-10 forward stops to operate automatic adjusters and equalize adjustment.

➡ **Bring vehicle to complete standstill at each stop. Incomplete, rolling stops will not activate automatic adjusters.**

CHASSIS ELECTRICAL   AIR BAG (SUPPLEMENTAL RESTRAINT SYSTEM)

GENERAL INFORMATION

✳✳ CAUTION

These vehicles are equipped with an air bag system. The system must be disarmed before performing service on, or around, system components, the steering column, instrument panel components, wiring and sensors. Failure to follow the safety precautions and the disarming procedure could result in accidental air bag deployment, possible injury and unnecessary system repairs.

SERVICE PRECAUTIONS

Disconnect and isolate the battery negative cable before beginning any airbag system component diagnosis, testing, removal, or installation procedures. Allow system capacitor to discharge for two minutes before beginning any component service. This will disable the airbag system. Failure to disable the airbag system may result in accidental airbag deployment, personal injury, or death.

Do not place an intact undeployed airbag face down on a solid surface. The airbag will propel into the air if accidentally deployed and may result in personal injury or death.

When carrying or handling an undeployed airbag, the trim side (face) of the airbag should be pointing away from the body to minimize possibility of injury if accidental deployment occurs. Failure to do this may result in personal injury or death.

Replace airbag system components with OEM replacement parts. Substitute parts may appear interchangeable, but internal differences may result in inferior occupant protection. Failure to do so may result in occupant personal injury or death.

Wear safety glasses, rubber gloves, and long sleeved clothing when cleaning powder residue from vehicle after an airbag deployment. Powder residue emitted from a deployed airbag can cause skin irritation. Flush affected area with cool water if irritation is experienced. If nasal or throat irritation is experienced, exit the vehicle for fresh air until the irritation ceases. If irritation continues, see a physician.

Do not use a replacement airbag that is not in the original packaging. This may result in improper deployment, personal injury, or death.

The factory installed fasteners, screws and bolts used to fasten airbag components have a special coating and are specifically designed for the airbag system. Do not use substitute fasteners. Use only original equipment fasteners listed in the parts catalog when fastener replacement is required.

During, and following, any child restraint anchor service, due to impact event or vehicle repair, carefully inspect all mounting hardware, tether straps, and anchors for proper installation, operation, or damage. If a child restraint anchor is found damaged in any way, the anchor must be replaced. Failure to do this may result in personal injury or death.

Deployed and non-deployed airbags may or may not have live pyrotechnic material within the airbag inflator.

Do not dispose of driver/passenger/curtain airbags or seat belt tensioners unless you are sure of complete deployment. Refer to the Hazardous Substance Control System for proper disposal.

Dispose of deployed airbags and tensioners consistent with state, provincial, local, and federal regulations.

After any airbag component testing or service, do not connect the battery negative cable. Personal injury or death may result if the system test is not performed first.

If the vehicle is equipped with the Occupant Classification System (OCS), do not connect the battery negative cable before performing the OCS Verification Test using the scan tool and the appropriate diagnostic information. Personal injury or death may result if the system test is not performed properly.

Never replace both the Occupant Restraint Controller (ORC) and the Occupant Classification Module (OCM) at the same time. If both require replacement, replace one, then perform the Airbag System test before replacing the other.

Both the ORC and the OCM store Occupant Classification System (OCS) calibration data, which they transfer to one another when one of them is replaced. If both are replaced at the same time, an irreversible fault will be set in both modules and the OCS may malfunction and cause personal injury or death.

If equipped with OCS, the Seat Weight Sensor is a sensitive, calibrated unit and must be handled carefully. Do not drop or handle roughly. If dropped or damaged, replace with another sensor. Failure to do so may result in occupant injury or death.

If equipped with OCS, the front passenger seat must be handled carefully as well. When removing the seat, be careful when setting on floor not to drop. If dropped, the sensor may be inoperative, could result in occupant injury, or possibly death.

If equipped with OCS, when the passenger front seat is on the floor, no one should sit in the front passenger seat. This uneven force may damage the sensing ability of the seat weight sensors. If sat on and damaged, the sensor may be inoperative, could result in occupant injury, or possibly death.

DISARMING THE SYSTEM

✳✳ WARNING

Always wear eye protection when servicing a vehicle. Failure to follow this instruction may result in serious personal injury.

✳✳ WARNING

Never probe the electrical connectors on air bag, Safety Canopy® or side air curtain modules. Failure to follow this instruction may result in the accidental deployment of these modules, which increases the risk of serious personal injury or death.

✳✳ WARNING

Do not handle, move or change the original horizontal mounting position of the restraints control module (RCM) while the RCM is connected and the ignition switch is ON. Failure to follow this instruction may result in the accidental deployment of the Safety Canopy® and cause serious personal injury or death.

✳✳ WARNING

To reduce the risk of accidental deployment, do not use any memory saver devices. Failure to follow this instruction may result in serious personal injury or death.

To avoid serious or fatal injury on vehicles equipped with airbags, disable the Supplemental Restraint System (SRS) before attempting any steering wheel, steering column, airbag, seat belt tensioner, impact sensor or instrument panel component diagnosis or service. Disconnect and isolate the battery negative (ground) cable, then wait two minutes for the system capacitor to discharge before performing further diagnosis or service. This is the only sure way to disable the SRS. Failure to take the proper precautions could result in accidental airbag deployment.

ARMING THE SYSTEM

Connect the negative battery cable.

CLOCKSPRING CENTERING

❊❊ WARNING

To avoid serious or fatal injury on vehicles equipped with airbags, disable the Supplemental Restraint System (SRS) before attempting any steering wheel, steering column, airbag, seat belt tensioner, impact sensor or instrument panel component diagnosis or service. Disconnect

and isolate the battery negative (ground) cable, then wait two minutes for the system capacitor to discharge before performing further diagnosis or service. This is the only sure way to disable the SRS. Failure to take the proper precautions could result in accidental airbag deployment.

➡ **Before starting this procedure, be certain to turn the steering wheel until the front wheels are in the straight-ahead position.**

1. Place the front wheels in the straight-ahead position.
2. Remove the clockspring from the steering column.

3. Rotate the clockspring rotor clockwise to the end of its travel. Do not apply excessive torque.
4. From the end of the clockwise travel, rotate the rotor about two and one-half turns counterclockwise.
5. The engagement dowel and yellow rubber boot should end up at the bottom, and the arrows on the clockspring rotor and case should be in alignment.
6. The clockspring is now centered. Secure the clockspring rotor to the clockspring case to maintain clockspring centering until it is reinstalled on the steering column.
7. The front wheels should still be in the straight-ahead position. Reinstall the clockspring onto the steering column.

DRIVE TRAIN

TRANSFER CASE ASSEMBLY

DRAINING & FILLING

See Figure 5.

1. Raise the vehicle.
2. Position drain pan under transfer case.
3. Remove drain and fill plugs and drain lubricant completely.
4. Install drain plug. Tighten plug to 15–25 ft. lbs. (20–34 Nm).
5. Remove drain pan.
6. Fill transfer case to bottom edge of fill plug opening with Mopar® ATF +4, Automatic Transmission fluid.
7. Install and tighten fill plug to 15–25 ft. lbs. (20–34 Nm).
8. Lower the vehicle.

FRONT DRIVESHAFT

REMOVAL & INSTALLATION

See Figure 6.

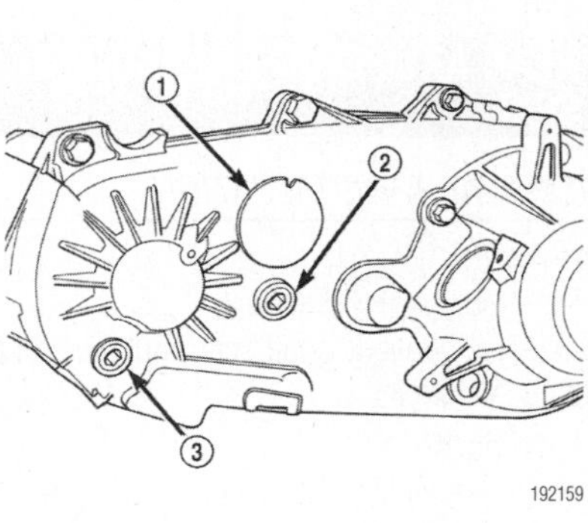

1. With vehicle in neutral, position vehicle on hoist.
2. Remove skid plate if equipped.
3. Mark a reference line across propeller shaft flange and pinion flange.
4. Remove exhaust crossover bolts from exhaust manifolds and lower crossover.
5. Remove boot clam from CV joint.
6. Remove drive shaft flange bolts.
7. Slide propeller shaft off the transfer case and remove shaft.

To install:

8. Install Constant Velocity (CV) boot clamp. Do not crimp the boot clamp at this time.
9. Slide the propeller shaft onto transfer case.
10. Align propeller shaft and pinion flange reference marks.

Install propeller shaft flange bolts and tighten to 85 ft. lbs. (115 Nm).

➡ **Flange bolts incorporate a Loctite® patch, new bolts should be used. If new bolts are not available, clean bolts and apply Mopar® Lock and Seal Adhesive, or equivalent to the threads.**

❊❊ CAUTION

Failure to follow these instruction may result in a driveline vibration.

11. Crimp the CV boot clamp.
12. Install skid plate, if equipped.

FRONT HALFSHAFT

REMOVAL & INSTALLATION

See Figure 7.

1. With vehicle in neutral, position vehicle on hoist.
2. Remove skid plate, if equipped.
3. Remove hub nut from the half shaft.
4. Remove brake caliper and rotor .
5. Remove wheel speed sensor if equipped.
6. Remove hub bearing bolts from the knuckle.
7. Remove hub bearing and brake shield from knuckle.
8. Support half shaft at the C/V joint housings.
9. Position two pry bars behind the inner C/V housing and disengage the C/V joint from the axle.
10. Remove half shaft from vehicle.

To install:

11. Apply a light coating of wheel bearing grease on the axle splines.
12. Insert half shaft into steering knuckle and onto the axle. Verify shaft snap-ring

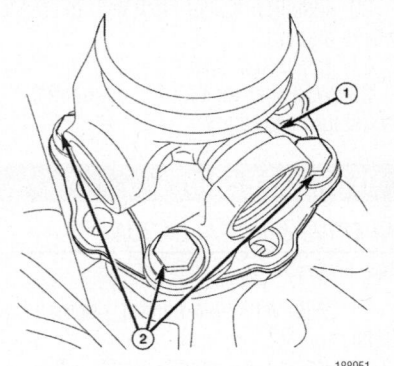

Fig. 5 Locating the I.D. tag (1), fill plug (2) and drain plug (3)

192159

Fig. 6 Remove drive shaft (1) flange bolts (2)

188951

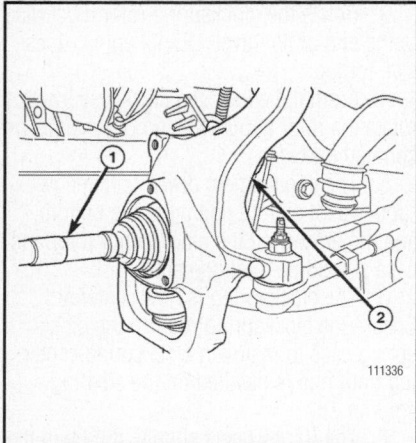

Fig. 7 Removing the halfshaft (1) from the knuckle (2)

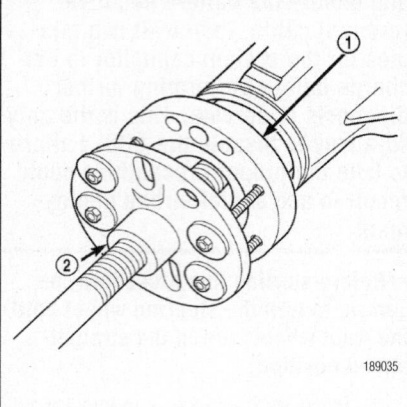

Fig. 8 Hold flange (1) with Holder (2) and four bolts and washers

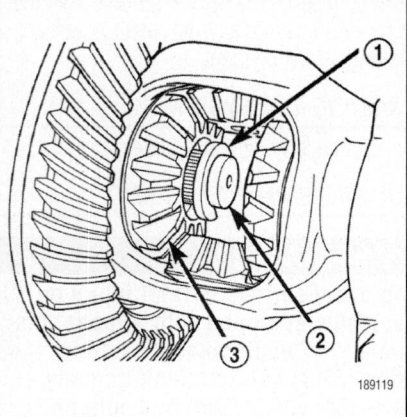

Fig. 9 Remove the C-lock (1), axle shaft (2) and gear (3)

engages with the groove on the inside of the joint housing.

13. Clean hub bearing bore and hub bearing mating surface. Lightly coat mating surfaces with grease.

14. Install hub bearing onto the axle half shaft and into steering knuckle. Tighten hub bearing bolts to 120 ft. lbs. (163 Nm).

15. Install wheel speed sensor, if equipped.

16. Install brake rotor and caliper adapter with caliper.

17. Install half shaft nut. Apply brakes and tighten shaft nut to 185 ft. lbs. (251 Nm).

18. Install skid plate, if equipped.

FRONT PINION SEAL

REMOVAL & INSTALLATION

See Figure 8.

1. Remove both half shafts.

2. Mark propeller shaft and pinion flange for installation reference.

3. Remove front propeller shaft.

4. Rotate pinion flange three to four times, to verify pinion rotates smoothly.

5. Record pinion torque to rotating with an inch pound torque wrench for installation reference.

6. Hold flange with Holder and four bolts and washers.

7. Remove pinion nut.

8. Mark a line across pinion shaft and flange for installation reference.

9. Remove flange with Puller.

10. Remove pinion seal with a seal pick.

To install:

11. Apply a light coating of gear lubricant on the lip of pinion seal.

12. Install seal with Installer and Handle.

13. Position flange on pinion shaft with reference marks aligned.

14. Install flange with Installer and holder.

15. Hold companion flange with Holder.

16. Install new pinion nut and tighten pinion nut to 200 ft. lbs. (271 Nm).

➡ **Do not exceed minimum tightening torque 200 ft. lbs. (271 Nm) when tighten pinion nut at this point.**

17. Record pinion torque to rotate, with a torque wrench. Pinion torque to rotating should be equal to recorded reading plus an additional 5 inch lbs.

18. If pinion torque to rotating is low, tighten pinion nut in 5 ft. lbs. increments until pinion torque to rotate is achieved.

❋❋ CAUTION

Never loosen pinion nut to decrease pinion bearing rotating torque. If pinion torque to rotating or maximum tightening torque 350 ft. lbs. (474 Nm) is exceeded a new collapsible spacer must be installed.

19. Failure to follow these instructions will result in damage to the axle.

20. Install propeller shaft with reference marks aligned.

21. Install half shafts.

22. Add gear lubricant to differential housing if necessary.

REAR AXLE SHAFT

REMOVE & INSTALLATION

See Figure 9.

1. With vehicle in neutral, position on hoist.

2. Remove rear brake components.

3. Remove differential housing cover and drain lubricant.

4. Rotate differential case so pinion

mate shaft lock screw is accessible. Remove lock screw and pinion mate shaft from differential case.

5. Push axle shaft inward and remove C-lock from the axle shaft.

6. Remove the axle shaft.

To install:

7. Lubricate bearing bore and seal lip with gear lubricant.

8. Install axle shaft through seal, bearing and engage into side gear splines.

➡ **Do not damaging axle shaft seal during axle installation.**

9. Install C-lock in axle shaft, then push axle shaft outward to seat C-lock in side gear.

10. Install pinion shaft into differential case and through thrust washers and differential pinions.

11. Align hole in shaft with hole in the differential case and install lock screw with Loctite® on the threads. Tighten lock screw to 8 ft. lbs. (11 Nm).

12. Install differential cover and fill with gear lubricant.

13. Install rear brake components.

REAR AXLE SHAFT BEARING & SEAL

REMOVAL & INSTALLATION

See Figure 10.

1. Remove the axle shaft.

2. Remove axle shaft seal from axle tube with a seal pick.

To install:

3. Remove any old sealer/burrs from axle tube.

4. Coat new seal lip with axle lubricant and install seal with Installer and Handle.

5. Install the axle shaft.

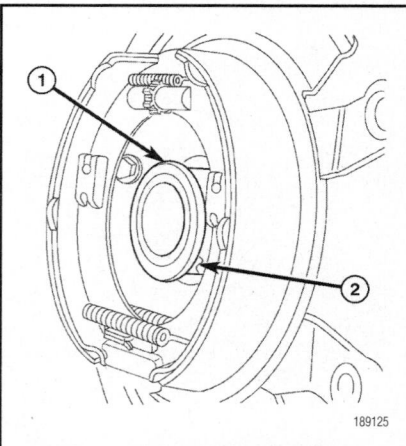

Fig. 10 Remove axle shaft seal (1) from axle tube (2)

6. Remove any old sealer/burrs from axle tube.

7. Coat new seal lip with axle lubricant and install seal with Installer and Handle.

8. Install the axle shaft.

REAR DRIVESHAFT

REMOVAL & INSTALLATION

See Figure 11.

1. With vehicle in neutral, position vehicle on hoist.

2. Mark propeller shaft pinion flange and propeller shaft flange with installation reference marks.

3. If equipped with manual transmission, mark manual transmission flange and propeller shaft flange for installation reference.

4. If equipped with a center bearing

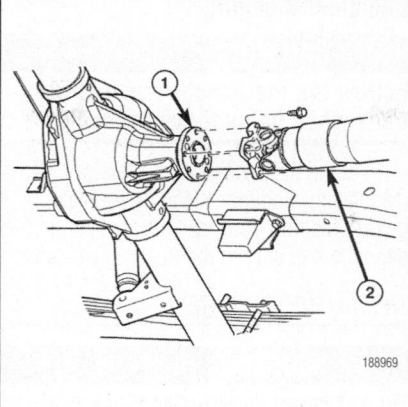

Fig. 11 Remove pinion flange (1) bolts from propeller shaft (2)

mark an outline of the center bearing on the center bearing bracket for installation reference. Then support propeller shaft and remove mounting bolts.

5. Remove pinion flange bolts from propeller shaft.

6. Slide propeller shaft back off automatic transmission/transfer case output shaft, then mark propeller shaft and transmission/transfer case output shaft for installation reference.

7. If equipped with manual transmission remove flange bolts.

8. Remove the propeller shaft from vehicle.

> ✳✳ **CAUTION**
> **Failure to follow these instructions may result in a driveline vibration.**

To install:

→ Flange bolts incorporate a Loctite® patch, new bolts should be used. If new bolts are not available, clean bolts and apply Mopar® Lock and Seal Adhesive, or equivalent to the threads.

> ✳✳ **CAUTION**
> **Failure to follow these instructions may result in a driveline vibration.**

9. Slide slip yoke onto automatic transmission/transfer case output shaft with reference marks aligned.

10. If equipped with manual transmission, align transmission flange and propeller shaft reference marks. Install flange bolts and tighten to 85 ft. lbs. (115 Nm).

11. If two piece propeller shaft, align center bearing (1) with reference marks on center bearing bracket and tighten bolts to 40 ft. lbs. (54 Nm).

12. Align reference marks on propeller shaft and pinion flange. Install companion flange (1) bolts and tighten to 85 ft. lbs. (115 Nm).

> ✳✳ **CAUTION**
> **Failure to follow these instructions may result in a driveline vibration.**

REAR PINION SEAL

REMOVAL & INSTALLATION

Refer to Front Pinion Seal.

ENGINE COOLING

ENGINE COOLANT

DRAIN PROCEDURE

See Figure 12.

> ✳✳ **WARNING**
> **Always allow the engine to cool before opening the cooling system. Do not unscrew the coolant pressure relief cap when the engine is operating or the cooling system is hot. The cooling system is under pressure; steam and hot liquid can come out forcefully when the cap is loosened slightly. Failure to follow these instructions may result in serious personal injury.**

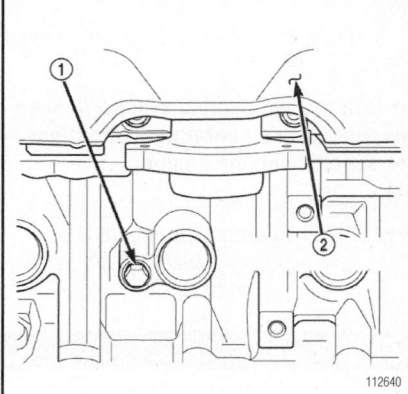

Fig. 12 Locating the cylinder block drain plug (1)

> ✳✳ **WARNING**
> **Do not remove cylinder block drain plugs or loosen radiator draincock with system hot and under pressure. serious burns from coolant can occur.**

→DO NOT WASTE reusable coolant. If solution is clean, drain coolant into a clean container for reuse.

1. Remove the radiator pressure cap.
2. Loosen the radiator petcock.
3. Remove cylinder block drain plugs.

CLEANING PROCEDURE

Cleaning

Drain the cooling system and refill with water. Run the engine with the radiator cap installed until the upper radiator hose is hot. Stop the engine and drain the water from the system. If the water is dirty, fill the system with water, run the engine and drain the system. Repeat until the water drains clean.

Reverse Flushing

Reverse flushing of the cooling system is the forcing of water through the cooling system. This is done using air pressure in the opposite direction of normal coolant flow. It is usually only necessary with very dirty systems with evidence of partial plugging.

Reverse Flushing Radiator

Disconnect the radiator hoses from the radiator inlet and outlet. Attach a section of radiator hose to the radiator bottom outlet fitting and insert the flushing gun. Connect a water supply hose and air supply hose to the flushing gun.

❉❉ CAUTION

Internal radiator pressure must not exceed 144.79 kPa (21 psi) as damage to radiator may result.

Allow the radiator to fill with water. When the radiator is filled, apply air in short blasts. Allow the radiator to refill between blasts. Continue this reverse flushing until clean water flows out through the rear of the radiator cooling tube passages.

Reverse Flushing Engine

Drain the cooling system. Remove the thermostat housing and thermostat. Install the thermostat housing. Disconnect the radiator upper hose from radiator and attach the flushing gun to the hose. Disconnect the radiator lower hose from the water pump and attach a lead-away hose to the water pump inlet fitting.

Connect the water supply hose and the air supply hose to the flushing gun. Allow the engine to fill with water. When the engine is filled, apply air in short blasts, allowing the system to fill between air blasts. Continue until clean water flows through the lead away hose.

Remove the lead away hose, flushing gun, water supply hose and air supply hose. Remove the thermostat housing and install the thermostat. Install the thermostat housing with a replacement gasket. Refer to Thermostat Replacement. Connect the radiator hoses. Refill the cooling system with correct antifreeze/water mixture.

Chemical Cleaning

❉❉ CAUTION

Follow the manufacturer's instructions when using these products.

In some instances, use a radiator cleaner (Mopar(tm) Radiator Kleen or equivalent) before flushing. This softens scale and other deposits and aids in the flushing operation.

REFILL PROCEDURE

❉❉ WARNING

Do not remove cylinder block drain plugs or loosen radiator draincock with system hot and under pressure. Serious burns from coolant can occur.

1. Install cylinder block drain plugs. Coat the threads with Mopar® Thread Sealant with Teflon.
2. Close radiator petcock.
3. Fill cooling system with a 50/50 mixture of water and.
4. Fill coolant reserve/overflow tank to MAX mark.
5. Start and operate engine until thermostat opens (upper radiator hose warm to touch).
6. If necessary, add antifreeze mixture, to the coolant reserve/overflow tank. This is done to maintain coolant level between the MAX and MIN marks. The level in the reserve/overflow tank may drop below the MIN mark after three or four warm-up and cool-down cycles.

FLUSHING

1. Drain the cooling system.
2. Remove the thermostat. For additional information, refer to Thermostat in this section.
3. Install the thermostat housing without the thermostat.

➡ **Refer to the cooling system flusher manufacturer's operating instructions for specific vehicle hook-up.**

4. Use an appropriate cooling system flusher to flush the engine and radiator.
5. Use premium cooling system flush.
6. Install the thermostat.

ENGINE FAN

REMOVAL & INSTALLATION

See Figure 13.

1. Partially drain the cooling system.
2. Remove the upper radiator hose.

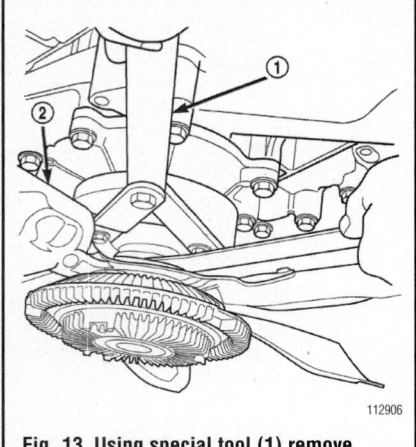

Fig. 13 Using special tool (1) remove from the water pump (2)

3. Remove the air filter housing assembly.
4. Using Tool and adapter pins, remove fan/viscous fan drive assembly from water pump. Do not attempt to remove fan/viscous fan drive assembly from vehicle at this time.
5. Position the fan/fan drive assembly in the radiator shroud.
6. Remove the two shroud mounting screws.
7. Remove the radiator shroud and fan drive assembly.
8. After removing fan blade/viscous fan drive assembly, do not place viscous fan drive in horizontal position. If stored horizontally, silicone fluid in the viscous fan drive could drain into its bearing assembly and contaminate lubricant.
9. Remove four bolts securing fan blade assembly to viscous fan drive .

To install:

10. Install fan blade assembly to viscous fan drive. Tighten bolts to 17 ft. lbs. (23 Nm) torque.
11. Position fan blade/viscous fan drive assembly into the radiator shroud.
12. Install the radiator shroud and fan drive assembly into the vehicle.
13. Install fan shroud retaining screws. Tighten screws to 50 inch lbs. (6 Nm).
14. Install fan blade/viscous fan drive assembly to water pump shaft .
15. Install the upper radiator hose.
16. Fill the cooling system.
17. Connect the battery negative cable.

RADIATOR

REMOVAL & INSTALLATION

1. Disconnect the battery negative cable.

2. Drain the cooling system.

3. Remove the pushpins and the upper condenser/radiator seal.

4. Remove the upper radiator hose.

5. Disconnect power steering hoses from power steering fluid cooler.

6. If equipped, disconnect transmission oil cooler lines.

7. Remove the overflow tube.

8. Remove the radiator fan shroud from the radiator and position over the radiator fan.

9. Raise the vehicle.

10. Disconnect the power steering cooler lines.

11. Remove the lower radiator hose.

12. Lower the vehicle.

13. Remove the upper radiator mounting bolts.

14. Remove the radiator.

15. Remove power steering fluid oil cooler from the radiator, if necessary.

16. Remove A/C condenser from radiator.

To install:

17. The radiator has two isolator pins on bottom of both tanks. These fit into alignment holes in radiator lower support .

18. Install A/C condenser, if removed.

19. Install power steering cooler, if removed.

20. Install transmission oil cooler if removed.

21. Install the upper radiator mount

22. Position isolator pins into alignment holes in radiator lower support.

23. Install upper radiator support. Tighten bolts to 17 ft. lbs. (23 Nm).

24. Install LH and RH radiator side seals.

25. Install upper radiator hose.

26. Install overflow tube.

27. Install radiator shroud.

28. Install power steering cooler lines.

29. If equipped, install transmission cooler lines.

30. Install lower radiator hose.

31. Lower vehicle.

32. Fill radiator .

33. Connect battery negative cable.

34. Start and warm the engine. Check for leaks.

THERMOSTAT

REMOVAL & INSTALLATION

See Figure 14.

1. Disconnect the negative battery cable.

2. Drain the cooling system.

3. Raise and support the vehicle.

4. 4.7L only: Remove the splash shield.

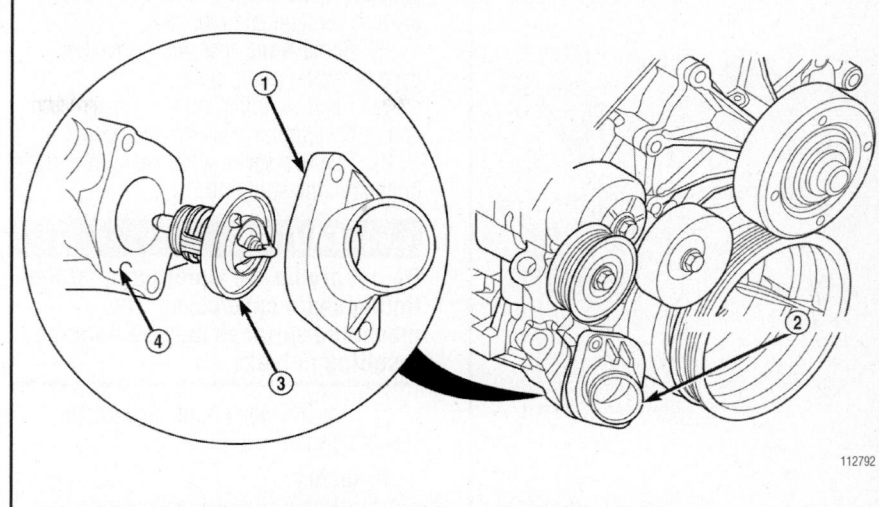
Fig. 14 Thermostat housing (1), lower radiator hose (2) and thermostat (3)

5. Remove the lower radiator hose the thermostat housing.

6. Remove the thermostat housing mounting bolts, thermostat housing and thermostat.

To install:

7. Clean the mating areas of timing chain cover and thermostat housing.

8. Install thermostat (spring side down) into recessed machined groove on timing chain cover .

9. Position the thermostat housing on timing chain cover.

10. Install two housing-to-timing chain cover bolts. Tighten bolts to 112 inch lbs. (13 Nm) torque.

✳✳ CAUTION

Housing must be tightened evenly and thermostat must be centered into recessed groove in timimg chain cover. If not, it may result in a cracked housing, damaged timing chain cover threads or coolant leaks.

11. Install lower radiator hose on thermostat housing.

12. Install splash shield.

13. Lower the vehicle.

14. Fill the cooling system.

15. Connect negative battery cable to battery.

16. Start and warm the engine. Check for leaks.

WATER PUMP

REMOVAL & INSTALLATION

See Figures 15 and 16.

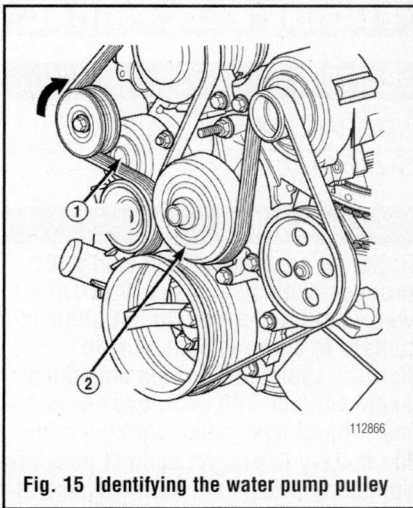
Fig. 15 Identifying the water pump pulley

➡ The water pump on 3.7L/4.7L engines is bolted directly to the engine timing chain case cover.

1. Disconnect negative battery cable.

2. Drain cooling system.

3. Remove fan/viscous fan drive assembly from water pump. Do not attempt to remove fan/viscous fan drive assembly from vehicle at this time.

4. If water pump is being replaced, do not unbolt fan blade assembly from thermal viscous fan drive.

5. Remove two fan shroud-to-radiator screws.

6. Remove fan shroud and fan blade/viscous fan drive assembly from vehicle.

7. After removing fan blade/viscous fan drive assembly, do not place thermal viscous fan drive in horizontal position. If stored horizontally, silicone fluid in viscous

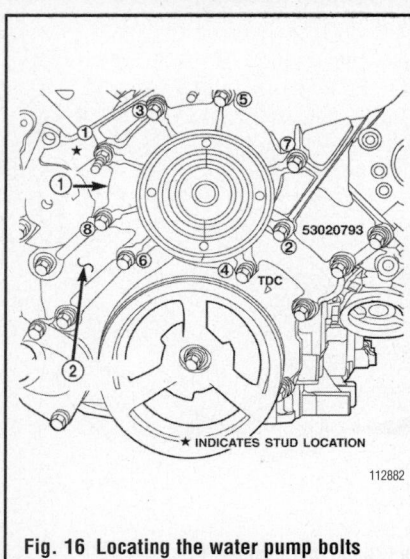

Fig. 16 Locating the water pump bolts

fan drive could drain into its bearing assembly and contaminate lubricant.

8. Remove the accessory drive belt from the water pump pulley.

9. Remove upper radiator hose clamp and remove upper hose at water pump.

10. Remove seven water pump mounting bolts and one stud bolt.

❊❊ CAUTION

Do not pry on the water pump at the timing chain case/cover. The machined surfaces may be damaged resulting in leaks.

11. Remove water pump and gasket. Discard gasket.

To install:

12. Clean the gasket mating surfaces.

13. Using a new gasket, position the water pump and install the mounting bolts as shown. Tighten water pump mounting bolts to 43 ft. lbs. (58 Nm).

14. Spin the water pump to be sure that the pump impeller does not rub against the timing chain case/cover.

15. Connect the upper radiator hose to the water pump.

16. Install the accessory drive belt.

17. Position the fan shroud and the fan blade/viscous fan drive assembly.

18. Install the two fan shroud-to-radiator screws.

19. Make sure there is 1.0 inches between the tips of the fan blades and fan shroud.

20. Install the fan blade/viscous fan drive assembly to the water pump shaft.

21. Evacuate air and refill cooling system.

22. Connect the negative battery cable.

23. Check the cooling system for leaks.

ENGINE ELECTRICAL

BATTERY

REMOVAL & INSTALLATION

See Figure 17.

❊❊ WARNING

Batteries contain sulfuric acid and produce explosive gases. Work in a well-ventilated area. Do not allow the battery to come in contact with flames, sparks or burning substances. Avoid contact with skin, eyes or clothing. Shield eyes when working near the battery to protect against possible splashing of acid solution. In case of acid contact with skin or eyes, flush immediately with water for a minimum of 15 minutes, then get prompt medical attention. If acid is swallowed, call a physician immediately. Failure to follow these instructions may result in serious personal injury.

❊❊ WARNING

Always deplete the backup power supply before repairing or installing any new front or side air bag supplemental restraint system (SRS) component and before servicing, removing, installing, adjusting or striking components near the front or side impact sensors or the restraints control module (RCM). Nearby components include doors, instrument panel, console, door latches, strikers, seats and hood latches.

➡ **To deplete the backup power supply energy, disconnect the battery ground cable and wait at least 1 minute. Be sure to disconnect auxiliary batteries and power supplies (if equipped).**

❊❊ WARNING

Failure to follow these instructions may result in serious personal injury or death in the event of an accidental deployment.

❊❊ WARNING

Always lift a plastic-cased battery with a battery carrier or with hands on opposite corners. Excessive pressure on the battery end walls may cause acid to flow through the vent caps, resulting in personal injury and/or damage to the vehicle or battery.

➡ **When the battery (or PCM) is disconnected and connected, some abnormal drive symptoms may occur while the vehicle relearns its adaptive strategy. The charging system setpoint may also vary. The vehicle may need to be driven to relearn its strategy.**

1. Turn the ignition switch to the Off position. Be certain that all electrical accessories are turned off.

2. Loosen the battery negative cable terminal clamp pinch-bolt hex nut.

3. Disconnect the battery negative cable terminal clamp from the battery negative terminal post. If necessary, use a battery termi-

BATTERY SYSTEM

nal puller to remove the terminal clamp from the battery post.

4. Loosen the battery positive cable terminal clamp pinch-bolt hex nut.

5. Disconnect the battery positive cable terminal clamp from the battery positive terminal post. If necessary, use a battery terminal puller to remove the terminal clamp from the battery post.

6. Remove the battery thermal guard.

7. Remove the battery hold down and bolt from the battery.

8. Remove the battery from the vehicle.

To install:

9. Clean and inspect the battery case, terminal posts and battery cable clamps.

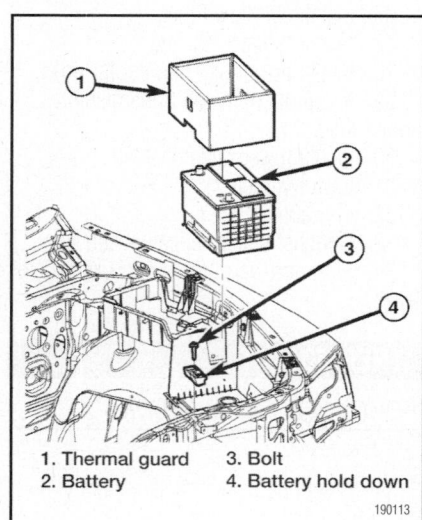

1. Thermal guard	3. Bolt
2. Battery	4. Battery hold down

Fig. 17 Exploded view of the battery assembly

10. Position the battery into the vehicle. Ensure that the battery positive and negative terminal posts are correctly positioned. The battery cable terminal clamps must reach the correct battery terminal post without stretching the cables.

11. Install the thermal guard and slide battery toward fender.

12. Install the battery hold down and bolt onto the battery. Tighten the bolt to 40 inch lbs. (4.5 Nm).

✳✳ CAUTION

Be certain that the battery cable terminal clamps are connected to the correct battery terminal posts.

13. Reverse battery polarity may damage electrical components of the vehicle.

14. Connect the battery positive cable terminal clamp (2) to the battery positive terminal post. Tighten the battery terminal clamp pinch-bolt hex nut to 45 inch (5 Nm).

15. Connect the battery negative cable terminal clamp (4) to the battery negative terminal post. Tighten the battery terminal clamp pinch-bolt hex nut to 45 inch (5 Nm).

16. Apply a thin coating of petroleum jelly or chassis grease to the exposed surfaces of the battery cable terminal clamps and the battery terminal posts.

BATTERY RECONNECT/RELEARN PROCEDURE

✳✳ WARNING

Batteries contain sulfuric acid and produce explosive gases. Work in a well-ventilated area. Do not allow the battery to come in contact with flames, sparks or burning substances. Avoid contact with skin, eyes or clothing. Shield eyes when working near the battery to protect against possible splashing of acid solution. In case of acid contact with skin or eyes, flush immediately with water for a minimum of 15 minutes, then get prompt medical attention. If acid is swallowed, call a physician immediately. Failure to follow these instructions may result in serious personal injury.

✳✳ WARNING

Always deplete the backup power supply before repairing or installing any new front or side air bag supplemental restraint system (SRS) component and before servicing, removing, installing, adjusting or striking components near the front or side impact sensors or the restraints control module (RCM). Nearby components include doors, instrument panel, console, door latches, strikers, seats and hood latches.

To deplete the backup power supply energy, disconnect the battery ground cable and wait at least 1 minute. Be sure to disconnect auxiliary batteries and power supplies (if equipped). Failure to follow these instructions may result in serious personal injury or death in the event of an accidental deployment.

✳✳ WARNING

Always lift a plastic-cased battery with a battery carrier or with hands on opposite corners. Excessive pressure on the battery end walls may cause acid to flow through the vent caps, resulting in personal injury and/or damage to the vehicle or battery.

➡**When the battery (or PCM) is disconnected and connected, some abnormal drive symptoms may occur while the vehicle relearns its adaptive strategy. The charging system setpoint may also vary. The vehicle may need to be driven to relearn its strategy.**

ENGINE ELECTRICAL

ALTERNATOR

REMOVAL & INSTALLATION

See Figure 18.

1. Disconnect negative battery cable at battery.

2. Remove the alternator drive belt.

3. Unsnap the plastic insulator cap from B+ output terminal.

4. Remove the B+ terminal mounting nut at rear of generator. Disconnect terminal from generator.

5. Disconnect field wire connector at rear of generator by pushing on connector tab.

6. Remove 1 rear vertical generator mounting bolt.

7. Remove 2 front horizontal generator mounting bolts.

8. Remove the generator from vehicle.

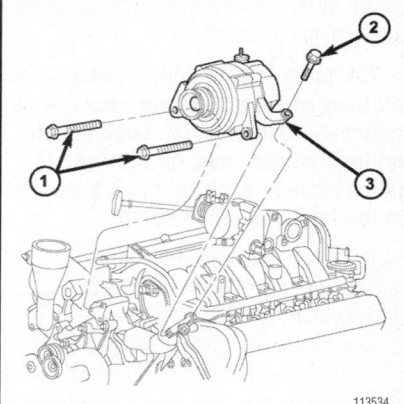

113534

Fig. 18 Removing the rear bolt (1), front bolts (2) and alternator (3)

To install:

9. Position generator to engine and install 2 horizontal bolts and 1 vertical bolt.

10. Tighten all 3 bolts.

CHARGING SYSTEM

11. Snap the field wire connector into rear of generator.

12. Install the B+ terminal eyelet to generator output stud. Tighten mounting nut. Refer to Torque Specifications.

✳✳ CAUTION

Never force a belt over a pulley rim using a screwdriver. The synthetic fiber of the belt can be damaged.

✳✳ CAUTION

When installing a serpentine accessory drive belt, the belt must be routed correctly. The water pump may be rotating in the wrong direction if the belt is installed incorrectly, causing the engine to overheat.

13. Install the generator drive belt.

14. Install negative battery cable to battery.

IGNITION COIL

REMOVAL & INSTALLATION

See Figure 19.

➡ An individual ignition coil is used for each pair of spark plugs. Each coil attaches directly to the top of the eight upper bank of spark plugs. Secondary cables connect each coil to the eight lower bank of spark plugs. The coils themselves fit into machined holes in the cylinder head. Each coil also has its own individual electrical connector.

➡ A mounting bolt secures each coil assembly to the top of the intake manifold. The bottom of the coil assembly is equipped with a rubber boot to seal the spark plug to the coil. Inside each rubber boot is a spring. The spring is used for a mechanical contact between the coil and the top of the upper bank of spark plugs. These rubber boots and springs are a permanent part of the coil assembly and are not serviced separately. The rubber boot is also used to seal the coil at the opening into the cylinder head.

1. Depending on which coil is being removed, the throttle body air intake tube or intake box may need to be removed to gain access to coil.
2. Disconnect coil electrical connector(s).
3. Clean area at base of coil with compressed air before removal.
4. Remove coil mounting bolt.
5. Disconnect spark plug wire from coil.
6. Carefully pull up coil from cylinder head opening with a slight twisting action.
7. Remove coil from vehicle.

   To install:

8. Using compressed air, blow out any dirt or contaminants from around top of spark plug.
9. Check condition of coil o-ring and replace as necessary. To aid in coil installation, apply silicone to coil o-ring.
10. Position ignition coil into cylinder head opening and push onto spark plug.
11. Tighten coil mounting bolt to 106 inch lbs (12 Nm).
12. Connect coil electrical connector.

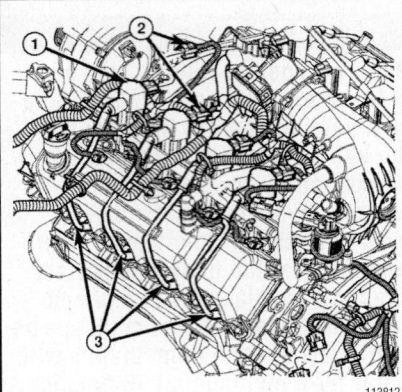

Fig. 19 Locating the ignition coil (1), electrical connector (2) and secondary cable (3)

13. Connect spark plug wires.
14. If necessary, install throttle body air tube.

IGNITION TIMING

ADJUSTMENT

Ignition timing is not adjustable.

SPARK PLUGS

REMOVAL & INSTALLATION

1. Remove the necessary air filter tubing and air intake components at the top of the engine at the throttle body.

➡ The three spark plugs located on the left bank of the engine are under three individual ignition coils. Each individual ignition coil must be removed to gain access to each spark plug located on the left bank of the engine.

2. Prior to removing the ignition coil, spray compressed air around the coil base at the cylinder head.
3. Remove the ignition coil check the condition of ignition coil O-ring and replace as necessary.
4. Prior to removing the spark plug, spray compressed air into the cylinder head opening. This will help prevent foreign material from entering combustion chamber.

5. Remove the spark plug from the cylinder head using a quality thin wall socket with a rubber or foam insert.
6. Inspect the spark plug condition.

INSPECTION

1. Inspect the spark plug for a bridged gap.
   a. Check for deposit build-up closing the gap between the electrodes. Deposits are caused by oil or carbon fouling.
   b. Install a new spark plug.
2. Check for oil fouling.
   a. Check for wet, black deposits on the insulator shell bore electrodes, caused by excessive oil entering the combustion chamber through worn rings and pistons, excessive valve-to-guide clearance or worn or loose bearings.
   b. Correct the oil leak concern.
   c. Install a new spark plug.
3. Inspect for carbon fouling. Look for black, dry, fluffy carbon deposits on the insulator tips, exposed shell surfaces and electrodes, caused by a spark plug with an incorrect heat range, dirty air cleaner, too rich a fuel mixture or excessive idling.
   a. Install new spark plugs.
4. Inspect for normal burning.
   a. Check for light tan or gray deposits on the firing tip.
5. Inspect for pre-ignition, identified by melted electrodes and a possibly damaged insulator. Metallic deposits on the insulator indicate engine damage. This may be caused by incorrect ignition timing, wrong type of fuel or the unauthorized installation of a heli-coil insert in place of the spark plug threads.
   a. Install a new spark plug.
6. Inspect for overheating, identified by white or light gray spots and a bluish-burnt appearance of electrodes. This is caused by engine overheating, wrong type of fuel, loose spark plugs, spark plugs with an incorrect heat range, low fuel pump pressure or incorrect ignition timing.
   a. Install a new spark plug.
7. Inspect for fused deposits, identified by melted or spotty deposits resembling bubbles or blisters. These are caused by sudden acceleration.
   a. Install new spark plugs.

STARTER

REMOVAL & INSTALLATION

Manual Transmission

See Figure 20.

1. Disconnect and isolate negative battery cable.
2. Raise and support vehicle.

➡ **If equipped with 4WD and certain transmissions, a support bracket is used between front axle and side of transmission. Remove 2 support bracket bolts at transmission. Pry support bracket slightly to gain access to lower starter mounting bolt.**

3. Remove one bolt and one nut if equipped with a manual transmission.
4. Move starter motor towards front of vehicle far enough for nose of starter pinion housing to clear housing. Always support starter motor during this process, do not let starter motor hang from wire harness.
5. Tilt nose downwards and lower starter motor far enough to access and remove nut (2) that secures battery positive cable wire harness connector eyelet to solenoid battery terminal stud. Do not let starter motor hang from wire harness.
6. Remove the battery positive cable wire harness connector eyelet from solenoid battery terminal stud.
7. Disconnect the battery positive cable wire harness connector from solenoid terminal connector receptacle.
8. Remove the starter motor.

To install:

9. Connect solenoid wire to starter motor (snaps on).

10. Position the battery cable to solenoid stud. Install and tighten battery cable eyelet nut. Refer to
11. Torque Specifications. Do not allow starter motor to hang from wire harness.
12. Position the starter motor to transmission.
13. Install and tighten the lock washer nut and bolt.
14. Lower the vehicle.
15. Connect negative battery cable.

Automatic Transmission

See Figure 21.

1. Disconnect and isolate negative battery cable.
2. Raise and support vehicle.

➡ **If equipped with 4WD and certain transmissions, a support bracket is used between front axle and side of**

transmission. **Remove 2 support bracket bolts at transmission. Pry support bracket slightly to gain access to lower starter mounting bolt.**

3. Remove two bolts if equipped with an automatic transmission.
4. Move starter motor towards front of vehicle far enough for nose of starter pinion housing to clear housing. Always support starter motor during this process, do not let starter motor hang from wire harness.
5. Tilt nose downwards and lower starter motor far enough to access and remove nut that secures battery positive cable wire harness connector eyelet to solenoid battery terminal stud. Do not let starter motor hang from wire harness.
6. Remove the battery positive cable wire harness connector eyelet from solenoid battery terminal stud.
7. Disconnect the battery positive cable

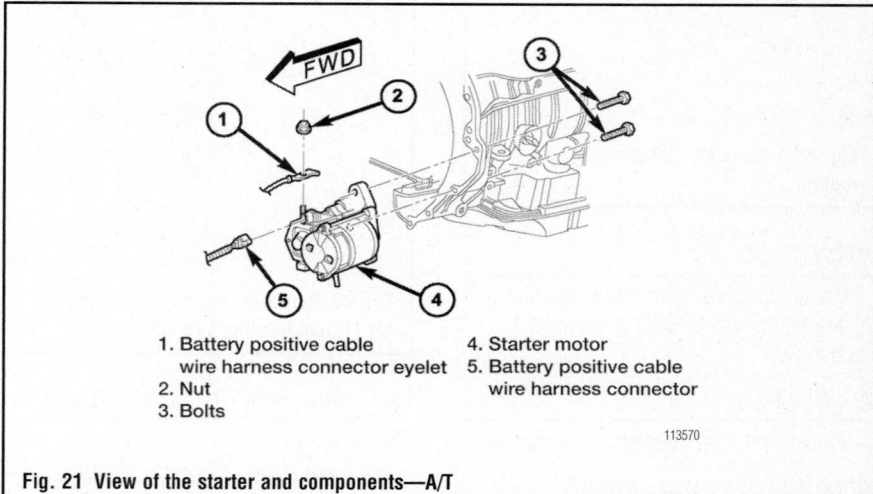

1. Battery positive cable wire harness connector eyelet
2. Nut
3. Bolts
4. Starter motor
5. Battery positive cable wire harness connector

113570

Fig. 21 View of the starter and components—A/T

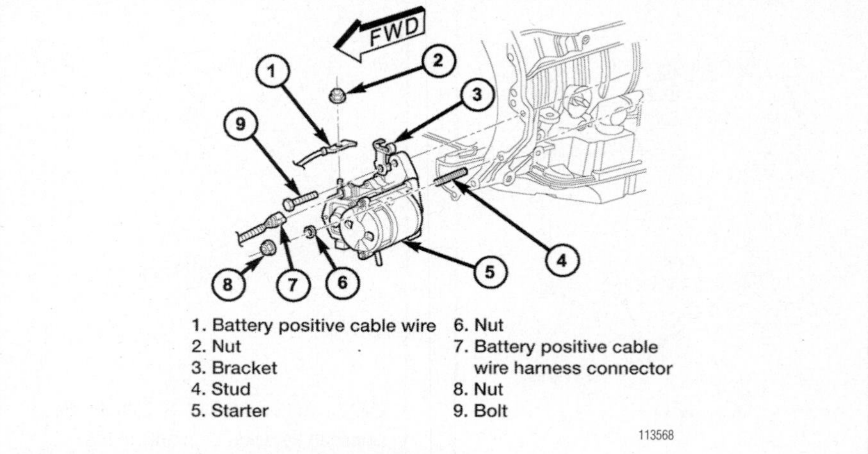

wire harness connector from solenoid terminal connector receptacle.
8. Remove the starter motor.

To install:

9. Connect solenoid wire to starter motor (snaps on).
10. Position the battery cable to solenoid stud. Install and tighten battery cable eyelet nut. Do not allow starter motor to hang from wire harness.
11. Position the starter motor to transmission.
12. If equipped with automatic transmission, slide cooler tube bracket into position.
13. Install and tighten both bolts.
14. Lower the vehicle.
15. Connect negative battery cable.

1. Battery positive cable wire
2. Nut
3. Bracket
4. Stud
5. Starter
6. Nut
7. Battery positive cable wire harness connector
8. Nut
9. Bolt

113568

Fig. 20 View of the starter and components—M/T

ENGINE MECHANICAL

➡ Disconnecting the negative battery cable may interfere with the functions of the on board computer systems and may require the computer to undergo a relearning process, once the negative battery cable is reconnected.

ACCESSORY DRIVE BELTS

ACCESSORY BELT ROUTING
See Figure 22.

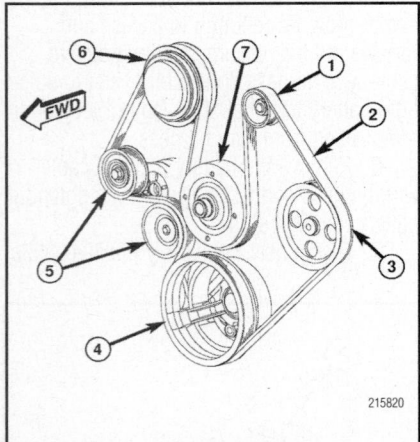

Fig. 22 3.7L and 4.7L accessory belt routing

INSPECTION
Inspect for glazing, cracking, splitting, delaminating and shredding. Replace as necessary.

ADJUSTMENT
Adjustment is not possible or necessary.

REMOVAL & INSTALLATION

✷✷ CAUTION
Do not let tensioner arm snap back to the freearm position, severe damage may occur to the tensioner.

1. Disconnect the negative battery cable.
2. Rotate the belt tensioner until it contacts the stop.
3. Remove the accessory drive belt, then slowly rotate the tensioner into the freearm position.
4. Install new belt. Route the belt around all pulleys except the idler pulley. Rotate the tensioner arm until it contacts it's stop position. Route the belt around the idle and slowly let the tensioner rotate into the belt. Make sure the belt is seatedonto all pulleys.
5. With the drive belt installed, inspect

the belt wear indicator. On 4.7L Engines only, the gap between the tang and the housing stop must not exceed 0.94 inches. If the measurement exceeds this specification replace the serpentine accessory drive belt.

AIR CLEANER

REMOVAL & INSTALLATION
See Figure 23.

1. Loosen clamp and disconnect air duct at air cleaner cover.
2. Lift entire housing assembly from 4 locating pins.
3. To install, reverse the removal procedure.

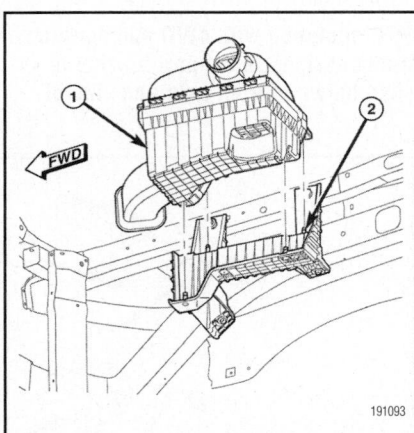

Fig. 23 Removing the air cleaner assembly (1) and locating pins (2)

FILTER/ELEMENT REPLACEMENT
See Figure 24.

1. Loosen clamp and disconnect air duct at air cleaner cover.

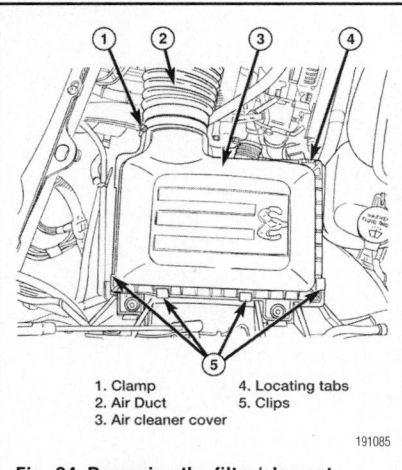

1. Clamp
2. Air Duct
3. Air cleaner cover
4. Locating tabs
5. Clips

Fig. 24 Removing the filter/element

2. Pry over 4 spring clips from housing cover (spring clips retain cover to housing).
3. Release housing cover from locating tabs on housing and remove cover.
4. Remove air cleaner element (filter) from housing.
5. Clean the inside of housing before replacing element.
6. To install, reverse the removal procedure.

CAMSHAFT AND VALVE LIFTERS

INSPECTION
1. Inspect the cylinder head for out-of-flatness, using a straightedge and a feeler gauge. If tolerances exceed 0.002 inches replace the cylinder head.
2. Inspect the valve seats for damage. Service the valve seats as necessary.
3. Inspect the valve guides for wear, cracks or looseness. If either condition exist, replace the cylinder head.

REMOVAL & INSTALLATION

3.7L Engine
See Figures 25 and 26.

➡ Procedure is for the left camshaft, right camshaft procedure is similar.

✷✷ CAUTION
When the timing chain is removed and the cylinder heads are still installed, Do not forcefully rotate the camshafts or crankshaft independently of each other. Severe valve and/or piston damage can occur.

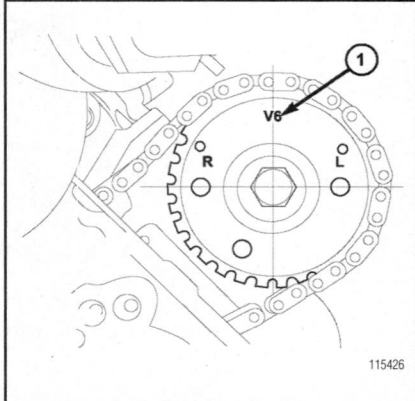

Fig. 25 Set engine to TDC cylinder No. 1, camshaft sprocket V6 marks at the 12 o'clock position

> ✸✸ **CAUTION**
>
> When removing the cam sprocket, timing chains or camshaft, Failure to use Wedge Locking Tool Locking Tool, Wedge will result in hydraulic tensioner ratchet over extension, requiring timing chain cover removal to reset the tensioner ratchet.

1. Remove the valve covers.
2. Set engine to TDC cylinder No. 1, camshaft sprocket V6 marks at the 12 o'clock position.
3. Mark one link on the secondary timing chain on both sides of the V6 mark on the camshaft sprocket to aid in installation.

> ✸✸ **CAUTION**
>
> Do not hold or pry on the camshaft target wheel (Located on the right side camshaft sprocket) for any reason, Severe damage will occur to the target wheel resulting in a vehicle no start condition.

4. Loosen but DO NOT remove the camshaft sprocket retaining bolt. Leave the bolt snug against the sprocket.

➡ The timing chain tensioners must be secured prior to removing the camshaft sprockets. Failure to secure tensioners will allow the tensioners to extend, requiring timing chain cover removal in order to reset tensioners.

> ✸✸ **CAUTION**
>
> Do not force the wedge past the narrowest point between the chain strands. Damage to the tensioners may occur.

5. Position Wedge Locking Tool between the timing chain strands, tap the tool to securely wedge the timing chain against the tensioner arm and guide.
6. Hold the camshaft with the Spanner Wrench and Adapter Pins while removing the camshaft sprocket bolt.
7. Using Camshaft Holder, remove the sprocket and gently allow the camshaft to rotate 5° clockwise until the camshaft is in the neutral position (no valve load).
Starting at the outside working inward, loosen the camshaft bearing cap retaining bolts 1/2 turn at a time. Repeat until all load is off the bearing caps.

> ✸✸ **CAUTION**
>
> Do not stamp or strike the camshaft bearing caps. severe damage will occur to the bearing caps.

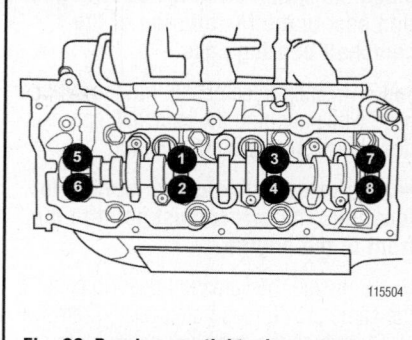

Fig. 26 Bearing cap tightening sequence

➡ When the camshaft is removed the rocker arms may slide downward, mark the rocker arms before removing camshaft.

8. Remove the camshaft bearing caps and the camshaft.

To install:

9. Lubricate the camshaft journals with clean engine oil.

➡ Position the left side camshaft so that the camshaft sprocket dowel is near the 1 o'clock position, This will place the camshaft at the neutral position easing the installation of the camshaft bearing caps.

10. Position the camshaft into the cylinder head.
11. Install the camshaft bearing caps, hand tighten the retaining bolts.

➡ Caps should be installed so that the stamped numbers on the caps are in numerical order, (1 through 4) from the front to the rear of the engine. All caps should be installed so that the stamped arrows on the caps point toward the front of the engine.

12. Working in 1/2 turn increments, tighten the bearing cap retaining bolts starting with the middle cap working outward.
13. Tighten the camshaft bearing cap retaining bolts to 100 inch lbs. (11 Nm).
14. Position the camshaft drive gear into the timing chain aligning the V6 mark between the two marked chain links (Two links marked during removal).
15. Using the Camshaft Holder, rotate the camshaft until the camshaft sprocket dowel is aligned with the slot in the camshaft sprocket. Install the sprocket onto the camshaft.

> ✸✸ **CAUTION**
>
> Remove excess oil from the camshaft sprocket retaining bolt, failure to do

so can cause bolt over-torque resulting in bolt failure.

16. Remove excess oil from bolt, then install the camshaft sprocket retaining bolt and hand tighten.
17. Remove the Wedge Locking Tool.
18. Using Spanner Wrench with adapter pins, tighten the camshaft sprocket retaining bolt to 90 ft. lbs. (122 Nm).
19. Install the cylinder head cover.

4.7L Engine

Left Camshaft

See Figures 27 and 28.

1. Remove the cylinder head cover.

> ✸✸ **CAUTION**
>
> When the timing chain is removed and the cylinder heads are still installed, Do not forcefully rotate the camshafts or crankshaft independently of each other. Severe valve and/or piston damage can occur.

2. Set #1 cylinder to TDC and align the camshaft sprocket V8 mark to the 12 o'clock position.
3. Mark the link on the secondary timing chain that is aligned with the two dots on the camshaft sprocket as shown to aid in installation.

> ✸✸ **CAUTION**
>
> When removing the camshaft sprocket, timing chains or camshaft, the timing chain tensioner must be secured, failure to use Locking Wedge Wedge, Locking will result in hydraulic tensioner ratchet over extension, requiring timing chain cover removal to reset the tensioner ratchet.

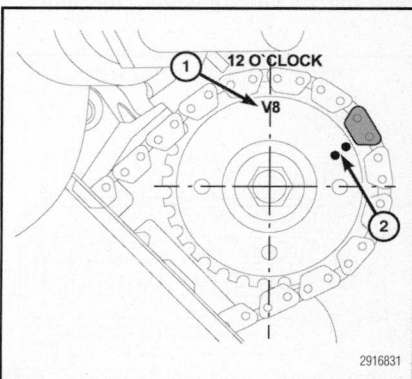

Fig. 27 Set #1 cylinder to TDC and align the camshaft sprocket V8 mark (1) to the 12 o'clock position

✳✳ CAUTION

Do not force Locking Wedge Wedge, Locking past the narrowest point between the chain strands. Damage to the tensioners may occur.

4. Position Locking Wedge between the timing chain strands, gently tap the wedge into position and secure the timing chain against the tensioner arm and guide.

5. Using Spanner Wrench with Adapter Pins, secure the camshaft sprocket and remove the camshaft sprocket bolt.

6. Position Camshaft Holder onto the camshaft.

7. Using the Camshaft Holder, hold the camshaft while removing the camshaft sprocket.

8. Using Camshaft Holder, gently allow the camshaft to rotate 15° clockwise until the camshaft is in the neutral position (no valve load).

✳✳ CAUTION

Do not stamp or strike the camshaft bearing caps or severe engine damage may result.

➡ When the camshaft is removed the rocker arms may slide downward, mark the rocker arms before removing camshaft.

9. Using the sequence shown, loosen the camshaft bearing cap retaining bolts 1/2 turn at a time until all load is off the bearing caps and remove bolts.

10. Remove the camshaft bearing caps and the camshaft.

To install:

11. Lubricate the camshaft journals with clean engine oil.

➡ **Position the left side camshaft so that the camshaft sprocket dowel is near the 1 o'clock position, this will**

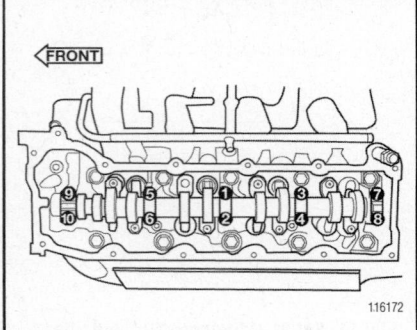

Fig. 28 Camshaft removing and tightening sequence—LH and RH camshafts

place the camshaft at the neutral position easing the installation of the camshaft bearing caps.

12. Install the camshaft into the cylinder head while aligning the camshaft sprocket dowel near the 1 o'clock position.

➡ **The camshaft caps are marked for location. The arrow must point to the front of the engine.**

13. Install the camshaft bearing caps in the same position as noted during removal.

14. Install the camshaft bearing cap retaining bolts hand tight.

15. Using the sequence shown, working in 1/2 turn increments, tighten the bearing cap retaining bolts to 8 ft. lbs. (11 Nm).

16. Check the camshaft end play.

17. Position the camshaft drive gear into the timing chain while aligning the two dots on the camshaft sprocket with the chain link marked during removal.

18. Using Camshaft Holder, rotate the camshaft until the camshaft sprocket dowel is aligned with the slot in the camshaft sprocket.

19. Position the sprocket onto the camshaft.

✳✳ CAUTION

Remove excess oil from the camshaft sprocket retaining bolt, failure to do so can cause bolt over-torque resulting in bolt failure.

20. Remove excess oil from the camshaft sprocket retaining bolt.

21. Install the camshaft sprocket retaining bolt hand tight.

22. Remove the timing chain Locking Wedge.

23. Using Spanner Wrench with Adapter Pins, secure the camshaft sprocket and tighten the retaining bolt to 90 ft. lbs. (122 Nm).

24. Install the cylinder head cover

Right Camshaft

See Figures 28 and 29.

1. Remove the cylinder head cover(s).

✳✳ CAUTION

When the timing chain is removed and the cylinder heads are still installed, Do not forcefully rotate the camshafts or crankshaft independently of each other. Severe valve and/or piston damage can occur.

2. Set #1 cylinder to TDC and align the camshaft sprocket V8 mark to the 12 o'clock position.

3. Mark the link on the secondary timing chain that is aligned with the two dots on the camshaft sprocket as shown to aid in installation.

✳✳ CAUTION

Do not hold or pry on the camshaft target wheel for any reason, severe damage will occur to the target wheel resulting in a vehicle no start condition.

✳✳ CAUTION

When removing the camshaft sprocket, timing chains or camshaft, the timing chain tensioner must be secured, failure to use Locking Wedge Wedge, Locking will result in hydraulic tensioner ratchet over extension, requiring timing chain cover removal to reset the tensioner ratchet.

✳✳ CAUTION

Do not force Locking Wedge Wedge, Locking past the narrowest point between the chain strands. Damage to the tensioners may occur.

4. Position Locking Wedge between the timing chain strands, gently tap the wedge into position and secure the timing chain against the tensioner arm and guide.

5. Using Spanner Wrench with Adapter Pins, secure the camshaft sprocket and remove the camshaft sprocket bolt.

6. Disconnect the electrical connector to the Camshaft Position Sensor (CMP).

7. Remove the CMP sensor retaining bolt

8. Using a slight rocking motion, carefully remove the CMP sensor.

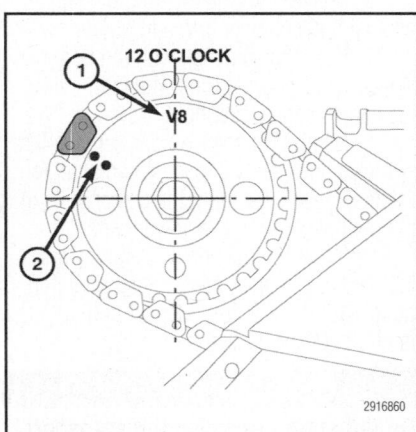

Fig. 29 V8 mark (1), chain and alignment marks (2)

9. Check the condition of the CMP sensor O-ring, replace as necessary.

10. Position Camshaft Holder onto the camshaft.

11. Using Camshaft Holder, hold the camshaft while removing the camshaft sprocket.

12. Using Camshaft Holder, gently allow the camshaft to rotate 45° counterclockwise until the camshaft is in the neutral position (no valve load).

✳✳ CAUTION

Do not stamp or strike the camshaft bearing caps or severe engine damage may result.

➡ **When the camshaft is removed the rocker arms may slide downward, mark the rocker arms before removing camshaft.**

13. Using the sequence shown, loosen the camshaft bearing cap retaining bolts 1/2 turn at a time until all load is off the bearing caps and remove bolts.

14. Remove the camshaft bearing caps and the camshaft.

To install:

15. Lubricate the camshaft journals with clean engine oil.

➡ **Position the right side camshaft so that the camshaft sprocket dowel is near the 10 o'clock position, this will place the camshaft at the neutral position easing the installation of the camshaft bearing caps.**

16. Install the camshaft into the cylinder head while aligning the camshaft sprocket dowel near the 10 o'clock position.

➡ **The camshaft caps are marked for location. The arrow must point to the front of the engine.**

17. Install the camshaft bearing caps in the same position as noted during removal.

18. Install the camshaft bearing cap retaining bolts hand tight.

19. Using the sequence, working in 1/2 turn increments, tighten the bearing cap retaining bolts to 8 ft. lbs. (11 Nm).

20. Check the camshaft end play.

21. Position the camshaft drive gear into the timing chain while aligning the two dots on the camshaft sprocket with the chain link marked during removal.

22. Using Camshaft Holder, rotate the camshaft until the camshaft sprocket dowel is aligned with the slot in the camshaft sprocket.

23. Position the sprocket onto the camshaft.

✳✳ CAUTION

Remove excess oil from the camshaft sprocket retaining bolt, failure to do so can cause bolt over-torque resulting in bolt failure.

24. Remove excess oil from the camshaft sprocket retaining bolt.

25. Install the camshaft sprocket retaining bolt hand tight.

26. Remove the timing chain Locking Wedge.

27. Using Spanner Wrench with Adapter Pins, secure the camshaft sprocket and tighten the retaining bolt to 90 ft. lbs. (122 Nm).

28. Install the cylinder head cover.

➡ **Before installing the CMP sensor into the cylinder head, the machined hole must be clean of any dirt or debris.**

29. Clean machined hole in the cylinder head.

30. Apply a small amount of engine oil to CMP sensor O-ring.

31. Install the CMP sensor into the cylinder head with a slight rocking motion. Do not twist sensor into position as damage to O-ring may result.

✳✳ CAUTION

Before tightening sensor mounting bolt, be sure sensor is completely flush to cylinder head. If sensor is not flush, damage to sensor mounting tang may result.

32. Install the retaining bolt and tighten to 9 ft. lbs. (12 Nm).

33. Connect the electrical connector to the CMP sensor.

CATALYTIC CONVERTER

REMOVAL & INSTALLATION
See Figure 30.

✳✳ CAUTION

When servicing or replacing exhaust system components, disconnect the oxygen sensor connector(s). Allowing the exhaust to hang by the oxygen sensor wires will damage the harness and/or sensor.

1. Raise and support the vehicle.
2. Saturate all exhaust bolts and nuts with Mopar® Rust Penetrant. Allow 5 minutes for penetration.
3. Disconnect the oxygen sensor electrical connectors.

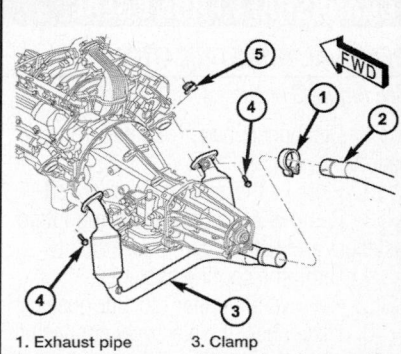

1. Exhaust pipe　3. Clamp
2. Catalytic converter　4. Extension pipe to muffler

Fig. 30 View of the catalytic converter and components

4. Remove the catalytic converter-to-manifold bolts.
5. Remove the catalytic converter to the exhaust pipe clamp.
6. If present, grind tack weld.
7. Remove the catalytic converter. You may have to loosen up other sections of the exhaust system.

To install:

✳✳ CAUTION

When servicing or replacing exhaust system components, disconnect the oxygen sensor connector(s). Allowing the exhaust to hang by the oxygen sensor wires will damage the harness and/or sensor.

➡**The band clamps are not reusable. After removal, they must be replaced with new one.**

8. Make sure the catalytic converter pipe is free of burrs.
9. Insert the catalytic converter into the exhaust pipe.
10. Make sure the alignment tang is fully seated in the alignment slot.
11. If other sections of the exhaust system where loosened in removal, refer to that information for the tightening procedures.
12. At the catalytic converter-to-extension pipe connection, install new clamp and nuts. Tighten the clamp nuts to 45 ft. lbs. (61 Nm) torque.
13. Lower the vehicle.
14. Start the engine, inspect for exhaust leaks. Repair exhaust leaks as necessary.
15. Check the exhaust system for contact with the body panels. Make the necessary adjustments, if necessary.

CRANKSHAFT FRONT SEAL

REMOVAL & INSTALLATION

See Figure 31.

1. Disconnect negative cable from battery.
2. Remove the accessory drive belt.
3. Remove A/C compressor mounting fasteners and set the compressor aside.
4. Drain the cooling system.
5. Remove the upper radiator hose.
6. Disconnect the electrical connector for fan mounted inside radiator shroud.
7. Remove the radiator cooling fan.
8. Remove crankshaft damper bolt.
9. Remove the damper using the Crankshaft Insert and Three Jaw Puller. Using the Seal Remover, remove crankshaft front seal.

To install:

☀ CAUTION

To prevent severe damage to the Crankshaft, Damper or Damper Installer Installer, Damper, thoroughly clean the damper bore and the crankshaft nose before installing Damper.

10. Using the Seal Installer and Damper Installer, install the crankshaft front seal.
11. Install the vibration damper.
12. Install the radiator cooling fan and shroud.
13. Install the upper radiator hose.
14. Install A/C compressor and tighten fasteners to 30 ft. lbs. (40 Nm).
15. Install the accessory drive belt.
16. Refill the cooling system.
17. Connect the negative battery cable to battery.

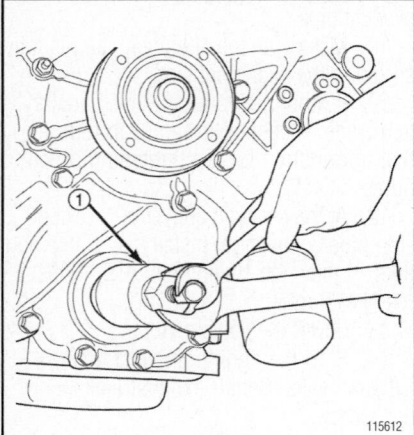

Fig. 31 Removing the crankshaft front seal using the seal remover (1)

CYLINDER HEAD

REMOVAL & INSTALLATION

3.7L Engine

Left

See Figures 32 and 33.

1. Disconnect the negative battery cable.
2. Raise and support the vehicle.
3. Disconnect the exhaust pipe at the left exhaust manifold.
4. Drain the engine coolant.
5. Lower the vehicle.
6. Remove the intake manifold.
7. Remove the master cylinder and booster assembly.
8. Remove the cylinder head cover.
9. Remove the fan shroud and fan blade assembly.
10. Remove the accessory drive belt.
11. Remove the power steering pump.
12. Rotate the crankshaft until the damper timing mark is aligned with TDC indicator mark.
13. Verify the V6 timing mark on the camshaft sprocket is at the 12 o'clock position, with the No. 1 cylinder at TDC on the exhaust stroke. Rotate the crankshaft one turn if necessary.
14. Remove the vibration damper.
15. Remove the timing chain cover.
16. Lock the secondary timing chains to the idler sprocket using the Secondary Camshaft Chain Holder.

➡ **Mark the secondary timing chain prior to removal to aid in installation.**

17. Mark the secondary timing chain, one link on each side of the V6 timing mark on the camshaft drive gear.
18. Remove the left side secondary chain tensioner.
19. Remove the cylinder head access plugs.

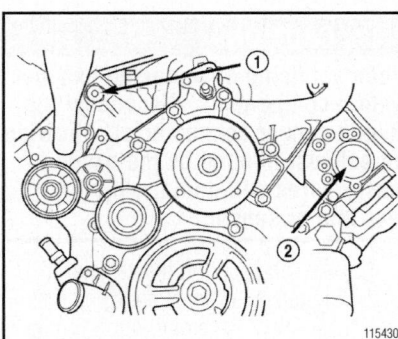

Fig. 32 Remove the cylinder head access plugs (1 and 2)

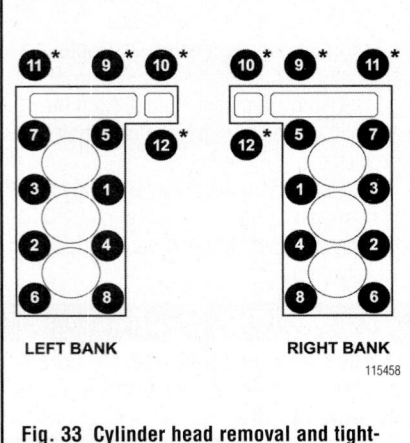

Fig. 33 Cylinder head removal and tightening sequence

20. Remove the left side secondary chain guide.
21. Remove the retaining bolt and the camshaft drive gear.

☀ CAUTION

Do not allow the engine to rotate. Severe damage to the valve train can occur.

☀ CAUTION

Do not overlook the four smaller bolts at the front of the cylinder head. Do not attempt to remove the cylinder head without removing these four bolts. The locations are identified with an *.

➡ **The cylinder head is attached to the cylinder block with twelve bolts.**

22. Using the sequence shown, remove the cylinder head retaining bolts.
23. Remove the cylinder head and gasket. Discard the gasket.

☀ CAUTION

Do not lay the cylinder head on its gasket sealing surface, due to the design of the cylinder head gasket, any distortion to the cylinder head sealing surface may prevent the gasket from properly sealing resulting in leaks.

To install:

➡ **The cylinder head bolts are tightened using a torque plus angle procedure. The bolts must be examined BEFORE reuse. If the threads are necked down the bolts should be replaced.**

24. Necking can be checked by holding a straight edge against the threads. If all the threads do not contact the scale, the bolt should be replaced.

✳✳ CAUTION

When cleaning cylinder head and cylinder block surfaces, DO NOT use a metal scraper, high speed scotch brite or rolock tool because the surfaces could be cut or ground. Use only a wooden or plastic scraper.

25. Clean the cylinder head and cylinder block mating surfaces.
26. Position the new cylinder head gasket on the locating dowels.

✳✳ CAUTION

When installing cylinder head, use care not damage the tensioner arm or the guide arm.

27. Position the cylinder head onto the cylinder block. Make sure the cylinder head seats fully over the locating dowels.

➡ The four smaller cylinder head mounting bolts require sealant to be added to them before installing. Failure to do so may cause leaks. The locations are identified with an *.

28. Lubricate the cylinder head bolt threads with clean engine oil and install the eight M11 bolts.
29. Coat the four M8 cylinder head bolts with Mopar® Lock and Seal Adhesive then install the bolts.

➡ The cylinder head bolts are tightened using an angle torque procedure, however, the bolts are not a torque-to-yield design.

30. Tighten the bolts in sequence using the following steps and torque values:
   a. Step 1: Tighten bolts 1-8, 20 ft. lbs. (27 Nm).
   b. Step 2: Verify that bolts 1-8, all reached 20 ft. lbs. (27 Nm), by repeating step 1 without loosening the bolts. Tighten bolts 9 thru 12 to 10 ft.lbs. (14 Nm).
   c. Step 3: Tighten bolts 1-8, 90 degrees.
   d. Step 4: Tighten bolts 1-8, 90 degrees, again. Tighten bolts 9-12, 19 ft. lbs. (26 Nm)
31. Position the secondary chain onto the camshaft drive gear, making sure one marked chain link is on either side of the V6 mark on the gear then using Camshaft Holder position the gear onto the camshaft.

✳✳ CAUTION

Remove the excess oil from camshaft sprocket retaining bolt before reinstalling bolt. Failure to do so may cause over-torqueing of bolt resulting in bolt failure.

32. Install the camshaft drive gear retaining bolt.
33. Install the left side secondary chain guide.
34. Install the cylinder head access plug.
35. Re-set and install the left side secondary chain tensioner.
36. Remove the Secondary Camshaft Chain Holder.
37. Install the timing chain cover.
38. Install the crankshaft damper. Tighten damper bolt 130 ft. lbs. (175 Nm).
39. Install the power steering pump.
40. Install the fan blade assembly and fan shroud.
41. Install the cylinder head cover.
42. Install the master cylinder and booster assembly.
43. Install the intake manifold.
44. Refill the cooling system.
45. Raise the vehicle.
46. Install the exhaust pipe onto the left exhaust manifold.
47. Lower the vehicle.
48. Connect the negative cable to the battery.
49. Start the engine and check for leaks.

Right

See Figure 33.

1. Disconnect battery negative cable.
2. Raise the vehicle on a hoist.
3. Disconnect the exhaust pipe at the right side exhaust manifold.
4. Drain the engine coolant.
5. Lower the vehicle.
6. Remove the intake manifold.
7. Remove the cylinder head cover.
8. Remove the radiator fan.
9. Remove oil fill housing from cylinder head.
10. Remove accessory drive belt.
11. Rotate the crankshaft until the damper timing mark is aligned with TDC indicator mark.
12. Verify the V6 mark on the camshaft sprocket is at the 12 o'clock position. Rotate the crankshaft one turn if necessary.
13. Remove the crankshaft damper.
14. Remove the timing chain cover.
15. Lock the secondary timing chains to the idler sprocket using Special Tool Timing Chain Holding Fixture.

➡ Mark the secondary timing chain prior to removal to aid in installation.

16. Mark the secondary timing chain, one link on each side of the V6 mark on the camshaft drive gear.
17. Remove the right side secondary chain tensioner.
18. Remove the cylinder head access plug.
19. Remove the right side secondary chain guide.

✳✳ CAUTION

The nut on the right side camshaft sprocket should not be removed for any reason, as the sprocket and camshaft sensor target wheel is serviced as an assembly. If the nut was removed retorque nut to 44 inch lbs. (5 Nm).

20. Remove the retaining bolt and the camshaft drive gear.

✳✳ CAUTION

Do not allow the engine to rotate. severe damage to the valve train can occur.

✳✳ CAUTION

Do not overlook the four smaller bolts at the front of the cylinder head. Do not attempt to remove the cylinder head without removing these four bolts.

✳✳ CAUTION

Do not hold or pry on the camshaft target wheel for any reason. A damaged target wheel can result in a vehicle no start condition.

➡ The cylinder head is attached to the cylinder block with twelve bolts.

21. Remove the cylinder head retaining bolts.
22. Remove the cylinder head and gasket. Discard the gasket.

To install:

➡ The cylinder head bolts are tightened using a torque plus angle procedure. The bolts must be examined BEFORE reuse. If the threads are necked down the bolts should be replaced.

Necking can be checked by holding a straight edge against the threads. If all the threads do not contact the scale, the bolt should be replaced.

※※ **CAUTION**

When cleaning cylinder head and cylinder block surfaces, DO NOT use a metal scraper, high speed scotch brite or rolock tool because the surfaces could be cut or ground. Use only a wooden or plastic scraper.

23. Clean the cylinder head and cylinder block mating surfaces.
24. Position the new cylinder head gasket on the locating dowels.

※※ **CAUTION**

When installing cylinder head, use care not damage the tensioner arm or the guide arm.

25. Position the cylinder head onto the cylinder block. Make sure the cylinder head seats fully over the locating dowels.

➡ **The four M8 cylinder head mounting bolts require sealant to be added to them before installing.**

26. Failure to do so may cause leaks.
27. Lubricate the cylinder head bolt threads with clean engine oil and install the eight M10 bolts.
28. Coat the four M8 cylinder head bolts with Mopar Lock and Seal Adhesive then install the bolts.

➡ **The cylinder head bolts are tightened using an angle torque procedure, however, the bolts are not a torque-to-yield design.**

29. Tighten the bolts in sequence using the following steps and torque values:

a. Step 1: Tighten bolts 1-8, 20 ft. lbs. (27 Nm).

b. Step 2: Verify that bolts 1-8, all reached 20 ft. lbs. (27 Nm), by repeating step 1 without loosening the bolts. Tighten bolts 9 thru 12 to 10 ft.lbs. (14 Nm).

c. Step 3: Tighten bolts 1-8, 90 degrees.

d. Step 4: Tighten bolts 1-8, 90 degrees, again. Tighten bolts 9-12, 19 ft. lbs. (26 Nm)

※※ **CAUTION**

The nut on the right side camshaft sprocket should not be removed for any reason, as the sprocket and camshaft sensor target wheel is serviced as an assembly. If the nut was removed retorque nut to 60 inch lbs. (5 Nm).

30. Position the secondary chain onto the camshaft drive gear, making sure one marked chain link is on either side of the V6 mark on the gear then using Camshaft Holder , position the gear onto the camshaft.

※※ **CAUTION**

Remove the excess oil from camshaft sprocket retaining bolt before reinstalling bolt. Failure to do so may cause over-torquing of bolt resulting in bolt failure.

31. Install the camshaft drive gear retaining bolt.
32. Install the right side secondary chain guide.
33. Install the cylinder head access plug.
34. Re-set and install the right side secondary chain tensioner.
35. Remove Camshaft Holder .
36. Install the timing chain cover.
37. Install the crankshaft damper. Tighten damper bolt 130 ft. lbs. (175 Nm).
38. Install accessory drive belt.
39. Install the radiator fan and shroud.
40. Install the cylinder head cover.
41. Install the intake manifold..
42. Install oil fill housing onto cylinder head.
43. Refill the cooling system.
44. Raise the vehicle.
45. Install the exhaust pipe onto the right exhaust manifold.
46. Lower the vehicle.
47. Reconnect battery negative cable.
48. Start the engine and check for leaks.

4.7L Engines

See Figure 34.

➡**Procedure is for the Left cylinder head, the right cylinder head procedure is similar.**

1. Disconnect the negative cable from the battery.
2. Raise the vehicle on a hoist.
3. Disconnect the exhaust pipe at the left side exhaust manifold.
4. Drain the engine coolant..
5. Lower the vehicle.
6. Remove the intake manifold.
7. Remove the master cylinder and booster assembly.
8. Remove the cylinder head cover.
9. Remove the fan shroud and fan blade assembly.
10. Remove accessory drive belt.
11. Remove the power steering pump and set aside.

12. Rotate the crankshaft until the damper timing mark is aligned with TDC indicator mark.
13. Verify the V8 mark on the camshaft sprocket is at the 12 o'clock position. Rotate the crankshaft one turn if necessary.
14. Remove the crankshaft damper.
15. Remove the timing chain cover.
16. Lock the secondary timing chains to the idler sprocket using Special Tool.

➡ **Mark the secondary timing chain prior to removal to aid in installation.**

17. Mark the secondary timing chain, one link on each side of the V8 mark on the camshaft drive gear.
18. Remove the left side secondary chain tensioner.
19. Remove the cylinder head access plug.
20. Remove the left side secondary chain guide.
21. Remove the retaining bolt and the camshaft drive gear.

※※ **CAUTION**

Do not allow the engine to rotate. Severe damage to the valve train can occur.

※※ **CAUTION**

Do not overlook the four smaller bolts at the front of the cylinder head. Do not attempt to remove the cylinder head without removing these four bolts.

➡ **The cylinder head is attached to the cylinder block with fourteen bolts.**

22. Remove the cylinder head retaining bolts using the sequence provided.
23. Remove the cylinder head and gasket. Discard the gasket.

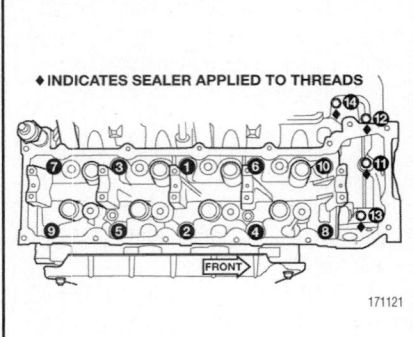

◆INDICATES SEALER APPLIED TO THREADS

171121

Fig. 34 Cylinder head removal and tightening sequence

✳✳ CAUTION

Do not lay the cylinder head on its gasket sealing surface, due to the design of the cylinder head gasket any distortion to the cylinder head sealing surface may prevent the gasket from properly sealing resulting in leaks.

To install:

➡ The cylinder head bolts are tightened using a torque plus angle procedure. The bolts must be examined BEFORE reuse. If the threads are necked down the bolts should be replaced.

24. Necking can be checked by holding a straight edge against the threads. If all the threads do not contact the scale, the bolt should be replaced.

✳✳ CAUTION

When cleaning cylinder head and cylinder block surfaces, DO NOT use a metal scraper, high speed scotch brite or rolock tool because the surfaces could be cut or ground. Use only a wooden or plastic scraper.

25. Clean the cylinder head and cylinder block mating surfaces.
26. Position the new cylinder head gasket on the locating dowels.

✳✳ CAUTION

When installing cylinder head, use care not damage the tensioner arm or the guide arm.

27. Position the cylinder head onto the cylinder block. Make sure the cylinder head seats fully over the locating dowels.

➡ The four M8 cylinder head mounting bolts (11 - 14) require sealant to be added to them before installing. Failure to do so may cause leaks.

28. Lubricate the cylinder head bolt threads with clean engine oil and install the ten M11 bolts.
29. Coat the four M8 cylinder head bolts with Mopar® Thread Sealant with PTFE then install the bolts.

➡ The cylinder head bolts are tightened using an angle torque procedure.

30. Tighten the bolts in sequence using the following steps and torque values:
    a. Tighten bolts 1 - 10 to 20 ft. lbs. (27 Nm).
    b. Verify that bolts 1 - 10 have all

reached 20 ft. lbs. (27 Nm), by repeating step 1 without loosening the bolts.
    c. Tighten bolts 11 - 14 to 89 inch lbs. (14 Nm).
    d. Rotate bolts 1 - 10 an additional 90°.
    e. Rotate bolts 1 - 10 an additional 90° again.
    f. Tighten bolts 11 - 14 to 19 ft. lbs. (26 Nm).

31. Position the secondary chain onto the camshaft drive gear, making sure one marked chain link is on either side of the V8 mark on the gear and position the gear onto the camshaft.
32. Install the camshaft drive gear retaining bolt.
33. Install the left side secondary chain guide.
34. Install the cylinder head access plug.
35. Re-set and Install the left side secondary chain tensioner.
36. Remove the Special Tool.
37. Install the timing chain cover.
38. Install the crankshaft damper.
39. Install the power steering pump.
40. Install the fan blade assembly and fan shroud.
41. Install the cylinder head cover.
42. Reinstall the master cylinder and booster assembly .
43. Install the intake manifold.
44. Refill the cooling system.
45. Raise the vehicle.
46. Install the exhaust pipe onto the left exhaust manifold.
47. Lower the vehicle.
48. Connect the negative cable to the battery.
49. Start the engine and check for leaks.

ENGINE ASSEMBLY

REMOVAL & INSTALLATION

ENGINE OIL & FILTER

OIL

➡The engine oil level indicator is located at the right rear of the engine.

Crankcase Oil Level Inspection

✳✳ CAUTION

Do not overfill crankcase with engine oil, pressure loss or oil foaming can result.

1. Inspect engine oil level approximately every 800 kilometers (500 miles). Unless the engine has exhibited loss of oil pres-

sure, run the engine for about five minutes before checking oil level. Checking engine oil level on a cold engine is not accurate.
2. To ensure proper lubrication of the engine, the engine oil must be maintained at an acceptable level. The acceptable levels are indicated between the ADD and SAFE marks on the engine oil dipstick.
3. Position vehicle on level surface.
4. With engine OFF, allow approximately ten minutes for oil to settle to bottom of crankcase, remove engine oil dipstick.
5. Wipe dipstick clean.
6. Install dipstick and verify it is seated in the tube.
7. Remove dipstick, with handle held above the tip, take oil level reading.
8. Add oil only if level is below the ADD mark on dipstick.

Engine Oil Change

1. Change engine oil at mileage and time intervals described in Maintenance Schedules.
2. Run engine until achieving normal operating temperature.
3. Position the vehicle on a level surface and turn engine off.
4. Hoist and support vehicle on safety stands.
5. Remove oil fill cap.
6. Place a suitable drain pan under crankcase drain.
7. Remove drain plug from crankcase and allow oil to drain into an oil drain pan. Inspect drain plug threads for stretching or other damage. Replace drain plug if damaged.
8. Install drain plug in crankcase. Torque to 25 ft. lbs. (34 Nm).
9. Lower vehicle and fill crankcase with specified type and amount of engine oil described in this section.
10. Install oil fill cap.
11. Start engine and inspect for leaks.
12. Stop engine and inspect oil level.

Used Engine Oil Disposal

Care should be exercised when disposing used engine oil after it has been drained from a vehicle engine. Refer to the WARNING at beginning of this section.

FILTER

See Figures 35 and 36.

All engines are equipped with a high quality full-flow, disposable type oil filter. Chrysler Corporation recommends a Mopar® or equivalent oil filter be used.

1. Position a drain pan under the oil filter.

2. Using a suitable oil filter wrench, loosen the filter.

3. Rotate the oil filter counterclockwise to remove it from the cylinder block oil filter boss.

4. When filter separates from cylinder block oil filter boss, tip gasket end upward to minimize oil spill.

5. Remove filter from vehicle.

➡ **Make sure filter gasket was removed with filter.**

6. With a wiping cloth, clean the gasket sealing surface of oil and grime.

To install:

7. Lightly lubricate oil filter gasket with engine oil.

8. Thread filter onto adapter nipple. When gasket makes contact with sealing surface, hand tighten filter one full turn, do not over tighten.

9. Add oil, verify crankcase oil level and start engine. Inspect for oil leaks.

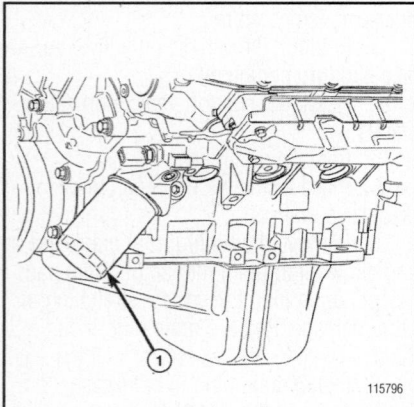

Fig. 35 Removing the oil filter—3.7L engine

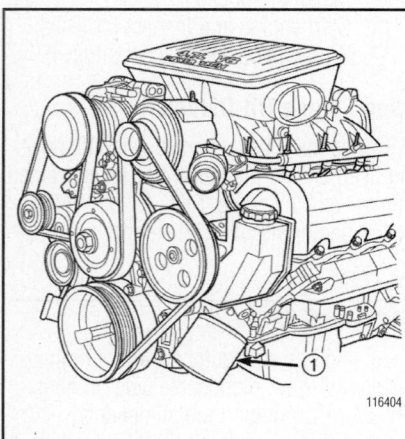

Fig. 36 Removing the oil filter (1)—4.7L engine

10. Lightly lubricate oil filter gasket with clean engine oil.

11. Thread filter onto adapter nipple. When gasket makes contact with sealing surface, hand tighten filter one full turn, do not over tighten.

12. Add oil, verify crankcase oil level and start engine. Inspect for oil leaks.

EXHAUST MANIFOLD

REMOVAL & INSTALLATION

3.7L Engine

1. Right manifold:
   a. Disconnect the negative cable from the battery.
   b. Raise and support the vehicle.
   c. Remove the bolts and nuts attaching the exhaust pipe to the engine exhaust manifold.
   d. Lower the vehicle.
   e. Remove the exhaust heat shield.
   f. Remove bolts, nuts and washers attaching manifold to cylinder head.
   g. Remove the manifold and gasket from the cylinder head.
2. Left exhaust manifold:
   a. Disconnect the negative cable from the battery.
   b. Raise and support the vehicle.
   c. Remove the bolts and nuts attaching the exhaust pipe to the engine exhaust manifold.
   d. Lower the vehicle.
   e. Remove the exhaust heat shields.
   f. Remove bolts, nuts and washers attaching manifold to cylinder head.
   g. Remove the manifold and gasket from the cylinder head.

To install:

✳✳ CAUTION

If the studs came out with the nuts when removing the engine exhaust manifold, install new studs. Apply sealer on the coarse thread ends. Water leaks may develop at the studs if this precaution is not taken.

   h. Position the engine exhaust manifold and gasket on the two studs located on the cylinder head. Install conical washers and nuts on these studs.
   i. Install remaining conical washers. Starting at the center arm and working outward, tighten the bolts and nuts to 18 ft. lbs. (25 Nm).
3. Install the exhaust heat shields.
4. Raise and support the vehicle.

✳✳ CAUTION

Over tightening heat shield fasteners, may cause shield to distort and/or crack.

5. Assemble exhaust pipe to manifold and secure with bolts, nuts and retainers. Tighten the bolts and nuts to 25 ft. lbs. (34 Nm).

4.7L Engine

Right Manifold

See Figure 37.

1. Disconnect the negative battery cable.
2. Remove the air cleaner assembly.
3. Remove the accessory drive belt.
4. Remove A/C compressor.
5. Remove A/C accumulator support bracket retainers.
6. Drain the coolant below heater hose level.
7. Remove the heater hoses at the engine and position aside.
8. Remove the exhaust manifold heat shield retaining nuts and remove the heat shield.
9. Remove the upper exhaust manifold retaining bolts.
10. Raise and support the vehicle.

✳✳ CAUTION

When servicing or replacing exhaust system components, disconnect the oxygen sensor connector(s). Allowing the exhaust to hang by the oxygen sensor wires will damage the harness and/or sensor.

11. Saturate the exhaust pipe/catalytic converter assembly flanged nuts at the exhaust manifold with heat valve lubricant, allow 5 minutes for penetration.
12. Disconnect the exhaust pipe/catalytic converter at the exhaust manifold.
13. Remove the starter.
14. Remove the lower exhaust manifold retaining bolts.

➡ **The exhaust manifold is removed from below the engine compartment.**

15. Remove the exhaust manifold and gasket.

➡**Refer to illustration for torque values.**

16. To install, reverse the removal procedure.

Left Manifold

See Figure 38.

1. Disconnect the negative battery cable.
2. Remove the engine cover.

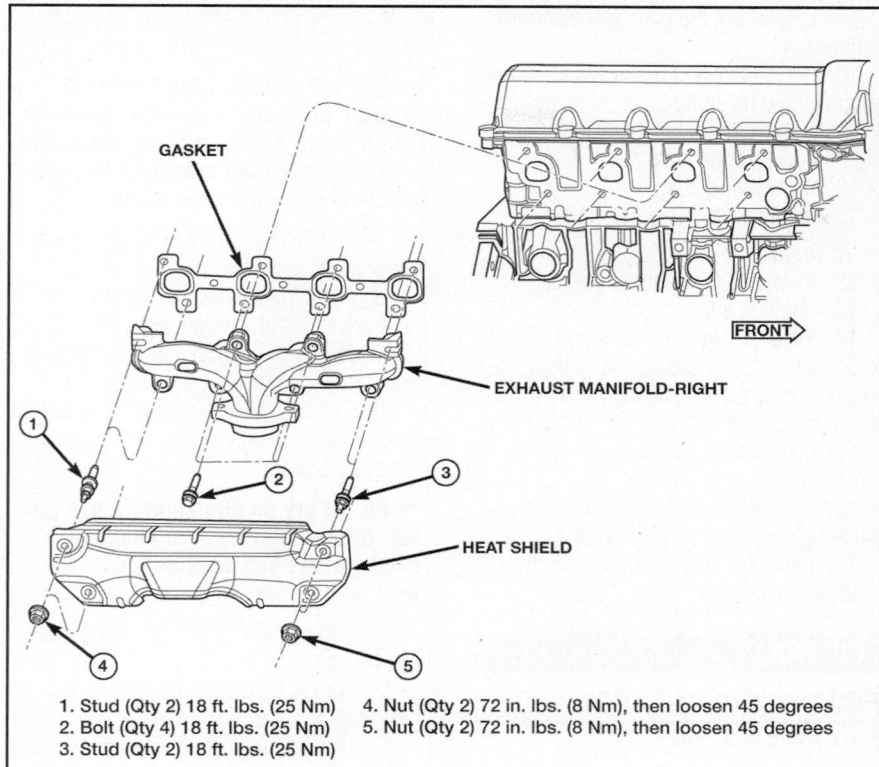

1. Stud (Qty 2) 18 ft. lbs. (25 Nm)
2. Bolt (Qty 4) 18 ft. lbs. (25 Nm)
3. Stud (Qty 2) 18 ft. lbs. (25 Nm)
4. Nut (Qty 2) 72 in. lbs. (8 Nm), then loosen 45 degrees
5. Nut (Qty 2) 72 in. lbs. (8 Nm), then loosen 45 degrees

116474

Fig. 37 Exploded view of the right exhaust manifold

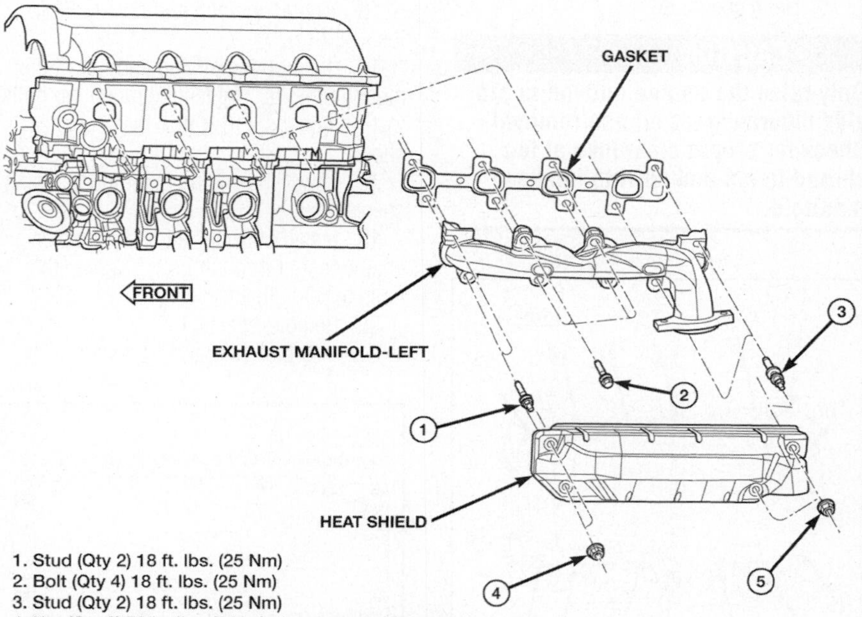

1. Stud (Qty 2) 18 ft. lbs. (25 Nm)
2. Bolt (Qty 4) 18 ft. lbs. (25 Nm)
3. Stud (Qty 2) 18 ft. lbs. (25 Nm)
4. Nut (Qty 2) 72 in. lbs. (8 Nm), then loosen 45 degrees
5. Nut (Qty 2) 72 in. lbs. (8 Nm), then loosen 45 degrees

116476

Fig. 38 Exploded view of the left exhaust manifold

3. Remove the front two exhaust manifold heat shield retaining nuts.
4. Raise and support the vehicle.

✲✲ CAUTION

When servicing or replacing exhaust system components, disconnect the oxygen sensor connector(s). Allowing the exhaust to hang by the oxygen sensor wires will damage the harness and/or sensor.

5. Saturate the exhaust pipe/catalytic converter assembly flanged nuts at the exhaust manifold with heat valve lubricant, allow 5 minutes for penetration.
6. Disconnect the exhaust pipe at the exhaust manifold.
7. Remove the rear heat shield retaining nuts and remove the heat shield.
8. Lower the vehicle.
9. Remove the upper exhaust manifold retaining bolts.

➡ **The exhaust manifold is removed from below the engine compartment**

10. Raise and support the vehicle.
11. Remove the lower exhaust manifold retaining bolts.
12. Remove the exhaust manifold and gasket.
13. Clean the mating surfaces.

➡**Refer to illustration for torque values.**

14. To install, reverse the removal procedure.

INTAKE MANIFOLD

REMOVAL & INSTALLATION

3.7L Engine

See Figure 39.

1. Bleed the fuel system.
2. Disconnect the negative cable from battery.
3. Remove the resonator assembly and air inlet hose.
4. Drain the cooling system below coolant temperature sensor level.
5. Disconnect the electronic throttle control (ETC) connector.
6. Disconnect electrical connectors for the following components:
   a. Coolant Temperature Sensor.
   b. Manifold Absolute Pressure (MAP) Sensor.
7. Disconnect vapor purge hose, brake booster hose, and positive crankcase ventilation (PCV) hose.

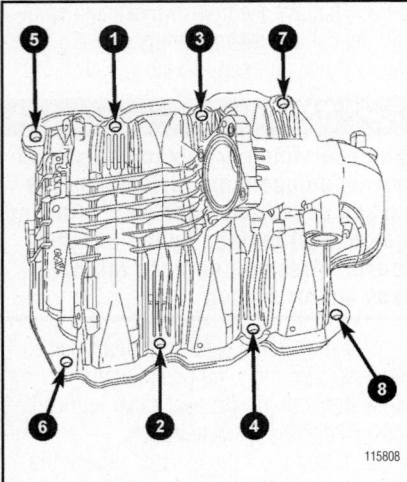

Fig. 39 Intake manifold removal and tightening sequence

8. Disconnect and remove ignition coil towers.

9. Remove the top oil dipstick tube retaining bolt.

10. Remove the EGR tube.

11. Remove fuel rail.

12. Remove throttle body assembly.

13. Remove the intake manifold retaining fasteners in reverse order of tightening sequence.

14. Remove the intake manifold.

To install:

15. Install the intake manifold seals.

16. Install the intake manifold.

17. Install the intake manifold retaining bolts and tighten in sequence shown to 106 inch lbs. (12 Nm).

18. Install the throttle body-to-intake manifold O-ring.

19. Install the throttle body to intake manifold.

20. Install the four mounting bolts. Tighten bolts to 60 inch lbs. (7 Nm).

21. Install the electrical connector.

22. To complete the installation, reverse the remaining removal procedure.

23. Using the scan tool, perform the ETC Relearn function.

4.7L Engine

1. Remove the resonator assembly and air inlet hose.

2. Bleed fuel system.

3. Disconnect negative cable from battery.

4. Disconnect electrical connectors for the following components:

5. Electronic Throttle Control (ETC).

6. Coolant Temperature (CTS) Sensor remove spark plug wires.

7. Disconnect the generator electrical connections.

8. Disconnect and remove ignition coils and manifold retaining bolts.

9. Remove top oil dipstick tube retaining bolt and ground strap.

10. Remove fuel rail.

11. Remove the intake manifold.

To install:

12. Install intake manifold gaskets.

13. Position intake manifold.

14. Install the ignition coils and manifold retaining bolts and torque from the center bolts, moving front to back in a crisscross pattern to 106 inch lbs. (12 Nm).

15. Install throttle body assembly, if removed.

16. To complete the installation, reverse the remaining removal procedure.

17. Using the scan tool, perform the ETC Relearn function.

OIL PAN

REMOVAL & INSTALLATION

See Figures 40 and 41.

1. Disconnect the negative battery cable.

2. Install engine support fixture special tool. Do not raise engine at this time.

3. Remove both left and right side engine mount through bolts.

4. Remove the structural dust cover.

5. Drain engine oil.

✵✵ CAUTION

Only raise the engine enough to provide clearance for oil pan removal. Check for proper clearance at fan shroud to fan and cowl to intake manifold.

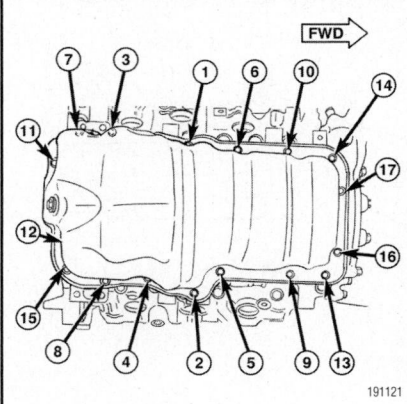

Fig. 40 Oil pan removal and tightening sequence—3.7L engines

6. Raise engine using special tool to provide clearance to remove oil pan.

➡ **On 4WD vehicles, the front axle must be lowered, to provide clearance for oil pan removal. It is not necessary to remove the front axle from the vehicle, or remove the axle shafts.**

7. For 4WD Vehicles Remove the pinion bracket.

8. For 4WD Vehicles Disconnect the front driveshaft at the front axle.

9. For 4WD Vehicles Remove the front axle mounting bolts.

10. For 4WD Vehicles Lower axle using suitable jack enough to provide clearance to remove oil pan.

➡ **Do not pry on oil pan or oil pan gasket. Gasket is integral to engine windage tray and does not come out with oil pan.**

11. Remove the oil pan mounting bolts and oil pan.

12. Unbolt oil pump pickup tube and remove tube.

13. Inspect the integral windage tray and gasket and replace as needed.

To install:

14. Clean the oil pan gasket mating surface of the bedplate and oil pan.

15. Position the oil pan gasket and pickup tube with new o-ring. Install the mounting bolt and nuts.

16. Tighten the bolt and nuts to 20 ft. lbs. (28 Nm).

17. Position the oil pan and install the mounting bolts. Tighten the mounting bolts to 140 inch lbs. (16 Nm) in the sequence shown.

18. Lower the engine into mounts using special tool.

19. Install both the left and right side engine mount through bolts. Tighten the bolts to 50 ft. lbs. (68 Nm)

20. Remove special tool

21. Install structural dust cover.

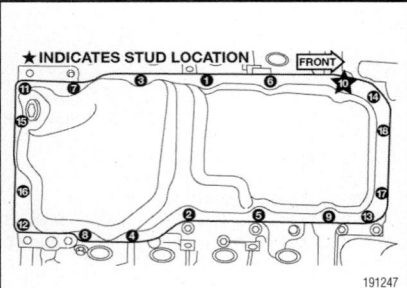

Fig. 41 Oil pan removal and tightening sequence—4.7L engines

➥ **On 4WD vehicles, the front axle must be lowered, to provide clearance for oil pan removal. It is not necessary to remove the front axle from the vehicle, or remove the axle shafts.**

22. For 4WD Vehicles Raise axle using suitable jack.

23. For 4WD Vehicles Install the front axle mounting bolts.

24. For 4WD Vehicles Install the pinion bracket.

25. For 4WD Vehicles Install the front driveshaft to the front axle.

26. Fill engine oil.

27. Reconnect the negative battery cable.

28. Start engine and check for leaks.

OIL PUMP

REMOVAL & INSTALLATION

See Figure 42.

1. Remove the oil pan and pick-up tube.

2. Remove the timing chain cover.

3. Remove the timing chains and tensioners.

4. Remove the four bolts, primary timing chain tensioner and the oil pump.

To install:

5. Position the oil pump onto the crankshaft and install one oil pump retaining bolt.

6. Position the primary timing chain tensioner and install three retaining bolts.

7. Tighten the oil pump and primary timing chain tensioner retaining bolts to 20 ft. lbs. (28 Nm) in the sequence shown.

8. To complete the installation, reverse the remaining removal procedure.

REAR MAIN SEAL

REMOVAL & INSTALLATION

See Figures 43 and 44.

1. If being performed in vehicle, remove the transmission.

2. Remove the flexplate.

➥ **The crankshaft oil seal CAN NOT be reused after removal.**

➥ **The Seal Remover tool must be installed deeply into the seal. Continue to tighten the removal tool into the seal until the tool cannot be turned farther. Failure to install tool correctly the first time will cause tool to pull free of seal without removing seal from engine.**

3. Using Seal Remover, remove the crankshaft rear oil seal.

To install:

4. Lubricate the crankshaft flange with engine oil.

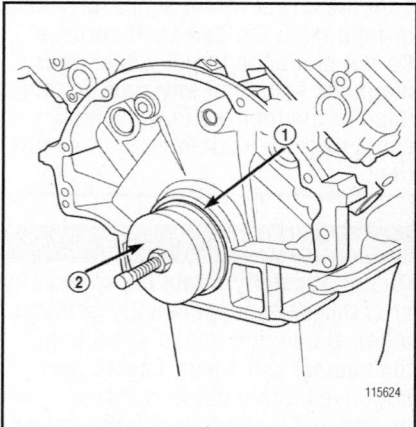

Fig. 43 Using the seal remover (2) remove the crankshaft rear oil seal (1)

5. Position the magnetic seal guide onto the crankshaft rear face. Then position the crankshaft rear oil seal onto the guide.

6. Using Crankshaft Rear Oil Seal Installer and Driver Handle, with a hammer, tap the seal into place.

7. Continue to tap on the driver handle until the seal installer seats against the cylinder block crankshaft bore.

8. Install the flexplate.

9. Install the transmission.

TIMING CHAIN FRONT COVER

REMOVAL & INSTALLATION

See Figure 45.

1. Disconnect the battery negative cable.

2. Drain the cooling system.

3. Remove electric cooling fan and fan shroud assembly.

4. Remove the radiator fan.

5. Disconnect both heater hoses at timing cover.

6. Disconnect lower radiator hose at engine.

7. Remove accessory drive belt tensioner assembly.

8. Remove crankshaft damper.

9. Remove the alternator.

10. Remove the A/C compressor.

✳✳ CAUTION

The 3.7L engine uses an anaerobic sealer instead of a gasket to seal the front cover to the engine block, from the factory. For service, Mopar® Grey Engine RTV sealant must be substituted.

➥ **It is not necessary to remove the water pump for timing cover removal.**

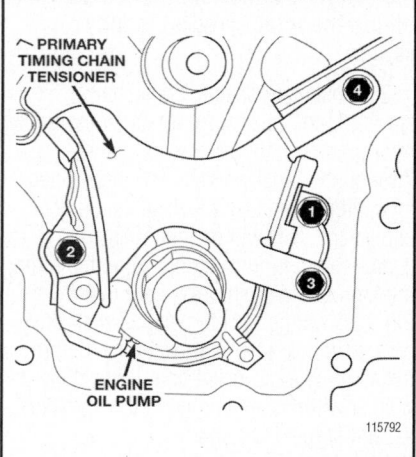

Fig. 42 Oil pump tightening sequence

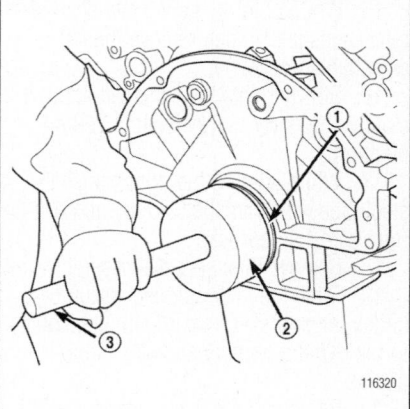

Fig. 44 Seal (1), Crankshaft Rear Oil Seal Installer (2) and driver handle (3)

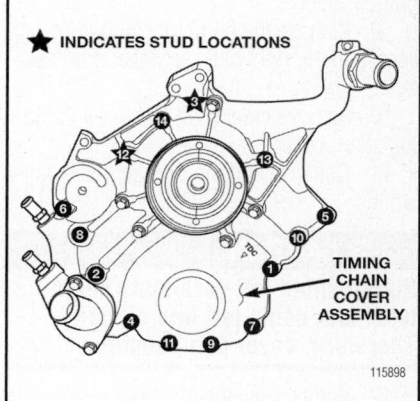

Fig. 45 Timing chain cover removal and tightening sequence

11. Remove the bolts holding the timing cover to engine block.

12. Remove the timing cover.

To install:

➡ The 3.7L uses a special anaerobic sealer instead of a gasket to seal the timing cover to the engine block, from the factory. For service repairs, Mopar® Engine RTV must be used as a substitute.

13. Inspect the water passage o-rings for any damage, and replace as necessary.

14. Apply Mopar® Engine RTV sealer to front cover using a 3 to 4 mm thick bead.

15. Install cover. Tighten fasteners in sequence as shown in to 43 ft. lbs. (58 Nm).

16. To complete installation, reverse the remaining removal procedure.

TIMING CHAIN & SPROCKETS

REMOVAL & INSTALLATION

See Figure 46.

➡Procedure is for V6, V8 procedure is similar.

1. Disconnect negative cable from battery.

2. Drain cooling system.

3. Remove right and left cylinder head covers.

4. Remove radiator fan.

5. Rotate engine until timing mark on crankshaft damper aligns with TDC mark on timing chain cover

6. Make sure the camshaft sprocket "V6" marks are at the 12 o'clock position (No. 1 TDC exhaust stroke).

7. Remove power steering pump. (Refer to Power Steering Pump

8. Remove access plugs from left and right cylinder heads for access to chain guide fasteners.

9. Remove the oil fill housing to gain access to the right side tensioner arm fastener.

10. Remove crankshaft damper and timing chain cover

11. Collapse and pin primary chain tensioner.

✷✷ CAUTION

Plate behind left secondary chain tensioner could fall into oil pan. Therefore, cover pan opening.

12. Remove secondary chain tensioners.

13. Remove camshaft position sensor.

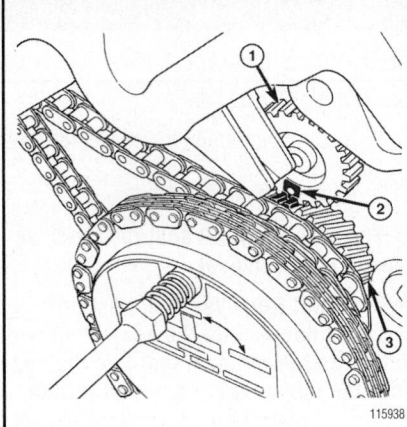

Fig. 46 Counterbalance shaft drive gear (1), timing mark (2) and idler sprocket gear (3)

✷✷ CAUTION

Care should be taken not to damage the camshaft target wheel. Do not hold the target wheel while loosening or tightening the camshaft sprocket. Do not place the target wheel near a magnetic source of any kind. A damaged or magnetized target wheel could cause a vehicle no start condition.

✷✷ CAUTION

Do not forcefully rotate the camshafts or crankshaft independently of each other. Damaging intake valve to piston contact will occur. Ensure the negative battery cable is disconnected and isolated to guard against accidental starter engagement.

14. Remove left and right camshaft sprocket bolts.

15. While holding the left camshaft steel tube Camshaft Holder, remove the left camshaft sprocket.

16. Slowly rotate the camshaft approximately 5 degrees clockwise to a neutral position.

17. While holding the right camshaft steel tube with Camshaft Holder, remove the right camshaft sprocket.

18. Remove idler sprocket assembly bolt.

19. Slide the idler sprocket assembly and crank sprocket forward simultaneously to remove the primary and secondary chains.

20. Remove both pivoting tensioner arms and chain guides.

21. Remove primary chain tensioner.

To install:

22. Using a vise, lightly compress the secondary chain tensioner piston until the piston step (5) is flush with the tensioner body. Using a pin or suitable tool, release ratchet pawl (4) by pulling pawl back against spring force through access hole on side of tensioner. While continuing to hold pawl back, Push ratchet device to approximately 2 mm from the tensioner body. Install Tensioner Pins into hole on front of tensioner. Slowly open vise to transfer piston spring force to lock pin.

23. Position primary chain tensioner over oil pump and insert bolts into lower two holes on tensioner bracket. Tighten bolts to 20 ft. lbs. (28 Nm).

24. Install right side chain tensioner arm. Install Torx® bolt. Tighten Torx® bolt to 20 ft. lbs. (28 Nm).

25. Install the left side chain guide. Tighten the bolts to 20 ft. lbs. (28 Nm).

26. Install left side chain tensioner arm, and Torx® bolt. Tighten Torx® bolt to 20 ft. lbs. (28 Nm).

27. Install the right side chain guide. Tighten the bolts to 20 ft. lbs. (28 Nm).

28. Install both secondary chains onto the idler sprocket. Align two plated links on the secondary chains to be visible through the two lower openings on the idler sprocket (4 o'clock and 8 o'clock). Once the secondary timing chains are installed, Secondary Camshaft Chain Holder to hold chains in place for installation.

29. Align primary chain double plated links with the timing mark at 12 o'clock on the idler sprocket. Align the primary chain single plated link with the timing mark at 6 o'clock on the crankshaft sprocket.

30. Lubricate idler shaft and bushings with clean engine oil.

➡ The idler sprocket must be timed to the counterbalance shaft drive gear before the idler sprocket is fully seated.

31. Install all chains, crankshaft sprocket, and idler sprocket as an assembly. After guiding both secondary chains through the block and cylinder head openings, affix chains with a elastic strap or equivalent. This will maintain tension on chains to aid in installation. Align the timing mark on the idler sprocket gear to the timing mark on the counterbalance shaft drive gear, then seat idler sprocket fully. Before installing idler sprocket bolt, lubricate washer with oil, and tighten idler sprocket assembly retaining bolt to 25 ft. lbs. (34 Nm).

➡ **It will be necessary to slightly rotate camshafts for sprocket installation.**

32. Align left camshaft sprocket "L" dot to plated link on chain.

33. Align right camshaft sprocket "R" dot to plated link on chain.

✳✳ CAUTION

Remove excess oil from the camshaft sprocket bolt. Failure to do so can result in over-torque of bolt resulting in bolt failure.

34. Remove Secondary Camshaft Chain Holder, then attach both sprockets to camshafts. Remove excess oil from bolts, then install sprocket bolts, but do not tighten at this time.

35. Verify that all plated links are aligned with the marks on all sprockets and the "V6" marks on camshaft sprockets are at the 12 o'clock position.

✳✳ CAUTION

Ensure the plate between the left secondary chain tensioner and block is correctly installed.

36. Install both secondary chain tensioners. Tighten bolts to 20 ft. lbs. (28 Nm).

➡ **Left and right secondary chain tensioners are not common.**

37. Remove all locking pins from tensioners.

✳✳ CAUTION

After pulling locking pins out of each tensioner, DO NOT manually extend the tensioner(s) ratchet. Doing so will over tension the chains, resulting in noise and/or high timing chain loads.

38. Using Spanner Wrench, with Adaptor Pins, tighten left camshaft sprocket bolts to 90 ft. lbs. (122 Nm).

39. Using Spanner Wrench, with Adaptor Pins, tighten right camshaft sprocket bolts to 90 ft. lbs. (122 Nm).

40. Rotate engine two full revolutions. Verify timing marks are at the follow locations:

    a. primary chain idler sprocket dot is at 12 o'clock

    b. primary chain crankshaft sprocket dot is at 6 o'clock

    c. secondary chain camshaft sprockets "V6" marks are at 12 o'clock

    d. balance shaft drive gear dot is aligned to the idler sprocket gear dot

41. Lubricate all three chains with engine oil.

42. After installing all chains, it is recommended that the idler gear end play be checked. The end play must be within 0.004 - 0.010 inches. If not within specification, the idler gear must be replaced.

43. To complete the installation procedure, reverse the remaining removal procedure.

44. Connect negative cable to battery.

VALVE COVERS

REMOVAL & INSTALLATION

3.7L Engine

See Figure 47.

➡**The gasket may be used again, providing no cuts, tears, or deformation has occurred.**

➡**Left side shown, right side similar.**

1. Disconnect negative cable from battery.

2. Remove the resonator assemble and air inlet hose.

3. Disconnect injector connectors and un-clip the injector harness.

4. Route injector harness in front of cylinder head cover.

5. Disconnect the left side breather tube and remove the breather tube.

6. Remove the cylinder head cover mounting bolts.

7. Remove cylinder head cover and gasket.

To install:

✳✳ CAUTION

Do not use harsh cleaners to clean the cylinder head covers. Severe damage to covers may occur.

➡**The gasket may be used again, provided no cuts, tears, or deformation has occurred.**

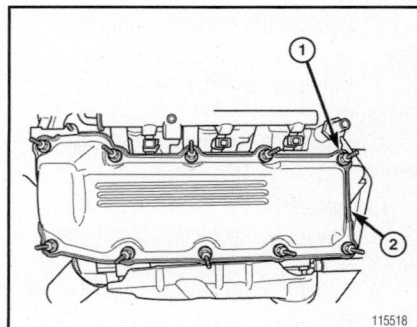

Fig. 47 Removing the mounting bolts (1) and valve cover (2)

115518

8. Clean the cylinder head cover and both sealing surfaces. Inspect and replace gasket as necessary.

9. Install the cylinder cover.

10. Tighten the cylinder head cover bolts and double ended studs to 9 ft. lbs. (12 Nm).

11. Install the left side breather and connect breather tube.

12. Connect the fuel injector electrical connectors and injector harness retaining clips.

13. Install the resonator and air inlet hose.

14. Connect negative battery cable.

4.7L Engine

Left Side

1. Disconnect negative cable from battery.

2. Remove the resonator assemble and air inlet hose.

3. Remove the spark plug wires.

4. Route injector harness in front of cylinder head cover.

5. Disconnect the left side breather tube and remove the breather tube.

6. Remove the cylinder head cover mounting bolts.

7. Remove the cylinder head cover and gasket.

➡**The gasket may be used again, provided no cuts, tears, or deformation has occurred.**

To install:

✳✳ CAUTION

Do not use harsh cleaners to clean the cylinder head covers. Severe damage to covers may occur.

8. Clean cylinder head cover and both sealing surfaces. Inspect and replace gasket as necessary.

9. Install cylinder head cover and hand start all fasteners. Verify that all studs are in the correct location as shown.

10. Tighten cylinder head cover bolts and double ended studs to 105 inch lbs. (12 Nm).

11. Install left side breather and connect breather tube.

12. Install the spark plug wires.

13. Install the resonator and air inlet hose.

14. Connect negative cable to battery.

Right Side

1. Disconnect the battery negative cable.

2. Remove air cleaner assembly, resonator assembly and air inlet hose.

3. Drain the cooling system.

4. Remove the accessory drive belt.

5. Remove air conditioning compressor retaining bolts and move compressor to the left.

6. Remove the heater hoses.

7. Disconnect and remove positive crankcase ventilation (PCV) hose.

8. Remove oil fill tube.

9. Remove the spark plug wires.

10. Remove the right rear breather tube and filter assembly.

11. Remove the cylinder head cover retaining bolts.

12. Remove the cylinder head cover.

To install:

13. Clean cylinder head cover and both sealing surfaces. Inspect and replace gasket as necessary.

14. Install cylinder head cover and hand start all fasteners.

15. Tighten cylinder head cover bolts and double ended studs to 9 ft. lbs. (12 Nm).

16. To complete installation, revere the remaining removal procedure.

17. Connect the battery negative cable.

ENGINE PERFORMANCE & EMISSION CONTROLS

CAMSHAFT POSITION (CMP) SENSOR

LOCATION

The Camshaft Position Sensor (CMP) is bolted to the front/top of the right cylinder head.

REMOVAL & INSTALLATION

See Figures 48 and 49.

1. Disconnect the negative battery cable.

2. Disconnect the Camshaft Position (CMP) sensor electrical connector.

3. Remove the bolt and the CMP sensor and discard the O-ring seal. Carefully twist sensor from cylinder head.

➡ **Lubricate the new O-ring seal with clean engine oil prior to installation.**

➡ **Before tightening sensor mounting bolt, be sure sensor is completely flush to cylinder head. If sensor is not flush, damage to sensor mounting tang may result.**

4. To install, reverse the removal procedure. Install sensor into cylinder head with a slight rocking and twisting action

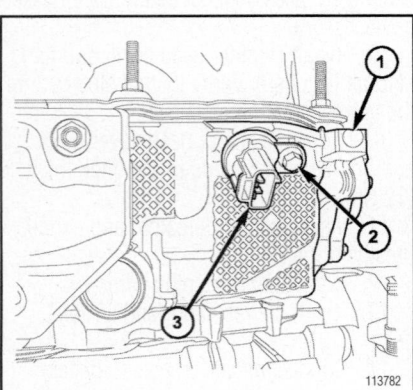

Fig. 48 Removing the CMP sensor (3), bolt (2) from the cylinder head (3)—3.7L engine

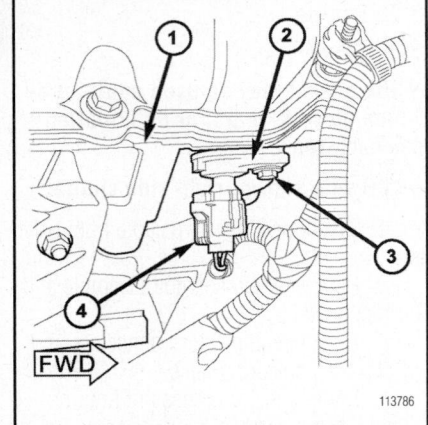

Fig. 49 Removing the CMP sensor—4.7L engine

CRANKSHAFT POSITION (CKP) SENSOR

LOCATION

The Crankshaft Position (CKP) sensor is mounted into the right rear side of the cylinder block. It is positioned and bolted into a machined hole.

REMOVAL & INSTALLATION

See Figures 50 and 51.

1. Raise the vehicle.

2. Disconnect the sensor electrical connector.

3. Remove the sensor mounting bolt.

4. Carefully twist the sensor from cylinder block.

5. Check the condition of sensor o-ring.

To install:

6. Clean out machined hole in engine block.

7. Apply a small amount of engine oil to sensor o-ring.

8. Install sensor into engine block with a slight rocking and twisting action.

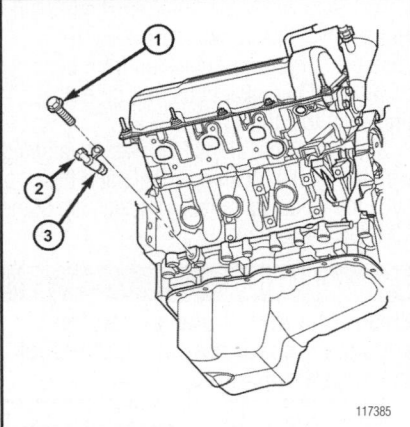

Fig. 50 Removing the bolt (1), sensor (2) and O-ring (3)—3.7L engines

✳✳ CAUTION

Before tightening sensor mounting bolt (1), be sure sensor is completely flush to cylinder block. If sensor is not flush, damage to sensor mounting tang may result.

9. Install mounting bolt and tighten to 21 ft. lbs. (28 Nm) torque.

10. Connect the electrical connector to sensor.

11. Lower the vehicle.

ELECTRONIC CONTROL MODULE (ECM)

LOCATION

The PCM is attached to the right-inner corner of the engine compartment.

REMOVAL & INSTALLATION

See Figure 52.

✳✳ CAUTION

Certain ABS systems rely on having the Powertrain Control Module (PCM) broadcast the Vehicle Identification Number (VIN) over the bus network.

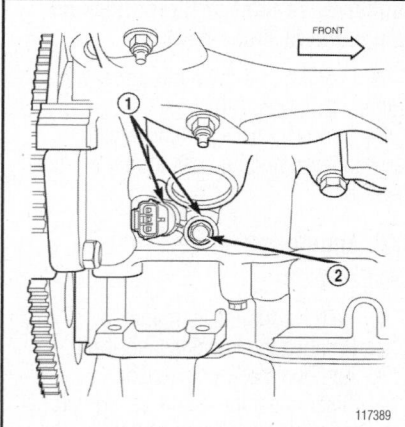

Fig. 51 Removing the bolt (2) and sensor (1)—4.7L engine

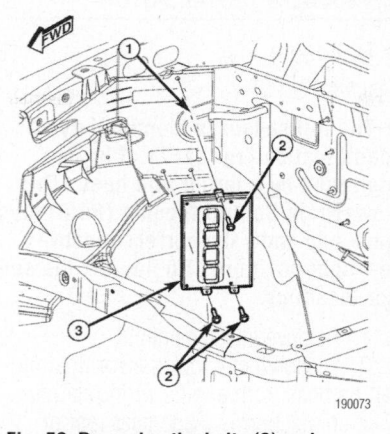

Fig. 52 Removing the bolts (2) and PCM (3)

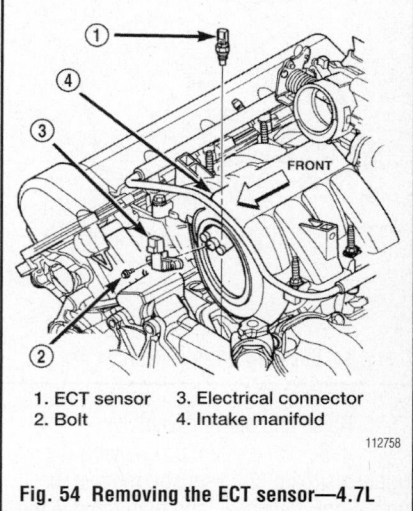

1. ECT sensor   3. Electrical connector
2. Bolt   4. Intake manifold

Fig. 54 Removing the ECT sensor—4.7L Engine

To prevent problems of DTCs and other items related to the VIN broadcast, it is recommend that you disconnect the ABS CAB (controller) temporarily when replacing the PCM. Once the PCM is replaced, write the VIN to the PCM using a diagnostic scan tool. This is done from the engine main menu. Arrow over to the second page to "1. Miscellaneous". Select "Check VIN" from the choices. Make sure it has the correct VIN entered before continuing. When the VIN is complete, turn off the ignition key and reconnect the ABS module connector. This will prevent the setting of DTCs and other items associated with the lack of a VIN detected when you turn the key ON after replacing the PCM.

✳✳ **CAUTION**

Use a diagnostic scan tool to reprogram the new PCM with the vehicles original identification number (VIN) and the vehicles original mileage. If this step is not done, a Diagnostic Trouble Code (DTC) may be set.

➡ To avoid possible voltage spike damage to the PCM, ignition key must be off, and negative battery cable must be disconnected before unplugging PCM connectors.

1. Disconnect and isolate the negative battery cable.
2. Carefully unplug the four 38-way connectors from PCM.
3. Remove three PCM mounting bolts, and position ground strap. Remove PCM from vehicle.

4. To install, reverse the removal procedure.
5. Use the diagnostic scan tool to reprogram new PCM with vehicles original Identification Number (VIN) and original vehicle mileage. If this step is not done, a Diagnostic Trouble Code (DTC) may be set.

ENGINE COOLANT TEMPERATURE (ECT) SENSOR

REMOVAL & INSTALLATION

See Figures 53 and 54.

1. Drain the cooling system.
2. Disconnect the Engine Coolant Temperature (ECT) sensor electrical connector.
3. Remove the clip and the ECT sensor.
4. To install, reverse the removal procedure.
5. Apply thread sealant to the ETC sensor threads.
6. Tighten the sensor to 20 ft. lbs. (27 Nm).

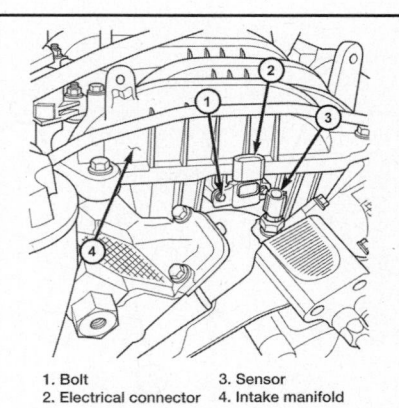

1. Bolt   3. Sensor
2. Electrical connector   4. Intake manifold

Fig. 53 Removing the ECT sensor—3.7L Engine

HEATED OXYGEN (HO2S) SENSOR

LOCATION

See Figures 55 and 56.

REMOVAL & INSTALLATION

✳✳ **CAUTION**

Never apply any type of grease to the oxygen sensor electrical connector, or attempt any repair of the sensor wiring harness.

✳✳ **WARNING**

The exhaust pipes and catalytic converter become very hot during engine operation. Allow the engine to cool before removing the oxygen sensor.

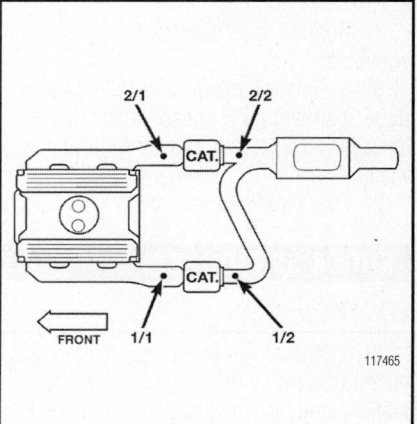

Fig. 55 Locating HO2S sensors—4 sensor system

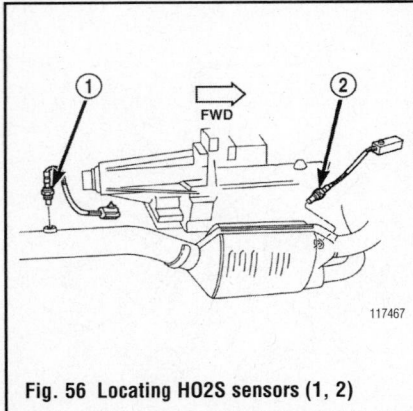

Fig. 56 Locating HO2S sensors (1, 2)

1. Raise and support vehicle.
2. 4-Sensor System If removing the right-upstream (2/1) sensor, remove the right-front tire/wheel, and then remove the plastic inner fender liner.
3. Disconnect wire connector from O2S sensor.

✳✳ WARNING

When disconnecting the oxygen sensor electrical connector, do not pull directly on the wire going into the sensor. The sensor wiring can be damaged resulting in sensor failure.

4. Remove the O2S sensor with an oxygen sensor removal and installation tool.
5. Clean threads in exhaust pipe using appropriate tap.

To install:

➡ Threads of new oxygen sensors are factory coated with anti-seize compound to aid in removal. **DO NOT add any additional anti-seize compound to threads of a new oxygen sensor.**

6. Install O2S sensor. Tighten to 30 ft. lbs. (41 Nm) torque.
7. Connect O2S sensor wire connector.
8. 4-Sensor System: If installing the right-upstream (2/1) sensor, install plastic inner fender liner, and right-front tire/wheel.
9. Lower vehicle.

KNOCK SENSOR (KS)

LOCATION

3.7L engine: The two knock sensors are bolted into the cylinder block under the intake manifold. The two sensors share a common wiring harness using one electrical connector. Because of this, they must be replaced as a pair.

REMOVAL & INSTALLATION

3.7L Engine
See Figure 57.

➡ The left sensor is identified by an identification tag (LEFT). It is also identified by a larger bolt head. The Powertrain Control Module (PCM) must have and know the correct sensor left/right positions. Do not mix the sensor locations.

1. Remove intake manifold.
2. Disconnect knock sensor dual pig-tail harness from engine wiring harness. This connection is made near rear of engine.
3. Remove both sensor mounting bolts. Note foam strip on bolt threads. This foam is used only to retain the bolts to sensors for plant assembly. It is not used as a sealant. Do not apply any adhesive, sealant or thread locking compound to these bolts.
4. Remove sensors from engine.

To install:
5. Thoroughly clean the knock sensor mounting holes.
6. Install the sensors into cylinder block.

➡ Over or under tightening the sensor mounting bolts will affect knock sensor performance, possibly causing improper spark control. Always use the specified torque when installing the knock sensors. The torque for the knock senor bolt is relatively light for an 8 mm bolt.

➡ Note foam strip on bolt threads. This foam is used only to retain the bolts to sensors for plant assembly. It is not used as a sealant. Do not apply any

adhesive, sealant or thread locking compound to these bolts.

7. Install and tighten mounting bolts. Tighten 15 ft. lbs. (20 Nm).
8. Connect knock sensor wiring harness to engine harness at rear of intake manifold.

4.7L Engine
See Figure 58.

1. Remove the intake manifold.
2. Remove the knock sensor bolt.
3. Remove the knock sensor.
4. Disconnect the knock sensor wiring harness to the engine harness at the rear of the intake manifold by pressing on lock tab.
5. Thoroughly clean the knock sensor mounting hole.

To install:
6. Thoroughly clean knock sensor mounting hole.
7. Postion knock sensor in place.

➡ Over or under tightening the sensor mounting bolts will affect knock sensor performance, possibly causing improper spark control. Always use the specified torque when installing the knock sensors.

➡ Note foam strip on bolt threads. This foam is used only to retain the bolts to sensors for plant assembly. It is not used as a sealant. Do not apply any adhesive, sealant or thread locking compound to these bolts.

8. Tighten knock sensor to 15 ft. lbs. (20 Nm).
9. Connect knock sensor wiring harness to engine harness (4) at rear of intake manifold.

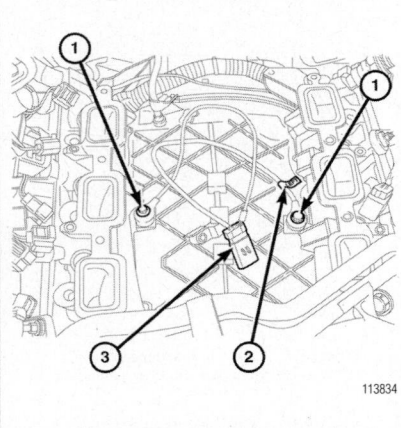

Fig. 57 Removing the sensors (1), tag (2) and harness (30

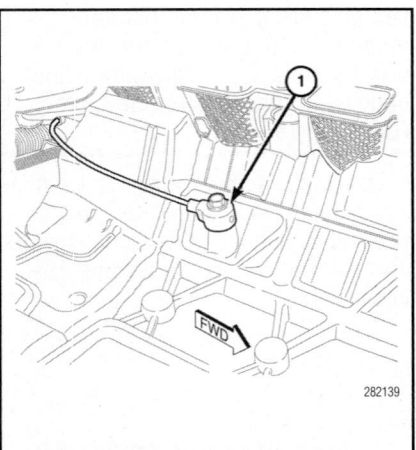

Fig. 58 Removing the knock sensor (1)— 4.7L engine

MANIFOLD ABSOLUTE PRESSURE (MAP) SENSOR

LOCATION

The Manifold Absolute Pressure (MAP) sensor (7) is mounted into the front of the intake manifold (1).

REMOVAL & INSTALLATION

See Figure 59.

1. Disconnect the electrical connector at sensor.
2. Clean the area around MAP sensor.
3. Remove one sensor mounting screw.

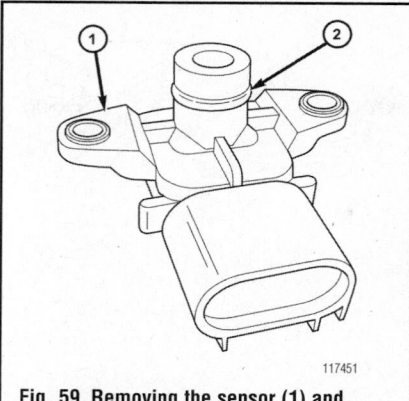

Fig. 59 Removing the sensor (1) and O-ring (2)

117451

4. Remove MAP sensor from intake manifold by slipping it from locating pin.
5. Check the condition of the sensor o-ring.
6. To install, reverse the removal procedure.

THROTTLE POSITION SENSOR (TPS)

LOCATION

The TPS is integrated with the throttle body.

FUEL   GASOLINE FUEL INJECTION SYSTEM

FUEL SYSTEM SERVICE PRECAUTIONS

Safety is the most important factor when performing not only fuel system maintenance but any type of maintenance. Failure to conduct maintenance and repairs in a safe manner may result in serious personal injury or death. Maintenance and testing of the vehicle's fuel system components can be accomplished safely and effectively by adhering to the following rules and guidelines.

• To avoid the possibility of fire and personal injury, always disconnect the negative battery cable unless the repair or test procedure requires that battery voltage be applied.

• Always relieve the fuel system pressure prior to disconnecting any fuel system component (injector, fuel rail, pressure regulator, etc.), fitting or fuel line connection. Exercise extreme caution whenever relieving fuel system pressure to avoid exposing skin, face and eyes to fuel spray. Please be advised that fuel under pressure may penetrate the skin or any part of the body that it contacts.

• Always place a shop towel or cloth around the fitting or connection prior to loosening to absorb any excess fuel due to spillage. Ensure that all fuel spillage (should it occur) is quickly removed from engine surfaces. Ensure that all fuel soaked cloths or towels are deposited into a suitable waste container.

• Always keep a dry chemical (Class B) fire extinguisher near the work area.

• Do not allow fuel spray or fuel vapors to come into contact with a spark or open flame.

• Always use a back-up wrench when loosening and tightening fuel line connection fittings. This will prevent unnecessary stress and torsion to fuel line piping.

• Always replace worn fuel fitting O-rings with new Do not substitute fuel hose or equivalent where fuel pipe is installed.

Before servicing the vehicle, make sure to also refer to the precautions in the beginning of this section as well.

RELIEVING FUEL SYSTEM PRESSURE

✲✲ WARNING

Do not smoke, carry lighted tobacco or have an open flame of any type when working on or near any fuel-related component. Highly flammable mixtures are always present and may be ignited. Failure to follow these instructions may result in serious personal injury.

✲✲ WARNING

Before working on or disconnecting any of the fuel tubes or fuel system components, relieve the fuel system pressure to prevent accidental spraying of fuel. Fuel in the fuel system remains under high pressure, even when the engine is not running. Failure to follow this instruction may result in serious personal injury.

✲✲ WARNING

Do not carry personal electronic devices such as cell phones, pagers or audio equipment of any type when working on or near any fuel-related

component. Highly flammable mixtures are always present and may be ignited. Failure to follow these instructions may result in serious personal injury.

✲✲ WARNING

When handling fuel, always observe fuel handling precautions and be prepared in the event of fuel spillage. Spilled fuel may be ignited by hot vehicle components or other ignition sources. Failure to follow these instructions may result in serious personal injury.

➡Use the following procedure if the fuel injector rail is, or is not equipped with a fuel pressure test port.

1. Remove the fuel fill cap.
2. Remove the fuel pump relay from the Integrated Power Module (IPM). For relay location, refer to the label on the underside of the IPM cover.
3. Start and run the engine until it stalls.
4. Attempt restarting engine until it will no longer run.
5. Turn the ignition key to the OFF position.
6. Place a rag or towel below the fuel line quick-connect fitting at the fuel rail.
7. Disconnect the quick-connect fitting at the fuel rail.
8. Return the fuel pump relay to the IPM.

➡One or more Diagnostic Trouble Codes (DTC's) may have been stored in the PCM memory due to the fuel pump relay removal. A diagnostic scan tool must be used to erase a DTC.

FUEL FILTER

REMOVAL & INSTALLATION

The fuel filter mounts inside the fuel pump module and is a non-serviceable part.

FUEL INJECTORS

REMOVAL & INSTALLATION
See Figure 60.

> ❊❊ **WARNING**
>
> **Do not smoke, carry lighted tobacco or have an open flame of any type when working on or near any fuel-related component. Highly flammable mixtures are always present and may be ignited. Failure to follow these instructions may result in serious personal injury.**

> ❊❊ **WARNING**
>
> **Do not carry personal electronic devices such as cell phones, pagers or audio equipment of any type when working on or near any fuel-related component. Highly flammable mixtures are always present and may be ignited. Failure to follow these instructions may result in serious personal injury.**

> ❊❊ **WARNING**
>
> **Before working on or disconnecting any of the fuel tubes or fuel system components, relieve the fuel system pressure to prevent accidental spraying of fuel. Fuel in the fuel system remains under high pressure, even when the engine is not running. Failure to follow this instruction may result in serious personal injury.**

> ❊❊ **WARNING**
>
> **When handling fuel, always observe fuel handling precautions and be prepared in the event of fuel spillage. Spilled fuel may be ignited by hot vehicle components or other ignition sources. Failure to follow these instructions may result in serious personal injury.**

> ❊❊ **WARNING**
>
> **Always disconnect the battery ground cable at the battery when working on an evaporative emission (EVAP) sys-**

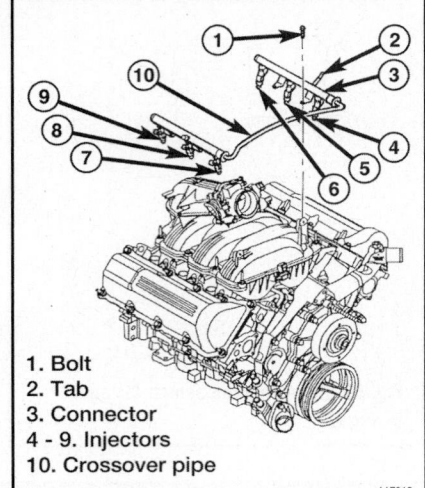

1. Bolt
2. Tab
3. Connector
4 - 9. Injectors
10. Crossover pipe

117319

Fig. 60 View of the fuel rail assembly—3.7L engine shown, 4.7 similar

tem or fuel-related component. Highly flammable mixtures are always present and may be ignited. Failure to follow these instructions may result in serious personal injury.

> ❊❊ **CAUTION**
>
> **The left and right fuel rails are replaced as an assembly. Do not attempt to separate rail halves at connector tubes. Due to design of tubes, it does not use any clamps. Never attempt to install a clamping device of any kind to tubes. When removing fuel rail assembly for any reason, be careful not to bend or kink tubes.**

1. Remove fuel tank filler tube cap.
2. Perform Fuel System Pressure Release Procedure.
3. Remove negative battery cable at battery.
4. Remove air duct at throttle body air box.
5. Remove air box at throttle body.
6. Remove air resonator mounting bracket at front of throttle body (2 bolts).
7. Disconnect fuel line latch clip and fuel line at fuel rail. A tool may be necessary for fuel line disconnection.
8. Remove the necessary vacuum lines at throttle body.
9. Disconnect the electrical connectors at all 6 fuel injectors. Refer to graphic. Push red colored slider away from injector. While pushing slider, depress tab and remove connector from injector. The factory fuel injection wiring harness is numerically

tagged (INJ 1, INJ 2, etc.) for injector position identification. If the harness is not tagged, note wiring location before removal.
10. Disconnect electrical connectors at all throttle body sensors.
11. Remove the 6 ignition coils.
12. Remove four fuel rail mounting bolts.
13. Gently rock and pull left side of fuel rail until fuel injectors just start to clear machined holes in cylinder head. Gently rock and pull right side of rail until injectors just start to clear cylinder head holes.
14. Repeat this procedure (left/right) until all injectors have cleared cylinder head holes.
15. Remove fuel rail (with injectors attached) from engine.
16. Disconnect clip(s) that retain fuel injector(s) to fuel rail.

To install:

17. Install fuel injector(s) into fuel rail assembly and install retaining clip(s).
18. If same injector(s) is being reinstalled, install new o-ring(s).
19. Apply a small amount of clean engine oil to each injector o-ring. This will aid in installation.
20. Clean out fuel injector machined bores in intake manifold.
21. Apply a small amount of engine oil to each fuel injector o-ring. This will help in fuel rail installation.
22. Position fuel rail/fuel injector assembly to machined injector openings in cylinder head.
23. Guide each injector into cylinder head. Be careful not to tear injector o-rings.
24. Push right side of fuel rail down until fuel injectors have bottomed on cylinder head shoulder. Push left fuel rail down until injectors have bottomed on cylinder head shoulder.
25. Install four fuel rail mounting bolts and tighten. Refer to torque specifications.
26. Install the 6 ignition coils.
27. Connect the electrical connectors to throttle body.
28. To complete installation, reverse the remaining removal procedure.
29. Start engine and check for leaks.

FUEL PUMP

REMOVAL & INSTALLATION
See Figure 61.

> ❊❊ **WARNING**
>
> **Do not smoke, carry lighted tobacco or have an open flame of any type when working on or near any fuel-related component. Highly flamma-**

ble mixtures are always present and may be ignited. Failure to follow these instructions may result in serious personal injury.

> ⁂ **WARNING**
>
> Do not carry personal electronic devices such as cell phones, pagers or audio equipment of any type when working on or near any fuel-related component. Highly flammable mixtures are always present and may be ignited. Failure to follow these instructions may result in serious personal injury.

> ⁂ **WARNING**
>
> Before working on or disconnecting any of the fuel tubes or fuel system components, relieve the fuel system pressure to prevent accidental spraying of fuel. Fuel in the fuel system remains under high pressure, even when the engine is not running. Failure to follow this instruction may result in serious personal injury.

> ⁂ **WARNING**
>
> When handling fuel, always observe fuel handling precautions and be prepared in the event of fuel spillage. Spilled fuel may be ignited by hot vehicle components or other ignition sources. Failure to follow these instructions may result in serious personal injury.

> ⁂ **WARNING**
>
> Always disconnect the battery ground cable at the battery when working on an evaporative emission (EVAP) system or fuel-related component. Highly flammable mixtures are always present and may be ignited. Failure to follow these instructions may result in serious personal injury.

1. Drain and remove fuel tank.
2. Note the rotational position of module before attempting removal. An indexing arrow is located on top of module for this purpose.
3. Position Lockring Remover/Installer into notches on outside edge of lockring.
4. Install 1/2 inch drive breaker bar to Lockring Remover/Installer.
5. Rotate breaker bar counter-clockwise to remove lockring.

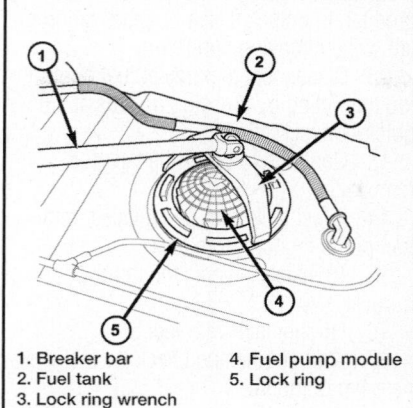

1. Breaker bar
2. Fuel tank
3. Lock ring wrench
4. Fuel pump module
5. Lock ring

117297

Fig. 61 Removing the fuel pump module

6. Remove the lockring. The module will spring up slightly when lockring is removed.
7. Remove the module from fuel tank. Be careful not to bend float arm while removing.

To install:

8. Using a new seal (gasket), position the fuel pump module into opening in fuel tank.
9. Position the lockring over top of fuel pump module.
10. Rotate module until embossed alignment arrow points to center alignment mark. This step must be performed to prevent float from contacting side of fuel tank. Also be sure fuel fitting on top of pump module is pointed to drivers side of vehicle.
11. Install the lockring Remover/Installer to lockring.
12. Install the 1/2 inch drive breaker (1) into lockring Remover/Installer
13. Tighten the lockring (clockwise) until all seven notches have engaged.
14. Install the fuel tank.

FUEL TANK

DRAINING

> ⁂ **WARNING**
>
> Do not smoke, carry lighted tobacco or have an open flame of any type when working on or near any fuel-related component. Highly flammable mixtures are always present and may be ignited. Failure to follow these instructions may result in serious personal injury.

> ⁂ **WARNING**
>
> Do not carry personal electronic devices such as cell phones, pagers or audio equipment of any type when working on or near any fuel-related component. Highly flammable mixtures are always present and may be ignited. Failure to follow these instructions may result in serious personal injury.

> ⁂ **WARNING**
>
> Before working on or disconnecting any of the fuel tubes or fuel system components, relieve the fuel system pressure to prevent accidental spraying of fuel. Fuel in the fuel system remains under high pressure, even when the engine is not running. Failure to follow this instruction may result in serious personal injury.

> ⁂ **WARNING**
>
> When handling fuel, always observe fuel handling precautions and be prepared in the event of fuel spillage. Spilled fuel may be ignited by hot vehicle components or other ignition sources. Failure to follow these instructions may result in serious personal injury.

> ⁂ **WARNING**
>
> Always disconnect the battery ground cable at the battery when working on an evaporative emission (EVAP) system or fuel-related component. Highly flammable mixtures are always present and may be ignited. Failure to follow these instructions may result in serious personal injury.

Two different procedures may be used to drain fuel tank: through the fuel fill fitting on tank, or using a diagnostic scan tool to activate the fuel pump relay.

The quickest draining procedure involves removing the rubber fuel fill hose at the fuel tank fill fitting.

As an alternative procedure, the electric fuel pump may be activated allowing tank to be drained at fuel rail connection. Refer to scan tool for fuel pump activation procedures. Before disconnecting fuel line at fuel rail, release fuel pressure.

If electric fuel pump is not operating, fuel must be drained through fuel fill fitting at tank. Refer to following procedures.

1. Release fuel system pressure.
2. Raise vehicle.
3. Remove left-rear tire/wheel.
4. Remove plastic fender liner in front of left-rear tire/wheel.
5. Thoroughly clean area around fuel fill fitting and rubber fuel fill hose at fuel tank.
6. Models with standard cabs: Loosen clamps and disconnect rubber fuel fill hose at fuel tank fitting. Using an approved gas holding tank, drain fuel tank through this fitting.
7. Models with extended cabs: Loosen clamps and disconnect rubber fuel fill hose at fuel tank fitting. Using an approved gas holding tank, drain fuel tank through this fitting.

REMOVAL & INSTALLATION

See Figure 62.

1. With vehicle in NEUTRAL, position it on a hoist.
2. Release the fuel system pressure.
3. Drain the fuel tank.
4. Disconnect vent line from tank.
5. Remove clamp and disconnect fill hose at fuel fill tube.
6. If equipped, remove fuel tank skid plate.
7. Disconnect electrical connector at ESIM switch.
8. Disconnect the ESIM, ORVR and EVAP lines at front of tank.
9. Support tank with a hydraulic jack.
10. Remove two fuel tank strap nuts and remove both tank support straps.
11. Carefully lower tank a few inches and disconnect fuel pump module electrical connector at top of tank. To disconnect elec-

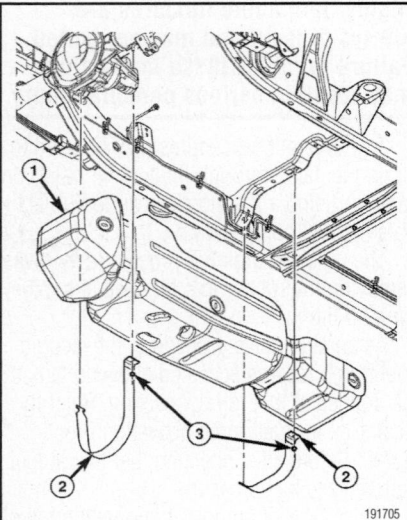

Fig. 62 Removing the tank (1), straps (2) and nuts (3)

trical connector: Push upward on red colored tab to unlock. Push on black colored tab while removing connector.
12. Disconnect fuel line at fuel pump module fitting by pressing on tabs at side of quick-connect fitting.
13. Continue to lower the tank for removal.
14. If fuel tank is to be replaced, remove fuel pump module from tank.
15. To install, reverse the removal procedure.
16. Fill fuel tank with fuel.
17. Start engine and check for fuel leaks near top of module.

IDLE SPEED

ADJUSTMENT

Idle speed adjustment is not necessary or possible.

THROTTLE BODY

REMOVAL & INSTALLATION

➡**Using a diagnostic scan tool, record any previous DTC's (Diagnostic Trouble Codes).**

➡**Never have the ignition key in the ON position when checking the throttle body shaft for a binding condition. This may set DTC's.**

3.7L Engine

See Figure 63.

A (factory adjusted) set screw is used to mechanically limit the position of the throttle body throttle plate. Never attempt to adjust the engine idle speed using this screw. All idle speed functions are controlled by the Powertrain Control Module (PCM).

1. Disconnect and isolate negative battery cable at battery.
2. Remove air intake tube at throttle body flange.
3. Disconnect throttle body electrical connector.
4. Disconnect the necessary vacuum lines at throttle body.
5. Remove the four throttle body mounting bolts.
6. Remove the throttle body from intake manifold.
7. Check the condition of old throttle body-to-intake manifold o-ring.

To install:

8. Check condition of throttle body-to-intake manifold O-ring. Replace as necessary.

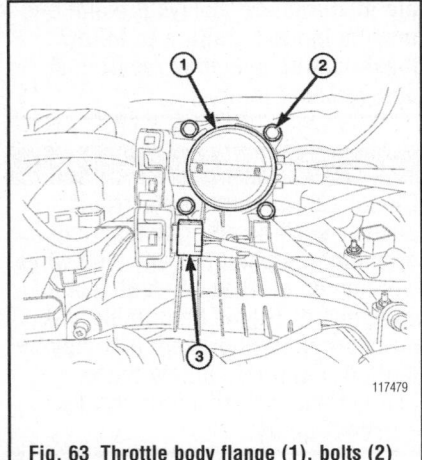

Fig. 63 Throttle body flange (1), bolts (2) and electrical connector (3)

9. Clean mating surfaces of throttle body and intake manifold.
10. Install O-ring between throttle body and intake manifold.
11. Position throttle body to intake manifold.
12. Install all throttle body mounting bolts finger tight.

✳✳ CAUTION

The throttle body mounting bolts MUST be tightened to specifications. Over tightening can cause damage to the throttle body or the intake manifold.

13. Obtain a torque wrench. Tighten mounting bolts in a mandatory torque criss-cross pattern sequence to 65 inch lbs. (7.5 Nm).
14. Install electrical connector.
15. Install necessary vacuum lines.
16. Install air cleaner duct at throttle body.
17. Connect negative battery cable.
18. Using the diagnostic scan tool, erase all previous DTC's and perform the ETC Relearn function.

4.7L Engine

See Figure 64.

1. Disconnect and isolate negative battery cable at battery.
2. Remove air duct and air resonator box at throttle body.
3. Disconnect throttle body electrical connector.
4. Disconnect the necessary vacuum lines at throttle body.
5. Remove the four throttle body mounting bolts.
6. Remove the throttle body from intake manifold.

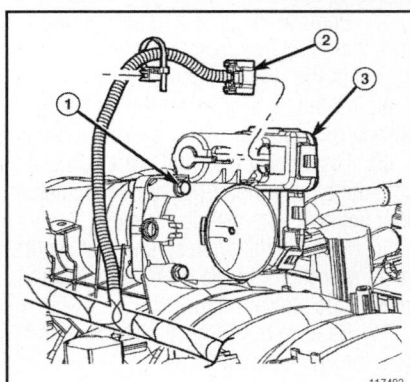

Fig. 64 Remove the mounting bolts (1), electrical connector (2) and throttle body (3)

7. Check the condition of old throttle body-to-intake manifold o-ring.

To install:

8. Check condition of throttle body-to-intake manifold O-ring. Replace as necessary.

9. Clean mating surfaces of throttle body and intake manifold.

10. Install throttle body-to-intake manifold O-ring.

11. Install all throttle body mounting bolts finger tight.

✳✳ CAUTION

The throttle body mounting bolts MUST be tightened to specifications. Over tightening can cause damage to the throttle body or the intake manifold.

12. Obtain a torque wrench. Tighten mounting bolts in a mandatory torque criss-cross pattern sequence to 65 inch lbs. (7.5 Nm).

13. Install electrical connector.

14. Install necessary vacuum lines.

15. Install air cleaner duct and plenum at throttle body.

16. Connect negative battery cable.

17. Using the diagnostic scan tool, erase all previous DTC's and perform the ETC Relearn function.

HEATING & AIR CONDITIONING SYSTEM

BLOWER MOTOR

REMOVAL & INSTALLATION

See Figure 65.

✳✳ CAUTION

Disable the airbag system before attempting any steering wheel, steering column or instrument panel component diagnosis or service. Disconnect and isolate the negative battery (ground) cable and wait two minutes for the airbag system capacitor to discharge before performing further diagnosis or service. This is the only sure way to disable the airbag system. Failure to follow these instructions may result in accidental airbag deployment and possible serious or fatal injury.

1. Disconnect and isolate the negative battery cable.

2. Disconnect the wire harness connector from the blower motor.

3. Remove the three screws that secure the blower motor to the HVAC housing.

4. Remove the blower motor from the HVAC housing.

5. To install, reverse the removal procedure.

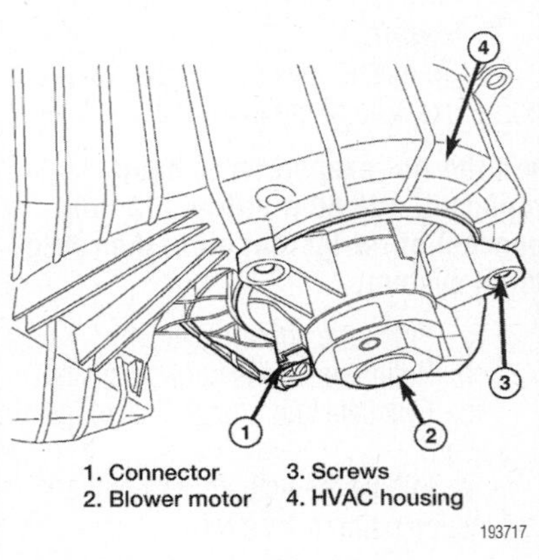

HEATER CORE

REMOVAL & INSTALLATION

See Figure 66.

✳✳ WARNING

Disable the airbag system before attempting any steering wheel, steering column or instrument panel component diagnosis or service. Disconnect and isolate the negative battery (ground) cable and wait two minutes for the airbag system capacitor to discharge before performing further diagnosis or service. This is the only sure way to disable the airbag system. Failure to follow these instructions may result in accidental airbag deployment and possible serious or fatal injury.

✳✳ WARNING

The heater core tubes are not serviced separately from the heater core. The heater core tubes should not be repositioned, loosened or removed from the heater core. Failure to follow these instructions may result in a coolant leak and possible serious or fatal injury.

1. Disconnect and isolate the negative battery cable.

2. Recover the refrigerant from the refrigerant system.

3. Drain the engine cooling system.

✳✳ WARNING

To avoid personal injury or death, never strike or drop the occupant restraint controller, as it can damage the impact sensor or affect its calibration. The occupant restraint controller contains the impact sensor, which enables the system to deploy the supplemental restraints. If an airbag control module is accidentally dropped during service, the module must be scrapped and replaced with a new unit. Failure to observe this warning could result in accidental, incomplete, or improper supplemental restraint deployment.

1. Connector   3. Screws
2. Blower motor   4. HVAC housing

Fig. 65 Removing the blower motor

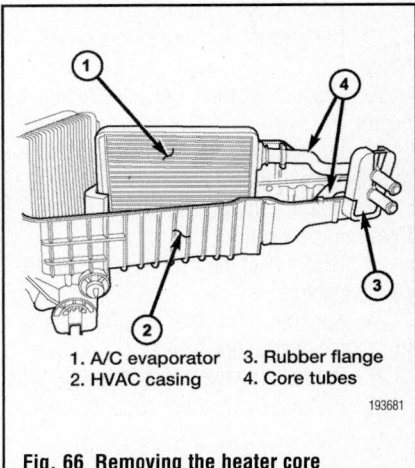

1. A/C evaporator   3. Rubber flange
2. HVAC casing   4. Core tubes

Fig. 66 Removing the heater core

✳✳ CAUTION

On vehicles equipped with the Occupant Classification System (OCS), never replace both the Occupant Restraint Controller (ORC) and the Occupant Classification Module (OCM) at the same time. If both require replacement, replace one. Then perform the supplemental restraint verification test before replacing the other. Both the ORC and the OCM store OCS calibration data, which they transfer to one another when one of them is replaced. If both are replaced at the same time, an irreversible fault will be set in both modules.

4. Remove the instrument panel from the passenger compartment

5. Remove the floor console.

6. Remove the driver side door sill trim cover.

7. Remove the steering column opening cover.

8. Position the front wheels straight ahead.

9. Remove the steering column tilt lever knob.

10. Remove the column shrouds.

11. Disconnect the brake switch electrical connector.

12. Disconnect the wiring harness to the column.

13. Disconnect the gearshift cable from vehicle..

14. Remove the upper steering shaft coupler bolt from the column.

15. Remove the four steering column mounting nuts.

16. Remove the steering column assembly from the vehicle.

17. Remove the bolts from the pedal support.

18. Remove the defroster grille.

19. Remove the five upper fence line bolts

20. Disconnect the HVAC electrical connector.

21. Loosen the screws and disconnect the electrical connectors.

22. Remove the bolt and the ground from the left a-pillar.

23. Disconnect the ABS module electrical connectors.

24. Separate the center wire harness from the center support.

25. Remove the two center support bolts.

26. Remove the two left support bolts.

27. Remove the passenger door sill trim cover.

28. Remove the passenger side end cap.

29. Disconnect the antenna cable.

30. Remove the bolt and nut and disconnect the grounds.

31. Disconnect the antenna amplifier connector, if equipped.

32. Remove the right side support bolts and with the help of another person, remove the instrument panel assembly from the vehicle.

33. Remove the two bolts that secure the HVAC housing to the passenger compartment side of the dash panel.

34. If equipped with 3.7L engine and automatic transmission, remove the number six cylinder ignition coil and retaining stud to gain access to the center HVAC housing nut in the engine compartment.

35. If equipped with 4.7L engine, remove the intake manifold to gain access to the center HVAC housing nut in the engine compartment.

36. Disconnect the A/C liquid line and the A/C accumulator from the A/C evaporator and install plugs into or caps over the fittings and evaporator tubes..

37. Disconnect the heater hoses from the heater core tubes and install plugs into or caps over the heater core tubes.

38. Remove the three nuts that secure the HVAC housing and the fresh air inlet screen to the engine compartment side of the dash panel.

39. Pull the HVAC housing assembly rearward so that the mounting studs and condensate drain tube clear the dash panel and remove the HVAC housing from the passenger compartment.

40. If required, remove the fresh air inlet screen from the dash panel.

41. Remove the HVAC housing and place it on a workbench.

42. Disconnect the HVAC wire harness from the mode door actuators located on the driver side end of the HVAC housing.

43. Remove the screws that secure the mode door actuators to the HVAC housing and remove the actuators.

44. Disconnect the HVAC wire harness from the evaporator temperature sensor and the blend door actuator located on the top of the HVAC housing.

45. Remove the screws that secure the blend door actuator to the HVAC housing and remove the actuator.

46. Remove the evaporator temperature sensor from the HVAC housing.

47. Remove the lever and linkage rod from the blend door pivot shaft located on the top of the HVAC housing.

48. Carefully disconnect the lever and linkage rod from the blend door pivot lever.

49. Disconnect the HVAC wire harness from the blower motor resistor, recirculation door actuator, and the blower motor.

50. Remove the three screws that secure the blower motor to the HVAC housing and remove the blower motor.

51. Remove the HVAC wiring harness from the HVAC housing.

52. Remove the four screws that secure the air inlet housing to the top of the HVAC housing and remove the air inlet housing.

53. If required, disassemble the air inlet housing

➡If the foam seal on the panel/defrost outlet is deformed or damaged, it must be replaced.

54. Remove the foam seal from the panel/defrost outlet located on the top of the HVAC housing.

55. Remove the six screw that secure the panel/defrost outlet to the top of the HVAC housing and remove the outlet.

56. Remove the panel-air door from the opening located at the top of the HVAC housing.

57. Remove the three screws that secure the floor distribution duct to the bottom of the HVAC housing and remove the duct.

58. Remove the three foam seals from the HVAC housing.

59. Remove the two metal clips eleven screw that secure the upper and lower HVAC housing halves together and separate the housing halves.

60. Carefully lift the heater core out of the lower half of the HVAC housing.

➡If the foam seal around the heater core is deformed or damaged, the seal must be replaced.

To install:

61. To install, reverse the removal procedure. Take note of the following:

➡If the A/C evaporator is being replaced, add 60 milliliters (2 fluid ounces) of refrigerant oil to the refrigerant system.

a. Flush the cooling system

b. Refill the engine cooling system.

c. Evacuate and charge the refrigerant system.

d. Initiate the Actuator Calibration function using a scan tool.

STEERING

POWER STEERING GEAR

REMOVAL & INSTALLATION

See Figure 67.

1. Siphon out as much power steering fluid as possible from the pump.
2. Lock the steering wheel.
3. Raise and support the vehicle.
4. Remove the front tires.
5. Remove the nuts from the tie rod ends.
6. Separate tie rod ends from the knuckles with Puller C3894-A
7. Remove the steering gear pinch bolt.
8. Remove the lower steering coupling from the steering gear.
9. Turn the steering gear to the full right position.

➡**Protect the end of hoses to prevent contamination to the system and damage to the o-rings.**

10. Remove the power steering lines from the gear.
11. Remove the steering gear mounting bolts and nuts.
12. Tip the gear forward to allow clearance and move to the right then tip the gear downward on the left side to remove from the vehicle.

To install:

➡**Before installing gear inspect bushings and replace if worn or damaged.**

13. Install gear to the vehicle and tighten mounting nuts and bolts to 190 ft. lbs. (258 Nm).
14. Install power steering lines to steer-

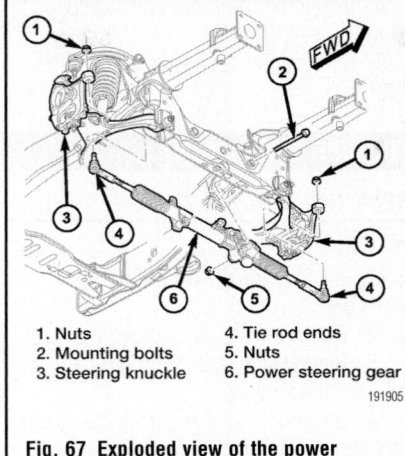

1. Nuts
2. Mounting bolts
3. Steering knuckle
4. Tie rod ends
5. Nuts
6. Power steering gear

191905

Fig. 67 Exploded view of the power steering gear

ing gear and tighten the pressure hose to 23 ft. lbs. (31 Nm) and tighten the return hose to 27 ft. lbs. (37 Nm).

15. Slide the shaft coupler onto gear. Install new bolt and tighten to 42 ft. lbs. (57 Nm).
16. Clean tie rod end studs and knuckle tapers.
17. Install tie rod ends into the steering knuckles and tighten the nuts to 60 ft. lbs. (81 Nm).
18. Install the front tires.
19. Remove the support and lower the vehicle.
20. Unlock the steering wheel.
21. Fill system with fluid.
22. Adjust the toe position.

POWER STEERING PUMP

REMOVAL & INSTALLATION

See Figure 68.

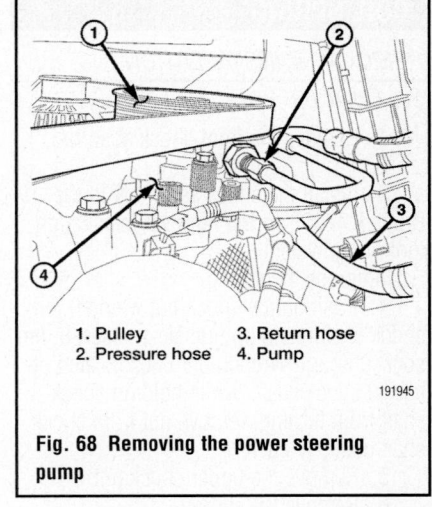

1. Pulley
2. Pressure hose
3. Return hose
4. Pump

191945

Fig. 68 Removing the power steering pump

1. Drain and siphon the power steering fluid from the pump.
2. Remove the serpentine drive belt.
3. Remove the reservoir return hose at the reservoir.
4. Remove the pressure hose from the pump.
5. Remove 3 pump mounting bolts through pulley access holes.
6. Remove the pump from the engine.

To install:

7. Align the pump with the mounting holes on the engine.
8. Install 3 pump mounting bolts through the pulley access holes. Tighten the bolts to 21 ft. lbs. (28 Nm).
9. Install the pressure hose to the pump. Tighten the tube nut to 23 ft. lbs. (31 Nm).
10. Install the reservoir return hose to the reservoir.
11. Install the serpentine drive belt.
12. Fill the power steering pump

COIL SPRING

REMOVAL & INSTALLATION

See Figure 69.

1. Remove the front shock absorber.
2.
3. Install the shock assembly in the Branick 7200® spring removal/installation tool or equivalent.
Compress the spring.
4. Position the shock nut wrench), on shock shaft retaining nut. Next, insert 8 mm socket though Wrench onto hex located on end of shock shaft. While holding shock shaft from turning, remove nut from shock shaft using Wrench.
5. Remove the upper shock nut.
6. Remove the shock.
7. Remove the shock upper mounting plate.
8. Remove and inspect the upper and lower spring isolators.
9. To install, reverse the removal procedure.
10. Tighten the nut to 33 ft. lbs. (45 Nm).

CONTROL LINKS

REMOVAL & INSTALLATION

1. Raise and support the vehicle.
2. Remove the lower nut.
3. Remove the upper nut, retainers and grommets from the stabilizer bar.
4. Remove the stabilizer link from the vehicle.
5. Install the stabilizer link to the vehicle.
6. Install the retainers, grommets and upper nut to the stabilizer bar and Tighten to 17 ft. lbs. (23 Nm).

7. Install the lower nut and Tighten to 75 ft. lbs. (102 Nm).
8. Remove the support and lower the vehicle.

LOWER BALL JOINT

REMOVAL & INSTALLATION

See Figure 70.

1. Remove the tire and wheel assembly.
2. Remove the brake caliper and rotor.
3. Remove the outer tie rod retaining nut from the knuckle.
4. Separate the tie rod from the steering knuckle using puller.
5. Remove the upper ball joint nut, then separate the upper ball joint from the knuckle using puller.
6. Remove the lower ball joint nut, then separate the lower ball joint from the steering knuckle using puller.
7. Remove the steering knuckle.
8. Move the halfshaft to the side and support the halfshaft out of the way 4WD only.
9. Remove the snap ring from the ball joint flange.

➡ **Extreme pressure lubrication must be used on the threaded portions of the tool. This will increase the longevity of the tool and insure proper operation during the removal and installation process .**

10. Press the ball joint from the lower control arm using special tools :
    a. Press.
    b. Remover/Driver.
    c. Remover/Installer/Receiver.

To install:

11. Reverse the removal procedure.
12. Install the tie rod end into the steering knuckle (5), then install the retaining nut and tighten to 80 ft. lbs. (108 Nm).
13. Tighten the halfshaft nut to 185 ft. lbs. (251 Nm), if equipped.
14. Check the vehicle ride height
15. Perform a wheel alignment.

LOWER CONTROL ARM

REMOVAL & INSTALLATION

See Figure 71.

1. Raise and support the vehicle.
2. Remove the wheel and tire assembly.
3. Remove the disc brake caliper assembly..
4. Remove the disc brake rotor.
5. Disconnect the wheel speed sensor at the wheel well.
6. Remove tie rod end jam nut.
7. Disconnect the tie rod from the knuckle using remover.
8. Remove the front halfshaft nut 4WD.
9. Remove the upper ball joint nut.
10. Separate the upper ball joint from the steering knuckle with Remover.
11. Remove the lower ball joint nut. Separate the lower ball joint from the steering knuckle with puller.
12. Remove the steering knuckle..
13. Remove the stabilizer bar link..
14. Remove the shock absorber lower bolt and nut .
15. Remove the lower control arm bolts, nuts and washers.
16. Remove the lower control arm from the vehicle.

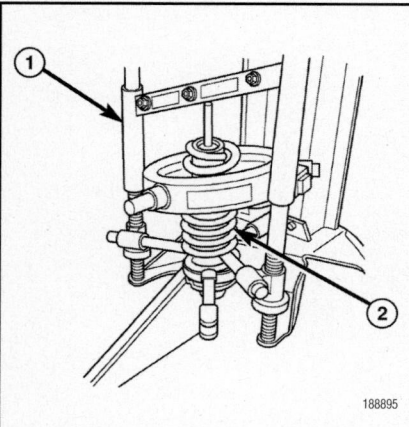

Fig. 69 Using the spring compressor (1) and spring (2)

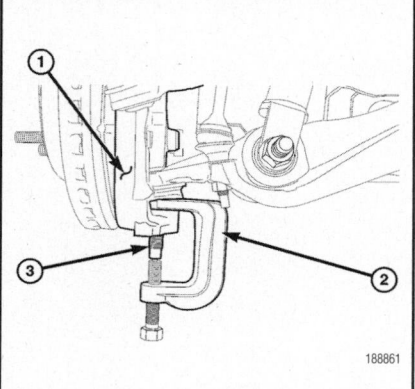

Fig. 70 Remove the lower ball joint nut, then separate the lower ball joint (3) from the steering knuckle (1) using puller (3)

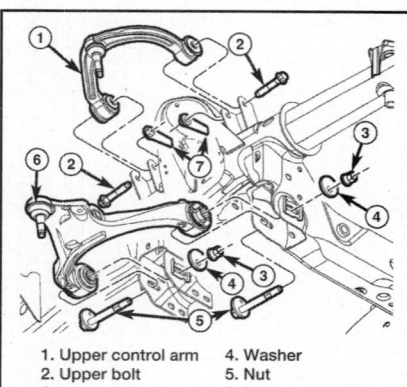

1. Upper control arm
2. Upper bolt
3. Lower bolt
4. Washer
5. Nut
6. Lower control arm

Fig. 71 Exploded view of the lower and upper control arm assembly

To install:

17. Position the lower control arm at the frame rail brackets. Install the pivot bolts washers and nuts. Tighten the nuts finger-tight.

➡**The ball joint stud taper must be CLEAN and DRY before installing the knuckle. Clean the stud taper with mineral spirits to remove dirt and grease.**

18. Install the steering knuckle.
19. Insert the lower ball joint into the steering knuckle. Install and tighten the retaining nut to 95 ft. lbs. (129 Nm).
20. Install the shock absorber.
21. Install the front halfshaft nut.
22. Insert the upper ball joint into the steering knuckle. Install and tighten the retaining nut to 70 ft. lbs. (95 Nm).
23. Install the stabilizer bar link.
24. Tighten the lower control arm pivot nut and bolts to 110 ft. lbs. (149 Nm).
25. Insert the outer tie rod end into the steering knuckle. Install and tighten the retaining nut to 80 ft. lbs. (108 Nm).
26. To complete installation, reverse the remaining removal procedure.
27. Check the vehicle ride height
28. Perform a wheel alignment.

STABILIZER BAR

REMOVAL & INSTALLATION

See Figure 72.

1. Remove the stabilizer link upper nut and remove the retainers and grommets.
2. Remove the stabilizer bar retainer bolts also remove the retainers from the frame sway bar and remove the bar.
3. If necessary, remove the bushings from the stabilizer bar.

To install:

4. If removed, install the bushings on the stabilizer bar.
5. Position the stabilizer bar on the frame crossmember brackets and install the bracket and bolts finger-tight.

➡**Check the alignment of the bar to ensure there is no interference with the either frame rail or chassis component. Spacing should be equal on both sides.**

6. Install the stabilizer bar to the stabilizer link and install the grommets and retainers.
7. Install the nuts to the stabilizer link and tighten to 17 ft. lbs. (23 Nm).
8. Tighten the bracket bolts to the frame to 45 ft. lbs. (61 Nm).

STEERING KNUCKLE

REMOVAL & INSTALLATION

See Figure 73.

1. Raise and support the vehicle.
2. Remove the wheel and tire assembly.
3. Remove the brake caliper, rotor shield and ABS wheel speed sensor if equipped
4. Remove the front halfshaft nut 4WD only.
5. Remove the tie rod end nut.
6. Separate the tie rod from the knuckle with puller.
7. Remove the upper ball joint nut.
8. Separate the ball joint from the knuckle with puller.
9. Install an hydraulic jack to support the lower control arm
10. Remove the lower ball joint nut
11. Separate the ball joint from the knuckle with puller and remove the knuckle.

12. Remove the hub/bearing bolts from the knuckle.
13. Remove the steering knuckle.

To install:

➡**The ball joint stud tapers must be CLEAN and DRY before installing the knuckle. Clean the stud tapers with mineral spirits to remove dirt and grease.**

14. Install the hub/bearing to the steering knuckle and tighten the bolts to 120 ft. lbs. (163 Nm).
15. Install the knuckle onto the upper and lower ball joints.
16. Install the upper ball joint nut. Tighten the nut to 70 ft. lbs. (95 Nm).
17. Install the lower ball joint nut. Tighten the nut to 95 ft. lbs. (129 Nm).
18. Remove the hydraulic jack from the lower control arm.
19. Install the tie rod end and tighten the nut to 80 ft. lbs. (108 Nm).
20. Install the front halfshaft into the hub/bearing 4WD only.
21. Install the halfshaft nut and tighten to 185 ft. lbs. (251 Nm) 4WD only.
22. To complete installation, reverse the remaining removal procedure.
23. Check the vehicle ride height
24. Perform a wheel alignment.

STRUT & SPRING ASSEMBLY

REMOVAL & INSTALLATION

See Figure 74.

1. Remove the upper shock nuts.
2. Raise and support the vehicle.
3. Remove the tire and wheel assembly.
4. Remove the disc brake caliper mounting bolts.
5. Remove the wheel speed sensor routing clip.
6. Remove the upper ball joint nut and separate the ball joint from the knuckle using special tool.
7. Support the lower control arm outboard end.
8. Remove the stabilizer link lower nut and then separate the stabilizer link from the lower control arm to gain access to the lower shock nut.
9. Remove the lower shock bolt and nut.
10. Remove the shock assembly.

To install:

➡**All suspension components should be tighten with the weight of the vehicle on them (curb height).**

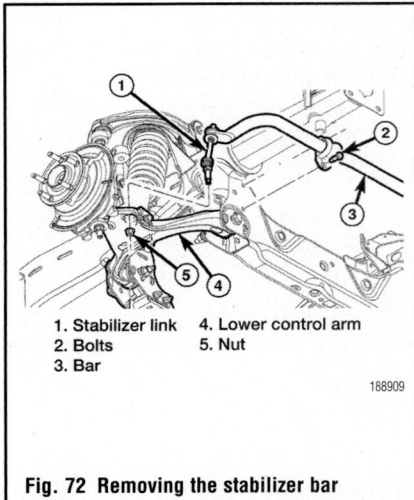

1. Stabilizer link   4. Lower control arm
2. Bolts
3. Bar

188909

Fig. 72 Removing the stabilizer bar

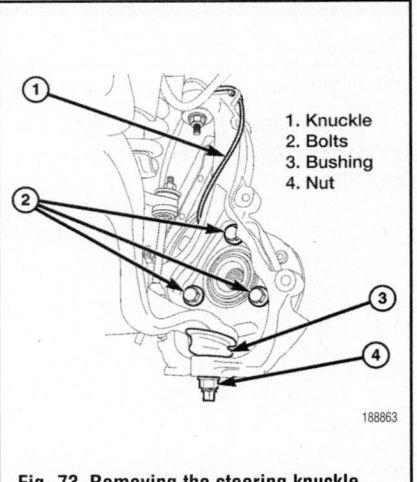

1. Knuckle
2. Bolts
3. Bushing
4. Nut

188863

Fig. 73 Removing the steering knuckle

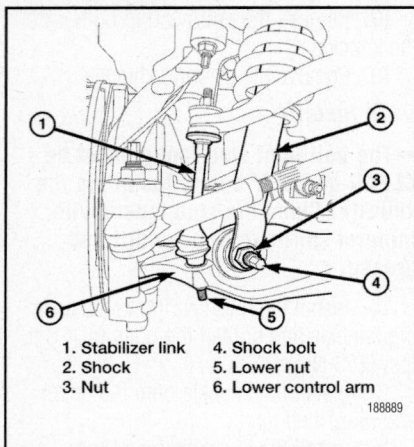

1. Stabilizer link **4.** Shock bolt
2. Shock **5.** Lower nut
3. Nut **6.** Lower control arm

188889

Fig. 74 Removing the strut and spring assembly

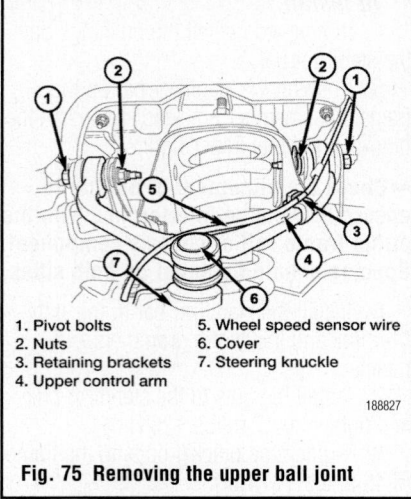

1. Pivot bolts **5.** Wheel speed sensor wire
2. Nuts **6.** Cover
3. Retaining brackets **7.** Steering knuckle
4. Upper control arm

188827

Fig. 75 Removing the upper ball joint

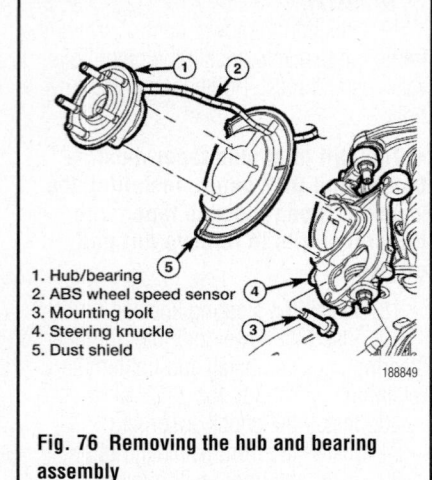

1. Hub/bearing
2. ABS wheel speed sensor
3. Mounting bolt
4. Steering knuckle
5. Dust shield

188849

Fig. 76 Removing the hub and bearing assembly

11. Install the upper part of the shock into the frame bracket.

12. Install the upper shock module nuts. Tighten to 45 ft. lbs. (61 Nm).

13. Install the lower part of the shock module into the lower control arm shock bushing.

14. Position the shock module to lower control. Install bolt so head of bolt is facing rear of vehicle and hand start nut. Tighten the bolt AND nut to 155 ft. lbs. (210 Nm).

15. Install the stabilizer link lower nut to the lower control arm.

16. Insert ball joint in steering knuckle and tighten ball joint nut to 70 ft. lbs. (95 Nm).

17. Reposition the wheel speed wire into the retaining brackets.

18. Install the caliper slide pin bolts. Tighten to 24 ft. lbs. (32 Nm).

19. Remove the support from the lower control arm outboard end.

20. Install the tire and wheel assembly.

21. Remove the support and lower the vehicle.

UPPER CONTROL ARM

REMOVAL & INSTALLATION

See Figure 75.

1. Raise and support vehicle.

2. Remove wheel and tire assembly.

3. Remove the nut from upper ball joint.

4. Separate upper ball joint from the steering knuckle with puller

5. Remove the wheel speed sensor wire from the retaining brackets to the upper control arm.

6. Remove the control arm pivot bolts and nuts and remove control arm.

To install:

7. Position the control arm into the frame brackets. Install bolts and nuts. Tighten to 130 ft. lbs. (176 Nm).

8. Reposition the wheel speed wir into the retaining brackets.

9. Insert ball joint in steering knuckle and tighten ball joint nut to 70 ft. lbs. (95 Nm).

10. Install the wheel and tire assembly.

11. Remove the support and lower vehicle.

12. Perform a wheel alignment.

WHEEL BEARINGS

REMOVAL & INSTALLATION

See Figure 76.

1. Raise and support the vehicle.

2. Remove the wheel and tire assembly.

3. Remove the brake caliper and rotor.

4. Remove the ABS wheel speed sensor if equipped.

5. Remove the halfshaft nut 4X4 only.

➡ Do not strike the knuckle with a hammer to remove the tie rod end or the ball joint. Damage to the steering knuckle will occur.

6. Pull down on the steering knuckle to separate the halfshaft from the hub/bearing. 4WD only.

7. Remove the three hub/bearing mounting bolts from the steering knuckle.

8. Slide the hub/bearing out of the steering knuckle.

9. Remove the brake dust shield.

To install:

10. Install the brake dust shield.

11. Install the hub/bearing into the steering knuckle and tighten the bolts to 120 ft. lbs. (163 Nm).

12. Install the brake rotor and caliper.

13. Install the ABS wheel speed sensor if equipped.

14. Install the halfshaft nut and tighten to 185 ft. lbs. (251 Nm), 4WD only.

15. Install the wheel and tire assembly.

16. Remove the support and lower vehicle.

LEAF SPRING

REMOVAL & INSTALLATION

See Figure 77.

➡ **The rear of the vehicle must be lifted only with a jack or hoist. The lift must be placed under the frame rail cross-member located aft of the rear axle. Use care to avoid bending the side rail flange.**

1. Raise the vehicle at the frame.
2. Use a hydraulic jack to relieve the axle weight.
3. Remove the wheel and tire assemblies.
4. Remove the nuts, the U-bolts and spring plate from the axle.
5. Loosen and remove the bolt and then remove the flag nut through the access hole in the bracket from the spring front eye.
6. Remove the nut and bolt that attaches the spring shackle to the rear frame bracket.
7. Remove the spring from the vehicle.
8. Remove the shackle from the spring.

To install:

9. Install the spring shackle on the spring finger tight.
10. Position the spring on the rear axle pad. Make sure the spring center bolt is inserted in the pad locating hole.
11. Align front spring eye with the bolt hole in the front frame bracket. Install the spring eye bolt and flag nut through the access hole in the frame and tighten the bolt finger-tight.
12. Align spring shackle eye with the bolt hole in the rear frame bracket. Install the bolt and nut and tighten the spring shackle eye nut finger-tight.
13. Install the U-bolts, spring plate and nuts.
14. Tighten the U-bolt nuts to 110 ft. lbs. (149 Nm).
15. Install the wheel and tire assemblies.
16. Remove the support stands from under the frame rails. Lower the vehicle until the springs are supporting the weight of the vehicle.
17. Tighten the front spring eye bolt and flagnut to 125 ft. lbs. (170 Nm).
18. Tighten the rear spring eye to shackle bolt and nut and the shackle to frame bolt and nut to 125 ft. lbs. (170 Nm).

STRUT ASSEMBLY

REMOVAL & INSTALLATION

See Figures 78 and 79.

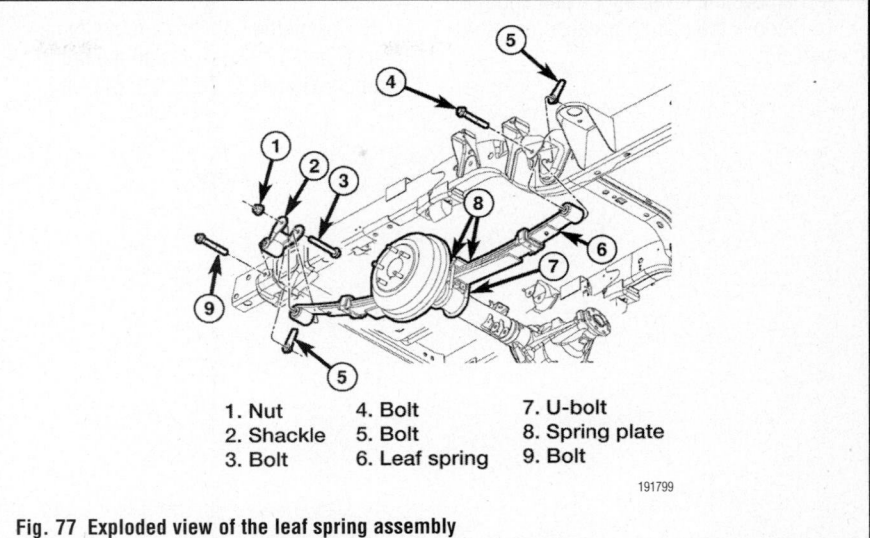

1. Nut	4. Bolt	7. U-bolt
2. Shackle	5. Bolt	8. Spring plate
3. Bolt	6. Leaf spring	9. Bolt

191799

Fig. 77 Exploded view of the leaf spring assembly

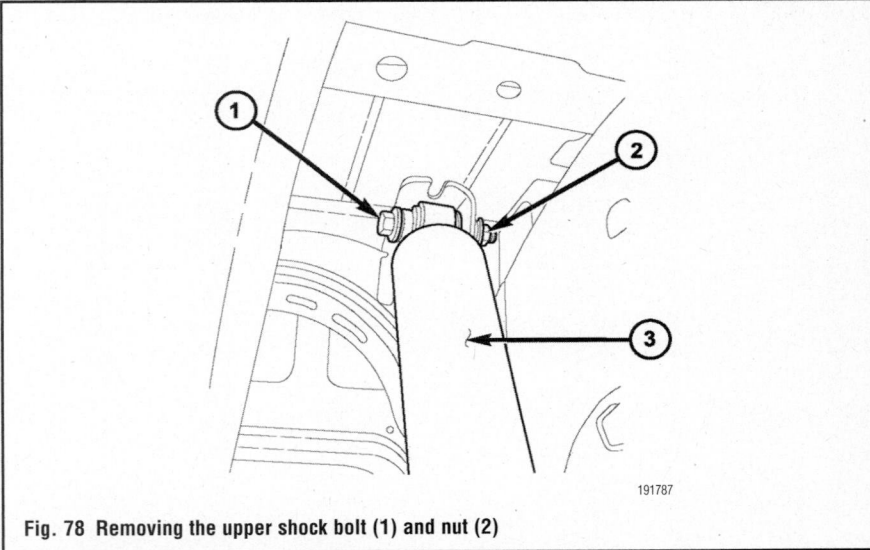

191787

Fig. 78 Removing the upper shock bolt (1) and nut (2)

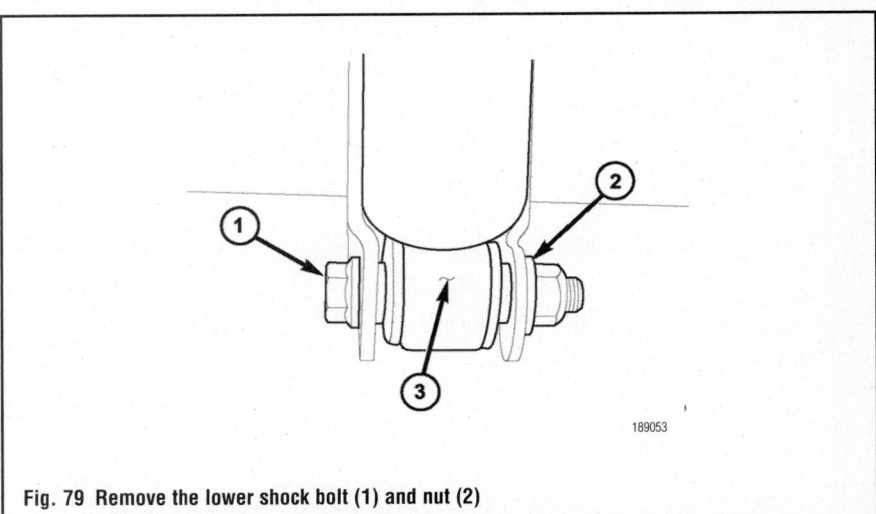

189053

Fig. 79 Remove the lower shock bolt (1) and nut (2)

1. Raise vehicle and support the axle.
2. Remove the upper shock bolt and nut.
3. Remove the lower shock bolt and nut.
4. Remove the rear shock absorber from the vehicle.

To install:

5. Position the shock absorber to the vehicle.
6. Install the bolt through the frame bracket and the shock. Install the nut to the top bolt. Tighten to 70 ft. lbs. (95 Nm).

7. Install the bolt through the axle bracket and the shock. Install the nut to the bolt. Tighten to 70 ft. lbs. (95 Nm).
8. Remove the support and lower the vehicle.

CHRYSLER, DODGE AND JEEP

Diagnostic Trouble Codes

DIAGNOSTIC TROUBLE CODES

OBD II VEHICLE APPLICATIONS

CHRYSLER CORP.

300
2010–2011
- 2.7L . . . . .VIN D
- 3.6L . . . . .VIN G
- 3.5L . . . . .VIN V
- 5.7L . . . . .VIN T
- 6.1L . . . . VIN W

Avenger
2010–2011
- 2.4L . . . . .VIN B
- 2.7L . . . . .VIN D
- 3.5L . . . . .VIN V
- 3.6L . . . . .VIN G

Caliber
2010–2011
- 2.0L . . . . .VIN A
- 2.4L . . . . .VIN B

Challenger
2010–2011
- 3.5L . . . . .VIN V
- 3.6L . . . . .VIN G

- 5.7L . . . . .VIN T
- 6.1L . . . . .VIN W
- 6.4L . . . . .VIN J

Charger
2010–2011
- 2.7L . . . . .VIN D
- 3.6L . . . . .VIN G
- 3.5L . . . . .VIN V
- 5.7L . . . . .VIN T
- 6.1L . . . . .VIN W

Commander
2010
- 3.7L . . . . .VIN K
- 4.7L . . . . .VIN P
- 5.7L . . . . .VIN T

Compass
2010–2011
- 2.0L . . . . .VIN A
- 2.4L . . . . .VIN B

Grand Caravan
2010–2011
- 3.3L . . . . .VIN E
- 3.6L . . . . .VIN G
- 3.8L . . . . VIN 1
- 4.0L . . . . .VIN X

Patriot
2010–2011
- 2.0L . . . . .VIN A
- 2.4L . . . . .VIN B

Sebring, Sebring Convertible
2010–2011
- 2.4L . . . . .VIN B
- 2.7L . . . . .VIN D
- 3.5L . . . . .VIN V
- 3.6L . . . . .VIN G

Town & Country
2010–2011
- 3.3L . . . . .VIN E
- 3.6L . . . . .VIN G
- 3.8L . . . . VIN 1
- 4.0L . . . . .VIN X

OBD II Trouble Code List (P0XXX Codes)

DTC	Trouble Code Title, Conditions, Possible Causes
DTC: P0003	**-FUEL QUANTITY CONTROL CIRCUIT LOW:** With the ignition on and the ECM command of the Fuel Quantity Solenoid off. The ECM detects that the (K365) Fuel Quantity Solenoid Control circuit voltage is shorted to ground for 0. 2 seconds.
DTC: P0004	**-FUEL QUANTITY CONTROL CIRCUIT HIGH:** With the ignition on and the ECM command of the Fuel Quantity Solenoid on. The ECM detects excessive current on the (K365) Fuel Quantity Solenoid Control circuit for 0. 2 of a second.
DTC: P000A	**-BANK 1 CAMSHAFT 1 POSITION SLOW RESPONSE:** Variable Valve Timing (VVT) rationality is monitored under the following conditions:(1) Cam phasing is commanded; (2) Oil temperature is between -12°C to 139° C (10° F to 282° F); (3) Battery voltage is greater than10 volts; (3) Engine speed is at least 650 to 1400 rpm, depending on oil temperature; (4) No CMP sensor, CKP sensor, or OBDI plausibility errors. Before VVT can be enabled, reference adaptation must be completed. The actual camshaft phasing position does not match the desired camshaft phasing position during camshaft phasing position changes.
DTC: P000A	**-BANK 1 CAMSHAFT 1 POSITION SLOW RESPONSE:** Variable Valve Timing (VVT) rationality is monitored under the following conditions:(1) Cam phasing is commanded off of the default (lockpin) position;(2) Oil temperature is between -12°C to 139°C (10°F to 282°F); (3)Battery voltage is greater than 10. 0 Volts; (3) Engine speed is at least 650 to 1400 rpm, depending on oil temperature; (4) No CMP Sensor, CKP Sensor or OBDI plausibility errors. Before VVT can be enabled, reference adaptation must be completed. The actual Camshaft phasing position does not match the desired Camshaft phasing position during Camshaft phasing position changes.
DTC: P000B	**-BANK 1 CAMSHAFT 2 POSITION SLOW RESPONSE:** Variable Valve Timing (VVT) rationality is monitored under the following conditions:(1) Cam phasing is commanded off of the default (lockpin) position;(2) Oil temperature is between -12° C to 139° C (10° F to 282° F);(3) Battery voltage is greater than 10 Volts; (3) Engine speed is at least 650 to 1400 rpm, depending on oil temperature; (4) No CMP sensor, CKP sensor or OBDI plausibility errors. Before VVT can be enabled, reference adaptation must be completed. The actual camshaft phasing position does not match the desired camshaft phasing position during camshaft phasing position changes.
DTC: P000B	**-BANK 1 CAMSHAFT 2 POSITION SLOW RESPONSE:** Variable Cam Timing (VCT) phasing accuracy is monitored under the following conditions: (1) Engine speed is at least 150 rpm; (2) No CMP sensor or CKP sensor plausibility errors. This is performed even when phasing control is not enabled, to verify the actuator is keeping the camshaft at the default (lockpin) phase. The actual measured camshaft phase does not match the desired camshaft phasing set point. Two Trip Fault. Three good trips to turn off the MIL.
DTC: P000B	**-BANK 1 CAMSHAFT 2 POSITION SLOW RESPONSE:** The Variable Cam Timing (VCT) phasing accuracy is monitored under the following conditions: (1) Engine speed is at least 150 rpm. (2) No CMP sensor or CKP sensor plausibility errors. This is performed even when phasing control is not enabled, to verify the actuator is keeping the camshaft at the default (lockpin) phase. The actual measured camshaft phase does not match the desired camshaft phasing set point. Two Trip Fault. Three good trips to turn off the MIL.
DTC: P000B	**-BANK 1 CAMSHAFT 2 POSITION SLOW RESPONSE:** Variable Valve Timing (VVT) rationality is monitored under the following conditions:(1) Cam phasing is commanded; (2) Oil temperature is between -12°C to 139° C (10° F to 282° F); (3) Battery voltage is greater than10 Volts; (3) Engine speed is at least 650 to 1400 rpm, depending on oil temperature; (4) No CMP sensor, CKP sensor, or OBDI plausibility errors. Before VVT can be enabled, reference adaptation must be completed. The actual camshaft phasing position does not match the desired camshaft phasing position during camshaft phasing position changes.
DTC: P000C	**-BANK 2 CAMSHAFT 1 POSITION SLOW RESPONSE :** Variable Valve Timing (VVT) rationality is monitored under the following conditions:(1) Cam phasing is commanded off of the default (lockpin) position;(2) Oil temperature is between -12° C to 139° C (10° F to 282° F);(3) Battery voltage is greater than 10 Volts; (3) Engine speed is at least 650 to 1400 rpm, depending on oil temperature; (4) No CMP sensor, CKP sensor or OBDI plausibility errors. Before VVT can be enabled, reference adaptation must be completed. The actual camshaft phasing position does not match the desired camshaft phasing position during camshaft phasing position changes.
DTC: P000D	**-BANK 2 CAMSHAFT 2 POSITION SLOW RESPONSE:** Variable Valve Timing (VVT) rationality is monitored under the following conditions:(1) Cam phasing is commanded off of the default (lockpin) position;(2) Oil temperature is between -12° C to 139° C (10° F to 282° F);(3) Battery voltage is greater than 10 Volts; (3) Engine speed is at least 650 to 1400 RPM, depending on oil temperature; (4) No CMP sensor, CKP sensor or OBDI plausibility errors. Before VVT can be enabled, reference adaptation must be completed. The actual camshaft phasing position does not match the desired camshaft phasing position during camshaft phasing position changes.
DTC: P0010	**-BANK 1 CAMSHAFT 1 POSITION ACTUATOR CIRCUIT OPEN:** With the engine running and battery voltage greater than 10. 4 Volts. The Powertrain Control Module (PCM) detects that the actual state of the VVT Intake Solenoid does not match the intended state.

DTC	Trouble Code Title, Conditions, Possible Causes
DTC: P0010	**-BANK 1 CAMSHAFT 1 POSITION ACTUATOR CIRCUIT OPEN:** With the engine running and battery voltage greater than 10. 4 volts. The Powertrain Control Module (PCM) detects that the actual state of the Camshaft1/1 Position Solenoid does not match the intended state.
DTC: P0013	**-BANK 1 CAMSHAFT 2 POSITION ACTUATOR CIRCUIT OPEN:** With the engine running and battery voltage greater than 10. 4 volts. The Powertrain Control Module (PCM) detects that the actual state of the Camshaft1/2 Position Solenoid does not match the intended state.
DTC: P0013	**-BANK 1 CAMSHAFT 2 POSITION ACTUATOR CIRCUIT OPEN:** With the battery voltage is between 11 and 18 volts with the engine running. The PCM detects that the actual voltage of the Variable Cam Timing (VCT) Solenoid Control circuit does not match the intended state. Two Trip Fault. Three good trips to turn off the MIL.
DTC: P0014	**-EXHAUST TARGET ERROR BANK 1:** Variable Cam Timing (VCT) rationality is monitored under the following conditions: (1) Cam phasing is commanded off of the default (lockpin) position; (2) Oil temperature is between -12° C to 139° C (10° F to 282° F); (3) Battery voltage is greater than 10 Volts; (3) Engine speed is at least 650 to 1400 rpm, depending on oil temperature; (4) No CMP sensor, CKP sensor or OBDI plausibility errors. Before VCT can be enabled, reference adaptation must be completed. The actual camshaft phasing position is not moving towards the desired camshaft phasing position during steady state operation.
DTC: P0016	**-CRANKSHAFT/CAMSHAFT TIMING MISALIGNMENT:** Engine cranking and Engine running Powertrain Control Module detects an error when the camshaft position is out of phase with the crankshaft position. One Trip Fault. Three good trips to turn off the MIL.
DTC: P0016	**-CRANKSHAFT/CAMSHAFT TIMING MISALIGNMENT:** With the engine speed between 480 and 6816 RPM and no CMP or CKP sensor DTCs detected. Powertrain Control Module detects an error when the camshaft position is out of phase with the crankshaft position. One Trip Fault. Three good trips to turn off the MIL.
DTC: P0017	**-CRANKSHAFT/CAMSHAFT 1/2 TIMING MISALIGNMENT:** Engine cranking and Engine running Powertrain Control Module (PCM) detects an error when the camshaft position is out of phase with the crankshaft position. One Trip Fault. Three good trips to turn off the MIL.
DTC: P0018	**-CRANKSHAFT/CAMSHAFT TIMING MISALIGNMENT:** Engine cranking and Engine running Powertrain Control Module (PCM) detects an error when the camshaft position is out of phase with the crankshaft position. One Trip Fault. Three good trips to turn off the MIL.
DTC: P0019	**-CRANKSHAFT/CAMSHAFT TIMING MISALIGNMENT:** Engine cranking and Engine running Powertrain Control Module (PCM) detects an error when the camshaft position is out of phase with the crankshaft position. One Trip Fault. Three good trips to turn off the MIL.
DTC: P0020	**-BANK 2 CAMSHAFT 1 POSITION ACTUATOR CIRCUIT:** Variable Valve Timing (VVT) rationality is monitored under the following conditions:(1) Cam phasing is commanded off of the default (lockpin) position;(2) Oil temperature is between -12°C to 139°C (10°F to 282°F); (3)Battery voltage is greater than 10 Volts; (3) Engine speed is at least650 to 1400 RPM, depending on oil temperature; (4) No CMP sensor, CKP sensor or OBDI plausibility errors. Before VVT can be enabled, reference adaptation must be completed. The PCM detects that the Camshaft 2/1 Control circuit is open.
DTC: P0023	**-BANK 2 CAMSHAFT 2 POSITION ACTUATOR CIRCUIT OPEN:** Variable Valve Timing (VVT) rationality is monitored under the following conditions:(1) Cam phasing is commanded off of the default (lockpin) position;(2) Oil temperature is between -12°C to 139°C (10°F to 282°F); (3)Battery voltage is greater than 10 Volts; (3) Engine speed is at least650 to 1400 RPM, depending on oil temperature; (4) No CMP sensor, CKP sensor or OBDI plausibility errors. Before VVT can be enabled, reference adaptation must be completed. The PCM detects that the Camshaft 2/2 Control circuit is open.
DTC: P0030	**-O2 SENSOR 1/1 HEATER CIRCUIT:** With the ignition on and the Oxygen Sensor Heater command on. The ECM detects an implausible voltage on the (K99) O2 1/1 Heater Control circuit for 2. 0 seconds.
DTC: P0031	**-O2 SENSOR 1/1 HEATER CIRCUIT LOW:** With the engine running and battery voltage greater than 10. 4 Volts. The Powertrain Control Module (PCM) detects that the Oxygen Sensor 1/1 Heater Control circuit is shorted low.
DTC: P0031	**-O2 SENSOR 1/1 HEATER CIRCUIT LOW:** With the ignition on and the Oxygen Sensor Heater command on. The ECM detects that the (K99) O2 1/1 Heater Control circuit is shorted to ground for 2. 0 seconds.
DTC: P0031	**-O2 SENSOR 1/1 HEATER CIRCUIT LOW:** Continuously during O2 heater operation with battery voltage between 10. 4 and 15. 75 Volts. The PCM detects that the O2 sensor heater element input is below the minimum acceptable voltage. One trip fault. Three good trips to turn off the MIL.
DTC: P0032	**-O2 SENSOR 1/1 HEATER CIRCUIT HIGH:** With the engine running and battery voltage greater than 10. 4 volts. The Powertrain Control Module (PCM) detects that the Oxygen Sensor 1/1 heater control circuit is shorted high.

DTC	Trouble Code Title, Conditions, Possible Causes
DTC: P0032	**-O2 SENSOR 1/1 HEATER CIRCUIT HIGH:** With the ignition on and the Oxygen Sensor Heater command on. The ECM detects that the (K99) O2 1/1 Heater Control circuit is shorted to voltage for 2. 0 seconds.
DTC: P0032	**-O2 SENSOR 1/1 HEATER CIRCUIT HIGH:** Continuously during O2 heater operation with battery voltage between 10. 4 and 15. 75 Volts. The Powertrain Control Module (PCM) detects that the O2 sensor heater element input is above the maximum acceptable voltage. One trip fault. Three good trips to turn off the MIL.
DTC: P0037	**-O2 SENSOR 1/2 HEATER CIRCUIT LOW:** Continuously during O2 heater operation with battery voltage between 10. 4 and 15. 75 Volts. The Powertrain Control Module (PCM) detects that the O2 Sensor 1/2 heater element input is below the minimum acceptable voltage. One trip fault. Three good trips to turn off the MIL.
DTC: P0038	**-O2 SENSOR 1/2 HEATER CIRCUIT HIGH:** Continuously during O2 heater operation with battery voltage between 10. 4 and 15. 75 volts. The Powertrain Control Module (PCM) detects that the O2 sensor heater element input is above the maximum acceptable voltage. One trip fault. Three good trips to turn off the MIL.
DTC: P0045	**TURBOCHARGER BOOST CONTROL CIRCUIT/OPEN:** With the ignition on and the Boost Pressure Servo Motor command off. The ECM detects that the (X635) Boost Pressure Servo Motor Control circuit is open for 2. 0 seconds.
DTC: P0046	**TURBOCHARGER BOOST CONTROL CIRCUIT PERFORMANCE:** With the ignition on and the Boost Pressure Servo Motor command on. The ECM detects that the (X635) Boost Pressure Servo Motor Control circuit voltage is implausible.
DTC: P0047	**TURBOCHARGER BOOST CONTROL CIRCUIT LOW:** With the ignition on and the Boost Pressure Servo Motor command off. The ECM detects that the (X635) Boost Pressure Servo Motor Control circuit is shorted to ground for 5. 3 seconds.
DTC: P0048	**TURBOCHARGER BOOST CONTROL CIRCUIT HIGH:** With the ignition on and the Boost Pressure Servo Motor command on. The ECM detects that the (X635) Boost Pressure Servo Motor Control circuit is shorted to voltage for 2. 0 seconds.
DTC: P0051	**-O2 SENSOR 2/1 HEATER CIRCUIT LOW:** Continuously during O2 heater operation with battery voltage between 10. 4 and 15. 75 Volts. The Powertrain Control Module (PCM) detects that the O2 Sensor 2/1 heater element input is below the minimum acceptable voltage. One trip fault. Three good trips to turn off the MIL.
DTC: P0052	**-O2 SENSOR 2/1 HEATER CIRCUIT HIGH:** Continuously during O2 heater operation with battery voltage between 10. 4 and 15. 75 volts. The PCM detects that the O2 sensor heater element input is above the maximum acceptable voltage. One trip fault. Three good trips to turn off the MIL.
DTC: P0057	**-O2 SENSOR 2/2 HEATER CIRCUIT LOW:** Continuously during O2 heater operation with battery voltage between 10. 4 and 15. 75 volts. The PCM detects that the O2 sensor heater element input is below the minimum acceptable voltage. One trip fault. Three good trips to turn off the MIL.
DTC: P0058	**-O2 SENSOR 2/2 HEATER CIRCUIT HIGH:** Continuously during O2 heater operation with battery voltage between 10. 4 and 15. 75 volts. The PCM detects that the O2 sensor heater element input is above the maximum acceptable voltage. One trip fault. Three good trips to turn off the MIL.
DTC: P0069	**-MANIFOLD PRESSURE/BAROMETRIC PRESSURE CORRELATION:** Engine speed is below 720 RPM. Intake Air Temperature is between 9. 96°C and 84. 9°C. There are no Sensor Reference Voltage DTC's. There are no other Boost Pressure related DTC's. There are no Inlet Pressure Sensor DTC's. The difference between the Boost Pressure Sensor Signal and the Atmospheric/Barometric Pressure Sensor Signal is greater than 150 hpa (2. 175 psi.) for at least 6. 0 seconds.
DTC: P006D	**-BAROMETRIC PRESSURE - INLET AIR PRESSURE CORRELATION:** With the ignition on. No other IAT DTC's present in the ECM. Engine speed below 800 rpm. The difference between the Inlet Pressure Sensor signal and the Atmospheric Pressure Sensor signal is 45 hpa (0. 65 psi) for 5. 0 seconds.
DTC: P0070-11	**-AMBIENT AIR TEMPERATURE SENSOR CIRCUIT - CIRCUIT SHORT TO GROUND:** With the ignition on. Battery voltage greater than 10. 4 volts. The Body Control Module (BCM) detects the Ambient Air Temperature Sensor input voltage is below the minimum acceptable value.
DTC: P0070-15	**-AMBIENT AIR TEMPERATURE SENSOR CIRCUIT - CIRCUIT SHORT TO BATTERY OR OPEN:** With the ignition on. Battery voltage greater than 10. 4 volts. The Body Control Module (BCM) detects the Ambient Air Temperature Sensor input voltage is above the maximum acceptable value.

DTC	Trouble Code Title, Conditions, Possible Causes
DTC: P0071	**-AMBIENT AIR TEMPERATURE SENSOR PERFORMANCE:** With engine off time greater than 480 minutes and ambient temperature greater than - 7° C (19. 4° F). After a calibrated amount of cool down time, the PCM compares the AAT, ECT, and IAT Sensor values. If one sensor value is not within 10° C (18° F) of the other temperature sensors for two consecutive trips, a DTC will set. Three good trips to turn off the MIL.
DTC: P0071	**-AMBIENT AIR TEMPERATURE SENSOR PERFORMANCE:** Engine off time is greater than 480 minutes and the vehicle has been driven for one minute over 35 mph. Ambient temperature is greater than -64° C (-83° F). The PCM compares the ambient, engine coolant, and intake air temperature sensor values. If engine coolant and intake air temperature sensors agree with each other but ambient air temperature does not agree with them, the ambient air temperature sensor is declared as irrational. Two Trip Fault. Three good trips to turn off the MIL.
DTC: P0072	**-AMBIENT AIR TEMPERATURE SENSOR CIRCUIT LOW:** With the ignition on and battery voltage greater than 10. 4 volts. The PCM detects that the Ambient Air Temperature Sensor input voltage is below the minimum acceptable value.
DTC: P0072	**-AMBIENT AIR TEMPERATURE SENSOR CIRCUIT LOW:** With the ignition on and battery voltage greater than 10. 4 volts. The PCM detects that the Ambient Air Temperature Sensor input voltage is below the minimum acceptable value.
DTC: P0073	**-AMBIENT AIR TEMPERATURE SENSOR CIRCUIT HIGH:** With the ignition on. Battery voltage greater than 10 volts. The Ambient Temperature Sensor voltage is greater than maximum acceptable value. One Trip Fault. Three good trips to turn off the MIL.
DTC: P0073	**-AMBIENT AIR TEMPERATURE SENSOR CIRCUIT HIGH:** With the ignition on and battery voltage greater than 10. 4 volts. The Powertrain Control Module (PCM) detects that the Ambient Air Temperature Sensor input voltage is above the maximum acceptable value.
DTC: P0087	**-FUEL RAIL PRESSURE TOO LOW:** With the engine running. The ECM determines that the fuel rail pressure is too low for a given engine speed and load.
DTC: P0088	**-FUEL RAIL PRESSURE TOO HIGH:** With the engine running. The ECM determines that the fuel rail pressure is too high for a given engine speed and load.
DTC: P0089	**-FUEL PRESSURE 1 CONTROL PERFORMANCE:** With the ignition on and the Fuel Pressure Solenoid command on. The ECM detects a fault on the (K370) Fuel Pressure Solenoid Control circuit for 0. 28 of a second.
DTC: P0090	**-FUEL PRESSURE 1 CONTROL CIRCUIT/OPEN:** With the ignition on and the Fuel Pressure Solenoid command off. The ECM detects that the (K370) Fuel Pressure Solenoid Control circuit is open for 0. 28 of a second.
DTC: P0091	**-FUEL PRESSURE 1 CONTROL CIRCUIT LOW:** With the ignition on and the Fuel Pressure Solenoid command off. The ECM detects that the (K370) Fuel Pressure Solenoid Control circuit is shorted to ground for 0. 22 second.
DTC: P0092	**-FUEL PRESSURE 1 CONTROL CIRCUIT HIGH:** With the ignition on and the Fuel Pressure Solenoid command on. The ECM detects excessive current on the (K370) Fuel Pressure Solenoid Control circuit for 0. 28 of a second.
DTC: P0100	**-MASS AIR FLOW SENSOR:** With the ignition on. The ECM detects that the (K157) Mass Air Flow Sensor Signal circuit or the (K362) Inlet Air Temperature Sensor Signal circuit voltage is not within a valid range.
DTC: P0102	**-MASS AIR FLOW SENSOR CIRCUIT LOW:** With the ignition on. The Mass Air Flow Sensor Signal is below the valid operating range.
DTC: P0103	**-MASS AIR FLOW SENSOR CIRCUIT HIGH:** With the ignition on. The Mass Air Flow Sensor Signal is above the valid operating range.
DTC: P0107	**-MANIFOLD ABSOLUTE PRESSURE SENSOR CIRCUIT LOW:** Engine speed between 600 to 3500 RPM. Battery voltage greater than 10 Volts. The MAP sensor signal voltage is below the minimum acceptable value. One Trip Fault. Three good trips to turn off the MIL. MIL will illuminate and the ETC light will flash if equipped.
DTC: P0107	**-MANIFOLD ABSOLUTE PRESSURE SENSOR CIRCUIT LOW:** Engine speed between 600 to 3500 RPM. Battery voltage greater than 10 volts. The PCM detects that the MAP Sensor input voltage is below the minimum acceptable value. One Trip Fault. Three good trips to turn off the MIL. The MIL will illuminate and the ETC light will flash if equipped.
DTC: P0107	**-MANIFOLD ABSOLUTE PRESSURE SENSOR CIRCUIT LOW:** With the ignition on and battery voltage greater than 10. 4 Volts. The Powertrain Control Module (PCM) detects that the MAP Sensor input voltage is below the minimum acceptable value.

DTC	Trouble Code Title, Conditions, Possible Causes
DTC: P0108	**-MANIFOLD ABSOLUTE PRESSURE SENSOR CIRCUIT HIGH:** With the ignition on and battery voltage greater than 10. 4 volts. The Powertrain Control Module (PCM) detects that the Manifold Absolute Pressure (MAP) Sensor input voltage is above the maximum acceptable value.
DTC: P0108	**-MANIFOLD ABSOLUTE PRESSURE SENSOR CIRCUIT HIGH:** Engine speed between 600 to 3500 RPM. Battery voltage greater than 10. 37 volts. The MAP sensor signal voltage is greater than the maximum allowable voltage One trip fault. Three good trips to turn off the MIL. MIL is illuminated and the ETC light is flashing, if equipped.
DTC: P0111	**-INTAKE AIR TEMPERATURE SENSOR PERFORMANCE:** With the engine off time greater than 480 minutes and ambient temperature greater than -7° C (19. 4° F). After a calibrated amount of cool down time, the Powertrain Control Module (PCM) compares the Ambient Air Temperature (AAT), Engine Coolant Temperature (ECT), and Intake Air Temperature (IAT) Sensor values. If one sensor value is not within 10° C (18° F) of the other temperature sensors for two consecutive trips, a DTC will set. Three good trips to turn off the MIL.
DTC: P0111	**-INTAKE AIR TEMPERATURE SENSOR RATIONALITY:** The engine off time is greater than 480 minutes. Ambient Temperature if greater than -64° C (-83° F). Once the vehicle is soaked for a calibrated engine off time and then driven over calibrated speed and load conditions for some calibrated time, the PCM compares the ambient, engine coolant, and intake air temperature sensor values. If engine coolant and ambient air temperature sensors agree with each other but intake air temperature does not agree with them, the intake air temperature sensor is declared as irrational. Two Trip Fault. Three good trips to turn off the MIL.
DTC: P0112	**-INTAKE AIR TEMPERATURE SENSOR CIRCUIT LOW:** With the ignition on and the battery voltage greater than 10. 4 Volts. The Powertrain Control Module (PCM) detects that the Intake Air Temperature (IAT) Sensor input voltage is below the minimum acceptable value.
DTC: P0112	**-INTAKE AIR TEMPERATURE SENSOR CIRCUIT LOW:** With the ignition on and battery voltage greater than 10. 4 Volts. When the Inlet Air Temp Sensor Signal circuit voltage is less than the minimum acceptable value. One trip failure. Three good trips to clear the MIL.
DTC: P0113	**-INTAKE AIR TEMPERATURE SENSOR CIRCUIT HIGH:** With the ignition on. Battery voltage greater than 10. 4 volts. The PCM detects that the Intake Air Temperature Sensor input voltage is above the maximum acceptable value. One Trip Fault. Three good trips to turn off the MIL.
DTC: P0113	**-INTAKE AIR TEMPERATURE SENSOR CIRCUIT HIGH:** With the ignition on and the battery voltage greater than 10. 4 Volts. The Powertrain Control Module (PCM) detects that the Intake Air Temperature (IAT) Sensor input voltage is above the maximum acceptable value.
DTC: P0113	**-INTAKE AIR TEMPERATURE SENSOR CIRCUIT HIGH:** With the ignition on. The (K21) Intake Air Temperature Sensor Signal circuit voltage is above 4. 96 volts for 2. 0 seconds.
DTC: P0116	**-ENGINE COOLANT TEMPERATURE SENSOR CIRCUIT PERFORMANCE:** Engine off time is greater than 480 minutes and the vehicle has been driven for one minute over 35 mph. Ambient temperature is greater than -64° C (-83° F). Once the vehicle is soaked for a calibrated engine off time and then driven over calibrated speed and load conditions for some calibrated time, the PCM compares the ambient, engine coolant, and intake air temperature sensor values. If ambient air and intake air temperature sensors agree with each other but engine coolant temperature does not agree with them, the engine coolant temperature sensor is declared as irrational. Two Trip Fault. Three good trips to turn off the MIL.
DTC: P0116	**-ENGINE COOLANT TEMPERATURE SENSOR PERFORMANCE:** With the ignition on. The Engine Control Module (ECM) detects an implausible voltage on the (K2) Engine Coolant Temperature Sensor Signal circuit.
DTC: P0117	**-ENGINE COOLANT TEMPERATURE SENSOR CIRCUIT LOW:** With the ignition on. The (K2) Engine Coolant Temperature Sensor Signal circuit voltage is below 0. 18 volt for 0. 5 second.
DTC: P0117	**-ENGINE COOLANT TEMPERATURE SENSOR CIRCUIT LOW:** With the ignition on. Battery voltage greater than 10. 4 volts. The PCM detects that the Engine Coolant Temperature Sensor input voltage is below the minimum acceptable value. One Trip Fault. Three good trips to clear the MIL. The MIL and ETC light will illuminate if equipped.
DTC: P0117	**-ENGINE COOLANT TEMPERATURE SENSOR CIRCUIT LOW:** With the ignition on. Battery voltage greater than 10. 4 Volts. The Powertrain Control Module (PCM) detects that the Engine Coolant Temperature Sensor input voltage is below the minimum acceptable value. One Trip Fault. Three good trips to clear the MIL. The MIL and ETC light will illuminate if equipped.
DTC: P0118	**-ENGINE COOLANT TEMPERATURE SENSOR CIRCUIT HIGH:** With the ignition on. Battery voltage greater than 10. 4 volts. The PCM detects that the Engine Coolant Temperature Sensor input voltage is above the maximum acceptable value. One Trip Fault. Three good trips to turn off the MIL. The MIL and ETC light will illuminate if equipped.

DTC	Trouble Code Title, Conditions, Possible Causes
DTC: P0118	**-ENGINE COOLANT TEMPERATURE SENSOR CIRCUIT HIGH:** With the ignition on. The (K2) Engine Coolant Temperature Sensor Signal circuit voltage is above 4. 97 volts for 0. 5 second.
DTC: P0121	**THROTTLE POSITION SENSOR 1 PERFORMANCE:** With the ignition on and battery voltage greater than 10. 4 volts. The Powertrain Control Module (PCM) detects that the Throttle Position Sensor 1 circuit input voltage is implausible.
DTC: P0121	**THROTTLE POSITION SENSOR 1 PERFORMANCE:** With the engine running and no TPS or MAP sensor DTCs present. The Powertrain Control Module (PCM) detects that the sensor input voltage does not fall within a valid range based on engine speed and load. Two Trip Fault. (Electronic Throttle Control) ETC light will illuminate. P2135 should set with this code also.
DTC: P0122	**TPS/APP CIRCUIT LOW:** Continuously with the ignition on and engine running. This DTC will set if the monitored TPS voltage drops below . 078 of a volt for the period of 0. 48 of a second.
DTC: P0122	**THROTTLE POSITION SENSOR 1 CIRCUIT LOW:** With the ignition on and battery voltage greater than 10. 4 volts. The Powertrain Control Module (PCM) detects that the Throttle Body input voltage is below the maximum acceptable value.
DTC: P0122	**THROTTLE POSITION SENSOR 1 CIRCUIT LOW:** With the ignition on. Battery voltage greater than 10 volts. Throttle Position Sensor voltage at the PCM is less than 0. 16 of a volt for 0. 7 of a second. One Trip Fault. Three good trips to turn off the MIL. ETC light will illuminate.
DTC: P0122	**THROTTLE POSITION SENSOR 1 CIRCUIT LOW:** With the ignition on and battery voltage greater than 10. 4 volts. The Powertrain Control Module (PCM) detects that the Throttle Position Sensor 1 input voltage is below the minimum acceptable value.
DTC: P0123	**TPS/APP CIRCUIT HIGH:** Continuously with the ignition on and engine running. This DTC will set if the monitored TPS voltage rises above 4. 94 volts for the period of 0. 48 of a second.
DTC: P0123	**THROTTLE POSITION SENSOR 1 CIRCUIT HIGH:** With the ignition on and battery voltage greater than 10. 4 volts. The Powertrain Control Module (PCM) detects that the Throttle Position Sensor 1 input voltage is above the maximum acceptable value.
DTC: P0123	**THROTTLE POSITION SENSOR 1 CIRCUIT HIGH:** With the ignition on. Battery voltage greater than 10 Volts. Throttle Position Sensor No. 1 voltage is greater than 4. 8 Volts for 25 ms. One Trip Fault. ETC light will illuminate.
DTC: P0124	**TPS/APP INTERMITTENT:** Continuously with the ignition on and engine running. This DTC will set if the monitored TPS throttle angle between the angles of 6° and 120° and the degree change is greater than 5° within a period of less than 7. 0 msec.
DTC: P0125	**-INSUFFICIENT COOLANT TEMP FOR CLOSED-LOOP FUEL CONTROL:** With battery voltage greater than 10. 4 volts and after engine is started. The engine temperature does not go above -10° C (15° F). Failure time depends on start-up coolant temperature and ambient temperature. (i.e. two minutes for a start temp of -10° C (15° F) or up to 10 minutes for a vehicle with a start-up temp of -28° C (5° F). Two Trip Fault. Three good trips to turn off the MIL.
DTC: P0128	**THERMOSTAT RATIONALITY:** With the engine running, start up coolant temperature between −8° C (17. 6° F) and 50° C (122° F), the difference between ambient temperature and coolant temperature less than 10° C (50° F) and average vehicle speed greater than 16 kph (10 mph) for more than 18% of vehicle run time. The Powertrain Control Module (PCM) detects that the actual engine coolant temperature does not reach the predicted engine coolant temperature within a specific time. Two trip fault. Three good trips to turn off the MIL.
DTC: P0128	**THERMOSTAT RATIONALITY:** With the engine running, ambient temperature between -8° C (17. 6° F) and 50° C (122° F), start up coolant temperature less than 50° C (122° F), and average vehicle speed greater than 16 kph (10 mph) until coolant temperature reaches 85° C (185° F). The PCM detects that the actual engine coolant temperature falls too far below the predicted engine coolant temperature and the predicted coolant temperature reaches the predicted target value before the actual coolant temperature reaches the actual coolant temperature target value. Two trip fault. Three good trips to turn off the MIL.
DTC: P0129	**-BAROMETRIC PRESSURE OUT-OF-RANGE LOW:** With the ignition key on. No Cam or Crank signal within 75 ms. Engine speed less than 250 RPM. The PCM senses the voltage from the MAP sensor to be less than 2. 2 volts but above 0. 04 of a volt for 300 milliseconds. One Trip Fault. Three good trips to turn off the MIL. MIL is illuminated and the ETC lamp will flash.

DTC	Trouble Code Title, Conditions, Possible Causes
DTC: P0129	**-BAROMETRIC PRESSURE OUT-OF-RANGE LOW:** With engine speed within 64 RPM of target idle, MAP sensor voltage between . 04 of a volt and 4. 96 volts, no vehicle speed, and the throttle closed. Each time the Powertrain Control Module (PCM) detects that the MAP sensor value is greater than a calibrated value for BARO, a counter is incremented. If the counter reaches a calibrated limit, the test fails. One trip fault. Three good trips to turn off the MIL.
DTC: P012C	**TURBO INLET AIR PRESSURE SENSOR CIRCUIT LOW:** With the ignition on. The (K68) Inlet Air Pressure Sensor Signal circuit voltage is below 0. 35 volt for 2. 0 seconds.
DTC: P012D	**TURBO INLET AIR PRESSURE SENSOR CIRCUIT HIGH:** With the ignition on. The (K68) Inlet Air Pressure Sensor Signal circuit voltage is above 4. 41 volts for 2. 0 seconds.
DTC: P0130	**-O2 SENSOR 1/1 CIRCUIT OPEN:** With the ignition on and the O2 1/1 Sensor at operating temperature. The ECM detects an open on the (Z43) O2 1/1 Negative Current Control circuit for 2. 0 seconds.
DTC: P0131	**-O2 SENSOR 1/1 CIRCUIT LOW:** Engine running for less than 30 seconds and the O2 Sensor Heater Temperature is less than 251° C (484° F) with battery voltage greater 10. 4 volts. The PCM detects that the 1/1 Oxygen Sensor signal voltage is below the minimum acceptable value. The DTC will set as Pending after one trip and Active after two trips. Three good trips to turn off the MIL.
DTC: P0131	**-O2 SENSOR 1/1 CIRCUIT LOW:** With the ignition on and the O2 1/1 Sensor at operating temperature. The ECM detects a short to ground on the (Z43) O2 1/1 Negative Current Control circuit for 2. 0 seconds.
DTC: P0132	**-O2 SENSOR 1/1 CIRCUIT HIGH:** With the Oxygen Sensor 1/1 heater temperature greater than 496° C (925° F) and the battery voltage greater than 10. 4 volts. The Powertrain Control Module (PCM) detects that the Oxygen Sensor 1/1 voltage is greater than 3. 99 volts for 40 seconds. One Trip Fault. Three good trips to turn off the MIL.
DTC: P0132	**-O2 SENSOR 1/1 CIRCUIT HIGH:** Continuously with the engine running, no O2 sensor heater DTCs present, 1/1 Oxygen Sensor heater temperature within a specific range, and battery voltage greater than 10. 4 volts. The Oxygen Sensor voltage is above the maximum acceptable value. The DTC will set as Pending after one trip and Active after two trips. Three good trips to turn off the MIL.
DTC: P0133	**-O2 SENSOR 1/1 SLOW RESPONSE:** With the ECT above 70° C (158° F), engine RPM between 1400 and 2300, vehicle speed between 64 and 96 kph (40 and 60 mph), and engine run time greater than three minutes. The Powertrain Control Module (PCM) detects that the oxygen sensor signal does not switch adequately during monitoring. Two Trip Fault. Three good trips to turn off the MIL.
DTC: P0134	**-O2 SENSOR 1/1 SIGNAL INACTIVE:** With the ignition on and the O2 1/1 Sensor at operating temperature. The ECM detects an implausible voltage on the (Z43) O2 1/1 Negative Current Control circuit for 2. 0 seconds.
DTC: P0135	**-O2 SENSOR 1/1 HEATER PERFORMANCE:** Engine running and heater duty cycle greater than 0%. Battery voltage greater than 11. 0 volts. The PCM detects no temperature change in the O2 sensor heater element when the heater circuit is active. The heater temperature is obtained by measuring the heater resistance and calculating the heater temperature. Two trip fault. Three good trips to turn off the MIL.
DTC: P0135	**-O2 SENSOR 1/1 HEATER PERFORMANCE:** Continuously during O2 sensor heater operation with battery voltage between 10. 4 and 15. 75 volts and no O2 sensor circuit DTCs present. The PCM detects no temperature change in the O2 sensor heater element when the heater circuit is active. The heater temperature is obtained by measuring the heater resistance and calculating the heater temperature. Two trip fault. Three good trips to turn off the MIL.
DTC: P0135	**-O2 SENSOR 1/1 HEATER PERFORMANCE:** With the ignition on and the Oxygen Sensor Heater command on. The ECM detects an implausible voltage on the (K99) O2 1/1 Heater Control circuit for 2. 0 seconds.
DTC: P0137	**-O2 SENSOR 1/2 CIRCUIT LOW:** Engine running for less than 30 seconds and the O2 Sensor Heater Temperature is less than 251° C (484° F) with battery voltage greater 10. 99 Volts. The Powertrain Control Module (PCM) detects that the 1/2 Oxygen Sensor signal voltage is below minimum acceptable value. The DTC will set as Pending after one trip and Active after two trips. Three good trips to turn off the MIL.
DTC: P0138	**-O2 SENSOR 1/2 CIRCUIT HIGH:** Continuously with the engine running, no O2 sensor heater DTCs present, 1/2 Oxygen Sensor heater temperature within a specific range, and battery voltage greater than 10. 4 volts. The PCM detects that the 1/2 Oxygen Sensor voltage is greater than the maximum acceptable value for a specific amount of time, based on O2 sensor heater temperature. The DTC will set as Pending after one trip and Active after two trips. Three good trips to turn off the MIL.

DTC	Trouble Code Title, Conditions, Possible Causes
DTC: P0139	**-O2 SENSOR 1/2 SLOW RESPONSE:** With engine run time greater than five minutes, the coolant temperature greater than 75 C (167 F), vehicle speed greater than 64 kph (40 mph) and the vehicle in decel fuel shut-off (coasting with the accelerator pedal fully released). The O2 signal voltage does not switch quickly enough from rich to lean when the fuel is turned off during a coast with the throttle closed. Two Trip Fault. Three good trips to turn off the MIL.
DTC: P0139	**-O2 SENSOR 1/2 SLOW RESPONSE:** Vehicle is started and driven between 32 and 88. 5 km/h (20 and 55 mph) with the Throttle open for a minimum of 120 seconds. Coolant greater than 70° C (158° F). Catalytic Converter Temp greater than 600° C (1112° F) and Evap Purge is active. The PCM detects that the oxygen sensor signal switches from lean to rich less than 16 times within 20 seconds during monitoring. Two Trip Fault. Three good trips to turn off the MIL.
DTC: P013A	**-O2 SENSOR 1/2 SLOW RESPONSE - RICH TO LEAN:** With the engine running, vehicle speed above 96 kph (60 mph), throttle open for a minimum of 120 seconds, ECT greater than 70° C (158° F), catalytic converter temperature greater than 600° C (1112° F), and downstream oxygen sensor in a rich state. During a decel fuel shutoff event, the downstream oxygen sensor should switch from rich to lean within a specific time. The PCM monitors the downstream O2 sensor. If the PCM does not detect a rich to lean switch within a specific time during a decel fuel shutoff event, the monitor will fail. One trip fault. Three good trips to turn off the MIL.
DTC: P0140	**-O2 SENSOR 1/2 NO ACTIVITY DETECTED:** With the engine running, vehicle speed between 32 and 88 kph (20 and 55 mph), throttle open for a minimum of 120 seconds, ECT greater than 70° C (158° F), Catalytic Converter Temperature greater than 600° C (1112° F) and EVAP Purge active. The Powertrain Control Module (PCM) detects that the oxygen sensor signal switches from lean to rich less than 16 times within 20 seconds during monitoring. Two Trip Fault. Three good trips to turn off the MIL.
DTC: P0140	**-O2 SENSOR 1/2 SIGNAL INACTIVE:** For six minutes after engine start up and the vehicle speed between 20 and 55 MPH. The O2 signal voltage does not switch lean or rich during monitoring for at least2 to 4 minutes. Two Trip Fault. Three good trips to turn off the MIL.
DTC: P0141	**-O2 SENSOR 1/2 HEATER PERFORMANCE:** Continuously during O2 sensor heater operation with battery voltage between 10. 4 and 15. 75 volts and no O2 sensor circuit DTCs present. The PCM detects no temperature change in the O2 sensor heater element when the heater circuit is active. The heater temperature is obtained by measuring the heater resistance and calculating the heater temperature. Two trip fault. Three good trips to turn off the MIL.
DTC: P0151	**-O2 SENSOR 2/1 CIRCUIT LOW:** With the engine running, battery voltage greater than 10. 4 volts, and no O2 sensor heater DTCs present. The PCM detects that the 2/1 Oxygen Sensor signal voltage is below approximately 1. 5 volts for 2. 8 seconds after engine startup. The DTC will set as Pending after one trip and Active after two trips. Three good trips to turn off the MIL.
DTC: P0151	**-O2 SENSOR 2/1 CIRCUIT LOW:** Engine running for less than 30 seconds and the O2 Sensor Heater Temperature is less than 251° C (484° F) with battery voltage greater 10. 99 volts. The PCM detects that the 2/1 Oxygen Sensor signal voltage is below the minimum acceptable value. The DTC will set as Pending after one trip and Active after two trips. Three good trips to turn off the MIL.
DTC: P0152	**-O2 SENSOR 2/1 CIRCUIT HIGH:** Continuously with the engine running, no O2 sensor heater DTCs present, 2/1 Oxygen Sensor heater temperature within a specific range, and battery voltage greater than 10. 4 volts. The PCM detects that the 2/1 Oxygen Sensor voltage is greater than the maximum acceptable value for a specific amount of time, based on O2 sensor heater temperature. The DTC will set as Pending after one trip and Active after two trips. Three good trips to turn off the MIL.
DTC: P0153	**-O2 SENSOR 2/1 SLOW RESPONSE:** With the ECT is above 70 °C (158 °F), engine RPM between 1400 and 2300, vehicle speed between 64 and 96 kph (40 and 60 mph) and engine run time greater than three minutes. The Powertrain Control Module (PCM) detects that the Oxygen Sensor signal does not switch adequately during monitoring. Two Trip Fault. Three good trips to turn off the MIL.
DTC: P0153	**-O2 SENSOR 2/1 SLOW RESPONSE:** Vehicle is started and driven between 32 and 88. 5 km/h (20 and 55 mph) with the Throttle open for a minimum of 120 seconds. Coolant greater than 70° C (158° F). Catalytic Converter Temp greater than 600° C (1112° F) and EVAP Purge is active. The PCM detects that the oxygen sensor signal switches from lean to rich less than 16 times within 20 seconds during monitoring. Two Trip Fault. Three good trips to turn off the MIL.
DTC: P0155	**-O2 SENSOR 2/1 HEATER PERFORMANCE:** Engine running and heater duty cycle greater than 0%. Battery voltage greater than 11. 0 volts. No sensor output is received when the PCM powers up the sensor heater. Two trip fault. Three good trips to turn off the MIL.

DTC	Trouble Code Title, Conditions, Possible Causes
DTC: P0155	**-O2 SENSOR 2/1 HEATER PERFORMANCE:** Continuously during O2 sensor heater operation with battery voltage between 10. 4 and 15. 75 volts and no O2 sensor circuit DTCs present. The PCM detects no temperature change in the O2 sensor heater element when the heater circuit is active. The heater temperature is obtained by measuring the heater resistance and calculating the heater temperature. Two trip fault. Three good trips to turn off the MIL.
DTC: P0157	**-O2 SENSOR 2/2 CIRCUIT LOW:** With the engine running, battery voltage greater than 10. 4 volts, and no O2 sensor heater DTCs present. The PCM detects that the 2/2 Oxygen Sensor signal voltage is below approximately 1. 5 volts for 2. 8 seconds after engine startup. The DTC will set as Pending after one trip and Active after two trips. Three good trips to turn off the MIL.
DTC: P0157	**-O2 SENSOR 2/2 CIRCUIT LOW:** Engine running for less than 30 seconds and the O2 Sensor Heater Temperature is less than 251° C (484° F) with battery voltage greater 10. 99 volts. The PCM detects that the 2/2 Oxygen Sensor signal voltage is below the minimum acceptable value. The DTC will set as Pending after one trip and Active after two trips. Three good trips to turn off the MIL.
DTC: P0158	**-O2 SENSOR 2/2 CIRCUIT HIGH:** Continuously with the engine running, no O2 Sensor Heater DTCs present, Oxygen Sensor 2/2 heater temperature within a specific range and battery voltage greater than 10. 4 Volts. The Powertrain Control Module (PCM) detects that the Oxygen Sensor 2/2 voltage is greater than the maximum acceptable value for a specific amount of time, based on O2 sensor heater temperature. The DTC will set as Pending after one trip and Active after two trips. Three good trips to turn off the MIL.
DTC: P0159	**-O2 SENSOR 2/2 SLOW RESPONSE:** Vehicle is started and driven between 32 and 88. 5 km/h (20 and 55 mph) with the Throttle open for a minimum of 120 seconds. Coolant greater than 70° C (158° F). Catalytic Converter Temp greater than 600° C (1112° F) and Evap Purge is active. The oxygen sensor signal voltage switches less than 16 times from lean to rich within 20 seconds during monitoring. Two Trip Fault. Three good trips to turn off the MIL.
DTC: P0159	**-O2 SENSOR 2/2 SLOW RESPONSE:** With the engine running, vehicle speed above 96 kph (60 mph), throttle open for a minimum of 120 seconds, ECT greater than 70°C (158°F), Catalytic Converter temperature greater than 600°C (1112°F), and downstream oxygen sensor in a rich state. During a decel fuel shutoff event, the downstream oxygen sensor should switch from rich to lean within a specific time. The Powertrain Control Module (PCM) monitors the Downstream O2 Sensor. If the PCM does not detect a rich to lean switch within a specific time during a decel fuel shutoff event, the monitor will fail. One trip fault. Three good trips to turn off the MIL.
DTC: P0160	**-O2 SENSOR 2/2 NO ACTIVITY DETECTED:** Vehicle is started and driven between 32 and 88. 5 km/h (20 and 55 mph) with the Throttle open for a minimum of 120 seconds. Coolant greater than 70° C (158° F). Catalytic Converter Temp greater than 600° C (1112° F) and EVAP Purge is active. The oxygen sensor signal voltage switches less than 16 times from lean to rich within 20 seconds during monitoring. Two Trip Fault. Three good trips to turn off the MIL.
DTC: P0161	**-O2 SENSOR 2/2 HEATER PERFORMANCE:** Continuously during O2 sensor heater operation with battery voltage between 10. 4 and 15. 75 volts and no O2 sensor circuit DTCs present. The PCM detects no temperature change in the O2 sensor heater element when the heater circuit is active. The heater temperature is obtained by measuring the heater resistance and calculating the heater temperature. Two trip fault. Three good trips to turn off the MIL.
DTC: P0161	**-O2 SENSOR 2/2 HEATER PERFORMANCE:** Engine running and heater duty cycle greater than 0%. Battery voltage greater than 11. 0 volts. No sensor output is received when the PCM powers up the sensor heater. Two trip fault. Three good trips to turn off the MIL.
DTC: P0171	**-FUEL SYSTEM 1/1 LEAN:** With the engine running in closed loop mode, the ambient/battery temperature above -6. 7°C (20°F) and altitude below 2590. 8 m (8500 ft). If the PCM multiplies short term compensation by long term adaptive and a certain percentage is exceeded for two trips, a freeze frame is stored, the MIL illuminates and a trouble code is stored. Two Trip Fault. Three good trips to turn off the MIL.
DTC: P0171	**-FUEL SYSTEM 1/1 LEAN:** With the engine running in closed loop, the ambient/battery temperature above -7° C (20° F) and altitude below 8500 ft. The Powertrain Control Module (PCM) monitors the Adaptive Memory factor (a combination of Short Term Adaptive and Long Term Adaptive). If the total fuel addition exceeds a calibrated threshold for an extended period, a fuel system lean fault is stored. If the total fuel subtraction exceeds a calibrated threshold, a fuel system rich fault is stored. Two Trip Fault. Three good trips to turn off the MIL.
DTC: P0174	**-FUEL SYSTEM 2/1 LEAN:** With the engine running in closed loop mode, the ambient/battery temperature above -6. 7°C (20°F) and altitude below 2590. 8 m (8500 ft). If the Powertrain Control Module (PCM) multiplies short term compensation by long term adaptive and a certain percentage is exceeded for two trips, a freeze frame is stored, the MIL illuminates and a trouble code is stored. Two Trip Fault. Three good trips to turn off the MIL.

DTC	Trouble Code Title, Conditions, Possible Causes
DTC: P0174	**-FUEL SYSTEM 2/1 LEAN:** With the engine running in closed loop mode, the ambient/battery temperature above -6. 7°C (20°F) and altitude below 2590. 8 m (8500 ft). If the PCM multiplies short term compensation by long term adaptive and a certain percentage is exceeded for two trips, a freeze frame is stored, the MIL illuminates and a trouble code is stored. Two Trip Fault. Three good trips to turn off the MIL.
DTC: P0175	**-FUEL SYSTEM 2/1 RICH:** With the engine running in closed loop mode, the ambient/battery temperature above -6. 7°C (20°F) and altitude below 2590. 8 m (8500 ft). If the PCM multiplies short term compensation by long term adaptive and a purge fuel multiplier and the result is below a certain value for 30 seconds over two trips, a freeze frame is stored, the MIL illuminates and a trouble code is stored. Two Trip Fault. Three good trips to turn off the MIL.
DTC: P0182	**-FUEL TEMPERATURE SENSOR CIRCUIT LOW:** With the ignition on. The (K156) Fuel Temperature Sensor Signal circuit voltage is below 0. 12 volt for 0. 6 second.
DTC: P0183	**-FUEL TEMPERATURE SENSOR CIRCUIT HIGH:** With the ignition on. The (K156) Fuel Temperature Sensor Signal circuit voltage is above 4. 96 volts for 0. 6 second.
DTC: P0192	**-FUEL RAIL PRESSURE SENSOR LOW:** With the ignition on. The (K181) Fuel Pressure Sensor Signal circuit voltage is below 0. 25 volt for 0. 14 second.
DTC: P0193	**-FUEL RAIL PRESSURE SENSOR HIGH:** With the ignition on. The (K181) Fuel Pressure Sensor Signal circuit voltage is above 4. 75 volts for 0. 14 second.
DTC: P0196	**-ENGINE OIL TEMPERATURE SENSOR CIRCUIT PERFORMANCE:** With engine off time greater than 480 minutes and ambient temperature greater than -7° C (19. 4° F). After a calibrated amount of cool down time, the Powertrain Control Module (PCM) compares the AAT, ECT and IAT Sensor values. If the general temperature rationality passes, the PCM compares the Oil Temperature Sensor value to a threshold based on the other temp sensor values. If the difference is greater than a calibrated value, the diagnostic fails.
DTC: P0197	**-ENGINE OIL TEMPERATURE SENSOR CIRCUIT LOW:** With the ignition on. Battery voltage greater than 10. 4 volts. The Engine Oil Temperature sensor circuit voltage at the PCM is less than the calibrated amount. One Trip Fault. Three good trips to clear the MIL.
DTC: P0197	**-ENGINE OIL TEMPERATURE SENSOR CIRCUIT LOW:** With the ignition on. The (G224) Oil Temperature Sensor Signal circuit voltage is below 0. 18 of a Volt for 0. 5 of a second.
DTC: P0198	**-ENGINE OIL TEMPERATURE SENSOR CIRCUIT HIGH:** With the ignition on. The (G224) Oil Temperature Sensor Signal circuit voltage is above 4. 95 volts for 0. 5 second.
DTC: P0198	**-ENGINE OIL TEMPERATURE SENSOR CIRCUIT HIGH:** With the ignition on. Battery voltage greater than 10. 4 volts. The Engine Oil Temperature sensor circuit voltage at the PCM is greater than the calibrated amount. One Trip Fault. Three good trips to turn off the MIL.
DTC: P0201	**-FUEL INJECTOR 1 CIRCUIT / OPEN:** With the engine running. The ECM detects an open in the Fuel Injector 1 circuit.
DTC: P0201	**-FUEL INJECTOR 1 CIRCUIT/OPEN:** With the engine running, battery voltage greater than 12 volts, and engine RPM less than 3000. The Powertrain Control Module (PCM) monitors the continuity of the injector circuits as well as the voltage spike created by the collapse of the magnetic field in the injector coil. Any condition that reduces the maximum current flow or the magnitude of the voltage spike can cause this DTC to set.
DTC: P0201	**-FUEL INJECTOR 1 CIRCUIT:** With battery voltage greater than 10 volts. Auto Shutdown Relay energized. Engine speed less than 3000 rpm. The PCM monitors the continuity of the injector circuits as well as the voltage spike created by the collapse of the magnetic field in the injector coil. Any condition that reduces the maximum current flow or the magnitude of the voltage spike can cause this DTC to set.
DTC: P0202	**-FUEL INJECTOR 2 CIRCUIT / OPEN:** With the engine running. The ECM detects an open in the Fuel Injector 2 circuit.
DTC: P0202	**-FUEL INJECTOR 2 CIRCUIT:** With battery voltage greater than 10 volts. Auto Shutdown Relay energized. Engine speed less than 3000 rpm. The PCM monitors the continuity of the injector circuits as well as the voltage spike created by the collapse of the magnetic field in the injector coil. Any condition that reduces the maximum current flow or the magnitude of the voltage spike can cause this DTC to set.
DTC: P0202	**-FUEL INJECTOR 2 CIRCUIT/OPEN:** With the engine running, battery voltage greater than 12 volts, and engine RPM less than 3000. The Powertrain Control Module (PCM) monitors the continuity of the injector circuits as well as the voltage spike created by the collapse of the magnetic field in the injector coil. Any condition that reduces the maximum current flow or the magnitude of the voltage spike can cause this DTC to set.

DTC	Trouble Code Title, Conditions, Possible Causes
DTC: P0203	**-FUEL INJECTOR 3 CIRCUIT:** With battery voltage greater than 10 volts. Auto Shutdown Relay energized. Engine speed less than 3000 rpm. The PCM monitors the continuity of the injector circuits as well as the voltage spike created by the collapse of the magnetic field in the injector coil. Any condition that reduces the maximum current flow or the magnitude of the voltage spike can cause this DTC to set.
DTC: P0203	**-FUEL INJECTOR 3 CIRCUIT/OPEN:** With the engine running, battery voltage greater than 12 volts, and engine RPM less than 3000. The Powertrain Control Module (PCM) monitors the continuity of the injector circuits as well as the voltage spike created by the collapse of the magnetic field in the injector coil. Any condition that reduces the maximum current flow or the magnitude of the voltage spike can cause this DTC to set.
DTC: P0204	**-FUEL INJECTOR 4 CIRCUIT/OPEN:** With the engine running, battery voltage greater than 12 volts, and engine RPM less than 3000. The Powertrain Control Module (PCM) monitors the continuity of the injector circuits as well as the voltage spike created by the collapse of the magnetic field in the injector coil. Any condition that reduces the maximum current flow or the magnitude of the voltage spike can cause this DTC to set.
DTC: P0204	**-FUEL INJECTOR 4 CIRCUIT:** With battery voltage greater than 10 volts. Auto Shutdown Relay energized. Engine speed less than 3000 rpm. The PCM monitors the continuity of the injector circuits as well as the voltage spike created by the collapse of the magnetic field in the injector coil. Any condition that reduces the maximum current flow or the magnitude of the voltage spike can cause this DTC to set.
DTC: P0205	**-FUEL INJECTOR 5 CIRCUIT/OPEN:** With the engine running, battery voltage greater than 12 volts, and engine RPM less than 3000. The Powertrain Control Module (PCM) monitors the continuity of the injector circuits as well as the voltage spike created by the collapse of the magnetic field in the injector coil. Any condition that reduces the maximum current flow or the magnitude of the voltage spike can cause this DTC to set.
DTC: P0205	**-FUEL INJECTOR 5 CIRCUIT:** With battery voltage greater than 10 volts. Auto Shutdown Relay energized. Engine speed less than 3000 rpm. The PCM monitors the continuity of the injector circuits as well as the voltage spike created by the collapse of the magnetic field in the injector coil. Any condition that reduces the maximum current flow or the magnitude of the voltage spike can cause this DTC to set.
DTC: P0206	**-FUEL INJECTOR 6 CIRCUIT/OPEN:** With the engine running, battery voltage greater than 12 volts, and engine RPM less than 3000. The Powertrain Control Module (PCM) monitors the continuity of the injector circuits as well as the voltage spike created by the collapse of the magnetic field in the injector coil. Any condition that reduces the maximum current flow or the magnitude of the voltage spike can cause this DTC to set.
DTC: P0206	**-FUEL INJECTOR 6 CIRCUIT:** With battery voltage greater than 10 volts. Auto Shutdown Relay energized. Engine speed less than 3000 rpm. The PCM monitors the continuity of the injector circuits as well as the voltage spike created by the collapse of the magnetic field in the injector coil. Any condition that reduces the maximum current flow or the magnitude of the voltage spike can cause this DTC to set.
DTC: P0207	**-FUEL INJECTOR 7 CIRCUIT/OPEN:** With the engine running, battery voltage greater than 12 volts, and engine RPM less than 3000. The Powertrain Control Module (PCM) monitors the continuity of the injector circuits as well as the voltage spike created by the collapse of the magnetic field in the injector coil. Any condition that reduces the maximum current flow or the magnitude of the voltage spike can cause this DTC to set.
DTC: P0207	**-FUEL INJECTOR 7 CIRCUIT:** With battery voltage greater than 10 volts. Auto Shutdown Relay energized. Engine speed less than 3000 rpm. The PCM monitors the continuity of the injector circuits as well as the voltage spike created by the collapse of the magnetic field in the injector coil. Any condition that reduces the maximum current flow or the magnitude of the voltage spike can cause this DTC to set.
DTC: P0208	**-FUEL INJECTOR 8 CIRCUIT:** With battery voltage greater than 10 volts. Auto Shutdown Relay energized. Engine speed less than 3000 rpm. The PCM monitors the continuity of the injector circuits as well as the voltage spike created by the collapse of the magnetic field in the injector coil. Any condition that reduces the maximum current flow or the magnitude of the voltage spike can cause this DTC to set.
DTC: P0208	**-FUEL INJECTOR 8 CIRCUIT/OPEN:** With the engine running, battery voltage greater than 12 volts, and engine RPM less than 3000. The Powertrain Control Module (PCM) monitors the continuity of the injector circuits as well as the voltage spike created by the collapse of the magnetic field in the injector coil. Any condition that reduces the maximum current flow or the magnitude of the voltage spike can cause this DTC to set.
DTC: P0218	**-HIGH TEMPERATURE OPERATION ACTIVATED:** Whenever the engine is running. Immediately after a Overheat shift schedule is activated when the Transmission temperature exceeds 127° C or 260° F.
DTC: P0219	**-ENGINE OVERSPEED:** Ignition on, engine running with the transmission in a valid forward gear. No active CAN Bus DTCs present. Monitored engine speed over the CAN Bus is greater than 6800 rpm for the period of 100 msecs.

DTC	Trouble Code Title, Conditions, Possible Causes
DTC: P0219	**-ENGINE OVERSPEED:** Continuously with the ignition on, engine running, with the transmission in gear with a valid Engine RPM message received at least once, and the CAN Bus Circuit and Engine CAN Message Missing are not active. Engine speed is greater than a calibrated limit (see table).
DTC: P0221	**THROTTLE POSITION SENSOR 2 CIRCUIT PERFORMANCE:** With the ignition on and battery voltage greater than 10. 4 volts. The Powertrain Control Module (PCM) detects that the Throttle Position Sensor (TPS) 2 circuit input voltage is implausible.
DTC: P0221	**THROTTLE POSITION SENSOR 2 CIRCUIT PERFORMANCE:** With the engine running and no TPS or MAP sensor DTCs present. TP Sensor signals do not correlate to the MAP Sensor signal. Two Trip Fault. ETC light will illuminate. P2135 should set with this code also.
DTC: P0222	**THROTTLE POSITION SENSOR 2 CIRCUIT LOW:** With the ignition on. Battery voltage greater than 10 volts. The PCM detects that the TP Sensor 2 voltage is lower than the acceptable value. One Trip Fault. Three good trips to turn off the MIL. The ETC light will illuminate.
DTC: P0222	**THROTTLE POSITION SENSOR 2 CIRCUIT LOW:** With the ignition on. Battery voltage greater than 10 volts. Throttle Position Sensor voltage at the PCM is less than 0. 16 of a volt for 0. 7 of a second. One Trip Fault. Three good trips to turn off the MIL. ETC light will illuminate.
DTC: P0223	**THROTTLE POSITION SENSOR 2 CIRCUIT HIGH:** With the ignition on. Throttle Position Sensor No. 2 Signal circuit voltage is greater than the maximum acceptable value. One Trip Fault. ETC light will illuminate.
DTC: P0223	**THROTTLE POSITION SENSOR 2 CIRCUIT HIGH:** With the ignition on and battery voltage greater than 10. 4 volts. The Powertrain Control Module (PCM) detects that the Throttle Position Sensor (TPS) 2 input voltage is above the maximum acceptable value.
DTC: P0234	**TURBOCHARGER OVERBOOST CONDITION:** With the engine running and the ECM attempting to govern turbocharger boost pressure. The Boost Pressure Sensor indicates actual turbocharger boost is greater than the ECM setpoint for engine boost.
DTC: P0237	**TURBO BOOST PRESSURE SENSOR CIRCUIT LOW:** With the ignition on. The (K37) Boost Pressure Sensor Signal circuit voltage is below 0. 29 volt for 0. 5 second.
DTC: P0238	**TURBO BOOST PRESSURE SENSOR CIRCUIT HIGH:** With the ignition on. The (K37) Boost Pressure Sensor Signal circuit voltage is above 4. 70 volts for 2. 0 seconds.
DTC: P0261	**-FUEL INJECTOR 1 CIRCUIT LOW:** With the engine cranking or running. The ECM detects a short to ground on a Fuel Injector Control circuit.
DTC: P0262	**-FUEL INJECTOR 1 CIRCUIT HIGH:** With the engine cranking or running. The ECM detects a short to voltage on a Fuel Injector Control circuit.
DTC: P0263	**-CYLINDER 1 CONTRIBUTION/BALANCE:** With the ignition on. The Engine Control Module (ECM) detects an internal failure.
DTC: P0264	**-FUEL INJECTOR 2 CIRCUIT LOW:** With the engine cranking or running. The ECM detects a short to ground on a Fuel Injector Control circuit.
DTC: P0265	**-FUEL INJECTOR 2 CIRCUIT HIGH:** With the engine cranking or running. The ECM detects a short to voltage on a Fuel Injector Control circuit.
DTC: P0266	**-CYLINDER 2 CONTRIBUTION/BALANCE:** With the ignition on. The Engine Control Module (ECM) detects an internal failure.
DTC: P0267	**-FUEL INJECTOR 3 CIRCUIT LOW:** With the engine cranking or running. The ECM detects a short to ground on a Fuel Injector Control circuit.
DTC: P0268	**-FUEL INJECTOR 3 CIRCUIT HIGH:** With the engine cranking or running. The ECM detects a short to voltage on a Fuel Injector Control circuit.
DTC: P0269	**-CYLINDER 3 CONTRIBUTION/BALANCE:** With the ignition on. The Engine Control Module (ECM) detects an internal failure.
DTC: P0270	**-FUEL INJECTOR 4 CIRCUIT LOW:** With the engine cranking or running. The ECM detects a short to ground on a Fuel Injector Control circuit.
DTC: P0271	**-FUEL INJECTOR 4 CIRCUIT HIGH:** With the engine cranking or running. The ECM detects a short to voltage on a Fuel Injector Control circuit.

DTC	Trouble Code Title, Conditions, Possible Causes
DTC: P0272	**-CYLINDER 4 CONTRIBUTION/BALANCE:** With the ignition on. The Engine Control Module (ECM) detects an internal failure.
DTC: P0273	**-FUEL INJECTOR 5 CIRCUIT LOW:** With the engine cranking or running. The ECM detects a short to ground on a Fuel Injector Control circuit.
DTC: P0274	**-FUEL INJECTOR 5 CIRCUIT HIGH:** With the engine cranking or running. The ECM detects a short to voltage on a Fuel Injector Control circuit.
DTC: P0275	**-CYLINDER 5 CONTRIBUTION/BALANCE:** With the ignition on. The Engine Control Module (ECM) detects an internal failure.
DTC: P0276	**-FUEL INJECTOR 6 CIRCUIT LOW:** With the engine cranking or running. The ECM detects a short to ground on a Fuel Injector Control circuit.
DTC: P0277	**-FUEL INJECTOR 6 CIRCUIT HIGH:** With the engine cranking or running. The ECM detects a short to voltage on a Fuel Injector Control circuit.
DTC: P0278	**-CYLINDER 6 CONTRIBUTION/BALANCE:** With the ignition on. The Engine Control Module (ECM) detects an internal failure.
DTC: P0298	**-ENGINE OIL TEMPERATURE TOO HIGH:** The engine oil temperature has dropped below a calibrated value. Engine start up. The Engine Oil temperature rises faster than a calibrated modeled temperature. When the actual oil temperature exceeds the high boundary of the calibrated modeled temperature for three minutes the fault is set. Two trip fault. Three good trips to turn off the MIL.
DTC: P0299	**TURBOCHARGER UNDERBOOST CONDITION:** With the engine running and the ECM attempting to govern turbocharger boost pressure. The Boost Pressure Sensor indicates actual turbocharger boost is less than the ECM setpoint for engine boost.
DTC: P0300	**-MULTIPLE CYLINDER MISFIRE:** Any time the engine is running and the adaptive numerator has been successfully updated. The threshold to set the fault is application specific; it is tied to the level of misfire that will cause emissions to increase to 1. 5 times the standard or in some cases 1%. It is always a two trip fault above the calibrated RPM. It takes one soft fail to set a malfunction and two trips to set the MIL. Three good trips to turn off the MIL.
DTC: P0301	**-CYLINDER 1 MISFIRE:** Any time the engine is running and the adaptive numerator has been successfully updated. The threshold to set the fault is application specific; it is tied to the level of misfire that will cause emissions to increase to 1. 5 times the standard or in some cases 1%. It is always a two trip fault above the calibrated RPM. It takes 1 soft fail to set a malfunction and two trips to set the MIL. Three good trips to turn off the MIL.
DTC: P0302	**-CYLINDER 2 MISFIRE:** Any time the engine is running, and the adaptive numerator has been successfully updated. The threshold to set the fault is application specific; it is tied to the level of misfire that will cause emissions to increase to 1. 5 times the standard or in some cases 1%. It is always a two trip fault above the calibrated RPM. It takes one failure to set a Pending Fault and two trips to set the MIL. Three good trips to turn off the MIL.
DTC: P0303	**-CYLINDER 3 MISFIRE:** Any time the engine is running and the adaptive numerator has been successfully updated. The threshold to set the fault is application specific; it is tied to the level of misfire that will cause emissions to increase to 1. 5 times the standard or in some cases 1%. It is always a two trip fault above the calibrated RPM. It takes one soft fail to set a malfunction and two trips to set the MIL. Three good trips to turn off the MIL.
DTC: P0304	**-CYLINDER 4 MISFIRE:** Any time the engine is running, and the adaptive numerator has been successfully updated. The threshold to set the fault is application specific; it is tied to the level of misfire that will cause emissions to increase to 1. 5 times the standard or in some cases 1%. It is always a two trip fault above the calibrated RPM. It takes one failure to set a Pending Fault and two trips to set the MIL. Three good trips to turn off the MIL.
DTC: P0305	**-CYLINDER 5 MISFIRE:** Any time the engine is running and the adaptive numerator has been successfully updated. The threshold to set the fault is application specific; it is tied to the level of misfire that will cause emissions to increase to 1. 5 times the standard or in some cases 1%. It is always a two trip fault above the calibrated RPM. It takes 1 soft fail to set a malfunction and two trips to set the MIL. Three good trips to turn off the MIL.

DTC	Trouble Code Title, Conditions, Possible Causes
DTC: P0306	**-CYLINDER 6 MISFIRE:** Any time the engine is running, and the adaptive numerator has been successfully updated. The threshold to set the fault is application specific; it is tied to the level of misfire that will cause emissions to increase to 1. 5 times the standard or in some cases 1%. It is always a two trip fault above the calibrated RPM. It takes one fail to set a Pending Fault and two trips to set the MIL. Three good trips to turn off the MIL.
DTC: P0307	**-CYLINDER 7 MISFIRE:** Any time the engine is running and the adaptive numerator has been successfully updated. The threshold to set the fault is application specific; it is tied to the level of misfire that will cause emissions to increase to 1. 5 times the standard or in some cases 1%. It is always a two trip fault above the calibrated RPM. It takes 1 soft fail to set a malfunction and two trips to set the MIL. Three good trips to turn off the MIL.
DTC: P0308	**-CYLINDER 8 MISFIRE:** Any time the engine is running, and the adaptive numerator has been successfully updated. The threshold to set the fault is application specific; it is tied to the level of misfire that will cause emissions to increase to 1. 5 times the standard or in some cases 1%. It is always a two trip fault above the calibrated RPM. It takes 1 soft fail to set a malfunction and two trips to set the MIL. Three good trips to turn off the MIL.
DTC: P0315	**-NO CRANK SENSOR LEARNED:** Under closed throttle decel and A/C off. ECT above 75° C (167° F). Engine start time is greater than 50 seconds. One of the CKP sensor target windows has more than 2% variance from the reference. One Trip Fault. Three good trips to turn off the MIL.
DTC: P0315	**-NO CRANK SENSOR LEARNED:** During deceleration, when fuel is cut off by the Powertrain Control Module (PCM). The Powertrain Control Module (PCM) measures the variation between crankshaft position reference points. The measurements are compared to an ideal reference that is stored in the PCM. If the variation exceeds a calibrated percentage, a fault is stored. One Trip Fault. Three good trips to turn off the MIL.
DTC: P0325	**-KNOCK SENSOR 1 CIRCUIT:** This monitor runs above 2000 RPM, under open throttle conditions. The Knock diagnostic does not run at idle or during decelerations. The high voltage test runs all the times the engine is running. The Powertrain Control Module (PCM) detects that the Knock Sensor input voltage is: Above 4. 0 Volts, less than or equal to 1. 0 Volt with engine RPM at or above 2200 or equal to 0. 0 Volts with engine RPM below 2200. Two Trip Fault. Three good trips to turn off the MIL.
DTC: P0330	**-KNOCK SENSOR 2 CIRCUIT:** This monitor runs above 2000 RPM, under open throttle conditions. The Knock diagnostic does not run at idle or during decelerations. The high voltage test runs all the times the engine is running. The Powertrain Control Module (PCM) detects that the Knock Sensor input voltage is: Above 4. 0 Volts, less than or equal to 1. 0 Volt with engine RPM at or above 2200 or equal to 0. 0 Volts with engine RPM below 2200. Two Trip Fault. Three good trips to turn off the MIL.
DTC: P0335	**-CRANKSHAFT POSITION SENSOR CIRCUIT:** Engine cranking. No CKP signal is present during engine cranking and at least eight Camshaft Position Sensor signals have occurred. One Trip Fault. Three good trips to turn off the MIL.
DTC: P0336	**-CRANKSHAFT POSITION SENSOR PERFORMANCE:** Engine cranking. No CKP signal is present during engine cranking and at least eight Camshaft Position Sensor signals have occurred. One Trip Fault. Three good trips to turn off the MIL.
DTC: P0336	**-CRANKSHAFT POSITION SENSOR PERFORMANCE:** With the engine cranking or running. The Engine Control Module (ECM) does not receive a signal from the Crankshaft Position Sensor when the Camshaft Position Sensor indicates engine rpm.
DTC: P0339	**-CRANKSHAFT POSITION SENSOR INTERMITTENT:** While cranking the engine and with the engine running. When the CKP Sensor failure counter reaches 20. One Trip Fault. Three good trips to turn off the MIL.
DTC: P0339	**-CRANKSHAFT POSITION SENSOR INTERMITTENT:** With the ignition on and battery voltage greater than 10. 4 volts. The Powertrain Control Module (PCM) detects that the Crankshaft Position Sensor input voltage is implausible.
DTC: P0340	**-CAMSHAFT POSITION SENSOR CIRCUIT:** During engine cranking and with the engine running. Battery voltage greater than 10 volts. At least 5 seconds or 2. 5 engine revolutions have elapsed with crankshaft position sensor signals present but no camshaft position sensor signal. One Trip Fault. Three good trips to turn off the MIL.
DTC: P0340	**-CAMSHAFT POSITION SENSOR CIRCUIT - BANK 1 SENSOR 1:** With the ignition on and the battery voltage greater than 10. 4 volts. The Powertrain Control Module (PCM) detects that the Camshaft Position (CMP) Sensor input voltage is implausible. One Trip Fault. Three good trips to turn off the MIL.

DTC	Trouble Code Title, Conditions, Possible Causes
DTC: P0340	**-CAMSHAFT POSITION SENSOR CIRCUIT:** During engine cranking and with the engine running. Battery voltage greater than 10 Volts. At least five seconds or 2. 5 engine revolutions have elapsed with crankshaft position sensor signals present but no camshaft position sensor signal. One Trip Fault. Three good trips to turn off the MIL.
DTC: P0341	**-CAMSHAFT POSITION SENSOR PERFORMANCE:** With the engine cranking or running The Engine Control Module (ECM) does not receive a signal from the Camshaft Position Sensor when the Crankshaft Position Sensor indicates engine rpm.
DTC: P0344	**-CAMSHAFT POSITION SENSOR INTERMITTENT:** With the ignition on and the battery voltage greater than 10. 4 volts. The Powertrain Control Module (PCM) detects that the Camshaft Position (CMP) Sensor input voltage is implausible. One Trip Fault. Three good trips to turn off the MIL.
DTC: P0344	**-CAMSHAFT POSITION SENSOR INTERMITTENT:** While cranking the engine and engine running. When the failure counter reaches 20. One Trip Fault. Three good trips to turn off the MIL.
DTC: P0349	**-CAMSHAFT 1/3 POSITION SENSOR INTERMITTENT:** While cranking the engine and engine running. When the failure counter reaches 20. One Trip Fault. Three good trips to turn off the MIL.
DTC: P0365	**-CAMSHAFT POSITION SENSOR CIRCUIT - BANK 1 SENSOR 2:** With the engine running or cranking. The Powertrain Control Module (PCM) receives either no signal or an incorrect signal from the Camshaft 1/2 Position Sensor.
DTC: P0365	**-CAMSHAFT 1/2 POSITION SENSOR CIRCUIT:** During engine cranking and with the engine running. Battery voltage greater than 10. 0 Volts. At least five seconds or 2. 5 engine revolutions have elapsed with Crankshaft Position Sensor signals present but no camshaft position sensor signal. One Trip Fault. Three good trips to turn off the MIL.
DTC: P0369	**-CAMSHAFT POSITION SENSOR INTERMITTENT - BANK 1 SENSOR 2:** With the engine cranking or running. The Powertrain Control Module (PCM) detects an intermittent signal error from the Camshaft 1/2 Position Sensor. One Trip Fault. Three good trips to turn off the MIL.
DTC: P0369	**-CAMSHAFT 1/2 POSITION SENSOR INTERMITTENT:** While cranking the engine and engine running. When the failure counter reaches 20. One Trip Fault. Three good trips to turn off the MIL.
DTC: P0390	**-CAMSHAFT 1/4 POSITION SENSOR CIRCUIT:** During engine cranking and with the engine running. Battery voltage greater than 10. 0 Volts. At least five seconds or 2. 5 engine revolutions have elapsed with Crankshaft Position Sensor signals present but no camshaft position sensor signal. One Trip Fault. Three good trips to turn off the MIL.
DTC: P0394	**-CAMSHAFT 1/4 POSITION SENSOR INTERMITTENT:** While cranking the engine and engine running. When the failure counter reaches 20. One Trip Fault. Three good trips to turn off the MIL.
DTC: P0401	**- EGR SYSTEM PERFORMANCE:** With the engine running. The Engine Control Module (ECM) detects and EGR flow problem for eight seconds
DTC: P0401	**-EGR SYSTEM PERFORMANCE:** Engine running for greater than two minutes with the Engine Coolant Temp greater than 70° C (158° F). EGR active. Less than 8500 feet. Ambient temperature greater than -6° C (20° F). The PCM closes the EGR valve while monitoring the O2 Sensor signal. Once a closed EGR fueling sample has been established the PCM then ramps in EGR and additional fueling while monitoring the O2 sensor signal in the open state. A fueling sample is again established. The PCM then compares the different O2 Sensor signal readings (fueling samples). If a larger than expected variation is detected, a soft failure is recorded. Three soft failures set a one trip failure. After two failed trips, a DTC is set and the MIL is illuminated.
DTC: P0402	**- EGR EXCESSIVE FLOW DETECTED:** With the engine running. The ECM detects and EGR flow problem for 8. 0 seconds
DTC: P0403	**-EGR SOLENOID CIRCUIT:** Engine running. Battery voltage greater than 10 volts. The EGR solenoid control circuit is not in the expected state when requested to operate by the PCM. One Trip Fault.
DTC: P0404	**-EGR POSITION SENSOR RATIONALITY OPEN:** Engine running. The EGR flow or valve movement is not what is expected. A rationality error has been detected from the EGR Close Position Performance. Two trip fault.

DTC	Trouble Code Title, Conditions, Possible Causes
DTC: P0405	**-EGR POSITION SENSOR CIRCUIT LOW:** With the ignition on. Battery voltage above 10. 0 volts. EGR Position Sensor Signal is less than the minimum acceptable value. One trip Fault.
DTC: P0406	**-EGR POSITION SENSOR CIRCUIT HIGH:** With the ignition on. Battery voltage greater than 10 volts. EGR position sensor signal is greater than the maximum acceptable value. One trip Fault.
DTC: P0406	**-EGR POSITION SENSOR CIRCUIT HIGH:** With the ignition on. Battery voltage greater than 10 Volts. EGR position sensor signal is greater than 4. 5 Volts. One trip Fault.
DTC: P0407	**-EGR AIRFLOW THROTTLE POSITION SENSOR CIRCUIT LOW:** With the ignition on. The (K312) EGR Airflow Control Valve Position Sensor Signal circuit voltage is below 0. 07 volt for 0. 30 second.
DTC: P0408	**-EGR AIRFLOW THROTTLE POSITION SENSOR CIRCUIT HIGH:** With the ignition on. The (K312) EGR Airflow Control Valve Position Sensor Signal circuit voltage is above 4. 7 volts for 0. 30 seconds.
DTC: P0411	**-SECONDARY AIR INJECTION SYSTEM INCORRECT FLOW DETECTED:** The Secondary Air Pump is on. Actual air flow is less than the expected air flow.
DTC: P0418	**-SECONDARY AIR INJECTION SYSTEM CONTROL CIRCUIT:** With the engine running, battery voltage greater than 10. 4 volts, and the control circuit active. The Powertrain Control Module (PCM) detects that the control circuit voltage is not within a specified range based on operating conditions.
DTC: P0420	**-CATALYST EFFICIENCY (BANK 1):** The monitor will run at between 1400 and 2300 RPM and MAP vacuum between 40 to 70 kPa (15. 0 and 21. 0 (Hg)). If the final State of Change index is within the calibrated fail threshold. Two trip fault. Three good trips to turn off the MIL.
DTC: P0420	**-CATALYST EFFICIENCY (BANK 1):** With the ECT above 70 C (158 F), engine RPM between 1400 and 2300, vehicle speed between 64 and 96 kph (40 and 60 mph), and engine run time greater than 3 minutes. If the final state of change index is within the calibrated fail threshold. Two trip fault. Three good trips to turn off the MIL.
DTC: P0420	**-CATALYST EFFICIENCY (BANK 1):** The monitor will run at between 1400 and 2300 RPM. It also runs between 40 and 70 kPa. If the final State of Change index is within the calibrated fail threshold. Two trip fault. Three good trips to turn off the MIL.
DTC: P0426	**-CATALYST TEMPERATURE SENSOR CIRCUIT PERFORMANCE - BANK 1 SENSOR 1:** At ignition on before engine crank. With no Intake Air Temp sensor DTCs The Engine Control Module (ECM) detects that the (K352) Pre-Catalyst Exhaust Temperature Sensor Signal circuit voltage is implausible.
DTC: P0430	**-CATALYST EFFICIENCY (BANK 2):** The monitor will run at between 1400 and 2300 RPM and MAP vacuum between 40 to 70 kPa (15. 0 and 21. 0 (Hg)). . If the final State of Change index is within the calibrated fail threshold. Two trip fault. Three good trips to turn off the MIL.
DTC: P0440	**-GENERAL EVAP SYSTEM FAILURE:** Engine running after a cold start with the difference between ECT and AAT is less than 10° C (19° F). Fuel Level between 12% and 88% full. Manifold vacuum greater than a calculated minimum value. Ambient Temperature between 4° C and 32° C (39° F and 89° F). When the monitor conditions are met, the Powertrain Control Module (PCM) will ramp in purge flow. If the PCM does not sense an ESIM switch closure after a calculated amount of purge flow accumulation, an error is detected. Two Trip Fault. Three good trips to turn off the MIL.
DTC: P0441	**-EVAP PURGE SYSTEM PERFORMANCE:** After the Evaporative System small leak test has passed, with the engine running, ambient temperature between 4° C (39° F) and 35° (95° F), with the engine at idle after a calibrated amount of drive time has accumulated. If the Powertrain Control Module (PCM) detects that the purge vapor ratio and the ESIM switch closed ratio are below a calculated value, the PCM commands the purge solenoid to flow at a specified rate to update the purge vapor ratio. If the ratio remains below a specified value, a one trip failure is recorded. Two Trip Fault. Three good trips to turn off the MIL.
DTC: P0441	**-EVAP PURGE SYSTEM PERFORMANCE:** With the engine running, after the Evap System small leak test has passed. If the PCM detects that the purge vapor ratio and the ESIM switch closed ratio are below a calculated value, the PCM commands the purge solenoid to flow at a specified rate to update the purge vapor ratio. If the ratio remains below a specified value, a one trip failure is recorded. Two Trip Fault. Three good trips to turn off the MIL.
DTC: P0443	**-EVAP PURGE SOLENOID CIRCUIT:** The ignition on or engine running. Battery voltage greater than 10 volts. The Powertrain Control Module (PCM) will set a trouble code if the actual state of the solenoid does not match the intended state. One Trip Fault. Three good trips to turn off the MIL.

DTC	Trouble Code Title, Conditions, Possible Causes
DTC: P0443	**-EVAP PURGE CONTROL CIRCUIT:** With the engine run time above a calibrated value, battery voltage greater than 10. 4 Volts, ECT within a specific range, and the Evap Purge Solenoid control active. This PCM compares the circuit feedback to a calibrated closed range when the circuit is de-energized or to a calibrated open range when the circuit is energized. If the value is determined to be out of the calibrated range in either the de-energized or energized state for more than a calibrated amount of time, this DTC will set.
DTC: P0452	**-EVAP PRESSURE SWITCH STUCK CLOSED:** Immediately after the ignition has been turned off. At key off, the Powertrain Control Module (PCM) energizes the Purge Solenoid for a calibrated amount of time (30 seconds maximum) and stores the state of the ESIM switch. The state is evaluated again at the next key on. If the PCM does not detect that the ESIM switch is open, an error is detected. Two Trip Fault. Three good trips to turn off the MIL.
DTC: P0455	**-EVAP PURGE SYSTEM LARGE LEAK:** With the engine running, during a cold start test with the fuel level above 12%, ambient temperature between 4° C and 32° C (39° F and 89° F) and the fuel system in closed loop. The test runs when the small leak test is maturing. The Powertrain Control Module (PCM) activates the Evap Purge solenoid to pull the Evaporative system into a vacuum to close the ESIM switch. Once the ESIM switch is closed, the PCM turns the Evap Purge solenoid off to seal the Evaporative system. If the ESIM switch reopens before the calibrated amount of time, a large leak error is detected. Two Trip Fault. Three good trips to turn off the MIL.
DTC: P0456	**-EVAP PURGE SYSTEM SMALL LEAK:** With the ignition off, fuel level less than 88%, ambient temperature between 4° C and 43° C (39° F and 109° F) and the fuel system in closed loop. As temperatures change, a vacuum is created in the fuel tank and Evaporative System. With the Evaporative System sealed, the Powertrain Control Module (PCM) monitors the ESIM Switch. If the ESIM Switch does not close within a calibrated time, an error is detected by the PCM. One Trip Fault. Three good trips to turn off the MIL.
DTC: P0457	**-LOOSE FUEL CAP:** Ignition on. Ambient Temperature between 4° C and 32° C (39° F and 89° F). Close Loop fuel system. Test runs after the medium leak test is inconclusive and the PCM has senses a fuel increase. The Powertrain Control Module (PCM) activates the Evap Purge Solenoid to pull the Evap system into a vacuum to close the ESIM switch. Once the ESIM switch is closed, the PCM turns the Evap Purge Solenoid off to seal the Evap system. If the ESIM switch reopens before the calibrated amount of time after a fuel tank fill, an error is detected. Two Trip Fault. Three good trips to turn off the MIL.
DTC: P0460	**-FUEL LEVEL SENSOR 1 CIRCUIT:** With the ignition on. The ECM does not receive a valid fuel level signal message from the Instrument Cluster (CCN) for 2. 0 seconds.
DTC: P0460-11	**-FUEL LEVEL SENSOR 1 - CIRCUIT SHORT TO GROUND:** With the ignition on. Battery voltage greater than 10. 4 volts. The Body Control Module (BCM) detects that the Fuel Level Sensor input voltage is below the minimum acceptable value.
DTC: P0460-15	**-FUEL LEVEL SENSOR 1 - CIRCUIT SHORT TO BATTERY OR OPEN:** With the ignition on. Battery voltage greater than 10. 4 volts. The Body Control Module (BCM) detects that the Fuel Level Sensor input voltage is above the maximum acceptable value.
DTC: P0461	**-FUEL LEVEL SENSOR 1 PERFORMANCE:** TEST No. 1: With the ignition on, the fuel level is compared to the previous key down after a 20 second delay. TEST No. 2: The PCM monitors the fuel level at ignition on. TEST No. 1: If the PCM does not see a difference in fuel level of greater than 0. 1 Volt the test will fail. TEST No. 2: If the PCM does not see a change in the fuel level over a set amount of miles the test will fail. Two trip fault. Three good trips to turn off the MIL.
DTC: P0461	**-FUEL LEVEL SENSOR 1 PERFORMANCE:** TEST No. 1: With the ignition on, the fuel level is compared to the previous key down after a 20 second delay. TEST No. 2: The PCM monitors the fuel level at ignition on. TEST No. 1: If the PCM does not see a difference in fuel level of greater than 0. 1 volt the test will fail. TEST No. 2: If the PCM does not see a change in the fuel level of . 1765 over a set amount of miles the test will fail. Three good trips to turn off the MIL.
DTC: P0462	**-FUEL LEVEL SENSOR 1 CIRCUIT LOW:** Ignition on and battery voltage above 10. 4 Volts. The Fuel Level Sensor signal voltage goes below the minimum acceptable value. One Trip Fault. Three good trips to turn off the MIL.
DTC: P0463	**-FUEL LEVEL SENSOR 1 CIRCUIT HIGH:** With the ignition on. The Cluster detects that the Fuel Level Sensor input voltage is above the maximum acceptable value.
DTC: P0463	**-FUEL LEVEL SENSOR 1 HIGH CIRCUIT:** With the ignition on. The CAN Bus message from the Instrument Cluster indicates Fuel Level Sensor 1 voltage is above 2. 51 Volts.
DTC: P0463	**-FUEL LEVEL SENSOR 1 CIRCUIT HIGH:** Ignition on and battery voltage above 10. 4 volts. The fuel level sensor signal voltage at the PCM goes above the maximum acceptable value. One Trip Fault. Three good trips to turn off the MIL.

DTC	Trouble Code Title, Conditions, Possible Causes
DTC: P0471	**-EXHAUST PRESSURE SENSOR 1 PERFORMANCE:** Engine speed is below 670 rpm. There are no other Exhaust Pressure Sensor DTCs. There are no Atmospheric/Barometric Pressure Sensor DTCs. The difference between the Exhaust Pressure Sensor Signal and the Atmospheric/Barometric Pressure Signal is greater than 400 hpa (5. 8 psi.) for at least 3. 0 seconds.
DTC: P0472	**-EXHAUST PRESSURE SENSOR 1 LOW:** With the ignition on. The Exhaust Gas Pressure Sensor Signal circuit voltage is below 4. 58 volts for 2. 0 seconds.
DTC: P0473	**-EXHAUST PRESSURE SENSOR 1 HIGH:** With the ignition on. The Exhaust Gas Pressure Sensor Signal circuit voltage is below 0. 25 volt for 2. 0 seconds.
DTC: P0480	**-COOLING FAN 1 CONTROL CIRCUIT:** With the ignition on. Battery voltage greater than 10 Volts. The ECM receives a CAN Bus message from the FCM indicating an open or shorted circuit on the Radiator Fan Relay Control circuit.
DTC: P0480	**-COOLING FAN 1 CONTROL CIRCUIT:** With the ignition on. Battery voltage greater than 10 volts. An open or shorted circuit is detected in the Low/High Rad Fan Control circuit. One Trip Fault. Three good trips to turn off the MIL.
DTC: P0480	**-COOLING FAN 1 CONTROL CIRCUIT:** With the ignition on and the battery voltage greater than 10 volts. The Powertrain Control Module (PCM) receives a Controller Area Network (CAN) Bus message from the Totally Integrated Power Module (TIPM) with TIPM indicating an open or shorted circuit on the Radiator Fan Relay Control circuit. One Trip Fault. Three good trips to turn off the Malfunction Indicator Lamp (MIL).
DTC: P0481	**-COOLING FAN 2 CONTROL CIRCUIT:** With the ignition on. Battery voltage greater than 10. 0 Volts. The Powertrain Control Module (PCM) is requesting the Totally Integrated Power Module (TIPM) to turn on the Cooling Fan and it is not operating.
DTC: P0481	**-COOLING FAN 2 CONTROL CIRCUIT:** With the ignition on and the battery voltage greater than 10 volts. The Powertrain Control Module (PCM) receives a Controller Area Network (CAN) Bus message from the Totally Integrated Power Module (TIPM) indicating an open or shorted circuit on the Radiator Fan High Relay Control circuit. One Trip Fault. Three good trips to turn off the Malfunction Indicator Lamp (MIL).
DTC: P0487	**-EGR AIRFLOW THROTTLE CONTROL CIRCUIT A OPEN:** With the engine running and the EGR Airflow Control Valve Motor command off. The Engine Control Module (ECM) detects an open (K314) EGR Airflow Control Valve Motor (+) circuit for 0. 5 second.
DTC: P0488	**-EGR AIRFLOW THROTTLE CONTROL CIRCUIT PERFORMANCE:** With the engine running and the EGR Airflow Control Valve Motor command on. The Engine Control Module (ECM) detects an implausible voltage on the (K314) EGR Airflow Control Valve Motor (+) circuit.
DTC: P0489	**-EGR CONTROL CIRCUIT LOW:** With the ignition on and the EGR Solenoid command off. The ECM detects a short to ground on the (K34) EGR Solenoid Control circuit for 2. 3 seconds.
DTC: P0490	**-EGR CONTROL CIRCUIT HIGH:** With the ignition on and the EGR Solenoid command on. The ECM detects excessive current on the (K34) EGR Solenoid Control circuit for 2. 0 seconds.
DTC: P0491	**-SECONDARY AIR INJECTION SYSTEM INSUFFICIENT FLOW:** After the diagnostics for air injection system stuck closed (P2441) and stuck off (P2445) have passed. ECT above 0° C (32° F), ambient air temperature within approximately 2 degrees of ECT, actual air flow is less than or equal to model air flow, and Secondary Air Flow diagnostic counter above 150 (approximately 4. 5 seconds). Actual air flow is less than model air flow, and the difference between model air flow and actual air flow is greater than 10 kg/h.
DTC: P0501	**-VEHICLE SPEED SENSOR 1 PERFORMANCE:** With the engine running, transmission not in park or neutral, brakes not applied, and engine RPM greater than 1500. This code will set if no vehicle speed signal is received from the ABS Module for more than 11 seconds for two consecutive trips. Two Trip Fault. Three good trips to turn off the MIL.
DTC: P0501	**-VEHICLE SPEED SENSOR 1 PERFORMANCE:** Continuously with the ignition on. The DTC will set if multiple ABS wheel speed signals are invalid.
DTC: P0503	**-VEHICLE SPEED SENSOR 1 ERRATIC (MTX NONABS):** With the ignition on and battery voltage greater than 10. 4 volts. The Powertrain Control Module (PCM) detects an implausible voltage on the Vehicle Speed Sensor circuit.
DTC: P0503	**-VEHICLE SPEED SENSOR 1 ERRATIC (EXC MTX NONABS):** With the engine running, transmission not in park or neutral, brakes not applied, and engine rpm greater than 1500. This code will set if no vehicle speed signal is received from the ABS Module for more than 11 seconds for 2 consecutive trips. Two Trip Fault. Three good trips to turn off the MIL.

DTC	Trouble Code Title, Conditions, Possible Causes
DTC: P0503	**-VEHICLE SPEED SENSOR 1 ERRATIC:** Ignition on and battery voltage greater than 10 volts. Transmission in Drive or Reverse. This code will set if no vehicle speed signal is received from the ABS Module up to 120 seconds for 2 consecutive trips. One Trip Fault. Three good trips to turn off the MIL.
DTC: P0504	**-BRAKE SWITCH SIGNAL CIRCUITS PLAUSIBILITY WITH REDUNDANT CONTACT:** With the ignition on. The Primary Brake Switch Signal and Secondary Brake Switch Signal inputs to the ECM do not agree for 2 minutes.
DTC: P0506	**-IDLE SPEED PERFORMANCE LOWER THAN EXCEPTED:** With the engine idling in drive, the brake applied, engine run time above a minimum calibrated value, and no VSS, MAF/MAP, ECT, TPS, ETC, CKP Sensor, fuel system, or injector DTCs present. Engine speed is 100 RPM or more below target idle speed for 30 seconds. Two Trip Fault. Three good trips to turn off the MIL.
DTC: P0506	**-IDLE SPEED PERFORMANCE LOWER THAN EXPECTED:** With the engine idling in drive, the brake applied, engine run time below a calibrated minimum value, and no VSS, MAF/MAP, ECT, TPS, ETC, CKP Sensor, fuel system, or injector DTCs present. Engine speed is 100 RPM or more below target idle speed for 30 seconds. Two Trip Fault. Three good trips to turn off the MIL.
DTC: P0507	**-IDLE SPEED PERFORMANCE HIGHER THAN EXCEPTED:** With the engine idling in drive, the brake applied, engine run time above a minimum calibrated value, and no VSS, MAF/MAP, ECT, TPS, ETC, CKP Sensor, fuel system, or injector DTCs present. Engine speed is 200 RPM or more above idle speed for 7 seconds. Two Trip Fault. Three good trips to turn off the MIL.
DTC: P050B	**-COLD START IGNITION TIMING PERFORMANCE:** Cold start condition. Ambient Air temperature between -7° C and 50° C (19. 4° F and 122° F). Engine Coolant temperature between -7° C and 50° C (19. 4° F and 122° F). The difference between the Ambient Air temp and ECT temp at Start is equal to or less than 10° C (50° F). Engine running at idle only. Engine RPM is 50 RPM or more (depending on vehicle specifications), below idle speed for at least 3 seconds and the average spark advance is above the threshold, too much spark advance, for a specified time limit. Two trip fault. Three good trips to turn off the MIL.
DTC: P050B	**-COLD START IGNITION TIMING PERFORMANCE:** During a cold start condition, with the difference between the AAT and ECT at startup below 10° C, and the engine running at idle. The PCM detects that engine speed is 50 RPM or more (depending on vehicle specifications) below target idle speed for more than 3 seconds, and the average spark advance is above the failure threshold for more than the specified limit. Two trip fault. Three good trips to turn off the MIL.
DTC: P050D	**-COLD START ROUGH IDLE:** Cold start condition. Ambient Air temperature between -7° C and 50° C (19. 4° F and 122° F). Engine Coolant temperature between -7° C and 50° C (19. 4° F and 122° F). The difference between the Ambient Air temp and ECT temp at Start is equal to or less than 10° C (50° F). Engine running at idle only. If a rough idle is detected and the Dynamic Crankshaft Fuel Control remains or returns to the high limit window for a calibrated time. Two trip fault.
DTC: P0513	**-INVALID SKIM KEY:** Ignition on. The Powertrain Control Module (PCM) detects an invalid SKREEM key. One Trip Fault.
DTC: P0520	**-ENGINE OIL PRESSURE SENSOR CIRCUIT:** Ignition on, engine not running. The Powertrain Control Module (PCM) senses the oil pressure is out of the calibrated range. One Trip fault.
DTC: P0520	**-OIL PRESSURE TOO LOW:** Ignition on, engine not running. The Powertrain Control Module (PCM) senses the oil pressure is out of the calibrated range. One Trip fault.
DTC: P0521	**-ENGINE OIL PRESSURE SENSOR PERFORMANCE:** Engine running. The engine oil pressure never reaches the calibrated specification with the engine RPM at 1250. One trip fault.
DTC: P0522	**-OIL PRESSURE SENSOR CIRCUIT LOW:** With the ignition key on and battery voltage above 10. 4 Volts. The Oil Pressure Sensor voltage at Powertrain Control Module (PCM) goes below the minimum acceptable value. One Trip Fault. Three good trips to turn off the MIL.
DTC: P0522	**-ENGINE OIL PRESSURE SENSOR CIRCUIT LOW:** At engine start-up. The ECM detects that the (G6) Oil Pressure Sensor Signal circuit is below 0. 2 volt for 0. 5 second.
DTC: P0523	**-ENGINE OIL PRESSURE SENSOR CIRCUIT HIGH:** At engine start-up. The ECM detects that the (G6) Oil Pressure Sensor Signal circuit is above 4. 88 volts for 0. 5 second.
DTC: P0523	**-ENGINE OIL PRESSURE SENSOR CIRCUIT HIGH:** With the ignition on. Battery voltage greater than 10 Volts. The Engine Oil pressure signal is greater than the calibrated amount. One Trip Fault.

DTC	Trouble Code Title, Conditions, Possible Causes
DTC: P0524	**- ENGINE OIL PRESSURE IS TOO LOW:** With the engine running. The Oil Pressure Sensor indicates low oil pressure for 5 seconds.
DTC: P0524	**-ENGINE OIL PRESSURE TOO LOW:** Engine running. The engine oil pressure never reaches the calibrated specification to allow the MDS activation. One trip fault.
DTC: P0532	**-A/C PRESSURE SENSOR CIRCUIT LOW:** Engine running, AC is learned, and AC Clutch Relay energized. The A/C pressure transducer signal voltage at the PCM goes below the minimum acceptable value. One Trip Fault. Three good trips to turn off the MIL.
DTC: P0532	**-A/C PRESSURE SENSOR CIRCUIT LOW:** With the ignition on and battery voltage greater than 10. 4 volts. The Powertrain Control Module (PCM) detects that the A/C Pressure Sensor input voltage is below the minimum acceptable value.
DTC: P0533	**-A/C PRESSURE SENSOR CIRCUIT HIGH:** Engine running and the A/C Clutch Relay energized. The A/C pressure transducer signal at the PCM goes above the maximum acceptable value. One trip Fault. Three good trips to turn off the MIL.
DTC: P0533	**-A/C PRESSURE SENSOR CIRCUIT HIGH:** With the ignition on and battery voltage greater than 10. 4 volts. The Powertrain Control Module (PCM) detects that the A/C Pressure Sensor input voltage is above the maximum acceptable value.
DTC: P053A	**-CRANKCASE VENT HEATER CONTROL CIRCUIT OPEN:** With the ignition on and the Crankcase Vent Heater command off. The ECM does not detect voltage on the (N116) Crankcase Vent Heater Control circuit for 2. 0 seconds.
DTC: P053B	**-CRANKCASE VENT HEATER CONTROL CIRCUIT LOW:** With the ignition on and the Crankcase Vent Heater command off. The ECM detects a short to ground on the (N116) Crankcase Vent Heater Control circuit for 2. 0 seconds.
DTC: P053C	**-CRANKCASE VENT HEATER CONTROL CIRCUIT HIGH:** With the ignition on and the Crankcase Vent Heater command on. The ECM detects excessive current on the (N116) Crankcase Vent Heater Control circuit for 2. 0 seconds.
DTC: P0545	**-EXHAUST GAS TEMPERATURE SENSOR CIRCUIT LOW - BANK 1 SENSOR 1:** With the ignition on. The ECM detects that the (K352) Pre-Catalyst Exhaust Temperature Sensor Signal circuit is shorted to ground.
DTC: P0546	**-EXHAUST GAS TEMPERATURE SENSOR CIRCUIT HIGH - BANK 1 SENSOR 1:** With the ignition on. The ECM detects that the (K352) Pre-Catalyst Exhaust Temperature Sensor Signal circuit is open shorted to voltage.
DTC: P054A	**-CAMSHAFT POSITION TIMING OVER - ADVANCED-BANK1:** Engine cranking and engine running If the Camshaft Position Signal (angular variation) is more than 15° of the Crankshaft Position Signal, this DTC is set.
DTC: P054C	**-CAMSHAFT POSITION TIMING OVER - ADVANCED-BANK 2:** Engine cranking and engine running If the Camshaft Position Signal (angular variation) is more than 15° of the Crankshaft Position Signal, this DTC is set.
DTC: P0562	**-ECM VOLTAGE TOO LOW:** With the ignition on or the engine running. The ECM detects battery voltage of 8. 0 volts or less for 5. 0 seconds.
DTC: P0562	**-BATTERY VOLTAGE LOW:** With engine running for more than 30 seconds. Battery voltage at the Powertrain Control Module (PCM) is less than 11. 7 Volts for a set period of time. One Trip Fault.
DTC: P0562	**-BATTERY VOLTAGE LOW:** With the engine running and the PCM has closed the Transmission Control Relay. If the battery voltage of the Transmission Control Output circuit(s) to the PCM is less than 10. 0 volts for the period of 15 seconds. **NOTE: P0562 generally indicates a gradually falling battery voltage or a resistive connection(s) to the PCM. The DTC will also set if the battery voltage sensed at the PCM is less than 6. 5v for 200ms or where Transmission Control Output circuit(s) is less than 7. 2v for 200ms.**
DTC: P0562	**-BATTERY VOLTAGE LOW:** The engine running. The engine speed greater than 1000 RPM. Battery voltage is less than 6. 0 Volts. One Trip Fault.
DTC: P0563	**-BATTERY VOLTAGE HIGH:** Continuously with the ignition on. When the monitored battery voltage rises above 16. 9 volts.
DTC: P0563	**-BATTERY VOLTAGE HIGH:** Continuously with the ignition in the run position. When the monitored battery voltage rises above 16. 0 volts.

DTC	Trouble Code Title, Conditions, Possible Causes
DTC: P0563	**-BATTERY VOLTAGE HIGH:** With the ignition on. Engine RPM greater than 1000 RPM. With no other charging system codes set. Battery voltage is 1 Volt greater than desired voltage for more than 10 seconds. Battery voltage greater than 15. 75 Volts. One Trip Fault. Three good trips to turn off the MIL.
DTC: P0571	**-BRAKE SWITCH 1 PERFORMANCE:** Ignition on. If the output of Brake Switch No. 1 to the PCM looks like it is not applied, while Brake Lamp Switch Output circuit is applied the fault will mature in 60ms. One Trip Fault.
DTC: P0571	**-BRAKE SWITCH 1 PERFORMANCE:** Ignition on and battery voltage above 10. 4 Volts. If the output of Brake Switch to the PCM looks like it is not applied, while Brake Lamp Switch Output circuit is applied. One Trip Fault.
DTC: P0571	**-BRAKE SWITCH 1 PERFORMANCE:** After initial start and any time the shift lever is changed from park to drive. System voltage between 9. 0 and 16 volts. No active CAN Bus DTCs present. Vehicle speed is greater than 30 Km/h (18. 5 mph) for at least 10 seconds. The brake switch status does not change during a drive cycle with a vehicle speed greater than 30 Km/h (18. 5 mph) for the period of 10 seconds. It takes two consecutive problem identification trips to mature the fault. After two consecutive trips, the MIL is illuminated on the next key on cycle (start of a third trip).
DTC: P0572	**-BRAKE SWITCH 1 STUCK ON:** With the ignition on, battery voltage greater than 10. 4 volts, and ambient temperature above -23 C. The PCM detects that the state of Brake Signal 1 does not change as expected.
DTC: P0572	**-BRAKE SWITCH 1 STUCK ON:** With the gear selector in drive, vehicle speed above a minimum value, and battery voltage greater than 10. 4 volts. The Powertrain Control Module (PCM) detects that the actual state of Brake Signal 1 or Brake Signal 2 does not match the desired state during monitoring. Two trip fault.
DTC: P0573	**-BRAKE SWITCH 1 STUCK OFF:** With the ignition on, battery voltage greater than 10. 4 volts, ambient temperature above -23 C. The PCM detects that the state of Brake Signal 1 does not change as expected.
DTC: P0573	**-BRAKE SWITCH 1 STUCK OFF:** When vehicle speed cycles from 0 kph to 48 kph (30 mph) at least 10 times. When the PCM recognizes Brake Switch No. 1 is stuck in the high/off position. Two Trip Fault. Three good trips to turn off the MIL.
DTC: P0578	**-SPEED CONTROL SWITCH 1 STUCK:** With the ignition on and no other Speed Control Switch DTCs present. The S/C Switch Sense 1 signal indicates that a switch is pressed continuously for 60 seconds.
DTC: P0579	**-SPEED CONTROL SWITCH 1 PERFORMANCE:** With the ignition key on. Speed Control (S/C) switch voltage output is not out of range but it does not equal any of the values for any of the button positions. One trip fault.
DTC: P0579	**-SPEED CONTROL SWITCH 1 PERFORMANCE:** With the ignition on. The S/C Switch Sense 1 signal is invalid for 60 seconds.
DTC: P0579-00	**-SPEED CONTROL SWITCH 1 PERFORMANCE:** Continuously with the ignition on. The Steering Column Control Module (SCCM) has detected that a non-permissible combination has occurred in the Right Steering Wheel Switch (Speed Control Switch).
DTC: P0580	**-SPEED CONTROL SWITCH 1 CIRCUIT LOW:** Continuously with the ignition on. Fault signifies when the switch voltage is shorted low.
DTC: P0580	**-SPEED CONTROL SWITCH 1 CIRCUIT LOW:** With the ignition on and battery voltage greater than 10. 4 Volts. The S/C Signal1 voltage is below a calibrated threshold for 0. 06 second.
DTC: P0580-00	**-SPEED CONTROL SWITCH 1 CIRCUIT LOW:** Continuously with the ignition on. Fault signifies when the switch voltage is shorted low.
DTC: P0581	**-SPEED CONTROL SWITCH 1 CIRCUIT HIGH:** Continuously with the ignition on. Fault signifies when the switch voltage is shorted high.
DTC: P0581	**-SPEED CONTROL SWITCH 1 CIRCUIT HIGH:** With the ignition key on. Speed Control (S/C) switch input above the maximum acceptable voltage at the Powertrain Control Module (PCM). One trip fault.
DTC: P0581-00	**-SPEED CONTROL SWITCH 1 CIRCUIT HIGH:** Continuously with the ignition on. Fault signifies when the switch voltage is shorted high.

DTC	Trouble Code Title, Conditions, Possible Causes
DTC: P0585	**-SPEED CONTROL SWITCH 1/2 CORRELATION:** With the ignition on and no other S/C Switch DTCs present. The (V71) S/C Switch No. 1 Signal and (V72) S/C Switch No. 2 Signal do not indicate the same S/C Switch position.
DTC: P0585	**-SPEED CONTROL SWITCH 1/2 CORRELATION:** Ignition on. Speed Control (S/C) switch inputs are not coherent with each other. Example: Powertrain Control Module (PCM) is reading Switch No. 1 as Accel and Switch No. 2 as Coast at the same time. One trip fault.
DTC: P0585	**-SPEED CONTROL SWITCH 1/2 CORRELATION:** Continuously with the ignition on. The Steering Column Control Module (SCCM) has detected that a non-permissible combination has occurred in the Speed Control Switch.
DTC: P0585-00	**-SPEED CONTROL SWITCH 1/2 CORRELATION:** Continuously with the ignition on. The Steering Column Control Module (SCCM) has detected that a non-permissible combination has occurred in the Speed Control Switch.
DTC: P0590	**-SPEED CONTROL SWITCH 2 STUCK:** With the ignition on and no other Speed Control Switch DTCs present. The S/C Switch Sense 2 signal indicates that a switch is pressed continuously for 60 seconds.
DTC: P0591	**-SPEED CONTROL SWITCH 2 PERFORMANCE:** With the ignition on. The S/C Switch Sense 2 signal is invalid for 60 seconds.
DTC: P0591	**-SPEED CONTROL SWITCH 2 PERFORMANCE:** With the ignition key on. Cruise switch voltage output is not out of range but it does not equal any of the values for any of the button positions. One trip fault.
DTC: P0591	**-SPEED CONTROL SWITCH 2 PERFORMANCE:** With the ignition key on. Speed Control (S/C) switch voltage output is not out of range but it does not equal any of the values for any of the button positions. One trip fault.
DTC: P0591-00	**-SPEED CONTROL SWITCH 2 PERFORMANCE:** Continuously with the ignition on. The Steering Column Control Module (SCCM) has detected that a non-permissible combination has occurred in the Speed Control Switch.
DTC: P0592	**-SPEED CONTROL SWITCH 2 CIRCUIT LOW:** With the ignition on. The S/C Switch Sense 2 voltage is below 0. 39 of a Volt for 0. 06 of a second.
DTC: P0592	**-SPEED CONTROL SWITCH 2 CIRCUIT LOW:** With the ignition key on. Speed Control (S/C) switch input No. 2 is below the minimum acceptable voltage at the Powertrain Control Module (PCM). One trip fault.
DTC: P0592-00	**-SPEED CONTROL SWITCH 2 CIRCUIT LOW:** Continuously with the ignition on. Fault signifies when the switch voltage is shorted low.
DTC: P0593	**-SPEED CONTROL SWITCH 2 CIRCUIT HIGH:** With the ignition key on. Speed Control Switch No. 2 input above the maximum acceptable voltage at the PCM. One trip fault.
DTC: P0593	**-SPEED CONTROL SWITCH 2 CIRCUIT HIGH:** Continuously with the ignition on. Fault signifies when the switch voltage is shorted high.
DTC: P0593-00	**-SPEED CONTROL SWITCH 2 CIRCUIT HIGH:** Continuously with the ignition on. Fault signifies when the switch voltage is shorted high.
DTC: P0600	**-SERIAL COMMUNICATION LINK:** With the ignition on. Internal Bus communication failure between processors. One Trip Fault. Three Global Good Trips to clear.
DTC: P0600	**-SERIAL COMMUNICATION LINK:** With the ignition on. The Powertrain Control Module (PCM) detects an internal failure.
DTC: P0601	**-INTERNAL MEMORY CHECKSUM INVALID:** With the ignition on. Internal checksum for software failed, does not match calculated value. One Trip Fault, Three Good Trips to clear.
DTC: P0601	**-INTERNAL MEMORY CHECKSUM INVALID:** With the ignition on. The Powertrain Control Module (PCM) detects an internal failure.
DTC: P0602	**-CONTROL MODULE PROGRAMING ERROR/NOT PROGRAMMED:** After an initial vehicle start with a system voltage between 9. 0 and 16. 0 volts. Transmission Control Module (TCM) does not receive valid vehicle information from the Front Control Module (FCM) for the period of 5 seconds.

DTC	Trouble Code Title, Conditions, Possible Causes
DTC: P0602	**-CONTROL MODULE PROGRAMMING ERROR/NOT PROGRAMMED:** Check for generic software is made at power-up. If generic software is found , the MIL will light immediately. This DTC is designed to signal the technician that the controller still has generic software installed.
DTC: P0602	**-CONTROL MODULE PROGRAMMING ERROR/NOT PROGRAMMED:** Continuously with the ignition on. If the TCM detects that the variables that dictate the vehicle application are not present.
DTC: P0604	**-INTERNAL CONTROL MODULE RAM:** One time after the controller is reset (ignition turned to the RUN position). Whenever the Powertrain Control Module (PCM) detects an internal controller problem.
DTC: P0604	**-INTERNAL CONTROL MODULE RAM:** Continuously with the ignition on. If the TCM detects an error with the controllers Random Access Memory (RAM).
DTC: P0605	**-INTERNAL CONTROL MODULE ROM:** One time after the ignition switch is turned to the run position. The read value does not match the written value in any ROM location. **Possible causes:** • TRANSMISSION CONTROL MODULE (TCM) - INTERNAL ERROR
DTC: P0605	**-INTERNAL CONTROL MODULE ROM:** One time after the ignition key is turned to the run position. If the ROM checksum does not match a known constant. **Possible causes:** • PCM - INTERNAL ERROR

DTC: P0605	**-INTERNAL CONTROL MODULE ROM:**
	One time after the controller is reset (ignition turned to the RUN position). Whenever the Powertrain Control Module (PCM) detects an internal controller problem.
	Possible causes:
	    • POWER OR GROUND CIRCUIT
	    • POWERTRAIN CONTROL MODULE (PCM)

DTC: P0606	**-INTERNAL ECM PROCESSOR:** With the ignition on. The Powertrain Control Module (PCM) detects an internal failure. **Possible causes:** • POWERTRAIN CONTROL MODULE (PCM)
DTC: P0606	**-INTERNAL ECM PROCESSOR:** Engine running. When the Powertrain Control Module (PCM) recognizes an internal failure to communicate with the ECM or the CMP and CKP Sensor count periods are too short. One trip fault. ETC light is flashing. **Possible causes:** • POWERTRAIN CONTROL MODULE (PCM)

DTC: P0607	**-ECU INTERNAL PERFORMANCE:**
	With the ignition on. The Engine Control Module (ECM) detects an internal failure.
	Possible causes:
	    • INTERMITTENT DTC
	    • ENGINE CONTROL MODULE (ECM)

DTC: P0607	**-ECU INTERNAL PERFORMANCE:** Continuously with the ignition in the run position. If the Shift Lever Assembly controller detects an invalid calibration (checksum value). **Possible causes:** • SHIFTER LEVER ASSEMBLY

DTC: P060B	**-ETC A/D GROUND PERFORMANCE:**
	When the Throttle Motor is powered. When ASD reading does not return to ground within a set period of time of test activation, this fault sets. The test typically runs a couple of times per second, and is the reason why APP2 signal spikes to ground a couple of times per second in normal running. Reprogramming the module may not always fix this fault. One trip fault. ETC lamp will illuminate.
	Possible causes:
	    • PCM NEEDS TO BE PROGRAMMED
	    • POWERTRAIN CONTROL MODULE (PCM)

DTC: P060B	**-ETC A/D GROUND PERFORMANCE:** With the ignition on. When the A/D reading does not return to ground within a set period of time during test activation, this DTC will set. Reprogramming the module may not fix this DTC. ETC lamp will flash. **Possible causes:** • POWERTRAIN CONTROL MODULE (PCM)

DTC	Trouble Code Title, Conditions, Possible Causes
DTC: P060B	**-INTERNAL CONTROL MODULE A/D PROCESSING PERFORMANCE:** One time after the ignition switch is turned to the run position. The TCM has detected an error with the internal processor. **Possible causes:** • TRANSMISSION CONTROL MODULE (TCM) - INTERNAL ERROR
DTC: P060D	**-ETC LEVEL 2 APP PERFORMANCE:** Throttle motor is powered and no matured faults related to APP Sensors. When secondary software determines that APPS 1 and APPS 2 signals do not match for a period of time. One trip fault. ETC lamp will flash. **Possible causes:** • PCM NEEDS TO BE PROGRAMMED • POWERTRAIN CONTROL MODULE (PCM)
DTC: P060D	**-ETC LEVEL 2 APP PERFORMANCE:** With the ignition on. When secondary software determines that the APPS 1 and APPS 2 signals do not match for a period of time. ETC lamp will flash **Possible causes:** • POWERTRAIN CONTROL MODULE (PCM)
DTC: P060E	**-ETC LEVEL 2 TPS PERFORMANCE:** With the ignition on. When secondary software determines that the TPS 1 and TPS 2 signals do not match for a period of time. ETC lamp will flash. **Possible causes:** • POWERTRAIN CONTROL MODULE (PCM)
DTC: P060E	**-ETC LEVEL 2 TPS PERFORMANCE:** Throttle motor is powered and no matured faults related to TP Sensors. When secondary software determines that TPS 1 and TPS 2 signals do not match for a period of time. One trip fault. ETC lamp will flash. **Possible causes:** • PCM NEEDS TO BE PROGRAMMED • POWERTRAIN CONTROL MODULE (PCM)
DTC: P060F	**-ETC LEVEL 2 ECT PERFORMANCE:** Throttle motor is powered and no matured faults related to the Engine Coolant Temp Sensor. When secondary software determines that the Coolant Temperature is implausible for a period of time. One trip fault. ETC lamp will flash. **Possible causes:** • PCM NEEDS TO BE PROGRAMMED • POWERTRAIN CONTROL MODULE (PCM)
DTC: P060F	**-ETC LEVEL 2 ECT PERFORMANCE:** With the ignition on. When secondary software determines that the Coolant Temperature is implausible for a period of time. ETC lamp will flash. **Possible causes:** • POWERTRAIN CONTROL MODULE (PCM)
DTC: P0610	**-ECU VEHICLE OPTIONS MISMATCH:** With the ignition on. The Engine Control Module (ECM) detects an internal failure. **Possible causes:** • INTERMITTENT DTC • ENGINE CONTROL MODULE (ECM)
DTC: P0610	**-ECU VEHICLE OPTIONS MISMATCH:** One time at initial ignition on with system voltage between 9. 0 and 16. 0 volts. FCM/TIPM variant data received more than once over the CAN Bus. FCM/TIPM variant data is in a valid range. Vehicle Configuration Learn Routine not finished. The vehicle option data received over the CAN Bus does not match the data stored in the EEPROM of the TCM. It takes one trip of problem identification to set the MIL. **Possible causes:** • USED CONTROLLER INSTALLED WITH WRONG CONFIGURATION • FCM/TIPM NOT PROPERLY PROGRAMED OR WAS REPLACED AND NOT PROGRAMED • NEW TCM INSTALLED • TRANSMISSION CONTROL MODULE
DTC: P0613	**-INTERNAL TRANSMISSION PROCESSOR:** After the ignition is turned to the run position and every 60 seconds thereafter. Either of the following conditions occur 3 times in less than 590 milliseconds: The watchdog line remains high after the watchdog test The transmission relay coil is detected as energized and remains on after the watchdog delay expires. **Possible causes:** • PCM - INTERNAL ERROR

DTC	Trouble Code Title, Conditions, Possible Causes
DTC: P0613	**-INTERNAL TRANSMISSION PROCESSOR:** Continuously with the ignition on. If the TCM detects an error with the controllers processor. **Possible causes:** • TRANSMISSION CONTROL MODULE
DTC: P0613	**-INTERNAL TRANSMISSION PROCESSOR:** 1) One time after the controller is reset (ignition turned to the RUN position) and every 60 seconds thereafter. The Delay Test is executed after a reset only. 2) Two seconds after an invalid test. If either of the following conditions occur three times:1) The watchdog fault line remains high after the period has elapsed for the too early - too late watchdog test. 2) The Transmission Control Relay remains on after the watchdog delay expired. **Possible causes:** • POWER OR GROUND CIRCUIT • POWERTRAIN CONTROL MODULE (PCM)
DTC: P0615	**-STARTER CONTROL CIRCUIT - OPEN:** With the engine running and battery voltage greater than 10. 4 volts. The Powertrain Control Module (PCM) detects that the actual state of the starter control does not match the intended state. **Possible causes:** • (T752) STARTER CONTROL CIRCUIT SHORTED TO VOLTAGE • (T752) STARTER CONTROL CIRCUIT SHORTED TO GROUND • (T752) STARTER CONTROL CIRCUIT OPEN OR HIGH RESISTANCE • TOTALLY INTEGRATED POWER MODULE (TIPM) • POWERTRAIN CONTROL MODULE (PCM)
DTC: P0615	**-STARTER CONTROL CIRCUIT/OPEN:** With the ignition on and the Starter Relay command off. The ECM does not detect voltage on the (T752) Engine Starter Motor Relay Control circuit for 1. 0 second. **Possible causes:** • INTERMITTENT DTC • (T752) ENGINE STARTER MOTOR RELAY CONTROL CIRCUIT SHORTED TO GROUND • (T752) ENGINE STARTER MOTOR RELAY CONTROL CIRCUIT OPEN OR HIGH RESISTANCE • (T751) FUSED IGNITION SWITCH OUTPUT (START) CIRCUIT OPEN OR HIGH RESISTANCE • STARTER RELAY • ENGINE CONTROL MODULE (ECM)
DTC: P0616	**-STARTER CONTROL CIRCUIT LOW:** With the ignition on and the Starter Relay command off. The ECM detects a short to ground on the (T752) Engine Starter Motor Relay Control circuit for 1. 0 second. **Possible causes:** • INTERMITTENT DTC • (T752) ENGINE STARTER MOTOR RELAY CONTROL CIRCUIT SHORTED TO GROUND • (T752) ENGINE STARTER MOTOR RELAY CONTROL CIRCUIT OPEN OR HIGH RESISTANCE • STARTER RELAY • ENGINE CONTROL MODULE (ECM)
DTC: P0616	**-STARTER CONTROL CIRCUIT LOW :** With the ignition on. Battery voltage greater than 10 volts. A shorted condition is detected in the Starter Control Output circuit. One Trip Fault. Three good trips to turn off the MIL. **Possible causes:** • (T752) STARTER RELAY CONTROL CIRCUIT SHORTED TO GROUND • (T752) STARTER RELAY CONTROL CIRCUIT OPEN • STARTER RELAY • POWERTRAIN CONTROL MODULE (PCM) • TOTALLY INTEGRATED POWER MODULE (TIPM)
DTC: P0617	**-STARTER CONTROL CIRCUIT HIGH:** With the ignition on and the Starter Relay command on. The ECM detects a short circuit on the (T752) Engine Starter Motor Relay Control circuit for at 1. 0 second. **Possible causes:** • INTERMITTENT DTC • (T752) ENGINE STARTER MOTOR RELAY CONTROL CIRCUIT SHORTED TO VOLTAGE • (T752) ENGINE STARTER MOTOR RELAY CONTROL CIRCUIT SHORTED TO THE (T751) FUSED IGNITION SWITCH OUTPUT (START) CIRCUIT • (T752) ENGINE STARTER MOTOR RELAY CONTROL CIRCUIT OPEN OR HIGH RESISTANCE • STARTER RELAY • ENGINE CONTROL MODULE (ECM)

DTC	Trouble Code Title, Conditions, Possible Causes
DTC: P061A	**-ETC LEVEL 2 TORQUE PERFORMANCE:** Throttle motor is powered. When secondary software determines that the customer requested output is not being achieved by the engine for a period of time. One trip fault. ETC lamp will flash. **Possible causes:** • PCM NEEDS TO BE PROGRAMMED • POWERTRAIN CONTROL MODULE (PCM)
DTC: P061A	**-ETC LEVEL 2 TORQUE PERFORMANCE:** With the ignition on. When secondary software determines that the requested output is not being achieved by the engine for a period of time. ETC lamp will flash. **Possible causes:** • POWERTRAIN CONTROL MODULE (PCM)
DTC: P061C	**-ETC LEVEL 2 RPM PERFORMANCE:** With the ignition on. When secondary software determines that the engine speed is implausible for a period of time. ETC lamp will flash. **Possible causes:** • POWERTRAIN CONTROL MODULE (PCM)
DTC: P061C	**-ETC LEVEL 2 RPM PERFORMANCE:** Throttle motor is powered and no camshaft or crankshaft electrical signal related DTCs are set. When secondary software determines that the engine speed is implausible for a period of time. One trip fault. ETC lamp will flash. **Possible causes:** • PCM NEEDS TO BE PROGRAMMED • POWERTRAIN CONTROL MODULE (PCM)
DTC: P0622	**-GENERATOR FIELD CONTROL CIRCUIT:** With the ignition on. Engine running. When the PCM tries to regulate the generator field with no result during monitoring. One Trip Fault. Three good trips to turn off the MIL. **Possible causes:** • (K20) GEN FIELD CONTROL CIRCUIT SHORTED TO VOLTAGE • (K20) GEN FIELD CONTROL CIRCUIT OPEN • (K20) GEN FIELD CONTROL CIRCUIT SHORTED TO GROUND • GENERATOR • POWERTRAIN CONTROL MODULE (PCM)
DTC: P0622	**-GENERATOR FIELD CONTROL CIRCUIT:** With the engine running and battery voltage greater than 10. 4 volts. The Powertrain Control Module (PCM) detects that the actual state of the generator field control does not match the intended state. **Possible causes:** • (K20) GEN FIELD CONTROL CIRCUIT SHORTED TO VOLTAGE • (K20) GEN FIELD CONTROL CIRCUIT SHORTED TO GROUND • (K20) GEN FIELD CONTROL CIRCUIT OPEN OR HIGH RESISTANCE • GENERATOR • POWERTRAIN CONTROL MODULE (PCM)
DTC: P0627	**-FUEL PUMP CONTROL CIRCUIT OPEN:** With the ignition on and the Fuel Pump Relay command off. The ECM does not detect voltage on the (K31) Fuel Pump Relay Control circuit for 2. 0 seconds. **Possible causes:** • (K31) FUEL PUMP RELAY CONTROL CIRCUIT SHORTED TO GROUND • (K31) FUEL PUMP RELAY CONTROL CIRCUIT OPEN OR HIGH RESISTANCE • (A15) FUSED ASD RELAY OUTPUT CIRCUIT OPEN OR HIGH RESISTANCE • FUEL PUMP RELAY • ENGINE CONTROL MODULE (ECM)
DTC: P0627	**-FUEL PUMP RELAY CIRCUIT:** With the ignition on. Battery voltage greater than 10. 4 volts. An open or shorted condition is detected in the fuel pump relay control circuit. One Trip Fault. Three good trips to turn off the MIL. **Possible causes:** • INTERNAL FUSED B+ CIRCUIT • (F202) FUSED IGNITION SWITCH CIRCUIT • (K31) FUEL PUMP RELAY CONTROL CIRCUIT OPEN • (K31) FUEL PUMP RELAY CONTROL CIRCUIT SHORTED TO GROUND • FUEL PUMP RELAY • POWERTRAIN CONTROL MODULE (PCM)

DTC	Trouble Code Title, Conditions, Possible Causes

DTC: P0627	**-FUEL PUMP CONTROL CIRCUIT/OPEN:**
	With the engine running and the battery voltage greater than 10. 4 Volts. The Powertrain Control Module (PCM) detects that the actual state of the fuel pump control does not match the intended state.
	Possible causes:
	  • (A109) FUSED B(+) CIRCUIT OPEN OR HIGH RESISTANCE
	  • (F950) RUN/START RELAY OUTPUT CIRCUIT OPEN OR HIGH RESISTANCE
	  • (K31) FUEL PUMP RELAY CONTROL CIRCUIT SHORTED TO VOLTAGE
	  • (K31) FUEL PUMP RELAY CONTROL CIRCUIT SHORTED TO GROUND
	  • (K31) FUEL PUMP RELAY CONTROL CIRCUIT OPEN OR HIGH RESISTANCE
	  • FUEL PUMP RELAY
	  • POWERTRAIN CONTROL MODULE (PCM)

DTC: P0628	**-FUEL PUMP CONTROL CIRCUIT LOW:**
	With the ignition on and the Fuel Pump Relay command off. The ECM detects a short to ground on the (K31) Fuel Pump Relay Control circuit for 2. 0 seconds.
	Possible causes:
	  • (K31) FUEL PUMP RELAY CONTROL CIRCUIT SHORTED TO GROUND
	  • (K31) FUEL PUMP RELAY CONTROL CIRCUIT OPEN OR HIGH RESISTANCE
	  • FUEL PUMP RELAY
	  • ENGINE CONTROL MODULE (ECM)

DTC: P0628	**-FUEL PUMP CONTROL CIRCUIT LOW:**
	With the engine running and the battery voltage greater than 10. 4 Volts. The Powertrain Control Module (PCM) detects that the fuel pump control circuit is low.
	Possible causes:
	  • (K31) FUEL PUMP CONTROL CIRCUIT SHORTED TO GROUND
	  • (K31) FUEL PUMP CONTROL CIRCUIT OPEN OR HIGH RESISTANCE
	  • TOTALLY INTEGRATED POWER MODULE (TIPM)
	  • POWERTRAIN CONTROL MODULE (PCM)

DTC: P0629	**-FUEL PUMP CONTROL CIRCUIT HIGH:**
	With the ignition on and the Fuel Pump Relay command on. The ECM detects a short circuit on the (K31) Fuel Pump Relay Control circuit for 2. 0 seconds.
	Possible causes:
	  • (K31) FUEL PUMP RELAY CONTROL CIRCUIT SHORTED TO VOLTAGE
	  • (K31) FUEL PUMP RELAY CONTROL CIRCUIT SHORTED TO THE (A15) FUSED ASD RELAY OUTPUT CIRCUIT
	  • (K31) FUEL PUMP RELAY CONTROL CIRCUIT OPEN OR HIGH RESISTANCE
	  • FUEL PUMP RELAY
	  • ENGINE CONTROL MODULE (ECM)

DTC: P062C	**-ETC LEVEL 2 MPH PERFORMANCE:**
	Throttle motor is powered and no vehicle speed related DTCs have matured. When secondary software determines that the vehicle speed is implausible for a period of time. One trip fault. ETC lamp will flash.
	Possible causes:
	  • PCM NEEDS TO BE PROGRAMMED
	  • POWERTRAIN CONTROL MODULE (PCM)

DTC: P062C	**-ETC LEVEL 2 MPH PERFORMANCE:** With the ignition on. When secondary software determines that the vehicle speed is implausible for a period of time. ETC lamp will flash. **Possible causes:** • POWERTRAIN CONTROL MODULE (PCM)
DTC: P062F	**-INTERNAL CONTROL MODULE EEPROM ERROR:** One time after the ignition switch is turned to the run position. The TCM has detected an error with the internal processor. **Possible causes:** • TRANSMISSION CONTROL MODULE (TCM) - INTERNAL ERROR

DTC: P0630	**-VIN NOT PROGRAMMED IN PCM:**
	At initialization. The VIN has not been programmed into the Powertrain Control Module (PCM). One Trip Fault. Three good trips to turn off the MIL.
	Possible causes:
	  • VIN NOT PROGRAMMED IN THE POWERTRAIN CONTROL MODULE (PCM)
	  • POWERTRAIN CONTROL MODULE (PCM)

DTC	Trouble Code Title, Conditions, Possible Causes
DTC: P0632	**-ODOMETER NOT PROGRAMMED IN PCM:** Ignition on. The vehicle mileage is not programmed into the Powertrain Control Module (PCM). One Trip Fault. Three good trips to turn off the MIL. **Possible causes:** • MILEAGE NOT PROGRAMMED IN THE POWERTRAIN CONTROL MODULE (PCM) • POWERTRAIN CONTROL MODULE (PCM)
DTC: P0633	**-SKIM SECRET KEY NOT STORED IN PCM:** Ignition on. The Secret Key information has not been programmed into the Powertrain Control Module (PCM). One Trip Fault. Three good trips to turn off the MIL. **Possible causes:** • SECRET KEY INFORMATION NOT PROGRAMMED IN THE POWERTRAIN CONTROL MODULE (PCM) • POWERTRAIN CONTROL MODULE (PCM)
DTC: P0633	**-SKIM SECRET KEY NOT STORED IN PCM:** Ignition on. The Secret Key information has not been programmed into the Powertrain Control Module (PCM). One Trip Fault. Three good trips to turn off the MIL. **Possible causes:** • PROGRAMMING SECRET KEY INTO THE PCM • POWERTRAIN CONTROL MODULE (PCM)
DTC: P063A	**-GENERATOR VOLTAGE SENSE CIRCUIT:** The engine running. The engine speed greater than 1157 RPM. The Powertrain Control Module (PCM) recognizes the alternator output voltage is less than the Battery feed circuit voltage. One trip failure. The Generator light will illuminate. The fault will be checked again on the next key cycle. **Possible causes:** • EXCESSIVE RESISTANCEIN THE (A804) GENERATOR SENSE CIRCUIT • (A804) GENERATOR SENSECIRCUIT SHORTED TO GROUND • GENERATOR • POWERTRAIN CONTROL MODULE (PCM)
DTC: P063A	**-GENERATOR VOLTAGE SENSE CIRCUIT:** With the engine running and battery voltage greater than 10. 4 volts. The Powertrain Control Module (PCM) detects no change when attempting to regulate the generator output. **Possible causes:** • (A804) GEN SENSE CIRCUIT SHORTED TO VOLTAGE • (A804) GEN SENSE CIRCUIT SHORTED TO GROUND • (A804) GEN SENSE CIRCUIT OPEN OR HIGH RESISTANCE • GENERATOR • POWERTRAIN CONTROL MODULE (PCM)
DTC: P0641	**-SENSOR REFERENCE VOLTAGE 1 CIRCUIT:** Ignition on with system voltage between 9. 0 and 16. 0 volts. When the monitored input voltage from primary pressure sensor and secondary pressure sensor is less than 0. 005 volts for a continuous period of 5. 0 seconds. **Possible causes:** • (T72) 5-VOLT SUPPLY CIRCUIT OPEN • (T72) 5-VOLT SUPPLY CIRCUIT SHORT TO GROUND • INTERNAL TRANSMISSION • TRANSMISSION CONTROL MODULE
DTC: P0642	**-SENSOR REFERENCE VOLTAGE 1 CIRCUIT LOW:** With the ignition on. The Powertrain Control Module (PCM) detects that the 5 volt supply circuit voltage is below the minimum acceptable value. One Trip Fault. ETC light is flashing. **Possible causes:** • 5-VOLT SUPPLY CIRCUIT SHORTED TO GROUND • ACCELERATOR PEDAL POSITION SENSOR • A/C PRESSURE TRANSDUCER • CRANKSHAFT POSITION SENSOR • THROTTLE BODY • POWERTRAIN CONTROL MODULE (PCM)

DTC	Trouble Code Title, Conditions, Possible Causes
DTC: P0642	**-SENSOR REFERENCE VOLTAGE 1 CIRCUIT LOW:** With the ignition on. The ECM detects a low voltage on the Sensor Supply #1 circuit for 0. 10 of a second. **Possible causes:** • 5-VOLT SUPPLY CIRCUIT SHORTED TO GROUND • CRANKSHAFT POSITION SENSOR • BOOST PRESSURE SENSOR • FUEL PRESSURE SENSOR • ENGINE CONTROL MODULE
DTC: P0642	**-SENSOR REFERENCE VOLTAGE 1 CIRCUIT LOW:** Ignition on. When the Powertrain Control Module (PCM) recognizes the Primary 5-Volt Supply circuit voltage is too low. One Trip Fault. ETC light is flashing. **Possible causes:** • (F855) 5-VOLT SUPPLY CIRCUIT SHORTED TO GROUND • (K854) 5-VOLT SUPPLY CIRCUIT SHORTED TO GROUND • CRANKSHAFT POSITION SENSOR • OIL PRESSURE SENSOR • THROTTLE BODY ASSEMBLY • A/C PRESSURE TRANSDUCER • ACCELERATOR PEDAL POSITION (APP) SENSOR • POWERTRAIN CONTROL MODULE (PCM)
DTC: P0643	**-PRIMARY 5-VOLT SUPPLY CIRCUIT HIGH:** Ignition on. When the Powertrain Control Module (PCM) recognizes the Primary 5-Volt Supply circuit voltage is too high. One Trip Fault. ETC light is flashing. **Possible causes:** • (F855) 5-VOLT SUPPLY SHORTED TO VOLTAGE • (K854) 5-VOLT SUPPLY CIRCUIT SHORTED TO VOLTAGE • POWERTRAIN CONTROL MODULE (PCM)
DTC: P0643	**-SENSOR REFERENCE VOLTAGE 1 CIRCUIT HIGH:** Continuously with the ignition on and no overvoltage condition exist. When the monitored sensor voltage is not within specified limits and rises above 7. 2 volts. **Possible causes:** • (T72) SENSOR SUPPLY VOLTAGE CIRCUIT SHORT TO VOLTAGE • (T72) SENSOR SUPPLY VOLTAGE CIRCUIT SHORT TO OTHER CIRCUITS • TRANSMISSION CONTROL MODULE
DTC: P0643	**-SENSOR REFERENCE VOLTAGE 1 CIRCUIT HIGH:** Ignition on. When the Powertrain Control Module (PCM) recognizes the Primary 5-Volt Supply circuit voltage is too high. One Trip Fault. ETC light is flashing. **Possible causes:** • (F855) 5-VOLT SUPPLY SHORTED TO VOLTAGE • (K852) 5-VOLT SUPPLY SHORTED TO VOLTAGE • POWERTRAIN CONTROL MODULE (PCM)
DTC: P0643	**-SENSOR REFERENCE VOLTAGE 1 TOO HIGH:** With the ignition on. The ECM detects a short to voltage on the Sensor Supply #1 circuit for 0. 10 of a second. **Possible causes:** • (K350) FUEL PRESSURE SENSOR 5 VOLT SUPPLY CIRCUIT SHORTED TO VOLTAGE • (K356) BOOST PRESSURE SENSOR 5 VOLT SUPPLY CIRCUIT SHORTED TO VOLTAGE • (K853) CRANKSHAFT POSITION SENSOR 5 VOLT SUPPLY CIRCUIT SHORTED TO VOLTAGE • ENGINE CONTROL MODULE (ECM)
DTC: P0645	**-A/C CLUTCH RELAY CIRCUIT:** With the ignition on. Battery voltage greater than 10. 0 Volts. A/C is being requested. An open or shorted condition is detected in the A/C Clutch Relay control circuit. One Trip Fault. Three good trips to turn off the MIL.
DTC: P0645	**-A/C CONTROL CIRCUIT/OPEN:** With the engine running and battery voltage greater than 10. 4 volts. The Powertrain Control Module (PCM) detects that the A/C Compressor control circuit voltage is not within an acceptable range.
DTC: P0646	**-A/C CLUTCH CONTROL CIRCUIT 2 LOW:** With the ignition on. Battery voltage greater than 10 volts. A/C Switch on. A shorted condition is detected in the A/C clutch control circuit. One Trip Fault. Three good trips to turn off the MIL.

DTC	Trouble Code Title, Conditions, Possible Causes
DTC: P0646	**-A/C CLUTCH CONTROL CIRCUIT LOW:** With the ignition on and the A/C Clutch Relay command off. The ECM detects a short to ground on the (C13) A/C Clutch Relay Control circuit for 1. 0 second.
DTC: P0647	**-A/C CLUTCH CONTROL CIRCUIT HIGH:** With the ignition on and the A/C Clutch Relay command on. The ECM detects a short circuit on the (C13) A/C Clutch Relay Control circuit for 1. 0 second.
DTC: P0647	**-A/C CLUTCH CONTROL CIRCUIT 2 HIGH:** With the ignition on. Battery voltage greater than 10 volts. A/C Switch on. A shorted high or open condition has been detected in the A/C Clutch Control output circuit by the TIPM. One Trip Fault. Three good trips to turn off the MIL.
DTC: P0652	**-SENSOR REFERENCE VOLTAGE 2 CIRCUIT LOW:** Ignition on. When the Powertrain Control Module (PCM) recognizes the Secondary 5-Volt Supply circuit voltage is too low. One Trip Fault. ETC light is flashing.
DTC: P0652	**-SENSOR REFERENCE VOLTAGE 2 CIRCUIT LOW:** With the ignition on. The Powertrain Control Module (PCM) detects that the 5 volt supply circuit voltage is below the minimum acceptable value. One Trip Fault. ETC light is flashing.
DTC: P0653	**-SENSOR REFERENCE VOLTAGE 2 CIRCUIT HIGH:** With the ignition on. The Powertrain Control Module (PCM) detects that the 5 volt supply circuit voltage is above the maximum acceptable value. One Trip Fault. ETC light is flashing.
DTC: P0653	**-SENSOR REFERENCE VOLTAGE 2 TOO HIGH:** With the ignition on. The ECM detects a short to voltage on the Sensor Supply #2 circuit for 0. 10 of a second.
DTC: P0657	**-SOLENOID SUPPLY VOLTAGE CIRCUIT:** With the ignition on. The ECM receives a CAN Bus message indicating the presence of a DTC in the TCM.
DTC: P0657	**-SOLENOID SUPPLY VOLTAGE CIRCUIT:** When the output is active and no under voltage condition exists. When the monitored supply voltage and battery voltage differ by 3. 6 volts.
DTC: P065A	**-GENERATOR PERFORMANCE:** With the engine running. The ECM detects that the Generator output is not within specifications.
DTC: P0671	**-CYLINDER 1 GLOW PLUG CIRCUIT:** With the ignition on and the Glow Plug Module Glow Plug command on. The Cylinder 1 Glow Plug circuit is open or shorted for 0. 5 seconds.
DTC: P0672	**-CYLINDER 2 GLOW PLUG CIRCUIT:** With the ignition on and the Glow Plug Module Glow Plug command on. The Cylinder 2 Glow Plug circuit is open or shorted for 0. 5 seconds.
DTC: P0673	**-CYLINDER 3 GLOW PLUG CIRCUIT:** With the ignition on and the Glow Plug Module Glow Plug command on. The Cylinder 3 Glow Plug circuit is open or shorted for 0. 5 seconds.
DTC: P0674	**-CYLINDER 4 GLOW PLUG CIRCUIT:** With the ignition on and the Glow Plug Module Glow Plug command on. The Cylinder 4 Glow Plug circuit is open or shorted for 0. 5 seconds.
DTC: P0675	**-CYLINDER 5 GLOW PLUG CIRCUIT:** With the ignition on and the Glow Plug Module Glow Plug command on. The Cylinder 5 Glow Plug circuit is open or shorted for 0. 5 seconds.
DTC: P0676	**-CYLINDER 6 GLOW PLUG CIRCUIT:** With the ignition on and the Glow Plug Module Glow Plug command on. The Cylinder 6 Glow Plug circuit is open or shorted for 0. 5 seconds.
DTC: P0685	**-AUTO SHUTDOWN RELAY CONTROL CIRCUIT:** With ignition on. Battery voltage above 10 volts. The actual ASD state is not equal to the desired ASD state. One Trip Fault. Three good trips to turn off the MIL.
DTC: P0685	**-ASD CONTROL CIRCUIT:** When the ignition is turned off, during after-run mode of operation. The Powertrain Control Module (PCM) determines that the ASD Relay has shut off before the AFTER-RUN mode of operation has been completed.

DTC	Trouble Code Title, Conditions, Possible Causes
DTC: P0688	**-AUTO SHUTDOWN RELAY SENSE CIRCUIT LOW:** With ignition key on. Battery voltage greater than 10 volts. No voltage sensed at the PCM when the ASD relay is energized. One Trip Fault. Three good trips to turn off the MIL.
DTC: P0688	**-ASD RELAY CONTROL SENSE:** With ignition key on. Battery voltage greater than 10. 0 Volts. The Powertrain Control Module (PCM) detects an open or short to ground in the (K51) ASD Relay control circuit. One Trip Fault. Three good trips to turn off the MIL.
DTC: P0689	**-AUTO SHUTDOWN RELAY SENSE CIRCUIT LOW:** Ignition on. Battery voltage between 9 and 16 volts and the ASD Relay is powered on. The ASD Output circuit voltage drops below an acceptable value at the FCM. The circuit is continuously monitored.
DTC: P068A	**-ECM RELAY OFF TOO EARLY:** When the ignition is turned off, during after-run mode of operation. The internal ECM timer determines that the ASD Relay has shut off before the AFTER-RUN mode of operation has been completed.
DTC: P068B	**-ECM RELAY OFF TOO LATE:** When the ignition is turned off, during AFTER-RUN mode of operation. The internal ECM timer determines that the ASD Relay remained on for 2. 0 seconds once AFTER-RUN mode of operation has been completed.
DTC: P0690	**-AUTO SHUTDOWN RELAY SENSE CIRCUIT HIGH:** With the ignition on and battery voltage greater than 10 volts. If the FCM detects high voltage on the ASD Relay Sense circuit for more than 3. 5 seconds.
DTC: P0691	**-COOLING FAN 1 CONTROL CIRCUIT LOW:** With the ignition on. Battery voltage greater than 10 volts. The Powertrain Control Module (PCM) is requesting the Totally Integrated Power Module (TIPM) to turn on the Cooling Fan On low speed and it is not operating. The TIPM detects an open in the Low/High Rad Fan Relay Control circuit. One Trip Fault. Three good trips to turn off the MIL.
DTC: P0692	**-COOLING FAN 1 CONTROL CIRCUIT HIGH:** With the ignition on. Battery voltage greater than 10 volts. The Powertrain Control Module (PCM) is requesting the Totally Integrated Power Module (TIPM) to turn on the Cooling Fan On low speed and it is not operating. The TIPM detects a shorted condition in the Low/High Rad Fan Relay Control circuit. One Trip Fault. Three good trips to turn off the MIL.
DTC: P0693	**-COOLING FAN 2 CONTROL CIRCUIT LOW:** With the ignition on. Battery voltage greater than 10 volts. Radiator fan off. The Powertrain Control Module (PCM) requests the Totally Integrated Power Module (TIPM) to turn on the radiator fan and it is not operating. The TIPM detects an open in the coil control circuit of both the radiator fan high relay (20) and radiator fan high/low control relay (19). One trip fault. Three good trips to turn off the Malfunction Indicator Lamp (MIL).
DTC: P0694	**-COOLING FAN 2 CONTROL CIRCUIT HIGH:** With the ignition on. Battery voltage greater than 10 volts. Engine running and above normal temperature. The Powertrain Control Module (PCM) requests the Totally Integrated Power Module (TIPM) to turn on the radiator fan and it is not operating. The TIPM detects a short to voltage in the coil control circuit of either the radiator fan high relay (20) or radiator fan high/low control relay (19). One trip fault. Three good trips to turn off the Malfunction Indicator Lamp (MIL).
DTC: P0698	**-SENSOR REFERENCE VOLTAGE 3 CIRCUIT LOW:** With the ignition on. The ECM detects low voltage on the Sensor Supply #3 circuit for 0. 10 of a second.
DTC: P0699	**-SENSOR REFERENCE VOLTAGE 3 CIRCUIT HIGH:** With the ignition on. The ECM detects a short to voltage on the Sensor Supply #3 circuit for 0. 10 seconds.
DTC: P06DA	**- DUAL STAGE OIL PUMP CIRCUIT:** With the battery voltage is between 11 and 18 Volts with the engine running. The Powertrain Control Module (PCM) detects that the actual voltage of the oil pump solenoid control circuit does not match the intended state. One Trip Fault. Three good trips to turn off the MIL.
DTC: P06DA	**-ENGINE OIL PRESSURE CONTROL CIRCUIT OPEN:** With the engine running. The Powertrain Control Module (PCM) detects and open on the (G62) Variable Oil Pump Control circuit for 1. 5 seconds.
DTC: P06DD	**-DUAL STAGE OIL PUMP STUCK LOW:** Based upon Engine oil temperature, the monitor runs when engine speed (RPM) is over a calibrated value. The cooler the engine oil, the lower is the enable engine speed (Minimum 1000rpm). To evaluate the dual stage oil pump, fully warm up the engine. To run DUAL STAGE OIL PUMP STUCK LOW (P06DD), drive vehicle with engine speed over 3500 rpm. The Powertrain Control Module (PCM) senses the oil pressure is less than a low threshold for 5 seconds. One Trip fault.

DTC	Trouble Code Title, Conditions, Possible Causes
DTC: P06DE	**-DUAL STAGE OIL PUMP STUCK HIGH:** Based upon Engine oil temperature, the monitor runs when engine speed (RPM) is over a calibrated value. The cooler the engine oil, the lower is the enable engine speed (Minimum 1000rpm). To evaluate dual stage oil pump, fully warm up the engine. To run DUAL STAGE OIL PUMP STUCK HIGH (P06DE), drive vehicle over 2500 rpm. The Powertrain Control Module (PCM) senses the oil pressure is more than a high threshold for 50 seconds . One Trip fault.
DTC: P0700	**TRANSMISSION CONTROL SYSTEM (MIL REQUEST):** With the ignition on. The ECM receives a CAN Bus message indicating the presence of a DTC in the TCM.
DTC: P0700	**TRANSMISSION CONTROL SYSTEM (MIL REQUEST):** Ignition on and battery voltage greater than 10 volts. An active DTC is stored in the TCM. One Trip Fault. Three good trips to turn off the MIL.
DTC: P0703	**-BRAKE SWITCH 2 PERFORMANCE:** Ignition on and battery voltage above 10. 4 Volts. When the Powertrain Control Module (PCM) recognizes Brake Switch voltage is not equal to the applied value at the PCM when Brake Switch is applied. This could be a normal condition. If this condition is seen repeatedly by the PCM the fault is set. Cruise will not work for the rest of the key cycle.
DTC: P0703	**-BRAKE SWITCH 2 PERFORMANCE:** Ignition on. When the PCM recognizes Brake Switch No. 2 voltage is not equal to the applied value at the PCM when Brake Switch No. 1 is applied. This could be a normal condition. If this condition is seen repeatedly by the PCM the fault is set. Cruise will not work for the rest of the key cycle.
DTC: P0706	**TRANSMISSION RANGE SENSOR RATIONALITY:** Continuously with the ignition on. The DTC will set if the controller detects an invalid PRNDL code which lasts for more than 0. 042 of a second.
DTC: P0706	**TRANSMISSION RANGE SENSOR RATIONALITY:** Continuously with the ignition on. The DTC will set if the controller detects an invalid PRNDL code which lasts for more than 0. 042 seconds.
DTC: P0706	**TRANSMISSION RANGE SENSOR RATIONALITY:** Continuously with the ignition on in the run position. The DTC will set if an invalid PRNDL code exists for more than 100 milliseconds within one second of power-up or if the PRNDL code error does not correct itself when (or before) the shift lever is moved to a different position (P, R, N, or OD), or if the PCM sees the PRNDL code rapidly (within 7 ms) jump across more than three shift lever detent positions.
DTC: P0706	**TRANSMISSION RANGE SENSOR RATIONALITY:** With the ignition on. The ECM receives a CAN Bus message indicating the presence of a DTC in the TCM.
DTC: P0707	**TRANSMISSION RANGE SENSOR CIRCUIT LOW:** Ignition on with system voltage between 9. 0 and 16. 0 volts. Vehicle speed above 10 Km/h (6 mph). No other Transmission Range Sensor (TRS) DTCs present. If a continuous input signal loss is read by the TCM from the TRS for the period of 5 seconds. It takes two consecutive one trips of problem identification to light the MIL.
DTC: P0708	**TRANSMISSION RANGE SENSOR CIRCUIT HIGH:** Ignition on with system voltage between 9. 0 and 16. 0 volts. No other Transmission Range Sensor (TRS) DTCs present. When the Transmission Control Module (TCM) receives more than one Transmission Range Sensor (TRS) signal from the TRS continuously for the period of 2. 0 seconds.
DTC: P0710	**TRANSMISSION TEMPERATURE SENSOR CIRCUIT:** Continuously with the ignition on. When the TCM detects an open circuit when in Reverse or any forward drive position the DTC will set.
DTC: P0711	**TRANSMISSION TEMPERATURE SENSOR PERFORMANCE:** Condition one : Transmission in a valid forward gear. System voltage between 9. 0 and 16. 0 Volts. Vehicle speed greater than 10 Km/h (6 mph). Accelerator Pedal Position (APP) greater than 12. 5%. Engine rpm greater than 450 rpm. Condition two: Ignition off for greater than 8 hours. Difference between the engine coolant temperature and the intake temperature is less than 3° C (37° F). No other temperature sensor or sensor ground DTCs present. Condition one: No change in the Transmission oil temperature the period of 10 minutes. Condition two: Transmission oil temperature is 40° C (104° F) different than the average temperature which consists of the combined average of the Engine Coolant temperature, Intake Temperature, Oil Temperature, and Ambient Temperature for the period of 5 seconds.

DTC	Trouble Code Title, Conditions, Possible Causes
DTC: P0711	**TRANSMISSION TEMPERATURE SENSOR PERFORMANCE:** Continuously with the ignition on and engine running. DTC will set when the transmission temperature does not reach a normal operating temperature within a given time frame. Time is variable due to ambient temperature. Approximate DTC set time is 10 to 35 minutes. The following are starting temperature to warm up times to set this **DTC:** starting temperature -40° C (-40° F) warm up time 35 minutes, starting temperature -28° C (-20° F) 25 minutes, starting temperature -6. 6° C (20° F) 20 minutes, starting temperature 15. 5 ° C (60° F) 10 minutes. When the fault is set, calculated temperature is substituted for measured temperature, however the DTC is stored only after three consecutive occurrences.
DTC: P0712	**TRANSMISSION TEMPERATURE SENSOR LOW:** Continuously with the ignition on and engine running. The DTC will set when the monitored Temperature Sensor voltage drops below 0. 078 of a volt for the period of 1. 45 seconds. When the fault is set, calculated temperature is substituted for measured temperature, however the fault code is stored only after three consecutive occurrences of the problem identification.
DTC: P0712	**TRANSMISSION TEMPERATURE SENSOR LOW:** Ignition on with battery voltage between 9. 0 and 16. 0 Volts. Vehicle speed greater than 10 Km/h (6 mph). No secondary speed sensor or sensor ground DTCs detected. Indicated temperature is greater than 180° C (356° F) for the continuous period of five seconds.
DTC: P0712	**TRANSMISSION TEMPERATURE SENSOR LOW:** Continuously with the ignition on and engine running. The DTC will set when the monitored Temperature Sensor voltage drops below 0. 078 of a volt for the period of 0. 45 of a second.
DTC: P0712	**TRANSMISSION TEMPERATURE SENSOR LOW:** Continuously with the ignition on and engine running. The DTC will set when the monitored Temperature Sensor voltage drops below 0. 078 volts for the period of 1. 45 seconds. When the fault is set, calculated temperature is substituted for measured temperature, however the fault code is stored only after three consecutive occurrences of the fault.
DTC: P0713	**TRANSMISSION TEMPERATURE SENSOR HIGH:** Continuously with the ignition on and engine running. The DTC will set when the monitored Temperature Sensor voltage rises above 4. 94 volts for the period of 1. 45 seconds. When the fault is set, calculated temperature is substituted for measured temperature, however the fault code is stored only after three consecutive occurrences of the fault.
DTC: P0713	**TRANSMISSION TEMPERATURE SENSOR HIGH:** Ignition on engine running with battery voltage between 9. 0 and 16. 0 Volts. Vehicle speed greater than 10 Km/h (6 mph). No secondary speed sensor or sensor ground DTCs present. Indicated temperature drops below -40° C (-40° F) for the continuous period of 5. 0 seconds.
DTC: P0714	**TRANSMISSION TEMPERATURE SENSOR INTERMITTENT:** Continuously with the ignition on and the Transmission Temperature below 170 °C (338 °F). When the TCM detects the Temperature sensor input changes more than 10 °C (18 °F) between each 20 msec sensor read.
DTC: P0714	**TRANSMISSION TEMPERATURE SENSOR INTERMITTENT:** Continuously with the ignition on and engine running. The DTC will set when the monitored Temperature Sensor voltage fluctuates or changes abruptly within a predetermined period of time.
DTC: P0715	**-INPUT SPEED SENSOR 1 CIRCUIT:** The transmission gear ratio is monitored continuously while the transmission is in gear. If there is an excessive change in the Input rpm in any valid gear (R, 1st, 2nd, 3rd, or 4th).
DTC: P0716	**-INPUT SPEED SENSOR 1 CIRCUIT PERFORMANCE:** The transmission gear ratio is monitored continuously while the transmission is in gear. If there is an excessive change in the Input rpm in any valid gear (R, 1st, 2nd, 3rd, or 4th).
DTC: P0716	**-INPUT SPEED SENSOR 1 CIRCUIT PERFORMANCE:** Ignition on, engine running with the transmission in a valid forward gear. System voltage between 9. 0 and 16. 0 volts Vehicle speed greater than 10 Km/h (6 mph). Accelerator Pedal Position (APP) greater than 12. 5%. Engine rpm greater than 450 rpm with TCC lock-up enabled. No DTCs from the following: TCC Solenoid Lock-up solenoid Step motor Input or Output Speed Sensor No Signal Transmission Range Sensor (TRS)Sensor Ground CAN Engine speed minus the primary speed is greater than 1000 rpm. Secondary speed multiplied by the estimated ratio, minus the Primary speed is greater than 1000 rpm. Engine speed minus the Secondary speed, multiplied by the estimated ratio is less than 1000 rpm.
DTC: P0717	**-INPUT SPEED SENSOR 1 CIRCUIT NO SIGNAL:** Engine speed greater than 450 RPM with none of the following DTCs present: engine speed, TCM under voltage, output speed sensor, and/or rear wheel speed DTCs. Also required are all wheel speeds above 250 RPM and no wheel slip detected (signal from the ABS system). If the Input Speed Sensor 1 (N2) signal is equal to 0 RPM.

DTC	Trouble Code Title, Conditions, Possible Causes
DTC: P0717	**-INPUT SPEED SENSOR 1 CIRCUIT NO SIGNAL:** Ignition on, engine running with system voltage between 9. 0 and 16. 0 volts. No detected Primary Speed Sensor and/or Sensor ground DTCs. Condition one: Input speed rpm is less than 150 rpm with a Output speed rpm greater than 1000 rpm for the period of 5 seconds. Condition two: Input speed rpm last value is greater than 1000 rpm where as the Input speed rpm current value is zero rpm for the period of 500 msec. Condition three: Both the Input and Output Speed sensors are less than 150 rpm with a actual vehicle speed greater than 10 Km/h. **(NOTE: this is an indication of either the power supply to both sensors is open or the C106 connector is disconnected.)**
DTC: P0720	**-OUTPUT SPEED SENSOR CIRCUIT:** The transmission gear ratio is monitored continuously while the transmission is in gear. If there is an excessive change in output RPM in any gear. This DTC can take up to five minutes of problem identification before illuminating the MIL.
DTC: P0721	**-OUTPUT SPEED SENSOR CIRCUIT PERFORMANCE:** The transmission gear ratio is monitored continuously while the transmission is in gear. If there is an excessive change in output RPM in any gear. This DTC can take up to five minutes of problem identification before illuminating the MIL.
DTC: P0721	**-OUTPUT SPEED SENSOR CIRCUIT PERFORMANCE:** The transmission gear ratio is monitored continuously while the transmission is in gear. If there is an excessive change in the Output rpm in any gear.
DTC: P0721	**-OUTPUT SPEED SENSOR CIRCUIT PERFORMANCE:** Ignition on, engine running with the transmission in a valid forward gear. System voltage between 9. 0 and 16+. 0 volts. Vehicle speed greater than 10 Km/h (6 mph). Accelerator Pedal Position (APP) greater than 12. 5%. Engine rpm greater than 450 rpm with TCC lock-up enabled. No active DTCs from the following: Torque Convertor Clutch (TCC)Lock-up Solenoid CAN Bus Step Motor Input or Output Speed Sensor No Signal Transmission Range Sensor (TRS)Sensor Ground
DTC: P0721	**-OUTPUT SPEED SENSOR CIRCUIT PERFORMANCE:** Ignition on, engine running with the transmission in a valid forward gear. System voltage between 9. 0 and 16. 0 volts Vehicle speed greater than 10 Km/h (6 mph). Accelerator Pedal Position (APP) greater than 12. 5%. Engine rpm greater than 450 rpm with TCC lock-up enabled. No DTCs from the following: TCC Solenoid Lock-up solenoid Step motor Input or Output Speed Sensor No Signal Transmission Range Sensor (TRS)Sensor Ground CAN Engine speed minus the primary speed is greater than 1000 rpm. Secondary speed multiplied by the estimated ratio, minus the Primary speed is greater than 1000 rpm. Engine speed minus the Secondary speed, multiplied by the estimated ratio is less than 1000 rpm.
DTC: P0722	**-OUTPUT SPEED SENSOR CIRCUIT NO SIGNAL:** Ignition on, engine running with system voltage between 9. 0 and 16. 0 volts. No detected Primary Speed Sensor DTCs. Condition one: Output speed rpm is less than 150 rpm with a Input speed rpm greater than 1000 rpm for the period of 5 seconds. Condition two: Vehicle speed is greater than 20 Km/h (12. 5 mph) calculated by the last secondary speed with the current Output Speed value equals to 0 rpm for the period of 500 msec. Condition three: Both the Input and Output Speed sensors are less than 150 rpm with a actual vehicle speed greater than 10 Km/h. **(NOTE: this is an indication of either the power supply to both sensors is open or the C106 connector is disconnected.)**
DTC: P0725	**-ENGINE SPEED SENSOR CIRCUIT:** Whenever the engine is running. The Engine RPM is less than 390 or greater than 8000 for more than 2 seconds while the engine is running.
DTC: P0726	**-ENGINE SPEED INPUT CIRCUIT RANGE/PERFORMANCE:** Continuously every 7 msec with the ignition on and engine running. This DTC will set when the calculated engine speed is less than 390 rpm with the engine running, or greater than 8000 rpm, for the period of 2. 0 seconds. The PCM will place the Transmission in Limp-in when this DTC is set. **NOTE: This is not a Transmission Input Speed Sensor DTC.**
DTC: P0726	**-ENGINE SPEED INPUT CIRCUIT RANGE/PERFORMANCE:** Whenever the engine is running. The Engine RPM is less than 390 or greater than 8000 for more than two seconds while the engine is running.
DTC: P0729	**-GEAR RATIO ERROR IN 6TH:** The Transmission gear ratio is monitored continuously while the transmission is in gear. If the ratio of the Input RPM to the Output RPM does not match the current gear ratio when compared to the known gear ratio.
DTC: P0730	**-INCORRECT GEAR RATIO:** If the difference between the transmission estimated pulley speed and the measured primary pulley speed is greater than 1000 rpm (belt slipping)for the continuous period of 5. 0 seconds.
DTC: P0730	**-INCORRECT GEAR RATIO:** With the ignition on. The ECM receives a CAN Bus message indicating the presence of a DTC in the TCM.

DTC	Trouble Code Title, Conditions, Possible Causes
DTC: P0731	**-GEAR RATIO ERROR IN 1ST:** The Transmission gear ratio is monitored continuously while the transmission is in gear. If the ratio of the Input RPM to the Output RPM does not match the current gear ratio when compared to the known gear ratio.
DTC: P0731	**-GEAR RATIO ERROR IN 1ST:** Continuously with the ignition on, engine running, and after the transmission has achieved the proper gear ratio. If the ratio of the Input rpm to the Output rpm does not match the current gear ratio. This DTC can take up to five minutes of problem identification before illuminating the MIL
DTC: P0732	**-GEAR RATIO ERROR IN 2ND:** Continuously with the ignition on, engine running, and after the transmission has achieved the proper gear ratio. If the ratio of the Input rpm to the Output rpm does not match the current gear ratio. This DTC can take up to five minutes of problem identification before illuminating the MIL
DTC: P0732	**-GEAR RATIO ERROR IN 2ND:** The Transmission gear ratio is monitored continuously while the transmission is in gear. If the ratio of the Input RPM to the Output RPM does not match the current gear ratio when compared to the known gear ratio.
DTC: P0733	**-GEAR RATIO ERROR IN 3RD:** The Transmission gear ratio is monitored continuously while the transmission is in gear. If the ratio of the Input RPM to the Output RPM does not match the current gear ratio when compared to the known gear ratio.
DTC: P0733	**-GEAR RATIO ERROR IN 3RD:** Continuously with the ignition on, engine running, and after the transmission has achieved the proper gear ratio. If the ratio of the Input rpm to the Output rpm does not match the current gear ratio. This DTC can take up to five minutes of problem identification before illuminating the MIL
DTC: P0734	**-GEAR RATIO ERROR IN 4TH:** Continuously with the ignition on, engine running, and after the transmission has achieved the proper gear ratio. If the ratio of the Input rpm to the Output rpm does not match the current gear ratio. This DTC can take up to five minutes of problem identification before illuminating the MIL.
DTC: P0734	**-GEAR RATIO ERROR IN 4TH:** The Transmission gear ratio is monitored continuously while the transmission is in gear. If the ratio of the Input RPM to the Output RPM does not match the current gear ratio when compared to the known gear ratio.
DTC: P0735	**-GEAR RATIO ERROR IN 5TH:** The Transmission gear ratio is monitored continuously while the transmission is in gear. If the ratio of the Input RPM to the Output RPM does not match the current gear ratio when compared to the known gear ratio.
DTC: P0735	**-GEAR RATIO ERROR IN 5TH:** Continuously with the ignition on, engine running, and after the transmission has achieved the proper gear ratio. If the ratio of the Input rpm to the Output rpm does not match the current gear ratio. This DTC can take up to five minutes of problem identification before illuminating the MIL.
DTC: P0736	**-GEAR RATIO ERROR IN REVERSE:** The Transmission gear ratio is monitored continuously while the transmission is in gear. If the ratio of the Input RPM to the Output RPM does not match the current gear ratio when compared to the known gear ratio.
DTC: P0736	**-GEAR RATIO ERROR IN REVERSE:** Continuously with the ignition on, engine running, and after the transmission has achieved the proper gear ratio. If the ratio of the Input rpm to the Output rpm does not match the current gear ratio. This DTC can take up to five minutes of problem identification before illuminating the MIL
DTC: P0740	**TCC OUT OF RANGE:** The Torque Converter Clutch (TCC) is in FEMCC or PEMCC, Transmission temperature is hot, Engine temperature is greater than 38° C or 100° F, Transmission Input Speed greater than engine speed, TPS less than 30°, and brake not applied. The TCC is modulated by controlling the duty cycle of the L/R Solenoid until the difference between the Engine RPM and the Transmission Input Speed RPM or duty cycle is within a desired range. The DTC is set after the period of 10 seconds and 3 occurrences of either: FEMCC - with slip greater than 100 RPM or PEMCC - duty cycle greater than 85%.
DTC: P0740	**TCC OUT OF RANGE:** During Electronically Modulated Converter Clutch (EMCC) Operation. Transmission must be in EMCC, with input speed greater than 1750 rpm. L/RTCC Solenoid achieves the maximum duty cycle and cannot pull engine speed within 60 rpm of input speed. Also when the transmission is in FEMCC and the engine slips TCC more than 100 rpm for 10 seconds. This DTC can take up to five minutes of problem identification before illuminating the MIL.

DTC	Trouble Code Title, Conditions, Possible Causes
DTC: P0741	**TORQUE CONVERTER CLUTCH CIRCUIT PERFORMANCE:** Ignition on, engine running with the transmission in a valid forward gear. System voltage between 9. 0 and 16. 0 Volts. Vehicle speed greater than 10 Km/h (6 mph). Accelerator Pedal Position (APP) greater than 12. 5%. Engine rpm greater than 450 rpm with TCC lock-up enabled. TCC Lock up command is ON (True). No active DTCs from the following: Step motor, Line Pressure Solenoid Secondary Solenoid Input or Output Speed Sensor Primary or Secondary Pressure Sensor CAN Bustle DTC is detected If the Torque Convertor Clutch (TCC) slip monitored by the Transmission Control Module (TCM) is greater than a predetermined value for the period of 30 seconds. **NOTE: This is not an electrical fault but a mechanical malfunction such as a control valve sticking in its bore or a TCC Solenoid hydraulic malfunction. It takes two consecutive problem identification trips for the DTC to mature and illuminate the MIL.**
DTC: P0741	**TORQUE CONVERTER CLUTCH CIRCUIT PERFORMANCE:** Ignition on, TCM not in initialization phase, no input speed sensor 1 or 2 (N2-N3) DTCs, no CAN bus or ECM DTCs, no CAN engine speed signal or engine torque signal not implausible DTCs, engine speed greater than 450 rpm, no shift in progress, gear 1, 2, 3, 4 or 5 engaged, and the TCM torque converter status is SLIP While in Slip Mode operation, the TCM detects TCC slippage greater than a calibrated value.
DTC: P0742	**TORQUE CONVERTER CLUTCH STUCK ON:** Ignition on, TCM not in initialization phase, No input speed sensor 1 or 2 (N2-N3) DTCs, No CAN bus or ECM DTCs, No CAN engine speed signal or engine torque signal not implausible DTCs, Engine speed greater than 450 rpm, No shift in progress, Gear 1, 2, 3, 4 or 5 engaged, and the TCM torque converter status is OPEN Engine RPM (Turbine Speed) is greater than 30 RPM when engine torque less than 100 Nm (74. 0 ft. lbs.) for period of 1. 0 second.
DTC: P0743	**TCC SOLENOID CIRCUIT:** Continuously with the ignition on, engine running, with the transmission in gear, the TCC Solenoid is inactive, or when the TCC Solenoid is active and controlled above 25% duty cycle, with the Solenoid Supply voltage active. If the TCM detects on the TCC Solenoid control circuit a open, short to ground, short to voltage, internal short in the TCC Solenoid or open in the TCC Solenoid.
DTC: P0743	**TCC SOLENOID CIRCUIT:** With the ignition on. The ECM receives a CAN Bus message indicating the presence of a DTC in the TCM.
DTC: P0746	**-LINE PRESSURE SOLENOID PERFORMANCE:** Ignition on, engine running with the transmission in a valid forward gear. Vehicle speed greater than 10 Km/h (6 mph). Accelerator Pedal Position (APP) greater than 12. 5%. Engine rpm greater than 450 rpm. Primary Pulley Speed greater than 500 rpm. No active DTCs from the following: Line Pressure Solenoid Temperature Sensor Primary or Secondary Pressure Sensor Transmission Range Sensor Step Motor Secondary Solenoid electrical Input and Output Speed Sensor Torque Convertor Clutch CAN Bus Over Temperature Condition Condition one: Gear ratio is greater than 2. 7 - 2 for the period of 0. 2 seconds (first trip). Condition two: Gear ratio is greater than 3. 5 - 1 for the period of 0. 1 seconds (second trip).
DTC: P0748	**-MODULATOR PRESSURE SOLENOID CIRCUIT:** With the ignition on. The ECM receives a CAN Bus message indicating the presence of a DTC in the TCM.
DTC: P0748	**-MODULATOR PRESSURE SOLENOID CIRCUIT:** Continuously with the ignition on, engine running, the Modulating Pressure Control Solenoid Valve is either off, or active with 25-75% duty cycle, with no Solenoid Supply Voltage DTCs present. When the Modulating Pressure Control Solenoid Valve is turned on and the Solenoid driver detects an error (the measured current is too different then the target current) or when the solenoid is off and a short to ground is detected.
DTC: P0750	**-LR SOLENOID CIRCUIT:** Initially at power-up, then every 10 seconds thereafter. The solenoid circuits will also be tested immediately after a gear ratio or pressure switch error is detected. After three consecutive solenoid continuity test failures, or one failure if test is run in response to a gear ratio or pressure switch error. This DTC is strictly an electrical fault and cannot be caused by any internal transmission failure other than an open in the Transmission Solenoid/TRS Assembly. If the Transmission Solenoid/TRS Assembly is in need of replacement — do not replace the Valve Body.
DTC: P0750	**-LR SOLENOID CIRCUIT:** Initially at ignition on, then every 10 seconds thereafter. The solenoids will also be tested immediately after a gear ratio error or pressure switch error is detected. Three consecutive solenoid continuity test failures, or one failure if test is run in response to a gear ratio or pressure switch error.
DTC: P0752	**-1-2/4-5 SOLENOID:** When both the 1-2/4-5 Solenoid and the Solenoid Supply voltage is active. When 1-2/4-5 Solenoid is turned on and the TCM detects any of the following in the 1-2/4-5 Solenoid or circuit: open, short to ground, short to voltage, or the solenoid driver in the TCM.
DTC: P0753	**-1/2 4/5 SOLENOID CIRCUIT:** With the ignition on. The ECM receives a CAN Bus message indicating the presence of a DTC in the TCM.
DTC: P0753	**-1-2/4-5 SOLENOID CIRCUIT:** When both the 1-2/4-5 Solenoid and the Solenoid Supply voltage is active. When 1-2/4-5 Solenoid is turned on and the TCM detects any of the following in the 1-2/4-5 Solenoid or circuit: open, short to ground, short to voltage, or the solenoid driver in the TCM.

DTC	Trouble Code Title, Conditions, Possible Causes
DTC: P0755	**-2/4 SOLENOID CIRCUIT:** Initially at ignition on, then every 10 seconds thereafter. The solenoids will also be tested immediately after a gear ratio error or pressure switch error is detected. Three consecutive solenoid continuity test failures, or one failure if test is run in response to a gear ratio or pressure switch error.
DTC: P0755-2C	**- SOLENOID CIRCUIT:** Initially at power-up, then every 10 seconds thereafter. The solenoid circuits will also be tested immediately after a gear ratio or pressure switch error is detected. After three consecutive solenoid continuity test failures, or one failure if test is run in response to a gear ratio or pressure switch error. This DTC is strictly an electrical fault and cannot be caused by any internal transmission failure other than an open in the Transmission Solenoid/TRS Assembly. If the Transmission Solenoid/TRS Assembly is in need of replacement — do not replace the Valve Body.
DTC: P0757	**-2-3 SOLENOID:** When both the 2-3 Solenoid and the Solenoid Supply voltage is active. When 2-3 Solenoid is turned on and the TCM detects any of the following in the 2-3 Solenoid or circuit: open, short to ground, short to voltage, or the solenoid driver in the TCM.
DTC: P0758	**-2/3 SOLENOID CIRCUIT:** With the ignition on. The ECM receives a CAN Bus message indicating the presence of a DTC in the TCM.
DTC: P0758	**-2-3 SOLENOID CIRCUIT:** When both the 2-3 Solenoid and the Solenoid Supply voltage is active. When 2-3 Solenoid is turned on and the TCM detects any of the following in the 2-3 Solenoid or circuit: open, short to ground, short to voltage, or the solenoid driver in the TCM.
DTC: P075A	**-LC SOLENOID CIRCUIT:** Initially at ignition on, then every 10 seconds thereafter. The solenoids will also be tested immediately after a gear ratio error or pressure switch error is detected. Three consecutive solenoid continuity test failures, or one failure if test is run in response to a gear ratio or pressure switch error.
DTC: P0760	**-OD SOLENOID CIRCUIT:** Initially at power-up, then every 10 seconds thereafter. The solenoid circuits will also be tested immediately after a gear ratio or pressure switch error is detected. After three consecutive solenoid continuity test failures, or one failure if test is run in response to a gear ratio or pressure switch error. This DTC is strictly an electrical fault and cannot be caused by any internal transmission failure other than an open in the Transmission Solenoid/TRS Assembly. If the Transmission Solenoid/TRS Assembly is in need of replacement — do not replace the Valve Body.
DTC: P0760	**-OD SOLENOID CIRCUIT:** Initially at ignition on, then every 10 seconds thereafter. The solenoids will also be tested immediately after a gear ratio error or pressure switch error is detected. Three consecutive solenoid continuity test failures, or one failure if test is run in response to a gear ratio or pressure switch error.
DTC: P0762	**-3-4 SOLENOID:** When both the 3-4 Solenoid and the Solenoid Supply voltage is active. When 3-4 Solenoid is turned on and the TCM detects any of the following in the 3-4 Solenoid or circuit: open, short to ground, short to voltage, or the solenoid driver in the TCM.
DTC: P0763	**-3/4 SOLENOID CIRCUIT:** With the ignition on. The ECM receives a CAN Bus message indicating the presence of a DTC in the TCM.
DTC: P0763	**-3-4 SOLENOID CIRCUIT:** When both the 3-4 Solenoid and the Solenoid Supply voltage is active. When 3-4 Solenoid is turned on and the TCM detects any of the following in the 3-4 Solenoid or circuit: open, short to ground, short to voltage, or the solenoid driver in the TCM.
DTC: P0765	**-UD SOLENOID CIRCUIT:** Initially at ignition on, then every 10 seconds thereafter. The solenoids will also be tested immediately after a gear ratio error or pressure switch error is detected. Three consecutive solenoid continuity test failures, or one failure if test is run in response to a gear ratio or pressure switch error.
DTC: P0765	**-UD SOLENOID CIRCUIT:** Initially at power-up, then every 10 seconds thereafter. The solenoid circuits will also be tested immediately after a gear ratio or pressure switch error is detected. After three consecutive solenoid continuity test failures, or one failure if test is run in response to a gear ratio or pressure switch error. This DTC is strictly an electrical fault and cannot be caused by any internal transmission failure other than an open in the Transmission Solenoid/TRS Assembly. If the Transmission Solenoid/TRS Assembly is in need of replacement — do not replace the Valve Body.
DTC: P076A-DC	**- SOLENOID CIRCUIT:** Initially at ignition on, then every 10 seconds thereafter. The solenoids will also be tested immediately after a gear ratio error or pressure switch error is detected. Three consecutive solenoid continuity test failures, or one failure if test is run in response to a gear ratio or pressure switch error.

DTC	Trouble Code Title, Conditions, Possible Causes
DTC: P0770-4C	**- SOLENOID CIRCUIT:** Initially at power-up, then every 10 seconds thereafter. The solenoid circuits will also be tested immediately after a gear ratio or pressure switch error is detected. After three consecutive solenoid continuity test failures, or one failure if test is run in response to a gear ratio or pressure switch error. This DTC is strictly an electrical fault and cannot be caused by any internal transmission failure other than an open in the Transmission Solenoid/TRS Assembly. If the Transmission Solenoid/TRS Assembly is in need of replacement — do not replace the Valve Body.
DTC: P0776	**-SECONDARY PRESSURE SOLENOID STUCK OFF (HIGH PRESSURE):** Ignition on, engine running with the transmission in a valid forward gear. Vehicle speed greater than 10 Km/h (6 mph). Accelerator Pedal Position (APP) greater than 12. 5%. Engine rpm greater than 450 rpm with a transmission fluid temperature greater than 20° C (68° F)No active DTCs from the following: Line Pressure Solenoid Lock-up Solenoid Primary or Secondary Pressure Sensor Transmission Range Sensor Step Motor Secondary Solenoid electrical Input and Output Speed Sensor Torque Convertor Clutch CAN Bus Over Temperature Condition When the difference between actual secondary pressure compared to the target (desired) secondary pressure is greater than 1200 Kpa (174 psi) for the period of 30 seconds. It takes two consecutive problem identified trips to set the DTC.
DTC: P0777	**-SECONDARY PRESSURE SOLENOID STUCK ON (LOW PRESSURE):** Ignition on, engine running with the transmission not in neutral or park. Transmission fluid temperature greater than -20° C (-4° F). Brake Switch in the OFF mode. Change rate of vehicle speed greater than 24 Km/h (15 mph). Change rate of accelerator pedal position less than ± 6. 25%. Engine rpm greater than 450 rpm with a transmission fluid temperature greater than 20° C (68° F). No active DTCs from the following: Line Pressure Solenoid Primary or Secondary Pressure Sensor Step Motor Secondary Solenoid electrical Input and Output Speed Sensor CAN Bus When the secondary pressure goes down gradually below a predetermined value during a drive cycle. The DTC could be due to the failure of the secondary pressure control system, secondary pressure solenoid performance or line pressure solenoid. There are two possible setting conditions to set this DTC.
DTC: P0778	**-SHIFT PRESSURE SOLENOID CIRCUIT:** With the ignition on. The ECM receives a CAN Bus message indicating the presence of a DTC in the TCM.
DTC: P0778	**-SHIFT PRESSURE SOLENOID CIRCUIT:** When the Shift Pressure Solenoid is: off, or active with 25-75% duty cycle, and the Solenoid Supply voltage is active. When Shift Pressure Solenoid is turned on and the TCM detects any of the following in the Shift Pressure Solenoid or circuit: open, short to ground, short to voltage, or the solenoid driver in the TCM.
DTC: P0791	**TRANSFER SPEED SENSOR CIRCUIT:** The transmission gear ratio is monitored continuously while the transmission is in gear. If there is an excessive change in the Transfer RPM in any gear.
DTC: P0792	**-COMPOUNDER SPEED RATIO ERROR:** The transmission gear ratio is monitored continuously while the transmission is in gear. If there is an excessive change in the Output RPM in any gear.
DTC: P0801	**-REVERSE GEAR LOCKOUT CIRCUIT OPEN OR SHORTED:** Engine running. Battery voltage greater than 10 volts. Reverse Lockout Solenoid Control circuit is not in the expected state when requested to operate by the Powertrain Control Module (PCM). One trip fault.
DTC: P0803	**-SKIP SHIFT CONTROL SOLENOID CIRCUIT:** Engine running. Battery voltage greater than 10 volts. The Skip Shift Solenoid Control Circuit is not in the expected state when requested to operate by the Powertrain Control Module (PCM). One Trip Fault.
DTC: P080B	**-SKIP SHIFT RATIONALITY:** Engine RPM greater than 1300. Transmission in 1st gear. Skip shift requested between 15 - 25 mph. The Skip Shift solenoid control circuit is not in the expected state when requested to operate by the PCM.
DTC: P0815-2A	**-UPSHIFT SWITCH - STUCK:** With the ignition on. The Upshift Switch has been pressed for greater than 20 seconds.
DTC: P0826	**-UP/DOWN SHIFT SWITCH CIRCUIT:** Ignition on with a system voltage between 9. 0 and 16 volts. Upshift and Downshift requested simultaneously while in the Drive position or the Upshift and/or Downshift request during while not in the Drive position for the period of 1. 0 second.
DTC: P0830	**-CLUTCH UPSTOP SWITCH STUCK ON:** Engine running. Battery voltage greater than 10. 4 Volts. The Powertrain Control Module (PCM) receives a signal from the Clutch Interlock Switch indicating that the clutch pedal is depressed while the vehicle is driven.
DTC: P0835	**-CLUTCH UPSTOP SWITCH STUCK OFF:** Engine running. Battery voltage greater than 10. 4 Volts. The Powertrain Control Module (PCM) receives a signal from the Clutch Interlock Switch indicating that the clutch pedal is not depressed when the vehicle is started.

DTC	Trouble Code Title, Conditions, Possible Causes
DTC: P083A	**-LC HYDRAULIC PRESSURE TEST:** In any forward gear with engine speed above 1000 rpm, shortly after a shift and every minute thereafter. After a shift into a forward gear, with engine speed greater than 1000 rpm, the Powertrain Control Module (PCM) momentarily turns on element pressure to the clutch circuits that don't have pressure to verify that the correct pressure switch closes. If the pressure switch does not close 2 times the DTC will set.
DTC: P083B	**-LC PRESSURE SWITCH RATIONALITY:** Whenever the engine is running. The DTC is set if one of the pressure switches are open or closed at the wrong time in a given gear. If the problem is identified for 3 successive key starts, the transmission will go into Limp-in mode and the MIL will turn on after 10 seconds of vehicle operation.
DTC: P0841	**-LR PRESSURE SWITCH RATIONALITY:** Whenever the engine is running. The DTC is set if one of the pressure switches are open or closed at the wrong time in a given gear. If the problem is identified for 3 successive key starts, the transmission will go into Limp-in mode and the MIL will turn on after 10 seconds of vehicle operation.
DTC: P0841	**-LR PRESSURE SWITCH RATIONALITY:** Continuously with the ignition on and engine running. The DTC will set if the L/R Pressure Switch reads open or closed at the wrong time in a given gear.
DTC: P0842	**-PRIMARY OIL PRESSURE SENSOR CIRCUIT LOW:** Ignition on, system voltage between 9. 0 and 16. 0 Volts. Transmission temperature greater than -20° C (-4° F)No active DTCs from the following: Primary Oil Pressure Sensor High Sensor ground When the monitored voltage drops below 0. 09 Volts for the period of five seconds.
DTC: P0843	**-PRIMARY OIL PRESSURE SENSOR CIRCUIT HIGH:** Ignition on, system voltage between 9. 0 and 16. 0 volts. Transmission temperature greater than -20° C (-4° F)No active DTCs from the following: Primary Oil Pressure Sensor Low Sensor ground When the monitored voltage rises above 4. 7 volts for the period of five seconds.
DTC: P0845	**-2/4 HYDRAULIC PRESSURE TEST:** In any forward gear with engine speed above 1000 rpm, shortly after a shift and every minute thereafter. After a shift into a forward gear, with engine speed greater than 1000 rpm, the PCM momentarily turns on element pressure to the clutch circuits that don't have pressure to verify that the correct pressure switch closes. If the pressure switch does not close 2 times the DTC sets
DTC: P0845-2C	**- HYDRAULIC PRESSURE TEST:** In any forward gear with engine speed above 1000 RPM shortly after a shift and every minute thereafter. After a shift into a forward gear, with engine speed above 1000 RPM, the PCM momentarily turns on element pressure to the Clutch circuits that don't have pressure to identify the correct Pressure Switch closes. If the Pressure Switch does not close two times, the DTC sets.
DTC: P0846	**-2/4 PRESSURE SWITCH RATIONALITY:** Whenever the engine is running. The DTC is set if one of the pressure switches are open or closed at the wrong time in a given gear. If the problem is identified for 3 successive key starts, the transmission will go into Limp-in mode and the MIL will turn on after 10 seconds of vehicle operation.
DTC: P0846-2C	**- PRESSURE SWITCH RATIONALITY:** Continuously with the ignition on, engine running, with the transmission in gear. The DTC is set if the 2C Pressure Switch reads open or closed at the wrong time in a given gear.
DTC: P0847	**-SECONDARY OIL PRESSURE SENSOR CIRCUIT LOW:** Ignition on, system voltage between 9. 0 and 16. 0 Volts. Transmission temperature greater than -20° C (-4° F)No active DTCs from the following: Primary Oil Pressure Sensor High Sensor ground When the monitored voltage drops below 0. 09 Volts for the period of five seconds.
DTC: P0848	**-SECONDARY OIL PRESSURE SENSOR CIRCUIT HIGH:** Ignition on, system voltage between 9. 0 and 16. 0 Volts. Transmission temperature greater than -20° C (-4° F). No active DTCs from the following: Secondary Oil Pressure Sensor Low Sensor ground When the monitored voltage rises above 4. 7 Volts for the period of five seconds.
DTC: P084A-DC	**- HYDRAULIC PRESSURE TEST:** In any forward gear with engine speed above 1000 rpm, shortly after a shift and every minute thereafter. After a shift into a forward gear, with engine speed greater than 1000 rpm, the PCM momentarily turns on element pressure to the clutch circuits that don't have pressure to verify that the correct pressure switch closes. If the pressure switch does not close 2 times the DTC sets
DTC: P084B-DC	**- PRESSURE SWITCH RATIONALITY:** Whenever the engine is running. The DTC is set if one of the pressure switches are open or closed at the wrong time in a given gear. If the problem is identified for 3 successive key starts, the transmission will go into Limp-in mode and the MIL will turn on after 10 seconds of vehicle operation.

DTC	Trouble Code Title, Conditions, Possible Causes
DTC: P0850	**-PARK/NEUTRAL SWITCH PERFORMANCE:** Continuously with the transmission in Park, Neutral, or Drive and NOT in Limp-in mode. This code will set if the PCM detects an incorrect Park/Neutral switch state for a given mode of vehicle operation. Two trip fault. Three good trips to turn off the MIL.
DTC: P0850	**-PARK/NEUTRAL SWITCH PERFORMANCE:** Continuously with the transmission in Park, Neutral, or Drive and NOT in Limp-in mode. This code will set if the PCM detects an incorrect Park/Neutral switch state for a given mode of vehicle operation. One trip fault. Three good trips to turn off the MIL.
DTC: P0868	**-LINE PRESSURE LOW:** Continuously while driving in a forward gear. The Powertrain Control Module (PCM) continuously monitors Actual Line Pressure and compares it to Desired Line Pressure. If the Actual Line Pressure is more than 69 kPa (5 psi) below Desired Line Pressure while the PCS duty cycle is at or near its minimum value, this DTC will set.
DTC: P0868	**-LINE PRESSURE LOW:** Continuously while driving in a forward gear. The PCM continuously monitors Actual Line Pressure and compares it to Desired Line Pressure. If the Actual Line Pressure is more than 10 psi below Desired Line Pressure, this DTC will set.
DTC: P0869	**-LINE PRESSURE HIGH:** Continuously while driving in a forward gear. The Powertrain Control Module (PCM) continuously monitors Actual Line Pressure. If the Actual Line Pressure reading is greater than the highest Desired Line Pressure ever used in the current gear, while the Pressure Control Solenoid duty cycle is at or near its maximum value (which should result in minimum line pressure), the DTC will set.
DTC: P0869	**-LINE PRESSURE HIGH:** Continuously while driving in a forward gear. The Powertrain Control Module (PCM) continuously monitors Actual Line Pressure. If the Actual Line Pressure reading is greater than 827 kPa (120 psi), while the Pressure Control Solenoid duty cycle is at or near its maximum value (which should result in minimum line pressure) for 3. 5 seconds continuously, the DTC will set.
DTC: P0870	**-OD HYDRAULIC PRESSURE TEST:** In any forward gear with engine speed above 1000 rpm, shortly after a shift and every minute thereafter. After a shift into a forward gear, with engine speed greater than 1000 rpm, the PCM momentarily turns on element pressure to the clutch circuits that don't have pressure to identify the correct pressure switch closes. If the pressure switch does not close 2 times the DTC sets.
DTC: P0871	**-OD PRESSURE SWITCH RATIONALITY:** Whenever the engine is running. The DTC is set if one of the pressure switches are open or closed at the wrong time in a given gear. If the problem is identified for 3 successive key starts, the transmission will go into Limp-in mode and the MIL will turn on after 10 seconds of vehicle operation.
DTC: P0875	**-UD HYDRAULIC PRESSURE TEST:** In any forward gear with engine speed above 1000 RPM shortly after a shift and every minute thereafter. After a shift into a forward gear, with engine speed above 1000 RPM, the Powertrain Control Module (PCM) momentarily turns on element pressure to the Clutch circuits that don't have pressure to identify the correct Pressure Switch closes. If the Pressure Switch does not close two times, the DTC sets.
DTC: P0876	**-UD PRESSURE SWITCH RATIONALITY:** Continuously with the ignition on and engine running. This DTC is set if the UD pressure switch is in the wrong state for the current gear. For example, this code would be set if the UD pressure switch remained off while the transmission was in second gear.
DTC: P0882	**TCM POWER INPUT LOW:** When the ignition is turned from "OFF" position to "RUN" position and/or the ignition is turned from "START" position to "RUN" position. This DTC is set when there is less than 3. 0 volts present at the transmission control output circuits located in the Powertrain Control Module (PCM) when the Transmission Control System requests the power up of those circuits.
DTC: P0882	**TCM POWER INPUT LOW:** When the ignition is turned from "OFF" position to "RUN" position and/or the ignition is turned from "START" position to "RUN" position. This DTC is set when there is less than 3. 0 volts present at the transmission control output circuits located in the Powertrain Control Module (PCM) when the Transmission Control System request the power up of those circuits. **NOTE: Due to the integration of the Transmission Control Module and the Powertrain Control Module, both systems have their own power and ground circuits. .**
DTC: P0883	**TCM POWER INPUT HIGH:** When the ignition is turned from "OFF" position to "RUN" position and/or the ignition is turned from "START" position to "RUN" position. This DTC is set if the Powertrain Control Module senses greater than 3. 0 volts on the Transmission Control Relay Output circuits prior to a request from the PCM to energize the Transmission Control Relay.
DTC: P0884	**-POWER UP AT SPEED:** One time after each controller reset. **NOTE: the Transmission Control Module is integrated with Powertrain Control Module. The Transmission Control Module has separate powers and grounds specifically to its portion of the PCM.** This DTC will set if the PCM powers up and senses the vehicle in a valid forward gear (no PRNDL DTCs) with an output speed above 800 rpm, approximately 32 km/h or 20 mph.

DTC	Trouble Code Title, Conditions, Possible Causes
DTC: P0884	**-POWER UP AT SPEED:** When Powertrain Control Module initially powers up. Due to the integration of the Powertrain and Transmission Control Modules, the transmission part of the PCM has its own specific power and ground circuits. This DTC will set if the PCM powers up and senses the vehicle in a valid forward gear, with no PRNDL DTCs, and an output speed above 800 rpm, approximately 32Km/h or 20 mph.
DTC: P0888	**TRANSMISSION RELAY ALWAYS OFF:** When the ignition is turned from "OFF" position to "RUN" position and/or the ignition is turned from "START" position to "RUN" position. This DTC is set when there is less than 3. 0 volts present at the transmission control output circuits located in the Powertrain Control Module (PCM) when the Transmission Control System requests the power up of those circuits.
DTC: P0888	**TRANSMISSION RELAY ALWAYS OFF:** When the ignition is turned from "OFF" position to "RUN" position and/or the ignition is turned from "START" position to "RUN" position. This DTC is set when there is less than 3. 0 volts present at the transmission control output circuits located in the Powertrain Control Module (PCM) when the Transmission Control System request the power up of those circuits. **NOTE: Due to the integration of the Transmission Control Module and the Powertrain Control Module, both systems have their own power and ground circuits. .**
DTC: P0890	**-SWITCHED BATTERY:** One time after a reset (ignition key turned to the RUN position or after cranking engine). A fault is set if voltage greater than 4. 5 volts is detected for 7 msec on any of the pressure switch circuits before the relay is energized. The transmission is placed in Limp-In. The MIL is on after 10 seconds. of vehicle operation.
DTC: P0890	**-SWITCHED BATTERY:** One time after a reset (ignition turned to the RUN position or after cranking engine). A fault is set if the sensed voltage on any of the pressure switch circuits is greater than 4. 5 volts for the period of 7 msec before a request by the Transmission Control System requests the Transmission Control Output circuit to be energized. The transmission is placed in Limp-In and the MIL is illuminated after 10 seconds of vehicle operation.
DTC: P0891	**TRANSMISSION RELAY ALWAYS ON:** When the ignition is turned from "OFF" position to "RUN" position and/or the ignition is turned from "START" position to "RUN" position. This DTC is set if the Powertrain Control Module senses greater than 3. 0 volts on the Transmission Control Relay Output circuits prior to a request from the PCM to TIPM to energize the Transmission Output circuits.
DTC: P0897	**TRANSMISSION FLUID DETERIORATED:** Each transition from full EMCC to partial EMCC for A/C bump prevention. DTC set if 20 occurrences of a turbine acceleration sum. Fault Set Time: 20 transitions from full EMCC to partial EMCC. Transmission will not use partial EMCC. Established for A/C bump prevention.
DTC: P0928	**-BTSI CONTROL CIRCUIT:** Continuously with the ignition on. The Diagnostic trouble Code (DTC) will set if the high side driver detects a short to ground for 10 seconds.
DTC: P0928	**-BTSI CONTROL CIRCUIT:** With the ignition on. The Cluster detects a fault on the (K321) Brake Transmission Shift Interlock Solenoid Unlock circuit.
DTC: P0928	**-BTSI CONTROL CIRCUIT:** Continuously with the ignition on. The DTC will set if the high side driver detects a short to ground for 10 seconds.
DTC: P0928-11	**-BTSI CONTROL - CIRCUIT SHORT TO GROUND:** With the ignition on. Brake pedal applied. The BCM detects a short to ground on the (K321) BTSI Control circuit for more than one second.
DTC: P0930	**-BTSI CONTROL CIRCUIT LOW :** Continuously with the ignition on. The DTC will set if the high side driver detects a short to ground for 10 seconds.
DTC: P0930	**-BTSI CONTROL CIRCUIT LOW:** Continuously with the ignition on. The DTC will set if the high side driver detects a short to ground for 10 seconds.
DTC: P0930	**-BTSI CONTROL CIRCUIT LOW:** With the ignition in the Unlock or Run position and the driver's foot applied to the brake pedal. The Instrument Cluster detects a low value on the BTSI Solenoid Control circuit.
DTC: P0931	**-BTSI CONTROL CIRCUIT HIGH :** Continuously with the ignition key on. The DTC will set if the high side driver detects an open load for 10 seconds.
DTC: P0931	**-BTSI CONTROL CIRCUIT HIGH - COLUMN SHIFT:** Continuously with the ignition key on. The DTC will set if the high side driver detects an open load for 10 seconds.
DTC: P0931	**-BTSI CONTROL CIRCUIT HIGH:** With the ignition in the Unlock or Run position and the driver's foot applied to the brake pedal. The Instrument Cluster detects a high value on the BTSI Solenoid Control circuit.

DTC	Trouble Code Title, Conditions, Possible Causes
DTC: P0932	**-LINE PRESSURE SENSOR CIRCUIT:** Continuously with the ignition on, engine running, with the transmission in gear. The Powertrain Control Module (PCM) continuously monitors Actual Line Pressure and compares it to Desired Line Pressure. If the Actual Line Pressure reading is more than 172. 4 kPa (25 psi) higher than the Desired Line Pressure, but is less than the highest Line Pressure ever used in the current gear, the DTC sets.
DTC: P0933	**-HYDRAULIC PRESSURE SENSOR RANGE/PERFORMANCE:** Continuously with the ignition on, engine running, with the transmission in gear. The Powertrain Control Module (PCM) continuously monitors Actual Line Pressure and compares it to Desired Line Pressure. If the Actual Line Pressure reading is more than 172. 4 kPa (25 psi) higher than the Desired Line Pressure, but is less than the highest Line Pressure ever used in the current gear, the DTC sets.
DTC: P0934	**-LINE PRESSURE SENSOR CIRCUIT LOW:** Continuously with the ignition on and engine running. This DTC will set when the monitored Line Pressure Sensor voltage is less than or equal to 0. 35 of a volt for 0. 18 of a second.
DTC: P0935	**-LINE PRESSURE SENSOR CIRCUIT HIGH:** Continuously with ignition on and engine running. This DTC will set if the monitored Line Pressure Sensor voltage is greater than or equal to 4. 75 volts for the period of 0. 18 of a second.
DTC: P0944	**-LOSS OF HYDRAULIC PUMP PRIME:** If the transmission is slipping in any forward gear and all the pressure switches are not indicating pressure, a loss of prime test is run. If the transmission begins to slip in a forward gear and all the pressure switch(s) that should be closed are open a loss of prime test begins. Available elements are turned on by the Powertrain Control Module (PCM) to see if pump prime exists. The DTC sets if no pressure switch(s) respond.
DTC: P0944	**-LOSS OF HYDRAULIC PUMP PRIME:** Every 350 msec the transmission begins to slip in any forward gear, and the pressure switch or switches that should be closed for a given gear are open, a loss of prime test begins. All available elements (in 1st gear LR, 2/4 and OD, in 2nd, 3rd, and 4th gear 2/4 and OD) are turned on by the Powertrain Control Module (PCM) to see if pump prime exists. The code is set if none of the pressure switches respond. The PCM will continue to run the loss of prime test until pump pressure returns. The vehicle will not move or the transmission will slip. Normal operation will continue if pump prime returns.
DTC: P0952	**-AUTOSTICK INPUT CIRCUIT LOW:** Whenever the engine is running. The transmission is not in the AutoStick® position and the upshift or downshift is reporting closed - below 0. 3 of a volt or if both switches are reported closed at the same time.
DTC: P0957	**-AUTOSTICK CIRCUIT LOW:** Whenever the engine is running. The transmission is not in the AutoStick® position and the upshift or downshift is reporting closed - below 0. 71 of a volt or if both switches are reported closed at the same time.
DTC: P0957	**-AUTOSTICK CIRCUIT LOW:** Ignition on and engine running and after 0. 5 seconds. When the monitored AutoStick Up/Down Sense circuit voltage drops below 0. 35 volts.
DTC: P0958	**-AUTOSTICK CIRCUIT HIGH:** Ignition on and engine running and after 0. 5 of a second. When the monitored AutoStick Up/Down Sense circuit voltage rises above 4. 75 volts.
DTC: P0962	**-PRESSURE CONTROL SOLENOID A CONTROL CIRCUIT LOW:** Ignition on with a system voltage between 9. 0 and 16. 0 volts. If the monitored line pressure solenoid voltage is less than 70% of the target line pressure solenoid voltage for the period of 1. 0 second.
DTC: P0963	**-PRESSURE CONTROL SOLENOID A CONTROL CIRCUIT HIGH:** Ignition on with a system voltage between 9. 0 and 16. 0 volts. No Line Pressure Solenoid Circuit Low DTC present. When the target line pressure solenoid current is greater than 0. 75 of an amp while the monitored line pressure solenoid current is less than 0. 4 of an amp for the period of five seconds.
DTC: P0966	**-PRESSURE CONTROL SOLENOID B CONTROL CIRCUIT LOW:** Ignition on with a system voltage between 9. 0 and 16. 0 volts. If the monitored secondary pressure solenoid voltage is less than 70% of the target secondary pressure solenoid voltage for the period of 1. 0second.
DTC: P0967	**-PRESSURE CONTROL SOLENOID B CONTROL CIRCUIT HIGH:** Ignition on with a system voltage between 9. 0 and 16. 0 volts. No Secondary Pressure Solenoid Low DTC present. When the target secondary pressure solenoid current is greater than 0. 75 of an amp while the monitored secondary pressure solenoid current is less than0. 4 of an amp for the period of five seconds.
DTC: P0987-4C	**- HYDRAULIC PRESSURE TEST:** In any forward gear with engine speed above 1000 rpm shortly after a shift and every minute thereafter. After a shift into a forward gear, with engine speed above 1000 rpm, the Powertrain Control Module (PCM) momentarily turns on element pressure to the Clutch circuits that don't have pressure to identify the correct Pressure Switch closes. If the Pressure Switch does not close two times, the DTC sets.

DTC	Trouble Code Title, Conditions, Possible Causes
DTC: P0988-4C	**- PRESSURE SWITCH RATIONALITY:** Continuously with the ignition on, engine running, with the transmission in gear. The DTC is set if the 4C Pressure Switch reads open or closed at the wrong time in a given gear .
DTC: P0992	**-2/4/OD HYDRAULIC PRESSURE TEST:** In any forward gear with engine speed above 1000 rpm, shortly after a shift and every minute thereafter. After a shift into a forward gear, with engine speed greater than 1000 rpm, the PCM momentarily turns on element pressure to the clutch circuits that do not have pressure to identify that the correct pressure switch closes. If the pressure switch does not close 2 times the DTC sets.

OBD II Trouble Code List (P1XXX Codes)

DTC	Trouble Code Title, Conditions, Possible Causes
DTC: P1009-00	**-HUMIDITY SENSOR MODULE:** With the ignition on. The Humidity Sensor detects an internal failure.
DTC: P1103-DC	**- TO AC CONVERTER SWITCH STUCK:** With the ignition on. If the Instrument Cluster/Cabin Compartment Node (CCN) senses the Inverter switch input for more than 10 seconds.
DTC: P1115	**-GENERAL TEMPERATURE RATIONALITY:** With the ignition on and battery voltage greater than 10 volts. AAT, ECT, and IAT sensor inputs are compared during a cold start. After start up, the values are monitored. If one of the readings is not plausible for two consecutive trips, a DTC is stored. Three good trips turns off the MIL.
DTC: P1115	**-GENERAL TEMPERATURE RATIONALITY:** Engine off time is greater than 480 minutes and the vehicle has been driven for one minute over 35 mph. Ambient temperature is greater than -64° C (-83° F). Once the vehicle is soaked for a calibrated engine off time and then driven over calibrated speed and load conditions for some calibrated time, the PCM compares the ambient air, engine coolant, and intake air temperature sensor values. If the values of all the three sensors disagree with one another, a general temperature sensor irrationality is declared. Two Trip Fault. Three good trips to turn off the MIL.
DTC: P1128	**-CLOSED LOOP FUELING NOT ACHIEVED - BANK 1:** Engine running in closed loop mode. Enable conditions are met and the 02 sensor has not been in closed loop control at least once on each of the two consecutive trips, the MIL illuminates and the DTC is set. Two Trip Fault. Three good trips to turn off the MIL
DTC: P1128	**-CLOSED LOOP FUELING NOT ACHIEVED - BANK 1:** With engine run time and coolant temperature above a calibrated value. The Powertrain Control Module (PCM) detects a condition where the vehicle has remained in open loop fuel control, from a start-up condition, longer than a calibrated amount of time, when conditions would have otherwise expected closed loop operation. Two Trip Fault. Three good trips to turn off the MIL.
DTC: P1129	**-CLOSED LOOP FUELING NOT ACHIEVED - BANK 2:** Engine running in closed loop mode. Enable conditions are met and the 02 sensor has not been in closed loop control at least once on each of the two consecutive trips, the MIL illuminates and the DTC is set. Two Trip Fault. Three good trips to turn off the MIL
DTC: P113D	**-02 SENSOR 1/1 SLOW RESPONSE:** With the Engine Coolant Temperature (ECT) at least 60°C (140°F), engine RPM between1000 and 2750, minimum engine run time of 20 seconds and Manifold Absolute Pressure (MAP) reading is between 21 - 96 Kpa (6. 2 - 28. 3in Hg). The Powertrain Control Module (PCM) detects that the Oxygen Sensor signal does not switch adequately at high frequency. Two Trip Fault. Three good trips to turn off the MIL.
DTC: P113D	**-02 SENSOR 1/1 SLOW RESPONSE:** With the Engine Coolant Temperature (ECT) at least 60°C (140°F), engine RPM between 1000 and 2750, minimum engine run time of 20 seconds and Manifold Absolute Pressure (MAP) reading is between 21 - 96 Kpa (6. 2 - 28. 3 in Hg). The Powertrain Control Module (PCM) detects that the Oxygen Sensor signal does not switch adequately at high frequency. Two Trip Fault. Three good trips to turn off the MIL. .
DTC: P113E	**-02 SENSOR 2/1 SLOW RESPONSE (HIGH FREQUENCY):** With the ECT at least 60°C (140°F), engine RPM between 1000 and 2750, minimum engine run time of 20 seconds and Manifold Absolute Pressure (MAP) readings between 21 - 96 Kpa (6. 2 - 28. 3 in Hg). The Powertrain Control Module (PCM) detects that the Oxygen Sensor signal does not switch adequately at high frequency. Two Trip Fault. Three good trips to turn off the MIL.
DTC: P1239	**-ENGINE OIL TEMPERATURE TOO LOW:** The engine oil temperature has dropped below a calibrated temperature value. Engine start up. The Engine Oil temperature rises slower than a calibrated modeled temperature. When the actual oil temperature falls below the low boundary of the calibrated modeled temperature for three minutes the fault is set. Two trip fault. Three good trips to turn off the MIL.

DTC	Trouble Code Title, Conditions, Possible Causes
DTC: P1270	**-INTAKE MANIFOLD RUNNER (SWIRL) PERFORMANCE:** With the ignition on and the Intake Swirl Servo Motor command on. The Engine Control Module (ECM) detects that the (N117) Intake Swirl Servo Motor Control circuit voltage is implausible.
DTC: P1272	**-A/C CLUTCH CONTROL CIRCUIT 2 LOW :** With the ignition on. Battery voltage greater than 10 volts. A/C Switch on. A shorted condition is detected in the A/C clutch control circuit. One Trip Fault. Three good trips to turn off the MIL.
DTC: P1273	**-A/C CLUTCH CONTROL CIRCUIT 2 HIGH:** With the ignition on. Battery voltage greater than 10 volts. A/C Switch on. A shorted high condition has been detected in the A/C Clutch Control output circuit by the TIPM. One Trip Fault. Three good trips to turn off the MIL.
DTC: P1274	**-A/C CLUTCH CONTROL CIRCUIT 2 OPEN:** With the ignition on. Battery voltage greater than 10. 4 volts. TIPM requesting A/C Clutch operation. An open condition has been detected in the A/C Clutch Control Output circuit by the TIPM. One Trip Fault. Three good trips to turn off the MIL.
DTC: P1276-11	**-STARTER CONTROL 2 - CIRCUIT SHORT TO GROUND:** Battery voltage greater than 10. 4 volts. Body Control Module (BCM) commanding Starter operation. The BCM detects a lower than expected voltage level on the starter relay control circuit for more than one second.
DTC: P1277	**-STARTER CONTROL CIRCUIT 2 LOW:** With the ignition on. Battery voltage greater than 10. 4 volts and Main Relay is on. Totally Integrated Power Module (TIPM) requesting Starter operation. Actual Starter state is not equal to desired state. One Trip Fault. Three good trips to turn off the Malfunction Indicator Lamp (MIL).
DTC: P1278	**-STARTER CONTROL CIRCUIT 2 HIGH:** With the ignition on. Battery voltage greater than 10. 4 volts and Main Relay is on. Totally Integrated Power Module (TIPM) requesting Starter operation. Actual Starter state is not equal to desired state. One Trip Fault. Three good trips to turn off the MIL.
DTC: P1279	**-STARTER CONTROL CIRCUIT 2 OPEN:** With the ignition on. Battery voltage greater than 10. 4 volts and Main Relay is on. Totally Integrated Power Module (TIPM) requesting Starter operation. Actual Starter state is not equal to desired state. One Trip Fault. Three good trips to turn off the MIL.
DTC: P127A	**-STARTER CONTROL CIRCUIT 2 OVERCURRENT:** With the ignition on. Battery voltage greater than 10. 4 volts and Main Relay is on. Totally Integrated Power Module (TIPM) requesting Starter operation. An overcurrent condition is detected in the Starter control output circuit. One Trip Fault. Three good trips to turn off the MIL.
DTC: P127C	**-FUEL PUMP CONTROL CIRCUIT 2 LOW:** With the ignition on. The battery voltage greater than 10. 4 volts and the Main Relay on. Totally Integrated Power Module (TIPM) requesting Fuel Pump operation. The actual Fuel Pump state is not equal to the desired state. One Trip Fault. Three good trips to turn off the Malfunction Indicator Lamp (MIL).
DTC: P127D	**-FUEL PUMP CONTROL CIRCUIT 2 HIGH:** With the ignition on. The battery voltage greater than 10. 4 volts and the Main Relay on. Totally Integrated Power Module (TIPM) requesting Fuel Pump operation. Actual Fuel Pump state is not equal to the desired state. One Trip Fault. Three good trips to turn off the MIL.
DTC: P127E	**-FUEL PUMP CONTROL CIRCUIT 2 OPEN:** With the ignition on. Battery voltage greater than 10. 4 volts and the Main relay is on. Totally Integrated Power Module (TIPM) requesting Fuel Pump operation. Actual Fuel Pump state is not equal to desired state. One Trip Fault. Three good trips to turn off the MIL.
DTC: P127F	**-FUEL PUMP CONTROL CIRCUIT 2 OVERCURRENT:** With the ignition on. The battery voltage greater than 10. 4 volts. Totally Integrated Power Module (TIPM) requesting fuel pump operation. An overcurrent condition is detected in the Fuel Pump control output circuit. One Trip Fault. Three good trips to turn off the MIL.
DTC: P128B	**TCM POWER CONTROL CIRCUIT 2 LOW:** With the ignition on. Battery voltage greater than 10. 0 volts. A shorted condition is detected in the Transmission Control Output circuit.
DTC: P128B	**TCM POWER CONTROL CIRCUIT 2 LOW:** With the ignition on. Battery voltage greater than 10. 0 volts. The Totally Integrated Power Module (TIPM) has detected a short to ground condition in the Transmission Control Output circuit.
DTC: P128C	**TCM POWER CONTROL CIRCUIT 2 HIGH - 41TE NGC:** With the ignition on with the battery voltage greater than 10. 0 volts. The Totally Integrated Power Module (TIPM) has detected voltage on the Transmission Control Output circuit when none should be present.

DTC	Trouble Code Title, Conditions, Possible Causes
DTC: P128C	**TCM POWER CONTROL CIRCUIT 2 HIGH:** With the ignition on. Battery voltage greater than 10 volts. A shorted condition is detected in the TIPM Transmission Control Output circuit.
DTC: P128D	**TCM POWER CONTROL CIRCUIT 2 OPEN:** With the ignition on. Battery voltage greater than 10 volts. An open condition of the Transmission Control Output circuit is detected by the Totally Integrated Power Module (TIPM).
DTC: P128D	**TCM POWER CONTROL CIRCUIT 2 OPEN:** With the ignition on. Battery voltage greater than 10. 0 volts. The Totally Integrated Power Module (TIPM) has detected an open condition on the Transmission Control Output circuit.
DTC: P128E	**TCM POWER CONTROL CIRCUIT 2 OVERCURRENT:** With the ignition on. Battery voltage greater than 10 volts. An overcurrent condition is detected in the TCM Power Control circuit. One Trip Fault. Three good trips to turn off the MIL.
DTC: P128E	**TCM POWER CONTROL CIRCUIT 2 OVERCURRENT:** With the ignition on. Battery voltage greater than 10. 0 volts. The Totally Integrated Power Module (TIPM) has detected an overcurrent condition in the Transmission Control Output circuit.
DTC: P1404	**-EGR POSITION SENSOR RATIONALITY CLOSED:** Engine running. The EGR flow or valve movement is not what is expected. A rationality error has been detected for the EGR Open Position Performance. Two trip fault.
DTC: P1411	**-CYLINDER 1 REACTIVATION CONTROL PERFORMANCE:** Transition from 8 to 4 cylinder mode. The MDS fails to active and take place for cylinder 1. One trip fault.
DTC: P1411	**-CYLINDER 1 REACTIVATION CONTROL PERFORMANCE:** Transition from 4 to 8 cylinder mode. The MDS fails to disengage for cylinder 1.
DTC: P1414	**-CYLINDER 4 REACTIVATION CONTROL PERFORMANCE:** Transition from 4 to 8 cylinder mode. The MDS fails to disengage for cylinder 4.
DTC: P1414	**-CYLINDER 4 REACTIVATION CONTROL PERFORMANCE:** Transition from 8 to 4 cylinder mode. The MDS fails to active and take place for cylinder 4. One trip fault.
DTC: P1416	**-CYLINDER 6 REACTIVATION CONTROL PERFORMANCE:** Transition from 8 to 4 cylinder mode. The MDS fails to active and take place for cylinder 6. One trip fault.
DTC: P1416	**-CYLINDER 6 REACTIVATION CONTROL PERFORMANCE:** Transition from 4 to 8 cylinder mode. The MDS fails to disengage for cylinder 6.
DTC: P1417	**-CYLINDER 7 REACTIVATION CONTROL PERFORMANCE:** Transition from 8 to 4 cylinder mode. The MDS fails to active and take place for cylinder 7. One trip fault.
DTC: P1417	**-CYLINDER 7 REACTIVATION CONTROL PERFORMANCE:** Transition from 4 to 8 cylinder mode. The MDS fails to disengage for cylinder 7.
DTC: P1452	**-DIFFERENTIAL PRESSURE SENSOR HOSE PERFORMANCE:** With the engine running. Differential Pressure Sensor signal indicates (–)10 hpa for 15. 0 seconds.
DTC: P1453	**-DIFFERENTIAL PRESSURE SENSOR HOSE BLOCKED:** With the engine running. The ECM detects differential pressure that are lower than expected for certain engine operating conditions for 2. 0 seconds.
DTC: P1454	**-DIFFERENTIAL PRESSURE SENSOR FLOW TOO HIGH:** With the engine running. The ECM detects incorrect exhaust flow through the particulate filter during certain engine operating conditions.
DTC: P1462	**-FUEL LEVEL OUTPUT CIRCUIT LOW:** With the ignition switch on. The Vehicle System Integration Module (VSIM) has detected the Fuel Level Status Signal circuit below a calibrated value.
DTC: P1463	**-FUEL LEVEL OUTPUT CIRCUIT HIGH:** With the ignition switch on. The Vehicle System Integration Module (VSIM) has detected the Fuel Level Status Signal circuit above a calibrated value.
DTC: P1501	**-VEHICLE SPEED SENSOR 1/2 CORRELATION - DRIVE WHEELS:** Ignition on and vehicle moving. Cruise is learned and customer is trying to use the Cruise. The PCM recognizes rear wheel speed is greater than front wheel speed. One trip fault.

DTC	Trouble Code Title, Conditions, Possible Causes
DTC: P1501	**-VEHICLE SPEED SENSOR 1/2 CORRELATION - DRIVE WHEELS:** With the ignition on and battery voltage greater than 10. 4 volts. The Powertrain Control Module (PCM) detects an implausible voltage on the Vehicle Speed Sensor circuit.
DTC: P1502	**-VEHICLE SPEED SENSOR 1/2 CORRELATION - NON DRIVE WHEELS:** Ignition on and vehicle moving. Brake pedal must not be applied. The PCM recognizes front axle speed is greater than rear axle speed. One trip fault.
DTC: P1502	**-VEHICLE SPEED SENSOR 1/2 CORRELATION - NON-DRIVE WHEELS:** With the engine running, transmission not neutral, brakes not applied, and engine RPM greater than 1500. This code will set if the Powertrain Control Module (PCM) receives an implausible vehicle speed signal from the Totally Integrated Power Module (TIPM).
DTC: P1504	**-VEHICLE SPEED OUTPUT CIRCUIT LOW:** With the ignition switch on. The Vehicle System Integration Module (VSIM) has detected the Vehicle Speed Signal circuit below a calibrated value.
DTC: P1505	**-VEHICLE SPEED OUTPUT CIRCUIT HIGH:** With the ignition switch on. The Vehicle System Integration Module (VSIM) has detected the Vehicle Speed Signal circuit above a calibrated value.
DTC: P150D	**-COLD START ROUGH IDLE - OPEN THROTTLE START:** Any time the engine is running and the adaptive numerator has been successfully updated. If the PCM detects that the variation in crankshaft speed between each cylinder exceeds a calibrated value, based on engine rpm and load, a fault is set.
DTC: P1513	**-STARTER REQUEST SWITCH STUCK:** With the ignition on and battery voltage greater than 10. 4 volts. The Powertrain Control Module (PCM) detects voltage on the (F963) Start Enable circuit for a specified time after the engine is running.
DTC: P1519	**-CRUISE CONTROL FRONT DISTANCE SENSOR LENS CRACKED MISSING:** Continuously monitored with the ignition in run and the Adaptive Cruise Control(ACC) Module in normal mode. ACC Module detects that the lens is damaged or missing. The ACC module will disable the ACC system and the SERVICE ACC message will display in the Cabin Compartment Node (CCN). Once the Diagnostic Trouble Code (DTC) goes to stored, the ACC system will return to normal operation. The DTC will be cleared after the ACC Module sees 100 consecutive key cycles of the STOREDDTC.
DTC: P1521	**-INCORRECT ENGINE OIL TYPE:** Engine Running. Using the oil pressure, oil temperature and other vital engine inputs the Powertrain Control Module (PCM) can determine the engine oil viscosity. Incorrect viscosity will affect the operation of the MDS by delaying cylinder activation .
DTC: P1524	**-OIL PRESSURE OUT OF RANGE - CAMSHAFT ADVANCE/RETARD DISABLED:** Engine running. RPM greater than or equal to 1100. Oil temperature less than or equal to 100° C (212° F)The engine oil pressure never reaches the calibrated specification to allow the VCT activation. One trip fault.
DTC: P1572	**-BRAKE PEDAL STUCK ON:** With the ignition on and battery voltage greater than 10. 4 Volts. The Powertrain Control Module (PCM) detects that the state of brake switch does not change as expected.
DTC: P1572	**-BRAKE PEDAL STUCK ON:** Ignition on. In plant mode only. PCM recognizes the Brake Pedal could not electrically indicate the applied (On) position with both switch inputs. One trip fault.
DTC: P1572	**-BRAKE PEDAL STUCK ON:** With the gear selector in drive, vehicle speed above a minimum value, and battery voltage greater than 10. 4 volts. The Powertrain Control Module (PCM) recognizes the Brake Pedal could not electrically indicate the applied (On) position with both switch inputs. One trip fault.
DTC: P1573	**-BRAKE PEDAL STUCK OFF:** Ignition on, In plant mode passed the Applied test. PCM recognizes the Brake Pedal could not electronically indicate the released (Off) position with both switches. If P1572 sets, P1573 will also set. One trip fault.
DTC: P1573	**-BRAKE PEDAL STUCK OFF:** Ignition on and battery voltage above 10. 4 Volts. The Powertrain Control Module (PCM) recognizes the Brake Pedal could not electronically indicate the released (Off) position with both switches. If P1572 sets, P1573 will also set. One trip fault.
DTC: P1573	**-BRAKE PEDAL STUCK OFF:** With the ignition on and battery voltage greater than 10. 4 Volts. The Powertrain Control Module (PCM) detects that the state of Brake Signal 2 does not change as expected.
DTC: P1593	**-SPEED CONTROL SWITCH 1/2 STUCK:** With the ignition on and battery voltage greater than 10. 4 volts. The Powertrain Control Module (PCM) detects that the (V71) S/C Signal 1 voltage does not match the (V72) S/C Signal 2 voltage.

DTC	Trouble Code Title, Conditions, Possible Causes
DTC: P1593	**-SPEED CONTROL SWITCH 1 STUCK:** Ignition on. Cruise Switch inputs are not coherent with each other. Example: The Powertrain Control Module (PCM) is reading Switch No. 1 as Accel and Switch No. 2 as Coast at the same time. One trip fault.
DTC: P1593	**-SPEED CONTROL SWITCH 1/2 STUCK:** Ignition on. One of the S/C Switches is mechanically stuck in the On/Off, Resume/Accel, or Set position for too long. One trip fault.
DTC: P1593	**-SPEED CONTROL SWITCH 1/2 STUCK:** Continuously with the ignition on. Fault signifies when the switch voltage does not register a valid cruise position.
DTC: P1593-2A	**-SPEED CONTROL SWITCH 1/2 STUCK:** Continuously with the ignition on. Fault signifies any Speed Control Switch is held/stuck for greater than 120 seconds.
DTC: P1602	**-PCM NOT PROGRAMMED:** Ignition on and battery voltage greater than 10 volts. The Powertrain Control Module (PCM) has not been programmed.
DTC: P1607	**-PCM INTERNAL SHUTDOWN TIMER SLOW RATIONALITY:** The Powertrain Control Module (PCM) internal timer is continuously monitored. Upon power up, the Powertrain Control Module (PCM) compares the change in engine coolant temp sensor since last engine shut down and compares it to the amount of time the engine was turned off. If not enough time has occurred to account for the difference in engine coolant temperature then the fault will set. Two Trip Fault. Three good trips to turn off the MIL.
DTC: P1607	**-PCM INTERNAL SHUTDOWN TIMER SLOW RATIONALITY:** With the engine running after a cycle when a complete engine warm up was achieved, the difference between engine coolant temperature and ambient air temperature less than or equal to 10° C (50° F), and battery voltage greater than 10 volts. This DTC sets if the engine coolant temp does not drop enough or drops too much during engine off time. This DTC may also set if the controller timer is inaccurate. Two Trip Fault. Three good trips to turn off the MIL.
DTC: P160A	**-ECU OVERTEMPERATURE:** Continuously monitored with the engine running, the Adaptive Cruise Control (ACC)Module voltage at battery voltage, and the ACC Module in normal mode. ACC Module detects ambient temperatures greater than 85°C (185°F). The ACC module will disable the ACC system and the ACC UNAVAILABLE message will displaying the Cabin Compartment Node (CCN). Once the Diagnostic Trouble Code(DTC) goes to stored, the ACC system will return to normal operation. The DTC will be cleared after the ACC Module sees 100 consecutive key cycles of the STORED DTC.
DTC: P1614	**-ECU RESET/RECOVERY OCCURRED:** Continuously monitored with the engine running and the Adaptive Cruise Control (ACC) Module in normal mode. The power supply was interrupted for less than 100 ms. The ACC module will disable the ACC system and the ACC UNAVAILABLE message will displaying the Cabin Compartment Node (CCN). Once the Diagnostic Trouble Code (DTC) goes to stored, the ACC system will return to normal operation. The DTC will be cleared after the ACC Module sees 100consecutive key cycles of the STORED DTC.
DTC: P1618	**-SENSOR REFERENCE VOLTAGE 1 ERRATIC:** With the ignition on. The Powertrain Control Module (PCM) detects that the 5 volt supply circuit voltage is below the minimum acceptable value. One Trip Fault. ETC light is flashing.
DTC: P1618	**-SENSOR REFERENCE VOLTAGE 1 CIRCUIT ERRATIC:** With the ignition on. The Powertrain Control Module (PCM) detects an excessive voltage variation on the5-Volt supply circuit.
DTC: P1618	**-SENSOR REFERENCE VOLTAGE 1 CIRCUIT ERRATIC:** Ignition on. When the PCM recognizes the Primary 5-volt Supply circuit voltage is varying too much too quickly. One Trip Fault. ETC light is flashing.
DTC: P1618	**-SENSOR REFERENCE VOLTAGE 1 CIRCUIT ERRATIC:** Ignition on. When the Powertrain Control Module (PCM) recognizes the Primary 5-Volt Supply circuit voltage is varying too much too quickly. One Trip Fault. ETC light is flashing.
DTC: P161A	**-ECU IN-PLANT MODE ACTIVE:** Continuously monitored with the ignition key in run, the Adaptive Cruise Control (ACC) Module voltage at battery voltage, and the ACC Module in normal mode. ACC Module is in the In-Plant mode. The ACC module will disable the ACC system and the ACC PLANT MODE message will display in the Cabin Compartment Node (CCN). Once the Diagnostic Trouble Code (DTC) goes to stored, the ACC system will return to normal operation. After a successful learning process, the active DTC will be cleared automatically.
DTC: P161B	**-BATTERY DISCONNECT / TCM INTERNAL:** One time at every ignition on cycle. When the calculated checksum does not equal the stored checksum configuration or loss of power to the controller. It takes one trip of problem identification to set the MIL.
DTC: P1628	**-SENSOR REFERENCE VOLTAGE 2 ERRATIC:** With the ignition on. The Powertrain Control Module (PCM) detects that the 5 volt supply circuit voltage is below the minimum acceptable value. One Trip Fault. ETC light is flashing.

DTC	Trouble Code Title, Conditions, Possible Causes
DTC: P1628	**-SENSOR REFERENCE VOLTAGE CIRCUIT ERRATIC:** With the ignition on. The Powertrain Control Module (PCM) detects an excessive voltage variation on the 5-Volt supply circuit.
DTC: P1629	**TCM INTERNAL - SOLENOID SUPPLY/ WATCHDOG:** Continuously with the ignition on. If the TCM detects voltage on the Solenoid Supply Voltage circuit when the TCM request the circuit to be off.
DTC: P1631	**TCM INTERNAL- PROCESSOR CLOCK PERFORMANCE:** Continuously with the ignition on. If the TCM detects an error with the controllers internal clock.
DTC: P1632	**TCM INTERNAL - TEST INTERNAL WATCHDOG PERFORMANCE:** Continuously with the ignition on. If the TCM detects an error with the controllers internal watchdog.
DTC: P1633	**TCM INTERNAL - TEST EXTERNAL WATCHDOG PERFORMANCE:** Continuously with the ignition on. If the TCM detects an error with the controllers external watchdog failed the power up test.
DTC: P1634	**TCM INTERNAL- INTERNAL WATCHDOG PERFORMANCE:** Continuously with the ignition on. If the TCM microprocessor internal watchdog detects an error.
DTC: P1636	**TCM INTERNAL- EXTERNAL WATCHDOG PERFORMANCE:** Continuously with the ignition on. If the TCM watch dog circuitry external to the microprocessor detects an error.
DTC: P1637	**TCM INTERNAL-EEPROM PERFORMANCE:** Continuously with the ignition on. If the TCM indicates that there is an internal error with the controllers Random Access Memory.
DTC: P1638	**TCM INTERNAL-CAN 1 RAM PERFORMANCE:** Continuously with the ignition on. If the TCM detects an internal error with the controllers Random Access Memory (RAM) on the CAN controller 1 section of the microprocessor.
DTC: P1639	**TCM INTERNAL-CAN 2 RAM PERFORMANCE:** Continuously with the ignition on. If the TCM detects an internal error with the controllers Random Access Memory (RAM) on the CAN controller 2 section of the microprocessor.
DTC: P1644	**-INCORRECT VARIANT/CONFIGURATION:** Continuously with the ignition on. If the TCM detects that the variables that dictate the vehicle application are not present.
DTC: P1644	**-INCORRECT VARIANT/CONFIGURATION:** Continuously monitored with the engine running, the Adaptive Cruise Control (ACC) Module voltage at battery voltage, and the ACC Module in normal mode. Current and original Vehicle Configuration do not match. The ACC module will disable the ACC system and the SERVICE ACC message will displaying the Cabin Compartment Node (CCN). Once the DTC goes to stored, the ACC system will return to normal operation. After a successful learning process, the active DTC will be cleared automatically.
DTC: P1648	**-GLOW PLUG MODULE INTERNAL:** With the ignition on. The Glow Plug Control Module reports an internal fault to the ECM.
DTC: P1649	**-GLOW PLUG MODULE POWER SUPPLY CIRCUIT:** With the ignition on and the Glow Plugs commanded on. The Glow Plug Control Module reports a power supply circuit fault to the ECM.
DTC: P164A	**-MIL OUTPUT CIRCUIT LOW:** With the ignition switch on. The Vehicle System Integration Module (VSIM) has detected the Malfunction Indicator Signal circuit below a calibrated value.
DTC: P164B	**-MIL OUTPUT CIRCUIT HIGH:** With the ignition switch on. The Vehicle System Integration Module (VSIM) has detected the Malfunction Indicator Signal circuit above a calibrated value.
DTC: P1661	**-SENSOR GROUND REFERENCE CIRCUIT:** With the ignition on and a system voltage between 9. 0 and 16. 0 volts. When all are present for the period of 200 msec:
DTC: P1666	**-CRUISE CONTROL MODULE INTERNAL:** Continuously monitored with the engine running, the Adaptive Cruise Control (ACC) Module voltage at battery voltage, and the ACC Module in normal mode. Internal ACC Module failure detected. The ACC module will disable the ACC system and the SERVICE ACC message will display in the Cabin Compartment Node (CCN). Once the Diagnostic Trouble Code (DTC) goes to stored, the ACC system will return to normal operation. The DTC will be cleared after the ACC Module sees 100 consecutive key cycles of the STORED DTC.

DTC	Trouble Code Title, Conditions, Possible Causes
DTC: P1678	**-ECU SENSOR ADJUSTMENT REQUIRED:** Continuously monitored with the engine running, the Adaptive Cruise Control (ACC) Module voltage at battery voltage, and the ACC Module in normal mode. There is horizontal misalignment between Sensor Axis and the vehicle driving axis that is greater than the performance threshold. The ACC module will disable the ACC system and the SERVICE ACC message will display in the Cabin Compartment Node (CCN). The DTC will be cleared after the ACC Module sees 100 consecutive key cycles of the STOREDDTC.
DTC: P1679	**-CALIBRATION NOT LEARNED:** Ignition on with a system voltage between 9. 0 and 16. 0 volts. The TCM is unable to read the hydraulic calibration data stored in the TCM EEPROM for the period of 5. 0 seconds.
DTC: P167A	**-CALIBRATION MISMATCH:** One time at initial ignition on with a system voltage between 9. 0 and 16. 0 volts. If the TCM stored calibration does not match the EEPROM assembly in the transmission. This DTC requires only one problem identification to set the MIL.
DTC: P1684	**-BATTERY WAS DISCONNECTED:** Whenever the ignition is in the Run/Start position. This DTC will set whenever Powertrain Control Module (PCM) is disconnected from Fused B(+) or ground. It will also be set using the scan tool to perform a Battery Disconnect and/or Quick Learn procedure.
DTC: P1684	**-BATTERY WAS DISCONNECTED:** After a reset (ignition turned to the RUN position). The checksum of the battery backed RAM does not match the stored checksum. Set Time: Less than 7 msec.
DTC: P1685	**-SKIM SYSTEM:** With the ignition on. A communication error occurs between the ECM and SKREEM.
DTC: P1696	**-EEPROM MEMORY WRITE DENIED/INVALID:** Continuously with the ignition on. An attempt to program/write to the internal EEPROM failed, Also checks at power down. One Trip Fault. Three good trips to turn off the MIL.
DTC: P1696	**-EEPROM MEMORY WRITE DENIED/INVALID:** Continuously with the ignition on. An attempt to program/write to the internal EEPROM failed, Also checks at power down. One Trip Fault. Three good trips to turn off the MIL.
DTC: P1697	**-EMR (SRI) MILEAGE NOT STORED:** Ignition on and battery voltage greater than 10 volts. The SRI Mileage has not been programmed into the PCM.
DTC: P1697	**-EMR (SRI) MILEAGE NOT STORED:** Continuously with the ignition on. The Powertrain Control Module (PCM) Odometer mileage has not been programmed into the PCM.
DTC: P1702	**-PRIMARY OIL PRESSURE SENSOR / SECONDARY OIL PRESSURE SENSOR CORRELATION:** Ignition on, system voltage between 9. 0 and 16. 0 volts. Engine running with the transmission in Drive. Vehicle speed greater than 10. 0 Km/h (6. 0 mph). Accelerator Pedal Position (APP) greater than 12. 5%. Engine rpm greater than 450 rpm. No active DTCs from the following: Primary or Secondary Pressure Sensor Transmission Temperature Sensor TCC Lock Up Solenoid Step Motor Input or Output Speed Sensor Transmission Range Sensor (TRS)Line Pressure Solenoid Secondary Pressure Solenoid Condition one: Reported primary pressure is less than the lower limit of the primary pressure correlated with the reported secondary pressure for more than five seconds. Condition two: Reported primary pressure is greater than the upper limit of the primary pressure correlated with the reported secondary pressure for more than five seconds.
DTC: P1704	**-INPUT SPEED SENSOR 1 OVERSPEED:** Continuously with the ignition on, engine running, transmission in gear, and Input Speed Sensor 1 (N2) greater than 0 RPM. If the RPM of the Input Speed Sensor 1 (N2) is greater than 7700 RPM.
DTC: P1705	**-INPUT SPEED SENSOR 2 OVERSPEED:** Continuously with the ignition on, engine running, transmission in gear, and Input Speed Sensor 2 (N3) greater than 0 RPM If the RPM of the Input Speed Sensor 2 (N3) is greater than 7700 RPM.
DTC: P170A	**-PARK/NEUTRAL OUTPUT CIRCUIT LOW:** With the ignition switch on. The Vehicle System Integration Module (VSIM) has detected the P/N Switch Sense circuit below a calibrated value.
DTC: P170B	**-PARK/NEUTRAL OUTPUT CIRCUIT HIGH:** With the ignition switch on. The Vehicle System Integration Module (VSIM) has detected the P/N Switch Sense circuit above a calibrated value.
DTC: P170C	**-ENGINE RPM OUTPUT CIRCUIT LOW:** With the ignition switch on. The Vehicle System Integration Module (VSIM) has detected the Engine Running Status Signal circuit below a calibrated value.

DTC	Trouble Code Title, Conditions, Possible Causes
DTC: P170D	**-ENGINE RPM OUTPUT CIRCUIT HIGH:** With the ignition switch on. The Vehicle System Integration Module (VSIM) has detected the Engine Running Status Signal above a calibrated value.
DTC: P1713	**-RESTRICTED MANUAL VALVE IN T2 RANGE:** Ignition on, engine running with the gear shift selector in a valid forward gear. This DTC sets whenever Transmission control system detects the manual valve is in the T2 range when it should be in OD. This is mainly an informational DTC.
DTC: P1715	**-RESTRICTED MANUAL VALVE IN T3 RANGE:** Whenever the PRNDL code indicates Temp 3. This DTC sets when conditions for the DTC P1776 are satisfied or three unsuccessful attempts to engage 1st gear while the shifter is in the temp 3 zone. This indicates a restricted port at the manual valve because the shifter is not fully engaged in the drive position.
DTC: P1718	**-EEPROM INTEGRITY FAILURE:** Continuously with the ignition on. An attempt to program/write to the internal EEPROM failed, Also checks at power down. One Trip Fault. Three good trips to turn off the MIL.
DTC: P1723	**-LOCK UP / SELECT CONTROL CIRCUIT:** Ignition on with a system voltage between 9. 0 and 16. 0 volts. If the TCC ON/OFF Solenoid status does not match the TCM requested ON/OFF status for the period of 200 msec the DTC will set. It takes two consecutive problem identification trips to illuminate the MIL.
DTC: P1729	**TRANSMISSION RATIO CONTROL CIRCUIT:** If the Step motor ON/OFF status does not match the TCM requested ON/OFF status for the period of 200 msec the DTC will set. It takes two consecutive problem identification trips to illuminate the MIL.
DTC: P1729	**TRANSMISSION RATIO CONTROL CIRCUIT:** If the Step motor ON/OFF status does not match the TCM requested ON/OFF status for the period of 200 msec the DTC will set. It takes two consecutive problem identification trips to illuminate the MIL.
DTC: P172A-00	**-GEAR SELECTOR SWITCH:** With the ignition on. The Gear Selector Switch has set an internal failure status.
DTC: P1736	**-GEAR RATIO ERROR IN 2ND PRIME:** Continuously with the ignition on, engine running, and after the transmission has achieved the proper gear ratio. If the ratio of the Input rpm to the Output rpm does not match the current gear ratio. This DTC can take up to five minutes of problem identification before illuminating the MIL
DTC: P1741	**-GEAR RATIO ERROR IN 4 PRIME:** The Transmission gear ratio is monitored continuously while the transmission is in gear. If the ratio of the Input RPM to the Output RPM does not match the current gear ratio when compared to the known gear ratio.
DTC: P1744	**TORQUE CONVERTER LOCK-UP CLUTCH HEAT CONTROL:** Ignition on, engine running with the transmission in a valid forward or reverse gear. No inhibitor switch, secondary speed sensor, or engine speed DTCs present. The DTC will set if an Engine stall speed condition is detected for the period of 18 seconds.
DTC: P1745	**TRANSMISSION LINE PRESSURE TOO HIGH FOR TOO LONG:** Continuously with ignition on. If the transmission has been operating in an open-loop line pressure control for 3220 kilometers (2000 miles) or 1000 2-3 upshifts.
DTC: P1771	**-INADEQUATE ELEMENT VOLUME 2/4:** Whenever the engine is running. The 2/4 Clutch Volume Index (CVI) is updated during a 3-1 or 2-1 manual downshift with throttle angle below 5 degrees. Transmission temperature must be at least 43° C (110° F). When the 2/4 Clutch Volume Index (CVI) falls below a calibrated value.
DTC: P1775	**-SOLENOID SWITCH VALVE LATCHED IN TCC POSITION:** During an attempted shift into 1st gear. This DTC is set if three unsuccessful attempts are made to shift the Solenoid Switch Valve (SSV) into the downshifted position in one given ignition start. This DTC can take up to five minutes to mature before illuminating the MIL.
DTC: P1775	**-SOLENOID SWITCH VALVE LATCHED IN TCC POSITION:** Prior to a shift into 1st gear. Transmission temperature must be hot. DTC is set after six unsuccessful attempts to shift into 1st gear.
DTC: P1776	**-SOLENOID SWITCH VALVE LATCHED IN LR POSITION:** Every 7 ms when doing PEMCC or FEMCC. Must be in partial or full EMCC. The DTC is set if L/R pressure is detected high for the fourth time.
DTC: P1776	**-SOLENOID SWITCH VALVE LATCHED IN LR POSITION:** Continuously when performing partial or full EMCC - PEMCC or FEMCC. If the transmission senses the L/R pressure switch closing while performing PEMCC or FEMCC. This DTC will set after two unsuccessful attempts to perform PEMCC or FEMCC. This DTC can take up to five minutes of problem identification before illuminating the MIL.

DTC	Trouble Code Title, Conditions, Possible Causes
DTC: P1790	**-FAULT IMMEDIATELY AFTER SHIFT:** After a Gear Ratio Error code is stored. After a Gear Ratio Error DTC has already been set. The DTC is set if the fault happened within 1. 3 seconds of a shift. The DTC set time will vary from 1. 214 seconds to 15 seconds.
DTC: P1794	**-SPEED SENSOR GROUND ERROR:** Every 7ms after a controller reset with transmission in neutral. After a PCM reset in neutral and Input and Output sensor ratio equals 2. 50 to 1. 0 ±50. 0 rpm.
DTC: P1794	**-SPEED SENSOR GROUND ERROR:** Every 7ms after a controller reset with transmission in neutral. After a PCM reset in neutral and Input and Output sensor ratio equals 2. 50 to 1. 0 ±50. 0 rpm.
DTC: P1794	**-SPEED SENSOR GROUND ERROR:** Every 7 msec after a controller reset with transmission in neutral. After a Powertrain Control Module (PCM) reset in neutral and Input and Output sensor ratio equals 2. 50 to 1. 0 (± 50. 0 rpm).
DTC: P1794	**-SPEED SENSOR GROUND ERROR:** The gear ratio is monitored continuously while the Transmission is in gear. After a controller reset in neutral and a ratio of input to output, of 1 to 2. This DTC can take up to five minutes of problem identification before illuminating the MIL.
DTC: P1797	**-MANUAL SHIFT OVERHEAT:** Continuously with engine running. If the Engine Temperature exceeds 123° C (255° F) or the Transmission Temperature exceeds 135° C (275° F) while in AutoStick® mode. **NOTE: Aggressive driving or driving in Low for extended periods of time will set this DTC.**
DTC: P1797	**-MANUAL SHIFT OVERHEAT:** Continuously with engine running. If the Engine Temperature exceeds 123° C (255° F) or the Transmission Temperature exceeds 135° C (275° F). **NOTE: Aggressive driving or driving in low for extended periods of time will set this DTC.**
DTC: P1897	**-LEVEL 1 RPM BUS UNLOCK:** Engine running. When the Powertrain Control Module (PCM) recognizes an internal failure to communicate with the Front Control Module (FCM) or the Camshaft Position (CMP) Sensor and Crankshaft Position (CKP) Sensor count periods are too short. One trip fault. ETC light is flashing.
DTC: P198A	**-AWD SYSTEM PERFORMANCE:** Ignition on, no CAN DTCs from either the AWD control module or the TIPM. Condition One: Received On/Off-road signal pattern but not an existing pattern for the period of 20 seconds. Condition Two: Received On/Off-road signal pattern but not a proper pattern for the period of 60 seconds.
DTC: P1C4E	**-FAULT IN ABS/ESP MODULE:** Ignition on and battery voltage greater than 10. 0 Volts. An active DTC is stored in the ABS/ESP Module. One Trip Fault. Three good trips to turn off the MIL.

OBD II Trouble Code List (P2XXX Codes)

DTC	Trouble Code Title, Conditions, Possible Causes
DTC: P2002	**-DIESEL PARTICULATE FILTER EFFICIENCY BELOW THRESHOLD:** With the engine running. The ECM detects incorrect exhaust flow through the particulate filter during certain engine operating conditions.
DTC: P2004	**-INTAKE MANIFOLD RUNNER CONTROL STUCK OPEN:** With the engine running, when the valve closes, below a calibrated RPM, depending upon pedal position. The Powertrain Control Module (PCM) detects that the position feedback of the Manifold Flow Valve Position Sensor is not within range of the adapted value learned during in-plant initialization or after a non volatile memory reset (adaptive memory clear).
DTC: P2006	**-INTAKE MANIFOLD RUNNER CONTROL STUCK CLOSED:** With the engine running, when the valve opens, above a calibrated RPM depending upon pedal position. The Powertrain Control Module (PCM) detects that the position feedback of the Manifold Flow Valve Position Sensor is not within range of the adapted value learned during in-plant initialization or after a non volatile memory reset (adaptive memory clear).
DTC: P2008	**-SHORT RUNNER VALVE (SRV) CONTROL CIRCUIT:** With the engine run time above a calibrated value, battery voltage greater than 10. 4 Volts, ECT within a specific range and the Short Runner Valve Assembly control active. This Powertrain Control Module (PCM) compares the circuit feedback to a calibrated closed range when the circuit is de-energized or to a calibrated open range when the circuit is energized. If the value is determined to be out of the calibrated range in either the de-energized or energized state for more than a calibrated amount of time, this DTC will set.

DTC	Trouble Code Title, Conditions, Possible Causes
DTC: P2008	**-INTAKE MANIFOLD RUNNER (SWIRL) CONTROL CIRCUIT OPEN:** With the ignition on and the Intake Swirl Servo Motor command off. The ECM does not detect voltage on the (N117) Intake Swirl Servo Motor Control circuit for 2. 0 seconds.
DTC: P2008	**-INTAKE MANIFOLD RUNNER (SWIRL) CONTROL CIRCUIT/OPEN:** With the engine running and battery voltage greater than 10. 4 volts. The Powertrain Control Module (PCM) detects that the Manifold Flow Valve control circuit voltage is not within an acceptable range.
DTC: P2009	**-INTAKE MANIFOLD RUNNER (SWIRL) CONTROL CIRCUIT LOW:** With the ignition on and the Intake Swirl Servo Motor command off. The ECM detects a short to ground on the (N117) Intake Swirl Servo Motor Control circuit for 2. 3 seconds.
DTC: P2010	**-INTAKE MANIFOLD RUNNER (SWIRL) CONTROL CIRCUIT HIGH:** With the ignition on and the Intake Swirl Servo Motor command on. The ECM detects excessive current on the (N117) Intake Swirl Servo Motor Control circuit for 2. 0 seconds.
DTC: P2015	**-INTAKE MANIFOLD RUNNER POSITION SENSOR PERFORMANCE:** With the ignition on and battery voltage greater than 10. 4 volts. The Powertrain Control Module (PCM) detects an implausible voltage on the Manifold Flow Valve circuit.
DTC: P2016	**-INTAKE MANIFOLD RUNNER POSITION SENSOR CIRCUIT LOW:** With the ignition on and battery voltage greater than 10. 4 volts. The Powertrain Control Module (PCM) detects that the Manifold Flow Valve (MFV) Position Sensor input voltage is below the minimum acceptable value.
DTC: P2016	**-SHORT RUNNER VALVE (SRV) POSITION SENSOR CIRCUIT LOW:** With the ignition on and battery voltage greater than 10. 4 Volts. The Powertrain Control Module (PCM) detects that the PWM signal from the Short Runner Valve position sensor circuit is below the minimum acceptable value.
DTC: P2017	**-SHORT RUNNER VALVE (SRV) POSITION SENSOR CIRCUIT HIGH:** With the ignition on and battery voltage greater than 10. 4 Volts. The Powertrain Control Module (PCM) detects that the PWM signal from the Short Runner Valve Position sensor is greater than the maximum acceptable value.
DTC: P2017	**-INTAKE MANIFOLD RUNNER POSITION SENSOR CIRCUIT HIGH:** With the ignition on and battery voltage greater than 10. 4 volts. The Powertrain Control Module (PCM) detects that the MFV Position Sensor input voltage is above the maximum acceptable value.
DTC: P2032	**-EXHAUST GAS TEMPERATURE SENSOR CIRCUIT LOW - BANK 1 SENSOR 2:** With the ignition on. The ECM detects that the (K353) Post-Catalyst Exhaust Temperature Sensor Signal circuit is shorted to ground.
DTC: P2033	**-EXHAUST GAS TEMPERATURE SENSOR CIRCUIT HIGH - BANK 1 SENSOR 2:** With the ignition on. The ECM detects that the (K353) Post-Catalyst Exhaust Temperature Sensor Signal circuit is shorted to voltage.
DTC: P2065-11	**-FUEL LEVEL SENSOR 2 - CIRCUIT SHORT TO GROUND:** With the ignition on. Battery voltage greater than 10. 4 volts. The Body Control Module (BCM) detects that the Fuel Level Sensor 2 input voltage is below the minimum acceptable value.
DTC: P2065-15	**-FUEL LEVEL SENSOR 2 - CIRCUIT SHORT TO BATTERY OR OPEN:** With the ignition on. Battery voltage greater than 10. 4 volts. The Body Control Module (BCM) detects that the Fuel Level Sensor 2 input voltage is above the maximum acceptable value.
DTC: P2066	**-FUEL LEVEL SENSOR 2 PERFORMANCE:** With engine run time greater than three minutes and Fuel Level Sensor 1 reading high. The Powertrain Control Module (PCM) detects no change in Fuel Level Sensor 2 circuit voltage after a significant amount of fuel should have been consumed based on a calculated value and the vehicle operating conditions.
DTC: P2067	**-FUEL LEVEL SENSOR 2 CIRCUIT LOW:** With the ignition on. The Cluster detects that the Fuel Level Sensor input voltage is below the minimum acceptable value.
DTC: P2068	**-FUEL LEVEL SENSOR 2 CIRCUIT HIGH:** With the ignition on. The Cluster detects that the Fuel Level Sensor input voltage is above the maximum acceptable value.
DTC: P2068	**-FUEL LEVEL SENSOR 2 CIRCUIT HIGH:** With the ignition on and battery voltage greater than 10. 4 Volts. The Fuel Level Sensor 2 input voltage is above the maximum acceptable value.

DTC	Trouble Code Title, Conditions, Possible Causes
DTC: P2072	**-ELECTRONIC THROTTLE CONTROL SYSTEM - ICE BLOCKAGE:** With the ignition on and battery voltage greater than 10. 4 volts. The Powertrain Control Module (PCM) detects that the throttle plate is stuck during extremely cold ambient temperature operation. The PCM will initiate a throttle de-icing procedure, and if the throttle blade still doesn't move, this DTC will set. The MIL will not illuminate. The vehicle will be in Limp home condition, limiting rpm and vehicle speed.
DTC: P2072	**-ELECTRONIC THROTTLE CONTROL SYSTEM - ICE BLOCKAGE:** Ignition on. The PCM recognizes the Throttle plate is stuck during extremely cold Ambient Temperature operation. The throttle plate goes through a de-icing procedure. If the throttle blade still doesn't move this fault sets. The MIL will not illuminate. ETC light will illuminate. The vehicle will be in Limp home condition, limiting rpm and vehicle speed.
DTC: P2080	**-EXHAUST GAS TEMPERATURE SENSOR CIRCUIT PERFORMANCE - BANK 1 SENSOR 1:** At ignition on before engine crank. With no Intake Air Temp sensor DTC's The Engine Control Module (ECM) detects that the (K352) Pre-Catalyst Exhaust Temperature Sensor Signal circuit voltage is implausible.
DTC: P2084	**-EXHAUST GAS TEMPERATURE SENSOR CIRCUIT PERFORMANCE - BANK 1 SENSOR 2:** With the ignition on. The Engine Control Module (ECM) detects that the (K353) Post-Catalyst Exhaust Temperature Sensor Signal circuit voltage is implausible.
DTC: P2096	**-DOWNSTREAM FUEL TRIM SYSTEM 1 LEAN:** With the engine running in closed loop, the ambient/battery temperature above -7° C (20° F) and altitude below 8500 ft. The conditions that cause this diagnostic to fail is when the upstream O2 sensor becomes biased from an exhaust leak, O2 sensor contamination, or some other extreme operating condition. The downstream O2 sensor is considered to be protected from extreme environments by the catalyst. The Powertrain Control Module (PCM) monitors the downstream O2 sensor feedback control, called downstream fuel trim, to detect any shift in the upstream O2 sensor target voltage from nominal target voltage. The value of the downstream fuel trim is compared with the lean thresholds. Every time the value exceeds the calibrated threshold, a fail timer is incremented and mass flow through the exhaust is accumulated. If the fail timer and accumulated mass flow exceed the fail thresholds, the test fails and the diagnostic stops running for that trip. If the test fails on consecutive trips, a DTC is set.
DTC: P2097	**-DOWNSTREAM FUEL TRIM SYSTEM 1 RICH:** With the engine running in closed loop, the ambient/battery temperature above -7° C (20° F) and altitude below 8500 ft. The conditions that cause this diagnostic to fail is when the upstream O2 sensor becomes biased from an exhaust leak, O2 sensor contamination, or some other extreme operating condition. The downstream O2 sensor is considered to be protected from extreme environments by the catalyst. The Powertrain Control Module (PCM) monitors the downstream O2 sensor feedback control, called downstream fuel trim, to detect any shift in the upstream O2 sensor target voltage from nominal target voltage. The value of the downstream fuel trim is compared with the rich thresholds. Every time the value exceeds the calibrated threshold, a fail timer is incremented and mass flow through the exhaust is accumulated. If the fail timer and accumulated mass flow exceed the fail thresholds, the test fails and the diagnostic stops running for that trip. If the test fails on consecutive trips, a DTC is set.
DTC: P2097	**-DOWNSTREAM FUEL TRIM SYSTEM 2 RICH:** With the engine running in closed loop, the ambient/battery temperature above -7°C (20°F) and altitude below 8500 ft. The conditions that cause this diagnostic to fail is when the upstream O2 Sensor becomes biased from an exhaust leak, O2 Sensor contamination, or some other extreme operating condition. The downstream O2 Sensor is considered to be protected from extreme environments by the catalyst. The Powertrain Control Module (PCM) monitors the downstream O2 Sensor feedback control, called downstream fuel trim, to detect any shift in the upstream O2 Sensor target voltage from nominal target voltage. The value of the downstream fuel trim is compared with the lean thresholds. Every time the value exceeds the calibrated threshold, a fail timer is incremented and mass flow through the exhaust is accumulated. If the fail timer and accumulated mass flow exceed the fail thresholds, the test fails and the diagnostic stops running for that trip. If the test fails on consecutive trips, a DTC is set.
DTC: P2098	**-DOWNSTREAM FUEL TRIM SYSTEM 2 LEAN:** With the engine running in closed loop mode, the ambient/battery temperature above -6. 7°C (20°F) and altitude below 2590. 8 m (8500 ft) and fuel level greater than 15%. The conditions that cause this diagnostic to fail is when the upstream O2 sensor becomes biased from an exhaust leak, O2 sensor contamination, or some other extreme operating condition. The downstream O2 sensor is considered to be protected from extreme environments by the catalyst. The PCM monitors the downstream O2 sensor feedback control, called downstream fuel trim, to detect any shift in the upstream O2 sensor target voltage from nominal target voltage. The value of the downstream fuel trim is compared with the lean thresholds. Every time the value exceeds the calibrated threshold, a fail timer is incremented and mass flow through the exhaust is accumulated. If the fail timer and accumulated mass flow exceed the fail thresholds, the test fails and the diagnostic stops running for that trip. If the test fails on consecutive trips, a DTC is set.

DTC	Trouble Code Title, Conditions, Possible Causes
DTC: P2099	**-DOWNSTREAM FUEL TRIM SYSTEM 2 RICH:** With the engine running in closed loop mode, the ambient/battery temperature above -6. 7°C (20°F) and altitude below 2590. 8 m (8500 ft). The conditions that cause this diagnostic to fail is when the upstream O2 sensor becomes biased from an exhaust leak, O2 sensor contamination, or some other extreme operating condition. The downstream O2 sensor is considered to be protected from extreme environments by the catalyst. The PCM monitors the downstream O2 sensor feedback control, called downstream fuel trim, to detect any shift in the upstream O2 sensor target voltage from nominal target voltage. The value of the downstream fuel trim is compared with the lean thresholds. Every time the value exceeds the calibrated threshold, a fail timer is incremented and mass flow through the exhaust is accumulated. If the fail timer and accumulated mass flow exceed the fail thresholds, the test fails and the diagnostic stops running for that trip. If the test fails on consecutive trips, a DTC is set.
DTC: P2100	**-ELECTRONIC THROTTLE CONTROL MOTOR CIRCUIT:** With the ignition on and the ETC Motor is not in Limp mode. When the Powertrain Control Module (PCM) detects an internal error or a short between the ETC Motor (+) and ETC Motor (-) circuits in the ETC Motor Driver. One trip fault. ETC light is flashing.
DTC: P2101	**-ELECTRONIC THROTTLE CONTROL MOTOR PERFORMANCE:** With the engine running, ETC motor not in limp home mode, and TPS adaptation complete. The Powertrain Control Module (PCM) detects too large of an error between the actual position of the throttle plate and the desired set point. One trip fault. The DTC will set within 5 seconds. Three good trips to turn off the MIL ETC light is flashing.
DTC: P2106	**-ELECTRONIC THROTTLE CONTROL SYSTEM - FORCED LIMITED POWER:** Ignition on. This DTC sets for OBDII MIL illumination purposes. This DTC will always have associated DTCs indicating a system failure. Engine speed is being limited and/or throttle motor is power free. ETC light is flashing.
DTC: P2107	**-ELECTRONIC THROTTLE CONTROL MODULE PROCESSOR:** With the ignition on. Internal Powertrain Control Module (PCM) failure. Module will attempt to reset, so you will be able to hear the throttle relearning. If the condition is continuous, the vehicle may not be drivable. One trip fault. ETC light is flashing.
DTC: P2107	**-ELECTRONIC THROTTLE CONTROL MODULE PROCESSOR:** With the ignition on and the ETC Motor is not in Limp Home mode. When the Powertrain Control Module (PCM) detects an internal error or a short between the ETC Motor - and ETC Motor + circuits in the ETC Motor Driver. One trip fault. ETC light is flashing.
DTC: P2108	**-ELECTRONIC THROTTLE CONTROL MODULE PERFORMANCE:** Ignition on. Internal PCM failure. Customer may experience an extended cranking condition with limited driving and a rough idle. One trip fault and the code will set within 5 seconds. ETC light is flashing.
DTC: P2110	**-ELECTRONIC THROTTLE CONTROL - FORCED LIMITED RPM:** Ignition on and ETC motor is working. When the Powertrain Control Module (PCM) requests to limit engine speed if PWM is too high for 20. five seconds and before P2118 sets. One trip fault and the code will set within five seconds. ETC light is illuminated.
DTC: P2110	**-ELECTRONIC THROTTLE CONTROL SYSTEM - FORCED LIMITED RPM:** With the ignition on and the ETC Motor not in Limp Home mode. When the Powertrain Control Module (PCM) requests to limit engine speed if PWM is too high for 20. five seconds and before P2118 sets. One trip fault and the code will set within five seconds. ETC light is illuminated.
DTC: P2110	**-ELECTRONIC THROTTLE CONTROL - FORCED LIMITED RPM:** Ignition on and ETC motor is working. When the Powertrain Control Module (PCM) requests to limit engine speed if PWM is too high for 20. five seconds and before P2118 sets. One trip fault and the code will set within five seconds. ETC light is illuminated.
DTC: P2111	**-ELECTRONIC THROTTLE CONTROL - UNABLE TO CLOSE:** Ignition on and battery voltage greater than 10 volts. Just after key on, the throttle is opened and closed to test the system. If the TP Sensor does not return to Limp Home Position at the end of this test, this DTC will set. One trip fault and the code will set within 5 seconds. ETC light is flashing.
DTC: P2112	**-ELECTRONIC THROTTLE CONTROL - UNABLE TO OPEN:** Ignition on and battery voltage greater than 10. 0 Volts. Just after key on, the throttle is opened and closed to test the system. If the TP Sensor does not return to Limp Position at the end of this test, this DTC will set. One trip fault and the code will set within five seconds. ETC light is flashing.
DTC: P2112	**-ELECTRONIC THROTTLE CONTROL SYSTEM - UNABLE TO OPEN:** With the ignition on and the ETC Motor not in Limp Home mode. When the Powertrain Control Module (PCM) detects an error in the ETC Motor Driver or throttle position.
DTC: P2112	**-ELECTRONIC THROTTLE CONTROL - UNABLE TO OPEN:** Ignition on and battery voltage greater than 10 volts. Just after key on, the throttle is opened and closed to test the system. If the Powertrain Control Module (PCM) detects that the TP Sensor does not move from Limp Home Position, this DTC will set. One trip fault. The DTC will set within five seconds. ETC light is flashing.

DTC	Trouble Code Title, Conditions, Possible Causes
DTC: P2115	**-ACCELERATOR PEDAL POSITION SENSOR 1 MINIMUM STOP PERFORMANCE:** With the igniting on. During in-plant testing, the APPS is checked to make sure the minimum and maximum values can be reached. The PCM performs the diagnostic test for this DTC after the diagnostic test for P2166 has passed. APPS 1 has failed to achieve the required minimum value during In-Plant testing. One trip fault and the code will set within 5 seconds. Engine will only idle.
DTC: P2115	**-ACCELERATOR PEDAL POSITION SENSOR 1 MINIMUM STOP PERFORMANCE:** Ignition on. During in plant mode the APP Sensors need to be checked to make sure that idle and full pedal travel can be reached on both sensors. The test for P2115 is only enabled once test for P2166 has passed. APPS No. 1 has failed to achieve the required minimum value during In Plant testing. One trip fault and the code will set within 5 seconds. Engine will only idle. ETC light is illuminated.
DTC: P2116	**-ACCELERATOR PEDAL POSITION SENSOR 2 MINIMUM STOP PERFORMANCE:** Ignition on. During in plant mode the APP Sensors need to be checked to make sure that idle and full pedal travel can be reached on both sensors. The test for P2116 is only enabled once test for P2167 has passed. APPS No. 2 has failed to achieve the required minimum value during In Plant testing. One trip fault and the code will be stored within 5 seconds. Engine will only idle. ETC light is illuminated.
DTC: P2116	**-ACCELERATOR PEDAL POSITION SENSOR 2 MINIMUM STOP PERFORMANCE:** With the igniting on. During in-plant testing, the APPS is checked to make sure the minimum and maximum values can be reached. The PCM performs the diagnostic test for this DTC after the diagnostic test for P2167 has passed. APPS 2 has failed to achieve the required minimum value during In-Plant testing. One trip fault and the code will be stored within 5 seconds. Engine will only idle.
DTC: P2118	**-ELECTRONIC THROTTLE CONTROL MOTOR CIRCUIT:** With the ignition on and the ETC Motor is not in Limp mode. When the Powertrain Control Module (PCM) detects an internal error or a short between the ETC Motor (+) and ETC Motor (-) circuits in the ETC Motor Driver. One trip fault. ETC light is flashing.
DTC: P2121	**-ACCELERATOR PEDAL POSITION SENSOR 1 PERFORMANCE:** With the ignition on. APP Sensor #1 and APP Sensor #2 signals do not agree.
DTC: P2122	**-ACCELERATOR PEDAL POSITION SENSOR 1 CIRCUIT LOW:** With the ignition on and battery voltage greater than 10. 4 volts. The Powertrain Control Module (PCM) detects that the APP Sensor 1 input voltage is below the minimum acceptable value.
DTC: P2122	**-ACCELERATOR PEDAL POSITION SENSOR 1 CIRCUIT LOW:** With the ignition on and no other APPS No. 1 DTCs present. When the APP Sensor No. 1 voltage is too low. Engine will additionally idle if the brake pedal is pressed or has failed. Acceleration rate and Engine output are limited. One trip fault and the code will set within 5 seconds. ETC light is flashing.
DTC: P2123	**-ACCELERATOR PEDAL POSITION SENSOR 1 CIRCUIT HIGH:** With the ignition on and no other APPS No. 1 DTCs present. When APP Sensor No. 1 voltage is too high. Engine will additionally idle if the brake pedal is pressed or has failed. Acceleration rate and Engine output are limited. One trip fault and the code will set within five seconds. ETC light is flashing.
DTC: P2123	**-ACCELERATOR PEDAL POSITION SENSOR 1 CIRCUIT HIGH:** With the ignition on and battery voltage greater than 10. 4 volts. The Powertrain Control Module (PCM) detects that the APP Sensor 1 input voltage is above the maximum acceptable value.
DTC: P2127	**-ACCELERATOR PEDAL POSITION SENSOR 2 CIRCUIT LOW:** With the ignition on and no other APPS No. 2 DTCs present. When the APP Sensor No. 2 voltage is too low. Engine will only idle if the Brake pedal is Pressed or has failed. Acceleration rate and Engine output are limited. One trip fault and the code will set within 5 seconds. ETC light is flashing.
DTC: P2127	**-ACCELERATOR PEDAL POSITION SENSOR 2 CIRCUIT LOW:** With the ignition on. The APP Sensor #2 Signal circuit is below 0. 097 volts for 0. 32 seconds.
DTC: P2128	**-ACCELERATOR PEDAL POSITION SENSOR 2 CIRCUIT HIGH:** With the ignition on and no other APPS No. 2 DTCs present. When APP Sensor No. 2 voltage is too high. Idle is additionally forced any time the brake is applied or failed. Acceleration rate and Engine output are limited. One trip fault and the code will set within five seconds. ETC light is flashing.
DTC: P2135	**THROTTLE POSITION SENSOR 1/2 CORRELATION:** With the ignition on and no other DTCs present for TP Sensor No. 1 or No. 2. The Powertrain Control Module (PCM) recognizes TP Sensors No. 1 and No. 2 are not coherent. One trip fault and the code will set within five seconds. ETC light is illuminated.
DTC: P2135	**THROTTLE POSITION SENSOR 1/2 CORRELATION:** With the engine running and no TPS or MAP sensor DTCs present. The Powertrain Control Module (PCM) recognizes TP Sensors No. 1 and No. 2 are not coherent. One trip fault and the code will set within five seconds. ETC light is illuminated.

DTC	Trouble Code Title, Conditions, Possible Causes
DTC: P2135	**THROTTLE POSITION SENSOR 1/2 CORRELATION:** With the ignition on, battery voltage greater than 10. 4 volts, and no other TP Sensor DTCs present. The Powertrain Control Module (PCM) detects that the TP Sensor voltages are not plausible. One trip fault and the code will set within five seconds. ETC light is illuminated.
DTC: P2138	**-ACCELERATOR PEDAL POSITION SENSOR 1/2 CORRELATION:** With the ignition on and no APPS No. 1 and APPS No. 2 DTC present. APPS values No. 1 and No. 2 are not coherent. Idle is additionally forced when the brake pedal is pressed or failed. Acceleration rate and Engine output are limited. One trip fault and the code will set within 5 seconds. ETC light is flashing.
DTC: P2138	**-ACCELERATOR PEDAL POSITION SENSOR 1/2 CORRELATION:** With the ignition on, battery voltage greater than 10. 4 Volts, and no APPS 1 and APPS 2 DTCs present. The Powertrain Control Module (PCM) detects that the correlation between APPS 1 and APPS 2 is not plausible. Idle may be affected when the brake pedal is pressed or if a brake switch circuit error is present. Acceleration rate and engine output are limited. One trip fault and the code will set within five seconds. ETC light is flashing.
DTC: P213A	**-EGR AIRFLOW THROTTLE CONTROL CIRCUIT B OPEN:** With the engine running and the EGR Airflow Control Valve Motor command off. The ECM does not detect voltage on the (K315) EGR Airflow Control Valve Motor (-) circuit for 0. 5 second.
DTC: P213C	**-EGR AIRFLOW THROTTLE CONTROL CIRCUIT B LOW:** With the engine running and the EGR Airflow Control Valve Motor command off. The (K315) EGR Airflow Control Valve Motor (-) circuit is shorted to ground for 0. 2 second.
DTC: P213D	**-EGR AIRFLOW THROTTLE CONTROL CIRCUIT B HIGH:** With the engine running and the EGR Airflow Control Valve Motor command on. The (K315) EGR Airflow Control Valve Motor (-) circuit is shorted to voltage for 0. 2 seconds.
DTC: P2141	**-EGR AIRFLOW THROTTLE CONTROL CIRCUIT A LOW:** With the engine running and the EGR Airflow Control Valve Motor command off. The (K314) EGR Airflow Control Valve Motor (+) circuit is shorted to ground for 0. 2 second.
DTC: P2142	**-EGR AIRFLOW THROTTLE CONTROL CIRCUIT A HIGH:** With the engine running and the EGR Airflow Control Valve Motor command on. The (K314) EGR Airflow Control Valve Motor (+) circuit is shorted to voltage for 0. 2 second.
DTC: P2146	**-FUEL INJECTOR GROUP 1 SUPPLY VOLTAGE CIRCUIT OPEN:** With the engine running. The ECM detects an open circuit error on a fuel injector high-side control circuit.
DTC: P2147	**-FUEL INJECTOR GROUP 1 SUPPLY VOLTAGE CIRCUIT LOW:** With the engine running. The ECM detects a short to ground error on the injector high-side control circuit.
DTC: P2148	**-FUEL INJECTOR GROUP 1 SUPPLY VOLTAGE CIRCUIT HIGH:** With the engine running. The ECM detects a short to voltage error on one of the injector high-side control circuits.
DTC: P2149	**-FUEL INJECTOR GROUP 2 SUPPLY VOLTAGE CIRCUIT OPEN:** With the engine running. The ECM detects an open circuit error on a fuel injector high-side control circuit.
DTC: P2150	**-FUEL INJECTOR GROUP 2 SUPPLY VOLTAGE CIRCUIT LOW:** With the engine running. The ECM detects a short to ground error on the injector high-side control circuit.
DTC: P2151	**-FUEL INJECTOR GROUP 2 SUPPLY VOLTAGE CIRCUIT HIGH:** With the engine running. The ECM detects a short to voltage error on one of the injector high-side control circuits.
DTC: P2161	**-VEHICLE SPEED SENSOR 2 ERRATIC:** Ignition on. PCM recognizes Vehicle speed input No. 2 erratic or high. VSS No. 2 is based on the average of the Front Wheel Speeds. One trip fault and the code will set within 5 seconds. No MIL and No ETC light. Cruise is disabled.
DTC: P2161	**-VEHICLE SPEED SENSOR 2 ERRATIC (with ABS):** With engine run time greater than 5 seconds, ECT above -8° C (17. 6° F), transmission not in park or neutral, brakes not applied, engine rpm greater than 1500, and no ECT, MAP, TPS, ETC, or brake switch stuck DTCs present. The Powertrain Control (PCM) receives an erratic vehicle speed signal. One Trip Fault. Three good trips to turn off the MIL.
DTC: P2166	**-ACCELERATOR PEDAL POSITION SENSOR 1 MAXIMUM STOP PERFORMANCE:** Ignition on. During in plant mode the APP Sensors need to be checked to make sure that idle and full pedal travel can be reached on both sensors. APPS No. 1 has failed to achieve the required maximum value during In Plant testing. One trip fault and the code will set within five seconds. Engine will only idle. ETC light will illuminate.

DTC	Trouble Code Title, Conditions, Possible Causes
DTC: P2167	**-ACCELERATOR PEDAL POSITION SENSOR 2 MAXIMUM STOP PERFORMANCE:** With the igniting on. During in-plant testing, the APP Sensors need to be checked to make sure the minimum and maximum values can be reached. APPS 2 has failed to achieve the required maximum value during In-Plant testing. One trip fault and the code will be stored within five seconds. Engine will only idle.
DTC: P2167	**-ACCELERATOR PEDAL POSITION SENSOR 2 MAXIMUM STOP PERFORMANCE:** Ignition on. During in plant mode the APP Sensors need to be checked to make sure that idle and full pedal travel can be reached on both sensors. APPS No. 2 has failed to achieve the required maximum value during In Plant testing. One trip fault and the code will set within five seconds. Engine will only idle. ETC light will illuminate.
DTC: P2172	**-HIGH AIRFLOW/VACUUM LEAK DETECTED (INSTANTANEOUS ACCUMULATION):** Ignition on and engine running with no MAP Sensor DTCs. A large vacuum leak has been detected or both of the TP Sensors have failed based on their position being 2. 5 Volts and the calculated MAP value is less than the actual MAP minus an Offset value. One trip fault and the code will set within five seconds. ETC light will flash.
DTC: P2173	**-HIGH AIRFLOW/VACUUM LEAK DETECTED (SLOW ACCUMULATION):** Ignition on and engine running with no MAP Sensor DTCs. A large vacuum leak has been detected or both of the TP Sensors have failed based on their position being 2. 5 Volts and the calculated MAP value is less than the Gas Flow Adaptation value is too high. One trip fault the code will set within 5 seconds. ETC light will flash.
DTC: P2174	**-LOW AIRFLOW/RESTRICTION DETECTED (INSTANTANEOUS ACCUMULATION):** Ignition on and engine running with no MAP Sensor DTCs. The Powertrain Control Module (PCM) calculated MAP value is greater than actual MAP value plus an offset value. One trip fault. Three good trips to turn of the mil. ETC light will flash.
DTC: P2175	**-LOW AIRFLOW/RESTRICTION DETECTED (SLOW ACCUMULATION):** Ignition on and engine running with no MAP Sensor DTCs. PCM calculated MAP value is greater than actual MAP value plus an offset value. One trip fault and the code will set within 5 seconds. Three good trips to turn of the mil. ETC light will flash.
DTC: P2175	**-LOW AIRFLOW/RESTRICTION DETECTED (SLOW ACCUMULATION):** Ignition on and engine running with no MAP Sensor DTCs. The Powertrain Control Module (PCM) calculated MAP value is greater than actual MAP value plus an offset value. One trip fault and the code will set within five seconds. Three good trips to turn of the mil. ETC light will flash.
DTC: P2181	**-COOLING SYSTEM PERFORMANCE:** Ignition on, Engine running, and no ECT DTCs present. PCM recognizes that the ECT has failed its self coherence test. The coolant temp should only change at a certain rate, if this rate is too slow or too fast this fault will set. One trip fault. Three good trips to clear MIL. ETC light will illuminate on first trip failure.
DTC: P219A	**-AIR-FUEL RATIO CYLINDER IMBALANCE BANK 1:** Engine Coolant Temperature (ECT) is greater than 70°C (158°F), Engine run time of 90 seconds, engine RPM 1000 - 2700, engine load 30 - 90% and in flex fuel vehicles the Fuel Adaptive Learned must be completed. DTC P113D is not set and the high frequency content of the O2 sensor exceeds a calibrated amount. Two Trip Fault. Three good trips to turn off the MIL.
DTC: P219B	**-AIR-FUEL RATIO CYLINDER IMBALANCE BANK 2:** Engine Coolant Temperature (ECT) is greater than 70°C (158°F), Engine run time of 90 seconds, engine RPM 1000 - 2700, engine load 30 - 90% and in flex fuel vehicles the Fuel Adaptive Learned must be completed. DTC P113E is not set and the high frequency content of the O2 Sensor exceeds a calibrated amount. Two Trip Fault. Three good trips to turn off the MIL.
DTC: P2231	**-O2 SENSOR 1/1 SIGNAL CIRCUIT SHORTED TO HEATER CIRCUIT:** With the ignition on. The ECM detects a short between the (Z43) O2 1/1 Negative Current Control circuit and the (K99) O2 1/1 Heater Control circuit.
DTC: P2237	**-O2 SENSOR 1/1 PUMP CELL CURRENT CIRCUIT OPEN:** With the ignition on and the O2 1/1 Sensor at operating temperature. The ECM detects an open on the (K43) O2 1/1 Positive Current Control circuit for 2. 0 seconds.
DTC: P2238	**-O2 SENSOR 1/1 PUMP CELL CURRENT CIRCUIT LOW:** With the ignition on and the O2 1/1 Sensor at operating temperature. The ECM detects a short to ground on the (K43) O2 1/1 Positive Current Control circuit for 2. 0 seconds.
DTC: P2239	**-O2 SENSOR 1/1 PUMP CELL CURRENT CIRCUIT HIGH:** With the ignition on and the O2 1/1 Sensor at operating temperature. The ECM detects a short to voltage on the (K43) O2 1/1 Positive Current Control circuit for 2. 0 seconds.
DTC: P2243	**-O2 SENSOR 1/1 REFERENCE VOLTAGE CIRCUIT OPEN:** With the ignition on and the O2 1/1 Sensor at operating temperature. The ECM detects an open on the (K41) O2 1/1 Reference Signal circuit for 2. 0 seconds.

DTC	Trouble Code Title, Conditions, Possible Causes
DTC: P2244	**-O2 SENSOR 1/1 REFERENCE VOLTAGE PERFORMANCE:** With the ignition on and the O2 1/1 Sensor at operating temperature. The ECM detects an implausible voltage on the (K41) O2 1/1 Reference Signal.
DTC: P2245	**-O2 SENSOR 1/1, 2/1 REFERENCE VOLTAGE CIRCUIT LOW:** Continuously after 15 seconds of engine runtime, no O2 Sensor Heater DTCs present and battery voltage greater than 10. 4 Volts. The Oxygen Sensor reference voltage is below 0. 9 Volt for 60 seconds. The DTC will set as Pending after one trip and Active after two trips. Three good trips to turn off the MIL.
DTC: P2245	**-O2 SENSOR 1/1 REFERENCE VOLTAGE CIRCUIT LOW:** With the ignition on and the O2 1/1 Sensor at operating temperature. The Powertrain Control Module (PCM) detects a short to ground on the (K41) O2 Sensor 1/1 Reference Signal circuit for 2. 0 seconds.
DTC: P2246	**-O2 SENSOR 1/1 REFERENCE VOLTAGE CIRCUIT HIGH:** With the ignition on and the O2 Sensor 1/1 at operating temperature. The Powertrain Control Module (PCM) detects a short to voltage on the (K41) O2 Sensor 1/1 Reference Signal circuit for 2. 0 seconds.
DTC: P2246	**-O2 SENSOR 1/1, 2/1 REFERENCE VOLTAGE CIRCUIT HIGH:** Engine running for 15 seconds, O2 Sensors at operating temperature and battery voltage greater 10. 4 Volts. The PCM detects that the (K902) Reference Signal voltage is greater than 3. 9 Volts for nine seconds.
DTC: P2270	**-O2 SENSOR 1/2 SIGNAL BIASED LEAN:** With the engine running, the odometer greater than the minimum mileage allowable for catalyst break-in, and no global or monitor conflicts or disabling conditions present. The test will only run if the monitor has not already run and passed or failed. The Powertrain Control Module (PCM) detects that the sensor does not output a voltage greater than a calibrated high voltage value and less than a calibrated low voltage value within a specific time period. If the voltage pass values are not achieved after the total accumulated test time, a pending fault will be set. An active fault is matured on a second trip failure. Three good trips will turn off the MIL.
DTC: P2271	**-O2 SENSOR 1/2 SIGNAL STUCK RICH:** With the engine running, vehicle speed above 96 kph (60 mph), throttle open for a minimum of 120 seconds, ECT greater than 70° C (158° F), catalytic converter temperature greater than 600° C (1112° F) and downstream oxygen sensor in a rich state. During a decel fuel shutoff event, the downstream oxygen sensor should switch from rich to lean within a specific time. The PCM monitors the downstream O2 sensor. If the PCM does not detect a rich to lean switch within a specific time during a decel fuel shutoff event, the monitor will fail. Two trip fault. Three good trips to turn off the MIL.
DTC: P2271	**-O2 SENSOR 1/2 SIGNAL BIASED RICH:** With the engine running, the odometer greater than the minimum mileage allowable for catalyst break-in, and no global or monitor conflicts or disabling conditions present. The test will only run if the monitor has not already run and passed or failed. The Powertrain Control Module (PCM) detects that the sensor does not output a voltage greater than a calibrated high voltage value and less than a calibrated low voltage value within a specific time period. If the voltage pass values are not achieved after the total accumulated test time, a pending fault will be set. An active fault is matured on a second trip failure. Three good trips will turn off the MIL.
DTC: P2273	**-O2 SENSOR 2/2 SIGNAL STUCK RICH:** With the engine running, vehicle speed above 96 kph (60 mph), throttle open for a minimum of 120 seconds, ECT greater than 70 C (158 F), catalytic converter temperature greater than 600 C (1112 F), and downstream oxygen sensor in a rich state. During a decel fuel shutoff event, the downstream oxygen sensor should switch from rich to lean within a specific time. The PCM monitors the downstream O2 sensor. If the PCM does not detect a rich to lean switch within a specific time during a decel fuel shutoff event, the monitor will fail. Two trip fault. Three good trips to turn off the MIL.
DTC: P2280	**-AIR FILTER RESTRICTION:** With the engine running. The ECM compares mass airflow volume/engine rpm to atmospheric pressure. The ECM detects a 50% or more drop in airflow through the air filter for five minutes.
DTC: P2299	**-BRAKE PEDAL POSITION/ACCELERATOR PEDAL POSITION INCOMPATIBLE:** Ignition on. No Break or APPS faults present. The PCM recognizes a brake application following the APPS showing a fixed pedal opening. Temporary or permanent. Internally the PCM will reduce throttle opening below driver demand. One trip fault and the code will be set within five seconds. ETC light will illuminate, the light will only stay illuminated while DTC is active.
DTC: P2299	**-BRAKE PEDAL POSITION/ACCELERATOR PEDAL POSITION INCOMPATIBLE:** With the engine running (engine speed above 570 rpm). No other APP or Brake Signal DTCs. Vehicle speed above 3 km/h. The ECM detects a brake signal input (brakes applied) and Accelerator Pedal Position above 3% at the same time for 15. 0 seconds.
DTC: P2302	**-IGNITION COIL 1 SECONDARY CIRCUIT - INSUFFICIENT IONIZATION:** With the engine running. The Powertrain Control Module (PCM) detects the secondary ignition burn time is incorrect or not present. One trip fault. Three good trips to turn off the Malfunction Indicator Lamp (MIL).
DTC: P2302	**-IGNITION COIL 1 SECONDARY CIRCUIT - INSUFFICIENT IONIZATION:** Engine running and battery voltage greater than 10. 0 Volts. If the Powertrain Control Module (PCM) detects that the secondary ignition burn time is incorrect, too short, or not present, an error is detected. One Trip Fault. Three good trips to turn off the MIL.

DTC	Trouble Code Title, Conditions, Possible Causes
DTC: P2305	**-IGNITION COIL 2 SECONDARY CIRCUIT - INSUFFICIENT IONIZATION:** Engine running and battery voltage greater than 10. 0 Volts. If Powertrain Control Module (PCM) detects that the secondary ignition burn time is incorrect, too short, or not present, an error is detected. One Trip Fault. Three good trips to turn off the MIL.
DTC: P2308	**-IGNITION COIL 3 SECONDARY CIRCUIT- INSUFFICIENT IONIZATION:** Engine running and battery voltage greater than 10 volts. If PCM detects that the secondary ignition burn time is incorrect, to short, or not present, an error is detected. One Trip Fault. Three good trips to turn off the MIL.
DTC: P2311	**-IGNITION COIL 4 SECONDARY CIRCUIT- INSUFFICIENT IONIZATION:** Engine running and battery voltage greater than 10 volts. If PCM detects that the secondary ignition burn time is incorrect, too short, or not present, an error is detected. One Trip Fault. Three good trips to turn off the MIL.
DTC: P2314	**-IGNITION COIL 5 SECONDARY CIRCUIT- INSUFFICIENT IONIZATION:** Engine running and battery voltage greater than 10 volts. If PCM detects that the secondary ignition burn time is incorrect, to short, or not present, an error is detected. One Trip Fault. Three good trips to turn off the MIL.
DTC: P2317	**-IGNITION COIL 6 SECONDARY CIRCUIT- INSUFFICIENT IONIZATION:** Engine running and battery voltage greater than 10 volts. If PCM detects that the secondary ignition burn time is incorrect, to short, or not present, an error is detected. One Trip Fault. Three good trips to turn off the MIL.
DTC: P2320	**-IGNITION COIL 7 SECONDARY CIRCUIT - INSUFFICIENT IONIZATION:** With the engine running. The Powertrain Control Module (PCM) detects the secondary ignition burn time is incorrect or not present. One trip fault. Three good trips to turn off the Malfunction Indicator Lamp (MIL).
DTC: P2323	**-IGNITION COIL 8 SECONDARY CIRCUIT - INSUFFICIENT IONIZATION:** With the engine running. The Powertrain Control Module (PCM) detects the secondary ignition burn time is incorrect or not present. One trip fault. Three good trips to turn off the Malfunction Indicator Lamp (MIL).
DTC: P242F	**-DIESEL PARTICULATE FILTER RESTRICTION - ASH ACCUMULATION:** With the engine running. The Differential Pressure Sensor signal indicates partial clogging of the particulate filter due to the accumulation of ash or other debris.
DTC: P2431	**-SECONDARY AIR INJECTION SYSTEM AIR FLOW SENSOR CIRCUIT PERFORMANCE:** Engine Coolant Temperature (ECT) above 0° C (32° F), ambient air temperature within approximately two degrees of ECT, actual air flow is less than or equal to model airflow, and Secondary Air Flow diagnostic counter above 100 (approximately three seconds). Secondary Air Pump Control circuit active. The Powertrain Control Module (PCM) detects that the measured air flow is below a calculated minimum value, above a calculated maximum value, or there is no difference between the minimum measured air flow value and the maximum measured air flow value during monitoring.
DTC: P2432	**-SECONDARY AIR INJECTION SYSTEM AIR FLOW SENSOR CIRCUIT LOW:** With the engine running and battery voltage greater than 10 volts. The Powertrain Control Module (PCM) detects that the sensor input voltage is below the minimum acceptable value.
DTC: P2433	**-SECONDARY AIR INJECTION SYSTEM AIR FLOW SENSOR CIRCUIT HIGH:** With the engine running and battery voltage greater than 10 volts. The Powertrain Control Module (PCM) detects that the sensor input voltage is above the maximum acceptable value.
DTC: P2440	**-AIR PUMP SWITCH VALVE STUCK OPEN:** Engine Coolant Temperature (ECT) above 0 C (32 F), intake temperature (IAT) within approximately 2 degrees of ECT. Measured airflow during pump actuation greater than a calibrated value (approximately 45 kg/h). Monitoring begins six seconds after the air injection pump turns off. The Powertrain Control Module (PCM) detects that the difference between minimum and maximum secondary airflow during monitoring (with the pump off) is greater than 6 kg/h.
DTC: P244B	**-DIESEL PARTICULATE FILTER DIFFERENTIAL PRESSURE TOO HIGH:** With the engine running. The ECM detects excessive pressure at the particulate filter.
DTC: P2453	**-DIESEL PARTICULATE FILTER DIFFERENTIAL PRESSURE SENSOR CIRCUIT PERFORMANCE:** At the beginning of engine crank. The Differential Pressure Sensor Signal is below negative 40 hpa or above positive 40 hpa.
DTC: P2454	**-DIESEL PARTICULATE FILTER DIFFERENTIAL PRESSURE SENSOR CIRCUIT LOW:** With the ignition on. The (K355) Exhaust Differential Pressure Sensor signal is below 0. 24 volts for 2. 0 seconds.
DTC: P2455	**-DIESEL PARTICULATE FILTER DIFFERENTIAL PRESSURE SENSOR CIRCUIT HIGH:** With the ignition on. The (K355) Exhaust Differential Pressure Sensor signal is above 4. 96 volts for 2. 0 seconds.
DTC: P2503	**-CHARGING SYSTEM OUTPUT LOW:** The engine running. The engine RPM is high enough to assure sufficient generator current output to satisfy the electrical loads. The battery sensed voltage is less than the target charging voltage, during engine operation, for a calibrated amount of time. One Trip Fault. Generator light will illuminate.

DTC	Trouble Code Title, Conditions, Possible Causes
DTC: P2503	**-CHARGING SYSTEM OUTPUT LOW:** With the engine speed greater than 1157 RPM. The Powertrain Control Module (PCM) detects that battery voltage is 1 volt below charging goal voltage for 13. 47 seconds. The PCM compares sensed battery voltage with the field driver on and off. If the voltages are the same, this code will set. One Trip Fault. Three good trips to turn off the MIL.
DTC: P2504	**-CHARGING SYSTEM OUTPUT HIGH:** The engine running. The engine speed greater than 1157 RPM. The alternator B+ voltage sense circuit voltage reading exceeds the direct Battery B+ sense circuit. The Generator Output terminal is not connected to the Battery B+ post. One trip fault.
DTC: P2504	**-CHARGING SYSTEM OUTPUT HIGH:** With the engine speed greater than 1157 RPM. The Powertrain Control Module (PCM) compares sensed battery voltage with the Generator Sense circuit voltage. If the Generator Sense circuit voltage if greater than sensed battery voltage, this DTC will set. One Trip Fault. Three good trips to turn off the MIL.
DTC: P2533	**-IGNITION SWITCH RUN/START POSITION CIRCUIT:** With the ignition on and the battery voltage greater than 10. 4 Volts. The Powertrain Control Module (PCM) detects and open or shorted condition in the Ignition Switch Run/Start circuit.
DTC: P258A	**-ELECTRIC VACUUM PUMP CIRCUIT:** With ignition on. Battery voltage above 10. 0 Volts. The actual EVP state is not equal to the desired EVP state. One Trip Fault. Three good trips to turn off the MIL.
DTC: P258D	**-ELECTRONIC VACUUM PUMP PERFORMANCE:** With the ignition on and engine running. Minimum Manifold Absolute Pressure (MAP) reading is 15 kpa (4. 4 in Hg). EVP minimum vacuum is -35 kpa (-10 in Hg) and the EVP cannot create 3 kpa (1. 0 inHg) or the system cannot increase the vacuum from -35 kpa (-10 in Hg) to -38 kpa (-11 in Hg). Two trip fault. Three good trips to turn off the MIL.
DTC: P2610	**-PCM INTERNAL SHUTDOWN TIMER FAST RATIONALITY:** With the engine running after a cycle when a complete engine warm up was achieved, the difference between engine coolant temperature and ambient air temperature greater than 10° C (50° F), after a minimum temperature drop of 10° C (50° F) during ignition off, and battery voltage greater than 10 volts. The PCM detects that the engine coolant temperature drops a specified amount during the measured engine off time. Two trip fault. Three good trips to turn off the MIL.
DTC: P2627	**-O2 SENSOR 1/1 PUMP CELL CURRENT TRIM CIRCUIT LOW:** With the ignition on. The ECM detects a short to ground on the (K902) O2 1/1 Pump Cell Current Trim circuit for 2. 0 seconds.
DTC: P2628	**-O2 SENSOR 1/1 PUMP CELL CURRENT TRIM CIRCUIT HIGH:** With the ignition on. The ECM detects a short to voltage on the (K902) O2 1/1 Pump Cell Current Trim circuit for 2. 0 seconds.
DTC: P2638	**TORQUE MANAGEMENT FEEDBACK SIGNAL PERFORMANCE:** Engine intervention active for at least 20 ms, no engine torque errors, engine torque demand is greater than 0. Torque Reduction acknowledge bit - not set, no shift aborts, the error flag Torque Reduction Acknowledge is not set, Powertrain controller not supporting torque requests.
DTC: P2700	**-INADEQUATE ELEMENT VOLUME LR:** Whenever the engine is running. The L/R clutch volume index (CVI) is updated during a 3-1 or 2-1 manual downshift with throttle angle below 5 degrees. Transmission temperature must be at least 43° C (110° F). When the L/R clutch volume index (CVI) falls below 16.
DTC: P2701	**-INADEQUATE ELEMENT VOLUME 2C:** Whenever the engine is running. The 2C clutch volume index (CVI) is updated during a 3-2 kickdown with throttle angle between 10 and 54 degrees. Transmission temperature must be at least 43° C (110° F). When the 2C CVI falls below 5.
DTC: P2702	**-INADEQUATE ELEMENT VOLUME OD:** Whenever the engine is running. The OD clutch volume index (CVI) is updated during a 2-3 upshift with throttle angle between 10 and 54 degrees. Transmission temperature must be at least 43° C (110° F). When the OD CVI falls below 5.
DTC: P2703	**-INADEQUATE ELEMENT VOLUME UD:** Whenever the engine is running. The UD clutch volume index (CVI) is updated during a 4-3 kickdown with throttle angle between 10 and 54 degrees. Transmission temperature must be at least 43° C (110° F). When the UD CVI falls below 11.
DTC: P2704	**-INADEQUATE ELEMENT VOLUME 4C:** Whenever the engine is running. The 4C clutch volume index (CVI) is updated during a 3-4 upshift with throttle angle between 10 and 54 degrees. Transmission temperature must be at least 43° C (110° F). When the 4C CVI falls below 5.

DTC	Trouble Code Title, Conditions, Possible Causes
DTC: P2706	**-MS SOLENOID CIRCUIT:** Initially at power-up, then every 10 seconds thereafter. The solenoid circuits will also be tested immediately after a gear ratio or pressure switch error is detected. After three consecutive solenoid continuity test failures, or one failure if test is run in response to a gear ratio or pressure switch error. **NOTE: This DTC is strictly an electrical fault and does not apply to any internal transmission failures.**
DTC: P2706	**-MS SOLENOID CIRCUIT:** Initially at power-up, then every 10 seconds thereafter. The solenoid circuits will also be tested immediately after a gear ratio or pressure switch error is detected. After three consecutive solenoid continuity test failures, or one failure if test is run in response to a gear ratio or pressure switch error. This DTC is strictly an electrical fault and cannot be caused by any internal transmission failure other than an open in the Transmission Solenoid/TRS Assembly. If the Transmission Solenoid/TRS Assembly is in need of replacement — do not replace the Valve Body.
DTC: P273A	**-INADEQUATE ELEMENT VOLUME LC:** Whenever the engine is running. The LC Clutch Volume Index (CVI) is updated during a 3-1 or 2-1 manual downshift with throttle angle below 5 degrees. Transmission temperature must be at least 43° C (110° F). When the LC CVI falls below a calibrated value.
DTC: P273B	**-INADEQUATE ELEMENT VOLUME DC:** Whenever the engine is running. The DC LC Clutch Volume Index (CVI) is updated during a 3-1 or 2-1 manual downshift with throttle angle below 5 degrees. Transmission temperature must be at least 43° C (110° F). When the DC CVI falls below a calibrated value.
DTC: P2748	**-INPUT SPEED SENSOR 1/2 CORRELATION:** With the ignition on. The ECM receives a CAN Bus message indicating the presence of a DTC in the TCM.
DTC: P2763	**TORQUE CONVERTER CLUTCH PRESSURE CONTROL CIRCUIT HIGH:** Battery voltage is greater than 7. 0 volts. TCC duty cycle is greater than 42%. Torque converter is in Lock Up or Partial Lock Up. The PCM detects the EMCC VFS voltage is above a calibrated threshold for 1. 785 seconds.
DTC: P2764	**TORQUE CONVERTER CLUTCH PRESSURE CONTROL CIRCUIT LOW:** TCC duty cycle is less than 8%. Torque converter is not in Lock Up or Partial Lock Up. The PCM detects the EMCC VFS voltage is below a calibrated threshold for 357 ms.
DTC: P2767	**-INPUT SPEED SENSOR 2 CIRCUIT NO SIGNAL:** Engine speed greater than 450 RPM with none of the following DTCs present: engine speed, TCM under voltage, output speed sensor, and/or rear wheel speed DTCs. Also required are all wheel speeds above 250 RPM and no wheel slip detected (signal from the ABS system). If the Input Speed Sensor 2 (N3) signal is equal to 0 RPM.
DTC: P2769	**TORQUE CONVERTER CLUTCH CIRCUIT LOW:** Ignition on, engine running with the transmission in a valid forward gear. Vehicle speed greater than 10 Km/h (6 mph). Accelerator Pedal Position (APP) greater than 12. 5%. Engine rpm greater than 450 rpm with TCC lock-up enabled. TCC Lock up command is ON (True). No DTCs active from the following: Step motor Line Pressure Solenoid, Secondary Solenoid Input and Output Speed Sensor Primary or Secondary Pressure Sensor CAN Bus If the actual voltage is 70% of the target voltage for the period of 1. 0 second. It takes two consecutive problem identification trips for the DTC to mature and illuminate the MIL.
DTC: P2770	**TORQUE CONVERTER CLUTCH CIRCUIT HIGH:** Ignition on, engine running with the transmission in a valid forward gear. Vehicle speed greater than 10 Km/h (6 mph). Accelerator Pedal Position (APP) greater than 12. 5%. Engine rpm greater than 450 rpm with TCC lock-up enabled. TCC Lock up command is ON (True). No active DTCs from the following: Torque Convertor Clutch Circuit Low, Step motor, Line Pressure Solenoid, Secondary Solenoid, Input and Output Speed Sensor, Primary or Secondary Pressure Sensor, or CAN BUS. If the target current is greater than 0. 75 amps and the monitored current is less than 0. 4 amps for the period of 5 seconds. It takes two consecutive problem identification trips for the DTC to mature and illuminate the MIL.
DTC: P2775	**-AUTOSTICK UPSHIFT SWITCH CIRCUIT PERFORMANCE (COLUMN SHIFT):** When in AutoStick®mode. When the expected AutoStick® switch state is not correctly sensed by the Electronic Shift Module (ESM). If the upshift switch signal is detected as active in a gear position other than drive or when both the upshift and downshift signals are active at the same time.
DTC: P2775	**-AUTOSTICK UPSHIFT SWITCH CIRCUIT PERFORMANCE:** Continuously with the ignition in the run position. When the expected switch state is not correctly sensed by the Shift Lever Assembly. If the upshift switch signal is detected as active in gear position other than drive.
DTC: P2779	**-AUTOSTICK DOWNSHIFT SWITCH CIRCUIT PERFORMANCE:** Continuously when the ignition is in the run position. When the expected switch state is not correctly sensed by the Shifter Lever Assembly (SLA) Electronic Shift Module (ESM). If the Downshift switch signal is detected as active in gear position other than drive.
DTC: P2779	**-AUTOSTICK DOWNSHIFT SWITCH CIRCUIT PERFORMANCE (COLUMN SHIFT):** When in AutoStick®mode. When the expected AutoStick® switch state is not correctly sensed by the Electronic Shift Module (ESM). If the upshift switch signal is detected as active in a gear position other than drive or when both the upshift and downshift signals are active at the same time.

DTC	Trouble Code Title, Conditions, Possible Causes
DTC: P2783	**TORQUE CONVERTER TEMPERATURE TOO HIGH:** When the solenoid supply voltage is active. With no reporting Input Speed Sensor 1 or 2 (N2 - N3), CAN Bus, PCM, CAN Engine, and/or CAN Engine Speed DTCs present. Torque Converter Clutch in slip mode. When the friction loss factor reaches threshold.
DTC: P2784	**-INPUT SPEED SENSOR 1/2 CORRELATION:** Engine speed greater than 450 RPM, no engine speed DTCs, no TCM under voltage system operation, no output speed sensor DTCs (CAN signal from the ABS system), all wheel speeds above 250 RPM (CAN signal from the ABS system), no rear wheel speed DTCs (signal from the ABS system), and no wheel slip detected (CAN signal from the ABS system), no shifting operation, Input Speed Sensor 2 (N3) greater than 800 RPM and Input Speed Sensor 1 (N2) greater than 0 RPM and the TCM not in reset. If the speed difference between the Input Speed Sensors 1 and 2 (N2 - N3) is greater than 150 RPM.
DTC: P2A00	**-O2 SENSOR 1/1 CIRCUIT PERFORMANCE:** With the ignition on. The ECM detects an open or implausible voltage on the (Z43) O2 1/1 Negative Current Control for 2. 0 seconds.

OBD II Trouble Code List (P3XXX Codes)

DTC	Trouble Code Title, Conditions, Possible Causes
DTC: P3400	**-MDS RATIONALITY BANK 1:** Transition from 4 to 8 cylinder mode. O2 sensor readings on Bank 1 side indicate a lean condition while in 4 cylinder mode.
DTC: P3400	**-MDS RATIONALITY BANK 1:** Transition from 8 to 4 cylinder mode. O2 sensor readings on Bank 1 side indicate a lean condition while in 4 cylinder mode. One trip fault.
DTC: P3401	**-MDS SOLENOID 1 CIRCUIT:** Transition from 8 to 4 cylinder mode. When the PCM recognizes a problem with the Solenoid Control circuit. One trip fault.
DTC: P3401	**-MDS SOLENOID 1 CIRCUIT:** Transition from 8 to 4 cylinder mode. When the Powertrain Control Module (PCM) recognizes an open or shorted condition with the Solenoid Control circuit.
DTC: P3402	**-CYLINDER 1 DEACTIVATION CONTROL PERFORMANCE:** Transition from 8 to 4 cylinder mode. The MDS fails to disengage for cylinder 1. One trip fault.
DTC: P3402	**-CYLINDER 1 DEACTIVATION CONTROL PERFORMANCE:** Transition from 8 to 4 cylinder mode. The MDS fails to engage for cylinder 1.
DTC: P3425	**-MDS SOLENOID 4 CIRCUIT:** Transition from 8 to 4 cylinder mode. When the Powertrain Control Module (PCM) recognizes a problem with the Solenoid Control circuit.
DTC: P3425	**-MDS SOLENOID 4 CIRCUIT:** Transition from 8 to 4 cylinder mode. When the PCM recognizes a problem with the Solenoid Control circuit. One trip fault.
DTC: P3426	**-CYLINDER 4 DEACTIVATION CONTROL PERFORMANCE:** Transition from 8 to 4 cylinder mode. The MDS fails to engage for cylinder 4.
DTC: P3426	**-CYLINDER 4 DEACTIVATION CONTROL PERFORMANCE:** Transition from 8 to 4 cylinder mode. The MDS fails to engage for cylinder 4. One trip fault.
DTC: P3426	**-CYLINDER 4 DEACTIVATION CONTROL PERFORMANCE:** Transition from 8 to 4 cylinder mode. The MDS fails to disengage for cylinder 4. One trip fault.
DTC: P3441	**-MDS SOLENOID 6 CIRCUIT:** Transition from 8 to 4 cylinder mode. When the PCM recognizes a problem with the Solenoid Control circuit. One trip fault.
DTC: P3442	**-CYLINDER 6 DEACTIVATION CONTROL PERFORMANCE:** Transition from 8 to 4 cylinder mode. The MDS fails to disengage for cylinder 6. One trip fault.
DTC: P3442	**-CYLINDER 6 DEACTIVATION CONTROL PERFORMANCE:** Transition from 8 to 4 cylinder mode. The MDS fails to engage for cylinder 6.
DTC: P3449	**-MDS SOLENOID 7 CIRCUIT:** Transition from 8 to 4 cylinder mode. When the Powertrain Control Module (PCM) recognizes a problem with the Solenoid Control circuit.
DTC: P3449	**-MDS SOLENOID 7 CIRCUIT:** Transition from 8 to 4 cylinder mode. When the PCM recognizes a problem with the Solenoid Control circuit. One trip fault.

DTC	Trouble Code Title, Conditions, Possible Causes
DTC: P3450	**-CYLINDER 7 DEACTIVATION CONTROL PERFORMANCE:** Transition from 8 to 4 cylinder mode. The MDS fails to disengage for cylinder 7. Two trip fault.
DTC: P3450	**-CYLINDER 7 DEACTIVATION CONTROL PERFORMANCE:** Transition from 8 to 4 cylinder mode. The MDS fails to engage for cylinder 7.
DTC: P3497	**-MDS RATIONALITY BANK 2:** Transition from 4 to 8 cylinder mode. O2 sensor readings on Bank 2 side indicate a lean condition while in 4 cylinder mode.
DTC: P3497	**-MDS RATIONALITY BANK 2:** Transition from 8 to 4 cylinder mode. O2 sensor readings on Bank 2 side indicate a lean condition while in 4 cylinder mode. One trip fault.

ABS: Anti-lock braking system. An electro-mechanical braking system which is designed to minimize or prevent wheel lock-up during braking.

ABSOLUTE PRESSURE: Atmospheric (barometric) pressure plus the pressure gauge reading.

ACCELERATOR PUMP: A small pump located in the carburetor that feeds fuel into the air/fuel mixture during acceleration.

ACCUMULATOR: A device that controls shift quality by cushioning the shock of hydraulic oil pressure being applied to a clutch or band.

ACTUATING MECHANISM: The mechanical output devices of a hydraulic system, for example, clutch pistons and band servos.

ACTUATOR: The output component of a hydraulic or electronic system.

ADVANCE: Setting the ignition timing so that spark occurs earlier before the piston reaches top dead center (TDC).

ADAPTIVE MEMORY (ADAPTIVE STRATEGY): The learning ability of the TCM or PCM to redefine its decision-making process to provide optimum shift quality.

AFTER TOP DEAD CENTER (ATDC): The point after the piston reaches the top of its travel on the compression stroke.

AIR BAG: Device on the inside of the car designed to inflate on impact of crash, protecting the occupants of the car.

AIR CHARGE TEMPERATURE (ACT) SENSOR: The temperature of the airflow into the engine is measured by an ACT sensor, usually located in the lower intake manifold or air cleaner.

AIR CLEANER: An assembly consisting of a housing, filter and any connecting ductwork. The filter element is made up of a porous paper, sometimes with a wire mesh screening, and is designed to prevent airborne particles from entering the engine through the carburetor or throttle body.

AIR INJECTION: One method of reducing harmful exhaust emissions by injecting air into each of the exhaust ports of an engine. The fresh air entering the hot exhaust manifold causes any remaining fuel to be burned before it can exit the tailpipe.

AIR PUMP: An emission control device that supplies fresh air to the exhaust manifold to aid in more completely burning exhaust gases.

AIR/FUEL RATIO: The ratio of air-to-gasoline by weight in the fuel mixture drawn into the engine.

ALDL (assembly line diagnostic link): Electrical connector for scanning ECM/PCM/TCM input and output devices.

ALIGNMENT RACK: A special drive-on vehicle lift apparatus/measuring device used to adjust a vehicle's toe, caster and camber angles.

ALL WHEEL DRIVE: Term used to describe a full time four wheel drive system or any other vehicle drive system that continuously delivers power to all four wheels. This system is found primarily on station wagon vehicles and SUVs not utilized for significant off road use.

ALTERNATING CURRENT (AC): Electric current that flows first in one direction, then in the opposite direction, continually reversing flow.

ALTERNATOR: A device which produces AC (alternating current) which is converted to DC (direct current) to charge the car battery.

AMMETER: An instrument, calibrated in amperes, used to measure the flow of an electrical current in a circuit. Ammeters are always connected in series with the circuit being tested.

AMPERAGE: The total amount of current (amperes) flowing in a circuit.

AMPLIFIER: A device used in an electrical circuit to increase the voltage of an output signal.

AMP/HR. RATING (BATTERY): Measurement of the ability of a battery to deliver a stated amount of current for a stated period of time. The higher the amp/hr. rating, the better the battery.

AMPERE: The rate of flow of electrical current present when one volt of electrical pressure is applied against one ohm of electrical resistance.

ANALOG COMPUTER: Any microprocessor that uses similar (analogous) electrical signals to make its calculations.

ANODIZED: A special coating applied to the surface of aluminum valves for extended service life.

ANTIFREEZE: A substance (ethylene or propylene glycol) added to the coolant to prevent freezing in cold weather.

ANTI-FOAM AGENTS: Minimize fluid foaming from the whipping action encountered in the converter and planetary action.

ANTI-WEAR AGENTS: Zinc agents that control wear on the gears, bushings, and thrust washers.

ANTI-LOCK BRAKING SYSTEM: A supplementary system to the base hydraulic system that prevents sustained lock-up of the wheels during braking as well as automatically controlling wheel slip.

ANTI-ROLL BAR: See stabilizer bar.

ARC: A flow of electricity through the air between two electrodes or contact points that produces a spark.

ARMATURE: A laminated, soft iron core wrapped by a wire that converts electrical energy to mechanical energy as in a motor or relay. When rotated in a magnetic field, it changes mechanical energy into electrical energy as in a generator.

ATDC: After Top Dead Center.

ATF: Automatic transmission fluid.

ATMOSPHERIC PRESSURE: The pressure on the Earth's surface caused by the weight of the air in the atmosphere. At sea level, this pressure is 14.7 psi at 32°F (101 kPa at 0°C).

ATOMIZATION: The breaking down of a liquid into a fine mist that can be suspended in air.

AUXILIARY ADD-ON COOLER: A supplemental transmission fluid cooling device that is installed in series with the heat exchanger (cooler), located inside the radiator, to provide additional support to cool the hot fluid leaving the torque converter.

AUXILIARY PRESSURE: An added fluid pressure that is introduced into a regulator or balanced valve system to control valve movement. The auxiliary pressure itself can be either a fixed or a variable value. (See balanced valve; regulator valve.)

AWD: All wheel drive.

AXIAL FORCE: A side or end thrust force acting in or along the same plane as the power flow.

AXIAL PLAY: Movement parallel to a shaft or bearing bore.

AXLE CAPACITY: The maximum load-carrying capacity of the axle itself, as specified by the manufacturer. This is usually a higher number than the GAWR.

AXLE RATIO: This is a number (3.07:1, 4.56:1, for example) expressing the ratio between driveshaft revolutions and wheel revolutions. A low numerical ratio allows the engine to work easier because it doesn't have to turn as fast. A high numerical ratio means that the engine has to turn more rpm's to move the wheels through the same number of turns.

BACKFIRE: The sudden combustion of gases in the intake or exhaust system that results in a loud explosion.

BACKLASH: The clearance or play between two parts, such as meshed gears.

BACKPRESSURE: Restrictions in the exhaust system that slow the exit of exhaust gases from the combustion chamber.

BAKELITE®: A heat resistant, plastic insulator material commonly used in printed circuit boards and transistorized components.

BALANCED VALVE: A valve that is positioned by opposing auxiliary hydraulic pressures and/or spring force. Examples include mainline regulator, throttle, and governor valves. (See regulator valve.)

BAND: A flexible ring of steel with an inner lining of friction material. When tightened around the outside of a drum, a planetary member is held stationary to the transmission/transaxle case.

BALL BEARING: A bearing made up of hardened inner and outer races between which hardened steel balls roll.

BALL JOINT: A ball and matching socket connecting suspension components (steering knuckle to lower control arms). It permits rotating movement in any direction between the components that are joined.

BARO (BAROMETRIC PRESSURE SENSOR): Measures the change in the intake manifold pressure caused by changes in altitude.

BAROMETRIC MANIFOLD ABSOLUTE PRESSURE (BMAP) SENSOR: Operates similarly to a conventional MAP sensor; reads intake manifold pressure and is also responsible for determining altitude and barometric pressure prior to engine operation.

BAROMETRIC PRESSURE: (See atmospheric pressure.)

BALLAST RESISTOR: A resistor in the primary ignition circuit that lowers voltage after the engine is started to reduce wear on ignition components.

BATTERY: A direct current electrical storage unit, consisting of the basic active materials of lead and sulfuric acid, which converts chemical energy into electrical energy. Used to provide current for the operation of the starter as well as other equipment, such as the radio, lighting, etc.

BEAD: The portion of a tire that holds it on the rim.

BEARING: A friction reducing, supportive device usually located between a stationary part and a moving part.

BEFORE TOP DEAD CENTER (BTDC): The point just before the piston reaches the top of its travel on the compression stroke.

BELTED TIRE: Tire construction similar to bias-ply tires, but using two or more layers of reinforced belts between body plies and the tread.

BEZEL: Piece of metal surrounding radio, headlights, gauges or similar components; sometimes used to hold the glass face of a gauge in the dash.

BIAS-PLY TIRE: Tire construction, using body ply reinforcing cords which run at alternating angles to the center line of the tread.

BI-METAL TEMPERATURE SENSOR: Any sensor or switch made of two dissimilar types of metal that bend when heated or cooled due to the different expansion rates of the alloys. These types of sensors usually function as an on/off switch.

BLOCK: See Engine Block.

BLOW-BY: Combustion gases, composed of water vapor and unburned fuel, that leak past the piston rings into the crankcase during normal engine operation. These gases are removed by the PCV system to prevent the buildup of harmful acids in the crankcase.

BOOK TIME: See Labor Time.

BOOK VALUE: The average value of a car, widely used to determine trade-in and resale value.

BOOST VALVE: Used at the base of the regulator valve to increase mainline pressure.

BORE: Diameter of a cylinder.

BRAKE CALIPER: The housing that fits over the brake disc. The caliper holds the brake pads, which are pressed against the discs by the caliper pistons when the brake pedal is depressed.

BRAKE HORSEPOWER (BHP): The actual horsepower available at the engine flywheel as measured by a dynamometer.

BRAKE FADE: Loss of braking power, usually caused by excessive heat after repeated brake applications.

BRAKE HORSEPOWER: Usable horsepower of an engine measured at the crankshaft.

BRAKE PAD: A brake shoe and lining assembly used with disc brakes.

BRAKE PROPORTIONING VALVE: A valve on the master cylinder which restricts hydraulic brake pressure to the wheels to a specified amount, preventing wheel lock-up.

BREAKAWAY: Often used by Chrysler to identify first-gear operation in D and 2 ranges. In these ranges, first-gear operation depends on a one-way roller clutch that holds on acceleration and releases (breaks away) on deceleration, resulting in a freewheeling coast-down condition.

BRAKE SHOE: The backing for the brake lining. The term is, however, usually applied to the assembly of the brake backing and lining.

BREAKER POINTS: A set of points inside the distributor, operated by a cam, which make and break the ignition circuit.

BRINNELLING: A wear pattern identified by a series of indentations at regular intervals. This condition is caused by a lack of lube, overload situations, and/or vibrations.

BTDC: Before Top Dead Center.

BUMP: Sudden and forceful apply of a clutch or band.

BUSHING: A liner, usually removable, for a bearing; an anti-friction liner used in place of a bearing.

CALIFORNIA ENGINE: An engine certified by the EPA for use in California only; conforms to more stringent emission regulations than Federal engine.

CALIPER: A hydraulically activated device in a disc brake system,

which is mounted straddling the brake rotor (disc). The caliper contains at least one piston and two brake pads. Hydraulic pressure on the piston(s) forces the pads against the rotor.

CAPACITY: The quantity of electricity that can be delivered from a unit, as from a battery in ampere-hours, or output, as from a generator.

CAMBER: One of the factors of wheel alignment. Viewed from the front of the car, it is the inward or outward tilt of the wheel. The top of the tire will lean outward (positive camber) or inward (negative camber).

CAMSHAFT: A shaft in the engine on which are the lobes (cams) which operate the valves. The camshaft is driven by the crankshaft, via a belt, chain or gears, at one half the crankshaft speed.

CAPACITOR: A device which stores an electrical charge.

CARBON MONOXIDE (CO): A colorless, odorless gas given off as a normal byproduct of combustion. It is poisonous and extremely dangerous in confined areas, building up slowly to toxic levels without warning if adequate ventilation is not available.

CARBURETOR: A device, usually mounted on the intake manifold of an engine, which mixes the air and fuel in the proper proportion to allow even combustion.

CASTER: The forward or rearward tilt of an imaginary line drawn through the upper ball joint and the center of the wheel. Viewed from the sides, positive caster (forward tilt) lends directional stability, while negative caster (rearward tilt) produces instability.

CATALYTIC CONVERTER: A device installed in the exhaust system, like a muffler, that converts harmful byproducts of combustion into carbon dioxide and water vapor by means of a heat-producing chemical reaction.

CENTRIFUGAL ADVANCE: A mechanical method of advancing the spark timing by using flyweights in the distributor that react to centrifugal force generated by the distributor shaft rotation.

CENTRIFUGAL FORCE: The outward pull of a revolving object, away from the center of revolution. Centrifugal force increases with the speed of rotation.

CETANE RATING: A measure of the ignition value of diesel fuel. The higher the cetane rating, the better the fuel. Diesel fuel cetane rating is roughly comparable to gasoline octane rating.

CHECK VALVE: Any one-way valve installed to permit the flow of air, fuel or vacuum in one direction only.

CHOKE: The valve/plate that restricts the amount of air entering an engine on the induction stroke, thereby enriching the air/fuel ratio.

CHUGGLE: Bucking or jerking condition that may be engine related and may be most noticeable when converter clutch is engaged; similar to the feel of towing a trailer.

CIRCLIP: A split steel snapring that fits into a groove to hold various parts in place.

CIRCUIT BREAKER: A switch which protects an electrical circuit from overload by opening the circuit when the current flow exceeds a pre-determined level. Some circuit breakers must be reset manually, while most reset automatically.

CIRCUIT: Any unbroken path through which an electrical current can flow. Also used to describe fuel flow in some instances.

CIRCUIT, BYPASS: Another circuit in parallel with the major circuit through which power is diverted.

CIRCUIT, CLOSED: An electrical circuit in which there is no interruption of current flow.

CIRCUIT, GROUND: The non-insulated portion of a complete circuit used as a common potential point. In automotive circuits, the ground is composed of metal parts, such as the engine, body sheet metal, and frame and is usually a negative potential.

CIRCUIT, HOT: That portion of a circuit not at ground potential. The hot circuit is usually insulated and is connected to the positive side of the battery.

CIRCUIT, OPEN: A break or lack of contact in an electrical circuit, either intentional (switch) or unintentional (bad connection or broken wire).

CIRCUIT, PARALLEL: A circuit having two or more paths for current flow with common positive and negative tie points. The same voltage is applied to each load device or parallel branch.

CIRCUIT, SERIES: An electrical system in which separate parts are connected end to end, using one wire, to form a single path for current flow.

CIRCUIT, SHORT: A circuit that is accidentally completed in an electrical path for which it was not intended.

CLAMPING (ISOLATION) DIODES: Diodes positioned in a circuit to prevent self-induction from damaging electronic components.

CLEARCOAT: A transparent layer which, when sprayed over a vehicle's paint job, adds gloss and depth as well as an additional protective coating to the finish.

CLUTCH: Part of the power train used to connect/disconnect power to the rear wheels.

CLUTCH, FLUID: The same as a fluid coupling. A fluid clutch or coupling performs the same function as a friction clutch by utilizing fluid friction and inertia as opposed to solid friction used by a friction clutch. (See fluid coupling.)

CLUTCH, FRICTION: A coupling device that provides a means of smooth and positive engagement and disengagement of engine torque to the vehicle powertrain. Transmission of power through the clutch is accomplished by bringing one or more rotating drive members into contact with complementing driven members.

COAST: Vehicle deceleration caused by engine braking conditions.

COEFFICIENT OF FRICTION: The amount of surface tension between two contacting surfaces; identified by a scientifically calculated number.

COIL: Part of the ignition system that boosts the relatively low voltage supplied by the car's electrical system to the high voltage required to fire the spark plugs.

COMBINATION MANIFOLD: An assembly which includes both the intake and exhaust manifolds in one casting.

COMBINATION VALVE: A device used in some fuel systems that routes fuel vapors to a charcoal storage canister instead of venting them into the atmosphere. The valve relieves fuel tank pressure and allows fresh air into the tank as the fuel level drops to prevent a vapor lock situation.

COMBUSTION CHAMBER: The part of the engine in the cylinder head where combustion takes place.

COMPOUND GEAR: A gear consisting of two or more simple gears with a common shaft.

COMPOUND PLANETARY: A gearset that has more than the three elements found in a simple gearset and is constructed by combining members of two planetary gearsets to create additional gear ratio possibilities.

COMPRESSION CHECK: A test involving removing each spark plug and inserting a gauge. When the engine is cranked, the gauge will record a pressure reading in the individual cylinder. General operating condition can be determined from a compression check.

COMPRESSION RATIO: The ratio of the volume between the piston and cylinder head when the piston is at the bottom of its stroke (bottom dead center) and when the piston is at the top of its stroke (top dead center).

COMPUTER: An electronic control module that correlates input data according to prearranged engineered instructions; used for the management of an actuator system or systems.

CONDENSER: An electrical device which acts to store an electrical charge, preventing voltage surges.
2. A radiator-like device in the air conditioning system in which refrigerant gas condenses into a liquid, giving off heat.

CONDUCTOR: Any material through which an electrical current can be transmitted easily.

CONNECTING ROD: The connecting link between the crankshaft and piston.

CONSTANT VELOCITY JOINT: Type of universal joint in a halfshaft assembly in which the output shaft turns at a constant angular velocity without variation, provided that the speed of the input shaft is constant.

CONTINUITY: Continuous or complete circuit. Can be checked with an ohmmeter.

CONTROL ARM: The upper or lower suspension components which are mounted on the frame and support the ball joints and steering knuckles.

CONVENTIONAL IGNITION: Ignition system which uses breaker points.

CONVERTER: (See torque converter.)

CONVERTER LOCKUP: The switching from hydrodynamic to direct mechanical drive, usually through the application of a friction element called the converter clutch.

COOLANT: Mixture of water and anti-freeze circulated through the engine to carry off heat produced by the engine.

CORROSION INHIBITOR: An inhibitor in ATF that prevents corrosion of bushings, thrust washers, and oil cooler brazed joints.

COUNTERSHAFT: An intermediate shaft which is rotated by a mainshaft and transmits, in turn, that rotation to a working part.

COUPLING PHASE: Occurs when the torque converter is operating at its greatest hydraulic efficiency. The speed differential between the impeller and the turbine is at its minimum. At this point, the stator freewheels, and there is no torque multiplication.

CRANKCASE: The lower part of an engine in which the crankshaft and related parts operate.

CRANKSHAFT: Engine component (connected to pistons by connecting rods) which converts the reciprocating (up and down) motion of pistons to rotary motion used to turn the driveshaft.

CURB WEIGHT: The weight of a vehicle without passengers or payload, but including all fluids (oil, gas, coolant, etc.) and other equipment specified as standard.

CURRENT: The flow (or rate) of electrons moving through a circuit. Current is measured in amperes (amp).

CURRENT FLOW CONVENTIONAL: Current flows through a circuit from the positive terminal of the source to the negative terminal (plus to minus).

CURRENT FLOW, ELECTRON: Current or electrons flow from the negative terminal of the source, through the circuit, to the positive terminal (minus to plus).

CV-JOINT: Constant velocity joint.

CYCLIC VIBRATIONS: The off-center movement of a rotating object that is affected by its initial balance, speed of rotation, and working angles.

CYLINDER BLOCK: See engine block.

CYLINDER HEAD: The detachable portion of the engine, usually fastened to the top of the cylinder block and containing all or most of the combustion chambers. On overhead valve engines, it contains the valves and their operating parts. On overhead cam engines, it contains the camshaft as well.

CYLINDER: In an engine, the round hole in the engine block in which the piston(s) ride.

DATA LINK CONNECTOR (DLC): Current acronym/term applied to the federally mandated, diagnostic junction connector that is used to monitor ECM/PC/TCM inputs, processing strategies, and outputs including diagnostic trouble codes (DTCs).

DEAD CENTER: The extreme top or bottom of the piston stroke.

DECELERATION BUMP: When referring to a torque converter clutch in the applied position, a sudden release of the accelerator pedal causes a forceful reversal of power through the drivetrain (engine braking), just prior to the apply plate actually being released.

DELAYED (LATE OR EXTENDED): Condition where shift is expected but does not occur for a period of time, for example, where clutch or band engagement does not occur as quickly as expected during part throttle or wide open throttle apply of accelerator or when manually downshifting to a lower range.

DETENT: A spring-loaded plunger, pin, ball, or pawl used as a holding device on a ratchet wheel or shaft. In automatic transmissions, a detent mechanism is used for locking the manual valve in place.

DETENT DOWNSHIFT: (See kickdown.)

DETERGENT: An additive in engine oil to improve its operating characteristics.

DETONATION: An unwanted explosion of the air/fuel mixture in the combustion chamber caused by excess heat and compression, advanced timing, or an overly lean mixture. Also referred to as "ping".

DEXRON®: A brand of automatic transmission fluid.

DIAGNOSTIC TROUBLE CODES (DTCs): A digital display from the control module memory that identifies the input, processor, or output device circuit that is related to the powertrain emission/driveability malfunction detected. Diagnostic trouble codes can be read by the MIL to flash any codes or by using a handheld scanner.

DIAPHRAGM: A thin, flexible wall separating two cavities, such as in a vacuum advance unit.

DIESELING: The engine continues to run after the car is shut off; caused by fuel continuing to be burned in the combustion chamber.

DIFFERENTIAL: A geared assembly which allows the transmission of motion between drive axles, giving one axle the ability to rotate faster than the other, as in cornering.

DIFFERENTIAL AREAS: When opposing faces of a spool valve are acted upon by the same pressure but their areas differ in size, the face with the larger area produces the differential force and valve movement. (See spool valve.)

DIFFERENTIAL FORCE: (See differential areas)

DIGITAL READOUT: A display of numbers or a combination of numbers and letters.

DIGITAL VOLT OHMMETER: An electronic diagnostic tool used to measure voltage, ohms and amps as well as several other functions, with the readings displayed on a digital screen in tenths, hundredths and thousandths.

DIODE: An electrical device that will allow current to flow in one direction only.

DIRECT CURRENT (DC): Electrical current that flows in one direction only.

DIRECT DRIVE: The gear ratio is 1:1, with no change occurring in the torque and speed input/output relationship.

DISC BRAKE: A hydraulic braking assembly consisting of a brake disc, or rotor, mounted on an axle shaft, and a caliper assembly containing, usually two brake pads which are activated by hydraulic pressure. The pads are forced against the sides of the disc, creating friction which slows the vehicle.

DISPERSANTS: Suspend dirt and prevent sludge buildup in a liquid, such as engine oil.

DOUBLE BUMP (DOUBLE FEEL): Two sudden and forceful applies of a clutch or band.

DISPLACEMENT: The total volume of air that is displaced by all pistons as the engine turns through one complete revolution.

DISTRIBUTOR: A mechanically driven device on an engine which is responsible for electrically firing the spark plug at a pre-determined point of the piston stroke.

DOHC: Double overhead camshaft.

DOUBLE OVERHEAD CAMSHAFT: The engine utilizes two camshafts mounted in one cylinder head. One camshaft operates the exhaust valves, while the other operates the intake valves.

DOWEL PIN: A pin, inserted in mating holes in two different parts allowing those parts to maintain a fixed relationship.

DRIVELINE: The drive connection between the transmission and the drive wheels.

DRIVE TRAIN: The components that transmit the flow of power from the engine to the wheels. The components include the clutch, transmission, driveshafts (or axle shafts in front wheel drive), U-joints and differential.

DRUM BRAKE: A braking system which consists of two brake shoes and one or two wheel cylinders, mounted on a fixed backing plate, and a brake drum, mounted on an axle, which revolves around the assembly.

DRY CHARGED BATTERY: Battery to which electrolyte is added when the battery is placed in service.

DVOM: Digital volt ohmmeter

DWELL: The rate, measured in degrees of shaft rotation, at which an electrical circuit cycles on and off.

DYNAMIC: An application in which there is rotating or reciprocating motion between the parts.

EARLY: Condition where shift occurs before vehicle has reached proper speed, which tends to labor engine after upshift.

EBCM: See Electronic Control Unit (ECU).

ECM: See Electronic Control Unit (ECU).

ECU: Electronic control unit.

ELECTRODE: Conductor (positive or negative) of electric current.

ELECTROLYSIS: A surface etching or bonding of current conducting transmission/transaxle components that may occur when grounding straps are missing or in poor condition.

ELECTROLYTE: A solution of water and sulfuric acid used to activate the battery. Electrolyte is extremely corrosive.

ELECTROMAGNET: A coil that produces a magnetic field when current flows through its windings.

ELECTROMAGNETIC INDUCTION: A method to create (generate) current flow through the use of magnetism.

ELECTROMAGNETISM: The effects surrounding the relationship between electricity and magnetism.

ELECTROMOTIVE FORCE (EMF): The force or pressure (voltage) that causes current movement in an electrical circuit.

ELECTRONIC CONTROL UNIT: A digital computer that controls engine (and sometimes transmission, brake or other vehicle system) functions based on data received from various sensors. Examples used by some manufacturers include Electronic Brake Control Module (EBCM), Engine Control Module (ECM), Powertrain Control Module (PCM) or Vehicle Control Module (VCM).

ELECTRONIC IGNITION: A system in which the timing and firing of the spark plugs is controlled by an electronic control unit, usually called a module. These systems have no points or condenser.

ELECTRONIC PRESSURE CONTROL (EPC) SOLENOID: A specially designed solenoid containing a spool valve and spring assembly to control fluid mainline pressure. A variable current flow, controlled by the ECM/PCM, varies the internal force of the solenoid on the spool valve and resulting mainline pressure. (See variable force solenoid.)

ELECTRONICS: Miniaturized electrical circuits utilizing semiconductors, solid-state devices, and printed circuits. Electronic circuits utilize small amounts of power.

ELECTRONIFICATION: The application of electronic circuitry to a mechanical device. Regarding automatic transmissions, electrification is incorporated into converter clutch lockup, shift scheduling, and line pressure control systems.

ELECTROSTATIC DISCHARGE (ESD): An unwanted, high-voltage electrical current released by an individual who has taken on a static charge of electricity. Electronic components can be easily damaged by ESD.

ELEMENT: A device within a hydrodynamic drive unit designed with a set of blades to direct fluid flow.

ENAMEL: Type of paint that dries to a smooth, glossy finish.

END BUMP (END FEEL OR SLIP BUMP): Firmer feel at end of shift when compared with feel at start of shift.

END-PLAY: The clearance/gap between two components that allows for expansion of the parts as they warm up, to prevent binding and to allow space for lubrication.

ENERGY: The ability or capacity to do work.

ENGINE: The primary motor or power apparatus of a vehicle, which converts liquid or gas fuel into mechanical energy.

ENGINE BLOCK: The basic engine casting containing the cylinders, the crankshaft main bearings, as well as machined surfaces for the mounting of other components such as the cylinder head, oil pan, transmission, etc.

ENGINE BRAKING: Use of engine to slow vehicle by manually downshifting during zero-throttle coast down.

ENGINE CONTROL MODULE (ECM): Manages the engine and incorporates output control over the torque converter clutch solenoid. (Note: Current designation for the ECM in late model vehicles is PCM.)

ENGINE COOLANT TEMPERATURE (ECT) SENSOR: Prevents converter clutch engagement with a cold engine; also used for shift timing and shift quality.

EP LUBRICANT: EP (extreme pressure) lubricants are specially formulated for use with gears involving heavy loads (transmissions, differentials, etc.).

ETHYL: A substance added to gasoline to improve its resistance to knock, by slowing down the rate of combustion.

ETHYLENE GLYCOL: The base substance of antifreeze.

EXHAUST MANIFOLD: A set of cast passages or pipes which conduct exhaust gases from the engine.

FAIL-SAFE (BACKUP) CONTROL: A substitute value used by the PCM/TCM to replace a faulty signal from an input sensor. The temporary value allows the vehicle to continue to be operated.

FAST IDLE: The speed of the engine when the choke is on. Fast idle speeds engine warm-up.

FEDERAL ENGINE: An engine certified by the EPA for use in any of the 49 states (except California).

FEEDBACK: A circuit malfunction whereby current can find another path to feed load devices.

FEELER GAUGE: A blade, usually metal, of precisely predetermined thickness, used to measure the clearance between two parts.

FILAMENT: The part of a bulb that glows; the filament creates high resistance to current flow and actually glows from the resulting heat.

FINAL DRIVE: An essential part of the axle drive assembly where final gear reduction takes place in the powertrain. In RWD applications and north-south FWD applications, it must also change the power flow direction to the axle shaft by ninety degrees. (Also see axle ratio.)

FIRING ORDER: The order in which combustion occurs in the cylinders of an engine. Also the order in which spark is distributed to the plugs by the distributor.

FIRM: A noticeable quick apply of a clutch or band that is considered normal with medium to heavy throttle shift; should not be confused with harsh or rough.

FLAME FRONT: The term used to describe certain aspects of the fuel explosion in the cylinders. The flame front should move in a controlled pattern across the cylinder, rather than simply exploding immediately.

FLARE (SLIPPING): A quick increase in engine rpm accompanied by momentary loss of torque; generally occurs during shift.

FLAT ENGINE: Engine design in which the pistons are horizontally opposed. Porsche, Subaru and some old VW are common examples of flat engines.

FLAT RATE: A dealership term referring to the amount of money paid to a technician for a repair or diagnostic service based on that particular service versus dealership's labor time (NOT based on the actual time the technician spent on the job).

FLAT SPOT: A point during acceleration when the engine seems to lose power for an instant.

FLOODING: The presence of too much fuel in the intake manifold and combustion chamber which prevents the air/fuel mixture from firing, thereby causing a no-start situation.

FLUID: A fluid can be either liquid or gas. In hydraulics, a liquid is used for transmitting force or motion.

FLUID COUPLING: The simplest form of hydrodynamic drive, the fluid coupling consists of two look-alike members with straight radial varies referred to as the impeller (pump) and the turbine. Input torque is always equal to the output torque.

FLUID DRIVE: Either a fluid coupling or a fluid torque converter. (See hydrodynamic drive units.)

FLUID TORQUE CONVERTER: A hydrodynamic drive that has the ability to act both as a torque multiplier and fluid coupling. (See hydrodynamic drive units; torque converter.)

FLUID VISCOSITY: The resistance of a liquid to flow. A cold fluid (oil) has greater viscosity and flows more slowly than a hot fluid (oil).

FLYWHEEL: A heavy disc of metal attached to the rear of the crankshaft. It smoothes the firing impulses of the engine and keeps the crankshaft turning during periods when no firing takes place. The starter also engages the flywheel to start the engine.

FOOT POUND (ft. lbs., lbs. ft. or sometimes, ft. lb.): The amount of energy or work needed to raise an item weighing one pound, a distance of one foot.

FREEZE PLUG: A plug in the engine block which will be pushed out if the coolant freezes. Sometimes called expansion plugs, they protect the block from cracking should the coolant freeze.

FRICTION: The resistance that occurs between contacting surfaces. This relationship is expressed by a ratio called the coefficient of friction (CL).

FRICTION, COEFFICIENT OF: The amount of surface tension between two contacting surfaces; expressed by a scientifically calculated number.

FRONT END ALIGNMENT: A service to set caster, camber and toe-in to the correct specifications. This will ensure that the car steers and handles properly and that the tires wear properly.

FRICTION MODIFIER: Changes the coefficient of friction of the fluid between the mating steel and composition clutch/band surfaces during the engagement process and allows for a certain amount of intentional slipping for a good "shift-feel".

FRONTAL AREA: The total frontal area of a vehicle exposed to air flow.

FUEL FILTER: A component of the fuel system containing a porous paper element used to prevent any impurities from entering the engine through the fuel system. It usually takes the form of a canister-like housing, mounted in-line with the fuel hose, located anywhere on a vehicle between the fuel tank and engine.

FUEL INJECTION: A system replacing the carburetor that sprays fuel into the cylinder through nozzles. The amount of fuel can be more precisely controlled with fuel injection.

FULL FLOATING AXLE: An axle in which the axle housing extends through the wheel giving bearing support on the outside of the housing. The front axle of a four-wheel drive vehicle is usually a full floating axle, as are the rear axles of many larger (1 ton and over) pick-ups and vans.

FULL-TIME FOUR-WHEEL DRIVE: A four-wheel drive system that continuously delivers power to all four wheels. A differential between the front and rear driveshafts permits variations in axle speeds to control gear wind-up without damage.

FULL THROTTLE DETENT DOWNSHIFT: A quick apply of accelerator pedal to its full travel, forcing a downshift.

FUSE: A protective device in a circuit which prevents circuit overload by breaking the circuit when a specific amperage is present. The device is constructed around a strip or wire of a lower amperage rating than the circuit it is designed to protect. When an amperage higher than that stamped on the fuse is present in the circuit, the strip or wire melts, opening the circuit.

FUSIBLE LINK: A piece of wire in a wiring harness that performs the same job as a fuse. If overloaded, the fusible link will melt and interrupt the circuit.

FWD: Front wheel drive.

GAWR: (Gross axle weight rating) the total maximum weight an axle is designed to carry.

GCW: (Gross combined weight) total combined weight of a tow vehicle and trailer.

GARAGE SHIFT: initial engagement feel of transmission, neutral to reverse or neutral to a forward drive.

GARAGE SHIFT FEEL: A quick check of the engagement quality and responsiveness of reverse and forward gears. This test is done with the vehicle stationary.

GEAR: A toothed mechanical device that acts as a rotating lever to transmit power or turning effort from one shaft to another. (See gear ratio.)

GEAR RATIO: A ratio expressing the number of turns a smaller gear will make to turn a larger gear through one revolution. The ratio is found by dividing the number of teeth on the smaller gear into the number of teeth on the larger gear.

GEARBOX: Transmission

GEAR REDUCTION: Torque is multiplied and speed decreased by the factor of the gear ratio. For example, a 3:1 gear ratio changes an input torque of 180 ft. lbs. and an input speed of 2700 rpm to 540 Ft. lbs. and 900 rpm, respectively. (No account is taken of frictional losses, which are always present.)

GEARTRAIN: A succession of intermeshing gears that form an assembly and provide for one or more torque changes as the power input is transmitted to the power output.

GEL COAT: A thin coat of plastic resin covering fiberglass body panels.

GENERATOR: A device which produces direct current (DC) necessary to charge the battery.

GOVERNOR: A device that senses vehicle speed and generates a hydraulic oil pressure. As vehicle speed increases, governor oil pressure rises.

GROUND CIRCUIT: (See circuit, ground.)

GROUND SIDE SWITCHING: The electrical/electronic circuit control switch is located after the circuit load.

GVWR: (Gross vehicle weight rating) total maximum weight a vehicle is designed to carry including the weight of the vehicle, passengers, equipment, gas, oil, etc.

HALOGEN: A special type of lamp known for its quality of brilliant white light. Originally used for fog lights and driving lights.

HARD CODES: DTCs that are present at the time of testing; also called continuous or current codes.

HARSH(ROUGH): An apply of a clutch or band that is more noticeable than a firm one; considered undesirable at any throttle position.

HEADER TANK: An expansion tank for the radiator coolant. It can be located remotely or built into the radiator.

HEAT RANGE: A term used to describe the ability of a spark plug to carry away heat. Plugs with longer nosed insulators take longer to carry heat off effectively.

HEAT RISER: A flapper in the exhaust manifold that is closed when the engine is cold, causing hot exhaust gases to heat the intake manifold providing better cold engine operation. A thermostatic spring opens the flapper when the engine warms up.

HEAVY THROTTLE: Approximately three-fourths of accelerator pedal travel.

HEMI: A name given an engine using hemispherical combustion chambers.

HERTZ (HZ): The international unit of frequency equal to one cycle per second (10,000 Hertz equals 10,000 cycles per second).

HIGH-IMPEDANCE DVOM (DIGITAL VOLT-OHMMETER): This styled device provides a built-in resistance value and is capable of limiting circuit current flow to safe milliamp levels.

HIGH RESISTANCE: Often refers to a circuit where there is an excessive amount of opposition to normal current flow.

HORSEPOWER: A measurement of the amount of work; one horsepower is the amount of work necessary to lift 33,000 lbs. one foot in one minute. Brake horsepower (bhp) is the horsepower delivered by an engine on a dynamometer. Net horsepower is the power remaining (measured at the flywheel of the engine) that can be used to turn the wheels after power is consumed through friction and running the engine accessories (water pump, alternator, air pump, fan etc.)

HOT CIRCUIT: (See circuit, hot; hot lead.)

HOT LEAD: A wire or conductor in the power side of the circuit. (See circuit, hot.)

HOT SIDE SWITCHING: The electrical/electronic circuit control switch is located before the circuit load.

HUB: The center part of a wheel or gear.

HUNTING (BUSYNESS): Repeating quick series of up-shifts and downshifts that causes noticeable change in engine rpm, for example, as in a 4-3-4 shift pattern.

HYDRAULICS: The use of liquid under pressure to transfer force of motion.

HYDROCARBON (HC): Any chemical compound made up of hydrogen and carbon. A major pollutant formed by the engine as a by-product of combustion.

HYDRODYNAMIC DRIVE UNITS: Devices that transmit power solely by the action of a kinetic fluid flow in a closed recirculating path. An impeller energizes the fluid and discharges the high-speed jet stream into the turbine for power output.

HYDROMETER: An instrument used to measure the specific gravity of a solution.

HYDROPLANING: A phenomenon of driving when water builds up under the tire tread, causing it to lose contact with the road. Slowing down will usually restore normal tire contact with the road.

HYPOID GEARSET: The drive pinion gear may be placed below or above the centerline of the driven gear; often used as a final drive gearset.

IDLE MIXTURE: The mixture of air and fuel (usually about 14:1) being fed to the cylinders. The idle mixture screw(s) are sometimes adjusted as part of a tune-up.

IDLER ARM: Component of the steering linkage which is a geometric duplicate of the steering gear arm. It supports the right side of the center steering link.

IMPELLER: Often called a pump, the impeller is the power input (drive) member of a hydrodynamic drive. As part of the torque converter cover, it acts as a centrifugal pump and puts the fluid in motion.

INCH POUND (inch lbs.; sometimes in. lb. or in. lbs.): One twelfth of a foot pound.

INDUCTANCE: The force that produces voltage when a conductor is passed through a magnetic field.

INDUCTION: A means of transferring electrical energy in the form of a magnetic field. Principle used in the ignition coil to increase voltage.

INITIAL FEEL: A distinct firmer feel at start of shift when compared with feel at finish of shift.

INJECTOR: A device which receives metered fuel under relatively low pressure and is activated to inject the fuel into the engine under relatively high pressure at a predetermined time.

INPUT: In an automatic transmission, the source of power from the engine is absorbed by the torque converter, which provides the power input into the transmission. The turbine drives the input(turbine)shaft.

INPUT SHAFT: The shaft to which torque is applied, usually carrying the driving gear or gears.

INTAKE MANIFOLD: A casting of passages or pipes used to conduct air or a fuel/air mixture to the cylinders.

INTERNAL GEAR: The ring-like outer gear of a planetary gearset with the gear teeth cut on the inside of the ring to provide a mesh with the planet pinions.

ISOLATION (CLAMPING) DIODES: Diodes positioned in a circuit to prevent self-induction from damaging electronic components.

IX ROTARY GEAR PUMP: Contains two rotating members, one shaped with internal gear teeth and the other with external gear teeth. As the gears separate, the fluid fills the gaps between gear teeth, is pulled across a crescent-shaped divider, and then is forced to flow through the outlet as the gears mesh.

IX ROTARY LOBE PUMP: Sometimes referred to as a gerotor type pump. Two rotating members, one shaped with internal lobes and the other with external lobes, separate and then mesh to cause fluid to flow.

JOURNAL: The bearing surface within which a shaft operates.

JUMPER CABLES: Two heavy duty wires with large alligator clips used to provide power from a charged battery to a discharged battery mounted in a vehicle.

JUMPSTART: Utilizing the sufficiently charged battery of one vehicle to start the engine of another vehicle with a discharged battery by the use of jumper cables.

KEY: A small block usually fitted in a notch between a shaft and a hub to prevent slippage of the two parts.

KICKDOWN: Detent downshift system; either linkage, cable, or electrically controlled.

KILO: A prefix used in the metric system to indicate one thousand.

KNOCK: Noise which results from the spontaneous ignition of a portion of the air-fuel mixture in the engine cylinder caused by overly advanced ignition timing or use of incorrectly low octane fuel for that engine.

KNOCK SENSOR: An input device that responds to spark knock, caused by over advanced ignition timing.

LABOR TIME: A specific amount of time required to perform a certain repair or diagnostic service as defined by a vehicle or after-market manufacturer .

LACQUER: A quick-drying automotive paint.

LATE: Shift that occurs when engine is at higher than normal rpm for given amount of throttle.

LIGHT-EMITTING DIODE (LED): A semiconductor diode that emits light as electrical current flows through it; used in some electronic display devices to emit a red or other color light.

LIGHT THROTTLE: Approximately one-fourth of accelerator pedal travel.

LIMITED SLIP: A type of differential which transfers driving force to the wheel with the best traction.

LIMP-IN MODE: Electrical shutdown of the transmission/ transaxle output solenoids, allowing only forward and reverse gears that are hydraulically energized by the manual valve. This permits the vehicle to be driven to a service facility for repair.

LIP SEAL: Molded synthetic rubber seal designed with an outer sealing edge (lip) that points into the fluid containing area to be sealed. This type of seal is used where rotational and axial forces are present.

LITHIUM-BASE GREASE: Chassis and wheel bearing grease using lithium as a base. Not compatible with sodium-base grease.

LOAD DEVICE: A circuit's resistance that converts the electrical energy into light, sound, heat, or mechanical movement.

LOAD RANGE: Indicates the number of plies at which a tire is rated. Load range B equals four-ply rating; C equals six-ply rating; and, D equals an eight-ply rating.

LOAD TORQUE: The amount of output torque needed from the transmission/transaxle to overcome the vehicle load.

LOCKING HUBS: Accessories used on part-time four-wheel drive systems that allow the front wheels to be disengaged from the drive train when four-wheel drive is not being used. When four-wheel drive is desired, the hubs are engaged, locking the wheels to the drive train.

LOCKUP CONVERTER: A torque converter that operates hydraulically and mechanically. When an internal apply plate (lockup plate) clamps to the torque converter cover, hydraulic slippage is eliminated.

LOCK RING: See Circlip or Snapring

MAGNET: Any body with the property of attracting iron or steel.

MAGNETIC FIELD: The area surrounding the poles of a magnet that is affected by its attraction or repulsion forces.

MAIN LINE PRESSURE: Often called control pressure or line pressure, it refers to the pressure of the oil leaving the pump and is controlled by the pressure regulator valve.

MALFUNCTION INDICATOR LAMP (MIL): Previously known as a check engine light, the dash-mounted MIL illuminates and signals the driver that an emission or driveability problem with the powertrain has been detected by the ECM/PCM. When this occurs, at least one diagnostic trouble code (DTC) has been stored into the control module memory.

MANIFOLD ABSOLUTE PRESSURE (MAP) SENSOR: Reads the amount of air pressure (vacuum) in the engine's intake manifold system; its signal is used to analyze engine load conditions.

MANIFOLD VACUUM: Low pressure in an engine intake manifold formed just below the throttle plates. Manifold vacuum is highest at idle and drops under acceleration.

MANIFOLD: A casting of passages or set of pipes which connect the cylinders to an inlet or outlet source.

MANUAL LEVER POSITION SWITCH (MLPS): A mechanical switching unit that is typically mounted externally to the transmission/transaxle to inform the PCM/ECM which gear range the driver has selected.

MANUAL VALVE: Located inside the transmission/transaxle, it is directly connected to the driver's shift lever. The position of the manual valve determines which hydraulic circuits will be charged with oil pressure and the operating mode of the transmission.

MANUAL VALVE LEVER POSITION SENSOR (MVLPS): The input from this device tells the TCM what gear range was selected.

MASS AIR FLOW (MAF) SENSOR: Measures the airflow into the engine.

MASTER CYLINDER: The primary fluid pressurizing device in a hydraulic system. In automotive use, it is found in brake and hydraulic clutch systems and is pedal activated, either directly or, in a power brake system, through the power booster.

MacPherson STRUT: A suspension component combining a shock absorber and spring in one unit.

MEDIUM THROTTLE: Approximately one-half of accelerator pedal travel.

MEGA: A metric prefix indicating one million.

MEMBER: An independent component of a hydrodynamic unit such as an impeller, a stator, or a turbine. It may have one or more elements.

MERCON: A fluid developed by Ford Motor Company in 1988. It contains a friction modifier and closely resembles operating characteristics of Dexron.

METAL SEALING RINGS: Made from cast iron or aluminum, their primary application is with dynamic components involving pressure sealing circuits of rotating members. These rings are designed with either butt or hook lock end joints.

METER (ANALOG): A linear-style meter representing data as lengths; a needle-style instrument interfacing with logical numerical increments. This style of electrical meter uses relatively low impedance internal resistance and cannot be used for testing electronic circuitry.

METER (DIGITAL): Uses numbers as a direct readout to show values. Most meters of this style use high impedance internal resistance and must be used for testing low current electronic circuitry.

MICRO: A metric prefix indicating one-millionth (0.000001).

MILLI: A metric prefix indicating one-thousandth (0.001).

MINIMUM THROTTLE: The least amount of throttle opening required for upshift; normally close to zero throttle.

MISFIRE: Condition occurring when the fuel mixture in a cylinder fails to ignite, causing the engine to run roughly.

MODULE: Electronic control unit, amplifier or igniter of solid state or integrated design which controls the current flow in the ignition primary circuit based on input from the pick-up coil. When the module opens the primary circuit, high secondary voltage is induced in the coil.

MODULATED: In an electronic-hydraulic converter clutch system (or shift valve system), the term modulated refers to the pulsing of a solenoid, at a variable rate. This action controls the buildup of oil pressure in the hydraulic circuit to allow a controlled amount of clutch slippage.

MODULATED CONVERTER CLUTCH CONTROL (MCCC): A pulse width duty cycle valve that controls the converter lockup apply pressure and maximizes smoother transitions between lock and unlock conditions.

MODULATOR PRESSURE (THROTTLE PRESSURE): A hydraulic signal oil pressure relating to the amount of engine load, based on either the amount of throttle plate opening or engine vacuum.

MODULATOR VALVE: A regulator valve that is controlled by engine vacuum, providing a hydraulic pressure that varies in relation to engine torque. The hydraulic torque signal functions to delay the shift pattern and provide a line pressure boost. (See throttle valve.)

MOTOR: An electromagnetic device used to convert electrical energy into mechanical energy.

MULTIPLE-DISC CLUTCH: A grouping of steel and friction lined plates that, when compressed together by hydraulic pressure acting upon a piston, lock or unlock a planetary member.

MULTI-WEIGHT: Type of oil that provides adequate lubrication at both high and low temperatures.

needed to move one amp through a resistance of one ohm.

MUSHY: Same as soft; slow and drawn out clutch apply with very little shift feel.

MUTUAL INDUCTION: The generation of current from one wire circuit to another by movement of the magnetic field surrounding a current-carrying circuit as its ampere flow increases or decreases.

NEEDLE BEARING: A bearing which consists of a number (usually a large number) of long, thin rollers.

NITROGEN OXIDE (NOx): One of the three basic pollutants found in the exhaust emission of an internal combustion engine. The amount of NOx usually varies in an inverse proportion to the amount of HC and CO.

NONPOSITIVE SEALING: A sealing method that allows some minor leakage, which normally assists in lubrication.

O2 SENSOR: Located in the engine's exhaust system, it is an input device to the ECM/PCM for managing the fuel delivery and ignition system. A scanner can be used to observe the fluctuating voltage readings produced by an O2 sensor as the oxygen content of the exhaust is analyzed.

O-RING SEAL: Molded synthetic rubber seal designed with a circular cross-section. This type of seal is used primarily in static applications.

OBD II (ON-BOARD DIAGNOSTICS, SECOND GENERATION): Refers to the federal law mandating tighter control of 1996 and newer vehicle emissions, active monitoring of related devices, and standardization of terminology, data link connectors, and other technician concerns.

OCTANE RATING: A number, indicating the quality of gasoline based on its ability to resist knock. The higher the number, the better the quality. Higher compression engines require higher octane gas.

OEM: Original Equipment Manufactured. OEM equipment is that furnished standard by the manufacturer.

OFFSET: The distance between the vertical center of the wheel and the mounting surface at the lugs. Offset is positive if the center is outside the lug circle; negative offset puts the center line inside the lug circle.

OHM'S LAW: A law of electricity that states the relationship between voltage, current, and resistance. Volts = amperes x ohms

OHM: The unit used to measure the resistance of conductor-to-electrical flow. One ohm is the amount of resistance that limits current flow to one ampere in a circuit with one volt of pressure.

OHMMETER: An instrument used for measuring the resistance, in ohms, in an electrical circuit.

ONE-WAY CLUTCH: A mechanical clutch of roller or sprag design that resists torque or transmits power in one direction only. It is used to either hold or drive a planetary member.

ONE-WAY ROLLER CLUTCH: A mechanical device that transmits or holds torque in one direction only.

OPEN CIRCUIT: A break or lack of contact in an electrical circuit, either intentional (switch) or unintentional (bad connection or broken wire).

ORIFICE: Located in hydraulic oil circuits, it acts as a restriction. It slows down fluid flow to either create back pressure or delay pressure buildup downstream.

OSCILLOSCOPE: A piece of test equipment that shows electric impulses as a pattern on a screen. Engine performance can be analyzed by interpreting these patterns.

OUTPUT SHAFT: The shaft which transmits torque from a device, such as a transmission.

OUTPUT SPEED SENSOR (OSS): Identifies transmission/transaxle output shaft speed for shift timing and may be used to calculate TCC slip; often functions as the VSS (vehicle speed sensor).

OVERDRIVE: (1.) A device attached to or incorporated in a transmission/transaxle that allows the engine to turn less than one full revolution for every complete revolution of the wheels. The net effect is to reduce engine rpm, thereby using less fuel. A typical overdrive gear ratio would be .87:1, instead of the normal 1:1 in high gear. (2.) A gear assembly which produces more shaft revolutions than that transmitted to it.

OVERDRIVE PLANETARY GEARSET: A single planetary gearset designed to provide a direct drive and overdrive ratio. When coupled to a three-speed transmission/transaxle configuration, a four-speed/overdrive unit is present.

OVERHEAD CAMSHAFT (OHC): An engine configuration in which the camshaft is mounted on top of the cylinder head and operates the valve either directly or by means of rocker arms.

OVERHEAD VALVE (OHV): An engine configuration in which all of the valves are located in the cylinder head and the camshaft is located in the cylinder block. The camshaft operates the valves via lifters and pushrods.

OVERRUNCLUTCH: Another name for a one-way mechanical clutch. Applies to both roller and sprag designs.

OVERSTEER: The tendency of some vehicles, when steering into a turn, to over-respond or steer more than required, which could result in excessive slip of the rear wheels. Opposite of under-steer.

OXIDATION STABILIZERS: Absorb and dissipate heat. Automatic transmission fluid has high resistance to varnish and sludge buildup that occurs from excessive heat that is generated primarily in the torque converter. Local temperatures as high as 6000F (3150C) can occur at the clutch plates during engagement, and this heat must be absorbed and dissipated. If the fluid cannot withstand the heat, it burns or oxidizes, resulting in an almost immediate destruction of friction materials, clogged filter screen and hydraulic passages, and sticky valves.

OXIDES OF NITROGEN: See nitrogen oxide (NOx).

OXYGEN SENSOR: Used with a feedback system to sense the presence of oxygen in the exhaust gas and signal the computer which can use the voltage signal to determine engine operating efficiency and adjust the air/fuel ratio.

PARALLEL CIRCUIT: (See circuit, parallel.)

PARTS WASHER: A basin or tub, usually with a built-in pump mechanism and hose used for circulating chemical solvent for the purpose of cleaning greasy, oily and dirty components.

PART-TIME FOUR WHEEL DRIVE: A system that is normally in the two wheel drive mode and only runs in four-wheel drive when the system is manually engaged because more traction is desired. Two or four wheel drive is normally selected by a lever to engage the front axle, but if locking hubs are used, these must also be manually engaged in the Lock position. Otherwise, the front axle will not drive the front wheels.

PASSIVE RESTRAINT: Safety systems such as air bags or automatic seat belts which operate with no action required on the part of the driver or passenger. Mandated by Federal regulations on all vehicles sold in the U.S. after 1990.

PAYLOAD: The weight the vehicle is capable of carrying in addition to its own weight. Payload includes weight of the driver, passengers and cargo, but not coolant, fuel, lubricant, spare tire, etc.

PCM: Powertrain control module.

PCV VALVE: A valve usually located in the rocker cover that vents crankcase vapors back into the engine to be reburned.

PERCOLATION: A condition in which the fuel actually "boils," due to excessive heat. Percolation prevents proper atomization of the fuel causing rough running.

PICK-UP COIL: The coil in which voltage is induced in an electronic ignition.

PING: A metallic rattling sound produced by the engine during acceleration. It is usually due to incorrect ignition timing or a poor grade of gasoline.

PINION: The smaller of two gears. The rear axle pinion drives the ring gear which transmits motion to the axle shafts.

PINION GEAR: The smallest gear in a drive gear assembly.

PISTON: A disc or cup that fits in a cylinder bore and is free to move. In hydraulics, it provides the means of converting hydraulic pressure into a usable force. Examples of piston applications are found in servo, clutch, and accumulator units.

PISTON RING: An open-ended ring which fits into a groove on the outer diameter of the piston. Its chief function is to form a seal between the piston and cylinder wall. Most automotive pistons have three rings: two for compression sealing; one for oil sealing.

PITMAN ARM: A lever which transmits steering force from the steering gear to the steering linkage.

PLANET CARRIER: A basic member of a planetary gear assembly that carries the pinion gears.

PLANET PINIONS: Gears housed in a planet carrier that are in constant mesh with the sun gear and internal gear. Because they have their own independent rotating centers, the pinions are capable of rotating around the sun gear or the inside of the internal gear.

PLANETARY GEAR RATIO: The reduction or overdrive ratio developed by a planetary gearset.

PLANETARY GEARSET: In its simplest form, it is made up of a basic assembly group containing a sun gear, internal gear, and planet carrier. The gears are always in constant mesh and offer a wide range of gear ratio possibilities.

PLANETARY GEARSET (COMPOUND): Two planetary gearsets combined together.

PLANETARY GEARSET (SIMPLE): An assembly of gears in constant mesh consisting of a sun gear, several pinion gears mounted in a carrier, and a ring gear. It provides gear ratio and direction changes, in addition to a direct drive and a neutral.

PLY RATING: A. rating given a tire which indicates strength (but not necessarily actual plies). A two-ply/four-ply rating has only two plies, but the strength of a four-ply tire.

POLARITY: Indication (positive or negative) of the two poles of a battery.

PORT: An opening for fluid intake or exhaust.

POSITIVE SEALING: A sealing method that completely prevents leakage.

POTENTIAL: Electrical force measured in volts; sometimes used interchangeably with voltage.

POWER: The ability to do work per unit of time, as expressed in horsepower; one horsepower equals 33,000 ft. lbs. of work per minute, or 550 ft. lbs. of work per second.

POWER FLOW: The systematic flow or transmission of power through the gears, from the input shaft to the output shaft.

POWER-TO-WEIGHT RATIO: Ratio of horsepower to weight of car.

POWERTRAIN: See Drivetrain.

POWERTRAIN CONTROL MODULE (PCM): Current designation for the engine control module (ECM). In many cases, late model vehicle control units manage the engine as well as the transmission. In other settings, the PCM controls the engine and is interfaced with a TCM to control transmission functions.

Ppm: Parts per million; unit used to measure exhaust emissions.

PREIGNITION: Early ignition of fuel in the cylinder, sometimes due to glowing carbon deposits in the combustion chamber. Preignition can be damaging since combustion takes place prematurely.

PRELOAD: A predetermined load placed on a bearing during assembly or by adjustment.

PRESS FIT: The mating of two parts under pressure, due to the inner diameter of one being smaller than the outer diameter of the other, or vice versa; an interference fit.

PRESSURE: The amount of force exerted upon a surface area.

PRESSURE CONTROL SOLENOID (PCS): An output device that provides a boost oil pressure to the mainline regulator valve to control line pressure. Its operation is determined by the amount of current sent from the PCM.

PRESSURE GAUGE: An instrument used for measuring the fluid pressure in a hydraulic circuit.

PRESSURE REGULATOR VALVE: In automatic transmissions, its purpose is to regulate the pressure of the pump output and supply the basic fluid pressure necessary to operate the transmission. The regulated fluid pressure may be referred to as mainline pressure, line pressure, or control pressure.

PRESSURE SWITCH ASSEMBLY (PSA): Mounted inside the transmission, it is a grouping of oil pressure switches that inputs to the PCM when certain hydraulic passages are charged with oil pressure.

PRESSURE PLATE: A spring-loaded plate (part of the clutch) that transmits power to the driven (friction) plate when the clutch is engaged.

PRIMARY CIRCUIT: The low voltage side of the ignition system which consists of the ignition switch, ballast resistor or resistance wire, bypass, coil, electronic control unit and pick-up coil as well as the connecting wires and harnesses.

PROFILE: Term used for tire measurement (tire series), which is the ratio of tire height to tread width.

PROM (PROGRAMMABLE READ-ONLY MEMORY): The heart of the computer that compares input data and makes the engineered program or strategy decisions about when to trigger the appropriate output based on stored computer instructions.

PULSE GENERATOR: A two-wire pickup sensor used to produce a fluctuating electrical signal. This changing signal is read by the controller to determine the speed of the object and can be used to measure transmission/transaxle input speed, output speed, and vehicle speed.

PSI: Pounds per square inch; a measurement of pressure.

PULSE WIDTH DUTY CYCLE SOLENOID (PULSE WIDTH MODULATED SOLENOID): A computer-controlled solenoid that turns on and off at a variable rate producing a modulated oil pressure; often referred to as a pulse width modulated (PWM) solenoid. Employed in many electronic automatic transmissions and transaxles, these solenoids are used to manage shift control and converter clutch hydraulic circuits.

PUSHROD: A steel rod between the hydraulic valve lifter and the valve rocker arm in overhead valve (OHV) engines.

PUMP: A mechanical device designed to create fluid flow and pressure buildup in a hydraulic system.

QUARTER PANEL: General term used to refer to a rear fender. Quarter panel is the area from the rear door opening to the tail light area and from rear wheel well to the base of the trunk and roof-line.

RACE: The surface on the inner or outer ring of a bearing on which the balls, needles or rollers move.

RACK AND PINION: A type of automotive steering system using a pinion gear attached to the end of the steering shaft. The pinion meshes with a long rack attached to the steering linkage.

RADIAL TIRE: Tire design which uses body cords running at right angles to the center line of the tire. Two or more belts are used to give tread strength. Radials can be identified by their characteristic sidewall bulge.

RADIATOR: Part of the cooling system for a water-cooled engine, mounted in the front of the vehicle and connected to the engine with rubber hoses. Through the radiator, excess combustion heat is dissipated into the atmosphere through forced convection using a water and glycol based mixture that circulates through, and cools, the engine.

RANGE REFERENCE AND CLUTCH/BAND APPLY CHART: A guide that shows the application of clutches and bands for each gear, within the selector range positions. These charts are extremely useful for understanding how the unit operates and for diagnosing malfunctions.

RAVIGNEAUX GEARSET: A compound planetary gearset that features matched dual planetary pinions (sets of two) mounted in a single planet carrier. Two sun gears and one ring mesh with the carrier pinions.

REACTION MEMBER: The stationary planetary member, in a planetary gearset, that is grounded to the transmission/transaxle case through the use of friction and wedging devices known as bands, disc clutches, and one-way clutches.

REACTION PRESSURE: The fluid pressure that moves a spool valve against an opposing force or forces; the area on which the opposing force acts. The opposing force can be a spring or a combination of spring force and auxiliary hydraulic force.

REACTOR, TORQUE CONVERTER: The reaction member of a fluid torque converter, more commonly called a stator. (See stator.)

REAR MAIN OIL SEAL: A synthetic or rope-type seal that prevents oil from leaking out of the engine past the rear main crankshaft bearing.

RECIRCULATING BALL: Type of steering system in which recirculating steel balls occupy the area between the nut and worm wheel, causing a reduction in friction.

RECTIFIER: A device (used primarily in alternators) that permits electrical current to flow in one direction only.

REDUCTION: (See gear reduction.)

REGULATOR VALVE: A valve that changes the pressure of the oil in a hydraulic circuit as the oil passes through the valve by bleeding off (or exhausting) some of the volume of oil supplied to the valve.

REFRIGERANT 12 (R-12) or 134 (R-134): The generic name of the refrigerant used in automotive air conditioning systems.

REGULATOR: A device which maintains the amperage and/or voltage levels of a circuit at predetermined values.

RELAY: A switch which automatically opens and/or closes a circuit.

RELAY VALVE: A valve that directs flow and pressure. Relay valves simply connect or disconnect interrelated passages without restricting the fluid flow or changing the pressure.

RELIEF VALVE: A spring-loaded, pressure-operated valve that limits oil pressure buildup in a hydraulic circuit to a predetermined maximum value.

RELUCTOR: A wheel that rotates inside the distributor and triggers the release of voltage in an electronic ignition.

RESERVOIR: The storage area for fluid in a hydraulic system; often called a sump.

RESIN: A liquid plastic used in body work.

RESIDUAL MAGNETISM: The magnetic strength stored in a material after a magnetizing field has been removed.

RESISTANCE: The opposition to the flow of current through a circuit or electrical device, and is measured in ohms. Resistance is equal to the voltage divided by the amperage.

RESISTOR SPARK PLUG: A spark plug using a resistor to shorten the spark duration. This suppresses radio interference and lengthens plug life.

RESISTOR: A device, usually made of wire, which offers a preset amount of resistance in an electrical circuit.

RESULTANT FORCE: The single effective directional thrust of the fluid force on the turbine produced by the vortex and rotary forces acting in different planes.

RETARD: Set the ignition timing so that spark occurs later (fewer degrees before TDC).

RHEOSTAT: A device for regulating a current by means of a variable resistance.

RING GEAR: The name given to a ring-shaped gear attached to a differential case, or affixed to a flywheel or as part of a planetary gear set.

ROADLOAD: grade.

ROCKER ARM: A lever which rotates around a shaft pushing down (opening) the valve with an end when the other end is pushed up by the pushrod. Spring pressure will later close the valve.

ROCKER PANEL: The body panel below the doors between the wheel opening.

ROLLER BEARING: A bearing made up of hardened inner and outer races between which hardened steel rollers move.

ROLLER CLUTCH: A type of one-way clutch design using rollers and springs mounted within an inner and outer cam race assembly.

ROTARY FLOW: The path of the fluid trapped between the blades of the members as they revolve with the rotation of the torque converter cover (rotational inertia).

ROTOR: (1.) The disc-shaped part of a disc brake assembly, upon which the brake pads bear; also called, brake disc. (2.) The device mounted atop the distributor shaft, which passes current to the distributor cap tower contacts.

ROTARY ENGINE: See Wankel engine.

RPM: Revolutions per minute (usually indicates engine speed).

RTV: A gasket making compound that cures as it is exposed to the atmosphere. It is used between surfaces that are not perfectly machined to one another, leaving a slight gap that the RTV fills and in which it hardens. The letters RTV represent room temperature vulcanizing.

RUN-ON: Condition when the engine continues to run, even when the key is turned off. See dieseling.

SEALED BEAM: A automotive headlight. The lens, reflector and filament from a single unit.

SEATBELT INTERLOCK: A system whereby the car cannot be started unless the seatbelt is buckled.

SECONDARY CIRCUIT: The high voltage side of the ignition system, usually above 20,000 volts. The secondary includes the ignition coil, coil wire, distributor cap and rotor, spark plug wires and spark plugs.

SELF-INDUCTION: The generation of voltage in a current-carrying wire by changing the amount of current flowing within that wire.

SEMI-CONDUCTOR: A material (silicon or germanium) that is neither a good conductor nor an insulator; used in diodes and transistors.

SEMI-FLOATING AXLE: In this design, a wheel is attached to the axle shaft, which takes both drive and cornering loads. Almost all solid axle passenger cars and light trucks use this design.

SENDING UNIT: A mechanical, electrical, hydraulic or electromagnetic device which transmits information to a gauge.

SENSOR: Any device designed to measure engine operating conditions or ambient pressures and temperatures. Usually electronic in nature and designed to send a voltage signal to an on-board computer, some sensors may operate as a simple on/off switch or they may provide a variable voltage signal (like a potentiometer) as conditions or measured parameters change.

SERIES CIRCUIT: (See circuit, series.)

SERPENTINE BELT: An accessory drive belt, with small multiple v-ribs, routed around most or all of the engine-powered accessories such as the alternator and power steering pump. Usually both the front and the back side of the belt comes into contact with various pulleys.

SERVO: In an automatic transmission, it is a piston in a cylinder assembly that converts hydraulic pressure into mechanical force and movement; used for the application of the bands and clutches.

SHIFT BUSYNESS: When referring to a torque converter clutch, it is the frequent apply and release of the clutch plate due to uncommon driving conditions.

SHIFT VALVE: Classified as a relay valve, it triggers the automatic shift in response to a governor and a throttle signal by directing fluid to the appropriate band and clutch apply combination to cause the shift to occur.

SHIM: Spacers of precise, predetermined thickness used between parts to establish a proper working relationship.

SHIMMY: Vibration (sometimes violent) in the front end caused by misaligned front end, out of balance tires or worn suspension components.

SHORT CIRCUIT: An electrical malfunction where current takes the path of least resistance to ground (usually through damaged insulation). Current flow is excessive from low resistance resulting in a blown fuse.

SHUDDER: Repeated jerking or stick-slip sensation, similar to chuggle but more severe and rapid in nature, that may be most noticeable during certain ranges of vehicle speed; also used to define condition after converter clutch engagement.

SIMPSON GEARSET: A compound planetary gear train that integrates two simple planetary gearsets referred to as the front planetary and the rear planetary.

SINGLE OVERHEAD CAMSHAFT: See overhead camshaft.

SKIDPLATE: A metal plate attached to the underside of the body to protect the fuel tank, transfer case or other vulnerable parts from damage.

SLAVE CYLINDER: In automotive use, a device in the hydraulic clutch system which is activated by hydraulic force, disengaging the clutch.

SLIPPING: Noticeable increase in engine rpm without vehicle speed increase; usually occurs during or after initial clutch or band engagement.

SLUDGE: Thick, black deposits in engine formed from dirt, oil, water, etc. It is usually formed in engines when oil changes are neglected.

SNAP RING: A circular retaining clip used inside or outside a shaft or part to secure a shaft, such as a floating wrist pin.

SOFT: Slow, almost unnoticeable clutch apply with very little shift feel.

SOFTCODES: DTCs that have been set into the PCM memory but are not present at the time of testing; often referred to as history or intermittent codes.

SOHC: Single overhead camshaft.

SOLENOID: An electrically operated, magnetic switching device.

SPALLING: A wear pattern identified by metal chips flaking off the hardened surface. This condition is caused by foreign particles, overloading situations, and/or normal wear.

SPARK PLUG: A device screwed into the combustion chamber of a spark ignition engine. The basic construction is a conductive core inside of a ceramic insulator, mounted in an outer conductive base. An electrical charge from the spark plug wire travels along the conductive core and jumps a preset air gap to a grounding point or points at the end of the conductive base. The resultant spark ignites the fuel/air mixture in the combustion chamber.

SPECIFIC GRAVITY (BATTERY): The relative weight of liquid (battery electrolyte) as compared to the weight of an equal volume of water.

SPLINES: Ridges machined or cast onto the outer diameter of a shaft or inner diameter of a bore to enable parts to mate without rotation.

SPLIT TORQUE DRIVE: In a torque converter, it refers to parallel paths of torque transmission, one of which is mechanical and the other hydraulic.

SPONGY PEDAL: A soft or spongy feeling when the brake pedal is depressed. It is usually due to air in the brake lines.

SPOOLVALVE: A precision-machined, cylindrically shaped valve made up of lands and grooves. Depending on its position in the valve bore, various interconnecting hydraulic circuit passages are either opened or closed.

SPRAG CLUTCH: A type of one-way clutch design using cams or contoured-shaped sprags between inner and outer races. (See one-way clutch.)

SPRUNG WEIGHT: The weight of a car supported by the springs.

SQUARE-CUT SEAL: Molded synthetic rubber seal designed with a square- or rectangular-shaped cross-section. This type of seal is used for both dynamic and static applications.

SRS: Supplemental restraint system

STABILIZER (SWAY) BAR: A bar linking both sides of the suspension. It resists sway on turns by taking some of added load from one wheel and putting it on the other.

STAGE: The number of turbine sets separated by a stator. A turbine set may be made up of one or more turbine members. A three-element converter is classified as a single stage.

STALL: In fluid drive transmission/transaxle applications, stall refers to engine rpm with the transmission/transaxle engaged and the vehicle stationary; throttle valve can be in any position between closed and wide open.

STALL SPEED: In fluid drive transmission/transaxle applications, stall speed refers to the maximum engine rpm with the transmission/transaxle engaged and vehicle stationary, when the throttle valve is wide open. (See stall; stall test.)

STALL TEST: A procedure recommended by many manufacturers to help determine the integrity of an engine, the torque converter stator, and certain clutch and band combinations. With the shift lever in each of the forward and reverse positions and with the brakes firmly applied, the accelerator pedal is momentarily pressed to the wide open throttle (WOT) position. The engine rpm reading at full throttle can provide clues for diagnosing the condition of the items listed above.

STALL TORQUE: The maximum design or engineered torque ratio of a fluid torque converter, produced under stall speed conditions. (See stall speed.)

STARTER: A high-torque electric motor used for the purpose of starting the engine, typically through a high ratio geared drive connected to the flywheel ring gear.

STATIC: A sealing application in which the parts being sealed do not move in relation to each other.

STATOR (REACTOR): The reaction member of a fluid torque converter that changes the direction of the fluid as it leaves the turbine to enter the impeller vanes. During the torque multiplication phase, this action assists the impeller's rotary force and results in an increase in torque.

STEERING GEOMETRY: Combination of various angles of suspension components (caster, camber, toe-in); roughly equivalent to front end alignment.

STRAIGHT WEIGHT: Term designating motor oil as suitable for use within a narrow range of temperatures. Outside the narrow temperature range its flow characteristics will not adequately lubricate.

STROKE: The distance the piston travels from bottom dead center to top dead center.

SUBSTITUTION: Replacing one part suspected of a defect with a like part of known quality.

SUMP: The storage vessel or reservoir that provides a ready source of fluid to the pump. In an automatic transmission, the sump is the oil pan. All fluid eventually returns to the sump for recycling into the hydraulic system.

SUN GEAR: In a planetary gearset, it is the center gear that meshes with a cluster of planet pinions.

SUPERCHARGER: An air pump driven mechanically by the engine through belts, chains, shafts or gears from the crankshaft. Two general types of supercharger are the positive displacement and centrifugal type, which pump air in direct relationship to the speed of the engine.

SUPPLEMENTAL RESTRAINT SYSTEM: See air bag.

SURGE: Repeating engine-related feeling of acceleration and deceleration that is less intense than chuggle.

SWITCH: A device used to open, close, or redirect the current in an electrical circuit.

SYNCHROMESH: A manual transmission/transaxle that is equipped with devices (synchronizers) that match the gear speeds so that the transmission/transaxle can be downshifted without clashing gears.

SYNTHETIC OIL: Non-petroleum based oil.

TACHOMETER: A device used to measure the rotary speed of an engine, shaft, gear, etc., usually in rotations per minute.

TDC: Top dead center. The exact top of the piston's stroke.

TEFLON SEALING RINGS: Teflon is a soft, durable, plastic-like material that is resistant to heat and provides excellent sealing. These rings are designed with either scarf-cut joints or as one-piece rings. Teflon sealing rings have replaced many metal ring applications.

TERMINAL: A device attached to the end of a wire or cable to make an electrical connection.

TEST LIGHT, CIRCUIT-POWERED: Uses available circuit voltage to test circuit continuity.

TEST LIGHT, SELF-POWERED: Uses its own battery source to test circuit continuity.

THERMISTOR: A special resistor used to measure fluid temperature; it decreases its resistance with increases in temperature.

THERMOSTAT: A valve, located in the cooling system of an engine, which is closed when cold and opens gradually in response to engine heating, controlling the temperature of the coolant and rate of coolant flow.

THERMOSTATIC ELEMENT: A heat-sensitive, spring-type device that controls a drain port from the upper sump area to the lower sump. When the transaxle fluid reaches operating temperature, the port is closed and the upper sump fills, thus reducing the fluid level in the lower sump.

THROTTLE POSITION (TP) SENSOR: Reads the degree of throttle opening; its signal is used to analyze engine load conditions. The ECM/PCM decides to apply the TCC, or to disengage it for coast or load conditions that need a converter torque boost.

THROTTLE PRESSURE/MODULATOR PRESSURE: A hydraulic signal oil pressure relating to the amount of engine load, based on either the amount of throttle plate opening or engine vacuum.

THROTTLE VALVE: A regulating or balanced valve that is controlled mechanically by throttle linkage or engine vacuum. It sends a hydraulic signal to the shift valve body to control shift timing and shift quality. (See balanced valve; modulator valve.)

THROW-OUT BEARING: As the clutch pedal is depressed, the throwout bearing moves against the spring fingers of the pressure plate, forcing the pressure plate to disengage from the driven disc.

TIE ROD: A rod connecting the steering arms. Tie rods have threaded ends that are used to adjust toe-in.

TIE-UP: Condition where two opposing clutches are attempting to apply at same time, causing engine to labor with noticeable loss of engine rpm.

TIMING BELT: A square-toothed, reinforced rubber belt that is driven by the crankshaft and operates the camshaft.

TIMING CHAIN: A roller chain that is driven by the crankshaft and operates the camshaft.

TIRE ROTATION: Moving the tires from one position to another to make the tires wear evenly.

TOE-IN (OUT): A term comparing the extreme front and rear of the front tires. Closer together at the front is toe-in; farther apart at the front is toe-out.

TOP DEAD CENTER (TDC): The point at which the piston reaches the top of its travel on the compression stroke.

TORQUE: Measurement of turning or twisting force, expressed as foot-pounds or inch-pounds.

TORQUE CONVERTER: A turbine used to transmit power from a driving member to a driven member via hydraulic action, providing changes in drive ratio and torque. In automotive use, it links the driveplate at the rear of the engine to the automatic transmission.

TORQUE CONVERTER CLUTCH: The apply plate (lockup plate) assembly used for mechanical power flow through the converter.

TORQUE PHASE: Sometimes referred to as slip phase or stall phase, torque multiplication occurs when the turbine is turning at a slower speed than the impeller, and the stator is reactionary (stationary). This sequence generates a boost in output torque.

TORQUE RATING (STALL TORQUE): The maximum torque multiplication that occurs during stall conditions, with the engine at wide open throttle (WOT) and zero turbine speed.

TORQUE RATIO: An expression of the gear ratio factor on torque effect. A 3:1 gear ratio or 3:1 torque ratio increases the torque input by the ratio factor of 3. Input torque (100 ft. lbs.) x 3 = output torque (300 ft. lbs.)

TRACTION: The amount of usable tractive effort before the drive wheels slip on the road contact surface.

TORSION BAR SUSPENSION: Long rods of spring steel which take the place of springs. One end of the bar is anchored and the other arm (attached to the suspension) is free to twist. The bars' resistance to twisting causes springing action.

TRACK: Distance between the centers of the tires where they contact the ground.

TRACTION CONTROL: A control system that prevents the spinning of a vehicle's drive wheels when excess power is applied.

TRACTIVE EFFORT: The amount of force available to the drive wheels, to move the vehicle.

TRANSAXLE: A single housing containing the transmission and differential. Transaxles are usually found on front engine/front wheel drive or rear engine/rear wheel drive cars.

TRANSDUCER: A device that changes energy from one form to another. For example, a transducer in a microphone changes sound energy to electrical energy. In automotive air-conditioning controls used in automatic temperature systems, a transducer changes an electrical signal to a vacuum signal, which operates mechanical doors.

TRANSMISSION: A powertrain component designed to modify torque and speed developed by the engine; also provides direct drive, reverse, and neutral.

TRANSMISSION CONTROL MODULE (TCM): Manages transmission functions. These vary according to the manufacturer's product design but may include converter clutch operation, electronic shift scheduling, and mainline pressure.

TRANSMISSION FLUID TEMPERATURE (TFT) SENSOR: Originally called a transmission oil temperature (TOT) sensor, this input device to the ECM/PCM senses the fluid temperature and provides a resistance value. It operates on the thermistor principle.

TRANSMISSION INPUT SPEED (TIS) SENSOR: Measures turbine shaft (input shaft) rpm's and compares to engine rpm's to determine torque converter slip. When compared to the transmission output speed sensor or VSS, gear ratio and clutch engagement timing can be determined.

TRANSMISSION OIL TEMPERATURE (TOT) SENSOR: (See transmission fluid temperature (TFT) sensor.)

TRANSMISSION RANGE SELECTOR (TRS) SWITCH: Tells the module which gear shift position the driver has chosen.

TRANSFER CASE: A gearbox driven from the transmission that delivers power to both front and rear driveshafts in a four-wheel drive system. Transfer cases usually have a high and low range set of gears, used depending on how much pulling power is needed.

TRANSISTOR: A semi-conductor component which can be actuated by a small voltage to perform an electrical switching function.

TREAD WEAR INDICATOR: Bars molded into the tire at right angles to the tread that appear as horizontal bars when $1/16$ in. of tread remains.

TREAD WEAR PATTERN: The pattern of wear on tires which can be "read" to diagnose problems in the front suspension.

TUNE-UP: A regular maintenance function, usually associated with the replacement and adjustment of parts and components in the electrical and fuel systems of a vehicle for the purpose of attaining optimum performance.

TURBINE: The output (driven) member of a fluid coupling or fluid torque converter. It is splined to the input (turbine) shaft of the transmission.

TURBOCHARGER: An exhaust driven pump which compresses intake air and forces it into the combustion chambers at higher than atmospheric pressures. The increased air pressure allows more fuel to be burned and results in increased horsepower being produced.

TURBULENCE: The interference of molecules of a fluid (or vapor) with each other in a fluid flow.

TYPE F: Transmission fluid developed and used by Ford Motor Company up to 1982. This fluid type provides a high coefficient of friction.

TYPE 7176: The preferred choice of transmission fluid for Chrysler automatic transmissions and transaxles. Developed in 1986, it closely resembles Dexron and Mercon. Type 7176 is the recommended service fill fluid for all Chrysler products utilizing a lockup torque converter dating back to 1978.

U-JOINT (UNIVERSAL JOINT): A flexible coupling in the drive train that allows the driveshafts or axle shafts to operate at different angles and still transmit rotary power.

UNDERSTEER: The tendency of a car to continue straight ahead while negotiating a turn.

UNIT BODY: Design in which the car body acts as the frame.

UNLEADED FUEL: Fuel which contains no lead (a common gasoline additive). The presence of lead in fuel will destroy the functioning elements of a catalytic converter, making it useless.

UNSPRUNG WEIGHT: The weight of car components not supported by the springs (wheels, tires, brakes, rear axle, control arms, etc.).

UPSHIFT: A shift that results in a decrease in torque ratio and an increase in speed.

VACUUM: A negative pressure; any pressure less than atmospheric pressure.

VACUUM ADVANCE: A device which advances the ignition timing in response to increased engine vacuum.

VACUUM GAUGE: An instrument used for measuring the existing vacuum in a vacuum circuit or chamber. The unit of measure is inches (of mercury in a barometer).

VACUUM MODULATOR: Generates a hydraulic oil pressure in response to the amount of engine vacuum.

VALVES: Devices that can open or close fluid passages in a hydraulic system and are used for directing fluid flow and controlling pressure.

VALVE BODY ASSEMBLY: The main hydraulic control assembly of the transmission/transaxle that contains numerous valves, check balls, and other components to control the distribution of pressurized oil throughout the transmission.

VALVE CLEARANCE: The measured gap between the end of the valve stem and the rocker arm, cam lobe or follower that activates the valve.

VALVE GUIDES: The guide through which the stem of the valve passes.

The guide is designed to keep the valve in proper alignment.

VALVE LASH (clearance): The operating clearance in the valve train.

VALVE TRAIN: The system that operates intake and exhaust valves, consisting of camshaft, valves and springs, lifters, pushrods and rocker arms.

VAPOR LOCK: Boiling of the fuel in the fuel lines due to excess heat. This will interfere with the flow of fuel in the lines and can completely stop the flow. Vapor lock normally only occurs in hot weather.

VARIABLE DISPLACEMENT (VARIABLE CAPACITY) VANE PUMP: Slipper-type vanes, mounted in a revolving rotor and contained within the bore of a movable slide, capture and then force fluid to flow. Movement of the slide to various positions changes the size of the vane chambers and the amount of fluid flow. **Note:** GM refers to this pump design as variable displacement, and Ford terms it variable capacity.

VARIABLE FORCE SOLENOID (VFS): Commonly referred to as the electronic pressure control (EPC) solenoid, it replaces the cable/linkage style of TV system control and is integrated with a spool valve and spring assembly to control pressure. A variable computer-controlled current flow varies the internal force of the solenoid on the spool valve and resulting control pressure.

VARIABLE ORIFICE THERMAL VALVE: Temperature-sensitive hydraulic oil control device that adjusts the size of a circuit path opening. By altering the size of the opening, the oil flow rate is adapted for cold to hot oil viscosity changes.

VARNISH: Term applied to the residue formed when gasoline gets old and stale.

VCM: See Electronic Control Unit (ECU).

VEHICLE SPEED SENSOR (VSS): Provides an electrical signal to the computer module, measuring vehicle speed, and affects the torque converter clutch engagement and release.

VESPEL SEALING RINGS: Hard plastic material that produces excellent sealing in dynamic settings. These rings are found in late versions of the 4T60 and in all 4T60-E and 4T80-E transaxles.

VISCOSITY: The ability of a fluid to flow. The lower the viscosity rating, the easier the fluid will flow. 10 weight motor oil will flow much easier than 40 weight motor oil.

VISCOSITY INDEX IMPROVERS: Keeps the viscosity nearly constant with changes in temperature. This is especially important at low temperatures, when the oil needs to be thin to aid in shifting and for cold-weather starting. Yet it must not be so thin that at high temperatures it will cause excessive hydraulic leakage so that pumps are unable to maintain the proper pressures.

VISCOUS CLUTCH: A specially designed torque converter clutch apply plate that, through the use of a silicon fluid, clamps smoothly and absorbs torsional vibrations.

VOLT: Unit used to measure the force or pressure of electricity. It is defined as the pressure needed to move one amp through the resistance of one ohm.

VOLTAGE: The electrical pressure that causes current to flow. Voltage is measured in volts (V).

VOLTAGE, APPLIED: The actual voltage read at a given point in a circuit. It equals the available voltage of the power supply minus the losses in the circuit up to that point.

VOLTAGE DROP: The voltage lost or used in a circuit by normal loads such as a motor or lamp or by abnormal loads such as a poor (high-resistance) lead or terminal connection.

VOLTAGE REGULATOR: A device that controls the current output of the alternator or generator.

VOLTMETER: An instrument used for measuring electrical force in units called volts. Voltmeters are always connected parallel with the circuit being tested.

VORTEX FLOW: The crosswise or circulatory flow of oil between the blades of the members caused by the centrifugal pumping action of the impeller.

WANKEL ENGINE: An engine which uses no pistons. In place of pistons, triangular-shaped rotors revolve in specially shaped housings.

WATER PUMP: A belt driven component of the cooling system that mounts on the engine, circulating the coolant under pressure.

WATT: The unit for measuring electrical power. One watt is the product of one ampere and one volt (watts equals amps times volts). Wattage is the horsepower of electricity (746 watts equal one horsepower).

WHEEL ALIGNMENT: Inclusive term to describe the front end geometry (caster, camber, toe-in/out).

WHEEL CYLINDER: Found in the automotive drum brake assembly, it is a device, actuated by hydraulic pressure, which, through internal pistons, pushes the brake shoes outward against the drums.

WHEEL WEIGHT: Small weights attached to the wheel to balance the wheel and tire assembly. Out-of-balance tires quickly wear out and also give erratic handling when installed on the front.

WHEELBASE: Distance between the center of front wheels and the center of rear wheels.

WIDE OPEN THROTTLE (WOT): Full travel of accelerator pedal.

WORK: The force exerted to move a mass or object. Work involves motion; if a force is exerted and no motion takes place, no work is done. Work per unit of time is called power. Work = force x distance = ft. lbs. 33,000 ft. lbs. in one minute = 1 horsepower

ZERO-THROTTLE COAST DOWN: A full release of accelerator pedal while vehicle is in motion and in drive range.

Commonly Used Abbreviations

2

2WD	Two Wheel Drive

4

4WD	Four Wheel Drive

A

A/C	Air Conditioning
ABDC	After Bottom Dead Center
ABS	Anti-lock Brakes
AC	Alternating Current
ACL	Air cleaner
ACT	Air Charge Temperature
AIR	Secondary Air Injection
ALCL	Assembly Line Communications Link
ALDL	Assembly Line Diagnostic Link
AT	Automatic Transaxle/Transmission
ATDC	After Top Dead Center
ATF	Automatic Transmission Fluid
ATS	Air Temperature Sensor
AWD	All Wheel Drive

B

BAP	Barometric Absolute Pressure
BARO	Barometric Pressure
BBDC	Before Bottom Dead Center
BCM	Body Control Module
BDC	Bottom Dead Center
BPT	Backpressure Transducer
BTDC	Before Top Dead Center
BVSV	Bimetallic Vacuum Switching Valve

C

CAC	Charge Air Cooler
CARB	California Air Resources Board
CAT	Catalytic Converter
CCC	Computer Command Control
CCCC	Computer Controlled Catalytic Converter
CCCI	Computer Controlled Coil Ignition
CCD	Computer Controlled Dwell
CDI	Capacitor Discharge Ignition
CEC	Computerized Engine Control
CFI	Continuous Fuel Injection
CIS	Continuous Injection System
CIS-E	Continuous Injection System - Electronic
CKP	Crankshaft Position
CL	Closed Loop
CMP	Camshaft Position
CPP	Clutch Pedal Position
CTOX	Continuous Trap Oxidizer System
CTP	Closed Throttle Position
CVC	Constant Vacuum Control
CYL	Cylinder

D

DBC	Dual Bed Catalyst
DC	Direct Current
DFI	Direct Fuel Injection
DIS	Distributorless Ignition System
DLC	Data Link Connector
DMM	Digital Multimeter
DOHC	Double Overhead Camshaft
DRB	Diagnostic Readout Box
DTC	Diagnostic Trouble Code
DTM	Diagnostic Test Mode
DVOM	Digital Volt/Ohmmeter

E

EBCM	Electronic Brake Control Module
ECM	Engine Control Module
ECT	Engine Coolant Temperature
ECU	Engine Control Unit or Electronic Control Unit
EDIS	Electronic Distributorless Ignition System
EEC	Electronic Engine Control
EEPROM	Electrically Erasable Programmable Read Only Memory
EFE	Early Fuel Evaporation
EGR	Exhaust Gas Recirculation
EGRT	Exhaust Gas Recirculation Temperature
EGRVC	EGR Valve Control
EPROM	Erasable Programmable Read Only Memory
EVAP	Evaporative Emissions
EVP	EGR Valve Position

F

FBC	Feedback Carburetor
FEEPROM	Flash Electrically Erasable Programmable Read Only Memory
FF	Flexible Fuel
FI	Fuel Injection
FT	Fuel Trim
FWD	Front Wheel Drive

G

GND	Ground

H

HAC	High Altitude Compensation
HEGO	Heated Exhaust Gas Oxygen sensor
HEI	High Energy Ignition
HO2 Sensor	Heated Oxygen Sensor

I

IAC	Idle Air Control
IAT	Intake Air Temperature
ICM	Ignition Control Module
IFI	Indirect Fuel Injection
IFS	Inertia Fuel Shutoff
ISC	Idle Speed Control
IVSV	Idle Vacuum Switching Valve

Commonly Used Abbreviations

K

KOEO	Key On, Engine Off
KOER	Key ON, Engine Running
KS	Knock Sensor

M

MAF	Mass Air Flow
MAP	Manifold Absolute Pressure
MAT	Manifold Air Temperature
MC	Mixture Control
MDP	Manifold Differential Pressure
MFI	Multiport Fuel Injection
MIL	Malfunction Indicator Lamp or Maintenance
MST	Manifold Surface Temperature
MVZ	Manifold Vacuum Zone

N

NVRAM	Nonvolatile Random Access Memory

O

O2 Sensor	Oxygen Sensor
OBD	On-Board Diagnostic
OC	Oxidation Catalyst
OHC	Overhead Camshaft
OL	Open Loop

P

P/S	Power Steering
PAIR	Pulsed Secondary Air Injection
PCM	Powertrain Control Module
PCS	Purge Control Solenoid
PCV	Positive Crankcase Ventilation
PIP	Profile Ignition Pick-up
PNP	Park/Neutral Position
PROM	Programmable Read Only Memory
PSP	Power Steering Pressure
PTO	Power Take-Off
PTOX	Periodic Trap Oxidizer System

R

RABS	Rear Anti-lock Brake System
RAM	Random Access Memory
ROM	Read Only Memory
RPM	Revolutions Per Minute
RWAL	Rear Wheel Anti-lock Brakes
RWD	Rear Wheel Drive

S

SBC	Single Bed Converter
SBEC	Single Board Engine Controller
SC	Supercharger
SCB	Supercharger Bypass
SFI	Sequential Multiport Fuel Injection
SIR	Supplemental Inflatible Restraint
SOHC	Single Overhead Camshaft
SPL	Smoke Puff Limiter
SPOUT	Spark Output
SRI	Service Reminder Indicator
SRS	Supplemental Restraint System
SRT	System Readiness Test
SSI	Solid State Ignition
ST	Scan Tool
STO	Self-Test Output

T

TAC	Thermostatic Air Clearner
TBI	Throttle Body Fuel Injection
TC	Turbocharger
TCC	Torque Converter Clutch
TCM	Transmission Control Module
TDC	Top Dead Center
TFI	Thick Film Ignition
TP	Throttle Position
TR Sensor	Transaxle/Transmission Range Sensor
TVV	Thermal Vacuum Valve
TWC	Three-way Catalytic Converter

V

VAF	Volume Air Flow, or Vane Air Flow
VAPS	Variable Assist Power Steering
VRV	Vacuum Regulator Valve
VSS	Vehicle Speed Sensor
VSV	Vacuum Switching Valve

W

WOT	Wide Open Throttle
WU-TWC	Warm Up Three-way Catalytic Converter

CHILTON LABOR GUIDE

Chilton's labor times are so trusted, even a competing publisher uses them!

The *Chilton 2012 Labor Guide* features new models and new labor operations in order to stay current with new technologies. Labor times have also been refined for normal and severe maintenance schedules, if applicable. The 2012 edition provides repair times for 1981-current import and domestic vehicles. Chilton's editors consider warranty times, component locations, component type, the environment in which technicians work, the training they receive, and the tools they use when calculating a labor time. To allow for vehicle age, operating conditions, and type of service, the *Chilton 2012 Labor Guide* provides standard and severe service times, plus OEM warranty times. Vehicle makes and models conform to current Automotive Aftermarket Industry Association (AAIA) standards.

978-1-4354-6155-0 Chilton 2012 Labor Guide Manual Set (Domestic & Import)
978-1-4354-6154-3 Chilton 2012 Labor Guide CD-ROM (Domestic & Import)

CD-ROM FEATURES

- ❍ access labor times for 1981-current models import and domestic vehicle models
- ❍ save time with automatically calculated labor charges, taxes, & parts as total job is estimated
- ❍ create professional estimates for your customer and worksheets for your technicians, printing them whenever needed
- ❍ keep track of customers, prior estimates, and your own parts or package jobs with less paper
- ❍ choose part names for estimates from an industry standard database to reduce typing
- ❍ estimate and track your work status with improved forms
- ❍ communicate easily with customers using re-designed printouts which show all labor and parts in an easy-to-read format.
- ❍ simplify adding parts to your estimate or work order with a helpful parts list
- ❍ locate information quick with a keyword search engine
- ❍ quickly locate work requests by day, week and month using the calendar feature

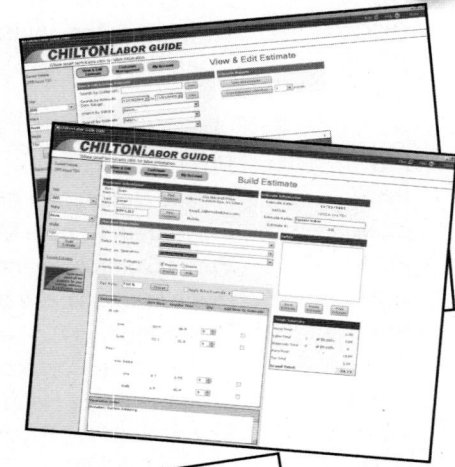

Manual FEATURES

- ❍ more than 2,500 pages of updated Chilton labor times split into two volumes includes vehicle information from 1981 to current models
- ❍ trusted by more service professionals than any other labor guide
- ❍ less flipping though pages with separate domestic and imported vehicle manuals and more specific vehicle groups
- ❍ convenient tabs display contents by manufacturer and model
- ❍ easy-to-find manufacturers are arranged alphabetically within each volume
- ❍ search using two-indexes - labor operations and systems - in each model group
- ❍ page numbers include manufacturer code so you know where you are in the book

CHILTON®PRO.COM

WHERE SMART TECHNICIANS CLICK FOR SERVICE INFORMATION

ChiltonPRO is the alternative for professional technicians who want a cost-effective electronic automotive repair system. It combines Chilton's famous automotive repair information into one solution covering more than 60 years of domestic and imported vehicles. The information is delivered online and is updated regularly throughout the year.

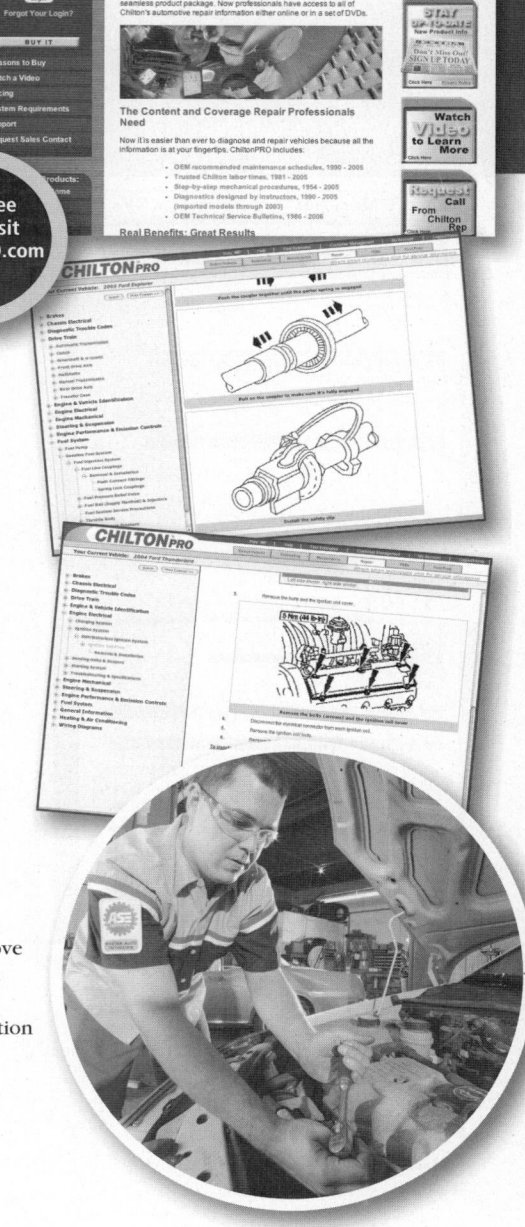

Online Monthly Payment
ISBN: 978-14180-3002-5

Online Annual Payment
ISBN: 978-14180-2876-3

For a free demo visit ChiltonPRO.com

ChiltonPRO FEATURES

- ○ make repairs even easier with videos & animations which explain system operations & contribute to technician knowledge
- ○ create better estimates using labor times developed with real-world factors
- ○ save money by accurately identifying and solving engine performance problems
- ○ save time with expert guidance through OBDII diagnostics
- ○ increase efficiency by understanding system operation through detailed explanations and theory
- ○ increase profits using Technical Service Bulletins (TSBs) to ensure that work is not going unperformed
- ○ execute effective repairs by viewing cutaway diagrams and actual photos
- ○ make better use of your time with information that can be found quicker using AAIA standards for year, make, and model
- ○ increase confidence levels by always being able to print what you need
- ○ eliminate guesswork with quick reference to critical specifications in helpful tables

Coverage Includes:

- OEM recommended maintenance schedules, 1990–current
- trusted Chilton labor times, 1981–current
- step-by-step mechanical procedures, 1940s–current
- diagnostics designed by instructors, 1990–current
- More than 75,000 OEM Technical Service Bulletins issued during the past 20 years

System Requirements:
Web browser

- Internet Explorer 7.0 or above (recommended)
- Firefox 3.6 or 4 or Safari
- High-speed internet connection
- Adobe Flash Player
- Adobe Reader
- Windows XP or above

CHILTON®ESTIMATING

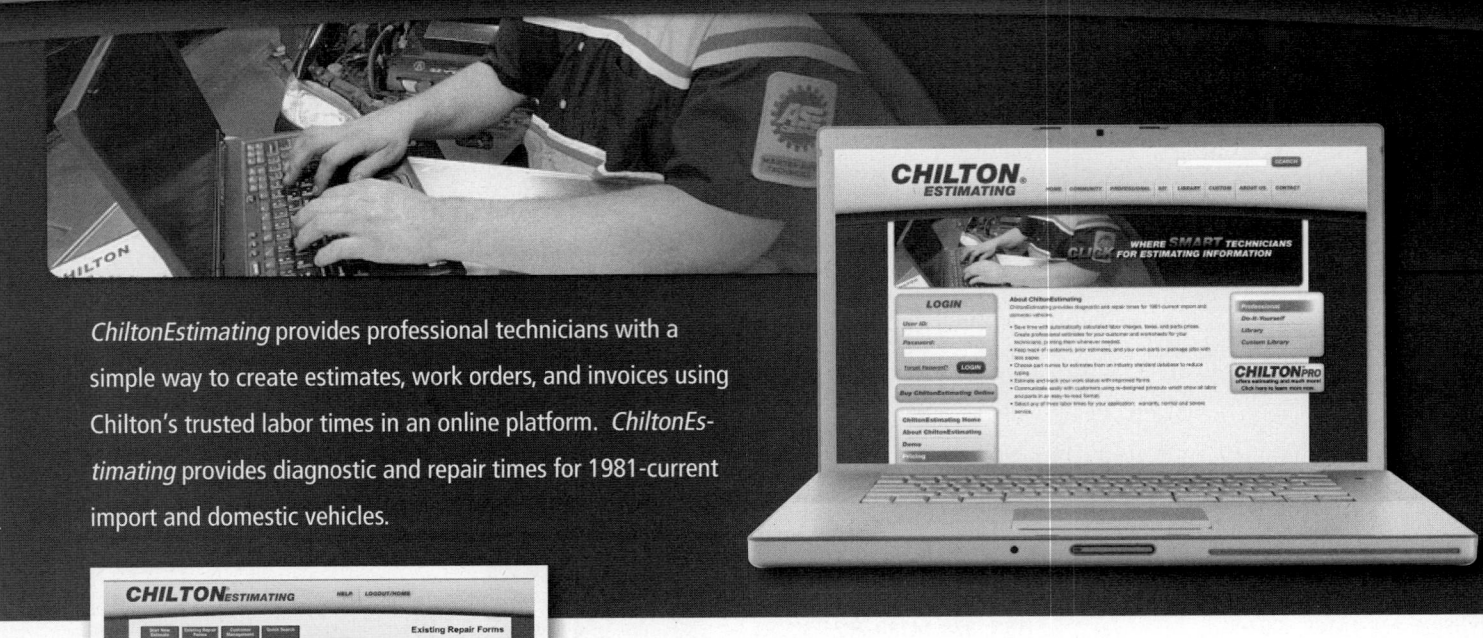

ChiltonEstimating provides professional technicians with a simple way to create estimates, work orders, and invoices using Chilton's trusted labor times in an online platform. *ChiltonEstimating* provides diagnostic and repair times for 1981-current import and domestic vehicles.

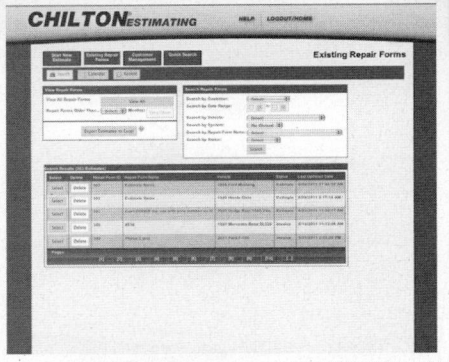

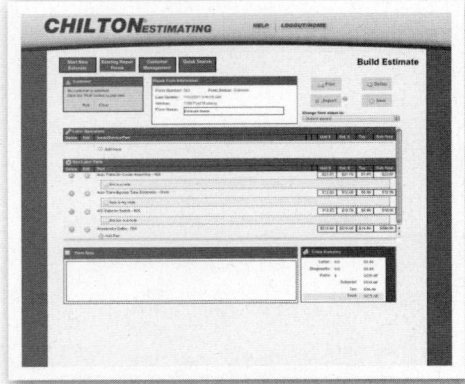

○ Access up-to-date information immediately. *ChiltonEstimating* is continuously updated!

○ Enjoy a hassle-free product with nothing to download and nothing to install.

○ Never fret over lost or damaged software or books again.

○ Secure your valuable customer data on our server, which won't be lost if your computer crashes.

○ Easily access the program from any web-enabled computer.

○ Work on more than one job at a time using *ChiltonEstimating's* two shop-user accounts.

○ Download all customer contact information easily for marketing purposes.

○ Cancel your subscription at any time by going to the "My Account" tab. No contract or obligation required. Customer data will be available to download for up to six months after a subscription has expired.

○ Save time with automatically calculated labor charges, taxes, and parts prices. Create professional estimates for your customer and worksheets for your technicians, printing them whenever needed.

○ Keep track of customers, prior estimates, and your own parts or package jobs with less paper.

○ Choose part names for estimates from an industry standard database to reduce typing.

○ Estimate and track your work status with improved forms.

○ Communicate easily with customers using re-designed printouts which show all labor and parts in an easy-to-read format.

○ Select any of three labor times for your application: warranty, normal and severe service.

System Requirements:
Web browser
- Internet Explorer 7.0 or above (recommended)
- Firefox 3.6 or 4 or Safari
- High-speed internet connection
- Adobe Flash Player
- Adobe Reader
- Windows XP or above

ONLINE **www.chilton.cengage.com**   TO PLACE AN ORDER CALL **1-800-347-7707**

CHILTON SERVICE MANUALS

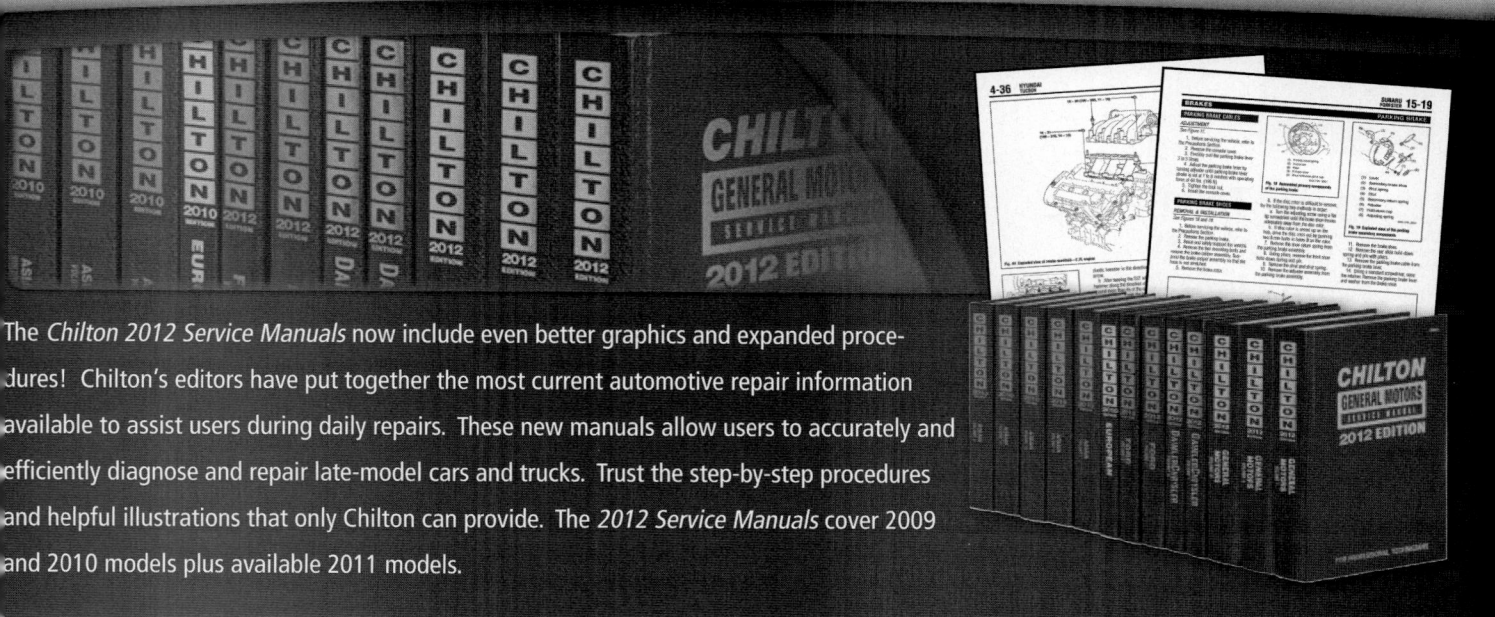

The *Chilton 2012 Service Manuals* now include even better graphics and expanded procedures! Chilton's editors have put together the most current automotive repair information available to assist users during daily repairs. These new manuals allow users to accurately and efficiently diagnose and repair late-model cars and trucks. Trust the step-by-step procedures and helpful illustrations that only Chilton can provide. The *2012 Service Manuals* cover 2009 and 2010 models plus available 2011 models.

KEY FEATURES

- organized by vehicle manufacturer
- provides thousands of pages of expertly written content
- access new year, make, and model information without repeating previous edition's content
- comprehensive, technically detailed content, including exploded view illustrations, diagnostics and specification charts, arranged alphabetically by model group for quick, easy

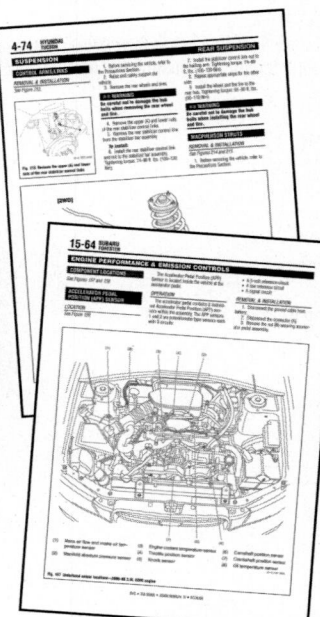

2012 EDITIONS

Chilton 2012 Chrysler
Service Manuals
ISBN: 978-1-1336-2576-6
Part No. 222576

Chilton 2012 Ford Service Manuals
ISBN: 978-1-1336-2575-9
Part No. 222575

Chilton 2012 General
Motor Service Manuals
ISBN: 978-1-1336-2574-2
Part No. 222574

2010 EDITIONS

2010 Asian Service Manual Vol. 1
ISBN 978-1-1110-3764-2
Part No. 163764

2010 Asian Service Manual Vol. 2
ISBN 978-1-1110-3765-9
Part No. 163765

2010 Asian Service Manual Vol. 3
ISBN 978-1-1110-3766-6
Part No. 163766

2010 Asian Service Manual Vol. 4
ISBN 978-1-1110-3767-3
Part No. 163767

2010 Asian Service Manual Vol. 5
ISBN 978-1-1110-3768-0
Part No. 163768

2010 European Service Manual
ISBN 978-1-1110-3769-7
Part No. 163769

2010 Chrysler Service Manual,
Volumes 1 & 2
ISBN 978-1-1110-3654-6
Part No. 163654

2010 Ford Service Manual,
Vols. 1 & 2
ISBN 978-1-1110-3657-7
Part No. 163657

2010 General Motors Service
Manuals, Vols. 1, 2, & 3
ISBN 978-1-111-03661-4
Part No. 163661

2008 EDITIONS

2008 Chrysler Service Manual,
Vols. 1 & 2
ISBN 978-1-4283-2204-2
Part No. 142204

2008 Ford Service Manuals,
Vols. 1 & 2
ISBN 978-1-4283-2208-0
Part No. 142208

2008 Edition General Motors
Service Manuals, Vols. 1 & 2
ISBN 978-1-4283-2211-0
Part No. 142211

2008 Asian Service Manuals,
Vols. 1-4
ISBN 978-1-4283-2214-1
Part No. 142214

2008 Asian Service Manual, Vol. 1
ISBN 978-1-4283-2215-8
Part No. 142215

2008 Asian Service Manual, Vol. 2
ISBN 978-1-4283-2216-5
Part No. 142216

2008 Asian Service Manual, Vol. 3
ISBN 978-1-4283-2217-2
Part No. 142217

2008 Asian Service Manual, Vol. 4
ISBN 978-1-4283-2218-9
Part No. 142218

2008 European Service Manual
ISBN 978-1-4283-2220-2
Part No. 142220

Chilton® Mechanical Service Manuals–Perennial Editions

These manuals contain repair and maintenance information for all major systems. Included are repair and overhaul procedures using thousands of illustrations.

CHILTON AUTO REPAIR MANUALS
1998-2002
ISBN 978-0-8019-9362-6/Part No. 9362
Covers all popular American and Canadian cars. An added feature includes scheduled maintenance interval charts.
1993-97
ISBN 978-0-8019-7919-4/Part No. 7919
Covers all popular American and Canadian cars.
1980-87
ISBN 978-0-8019-7670-4/Part No. 7670
Covers all popular American and Canadian cars.

CHILTON IMPORT AUTO REPAIR MANUALS
1998-2002
ISBN 978-0-8019-9363-3/Part No. 9363
Covers all popular Import cars. An added feature includes scheduled maintenance intervals charts.
1993-97
ISBN 978-0-8019-7920-0/Part No. 7920
Covers all popular Import cars.
1988-92
ISBN 978-0-8019-7907-1/Part No. 7907
Covers all popular Import cars.
1980-87
ISBN 978-0-8019-7672-8/Part No. 7672
Covers all popular Import cars.

CHILTON TRUCK AND VAN REPAIR MANUALS
1998-2002
ISBN 978-0-8019-9364-0/Part No. 9364
Covers popular U.S., Canadian, and Import Pick-Ups, Vans, and 4WDs. An added feature includes scheduled maintenance interval charts.

1993-97
ISBN 978-0-8019-7921-7/Part No. 7921
Covers popular U.S., Canadian, and Import Pick-Ups, Sport-Utilities, Vans, RVs and 4 wheel drives.
1991-95
ISBN 978-0-8019-7911-8/Part No. 7911
Covers popular U.S., Canadian, and Import Pick-Ups, Vans, RVs and 4 wheel drives.
1986-90
ISBN 978-08019-7902-6/Part No. 7902
Covers popular U.S., Canadian, and Import Pick-Us, Vans, RVs and 4 wheel drives.
1979-86
ISBN 978-08019-7655-1/Part No. 7655
Covers popular U.S., Canadian, and Import Pick-Ups, Vans, RVs and 4 wheel drives.

CHILTON SUV REPAIR MANUAL
1998-2002
ISBN 978-08019-9365-7/Part No. 9365
Covers popular U.S., Canadian, and import SUVs. An added feature includes scheduled maintenance intervals charts.

COLLECTOR'S SERIES
CHILTON AUTO REPAIR MANUAL 1964-1971
ISBN 978-08019-5974-5/Part No. 5974
1971-1978
ISBN 978-08019-7012-2/Part No. 7012

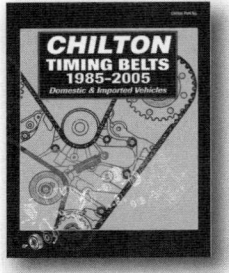

ISBN 978-1-4018-9880-9
Part No. 129880
544 pp, 8" x 11", SC, ©2006

Chilton Timing Belts, 1985-2005

Timing belt procedures can represent increased profits for automotive repair shops and service stations, and this manual contains all the information automotive technicians need to properly service timing belts on domestic and imported cars, vans, and light trucks through 2005 models. Clear, straightforward procedures, illustrations, and specifications help to communicate 20 years of vehicle applications for fast, accurate inspection, replacement, and tensioning of timing belts. Users will learn how to perform key procedures quickly and safely, while learning the correct labor time to charge for the service.

ALSO AVAILABLE:
Quick-Reference Manuals
The Chilton Professional Series offers *Quick-Reference Manuals* for the automotive professional, providing complete coverage on repair and maintenance, adjustments, and diagnostic procedures for specific systems and components.

KEY FEATURES
- step-by-step procedures
- detailed illustrations and exploded views
- easy-to-use manufacturer and model indexing
- handy specifications or data charts

Heater Core Service 1990-2000,
ISBN 978-0-8019-9311-4
Part No. 9311

Brake Specifications and Service 1990-2000
ISBN 978-0-8019-9312-1
Part No. 9312

Electric Cooling Fans, Accessory Drive Belts &
Water Pumps, 1995-1999,
ISBN 978-0-8019-9126-4
Part No. 9126

Powertrain Codes & Oxygen Sensors, 1990-1999,
ISBN 978-0-8019-9127-1
Part No. 9127

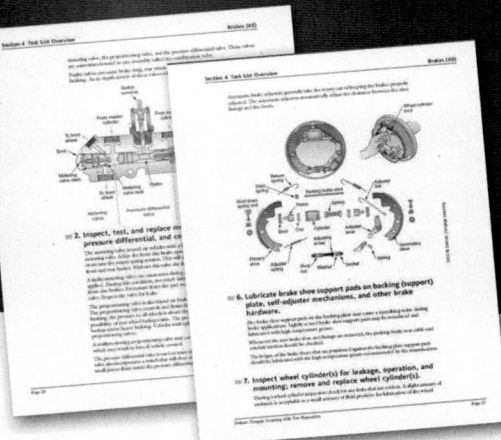

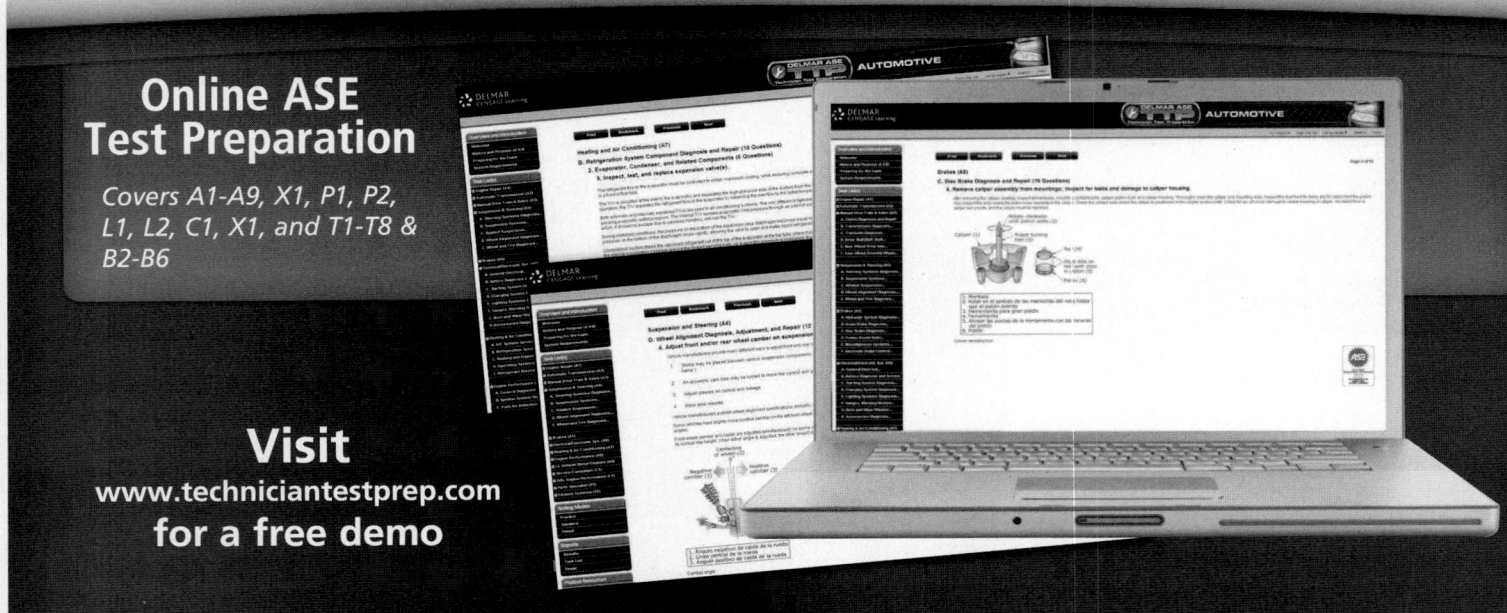
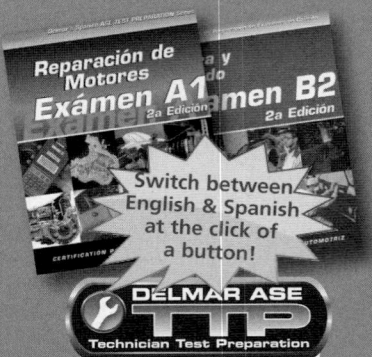

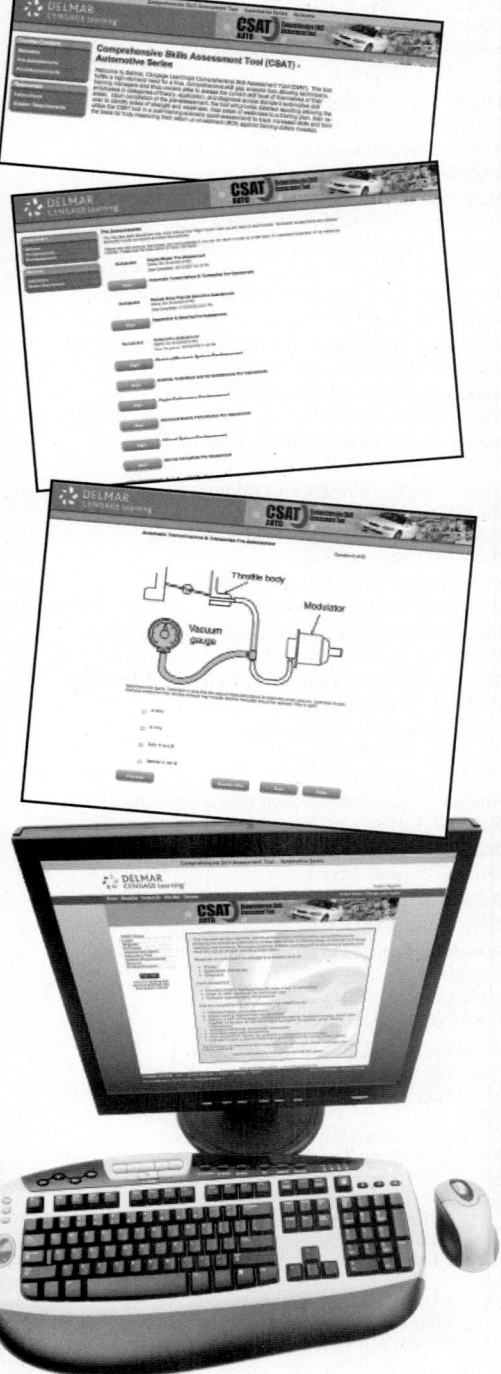

CSAT-Automotive Series

The online *Comprehensive Skill Assessment Tool-Automotive Series* helps instructors and trainers implement the necessary training programs for individual areas needing improvement over various key automotive topics. As a true skill gap analysis tool, within each key topic, strategic learning areas are measured for knowledge of theory, hands-on application, and diagnostic skill. Areas of strength and areas needing improvement are identified. The combined phases of education and training, and post-assessment allow instructors to track skill level growth and target specific areas needing development.

Courses Available in the CSAT Automotive Series

Parts Specialist
ISBN 978-1-4180-3225-8

Service Consultant
ISBN 978-1-4180-3223-4

Advanced Engine Performance
ISBN 978-1-4180-0073-8

Brakes
ISBN 978-1-4180-0069-1

Electrical/Electronic Systems
ISBN 978-1-4180-0070-7

Engine Performance
ISBN 978-1-4180-0072-1

Engine Repair
ISBN 978-1-4180-0065-3

Exhaust Systems
ISBN 978-1-4180-0074-5

Heating and Air Conditioning
ISBN 978-1-4180-0071-4

Manual Drive Train & Axles
ISBN 978-1-4180-0067-7

Suspension & Steering
ISBN 978-1-4180-0068-4

Transmissions & Transaxles
ISBN 978-1-4180-0066-0

All-in-One (contains questions from all eight core automotive areas in one product)
ISBN 978-1-4354-2825-6

FEATURES

- available tests include Engine Repair, Transmissions and Transaxles, Manual Drive Train and Axles, Suspension and Steering, Brakes, Electrical/Electronic Systems, Heating and Air Conditioning, Engine Performance, Advanced Engine Performance, and Exhaust Systems
- can be utilized by companies to measure the technical skill level of individuals against an "ideal" to identify areas of strength and creates a skill gap analysis to help users address areas needing improvement
- questions are written and reviewed by experts in the industry and offer users the opportunity to receive instant feedback
- account set-up that enables instructors and trainers to assess and track the results of individual students
- acts as a true return on investment (ROI) tool for companies to ensure they invest their training dollars in the most appropriate areas

Visit www.skillanalysis.com
for a free demo!

Professional Automotive Technician Training Series: PATTS

Delmar

Delmar, the leader in providing first-rate educational materials for automotive technicians, now offers this exciting self-paced learning series. Choose the delivery method that best suits your needs—CD-ROM or Web-based product – and receive more than 8.5 hours worth of quality instruction. Combining theory, diagnosis, and repair information into one easy-to-use training tool, this highly interactive product helps technicians receive the most applicable delivery method for their needs, regardless of technical infrastructure.

KEY FEATURES

- attention-grabbing animations and learner interactions keep users interested and engaged throughout the course of the program
- bookmarking technology enables users to track their progress from beginning to end
- periodic progress checks and end-of-section reviews are integrated throughout to ensure the highest level of retention
- a certificate of completion can be printed by users achieving a score of 80% or higher on the final review of the course
- all material is completely AICC and SCORM compliant
- all material follows the latest ASE and NATEF standards

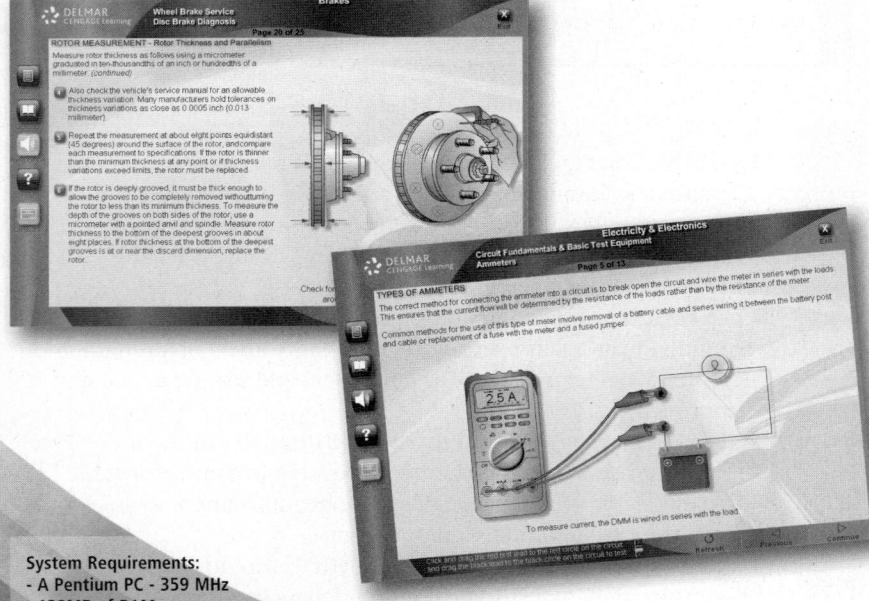

System Requirements:
- A Pentium PC - 359 MHz
- 128MB of RAM
- Windows 2000, Windows XP, Windows Vista
- Graphics adapter with Minimum 1024 x 768 display resolution, 32 bit depth
- Minimum Display Resolution 1024 x 768
- High Speed Internet Connection
- Internet Explorer 6, 7, or Firefox 2
- Not Mac Compatible

Basic Automotive Service and Maintenance Web Based Training
ISBN 978-1-4180-4101-4

Basic Automotive Service and Maintenance Computer Based Training
ISBN 978-1-4180-4100-7

Electricity and Electronics Web Based Training
ISBN 978-1-4180-4242-4

Electricity and Electronics Computer Based Training
ISBN 978-1-4180-4241-7

Brakes Web Based Training
ISBN 978-1-4180-4236-3

Brakes Computer Based Training
ISBN 978-1-4180-4235-6

Engine Performance Web Based Training
ISBN 978-1-4180-4240-0

Engine Performance Computer Based Training
ISBN 978-1-4180-4239-4

Suspension and Steering Web Based Training
ISBN 978-1-4180-4238-7

Suspension and Steering Computer Based Training
ISBN 978-1-4180-4237-0

Automatic Transmissions Web Based Training
ISBN 978-1-4180-4244-8

Automatic Transmissions Computer Based Training
ISBN 978-1-4180-4243-1

Service Consultant Web Based Training
ISBN 978-1-4180-4249-3

Service Consultant Computer Based Training
ISBN 978-1-4180-4247-9

Engine Repair Web Based Training
ISBN 978-1-4180-4254-7

Engine Repair Computer Based Training
ISBN 978-1-4180-4253-0

Parts Specialist Web Based Training
ISBN 978-1-4180-4252-3

Parts Specialist Computer Based Training
ISBN 978-1-4180-4250-9

Heating and Air Conditioning Web Based Training
ISBN 978-1-4180-4246-2

Heating and Air Conditioning Computer Based Training
ISBN 978-1-4180-4245-5

Manual Transmissions Web Based Training
ISBN 978-1-4180-4256-1

Manual Transmissions Computer Based Training
ISBN 978-1-4180-4255-4

Advanced Engine Performance Web Based Training
ISBN 978-1-4283-2098-7

Advanced Engine Performance Computer Based Training
ISBN 978-1-4283-2097-0

New Courses!

Fuels, Emissions, and Exhaust Computer Based Training
ISBN 978-1-4354-4148-4

Fuels, Emissions, and Exhaust Web Based Training
ISBN 978-1-4354-4147-7

Hybrid, Electric, and Fuel-Cell Vehicles Web Based Training
ISBN 978-1-4354-4144-6

Hybrid, Electric, and Fuel-Cell Vehicles Computer Based Training
ISBN 978-1-4354-4143-9

Visit www.techniciantraining.com for a free demo!